The Zohar
in English

Translated by Maurice Simon,
Harry Sperling, and Paul P. Levertoff
Introduction by Joshua Abelson
Foreword and Edited by Tzvee Zahavy

The Zohar in English

Based on the edition of London: The Soncino Press, 1931.
Vol. 1 translated by Harry Sperling and Maurice Simon with an introduction by Dr. J. Abelson.
Vol. 3 translated by Harry Sperling, Maurice Simon, and Paul P. Levertoff; v. 4, by Maurice Simon and Paul P. Levertoff.
Vols. 1–2, Genesis; v. 3–4, Exodus, Leviticus I-XI; v. 5, Leviticus XII-XXVII, Numbers, Deuteronomy.

1. Cabala. 2. Bible. O. T. Pentateuch-Commentaries,
I. Sperling, Harry, 1880 tr. I. Simon, Maurice, b. 1874, tr. II. Levertoff, Paul Philip, 1878 tr. III
BM525.Z6 296 32–4409
Library of Congress 02:371 CCSC/sr

Cover designed with Kindle Cover Creator. Cover photo credit: Mick Haupt on Unsplash

Tzvee Zahavy
Website at www.tzvee.com

Printed in the United States of America
First Printing: 2022

Contents

FOREWORD

By Tzvee Zahavy

The Context of Jewish Mysticism

Mystical ideas had been a part of Jewish belief since its earliest times. But only in the Middle Ages did the doctrines of Jewish mysticism come to full flower.

Mysticism focuses on the perceived experience of God and the extreme feeling of the participant. The mystical "moment" is far from a routine and quiet contemplation. It is an alive and vibrant dimension of religious life.

Gershom Scholem, a leading authority on the subject of Jewish mysticism, emphasized another side to the world of religious mysticism—the role of tradition in mysticism. Scholem demonstrated how firmly mysticism was grounded in a specific and complex belief system. He divided the religious experience of humankind into two stages.

In the first stage, God surrounds man in nature. No gap is felt between man and God; therefore there is no room for mystical experience and, indeed, no need for it.

In the second stage, humanity is separated from God. Only God's voice through revelation can link persons to the Divine.

The myths of religion give concrete form to expressions of the main ideas of religion: creation, revelation, and redemption. Mysticism within a religion, then, can make use of these ideas developed in history and give them, according to Scholem, new and different meanings reflecting the characteristic feature of mystical experience, the direct contact between the individual and God.

Mysticism in the second stage becomes inexorably linked with the traditions of a religious system. Jewish mysticism at this stage of development is called kabbalah (tradition). It combines elements of teachings available to all who wish to learn them and a host of secret doctrines accessible to only a few elite initiates. (*Major Trends in Jewish Mysticism*, 1946)

Mysticism has developed in every generation of Jewish history, from Rabbi Aqiba in the first century to the present. Some concerns are common to all eras of Jewish mysticism. Two such issues are the desire to know the attributes of God and the search for the symbolic meanings of the Torah.

Mystics have suggested alternative readings to the stories of the Torah. A mystic who reads the story of the exodus from Egypt might interpret it to be a narrative of a different sort of journey: the release from one's inner Egypt, the bondage of the human situation. In addition, Jewish mysticism has often dealt with eschatological ideas (those concerned with the final events of mankind or of the world) and cosmogonic notions (those concerned with the creation or origin of the world).

In the Middle Ages Jewish mysticism burst forth in defiance of the pressures of the times. True, the Jews remained concerned with Talmudic precepts and ritual, but they turned with fervor to mystical and messianic teachings in search of a way to understand the implications of their historical conditions.

Some historians think that the bleak historical circumstances of the riots, expulsions, and persecutions of the twelfth through the sixteenth centuries forced many Jewish thinkers to retreat into the complicated and esoteric realms of mystical contemplation.

The Jews of the Rhineland, for example, sent a query to one of the leading rabbis of the day regarding two seemingly unrelated issues. First, they inquired about a mundane matter – the proper way to slaughter an animal so that the meat would be kosher (fit to eat according to dietary laws). Second, they wanted to know about a profound issue – when the Messiah would come to redeem the Jewish people.

Mysticism flourished in both of the major cultural spheres of Judaism: in the Ashkenazic (central European) and the Sephardic (Spanish and North African) worlds. In early times the main focus of mystical tradition was on the doctrines concerning the creation of the world by God.

The expulsion of the Jews from Spain in 1492 had a great impact on the Jewish community. After this event the emphasis of Jewish mysticism shifted to issues relating to the redemption of the people, not the creation of the universe.

The kabbalah of Isaac Luria (also called the Ari) had a great effect on Jews of this time. Luria taught that Jews themselves could bring about the redemption of the nation and the world. Further, through the observance of the mitzvot (commandments), Jews could alter the course of history. His doctrines attributed a universal significance to rabbinic Judaism. To express these doctrines Lurianic kabbalah developed a symbolic language. It taught that to bring redemption to the world, Jews had to rescue the "sparks of light" by fulfilling God's will to change the "flow of primal light".

The development of kabbalah took a significant turn at the juncture of the sixteenth century when mystical thought became linked with messianic yearnings. This connection changed the character of Jewish mysticism by transforming the kabbalah from a strictly doctrinal system to a more salvific worldview.

In the seventeenth century, mysticism was carried forward to its ultimate logical conclusion by Shabbetai Zevi, a false messiah. In later historical periods, Zionism and Reform Judaism developed further the doctrines of a utopian non-mystical salvation.

The Zohar Today

Where does the Zohar fit today in the diverse universe of Jewish expressions? And what is its relevance today to Jews and to others seeking to unravel the mysteries of God and the universe and the challenges all humans confront day to day and throughout our difficult recent epochs?

I propose first a personal answer. My father Rabbi Zev Zahavy became an ordained rabbi during the years of the Holocaust. I asked him once how he maintained his firm faith in God and Judaism after living through the times of awful sufferings and deaths of those years of his lifetime.

He told me that he found helpful answers in two places: in his philosophical approach to the cosmology of the universe and in his deep study of the Judaic kabbalah. He wrote about both in his masterful sermons over the years that he served in the rabbinate, and in two books that he published.[1]

Many thoughtful Jews like my father sought out answers to life's mysteries in the works of Jewish mysticism. But know well that Orthodox Jews and rabbis were not and are not the only people who have searched for answers and meanings in mystical books like the Zohar.

In recent years a wider public has been able to read and interpret these marvelous texts sometimes through study of the original book in Aramaic and often via translations into English with the help of learned analyses and summaries.

In the past generation some celebrities both Jewish and not, some from the world of entertainment and the arts, have brought in recent times wider attention to the Zohar and Kabbalah.

Performers like the popular singers Madonna and Arianna Grande for instance have engaged in Zohar study and found creative inspiration in its texts. Madonna, a famous disciple of the Kabbalah Center, claims to have integrated Kabbalistic themes and ideas in her songs, performances, video-clips, and in her children's books.

In 2006 I observed on my blog[2] that, superstar singer and dancer Madonna is not a Jew. She was born and brought up Catholic. However she was linked in the past to the Jewish mystical practice of Kabbalah.

On Madonna's 2005 album, "Confessions on a Dance Floor"[3] the tenth track is controversial because it is called *Isaac* and contains allusions to the Kabbalah. Rabbis in Israel (mistakenly) thought Madonna was trying to cash in on the good name of Isaac Luria, the Ari, the great founder of Lurianic Kabbalah. So those good men condemned the singer and the album. It turns out that the singer named this song in homage to her quite living London spiritual guide, a Mr. Yitzhak Sinwani—Isaac is his English name. There are elements of Jewish chant in this song with strings and guitars and guts and emotion—with a spiritual vibe. Yitzhak Sinwani of the London Kabbalah Centre does sing several stanzas on the song in Aramaic and provides the soft-spoken English coda at its end. Madonna said to the press that the Aramaic chant by Yitzhak in the song made her cry. "I had tears in my eyes and did not even know what he was singing about," she told AOL. "Then he told me and I cried even more."

In fact, this is not the Zohar or traditional Kabbalah. It is a pop-star Madonna stringing together poetically some lines about heaven and angels and light and doors that are locked. Everyone that sings of light in heaven is not a Kabbalist. And locked doors of the heart are a classic Madonna theme. *Open Your Heart* is a Madonna standard from her *True Blue* album of 1986. *Im ninalu* is in fact the title of a Hebrew and Jewish-Yemenite piyyut written by the 17th century Yemeni poet Rabbi Shalom Shabazi[4].

Another celebrity artist, Ariana Grande, in 2022 more popular by far than the super celebrity Madonna, said in the recent past about her once meeting Madonna (as told to V Magazine when Grande was 22 years old): "Grande befriended

---

[1] *Whence and Wherefore: The Cosmological Destiny of Man Scientifically and Philosophically Considered*, NY, 1978 republished through Amazon publishing in 2021 and *Idra Zuta Kadisha: The Lesser Holy Assembly. Aramaic Text and English Translation*, NY, 1977

[2] Blog link: https://tzvee.blogspot.com/2005/12/madonna-still-not-kabbalist.html

[3] Album link: http://www.amazon.com/Confessions-On-A-Dance-Floor/dp/B0011Z0YFE?ie=UTF8&tag=zahavyinc&link_code=btl&camp=213689&creative=392969

[4] https://he.wikipedia.org/wiki/%D7%90%D7%9D_%D7%A0%D7%A0%D7%A2%D7%9C%D7%95

Madonna because of their shared interest in the mystical religion..." "I practice Kabbalah as well, so that was one of the first things she (Madonna) mentioned, because I had my Zohar in my pocket."[5]

Yes, there are published mini-Zohar book editions—partial texts for sale—that indeed will fit in one's pocket. This edition that you hold in your hands is not one of those small volumes.

INTRODUCTION TO THE ZOHAR

By Dr. Joshua Abelson

If the world's literature holds any book which might truly be described as being sealed with seven seals, that book is the Zohar. What with the difficulties and obscurities clustering round its origin and authorship, what with the baffling obscurities of its language, style, and contents, and what with the problems that must inevitably be presented by a book which is not a homogeneous work but a compilation pieced together at times and under circumstances which are by no means clear, the task of bringing out, for the first time, a complete English translation needs not only learning but much moral courage as well.

No one will deny that an English rendering of such a pivotal Hebrew work as the Zohar is long overdue. For the Zohar is the fundamental book of Jewish Cabbalism. It is the premier textbook of medieval Jewish mysticism. If, as Professor Rufus Jones has so finely said, 'mysticism is religion in its most acute, intense, and living stage', then it follows that Jewish mysticism as enshrined and taught in the Zohar represents Judaism in its 'most acute, intense, and living stage'. This is no small prerogative. But how are both Jews and Christians to get to know these quintessential characteristics of the Jewish religion if they are locked up and secreted in a book whose language, style, and contents no one but a deeply accomplished Hebraist can comprehend? As a matter of fact, Jews are not infrequently blamed for what is regarded on their part as some mysterious desire to keep their spiritual and literary treasures all to themselves, stored away in the trappings of a strange language like Rabbinic Hebrew or Aramaic, and hence inaccessible to the average honest seeker after knowledge. This translation will, it is to be hoped, serve to remedy the defect as well as to roll away the implied reproach.

The Zohar is in form a Commentary on the Pentateuch, and its language is partly Aramaic and partly Hebrew. It purports to be a record of discourses carried on between Rabbi Simeon ben Yohai, who lived in the second century of the common era, and certain contemporary Jewish mystical exegetes. There is a story in the Talmud that Simeon and his son, in order to escape the fury of the Roman persecution, hid themselves in a cave for thirteen years, during which they gave themselves up to those mystical speculations on God, Torah, and the universe which compose the Zohar. Simeon came thus to be regarded as the author of the Zohar. But scholarship and research have forced us to dismiss this sup position as nothing more than legend. Even the most superficial perusal of any section of the Zohar will convince the reader of the absurdity of this view of its high antiquity. The merest tyro in Rabbinic literature will find in the Zohar a great many Rabbinic comments and observations which belong without question to a period (and periods) later than that in which Simeon ben Yohai lived. A legend of a more elaborate type, and one which modern critics have been much more ready to accept, attributes the Zohar to a thirteenth-century Cabbalistic writer, Moses de Leon, of Granada in Spain, who certainly was the first to make it known to the general public. Moses de Leon published the Zohar as the work of Simeon ben Yohai, professing to have transcribed the copies which he issued from an ancient manuscript which had come into his possession. After his death, however, his widow confessed that her husband possessed no such manuscript, and that he wrote the work himself. When asked why he did not publish the book in his own name but chose that of Simeon ben Yohai, she replied that her husband always said that a book by a miracle-working Rabbi like Simeon ben Yohai would prove more lucrative than a book bearing his own name.

Though the widow's story bristles with contradictions and absurdities, many Jewish writers and scholars have maintained that de Leon was the sole author of the Zohar. On the other hand, many books have been written, mainly in Hebrew, to show that the Zohar is a work of great antiquity and that its authorship can very properly and suitably be attributed to the ancient Sage, Simeon ben Yohai. But neither of these views can hold water in the light of all the facts as we know them. No student of the Zohar, indeed no competent assessor of literature generally, can believe that it ever could have emanated from the brain of one man. To call it a book is to misname it. It is a literature—a literature of immense variety and compass. It embraces so many diverse themes, it holds within its folds such a number of views and doctrines which are often mutually irreconcilable, that it cannot possibly be the production of one individual, however gifted. And to credit a Rabbi of the second century with the authorship of a book which describes the sayings and doings of men who lived long after his time, is to adopt a standpoint which no one in these times will seriously countenance.

---

[5] Grande, 22, told this to V Magazine as reported here: https://www.indiatvnews.com/lifestyle/news/ariana-grande-bonds-with-madonna-over-kabbalah-5566.html

The Zohar in English

The Zohar is a congeries of treatises, texts, extracts or fragments of texts, belonging to different periods, but all resembling one another in their method of mystical interpretation of the Torah as well as in the baffling anonymity in which they are shrouded. The ways in which these component parts are pieced together strikes one as arbitrary in the extreme. They often appear to bear little or no relation to that which precedes or follows. The arrangement is all so destitute of design that it might have been done by the printers and publishers of the first edition whenever they felt that it suited their convenience or whenever they happened to come across some anonymous fragments which, in their unlearned opinion, could be suitably interpolated at a certain point in the main text.

From a survey of the whole subject, one is drawn irresistibly to the conclusion that the Zohar, so far from being a homogeneous work, is a compilation of a mass of material drawn from many strata of Jewish and non-Jewish mystical thought and covering numerous centuries. Many of both its fundamental and subsidiary teachings are to be found in the oldest portions of the Babylonian and Palestinian Talmuds, as well as in that large mass of Jewish Apocalyptic literature which was produced in the centuries immediately before and after the destruction of the second Temple. Discussions on Jewish law and Biblical interpretations (which are often almost verbal repetitions of passages to be found in the two recensions of the Talmud), speculations on theology, theosophy, and cosmogony which have their counterpart in Hellenistic literature and which sometimes show resemblances to certain ideas contained in the Zend Avesta a fact which has induced some scholars to find a good deal of the background of the Zohar in the religion of ancient Zoroastrianism-the allegorical type of exegesis of which Philo is the leading exponent, Gnostic theories concerning the relation between the human and the divine, echoes of medieval beliefs regarding astrology, physiognomy, necromancy, magic, and metempsychosis which are alien to the Jewish spirit, all these elements jostle one another at random in the pages of the Zohar. A veritable storehouse of anachronisms, incongruities and surprises!

And yet, with all its faults, the Zohar appeals to many Jews in a way that makes them regard it as the most sacred of sacred books! For it mirrors Judaism as an intensely vital religion of the spirit. More overpoweringly than any other book or code, more even than the Bible, does it give to the Jew the conviction of an inner, unseen, spiritual universe an eternal moral order.

The constituent parts of the Zohar are as follows: There is (i) the main portion which bears the general title of 'Sefer Ha-Zohar'. To this are attached (ii) the 'Sifra-di-Tseniuta' ('The Book of the Veiled Mystery'), consisting of five chapters inserted in the Book of Exodus and dealing with the mysteries of creation, the human soul and the relation between spirit and matter. (iii) 'Sitré Torah' ('Secrets of the Torah'), treating largely of Cabbalistic angelology and the mysteries clustering round the Divine Name and the Divine Unity. (iv) 'Raya Mehemna' ('The True Shepherd', Pastor Fidelis), which, besides dealing with topics similar to the foregoing, lays down definite precepts and rules of conduct, the exegesis being usually introduced with the words 'The true shepherd saith'-the true shepherd being Moses. (v) 'Midrash Ha-ne'lam' ('Recondite Exposition'), which contains a great deal of Scriptural exposition by the method of 'Gematria', i.e. the permutations and combinations of the letters of the Hebrew alphabet and the Hebrew numerals. It also contains some allegorical exegesis of Scripture reminding one of the methods of Philo. (vi) 'Tosefta' ('Additions'), some stray fragmentary supplements to the main exegesis of the Zohar in which are contained references to the Sefiroth. (vii) 'Hekaloth' ('halls' or 'palaces'), wherein are pictured with a dazzling literality the abodes of paradise and hell, the dwelling-places of the varying grades of the angelic hosts and their dealings with the souls of men. There are also in this section several recondite allusions to astrology and magic. (viii) The Idra Rabba ('Greater Synod') and Idra Zuta ('Lesser Synod'), which are amplifications of (ii). Speaking generally, none of these sections can be said to differ very greatly from any other or from the main body of the Zohar, either in style or contents. There is considerable overlapping. There is also a frequent repetition of the same theme, the same treatment, even the same words.

The first printed edition of the Zohar appeared almost simultaneously in two different places, viz. Mantua and Cremona, in 1588-90. Later editions are those of Lublin, 1623; Amsterdam, 1714 and 1805; Constantinople, 1736; and Venice. The Mantua edition, with a long and elaborate Introduction by Isaac de Lattes, has always had the greatest vogue, nearly all subsequent editions being based upon the Mantua text. An interesting fact is that almost simultaneously with the publication of the first Mantua edition-but to all appearance quite independently of it-there was issued from the same press the Tikkuné Ha-Zohar ("Emendations to the Zohar"), a book written in Aramaic and with the same kind of subject-matter as the Zohar. Another similar work which has always enjoyed great popularity, and which first saw the light at Salonika in 1597, is the Zohar Hadash ("The New Zohar"), which is an independent mystical commentary on the same lines as the Zohar, but embracing, in addition to the Pentateuch, the 'Five Megilloth' (Scrolls), viz. the Song of Songs, Ruth, Lamentations, Ecclesiastes, and Esther.

The Zohar humbly professes to be no more than a Commentary on the Pentateuch; and it might hence be interesting to hear its own expressed views on the correct method of Biblical exegesis. It says: "Woe unto those who see in the Law nothing but simple narratives and ordinary words!" Were this really the case, then could we, even today, compose a Law equally worthy of admiration. But it is all quite otherwise.... Every word of the Law contains an elevated sense and a sublime mystery. The narratives of the Law are but the raiment in which it is swathed. Woe unto him who mistakes the raiment for the Law itself! It was to avert such a calamity that David prayed, "Open mine eyes that I might behold wondrous things out of thy Law". Another passage states similarly, but even more strikingly: 'If the Law merely consisted of ordinary words and narratives like the stories of Esau, Hagar, and Laban, or like the words which were spoken by Balaam's ass or by Balaam himself, why should it have been called the Law of Truth, the perfect Law, the faithful testimony of God?'

These statements may well be regarded as a sort of rationale of the aim and purpose of the Zoharic exegesis; and they summarise the basic characteristics of all schools of Cabbalistic interpretation, both before and after the Zohar. Indeed, herein may be said to lie the undying service which Cabbalism has rendered to Judaism, whether as creed or as life. A too literal interpretation of the words of Scripture giving Judaism the appearance of being nothing more than an ordered legalism, an apotheosis of the 'letter which killeth', a formal and petrified system of external commands bereft of all spirit and denying all freedom to the individual—these have been, and are still in some quarters, the blemishes and shortcomings cast in the teeth of Rabbinic Judaism. The supreme rebutter of such taunts and objections is Cabbalah. The arid field of Rabbinism was always kept well-watered and fresh by the living streams of Cabbalistic lore. Mystic schools and mystic circles flourished at nearly every important epoch of Jewish history, and the object of their studies was to penetrate to the true meaning hidden beneath the letter of Scripture. Some of the foremost Jewish legalists were also pronounced Cabbalists. And this esoteric study of the Law which is the quintessence of Cabbalah gave to its devotees not a shackled creed comprehended in formulæ, but a religion of intense spiritual possibilities, rendering the Jew capable of a vivid sense of the nearness of God and filling him with a constant longing for communion with Him.

Illustrations of the way in which the Zohar penetrates the outer shell of Scripture in order to extract the esoteric kernel within could be quoted, did not space forbid, in great abundance. I will only refer here to some specimens of Zoharic exegesis on the Psalms which are frequently interspersed in the exegesis on the Pentateuchal books. Thus, Psalm XXXIII, 6, says: "By the word of the Lord were the heavens made; and all the hosts of them by the breath of his mouth." This verse gives the impetus to a whole series of mystic axioms proving that the world rests on Divine spirit. The 'upper universe' resembles the 'lower universe', and both find their unity in God. Earth is a copy of Heaven. Heaven is a copy of earth. They are no duality but an absolute unity. Any other view of the universe is irreligious because it makes an *alma deperuda* (a world of division), an idea which, by the way, is paralleled by Blake's argument that the universe as we know it, i.e. the sheer material unspiritual universe, is the result of the fall of the one life from unity into division. Again, Psalm CXLV, 18, declares: "The Lord is near unto all them that call upon him, to all that call upon him in truth." What is the meaning of the phrase 'in truth', asks the Zohar? And the reply is 'a knowledge of how to declare the Divine Unity in prayer. For in this knowledge consists the service of the Holy King; and whosoever knows how to declare the Divine Unity is a helper in establishing that one unique nation of whom it is said, "And who is like thy people Israel, one unique nation in the earth?" And when all those who know how to declare the Divine Unity do so in the right way, then are all the walls of darkness cleft in twain. The face of the Heavenly King is revealed. There is light unto all. The "realms above" as well as the "realms below" draw unto themselves blessings without end. In these quaintly original remarks on the effects wrought by prayer, there are many points which are of fundamental importance in Jewish mystical teaching of all ages. The declaration of the Divine Unity in prayer does not mean merely the clear and unequivocal pronouncement of the word Echad (One). It goes. much deeper. It implies the conviction that all things should be regarded as so many manifestations of the Divine whose vivifying power is never for an instant withdrawn from the world which it animates. To pray is thus, in the last resort, to become absorbed in God; and only in the enjoyment of such an experience does man find light, truth, and bliss, both for himself and for others. This type of theological doctrine comes to the front more particularly in the later Cabbalists, i.e. the Hassidic literature, starting with Israel Baalshem.

The fundamental note in the Zohar's treatment of the Divine nature is the attempt to combine the transcendent and immanent aspects of the Deity in a single concept. Not that it does this with a strictly scientific consistency. Far from it. God, in the Zohar, is the great Unknowable, the Supreme Incomprehensible. God is exalted above human understanding; the depths of the Divine wisdom are beyond human penetration. To quote the words of the Idra Rabba, 'God is the most ancient of the ancient, the mystery of mysteries, the unknown of the unknown'. Here we have the doctrine of the Divine Transcendency par excellence. Nevertheless, God in the Zohar is very knowable, very fathomable. The universe as well as man's heart reveal His infinite power and infinite love. Nay, even the human organs and limbs reflect certain static and dynamic characteristics of Deity. The world is an image of the Divine. There is a constant and conscious interaction between 'the above' (the celestial kingdom) and 'the below' (the mundane kingdom). Here we have the doctrine of the Divine immanence par excellence. It is the ceaseless interweaving of these two doctrines in the pages of the Zohar that supplies the book with its uncompromisingly spiritual atmosphere. Without this combination, the Zohar would be a false presentation of Judaism. Had it emphasized exclusively a 'mysterious' and 'unknowable' Deity, it would but have supplied one more weapon to the armoury of the Pauline critics of a 'legalistic' Judaism. On the other hand, an unbalanced insistence on the doctrine that the world is but a manifestation or mirror of a Divine life pulsating everywhere would lead men away to a Spinozistic pantheism a creed which is at out-and-out variance with the postulates of Jewish theism. The transcendent God of the Cabbalah, called the En Sof (the limitless one), becomes immanent in the cosmos by a species of 'flowings forth' or emanations, which in their turn give rise to 'four universes', viz. (a) Atsiluth; (b) Beriah; (c) Yetsirah; (d) Asiah, i.e. Emanation, Creation, Formation, and Action, respectively. These 'four universes' are apportioned among 'Ten Sefiroth', which are named as follows: (a) Kether (The Crown); (b) Hokmah (Wisdom); (c) Binah (Understanding); (d) Hesed (Mercy); (e) Geburah (Force or Severity); (f) Tifereth (Beauty); (g) Nezaḥ (Victory); (h) Hod (Glory); (i) Yesod (Foundation); (j) Malkuth (Kingdom); These names are, on the surface, largely arbitrary and conventional; and as for the way in which these 'Ten Sefiroth' are allocated to the worlds of Cabbalism— this is an extremely complicated theme into the consideration of which it is not possible to enter in the limited space of an Introduction such as this.

The feature in the Jewish Cabbalistic literature which is calculated to recommend it for all time to the admiration of scholars and thinkers is the high place which it accords to the human soul. The Zohar is replete with references to the dominating part played by man's soul in the furtherance of his own good, as well as in the development of all these 'universes' with whose workings man is so intensely and inevitably bound up. Man is man only because of his soul. On this point the Zohar is far more definite and uncompromising than the Bible and the Talmud. A statement like 'For dust thou art and unto dust shalt thou return' (Genesis III, 19) would be quite out of keeping with Zoharic theology. And so would the remark of the pessimist Ecclesiastes: 'And the preeminence of man over beast is nought, for all is vanity' (Eccl. III, 19). The whole atmosphere cast by the Zohar around these spiritual problems is far warmer and lighter, more cheering and more encouraging. The Mishnah (Aboth III, 1) declares, 'Know whence thou camest: from a putrefying drop; and whither thou art going: to a place of dust, worms, and maggots.' Man's origin is envisaged by the Zohar in a far more refined and poetic outlook than this; and as for man's destiny in the hereafter, it is no mere period of judgement before a Heavenly Tribunal, but a series of progressive spiritual experiences in many forms until at the last there is a union of the soul with the Divine source whence it emanated.

Man, says the Zohar, was 'created' on the 'sixth day', because he is, in himself, a noble epitome of the cosmos. And he is this by reason of the infinite association of his soul with the Sefiroth. The 'upper' and the 'lower' world both find their meeting point in him. He is a *Shekinta Ta-ta-aa*, i.e. a Divine Presence on earth.

The Soul, as a spiritual entity playing the highest of high parts in man's relations with the Unseen, is well brought to the front in all branches of the medieval Cabbalah. The Zohar warns us against thinking that man is made up solely of flesh and skin, veins and sinews. Man's skin typifies the firmament, which extends everywhere and covers everything. His flesh typifies the evil side of the universe, i.e. the elements which are purely exterior, of sense. The sinews and veins symbolise the 'Celestial chariot' (the Merkabah), being the interior forces of man which are the servitors of God. But all these are merely an outward covering. In the kingdom of man's soul there are processes going on which are the exact counter part of those going on in the 'upper world'. The soul is threefold. There is (i) Neshamah, which is the highest phase of its existence. (ii) Ruah, which is the seat of good and evil, the abode of the moral attributes. (iii) Nefesh, which is the grosser side of spirit and is *en rapport* with the body and the cause of all the movements and instincts of the physical life. Each of these three constituents of the soul has its source in some one or other of the ten Sefiroth.

The soul enjoyed a heavenly pre-existence. This idea is already found in the Talmud and is deduced from certain passages in the Hebrew Bible. Whether the old Rabbis discovered the idea independently, or whether they merely adapted it from the teaching of Plato is a moot point. Complementary to this doctrine of pre-existence is that of the transmigration of the soul-metempsychosis—which is taught in the Zohar by way of a solution of the eternally vexing problem of why the wicked prosper. The famous post Zoharic Cabbalist, Isaac Luria (1534-72), was of opinion that all souls were born with Adam, and that every human being received at birth, through Divine intervention, the soul that fitted it. All souls born with Adam constituted originally one and one only great soul. When Adam sinned through disobedience, this one comprehensive soul born with him and of which every future human being was, at birth, to receive a microscopic fragment, became involved in sin. But all these tainted souls possess the potentiality and hence have the duty of cleansing themselves and working themselves up to a high level of destiny. This tenet was widely held by the Cabbalists and suggested to them their many strange theories about the chequered wanderings of the soul. The soul's dross cannot be cast off in the course of one lifetime. It must pass through many bodies and experience many terrestrial existences, each one higher than the other, before it can reach the pinnacle of perfection—union with God— which is its predestined end.

The Cabbalistic successors of Luria went even further, and said that souls wandered on earth and could sometimes enter the bodily framework of some living person, so as to help him to fulfil certain religious duties which he had neglected.

INTRODUCTION TO THE ZOHAR

The soul, says the mystic of all ages and creeds, seeks to enter consciously into the Presence of God. And this idea of the soul's unquenchable yearning to be united with its Divine source is reiterated under many forms in all parts of the Zohar and lends to it a charm as well as a lightness of touch which serve as a relief to the excessively sombre and solemn tone of most of the book. It is the poetry of the Zohar. Man's intimacy with God, the soul's union with Him, are described in sexual terminology. It is the union of the male with the female. The symbolism is sometimes liable to strike the reader as offensively crude in some of its details; and the Zohar has more than once had to suffer for this the cheap sneers of detractors. But this is only the result of shallow knowledge and false perspective. On deeper study and reflection these sexual references will be found to be just as admissible as are the sexual similes and analogies which pervade the writings of the most refined and elegant of poets and romancers. For the Zohar speaks throughout of cosmic union—a coming together, a fusion, of all the manifold universes 'above' and 'below'. The worlds above are 'married' to the worlds below. And man, who, mainly by reason of his soul, is a denizen of these multiple worlds, becomes, whilst striving after communion with the Divine, a sharer in these cosmic acts of intercourse. Of course, it will be recollected. that the amorous sentiments which find such bold expression in the Old Testament book of the Song of Songs were made to bear a strongly allegoric-mystic interpretation in the old homilies of the Midrashic literature. And there can be little doubt that these pictures of conjugal relations as applied to express man's consummated longing for the Divine must have largely prepared the way for those numerous and often obscure allusions which constitute what has been called the 'sex-mystery' of the Zohar.

That much of the mystic speculation to be found in the Zohar dates back to the early centuries before and after the destruction of the second Temple is a point upon which there is now unanimous agreement amongst scholars. The early Jewish Apocalyptic and magical literature, the Palestinian and Babylonian Talmuds, the huge and variegated crop of Midrashic literature which continued to spring up for many years after the completion of the Talmud—all these monuments of early Jewish interpretative activity scintillate with mystic allusions which found incorporation in many modified forms in the pages of the Zohar. Much of this early speculation was never committed to writing. It was transmitted orally from generation to generation. Herein, by the way, lies the meaning of Cabbalah: oral tradition. And the Zohar was probably the first important book in which these floating traditions were preserved in writing. Schools and circles wherein Cabbalah was meditated upon had started as early as the sixth century in Galilee, and these, after disappearing for some centuries owing to the fluctuating fortunes of the Jews, were revived in the twelfth and thirteenth centuries under the influence of such great Talmudic luminaries as Moses Nahmanides, Solomon ben Adrath, and others. In the middle of the sixteenth century, Isaac Luria, who had learnt Cabbalah in Egypt, founded a new mystical school at Safed, in Galilee, then the centre of Jewish learning. He gathered round him a host of disciples, many of them, like Elijah de Vidas and Joseph Hagiz, being themselves distinguished writers of Cabbalistic works. Luria himself wrote nothing. His utterances were taken down in writing by his most prominent disciple, Hayyim Vital Calabreze, whose book *Ets Hayyim* shows how Luria developed many of the leading ideas of the Zohar and inaugurated a new mystic system in Judaism, a system wherein Messianic theology and Messianic expectations held a central place. Luria's enlarged and elaborated conceptions of Cabbalah found numerous enthusiastic disciples; and the Zohar, as the result of a too extravagant emphasis on certain Messianic comments contained within it, emerged, by an unhappy fate, as the source whence the pseudo-Messiah, Sabbatai Zevi (1626-76), presumed to have drawn the warrant for his dramatically pretentious career.

It goes without saying that the mysticism of the Zohar, emphasizing as it does the efficacy of prayer, must have influenced considerably the Hebrew Prayer Book, as well as the Divine Service of the Synagogue and certain aspects of Jewish ceremonial observance. Much of the extravagant Zoharic angelology came to find a place in the liturgy, as also much Zoharic doctrine concerning the secrets of the supra-mundane universe and the mysteries, both painful and pleasurable, of the life hereafter. Many mystical formulas, mystical names and symbols intermixed with many arithmetical and astrological references, also became interpolated within the pages of the Prayer Book. Most of this highly pictorial type of prayer material has been eliminated from the modern worship of the Synagogue because of its incongruity with the prevailing conceptions of the Deity; but in spite of this weeding-out, it may still be said that our Jewish liturgy of today scintillates with many a Zoharic phrase and idea which are a decided gain to the spirituality of Jewish home or synagogue ritual. One is inclined to differ in this respect from Leopold Zunz when he says: Although the more respectable mystics did something for spiritual religion and for devotion as opposed to thoughtless formalism, yet the liturgy lost more than it gained by their influence' (D. Ritus, p. 24). The ceremony of blowing the Shofar on Rosh Ha-Shanah gains rather than loses in impressiveness by the accompanying Zoharic prayers which ask that 'the angels emanating from the Shofar may bring the prayers of Israel to the Divine hearing.' Taken literally, the idea jars, of course, on our intelligence. But the Zoharic mysticism, like the mysticism of all other religions and literatures, demands the higher interpretation. And on this basis the blowing of the Shofar, far from being a mere stereotyped act of observance of the letter of the Law, rises to become the outward expression of one more of the many mystical beliefs in the unseen spiritual agencies uniting the human with the Divine—an outstanding Zoharic doctrine. Similarly in the case of the prayer, *B'rich Sh'meh Ve'athreh*, recited before the Reading of the Law on Sabbaths and Festivals. The Zohar introduces it with these words: "When the scroll is taken out in the assembly to read therein, the Gates of the heavens of mercy open and the celestial love awakes." The prayer is a truly noble one, teeming with a vivid, sense of the nearness of God, combined with an ever-felt and never-satisfied longing for communion with Him by means of the Torah—a thought which is ubiquitous in the Zohar. A modified and modernised adoption of a little more Zoharic sentiment to the Jewish liturgy of today would be a welcome improvement! By thus introducing a tinge of 'Ecstasy', of direct intuition of God, into Jewish prayer; by making it less of a merely external religious exercise and more of a means for transcending earthly affairs for a time, there would be restored to prayer something of the position it must have occupied in the days of the Hebrew Psalmist, as well as something of the intensely individual and devotional part which it played in the neo-Hassidic mysticism of the eighteenth century.

Besides influencing the liturgy, the Zohar, as is only to be expected from a book which stimulates the imagination and the feelings, has left numerous traces in the medieval religious poetry outside the synagogue. Its allegorism, its symbolism, its erotic terminology, proved excellent material for portraying the ceaseless yearnings of the human heart for union with the Infinite; and the reader is often startled at the ingenuity with which many a simple and innocent Biblical word or phrase is poetically worked up to indicate the physical as well as the spiritual mysteries which surround the Deity and the effort of man to become finally absorbed in Him by means of prayer, Torah study and contemplation.

For some centuries after its first appearance, the Zohar was generally regarded by the Jews as an integral part of the literature of Torah, like the Talmud and the Midrash, and, like them, it was considered one of the subjects of religious study, of talmud torah. It was, in fact, generally known as the 'Midrash of R. Simeon ben Yohai'. Unlike the Talmud, however, it was what might be called an optional subject in the curriculum of Torah study; a man could be a great Jewish scholar without knowing anything of the Zohar or the Cabbalah. Still, there was a merit in studying them also. A breach, however, arose between the Talmudists and the Cabbalists. after the failure of the Messianic movement of Sabbatai Zevi in the middle of the seventeenth century. The extravagances of Zevi and his followers were largely inspired by the Zohar, and this work in consequence fell into suspicion and disfavour with a large number of Talmudists. This antipathy to the Zohar found its culmination in a treatise (in *Mitpahat Sefarim*) written in the middle of the eighteenth century by the great Talmudical scholar, Jacob Emden of Altona, in which it is denounced as being for the most part the work of an impostor. Emden was led to investigate the Zohar through his desire to extirpate the Shabbetaean heresy which still lingered in his day. His examination of the Zohar shows considerable critical acumen, and his conclusions have been adopted by a large number of orthodox Jews.

The place to be assigned to the Zohar in the scheme of Jewish study is also one of the fundamental points at issue between the sect of Hassidim, founded by Israel Baalshem in the eighteenth century, and their opponents in Poland and Lithuania, known as the 'Mithnagedim'. The controversy between the two sects is interesting not only in itself but also for the light it sheds upon many aspects of the Jewish religious and social life of those times. It was a struggle for supremacy between Rabbinic orthodoxy, based upon the authority of the Talmud, and the mystic-emotional-spiritual Judaism founded upon the Zoharic interpretation of the Torah. It was a contest between two principles in Judaism, the formalism of dogmatic ritual and the direct religious sentiment. Whilst Rabbinical orthodoxy, without rejecting the Zohar, regarded the ideal Jewish life as one of obedience to law founded upon the study of the Talmud and the Codes, Hassidic Judaism based itself upon the Zohar, maintaining that the quintessence of the Jewish religion lay in the cultivation of a sincere love of God, combined with a warm faith and deep belief in the efficacy of prayer. This does not imply that the Hassidim despised Talmudic scholarship or flouted the traditional Rabbinic ordinances. What it does imply is that Hassidism aimed at altering the centre of gravity of the Jewish religious life by introducing into it a new 'spirituality'. This 'spirituality' derived from the Zohar consisted in the conviction that there is an unbroken intercourse between the world of the Deity and the world of humanity; that these worlds have a reciprocal influence upon one another; and that prayer should be an ecstatic communion with God, so as to unite the human life with Him who is 'the life of all worlds'. It is not given to all men to attain this exalted state. But the man who attains it is, in the Hassidic sense, the Tsaddik who, as a result, possesses a degree of prophetic insight and a power to work miracles.

The study of the Zohar, as well as of the Cabbalistic writings which succeeded it, attracted a great many noted Christian scholars of the past. William Postel, who translated the *Sefer Yetsirah* into Latin (Paris, 1552), seems to have been the first Christian to introduce the mysteries of the Cabbalah to the learned circles of Europe. But the first Christian into whose hands the Zohar came was Pico della Mirandola, who wrote short theses in Latin about it. He was, too, the first Christian to declare that the Zohar contains. elements which are capable of a Christian construction. He seems to have believed that the doctrines concerning the Trinity, Original Sin, and the Incarnation could be deduced from its pages. John Reuchlin, another ardent student of Jewish occultism, wrote *De Arte Cabalistica*, which he dedicated to Leo X, and the object of which was to prove from the post-Zoharic writers on Cabbalism that the Messiah had already appeared. Petrius Galatinus, a contemporary of Reuchlin, published, in 1516, *De Arcanis Catholicae Veritatis*, in which the Zoharic teachings are made to reflect many of the cardinal doctrines of Christianity. The complete list of all the other Christian students would be too long to mention here. Outstanding names are those of Alabaster, Gasparellus, and Athanasius Kircher. But the greatest of all these was Knorr von Rosenroth, whose *Kabbalah Denudata*, first published at Sulzbach in 1677-8 and translated into English by S. L. Macgregor Mathers (London, 1887), contains much valuable material and has proved particularly useful to Christian scholars unable to read the Hebrew and Aramaic originals. A new French translation of the whole of the Zohar has recently been made by M. Jean de Pauly and published posthumously by M. Emil Lafuma-Giraud (1906). Grateful reference is also due to the many writings on all aspects of the Zohar by the celebrated scholar, Mr. Arthur Edward Waite.

It is unnecessary to mention here that many of the leading Jewish theologians of the nineteenth century have done much in the way of giving an enlightened and objective presentation of the mysterious and uncanny world in which the Zohar lives and moves and has its being. Adolph Franck's *La Kabbale*, first published in Paris in 1843, contains long and representative extracts from the Zohar in a beautifully phrased French translation. In German there are numerous monographs and partial translations by Zunz, Jost, Jellinek, Joel, Graetz, and Steinschneider. In Hebrew, Rapaport, Harkavy, and others have made important contributions. During the present century there has been a distinct revival of interest in the literature of the Hassidim from the time of Baalshem, and much has been written by Kahana, Horodetsky, Dubnow, and others, mainly in Hebrew, to show that these devotees of the mystic side of Jewish life and religion were not, as is popularly supposed, half-crazy visionaries living in a universe peopled by the figments of their own degenerate brains, but men of intellect, scholarship, and sound sense who aimed at bringing back to Jewish organised communal life a breath of that mystic sentiment and emotion which are the aromatic life-essence of religion, and which are indispensable to Judaism if it is to continue to play its predestined part of bringing mankind 'under the wings of the Shekinah'.

It has been said that every man is born either a Platonist or an Aristotelian. This means that there is an innate predisposition in every one of us to assimilate certain fixed forms of thought from which we cannot be diverted, no matter what future training, education, or experience we may receive. The Jews during the Middle Ages, both before and after the appearance of the Zohar, were (largely through the influence of Maimonides) amongst the staunchest supporters of Aristotle. Whilst the Aristotelian philosophy stands immortalised in the writings of the leading Jewish theologians of medieval times, the philosophy of Plato finds but a mere handful of exponents, eminent though these be. Hence there has arisen the commonly accepted belief that Jews are by nature rationalists rather than mystics. Is this belief correct? Does it square with the facts? I think not. Judaism is unquestionably and supremely a religion of reason. But, paradoxically enough, it only made its appeal to the Jew and held him tightly in its grip because he was—and is—by nature and inclination a mystic. The *Moreh Nebuchim* of Maimonides was the great Jewish philosophical exposition in the Middle Ages, of the 'Supremacy of Reason' in Judaism. But the Jew in the mass knew it not. It was never a people's book. But the Zohar was a people's book. It struck a chord in whose music the Jew heard:

The bubblings of the springs that feed the world.

And the impress went down to the roots of his being. However much in accord with reason Judaism may have appeared to the Jew, there were always crises and catastrophes in which he felt that reason failed to solve the tantalising problems involved problems of pain and suffering, of reward and punishment, of the relation between the human and the Divine, of the life here and the life hereafter. The Jew, as a pure rationalist, would have quailed in the face of these enigmas; and Judaism might by now have been but a pale memory. But the Jew believed and lived not by logic but by love, not by ratiocination but by intuition. It was by these standards that he was led on:

To see one changeless Life in all the Lives, And in the Separate, One Inseparable.

In his great book *Belief in God*, Canon Gore says: 'It is by feeling or intuition that the supreme artist gains his profound vision of experience and of God.' The Jew was this supreme artist. For was he not of the spiritual lineage of the Psalmist, who said: 'My heart and my flesh sing for joy unto the living God. With my whole heart have I sought thee; O let me not err from thy commandments'? Though he could not know God, he nevertheless felt that it was given to him to transcend the crushing weight of earthly affairs, to be raised above the grosser hindrances of sense and to become an organ reflecting the Divine life. Such is the standpoint of the true mystic of all the ages. The Jew had it in overflowing measure. And the Jewish book which first and more than any other crystallised these feelings and gave them their overpowering momentum was the Zohar.

DR. JOSHUA ABELSON
Leeds. September 1931

TRANSLATORS' PREFACE

The aim of this translation is, on the one hand, to make the Zohar accessible to English readers, and on the other hand, to afford assistance to those who struggle with its intricacies in the original. For the sake of the latter a good deal has been included which, as far as the former are concerned, might perhaps have been spared, especially if they have never studied the Hebrew Bible. The greater part, however, will probably be intelligible enough, even to those who have no knowledge of Hebrew.

The printed Hebrew editions of the Zohar contain intercalations from other, allied, works, which are paged along with the Zohar itself. These are not included in the present translation, which confines itself to what may be called the Zohar proper. Certain individual passages have also been omitted for reasons given where they occur. There are also minor omissions (indicated by the ellipsis sign...) of passages containing plays upon Hebrew words and similar matter unsuitable for translation. With these qualifications, the translation may be regarded as complete for the part of the text covered by the first volume, viz. up to the end of Vayera (p. 120b).

Certain parts of the Zohar—notably the comments on the opening sections of Genesis—are highly enigmatical, and in the absence of an authentic tradition their true meaning is a matter of conjecture. An attempt has been made to give a faithful translation of these also, accounting for practically every word in the original. The result has perhaps been to reproduce only too faithfully the tenebrosity of the original, for which the reader may not be thankful. But he will know, at any rate, that he is getting the authentic Zohar and not the translators' own ideas; and he or she may find assistance in an appendix and a glossary in which the translators indicate their own view of the general trend and purpose of these passages.

In printing the Biblical quotations with which the Zohar abounds, a device has been adopted which it is hoped the reader will find useful. The main text-headings, that is to say, the verses from the Pentateuch which the Zohar sets out to expound in regular order, are printed in capitals. The subsidiary text-headings, that is to say, other verses from the Bible which are made the subject of disquisitions illustrative of the main text, are printed (in this edition) in the ordinary type face. Repetitions of these texts, or incidental quotations, are printed in ordinary type between quotation marks. This distinction will help the reader to see with what subject the Zohar is dealing at any point.

A further effort has been made in this version to bring order and system into the text by careful paragraphing and by a judicious use of parentheses. (It should be remembered that in the original text not only these aids, but even punctuation marks, including full stops, are inserted very sparingly, and then not infrequently at the wrong place.) The result, it is hoped, will be to show that the Zohar is by no means such a jumble as is usually supposed, that with all its discursiveness it follows a well-defined course, and that there is a reason why most of its reflections are inserted just where they are and not somewhere else.

The Biblical references are in all cases to the Hebrew text (or to the American Jewish translation). The renderings have been taken where possible from this version or the English Revised Version. In many cases, however, it has been necessary to give the Hebrew quite a different rendering, in order to make it accord with the lesson which the Zohar seeks to derive from it—often in lordly disregard of the context or even the rules of grammar.

Text and Translation

The translation has been made in the main from the Mantuan text of the Zohar, but occasionally a reading has been adopted from the Amsterdam text. The paging numbers of the Mantuan text have been inserted directly into the translation where they occur in the text in the format e.g., "Zohar: Bereshith, Section 1, Page 1b".

Inasmuch as the Vilna edition, itself, is largely based on the Mantua edition, the discrepancies should be comparatively few. However, there are passages which vary to a greater or a lesser degree. We have noted most of these variances on the appropriate pages. The notes indicating a discrepancy between the Hebrew text and this translation edition are labeled "Note". When an omission or discrepancy is described by the number of lines in the Hebrew, this is always just an approximation.

In addition, this translation has omitted a number of passages because the translators believed they were too complex or involved to be translated into understandable English, or because there were questions concerning the reliability of the text. Such passages are marked either by a long sequence of periods, or, most often, by a note indicating the reason for the omission. These notes are labeled "Tr. note".

The English text here is that of the five-volume edition of the Soncino Zohar. Two terminology changes have been made in this text: the term "Tetragrammaton" has been substituted for the four-letter Hebrew term for the Deity and its English equivalents, and the term "Kah" has been substituted for the two-letter Hebrew term for the Deity. The British spellings of "colour", "centre", etc. have been retained throughout. For the convenience of the reader, the footnotes have been embedded into the body of the text in brackets, and are labeled "Tr. note".

Transliteration

The transliteration of Hebrew words is the generally accepted scholarly and academic one. It does not correspond to the modern Israeli usage, and thus we have "Bereshith" instead of "Bereshit". In addition, to simplify this edition, the 'h' with a dot underneath it (signifying "chet") appears as an ordinary 'h'. The accent over the letter 'e' indicating the "ay" sound is also not shown. Thus, the fifth letter of the Hebrew alphabet appears as He.

Other Sections of the Zohar

This translation presents the main body of the Zohar in which its principal doctrines are expounded, as well as part of the Raya Mehemna. The Raya Mehemna consists of several different passages, which appear to the side of the main Zohar on various pages. Much of it is not translated. In the present version, these passages are placed in a chapter, titled "Raya Mehemna". Each passage starts with a page title identifying where it goes, and the translation of the main text at that place has a note indicating where the Raya Mehemna appeared in the original text. Other portions of the Zohar, e.g., the Tikkunai Zohar are not included in this edition.

Zohar Section 1: Genesis

Zohar: Bereshith, Section 1, Page 1a

PROLOGUE

[Tr. note: This chapter, a preliminary exposition of Gen. I, serves to introduce the reader to the circle of R. Simeon and his colleagues, and to give him an idea of the scope and nature of their discussions. It is somewhat more discursive and fanciful than the main body of the Zohar.]

Rabbi Hizkiah opened his discourse with the text: As a lily among thorns, etc. (S.S. II, 2). 'What', he said, 'does the lily symbolise? It symbolises the Community of Israel. As the lily among thorns is tinged with red and white, so the Community of Israel is visited now with justice and now with mercy; as the lily possesses thirteen leaves, so the Community of Israel is vouchsafed thirteen categories of mercy which surround it on every side. For this reason, the term Elohim (God) mentioned here (in the first verse of Genesis) is separated by thirteen words from the next mention of Elohim, symbolising the thirteen categories of mercy which surround the Community of Israel to protect it. The second mention of Elohim is separated from the third by five words, representing the five strong leaves that surround the lily, symbolic of the five ways of salvation which are the "five gates". This is alluded to in the verse, "I will lift up the cup of salvation" (Ps. CXVI, 13). This is the "cup of benediction", which has to be raised by five fingers and no more, after the model of the lily, which rests on five strong leaves in the shape of five fingers. Thus the lily is a symbol of the cup of benediction. Immediately after the third mention of Elohim appears the light which, so soon as created, was treasured up and enclosed in that brith (covenant) which entered the lily and fructified it, and this is what is called "tree bearing fruit wherein is the seed thereof": and this seed is preserved in the very sign of the covenant. And as the ideal covenant was formed through forty-two copulations, so the engraven ineffable name is formed of the forty-two letters of the work of creation.

IN THE BEGINNING. R. Simeon opened his discourse with the text: The blossoms appeared on the earth, etc. (S. S. II, 12). '"The blossoms", he said, 'refer to the work of creation. "Appeared on the earth",': when? On the third day, as it is written, "And the earth brought forth": they thus then appeared on the earth. "The time of pruning is come" alludes to the fourth day in which "the pruning of the overbearing" (Is. XXV, 5) took place. "And the voice of the turtle" alludes to the fifth day, as it is written, "Let the waters swarm, etc., to produce living creatures". "Is heard" points to the sixth day, as it is written, "Let us make man" (namely him who was destined to say first "we will do" and then "we will hear", for the expression

Zohar: Bereshith, Section 1, Page 1b

in our text, na'aseh, "Let us make man", finds its echo in the expression "na'aseh (we will do) and hear" (Exod. XXIV, 7)); "In our land" implies the day of the Sabbath, which is a copy of the "land of the living" (the world to come, the world of souls, the world of consolations). The following is an alternative exposition: "The blossoms" are the patriarchs who pre-existed in the thought of the Almighty and later entered the world to come, where they were carefully preserved; from thence they issued secretly to become incarnate in the true prophets. Thus when Joseph entered the Holy Land he planted them there, and thus they "appeared on the earth" and revealed themselves there. When do they become visible? When the rainbow betokens that "the time of pruning is come", to wit, the time when the sinners are due to be cut off from the world; and they only escape because "the blossoms appear on the earth": if not for their appearance the sinners would not be left in the world and the world itself would not exist. And who is it that upholds the world and causes the patriarchs to appear? It is the voice of tender children studying the Torah; and for their sakes the world is saved.'

IN THE BEGINNING. R. Eleazar opened his discourse with the text: Lift up your eyes on high and see: who hath created these? (Is. XL, 26). '"Lift up your eyes on high": to which place? To that place to which all eyes are turned, to wit, Petah 'Enaim ("eye-opener"). By doing so, you will know that it is the mysterious Ancient One, whose essence can be sought, but not found, that created these: to wit, Mi (Who?), the same who is called "from (Heb. mi) the extremity of heaven on high", because everything is in His power, and because He is ever to be sought, though mysterious and unrevealable, since further we cannot enquire. That extremity of heaven is called Mi, but there is another lower extremity which is called Mah (What?). The difference between the two is this. The first is the real subject of enquiry, but after a man by means of enquiry and reflection has reached the utmost limit of knowledge, he stops at Mah (What?), as if to say, what knowest thou? what have thy searchings achieved? Everything is as baffling as at the beginning. In allusion to this, it is written "I, Mah, testify against thee, etc." (Lam. II, 13). When the Temple was destroyed a voice went forth and said: "I, Mah, have testified against thee day by day from the days of old," as it is written, "I called heaven and earth to witness against you." (Deut. XXX, 19.) Further, I, Mah, likened myself to thee; I crowned thee with holy crowns, and made thee ruler over the earth, as it is written, "Is this the city that men call the perfection of beauty? etc." (Lam. II, 15), and again, "I called thee Jerusalem that is builded as a city compact together". Further, I, Mah, am equal to thee; in the same plight in which thou, Jerusalem, art here, so I am, as it were, above; just as the holy people does not go up to thee any more in sacred array, so, I swear to thee, I will not ascend on high until the day when thy throngs will again stream to thee here below. And this may be thy consolation, inasmuch as to this extent I am thy equal in all things. But now that thou art in thy present state "thy breach is great like the sea" (Ibid. 13). And lest thou sayest there is for thee no abiding and no healing, "Mi will heal thee" (Ibid.). Of a surety the veiled One, the most High, the sum of all existence will heal thee and uphold thee-Mi, the extremity of heaven above, Mah, as far as the extremity of heaven below. And this is the inheritance of Jacob, he being the "bolt that passes from extremity to extremity" (Exod. XXVI, 28), that is, from the higher, identical with Mi, to the lower, identical with Mah, as he occupies a position in the middle. Hence "Mi (Who) created these".'

Said R. Simeon, 'Eleazar, son of mine, cease thy discourse, that there may be revealed the higher mysteries which remain sealed for the people of this world.' R. Eleazar then fell into silence. R. Simeon wept a while and then said: 'Eleazar, what is meant by the term "these"? Surely not the stars and the other heavenly bodies, since they are always visible, and were created through Mah, as we read, "By the word of the Lord were the heavens made" (Ps. XXXIII, 6). Nor can it imply the things inaccessible to our gaze, since the vocable "these" obviously points to things that are revealed. This mystery remained sealed until one day, whilst I was on the sea-shore, Elijah came and said to me, "Master, what means 'Mi (Who?) created these?' "I said to him, "That refers to the heavens and their hosts, the works of the Holy One, blessed be He, works through the contemplation of which man comes to bless Him, as it is written, 'When I behold thy heavens, the work

Zohar: Bereshith, Section 1, Page 2a

of thy fingers, etc. O Lord our God, how glorious is thy name in all the earth!'" (Ps. VIII, 4-10). Then he said to me, "Master, the Holy One, blessed be He, had a deep secret which He at length revealed at the celestial Academy. It is this. When the most Mysterious wished to reveal Himself, He first produced a single point which was transmuted into a thought, and in this He executed innumerable designs, and engraved innumerable gravings. He further graved within the sacred and mystic lamp a mystic and most holy design, which was a wondrous edifice issuing from the midst of thought.

This is called MI, and was the beginning of the edifice, existent and non-existent, deep-buried, unknowable by name. It was only called MI (Who?). It desired to become manifest and to be called by name. It therefore clothed itself in a refulgent and precious garment and created ELeH (these), and ELeH acquired a name. The letters of the two words intermingled, forming the complete name ELoHIM (God). (When the Israelites sinned in making the golden calf, they alluded to this mystery in saying 'Eleh (these are) thy Gods, O Israel' (Exod. XXXII, 4).) And once MI became combined with ELeH, the name remained for all time. And upon this secret the world is built." Elijah then flew away and vanished out of my sight. And it is from him that I became possessed of this profound mystery.' R. Eleazar and all the companions came and prostrated themselves before him, weeping for joy and saying, 'If we had come into the world only to hear this we should have been content.' R. Simeon said further: 'The heavens and their hosts were created through the medium of Mah (What?), as it is written, "When I behold thy heavens, the work of thy fingers, etc... ' O Lord our God (Adon), Mah, glorious is thy name in all the earth, whose majesty is rehearsed above the heavens." (Ps. VIII, 4, 2). God is "above the heavens" in respect of His name, for He created a light for His light, and one formed a vestment to the other, and so He ascended into the higher name; hence "In the beginning Elohim (God) created", that is, the supernal Elohim. Whereas Mah was not so, nor was it built up until these letters Eleh (from the name Elohim) were drawn from above below, and the Mother lent the Daughter her garments and decked her out gracefully with her own adornments. When did she so adorn her? When all the males (of Israel) appeared before her in accordance with the command "all thy males shall appear before the Lord (Adon) God" (Exod. XXXIV, 23). This term Lord (Adon) is similarly used in the passage "Behold the Ark of the covenant of the Lord (Adon) of all the earth" (Jos. III, 11). Then the letter He (of Mah) departed and her place was taken by Yod (making Mi), and then she decked herself in male garments, harmonizing with "every male in Israel". Other letters, too, Israel drew from on high to that place. Thus it says: "These (Eleh) I remember" (Ps. XLII, 5), i.e., I make mention with my mouth and I pour out my tears, and thus "I make them (the letters) flit" from on high "unto the house of Elohim" (Ibid.) to be Elohim (God) after his form. And with what? "With the voice of song and praise and amidst a festive throng" (Ibid.)' Said R. Eleazar, 'My keeping silence was the means of building the sanctuary above and the sanctuary below. Verily "speech is worth a sela, silence two". Speech is worth a sela, namely, my exposition and remarks on the subject; but silence is worth two, since through my silence two worlds were built together.'

R. Simeon said: 'We will go on to expound the conclusion of the verse, viz. He who bringeth forth by number their host (Is. XL, 26). There are two grades which have to be distinguished, one of Mah and one of Mi-one of the higher and the other of the lower sphere. The higher is singled out here in the words, "He who bringeth forth by number their host". "He who" expresses something definite and absolute, a being universally recognized and without equal. (Corresponding to this is the expression "He who bringeth forth bread from the earth": here also "He who" implies the universally acknowledged one, though here visualised as the lower grade; the two, however, are one.) "By number": six hundred thousand are they, and they have in turn produced according to their kinds beyond all number. "All of them", whether the six hundred -thousand or the rest of the hosts, "He calls by name". This cannot mean by their names, for if it were so, it should have been written "by names". What it means is that as long as this grade did not assume a name, and was still called Mi, it was unproductive, and did not bring into actuality the latent forces within it, each according to its kind. But as soon as it created ELeH (these), and assumed its rightful name and was called ELoHIM (God), then, by force of that name, it produced them in their complete form. This is the meaning of "calls by name", to wit, He proclaimed His own name so as to bring about the emergence of each sort of being in its full form. (Analogous to this we read, "See, I have called by name" (Exod. XXXI, 2), to wit, I have bestowed my name on Bezalel (in the shadow of God) so that his work should emerge in perfection. Further, the words "by the abundance of powers,' (Is. XL, 26) refer to the supreme grade whereto all the volitions ascend

Zohar: Bereshith, Section 1, Page 2b

by a mysterious path. "And mighty of strength": the word "strength" (KoaH) symbolizes the supernal World which assumed the name Elohim (God), as already said. "No one is missing" of the six hundred thousand which emerged by the power of the Name. And because no one is missing, therefore whenever Israelites died on account of a national sin, the people were afterwards numbered, and it was found that the number of six hundred thousand had not been diminished even by one, so that the likeness to the supernal prototype was still complete; just as no one was missing above, so no one was missing here below.

IN THE BEGINNING. Rab Hamnuna the Venerable said: 'We find here a reversal of the order of the letters of the Alphabet, the first two words Bereshith bara-"in-the-beginning He-created"-commencing with beth, whereas the two words following, Elohim eth-"God the" commence with aleph. The reason is as follows. When the Holy One, blessed be He, was about to make the world, all the letters of the Alphabet were still embryonic, and for two thousand years the Holy One, blessed be He, had contemplated them and toyed with them. When He came to create the world, all the letters presented themselves before Him in reversed order. The letter Tau advanced in front and pleaded: May it please Thee, O Lord of the world, to place me first in the creation of the world, seeing that I am the concluding letter of EMeTh (Truth) which is engraved upon Thy seal, and seeing that Thou art called by this very name of EMeTh, it is most appropriate for the King to begin with the final letter of EMeTh and to create with me the world. The Holy One, blessed be He, said to her: Thou art worthy and deserving, but it is not proper that I begin with thee the creation of the world, since thou art destined to serve as a mark on the foreheads of the faithful ones (vide Ezek. IX, 4) who have kept the Law from Aleph to Tau, and through the absence of this mark the rest will be killed; and, further, thou formest the conclusion of MaWeTh (death). Hence thou art not meet to initiate the creation of the world. The Shin then came to the fore and pleaded: O Lord of the world, may it please Thee to begin with me the world, seeing that I am the initial letter of Thy name ShaDDaI (Almighty), and it is most fitting to create the world through that Holy Name. Said He in reply: Thou art worthy, thou art good, thou art true, but I may not begin through thee the creation of the world, since thou formest part of the group of letters expressing forgery, ShekeR (falsehood), which is not able to exist unless the Koph and Resh draw thee into their company. (Hence it is that a lie, to obtain credence, must always commence with something true. For the shin is a letter of truth, that letter by which the Patriarchs communed with God; but koph and resh are letters belonging to the evil side, which in order to stand firm attach to themselves the shin, thus forming a conspiracy (QeSheR).) Having heard all this, the shin departed. Enters the Zade and says: O Lord of the world, may it please Thee to create with me the world, inasmuch as I am the sign of the righteous (Zadikim) and of Thyself who art called righteous, as it is written, "For the Lord is righteous, he loveth righteousness" (Ps. XI, 7), and hence it is meet to create the world with me. The Lord made answer: O Zade, thou art Zade, and thou signifiest righteousness, but thou must be concealed, thou mayest not come out in the open so much lest thou givest the world cause for offence. For thou consistest of the letter nun surmounted by the letter yod (representing together the male and the female principles). And this is the mystery of the creation of the first man, who was created with two faces (male and female combined). In the same way the nun and the yod in the zade are turned back-to-back and not face to face, whether the zade is upright or turned downwards. The Holy One, blessed be He, said to her further, I will in time divide thee in two, so as to appear face to face, but thou wilt go up in another place. She then departed. The letter Pe presented herself and pleaded thus: May it please Thee, O Lord of the world, to create through me the world, seeing that I signify redemption and deliverance (Purkana, Peduth), which Thou art to vouchsafe to the world. It is, hence, meet that through me the world be created. The Lord answered: Thou art worthy, but thou representest transgression (Pesha), and moreover thou art shapen like the serpent, who had his head curled up within his body, symbolic of the guilty man who bends his head and extends his hand. The letter 'Ayin was likewise refused as standing for iniquity ('Awon), despite her plea that she represents humility. ('Anavah). Then the Samekh appeared and said: O Lord

Zohar: Bereshith, Section 1, Page 3a

of the world, may it please Thee to create through me the world, inasmuch as I represent upholding (Semikah) of the fallen, as it is written, "The Lord upholdeth all that fall" (Ps. CXLV, 14). The Lord answered her: This is just the reason why thou shouldst remain in thy place, for shouldst thou leave it, what will be the fate of the fallen, seeing that they are upheld by thee? She immediately departed. The Nun entered and pleaded her merits as being the initial letter in "Fearful (Nora) in praises" (Ex. XV, 11), as well as in "Comely (Nawa) is praise for the righteous" (Ps. XXXIII, 1). The Lord said: O Nun, return to thy place, for it is for thy sake (as representing the falling, Nofelim) that the Samekh returned to her place. Remain, therefore, under her support. The Nun immediately returned to her place. The Mim came up and said: O Lord of the world, may it please Thee to create by me the world, inasmuch as I commence the word Melekh (King) which is Thy title. The Lord replied: It is so assuredly, but I cannot employ thee in the creation of the world for the reason that the world requires a King. Return, therefore, to thy place, thou along with the Lamed and the Kaph, since the world cannot exist without a MeLeKh (King). At that moment, the Kaph descended from its throne of glory and quaking and trembling said: O Lord of the universe, may it please Thee to begin through me the creation of the world, seeing that I am Thine own Kabod (honour). And when Kaph descended from its throne of glory, two hundred thousand worlds began to shake, the throne trembled, and all the worlds quaked and were about to fall in ruins. Said to her the Holy One, blessed be His Name: Kaph, Kaph, what doest thou here? I will not create the world with thee. Go back to thy place, since thou standest for extermination (Kelayah). Return, then, to thy place and remain there. Immediately she departed and returned to her own place. The letter Yod then presented herself and said: May it please Thee, O Lord, to vouchsafe me first place in the creation of the world, since I stand first in the Sacred Name. The Lord said to her: It is sufficient for thee that thou art engraven and marked in Myself and that thou art the channel of My will; thou must not be removed from My Name. The Teth then came up and said: O Lord of the universe, may it please Thee to place me at the head in the creation of the world, since through me Thou art called Good (Tob) and upright. The Lord said to her: I will not create the world through thee, as the goodness which thou representest is hidden and concealed within thyself, as it is written, "O how abundant is thy goodness which thou hast laid up for them that fear thee" (Ps. XXXI, 20). Since then it is treasured within thyself, it has no part in the world which I am going to create, but only in the world to come. And further, it is because thy goodness is hidden within thee that the gates of the Temple sank into the ground, as it is written, "Sunk (Tabe'u) in the ground are her gates" (Lam. II, 9). And furthermore, the letter Heth is at thy side, and when joined you make sin (HeT). (It is for that reason that these two letters are not to be found in the names of any of the tribes.) She departed immediately. Then the Zayin presented herself and put forth her claim, saying, O Lord of the World, may it please Thee to put me at the head of the creation, since I represent the observance of the Sabbath, as it is written, "Remember (Zakhor) the day of the Sabbath to keep it holy" (Ex. XX, 8). The Lord replied: I will not create the world through thee, since thou representest war, being in shape like a sharp-pointed sword, or a lance. The Zayin immediately departed from His presence. The Vau entered and put forth her claim, saying: O Lord of the world, may it please Thee to use me first in the creation of the world, inasmuch as I am one of the letters of Thy name. Said the Lord to her: Thou, Vau, as well as He', suffice it to you that you are of the letters of My name, part of the mystery of My name, engraven and impressed in My name. I will therefore not give you first place in the creation of the world. Then appeared the letter Daleth as well as the letter Gimel and put forth similar claims. The Lord gave them a similar reply, saying: It should suffice you to remain side by side together, since "the poor will not cease from the land" (Deut. XV, 11), who will thus need benevolence. For the Daleth signifies poverty (Dalluth) and the Gimel beneficence (Gemul). Therefore separate not from each other, and let it suffice you that one maintains the other. The Beth then entered and said: O Lord of the world, may it please Thee to put me first in the creation of the world, since I represent the benedictions (Berakhoth) offered to Thee on high and below. The Holy One, blessed be He, said to her: Assuredly, with thee I will create the world, and thou shalt form the beginning in the creation of the world. The letter Aleph remained in her place without presenting herself. Said the Holy One, blessed be His name: Aleph, Aleph, wherefore comest thou not before Me like the rest of the letters? She answered: Because I saw all the other letters leaving Thy presence without any success. What, then, could I achieve there? And further, since

Zohar: Bereshith, Section 1, Page 3b

Thou hast already bestowed on the letter Beth this great gift, it is not meet for the Supreme King to take away the gift which He has made to His servant and give it to another. The Lord said to her: Aleph, Aleph, although I will begin the creation of the world with the beth, thou wilt remain the first of the letters. My unity shall not be expressed except through thee, on thee shall be based all calculations and operations of the world, and unity shall not be expressed save by the letter Aleph. Then the Holy One, blessed be His name, made higher-world letters of a large pattern and lower-world letters of a small pattern. It is therefore that we have here two words beginning with beth (Bereshith bara) and then two words beginning with aleph (Elohim eth). They represent the higher-world letters and the lower-world letters, which two operate, above and below, together and as one.'

BERESHITH (In the beginning). Said R. Yudai: 'What is the meaning of Bereshith? It means "with Wisdom", the Wisdom on which the world is based, and through this it introduces us to deep and recondite mysteries. In it, too, is the inscription of six chief supernal directions, out of which there issues the totality of existence. From the same there go forth six sources of rivers which flow into the Great Sea. This is implied in the word Bereshith, which can be analysed into BaRa-SHiTH (He created six). And who created them? The Mysterious Unknown.' R. Hiya and R. Yose were walking along the road. When they reached the open country, R. Hiya said to R. Yose, 'What you said about Bereshith signifying bara-shith (created six) is certainly correct, since the Torah speaks of six primordial days and not more. The others are hinted at but not disclosed; nevertheless, from what is told us we can perceive the following. The Holy and Mysterious One graved in a hidden recess one point. In that He enclosed the whole of Creation as one who locks up all his treasures in a palace, under one key, which is therefore as valuable as all that is stored up in that palace; for it is the key which shuts and opens. In that palace there are hidden treasures, one greater than the other. The palace is provided with fifty mystic gates. They are inserted in its four sides to the number of forty-nine. The one remaining gate is on none of its sides and it is unknown whether it is on high or below: it is hence called the mysterious gate. All these gates have one lock, and there is one tiny spot for the insertion of the key, which is only marked by the impress of the key. It is this mystery which is implied in the words "In the beginning created God", "In the beginning" (Bereshith): this is the key which encloses the whole and which shuts and opens. Six gates are controlled by this key which opens and shuts. At first it kept the gates closed and impenetrable; this is indicated by the word Bereshith, which is composed of a revealing word (shith) with a concealing word (bara). Bara is always a word of mystery, closing and not opening,' Said R. Yose: 'Assuredly it is so, and I have heard the Sacred Lamp say the same, to wit, that bara is a term of mystery, a lock without a key, and as long as the world was locked within the term bara it was not in a state of being or existence. Over the whole there hovered Tohu (chaos), and as long as Tohu dominated, the world was not in being or existence. When did that key open the gates and make the world fruitful? It was when Abraham appeared, as it is written, "These are the generations of the heavens and of the earth behibaream" (when they were created) (Gen. II, 4). Now, BeHiBaReAm is an anagram of BeABeRaHaM (through Abraham), implying that what was hitherto sealed up and unproductive in the word bara has by a transposition of letters become serviceable, there has emerged a pillar of fruitfulness: for BaRa has been transformed into AiBeR (organ), which is the sacred foundation on which the world rests. Further, in the same way, as Ai Bra Ha M contains Ai Be R, a transformation of BaRA, so it is with the splendour of the name of the Most High and most Concealed One. This is implied in the words MI BaRA AiLeH. Add the other sacred name MaH. Transpose BaRA into AiBeR. We have AiLeH on one side and AiBeR on the other side. Add the He (of MaH) to AiBeR and the Yod (of MI) to AiLeH. When we take now the Mim of both MI and MaH and join each to each we have complete the sacred name AeLoHiM and also the name

Zohar: Bereshith, Section 1, Page 4a

ABRaHaM. According to another view, the Holy One, blessed be He, took MI and joined it to AiLeH, so that there was shaped AeLoHiM; similarly He took MaH and joined it to AiBeR and there was shaped ABRaHaM. And thus He made the world unfold itself, and made the name complete, as it had not been hitherto. This is meant by the verse "These are the generations (i.e. unfoldings) of the heaven and of the earth BeHiBaReaM (when they were created)". That is, the whole creation was in suspense until the name of ABRaHaM was created, and as soon as the name of Abraham was completed the Sacred Name was completed along with it, as it says further, "in the day that the Lord God made earth and heaven".'

R. Hiya then prostrated himself on the earth, kissed the dust, and said weeping: 'Dust, Dust, how stiffnecked art thou, how shameless art thou that all the delights of the eye perish within thee! All the beacons of light thou consumes and grindest into nothingness. Fie on thy shamelessness! That Sacred Lamp that illuminated the world, the mighty spiritual force by whose merits the world exists, is consumed by thee. Oh, R. Simeon, thou beacon of light, source of light to the world, how hast thou turned to dust, thou leader of the world whilst alive!' After falling for a moment into a reverie, he continued, 'O dust, dust! pride not thyself, for the pillars of the world will not be delivered into thy power, nor will R. Simeon perish within thee.'

R. Hiya then arose weeping and set out in company with R. Yose. He fasted from that day for forty days, in order that he might see R. Simeon. 'Thou canst not see him' was all the answer to his supplication. He then fasted another forty days, at the end of which he saw in a vision R. Simeon and his son R. Eleazar discussing the very subject which R. Yose had just explained to him, while thousands were looking on and listening. Meanwhile, there appeared a host of huge winged celestial beings upon whose wings R. Simeon and his son R. Eleazar were borne aloft into the heavenly Academy, whilst those beings remained at the threshold, awaiting them. Their splendour was constantly renewed, and they radiated a light exceeding that of the sun. R. Simeon then opened his mouth and said, 'Let R. Hiya enter and behold what the Holy One, blessed be He, has prepared for the rejoicing of the righteous in the world to come. Happy is he who enters here without misgiving, and happy is he who is established as a strong pillar in the world to come.' On entering he (R. Hiya) noticed that R. Eleazar and the other great scholars that were sitting near him stood up. He drew back in some embarrassment, and sat down at the feet of R. Simeon. A voice thereupon went forth, saying, 'Lower thine eyes, raise not thy head and do not look.' He lowered his eyes and discerned a light shining afar. The voice went forth again, saying 'O, ye unseen celestials, ye open-eyed who sweep to and fro throughout the world, behold and see! O, ye terrestrial beings who are sunk deep in slumber, awake! Who among you laboured to turn darkness into light and bitter into sweet before you entered here? Who among you awaited every day the light that shall break forth what time the King shall visit his beloved gazelle, when He will be glorified and called King by all the kings of the world? He who did not thus wait every day in the world below will have no share here.' Meanwhile he beheld a number of his colleagues gather round, even all the mighty pillars of wisdom, and he saw them ascend to the heavenly Academy, while others in turn descended. At the head of them all he saw the chief of the winged angels, who approached him and solemnly declared that he had heard 'from behind the curtain' that the King visits each day and remembers his gazelle which is trodden in the dust, and that at the moment He does so He strikes the three hundred and ninety heavens so they all quake and tremble

Zohar: Bereshith, Section 1, Page 4b

before Him: for her fate He sheds tears hot as burning fire, which fall into the great sea. From these tears arises and is sustained the presiding genius of the sea, who sanctifies the name of the Holy King, and who has pledged himself to swallow up all the waters of the creation and to gather them all within himself on that day when all the nations shall assemble against the holy people, so that they shall be able to pass on dry land. Anon he heard a voice proclaiming, 'Make room, make room, for King Messiah is coming to the Academy of R. Simeon.' For all the righteous there have been heads of Academies on earth, and have become disciples of the heavenly Academy, and the Messiah visits all these Academies and puts his seal on all the expositions that issue from the mouths of the teachers. The Messiah then entered wearing heavenly diadems, with which he had been crowned by the heads of the Academy. All the colleagues stood up, along with R. Simeon, from whom a light shot up to the empyrean. The Messiah said to him, 'Happy art thou, for thy teaching mounts on high in the form of three hundred and seventy illuminations, and each illumination subdivides itself into six hundred and thirteen arguments, which go up and bathe themselves in streams of pure balsam. And the Holy One, blessed be He, Himself places His seal on the teaching of thy Academy and of the Academy of Hezekiah, King of Judah, and of the Academy of Ahijah of Shiloh. I come not to set my seal in thy Academy, since it is the chief of the winged angels who comes here; for I know that he does not visit any but thy Academy.' After that R. Simeon told him what the chief of the winged angels had so solemnly declared. Thereupon the Messiah fell a-quaking, and he cried aloud, and the heavens quivered, and the great sea quaked and the Leviathan trembled, and the world was shaken to its foundations. His eye then fell upon R. Hiya, who was sitting at the feet of R. Simeon. 'Who has brought here this man,' he asked, 'who still wears the raiment of the other world?' R. Simeon answered, 'This is the great R. Hiya, the shining lamp of the Torah.' 'Let him then,' said the Messiah, 'be gathered in, together with his sons, and let them become members of the Academy.' R. Simeon said, 'Let a time of grace be granted to him.' A time of grace was then granted to him, and he went forth from thence trembling, with tears running from his eyes, saying as he wept, 'Happy is the portion of the righteous in that world and happy is the portion of the son of Yohai who has merited such glory. It is concerning such as he that it is written, "That I may cause those who love me to inherit a lasting possession; and their treasures will I fill" (Prov. VIII, 21.)'

IN THE BEGINNING. R. Simeon opened his discourse with the text: And I put my words in thy mouth (Is. LI, 16). He said: 'How greatly is it incumbent on a man to study the Torah day and night! For the Holy One, blessed be He, is attentive to the voice of those who occupy themselves with the Torah, and through each fresh discovery made by them in the Torah a new heaven is created. Our teachers have told us that at the moment when a man expounds something new in the Torah, his utterance ascends before the Holy One, blessed be He, and He takes it up and kisses it and crowns it with seventy crowns of graven and inscribed letters. When a new idea is formulated in the field of the esoteric wisdom, it ascends and rests on the head of the "Zaddik, the life of the universe", and then it flies off and traverses seventy thousand worlds until it ascends to the "Ancient of Days". And inasmuch as all the words of the "Ancient of Days" are words of wisdom comprising sublime and hidden mysteries, that hidden word of wisdom that was discovered here when it ascends is joined to the words of the "Ancient of Days", and becomes an integral part of them, and enters into the eighteen mystical worlds, concerning which we read "No eye hath seen beside thee, O God" (Ibid. LXIV, 3). From thence they issue and fly to and fro, until finally arriving, perfected and completed, before the "Ancient of Days". At that moment the "Ancient of Days" savours that word of wisdom, and finds satisfaction therein above all else. He takes that word and crowns it with three hundred and seventy thousand crowns, and it flies up and down until it is made into a sky. And so each word of wisdom is made into a sky which presents itself fully formed before the "Ancient of Days", who calls them "new heavens", that is, heavens created out of the mystic ideas of the sublime wisdom. As for the other new expositions of the Torah, they present themselves before

Zohar: Bereshith, Section 1, Page 5a

the Holy One, blessed be He, and ascend and become "earths of the living", then they descend and become absorbed into one earth, whereby a new earth emerges through that new discovery in the Torah. This is implied in the verse, "For as the new heavens and the new earth, which I am making, rise up before me, etc." (Ibid. LXVI, 22). It is not written "I have made", but "I am making", signifying continual creation out of the new ideas discovered in the Torah. Further, it is written,

"And I have placed my words in thy mouth, and with the shadow of my hand have I covered thee, to plant a heaven and to lay the foundations of an earth" (Ibid. LI, 16). It does not say "the heaven", but "a heaven". 'Said R. Eleazar: 'What signifies "with the shadow of my hand have I covered thee"?' He replied: 'When the Torah was delivered to Moses, there appeared myriads of heavenly angels ready to consume him with their fiery breath, but the Holy One, blessed be He, sheltered him. Similarly now when the new word ascends and is crowned and presents itself before the Holy One, blessed be He, He covers and protects that word, and also shelters the author of that word, so that the angels should not become aware of him and so be filled with jealousy, until that word is transformed into a new heaven and a new earth. That is the meaning of the passage, "and with the shadow of my hand have I covered thee, to plant a heaven and to lay the foundations of an earth". From this we learn that each word of which the purpose is not obvious contains some lesson of special value, as it is written: "And with the shadow of my hand have I covered thee." Why is it covered and hidden from our view? For an ulterior purpose, to wit, "to plant a heaven and to lay the foundation of an earth", as already explained. The verse continues: "And to say to Zion thou art 'Ami, my people" (Ibid.). This means, to say to those gates of study and those words of Zion (distinction) "thou art 'Ami". The word 'Ami (my people) may be read 'Imi (with me), meaning "to be a collaborator with Me"; for just as I made heaven and earth by a word, as it says: "By the word of the Lord the heavens were made" (Ps. XXXIII, 6), So dost thou. Happy are those who devote themselves to the study of the Torah! You should not think, however, that all this applies even to one who is no true scholar. Not so. When one who is a stranger to the mysteries of the Torah makes pseudo-discoveries based on an incomplete understanding, that "word" rises, and is met by the perverse One, the Demon of the false tongue, who emerges from the cavern of the great abyss and makes a leap of five hundred parasangs to receive that word. He takes it and returns with it to his cavern, and shapes it into a spurious heaven which is called Tohu (chaos). That Demon then traverses in one swoop the whole of that heaven, a space of six thousand parasangs. As soon as that heaven is formed, the Harlot emerges, and lodges herself in it, and joins forces with it, and issuing from thence she slays thousands and tens of thousands. For as long as she is lodged in that heaven she has authority and power to swoop through the world in the twinkling of an eye. This is implied in the words, "Woe unto them that draw iniquity with cords of vanity" (Is. V, 18). The word for "iniquity", 'Avon, being of the masculine gender, designates the Demon. In the next part of the verse, "and sin, as it were, with a cart rope", the word for "sin", hattaah, being of the feminine gender, signifies the female, the Harlot who rushes to execute slaughter on the sons of men. Concerning her we also read, "For she hath caused to fall many deadly wounded" (Prov. VII, 26), namely, that hattaah (sin) who slays the sons of men. And the ultimate cause is the unripe scholar who is not qualified to teach and yet does so. May God save us from him!' Said R. Simeon to the colleagues: 'I beseech you not to let fall from your mouth any word of the Torah of which you are not certain and which you have not learnt correctly from a "great tree", so that you may not be the cause of that Harlot slaying multitudes of the sons of men.' They answered in unison, 'God forbid, God forbid!' R. Simeon proceeded: 'See now, it was by means of the Torah that the Holy One created the world. That has already been derived from the verse, "Then I was near him as an artisan, and I was daily all his delight" (Prov. VIII, 30). He looked at the Torah once, twice, thrice, and a fourth time. He uttered the words composing her and then operated through her. That is a lesson for men, how to study the Torah properly. This lesson is indicated by the verse, "Then did he see, and declare it; he established it, yea, and searched it out." (Jób. XXVIII, 27). Seeing, declaring, establishing and searching out correspond to these four operations which the Holy One, blessed be He, went through before entering on the work of creation. Hence the account of the creation commences with the four words Bereshith Bara Aelohim Aith ("In-the-beginning created God the"), before mentioning "the heavens", thus signifying the four times which the Holy One, blessed be He, looked into the Torah before He performed His work.'

R. Eleazar was journeying to visit his father-in-law, R. Yose, son of R. Simeon son of Lakunya.

Zohar: Bereshith, Section 1, Page 5b

He was accompanied by R. Abba, and another man was leading their baggage-ass behind them. Said R. Abba, 'Let us open a discourse on the Torah, the time and place being propitious.' R. Eleazar then began thus: 'It is written: Ye shall keep my Sabbaths (Lev. XIX, 30). Consider this: the Holy One, blessed be He, created the world in six days and each day revealed a part of His work, and functioned through the energy imparted to it. But none of the work was actually disclosed nor the energy functioning until the fourth day. The first three days were undisclosed and imperceptible, but when the fourth day came the product and energy of all of them was brought out into the open. Fire, water, and air, as three primordial elements, were still in suspense, their activity not having become visible until the earth disclosed them and so made knowable the workmanship of each one of them. You may object that in the account of the third day it is written, "Let the earth put forth grass", as well as "And the earth put forth". The answer is that, though ascribed to the third day, this actually took place on the fourth day, and it was included in the account of the third day merely to indicate the unbroken continuity of the creation. From the fourth day onwards He disclosed His work and produced an artificer for the function of each one (for the fourth day is the symbol of the fourth leg of the celestial Throne). Furthermore, the activities of all the days, whether of the first or the second triad, were made dependent on the day of the Sabbath, as it is written, "And on the seventh day God finished." This is the Sabbath, and this is the fourth foot of the celestial Throne. What, then, you may ask, is implied in "My Sabbaths ye shall observe", which seems to point to two Sabbaths? The answer is that the plural form indicates the eve of Sabbath and the Sabbath itself, which merge into each other without a break.'

At this point the driver who was following them interposed with the question: 'What is meant by "And ye shall reverence my sanctuary" (Ibid.)?' R. Abba replied: 'This designates the sanctity of the Sabbath.' 'What then,' he said, 'is the sanctity of the Sabbath?' 'It is the sanctity which was conferred upon it from above.' 'If that is so' (argued the stranger) 'thou makest the Sabbath to possess no sanctity of its own but only such as rests on it from above.' 'It is indeed so' (said R. Abba), 'as it is written, "And call the Sabbath a delight, and the holy of the Lord honourable" (Is. LVIII, 13), where the "Sabbath" and the "holy of the Lord" are mentioned each separately.' 'What, then, is the "holy of the Lord"?' 'It is the holiness which descends from above to rest on it.' 'But' (argued the stranger) 'if the holiness emanating from on high is called "honourable", evidently the Sabbath itself is not so called, and yet it is written, "And thou shalt honour it" (Ibid.).' Said R. Eleazar to R. Abba, 'Cease arguing with that man, for he seems to know some mystery of which we are ignorant.' They then said to him: 'Say what thou hast to say.' He commenced thus: 'It is written: 'eth Shabthothai ("My sabbaths") (Lev. XIX, 30). The particle eth indicates that in the precept of the Sabbath is to be included the limit of the Sabbath walk, which is two thousand cubits in all directions. "My Sabbaths" is a reference to the higher Sabbath and the lower Sabbath, which are two joined together as one. There was still one Sabbath left unmentioned. Feeling humiliated, she pleaded before the Creator, saying, "O Lord of the universe, since the time when Thou didst create me, I have been called merely 'day of Sabbath', but surely a day must have for companion a night." Said the Lord to her, "O my daughter, thou art Sabbath, and Sabbath I will call thee. But I will confer on thee an even more glorious crown." He then made proclamation, "And ye shall fear my sanctuary" (Ibid.). This is a reference to the Sabbath of the eve of Sabbath, which inspires fear, and upon which fear rests. And it is the Holy One, blessed be He, Himself who identified Himself with her, saying "I am the Lord" (Ibid.). I have further heard' (continued the stranger) 'the following exposition from my father. He stressed the particle eth as signifying the limit of the Sabbath walk. "My Sabbaths," he said, denotes the circle and the square within [Tr. note: The circle, square, and point were used by the Cabbalists to symbolise the three highest Sefiroth], and corresponding to these two the sanctification recital consists of two parts, one the verses Genesis II, 1-3, commencing Vaikhulu (and were completed) and the other the sanctification proper (Kiddush). Vaikhulu contains thirty-five words, and the Kiddush contains thirty-five words, making together seventy, corresponding to the seventy names of the Holy One, blessed be He, by which the congregation of Israel is crowned. On account of this circle and square, the Sabbaths here referred to come under the injunction of the word "keep" used in the second version of the Ten Commandments (Deut. V, 12) as it is written here, "ye shall keep my Sabbaths". For the other, the highest Sabbath does not come under the injunction of Shamor (keep), but is under that of Zakhor (remember), which is used in the first version of the Ten Commandments (Exod. XX, 8), since the Supreme King is hinted at in the word Zakhor (remember). For this reason He is called "the King with whom Peace dwells", and His peace is within the injunction of zakhor (remember). And this is why there is no contention in the supernal realm, because of the twofold peace here below, one for Jacob and one for Joseph, as it is written, "Peace, Peace, to him that is far off and to him that is near" (Is. LVII, 19): "to him that is far off" refers to Jacob

Zohar: Bereshith, Section 1, Page 6a

"and to him that is near" refers to Joseph. "To him that is far" is parallel to "From afar the Lord appeared unto me" (Jer. XXXI, 3), as well as to "And his sister stood afar off" (Exod. II, 4); "and to him that is near" is parallel to "new gods who came up since a near time" (Deut. XXXII, 17). "From afar" signifies the supernal point which is situated in His palace, and in regard to which it is said "ye shall keep", thus bringing it under the injunction of shamor (keep). "And my sanctuary ye shall fear" refers to the point which is situated in the centre and which is most to be feared, as the penalty of transgression is death, as it is written, "Everyone that profaneth it shall surely be put to death" (Ex. XXXI, 14); i.e. those who penetrate into the space of the circle-square, treading on the spot where the central point is situated and damaging it-these shall surely be put to death. Of this it is written, "Ye shall fear." That point is called Ani (I) (Lev. XIX, 30), and upon it rests the unknown, the Most High, the unrevealed One which is Tetragrammaton (the Lord), both being one.' R. Eleazar and R. Abba came up to the stranger and kissed him. They said: 'With all this profound knowledge thou hast displayed, is it meet that thou shouldst journey behind us? Who art thou?' they asked him. 'Do not ask,' he said, 'but let us proceed on our way and together let us discourse on the Torah. Let each one say some word of wisdom to illumine our way.' They asked him, 'Who charged thee to make this journey as an ass-driver?' He said to them, 'The letter Yod waged war with the letters Kaph and Samekh, to make them join me. The Kaph refused to leave its place, since it could not exist for a moment elsewhere. The Samekh refused to move from its place lest it should cease to support those that fall. The Yod then came to me all alone and kissed and embraced me. He wept with me and said, "My son, what shall I do for thee? I will go and load myself with a plenitude of good things and of precious, sublime and mystic symbols, and then I will come to thee and help thee and put thee in possession of two celestial letters superior to those that have departed, to wit the word Yesh (plentifulness), consisting of a celestial Yod and a celestial Shin, so that thou wilt become possessed of stores of riches of all kinds. Go then, my son, and load thy ass." This is why I am travelling in this manner.' R. Eleazar and R. Abba rejoiced; they also wept and said to him, 'Go, ride in front and we will follow thee on the ass.' He said to them, 'Have I not told you that it is the command of the King that I should continue thus until he who will ride on an ass shall appear?' They said to him, 'Thou hast not told us thy name, nor thy habitation.' He answered, 'My habitation is a good one and an exalted one for me-a mighty and imposing tower suspended in the air. In that tower there reside the Holy One, blessed be He, and a certain poor man: and that is my place of habitation. But I have left it and am become an ass-driver.' R. Abba and R. Eleazar gazed at him, and he discoursed to them words as sweet as manna and honey. They said to him, 'If thou wouldst tell us the name of thy father we would kiss the dust of thy feet.' He said to them, 'Why so? It is not my habit to pride myself on a knowledge of the Torah, but my father inhabited the great sea, he was a huge fish who embraced the great sea from one end to the other; he was mighty and noble and ancient of days so that he would swallow up all the other fishes in the sea and then release them again alive and filled with all the good things of the world. Like a mighty swimmer he could traverse the whole sea in one second. He shot me out like an arrow in the hand of a bowman and hid me in the place I told you of, and he himself returned to his place and is hid in that sea.' R. Eleazar pondered a little and said, 'Thou art the son of the sacred lamp, thou art the son of the venerable Rab Hamnuna, thou art the son of the light of the Torah, and yet thou drivest behind us!' They both wept together and they kissed him and went forward on their way. They further said to him, 'May our master be pleased to let us know his name.' He thereupon began to discourse on the verse: And Benaiah the son of Jehoiada, etc. (II Sam. XXIII, 20). 'This verse', he said, 'has been well explained-in addition to its literal meaning-to signify high mysteries of the Torah. "Benaiah the son of Jehoiada" (i.e. son of God, son of knowing-God) contains an allusion to wisdom, and is a symbolic appellation which influences its bearer. "The son of a living man" indicates the "Zaddik, the life of the universe". "Mighty of deeds" signifies the Master of all actions and of all celestial hosts, since all proceed from him; He is the "Lord of hosts", the insignia of all His hosts, yet distinguished and exalted above all. He is "mighty of deeds, from Kabzeel", as if to say: "that great and most mighty tree, from what place comes it, from what grade does it issue? From Kabzeel" (lit. gathering of God), from the highest and hidden grade

Zohar: Bereshith, Section 1, Page 6b

where "no eye hath ever seen, etc." (Is. LXIV, 3), a grade which contains the whole and which is the focus of the supernal light, and from which everything issues. That light is the sacred and hidden temple (Hekal) wherein is concentrated that divine essence from which all the worlds draw sustenance, and all divine hosts are nourished and so subsist. "He smote the strong lion of Moab" is a reference to the two Temples that existed for His sake and drew their strength from Him, namely, the first Temple and the second Temple. But as soon as He departed, the flow of blessing from above ceased; "He", as it were, "smote" them, destroyed them, made an end of them, and the sacred Throne was overturned, as it is written, "as I was among the captives" (Ezek. I, 1), implying that that divine essence called "I" was in captivity. "On the river Khebar" (Ibid.) (Khebar=long ago) means the stream that was once flowing, but the waters and sources of which were cut off so that it flows no more as formerly. The same is implied in the verse "and the river faileth and drieth up" (Job. XIV, 11): "faileth", referring to the first Temple, and "drieth up" to the second Temple. And so "He smote the two strong lions of Moab" (Moab: Meab, of the father), namely the Temples of the Father in heaven, by whom they were now destroyed, so that all lights which illuminated Israel were now darkened. Further, "He went down and smote the lion": formerly when that stream flowed down to here below, Israel was free from care, offering peace-offerings and sin-offerings to atone for his soul; and from on high descended the image of a lion visible to all, crouching on his prey, consuming the offerings like a mighty giant. All the dogs kept themselves out of sight, fearing to venture abroad. But when sin prevailed, He descended to the regions here below and slew that lion, not desiring any more to provide his portion as formerly. He, as it were, slew him: "He smote the lion", most assuredly, "into the pit", that is to say, in the sight of the "evil monster". The same evil monster, seeing this, sent a dog to consume the offerings. The name of the lion is Ariel, as his face is that of a lion; and the name of the dog is Baladon (not-man), for it is a dog and has the face of a dog. "In a day of snow", that is, in the day when on account of Israel's sins sentence was pronounced by the Court on high. (The same is implied in the verse "She is not afraid of the snow for her household" (Prov. XXXI, 21), that is to say, of the judgement on high; why so? "for all her household are clothed with scarlet", and hence can endure the strongest fire.) Such is the mystical meaning of this verse. The next verse reads: "And he smote an Egyptian, a man of good appearance, etc." The mystical meaning of this verse is that every time Israel sins, God leaves them and withholds from them all the blessings and all the lights which illumined them. "He smote an Egyptian": this signifies the light of Israel's great luminary, to wit, Moses, who is called an Egyptian, as it is written, "And they said, an Egyptian delivered us, etc." (Exod. II, 19), for there he was born, there he was brought up and there he was vouchsafed the higher light. "A man of good appearance" (mar'eh) also signifies Moses, of whom it is written "ou-mar'eh (by clear appearance) and not in dark speeches" (Num. XII, 8); so too "man" (ish), as he is called "man of God" (Deut. XXXIII, 1), the husband, as it were, of the Divine glory, leading it whereso he would upon the earth, a privilege no other man had ever enjoyed. "And the Egyptian had a spear in his hand," to wit, the divine rod that was delivered into his hand, as we read: "With the rod of God in my hand" (Exod. XVII, 9), which is the same rod that was created in the twilight of the Eve of Sabbath, and on which there was engraven the Divine Name in sacred letters. With the same rod Moses sinned by smiting the rock, as we read: "And he smote the rock with his rod twice" (Num. XX, 11). The Holy One, blessed be He, said to him "I have not given the rod for that purpose; by thy life, from henceforward it will not be in thy hand any more." Immediately "He went down to him with a rod", i.e. He judged him rigidly, "and plucked the spear out of the Egyptian's hand," for from that moment he lost it and never more regained it. "And slew him with his spear," i.e. through the sin of smiting the rock with that rod he died without entering the Holy Land, and thereby that illumination was withheld from Israel. "He was more honourable than the thirty" (II Sam. XXIII, 23) alludes to the thirty celestial years from which he was taken to be sent down below. "But he attained not to the first three", that is, they (the patriarchs) came to him and gave him whatever he craved, but he did not come to them; and although he did not enter into their number, yet "David put him into his service", that is, David never detached him from his heart,

Zohar: Bereshith, Section 1, Page 7a

nor will there ever be any separation between the two. David turned his heart towards him, but he did not turn his towards David, in the same manner as the moon addresses her praises and hymns towards the sun, drawing him to herself to set up, as it were, his abode with her. This is implied in the words "And David put him into his service".'

R. Eleazar and R. Abba prostrated themselves before the stranger. Of a sudden they saw him not. They arose and looked on every side, but they saw him not. They sat down and wept and were unable to exchange a word. After a while R. Abba said: 'It is assuredly true as we have been taught, that whenever the righteous on their journey busy themselves with expositions of the Torah, they are favoured by visits from the other world; for it is clear that it was the venerable

Rab Hamnuna who appeared to us from the other world to reveal to us all these things, and now before we could recognize him, he has vanished.' They arose and tried to drive the asses, but could not make them go, and again tried, but could not. They became frightened and left the animals behind. That spot is called until this day 'Asses' place.

R. Eleazar commenced to discourse thus: O how great is the abundance of thy goodness which thou hast laid up for them that fear thee, etc. (Ps. XXXI, 20). 'How great is the heavenly bounty which the Holy One, blessed be He, hath reserved for those who excel in righteousness, who shun sin and devote themselves to the study of the Torah, when they ascend to the world to come. It is not written simply "thy goodness", but "abundance of thy goodness", the same expression as in the verse "They utter the fame of the abundance of thy goodness" (Ps. CXLV, 7), to wit, the delight which the righteous enjoy in the world to come in the presence of the Everlasting who is "abundant in goodness towards the house of Israel" (Is. LXIII, 7). We may also find enshrined in this passage a mystery of wisdom, in which all other mysteries are enclosed. We translate: "O Mah, great is thy goodness, etc." Mah ("How" or "What") has already been explained. Rab ("abundant" or "great") alludes to the strong and mighty tree: there is another and a smaller tree, but this one is tall, reaching into the highest heaven. "Thy goodness" alludes to the light that was created on the first day. "Which thou hast laid up for those who fear thee", since He has treasured it up for the righteous in the world to come: "which thou hast wrought" alludes to the higher Gan-Eden (Garden-of-Eden, Paradise), as it is written, "The place, O Lord, which thou hast wrought for thy dwelling" (Exod. XV, 17), to wit, "Thou hast wrought for them that trust in thee". "In the sight of the sons of men" alludes to the lower Gan-Eden where all the righteous abide, as spirits clad in a resplendent vesture resembling their corporeal figure in this world; this is meant by "in the sight of man", i.e. presenting the likeness of the people of this world. They stay there for a time, then rise in the air and ascend to the celestial Academy, which is the Gan-Eden above; then they rise again and bathe in the dewy rivers of pure balsam, and then descend and remain below, and sometimes they appear to men to perform for them miracles in the manner of angels, as we have just seen the light of the "Sacred Lamp", without, however, being vouchsafed an insight into the mysteries of Wisdom, so far as we could have wished.' R. Abba said: 'It is written, "And Manoah said unto his wife, We shall surely die, because we have seen God" (Judg. XIII, 22). Although Manoah was ignorant of the object of the apparition, he nevertheless argued, "Since it is written ' for man shall not see me and live ' (Exod. XXXIII, 20), and as we certainly saw Him, we shall therefore die." And we were privileged to see that light which accompanied us, and we are still alive, because the Holy One, blessed be He, sent it to us in order to reveal to us the mysteries of Wisdom. Happy is our portion!'

They continued their journey and reached a certain hill at sunset. The branches of the trees on the hill began to shake and rustle and broke forth into hymns. Whilst walking, they heard a resounding voice proclaim: 'Holy sons of God, who are interspersed among the living of yonder world, ye who are the lamps of the Academy, reassemble into your places to regale yourselves, under the guidance of your Master, in the study of the Torah.' In fear and trembling they stopped and sat down. Meanwhile, a voice went forth again and proclaimed: 'O, ye mighty rocks, exalted hammers, behold the Lord, lo, Him whose appearance is as a broidered pattern of many colours, mounted on His throne: enter then into your place of assembly.' At that moment they heard a loud and mighty sound issuing from between the branches of the trees, and they uttered the verse: 'The voice of the Lord breaketh the cedars' (Ps. XXIX, 5). R. Eleazar and R. Abba fell upon their faces and a great fear came over them. They then arose in haste and went on their way, and heard nothing more. They left the hill, and when they reached the house of R. Simeon the son of Lakunya they saw there R. Simeon the son of Yohai, and they rejoiced

Zohar: Bereshith, Section 1, Page 7b

exceedingly. R. Simeon said to them, 'Assuredly ye traversed a path of heavenly miracles and wonders, for as I was sleeping just now I had a vision of you and of Benaiah the son of Jehoiada, who was sending you two crowns by the hand of a certain elder to crown you withal. Assuredly the Holy One, blessed be He, was on that path. Further, I saw your faces as if transfigured.'

R. Yose remarked: 'Well have ye said that "the sage is superior to the prophet".' R. Eleazar then approached and put his head between the knees of his father and told him all that had happened to them. R. Simeon trembled and wept. '"O Lord, I have the report of thee, and I am afraid"' (Habak. III, 2), he said. 'This verse did Habakkuk exclaim at the time when he reflected on his own death and his resurrection through Elisha. Why was he named HaBaKkuK? Because it is written, "At this season when the time cometh round, thou shalt be embracing (HoBeKeth) a son" (II Kings IV, 16), and he-Habakkuk-was the son of the Shunammite. He received indeed two embracings, one from his mother and one from Elisha, as it is written, "and he put his mouth upon his mouth" (Ibid. 34). In the Book of King Solomon I have found the following: He (Elisha) traced on him the mystic appellation, consisting of seventy-two names. For the alphabetical letters that his father had at first engraved on him had flown off when the child died; but when Elisha embraced him he engraved on him anew all those letters of the seventy-two names. Now the number of those letters amounts to two hundred and sixteen, and they were all engraved by the breath of Elisha on the child so as to put again into him the breath of life through the power of the letters of the seventy-two names. And Elisha named him Habakkuk, a name of double significance, alluding in its sound to the twofold embracing, as already explained, and in its numerical value (H. B. K. V. K. =8. 2. 100. 6. 100) to two hundred and sixteen, the number of the letters of the Sacred Name. By the words his spirit was restored to him and by the letters his bodily parts were reconstituted. Therefore the child was named Habakkuk, and it was he who said: "O Lord, I have heard the report of thee, and I am afraid" (Habak. III, 2), that is to say, I have heard what happened to me, that I tasted of the other world, and am afraid. He then commenced to supplicate for himself, saying, "O Lord, Thy work" which Thou hast accomplished for me, "in the midst of the years", I pray, "let its life be". For he who is bound up with the cycles of past years has life bound up with him. "In the midst of the years make it known", to wit, that stage in which there is no life.' R. Simeon then wept and said: 'I also from what I have heard am seized with fear of the Holy One, blessed be He.' He then raised his hands above his head and said, 'What a privilege it was for you to see face to face the venerable Rab Hamnuna, the light of the Torah-a privilege I have not been granted.' He then fell on his face and saw him uprooting mountains, and kindling the lights in the temple of the Messiah. R. Hamnuna, addressing him, said, 'Master, in this other world thou wilt be the neighbour of the teachers of the Law in the presence of the Holy One, blessed be He.' From that time onward R. Simeon named R. Eleazar his son and R. Abba Peniel (face of God), in allusion to the verse, "For I have seen God face to face" (Gen. XXXII, 31).

IN THE BEGINNING. R. Hiya opened his discourse thus: The beginning of wisdom is the fear of the Lord; A good understanding have all they that do hereafter. His praise endureth forever (Ps. CXI, 10). He said: 'Instead of "the beginning of wisdom" it would be more appropriate to say, "the end of wisdom is the fear of the Lord", since the fear of the Lord is the final object of wisdom. The Psalmist, however, speaks of the highest order of wisdom, which can only be reached through the gate of the fear of God. This is implied in the verse "Open to me the gates of righteousness. This is the gate of the Lord..." (Ps. CXVIII, 19-20). Assuredly, without entering through that gate one will never gain access to the most high King. Imagine a king greatly exalted who screens himself from the common view behind gate upon gate, and at the end, one special gate, locked and barred. Saith the king: He who wishes to enter into my presence must first of all pass through that gate. So here the first gate to super-Wisdom is the fear of God; and this is what is meant by reshith (beginning). The letter Beth (=2) indicates two things joined together, namely two points, one shrouded in mystery and one capable of being revealed; and as they are inseparable they therefore are both joined in the single term reshith (beginning), i.e. they are one and not two, and he who takes away the one takes away the other as well. For He and His name are one, as it is written "That they may know that thou and thy name of Lord art alone" (Ps. LXXXIII, 19). Why is this first gate called "the fear of the Lord"? Because it is the tree of good and evil. If a man deserves well it is good, and if he deserves ill it is evil.

Zohar: Bereshith, Section 1, Page 8a

Hence in that place abides fear, which is the gateway to all that is good. "Good" and "understanding" are two gates which are as one.' R. Yose said: 'The term "A good understanding" alludes to the tree of life which is the knowledge of good without evil. "To all that do hereafter": these are "the sure mercies of David" (Is. LV, 3), viz. they who support the study of the Torah. For they who support the study of the Torah are, we may say, doing something, whereas those who are merely occupied in its study are for the time being not doing. Through this activity "his praise endureth forever", and the Throne abides on its base securely.'

R. Simeon was sitting and studying the Torah during the night when the bride was to be joined to her husband. [Tr. note: i.e. the eve of Pentecost.] For we have been taught that all the members of the bridal palace, during the night preceding her espousals, are in duty bound to keep her company and to rejoice with her in her final preparations for the great day: to study all branches of the Torah, proceeding from the Law to the Prophets, from the Prophets to the Holy Writings, and then to the deeper interpretations of Scripture and to the mysteries of Wisdom, as all these represent her preparations and her adornments. The bride, indeed, with her bridesmaids, comes up and remains with them, adorning herself at their hands and rejoicing with them all that night. And on the following day she does not enter under the canopy except in their company, they being called the canopy attendants. And when she steps under the canopy the Holy One, blessed be He, enquires after them and blesses them and crowns them with the bridal crown: happy is their portion!

Hence R. Simeon and all the companions were chanting the Scripture with exultation, each one of them making new discoveries in the Torah. Said R. Simeon to them, 'O my sons, happy is your portion, for on the morrow the bride will not enter the bridal canopy except in your company; for all those who help to prepare her adornments to-night will be recorded in the book of remembrance, and the Holy One, blessed be He, will bless them with seventy blessings and crown them with crowns of the celestial world.' R. Simeon opened his discourse thus: The heavens declare the glory of God, etc. (Ps. XIX, 2). He said: 'The inner meaning of this verse is as follows. When the bride awakes on the morn of her wedding day, she begins to prepare her ornaments and decorations with the aid of the companions who have rejoiced with her all that night, as she with them. On that day there assemble in her honour hosts upon hosts, awaiting each one of those who have helped in her adornment on the previous night. As soon as the bride beholds her spouse, "the heavens declare the glory of God". "The heavens" are the bridegroom, who enters under the bridal canopy. "Declare" (meSaPeRim) signifies that they radiate a brilliance like that of a sapphire, sparkling and scintillating from one end of the world to the other. "The glory of El" (God) signifies the glory of the bride which is called El (God), as it is written "and El (God) hath indignation every day" (Ps. VII, 12); all the days of the year it is called El (God), but now when she enters under the bridal canopy it is called Glory. It is also at the same time still called El (God), signifying glory on glory, splendour on splendour, and dominion on dominion. Thus, at that time when heaven enters into the canopy and irradiates her, all those companions who joined in her adornment have their names recorded there above, as it is written, "and the firmament showeth his handiwork" (Ibid. XIX, 2), the words "his handiwork" being an allusion to those who have entered into a covenant with the bride. The confederates of the covenant are called "the works of his hands", as we read "the work of our hands establish thou it" (Ps. XC, 17) This is an allusion to the covenant that is engraven on man's body.'

Rab Hamnuna discoursed thus: Suffer not thy mouth to bring thy flesh into guilt (Eccl. V, 5). 'This is a warning to man not to utter with his mouth words that might suggest evil thoughts and so cause to sin the sacred body on which is stamped the holy covenant. For he who does this is dragged into Gehinnom. The angel presiding over Gehinnom is called Duma, and there are tens of thousands of angels of destruction under him. He stands at its door, but those who have carefully guarded the sign of the holy covenant he has no power to touch. David, after his affair with Uriah, was in great fear. Duma entered into the presence of the Holy One, blessed be He, and said:

Zohar: Bereshith, Section 1, Page 8b

"O Lord of the universe, it is written in the Torah: 'And the man that committeth adultery with another man's wife, etc.' (Lev. XX, 10), and it is also written 'And with thy neighbour's wife, etc.' (Ibid. XVIII, 20). Now, David has misused the sign of the holy covenant; what shall be done to him?" Said the Holy One, blessed be His name: "David is pure, and the holy covenant remains untouched inasmuch as at the creation of the world it was revealed before Me that Bath-Sheba was assigned to him."

'"If before Thee it was revealed, yet it was not revealed to him."

'And further, what was done was done lawfully, since every one who goes out to war first gives a bill of divorcement to his wife."

'"Even so, he ought to have waited three months, which he did not."

'"That rule only applies where there is a risk that she may be pregnant. In this case, however, it is known to Me that Uriah never came in unto her, in witness whereof My name is sealed in his, as he is sometimes called URiYaH and sometimes URiYaHU to show that he never had intercourse with her."

'"O Lord of the universe, I must repeat my plea. If to Thee it was manifest that Uriah never came in unto her, was it manifest unto David? He ought then to have waited three months. Further, if David was aware that he never came near her, why then did he send an order to him to go home and visit his wife, as it is written, 'Go down to thy house and wash thy feet' (II Sam. XI, 8)?"

'"He certainly was not aware of it, and indeed he waited even more than three months, namely, four months, as we have been taught: The twenty-fifth day of Nisan David called the people to arms, and the people assembled under Joab on the seventh of Sivan, when they went and smote the Ammonites. They remained there the months of Sivan, Tamuz, Ab, and Elul, and on the twenty-fourth of Elul happened the incident of Bath-Sheba. And on the day of Kippur (Atonement) the Holy One, blessed be He, forgave him that sin. According to another account, on the seventh day of Adar David called the people to arms, and they assembled on the fifteenth of Iyar, and on the fifteenth of Elul happened the incident of Bath-Sheba, and the day of Kippur he was vouchsafed the message: 'The Lord also hath put away thy sin: thou shalt not die' (Ibid. XII, 13), to wit, thou shalt not die at the hand of Duma."

'"O Lord of the universe, I have still one argument, that he himself pronounced his doom, saying: 'As the Lord liveth, the man that hath done this deserveth to die' (Ibid. 5). He thereby condemned himself, and my charge against him stands."

'"Thou hast no power over him since he made confession to Me and said 'I have sinned against the Lord', although he was not guilty. As for his sin in the matter of Uriah, I prescribed a penalty for him which he suffered immediately.

'Duma returned then crestfallen to his place. It is in regard to this that David said: "Unless the Lord had been my help, but a little would have been wanting that my soul had dwelt in duma" (silence) (Ps. XCIV, 17). That is, if the Lord had not been my advocate, "it wanted but little, etc." Only by the hairbreadth which is between me and the "Sinister Power" did my soul escape from the clutches of Duma A man should therefore be on his guard not to let slip an incautious word like David, since he will not be able to plead with Duma "that it was an error" (Eccl. V, 5), like David, who was vindicated by the Holy One, blessed be His Name; "wherefore should God be angry at thy voice, and destroy the work of thy hands?" (Ibid.), i.e., the flesh of the holy covenant which the man has defiled and which, as a punishment, is stretched in Gehinnom at the hand of Duma.'

[R. Simeon resumed:] 'The words "And the firmament showeth his handiwork" (Ps. XIX, 2) are an allusion to the companions who kept the bride company and are the custodians of her covenant. Every one of them He telleth and inscribeth. The "firmament" here mentioned is that one wherein are the sun, the moon, the stars, and constellations, and which constitutes the Recording Book. He telleth and inscribeth every one of them as denizens of the heavenly Palace, whose desires shall always be accomplished. "Day unto day uttereth speech" (Ibid. 3); each sacred day of the heavenly days utters the praises of the companions and repeats each word of exposition which was exchanged between them: day unto day expresses that word and extols it. "And night unto night revealeth knowledge" (Ibid.): that is, all the forces ruling in the night extol to one another the deep knowledge of the companions, and become their devoted friends. "There is no speech, there are no words, neither is their voice heard" (Ibid. 4): this refers to worldly conversation, which is not heard by the holy King, nor does He desire to hear it. But as for those words of wisdom, "their line is gone out through all the earth" (Ibid. 5), they trace

Zohar: Bereshith, Section 1, Page 9a

the measure and the plan of all celestial and all terrestrial habitations: it is indeed through those words that the heavens were made, and it is through the praises sung in those words that the earth was made. Nor think that they rest only in one spot: we are told "and their words to the end of the earth" (Ibid.). Who, then, inhabits the heavens made by them? "In them hath he set a tent for the sun" (Ibid.): the sacred sun has made his habitation in them and is crowned in them. Thus we read "And he is as a bridegroom coming out of his chamber" (Ibid. 6), gaily coursing through those heavens. When he emerges from them and hastens to another tower in another place, "his going forth is from the end of the heavens" (Ibid. 7), he issues from the supernal world, which is as the "extremity of heaven" above. "His circuit" (Ibid.) is the extremity of heaven" below, viz. the circuit of the year, which goes completely round and extends from the heaven to our firmament. "And there is nothing hid from his heat" (Ibid.), i.e. from the heat of this circuit, and from the circuit of the sun, which embraces every side; from this "nothing is hid", i.e. no one of all the upper grades is hid from him, since all come round to him, and not one is hidden "from his heat" when he returns to them in full strength. All this praise and laudation is on account of the Torah (Law), as we read, "The Law of the Lord is perfect, etc." (Ibid. 8-10). We find in this passage six times the mention of the Lord (tetragrammaton) as well as six verses from "The heavens declare" up to "The Law of the Lord is perfect". Likewise the first word of the Torah, Bereshith (in the beginning) consists of six letters, and the rest of the first verse, "created God the heaven and-the earth", also consists of six words. The six verses of our text correspond to the six letters, and the six mentions of the Name correspond to the six words.'

Whilst they were sitting there entered his son, R. Eleazar, and R. Abba. He said to them: 'Of a certainty the face of the Shekinah has arrived, and it is for this reason that I named you Peniel, because you have seen the Shekinah face to face. And now that you have learnt the secret of the verse concerning Benaiah the son of Jehoiada, an exposition indeed emanating from the Ancient and Holy One, as well as of the verse following, I am going to expound to you another even more mysterious verse in another passage.' He then opened his discourse thus: 'It is written, And he slew an Egyptian, a man of great stature, five cubits high (I Chr. XI, 23). There is here the same hidden meaning as in the verses just mentioned. By "the Egyptian" is meant that well-known figure who was "very great in the land of Egypt in the eyes of the servants, etc." (Exod. XI, 3). He was great and honoured, as Rab Hamnuna explained. In the heavenly Academy, however, the words ish middah (man of dimension) were explained as "one whose dimensions extended from one end of the world to the other", which were the dimensions of the first man, Adam. Those "five cubits", then, must have been such as to extend from one end of the world to the other. To return, however: "And in the Egyptian's hand was a spear like a weaver's beam" (I Chr. XI, 23). This alludes to the divine rod which was in Moses' hand, and on which there was engraved the divine ineffable Name radiating in various combinations of letters. These same letters were in possession of Bezalel, who was called "weaver", and his school, as it is written: "Them hath he filled with wisdom of heart... of the craftsman and the skilled workman, and the weaver, etc." (Exod. XXXV, 35). So that rod had engraved on it the ineffable Name on every side, in forty-two various combinations, which were illumined in different colours. The rest of the verse is as he already explained. Happy is his portion! Come, dear friends, come and let us renew the preparations of the bride in this night. For everyone who keeps vigil with her in this night will be guarded above and below and will complete the year in peace. It is of them that it is written: "The angel of the Lord encampeth round about them that fear him and delivereth them: O consider and see that the Lord is good." (Ps. XXXIV, 8-9).'

R. Simeon opened his discourse thus: 'It is written, In the beginning God created. This verse must be well laid to heart, for he who affirms that there is another god will be destroyed from the world. It is written: Thus shall ye say unto them: The gods that have not made the heavens and the earth, these shall perish from the earth and from under the heavens. (Jer. X, 11). Why has this verse

Zohar: Bereshith, Section 1, Page 9b

been written in Aramaic, with the exception of the last word? It cannot be because the holy angels do not pay attention to Aramaic and do not understand it, for then all the more was it appropriate for this verse to be written in

Hebrew, so that the angels should acknowledge its doctrine. The true reason certainly is that the angels, since they do not understand Aramaic, shall not come to be jealous of man and do him evil. For in this verse the holy angels are comprised, as they are called Elohim (gods, powers), and yet they have not made heaven or earth. Instead of wearka (and the earth) there should have been written the proper Aramaic word wear'a. Arka, however, is one of the seven nether earths, the place inhabited by the descendants of Cain. When Cain was banished from the face of the earth, he descended into that land and there propagated his kind. That earth consists of two sections, one enveloped in light, the other in darkness, and there are two chiefs, one ruling over the light, the other over the darkness. These two chiefs were at perpetual war with each other, until the time of Cain's arrival, when they joined together and made peace; and therefore they are now one body with two heads. These two chiefs were named 'Afrira and Kastimon. They, moreover, bear the likeness of holy angels, having six wings. One of them had the face of an ox and the other that of an eagle. But when they became united they assumed the image of a man. In time of darkness they change into the form of a two-headed serpent, and crawl like a serpent, and swoop into the abyss, and bathe in the great sea. When they reach the abode of Uzza and Azael they stir them up and rouse them. These then leap into the "dark mountains", thinking that their day of judgement has come before the Holy One, blessed be His Name. The two chiefs then swim about in the great sea, and when night comes they fly off to Na'amah, the mother of the demons (shedim), by whom the first saints were seduced; but when they think to approach her she leaps away six thousand parasangs, and assumes all shapes and forms in the midst of the sons of men, so that the sons of men may be led astray after her. These two chiefs then fly about through the world, and return to their abode, where they arouse sensual desires in the descendants of Cain to bear children. The heaven above that earth is not like ours, nor are the seasons of seed and harvest the same as ours, but they only return after cycles of many years. "These Elohim", then, "who have not made heaven and earth [may] perish from" the upper earth of the universe, so that they should have no dominion there, should not traverse it and should not cause men to pollute themselves "through anything that chanceth by night"; and for that "they will perish from the earth and from underneath the heaven" which were made in the name of Eleh, as has been explained above. It is for that reason that this verse has been written in Aramaic, so that the angels should not think that they are alluded to and so bring accusations against us. This, too, is the secret of the last word, to wit, Eleh, which being a sacred name, could not be altered into Aramaic.'

R. Eleazar said to his father: 'Regarding what is written in the same passage, Who will not fear thee, O King of the Gentiles? For it befitteth thee (Jer. X, 7), is this such a high eulogy?' His father said to him: 'Eleazar, my son, this passage has been variously explained, but for its full meaning we must go to its continuation, which reads: For among all the wise men of the Gentiles, and in all their royalty, there is none like unto thee. (Ibid.) The purpose of this verse is to express the view of the sinners, who fancy that God does not know their thoughts, and to answer them according to their folly. Once,' he continued, 'a Gentile philosopher came to visit me and argued with me thus: You say that your God rules in all the heights of heaven, and that all the heavenly hosts and legions cannot approach Him and do not know His place. If so, then this verse, saying "For among all the wise men of the Gentiles, and in all their royalty there is none like unto thee", does not extol Him very highly, for what special glory is there for Him not to find among perishable men His like?

Zohar: Bereshith, Section 1, Page 10a

And further, you infer from the passage which says "And there hath not arisen a prophet since in Israel like unto Moses" (Deut. XXXIV, 10), that only in Israel hath there not arisen, but among the other nations of the world there did arise one like him; and on this analogy I am justified in inferring that only among the wise of the Gentiles there is none like Him, but among the wise of Israel there is. If that is so, such a God, the like unto whom is to be found among the wise men of Israel, cannot be all-powerful. Look closely into the verse and you will find that it bears out my inference. I replied to him: Indeed, what you say is actually true. Who raises the dead to life? Only the Holy One alone, blessed be He; yet Elijah and Elisha came and raised the dead to life. Who causes rain to fall? Only the Holy One alone, blessed be He; yet Elijah came and kept back the rain and then made it descend again, through his prayer. Who made heaven and earth? The Holy One alone, blessed be He; yet Abraham came and they were firmly established for his sake. Who regulates the course of the sun? None but the Holy One, blessed be He; yet Joshua came and ordered it to stand still in its place and it stood still, as it is written, "And the sun stood and the moon stayed" (Jos. X, 13). The Holy One blessed be He, issues decrees, but similarly Moses issued decrees, and they were fulfilled. Further, the Holy One, blessed be He, pronounces judgements and the righteous of Israel annul them, as it is written, "The righteous ruleth the fear of God" (II Sam. XXIII, 3). And further, He commanded them to follow literally in His ways, and to be like Him in every way. That philosopher then went to K'far Shekalim and became a proselyte, and was given the name of Yose Katina (humble), and he studied the Torah diligently until he became one of the most learned and pious men of that place.'

'Now,' continued R. Simeon, 'we must look more closely into this verse. We remark at once that another passage says: "All the nations are as nothing before him" (Is. XL, 17). What special glorification is then here expressed? Is He only the King of the Gentiles and not the King of Israel? the explanation is this. We find in every place in the Scriptures that the

Holy One, blessed be He, has desired to be glorified only by Israel and has attached His name to Israel only; so it is written: "The God of Israel", "the God of the Hebrews" (Exod. V, 1, 3), and further: "Thus saith the Lord, the King of Israel" (Is. XLIV, 6). The nations of the world therefore said: We have another Patron in heaven, since your King has dominion only over you alone and not over us. Hence the verse comes and says: "Who would not fear thee, O King of the Gentiles? Forasmuch as among all the wise men of the nations", alluding thereby to the great chiefs in heaven appointed over the Gentiles. The expression "and in all their royalty there is none like unto thee" alludes to the celestial government, inasmuch as there are four rulers on high who, by the will of God, rule over all the other nations; and for all that, not one of these has the power to do the smallest thing except as He commands them, as it is written: "And he doth according to his will in the host of heaven, and among the inhabitants of the earth" (Dan. IV, 32). "The wise ones of the Gentiles" are, then, the heavenly superintendents from whom they draw their wisdom; and the phrase "and in all their royalty" implies the heavenly over-lords of the nations, as has just been explained. This is the plain meaning of the passage. But in ancient books I have found it expounded as follows. Although these heavenly hosts and legions (who are "the wise of the nations and their royalty") have the control of the affairs of this world and have each their mission allotted to them, who of them can accomplish the least thing "like unto thee"? For Thou excellest in Thy work on high and below above all of them. "There is not like unto thee, O Lord", that is, What Holy Unknown is there who acts and is like Thee above and below, and is on an equality with Thee in all respects? The work of the Holy King is heaven and earth, but "they are vanity, and their costly idols cannot profit" (Is. XLIV, 9). Of the Holy One, blessed be He, it is written, "In the beginning God created etc.", but of the lower royalty it is written "And the earth was chaos and confusion".'

Said R. Simeon to the companions: 'Come all you that participate in this bridal festivity, let each one of you prepare a decoration for the bride.' To R. Eleazar his son he said: 'Eleazar, offer a present to the heavenly bride so that on the morrow thou mayest be deemed worthy to behold her when she enters under the bridal canopy amidst the songs and hymns of the heavenly retinue.' R. Eleazar then opened his discourse thus: Who is this that cometh up ('Olah) out of the wilderness? (S. S. III, 6). The words Mi (Who?) and zoth (this) denote the separate holinesses of the two worlds joined in firm bond and union; and this union is said to be 'olah (a burnt-offering), and so holy of holies. For Mi is holy of holies, and zoth through its union with this becomes a burnt-offering ('olah), which is holy of holies. "Out of the wilderness,': because she had to come forth from there in order to become the heavenly bride and to enter under the nuptial canopy. Further, the term midbar (wilderness) signifies speech, as we read, "and thy speech (oumidbarekh) is comely" (Ibid. IV, 3): by that midbar which is the utterance

Zohar: Bereshith, Section 1, Page 10b

of the lips she goes up. Further, we have been taught as follows: It is written "these mighty gods; these are the gods that smote the Egyptians with all manner of plagues in the wilderness" (bamidbar) (I Sam. IV, 8). What does this verse mean? Was it only in the wilderness that the Lord showed them all His great deeds, and not in inhabited country? Not so, only the term bamidbar means "by means of the word", analogous to the expression "and thy speech (oumidbarekh) is comely" (S. S. IV, 3), or to the expression "and from the word (oumimidbar) did the mountains arise" (Ps. LXX, 7). Similarly here, "she rises up out of the word", that is, by means of uttered words she mounts up and nestles between the wings of the Mother, and then by the same means she descends and rests on the heads of the holy people. Her ascent is effected thus. At the beginning of the day, when a man rises in the morning, it is his duty to bless his Master as soon as he opens his eyes. The pious men of old used to have by them a cup of water, and when they awoke in the night they washed their hands and rose and occupied themselves in the study of the Torah, having first pronounced the appropriate blessing. When the cock crows it is precisely midnight, and at that moment the Holy One, blessed be He, is to be found in company with the righteous in the Garden of Eden (Gan-Eden). It is therefore proper then to pronounce the benediction and study the Torah; but one may not pronounce the benediction with unclean hands. So, too, at any time that one rises up from his sleep. For whilst a man is asleep his soul departs from him and an impure spirit comes forth and settles on his hands and defiles them: hence one may not pronounce a blessing without first washing them. Why then, one may ask, is it forbidden, after one has been in a privy, to pronounce a blessing or to read even one word of the Torah, even in the daytime, without washing the hands, although one has not been asleep, so that one's soul did not depart, and one's hands have not been defiled by an evil spirit? Why is it forbidden even if one's hands are quite clean? The answer is: woe to those who pay no heed to the majesty of their Master, and do not realise on what this world is founded. There is in every privy a spirit which feasts on filth and excrement, and settles forthwith on the fingers of a man's hands.'

R. Simeon further discoursed as follows: 'He who rejoices on the festivals but does not give to the Holy One, blessed be He, His due share, is selfish, the Satan tries to injure him and accuses him before heaven, compasses his downfall, and causes him endless trouble. To give the portion of the Holy One, blessed be He, means to make glad the poor, according to one's ability. For on these days the Holy One, blessed be He, goes to look at those broken vessels of His: He comes to them, and, seeing that they have nothing with which to rejoice on the festival, He weeps over them and reascends on high with intent to destroy the world. The members of the heavenly Academy then present themselves before Him and plead: "O Lord of the universe, Thou art called gracious and merciful, let Thy compassion be moved upon Thy children." The Lord makes answer: "Verily I have made the world only on the foundation of mercy, as it is written: 'I have said, the world is built on mercy' (Ps. LXXXIX, 3), and the world is established on it." Then the heavenly angels proceed: "O Master of the universe, behold so-and-so, who eats and drinks and is in a position to give charity but neglects to do so." Then the Accuser comes and, having claimed and obtained permission, sets out in pursuit of that man. Whom have we in the world greater than Abraham, whose benevolence extended to all creatures? Once, we are told, he prepared a feast, as it is written: "And the child grew, and was weaned. And Abraham made a great feast on the day that Isaac was weaned" (Gen XXI, 8). To that feast Abraham invited all the great men of the age. Now we have been taught that whenever a banquet is given, the Accuser comes to spy out whether the owner has first dispensed charity and invited poor people to his house. If he finds that it is so, he departs without entering the house. But if not, he goes in and surveys the merry-making, and having taken note that no charity had been sent to the poor nor had any been invited to the feast, he ascends above and brings accusations against the owner. Thus, when Abraham invited to his feast the great men of the age, the Accuser came and appeared at the door in the guise of a poor man, but no one took notice of him. Abraham was attending on the kings and magnates; Sarah was giving suck to all their babes; for people did not believe that she had born a child, and said that it was only a foundling from the street, and so all the guests brought their infants with them, and Sarah suckled them in the presence of all, as it is written, "Who would have said

Zohar: Bereshith, Section 1, Page 11a

unto Abraham that Sarah should give children suck?" (Ibid. 7) (note the plural "children"). The Accusing Angel was still standing at the door when Sarah said: "God hath made laughter for me" (Ibid. 6). The Accusing Angel then presented himself before the Holy One, blessed be He, and said to Him: "O Master of the world, Thou hast said 'Abraham is my friend'; behold, he has made a feast and has not given anything to Thee nor to the poor, nor hath he offered up to Thee so much as one pigeon; and further, Sarah said that Thou hast made mock of her." The Lord made answer: "Who in this world can be compared to Abraham?" Nevertheless the Accusing Angel did not stir from thence until he had spoilt all the festivity; and the Lord after that commanded Abraham to offer up Isaac as an offering, and it was decreed that Sarah should die from anguish on account of her son's danger-all this because Abraham did not give anything to the poor.'

R. Simeon further discoursed thus: 'It is written, Then Hezekiah turned his face to the wall, and prayed unto the Lord. (Is. XXXVIII, 2.) Observe how powerful is the might of the Torah, and how it surpasses any other force. For whoso occupies himself in the study of the Torah has no fear of the powers above or below, nor of any evil haps of the world. For such a man cleaves to the tree of life, and derives knowledge from it day by day, since it is the Torah that teaches man to walk in the true path, and gives him counsel how to repent and return to his Master so that He may annul the evil decreed against him; nay, even if it has been further decreed that it shall not be annulled, yet it is annulled and no longer threatens that man in this world. Hence it is incumbent upon a man to occupy himself in the study of the Torah day and night without cessation, in accordance with the text, "and thou shalt meditate therein day and night" (Jos. I, 8); and if he abandons such study, it is as though he abandoned the tree of life. Here, then, is a wise counsel for man. When a man goes to bed of a night, he should acknowledge wholeheartedly the kingship of heaven, and should entrust his soul to the keeping of heaven: he will then immediately be guarded against all diseases and evil spirits, and they will have no power over him. In the morning, when he rises from his bed, he should bless his Master, proceed to His house, bow down before His sanctuary with awe, and then offer up his prayer. For this, he must take counsel of the holy patriarchs, as it is written: "But as for me, in the abundance of thy lovingkindness will I come into thy house: I will bow down towards thy holy temple in the fear of thee" (Ps. V, 8). This verse has been interpreted to imply that a man should not enter the Synagogue without first taking counsel of Abraham, Isaac, and Jacob, for the reason that it is they who instituted prayer to the Holy One, blessed be He. Thus, in the verse just mentioned, the words "but as for me, in the abundance of thy lovingkindness will I come into thy house" are an allusion to Abraham; "I will bow down towards thy temple", to Isaac; "in the fear of thee", to Jacob. It is fitting, then, to invoke their names first and then enter the synagogue to offer up one's prayer. Of such a one it is written: "And he said unto me, Thou art my servant, Israel, in whom I will be glorified" (Is. XLIV, 3).

R. Phineas was a frequent visitor at the house of R. Rehumai, who lived on the shore of the lake of Gennesareth. He was a man of note, well advanced in years, and had lost his sight. Said he one day to R. Phineas: 'Verily I have heard that our colleague Yohai possesses a precious jewel. [Tr. note: His son, R. Simeon.] I did look at that jewel, and it flashed like the radiance of the sun when he emerges from his sheath, and flooded the world with a light which radiated from heaven to earth and spread to the whole world, until the Ancient of Days was duly enthroned. That light is wholly contained in thy household, and from that light there emanates a tiny and tenuous ray which is shed abroad and illumines the whole world. Happy is thy portion! Go forth, my son, go forth and try to find that gem which illumines the world, for the hour is propitious.' R. Phineas took his leave and embarked in a boat in the company of two other men. He noticed two birds which were flying to and fro over the sea, and cried to them: 'Birds, birds, ye that fly about over the sea, have ye seen anywhere the resting-place of the son of Yohai?' He paused a while and then said: 'Birds, birds, go your way and bring me answer.' They flew away and disappeared in the distance, but before R. Phineas left the boat they returned, and one of them was holding in its mouth a written note stating that the son of Yohai had left the cave together with his son Eleazar. R. Phineas then went to visit him, and found him sadly changed, with his body full of sores. He wept

Zohar: Bereshith, Section 1, Page 11b

and said: 'Woe unto me that I see thee thus!' He replied: 'Happy is my portion that thou seest me thus, for otherwise I would not be what I am.' R. Simeon then opened his discourse on the precepts of the Torah. He said: 'The precepts of the Torah which the Holy One has given to Israel are all laid down in the first chapter of Genesis in summary. In the Beginning God created. [Tr. note: The remainder of this chapter is more in the style of the Raya Mehemnah than of the Zohar.] This contains the first precept of all, to wit, the fear of the Lord, as it is written: "The fear of the Lord is the beginning of wisdom" (Ps. CXI, 10), as well as: "The fear of the Lord is the beginning of knowledge" (Prov. I, 7). It is the beginning and the gateway of faith, and on this precept the whole world is established. There are three types of fear: two have no proper root, while the third is the real fear. There is the man who fears the Holy One, blessed be He, in order that his children may live and not die, or lest he be punished in his body or his possessions; and so he is in constant fear. Evidently this is not the genuine fear of God. Another man fears the Holy One, blessed be He, because he is afraid of punishment in the other world and the tortures of Gehinnom. This is a second type which is not genuine fear. The genuine type is that which makes a man fear his Master because He is the mighty ruler, the rock and foundation of all worlds, before whom all existing things are as nought, as it has been said: "and all the inhabitants of the earth are as nought" (Dan. IV, 32), and place his goal in that spot which is called yir'ah (fear).' R. Simeon here wept and said: 'Woe to me if I tell and woe to me if I do not tell! If I tell, then the wicked will know how to worship their Master; and if I do not tell, then the companions will be left in ignorance of this discovery. Corresponding to the "holy fear" there is an "evil fear" below which scourges and accuses, and which is a lash for punishing the wicked. Now he whose fear is of punishment and accusation is not endowed with that fear of God which leads to life. The fear which rests upon him is that evil fear of the lash, but not the fear of the Lord. For this reason the spot which is called "the fear of the Lord" is also called "the beginning of knowledge". Hence this precept is laid down here, as it is the principle and root of all the other precepts of the Torah. He who cherishes fear observes the whole Torah, and he who does not cherish fear does not observe the other precepts of the Torah, since it is the gate of all. Therefore it is written: Bereshith, through a beginning, that is, fear, God created heaven and earth. For he who transgresses this transgresses all the precepts of the Torah; and his punishment is to be scourged by the evil lash. This is implied in the words: "And the earth was chaos and confusion (tohu wabohu), and darkness was upon the face of the abyss." This is an allusion to the four kinds of punishment which are meted out to the wicked: tohu (chaos) alludes to strangulation, as it is written: "a line of (tohu) chaos" (Is. XXXIV, 11), meaning a measuring cord. Bohu (confusion) alludes to stoning ("stones of confusion", ibid.) by the stones which are sunk in the great abyss for the punishment of the wicked; "Darkness" is burning, as it is written: "And it came to pass, when ye heard the voice out of the midst of the darkness, while the mountain did burn with fire,' (Deut. V, 20), also: "and the mountain burned with fire into the heart of heaven and darkness, etc. "(Ibid. IV, 11): this is the fire that rests on the heads of the wicked to consume them. The "wind" alludes to beheading by the sword, which whirls round the wicked like a tempest, as it is said: "and the flaming sword which is turned every way" (Gen. III, 24). These punishments are meted out to those who transgress the precepts of the Torah, and the words which allude to them follow immediately after the word "beginning", which symbolises the fear of God, which is the summary of all the precepts. Then follow all the other precepts of the Torah.

'The second precept is the one which is indissolubly bound up with the precept of fear, namely, love; that a man should love his Master with a perfect love, that which is called "great love". This is implied in the command: "walk before me, and be thou wholehearted" (Gen. XVII, 1), to wit, in love. This is implied also in the verse: And God said, Let there be light, which alludes to the perfect love, called great love. Herein, then, is the precept for man to love his Master truly.' Said R. Eleazar, 'Father, I have heard a definition of perfect love.' His father said to him 'Expound it, my son, whilst R. Phineas is present, for he truly practises it.' R. Eleazar then explained thus: '"Great love" is the love which is complete through the union of two phases, without which it is not

Zohar: Bereshith, Section 1, Page 12a

genuine love; and this is signified by the dictum that the love of the Holy One, blessed be He, has two aspects. There is, for instance, the man who loves Him because he has riches, length of life, children, power over his enemies, success in all his undertakings-all of these form the motive of his love. Should the Holy One, blessed be He, turn the wheel of fortune against him and bring suffering upon him, he will change and his love will be no more. This kind of love has no root. Perfect love is the kind which remains steadfast in both phases, whether of affliction or prosperity. The right way of loving one's Master is expressed in the traditional teaching which says: "even if he deprive thee of thy life". This is, then, perfect love, embracing two phases. It was for this reason that the light of creation which first emerged was afterwards withdrawn. When it was withdrawn suffering emerged, in order that there might be this perfect love.' R. Simeon embraced his son and kissed him; R. Phineas also came and kissed him and blessed him, saying: 'Of a surety, the Holy One, blessed be He, sent me hither, and this is the meaning of the "tiny light" which I was told was somewhere in my household and would illumine the whole world.' Said R. Eleazar: 'Assuredly, fear must not be forgotten in any of the precepts, least of all in this precept of love, which requires the association of fear. How is this to be achieved? In this way. Love, as has been said, may in one phase be inspired by favours, such as riches, length of life, children, plenty, and affluence. In such cases a man should be ever haunted by the fear lest sin may cause a reversal. Of such a one it is written: "Happy is the man that feareth always" (Prov. XXVIII, 14), since he combines fear and love. The "adverse influence" (sitra ahra) which brings suffering and chastisement is therefore necessary in the world, since it rouses in man fear: for through chastisement a man becomes filled with the true fear of God, and does not harden his heart; for if he does, then "he that hardeneth his heart shall fall into evil" (Ibid.), to wit, into the hands of that "adverse influence" which is called "evil". Thus we have a love which is complete in both phases, and from this results a true and perfect love.

'The third precept is to acknowledge that there is a God, all-powerful and ruler of the universe, and to make due proclamation of his unity every day, as extending in the six supernal directions, and to unify them all through the six words contained in the Shema Israel, and in reciting these to devote oneself wholly to God. The word Ehad therefore must be dwelt on to the length of six words. This is implied in the passage, Let the waters under the heaven be gathered together unto one place: that is, let the grades beneath the heaven be unified in it so as to form one whole, perfect in all the six directions. With God's unity one must further associate fear, for which reason one must dwell on the daleth, the last letter of Ehad, the daleth being for that reason written larger than the other letters. And this is implied in the words "and let the dry land be seen", that is, let the daleth, which is a "dry land", be associated with that unity. After forming this union on high it is necessary to repeat the process for the lower world through all its multiplicity in the six lower directions. This is expressed in the verse we recite after the Shema, viz. "Blessed-be the-name-of the-glory-of His-Kingdom for-ever and-ever", which contains another six words expressive of the unity. In this way, what was dry land becomes fertile soil to produce fruits and flowers and trees. This is implied in the passage: "And God called the dry land earth", that is, by the manifestation of God's unity here below the earth was duly perfected. It is for this reason that in the account of the third day the expression "that it was good" appears twice, once for the manifestation of the unity above and once for the manifestation of the unity below. As soon as that unity was made manifest at both ends, the text says "Let the earth put forth grass", that is, the earth was then fitted to produce fruits and flowers according to its capacity.

'The fourth precept is to acknowledge that the Lord is God, as we read: "Know this day, and lay it to thy heart that the Lord, he is God" (Deut. IV, 39); namely, to combine the name Elohim (God) with the name Tetragrammaton (Lord) in the consciousness that they form an indivisible unity. And this is the inner meaning of the text: Let there be lights in the firmament of heaven. The omission of the vau from the word emoroth (lights) points to complete unity, to the black light and the white light being only two manifestations of one indivisible light.

Zohar: Bereshith, Section 1, Page 12b

The same is symbolised by the "white cloud by day" and the "cloud of fire by night" (Exod. XIII, 21); the two phases of day and night are complementary to each other, both forming one whole, in order-as we read-"to give light upon earth". Herein consisted the sin of the primeval serpent who united below but divided above, and so caused the mischief we still lament. The right way, on the contrary, is to recognise diversity below but unity above, so that the black light becomes wholly merged above and afterwards unified in respect of its diverse elements, and so is kept away from the evil power. It is therefore necessary for man to acknowledge that "God" and "the Lord" are one and the same without any cleavage whatever: "The Lord he is God" (I Kings XVIII, 39); and when mankind will universally acknowledge this absolute unity, the evil power (sitra ahra) itself will be removed from the world, and exercise no more influence on earth. This is hinted in the word meoroth, which is made up of or (light), surrounded by moth (death), just as the brain, symbolic of light, is enveloped in a membrane symbolic of the baneful power (sitra ahra) which is death. Should the light (or) be removed, the letters on either side would coalesce and form death (moth)....

'The fifth precept. It is written: And God said, Let the waters swarm with the movement of living creatures. This verse contains three precepts-to labour in the study of the Torah, to beget children, and to circumcise a male child on the eighth day by removing the foreskin. It behoves a man to labour in the study of the Torah, to strive to make progress in it daily, so as thereby to fortify his soul and his spirit: for when a man occupies himself in the study of the Torah, he becomes endowed with an additional and holy soul, as it is written: "the movement of living creatures", that is, a soul (nefesh) derived from the holy centre called "living" (hayah). Not so is it with the man who does not occupy himself with the study of the Torah: such a man has no holy soul, and the heavenly holiness does not rest upon him. But when a man earnestly studies the Torah, then the motion of his lips wins for him that "living soul" and he becomes as one of the holy angels, as it is written: "Bless the Lord, ye angels of his" (Ps. CIII, 20), to wit, those who occupy themselves in the study of the Torah, and who are therefore called His angels on earth. The same are alluded to in the words: "and let birds fly on the earth". So much for his reward in this world. As regards the other world, we have been taught that the Holy One, blessed be He, will provide them with wings as of eagles, enabling them to fly across the whole universe, as it is written: "But they that wait for the Lord shall renew their strength, then shall mount up with wings as eagles" (Is. XLIV, 31). This, then, is the interpretation of that which is written: "Let the waters swarm with the movement of living creatures": the Torah, which is symbolised by water, possesses the virtue of implanting in her devotees a mobile soul derived from the place called "living" (hayah), as has already been said. David alluded to this when he said: "Create in me a clean heart, O God", so that I may be devoted to the Torah, and thus "renew a steadfast spirit within me" (Ps. LI, 12).

'The sixth precept is to be fruitful and multiply. For he who performs this precept causes the stream (of existence) to be perennially flowing so that its waters never fail, and the sea is full on every side, and new souls are created and emerge from the "tree" (of life) and the celestial hosts are increased in company with those souls. This is implied in the words: Let the waters swarm with the movement of living souls. This is an allusion to the holy and imperishable covenant, to the perennially rushing stream, the waters of which continually swell and produce new swarms of souls for that "living" (hayah). Along with the souls as they arise there appear many winged beings who fly about all over the world, and whenever a soul descends into this world the winged being that issued together with it from that tree accompanies it. Two accompany each soul, one on its right hand, and one on its left. If the man is worthy they constitute themselves his guardians, as it is written: "For he will give his angels charge over thee" (Ps. XCI, 11), but if not, they act as his accusers.' Said R. Phineas: 'Three

Zohar: Bereshith, Section 1, Page 13a

is the number of angels who keep guard over a man who is worthy, as it is written: "If there be for him an angel, an intercessor, one among a thousand, to vouch for man's uprightness" (Job. XXXIII, 23). "If there be for him an angel" signifies one; "an intercessor" signifies another one; "one among a thousand to vouch for man's uprightness" is a third one.' R. Simeon said: 'Five angels, since it is written further: "And He is gracious unto him, and saith". "And he is gracious unto him" implies one, "and saith" implies another one.' R. Phineas replied: 'It is not so, as the expression "And he is gracious unto him" refers only to the Holy One, blessed be He, no one else having the power to dispense grace.' Said R. Simeon: 'You are right. Now' (he continued) 'he who refrains from propagating his kind derogates, if one might say so, from the general form in which all individual forms are comprehended, and causes that river to cease its flow and impairs the holy covenant on all sides. Of such a one it is written, "And they shall go forth and look upon the carcasses of the men that have rebelled against me" (Is. LXVI, 24)-' against me" assuredly. This is the punishment for the body, and as for his soul, she will not enter at all "within the curtain", and will be banished from the next world.

'The seventh precept is to circumcise the male child on the eighth day after birth and thereby to remove the defilement of the foreskin. The "living" (hayah) of which we have spoken forms the eighth grade in the scale, and hence the soul which has flown away from it must appear before it on the eighth day. And in this way it is made clear that this is really a "living soul", emanating from that holy "living" and not from the "unholy region". And this is alluded to in the words: Let the waters swarm, which in the Book of Enoch are explained thus: Let the water of the holy seed be stamped with the stamp of the "soul of the living", which is the form of the letter yod impressed on the holy flesh in preference to all other marks. The words, "and let winged beings fly on the earth" are a reference to Elijah, who traverses the universe in four swoops in order to be present at the initiation of the child into the holy covenant. It is proper to prepare for him a seat and to proclaim, "This is the throne of Elijah"; otherwise he will not be present. The words "And the Lord created the two great fishes" refer to the two operations, circumcision and uncovering, which represent the male and female principles; "and every living soul that moves" refers to the stamping of the sign of the holy covenant, which is a holy living soul, as has been explained. "Wherewith the waters swarmed": to wit, the supernal waters which were drawn towards that distinguishing mark. And it is for that reason that the Israelites were stamped with that sign of holiness and purity; for just as the supernal holy beings are marked in such a way as to distinguish between the "holy region" and the impure "unholy region", so the Israelites are marked in order to distinguish between the holy people and the idolatrous nations who are derived from the impure "unholy region", as has been already explained. And in the same way as the Israelites themselves are marked, so are the clean animals and birds permitted to them for food marked off from the other animals and birds eaten by the Gentiles. Happy the portion of Israel!

'The eighth precept is to love the proselyte who comes to be circumcised and to be brought under the wings of the "Divine Presence" (Shekinah), which takes under its wings those who separate themselves from the impure "unholy region" and come near unto her, as it is written: Let the earth bring forth a living soul according to its kind. Think not that the same "living soul" which is found in Israel is assigned to all mankind. The expression "after its kind" denotes that there are many compartments and enclosures one within the other in that region which is called "living", beneath its wings. The right wing has two compartments, which branch out from it for two other nations who approach Israel in monotheistic belief, [Tr. note: Al. "are most closely related to Israel."] and therefore have entrance into these compartments. Underneath the left wing there are two other compartments which are divided between two other nations, namely Ammon and Moab. All these are included in the term "soul of the living". There are besides under each wing other concealed enclosures and divisions from whence there emanate souls which are assigned to all the proselytes who enter the fold-these are indeed termed "living soul", but "according to its kind": they all enter under the wings of the Shekinah, and no farther. The soul of Israel, on the other hand, emanates from the very body of that tree and from thence flies off into the very bowels of that earth. This is hinted in the words: "For ye shall be a delightsome land" (Mal. III 12). It is for that reason that Israel is called a "darling son", for whom the bowels, as it were, of the Shekinah yearn, and that the children of Israel are called "those who are born from the womb", and not merely from the outer wings. Furthermore,

Zohar: Bereshith, Section 1, Page 13b

the proselytes have no portion in the celestial tree, much less in the body of it; their portion is only in the wings and no more. The righteous proselytes, therefore, rest underneath the wings of the Shekinah and are united to it there, but penetrate no further, as has already been explained. Therefore we read: Let the earth bring forth a living soul according to its kind, namely, cattle, and creeping thing, and beast of the earth after its kind, that is to say, all derive their soul from that source called "living", but each according to its kind, from the grade appropriate to itself.

'The ninth precept is to show kindness to the poor and to provide them with their needs, as it is written: Let us make man in our image, after our likeness; that is, "let us make man", as a compound being, including the male and female, "in our image", to wit, the rich; "after our likeness", to wit, the poor. For the rich are from the male side and the poor from the female. For as the male and the female act in cooperation, showing compassion to each other and mutually exchanging benefits and kindnesses, so must man here below act rich and poor in co-operation, bestowing gifts upon each other and showing kindness to each other. We have seen the following mystical observation in the Book of King Solomon. He who of his own impulse shows pity to the poor will retain forever unchanged the original form of the first man, and by that impress of the likeness of Adam he will exercise dominion over all creatures of the world. This is implied in the words: "And the fear of you and the dread of you shall be upon every beast of the earth, etc." (Gen. IX, 2), that is, all and every one will be in fear and in dread of that image which characterises man. For this is a noble precept, by means of which man can rise in the image of Adam above all other creatures. This we know from Nebuchadnezzar who, in spite of the dream that he had seen, as long as he showed mercy to the poor suffered no evil effects; but as soon as he selfishly neglected the poor, what do we read about him? "While the word was in the King's mouth, etc." (Dan. IV, 28), his image changed and he was driven from men....

'The tenth precept is to put on tephillin (phylacteries), and thereby to attain in oneself the perfection of the divine image, according to that which is written: And the Lord created man in His own image.'

R. Simeon discoursed in this connection on the text "Thy head upon thee is like Carmel" (S. S. VII, 6). 'This verse,' he said, 'has already been explained in a way, but its true meaning is as follows: "Thy head upon thee is like Carmel" alludes to the phylactery worn on the head above, containing four sections of the Torah which represent each one of the four letters of the Divine Name (Tetragrammaton) of the most high King. Our teachers have told us that the verse: "that the name of the Lord is called upon thee, and they shall be afraid of thee" (Deut. XXVIII, 10) alludes to the phylactery worn on the head which represents the Divine Name in order of its letters. Thus, the first section, "Sanctify unto me all the first-born, etc." (Exod. XIII, 2) represents the Yod, which is the first of all the supernal sanctities; "whatsoever openeth the womb" (Ibid.) is an allusion to the slender stroke underneath the yod which opens the womb to bring forth fitting fruit. The second section, "And it shall be when the Lord shall bring thee, etc." (Ibid. 5) represents the He, significant of the palace the womb of which was opened by the Yod. It is through fifty mysterious gates and forecourts and enclosures that the Yod makes an opening and enters that palace, causing the sound to issue from the great Shofar. For the Shofar was closed on all sides and the Yod came and opened it to cause the emission of its sound; and as soon as he opened it he emitted a blast as a signal for the freeing of the slaves. It was at the blowing of that Shofar that the Israelites went forth from Egypt. And the same will be repeated at the end of days. Indeed, every deliverance is preceded by the blowing of that Shofar. Hence the deliverance from Egypt is included in this section, since it resulted from that Shofar when under the pressure of the Yod it opened its womb and produced its sound as a signal for the deliverance of the slaves. So much as regards the He, the second letter of the Divine Name. The third section contains the mystery of the unity in the proclamation: "Hear, O Israel, etc." (Deut. VI, 4), and is represented by the Vau, which is the summary of all, expressive of absolute unity, combining and absorbing all. The fourth section "And it shall come to pass if ye shall hearken, etc." (Ibid. XI, 13-21) presents the two influences

Zohar: Bereshith, Section 1, Page 14a

to which the Congregation of Israel-the manifestation of God's power below-is subjected. This, then, is represented by the second He, which takes up the previous letters and contains them. The phylacteries are thus literally the counterpart of the letters of the Divine Name. Hence "Thy head upon thee is like Carmel" is an allusion to the phylactery worn on the head; and the "hair (dallath, lit. poverty) of the head" signifies the phylactery worn on the hand, which is poor in comparison to that worn on the head above, but which nevertheless has its own perfection like that which it symbolises above. "The King is held captive in the tresses thereof", that is, the heavenly King is duly enshrined in these compartments of the Tephillin through the Divine Name therein contained in manner due. Thus he who equips himself with them is a man made in the image of God, for just as the letters of Holy Name are united to express the divine essence, so in a degree they are united by him (through the phylacteries). "Male and female he created them" is a reference to the phylactery of the head and the phylactery of the hand, which together make one whole.

'The eleventh precept is to give the tithe of the produce of the land. This includes two precepts, one the tithing of the land and the other the giving of the first fruits of the trees; for it is written: Behold I have given you every herb yielding seed, which is upon the face of all the earth. The expression "I have given" is applied to tithe in the passage: "And unto the children of Levi, behold, I have given all the tithe in Israel" (Num. XVIII, 21), and it is written besides: "And all the tithe of the land, whether of the seed of the land, or of the fruit of the tree, is the Lord's" (Lev. XXVII, 30).

'The twelfth precept is to bring as an offering the fruits of the tree, which is alluded to in the words: and every tree in which is the fruit of a tree yielding seed, that is, although whatever is consecrated to God may not be eaten by man, yet God permitted them (the Levites) to enjoy all His tithe and the first fruit of the tree. I have given to you; that is, to you and not to the generations in the future.

'The thirteenth precept is to redeem the first-born son so as to attach him firmly to life. Forevery man is attended by two angels, one of life and one of death, and by redeeming his first-born son the father ransoms him from the angel of death, who therefore has no power over him. This is hinted in the words: And God saw everything that he had made, to wit, creation as a whole, and, behold it was good; this alludes to the angel of death. Through the act of redemption, then, the life-angel is strengthened, whilst the death-angel is weakened. By means of this redemption the child obtains life, as has already been stated; the evil power leaves him and has no more hold on him.

'The fourteenth precept is to observe the Sabbath day, which was the day of rest from all the works of Creation. This precept comprises two parts, one to rest on the Sabbath, and one to invest it with holiness. We have to observe that day as a day of rest, as has already been said, for the reason that it was a day of rest from the beginning, the whole work of Creation having been completed before this day was sanctified. After the day was sanctified there was left a residue of spirits for which no bodies had been created. Why, it may be asked, could not God have waited to sanctify the day until He had created bodies for those spirits? The reason is that from the tree of the knowledge of good and evil there went forth the "evil power" to seize control of the world, and so a number of diverse spirits set out to acquire for themselves bodies by force. As soon as the Holy One, blessed be He, saw this, He raised out of the tree of life a wind that blew and lashed against the other tree so that the "beneficent power" arose and the day was sanctified. For the creation of bodies and the stirring of spirits on that night comes about under the influence of the "beneficent power" and not of the "evil power". Had the "evil power" forestalled on that night the "beneficent power", the world could not exist, on account of the evil spirits, for an instant. But the Holy One, blessed be He, provided the cure in advance; He hastened the sanctification of the day before the evil power prevailed, and so the world was established, and instead of the evil power becoming master of the world as it thought to be, on that night it was the "beneficent power" which obtained the victory, and therefore sacred bodies and spirits are being built up on that night under the influence of the "beneficent power". It is for that reason that the marital intercourse of the wise and learned men who know this

Zohar: Bereshith, Section 1, Page 14b

is weekly, from Sabbath to Sabbath. It is, moreover, the night on which the "evil power", being supplanted by the "beneficent power", roams about the world, accompanied by his many hosts and legions, and pries into all places where people perform their conjugal intercourse immodestly and by the light of a candle, with the result that the children born of such intercourse are epileptics, being possessed by spirits of that "evil power," which are the nude spirits of the wicked, called demons (shedim); these are pursued and killed by the demon Lilith. As soon as the day is sanctified the evil power becomes weakened and withdraws into hiding all the night and day of the Sabbath, with the exception of Assimon and his band, who roam about to spy out indecent intercourses and then go and hide themselves in the cave of the great abyss. As soon as Sabbath ends, innumerable hosts and companies of them commence to fly and roam to and fro through the world, and it is to ward them off that the recitation of the Hymn against Calamities (Ps. XCI) has been instituted, so as to destroy their power over the holy people. When, after issuing precipitately to obtain dominion over the holy people, they see them engaged in prayer and hymns, reciting the "Separation" (Habdalah) in the course of the prayer and afterwards over the cup, they flee and wander about until they reach the wilderness. May the Merciful One deliver us from them and from the evil power! Our teachers, of blessed memory, said: There are three persons who bring evil upon themselves. One is the man who utters a curse against himself; a second, he who throws on the floor pieces of bread of the size of an olive; the third, he who lights his candle at the close of the Sabbath before the congregation has reached the recital of the "Sanctification" at the close of the service, for thereby he causes the fire of Gehinnom to be kindled by that light before its time. There is a place in Gehinnom assigned for those who profane the Sabbath, and those who undergo there their punishment curse the man who has lighted a candle before the time and pronounce against him the verse: "Behold the Lord will hurl thee up and down with a man's throw, yea, he will wind thee round and round" (Is. XXII, 17). For it is not lawful to kindle a light at the close of the Sabbath before Israel has pronounced the "Separation Blessing" in the prayer and the "Separation Blessing" over the cup, as until that time it is still Sabbath, and the sanctity of the Sabbath still rests on us. At the moment, however, when we recite the "Separation Blessing" over the cup, all the armies and camps which have charge over the weekdays return each to its place and to its appointed service. For with the entrance of the Sabbath and at the moment when it is sanctified, holiness awakens and spreads its dominion over the world, and worldliness is divested of its rule, and until the close of the Sabbath they do not return to their place; and even when the Sabbath closes they do not return to their places until the Israelites pronounce the words, "Blessed art Thou, O Lord, who separatest the holy from the profane." Then holiness withdraws and the armies appointed over the weekdays rouse themselves and return each to its place and office. But yet they do not assume control until they become illumined through the light of the candle, for which reason they are called "fiery lights", because they spring from the fiery element, which gives them the power to rule over the terrestrial world. All this is only when a man lights a candle before the congregation has finished the recital of the "Sanctification" at the close of prayer. But when he waits until the close of that recital, the wicked in Gehinnom acknowledge the justice of the Holy One, blessed be He, and confirm for that man the blessings which the congregation recite in the words "So God give thee of the dew of heaven, etc." (Gen. XXVII, 28), as well as: "Blessed shalt thou be in the field, etc." (Deut. XXVIII, 3).

'"Happy is he that considereth the poor, the Lord will deliver him in the day of evil" (Ps. XLI, 2). We should have expected "in the evil day"; but the expression "the day of evil" alludes to the day when the "evil power" obtains permission to seize man's soul. Hence, "Happy is he that considereth the poor", to wit, the man sick of soul, so as to heal him of his sins before the presence of the Holy One, blessed be He. According to an alternative interpretation, "the day of evil" alludes to the last day of judgement of the world from which such a one will be delivered, as it says: "in the day of evil the Lord will deliver him", to wit, the day when the world is placed in the power of that evil one to chastise it.' [Tr. note: The text breaks off here abruptly.]

Zohar: Bereshith, Section 1, Page 15a

BERESHITH

[Tr. note: v. Appendix I.]

At the outset the decision of the King made a tracing in the supernal effulgence, a lamp of scintillation, [Tr. note: al. 'darkness'; al. 'measurement'.] and there issued within the impenetrable recesses of the mysterious limitless a shapeless nucleus [Tr. note: al. 'vapour'.] enclosed in a ring, neither white nor black nor red nor green nor of any colour at all. When he took measurements, he fashioned colours to show within, and within the lamp there issued a certain effluence from which colours were imprinted below. The most mysterious Power enshrouded in the limitless clave, as it were, without cleaving its void, remaining wholly unknowable until from the force of the strokes there shone forth a supernal and mysterious point. Beyond that point there is no knowable, and therefore it is called Reshith (beginning), the creative utterance which is the starting point of all.

It is written: And the intelligent shall shine like the brightness of the firmament, and they that turn many to righteousness like the stars forever and ever (Dan. XII, 3). There was indeed a "brightness" (Zohar). The Most Mysterious struck its void, and caused this point to shine. This "beginning" then extended, and made for itself a palace for its honour and glory. There it sowed a sacred seed which was to generate for the benefit of the universe, and to which may be applied the Scriptural words "the holy seed is the stock thereof" (Is. VI, 13). Again there was Zohar, in that it sowed a seed for its glory, just as the silkworm encloses itself, as it were, in a palace of its own production which is both useful and beautiful. Thus by means of this "beginning" the Mysterious Unknown made this palace. This palace is called Elohim, and this doctrine is contained in the words, "By means of a beginning (it) created Elohim." The Zohar is that from which were created all the creative utterances through the extension of the point of this mysterious brightness. Nor need we be surprised at the use of the word "created" in this connection, seeing that we read further on, "And God created man in his image" (Gen. I, 27). A further esoteric interpretation of the word Bereshith is as follows. The name of the starting point of all is Ehyeh (I shall be). The holy name when inscribed at its side is Elohim, but when inscribed by circumscription [Tr. note: i.e. between the two Ehyeh's. v. Ex. III, 4.] is Asher, the hidden and recondite temple, the source of that which is mystically called Reshith. The word Asher (i.e. the letters, Aleph, Shin, Resh from the word Bereshith) is anagrammatically Rosh (head), the beginning which issues from Reshith. So when

Zohar: Bereshith, Section 1, Page 15b

the point and the temple were firmly established together, then Bereshith combined the supernal Beginning with Wisdom. Afterwards the character of that temple was changed, and it was called "house" (bayith). The combination of this with the supernal point which is called rosh gives Bereshith, which is the name used so long as the house was uninhabited. When, however, it was sown with seed to make it habitable, it was called Elohim, hidden and mysterious. The Zohar was hidden and withdrawn so long as the building was within and yet to bring forth, and the house was extended only so far as to find room for the holy seed. Before it had conceived and had extended sufficiently to be habitable, it was not called Elohim, but all was still included in the term Bereshith. After it had acquired the name of Elohim, it brought forth offspring from the seed that had been implanted in it.

What is this seed? It consists of the graven letters, the secret source of the Torah, which issued from the first point. That point sowed in the palace certain. three vowel-points, holem, shureq, and hireq, which combined with one another and formed one entity, to wit, the Voice which issued through their union. When this Voice issued, there issued with it its mate which comprises all the letters; hence it is written Eth hashammaim (the heavens), to wit, the Voice and its mate. This Voice, indicated by the word "heaven", is the second Ehyeh of the sacred name, the Zohar which includes all letters and colours, in this manner. Up to this point the words, "The Lord our God the Lord" (Tetragrammaton Elohenu Tetragrammaton) represent three grades corresponding to this deep mystery of Bereshith bara Elohim. Bereshith represents the primordial mystery. Bara represents the mysterious source from which the whole expanded. Elohim represents the force which sustains all below. The words eth hashammaim indicate that the two latter are on no account to be separated, and are male and female together. The word eth consists of the letters aleph and tau, which include between them all the letters, as being the first and last of the alphabet. Afterwards he was added, so that all the letters should be attached to he, and this gave the name attah (Thou); hence we read "and Thou (ve-attah) keepest all of them alive" (Neh. IX, 6). Eth again alludes to Adonai (Lord), who is so called. Hashammaim is Tetragrammaton in its higher signification. The next word, ve-eth, indicates the firm union of male and female; it also alludes to the appellation ve-Tetragrammaton (and the Lord), both explanations coming to the same thing. Ha-aretz (the earth) designates an Elohim corresponding to the higher form, to bring forth fruit and produce. This name is here found in three applications, and thence the same name branches out to various sides.

Up to this point only extend the allusions to the Most Mysterious who carves out and builds and vivifies in mysterious ways, through the esoteric explanation of one verse. From this point onwards bara shith, "he created six", from the end of heaven to the end thereof, six sides which extend from the supernal mystic essence, through the expansion of creative force from a primal point. Here has been inscribed the mystery of the name of forty-two letters.

And the intelligent shall shine (Dan. XII, 3). This "shining" corresponds to the movement given by the accents and notes to the letters and vowel-points which pay obeisance to them and march after them like troops behind their kings. The letters being the body and the vowel-points the animating spirit, together they keep step with the notes and come to a halt with them. When the chanting of the notes marches forward, the letters with their vowel-points march behind them, and when it stops they also stop. So here: "the intelligent" correspond to the letters and the vowel-points; "the brightness" to the notes; "the firmament" to the flow of the chant through the succession of notes; while "they that turn to righteousness" correspond to the pausal notes, which stop the march of the words and bring out clearly the sense. These "cause to shine" letters and vowels, so that they all flow together in their own mystical manner through secret paths. From this impetus the whole was extended. Again, the words "and the intelligent shall shine as the brightness of the firmament" may be referred to the pillars and sockets of the "celestial palanquin" (apiryon). [Tr. note: v. p. 110.] The "wise and intelligent" as the supernal pillars and sockets, since they ponder with understanding all things needful for the upholding of the palace. This use of the term "intelligent" (maskilim) has its parallel in the passage: "Blessed is he that considereth (maskil) the poor" (Ps. XLI, 2). "They will shine", for if they do not shine and give light, they cannot well consider and ponder the needs of the palace. "As the brightness of the firmament",

Zohar: Bereshith, Section 1, Page 16a

namely, of that firmament which rests upon those "intelligent" we have mentioned, and of which it is written, "And over the head of the Hayyah there was the likeness of a firmament, like the colour of the terrible ice" (Ezek. I, 22). "The brightness" is that which illumines the Torah, and which illumines also the heads of the Hayyah, those heads being the "intelligent", who shine continually and ever contemplate the "firmament" and the light which issues therefrom, to wit, the light of the Torah which radiates perpetually without cease.

NOW THE EARTH HAD BEEN VOID AND WITHOUT FORM. The word hoithah (was), being a pluperfect, implies that the earth had been previously. There was snow in the midst of water, from the action of which was produced a slime. Then a mighty fire beat upon it and produced in it a refuse. So it was transformed and became Tohu (chaos), the abode of slime, the nest of refuse, and also Bohu (formlessness), the finer part which was sifted from the Tohu and rested on it. The word "darkness" in the text alludes to this mighty fire. This darkness covered the Tohu, namely the refuse, and was buoyed up by it. The "spirit of God" is a holy spirit that proceeded from Elohim Hayyim (living God), and this "was hovering over the face of the waters". When this wind blew, a certain film detached itself from the refuse, like the film which remains on the top of boiling broth when the froth has been skimmed off two or three times. When Tohu had thus been sifted and purified, there issued from it "a great and strong wind rending the mountains and breaking in pieces the rocks", like that which Elijah saw (I Kings XIX, 11, 12). Similarly Bohu was sifted and purified, and there issued from it earthquake, as with Elijah. 'I'hen what we call "darkness" was sifted, and there was contained in it fire, just as to Elijah there appeared "after the earthquake fire". When what we call "spirit" was sifted, there was contained in it a still, small voice. Tohu is a place which has no colour and no form, and the esoteric principle of "form" does not apply to it. It seems for a moment to have a form, but when looked at again it has no form. Everything has a "vestment" except this. Bohu, on the other hand, has shape and form, namely, stones immersed in the chasm of Tohu, but sometimes emerging from the chasm in which they are sunk, and drawing therefrom sustenance for the world. Through the form of their vestment they draw sustenance from above to below, and ascend from below above, and therefore they are hollow and strong. These are suspended in the expanse; that is to say, sometimes they are suspended in the expanse when they rise out of the chasm, and sometimes they are hidden, to wit, on the "day of cloud", when they draw waters from the abyss to supply therewith Tohu, for then there is joy that Tohu was spread in the universe. "Darkness" is a black fire, strong in colour. There is a red fire, strong in visibility; a yellow fire, strong in shape; and a white fire, the colour which includes all. "Darkness" is the strongest of all fires, and this it was which took hold of Tohu. "Darkness" is fire, but fire is not darkness, save when it takes hold of Tohu. The symbol for this is, "his eyes were dim so that he could not see, and he called Esau, etc." (Gen. XXVII, 1). Here, too, "the countenance of the evil one was darkened" because it countenanced the evil one. Hence this fire is called "darkness" because it rested upon Tohu and took hold of it; this is the inner meaning of the words "and darkness on the face of the abyss". "Spirit" is the voice which rests on Bohu, and grasps it and guides it as required. This is symbolised in the words "The voice of the Lord is on the waters" (Ps. XXIX, 3); and so, too, "the spirit of the Lord was hovering over the face of the waters". By "face of the waters" is meant stones sunk in the abyss, so called because waters issue from them. Thus each was provided as befitted. Tohu is under the aegis of the name Shaddai; Bohu, under that of Zebaoth; Darkness, under that of Elohim; Spirit, under that of Tetragrammaton. We now understand what happened to Elijah: "there was a strong wind breaking the mountains, but the Lord was not in the wind", because this name was not in it, since Shaddai presides over it through the mystic nature of Tohu. "After the wind there was a quaking, but the Lord was not in the quaking", since over it presides the name of Zebaoth, through the mystic nature of Bohu (which is called "quaking" (ra'ash), because it quakes continually. "After the quaking there was a fire, but the Lord was not in the fire", because over it presides the name Elohim from the side of darkness. "And after the fire there was a small still voice"; and here at last was found the name Tetragrammaton. There are in this verse four clauses corresponding to the four so-called "sections of the body" and "limbs" which, being four, are resolvable into twelve. Here, too, is the graven name of twelve letters which was transmitted to Elijah in the cave.

Zohar: Bereshith, Section 1, Page 16b

[Note: The first 27 lines of the English translation do not correspond to the Hebrew text. Line 28 of the English text corresponds to the passage beginning on line 5 of the Hebrew text.]

AND GOD SAID, LET THERE BE LIGHT; AND THERE WAS LIGHT. From this point we can begin to discover hidden things relating to the creation of the world in detail. For up to this point the Creation has been described in general, and lower down the general description is repeated, so that we have a combination of general-particular-general. [Tr. note: i.e. according to the Rabbinical system of hermeneutics, the 'general' (heaven-and-earth) is of the same nature as the 'particular' (days), being like them the product of a 'saying']. Up to this point the whole was suspended in the void in direct dependence on the limitless. When, however, energy had been extended through the supernal palace alluded to in the name Elohim, the term "saying" is used in connection with it, in the words "And God said". For to that which is beyond no detailed "saying" is ascribed; for although the word Bereshith is a creative utterance (maamar), the actual words "and said" are not used in connection with it. This expression "and said" (vayomer) opens the door to inquiry and understanding. We define this "saying" as an energy that was culled, as it were, in silence from the mystic limitless through the mystic power of thought. Hence "and God said" means that now the above-mentioned palace generated from the holy seed with which it was pregnant. While it brought forth in silence, that which it bore was heard without. That which bore, bore in silence without making a sound, but when that issued from it which did issue, it became a voice which was heard without, to wit, "Let there be light." Whatever issued came forth under this category. The word Yehi (let there be) indicates that the union of the Father and Mother symbolised by the letters Yod He became now a starting-point (symbolised by the second Yod) for further extension.

LIGHT, AND THERE WAS LIGHT. These words imply that there had already been light. This word, awr (light), contains in itself a hidden significance. The expansive force proceeding from the hidden recesses of the secret supernal ether opened a path and produced from itself a mysterious point (or, rather, the En Sof (Limitless) clave its own ether and disclosed this point), Yod. When this expanded, that which was left of the mysterious AWIR (ether) was found to be AWR (light). When the first point had developed from it, it showed itself upon it, touching and yet not touching it. When it expanded, it emerged into being, and thus was light (awr) left from ether (awir); and this is what we mean by saying that it "had been" previously; and so it remained. It went up and was stored away, and there was left of it one dot, which continually approaches by invisible paths the other point, touching and yet not touching, illuminating it in the manner of the first point from which it issued. Therefore the whole is linked together, and it illumines both one and the other. When it ascends, all ascend and are attached to it, and it reaches the place of En Sof, where it is stored away, and all becomes one. This dot of the word Awr is Light. It extended, and there shone forth in it seven letters of the alphabet, which did not solidify and remained fluid. Afterwards Darkness issued, and there issued in it seven other letters of the alphabet, and they too were not solidified and remained fluid. There then issued the Firmament, which prevented discord between the two sides. In it there issued eight other letters, making twenty-two in all. Seven letters jumped from one side and seven from the other, and all were graven in this Firmament, where they remained for a time fluid. When the firmament solidified, the letters were also solidified, and took material shape. Thus there was graven there the Torah to shine abroad. "Let there be light": to wit, El Gadol (great God), that which emerged from the primal ether. "And there was": this signifies Darkness, which is called Elohim. "Light": signifying that the Left was included in the Right, and so from that which we call El was produced Elohim. Right was included in Left and Left in Right.

AND GOD SAW THE LIGHT THAT IT WAS GOOD. This is the Central Column: Ki Tob (that it was good) threw light above and below and on all other sides, in virtue of Tetragrammaton, the name which embraces all sides. AND GOD DIVIDED: He put away strife, so that the whole was in perfect order. AND GOD CALLED. The word called here means called to" or "invited". God summoned to issue forth from this complete Light which was in the centre a certain radiance which is the foundation of the world, and on which worlds are established. From that complete Light, the Central Pillar, extended the foundation, the Life of worlds, which is day from the side of the Right. AND THE DARKNESS HE CALLED NIGHT. He summoned to issue from the side of Darkness a kind of female moon which rules over the night and is called night, and is associated with Adonai, the Lord of all the earth. The Right entered into the complete Pillar of the centre united with the Left, and the primal point thereupon ascended on high and there seized

Zohar: Bereshith, Section 1, Page 17a

the energy of three dots, the holem, the shureq, and the hireq, the seed of holiness (for no seed has been sown save from this source).

The whole was then united in the Central Pillar, and it produced the foundation of the world, which therefore is called Kol (all), because it embraces the whole in the radiation of desire. Meanwhile the Left flamed forth with its full power, producing at all points a kind of reflection, and from this fiery flame came forth the female moonlike essence. This flaming was dark because it was from Darkness. These two sides produced these two grades, one male and one female. Unity was retained in the Central Pillar from that surplus of light which was in it. For since that Central Pillar was complete in itself and made peace on all sides, additional light was lent to it from above and from all sides through the universal joy in it. From that additional joy came forth the foundation of worlds, which was also called Musaf (additional). From this issue all the lower powers and spirits and holy souls, alluded to in the expressions, "Lord of hosts" (Tetragrammaton Zebaoth) and "God the God of spirits" (Num. XVI, 22). "Night" is "the Lord of all the earth" from the side of the left, from Darkness. It was because the desire of Darkness was to merge itself in the Right, and it was not strong enough, that night spread from it. When night began to spread, and before it was complete, Darkness went and merged itself in the right, and the night was left defective. Just as it is the desire of Darkness to merge itself in Light, so it is the desire of night to merge itself in day. Darkness abated its light, and therefore it produces a grade which was defective and not radiant. Darkness does not radiate save when it is merged in Light. So night which issued from it is not light save when it is merged in day. The deficiency of night is only compensated by the Musaf. What is added in one place is subtracted from the other. The Musaf contained a symbolism of the supernal point and of the Central Pillar, and therefore two letters were added in respect of it which were lacking in respect of the night, viz. the vau yod of vayikra (and he called). Herein is an allusion to the name of seventy-two letters, the tracing of the supernal crown.

AND GOD SAID, LET THERE BE A FIRMAMENT IN THE MIDST OF THE WATERS. Here in the particular (day) there is an allusion to the separation of the upper from the lower waters through that which is called "the Left". Here, too, discord was created through that which is called "the Left". For up to this point the text has alluded to the right, but now it alludes to the left; and therefore there was an increase of discord between this and the right. It is the nature of the right to harmonize the whole, and therefore the whole is written with the right, since it is the source of harmony. When

40

the Left awoke there awoke discord, and through that discord the wrathful fire was reinforced and there emerged from it the Gehinnom, which thus originated from the left and continues there.

Moses in his wisdom pondered over this and drew a lesson from the work of creation. In the work of creation there was an antagonism of the left against the right, and the division between them allowed the Gehinnom to emerge and to fasten itself to the left. Then the Central Column, which is the third day, intervened and allayed the discord between the two sides, so that the Gehinnom descended below, and the Left became absorbed in the Right and there was peace over all. Similarly the quarrel of Korah with Aaron was an antagonism of the left against the right. Moses, reflecting on what had happened during the Creation, said: 'It seems proper to me to compose the difference between the right and the left.' He therefore endeavoured to effect an accord between the two. The left, however, was not willing, and Korah proved obdurate. Moses thereupon said: 'Assuredly the Gehinnom is embittering this quarrel. The left ought to strive upwards and absorb itself in the right. Korah has no wish to attach himself to the higher influences and to merge himself in the right. Let him, then, descend below in the impetus of his wrath.' The reason why Korah refused to allow the quarrel to be composed by the intervention of Moses was that he had not entered upon it for a truly religious motive, and that he had scant regard for the glory of God, and refused to acknowledge His creative power. When Moses perceived that he had thus placed himself outside the pale, he "was very wroth" (Num. XVII, 15). He was "wroth" because he was not able to compose the quarrel; he was "very wroth" because they denied the creative power of God. Korah denied

Zohar: Bereshith, Section 1, Page 17b

this power wholly, both in the higher and the lower sphere, as implied in the phrase: "when they strove against the Lord" (Num. XXVI, 9). Hence Korah clave to that which was meet for him. A dispute that was composed on the pattern of the supernal dispute, that became more and not less worthy as it proceeded, and that perpetuated itself rightfully, was that between Shammai and Hillel. The Holy One, blessed be He, approved of their dispute, for the reason that its motive was lofty and that it therefore resembled that which took place at the Creation. Hence, like the latter, the dispute between Shammai and Hillel has survived to this day. Korah, on the other hand, denied the Creation, fought against heaven itself and sought to confute the words of the Torah. He certainly was of the following of the Gehinnom, and therefore remained attached to it. All this is brought out in the Book of Adam. It says there that when Darkness asserted itself, it did so with fury, and created the Gehinnom, which attached itself to it in that quarrel we have mentioned. But as soon as the wrath and the fury abated there arose a quarrel of another kind, to wit, a quarrel of love. Thus the dispute fell into two distinct parts. It is the way of the righteous to enter on a dispute stiffly and end it amicably. Korah continued the dispute as he began it, in wrath and passion; and therefore clung to Gehinnom. Shammai conducted his dispute in that spirit of calm which should follow on the first burst of passion; it therefore became a quarrel of love and obtained the approval of Heaven. This is indicated by our text. It says first: "Let there be a firmament in the midst of the waters, and let it divide, etc." This refers to the beginning of quarrel, the outburst of passion and violence. There was a desire for reconciliation, but meanwhile the Gehinnom arose before the wrath and passion cooled down. Then "God made the firmament, etc."; that is, there emerged a quarrel of love and affection which made for the permanence of the world. And in this category is the dispute between Shammai and Hillel, the result of which was that the Oral Law approached in a loving mood the Written Law, so that they mutually supported each other.

As regards separation, it always proceeds from the left. Here it is written, "and let it separate", as well as, "and he separated"; and in connection with Korah it is written, "Is it a small thing unto you that the God of Israel hath separated you from the congregation of Israel, etc."; and it is also written, "At that time the Lord separated the tribe of Levi" (Deut. X, 8). In all these texts we find separation associated with the second (day or tribe), which is the place of the left. It may be objected that Levi was the third and not the second tribe; separation, then, should have been associated, not with Levi, but with Simeon, he being the second.

The answer is that in the eyes of Jacob (who, on the first night of his nuptials, was unaware that Leah was substituted for Rachel) Levi was the second (from Leah). Hence the separation of the tribe of Levi was perfectly correct. There is a "separation" on every outgoing of the Sabbath, between the powers that have sway on week-days and on the Sabbath respectively. As soon as the Sabbath ends, there ascends from the Gehinnom, from the grade called Sheol, a party of evil spirits who strive to mingle among the seed of Israel and to obtain power over them. But when the children of Israel perform the ceremonies of the myrtle and the cup of blessing, and recite the separation prayer (Habdalah), that evil spirit departs to his place in Sheol, the region where Korah and his accomplices abide, as it is written: "And they and all that appertained to them went down alive into the Sheol" (pit) (Num. XVI, 33). These, too, did not descend to the Sheol before the Israelites had performed a separation (Habdalah), as it is said: "Separate yourselves from among this congregation" (Ibid. 21). "Separation" is thus associated with the second, which is symbolic of the left, at its first impetus, when it first enters on a quarrel in wrath and violence, giving birth to Gehinnom before the fury subsides. It was on the second that, before the discord was allayed, the Gehinnom was created. Then also were created all the angels

41

who revolted against their Master, and whom the fire of the Gehinnom consumed and destroyed; likewise all those others who vanish away and do not endure and are consumed by fire.

LET THERE BE A FIRMAMENT: i.e. let there be a gradual extension. Thereupon El (God), the "right cluster", [Tr. note: al. 'shoulder': in either case a designation of the grade Hesed (kindness).] El Gadol (Great God), spread forth from the midst of the waters to complete this name El and to combine with this extension, and so El was extended into Elohim (=El+H, Y, M). These H, Y, M, extended and became reversed so as to form lower waters, Y, M, H. This extension which took place on the second day is the upper waters. The he, yod, mim, form hayam (the sea), which is the upper waters. The reversal of these letters, yamah (seaward), is the lower waters. When they were firmly established, all became one whole, and this name was extended to a number of places. The upper waters are male and the lower waters female. At first they were commingled, but afterwards they were differentiated into upper and lowers waters. This is the meaning of "Elohim upper waters", and this is the meaning of "Adonai lower waters"; and this is the meaning of upper He and lower He. It is further written: AND GOD MADE THE FIRMAMENT. That is to say, this extension took this name. Elohim is the upper waters, and the lower waters

Zohar: Bereshith, Section 1, Page 18a

are Adonai; nevertheless, since the upper waters were completed by the lower, this name spread to the whole.

Even after the separation between the waters, the discord did not cease till the third day, when peace was restored and everything was settled in its place. It is on account of this strife, necessary as it was for the existence of the world, that the phrase "that it was good" is not applied to the work of the second day, because it was not completed. So long as the upper and lower waters were commingled, there was no production in the world: this could only be when they were separated and made distinct. They then produced, and in this way, although on the second day there was separation and discord, the third day brought complete harmony. This is the name which is graven with the lettering the Tetragrammaton, to reconcile the upper with the lower waters, the upper with the lower He; the insertion of the Vau between them harmonises the two sides. Symbolic of this is the crossing by the Israelites of the Jordan (Josh. III, 16): "the waters (of the Jordan)" corresponds to the upper waters; "rose up in one heap" corresponds to the lower waters, which descended into the sea, whilst the Israelites passed between the two.

Five "firmaments" are mentioned in this section, and the Life of the World passes among them and leads them, and they are all interwoven. But for this discord, however, which was composed by the mediator, they would not have been intertwined or harmonised. They correspond to the five hundred years to which the Tree of Life clings in order to become a source of growth and fruitfulness to the world. All the waters of creation which issue from the original source branch out from its foot. King David similarly takes the whole and subsequently distributes it, as we read: "And he distributed among all the people, even among the whole multitude, etc." (II Sam. VI, 19); likewise we read: "That thou givest them they gather" (Ps. CIV, 28); also: "She rises also while it is yet night, and giveth meat to the household (Prov. XXXI, 15).

At the time when discord was stirred by the violence of the left, the Avenging Spirit was reinforced. There issued from it (two) demons which immediately became solidified without any moisture, one male and one female. From them were propagated legions of demons, and to this is due the inveteracy of the unclean spirit in all those demons. It is they who are symbolised by the foreskin (orlah); the one is called Ef'eh (adder) and the other is called Nahash (serpent), the two, however, being but one. The Ef'eh bears offspring from the Nahash after a period of seven years' gestation. Herein is the mystery of the seven names borne by the Gehinnom as well as by the "evil tempter" (yetser-hara'); and from this source impurity has been propagated in many grades through the universe. All this proceeds from the mystic power of the left, which dispenses good and evil, thereby rendering the world habitable. Here we have the engraven Name of eighteen letters, which presides over the gentle and beneficent rains for the well-being of the world.

AND GOD SAID, LET THE WATERS FLOW: The word flow (yikavvu) implies that they were to go in a line (kav) so as to take a straight path. For from the first mystic point the Whole issues in secret, until it reaches and is gathered into the supernal Palace, and from there it issues in a straight line to the other grades, until it comes to that place which collects the whole in a union of male and female; this is the "Life of worlds." THE WATERS: to wit, those that issue from on high, from under the upper He'. FROM UNDER THE HEAVEN: this is the lesser Vau (hence the word yikavva is spelt with two vau's, one for "the heaven" and one for "under the heaven"). In consequence: LET THE DRY LAND APPEAR. This is the lower He. This is disclosed and all the rest is undisclosed; from this last we conclude by inference to that which is undisclosed. TO ONE PLACE: so called because it is here that the whole of the upper World is linked into one.

It is written: The Lord (Tetragrammaton) is one and his name is One (Zech. XIV, 9). Two unifications are here indicated, one of the upper World in its grades, and one of the lower World in its grades. The unification of the upper World is consummated at this point. The Life of Worlds was there firmly based, and through its unity the upper World was bound together, and therefore it is called "one place". All grades and all members were gathered there and became in it one without any separation; nor is there any grade in which they are embraced in one unification save this. In it, too, they all mysteriously conceal themselves in one desire. In this grade the disclosed World is linked with the undisclosed. The disclosed World is similarly unified below, and the disclosed World is, in fact, a lower world. Hence such expressions as: "I saw the Lord" (Is. VI, 1), "And they saw the God of Israel" (Ex. XXIV, 10), "And the glory of the Lord appeared" (Num. XIV, 10: XVII, 7), "So was the appearance of the brightness round about; this was the appearance of the likeness of the glory of the Lord" (Ezek. I, 28). This, too, is the inner meaning of the words here, "and let the dry land appear". The same is referred to in the words, "My bow I have set in the cloud" (Gen. IX, 13): to wit, from the day on which the world was created. On the day

of cloud, when the bow, "the appearance of the likeness of the glory of the Lord" appeared, the Left arose in might. Then "Rachel went forth and had pain in childbirth". With her appeared Michael on one side, Raphael on another, and Gabriel on a third, these being the colours which appeared in the "likeness". Hence "the appearance of the brightness round about", to wit, the radiance which is hidden in the pupil of the eye, becomes "the appearance of the likeness of the glory of the Lord", to wit, corresponding colours, so that the lower unity is formed in correspondence with the upper unity. This is signified by the formula, "The Lord our God the Lord" (Deut. VI, 4). The mysterious and undisclosed colours which are linked "in one place" form one higher unity; the colours of the bow below in which are united white, red, and yellow, corresponding to those other mysterious colours, form another unity, signified by the formula "and his name is One". Further, the form "Blessed be the name of the glory of his kingdom forever and ever" signifies the lower unity, while the upper unity is signified by the form "Hear, O Israel, the Lord our God the Lord is one." These forms correspond, each having six words. [Tr. note: i.e. in the original Hebrew.]...

LET THE EARTH PUT FORTH GRASS, HERB, ETC. At this behest the "earth" put forth a host through those waters which were gathered together in one place and flowed mysteriously through it, so that there issued in it hidden celestial beings and sacred existences which are upheld and sustained and constantly renewed by the faithful among mankind through the worship they offer to their Master. This mystery is indicated by the verse: "Who causest the grass to spring up for the B'hema" (cattle), etc. (Ps. CIV, 14). This refers to Behemoth that crouches on a thousand mountains and for whom these mountains produce each day what is here called "grass", by which is meant those angelic beings whose existence is ephemeral, and who were created on the second day as destined food for that Behemoth, which is "fire consuming fire". The Psalmist continues, "and herb for the service of man", indicating by "herb" the angelic orders named Ofanim (wheels), Hayyoth (animal-shaped), and Cherubim, all of whom are upheld, sustained, and confirmed whenever mortal beings come to worship their Master with sacrifices and prayers, in which consists the "service of man", and as they are reinforced by virtue of that service of man, there springs up food and sustenance for the world, as it is written: "to bring forth bread out of the earth" (Ibid.). The same is implied here by the words HERB YIELDING SEED. For "grass" does not yield seed, but is only destined for food for the sacred fire, whereas "herb" helps to maintain the world. All this has for its purpose "to bring forth bread from the earth", i.e. to provide, by virtue of the service offered to their Master by human beings, food and sustenance out of the earth for this world, so that the heavenly blessings should descend on mankind. FRUIT TREE BEARING FRUIT. One degree above another, these combining male and female. Just as "fruit tree" produced the host of "trees bearing fruit", so the latter in turn produced "Cherubim and Pillars". "Pillars" are those that go up in the smoke of the sacrifices and derive their strength therefrom, and hence are called "pillars of smoke", and all of them exist permanently for the "service of man", whereas the "grass" has no permanence, being destined to be consumed as food, as it is written: "Behold now Behemoth, which I made with thee; he eateth grass as an ox" (Job XL, 15). The words "fruit tree bearing fruit" indicate the form of male and female in combination. Their faces are "like the face of a man" (Ezek. I, 10), but they are not like the Cherubim, having large faces covered with beards, whereas the Cherubim have little faces like those of tender children.

All forms are comprised in these, because they are "large faces". On them are traced forms like the tracings of the Divine Name on the four cardinal points, East, West, North, and South. Michael is imprinted on the South, and all faces are turned towards him, viz. "the face of a man... the face of a lion... the face of an ox... the face of an eagle" (Ibid.). "Man" implies the union of male and female, without which the name "man" (Adam) is not applied. By him are formed the figures of the chariot of God, as it is written: "(On) the chariot of God are myriads of thousands of Shin'an (angels)" (Ps. LXVIII, 15): the word SHiN'AN expresses by means of its initials all the figures, the Shin standing for Shor (ox), the Nun for Nesher (eagle), and the Aleph for Aryeh (lion), and the final Nun representing by its shape man,

who walks erect, and who mystically combines male and female. All those thousands and myriads of angels issue from those symbolised by the name Shin'an, and from these types they diverge in their several groups, each to its appropriate side. These four are all interlaced and intertwined in one another, to wit, ox, eagle, lion, man. Their activity is directed by four graven names, which they ascend to contemplate. "Ox" ascends to seek guidance and gaze in the face of "Man". There ascends with him a certain name crowned and engraved in two mystic forms, which represent the name El (God). Then it turns back and the throne engraves and traces it and it is imprinted thereon to be under the guidance of this mystic name. "Eagle" ascends to seek guidance and gaze in the face of "Man". There ascends with it another name, which is crowned and engraved in two mystic forms, to shine forth and to mount and be crowned on high; this represents the attribute "Great". Then it turns back and the throne engraves it and it is imprinted thereon to be under the guidance of this mystic name. "Lion" ascends to seek guidance and to gaze in the face of "Man". Another name ascends with it and is crowned and engraved in two mystic forms to be endowed with strength and power, representing the attribute of "Mighty". It turns back and the throne engraves it and it is imprinted thereon to be under the guidance of this mystic name. "Man" contemplates all of them, and all ascend and contemplate him. Thus they all become engraved in this form in the one mystic name known as "Tremendous" (Nora). Thus it is written concerning them, "And the likeness of their faces is as the face of man" (Ezek. I, 10). They are all embraced in that likeness, and that likeness embraces them all. In virtue of all this the Holy One, blessed be He, is called the Great, Mighty, and Tremendous God, since these names are engraved above on the supernal chariot which is comprised in the four letters of the Tetragrammaton, which is the name that comprises all. These likenesses are engraved on the throne, and the throne is decorated with them, one to the right, one to the left, one in front, and one behind, corresponding to the four quarters of the world. The throne when it ascends is stamped with these four likenesses. These four supernal names bear along the throne, and the throne is comprised in them, and collects a harvest of longing desires. When it has collected these desires, it descends with its burden like a tree laden with branches on all sides and full of fruit. As soon as it descends, these four likenesses come forth in their several shapes emitting bright flashes which scatter seed over the world. Hence it is written, "herb yielding seed", because these scatter seed over the world. But of the issuing forth of the likeness of man which comprises all the other likenesses it is written, "fruit tree yielding fruit after its kind, the seed of which is in it on the earth". It produces no seed save for propagation. The term "in it" should be noticed. It teaches us that man may not emit his seed idly. This is hinted in the word "verdure", which does not "yield seed", and hence has no permanency like the others, not having any likeness which can be shaped or engraved in any manner at all. Such things show themselves but to vanish: they have not acquired form and likeness, and have no permanency; they exist only for a moment and then are consumed in that fire which devours fire, and are continually renewed and devoured.

Man here below possesses an ideal form and likeness, but he is not so permanent as those supernal beings. These are formed in their proper shape without any outer covering to modify it. Hence they are changeless; whereas man below assumes form through the medium of an outer covering. Hence he endures for a while, and every night the spirit is divested of that garment and ascends and is consumed by that consuming fire, and then reverts to its former state and takes the same outer shape again. Hence they have not the same permanency as those supernal forms, and in allusion to this it is written, "new every morning" (Lam. III, 23), i.e. human beings who are renewed every day.

Zohar: Bereshith, Section 1, Page 19b

The reason is that "great is thy faithfulness" (Ibid.)—great and not little. "Great is thy faithfulness": assuredly great, since it can support all the creatures of the world and comprise them all in itself, upper and lower alike. It is of infinite expanse, it absorbs all and becomes no fuller. This is alluded to in the verse, "All the rivers run into the sea, yet is the sea not full, etc." (Eccl. I, 7). They run into the sea, and the sea receives and swallows them and is not filled, and then it restores them to their former state. Hence "great is thy faithfulness". In the account of this (third) day it is written twice "that it was good", the reason being that this day became intermediary between two opposing sides, and removed discord. It said to this side "good", and to the other side "good", and reconciled the two. Hence we find twice written in the account of it, "and he said". Connected with this day is the secret of the name of four letters engraved and inscribed, which can be made into twelve (by permutations), corresponding to the four images on the four sides inscribed on the holy throne.

AND GOD SAID, LET THERE BE LIGHTS, ETC. The word for "lights" (meoroth) is written defectively, as if me'eroth (curses), for the reason that the children's disease, croup, was through them created. For after the primordial light was withdrawn there was created a "membrane for the marrow", a k'lifah, and this k'lifah expanded and produced another. As soon as this second one came forth she went up and down till she reached the "little faces". [Tr. note: v. p 79.] She desired to cleave to them and to be shaped as one of them, and was loth to depart from them. But the Holy One, blessed be He, removed her from them and made her go below. When He created Adam and gave him a partner, as soon as she saw Eve clinging to his side and was reminded by his form of the supernal beauty, she flew up from thence and tried as before to attach herself to the "little faces". The supernal guardians of the gates, however, did not permit her. The Holy One, blessed be He, hid her and cast her into the depths of the sea, where she abode until the time that Adam and his wife sinned. Then the Holy One, blessed be He, brought her out from the depth of the sea and gave her power over all those children, the "little faces" of the sons of men, who are liable to punishment for the sins of their fathers. She then wandered up and down the world. She approached the gates of the terrestrial paradise, where she saw the Cherubim, the guardians of the gates of Paradise, and sat down near the flashing sword, to which she was akin in origin. When she saw the flashing sword revolving, she fled and wandered about the world and, finding children liable to punishment, she maltreated and killed them. All this is on account of the action of the moon in diminishing her (original) light. When Cain was born this k'lifah tried for a time without success to attach herself to him, but at length she had intercourse with him and bore spirits and demons. Adam for a hundred and thirty years had intercourse with female spirits until Naamah was born. She by her beauty led astray the "sons of God", Uzza and Azael, and she bore them children, and so from her went forth evil spirits and demons into the world. She wanders about at nighttime, vexing the sons of men and causing them to defile themselves. Wherever these spirits find people sleeping alone in a house, they hover over them, lay hold of them and cleave to them, inspire desire in them and beget from them. They further inflict diseases on them without their being aware-all this through the diminution of the moon. When the moon was restored, the letters of meoroth (lights) were reversed to form imrath (word), as it is written, "the word (imrath) of the Lord is tried, he is a shield to those that trust in him" (Ps. XVIII, 31), i.e. He is a shield against all those evil spirits and demons that wander about the world at the waning of the moon, unto those that hold fast to their faith in the Holy One, blessed be He. King Solomon, when he "penetrated into the depths of the nut garden" (as it is written, "I descended into the nut garden", S. S. VI, 11), took a nut-shell (klifah) and drew an analogy from its layers to these spirits which inspire sensual desires in human beings, as it is written, "and the delights of the sons of men (are from) male and female demons" (Eccl. II, 8). This verse also indicates that the pleasures in which men indulge in the time of sleep give birth to multitudes of demons. The Holy One, blessed be He, found it necessary to create all these things in the world to ensure its permanence, so that there should be, as it were, a brain with many membranes encircling it. The whole world is constructed on this principle, upper and lower, from the first mystic point up to the furthest removed of all the stages. They are all

Zohar: Bereshith, Section 1, Page 20a

coverings one to another, brain within brain and spirit within spirit, so that one is a shell to another. The primal point is the innermost light of a translucency, tenuity, and purity passing comprehension. The extension of that point becomes a "palace" (Hekal), which forms a vestment for that point with a radiance which is still unknowable on account of its translucency. The "palace" which is the vestment for that unknowable point i s also a radiance which cannot be comprehended, yet withal less subtle and translucent than the primal mystic point. This "palace" extends into the primal Light, which is a vestment for it. From this point there is extension after extension, each one forming a vestment to the other, being in the relation of membrane and brain to one another. Although at first a vestment, each stage becomes a brain to the next stage. The same process takes place below, so that on this model man in this world combines brain and shell, spirit and body, all for the better ordering of the world. When the moon was in connection with the sun, she was luminous, but as soon as she separated from the sun and was assigned the charge of her own hosts, she reduced her status and her light, and shells upon shells were created for covering the brain, and all for the benefit of the brain. Hence meoroth is written defectively. All this was for the benefit of the world, and hence it is written, "to give light upon the earth".

AND GOD MADE THE TWO GREAT LIGHTS. The word "made" signifies the due expansion and establishment of the whole. The words "the two great lights" show that at first they were associated as equals, symbolising the full name Tetragrammaton Elohim (although the latter part is not revealed, but is known inferentially). The word "great" shows that at their creation they were dignified with the same name, so that through them the name of the Whole was called Mazpaz Mazpaz, [Tr. note: If the Hebrew alphabet is inverted, M= Y, Z=H, P=V.] the two highest names of the thirteen categories of mercy. [Tr. note: v. Ex.XXXIV, 6.] These were invested with greater dignity, and they are placed at the head because they derive from on high and ascend for the benefit of the world and for the preservation of worlds. Similarly the two lights ascended together with the same dignity. The moon, however, was not at ease with the sun, and in fact each felt mortified by the other. The moon said "Where dost thou pasture?" (S. S. I, 7). The sun said "Where dost thou make thy flock to rest at noon? (Ibid.) How can a little candle shine at midday?" God thereupon said to her, "Go and diminish thyself." She felt humiliated and said, "Why should I be as one that veileth herself?" (Ibid.). God then said, "Go thy way forth in the footsteps of the flock." Thereupon she diminished herself so as to be head of the lower ranks. From that time she has had no light of her own, but derives her light from the sun. At first they were on an equality, but afterwards she diminished herself among all those grades of hers, although she is still head of them; for a woman enjoys no honour save in conjunction with her husband. The "great light" corresponds to Tetragrammaton, and the "lesser light" to Elohim, which is the last of the degrees and the close of the Thought. At first it was inscribed above among the letters of the sacred Name, in the fourth letter thereof, but afterwards it took a lower rank with the name Elohim; nevertheless, it still ascends in all directions above in the letter He in the union of the letters of the sacred Name. Afterwards degrees extended on this side and on that. The degrees that extended upwards were called "the dominion of the day", and the degrees that extended downwards were called "the dominion of the night". "The stars" are the remainder of the forces and the hosts which, countless in number, are all suspended in that "firmament of the heaven" which is the "life of the universe", as it is written, "and God placed them in the firmament of the heaven to give light upon the earth." This is the lower earth, which derives light from them as they from above. On this (the fourth) day the kingdom of David was established, the fourth leg and support of the (divine) throne, and the letters (of the divine Name) were firmly fixed in their places. Yet withal until the sixth day, when the likeness of man was fully formed, the throne was not firmly fixed in its place; but then at last both the upper and the lower thrones were established, and all the worlds were settled in their places, and all the letters were fixed

Zohar: Bereshith, Section 1, Page 20b

in their spheres by the extension of the primordial vapour. The fourth day was "rejected of the builders", because on it this luminary degraded itself and abated its radiance, and the outer shells were reinforced. All those radiating lights are suspended in that firmament of the heaven, that by them the throne of David may be established.

Those lights are formative agents in the lower world to perfect the shape of all those who are included in the term "man". This is the name given to every interior shape; and thus every shape which is comprised in this extension is called "man", which properly indicates man's spirit emanating from the realm of holiness, to which his body is a vestment, as we read, "Thou clothest me in skin and flesh" (Job X, 11). Hence we often meet the expression "flesh of man", implying that the real man is within and the flesh which is his body is only a vestment. The lower beings which have been compounded with this spirit assume shapes which are clothed in another vestment, such as the forms of clean animals, ox, sheep, goat, deer, etc. They would fain partake of the vestment of man, corresponding to their inner nature, but their forms are covered by the name applied to their bodies; so we find "flesh of ox", "ox" being the inner element of that body, while the "flesh" is the vestment; and so with all. Similarly with the "other side": the spirit which is found in the idolatrous nations issues from the realm of uncleanliness and is not, properly speaking, "man"; therefore it is not covered by this name and has no portion (in the future world). Its body, which is the vestment of that unclean thing, is unclean flesh, and the spirit is unclean within the flesh that clothes it. Therefore as long as that spirit is within that body it is called "unclean". When the spirit emerges from that covering it is not called "unclean", and the vestment does not bear the name of man. The lower beings compounded with this spirit assume shapes which clothe themselves in another vestment, such as the forms of unclean animals, of which the Law says "this shall be unclean to you", such as the pig and unclean birds, and beasts of that side. The spirit is covered by the name of the body in which it is clothed, and the body is called "flesh of pig"—pig within the flesh which clothes it. Consequently these two groups are sharply separated, one side being embraced under the category "man" and the other under the category "unclean", and the individuals flock each to its kind and return to their kind. Thus the supernal lights radiate in that "firmament of the heaven" to fashion in the lower world the requisite shapes, as it is written, "and God set them in the firmament of the heaven... and to rule by day and by night".

It is fit and proper that two lights should rule, the greater light by day and the lesser light by night. The lesson we derive is that the male rules by day to regulate his household and to bring food and sustenance into it. When night arrives, the female takes command, and she rules the house, as it is written, "she rises while it is still night and giveth food to her house" (Prov. XXXI, 15)-she and not he. Thus the dominion of the day belongs to the male and the dominion of the night to the female. Further it is written, AND THE STARS. As soon as the wife has given her orders and retired with her husband, the direction of the house is left to the maidens, who remain in the house to look after all its requirements. Then when day comes the man again duly takes command.

"And God made the two lights." There are two kinds of luminaries. Those which ascend above are called "luminaries of light", and those which descend below are called "luminaries of fire". These latter belong to the lower sphere and rule over the weekdays. It is for this reason that at the expiry of Sabbath a blessing is said over the lamp, because rule is then restored to these luminaries. Man's fingers symbolise the mystic grades of the upper world, which are divided into front and back. The latter are outside, and are symbolised by the finger-nails, and therefore it is

Zohar: Bereshith, Section 1, Page 21a

permissible to look at the finger-nails at the expiry of Sabbath by the light of the candle. But it is not permissible to look at the fingers from the inside by the light of the candle. This is hinted in the verse, "Thou shalt see me from the back, thou shalt not see my face" (Ex. XXXIII, 23). Therefore a man should not look at his fingers from the inside when he recites the blessing "Creator of the light of the fire". On the Sabbath day God rules alone by means of those inner grades upon His throne of glory, and all of them are comprised in Him and He assumes dominion. Therefore on this day He accorded rest to all worlds. As part of the legacy of this day the holy and unique people has inherited the "luminaries of light" from the side of the Right, which is the primal light that was on the first day. For on the Sabbath day those luminaries of light shine alone and have dominion, and from them everything is illumined below. When Sabbath expires the luminaries of light are withdrawn and the luminaries of fire assume sway each in its place. They rule from the expiry of one Sabbath till the commencement of the next. For this reason it is proper to use the light of the lamp at the expiry of Sabbath.

It is said of the Hayyoth that "they run to and fro" (Ezek. I, 14), and so no eye can follow them. The Hayyoth which disclose themselves are those in the midst of which there is an Ofan (wheel), which is Metatron, who is more exalted than all the other hosts. The Hayyoth which are never disclosed are those which are under the two undisclosed letters Yod, He', which rule over Vau, He', these being the pedestal of the former. The most mysterious and incomprehensible essence rules over all and is mounted upon all. The Hayyoth which disclose themselves are below those which remain undisclosed and derive light from them and follow them. The celestial Hayyoth are all comprised in the "firmament of the heaven", and are referred to in the words "let there be lights in the firmament of the heaven", "and they shall be for lights in the firmament of the heaven". They are all suspended in that firmament. But there is also a firmament above the heavens of which it is written, "and a likeness upon the heads of the Hayyah, a firmament like the ice, etc." (Ezek. I, 22). This is the first He' beyond which it is impossible for the human mind to penetrate, because what is further is enveloped in the thought of God, which is elevated above the comprehension of man. If that which is within the Thought cannot be comprehended, how much less the Thought itself! What is within the Thought no one can conceive, much less can one know the En Sof, of which no trace can be found and to which thought cannot reach by any means. But from the midst of the impenetrable mystery, from the first descent of the En Sof there glimmers a faint undiscernible light like the point of a needle, the hidden recess of thought, which even yet is not knowable until there extends from it a light in a place where there is some imprint of letters, and from which they all issue. First of all is Aleph, the beginning and end of all grades, that on which all the grades are imprinted and which yet is always called "one", to show that although the Godhead contains many forms, it is still only one. This is the letter on which depend both the lower and the upper entities. The top point of the Aleph symbolises the hidden supernal thought, in which is contained potentially the extension of the supernal firmament. When Aleph issues from that firmament in a form symbolising the commencement of Thought, there issue in its middle bar six grades, corresponding to the hidden supernal Hayyoth which are suspended from the Thought. One is the light which shone and was withdrawn. This is the "heat of the day" which Abraham felt when he was sitting at "the door of his tent", the door which opens the way from below to above, and on which shone "the heat of the day". A second light is that which fades away at eventide, to restore which was the object of Isaac's prayer, as it is written, "Isaac went forth into the field to meditate at eventide" (Gen. XXIV, 63). A third light is that which combines these other two,

Zohar: Bereshith, Section 1, Page 21b

and shines for healing, and it is hinted at in the verse which says of Jacob that "the sun rose upon him, etc." (Gen. XXXII, 32). Of a surety it was after he had attained the degree of "eventide". From this point he was "halting on his thigh", i.e. he attained imperfectly to the conception of the "strength (Nezah) of Israel". It is written "on his thigh" and not "on his thighs"; this is the fourth degree, by which no prophet was inspired till Samuel came, of whom it is written, "and also the strength (Nezah) of Israel, etc." (I Sam. XV, 29). Thus he restored to its pristine strength that which was weak from the time that Jacob was injured by the guardian angel of Esau. "He touched the hollow of his thigh." When he came to Jacob, he derived strength from that "eventide" which is associated with the attribute of stern justice. Jacob, however, being embraced in that grade, was proof against him. "He saw that he could not prevail against him and he touched the hollow of his thigh." He found a weak spot in the thigh, because that is outside of the trunk, which is the symbolical name of Jacob, whose body was therefore under the protection of two degrees symbolised by the name "man". So when the angel found a point of attack outside the trunk, straightway "the hollow of Jacob's thigh sank", and no man received prophetic inspiration from that source till Samuel came. Joshua derived prophetic inspiration from the majesty of Moses, as it is written, "thou shalt confer of thy majesty upon him" (Num. XXVII, 20); this, then, is the fifth grade. Nezah is the left thigh, the grade of Jacob, and therefore David came and united it with the right, as it is written, "bliss in thy right hand is Nezah". The reason why Jacob's thigh was weak was because the side of impurity touched it and deprived it of its strength; and it remained weak till the time of Samuel. Hence Samuel spoke of the Nezah of Israel; and hence, too, he spoke always with severity. Later, however, God brought him under the aegis of Hod, after he had anointed kings. On this account he is ranked with Moses and Aaron, since he combined two lower grades, as they combined two upper grades, though all the grades are linked with one another. [Tr. note: Here in the text follows a passage (up to behai' alma, p. 22a) dealing with the prophetic grades of Moses and Jacob as typified respectively by the 'Jubilee' and the 'Shemitah'. It has been omitted from the translation as being both highly technical and in the nature of a digression.]

Zohar: Bereshith, Section 1, Page 22a

[Note: The first 16 lines of the Hebrew text do not appear in our translation]

All those supernal lights exist in their image below, some of them in their image below upon the earth; but in themselves they are all suspended in the "firmament of the heaven". Here is the secret of two names combined which are completed by a third and become one again.

AND GOD SAID, LET US MAKE MAN. [Tr. note: The commentator, Derekh Emeth, remarks that from here to 29a (Bereshith teninan) is obviously, from its style, not an intrinsic part of the Zohar. It seems, however, to fill a gap in the Zoharic exposition, and therefore most of it has been translated.]

It is written, "The secret of the Lord is to them that fear him" (Ps. XXV, 14). That most reverend Elder opened an exposition of this verse by saying 'Simeon Simeon, who is it that said: "Let us make man?" Who is this Elohim?' With these words the most reverend Elder vanished before anyone saw him. R. Simeon, hearing that he had called him plain "Simeon", and not "Rabbi Simeon", said to his colleagues: 'Of a surety this is the Holy One, blessed be He, of whom it is written: "And the Ancient of days was seated" (Dan. VII, 9). Truly now is the time to expound this mystery, because certainly there is here a mystery which hitherto it was not permitted to divulge, but now we perceive that permission is given.' He then proceeded: 'We must picture a king who wanted several buildings to be erected, and who had an architect in his service who did nothing save with his consent. The king is the supernal Wisdom above, the Central Column being the king below: Elohim is the architect above, being as such the supernal Mother, and Elohim is also the architect below, being as such the Divine Presence (Shekinah) of the lower world. Now a woman may not do anything without the consent of her husband. When he desired anything built in the way of emanation (aziluth), the Father said to the Mother by means of the Word (amirah), "let it be so and so", and straightway it was so, as it is written, "And he said, Elohim, let there be light, and there was light": i.e. one said to Elohim, let there be light: the master of the building gave the order, and the architect carried it out immediately; and so with all that was constructed in the way of emanation. When he came to the "world of separation", which is the sphere of individual beings, the architect said to the master of the building: "Let us make man in our image, according to our likeness." Said the master of the building: "Truly, it is well that he should be made, but he will one day sin before thee, because he is foolish: so it is written, 'A wise son rejoiceth his father, and a foolish son is a heaviness to his mother' (Prov. X, 1)." She replied: "Since his guilt is referred to the mother and not the father, I desire to create him in my likeness." Hence it is written, "And Elohim created man in his image", the Father not being willing to share in his creation. Thus in reference to his sin it is written,

Zohar: Bereshith, Section 1, Page 22b

"and through your transgression your Mother is dismissed" (Is. L, 1). Said the king to the mother, "Did I not tell thee that he was destined to sin?" At that time he drove him out and drove out his mother with him; and so it is written, "A wise son rejoiceth his father and a foolish son is the heaviness of his mother." The wise son is Man formed by emanation, and the foolish son is man formed by creation (beriah).'

The colleagues here interrupted and said, 'Rabbi, Rabbi, is there such a division between Father and Mother that from the side of the Father Man has been formed in the way of emanation, and from the side of the Mother in the way of creation?' He replied, 'My friends, it is not so, since the Man of emanation was both male and female, from the side of both Father and Mother, and that is why it says, "And God said, Let there be light, and there was light": "let there be light" from the side of the Father, "and there was light" from the side of the Mother; and this is the man "of two faces". This "man" has no "image and likeness". Only the supernal Mother had a name combining light and darkness–light, which was the supernal vestment and which God created on the first day and then stored away for the righteous, and darkness, which was created on the first day for the wicked. On account of the darkness, which was destined to sin against the light, the Father was not willing to share in man's creation, and therefore the Mother said: "let us make man in our image after our likeness". "In our image" corresponds to light, "after our likeness", to darkness, which is a vestment to light in the same way that the body is a vestment to the soul, as it is written, "Thou didst clothe me with skin and flesh." ' He then paused, and all the colleagues rejoiced and said: "Happy is our lot that we have been privileged to hear things which were never disclosed till now.'

R. Simeon then proceeded, taking as his text: See now that I, I am he, and Elohim is not with me, etc. (Deut. XXXII, 39). He said: 'Friends, here are some profound mysteries which I desire to reveal to you now that permission has been given to utter them. Who is it that says, "See now that I, I am he"? This is the Cause which is above all those on high, that which is called the Cause of causes. It is above those other causes, since none of those causes does anything till it obtains permission from that which is above it, as we pointed out above in respect to the expression, "Let us make man". "Us" certainly refers to two, of which one said to the other above it, "let us make", nor did it do anything save with the permission and direction of the one above it, while the one above did nothing without consulting its colleague. But that which is called "the Cause above all causes", which has no superior or even equal, as it is written, "To whom shall ye liken me, that I should be equal?" (Is. XL, 25), said, "See now that I, I am he, and Elohim is not with me", from whom he should take counsel, like that of which it is written, "and God said, Let us make man".' The colleagues here interrupted him and said, 'Rabbi, allow us to make a remark. Did you not state above that the Cause of causes said to the Sefirah Kether, "Let us make man"?' He answered, 'You do not listen to what you are saying. There is something that is called "Cause of causes", but that is not the "Cause above all causes" which I mentioned, which has no colleague of which it should take counsel, for it is unique, prior to all, and has no partner. Therefore it says: "See now that I, I am he, and Elohim is not with me", of which it should take counsel, since it has no colleague and no partner, nor even number, for there is a "one" which connotes combination, such as male and female, of whom it is written, "for I have called him one" (Is. LI, 2); but this is one without number and without combination, and therefore it is said: "and Elohim is not

48

with me".' They all rose and prostrated themselves before him, saying, 'happy the man whose Master agrees with him in the exposition of hidden mysteries which have not been revealed to the holy angels.'

He proceeded: 'Friends, we must expound the rest of the verse, since it contains many hidden mysteries. The next words are: I kill and make alive, etc. That is to say, through the Sefiroth on the right side I make alive, and through the Sefiroth on the left side I kill; but if the Central Column does not concur, sentence cannot be passed, since they form a court of three. Sometimes,

Zohar: Bereshith, Section 1, Page 23a

even when they all three agree to condemn, there comes the right hand which is outstretched to receive those that repent; this is the Tetragrammaton, and it is also the Shekinah, which is called "right hand", from the side of Hesed (kindness). When a man repents, this hand saves him from punishment. But when the Cause which is above all causes condemns, then "there is none that delivers from my hand".' Withal the colleagues explained the word Elohim in this verse as referring to other gods, and the words "I kill and make alive" as meaning "I kill with my Shekinah him who is guilty, and preserve by it him who is innocent." What, however, has been said above concerning the Supreme Cause is a secret which has been transmitted only to wise men and prophets. See now how many hidden causes there are enveloped in the Sefiroth and, as it were, mounted on the Sefiroth, hidden from the comprehension of human beings: of them it is said, "for one higher than another watcheth" (Eccl. V, 7). There are lights upon lights, one more clear than another, each one dark by comparison with the one above it from which it receives its light. As for the Supreme Cause, all lights are dark in its presence.

Another explanation of the verse "Let us make man in our image after our likeness" was given by the colleagues, who put these words into the mouth of the ministering angels. Said R. Simeon to them, 'Since they know what has been and what will be, they must have known that he was destined to sin. Why, then, did they make this proposal? Nay more, Uzza and Azael actually opposed it. For when the Shekinah said to God "Let us make man", they said, "What is man that thou shouldst know him? Why desirest thou to create man, who, as thou knowest, will sin before thee through his wife, who is the darkness to his light, light being male and darkness female?" The Shekinah answered them: "You yourselves shall commit the very crime of which you accuse him"; and so it is written, "and the sons of God saw the daughters of man that they were comely", and they went astray after them and were degraded by the Shekinah from their holy estate.' Said the colleagues: 'Rabbi, after all, Uzza and Azael were not wrong, because man was really destined to sin through woman.' He replied, 'What the Shekinah said was this: "You have spoken worse of man than all the rest of the heavenly host. If you were more virtuous than man, you would have a right to accuse him. But whereas he will sin with one woman, you will sin with many women, as it is written, 'and the sons of God saw the daughters of man'-not a daughter, but daughters; and further, if man sinned, he was ready to repent and to return to his Master and repair his wrong." ' Said the colleagues, 'If so, why was he after all created?' He replied: 'If God had not created man in this way, with good and evil inclination, which correspond to light and darkness, created man would have been capable neither of virtue, nor of sin; but now that he has been created with both, it is written, "see, I have set before thee this day life and death" ' (Deut. XXX, 19). They said to him: 'Still, why all this? Would it not have been better that he should not have been created and so not have sinned, thereby causing so much mischief above, and that he should have had neither punishment nor reward?' He replied: 'It was just and right that he should be created in this way, because for his sake the Torah was created in which are inscribed punishments for the wicked and rewards for the righteous, and these are only for the sake of created man.' They said: 'Of a truth we have heard now what we never knew before. Certainly God created nothing which was not required.' What is more, the created Torah

Zohar: Bereshith, Section 1, Page 23b

is a vestment to the Shekinah, and if man had not been created, the Shekinah would have been without a vestment like a beggar. Hence when a man sins it is as though he strips the Shekinah of her vestments, and that is why he is punished; and when he carries out the precepts of the Law, it is as though he clothes the Shekinah in her vestments. Hence we say that the fringes (tsitith) worn by the Israelites are to the Shekinah in captivity like the poor man's garments, of which it is said, "for that is his only covering, it is his garment for his skin, wherein shall he sleep?" (Ex. XXII, 26).

Prayer which is not whole-hearted is pursued by numbers of destructive angels, according to the Scriptural expression: "all her pursuers have overtaken her, etc." (Lam. I, 3). Therefore it is well to preface one's prayer with the verse, "but he is merciful and forgiveth iniquity, etc." (Ps. LXXVIII, 38). The word "iniquity" signifies Samael, who is the serpent; "he will not destroy" signifies the destroyer; "he turneth his anger away" refers to the demon Af (anger); "and doth not stir up all his wrath" refers to the demon Hemah (wrath). To these powers are attached many destructive angels, which are under seven chiefs with seventy under-chiefs, dispersed in every firmament, and under them are myriads of others. When an Israelite wearing fringes and phylacteries prays with devotion, then the words of the Scripture are fulfilled: "All the peoples of the earth shall see that the name of the Lord is called upon thee and they shall fear thee" (Deut. XXVIII, 10). We have agreed that "the name of the Lord" refers to the phylactery of the head; and when the destructive angels see the name of Tetragrammaton on the head of him who is praying, they at once take to flight, as it is written, "a thousand shall fall at thy side" (Ps. XCI, 7).

Jacob foresaw the oppression of the last captivity in the end of days, and therefore "he prayed in that place and tarried there because the sun had set" (Gen. XXVIII, 11), i.e. the night of captivity had come. David, referring to the captivity, said "hungry and weary and thirsty in the wilderness". He saw the Shekinah parched and withered and dried, and was in deep sorrow on its behalf. When he saw Israel returning in joy, he composed ten kinds of chants, and at the end of all he exclaimed: "A prayer for the poor man when he fainteth" (Ps. CII, 1). This is the prayer which comes before God before all the others. Which is the "prayer of the poor man"? This is the evening prayer, which is single, without a husband; and because she is without a husband she is poor and dry. Like her is the just man, poor and parched; this is the seed of Jacob, which is in subjection to all nations and resembles the evening prayer, which typifies the night of captivity. The Sabbath prayer is a kindness to this poor man. Therefore a man when reciting the Amidah prayer during the weekdays should stand like a poor man at the king's gate on account of the Shekinah, and he should clothe it with the vestment of the fringes, and he should stand in his phylacteries like a beggar at the gate when he begins with the word Adonai (Lord). When he opens his mouth to utter the evening prayer an eagle comes down on the weekdays to take up on its wings the evening prayer. This is the angel called Nuriel when coming from the side of Hesed (Kindness), and Uriel when coming from the side of Geburah (Force), because it is a burning fire. For the morning prayer also a lion comes down to receive it in his winged arms: this is Michael. For the afternoon prayer an ox comes down to take it with his arms and horns: this is Gabriel. On Sabbath God himself comes down with the three patriarchs to welcome his only daughter. At that moment the celestial beings who are called by the name of the Lord exclaim "Lift up your heads, O ye gates, and be exalted, ye everlasting doors," and straightway the doors of seven palaces fly open. The first palace is the palace of love; the second, of fear; the third, of mercy; the fourth, of prophecy through the clear mirror;

Zohar: Bereshith, Section 1, Page 24a

the fifth, of prophecy through the hazy mirror; the sixth, of righteousness; the seventh, of justice. [Tr. note: From here to razin t'mirin on 24b is a dissertation on the relation of prayer to the various Sefiroth, involving much manipulation of Hebrew letters and vowel-points, and therefore unsuitable for translation.]

Zohar: Bereshith, Section 1, Page 24b

[Note: The translation resumes on line 29 of the Hebrew text.]

THESE ARE THE GENERATIONS OF THE HEAVENS AND THE EARTH. We have laid down that the expression "these are" denotes that those mentioned before are henceforth of no account. In this case what is referred to is the products of tohu (emptiness) hinted at in the second verse of the first chapter, "and the earth was tohu and bohu". These it is of which we have learnt that "God created worlds and destroyed them". On account of this the earth was "dazed" (tohah) and "bewildered" (bohah), as if to say, "How could God create worlds to destroy them? It were better not to create them." Similarly it is said of the heavens, "the heavens have vanished like smoke" (Is. LI, 6). But in fact we have here an indication of what is meant by the expression "destroyed them" showing that God does not really destroy the works of His hands. The explanation is this. God created the world by means of the Torah, that is to say, in so far as it is called Reshith. By this Reshith He created the heavens and the earth, and He supports them by it, because the word Bereshith contains the word brith (covenant); this covenant is referred to in the verse: "Were it not for my covenant with the day and night, I had not appointed the ordinances of heaven and earth" (Jer. XXXIII, 25). This heaven is that of which it is said "the heavens are the heavens of the Lord" (Ps. CXV, 16), and this earth is the "land of the living" comprising seven lands of which David said: "I will walk before the Lord in the lands of the living" (Ibid. CXVI, 9). Afterwards He created a heaven and an earth

Zohar: Bereshith, Section 1, Page 25a

resting on Tohu (emptiness), and having no foundation, i.e. "covenant", to support them. For this reason God sought to give to the nations of the world the Law containing the covenant of the circumcision, but they were not willing to accept it, and consequently the earth remained parched and desolate. Hence we read: "Let the waters be gathered to one place, and let the dry land appear." By "the waters" we understand in this connection the Torah; by "one place" we understand Israel, whose souls are attached to that place of which it is written, "blessed is the glory of the Lord from his place". The glory of the Lord is the lower Shekinah; "his place" is the upper Shekinah; and since their souls are from that quarter, the name of the Lord rests upon them, and it is said of them, "for the portion of the Lord is his people". In this way "the waters were gathered to one place". The Torah is the salvation of the world, and the Gentiles who did not accept it were left dry and parched. It is in this way that God created worlds and destroyed them, viz. those who do not keep the precepts of the Law; not that He destroys His own works, as some fancy. For why indeed should He destroy His sons, of whom it is written: behibar'am (when they were created) in this passage, which may be analysed into behe'beraam, "He created them by means of He" (symbolising the attribute of mercy)? This refers to those of the

Gentiles who embrace Judaism. Moses, before leaving Egypt, sought to enroll proselytes, thinking that they were of those who had been thus created through the letter He', but they were not sincere, and therefore they caused him to be degraded, as it is written, "Go, get thee down, for the people (i.e. thy proselytes) have dealt corruptly" (Ex. XXXII, 7). There are five sections among the "mixed multitude", Nefilim, Gibborim, Anakim, Refaim, and Amalekites. The Amalekites are those who are left from the time of the Flood, from those of whom it is written, "and he blotted out all living substance"; those who have been left from this class in this fourth captivity make themselves leaders by main force, and are scourges to Israel; of them it is written, "for the earth was full of violence because of them". These are the Amalekites. Of the Nefilim (lit. fallen ones) it is said: "and the sons of God saw the daughters of man that they were fair" (Ibid.). These form a second category of the Nefilim, already mentioned above, in this way When God thought of making man, He said: "Let us make man in our image, etc." i.e. He intended to make him head over the celestial beings, who were to be his deputies, like Joseph over the governors of Egypt (Gen. XLI, 41). The angels thereupon began to malign him and say, "What is man that Thou shouldst remember him, seeing that he will assuredly sin before Thee." Said God to them, "If ye were on earth like him, ye would sin worse." And so it was, for "when the sons of God saw the daughters of man", they fell in love with them, and God cast them down from heaven. These were

Zohar: Bereshith, Section 1, Page 25b

Uzza and Azael; from them the "mixed multitude" derive their souls, and therefore they also are called nefilim, because they fall into fornication with fair women. For this, God casts them out from the future world, in which they have no portion, and gives them their reward in this world, as it is written, "He repays his enemies to their faces" (Deut. VII, 10). The Gibborim (mighty ones) are those of whom it is written: "they are the mighty ones... men of name" (Gen. VI, 4). They come from the side of those who said "Come, let us build a city and make to us a name" (Gen. XI, 4). These men erect synagogues and colleges, and place in them scrolls of the law with rich ornaments, but they do it not for the sake of God, but only to make themselves a name, and in consequence the powers of evil prevail over Israel (who should be humble like the dust of the earth), according to the verse: "and the waters prevailed very much upon the earth" (Gen. VII, 19). The Refaim (lit. weak ones), the fourth section of the "mixed multitude", are those who, if they see Israel in trouble, abandon them, even though they are in a position to help them, and they also neglect the Torah and those who study it in order to ingratiate themselves with the non-Jews. Of them it is said, "They are Refaim (shades), they shall not arise" (Is. XXVI, 14); when redemption shall come to Israel, "all their memory shall perish" (Ibid.). The last section, the Anakim (lit. giants), are those who treat with contumely those of whom it is written, "they shall be as necklaces (anakim) to thy neck". Of them it is said, "the Refaim are likewise counted as Anakim", i.e. they are on a par with one another. All these tend to bring the world back to the state of "tohu and bohu", and they caused the destruction of the Temple. But as "tohu and bohu" gave place to light, so when God reveals Himself they will be wiped off the earth. But withal redemption will not be complete until Amalek will be exterminated, for against Amalek the oath was taken that "the Lord will have war against Amalek from generation to generation" (Ex. XVII,16).

The following is another explanation of the words: "These are the generations of heaven and earth." The expression "these are" here corresponds to the same expression in the text: "these are thy gods, O Israel" (Ex. XXXII, 4). When these shall be exterminated, it will be as if God had made heaven and earth on that day; hence it is written, "on the day that God makes heaven and earth". At that time God will reveal Himself with the Shekinah and the world will be renewed, as it is written, "for as the new earth and the new heaven, etc." (Is. LXVI, 22); At that time "the Lord shall cause to spring from the ground every pleasant tree, etc.", but before these are exterminated the rain of the Torah will not descend, and Israel, who are compared to herbs and trees, cannot shoot up, as is hinted in the words: "no shrub of the field was yet in the earth, and no herb of the field, etc." (Gen. II, 5), because "there was no man", i.e. Israel were not in the Temple, "to till the ground" with sacrifices. According to another explanation, the words "no shrub of the field was yet in the earth" refer to the first Messiah, and the words "no herb of the field had yet sprung up" refer to the second Messiah. Why had they not shot forth? Because Moses was not there to serve the Shekinah-Moses, of whom it is written, "and there was no man to till the ground". This is also hinted at in the verse "the sceptre shall not depart from Judah nor the ruler's staff from between his feet", "the sceptre" referring to the Messiah of the house of Judah, and "the staff" to the Messiah of the house of Joseph. "Until Shiloh cometh": this is Moses, the numerical value of the two names Shiloh and Moses being the same. It is also possible to refer the "herbs of the field" to the righteous or to the students of the Torah... [Note: The last 8 lines of the Hebrew text do not appear in our translation.]

Zohar: Bereshith, Section 1, Page 26a

[Note: The Hebrew text of this page does not correspond entirely to the English translation.]

AND THE LORD GOD FORMED MAN. "Man" here refers to Israel, whom God shaped at that time both for this world and for the future world. Further, the word vayizer (and he formed) implies that God brought them under the aegis of His own name by shaping the two eyes like the letter Yod and the nose between like the letter Vau Forthwith at that time He planted Israel in the holy Garden of Eden, as it is said: "and the Lord God planted" (Gen. II, 8). The two names here refer to the Father and the Mother; the "Garden" is the Shekinah on earth, and "Eden" is the supernal Mother; "the man" is the Central Column; the Shekinah was to be his plantation, his spouse who was never to depart from him and was to be his perpetual delight. Thus God at that time planted Israel as a holy shoot, as it is written, "the branch of my planting, the work of my hands, in which I glory".

AND THE LORD GOD CAUSED TO GROW. The two names may be referred to the Father and the Mother; "every pleasant tree" refers to the Zaddik; "good to eat" refers to the Central Column, through which He provided food for all, and from which alone the Zaddik is nourished, as the Shekinah from him. These have no need of the lower world, but, on the contrary, all below are nourished from him. For in this period of captivity the Shekinah and "the Life of the universe" are only nourished by the eighteen blessings of Israel's prayer, but at the time he will be food for all. AND THE TREE OF LIFE. This means that at that time the Tree of Life will be planted in the Garden, so that "he shall take also of the Tree of Life and eat and live forever" (Gen. III, 22). The Shekinah will no longer be in the power of the "evil influence", i.e. the mixed multitude who are "the tree of the knowledge of good and evil", and shall no longer receive into itself anyone unclean, to fulfil what is written, "the Lord alone shall lead him and there shall be no strange god with him" (Deut. XXXII, 12). For this reason proselytes will no longer be admitted in the days of the Messiah. The Shekinah will be like a vine on which there cannot be grafted any shoot from another species, and Israel shall be "every tree pleasant to see", and their former beauty shall be restored to them, of which we are told: "He cast from heaven to earth the beauty of Israel" (Lam. II, 1). "The tree of the knowledge of good and evil" shall be thrust from them and shall not cleave to them or mingle with them, for of Israel it is said: "and of the tree of the knowledge of good and evil ye shall not eat". This tree is the "mixed multitude", and God pointed out to them that through mixing with them they suffered two losses, of the first and of the second Temple, as it is said: "and on the day that thou eatest of it thou shalt surely die". They caused the Zaddik to be left parched and desolate by the loss of the first Temple, which is the Shekinah in heaven, and by the loss of the second Temple, which is the Shekinah on earth. Hence it is written, "and the river shall be drained dry"; i.e. the river vau shall dry in the lower he, so as to deprive it of the flow of yod issuing from En-Sof. But as soon as Israel shall go forth from captivity, that is, the holy people alone, then that river which was dried up shall become "the river that goes forth from Eden to water the garden". This river is the Central Column; "goes forth from Eden" is the supernal Mother; "to water the garden" is the Shekinah on earth. In reference to that time it is said of Moses and Israel, "Then thou shalt delight in the Lord", and the words shall be fulfilled, "then Moses shall sing" (Ex. XV, 1).

Zohar: Bereshith, Section 1, Page 26b

[Note: The Hebrew text of this page does not correspond entirely to the English translation.]

... Further, the river "shall part from thence and become four heads" (Gen. II, 10). The first of these is Hesed (Kindness), which is the right arm. From this shall drink the camp of Michael, and with it the tribe of Judah and his two accompanying tribes. The second is Geburah (Force), and from it shall drink the camp of Gabriel, and with it the tribe of Dan and his two accompanying tribes. The third is Nezah (Victory), the right leg, and from it shall drink the camp of Nuriel, and with it the tribe of Reuben and his two accompanying tribes. The fourth is Hod (Majesty), the "left leg" (referred to in what was said of Jacob, that "he halted on his left thigh"), and from it shall drink the camp of Raphael, whose mission is to heal the ills of the captivity, and with it the tribe of Ephraim and his two accompanying tribes. [Tr. note: Here follows a digression (up to abathreh, p. 27a) on a saying of R. Akiba about the esoteric study, too technical for translation into English.]

Zohar: Bereshith, Section 1, Page 27a

[Note: The Hebrew text of this page does not correspond entirely to the English translation.]

AND THE LORD GOD TOOK THE MAN AND PUT HIM IN THE GARDEN OF EDEN, ETC. From whence did he take him? He took him from the four elements which are hinted at in the verse "and from there it parted and became four heads". God detached him from these and placed him in the Garden of Eden. So does God do now to any man created from the four elements when he repents of his sins and occupies himself with the Torah; God takes him from his original elements, as it is said, "and from there he parts", i.e. he separates himself from the desires which they inspire, and God places him in his garden, which is the Shekinah, "to dress it", by means of positive precepts, "and to keep it", by means of negative precepts. If he keeps the law, he makes himself master of the four elements, and becomes a river from which they are watered, and they obey him and he is their ruler. But if he transgresses the law, they are watered from the bitterness of the tree of evil, which is the evil inclination, and all his limbs are full of bitterness; but when the members of the body are kept holy from the side of good, it may be said of them that "they came to Marah and were not able to drink waters from Marah, for they were bitter" (Ex. XV, 23). Similarly, the study of the Talmud is bitter compared with that of the esoteric wisdom, of which it is said, "And God showed him a tree" (Ibid.); this is a tree of life, and through it "the waters were sweetened". Similarly of Moses it is written, "And the staff of God was in his hand." This rod is Metatron, from one side of whom comes life and from the other death. When the rod remains a rod, it is a help from the side of good, and when it is turned into a serpent it is hostile, so that "Moses fled from it", and God delivered it into his hand. This rod typifies the Oral Law which prescribes what is permitted and what is forbidden. When Moses struck the rock God took it back from him, and "he went down to him with a rod" (II Sam. XXXIII, 21), to smite him with it, the "rod" being the evil inclination, which is a serpent, the cause of the captivity. A further lesson can be derived from the words "and from there it parted": happy is the man who devotes himself to the Torah, for when God takes him from this body, from the four elements, he is detached from them and ascends to become the head

Zohar: Bereshith, Section 1, Page 27b

of the four Hayyoth, as it is written, "and they shall bear thee on their hands" (Ps. XCI, 12).

AND THE LORD GOD COMMANDED THE MAN, SAYING. It is agreed that the term "command" in the Scripture always has reference to the prohibition of idolatry. This sin has its root in the liver, which is the seat of anger, and it has been laid down that "to fall into a passion is like worshipping idols". The expression "the man" designates bloodshed, on the analogy of the verse: "by man shall his blood be shed" (Gen. IX, 6). This sin has its root in the gall, the sword of the angel of death, after the verse: "her latter end is bitter like gall, piercing like a two-edged sword" (Prov. V, 4). The expression "saying" refers to incest, which has its root in the spleen, as it is written, "Such is the way of the adulterous woman, she eats and wipes her mouth" (Ibid. XXX, 20). Although the spleen has no mouth or suckers, yet it absorbs the black turbid blood of the liver; so the adulterous woman wipes her mouth and leaves no trace. The murderer is incited by the bile and sucks from the blood of the heart. All who see bile recoil from it, but unchastity is covered in darkness, in the black blood of the spleen. Whoever sins by murder, idolatry, and incest bans his soul through the liver, the gall, and the spleen, and is punished in Gehinnom in these three members, through three chief demons, Mashith (destroyer), Af (anger), and Hemah (wrath)....

Before Israel went into captivity, and while the Shekinah was still with them, God commanded Israel: "thou shalt not uncover thy mother's nakedness" (Lev. XVIII, 7), and this captivity is the uncovering of the nakedness of the Shekinah, as it is written, "On account of your sins your mother has been put away" (Is. L, 1), i.e. for the sin of unchastity Israel has been sent into captivity and the Shekinah also, and this is the uncovering of the Shekinah. This unchastity is Lilith, the mother of the "mixed multitude". It is they who separate the two He's of the sacred name, and prevent the Vau from entering between them; so it is written, "the nakedness of a woman and her daughter thou shalt not uncover", referring to the upper and lower Shekinah. When the "mixed multitude" are between the one He and the other, the Holy One, blessed be He, cannot link them together, and consequently "the river becomes dry and parched"-dry in the upper He and parched in the lower He, in order that the "mixed multitude" may not be nourished by the Vau, which is the Tree of Life. Therefore the Vau does not link together the two He's when the mixed multitude is between them, and the letter Yod is not able to draw near to the second He'; thus the precept "thou shalt not uncover the nakedness of thy daughter-in-law" is transgressed. Further, they separate the Yod from the upper He, and so break the command "thou shalt not uncover the nakedness of thy father's wife", the Yod being the father, the first He the mother, Vau the son and the second He the daughter. Therefore it is ordained with regard to the upper He, "thou shalt not uncover the nakedness of thy father's wife"; "the nakedness of thy sister the daughter of thy father" refers to the lower He; "her son's daughter and her daughter's daughter" refers to the He and He which are the children of He; "the nakedness of the father's brother" refers to the Yod, which is the product of the letter Yod, a brother to Vau. In a word, when the "mixed multitude" are mingled with Israel, the letters of the name Tetragrammaton cannot be joined and linked together; but as soon as they are removed from the world, then it is said of the letters of God's name that "On that day the Lord shall be one and his name one" (Zech. XIV, 9). This is why Adam, who is Israel, is closely linked with the Torah, of which it is said, "It is a tree of life to those who take hold on it"; this tree is the Matron, the Sefirah Malkhuth (Kingship), through their connection with which Israel are called "sons of kings". On this account God said, "It is not good that the man should be alone; I will make him an help meet for him" (Gen. II, 18). This help is the Mishnah (the oral Law), the handmaid of the Shekinah. If Israel deserve well, it is a help to them in the captivity from the side of the permitted, the clean, and the proper; if they do not deserve well, it is a hindrance to them from the side of the unclean, the unfit, and the forbidden, the clean, the permitted, and the fit signifying the good inclination, and the unfit, the unclean, and the forbidden signifying the evil inclination. Thus the Mishnah resembles the woman, who has both pure and impure blood of menstruation. But the Mishnah is not the spouse of his real union, for real union is denied to him until the "mixed multitude" shall be removed from the earth. On account of this Moses was buried outside of the Holy Land....

Zohar: Bereshith, Section 1, Page 28a

[Note: The English translation resumes at the end of line 2 of the Hebrew text.]

AND THE LORD GOD FORMED FROM THE GROUND ALL THE BEASTS OF THE FIELD AND ALL THE FOWL OF THE HEAVEN. Said R. Simeon, 'Alas for the stupidity and the blindness of men who do not perceive the mysteries of the Torah, and do not know that by "the beasts of the field and the fowl of the heaven" are designated the unlearned. Even those of them who are "a living soul" are of no service in the Captivity to the Shekinah or to Moses who is with her, for all the time that she is in exile he does not quit her.' Said R. Eleazar, 'Are we justified in applying what is said of Adam to

Moses and Israel?' R. Simeon answered: 'My son, is it you who speak thus? Have you forgotten the text, "He announceth the end from the beginning" (Is. XLVI, 10)?' He replied: 'You are certainly right; and that is why we are told that Moses did not die, and that he was called Adam; and in reference to him in the last captivity it is written, "and for Adam he found no help", but all was "against him". So, too, of the Central Column it is written, "and for the man he found no help", viz. to bring the Shekinah out of captivity; therefore it is written, "And he turned this way and that and saw that there was no man" (Ex. II, 12), Moses being after the pattern of the Central Column. At that time "the Lord God caused a deep sleep to fall upon the man" (Gen. II, 21). "Lord God" designates the Father and the Mother; the "deep sleep" is the "captivity", as it is said, "and a deep sleep fell upon Abraham" (Ibid. XV, 12). "And he took one of his sides." Whose sides? What is referred to is the maidens of the Matron. The Father and the Mother took one of these, a white side, fair as the moon, "and closed up the place with flesh"; this is the flesh of which it is written, "seeing that he also is flesh" (Gen. VI, 3), which refers to Moses.

AND THE LORD GOD BUILT THE SIDE. Here is an allusion to the law of the deceased husband's brother, in regard to whom the Sages said, "If he refuses to build once, he shall not build any more", as it is written, "thus shall be done to the man who shall not build his brother's house" (Deut. XXV, 9). But of God it is written, "And the Lord God built", i.e. the Father and the Mother built the son, as it is written, "God buildeth Jerusalem", i.e. Vau, which is the son, is built by Yod He, which are the Father and Mother. Hence it says, "And the Lord God built the side which he had taken from the man", viz. the Central Column, "and brought it to the man", i.e. he brought to the side which he had taken from He its maiden, and of her it is said, "And I shall be to her, saith the Lord, a wall of fire round about" (Zech. II, 9). It is because the future Temple will be built on this rock by the hands of the Holy One, blessed be He, that it will endure for all generations. Of this Temple it is written, "greater shall be the glory of this latter house than of the former", for the former was built by the hands of man, but this one shall be built by the hands of the Holy One, blessed be He.... The words "and the Lord God built the side" can also be applied to Moses, in so far as he is from the side of Hesed (Kindness). "And he closed the place of it with flesh": flesh being red, symbolises Geburah (Force), and so in Moses both were combined. THIS TIME BONE OF MY BONE AND FLESH OF MY FLESH. This is said of the Shekinah, the betrothed maiden, by the Central Column, as though to say, "I know that this is bone of my bone and flesh of my flesh; so this of a surety shall be called woman, from the supernal realm, which is Mother, for she was taken from the realm of the Father, which is Yod." And as with the Central Column, so with Moses below. At that time every Israelite will find his twin-soul, as it is written, "I shall give to you a new heart, and a new spirit I shall place within you" (Ezek. XXXVI, 26), and again, "And your sons and your daughters shall prophesy" (Joel III, 1); these are

Zohar: Bereshith, Section 1, Page 28b

the new souls with which the Israelites are to be endowed, according to the dictum, "the son of David will not come until all the souls to be enclosed in bodies have been exhausted", and then the new ones shall come. At that time the mixed multitude shall pass away from the world, and it will be possible to say of Moses and of Israel, each in reference to his twin-soul, "and the man and his wife were both naked and were not ashamed", because unchastity shall pass away from the world, namely those who caused the captivity, the mixed multitude. Of them it is further said, AND THE SERPENT WAS MORE SUBTLE THAN ANY BEAST OF THE FIELD WHICH THE LORD GOD HAD MADE; i.e. they are more subtle for evil than all the Gentiles, and they are the offspring of the original serpent that beguiled Eve. The mixed multitude are the impurity which the serpent injected into Eve. From this impurity came forth Cain, who killed Abel.... From Cain was descended Jethro, the father-in-law of Moses, as it is written, "And the sons of the Kenite the father-in-law of Moses" (Jud. I, 16), and according to tradition he was called Kenite because he originated from Cain. Moses, in order to screen the reproach of his father-in-law, sought to convert the "mixed multitude" (the descendants of Cain), although God warned him, saying, "They are of an evil stock; beware of them." Through them Moses was banished from his proper place and was not privileged to enter the land of Israel, for through them he sinned in striking the rock when he was told to speak to it (Num. XX, 8); it was they who brought him to this. And withal God takes account of a good motive, and since Moses' motive in converting them was good, as has been said, therefore God said to him, "I shall make thee a nation greater and mightier than he" (Ibid. XIV, 12). In regard to them it is written, "Whoso hath sinned against me, him will I blot out of my book" (Ex. XXXII, 33), for they are of the seed of Amalek, of whom it is said, "thou shalt blot out the memory of Amalek" (Deut. XXV, 19): it was they who caused the two tablets of the Law to be broken, whereupon, AND THE EYES OF BOTH OF THEM WERE OPENED AND THEY KNEW THAT THEY WERE NAKED, i.e. Israel became aware that they were sunk in the mire of Egypt, being without Torah, so that it could be said of them "and thou wast naked and bare".... Next it says, AND THEY SEWED FIG LEAVES, that is to say, they sought to cover themselves with various husks from the "mixed multitude"; but their real covering is the fringes of the Tzitzith and the straps of the phylacteries, of which it is said, AND THE LORD GOD MADE FOR THE MAN AND HIS WIFE COATS OF SKIN AND COVERED THEM; this refers more properly to the phylacteries, while the fringes are designed in the words AND THEY MADE FOR THEMSELVES GIRDLES. AND THEY HEARD THE VOICE OF THE LORD GOD, ETC. This alludes to the time when Israel came to Mount Sinai as it is written, "Hath a people heard the voice of God speaking from the midst of the fire, etc." The mixed multitude then perished, those who said to Moses, "Let not God speak with us lest we die" (Ex. XX, 16). These are the prototypes of the unlearned (Am haaretz), of whom it is said, "cursed is he that lieth with any manner of beast" (Deut. XXVII, 21), because they are from the side of the serpent, of which it is said, "cursed art thou from among all the beasts" (Gen. III, 14). Various impurities are mingled in the composition of Israel, like animals among men. One kind is from the side of the serpent; another from the side of the Gentiles, who are compared to the beasts of the field; another from the side of mazikin (goblins), for the souls

Zohar: Bereshith, Section 1, Page 29a

of the wicked are literally the mazikin (goblins) of the world; and there is an impurity from the side of the demons and evil spirits; and there is none so cursed among them as Amalek, who is the evil serpent, the "strange god". He is the cause of all unchastity and murder, and his twin-soul is the poison of idolatry, the two together being called Samael (lit. poison-god). There is more than one Samael, and they are not all equal, but this side of the serpent is accursed above all of them.

AND THE LORD GOD CALLED TO THE MAN AND SAID, WHERE ART THOU? The word aiekah (where art thou) has the same letters as the word aikah (how), which commences the book of Lamentations, and thus foreshadows the destruction of the Temple and the lamentation over it. But in the days to come God will sweep away all evil growths from the world, as it is written, "He hath swallowed up death forever" (Is. XXV, 8), and everything shall be restored to its rightful place, as it is written, "On that day the Lord shall be one and his name one" (Zech. XIV, 9).

IN THE BEGINNING. [Tr. note: v. Appendix, p. 383.] We have been taught that wherever the name Solomon occurs in the Song of Songs, it refers to "the King to whom peace belongs", while the term "king", simply, refers to the Female. The lower is contained in the upper, and the mnemonic is that the lower is heir to the upper, so that both are as one, together constituting beth (=bayith, house), as it is written, "With wisdom a house (bayith) is builded" (Prov. XXIV, 3). Now it is written: The king Solomon made him a palanquin of the trees of Lebanon (S. S. III, 9). The "palanquin" is the maintenance of the lower world through the agency of the upper world. Before God created the world, His name was enclosed within Him, and therefore He and His name enclosed within Him were not one. Nor could this unity be effected until He created the world. Having, therefore, decided to do so, He traced and built, but the aim was not attained until He enfolded Himself in a covering of a supernal radiance of thought and created therefrom a world. He produced from the light of that supernal radiance mighty cedars of the upper world, and placed His chariot on twenty-two graven letters which were carved into ten utterances and infixed there. Hence it is written, "from the trees of Lebanon", and it is also written, "the cedars of Lebanon which he hath planted" (Ps. CIV, 16). It says in our text, "King Solomon made for himself." The words "for himself" indicate that He made it for His own behoof, for His own advantage, to display His glory, to show that He is one and His name one, as it is written, "and they shall know that it is thou alone whose name is the Lord" (Ps. LVIII, 19). Through the blows of His light various realms were made intelligible. He glanced at this side above, He glanced to the right, He turned to the left and descended below, and so to all four cardinal points. Thus His kingdom spread above and below and in all four directions, since a certain supernal stream flowed downwards and formed a great sea, as it says, "all the rivers flow into the sea and the sea is not full" (Eccl. I, 7), for it gathers the Whole and draws it into its midst, as it is written, "I am the rose of Sharon" (S. S. II, 1), Sharon being the basin of the great sea which draws to itself all the waters of the World and absorbs them. Thus the one discharges and the other collects, and one shines through the other in a specified manner. Of this relationship it is written, "By wisdom is the house built"; hence the beth (=2) of Bereshith, implying that the upper house is built in wisdom and the lower one also. The upper house, which is the greater, makes the world habitable, and is called Elohim; the lower one is called simply "king". It is written, "The king shall rejoice in Elohim" (Ps. LXIII, 12): to wit, when the supernal Geburah (Force) bestirs itself to embrace him and draw him to himself, so that all should be one. Again, the words may be taken to refer to the gladness of the stream which issues in one hidden and secret path and enters as two which are one, thus rendering the world complete and whole. Or again, "The king shall rejoice in Elohim", i.e. the lower world rejoices in the upper recondite world which sent forth life to all, which was called the life of the king. This is the foundation

Zohar: Bereshith, Section 1, Page 29b

of the house. This house built the house of the world, and built a world. This is what is meant by "in the beginning God created": "in the beginning", to wit, in Wisdom.

When it collected the whole into itself, it became the great sea, a sea of which the waters were congealed, those waters which had flowed in from the upper source, as we indicate by the verse, "From the womb of Whom (Mi) came forth the ice" (Job. XXXVIII, 29), its waters congealing in it in order to draw in others. This ice was a frozen sea the waters of which did not flow until the force of the South reached it and drew it to itself. Then the waters which were congealed in the side of the North were relaxed and commenced to flow; for it was on the side of the North that the waters were frozen, and on the side of the South that they thawed and began to flow, in order to water all the "beasts of the field", as it is written, "they give water to all the beasts of the field" (Ps. CIV, 11). These are called hare bather (mountains of separation), and all are watered when the side of the South begins to approach and to make the water flow. Through the streaming of this supernal energy all were in gladness. When it so pleased the thought of the Most Mysterious, a river flowed forth therefrom, and when one joined the other by a path which cannot be traced either above or below, herein was the beginning of all, and Beth (= second), which is plain "king", was completed from this beginning, and one was like the other. With this energy God created the heavens, a hidden point the waters of which flow forth without, and produced therefrom a voice which is called the voice of the Shofar. Hence it says, "God created the heavens", to wit, the voice of the Shofar. The heavens control the life of the supernal King upon the earth (as indicated by the catchword, "the son of Jesse is alive upon the earth", since life depends upon the son of Jesse). It is through Vau that life flows to it, and it controls all and the earth is fed therefrom; hence it is written, "and (v-) the earth", the vau being added to control the sustenance of the earth. The word eth refers to something in the upper world, to wit, the power of the totality of the twenty-two letters, which Elohim produced and gave to the heavens (as it says, "with the crown with which his mother crowned him on the day of his espousals"); hence, "the (eth) heavens", to associate and combine one with the other, so as to be established together by the "life of the king", that the heavens should be fed therefrom. The words "and (ve-eth) the earth" indicate the union of male and female, which were traced with individual letters, and the "life of the king" which flowed from the heavens, the heavens pouring them forth to maintain the earth and all its denizens.

In this way the so-called supernal Elohim made a heaven and earth for permanency, and produced them together by the supernal energy, the starting-point of all. The supernal essence then descended to a lower grade, and this latter made a heaven and earth below. The whole process is symbolised by the letter beth. There are two Worlds and they created worlds, one an upper world and one a lower world, one corresponding to the other; one created heaven and earth and the other created heaven and earth. In this way the letter beth signifies two further worlds; one produced two worlds and the other produced two worlds; and all through the energy of the supernal reshith. When the upper descended into the lower, it was filled from the channel of a certain grade which rested on it, corresponding to that hidden, secret and recondite path above, the difference being that one is a narrow path and the other a way. The one below is a way, like "the way of the righteous which is as a shining light" (Prov. IV, 18), whereas the one above is a narrow path, like. "the track which the vulture knoweth not" (Job XXVIII, 7). The mnemonic for the whole is the verse, "who maketh a way in the sea and a path in the mighty waters" (Is. XLIII, 16); and similarly it is written, "Thy way is in the sea and thy path is in great waters".

When the upper world was filled and became pregnant, it brought forth two children together, a male and a female, these being heaven and earth after the supernal pattern. The earth is fed from the waters of the heaven which are poured into it. These upper waters, however, are male, whereas the lower are female, and the lower are fed from the male and the lower waters call to the upper, like a female that receives the male, and pour out water to meet the water of the male to produce seed. Thus the female is fed from the male, as it is written, "and the earth", with the addition of vau, as we have explained.

Letters were imprinted

Zohar: Bereshith, Section 1, Page 30a

on the fabric of the Whole, on the upper and on the lower fabric. Afterwards the letters were distinguished and inscribed in the Scripture-beth in Bereshith bara, and aleph in Elohim eth. Beth is female, aleph male. As beth created, so aleph produced letters. "The heavens" are the totality of twenty-two letters. The letter he produced the heavens to give them life and to water them and the earth. The letter vau produced the earth to give it food and to provide for it its requirements. The word ve-eth (and) signifies that vau took eth, which embraces the twenty two letters, and the earth absorbed them, as it is written, "all the rivers go to the sea", and was thus fed. Thus the heavens and the earth are united and the earth is fed. When the flaming fire goes forth and the Left is awakened, smoke also goes up, as it says, "Now mount Sinai was altogether on smoke, because the Lord descended upon it in fire" (Ex. XIX, 18); because when fire descends, smoke and fire are intermingled, and so the whole is on the side of the left. This is the inner meaning of the verse, "Yea, my hand hath laid the foundations of the earth, and my right hand hath spread out the heavens" (Is. XLVIII, 13), i.e. by the power of the Right above; for the heavens are male and the male comes from the side of the right, and the female from the side of the left.

It says: Lift up your eyes on high and see, Who hath created these (Is. XL, 26). This is the limit of inquiry. For Wisdom was completed from ayin (nothing), which is no subject of inquiry, since it is too deeply hidden and recondite to be comprehended. From the point at which its light begins to extend it is the subject of inquiry, although it is still more recondite than anything beneath, and it is called the interrogative pronoun, "Who?" Hence, "Who (Mi) created these", and also, "From the womb of Whom (Mi) came forth the ice"; as much as to say, that about which we can inquire but find no answer. We have analysed the word Bereshith into the letter beth and the word reshith. Is reshith a creative utterance, or are we to say that Bereshith is the creative utterance? The truth is that so long as its energy had not emerged and spread and everything was still latent in it, it was Bereshith, and that was a creative utterance. But when being emerged and spread from it, it was called reshith, and that became a creative utterance. Similarly, the interrogative Mi created eleh (these); but subsequently when it extended and completed itself, it became Yam (sea), and created a lower world after the pattern of the upper, the two being represented by the letter beth (= 2). It is written: While the king sat at his table, my spikenard sent forth its fragrance (S. S. I, 12). This describes how the King delights himself in the company of the lower king, in their affectionate companionship in the celestial Eden, in that hidden and concealed path which is filled from him and issues in certain specified streams. "My spikenard gave its fragrance": this is the lower king, who created a lower world after the pattern of the upper. So there goes up a goodly fragrance to direct and to perform, and it acquires power and shines with supernal light.

The world was created in two fashions, with the right and with the left, in six supernal days. Six days were created to illumine, as it says, "for into six days the Lord made the heavens and the earth", and they trod out paths and made sixty openings into the great abyss, to conduct the waters of the streams into the abyss. Hence the Rabbinic dictum that "the openings (under the altar) were from the six days of creation", and they brought peace to the world.

AND THE EARTH WAS VOID AND WITHOUT FORM. This describes the original state-as it were, the dregs of ink clinging to the point of the pen-in which there was no subsistence, until the world was graven with forty-two letters, all of which are the ornamentation of the Holy Name. When they are joined, letters ascend

Zohar: Bereshith, Section 1, Page 30b

and descend, and form crowns for themselves in all four quarters of the world, so that the world is established through them and they through it. A mould was formed for them like the seal of a ring; when they went in and issued, and the world was created, and when they were joined together in the seal, the world was established. They struck against the great serpent, and penetrated under the chasms of the dust fifteen hundred cubits. Afterwards the great deep arose in darkness, and darkness covered all, until light emerged and cleft the darkness and came forth and shone, as it is written, "He uncovereth deep things out of darkness, and bringeth out to light the shadow of death" (Job XII, 22). The waters were weighed in a balance. Fifteen hundred times three fingers flowed into the balance, half for preservation and half to go below. At first one side of the balance rose and the other fell. When, however, the lower side was raised by the hand, the balance was even and did not incline to left or right; hence it is written, "Who hath measured the waters in the hollow of his hand?" (Is. XL, 12). At first all the powers of the earth were latent and not productive, and the waters were frozen in it and did not flow. They only spread abroad when a light from above was shed upon the earth, for when this struck it with its rays its powers were released. So it says, "And God said, Let there be light, and there was light." This is the supernal primordial light which was already existing; from this came forth all powers and forces, and through this the earth was firmly established and subsequently brought forth its products. When this light shone on what was below, its radiance spread from one end of the world to the other; but when it observed the sinners of the world, it hid itself away, and issued only by secret paths which cannot be discovered.

AND GOD SAW THE LIGHT THAT IT WAS GOOD. We have learnt that every dream which contains the term tob (good) presages peace above and below, provided the letters are seen in their proper order... [Tr. note: Here follow some lines on the inner significance of the letters of the word tob, viz. teth, representing the ninth grade (from the end, i.e. Wisdom) vau, the heavens, and beth, the two worlds.] These three letters were afterwards combined to signify "the Righteous one (Zaddik) of the world", as it is written, "Say of the righteous one that he is good", because the supernal radiance is contained therein.

IN THE BEGINNING GOD CREATED. The word reshith (beginning) refers to the supernal Wisdom; the letter beth (i.e. bayith, house) designates the world, which is watered from that stream which enters it, and which is alluded to in the verse, "A stream went forth from Eden to water the garden." This stream gathers all the waters from a supernal hidden source, and flows perennially to water the Garden. (This hidden source is the First Temple.) In reshith all the letters were enclosed by a secret path hidden within it. From this source went forth two entities, as it is written, "the heavens and the earth". The earth was at first included in the heavens, and they emerged together, clinging to one another. When the first illumination came, the heavens took the earth and put it in its place. Thereupon the earth, being separated

Zohar: Bereshith, Section 1, Page 31a

[Note: The text of our translation varies somewhat from that of the Hebrew.]

from the side of the heavens, was amazed and dumbfounded, desiring to cleave to the heavens as before, because she saw the heavens bathed in light while she was enveloped in darkness. At length, however, the celestial light descended upon her, and from her place she looked at the heavens face to face; and so the earth was firmly established. Light came forth on the right side and darkness on the left, and God afterwards separated them in order again to unite them, as it is written, "And God divided the light from the darkness." This does not mean that there was an absolute separation, but that day came from the side of light, which is the right, and night from the side of darkness, which is the left, and that, having emerged together, they were separated in such a way as to be no longer side by side but face to face, in which guise they clung to one another and formed one, the light being called day and the darkness night, as it says, "And God called the light day and the darkness he called night." This is the darkness that is attached to night, which has no light of its own, although it comes from the side of the primordial fire which is also called "darkness". It remains dark until it is illumined from the side of day. Day illumines night, and night will not be light of itself until the time of which it is written, "the night shineth as the day, the darkness is even as the light" (Ps. CXXXIX, 12).

[Tr. note: There is a lacuna in the text.]

R. Eleazar came forward first and expounded the verse: The voice of the Lord is upon the waters: the God of glory thundereth, even the Lord upon many waters (Ps. XXIX, 3). He said, '"The voice of the Lord" is the supernal voice presiding over the waters, which flow from grade to grade until they are all collected in one place and form one gathering. It is this voice which sends them forth each in its course, like a gardener who conducts water through various channels to the requisite spots. "The God of glory thundereth": this is the side that issues from Geburah (Force), as it is written, "Who can understand the thunder of his mighty deeds (geburotov)?" (Job. XXVI, 14). "The Lord upon many waters": this is the supernal Wisdom, which is called Yod, and which is "upon the many waters", the secret source that issues therefrom.'

R. Simeon explained the difference, and said: 'It is written, "Close by the border shall the rings be, for places for the staves" (Ex. XXV, 27). The "border" is a secret place accessible only by one narrow path known to a few. It is, therefore, filled with gates and lit with lamps. This is the future world, which, being hidden and stored away, is called misgereth (border, lit. closed). The "rings" are the supernal chain of water, air, and fire, which are linked with one another and emerge from one another like so many rings of a chain. They all turn to the "border", with which is connected that supernal stream which waters them, and with which they are thus connected. Further, these supernal rings are "places for the staves", to wit, the lower chariots, of which some are from the side of fire, some of water, and some of air, so that they should be a chariot to the ark. Hence anyone who approaches should proceed only as far as the staves, but should not penetrate further, save those who are qualified to minister within, and to whom permission has been given to enter for that purpose.'

R. Yose propounded the question: 'What are the "six days of Bereshith" of which the Rabbis speak so often?' R. Simeon answered: 'These are, in truth, "the cedars of Lebanon which he has planted". As the cedars spring from Lebanon, so these six days spring from Bereshith. These are the six supernal days which are specified in the verse: "Thine, O Lord, are the Greatness (Gedulah), the Might (Geburah), the Beauty (Tifereth), the Victory (Nezah), and the Majesty (Hod)" (I Chron. XXIX, 11). The words "For all" refer to the Zaddik (righteous one), who is Yesod (foundation of the world)....

Zohar: Bereshith, Section 1, Page 31b

The word Bereshith we interpret to mean "the second, i.e. Hokmah (Wisdom) is the starting-point", because the supernal Kether (Crown), which is really first, is too recondite and therefore is not counted; hence the second is the starting-point. Again, the word be-reshith indicates that there are two reshith's, because as the upper Wisdom is a reshith (starting-point), so the lower Wisdom is a reshith. Further, we reckon Bereshith as a maamar (creative utterance), and six days issued from it and are comprised in it, and bear the names of those others. The next words, Created Elohim, are analogous to the verse "and a river went forth from Eden to water the garden", i.e. to water it and keep it and attend to all its needs. Thus this Elohim is Elohim Hayyim (the living God), and we render ''Bereshith created Elohim'' by means of that stream, as the agent for producing the world and vivifying it. Further, the two words eth hashamaim (the heavens) signify the fitting union of male and female. After this a lower world was created through the agency of the heavens, and through it Elohim gave being to all. More precisely, the heavens produced eth, which is the Whole. When the Whole was settled in its place, this last link in the chain became in turn a starting-point (reshith), through which Elohim released the stream, and the waters began to flow to the lower world, so that we can now render "by means of reshith God created", viz. the lower world; by its means He produced radiances and gave being to all.' R. Judah said: 'In allusion to this it is written, "should the axe boast itself against him that heweth therewith?" (Is. X, 15). Surely it is the craftsman who is entitled to boast. So here, seeing that by means of this reshith the supernal Elohim created the heavens, it is God to whom the glory belongs. '

AND GOD SAID, LET THERE BE LIGHT, AND THERE WAS LIGHT. This is the original light which God created. This is the light of the eye. It is the light which God showed to Adam, and through which he was able to see from one end of the world to the other. It was the light which God showed to David, who on seeing it burst forth into praise, saying, "Oh, how abundant is thy goodness which thou hast laid up for them that fear thee" (Ps. XXXI, 20). It is the light through which God showed to Moses the Land of Israel -from Gilead to Dan. When God foresaw that three sinful generations would arise, namely the generation of Enosh, the generation of the Flood, and the generation of the Tower of Babel, He put it away so that they should not enjoy it, and gave it to Moses for the first three months after he was born when his mother hid him. When he was brought before Pharaoh God withdrew it from him, and only restored it to him when he stood upon the mountain of Sinai to receive the Torah. From that time he had the use of it for the rest of his life, so that the Israelites could not approach him till he put a veil over his face (Ex. XXXIV, 30).

LET THERE BE LIGHT, AND THERE WAS LIGHT. Anything to which the term vayehi (and there was) is applied is found in this world and the next world. R. Isaac said: 'The radiance which God produced at the time of the Creation illumined the world from one end to the other, but was withdrawn, in order that the sinners of the world might not enjoy it, and it is treasured up for the righteous, i.e. for the Zaddik,

Zohar: Bereshith, Section 1, Page 32a

as it is written, "light is sown for the Zaddik" (Ps. XCVII, 11); then worlds will be firmly established and all will form a single whole, but until the time when the future world shall emerge this light is hidden and stored up. This light issued from the darkness which was carved out by the strokes of the Most Recondite; and similarly from that light which was stored away there was carved out through some hidden process the lower-world darkness in which light resides. This lower darkness is what is called "night" in the verse, "and the darkness he called night" (Gen. I, 5). Hence the Rabbinical exposition of the text: "He uncovereth deep things out of darkness" (Job. XII, 22)', on which R. Yose said: 'This cannot be the original darkness, since all the supernal crowns contained therein are still undisclosed, and we call them "deep things". The term "uncovereth" can be applied to those supernal mysteries only in so far as they are contained in that darkness which is in the category of night. For all those deep and hidden things which issue from (God's) thought and are taken up by the Voice are not disclosed till the Word reveals them. This Word is Speech, and this Speech is called Sabbath, because this Speech seeks to dominate and not to let any other do so. It is this Speech which comes from the side of darkness that discloses hidden things from that darkness.' Said R. Isaac: 'If so, what is the meaning of the text, "And God divided the light from the darkness"?' He replied: 'Light produced day and darkness produced night. Afterwards He joined them together and they were one, as it is written, "And there was evening and there was morning one day", i.e. night and day were called one. As for the words, "And God divided the light from the darkness", this means that He prevented dissension between them.' Said R. Isaac: 'Up to this point the male principle was represented by light and the female by darkness; subsequently they were joined together and made one. The difference by means of which light is distinguished from darkness is one of degree only; both are one in kind, as there is no light without darkness and no darkness without light; but though one, they are different in colour.' R. Simeon said: 'The world is created and established on the basis of a covenant, as it is written, "If not for my covenant with the day and night, I had not appointed the ordinances of heaven and earth" (Jer. XXXIII, 25).This covenant is the Zaddik (righteous one), the foundation of the world, and therefore the world is established on the covenant of day and night together, as stated in our text, the "ordinances of heaven" being those which flow and issue forth from the celestial Eden.' R. Simeon discoursed here on the text: From the (place of) the voice of those who mediate between the water drawers, there they shall rehearse the kindnesses of the Lord, etc. (Judges V, 11). 'This voice', he said, 'is the voice of Jacob, which rests between those who draw waters from on high, and takes hold of both sides and unites them in itself. "There they shall rehearse the kindnesses of the Lord": i.e. there is the place for faith to cleave fast; there the kindnesses of the Lord draw sustenance. The verse proceeds: "The kindnesses of him who is generous to Israel." This is the "Righteous One of the world", who is everlasting and holy, and who draws in to Himself the stream of the Whole and disperses the supernal waters into the great sea. "In Israel": because Israel inherited this covenant, and God gave it to them for an everlasting inheritance. When Israel deserted it through performing the ceremony of circumcision without drawing back the flesh, there was applied to them the verse, "then the people of the Lord went down to the gates" (Ibid.): these are the gates of righteousness in which they sat without entering further. Of that time

Zohar: Bereshith, Section 1, Page 32b

it is written, "and the children of Israel forsook the Lord" (Judges II, 12), until Deborah came and restored the proper performance of the ceremony. Hence Deborah speaks of herself as a "mother in Israel", to indicate that she brought down the supernal waters from above to establish both worlds through Israel, thus showing that the world rests only on this covenant. We see from all this how three issue from one and one is established on three; one enters between two, two give suck to one, and one feeds many sides, and so all are one. Hence it is written, "and there was evening and there was morning one day", i.e. a day that embraces both evening and morning, thus indicating the covenant of day and night and rendering the whole a unity.'

AND GOD SAID, LET THERE BE A FIRMAMENT IN THE MIDST OF THE WATERS, AND LET IT DIVIDE WATERS FROM WATERS. R. Judah said: 'There are seven firmaments above, all in the realm of supernal holiness, and the Holy Name is completed through them. The firmament mentioned here is in the midst of the waters; it rests upon other Hayyoth, separating the upper from the lower waters. The lower waters call to the upper and drink them in through the medium of this firmament, because all the upper waters are collected in it, and it then transmits them to these Hayyoth, and so they draw from there. It is written: "A garden shut up is my sister, my bride, a spring shut up, a fountain sealed" (S. S. iv, 12).

59

This firmament is called a "garden shut up", because the whole is enclosed and embraced in it. It is called a "spring shut up", because the supernal stream as it courses enters it but cannot issue, the waters being congealed. For the north wind blows on them, and so they become congealed and cannot issue, being made into ice; nor would they ever issue were it not for a wind from the South which breaks up the ice. The appearance of this highest firmament is like that of the ice which collects all the waters. Similarly it collects waters and separates the upper from the lower waters. When we said above that it was in the middle, this refers to that firmament which was produced from this one, but this one is above and rests on the heads of the Hayyoth.' Said R. Isaac: 'There is a membrane in the inside of the human body which separates the upper from the lower part of the trunk, and which imbibes from the upper part and distributes to the lower part; so is this firmament between the waters. ' R. Abba illustrated from the text:

'Who lays the beams of his upper chambers in the waters, etc." (Ps. CIV, 3), the "waters" mentioned here being the supernal waters through which the "house" was built up, as it is written, "through wisdom a house is builded and through understanding it is established" (Prov. XXIV, 3). In the following clause, "Who makes the clouds his chariot", R. Yesa divided the word abim (clouds) into ab (cloud), and yam (sea), interpreting it to mean "the cloud", viz. darkness from the Left, "resting on this sea". "Who walketh upon the wings of the wind": this is the spirit of the supernal sanctuary.... R. Yose said: 'It is written, "and he meteth out waters by measure" (middah), implying that God literally measured them out, so that they were for the well-being of the world when they came from the side of Geburah (Force).' R. Abba said: 'When the scholars of old came to this place, they used to say: "The lips of the wise move but they say nothing lest they bring down punishment on themselves".' R. Eleazar said: 'The first of the letters was flitting over the face of the ethereal expanse, and was crowned above and below, and went up

Zohar: Bereshith, Section 1, Page 33a

and down, and the waters were graven into their shapes and were settled in their places, and enfolded in one another; and so all the letters were combined with one another and crowned with one another until a firm building was erected on them. When they were all built and crowned, the upper waters and the lower waters, which were still mingled together, produced the habitation of the world. And the waters continued going up and down until this firmament came into being and separated them. The division took place on the second (day), on which was created Gehinnom, which is a blazing fire, and which is destined to rest upon the heads of sinners.' Said R. Judah: 'From this we learn that every division (of opinion) in which both sides act for the glory of heaven endures, since here we have a division which was for the sake of heaven. Through the firmament the heavens were established, as it is written, "and God called the firmament heaven", since this divides the more from the less holy, like the curtain in the Tabernacle.'

LET THE WATERS UNDER THE HEAVEN BE GATHERED: i.e. those "under the heaven" only. TO ONE PLACE: i.e. to the place which is called "one", namely, the lower sea, which completes the formation of One, and without which God would not be called One. R. Yesa said: "'One place" is the place of which it is written, "my covenant of peace shall not be removed" (Is. LIV, 10), for this takes the Whole and casts it into the sea, whereby the earth is established, as it is written, AND LET THE DRY LAND APPEAR, which is the earth, as it is written, AND GOD CALLED THE DRY LAND EARTH. The earth is called "dry" because it is "bread of the poor one" (Yesod), and it remains dry until this place fills it, and then the waters commence to flow from their sources.'

AND THE GATHERING TOGETHER OF THE WATERS CALLED HE SEAS. This is the upper reservoir of the waters where they are all collected and from which they all flow and issue forth. R. Hiya said: 'The gathering place of the waters is the Zaddik (righteous one), because it is written in connection with it, AND GOD SAW THAT IT WAS GOOD, and it is written elsewhere, "say ye of the righteous that he is good" (Is. III, 10).' R. Yose said: 'This Zaddik is also referred to in the words, "he called seas", because he takes all the streams and sources and rivers and he is the source of all; hence he is called "waters". Hence it says: AND GOD SAW THAT IT WAS GOOD. And since the Zaddik is designated with the words "that it is good", there is a gap between the first and the third days, and on the day between it is not written, "that it was good", since on the third day the earth brought forth produce from the impulse of that Zaddik, as it is written, AND GOD SAID, LET THE EARTH PUT FORTH GRASS, HERB YIELDING SEED, AND FRUIT TREE BEARING FRUIT AFTER ITS KIND. By "fruit tree" is meant the tree of the knowledge of good and evil, which put forth blossoms and fruit. "Bearing fruit" is the Zaddik, the basis of the world. "After its kind" means that all human beings who have in them the spirit of holiness which is the blossom of that tree are stamped as being of its kind. This stamp is the covenant of holiness, the covenant of peace, and the faithful enter into that kind and do not part from it. The Zaddik generates, and that tree conceives and brings forth fruit after his kind, i.e. after the kind of the producer, so as to be like him. Blessed he that resembles these his mother and his father. The holy seal is therefore set upon him on the eighth day that he may resemble his "mother" (who is the eighth grade), and the flesh is turned back to show the holy seal in order that he may resemble the "father". So by "fruit tree" we understand the mother, by "producing" the father, by "fruit" the holy covenant, and by "to its kind", the resemblance to the father. WHOSE SEED IS IN IT UPON THE EARTH. Instead of zar'o (whose seed), we may read zera'vau (the seed of Vau), which has literally been cast upon the earth. Blessed is the lot of

Israel, who are holy and resemble the holy angels, wherefore it is written, "and thy people are all righteous" (Is. LX, 21), truly righteous, for from such they issue and such they resemble. Happy they in this world and in the world to come.'

R. Hiya said: 'It is written, "God maketh the earth by his strength" (Jer. X, 12). He who "maketh the earth" is the Holy One, blessed be He, above; "by his strength" means by the Zaddik; "he establishes the universe", this is the earth beneath; "by his wisdom,', refers to Zedek (justice). Also it is written, "makes the earth", and not "made", because God constantly regulates the earth and its activities through the agency of His "strength", as just explained... ' R. Isaac said: 'It is written, "By the word of the Lord the heavens were made and by the breath of his mouth all their hosts." The "heavens" mentioned here are the lower heavens, which were made by the word of the upper heavens, through the spirit which sent forth a voice until it reached that stream which issues and flows perennially. By "all their hosts" is meant the lower world, which exists through that "breath", which is male. A similar lesson is derived from the verse, "Who watereth the mountains from his upper chambers, the earth is full of the fruit of thy works" (Ps. CIV, 13). The "upper chambers" we have already explained, and the term can be further illustrated by the verse, "Who lays the beams of his upper chambers in the waters." The expression "the fruit of thy works" alludes to that stream which ever flows and issues forth; hence it is written, "Yielding fruit whose seed is in it," as explained.'

LET THERE BE LIGHTS IN THE FIRMAMENT OF THE HEAVEN TO GIVE LIGHT UPON THE EARTH. The word meoroth (lights) is written defectively. R. Hizkiah says that this indicates that this firmament is the home of the rigour of justice. R. Yose says that the defective spelling indicates the lowest, namely the moon, which is the cause of croup in children. It is also the cause of other misfortunes, because it is the smallest of all the luminaries, and sometimes it is obscured and receives no light at all. IN THE FIRMAMENT OF HEAVEN. This is the firmament which includes all the others, since it receives all lights and it illumines the one which has no light of its own. R. Isaac said: 'Even that firmament which has no light of its own is called by us "the kingdom of heaven" and "the land of Israel" and "the land of the living". It is the heaven which illumines this firmament. Hence the word meoroth is written defectively, to show that without Vau there would be death to the world. Everything is included in it, and through it Lilith also finds a place in the world. (We derive this from the recurrence of the word "there" in the sentences: "the small and the great are there" (Job. III, 19). "The Lord shall be with us there in majesty" (Is. XXXIII, 21), and "Lilith reposeth there" (Is. XXXIV, 14).') R. Eleazar said: 'The word meoroth (lights), being written defectively, indicates a shining body which has no light of its own, but only reflects the light of other more luminous bodies. It is written: "Behold, the ark of the covenant, the Lord of all the earth" (Josh. III, 11). The ark here is the "unclear mirror"; the covenant is the "clear mirror". The ark is the receptacle for the Written Torah, whereas the covenant is the sun that illumines it. The covenant is the "lord of all the earth"; and on its account the ark is also called

Adon (lord), which is the same as Adonai (the Lord). Observe that stars and planets exist through a covenant which is the firmament of the heaven, in which they are inscribed and engraved.' R. Yesa the Elder used to explain thus: 'The words "let there be lights" refer to the moon, which is suspended in the firmament of the heaven. The words "and let them be for lights" indicate the sun. "They shall be for seasons", because seasons, holydays, new-moons and Sabbaths are determined by them. There are seven planets corresponding to seven firmaments, and by all the world is regulated. The supernal world is above them. There are two worlds, an upper world and a lower world, the lower being on the pattern of the upper. There is a higher king and a lower king. It is written: "The Lord reigneth, the Lord hath reigned, the Lord will reign forevermore", i.e. "the Lord reigneth" above, "the Lord hath reigned" in the middle, "the Lord will reign" below.' R. Aha said: '"The Lord" refers to the supernal Wisdom; "reigneth", to the supernal world which is the world to come. "The Lord hath reigned" refers to the "beauty of Israel"; "the Lord will reign" signifies the ark of the covenant. At another time David reversed the order and said, "The Lord is king forever and ever" (Ps. X, 16), i.e. "the Lord is king", below, "forever", in the middle, "and ever", above, for there is the reunion and the perfection of all. God "is king" above, and "will reign" below.' R. Abba said: 'All those lights are collected in the firmament of the heaven to give light on the earth. What is this firmament that gives light upon the earth? It is, of course, that stream which flows and issues forth from Eden, as it is written, "And a river went forth from Eden to water the garden." For when the moon is dominant and is illumined by that stream which flows and issues forth, all the lower heavens and their hosts receive increased light, and the stars which have charge of the earth all function and cause plants and trees to grow, and enrich the earth, and even the waters and the fishes of the sea are more productive. Many emissaries of divine justice also traverse the world, because all are in good spirits and full of energy when there is gladness in the king's palace, and even the beings which hover on the outskirts are glad and fly about the world; and therefore it is necessary to take special care of young children.'

AND GOD SET THEM IN THE FIRMAMENT OF THE HEAVEN. R. Aha said: 'When all of them were there they rejoiced in one another. Then the moon diminished its light in presence of the sun; all the light which it receives from the sun is to shine upon the earth, as it is written, "to give light upon the earth".' R. Isaac said: 'It is written, "The light of the moon shall be as the light of the sun, and the light of the sun as the light of the seven days" (Is. XXX, 26). These seven days are the seven days of the Creation.' R. Judah said: 'They are the seven days of the consecration of the Tabernacle, when the world was restored to its original completeness, and the moon was not impaired by the evil serpent. This will again be at the time when "God shall swallow up death forever" (Is. XXV, 8), and then "the Lord will be one and his name one".'

LET THE WATERS SWARM WITH SWARMS OF LIVING CREATURES. R. Eleazar said: 'These are the lower waters, which brought forth species corresponding to those above, so that there was a lower order and a higher order.' R. Hiya said: 'It was the upper waters which brought forth a "living soul", to wit, the soul of the first man, as it is written, "and the man became a living soul" (Gen. II, 7).' AND FOWL TO FLY ABOVE THE EARTH. These are the emissaries from the upper world which appear to men in visible shape. For there are others of whose existence man knows only by conjecture.

These latter are referred to in the next verse in the words, "every winged fowl after its kind". The words "after its kind" are used in connection with the latter and not with the former, because the latter never take the forms of another species, whereas the former do. Nevertheless, they do differ one from another.

AND GOD CREATED THE GREAT SEA MONSTERS. These are the Leviathan and its female. AND EVERY LIVING CREATURE THAT CREEPETH. This is the soul of the creature which creeps to the four quarters of the globe, to wit, Lilith. WHEREWITH THE WATERS SWARMED, AFTER ITS KIND. It is the waters which nourish them. For when the wind blows from the South, the waters are released and flow to all sides, and ships pass to and fro, as it is written, "there go the ships, there is Leviathan whom thou hast formed to sport therein" (Ps. CIV, 26). EVERY WINGED FOWL AFTER ITS KIND: this refers, as already said, to the angels, as in the verse, "for a bird of the air shall carry the voice, and that which hath wings shall tell the matter" (Eccl. X, 20),' R. Yose said: 'They all have six wings, and never change their shape; hence it is written of them, "to their kind". i.e. that they are always angels. It is these who sweep through the world with six beats of their wings, who observe the actions of men and record them above; hence the Scripture says, "even in thy thought curse not the king, etc." (Ibid.).' R. Hizkiah said: 'Just as it is written here, "living creature that creepeth", so elsewhere (Ps. CIV, 20) it is written, "wherein creep all the beasts (haytho) of the field." Just as here we interpret the word hayah of Lilith, so there we interpret the word haytho of the Hayyoth. For they all have sway when she has sway; they commence to chant at each of the three watches of the night and go on without cessation, and of them it is written, "Ye that are the Lord's remembrancers, take ye no rest" (Is. LXII, 6).

R. Simeon arose and spoke thus: 'My meditation disclosed to me that when God came to create man, all creatures trembled above and below. The sixth day was proceeding on its course when at length the divine decision was formed. Then the source of all lights shone forth and opened the gate of the East, for thence light issues. The South displayed in full power the light which it had inherited from the commencement, and joined hands with the East. The East took hold of the North, and the North awoke and spread forth and called aloud to the West to come and join him. Then the West went up into the North and united with it, and afterwards the South took hold of the West, and the South and the North, which are the fences of the Garden, surrounded it. Then the East approached the West, and the West was rejoiced and said to the others, "Let us make man in our image, after our likeness", embracing like us the four quarters and the higher and the lower. Then the East united with the West and produced him. Hence our Sages have said that man emerged from the site of the Temple. Further, the words "let us make man" may be taken to signify that God imparted to the lower beings who came from the side of the upper world the secret of forming the divine name "Adam", which embraces the upper and the lower in virtue of its three letters, aleph, daleth, and mim final. When these three letters descended below, together in their complete form, the name Adam was found to comprise male and female. The female was attached to the side of the male until God cast him into a deep slumber, during which he lay on the site of the Temple. God then sawed her off from him and adorned her like a bride and brought her to him, as it is written, "And he took one of his sides and closed up the place with flesh." (Gen. II, 21). I have found it stated in an old book that the word "one" here means "one woman", to wit, the original Lilith, who was with him and who conceived from him. Up to that time, however, she was not a help to him, as it is written, "but for Adam there was not found an help meet for him." Observe that Adam came last of all, it being fitting that he should find the world complete on his appearance.'

AND NO PLANT OF THE FIELD WAS YET IN THE EARTH ETC. R. Simeon said further: 'These are

the great trees which were planted out later, but as yet were tiny. We have stated that Adam and Eve were created side by side. Why were they not created face to face? Because "the Lord God had not yet caused it to rain upon the earth" (Gen. II. 5), and the union of heaven and earth was not yet firmly established. When the lower union was perfected and Adam and Eve were turned face to face, then the upper union was consummated. We know this from the case of the

Tabernacle, of which we have learnt that another tabernacle was erected with it, and that the upper one was not raised till the lower one was raised; and similarly here. Further, since all was not yet in order above, Adam and Eve were not created face to face. The order of verses in the Scripture proves this: for first we read, "For the Lord God had not caused it to rain upon the earth", and then "there was not a man to till the ground", the meaning being that man was still defective, and only when Eve was perfected was he also perfected. This is further indicated by the fact that in the word vayisgor (and he closed) the letter samekh, which means "support", occurs for the first time in this section, as if to say that they now supported one another, as male and female. Similarly the lower and the upper world mutually support one another. For until the lower world was completed, that other world of which we have spoken was not completed. When this lower world was turned face to face to the upper, it became a support to the upper, for previously the work had been defective, because "the Lord God had not caused rain to fall upon the earth". Next, A MIST WENT UP FROM THE GROUND, to repair the deficiency below, by "watering the whole face of the ground". The rising of the mist signifies the yearning of the female for the male. According to another explanation, we supply the word "not" from the previous clause after "mist", the meaning being that God did not send rain because a mist had not gone up, etc., it being necessary for the impulse from below to set in motion the power above. So vapour first ascends from the earth to form the cloud. Similarly, the smoke of the sacrifice rises and creates harmony above, so that all unite, and in this way there is completion in the supernal realm. The impulse commences from below, and from this all is perfected. If the Community of Israel did not give the first impulse, the One above would not move to meet her, for by the yearning from below completion is effected above.'

THE TREE OF LIFE ALSO IN THE MIDST OF THE GARDEN, AND THE TREE OF THE KNOWLEDGE OF GOOD AND EVIL. The Tree of Life, according to a tradition, extends over five hundred years' journey, and all the waters of Creation issue from its foot. This tree was in the middle of the Garden, and it collected all the waters of Creation, which afterwards flowed from it in different directions. For the perennially flowing stream rests upon this Garden and enters it, and the waters issuing from it divide into numbers of streams below which water the "beasts of the field", just as the waters originally issued from the supernal world and watered the celestial "mountains of pure balsam". THE TREE OF GOOD AND EVIL: This tree was not in the middle. It is called by this name because it draws sustenance from two opposite sides, which it distinguishes as clearly as one distinguishes sweet and bitter, and therefore it is called "good and evil". All those other plants rest upon it. Other supernal plants are also attached to it, which are called "cedars of Lebanon"; these are the six supernal days, the six days of the Creation which we have mentioned, which were indeed saplings which God first planted and then transferred to another place,

Zohar: Bereshith, Section 1, Page 35b

where they were firmly established. R. Abba here remarked: 'How do we know that Adam and Eve were also planted out? From the verse, "the branch of my planting, the work of my hands, wherein I glory" (Is. LX, 21). They are called "the work of God's hands,' because no other creatures were concerned in their formation. We have been taught that the plants at first were like the antennae of grasshoppers, and their light was feeble, until they were planted and firmly established, when their light was augmented and they were called "cedars of Lebanon". Adam and Eve also when they were first planted were not swathed in light nor did they emit a sweet odour; of a surety they were uprooted and replanted and duly established.'

AND THE LORD GOD COMMANDED. According to our teachers, the word "commanded" here contains a prohibition of idolatry; "the Lord", of blasphemy; "God", of the perversion of justice; "the man", of murder; "saying", of adultery and incest; "from all the trees of the garden", of robbery; "thou mayest freely eat", of eating flesh from a living animal; and so we agree. OF ALL THE TREES OF THE GARDEN THOU SHALT SURELY EAT. This means that he was permitted to eat them all together, for, as we see, Abraham ate, Isaac and Jacob ate, and all the prophets ate and remained alive. This tree, however, was a tree of death, in so far that he who ate it by itself was bound to die, since he took poison. Hence it says, IN THE DAY THAT THOU EATEST THEREOF THOU SHALT SURELY DIE, because thereby he would be separating the shoots. R. Judah asked R. Simeon: 'What is the meaning of the dictum of the teachers, that Adam drew his foreskin?' He said: 'It means that he removed the holy covenant from its place; he abandoned the holy covenant and clung to the orlah and allowed himself to be seduced by the serpent.' The words OF THE FRUIT OF THE TREE (Gen. III, 3) signify the woman, of whom it is written, "Her feet go down to death, her steps take hold of the nether world" (Prov. V, 5). On this tree there was fruit, but not on a certain other. R. Yose said: 'That tree which we mentioned was nurtured and fostered from above, and rejoiced thereat, as it says: "A river went forth from Eden to water the garden." The "garden" designates woman; this river entered it and watered it, and up to this point there was complete unity, for it is from this point onward that there is separation, as it is written, "and from there it parted".'

AND THE SERPENT. R. Isaac said: 'This is the evil tempter'. R. Judah said that it means literally a serpent. They consulted R. Simeon, and he said to them: 'Both are correct. It was Samael, and he appeared on a serpent, for the ideal form of the serpent is the Satan. We have learnt that at that moment Samael came down from heaven riding on this serpent, and all creatures saw his form and fled before him. They then entered into conversation with the woman, and the two brought death into the world. Of a surety Samael brought curses on the world through Wisdom and destroyed the first tree that God had created in the world. This responsibility rested on Samael until another holy tree came, namely Jacob, who wrested the blessings from him, in order that Samael might not be blessed above and Esau below. For Jacob was the reproduction of Adam, and he had the same beauty as Adam. Therefore as Samael withheld blessings from the first tree, so Jacob, who was such another tree as Adam, withheld blessings, both upper and lower, from Samael; and in doing so Jacob but took back his own. It is written: AND THE SERPENT WAS SUBTLE. This serpent is the evil tempter and the angel of death. It is because the serpent is the angel of death that it brought death to the world.' AND HE SAID TO THE WOMAN, YEA (af). R. Yose said: He commenced with af, and he brought af (wrath) upon the world. He said

Zohar: Bereshith, Section 1, Page 36a

to the woman: "With this tree God created the world; eat therefore of it, and ye shall be like God, knowing good and evil, for through this knowledge he is called God."' Said R. Judah: 'This was not the way he spoke, for had he said that God created the world through this tree, he would have spoken correctly, for the tree was really "like the axe in the hand of him that hews with it". What he said, however, was that God ate of the tree and so built the world. "Therefore," he went on, "eat you of it and you shall create worlds. It is because God knows this that He has commanded you not to eat of it, forevery artisan hates his fellow of the same craft." ' R. Isaac said: 'The speech of the serpent was one tissue of falsehoods. His first remark, "Surely God hath said that ye shall not eat of all the trees of the garden" was a lie, because God had said, "of all the trees of the garden thou shalt surely eat", and all was permitted to him.' R. Yose said: 'With reference to the dictum quoted above, that God prohibited to Adam idolatry, injustice, murder, incest, and so forth, why should all this have been necessary, seeing that Adam was still alone in the world? The answer is that all these prohibitions had reference to the tree alone, and were applicable to it. For whoever takes of it causes separation and associates himself with the lower hordes which are attached to it. He renders himself guilty of idolatry, murder, and adultery. Of idolatry, because he acknowledges the superior chieftains; of bloodshed, because that is inspired by this tree, which is of the side of Geburah (Force), under the charge of Samael; and of adultery, because the tree is of the female principle and is called "woman", and it is forbidden to make an appointment with a woman without her husband, for fear of suspicion of adultery. Hence all the prohibitions had reference to this tree, and when he ate of it he transgressed them all.' R. Judah said: 'The way in which the serpent seduced Eve was as follows. He said to her: "See, I have touched the tree and yet am not dead; you also put your hand on it and you will not die" (for it was he who added on his own account the words neither shall ye touch it).

AND THE WOMAN SAW THAT IT WAS GOOD. R. Isaac said that 'saw here means "perceived", to wit, through the pleasant odour that the tree emitted, which inspired in her a desire to eat of it. R. Yose said that she really "saw". Said R. Judah to him, 'How can this be, seeing that it says later that "their eyes were opened"? ' He answered: 'This "seeing" means really that she made a mental picture of the tree, seeing it and yet not seeing. THAT IT WAS GOOD. She saw that it was good, but this was not enough for her, so SHE TOOK OF ITS FRUIT, but not of the tree itself; she thus attached herself to the place of death, and brought death upon the world, and separated life from death. This sin, too, is the cause of the menstruation which keeps a woman apart from her husband.' (The Voice should never be separated from the Utterance, and he who separates them becomes dumb, and, being bereft of speech, returns to dust. R. Simeon said: 'It is written: "I was dumb with silence, I held my peace, having no good things to say, and my sorrow was stirred" (Ps. XXXIX, 3). This is the exclamation of the Community of Israel in exile; for then Voice is separated from Utterance, and no word is heard, and therefore Israel is "dumb with silence, etc." And Israel further say: "To thee praise is silent" (Ps. LXV, 2), i.e. the psalm of David is silent in exile and without voice.) According to a tradition, Eve pressed grapes and gave to Adam, and in this way brought death into the world. For death is attached to this tree. Its sway is by night,

Zohar: Bereshith, Section 1, Page 36b

and during that time all creatures taste of death save those faithful ones who first entrust their souls to God, so that they are in due course restored to their place; hence it is written, "And thy faithfulness is at night" (Ps. XCII, 3).'

AND THE EYES OF BOTH OF THEM WERE OPENED. R. Hiya says, their eyes were opened to the evil of the world, which they had not known hitherto. Then they knew that they were naked, since they had lost the celestial lustre which had formerly enveloped them, and of which they were now divested. AND THEY SEWED FIG LEAVES. They strove to cover themselves with the (delusive) images from the tree of which they had eaten, the so-called "leaves of the tree". AND THEY MADE THEMSELVES GIRDLES. R. Yose said: 'When they obtained knowledge of this world and attached themselves to it, they observed that it was governed by those "leaves of the tree". They therefore sought in them a stronghold in this world, and so made themselves acquainted with all kinds of magical arts, in order to gird themselves with weapons of those leaves of the tree, for the purpose of self-protection.' R. Judah said: 'In this way three came up for judgement and were found guilty, and the terrestrial world was cursed and dislodged from its estate on account of the defilement of the serpent, until Israel stood before Mount Sinai.' Afterwards God clothed Adam and Eve in garments soothing to the skin, as it is written, HE MADE THEM COATS OF SKIN ('or). At first they had had coats of light ('or), which procured them the service of the highest of the high, for the celestial angels used to come to enjoy that light; so it is written, "For thou hast made him but little lower than the angels, and crownest him with glory and honour" (Ps. VIII, 6). Now after their sins they had only coats of skin ('or), good for the body but not for the soul.

When they begat children, the first-born was the son of the (serpent's) slime. For two beings had intercourse with Eve, and she conceived from both and bore two children. Each followed one of the male parents, and their spirits parted, one to this side and one to the other, and similarly their characters. On the side of Cain are all the haunts of the evil species, from which come evil spirits and demons and necromancers. From the side of Abel comes a more merciful class, yet not wholly beneficial-good wine mixed with bad. The right kind was not produced until Seth came, who is the first ancestor of all the generations of the righteous, and from whom the world was propagated.

From Cain come the shameless and wicked sinners of the world. R. Eleazar said: 'When Cain sinned, he was in great terror because he saw before him figures like armed warriors coming to kill him. When he repented, he said: BEHOLD THOU HAST DRIVEN ME OUT THIS DAY FROM THE FACE OF THE GROUND, AND FROM THY FACE SHALL I BE HID. By these words he meant: "I shall be kept away from my proper building." R. Abba said: 'The word "face" here has the same meaning as in the verse, "and he hid not his face from him" (Ps. XXII, 25), i.e. providential care. Consequently he said, WHOSOEVER FINDETH ME SHALL SLAY ME. Therefore THE LORD APPOINTED A SIGN FOR CAIN. This sign was one of the twenty-two letters of the Torah, and God set it upon him to protect him.' R. Judah said: 'Cain rose up against Abel and killed him because he inherited his nature from the side of Samael, who brought death into the world. He was jealous of Abel on account of his female, as indicated by the words, "and it came to pass when they were in the field", the word "field" signifying woman.' On R. Hiya objecting that, according to the text, Cain was wroth because his offering was not accepted, R. Judah answered that this was a further reason. R. Judah further expounded the words, "If thou doest well, shall there not be an uplifting?" 'The word "uplifting",' he said, 'means the dignity which is due to a first-born, provided his actions warrant it. In the next clause, "If thou doest not well, sin coucheth at the door", this door

Zohar: Bereshith, Section 1, Page 37a

is the door on high from which issue the chastisements for evil deeds in this world. The "sin" which couches at that door is the angel of death, who is ready to punish thee. The word "door" (petah, lit. opening) further contains an allusion to the New Year, the day of judgement, on which Adam was born.' "Unto thee is his desire", i.e. he will not be content until thou art destroyed. "And thou shalt rule over him": the word "thou" contains a mystic allusion to the Almighty, who is also called "Thou". There is a dictum that God is supreme only when the wicked are destroyed, but our text indicates that when the angel of death destroys them, God "rules over him" to prevent him from ruining the world. R. Judah, however, explained the words "thou shalt rule over him" to mean "through repentance".

R. Yose said: 'When the descendants of Cain spread through the world, they used to cut up the soil, and they had traits in common both with the upper and the lower beings.' R. Isaac said: 'When Uzza and Azael fell from the abode of their sanctity above, they saw the daughters of mankind and sinned with them and begat children. These were the Nefilim (giants), of whom it is said, THE NEFILIM WERE IN THE EARTH (Gen. VI, 4).' R. Hiya said: 'The descendants of Cain were "the sons of God" (Ibid. 2). For Cain was born from Samael and his aspect was not like that of other human beings, and all who came from his stock were called "sons of God".' R. Judah said that the Nefilim were also called so. THE SAME WERE THE MIGHTY MEN. There were sixty on the earth, corresponding to the number above, as it is written, "Threescore mighty men are about it" (S.S. III, 7). WHICH WERE OF OLD, THE MEN OF NAME. R. Yose saw in the word "name" an indication that they were from the upper world, while R. Hiya saw in the word me'olam ("of old" or "from the world") an indication that they were from the terrestrial world, and that from there God moved them.

R. Yesa asked the meaning of the words THIS IS THE BOOK OF THE GENERATIONS OF ADAM (Gen. V, 1). Said R. Abba to him: 'There is here a very recondite allusion. According to the Rabbinical dictum, "three books are opened on New Year, one of the wholly righteous,

Zohar: Bereshith, Section 1, Page 37b

etc." One is the supernal book from which issued the Whole, and from which issues also writing. The middle book unites the higher and the lower; it embraces all sides and is called the Written Torah of the first man. The third book is called that of the generations of man, and this is the book of the completely righteous. IN THE DAY THAT GOD CREATED MAN IN THE LIKENESS OF GOD: for thereby indeed the whole was completed above and below, and both were established after one pattern. MALE AND FEMALE HE CREATED THEM: the one included in the other. R. Abba said: 'God did indeed send down a book to Adam, from which he became acquainted with the supernal wisdom. It came later into the hands of the "sons of God", the wise of their generation, and whoever was privileged to peruse it could learn from it supernal wisdom. This book was brought down to Adam by the "master of mysteries", preceded by three messengers. When Adam was expelled from the Garden of Eden, he tried to keep hold of this book, but it flew out of his hands. He thereupon supplicated God with tears for its return, and it was given back to him, in order that wisdom might not be forgotten of men, and that they might strive to obtain knowledge of their Master. Tradition further tells us that Enoch also had a book, which came from the same place as the book of the generations of Adam.... [Tr. note: Here follows a highly allusive passage identifying Enoch with "the lad" (v. Prov. XXII, 6), i.e. Metatron.] This is the source of the book known as "the book of Enoch". When God took him, He showed him all supernal mysteries, and the Tree of Life in the midst of the Garden and its leaves and branches, all of which can be found in his book. Happy are those of exalted piety to whom the supernal wisdom has been revealed, and from whom it will not be forgotten forever, as it says, "The secret of the Lord is with them that fear him, and his secret to make them know it." ‘

AND THE LORD SAID, MY SPIRIT SHALL NOT STRIVE WITH MAN FOREVER, FOR THAT HE ALSO IS FLESH. R. Aha said: ‘At that time the stream which perennially flows used to draw forth the celestial spirit from the tree of life and pour it into the tree which harbours death, and so the spirit was continued in the body of men for great length of days, until they turned out bad and inclined to sin. Then the celestial spirit departed from that tree at the moment of the soul's entry into the sons of men.’ R. Eleazar said that the word beshagam (for that he) signifies Moses, who caused the moon to shine, and this enabled men to abide in the world for great length of days. AND HIS DAYS SHALL BE A HUNDRED AND TWENTY YEARS.

This is an allusion to Moses, through whose agency the Law was given and who thus bestowed life on men from the tree of life. And in truth had Israel not sinned, they would have been proof against death, since the tree of life had been brought down to them. All this was through Moses, who is called beshagam, and hence we have learnt: Moses did not die, but he was gathered in

Zohar: Bereshith, Section 1, Page 38a

from the world, and caused the moon to shine", being in this respect like the sun, which also after setting does not expire, but gives light to the moon. According to another explanation we translate, "for that it, to wit, the spirit, is also flesh", i.e. it is long converted into flesh, in the sense of following the body and seeking the pleasures of this world.

R. Isaac said: ‘The generations which followed in the steps of Seth were all pious and righteous. Subsequently, as mankind spread and multiplied, they learnt the arts of war, which they practised until Noah came and taught them the arts of peace and agriculture; for at first they used not to sow or reap, but afterwards they found this necessary, as it is written, "While the earth remaineth, seedtime and harvest, etc. (Gen. VIII, 22).’

R. Eleazar said: ‘God will one day re-establish the world and strengthen the spirit of the sons of men so that they may prolong their days forever, as it is written, "For as the days of a tree shall be the days of

my people, etc." (Is. LXV, 22), and also, "He hath swallowed up death forever, and the Lord God will wipe away tears from all faces, and the reproach of his people shall he take away from off all the earth, for the Lord hath spoken it" (Ibid. XXV, 8). [Tr. note: Here closes the second exposition of the section Bereshith. A third commences on the fifth line of p. 39b, goes on to the eighth line of p. 40a, and is then interrupted and resumed towards the end of p. 45b. Pp. 38a-39b and 40a-45b contain a dissertation, or rather three allied dissertations, on the abodes of the righteous in Paradise, and of the angels (Hekaloth and Medorin), and on the halls of prayer (also called Hekaloth). These really constitute a separate work called Hekaloth, and therefore have not been included in this translation.]

Zohar: Bereshith, Section 1, Pages 38b-39a

[Note: Pages not translated in our text as explained in the Translator's note on page 37b.]

Zohar: Bereshith, Section 1, Page 39b

IN THE BEGINNING. [Tr. note: Gen. I, 1.] R. Judah said: There were two houses, the first house and the second house, one higher and one lower. There are two he's, one higher and one lower; all, however, form only one. The higher beth opens the gates to every side, and when combined with reshith forms the "beginning" in the list of the component parts of the building. R. Isaac said in the name of R. Eleazar: ‘This Bereshith is the comprehensive form in which all forms are embraced. This is the inner meaning of the words, "this was the appearance of the likeness of the glory of the Lord" (Ezek. I, 28); to wit, the appearance in which the six others are discernible. Hence we analyse the word Bereshith into bara shith (created six). When the six colours enter into this appearance, it makes itself ready to reflect them, and through them to keep the world going. Yet the credit for this must be ascribed not to this grade alone, but to all the six.’ R. Yose quoted here the verse, The flowers appear on the earth, the time of singing is come, and the voice of the turtle is heard in our land (S. S. II,12). ‘"The flowers",’ he said, ‘allude to the six grades. The words "they appear on the earth" mean that they are forms which are reflected by the grade so called. It is then that "the time of singing is come", to wit, of praise and laudation.’ R. Abba said: ‘The uppermost world is shrouded in mystery and all its attributes likewise, because it forms a day separate from all other days. When it created and produced, it produced those other six. On account of its incomprehensibility, the Scripture opens with the word Bereshith, "it created six", without saying what created. But when it came to the lower creation, it gave a name to the creator, who was now discoverable, and said: "Elohim created the heavens and the earth." Thus the first, which is the higher, remains shrouded in mystery, while the lower is disclosed, so that the work of the Holy One, blessed be He, should be ever both hidden and disclosed. Similarly, the holy name is also, in the esoteric doctrine, both hidden and disclosed.'

THE (eth) HEAVENS: the particle eth indicates that the lower heavens were also created for the lower world. Similarly, the word ve-eth in AND THE EARTH points to the lower earth and all its products after the supernal pattern.

NOW THE EARTH WAS FORMLESS AND VOID, as we have explained. "The earth" here is the upper earth, which has no light of its own. It "was" at first in its proper state, but now "void and without form", having diminished itself and its light. Tohu (formlessness), bohu (void), "darkness", and "spirit" were the four elements of the world which were comprised in it. Hence, "the earth was formless and void and darkness and spirit".

Zohar: Bereshith, Section 1, Pages 40a-45a

[Note: Pages not translated in our text as explained in the Translator's note on page 37b.]

Zohar: Bereshith, Section 1, Page 45b

[Note: Our translation resumes 3 lines from the bottom of the Hebrew text for this page.]

AND GOD SAID, LET THERE BE LIGHT R. Isaac said: 'We learn from these words that God uprooted those shoots of which we have spoken [Tr. note: v. p. 131] and replanted them; hence the expression "and there was light", implying that light had already existed.'

R. Judah confirmed this idea from the verse "light is sown for the Zaddik" (Ps. XCVII, 11), this being the one mentioned in the verse "Who aroused Righteousness (zedek) from the East, etc." (Is. XLI, 2).

AND GOD SAW THE LIGHT AND DIVIDED. Said R. Isaac: 'This implies, as we have explained, that he foresaw the works of the wicked and stored the light away.' R. Abba said: 'He saw its radiance flashing from one end of the world to the other, and concluded that it was better

Zohar: Bereshith, Section 1, Page 46a

to store it away in order that sinners might not have the benefit of it.' R. Simeon said: 'The expression "God saw the light that it was good" means really "God decided that the light should be only good", that is, that it should never be an instrument of wrath (cf. "that it was good in the eyes of the Lord to bless Israel", Num. XXIV, 1); and this is proved by the end of the verse, "And God divided the light from the darkness." For although He afterwards united light and darkness, yet this light continued to emanate from the supernal radiance, and through that radiance to bring gladness to all. This also is the Right Hand through which the most deeply graven letters [Tr. note: The letters Yod, He, Vau, of the sacred name.] are crowned, as has been explained. The treasuring up of this primal light is referred to in the verse, "How great is thy goodness which thou hast laid up for them that fear thee, which thou hast wrought for them that trust in thee" (Ps. XXXI, 20).

AND THERE WAS EVENING AND THERE WAS MORNING, ONE DAY: evening from the side of darkness and morning from the side of light; and because they are joined together, the Scripture speaks of "one day". R. Judah said: 'The reason why it is written "and there was evening and there was morning" for each day is to show that there is no day without night and no night without day, and the two cannot be separated.' R. Yose said: 'The day in which the primal light emerged extended into all the other days; hence the word "day" is repeated with all of them.' R. Eleazar said: 'We learn this from the fact that the term "morning" is used in connection with all of them, and "morning" proceeds only from the side of the primal light.' R. Simeon said: 'The first day accompanies all the others, and all are embraced in it, to show that there is no break between them and they all merge into one another.' Another explanation of the words "let there be light" is: "let there be an extending of this light downwards, to form the angels, who were created on the first day, and who have permanent existence on the right side." Further, the word eth in the fourth verse may be taken to indicate that the "unclear mirror" was created along with the "clear mirror". R. Eleazar says that it points to the creation of all the angels, who proceed from the side of light and who all continue to shine as brightly as at first.

LET THERE BE A FIRMAMENT IN THE MIDST OF THE WATERS. R. Judah said: 'By this the "upper waters" were separated from the "lower waters", the firmament being an extending of the waters, as has been explained. Similarly, "let it divide", to wit, the "upper waters" from the "lower waters".'

AND GOD MADE THE FIRMAMENT: the word made indicates that God exercised upon it particular care, and invested it with great power. R. Isaac said: 'On the second day was created Gehinnom for sinners; on the second day, too, was created conflict. On the second day the work begun was not finished, and therefore the words "and it was good" are not used in connection with it. Not till the third day was the work of the second finished; hence in the account of that day we find twice the expression "that it was good", once in reference to its own proper work, and once in reference to that of the second day. On the third day the deficiency of the second day was made good: discord was removed on it, and mercy was extended to the sinners in Gehinnom, the flames of which were moderated. Hence the second day is embraced in and completed by the third.' While studying one day with R. Simeon, R. Hiya said to him: 'You say that light was on the first day and darkness on the second, and the waters separated and discord arose on it–why was not the whole work finished on the first day, when the Right still comprised the Left?' He answered: 'That is the very reason why there was discord, and hence it was necessary for the third day to intervene and to restore their amity.'

LET THE EARTH PUT FORTH GRASS: this indicates the union of the upper with the lower waters so as to bear fruit. The upper waters generate, and the lower call to them as the female to the male, because the upper waters are male and the lower female. R. Simeon said: 'All this takes place both above and below.' Said R. Yose, 'If so, seeing that we have posited Elohim hayyim (living God) above, are we to posit plain Elohim below? Not so, but the truth is that generation is only below

Zohar: Bereshith, Section 1, Page 46b

(according to our explanation of the words "these are the generations of the heavens and the earth when they were created (behibaream)", or, as we explain, "which were created with he"), while the one above is the father of all; the other is a creation, and therefore it is the earth which brought forth products (toledoth), being made pregnant like a female by a male.' R. Eleazar said: 'All forces were latent in the earth from the first, but it did not bring forth its products till the sixth day, as it is written, "let the earth bring forth living soul". True, it is written that on the third day "the earth brought forth grass", but this only means that it brought its forces into a state of preparedness, and all its products remained latent in it till the due time. First it was "void and without form", then it was duly prepared and furnished with seeds and with grass, plants, and trees, and finally it put them forth. Similarly the luminaries did not emit their light till the due time.'

LET THERE BE LIGHTS IN THE FIRMAMENT OF THE HEAVEN. The omission of the vau from the word meoroth (so that it can be read meeroth (curses)) indicates the inclusion of the evil serpent which befouled the moon and separated it from the sun, thus causing the earth to be cursed (Gen. III, 17). The word yehi, being in the singular, shows that the word 'lights' refers to the moon, while 'the firmament of the heaven' refers to the sun. Thus the whole expression indicates that both were meant to be coupled together so as to illumine worlds both above and below, as shown by the expression 'above' ('al) the earth. All calculation (of time) is by the moon. R. Simeon said: 'Measurements and the determination of seasons and intercalary days are all made by the moon, and not by the higher spheres.' Said R. Eleazar to him: ' Is that so? Do not our colleagues make all kinds of calculations and measurements (by the higher spheres)?' He answered, 'No. Calculation is made by the moon, and this is a basis for proceeding further.' R. Eleazar further objected that it is written 'and they shall be for signs'.

R. Simeon answered that the word for signs (othoth) is written defectively (showing that only one is meant), while the expression 'they shall be' alludes to the many phases of the moon, which make it as it were a storehouse full of various objects, though it is always the one moon which is the basis of reckoning. Consider this. There is a certain point which is the beginning of number, and which cannot be further analysed. There is one point above, unrevealed and unknowable, which is the starting-point for numbering all entities hidden and recondite. Corresponding to it there is a point below which is knowable and which is the starting-point for all calculation and numbering; here, consequently, is the place for all measurements and determinations of seasons and intercalary days and festivals and holy-days and Sabbaths. Israel who cleave to God reckon by the moon, and so they ascend above, as it is written, 'and ye who clave unto the Lord your God, etc.' (Deut. IV, 4).

LET THE WATERS TEEM WITH SWARM OF LIVING CREATURES. R. Eleazar said: 'We have already explained that these (lower) waters teemed and produced, like those above; and so it is agreed. AND BIRDS TO FLY ABOVE THE EARTH. The form yeofef (to fly) is peculiar. R. Simeon said: 'There is here a mystic allusion. "Birds" refers to the angel Michael, of whom it is written, "And one of the Seraphim flew to me" (Is. VI, 6). "To fly" refers to Gabriel, of whom it is written, "The man Gabriel whom I had seen at first in a vision being caused to fly quickly." (Dan. IX, 21). UPON THE EARTH: R. Abba says, This is Raphael (lit. healer of God), who is charged to heal the earth, and through whom the earth is healed so as to furnish an abode for man, whom also he heals of his maladies. ON THE FACE OF THE FIRMAMENT OF THE HEAVEN: this is Uriel. (All these names can be found in the text.) Hence the text proceeds: AND GOD CREATED THE GREAT SEA-MONSTERS. Said R. Eleazar: 'These are the seventy great chieftains appointed for the seventy nations, and for this they were created, to be in control of the earth. AND EVERY LIVING CREATURE THAT MOVETH: these designate Israel, whose

Zohar: Bereshith, Section 1, Page 47a

souls actually are derived from the 'living' (hayah) of which we have spoken, and who are called 'one nation on the earth'. WHICH THE WATERS BROUGHT FORTH ABUNDANTLY AFTER THEIR KINDS. This designates those who study the Torah. AND EVERY WINGED FOWL AFTER ITS KIND: these are the righteous among them, in virtue of whom they are 'living soul'. According to another explanation, these are the angels sent as God's messengers into the world, of whom we have already spoken. R. Abba said that 'living soul' designates Israel because they are children to the Almighty, and their souls, which are holy, come from Him. From whence, then, come the souls of other peoples? R. Eleazar said: 'They obtain souls from those sides of the left which convey impurity, and therefore they are all impure and defile those who have contact with them.'

AND THE LORD SAID, LET THE EARTH BRING FORTH LIVING SOUL, ETC. This includes all the other animals (except man), each after its kind. R. Eleazar said: 'The repetition of the words "after its kind" confirms what we have said before, that "living soul" refers to Israel, who have holy living souls from above, and "cattle and creeping thing and beast of the earth" to he other peoples who are not "living soul", but who are as we have said.' LET US MAKE MAN IN OUR IMAGE, AFTER OUR LIKENESS, i.e. partaking of six directions, compounded of all, after the supernal pattern, with limbs arranged so as to suggest the esoteric Wisdom, altogether an exceptional creature. 'Let us make man': the word adam (man) implies male and female, created wholly through the supernal and holy Wisdom. 'In our image, after our likeness': the two being combined, so that man should be unique in the world and ruler over all.

AND GOD SAW ALL (eth kol) THAT HE HAD MADE, AND BEHOLD, IT WAS VERY GOOD. Here the word 'very' makes good the omission of the words 'that it was good' in the account of the second day. On the second day death was created, and, according to our colleagues, the expression 'very good' refers to death, 'And God saw, etc.' Assuredly He had seen all before, but the Scripture here indicates by the accusative particle eth that God now saw also all the generations which were to be, and everything which was to happen in the world in each generation before it came into existence. 'Which he had made': these words indicate all the works of the creative period (recounted in the section Bereshith), in which was created the foundation and basis of all that was to be and come to pass in the world subsequently. God foresaw all, and placed all potentially in the work of the creation. The word ha-shishi (the sixth) here contains the definite article, which was not used in numbering the other days. This is to indicate that when the world was finished the male and female were united so as to form a single whole - he' with 'sixth', which is the foundation. 'Were finished': this indicates that they were completed in every detail; they were completed from every side, and fully equipped with everything.

R. Eleazar discoursed on the text: How great is thy goodness which thou hast laid up for them that fear thee, thou hast wrought for them that put their trust in thee, before the sons of men (Ps. XXXI, 20). He said: 'God created man in the world and gave him the faculty to perfect himself in His service and to direct his ways so as to merit the enjoyment of that celestial light which God has hidden and reserved for the righteous, as it is written, "Eye has not seen, O Lord, besides thee what thou wilt do for him that waits for thee" (Is. LXIV, 3). It is through the Torah that man can make himself worthy of that light. For whoever studies the Torah every day is earning a share in the future world, and is even accounted a builder of worlds, because through the Torah the world has been built and completed; so the Scripture says, "The Lord founded the earth with Wisdom (i.e. the Torah), he established the heavens with Understanding" (Prov. III, 19), and again, "And I (the Torah) was a craftsman with him, and I was his delight every day" (Ibid. VIII, 30). Thus whoever studies the Torah completes the world and preserves it. Further, God made the world through a breath, and through a breath it is preserved-the breath of those who assiduously study the Torah, and still more the breath of school-children, when reciting their lesson. By "great goodness" in this verse is meant the stored-up blessing, and by "those that fear Thee", those that fear sin. "Thou hast wrought for them that trust in Thee": the implied object of "wrought" is the work of creation.' R. Abba says, it is the Garden of Eden, which God has cunningly wrought upon the earth after the supernal pattern for the righteous to seize and hold

Zohar: Bereshith, Section 1, Page 47b

hence it is written "before the sons of men", since this one is in the presence of men, while the other is in the presence of the holy angels. R. Simeon said: 'The Garden of Eden above is said to be "before the sons of men" because in it are gathered the righteous who perform the will of their Master'.

AND WERE FINISHED: implying that all the work which was to be done, both above and below, was finished. THE HEAVEN AND THE EARTH: above and below. R. Simeon said: 'These words designate the general fabric of the Written Law, and the general fabric of the Oral Law. The words AND ALL THEIR HOSTS designate the details of the Torah, the seventy alternative explanations of the Torah; while the words AND THEY WERE COMPLETED imply that the two Torahs are complementary to one another. Or again, "heaven and earth" may be interpreted as the general and the particular, and "all their hosts" as the inner meanings of the Torah, its rules concerning clean and unclean, etc. AND GOD FINISHED BY MEANS OF THE SEVENTH DAY: this is the Oral Law, which is the "seventh day", and through which the world was completed and the whole is preserved. HIS WORK WHICH HE HAD MADE, but not the whole of HIS work, because it was the Written Torah which produced the Whole through the power of the Writing which issued from Wisdom. The words "on the seventh day" are used here three times, viz. "and God finished on the seventh day", "and he rested on the seventh day", and "and God blessed the seventh day". The "seventh day" in the first of these quotations is the Oral Torah, because with this seventh day the world was completed, as we have said. "And he rested on the seventh day" refers to the "Foundation of the world". In the book of R. Yeba the Elder it says that this is the Jubilee, and hence it is written here "from the whole of his work" because the Whole issues from it. We, however, interpret it of the Foundation, because this is the chief source of rest and contentment. And "God blessed the seventh day" refers to the

High Priest, who blesses all, and who always takes the first share, as we have learnt: "The High Priest takes the first share, and blessings open with him, and he is called seventh." R. Yesa the Elder says: These two mentions of the "seventh day" refer one to the Foundation of the world and one to the Column of the centre. AND HE SANCTIFIED IT: the word otho (it) means also "his sign" (cf. II Sam. XV, 25), and so refers to the place in which the sign of the covenant is fixed. This is the abode of all the celestial sanctifications, and from it they descend upon the community of Israel to bestow upon it all kinds of luxuries and dainties. This may be illustrated from the verse "From Asher his bread is fat, and he shall give the dainties of a king" (Gen. XLIX, 20). "Asher" we interpret as the perfect covenant. "His bread is fat" means that what was bread of affliction has been converted into bread of luxury. The "king" is the community of Israel, to whom it gives all the luxuries in the world. FOR ON IT HE RESTED: in it all find rest and contentment, upper and lower, and in it is the Sabbath for rest. WHICH GOD CREATED TO MAKE: As "remembering" finds its fulfilment in "keeping", so here "creating" is implemented by "making", to establish firmly the work of the world; "to make" indicates the world's artificer, through whom the whole is carried on.' R. Simeon further explained the verse as follows. He said: 'It is written, Who keepeth the covenant and the kindness (Deut. V, 10). "Who keepeth" indicates the community of Israel; "the covenant" indicates the Foundation of the world; "kindness" indicates Abraham. The community of Israel is that which keeps the covenant and the kindness, and it is called "keeper of Israel", and guards the gate of the Whole, and on it depend all the works of the world. This it is which "God created to make", i.e. to perfect and finish off the whole, and to bring forth spirits and souls and even spirits and demons. Do not think that these also are not for the good of the world, for they serve for the punishment of the wicked, whom they find out and admonish; for he who proceeds towards the left becomes entangled in the left side, and is set upon by them. Hence they are of use.

'We read that God said with regard to Solomon, "I will chasten him with the rod of men and with the plagues of the children of men" (II Sam. VII, 14). These "plagues of the children of men" are the demons. They were created just at the moment when the Sabbath was sanctified. [Tr. note: v. p. 59.] and they were left spirit without body. These are the creatures which were not

Zohar: Bereshith, Section 1, Page 48a

finished; they are from the left, dross of gold, and because they were not finished and remained defective, the holy name is not mentioned in connection with them, and they do not cleave to it, and are in great terror of it. The holy name does not rest upon anything defective. Hence a man who departs from life defective through not having left a son behind him cannot attach himself to the holy name, and is not admitted within the curtain, because he is defective, and a tree which has been uprooted must be planted over again; for the holy name is perfect on every side, and no defect can attach to it. Those creatures we have mentioned are rejected both above and below, and therefore they have no sure place either above or below. It is these which are meant by the words" which God created to make", i.e. they were not made into finished beings either above or below. You may ask, seeing that they are spirits, why were not these beings finished off above? The answer is that they were not finished below on the earth, and therefore they were not finished above. They all have their origin in the side of the left; they are invisible to men and hover round them to do them mischief. They have three features in common with the angels and three in common with human beings, as has been laid down elsewhere. After they had been created, they were left behind the millstones of the chasm of the great abyss during the night and the day of Sabbath. When the sanctity of the day expired, they came out into the world in their unfinished state and commenced flying about in all directions. They became a great danger to the world, because with them the whole of the left side roused itself and the fire of Gehinnom began to flash, and all the denizens of the left side commenced to roam about the world. They sought to clothe themselves in bodies, but were not able. Hence we require protection against them, and therefore the recital of the "hymn of accidents" (Ps. XCI) has been prescribed forevery occasion when danger is threatened from them. For when the Sabbath is sanctified on Friday evening, a tabernacle of peace descends from heaven and is spread over the world. This tabernacle of peace is the Sabbath, and when it comes down, all evil spirits and demons and all the creatures which defile hide themselves within the orifice of the millstones of the chasm of the great abyss. For when sanctity spreads over the world, the spirit of uncleanliness remains inactive, since the two shun one another. Hence the world is under special protection (on the Sabbath eve), and we do not require to say the prayer "who keepeth his people Israel forever, amen". This prayer has been prescribed for week-days, when protection is needed. But on Sabbath a tabernacle of peace is spread over the world, which is thus sheltered on all sides. Even the sinners in Gehinnom are protected, and all beings are at peace, both in the upper and lower spheres, and therefore we conclude our prayer this day with the words "who spreads a tabernacle of peace over us and over all his people Israel and over Jerusalem". (The reason why Jerusalem is mentioned is because it is the abode of the tabernacle.) Thus it behooves us to invite that tabernacle to spread itself over us and to rest upon us and to shield us as a mother shields her children, so that we should feel secure on every side. See now, when Israel by reciting this blessing invite this tabernacle of peace to their homes as a holy guest, a divine sanctity comes down and spreads its wings over Israel like a mother encompassing her children. Then all evil spirits disappear from the world, and Israel are at rest under the sheltering sanctity of their

Master. Further, this tabernacle of peace imparts new souls to her children. For souls have their abode in her and issue from her, and so when she comes down and spreads her wings over her children, it sheds a new soul on each one of them.' R. Simeon said further: 'It is on this account that, as we have learnt, Sabbath is a mirror of the future world. For this same reason, too, the Sabbatical year and the Jubilee mirror one another. This additional soul descends from the mystic force implied in the word zachor (remember) upon the tabernacle of peace, being taken

Zohar: Bereshith, Section 1, Page 48b

from the future world, and the tabernacle gives it to the holy people, who are gladdened by it and enabled to forget all worldly matters and all their troubles and sorrows, thus realising the words of the prophet, "on the day that the Lord shall give thee rest from thy sorrow, and from thy trouble, and from the hard service, etc." (Is. XIV, 3). Therefore on Friday night a man should have a full course meal, to show that this tabernacle of peace has been formed by a union of all principles, provided only that he leaves himself enough for one meal the next day, or, according to others (and this is more correct), for two meals. All the more so, of course, if he has more than enough left for the next day. For children two dishes are enough; [Tr. note: al. Two dishes should be the minimum.] and so the colleagues agreed. The function of lighting the Sabbath light has been entrusted to the women of the holy people: as the colleagues put it, "woman put out the light of the world and brought darkness, etc."; and so we agree. There is, however, a more esoteric reason. This tabernacle of peace is the Matron of the world, and the souls which are the celestial lamp abide in her. Hence it behoves the matron to kindle the light, because thereby she is attaching herself to her rightful place and performing her rightful function. A woman should kindle the Sabbath light with zest and gladness, because it is a great honour for her, and, further, she qualifies herself thereby to become the mother of holy offspring who will grow to be shining lights of learning and piety and will spread peace in the world, and she also procures long life for her husband. Hence she should be very careful to observe this ceremony. Observe that the words "remember" and "keep" in the commandment of the Sabbath (Ex. XX, 8, and Deut. V, 12). Both apply equally to the day and to the night; nevertheless "remember" has a more special application to the man and "keep" to the woman, whose chief observance is at night.'

AND THE LORD GOD BUILT (vayiven) THE SIDE WHICH HE HAD TAKEN FROM THE MAN, ETC. Said R. Simeon: 'It is written, God understandeth the way thereof and he knoweth the place thereof (Job XXVIII, 23). This verse may be taken in many ways. One is that the word "understood" (hevin) has the same sense as vayiven in the second chapter of Genesis. Hence the "side" here is the Oral Law, which forms a "way", as it is written, "who maketh a way in the sea" (Is. XLIII, 16). Similarly, "place" here can be interpreted as the Written Law, which is a source of knowledge. The double name "Lord God" is used to show that it was completed in all details, Hence it is called both Hohmah (wisdom) and Binah (understanding). "The side" (zela') is the unclear mirror, as it is written, "they rejoiced at my halting (be-zal'i) and gathered together" (Ps. XXXV, 15). "Which he took from the man": because the Oral Law issued from the Written Torah. INTO A WOMAN: to be linked with the flame of the left side, because the Torah was given from the side of Geburah. Further, ishah (woman) may be analysed into esh he (fire of he), signifying the union of the two. AND HE BROUGHT HER TO THE MAN: as much as to say that the Oral Torah must not be studied by itself, but in conjunction with the Written Torah, which then nourishes and supports it and provides all its needs. (We have similarly explained the words "and the earth".) We learn from this passage that when a man gives his daughter in marriage, up to the time of the wedding the father and mother are responsible for her upkeep, but once she is married the husband has to support her and provide all her necessaries. For it first says here that the Lord God built up the side, i.e. that the Father and Mother provided for her, but afterwards "he brought her to the man", that they might be closely united to one another, and the man might thenceforth provide all her requirements.

Zohar: Bereshith, Section 1, Page 49a

According to another explanation this verse has a deep esoteric meaning, viz. that the primal point is unknowable save to God, who "understands its way", i.e. the future world, while "He", i.e. the great inscrutable called hu (he) "knows its place".'

AND THE LORD GOD FORMED THE MAN. At this point he was completely formed so as to partake both of the Right and of the Left. We laid down before that he was wholly under the aegis of the good inclination: now God formed him with both good and evil inclination-with the good inclination for himself, and the evil inclination to turn towards the female. Esoterically speaking, we learn from here that the North is always attracted to the female and attaches itself to her, and therefore she is called isha (i.e. esh he', fire of he'). Observe this. The good inclination and the evil inclination are in harmony only because they share the female, who is attached to both, in this way: first the evil inclination sues for her and they unite with one another, and when they are united the good inclination, which is joy, rouses itself and draws her to itself, and so she is shared by both and reconciles them. Hence it is written, "and the Lord God formed man", the double name being made responsible both for the good and the evil inclination. THE MAN: as we have explained, male and female, together and not separated, so as to turn face to face. Hence it is written DUST FROM THE GROUND. The use of the word "ground" (adamah) here must be explained. When the wife is joined with the husband she is called by the name of the husband; thus the correlatives ish (man) and ishah, zaddik (righteous one), and zedek, 'ofer (buck) and 'efar, zebi (hart), and zibia. So, too, with the words asher (which) and asherah. It says, 'Thou shalt not plant thee an Asherah (grove) of any kind of tree beside the altar of the Lord thy God which (asher) thou shalt make thee.' Are we to suppose that anywhere else it is permitted? The truth is that the He' is called Asherah, after the name of its spouse, Asher, and the meaning of the verse is therefore: 'thou shalt not plant another asherah by the side of the altar which is established upon this.' Observe that throughout the Scriptures the worshippers of the sun are called servants of Baal and the worshippers of the moon servants of Asherah; hence the combination 'to Baal and Asherah.' If this is so (that Asherah is the name of the He'), why is it not used as a sacred name? The reason is that this name brings to mind the words of Leah, 'happy am I, for the daughters will call me happy (ishruni)', but this one is not 'called happy' by other nations, and another is set up in its place; nay more, it is written, 'all that honoured her despise her' (Lam. I, 8). But the real altar is one that is made of earth, as it is written, 'An altar of earth thou shalt make for me. Hence dust from the earth. AND HE BREATHED INTO HIS NOSTRILS THE BREATH OF LIFE. The breath of life was enclosed in the earth, which was made pregnant with it like a female impregnated by the male. So the dust and the breath were joined, and the dust became full of spirits and souls. AND THE MAN BECAME A LIVING SOUL. At the this point he attained his proper form, and became a man to support and nourish the living soul.

AND THE LORD GOD BUILT. Here also the full name of the Deity is used, indicating that the father and mother provided for her until she came to her husband. THE SIDE: 'black but comely'; she was the 'unclear mirror', but the father and mother tricked her out so as to make her acceptable to her husband. AND BROUGHT HER TO THE MAN. From this we learn that it is incumbent on the father and mother of the bride to transfer her to the charge of the bridegroom; so we read 'my daughter I have given to this man' (Deut. XXII, 16). From that point the husband is to come to her, since the house is hers; so it is written 'and he came to her' (Gen. XXIX, 23), 'and he came in to Rachel' (Ibid.). Of the father and mother it is written that they 'brought', but of the husband that he 'came', to show that he must obtain her permission. We make a similar reflection on the verse, 'And he prayed in the place and tarried there.' (Gen. XXVIII, 11), viz. that Jacob sought permission first. From this we learn that a man who desires his wife's society

Zohar: Bereshith, Section 1, Page 49b

must first entreat and coax her; and if he cannot persuade her, he must not stay with her, for their companionship must be loving and unconstrained. It says further of Jacob that 'he tarried there because the sun had set', which shows that sexual intercourse is forbidden during the day. Further it says that 'he took of the stones of the place and put it under his head'. From this we learn that even a king who has a bed of gold with precious coverings, if his wife prepares for him a bed of stones, must leave his own bed and sleep on the one which she prepares, as it is written, 'and he lay down in that place. Observe that it says here AND THE MAN SAID, THIS TIME, ETC., to show that he spoke to her lovingly so as to draw her to him and to win her affections. See how tender and coaxing is his language-'bone of my bone and flesh of my flesh'-to prove to her that they were one and inseparable. Then he began to sing her praises: THIS SHALL BE CALLED WOMAN, this is the peerless and incomparable one; this is the pride of the house, who surpasses all other women as a human being surpasses an ape. This one is perfect in all points, and alone merits the title of woman. Every word is inspired by love, like the verse 'Many daughters have done valiantly, but thou excellest them all' (Prov. XXXI, 29). THEREFORE A MAN SHALL LEAVE HIS FATHER AND HIS MOTHER AND CLEAVE TO HIS WIFE, AND THEY SHALL BE ONE FLESH: all this, too, was to win her affection and to draw her closer.

AND THE SERPENT WAS SUBTLE. After the man had addressed all these words to the woman, the evil inclination awoke, prompting him to seek to unite with her in carnal desire, and to entice her to things in which the evil inclination takes delight, until at last THE WOMAN SAW THAT THE TREE WAS GOOD FOR FOOD, AND THAT IT WAS A DELIGHT FOR THE EYES AND SHE TOOK OF THE FRUIT THEREOF AND ATE-giving ready admission to the evil inclination-AND GAVE ALSO UNTO HER HUSBAND WITH HER: it was she now who sought to awaken desire in him, so as to win his love and affection. This account shows the proceedings of human beings after the model of those above. Said R. Eleazar, 'If so, what are we to make of the evil inclination seizing the female above?' He said: 'It has already been observed that one set (Left and Right) is above and one set below, viz. the good inclination and the evil inclination; the good inclination on the right and the evil inclination on the left. The Left above seizes the female to join with her in the body, as it is written, "his left hand under my head, etc." (S. S. II, 6). In this way the passage can he interpreted as applying both above and below. The rest of the points are not at all recondite, and a child almost could elucidate them; and the colleagues have noted them.'

R. Simeon was once going to Tiberias accompanied by R. Yose and R. Judah and R. Hiya. On the way they saw R. Phineas coming towards them. When they met, they dismounted and sat down under a large tree. Said R. Phineas, 'Now that I am sitting here, I should like to hear some of those wonderful ideas to which you daily give utterance.' R. Simeon thereupon opened a discourse with the text, And he went on his journeys from the South even unto Bethel, unto the place where his tent was at first, between Bethel and Ai, (Gen. XIII, 3). He said: 'The word "journeys" is used here where we might have expected "journey", to indicate that the Shekinah was journeying with him. It is incumbent on a man to be ever "male and female", in order that his faith may be firm, and that the Shekinah may never depart from him. What, then, you will say, of a man who goes on a journey and, being absent from his wife, is no longer "male and female"? His remedy is to pray to God before he starts his journey, while he is still "male and female", in order to draw to himself the presence of his Master. When he has offered his prayer and thanksgiving and the Shekinah rests on him, then he can depart, for through his union with the Shekinah he has become "male and female" in the country as he was "male and female,' in the town, as it is written: "Righteousness (zedek, the female of zaddik) shall go before him and shall place his footsteps on the way" (Ps. LXXXV, 14). Observe this. All

Zohar: Bereshith, Section 1, Page 50a

the time that a man is on his travels he should be very careful of his actions, in order that the celestial partner may not desert him and leave him defective, through lacking the union with the female. If this was necessary when his wife was with him, how much more so is it necessary when a heavenly partner is attached to him? All the more so since this heavenly partner guards him on the way all the time until he returns home. When he does reach home again, it is his duty to give his wife some pleasure, because it is she who procured for him this heavenly partner. It is his duty to do this for two reasons. One is that this pleasure is a religious pleasure, and one which gives joy to the Shekinah also, and what is more, by its means he spreads peace in the world, as it is written, "thou shalt know that thy tent is in peace, and thou shalt visit thy fold and not sin" (Job. V, 24). (Is it a sin, it may be asked, if he does not visit his wife? The answer is that it is so because he thereby derogates from the honour of the celestial partner who was joined with him on account of his wife.) The other is, that if his wife becomes pregnant, the celestial partner imparts to the child a holy soul, for this covenant is called the covenant of the Holy One, blessed be He. Therefore he should be as diligent to procure this gladness as to procure the gladness of the Sabbath, which is the partner of the Sages. Hence "thou shalt know that thy tent is in peace", since the Shekinah comes with thee and abides in thy house, and therefore "thou shalt visit thy house and not sin", by performing with gladness the religious duty of conjugal intercourse in the presence of the Shekinah. In this way the students of the Torah who separate from their wives during the six days of the week in order to devote themselves to study are accompanied by a heavenly partner in order that they may continue to be "male and female". When Sabbath comes, it is incumbent on them to gladden their wives for the sake of the honour of the heavenly partner, and to seek to perform the will of their Master, as has been said. Similarly again, if a man's wife is observing the days of her separation, during all those days that he waits for her the heavenly partner is associated with him, so that he is still "male and female". When his wife is purified, it is his duty to gladden her through the glad performance of a religious precept. All the reasons we have mentioned above apply to this case also. The esoteric doctrine is that men of true faith should concentrate their whole thought and purpose on this one (the Shekinah). You may object that, according to what has been said, a man enjoys greater dignity when he is on a journey than when he is at home, on account of the heavenly partner who is then associated with him. This is not so. For when a man is at home, the foundation of his house is the wife, for it is on account of her that the Shekinah departs not from the house. So our teachers have understood the verse, "and he brought her to the tent of his mother Sarah" (Gen. XXIV, 67), to indicate that with Rebecca the Shekinah came to Isaac's house. Esoterically speaking, the supernal Mother is found in company with the male only at the time when the house is prepared, and the male and female are joined. Then the supernal Mother pours forth blessings for them. Similarly the lower Mother is not found in company with the male save when the house is prepared and the male visits the female and they join together; then the lower Mother pours forth blessings for them. Hence the man in his house is to be encompassed by two females, like the Male above. There is an allusion to this in the verse "Unto ('ad) the desire of the everlasting hills" (Gen. XLIX, 26). This 'ad is the object of the desire of the "everlasting hills", viz. the supreme female, who is to prepare for him and beatify and bless him, and the secondary female, who is to be conjoined with him and to be supported by him. Similarly below, when the man is married the desire of the "everlasting hills" is towards him, and he is beatified by two females, one of the upper and one of the lower world-the upper one to pour blessings upon him, and the lower one to be supported by him and to be conjoined with him. So much for the man in his house. When, however, he goes forth on a journey, while the celestial Mother still accompanies him, the lower wife is left behind: so when he comes back he has to take measures to encompass himself with two females, as we have said.' Said R. Phineas: 'Even the angels above would not dare to open

Zohar: Bereshith, Section 1, Page 50b

their mouths before thee.'

R. Simeon proceeded: 'In the same way the Torah is situated between two houses, one recondite and on high, and the other more accessible. The one on high is the "Great Voice" referred to in the verse, "a great voice which did not cease" (Deut. V, 19)'. This Voice is in the recesses and is not heard or revealed, and when it issues from the throat it utters the aspirate without sound and it flows on without ceasing, though it is so tenuous as to be inaudible. From this issues the Torah, which is the voice of Jacob. The audible voice issues from the inaudible. In due course speech is attached to it, and through the force of that speech it emerges into the open. The voice of Jacob, which is the Torah, is thus attached to two females, to this inner voice which is inaudible, and to this outer voice which is heard.

Strictly speaking, there are two which are inaudible and two which are heard. The two which are not heard are, first, the supernal Wisdom which is located in the Thought and is not disclosed or heard; and secondly the same Wisdom when it issues and discloses itself a little in a whisper which cannot be heard, being then called the "Great Voice", which is very tenuous and issues in a whisper. The two which are heard are those which issue from this source–the voice of Jacob and the articulation which accompanies it. This "Great Voice" which cannot be heard is a "house" to the supernal Wisdom (the female is always called "house"), and the articulation we have mentioned is a "house" to the Voice of Jacob, which is the Torah, and therefore the Torah commences with the letter beth, which is, as it were, a "house" to it.'

R. Simeon here drew a parallel between the creation of heaven and earth and of woman. '"In the beginning God created",' he said, 'corresponds to "And the Lord God built the side"; "the heavens" corresponds to "and he brought her to the man"; "and the earth" corresponds to "bone from my bone", since this one assuredly is "the land of the living".'

R. Simeon further gave an exposition of the verse: The Lord said unto my lord, Sit at my right hand until I make thine enemies thy footstool (Ps. CX, 1). "The Lord saith unto my lord": 'to wit, the upper grade said to the lower, "sit at my right hand", in order that the West should be linked with the South and the Left with the Right so as to break the power of the Gentiles. Or again, "The Lord" is (the celestial) Jacob, and "to my lord" is "the ark of the covenant, the lord of all the earth" (Josh. III, 11). According to another explanation, "the Lord" refers to the Jubilee and "my lord" to the Sabbatical Year (cf. Ex. XXI, 5, "I love my lord"). The words "sit at my right hand" are appropriate, because the Right is located in the Jubilee, and the Sabbatical Year craves to be linked with the Right. When it first came into being, the Sabbatical Year was not linked securely (to the supreme power) through either the Right or the Left. So when it sought to secure itself, the supreme power stretched forth its right arm to meet it and created this world. It is because it is from the side of the Left that it has no sure basis till the time of the seventh millennium, when at length it will be linked through the Right. Then the Sabbatical Year, between the Right and the Left, will be securely based, there will be a new heaven and a new earth, and it will not depart from there forever. According to this explanation, we must take the words "sit at my right hand" to refer only to a specified period, viz. "till I make thine enemies thy footstool", but not in perpetuity; for when that event has come to pass, it will not depart from there forever, as it is written, "for thou shalt spread abroad on the right hand and on the left" (Is. LIV, 3), all being united. Similarly we can interpret the text "the heavens and the earth" to mean that the higher Shekinah and the lower Shekinah will be joined in the union of male and female; this has already been explained, as the colleagues have noted.'

They now rose to depart, but R. Simeon said: 'I have still one thing more to tell you. It says in one place "For the Lord thy God is a consuming fire" (Deut. IV, 24), and in another place "Ye that clave to the Lord your God are all of you alive this day" (Deut. IV, 4). The apparent contradiction between these texts has already been discussed among the colleagues, but here is another explanation. It has already been established among the colleagues that there is a fire which consumes fire and destroys it, because there is one sort of fire stronger than another. Pursuing this idea, we may say that he who desires to penetrate to the mystery of the holy unity should contemplate the flame which rises from a burning coal or candle. The flame cannot rise save

Zohar: Bereshith, Section 1, Page 51a

from some concrete body. Further, in the flame itself there are two lights: one white and luminous, and the other black, or blue. The white light is the higher of the two and rises steadily. The black or blue light is underneath the other, which rests on it as on a pedestal. The two are inseparably connected, the white resting and being enthroned upon the black. (Herein is the inner significance of the fringe of blue.) This blue or black base is in turn attached to something beneath it which keeps it in flame and impels it to cling to the white light above. This blue or black light sometimes turns red, but the white light above never changes its colour. The lower light, which is sometimes black, sometimes blue, and sometimes red, is a connecting link between the white light to which it is attached above and to the concrete body to which it is attached below, and which keeps it alight. This light always consumes anything which is under it or which is brought in contact with it, for such is its nature, to be a source of destruction and death. But the white light which is above it never consumes or destroys and never changes. Therefore Moses said, "For the Lord thy God is a consuming fire", literally consuming all that is beneath him; that is why he said "thy God" and not "our God", because Moses was in that white light above which does not consume or destroy. Now observe. The impulse through which this blue light is set aflame and attaches itself to the white light comes only from Israel, who cleave to it from below. Further, although it is the nature of this blue or black light to consume everything that is in contact with it beneath, yet Israel are able to cleave to it from below and still exist; so it is written, "and ye that cleave to the Lord your God are all of you alive this day". Your God and not our God: to wit, that blue or black flame which consumes and destroys all that cleaves to it from below; yet you cleave and are still alive. Above the white light and surrounding it is still another light scarcely perceptible, symbolical of the supreme essence. Thus the ascending flame symbolises the highest mysteries of wisdom.'

R. Phineas approached and kissed him, saying, 'Blessed be God who led my steps here.' They then accompanied R. Phineas on his way for three miles. When they came back, R. Simeon said: 'What I told you before furnishes a symbol of the sacred unification. The second he of the holy name is the blue or black light which is attached to Yod, He, Vau, which are the white shining light. Sometimes this blue light is not he' but daleth; that is to say, when Israel do not cleave to it from below so as to make it burn and cling to the white light, it is daleth, but when they give it the impulse to cling to the white light, it is he. For where male and female are not found together, he is eliminated and only daleth is left (hence in Deut. XXII, 15, the word na'ar is used for "maiden" instead of na'arah, because she is not united with the male). But when the chain is complete, the he' cleaves to the white light and Israel cleave to it and feed its light without being destroyed. This is the secret of the sacrifice. The ascending smoke kindles the blue light, which then attaches itself

Zohar: Bereshith, Section 1, Page 51b

to the white light, so that the whole candle is completely alight. Since it is the nature of this blue light to destroy and consume everything which is in contact with it underneath, when the sacrifice is pleasing and the candle is completely alight, then, as in the case of Elijah, "the fire of the Lord descends and consumes the burnt-offering" (I Kings XVIII, 38), this being a manifestation that the chain is complete, the blue light both cleaving to the white light and consuming the fat and flesh of the burnt-offering beneath it, for it does not consume what is beneath it save when it ascends and attaches itself to the white light. Then there is peace in all worlds, and the whole forms a unity. When the blue light has consumed all that is beneath it, the priests, the Levites, and the laity assemble at its foot with chanting, with meditation, and with prayer, the lamp burns above them, the lights are welded into one, worlds are illumined, and both those above and those below are blessed. Hence it is that "ye, even while cleaving to the Lord your God, are all alive this day". The word athem (you) here is preceded by the letter vau (and), to show that whereas the fat and the flesh which cleave to the flame are destroyed by it, you cleave to it and are still alive.'

All colours seen in a dream are of good presage, except blue; this is ever consuming and destroying, being the tree in which death is located. It spreads over the lower world, and because all things are situated beneath it, therefore they are perishable. It is true that it also pervades the heaven, and there are many objects there which are imperishable. These, however, are constituted of this blue light, whereas the lower ones are of coarser material, and constitute a lower world on which the upper one rests. Hence the blue light consumes and destroys them.' [Tr. note: From this point to 52a ad fin. is a Cabbalistic interpolation on the origin of the Serpent.]

Zohar: Bereshith, Section 1, Page 52a

[Note: Our translation of the Hebrew text resumes with the fifth line from the bottom of page 52a]

AND THEY HEARD THE VOICE OF THE LORD GOD WALKING IN THE GARDEN. (Note the form mithalech (walking) instead of the usual mehalech.) Until he sinned, man was gifted with the wisdom of celestial illumination, and he did not for an instant quit the Tree of Life. But when he was seduced by his desire to know what was below, he weakly followed it until he became separated from the Tree of Life, and knew evil and forsook good: hence the Scripture says 'for thou art not a God that hath pleasure in wickedness,

Zohar: Bereshith, Section 1, Page 52b

evil shall not sojourn with thee' (Ps. V. 5). He who is drawn after evil may not abide with the Tree of Life. Before they sinned, the human pair used to hear a voice from above, and were endowed with the higher wisdom; they stood erect with heavenly radiance, and knew no fear. When they sinned, they were not able to stand up even before an earthly voice. A similar thing happened later with the Israelites. When Israel stood before Mount Sinai, the impurity of the serpent was removed from them, so that carnal passion was suppressed among them, and in consequence they were able to attach themselves to the Tree of Life, and their thoughts were turned to higher things and not to lower. Hence they were vouchsafed heavenly illuminations and knowledge which filled them with joy and gladness. Further, God girt them with cinctures of the letters of the Holy Name, which prevented the serpent from gaining power over them or defiling them as before. When they sinned by worshipping the calf, they were degraded from their high estate and lost their illumination, they were deprived of the protective girdle of the Holy Name and became exposed to the attacks of the evil serpent as before, and so brought death into the world. After their sin, it is related that 'Aaron and the children of Israel saw Moses, and behold, the skin of his face shone, and they were afraid to come nigh him' (Ex. XXXIV, 30). Before that, however, we are told that 'Israel saw the great hand' (Ibid. XIV, 31) on the Red Sea, and that at Mount Sinai they all saw celestial lights and were illumined with the vision of clear prophecy, as it is written, 'And all the people saw the voices' (Ibid. XX, 18), and by the Red Sea they saw God and did not fear, as it is written, 'This is my God and I will praise him' (Ibid. XV, 2). But after they sinned, they were not able to look even on the face of the deputy (Moses). How was this? Because 'the children of Israel were deprived of their ornament from Mount Sinai', to wit, of the armour with which they were girt on Mount Sinai in order that the evil serpent should not have power over them. After this had been stripped from them we read that 'Moses took the tent and pitched it without the camp, afar off from the camp' (Ibid. XXXIII, 7). R. Eleazar explained the connection thus: 'When Moses perceived that Israel had been deprived of their heavenly armour, he said, "Of a surety the evil serpent will now come to dwell among them, and if the sanctuary remains here among them it will be defiled", and he therefore took the tent and pitched it outside, far from the camp.' 'And he called it the tent of meeting.' It had been such before, but had been called the 'tent', simply. The epithet 'of meeting' was now given to it, according to R. Eleazar, in compliment, according to R. Abba, in disparagement. R. Eleazar defended his view on the ground that moed (meeting, appointed time) is the word used of the day when the moon is in full career, when its holiness is increased and it is free from defect; so here, Moses gave the tent this name to show that it had been removed from the contagion of the people. R. Abba argued that the simple name 'tent, has the same implication as in the verse 'a tent that shall not be removed, the stakes of which shall never be plucked up' (Is. XXXIII, 20), i.e. that it designates something which confers eternity on the world and saves it from death, whereas the epithet 'meeting' is used in the same sense as in the phrase 'a house of meeting for all flesh' (i.e. the grave, Job XXX, 23), and indicates that now the life which it conferred was only for a limited period. At first it was unimpaired, but now it was impaired; at first the sun and the moon were in continuous union, but now their union was only from season to season (moed); hence the name 'tent of season' (moed).

R. Simeon was one night studying the Torah in company with R. Judah, R. Isaac, and R. Yose. Said R. Judah to him: 'We read that "the Israelites took off their ornament from Mount Horeb", and we go on to assert that they thereby brought death upon themselves, and once more placed themselves in the power of the evil serpent from whose clutches they had previously escaped. This may be true of the Israelites; but what of Joshua, who had not sinned? Are we to say that he was deprived of the armour which he received with them, or not?

Zohar: Bereshith, Section 1, Page 53a

If not, why did he die like other people? If you say he was deprived, what was the reason, seeing that he had not sinned, as he was with Moses when the people sinned? And if you say that he did not receive the same crown on Mount Sinai as the rest of the people, again, what was the reason?' R. Simeon in reply quoted the text: For the Lord is righteous, he loveth righteousness, he is upright, men shall behold his face (Ps. XI, 7). He said: 'This verse has been variously explained by our colleagues, but it may be taken in this way. "For the Lord is righteous": to wit, He is righteous and His name is Righteous (Zaddik) and therefore He loves righteous deeds. He is also upright, as it is written, "righteous and upright is he" (Deut. XXXII, 4); and therefore all the inhabitants of the world behold His face, that they may amend their ways and walk in the straight path. For when God judges the world, He passes sentence only according to the conduct of the majority. Now when Adam sinned by eating of the forbidden tree, he caused that tree to become a source of death to all the world. He also caused imperfection by separating the Wife from her Husband. This imperfection was exhibited in the moon, until the time when Israel stood before Mount Sinai, when the moon was freed from its defect, and was in a position to shine continually. When Israel sinned by making the calf, the moon reverted to its former imperfection, and the evil serpent was able to seize her and draw her to him. When Moses saw that Israel had sinned and that they had been deprived of their holy armour, he knew full well that the serpent had seized the moon to draw her to him, and that she had become defective, and he therefore took her outside. Thus she has reverted to the defective state into which she was brought by the sin of Adam, and therefore no man can live permanently save Moses, who controls her, and whose death was due to a different cause. Hence she had not power to bestead permanently even Joshua, although he retained his holy armour; and it was therefore that Moses called her "tent of appointed time" (moed), to wit, the tent in which is an appointed time for all living. To speak more esoterically: there is a Right above and there is a Right below; there is a Left above and there is a Left below. There is a Right above in the realm of supernal holiness, and there is a Right below located in the "other side". There is a Left above in the realm of supernal holiness to procure indulgence for the moon, so as to link her to the holy place and enable her to shine. There is a Left below which estranges the upper realm from her and prevents her from reflecting the sun's light and drawing near to him. This is the side of the evil serpent, who, when this Left of the lower realm bestirs itself, draws the moon to himself and separates her from the upper world, so that her light is darkened. She then causes death to descend like a stream on all that is below; she cleaves to the serpent and departs from the Tree of Life, and so brings death on all the world. At such time the sanctuary is defiled till an appointed time when the moon is repaired and shines again. Hence the name "tent of appointed time" (moed), and hence it is that Joshua died only through the instigation of the serpent, which came up to the tent and rendered it imperfect as at first. This is the inner meaning of the verse, "And Joshua the son of Nun, a lad (naar), departed not from out the tent" (Ex. XXXIII, 11). Although he was a "lad" (i.e. attendant) beneath qualified to receive the (celestial) light, he did not depart from out the tent: he shared in its imperfection; although he still had the holy armour, yet when the moon became imperfect, he also was not delivered from the same power which caused that imperfection. Similarly when Adam sinned, God took from him the armour of the bright and holy letters with which he had been encompassed, and then he and his wife were afraid, perceiving that they had been stripped; so it says AND THEY KNEW THAT THEY WERE NAKED. At first they had been invested with those glorious crowns which gave them protection and exemption from death. When they sinned, they were stripped of them, and then they knew that death was calling them, that they had been deprived of their exemption, and that they had brought death on themselves and on all the world.'

BERESHITH

[Note: The beginning passage about fig leaves is not found in our Hebrew text.]

AND THEY SEWED FIG LEAVES TOGETHER. This means, as explained elsewhere, that they learnt all kinds of enchantments and magic, and clung to worldly knowledge, as has been said. At that moment the stature of man was diminished by a hundred cubits. Thus a separation took place (of man from God), man was brought to judgement, and the earth was cursed, all as we have explained.

AND HE DROVE OUT THE MAN. R. Eleazar said: We naturally suppose that "he" is the subject and "man" the object. The truth is, however, that "man" is the subject and the object is the accusative particle eth, so that we render "and the man drove out eth". Hence it is written, "And God sent him forth from the Garden of Eden", for the reason that he had divorced eth, as we have explained. AND HE PLACED: the subject is still "man"; it was he who fixed the Cherubim in this place, who closed the path to Paradise, who subjected the world to chastisement, and drew upon it curses from that day onward. THE FLAME OF A SWORD WHICH TURNED EVERY WAY: this refers to those beings who are ever in readiness to chastise the world, and who take all manner of shapes, being sometimes male, sometimes female, sometimes flaming fire and sometimes irresistible winds. All this is TO KEEP THE WAY OF THE TREE OF LIFE, so that man should not do any more mischief there. The "flaming sword" denotes those punitive spirits who heap fire on the heads of the wicked and sinners (in hell). They take various forms according to the offences of those who are punished. The word "flaming" (lahat) here has its analogy in the verse, "the day that cometh shall burn them up" (ve-lihat, Mal. III, 19). The "sword" is that mentioned in the verse, "The sword of the Lord is filled with blood, etc." (Is. XXXIV, 6).' R. Judah said: 'All those punitive spirits that we have mentioned, that assume so many various forms, are charged to maltreat and harry in this world the sinners who deliberately transgress the precepts of their Master. For when a man sins, he draws towards himself numbers of evil spirits and emissaries of punishment, before whom he quails in fear. Solomon was conversant with the mysteries of Wisdom, and God set upon his head the crown of royalty, and the whole world feared him. When, however, he sinned, he drew towards himself numbers of evil and punitive spirits, of whom he was much frightened, so that they were able to maltreat him and to take away his (precious) possessions. In truth, a man by his actions is always drawing to himself some emissary from the other world, good or evil according to the path which he treads. So Adam drew to himself an emissary of defilement who defiled him and all mankind after him. This was the evil serpent who is himself unclean and defiled the world. Our Sages have taught that when he draws the soul out of a man, there is left an unclean body which renders the whole house unclean, and all those that touch it, as it is written, "He that touches a dead body, etc." (Num. XXX, 11). The reason is that when he takes the soul and renders the body unclean, permission is given to all the unclean spirits, which are akin to the evil serpent, to rest upon it, and so the whole place where the evil serpent is present becomes defiled. Further, when men sleep on their beds at night-time and night spreads her wings over the world, they are having a foretaste of death, and in consequence the unclean spirit is let loose in the world, carrying pollution. In particular it rests upon a man's hands and defiles them, so that when he wakes up and his soul is restored to him, everything which he touches with his hands is rendered unclean. Hence a man should be careful when dressing not to take his garments from a person who has not washed his hands, because in this way he draws upon himself the unclean spirit and becomes defiled. This spirit is authorised to settle in every place where there is the merest trace of the side from which it issues. Hence a man should not let water be poured over his hands by one who has not yet washed his own hands, because in this way he draws on himself the unclean spirit, from contact with the one who pours water over him.

Therefore a man should be on his guard on every side against the side of this evil serpent, which otherwise will gain the better of him. God has promised one day to remove it from this world, as it is written, "I will cause the unclean spirit to pass out of the land" (Zech. XIII, 2), and also "He will swallow up death forever" (Is. XXV, 8).'

AND THE MAN KNEW EVE HIS WIFE. R. Abba discoursed in connection with this verse on the text: Who knoweth the spirit of man which goeth upwards, and the spirit of the beast which goeth downward to the earth? (Eccl. III, 21). He said: 'This verse can bear many constructions, and so it is with all the words of the Torah: they can all bear several meanings, and all good, and the whole Torah can be expounded in seventy ways, corresponding to seventy sides and seventy wings. We will, however, expound thus. When a man walks in the path of truth, he goes towards the right and attracts to himself a holy spirit from above, which in turn ascends with holy intent to attach itself to the upper world and to cleave to the supernal holiness. When, however, a man walks in the path of evil, he draws to himself an unclean spirit belonging to the left side, which renders him impure; so it is written, "ye shall not make yourselves unclean with them that ye should be defiled thereby" (Lev. XI, 43), i.e. he that first defiles himself is led further into defilement. Further, when a man walks in the right path and attracts to himself a spirit of holiness from above and cleaves to it, he also draws a spirit of holiness on to the son whom he bears into the world, so that he is like to be endowed with the sanctity of his Master (as it is written, "if ye sanctify yourselves, ye shall be holy" (Lev. XI, 44)). Contrariwise, when the man goes to the side of the left and draws to himself the impure spirit and clings to it, he also draws a spirit of uncleanliness on the son that issues from him, so that he is like to be defiled by the impurity of the left side. This is what is meant by the words, "Who knows the spirit of the sons of men, namely that one which ascends on high, etc." When a man cleaves to the right, the spirit mounts aloft, but when he cleaves to the left, the side of the left, which is the spirit of uncleanliness, descends from above and fixes its abode in a man's body, and the son whom he begets in that state of impurity is his son from that unclean spirit. Now Adam clave to that unclean spirit, and his wife clung to it at first and received defilement from it. Hence when Adam begat a son, that son was the son of the impure spirit. Thus there were two sons-one from the unclean spirit, and one after Adam had repented. Thus one was from the pure side and one from the impure.' R. Eleazar said: 'When the serpent injected his impurity into Eve, she absorbed it, and so when Adam had intercourse with her she bore two sons-one from the impure side and one from the side of Adam; and Abel bore a resemblance to the higher form and Cain to the lower. Hence it was that their ways in life were different. It was natural, too, that Cain, coming from the side of the angel of death, should kill his brother. He also adhered to his own side, and from him originate all the evil habitations and demons and goblins and evil spirits in the world.' R. Yose said: 'Cain was the nest (Qina) of the evil habitations which came into the world from the impure side. Afterwards both Cain and Abel brought sacrifices, each from his appropriate side; hence it is written, AND IT CAME TO PASS AT THE END OF DAYS THAT CAIN BROUGHT OF THE FRUIT OF THE GROUND, ETC. R. Simeon said: This "end of days" is the same as "the end of all flesh" (Gen. VI, 13), who is also the angel of death. Cain brought his offering from this "end of days"; this is indicated by the expression in the text "from the end" (mi-ketz).

Zohar: Bereshith, Section 1, Page 54b

CAIN BROUGHT OF THE FRUIT OF THE GROUND: this is parallel to "of the fruit of the tree" in God's words to Adam.' R. Eleazar said: 'We can apply to Cain the verse, "Woe to the wicked, it shall be ill with him, for the reward of his hands shall be done to him" (Is. III, 11). "The reward of his hands" refers to the angel of death, who is drawn towards them and clings to them so as to slay or defile them. Thus Cain offered from the side appropriate to him. AND ABEL ALSO BROUGHT OF THE FIRSTLINGS: to amplify the higher side which comes from the side of holiness. Hence THE LORD HAD RESPECT UNTO ABEL AND TO HIS OFFERING, BUT TO CAIN AND TO HIS OFFERING HE HAD NOT RESPECT, i.e. God did not accept it, and therefore CAIN WAS VERY WROTH AND HIS COUNTENANCE (presence) FELL, because his presence was not received, being from the side of the left. On the other hand, God received Abel, and therefore it is written, AND IT CAME TO PASS WHEN THEY WERE IN THE FIELD, ETC. 'Field is here a designation for woman; Cain was jealous of the twin sister that was born with Abel (according to the interpretation placed by us on the words "and she bore in addition", IV, 2).' IF THOU DOEST WELL, SHALL THERE NOT BE UPLIFTING?

This has already been explained, viz. the word se'eth (uplifting) means, according to R. Abba, 'thou shalt mount above and shalt not descend below'. R. Yose said: 'We accept this explanation, which is a good one, but I have also heard another, viz. "this attachment of the impure spirit shall depart (lit. be lifted) from thee and leave thee". If not, then SIN COUCHETH AT THE DOOR. By "door" is meant the heavenly tribunal which is the door through which all enter, as it is written, "open to me the doors of righteousness" (Ps. CXVIII, 19). By "sin coucheth" is meant that the side which clung to thee and was drawn towards thee is lying in watch for thee to exact punishment from thee.' Said R. Isaac: 'When Cain wanted to kill Abel, he did not know how to make him give up the ghost, and he bit him like a snake, as our colleagues have explained. God then cursed him, and he wandered about the world without being able to find any resting-place until, clapping his hands on his head, he repented before his Master. Then the earth found a place for him in one of its lower levels.' R. Yose said: 'The earth allowed him to stay on its surface, as it is written, "And the Lord set upon Cain a sign".' R. Isaac said: 'That is not so. The earth found a place for him in a certain lower level, as it is written, "Behold, thou hast driven me out this day from the face of the ground", implying that he was banished from the surface but not from underground. The level on which he found a resting-place was Arka, of the denizens of which it is written, "these shall perish from the earth and from beneath the heavens" (Jer. X, 11). There was fixed his habitation, and this is what is meant by the words, AND HE DWELT IN THE LAND OF NOD ON THE EAST OF EDEN. Said R. Isaac further: From the time that Cain killed Abel Adam separated from his wife. Two female spirits then used to come and have intercourse with him, and he bore from them spirits and demons that flit about the world. This need cause no surprise, because now also when a man dreams in his sleep, female spirits often come and disport with him, and so conceive from him and subsequently give birth. The creatures thus produced are called "plagues of mankind"; they appear always under the form of human beings, but they have no hair on their heads. It is they who are referred to in the verse, "and I shall chastise him with the rod of men and with the plagues of the sons of men" (II Sam. VII, 14). In the same way male spirits visit womenfolk and make them pregnant, so that they bring forth spirits which are also called "plagues of the sons of men".

After a hundred and thirty years, Adam again felt drawn

Zohar: Bereshith, Section 1, Page 55a

with desire towards his wife, and he begat from her a son whom he called Seth. This name symbolises an end, being composed of the two last letters of the alphabet in regular order.' R. Judah said: 'This name symbolised the reincarnation of the spirit which had been lost, being of the same letters as the word shath (set) in the sentence "God hath replaced (shath) for me another seed instead of Abel." R. Judah further said: The words AND HE BEGAT IN HIS OWN LIKENESS AFTER HIS IMAGE indicate that his other sons were not fully after his likeness, but that this one reproduced his qualities both of body and soul. This accords with what R. Simeon said in the name of R. Yeba, the Elder, that his other sons were engendered in defilement through the attachment of the serpent and of its rider, Samael, and therefore they were not a complete reproduction of Adam. We said before, it is true, that Abel was not from the same side as Cain; nevertheless, both were alike in this, that they were not endowed with the full human figure.' R. Yose said: 'This view is borne out by the language of the text, which in regard to the birth of Cain says, "And Adam knew his wife and she conceived and she bore Cain", and so of Abel, "and she again bore his brother Abel", but of Seth it says, "and he bore in his likeness after his image".' R. Simeon said: 'For a hundred and thirty years Adam separated from his wife, and during that time he begat many spirits and demons, through the force of the impurity which he had absorbed. When that impurity was exhausted, he turned once more to his wife and begat from her a son, of whom it is written, "he begat in his own likeness after his image". For when a man goes to the side of the left and walks in impurity, he draws to himself all kinds of impure spirits, and an unclean spirit clings to him and refuses to leave him, since these spirits cling only to those that cling to them first. Happy the righteous who walk in the straight path, they being the truly righteous; their children are also blessed, and of them it is written, "for the upright shall dwell in the earth" (Prov. II, 21).'

AND THE SISTER OF TUBAL CAIN WAS NAAMAH. R. Hiya said: 'Why does the Scripture particularly mention Naamah? The reason is that she was the great seducer not only of men, but also of spirits and demons.' R. Isaac said: 'The "sons of God" mentioned in the Scripture (Gen. VI, 4), who were Uzza and Azael, were seduced by her.' R. Simeon said: 'She was the mother of the demons, being of the side of Cain, and it is she who in company with Lilith brings epilepsy on children.' Said R. Abba to him: 'Did you not say before that her function is to seduce men?' He replied: 'That is so; she disports herself with men, and sometimes bears spirits from them. And she still exists to seduce men.' Said R. Abba to him: 'But do these demons not die like human beings? How then comes she to exist to the present day?' He replied: 'It is so. Lilith and Naamah and Iggereth, the daughter of Mahlath, who originated from their side, will all continue to exist until the Holy One, blessed be He, sweeps away the unclean spirit, as it is written, "I will cause the unclean spirit to pass out of the land" (Zech. XIII, 2).' Said R. Simeon: 'Alas for the blindness of the sons of men, all unaware as they are how full the earth is of strange and invisible beings and hidden dangers, which could they but see, they would marvel how they themselves can exist on the earth. This Naamah was the mother of the demons, and from her originate all those evil spirits which mix with men and arouse in them concupiscence, which leads them to defilement. It is because such a hap comes from the side of the unclean spirit that it entails the need of purification by ablution, as our colleagues have explained.'

THIS IS THE BOOK OF THE GENERATIONS OF ADAM, i.e. those who inherited his likeness. Said R. Isaac: 'God showed Adam the visages of all future generations, of all the wise men and all the kings that were destined to rule over Israel. When he saw David, who was destined to die as soon as he was born, he said, "I will lend him seventy years from my life", and so it came to pass. It was to this that David referred when he said: "For Thou, O Lord, hast made me glad

Zohar: Bereshith, Section 1, Page 55b

through thy work, I will triumph in the works of thy hands" (Ps. XCII, 5), the expression "work" and "works of thy hands" in this passage referring to Adam, who was made by God and not by flesh and blood. Hence Adam's days fell short by seventy years of the thousand which he ought by right to have lived. God also showed him the wise men of each generation. When he came to R. Akiba and saw his great learning, he rejoiced, but when he saw his martyrdom he was sorely grieved. Nevertheless, he exclaimed: "How precious in mine eyes are thy companions, O God, how mighty are the chiefs of them" (Ps. CXXXIX, 17). "This is the book": literally so, as we have explained, viz. that when Adam was in the Garden of Eden, God sent down to him a book by the hand of Raziel, the angel in charge of the holy mysteries. In this book were supernal inscriptions containing the sacred wisdom, and seventy-two branches of wisdom expounded so as to show the formation of six hundred and seventy inscriptions of higher mysteries. In the middle of the book was a secret writing explaining the thousand and five hundred keys which were not revealed even to the holy angels, and all of which were locked up in this book until it came into the hands of Adam. When Adam obtained it, all the holy angels gathered round him to hear him read it, and when he began they exclaimed: "Be thou exalted, O Lord, above the heavens, let thy glory be above all the earth" (Ps. LVII, 12). Thereupon the holy angel Hadarniel was secretly sent to say to him: "Adam, Adam, reveal not the glory of the Master, for to thee alone and not to the angels is the privilege given to know the glory of thy Master." Therefore he kept it by him secretly until he left the Garden of Eden. While he was there he studied it diligently, and utilised constantly the gift of his Master until he discovered sublime mysteries which were not known even to the celestial ministers. When, however, he transgressed the command of his Master, the book flew away from him. Adam then beat his breast and wept, and entered the river Gihon up to his neck, so that his body became all wrinkled and his face haggard. God thereupon made a sign to Raphael to return to him the book, which he then studied for the rest of his life. Adam left it to his son Seth, who transmitted it in turn to his posterity, and so on until it came to Abraham, who learnt from it how to discern the glory of his Master, as has been said. Similarly Enoch possessed a book through which he learnt to discern the divine glory.'

MALE AND FEMALE HE CREATED THEM. R. Simeon said: 'Profound mysteries are revealed in these two verses. [Tr. note: i.e. this one and Gen. I, 27.] The words "male and female he created them" make known the high dignity of man, the mystic doctrine of his creation. Assuredly in the way in which heaven and earth were created man was also created; for of heaven and earth it is written, "these are the generations of the heaven and the earth", and of man it is written, "these are the generations of man"; of heaven and earth it is written, "when they were created", and of man it is written, "on the day when they were created": "Male and female he created them." From this we learn that every figure which does not comprise male and female elements is not a true and proper figure, and so we have laid down in the esoteric teaching of our Mishnah. Observe this. God does not place His abode in any place where male and female are not found together, nor are blessings found save in such a place, as it is written, AND HE BLESSED THEM AND CALLED THEIR NAME MAN ON THE DAY THAT THEY WERE CREATED: note that it says them and their name, and not him and his name. The male is not even called man till he is united with the female.' R. Judah said: 'Since the destruction of the Temple, blessings have not reached the world, but they go astray every day, as it is written, "The righteous loses", to wit, the blessings which used to rest upon him, as it is written, "blessings on the head of the righteous". AND CALLED HIS NAME SETH. It is to Seth that all the generations which have survived in the world and all the truly righteous of the world trace their descent.' R. Yose said: 'The two last letters of the alphabet were left in their order after the others had been reversed

Zohar: Bereshith, Section 1, Page 56a

through Adam's transgression, and therefore when he repented he grasped at these two and called the son who was born in his likeness Seth, a name formed of the last two letters of the alphabet in proper order. Nevertheless, the other letters of the alphabet remained in the inverse order, and not till Israel stood before Mount Sinai did they recover their proper order as on the day when the heaven and earth were created, and the earth was once more securely established.' R. Abba said: 'On the day that Adam transgressed the command of his Master, heaven and earth were like to have been uprooted from their place, being based as they are only on the covenant, as it is written, "But for my covenant day and night, I had not set the statutes of heaven and earth" (Jer. XXXIII, 25), and Adam broke the covenant, as it is written, "And they like Adam transgressed the covenant" (Hos. VI, 7). And had not God foreseen that Israel would one day stand before Mount Sinai to confirm this covenant, the world would not have been preserved.' R. Hizkiah said: 'Whoever confesses his sin thereby procures forgiveness from God. See now, when God created the world, He made this covenant and established the world upon it, as it is written Bereshith, which we interpret as bara shith, "he created the foundation", to wit, the covenant on which the world rests, and which is also called shith, because it is a trough from which blessings flow forth to the world. Adam broke this covenant and removed it from its place. This covenant is symbolised by the small letter Yod, the root and foundation of the world. When Adam begat a son, he confessed his guilt and called the child Seth; he did not venture to insert a Yod and call him "Shith", because he had broken the covenant so symbolised. In recompense, God propagated mankind from Seth, and made him the forefather of all the righteous who have lived since. Note also this. When Israel stood before Mount Sinai, there entered between these two letters (shin and tau) a symbol of the covenant, to wit, the letter beth, and God gave to Israel the word formed of all three letters, which is SaBbaTH, as it is said: "And the children of Israel shall keep the Sabbath, to make the Sabbath throughout their generations a perpetual covenant." In this way these two letters finally obtained their original potency, which had remained in suspense until the world was brought into its complete state and the holy covenant entered between them.' R. Yose said: 'These two letters were indeed fully reinstated through the letter beth, but all the letters commenced to return to their proper order with the birth of Seth, and so in every generation until Israel stood before Mount Sinai, when they were finally restored.' R. Judah said: 'They had already been restored below, and in every generation the world was held together by the letters though they were not yet properly settled in their places; but when the Torah was given to Israel, then everything was put right.'

R. Eleazar said: 'In the time of Enosh, men were skilled in magic and divination, and in the art of controlling the heavenly forces. Adam had brought with him from the Garden of Eden the knowledge of "the leaves of the tree", but he and his wife and their children did not practise it. When Enosh came, however, he saw the advantage of these arts and how the heavenly courses could be altered by them, and he and his contemporaries studied them and practised magic and divination. From them these arts descended to the generation of the Flood and were practised for evil purposes by all the men of that time. Relying upon these arts, they defied Noah, saying that divine justice could never be executed upon them, since they knew a way to avert it. The practice of these arts commenced with Enosh, and hence it is said of his time, THEN WAS THE NAME OF THE LORD CALLED UPON PROFANELY. R. Isaac said: All the righteous men that were among them sought to restrain them, such as Jered, Methuselah, and Enoch, but without success, and the world became full of sinners who rebelled against their Master saying, "What is the Almighty that we should serve him?" (Job XXI, 15). This is not so foolish as it sounds, for they knew all the arts we have mentioned and all the ruling chieftains in charge of the world, and on this knowledge they relied, until at length God disabused them by restoring the earth to its primitive state

Zohar: Bereshith, Section 1, Page 56b

and covering it with water. Later, He again restored it and made it productive, since He looked upon it with mercy, as it is written, "The Lord sat at the Flood"–"the Lord" signifying the attribute of mercy. In the days of Enoch even children were acquainted with these mysterious arts.' Said R. Yesa: 'If so, how could they be so blind as not to know that God intended to bring the Flood upon them and destroy them?' R. Isaac replied: 'They did know, but they thought they were safe because they were acquainted with the angel in charge of fire and the angel in charge of water, and had means of preventing them from executing judgement on them. What they did not know was that God rules the world and that punishment proceeds from Him. They only saw that the world was entrusted to those chieftains and that everything was done through them, and therefore they took no heed of God and His works until the time came for the earth to be destroyed and the Holy Spirit proclaimed every day, "Let sinners be consumed out of the earth and let the wicked be no more" (Ps. CIV, 35). God gave them a respite all the time that the righteous men Jered, Methuselah, and Enoch were alive; but when they departed from the world, God let punishment descend upon them and they perished, as it says, "and they were blotted out from the earth" (Gen. VII, 23).'

AND ENOCH WALKED WITH GOD, AND HE WAS NOT, FOR GOD HAD TAKEN HIM. R. Yose illustrated this verse from the passage: While the king was still with his company at table, my spikenard sent forth its fragrance (S. S. I, 12). 'This verse', he said, 'can be expounded as referring to the ways of God. When God sees that a man who cleaves to Him and with whom He abides will one day degenerate, He takes him from the world prematurely, culling, as it were, the odour while it is still sweet; hence it is written, "while the King was with his company, my spikenard gave up its scent." The King is God; the company is the good man who cleaves to Him and walks in His ways; the spikenard indicates the good deeds on account of which he is removed from the world before his time. Of such a case did King Solomon say: "There is a vanity which is done upon the earth, that there be righteous men unto whom it happeneth according to the work of the wicked, etc." (Eccl. VIII, 14). How there are "righteous men to whom it happeneth according to the work of the wicked" we have just explained, viz. that because their deeds are good, God removes them from the world before their time and before they become liable to punishment. The rest of the verse, "there be wicked men to whom it happeneth according to the work of the righteous", means that God gives them a respite and is long-suffering with them. Thus the good die early in order that they may not degenerate, and the wicked live on in order that they may have a chance to repent, or in order that a virtuous progeny may issue from them. See now, Enoch was virtuous, but God saw that he would degenerate, and therefore gathered him in in time, as one "gathers lilies" (S. S. VI, 2) because of their good scent. "And he was not, for God had taken him." This means that he did not live to a great age like his contemporaries, because God took him before his time.' R. Eleazar said: 'God removed Enoch from the earth, and took him up to the highest heavens, and there presented to him wonderful treasures, including forty-five mystical key-combinations of graven letters which are used by the highest ranks of angels, as has been explained elsewhere.'

AND THE LORD SAW THAT THE WICKEDNESS OF MAN WAS VERY GREAT IN THE EARTH, AND THAT EVERY IMAGINATION OF THE THOUGHTS OF HIS HEART WAS ONLY EVIL CONTINUALLY. R. Judah quoted in this connection the verse: For thou art not a God who hath pleasure in wickedness, evil shall not sojourn with thee (Ps. V, 5). He said: 'One lesson that may be derived from this verse is that if a man cleaves to the evil imagination and follows after it, not only does he defile himself thereby, but he is led further into defilement, as has already been stated. The men of the time of the Flood committed all kinds of sin, but the measure of their guilt was not full until they wasted their blood (i.e. seed) upon the ground. We know this from the fact that the word ra' (evil) is used here,

Zohar: Bereshith, Section 1, Page 57a

and also in the verse, "and Er the son of Judah was evil (ra') in the sight of the Lord" (Gen. XXXVIII, 7).' Said R. Yose: 'Is not evil (ra') the same as "wickedness" (resha')?' He said: 'No. A man is called "wicked" (rasha') if he merely lifts his hand against his neighbour without doing him any harm, as it is written, "And he said to the wicked one (rasha'), why wilt thou smite thy neighbour?", the future tense (wilt smite) implying that he had not yet done anything to him. But only he is called "evil" (ra') who corrupts his way and defiles himself and the earth, and so lends force to the unclean spirit which is called ra' (whence it is said that "all their thoughts were for evil", ra'). Such a one will never enter the heavenly palace nor gaze upon the Shekinah, for by this sin the Shekinah is repelled from the world. We know this from Jacob, who, when the Shekinah departed from him, concluded that there was some stain attaching to his offspring, on account of which the unclean spirit had acquired strength and the light of the moon had been impaired: for this sin defiles the sanctuary. If on this account the Shekinah departed from Jacob, how much more certain is it that it will depart from one who corrupts his way and defiles himself, so giving power to the unclean spirit. Hence when a man defiles himself he is called ra'. Further, when a man defiles himself, he is not favoured with visitation (in dreams) from the Holy One, blessed be He, but on the contrary he is subject at all times to the visits of the spirit called ra', as it is written, "he who sleeps sated (i.e. without evil passion) will not be visited by evil" (Prov. XIX, 23) (as much as to say that when he walks in the right path he will not be visited by Ra'.) Hence it is said of the men of the blood that their thoughts were only evil, and the Psalmist said, "evil shall not sojourn with thee". Those who commit this sin are called ra' and not rasha'. Hence, too, it is written, "Yea, though I walk through the valley of the shadow of death I will not fear evil (ra'), for thou art with me".'

AND IT REPENTED THE LORD THAT HE HAD MADE MAN UPON THE EARTH, AND IT GRIEVED HIM AT HIS HEART. R. Yose illustrated from the verse: Woe unto them that draw iniquity with cords of vanity, and sin as it were with a cart rope (Is. V, 18). He said: 'Those who "draw iniquity" are the men who sin before their Master every day, and in whose eyes the sins they commit are like gossamer threads, which are of no account and are not noticed by God. And so they go on until they make their guilt as strong as a cart rope which cannot be broken. See now, when the time comes for God to pass sentence on sinners, although they have provoked Him every day, He is yet unwilling to destroy them, and though He sees their deeds, He is yet indulgent towards them because they are the work of His hands, and therefore He gives them a respite. When at last He does come to execute judgement upon them, He is, as it were, grieved, since they are the work of His hands, although it is written, "Honour and majesty are before him, strength and joy are in his place" (Ps. XCVI, 6).' R. Yose said: 'Observe that it says, "He was grieved to his heart". The seat of the grief was the heart and no other place, "heart" having here the same sense as in the verse, "according to that which is in mine heart and in my mind" (I Sam. II, 35).'

R. Isaac said: 'The word "repented" here has the same sense as in the sentence, "And the Lord repented of the evil which he had said he would do unto his people" (Ex. XXXII, 14). R. Yesa says that the word niham, used of God, means "repent", as has been remarked, implying that God bethinks Himself that the sinners are the work of His hands, and therefore pities them and is grieved because they sin before Him. R. Hizkiah says that it means "is consoled", implying that when God resolves to destroy the wicked, He comforts Himself for their loss like one who resigns himself to the loss of some article, and once He has done so, justice takes its course and repentance no longer avails; for up to that point the decision may still be reversed. No only so, but judgement is executed with additional rigour, until the sinners are utterly destroyed. The text tells us as much; for the words "the Lord was comforted" indicate that God resigned Himself, and the words "he was grieved to his heart" that He allowed justice to take its course without mercy.' R. Hiya said: 'The words "God was comforted because he had made man" refer to the time when man was first created on the earth, in the supernal image, and God rejoiced because the angels praised Him saying,

Zohar: Bereshith, Section 1, Page 57b

'Thou hast made him (man) little lower than God, and crownest him with glory and honour" (Ps. VIII, 6). But afterwards when man sinned, then God "was grieved", because now the angels could say that they had been right in protesting against his creation, saying: "What is man that thou art mindful of him and the son of man that thou visitest him?" (Ibid. 5).' R. Judah said: 'God was grieved because the execution of judgement is always displeasing to Him. Thus we read that Jehoshaphat when going out to war "appointed those that should sing.... Give thanks unto the Lord, for his mercy endureth forever" (II Chron. XX, 21), and R. Isaac has explained that the reason why the words "for he is good" do not appear in this chant, as in other passages where it is given, is because He was about to destroy the works of His hands before Israel. Similarly, at the time when Israel crossed the Red Sea, when the angels came as usual to chant their praises before God on that night, God said to them: "The works of my hands are drowning in the sea, and will you chant praises?"; hence it says, "and this (angel) drew not near to that one all the night" (Ex. XIV, 20). Thus whenever destruction of the wicked takes place, there is grief for them above.' R. Abba said: 'God had already been grieved when Adam sinned before Him and transgressed His commandment. He said to him: "Woe to thee that thou hast weakened the heavenly power, for at this moment thou hast quenched a light"; and forthwith He banished him from the Garden of Eden, saying: "I put thee in the garden to bring offerings, but thou hast impaired the altar so that offerings cannot henceforth be brought on it; henceforth therefore it is thy doom to labour at the ground." '

God also decreed that he should die. Taking pity on him, however, God allowed him when he died to be buried near the Garden of Eden. For Adam had made a cave near the Garden, and had hidden himself there with his wife. He knew it was near the Garden, because he saw a faint ray of light enter it from there, and therefore he desired to be buried in it; and there he was buried, close to the gate of the Garden of Eden. So it is that when a man is about to depart from life, Adam, the first man, appears to him and asks him why and in what state he leaves the world. He says: "Woe to thee that through thee I have to die." To which Adam replies: "My son, I transgressed one commandment and was punished for so doing; see how many commandments of your Master, negative and positive, you have transgressed".' R. Hiya said:

82

'Adam exists to this day, and twice a day he sees the patriarchs and confesses his sins, and shows them the place where once he abode in heavenly glory. He also goes and looks at all the pious and righteous among his descendants who have attained to celestial glory in the Garden of Eden. All the patriarchs then praise God, saying: "How precious is thy lovingkindness, O God, and the children of men take refuge under the shadow of thy wings" (Ps. XXXVI, 8).' R. Yesa said: 'Adam appears to every man at the moment of his departure from life to testify that the man is dying on account of his own sins and not the sin of Adam, according to the dictum, "there is no death without sin". There are only three exceptions, namely, Amram, Levi, and Benjamin, who were deprived of life through the prompting of the primeval serpent; some add also, Jesse. These did not sin, and no ground could be assigned for their death save the prompting of the serpent, as we have said.

'All the generations contemporary with Noah committed their sins openly, in the sight of all. R. Simeon was one day walking through the gate of Tiberias when he saw some men drawing the bow tight over earthenware pots. He cried: "What! do these miscreants dare to provoke their Master thus openly?" He scowled at them, and they were thrown into the sea and drowned. Take note that every sin which is committed openly repels the Shekinah and causes her to remove her abode f rom this world. The contemporaries of Noah committed their sins openly and defiantly, and so they drove the Shekinah away from the world, in punishment for which God removed them from the world, in accordance with the maxim, "Take away the dross from the silver, and there cometh forth a vessel for the finer; take away the wicked from before the king, and his throne shall be established in righteousness" (Prov. XXV, 4 and 5).'

AND THE LORD SAID, MY SPIRIT SHALL NOT STRIVE WITH MAN FOREVER, FOR THAT HE ALSO IS FLESH. R. Eleazar said: 'When God created the universe, He ordained that this world should be served

from the world above. Hence when mankind are virtuous and walk in the right path, God puts in motion the spirit of life from above until it comes to the place where Jacob abides. From there the life descends further until the spirit reaches the world in which David is located; and from there blessings descend on all here below, who through the streaming of the spirit from above are able to maintain their existence. Now, however, that men sinned, the streaming ceased, so that the spirit of life no longer descended on this world for the benefit of its denizens. "For that he also is flesh,': i.e. in order that, through being shed over this world, the spirit might not benefit the serpent, the lowest of the grades, which might also have grasped hold of it; and the holy spirit ought not to mix with the unclean spirit. The reference in "he also" is to the primeval serpent, as in the verse, "the end of all flesh comes before me" (Gen. VI, 13), which R. Simeon explains to mean the angel of death. HIS DAYS SHALL BE A HUNDRED AND TWENTY YEARS: a period of grace for the continued union (of body and soul). THE NEFILIM WERE IN THE EARTH. R. Yose says, following a tradition, that these were Uzza and Azael, whom, as already mentioned, God deprived of their supernal sanctity. How, it may be asked, can they exist in this world? R. Hiya answers, that they were of the class of spirits referred to in the words "And birds which fly on the earth" (Gen. I, 20), and these, as we have said, appear to men in the form of human beings. If it is asked, how can they transform themselves? The answer is, as has been said, that they do in fact transform themselves into all kinds of shapes, because when they come down from heaven they become as concrete as air and take human shape. These are Uzza and Azael, who rebelled in heaven, and were cast down by God, and became corporeal on the earth and remained on it, not being able to divest themselves of their earthly form. Subsequently they went astray after women, and up to this day they exist and teach men the arts of magic. They begat children whom they called Anakim (giants), while the Nefilim themselves were called "sons of God", as has been elsewhere explained.

AND THE LORD SAID, I WILL DESTROY MAN WHOM I HAVE CREATED FROM THE FACE OF THE GROUND. R. Yose quoted in this connection the verse, For my thoughts are not your thoughts (Is. LV, 8). He said: 'When a man wants to take vengeance on another, he keeps his counsel and says nothing, for fear that, if he discloses his intention, the other will be on his guard and escape him. Not so God. Before punishing the world, God proclaims His intention once, twice, and three times, because there is none who can stay his hand and say to Him, "what doest Thou?", and in vain would one attempt to guard against Him. So now God said, "I will blot out man whom I have created from the face of the earth"; He proclaimed His intention to them by the hand of Noah, and warned them several times, but they would not listen. Then at last He executed judgement on them and exterminated them.

AND HE CALLED HIS NAME NOAH SAYING, THIS SHALL COMFORT US, ETC. How did Noah's father know this? In this way. When God cursed the earth, Adam said to Him,

"Sovereign of the Universe, how long shall the earth be subject to this curse?" God replied: "Until a descendant of yours shall be born circumcised, like yourself." So they waited until at last a child was born circumcised and marked with the holy sign. When his father saw this, and observed the Shekinah hovering over him, he called him Noah, [Tr. note: lit. 'rest'.] in anticipation of his future career. For up to his time men did not know the proper way to sow or reap or plough, and they used to work the ground with their hands. But when Noah came, he taught them the arts of husbandry, and devised for them the necessary implements. Hence it is written: "This one shall comfort us for our work and for the toil of our hands." It was indeed Noah who liberated the earth from its curse; for up to his time they used to sow wheat and reap thorns and thistles; hence Noah is called "a man of the ground" (Gen. IX, 20).' R. Judah said: 'The word ish (man) is applied to him because he was righteous, and through the sacrifice which he brought he liberated the earth from its curse. We see, then, how he received his name in anticipation of the future.' R. Judah once expounded the text: Come, behold the works of the Lord, [Tr. note: So our texts (Tetragrammaton) But it is obvious from what follows that the Zohar read Elohim (God).] who hath made desolations in the earth (Ps. XLVI, 9). 'If,' he said, 'it had been the works of Tetragrammaton, then they would have brought more life into the world, but being the works of Elohim, they made desolation in the world.' Said R. Hiya to him: 'As you have raised this point, I take leave to differ from you. In my opinion, whichever name is used the result is beneficial; and in this verse we should, as our colleagues have pointed out, read not shammoth (desolations), but shemoth (names).' R. Isaac said: 'You are both right. As R. Hiya says, if the world had been created through the name which connotes mercy (Tetragrammaton), it would have been indestructible; but since it has been created through the name which connotes justice (Elohim), "desolations have been placed in the earth", and rightly so, since otherwise the world would not be able to endure the sins of mankind. Consider also this. When Noah was born, they gave him a name which connoted consolation, in the hope that it would work out its own fulfilment for them. His relation to God, however, is expressed by the same letters in the reverse order, viz. HeN (favour), as it is written, "and Noah found favour in the eyes of the Lord'.' Said R. Yose: 'The names of the righteous influence their destiny for good, and those of the wicked for evil. Thus the anagram of Noah's name is hen (favour), and we find it written of him, "and Noah found favour in the eyes of the Lord"; whereas the anagram of the name of Er the (wicked) son of Judah is ra' (evil), and of him it is written, "and Er was evil in the sight of the Lord" (Gen. XXXVIII, 7). When Noah grew up, and saw how mankind were sinning before God, he withdrew himself from their society and sought to serve his Master, so as not to be led astray by them. He was especially diligent in the study of the book of Adam and the book of Enoch which we have mentioned, and from them he learnt the proper forms in which to worship God. This explains how it is that he knew it was incumbent upon him to bring an offering; it was these books which revealed to him the basis on which the existence of the world depends, to wit, the sacrifices, without which neither the higher nor the lower world can endure.'

R. Simeon was once travelling in company with his son R. Eleazar and R. Yose and R. Hiya. As they were going along steadily, R. Eleazar said, 'This is a favourable opportunity for hearing some explanation of the Torah.' R. Simeon thereupon commenced a discourse on the text: Also when the fool walketh by the way, his understanding faileth him, etc. (Eccl. X, 3). He said: 'If a man desires that his journey should be agreeable in the sight of God, he should, before he starts, take counsel of God and offer the appropriate prayer, according to the Rabbinical dictum based on the verse, "When righteousness goeth before him, then he shall set his feet on the way" (Ps. LXXXV, 14), for then the Shekinah is not parted from him. But of him who does not believe in his Master it is written,

Zohar: Bereshith, Section 1, Page 59a

"Also when the fool walketh in the way, his understanding (lit. heart) faileth him." By "heart" is here designated the Holy One, blessed be He, who will not accompany him on the way nor lend him His support, because he is a man who does not believe in his Master and did not seek His support before starting on the journey. Likewise on the journey itself he does not busy his thoughts with the Torah, and for this reason also it is said that "his heart faileth him", because he does not walk with his Master and is not found in His path. Further, "he saith to all, it is folly": that is, when he does hear a word of true doctrine, he says it is folly to pay attention to it; like the man who was asked about the sign of the covenant imprinted on the flesh, and replied that it was no article of faith, whereupon R. Yeba the Elder frowned on him and he became a heap of bones. We, therefore, being on this journey with the support of the Almighty, are beholden to discuss some point of Torah.' He thereupon took the text: Teach me thy way, O Lord, I will walk in thy truth, unite my heart to fear thy name (Ps. LXXXVI, 11). He said: 'This verse seems to conflict with the Rabbinical dictum that a man's whole career is in the hands of heaven, save his choice of virtue or vice. If this is so, how could David make such a request as this of God? What David really asked, however, was only that God should teach him His ways, that is, open his eyes to know the right and proper way; then he would himself be able to walk in the way of truth without turning aside right or left. As for the expression "my heart", this has the same significance as in the verse "the rock of my heart and my portion" (Ps. LXXIII, 26). All this I entreat, he said, in order to fear Thy name, to cleave to Thy fear and to keep to the straight path. The words "to fear thy name" refer to David's allotted place in which the fear of God is located. Consider this. Every man who fears God is secure in his faith, since he is whole-hearted in the service of his Master. But he who does not constantly fear his Master is not truly possessed of faith, nor is he accounted worthy of a share in the future world.' R. Simeon further discoursed on the text: But the path of the righteous is as the shining light, that shineth more and more unto the perfect day (Prov. IV, 18). He said: 'Happy are the righteous in this world and the world to come, since God desires to glorify them. For their path is as "the shining light," that is to say, that radiant light which God created at the beginning of things, and which He set aside for the righteous in the future world. This "shineth more and more", for its brightness continually augments. But of the wicked it is written, "The way of the wicked is as darkness, they know not at what they stumble" (Ibid. 19). In truth they do know; but they walk in a crooked path, and will not stop to reflect that one day God will judge them in the future world, and chastise them with the punishments of Gehinnom. Then they will bewail themselves every day, saying, "Woe to us that we did not incline our ears and listen." But as for the righteous, God will illumine them in the future world and will give them their due reward in a place which eye has never beheld, as it is written, "Eye hath not seen beside thee, O God, what thou wilt do for him that waits for thee" (Is. LXIV, 3). Also, "And they shall go forth and look upon the carcasses of the men that have transgressed against me" (Is. LXVI, 24); and again, "And ye shall tread down the wicked, for they shall be ashes under the soles of your feet" (Mal. III, 21). Happy are the righteous in this world and in the world to come; of them it is written, "the righteous shall forever inherit the earth" (Is. LX, 21), and also, "verily the righteous shall praise thy name, the upright shall dwell in thy presence" (Ps. CXL, 14). Blessed is the Lord forever, Amen and Amen.'

Zohar: Bereshith, Section 1, Page 59b

NOAH

THESE ARE THE GENERATIONS OF NOAH. R. Hiya opened with the text: And thy people are all righteous, they will inherit the land forever; the branch of my planting, the work of my hands wherein I glory (Is. LX, 21). He said: 'Happy are the people of Israel, who occupy themselves with the Torah and are familiar with its paths, through following which they will merit the world to come. For all Israelites have a portion in the world to come, for the reason that they observe the covenant on which the world is established, and of which it is said: "If my covenant be not (observed) day and night, it were as if I had not appointed the ordinances of heaven and earth" (Jer. XXXIII, 25). Hence Israel, who have accepted the covenant and observe it, have a portion in the world to come. Furthermore, they are therefore called righteous. We learn this from Joseph, who, by reason of his having observed the covenant, is known as "Joseph the righteous".'

R. Eleazar said: 'The term "These are", as we have learnt, always implies that something spoken of before in the text is now of no account. Now it is written above in the account of the Creation [Tr. note: Where also we find the expression 'these are the generations, (Gen. II, 4).] that "A river went out from Eden to water the garden and from thence it was parted, etc." (Gen. II, 10). That stream which flows perennially entered the Garden to water it from the supernal waters, and brought gladness to it, making it produce fruit and seed for the universal content; and so the stream gladdened the Garden, as it is written, "And he rested on the seventh day" (Ibid. 3). Thus the words "these are the generations" imply that this brought forth products and no other. So it was with Noah in the lower world. Noah was the sacred covenant below corresponding to that above, and hence is called "Man of the earth". The inner meaning which we learn from this is that Noah had need of an ark with which to become united in order thereby to preserve the seed of all species, as it is written, "To preserve seed". This ark is the Ark of the Covenant, and Noah with the ark below corresponded to a similar union above. The word "covenant" is used in connection with Noah, as it is written, "And I will establish my covenant with thee", and before the covenant was established with him he did not enter the ark, as it is written, "And I will establish my covenant with thee and thou shalt come into the ark." Thus his ark represented the Ark of the Covenant, and Noah and the ark together were a symbol of the supernal pattern. And since this covenant above brought forth products, so Noah below also bore generations. Hence it says, "These are the generations of Noah."

NOAH WAS A RIGHTEOUS MAN. Assuredly so, after the supernal pattern. It is written, "The Righteous one is the foundation of the world" (Prov. X, 25), and the earth is established thereon, for this is the pillar that upholds the world. So Noah was called Zaddik (righteous) below. All this is implied in the words NOAH WALKED WITH GOD, meaning that he never separated himself from Him, and acted so as to be a true copy of the supernal ideal, a "Zaddik the foundation of the world", an embodiment of the world's covenant of peace. And it is thus that NOAH FOUND FAVOUR IN THE EYES OF GOD. PERFECT HE WAS IN HIS GENERATIONS: this refers to his descendants; he perfected them all, and he was more virtuous than all of them. Again, the words "He was perfect" indicate that he was born circumcised (cf. of Abraham, "Walk before me and be perfect, i.e. circumcised" Gen. XVII, 1). IN HIS GENERATIONS: and not in those of his contemporaries, for all future generations issued from him only. Consider this. From the day that the world was created, Noah was the first man fitted to be joined in union with the ark and to enter it, and until they were joined the world had not yet reached a stable condition. But once this had happened we read "From these all the earth was overspread" (Gen. X, 32). These words are analogous to the expression "And from thence the river parted" (Ibid. II, 10), of the Garden of Eden, which indicate that from this point there was a parting and diffusion of progeny into all quarters of the world. The two cases are analogous in every way. Hence it says: "These are the generations"; assuredly "these", as it was he who was the foundation of the world that brought forth

Zohar: Bereshith, Section 1, Page 60a

generations to abide on the earth.' R. Abba then approached and kissed him, saying: 'The lion in his might has pierced through the rock and broken it asunder. Your exposition is certainly the right one, as can also be deduced from the measurements of the ark.'

THESE ARE THE GENERATIONS OF NOAH. R. Judah discoursed on the text: The good man is gracious and lendeth, he ordereth his affairs according to justice (Ps. CXII, 5). '"The good man" refers to the Holy One, Blessed be He, since He is called "good" (as well as "Man"), as it is written, "The Lord is good to all" (Ibid. CXLV, 9), as well as "The Lord is a man of war" (Exod. xv, 3). Thus God is gracious and lends to that quarter which has no possession of its own, but derives its sustenance from Him. This idea is further developed in the sentence "He ordereth his affairs according to justice", indicating that that quarter is granted sustenance only according to justice, as it is written, "Righteousness and justice are the foundation of thy throne" (Ps. LXXXIX, 15). According to another explanation, the "good man" refers to the Righteous one (Zaddik), as it is written, "Say ye of the righteous one that he is good" (Is. III, 10). R. Yose said that it refers to Noah, as it is written, "Noah was a righteous man." R. Isaac said that it refers to the Sabbath, since the psalm in praise of the Sabbath commences with the words "It is a good thing to give thanks unto the Lord" (Ps. XCII, 2).' R. Hiya said: 'It is the Zaddik who produces offspring in the world. Who constitute this offspring? The souls of the righteous, these being the fruit of the handiwork of the Holy One, blessed be He.'

R. Simeon said: 'When the Holy One, blessed be He, puts on his crowns, he receives them from above and from below: above, from the region of absolute remoteness; below, he is crowned by the souls of the righteous. The result is an increment of life-energy from above and below, embracing the place of the sanctuary on all sides, and causing the cisterns to become full and the sea to be replenished, and providing sufficiency for all. It is written: "Drink water out of thine own cistern, and running water out of thine own well" (Prov. V, 15). Why speak first of a cistern (bor), which is naturally waterless, and then of a well (beer), which is a fountain bubbling with water? In truth, both are one: this first refers to a certain region which is beset by poverty, and is thus called "cistern", as not possessing anything of its own save what is given to it: that region is called daleth (poverty, also the fourth letter of the alphabet). In time, however, it becomes a well, filled on all sides with bubbling water; it then typifies the letter he, being filled from on high

Zohar: Bereshith, Section 1, Page 60b

and bubbling up from below. It is filled from above in the way already explained, while its bubbling from below is from the souls of the righteous. (According to another interpretation, "drink water out of thine own cistern" refers to King David, who said, "Oh that one would give me water to drink of the cistern of Bethlehem" (II Sam. XXIII, 15); and "running waters" refers to Abraham; "out of the midst" refers to Jacob, he representing the centre; "thine own well" signifies Isaac, who is called "well of living waters". Thus in this verse is a reference to the sacred and honoured team of the three patriarchs with King David associated with them.) As the desire of the female towards the male only awakes when a certain spirit enters into her and the flow ascends to meet that of the male, so the congregation of Israel only conceives a longing for the Holy One, blessed be He, when it is permeated with the spirit of the righteous. It is then that its energy rises from below to meet the energy from above so as to form a perfect union. There flows from this a universal content, and it is then that the Holy One, blessed be He, walks familiarly among the souls of the righteous.

See now, all the offspring of the Garden of Eden did not issue from the Righteous one until he entered into that ark of which we have spoken and became one with it–that ark which contained all in embryo. Similarly Noah the righteous man did not beget offspring to populate the world until he entered the ark in which all (life) was gathered and safely stored and from which it afterwards emerged to multiply in the world and to have an abiding existence on earth. Had not these creatures been through the ark they would not have endured in the world. And all this was planned after the supernal pattern. As they emerged from the Ark there on high, so they emerged from the ark here below. And thus the world then obtained the character of permanency which it had not possessed before. Hence the expression "And running waters out of the midst of thy well", which is echoed by the verse "And Noah begat three sons." '

AND THE EARTH WAS CORRUPTED BEFORE GOD. Said R. Judah: 'What does the phrase "before God" signify? ' It signifies that they perpetrated their crimes openly in the eyes of all.' Said R. Yose: 'I interpret it in a reverse sense, namely, that at first "the earth was corrupted before God", that is, that they committed their sins secretly, so as to be known only to God but not to man. They finished, however, by coming out into the open, as it is written, AND THE EARTH WAS FILLED WITH VIOLENCE, indicating that there was not a place in the whole earth which did not witness their sins.' R. Abba said: 'From the time that Adam transgressed the command of his Master, all the succeeding generations were called "sons of Adam" in a derogatory sense, as much as to say, "the sons of the man who transgressed his Master's commands". But when Noah appeared, mankind were called by his name, to wit, "the generations of Noah", in an honourable sense, since he secured for them permanent existence in the world, and not "the generations of Adam", since he had caused them to be driven from the world and brought death to all.' Said R. Yose to him: 'But in a later passage (Gen. XI, 5) it is written, "and the Lord came down to see the city and the tower which the children of Adam had built"—Adam and not Noah.' R. Abba replied: 'It was because he was the first sinner. Better had it been for him that he should not have been created, so as not to be mentioned in this verse. See now, it is written: "A wise son causeth his father to rejoice" (Prov. X, 1). When a son is good, people mention his father's name with praise; but if he is bad, they mention his father with reproach. So it was with Adam. He transgressed the command of his Master, and therefore when later men arose who rebelled against their Master, they were designated by the Scripture "the sons of Adam", that is, the sons of the first man who rebelled against his Master and transgressed His commands. Hence "these are the generations of Noah"-these and not the former ones; these who entered into and emerged from the ark and brought forth generations to people the world; but they are not the generations of Adam, who emerged from the Garden of Eden without bringing any progeny forth from thence. For indeed, if Adam had brought offspring with him out of the Garden of Eden, these would never have been destroyed, the light of the moon would never have been darkened, and all would have lived forever; and not even the angels would have equaled them in illumination and wisdom, as we read, "In the image of God he created him" (Gen. I, 27). But since,

Zohar: Bereshith, Section 1, Page 61a

through his sin, he left the Garden by himself and bore offspring outside it, these did not endure in the world, and this ideal was, therefore, not realised.' Said R. Hizkiah: 'How could they have begotten children there, seeing that, had the evil inclination not enticed him to sin, Adam would have dwelt forever in the world by himself and would not have begotten children? In the same way, if Israel had not sinned by making the golden calf, they would not have borne children and no new generations would have come into the world" R. Abba replied: 'If Adam had not sinned, he would not have begotten children from the side of the evil inclination, but he would have borne offspring from the side of the holy spirit. But now, since all the children of men are born from the side of the evil inclination, they have no permanence and are but short-lived, because there is in them an element of the "other side". But if Adam had not sinned and had not been driven from the Garden of Eden, he would have begotten progeny from the side of the holy spirit-a progeny holy as the celestial angels, who would have endured to eternity, after the supernal pattern. Since, however, he sinned and begat children outside the Garden of Eden, these did not take root, even in this world, until Noah arose, who was a righteous man and entered the ark, so that from the ark there went forth all the future generations of mankind, who spread thence into the four quarters of the earth.'

AND GOD SAW THE EARTH AND BEHOLD IT WAS CORRUPT. It was corrupt because "all flesh had corrupted its way", in the sense we have explained. R. Hiya adduced the following text: And God saw their works that they turned from their evil way (Jonah III, 10). 'See now,' he said, 'when the sons of men are righteous and observe the commands of the Torah, the earth becomes invigorated, and a fullness of joy pervades it, because then the Shekinah rests upon the earth, and there is thus gladness above as well as below. But when mankind corrupt their way and do not observe the commands of the Torah, and sin before their Master, they, as it were, thrust the Shekinah out of the world, and the earth is thus left in a corrupt state. For the Shekinah being thrust out, another spirit comes and hovers over the world, bringing with it corruption. It is in this sense that we say that Israel "gives strength unto Elohim", that is, to the Shekinah, and thereby makes the world more secure. Should, however, Israel-God forbid-prove sinful, then, in the words of the Scripture, "God withdraws himself above the heavens" (Ps. LVII, 6). Why? Because "they have prepared a net for my footsteps, my soul is bent down", through their violence and causeless hatreds, "they have digged a pit before me" (Ibid. 7). The same thing happened with the generation of the Flood, whose violent acts led to mutual hatred and contention among them. We might think that the same applies to the Land of Israel. Our teachers, however, have laid down that no other spirit rests upon the Land of Israel, nor has it any guardian angel save God alone. There was, however, one occasion when another spirit did rest upon it in order to destroy the people. That was in the time of David, when, as it is written, "David saw the angel of the Lord... having a drawn sword in his hand stretched out over Jerusalem" (I Chron. XXI, 16), and thus destruction came upon the land.' R. Eleazar said: 'Even then it was the Holy One, blessed be He, Himself, the term "angel" here having the same meaning, as in the passages "the angel who redeemed me" (Gen. XLVIII, 16), and the angel of God removed (Ex. XIV, 19). Be it for good or for ill, the Holy One, blessed be He, always has sway over it personally. For good, so that it should not be delivered into the hands of the "higher chieftains", and so that all the inhabitants of the world should be ashamed of their wicked deeds; for ill, so that the nations should not have the gratification of ruling over it. It is true, the Scripture says in one place, "For she hath seen that the heathen are entered into her sanctuary" (Lam. I, 10), and have destroyed the House, from which it may be inferred that if those alien chiefs had not had sway, the Temple would not have been destroyed. This, however, must not be stressed; for the Scripture also says, "For thou hast done it" (Ibid. I, 21), and "The Lord hath done what he hath devised" (Ibid. II, 17).' R. Hiya continued: 'It is written here, in connection with Noah, "And God saw the earth and behold it was corrupt." Contrast with this the verse "And God saw their deeds, and they had repented of their evil ways" (Jonah III, 10). There the earth called to God, reaching out towards heaven, and beautifying her face, as it were, like a woman trying to please her husband; so the earth tried to please God by raising up for Him righteous children. But here, when the generation of the Flood did not repent of their sins, it is written, "And God saw the earth, and behold it was corrupt", like a faithless wife who hides her face from before her husband. But when mankind committed sin upon sin openly and flagrantly, then the earth became brazen-faced like an abandoned female without any sense of shame, as it is said on another occasion, "And the earth was defiled under its inhabitants" (Is. XXIV, 5). Hence this is the connection here: "God saw that the earth was corrupted", why? "Because all

flesh had corrupted their way upon the earth".'

R. Eleazar went to see R. Yose, the son of R. Simeon, the son of Lakunia, his father-in-law. The latter, as soon as he saw him, spread out for him a carpet under a canopy, on which they sat down. He asked his son-in-law, 'Did you happen to hear from your father the interpretation of the verse: The Lord hath done that which he devised, he hath performed his word that he commanded in the days of old (Lam. II, 17)?' He answered, 'Our colleagues have interpreted it thus. They take the words bitza imratho ("He hath performed his word") to mean "He rent his purple cloak"- that cloak which "he commanded from days of old", that is, which He had appointed from the beginning of things. On the day the Temple was destroyed He rent that purple cloak which was His glory and ornament.' Said R. Yose: 'What of the words "the Lord hath done that which he (had already) devised"? Does a king devise evil against his sons before they sin?' R. Eleazar replied: 'Imagine a king who possessed a precious vase, and who, being constantly apprehensive lest it should be broken, had it ever under his eyes, and never lost sight of it for a moment. One day his son came and provoked him to anger, so that in his rage he took up the vase and broke it in pieces. In this way the Lord "hath done that which he had already devised". From the day when the Temple was built, the Holy One, blessed be He, used to contemplate it fondly, and every time He came to the sanctuary, He used to put on the purple cloak we have mentioned. But when Israel sinned, and provoked their King, the Temple was destroyed, and the mantle was rent. Only on that occasion did God mourn the destruction of the wicked, but at any other time the Holy One, blessed be He, takes joy in nothing so much as in the destruction of the world's sinners, and of those who have provoked Him to anger, as it is written, "And when the wicked perish there is joy" (Prov. XI, 10). So throughout the generations, whenever justice is executed on sinners, there is joy and thanksgiving before the Holy One, blessed be He. But, you may say, is there not a dictum of the Rabbis that the Holy One, blessed be He, does not rejoice when he executes judgement on sinners? The truth is that He does take joy in the destruction of the wicked, but only when He has been longsuffering with them and they have still remained unrepentant. But if He exacts punishment from them before that time, before the measure of their sins has been completed (cf. "For the iniquity of the Amorite is not yet full", Gen. XV, 16), then there is no joy before Him, but, on the contrary, He is grieved at their destruction. Another difficulty here arises: if their time has not come, why should punishment be at all inflicted on them? But, indeed, they themselves are to blame for this. For the Holy One, blessed be He, never inflicts punishment on the wicked before the full time, except when they interfere with Israel in order to do them harm. It is then that He inflicts punishment upon them before the full time, and it is then that their destruction grieves Him. It was for this reason that He drowned the Egyptians in the Red Sea, and destroyed the enemies of Israel in the days of Jehoshaphat, and inflicted punishment on others; they were all destroyed before the full time on account of Israel. But if the time of respite expires without their showing any sign of repentance, then their destruction is a cause of joy and glory before Him. Nevertheless, it was not so with the destruction of the Temple; for on that occasion, although Israel had filled up the cup of provocation, there was no joy before Him, and since that time there has been no joy, neither above nor below.'

FOR YET SEVEN DAYS, AND I WILL CAUSE IT TO RAIN UPON THE EARTH FORTY DAYS AND FORTY NIGHTS. R. Judah said: 'What is the point of mentioning the exact period? The answer is that forty is the appropriate number for the punishment of sinners, in accordance with the ordinance, "Forty stripes he may give him, he shall not exceed" (Deut. XXV, 3). Further, this number corresponds to the four quarters of the world, so that there were ten for each quarter. For since man was created from the four quarters of the world, and the decree went forth, "And I will blot out every living substance that I have made from the face of the earth", forty were required for this purpose.' R. Isaac studied regularly with R. Simeon. One day he asked him: 'With reference to the passage "And the earth was corrupt",

if men sinned, why should the earth be called corrupt?'

R. Simeon replied: 'We find a parallel in the passage, "And the land was defiled, therefore I did visit the iniquity thereof upon it" (Lev. XVIII, 25), where the same problem arises. The explanation is that mankind constitutes the essence of the earth, so that they infect the earth with their own corruption. This is made clear by the language of the Scripture in the passage, "And God saw the earth, and behold it was corrupt, for all flesh had corrupted their way upon the earth." For indeed all the other sins of man, involving but his own corruption, admit of repentance. But the sin of onanism is one by which man corrupts both himself and the earth; and of such a one it is written, "The stain of thine iniquity remains before me" (Jer. II, 22), also "For thou art not a God that hath pleasure in wickedness, evil shall not sojourn with thee" (Ps. V, 5), and it is further written, "And Er, Judah's firstborn, was wicked in the sight of the Lord, and the Lord slew him" (Gen. XXXVIII, 7), as explained elsewhere.' R. Judah further asked, "Why did the Holy One, blessed be He, punish the world with water, and not with fire or any other element?' R. Simeon replied: 'There is a mystical reason, based on the fact that they "corrupted their ways". As their sin consisted in not allowing the upper and lower waters to meet in conjunction, as they ought, so were they punished with water. Further, the waters of the Deluge were burning hot, and caused their skins to peel off, this being a meet punishment for the sin they committed in wasting the warm fluid. It was all measure for measure. The words in the text, "All the fountains of the great deep were broken open" refer to the lower waters, and the words "And the windows of Heaven were opened" refer to the upper waters. Thus were the two waters combined as a fit punishment for their sins.'

R. Hiya and R. Judah, while once going on their travels, came to some huge mountains, in the ravines of which they found human bones left over from the generation of the Flood. They measured a bone and found to their amazement that it was three hundred paces long. They said: 'This bears out what our colleagues have said, that the men of the time of the Flood did not fear the vengeance of the Holy One, blessed be He, as it is written, "They said unto God, Depart from us, for we desire not the knowledge of thy ways" (Job XXI, 14), and that one of the things they did was to stop up with their feet the fountains of the deep, until the waters which bubbled up became too hot for them to endure, so that they finally succumbed and fell to the ground and died.'

AND NOAH BEGAT THREE SONS. [Tr. note: This paragraph is out of place. It should properly follow "begat three sons" on Zohar: Bereshith, Section 1, Page 60b.] Said R. Hiya to R. Judah: 'Let me tell you what I have heard regarding this text. A man once entered the recesses of a cavern, and there issued two or three children together, who differed from one another in their character and conduct: one was virtuous, a second vicious, and a third average. Similarly we find three strands of spirit which flit about and are taken up into three different worlds. The neshamah (spiritual soul) emerges and enters between the gorges of the mountains, where it is joined by the ruah (intellectual spirit). It descends then below where the nefesh (vital spirit) joins the ruah, and all three form a unity.' R. Judah said: 'The nefesh and the ruah are intertwined together, whereas the neshamah resides in a man's character–an abode which cannot be discovered or located. Should a man strive towards purity of life, he is aided thereto by a holy neshamah, whereby he is purified and sanctified and attains the title of "saint". But should he not strive for righteousness and purity of life, he is animated only by the two grades, nefesh and ruah, and is devoid of a holy neshamah. What is more, he who commences to defile himself is led further into defilement, and heavenly help is withdrawn from him. Thus each is led along the path which he chooses.'

Zohar: Bereshith, Section 1, Page 62b

AND GOD SAID TO NOAH, THE END OF ALL FLESH IS COME BEFORE ME. R. Judah illustrated this passage from the verse: Lord, make me know mine end, and the measure of my days what it is; let me know how short lived I am (Ps. XXXIX, 5). He said: 'David said before the Holy One, blessed be He, "There are two 'ends', one on the right and one on the left, these being the two paths by which men proceed towards the other world." The end on the right is referred to in the words "at the end of the right" (Daniel XII, 13); and the end on the left in the words "He setteth an end to darkness, and the ending of all things does he search out" (Job XXVIII, 3). "End" here is the angel of destruction, who is also the serpent, and who is called "End of all flesh". When the doom of destruction is hanging over the world, this "searches out" and explores every avenue through which it can bring accusations against the world so as to reduce men to despair.

Zohar: Bereshith, Section 1, Page 63a

The term "end of the right", as already said, is based on the phrase "at the end of the right" in the book of Daniel. The Holy One, blessed be He, said to Daniel, "Thou shalt go towards the end, and wilt rest" (Dan. XII, 13). Daniel asked: "Rest in this world or in the next world?" "Rest in the next world", was the answer (cf. "They will rest in their beds", Is. LVII, 2), "and thou shalt stand up to thy lot at the end of days". Daniel asked, "Shall I be among the resurrected or not?" God answered, "And thou wilt stand up." Daniel then said, "I know full well that the dead will rise up in various classes, some righteous and some wicked, but I do not know among whom I shall be found." God answered, "To thy lot." Daniel then said, "As there is a right end and a left end, I do not know whether I shall go to the right end (l'qets hayamin) or to the end of days (l'qets hayamim)." The answer was, "To the end of the right (l'qets hayamin)." Similarly, David said to the Holy One, blessed be He, "make me to know my end", that is, he wished to know to which end he was allotted, and his mind was not at rest till the good tidings reached him, "Sit at my right hand" (Ps. CX, 1). So to Noah also the Holy One, blessed be He, said, "The end of all flesh is come before me." The term "end", as we have seen, alludes to the angel of death, who reduces men to despair, and who is indeed the end of all flesh. "Is come before me": from this we learn that though the wicked go half-way to meet him and draw him to themselves, yet only after he receives authorisation does he take a man's soul: he cannot take it before. Hence we read "is come before me", to wit, to obtain permission to darken the faces of mankind, and so "I will destroy them with the earth". Hence the command given to Noah, MAKE THEE AN ARK OF GOPHER WOOD, to save thyself therein and so that he should not have power over thee. There was also another reason. We have a dictum that when death rages in a town or in the world at large, no man should show himself in the street, because the destroying angel is then authorised to kill indiscriminately. Hence the Holy One, blessed be He, said to Noah, "It behoves thee to take heed to thyself and not show thyself before the destroyer, so that he may have no power over thee." You may perhaps say that there was not here any destroying angel, but only the onrush of the overwhelming waters. This is not so; no doom is ever executed on the world, whether of annihilation or any other chastisement, but the destroying angel is in the midst of the visitation. So here there was indeed a flood, but this was only an embodiment of the destroyer who assumed its name. Hence the command given to Noah to hide himself and not to show himself abroad. But, you may object further, the ark was exposed to full view in the midst of the world through which the destroyer was roaming. The answer is that this made no difference, since, as long as the face of a man is not seen by the destroyer, he has no power over him. We learn this from the precept given at the time of the Exodus, "and none of you shall go out of the door of his house until the morning" (Ex. XII, 22), the reason being that the destroyer was then abroad with power to destroy anyone who showed himself. For the same reason Noah withdrew himself and all under his charge into the ark, so that the destroyer had no power over him.'

R. Hiya and R. Yose in the course of their travels came to the mountains of Kurdistan, and observed there some deep ravines which had been left from the Flood. Said R. Hiya: 'These ravines are vestiges of the days of the Flood, and the Holy One, blessed be He, has left them throughout the generations so that the sins of the wicked should not be blotted out from before Him. For just as God causes the memory of those who do His will to endure on high and here below from generation to generation, so He ordains that the evil memory of the sins of the wicked who have not obeyed Him shall not pass away but remain for all generations, as it is written, "The stain of thine iniquity remains before me" (Jer. II, 22).'

R. Yose discoursed on the text: Cry thou with a shrill voice, oh daughter of Gallim! Hearken, oh Laish! Oh thou poor Anathoth! (Is. X, 30). He said: 'Our companions have already interpreted this verse in their own way, but in truth it refers to the Community of Israel, called "the daughter of springs" (Gallim), on the analogy of the expression, "A spring (gal) shut up" (S.S. IV, 12). The term "spring" has special reference to those streams that converge and flow into the Garden, as it is written, "Thy shoots are a garden (pardes) of pomegranates" (Ibid. 13). The term laisha is akin to the term laish in "the lion (laish) perisheth for lack of prey" (Job IV, 11). Why is the Community of Israel called "lion"? It might be in allusion to "the lion which is mighty among beasts" (Prov. XXX, 30), or again to "the lion perisheth for lack of prey". But indeed, the two aspects are combined in it. At one time it is laish (he lion), filled with the lower-world energy emanating from the higher-world energy; and then again it is reduced to the state of "a lion perishing for lack of prey", when the rivers dry up and do not come to replenish her, at which time she is rather called laisha (lioness).

Zohar: Bereshith, Section 1, Page 63b

The name laisha is further explained by the words which immediately follow, aniah anathoth, which properly mean 'poorest of the poor". The word anathoth is found with a similar meaning in the passage "of the priests that were in Anathoth" (Jer. I, 1). Another example of the word used in this sense is in the verse "Anathoth, get thee unto thine own fields" (I Kings II, 26). The meaning of this verse is as follows. So long as King David was alive, Abiathar was wealthy and prosperous; but after David died, Solomon ordered him to get to his own fields, calling him "Anathoth". Why did he give him this name? It cannot be because this was the name of the town he came from, since it is written, "and one of the sons of Ahimelech the son of Ahitub, named Abiathar, escaped" (I Sam. XXII, 20), which proves that he belonged to Nob, the city of the priests. Some, indeed, are of opinion that Anathoth and Nob are two names of the same place, the name "Anathoth" having been given to it on account of the poverty and destitution to which it had been reduced by Saul through the slaughter of all its priestly inhabitants. This, however, is incorrect, as Anathoth was distinct from Nob. The real reason why Solomon called Abiathar "Anathoth" is to be found in the words "and because thou wast afflicted (hithanitha) in all wherein my father was afflicted" (I Kings II, 26); thus the name "Anathoth" alludes to the poverty and affliction which he underwent in the time of David.'

R. Hiya said: 'The world was in a state of poverty and misery from the time Adam transgressed the command of the Almighty until Noah came and offered up a sacrifice, when its prosperity returned.' R. Yose said: 'The world was not properly settled, nor was the earth purged from the defilement of the serpent, until Israel stood before Mount Sinai, where they laid fast hold of the Tree of Life, and so established the world firmly. Had not Israel backslided and sinned before the Holy One, blessed be He, they would never have died, since the scum of the serpent had been purged out of them. But as soon as they sinned, the first tablets of the Law were broken-those tablets which spelt complete freedom, freedom from the serpent who is the "end of all flesh". When the Levites rose up to slay the guilty, the evil serpent went in front of them, but he had no power over Israel, because they were girt with a certain armour which protected them against his attacks. When, however, God said to Moses, "Therefore now put off thy ornaments from thee" (Ex. XXXIII, 5), this was the signal that they were placed in the power of the serpent (this is indicated by the form vayithnaselu, which shows that they were stripped by the hand of another). The ornaments referred to are those which they received at Mount Horeb at the time when the Torah was given to Israel.' R. Hiya said: 'Why did not Noah, being a righteous man, cause death to vanish from the world? The reason is that the scum of the serpent had not yet been removed from the world, and further, that his generation did not believe in the Holy One, blessed be He, and all of them clung to the "lower leaves of the tree", and were clothed with an unclean spirit. Furthermore, they persisted in their sins, and followed their evil inclination as before, and the holy Torah, which is the Tree of Life, had not yet been brought down to the earth. Moreover, Noah himself drew death into the world, through his own sin, of which it is written, "And he drank of the wine and was drunken, and he was uncovered within his tent" (Gen. IX, 21), as elsewhere explained.' As they were going along they saw a man coming towards them. Said R. Yose: 'This man is a Jew.' When he came up to them they asked him who he was. He said: 'I am on a religious errand from the village of Ramin, where I live. As it is near the Feast of Tabernacles, we require a palm branch with its accessories. I am therefore on my way to pluck them.' They all then walked on together. The Judean said to them: 'In regard to these four plants which we take in order to propitiate the Almighty, have you heard why we require them precisely on the Feast of Tabernacles?' Said R. Yose to him: 'Our colleagues have already discussed this question. But if you have any explanation of your own, tell us.' He replied: 'The place where we live is indeed only a little hamlet, but all its inhabitants diligently study the Torah under the guidance of a learned teacher, R. Isaac the son of Yose by name, of Mehozah, who every day gives us some fresh explanation of points in the Torah. Regarding this festival, he explained that this is the fitting period for Israel to obtain dominion over the chiefs who have charge of the nations of the Gentiles, and who are called by them "the proud waters" (Ps. CXXIV, 6). In order to obtain dominion over them, we come with a symbolic representation of the Divine name by means of the four plants, which we also take for the purpose of placating the Almighty

Zohar: Bereshith, Section 1, Page 64a

so as to procure for ourselves a plenitude of sacred waters with which to pour a libation on the altar. He further told us that on the New Year there is in the world "a first stirring". What is meant by "a first stirring"? This is the lower-world tribunal which bestirs itself to bring the world to judgement, as God then sits in judgement over the world. This tribunal continues in session until the Day of Atonement, when the face of the moon is bright, and the slanderous serpent leaves the world alone, being occupied with the he-goat which has been offered to him-an appropriate offering, as the goat is from the "impure region". Being occupied with that goat, he does not come near the sanctuary. This goat performs the same function as the goat offered up on the New Moon, with which also the serpent occupies himself, allowing the moon to grow bright. In consequence, all Israel find favour in the eyes of the Almighty, and their guilt is removed. He further discoursed to us on another mystery which it is not permitted to disclose save to those of excelling wisdom, saintliness, and piety.' 'What is it?' asked R. Yose. 'I cannot say unless I first test you,' replied the Jew. They then proceeded on their way, and after a time he said: 'When the moon approaches the sun, the Holy One, blessed be He, stirs up the northern side, and it grasps the moon lovingly and draws her towards itself. Then the South awakens from the other side, and the moon rises and joins the East. She thus draws sustenance from two sides, and noiselessly receives blessings; and thus it is that the moon is blessed and attains her fullness. Now as there is a symbolical attribution of members to the (supernal) Adam, so there is to the (supernal) Female, and so, too, there is the symbolism of another Adam under the moon, and also of a Female. As the Left Arm above grasps the Female and lovingly draws her to him, so below the serpent, which is the left arm of the unclean spirit, and joined with it he that rides on it, draw near to the moon and draw her tightly to them, so that she becomes defiled. Israel, therefore, here below offer up a goat, to which the serpent is drawn away. The moon then purges herself, ascends on high, and unites herself to the higher sphere to receive blessing, and her lower face, which was darkened, becomes bright. So here on the Day of Atonement, since the evil serpent is occupied with the he-goat, the moon breaks loose from him, and earnestly pleads the cause of Israel, and watches over them like a mother over her children, so that the Holy One, blessed be He, blesses them from above and forgives their sins. Afterwards, when Israel celebrate the Feast of Tabernacles, the "right side" is awakened on high, so that the moon may attach herself to it and her face may become completely bright. She then shares out blessings to all those presiding chiefs of the lower world, so that they may be fully occupied with their own portions, and not attempt to draw sustenance from the side from which Israel obtained their portion. The same thing happens here below. When all the other nations receive their blessings, they are fully occupied with their own portions, and so do not come and meddle with Israel or covet the portion of their heritage. Israel for this reason cause blessings to flow to all those presiding chiefs, in order that they may be absorbed with their own portions and not meddle with that of Israel. And when the moon obtains her due fill of blessings, Israel come and draw sustenance from her all by themselves; and of this it is written, "on the eighth day there shall be to you a solemn gathering" (atsereth, Num. XXIX, 35). This "gathering" indicates the gathering of all the blessings from above, from which no other nation draws sustenance save Israel; hence "there shall be to you a gathering", to you, and not to the other nations and presiding chiefs. And for this reason Israel entreats Heaven to grant a plenitude of rain, so as to accord the nations their share of blessings, that they may be fully occupied therewith, and not meddle in the festivity of Israel, who imbibe the superior blessings. Concerning this day it is written, "My beloved is mine and I am his" (S. S. II, 16), and there is no third one with us. The following parable will make this clearer. A king once invited his favourite to a special feast on an appointed day, thus making known to him

Zohar: Bereshith, Section 1, Page 64b

that he stood high in the favour of the king. The king, however, was apprehensive lest in the midst of the feast all the governors of his provinces might put in an appearance, sit down to table, and partake of the repast intended for his beloved friend. What did he do?

He first treated his governors and ministers to a repast of meat and vegetables. Afterwards he sat down with his favourite to that special banquet where all the finest delicacies of the world were spread before them; and whilst alone with the king the favourite laid before him all his petitions and requests, which the king granted. Thus the king enjoyed the company of his friend alone and undisturbed. So it is with Israel in their relation to the Holy One, blessed be He, and hence it is written, "the eighth day shall be to you a gathering".' Said R. Hiya and R. Yose: 'The Holy One, blessed be He, has led our footsteps in the right path. Happy those who occupy themselves with the Torah.' With these words they came up to him and embraced him. R. Yose applied to him the verse, "And all thy children shall be taught of the Lord, and great shall be the peace of thy children" (Is. LIV, 13).

When they came to a certain field, the stranger discoursed thus. 'In the account of the destruction of Sodom and Gomorrah it is written, "And the Lord (Tetragrammaton) caused to rain, etc." (Gen. XIX, 24), whereas throughout the narrative of the Flood the term Elohim (God) isused exclusively. What is the reason for this difference? We have been taught that the term V-Tetragrammaton (and the Lord), wherever written indicates the Deity presiding over his Court of Justice, whereas the term Elohim (God) is used when the Deity judges alone. Now the destruction of Sodom was limited to one locality, and did not involve the whole world, hence it was decreed in open court, as indicated by the term V-Tetragrammaton (and the Lord); whereas the Flood overwhelmed the whole world, and therefore had to be decreed by the Deity alone, in concealment, as it were; hence the term Elohim. (As for Noah and his companions, they were only saved through being carefully concealed from sight.) In this light we explain the verse "The Lord sat at the Flood" (Ps. XXIX, 10), that is, He sat as it were all by Himself, on the analogy of the expression "He shall sit alone" (Lev. XIII, 46). Now it is because Noah was completely hidden from sight that, after the world had suffered its doom and the wrath of the Deity had been appeased, we read AND GOD (ELOHIM) REMEMBERED NOAH, for Noah having been so long out of sight had to be specially brought to mind. From this passage we derive the mystical doctrine that the Holy One, blessed be He, i s sometimes discoverable and sometimes undiscoverable. He is discoverable when presiding over the lower Court. He remains undiscoverable in the spot whence all blessings flow. Hence those possessions of a man which are hidden from sight are receptive of the heavenly blessing; whereas things which are exposed to view attract the notice of the accuser, and are subject to the influence of him who is named "Evil of eye". There is a deep mystery which connects all this with the supernal pattern.' R. Yose, with tears in his eyes, said: 'Happy is the generation in which R. Simeon flourishes, for it is through his merit that we have been privileged to hear so sublime a discourse as this.' R. Yose said further, 'God must have sent that man on this road to impart to us these ideas.' When they came to R. Simeon and repeated to him all they had heard, he said, 'Of a truth he spoke well.'

R. Eleazar, studying one day with his father, R. Simeon, asked him, 'Did the "End of all flesh" derive nourishment from the sacrifices which Israel used to offer on the altar?' His father replied: 'All alike derived sustenance from them, both above and below. Consider this. The priests, the Levites, and the Israelites are called Adam (Man), through the unison of the holy liturgies which proceed from them. Whenever a sheep or a lamb, or any animal, was brought as an offering, it was required of those who brought it, before it was offered on the altar, to recite over it all sins and evil intentions and thoughts, and to make confession of them, and it is thus that the creature is designated a b'hemah (animal) throughout, in that it carries these sins and evil thoughts. As in the case of the Azazel (scapegoat) offering it is written, "And he shall confess over him all the iniquities of the children of Israel, etc." (Lev. XVI, 21), So it is here: the one offering brought on the altar bears a twofold burden. Consequently each part goes to its fitting place, the one qua "man" and the other qua "beast", as we read, "Man and beast thou dost save, O Lord" (Ps. XXXVI, 7). Baked meal-offering or other meal-offerings are the means of invoking the Holy Spirit on the service of the priests, the song of the Levites, and the prayer of the Israelites; and from the smoke that rises up from the oil and the flour all the accusers replenish themselves,

Zohar: Bereshith, Section 1, Page 65a

so that they are powerless to pursue the indictment which has been delivered into their hands. Thus we see that things have been so arranged in the mystery of faith that the adversary should have his share in the holy things, and that the requisite portion should ascend even to the Limitless.'

R. Simeon said: 'When praying, I raise my hand on high, that when my mind is concentrated on the highest, there is higher still that which can never be known or grasped, the starting-point that is absolutely concealed, that produced what it produced while remaining unknowable, and irradiated what it irradiated while remaining undisclosed. It is the desire of the upward-striving thought to pursue after this and to be illumined by it. In the process a certain fragment is detached, and from that fragment, through the pursuit of the upward-striving thought, which reaches and yet does not reach it, there is a certain illumination. The upward-striving thought is thus illumined by a light undisclosed and unknowable even to that thought. That unknowable light of Thought impinges on the light of the detached fragment which radiates from the unknowable and undisclosed, so that they are fused into one light, from which are formed nine Palaces (Hekaloth). These Palaces are neither lights nor spirits nor souls, neither is there anyone who can grasp them. The longing of the nine illuminations which are all centred in the Thought-the latter being indeed counted as one of them-is to pursue these Palaces at the time when they are stationed in the thought, though they are not (even then) grasped or known, nor are they attained by the highest effort of the mind or the thought. All the mysteries of faith are contained in those Palaces, and all those lights which proceed from the mystic supreme Thought are called EN SOF (Limitless). Up to this point the lights reach and yet do not reach: this is beyond the attainment of mind and thought. When Thought illumines, though from what source is not known, it is clothed and enveloped in Binah (understanding), and then further lights appear and one is embraced with the other until all are intertwined. The symbolism of the sacrifices consists, then, in this. When the whole ascends one part is knit with the other and its elements shine through one another, so that all ascend and the thought is embraced in the limitless. The light from which the upward-striving thought is illumined is called En-Sof, and from it all radiation proceeds and on it is based the whole of existence. Happy the portion of the righteous in this world and in the world to come. In regard, then, to the "end of all flesh", just as there is unison above with joy (at the time of the sacrifice), so also below there is joy and appeasement. There is thus satisfaction both above and below, and the Mother of Israel watches lovingly over her children. Consider this. At every New Moon the "End of all flesh" is given a portion over and above that of the daily offering, so as to divert his attention from Israel, who are thus left entirely to themselves and in full freedom to commune with their King. This extra portion comes from the he-goat (sa'ir), being the portion of Esau, who is also called sa'ir, as it is written, "Behold Esau my brother is a hairy (sa'ir) man" (Gen. XXVII, 11). Esau thus has his portion and Israel their portion. Hence it is written, "For the Lord hath chosen Jacob unto himself, and Israel for his own treasure" (Ps. CXXXV, 4). Consider this point. The whole desire of this "End of all flesh" is for flesh only, and the tendency of flesh is ever towards him; it is for this reason that he is called "End of all flesh". Such power, however, as he does obtain is only over the body and not over the soul. The soul ascends to her place, and the body is given over to its place, in the same way as in an offering the devotion of him who offers ascends to one place, and the flesh to another. Hence the righteous man is, of a truth, himself an offering of atonement. But he who is not righteous is disqualified as an offering, for the reason that he suffers from a blemish, and is therefore like the defective animals of which it is written, "they shall not be accepted for you" (Lev. XXII, 25). Hence it is that the righteous are an atonement and a sacrifice for the world.'

Zohar: Bereshith, Section 1, Page 65b

[Note: The first 4 lines of the Hebrew text do not appear in our translation.]

AND NOAH WAS SIX HUNDRED YEARS OLD. Why is Noah's age specified here? The reason is that if he had not reached this age, he would not yet have been qualified to enter the ark and become united with it. Hence, after the measure of the world's sins had been completed, God respited them until Noah, having lived to the age of six hundred years, reached his full development and attained the condition of "a man righteous and perfect". Then it was that he entered the ark, and reproduced the supernal pattern.

AND I, BEHOLD I DO BRING THE FLOOD OF WATERS. Note the repetition of the term "behold I" after "I". The explanation is as follows: Wherever the term ani (I) is used of the Deity, it signifies, as it were, the relation of a body to a soul which inspires it. For this reason it is figuratively called "the sign of the covenant" in the passage "I (ani) behold (am) my covenant with thee" (Gen. XVII, 4), i.e. "I" who am manifest and in course of becoming known; "I" the throne to the Essence on high; "I" who exact vengeance from generation to generation. The word va'ani (and I) embodies male and female in conjunction; afterwards the male is noted separately, as being held in readiness to execute judgement, in the word "behold I" (hineni). I DO BRING THE FLOOD OF WATERS. If "flood', why also waters? The truth is that the term "flood" here indicates the angel of death, who was the chief agent of destruction, although he used the waters as his instrument. With reference to the word ani, our teachers have explained that the expression "I am (ani) the Lord" is equivalent to "I am faithful to recompense the righteous and to punish the wicked"; hence Scripture always uses the term ani (I) in recording God's promise to the righteous to reward them and His threat to the wicked to punish them in the world to come. TO DESTROY ALL FLESH: to wit, through the world's destroying angel, as already explained; the same that is referred to in the verse "And he will not suffer the destroyer to come into your houses to smite you" (Ex. XII, 23). Hence "to destroy all flesh" means, from the side of "the end of all flesh". For as soon as the time of grace expired which God granted them till Noah should reach the age of six hundred years, then the moment arrived to "destroy all flesh".

R. Simeon discoursed on the text: I said, I shall not see the Lord, even the Lord in the land of the living; I shall behold man no more with the inhabitants of the world (Is. XXXVIII, 11). 'How obtuse,' he said, 'are the sons of men who do not know nor pay heed to the words of the Torah, but think only of worldly matters, so that the spirit of wisdom is forgotten of them. For when a man departs from this world, and goes to give an account to his Master of all his actions in this world while body and soul were still joined together, he sees many strange things on his way, and at length meets Adam, the first man, sitting at the gate of the Garden of Eden, ready to welcome with joy all those who have observed the commands of their Master. Round him are many righteous men, those who in this life have kept clear of the path to Gehinnom and followed the path to the Garden of Eden. It is these who are here called "inhabitants of the world"'. The word used for "world" here is not the usual holed, but hadel. The reason is that holed is akin to huldah (mole), a creature whose characteristic it is laboriously to heap up provision and leave it to it knows not whom. The term hodel, on the other hand, is derived from a root signifying "avoidance", and thus is a description of the righteous who avoid and keep far from the ways of Gehinnom and cling to those leading to the Garden of Eden. According to another interpretation, the expression "inhabitants of hodel" designates penitents who have resolutely kept clear of their former sins, and since Adam was the first penitent, he was given charge of all penitents, those who are called "sons of hodel" (avoidance), and he therefore sits at the gate of the Garden of Eden, welcoming with joy and gladness the righteous who take the path to the Garden of Eden. It says further in the same passage: "I will not see God". Naturally one cannot see God, but the expression is explained by the concluding words, "God in the land of the living". When souls ascend to the place of the "bundle of life" (v. I Sam. XXV, 29), they feast their eyes on the beams of the "refulgent mirror" which radiates

Zohar: Bereshith, Section 1, Page 66a

from the most sublime region. And were the soul not clothed in the resplendency of another (i.e. nonfleshly) garment, it would not be able to approach that effulgence. The esoteric doctrine is that in the same way as the soul has to be clothed in a bodily garment in order to exist in this world, so is she given an ethereal supernal garment wherewith to exist in the other world, and to be enabled to gaze at the effulgence of life radiating from that "land of the living". Hence it is that Moses was not able to draw near to the place of God and to fix his gaze on what was to be seen there until he was first enveloped in another garment, as we read: "And Moses entered into the midst of the cloud, and went up into the mount" (Ex. XXIV, 18), that is, he enveloped himself in the cloud, as in a garment, and then he "drew near into the thick darkness where God was" (Ex. XX, 18), and "was in the mount forty days and forty nights" (Ibid. XXIV, 18), and was able to see what he did see. In similar fashion the souls of the righteous in the other world clothe themselves in garments belonging to that world, so that they can endure to gaze on the light which is diffused in that "land of the living". This is what Hezekiah meant when he said "God, God in the land of the living" (Is. XXXVIII, 11). He was afraid that he would be found unworthy to gaze on that light because he had allowed the lifegiving stream to cease with him, through not begetting children. In his further words, "I shall behold Adam no more" (Ibid.), there is a reference to Adam the first man, as has already been explained. He spoke in this strain because the prophet had told him, "for thou shalt die and not live" (Ibid. 1), "die", that is, in this world, and "not live" in the other world. For he who does not beget children in this world is denied all the blissfulness we have mentioned, and he is not privileged to contemplate the glorious effulgence. If this was the case with Hezekiah, who came of pious ancestors, and was himself worthy, righteous and pious, how much more so must it be the case with one who has no such ancestral merit to support him, and has himself sinned before his Master? That garment of which we have spoken is the same which the companions call "the robe of the sages", with which they are clothed in the other world. Happy the portion of the righteous, for whom the Holy One, blessed be He, has treasured up blessings and delights in the other world! Of them it is written, "Eye hath not seen besides thee, O God, what thou shalt do for him that waiteth for thee" (Is. LXIV, 3).'

AND I, BEHOLD I, DO BRING THE FLOOD OF WATERS UPON THE EARTH. R. Judah discoursed on the text: These are the waters of strife, wherein the children of Israel strove with the Lord and he was sanctified in them (Num. XX, 13). He said: 'As this was not the only occasion when the children of Israel strove with the Lord, why is the epithet of "strife" attached to these waters in particular? The reason is that these waters gave added strength and confidence to the accusers. For there are sweet waters and bitter waters, clear waters and turbid waters, waters of peace and waters of strife. These were waters of strife, because through them Israel drew upon themselves the unwelcome visitor through whom they became defiled; this is indicated in the word vayiqadesh.' Said R. Hizkiah: 'If this is so, we should have the plural vayiqadeshu (and they were defiled). The truth is that the singular refers not to the Israelites but to the moon, and the word vayiqadesh is not used here in a good sense.' R. Yose said: 'Woe to the wicked who will not repent of their sins before the Almighty while they are still in this world. For when a man repents of his sins and feels remorse for them, the Holy One, blessed be He, forgives them. But those who cling to their sins and refuse to repent of them will in the end descend to Gehinnom and never come up again. Thus because the generation of Noah were stubborn of heart and flaunted their sins openly and defiantly, the Holy One, blessed be He, punished them as here described.' Said R. Isaac: 'When a man sins in secret, if he repents, the Holy One, blessed be He, being merciful, relents and forgives him; but if not, He then publishes his sins before the world. We learn this from the treatment of the faithless wife (Sotah). [Tr. note: v. Numbers v.] Similarly here, the wicked were exterminated in sight of all. The manner of their death was as follows: scalding water spurted up from the abyss, and as it reached them it first burnt the skin from the flesh, and then the flesh from the bones; the bones then came asunder, no two remaining together, and thus they were completely blotted out.' R. Isaac said: 'The words "they were blotted out from the earth" is analogous to the expression "let them be blotted out of the book of the living" (Ps. LXIX, 29), thus indicating that they will not participate in the resurrection and will not rise in the Day of Judgement.'

Zohar: Bereshith, Section 1, Page 66b

AND I WILL ESTABLISH MY COVENANT WITH THEE, R. Eleazar said: 'From this we learn that there is an establishment of the covenant on high co-ordinate with the establishment of the covenant here below. This we deduce from the expression "with thee".' R. Eleazar further said: 'We also learn from here that when there are righteous men in this world, the universe is more firmly established both above and below.' R. Simeon said: 'A recondite principle is here enshrined. As the desire of the male towards the female is intensified by jealousy, so is the desire of the Most High towards the Shekinah. Thus, when there is a righteous man in the world, the Shekinah attaches herself to him and never leaves him. This creates, as it were, jealousy on high, which provokes love towards her in the same way as the male is incited to love the female through jealousy; this is implied in the expression "And I will establish my covenant with thee", as much as to say: "Desire hath awakened through you." The same idea is contained in the words "but my covenant will I establish with Isaac" (Gen. XVII, 21). AND I WILL ESTABLISH MY COVENANT WITH THEE: in other words: "Thou shalt be the embodiment of my covenant in the world. and then: AND THOU SHALT COME INTO THE ARK. For had not Noah been righteous, he could not have entered the ark, as only the Righteous one (Zaddik) can become united with the ark, as has been explained.' R. Eleazar said: 'As long as men remain attached to that ark and do not loosen their hold of it, there is no nation or language in the world that can harm them. Noah too kept fast hold of the covenant and observed it, and therefore the Holy One, blessed be He, preserved him; but all his contemporaries who did not keep the covenant were destroyed.' As has already been stated, the manner of their destruction corresponded exactly to the character of their crimes.

R. Judah studied regularly with R. Simeon. On one occasion they discussed the verse: And he repaired (lit. healed) the altar of the Lord that was thrown down (I Kings XVIII, 30). 'What', they asked, 'is meant by the term vayrappe (and he healed)?' 'The answer is this. In the days of Elijah, all Israel forsook the Holy One, blessed be He, and neglected the holy covenant. When Elijah became aware that the children of Israel had entirely neglected the covenant, he set himself to rectify the evil and to restore the covenant to its former vogue. Hence the expression, "And he healed the altar of the Lord that was thrown down", to wit, the established covenant that was utterly neglected. It is further written: "And Elijah took twelve stones according to the number of the tribes of the sons of Jacob" (this being the appropriate means of repairing the altar of the Lord), "unto whom the word of the Lord came saying, Israel shall be thy name" (Ibid. 31), implying that Israel was to be the name by which he could ascend on high and restore the covenant in its place. It is for this reason that Elijah said expressly, "for the children of Israel have forsaken thy covenant" (Ibid. XIX, 10), and, as a consequence, "thrown down thine altars" (Ibid.). Take note that as long as Israel observe the holy covenant, they thereby effect the stabilisation of the world above and below, as it is written: "If my covenant be not (observed) day and night, the ordinances of heaven and earth were as if I had not appointed them." (Jer. XXXIII, 25). The repairing, then, of the shattered altar was truly a healing, as it had for its purpose the reintegration of the spot to which faith attaches itself. Similarly with Phineas at the time when he was filled with zeal to punish the crime of Zimri: he also re-established the covenant in its place, and hence God said to him, "Behold, I give unto him my covenant of peace" (Num. XXV, 12). This does not mean that the covenant was on account of Phineas, or that he was in conflict with the covenant, but that now it was firmly attached to its place. This is shown by the combination of the words "covenant,' and "peace", as if to say, "Behold I give to him the peaceful confirmation of the covenant in its place", from which it had been torn by the transgressors. Hence, too, "and it shall be unto him and to his seed after him the covenant of an everlasting priesthood, because he was jealous for his God".' (Ibid. 13). R. Simeon said: 'There is no sin in the world which so much provokes the anger of the Almighty as the sin of neglecting the covenant, as we read, "a sword that shall execute the vengence of the covenant" (Lev. XXVI, 25). The proof is that in the generation of the Flood the measure of sin was not filled up until mankind became (sexually) perverted and destroyed their seed. And although they defrauded each other, as it is written,

Zohar: Bereshith, Section 1, Page 67a

"And the earth was filled with violence", [Tr. note: lit. 'fraud', 'overreaching'.] and again "for the earth is filled with violence through them", yet it was because "the earth was corrupt before God" that the doom was finally pronounced, "behold I will destroy (lit. corrupt) them". Thus they suffered measure for measure: they were doomed to corruption for having corrupted and perverted their ways. According to another view, it was the sin of violence which finally completed the measure of their guilt, as they used to overreach one another and were thus wicked both towards Heaven and towards their fellow men. For many are the guardians on high charged to lend ear to those who cry out for justice against their oppressors. Hence the words FOR THE EARTH IS FILLED WITH VIOLENCE THROUGH THEM are immediately followed by the words AND BEHOLD I WILL DESTROY THEM WITH THE EARTH. AND THE LORD SAID UNTO NOAH, COME THOU AND ALL THY HOUSE. Said R. Simeon: 'How is it that throughout this passage God is always designated Elohim save in this place, where we find the name Tetragrammaton, significant of the attribute of mercy? There is here an inner meaning which is at the same time a lesson. The lesson is that a woman should not admit a guest into her house without the consent of her husband. So here, when Noah wished to enter the ark, and to become united with her, it was not becoming for her to admit him before her Master gave his permission to enter and said: "Come thou and all thy house into the ark." Hence the name Tetragrammaton is used here, to designate what we call the husband of the ark. Similarly we learn that neither may the guest enter the house save with the consent of the husband, who is the master of the house, and hence it was only later that NOAH WENT IN. Note again the words: FOR THEE I HAVE SEEN RIGHTEOUS BEFORE ME IN THIS GENERATION. We learn from this the lesson that a man should not admit into his house any guest whom he suspects of wrong-doing, but only such a one as is above all suspicion in his eyes. It was in accordance with this principle that God said unto Noah, "Come thou and all thy house into the ark, for thee have I seen righteous before me in this generation." We further learn that special permission must be obtained for the guest's household, as it is written: "Come thou and thy house".'

R. Judah discoursed on the verse: Of David a psalm. The earth is the Lord's and the fulness thereof (Ps. XXIV, 1). He said: 'We have been taught that the heading "Of David a psalm" in the Book of Psalms implies that David began to compose of himself and thereby induced the Holy Spirit to rest on him, whereas the heading "A psalm of David" implies the opposite, viz. that the Holy Spirit rested on him first, and under its inspiration he was moved to song. "The earth" here refers to the holy land of Israel, and by the words "and the fulness thereof" is meant the Shekinah, which is associated with fulness in the verses "for the glory of the Lord filled the house of the Lord" (I Kings VIII, 2), and again, "and the glory of the Lord filled the tabernacle" (Ex. XL, 35). This last passage means literally "the glory of the Lord was full" (male), i.e. full to overflowing, full from all sides both from the sun and the moon like a storehouse filled with all kinds of good things. Similar is the sense of the words "and the fulness thereof" here. The words "the world and they that dwell therein" refer to the rest of the world. According to another view, the words "the earth and the fulness thereof" refer to the supernal Holy Land in which is the delight of the Holy One, blessed be He, and the words "the fulness thereof" refer to the souls of the righteous who fill this earth. What is meant by "the righteous filling the earth" is this. When the righteous multiply in the world, then the earth is truly productive and filled with goodness. But when the wicked multiply in the world, then it may be said that "the waters cease from the sea, and the river is drained dry" (Job XIV, 11), the "sea" being the Holy Land, which is watered by the supernal stream.'

R. Judah further said: 'When the sinners were destroyed in the time of Noah, God was very anxious for the preservation of the world, but could see no one who might save it from His wrath; for the whole efforts of Noah were required to save himself and to repeople the world. So it is written: FOR THEE HAVE I SEEN RIGHTEOUS BEFORE ME IN THIS GENERATION, i.e. he was righteous only by comparison with his contemporaries.' R. Yose said:

Zohar: Bereshith, Section 1, Page 67b

'The words "in this generation" are a tribute to Noah, as much as to say, surrounded as he was by that wicked generation, he yet remained as righteous and perfect a man as if he had lived in the generation of Moses. But he could not save the world, for the reason that there were not to be found ten righteous men in it (similarly we read of Sodom, "peradventure ten shall be found there", Gen. XVIII, 32), but only Noah and his three sons with their womenfolk.' R. Eleazar asked R. Simeon, his father: 'We have been taught that when the world becomes full of sin and is doomed to destruction, woe is then to the righteous man who is found in it, for he is first made answerable for its sins. How, then, was Noah able to escape the general doom?' His father replied: 'It has already been said that the Holy One, blessed be He, desired to people the world anew through him when he should issue from the ark. And further, the general doom could not reach him because he was securely stored away in the ark and concealed from sight, thus fulfilling the verse, "Seek righteousness, seek humility, it may be ye shall be hid in the day of the Lord's anger" (Zeph. II, 3). Because Noah sought righteousness, he was permitted to enter the ark, and thus "was hid in the day of the Lord's anger", and was placed beyond the reach of the Adversary.' The word vayimahu (and they were blotted out) contains a hint to the "saints of the Most High" [Tr. note: v. Daniel VII, 18.] of the secret power of the sacred letters of the alphabet, and their destructive potency when used in the reverse order.

R. Isaac expounded here the verse: He who caused his glorious arm to go at the right hand of Moses, that divided the water before him to make himself an everlasting name (Is. LXIII, 12). 'In these words', he said, 'is a reference to the merit of Abraham, which was the "right hand" and the "glory" of Moses and divided the water before him, in order that he might "make himself an everlasting name". Observe the difference between Moses and other men. When God said to Moses, "now therefore let me alone... and I will make of thee a great nation, etc." (Ex. XXXII, 10), Moses said immediately, "Shall I abandon Israel for my own advantage? The world will say that I killed Israel and did to them as Noah did to his generation. For when God bade Noah save himself and his household in the ark from the universal destruction at the time of the Flood, he did not intercede on behalf of his generation, but let them perish." It is for this reason that the waters of the Flood are named after him, as it is written, "for this is as the waters of Noah unto me" (Is. LIV, 9). Moses thus said: "Everyone will think that I killed them because the Lord promised to make me a great nation. It is therefore better that I should die and that Israel should not be destroyed." Immediately, therefore, he besought mercy for his people, and mercy was indeed vouchsafed to them.' R. Isaac said further: 'How come Moses to begin his intercession with the words, "Why, O Lord, doth thy wrath wax hot against thy people?" (Ex. XXXII, 11) How could Moses ask such a question, knowing as he did that they had worshipped a strange god, as we read "they have made them a molten calf and have worshipped it, etc." (Ibid. 8)? In truth we are taught here that when endeavouring to appease a man who is angry with his neighbour for an offence committed against him, one should not magnify the offence, but, on the contrary, should seek to minimise it: whereas subsequently, when speaking to the offending person himself, one should emphasise the enormity of the offence, as Moses did when he said to Israel, "Ye have sinned a great sin" (Ibid. 30). Moses went so far in his intercession as to offer his own life, as it is written, "and if not, blot me, I pray thee, out of thy book which thou hast written" (Ibid. 32), with the result that the Holy One, blessed be He, forgave them, as it is written, "and the Lord repented of the evil" (Ibid. 14). But Noah did not do so, but was intent on saving himself only, leaving the world to its fate. Thus, whenever the world is called to strict account, the Holy One, blessed be He, says, "Alas that there is no one to be found like Moses, as it is written, 'and his people remember... the days of Moses; where is he that brought us up out of the sea, etc.?'" (Is. LXIII, 11). Moses is called "he that brought them up out of the sea" because their deliverance at that time was due to his prayer, as we read, "and the Lord said to Moses, Wherefore criest thou unto me?" (Ex. XIV, 15). So, too, the words which follow, "where is he that put his holy spirit in the midst of them?" refer to Moses who planted

Zohar: Bereshith, Section 1, Page 68a

the Shekinah in the midst of Israel. So, too, the words, "Who led them through the deeps", when the waters were cleft, and they went through the deeps on dry land. The whole achievement is ascribed to Moses because he risked his life for Israel.'

Said R. Judah: 'Although Noah was a righteous man, he was not so pious that God should think fit to save the world for his sake. Observe that Moses pleaded not his own merit, but that of the ancient patriarchs. Noah, however, did not possess this resource. Nevertheless, after God had said to him "and I will establish my covenant with thee", he should have entreated mercy for his fellow men, and should then have offered up the sacrifice which he brought later, in order to appease God's anger against the world.' Said R. Judah: 'What could he do? He was in fear for his own life, lest he should perish along with the wicked, whose iniquities and provocations he had observed for so long.' R. Isaac said: 'When the wicked spread, it is the righteous man in their midst who first suffers for their sins, as it is written, "and from my sanctuary ye should commence" (Ez. IX, 6), where the word mimiqdashi (my sanctuary) may be read-so tradition tells us-as mimqudashai (my saintly ones). How is it, then, that God saved Noah from the midst of the sinners? It was in order to people the world anew through him, as he was a righteous man, meet for this purpose; and further, he daily warned the people, who, however, disregarded his warning, so that to him may be applied the words, "yet if thou warn the wicked... but thou hast delivered thy soul" (Ezek. III, 19). From this we learn that he who warns the wicked, even if his warning is disregarded, saves himself and is not involved in the punishment which befalls them. If it is asked, how long should one go on warning, the answer is, till he is peremptorily forbidden. This is the point fixed by the colleagues.'

When R. Yose was studying regularly with R. Simeon, he one day said to him: 'What was the motive of the Almighty in extirpating all the animals of the field and the birds of the air along with the wicked among men? If men sinned, what wrong had the animals and birds and other creatures committed? ' R. Simeon answered: 'The reason is given in the words, "For all flesh had corrupted their way upon the earth." This indicates that the whole of the animal world had become corrupted and had confounded their species. Observe that it was the wicked among mankind who brought about the unnatural intercourse in the animal world, and who sought thereby to undo the work of creation: they made the rest of creation pervert their ways in imitation of themselves. Said God to them: "You seek to undo the work of my hands; your wish shall be fully granted, for every living thing that I have made will I blot out from the face of the earth. I will reduce the world to water, to its primitive state, and then I will form other creatures more worthy to endure." '

AND NOAH WENT IN AND HIS SONS AND HIS WIFE AND HIS SONS' WIVES WITH HIM. R. Hiya quoted in this connection the verse: Can any hide himself in secret places that I shall not see him? saith the Lord (Jer. XXIII, 24). 'How blind and obtuse are the sons of men who regard not and know not the honour of their Master, of whom it is written, "Do not I fill heaven and earth?" (Ibid.). And yet men imagine that they can hide their sins, saying, "Who seeth us? And who knoweth us?" (Is. XXIX, 15). Where, indeed, can they hide themselves? There was once a king who built a palace and constructed underneath it secret subterranean chambers. One day the courtiers rose in revolt against the king, who thereupon laid siege to the palace with his army. The rebels sought safety by hiding in the subterranean passages and chambers. Said the king: "It is I who constructed these secret places, and do you think to escape from me by hiding there?" So God says to the wicked, "Can anyone hide himself in secret places that I shall not see him?" As much as to say, "I have created all chasms and caverns, I have made darkness and light; how, then, can you think to hide yourselves from Me?" Observe this. When a man sins before his Master and uses all devices to conceal himself, the Holy One, blessed be He, chastises him openly. Should, however, the man purify himself of his sins, God will then shield him so that he shall not be visible in the day of the fierce wrath of the Lord. For assuredly a man should take care

Zohar: Bereshith, Section 1, Page 68b

not to make himself visible to the destroying angel when he swoops down upon the world, and not to attract his notice, since he is authorised to destroy whosoever comes within his view. This accords with a remark of R. Simeon, that a man possessed of an evil eye carries with him the eye of the destroying angel; hence he is called "destroyer of the world", and people should be on their guard against him and not come near him, so that they should not be injured by him; it is actually forbidden to come near him in the open. If, therefore, it is necessary to beware of a man with an evil eye, how much more should one beware of the angel of death? An example of a man with an evil eye was Balaam, of whom it is written, "thus saith the man whose eye is closed" [Tr. note: So the Rabbinical interpretation of the word sh'thum.] (Num. XXIV, 3); this means that he was possessed of an evil eye, and on whatsoever he fixed his gaze he drew thereon the destroying spirit. Knowing this, he sought to fix his gaze on Israel, in order that he might destroy everything upon which his look should fall. Thus it is written, "And Balaam lifted up his eye" (Ibid. 2), indicating that he raised one eye and lowered the other, so that his evil eye should fall upon Israel. Israel, however, were immune; for it is written, "and he saw Israel dwelling tribe by tribe" (Ibid.), that is, he saw the Shekinah hovering over them and kept in position by the twelve tribes beneath, and his eye had no more power over them. "How," he said, "can I prevail against them, seeing that the holy spirit from on high rests on them and shields them with her wings?" This is indicated in the words, "He couched, he lay down as a lion, who shall rouse him up?" (Ibid. 9); that is, who shall raise Him from over them so that they shall be exposed to the influence of the evil eye? In the same manner the Holy One, blessed be He, sought to shield Noah, and to hide him from the evil eye, so that the impure spirit should have no power over him, and do him no harm.'

AND NOAH WENT IN, as has already been said, to hide himself from all eyes, BECAUSE OF THE WATERS OF THE FLOOD, which were already pressing him hard. Said R. Yose: He saw the angel of death coming, and so he went into hiding for a twelvemonth.' Why for a twelvemonth? On this point R. Isaac and R. Judah differed. One said it was because a twelvemonth is the fixed term of punishment in Gehinnom for the guilty. The other said that it was in order that the righteous Noah might complete his twelve degrees and the other degrees which it was fitting that he should bring with him out of the ark. R. Judah asked: 'Seeing that for six months the wicked (in Gehinnom) are punished by water and another six months by fire, why did the waters prevail for twelve months?' R. Yose answered: 'The punishments of Gehinnom, water and fire, were here let loose together. Rain descended upon them from above, and at the same time scalding waters, hot as fire, gushed up from below. Their punishment was thus the same as that in Gehinnom, which consists of fire and water, and it continued until they were utterly destroyed. Meanwhile Noah was hidden in the ark, concealed from sight, so that the destroyer could not come near him, while the ark floated on the face of the waters, as we read: AND THEY BORE UP THE ARK, AND IT WAS LIFTED ABOVE THE EARTH. For forty days they suffered punishment, as it is written, AND THE FLOOD WAS FORTY DAYS UPON THE EARTH, and for the rest of the time they were gradually being exterminated, as it is written, AND THEY WERE BLOTTED OUT FROM THE EARTH. Woe to those sinners, since they will not rise from the dead on the day of the last judgement. This is indicated by the expression "and they were blotted out", which contains the same idea as the verse "Thou hast blotted out their name forever and ever" (Ps. IX, 6).'

AND THEY BORE UP THE ARK, AND IT WAS LIFTED UP ABOVE THE EARTH. R. Abba connected this text with the verse: Be thou raised above the heavens, O Elohim, thy glory be above all the earth (Ps. LVII, 6). 'Woe,' he said, 'to the sinners who daily provoke their Master, and through their sins repel the Shekinah and cause it to disappear from the world, wherefore the Scripture says: "Be thou raised above the heavens, O Elohim" (the Shekinah being called Elohim). So here, the words, "and they bore up the ark" indicate that they thrust her forth, and the words, "it was lifted up above the earth", that she found no more rest in the world, and so departed altogether from it. And in the absence of the Shekinah there is no one to take thought for the world, with the result that divine justice is exercised upon it with rigour. But when the wicked are blotted out and removed from the world, the Shekinah again takes up her abode therein.' R. Yose put to R. Abba the question: 'Why, after the sinners in the land of Israel were wiped out, did the Shekinah not return to her former habitation?' R. Abba replied: 'It is because the remnant of the righteous did not remain there, for wherever these went the Shekinah descended and made

Zohar: Bereshith, Section 1, Page 69a

her habitation with them. We thus see that in a strange land she does not separate from them; how much more would she cling to them had they remained in the Holy Land! All sins of mankind repel the Shekinah, particularly the sin of him who corrupts his way upon the earth. Therefore such a one will not see the face of the Shekinah, and will not gain entrance to the celestial Palace. For when the day comes on which the Holy One, blessed be He, will raise the dead to life, He will physically re-create all those dead who have been buried in strange lands. For if but one bone of them is left in the earth, this will be like the lump of leaven which causes the dough to rise, and on it the Holy One, blessed be He, will build up the whole body. But God will not restore their souls [Tr. note: The neshamah (v. pp. 203, 278).] to them save in the land of Israel, as it is written, "Behold I will open your graves, and cause you to come up out of your graves, O my people, and I will bring you into the land of Israel" (to which they will roll through subterranean passages), and then "I will put my spirit in you and you shall live" (Ezek. XXXVII, 12, 14). We see thus that only in the land of Israel will souls be provided for the resurrected. But those will be excluded who defile themselves and defile the earth, and of them it is written, "and they were blotted out of the earth". The word "earth" we take to mean here "the land of the living" (although some of the ancient sages question this), and the whole expression is analogous to the verse, "let them be blotted out of the book of the living" (Ps. LXIX, 29).'

R. Simeon said to him: 'Undoubtedly they will have no portion in the world to come, since the expression "and they were blotted out of the earth" is the exact opposite of the expression "they shall inherit the land forever" (Is. LX, 21); but they will be called up for judgement, as it is with reference to them that the Scripture says, "and many of them that sleep in the dust of the earth shall awake, some to everlasting life, and some to reproaches and everlasting abhorrence" (Dan. XII, 2).'

AND HE BLOTTED OUT EVERY (eth-kol) LIVING SUBSTANCE WHICH WAS UPON THE FACE OF THE EARTH. Said R. Abba: 'The particle eth signifies the inclusion of all those higher chieftains who control and superintend the earth: these are "the substance which was upon the face of the earth". For whenever the Holy One, blessed he He, executes judgement on the earth, those higher chieftains are brought to justice first, and only in the next place those who abide beneath the shelter of their wings. This is illustrated in the passage, "the Lord will punish the host of the high heavens on high", and then "and the kings of the earth upon the earth" (Is. XXIV, 21). The punishment of these chieftains is, to be driven through burning fire, as it is written, "for the Lord thy God is a devouring fire, a jealous God" (Deut. IV, 24); that is, fire consuming fire. The "living substance" of the upper regions were thus passed through fire, and those under their control through water; and so, first, HE BLOTTED OUT EVERY LIVING SUBSTANCE WHICH WAS UPON THE FACE OF THE GROUND, and then, BOTH MAN AND CATTLE AND FOWL OF THE HEAVEN, AND THEY WERE BLOTTED OUT FROM THE EARTH-to wit, all those beneath. AND NOAH ONLY WAS LEFT; the particle ach (only) shows that absolutely nothing was left save what was in the ark'. R. Yose said: 'It indicates that even Noah was not left intact, as he was injured by a blow from a lion, as elsewhere explained.'

AND GOD REMEMBERED NOAH AND EVERY LIVING THING AND ALL THE CATTLE THAT WERE WITH HIM IN THE ARK. R. Hiya quoted in this connection the verse: A prudent man seeth evil and hideth himself (Prov. XXII, 3) 'This verse,' he said, 'refers to Noah, who went into the ark and hid himself there, not, however, before the waters forced him in. It has already been said that before he entered the ark he caught sight of the angel of death going among the people and encircling them. As soon as he espied him, he went into the ark and hid himself there. Thus, "the prudent man saw evil and hid himself", i.e. Noah saw the angel of death and hid himself from him, going into the ark, as the Scripture says, "because of the waters of the flood".' R. Yose said that the reference of the verse is to what has been said above, viz. that when death is raging in the world the prudent man goes into hiding and does not venture abroad, so as not to be seen by the destroying angel, who, once he has obtained leave, will destroy whomsoever he meets at large, and whoever passes before him in the open, as the latter part of the verse expresses it, "but the thoughtless pass on and are punished". According to another interpretation, the word abroo (pass on) means here "transgress", i.e. they transgress the precept of self-preservation and are therefore punished. According to yet another interpretation, while the first half of the verse refers to Noah, the second half refers to his contemporaries. When he had remained a sufficient time under cover,

Zohar: Bereshith, Section 1, Page 69b

the Scripture says that GOD REMEMBERED NOAH. Said R. Simeon: Observe that all the time that judgement was being executed there was no remembering, but only after the chastisement had been completed and the wicked had been exterminated do we find mention of remembering. For as long as judgement hangs over the worlds there is no communion of man with God, and the destroying angel is rampant. But as soon as judgement has run its course and wrath has been allayed, everything returns to its previous state. Hence we read "and God remembered Noah", remembrance being centred in him since he was entitled "righteous".'

It is written: [Tr. note: Here, apparently, there should be a text-heading: AND GOD MADE A WIND PASS OVER EARTH, AND THE WATERS WERE ASSUAGED] Thou rulest the proud swelling of the sea, when the waves thereof arise, thou

99

stillest them (Ps. LXXXIX, 10). When the stormy waves of the sea mount on high, and beneath them yawn the chasms of the deep, the Holy One, blessed be He, sends down a thread from the "right side" which in some mysterious way restrains the mounting waves and calms the rage of the sea. How is it that when Jonah was cast into the sea, and had been swallowed by a fish, his soul did not at once leave his body? The reason is that the Holy One, blessed be He, has dominion over the swelling of the sea, which is a certain thread from the "left" that causes the sea to heave, and rises with it. And if not for the thread of the "right side" it would never be removed, for as soon as this thread descends into the sea, and is fairly grasped by it, then the waves of the sea are stirred up, and begin to roar for prey, until the Holy One, blessed be He, thrusts them back to their own place, as it says, "when the waves thereof arise, thou stillest them". (According to another interpretation, the term teshabhem (thou stillest them), is related to the word shabah (praise), and signifies here, "thou praisest them", because they mount to the top in their eagerness to see the outer world. The lesson to be learnt from this is that he who manifests an eagerness to examine things and to acquire new knowledge, although he lacks talent, merits praise and receives praise from all around him.) R. Judah said: 'While Noah was in the Ark, he was apprehensive lest God should never more remember him. He was, however, wrong, for after judgement had been executed, and the wicked had perished from the world, the Scripture tells us that GOD REMEMBERED NOAH. Said R. Eleazar: When the world is being called to account, it is not advisable that a man should have his name mentioned on high, for the mention of his name will be a reminder of his sins, and will cause him to be brought under scrutiny. This we learn from the words of the Shunammitess. It was on New Year's day, when God sits in judgement on the world, that Elisha asked her, "Wouldst thou be spoken for to the king?" (II Kings IV, 13), i.e. to the Holy One, blessed be He, for on that day He is, in a special sense, King, Holy King, King of Judgement. She answered, "I dwell among my own people" (Ibid.), as much as to say, "I do not wish to be remembered and to have attention drawn to me, save among my own people." He who keeps himself in the midst of his own people does not draw attention upon himself, and so escapes criticism. In the same way, as long as the heavenly wrath was raging in the world, Noah was not remembered; but as soon as judgement had been executed, then, as we read, "God remembered Noah".'

R. Hizkiah was going from Cappadocia to Lud, when R. Yesa met him. Said the latter to him, 'I am surprised at your walking all alone, seeing that we have been taught that no man should proceed on a journey unaccompanied.' R. Hizkiah replied, 'There is a youth accompanying me, and he is following on.' Said R. Yesa, 'I am still more surprised to find that you have for a companion one with whom you could not discuss points of the Torah, since we have been taught that he who makes a journey unaccompanied by discussions on; the Torah exposes himself to danger.' R. Hizkiah replied, 'It is certainly so.' Meanwhile the youth came up with them. Said R. Yesa to him, 'My son, where do you come from?' The lad answered, 'From the town of Lud, and when I heard that this learned man was proceeding thither, I offered him my service and company.' 'My son,' said R. Yesa, 'do you know any Torah-exposition?' 'I do,' was the reply, 'as my father used to teach me the section of the sacrifices, and I also used to listen attentively to the expositions he gave to my elder brother.' At the invitation of R. Yesa, he then commenced to discourse as follows.

AND NOAH BUILDED AN ALTAR UNTO THE LORD; AND TOOK OF EVERY CLEAN BEAST, AND OF EVERY CLEAN FOWL, AND OFFERED BURNT OFFERINGS ON THE ALTAR. The altar that Noah made was the very same on which Adam, the first man, offered up sacrifice. Why did Noah bring burnt offerings,

Zohar: Bereshith, Section 1, Page 70a

seeing that a burnt offering is brought only to counteract wrongful thoughts? Was, then, Noah guilty of such? In truth, Noah did harbour wrongful thoughts, since he said to himself, "Behold, the Holy One, blessed be He, has decreed the destruction of the world, and who knows but that through my being saved I have used up all the merit which I had accumulated?" He therefore hastened to build an altar unto the Lord. The altar was the very same on which Adam, the first man, offered up sacrifice, but as the wicked had wrenched it from its place, Noah had to rebuild it. AND OFFERED BURNT OFFERINGS. It is written olath (burnt offering) defectively, which would indicate only one. This is explained by reference to the verse, "it is a burnt offering, a fire offering for sweet savour to the Lord" (Lev. I, 17). A burnt offering has to be male, not female, as it says: "he shall offer it a male, without blemish" (Lev. I, 3). The word "fire offering" (isheh) seems to be superfluous, as we know there was fire on the altar. We should therefore read ishah (lit. woman), and we learn from this that the female element must not be parted from the male, which is offered through it, so that the two are united. It was right for Noah to bring a burnt offering, since God had set him in the place of a male in relation to the ark. "The burnt offering is isheh", to wit, esh he (fire of he), indicating that the Left is joined with the Female (since the female is from the left and the male from the right) through the clinging of one to the other. Hence the female is called isheh, indicating the bond of love in which the Left is joined to her, so as to mount with her on high and be united with her there. Hence the words "a burnt offering, a fire offering", indicate the bond of the male and female.

AND THE LORD SMELLED THE SAVOUR OF APPEASEMENT. It is also written "a fire offering, a savour of appeasement" (Lev. I, 13). With reference to the term "fire offering" we have heard the following. Fire and smoke are joined together, there being no smoke without fire, as it is written: "Now Mount Sinai was altogether on smoke, because the Lord descended upon it in fire" (Ex. XIX, 18). It is in this way. Fire, being very tenuous, issues from an inmost part, and then takes hold of some substance outside which is less tenuous, and by the junction of the two smoke is engendered: the reason being that fire has taken hold of something catching. An example is the warm breath that issues from the nostrils. Hence it is written, "They shall put incense in thy nose" (Deut. XXXIII, 10), i.e. they shall act so as to cause the fire to recede to its place, since through the smell of the incense the nose contracts inwardly, till the whole odour is drawn in and brought near to the thought, producing a pleasing sensation. Hence there results "a savour of appeasement", when the anger is appeased and calm is restored, since the smoke has been gathered in and condensed in the fire, and the fire has seized the smoke and both have been drawn further and further back until the anger is assuaged and a reunion is formed, called "appeasement": an appeasement of the spirit, a universal rejoicing, a radiance of lamps, a brightening of faces, and thus, AND THE LORD SMELT THE SAVOUR OF APPEASEMENT as one who smells and draws in the savour to the innermost spot.'

R. Yesa then approached the lad and kissed him, saying, 'To think that all these precious goods were in thy possession and I was unaware of it.' He further said, 'I will go out of my way to remain in thy company.' Whilst they proceeded R. Hizkiah said, 'On this road we are accompanied by the Shekinah. Let us, then, go forward confidently, since no harm can befall us on the way.' He then took hold of the lad's hand and they went along. They then said to him, 'Repeat to us one of those Scriptural expositions you have heard from your father.' The lad then began a discourse on the text: Let him kiss me with the kisses of his mouth (S. S. I, 2). 'This,' he said, 'is a more burning desire, in which affection issues from the mouth with a fire unlike that which issues from the nostrils. For when mouth is joined with mouth to kiss, fire issues from the strength of affection, accompanied by radiance of the countenance, by rejoicing on both sides and by gladsome union. "For thy love is better than wine" (Ibid.), to wit, than that wine which exhilarates and brightens the countenance, which makes the eyes sparkle and induces good feeling; not the wine that intoxicates, induces rage, beclouds the countenance, and inflames the eyes, the wine of rage. It is because this wine is exhilarating and cheering and induces love and affection that a libation of it is offered every day on the altar, of just such a quantity

Zohar: Bereshith, Section 1, Page 70b

as would induce in him who drinks it a cheerful mood and a spirit of contentment, as it is written, "And the drink offering thereof shall be a fourth part of a hin" (Num. XXVIII, 7). "For thy love is better than wine" alludes thus to the wine that induces love and desire. And as here below, so is love awakened on high. For there are two lamps, and when the light of the one on high is extinguished, by the smoke that rises from the one below it is relit.' Said R. Hizkiah: 'Assuredly it is so, the lower and the upper world are interdependent; and since the destruction of the Temple there are no blessings, either on high or below, which proves their interdependence.' R. Yose said: 'Not only are there no blessings, but there are everywhere curses, as the supply of sustenance is now drawn from the "sinister side". Why so? Because Israel do not dwell now in the land, and thus do not perform the holy service which is required for lighting the (celestial) lamps and so obtaining blessings. Hence they are to be found neither on high nor here below, and the world is out of gear.'

I WILL NOT AGAIN CURSE THE GROUND ANY MORE FOR MAN'S SAKE. R. Hizkiah asked, 'What does this verse mean?' R. Yesa replied: 'I have heard from R. Simeon the following. So long as the supernal fire is gathering force, the smoke, which is the execution of judgement here below, rages more and more fiercely and is more and more destructive; for once the fire starts, there is no keeping it back until the judgement has been fully executed. But when punishment below is not intensified by punishment from above, it burns itself out without bringing the world to ruin. Hence it is written, lo osif (I will not add) as much as to say, "I will not lend any additional force and volume to the punishment below".'

Said the young lad, 'I have heard that the expression "for man's sake" alludes to the utterance, "cursed is the ground for thy sake" (Gen. III, 17). For at the time when the earth was cursed for the sin of Adam, full dominion over her was granted to that evil serpent, the destroyer and exterminator of the world and its inhabitants. From the day, however, that Noah offered up sacrifices, and the Holy One, blessed be He, smelt their sweet savour, the earth was liberated from the dominion of the serpent and threw off his defilement. It is for this same reason that Israel bring offerings, so as to keep bright the countenance of the earth.' Said R. Hizkiah, 'This is correct, but nevertheless this liberation remained in suspense until Israel stood at Mount Sinai.' R. Yesa said: 'The Holy One, blessed be He, had already diminished the moon and allowed the serpent to obtain sway, but on account of the sin of Adam she was actually cursed in order that the whole world might be cursed. But on that day the earth was freed of that curse, whilst the moon remained in her diminished state, save during the time when offerings are brought and Israel dwell in their own land.' R. Yesa asked the child, 'What is your name?' He replied, 'Abba'. He said to him, 'Abba (=father, chief) you shall be in everything, in wisdom and in years.' He further applied to him the verse. "Thy father and thy mother will be glad, and she that bore thee will rejoice" (Prov. XXIII, 25). R. Hizkiah said: 'The Holy One, blessed be He, will one day sweep away the unclean spirit, as it is written, "And the unclean spirit I will cause to pass out of the land" (Zech. XIII, 2), and further, "He will swallow up death forever, and the Lord God will wipe away tears from all faces, and the reproach of his people will he take away from off all the earth, for the Lord hath spoken it" (Is. XXV, 8). The Holy One, blessed be He, will also one day restore the moon to its full light, and dissipate the darkness brought on her by the evil serpent, as it is written, "And the light of the moon shall be as the light of the sun, and the light of the sun shall be sevenfold, as the light of the seven days" (Ibid. XXX, 26), the reference here being to the primordial light which the Holy One, blessed be He, stored away during the period of the creation.'

AND GOD (Elohim) BLESSED NOAH AND HIS SONS, AND SAID UNTO THEM: BE FRUITFUL AND MULTIPLY, ETC. R. Abba began his discourse with the text: The blessing of the Lord, it maketh rich, and no pain shall be added thereto (Prov. X, 22). '"The blessing of the Lord" is bound up with the Shekinah, as she is in charge of the blessings of the world, and from her flow blessings for all. Observe that at first (Gen. VII, 1) it was written, AND Tetragrammaton SAID TO NOAH, COME THOU AND ALL THY HOUSE INTO THE ARK, which conforms with what was said before, that the master of the house gave him permission to enter; whereas afterwards it was the wife who speeded him out of the ark, as it is written, AND ELOHIM (=Shekinah) SPOKE UNTO NOAH, SAYING: GO FORTH FROM THE ARK. From here we learn that it is the master

Zohar: Bereshith, Section 1, Page 71a

of the house that takes in the guest and it is the wife that speeds him forth, but that she may not herself bid him enter. We learn further from here that it is proper for the guest on departing to leave presents for the mistress of the house, as she is always in the house and supervises it. It is fitting to give her those presents, not in her own hand directly, but through the agency of her husband, so as to enhance their mutual affection. This we deduce from the text: AND HE TOOK OF EVERY CLEAN BEAST AND HE OFFERED BURNT OFFERINGS ON THE ALTAR. These were the presents for her which he gave, as it were, into the hands of the husband in order to enhance his love for his consort. Noah then received a blessing, as it is written, "And God blessed Noah and his sons, and said unto them, Be fruitful and multiply, etc." All this is illustrated by the text, "The blessing of the Lord, it maketh rich." As for the words "and no pain shall be added thereto", these allude to the pain mentioned in the passage "in pain shalt thou eat of it" (Gen. III, 17), that is, in pain and perturbation, with sad and gloomy looks, since the moon was darkened, and so blessings were no more. Again "in pain" refers to the side of the impure spirit who kept back blessings from the world. But now "No pain will be added thereto"; the word "add" (yosif) here shows the inner meaning of the words, "I will not again (osif, lit. add) curse the earth any more."

AND THE FEAR OF YOU AND THE DREAD OF YOU SHALL BE UPON EVERY BEAST OF THE EARTH: as much as to say, "Henceforward you will assume the facial impress of man"; for up to that time their facial impress was not that of human beings. For at first: "in the image of God created he him" (Gen. I, 27), also "in the likeness of God made he him" (Ibid. V, 1); but when they sinned, their facial impress was changed from the supernal prototype, and through this transformation they became afraid of the beasts of the field. Whereas formerly all the creatures of the world, when looking up towards man, encountered the supernal sacred impress and thus were filled with fear and trembling, now after they sinned their appearances were transformed, and it was men who feared and dreaded the rest of the animal world. Thus it is that all who are mindful of their Master, who keep themselves from sin and do not transgress the precepts of the Torah, retain their visage unaltered from the supernal prototype, and hence all the creatures of the world fear them and tremble before them. But when men transgress the precepts of the Torah, their visages change, and they fear the other creatures and tremble before them; the beasts of the field obtain dominion over men because they do not see any more in them the true supernal image. Hence, now that the world was reinstated in its former position, He bestowed on them His blessing and granted them dominion over all the creatures, as we read: AND UPON ALL THE FISHES OF THE SEA: INTO YOUR HAND ARE THEY DELIVERED; that is, all, even to the fishes of the sea.'

R. Hiya said: ' It is written "into your hand were they delivered" (nithanu), i.e. originally, for when the Holy One, blessed be He, created the world, He delivered all in man's hand, as it is written, "and have dominion over the fish of the sea, and over the fowl of the air, etc." (Gen. I, 28).' In reference to the words "And God blessed Noah", R. Hizkiah discoursed on the text: Of David, Maskil. Happy is he whose transgression is forgiven, whose sin is covered (Ps. XXXII, 1). He said: 'This verse contains deep mysteries of wisdom. For we have been taught that David, in offering praise to the Holy One, blessed be He, made use of ten varieties of praise, one of which was Maskil, which is one of the ten grades (of illumination), and the word here implies that David qualified himself to attain that grade. The verse proceeds: "Happy is he whose transgression is forgiven, whose sin is covered." The words nesui pesha mean literally "whose transgression is uplifted". That is to say, when the Holy One, blessed be He, weighs the sins and the merits of men in the balance, happy then is he whose sins rise and mount in the one scale whilst his merits sink down the other. "Whose sin is covered": i.e. when the world is being chastised, that man will be concealed so that the destroyer will have no power over him, in the same way that Noah was concealed by the Holy One, blessed be He, so that he escaped the consequences that Adam's sin drew upon the world. For that sin transferred dominion from man to the other creatures, making him fear them, and thus reversing the true order of things. Therefore when Noah went forth from the ark, the Holy One, blessed be He, blessed him, as it is written, "And God blessed Noah and his sons, etc."

AND YOU, BE YE FRUITFUL AND MULTIPLY. The women do not seem to have been included in this blessing, as it was only addressed to Noah and his sons. R. Simeon, however, said that the term ve-athem (and you) includes both male

Zohar: Bereshith, Section 1, Page 71b

and female. And further, the particle eth preceding "his sons" signifies the inclusion of their spouses. It is because the women were included that God said: "Do you be fruitful and multiply", to propagate your kind. On this occasion the Holy One, blessed be He, gave them seven precepts of the Torah-to them and to all their successors, until Israel stood at Mount Sinai, when they received all the precepts of the Torah in one code.'

AND GOD SAID TO NOAH... THIS IS THE TOKEN OF THE COVENANT WHICH I MAKE BETWEEN ME AND YOU... I HAVE SET MY RAINBOW IN THE CLOUD. The past tense "I have set" shows that the bow had already been there. In connection with this passage R. Simeon discoursed on the verse: And above the firmament that was over their heads was the likeness of a throne, as the appearance of a sapphire stone (Ezek. I, 26). 'Before this verse,' he said, 'we find the words, "And when they went I heard the noise of their wings like the noise of great waters, like the voice of the Almighty" (Ibid. 24). These are the four sacred and mighty beings called Hayyoth (animals), by whom the firmament is upheld, and whose wings are usually joined together to cover their bodies. When, however, they spread out their wings, a volume of sound swells forth, and they break out into songs of praise, "as the voice of the Almighty", which never becomes silent, as it is written, "so that my glory may sing praise to thee, and not be silent" (Ps. XXX, 13). The tenour of their praises is, "The Lord hath made known his salvation, his righteousness hath he revealed in the sight of the nations" (Ps. XCVIII, 2). It says further: "A noise of tumult like the noise of a host" (Ezek. I, 24), i.e. like the sound of the holy camps when all the supernal armies assemble on high. What is it they declaim? "Holy, holy, holy, is the Lord of Hosts, the whole earth is full of his glory" (Is. VI, 3). They turn to the south and say "holy", they turn to the north and say "holy", they turn to the east and say "holy", they turn to the west and say "blessed". And that firmament rests upon their heads, and in whatever direction it turns, their faces turn also. They turn their faces to the four cardinal points, and all revolve in a circle. The firmament is imprinted, at the four corners of a square, with four figures, of a lion, an eagle, an ox, and a man; and the face of a man is traced in all of them, so that the face of Lion is of Man, the face of Eagle is of Man, and the face of Ox is of Man, all being comprehended in him. Hence it is written: "As for the likeness of their faces, they had the face of a man" (Ezek. I, 10). Eurther, the firmament with its enclosed square contains the gamut of all the colours. Outstanding are four colours, each engraved with four translucent signs, both higher and lower. These when decomposed become twelve. They are green, red, white, and sapphire, which is made up of all these colours. Hence it is written, "As the appearance of the bow that is in the cloud in the day of rain, so was the appearance of the brightness round about. This was the appearance of the likeness of the glory of the Lord" (Ibid. I, 28): containing, that is to say, all shades of all colours. The same is referred to in the text I HAVE SET MY BOW IN THE CLOUD. The bow here has a parallel in the text, "But his bow abode firm" (Gen. XLIX, 24), i.e. the covenant of Joseph, because he was a righteous man, had for its symbol the bow, since the bow is linked with the covenant, and the covenant and the righteous are integral in one another. And because Noah was righteous, the sign of his covenant was the bow. (The word vayophozu, mentioned in connection with Joseph, is akin to the term paz (fine gold) in the passage, "More to be desired are they than gold, yea, than much fine gold" (Ps. XIX, 11), and it means that his arms shone with the lustre of the most desirable substance, they shone with the light supernal, since he had observed the covenant; hence he is named "Joseph the righteous".) And the rainbow is therefore called "covenant" because they embrace one another. Like the firmament it is a supernal resplendent glory, a sight of all sights, resembling the hidden one (the Shekinah), containing colours undisclosed and unrevealable. Hence it is not permitted to gaze at the rainbow when it appears in the heavens, as that would be disrespectful to the Shekinah, the hues of the rainbow here below being a replica of the vision of the supernal splendour, which is not for man's gaze. Hence when the earth saw the rainbow as a holy covenant, it was once more firmly established, and therefore God said, AND IT SHALL BE FOR A TOKEN OF A COVENANT BETWEEN GOD, ETC. The three primary colours and the one compounded of them, which we mentioned before, are all one symbol, and they all show themselves in the cloud. "And above the firmament that was over their heads was the likeness of a throne, as the appearance of a sapphire stone" (Ezek. I, 26). This alludes to the "foundation stone" (eben shethiah), which is the central point of the universe and on which stands the Holy of Holies. "The likeness of a throne", i.e. the supernal holy throne, possessing four supports, and which is symbolic of the Oral Law. "And upon the likeness of the throne was the likeness as the appearance of a man upon it above" (Ibid.); this symbolises the Written Law. From here we learn that copies of the Written Law should rest

Zohar: Bereshith, Section 1, Page 72a

on copies of the Oral Law (and not vice versa), because the latter is the throne to the former. "As the appearance of a man" refers to the image of Jacob, who sits on it.'

R. Judah one night, whilst staying at an inn in Matha-Mehasia, rose at midnight to study the Torah. At the time there happened to be there a certain Judean traveller who had with him two sacks of clothes. R. Judah began to expound the verse, "And this stone which I have set up for a pillar shall be God's house" (Gen. XXVIII, 22). 'That stone', he said, 'was the foundation stone out of which the world evolved, and on which the Temple was built.' The Judean raised his head and said, 'How is this possible? This foundation stone was created before the world, to be the point from which the world evolved, and yet you say that it is referred to in the verse, "and this stone which I have set up for a pillar", which indicates that Jacob put it there, this being the same stone of which it is said, "and he took the stone that he had put under his head" (Ibid. 18). A further difficulty is that Jacob was in Bethel, whereas the foundation stone is in Jerusalem.' R. Judah, without turning his head, recited the verse, "Prepare to meet thy God, O Israel" (Amos IV, 12), and also "Be attentive and hearken, O Israel" (Deut. XXVII, 9). 'We learn from here, he said, 'that the study of the Torah must be approached with proper preparation, not only of the mind but also of the body.' The Judean then arose and put on his garments, and seating himself beside R. Judah, said, 'Happy are ye righteous who give yourselves up to the study of the Torah day and night.' Said R. Judah to him, 'Now that you have properly attired yourself, say what you have to say, so that we may join together, as the study of the Torah requires a seemly garb as well as an attentive mind. Otherwise I could just as well lie in my bed and meditate. But we have been taught that even a single person who sits and studies the Torah has for his companion the Shekinah; and how could the Shekinah be here whilst I am in bed? Furthermore, the words of the Torah must be clearly articulated. Moreover, when a man gets up to study at midnight, at the time when the Holy One, blessed be He, comes to disport Himself with the righteous in the Garden of Eden, He and all the righteous in the Garden are listening to the words that issue from his mouth. Since that is so, that the Holy One, blessed be He, and all the righteous feel delight in listening to the words of the Torah at this time, should I remain lying in bed?' He then said to him, 'Now say what you have to say.'

The Judean then said, 'Regarding your remark that Jacob's stone was the foundation stone, I have asked you, first, how can that be, seeing that the foundation stone preceded the creation of the world, and was the one from which the world evolved, whereas Jacob's stone was put by him in its place, as it is written, "and the stone which I have put", also, "And he took the stone that he had put under his head." And secondly, how can the two be identified, seeing that Jacob was in Bethel and that the stone was in Jerusalem?'

R. Judah answered, 'The whole land of Israel was folded up beneath him, so that that stone was underneath him.' The Judean repeated his question, quoting again the expressions 'that he put'-'the stone which I had put'. Said R. Judah to him, 'If you know a better answer, say it.' The Judean then discoursed as follows.

'It is written, As for me, I shall behold thy face in righteousness; I shall be satisfied when I awake with thy likeness (Ps. XVII, 15). King David felt great affection and attachment for this stone: it was of it that he said, "The stone which the builders rejected is become the corner stone" (Ibid. CXVIII, 22). And whenever he desired to gaze at the reflection of the glory of his Master, he first took that stone in his hand and then he entered, as whoever wishes to appear before his Master can only do so through that stone, as it is written, "Herewith shall Aaron come into the holy place" (Lev. XVI, 3). It was David's boast that "As for me, I shall behold thy face in righteousness", and he exerted himself in every way to appear before Him on high in proper guise by means of that stone. Now, Abraham instituted morning prayer and taught the world the character of his Master, and made that hour a propitious one for prayer. Isaac instituted afternoon prayer (minhah) and taught the world that there is a supreme Judge who can either pardon or condemn the world. Jacob instituted evening prayer. And it was in reference to this prayer, which he instituted for the first time as a proper method of propitiation, that he said in his own praise,

[Note: The last four lines of the Hebrew text do not appear in our translation.]

Zohar: Bereshith, Section 1, Page 72b

"And this stone which I had put for a pillar", as up to that time no one had erected one like it. This is implied in the expression, "and he put it as a matsebah" (erection, upstanding), implying that he set up again something which had been prostrate. He also "poured oil on its head", thus doing more than anyone else to restore it.' R. Judah thereupon embraced the Judean, saying, 'You have all this knowledge, and yet you occupy yourself with commerce and neglect that which gives life eternal!' He answered, 'Times are pressing, and I have two sons at school, and I have to work to provide their food and payment for their tuition, so that they may continue diligently to study the Torah.' He then resumed his discourse, taking the text: "And Solomon sat upon the throne of David his father, and his kingdom was established firmly" (I Kings II, 12). He said: 'What great achievement, it may be asked, is here ascribed to Solomon? The truth is that he prepared the foundation stone and set over it the Holy of Holies, and for this his kingdom was established firmly.'

The stranger further said: 'It is written: "And I will look upon it (the rainbow) that I may remember the everlasting covenant." This means that God's desire is constantly for the bow, and that he who is not visible therein will not enter into the presence of his Master. The inner meaning of the words, "And I will look upon it", is to be found in the words, "and set a mark upon the foreheads, etc." (Ezek. IX, 4), so as to be clearly visible.' (According to others, the mark was symbolic of the holy mark in the flesh.) R. Judah said, 'This is assuredly so, but the rainbow that appears in the sky has a profound mystic significance, and when Israel will go forth from exile that rainbow is destined to be decked out in all the finery of its colours, like a bride who adorns herself for her husband.' The Judean said to him, 'This is what my father said to me when he was on the point of departing this world: "Do not expect the coming of the Messiah until the rainbow will appear decked out in resplendent colours which will illumine the world. Only then expect the Messiah." We learn this from the words, "And I will look upon it, that I may remember the everlasting covenant" (Gen. IX, 16). That is, at present the bow appears in dull colours, since it is only designed as a reminder that there shall be no return of the Flood; but at that time it will appear in its full panoply of colours as a bride does for her husband, and that will be "to remember the everlasting covenant"' The Holy One, blessed be He, will remember the covenant which is in exile and He will raise her from the dust, as it is written, "and they will seek the Lord their God and David their king" (Hos. III, 4); also, "But they shall serve the Lord their God, and David their king, whom I will raise unto them" (Jer. XXX, 9), i.e. raise from the dust, in accordance with the text: "I will raise up the tabernacle of David that is fallen" (Amos IX, 11). The "everlasting covenant" will thus be remembered to be raised from the dust. My father also said that it is for that reason that in Scripture the redemption of Israel and the remembrance of the rainbow are mentioned together, as it is written: "For as I have sworn that the waters of Noah should no more go over the earth, so have I sworn that I would not be wroth with thee, nor rebuke thee" (Is. LIV, 9).'

AND THE SONS OF NOAH THAT WENT FORTH FROM THE ARK WERE SHEM, AND HAM, AND JAPHETH. R. Eleazar asked why the Scripture inserts the words "who went forth from the ark". Did, then, Noah have other sons who did not go forth from the ark? R. Abba said: "Yes: the children whom his sons bore afterwards; and the Scripture points out that these did not go forth from the ark.' R. Simeon said: 'Had I been alive when the Holy One, blessed be He, gave mankind the book of Enoch and the book of Adam, I would have endeavoured to prevent their dissemination, because not all wise men read them with proper attention, and thus extract from them perverted ideas, such as lead men astray from the Most High to the worship of strange powers. Now, however, the wise who understand these things keep them secret, and thereby fortify themselves in the service of their Master.'

Zohar: Bereshith, Section 1, Page 73a

Of the three sons of Noah that went forth from the ark, Shem, Ham, and Japheth, Shem is symbolic of the right side, Ham of the left side, whilst Japheth represents the "purple", which is a mixture of the two. AND HAM WAS THE FATHER OF CANAAN. Ham represents the refuse and dross of the gold, the stirring and rousing of the unclean spirit of the ancient serpent. It is for that reason that he is designated the "father of Canaan", namely, of Canaan who brought curses on the world, of Canaan who was cursed, of Canaan who darkened the faces of mankind. For this reason, too, Ham is given a special mention in the words, "Ham, the father of Canaan", that is, the notorious world-darkener, whereas we are not told that Shem was the father of such-a-one, or that Japheth was the father of such-a-one. No sooner is Ham mentioned, than he is pointed to as the father of Canaan. Hence when Abraham came on the scene, it is written, "And Abraham passed through the land" (Gen. XII, 6), for this was before the establishment of the patriarchs and before the seed of Israel existed in the world, so that the land could not yet be designated by this honoured and holy name. Observe that when Israel were virtuous the land was called by their name, the Land of Israel; but when they were not worthy it was called by another name, to wit, the Land of Canaan. Hence it is written: AND HE SAID, CURSED BE CANAAN, A SERVANT OF SERVANTS SHALL HE BE UNTO HIS BRETHREN, for the reason that he brought curses on the world, in the same way as the serpent, against whom was pronounced the doom, "Cursed art thou among all cattle" (Gen. III, 14).

THESE THREE WERE THE SONS OF NOAH. By these was established the whole world, and also the higher symbolism. AND OF THESE WAS THE WHOLE EARTH OVERSPREAD. Herein is a mystical allusion to the three supernal colours. For when that river that flows perennially watered the Garden by the power of those three supernal influences, there spread forth those terrestrial colours here below, each combined with the others, which show that the glory of the Holy One, blessed be He, extends through all the heights and the depths, and that He is one above and below.

R. Eleazar said: 'These three colours are themselves displayed in all those who issue from the side of holiness, and their reflection falls upon all those who issue from the side of the other spirit. And if you ponder the mystery of grades, you will find how the colours radiate to all sides until they enter the lower sphere through those twenty-seven mystic channels which are the sides of the doors that stop up the abyss. All this is known to the adepts in mystic lore. Happy the portion of the righteous whom the Holy One delights to honour and to whom He reveals the sublime mysteries of wisdom. Of them it is written: "The counsel of the Lord is with them that fear Him" (Ps. XXV, 14).' R. Eleazar here quoted the verse: "O Lord, thou art my God, I will exalt thee, I will praise thy name, for thou hast done wonderful things, even counsels of old, in faithfulness and truth" (Is. XXV, 1). 'How greatly', he said, 'it behoves men to reflect on the glory of the Holy One, blessed be He, and to offer up songs of praise to His glory, for when one knows how to offer praise to his Master in the manner appropriate, the Holy One, blessed be He, accomplishes his will. Such a man, furthermore, causes an increase of blessings on high and below. He, therefore, who knows how to offer praise to his Master and to proclaim His unity is held in affection on high and is beloved below; the Holy One, blessed be He, is proud of him, and of him it is written: "And he said unto me, thou art my servant, Israel, in whom I will be glorified" (Is. XLIX, 3).'

AND NOAH THE HUSBANDMAN BEGAN AND PLANTED A VINEYARD. R. Judah and R. Yose differed as to the origin of this vine. One said that it came from the Garden of Eden and Noah now planted it here. The other said that it had been on the earth before the Flood and Noah had plucked it and now replanted it. On the same day it blossomed, ripened, and brought forth grapes. Noah then pressed out from them wine, drank of it and became drunken. R. Simeon said: 'There is a mystical allusion in this verse. When Noah began to probe into the sin of Adam, not for purpose of practising it but in order to understand it, and so warn the world against it, he pressed grapes in order to make researches into that vineyard. But when he reached that point he was "drunken and uncovered"–he lost his (mental) balance and uncovered the breach of the world which hitherto had been closed up. WITHIN HIS TENT. It is written oholoh (lit. her tent), an allusion to the idea contained in the passage, "And come not

Zohar: Bereshith, Section 1, Page 73b

nigh the door of her house" (Prov. V, 8), "her tent" implying the tent of that vineyard. The same explanation applies to the case of the sons of Aaron, who, we have been taught, were drunk from wine (when they sinned). Who then, gave them wine at that place to drink? And is it conceivable that they would dare to get drunk at such a time? But in reality the wine which made them drunk was this same wine of Noah, as it is written, "and they offered strange fire before the Lord" (Lev. X, 1), an analogous term to which is found in the passage, "That they may keep thee from the strange woman" (Prov. VII, 5): all these terms allude to one and the same thing. The same sense, then, underlies the verse, "And he drank of the wine and was drunken, and he was uncovered within his tent." This, as explained, was observed by Ham, the father of Canaan, and Canaan seized the opportunity to work his will by removing from that righteous man the mystical symbol of the covenant; for this, according to tradition, is what he did. Therefore Noah said, CURSED BE CANAAN. since through him the curse returned to the world. A SLAVE OF SLAVES HE SHALL BE: these words correspond to those addressed to the serpent: "cursed art thou from all cattle, etc." (Gen. III, 14). Hence, while all others will be saved in the world to come, he will not be saved; all others will obtain their freedom, but not he. This is a mystery known to the adepts in the ways and paths of the Torah.'

R. Simeon further discoursed, beginning with the verse: For I know my transgressions, and my sin is ever before me (Ps. LI, 5). He said: 'How much must a man be on his guard against sinning before the Holy One, blessed be He, for each sin committed by man is recorded on high, and is not blotted out save by much repentance, as it is said, "For though thou wash thee with nitre, and take thee much soap, yet thine iniquity is marked before me" (Jer. II, 22). For when a man commits a sin once before God, it leaves a mark, and when he repeats the same sin that mark is deepened, and after a third time it becomes a stain spreading from one side to the other, as expressed in the words, "thine iniquity is become a stain before me" (Ibid.). When David committed his great sin in taking Bath-Sheba, he thought that it would leave its mark forever, but the message came to him, "The Lord also hath put away thy sin, thou shalt not die" (II Sam. XII, 13); i.e. the stain has been removed.' R. Abba put this question to R. Simeon: 'Since we have been taught that Bath-Sheba was destined for King David from the day of the creation, how comes it that the Holy One, blessed be He, first gave her to Uriah the Hittite?' R. Simeon replied: 'Such is the way of the Holy One, blessed be He; although a woman is destined for a certain man, He first allows her to be the wife of another man until his time arrives. As soon as that time arrives, he departs from the world to make way for the other, although the Holy One, blessed be He, is loath to remove him from the world to make way for the other man before his time arrives. This is the inner reason why Bath-Sheba was given to Uriah first. Now reflect and you will find the reason for the Holy Land having been given to Canaan before Israel came there. You will find that the inner reason underlying the two is the same. Observe, further, that David, although he confessed his sin and repented, could not obliterate from his heart and mind the memory of the sins that he had committed, especially of that concerning Bath-Sheba, and was always apprehensive lest one of them would prove a stumbling-block to him in the hour of danger. Hence he never removed them from his thoughts. According to another interpretation, the words "For I know my transgressions" indicate his knowledge of the diverse grades to which the various sins of men are to be referred, while the words "and my sin" (hatathi=my failing) refer to the defect of the moon, which did not emerge from her impurity until the time of Solomon, when her light once more became whole, so that the world became firmly established and Israel dwelt secure, as it is written: "And Judah and Israel dwelt safely, every man under his vine and under his fig tree" (I Kings V, 5). Nevertheless, as David said, "My deficiency is ever before me", and that will not be obliterated from the world until the Messiah will come, as it is said: "And the unclean spirit I will cause to pass out from the earth" (Zech. XIII, 2).'

HE WAS A MIGHTY HUNTER BEFORE THE LORD; WHEREFORE IT IS SAID: LIKE NIMROD A MIGHTY HUNTER BEFORE THE LORD. Truly he was a man of might, because he was clad in the garments of Adam, and was able by means of them to lay snares for mankind and beguile them. R. Eleazar said: 'Nimrod used to entice people into idolatrous worship by means of those garments, which enabled him to conquer the world and proclaim himself its ruler, so that mankind offered him worship. He was called "Nimrod", for the reason that he rebelled (marad=rebel) against the most high King above, against the higher angels and against the lower angels.'

Zohar: Bereshith, Section 1, Page 74a

R. Simeon said: 'Our colleagues are acquainted with a profound mystery concerning these garments.'

AND THE WHOLE EARTH WAS OF ONE LANGUAGE AND OF ONE SPEECH. R. Simeon began his discourse with the verse: And the house in its being built, was built of stone made ready at the quarry; and there was neither hammer nor axe nor any tool of iron heard in the house in its being built (I Kings VI, 7). He said: The phrase "in its being built" (behibbonotho) implies self-building, as though without the hands of artisans. Were not, then, Solomon with all his workpeople engaged in the work of building? It was here as with the candlestick, in regard to which we read, "And thou shalt make... of beaten work will the candlestick be made" (Ex. XXV, 31). If the candlestick was to be made of itself, why say "thou shalt make it"? In reality it was made of itself, by a miracle. So soon as the artisans set their hands to the work, it showed them how to proceed in a manner quite novel to them, the reason being that the blessing of the Almighty rested on their hands; and similarly here, in the building of the Sanctuary. It was built of its own accord, though seemingly by the hands of the labourers; it showed the workers a design which guided their hands and from which they did not turn their eyes until the whole building of the house was completed. Further it says: "Of stone made ready at the quarry" (I Kings VI, 7). The word sh'lemah (made ready, complete) is written defectively, as though sh'lomoh (Solomon), for truly it was of Solomon; while massa (lit. transporting) implies that the hands of the workers were moved involuntarily, so that they did they knew not what. "And there was neither hammer nor axe nor any tool of iron heard in the house in its being built" (Ibid.), because the shamir (stone-cutting insect) performed all the splitting without any sound being heard. No cutting-tools were thus required, the whole work being accomplished by a miracle.' Said R. Simeon, 'How precious are the words of the Torah! Happy is the portion of him who occupies himself with them and knows how to follow the path of truth! The Scripture says, "And the house in its being built." When the Holy One, blessed be He, wills that His glory should be glorified, there issues from His thought a determination that it should spread forth; whereupon it spreads from the undiscoverable region of thought until it rests in garon (throat), a spot through which perennially flows the mystic force of the "spirit of life". When the thought, after its expansion, comes to rest in that place, it is called Elohim hayyim (living God). It then seeks to spread and disclose itself still further, and there issue from that spot fire, air, and water, all compounded together. There also emerges "Jacob, the perfect man", symbolic of a certain voice that issues and becomes audible. Thus the thought that was hitherto undisclosed and withdrawn in itself is now revealed through sound. In the further extension and disclosure of the thought, the voice strikes against the lips, and thus comes forth speech which is the culmination of the whole and in which the thought is completely disclosed. It is thus clear that all is composed of that undisclosed thought which was withdrawn into itself, and that the whole is one essence. When the expansion has reached that stage, and speech has been generated by the force of that voice, then "the house in its being built", i.e. throughout the whole process of its construction, "is of complete stones", as has been explained. The word "transported" means that the thought issues from within and commences to transport itself outside; it issues from above and commences to transport itself below. "And there was neither hammer nor axe nor any tool of iron": this alludes to the lower grades, which all depend upon the Thought, and which are not heard or admitted inside when the Thought ascends on high to draw fresh sustenance. When she does so, all of them rejoice and draw sustenance and are filled with blessings. At that time all worlds are sustained as one unity without any division whatever. After they have taken their several portions they all disperse, each to its side and to its assigned function.

Zohar: Bereshith, Section 1, Page 74b

Hence it says: "And the whole earth was of one language", and afterwards, "and it came to pass as they journeyed miquedem" (lit. from before), i.e. from that which is the starting-point of the world, "that they found a valley in the land of Shin'ar", for from there they spread out in all directions, and that spot is the starting-point of differentiation. It may be objected that differentiation started later, as we read, "a river went forth from Eden to water the garden, and from there it parted". The truth is that when they move from the first spot there is separation, and when they gather together to draw sustenance there is no separation, and when they journey again there is separation. Hence it is written, "And it came to pass when they journeyed from the East that they found a valley", as has been explained.'

AND THE WHOLE EARTH WAS OF ONE LANGUAGE AND ONE SPEECH, i.e. the world was still a unity with one single faith in the Holy One, blessed be He. BUT AFTERWARDS THEY JOURNEYED AWAY miquedem (lit. from before), that is, from the One who is before all, from the foot of the world, who was the object of universal faith. AND THEY FOUND A PLAIN, that is, they made a discovery, by means of which they shook off their faith in the Most High. So it is written of Nimrod: AND THE BEGINNING OF HIS KINGDOM WAS BABEL, this being the starting-point from which he commenced to attach himself to other powers. Similarly here, "they found a plain in the land of Shin'ar", a place in which they conceived the idea of forsaking the Supernal Power for another power.

AND THEY SAID: COME, LET US BUILD US A CITY, AND A TOWER, WITH ITS TOP IN HEAVEN, AND LET US MAKE US A NAME. R. Hiya began his discourse with the text: And the wicked are like the driven sea (Is. LVII, 20). 'When can the sea be said to be "driven"? When it becomes violently disturbed and sways this way and that and is driven from its bed; it is then like a drunken man, reeling and staggering and heaving up and down. "For it cannot rest, and its waters cast up mire and dirt" (Ibid.), i.e. it throws up all the dirt and foul matter of the sea on to the shore. So it is with the wicked who leave the straight path and reel and stagger in the crooked roads they have taken, like a man drunk with wine. And what is more, with every word which they utter in their rage there issues from their mouth filth and abomination so that they are utterly defiled.

Zohar: Bereshith, Section 1, Page 75a

See now, they said: "Come let us build a city, and a tower, with its top in heaven." Underlying these words there was a plan of rebellion against the Holy One, blessed be He. It was a foolish scheme, born out of the stupidity of their heart.' R. Abba said, 'Foolish they certainly were, but at the same time they had a crafty design to rid themselves of the Supreme Power and to transfer His glory to another. Throughout, there is an allusion to the mysteries of religion. Thus, the words "Come, let us build a city and a tower" mean that when they reached that plain, which signifies the "strange power", and there was revealed to them the place of its dominion, which extends particularly over "the fishes of the sea", they said, "Here is a place where the beings of the lower world can abide in comfort." At once they said: "Come, let us build a city, and a tower, and let us make us a name." This place, they said, shall be to us a centre of worship, and no other; so "let us build a city and a tower"; what need is there for us to go up to the regions on high where we cannot derive any enjoyment? Behold, here is a place all made ready for us. Further they said: AND LET US MAKE A NAME, that is, an object of worship, LEST WE BE SCATTERED ABROAD, i.e. to other grades and different quarters of the world.

AND THE LORD CAME DOWN TO SEE THE CITY AND THE TOWER. This is one of the ten occasions on which the Shekinah descended to earth. "To see" here means "to consider methods of punishment", as in the verse, "May the Lord see and judge" (Gen. XVI, 5). It is not written, "to see the people", but "to see the city and the tower". Why so? Because when the Holy One, blessed be He, sets out to execute judgement, He first surveys the upper ranks and then the lower ranks, and since this action of mankind affected also the regions on high, the first consideration was directed to those on high. This is implied in the words, "to see the city and the tower which the sons of man (Adam) built". Mankind are here called "sons of Adam", because it was Adam, the first man, who rebelled against his Master and brought death into the world. R. Simeon began his discourse with the verse: Thus

Zohar: Bereshith, Section 1, Page 75b

saith the Lord God: The gate of the inner court that looketh towards the east shall be shut the six working days; but on the Sabbath day it shall be opened, and in the day of the new moon it shall be opened (Ezek. XLVI, 1). He said: 'If this verse is attentively considered, it is found to contain an allusion with which we are familiar. The reason why the gate is to be shut on the six working days is in order that the profane should not make use of the sacred; "but on the Sabbath day it shall be opened and on the day of the new moon it shall be opened", since in this case the sacred makes use of the sacred, and so the moon comes then to form a junction with the sun. The reason why that gate is not to be opened on the six working days is because from them this lower world draws sustenance, and they have control of the whole world with the exception of the Land of Israel: that land cannot be touched by them because the gate is shut. But on the Sabbath day and on the day of the new moon they are removed from control because the gate is open, and the world is in festivity and derives its sustenance from there, and is not under any other power. But think not that the six days have the sole dominion, even when they are in control, for we are told that that gate "looketh towards the east", i.e. the Eternal; for the Eternal, even before they assumed control, had the world under His observation, only the gate is not to be opened, so that the world should not receive sustenance from the sacred source save on Sabbath and new moons. Indeed, all the days are attached to the Sabbath day, from which they draw their sustenance, and on which all the gates are opened, and rest is vouchsafed to all on high and below. Similarly here, THE LORD CAME DOWN TO SEE, i.e. He descended from the sacred to the profane, in order to survey what they had built and what steps they had taken to establish an idolatrous worship.'

R. Isaac was once studying with R. Simeon and put to him the question: 'How could these people have been so foolish as to raise a rebellion against the Holy One, blessed be He, and what is more, with such unanimity?' R. Simeon replied: 'That has already been explained, and the answer is indicated in the words, "And it came to pass when they journeyed miqedem" (from the Eternal), which means that they proceeded downwards, from above to below, from the Land of Israel to Babel. They said that that was just the right place to which to attach themselves, since there the divine chastisement could be successfully resisted. There, too, the whole world could obtain nourishment in abundance, for from the higher realm sustenance could only be procured with difficulty. And furthermore, they said, we will ascend into heaven and make war against it so as to prevent it bringing a flood on the world as before.'

AND THE LORD SAID: BEHOLD, THEY ARE ONE PEOPLE, AND THEY HAVE ALL ONE LANGUAGE, i.e. being united they may indeed succeed in their undertaking. Let, therefore, all the grades be dispersed, each in its own direction, and in this way mankind below will also be dispersed. Hence it is written: AND THE LORD SCATTERED THEM ABROAD FROM THENCE. Why was their language confounded? Because they all spoke the holy tongue, and this was of help to them. For in the utterance of prayer, it is Hebrew words which fully express the purpose of the heart, and thus help to the attainment of the desired goal; hence their tongue was confounded in order that they might not be able to express their desires in the holy tongue. Since the angels on high do not understand any language save the sacred language, therefore as soon as the language of the rebels was confounded they lost the source of their power. For whatever men utter below in the holy tongue all the hosts of heaven understand and take heed of, but any other language they do not understand. Hence as soon as the language of the builders was confounded THEY LEFT OFF TO BUILD THE CITY, since their strength was broken and they were unable to achieve their purpose. We read, "Blessed be the name of God from everlasting even unto everlasting; for wisdom and might are his" (Dan. II, 20). Truly His: for whenever the Holy One, blessed be He, allowed the deep mysteries of wisdom to be brought down into the world, mankind were corrupted by them and attempted to declare war on God. He gave supernal wisdom to Adam, but Adam utilised the wisdom disclosed to him

Zohar: Bereshith, Section 1, Page 76a

to familiarise himself with the lower grades also, until in the end he attached himself to the yetzer-hara (evil tempter), and the fountains of wisdom were closed to him. After he repented before his Master, parts of that wisdom were again revealed to him, in that same book, but through that same knowledge people came later on to provoke God. He gave wisdom to Noah, who, indeed, worshipped by means of it the Holy One, blessed be He, but afterwards "he drank of the wine and was drunken and uncovered", as already explained. He gave wisdom to Abraham, who by means of it served the Holy One, blessed be He, but then he gave birth to Ishmael, who provoked the Holy One, blessed be He. The same with Isaac, from whom Esau was born. As for Jacob, he married two sisters. He gave wisdom to Moses, of whom it is written: "He is trusted in all my house" (Num. XII, 7). There was none like Moses, a faithful servant, who was cognisant of all the grades, but whose heart was not seduced by any one of them from firm faith in the highest. He gave profound wisdom to Solomon, who called himself l'ithiel, l'ithiel v'ukhal (Prov. XXX, 1), as much as to say: "God is with me, and since wisdom is His, v'ukhal, I am able to do my own will." But afterwards "the Lord raised up an adversary for Solomon" (I Kings XI, 14). Thus we see that in virtue of the fragments which those people retained from that wisdom of the ancients, they provoked the Holy One, blessed be He, built a tower, and did various kinds of mischief, until they were scattered over the face of the earth, and there was no wisdom left with them for any purpose at all. But in the future the Holy One, blessed be He, will cause wisdom to be disseminated in the world, and the peoples will worship Him, as it is written: "And I will set my spirit within you" (Ezek. XXXVI, 27), but-in contrast with the generations of old, who used it for the ruin of the world-"I will cause you", the verse continues, "to walk in my statutes and ye shall keep mine ordinances, and do them" (Ibid.).

As R. Yose and R. Hiya were once walking together, R. Yose said: ʻLet us begin some discourse on the Torah, and evolve some new idea.ʼ R. Yose thereupon began with the verse: For the Lord thy God walketh in the midst of thy camp, to deliver thee, and to give up thine enemies before thee; therefore shall thy camp be holy, that he see no unseemly thing in thee, and turn away from thee (Deut. XXIII, 15). He said: ʻThe term for "walketh" is here mithhalekh, as in the passage, "walking (mithhalekh) in the garden towards the cool of the day" (Gen. III, 8) (in connection with Adam's eating of the forbidden tree). Mithhalekh is the term for the female, and corresponding to it for the male is the term mehalech. This is the same power that went in front of Israel whilst they were going through the wilderness, as it is written: "And the Lord went before them by day" (Ex. XIII, 21). It is this same power that goes in front of a man when he is on a journey, as it is written: "Righteousness shall go before him, and shall make his footsteps a way" (Ps. LXXXV, 14). It walks in front of a man when he is virtuous in order "to deliver thee and to give up thine enemies before thee", to wit, to rescue a man when journeying from the power of "the other one". Hence it is incumbent on a man to guard himself against sin and to purify himself. How purify himself? In the manner indicated in the words, "therefore shall thy camp be holy". The word qadosh (holy) here is singular, which shows that by the word "camp" we may understand the members of which the body is composed; these are "thy camp" which is to be "holy". By the term "unseemly thing" is indicated indecency, which is a thing most hateful to the Holy One, blessed be He. Further, the term dabar (thing, lit. word) alludes to the obscene word by which sinners besmirch and befoul themselves. Why all this? Because "He walketh before thee". If thou be remiss in regard to this, He will immediately "turn away from thee". Now, since we are walking along before Him in the road, let us occupy ourselves with words of the Torah. For when the Torah forms a crown over a man's head, the Shekinah does not depart from him.ʼ

R. Hiya then discoursed as follows: ʻIt is written: "And the Lord said: Behold they are one people, and they have all one language"ʼ After this we read: "And it came to pass as they journeyed miqedem." The term miqedem signifies "away from the Ancient One (qadmon) of the world". "That they found." We should have expected "saw"; but the word "found" is used to indicate that they found remnants of the secret wisdom that had been left there by the generation of the Flood, and with that they made their attempt to provoke the Holy One, blessed be He. As they said,

Zohar: Bereshith, Section 1, Page 76b

so they did. Note what is written, "Behold, they are one people and they have all one language." Being of one mind, of one will, and speaking one language, "nothing will be withholden from them which they purpose to do". But, said God, I know what to do; I will confound for them the grades on high and their language below, and thus their work will stop. Now, seeing that, because they were all of one mind and one will and spoke the holy tongue, it is written of them "nothing will be withholden from them which they purpose to do", and the supernal judgement was powerless against them, how much more must this apply to us or any other of the companions who are occupied in the study of the Torah!' R. Yose said: 'From here we learn that quarrelsome folk soon come to grief. For we see here that as long as the peoples of the world lived in harmony, being of one mind and one will, although they rebelled against the Holy One, blessed be He, the supernal judgement could not touch them; but as soon as they were divided, "the Lord scattered them abroad". Of the world to come, however, it is written: "For then will I turn to the peoples a pure language, that they may all call upon the name of the Lord, to serve him with one consent" (Zeph. III, 9); also: "And the Lord shall be King over all the earth; in that day shall the Lord be one, and his name one" (Zech. XIV, 9). Blessed be the Lord forever. Amen and Amen!'

LECH LECHA

R. Abba introduced this portion with a discourse on the text: Hearken to me, ye obstinate of heart who are far from righteousness (Is. XLVI, 12). He said: 'How obstinate is the heart of sinners who see the paths and ways of the Torah and pay no heed to them, but harden their hearts and do not return in repentance to their Master, wherefore they are called "obstinate of heart". Also "far from righteousness", because they keep themselves far from the Torah. R. Hizkiah says, that it is because they keep themselves far from God; they refuse to draw near to God and therefore they are far from righteousness. And because they are far from righteousness, therefore they are far from peace, and they have no peace, as it is written. "There is no peace, saith the Lord, unto the wicked" (Is. XLVIII, 22). The reason is that they are far from righteousness. See now, Abraham sought to draw near to God, and he succeeded. So it is written, "Thou didst love righteousness and hate wickedness" (Ps. XLV, 8), and it is further written, "Abraham who loves me" (Is. XLI, 8), i.e. Abram is said to have "loved God" because he loved righteousness; this was Abram's love of God, in which he excelled

Zohar: Bereshith, Section 1, Page 77a

all his contemporaries, who were obstinate of heart and far from righteousness, as has been said.'

R. Yose opened with the text: How amiable are thy tabernacles, O Lord of Hosts (Ps. LXXXIV, 2). He said: 'It behoves men to consider well the importance of the service of the Holy One, blessed be He. For the mass of mankind do not know or reflect what it is that keeps the world or themselves in existence. For when God created the world, He made the heavens of fire and water mingled together but not compact, and afterwards they were made compact and firm by a divine spirit. From there God planted forth the world to rest upon supports, which themselves are kept up only by that spirit. When that spirit departs they all quiver and shake and the world trembles, as it is written, "Who shaketh the earth out of her place and the pillars thereof tremble" (Job IX, 6). The whole is based upon the Torah. Thus when Israel devotes itself to the Torah the world is firmly established and they are secure and the supports are firmly fixed in their places. See now, at the moment when midnight arrives and the Holy One, blessed be He, enters the Garden of Eden to disport Himself with the righteous, all the trees in the Garden sing praises before Him, as it is written, "Then sing the trees of the wood for joy before the Lord" (I Chron. XVI, 33). A herald proclaimeth lustily: "To you we speak, exalted holy ones; who is there among you whose ears are quick to hear and whose eyes are open to see and whose heart is alert to perceive, what time the spirit of all spirits culls the sweet effluence of the inner soul, and a voice goes forth from there saying, Disperse, ye hosts, to the four corners of the world?" Then

One mounts to one side.

One descends on that side.

One enters between the two.

Two crown themselves with a third.

Three enter into one.

One produces various colours.

Six of them descend on one side and six of them on the other.

Six enter into twelve.

Twelve bestir themselves to form twenty-two.

Six are comprised in ten.

Ten are fixed in one.

Woe to those that sleep with eyes fast closed and do not know or consider how they will arise in the Day of Judgement; for reckoning is exacted

Zohar: Bereshith, Section 1, Page 77b

when the body is defiled, and the soul flits over the face of the transparent ether, now up and now down, and if the gates are not opened it is tossed about like a stone from the sling. Woe to them! Who shall plead for them? For they shall not be admitted to this joyaunce, among the delightful habitations of the righteous their places shall be missing, they shall be delivered into the hands of Duma, they shall descend and not ascend. Of them it is written, "As the cloud is consumed and vanisheth away, so he that goeth down to Sheol shall come up no more" (Job VII, 9). At that moment a certain flash springs forth from the side of the North and strikes the four quarters of the world and comes down and alights between the wings of the cock, which is thereby awakened and begins to crow. But none are stirred save those truly pious ones who rise and remain awake and study the Torah, and then the Holy One, blessed be He, and all the righteous in the Garden of Eden listen to their voices, as it is written, "Thou that dwellest in the gardens, the companions hearken for thy voice, cause me to hear it" (S. S. VIII, 13).

AND THE LORD SAID TO ABRAM. Just before this it is written, "And Haran died in the presence of Terah his father" (Gen. XI, 28). The connection is as follows. Up to that time no one had ever died in the lifetime of his father. Haran, however, was killed at the time when Abram was cast into the furnace. Then it says, "And Terah took Abram his son and Lot the son of Haran, etc.... and they went forth with them from Ur of the Chaldees." We should expect "and they went forth with him", referring to Terah; why, then, does it say "with them"? The reason is that Terah and Lot went forth with Abram and Sara, who led the way in departing from that sinful district; for when Terah saw that Abram was rescued from the fire, he began to be guided by Abram, and therefore we read, "and they went forth with them", i.e. Terah and Lot with Abram and Sara. Also it was "to go into the land of Canaan", where they wanted to go. We learn further from this text that whoever makes an effort to purify himself receives assistance from above. For no sooner is it written, "to go to the land of Canaan" than we read "and God said to Abram, Get thee forth"; this message was not given to him until he made the first move himself. For the upper world is not stirred to act until an impulse is given from the lower world. The prototype of this process is that the blackish light is not caught up by the white light until it has first itself begun to mount; [Tr. note: v. p. 163] but when it does so, forthwith the white light rests upon it, and therefore it is written, "O Lord, keep not thou silence, hold not thy peace and be not still, O God" (Ps. LXXXIII, 2), in order that the white light may never be withheld from the world. So, too, it says, "Ye that are the Lord's remembrancers, keep not silence" (Is. LXII, 6), in order to give the impulse from below for the influence to descend from the upper world. Similarly the prophetic spirit rests upon man only when he has first bestirred himself to receive it. So here, too, when once Abram and his family had left Ur of the Chaldees, then God said to him, "Get thee forth"; the word "thee" here, says R. Eleazar, means "for thine own advantage, to prepare thyself, to perfect thy degree". "Get thee forth": that is, it is not fitting for thee to remain here among these sinners. The real truth of the matter is this.

Zohar: Bereshith, Section 1, Page 78a

God inspired Abram with a spirit of wisdom so that he was able to discover by means of certain tests the characters of all the inhabited countries of the world. He surveyed them and weighed them in the balance, and discovered the (heavenly) powers to which each is entrusted. When he came to the central point of the inhabited world he tried to weigh it, but obtained no response. He tried to find the power to which it was entrusted, but could not grasp it, though he weighed again and again. He noted that from that point the whole world was planted out, and he once more tested and weighed and found that the upper power in charge of it was one which could not be gauged, that it was recondite and hidden, and not like the (powers in charge of) the outlying parts of the inhabited world. He once more reflected, and came to the conclusion that as the whole world had been planted out in all directions from that point in the centre, so the power in charge of it was the one from which issued all the powers in charge of the other quarters of the world and to which they were all attached: hence "they went forth with them from Ur of the Chaldees to go to the land of Canaan". He then once more reflected and weighed in the balance and tested to find out the real truth about that place, but he could not get to the root of it. He felt himself baffled by the obscurity which surrounded it, and therefore "they came to Haran and abode there". The reason, as we have seen, is that Abraham was able to test all the upper powers that rule the world in all the quarters of the inhabited section, and did actually test them and find out which of the guiding powers among the stars and constellations had sway over which, and he weighed successfully all the inhabited parts of the globe. But when he came to this place he was met with a baffling obscurity which he could not penetrate. When God, however, perceived his efforts and his desire, He straightway revealed Himself to him and said: GET THEE FORTH, so as to know thyself and prepare thyself, FROM THY LAND: from that side of the inhabited world to which thou wast hitherto attached, AND FROM THY KINDRED, from that wisdom wherewith thou didst cast thy horoscope, noting the hour and second of thy birth and the star that was then in the ascendant, AND FROM THY FATHER'S HOUSE, that thou shouldst not heed thy father's house, even if thou couldst hope in virtue of thy father's house for some prosperity in this world;

therefore get thee gone from this wisdom and from this consideration. That this explanation is right may be proved thus. They had left Ur of the Chaldees and were in Haran. Why, then, should God say to Abram, "Get thee forth from thy land and from thy kindred"? It must therefore be as we have explained.TO THE LAND WHICH I SHALL SHOW THEE: i.e. I shall show thee that which thou wast not able to discover; the power of that land so recondite and obscure.

AND I SHALL MAKE THEE A GREAT NATION, ETC. "I shall make thee", in compensation for "get thee gone"; AND I SHALL BLESS THEE, in compensation for "from my land"; AND I WILL MAKE GREAT THY NAME, in compensation for 'and from thy kindred'; AND BE A BLESSING, in compensation for "and from thy father's house". R. Simeon said: "I shall make thee a great nation"; from the side of the Right; "and I shall bless thee", from the side of the Left; "and I shall make great thy name", from the realm of the Centre; "and be thou a blessing", from the side of the Land of Israel. Here we have an allusion to the throne resting on four supports, all of which were comprised in Abram. From this point blessings are transmitted to others also, who are sustained from here, as it is written, I SHALL BLESS THEM THAT BLESS THEE,

Zohar: Bereshith, Section 1, Page 78b

AND CURSE THEM THAT CURSE THEE, AND ALL THE FAMILIES OF THE EARTH SHALL BE BLESSED IN THEE. R. Eleazar was sitting one day before his father, R. Simeon, and with him were R. Judah and R. Isaac and R. Hizkiah. Said R. Eleazar to R. Simeon: In reference to this verse, GET THEE FORTH FROM THY LAND AND FROM THY KINDRED, since they all went forth, why was not Abram told that they should go? For though Terah was an idolater, yet since he had the good impulse to go forth with Abram, and since, as we know, God delights in the repentance of sinners, and Terah actually began the journey, why is it not written "get ye forth"? Why was it said to Abram alone "get thee forth"? R. Simeon replied: If you think that Terah left Ur of the Chaldees in order to repent of his past life, you are mistaken. The truth is that he was running away for his life, as his fellow-countrymen wanted to kill him. For when they saw that Abram was delivered (from the fiery furnace) they said to Terah, "It is you who misled us with those idols of yours", and it was through fear of them that Terah left. When he reached Haran he did not go any further, as it is written, "And Abram went as the Lord had said to him, and Lot went with him", but Terah is not mentioned. R. Simeon expounded in this connection the text, "And from the wicked their light is withholden, and the high arm is broken" (Job XXXVIII, 15). The words "and from the wicked their light is withholden", he said, can be referred to Nimrod and his contemporaries, from whom Abram, who was their light, departed. Or we may refer them to Terah and his household, whose light was Abram. It does not say "light", but "their light", viz. the light that was with them. "The high arm is broken" refers to Nimrod, who led astray the whole of mankind. Therefore it is written lech lecha (lit. go for thyself), to give light to thyself and to all that shall follow thee from now onwards. R. Simeon further discoursed on the text, "Now they see not the light; it is bright in the skies, and a wind passeth and cleanseth them" (Job XXXVII, 21). "Now they see not the light", i.e. Abram's family saw not the light when God said to Abram, "Get thee forth from thy land and from thy kindred and from thy father's house". "It is bright in the skies" means that God willed to make Abram cleave to that supernal light and to shine there. "A wind passeth and cleanseth them": because subsequently Terah and all his household repented, as it is said, "and the souls which they had saved (lit. made) in Haran", referring to Terah's household, and further, "and thou shalt come to thy fathers in peace" (Gen. XV, 15), which shows that Terah joined Abram.

SO ABRAM WENT AS THE LORD HAD SPOKEN TO HIM, ETC. Said R. Eleazar: 'It is not written "and Abram went forth", but simply "Abram went"; the first step was "going forth", as it is written, "and they went forth (vayez'u) from Ur of the Chaldees" (Gen. XI, 31), but the second step was "going", corresponding to God's command "Go (lech) thou" (Ibid. XII, 1). AS THE LORD HAD SPOKEN TO HIM: i.e. because he had received all those promises. AND LOT WENT WITH HIM: i.e. he attached himself to him to learn his ways, and in spite of this he did not learn them too well.' Said R. Eleazar: 'Happy are the righteous who learn the ways of the Holy One, blessed be He, to walk in them and to go in fear of that Day of Judgement when man will be called to account before God.' To illustrate this, R. Eleazar expounded the text: "By his hand every man sealeth, that all men may acknowledge their works" (Job. XXXVII, 7). He said:

Zohar: Bereshith, Section 1, Page 79a

'On the day when man's time arrives to depart from the world, when the body is broken and the soul seeks to leave it, on that day man is privileged to see things that he was not permitted to see before, when the body was in full vigour. Three messengers stand over him and take an account of his life and of all that he has done in this world, and he admits all with his mouth and signs the account with his hand as it is written, "every man sealeth with his hand": the whole account is signed with his hand so that he should be judged in the next world for all his actions, former and later, old and new, not one of them is forgotten (as it is written, "that every man should acknowledge his works"); and for all the deeds which he committed with his body and his spirit in this world he gives an account with his body and spirit before he leaves the world. For just as sinners are stiff-necked in this world, so they are stiff-necked even at the moment when they are on the point of departing from the world. Happy, therefore, is the man who learns in this world the ways of God to walk in them. But sinners, even though they observe the righteous, are too stiffnecked to learn from them. Therefore it behoves the righteous to importune them and, even though the sinner be stiffnecked, not to relax his hold of him, for if he let him go, he may depart and destroy the world. We see this from the case of Gehazi when driven out by Elisha. So, too, with Lot: as long as Abram was with him, he did not associate with the wicked, but as soon as he left him, what do we find? "So Lot chose him all the plain of Jordan"; and further, "and he moved his tent as far as Sodom", the inhabitants of which "were wicked and sinners against the Lord exceedingly". Said R. Abba to R. Eleazar, 'With reference to your observation that the text says "Abraham went", and not "went forth", what do you make of the end of the verse which says "when he went forth from Haran"?' Said R. Eleazar: 'The words "from Haran" are important; the journey was in the first instance a "going forth" from the land of his kindred. AND ABRAM TOOK SARAI HIS WIFE. The word "took" signifies that he pleaded with her and persuaded her. For a man is not permitted to take his wife with him to another country without her consent. The word "take" is used in a similar sense in the texts "Take Aaron" (Num. XX, 25), and "Take the Levites" (Ibid. III, 45). So Abram spoke persuasively to Sarai, pointing out to her how wicked were the ways of their contemporaries. Further, Abram took LOT HIS BROTHER'S SON. Abram s reason for taking Lot with him was that he foresaw through the Holy Spirit that David was destined to issue from him. AND THE SOULS THAT THEY HAD GOTTEN IN HARAN: these were the male and female proselytes whose souls they had saved. Abram converted the men and Sarai the women, and therefore they are spoken of as if they had made them.' Said R. Abba: 'If so, they must have been a great crowd, if you say that they all went with him.' Said R. Eleazar: 'That is so; and therefore the whole company that went with him were called

Zohar: Bereshith, Section 1, Page 79b

"the people of the God of Abraham", and he travelled through the land without fear, as it is written, "And Abram passed through the land".' Said R. Abba to him: 'I interpret differently, viz. that the particle eth here signifies the augmentation of his merit by that of the souls that went with him, since one who puts another in the path of righteousness ever reaps benefit from his merit also. So it was the merit of those souls which were "made" in Haran that accompanied Abram.'

GET THEE FORTH. R. Simeon said: What is the reason that the first communion which God held with Abraham commenced with the words "Get thee forth" (lech lecha)? It is that the numerical value of the letters of the words lech lecha is a hundred, and hence they contained a hint to him that he would beget a son at the age of a hundred. See now, whatever God does upon the earth has some inner and recondite purpose. Abram was not cleaving to God as closely as he should have done, and therefore God said to him, "Get thee forth", alluding thereby to the place where he would be able to draw near to God, which was the first grade for entering before God; hence "get thee forth". Abram could not attain to this grade until he had entered the promised land; but there he was destined to attain it. Similarly with David, of whom it is written, "And David inquired of the Lord saying, Shall I go up into any of the cities of Judah? And the Lord said unto him, Go up. And David said, Whither shall I go up? And he said, Unto Hebron." (II Sam. II, 1). Seeing that Saul was dead and the kingship belonged of right to David, why was he not at once declared king over all Israel? Here again there was an inner purpose: David was not qualified to become king until he had attached himself to the patriarchs who were buried in Hebron, and therefore he stayed there seven years in order to qualify himself completely for the kingship. Thus all was done with an inner purpose, and in order that there should be no flaw in his kingship. Similarly Abram did not enter into the covenant of God until he entered the land. Observe that the text says "And Abram passed through the land", where we should have expected "went through". We have here an allusion to the holy name of seventy-two letters with which the world is sealed, all of which are in this name. We read here "and he passed ", and in another place we find "And the Lord passed by before him and proclaimed" (Ex. XXXIV, 6). In the book of the venerable R. Yesa we find: It is written here "And Abram passed through the land", and in another place it says "I will make all my goodness pass before thee" (Ex. XXXIII, 19), this being an allusion to the holiness of the land which emanates from a heavenly source.

UNTO THE PLACE OF SHECHEM, UNTO THE OAK OF MORETH, i.e. from one sphere to the other, as befitted. AND THE CANAANITE WAS THEN IN THE LAND. This confirms what has previously been said, that up to that time the wicked serpent that was cursed and brought curses on the world held sway over the land, as it is written, "Cursed is Canaan, a servant of servants shall he be unto his brethren" (Gen. IX, 25), and of the serpent, "Cursed art thou above all cattle" (Gen. III, 14). It was in that land that Abram drew near to God. For it is written here AND THE LORD APPEARED UNTO ABRAM: here was revealed to him what

Zohar: Bereshith, Section 1, Page 80a

he could not previously find out, the hidden force that ruled over the (holy) land, and so HE BUILT THERE AN ALTAR TO THE LORD WHO APPEARED TO HIM. The words "who appeared to him", which seem to be superfluous, indicate that here was revealed to him that grade which rules over the land, and that he entered into it and was confirmed in it.

AND HE REMOVED FROM THENCE UNTO THE MOUNTAIN: The word ha-harah (to the mountain) can be rendered "to the mountain of he", implying that he now became acquainted with this and with all the grades planted there. AND PITCHED HIS TENT: here, again, the letter he in the word aholoh (his tent) indicates that he purified himself and acknowledged the kingship of heaven in all the grades attached to it. He acquired the certainty that God rules over all, and so he built an altar. There were, in fact, two altars, because here it was revealed to him that God is ruler over all, and he became acquainted with the higher wisdom, which he had not known previously. He therefore built two altars, one for the grade (of the Godhead) which was already known to him, and one for the grade which was still concealed. This can be seen from the text: it first says "And he built there an altar to the Lord who appeared to him", and afterwards it says "and he built an altar to the Lord", simply-with an allusion to the higher wisdom. Thus Abram proceeded from grade to grade until he reached his own rightful grade, as it is written, "And Abram journeyed, going on still toward the South", the South (typifying wisdom) being the allotted portion of Abram, and there he finally fixed himself.

AND THERE WAS A FAMINE IN THE LAND: because up to now the power in charge of the land had not endowed the land with strength to produce food, since as yet it (the land) had not attained its complete development. So, seeing that the power in charge of the land was not endowing it with its rightful force and energy, ABRAM WENT DOWN TO EGYPT TO SOJOURN THERE. How did Abram know that the land was still defective? Because it was said to him, UNTO THY SEED WILL I GIVE THIS LAND. From this Abram knew that the land would not be invested with its appropriate holiness save through the grades of holiness which would be exhibited by his offspring.

AND ABRAM WENT DOWN TO EGYPT TO SOJOURN THERE. Why to Egypt? Because it is compared to the Garden of the Lord, as it is written, "Like the garden of the Lord, like the land of Egypt". For there a certain stream (from the Garden) which is on the right descends and flows, as it is written, "The name of the one was Pishon, that it is which compasseth the whole land of Havilah where there is gold" (Gen. II, 11). When Abram knew God and became perfect in faith, he sought to acquaint himself with all those grades (of wisdom) which are attached to the lower world, and since Egypt derived from the Right, he went down to Egypt. (We remark here that famine comes only when mercy ceases to temper justice.)

NOW IT CAME TO PASS THAT WHEN HE WAS COME NEAR TO ENTER INTO EGYPT. The word hikrib (came near) literally means "brought near"; as much as to say that he brought himself fittingly near to God. TO ENTER INTO EGYPT: i.e. to examine those other (worldly) grades so as to know how to avoid them and to shun the ways of the Egyptians. R. Judah said: 'Consider this. Because Abram went down to Egypt without first obtaining God's consent (for nowhere is it written that God told Abram to go down to Egypt), therefore his descendants were enslaved to the Egyptians four hundred years.' All that night he was filled with anxiety concerning Sarai, AND HE SAID TO SARAI HIS WIFE, BEHOLD NOW I KNOW THAT THOU ART A FAIR WOMAN TO LOOK UPON. Did he then not know it before? This confirms what we have learnt, that up to that time Abram had never looked closely at the features of Sarai on account of the excessive modesty which ruled their intercourse, but when he approached Egypt they were disclosed, and he saw how fair she was. According to another explanation, he knew it through the fact that, contrary to the usual experience, she looked as beautiful as ever after the fatigues of the journey. Another explanation is that Abram said so because he saw with her the Shekinah. It was on this account that Abram made bold to say subsequently, "she is my sister", with a double meaning: one literal, the other figurative, as in the words "say to Wisdom, thou art my sister" (Prov. VII, 4). SAY NOW THOU ART MY SISTER. R. Yesa said: 'Abram knew that all the Egyptians were full of lewdness. It may therefore

Zohar: Bereshith, Section 1, Page 82a

seem surprising that he was not apprehensive for his wife and that he did not turn back without entering the country. But the truth is that he saw with her the Shekinah and was therefore confident. THAT IT MAY BE WELL WITH ME FOR THY SAKE: these words were addressed to the Shekinah, as if to say: "that God may entreat me well for thy sake. AND THAT MY SOUL MAY LIVE BECAUSE OF THEE: because through this (the Shekinah) man ascends and becomes privileged to enter on the path of life.'

NOW IT CAME TO PASS THAT WHEN ABRAM WAS COME TO EGYPT THE EGYPTIANS BEHELD THE WOMAN THAT SHE WAS VERY FAIR. R. Judah said: He brought her in a box, and they opened it to levy duty. When it was opened a light like that of the sun shone forth, as it says "that she was very fair". The word "very" indicates that they saw in the box another figure; for when they took her out, they saw a figure in the box as before. Hence the Scripture repeats, AND THE PRINCES OF PHARAOH SAW HER, and on this account THEY PRAISED HER TO PHARAOH.' R. Isaac said: 'Woe to the sinners of the world who do not know and do not observe the work of the Holy One, blessed be He, nor do they reflect that all which takes place in the world is from God, who knows from the outset what will be at the end, as it is written, "declaring the end from the beginning" (Is. XLVI, 10). He looks ahead and lays a train now for developments in the distant future. Thus had not Sarai been taken to Pharaoh, he would not have been plagued, and it was his castigation which caused the subsequent castigation of the Egyptians. The word "great" is applied here to the plagues inflicted on Pharaoh and also to the "signs and wonders which God showed upon Egypt" (Deut. VI, 22), to indicate that here, as there, were ten plagues, and that just as God performed wonders for Israel by night, so He performed wonders for Sarai by night.' R. Yose expounded the text: Thou, O Lord, art a shield about me, my glory and the lifter up of mine head (Ps. III, 4). He said: 'What David meant was: "though the whole world should come to make war on me, thou, O Lord, art a shield about me". David further said to God: "Sovereign of the Universe, wherefore do not the Israelites conclude one of their blessings with my name as they do with the name of Abraham, [Tr. note: The first blessing of the Amidah.] of whom it is written 'I am thy shield' (Gen. XV, 1)?" God replied: "Abraham I have already tried and tested and found to be wholly steadfast." Said David: "If so, 'examine me, O Lord, and prove me, try my reins and my heart' (Ps. XXVI, 2)." When he sinned in the matter of Bathsheba, David remembered what he had said, and he exclaimed "'Thou hast proved mine heart, thou hast visited me in the night, thou hast tried me and hast not found, my thoughts should not have passed my mouth' (Ps. XVII, 3). I said, Examine me, O Lord, and prove me, and thou hast proved my heart; I said, Try my reins, and thou hast tried me; but thou hast not found me as I should be; would that what was in my mind had not passed my lips." (And with all this the Israelites do conclude a blessing with his name. [Tr. note: The third blessing after the Haftarah.]) Therefore David said: "'Thou, O Lord, art a shield about me, my glory and the lifter up of my head': this grade assuredly is my glory with which I am crowned." '

AND PHARAOH GAVE MEN CHARGE CONCERNING HIM, AND THEY SENT HIM ON HIS WAY. Assuredly God is a shield to the righteous to save them from falling into the power of men, and so God shielded Abram that the Egyptians should not have power to harm him and his wife. For the Shekinah did not leave Sarai all that night. When Pharaoh tried to approach her, the angel came and smote him. Whenever Sarai said "smite", he smote, and meanwhile Abram firmly trusted in God that He would allow no harm to come to Sarai, as it is written, "the righteous are bold as a lion" (Prov. XXVIII, 1). This is one of the trials which Abram endured without complaining against God. R. Isaac said that God purposely refrained from telling Abram to go down to Egypt, and allowed him to go of his own accord, in order that people might not be able to say that after making him go there He brought trouble on him through his wife. R. Isaac here expounded the text The righteous shall flourish like the palm tree, he shall grow like the cedar in Lebanon (Ps. XCII, 13). 'Why is the righteous man compared to a palm tree? Because just as, if a palm tree is cut down, it takes a long time for one to grow again, so if the world loses a righteous man, it is a long time before another arises in his place. Further, just as a palm tree does not grow unless the male be accompanied by the female, so the righteous cannot flourish save when they are male and female together, like Abram and Sarai. Again, "he shall grow like a cedar in Lebanon": just as a cedar is pre-eminent and all can sit under it, so the righteous man is pre-eminent and all sit under him. The world is supported upon one righteous one, as it is written, "the righteous is the foundation of the world" (Prov. X, 25).' Said R' Judah, 'Is it not a dictum of the Rabbis that the world rests on seven supports, as it is written, "Wisdom hath hewn out her seven pillars" (Prov. IX, 1)?' R. Yose replied: 'That is so, but those others depend on one

Zohar: Bereshith, Section 1, Page 82b

who is the real support of the world. This is the Zaddik who waters and refreshes the world and feedeth all, and of whom it is written, "Say of the Zaddik that he is good, for (through him) they eat of the fruit of their works" (Is. III, 10), and again, "The Lord is good to all and his tender mercies are over all his works" (Ps. CXLV, 9).'

R. Isaac said: 'The Scripture tells us that "a river went forth from Eden to water the garden" (Gen. II, 10). It is this river which is the support upon which the world rests. It waters the Garden and causes it to bear fruits which spring up and blossom in the world, and which uphold the world and make possible the study of the Torah. What are these fruits? They are the souls of the righteous which are the fruit of God's handiwork. Therefore every night the souls of the righteous mount on high, and at the hour of midnight the Holy One, blessed be He, comes to the Garden of Eden to disport Himself with them. With which of them? R. Yose said, with all: both with those whose abode is in the other world and with those who are still in their dwellings in this world-with all of them God disports Himself at midnight. For the world on high requires to be stirred by the impulse of the lower world, and so when the souls of the righteous leave this world and mount on high, they all clothe themselves with a supernal light, with a resplendent figure, and God disports Himself with them and delights in them, since they are the fruit of His handiwork, and for this reason Israel who are possessed of holy souls are called sons to the Holy One, blessed be He, as it is written, "Ye are sons to the Lord your God" (Deut. XIV, 1), that is, the fruit of His handiwork.' Said R. Yesa, 'You say that God disports Himself also with the souls in this world: how is this?' He answered, 'At midnight all the truly righteous arise to read the Torah and to sing psalms, and we have learnt that the Holy One, blessed be He, and all the righteous in the Garden of Eden listen to their voices, and in consequence a certain grace is imparted to them by day; so it is written, "The Lord will command his grace in the day-time, and in the night his song shall be with me" (Ps. XLII, 9). Hence it is that the praises which are sung at night constitute the most perfect praise. So when God was slaying the first-born in Egypt, the Israelites in their houses were singing praises and psalms to Him. See now, King David too used to get up in the middle of the night, as it is written, "At midnight I will rise to give thanks to thee" (Ps. CXIX, 62). He did not remain sitting or lying in his bed, but he literally rose and stood up to compose psalms and praises. Therefore it is that King David lives forever, and even in the days of the King Messiah he will be king, according to the dictum: "If the King Messiah will be from the living, David will be his name, and if he will be from the dead, David will be his name. "He, as it were, awoke the dawn, as it is written, "Awake, my glory, awake, psaltery and harp; I myself will awake right early" (Ps. LVII, 9).

115

In the night when Sarai was with Pharaoh, the angels came to sing praises before God, but God said to them, "Go all of you, and deal heavy blows on Egypt, in anticipation of what I intend to do subsequently"; hence it is written, "And the Lord smote Pharaoh with great plagues." Then, PHARAOH CALLED ABRAM, ETC. What gave him this idea, seeing that God did not say anything to him as He did later to Abimelech, as when He said, "And now restore the man's wife, for he is a prophet", etc. (Gen. XX, 7)?' Said R. Isaac, 'The answer is contained in the words BECAUSE OF SARAI ABRAM'S WIFE: the angels as they smote him said "this blow is because of Sarai Abram's wife" and no more, and then he knew that she was Abram's wife, and straightway "Pharaoh called Abram and said, etc." AND PHARAOH GAVE MEN CHARGE CONCERNING HIM: why so? In order that no man should come near to hurt them. AND THEY BROUGHT HIM ON THE WAY: i.e. they conducted him through the land of Egypt. Said God to him: So art thou destined to do to his descendants: thou shalt conduct them from thy land, as it is written, "And it came to pass when Pharaoh let go (beshallach, lit. escorted) the people" (Ex. XIII, 17).' R. Abba said: 'All this happened to Abram and he had to go through all this only in order that he and Sarai might acquire a great name in the world.

Zohar: Bereshith, Section 1, Page 83a

For even in Egypt, a country of magicians from whom no man could escape, Abram distinguished himself, and he raised himself there to a higher eminence, as it is written, AND ABRAM WENT UP OUT OF EGYPT. To where did he ascend? INTO THE SOUTH.' Said R. Simeon: 'Observe that these words have an inner meaning, and indicate to us that Abram went down to the "lower degrees" in Egypt, and probed them to the bottom, but clave not to them and returned unto his Master. He was not like Adam, who, when he descended to a certain grade, was enticed by the serpent and brought death upon the world; nor was he like Noah, who, when he descended to a certain grade, was enticed and "drank of the wine and became drunk and was uncovered in the midst of his tent" (Gen. IX, 21). Unlike them, Abram came up again and returned to his place, to the upper grade to which he had been attached previously. This whole incident is related in order to show that he was steadfast in his attachment to Wisdom, and was not seduced, and returned to his former condition. "Into the South": this is the higher grade to which he was attached at first, as it is written, "going on still to the South". The inner significance of this narrative is that if Abram had not gone down to Egypt and been tested there, his portion would not have been in the Lord. Similarly with his descendants, whom God desired to make a unique and perfect people and to bring near to Himself: if they had not first gone down to Egypt and been tested there, they would not have been God's chosen people. Similarly, too, if the Holy Land had not been first given to Canaan to rule over, it would not have become the lot and portion of the Holy One, blessed be He. In all these facts the same mystical purpose is to be observed.'

R. Simeon was once on a journey in company with his son R. Eleazar and R. Abba and R. Judah. As they were going along, R. Simeon said: 'I marvel how indifferent men are to the words of the Torah and the problem of their own existence!' He proceeded to discourse on the text: With my soul have I desired thee in the night, yea, with my spirit within me will I seek thee early (Is. XXVI, 9). He said: 'The inner meaning of this verse is as follows. When a man lies down in bed, his vital spirit (nefesh) leaves him and begins to mount on high, leaving with the body only the impression of a receptacle which contains the heartbeat. The rest of it tries to soar from grade to grade, and in doing so it encounters certain bright but unclean essences. If it is pure and has not defiled itself by day, it rises above them, but if not, it becomes defiled among them and cleaves to them and does not rise any further. There they show her certain things which are going to happen in the near future: and sometimes they delude her and show her false things. Thus she goes about the whole night until the man wakes up, when she returns to her place. Happy are the righteous to whom God reveals His secrets in dreams, so that they may be on their guard against sin! Woe to the sinners who defile their bodies and their souls! As for those who have not defiled themselves during the day, when they fall asleep at night their souls begin to ascend, and first enter those grades which we have mentioned, but they do not cleave to them and continue to mount further. The soul which is privileged thus to rise finally appears before the gate of the celestial palace, and yearns with all its might to behold the beauty of the King and to visit His sanctuary. This is the man who ever hath a portion in the world to come, and this is the soul whose yearning when she ascends is for the Holy One, blessed be He, and who does not cleave to those other bright essences, but seeks out the holy essence in the place from which she (originally) issued. Therefore it is written, "With my soul have I desired thee in the night", to pursue after thee and not to be enticed away after false powers. Again, the words "With my soul have I desired thee

Zohar: Bereshith, Section 1, Page 83b

in the night" refer to the soul (nefesh) which has sway by night, while the words "with my spirit within me will I seek thee early" refer to the spirit (ruah) which has sway by day. "Soul "(nefesh) and "spirit" (ruah) are not two separate grades, but one grade with two aspects. There is still a third aspect which should dominate these two and cleave to them as they to it, and which is called "higher spirit" (neshamah). (All these grades are arranged in wisdom, and contemplation of them throws light on the higher Wisdom.) This spirit enters into them and they cleave to it, and when it dominates, such a man is called holy, perfect, wholly devoted to God.

"Soul" (nefesh) is the lowest stirring, it supports and feeds the body and is closely connected with it. When it sufficiently qualifies itself, it becomes the throne on which rests the lower spirit (ruah), as it is written, "until the spirit be poured on us from on high" (Is. XXXII, 15). When both have prepared themselves sufficiently, they are qualified to receive the higher spirit (neshamah), to which the lower spirit (ruah) becomes a throne, and which is undiscoverable, supreme over all. Thus there is throne resting on throne, and a throne for the highest. From observing these grades of the soul, one obtains an insight into the higher Wisdom, and it is wholly through Wisdom that in this way certain mysteries are connected together. For nefesh is the lowest stirring to which the body cleaves, like the dark light at the bottom of the candle-flame which clings to the wick and exists only through it. When fully kindled it becomes a throne for the white light above it. When both are fully kindled, the white light becomes a throne for a light which cannot be fully discerned, an unknown something resting on that white light, and so there is formed a complete light. So with the man who attains perfection and is called "holy", as in the verse "for the holy ones that are in the earth". And so also in the upper world. Hence at the time when Abram entered the land God appeared to him and he received there a nefesh, and built an altar to the corresponding grade (of divinity). Then "he journeyed to the South", receiving a ruah. Finally he rose to the height of cleaving to God through the medium of the neshamah, whereupon he "built an altar to the Lord", indicating the most recondite grade corresponding to the neshamah. He then found that it was requisite for him to test himself and endow himself with grades, so he went down to Egypt. There he preserved himself from being seduced by those bright essences, and after testing himself he returned to his place: he "went up" from Egypt literally, strengthened and confirmed in faith, and reached the highest grade of faith. Thenceforth Abram was acquainted with the higher Wisdom and clung to God and became the right hand of the world. Hence it says AND ABRAM WAS VERY RICH IN CATTLE, IN SILVER, AND IN GOLD: "very rich", from the side of the East; "in cattle", from the side of the West; "in silver", from the side of the South; "in gold", from the side of the North.' R. Eleazar and R. Abba and all the companions thereupon came and kissed his hands. R. Abba wept and said, 'Alas, alas, when thou departest from the world, who shall cause the light of the Torah to shine forth? Happy the lot of the companions who hear these words of the Torah from thy mouth,' Said R. Simeon, Let us proceed.

AND HE WENT ON HIS JOURNEYS, i.e. to revisit his place and his grades, until he reached the first grade where the first revelation had taken place. "On his journeys": all those grades, grade after grade, as has been said.

Zohar: Bereshith, Section 1, Page 84a

EVEN TO BETHEL: to prepare his place and to combine "the South" and "Bethel" in a complete unity, since from the South to Bethel comprised the whole gamut of Wisdom. UNTO THE PLACE WHERE HIS TENT HAD BEEN AT THE BEGINNING, to wit, Bethel, the "perfect stone". The spot is further defined as THE PLACE OF THE ALTAR WHICH HE HAD MADE THERE AT THE FIRST, as it was said, "to the Lord who appeared unto him", and therefore now ABRAM CALLED ON THE NAME OF THE LORD, in proof that he had attained to perfect faith. Note this. At first Abram proceeded from the lower to the higher, as it is written, "And the Lord appeared to Abram", and again, "to the Lord who appeared to him", and then "going on his journeys to the South"-grade after grade until he was endowed with the South which was his rightful portion. From thence he began to reverse the process and descended from the higher to the lower, so as to fix all in its proper place. On the return journey, too, the mention of his stages contains an allusion to the higher Wisdom. It is written, "And he went on his journeys from the South", i.e. from the side of the Right, from the very beginning of the upper world, the mysterious and recondite, reaching to the Limitless (En Sof), and then descended stage by stage "from the South to Bethel", where "Abram called on the name of the Lord", i.e. he affixed the unity to its proper place, viz. "the place of the altar which he had made there at the first": i.e. he had taken it from the lower to the upper grade, and now he brought it down by stages from the upper to the lower in order that it should not depart from those upper grades nor they from it and the whole should constitute an indissoluble unity. Then was Abram fully endowed, and he became the lot and the portion of God in real truth. Happy are the righteous who are crowned in God as God in them! Happy in this world and happy in the world to come! Of them it is written, "Thy people shall be all righteous, they shall inherit the earth forever" (Is. LX, 21); and again, "The path of the righteous is as the shining light, that shineth more and more unto the perfect day" (Prov. IV, 18).

The travellers went on until they came to a field, where they sat down. R. Simeon then discoursed on the text: Turn unto me and have mercy upon me (Ps. LXXXVI, 16). He said: 'This verse deserves careful study, for although we have already explained it more than once, yet it has still an inner meaning. How could David say to God, "Turn to me "? The truth is that he was referring to the grade with which he was endowed. Similarly he said Give thy strength to thy servant (Ibid.). The word "strength" refers to the supernal Force (Geburah), as in the verse "And he gave strength to his king" (Is. II, 19). The word "king", used thus without qualification, refers to the Messiah, as also does the word "servant" in this passage. And save the son of thy handmaid. Why does he call himself the son of his mother and not of his father Jesse? This bears out what we have laid down, that when a man comes to ask something of heaven, he should only say that of which he is certain; hence he mentioned his mother and not his father. And further, tradition refers this verse to the Messiah, as we have said.' R. Simeon proceeded: AND THERE WAS A STRIFE BETWEEN THE HERDMEN OF ABRAM'S CATTLE. The omission of the letter Yod from the word rib (strife) indicates that Lot desired to revert to the idolatry of the inhabitants of the Country; this is confirmed by the end of the verse AND THE CANAANITE AND THE PERIZZITE DWELT THEN IN THE LAND. That Lot actually did revert to idolatry we know from the words AND LOT JOURNEYED FROM THE EAST: the word mi-qedem (from the East) is equivalent to mi-qadmono (from the Ancient One) of the world (similarly it says of the men who built the Tower of Babel that they journeyed "from the East", Gen. XI, 1). As soon as Abram saw that this was in Lot's mind, straightway HE SAID TO LOT... SEPARATE THYSELF, I PRAY THEE, FROM ME; as if to say, thou art not worthy to associate with me. So Abram separated from him and refused to accompany or join him, since whoever associates with a sinner eventually follows in his footsteps and so brings punishment

Zohar: Bereshith, Section 1, Page 84b

upon himself. We know this from Jehoshaphat, who through joining with Ahab would have brought punishment on himself had he not been saved by the merit of his ancestors. Therefore Abram refused to accompany Lot; and for all that Lot did not turn from his evil course, but CHOSE HIM ALL THE PLAIN OF THE JORDAN and journeyed mi-qedem, i.e. departed from the Ancient One of the world, and did not seek to perfect himself in faith like Abram. SO ABRAM DWELLED IN THE LAND OF CANAAN, to cleave to the place where faith could be strengthened and to learn wisdom in order to cleave to his Master, whereas LOT DWELLED IN THE CITIES OF THE PLAIN and MOVED HIS TENT AS FAR AS SODOM, with those godless sinners who had abandoned faith, as it is written, NOW THE MEN OF SODOM WERE WICKED AND SINNERS AGAINST THE LORD EXCEEDINGLY. Thus each went his own way. Happy are the companions who devote themselves to the Torah day and night and seek converse with God; of them it is written, "Ye that cleave unto the Lord your God are alive every one of you this day" (Deut. IV, 4).'

AND THE LORD SAID TO ABRAM AFTER THAT LOT WAS SEPARATED FROM HIM. In connection with this verse R. Abba discoursed on the following text: Jonah rose up to flee to Tarshish from the presence of the Lord (Jonah, I, 3). He said: 'Woe to the man who seeks to hide himself from God, of whom it is written, "Do I not fill heaven and earth, saith the Lord?" (Jer. XXIII, 24). Why, then, did Jonah seek to flee from Him? The reason is to be found in the verse "My dove that art in the clefts of the rock, in the coverts of the steep place" (S. S. II, 14). "My dove" refers to the community of Israel; "the clefts of the rock" refers to Jerusalem, which is firm and eminent like a rock; "the coverts of the steep place" refer to the place which is called "holy of holies", the heart of the world. It is called "coverts" because there the Shekinah is concealed like a woman who converses only with her husband and never goes out. The community of Israel does not dwell outside its own place save in the time of exile, and because it is in exile, therefore other nations enjoy greater prosperity. When Israel were in their own land everything was as it should be, the heavenly throne was fully spread over them, and the liturgy which they performed pierced through the ether and ascended on high to its place. For Israel alone was qualified to serve God in that land, and therefore the Gentiles kept aloof, since they did not rule over it as now, but were nourished only by the "residue". You may say, How do you reconcile this with the fact that a number of (foreign) kings ruled over it at the time when the Temple still existed. The answer is that in the time of the first Temple, before Israel defiled the land, the Gentiles did not rule over it but were nourished from the "residue". But when Israel sinned and defiled the land, they, as it were, drove the Shekinah from its place, and it went to another place, and therefore other nations were allowed to rule over the land. For no angel has control of the land of Israel, but only God. When Israel sinned and burned incense to other gods in the Holy Land, the Shekinah was driven from its place, and other gods were associated with it, and so other nations obtained dominion and the prophets died out, and all the higher grades ceased to rule, and dominion was not withdrawn from other nations, because they drew the Shekinah to themselves. Hence in the time of the second Temple the rule of the other nations did not cease, and even less so in the period of the Exile, when the Shekinah found herself among other nations where other chieftains exercise dominion, deriving their sustenance from the Shekinah, which has consorted with them. Thus we see that

Zohar: Bereshith, Section 1, Page 85a

when Israel dwelt in their own land and maintained the Temple service, the Shekinah remained among them in privacy, and did not issue from her house openly. Therefore all the prophets who lived in those times drew their inspiration only from her place, as we have said. That was the reason why Jonah fled from the Holy Land, namely, that the prophetic inspiration should not come to him, and he should not have to take the Lord's message. But, you may say, did not the Shekinah reveal itself (to Ezekiel) in Babylon, which is outside the Holy Land? The answer is that, according to an authentic tradition, the words "came expressly" used at the beginning of Ezekiel's prophecy indicate that this was without precedent from the day when the Temple was built, and this prophecy was for a special emergency. Further, the incident took place on the river Khebar (khebar=of old), so called because it was qualified for this from the beginning of the world, and the Shekinah had been constantly revealed on it, as it is written, "And a river went out from Eden to water the garden and from there it parted, etc." (Gen. II, 10). This was one of the four rivers, and there the Shekinah was revealed exceptionally to relieve Israel in their emergency; but at other times it did not appear there. Therefore Jonah left the Holy Land in order that the Shekinah might not rest upon him or appear to him, and hence it says "from the presence of the Lord", and again, "for the men knew that he fled from the presence of the Lord" (Jon. I, 10). What is the point of all this? It is that just as, in the case of Jonah, the Shekinah did not reveal itself save in the fitting place, so in the case of Abram it did not reveal itself save when he was in fitting company. For from the day when Lot made up his mind to become a renegade, the Holy Spirit departed from Abram; but when Lot left him, straightway the Holy Spirit rested upon him: so it is written, AND THE LORD SAID UNTO ABRAM AFTER THAT LO T WAS SEPARATED FROM HIM. Furthermore, when Abram saw that Lot had reverted to his sinful ways, he was afraid and said to himself, "Perhaps through associating with this man I have lost the holy heritage with which God has endowed me"; hence, when Lot left him, God said to him, LIFT UP NOW THINE EYES AND LOOK FROM THE PLACE WHERE THOU ART. "The place where thou art" means "the place to which thou didst cleave before, and in which thou wast endowed with perfect faith". NORTHWARD AND SOUTHWARD AND EASTWARD AND WESTWARD: These are the same as the "journeys" referred to in verse 3, indicating, like them, the "higher degrees". Abram now received tidings that that perfect faith which he had acquired on his first passage through the land would not depart from him and his descendants forever; hence it is written, FOR THE LAND WHICH THOU SEEST, TO THEE WILL I GIVE IT AND TO THY SEED FOREVER: the words which thou seest" indicate the first grade which he had acquired originally, and which now included and exhibited all the other grades.'

R. Eleazar was once at an inn at Lud, where R. Hizkiah also happened to be. In the course of the night he got up to study the Torah, as did also R. Hizkiah. On seeing him, he said, 'An inn like this is always a meeting-place for the companions.' He then began to discourse on the text: As the apple tree among the trees of the wood, so is my beloved among the sons (S. S. II, 3). 'The apple tree,' he said, 'indicates the Holy One, blessed be He, being more delightful than all the other trees, and distinguished among them by its colours. So none can compare with Him; therefore "I delighted in his shadow"–in his shadow and not in that of the other guardian-angels, even from the time when Abram was in the world, Abram, who was attached to God in love, as it is written, "Abraham my friend" (Is. XLI, 8). His fruit was sweet to my taste refers to Isaac, who was a holy fruit. The words "In his shadow I delighted and sat down" may also be referred to Jacob, and the words "and his fruit was sweet to my taste" to Joseph, who produced holy fruit in the world.

Zohar: Bereshith, Section 1, Page 85b

It is also possible to understand the words "Like an apple tree among the trees of the wood" of Abraham, who smelt sweetly like an apple tree, who was distinguished in faith above all his contemporaries, and who was marked out as unique both above and below, as it is written, "Abraham was one" (Ezek. XXXIII, 24). He was so called because no one else of his contemporaries attained to the virtue of faith in God.' Said R. Hizkiah to him: 'What of the words "And the souls which they made in Haran"?' He replied: 'These did not reach the higher grades which Abraham acquired.' later on he said to him: 'Another thing I have been told is that Abraham was not called "one" until he had associated with himself Isaac and Jacob. When he had done this and when all three were patriarchs, then Abraham was called "one", and then he became the apple tree distinguished above all the rest of the world.' He said: 'Your explanation is good. According to another explanation, the words "the apple tree", "my beloved", and "in his shadow" all equally indicate the Holy One, blessed be He. "I delighted and sat": to wit, on the day when God revealed Himself on Mount Sinai and Israel received the Torah and said, "We will do and we will hearken" (Ex. XXIV, 7). "His fruit is sweet to my taste" refers to the words of the Torah which are called "sweeter than honey and the honeycomb" (Ps. XIX, 11). Another explanation refers the "fruit" to the souls of the righteous, who are the fruit of the handiwork of the Almighty and abide with Him above. Listen to this. All the souls in the world, which are the fruit of the handiwork of the Almighty, are all mystically one, but when they descend to this world they are separated into male and female, though these are still conjoined. When they first issue forth, they issue as male and female together. Subsequently, when they descend (to this world) they separate, one to one side and the other to the other, and God afterwards mates them–God and no other, He alone knowing the mate proper to each. Happy the man who is upright in his works and walks in the way of truth, so that his soul may find its original mate, for then he becomes indeed perfect, and through his perfection the whole world is blessed.' Said R. Hizkiah: 'I have heard the following explanation of the verse "From me is thy fruit found" (Hos. XIV, 9). The Holy One, blessed be He, said to the Community of Israel, "From me assuredly is thy fruit found"–not my fruit, but thy fruit: the desire of the female produces a vital spirit and is embraced in the vehemence of the male, so that soul is joined with soul and they are made one, each embraced in the other. Afterwards they become two in this world, and thus through the force of the male is produced the fruit of the female. According to another explanation, the fruit of the male is produced through the desire of the female, since if not for the desire of the female for the male no fruit would ever be produced.'

NOW IT CAME TO PASS IN THE DAYS OF AMRAFEL KING OF SHINAR. R. Yose expounded in this connection the text: Who hath raised up one from the East, whom Righteousness calleth to follow him? (Is. XLI, 2). He said: 'This verse has been explained in various ways, but it also contains an esoteric allusion. God, we have learnt, has made seven firmaments on high, all of which acknowledge the glory of the Almighty and are capable of pointing the lesson of true faith. Now there is above these seven a hidden firmament which guides and illumines them. Of this one we cannot discover the true nature, however much we inquire and therefore it is designated by the interrogative particle Mi (Who), as has been pointed out: hence the Scripture says: "From the womb of Whom (Mi) came forth the ice" (Job XXXVIII, 29), which has been explained to refer to the highest firmament

Zohar: Bereshith, Section 1, Page 86a

over the other seven. At the bottom again there is a firmament, the lowest of all, which has no light; and on that account the highest firmament joins with it in such a way as to insert in it the two letters of its own name, so that it is called Yam (sea), being, as it were, the sea of that highest firmament, because all the other firmaments serve as streams (to convey its light), and flow into this lowest one as into a sea; and it thereupon produces fruits and fishes after their kind, and in reference to this David said; "Lo, the sea great and wide, wherein are things creeping innumerable both small and great beasts" (Ps. CIV, 25). We now see what is meant by the words "Who raised up from the East". The one raised up was Abraham. The words "Righteousness calleth him to follow him" refer to the lowest firmament which has become "sea". It is this which "giveth nations before him", which executes vengeance and overthrows the enemy. "He giveth nations before him": these are the peoples of the earth. "And maketh him to rule over kings": these are the guardian-angels of the nations above, for when God executes judgement on a people, He does so both below and above. "He pursueth them and passeth on safely" (Is. XLI, 3): this is Abram who pursued them while God passed before him and slew them, as it says, "Peace passeth on" (Ibid.), "Peace" referring to God. "Even by a way that he had not gone by his feet": if not with his feet, how then did Abram go-on the clouds or with horses and chariots? No: what it means is that it was not an angel or a messenger, but God Himself, that went before Abram, the word "feet" here referring to the angels, who are subject to God, as in the verse "And his feet shall stand in that day" (Zech. XIV, 4). Another explanation of the verse is as follows. When God "awoke" the world to bring Abram and to draw him near to Himself, this was because Jacob was destined to issue from him and to establish twelve tribes who should all be righteous in the sight of God. "Whom he calleth in righteousness": because God was calling him constantly from the day that the world was created, as it is written, "calling the generations from the beginning" (Is. XLI, 4). "To his foot": i.e. to attach him to His service and to bring him near to Himself. R. Judah says: "Who aroused from the East" this refers to Abraham, who received his first impulse to seek God from the East. For when he saw the sun issuing in the morning from the East, he was first moved to think that that was God, and said "this is the King that created me", and worshipped it the whole day. In the evening when the sun went down and the moon commenced to shine, he said, "Verily this rules over the orb which I worshipped the whole day, since the latter is darkened before it and does not shine any more." So he served the moon all that night. In the morning when he saw the darkness depart and the East grow light, he said, "Of a surety there is a king who rules over all these orbs and orders them." So when God saw Abram's longing to find Him, He revealed Himself unto him and spoke with him, as it is written, "Righteousness called to him to follow him."'

R. Isaac explained in connection with Abraham the verse: I am the Lord speaking righteousness, declaring what is right (Is. XLV, 19).

Zohar: Bereshith, Section 1, Page 86b

He said: 'All God's words are truth and His acts are righteousness. For when God first created the world it was unstable and rocked to and fro. Said God to the world, Wherefore rockest thou? It answered: Sovereign of the Universe, I cannot be firm, because I have no foundation on which to rest. God thereupon said: Behold, I intend to raise up in thee a righteous man, Abraham, who will love Me. Hearing this, the world straightway became firmly established; therefore it is written, "these are the generations of the heavens and the earth behibaream (when they were created), which by a transposition of letters becomes beabraham (for the sake of Abraham).' R. Hiya enlarged upon the words "declaring what is right". He said: 'The world continued to remonstrate with God, saying, "From this Abraham will issue descendants [Tr. note: The peoples of Ishmael and Esau.] who will destroy the Temple and burn the Law." God replied: "He will also have one descendant, namely Jacob, who will be the father of twelve tribes who will all be righteous." Forthwith the world was established for his sake, and therefore God is said to be "declaring (the advent of) things that are right".' R. Eleazar said: 'It has been noted that there is a difference between "speaking" (dober) and "declaring" (maggid). "Speaking" is from a revealed source, an outer grade, not of the highest; therefore it is applied here to "righteousness" (zedek). But "declaring" indicates the inner grade which controls that belonging to "speaking"; hence it says here "declaring things that are right" (mesharim), these referring to the higher grade in which is that of Jacob.' Said R. Isaac to him, 'Is there not a text "he declares to you his covenant" (Deut. IV, 13)?' He replied: 'The "covenant" also is a grade superior to that referred to in the expression "speaking righteousness". One must be careful too to note that although "speaking" is lower than "declaring", it still actually designates a high grade and is very pregnant in signification.'

R. Eleazar was once on the way to visit his father-in-law along with R. Hiya and R. Yose and R. Hizkiah. Said R. Eleazar, 'It is borne in upon me that stirring above is produced only in response to an impulse from below, and depends upon the longing of that below.' He illustrated this from the text: O God, keep thou not silence, hold not thy peace, and be not still, O God (Ps. LXXXIII, 2), which he expounded thus. 'David said: "O God, keep thou not silence." These words represent an impulse to Elohim to exert His sway. David said in effect: "Elohim, cease not to rouse the Highest and to associate thyself with the Right." Wherefore so? Because "thine enemies make a tumult, etc.", they have consulted together with one consent, against Thee do they make a covenant. "Therefore, O God, be not silent," as explained. For when Elohim is joined with the Right, then the enemies are crushed, as it is written, "Thy right hand, O Lord, is glorious in power, thy right hand, O Lord, dasheth in pieces the enemy." Note that, when all those kings joined together to make war on Abram, they designed to make away with him. But so soon as they got possession of Lot, his brother's son, they went off (as it is written, AND THEY TOOK LOT, ABRAM'S BROTHER'S SON, AND HIS GOODS AND DEPARTED), the reason being that Lot closely resembled Abram, so that thinking they had Abram, they went off. The reason of their enmity to Abram was that Abram weaned men from idolatry and taught them to worship God. Also God incited them to make their invasion in order to aggrandise Abram and to attract him to his service. Esoterically speaking, when Abram started to pursue them, then God "did not keep silent" until the whole was linked up with Abram; then when the whole was linked up with Abram, then all those kings were crushed before him, as we have said.' AND MELCHIZEDEK KING OF SALEM BROUGHT FORTH BREAD AND WINE. R. Simeon adduced here the text "In Salem also is his tabernacle" (Ps. LXXVI, 3). He said: 'When God decided to create the world, He first produced a flame of a scintillating lamp. He blew spark against spark, causing darkness and fire, and produced from the recesses

Zohar: Bereshith, Section 1, Page 87a

of the abyss a certain drop which He joined with the flame, and from the two He created the world. The flame ascended and encircled itself with the Left, and the drop ascended and encircled itself with the Right. They then crossed and changed places, going up and down alternately until they were closely interlocked, and there issued from between them a full wind. Then those two sides were made one, and the wind was set between them and they were entwined with one another, and so there was harmony above and harmony below; the grade was firmly established, the letter he was crowned with vau and vau with he, and so he ascended and was joined in a perfect bond. This is alluded to in the words "Melchizedek (lit. king of righteousness) king of Salem" (lit. completeness), i.e. the king who rules with complete sovereignty. When is he completely king? On the Day of Atonement, when all faces are illumined. According to another explanation, "Melchizedek" alludes to the lower world, and "king of Salem" to the upper world; and the verse indicates that both are intertwined inseparably, two worlds like one, so that the lower world also is the whole, and the whole is one. "Brought forth bread and wine": signifying that both of these are in it. AND HE WAS PRIEST OF GOD MOST HIGH: i.e. one world ministers to the other. "Priest" refers to the Right, and "Most High God,' to the upper world; and hence a priest is required to bless the world. For this lower world receives blessings when it is associated with a High Priest; hence there is a special force in the words "and he blessed him and said, Blessed is Abram to the Most High God". After this model it behoves the priest on earth to intertwine his fingers when blessing in the synagogue in order that he may be linked with the Right and that the two worlds may be linked together. BLESSED IS ABRAM. The words of the text are a prototype of the formula of blessing (used by the Israelites). "Blessed is Abram" (in the sense we have given to it) corresponds to "blessed art Thou ". "To the Most High God" corresponds to "O Lord our God". "Possessor of heaven and earth" corresponds to "king of the universe. Further, AND HE BLESSED HIM indicates the course of blessing from below to above; BLESSED IS THE MOST HIGH GOD indicates from above to below. AND HE GAVE HIM A TENTH OF ALL: so that he should cleave to the place where the link was formed with the lower world.'

As they were going along they came across R. Yesa and a certain Judean with him who was explaining the text "To David: Unto thee, O Lord, do I lift up my soul" (Ps. XXV, 1). He said: 'Why is the inscription of this psalm simply "to David" and not "A Psalm of David"? It is because the real meaning is "for the sake of David", i.e. of his grade. "Unto thee, O Lord", i.e. upward-striving; "my soul", i.e. David himself, his original grade; "I lift up": to wit, I cause to ascend, since David was ever striving to rise to a higher grade and to link himself to it firmly. Similarly it was for the sake of his grade that David uttered the words "To David: Bless the Lord, O my soul" (where the word eth indicates his desire to be linked above) "and all that is within me bless his holy name" (Ps. CIII, 1), referring to the "beasts of the field" which are called "inwards".' Said R. Eleazar to R. Yesa, 'I see that you have come in company with the Shekinah.' He said, "Assuredly it is so. I have been walking with him three parasangs, and he has told me ever so many excellent things. I hired him as a porter, not knowing that he was the shining light which I have discovered him to be.' R. Eleazar then said to the man, 'What is your name?' He said: 'Joezer'. Whereupon he said: 'Let Joezer and Eleazar sit together.' So they sat down on a rock

Zohar: Bereshith, Section 1, Page 87b

in that field. The Judean then commenced to discourse on the text "I, even I, am he that blotteth out thy transgressions, for mine own sake, and thy sins I will not remember" (Is. XLIII, 25). He said: 'The word "I" occurs here twice: once in reference to Sinai (cf. "I am the Lord thy God", Ex. XX, 2), and the other in reference to the creation of the world (cf. "I have made the earth and created man upon it", Is. XLV, 12), to show that there is no division between the upper and lower worlds. "That blotteth out thy transgressions": not merely removing them, so that they shall never be seen more. "For mine own sake": i.e. for the sake of the mercy which I dispense, as it is written, "For the Lord thy God is a merciful God" (Deut. IV, 31). Another explanation of the words "that blotteth out thy transgressions for mine own sake" is as follows. Sinners in this world impair the influence of the upper world, for when they sin, mercy and the supernal light depart, and the stream of blessing does not descend to this world, and this grade (of mercy) does not take up the blessings from above in order to convey them to the lower world. Hence God acts "for His own sake", in order that the stream of blessing should not be withheld. Similarly it is written, "See now that I, I am he" (Deut. XXXII, 39), to show that there is no division between the upper and the lower. See now, in this way, when there are righteous men in the world, blessings are sent to all worlds. When Abram came, blessings were sent to the world, as it is written, "And I shall bless thee, and be thou a blessing, i.e. that blessing should be found both above and below for his sake. When Isaac came he taught the world that there is a judge executing judgement above to punish the wicked, and he invoked justice upon the world in order that its inhabitants might fear God. When Jacob came he obtained mercy for the world and perfected men's faith in God. Hence in the days of Abram MELCHIZEDEK KING OF SALEM (salem=completeness), i.e. God whose throne was then established in its place and whose sovereignty therefore became complete, BROUGHT OUT BREAD AND WINE, i.e. produced the appropriate food for the whole world, and did not withhold blessing from all the worlds; from the upper grades He brought forth food and blessings for all the worlds. AND HE WAS A PRIEST TO THE MOST HIGH GOD, the whole thus being in the most perfect order; to show that as the wicked upset the world and cause blessing to be withheld, so the righteous bring blessing to the world and for their sakes all its inhabitants are blessed. AND HE GAVE HIM A TENTH OF ALL, to wit, of those blessings which issue from "all", the source of all the blessings which descend upon the world. According to another explanation, God gave Abram a tenth, namely, the grade [Tr. note: Malkuth.] in which all the sources of faith and blessing are established, and which is the tenth, one out of ten and ten out of a hundred; and from this point onwards Abram was fully confirmed from above.' Said R. Eleazar to him: 'What you say is right.' R. Eleazar further asked him what his business was. He said: 'I was a teacher of children in my town till R. Yose came, when they left me and went to him. Nevertheless the townsfolk used to pay me my salary as before. Not wishing, however, to take money for nothing, I entered into the service of this Sage.' Said R. Eleazar: 'This is a case where my father's blessings are required.' They went to R. Simeon, and the Judean used to study all day before him. One day he was studying the subject of washing the hands, and said: 'Whoever does not wash his hands as required, although he is punished in the next world is also punished in this world, because he endangers his health. And similarly, he who washes his hands as required procures for himself blessings above which rest upon his hands, and is also blessed with wealth.'

Zohar: Bereshith, Section 1, Page 88a

[Note: The first 5 lines of the English translation do not appear in our Hebrew text]

Afterwards R. Simeon caught sight of him washing his hands and using a great quantity of water, and he exclaimed: 'Fill his hands with thy blessings.' And so it came to pass, since he found a treasure and grew rich, and he used to study the Torah and give sustenance to the poor every day and smile upon them benignantly, so that R. Simeon applied to him the verse "And thou shalt rejoice in the Lord and glory in the Holy One of Israel." '

AFTER THESE THINGS. R. Judah discoursed on the text: I am my beloved's and his desire is towards me (S. S. VII, 11). He said: 'The inner meaning of this verse is that the stirring below is accompanied by a stirring above, for there is no stirring above till there is a stirring below. Further, blessings from above descend only where there is some substance and not mere emptiness. We learn this from the wife of Obadiah to whom Elisha said, "Tell me, what hast thou in the house" (II Kings, IV, 2), meaning that blessings from above would not descend on an empty table or an empty place. When she said: "Thy handmaid hath nothing in the house save a cruse of oil"-only enough to smear her little finger-he said to her: "You have relieved me, for I did not see how blessings were to descend from above on to an empty place, but since you have some oil, this will provide a place sufficient for the purpose." (The connection of "oil" with "blessing" is found in Psalm CXXXIII, where it says "like the good oil' etc., and then "for there the Lord commanded the blessing, life forevermore". It is true, the immediate comparison in the passage is with dew, not oil, but the two mean the same thing, as this dew was distilled by God from the supernal oil. Wine and oil belong respectively to the Left and the Right sides, and from the Right side blessings descend on the world, and from there the holy kingdom is anointed. Thus because it was fixed upon below, oil was first prepared above as the source of blessings. From the stirring

Zohar: Bereshith, Section 1, Page 88b

of this supernal oil the lower oil was poured on David and Solomon to bring blessings on their descendants. This is derived from a collation of the text "and the oil stood", in II Kings IV, 6, with the text "the root of Jesse which standeth for an ensign of the nations", Is. XI, 10.)

We derive the same lesson from the fact that the table of shew-bread, from which issued blessings, was not to be left empty a single moment; and on that account we do not say grace over an empty table, since blessings from above do not rest on an empty table. To resume, then, the verse "I am my beloved's and towards me is his desire" indicates that "first of all I am my beloved's, and then, in consequence, his desire is towards me; first I prepare for him a place, and then his desire is towards me". The verse may also be explained by reference to the dictum that the Shekinah is not found in the company of sinners, but when a man exerts himself to purify himself and to draw near to God, then the Shekinah rests on him. So "I am my beloved's" to begin with, and then "his desire is towards me".'

AFTER THESE THINGS, i.e. after Abram pursued the kings and God slew them, Abram felt some qualms lest he had perchance forfeited some of his reward for converting men to the service of God, seeing that now some of his fellow creatures had been killed through him. Therefore God said to him: FEAR NOT, ABRAM, I AM THY SHIELD, THY REWARD IS EXCEEDING GREAT: you have received a reward for them, for none of them shall ever be accounted innocent. THE WORD OF THE LORD CAME UNTO ABRAM IN A VISION SAYING. Vision is the grade in which all figures are beheld. R. Simeon said: 'Up to the time when Abram was circumcised, only one grade spoke with him; namely Vision, which is also mentioned in the verse "who seeth the vision of Shaddai" (Num. XXIV, 4). After his circumcision, all grades combined with this grade, and in this way God spoke with him.

Zohar: Bereshith, Section 1, Page 89a

It may be objected that according to our interpretation the verses "and the Lord appeared to Abram", "and Abram journeyed to the South", "and he built there an altar", indicate that he had attained to these higher grades; how, then, can you say that before he was circumcised these grades did not combine with this one to speak with him? The answer is that previously God gave wisdom to Abraham to cleave to Him and to know the true meaning of faith, but only this lower grade actually spoke with him; but when he was circumcised, all the higher grades joined this lower grade to speak with him, and thus Abraham reached the summit of perfection. See now, before a man is circumcised he is not attached to the name of God, but when he is circumcised he enters into the name and is attached to it. Abram, it is true, was attached to the name before he was circumcised, but not in the proper manner, but only through God's extreme love for him; subsequently He commanded him to circumcise himself, and then he was vouchsafed the covenant which links all the supernal grades, a covenant of union which links the whole together so that every part is intertwined. Hence, till Abram was circumcised, God's word with him was only in a vision, as has been said.'

Consider this. When God created the world, it was created only through a covenant, as it is written, "Bereshith (b'rith esh, covenant of fire), God created"; and it is further written, "If my covenant of day and night stand not, if I have not appointed the ordinances of heaven and earth" (Jer. XXXIII, 25), since there is a covenant of union that day and night shall not be separated. R. Eleazar said: 'When God created the world, it was on condition that if Israel when they came into the world should accept the Torah, it would be well, but if not, then the world should revert to chaos. Nor was the world firmly established until Israel stood before Mount Sinai and accepted the Torah. From that day God has been creating fresh worlds, to wit, the marriages of human beings, for from that time God has been making matches and proclaiming "the daughter of so-and-so for so-and-so"; these are the worlds which He creates.'

I AM A SHIELD TO THEE: this "I is the first grade to which he was attached at the start.

Zohar: Bereshith, Section 1, Page 90a

AND ABRAM SAID, O LORD GOD: the two names indicate the union of the upper and the lower world. WHAT WILT THOU GIVE TO ME, SEEING THAT I GO CHILDLESS? i.e. not having a son, and we have learnt that he who has no son is called childless. The words "What wilt thou give to me" would seem to indicate some want of faith on the part of Abraham, but this is not so. God said to him: "I am thy shield," to wit, in this world, "thy reward is very great", to wit, in the next world. Abram, however, knew from the wisdom which he had acquired that a man who has not begotten a son is not rewarded with the future world, and he therefore said, "How canst thou give me (such a reward), seeing that I have not merited it?" (Hence we learn that a man who is not vouchsafed sons in this world is not granted in the future world the privilege of entering within the curtain.) Abram saw from his horoscope that he was fated not to have children; therefore HE BROUGHT HIM FORTH ABROAD; that is, God said to him: "Take no notice of that, for through my name thou shalt have a son; hence it says SO (Koh) SHALL THY SEED BE. The word Koh indicates the Holy Name, which was now linked to him from that side. It is the gateway of prayer through which a man obtains his request; it is the side which comes from the side of Geburah (might), from which Isaac also came. The side of Geburah is called Koh, because from it come fruit and produce to the world, and not from the side of the stars and constellations. AND HE BELIEVED IN THE LORD: he clave to the higher and not the lower; he believed in the Lord and not in stars and constellations: in the Lord who had promised to give him great recompense in the future world. "He believed in the Lord": namely in the grade which was vouchsafed him, that from there seed would come to him to bear children in the world. AND HE COUNTED IT TO HIMSELF FOR KINDNESS: i.e. although this koh was pure justice, Abram counted it as mercy. Another explanation is that he linked the upper with the lower to join them together, in this way. According to tradition, God told Abram that he would not beget till his name had been changed to Abraham. The question has been asked, did he not beget Ishmael while he was still Abram? The answer is that he did not beget the son who was promised him while he was still Abram. Then he only bore for the lower world, but when he obtained the name Abraham and entered into the covenant he bore for the upper world. Hence Abram did not bear for the upper union, but Abraham did, as we have said, and he was linked above through Isaac.'

Zohar: Bereshith, Section 1, Page 90b

NOW WHEN ABRAM WAS NINETY-NINE YEARS OLD, ETC. In connection with this verse R. Abba discoursed on the text: For who is God save the Lord, and who is a rock save our God? (II Sam. XXII, 32). He said: 'These words of King David may be paraphrased: What (heavenly) ruler or chieftain is there who can do anything without the Lord, anything save what he has been commanded by the Holy One, blessed be He, since all are subject to Him and cannot do anything of themselves? And what mighty power is there that has any force in himself save what he derives from our God? Another explanation is that a vision shown by the stars is not like a vision shown by God, for they show a thing and God changes it. And again, "Who is a rock (tsur) save our God?" i.e. there is no fashioner (tsayar) who fashions form within form and finishes it in all its details and inserts in it the heavenly soul which bears likeness to the Deity. See now when desire brings man and woman together, there issues from their union a son in whom both their forms are combined, because God has fashioned him in a mould partaking of both. Therefore a man should sanctify himself at such time, in order that the form may be as perfect as possible.' Said R. Hiya, 'How great are the works of the Holy One, blessed be He, for man is fashioned as a microcosm of the world, and every day God creates a world by bringing the proper couples together, and He fashions the forms of the offspring before they are born. See now what R. Simeon has told us, in explanation of the verse "This is the book of the generations of Adam", that God showed Adam every generation and its students, etc. This does not simply mean that he saw through the spirit of prophecy that they were destined to come into the world, like one who in wisdom foresees the future, but it means that he literally saw with his eyes the form in which they were destined to exist in the world. He was able to do this because from the day on which the world was created all the souls which were destined to come to life among mankind were existing before God in that very form which they were destined to assume

Zohar: Bereshith, Section 1, Page 91a

on earth (in the same way that the righteous after death are clothed in a form similar to that which they wore in this world), and so Adam saw them with his eyes. Nor can it be thought that after he saw them they disappeared, for all God's creations exist before Him permanently until they descend below. Similarly when Moses said "with him that standeth here this day with us, etc." (Deut. XXIX, 14), we understand him to have indicated that all who were yet to be born were there. (This point demands a little more consideration. The words of the text are, "him that standeth here... and him that is not here with us this day". The word "standeth" is omitted from the second half of the clause to show that the future generations were in fact standing there, but they were not visible. It may be asked, why were they not visible here in the same way that they were visible to Adam, seeing that here there was more reason. The reason is that when the Torah was given to Israel, they beheld and gazed upon other sights and other grades, and they yearned to contemplate the glory of their Master, and therefore they had no eyes but for that.) The same idea is expressed in the words of the Psalmist, "Thine eyes did see mine unperfect substance" (Ps. CXXXIX, 16), viz. the other celestial form resembling the one on earth. Thus we understand the words "Who is a tsur like our God", i.e. who is so excellent a fashioner (tsayar) as God who fashioned all. It is also possible to explain the words "For who is God besides the Lord, etc." in a more esoteric way. The word for "God" here is El, which signifies the union of all grades. Now there is a text "El hath indignation every day" (Ps. VII, 12), which might lead us to suppose that it designates a separate grade. Hence it says here "Who is El without Tetragrammaton", indicating that El is never alone disjoined from Tetragrammaton; and similarly there is no "Rock" (signifying the attribute of justice) "without our God".'

Until Abram was circumcised, God spoke to him only in a vision, as it says above, "The word of the Lord came unto Abram in a vision" (Gen. XV, 1). By "vision" we understand the grade in which all figures are apparent, and which symbolises the covenant. This seems to contradict what was said before, that till Abram was circumcised he was addressed only by that grade to which the other grades are not attached. The truth is that this grade is indeed the reflection of all the higher grades, and was rendered possible through that reflection; it reflects all the colours (symbolic of the divine attributes)-white at the right, red at the left, and a further colour compounded of all colours. In this reflection God stood over Abram and spoke with him, although he was not circumcised. Of Balaam it is said that he saw "the vision of Shaddai" (Num. XXIV, 4), and of Abraham that God spoke to him "in a vision", simply. The difference is that Balaam saw only those (angels) below the Almighty, whereas Abram saw the He in which all the celestial figures are reflected. Till Abram was circumcised, he was addressed only by that degree which we have mentioned; after he was circumcised, then THE LORD APPEARED UNTO ABRAM, i.e. all the other

Zohar: Bereshith, Section 1, Page 91b

grades appeared over this grade, and this grade addressed him without reserve. Thus when Abram was circumcised he emerged from the unripe state and entered into the holy covenant, and was crowned with the sacred crown, and entered into the covenant on which the world is based, and thus the world was firmly established for his sake. For it is written, "But for my covenant, I had not set the ordinances of heaven and earth", and also "There are the generations of heaven and earth when they were created"-the word behibaream (when they were created) can be read anagrammatically both beabraham (for the sake of Abraham) and b'he b'raam (he created them with He), and both come to the same thing.

When God showed Adam all future generations, he saw them all in the Garden of Eden in the form which they were destined to assume in this world. When he saw David-so we have been told-with no span of life at all apportioned to him, he was grieved, and gave him seventy years of his own; that is why Adam lived seventy years short of the thousand, the rest being given to David. The fact of David's only having seventy years from Adam, the first man, symbolises something in the higher world, as does everything here below.

Note that all the figures of souls that are to be born stand before God in pairs, and afterwards when they come to this world God mates them. R. Isaac says: 'God announces, The daughter of so-and-so for so-and-so.' R. Yose said: 'How can that be, seeing that, as the Scripture tells us, "there is nothing new under the sun"?' R. Judah said: 'It is true that God creates nothing new under the sun; but this is done above.' R. Yose further asked: 'Why is there a proclamation, seeing that, as we have been told by R. Hizkiah in the name of R. Hiya, a man's wife is assigned to him at the very moment when he is born?' Said R. Abba: 'Happy are the righteous whose souls are beatified before the Holy King before they come into this world. For we have learnt that when God sends souls into the world they are formed into pairs of male and female, and thus united are placed in the hands of an emissary who has charge of conception, and whose name is Night. After that they are separated, and subsequently taken down among mankind (not always both at the same time). When their time of marriage arrives, God, who knows each spirit and soul, joins them as at first, and proclaims their union. Thus when they are joined they become one body and one soul, right and left in unison, and in this way "there is nothing new under the sun". You may object that there is also a dictum that "a man only obtains the wife he deserves". This is so, the meaning being that if he leads a virtuous life he is privileged to marry his own true mate, whose soul emerged at the same time as his.' R. Hiya asked: 'Where should a man of good character look for his soul-mate?' He replied: 'There is a dictum that a man should sell all his property in order to obtain in marriage a daughter of a scholar, for the special treasure of God is deposited with the learned in the Torah. We have also learnt in the esoteric Mishnah that one whose soul is a second time on earth can through prayer anticipate another in marrying a woman who is really destined for him; this is the meaning of the warning of the colleagues, "it is permissible to affiance a woman on the festival, lest another through prayer anticipate him"; and they were right. The word "another" is used significantly; and it is for this reason that marriages constitute a difficult task for the Almighty, for in all cases "the ways of the Lord are right" (Hos. XIV, 10).'

R. Judah sent a question to R. Eleazar. 'I know', he said, 'about marriages in heaven, but I would like to ask, from where do those whose souls are a second time on earth obtain their mates?' The reply R. Eleazar sent him was this: 'It is written: "How shall we do for wives for them that remain?" (Jud. XXI, 7), and again, "and you shall catch every man his wife, etc." (Ibid. 21). This story of the Benjaminites shows us how it can be done, and hence the dictum "lest another anticipate him through his prayers".'

Zohar: Bereshith, Section 1, Page 92a

Said R. Judah: 'No wonder we say that marriages constitute a difficult problem for the Almighty! Happy the lot of Israel who learn from the Torah the ways of God and all hidden things, and even the most secret of His mysteries! "The Law of the Lord is perfect", says the Scripture. Happy the lot of him who occupies himself with the Torah without cessation, for if a man abandons the Torah for one moment, it is as if he abandoned eternal life, as it says, "For it is thy life and the length of thy days" (Deut. XXX, 20), and again, "For length of days and years of life and peace shall they add to thee" (Prov. III, 2).'

NOW ABRAM WAS NINETY YEARS OLD, ETC. R. Yose discoursed on the text: Thy people are all righteous, they shall inherit the land forever (Is. LX, 21). He said: 'Happy are Israel above all peoples, in that the Holy One, blessed be He, has called them righteous. For so we have learnt from tradition that there are a hundred and twenty-eight thousand winged creatures who flit about over the world ready to catch up any voice that they hear; for, as tradition tells us, there is nothing done in the world which does not produce a certain sound, and this soars to the firmament and is caught up by those winged creatures, who carry it aloft to be judged, whether for good or ill, as it is written, "For a bird of the heaven shall carry the voice and that which hath wings shall tell the matter" (Eccl. X, 20).' At what time do they judge the voice? R. Hiya said: 'At the time when a man is asleep in his bed, when his soul leaves him and testifies against him; it is then that the voice is judged, for so it says, "from her that lieth in thy bosom keep the doors of thy mouth" (Mich. VII, 5), because it is she who testifies against a man.' R. Judah said: 'Whatever a man does in the day his soul testifies against him at night.' We have learnt as follows: R. Eleazar says: 'At the beginning of the first hour of the night, when the day is expiring and the sun going down, the keeper of the keys of the sun finishes his process through the twelve gates that were open in the day, and they are all closed. A herald then proclaims to the guardians of the gates, "Each one to his place to lock the gates." When the herald has finished, all of them come together and go aloft without uttering a sound. Then the accusing angels below begin to stir and to fly about the world, and the moon begins to shine and the trumpeters sound a blast. At the second blast, the angels of song start up and chant before their Lord. Emissaries of chastisement also start up, and punishment commences in the world. Then the souls of men who are sleeping give their testimony and are declared guilty, but the Holy One, blessed be He, deals kindly with men and allows the soul to return to its place. At midnight, when the cock crows, a wind blows from the North, but at the same time a current from the South arises and strikes against it, causing it to subside. Then the Holy One, blessed be He, rises as is His wont to disport himself with the righteous in the Garden of Eden. Happy the portion of the man who rises at that hour to study with zest the Torah, for the Holy One, blessed be He, and all the righteous listen to his voice; for so it is written, "Thou that dwellest in the gardens, the companions hearken for thy voice, cause me to hear it" (S. S. VIII, 13). Nay more, God draws round him a certain thread of grace which secures him the protection both of the higher and the lower angels, as it is written, "By day the Lord will command his grace, and at night I shall chant his song" (Ps. XLII, 9).'

R. Hizkiah said: 'Whoever studies the Torah at that hour has constantly a portion in the future world.' Said that R. Yose to him: 'What do you mean by "constantly"?' He replied: 'I have learnt that at midnight, when the Holy One, blessed be He, enters the Garden of Eden, all the plants of the Garden are watered more plenteously by the stream which is called

Zohar: Bereshith, Section 1, Page 92b

"the ancient stream" and "the stream of delight", the waters of which never cease to flow. When a man rises and studies the Torah at this hour, the water of that stream is, as it were, poured on his head and he is watered by it along with the other plants of the Garden of Eden. Moreover, because all the righteous in the Garden listen to him, he is given a right to be watered by that stream, and in this way he has a portion constantly in the future world.'

R. Abba was journeying from Tiberias to meet other learned scholars at the house of his father-in-law. He was accompanied by his son, R. Jacob. Coming to Kfar Tarsha, they decide to spend the night there. Said R. Abba to his host, 'Have you a cock here?' He said, 'Why?' 'Because,' he said, 'I want to get up precisely at midnight.' He answered; 'You have no need of a cock for that. I have a water-clock by my bed from which the water issues drop by drop till exactly midnight, when all the water is emptied and the wheel swings back with a great noise which wakens the whole house. I made it for the sake of a certain old man who used to get up every night at midnight to study the Torah.' Said R. Abba, 'Blessed be God for sending me here.' At midnight the wheel of the water-clock swung back, and R. Abba and R. Jacob got up. They heard the voice of their host, who was sitting in the lower part of the house with his two sons and saying: 'It is written: Midnight I will rise to give thanks to thee because of thy righteous judgments (Ps. CXIX, 62). Since the word "at" is omitted, we may take "Midnight" as an appellation of the Holy One, blessed be He, who is addressed thus by David because He is to be found with His retinue at midnight, that being the hour when He enters the Garden of Eden to converse with the righteous.' Said R. Abba to R. Jacob: 'Truly we have now an opportunity to associate with the Shekinah.' So they went and sat by him, and said to him, 'Repeat what you just said, for it is excellent. Where did you get it from?' He replied: 'I learnt it from my grandfather. [Tr. note: Al. 'Old visitor'.] He told me that during the first three hours of the night the accusing angels below are actively going about the world, but at midnight precisely God enters the Garden of Eden and the accusations below cease. These nightly ceremonies above take place only at midnight precisely; we know this from what it says of Abraham, that "the night was divided for them" (Gen. XIV, 15); also from the words "and it came to pass at the middle of the night" in the account of the Exodus (Ex. XII, 29), and from many other places in the Scripture. David knew this, because-so the old man told me-his kingship depended on this; and therefore he used to rise at this hour and chant praises, and for this reason he addressed God as "Midnight". He also said, "I rise to give thanks to Thee for Thy righteous judgements" because this is the fount of justice, and the judgements of earthly kings derive from here; therefore David never neglected to rise and sing praises at this hour.' R. Abba came and kissed him, saying, 'Of a surety it is so. Blessed be God who has sent me here! For night is the time of judgement in every place, as we have fully established, and as has been discussed in the presence of R. Simeon.' The young son of the inn-keeper thereupon asked: 'If so, why does it say "midnight"?' He replied: 'It is laid down that the heavenly Majesty rises at midnight.' Said the boy: 'I can give another explanation.' Said R. Abba: 'Speak, my child; for the voice of the Lamp [Tr. note: R. Simeon.] will speak through thy mouth.' He thereupon said: 'What I have heard is this. Night is in truth the time of the royal judgement, and that judgement extends to all parts alike. Midnight, however, is fed from two sides, from justice and from clemency; only the first half of the night is the time of judgement, but the second half is illumined from the side of clemency (hesed). Therefore David said "Midnight".' R. Abba rose and placed his hands on his head and blessed him. He said: 'I thought indeed that wisdom was to be found only in a few favoured pious ones. Now I see that even children in the generation of R. Simeon are endowed with heavenly wisdom. Happy art thou, R. Simeon! Woe to the generation when thou departest from it!'

So they sat till

morning studying the Torah. R. Abba then discoursed on the text: Thy people are all righteous, they shall forever inherit the earth, a branch of my planting, etc. (Is. LX, 21). He said: 'Our colleagues have pointed out that these words cannot be taken literally, seeing how many sinners there are in Israel who transgress the precepts of the Law. The meaning is, as we have learnt in the esoteric teaching of our Mishnah: "Happy are Israel who bring an acceptable offering to the Almighty by circumcising their sons on the eighth day. They thereby become the portion of the 'Zaddik (Righteous One) who is the foundation of the world', and are called righteous; and therefore 'they shall forever inherit the earth'. They are 'the branch of my planting': that is, a branch of those shoots which God planted in the Garden of Eden, and of which the 'earth' mentioned here is one; hence Israel have a goodly portion in the future world, as it is written 'the righteous shall inherit the earth' (Ps. XXXVII, 29)." We have further learnt: "The reason why the name Abraham occurs for the first time in connection with the circumcision is that when he was circumcised he became associated with the letter He, and the Shekinah rested on him." ' Said R. Abba: 'Happy are Israel in that God has chosen them from all peoples and has given them this sign of the covenant; for whoever has this sign of the covenant will not descend to Gehinnom if he guards it properly, not subjecting it to another power or playing false with the name of the King; for to betray this sign is to betray the name of God, as it is written, "they have dealt treacherously against the Lord in that they have born strange children" (Hos. V, 7).' Said R. Abba further: 'When a man takes up his son to initiate him in this covenant, God calls to the ministering angels and says, "See what a creature I have made in the world." At that moment Elijah traverses the world in four sweeps and presents himself there; and for this reason we have been taught that it behoves the father to prepare an extra chair for his honour, and to say "this is the chair of Elijah"; and if he neglects to do so, Elijah does not visit him nor go up and testify before the Almighty that the circumcision has taken place. Why has Elijah to testify? For this reason. When God said to him "What dost thou here, Elijah?" (I Kings XIX, 9), he answered, "I have been very jealous for the Lord, the God of Hosts, for the children of Israel have forsaken thy covenant." Said God to him: "As thou livest, wherever my sons imprint this sign upon their flesh, thou shalt be there, and the mouth which charged Israel with forsaking the covenant shall testify that they are observing it." Our teachers have also taught that the reason why Elijah was punished was because he brought false charges against God's children.'

By this time it was full daylight and they rose to go, but the host came to them and said: 'Will you not finish the subject on which you were engaged tonight?' They said to him: 'What do you mean?' He said: 'Tomorrow you have a chance of seeing the sponsor of the covenant, [Tr. note: Elijah.] for tomorrow is the celebration of the circumcision of my son, and my wife begs you to stay.' Said R. Abba: 'We are invited to a pious act, and if we stay, it will be to behold the divine presence.' They accordingly stayed the whole of that day.

When night came the host brought together all his friends and they studied the Torah all that night and not one of them slept. Said the host to them, 'May it please you that each one should give an exposition of the Torah.'

Then one began on the text: For that there was an uncovering of flesh in Israel, for that the people offered themselves willingly, bless ye the Lord (Jud. V, 2). He said: 'The reason why Deborah and Barak commenced their song with these words was as follows. The world, as we have been taught, rests only upon this covenant of circumcision, according to the verse in Jeremiah (XXXIII, 25), "If not for my covenant day and night, I had not set the ordinances of heaven and earth." Hence as long as Israel observe this covenant, the heaven and earth go on in their appointed course. But if Israel neglect this covenant, then heaven and earth are disturbed, and blessing is not vouchsafed to the world. Now in the time of the Judges the Gentiles gained power over Israel only because they neglected this covenant, to this extent, that they did not uncover the flesh after circumcision: this is indicated by the words, "And the children of Israel forsook the Lord." Hence God delivered them into the hand of Sisera, until Deborah came and made all Israel vow to circumcise properly; then their enemies fell before them. Similarly, as we have learnt, God said to Joshua, "Do you not know that the Israelites are not circumcised properly, as the flesh has not been uncovered; how then can you expect to lead them into the land and subdue their enemies?" Hence God said to him, "Circumcise again the children of Israel a second time" (Josh. V, 2); and until the uncovering was performed, they did not enter the land and their enemies were not subdued. So here, when Israel vowed to observe this sign, their enemies were overcome and blessing returned to the land.'

Another one then discoursed on the text: And it came to pass on the way at the lodging place that the Lord met him and sought to kill him. He said: 'By "him" is here meant Moses. Said God to him: "How can you think to bring Israel out of Egypt and to humble a great king, when you have forgotten my covenant, since your son is not circumcised?" Forthwith "he sought to slay him": that is, as we have learnt, Gabriel came down in a flame of fire to destroy him, having the appearance of a burning serpent which sought to swallow him. The form of a serpent was chosen as emblematical of the king of Egypt, who is compared to a serpent (Ezek. XXIX, 3). Zipporah, however, saw in time and circumcised her son, so that Moses was released; so it is written, "And Zipporah took a flint and cut off the foreskin of her son", being guided by a sudden inspiration.'

Another then discoursed on the text: And Joseph said to his brethren, Come near to me, I pray you, and they came near (Gen. XLV, 4). He said: 'Seeing that they were already standing by him, why did he tell them to come near? The reason was that when he said to them "I am Joseph your brother", they were dumbfounded, seeing his royal state, so he showed them the sign of the covenant and said to them: "It is through this that I have attained to this estate, through keeping this intact." From this we learn that whoever keeps intact this sign of the covenant is destined for kingship. Another example is Boaz, who said to Ruth, "As the Lord liveth, lie down until the morning" (Ruth III, 13). By this adjuration he exorcised his passion, and because he guarded the covenant he became the progenitor of the greatest lineage of kings, and of the Messiah, whose name is linked with that of God.'

Another then discoursed on the text: Though an host should encamp against me,... in this (zoth) will I be confident (Ps. XXVII, 3). He said: 'We have learnt that the word zoth (this) alludes to the sign of the covenant, which is always on a man's person and also has its counterpart above. If so, it may be said, why should David alone be confident in it and not everyone else? The answer is that this zoth was attached to him in a peculiar degree, being the crown of the kingdom [Tr. note: i.e. of the Sefirah Malkuth, of which David's throne was the counterpart below.]. It was because David did not guard it properly that the kingship

Zohar: Bereshith, Section 1, Page 94a

was taken from him for so long a time. For this zoth symbolises also the supernal Kingdom and Jerusalem the holy city, and when David sinned a voice went forth and said: "David, thou shalt now be disjoined from that with which thou wast united; thou art banished from Jerusalem and the kingship is taken from thee"; thus he was punished in that wherein he had sinned. And if David could be so punished, how much more so other men?' Another then discoursed on the text: Unless the Lord had been my help, my soul had soon dwelt in silence (duma) (Ps. XCIV, 17). He said: 'We have learnt that that which saves Israel from descending to Gehinnom and being delivered into the hands of Duma like other nations is this same covenant. For so we have learnt, that when a man leaves this world, numbers of angels swoop down to seize him, but when they behold this sign of the holy covenant they leave him and he is not delivered into the hands of Duma, so as to be sent down to Gehinnom. Both upper and lower (angels) are afraid of this sign, and no torture is inflicted on the man who has been able to guard this sign, because thereby he is attached to the name of the Holy One, blessed be He. So with David, when he was dethroned and driven from Jerusalem, he was afraid that he would be delivered into the hands of Duma and die in the future world, until the message came to him, "The Lord also hath put away thy sin, thou shalt not die" (II Sam. XII, 13). Then it was that he exclaimed "Unless the Lord had been my help, etc." '

Another one then discoursed as follows: 'What did David mean by saying (when fleeing from before Absalom): and he shall show me both himself (otho) and his habitation (II Sam. XV, 25)?' He said: 'Who is there that can see God? In truth the word otho here means not "him" but "his sign", and it is as we have learnt, that when David's punishment was decreed, and he knew that it was for not having guarded properly this sign (which is the sum and substance of all, and without the due observance of which no one can be called righteous), he prayed that God should show him this sign, fearing that it had parted from him, because on it depended both his throne and Jerusalem; hence he joined the sign and the habitation, meaning that the kingdom conferred by this sign should be restored to its place.'

Another then discoursed on the text: From my flesh shall I see God (Job XIX, 26). He said: 'The words "my flesh" are to be literally taken as the place where the covenant is imprinted, as we have learnt: "Whenever a man is stamped with this holy imprint, through it he sees God", because the soul (neshamah) is attached to this spot. So if he does not guard it, then of him it is written, "they lose the soul (neshamah) given by God" (Job IV, 9). If, however, he guards it, then the Shekinah does not depart from him. He cannot be sure of it till he is married, when at last the sign enters into its place. When the man and wife are joined together and are called by one name, then the celestial favour rests upon them, the favour (Hesed) which issues from the supernal Wisdom and is embraced in the male, so that the female also is firmly established. Further, it has been pointed out that the word for "God" in this passage, viz. Eloah, may be divided into El, signifying the radiance of Wisdom, the letter Vau, signifying the male, and the letter He, signifying the female; when they are joined, the name Eloah is used, and the holy neshamah is united to this spot. And since all depends on this sign, therefore it is written, "and from my flesh I shall see Eloah". Happy are Israel, the holy ones, who are linked to the Holy One, blessed be He, happy in this world and happy in the next: of them it is written, "Ye that cleave unto the Lord your God, are alive every one of you this day" (Deut. IV, 4).'

Said R. Abba: 'I marvel that with so much learning you are still living in this village.' They said to him: 'If birds are driven from their homes,

Zohar: Bereshith, Section 1, Page 94b

they do not know where to fly, as it is written, "As a bird that wandereth from her nest, so is a man that wandereth from his place" (Prov. XXVII, 8). It is in this place that we have learnt the Torah, because it is our habit to sleep half the night and to study the other half. And when we rise in the morning the smell of the fields and the sound of the rivers seem to instil the Torah into us, and so it becomes fixed in our minds. Once this place was visited with punishment for neglect of the Torah, and a number of doughty scholars were carried off. Therefore we study it day and night, and the place itself helps us, and whoever quits this place is like one who quits eternal life.' R. Abba thereupon lifted up his hands and blessed them. So they sat through the night, until at last they said to some boys who were with them: 'Go outside and see if it is day, and when you come back let each one of you say some piece of Torah to our distinguished guest.' So they went out and saw that it was day. One of them said: 'On this day there will be a fire from above.' 'And on this house,' said another. Said a third: 'There is an elder here who this day will be burnt with fire.' 'God forbid,' said R. Abba, who was greatly perturbed, and did not know what to say. 'A cord of the (divine) will has been grasped on earth,' he exclaimed. And it was indeed so; for on that day the companions beheld the face of the Shekinah, and were surrounded with fire. As for R. Abba, his countenance was aflame with the intoxication of the Torah. It is recorded that all that day they did not leave the house, which was enveloped in smoke, and they propounded new ideas as if they had on that day received the Torah on Mount Sinai. When they rose they did not know whether it was day or night. Said R. Abba: 'While we are here, let each one of us say some new word of wisdom in order to make a fitting return to the master of the house, who is making the celebration.'

Thereupon one opened with the text: Blessed is the man whom thou choosest and causest to approach unto thee, that he may dwell in thy courts; we shall be satisfied with the goodness of thy house, the holy place of thy temple (Ps. LXV, 5). 'This verse', he said, 'speaks first of courts, then of house, then of temple. These are three grades, one within the other and one above the other. At first a man "dwells in thy courts", and of him it may be said "he that is left in Zion and he that remaineth in Jerusalem shall be called holy" (Is. IV, 3). As a next step "we are satisfied with the goodness of thy house", which is explained by the text "a house shall be built through Wisdom". (Note that it does not say "Wisdom shall be built as a house", which would imply that Wisdom itself is called "house", but "by Wisdom", with allusion to the verse "a river went forth from Eden to water the Garden".) Lastly, "the holy place of thy temple" (hekal) is the culmination of all, as we have been taught: the word hekal (temple) may be divided into he and kol (all), implying that both are in it in complete union. The opening words of the verse, "Blessed is the man whom thou choosest and causest to approach thee", indicate that whoever brings his son as an offering before God pleases God therewith, so that God draws him near and places his abode in two courts. which He joins so as to form one (hence the plural "courts"). Hence when the pious men who lived in this place in former times made this offering of their children, they used to begin by exclaiming, "Blessed he whom thou choosest and bringest near, he shall dwell in thy courts", while the company present replied, "We shall be satisfied with the goodness of thy house, the holy place of thy temple." Afterwards the celebrant said the blessing, "who sanctified us with his commandments and commanded us to initiate the child in the covenant of our father Abraham", while those present responded, "As thou hast initiated him into the covenant, etc." This ritual is in accordance with the dictum: "A man should first pray for himself and then for his neighbour," as it is written, "and (the High Priest) shall make atonement for himself and for all the congregation of Israel"–for himself first and then for the congregation. To this custom we adhere, for so we think proper.' Said R. Abba: 'Assuredly it is so, and he who does not recite these words excludes himself from the ten canopies which God intends to raise for the righteous in the future world, and which all depend upon this. Hence it is that there are ten words in this verse, out of each of which, if recited with proper faith, is made a canopy. Happy your lot in this world and in the world to come, for the Torah is fixed in your hearts as if you had yourselves stood

Zohar: Bereshith, Section 1, Page 95a

at Mount Sinai when the Law was given to Israel.'

Another then discoursed on the text: An altar of earth thou shalt make unto me, and shalt sacrifice thereon thy burnt offerings and thy peace offerings, etc. (Ex. XX, 24). He said: 'We have learnt that whoever makes this offering of his son is esteemed no less worthy than if he had offered to God all the sacrifices in the world, and had built an altar before Him. Therefore it is fitting that he should make a kind of altar in the shape of a vessel full of earth over which the circumcision may be performed, that so God may reckon it to him as if he had sacrificed on it burnt offerings and peace offerings, sheep and oxen, and be even better pleased therewith; for so it is written in the latter half of the text: "in every place where I record my name I will come to thee and bless thee", where the words "I will record my name" refer to the circumcision, of which it is written, "The secret of the Lord is with them that fear him, and he will show them his covenant" (Ps. XXV, 14). So much for the altar of earth. In the next verse we read: "And if thou make me an altar of stone." This alludes to the proselyte who comes from a stubborn and stony-hearted people. The text proceeds: "thou shalt not build it of hewn stones". This means that the proselyte must enter into the service of God, and that he must not be circumcised until he puts out of his mind the alien worship which he practised hitherto, and removes the stoniness of his heart. For if he is circumcised before he does this, then he is like a statue which, though hewn into shape, still remains stone. Hence "thou shalt not build it of hewn stones", since if he is still obdurate, "thou hast lifted up thy tool upon it and hast polluted it"; i.e. the act of circumcision is of no use to him. Wherefore happy is the lot of him who brings this offering with gladness and pleases God thereby; and it is fitting that he should rejoice in this boon the whole of the day, as it is written, "For all those that put their trust in thee shall rejoice, they shall ever shout with joy, and they that love thy name shall exult in thee" (Ps. V, 12).'

Another then discoursed on the text: Now when Abram was ninety years (lit. year) and nine years old, the Lord appeared... and said unto him, I am God Almighty, walk before me, etc. (Gen. XVII, 1). 'This verse presents a number of difficulties. In the first place, it seems to imply that God only now appeared to Abram when he had attained this age, whereas God had already spoken to Abram on various occasions (v. Gen. XII, 1; XIII, 14; XV, 13). Again, the word "years" is mentioned twice, first in the singular (shanah) and then in the plural (shanim). The answer is, as our teachers have stated, that as long as Abram was closed in body, and therefore in heart, God did not fully reveal Himself to him, and hence it is not stated hitherto that God appeared to Abram. Now, however, God appeared to him because He was now about to expose in him this sign and holy crown, and further because God desired to bring forth from him holy seed, and this could not be so long as his flesh was closed; now, however, that he was ninety-nine years old and the time was drawing near for holy seed to issue from him, it was fitting that he himself should be holy first. Hence his age is stated on this occasion, and not on all the others when God spoke to him. Further, the expression "ninety year", instead of "ninety years", indicates that all his previous years counted for no more than one year, and that his life had been no life; but now that he had come to this point, his years were really years. Further we may ask, why is the term "God Almighty" (El Shaddai) used here for the first time? The reason is, as we have learnt, that God has made lower crowns which are not holy, and which, in fact, pollute, and with these are marked all who are not circumcised. The mark consists of the letters Shin and Daleth, [Tr. note: Forming the word Shed (demon).] and therefore they are polluted with the demons and cling to them. After circumcision, however, they escape from them and enter under the wings of the Shekinah, as they display the letter Yod, the holy mark and the sign of the perfect covenant,

Zohar: Bereshith, Section 1, Page 95b

and there is stamped upon them the name Shaddai (Almighty), complete in all its letters. Hence we find written in this connection, "I am El Shaddai." It says further: "Walk before me and be perfect", as much as to say: "Hitherto thou hast been defective, being stamped only with Shin Daleth: therefore circumcise thyself and become complete through the sign of Yod." And whoever is so marked is ready to be blessed through this name, as it is written, "And God Almighty (El Shaddai) shall bless thee" (Gen. XXVIII, 3), to wit, the source of blessings, that dominates the "lower crowns" and inspires fear and trembling in them all. Hence all that are not holy keep afar from one who is circumcised, and have no power over him. Moreover, he is never sent down to Gehinnom, as it is written, "Thy people are all righteous, they shall forever inherit the earth" (Is. LX, 21).' Said R. Abba: 'Happy are ye in this world and in the world to come! Happy am I that I am come to hear these words from your mouths! Ye are all holy, all the sons of the Holy God; of you it is written, "One shall say, I am the Lord's, and another shall call himself by the name of Jacob, and another shall subscribe with his hand unto the Lord and surname himself by the name of Israel" (Ibid. XLIV, 5). Everyone of you is closely attached to the holy King on high: ye are the mighty chieftains of that land which is called "the land of the living", the princes of which feed on the manna of holy dew.'

Another then discoursed on the text: Happy art thou, O land, when thy king is a son of freedom and thy princes eat in due season (Eccl. X, 17). 'Just before this it is written: "Woe to thee, O land, when thy king is a child, and thy princes eat in the morning." There is an apparent but not a real contradiction between these verses. The reference in the verse "happy art thou, O land," is to the supernal realm which has control over all the life above, and is therefore called "land of the living". Of this it is written, "a land which the Lord thy God careth for continually" (Deut. XI, 12), and again "a land where thou shalt eat bread without scarceness, thou shalt not lack anything in it" (Ibid. VIII, 9). Why so? Because "thy king is a son of freedom". By this is meant the Holy One, blessed be He, who is called a "son of freedom" because of the Jubilee, which is the source of freedom. It is true that, according to this explanation, we should expect to have in our text the word heruth (freedom) and not, as we actually find written, horin (free ones). The reason is, as we have learnt in our secret Mishnah, that when the Yod is united with the He, they produce "the river which issues from Eden to water the Garden" (Gen. II, 10). It is, in fact, misleading to say "when they unite", for they are indeed united, and therefore it is written ben horin. Hence "happy art thou, O land, when thy king is a ben horin, and thy princes eat in due season", with joy, with sanctity, and with God's blessing. On the other hand, "Woe to thee, O land, when thy prince is a child." This is the land of the lower world; for so we have learnt: "All the lands of the Gentiles have been committed to great chieftains who are appointed over them, and above all is he of whom it is written, 'I was a lad and am now old' "(Ps. XXXVII, 25), words which, according to tradition, were pronounced by the "Prince of the Globe". Hence, "Woe to thee, O land, when thy king is a lad": i.e. woe to the world which derives sustenance from this side; for when Israel are in captivity, they, as it were, derive their sustenance from an alien power. Further, "when thy princes eat in the morning"; i.e. in the morning only and not the whole day, or any other time of the day. For so we have learnt, that at sunrise when men go forth and bow down to the sun, wrath is suspended over the world, and at the time of the afternoon prayer also wrath is suspended over the world. Why is this? Because "thy king is a lad", viz. he who is called "lad". But you, truly pious ones, sainted to those above, do not derive sustenance from that side, but from that holy place above. Of you it is written: "Ye who cleave to the Lord are alive all of you this day" (Deut. IV, 4).'

R. Abba then discoursed on the text: Let me sing for my well beloved a song of my beloved touching his vineyard, etc. (Is. V, 1). He said: 'This passage presents many difficulties. In the first place it should rather be called a "reproof" than a "song". Then again why first "well beloved" and then "beloved"? Also, we find nowhere else mention of a place

called "Keren Ben Shemen" (horn of the son of oil). Our colleagues have expounded these verses in many ways, and all of them are good, but I explain them in this way. The word "well beloved" contains an allusion to Isaac, who was called so before he was born. For so we have learnt, that God showed great love for him in not allowing him to be born until Abraham his father had been circumcised and called perfect and had been completed by the addition to his name of the letter he. To Sarah, too, a he had been given. Here arises a question. We understand he for Sarah, but for Abram the added letter should have been not he but yod, he being a male. The reason is in truth a somewhat deep and recondite one. Abraham rose to the highest stage, and took as his additional letter the higher he, which symbolises the sphere of the male. For there are two symbolic he's, one higher and one lower, one associated with the male and the other with the female. Hence Abraham ascended with the he of the higher sphere, and Sarai descended with the he of the lower sphere. Further it is written, "thus (koh) shall be thy seed", and the word "seed" here, as we have learnt, is to be taken exactly (of Isaac). For it was he who entered into this covenant from his birth, and whoever enters from his birth really enters. It is for this reason that a proselyte who is circumcised is called "a proselyte of righteousness", because he does not come from the holy stock who have been circumcised; and therefore one who enters in this way is called by the name of the first pioneer "Abraham". Thus the letter he, too, was given to him; and if it had not also been given to Sarah, Abraham would of necessity have begotten on a lower level, in the same way as Koh, which begets on a lower level. But when he was given to Sarah, the two he's were joined together, and brought forth on a higher level, that which issued from them being yod; hence yod is the first letter of the name of Isaac, symbolising the male. From this point the male principle began to extend, and therefore it is written, "For in Isaac shall thy seed be called", and not in thee. Isaac bore on the higher level, as it is written, "Thou givest truth to Jacob" (Micah VII, 20), showing that Jacob completed the edifice. It may be asked: "Was Abraham attached only to this grade and no more?" If so, why does it say, "kindness (hesed) to Abraham"? (Ibid.) The answer is that hesed was his portion because he dealt kindly with mankind, but for bearing children, it was here that he was attached and here that he began. Hence it was that Abraham was not circumcised till he was ninety-nine years old; the inner reason for this is well known and has been explained in our Mishnah. For this reason, too, Isaac typifies stern justice, which was his portion, but for begetting he was called "kindness" (hesed). Hence Jacob crowned the edifice on this side and on that. In respect of the strivings of Abraham and Isaac for portions above he was the culmination; and in respect of the privilege which was granted to them to bear sons better than themselves he was also the culmination. Hence the Scripture says of him, "Israel in whom I glory" (Is. XLIX, 3). In him were united attributes both from the higher and the lower. Hence the word "song" is used in this passage. According to some, the word "well beloved" here refers to Abraham, who transmitted this inheritance; but it is more correct to refer it to Isaac, as I do. To proceed: "the song of my beloved to his vineyard" refers to the Holy One, blessed be He, who is commonly called "beloved" (dod), as in the verse, "My beloved is white and ruddy" (S. S. V, 10). Thus, my well beloved unites with my beloved, who is male, and from him springs forth a vineyard, as it is written, "My well beloved had a vineyard." The Scripture further says that this vineyard sprang forth in "Keren-Ben-Shemen". This "Keren" is the same as the "horn" (keren) of the Jubilee, and it is united with the male that is called ben shemen (son of oil), which is the same as ben horin (son of freedom). "Shemen" is mentioned because it is the source of the oil for lighting the lamps (of understanding). This oil makes faces shine and kindles lamps until it is gathered in a horn, which is then called "the horn of the Jubilee". For this reason Royalty is always anointed from a horn; and the reason why the kingdom of David endured was because he was anointed from a horn and was true to it. The next words are, "he put a fence round it and stoned it":

i.e. he removed from himself and from his portion all the celestial chieftains and champions, and all the "lower crowns", and chose this vineyard for his portion, as it is written, "For the Lord's portion is his people, Jacob is the lot of his inheritance" (Deut. XXXII, 9). Further, "He planted it with the choicest vine", as it says elsewhere, "I planted thee a noble vine, wholly a right seed" (Jer. II, 21). (The word kuloh (wholly) in this sentence is written with he to point the same lesson as the text "thus (koh) shall be thy seed".) Our text closes with the words: "He built a tower in the midst of it"-the "tower" is that mentioned in the verse, "The name of the Lord is a strong tower, the righteous runneth into it and is safe" (Prov. XVIII, 10) "and also hewed out a wine press therein": this is the "gate of righteousness" mentioned in the verse, "Open to me the gates of righteousness" (Ps. CXVIII, 19). We learn from this that every Israelite who is circumcised has the entry into both the tower and the gate. He who makes this offering of his son brings him under the aegis of the Holy Name. On this sign, too, are based the heaven and earth, as it is written, "But for my covenant day and night, I had not set the ordinances of heaven and earth" (Jer. XXXIII, 25). Our host of today has been privileged to see the Holy One, blessed be He, face to face this day. Happy we that we have lived to see this day, and happy thy portion with us. To this son that is born to thee I apply the words of the Scripture, "Every one that is called by my name... I have formed him, yea I have made him" (Is. XLIII, 7); also the verse, "and all thy children shall be taught of the Lord, etc." (Ibid. LIV, 13).'

They then rose and escorted R. Abba on his way for three miles. They said to him: 'Your host who made the ceremony deserves all the honour he has received, because his act was a doubly pious one.' He said: 'What do you mean?' They answered: 'This man's wife was formerly the wife of his brother, who died without children, and so he married her, and this being the first son, he calls him after the name of his dead brother.' [Tr. note: v. Deut. XXV, 5-10.] Said R. Abba: 'From now onwards his name shall be Iddi'; and in fact he grew up to be the well-known Iddi bar Jacob. R. Abba then gave them his blessing and continued his journey. When he reached home, he informed R. Eleazar of all that had happened, but was afraid to tell R. Simeon. One day as he was studying with R. Simeon, the latter said: 'It is written: "And Abraham fell on his face and God spoke with him saying, As for me, behold my covenant is with thee." This shows that until he was circumcised, he used to fall on his face when God spoke with him, but after he was circumcised he stood upright without fear. Further, the words "behold, my covenant is with thee" show that he found himself circumcised.' Said R. Abba to him: 'Perhaps your honour will permit me to relate some excellent ideas which I have heard on this subject.' 'Speak,' he said. 'But I am afraid,' continued R. Abba, 'that the people who told me may suffer through my telling.' 'God forbid!' said R. Simeon. 'Remember the verse: "He shall not be afraid of evil tidings, his heart is fixed trusting in the Lord".' He then told him what had happened, and related to him all that he had heard. Said R. Simeon: 'You mean to say that you knew all this and did not say a word to me? I order you during the next thirty days to do your very utmost to forget it. Does not the Scripture say: "Withhold not good from them to whom it is due, when it is in the power of thine hand to do it"?' And so it came to pass. R. Simeon further said: 'I order that with these explanations they shall be banished to Babylon, I mean to say, among our colleagues in Babylon.' R. Abba was sorely grieved at this. One day R. Simeon, seeing him, said: 'Your looks betray some inward sorrow.' He replied: 'I am not grieving for myself, but for them.' He answered: 'God forbid they should be punished for anything except for speaking too openly. For this let them go into exile among the colleagues and learn from them how to keep things to themselves; for these matters are not to be divulged save among ourselves, since the Holy One, blessed be He, has confirmed our ideas, and made us the instruments for disclosing them.' R. Yose said: 'It is written, "Then shall thy light break forth as the morning, etc." (Is. LVIII, 8). This means that the Holy One, blessed be He, will one day proclaim with regard to his sons: "Then shall thy light break forth as the morning, and thy healing shall spring forth speedily, and thy righteousness shall go before thee and the glory of the Lord shall be thy reward".'

VAYERA

Zohar: Bereshith, Section 1, Page 97a

AND THE LORD APPEARED UNTO HIM. R. Hiya commenced to discourse on the verse: The flowers appear on the earth, the time of song is come, and the voice of the turtle is heard in our land (S. S. II, 12). He said: 'When God created the world, He endowed the earth with all the energy requisite for it, but it did not put forth produce until man appeared. When, however, man was created, all the products that were latent in the earth appeared above ground. Similarly, the heaven did not impart strength to the earth until man came. So it is written, "All the plants of the earth were not yet on the earth, and the herbs of the field had not yet sprung up, for the Lord God had not caused it to rain upon the earth, and there was not a man to till the ground" (Gen. II, 5), that is to say, all the products of the earth were still hidden in its bosom and had not yet shown themselves, and the heavens refrained from pouring rain upon the earth, because man had not yet been created. When, however, man appeared, forthwith "the flowers appeared on the earth", all its latent powers being revealed; "the time of song was come", the earth being now ripe to offer up praises to the Almighty, which it could not do before man was created. "And the voice of the turtle is heard in our land": this is the word of God, which was not

Zohar: Bereshith, Section 1, Page 97b

in the world till man was created. Thus when man was there, everything was there. When man sinned, the earth was cursed, and all these good things left it, as it is written, "cursed is the earth for thy sake" (Gen. III, 17), and again, "when thou tillest the ground it shall not give its strength to thee" (Ibid. IV, 12), and again, "thorns and thistles it shall bring forth to thee" (Ibid. III, 18). When Noah came, he invented spades and hoes, but afterwards he sinned through drunkenness, and the rest of the world also sinned before God, and the strength of the earth deserted it. So matters continued until Abraham came. Then once more "the blossoms appeared in the earth", and all the powers of the earth were restored and displayed themselves. "The time of pruning (zamir) came", i.e. God told Abraham to circumcise himself. When at length the covenant existed in Abraham through the circumcision, then all this verse was fulfilled in him, the world was firmly established, and the word of the Lord came to him openly: hence it is written, AND THE LORD APPEARED UNTO HIM. Said R. Eleazar: 'Until Abraham was circumcised, God did not speak with him save from a lower grade, whereon, too, the higher grades were not resting. But when he was circumcised, straightway "the blossoms appeared in the earth", to wit, the lower grades which the earth put forth, thereby establishing that lower grade we have mentioned; further, "the time of pruning came", to wit, the pruning of the boughs of orlah; and to crown all, "the voice of the turtle was heard in the land", to wit, the voice which issues from the innermost

Zohar: Bereshith, Section 1, Page 98a

recess. This voice was now heard, and shaped the spoken words and gave them their perfect form. This is implied in the words here used, "and the Lord appeared to him". Already, before Abraham was circumcised, we are told that "the Lord appeared unto Abram" (Gen. XVII, 1), and if the word "him" in this sentence refers to Abraham, we may well ask, what advance had he made (in prophecy) by being circumcised? The answer is that the word "him" here has an inner meaning: it refers to the grade which now spoke with him. Now for the first time "the Lord appeared" to that grade; that is to say, the Voice was revealed, and associated itself with the Speech (dibbur) in conversing with him. Similarly in the words, AS HE SAT IN THE TENT DOOR IN THE HEAT OF THE DAY, the word "he" has an inner meaning, indicating that all the grades rested on this lower grade after Abraham was circumcised. Thus the words "And the Lord appeared unto him" contain a mystic allusion to that audible Voice which is united to Speech, and manifests itself therein. "As he sat in the tent door" refers to the supernal world which was at hand to illumine him. "In the heat of the day." That is, it was the right side, to which Abraham clave, that illumined. According to another exposition, "in the heat of the day" indicates the time when the grades approach each other, impelled by mutual desire.'

Zohar: Bereshith, Section 1, Page 98b

AND THERE APPEARED UNTO HIM. R. Abba said: 'Before Abraham was circumcised he was, as it were, covered over, but as soon as he was circumcised he became completely exposed to the influence of the Shekinah, which thereupon rested on him in full and perfect measure. The words "as he sat in the tent door" picture the supernal world hovering over this lower world. When is this? "In the heat of the day", that is, at a period when a certain Zaddik (righteous one) feels a desire to repose therein. Straightway "it lifts up its eyes and looks, and lo, three men stand over against it". Who are these three men? They are Abraham, Isaac, and Jacob, who stand over this lower grade, and from whom it

Zohar: Bereshith, Section 1, Page 99a

draws sustenance and nourishment. Thereupon "it sees and runs to meet them", since it is the desire of this lower grade to attach itself to them, and its joy is to be drawn after them. "And it bows down to the ground", to prepare a throne near them. Observe that the Almighty made King David one of the under-pillars of the supernal throne, the patriarchs being the other three. For he was a pedestal to them, yet when he is joined with them he becomes one of the pillars upholding the supernal throne; and on that account he reigned in Hebron for seven years, namely, in order that he might be closely associated with them, as explained elsewhere.'

R. Abba opened a discourse with the verse: Who shalt ascend into the mountain of the Lord? And who shall stand in his holy place? (Ps. XXIV, 3). 'Mankind', he said, 'little realise on what it is that they are standing whilst in this world' For the days as they pass ascend and range themselves before the Almighty-namely, all the days of men's existence in this world. For all these have been created, and they all present themselves on high. That they have been created we know from the words of Scripture, "The days were fashioned" (Ps. CXXXIX, 16). And when the time comes for the days to depart from this world, they all approach the Most High King, as it is written, "And the days of David drew nigh that he should die" (I Kings II, 1), and again, "And the days of Israel drew nigh that he should die" (Gen. XLVII, 29). Man, however, whilst in this world, considers not and reflects not what it is he is standing on, and each day as it passes he regards as though it has vanished into nothingness. When the soul departs this world she knows not by what path she will be made to travel; for it is not granted to all souls to ascend by the way that leads to the realm of radiance where the choicest souls shine forth.

Zohar: Bereshith, Section 1, Page 99b

For it is the path taken by man in this world that determines the path of the soul on her departure. Thus, if a man is drawn towards the Holy One, and is filled with longing towards Him in this world, the soul in departing from him is carried upward towards the higher realms by the impetus given her each day in this world.' R. Abba continued: 'I once found myself in a town inhabited by descendants of the "children of the East", and they imparted to me some of the Wisdom of antiquity with which they were acquainted. They also possessed some books of their Wisdom, and they showed me one in which it was written that, according to the goal which a man sets himself in this world, so does he draw to himself a spirit from on high. If he strives to attain some holy and lofty object, he draws that object from on high to himself below. But if his desire is to cleave to the other side, and he makes this his whole intent, then he draws to himself from above the other influence. They said, further, that all depends on the kind of speech, action, and intention to which a man habituates himself, for he draws to himself here below from on high that side to which he habitually cleaves. I found also in the same book the rites and ceremonies pertaining to the worship of the stars, with the requisite formulas and the directions for concentrating the thought upon them, so

Zohar: Bereshith, Section 1, Page 100a

as to draw them near the worshipper. The same principle applies to him who seeks to be attached to the sacred spirit on high. For it is by his acts, by his words, and by his fervency and devotion that he can draw to himself that spirit from on high. They further said that if a man follows a certain direction in this world, he will be led further in the same direction when he departs this world; as that to which he attaches himself in this world, so is that to which he will find himself attached in the other world: if holy, holy, and if defiled, defiled. If he cleaves to holiness he will on high be drawn to that side and be made a servant to minister before the Holy One among the angels, and will stand among those holy beings who are referred to in the words, "then I will give thee free access among these that stand by" (Zech. III, 7). Similarly if he clings here to uncleanness, he will be drawn there towards that side and be made one of the unclean company and be attached to them. These are called "pests of mankind", and when a man leaves this world they take him up and cast him into Gehinnom, in that region where judgement is meted out to those who have sullied themselves and soiled their spirits. After that he is made a companion of the unclean spirits and becomes a "pest of mankind" like one of them. I then said to them: My children, all this is similar to what we learn in our Torah, nevertheless you should keep away from these books so that your hearts should not

Zohar: Bereshith, Section 1, Page 100b

be led astray after those idolatrous services and after those "sides" mentioned here. Be on your guard lest, God forbid, you be led astray from the worship of the Holy One, since all these books mislead mankind. For the ancient children of the East were possessed of a wisdom which they inherited from Abraham, who transmitted it to the sons of the concubines, as it is written, "But unto the sons of the concubines that Abraham had, Abraham gave gifts, and he sent them away from Isaac his son, while he yet lived, eastward, unto the country of the children of the East" (Gen. XXV, 6). In course of time they followed the track of that wisdom into many (wrong) directions. Not so with the seed of Isaac, with the portion of Jacob. For it is written, "And Abraham gave all that he had unto Isaac" (Ibid. 5), this being the holy heritage of faith to which Abraham clave, and from the sphere of which issued Jacob, of whom it is written, "And, behold, the Lord stood beside him" (Gen. XXVIII, 13), and also, "And thou, Israel, my servant, etc." (Is. XLI, 8). Hence it behoves a man to follow the Holy One and to cleave to Him continually, as it is written, "and to him shalt thou cleave" (Deut. X, 20). It is written, "Who shall ascend into the mountain of the Lord?" and the answer is given, "He that hath clean hands and a pure heart" (Ps. XXIV, 3-4), that is, he that has not made with his hands vain shapes nor grasped with them wrongful objects, nor has he defiled himself through them like those who defile their bodies willfully. "And pure of heart": that is, he that averts his heart and mind from the "other side" and directs them towards the service of the Holy One. It says further: "Who hath not lifted up his soul unto falsehood... he shall receive a blessing from the Lord" (Ibid. 4-5);

Zohar: Bereshith, Section 1, Page 101a

that is to say, when he leaves this world his soul ascends furnished with good works which will enable him to obtain entry among the holy celestial beings, in accordance with the verse, "I shall walk before the Lord in the lands of the living" (Ps. CXVI, 9), for since "he hath not lifted his soul unto falsehood, he shall receive a blessing from the Lord, etc."

'When Abraham was still suffering from the effects of the circumcision, the Holy One sent him three angels, in visible shape, to enquire of his well-being. You may, perhaps, wonder how angels can ever be visible, since it is written, "Who makes his angels spirits" (Ps. CIV, 4). Abraham, however, assuredly did see them, as they descended to earth in the form of men. And, indeed, whenever the celestial spirits descend to earth, they clothe themselves in corporeal elements and appear to men in human shape. Now Abraham, although he was in great pain from his wound, ran forward to meet them so as not to be remiss in his wonted hospitality. R. Simeon said: 'Assuredly he saw them in their angelic forms, since it is written, AND HE SAID, ADONAI (my Lord), which shows that the Shekinah (one appellative of which is Adonai) had come with them, and that the angels accompanied her as her throne and pillars, because they are the three colours below her, and Abraham, now that he was circumcised, saw what he could not see before.'

Zohar: Bereshith, Section 1, Page 101b

At first he took them for men, but afterwards he became aware that they were holy angels who had been sent on a mission to him. This was when they asked him, WHERE IS SARAH THY WIFE? and announced to him the coming birth of Isaac. AND THEY SAID TO HIM: in the word elau (to him) there are dots over the letters aleph, yod, and vau, which spell out the word ayo (where is he?). This is a reference to the Holy One who is above. Again, the word thus formed ayo is followed by the word ayeh (where?), which is a feminine form of the same, to emphasise the bond of union between the male and the female, which is the secret of true faith. Where is that bond of union complete? The answer is, BEHOLD IN THE TENT: there it is found, and there is the all-in-all union. WHERE IS SARAH THY WIFE? Did not the celestial angels know that she was in the tent? The fact is that angels do not know of happenings in this world save what is necessary for their mission. This is borne out by the text, "For I will pass through the land of Egypt... I am the Lord" (Ex. XII, 12), which indicates that although the Holy One had many messengers and angels to perform His work, yet they would not have been able to distinguish between the germ of the first-born and of the later born-only the Almighty Himself could do this. Another example is the verse, "and set a mark upon the foreheads of the men etc." (Ezek. IX, 4), which proves that the angels require a mark, as otherwise they only know what is specially communicated to them, as, for instance, the sufferings which the Holy One is about to bring upon the world as a whole and which He proclaims throughout the seven heavens. Thus when the destroying angel is at large

Zohar: Bereshith, Section 1, Page 102a

in the world, a man should take shelter in his house, remain under cover and not show himself in the open, so that no hurt may befall him, as the Israelites were bidden in Egypt, "and none of you shall go out of the door of his house until the morning" (Ex. XII, 22). From the angels one can hide oneself, but not from God, of whom it is written, "Can any hide himself in secret places that I shall not see him? saith the Lord" (Jer. XXIII, 24). The angel asked: "Where is Sarah thy wife?" for the reason that he did not want to deliver the message in her presence; but as soon as Abraham said, "Behold, she is in the tent", he said: I WILL CERTAINLY RETURN UNTO THEE WHEN THE SEASON COMETH ROUND, AND, LO, SARAH THY WIFE SHALL HAVE A SON. Note the delicacy of the angels in not announcing anything to Abraham before he invited them to eat, so as not to make it appear that the invitation was a repayment for their good tidings. We thus read first, "and they did eat", and then, and they said unto him. AND THEY DID EAT: how so? Do celestial angels eat? The truth is that they only simulated eating in honour of Abraham. R. Eleazar said: 'They certainly did eat, in the sense of fire consuming fire invisibly; of a truth what Abraham offered them they ate, as it is from the side of Abraham that they obtain sustenance on high.'

Note that Abraham kept all his food in a state of ritual cleanliness, and therefore he personally waited on them whilst they were eating. He observed so strictly the laws regarding clean and unclean that no man in a state of ritual impurity was allowed to serve in his house until he had duly cleansed himself by bathing before nightfall or by abstention for

Zohar: Bereshith, Section 1, Page 102b

seven days, according to the degree of his defilement. And as Abraham prepared the means of purification for men in such a state, so did Sarah for women. The reason why Abraham did this was because he was himself pure and is designated "pure" (as it is written, "Who can bring forth a pure one from one impure?" (Job XIV, 4), which is a reference to Abraham, who was born of Terah). R. Simeon said that it was in order to confirm Abraham in his special grade, which is symbolised by water, that he set out to keep the world pure by means of water. The same symbolic meaning underlies the words uttered by him when he invited the angels to partake of food, to wit, "Let a little water be fetched", he wishing thereby to confirm himself in the degree symbol sed by water. He therefore endeavoured to purify people in all respects-to cleanse them from idolatry and to cleanse them from ritual impurity. In the same way Sarah purified the women. The result was that all in their house were in a state of ritual purity. Wherever Abraham took up his residence he used to plant a certain tree, but in no place did it flourish properly save in the land of Canaan. By means of this tree he was able to distinguish between the man who adhered to the Almighty and the man who worshipped idols. For the man who worshipped the true God the tree spread out its branches, and formed an agreeable shade over his head; whereas in the presence of one who clung to the side of idolatry the tree shrank within itself and its branches stood upright. Abraham thus recognised the erring man, admonished him, and did not desist until he had succeeded in making him embrace the true faith. Similarly the tree received under its shade those who were clean, and not those who were unclean; and when Abraham recognised the latter, he purified them by means of water. Moreover, there was a spring of water under that very tree, and when a man came who required immediate immersion, the waters rose and also the branches of the tree: and that was a sign for Abraham that that man needed immersion forthwith. On other occasions the water dried up: this was a sign to Abraham that that man could not be purified before the lapse of seven days. Note that Abraham, in offering his invitation to the angels, said, "and recline yourselves under the tree": this was for the purpose of testing them, in the same way as he tested by the same tree any wayfarer who came. By the word "tree", he also referred to the Holy One, blessed be He, who is the tree of life for all, as though to say, "recline yourselves under His shade, and not under the shelter of strange gods". Note that Adam transgressed through eating of the tree of knowledge of good and evil, and this brought death into the world. God then said, "and now, lest he put forth his hand, and take also the tree of life etc." (Gen. III, 22). But when Abraham came, he remedied the evil by means of that other tree, which is the tree of life, and by means of which he made known the true faith to the whole world.

AND HE SAID: I WILL CERTAINLY RETURN UNTO THEE WHEN THE SEASON COMETH ROUND, ETC. R. Isaac said: 'Instead of "I will return", we should have expected here "he will return", since the visitation of barren women is in the hand of the Almighty Himself and not in the hand of any messenger, according to the dictum: "Three keys there are which have not been entrusted to any messenger, namely, of child-birth, of the resurrection, and of rain." But the truth is that the words "I will return" were spoken by the Holy One, blessed be He, who was present there. This is corroborated by the use here of the term vayomer (and he said). For it is to be observed that wherever the verb vayomer (and he said), or vayiqra (and he called), occurs without a subject, then the implied subject is the Angel of the Covenant and no other. Examples are: "And he said, If thou wilt diligently hearken etc." (Ex. XV, 26); also: "And he called unto Moses" (Lev. I, 1); also: "And unto Moses he said" (Ex. XXIV, 1).

Zohar: Bereshith, Section 1, Page 103a

In all these passages, as well as in our present passage, the unspecified subject of the sentence is the Angel of the Covenant.

AND, LO, SARAH THY WIFE SHALL HAVE A SON. Why not "and thou shalt have a son"? In order that Abraham should not think that possibly he should be from Hagar, like the previous one. R. Simeon here discoursed on the text: A son honoureth his father, and a servant his master (Mal. I, 6). He said: 'A conspicuous example of a son honouring his father is presented by Isaac at the time when Abraham bound him on the altar with the intent of offering him up as a sacrifice. He was then thirty-seven years old, whilst his father was an old man; and though he could easily, by a single kick, have liberated himself, he let himself be bound like a lamb in order to do the will of his father. A servant's honouring his master is illustrated by Eliezer's conduct on the occasion when he was sent by Abraham to Haran; he there followed out all the wishes of his master and paid him great respect, as it is written, "And he said, I am Abraham's servant; and the Lord blessed my master Abraham" (Gen. XXIV, 34-35). Here was a man who had with him silver and gold and precious stones and camels and was himself of a goodly presence; yet he did not present himself as a friend of Abraham or one of his kin, but openly declared, "I am the servant of Abraham", in order to extol his master and make him an object of honour in the eyes of his hearers. Hence the prophet proclaims: "A son honoureth his father, and a servant his master", as much as to say, "but ye Israel my children, ye feel ashamed to declare that I am your father or that ye are my servants". Hence the verse proceeds: "If then I be a father, where is my honour?" (Mal. I, 6). So when it says of Isaac, "And lo, a son", it means, "truly a son, a son proper, not an Ishmael, but a son who will pay due respect and honour to his father". Further it is said, "And Sarah thy wife shall have a son", because Isaac was indeed a son to Sarah, since it was on his account that she died, on his account she suffered anguish of soul until her life departed, and, further, on his account she is exalted at the time when the Holy One sits in judgement on the world, for on that day the Israelites read the portion: "And the Lord remembered Sarah as he had said" (Gen. XXI, I), mentioning Sarah for the sake of Isaac. Truly he was "a son to Sarah". AND SARAH HEARD IN THE TENT DOOR, AND IT WAS BEHIND HIM. We should have expected "and she was behind him". But the inner meaning of the whole verse is that Sarah heard the "Door of the Tent", which is identical with the Holy One in the lower grade, making the declaration, and that "He", to wit, the Holy One in the supernal grade, "was behind him" (the door), confirming the declaration. During the whole of her lifetime Sarah never heard any utterance from the Holy One save on that occasion. According to another interpretation, the expression "and he was behind him" refers to Abraham, who was behind the Shekinah.'

NOW ABRAHAM AND SARAH WERE OLD, THEY HAD ARRIVED IN REGARD TO DAYS. The expression they had arrived (ba'u) in regard to days" is equivalent to "their days had approached their allotted term", Abraham being a hundred years old and Sarah ninety. We may compare the expression "for the day arrived" (ba), i.e. the day had declined towards evening. IT HAD CEASED TO BE WITH SARAH AFTER THE MANNER OF WOMEN: but at that moment she experienced a rejuvenation. Hence her remark AND MY LORD IS OLD, as much as to say that he was unfitted to beget children on account of age. R. Judah here began a discourse with the verse: Her husband is known in the gates, when he sitteth among the elders of the land (Prov. XXXI, 23). He said: 'The Holy One, blessed be He, is transcendent in His glory, He is hidden and removed far beyond all ken; there is no one in the world, nor has there ever been one, whom His wisdom and essence do not elude, since He is recondite and hidden and beyond all ken, so that neither the supernal nor the lower beings are able to commune with Him until they utter the words "Blessed be the glory of the Lord from his place" (Ezek. III, 12). The creatures of the earth think of Him as being on high, declaring, "His glory is above the heavens" (Ps. CXIII, 4), while the heavenly beings think of Him as being below, declaring, "His glory is over all the earth" (Ps. LVII, 12), until they both, in heaven and on earth, concur in declaring, "Blessed be the glory of the Lord from his place", because He is unknowable and no one can truly understand Him. This being so, how can you say, "Her husband is known in the gates"?

Zohar: Bereshith, Section 1, Page 103b

But of a truth the Holy One makes Himself known to every one according to the measure of his understanding and his capacity to attach himself to the spirit of Divine wisdom; and thus "Her husband is known", not "in the gates"

136

(bishe'arim), but, as we may also translate, "by measure", though a full knowledge is beyond the reach of any being.' R. Simeon said: 'The "gates" mentioned in this passage are the same as the gates in the passage, "Lift up your heads, O ye gates" (Ps. XXIV, 7), and refer to the supernal grades by and through which alone a knowledge of the Almighty is possible to man, and but for which man could not commune with God. Similarly, man's soul cannot be known directly, save through the members of the body, which are the grades forming the instruments of the soul. The soul is thus known and unknown. So it is with the Holy One, blessed be He, since He is the Soul of souls, the Spirit of spirits, covered and veiled from anyone; nevertheless, through those gates, which are doors for the soul, the Holy One makes Himself known. For there is door within door, grade behind grade, through which the glory of the Holy One is made known. Hence here "the tent door" is the door of righteousness, referred to in the words, "Open to me the gates of righteousness" (Ps. CXVIII, 19), and this is the first entrance door: through this door a view is opened to all the other supernal doors. He who succeeds in entering this door is privileged to know both it and all the other doors, since they all repose on this one. At the present time this door remains unknown because Israel is in exile; and therefore all the other doors are removed from them, so that they cannot know or commune; but when Israel return from exile, all the supernal grades are destined to rest harmoniously upon this one. Then men will obtain a knowledge of the precious supernal wisdom of which hitherto they wist not, as it is written, "And the spirit of the Lord shall rest upon him, the spirit of wisdom and understanding, the spirit of counsel and might, the spirit of knowledge and of the fear of the Lord" (Is. XI, 2). All these are destined to rest on this lower door which is the "tent door"; all too will rest upon the Messiah in order that he may judge the world, as it is written, "But with righteousness shall he judge the poor, etc." (Ibid. 4). Thus when the good tidings were brought to Abraham, it was that grade which brought them, as we have deduced from the fact that the word vayomer (and he said) is used without a specific subject in the passage "And he said, I will certainly return unto thee when the season cometh round."

'Observe how the great love of the Almighty towards Abraham was manifested in the fact that Isaac was not born to him until he was circumcised. In this way it was made certain that his seed should be holy, according to the words of the Scripture, "wherein is the seed thereof after its kind" (Gen. I, 12). For had Abraham begotten before he was circumcised, his seed would not have been holy, as it would have issued from the state of orlah, and thus would have clung to that state here below; but after Abraham's circumcision the seed issued from the state of holiness and became attached to supernal holiness, and he begat children in the higher plane and thus became attached to his grade in the manner fitting.' R. Eleazar asked one day of his father, R. Simeon: 'In regard to the name Isaac, why did the Holy One give him that name before he came into the world, by commanding "And thou shalt call his name Isaac" (Gen. XVII, 19)?' R. Simeon answered: 'We have elsewhere stated that through Isaac fire supplanted water. For water comes from the side of Geburah (Force), and it is further required of the Levites that they should entertain that side with hymns and songs on divers instruments. Hence Isaac was joyousness, because he issued from that side and became attached to it. Observe that the word Yitzhak (Isaac) means "laughter", to wit, rejoicing because water was changed to fire and fire to water; hence he was called Isaac, and hence the Holy One called him

so before he came into the world, and He announced that name to Abraham. You will see that in other cases the Holy One permitted the parents, even the mothers, to give names to their children. Here, however, the Holy One did not give permission to the mother to name the child, but only to Abraham, as it is written: "And thou shalt call his name Isaac"– thou and no other, so as to intermingle water with fire and fire with water and to range it on his side.'

Having related how Abraham was informed of the coming birth of Isaac, the Scripture proceeds: AND THE MEN ROSE UP FROM THENCE, AND LOOKED OUT TOWARD SODOM. Said R. Eleazar: 'Observe how merciful the Holy One, blessed be He, shows Himself towards all beings, and especially towards those who walk in His paths. For when He is about to execute judgement on the world, before doing so He puts in the way of His beloved the occasion of performing a good act. We have thus been taught that when the Holy One loves a man, He sends him a present in the shape of a poor man, so that he should perform some good deed to him, through the merit of which he shall draw to himself a cord of grace from the right side which shall wind round his head and imprint a mark on him, so that, when punishment falls on the world, the destroyer, raising his eyes and noticing the mark, will be careful to avoid him and leave him alone. So when the Holy One was about to execute judgement on Sodom, He first led Abraham to do a meritorious action by the present which He sent him, so as thereby to save Lot his brother's son from destruction. It is therefore written, "And God remembered Abraham, and sent Lot out of the midst of the overthrow" (Gen. XIX, 29). It does not say that God remembered Lot, since he was saved through the merit of Abraham. What God remembered was the kindness which Abraham had shown to those three angels. Similarly, the charitable deeds which a man performs are remembered by the Holy One at the time when punishment impends upon the world, forevery meritorious action is recorded on high, and when chastisement impends over that man the Holy One remembers the kindness he had performed with other men, as we read: "but charity delivereth from death" (Prov. XI, 4). The Holy One thus afforded Abraham in advance the occasion of a good action, so that by his merit he should deliver Lot from destruction.'

AND THEY LOOKED OUT TOWARD SODOM. This was immediately after "the men rose up from thence", that is, from the feast that Abraham had prepared for them, so performing a meritorious act. For although they were angels, his hospitality to them was a good action, since of the whole of the food offered them they left nothing over, purposely that Abraham should acquire merit thereby, as it is written, "and they did eat", the food having been consumed by their fire. It may be objected that the three angels were one of fire, one of water, and the third of air. The answer to this, however, is that they all partook of each other's essences, and hence "they did eat". Analogous to this is the passage "and they beheld God, and did eat and drink" (Ex. XXIV, 11). There it was truly eating, for they feasted themselves on the Shekinah. So here, "and they did eat" implies that they feasted themselves on that side to which Abraham was attached, and for that reason nothing remained of what Abraham put before them. For just as it behoves a man to partake of the cup of blessing (after a meal), that he merit the blessing from on high, so the angels also ate from what Abraham prepared for them that they might be privileged to feast on that which proceeds from the side of Abraham, for it is from that side that sustenance issues for all the celestial angels. AND THEY LOOKED OUT: with an impulse of mercy for the delivery of Lot. The word vayashqifu (and they looked out) here is analogous with its kindred word in "Look forth (hashqifah) from thy holy habitation" (Deut. XXVI, 15), and as there the implication is an exercise of mercy, so here. AND ABRAHAM WENT WITH THEM TO BRING THEM ON THE WAY; that is, to escort them. R Yesa said: 'This shows that Abraham was not aware that they were angels; for if he was, what need had he to see them off?' 'No,' answered R. Eleazar; 'although he knew, he kept to his usual custom with them, and saw them off. For it is highly incumbent on a man to escort a departing guest, for this crowns the good act. So whilst he was walking with them, the Holy One appeared to Abraham, as it is written, "And the Lord said, Shall I hide from Abraham that which I am doing?" The term V–Tetragrammaton (and the Lord) implies God with the attendance of the heavenly Court.

Zohar: Bereshith, Section 1, Page 104b

Thus we see that, when a man escorts his departing friend, he draws the Shekinah to join him and to accompany him on the way as a protection.' AND THE LORD SAID, SHALL I HIDE FROM ABRAHAM THAT WHICH I AM DOING? R. Hiya quoted here the verse: For the Lord God will do nothing, but he revealeth his counsel unto his servants the prophets (Amos III, 7). 'Happy,' he said, 'are those pious ones of the world in whom the Holy One finds delight, and whom He uses as His agents for all that He does in heaven or intends to do in this world, not hiding anything from them. For the Holy One desires to associate with Himself the righteous so that they may admonish and call the people to repentance in order that they may escape the punishment decreed by the judgement–seat on high, and, in any case, so that they should not be left with any loophole for complaining that the Holy One metes out punishment without justice.' R. Eleazar said: 'Woe to the guilty who are steeped in ignorance and refrain not from sin. Now, seeing that the Holy One, whose acts are truth and whose ways are justice, nevertheless does not execute His designs in the world before He reveals His intent to the righteous, so as not to give occasion to mankind for censuring His acts, how much more must the sons of men be on their guard so to act as not to leave any room for others to spread evil rumours against them. So it is written: "And ye shall be clean before the Lord and before Israel" (Num. XXXII, 22). It is thus incumbent on these righteous to act so that men shall not be able to complain against God, and to warn them betimes, if they are sinful, not to give an opening to the stern justice of God to descend upon them. And how are they to guard themselves? By repentance and good deeds.' R. Judah commented as follows: 'The Holy One, blessed be He, gave the whole land to Abraham

Zohar: Bereshith, Section 1, Page 105a

as an everlasting heritage, as it is written: "For all the land which thou seest, to thee I give it, etc." (Gen. XIII, 15). That he saw the whole land is indicated in the words which precede: "lift up now thine eyes from the place where thou art, northward, etc." (Ibid. 14). And now the Holy One found it necessary to uproot those places. He therefore said to Himself: "I have already given over the land to Abraham, he thus being the father of all its inhabitants [so it is written: 'for the father of a multitude of nations have I made thee' (Gen. XVII, 5)], and so it is not fitting for me to inflict punishment on the children without first giving warning to their father, to 'Abraham my friend' (Is. XLI, 8). Hence, AND THE LORD SAID, SHALL I HIDE FROM ABRAHAM, ETC.?

R. Abba said: Notice the unselfishness of Abraham. For although the Almighty notified him of the coming calamity, announcing VERILY, THE CRY OF SODOM AND GOMORRAH IS GREAT, and so on, and thus gave him a breathing–space before the final catastrophe, Abraham, nevertheless, did not plead for Lot to be delivered from the punishment. Why so? In order that it should not appear that he was asking a reward for his good deeds. But just for this reason did the Holy One send Lot forth and deliver him: it was for the sake of Abraham, as it is written, "And God remembered Abraham, and sent Lot out of the midst of the overthrow" (Gen. XIX, 29). In the same place it mentions "the cities in which Lot dwelt" to indicate that they were all guilty, without any redeeming features, save Lot. We learn also from this that any place inhabited by wicked people is doomed to destruction. Lot dwelt only in one of these cities, not in all of them, but it was due only to his presence that they were not all destroyed before. And this, too, was not due to Lot's own merits, but to the merits of Abraham.' As to this point, R. Simeon said: 'Note that any service rendered to a righteous man procures protection for the doer. Nay more, even if he himself is sinful, yet by rendering service to a righteous man he is bound to learn some of his ways and practise them. So you see that Lot, by reason of having kept company with Abraham, although he had not adopted all his ways, had learnt to show kindness to people in imitation of Abraham, and this it was that enabled those cities to exist so many years after Lot settled among them.'

[Note: The last 6 lines of the Hebrew text do not appear in our translation.]

Zohar: Bereshith, Section 1, Page 105b

[Note: The first 12 lines of the Hebrew text do not appear in our translation. The first portion of our translation up to "Seeing that Abraham" is apparently based on a variant reading.]

I WILL GO DOWN AND SEE: IF IT IS ACCORDING TO THE CRY OF IT, THEN MAKE YE AN EXTERMINATION. To whom was this command addressed? It cannot be to the angels, since that would mean that God was speaking to one party (Abraham) and giving command to another (the angels), which is not usual. The explanation is that it was really addressed to Abraham, in whose jurisdiction the cities were. But then why the plural, "make ye" ('asu) instead of the singular "make thou" ('ase)? The answer is that it was addressed both to Abraham and the Shekinah, which was all the time with him. According to another interpretation the command was given to the angels, who were standing there ready at hand to do execution. According to another interpretation, again, the proper reading is 'asu (they have made), and this accords with the translation of Onqelos. It says: "I will go down and see." Are not all things revealed before the Almighty that there was need for Him to go down and see? The expression, however, "I will go down", implies descent from the grade of mercy to that of rigour, and by "and see" is meant the consideration of the kind of punishment to be meted out to them. "Seeing" in the Scriptures can be both for good and for ill. An example of the former use is: "And God saw the children of Israel, and God took cognizance of them" (Ex. II, 25); an example of the latter is "I will go down and see", i.e. to determine the mode of punishment. In regard to all this God said, "Shall I hide from Abraham, etc."

SEEING THAT ABRAHAM WILL SURELY BECOME A GREAT AND MIGHTY NATION. How comes this blessing to be inserted here? It is to teach us that the Holy One, even when He sits in judgement on the world, does not change His nature, since whilst sitting in judgement on one He is displaying mercy to others, and all at one and the same moment. R. Judah objected that it is written: "But as for me, let my prayer be to thee, O Lord, in an acceptable time" (Ps. LXIX, 14), which would seem to show that there are with God acceptable moments and unacceptable, that at one time He grants audience, at another time He does not, that the Almighty is now accessible, now inaccessible; and this is corroborated by the verse: "Seek ye the Lord while he may be found, call ye upon him while he is near" (Is. LV, 6). In reply to this, R. Eleazar said that the verses cited apply to the prayers of an individual, whilst the lesson of our text applies to communal prayer; the former to a single locality, the latter to the world as a whole. Hence God here blessed Abraham because he was on a par with the whole world, as it is written: "These are the generations of the heaven and the earth when they were created" (Gen. II, 4), where the term behibaream (when they were created), by a transposition of letters, appears as beabraham (in Abraham). The numerical value of the letters of yihyah (will become) is thirty, which points to the traditional dictum that the Holy One provides for the world thirty righteous men in each generation in the same manner as He did for the generation of Abraham. R. Eleazar supported this from the verse: "He was more honourable than the thirty, but he attained not to the three" (II Sam. XXIII, 23). 'The thirty', he said, 'refers to the thirty righteous whom the Holy One has provided for the world without intermission; and Benaiah the son of Jehoiada of whom it is written "He was the most honourable of the thirty" was one of them. "But he attained not to the three": i.e. he was not equal to those other three [Tr. note: The Patriarchs.] on whom the world subsists, neither being counted among them nor being deemed worthy to be associated with them and to have an equal share with them. Now since there were thirty righteous in the time of Abraham, as the term yihyah indicates, therefore God blessed him in their company.'

God said to Abraham, "Verily, the cry of Sodom and Gomorrah is great", as much as to say: I have taken note of their behaviour towards their fellow-men, which causes all men to avoid setting foot in Sodom and Gomorrah. So it is written: "The stream made a chasm for strangers, so they are forgotten of the foot that passeth by; they are the poorest of men, they move away" (Job. XXVIII, 4). The stream divided to swallow up any stranger who ventured to enter Sodom; for if anyone was detected offering food or drink to a stranger, the people of the town would cast him into the deepest part of the river, as well as the recipient. Hence, "they are forgotten of the foot", i.e. men avoided it and never put foot into it; and as for those who happened to enter it–"they are the poorest of men, they move away", i.e. as no food or drink was given to them, their bodies became so emaciated that they scarcely looked any more like human beings, and hence "they moved away", i.e. people passed it by on one side. Even the birds of heaven

Zohar: Bereshith, Section 1, Page 106a

avoided it, as it is written, "that path no bird of prey knoweth" (Ibid. 7). A universal outcry therefore went up against Sodom and Gomorrah and all the other towns that behaved like them. It is written here: "According to the cry of it." Why not of them, since two cities are mentioned here? This is explained as follows. From the side underneath the Hail-Stone vapours ascend to the shoulder (of the Divine Throne), where they gather themselves into one drop, and then descend into the chasm of the great abyss. There five become merged into one. When the voices of all of them are clear they unite into one. Then a voice ascends from below and mingles with them, and the combined cry keeps on ascending and clamouring for justice, until at last the Holy One appears to investigate the accusation. Hence R. Simeon says that the "it" here refers to the sentence of judgement, which demands execution day by day. This conforms with the tradition that for many years the sentence of judgement continued to demand reparation for the sale of Joseph by his brethren. Hence here also her cry went up for justice, and therefore it is written, "according to the cry of her". The word which follows, habbaah (which is come), really means "which is coming", i.e. coming continually.

AND ABRAHAM DREW NEAR, AND SAID: WILT THOU INDEED SWEEP AWAY THE RIGHTEOUS WITH THE WICKED? R. Judah said: 'Was there ever seen such a merciful father as Abraham? Observe that in regard to Noah it is written, "And God said to Noah, The end of all flesh is come before me... Make thee an ark of gopher wood" (Gen. VI, 13-14), but Noah remained silent: he said nothing, nor did he beseech for mercy (for his fellow-men). Abraham, on the contrary, as soon as the Holy One made announcement to him, "Verily, the cry of Sodom and Gomorrah is great,... I will go down and see, etc.", immediately "drew near, and said: Wilt Thou indeed sweep away the righteous with the wicked?" ' Said R. Eleazar: 'Even Abraham's action is not beyond cavil. He was, indeed, better than Noah, who did nothing, whereas he pleaded earnestly for the righteous that they should not perish with the guilty, beginning his plea with the number of fifty righteous and descending to ten; then, however, he stopped, without completing his prayer for mercy for all, saying, as it were, "I do not wish to draw upon the recompense due to me for my good deeds." The perfect example is given by Moses, who as soon as the Holy One said to him, "they have turned aside quickly out of the way... they have made them a molten calf, and have worshipped it" (Ex. XXXII, 8), straightaway "besought the Lord his God, etc." (Ibid. 11), concluding with the words "and if not, blot me, I pray thee, out of thy book which thou hast written" (Ibid. 32). And although the whole people had sinned, he did not stir from his place until God said: "I have pardoned according to thy word." Abraham was inferior in that respect, since he only asked for mercy in the event that there should be found righteous men, but not otherwise. Thus there never was a man who was so sure a bulwark to his generation as Moses, the "faithful shepherd".'

AND ABRAHAM DREW NEAR, that is, he made ready to plead, AND SAID: PERADVENTURE THERE ARE FIFTY RIGHTEOUS WITHIN THE CITY. Abraham began with the number fifty, which is the entrance to understanding, and ended with ten, which number is the last of all the grades. R. Isaac said: 'Abraham stopped at ten as the number symbolic of the ten days of Penitence between New-Year and the Day of Atonement. Reaching that number, Abraham said, as it were, "After this there is no more room for penitence", and therefore he did not descend further.'

AND THE TWO ANGELS CAME TO SODOM AT EVEN, ETC. R. Yose pointed out that the preceding verse, "And the Lord went his way as soon as

Zohar: Bereshith, Section 1, Page 106b

he had left off speaking to Abraham", indicates that only when the Shekinah departed from Abraham, and Abraham returned to his place, did "the two angels come to Sodom at eve". (It says "two", because one of the angels departed with the Shekinah, leaving only two.) As soon as Lot saw them he ran after them. Why so? Did Lot, then, take into his house all wayfarers and offer them food and drink? Would not the townspeople have killed him, and meted out to him the same treatment as they did to his daughter? (For Lot's daughter once offered a piece of bread to a poor man, and when it was found out, the people of the town covered her body with honey, and left her thus exposed on the top of a roof until she was consumed by wasps.) The angels, however, came in the night, so that Lot thought that the townspeople would not notice it. Nevertheless, as soon as the visitors entered his house all the people assembled and surrounded the house.'

R. Isaac put the question, "Why did Lot run after them?" R. Hizkiah and R. Yesa each gave an answer. One said that it was because he observed in them a likeness to Abraham; and the other, because he noticed the Shekinah hovering over them. This view is supported by the fact that of Abraham also it is written, "And he ran to meet them from the tent door", and the words there are taken to mean that Abraham saw the Shekinah.

AND LOT SAW AND RAN TO MEET THEM... AND HE SAID, BEHOLD NOW, MY LORDS, TURN ASIDE, I PRAY YOU. The expression "turn aside", instead of "draw near", implies that he took them by a roundabout way, so that the people of the town should not see them. R. Hizkiah here discoursed on the verse: For he looketh to the ends of the earth, and seeth under the whole heaven (Job XXVIII, 24). 'How incumbent it is', he said, 'upon the sons of men to contemplate the works of the Almighty and to busy themselves in the study of the Torah day and night, for through him who thus busies himself the Almighty is glorified on high and below. The Torah indeed is a tree of life for all those who occupy themselves with it, affording them life in this world and

Zohar: Bereshith, Section 1, Page 107a

in the world to come. "For he looketh to the end of the land", to give them food and to satisfy all their needs; for He continually holds it under His eye, as it is written. "The eyes of the Lord thy God are always upon it, from the beginning of the year even unto the end of the year" (Deut. XI, 12). This is, again, the land of which it is written, "she bringeth her food from afar" (Prov. XXXI, 14), and then she provides food and sustenance for all those "beasts of the field", for so it is written, "she riseth also while it is yet night, and giveth meat to her household and a portion to her maidens" (Ibid. 15). It is further written: "Thou openest thy hand, and satisfiest every living thing with favour" (Ps. CXLV, 16). According to another interpretation, "He looketh to the ends of the earth" so as to survey the works of each man and to examine the doings of mankind throughout the world: "and seeth under the whole heaven", i.e. He scans and scrutinises each individual. Thus when the Holy One saw the works of Sodom and Gomorrah, He sent upon them those angels to destroy them.' Thereupon, as it is written, "Lot saw," to wit, the Shekinah. Not that anyone can see the Shekinah really, but he saw a resplendent halo about their heads, and therefore we read: "And he said, Behold now, my lords (Adonay)", as has been already explained, and it was on account of the halo, the reflection of the Shekinah, that he said, "turn aside, I pray you, into your servant's house, and tarry all night, and wash your feet". This was not the way that Abraham acted. For he first said: "wash your feet", and then: "and I will fetch a morsel of bread, etc." Lot, however, first said, "turn aside, I pray you, into your servant's house, and tarry all night", and then he said, AND WASH YOUR FEET AND YE SHALL RISE UP EARLY, AND GO ON YOUR WAY. His object was that the people should not become aware of their presence. AND THEY SAID, NAY, BUT WE WILL ABIDE IN THE BROAD PLACE ALL NIGHT. that being the custom for visitors to those cities, as no one would take them into his house. The verse proceeds: AND HE URGED THEM GREATLY. When the Holy One is about to execute judgement in the world, He sends one messenger for this purpose. Why, then, have we here two messengers, where one would have sufficed? The truth is that of the two angels one came to rescue Lot, and so only one was left to overthrow the city and destroy the soil.

THEN THE LORD CAUSED TO RAIN UPON SODOM AND UPON GOMORRAH, ETC. R. Hiya opened his discourse on this with the verse: Behold, the day of the Lord cometh, cruel, etc. (Is. XIII, 9). He said: 'The words "Behold, the day of the Lord cometh" refer to the lower Court. The term "cometh" has thus the same force as in the passage, "according to her cry which is come upon me", both implying that the lower power cannot execute judgement until it comes and appears on high and receives authorisation. So, too, in the verse, "the end of all flesh is come before me".

According to another interpretation, "behold the day of the Lord cometh" refers to the destroying angel here below when he comes to take the soul of man. Hence "cruel, and full of wrath and fierce anger, to make the earth a desolation", referring to Sodom and Gomorrah; "and to destroy the sinners thereof

Zohar: Bereshith, Section 1, Page 107b

out of it" (Ibid.), referring to the inhabitants of those cities. Immediately after we read, "For the stars of heaven and the constellations thereof, etc.", for He caused to rain upon them fire from heaven and exterminated them. Further on it is written: "I will make man more rare than fine gold, etc." (Ibid. 12), referring to Abraham, whom the Holy One exalted over all the peoples of the world.' R. Judah interpreted these verses as referring to the day on which the Temple was destroyed, as on that day both men and angels were plunged into gloom and the supernal and the lower realms and the heaven and the stars were darkened.

R. Eleazar, again, interpreted these verses as referring to the day when the Holy One will raise the community of Israel from the dust. That day will be a day of note both above and below, as it is written, "and there shall be one day, which shall be known as the Lord's" (Zech. XIV, 7); that day will be the day of vengeance, the day which the Holy One, blessed be He, has appointed for taking vengeance on the idolatrous nations. For whilst the Holy One is taking vengeance on the idolatrous nations, He "will make a man more precious than gold", to wit, the Messiah, who will be raised and glorified above all mankind, and to whom all mankind will pay homage and bow down, as it is written, "Before him those that dwell in the wilderness will bow down... the Kings of Tarshish and of the isles shall render tribute" (Ps. LXXII, 9-10). Observe that although this prophecy (in the book of Isaiah) was primarily intended for Babylonia, yet it has a general application, since this section commences with the words, "When the Lord shall have mercy on Jacob", and it is also written, "And peoples shall take them and bring them to their place."

AND THE LORD CAUSED TO RAIN UPON SODOM. The term V-Tetragrammaton (and the Lord) signifies the grade of the lower Court which requires authorisation from on high. R. Isaac said that God showed mercy in the midst of punishment, as it is written, "from Tetragrammaton (the Lord) out of heaven". The exercise of mercy is recorded in the words: AND IT CAME TO PASS, WHEN GOD DESTROYED THE CITIES OF THE PLAIN, THAT GOD REMEMBERED ABRAHAM, AND SENT LOT OUT, ETC., from whom in course of time issued two entire nations, and who was destined to have among his descendants King David and King Solomon. AND IT CAME TO PASS, WHEN THEY HAD BROUGHT THEM FORTH ABROAD, THAT HE SAID, ETC. This is another proof that when punishment overtakes the world a man should not-as has already been said-let himself be found abroad, since the executioner does not distinguish between the innocent and the guilty. For this reason, as has been explained, Noah shut himself in in the ark so as not to look out on the world at the time when judgement was executed. So also it is written, "And none of you shall go out of the door of his house until the morning" (Ex. XII, 22). Hence the angel said to Lot, ESCAPE FOR THY LIFE, LOOK NOT BEHIND THEE, ETC. R. Isaac and R. Judah were once walking on the road together. The latter remarked: 'Both the punishment of the Flood and the punishment of Sodom were of the kinds meted out in Gehinnom, where sinners are punished by water and by fire.' R. Isaac said: 'That Sodom suffered the punishment of Gehinnom is shown by the words of the Scripture, "And the Lord caused to rain upon Sodom and upon Gomorrah brimstone and fire from the Lord out of heaven", the former proceeding from the side of water and the latter from the side of fire, both being punishments of Gehinnom inflicted upon sinners there.'

R. Judah then said to him: 'The punishment of sinners in Gehinnom lasts twelve months, after which the Holy One raises them out of Gehinnom, where they have undergone purification. They remain then sitting at the gate of Gehinnom, and when they see sinners enter there to be punished, they beseech mercy for them. In time the Holy One takes pity on them and causes them to be brought to a certain place reserved for them. From that day onward the body rests in the dust and the soul is accorded

Zohar: Bereshith, Section 1, Page 108a

her proper place. Observe that, as has been stated, even the generation of the Flood were punished with nothing else but with fire and water: cold water descended from above, whilst seething water bubbled up from below mingled with fire. They thus underwent the two punishments regularly meted out from on high; and so was Sodom also punished, namely, by brimstone and fire.' R. Isaac asked him: 'Will the generation of the Flood arise on the Day of Judgement?' R. Judah said: 'That question has already been discussed elsewhere; as regards the people of Sodom and Gomorrah, we can say that they will not arise. This is proved from the words of the Scripture, "and the whole land thereof is brimstone, and salt, and a burning that is not sown, nor beareth, nor any grass groweth therein, like the overthrow of Sodom and Gomorrah... which the Lord overthrew in his anger, and in his wrath" (Deut. XXIX, 22), where the words "which the Lord overthrew" refer to this world, and the words "in his anger,' to the world to come, while the words, "and in his wrath" refer to the time when the Holy One will bring the dead to life.' R. Isaac then said to him: 'Observe that just as the soil of their land was destroyed to all eternity, so were the inhabitants themselves destroyed to all eternity. And observe further how the justice of the Holy One metes out measure for measure: as they did not quicken the soul of the poor with food or drink, just so will the Holy One not restore them their souls in the world to come. And further, just as they neglected the exercise of charity which is called life, so has the Holy One withholden from them life in this world and in the world to come. And as they closed their roads and paths to their fellow-men, so has the Holy One closed to them the roads and paths of mercy in this world and in the world to come.' R. Abba said: 'All men will rise up from the dead and will appear for judgement. Of these it is written, "and some to reproaches and everlasting abhorrence" (Dan. XII, 2). God, however, is the fountain of mercy, and since He punished them in this world and they suffered for their sins, they have no longer to suffer all the punishments of the next world. '

R. Hiya said: 'It is written: "And he sent Lot out of the midst of the overthrow, when he overthrew the cities in which Lot dwelt." The expression "the cities in which Lot dwelt" indicates that he tried to settle in each of the cities in turn, but none would keep him save Sodom, the king of which allowed him residence

Zohar: Bereshith, Section 1, Page 108b

for the sake of Abraham. This is borne out by the passage, "and Lot dwelt in the cities of the plain, and moved his tent as far as Sodom" (Gen. XIII, 12). BUT HIS WIFE LOOKED BACK FROM BEHIND HIM. We should have expected "from behind her". It means, however, "From behind the Shekinah". R. Yose said that it means "from behind Lot", as the destroying angel followed him. How, it may be asked, could he follow him, seeing that he had sent him away? The fact is that the angel kept behind Lot, destroying on the way, but he did not touch any spot till Lot had passed it. Hence he said, "look not behind thee", implying "for behind thee I am doing my work of destruction". But his wife looked back from behind him, thus turning her face to the destroying angel, and she became a pillar of salt; for as long as the destroying angel does not see the face of a man he does not harm him; but as soon as Lot's wife turned her face to look at him she became a pillar of salt.'

R. Eleazar and R. Yose were one day studying the verse: "A land which in it thou shalt eat bread without scarceness, which in it thou shalt not lack anything" (Deut. VIII, 9). Said R. Eleazar: 'The repetition of the term bah (in it) is to be noted. The reason is, as has been stated, that the Holy One has assigned all nations and countries to (celestial) chieftains and envoys, with the exception of the Land of Israel, which is under the governance of no angel or chieftain, but only under that of God Himself. For this reason He brought the people who have no ruler save Him into the land which has no ruler save Him. For the Holy One provides sustenance there first, and only then to the rest of the world. All the idolatrous nations suffer scarceness, but not so the Land of Israel: the Land of Israel receives the first supply, the residue being left for the rest of the world. Hence "A land which in it thou shalt eat bread without scarceness", and in a rich abundance:

"in it" but in no other place; in it is the home of true faith and on it rests the heavenly blessing. Hence it is said that Sodom and Gomorrah were "like the garden of the Lord, like the land of Egypt" (Gen. XIII, 10),

Zohar: Bereshith, Section 1, Page 109a

that is, possessing luxurious abundance. So was Egypt also: as the garden of the Lord does not need to be watered by man, neither did Egypt, being amply supplied by the river Nile, which periodically rises and irrigates the whole land. The Scripture says in one place that "it shall be, that whoso of the families of the earth goes not unto Jerusalem... upon them there shall be no rain" (Zech. XIV, 17), i.e. as a punishment; but the passage continues: "And if the family of Egypt go not up, and come not... there shall be the plague wherewith the Lord will smite the nations" (Ibid. 18). Observe that it is not written "upon them there shall be no rain", for the reason, that it never rains in Egypt, nor is there any need of rain there: hence, their punishment will be "the plague wherewith the Lord will smite all the nations". Similarly of Sodom it is written that "it was well watered everywhere" (Gen. XIII, 10); it possessed all the luxuries of the world, and its inhabitants were unwilling that other people should share them.' R. Hiya said: 'They deserved punishment both for their immorality and their uncharitableness. For whoever grudges assistance to the poor does not deserve to exist in this world, and he also forfeits the life of the world to come. Contrariwise, whoever is generous towards the poor deserves to exist in the world, and it is for his sake that the world exists, and the fulness of life is reserved for him in the world to come.'

AND LOT WENT UP OUT OF ZOAR, AND DWELT IN THE MOUNTAIN, AND HIS TWO DAUGHTERS WITH HIM, ETC. For what reason? Because Zoar was too near Sodom: hence he moved away further. R. Isaac discoursed on the verse: And they are turned round about by his devices, according to their work, etc. (Job XXXVII, 12). 'This means', he said, 'that the Holy One, blessed be He, constantly turns the wheel of events, bringing hidden things to the top, and then again giving another turn and shaping things differently; and thus "by his devices" He is ever scheming and planning how to effect the change, and make a new pattern.

Zohar: Bereshith, Section 1, Page 109b

All is "according to their work", i.e. the variation takes place in accordance to the works and deeds of man. The verse continues: "according as he commandeth them upon the face of the habitable world", that is, it is in accordance with man's works that God shapes the course of events, in all that He ordains on the face of the world.' R. Eleazar interpreted the words "and they are turned round about by His devices", in the following manner. 'The Holy One guides the course of events so as to bring to pass a seemingly stable state of things; but when the sons of men imagine that all before them is fixed and firmly established, then the Holy One turns His works into something altogether different from their former state. Further,' he said, 'we may translate not "devices", but "device", i.e. "instrument", and compare God to a potter who, in turning his wheel, constantly fashions new vessels according to his fancy. So is the Holy One constantly reshaping His works, the instrument which constitutes His potter's wheel, so to speak, being the lower world Judgement Court. And all is done in accordance with man's works. If they are good, the wheel revolves to the right, making the course of events highly favourable to them; and however long the wheel revolves, punishment never settles on that side. Should men, however, turn to evil ways

Zohar: Bereshith, Section 1, Page 110a

the Holy One imparts to His device a spin to the left, and all things now take a direction to the left, and the wheel gives to events a course unfavourable to the sons of men. So it goes on until they become penitent and retrace their evil ways. But the motive power of the wheel is centred in the works of man; hence the phrase, "by His device, according to their work", there being no permanency. In this case too God manipulated events so as to attain a certain end, and all that happened had its roots in the supernal sphere. God had brought Abraham near to Him, and there issued from him Ishmael. Ishmael was born before Abraham was circumcised, that is, before he was made perfect through the sign of the holy covenant. Then the Holy One, blessed be He, so devised that Abraham circumcised himself and entered the covenant and acquired his complete name of Abraham, and was crowned by the supernal he with the symbolical issuing of water from wind. As soon as the symbolism was completed and Abraham was circumcised, there issued from him Isaac, who was the holy seed and who was attached to the supernal spheres as symbolising fire from water, and who was not in any way linked to the "other side". From Lot, again, and from his daughters there came forth two disparate nations who became attached to the side appropriate to them. We see here, again, how the Almighty contrives

Zohar: Bereshith, Section 1, Page 110b

the course of things, turning them about so that everything should fit into the general scheme and fall into its proper place. For observe that it would have been more fitting for Lot that the Holy One should have produced these two nations from his union with his wife. It was, however, necessary that these nations should be attached to their predestined place, and for this wine had to play its part; and wine, indeed, was found ready at hand in that cavern. The mystical part played by wine here is similar to that regarding w hich we read, "and he drank of the wine, and was drunken" (Gen. IX, 21), as has already been explained elsewhere.

In regard to the names Moab and Ammon, R. Yose made the following comment. 'The first-born daughter was boldfaced enough to call her son "Moab", thereby proclaiming that he was meab, i.e. the issue of her own father; whereas THE YOUNGER SHE ALSO BORE A SON, AND CALLED HIS NAME BEN-AMMI: the mother out of delicacy gave him that name which being interpreted simply means "a son of my people", without betraying who his father was. Further, the words AND HE KNEW NOT WHEN SHE LAY DOWN, NOR WHEN SHE AROSE, occur twice in this passage, first in reference to the younger daughter, and then in reference to the elder. In the former case the word b'qumah (when she arose) occurring in it is written plene, i.e. with the letter vau, which, moreover, is provided with a dot; this is to signify that heaven, as it were, was an accomplice to the act which ultimately was to bring about the birth of the Messiah. Contrariwise, the similar word in reference to the younger one is written defectively, without the letter vau, for the reason that none of her issue had any part in the Holy One, blessed be He.' R. Simeon said: 'The underlying meaning of the words "and he knew not" is that he was unaware that the Holy One intended to raise from her King David and Solomon and all the other kings and, finally, the Messiah.' R. Simeon said further: 'The expression "when she arose" has its counterpart in the words used by Ruth, "and she rose up before one could discern another" (Ruth III, 14). For it was on that day that Lot's daughter could be said to have risen to the height of her destiny in that

Zohar: Bereshith, Section 1, Page 111a

Boaz became attached to one of her lineage in order "to raise up the name of the dead upon his inheritance", by means of which there were raised from her all those kings and the elect of Israel. Again, "And he knew not when she lay down" has its counterpart in the verse, "and she lay at his feet until the morning" (Ibid.). Observe the restraint of Abraham in not beseeching grace on behalf of Lot, even when the Holy One at first announced to him His determination to execute punishment on Sodom; nor after he BEHELD, AND, LO, THE SMOKE OF THE LAND WENT UP AS THE SMOKE OF A FURNACE did he intercede for Lot, or address to the Holy One any word about him. Neither did the Holy One mention this subject to Abraham, in order that the latter should not think that God had used up some of his merit in order to save Lot. It cannot be said that Lot was of no account in the eyes of Abraham, seeing that Abraham risked his life on his behalf in waging war against five powerful kings. But because of his love for the Almighty and, in addition, because he saw that Lot's conduct fell far short of the proper standard, Abraham did not plead that any indulgence should be shown to Lot for his sake. This is the reason why Abraham did not intercede on behalf of Lot either at the beginning or at the end.'

AND ABRAHAM JOURNEYED FROM THENCE TOWARD THE LAND OF THE SOUTH. All his journeyings were toward the side of the South,

Zohar: Bereshith, Section 1, Page 111b

which he preferred to the other sides, in that it is the side of Wisdom. AND ABRAHAM SAID OF SARAH, HIS WIFE, SHE IS MY SISTER. It is a dictum of our teachers that a man should not rely on miracles, and even if the Holy One, blessed be He, has once performed a miracle for him he should not count on it another time, for miracles do not happen every day. And whoever runs into obvious danger may thereby exhaust all his merit previously accumulated. This has been made clear in explanation of the verse, "I am not worthy of all the mercies, and of all the truth, etc." (Gen. XXXII, 11). Now, seeing that Abraham had already had once a miraculous deliverance when he journeyed into Egypt, why did he put himself now again into a similar difficulty by saying "she is my sister"? The answer is that Abraham did in no way rely on himself, but he saw the Shekinah constantly in the abode of Sarah, and that emboldened him to declare "she is my sister", in the sense of the verse "Say unto wisdom, Thou art my sister" (Prov. VII, 4).

AND GOD CAME TO ABIMELECH, ETC. Can that be? Does, then, the Holy One, blessed be He, come to the wicked? The same question is raised by the words, "and God came unto Balaam" (Num. XXII, 9), and again, "and God came to Laban" (Gen. XXXI, 24). In all these cases, however, it was, in fact, only a heavenly messenger who was dispatched to them, and who in executing their message assumed that divine name (Elohim), since they were emissaries of justice. Hence: AND GOD CAME TO ABIMELECH IN A DREAM OF THE NIGHT, AND SAID TO HIM, BEHOLD, THOU SHALT DIE BECAUSE OF THE WOMAN WHOM THOU HAST TAKEN, ETC. R. Simeon here discoursed on the verse: The lip of truth shall be established forever; but a lying tongue is but for a moment (Prov. XII, 19). 'The first part of the verse,' he said, 'alludes to Abraham, whose words on every occasion were truth; and the other part of the verse is an allusion to Abimelech. Twice Abraham said of Sarah, "she is my sister". On the first occasion he referred to the Shekinah, who was constantly with Sarah, and as Abraham

Zohar: Bereshith, Section 1, Page 112a

was of the right side he could indeed say of the Shekinah "she is my sister", using the term in the same mystic sense as in the verse, "my sister, my love, my dove, my undefiled" (S. S. V, 2). Abraham always called her "sister" because he was attached to her inseparably. Later he said: "And moreover she is my sister, the daughter of my father, but not the daughter of my mother." Was it really so? In truth he was alluding all the time to the Shekinah. At first he said, "she is my sister" in conformity with the admonition, "Say to wisdom, Thou art my sister." Then he amplified this by saying "moreover she is my sister, the daughter of my father", i.e. the daughter of Supernal Wisdom, for which reason she is called "my sister" and also Wisdom–"but not the daughter of my mother"–i.e. from the place where is the origin of all, most hidden and recondite. "And so she became my wife", i.e. by way of fondness and affection, in the sense of the verse "and his right hand embrace me" (S. S. II, 6). Thus all his words contained mystic allusions. Observe that on the first occasion, when they went down to Egypt, he called her "my sister" in order to cleave all the more firmly to the true faith, and not to be led astray after outer grades; similarly now he continued to declare "she is my sister" because he had not deviated from the true faith. For Abimelech and all the inhabitants of the land followed strange worship, and therefore Abraham, entering there, made bold to say "my sister", claiming thereby the same indissoluble kinship as between brother and sister. For the marital bond can be dissolved, but not that between brother and sister. So whereas all the people of that land were addicted to the worship of the stars and constellations, Abraham, the true believer, avowed "she is my sister", as much as to say, "We two will never separate." We can apply here the words, "and for his sister a virgin (Lev. XXI, 3), which were spoken of the priest, but esoterically signify the abode where Abraham reposes. It is written: The Lord thy God thou shalt fear; him shalt thou serve; and to him shalt thou cleave, and by his name shalt thou swear (Deut. X, 20). The accusative particle eth

Zohar: Bereshith, Section 1, Page 112b

points to the first grade, the region of the fear of God, and hence "thou shalt fear", for there a man must fear his master, it being the Court of Justice. The words "him shalt thou serve" point to a higher grade which rests upon the lower grade, the two being inseparable. This is the place of the holy covenant, the object of service. "And to him shalt thou cleave" refers to the region of complete union, to wit, the body which rests in the centre; "and by his name shalt thou swear" refers to the seventh of the grades. Abraham, therefore, clave to the true faith when he went down into Egypt and also when he went to the land of the Philistines. He was like a man who wanted to go down into a deep pit but was afraid he would not be able to come up again. He therefore fastened a rope above the pit, and having thus assured his ascent, he went down. In the same way Abraham, when he was about to go down to Egypt, first secured his faith firmly, and thus having something to hold by he went down there; and he did the same when he went into the land of the Philistines. "The lip of truth", then, "is established forever; but a lying tongue is but for a moment", the "lying tongue" referring to Abimelech, who said, IN THE SIMPLICITY OF MY HEART AND THE INNOCENCY OF MY HANDS HAVE I DONE THIS. But what was the reply he received? YEA, I KNOW THAT IN THE SIMPLICITY OF THY HEART THOU HAST DONE THIS. but no mention was made of innocency of hands. NOW THEREFORE RESTORE THE MAN'S WIFE, FOR HE IS A PROPHET.

R. Judah discoursed on the verse: He guardeth the feet of his pious ones, etc. (I Sam. II, 9). '"His pious one",' he said 'is Abraham, whom God constantly kept under watchful care, whilst the word "feet" is an allusion to his wife, with whom God sent the Shekinah to guard her. According to another interpretation, the Holy One continually accompanied Abraham so that no one should do him any harm. "But the wicked shall be put to silence by the darkness" (Ibid.). These are the kings whom the Holy One had slain on that night when Abraham pursued them; the night, as it were, united with darkness to slay them, so that while it was Abraham who pursued, it was the darkness that killed. So it is written: "And he divided himself against them by night, he and his servants, and he smote them" (Gen. XIV, 15). By "dividing" is here meant that the Holy One separated His attribute of mercy from that of justice in order to avenge Abraham. Instead of "and he smote them" we should have expected "and they smote them". But this is again a reference to the Holy One, "for man prevaileth not by strength", seeing that only Abraham and Eliezer were there.' R. Isaac put the question: 'Have we not been taught that a man should not court danger, in reliance on a miracle? And was not Abraham putting himself into extreme danger in pursuing the five kings and engaging in battle against them?' R. Judah replied: 'Abraham did not set out with the intention of joining battle, nor did he count upon a miracle. What impelled him to leave his house was the distress of Lot, whom he resolved to ransom, taking money with him for this purpose, and being prepared, in case he should not succeed, to die with him in captivity. But as soon as he set out he saw the Shekinah illumining the way before him, and hosts of angels encompassing him. Then it was that he began to pursue them, whilst the Holy One slew them. Hence the verse: "and the wicked are put to silence in darkness" (I Sam. II, 9).' R. Simeon said: 'The mystical interpretation of the verse is as follows: "He guardeth the feet of his pious ones"; this refers to Abraham. But when Abraham set out Isaac joined him and so the enemies fell before him. But had not Isaac been associated with Abraham, they would not have been exterminated. So it is written: "But the wicked shall be put to silence in darkness, for man prevaileth not by strength", indicating that although strength resides always in the right side, if not for the help of the left side (darkness), the opponents could not be overcome.' According to another interpretation, "He guardeth the feet of his pious ones" signifies that when a man truly loves God, then God reciprocates his love in all his doings and guards him in all his ways, as it is written, "The Lord shall guard thy going out and thy coming in, from this time forth and forever" (Ps. CXXI, 8). Observe how assiduous Abraham was in his love towards the Holy One; for wherever he went he had no regard whatever for himself

Zohar: Bereshith, Section 1, Page 113a

and sought only to cleave to the Almighty. Hence God guarded the feet of "his pious ones", the term "feet" referring to Abraham's wife, in regard to whom it is written, "Now Abimelech had not come near her", also "Therefore suffered I thee not to touch her." We find also written in the case of Pharaoh, "And the Lord plagued Pharaoh and his house with great plagues at the word of Sarai,' (Gen. XII, 17), implying that she, as it were, gave out the order and the Holy One administered the blows. Thus "He guardeth the feet of his pious ones." "But the wicked shall be put to silence in darkness": these are Pharaoh and Abimelech, to whom the Holy One administered punishment by night, while the words "For not by strength shall man prevail" refer to Abraham, on whose behalf God said, "Now therefore restore the man's wife, etc." '

AND THE LORD REMEMBERED SARAH AS HE HAD SAID, ETC. R. Hiya discoursed on the verse: And he showed me Joshua the High priest standing before the angel of the Lord, and Satan standing at his right hand to accuse him (Zech. III, 1). 'This verse,' he said, 'must be carefully pondered. "Joshua the high priest" is Joshua the son of Jehozedek; "the angel of the Lord" before whom he was standing is the region of the "bundle of the souls" of the righteous, which is known as "the angel of the Lord"; "Satan standing at his right hand to accuse him" is the evil tempter who roams to and fro through the world to snatch up souls and to lure beings to perdition, angels as well as human beings. Joshua had been cast by Nebuchadnezzar into the fire, along with the false prophets; and that was the moment seized by Satan to bring accusations against him on high in order that he should be burnt along with them. For this is the way of the Satan, to reserve his indictment for the hour of danger, or for a time when the world is in distress. At such a time he has authority both to accuse and to punish even without justice, as it says: "But there is that is swept away without a just cause" (Prov. XIII, 23). Satan then was standing "to accuse him", to wit, to plead that either they should all be delivered or all burnt in the fire. For when the angel of destruction obtains authorisation to destroy, he does not discriminate between innocent and guilty. It is for this reason that when punishment falls upon a town a man should flee from thence before he is overtaken. Here it was all the easier for the Satan, as the three were already joined as one in the fiery furnace, and he could thus demand a single treatment for them all, either to be burnt or to be saved. For a miracle is not performed

Zohar: Bereshith, Section 1, Page 113b

in halves, delivering half and leaving half to be destroyed, but the whole is either miraculously saved or left to its doom. ' Said R. Yose to him: 'Is it really so? Did not God divide the Red Sea for the Israelites so that they could pass on dry land, while the same waters swept round on the Egyptians and drowned them, so that here you have a miraculous deliverance and a divine punishment at one and the same point?' R. Hiya replied: 'This was precisely why the miracle of the Red Sea presented such difficulties to the Almighty. For when God does punish and miraculously deliver at the same time, it is usually not in the same place or the same house. If that does happen it constitutes a heavy task for Him. On the same principle the Holy One does not punish the guilty until the measure of their guilt is full, as it is written, "for the iniquity of the Amorite is not yet full" (Gen. XV, 16), and again, "in full measure, when thou sendest her away, thou dost contend with her" (Is. XXVII, 8). Satan, therefore, demanded that Joshua should be burnt along with the others, until he said to him, "The Lord rebuke thee, O Satan" (Zech. III, 2). Who said this? It was the angel of the Lord. The text, it is true, runs: "The Lord said to Satan, The Lord rebuke thee, O Satan." But observe that regarding Moses at the bush it is also written: "And the angel of the Lord appeared unto him in a flame of fire" (Ex. III, 2), whilst a little later it is written, "And when the Lord saw that he turned aside to see" (Ibid. 4). The truth is that sometimes the Scripture says "the angel of the Lord", sometimes simply "the angel", and sometimes again "the Lord". Hence here also it is written, "The Lord rebuke thee, O Satan," and not: "Behold, I rebuke thee." So whenever the Holy One sits on the Throne of Judgement to judge the world, Satan, the seducer of men and angels, is at hand to do mischief and to snatch up souls.'

R. Simeon was one day in the course of his studies examining the verse, "And the elders of that city shall take a heifer of the herd... and shall break the heifer's neck there in the valley" (Deut. XXI, 3-4). 'According to the law,' he said, 'the neck must be broken with a hatchet.' Said to him R. Eleazar: 'What is the need of all this?' R. Simeon then wept and said: 'Woe to the world which has been lured after this one. For from the day that the evil

Zohar: Bereshith, Section 1, Page 114a

serpent, having enticed Adam, obtained dominion over man and over the world, he has ever been at work seducing people from the right path, nor will the world cease to suffer from his machinations until the Messiah shall come, when the Holy One will raise to life those who sleep in the dust in accordance with the verse, "He will swallow up death forever, etc." (Is. XXV, 8), and the verse, "And I will cause the unclean spirit to pass out of the land" (Zech. XIII, 2). Meanwhile Satan dominates this world and snatches up the souls of the sons of men. Observe now the passage: "If one be found slain in the land, etc." (Deut. XXI, 1-9). Ordinarily it is through the angel of death that the souls of men pass out of their bodies, but with that man it was not so, but he that slew him made his soul depart from him before the time came for the angel of death to gather him in. Hence it is written: "And no expiation can be made for the land for the blood that is shed therein, but by the blood of him that shed it" (Num. XXXV, 33). Is it not enough for the world that

Satan should be continually on the watch to lead men astray and to formulate accusations against them, that one must needs increase his fury by depriving him of what is his due? But the Holy One is merciful towards His children, and so provided the offering of a calf as reparation for the soul of which Satan was deprived and as a means of pacifying the world's accuser. Herein is involved a deep mystery. The offerings of the ox, the cow, the calf, the heifer have all a deep mystical significance, and therefore we make reparation to him in the way mentioned in the text. Hence the declaration, "Our hands have not shed this blood, etc." (Deut. XXI, 7)-they have not shed this blood, and we have not caused his death; and by this means the accuser is thereby kept at a distance. All this constitutes good counsel given by the Holy One to the world. Observe that the same applies to New Year Day and to the Day of Atonement. That is the time when the world is on trial and Satan brings his accusations. Hence it is needful for Israel to give a blast on the trumpet and to emit a sound which is a compound of fire, water, and air; that sound ascends to the place of the Throne of Judgement, where the Court of Justice is sitting, and impinges on it and ascends further. As soon as the sound arrives from beneath, the voice of Jacob is reinforced on high, and the Holy One, blessed be He,

Zohar: Bereshith, Section 1, Page 114b

is stirred to mercy. For corresponding to the sound uniting fire, water, and air, which Israel emits here below, there goes forth a blast from on high. Through the two blasts, the one on high and the other below, the world is fortified and mercy prevails. The accuser then, who thought to prevail in judgement and to obtain sentence on the world, becomes confounded; his strength fails and he is unable to achieve anything. The Holy One then, sitting in judgement, joins mercy to justice, and so the world is judged by mercy, and not rigorously. Observe the verse: "Blow the horn at the new moon, at the time of its covering for our feast day" (Ps. LXXXI, 4). The word ba-keseh (at the covering) means the time when the moon is invisible. For at that time the evil serpent is in power and is able to do hurt to the world. But when mercy is aroused, the moon ascends and is removed from that place, and so the evil serpent is confounded, loses his power and is unable to approach there. Hence on New Year Day it is necessary to confound him, so that he should be like one awakening from sleep and still half-conscious. Again, on the Day of Atonement it is requisite to pacify and propitiate him by means of the scapegoat which is brought to him, whereby he is induced to undertake the defence of Israel. But on New Year Day he becomes confused, and is unable to do anything. He sees the stirring of mercy ascending from below, the awakening of mercy on high, and the moon between them, and he is thereby confounded, and remains bewildered and powerless, and so the Holy One dispenses His judgement to Israel in a spirit of mercy, and accords them as a time of grace those ten days between New Year Day and the Day of Atonement, for the acceptance of all those who repent of their sins and for forgiveness of their iniquities, by giving them a respite till the Day of Atonement. The Holy One had thus given Israel all these commandments to save them from falling into the wrong hands and from being judged with rigour, so that they should all come out innocent on earth,

Zohar: Bereshith, Section 1, Page 115a

through His mercy which is like the mercy of a father towards his children. All depends on actions and words, as we have explained.'

AND THE LORD VISITED SARAH AS HE HAD SAID: thus fulfilling the words, "I will certainly return unto thee when the season cometh round; and, lo, Sarah thy wife shall have a son" (Gen. XVIII, 10). A tradition teaches us that the term paqad (visited) is written in connection with women, and the term zakhar (remembered) in connection with men. Hence here it is written "And the Lord visited Sarah as he had said." The expression "as he had said" proves that the words "and he said", in the passage in Gen. XVIII, 10, refer to the Lord Himself, and no messenger. AND THE LORD DID UNTO SARAH AS HE HAD SPOKEN. Since the text has already said, "and the Lord visited Sarah", what need is there to add, "and he did unto Sarah"? The reason is this. It is one of our doctrines that the "fruit of the handiwork" of the Almighty springs from that river which flows forth from Eden. This "fruit of God's handiwork" is the souls of the righteous, and it is also the allotment (mazzal) [Tr. note: Lit. 'luck'; also 'flowing'.] from which flow all good fortune and rains of blessing, as it is written, "to water the garden" (Gen. II, 10), that is, to cause the stream to flow from on high and irrigate and fertilise the world below. For mankind depends on that allotment and not on any other source. Hence, besides "visiting" Sarah, God also "did" something in the region on high, since everything depends on that. Hence the two stages of "visiting" and "doing", with the name of "the Lord" mentioned with each, the whole forming one process.'

R. Eleazar discoursed on the verse: Lo, children are a heritage of the Lord, the fruit of the womb is a reward (Ps. CXXVII, 3). 'The meaning', he said, 'is that children confer on a man the heritage of the Lord, by which he attaches himself to the Lord to all time. For the man who is privileged to have children in this world will through them be worthy to enter "behind the partition" in the world to come; and by leaving a son in this world a man's merits are enhanced in the world to come, and through him he enters into the "heritage of the Lord". What is the "heritage of the Lord"? It is the "land of the living", a name by which the Land of Israel is called, as is proved from the words of King David, "for they have driven me out this day that I should not cleave unto the heritage of the Lord, saying, Go serve other gods" (I Sam. XXVI, 19). Hence: "Lo, children are a heritage of the Lord",

Zohar: Bereshith, Section 1, Page 115b

that is, it is children who make a man worthy of the heritage of the Lord. "The fruit of the womb is a reward" refers to reward in the next world, for by the fruit of the womb a man merits the world to come. Again, "a heritage of the Lord are children", that is, the heritage of the fruit of the works of the Holy One is from above, from the tree of life, for it is from thence that a man is blessed with children, as we read, "From me is thy fruit found" (Hos. XIV, 9). "Happy is the man that hath his quiver full of them; they shall not be put to shame, etc." (Ps. CXXVII, 5): happy in this world and happy in the world to come. "They will not be put to shame when they speak with their enemies in the gate": who are the "enemies in the gate"? They are the accusing angels. For when a man departs from this world, there are numbers of such accusing angels who try to block his way and prevent him from reaching his place. But he passes through "the gate" because he has left hostages in this world by virtue of whom he is found worthy of a place in the next world. Thus, "they shall not be put to shame when they speak with their enemies in the gate".'

R. Judah and R. Yose were walking on the road. Said R. Judah to R. Yose: 'Open thy lips and say something in exposition of the Torah, since the Shekinah is accompanying thee. For whenever the Torah is studied earnestly, the Shekinah comes and joins, and all the more so on the road, where the Shekinah comes in anticipation, preceding those who cleave to their faith in thc Holy One, blessed be He.' R. Yose then began to discourse on the verse: Thy wife shall be as a fruitful vine in the innermost parts of thy house; thy children like olive plants, round about thy table (Ps. CXXVIII, 3). 'So long', he said, 'as a woman abides in the innermost parts of the house, she remains chaste and is fit to bear worthy children. She is like a vine, for just as a vine is never grafted with another kind but only with its own, so the worthy woman does not bear offspring from a strange man but only from her husband. Her reward is

Zohar: Bereshith, Section 1, Page 116a

to have "children like olive plants, round about thy table". Just as the leaves of olive trees do not fall off but remain firmly attached to the twigs all the year round, so shall "thy children be like olive plants, round about thy table." The text proceeds: "Behold, surely thus shall the man be blessed that feareth the Lord" (Ibid. 4). The term "surely" seems to be superfluous. It indicates, however, a further lesson, viz. that so long as the Shekinah stayed modestly in her own place, if one may be permitted the expression, then it could be said of her, "thy children like olive plants, round about thy table", referring to Israel during the time that they dwelt in the Land of Israel; "round about thy table" they were, eating and drinking and bringing offerings and feasting before the Holy One, blessed be He: both all those on high and all those below were blessed through them. But when the Shekinah departed, Israel were driven from the table of their father, and dispersed among the nations, and they continually cried out without anyone taking heed, excepting the Holy One, as it is written: "And yet for all that, when they are in the land of their enemies, etc." (Lev. XXVI, 44). We have seen how many saintly and holy men have perished through tyrannical decrees, all as part of Israel's punishment for not keeping the Law when they were in the Holy Land. It is written, "Because thou didst not serve the Lord thy God with joyfulness, and with gladness of heart, by reason of the abundance of all things" (Deut. XXVIII, 47). The words "because thou didst not serve with joyfulness" refer to the priests, who offered sacrifices and holocausts "with joyfulness"; "and with gladness of heart" alludes to the Levites; "by reason of the abundance of all things" is an allusion to the lay Israelites whose position was in the middle, and who received blessings from all sides. Again it is written, "Thou hast multiplied the nation, thou hast made great their joy" (Is. IX, 2), in allusion to the priests; "they joy before thee according to the joy in harvest" (Ibid.) indicates the lay Israelites whom the Holy One blesses with a good harvest of the field, from all of which they give a tenth; "as men rejoice when they divide the spoil" (Ibid.) refers to the Levites, who take a tenth from the threshing floor. According to another explanation: "Thou hast multiplied the nation" indicates Israel, who have faith in the Holy One; "Thou hast made great his joy" alludes to the first and supernal grade, to which Abraham attached himself, this being great and filled with joy; "they joy before thee"

Zohar: Bereshith, Section 1, Page 116b

at the time when they go up to attach themselves to Thee, "according to the joy in harvest", an allusion to the community of Israel, to which properly belongs the joy in harvest; "as men rejoice when they divide the spoil", a reference to the joy evinced by the rest of the lower powers and chariot-riders when they divide the spoil and fall upon their prey in the forefront of all.'

R. Judah discoursed on the verse: It is a time to work for the Lord; they have made void thy law (Ps. CXIX, 126). It has been laid down that the term 'eth (time) is a designation of the community of Israel. Why is the community of Israel designated "time" ('eth)? Because all things with her are regulated by times and periods, when to come near the Deity, when to receive light (from above), and when to commune, as we read, "But as for me, let my prayer be unto thee, O Lord, in an acceptable time" (Ps. LXIX, 14). Thus, "the community must be made unto the Lord", that is, it must be prepared and fitted to commune with God (so the word "made" is used in the verse "and David made himself a name" (II Sam. VIII, 13)), and this by means of those who labour in the study of the Torah. And why all this? Because "they have made void thy law", for if "they had not made void thy law" there would never have been any estrangement between the Holy One and Israel.' R. Yose said: 'In this way is explained the verse: "I the Lord will in its time hasten it" (Is. LX, 22). The word b'itah (in its time) may be resolved into b'eth he (in the time of the letter He), i.e. "when the time arrives for the He to rise up from the dust I will hasten it".' Said R. Yose further: 'Yet the community of Israel is to remain only one day in the dust and no more.' Said R. Judah: 'Tradition agrees with what you have said. But observe what we have learnt regarding this, namely, that when the community of Israel was exiled from its home, the letters of the Divine Name, became, if one may say so, separated, the He flying apart from the Vau. We can thus understand the sentence, "I was dumb with silence" (Ps. XXXIX, 3), as through the separation of the Vau from the He there was no Voice, and thus Utterance was silenced. She therefore lies in the dust all the day of the He, that is, the whole of the fifth thousand (although they were already in exile before the beginning of the fifth thousand, which is symbolised by the He); and when the sixth thousand, which is symbolised

Zohar: Bereshith, Section 1, Page 117a

by the Vau, begins, the Vale will resuscitate the He at six times ten (an allusion to the sixty souls), which means the Vau repeated ten times. The Vau will ascend to the Yod and redescend to the He. The Vau will be multiplied into the He ten times, making sixty, when it will raise the exiles from the dust. At every sixty years of the sixth thousand the He will mount a stage higher, acquiring greater strength. And after six hundred years of the sixth thousand there will be opened the gates of wisdom above and the fountains of wisdom below, and the world will make preparations to enter on the seventh thousand as man makes preparations on the sixth day of the week, when the sun is about to set. As a mnemonic to this we take the verse, "In the six hundredth year of Noah's life... all the fountains of the great deep were broken up" (Gen. VII, 11).' Said R. Yose to him: 'Your calculations lay down a much longer period than that arrived at by the companions, according to whom the exile of the community of Israel was only to last one day (i.e. a thousand years), as it says, "He hath made me desolate and faint all the day" (Lam. I, 13).' R. Judah said in reply: 'This is what I have learnt from my father concerning the mysteries of the letters of the Divine Name, and of the duration of the world as well as of the days of creation, all of which belongs to the same mystical doctrine. At that time the rainbow will appear in the cloud in radiant colours, like a woman that decks herself out for her husband, in fulfilment of the verse, "and I will look upon it, that I may remember the everlasting covenant" (Gen. IX, 16), a passage already explained elsewhere. "I will see it" with all its bright colours, and I will thus "remember the everlasting covenant". Who is the everlasting covenant? It is the community of Israel. The Vau will join the He, and will resuscitate her from the dust. When the Vau shall move to join the He, heavenly signs will appear in the world, and the Reubenites will make war against all the world; and so the community of Israel will be raised from the dust, for the Holy One will remember her. In this way the Holy One will have dwelt with her in exile years to the number of Vau times Yod, that is, six times ten, after which she will be raised, and vengeance will be executed on the world, and the lowly will be exalted.' Said R. Yose to him: 'All you say is right, being

Zohar: Bereshith, Section 1, Page 117b

mystically indicated by the letters, and we need not enter upon any other calculations regarding the end (qets). For in the book of the venerable R. Yeba we find the same calculation. The verse, "Then shall the land satisfy her Sabbaths" (Lev. XXVI, 34) is an allusion to the mystical implication of the Vau, as indicated in a subsequent verse, "And I will remember my covenant with Jacob" [Tr. note: The name Jacob is in this verse exceptionally spelt plene, i.e. with a vau. v. infra, p. 369.] (Ibid. 42), and then it says, "and I will remember the land" (Ibid.), indicating the community of Israel. The word "will satisfy" (tirzeh) signifies that the Holy One will be favourable to her. As for the "one day" of which the companions have spoken, it is assuredly all hidden with the Holy One, and it is all found in the mystery of the letters of the Divine Name; for R. Yose here has revealed the end of the exile by means of these letters.' Said R. Judah: 'Observe that also when Sarah was visited, it was the grade of the divine essence symbolised by the Vau that visited her, as it is written, "And (Va) the Lord visited Sarah", for all is contained in the mystery of the Vau, and through it all things are to be revealed.' Said R. Yose: 'We have still a long time to be in exile until the day arrives, but all depends on whether the people will repent of their sins, as appears from the passage, "I the Lord will hasten it in its time" (Is. LX, 22), i.e. if they will be worthy, "I will hasten it", and if not, then "in its time".' The two then proceeded on their way. Suddenly R. Yose said: 'It comes to my memory that in this place I was once sitting with my father and he said to me: "When you will reach the age of sixty years you are destined to find in this place a treasure of sublime wisdom." I have lived to reach that age, and I have not found the treasure, but I wonder if the words spoken by us just now are not the wisdom that he meant. He further said to me: "When the celestial flame reaches the spaces between your fingers, it will escape from you." I asked him: "How do you know this?" He replied: "I know it by the two birds that passed over your head." ' At this point R. Yose left him and entered a cavern,

Zohar: Bereshith, Section 1, Page 118a

149

at the farther end of which he found a book hidden in the cleft of a rock. He brought it out and caught sight of seventy-two tracings of letters which had been given to Adam the first man, and by means of which he knew all the wisdom of the supernal holy beings, and all those beings that abide behind the mill with turns behind the veil among the supernal ethereal essences, as well as all that is destined to happen in the world until the day when a cloud will arise on the side of the West and darken the world. R. Yose then called R. Judah and the two began to examine the book. No sooner had they studied two or three of the letters than they found themselves contemplating that supernal wisdom. But as soon as they began to go into the book more deeply and to discuss it, a fiery flame driven by a tempestuous wind struck their hands, and the book vanished from them. R. Yose wept, saying, 'Can it be, Heaven forefend, that we are tainted with some sin? Or are we unworthy to possess the knowledge contained therein?' When they came to R. Simeon they told him what had occurred. He said to them: 'Were you, perhaps, scrutinising those letters which dealt with the coming of the Messiah?' They answered: 'We cannot tell, as we have forgotten everything.' R. Simeon continued: 'The Holy One, blessed be He, does not desire that so much should be revealed to the world, but when the days of the Messiah will be near at hand, even children will discover the secrets of wisdom and thereby be able to calculate the millennium; at that time it will be revealed to all, as it is written, "For then will I turn to the peoples a pure language, etc." (Zeph. III, 9), the term az (then) referring to the time when the community of Israel will be raised from the dust and the Holy One will make her stand upright; then "will I turn to the peoples a pure language, that they may all call upon the Lord, to serve him with one consent" (Ibid.).'

Observe that although it is said of Abraham that he "journeyed still toward the South" (Gen. XII, 9), he did not attain to his rightful grade until Isaac was born. But as soon as Isaac was born, he attained this grade, through the close association and union

Zohar: Bereshith, Section 1, Page 118b

of the two. For that reason he, and no other, called him Isaac, in order that water and fire should be merged together. Hence: AND ABRAHAM CALLED THE NAME OF HIS SON THAT WAS BORN UNTO HIM, WHOM SARAH BORE TO HIM, ISAAC: to wit, the son that was born to him as fire born from water.

AND SARAH SAW THE SON OF HAGAR THE EGYPTIAN, WHOM SHE HAD BORN UNTO ABRAHAM, MAKING SPORT. R. Hiya said: 'After recording the birth of Isaac, the Scripture never mentions Ishmael by name so long as he was still in the house of Abraham: dross cannot be mentioned in the presence of gold. Hence Ishmael is referred to here as "the son of Hagar the Egyptian", as it was not fitting that his name should be mentioned in the presence of Isaac.' Said R. Isaac: 'The words "and Sarah saw" imply that she looked at him disdainfully, as being the son not of Abraham but of Hagar the Egyptian, and, furthermore, only Sarah regarded him so, but not Abraham, as we read that THE THING WAS VERY GRIEVOUS IN ABRAHAM'S SIGHT ON ACCOUNT OF HIS SON-not the son of Hagar, but his son.' R. Simeon said: 'The Scripture really speaks in praise of Sarah. For what she saw was that he was indulging in idolatrous practices. Hence she said: Surely, this is not the son of Abraham, who follows in the footsteps of Abraham, but the son of Hagar the Egyptian, who is reverting to the type of his mother. Hence: AND SHE SAID UNTO ABRAHAM: CAST OUT THIS BONDWOMAN AND HER SON; FOR THE SON OF THIS BONDWOMAN SHALL NOT BE HEIR WITH MY SON, EVEN WITH ISAAC. It cannot be supposed that Sarah was moved by jealousy of her or her son. For if so, the Holy One would not have supported her by saying, IN ALL THAT SARAH SAITH UNTO THEE, HEARKEN UNTO HER VOICE. The truth, therefore, is that she observed him worshipping idols, and performing the practices which his mother had taught him. Hence the words of Sarah, "For the son of this bondwoman shall not be heir", as much as to say: "I know that he will never enter the fold of the true faith and that he will have no portion with my son either in this world or in the world to come." Therefore God supported her, since He wished to keep the holy seed carefully separated, for that was the end for which He created the world, as Israel was already in His thought before the creation of the world. It was therefore that Abraham appeared in the world, so that the world could be sustained for his sake. Abraham and Isaac together upheld the world, yet they were not firmly established until Jacob came into the world. When Jacob appeared, both Abraham and Isaac became firmly established and the whole world with them. From Jacob the holy people gradually emerged into the world, and so the whole of existence became duly established according to the holy pattern. Hence God said, "In all that Sarah saith unto thee, hearken unto her voice; for in Isaac shall seed be called to thee", i.e. in Isaac and not in Ishmael.

The text proceeds: AND SHE DEPARTED AND STRAYED IN THE WILDERNESS OF BEERSHEBA.

The term vatetha (and she strayed) indicates idolatry, like the kindred term in the verse, "They are vanity, work of delusion (tha'athuim, lit. "goings astray") (Jer. X, 15). Thus it was only for the sake of Abraham that the Holy One did not abandon her or her son. Observe that on the previous occasion when she fled from Sarah, it was said to her: "The Lord hath heard thy affliction" (Gen. XVI, 11); but now since she went astray after idols, although she lifted up her voice and wept, yet it says, FOR GOD HATH HEARD THE VOICE OF THE LAD WHERE HE IS. The expression "where he is" we interpret to imply that he was still a minor in the eyes of the heavenly court. For whereas in the human court, here below, the age of liability is reached at thirteen years, in the heavenly court it is reached only at twenty years; before that

150

age, even if one is guilty, he is not punishable. Hence the phrase "where he is". Said R. Eleazar: 'If that be so, why should anyone be punished by dying before twenty? Before thirteen, it is true, he may die for the sins of his father, but why after thirteen?' R. Hiya replied: 'The Holy One has mercy on such a one so that he should die whilst still innocent, and obtain a reward in the other world, instead of dying in guilt and receiving punishment in that world.' R. Eleazar rejoined: 'But if he is already guilty before he reaches the age of

Zohar: Bereshith, Section 1, Page 119a

twenty years, what are we to say? Since he has died (before reaching the age of punishment), how will he be punished?' R. Simeon replied: 'It is of such that it is written, "But there is that is swept away without judgement" (Prov. XIII, 23). For when chastisement descends on the world, then such a one is struck down by the destroying angel without express sentence pronounced either by the heavenly or the earthly tribunal, while Providence is not keeping watch over him. It is also written of such a one: "His own iniquities shall ensnare (eth) the wicked, and he shall be holden with the cords of his sin" (Ibid. v. 22). The accusative particle eth amplifies the term "the wicked" so as to make it include one who has not yet come of legal age; of him, then, it is said, "His own iniquities shall ensnare the wicked", but not the heavenly tribunal, "and he shall be holden with the cords of his sin", but not by the earthly tribunal. Hence it says here: "For God hath heard the voice of the lad where he is." '

R. Simeon discoursed on the verse: And I will remember my covenant with Jacob, etc. (Lev. XXVI, 42). 'The name Jacob', he said, 'is here written in full, with the letter vau. For what reason? In the first place as an allusion to the grade of Wisdom, the realm where Jacob dwells. But the chief reason is because the passage speaks of the exile of Israel, intimating that the redemption of Israel will come about through the mystic force of the letter vau, namely, in the sixth millennium, and, more precisely, after six seconds and a half a time. When the sixtieth year shall have passed over the threshold of the sixth millennium, the God of heaven will visit the daughter of Jacob with a preliminary remembrance (p'qidah). Another six and a half years will then elapse, and there will be a full remembrance of her; then another six years, making together seventy-two years and a half. In the year sixty-six the Messiah will appear in the land of Galilee. A star in the east will swallow seven stars in the north, and a flame of black fire will hang in the heaven for sixty days, and there shall be wars towards the north in which two kings shall perish. Then all the nations shall combine together against the daughter of Jacob in order to drive her from the world. It is of that time that it is written: "And it is a time of trouble unto Jacob, but out of it he shall be saved" (Jer. XXX, 7). At that time all the souls in Guph will have been used up, and will need to be re-created. As a mnemonic of this we may use the verse: "All the souls of the house of Jacob that came into Egypt... all the souls were threescore and six" (Gen. XLVI, 26). In the year seventy-three all the kings of the world will assemble in the great city of Rome, and the Holy One will shower on them fire and hail and meteoric stones until they are all destroyed, with the exception of those who will not yet have arrived there. These will commence anew to make other wars. From that time the Messiah will begin to declare himself, and round him there will be gathered many nations and many hosts from the uttermost ends of the earth. And all the children of Israel will assemble in their various places until the completion of the century. The Vau will then join the He, and then "they shall bring all your brethren out of all the nations for an offering unto the Lord" (Is. LXVI, 20). The children of Ishmael will at the same time rouse all the peoples of the world to come up to war against Jerusalem, as it is written, "For I will gather all nations against Jerusalem to battle, etc." (Zech. XIV, 2), also, "The kings of the earth stand up, and the rulers take counsel together, against the Lord, and against his anointed" (Ps. II, 2); and further, "He that sitteth in heaven laugheth, the Lord hath them in derision" (Ibid. II, 4). Then the lesser Vau will rouse itself to unite (with the He) and renew the souls that had become old, so as to rejuvenate the world, as it is written, "May the glory of the Lord endure forever, let the Lord rejoice in his works" (Ps. CIV, 31). The first part of this verse signifies that God's glory will attach itself to the world, and the latter half that He will cause souls to descend into the world and make them into new beings, so as to join the world into one. Happy are those who will be left alive at the end of the sixth millennium to enter on the Sabbath. For that is the day set apart by the Holy One on which to effect the union of souls and to cull new souls to join those that are still on earth, as it is written, "And it shall come to pass, that he that is left in Zion, and he that remaineth in Jerusalem, shall be called holy, even every one that is written unto life in Jerusalem" (Is. IV, 3).'

AND IT CAME TO PASS AFTER THESE THINGS, THAT GOD DID PROVE ABRAHAM, AND SAID UNTO HIM: ABRAHAM, AND HE SAID: HERE AM I. R. Judah discoursed on the verse: Thou art my King, O God (Ps. XLIV, 5). 'This allocution', he said, 'signifies the complete union of all grades. "Command the salvation of Jacob" (Ibid.), to wit, the emissaries who perform God's behests

Zohar: Bereshith, Section 1, Page 119b

in the world, that they may be all from the side of mercy and not from the side of stern justice; since there are messengers from the side of mercy and others from the side of justice. Those belonging to the side of mercy never execute a mission of punishment in the world. It may be asked, how can we reconcile with this the case of the angel who appeared to Balaam, and of whom we have been taught that he was first a messenger of mercy and then was changed into one of severity. In reality the character of his mission was not changed, as he was throughout a messenger of mercy on behalf of Israel, to protect them and plead for them, but this meant punishment to Balaam. For this is the way of the Holy One, that when He confers kindness on one, the same kindness may result in punishment for another. Similarly here, the same messenger who was one of mercy for Israel turned into one of punishment for Balaam. Hence David prayed, "Command the salvation of Jacob", as much as to say: "When messengers are sent into the world, order such as are of the side of mercy." ' R. Abba said: 'The words "command the salvation of Jacob" allude to those in exile, for whose redemption David prayed. Further, Jacob was the crown of the patriarchs, but if not for Isaac he would not have appeared in the world; hence the request "command the salvation of Jacob" refers primarily to Isaac, since the saving of his life was the salvation of Jacob.'

AND IT CAME TO PASS. Said R. Simeon: 'We have been taught that the expression "and it came to pass in the days" indicates that some trouble is about to be narrated, while the expression "and it came to pass", even without the addition of "in the days", presages a certain tinge of distress. AFTER THESE WORDS: this means, after the lowest grade of all the supernal grades, which is called "words" (d'barim), as in the passage, "I am not a man of words" (Ex. IV, 10). THAT ELOHIM PROVED ABRAHAM, i.e. the evil tempter came to accuse him before the Holy One, blessed be He. The text here is rather surprising, for instead of Abraham we should have expected here to read, "God proved Isaac", seeing that he was already thirty-seven years of age, and no longer under his father's jurisdiction. He could thus easily have refused without rendering his father liable to punishment. The truth, however, is that it was requisite, in order that Abraham might attain to perfection, that he should be invested with the attribute of rigour, which he had not exhibited up to that time. Now, however, water was united with fire and fire with water, and it was possible for him to dispense rigorous justice and make it part of his character. The evil tempter thus came to accuse Abraham on the ground that he could not be said to have perfected himself until he should have exercised rigour against Isaac. But observe that although only Abraham is explicitly mentioned as being proved, Isaac, nevertheless, was also included in the trial, as is implied by the amplifying particle eth before "Avraham", which indicates Isaac. For Isaac was at that time in the grade of the lower Geburah (Force, Rigour); but after he had been bound and made ready to undergo the rigorous trial at the hand of Abraham, he was equipped in his own place together with Abraham, and so fire and water were joined and rose to a higher grade, and the discord was appeased. For who ever saw a father's heart turn from compassion to cruelty? But the object here was to assuage the discord between fire and water so that they should be settled in their places until Jacob appeared, when all was put in order, and the triad of the patriarchs was completed, and higher and lower creations were firmly established.

AND HE SAID, TAKE NOW THY SON. The word take does not mean "take forcibly", since Abraham was too old for that, but it has the same sense as in "take Aaron and Eleazar his son" (Num. XX, 25), signifying that he should use persuasion and gently lead him on to do the will of God. THY SON, THINE ONLY SON, WHOM THOU LOVEST. This

Zohar: Bereshith, Section 1, Page 120a

has been explained elsewhere. AND GET THEE INTO THE LAND OF MORIAH: the meaning is similar to that of the passage, "I will get me to the mountain of myrrh" (S. S. IV, 6), i.e. to become invigorated in the appropriate place.

ON THE THIRD DAY ABRAHAM LIFTED UP HIS EYES, AND SAW THE PLACE AFAR OFF. As we have already been told that Abraham went to the place, all this seems superfluous. But the truth is that "the third day" means the third generation, i.e. Jacob, and the words "he saw the place from afar" are parallel to the expression "from afar the Lord appeared unto me" (Jer. XXXI, 3). Or again, "the place" alludes to Jacob, of whom it is written, "and he took one of the stones of the place" (Gen. XXVIII, 11). For Abraham scrutinised the "third day", which is the third grade, and he beheld Jacob, who was destined to descend from him. "Afar off", to wit, at some distant time, and not soon. R. Eleazar said to R. Judah: 'What credit is herein ascribed to Abraham, if whilst about to bind Isaac he saw that Jacob was destined to descend from him?' R. Judah replied: 'Indeed Abraham did see Jacob, since even before that Abraham was endowed with the higher Wisdom; and now he scrutinised the third day, which is the third grade, in order to make sure. And indeed he did see him, but now only "from afar", for the reason that he was going to bind Isaac, and he did not wish to question the ways of the Holy One. "Afar off", that is, he saw him through a "dim glass" only, and therefore only partially; for if the "clear glass" had been resting upon the "dim glass", Abraham would have seen him properly. The "clear glass" did not function on this occasion, because this is the grade of Jacob, who, not yet being born, had not reached that grade; and also in order that Abraham's reward might be all the greater. AND THEY CAME TO THE PLACE WHICH GOD HAD TOLD HIM OF, ETC. Here it is intimated that although Abraham had some vision of Jacob, yet he said to himself, "Assuredly the Holy One knows another way which will serve.' Forthwith, therefore, ABRAHAM BUILT THE ALTAR THERE. Before this it is written: AND ISAAC SPOKE UNTO ABRAHAM HIS FATHER, AND SAID, MY FATHER. As explained elsewhere, the reason why Abraham did not respond to him immediately was because the normal compassion of a father towards a son left him, and hence he simply said: 'Here I am, my son", implying that the quality of mercy in him had been transmuted into rigour. AND ABRAHAM SAID. It is not written: "and his father said", which shows again that he was regarding him not as his father but as his adversary. GOD WILL PROVIDE FOR HIMSELF THE LAMB FOR A BURNT OFFERING, MY SON. He should have said: "provide for us", but what he meant was, "God will provide for Himself when necessary, but for the present it is going to be my son and nothing else." Forthwith, AND THEY WENT BOTH OF THEM TOGETHER. R. Simeon discoursed here on the verse: Behold, angels cry abroad, the angels of peace weep bitterly (Is. XXXIII, 7). 'These angels', he said, 'are superior angels who "cried abroad" because they no longer knew what to make of God's promise to Abraham at the time when "He brought him forth abroad" (Gen. XV, 5). The "angels of peace" are those other angels who were destined to go forth to meet Jacob, for whose sake the Holy One promised them peace, as it is written, "And Jacob went on his way, and the angels of God met him" (Ibid. XXXII, 2), and these are called "angels of peace". All these wept when they saw Abraham binding Isaac, the upper and the lower beings trembled and shook, and all on account of Isaac.

AND THE ANGEL OF THE LORD CALLED UNTO HIM... ABRAHAM, ABRAHAM. There is in the text a disjunctive mark between the two Abrahams, to show that the latter was not like the former; the latter

Zohar: Bereshith, Section 1, Page 120b

was the perfected Abraham, while the former was still incomplete. Similarly, in the passage where the name Samuel is repeated with a disjunctive line between (I Sam. III, 10), the second is the perfected Samuel, whilst the first was not yet so. The second Samuel was a prophet, but not the first. But when we come to "Moses, Moses" (Ex. III, 4), we do not find any pausal sign between, for the reason that from the day Moses was born the Shekinah never departed from him. R. Hiya said that the angel repeated Abraham's name in order to animate him with a new spirit, and spur him to a new activity with a new heart. R. Judah said: 'Isaac purified himself and in intention offered himself up to God, was at that moment etherealized and, as it were, he ascended to the throne of God like the odour of the incense of spices which the priests offered before Him twice a day; and so the sacrifice was complete. For Abraham felt distressed when the angel said to him, "Lay not thy hand upon the lad", thinking that his offering was not complete and that his labour, his preparations and the building of the altar had all been in vain. Straightway, however, ABRAHAM LIFTED UP HIS EYES AND LOOKED AND BEHELD BEHIND HIM A RAM, ETC. We have been taught that that ram was created at twilight (on the sixth day of Creation), and he was of the first year, as it is written, "one he-lamb of the first year" (Num. VII, 63), thus being according to requirement. But if so, how could he have been created at twilight? The truth is that from that time it was pre-ordained that that ram should be at hand at the moment when Abraham should require it. The same applies to all those things said to have come into being "at twilight", which in reality means that they were then predestined to appear at the requisite moment.

R. Judah further discoursed on the verse: In all their affliction he was afflicted, and the angel of his presence saved them (Is. LXIII, 9). He said: 'This is the translation of the k'ri, hut according to the k'thib we should translate, "He was not afflicted." The lesson to be derived from this variation is that Israel's affliction reaches the Holy One even in the place above which is beyond affliction or perturbation. "And the angel of his presence saved them." If He is together with them in their affliction, how can it be said that He saves them? Observe, however, that it is not written, "He saves them", but "he saved them", that is, He determined in advance to partake in their sufferings. For whenever Israel is in exile the Shekinah accompanies them, as it is written, "Then the Lord thy God will return (v'-shab) with thy captivity" (Deut. XXX, 3). According to another explanation, "The angel of his presence" signifies the Shekinah, which accompanies them in exile. Hence in the Scripture the words "and I have remembered my covenant" (Ex. VI, 5) are immediately followed by "and now, behold, the cry of the children of Israel is come unto me; moreover, I have seen" (Ex. III, 9). It is also written, "And God remembered his covenant" (Ibid. II, 24), referring to the Shekinah, "with Abraham" (Ibid.), symbolic of South-west, "with Isaac" (Ibid.), symbolic of North-west, "and with Jacob" (Ibid.), symbolising the complete and perfect union. The Holy One, blessed be He, will one day send forth a voice to proclaim to the world the words, "For he said, Surely, they are my people, children that will not deal falsely; so he was their saviour" (Is. LXIII, 8). Blessed be the Lord forevermore, Amen and Amen.'

Zohar: Bereshith, Section 1, Page 121a

HAYE SARAH

AND THE LIFE OF SARAH WAS A HUNDRED AND SEVEN AND TWENTY YEARS. R. Yose discoursed on the verse: And they took up Jonah, and cast him forth into the sea; and the sea ceased from its raging (Jonah I, 15). 'The question may here be asked,' he said, 'why it was the sea and not the earth that raged against him, seeing that he fled to prevent the Shekinah from resting upon him. In fact, however, it was appropriate that it should be so. Our teachers say that the sea resembles the sky and the sky resembles the Throne of Glory; hence the sea seized him and held him fast. For as he, in effect, fled from the sea, the sea was the proper agent to fill him with fear and trembling. "And they took up Jonah and cast him into the sea." Tradition says that as they took him up and plunged him into the water up to his thighs, the sea was assuaged, and when they lifted him up again the sea resumed its violence. This happened repeatedly, until finally

Jonah said: "Take me up, and cast me forth into the sea" (Ibid. I, 12). Forthwith they did so. No sooner was he cast forth into the sea than his soul took flight from him and ascended to the Throne of the King, before whom she was brought to judgement. She was then restored to Jonah, and then the fish swallowed him. The fish died, but afterwards came to life again.

This is the accepted explanation.

Zohar: Bereshith, Section 1, Page 121b

In the same way, every night when a man retires to his bed his soul leaves him and ascends to be judged before the King's tribunal. If she is found deserving to continue in her present state, she is allowed to return to this world. In the judgement, good and evil actions are not weighed in the same way. No account is taken of evil deeds which a man is likely to perpetrate in the future, for so it is written, "for God hath heard the voice of the lad where he is" (Gen. XXI, 17). But in regard to good actions, not only those already performed in the past are taken into consideration, but also those which a man is going to perform in the future; so that even if the present account would prove a man guilty, the Holy One in His bounty towards His creatures puts to his credit all his future good deeds, and the man is thus saved. Observe that when Jonah was cast forth into the sea, "the sea"–as we read–"stood still from raging". This means the supernal sea, which is said to "stand still" when its wrath is assuaged. For the heavenly tribunal, at a time when the world is under judgement, is like a pregnant woman who is convulsed with the pangs of childbirth, which cease, however, as soon as she is delivered of the child. Similarly the heavenly tribunal in time of judgement is agitated and convulsed, but once judgement is executed it becomes pacified and resumes with gladness its wonted calm, as it is written, "And when the wicked perish there is joy" (Prov. XI, 10). There is, indeed, a passage to the contrary, saying, "Have I any pleasure at all that the wicked should die?" (Ezek. XVIII, 23). This passage, however, speaks of those sinners who have not yet gone to the limit of provocation, whereas the previous passage speaks of those sinners whose measure is full.' AND THE LIFE OF SARAH WAS, ETC. How is it that the death of Sarah alone, among all women mentioned in the Bible, is recorded? R. Hiya said: 'Is that so? Do we not find it written, "And Rachel died, and was buried in the way to Ephrah" (Gen. XXXV, 19), and again, "and Miriam died there, etc." (Num. XX, 1), also, "and Deborah

Zohar: Bereshith, Section 1, Page 122a

Rebekah's nurse died" (Gen. XXXV, 8), and finally, "and Shuah's daughter the wife of Judah died" (Ibid. XXXVIII, 12)?' Said R. Yose: 'The problem is, why is the record of Sarah's years given with so much particularity, such as we find in the case of no other woman? Why, moreover, to Sarah alone of all the women of Scripture was a whole section of the Torah devoted? There is an esoteric reason, namely, that Sarah reached that grade on which depend all the years and the days of a son of man.' R. Yose discoursed on the verse: And the abundance of the earth is in all (ba-kol), and a king to a laboured field (Eccl. V, 8). 'The abundance of the earth,' he said, 'is certainly in kol (the Whole), as that is the source from whence issue spirits and souls, and from which beneficence is vouchsafed to the world. By "king" we have to understand the Holy One, blessed be He, the most high King, who, if the field be tilled and cultivated properly, attaches himself to it. What is this field? It is the field mentioned in the words, "as the smell of a field which the Lord hath blessed" (Gen. XXVII, 27).' R. Eleazar said: 'Herein are contained various deep esoteric ideas. The term "king" here is an allusion to the Shekinah, who does not dwell in a house unless the master of the house is married and is united to his wife for the purpose of bearing offspring; the Shekinah then brings forth souls to plant in that house. Hence the King, or Shekinah, is only attached to a cultivated field, but to no other. According to another explanation we translate, "a king is subjected to a field". "King" in this case is an allusion to the God-fearing woman of whom it is written, "but a woman that feareth the Lord, she shall be praised" (Prov. XXXI, 30), while "field" alludes to the strange woman of whom it says, "that they may keep thee from the strange woman" (Ibid. VII, 5). For there are fields and fields. There is the field in which abide all blessings and sanctities, and of which it is said, "as the smell of a field which the Lord hath blessed" (Gen. XXVII, 27); and there is another kind of field which is the abode of desolation, impurity, war and slaughter. And that king is sometimes enslaved to such a field, as it says, "For three things the earth doth quake... for a servant when he reigneth

Zohar: Bereshith, Section 1, Page 122b

and a handmaid that is heir to her mistress" (Prov. XXX, 21f). Such a king is plunged in darkness until he purifies himself and regains the supernal sphere. It is for that reason that a he-goat is offered up on New-Moon days, namely, because that field has been estranged from the Divine King, so that no blessings from that King could rest upon it; so when the other king is enslaved to the field, we may apply the words, "for in the field he found her, etc." (Deut. XXII, 27). Thus when Eve came into the world she attached herself to the serpent, who injected his impurity into her, so that she brought death into the world and to her husband. Then came Sarah, who, though she went down, came up again, and never attached herself to the serpent, as we read, "And Abram went up out of Egypt, he, and his wife, and all that he had" (Gen. XIII, 1). Of Noah, too, it is written, "And he drank of the wine, and was drunken; and he was uncovered within his tent" (Gen. IX, 21). And because Abraham and Sarah kept afar from the serpent, Sarah obtained life eternal for herself, her husband and all her descendants after her, who were bidden to "look unto the rock whence ye were hewn, and to the hole of the pit whence ye were digged" (Is. LI, 1). Hence the Scripture says, "and the life of Sarah was, etc.", a formula not used in the case of Eve or any other woman. For Sarah attached herself throughout to life, and thus life was made her own. AND THE LIFE OF SARAH WAS A HUNDRED YEARS AND TWENTY YEARS AND SEVEN YEARS. Each of these periods was marked by its own peculiar degree of virtue. R. Simeon said:

Zohar: Bereshith, Section 1, Page 123a

'There is an inner significance in the fact that with the other numbers the word for "years" (shanah) is in the singular, whereas with the number seven it is in the plural (shanim). The hundred forms a unit because the Holy One is united with the highest and most mysterious by the secret of the hundred benedictions pronounced each day. Similarly the number twenty symbolises the unity of the Thought with the Jubilee. Hence the singular shanah (year). Whereas the seven years correspond to the seven lower realms that issue separately from the mysterious supernal essence, and which, though they also form, in a sense, a unity, diverge in respect of the categories of justice and mercy into diverse sides and paths. This is not so in the supernal region. Hence, there we have "year", but here we have "years". But they are all called "life". Thus "the life of Sarah was" means "really was", having been created and established in the supernal regions.' R. Hiya said: 'It has been established that when Isaac was bound on the altar he was thirty-seven years old, and immediately after Sarah died, as it is written, "And Abraham came to mourn for Sarah, and to weep for her." Whence did he come? He came from Mount Moriah, after his binding of Isaac. These thirty-seven years from Isaac's birth to the time of his being bound were thus the real life of Sarah, as indicated in the expression "and the life of Sarah was (vayihyu)", the word VYHYV having the numerical value of thirty-seven.'

R. Yose discoursed on the verse: A Psalm. O sing unto the Lord a new song, for he hath done marvellous things; his right hand and his holy arm hath wrought salvation for him (Ps. XCVIII, 1). 'According to the companions, this verse was uttered by the cows, of whom it is said, "and the kine sang (vayisharnah) on the way" (I Sam. VI, 12). What they sang was this Psalm, commencing: "O sing unto the Lord a new song, for he hath done marvellous things." It should here be observed that while everything that the Holy One has created sings songs and praises before Him, both on high and here below, the chanting of these cows was not of the kind that falls within this mystical category, but was due to the fact that they were bearing the sacred ark; for as soon as the ark was removed from them they reverted to their brutishness and began lowing after the manner of other kine. Hence it was assuredly the feeling of the ark on their backs

Zohar: Bereshith, Section 1, Page 123b

that worked within them and made them utter song. The difference between "Psalm of David" and "To David a psalm" has been expounded elsewhere. Here, however, we have "Psalm" simply. The reason is that this Psalm is one destined to be sung by the Holy Spirit at the time when the Almighty will raise Israel from the dust. Hence the epithet "new song", since such a song will never have been chanted since the creation of the world.' Said R. Hiya: 'It is written, "there is nothing new under the sun" (Eccl. I, 9), whereas this song is going to be something new, and is going to happen under the sun. How can this be? The truth is that this is the moon, and is thus both "new" and "under the sun". Why will there be a new song? Because "He hath done marvellous things; his right hand and his holy arm hath wrought salvation for him." For whom?

Zohar: Bereshith, Section 1, Page 124a

For that grade that intones the chant, for on that grade He supports Himself, as it were, by His right hand and by His left hand. When will that Psalm be chanted? When the dead will come to life and rise from the dust; then there will be something new that had never yet been in the world.' Said R. Yose: 'When the Holy One will avenge Israel on the nations, then will this Psalm be chanted. For after the resurrection of the dead the world will be perfectly renewed, and will not be as before, when death prevailed in the world through the influence of the serpent, through whom the world was defiled and disgraced. Observe this. It is written, "And I will put enmity between thee and the woman" (Gen. III, 15). The term ebah (enmity) is akin to a similar word in the verse, "they are passed away as the ships of ebeh" (Job IX, 26), for on the great ocean there float numerous ships and boats of many kinds, and those in which the serpent sails are called "ships of ebeh" (enmity). The "woman" referred to here is the God-fearing woman; "thy seed" refers to the idolatrous nations; "her seed" to Israel; "he shall bruise thy head", to wit, the Holy One, who will one day destroy him, as it is written: "He will swallow up death forever" (Is. XXV, 8), and also, "and I will cause the unclean spirit to pass out of the land" (Zech. XIII, 2). "In the head" means in the time to come when the dead will come to life; for then the world will be the "head", since it will be established by the "head", that is, the supernal world. "In the heel" means now in this world, which is merely "heel" and not endowed with permanence, and so the serpent bites and mankind is in disgrace. See, now, a man's days were created and are located in the supernal grades, but when they draw to the end of their term, when they reach the Scriptural limit of threescore and ten (Ps. XC, 10), there remains then no grade any more for them to abide in, and so "their pride is but travail and vanity" (Ibid.), and they are as nought. Not so the days of the righteous.

Zohar: Bereshith, Section 1, Page 124b

They have a permanent abiding. Thus we read "And the life of Sarah was" (vayihyu, lit. "and they were" or "remained"); similarly, "And these are the days of the years of Abraham's life" (Gen. XXV, 7). You may object that similarly in the case of Ishmael it is written, "And these are the years of the life of Ishmael" (Ibid. 17). Ishmael, however, had in fact repented of his evil ways, and the days of his life thus attained permanency.' AND SARAH DIED IN KIRYATH-ARBA, ETC. R. Abba said: 'Of Sarah alone among all women do we find recorded the number of her days and years and the length of her life and the place where she was buried. All this was to show that the like of Sarah was not to be found among all the women of the world. You may object that we find a somewhat similar record in connection with Miriam, of whom it is written, "And Miriam died there, and was buried there" (Num. XX. 1). But the object there was to show the unworthiness of Israel, for whom water was made to flow forth only through the virtue of Miriam. Hence Miriam's death was not recorded with such full details as that of Sarah.'

R. Judah discoursed on the verse: Happy art thou, O land, when thy king is a free man (Eccl. X, 17). 'This verse,' he said, 'the companions have already explained, but further lessons may be derived from it. Happy are Israel, to whom the Holy One, blessed be He, gave the Torah, by the study of which all hidden paths should be made known to them and sublime mysteries should be revealed to them. The "land" here is "the land of life", and it is "happy" because its King showers upon it all the blessings pronounced upon it by the patriarchs. This is through the mystic influence of the Vau, who is always in readiness to pour on it blessing, and who is the "son of freedom" and "son of Jubilee", who obtains for slaves their freedom. He is a scion of the supernal world, and the author of all life, of all illuminations, and all exalted states. All this does the first-born son draw towards that land. Hence, "Happy art thou, O land." On the other hand, the words "Woe to thee, O land, when thy King is a boy" (Ibid.) refer to the nether earth and the nether world which draw their sustenance only from the dominion of the uncircumcised, and from that king called "boy". [Tr. note: Metatron.] Woe to the land that has to draw its sustenance in this manner! For this "boy"

Zohar: Bereshith, Section 1, Page 125a

possesses nothing of himself, but only such blessings as he receives at certain periods. But when these blessings are withheld from him, when the moon is impaired and darkness prevails, then woe to the world that needs to draw sustenance at that time! And how much the world has to endure before it obtains sustenance from him! 'Observe, now, that in the words "And Sarah died in Kiryath-arba" there is an inner meaning, to wit, that Sarah's death was not brought about by the tortuous serpent, which possessed no power over her as over the rest of mankind. For through him the people of the world have died since the sin of Adam, with the exception of Moses, Aaron, and Miriam, who died, as it is written, "by the mouth of the Lord" (although this expression is not used in connection with Miriam, out of respect for the Shekinah). The Scripture, however, here indicates that Sarah died not merely in, but by the hands of Kiryath-arba (lit. city of four), so called because it is the same as Hebron, where David joined the patriarchs. Her death thus was brought about by the hands of no one save Kiryath-arba.

'Observe that when the days of a man are firmly established in the supernal grades, that man has a permanent abiding in the world; but if not, those days gradually descend until they approach the grade wherein death resides. The angel of death then receives authority to take away the soul, traverses the world with one sweep, takes away the man's soul, and pollutes his body, which remains permanently unclean. Happy are the righteous who have not polluted themselves and in whom no pollution has remained. In the centre of the heaven there is an illumined path, which is the celestial dragon, and in it are fixed multitudes of little stars which are charged to keep watch over the secret deeds of human beings. In the same way myriads of emissaries go forth from the primeval celestial serpent, by whom Adam was seduced, to spy out the secret deeds

Zohar: Bereshith, Section 1, Page 125b

of mankind. Whoever, therefore, strives to live a life of purity is assisted from on high, and is encircled by the protecting hand of his Master, and is called saintly. On the other hand, when a man seeks to pollute himself, hosts of demons, who lie in wait for him, hover over him and surround and pollute him, so that he is called unclean. They all walk in front of him and cry, "unclean, unclean", as the Scripture says, "and he shall cry, Unclean, unclean" (Lev. XIII, 45).'

R. Isaac and R. Yose were walking from Tiberias to Lud. Said R. Isaac: 'I marvel at the wicked Balaam, how all his actions proceeded from the side of impurity. We here learn the mystical lesson that all species of witchcraft are linked up with, and proceed from, the primeval serpent who is the foul and unclean spirit. Hence all sorceries are called n'hashim (lit. serpents). And whoever becomes addicted to them pollutes himself, nay more, he has first to become polluted in order to attract to himself the side of the unclean spirit. For it is a dictum of our teachers that corresponding to the impulses of a man here are the influences which he attracts to himself from above. Should his impulse be towards holiness, he attracts to himself holiness from on high and so he becomes holy; but if his tendency is towards the side of impurity, he draws down towards himself the unclean spirit and so becomes polluted. For this reason, in order to draw towards himself the unclean spirit from that supernal serpent, the wicked Balaam besmirched himself nightly by bestial intercourse with his ass, and he would then proceed to his divinations and sorceries. To begin with he would take one of the familiar serpents, tie it up, break

its head, and extract its tongue. Then he would take certain herbs, and burn them as incense. He would then take the head of the serpent, split it into four sections, and offer it up as a second offering. Finally, he traced a circle round himself, mumbled some words, and made some gestures, until he became possessed of the unclean spirits, who told him all that they knew from the side of the heavenly dragon; and he thus continued his magical practices until he became possessed of the spirit of the primeval serpent. It is thus that we understand the passage, "he went not, as at the other times, to meet with n'hashim" (enchantments, lit. serpents) (Num. XXIV, 1).' Said R. Yose: 'Why is it that many kinds of magic and divination are only found in women?' R. Isaac replied: 'Thus I have learnt, that when the serpent had intercourse with Eve he injected defilement into her but not into her husband.' R. Yose then went up to R. Isaac and kissed him, saying, 'Many a time have I asked this question, but not until now have I received a real answer.' R. Yose further asked him: 'In which place and from whom did Balaam derive all his magical practices and knowledge?' R. Isaac replied: 'He learned it first from his father, but it was in the "mountains of the East", which are in an eastern country, that he obtained a mastery of all the arts of magic and divination. For those mountains are the abode of the angels Uzza and Azael whom the Holy One cast down from heaven, and who were chained there in iron fetters. It is they who impart to the sons of men a knowledge of magic. Hence the Scripture says: "From Aram Balak bringeth me, the King of Moab, from the mountains of the East" (Num. XXIII, 7).' 'But,' said R. Yose, 'is it not written, "and he went not as at the other times to meet with enchantments, but he set his face toward the wilderness" (Ibid. XXIV, 1)?' Said R. Isaac to him: 'The lower side, which comes from the unclean spirit above, was the unclean spirit prevailing in the wilderness when Israel made the calf in order to defile themselves therewith; and Balaam tried every device of magic

to uproot Israel, but without success.' Said R. Yose: 'You rightly said that when the serpent had carnal intercourse with Eve he injected into her defilement. We have, however, been taught that when Israel stood at Mount Sinai that defilement left them. But only Israel, who have received the Torah, were freed from it; whereas all the other nations, the idolaters, remained infected with it.' R. Isaac said: 'What you say is right. But observe that the Torah was only given to males, as it is written, "And this is the law which Moses set before the sons of Israel" (Deut. IV, 44), so that women are exempt from the precepts of the Torah. Furthermore, after they sinned they reverted to their former state of infection, of which it is more difficult for a woman to rid herself than for a man. Hence greater numbers of women are found to be addicted to magic and lasciviousness than men, as they come from the left side, and so are under the aegis of the divine rigour, and this side cleaves to them more than to men. Here is a proof of what I have just said, namely, that Balaam polluted himself first in order to draw unto himself the unclean spirit. During the period of a woman's menstruation a man must keep away from her, as then she is in close touch with the unclean spirit, and therefore at such a period she will be more successful in the use of magical arts than at any other time. Whatever thing she touches becomes unclean, and all the more so any man coming too near her. Happy are Israel, to whom the Holy One gave the Torah containing the precept, "and thou shalt not approach unto a woman to uncover her nakedness, as long as she is impure by her uncleanness" (Lev. XVIII, 19).' R. Yose asked: 'Why is one who attempts to interpret the chirping of birds called nahash (magician, also "serpent")?' R. Isaac replied: 'Because such a one certainly comes from the left side, as the unclean spirit hovers over such a bird and imparts to it

a knowledge of future events; and all unclean spirits are attached to the serpent (nahash)? from whom none can escape, since he is with everyone and will remain so until the time when the Holy One will remove him from the world, as already said, and as it is written, "He will swallow up death forever, and the Lord God will wipe away tears from all faces, etc." (Is. XXV, 8), and also, "and the unclean spirit I will cause to pass out of the land" (Zech. XIII, 2).'

R. Judah said: 'Abraham recognised the cave of Machpelah by a certain mark, and he had long set his mind and heart on it. For he had once entered that cave and seen Adam and Eve buried there. He knew that they were Adam and Eve because he saw the form of a man, and whilst he was gazing a door opened into the Garden of Eden, and he perceived the same form standing near it. Now, whoever looks at the form of Adam cannot escape death. For when a man is about to pass out of the world he catches sight of Adam and at that moment he dies. Abraham, however, did look at him, and saw his form and yet survived. He saw, moreover, a shining light that illumined the cave, and a lamp burning. Abraham then coveted that cave for his burial place, and his mind and heart were set upon it. Observe now with what tact Abraham made his request for a burial place for Sarah. He did not ask at first for the cave, neither did he indicate any desire to separate himself from the people of the land, but simply said: GIVE ME A POSSESSION OF A BURYING PLACE WITH YOU, THAT I MAY BURY MY DEAD OUT OF SIGHT. Although he addressed himself to the sons of Heth, we cannot suppose that Ephron was not present then, since it says: Now EPHRON WAS SITTING IN THE MIDST OF THE CHILDREN OF HETH.

Abraham, however, did not at first say anything to him, but spoke only to them, as it says: AND HE SPOKE TO THE CHILDREN OF HETH, ETC. Now it cannot be imagined that Abraham wished to be buried among them, among the impure, or that he desired to mix with them. But Abraham acted tactfully, giving a lesson to the

Zohar: Bereshith, Section 1, Page 127b

world. Though his whole desire was centred on that cave, he did not ask for it forthwith, but asked for something else of which he had no need, and he addressed his request to the others, not to Ephron himself. It was only after they said to him in the presence of Ephron: "Hear us, my lord; thou art a mighty prince among us, etc." that he said, "hear me, and entreat for me to Ephron the son of Zohar, that he may give me the cave of Machpelah, which he hath, etc." Abraham as much as said: Do not think that I wish to separate from you as being superior to you. No, in the midst of you I desire to be buried, for as I am fond of you I do not wish to keep aloof from you.'

R. Eleazar said: 'Abraham came to enter the cave in this way. He was running after that calf of which we read, "and Abraham ran unto the herd, and fetched a calf" (Gen. XVIII, 7), and the calf ran until it entered a cave, and then Abraham entered after it and saw what we have described. Further, Abraham used to offer up his prayer daily, and in so doing used to proceed as far as that field, which emitted heavenly odours. Whilst there he saw a light issuing from the cave, so that he prayed on that spot, and on that spot the Holy One communed with him. On that account Abraham now asked for it, having always longed for it since then. Why did not he ask for it before that time? Because the people would not have listened to him, as he had no obvious need for it. Now that he needed it, he thought it was time to demand it. Observe that had Ephron seen inside the cave what Abraham saw, he would never have sold it to him. But he never saw there anything, since such things are never revealed except to their rightful owner. It was thus revealed to Abraham and not to Ephron: to Abraham, who was its rightful owner, but not to Ephron,

Zohar: Bereshith, Section 1, Page 128a

who had no part or portion in it, and who therefore only saw darkness in it; and for that reason he sold it. Nay, he even sold him more than he had mentioned in his original request. For Abraham only said, "that he may give me the cave of Machpelah which he hath... for the full price let him give it to me", whereas Ephron said, "the field give I thee, and the cave that is therein", as he felt indifferent to the whole thing, not realising what it was. 'Observe that when Abraham entered the cave for the first time he saw there a bright light, and as he advanced, the ground lifted, revealing to him two graves. Adam then arose in his true form, saw Abraham and smiled at him. (Abraham thereby knew that there he was destined to be buried.) Abraham then said to him: "Could you tell me, is there not a tent for me close to you?" Adam replied: "The Holy One buried me here, and from that time until now I have been lying hid like a corn seed in the ground, until thou camest into the world. But from now there is salvation for me and for the world for thy sake. Hence it is written, AND THE FIELD AND THE CAVE THAT IS THEREIN AROSE, that is, there was literally an arising before the presence of Abraham, as up to that time nothing there had been visible, but now what had been hidden rose up, and thus the whole spot was devoted to its lawful purpose.' R. Simeon said: 'When Abraham brought Sarah in there for burial, Adam and Eve arose and refused to receive her. They said: "Is not our shame already great enough before the Holy One in the other world on account of our sin, which brought death into the world, that ye should come to shame us further with your good deeds?" Abraham made answer: "I am already destined to make atonement before the Almighty for thee, so that thou mayest nevermore be shamed before Him." Forthwith Abraham after this buried Sarah

Zohar: Bereshith, Section 1, Page 128b

his wife, to wit, after Abraham had taken upon himself this obligation. Adam then returned to his place, but not Eve, until Abraham came and placed her beside Adam, who received her for his sake. Hence the text says, AND AFTER THIS, ABRAHAM BURIED (eth) SARAH HIS WIFE: the augmenting particle eth indicates that the burial included, as it were, Eve. Thus they were all settled in their proper places. Hence the Scripture says, "These are the generations of heaven and earth when they were created (b'hibar'am)" (Gen. II, 4), which according to tradition, means "on account of Abraham" (b'Abraham). Now "the generations of the heaven and the earth" can only be Adam and Eve, they having been the direct issue of the heaven and earth and not of human parents, and it was they who became established through Abraham: before Abraham, Adam and Eve were not established in their places in the other world.'

R. Eleazar asked his father, R. Simeon, for an explanation of the term Machpelah (lit. "twofold", or "folded"). 'How is it,' he said, 'that first it is written "the cave of Machpelah", and subsequently "the cave of the field of Machpelah", implying that the field and not the cave was "Machpelah" (doubled)?' R. Simeon replied: 'The term Machpelah belongs properly neither to the cave nor to the field, but to something else with which both were connected. The cave belongs to the field, and the field to something else. For the whole of the Land of Israel and of Jerusalem is folded up beneath it, since it exists both above and below, in the same way as there is a Jerusalem both above and below, both of the same pattern. The Jerusalem above has a twofold attachment, above and below; similarly the Jerusalem below is linked to two sides, higher and lower. Hence it is folded in two; and that field partakes of the same character, seeing that it is therein situated. The same reference is contained in the passage, "as the smell of a field which the Lord hath blessed" (Gen. XXVII, 27), to wit, both above

Zohar: Bereshith, Section 1, Page 129a

and below. Hence its name, "field of folding", but not "folded field". Further, the esoteric implication of the term Machpelah relates it to the Divine Name, in which the letter He is doubled, though both are as one. It is, indeed, true that the cave was a twofold one, a cave within a cave, yet the name "cave of the field of Machpelah" has a different connotation, as already explained. Abraham, on his part, who knew its true character, in speaking to the children of Heth called it simply "cave of Machpelah", as if to imply merely "double cave", which it also was in fact. Scripture, however, describes it as "the cave of the field of Machpelah", this being its true description. For the Holy One has disposed all things in such a way that everything in this world should be a replica of something in the world above, and that the two should be united so that His glory should be spread above and below. Happy the portion of the righteous in whom the Holy One finds pleasure both in this world and in the world to come!' AND ABRAHAM WAS OLD, HE HAD COME INTO DAYS; AND THE LORD BLESSED ABRAHAM IN ALL THINGS. R. Judah discoursed on the verse: Happy is the man whom thou choosest and bringest near, that he may dwell in thy courts (Ps. LXV, 5). 'This verse', he said, 'may be explained as follows. Happy is the man whose ways are found right before the Holy One and in whom He finds pleasure so as to bring him near to Himself. Observe how Abraham strove to come nearer and nearer to Him, making Him the object of his longing the whole of his days. Not just one day, or just every now and then, but by his works advancing day by day from grade to grade, until he rose, when he was old, to the higher grades proper to him. Hence we read that when Abraham was old he "came into days", i.e. he entered into those supernal days, the days familiar in the doctrine of true faith. Further, "the Lord blessed Abraham in all things (ba-kol)", the region called kol (all) being the source whence issue all boons and blessings. Happy are the penitent who in the space of one day, one hour, nay, one second, can draw near to

Zohar: Bereshith, Section 1, Page 129b

the Holy One, as near as even the truly righteous in the space of many years. Abraham did not reach that high grade until he was old, as already said. So, too, David, of whom it is written, "and King David was old, he came into days" (I Kings I, 1). But the penitent immediately finds entrance, and is brought close to the Holy One, blessed be He.' R. Yose said: 'We have been taught that the place assigned to the penitent in the next world is one where even the wholly righteous are not permitted to enter, as the former are the nearest of all to the King; they are more devoted and strive more intently to draw near to the King. For there are many abodes prepared by the Holy One, blessed be He, for the righteous in the next world, each one according to his grade. It is written: "Happy is the man whom thou choosest, and bringest near, that he may dwell in thy courts", that is, those whom the Holy One brings near unto Him, those souls who mount from below on high so as to possess themselves of the heritage prepared for them; "that he may dwell in thy courts", to wit, the outer halls and grades, referred to in the words, "then I will give thee free access among these that stand by" (Zech. III, 7), i.e. a grade among the supernal holy angels. Those who attain that grade are messengers of the Lord, on an equality with the angels, and are constantly being used in the service of their Master, because in life they always strove to remain holy and keep afar from impurity. Contrariwise, whoever pollutes himself in this world draws to himself the spirit of uncleanness, and when his soul leaves him the unclean spirits pollute it, and its habitation is among them. For according to a man's strivings in this world is his habitation in the next world; hence such a man is polluted by the spirits of uncleanness and cast into Gehinnom. Thus whoever sanctifies himself and is on his guard against defilement in this world finds his habitation in the next world among the supernal holy

Zohar: Bereshith, Section 1, Page 130a

angels, where they carry out God's messages. These are they who abide in the court—"the court of the Tabernacle" (Ex. XXVII, 9). But there are others who penetrate further, of whom David said, "we will be satisfied with the goodness of thy house" (Ps. LXV, 5). (The use of the term "we" here instead of "he", as we should have expected, is explained by the dictum that in the Temple Court no seats are permitted save to the kings of the Davidic dynasty.) Still further within is a compartment reserved for the pious of a higher grade, referred to in the verse, "and those that were to pitch before the tabernacle eastward, before the tent of meeting toward the sunrising, were Moses and Aaron and his sons, etc." (Num. III, 38). Thus there is in the next world a gradation of glorious abodes and resplendent lights, each outshining the other.

'As the works of the righteous differ in this world, so do their places and lights differ in the next world. Further, it has been laid down that even in this world, when men sleep at night and their souls leave them and flit about through the world, not every one alike rises to behold the glory of the Ancient of Days, but each one in proportion to a man's constancy of attachment to God and to his good deeds. The soul of the man who is besmirched, when it leaves the body asleep, meets with throngs of unclean spirits of the infernal orders traversing the universe, who take her up and to whom she clings. They disclose to her events about to come to pass in the world; occasionally they delude her with false information. This has been already stated elsewhere. But the soul of the worthy man, when it leaves him in sleep, ascends and cleaves its way through the unclean spirits, which cry aloud, "Make way, make way! Here is one not belonging to our side!" The soul then ascends among the holy angels, who communicate to it some true information. When the soul is on its descent again, all those malignant bands are eager to meet it in order to obtain from it that information, in exchange for which they impart to it many other things. But the one thing it learnt from the holy angels is to those

Zohar: Bereshith, Section 1, Page 130b

other things as grain to chaff. This is a rare privilege for one whose soul is still in this world. Similar adventures await the souls when they altogether leave the body to depart from this world. In their attempt to soar upwards they have to pass through many gates at which bands of demons are stationed. These seize the souls that are of their side and deliver them into the hands of Duma in order that he may take them into Gehinnom. They then seize them again and ascend, and make proclamation concerning them, saying, "These are they who transgressed the commands of their Lord." They then sweep through the universe and bring the souls back to Gehinnom. This procedure goes on for the whole of the first twelve months. After that they are assigned each to its appropriate place. On the other hand, the worthy souls soar upwards, as already explained, and are assigned the places corresponding to their merits. Happy, therefore, are the righteous, for whom many boons are reserved in the next world. But for none is a more interior abode reserved than for those who penetrate into the divine mystical doctrines and enter each day into close union with their Divine Master. Of such it is written, "What no eye hath seen, O God, beside thee, that will he do for those who wait for him" (Is. LXIV, 3). The word "wait" here has a parallel in the verse, "now Elihu had waited to speak unto Job" (Job XXXII, 4), and refers to those who are importunate for any word of esoteric wisdom, who study it minutely and patiently to discover its true significance and so to gain knowledge of their Lord. These are those in whom their Master glorifies Himself each day, who enter the company of the supernal holy angels, and pass through all the celestial gates without let or hindrance. Happy their portion in this world and the next!

'In this way Abraham penetrated into the Divine Wisdom and united himself with his Divine Master after he had duly prepared himself by a life of pious deeds. He thus merited those supernal days, and received blessings from the region whence all blessings flow, as it is written, "And the Lord blessed Abraham ba-kol" (in all things), where the term kol is the designation of the river the waters of which never fail.' R. Hiya said: 'Observe that Abraham abstained from intermarrying with other nations and from attaching himself to idolatrous peoples. For the women of idolatrous nations pollute their husbands and those who come into close contact with them. But Abraham, having penetrated into the mystic doctrines of Wisdom, knew the source whence the unclean spirits emerge to traverse the universe, and it was for this reason that he adjured his servant not to take a wife for his son from other nations.'

R. Isaac discoursed on the verse: And the dust returneth to the earth as it was, and the spirit returneth unto God who gave it (Eccl. XII, 7). He said: 'When the Holy One, blessed be He, created Adam, He took his dust from the site of the Temple and built his body out of the four corners of the world, all of which contributed to his formation. After that He poured over him the spirit of life, as it says, "and he breathed into his nostrils the breath of life" (Gen. II, 7). Adam then arose and realised that he was both of heaven and of earth, and so he united himself to the Divine and was endowed with mystic Wisdom. Each son of man is, after the same model, a composite of the heavenly and the earthly; and all those who know how to sanctify themselves in the right manner in this world, when they beget a son cause the holy spirit to be drawn upon him from the region whence all sanctities emerge. Such are called the children of the Holy One; and as their bodies were formed in sanctity, so are they given a spirit from the supernal holy region. Observe that the day on which a man is about to depart from this world is a day of reckoning when the body and the soul in combination have to give an account of their works. The soul afterwards leaves him, and the body returns to the earth, both thus returning to their original source, where they will remain until the time when the Holy One will bring the dead to life again. Then God will cause the identical body and the identical soul to return to the world in their former state, as it is written, "Thy dead shall live, my dead bodies shall arise" (Is. XXVI, 19). The same soul is meanwhile stored up by the Holy One, thus returning to its original place, as it is written, "And the spirit returns to God who gave it" (Eccl. XII, 7). And at the time when the Holy One will raise the dead to life He will cause dew to descend upon them from His head. By means of that dew all will rise from the dust, as it says, "for thy dew is as the dew of lights" (Is. XXVI, 19), these being the supernal lights through which the Almighty will in future pour forth life upon the world. For

Zohar: Bereshith, Section 1, Page 131a

the tree of life exudes life unceasingly into the universe. Life in the present dispensation is cut short through the influence of the evil serpent, whose dominion is symbolised by the darkened moon. Under the same influence the celestial waters, as it were, fail, and life is not dispensed in the world in proper measure. At that time, however, the evil tempter, who is none other than the evil serpent, will be removed from the world by the Almighty and disappear, as it is written, "and I will cause the unclean spirit to pass out of the earth" (Zech. XIII, 2). After he disappears the moon will no more be obscured, and the waters of the celestial river will flow on perennially. Then will be fulfilled the prophecy,

"Moreover the light of the moon shall be as the light of the sun, and the light of the sun shall be sevenfold, as the light of the seven days, etc." (Is. XXX, 26).'

Said R. Hizkiah: 'If it be so that all the dead bodies will rise up from the dust, what will happen to a number of bodies which shared in succession the same soul?'

R. Yose answered: 'Those bodies which were unworthy and did not achieve their purpose will be regarded as though they had not been: as they were a withered tree in this world, so will they be regarded at the time of the resurrection. Only the last that had been firmly planted and took root and prospered will come to life, as it says, "For he shall be as a tree planted by the waters... but its foliage shall be luxuriant, etc." (Jer. XVII, 8). This alludes to the body that struck deep root, produced fruit and prospered. But of the former body which remained fruitless, which did not take root, which was unworthy and did not achieve its end, it is written, "For he shall be like a tamarisk in the desert, and shall not see when good cometh, etc." (Ibid. 6), i.e. he will not be included in the resurrection, and will not see the light stored up at the Creation for the delectation of the righteous, regarding which it says, "And God saw the light that it was good" (Gen. I, 4), and also, "But unto you that fear my name shall the sun of righteousness arise, etc." (Mal. III, 20). The Holy One will thus in the future raise the dead to life again, and the good principle will prevail in the world and the Evil One will vanish from the world, as already said, and the previous bodies will be as though they never had been.' Said R. Isaac: 'For such bodies the Holy One will provide other spirits, and if found worthy they will obtain an abiding in the world, but if not, they will be ashes under the feet of the righteous, as it is written, "and many of them that sleep in the dust of the earth shall awake, etc." (Dan. XII, 2). All then will rise up and will be ranged before the Holy One, who will enumerate them, as it were, as it says, "He that bringeth out their host by number" (Is. XL, 26). Observe that it has been laid down that the dead of the Land of Israel will be the first to rise, and of them it is written, "Thy dead shall live" (Ibid. XXVI, 19). On the other hand, the words "my dead bodies shall arise" (Ibid.) allude to the dead of other lands, since instead of "shall live" it says "shall arise". The living spirit, in fact, will only infuse the bodies in the Land of Israel. "Thy dead", then, "shall live". But the other dead bodies will rise without the spirit of life, and only after they shall have rolled themselves underground and reached the Land of Israel will they receive souls–only there, but not in other realms–so that they may be really resurrected.'

R. Eleazar and R. Yose were one night studying the Torah. Said R. Eleazar: 'Observe that at the time when the Holy One will bring the dead back to life, all the souls mustered before Him will bear each a form identical with the one it bore in this world. The Holy One will bring them down, and will call them by their names, as it says, "He calleth them all by name" (Ibid. XL, 26). Every soul will then enter into its own place, and the dead will be fully resurrected, and the world will thus reach its consummation. Of that time it is written, "And the reproach of his people will he take away from off all the earth" (Ibid. XXV, 8), which is a reference to the evil tempter, who darkens the faces of men and leads them astray.'

R. Yose, interposing, said: 'How is it that a man whilst the spirit of life is in him is not a source of defilement, whereas after his soul leaves him he becomes a source of defilement?' R. Isaac replied: 'Assuredly this is the law, and the explanation given is that the evil tempter, in the act of taking away the spirit of a man, defiles it, and thus the body is left in a state of defilement. This, however, is not the case with idolatrous nations. For since they carry defilement during life, as their souls are derived from the side of defilement, when this defilement is removed the body remains without any defilement whatever. For this reason

Zohar: Bereshith, Section 1, Page 131b

whoever forms an attachment with a woman of any of the idolatrous nations becomes defiled, and the offspring born from such an attachment receives a defiled spirit. It may be asked why, seeing that the father is an Israelite, the offspring should receive a defiled spirit. The reason is that as soon as the father attached himself to that woman, defilement entered into him. Now if the father became defiled through the unclean woman, how much more must the offspring born of her be defiled to its very spirit. Such a man, moreover, transgresses the precept of the Torah, contained in the words, "For thou shalt bow down to no other god; for the Lord whose name is Jealous, is a jealous God" (Ex. XXXIV, 14), i.e. He is jealous for the sanctity of the holy covenant.'

R. Eleazar said: 'Observe that, as has been stated elsewhere, our father Abraham, after he acquired Wisdom, determined to keep separate from all other nations and not to enter into matrimonial alliance with them. Hence we read: AND I WILL MAKE THEE SWEAR BY THE LORD, THE GOD OF HEAVEN AND THE GOD OF EARTH, THAT THOU SHALT NOT TAKE A WIFE FOR MY SON OF THE DAUGHTERS OF THE CANAANITES, ETC. The words "daughters of the Canaanites" are parallel to the expression "daughters of a strange god" (Mal. II, 11). So, too, the word "I" (Anokhi) which follows is a reference to the Deity, as in the verse, "I (Anokhi) made the earth." The purpose of this injunction was to save Isaac from being defiled by them. For whoever impairs the sanctity of the holy covenant by contact with a woman of an idolatrous nation causes the defilement of a certain other place, alluded to in the passage, "For three things the earth doth quake, etc." (Prov. XXX, 21). And although Abraham adjured his servant by the holy covenant, he did not feel

161

satisfied until he had made supplication on his behalf to the Holy One, blessed be He, saying: THE LORD, THE GOD OF HEAVEN... MAY HE SEND HIS ANGEL BEFORE THEE, ETC., to wit, the angel of the covenant", so that the covenant might be preserved in its sanctity, and not be defiled among the nations. He continued: BEWARE THOU THAT THOU BRING NOT MY SON BACK THITHER. Why so? Because Abraham knew that none among those nations had knowledge of the true God like himself, and so he desired that Isaac should not settle among them, but should continue to dwell with him, so that he might constantly learn the ways of the Holy One, and turn neither to the right nor to the left.' R. Yose said: 'Of a certainty the merits of Abraham stood his servant in good stead, for on the very day on which he set out he reached the fountain, as it says, AND I CAME THIS DAY UNTO THE FOUNTAIN.

R. Eleazar discoursed on the verse: Open thou mine eyes, that I may behold wondrous things out of thy law (Ps. CXIX, 18). 'How devoid of discernment,' he said, 'are those sons of men who abide in ignorance of the Torah and pay no regard to its study. For it is the Torah that spells life and freedom and felicity in this world and in the world to come. It is life in this world, earning for its devotees fulness of days, as it says, "the number of thy days I will fulfil" (Ex. XXIII, 26), as well as length of days in the world to come; for the Torah is the very fulness of life, life of bliss without any gloom; it is freedom in this world, complete freedom; for when a man applies himself to the study of the Torah all the nations of the world cannot prevail against him. Such a one also obtains deliverance from the angel of death, who has no power over him. (You may object, What of the martyrs who suffered in times of persecution, such as R. Akibah and his colleagues? These suffered, however, under a special decree from on high in accordance with a special purpose.) Assuredly, had Adam held fast to the tree of life, which is nothing else but the Torah, he would not have brought death upon himself and upon the rest of the world. Hence, in connection with the giving of the Law it is written, "Heruth (freedom) on the tables" (Ex. XXXII, 16), as explained elsewhere. And had Israel not sinned and forsaken the tree of life they would not have brought death anew into the world. Hence God could say to them, in the words of the Psalmist, "I said, Ye are godlike beings, and all of you sons of the Most High" (Ps. LXXXII, 6), but ye have done hurt to yourselves, and so: "verily like Adam shall ye die, etc." (Ibid.). Thus whoever applies himself to the study of the Torah is not subject to the power of the evil serpent, the darkener of the world.' R. Yesa put the question: 'If that is so, why did Moses die, he having committed no sin?' R. Eleazar replied: 'Moses assuredly died, but not by the power of the evil serpent, and so he was not defiled by his hands. Besides, from another aspect, he did not die,

Zohar: Bereshith, Section 1, Page 132a

but was only drawn up by the Shekinah and departed to eternal life, as has already been explained in connection with the passage, "And Benaiah the son of Jehoiada, the son of a living man, etc." (II Sam. XXIII, 20). [Tr. note: v. p. 6b.] Thus whoever applies himself to the study of the Torah attains perfect freedom: freedom in this world from the bondage of the idolatrous nations, and freedom in the next world, as no accusation will be brought against him there. For the Torah contains sublime and recondite truths, as it says, "she is more precious than rubies" (Prov. III, 11). Treasures innumerable are indeed concealed therein, so that David, when he considered the Torah in the spirit of wisdom, and realised how many wondrous truths unfold themselves therefrom, was moved to exclaim, "Open thou mine eyes, that I may behold wondrous things out of thy Law" (Ps. CXIX, 18). AND IT CAME TO PASS, THAT BEFORE HE HAD DONE SPEAKING, BEHOLD, REBEKAH WENT OUT.

Instead of "went out" (yozeth) we should have expected "came" (baah). The implication is that God brought her away from the people of the town, and made her an exception to them. AND SHE WENT DOWN TO THE FOUNTAIN. This fountain was none other than the well of Miriam; hence the word "to" here is expressed by the letter he (ha-'aynah). According to another explanation, the term "went out", like the similar term in the passage, "young maidens going out to draw water" (I Sam. IX, 11), implies modesty, that is, that they kept at home and only went out at a certain hour to draw water. This was the sign by which Abraham's servant recognised her. For when he reached Haran and met Rebekah "at the time of evening" it was the time of the afternoon prayer (minhah). Thus the moment when Isaac began the afternoon prayer coincided with the moment when the servant encountered Rebekah. So, too, it was at the very moment of his afternoon prayer that Rebekah came to Isaac himself. Thus all was fitly disposed through the working of the Divine Wisdom. It was as part of the same scheme that the servant came to the well of water, the inner significance of which is to be found in the passage, "Thou art a fountain of gardens, a well of living waters, and flowing streams from Lebanon" (S.S. IV, 15).

R. Simeon was once on his way to Tiberias in company with R. Abba. Said R. Simeon to him, 'Let us proceed, for I foresee that a man will come up to us who has something new to say, some new expositions of the Torah. ' Said R. Abba: 'Verily I know that wherever you go the Holy One sends you winged angels to entertain you.' When they had gone a little further, R. Simeon raised his eyes and saw a man running along. R. Simeon and R. Abba then sat down. When the man came up to them R. Simeon asked him, 'Whence art thou?' He said, 'I am a Judean and am coming from Cappadocia, and I am on my way to the abode of the son of Yohai, to whom the companions sent me in order to communicate certain decisions to which they have come.' R. Simeon said to him, 'Speak, my son.' The man asked, 'Art thou the son of Yohai?'

'I am,' was the reply. The man then said: 'It is an established rule that a man whilst praying should not let anything interpose between himself and the wall, as it is written, "then Hezekiah turned his face to the wall" (Is. XXXVIII, 2); and it is further forbidden to pass within four cubits of the man who stands in prayer, and they have now laid down that this means on any side save directly in front of him. Further, that a man may not pray standing behind his teacher, etc. These are the decisions of the companions.' The man then discoursed on the verse: Hear my prayer, O Lord, and give ear unto my cry; keep not silence at my tears (Ps. XXXIX, 13). 'Why', he asked, 'is the word for "hear" in this place written shim'ah instead of the usual sh'ma'? The truth is that the form sh'ma' is always addressed to the male aspect of the Deity, whereas the form shim'ah is addressed to the female aspect. Hence the term shim'ah is used because it is addressed to that grade which receives all the prayers of mankind, and, according to our tradition, weaves them into a crown which it puts on the head of the Zaddik, the life of the universe, referred to in the words, "Blessings upon the head of the Just One" (Prov. X, 6). Further, the words "Hear, O Lord, my prayer" allude to silent prayer, whereas the succeeding words "and give ear unto my cry" refer to prayer which a man cries aloud in his anguish, as we read, "and their cry came up to God" (Ex. II, 23). (The term shav'atham (their cry) indicates the raising of the voice and the raising of the eyes towards heaven; it is akin to the term sho'a (turning) in the passage "and turning (v'sho'a) to the mount" (Is. XXII, 5).) Such a prayer

Zohar: Bereshith, Section 1, Page 132b

breaks through all gates and ascends to heaven. "Keep not silence at my tears": prayerful tears ascend before the King, no gate can withstand them, and they are never turned away empty. Further, there are in this passage three grades of supplication: prayer, cry, and tears, corresponding to the three grades mentioned in the verse, "For I am a stranger with thee, a sojourner, as all my fathers were" (Ps. XXXIX, 13). First "a stranger", then "a sojourner", and last "as all my fathers", who were the basis of the world. Observe that there are two categories of prayer, one to be said standing and the other sitting, although they form but one whole. There are also two phylacteries, one for the arm and one for the head, corresponding to day and night, the two again making one whole. The sitting prayer corresponds to the arm phylactery, which prepares and adorns it like a bride before entering under the bridal canopy. So the prayer is surrounded and escorted, mystically speaking, by the chariots and legions mentioned in the prayer, "Creator of ministering spirits.... And the Ophanim and holy Hayoth... "This prayer, therefore, is recited sitting, but when the prayer approaches the Supreme King and He is about to receive it, then we are to stand up before the most high King, for then the male is united with the female. Hence there must be no interruption between the redemption benediction at the end of the sitting prayer and the beginning of the standing prayer. Also, since one is standing before the Supreme King, he must on concluding step backwards four cubits, which has been explained to be a divine measure. Thus, whatever part of the prayer is symbolic of the male principle has to be recited standing. Similarly the supplicant bends his knee at the utterance of barukh (blessed be), and erects himself to his full height at the utterance of the Divine Name, to symbolise the superiority of the male over the female. Observe, further, that we have laid down that one should not while praying stand immediately behind his teacher. The reason is this. It is written: "Thou shalt fear the (eth) Lord thy God" (Deut. VI, 13). The particle eth here indicates that the teacher is associated with God as the object of fear. Hence during prayer a man should not be faced with that object of fear, so that he may be filled exclusively with the fear of the Holy One alone without any adjunct. Isaac instituted afternoon prayer in the same way as Abraham instituted morning prayer. Each of them instituted the prayer corresponding with the grade to which he was attached. Hence the time for the afternoon prayer begins with the sun's decline towards the west, inasmuch as the period preceding that time, from the dawn onward, is termed day, as in the passage, "the mercy of God endureth the whole day" (Ps. LII, 3). Nor can it be said that "the whole day" lasts until darkness sets in, since it is written, "Woe unto us, for the day hath departed, for the shadows of the evening are stretched out" (Jer. VI, 4). This shows that the term "day" is limited to the time for receiving the morning prayer, of which it is written, "the mercy of God endureth the whole day", for at that time the sun is still on the east side. As soon as the sun declines in its passage towards the west, the time of the afternoon prayer sets in, as the day has already departed, and has given place to the shadows of the evening, when the quality of rigour asserts itself. "The day has departed", that is, the period when the grade of mercy (hesed) prevails, and "the shadows of the evening are stretched out", at what time there rages the grade of rigour, that very hour when the Sanctuary was destroyed and the Temple burnt down. For this reason tradition teaches us that a man should be careful not to miss the afternoon prayer, as then is the time when the world is under the aegis of rigour. Jacob instituted evening prayer ('arbith), thereby causing the letter Vau (symbolic of Jacob) to supplement the letter He (symbolic of Isaac), which is nourished by the Vau, having no light of its own. For that reason the evening prayer is optional, inasmuch as it is a continuation of the day prayer, having for its aim to illumine the obscurity of the night. That obscurity prevails until midnight, at which hour the Holy One disports Himself with the righteous in the Garden of Eden. Hence it is an opportune time for a man to busy himself in the study of the Torah, as already explained elsewhere. Observe that David in his psalms made allusion to the three periods of prayer, in the words, "Evening, and morning, and at noonday, do I meditate, and moan" (Ps. LV, 18). Here we have allusion to three periods, although David himself observed only two prayers, one alluded to in "do I meditate" and the second in "and moan". The first is the prayer of the morning, the period of mercy; hence "meditating" suffices. The second is the prayer of the afternoon, the period of rigour; hence, "and I do moan". At midnight David arose to chant songs and hymns,

Zohar: Bereshith, Section 1, Page 133a

as it is written, "and in the night his song is with me" (Ps. XLII, 9).'

R. Simeon then rose up and they proceeded on their way, the stranger accompanying them as far as Tiberias. On the way R. Simeon said: 'Observe that the members of the Great Synod [Tr. note: A body which, according to Rabbinic tradition, regulated the affairs of the Jewish community during the lifetime of Ezra and for some time afterwards.] instituted the prayers in correspondence to the fixed daily offerings, of which there were two, as it is written, "the one lamb shalt thou offer in the morning, and the other lamb shalt thou offer between the two evenings" (Num. XXVIII, 4), that is, at the two periods which coincide with the periods of prayer.' Said the stranger: 'Since originally it was the patriarchs who instituted the prayers, why should those instituted by Abraham and Isaac be of primary importance, while the one instituted by Jacob, who was the cream of the patriarchs, be only voluntary?' R. Simeon replied: 'The reason, as has been affirmed, is as follows: The two periods of the two earlier prayers have for their object only to unite Jacob to his heritage, but once this has been effected we need nothing further: as soon as the Woman is placed between the two arms and is joined to the Body, nothing more is needed. The two prayers are thus the two arms between which Jacob is united to the body, that is, to heaven, in accordance with the verse, "but thou, O Lord, art on high forevermore" (Ps. XCII, 9). All this contains deep mysteries known only to the initiated.' R. Abba and the Judean then approached R. Simeon and kissed his hand, after which R. Abba remarked: 'Until this day I always found here a difficulty, but now happy is my portion that I have been privileged to solve it!' AND ISAAC BROUGHT HER INTO THE TENT (OF) SARAH HIS MOTHER. R. Yose remarked: 'The letter he at the end of the word haohelah (into the tent) is a reference to the Shekinah, which now returned to the tent. For during the whole of Sarah's life the Shekinah did not depart from it, and a light used to burn there from one Sabbath eve to the other; once lit, it lasted all the days of the week. After her death the light was extinguished, but when Rebekah came the Shekinah returned and the light was rekindled. Thus the verse reads literally: "And he brought her into the tent-Sarah his mother", the last phrase implying that Rebekah was in all her works a replica of Sarah his mother.' R. Judah said: 'Just as Isaac was the very image of Abraham, so that whoever looked at Isaac said, "there is Abraham", and knew at once that "Abraham begat Isaac", so was Rebekah the very image of Sarah. She was thus, so to say, in the phrase of our text, "Sarah his mother".' R. Eleazar said: 'All this is truly said. But observe a deeper mystery here. For, verily, although Sarah died, her image did not depart from the house. It was not, however, visible for a time, but as soon as Rebekah came it became visible again, as it is written, "and he brought her into the tent-Sarah his mother", as much as to say, "and forthwith Sarah his mother made her appearance". No one, however, saw her save Isaac, and thus we understand the words, "and Isaac was comforted after his mother", that is, after his mother became visible and was installed in the house again.'

R. Simeon said: 'Why does the Scripture tell us with so much detail that Isaac TOOK REBEKAH, AND SHE BECAME HIS WIFE, AND HE LOVED HER? The last statement seems to be unnecessary, for naturally if she became his wife he loved her, as is the way of all men to love their wives. The explanation is that the attraction of the male to the female is derived from the left, as we read, "Let his left hand be under my head" (S. S. II, 6), the left being symbolic of night and darkness; hence although Abraham loved Sarah, the statement "and he loved her" is only mentioned in the case of Isaac (he being of the left). Of Jacob also it is written that he "loved Rachel" (Gen. XXIX, 18); but here the explanation is that this was due to the side of Isaac which was contained in him. Observe that Abraham, on seeing Sarah, only embraced her, and nothing more, whereas Isaac seized Rebekah and put his arm under her head, as it is written, "Let his left hand be under my head, and his right hand embrace me" (S. S. II, 6). Jacob afterwards had intercourse with his wives and begat twelve tribes. Observe, too, that all the patriarchs followed the same course,

Zohar: Bereshith, Section 1, Page 133b

in that each one of them espoused four women. Abraham had four spouses, besides Sarah and Hagar, two concubines, as is seen from the passage, "but unto the sons of the concubines that Abraham had" (Gen. XXV, 6). Isaac had four spouses, in that Rebekah, mystically speaking, combined in herself the virtues of four women. This is indicated in Scripture in the following manner: "And he took Rebekah" alludes to one; "and she became his wife" indicates a second; "and he loved her" indicates a third; "and Isaac was comforted for his mother" makes four. Correspondingly, Jacob had four spouses; and one mystic purpose guided them all.' R. Hiya said: 'Abraham and Isaac had each one wife for a union of holiness, the one Sarah, the other Rebekah, and Jacob had as many as both together twice over, namely four.' R' Simeon said: 'It practically comes to the same thing, since all was arranged by a divine dispensation to one and the same mystical purpose.' AND ABRAHAM TOOK ANOTHER WIFE, AND HER NAME WAS KETURAH. Keturah was none other than Hagar. For we know by tradition that though Hagar when she left Abraham went astray after the idols of her ancestors, yet in time she again attached herself to a life of virtue. Hence her name Keturah (lit. attached). Abraham then sent for her and took her to wife. From here we learn that a change of name acts as an atonement for sin, since that was the reason why her name was changed. The term vayoseph (lit. and he added) here indicates not that Abraham took another wife, but that he took again his former spouse whom he had driven out on account of Ishmael, and who had now abandoned her evil practices, and had made a change in her name symbolical of her change of life. Observe that R. Eleazar, in comment on the passage, "And Isaac brought her into the tent-Sarah his mother", said that the form of Sarah was there revealed, and Isaac was comforted by virtue of this, as he looked at her image every day. But Abraham, although he married again, never entered Sarah's tent nor allowed that woman to enter there, for a handmaid may not be heir to her mistress. No other woman, in fact, ever appeared in Sarah's tent save Rebekah. And although Abraham knew that Sarah's image revealed itself there, he left the tent entirely to Isaac to behold each day his mother's form. This is indicated in the verse, AND ABRAHAM GAVE ALL THAT HE HAD UNTO ISAAC, where the expression all that he had" indicates the form of Sarah that was installed in that dwelling. According to another explanation this verse indicates that Abraham transmitted to Isaac the exalted doctrine of the true faith, so that he should be attached to his rightful grade. BUT UNTO THE SONS OF THE CONCUBINES THAT ABRAHAM HAD ABRAHAM GAVE GIFTS What sort of gifts were they? They comprised the sides of the low grades, that is to say, the names of the powers of the unclean spirit, so as to complete the whole list of grades. (Isaac was raised above those grades by the power of the true faith.) "The sons of the concubines" are the sons of Keturah, who had formerly been a concubine and was now once more a concubine.' R. Hiya said that the term "concubines" here in the plural must be taken literally. AND HE SENT THEM AWAY FROM ISAAC HIS SON, so that they should not be on a par with Isaac. WHILE HE YET LIVED, that is, while Abraham was yet alive and vigorous, so that they should not complain against him after his death, and so that Isaac might strengthen himself in the side of rigour so as to prevail over them all and make them all submit to him. EASTWARD, UNTO THE EAST COUNTRY: for the reason that there are the haunts of the impure practitioners of magic and witchcraft. Observe this. It is written: "And Solomon's wisdom excelled the wisdom of all the children of the East" (I Kings V, 10). Herein is an allusion to the descendants of the very children of Abraham's concubines, who, as already said, inhabit the mountains of the East, where they instruct the sons of men in the arts of magic and divination. It was this very land of the East from which came Laban and Beor and his son Balaam, who were all magicians.'

R. Hizkiah discoursed on the verse: Who gave Jacob

Zohar: Bereshith, Section 1, Page 134a

for a spoil, and Israel to the robbers? Did not the Lord, he against whom we have sinned, and in whose ways they would not walk? (Is. XLII, 24). 'Observe,' he said, 'that since the destruction of the Temple, blessings have been withdrawn from the world, if one might say so, both on high and here below, so that all the lower grades are reinforced and exercise dominion over Israel on account of their sins. Now the verse just cited requires elucidation. For while it begins by speaking of Jacob and Israel in the third person, it goes off into the first, saying "he against whom we have sinned", and then reverts to the third person, saying "and they would not walk". The truth is that when the Sanctuary was destroyed and the Temple was burnt and the people driven into exile, the Shekinah left her home in order to accompany them into captivity. Before leaving, however, she took one last look at her House and the Holy of Holies, and the places where the priests and the Levites used to perform their worship. When she entered the land of exile she observed how the people were oppressed and trodden under foot by the nations, and she exclaimed, "Who gave Jacob for a spoil, etc.?" And the reply of the people was: "he against whom we have sinned". Then the Shekinah echoed back: "And in whose ways they would not walk." So in the days to come, when the Holy One, blessed be He, will remember His people, the community of Israel, the Shekinah will return from exile first and proceed to her House, as the holy Temple will be built first. The Holy One, blessed be He, will then say to the Community of Israel: "Shake thyself from the dust, arise and sit down, O Jerusalem" (Is. LII, 2). She will enquire, "Whereto shall I go, since my House is destroyed, my Temple is burnt with fire?" The Holy One, blessed be He, will then rebuild the Temple first, restore the Holy of Holies, build the city of Jerusalem and then raise her from the dust. So Scripture says: "The Lord doth build up Jerusalem" first, and then, "He gathereth together the dispersed of Israel", 134a<and afterwards, "Who healeth the broken in heart, and bindeth up their wounds" (Ps. CXLVII, 2, 3)-this being an allusion to the resurrection of the dead. Then will be fulfilled that which is written, "And I will put my spirit within you, and cause you to walk in my statutes, etc." (Ezek. XXXVI, 27). 'Blessed be the Lord forevermore!'

TOLDOTH

R. Hiya once discoursed on the text: "Who can express the mighty acts of the Lord, or make all his praise to be heard?" (Ps. CVI, 2). 'When God', he said, 'resolved to create the world, He used the Torah as the plan both of the whole and the parts. Hence Scripture says: "Then I was by him as a nursling, and I was

Zohar: Bereshith, Section 1, Page 134b

daily all delight" (Prov. VIII, 30), where the word 'amon (nursling) may also be read 'oman (architect, designer). When God was about to create man the Torah remonstrated, saying: "Should man be created and then sin and be brought to trial before Thee, the work of Thy hand will be in vain, for he will not be able to endure Thy judgement." Whereto God replied: "I had already fashioned repentance before creating the world." When God created the world, He said to it: "O world, world! Thou and thy order are founded only upon the Torah, and therefore I have created man in thee that he may apply himself to its study; otherwise I will turn thee into chaos again." Hence Scripture says: "I have made the earth and created man upon it" (Is. XLV, 12). The Torah in truth continually calls to the sons of men to devote themselves to its study, but none gives ear. Yet whoever labours in the Torah upholds the world, and enables each part to perform its function. For there is not a member in the human body but has its counterpart in the world as a whole. For as man's body consists of members and parts of various ranks all acting and reacting upon each other so as to form one organism, so does the world at large consist of a hierarchy of created things, which when they properly act and react upon each other together form literally one organic body. Thus the whole is organised on the scheme of the Torah, which also consists of sections and divisions which fit into one another and, when properly arranged together, form one organic body. This reflection led David to exclaim: "How manifold are thy works, O Lord! In wisdom hast thou made them all; the earth is full of thy creatures" (Ps. CIV, 24). The Torah contains all the deepest and most recondite mysteries; all sublime doctrines, both disclosed and undisclosed; all essences both of the higher and the lower grades, of this world and of the world to come are to be found there, but there is no one

Zohar: Bereshith, Section 1, Page 135a

to fathom its teachings. Hence it is written: "Who can express the mighty acts of the Lord, or make the whole of his praise to be heard?" (Ps. CVI, 2). Solomon thought to penetrate to the innermost meanings of the Torah, but it baffled him and he exclaimed: "I said, I will get wisdom, but it was far from me" (Eccl. VII, 23). David said: "Open thou mine eyes, that I may behold wondrous things out of thy law" (Ps. CXIX, 18). We read of Solomon that he "spoke three thousand proverbs; and his songs were a thousand and five" (I Kings V, 12), and tradition explains this to mean that each of his proverbs admitted of a thousand and five interpretations. Now if this could be said of the words of mere flesh and blood like Solomon, must we not perforce believe that each of the words of the Torah spoken by the Holy One, blessed be He, contains proverbs, songs, and hymns innumerable, sublime mysteries, and truths of Divine Wisdom? Hence: "Who can express the mighty acts of the Lord?".'

'We derive also another lesson from this verse. It is written "And these are the generations of Isaac" (Gen. XXV, 19), and a few verses before (Ibid. 12) the text says, "And these are the generations of Ishmael", and goes on to enumerate twelve princes. Seeing that Isaac had only two sons, we might think that in this respect Ishmael was superior to him. But in truth it is just in allusion to Isaac that Scripture exclaims: "Who can express the mighty acts of the Lord?" the term "mighty acts" being an allusion to Isaac. For Isaac begat Jacob, who in his own self excelled them all, and who further begat twelve tribes, through whom all both above and below were firmly established. Isaac was invested with the sanctity of the supernal world, whereas Ishmael was of the lower world. Hence it says: "Who can express the mighty acts of the Lord, or make the whole of his praise to be heard?" the latter clause alluding to Jacob, as much as to say: "When the sun joins the moon innumerable stars are thereby illuminated." AND THESE ARE THE GENERATIONS OF ISAAC, ABRAHAM'S SON. 'Why', asked R. Yose, 'should Isaac be referred to just here, and here only, as "Abraham's son"? The reason is that with the death of Abraham Isaac assumed the image of his father, so that anyone looking at him could say "This is surely Abraham", and thus would be convinced that "Abraham begat Isaac".'

R. Isaac rose from his bed one night

Zohar: Bereshith, Section 1, Page 135b

to study the Torah. R. Judah, who happened then to be in Caesarea, said to himself at the same time: 'I will go and join R. Isaac in the study of the Torah.' He accordingly set out along with his youthful son Hizkiah. As he was nearing R. Isaac's threshold he overheard him expound the verse: "And it came to pass after the death of Abraham, that God blessed Isaac his son; and Isaac dwelt by Beer-lahai-roi" (Gen. XXV, 11). 'The connection between the two parts of this verse', he said, 'is obscure, but may be explained as follows. It was necessary that God should bless Isaac, because Abraham had not blessed him, and the reason why Abraham had not blessed him was to prevent that blessing being transmitted to Esau. Hence the task of blessing fell, so to speak, to the Almighty. The text thus continues: "And Isaac dwelt by Beer-lahai-roi" (lit. the well of the living and seeing one), that is, as the Aramaic paraphrase has it, "the well where appeared the Angel of the Covenant", to wit, the Shekinah, to which Isaac became attached, thereby drawing upon himself the blessing of the Almighty.' At that point R. Judah knocked at R. Isaac's door, entered the room and joined him. R. Isaac said: 'Now, the Shekinah herself is in our presence.' Said R. Judah: 'Your exposition of the term beer-lahai-roi is quite correct, but there is more in it than you have said.' He then began to discourse thus. 'It is written: "A fountain of gardens, a well of living waters, and flowing streams from Lebanon" (S. S. IV, 1). "A fountain of gardens" is a description of Abraham; "a well of living waters" is a description of Isaac, of whom it is written: "And Isaac dwelt by the well of the living and seeing one (beer-lahai-roi)." The "well" is none other but the Shekinah; "the living one" is an allusion to the Righteous One who lives in the two worlds, that is, who lives above, in the higher world, and who also lives in the lower world, which exists and is illumined through him, just as the moon is only illumined when she looks at the sun. Thus the well of existence literally emanates from "the living one" whom "it sees", and when it looks at him it is filled with living waters. (The word "living" is similarly used in the verse,

Zohar: Bereshith, Section 1, Page 136a

"And Benaiah the son of Jehoiada, the son of a living man" (II Sam. XXIII, 20), i.e. a righteous man who illumines his generation as the living Deity above illumines the universe.) So the well constantly looks to the "living one" to be illumined. Further, the statement that Isaac dwelt by Beer-lahai-roi teaches the same lesson as the statement, "And Isaac was forty years old when he took Rebekah" (Gen. XXV, 20), and abode with her and was united with her, symbolising in this way the union of darkness with night, as it is written: "His left hand under my head" (S. S. II, 6). Observe now that after Abraham's death Isaac remained in Kiriath-arba; how, then, it may be asked, can it say that he dwelt in Beer-lahai-roi? The answer is, to indicate that Isaac attached himself and held fast to that well in order to awaken the attribute of mercy, as already explained.' R. Isaac discoursed on the verse: The sun shineth forth and the sun cometh in and hasteth to his place where he ariseth (Eccl. I, 5). '"The sun shineth forth" from the supernal place where he is established, in order to cast his lustre on the moon, which only reflects the light of the sun; "and cometh in" in order to join the moon. "He goeth toward the South" (Ibid. 1, 6), which is on the right and in which, therefore, his strength reposes (for all the strength of the body is on the right side); "and then turneth about to the North" (Ibid.), in order to impart light both to the one side and to the other. Further, "The wind turneth about continually and in its circuit" (Ibid.). Although the text here speaks of the wind and not of the sun, yet it is all one, and has the same inner meaning; all this is that the moon may be illumined from the sun and the two may be associated. Observe that when Abraham appeared in the world he embraced the moon and drew her near; when Isaac came he took fast hold of her and clasped her affectionately, as it says: "His left hand under my head" (S. S. II, 6). But when Jacob came the sun joined the moon and she became illumined, so that Jacob was found perfect on all sides, and the moon was encircled in light and attained completion through the twelve tribes.'

R. Judah discoursed on the verse: Behold, bless ye the Lord, all ye servants of the Lord, etc. (Ps. CXXXIV, 1). 'This verse tells us', he said, 'that only those are truly worthy to bless the Almighty who are the servants of the Lord. For although it is true that every

Zohar: Bereshith, Section 1, Page 136b

Israelite is regarded as fitted to bless the Almighty, yet only the servants of the Lord are worthy to offer those benedictions from which is diffused blessing in the upper and lower worlds. And who, then, are those servants of the Lord? "They that stand in the house of the Lord in the night seasons" (Ibid.), to wit, those who rise at midnight and keep vigil in the study of the Torah: these do "stand in the house of the Lord in the night seasons", as at that time the Holy One, blessed be He, comes to disport Himself with the righteous in the Garden of Eden. Since, then, we are passing the night in expounding the Torah, let us say something about Isaac, whom we have just mentioned.'

R. Isaac then began his discourse on the verse: AND ISAAC WAS FORTY YEARS OLD WHEN HE TOOK REBEKAH ETC. 'The number "forty" here', he said, 'has an esoteric significance, to wit, that Isaac when he took Rebekah comprised in himself the union of North and South and fire and water. Further, as the rainbow exhibits three colours, green, white, and red, so Rebekah was three years old when Isaac took her; and he begat offspring when he was sixty years old, this being a ripe age for producing a child like Jacob who should be endowed with all good qualities, according to God's design. THE DAUGHTER OF BETHUEL THE ARAMEAN, OF PADAN-ARAM, THE SISTER OF LABAN THE ARAMEAN. Why all these details, seeing that it has already been stated: "And Bethuel begat Rebekah etc."? (Gen. XXII, 23). It is to emphasise the fact that although she was brought up among sinful people, being the daughter of Bethuel, and a native of Padan-Aram, and the sister of Laban the Aramean, and thus came from a wicked environment, yet she did not follow their ways, but distinguished herself in good and righteous deeds. Here a difficulty arises. If we could say that Rebekah was then twenty years old or more, or even thirteen years old, then we could indeed commend her for not imitating the conduct of her surroundings; but since, as previously said, she was only a child of three years, how can we ascribe to her any merit on this account?'

R. Judah said in reply: 'Though she was but three years old, she had shown her character by what she did for Abraham's servant.' R. Isaac rejoined: 'In spite of all that she had done for him, one could not yet say positively that her character was really good.

Zohar: Bereshith, Section 1, Page 137a

But we learn this from another source. It is written, "As a lily among thorns, so is my love among the daughters" (S. S. II, 2). The lily may be taken as symbolic of the Community of Israel, which in the midst of its multitudes resembles a rose among thorns. But there is a more esoteric explanation of the verse, as follows. Isaac was derived from the side of

Abraham, who was the embodiment of supernal grace (Hesed), and acted graciously towards all creatures, though he himself represented the attribute of severity. Rebekah, on the other hand, originated from the side of severity, but broke away from her kith and kin and joined Isaac; and in spite of her origin, she was of a mild disposition and gracious bearing, so that in the midst of the severity which characterised Isaac she was "as a lily among thorns". And if not for her gentleness the world would not have been able to endure the severity inherent in Isaac. In this manner God constantly mates couples of opposing natures, one, for example, of a stern with one of a mild type, so that the world preserves its balance.'

R. Judah followed with a discourse on the text: AND ISAAC ENTREATED THE LORD FOR HIS WIFE. 'The term "entreated" (vaye'tar)', he said, 'implies prayer accompanied by offerings, on an analogy with a kindred term in the passage, "So the Lord was entreated for the land" (II Sam. XXIV, 25), where also the prayer was accompanied by offerings. It is written here first, "And Isaac entreated", and then "And the Lord let himself be entreated", indicating that a celestial fire descended to meet the fire ascending from below. According to another explanation, the term vaye'tar (and he entreated) is akin to vayehtar (and he dug), signifying that Isaac in his prayer dug a tunnel, as it were, leading right up to the supernal department appointed over fecundity. He thus rose above the planetary influences (mazzal) in the same way as Hannah in her prayer, of whom it is written: "And she prayed unto ('al', lit. upon) the Lord" (I Sam. I, 10) Similarly, the term vaye'ather (and he let himself be entreated) implies that the Lord Himself cleared a way for Isaac's prayer, with the result that "Rebekah his wife conceived". Observe that Isaac lived with his wife for twenty years without having children, the reason being that God delights in the prayer of the righteous, who thereby attain to higher sanctity and purification. He therefore withholds from them

their needs until they offer their supplications. Now observe that Abraham did not supplicate God for children, notwithstanding that Sarah was barren (for when he said "Behold, to me thou hast given no seed" (Gen. XV, 3), he did not mean it as a prayer, but as a mere statement of fact); but Isaac did offer up prayer on behalf of his wife, as he felt confident that he himself was not sterile. This confidence was based on his inspired knowledge that Jacob was destined to issue from him and produce twelve tribes, but he could not tell whether it would be from his present wife or from another. Hence he entreated the Lord for his wife, not for Rebekah.' The youthful son of R. Judah here asked his father: 'If that is so, why did not Isaac love Jacob as much as Esau, knowing as he did that the former would rear twelve tribes?' 'That is a good question,' said his father, 'and the answer is as follows. All creatures of the same kind love one another and are drawn to one another. Now we are told that Esau "came forth ruddy", a colour emblematic of severity. There was thus an affinity between Isaac, the representative of severity on high, and Esau, the embodiment of severity here below; and through this affinity Isaac loved him above Jacob. Hence we read: "And Isaac loved Esau, because he did eat of his hunting", where the term zayid (hunting) suggests the same idea as the similar term in the verse: "Like Nimrod a mighty hunter (gibbor zayid) before the Lord" (Gen. X, 9).'

R. Isaac said: 'It is written: AND THE CHILDREN STRUGGLED TOGETHER WITHIN HER; AND SHE SAID, IF IT BE SO, WHEREFORE DO I LIVE? AND SHE WENT TO ENQUIRE OF THE LORD. Whither did she go? To the Academy of Shem and Eber. "And the children struggled together within her", for there already Esau declared war against Jacob. The term vayithrozzu (and they struggled) is akin to a root meaning "to break", and thus it implies that they broke asunder and drifted away from each other. Observe that the one was of the side of him who rides the serpent, whilst the other was of the side of Him who rides on the sacred and perfect throne; of the side

of the sun that illumines the moon. And observe further that because Esau was drawn after that serpent, Jacob dealt with him crookedly like the serpent, who is cunning and goes crookedly, as we read: "And the serpent was more cunning etc." (Gen. III, 1). Jacob then dealt with him after the manner of the serpent in order to draw him further serpentward, so that he should separate further from himself and thus not have any share with him either in this world or in the world to come; and our teachers have said, "When a man comes to kill you, kill him first." It is written of Jacob: "In the womb he took his brother by the heel" (Hos. XII, 4), that is, he drew him downwards by [Tr. note: Al. "to the heel", i.e. to the lower grades.] the heel. So it says: AND HIS HAND HAD HOLD ON ESAU'S HEEL, i.e he put his hand on Esau's heel in order thereby to force him down. According to another explanation, the words "and his hand had hold" imply that he could not escape him entirely, but his hand was still clinging to his brother's heel. Esoterically speaking, the moon was obscured through the heel of Esau; hence it was necessary to deal with him cunningly, so as to thrust him downwards and make him adhere to the region assigned to him.' AND HE CALLED HIS NAME JACOB. It was God who called him so. (So, too, it is written lower down, "Hath he not rightly called his name Jacob?" (Gen. XXVII, 36) and not "his name was called".) God saw that the primeval serpent was full of guile to do mischief, and so when Jacob appeared He said: "Behold, here is one who can stand up to him", and therefore He called him Ya'kob, akin to the term vaya'kebeni (and he acted toward me with guile) (Gen. XXVII, 35). It has already been pointed out that the simple term vayikra (and he called), as when it says, "and he called unto Moses", points to the lowest grade (of the Sephiroth). At no time did Jacob receive a name from a human being. So in another passage we find: "And the God of Israel called him El (God)" (Gen. XXXIII, 20), signifying that the God of Israel called Jacob by the name of "El" (God), as though to say, "I am the God of the supernal world and be thou the God of the world below". Observe that Jacob knew that Esau was destined to ally himself to that tortuous serpent, and hence in all his dealings with him he conducted himself like another tortuous serpent,

Zohar: Bereshith, Section 1, Page 138b

using all cunning devices; and so it was meet. The same idea was expressed by R. Simeon when, in expounding the verse, "And God created the great fishes, and every living creature that creepeth" (Gen. I, 21), he said: 'The "great fishes" are symbolic of Jacob and Esau, and "every living creature that creepeth" symbolises all the intermediate grades.' Verily Jacob was endowed with cunning to enable him to hold his own with that other serpent; and so it was meet. For the same reason every New Moon a goat is to be offered up so as to draw the serpent to his own place and thus keep him away from the moon. The same applies to the Day of Atonement, when a goat is to be offered. All this is cunningly devised in order to gain dominion over him, and make him impotent to do mischief. So Scripture says: "And the goat shall bear upon him all their iniquities into a land which is cut off" (Lev. XVI, 22), where the goat (sa'ir = Seir), as already explained, symbolises Esau. In all dealings with him cunning and craft are employed, in accordance with the words of the Scripture: "And with the crooked thou dost show thyself subtle" (Ps. XVIII, 27); and as the evil serpent is resourceful and crafty, trying to mislead the heavenly as well as the earthly beings, Israel anticipate him and counter him with similar ruses and devices so as to prevent him from working his evil will; just as Jacob, who was endowed with the true faith, in all his actions towards Esau had no aim but to prevent the serpent from defiling the Sanctuary or even approaching it, and so achieving dominion over the world. There was however, no need either for Abraham or for Isaac to use such tortuous ways, seeing that Esau, who was of the side of the serpent, had not yet appeared in the world. But Jacob, being the master of the household, had to counter the serpent, and to give him no chance to tarnish the Sanctuary of Jacob. Hence Jacob had need of such shifts more than any other person. Israel, therefore, was chosen as the portion of the heritage of the Holy One, blessed be He, as it is written: "For the portion of the Lord is his people, Jacob the lot of his inheritance" (Deut. XXXII, 9).

AND THE BOYS GREW. It was the side of Abraham which gave them their vitality, and his merit was their support. He trained them in observing the precepts, for so we read: "For I have known him, to the end that he may command his children etc." (Gen. XVIII, 19). R. Eleazar said: 'Each one of them took his own way,

Zohar: Bereshith, Section 1, Page 139a

one to the side of true faith and the other to the side of idolatry; and they had already exhibited the same traits whilst in the womb of their mother, where each one of them inclined to his own side. Thus, whenever she was performing some good action or approaching a goodly spot in order to carry out some precept of the Torah, Jacob would gleefully thrust himself forward to come forth. But did she happen to pass near an idolatrous shrine, Esau would kick and struggle to come forth. Thus, when they were fully formed and emerged into the world, they separated, each one taking his own way and being drawn to the place befitting him.' AND ISAAC LOVED ESAU, FOR THE HUNTER'S CUNNING WAS IN HIS MOUTH. So we translate in accordance with what has been said above. A MAN OF THE FIELD: this means that he was a highwayman who robbed and murdered people, while all the time pretending to his father that he was abroad performing his prayers. Again, he was a fieldman in that his portion was not cast in inhabited land but in wild and desolate places. It may be asked, how came Isaac to be unaware of Esau's evil deeds, seeing that the Shekinah was with him, as is proved by the fact of his subsequently blessing Jacob. The truth is that the Shekinah, although continually with him, did not reveal to him Esau's evil career in order that Jacob should receive his blessing not by the will of Isaac, but solely by the will of the Holy One, blessed be He. So it was destined to be, and when Jacob entered into the presence of his father the Shekinah accompanied him, and Isaac thus felt that there was before him one who was worthy of being blessed; and blessed he was by the will of the Shekinah. AND JACOB SOD [COOKED] POTTAGE; AND ESAU CAME IN FROM THE FIELD, AND HE WAS FAINT. R. Eleazar said: According to the received explanation, the pottage of lentils was a sign of mourning for the death of Abraham. But if so, we should have expected Isaac to have prepared it. The deeper explanation, therefore, is that Jacob cooked

Zohar: Bereshith, Section 1, Page 139b

that pottage in virtue of his clear discernment of the side to which Esau adhered. Lentils form a red pottage which is cooling to hot blood. Hence Jacob purposely chose such a dish as a means of weakening the strength and power of Esau, and the effect was that Esau sold himself to Jacob as a slave and sold him his birthright. At that moment Jacob divined that for the sake of one he-goat that his descendants would bring as a sacrifice to Esau's grade, the latter would consent to be a slave to them and desist from attacking them.'

R. Judah said: 'Of a like manner were Jacob's dealings with Laban, who was a magician, as it says: "I have observed the signs, and the Lord hath blessed me for thy sake" (Gen. XXX, 27); and notwithstanding that Jacob is designated a "simple man", this means only that he was so in his dealings with anyone who deserved to be treated gently; but where cunning and severity were necessary, he could use these also. For he was of a twofold character, and to him could be applied the words: "With the merciful thou dost show thyself merciful. And with the crooked thou dost show thyself subtle" (Ps. XVIII, 26-27), just as required.' AND THERE WAS A FAMINE IN THE LAND, BESIDE THE FIRST FAMINE, ETC. R. Judah discoursed here on the verse: The Lord trieth the righteous; but the wicked and him that loveth violence his soul hateth (Ps. XI, 5). 'How goodly', he said, 'are the acts of the Holy One, blessed be He, all based upon justice and truth, as it says: "The Rock, his work is perfect; for all his ways are justice; a God of faithfulness and without iniquity, just and right is he" (Deut. XXXII, 4). For He did not punish Adam, the first man, until He had given him precepts to keep him in the right path and save him from defilement; and not until he was unmindful and transgressed the command of his Master was he punished.

Zohar: Bereshith, Section 1, Page 140a

Even then God did not exact the full penalty from him, but was long-suffering with him and permitted him to survive for one day-to wit, a thousand years-save seventy years which Adam presented of his allotted time to King David, who had none of his own. In like manner, the Almighty does not mete out punishment to a man in strict accordance with the evil deeds to which he is addicted, or else the world could not endure. God is thus long-suffering with the righteous, and even more so with the wicked. He is forbearing with the wicked in order that they may change in their ways in complete repentance and so establish themselves in this world and in the world to come, as Scripture says: "Have I any pleasure, saith the Lord God, in the death of the wicked, and not rather that he should return from his way and live" (Ezek. XVIII, 23), i.e. that he may live in this world and in the world to come. The Almighty is also forbearing with the wicked for the sake of the goodly seed which may spring from them for the benefit of the world, as there issued from Terah that goodly scion, Abraham, who was a blessing for the world. But with the righteous God is strict, as He knows that they will turn aside neither to the right nor to the left, and therefore He puts them to the test; not for His own sake, since He knows the firmness of their faith, but so as to glorify them the more. It was for this purpose that God-as we read-"proved (nissah) Abraham" (Gen. XXII, 1), or, as we may also translate, "He raised his banner aloft throughout the world" [for the term nissah (he proved) implies the lifting of an ensign, as it is written: "Lift up an ensign (nes) over the peoples" (Is. LXII, 10). The text continues: "The Lord trieth the righteous" (Ps. XI, 5). For what reason? Said R. Simeon: 'Because when God finds delight in the righteous, He brings upon them sufferings, as it is written: "Yet it pleased the Lord to crush him by disease" (Is. LIII, 10), as explained elsewhere. God finds delight in the soul but not in the body, as the soul resembles the supernal soul, whereas the body is not worthy to be allied to the supernal essences, although the image of the body is part of the supernal symbolism.

Zohar: Bereshith, Section 1, Page 140b

Observe that when God takes delight in the soul of a man, He afflicts the body in order that the soul may gain full freedom. For so long as the soul is together with the body it cannot exercise its full powers, but only when the body is broken and crushed. Again, "He trieth the righteous", so as to make them firm like "a tried stone", the "costly corner-stone" mentioned by the prophet (Is. XXVIII, 16). "But the wicked and him that loveth violence his soul hateth." So we would naturally translate; but this is hardly admissible, and it is more probable that the verse alludes to that grade whence all souls derive their existence, and tells us that "that grade hateth the soul of the wicked man", not wanting it at all, neither in this world nor in the world to come. When God created Adam He gave him a precept for his well-being and endowed him with wisdom through which he rose to the higher grades of contemplation. But when Adam turned his thoughts to the lower world, he let himself be enticed by the evil tempter and clung to him, so that all that he had observed of the glory of his Master vanished from his mind. After him Noah at first was a man righteous and devout; but afterwards he also went downwards, and seeing the wine-wine a day old, not yet refined-"he drank of the wine, and was drunken, and he was uncovered within his tent" (Gen. IX, 21). Then came Abraham, who contemplated the wisdom and glory of his Master. In his time "there was a famine in the land; and Abram went down into Egypt to sojourn there" (Ibid. XII, 10), but subsequently he "went up out of Egypt, he and his wife and all that he had, and Lot with him, into the South" (Ibid. XIII, 1). That is, he ascended again to his own former grade, so that he came out unscathed as he went in. Then came Isaac, of whom it is written: "And there was a famine in the land, beside the first famine, etc." He went into Gerar and afterwards ascended again from thence unscathed. Thus God proves the righteous in order to glorify them in this world and in the world to come. AND THE MEN OF THE PLACE ASKED HIM OF HIS WIFE; AND HE SAID: SHE IS MY SISTER. Like Abraham before him, he referred with these words to the Shekinah, which was with him as well as with Rebekah his wife; for like Abraham he carried out the injunction: "Say unto wisdom: Thou art my sister" (Prov. VII, 4). They were further entitled to call her sister in virtue of the verse, "My sister, my love, my dove, my undefiled" (S. S. V, 2), for it is for this that the righteous cleave to God.

AND IT CAME TO PASS, WHEN HE HAD BEEN THERE A LONG TIME... WITH REBEKAH HIS WIFE. The particle eth (with) indicates that it was the Shekinah that was with Rebekah. In any case it is not to be supposed that Abimelech saw Isaac having intercourse with his wife in the daytime, for this would be contrary to the dictum: "Israel are holy and they abstain from cohabitation in the daytime." But the truth is that Abimelech was an astrologer, and the window through which he looked was nothing but the planetary constellation. [The word "window" is similarly used in the passage: "Through the window she looked forth, and peered, the mother of Sisera" (Jud. V, 28).] Abimelech by this means discovered that, contrary to Isaac's assertion, Rebekah was his wife. SO ABIMELECH CALLED ISAAC, AND SAID, ETC. R. Yose said: 'Abimelech would have behaved toward Isaac as he behaved toward Abraham, were it not that God had reproved him in the previous case. Note that when Abraham said, "Surely the fear of God is not in this place" (Gen. XX, 11), his reason for thinking so was that the people lacked faith, and had they possessed faith, he would have had no need to act as he did.'

Zohar: Bereshith, Section 1, Page 141a

R. Eleazar said: 'The Shekinah does not abide outside the Holy Land, and that is what Abram meant by saying that "the fear of God is not in this place", namely, that this was not the place where the Shekinah could find abode. Isaac, however, held fast to the true faith under the inspiration of the Shekinah, which he saw residing, as it were, within his wife.' AND ABIMELECH CHARGED ALL THE PEOPLE, SAYING: HE THAT TOUCHETH THIS MAN OR HIS WIFE SHALL SURELY BE PUT TO DEATH. Observe how long a respite God gave to this wicked people for the sake of the kindness that Abimelech showed to Israel's first ancestors. It was on this account that Israel could not touch them till many generations had elapsed. Abimelech thus did well to show kindness to Abraham in saying to him: "Behold my land is before thee: dwell where it pleaseth thee" (Gen. XX, 1). R. Judah said: 'Woe to the wicked who when they do a kindness never do it perfectly. Ephron, for instance, first said to Abraham: "Nay, my lord, hear me: the field I give thee and the cave that is therein, I give it thee, etc." (Gen. XXIII, 11). But later on he said: "A piece of land worth four hundred shekels, etc." (Ibid. 15); and then we read: "And Abraham weighed to Ephron the silver... current money with the merchant" (Ibid. 16). Similarly here, at first Abimelech said: "He that toucheth this man, etc.", but later on he said, "Go from us, for thou art much mightier than we" (Gen. XXVI, 16).' R. Eleazar said to R. Judah: 'Abimelech's kindness to him consisted in his not taking anything from him, and sending him away with all his possessions intact, and then going after him to make a covenant with him.'

AND ISAAC DIGGED AGAIN THE WELLS, ETC. R. Eleazar said: 'In digging these wells Isaac acted fittingly, for he discerned from his knowledge of the mysteries of Wisdom that in this way he could attach himself more firmly to his faith. Abraham likewise made a point of digging a well of water. Jacob found the well already prepared for him, and he sat down by it. Thus they all looked for a well and strove through it to preserve their faith pure and undiminished. And nowadays Israel hold fast to the well through the symbolism of the precepts of the Torah, as when each day every Israelite performs the precept of the fringes in which he envelops himself, and of the phylacteries which he puts on his head and on his arm. All these have a deep symbolism, since God is found in the man who crowns himself with the phylacteries and envelops himself in the fringes. Hence, whoever does not envelop himself in the latter, nor crown himself with the former each day to invigorate himself in faith, makes it appear as though faith does not dwell within him, and fear of his Master has departed from him, and so his prayer is not as it should be. Hence our ancestors strengthened themselves in the true faith in digging the well, symbolic of the supernal well, which is the abode of the mystery of perfect faith.' AND HE REMOVED FROM THENCE, AND DIGGED ANOTHER WELL. R. Hiya discoursed on the verse: And the Lord will guide thee continually, and satisfy thy soul in brightness, and make strong thy bones (Is. LVIII, 11). 'The true believers', he said, 'have derived strength from this verse, where promise is made to them of the world to come, for the word "continually" includes both this world and the world to come. Again, the term "continually", which seems superfluous, is an allusion to the continual burnt-offering which is offered at dusk, and is held firm underneath the arm of Isaac and is symbolic of the world to come. The term "guiding" is similarly used by David in the verse: "He guideth me in straight paths for his name's sake" (Ps. XXIII, 3). "And satisfy thy soul in brightness"; this is the "clear mirror" from the contemplation of which all souls obtain delight and benefit. "And make strong thy bones": these words do not seem to harmonise with what has gone before, which we have interpreted of the souls of the righteous ascending on high. We interpret them, therefore, to allude to the resurrection of the dead, when the Holy One, blessed be He, will reconstitute the bones and restore the body to its former state. The soul will then derive stronger illumination from the "clear mirror", so as to illumine the body to the full extent of which it is capable. Hence: "And thou shalt be like a watered garden" (Is. LVIII, 11), that is, like the celestial garden whose supernal waters never fail, but flow on forever and ever;

Zohar: Bereshith, Section 1, Page 141b

"and like a spring of water, whose waters fail not" (Ibid.), alluding to the river that issues from Eden and flows on for all eternity. Observe that the "well of living waters" is a symbol within a symbol for guiding faith. There is the well which is the very source of the waters, and there is the well which is fed by that source of water. There are thus two grades, which are, however, really one with two aspects, male and female, in fitting union. The well and the issue of waters are one, designated by the name of "well", it being at once the supernal never-ceasing fountain and the well that is filled by it. And whoever gazes at that well gazes at the true object of faith. This is the symbol which the patriarchs transmitted in digging the well, in such a way as to indicate that the source and the well are indissoluble. AND HE CALLED ITS NAME REHOBOTH (lit. streets, broad places). By this he intimated that his descendants would one day tend that well in the fitting manner through the mystical potency of offerings and burnt-offerings (like Adam, when God "put him into the garden of Eden to dress it and keep it" (Gen. II, 15), to wit, by offerings and burnt-offerings), so that its springs should flow forth on every side, as Scripture says: "Let thy springs be dispersed abroad, and courses of water in the streets (rehoboth)" (Prov. V, 16). Hence here the name of Rehoboth (streets, broad places).'

R. Simeon here discoursed on the verse: WISDOM CRIETH ALOUD IN THE STREET, SHE UTTERETH HER VOICE IN THE BROAD PLACES (Prov. I, 20). 'This verse', he said, 'contains a deep mystical teaching. The term hokhmoth (lit. wisdoms) implies the superior Wisdom and the lesser Wisdom which is included in the superior Wisdom and abides therein. The superior Wisdom is an essence most recondite and concealed, unknown and unrevealed, as Scripture says: "Man knoweth not the price thereof, etc." (Job XXVIII, 13); and when it expands into a source of light, its illumination is that of the world to come, and that world is created by it: for so we have learned, that the world to come was created by the Yod, and there Wisdom remained hidden, the two being one. When God was crowned, it was through the mystery of the future world, as already said. There was joy at this illumination, but all was in silence without a sound being heard abroad. Wisdom then willed it to expand further, so that from that space there issued fire and water and air, as already said, from which there sprang up a voice which issued forth abroad and was heard, as already said. From that point onwards all is exterior (huz), whereas in the interior the voice is silent and not heard abroad. Once, however, the secret force has become audible, it is called "without" (huz). Hence it is incumbent on man to be zealous in searching after wisdom "in the wide places" (ba-rehoboth). This refers to the firmament, which contains all the luminous stars, and which constitutes the fountain of perennial waters, referred to in the verse: "And a river went forth from Eden to water the garden" (Gen. II, 10). And there "she uttereth her voice", both the superior and the lower Wisdom, which in truth are one. Solomon alluded to this in saying: "Prepare thy work without" (ba-huz), and make it ready for thee in the field" (Prov. XXIV, 27), where the word "without" is used as in the verse "Wisdom crieth out without", indicating the point from which man can commence to inquire and investigate, as it is written: "For ask now of the days past... and from one end of heaven unto another" (Deut. IV, 32). The "field" again is the "field which the Lord hath blessed" (Gen. XXVII, 27). When a man has penetrated into the mystery of Wisdom and perfected himself therein, then Solomon tells him to "build his house" (Prov. XXIV, 27), i.e. to cultivate his soul in his body, so as to attain perfection. Hence, when Isaac digged and prepared the well in peace he called it Rehoboth (wide places), and all was done in the right manner. Happy the righteous by whose works the Holy One sustains the world, as it says: "For the upright shall inhabit the land" (Prov. II, 21), where the term yishkenu (they will inhabit) may be read yashkinu (they shall cause to be inhabited).' AND IT CAME TO PASS, THAT WHEN ISAAC WAS OLD, AND HIS EYES WERE DIM. R. Simeon said: It is written: And God called the light day, and the darkness he called night (Gen. I, 5). This verse has already been expounded, but there is yet more to be learnt from it. For all the works of the Almighty are manifestations of truth and contain deep lessons; and all the words of the Torah assist faith and are deeply symbolical. Observe now that Isaac was not so fortunate as Abraham, whose eyes were not blinded nor dimmed. Herein is a profound lesson touching faith, as has already been explained elsewhere. By "the light" here is meant Abraham, who is the light of the day and whose light keeps on expanding

Zohar: Bereshith, Section 1, Page 142a

and growing stronger like that of the day. Hence it is written: "And Abraham was old, advancing in days" (Gen. XXIV, 1), that is, in illumination, and as he grew older his light continued to expand, so that he was "shining more and more unto the perfect day" (Prov. IV, 18). On the other hand, "the darkness" is a description of Isaac, who represents darkness and night, and hence when he was old his eyes were dim, so that he could not see. He had to become enveloped in darkness in order to become attached to his own proper grade.' R. Eleazar his son came and kissed his hand. He said: 'So far I understand. Abraham was bathed in light from the side of his grade; whereas Isaac became wrapt in darkness from the side of his grade. But why is it written of Jacob: "And the eyes of Israel were heavy for age" (Gen. XLVIII, 10)?' R. Simeon in answer said: 'It is written here "they were heavy", but not "they were dim"; and further, it is not written "for his old age", but "for old age", referring to the old age of Isaac, and implying that his eyes were heavy as a result of the side of Isaac, but still they were only so heavy as to prevent him seeing properly, but not entirely dim. Whereas Isaac's eyes were altogether dimmed, so that darkness settled upon him and night took hold of him, until to him could be applied the words, "And the darkness he called night." 'AND HE CALLED ESAU, HIS ELDER SON, who was derived from his own side of severe judgement, AND HE SAID: BEHOLD NOW, I AM OLD, I KNOW NOT THE DAY OF MY DEATH. R. Eleazar discoursed on the verse: Happy is the man whose strength is in thee, etc. (Ps. LXXXIV, 6). 'Happy is the man', he said, 'who holds fast to the Holy One and places his strength in Him. Like whom, for instance? Shall we say, like Hananiah, Mishael and Azariah, when they boldly said to the King of Babylon: "Behold, our God whom we serve is able to deliver us from the burning fiery furnace; and he will deliver us out of thine hand" (Dan. III, 17)? Not so; for if God had not stood by them to deliver them, His name would not have been acclaimed holy as they declared it to be. But they themselves realized their mistake, and so they corrected themselves and said: "But if not, be it known unto thee, O King, etc." (Ibid. 18), that is, whether our God deliver us or not, be it known unto thee that we will not serve thy gods, etc. Tradition tells us that Ezekiel said something to them which opened their eyes, namely, that God would not stand by them if they expected reward. It was then that they began all over again, saying: "But if not, be it known unto thee, O King, etc." A man, therefore, should not confidently affirm: "God will deliver me or will do for me this or that"; but he should endeavour to fulfil the precepts of the Law and to walk in the path of truth, and then put his full trust in Him that He will help him thereto. For assuredly whenever a man sets out to purify himself he is helped thereto from on high. A man should thus put his trust in God and not anywhere else. Hence the expression "whose strength is in thee". The next words, "in whose heart are paths", indicate that a man should purge his heart of all strange thoughts, so as to make it like a path that leads straight to the desired destination. According to another interpretation, the word "strength" alludes to the Torah, of which we read: "The Lord gives strength unto his people" (Ps. XXIX, 11). It is thus here indicated that a man should study the Torah in single-hearted devotion to the Almighty, and whoever labours in the Torah from worldly motives had better not have been born. The word mesilloth also may be translated not "highways" but "extollings" (cf. the verse "Extol (solu) him that rideth upon the skies" (Ps. LXVIII, 5)). It thus alludes to the man who labours in the Torah with the object of extolling God and making Him the only object of devotion in the world. Observe that Jacob performed all his actions for the sake of God, and therefore God was always with him and did not ever remove His Presence from him. We know this from the fact that although Jacob was not present when Isaac called Esau his son, the Shekinah told Rebekah, who in her turn told Jacob.' R. Yose said: 'Observe that had Esau, God forbid, been blessed there and then, Jacob would never have been able to assert himself; but all was directed by Providence, and everything fell into its right place.' AND REBEKAH LOVED JACOB, and so she sent for him and said to him: BEHOLD, I HEARD THY FATHER SPEAK UNTO ESAU THY BROTHER, SAYING... NOW THEREFORE, MY SON, HEARKEN TO MY VOICE, ETC. It was then the eve of Passover, a time when the evil tempter had to be removed, so as to restore to power the moon, to symbolise the true object

Zohar: Bereshith, Section 1, Page 142b

of faith. Rebekah therefore prepared two dishes. R. Judah said: 'Herein were foreshadowed the two he-goats which the children of Jacob were in the future to offer, one for the Lord and the other for Azazel on the Day of Atonement. We see thus Rebekah offering "two kids of the goats", one for the supernal grade and the other with the object of subduing the grade of Esau, so as to deprive him of any power over Jacob. Hence "two kids of the goats", both of which Isaac tasted and ate of. Similarly, when it says "And he brought him wine, and he drank", the word "brought" intimates that the wine was fetched from a distant region, namely, from the region of Esau. R. Eleazar said: 'There is an allusion here to that wine in which is all kind of exhilaration, since Isaac and his side required to be exhilarated.' AND REBEKAH TOOK THE CHOICEST GARMENTS OF ESAU, ETC. These were the garments of which Esau had despoiled Nimrod. They were precious garments which, originally belonging to Adam, in time came into the hands of Nimrod, who used them as his hunting dress, for so Scripture says: "He was a mighty hunter before the Lord" (Gen. X, 9). Then Esau went out into the field and made war against Nimrod, and slew him and possessed himself of those garments, as is hinted in the passage: "And Esau came in from the field, and he was faint" (Ibid. XXV, 29), that is, from killing, as in the passage, "for my soul fainteth before the murderers" (Jer. IV, 31). Now, Esau kept those garments in Rebekah's apartment, from whence he would fetch them whenever he went a-hunting. On that day, however, he went out into the field without them, and thus he stayed there longer than usual. Now when Esau put on those garments no aroma whatever was emitted from them, but when Jacob put them on they were restored to their rightful place, and a sweet odour was diffused from them. For Jacob inherited the beauty of Adam; hence those garments found in him their rightful owner and thus gave off their proper aroma. Said R. Yose: 'Can it really be so, that Jacob's beauty equaled that of Adam, seeing that, according to tradition, the fleshy part of Adam's heel outshone the orb of the sun? Would you, then, say the same of Jacob?' Said R. Eleazar in reply: 'Assuredly Adam's beauty was as tradition says, but only at first before he sinned, when no creature could endure to gaze at his beauty; after he sinned, however, his beauty was diminished and his height was reduced to a hundred cubits. Observe further that Adam's beauty is a symbol with which the true faith is closely bound up. This is hinted at in the passage: "And let the graciousness of the Lord our God be upon us" (Ps. XC, 17), as well as in the expression, "to behold the graciousness of the Lord" (Ibid. XXVII, 4). And Jacob assuredly participated of that beauty. The whole, then, is deeply symbolical.' AND HE SMELLED THE SMELL OF HIS RAIMENT, AND BLESSED HIM. Observe that it is not written "the raiment", but "his raiment". This is explained by the text "Who coverest thyself with light as with a garment" (Ps. CIV, 2). The word "his" may also be understood to indicate that it was only when Jacob put them on that the garments emitted their sweet odour; and it was only the sweet odour diffused by them that made Isaac bless him, for only then did he feel that there was before him one deserving of the blessings, since otherwise all these divine aromas would not have accompanied him. Hence the sequence of the verse: AND HE SMELLED THE SMELL OF HIS RAIMENT, AND BLESSED HIM, AND SAID: SEE THE SMELL OF MY SON IS AS THE SMELL OF THE FIELD WHICH THE LORD HATH BLESSED. The subject of the word "said" is, according to some, the Shekinah, according to others, Isaac himself. "The field which the Lord hath blessed" alludes to the "field of apple trees", the field which the patriarchs cherish and cultivate. SO GOD GIVE THEE OF THE DEW OF HEAVEN, AND OF THE FAT PLACES OF THE EARTH, AND PLENTY OF CORN AND WINE. R. Abba said: 'We may bring into connection with this passage the verse: "A song of Ascents. In my distress I called unto the Lord and he answered me" (Ps. CXX, 1). Many songs and hymns did David utter before the Almighty for the purpose of perfecting his grade and making himself a name, as Scripture says: "And David got him a name" (II Sam. VIII, 13). But this song David recited when he contemplated this incident of Jacob.' R. Eleazar said: 'It was Jacob who uttered this psalm at the moment when his father said to him: "Come near, I pray thee, that I may feel thee, my son, whether thou be my very son Esau or not." That was

Zohar: Bereshith, Section 1, Page 143a

a moment of great distress for Jacob, as he feared that his father would recognize him. We read, however: "And he discerned him not, because his hands were hairy, as his brother Esau's hands; so he blessed him." It was then that Jacob said: "In my distress I called unto the Lord, and he answered me. O Lord, deliver my soul from lying lips, from a deceitful tongue" (Ps. CXX, 1-2). The "lying lips" is a reference to the grade of Esau, which is so called because when the serpent brought curses into the world it was by means of cunning and crookedness. Observe that when Isaac said to Esau: "and go out into the field, and take me venison", he added, "I will bless thee before the Lord" (Gen. XXVII, 7). Now, had Isaac said simply, "that I may bless thee", there would have been no harm. But when he uttered the words "before the Lord", the Throne of Glory of the Almighty shook and trembled, saying: "Will the serpent now be released from his curses and Jacob become subject to them?".' At that moment the angel Michael, accompanied by the Shekinah, appeared before Jacob. Isaac felt all this, and he also saw the Garden of Eden beside Jacob, and so he blessed him in the presence of the angel. But when Esau entered there entered with him the Gehinnom, and thus we read: "And Isaac trembled very exceedingly", as until that time he had not thought that Esau was of that side. "And I have blessed him"– he then said–"yea, he shall be blessed". Jacob thus equipped himself with wisdom and cunning, so that the blessings reverted to himself who was the image of Adam, and were snatched from that serpent of "the lying lips" who acted and spoke deceitfully in order to lead astray the world and bring curses on it. Hence Jacob came with craft and misled his father with the object of bringing blessings upon the world, and to recover from the serpent what hitherto he had withheld from the world. It was measure for measure, as expressed in the verse: "Yea, he loved cursing, and it came unto him; and he delighted not in blessing, and it is far from him" (Ps. CIX, 17). Concerning him it is written: "Cursed art thou from among all cattle, and from among all beasts of the field" (Gen. III, 14). He remains in that curse forevermore, and Jacob came and took away from him the blessings; from the very days of Adam Jacob was destined to snatch from the serpent all those blessings, leaving him still immersed in the curses without the possibility of emerging from them. David also said concerning him: "What shall be given unto thee, and what shall be done more unto thee, thou deceitful tongue?" (Ps. CXX, 3). That is to say, of what benefit was it to the serpent that he brought curses upon the world? As the adage says: "The serpent bites and kills, and feels no satisfaction". "A deceitful tongue": in that he deceived Adam and his wife and brought evil upon them and upon the world, until Jacob came and took away from him all the blessings. "Sharp arrows of the mighty" (Ibid. 4) is an allusion to Esau, who nursed his hatred toward Jacob on account of these blessings, as we read: "And Esau hated Jacob because of the blessing, etc. SO GOD GIVE THEE OF THE DEW OF HEAVEN, AND OF THE FAT PLACES OF THE EARTH, that is to say, blessings from above and from below in conjunction. AND PLENTY OF CORN AND WINE, in consonance with the text: "yet have I not seen the righteous forsaken, nor his seed begging bread" (Ps. XXXVII, 25). This, as we have laid down, was uttered by the Prince of the world; hence "plenty of corn and wine". LET PEOPLES SERVE THEE: alluding to the time when King Solomon reigned in Jerusalem, as it is written: "And all the kings of the earth etc. And they brought every man his present" (II Chr. IX, 23-24). AND NATIONS BOW DOWN TO THEE, alludes to the time when the Messiah will appear, concerning whom it is written: "Yea, all kings shall prostrate themselves before him" (Ps. LXXII, 11). R. Judah said: 'The whole applies to the advent of the Messiah, of whom it is also written: "all nations shall serve him (Ibid.). BE (heveh) LORD OVER THY BRETHREN. The irregular form heveh (be), instead of heyeh or tihyeh, has a deep mystical signification, being composed, as it is, of the three letters which are the basis of faith: He at the first, Vau in the centre, then He following. Hence: "Be (heveh) lord over thy brethren", namely, to rule over them and subdue them at the time of King David. R. Yose said: 'These blessings apply to the time of the advent of the Messiah, since on account of Israel transgressing the precepts of the Torah Esau was able to take advantage of the blessing given to him, "thou shalt shake his yoke from off thy neck" (Gen. XXVII, 40).' R. Yose said: 'All these

TOLDOTH

blessings were from the side of Jacob's portion, so that Jacob only received what was his own. Isaac desired to transfer them to Esau, but God brought it to pass that Jacob came into his own. Observe the parallelism. When the serpent brought curses upon the world God said to Adam: "Because thou hast hearkened unto the voice of thy wife... cursed is the ground for thy sake, etc." (Gen. III, 17), meaning that it should not bring forth fruit or any vegetation in proper measure. Corresponding to this curse we have here the blessing, "of the fat of the earth". Again, there it is written: "In toil thou shalt eat it" (Ibid.): here comes the corrective, "of the dew of heaven". There it says: "Thorns also and thistles shall it bring forth unto thee" (Ibid. 18)–here, "and plenty of corn and wine". There we have "In the sweat of thy face thou shalt eat bread" (Ibid. 19)–here, "Let peoples serve, and nations bow down to thee", tilling the earth and cultivating the field, as it is written: "And aliens shall be your plowmen and your vine-dressers" (Is. LXI, 5). Jacob thus turned each curse into a blessing, and what he took was his own. God brought all this about so that Jacob should remain attached to his own place and portion, and that Esau should remain attached to his place and portion.'

R. Hizkiah questioned this exposition, saying: 'Do we not find that later on Esau received a similar blessing as regards the fat places of the earth and the dew of heaven, as we read: "Behold, of the fat places of the earth shall be thy dwelling, and of the dew of heaven from above"?' Said R. Simeon in reply: 'The two blessings are not alike, being from entirely different grades. As regards Jacob it is written: "So God give thee", whereas as regards Esau it is written merely: "Of the fat places of the earth shall be, etc."; as regards Jacob it is written: "of the dew of heaven and of the fat places of the earth", but as regards Esau, "of the fat places" and then "of the dew of heaven". The difference between the two goes very deep. For the "dew of heaven" promised to Jacob is the supernal dew that flows from the Ancient of Days, and is therefore called "dew of heaven", namely, of the upper heaven, dew that flows through the grade of heaven, to fall on the "field of consecrated apples". Also, the earth mentioned in Jacob's blessing alludes to the supernal "earth of the living". Jacob thus inherited the fruit of the supernal earth and the supernal heaven. Esau, on the other hand, was given his blessings on earth here below and in heaven here below. Jacob obtained a portion in the highest realm, but Esau only in the lowest. Further, Jacob was given a portion both above and below, but Esau only here below. And although he was promised, "And it shall come to pass when thou shalt break loose, that thou shalt shake his yoke from off thy neck" (Gen. XXVII, 40), this was only to be here below, but regarding the upper world it is written: "For the portion of the Lord is his people, Jacob the lot of his inheritance" (Deut. XXXII, 9).'

Observe that as soon as Jacob and Esau commenced to avail themselves of their blessings, the former possessed himself of his portion on high, and the latter of his portion here below. R. Yose the son of R. Simeon, the son of Laqunia, once said to R. Eleazar: 'Have you ever heard from your father how it comes about that the blessings given by Isaac to Jacob have not been fulfilled, while those given to Esau have all been fulfilled in their entirety?' R. Eleazar replied: 'All the blessings are to be fulfilled, including other blessings with which God blessed Jacob. For the time being, however, Jacob took his portion above and Esau here below. But in aftertime, when the Messiah will arise, Jacob will take both above and below and Esau will lose all, being left with no portion of inheritance or remembrance whatever. So Scripture says: "And the house of Jacob shall be a fire, and the house of Joseph a flame, and the house of Esau for stubble, etc." (Obad. I, 18), so that Esau will perish entirely, whilst Jacob will inherit both worlds, this world and the world to come. Of that time it is further written: "And saviours shall come up on Mount Zion to judge the mount of Esau; and the kingdom shall be the Lord's" (Ibid. I, 21), that is to say, the kingdom which Esau has taken in this world shall revert to God. For although God rules both above and below, yet for the time being He has given to all the peoples each a portion and an inheritance in this world; but at that time He will take away dominion from all of them, so that all will be His, as it is written, "And the kingdom shall be the Lord's". It will be the Lord's alone, as it is further written, "And the Lord shall be king over all the earth; in that day shall the Lord be One, and his name One" (Zech. XIV, 9).' AND IT CAME TO PASS AS JACOB WAS SCARCELY GONE OUT, ETC. R. Simeon said: 'The double form yazo yaza (lit. going out, went out) indicates that

the Shekinah went out with him. For it had entered along with Jacob, and had been with him when he received his blessings and had confirmed them. And when Jacob went out the Shekinah went out with him, and hence the twofold expression yazo yaza, implying a simultaneous going out of two.' AND ESAU HIS BROTHER CAME IN FROM HIS HUNTING. It was literally "his", devoid of any blessing, and the Holy Spirit cried out to Isaac: "Eat thou not the bread of him that hath an evil eye' (Prov. XXIII, 6). AND HE ALSO MADE SAVOURY FOOD.... LET MY FATHER ARISE. He spoke in a rough and overbearing manner, with no sign of politeness. Observe the difference between Jacob and Esau. Jacob spoke to his father gently and modestly, as it says: "He came to his father and said: My father." He was careful not to startle him, and said in a tone of entreaty: "Arise, I pray thee, sit and eat of my venison." But Esau said: "Let my father arise", as though he were not addressing him personally. Also, when Esau entered the Gehinnom accompanied him, so that Isaac shook with fear, as it says: "And Isaac trembled, greatly, exceedingly." The word "exceedingly" is added to show that no such fear and terror had ever assailed Isaac since the day he was born; and not even when he lay bound on the altar with the knife flashing before his eyes was he so affrighted as when he saw Esau enter and the Gehinnom enter with him. He then said: BEFORE THOU CAMEST, AND I HAVE BLESSED HIM. YEA, AND HE SHALL BE BLESSED, because he saw that the Shekinah had confirmed his blessings. According to another explanation, Isaac said: "And I have blessed him", and a heavenly voice answered: "Yea, and he shall be blessed." Isaac, indeed, wanted to curse Jacob, but the Holy One said to him: "O Isaac, thou wilt thereby be cursing thyself, since thou hast already pronounced over him the words, 'Cursed be every one that curseth thee, and blessed be every one that blesseth thee'." Observe that all, both above and below, confirmed these blessings, and even he who was the portion that fell to the lot of Esau consented to those blessings, and, moreover, actually himself blessed Jacob, as it is written: "And he said: Let me go for the day breaketh. And he said: I will not let thee go, except thou bless me" (Gen. XXXII, 27). The angel said "Let me go" because Jacob seized hold of him. You may wonder how could a man of flesh and blood take hold of an angel, who is pure spirit, as it is written: "Who makest spirits thy messengers, the flaming fire thy ministers" (Ps. CIV, 4). But the truth is that when the angels, the messengers of the Holy One, descend to earth, they make themselves corporeal, and put on a bodily vesture like to the denizens of this world. For it is fitting not to deviate from the custom of the place where one happens to be, as has already been explained. We find it thus written of Moses when he ascended on high: "And he was there with the Lord forty days and forty nights; he did neither eat bread, nor drink water" (Ex. XXXIV, 28), in order not to deviate from the custom of the place to which he went. Similarly we read, as an example of the behaviour of angels on descending here below: "And he stood by them under the tree, and they did eat" (Gen. XVIII, 8). So here, Jacob could only have wrestled with the angel after the latter had assumed a bodily vesture after the manner of a being of this world. The reason, too, why Jacob had to wrestle with him the whole of that night was because those beings possess dominion only in the night, and so, correspondingly, Esau dominates only during the exile, which is none other than night. During the night, therefore, the angel held fast to Jacob and wrestled with him; but as soon as day broke his strength waned, and he could no more prevail, so that Jacob got the upper hand, since Jacob's domination is in the daytime. (Hence it is written: "The burden of Dumah. One calleth unto me out of Seir: Watchman, what of the night? Watchman, what of the night?" (Is. XXI, 11). For the domination of Esau, who is identical with Seir, is only in the night.) The angel, therefore, feeling his strength ebb as the day broke, said: "Let me go, for the day breaketh." Jacob's answer, "I will not let thee go, except thou hast blessed me",

Zohar: Bereshith, Section 1, Page 144b

is peculiar, since we should have expected "except thou wilt bless me". By using the past tense, however, Jacob as much as said: "except thou acknowledge those blessings with which my father blessed me, and wilt not contend against me on account of them". The angel, we are told, thereupon said: "Thy name shall be called no more Jacob, but Israel; for thou hast striven with God and with men, and hast prevailed" (Gen. XXXII, 29). By the name Israel he meant to imply: "We must needs be subservient to thee, since thou art crowned with thy might above in a supernal grade." "Israel shall be thy name"; assuredly so, for "thou hast striven with Elohim". By this name he apparently referred to himself, but he really had a deeper meaning, viz. "Thou hast striven to associate thyself with God in a close union, as symbolised by the junction of the sun and the moon." Hence he did not say "thou hast prevailed over God", but "with God", i.e. to unite closely with God. R. Simeon here discoursed on the verse: When a man's ways please the Lord, he maketh even his enemies to be at peace with him (Prov. XVI, 7). 'How greatly', he said, 'is it incumbent on man to direct his path toward the Holy One, blessed be He, so as to observe the precepts of the Torah. For, according to our doctrine, two heavenly messengers are sent to accompany man in his path through life, one on the right and one on the left; and they are also witnesses to all his acts. They are called, the one, "good prompter", and the other, "evil prompter". Should a man be minded to purify himself and to observe diligently the precepts of the Torah, the good prompter who is associated with him will overpower the evil prompter, who will then make his peace with him and become his servant. Contrariwise, should a man set out to defile himself, the evil prompter will overpower the good prompter; and so we are agreed. Thus when a man sets out to purify himself, and his good prompter prevails, then God makes even his enemies to be at peace with him, that is to say, the evil prompter submits himself to the good prompter. Of this Solomon said: "Better is he that is lightly esteemed, and hath a servant" (Prov. XII, 9), the servant being the evil prompter. Hence inasmuch as Jacob put his trust in the Almighty, and all his actions were for His sake, God "made even his enemies to be at peace with him", to wit, Samael, who is the power and strength of Esau; and, he having made peace with Jacob and consented to the blessings, Esau also consented to them. For until Jacob was at peace with the chieftain of Esau, Esau was not at peace with Jacob. For in all cases power below depends on the corresponding power above.' AND ISAAC TREMBLED VERY EXCEEDINGLY, AND SAID: WHO THEN (epho) IS HE ...? The term epho (lit. here) is an allusion to the Shekinah that was present when Isaac blessed Jacob. Isaac thus as much as said: "Who is he that stood here and confirmed the blessings I conferred upon him? YEA, AND HE SHALL BE BLESSED, seeing that God approved of these blessings." R. Judah said: 'For having caused his father thus to tremble, Jacob was punished by being thrown into a similar tremor when his sons showed him Joseph's coat and said, "This have we found" (Gen. XXXVII, 32).' (Note that the word epho used by Isaac here is also used to herald the punishment of Jacob through the loss of Joseph, who, when sent to seek his brethren, said: "Where (epho) are they feeding the flock?" (Ibid. 16); and this although God approved of the blessings.) AND ISAAC TREMBLED A GREAT TREMBLING. The term great is echoed by the phrase "and this great fire" (Deut. XVIII, 6), thus intimating that the Gehinnom entered along with Esau. VERY EXCEEDINGLY ('ad me'od): the term me'od, on an analogy with the same term in the clause, "and behold, it was very (me'od) good" (Gen. I, 31), alludes to the angel of death; hence the exclamation: "Who then is he...?"

Zohar: Bereshith, Section 1, Page 145a

WHEN ESAU HEARD THE WORDS OF HIS FATHER, ETC. R. Hiya exclaimed: 'How much has Israel suffered on account of those tears which Esau shed before his father, in his desire to be blessed by him, out of the great regard he had for his father's words!' HAS ONE NOT RIGHTLY CALLED HIM JACOB? The form of the expression, instead of the more natural "has not his name been called", indicates the contempt with which Esau uttered the words. FOR HE HATH SUPPLANTED ME THESE TWO TIMES. The word "these" (ze) implies that the supplanting was of the same character on both occasions, since the word bekhorathi (my birthright) consists of the same letters as birkhathi (my blessing). The word ze has a similar force in the sentence: "Surely we had now (ze, lit. this) returned a second time" (Gen. XLIII, 10), where the letters of the word shavnu (we had returned) can be transposed to form boshnu (we are put to shame), as much as to say: "if we delay longer, we shall both return and be ashamed". Job made use of a similar wordplay when he said: "And thou holdest me for thine enemy" (oyeb) (Job XIII, 24), as much as to say: "Thou hast turned about Iyob (Job) into oyeb (enemy)." Similarly here, Esau said: "He first took my birthright (bekhorathi), and now he turned the same about into my blessing (birkhathi), which he has also taken from me." BEHOLD, I HAVE MADE HIM THY LORD... AND WHAT THEN SHALL I DO FOR THEE, MY SON? By the word epho (then, lit. here) he implied that there was no one there to approve of a blessing for him. Isaac thus blessed him with worldly goods; he surveyed his grade and said, "And by thy sword shalt thou live", as much as to say: "This is just what suits you, to shed blood and to make war." It was for this reason, as R. Eleazar explains, that he first said to him: "And what then shall I do for thee?", seeing that I behold in thee harshness, the sword and blood, but in thy brother the way of peace. Then he added "my son", as if to say, "my son thou surely art, and I transmit to thee all this". Hence, BY THY SWORD SHALT THOU LIVE AND THOU SHALT SERVE THY BROTHER. This has not yet been fulfilled, seeing that Esau has till now not yet served Jacob, since Jacob did not desire it at the time, and, indeed, himself many times called him "my master". The reason is that Jacob gazed into the distant future and therefore deferred the fulfilment of the blessings to the end of days, as already said.

As R. Hiya and R. Yose were once walking together, they noticed R. Jesse the Elder coming up behind them. So they sat down and waited for him until he came up to them. As soon as he joined them they said, 'Now we shall journey with godspeed.' As they proceeded, R. Hiya said: "'It is time to do for the Lord" (Ps. CXIX, 126).' R. Yose thereupon began to discourse on the verse: She openeth her mouth with wisdom, and the law of kindness is on her tongue (Prov. XXXI, 26). 'The word "wisdom"'; he said, 'signifies the Beth of the word bereshith (in the beginning), as already explained elsewhere. The Beth is closed in on one side and open on the other. It is closed in on one side as symbolic of that which is written: "And thou shalt see my back" (Ex. XXXIII, 23), and open on the other side so as to illumine the higher worlds. (It is also open on one side in order to receive from the higher worlds, like a hall in which guests gather.) For that reason it is placed at the beginning of the Torah, and was later on filled in. Again, "She openeth her mouth with wisdom", for so the word bereshith is rendered in the Chaldaic version, behokhmetha (with wisdom). "And the law of kindness (hesed) is on her tongue", i.e. in her subsequent utterances, as it is written: "And God said: Let there be light, and there was light." The "mouth" again is an allusion to the He, of the Divine Name, which contains the Whole, which is both unrevealed and revealed, and comprises both the higher and the lower emanations, being emblematic of both. "She openeth her mouth with wisdom", inasmuch as, though herself hidden and absolutely unknowable, as it says, "And it is hid from the eyes of all living, and kept close from the fowls of the air" (Job XXVIII, 21), yet when she begins to expand by means of the Wisdom to which she is attached and in which she resides, she puts forth a Voice which is the "law of kindness" (hesed). Or again, the "mouth" can be taken as alluding to the final He of the Divine Name, which is the Word that emanates from Wisdom, while the "law of kindness on her tongue" signifies the Voice which is above the Word, controlling it and guiding it,

Zohar: Bereshith, Section 1, Page 145b

since speech cannot be formed without voice, as has been agreed.'

R. Hiya then followed with a discourse on the verse: I wisdom dwell with prudence, and find out knowledge of devices (Prov. VIII, 12). '"Wisdom" here', he said, 'alludes to the Community of Israel; "prudence" signifies Jacob, the prudent man; and "knowledge of devices" alludes to Isaac, who used devices for the purpose of blessing Esau. But since wisdom allied itself with Jacob, who was possessed of prudence, it was he who was blessed by his father, so that all those blessings rested on him and are fulfilled in him and in his descendants to all eternity. Some have been fulfilled in this

177

world, and the rest will be fulfilled on the advent of the Messiah, when Israel will be one nation on earth and one people of the Holy One, blessed be He. So Scripture says: "And I will make them one nation on earth" (Ez. XXXVII, 22). And they will exercise dominion both on high and here below, as it is written: "And, behold, there came with the clouds of heaven one like unto a son of man" (Dan. VII, 13), alluding to the Messiah, concerning whom it is also written: "And in the days of those kings shall the God of heaven set up a kingdom, etc." (Ibid. II, 44). Hence Jacob desired that the blessings should be reserved for that future time, and did not take them up immediately.'

R. Jesse then followed with a discourse on the verse: But fear not thou, O Jacob my servant, neither be dismayed, O Israel, etc. (Jer. XLVI, 27). 'When Jacob', he said, 'rose to leave his father, he became aware that he would not be able to avail himself of the blessings till a long time had elapsed, and he was greatly dismayed. A voice then went forth and said: "But fear not thou, O Jacob... for I am with thee" (Ibid. 27-28), i.e. I will not forsake thee in this world. "For, lo, I will save thee from afar" (Ibid.), i.e. at the time for which thou hast reserved those blessings, "and thy seed from the land of their captivity" (Ibid.), that is to say: "Although Esau has already taken possession of his blessing and so will enslave thy children, I will free them from his hands, and then thy children will be masters over them." "And Jacob will return" (Ibid.), i.e. he will return to his blessings, "and he will be quiet and at ease" (Ibid.) from the kingdoms of Babylonia, Media, Greece, and Edom, which have enslaved Israel, "and none shall make him afraid" (Ibid.), forever and ever.'

The three then proceeded on their way, when R. Yose remarked: 'Truly all that God does in the world is an emblem of the divine Wisdom and is done with the object of manifesting Wisdom to the sons of men, so that they should learn from those works the mysteries of Wisdom, and all is accomplished according to plan. Further, all the works of God are the ways of the Torah, for the ways of the Torah are the ways of the Holy One, blessed be He, and no single word is contained in it but is an indication of ever so many ways and paths and mysteries of divine Wisdom. Did not Rabban Johanan evolve three hundred legal decisions, through esoteric allusions, from the verse: "And his wife's name was Mehetabel, the daughter of Matred, the daughter of Mezahab" (Gen. XXXVI, 39)-decisions which he revealed only to R. Eleazar? This shows that each incident recorded in the Torah contains a multitude of deep significations, and each word is itself an expression of wisdom and the doctrine of truth. The words of the Torah, then, are all sacred, revealing wondrous things, as we read: "Open thou mine eyes, that may behold wondrous things out of thy law" (Ps. CXIX, 18). Here is a proof. When the serpent had subverted Adam and his wife, and infected her with impurity, the world fell thereby in a state of defilement, and was laid under a curse, and death was brought into it. So the world had to be punished through him until the tree of life came and made atonement for man and prevented the serpent from ever again having dominion over the seed of Jacob. For each time the Israelites offered up a he-goat the serpent was subdued and led captive, as already said. Hence Jacob brought his father two he-goats (se'irim), one to subdue Esau, who was hairy (sa'ir), and the other to subdue the grade to which Esau was beholden and to which he adhered, as has been said already. And it is through this that the world will be preserved until a woman will appear after the pattern of Eve and a man after the pattern of Adam, who will circumvent and out maneuver

Zohar: Bereshith, Section 1, Page 146a

the evil serpent and him who rides on him, as explained elsewhere.'

R. Yose further discoursed as follows: And Esau was a cunning hunter... and Jacob was a perfect man, dwelling in tents (Gen. XXV, 27). 'In which way was he "perfect"? In that he was "dwelling in tents", i.e. that he held fast to the two sides, to that of Abraham and that of Isaac. In dealing with Esau he advanced from the side of Isaac, as already said, and in the spirit of the passage: "With the merciful thou dost show thyself merciful... and with the crooked thou dost show thyself subtle" (Ps. XVIII, 26-27). But when he came to receive the blessings, he came with help from on high, and with support from both Abraham and Isaac, and thus all was prescribed by wisdom, as already said above. For Jacob conquered the serpent with prudence and craft, but chiefly by means of the he-goat; and although the serpent and Samael are the same, yet he also conquered Samael by another method, as described in the passage, saying: "and there wrestled a man with him until the breaking of the day. And when he saw that he prevailed not against him" (Gen. XXXII, 25-26). Observe how great Jacob's merit must have been. For as his adversary was intent on destroying him completely, and that night was the night when the moon was created, it was doubly unpropitious for Jacob, who remained behind all alone. For we have been taught that a man should not go out alone in the night time; how much less then in the night when the lights were created, [Tr. note: i.e. the fourth night of the week.] since the moon is defective, and on such a night the evil serpent is specially powerful. Samael thus came and attacked him, in order to destroy him utterly. Jacob, however, had strong support on all sides, on the side of Isaac and on the side of Abraham, both of whom constituted the strength of Jacob. When Samael attacked Jacob's right he saw there Abraham equipped with the strength of day, being of the side of the Right, the same being Mercy (Hesed). When he attacked his left, he saw there Isaac with the strength of stern judgement. When he attacked in front, he found Jacob strong on either side by reason of those surrounding him, and thus we read: "And when he saw that he prevailed not against him, he touched the hollow of his thigh" (Gen. XXXII, 26), that is, a part that is outside of the trunk and one of its supports. Hence, "the hollow of Jacob's thigh was strained"

(Ibid.). When day appeared and night departed, Jacob's strength increased and Samael's waned, so that the latter said: "Let me go, for the moment of the recital of the morning hymn had arrived", and it was therefore necessary for him to depart. He thus confirmed Jacob's blessings and added to them one blessing more, as it says: "And he blessed him there" (Ibid. 30).

'Many were the blessings which Jacob received at different times. First he obtained blessings from his father, through the exercise of craft; then a blessing from the Shekinah, at the time when he returned from Laban, as we read, "And God (Elohim) blessed Jacob"; another blessing he received from that angel, the chieftain of Esau; and then his father blessed him when he set out for Padan-Aram, saying, "And God Almighty bless thee...." (Gen. XXVIII, 3). When Jacob saw himself equipped with all these blessings, he deliberated within himself, saying, "Of which of these blessings shall I avail myself now?" He decided to make use for the time being of the least of them, which was the last; for although in itself it was powerful, yet Jacob thought that it was not so strong in promises of dominion in this world as the others. Jacob hence said: "Let me take this blessing to use for the time being, and the others I will reserve against the time when I and my descendants after me will be in need of them-the time, that is, when all the nations will assemble to exterminate my offspring from the world." To Jacob may be applied the words of the Scripture: "All nations compass me about, verily, in the name of the Lord I will cut them off. They compass me about, yea, they compass me about.... They compass me about like bees, etc." (Ps. CXVIII, 10-12). Here we have three times the words "compass me about", corresponding to the three remaining benedictions: his father's first blessing, then God's blessing, and thirdly the blessing of the angel. Jacob said: "Those blessings will be needed at that time for use against all those kings and nations: I shall therefore reserve them for that time, but now to cope with Esau this blessing will suffice me." He was like a king who had at his disposal a numerous and powerful army with skilled leaders, able and ready to engage in warfare with the most powerful

Zohar: Bereshith, Section 1, Page 146b

adversary. Being once informed that a highway robber was infesting the country, he merely said, "Let my gate-keepers set out to deal with him." "Of all thy legions," he was asked, "hast thou no others to send but these gate-keepers?" "To cope with the robber these will suffice," he answered, "whereas all my legions and military leaders I have to keep in reserve for the time when I will need them to meet my powerful adversaries." Similarly Jacob said: "For dealing with Esau these blessings will suffice me, but the others I will keep in reserve against the time when my children will need them to withstand all those monarchs and rulers of the earth." When that time will come all those blessings will become operative, and the world will be established on a firm foundation. From that day onward that kingdom will gain the ascendancy over all other kingdoms, and it will endure forever, as it is written: "It shall break in pieces and consume all these kingdoms, but it shall stand forever" (Dan. II, 44). This is "the stone that was cut out of the mountain without hands, etc." (Ibid. 45). The same stone is alluded to in the words: "From thence, from the Shepherd, the stone of Israel" (Gen. XLIX, 24). This stone is the Community of Israel, alluded to in the verse: "And this stone, which I have set up for a pillar, etc." (Gen. XXVIII, 22).' R. Hiya cited the following verses in regard to Jacob's blessings: '"A remnant shall return, even the remnant of Jacob" (Is. X, 21). 'This is a reference', he said, 'to the remainder of the blessings. It is further written: "And the remnant of Jacob shall be in the midst of many peoples (i.e. all the peoples, and not Esau alone), as dew from the Lord, as showers upon the grass" (Micah V, 6).' R. Yesa said: 'It is written: "A son honoureth his father, and a servant his master" (Mal. I, 6). Such a son was Esau, for there was not a man in the world who showed so much honour to his father as he did, and this it was that procured him dominion in this world. The "servant honouring his master" is typified by Eliezer the servant of Abraham, as already explained elsewhere. So, too, the tears which Esau shed made Israel subject to him, until the time when they will return unto the Holy One with weeping and with tears, as it says, "They shall come with weeping, etc." (Jer. XXXI, 9). And then will be fulfilled the prophecy: "And saviours shall come up on Mount Zion, to judge the Mount of Esau, and the kingdom shall be the Lord's" (Ob. I, 21). Blessed be the Lord forevermore.'

VAYEZE

AND JACOB WENT OUT PROM BEER-SHEBA AND WENT TOWARD HARAN. R. Hiya drew a parallel between this statement and the verse: The sun ariseth, and the sun goeth down, and hasteth to his place where he ariseth (Eccles. I, 5). 'The sun arising', he said, 'is parallel to Jacob when in Beersheba; and "the sun going down" to Jacob on his way to Haran, when, as we read, "he tarried there all night, because the sun was set"; and as the "sun hasteth to his place

Zohar: Bereshith, Section 1, Page 147a

where he ariseth", so Jacob "lay down in that place to sleep". Observe that although the sun illumines all quarters of the world, yet he travels only in two directions, as we read: "He goeth toward the South, and turneth about unto the North" (Eccles. I, 6), one being the right and the other the left. Every day, too, he emerges from the East, turns to the South, then to the North, then toward the Western side, and finally is gathered unto the West. As the sun emerges from the East, so Jacob went out from Beer-sheba, and as the sun turns toward the West, so Jacob went toward Haran.' R.

Simeon said that Jacob "went forth" from the ambit of the Land of Israel, and he "went into" another sphere, as is implied in the sentence, "and he went toward Haran" (lit. strange, alien). R. Hiya said: 'When the sun goes down to the West, the West is called the place of the sun and his throne, the place in which he abides, and to which he gathers in all his radiance. This accords with the Rabbinic dictum that God puts on phylacteries, that is, He takes up all the supernal crowns, to wit the emblem of the supernal Father and the emblem of the supernal Mother (these being the phylactery worn on the head), and then He takes up the Right and the Left, thereby carrying the whole.' R. Eleazar said: 'The "Beauty of Israel" takes up the whole, and when the Community of Israel is drawn toward the world on high, it also carries the whole, the male world of the Holy One as well as the female world

Zohar: Bereshith, Section 1, Page 147b

of the Holy One; for just as all the lights radiate from the one, so the other carries the whole, one world being a representation of the other. Hence Beer-sheba (lit. well of seven) signifies the Jubilee year, be'er (well) symbolising a Sabbatical year; and the sun shines only from the Jubilee year. Hence "Jacob went out from Beer-sheba and went unto Haran", that is toward the West, which is identical with the Sabbatical year.' R. Simeon said: 'Beer-sheba symbolises the Sabbatical year, and Haran the year of 'orlah, inasmuch as he issued from the sphere of holiness into an alien sphere, since he was fleeing from his brother, as already explained.' But when he arrived at Bethel, which is still within the holy sphere, it is written: AND HE LIGHTED UPON THE PLACE. R. Hiya said: 'This is the place mentioned in the verse, "and he hasteth to his place' (Eccl. I, 5). AND TARRIED THERE ALL NIGHT, BECAUSE THE SUN CAME, i.e. came to illumine it, as it says: "he hasteth to his place where he shines".

AND HE TOOK OF THE STONES OF THE PLACE. This is an allusion to the twelve precious and wondrous stones of the upper layer, of which it is written, "Take you... twelve stones" (Josh. IV, 3), and underneath which there are thousands and myriads of hewn stones. Hence it says "of the stones", and not simply "the stones. AND PUT THEM UNDER HIS HEAD (lit. heads). The plural form shows that we should refer the "his" not to Jacob but to the place, and understand the "heads" to be the four cardinal points of the world: he arranged the stones three to the

Zohar: Bereshith, Section 1, Page 148a

North, three to the West, three to the South, and three to the East, and that place or spot was above them so that it should be established on them. Thereafter he LAY DOWN IN THAT PLACE TO SLEEP, for now that the couch was properly arranged, he, namely the sun, lay down on it. Thus the words "and he lay down in that place to sleep" are parallel to the text: "the sun ariseth and the sun comes in".'

Whilst R. Isaac was one day sitting at the entrance of the cave of Apikutha, a man passed by with his two sons. Said one of them to the other: 'The sun is most powerful when it is in the South, and were it not for the wind which tempers the heat, the world could not exist.' Said the younger brother: 'If not for Jacob, the world could not subsist. For when the unity of God is proclaimed by his sons with the verse, "Hear, O Israel, the Lord our God, the Lord is one" (Deut. VI, 4), which is an expression of perfect and absolute oneness, then Jacob their father joins them, and takes possession of his house, where he abides in close association with his fathers, so that male and female become united.' Said R. Isaac to himself: 'I will join them and listen to what they have to say.' He accordingly went along with them. The man then commenced to discourse on the verse: Arise, O Lord, unto thy resting place, thoa and the ark of thy strength (Ps. CXXXII, 8). 'David,' he said, 'when he uttered these words, was like a man saying to a king, "Let your Highness arise and proceed to his abode of rest." Moses also addressed God similarly when he said: "Arise, O Lord, and let thine enemies be scattered" (Num. X, 35). The difference between the two is this. Moses spoke like a man giving orders in his own household, and so, as it were, bade the Lord to make war against His enemies; whereas David solicited Him to retire to His place of rest, and in accordance with the rules of etiquette included in his invitation both the King and His Consort. Hence he said: "Arise, O Lord, unto thy resting place, thou and the ark of thy strength", so as not to separate them. From David's conduct on this occasion we learn that anyone who invites a king should strive to entertain him in some novel

Zohar: Bereshith, Section 1, Page 148b

fashion, so as to afford him special pleasure. If, for instance, it is the king's wont to be entertained by ordinary clowns and jester, he should provide for him specially refined and courtly entertainers. Thus, when David invited the King and His Consort, he replaced the customary entertainers of the King with a higher order.

So he said: "Let thy priests be clothed with righteousness, and let thy saints sing songs" (Ps. CXXXII, 9). Now the Levites were the regular musicians of the King, but David, having extended an invitation to Him, deviated from the normal practice and provided priests and saints to entertain Him. God said to him: "David, I do not wish to burden thee overmuch." Said David in reply: "O my Master, when Thou art in Thy palace, Thou doest according to Thy will, but now that I have invited Thee, it is for me to arrange matters, and it is my will to bring before Thee these, although it is not their usual task." From here we learn again that in his own house a man may arrange things as he pleases, but when invited out he must be at the command of his host, and conform to his desires. For when David substituted the priests for the Levites, God assented to his wish. David further said: "For thy servant David's sake turn not away the face of

180

thine anointed" (Ibid. 10), as much as to say: "Let not the arrangements I have made be annulled." God said to him: "David, even my vessels I will not make use of, but will use thine instead." Nor did God stir from there until He had bestowed upon him a multitude of gifts, as it is written: "The Lord swore unto David in truth; he will not turn back from it: of the fruit of thy body will I set upon thy throne" (Ibid. 11).' R. Isaac went up to the man and kissed him, saying: 'It was worth my while to come hither if only to hear this.'

The elder son of the man then discoursed thus: And Jacob went out from Beer-sheba, and went unto Haran. 'Jacob', he said, 'acted in conformity with the verse: "Therefore shall a man leave his father and his mother, and shall cleave unto his wife" (Gen. II, 24). Or again, his action may be regarded as symbolical of a later time when Israel left the Sanctuary and were driven into exile among the nations, as described in the text: "And gone is from the daughter of Zion all her splendour" (Lam. I, 6), as well as ill the passage, "Judah is gone into exile because of affliction" (Ibid. 3).' The younger son then began to discourse thus: And he lighted upon the place, and tarried there all night, etc. 'Even a king,' he said, 'when he desires to visit his consort, should coax her and use words of endearment, and not treat her as a mere chattel; and though he should have a golden couch with embroidered coverings in a grand palace, and she prepares for him a bed on a floor of stones with a straw mattress, it is incumbent on him to leave his own couch and lie down on hers, so as to give her satisfaction, and so that their hearts may be united, without any constraint. We learn this lesson from this text, which tells us that when Jacob went unto her, he "took from the stones of the place... and lay down in that place to sleep", showing that he loved even the stones of that place.' R. Isaac wept for joy, and said: 'Seeing that such pearls are in your possession, how can I help following you?' The man said to him: 'You must leave us, as we have to go to the town to celebrate the wedding of this my son.' R. Isaac then said: 'I must then needs go my own way.'

Zohar: Bereshith, Section 1, Page 149a

[Note: The English passage from the beginning of the page until "Said R. Isaac" is not found in our Hebrew text]

He then went and repeated the expositions he had heard to R. Simeon, who remarked: 'They indeed spoke well, and all they said about God has been affirmed by us. Moreover, these expositions come from the mouths of the descendants of R. Zadok the invalid. He was called invalid because he fasted forty years, praying that Jerusalem should not be destroyed in his life-time. He used to discover within each word of the Torah profound lessons, from which he deduced the proper rules for the conduct of life.' Said R. Isaac: 'Not many days elapsed before I again met that man, accompanied by his younger son. I said to him: "Where is your other son?" He said: "I had him married, and he is with his wife." Then, recognising me, he said: "I swear to you that I refrained from inviting you to the marriage of my son for three reasons: first, because I did not know you, and, since the style of an invitation must accord with the rank of the recipient, I was afraid lest you might happen to be a great man and I should unwittingly offend your dignity; secondly, I thought you might be in a hurry, and so I did not wish to inconvenience you; and thirdly, I did not wish to put you to shame in the presence of the company of guests, as it is a custom with us that whoever sits at table with the bride and bridegroom gives them presents and gifts." I said to him: "God give you credit for your good intentions." I further asked him his name, and he said: "Zadok the Little." On that occasion I learnt from him thirteen profound lessons in the Torah, and from his son I learnt three, one concerning prophecy, one concerning dreams, and one concerning the difference between prophecy and dreams. He said that prophecy is of the male world, whereas dreams are of the female world, and from the one to the other is a descent of six grades. Prophecy is from both the right side and the left side, but dreams are only from the left side. Dream branches out into many grades in reaching here below; hence dreams are universally diffused throughout the world, each man seeing the kind of dream that answers to his own grade. Prophecy, on the other hand, is confined to its own region.' [Note: The last 14 lines of the Hebrew text do not appear in our translation.]

Zohar: Bereshith, Section 1, Page 149b

AND HE DREAMED. It may be asked, how came Jacob, the holy man, the perfection of the Patriarchs, to have a vision only in a dream, and that in such a holy spot? The reason is that Jacob at that time was not yet married, and that Isaac was still alive. It is true that we find him subsequently saying: "and I saw in a dream" (Gen. XXXI, 10), at a time when he was already married. But that was due to the inferiority of the place, as well as to the fact that Isaac was still alive. So when he came into the Holy Land with all the tribes, with "the foundation of the house, the mother of the children rejoicing", we read, "and God spake unto Israel in the visions of the night" (Gen. XLVI, 2)-not "dream", but "visions", which are of another and higher grade. Dreams are transmitted through the medium of Gabriel, who is the sixth in rank of inspiration; but a vision comes through the grade of the Hayyah that rules in the night. True, it says in one place, "Gabriel, make this man to understand the vision" (Dan. VIII, 16). The reason there is that a dream is more precise than a vision, and may explain what is obscure in a vision, and therefore Gabriel was sent to explain to Daniel what was obscure in his vision. A "vision" (mar'eh=vision, or mirror) is so called because it is like a mirror, in which all images are reflected. (Thus we read: "And I appeared... as El Shaddai" (Ex. VI, 2), this grade being like a mirror which showed another form, since all supernal forms are reflected in it.) AND BEHOLD A LADDER SET UP ON THE EARTH. This ladder signifies the grade on which the other grades rest, to wit, the "Foundation of the world". AND THE TOP OF IT REACHED TO HEAVEN, so as to be attached to it. For this grade is the conclusion of the Body standing between the upper and the lower world in the same way as the sign of the covenant is situated at the end of the trunk of the body, between the thighs. AND BEHOLD, THE ANGELS OF GOD ASCENDING AND DESCENDING ON IT; this alludes to the Chieftains who have charge of all the nations, and who ascend and descend on that ladder. When Israel are sinful, the ladder is lowered and the Chieftains ascend by it; but when Israel are righteous, the ladder is removed and all the Chieftains are left below and are deprived of their dominion. Jacob thus saw in this dream the domination of Esau and the domination of the other nations. According to another explanation, the angels ascended and descended on the top of the ladder; for when the top was detached, the ladder was lowered and the Chieftains ascended, but when it was attached again, the ladder was lifted and they remained below. But it comes to the same thing.

It says of Solomon that "In Gibeon the Lord appeared to him in a dream by night" (I Kings III, 5).

Zohar: Bereshith, Section 1, Page 150a

Here we have "appearing" and "dream" combined, to show that there was there a mingling of two grades, a higher and a lower, the reason being that Solomon had not then yet attained his full development. But when he had perfected himself it is written of him, "And God gave Solomon wisdom" (Ibid. V, 9), also" And Solomon's wisdom excelled, etc." (Ibid. 10); for the moon then reached its fullness and the Temple was built, and thus Solomon saw wisdom eye to eye and had no need of dreams. After he sinned, however, he was beholden again to dreams as before. Hence it says that "God appeared unto him twice" (Ibid. XI, 9)-twice, that is, in dreams, for communications through wisdom he had every day. Moreover, the dream-medium of Solomon excelled that of all other men inasmuch as it was a mingling of grade with grade, of vision with vision. In his later days, however, darkness fell upon him on account of his sins, and the moon waned because he observed not the holy covenant and gave himself up to strange women. This was the condition God made with David, saying: "If thy children keep my covenant... their children also forever shall sit upon the throne" (Ps. CXXXII, 12), where the expression "forever" it of the same import as the phrase "as the days of the heaven above the earth" (Deut. XI, 21). And since Solomon did not keep the covenant properly, the moon began to wane, and so in the end he was beholden again to dreams; and likewise Jacob was beholden to dreams, as explained before. AND BEHOLD, THE LORD STOOD (nitsab) UPON IT, ETC. Here Jacob discerned the essential unity of the object of faith. This is implied in the term nitsab (firmly knit), which implies that Jacob saw all grades stationed as one on that ladder so as to be knit into one whole. And inasmuch as that ladder is situated between two sides, God said to him: I AM THE LORD, THE GOD OF ABRAHAM THY FATHER, AND THE GOD OF ISAAC, these two being respectively of the two sides, one of the right and the other of the left. According to another explanation, the Lord was standing over him, to wit, over Jacob, so as to form the Divine Chariot, with the Community of Israel, embodied in Jacob, as the uniting link in the midst, between the right and the left. That Jacob was in the midst is proved by the fact that the text here calls Abraham "thy father", but not Isaac, thus showing that Jacob was next to Abraham; and hence the text naturally continues: THE LAND WHEREON THOU LIEST, showing that the whole formed one sacred Chariot. Here Jacob saw that he was to be the crown of the patriarchs. The words "the God of thy father Abraham and the God of Isaac" show that Jacob was attached to either side and holding fast to both of them. But as long as he was not married this fact is not disclosed in the text, save to those who can read between the lines. After he married and begat children, however, it was openly stated, as it is written: "And he erected there an altar, and the God of Israel called him El (godlike)". From here we learn that whoever is incomplete below remains incomplete on high. Jacob was an exception, yet he too before marriage was not perfected openly; or rather, he only foresaw that he eventually would be perfected. It is true, God had already said to him, "And, behold, I am with thee, and will keep thee whithersoever thou goest." This, however, only implies that God's care and protection were always with him in the hour of need, in this world; but as regards the higher world, he was not sure of it till he had perfected himself. AND JACOB AWARENED OUT OF HIS SLEEP, AND HE SAID: SURELY THE LORD IS IN THIS PLACE, AND I KNEW IT NOT. How, we may ask, could he have known? The truth is, however, that he meant much the same as Saul when he said: "and I have not entreated the Presence of the Lord" (I Sam. XIII, 12). What Jacob really said was: "And I have not known Anokhi (I, i.e. the Shekinah)"; as much as to say: "Behold all this revelation has been vouchsafed to me whilst yet I have not reached the stage of a knowledge of Anokhi (I) and of entering under the wings of the Shekinah, so as to attain perfection". Similarly, Rebekah said: "If it be so, what boots me Anokhi (I)?" (Gen. XXV, 22), because she saw every day the splendour of the Shekinah,

Zohar: Bereshith, Section 1, Page 150b

but when she felt the pains of approaching childbirth, "she went to enquire of the Lord" (Ibid.), that is, she proceeded from the Shekinah grade to another grade, identical with the Lord (Tetragrammaton). Hence Jacob said: "Have I seen all this without knowing Anokhi?", because he was single, and had not yet come under the wings of the Shekinah. Straightway: AND HE WAS AFRAID, AND SAID: HOW FULL OF AWE IS THIS PLACE. The word "place" here has a twofold significance. It refers in the first instance to the place mentioned by Jacob in the preceding verse; but it also refers to the mark of the holy covenant, which should not be left inoperative. (These two significations, however, are only two aspects of one and the same idea.) Jacob then said: THIS IS NONE OTHER THAN THE HOUSE OF GOD, implying: This is not to remain idle; its covenant is not meant to exist in isolation. It is in sooth a godly abode, to be used for the promotion of fecundity and for receiving blessing from all the bodily organs. For indeed this is THE GATE OF HEAVEN, or, in other words, the gate of the Body, the gate assuredly through which pass the blessings downwards, so that it is attached both on high and below: on high, as being the gate of heaven, and below, as being none other than the house of God." Hence "he was afraid, and said: How full of awe is this place!" But mankind (it may be added) pay no regard to its preciousness, so as thereby to become perfect on high and here below.'

The father of the youth went up to him and kissed him. R. Isaac said: 'When I heard him speak thus, I wept and said: Blessed be the Merciful One who has not allowed divine Wisdom to perish from the world. I followed them until we entered the next town, a distance of three parasangs. Hardly had they arrived in the town when the man had his son affianced. I said to him: "You act upon your own words." I also repeated the remark of R. Simeon, that all these verses are allegorical and have a profound significance. When I repeated all this in the presence of R. Simeon, he remarked to me that I should not think that all this exposition was merely the youth's own idea: it contains recondite thoughts which bear the seal of divine Wisdom.'

AND JACOB VOWED A VOW, SAYING: IF GOD WILL BE WITH ME, ETC. Said R. Judah: After receiving all these promises, how could Jacob still say, If God will be with me, etc."? What Jacob meant, however, was this: "Some dreams are true and some not, so if this dream should come true, and God will really be with me as I have dreamt, then "the Lord shall be to me for God", that is, I shall draw blessings from the well-spring of the universal stream towards the region called Elohim.' For Israel being in the centre take first of the original well-spring, and after the bounty reaches them they pass it on toward that region. Hence we may render: "and the Lord shall be toward me, first, and afterwards the whole will be drawn toward Elohim": i.e. in the same way as Elohim will fulfil for me all these good promises, so will I draw toward Him from my region all those blessings and will make Him the all-comprehensive uniting force. When will that be? "When I come back to my father's house in peace", when I shall be settled in my own grade, in the grade of peace so as to make perfect my father's house, then "will the Lord be toward me, toward Elohim (God)".' According to another explanation, Jacob meant: "I desire to come back to my father's house in peace, because there is the Holy Land, and there I will become perfected, and the Lord shall be my God. In that place will I duly rise from this grade to another grade, and there I will engage myself in His worship." R. Hiya adduced here the verse: The tale of iniquities is too heavy for me; our transgressions, thou wilt pardon them (Ps. LXV, 4). 'The two halves of the verse', he said, 'do not seem to fit one another. The truth is, however, that David first prayed for himself and then for mankind in general, as though to say, "I know my own sins, but there are a great number of sinners in the world whose sins are much more grievous than mine; this being so, both mine

and theirs, all our transgressions, thou wilt pardon them." For when sinners become numerous in the world, they go up to the place where the records are kept, as it is written, "there is a sitting in judgement and the books are open" (Dan. VII, 10). That book stood, as it were, over the head of David, and hence he said, "The tale of iniquities is too heavy for me, and therefore", he went on, "our transgressions thou wilt pardon them". Jacob, being in a similar condition, felt distrustful, not of God, but of himself, and he feared lest his sins should prevent him from returning in peace and deprive him of God's providential care. THEN SHALL THE LORD BE MY GOD: i.e. should I return in peace, I shall not care even if the attribute of divine mercy becomes justice towards me, inasmuch as I will worship Him continually.' R. Aha said that Jacob's words amounted to saying: 'Now I have no need of severity, but when I will return to my father's house, I will link myself with that attribute also.' Said R. Yose: 'That is not so, but what Jacob ptactically said was: Now I require the attribute of divine justice to guard me (against my enemies) until I return in peace to my father's house, but then I will combine mercy with justice, and bind all attributes in a firm unity.'

AND THIS STONE, WHICH I HAVE SET UP FOR A PILLAR, SHALL BE GOD'S HOUSE: seeing that all will be then united into one, and this stone will be blessed from the right and from the left, from on high and from below, for the reason that I will give the tenth of everything. We should have expected here, instead of Elohim, the name Tetragrammaton, as in the text: "to prepare chambers in the house of the Lord (Tetragrammaton)" (II Chr. XXXI, 20), also: "Let us go unto the house of the Lord (Tetragrammaton)" (Ps. CXXII, 1). But in truth, the name Elohim here points to the tribunal which represents the attribute of justice on its two supernal sides, on the side of the Jubilee year, known as Living God (Elohim Hayyim), and on the side of Isaac, expressed simply by the term "God" (Elohim). R. Eleazar said: 'The Jubilee Year, although it dispenses judgement, is yet altogether pervaded with mercy and is the source of universal joy and gladness. But "the house of God (Elohim)" represents rigorous judgement only, on the side of the left, either for good, in consonance with the text, "His left hand be under my head" (S. S. II, 6), or for evil, as it says, "Out of the North the evil shall break forth upon all the inhabitants of the land" (Jer. I, 14). Well then may it be called "the house of God

(Elohim)".' R. Simeon said: '"The house of God (Elohim)" signifies the same as "the city of the great king" (Ps. XLVIII, 3). Verily the supernal world is not only "King", but a "Great King", and that is what is meant here.'

R. Hiya and R. Hizkiah were once sitting underneath a tree in the field of Ono. R. Hiya fell into a slumber and beheld Elijah. He said to him: 'The whole field is illumined with your presence.' Elijah answered: 'I am come to tell you that Jerusalem is about to be laid waste together with all the towns of the sages, for the reason that Jerusalem is the embodiment of judgement, and is preserved by judgement, and now judgement demands its destruction; and Samael has already been given power over it and over its mighty ones. I have therefore come to advise the sages thereof so that they may try to obtain for Jerusalem some years of grace. For so long as knowledge of the Torah is found therein it will be spared, the Torah being the tree of life by which all live. But when the study of the Torah ceases below, the tree of life disappears from the world. Hence so long as the sages cling to the Torah, Samael has no power over them, as Scripture says: "The voice is the voice of Jacob, but the hands are the hands of Esau" (Gen. XXVII, 22). The voice is the Torah, which is termed the voice of Jacob, and so long as that voice pours forth, the utterance also dominates and prevails (over the hands of Esau). Hence the study of the Torah should never cease.' R. Hiya

Zohar: Bereshith, Section 1, Page 151b

then awoke, and they went and told the sages. Said R. Jesse: 'We all know this, and so it is written: "Except the Lord keep the city, the watchman waketh in vain" (Ps. CXXVII, 1), as much as to say: "It is those who labour in the Torah who preserve the Holy City, and not the warriors and men of might".' AND HE LOOKED, AND BEHOLD A WELL IN THE FIELD, ETC. R. Judah discoursed on the verse: A psalm (mizmor= song, hymn) of David when he fled from Absalom his son (Ps. III, 1). 'The companions', he said, 'have been perplexed by the title "song" given to this psalm. When his own son rose up against him, David should rather have uttered a lamentation, since a little hurt from one's kin is worse than a great hurt from a stranger. The truth, however, is that David was apprehensive lest the punishment for his sons might be remitted to the next world, and so when he found that it was being exacted from him in this world he rejoiced. Further, he was comforted by the fact that many, superior to himself, had had to flee alone, like Jacob, who "fled into the field of Aram" (Hos. XII, 13), all alone, and Moses, who fled from the face of Pharaoh (Ex. II, 15), also alone; whereas he was accompanied by all the nobility and the valiant men of the land and the chiefs of Israel, who stood on his right hand and on his left to guard him on all sides. Seeing himself thus favoured, David broke out into song.' R. Judah further remarked: 'The fugitives mentioned above in the course of their wanderings all came across that well. Why not David also? The reason is that it was at that time at enmity with him, whereas it welcomed Jacob and Moses and was eager to approach them, and as soon as it saw them its waters rose to meet them, like a woman rejoicing to greet her husband. Why, it may be asked, was not Elijah when he fled also met by the well? The reason is that Elijah is beneath the well and not above it, as Moses and Jacob were, and hence he is an angel who executes messages. So when it says that "Jacob looked, and behold, a well in the field", there is here an inner meaning, to wit, that he discerned the supernal well which corresponds to the well below. This is borne out by the next words: THREE FLOCKS OF SHEEP LYING THERE BY IT. Since they were only

Zohar: Bereshith, Section 1, Page 152a

three, why is it written, "And thither were all the flocks gathered"? But in truth the three allude to the South, the East, and the North, the South on one side, the North on the other, and the East between them, all three standing by that well, holding fast to it and filling it. Why all this? FOR OUT OF THAT WELL THEY WATERED THE FLOCKS, the allusion being the same as in the text: "They give drink to all the Hayyoth of the field" (Ps. CIV, 11). Further, the words AND THITHER WERE ALL THE FLOCKS GATHERED, can be illustrated from the passage: "All the rivers run into the sea" (Eccl. I, 7). AND THEY ROLLED THE STONE FROM THE WELL'S MOUTH: i.e. they dispelled from it the rigidity of hard judgement, which congeals it as it were into stone, from which water cannot flow. For when those rivers arise, the South, which is on the right, gathers strength and prevents the North from solidifying the water. For a large river, with a great volume of water, does not become frozen and congealed so soon as a small river with a small volume of water. Hence when those rivers arrive, the South, which is the right, puts forth its strength and the waters thaw and are loosened, so as to flow onward and give drink to the flocks, as it says, "they water the Hayyoth of the field" (Ps. CIV, 11). Then "they put the stone back upon the well's mouth in its place", because the world has need of its judgement so as thereby to punish the guilty.

Observe that Jacob, when he sat by the well and saw the water rising up toward him, knew that there he would meet his destined wife; and so it was, as Scripture says: WHILE HE WAS YET SPEAKING WITH THEM, RACHEL CAME WITH HER FATHER S SHEEP. AND IT CAME TO PASS WHEN JACOB SAW RACHEL, ETC. It was the same with Moses, who, when he sat down by the well, as soon as he saw the water rising toward him knew that there he would meet his destined wife; and so indeed it turned out, as we read: "And the shepherds came and drove them away, etc." (Ex. II, 17), with the result that there he met with Zipporah.

Zohar: Bereshith, Section 1, Page 152b

It was the well that served as medium to both of them. Observe that in this section the term "well" (be'er) is mentioned seven times, which indicates the identification of this well with "Beer-Sheba" (the well of seven). In the narrative of Moses, on the other hand, the well is mentioned only once, when it says, "and he sat down by the well" (Ibid. 15). The reason is that Moses completely separated himself from his house here below, whereas Jacob did not separate himself at all. Moses adhered to one, the one of which we read: "My dove, my undefiled, is but one, she is the only one of her mother" (S. S. VI, 9). Moses thus was master of the house and ascended on high; hence of him it is written: "and he sat upon ('al) the well", whereas of Jacob it is merely written, "and he saw, and behold a well in the field".

[The following is an alternative exposition of this section. AND JACOB WENT OUT FROM BEER SHEBA, AND WENT TOWARD HARAN.] R. Abba discoursed on the verse: Happy are they that keep justice, that perform acts of charity (zedakah) at all times (Ps. CVI, 3). 'Happy are Israel', he said, 'to whom the Holy One, blessed be He, gave the Law of truth so that they should exert themselves in its study day and night, as whoever exerts himself in the study of the Torah achieves complete freedom, even from death, which can no more prevail over him, as already explained elsewhere. For whoever exerts himself in the study of the Torah and lays hold of it, lays hold of the tree of life; and whoever relaxes his hold of the tree of life, behold the tree of death overshadows him and takes hold of him. So Scripture says: "If thou relaxest in the day of adversity, thy strength is narrow indeed" (Prov. XXIV, 10), signifying that whoever relaxes in the study of the Torah, in the day of adversity his strength (Koah-KoH=the strength of KoH) is narrow indeed, to wit, the strength of KoH that continually follows on the right of the man that walks in the ways of the Torah, and forms his constant guard, so that the evil power is prevented from approaching him and is powerless to accuse him. But of him who turns aside from the ways of the Torah and relaxes his hold of it, it is said: "narrow indeed is the strength of KoH", as the evil power, represented by the left, obtains dominion over that man and thrusts aside that KoH, so that he has no room to move. According to another interpretation, the term "zar" (narrow) signifies here "adversary"; for when a man holds fast to the ways of the Torah he is beloved both on high and below, and is the favourite of the Holy One, blessed be He, as we read: "And the Lord loved him" (II Sam. XII, 24); but when a man turns aside from the ways of the Torah, then zar kohekoh, that is, the strength of KoH becomes his enemy, and makes the evil one obtain dominion over him so as to accuse him in this world and the world to come. For the evil one, who is the same as the evil tempter, dominates the world from many sides, and exercises great power therein; he is indeed the very same mighty serpent through whom Adam fell into sin, and who entices mankind to draw him unto themselves until he draws out their souls. Now his power is over the body, and when he obtains that power over the body, the soul departs because the body has become defiled. To obtain that dominion over the body, however, the evil one must receive authorisation. Further, many evil powers come forth from his side to dominate the world. According to our teachers, all the affairs of the world come under their rule, as he has subordinates and ministers who interfere in all the activities of the world. Hence he is called the "left end". For, as already explained, there is a right end and a left end; and this left end is identical with the "end of all flesh". It is called "the end of all flesh", but not "the end of all spirit". Each is an "end" in the mystical sense, but one presides over flesh, the other over spirit, the latter being the inner one, the former the outer one; one being right, the other left, one being holy, the other defiled, as already explained elsewhere. Now observe a deep and holy mystery of faith, the symbolism of the male principle and the female principle of the universe. In the former are comprised all holinesses and objects of faith, and all life, all freedom, all goodness, all illuminations

Zohar: Bereshith, Section 1, Page 153a

emerge from thence; all blessings, all benevolent dews, all graces and kindnesses–all these are generated from that side, which is called the South. Contrariwise, from the side of the North there issue a variety of grades, extending downwards, to the world below. This is the region of the dross of gold, which comes from the side of impurity and loathsomeness and which forms a link between the upper and nether regions; and there is the line where the male and female principles join, forming together the rider on the serpent, and symbolised by Azazel. Now from thence there spread many grades which dominate the world, all of them presenting sides of defilement and acting as chieftains and prefects in the world. Observe that Esau, when he emerged into the world, was red all over like a rose, and was hairy after the pattern of a goat (sa'ir), and from such a being came forth chieftains and prefects, fully armed, who dominate the world. This has already been explained elsewhere. Observe now the verse previously cited: "Happy are they that keep justice", to wit, they who keep the faith of the Holy One, blessed be He, since God is justice, so that a man should be on his guard not to turn aside but to keep to the way of justice, as God is justice and all His ways are justice. The verse proceeds: "that exercise charity (zedakah) at all times". The words "at all times" cannot be taken quite literally, but refer to those who endeavour to follow the ways of the Torah and dispense charity to those who are in need of it. For when charity is given to the poor, its effect is felt both on high and here below. For that charity ascends on high and reaches to the region of Jacob, who is the supernal chariot, and causes blessings to flow toward that region from the very fountain of fountains; and from that charity he causes blessings to flow in abundance to all the lower beings and to all chariots and hosts. All these are blessed and increase in illumination, as is befitting, for they all are comprehended within the term "time" ('eth). This, then, is the meaning of the words "that do charity in the whole of time". Observe that as long as Israel were in the Holy Land they drew the blessings from on high to below, but after they went forth from the Holy Land they came under a strange power and blessings were withheld from the world. Jacob was at first under sacred jurisdiction, but when he departed from the land he entered into a strange jurisdiction. And before he came under a strange jurisdiction the Holy One, blessed be He, appeared unto him in a dream, and he saw wonderful things, and holy angels accompanied him until he sat down by the well; and when he sat by the well the waters thereof rose toward him, as a portent that he would there meet his wife, and the same thing happened to Moses. The inward significance of the matter is that the well only rose when it saw its affinity, to form with him a union.'] AND JACOB WENT ON HIS JOURNEY, AND CAME TO THE LAND OF THE CHILDREN OF THE EAST (Gen. XXIX, 1). R. Abba said: 'Since Laban dwelt in Haran, why did Jacob go further on? That Laban dwelt in Haran we know from the verses: "And Jacob said unto them: My brethren, whence are ye? And they said: Of Haran are we. And he said: Know ye Laban the son of Nahor? And they said: We know him" (Ibid. 4-5). The truth, however, is that Jacob said to himself: "I wish to enter into communion with the Shekinah, or in other words, I desire to marry. Now, when the servant was sent to take a wife for my father, he found a well of water through which he met my father's destined wife. But, behold, in this place I have found neither spring, nor well, nor any water at all." Straightway he proceeded further, and came to "the land of the children of the East", where he found a well, as already said, and where he encountered his wife.' Said R. Eleazar: 'That place was assuredly Haran, but the well was in an outlying field, and that is why it says that "Rachel ran and told her father" (Ibid. 12).' R. Eleazar further remarked: 'Since Jacob had to find his wife by the well, why did he not meet there Leah, who was to be the mother of so many tribes? The answer is that it was not the will of God that Leah should be espoused to Jacob openly, and in fact he married her without his knowledge, as it is written: "And it came to pass in the morning that, behold, it was Leah" (Ibid. 25). It was also in order to rivet his eye and heart on the beauty of Rachel, so that he should establish his principal abode with her.

Zohar: Bereshith, Section 1, Page 153b

How did Jacob know that she was Rachel? We must suppose that the shepherds told him, as it is written, "and, behold, Rachel his daughter came with the sheep" (Ibid. 6).' AND HE SAID: I WILL SERVE THEE SEVEN YEARS FOR RACHEL THY YOUNGER DAUGHTER. Why should Jacob have mentioned seven years rather than ten months or one year? For one thing, Jacob did not want people to say that he lusted after Rachel's beauty. Also he knew that the wisdom of the moon requires a septennate; and all the seven supernal years hovered over Jacob before he married Rachel, so that his association with her should accomplish its true purpose. For Jacob, before his marriage, first made his own all those years, so that when at last he came to her he should be as it were the heaven to her earth. Hence it says: AND THEY SEEMED UNTO HIM BUT A FEW DAYS. The inner meaning of the word ahadim (few, lit. united) is that all those seven years resembled in his eyes those superior years that are bound together so as to form a complete whole and an inseparable unity. The verse continues: FOR THE LOVE HE HAD FOR HER, that is, his desire to reproduce the supernal pattern. R. Abba said: 'Jacob assuredly served seven years in order to join himself to the Sabbatical Year.' R. Eleazar said: 'Observe that the Jubilee Year, wherever mentioned, symbolises that which is undisclosed (to the human mind), whereas the Sabbatical Year symbolises the disclosed. So when Jacob had served the first seven years, a voice went forth and said: O Jacob, it is written: "from one world to the other world" (Ps. CVI, 48). The one world is the upper world, which is veiled, the category of the Jubilee Year. From thence is the starting point; for those which are veiled and undisclosed are from the category of the Jubilee Year.' Hence they were hidden from Jacob, who thus mistakenly thought that his own seven years were from the Sabbatical septennate. Their inwardness was hidden from him in order that he should make a beginning from the highest world, from the Jubilee cycle which is undisclosed. And after the years symbolic of the Jubilee cycle, which is undisclosed, had passed, he served the years of the Sabbatical septennate which are disclosed. He was thus crowned with the two worlds and laid hold of both of them.

Observe that Leah bore six sons and one daughter. That was in the order of things, since six world-directions were stationed above her, and so the six sons and one daughter formed a symbol of the grades. Rachel bore two righteous ones, and this was also in order, since the Sabbatical septennate is placed perpetually between two Righteous Ones, as it is written: "The righteous ones shall inherit the land" (Ps. XXXVII, 29), one Righteous One on high and one below. From the one on high there is a flowing out of upper waters, and from the one below there is a reciprocal welling up of water from the female principle toward the male principle in a perfect ecstasy. There are thus a Righteous One on this side and a Righteous One on that side; and as the male principle above is situated between two female principles, so the female principle below is situated between two Righteous Ones. Hence Joseph and Benjamin represent the two Righteous Ones. Joseph merited to be the (symbol of the) Righteous One on high in virtue of his having kept under guard the sign of the holy covenant. Benjamin was the Righteous One below, so that the Sabbatical septennate was crowned between Righteous Ones, to wit, Joseph the righteous and Benjamin the righteous.

It may be asked, was Benjamin indeed a righteous man? Yes, he was, in that he never in his life transgressed in regard to the sign of the holy covenant. It is true, however, that he was never exposed to a temptation like that of Joseph. If so, why was he called righteous? The reason is that during the whole time of Jacob's mourning for the loss of Joseph he abstained from conjugal intercourse. But, it may be said, when Joseph was carried off, was not Benjamin a mere child? What, then, is the point of saying that he abstained from conjugal intercourse? The answer is that he abstained from conjugal intercourse even after he was married. But again we may ask, how is this to be squared with the tradition that Joseph, when he came down to Egypt, asked him whether he had a wife and children, and he answered, "Yes, and they are all named in memory of my brother, to wit, Bela and Becher, and Ashbel, Gera, and Naaman, etc." (Gen. XLVI, 21). How, then, can it be said that he abstained from conjugal relations? The truth, however, is that Benjamin had no children at that time, but he had begotten them already when the brethren went (finally) to Egypt. Benjamin, then, assuredly observed conjugal abstinence all the time his father mourned for Joseph, saying: "Behold, my brother Joseph constituted the sign-of-the-holy-covenant of my father, that sign being the end of the bodily trunk. Now that he is lost I have to guard

Zohar: Bereshith, Section 1, Page 154a

the place of my brother". One may still object that at the time when Joseph was lost Benjamin had not yet proved himself righteous, and he did not, in fact, do so until the time when he withstood temptation. But the truth is that Jacob knew that Joseph would guard that place, and the others obtained that knowledge from Jacob. It was for that reason that he prolonged his stay with Laban until his body, as it were, was made complete, the completion being constituted by the sign of the holy covenant. Hence it is written: "And it came to pass when Rachel had borne Joseph, etc." (Ibid. XXX, 25), Jacob having said to Laban in so many words, "Now that my body has been made complete I am desirous of going." In this way Benjamin knew that his brother was righteous, and he trod in his footsteps. And after Joseph had been found he returned home, had conjugal intercourse, and begat children. God thus declared him righteous here below and Joseph righteous above.

It was thus in the order of things that Rachel bore two sons and Leah six sons and a daughter; and the first seven years were thus veiled from Jacob as they represented the Jubilee cycle; and whilst in intention serving the Sabbatical seven years, which are of the disclosed realm, Jacob in reality served the Jubilee cycle which belongs to the undisclosed realm. So Scripture says: "And Jacob served seven years for Rachel", the term seven years being unqualified, implying that he served for Rachel seven years of the supernal order, and he thus laid hold of both worlds. From here we learn that only through the disclosed can a man reach the undisclosed. If it is asked, how can the first seven years correspond to the Jubilee cycle, seeing that in regard to the latter it is written, "seven times seven years" (Lev. XXV, 8), and here there are no seven times, the answer is that the seven times are represented in the seven days of festivity with which Jacob celebrated his marriage with Leah. The number was thus made complete, since each day may be regarded as sevenfold, in harmony with the verse, "Seven times a day do I praise thee, because of thy righteous ordinances" (Ps. CXIX, 164), and the seven years were thus to be multiplied by the seven days. But, it may be said, Jacob should have first served the Sabbatical septennate and attached himself to the grade of the Sabbatical year. The answer is that since in intention he did serve them, the effect was the same as if he had served them in reality.' R. Abba then came up to R. Eleazar and kissed him, saying: 'Blessed be the Merciful One for the exposition of this verse. Concerning such a privilege, it is written: "The Lord was pleased for his righteousness' sake, to make the Torah great and glorious" (Is. XLII, 21).' R. Eleazar said further:' What has been said about Leah having borne six sons and one daughter and Rachel having borne two sons is assuredly correct; but how do the sons of the concubines fit into the scheme? They constitute, as it were, the four joints, the socalled hinder parts, alluded to in the statement: "and all their hinder parts were inward" (I Kings VII, 25). For the right arm contains three joints, the middle one of which is the largest and projects backwards, being as it were outside the body. There is a similar joint in the left arm, as well as in the right thigh and in the left thigh; and when the whole is properly arranged, all of them look inward, in fulfilment of the statement, "all their hinder parts were inward". Now all the other joints are in the line of the body, but these protrude outside the arms and the thighs. Correspondingly, the sons of the handmaids, although they are within the number, yet are not of the same rank as the sons of Rachel and Leah, and thus remain outside. According to another explanation, these four are the joints by which all the others are moved.' R. Abba remarked: 'So assuredly it is, and thus the whole is properly constructed.' AND THE LORD SAW THAT LEAH WAS HATED. R. Eleazar said: 'It is written: "Who sets aright the foundation ('aqereth, lit. barren woman) of the house, a joyful mother of children. Hallelukah" (Ps. CXIII, 9). "The foundation of the house" is an allusion to Rachel, whereas by "a joyful mother of children" is meant Leah. According to another explanation, the "foundation of the house" is an allusion to the Sabbatical year, which constitutes the basis of this world; and "a joyful mother of children" signifies the Jubilee year, on which depend the joy and gladness of all the worlds; and this verse comprehends them all in a sacred symbolism, and hence the concluding word, "Hallelukah". We can now understand why it says here that "Leah was hated". This seems strange, in view of the fact that children of a hated woman are of a

187

low type, whereas all Leah's children were of a high type. But the truth is that the Jubilee is a veiled world nothing of which

is disclosed to human intelligence; hence Jacob was wholly unaware of it. Now the lower world is intelligible, and is the starting point for the ascending grades. Just as the Supernal Wisdom is a starting point of the whole, so is the lower world also a manifestation of Wisdom, and a starting point of the whole. This world, therefore, is named "Thou" (attah), being symbolic of the Sabbatical year, and is intelligible, whereas the upper world, symbolic of the Jubilee, is named He (hu'=he, or it), as it is wholly veiled from human understanding. Hence there is an inner significance in the words "and he lay with her that (hu') night". Hence, too, it is written: "And the Levite shall serve hu (him)" (Num. XVIII, 23), so as to draw blessings forevery one from it, namely from the upper world, which remains forever veiled. Jacob, however, had no mind to attach himself to the undisclosed, but only to the disclosed, in harmony with the recondite meaning of the verse, "and he shall cleave to his wife" (Gen. II, 25). Also, from the words: "And the Lord saw that Leah was hated" we may learn that a man is not naturally tempted by his mother, and that hence he may remain alone with his mother in any place whatever without any scruple. Observe that it was for the sake of Jacob that the world became firmly established. (For though we have said elsewhere that it was for the sake of Abraham, the truth is that it was for the sake of Jacob that Abraham was firmly established, as it is written: "Thus saith the Lord, concerning the house of Jacob who redeemed Abraham" (Is. XXIX, 22).) For at first God built up worlds and destroyed them, and only when Jacob came did the worlds take their final form, and were not again demolished as heretofore. So Scripture says: "But now thus saith the Lord that created thee, O Jacob, and he that formed thee, O Israel" (Is. XLIII, 1). Israel is also called "son" to God, as it is written: "Israel is my son, my firstborn", also, "Let my son go that he may serve me" (Ex. IV, 22-23). There is also the same allusion in the verse: "What is his name, and what is his son's name, if thou knowest" (Prov. XXX, 4).' AND SHE CALLED HIS NAME REUBEN (lit. see, a son). She did not give him a more specific name, because he was to form a group with the other two, Simeon and Levi. The name Levi, being akin to the term loyoth (joining) (I Kings VII, 30), signifies the perfect combination of them into one scheme. R. Judah said that the same idea is implied in the phrase: "The excellency of dignity, and the excellency of power" (Gen. XLIX, 3), which is rendered in the Chaldaic paraphrase: "Birthright, priesthood, and kingdom", kingdom belonging to the side of power (Geburah). Hence the name Reuben, implying "son" (ben), simply. R. Abba said that the birth of that triad, as implied in the name Reuben, was the goal towards which Leah strove, as indicated in her utterance: "Now this time will my husband be joined unto me, because I have borne him three sons" (Gen. XXIX, 34), that is, three joined together as one. Observe now that the Heavenly Throne consists of our three patriarchs, to whom King David was subsequently joined, making together a tetrad, symbolic of the Divine Tetragrammaton. Correspondingly we have Reuben, Simeon, and Levi, to whom later on there was joined Judah, who inherited the kingship. Hence the significance of the passage: "This time will I praise the Lord. Therefore she called his name Judah. And she left off bearing", the reason being that now all the four supports of the Heavenly Throne were completed. (Why did she say: "this time will I praise the Lord" in regard to this son and not in regard to any of the others? The truth is that we learn from here that as long

as the Community of Israel is in exile the Divine Name remains incomplete.) Observe that with the birth of three sons the Heavenly Throne was not yet made complete until Judah was born; hence only then Leah said, "This time will I praise the Lord", and not in regard to any of the other sons; and hence again the term vatha'amod (and she left off, lit. stood), implying that the Heavenly Throne stood then firm on its supports. (This term also indicates that up to that point there is unity, but below that is the world of separation.) As for the two other sons born subsequently with the same characteristics, these were united with the others, constituting together a unity symbolic of the six directions of the world.

Observe further that all the twelve tribes are the integral parts of the Community of Israel in this world, to give full strength to the supernal light, enveloped in blackness, and restore the root principle of the Whole to its place. All the worlds are built on the same pattern; and through this relation the lower world was completed on the pattern of the upper world. By the birth of Issachar and Zebulun there was made complete the number six, symbolic of the six directions of the world. Then again the four sons of the handmaids were associated with them, they being, as it were, the four joints that were linked with them, as already explained. So Scripture says of them: "and their hinder parts were inward" (I Kings VII, 25), to wit, although they were the sons of the handmaids, yet they belonged inward. R. Hizkiah said: 'We have affirmed that what the lower world produces belongs to the category of separation, as it is written "and from thence it was parted" (Gen. II, 11). If so, what about Joseph and Benjamin? How can you say that they belonged to the same world as the others, since they did not issue from the upper world, and what the lower world brings forth is for the lower world and not for the upper world; and, if so, they are separated from the others, since it has been laid down that whatever the lower world produces belongs to the category of separation.' R. Abba came up and kissed him and said:

'This is a real difficulty, since it is true that the upper world becomes perfected by the twelve which properly belong to it. But it can be solved esoterically as follows. At every moment the Righteous One both leaves and enters the lower world. Hence he is built up in this place, while his root is above. Thus he is always present in the lower world.

Zohar: Bereshith, Section 1, Page 155b

It is written: "And it came to pass as her soul (nafshah) was in departing, for she died" (Gen. XXXV, 18). Now the Righteous One is both in and out of this lower world. When he enters it he does so as symbolised by Joseph the righteous; and when he leaves it he does so as symbolised by Benjamin. Hence it says in connection with the birth of Benjamin: "And it came to pass as her soul (nafshah) was in departing-for she died", where "her soul" alludes to the Righteous One that was departing, to wit, Benjamin. She called him Ben-oni (son of my sorrow), thinking that what she bore belonged to the lower world, the world of separation, thus leaving only eleven as belonging to the upper world. His father, however, called him Benjamin (son of the right hand) (Ibid.), implying that he ascended on high to the upper world; for when Joseph disappeared Benjamin took his place. Thus did the Righteous One both enter the lower world and leave it. Hence Joseph and Benjamin and all the others completed the number of twelve, who formed a unity after the supernal pattern.' THIS TIME WILL I PRAISE THE LORD. R. Simeon adduced here the verse: "I will praise the Lord with my whole heart (lebab), with the council of the upright, and with the congregation" (Ps. CXI, 1). 'The intensified form lebab (heart) is used here', he said, 'to show that David desired to praise the Lord with his whole being, including both his good prompter (yetser-tob) and his evil prompter (yetser-ra'), or, in other terms, the right side and the left side, the heart (lebab), being symbolic of South and North. By the phrase "with the council of the upright" David implied the other directions, making up the six directions of the world, after the supernal pattern; "the congregation" is a reference to the realm of Judah, the term 'edah (congregation) being akin to the term 'eduth (testimony) in the passage, "and my testimony (ve-'edothi) that I shall teach them" (Ps. CXXXII, 13), as well as to the vocable 'od (yet) in the passage, "but Judah yet ('od) ruleth with God, etc." (Hos. XII, 1). On the other hand, in the verse: "I will praise thee with my whole heart (libi) toward Elohim will I sing praise unto thee" (Ibid. CXXXVIII, 1), David addressed himself to one single realm, designated Elohim [Tr. note: The grade Malkuth, or Kingdom.], singing praises to the grade associated with the right side. Observe that Judah embraced all sides, having taken hold of the South as well as of the East; himself issuing from the left side, with his beginning in the North, he took hold of the South, since his turnings were to the right, and attached himself to the body. Hence Leah's words: "This time I will praise the Lord." The words, "And she stood still not to bear any more" imply that there was now a firm standing, that all was now in order, since the Heavenly Throne was now (with the birth of Judah) made complete.'

R. Simeon was once walking in the country when he met R. Abba and R. Hiya and R. Yose. When he saw them he said: 'We ought to have here some new expositions of the Torah. So the three of them sat down for a time. When he was about to go, each one of them in turn discoursed on a Scriptural text. R. Abba took the verse: And the Lord said unto Abram, after that Lot had separated from him: Lift up now thine eyes, etc. (Gen. XIII, 14). 'Did Abraham then', he asked, 'inherit only so much of land as was within his range of vision and no more -a mere three, four, or, at most, five parasangs? This would contradict the next verse saying: "for all the land which thou seest to thee I will give it" (Ibid. 15). But the truth is that in surveying the four directions of the world he saw the whole land, since the four directions embrace the whole world. Furthermore, God raised him high above the Land of Israel

Zohar: Bereshith, Section 1, Page 156a

and made him see how it is bound up with the four cardinal points. Abram thus looked over the whole of the land. In a similar way, whoever sees R. Simeon sees the whole world, sees the delight of the upper world and the lower world.' R. Hiya followed with the text: "The land whereon thou liest, to thee will I give it, and to thy seed" (Gen. XXVIII, 13). 'Did God, then', he asked, 'promise him no more than that spot, a mere four or five cubits? The truth, however, is that God at that moment folded up the whole of the land of Israel within those four cubits, so that that spot comprised the whole land. Now, if the whole land can be so concentrated, how much more truly may it be said that R. Simeon, who is the light of the world, is of equal worth with the whole world!' R. Yose then took the passage: "This time will I praise the Lord." 'Was it not', he asked, 'equally incumbent on her to praise God for the birth of her other sons? But the truth is that Judah, in virtue of being the fourth son, was the completion of the Heavenly Throne. Judah alone is thus the mainstay of the Heavenly Throne and is its truest support. For this very reason, moreover, was he called Judah (YHVDH), a word which contains the Divine Name with the addition of the letter Daleth (four), pointing to the four supports of the Heavenly Throne. With how much greater force can this be said of R. Simeon, who illumines the whole world with the light of the Torah, and who kindles the light of many lamps!' AND REUBEN WENT IN THE DAYS OF WHEAT HARVEST, AND FOUND MANDRAKES IN THE FIELD. R. Isaac discoursed on the verse: How manifold are thy works, O Lord! In wisdom hast thou made them all; the earth is full of thy creatures (Ps. CIV, 24). 'Who', he said, 'can count the works of the Almighty, inasmuch as there are hosts upon hosts, and legions upon legiouls of beings, each differing f rom the other, al l existing simultaneously? For just as the one hammer-blow causes sparks to fly off in all directions, so God brought into being simultaneously manifold species and hosts, each differing from the other, without number. The world was brought into being by a word and a breath together, as it is written: "By the word of the Lord were the heavens made, and all the host of them by the breath of his mouth" (Ps. XXXIII, 6). One is inoperative without the other, but from their combined action there came into being hosts upon hosts and legions upon legions, and all simultaneously. Now when God was about to create the world, He produced a secret spark from which there issued and radiated all the lights which are disclosed. First there spread from it those lights which constitute the upper world. Then it continued its radiation, and the Artificer made it into a light without brightness, and thus He made the lower world. And by reason of its being a light, but without illumination, it feels itself attracted towards

Zohar: Bereshith, Section 1, Page 156b

the upper world. Now it is that light without illumination which through its attachment to the upper world brought into being all those legions and hosts of existences, all the multitudinous species, of which it is written, "How manifold are thy works, etc." And whatever is on earth has its counterpart on high, there being no object, however small, in this world but what is subordinate to its counterpart above which has charge over it; and so whenever the thing below bestirs itself, there is a simultaneous stimulation of its counterpart above, as the two realms form one interconnected whole. This may be illustrated from the verse: GIVE ME, I PRAY THEE, OF THY SON'S MANDRAKES. It was not the mandrakes that made Rachel bear children, but God used them as an instrument for procuring the birth of a child, Issachar, who should hold fast to the Torah more than all the other tribes. For Rachel at first held fast to Jacob and did not let him go to Leah, as it is written: "Is it a small matter that thou hast taken away my husband?" But afterwards Rachel said: "Therefore he shall lie with thee to-night for thy son's mandrakes." Thus the mandrakes were responsible for the birth of Issachar, through whom the fragrance of the Torah ascended to the presence of the Almighty, in harmony with the words: "The mandrakes give forth fragrance" (S. S. VII, 14); and thus it is further written: AND HE LAY WITH HER THAT (hu) NIGHT, where the term hu (he) points assuredly to Him of the supernal world, which, as already explained, is hidden absolutely. For the Torah came forth from the upper world, which is everywhere pointed to by the vocable hu (He), indicating a realm undisclosed. Now Issachar took hold of the Torah, which is called the tree of life, meaning life of the upper world, which is called hu (he) and not attah (thou). It is clear that it was not the mandrakes that opened Rachel's womb, seeing that it is written "and God hearkened to her, and opened her womb"-God, and no other. For although the mandrakes are endowed with a certain power above, yet that power cannot influence the birth of children, inasmuch as children depend on fate (mazzal) and nothing else. However, the mandrakes also are a help to

Zohar: Bereshith, Section 1, Page 157a

women who are slow in child-bearing but not barren, the latter being under the influence of mazzal.' AND LEAH WENT OUT TO MEET HIM, AND SAID: THOU MUST COME IN UNTO ME, ETC. This language appears on the surface to be immodest, but really it is a proof of Leah's modesty that she said nothing in the presence of her sister, but went out to meet Jacob, and there told him in a low tone that, though he properly belonged to Rachel, yet I HAVE SURELY HIRED THEE, and have obtained permission from Rachel; and in order that he might not become confused in the sight of Rachel, she spoke to him outside and not in the house. Moreover, one door of Leah's tent faced on the road, and she brought him in by that door before he could enter into the tent of Rachel, so that she should not say anything in the presence of Rachel, which would have been immodest. She further reflected that should Jacob once enter Rachel's tent, it would not be right for her to make him leave it; she therefore intercepted him outside. Leah went to all this trouble because the Holy Spirit stirred within her, and she knew that all those holy tribes would issue from her; and she thus hastened the hour of union in her loving devotion to God, and under the same inspiration she called them by names with deep symbolical meanings.

As R. Hiya and R. Yose were once walking on the road, the latter said: 'Every time we walk together and discuss matters pertaining to the Torah, God performs for us miracles, and now that we have a long road before us let us occupy ourselves in the Torah and so God will join us.' R. Hiya then opened with the verse: In the first month, on the fourteenth day of the month at even, ye shall eat unleavened bread (Ex. XII, 18). 'This unleavened bread', he said, 'is called in another place "bread of affliction" (Deut. XVI, 3), an expression on which the companions have commented as follows. When Israel were in Egypt they were under an alien power; and when God desired to bring them near unto Himself, He assigned them the region of the bread of 'oni (affliction), the term 'oni admitting also of the reading 'ani (poor), and thus pointing to King David, who said of himself: "for I am poor ('ani) and needy" (Ps. LXXXVI, 1). Now this bread of affliction is called mazzah (unleavened bread), symbolic of the female principle, which without the male principle is, so to speak, in poverty. Thus Israel were first brought near the grade symbolised by mazzah. But afterwards God caused them to enter other grades, until the male principle joined the female principle, and so mazzah received the addition of the letter vau, symbolic of the male principle, and became converted into mizvah (command, precept). So Scripture says: "For this commandment" (Deut. XXX, 7): first mazzah (unleavened bread), then mizvah (commandment).'

Whilst they were going along they heard a voice saying: 'Ye tent-dwellers who take a crooked path, turn to the high ground and do not descend by the path leading downwards.' R. Yose said: 'This proves that God is guarding our way.' They then took the mountain path and ascended a hill that was situated between huge rocks, saying to themselves: 'Since God desires us to take this road, we are sure to see something of note, or experience some miracle.' They went on and sat down by a cleft in the rock, and were amazed to see a man suddenly emerge from it. 'Who art thou?' said R. Yose. 'I belong to the denizens of Arfa,' he answered. 'Are there human beings there?' they asked. 'Yes,' he answered, 'and they sow and reap. Some of them are of a strange appearance, different from my own; and the reason I ascended to you is to learn from you the name of the earth wherein ye dwell.' 'This earth', R. Yose replied, 'is called erez, namely, the erez (land) of life, of which it is written: "As for the earth (erez), out of it cometh bread" (Job XXVIII, 5), implying that only out of this earth cometh bread, but not out of any other, or if it does come, it is not bread of any of the seven kinds.' The man thereupon returned to his place, leaving them astonished. They said: 'Assuredly, God wishes to recall something to our minds through this incident.' R. Hiya then said: 'Assuredly so. Now in regard to the verse you have just cited, I remember that my grandfather pointed out to me an excellent idea in connection with the unleavened bread, namely, that God first gave Israel that bread from the land of life and afterwards He gave them bread from heaven; and so we have affirmed. He further said that a

Zohar: Bereshith, Section 1, Page 157b

man born into this world knows nothing until he tastes bread, and only then is there an awakening in him of intelligence and power of discernment. In the same way, when Israel left Egypt they were devoid of all knowledge until God made them taste bread of that earth called erez, of which it says: "As for the earth (erez), bread cometh of it'" Then Israel began to know and to recognise God. God, however, desired that they should know also of that place which is the fitting counterpart of this earth, but they were not able to do so until they tasted bread from that place, to wit, heaven, as it says: "I will cause to rain bread from heaven for you" (Ex. XVI, 4). It was only then that they attained to a knowledge and a vision of that realm. ' R. Yose came up to R. Hiya and kissed him, saying: 'Assuredly this was the reflection of which God desired to remind us. We learn, then, that the preliminary to Israel's knowledge was bread.' They then arose and proceeded on their way. Whilst walking they noticed two Damascene plums, a male and a female, which led R. Yose to remark: 'There is no species which is not divided into male and female. Further, whatever being exists on dry land has its counterpart in the sea.'

R. Yose discoursed on the verse: AND JACOB CAME FROM THE FIELD IN THE EVENING, AND LEAH WENT OUT TO MEET HIM. 'According to tradition,' he said, 'she knew of his coming through the braying of an ass, and hence Scripture says: "Issachar is an ass large-boned" (Gen. XLIX, 14), where the word garem (large-boned) can also be read garam (he caused), signifying that the ass was a cause of his birth. Leah said to herself: I assuredly know that should Jacob once enter Rachel's tent I shall not be able to get him out again. I will therefore await him here so that he may enter my tent. FOR I HAVE SURELY HIRED THEE WITH MY SON'S MANDRAKES. She mentioned the mandrakes to Jacob, because she thought this would predispose him in her favour, on account of their efficacy for childbirth. Jacob, however, knew that it did not depend on the mandrakes but on heaven. By the words "for I have surely hired thee", Leah may have referred to the Torah, which Jacob embodied. Or she may have meant literally his own self, as much as to say:

Zohar: Bereshith, Section 1, Page 158a

"I have hired thee so that I may bear thy very image." From here we learn that whoever studies diligently the Torah inherits the world to come and the inheritance of Jacob. For the name Issachar may be divided into the two words yesh sakher (there is a reward), found in the verse: "there is a reward to thy work" (Jer. XXXI, 16), and again: "There is (yesh) an inheritance for those that love me, and I will fill their treasures" (Prov. VIII, 21).' BECAUSE I HAVE BORNE HIM SIX SONS. R. Hizkiah said: 'The six sons prefigured the upward and downward and the four directions of space, and the purpose of prolonging the word ehad (in reciting the Shema) is to acclaim God as King on high and below and in the four directions of the world, and so truly one.'

R. Hizkiah further said: 'A distinction is to be drawn between "mountains of separation" (S. S. II, 17) and "mountains of spices" (Ibid. YllI, 14). The latter are typified by the six sons of Leah, who included within themselves the other six sons, thus constituting all the twelve, with Leah presiding, as it were, over them, in fulfilment of the passage: "the mother of the children is joyful. Praise ye the Lord" (Ps. CXIII, 9). It is therefore written "thou shalt not take the dam with the young" (Deut. XXII, 6), for the reason that she represents the undisclosed world, and hence: "thou shalt in any wise let the dam go, but the young thou mayest take unto thyself" (Ibid. 7), inasmuch as she symbolises the world that is absolutely concealed, while "the young thou mayest take unto thyself" in harmony with the verse: "For ask now of the days past, etc., and from the one end of heaven unto the other" (Ibid. IV, 22). Now, all these are called "mountains of spices", whereas all which is underneath is called "the mountains of separation", in allusion to the passage: "and from thence it was parted and became four heads" (Gen. II. 10).' R. Jesse said: 'The sons of the handmaids represented the four joints which were necessary for the perfecting of the whole.' R. Eleazar remarked: 'It was for that reason that these joints project outwards, despite the fact that they are all organic parts of the body, which otherwise is perfectly straight; and thus all the tribes ascend as a testimony on high, as Scripture says: "Whither the tribes went up, even the tribes of the Lord, as a testimony unto Israel, to give thanks unto the name of the Lord" (Ps. CXXII, 4).' R. Eleazar further cited the verse: AND IT CAME TO PASS WHEN RACHEL HAD BORNE JOSEPH, ETC. 'With the birth of Joseph, Jacob saw that the adversary of Esau had appeared, and he therefore made ready to depart. Observe further that Joseph gave, as it were, fixity to Jacob, corresponding to the Zaddik in whom the Body ends, and so he merited in particular to be called righteous. So when Jacob saw that the Body was made complete, his body conceived the desire to depart, the completion of the body being the sign of the covenant. But for all that it was Benjamin who completed the number of the twelve tribes. Why, then, it may be asked, did Jacob, knowing that the number of the tribes was not yet full, not wait for the birth of Benjamin to complete the number? The reason is that Jacob was guided by a further consideration. "It is clear", he said, "that if the number of the tribes will be completed here, then divine perfection will rest upon them in the appropriate manner; but in this land it is not desirable that they should attain perfection, but only in the Holy Land." The proof that all the twelve tribes together effect the full realisation of the lower world is to be seen in the fact that immediately Benjamin was born Rachel died, and this lower world fell into its proper place, and attained through them perfect realisation. Hence Benjamin had to be born in the Holy Land and not elsewhere. So Scripture says: "And as for me, when I came from Paddan, Rachel died unto me in the land of Canaan" (Gen. XLVIII, 7). Rachel thus died there, and her place was filled by this lower world, which assumed its rightful place in a completed House. But as long as Rachel was alive the lower world could not be made perfected through them. If it is asked why Leah did not die at the same time, the answer is that the House was in the lower world, and from it all were to be brought to full self-realisation, but it was not in the upper world. This was the reason that Leah did not die at that time. Moreover, all that concerned Leah is kept under a veil, as she typified the upper world, which is veiled and undisclosed; and this is another reason why Leah's death is not divulged like that of Rachel. It is in accordance, too, with this difference between the upper and the lower worlds that Leah was buried away fro n sight in the cave of Machpelah; whereas Rachel was buried by the open road. Hence it is that all blessings are from two worlds, the disclosed and the undisclosed, though the whole originates from the upper world; [Note: The last 3 lines of the Hebrew text do not appear in our translation.]

Zohar: Bereshith, Section 1, Page 158b

and when we offer blessings to God we invariably associate Him with the two worlds in such words as: "Blessed be the Lord, the God of Israel, from one world even unto the other world" (Ps. CVI, 48). It is for this reason that the upper world is named Hu (He), whereas the lower world is named Attah (Thou), because it is blessed from the upper world through the Righteous One. Thus Scripture says: "Blessed be the Lord out of Zion, who dwelleth in Jerusalem, etc." (Ps. CXXXV, 21): assuredly it is out of Zion that He is blessed. Observe that we similarly find the divine Name repeated twice in: "The Lord, the Lord... merciful and gracious" (Ex. XXIV, 6), alluding to the two worlds, the hidden and the revealed; and this explains the tonal pause between the two. But for all that, the one world and the other form together an absolute unity.' AND IT CAME TO PASS, WHEN RACHEL HAD BORNE JOSEPH, ETC. R. Judah said: 'Jacob, as a straightforward man, did not wish to leave save by the permission of Laban. In the end, it is true, he did depart without asking Laban's permission, but this was because he feared that Laban would not let him go, and in consequence the last of the twelve tribes would be born in an alien land. Hence, when he saw that the time had come for Benjamin to be born, he fled, as it is written: SO HE FLED WITH ALL THAT HE HAD. For as soon as Benjamin was born, the Shekinah attached herself to the company of the tribes and made her home with them. And Jacob, through his knowledge of the mystic symbolism, was aware that as soon as the twelve tribes should be complete the Shekinah would make them her adornment and attach herself to them, and that Rachel would die and the Shekinah would take possession of the House. Our tradition tells us that the lower world was assigned to Jacob in the same way as it was later to Moses, but this could not be accomplished until there were the full twelve tribes in the House to whom the Shekinah could attach herself. It was then that Rachel was removed, and the Shekinah took up her abode in the House with all the tribes, and become the foundation of the House. Assuredly, "He sets in her place the foundation of the House" (Ps. CXIII, 9). Jacob thus said: "The time has now arrived for the number of the twelve tribes to be completed, so that the upper world will be due to descend into the House to become attached to them, and this poor woman (Rachel) will be thrust out to make room for it. Should she die here, I shall never be able to get away. Moreover, this is not the land where it is fitting that the House should be made complete." Hence AND IT CAME TO PASS, ETC.' R. Simeon, on hearing all this exposition, said: 'Assuredly all R. Judah's expositions are excellent, but this excels them all. Jacob might indeed have departed at once, but he delayed until Rachel was pregnant with Benjamin. Then he fled without asking permission, so as not to linger there any more and so that his union with all the tribes might be effected in the fitting place.'

R. Abba said: 'We read of Moses that "he went and returned to Jethro his father-in-law, etc." (Ex. IV, 18). Now Moses, who was the shepherd of Jethro's flock and lived with him as Jacob with Laban, when he wished to go away first obtained his permission; why, then, did not Jacob, being so upright a man, obtain permission from Laban before leaving him? The truth is, as tradition teaches us, that Jacob feared lest Laban might employ all sorts of devices to make him remain with him longer, as he had done at first. Moses, however, had nothing of the kind to fear from Jethro. Laban was a magician, and in all his dealings with Jacob used magical arts. But Jacob did not wish to remain there any longer, since God had said to him: "Return unto the land of thy fathers, etc." (Gen. XXXI, 3). Jacob thus did not wish to stay and transgress the command of his Master.'

R. Abba further discoursed on the verse: For the Leader; of the sons of Korah, upon Alamoth. A song (Ps. XLVI, 1). 'This verse,' he said, 'if properly considered, will be found to contain a deep mystical allusion. And, indeed, all the songs and hymns sung by the sons of Korah were ancient songs and hymns sung anew; and all the songs and hymns sung by David and his associates contain deep allusions of wisdom. Now God has made the lower world after the pattern of the upper world, and all the arrangements laid down by David and Solomon and by all the true prophets were

Zohar: Bereshith, Section 1, Page 159a

after the supernal pattern. Observe that in the same manner as there are watches of the night on earth, so are there in heaven relays of angels who sing praises to their Master and intone hymns continually; they all stand ranged in rows, facing each other, and producing one harmony of song and praise. Thus the companions have interpreted the phrase "upon Alamoth. A song". The term "Alamoth", according to them, has a meaning similar to its homonym in the verse: "There are threescore queens, and fourscore concubines, and maidens ('alamoth) without number" (S. S. VI, 8), whilst the phrase "without number" finds its echo in the passage: "Is there any number in his armies?" (Job XXV, 3). Hence "maidens without number" all standing in rows upon rows, facing each other, to sing hymns and praises to their Master. These are called "the maidens of song" because there are other maidens who do not chant hymns like these. There are three orders (of singers) arrayed on each one of the four sides of the world, and each order again is subdivided into three sub-orders. l'he first order on the East contains thus three orders each with three sub-orders, amounting altogether to nine, each of which comprises thousands and tens of thousands of angels. All these nine orders are guided by a signal of engraved letters to which they constantly look up The same procedure is followed by the rest of the orders, all of whom are similarly guided by engraved letters. Furthermore, they are arrayed in a series of ranks one above the other, all of them chanting praises in unison; and when those letters soar high in the air the chief of them gives the command and a melodious chanting is raised. Then one letter flies up from the lower world, rising and descending, until two letters fly down to meet it; they then join together into a group of three, corresponding to the letters YHV, which are the three letters within the "illuminating mirror". The two supernal letters which rise aloft are intertwined the one within the other, expressing the union of mercy and severity. Hence they are two, and are of the upper world, symbolising the male principle. On the other hand, the one that ascended from below and joined them symbolises the female principle, and thus is embraced by the two, in the same way as the female is embraced by two arms, the right and the left, so that a unity is formed which is both male and female. For when the world was created it was the supernal letters that brought into being all the works of the lower world, literally after their own pattern. Hence, whoever has a knowledge of them and is observant of them is beloved both on high and below.' R. Simeon said: 'All these letters consist of male and female merging together into one union, symbolical of the upper waters and the lower waters, which also form one union. This is the type of perfect unity. Hence, whoever has a knowledge of them and is observant of them, happy is his portion in this world and in the world to come; as therein is contained the root principle of true and perfect unity. Now, the three orders on each side act in perfect unison, being truly symbolical of the supernal order. The second order on the South consists also of three orders each with three sub-orders, forming a total of nine, as said above. As for the letters, they are distributed on all the sides, so as to become united later, inasmuch as there are letters of the female principle and letters of the male principle, the two classes of which come together to form a unity symbolical of the mystery of the complete divine Name. The third order on the North also comprises three orders each with three sub-orders, amounting to nine. The total number of orders on all three sides thus amounts to twenty-seven,

Zohar: Bereshith, Section 1, Page 159b

corresponding to the twenty-seven letters, inclusive of the five final letters. These twenty-seven letters distributed over the three sides consist of nine letters of the female principle which join and become united with the other eighteen letters, as has been explained, all being carried out in proper order. Observe that after the pattern of the supernal letters there are other letters here below, the upper letters being large ones and the lower letters small ones, but both of the same pattern. And they both contain the mystery of the male principle and the female principle, which together form a perfect unity.' AND GOD (Elohim) REMEMBERED RACHEL.

The name Elohim is used here because Rachel was still dependent upon a "lucky star", and therefore also the term remembering (zakhar) is used here. Of Sarah, however, it is written that "the Lord visited (paqad) her" (Gen. XXI, 1), because she did not depend on a lucky star, and so in her case all forces were combined. The reason why in her case the term "visiting" (paqad) is used, is that "remembering" had already preceded, and the key to child-birth had already been handed over, as it were, to the lower-world force, God having declared: "But my covenant will I establish with

Isaac, whom Sarah shall bear unto thee at this time, etc." (Ibid. XVII, 21). Since, then, Isaac had been "remembered" in the higher sphere, he now was noticed within the sphere of the female principle under the process of "visiting", so as to effect a unity of both forces. R. Hiya here discoursed on the verse: And moreover I have heard the groaning of the children of Israel, whom the Egyptians keep in bondage; and I have remembered my covenant (Ex. VI, 5). 'The expression "remembering" is used here', he said, 'because it was a process taking place on high, above the starry course (mazzal), and in virtue of the male principle, coming on top of the process of "visiting", which operates in exile, here below, in virtue of the female principle. In a similar sense it is written: "And God remembered Rachel", which has a meaning similar to that of the passage "and I remembered my covenant". Now, if we say that the term "visiting" is used only of the female principle (the Shekinah), we are met with a difficulty in the text: "I have surely visited you". For how could the Shekinah speak thus, seeing that she was herself in exile, and, in fact, how could she appear to Moses at all? But in truth there is a deep significance in this passage. For as the sun, although his centre is in heaven, yet spreads his power and might throughout the earth, so that the whole earth is full of his glory, so, as long as the Temple was in existence, the whole earth, to wit, the Holy Land, was full of God's glory; but now that Israel is in exile, the Shekinah is on high, but still her might surrounds Israel so as to shield them, even when they are in a strange land. For the Shekinah is both here below and on high. The Shekinah on high abides in the twelve holy chariots and the twelve supernal Hayyoth; the lower Shekinah is among the twelve holy tribes, and thus the upper Shekinah and the lower Shekinah are intertwined, and both operate together and simultaneously. Now, when Israel is in exile, the upper Shekinah is not complete because the lower Shekinah is not complete, and that is what is meant by the Shekinah being in exile when Israel is in exile. It is like a king who has lost a son, and who as a sign of his mourning turns over his couch and spreads thistles and thorns on its underside and then lays himself down on it. Similarly when Israel went into exile and the Temple was destroyed, God took thorns and thistles and put them underneath Him, as it were, as it is written: "And the angel of the Lord appeared unto him in a flame of fire out of the midst of a thorn-bush" (Ex. III, 2), the reason being that Israel was in exile. It was now "visiting", as the "remembering" had taken place already, as it says: "And I remembered my covenant." First, then, there was a "remembering", which was now followed by a "visiting",

Zohar: Bereshith, Section 1, Page 160a

the "visiting" completing the previous "remembering". Similarly with Sarah it says: "And the Lord visited Sarah." But here in the case of Rachel, since she had not yet been "remembered" before, it does not say "visited" but "remembered", a term concerned with luck or fate (mazzal).'

R. Judah and R. Hizkiah were once going from Cappadocia to Lydia, the former riding whilst the latter was on foot. R. Judah dismounted and said: 'From now onward let us occupy ourselves with expositions of the Torah, in harmony with the injunction: "Ascribe ye greatness unto our God" (Deut. XXXII, 3).' Said R. Hizkiah: 'It is a pity we are not three, as then one could have expounded while the other two chimed in.' R. Judah rejoined: 'This only applies to the recital of benedictions, one mentioning the name of the Holy One, blessed be He, and the other two responding, in harmony with the verse: "When I proclaim the name of the Lord, ascribe ye greatness unto our God" (Ibid.); but in regard to the Torah, even two may sit together and praise the Almighty for the great boon of the Torah.' R. Hizkiah then asked: 'Why are three required for the recital of benedictions?' His companion replied: 'I have just explained, but in truth there is a mystic virtue in the number three for pronouncing the praises of the Almighty, as in this way the blessings are established through a supernal symbolism.' Whilst they were proceeding on their way, R. Judah said: 'We have learned that there is a remembering for good and a remembering for evil; a visiting for good and a visiting for evil. Examples of remembering for good are: "But I will for their sakes remember the covenant of their ancestors" (Lev. XXVI, 45); "And God remembered Noah" (Gen. VIII, 1); "And God remembered his covenant" (Ex. II, 24). An example of remembering for evil is: "So he remembered that they were but flesh" (Ps. LXXVIII, 39). Visiting for good we find in: "I have surely visited you" (Ex. III, 16); visiting for evil we find in, "Then will I visit their transgression with the rod, and their iniquity with strokes" (Ps. LXXXIX, 33). In all these verses there are mystic references. All those remembrances and visitations for good refer to grades of the true object of faith embracing male and female, the one under remembrance, the other under visiting, both being for good. Contrariwise, the remembrance and visitation for evil refer to the other side (sitra ahra), with allusions to strange gods, and similarly embracing male and female in one union: the one (male) under remembrance, the other (female) under visitation, both unceasingly intent on evil. There are thus two parallel and opposing influences. From the one there flows all the inspiration of true Faith and all supernal sanctifications; from the other flows whatever is evil, all kinds of death and all sorts and conditions of mischief in the world.' R. Hizkiah said: 'Assuredly it is so. Happy is he whose portion is firmly established on the good side, and who does not incline himself to the other side, but is delivered from them.' Said R. Judah: 'Assuredly it is so, and happy is he who is able to escape that side, and happy are those righteous who are able to wage war against that side.' R. Hizkiah asked: 'How?' R. Judah, in reply, began to discourse on the verse: For by wise guidance thou shalt make thy war, etc. (Prov. XXIV, 6). 'This war', he said, 'alludes to the war against the evil side, which man must combat and overcome, so as to be delivered from it. It was

194

in this way that Jacob dealt with Esau, who was on the other side, so as to outwit him by craft, as was necessary in order to keep the upper hand of him from the beginning to the end, as befitted. Moreover, the beginning and the end fitted into one another, the beginning being "my birthright" (bekhorathi), while the end concerned "my blessing" (birkhothi), so that the two victories were embodied in two vocables of similar sound. Happy thus is he who escapes them and obtains mastery over them. Observe, again, that remembrance and visitation for good go together in the true faith, and happy is he who strives after true faith in accordance with that which is written: "They shall walk after the Lord, who shall roar like a lion, etc." (Hos. XI, 10).' Said R. Hizkiah: 'Assuredly it is so. Observe that when a man prays, he should not say: "O remember me and visit me", since remembrance and visitation can be for evil as well as for

good, and the evil forces are ready to take the word out of the mouth of the suppliant, and thus to make remembrance of the sins of that man and bring punishment on him. Unless, indeed, he be a perfectly righteous man, so that when search is made for his sins he will be unaffected. It was so with Nehemiah when he said: "Remember me, O my God, for good" (Nehem. XIII, 25). Again, when a man prays, it is best that he should merge himself in the general mass of the community. We may take example from the Shunammitess and her answer to Elisha. It happened to be the day of the New-Year on which the heavenly Court sits in judgement over the world, and God is called King of Judgement, when Elisha spoke to her, and hence he asked her: "Wouldst thou be spoken for to the King?" (II Kings IV, 13). But she answered: "I dwell among mine own people" (Ibid.), as much as to say: "I have no desire to be marked out on high, but only to be counted among the multitude, and not to stand out apart from them." It is thus requisite for a man to mingle himself among the mass and not to isolate himself, so that no special notice may be takefl of his sins, as already explained.'

R. Judah discoursed on the verse: Have the gates of death been revealed to thee? Or hast thou seen the gates of the shadow of death? (Job. XXXVIII, 17). 'God', he said, 'addressed these words to Job when He saw him perplexed by the problem of divine justice. Job had said: "Though he slay me, yet will I trust in him (lo) (Ibid. XIII, 15). The word lo is written with an aleph, meaning "not", and is read as with a vau, meaning "in Him". God said in reply to him: "Am I the one that kills the sons of men? Have the gates of death been revealed to thee? And seest thou the gates of the shadows of death? There are ever so many gates open on that side, over which death ruleth, hidden away from the sons of men, who know them not." There are here mentioned both "death" and "the shadow of death". These are a pair, the one being the angel of death, the other his rider, [Tr. note: The grade Geburah.] who also is his protecting shadow and strength, the two being linked together and forming but one being. All the grades that issue from them and are attached to them form their "gates". Corresponding to the gates on high, of which it is written: "Lift up your heads, O ye gates, etc." (Ps. XXIV, 7), and which are called rivers and brooks flowing through the six directions of the world, there are these gates of death and the shadow of death emanating from the other side, forming certain grades that rule over the world. The "gates of death" and the "gates of the shadow of death" are female and male combined into one. Hence, in answer to Job's complaints: "As the cloud is consumed and vanisheth away, so he that goeth down to the grave shall come up no more" (Job VII, 8), and so forth, God said to him: "Are those gates revealed unto thee as being all in my power, and destined one day to be destroyed from off the world, as it is written: 'He shall swallow up death forever'? (Is. XXV, 8.)" ' AND GOD (Elohim) REMEMBERED RACHEL, AND GOD (Elohim) HEARKENED UNTO HER AND OPENED HER WOMB. The name Elohim (God) is mentioned here twice, once to represent the male world and the other the female world, the two having been necessary, since the birth of children depends on fate (mazzal). Now when Rachel was moved to name her son Joseph, saying, "The Lord add to me another son", Jacob knew that it was she that was destined to complete the number of the tribes, whilst she herself would not survive; hence he desired immediately to leave, but he could not carry out his wish. When, however, Benjamin was about to be born, Jacob fled and departed thence, so that the House should not be made complete and the world of holiness become bound up with it in a strange land. So Scripture says: "And the Lord said unto Jacob: Return unto the land of thy fathers, and to thy kindred; and I will be with thee" (Gen. XXXI, 3). God, in effect, said to him: "Until now Rachel was with thee, being the basis of the House; henceforward I will be with thee and will carry on the House with thee in its complement of the twelve tribes". The same idea is implied in the verse: "And as for me, when I came from Paddan, Rachel died unto me ('alai, lit. upon me") (Gen. XLVIII, 7). By the word 'alai (on me) Jacob meant to say, "it was on account of me and through me that she was thrust out and another one came and took over the house so as to inhabit it with me". AND HE SAID: APPOINT (naqebah) ME THE WAGES, AND I WILL GIVE IT. R. Isaac said: The term naquebah (appoint, akin to neqebah=female) signifies that the wicked Laban said to himself, "I see that Jacob has an eye only for females,

for the sake of whom he will serve me." He therefore said in effect: "Behold, a female shall be thy wage as before; tell me on what female thou hast cast thine eyes, and I will give her to thee in return for thy service." AND JACOB SAID: THOU SHALT NOT GIVE ME AUGHT. Jacob practically said: "Far be it from me! For in all my acts I am zealous for the glory of the Holy King, and hence thou shalt not give me aught, as my mind is not set on that, but if thou wilt do this thing for me, etc." · AND HE REMOVED THAT DAY THE HE-GOATS. R. Eleazar quoted here the verse: Lord, who shall sojourn in thy tabernacle.... He that walketh in perfection, and worketh righteousness, and speaketh truth in his heart (Ps. XV, 1-2). '"He that walketh in perfection",' he said, 'refers to Abraham, who, after he had circumcised himself, was called "perfect"; "and worketh righteousness" refers to Isaac; "and speaketh the truth" refers to Jacob, who indeed attached himself to the truth. If that is so, why then did he act towards Laban in this way? The reason is that Jacob wanted to see if the hour was propitious for him, for it is permissible for a man to test his luck before returning to his land. If he finds fortune favourable, well and good; but if not, let him not stir before his luck is in again. It is written: SO SHALL MY RIGHTEOUSNESS WITNESS AGAINST ME HEREAFTER, ETC., for he did not attempt to obtain from Laban anything for nothing, but he acted throughout honestly and uprightly, and, moreover, he asked Laban for permission to depart. Hence Laban himself said: I HAVE OBSERVED THE SIGNS, AND THE LORD HATH BLESSED ME FOR THY SAKE. For Laban tested Jacob by all manner of divinations, and found that he brought him luck; through Jacob he obtained each month a hundred sheep and a hundred lambs and a hundred he-goats more than his flock was wont to produce.' R. Abba said: 'Jacob brought him in a thousand sheep and a thousand lambs and a thousand he-goats extra every month. This is proved by the verse: FOR IT WAS LITTLE WHICH THOU HADST BEFORE I CAME, AND IT HATH INCREASED ABUNDANTLY: AND THE LORD HATH BLESSED THEE FOR MY SAKE. For a blessing from on high never results in less than a thousand of each kind. So that there was a surplus of a thousand in Laban's ewes, and the same in his lambs, and in his goats, until he acquired great wealth, and all through Jacob. But when Jacob came for his recompense, he only obtained ten of each kind, and even this he considered great riches. What a small part then did he take for himself of all that he contributed for the benefit of Laban, and even that he had to force from him, as it were, by means of the rods which he placed against the flock. Observe how Jacob in his simplicity did everything possible to satisfy Laban, and while bringing him all this wealth, he only asked for the spotted and speckled. But for all that Laban consented to this, he would not in the end let him have them, but he took ten of each kind and sent them to him through his sons, saying: "Take these, and whatever they will bear of the sort you said shall be yours." It is thus written: "And your father hath deceived me" (Gen. XXX, 7), and also, "and thou hast changed my wages ten times" (Ibid. 41), the term monim (times, akin to minim--kinds) indicating ten of each kind. So whatever agreement Laban made with Jacob, he went back on his word and took from him everything, until God had compassion on him, so that he wrested what was his own from him by force, as it were.' R. Eleazar remarked that all these verses contain deep lessons, based on what we have learned from tradition, to wit, that some blessings from above are obtained by action, some by speech, and others by devotion. So that whoever wishes to draw down to himself blessings must exercise prayer, which consists of speech and devotion; yet there are blessings that cannot be obtained by prayer, but only by action.

Observe that Jacob, the simple man, acted throughout with wisdom. AND HE SET THE RODS — we read— WHICH HE HAD PEELED OVER AGAINST THE FLOCKS IN THE GUTTERS IN THE WATERING TROUGHS. This was all done with esoteric wisdom so as to draw benedictions from the chief well-spring that waters all the supernal grades which were his lot and portion. The rods were symbolic of the grades embodying judgement, which he had "peeled", that is, the severity of which he had mollified. "In the gutters" (rehatim) finds its echo in the passage: "The king is bound to the gutters (rehatim)" (S. S. VII, 5),

Zohar: Bereshith, Section 1, Page 161b

indicating that the supernal King is tied and bound to those supernal aqueducts whence flow benedictions for all, "Flowing in the watering troughs"; to wit, in the rivers and brooks that flow on until they reach their final reservoir. Again, "where the flocks came to drink" is parallel with the verse: "They give drink to every animal of the field, the wild asses quench their thirst" (Ps. CIV, 11), both alluding to the reservoir, the gathering place of all the waters whereto all resort to drink. "And they were heated" (vayehamnah). When the north wind blows, the waters become frozen, they stop flowing, so that no one comes to drink of them. This is the time when judgement impends over the world, and the cold of the North freezes the waters. But when the south wind arises, the waters become warmer, and, the ice being melted, flow on their way, and all come to drink of them; for the southern warmth having caused the waters to thaw, all come to drink with relish the waters after they have been freed from the icy grip of the North. Thus all that Jacob did contained a deep symbolic purpose. Further it is written: AND JACOB TOOK RODS OF FRESH POPLAR, ETC. R. Eleazar discoursed here on the verse: For the Lord hath chosen Jacob unto himself and Israelfor his own treasure (Ps. CXXXV, 4). 'From the actual words of the original', he said, 'we could not tell whether it was the Lord who chose Jacob or vice-versa. That the former is meant we know from the parallel verse which says: "For the portion of the Lord is his people, Jacob the lot of his inheritance" (Deut. XXXII, 9). Nevertheless, it is also true that Jacob on his part, too, has chosen his heritage and his portion, and, rising above all intermediate grades, has taken for his lot "rods of fresh poplar" (libneh= white), symbolic of the white grade of the Right side, and "of the almond and of the plane-tree", symbolic of the red grade of the Left side; "and peeled with streaks in them", signifying that he removed severity from the Left, and linked the Left with the

Right, while he entered between and laid hold of both of them together, so that there resulted one united blend of two colours, but at the same time "making the white appear", i.e. predominate over the red. Why all this? So as to draw to the grade which was his own portion blessings from the universal well-spring, and to place that grade, which is the third, "in the gutters in the watering-troughs", as has been already explained. Now from these operations of Wisdom blessings flow to the lower world, and all worlds are watered and beatified, as it says: "In the morning he devoureth the prey" (Gen. XLIX, 27), and after that: "and at even he divideth the spoil" (Ibid.), so that the blessings pass

Zohar: Bereshith, Section 1, Page 162a

to all the lower worlds. Jacob, too, took his portion of those blessings that rested upon him in this world, inasmuch as he is the portion and lot of the Holy One, blessed be He.'

R. Jesse the Younger was a frequent visitor at the school of R. Simeon. Referring one day to the verse: "Blessings are upon the head of the righteous" (Prov. X, 6), he asked: 'Why does it say "upon the head of the righteous", and not simply "upon the righteous"?' R. Simeon in answer said: 'This is an allusion to the Holy Crown, as has been explained elsewhere. Or again, the "head of the righteous" can be an allusion to Jacob, who received the blessings and transmitted them to the Righteous One, from whom they were diffused to all sides, so that all worlds were blessed. We have, however, affirmed that "Righteous" is the name given to the place of the covenant whence there issue fountains abroad, and just as the aperture of a wine cask through which the wine is drawn is called the top or head of the cask, so is this spot called "the head of righteous", when it wells forth into the female. Furthermore, whoever succeeds in keeping unsullied the sign of the holy covenant, and observes the precepts of the Torah, is called righteous, and is so called from the crown of his head to the sole of his foot; and when blessings flow into the world they rest upon his head, from whence they are diffused throughout the world, through the medium of the holy and worthy sons whom he brings up.' R. Jesse further cited the verse, I have been young, and now am old; yet have I not seen the righteous forsaken (Ps. XXXVII, 25). 'These words,' he said, 'according to our teaching, were uttered by the Chieftain of the world, who concentrated in them more wisdom than most people would think.' R. Simeon said to him: 'My son, that is quite true, as it deals with the subject of holy union. It is a laudation of this unity, in which day is never found without night, for night is ever found in day. Now the Righteous One holds fast to the upper world and also to the lower world. As for the words "nor his seed begging bread", the meaning is that when the seed flows forward, he does not court the Female, since she abides with him and never parts from him, and hence is ever in a state of readiness for him. For the seed does not flow save when the Female is present,

Zohar: Bereshith, Section 1, Page 162b

and their mutual desires are blended into one indissoluble ecstasy. Hence he has no need to ask for consent.' R. Jesse remarked: 'This surely is not the case during the time of exile.' R. Simeon rejoined: 'As regards the seed it is, since it is written "his seed" but not he himself; that is, the outpouring of the blessings only occurs when there is close union of the female with the male. It may be asked then, does the assertion, "and I have not seen a righteous forsaken" apply to the time of exile? The truth is that the Righteous One is always closely bound to the upper world and so far is never abandoned. Thus at one time, that is, at the time of exile, the Righteous One is not forsaken from the side of the upper world, to which he holds fast, whilst at another time he is not forsaken from the two sides, holding fast to both, the upper and the lower worlds, so that in fact he is never forsaken.'

This Zaddik is also called "the firmament of the heaven" (Gen. I, 17). For there are two similar firmaments, one at the beginning and one at the end of the series of eight. The top one is the eighth firmament, the one in which there are set all the lesser and the greater stars. It is the undisclosed upper firmament which upholds the totality of things and from which all existence flows. This is the eighth firmament counting from below, and is thus the top one and the starting-point from which all things receive their existence. Correspondingly there is an eighth firmament counting from above, in which also are set all stars and lights and lamps. This firmament supports the whole and forms the end of the whole. Thus the top firmament and the end firmament are of the same pattern, forming together the river that flows on perennially so that the end is already enclosed in the beginning. Hence it says: "And God set them in the firmament of heaven." For what purpose? "To give light upon the earth." There is, however, a difference between the two firmaments, for while the upper one sustains and nourishes the upper world in which it is set and all those upper sides, the lower firmament sustains and nurtures the lower world and all those lower sides. It may be asked, what is meant here by the "upper world", seeing that the upper eighth firmament, which is hidden and undiscoverable, is itself the upper world and is so called? But the truth is that while it itself forms the upper world proper, all those that emanate from it are also designated by that name. It is the same with those that emanate from the lower world, they also being designated by its name. Yet all of them form one unity. Blessed be He forever and ever! It is written: The trees of the Lord have their fill, the cedars of Lebanon which he hath planted; Wherein the birds make their nests; as for the stork (hasidah), the fir trees are her house (Ps. CIV, 16-17). The allusion of Lebanon has been explained already elsewhere. The birds also are the two referred to in many places

The Zohar in English

as those from which there emerge hosts of other birds. They themselves, however, are superior, as emanating from Lebanon, which is in the supernal realm. They are hinted at in the words "Laban had two daughters". The "fir-trees" are the six supernal sons, symbolic of the six directions of the world, as already explained elsewhere. In them "the stork has made her house". Why is it called here by the feminine form hasidah (stork, lit. filled with mercy)? The truth is that this upper world is really of the female principle, but we usually give it a masculine name (hesed), inasmuch as in its unfolding it is the source whence all beneficence and all light come forth. And thus, as it is hasidah, there springs from it hesed (mercy), which is the primordial light referred to in the statement: "And God said, Let there be light" (Gen. I, 3). It is thus that region of which it says: "fir-trees are her house", where the word beroshim (fir-trees) may be read berashim (at the heads, or head), signifying that there is another world (Geburah) which has its habitation below and constitutes the Court of Justice of this world. It is to this that we can refer such expressions as: "And it repented the Lord... and it grieved him at his heart" (Ibid. v, 6), or "the fierce anger of the Lord", for in the realms above there resides only light spreading life all around. Hence the dictum: "there is no grief in the presence of God". Hence, too, it is written: "Serve the Lord with gladness; come before his presence with singing" (Ps. C, 2), the word "Lord" alluding to the upper world, and the word "presence" to the lower world. Happy are Israel in this world and in the world to come. So Scripture says: "Happy art thou, O Israel, who is like unto thee? A people saved by the Lord, the shield of thy help, and that is the sword of thy excellency! etc." (Deut. XXXIII, 29).

AND HE SET THE RODS WHICH HE PEELED IN THE GUTTERS, ETC. Said R. Eleazar: 'There are sinners who either neglect altogether the words of the Torah, or if they do cast an eye on them, think them mere foolishness. But in truth the foolishness is in their own minds, since all the words of the Torah are sublime and precious, and of every word it is written: "She is more precious than rubies; and all the things thou canst desire are not to be compared with her" (Prov. III, 15). Woe to all these foolish and senseless people, when the Holy One, blessed be He, will demand an account from them for the insult done to the Torah and they will be punished for having rebelled against their Master. So Scripture says: "For it is no empty thing for you" (Deut. XXXII, 47), implying that if it is an empty thing, its emptiness is from you yourselves, seeing that all the things one can desire are not to be compared with her. How can they say that the Torah is an empty thing seeing that Solomon said: ' ' If thou art wise, thou art wise for thyself" (Prov. IX, 12), implying that whoever becomes wise in the Torah benefits himself thereby? Thus the Torah is filled with all riches and no one can add thereto even one letter. "But if thou scornest, thou alone shalt bear it" (Ibid.), since the worth of the Torah will be in no wise diminished thereby, and the scorning will only recoil on the head of the scorner so as to cause him to perish in this world and in the world to come. Observe now. When the supernal letters are joined together and attach themselves to that grade which is the last of all the supernal holy grades, and it becomes filled from them and enriched with blessings from the upper world, this same grade is in readiness to "water all the flocks" according to their requirements, each one being watered both with judgement and mercy. Now Jacob desired to institute evening prayer and so restore the light of the moon and water her and enrich her with blessings on all sides. Hence it is written, "And he set the rods, etc." These rods signify severity and force, which issue from the supernal Geburah. So Jacob, in his desire to put himself right with that grade, "set the rods", that is, he removed all the influences of severity and force symbolised by the rods, and "placed them in the gutters", to wit, those four gutters [Tr. note: i.e. the four Hayyoth, v. Ezek. 1, 5.] that stand underneath "the well, which the princes digged" (Num. XXI, 18), the well which was filled from those supernal rivers and fountains; for when water comes forth out of that sacred well, these four receive the whole of it, they being called gutters (rehatim=swift runners) for that reason, and to that source

they all come to drink, taking of those implements of severity and force what is fitting for each. So it says: "over against the flocks". Further it is written, "and they conceived" (lit. grew hot); that is to say, when they are invested with power to punish, they become heated thereby, and then they set out to roam to and fro in the world and closely inspect the ways of men, whether for good or for evil. Further we read: "And the flocks became heated at the sight of the rods", inasmuch as these rods become hot and take charge of the judgements to be meted out to the world, and the sons of men receive their punishments through them, as we read: "The sentence is by the decree of the angels, and the decision by the word of the holy ones" (Dan. IV, 14).'

R. Hiya discoursed on the verse: My soul cleaveth unto thee; thy right hand holdeth me fast (Ps. LXIII, 9). 'King David', he said, 'could speak thus because his soul ever clave to God, and he had no care for worldly matters, and therefore God supported him and never let him go; and so it is with every man who cleaves to God. Or again, David may have meant these words as a prayer that his grade should be crowned in the supernal realm, for when that grade clings to the supernal grades to ascend after them, then the right hand of God lays hold of it, raises it, and unites it to itself, as we read: "And thy right hand would hold me" (Ps. CXXXIX, 10), also: "And his right hand should embrace me" (S. S. VIII, 3). Hence David's words: "Thy right hand holdeth me fast." Of him who does hold fast to the Holy One, blessed be He, it is written: "His left hand should be under my head, and his right hand should embrace me" (Ibid.), an expression indicative of perfect attachment and union.'

When the water pours into those gutters, they are filled on all four sides, so that all the flocks can be watered each from its proper side. Now when Jacob essayed to perfect his grade, he chose for himself the right side which befitted him, and allowed the left side which did not befit him to part from him, as it is written: "and he put his own droves apart, and put them not unto Laban's flocks". "Apart", that is, by himself, so that he should not avail himself of alien idols of the other sides. Happy the portion of Israel of whom it is written: "For thou art a holy people unto the Lord thy God, and the Lord hath chosen thee, etc." (Deut. XIV, 2). Now Jacob was the crown of the patriarchs and their epitome, summing them all up within himself, and he therefore set about to restore the light of the moon, as well as to institute the evening prayer; and all this work was well becoming him, as thereby he perfected all those sides of holiness which belonged to his side, and separated his portion from the portion of the other nations. The former are the supernal sides, sanctified with the supernal sanctities, whilst the latter are utterly defiled and unclean. So that Jacob, as already explained, "put his own droves apart"; that is, he prepared himself for the adoption of a faith which should keep him apart, as it is written: "and the Lord hafh chosen thee to be his own treasure out of all peoples" (Deut. XIV, 2); "and put them not unto Laban's flock", that is, he did not place his portion and lot with them. Jacob thus, being the perfection of the patriarchs, established the true faith, and separated his own portion and lot from that of other peoples. To such an action could be applied the words: "But ye that did cleave unto the Lord your God are alive every one of you this day" (Ibid. IV, 4). Said R. Abba: 'Happy is the portion of Israel, who are exalted above the idolatrous nations, in virtue of their grade being above on high, whereas the grade of the idolatrous people is down below. The former are of the side of holiness, the latter of the side of uncleanness; they are on the right, the others on the left. But when the Temple was destroyed, then it could be said, "He hath drawn back his right hand" (Lam. II, 3), wherefore also it is written: "Save me with thy right hand and answer me" (Ps. LX, 7); and the left side has since been gathering force and uncleanness, and will continue to do so until God shall rebuild the Temple and establish the world on its right foundation, and the right order shall be restored, and the side of uncleanness shall pass out of the world, as it says: "and I will cause the unclean spirit to pass out of the land" (Zech. XIII, 2),

Zohar: Bereshith, Section 1, Page 164a

also: "He will swallow up death forever" (Is. XXV, 8). God will then remain alone, as it is written: "And the idols shall utterly pass away" (Ibid. II, 18), also: "and the Lord alone shall be exalted in that day" (Ibid. 17). He alone, then, will be left, as it is written: "And there was no strange God with him" (Deut. XXXII, 12), the unclean host being then extirpated from the world, so that both in the upper world and in the lower world there will be no other left save God alone, with Israel, the holy people, worshipping Him. For Israel will then be designated holy, as it is written: "And it shall come to pass, that he that is left in Zion, and he that remaineth in Jerusalem, shall be called holy, even every one that is written unto life in Jerusalem" (Is. IV, 3). There will thus be one and only one King on high and below, and one and only one people to worship Him, as it is written: "And who is like thy people Israel, a nation one in the earth...?" (I Chron. XVII, 21).'

R. Isaac and R. Jesse were once walking together on the road. Said R. Jesse: 'Behold, the Shekinah is near us. Let us therefore engage in an exposition of the Torah, since whoso occupies himself with the Torah draws Her nearer to himself.' R. Isaac then began a discourse on the verse: The Lord liveth, and blessed be my Rock, and exalted be the God of my salvation (Ps. XVIII, 47). 'This verse', he said, 'has a recondite meaning We know that God is called "the living one". But this verse indicates that the perfectly righteous man also is called "living one", so that there is a righteous living one on high, and correspondingly a righteous living one here on earth. On high it is God who is called "living one", and here below it is the righteous man who is called "living one", as it is written: "And Benaiah the son of Jehoiada, the son of a living man" [Tr. note: According to the K'tib.] (II Sam. XXIII, 20). He was so called because he was a righteous man, and the righteous man is called "living one". The words "blessed by my Rock" have the same reference, since the Living One and the Blessed One are never parted, and when united are called "well of living waters"; the one flows in, and the other is filled therewith. "And exalted be the God of my salvation"; this indicates the supernal world, which is high and exalted over all, inasmuch as from it everything springs, even all the outpouring by which the well is filled, receiving therefrom blessings to spread light among all the dwellers of the lower world. And when the whole is filled properly, then "exalted will be the Rock of salvation".' R. Jesse then discoursed on the verse: He withdraweth not his eyes from the righteous; but with kings upon the throne he setteth them forever, and they are exalted (Job XXXVI, 7). 'When', he said, 'the domination of the wicked ceases and they perish from the world, then the righteous obtain dominion, as it says: "He preserveth not the life of the wicked, but giveth to the poor their right" (Ibid. 6). The words, "He withdraweth not from the righteous his eye" are parallel to the text, "The eyes of the Lord are toward the righteous" (Ps. XXXIV, 16). "But with kings upon the throne"; these are the kings who are, as it were, united to their thrones, and whom He setteth forever so that they remain immovably established. "And they are exalted", to wit, to rule over the world so that the throne remains firmly established on its supports. Or, again, it may mean that they raise the throne and set it up on high so that it should become united to its proper place and there should thus be a complete unity.'

Whilst they were proceeding on their way they caught sight of a man coming towards them, with a child riding on his shoulders. Said R. Isaac: 'This man is without doubt a Judean, and he wants to give people a chance to do a good action.' Said R. Jesse: 'Let us be the first to take advantage of the opportunity.' When he came up to them, R. Jesse asked him: 'Whereto is the saffron pot set on the path?' The man replied: 'So as to afford people an opportunity of doing a pious action; for I have two sons who were taken captive by a brigand who passed through my native town, and now I am on the road in order to afford people the opportunity of doing a good action.' The two thereupon availed themselves of the occasion and gave him food to eat. The Judean then began a discourse on the verse: My food which is presented unto me for an offering made by fire, of a sweet savour unto me, shall ye observe to offer unto me in due season (Num. XXVIII, 2). 'The offering brought unto the Holy One, blessed be He, every day,' he said, 'was for the purpose of feeding the world and providing sustenance both for the upper world and the lower world, inasmuch as the upper world moves in response to the lower world, with the result that every one is supplied according to his due. The words, "My food which is presented to me as an offering", are paralleled by the verse, "I have eaten my honeycomb with my honey; I have drunk my wine with my milk" (S. S. V, 1); and "made by fire" by the words: "Eat, O friends, drink, yea, drink abundantly, O beloved" (Ibid.). Now, if God assigns food above in order that therefrom food may be dispensed below, with how much more reason must he who offers food for the preservation of a soul be rewarded, in that God will bless him and direct to him sustenance from on high, so that the world will receive blessings for his sake!' R. Isaac remarked: 'Assuredly this is the inner meaning of the verse.' R. Jesse said: 'This incident assuredly bears out the admonition of the Sages that no man should ever treat slightingly another man, for this man has occasioned us a double privilege.'

The stranger then continued his discourse on the above verse, but in the name of

Zohar: Bereshith, Section 1, Page 164b

R. Eleazar. 'The accusative particle "eth" here,' he said, 'alludes to the Community of Israel; the "offering" is a connecting link (between high and low); "my food" is an allusion to the food that descends from on high in response to the stirring here below; "as a fire offering" includes all the other hosts which receive their necessary sustenance each one in proper measure; "of a sweet savour unto me" signifies the uniting of the whole in one bond of unity and good will so as to form an emblem of the upper world; "shall ye observe to offer unto me in due season" alludes to the time when Abraham bestirred himself to do the will of God, regarding which it is written: "And Abraham rose early in the morning" (Gen. XXII, 3), and also to the time when Isaac was bound on the altar, which was at eventide.' Said R. Jesse: 'In that case, we should rather have expected the plural "seasons".' The Judean in reply said: 'At the time of the sacrifice, fire and water are intermingled and become one, and hence it says "season" and not "seasons". The expression "ye shall observe to offer unto me" is used in connection with this offering only, the reason being that this offering ascends to the highest grade in an intermingling of the Right and the Left, symbolised by Abraham and Isaac.' Said R. Jesse: 'If only to hear this, it was worth our while coming here. Happy are Israel in this world and in the world to come! In regard to this it is written: "Thy people are all righteous, they shall inherit the land forever; the branch of my planting, the work of my hands, wherein I glory" (Is. LX, 21).' NOW LABAN WAS GONE TO SHEAR HIS SHEEP, ETC. R. Yose said: 'The teraphim were idols, so called out of contempt, the name being akin to the word toreph (obscenity). The proof that they were idols is found in Laban's question: "Wherefore hast thou stolen my gods?" as well as in Jacob's words: "With whomsoever thou findest thy gods, etc." For Laban was a great sorcerer who practised all kinds of magical arts, and it was by such means that he learnt all that he wished to know.' R. Hiya said that the powers of the idol were derived from wizardry; R. Yose, from divination. R. Judah said: 'They were derived from a close observance of the times and moments for striking and for holding off. At one moment the craftsman would use his hand to beat it into shape, and another he would relax. Hence the term teraphim, akin to hereph (relax) (II Sam. XXIV, 16). For when the craftsman was making it, the man who knew the proper seconds and hours stood over him, saying now "strike", and now "stay". There is no other work which requires to be timed in this way. Now, this magic idol was continually uttering evil counsel, and prompting to mischief. Rachel thus feared lest it should counsel her father to do mischief to Jacob, and by reason of her contempt for the idol she placed it underneath her, so that it was not able to speak; for whenever it was consulted they used to sweep and clean up before it. The teraphim were a male and a female image, and a number of ceremonies had to be.performed before them before they would speak. Hence Laban delayed three days before pursuing, as he was unaware of Jacob's flight, as it says: AND IT WAS TOLD LABAN ON THE THIRD DAY THAT JACOB WAS FLED .' R. Judah further said: 'Laban prepared himself in two ways: he equipped himself with all his magical arts and also with ordinary weapons in order to destroy Jacob, as it is written: "An Aramean was going to destroy my father" (Deut. XXVI, 5). So when God saw that he intended to destroy Jacob, He warned him, saying: TAKE HEED TO THYSELF THAT THOU SPEAK NOT TO JACOB EITHER GOOD OR BAD. This is borne out by Laban's words: IT IS IN THE POWER OF MY HAND TO DO YOU HURT, to wit, through his magical arts. Observe that Laban covered in one day a distance that took Jacob seven days, and all in order to destroy him utterly; first because he had fled, and secondly for the loss of the teraphim. Now, as regards Rachel, although her purpose was to wean her father from idolatry, yet she was punished by not surviving to bring up Benjamin or even to live with him a single hour; and all on account of the pain she caused her father, notwithstanding her good intention.' R. Isaac said: 'All this reproof which Jacob administered to Laban served to make him acknowledge the Holy One, blessed be He, as is proved from Laban's words: SEE, GOD IS WITNESS BETWIXT ME AND THEE. But observe that it is further written: THE GOD OF ABRAHAM, AND THE GOD OF NAHOR... JUDGE BETWIXT US. This indicates that, sinner as he was, he reverted to his former idolatrous worship, for after invoking the God of Abraham, he immediatey added "the God of Nahor".'

Zohar: Bereshith, Section 1, Page 165a

AND JACOB SWORE BY THE FEAR OF HIS FATHER ISAAC. Why by "the fear of Isaac" and not by the God of Abraham? Because he did not wish to trouble, as it were, the right-hand grade for the sake of Laban; furthermore, it is not right for a man to swear, even a true oath, by the most high realm. R. Yose said: 'Truly, Jacob's oath was most appropriate to the occasion. For he said to himself: "Behold, he has invoked the God of Abraham, but left out the name of my father; let me therefore make up the deficiency." Hence he swore by the "fear of his father Isaac". Another explanation is that Jacob desired to bring the grade of severity on to his side to assist him against Laban.' AND JACOB WENT ON HIS WAY, AND THE ANGELS OF GOD MET HIM. R. Abba discoursed on the verse: Male and female created he them, etc. (Gen. V, 2). 'How incumbent it is upon us', he said, 'to study intently the words of the Torah! Woe to those whose heart is obdurate and whose eyes are blinded! Behold, the Torah is calling unto them, saying: "Whoso is thoughtless, let him turn in hither; as for him that lacketh understanding, she saith to him: Come, eat, of my bread, and drink of the wine which I have mingled" (Prov. IX, 4-5). But there is no one to pay attention to her. Observe that this verse contains sublime mysteries, it has an inner and an outer meaning. Thus, one meaning is that the sun and moon are closely united, as is implied in the passage: "The sun and the moon stand still in her habitation" (Hab. III, 11); and another is that Adam and Eve were created as a united pair; and since they were coupled together, God blessed them. For blessing does not reside save in a spot where there are male and female. Observe that when Jacob set out on his journey to Haran he was all by himself, not yet having married. What does Scripture say of that occasion? "And he lighted upon (vayifga'=entreated) the place, etc." (Gen. XXVIII, 11), and he was only promised deliverance in a dream. But now that he was married and was coming with all the tribes, heavenly legions entreated and supplicated him, as it were, for we read: "And the angels of God met (vayifge'u=entreated) him." Whereas before it was he who entreated the "place", now it was they who entreated him, for the reason that it was for the sake of Jacob and the tribes that they were watered from the great sea. Moreover, whereas before he saw them only in a dream of the night, now he saw with open eyes and in full daylight, as it is written: AND JACOB SAID WHEN HE SAW THEM: THIS IS GOD'S CAMP, ETC.

Zohar: Bereshith, Section 1, Page 165b

How, it may be asked, did he recognise them? The answer is that they were the same angels whom he had seen in his dream. Hence he called them Mahaneum (two camps), indicating the camp which had appeared to him on high and the camp which appeared now below. Why did they appear unto him to entreat him? Because the Shekinah accompanied him in order to bear along his household, and she was also awaiting the birth of Benjamin so as to make her home with Jacob as pre-ordained. It is in allusion to this that Scripture says: "And Jacob shall again be quiet and at ease, and none shall make him afraid" (Jer. XXX, 10). Blessed be the Lord forevermore. Amen and Amen!'

VAYISHLAH

AND JACOB SENT MESSENGERS (lit. angels), ETC. R. Judah discoursed on the text: For he will give his angels charge over thee, to keep thee in all thy ways (Ps. XCI, 11). 'According to the companions,' he said, 'the moment a child is born into the world, the evil prompter straightway attaches himself to him, and thenceforth brings accusations against him, as it says, "sin coucheth at the door" (Gen. IV, 7), the term "sin" being a designation of the evil prompter, who was also called sin by King David in the verse: "and my sin is ever before me" (Ps. LI, 5). He is so called because he makes man every day to sin before his Master, never leaving him from the day of his birth till the end of his life. But the good prompter first comes to man only on the day that he begins to purify himself, to wit, when he reaches the age of thirteen years. From that time the youth finds himself attended by two companions, one on his right and the other on his left, the former being the good prompter, the latter the evil prompter. These are two veritable angels appointed to keep man company continually. Now when a man tries to be virtuous, the evil prompter bows to him, the right gains dominion over the left, and the two together join hands to guard the man in all his ways; hence it is written: "For he will give his angels charge over thee, to keep thee in all thy ways." '

R. Eleazar applied this verse to Jacob when God assigned to him companies of angels as an escort because he came with the full number of tribes, forming with them a godly company. Hence it says: "And Jacob went on his way, and the angels of God met him" (Gen. XXXII, 2), as already explained. Here, therefore, when he was delivered from the hands of Laban and dissociated himself from him, the Shekinah joined him, and sacred camps came to encircle him, so that

Zohar: Bereshith, Section 1, Page 166a

"Jacob said when he saw them, etc." (Ibid. 3). It was from these angels that he sent a mission to Esau, as it says: "And Jacob sent angels" (mal'akhim).' R. Isaac said: 'Why, in one place in the Psalms does it say "The angel of the Lord encampeth round about them that fear him and delivereth them" (Ps. XXXIV, 8), in the singular, and in another place, "For he will give his angels charge over thee" (Ibid. XCI, 11), in the plural? The reason is that the term "angels" is a reference to angels proper, whereas in the verse: "The angel of the Lord encampeth", the reference is to the Shekinah, as in the verse: "And the angel of the Lord appeared unto him in a flame of fire out of the midst of a bush" (Ex. III, 2). Thus "the angel of the Lord encampeth round about those who fear him" to deliver them; and when the Shekinah abides within a man, ever so many holy legions rally round him. David uttered this verse when he escaped from Achish the king of Gath, because the Shekinah encompassed him and delivered him from Achish and his people, and all those who assailed him. It is written in the same connection: "And he feigned himself mad (vaytholel) in their hands" (I Sam. XXI, 14). The term vaytholel here, in place of the more usual vayishtagea', contains an allusion to the kindred term used formerly by David when he said: "For I was envious of the madmen (holelim)" (Ps. LXXIII, 3). God thus said in effect to David: "As thou livest, since thou enviest madmen, thou thyself wilt yet be driven to play the madman"; and so it came to pass when he was brought before Achish and his life was in danger; he then "feigned himself mad (vaytholel) in their hand", that is, he behaved like one of those madmen (holelim) whom he had once envied; and only then did the Shekinah come to his rescue. How, it may be asked, could this be, seeing that the Shekinah abides only in her own heritage, the Holy Land? The answer is that from there only she bestows blessings, but for purposes of protection she is to be found elsewhere also. So here, when Jacob departed from Laban, all the holy legions surrounded him, so that he was not left by himself.'

R. Hizkiah asked: 'If that was so, how came Jacob, as stated later, to be "left alone" (Gen. XXXII, 25)?' Said R. Judah in reply: 'Because he exposed himself deliberately to danger, and therefore the angels deserted him. It was to this that he alluded when he said: "I am not worthy of all the mercies and of all the truth which thou hast shown unto thy servant" (Ibid. 11).' R. Isaac said that the reason why they departed was to leave him alone with the chieftain of Esau, who came down to him with divine permission; and they meanwhile went off to chant the hymns for which the hour was then due and to sing the praises of the Holy One, blessed be He, and afterwards they returned to Jacob. "Now I am become two camps": to wit, the camp of the Shekinah and his own household, so that he was complete on all sides, having his portion both with the white and with the red. R. Eleazar said: 'The sages have stated that on that night and at that hour the power of Esau was in the ascendant, and therefore Jacob was left alone, or, from another aspect, the sun was left alone, the light of the moon having been obscured. Nevertheless, the guardianship of Providence did not leave him entirely, so that his antagonist prevailed not against him, as it says: "And when he saw that he prevailed not against him...". He looked to Jacob's right, and there his gaze met Abraham; he turned to his left, and there he saw Isaac; he looked at Jacob's body, and he saw that it was a fusion of tht two sides, and so he touched the hollow of his thigh, which is a pillar adjoining the body but is outside the body. In this way, then, the angel encompassed Jacob on all sides to deliver him; and when the Shekinah came down to abide with him, there joined him multitudinous hosts and legions; and it was of those angels that he sent a party to Esau.' AND JACOB SENT ANGELS. Said R. Abba: What induced Jacob to make advances towards Esau? Would he not have done better to leave him alone? The truth is that Jacob said to himself: "I am well aware that Esau has great respect for his father and would never cause him any vexation, and so I know that I have no ground to fear him so long as my father is alive. Let me, therefore, effect a reconciliation with him whilst my father is alive." Straightway, then, Jacob "sent angels before him".' R. Simeon opened a discourse on the verse: Better is he that is lightly esteemed, and hath a servant, than he that playeth the man of rank, and lacketh bread (Prov. XII, 9). 'This verse', he said, 'speaks of the

Zohar: Bereshith, Section 1, Page 166b

evil prompter, who lays plots and unceasingly brings up accusations against a man. He puffs up a man's heart, encouraging him to arrogance and conceit, and induces him to twirl his hair and carry his head high, until he obtains an ascendancy over him and drags him down to Gehinnom. Better, therefore, is one who is "lightly esteemed" and who does not follow the evil prompter, but remains humble in heart and spirit and submits himself to the will of the Holy One, blessed be He. The evil prompter is bowed down before such a one, and so far is he from obtaining the mastery over the man that it is the man who obtains the mastery over him, as it says, "but thou mayest rule over him" (Gen. IV, 7). Such a man is better than he who "playeth the man of rank", who has a high opinion of himself, twirls his hair and is full of conceit, as already mentioned above, but "lacketh bread", to wit, the true faith, which is referred to as "the bread of his God" (Lev. XXI, 22) (Ibid. 6). Again, "he who is lightly esteemed" is exemplified in Jacob, who humbled himself before Esau so that the latter should in time become his servant, in fulfilment of the blessing: "Let people serve thee, and nations bow down to thee, etc." (Gen. XXVII, 29). For Jacob's time had not yet arrived, as he deferred it to the future, and in the immediate present he "esteemed himself lightly". But in the proper time "he that playeth the man of rank" will become the servant to him "that lacketh bread", to the man who was allotted "plenty of corn and wine" (Ibid. 28). Jacob knew that it was for the time being necessary for him to humble himself before Esau, and so made himself as one who "esteemed himself lightly". And, moreover, he displayed therein more craft and subtlety than in all his other dealings with Esau; and had Esau realised this, he would rather have taken his own life than come to such a pass. Jacob thus acted throughout with wisdom, and to him can be applied the words of Hannah: "They that strive with the Lord shall be broken in pieces... and he will give strength unto his king, etc." (I Sam. II. 10).' AND HE COMMANDED THEM, SAYING: THUS SHALL YE SAY UNTO MY LORD ESAU: THUS SAITH THY SERVANT JACOB: I HAVE SOJOURNED WITH LABAN, AND STAYED UNTIL NOW. He began by representing himself as Esau's servant, in order that the latter's thoughts might be diverted from the blessings which he had received from his father, and the enjoyment of which he was postponing for a future time, as already said. R. Judah said: 'What was Jacob's object in saying to Esau, "I have sojourned with Laban"? What had this to do with his message to Esau? The reason was that Laban the Aramean was famous throughout the world as a master magician and sorcerer whose spell no man could escape. He was, in fact, the father of Beor, who was the father of Balaam, mentioned in Scripture as "Balaam the son of Beor, the soothsayer" (Josh. XIII, 22). But for all Laban's skill and pre-eminence in sorcery and magic, he could not prevail over Jacob, though he employed all his arts to destroy him, as it says: "An Aramean designed to destroy my father" (Deut. XXVI, 5).' R. Abba said: 'All the world knew that Laban was the greatest of wizards and sorcerers and magicians, and that no one whom he wished to destroy could escape from him, and that it was from him that Balaam learnt all his skill-Balaam, of whom it is written: "for I know that he whom thou blessest is blessed, and he whom thou cursest is cursed" (Num. XXII, 6). Thus Laban and his magic were universally feared. Hence Jacob's first intimation to Esau was, "I have sojourned with Laban"; and lest Esau should think that it was merely a month, or, at most, a year, he added: "and I stayed until now"-a space of twenty years. And lest Esau should think that he had achieved nothing of consequence, he added: "And I have oxen and asses", these being the symbols of two grades of severity that are never combined together save to bring suffering on the world. (This is the underlying reason of the precept: "Thou shalt not plow with an ox and an ass together" (Deut. XXII, 10)). Further, "and flocks, and men-servants, and maid-servants", these being symbolic of the lower crowns whom God slew in Egypt, in the form of "the first-born of cattle, the first born of the captive" (Ex. XII, 29), and "the first-born of the maidservant" (Ibid. XI, 5). Straightway Esau was seized with fear and went forth to meet him. Indeed, he was as much afraid of Jacob as Jacob was afraid of him. Jacob was like a traveller who hears that robbers are lying in wait for him on the road. Meeting another man, he asks him to whom he belongs, and he replies: "I am a member of such and such a band of robbers". "Get thee hence," exclaims the wayfarer, "for I have about me a snake who kills anyone that approaches me." The man then returns to the chief of the brigands and warns him, saying: "A man is coming along this way who has about him a snake which bites anyone who approaches him

Zohar: Bereshith, Section 1, Page 167a

and kills him." Hearing this, the chief of the brigands says: "I had better go out to meet that man and make peace with him." When the wayfarer sees him coming be exclaims: "Woe is me, he is going to kill me." So he commences to bow and prostrate himself before him, whereupon the brigand regains his self-assurance, thinking: "If he had with him such a dangerous snake as he said, he would not have bowed so much to me. But since he does bow so much before me, I will not kill him." In the same way Jacob sent word to Esau, saying: "I have sojourned with Laban and stayed until now", as much as to say: "I have stayed with him twenty years, and I have brought with me a deadly snake who slays people with his bite." Esau, on hearing this said: "Woe is me, who can stand up before him?" for he was afraid that Jacob would kill him with his mouth. He therefore went forth to meet him and to make peace with him. But Jacob, we read, as soon as he saw him, "was greatly afraid and distressed", and when he approached him he commenced bowing and kneeling before him, as it says: "and bowed himself to the ground seven times, until he came near to his brother". Esau then said to himself: "Had he really been so well equipped as he said, he would not have bowed before me", and he again began to carry himself haughtily.

It is written in regard to Balaam: "And God came unto Balaam at night" (Num. XXII, 20). Similarly in regard to Laban it is written: "And God,came to Laban the Aramean in a dream of the night, and said unto him: Take heed to thyself that thou speak not to Jacob either good or bad" (Gen. XXXI, 24). Instead of the words "that thou speak not", we should have expected here "that thou do no evil to Jacob" But the truth is that Laban in his pursuit after Jacob did not intend to contend against him with armed force, as he was well aware that Jacob and his sons were more than a match for him, but he designed to kill him with the power of his mouth. Hence: "that thou speak not", and not "that thou do not". It is also written: "It is in the power of my hand to do you hurt" (Gen. XXXI, 29). Laban knew this from the warning given him, as he himself continued: "But the God of your father spoke to me, etc." (Ibid.). And this is the very testimony which God commanded the Israelites to pronounce, as it is written: "And thou shalt testify and say before the Lord thy God: An

Aramean intended to destroy my father, etc." (Deut. XXVI, 5). Of Balaam it is further written: "and he went not as at other times, to meet enchantments" (Num. XXIV, 1), this being his wont, since he was an adept in divinations. Laban also said: "I have observed the signs" (Gen. XXX, 27), that is to say, he tested Jacob's fortune by means of his divinations, and when he set out to destroy him he also intended to accomplish his end by the same power of magic and sorcery, but God did not permit him. And it was in allusion to this that Balaam his grandson said: "For there is no enchantment with Jacob, neither is there any divination with Israel" (Num. XXIII, 23), as much as to say: "Who can prevail against them, seeing that when my grandfather sought to destroy their ancestor by means of enchantments and sorceries, he did not succeed, as he was not permitted to curse him?" Laban, indeed, employed against Jacob all the ten kinds of magic and divination of the flashing of the underworld crowns, but could do him no hurt, as it is written: "and he changed my wages ten times, but God suffered him not to hurt me" (Gen. XXXI, 7), where the term monim (times) is akin to the term minim, signifying "kinds". These ten kinds of witchcraft are alluded to in the verse saying: "There shall not be found among you... one that useth divination, a soothsayer, or an enchanter, or a sorcerer, or a charmer, or one that consulteth a ghost or a familiar spirit, or a necromancer" (Deut. XVIII, 10-11). R. Yose said: 'Divination and enchantment are two different arts of the same potency. Balaam made use of divination against Israel, as it says: "with divinations in their hand" (Num. XXII, 7). Laban, on the other hand, used enchantments against Jacob, but neither of them succeeded. Hence Balaam said: "For there is no enchantment with Jacob, neither is there any divination with Israel" (Ibid. XXIII, 23), the first half of the verse alluding to the days of Laban, the other half to the time of Balaam himself. Balaam said in effect to Balak: "How can anyone prevail against them, seeing that all the divinations and sorceries residing in our crowns derive their potency from the flashing of the supernal sovereignty, which is attached to them, as it is written: 'The Lord his God is with them, and the shouting for the King is among them" (Ibid. 21).' R. Judah said: 'Far be it from us to imagine that Balaam knew aught of the supernal sanctity,

Zohar: Bereshith, Section 1, Page 167b

seeing that God did not choose any people or tongue to make use of His glory save His holy children, to whom he said: "sanctify yourselves therefore, and be ye holy" (Lev. XI, 44). Only those who are themselves holy are permitted to make use of holy things; and it is only Israel who are holy, as it is written: "For thou art a holy people" (Deut. XIV, 2), that is, thou alone art holy, but no other people. Contrariwise, those who are impure are brought into contact with impurity and become more impure, and of such it is written: "he is unclean; he shall dwell alone; without the camp shall his dwelling be" (Lev. XIII, 46); for impurity calls unto impurity, as it says: "and he shall cry unclean, unclean" (Ibid. 45), where the text admits of the rendering, "and unclean calls to unclean", that is, seeks out its own kind.'

R. Isaac said: 'Was it becoming for a holy man like Jacob to admit that he had contaminated himself with Laban and his enchantments? Was this anything to his credit?' R. Yose said to him: 'Although R. Judah has given an explanation, I agree with you that we should seek another. For we find a somewhat similar difficulty in Jacob's words: "I am Esau thy first-born" (Gen. XXVII, 19), where also we may ask: "Was it becoming for a righteous man like Jacob to assume the name of the impure Esau?" I will answer both these difficulties. There is a tonal pause after the word "I-am" (anokhi) in this passage, so that what Jacob really said was: "I am (who I am, but) Esau (is) thy first-born", as already explained elsewhere. Similarly here Jacob meant to say: "Do not pay any regard to the blessing which my father gave, nor imagine that it has been fulfilled in me. For he blessed me saying, 'be lord over thy brethren', whereas of a truth 'I am thy servant Jacob, to my lord Esau'. Again, he blessed me with 'plenty of corn and wine', but I have no stock of these, but 'oxen, and asses and flocks', and am only a shepherd in the field. Of the blessing 'of the dew of heaven, and of the fat places of the earth', nothing has been fulfilled in me, seeing that 'I have sojourned with Laban', being merely a sojourner, without so much as a house that I can call my own, let alone the fatness of the earth." The whole of Jacob's message was thus calculated to divert Esau's regard from those blessings, so that he should not quarrel with him over them.' R. Abba said: 'It is written of Jacob that he was "a perfect man, dwelling in tents" (Gen. XXV, 27). The designation "perfect man" was given him because he resided in the two supernal Tabernacles and embodied in himself both this side and that side, and thus was made complete. His language must not be construed into an admission that he had contaminated himself with the enchantments of Laban, and, with all due respect to R. Judah, his heart was pure and full of thankfulness for the kindness and the truth that God had shown him. Thus Jacob's message to Esau amounted to saying: "Everyone knows what kind of a man Laban is, and that no one can escape him. Yet I stayed with him twenty years, and though he contended with me and sought to destroy me, yet God delivered me from his hand." Jacob's purpose in all his words was to prevent Esau from thinking that the blessings had been fulfilled, and so from nursing a grudge against himself. Regarding such conduct Scripture says: "For the ways of the Lord are right, etc." (Hos. XIV, 10), also: "Thou shalt be whole-hearted with the Lord thy God" (Deut. XVIII, 13).' AND THE ANGELS RETURNED TO JACOB, SAYING: WE CAME TO THY BROTHER ESAU, AND MOREOVER HE COMETH TO MEET THEE, AND FOUR HUNDRED MEN WITH HIM. The word "Esau" after "thy brother" seems to be superfluous, since Jacob had no other brothers. It was, however, a hint to Jacob not to think that Esau had retraced his steps and entered on the path of rectitude, but that he was still the same wicked

Esau as of old. And moreover "he cometh to meet thee", and that not by himself, but having "four hundred men with him". Why all these details? Because God always delights in the prayer of the righteous, and He crowns Himself, as it were, with their supplications. So we affirm that the angel in charge of the prayers of Israel, Sandalphon by name, takes up all those prayers and weaves out of them a crown for the Living One of the worlds. All the more, then, must we believe that the prayers of the righteous, in which God takes delight, are made into a crown for Him. Seeing that Jacob had with him legions of holy angels, it may be asked why he was afraid. The truth is that the righteous rely not on their merits but on their prayers and supplications to their Master. R. Simeon said: 'The prayer of a congregation ascends to the Almighty, and He is crowned therewith, because it comprises many hues and directions, wherefore it is made into a crown to be placed on the head of the Righteous One, the Living One of the worlds; whereas the prayer of an individual is not many-sided and presents only one hue, and hence is not so complete and acceptable as the prayer of a congregation. Jacob was many-sided, and therefore God craved for his prayer, and hence it is written: "Then Jacob was greatly afraid and was distressed".' R. Judah cited here the verse: "Happy is the man that feareth alway; but he that hardeneth his heart shall fall into evil" (Prov. XXVIII, 14).

Zohar: Bereshith, Section 1, Page 168a

'Happy is the people of Israel', he said, 'in whom the Holy One, blessed be He, finds delight, and to whom He has given the Torah of truth that thereby they may merit life eternal. For whoso labours in the Torah is vouchsafed from heaven the best life, and is taken up into the life of the world to come, as it is written: "for that is thy life, and the length of thy days" (Deut. XXX, 20); also, "and through this thing ye shall prolong your days" (Ibid. XXXII, 47), implying life in this world and in the world to come.' R. Eleazar said: 'Whoever labours in the Torah for its own sake will not die through the agency of the evil prompter (the same being the serpent and the angel of death), inasmuch as he holds fast to the tree of life and relaxeth not. For this reason the bodies of the righteous who have laboured in the Torah remain undefiled after death, since the spirit of defilement does not hover over them. How came it, then, that Jacob, who was the tree of life itself, as it were, was afraid of Esau, who surely could not prevail against him? Had he not, too, the promise: "And, behold, I am with thee" (Gen. XXVIII, 15)? And had he not further protection in the escort of the host of holy angels, of whom it says, "and the angels of God met him" (Ibid. XXXII, 2)? The reason, however, of his fear was that he did not wish to rely on a miracle, as he did not consider himself deserving that a miracle should be wrought on his behalf. The cause of his self-mistrust was that he had not rendered filial service to his father and mother as he should have done, and that he had not devoted himself to the Torah, and, further, that he had married two sisters. But, in truth, a man should always go in fear and offer up prayer to the Almighty, as it says: "Happy is the man that feareth alway".

'It was the prayers offered up by the patriarchs that sustained the world, and by them are upheld all who dwell therein; and the merits of the patriarchs will never be forgotten, inasmuch as they form the support of the upper and the lower realms; and Jacob's support is firmer than that of all the others. Hence it is that when the children of Jacob are oppressed, God looks at the image of Jacob and is filled with pity for the world. This is hinted in the passage: "Then will I remember my covenant with Jacob" (Lev. XXVI, 42), where the name Jacob is spelt plene, with a vau, which is itself the image of Jacob. To look at Jacob was like looking at the "clear mirror". According to tradition, the beauty of Jacob was equal to that of Adam, the first man.' R. Yose said: 'I have heard it said that he who sees in his dream Jacob robed in his mantle enjoys length of life.'

R. Simeon said: 'We have learnt that no life-portion was originally assigned to David, but Adam gave him seventy years of his own; and so David lived seventy years, whilst Adam lived a thousand years less seventy; thus the first thousand years included the lives of both Adam the first man and King David. The Scripture', he said, 'alludes to this in the verse, "He asked life of thee, thou gavest it him; even length of days forever and ever" (Ps. XXI, 5). For when God created the Garden of Eden and placed in it the soul of King David, He saw that it possessed no life-portion of its own, and cast about for a remedy. So when He created Adam the first man, He said, "Here, indeed, is the remedy"; and so it was that from Adam were derived the seventy years that David lived. Further, each of the patriarchs conceded him some years of his own life, that is to say, Abraham and Jacob and Joseph, but not Isaac, because King David belonged to the same side as himself. Abraham allowed him five years of the hundred and eighty years which he was properly entitled to live, so that he lived only a hundred and seventy-five years, five years less than his due. Jacob was also due to live in this world as many years as Abraham, but he lived

Zohar: Bereshith, Section 1, Page 168b

only a hundred and forty-seven years. Thus, Abraham and Jacob between them conceded to David thirty three years. Then Joseph should have lived a hundred and forty-seven years like Jacob, his father, but he fell short of that number by thirty-seven years. These, with the other thirty-three, completed the seventy years allotted to David, which were thus transferred to him out of the lives of the patriarchs. The reason why Isaac did not transfer to him any years like the others was that he was himself wrapt in darkness, and David came from the side of darkness, and he who is in darkness possesses no light whatever, nor any life: it is for that reason that David possessed no life at all of his own. But those others, being possessed of light, could afford light to King David, who was beholden to them for light and for life, since of the dark side he had no life at all. Hence Isaac did not come into the reckoning. Why, it may be asked, was Joseph's contribution greater than those of the other two together? It was because Joseph was reckoned the equivalent of the other two, since he was called "the righteous", and he was better able than the others to illumine the moon, and hence he conceded to King David a greater share of life than all the others. 'To protect himself against Esau, Jacob resorted to prayer and did not rely upon his merit, since he desired to keep this in reserve for the benefit of his descendants in the future, and not to use it up now against Esau. Hence he now offered up his prayer to the Almighty, and did not rely upon his merits, nor ask for deliverance for their sake. Hence we read: AND HE SAID: IF ESAU COME TO THE ONE CAMP, AND SMITE IT, THEN THE CAMP WHICH IS LEFT SHALL ESCAPE. It was for this reason that he "divided the people that was with him... into two camps". Now the Shekinah never departed from the tent of Leah nor from the tent of Rachel. Jacob knew, therefore, that they were under the protection of the Almighty, and so he put the handmaids and their children foremost, saying to himself: "If Esau slays them, well, he will slay them, but as regards the others I have no fear, since the Shekinah is with them." Hence it says: THEN THE CAMP WHICH IS LEFT SHALL ESCAPE. Having taken this step, he next resorted to prayer, as it is written: And Jacob said, O GOD OF MY FATHER ABRAHAM, AND GOD OF MY FATHER ISAAC, O LORD, WHO SAIDST UNTO ME: RETURN UNTO THY COUNTRY, AND TO THY KINDRED, AND I WILL DO THEE GOOD. R. Yose discoursed on the verse: A prayer of the poor, when he fainteth (ya'atof) and poureth out his complaint before the Lord (Ps. CII, 1). He said: 'As has been laid down in many places, this psalm was composed by King David when he contemplated the plight of the poor man, and that was when he fled from his father-in-law. It was then that he composed a "prayer of the poor", as much as to say: "Behold, this is the prayer a poor man offers up to the Almighty, and one which should ascend in advance of all other prayers." The phrase, "a prayer of the poor", finds its parallel in the expression: "A prayer of Moses, the man of God" (Ibid. XC, 1), the one alluding to the phylactery of the head, the other to that of the arm, the two being inseparable and of equal importance. The reason why the prayer of the poor is admitted first into the presence of the Almighty is indicated in the verse: "For he hath not despised nor abhorred the lowliness of the poor, etc." (Ibid. XXII, 25). According to another exposition, the term "a prayer" is an allusion to Moses; "of the poor" to David; "when he fainteth" (ya'atof = is covered) to the moon when it is hidden and the sun is concealed from it. Observe that the prayer of other people is just a prayer, but the prayer of a poor man breaks through all barriers and storms its way to the presence of the Almighty. So Scripture says: "And it shall come to pass, when he cries unto me, that I will hear; for I am gracious" (Ex. XXII, 26); also: "I will surely hear their cry" (Ibid. 22). David continues: "and poureth out his complaint before the Lord", like one who protests against the judgements of the Almighty.'

R. Eleazar said: 'The prayer of the righteous is an object of joy for the Community of Israel,

Zohar: Bereshith, Section 1, Page 169a

who weave out of it a crown by which to adorn themselves before the Holy One, blessed be He. Hence God holds it in special affection: He longs, as it were, for the prayer of the righteous, when they are in straits, because they know how to appease their Master.'

Note the words of Jacob's prayer: O GOD OF MY FATHER ABRAHAM, AND GOD OF MY FATHER ISAAC, O LORD, WHO SAIDST UNTO ME: RETURN. Various strands are here fitly interwoven. "O God of my father Abraham" symbolises the Right; "God of my father Isaac" symbolises the Left; while by the words "Who saidst unto me" Jacob interwove himself between the two. I AM NOT WORTHY OF ALL THE MERCIES. The connection of those words with what precedes is as follows. Jacob said in effect: "Thou hast promised me to deal well with me, but I know that all thy promises are conditional. Now, behold, I possess no merits, so that I am not worthy of all the mercies and of all the truth which Thou hast shown unto Thy servant; and all that Thou hast done for me until this day Thou hast done not for sake of my merits but for Thine own sake. For behold, when first I crossed the Jordan, fleeing from Esau, I was all alone, but Thou hast shown unto me mercy and truth, in that I have now crossed with two companies." Up to this point Jacob was reciting the praises of the Almighty; he then proceeded to pray for his requirements. From Jacob all men can take example, when offering prayer, first to recite the praises of their Master, and only then to present their petition. So Jacob, after praising the Lord, continued: "Deliver me, I pray thee, from the hand of my brother, from the hand of Esau; for I fear him, lest he come and smite me, the mother with the children." Here, too, is a lesson that in praying a man should state in precise terms what he requires. Thus Jacob commenced: "Deliver me, I pray thee," and since it might be said that he had already been delivered from the hand of Laban, he added "from the hand of my brother"; and since, again, the term "brother" covers all relatives, he added "from the hand of Esau"; and yet again, lest it should be urged that he had no need of such a delivery, he continued: "for I fear him, lest he come and smite me, the mother with the children"; all this in order that there should be no possibility of misunderstanding. AND THOU SAIDST: I WILL SURELY DO THEE GOOD, ETC. We find King David closing a prayer with the words: "Let the words of my mouth and the meditation of my heart be acceptable before thee" (Ps. XIX, 15), the former of these clauses referring to what he had actually said explicitly, and the latter to his inner thoughts which he had only half expressed. This division of prayer into clearly expressed and half-expressed desires corresponds to a distinction in the divine grades, the clearly expressed prayer being addressed to the lower grade, the meditation of the heart to the higher and inner grade. Jacob divided his prayer similarly; first he stated what he desired distinctly, then he left his thought only half expressed, in the words alluding to the promise made to him, "and I will make thy seed as the sand of the sea, which cannot be numbered for multitude". There was here an underlying thought which was best left unexpressed. This division was necessary, as explained, so as to make the unification complete. Happy are the righteous who know how to express fittingly the praises of their Master, as a preliminary to their prayer. Of them it is written: "And he said unto me: Thou art my servant, Israel, in whom I will be glorified" (Is. XLIX, 3). AND JACOB WAS LEFT ALONE, ETC. R. Hiya discoursed on the verse: There shall no evil befall thee, neither shall any plague come nigh thy tent. (Ps. XCI, 10). 'When God', he said, 'created the world, He made on each day

Zohar: Bereshith, Section 1, Page 169b

the work appropriate for that day. This has already been explained. Now on the fourth day the lights were created; but the moon was created without light, since she diminished herself. This is implied in the phrase "Let there be lights", wherein the term meoroth (lights) is written defectively (less the letter vau), as it were me'eroth (curses); for as a result of the moon's diminution, occasion was granted to all spirits and demons and hurricanes and devils to exercise sway, so that all unclean spirits rise up and traverse the world seeking whom to seduce; they haunt ruined places, thick forests and deserts. These are all from the side of the unclean spirit, which, as has been said, issues from the crooked serpent, who is, indeed, the veritable unclean spirit, and whose mission is to seduce man after him. Hence it is that the evil prompter has sway in the world, following men about and employing all manner of ruses and seductions to turn them aside from the paths of the Holy One, blessed be He. And in the same way as he seduced Adam and thereby brought death into the world, so does he ever seduce men and cause them to defile themselves; and whoever allows himself to be defiled draws upon himself the unclean spirit and clings unto him, and numerous unclean influences are at hand to defile him, so that he remains polluted in this world and in the world to come. Contrariwise, should a man strive to purify himself, the unclean spirit is foiled and can no longer dominate him. Thus it is written: "No evil shall befall thee, neither shall any plague come nigh thy tent".' R. Yose said: '"Evil" here alludes to Lilith (night-demon), and "the plague" to the other demons, as has been explained elsewhere.' R. Eleazar said: 'It has been taught that a man should not go out alone at night, and especially when the time of the creation of the moon recurs and it is without light. For at that time the unclean spirit, which is the same as the evil spirit, is at large. Now, the term "evil" here is an allusion to the evil serpent, while "the plague" alludes to him who rides on the serpent, so that evil and plague work together. It is true, we have also been taught that the term "plague" signifies "the plagues of the sons of man", which issued from Adam. For during all those years that Adam kept away from his wife, unclean spirits came and conceived from him, and bore offspring, which are called "plagues of the offspring of Adam"; and it has been affirmed that when a man is sleeping and is not in control of himself, he is assailed by an unclean spirit and sometimes by a number of unclean female spirits who draw him unto themselves, conceive from him and give birth to spirits and demons. These sometimes appear in the form of human beings, save that they have no hair on their heads. It is therefore incumbent on a man to be on his guard against them and not to let himself be contaminated by them, but to follow the paths of the Torah. For there is no man falls asleep on his bed in the night-time but he has a foretaste of death, in that his soul (neshamah) departs from him; and since his body is left without the holy soul, an unclean spirit comes and hovers upon it and it becomes defiled. It has already been said elsewhere that a man should not pass his hands over his eyes when he wakes in the morning on account of the unclean spirit hovering over his hands. Now, although Jacob was beloved by the Almighty, yet when he was left alone a strange spirit immediately came and joined battle with him.' R. Simeon said: 'It is written of Balaam, "and he went shefi (to a bare height)" (Num. XXIII, 3). The word shefi signifies "alone", and it is also akin to the term shefifon, in the phrase "shefifon (a horned snake) in the path". So Balaam went alone, like a snake that goes alone and lurks in by-paths and lanes, with the object of attracting to himself the unclean spirit. For he who walks alone at certain periods, and in certain places, even in a town, attracts to himself the unclean spirit. Hence no one should ever go on a lonely road, even in a city, but only where people are about, nor should a man go out in the night-time, when people are no longer about. It is for a similar reason that it is written: "his body shall not remain all night upon the tree" (Deut. XXI, 23),

Zohar: Bereshith, Section 1, Page 170a

so as not to leave the dead body, which is alone, without the spirit, above ground in the night. The wicked Balaam, however, for that very reason went alone like the serpent, as already explained.' AND THERE WRESTLED (vaye'oveq) A MAN WITH HIM.

R. Joshua the son of Levi said: 'From the word behe'ovqo (in his wrestling) we learn that they raised a dust with their feet which reached the Throne of Glory, as this word finds a parallel in the phrase "the dust ('abaq) of his feet" (Nahum I, 3). The angel here mentioned was Samael, the chieftain of Esau, and it was right that his dust should rise to the Throne of Glory which is the seat of judgement.' R. Simeon said: 'This dust ('abaq) was not ordinary dust, but ashes, the residue of fire. It differs from dust proper in that it is sterile and unproductive, whereas dust ('afar) is that from which all fruit and vegetation spring and is common to the lower and higher existences.' R. Judah remarked: 'If so, how can we explain the passage: "He raiseth up the poor out of the dust" (I Sam. II, 8)?' R. Simeon replied: 'The dust possesses nothing of its own, hence it is from the dust that the poor man has to be raised who possesses nothing of his own either. At the same time the dust is the source of all fruitfulness and of all the produce of the world, and from it have been formed all things in the world, as it is written: "all are of the dust and all return to dust" (Eccl. III, 20), including, according to tradition, even the solar sphere. But the dust called abaq is forever barren, and hence, as the term vaye'obeq ("and he wrestled", or "raised the dust") implies, the man came up, riding, as it were, upon that dust, in order to contest Jacob's right.' UNTIL THE BREAKING OF THE DAY; this being the moment when his dominion passed away and vanished. The same will happen in the time to come. For the present exile is like the night, and in that night the barren dust rules over Israel, who are prostrate fo the dust; and so it will be until the light will appear and the day will break; then Israel will obtain power, and to them will be given the kingdom, as they are the saints of the Most High. So Scripture says: "And the kingdom and the dominion, and the greatness of the kingdoms under the whole heaven, shall be given to the people of the saints of the Most High; their kingdom is an everlasting kingdom, and all dominions shall serve and obey them" (Dan. VII, 27). AND HE SAID: LET ME GO, FOR THE DAY BREAKETH, AND HE SAID: I WILL NOT LET THEE GO, EXCEPT THOU BLESS ME. R. Judah discoursed on the verse: Who is she that looketh forth as the dawn, fair as the moon, clear as the sun, terrible as an army with banners? (S. S. VI, 10). 'This verse', he said, 'refers to Israel, at the time when the Holy One, blessed be He, will raise them up and bring them out of captivity. At that time he will first open for them a tiny aperture of light, then another somewhat larger, and so on until He will throw open for them the supernal gates which face on all the four quarters of the world. And, indeed, this process is followed by God in all that He does for Israel and the righteous among them. For we know that when a man has been long shut up in darkness it is necessary, on bringing him into the light, first to make for him an opening as small as the eye of a needle, and then one a little larger, and so on gradually until he can endure the full light. It is the same with Israel, as we read: "By little and little I will drive them out from before thee, until thou be increased, etc." (Ex. XXIII, 30). So, too, a sick man who is recovering cannot be given a full diet all at once, but only gradually. But with Esau it was not so. His light came at a bound, but it will gradually be withdrawn from him until Israel will come into their own and destroy him completely from this world and from the world to come. Because he plunged into the light all at once, therefore he will be utterly and completely exterminated. Israel's light, on the other hand, will come little by little, until they will become strong. God will illumine them forever. All then will ask: "Who is she that looketh forth like the dawn", this being a reference to the first tiny streak of the dawn, then "fair as the moon", the light of the moon being stronger than that of the dawn, and then "clear as the sun", that is, a still stronger light, and finally "terrible as an army with banners", expressive of the light in its full strength. For, just as when the dawn emerges from the darkness its light at first is faint, but gradually brightens till full daylight is reached, so when God will bestir Himself to shine upon the Community of Israel, He will first shed on them a streak of light like that of the daybreak which is still black, then increase it to make it "fair as the moon", then "clear as the sun", until it will be "tremendous as an army with banners", as already explained.'

Zohar: Bereshith, Section 1, Page 170b

[Note: The first 28 lines of the Hebrew text (until "Said R. Hiya) do not appear in our translation.]

Now in connection with Jacob it is not written: "for daybreak has come (ba')", but "for daybreak has gone up ('alah)". For at the moment when daybreak arrived, the Chieftain summoned all his strength and struck out at Jacob in order thereby to impart power to Esau; but as soon as the blackness of the dawn passed the light came on and Jacob's power increased; for his time had then arrived to come into the light, as it is written: "And the sun rose upon him as he passed over Peniel. In the next words, AND HE LIMPED UPON HIS THIGH, there is a hint that after Israel in exile have endured many sufferings and pains, when daylight rises upon them and they attain to rest and ease they will in their memory go through again their past sufferings and afflictions and will wonder how they could have endured them. So Jacob, after "the sun had risen upon him", was "limping upon his thigh", vexing himself for what had befallen. But when the blackness of the early dawn passed he made a great effort and grasped his opponent, whose strength at the same time gave out, his dominion being only during the night, whereas Jacob has ascendancy in the daytime. Hence he said: LET ME GO, FOR THE DAY BREAKETH, so that, as he might have added, "I am now in thy power".

R. Hiya said: 'Had Jacob's strength not failed him at that spot (the sinew that shrank) he would have prevailed against the angel so completely that Esau's power would then have been broken both on high and below.' R. Simeon remarked: 'Ezekiel the prophet said: "As the appearance of the bow that is in the cloud in the day of rain, so was the appearance of the brightness round about. This was the appearance of the likeness of the glory of the Lord. And when I saw it I fell upon my face, etc." (Ez. I, 28). This verse illustrates the difference between the other prophets and Moses, of whom it is written, "And there hath not arisen a prophet since in Israel like unto Moses" (Deut. XXXIV, 10). For Moses gazed into the clear mirror of prophecy, whereas all the other prophets looked into a hazy mirror.

VAYISHLAH

Moses received the divine message standing and with all his senses unimpaired, and he comprehended it fully, as it is written: "even manifestly, and not in dark speeches" (Num. XII, 8); whereas other prophets fell on their faces in a state of exhaustion and did not obtain a perfectly clear message. All those prophets thus failed to realise fully what God had in store for Esau in the future, with the exception of the prophet Obadiah, who, being himself a proselyte, originating from the side of Esau, was able to receive a full message with regard to Esau. The reason why all the prophets except Moses were thus weak was that "he touched the hollow of Jacob's thigh through the sinew of the thigh-vein"-the sinew that draws to the thigh all its energy; the energy of the thigh was thus broken, and Jacob remained "limping upon his thigh", and hence the rest of the prophets, with the exception of Moses, could not retain their faculties during a vision and grasp it fully. Now just as the prophets were thus weakened, so when scholars are not encouraged and no one gives them pecuniary support the Torah is forgotten from one generation to another and its strength is weakened, those who toil in it having no support, and the sinful kingdom increases in power with each day. Much evil therefore results; since, as the upholders of the Torah become weaker, strength is thereby gained by him who has no legs to stand upon. For when God said to the serpent, "upon thy belly shalt thou go" (Gen. III, 14), the serpent had his supports and legs cut off so that he was left with nothing to stand on. But when Israel neglect to support the Torah, they thereby provide him with supports and legs on which to stand firm and upright.

Many were the stratagems and cunning devices to which the serpent-rider resorted on that night against Jacob. For he well knew that "the voice is the voice of Jacob, but the hands are the hands of Esau" (Gen. XXVII, 22), so that whenever the voice of Jacob is interrupted, the hands of Esau are reinforced. He therefore cast about on all sides for means of interrupting his voice, but he found him strong on all sides, his arms strong on both sides and firmly upheld between them, and the Torah firmly entrenched therein. Seeing, therefore, that he could not prevail against him, he "touched the hollow of his thigh". For he knew that when the supports of the Torah are broken, the Torah itself is shaken; hence he thought that in this way he should reap the benefit of what their father had said, namely: "And it shall come to pass when thou shalt break loose, that thou shalt shake his yoke from thy neck" (Ibid. 40). His whole purpose in contending with Jacob was to break the force of the Torah, and when he saw that he could not strike at the Torah itself, he weakened the power of its upholders; for without upholders of the Torah there will be no "voice of Jacob", and the hands of Esau will operate. Jacob, on seeing this, as soon as day broke, seized hold of him and did not let him go, so that he blessed him and confirmed to him those blessings, and said to him: "Thy name shall be called no more Jacob (Ya'aqob=supplanter), but Israel (Yisrael=princehood and strength), so that no one can prevail against thee." Now, from that serpent issue numerous hosts which disperse themselves on every side to prowl about the world. It is incumbent, therefore, upon us to preserve in a complete state the sinew of the thigh-vein, for although the serpent-rider touched it, it retained its vitality, and we require its strength to establish ourselves in the world and to make good the words: "For thou hast striven with God and with men, and hast prevailed." When the adversary sees that that part is not broken or consumed, his own strength and courage is broken

and he can no more do any harm to the sons of Jacob. It is for that reason that we are forbidden to give that part (of an animal) to anyone to eat and may not benefit of it in any way. R' Jesse the elder connected the word "touched" in this clause with the same word in the verse: "He that toucheth the dead, even any man's dead body, etc." (Num. XIX, 11). 'Just as in the latter case', he said, 'there is defilement, so here defilement is implied, that part of the body being an object of defilement, so that we may not put it to any use whatever.' Blessed be the Merciful One who gave the Torah to Israel, whereby to merit this world and the world to come, as it is written: "Length of days is in her right hand; in her left hand are riches and honour" (Prov. III, 16). AND HE HIMSELF PASSED OVER BEFORE THEM, AND BOWED HIMSELF TO THE GROUND SEVEN TIMES, UNTIL HE CAME NEAR TO HIS BROTHER. Said R. Eleazar: It is written, "For thou shalt bow down to no other god, for the Lord, whose name is Jealous, is a jealous God" (Ex. XXXIV, 14). Now, Jacob was the consummation of the patriarchs, who was selected as the choicest portion of the Almighty, and was brought specially near to Him and was perfected above and below. How came it, then, that such a man should bow down to the wicked Esau, who was of the side of another god, so that bowing down to him was the same as bowing down to another god? The proverb, it is true, says, "When a fox is in honour, bow down to him." This, however, could not apply to Esau, who was like another god, belonging to that side and that portion to whom Jacob would in no way bow down. A similar difficulty arises with the verse: "And thus ye shall say: All hail! (lehay, lit. to the living one) and peace be both unto thee, and peace be to thy house, and peace be unto all that thou hast" (I Sam. XXV, 6). Now, inasmuch as, according to our teaching, it is forbidden to give the first greeting to a wicked man, how could David have sent such a message to Nabal? There, however, the explanation is that David in reality addressed his words to God, as is implied in the expression lehay (to the Living One), although Nabal misunderstood them as addressed to himself. Similarly, when we read: "And Israel bowed himself upon the bed's head" (Gen. XLVII, 31), we are not to suppose that he bowed down in worship to his son, but that his obeisance was directed towards the spot where the Shekinah rested. So in this passage, the words: "and he himself passed over before them" refer to the celestial Shekinah who went before Jacob in order to afford him the promised protection from on high. When Jacob became aware of this he thought it incumbent on him to make obeisance towards the Holy One, blessed be He, who was going, as it were, in front of him, and so "he bowed himself to the ground seven times, until he came near to his brother". Mark that it is not written, "and he bowed down to Esau", but simply "he bowed down", implying that he did so because he saw the Holy One, blessed be He, going before him, not that he made obeisance by way of worship to anyone else. Everything was thus in order. Happy are the righteous all of whose actions are for the glory of their Master, and with the object that they themselves should turn neither to the right nor to the left.' AND ESAU RAN TO MEET HIM, AND EMBRACED HIM, AND FELL ON HIS NECK AND KISSED HIM; AND THEY WEPT. The word zavaro (his neck) is used here instead of the more usual zavorav; while dots are placed over the letters of the word vayishoqehu (and he kissed him). Said R. Isaac: 'Many are the methods by which the Scripture conveys recondite allusions, yet with a common purpose. It is written: "But the wicked are like the troubled sea; for it cannot rest, and its waters cast up mire and dirt" (Is. LVII, 20). This verse may be applied to Esau, all of whose actions were wicked and sinful. His approaches to Jacob on this occasion were insincere, as is shown by the signs mentioned above. The "neck" here is an allusion to Jerusalem, which is indeed the neck of the universe, and the singular form zavaro is used instead of the regular dual form zavorav as a hint that the seed of Esau would one day fall upon and destroy one of the two Temples. Again, the dots above the word vayishaqehu (and he kissed him) indicate that he kissed him reluctantly. The verse: "but the kisses of an enemy are importunate" (Prov. XXVII, 6) has been applied by our teachers to Balaam, who, although he blessed Israel, did it against his will; but Esau provides another illustration.' R. Yose said: 'It is written: "For thou hast smitten all my enemies upon the cheek, thou hast broken the teeth of the wicked" (Ps. III, 8), and there is a tradition which reads here shirbabtha (thou hast lengthened) instead of shibbartha (thou hast broken), to indicate that Esau's teeth were suddenly lengthened to prevent him from biting.' We read further: AND THEY WEPT; both the one and the other with good cause,

Zohar: Bereshith, Section 1, Page 172a

as the companions have expounded. For Esau was so evilly disposed to Jacob that even at that very time he was planning how to afflict him and bring accusations against him in the distant future. Hence they wept: Jacob for fear lest he might not escape from his brother's onslaught, and Esau to think that his father was still alive, so that he was unable to do any harm to Jacob.' R. Abba said: 'Assuredly Esau's wrath was allayed at the moment he beheld Jacob, since his chieftain had confirmed Jacob's claims, and therefore it would have been vain for Esau to vent his wrath. For all the affairs of this world depend on what is done above, and whatever is agreed upon above is accepted below, and no power can be exercised below until power is granted above. Thus one world depends always on the other.' LET MY LORD, I PRAY THEE, PASS OVER BEFORE HIS SERVANT; AND I WILL JOURNEY ON GENTLY, ETC. R. Eleazar said: 'This bears out what we said before, namely, that Jacob did not wish as yet to avail himself of the first blessings that he received from his father, not one of which had so far been fulfilled, since he reserved them for the end of days when his descendants should need them in their struggle against the nations of the world. Hence, when Esau said: "Let us take our journey, and let us go", that is, "let us share together this world and rule it in partnership", Jacob replied: "Let my lord, I pray thee, pass over before his servant", as much as to say: "Have thou first thy dominion of this world, and I will journey on gently, and reserve myself for the world to come and for the latter days that flow on gently... 'until I come unto my lord unto Seir', i.e. I will endure subjection to thee until my time will come to rule over the mount of Esau, as it is written: 'And saviours shall come up on mount Zion to judge the mount of Esau; and the kingdom shall be the Lord's'" (Oba. I, 21).' AND JACOB JOURNEYED TO SUCCOTH, AND BUILT HIM A HOUSE, AND MADE BOOTHS FOR HIS CATTLE. THEREFORE THE NAME OF THE PLACE IS CALLED SUCCOTH. R. Hiya discoursed on the verse: Except the Lord build the house, etc., except the Lord keep the city, etc. (Ps. CXXVII, 1). He said: 'When God resolved to create the world, He produced out of the primordial lamp of scintillation a nucleus that flashed forth from the midst of darkness and remained on high while the darkness went below. It flashed along through a hundred paths and ways, some narrow and some broad, until the House of the world [Tr. note: By 'house of the world', here seems to be meant the 'world of emanation', which is 'central', as being least penetrable to the intelligence.] was made. This House forms the centre of the universe, and it has many doors and vestibules on all its sides, sacred and exalted abodes where the celestial birds build their nests, each according to its kind. From the midst of it rises a large tree, with mighty branches and abundance of fruit providing food for all, which rears itself to the clouds of heaven and is lost to view between three rocks, from which it again emerges, so that it is both above and below them. From this tree the house is watered. In this house are stored many precious and undiscovered treasures. Thus was the house built and completed. That tree is visible in the day-time but is hidden at night, whereas the house becomes manifest in the night and is hidden by day. As soon as darkness sets in and all the doors on all sides are closed, innumerable spirits fly about, desiring to know what is in it. They pass between the birds, bringing their credentials, they flit about and see many things, until the darkness by which the house is enveloped is aroused and sends forth a flame and strikes with mighty hammers, causing the doors to be opened, and splitting the rocks; then the flame goes up and down and strikes the world with blows that resound above and below. Then a

Zohar: Bereshith, Section 1, Page 172b

herald ascends, attaches himself to the ether, and makes proclamation. That ether emerges from the pillar of cloud of the inner altar, and spreads itself out into the four quarters of the world. A thousand thousand stand at the left side and a myriad of myriads stand at the right side. And the herald stands in his place and makes loud proclamation. Then innumerable are those who chant hymns and make obeisance; and two doors open, one on the South and one on the North. The house then is lifted up and is fastened between the two sides, whilst hymns are chanted and songs of praise ascend. Then some enter silently whilst the house is lit up on every side with six lights, brilliant and resplendent, and from thence flow out six rivers of balsam from which all the "animals of the field" are watered, as it says: "They give drink to every animal of the field, the wild asses quench their thirst, etc." (Ps. CIV, 11). They thus continue singing praises until daybreak. At daybreak, the stars, the constellations and their hosts all commence to chant songs of praise and hymns, as we read: "When the morning stars sang together, and all the sons of God shouted for joy" (Job XXXVIII, 7). Now observe the words: "Except the Lord build the house they labour in vain that build it." This is a reference to the Most High King who constantly builds the house and perfects it, but only when acceptable worship ascends from below in due form. Then again the words "Except the Lord keep the city, the watchman waketh but in vain" refer to the time when the darkness of the night sets in and armed companies roam to and fro in the world, and the doors are shut, and the city is guarded on all sides so that the uncircumcised and the unclean may not come near it. So it says: "For henceforth there shall no more come unto thee the uncircumcised and the unclean" (Is. LII, 1), since God will one day remove them from the world. Who, then, is the uncircumcised and who is the unclean? They are both one, the same that seduced Adam and his wife to follow him and so bring death into the world. He, too, will continue to defile this house until such time as the Holy One, blessed be He, will cause him to vanish from the world. Hence: "Except the Lord keep the city, etc."

Observe that Jacob "journeyed to Succoth", whereas Esau "returned that day on his way unto Seir", each one taking the road toward his own side. Esau betook himself toward the side of Seir, that is, toward the "strange woman", the strange god, which are both designated by the name Seir; whereas Jacob journeyed to Succoth (lit. tabernacles), a name indicative of the true faith. "And built him a house", to wit, the House of Jacob.' Said R. Eleazar: 'Here is an indication that Jacob instituted evening prayer. We read further: "and he made booths (succoth) for his cattle"; these were other tabernacles which he made for guarding them, but the former succoth were his own portion.' AND JACOB CAME PERFECT (shalem): perfect in every respect; the same allusion is contained in the words: "In Shalem (lit. in perfection) also he set his tabernacle" (Ps. LXXVI, 3). For faith became his constant companion when he attained perfection, when he was crowned in the spot appropriate to him; and then also that Tabernacle was crowned along with him who was the perfection of the patriarchs, being completed by his sons. He was thus perfect on all sides: perfect on high, perfect below, perfect in heaven and perfect on earth. Perfect on high in that he was the consummation of the patriarchs, the glory of Israel; perfect below, through his holy sons; perfect in heaven and perfect on earth, so that "in perfection also he set his tabernacle". AND DINAH THE DAUGHTER OF LEAH WENT OUT. The companions have remarked that there exist a variety of grades and sides on high, each one different from the other, serpents of all sorts, one kind endeavouring to gain dominion over the other and to devour prey, each according to its kind. From the side of the unclean spirit ever so many grades branch out, and all of them lie in wait to bring accusations against each other. Hence it is written: "Thou shalt not plow with an ox and an ass together" (Deut. XXII, 10), inasmuch as vhen these are joined together they bring accusations against mankind. Observe further that the great desire of the unclean grades is to find matter of charge against the holy sides. Thus, since Jacob was a holy man, they all lay in wait for him and contended with him. First the serpent bit him when he touched the hollow of his thigh, and now the ass bit him. Then it was Jacob himself who opposed the serpent, now it was Simeon and Levi, who belonged to the side

Zohar: Bereshith, Section 1, Page 173a

of stern judgement, who stood up against the ass and prevailed over him and completely subdued him, as we read: "And they slew Hamor (lit. ass) and Shechem his son with the edge of the sword." Now Simeon, who was under the zodiacal sign of ox (Taurus), set upon the ass so as to prevent the two from joining, as then the latter would have set upon him. All came to contend with Jacob, who, however, was delivered from them and afterwards obtained dominion over them. Then came the one who is designated ox, and made himself perfect among the asses, that is, among those who were of the side of the ass. For Joseph was designated ox, and of the Egyptian the Scripture says: "whose flesh is as the flesh of asses" (Ez. XXIII, 20). It was for this reason that the sons of Jacob later on fell among those asses, inasmuch as the ox was joined with them; and they bit them to the bone until Levi arose as on the former occasion, and scattered and subdued them, and utterly broke their force. He also removed the ox from them, as it is written: "And Moses took the bones of Joseph with him" (Ex. XIII, 19). Observe that when Simeon assailed the ass (Hamor) on the first occasion he first made them see blood -the blood of circumcision-and after that "they slew all the males". God dealt in the same way through the hand of the Levite, Moses, with those other asses, the Egyptians. He first showed them blood and afterwards "the Lord slew all the firstborn in the land of Egypt" (Ibid. XII, 29). In connection with Hamor it is writter: "They took their flocks and their herds and their asses, etc."; in connection with those other asses it is written: "jewels of silver and jewels of gold, and raiment" (Ibid. 35), also: "And a mixed multitude went up also with them; and flocks and herds, even very much cattle" (Ibid. 38). In the same way, too, as Simeon withstood this one ass, Levi withstood that company of asses. They all conspired against Jacob the holy man and essayed to bite him, but he together with his sons stood up against them and subdued them. But now that Esau is biting him and his children, who will stand up against him? Jacob and Joseph, one on one side and the other on the other side. So Scripture says: "And the house of Jacob shall be a fire, and the house of Joseph a flame, and the house of Esau for stubble, etc." (Oba. I, 18). AND THEY JOURNEYED; AND A TERROR OF GOD WAS UPON THE CITIES THAT WERE ROUND ABOUT THEM, AND THEY DID NOT PURSUE AFTER THE SONS OF JACOB. R. Yose said: 'They all came together, but when they commenced to gird on their arms a terror seized them and they left them alone. Hence "they did not pursue after the sons of Jacob".' PUT AWAY THE STRANGE GODS, ETC. These were the silver and gold vessels that they had taken from Shechem, and on which were engraved images of their gods. R. Judah said: 'Their idols themselves were made of silver and gold, and Jacob hid them there in order that his children should not make use of the side of idolatry, as a man is forbidden to have any benefit whatsoever from it;'As R. Judah and R. Hizkiah were once walking together on the road, the latter said: 'It is written: "And he took the crown of Malcam from off his head; and the weight thereof was a talent of gold, and in it were precious stones; and it was set on David's head" (II Sam. XII, 30). Now, we have been taught that "Milcom the abomination of the Ammonites" (I Kings XI, 5) is the same as Malcam in this verse. How, then, was this crown permitted to be set on David's head? And further, why is it called "abomination", whereas other idols are referred to as "gods of the peoples", "strange gods", and the like?' R. Judah replied: 'Indeed, other idols are also called abominations, as we read: "And ye have seen their abominable things and their idols" (Deut. XXIX, 16). As regards the identification of Malcam with Milcom, this is certainly correct; nevertheless David was able to use the crown of Malcam because Ittai the Gittite, before he became a proselyte, broke it, that is to say, he disfigured the image which was on it, and so made its use permissible, [Tr. note: According to the Rabbinical rule: "An idolater can render his idol null and void."] and it was set on David's head. The idol of the Ammonites was a serpent graven deep on that crown, and for that reason it was called abomination.' R. Isaac said that the order "put away the strange gods" referred to the other women who brought with them on their persons all their ornaments. Hence it is written: AND THEY GAVE UNTO JACOB ALL THE FOREIGN GODS, to wit, of those women. AND JACOB HID THEM

Zohar: Bereshith, Section 1, Page 173b

so that his people should not derive any benefit whatever from the side of idolatry.

Observe the complete devotion of Jacob to the Almighty, as shown by his words: AND LET US ARISE, AND GO UP TO BETH-EL, AND I WILL MAKE THERE AN ALTAR UNTO GOD, WHO ANSWERED ME IN THE DAY OF MY DISTRESS, AND WAS WITH ME IN THE WAY WHICH I WENT. From these last words we learn that it is incumbent on a man to praise God and to give Him thanks for any miracle or any kindness that He has shown him. Observe that first Jacob said: "let us arise and go up to Beth-El", thus associating his children with him; but then: "and I will make there an altar", and not "we will make". The reason was that this task devolved upon him alone, since it was he who had passed through all those tribulations from the time when he fled from his brother, whereas his sons were not born until after. Hence he did not associate them with him. R. Eleazar said: 'From here we learn that he to whom a miracle is vouchsafed must himself offer thanks; just as he who has eaten a meal should say grace, and not one who has eaten nothing.' AND HE BUILT THERE AN ALTAR, ETC. There is no mention here of libation or offering. The reason is that Jacob's intention was only to complete the grade which required completion, to wit, to join the lower grade, referred to by the word "altar", to the upper, referred to by the word "Lord". Hence he only built an altar and did not offer drink-offerings or burnt-offerings. AND CALLED THE PLACE EL-BETH-EL: a name analogous to the Most High Name, inasmuch as when there is a plenitude of light, then "like mother, like daughter, the two becoming one. BECAUSE THERE GOD WAS (lit. were) REVEALED UNTO HIM: the word Elohim (God) here is an allusion to the seventy who are always attendant on the Shekinah, there being seventy thrones round the Shekinah. Hence: "there God was revealed unto him", indicating the same place of which it is written: "And behold, the Lord stood beside him" (Gen. XXVIII, 13). AND GOD WENT UP FROM HIM IN THE PLACE WHERE HE SPOKE WITH HIM. R. Simeon said: From here we learn that Jacob formed the Holy Chariot together with the other patriarchs; further, that Jacob constitutes the supernal Holy Chariot which will restore the full light of the moon, and that he forms a Chariot by himself, as implied in the statement: "And God went up from him". It is written: "For what great nation is there, that hath God so nigh unto them, as the Lord our God is whensoever we call upon him?" (Deut. IV, 7). How dear', he exclaimed, 'must Israel be to the Almighty, seeing that there is no nation or language among all the idol-worshippers that has a god to hearken unto them, whereas the Holy One, blessed be He, is ready to receive the prayers and supplications of Israel in their hour of need, to hearken to their prayers for the sake of their grade.'

AND GOD SAID: THY NAME SHALL BE CALLED No MORE JACOB, BUT ISRAEL SHALL BE THY NAME; AND (he) CALLED HIS NAME ISRAEL. The subject of "and called" is the Shekinah, as in the expression: "And (he) called unto Moses": whereas the name "God" earlier in the sentence refers to the higher grade. The name Israel was given him in virtue of his having achieved perfection, and so by this name he was raised to a higher grade and was made perfect in that name. As R. Eleazar and R. Yose were once walking on the road, the latter said to R. Eleazar: 'Assuredly it is as you said, that Jacob was the consummation of the patriarchs and that he was attached to all the sides and so his name was called Israel. But how comes it that God afterwards again called him many times by the name of Jacob, and that he is commonly called Jacob just as before?' R. Eleazar replied: 'That is a good question. To find an answer, consider the verse: "The Lord will go forth as a mighty one, he will stir up jealousy like a warrior" (Is. XLII, 12). Why say as a mighty one, seeing that He is a mighty one; and why say like a warrior, seeing that He is a warrior? But the truth is that, as we have learned, the name Tetragrammaton (Lord) is everywhere expressive of the attribute of mercy. Now, assuredly,

Zohar: Bereshith, Section 1, Page 174a

God is named Tetragrammaton (Lord), as it is written: "I am the Lord Tetragrammaton" (Ibid. 8). Yet we see that at times His name is called Elohim (God), which is everywhere expressive of judgement. The explanation is that when the righteous are numerous among mankind, He is called by the name of Tetragrammaton (Lord), the name which implies mercy, but when sinners abound, He is called by the name of Elohim (God). Similarly with Jacob. When he is not among enemies, or in a strange land, his name is Israel, but when he is among enemies or in a strange land he is called Jacob.' R. Yose rejoined: 'This does not quite solve the difficulty, seeing that it is written: "thy name shall no more be called Jacob", and yet all the time we do call him Jacob; as for your remark that he is only called Jacob when among enemies or in a strange land, do we not find it written: "And Jacob dwelt in the land of his father's sojournings in the land of Canaan" (Gen. XXXVII, 1), which was not a strange land?' R. Eleazar replied: 'Just as the names "Lord" and "God" indicate different degrees, so the names Jacob and Israel indicate different degrees; and as for the words "thy name shall no more be called Jacob", that signifies merely that Jacob should not be his fixed name.' Said R. Yose: 'If that is so, how is it that the name of Abraham became fixed after God had said: "Neither shall thy name any more be called Abram, but thy name shall be Abraham" (Ibid. XVII, 5).' R. Eleazar replied: 'It is because there it is written: "but thy name shall be (vehayah), that is, always, whereas here it is written: "but Israel shall be (yihyeh) thy name", that is, at least on one occasion, if not oftener. When, however, his posterity were crowned with priests and Levites, and were raised to high degrees, he was invested with the name of Israel in perpetuity.'

Whilst they were walking, R. Yose said to R. Eleazar: 'It has been said that with Rachel's death the house was transferred to Her who required to be adorned with twelve tribes. Nevertheless, why should Rachel have died immediately after the birth of Benjamin?' R. Eleazar in reply said: 'It was in order that the Shekinah should be duly crowned and take her place in the house as "a joyful mother of children". With Benjamin, the Shekinah was equipped with the full twelve tribes, and with him the kingdom of heaven began to be made manifest on earth. Now the beginning of any manifestation is brought about with strain, and involves a doom of death before it can become established. Here, when the Shekinah was about to assume her rightful place and to take over the house, the doom fell upon Rachel. Similarly, when the kingdom was about to be made manifest on earth, it commenced with a judgement, and the kingdom was not established in its place until a doom had fallen upon Saul, in accordance with his deserts; and only then was it established. It is a general rule that beginnings are rough, whereas the subsequent course is smooth. Thus, on New Year's day (Rosh-hashana) the year opens with severity, as the whole world passes under judgement, each individual according to his deeds, but soon after comes relief and forgiveness and atonement. The reason is that the beginning is from the left side, and so it brings harsh judgements, until the right side is aroused and ease follows. In time to come God will first treat the idolatrous nations gently and indulgently, but afterwards with severity and stern judgement. So Scripture says: "The Lord will go forth as a mighty one, he will stir up jealousy as a warrior; he will cry, yea, he will shout aloud, he will prove himself mighty against his enemies" (Is. XLII, 13); which interpreted means that first He will manifest Himself as Tetragrammaton (the Lord), in His attribute of mercy, then as a mighty one, but not in His full might, then as a warrior, but not in His full war panoply, and finally, His whole might will become manifest against them in order to exterminate them, so that "he will cry, yea, he will shout aloud, he will prove himself mighty against his enemies." Again, it is written: "Then shall the Lord go forth, and fight against those nations, as when he fighteth in the day of battle" (Zech. XIV, 3). Also: "Who is this that cometh from Edom with crimson garments from Bozrah? etc." (Is. LXIII, 1)' AND IT CAME TO PASS, AS HER SOUL WAS IN DEPARTING FOR SHE DIED-THAT SHE CALLED HIS NAME BEN-ONI; BUT HIS FATHER CALLED HIM BENJAMIN. R. Judah discoursed on the verse: The Lord is good, a stronghold in the day of trouble; and he knoweth them that take refuge in him (Nahum I, 7). 'Happy', he said, 'is the man who finds his strength in the Holy One, blessed be He, since His strength is invincible. The Lord is indeed "good to all" (Ps. CXLV, 9), "a stronghold", wherein is salvation, as we read: "He is a stronghold of

Zohar: Bereshith, Section 1, Page 174b

salvation" (Ibid. XXVIII, 8); "in the day of trouble", to wit, in the day of Israel's oppression at the hand of other nations. Now of him who relaxes his hold of the Holy One, blessed be He, it is written: "If thou art faint in the day of adversity, thy strength is straitened" (Prov. XXIV, 10), and the only way of holding firmly to God is to hold firmly to the Torah; for whosoever holds firmly to the Torah holds firmly to the tree of life, and, as it were, adds strength to the community of Israel. But if he relaxes his hold of the Torah, then, as it were, he presses hard the Shekinah, which is the strength of the world. Again, when a man relaxes his hold of the Torah and walks in the wrong path, ever so many enemies are ready at hand to act as his accusers in the day of trouble, nay, even his own soul, which is his power and strength, turns against him, and becomes his enemy, so that it may be said of him "thy strength becomes an enemy" (zar=enemy, or straitened).' Said R. Abba: 'When a man follows the guidance of the Torah and walks in the straight path, many are the advocates that rise up to say a good word for him. Thus we read: "If there be for him an angel, an intercessor, one among a thousand, to vouch for man's uprightness; then he is gracious unto him, and saith: Deliver him from the pit, I have found a ransom" (Job XXXIII, 23, 24). These verses', continued R. Abba, 'present a difficulty. Is not everything revealed before God, that He should require an angel to point out to Him the good or bad that is found in a man, so that only when a man has defenders on his side to recall his merits before Him, and no accusers, then He is gracious unto him, and saith: "Deliver him from going down into the pit, I have found a ransom"? But the language of the text, if properly considered, contains the answer. For it would have sufficed to say: "If there be for him an angel"; who, then, is the "intercessor, one among a thousand"? It is one of the angels appointed to follow man on his left side. There are a thousand such, as it says, "A thousand may fall at thy side, and ten thousand at thy right hand" (Ps. XCI, 7). Now "one among a thousand" is a designation of the evil prompter, who is the outstanding figure of the thousand on the left, since he is the one who ascends on high and obtains authorisation. Hence, if a man walks in the way of truth and the evil prompter becomes his servant, according to the words, "Better is he that is lightly esteemed, and hath a servant" (Prov. XII, 9), then he ascends on high and becomes the man's advocate, pleading his merits before God, whereupon God says: "Deliver him from going down into the pit." Nevertheless, the evil prompter does not return empty-handed, since another man is delivered into his power, one whose sins he has already set forth, and this one is a ransom for the other man. This is what is meant by the words: "I (God) have found a compensation" (for thee, the accuser). According to another interpretation, the ransom consists in the merits of the man, through which he is freed from the pit and from death. It is therefore incumbent on a man to walk in the path of truth so that the accuser should be turned into his defender. A similar procedure is employed by Israel on the Day of Atonement, when they tender a he-goat to the evil prompter and so engage his attention until he ascends and gives testimony before the Almighty, in their favour. Thus Solomon says: "If thine adversary be hungry, give him bread to eat, and if he be thirsty, give him water to drink" (Ibid. XXV, 21), referring to the evil prompter. The words: "The Lord is good, a stronghold in the day of trouble" apply to Jacob when Esau came forward to accuse him, and the words: "and he knoweth them that put their trust in him" were exemplified when the trouble of Dinah befell him. Observe that the accuser attacks a man only in time of danger; and so it was on account of Jacob having delayed to fulfil his vows which he had made to God that the accuser came forward against him,

Zohar: Bereshith, Section 1, Page 175a

selecting the moment when Rachel's life was in danger. "Behold," he said, "Jacob has made vows and has not paid them; he has wealth and children and is short of nothing, yet he has not paid his vow that he made before Thee; and Thou hast not punished him." Then straightway "Rachel travailed and she had hard labour", the term "hard" indicating that a severe doom was issued on high at the instigation of the angel of death.' AND RACHEL DIED. We have seen that Jacob, at the time Esau came up to him, put the handmaids and their children foremost, and Leah and her children after, and Rachel and Joseph hindermost. Why did he put Rachel hindermost? Because he feared that the wicked Esau might observe her beauty and assail him on account of her. It is written further: "Then the handmaids came near, they and their children, and they bowed down. And Leah also and her children came near, and bowed down", the females before the males. But in regard to Rachel it is written: "and after came Joseph near and Rachel", that is, Joseph in front of his mother, so as to protect her. And here Rachel was punished at the hand of the evil prompter, who availed himself of the moment of danger and brought accusations against her; and Jacob was punished for not having paid his vow. Jacob felt this blow more acutely than all the other sufferings that befell him. That her death was due to him we learn from his words: "Rachel died upon me" (Gen. XLVIII, 7), or, as we may translate, "on account of me", i.e. through my not having paid my vows. R. Yose said: 'It is written: "the curse that is causeless shall come home" (Prov. XXVI, 2). This signifies that the curse of a righteous man, even if pronounced under a misapprehension, once uttered is caught up by the evil prompter to be used at a moment of danger. Now Jacob said to Laban: "With whomsoever thou findest thy gods, he shall not live" (Gen. XXXI, 32); and although he was unaware that it was Rachel who had stolen them, the Satan (adversary) who perpetually dogs the footsteps of the sons of men, seized on that utterance. Hence we are taught that a man should "never open his mouth for the Satan", inasmuch as the latter is sure to take hold of his utterance and use it to bring accusations on high and below; all the more so if it is the utterance of a righteous man or a sage. These, then, were the true causes of Rachel's death.' AND IT CAME TO PASS, AS HER SOUL DEPARTED-FOR SHE DIED. R. Abba said: 'What need is there to state that she died, after it says that her soul departed? The object is to make it clear that her soul did not return again to her body, as sometimes happens with some people. Thus we read: "And his spirit returned unto him"; also: "And their heart departed" (Gen. XLII, 28); or: "My soul departed" (S. S. V, 6); again: "until there was no soul left in him" (I Kings XVII, 17). But when Rachel's soul passed out, it did not return, and so she died.' AND SHE CALLED HIS NAME BEN-ONI (the son of my sorrow), in reference to the doom that was pronounced against her; but Jacob turned him round and attached him to the right (Benyamin=the son of the right hand), as the West (of which Benjamin was symbolic) needed to be bound up with the right. Thus, although he was Ben-oni (the son of sorrow), derived from the side of chastisement, yet was he also Benjamin (the son of the right), as the mother was bound up with the right and was buried by the road, as explained elsewhere. Rachel's death and burial-place are recorded, but neither the death nor the burial-place of Leah is recorded; and this although the matriarchs have a joint symbolism, which has been explained elsewhere. AND JACOB SET UP A PILLAR UPON HER GRAVE. R. Yose said: 'He did this in order that her burial-place should never be forgotten until the day when God shall raise the dead to life. This is borne out by the phrase: "unto this day", which means until that great day.' R. Judah said: 'It means, until the day when the Shekinah will return with the exiles of Israel to that spot, as it is written: "And there is hope for thy future, saith the Lord; and thy children shall return to their own border" (Jer. XXXI, 17). This is the oath which God swore unto her; and Israel are destined, when they return from exile, to stop at Rachel's grave and weep there as she wept over Israel's exile. It is thus written: "They shall come with weeping, and with supplications will I lead them" (Ibid. 9); also: "for thy work shall be rewarded" (Ibid. 16). And at that

Zohar: Bereshith, Section 1, Page 175b

time Rachel who lies on the way will rejoice with Israel and with the Shekinah. The Companions have thus expounded all this.' AND IT CAME TO PASS, WHILE ISRAEL DWELT IN THAT LAND, THAT REUBEN WENT AND LAY WITH BILHAH HIS FATHER'S CONCUBINE; AND ISRAEL HEARD OF IT. NOW THE SONS OF JACOB WERE TWELVE. R. Eleazar said: 'The term dwelt (sh'kon) indicates that Leah and Rachel had died by that time, and the house had been taken over by the new mistress (the Shekinah). In spite of the words of the text, we are not to suppose that Reuben really lay with Bilhah. The truth is that during the lives of Leah and Rachel the Shekinah hovered over them; and now that they had died the Shekinah never departed from the house, but took up there her abode, namely, in the tent of Bilhah; nor would it have been found there had not Jacob formed a new union of male and female. But Reuben, in his displeasure at seeing Bilhah filling his mother's place, came and disarranged the couch; and because the Shekinah rested on it, it is written, "And he lay with Bilhah".' R. Jesse said that Reuben laid himself down to sleep on that couch, thus showing disrespect to the Shekinah. Hence Reuben was not excluded from the list of the tribes; and so Scripture relates that "the sons of Jacob were twelve", commencing with Reuben, Jacob's firstborn, thus putting him at the head of the tribes.

R. Judah discoursed on the verse: For the ways of the Lord are right, and the just do walk in them; but transgressors stumble therein (Hos. XIV, 10). 'All the ways of God', he said, 'are right and true, but mankind know not and regard not what it is that keeps them alive. Hence "the just do walk in them", because they know the ways of God, and they devote themselves to the Torah; for whoever devotes himself to the Torah knows those ways and follows them without turning either to the right or the left. "But transgressors do stumble therein", to wit, the sinners, since they labour not in the Torah nor regard the ways of the Almighty, and know not in which way they are walking. And since they are thoughtless and do not study the Torah, they stumble in their ways in this world and in the world to come. Now the soul of one who has laboured in the study of the Torah, when it leaves this world, ascends by the ways and paths of the Torah-ways and paths familiar to them. They who know the ways and paths of the Torah in this world follow them in the other world when they leave this world. But those who do not study the Torah in this world and know not its ways and paths, when they leave this world know not how to follow those ways and paths, and hence stumble therein. They thus follow other ways which are not the ways of the Torah, and are visited with many chastisements. Of him who devotes himself to the Torah, on the other hand, it is written: "When thou liest down, it shall watch over thee; and when thou awakest, it shall talk with thee" (Prov. VI, 22). "When thou liest down", to wit, in the grave, the Torah shall watch over thee against the judgement of the other world; "and when thou awakest", that is, when the Holy One, blessed be He, will awake the spirits and souls so as to bring the dead to life again, it shall talk with thee, the Torah will speak in defence of the body, so that those bodies which laboured to keep the Torah as required will rise up. These it is who will be the first to rise up, and of whom it is written: "And many of them that sleep in the dust of the earth shall awake, some to everlasting life, etc." (Dan. XII, 2), for the reason that they occupied themselves with everlasting life, which is the Torah. Further, all the bodies of those who have devoted themselves to the Torah will be preserved, and the Torah will protect them, inasmuch as at that time the Holy One, blessed be He, will raise up a wind from all four quarters of the world, a wind specially prepared to bring to life all those who have laboured in the Torah so that they should live forever. It may be asked here, what of the dead who were revived by the prophet's invocation, "Come from the four winds, O breath" (Ez. XXXVII, 9), and who yet did not survive, but died a second time? The answer is that at that time, although the wind was compounded of all four winds, it did not come down to give them permanent life, but only to demonstrate the mode in which God will one day bring the dead to life, namely, by a wind

Zohar: Bereshith, Section 1, Page 176a

formed in this fashion. So that although those who were then resurrected turned again into bones, since their resurrection was only meant as a proof to the world that God will one day raise the dead to life, we may still believe that at the proper time the righteous will be resurrected for an everlasting life. For the Torah itself will stand by each one of those who have occupied themselves in the study of the Torah, recounting his merits before the Almighty.' R. Simeon said: 'All the words of the Torah, and all the doctrine of the Torah to which a man devotes his mind in this world, are ever before the Almighty, and at that time the Torah will recount how the man devoted himself to the Torah in this world, and thereat such men will all rise foreverlasting life, as we said already.' Thus, "the ways of the Lord are right, and the just do walk in them; but transgressors do stumble therein."

R. Hiya cited in this connection: "Now Eli was very old; and he heard all that his sons did unto all Israel, and how that they lay with the women that did service at the door of the tent of meeting" (I Sam. II, 22). 'Are we to believe', he said, 'that the priests of the Lord actually did such a thing? And what, in fact, were their sins as recorded by the Scripture? Merely that they "dealt contemptuously with the offering of the Lord" (Ibid. 17), and that "the custom of the priests with the people was that, when any man offered sacrifice....

Yea, before the fat was made to smoke, the priest's servant came, and said to the man that sacrificed: Give flesh to roast for the priest. Nay, but thou shalt give it to me now, and if not, I will take it by force" (Ibid. 16). In fact, they only took those portions that belonged to the priests, and it was only because they treated lightly the offerings that they were punished. Yet here Scripture states that "they lay with the women that did service at the door of the tent of meeting". Assuredly they could not have committed so grave a sin, and that in so sacred a place, without the whole of Israel arising and slaying them. The truth is that what they did was to prevent the women from entering and offering their prayers until the other sacrifices had been offered, because their offerings were of a kind in which the priests had no portion. It is this action of preventing them from entering the sanctuary which is described by the words: "they lay with the women, etc." Similarly, in the case of Reuben, we should not dream of taking literally the words "and he lay with Bilhah". What he did was to prevent her from performing her conjugal duty to his father, and this was the object of his disarranging his father's couch; and, moreover, he did it in the presence of the Shekinah; for the Shekinah is always present whenever marital intercourse is performed as a religious duty; and whoever obstructs such a performance causes the Shekinah to depart from the world. So Scripture says: "Because thou wentest up to thy father's bed; then profanedst thou that one that went up to my couch" (Gen. XLIX, 4). Hence it is written: "that Reuben went and lay with Bilhah, his father's concubine; and Israel heard of it. Now the sons of Jacob were twelve"; that is to say, they were all included in the number, and their merit was in no wise abated.'

R. Eleazar asked: 'Why do we find in this verse first the name Israel and then the name Jacob? The reason may be given as follows. Reuben said to himself: "My father was intended to raise twelve tribes and no more, yet now he is about to beget more children. Does he then wish to disqualify us and repiace us with others?" So straightway he disarranged the couch and prevented the intended intercourse, thereby slighting, as it were, the honour of the Shekinah that hovered over that couch. Hence it is written first "and Israel heard", since it was by that name that he was exalted among the twelve hidden ones which are the twelve pure rivers of balsam, and then "and the sons of Jacob were twelve", alluding to the twelve tribes by whom the Shekinah was adorned and whom the Torah again enumerated

Zohar: Bereshith, Section 1, Page 176b

as before, implying that they were all of them holy, all of them considered by the Shekinah worthy to behold the sanctity of their Master; for had Reuben really committed the act mentioned, he would not have been included in the number. For all that, he was punished by being deprived of the birthright and by its transference to Joseph, as we read: "And the sons of Reuben, the first-born of Israel-for he was the first-born; but forasmuch as he defiled his father's couch, his birthright was given unto the sons of Joseph" (I Chron. VI). We see from this how all that God does is planned with profound wisdom, and every act of a man leaves its imprint and is preserved before the Almighty. For on the night when Jacob went in to Leah, all his thoughts were centred upon Rachel, and from that intercourse, and from the first germ, and under that intention Leah conceived; and we have affirmed that had not Jacob been unaware of the deception, Reuben would not have entered into the number. It is for that reason that he did not receive a name of special significance, but was simply called Reuben (reu-ben=behold, a son). But for all that, the intended effect was produced, and the birthright reverted to the eldest son of Rachel, as originally purposed. Thus everything came right in the end, for all the works of the Almighty are based on truth and right.'

R. Hizkiah one day found R. Yose cooking a dish from which grease was dripping on to the fire, sending up a cloud of smoke. He said then to him: 'If the pillars of smoke which used once to ascend from the top of the altar had continued to go up like this smoke, wrath would not have descended on the world and Israel would not have been exiled from their land.' R. Yose then opened a discourse on the verse: Who is this that cometh out of the wilderness like pillars of smoke, perfumed with myrrh and frankincense, with all powders of the merchant (S. S. III, 6). 'When Israel', he said, 'were journeying in the wilderness, the Shekinah went in front of them, as it is written: "And the Lord went before them by day in a pillar of cloud, to lead them the way; and by night in a pillar of fire, to give them light" (Ex. XIII, 22). They on their side followed its guidance; wherefore it is written: "Thus saith the Lord: I remember thee the affection of thy youth, the love of thine espousals; how thou wentest after me in the wilderness, etc." (Jer. II, 2). The Shekinah was accompanied by all the clouds of glory, and when it journeyed the Israelites took up their march, as it says: "And whenever the cloud was taken up from over the tent, then after that the children of Israel journeyed, etc." (Num. IX, 17). And when the Shekinah ascended, the cloud also ascended on high, so that all men looked up and asked: "Who is this that cometh out of the wilderness like pillars of smoke?" For the cloud of the Shekinah looked like smoke because the fire which Abraham and his son Isaac kindled clung to it and never left it, and by reason of that fire it ascended both as cloud and smoke; but for all that it was "perfumed", or, as we may also translate, "bound up with myrrh and frankincense", that is, with the cloud of Abraham on the right and with the cloud of Isaac on the left. The words "with all powders of the merchant" allude to Jacob, or, according to another explanation, to Joseph, whose bier accompanied the Israelites in the wilderness, and the designation rokhel (merchant or tale-bearer) is given to him because he brought evil reports of his brethren to their father; or, again, because just as the seller of spices keeps his herbs and spices in bundles, so Joseph through one action kept the whole of the Torah, since all the precepts of the Torah are bound up with the preservation of the holy covenant in its integrity. The Shekinah was thus leagued with Abraham, Isaac, and Jacob together with Joseph, inasmuch as the two latter are one in essence, each one being the image of the other, as indicated in the words: "These are the offspring of Jacob: Joseph" (Gen. XXXVII, 2). Now, when the Israelites dwelt in their land and brought offerings, they all drew themselves nearer to God in manner due; and when the work of sacrifice was performed and the smoke of the altar ascended in a straight column, they knew that it had kindled

Zohar: Bereshith, Section 1, Page 177a

the lamp which they desired to kindle, and so all faces shone and all lamps were lit. But since the destruction of the Temple not a day passes but is visited with wrath and rage, as it says: "and God hath indignation every day" (Ps. VII, 12), and joy has departed from on high and from below, and Israel have gone into exile and are subject to other gods, and the words of Scripture have been fulfilled, saying: "and there thou shalt serve other gods" (Deut. XXVIII, 64). Why all this? "Because thou didst not serve the Lord thy God with joyfulness, and with gladness of heart, by reason of the abundance of all things. Therefore shalt thou serve thine enemy, etc., in want of all things" (Ibid. XXVIII, 47-48). And so it will be until God will arise and redeem them from among the nations, as we read: "then the Lord thy God will turn thy captivity, and have compassion upon thee, and will return and gather thee from all the peoples, whither the Lord thy God hath scattered thee. If any of thine that are dispersed be in the uttermost parts of heaven, from thence will the Lord thy God gather thee, etc." (Ibid. XXX, 3-4).' NOW THESE ARE THE GENERATIONS OF ESAU-THE SAME IS EDOM. The Scripture does not enumerate the sons of Esau until after it has recorded the death of Isaac, whereas Jacob's sons were enumerated long before. The reason for the distinction is this. Esau had neither portion nor inheritance nor lot in Isaac, but only Jacob and his sons. Jacob and his sons are therefore the portion of the Holy One, blessed be He, and they enter into the reckoning; but Esau, who was not of the portion of the side of true faith, made up his account, as it were, after the death of Isaac, and his portion parted and took its course to another region. Observe that after Isaac died and Esau retired to his own side, it is written: "And Esau took his wives... and went into a land away from his brother Jacob", that is, he relinquished to Jacob both the capital and the profit, or, in other words, the bondage of Egypt and the land, and he sold his own portion in the cave of Machpelah, and went away from the land and from the true faith, abandoning all completely. Observe, then, how much Jacob's portion was thus enhanced in every respect, in that Esau did not remain with him, but parted from him and went away to his own portion and lot, so that Jacob was left in possession of the heritage of his father and of his ancestors. Hence: "and he went into a land away from his brother Jacob", the last phrase indicating that he had no desire for Jacob's portion or inheritance or his meed of faith. Happy the portion of Jacob, of whom the Scripture says: "For the portion of the Lord is his people, Jacob the lot of his inheritance" (Ibid. XXXII, 9). AND THESE ARE THE KINGS THAT REIGNED IN THE LAND OF EDOM, BEFORE THERE REIGNED ANY KING OVER THE CHILDREN OF ISRAEL. R. Jesse discoursed on the verse: Behold, I make thee small among the nations, thou art greatly despised (Ob. I, 2). 'When God', he said, 'made the world, He divided it into seven regions corresponding to the seventy Chieftains whom He placed in charge over the seventy nations, assigning to each the nation appropriate to him, as we read: "He set the borders of the peoples, according to the number of the children of Israel" (Deut. XXXII, 8); and of all those Chieftains who were given charge over the other nations no one is so much despised before Him as the Chieftain of Esau. The reason of this is that the side of Esau is the side of defilement; and the side of defilement is despicable before the Holy One, blessed be He, as it springs from those base grades that are behind the empty millstones of the red custodians. Hence, God said to it: "Behold, I make thee small among the nations; thou art greatly despised", as it is written: "upon thy belly shalt thou go, and dust shalt thou eat all the days of thy life" (Gen. III, 14), and also: "cursed be thou from among all cattle, and from among all beasts of the field" (Ibid.) Observe that the lower grades form a hierarchy, one above the other, and each different from the other, yet all linked and interlocked with each other. So is kingdom separate from kingdom, yet is each linked to the other. All the grades are held, as it were, by one chain of a certain measurement, which in its turn is divided into three smaller chains which reach down and are tied to the stars and planets, so that each grade is assigned one

Zohar: Bereshith, Section 1, Page 177b

star or planet. Those stars in their turn operate under the grades above. Every grade has thus charge of its own proper region, and, when they diverge, a chain is formed by which each grade is bound to its proper side. The sides of the unclean grades, which are on the left side, diverge all of them into numerous ways and paths and distribute their power to thousands and myriads in the lower world; and in reference to this it was said to Edom: "Behold, I make thee small among the nations; thou art greatly despised." Now, in the text, "And these are the kings that reigned in the land of Edom", the words "in the land" indicate the side of his grade, that is, the grade of Esau, since it is written: "Esau-the same is Edom." All these things were thus from the side of the unclean spirit; and they were "before there reigned any king over the children of Israel", inasmuch as they embody the grades that stand first at the lower gates. It was this that Jacob had in mind when he said "Let my lord, I pray thee, pass over before his servant" (Gen. XXXIII, 14), since Esau's grades were the first to gain an entrance. They thus reigned before there was any king over Israel, for as yet the time had not arrived for the kingdom of heaven to enter into power and to league itself with the children of Israel. When it did, it began with the least of the tribes, which was Benjamin, as it says: "There is Benjamin, the youngest, ruling them, etc." (Ps. LXVIII, 28), and with him the kingdom began to advance. After that the kingdom came into its own place and was established, never to be removed.'

R. Hiya discoursed on the verses: Yet now hear, O Jacob my servant, and Israel, whom I have chosen; thus saith the Lord that made thee and formed thee from the womb, who will help thee: Fear not, O Jacob my servant, and thou Jeshurun, whom I have chosen (Is. XLIV, 1-2). 'Observe', he said, 'how God has promised Israel in many places to make them worthy of the world to come, as He has not chosen for his portion any other people or language, but only Israel. It was for this purpose that He gave them the Torah of truth, by whose means they may live virtuously and learn the ways of the Holy One, blessed be He, so that they may inherit the Holy Land; for whoever is thought worthy of the Holy Land has a portion in the world to come. So Scripture says: "Thy people also shall be all righteous, they shall inherit the land forever" (Ibid. LX, 21). Now, in the verses above quoted three grades are mentioned: first Jacob, then Israel, and finally Jeshurun. Jacob and Israel have been explained. Jeshurun suggests the word shur (row, side) and indicates that he has his rank on this side and on the other. The three names, though representing different grades, are really the same. Jacob is called "my servant" because sometimes he is like a servant who has orders from his master and is eager to execute his will. We read elsewhere: "the Lord that created thee, O Jacob, and he that formed thee, O Israel" (Ibid. XLIII, 1), and in the above verse we read: "Thus saith the Lord that made thee." We have thus herein the terms "crested", "formed", and "made", which represent different grades, one above the other, but which all are essentially one. Happy the portion of Israel in whom the Holy One, blessed be He, finds delight above all the nations who worship idols, of which it is written: "They are vanity, a work of delusion; in the time of their visitation they shall perish" (Jer. X, 15). That will come to pass on the day when God will destroy them from the world, so that He alone will remain, as it says: "And the Lord alone shall be exalted in that day" (Is. II, 11).'

R. Judah discoursed on the verse: Fear not, thou worm Jacob, and ye men of Israel; I help thee, saith the Lord, and thy Redeemer the Holy One of Israel (Ibid. XLI, 14). 'Observe', he said, 'that all the Gentiles have been placed by the Almighty under the charge of certain tutelary Chieftains, as already stated, and that they all follow their own gods, as it is written: "For all the peoples walk each one in the name of its god" (Micah IV, 5); and they are addicted to bloodshed and warfare, to robbery, violence, and fornication,

Zohar: Bereshith, Section 1, Page 178a

and other kinds of wickedness, and use all their power to injure and do harm. Israel, on their part, have no force or power to overcome them save in their mouth, like to the worm which has no strength or power except in its mouth, by which, however, it wears through everything. Hence Israel are called "worm". Or again, as the silkworm, that precious creature which produces from itself a fine thread out of which is woven the costliest kingly raiment, leaves behind before it dies a seed out of which it comes to life as before; so Israel, although they seemingly die, always re-emerge and persist in the world as before. So Scripture says: "Behold, as the clay in the potter's hand, so are ye in my hand, O house of Israel" (Jer. XVIII, 6). The term homer (clay) signifies in reality the material of glass which, when broken, can be refounded and made whole as before. "Fear not... men of Israel", they being the tree of life, for since the children have engrafted themselves on the tree of life, they will arise from the dust and will be established in the world as one united people to worship the Holy One, blessed be He, in harmony with the words: "That they may call upon the name of the Lord, to serve him with one consent" (Zeph. III, 9).'

R. Eleazar and R. Isaac were one day travelling on the road together when the time for the reading of the Shema arrived. R. Eleazar paused and recited the Shema and said his prayer. After he had finished, R. Isaac said to him: 'Have we not learnt that before a man starts on a journey he must first ask leave from his Master and offer up his prayer?' R. Eleazar said in reply: 'When I left it was not yet time either for the reading of the Shema or for saying prayers. Now that the sun has risen I have said my prayer. But all the same, before commencing my journey I did offer a prayer to Him and consulted Him, as it were. I, however, did not say this prayer because I have been occupied in studying the Torah since midnight, and from the early dawn up to now it was not yet the time for prayer, for while the morning is still dark the Wife is conversing with her Husband, being about to retire to her tent, where her maidens keep her company. Hence no man should then interrupt them and break in with other words. Now, however, that the sun has risen it is the time for prayer, as it is written: "They shall fear thee with the sunrise" (Ps. LXXII, 5), which indicates the close connection between fear of God, or devotion, and the light of the sun, which makes it incumbent on man not to part them, but to associate them together.' The two then proceeded on their way, until they arrived at a field, where they sat down. Raising their eyes, they saw a mountain, on the top of which they discerned strange creatures moving about. R. Isaac began to tremble. Said R. Eleazar to him: 'Why are you afraid?' He answered: 'Because this mountain looks so formidable and on it are strange creatures, which I fear will attack us.' R. Eleazar then said to him: 'Whoever is afraid of his sins has cause to fear. Those creatures are not of the dangerous kind that haunt the mountains.' He then began to discourse on the verse: AND THESE ARE THE CHILDREN OF ZIBEON: AIAH AND ANAH-THIS IS ANAH WHO FOUND THE YEMIM IN THE WILDERNESS. In regard to this verse,' he said, 'it is agreed that these yemim are not the same as the Emim mentioned in the verse: "The Emim dwelt therein aforetime... but the children of Esau succeeded them" (Deut. II, 10-11). They were an unnatural kind of being which was first created from the side of evil spirits and goblins at the moment when the Sabbath was about to be sanctified, and they remained unsubstantial and bodiless, since neither the sixth day nor the seventh day would own them.

Zohar: Bereshith, Section 1, Page 178b

When, however, Cain was driven from the face of the earth and dwelt in the land of Nod, they spread from his side and became corporeal, but not for any length of time. They are therefore called yamim (days), spelt in the same way as yemim here, without a yod, in allusion to the fact that they appear occasionally to men as they haunt the mountains, and for one moment in the day assume bodily shape, but forthwith lose it again. Anah found them and they taught him to bring bastards into the world. For Anah himself was a bastard, the offspring of an incestuous intercourse between Zibeon and his own mother; and this came about through the side of the unclean spirit that attached itself to him. Those and numerous other monstrous beings of many varieties are derived from that side and roam about in the wilderness and can be seen there, as the wilderness is a desolate place and therefore is a suitable haunt for them. For all that, whoever walks in the ways of the Holy One, blessed be He, and fears Him, has no cause to fear them.' The two then went on and ascended the mountain. Said R. Isaac: 'Are they found in all desert mountains like these?' Said R. Eleazar: 'That is so, but of all those who labour in the Torah it is written: "The Lord shall keep thee from all evil; he shall keep thy soul. The Lord shall guard thy going out and thy coming in, from this time forth and forever" (Ps. CXXI, 74).

R. Eleazar discoursed on the verse: Hallelukah (praise ye the Lord). I will give thanks unto the Lord with my whole heart, in the council of the upright, and in the congregation. (Ps. CXI, I). 'King David', he said, 'daily devoted himself to the worship of the Almighty, and he would rise at midnight and sing hymns and songs of praise and thanksgiving, so as to establish his place in the kingdom above. For as soon as the north wind began to blow at midnight he knew that the moment had come when God rose, as it were, to disport Himself with the righteous in the Garden of Eden; so he arose at that moment and busied himself with songs and thanksgivings until the morning. For, as we have affirmed, when the Holy One, blessed be He, appears in the Garden of Eden, He and all the righteous in the Garden of Eden listen to the voice of the suppliant, as we read: "The companions hearken for thy voice, cause me to hear it" (S. S. VIII, 13); and, moreover, a thread of grace is woven round him during the day, as it is written: "By day the Lord will command his lovingkindness, and in the night his song shall be with me" (Ps. XLII, 9). And furthermore, all the words of the Torah which one utters in the night ascend and are woven into a garland before the Almighty. King David therefore devoted himself during the night to the service of his Master. Observe the heading Hallelukah (praise ye the Lord), for we have learned that of all the titles that David affixed to his songs and hymns, the most excellent was Hallelukah, embracing as it does in one single word the name of God and the call to praise, the name being Kah, and the praise coming from the Community of Israel, who continually compose thanksgivings to the Holy One, blessed be He, as we read: "O God, there is no silence for thee; hold not thy peace, and be not still, O God" (Ps. LXXXIII, 2), because the Community of Israel continually arranges and offers up its thanksgivings to Him. Now we read further: "I will give thanks unto the Lord with my whole heart (lebab)", that is, as already explained, with the good and the evil prompter, who are always with a man: "in the council of the upright, and in the congregation" is an allusion to Israel, who are adorned with all grades-priests and Levites, the just and the pious. It is the same congregation of which we read: "God standeth in the congregation of God" (Ps. LXXXII, 1). Hence a man should continually offer praise to God, since He takes delight in songs and hymns, and when a man knows how to offer praise to God in the proper manner, He accepts his prayer and delivers him, as we read: "I will set him on high, because he hath known my name... With long life will I satisfy him, etc." (Ibid. XCI, 14-16).'

R. Yose discoursed on the verse: Thou art my hiding-place; thou wilt preserve me from the adversary; with songs of deliverance thou wilt compass me about. Selah (Ibid. XXXII, 7). 'It is God', he said, 'who is a hiding-place and a shield to the man that walks in the ways of the Torah; such a man is covered by the shadow of His wings so that no one can do him mischief. "Thou wilt preserve me from the adversary"; that is, from the adversary on high and from the adversary here below, both of whom are one and the same evil prompter,

Zohar: Bereshith, Section 1, Page 179a

who is the opponent above and the opponent below; and if not for the evil prompter, man would have no adversary in the world. "With songs of deliverance thou wilt compass me about" is an allusion to those songs that possess grades of potency to save; with which, therefore, "Thou wilt compass me about" to afford me deliverance when on a journey. (This verse is efficacious whether read forwards or backwards.) Observe that all the songs and hymns that David sang contain deep allusions of wisdom, because he composed them under the inspiration of the Holy Spirit, which alone it was that prompted him.'

R. Eleazar discoursed on the verse: Thou didst thrust sore at me that I might fall; but the Lord helped me (Ibid. CXVIII, 13). 'We should have expected', he said, '"they did thrust sore at me" instead of "thou didst, etc." But, in truth, this alludes to the "other side" that continually thrusts at a man, and tries to seduce him and lead him astray from God; the same is, indeed, the evil prompter who follows man about. It is to him that David addressed the words, "thou didst thrust sore at me", seeing that he endeavoured by means of all sorts of afflictions to turn him aside from God. David thus said: "Thou didst thrust sore at me-to cause me to fall into Gehinnom-but the Lord helped me-so that I was not delivered into thy hand." It is, hence, incumbent on a man to be on his guard against the evil prompter, so that he shall not obtain the mastery over him; such a man God guards in all his ways, as it is written: "Then shalt thou walk in thy way securely, and thou shalt not dash thy foot" (Prov. III, 23), also: "When thou goest thy step shall not be straitened; and if thou runnest thou shalt not stumble" (Ibid. IV, 12); and also: "But the path of the righteous is as the light of dawn, that shineth more and more unto the perfect day" (Ibid. v, 18).'

Said R. Judah: 'Happy are Israel whom the Holy One, blessed be He, preserves in this world and in the world to come, as it is written: "Thy people also shall be all righteous, they shall inherit the land forever" (Is. LX, 21). Blessed be the Lord, forevermore. Amen and Amen!'

VAYESHEB

AND JACOB DWELT IN THE LAND OF HIS FATHER'S SOJOURNINGS, IN THE LAND OF CANAAN. R. Hiya discoursed on the verse: Many are the ills of the righteous, but the Lord delivereth him out of them all (Ps. XXXIV, 20). 'Many, indeed', he said, 'are the adversaries with whom a human being has to contend from the day that God breathes into him a soul in this world. For as soon as he emerges into the light of day, the evil prompter is at hand in readiness to join him, according to our interpretation of the verse: "Sin coucheth at the door" (Gen. IV, 7). In proof whereof note that the beasts from the day they are born are able to take care of themselves, and avoid fire and similar dangers, whereas man, on the other hand, seems to feel at first a natural propensity to throw himself into the fire, the reason being that the evil prompter dwells within him and from the beginning lures him into evil ways. So Scripture says: "Better is a poor and wise child than an old and foolish king, who knoweth not how to receive admonition any more" (Eccl. IV, 13). The "child" here signifies the good prompter, who is so called because he is, as it were, a youngster by the side of man, whom he does not join till he is at the age of thirteen years, as elsewhere affirmed. He is better, then, than "an old and foolish king", to wit, the evil prompter, who is called king and ruler over the sons of men, and who is assuredly old, since, as already said, so soon as a man is born and sees the light of day he

Zohar: Bereshith, Section 1, Page 179b

attaches himself to him; and he is foolish, not knowing how to receive admonition, since, as Solomon says of him also, "the fool walketh in darkness" (Ibid. II, 14). Indeed, he comes from the very quarry of darkness, and light is forever a stranger to him.' R. Simeon said: 'It has been laid down that the "poor child" here is the good prompter, the same as he who said of himself: "I have been young, and now am old" (Ps. XXXVII, 25). He is called "poor child", as he has no

220

possession whatever of his own, and is called "youth" for the reason that he is constantly renewed in the same way as the moon; also he is wise, since wisdom dwells within him. He is better than the "old king", who is the evil prompter, as already said, since from his first emergence he has never rid himself of his impurity, and he is foolish in that all his steps are toward the evil ways, and he turns the sons of men from the right path, employing all kinds of pretexts to divert them from the good way to the evil. And he hastens to join man on the very day he is born, in order that man may come to believe in him, and that when the good prompter arrives later he may be loth to believe him and think him a burden. Similarly our teachers have defined a "cunning wicked man" to be one who comes first to the judge and pleads his cause before his opponent arrives; as Scripture says: "He that pleadeth his cause first seemeth just, etc." (Prov. XVIII, 17). In the same way the evil prompter is cunningly wicked, as we read: "And the serpent was more cunning, etc." (Gen. III, 1), and so he arrives first to take up his abode with man, and make his case plausible to him, so that when his fellow, that is, the good prompter, arrives, he finds himself obnoxious to man, and is not able to raise his head, as though he were bowed down with a heavy burden, because of that cunningly wicked one who has got the start of him. Hence the words of Solomon: "the poor man's wisdom is despised, and his words are not heard" (Eccl. IX, 16), because the other has anticipated him. Hence for a judge to receive the pleadings of one lit igant in the absence of the other is like acknowledging strange gods. But the way of the righteous judge is to wait till "his neighbour cometh and searcheth him out" (Prov. XVIII, 17). Similarly the righteous man is he who does not put credence in the evil prompter, but first waits for the arrival of the good prompter. For neglecting to do this the sons of man will stumble in the world to come. The righteous man, on the other hand, endures in this world many trials for not believing in and not associating himself with the evil prompter, but the Holy One, blessed be He, delivers him from all ills, as it says: "Many are the ills of the righteous, but the Lord delivereth him out of them all" (Ps. XXXIV, 20). For God finds delight in such a man and delivers him from all ills in this world and in the world to come. Happy is his portion! See how many ills befell Jacob in his effort not to be drawn to the evil prompter, and to keep himself far from his portion; and for this he endured many afflictions and ills without respite.' R. Hiya applied to Jacob the verse: I was not at ease, neither was I quiet, neither had I rest; but trouble came (Job. III, 26). 'How many ills and sufferings,' he said, 'one after another come upon the righteous in this world that they may merit the world to come. Jacob was one of them, and could say of himself, "I was not at ease" in the house of Laban, from whom I could not escape; "neither was I quiet" on account of Esau, through the pain inflicted on me by his Chieftain, and later on through fear of himself; "neither had I rest" in the affair of Dinah and Shechem; "but trouble came", to wit, the trouble and confusion of the loss of Joseph, which was the worst of all, on account of his love for Joseph.' AND JACOB DWELT IN THE LAND OF HIS FATHER'S SOJOURNINGS, IN THE LAND OF CANAAN.

Zohar: Bereshith, Section 1, Page 180a

R. Yose discoursed here on the verse: The righteous perisheth, and no man layeth it to heart, and godly men are taken away, none considering that the righteous is taken away from the evil to come (Is. LVII, 1). 'When God', he said, 'surveys the world and finds it misbehaving and meet for chastisement, He first removes from it any righteous man that is present in it, so that chastisement should be visited on all the others and there should be none to shield them. For as long as there is a righteous man in the world chastisement cannot befall it, as we learn from Moses, of whom it is written: "Therefore he said that he would destroy them, had not Moses his chosen stood before him in tbe breach, etc." (Ps. CVI, 23). God thus first removes the righteous from the world, and only then collects His account, as it were. We thus translate the conclusion of the verse: "the righteous is taken away before (mitne') the evil to come", that is, before the evil is due to befall. (According to another interpretation, "from the evil to come" is an allusion to the evil prompter.) Observe now that although the galuth was already due in the life-time of Jacob, yet because he was a righteous man-the perfection of the patriarchs-the sentence was postponed; for whilst he was alive punishment could not befall the world, and even the famine of Egypt ceased on his arrival. Neither did the exile really commence during the life-time of Joseph, since he was the image of his father, but as soon as he died the captivity began in earnest, as it says: "And Joseph died... come, let us deal wisely with them... and they made their lives bitter with hard service, in mortar and in brick, etc." (Ex. I, 6-14). Similarly, wherever a righteous man exists, God for his sake shields the world, and during his life-time no chastisement falls on the world; and so we affirm.' AND JACOB DWELT IN THE LAND OF HIS FATHER'S SOJOURNINGS. The term m' gure (sojournings) can be rendered "apprehensions", being akin to the term magor in the phrase magor misabib, "a terror on every side" (Jer. VI, 25), and so indicates that Jacob passed all his life in fear and anxiety. THESE ARE THE GENERATIONS OF JACOB: JOSEPH, ETC. When Jacob was brought to rest in Joseph, and so the sun was united with the moon, then there commenced a production of offspring, the progenitor being Joseph. For it is that perennially flowing stream which fructifies the earth and from which generations are propagated in the world. For the sun, even when he approaches the moon, cannot cause vegetation without the help of that grade which goes under the name of Righteous (Zaddik). It was, then, Joseph who was the grade of Jacob to bear fruit and bring forth offspring in the world. Hence: "These are the generations (tol'doth, lit. offspring) of Jacob: Joseph." Or, again, we may take the words to signify that whoever looked at Joseph thought he was looking at Jacob. Hence this form of expression is used only in connection with Joseph and not with any other of Jacob's sons-it is not written, for instance, "These are the offspring of Jacob: Reuben", the reason being that Joseph was the exact image of his father. BEING SEVENTEEN YEARS OLD. R. Abba said: This number of seventeen is significant, corresponding as it does to the seventeen years of joy and honour which Jacob lived in Egypt, with all his sons round him and Joseph as king, and which God vouchsafed him in return for the years during which he mourned for Joseph, and did not see him.'

R. Hiya discoursed on the text: Therefore hearken unto me, ye men of understanding: Far be it from God that he should do wickedness; and from the Almighty that he should commit iniquity. For the work

Zohar: Bereshith, Section 1, Page 180b

of man will he requite unto him, and cause every man to find according to his ways (Job XXXIV, 10-11). 'God,' he said, 'in creating the world, meant it to be based on justice, and all that is done in the world would be weighed in the scales of justice, were it not that, to save the world from perishing, God screened it with mercy, which tempers pure justice and prevents it from destroying the world. The world is thus governed in mercy and thereby is able to endure. But, you may ask, is not a man often punished by God undeservedly? The answer is, as has been affirmed, that when suffering befalls a righteous man, it is on account of the love which God bears to him. He crushes his body in order to give more power to his soul, so that He may draw him nearer in love. For it is needful that the body should be weak and the soul strong, that so a man may be beloved of God, as the Companions have affirmed, that the Holy One inflicts suffering on the righteous in this world in order that they may merit the world to come. But he who is weak of soul and strong of body is hated of God. It is because God has no pleasure in him that He inflicts no pain upon him in this world, but permits his life to flow smoothly along with ease and comfort, in that for any virtuous act he may perform he receives his reward in this world, so that no portion should be left him in the next world. This is in accordance with Onkelos's paraphrase of the text: "And he repayeth them that hate him to their face" (Deut. VII, 10), which reads: "And he repayeth them that hate him in this world." The righteous man, then, who is continually broken in body is the beloved of the Holy One, blessed be He.

Now various difficulties are raised by this statement. In the first place we know that the Shekinah does not dwell amid sad surroundings, but only where there is cheerfulness. For this reason Elisha said: "But now bring me a minstrel, and so it came to pass that when the minstrel played, the hand of the Lord came upon him" (II Kings III, 15), and we learn the same lesson from Jacob, from whom the Shekinah departed during the years that he was grieving for Joseph, but to whom it returned as soon as the glad tidings about Joseph reached him, when, as it says, "the spirit of Jacob their father revived" (Gen. XLV, 27). That being so, where, we may ask, is the cheerful spirit in the righteous man who is broken in body, seeing that he is tormented by his sufferings? And further, do we not know of many righteous men, beloved by the Almighty, who were never a prey to acute suffering or physical weakness? Why this discrimination? Why should these be physical wrecks and the others hale and hearty? One explanation given is that the latter were born of righteous parents, whereas the former, although themselves righteous, were not children of righteous parents. But the facts are against this, since we see many righteous men who are the sons of righteous parents, and who nevertheless are afflicted with bodily ills and are lifelong sufferers. But there is a deep mystery involved here, inasmuch as all the ways of God are based on truth and righteousness. In connection with this verse I have found in the books of the ancients a mystical doctrine, and next to it another mystical doctrine, both being in essence one and the same. It amounts to the following. There is a period when the moon is defective, judgement being visited upon her, and the sun being concealed from her. Now it is the moon that at all times and seasons releases souls to enter the sons of men-she having previously gathered them for the purpose. Of those souls, then, which she releases during the period that she is under sentence, every one will always be the victim of degradation and poverty and suffer other chastisements, irrespective of whether he be sinful or righteous. (Prayer, however, can avert any sentence of punishment.) But those souls which the moon sends forth when she is in the grade of completeness, and the perennially flowing stream plays about her, are destined to enjoy abundance of all good things-of riches, children, and bodily health-and all on account

Zohar: Bereshith, Section 1, Page 181a

of the allotment (mazzal) that flowed forth and joined itself to that grade in order to be perfected and blessed by it. We see thus that all things are dependent on allotment (mazzal), according to the dictum: "Children, life, and livelihood do not depend on a man's merits, but on mazzal." Hence all those who are sorely afflicted in this world in spite of being truly righteous suffer through the mischance of their soul; but in compensation the Holy One, blessed be He, has compassion on them in the world to come.' R. Eleazar said: 'All the acts of the Almighty are in accordance with justice, and His purpose is to purify that soul from the scum that adheres to it in this world, so as to bring it into the world to come. When the body is crushed the soul is purified, and so God brings pains and sufferings on the righteous man in this world in order that he may gain k life everlasting. In this regard it is written: "The Lord trieth the righteous, etc." (Ps. XI, 5).'

R. Simeon said: 'It is written: "Only he shall not go in unto the veil, nor come nigh unto the altar, because he hath a blemish; that he profane not my holy places, because I am the Lord who sanctify them" (Lev. XXI, 23). When the perennial stream releases human souls, and the Female becomes pregnant, they all range themselves within the edifice. Now all those that go forth at the period when the moon is defective by reason of the evil serpent, although pure and holy, become bruised and defective in whatever place they reach, and have to undergo pain and suffering. And these are the souls in whom the Holy One finds delight in spite of their being sad instead of joyful. Esoterically speaking they are a counterpart of something above, the body being impaired and the soul being within after the supernal pattern, each corresponding to each, and these are the souls that require to be renewed with the renewal of the moon, and hence it is written concerning them: "And it shall come to pass, that from one new moon to another, and from one Sabbath to another, shall all flesh come to worship before me" (Is. LXVI, 23), the word "all" signifying that these souls will be renewed wholly with the renewal of the moon. For they are partners, as it were, with the defective moon, for which reason she dwells in them always, without leaving them, in allusion to which the Scripture says: "I dwell... with him also that is of a contrite and humble spirit... to revive the heart of the contrite ones" (Is. LVII, 15), also: "The Lord is nigh unto them that are of a broken heart" (Ps. XXXIV, 19). These verses refer to those who are fellow–sufferers with the moon in her defect, and regarding whom it is fitly said, "to revive the heart of the contrite ones", that is, to make those who participated in the sufferings of the moon also participate in the new life to be bestowed on her in the future. Such sufferings undergone by them are called "sufferings in token of love". Happy is their portion in this world and in the world to come when they will be privileged to be partners with her, in allusion to which it is written: "For my brethren and companions' sakes, etc." (Ibid. CXXII, 8).'

R. Simeon further discoursed on the text: Behold, my servant shall prosper, he shall be exalted and lifted up, and shall be very high (Is. LII, 13). 'Happy is the portion of the righteous', he said, 'to whom the Holy One reveals the ways of the Torah that they may walk in them. This verse contains an esoteric meaning. When God created the world, He made the moon, and made her small, for she possesses no light of her own, but because she accepted her diminution she receives reflected light from the sun and from the other superior luminaries. Now, as long as the Temple existed, Israel were assiduous in bringing offerings, which together with all the other services performed by the priests, Levites, and Israelites had for their object to weave bonds of union and to cause luminaries to radiate. But after the Temple was destroyed there was a darkening of the lights, the moon ceased to receive light from the sun, the latter

having withdrawn himself from her, so that not a day passes but is full of grievous distress and afflictions. The time, however, will come for the moon to resume her primordial light, and in allusion to this it is written: "Behold, my servant will prosper." That is to say, there will be a stirring in the upper realms as of one who catches a sweet odour and stands alert. "He shall be exalted", from the side of the most exalted luminaries; "and lifted up", from the side of Abraham; "and shall be high", from the side of Isaac; "very", from the side of Jacob. At that time, then, the Holy One will cause a stirring on high with the object of enabling the moon to shine with her full splendour, as we read: "Moreover the light of the moon shall be as the light of the sun, and the light of the sun shall be sevenfold, as the light of the seven days" (Ibid. XXX, 26). There will thus be added to the moon an exalted spirit whereby all the dead that are in the dust will be awakened. This is the esoteric meaning of "my servant", viz. the one that has in his hand the key of his Master.

So, too, in the verse: "And Abraham said unto his servant, etc." (Gen. XXIV, 2), the servant is an allusion to the moon as already explained. Also, the servant is identical with Metatron, who is the servant and messenger of his Master, and who was, as we read further, the elder of his house, the same who is alluded to in the text: "I have been young, and now am old" (Ps. XXXVII, 25). "That ruled over all that he had"; this applies to the same Metatron by reason of his displaying the three colours, green, white, and red. "Put, I pray thee, thy hand under my thigh"; this is symbolic of the foundation of the world, for this servant was destined to bring to life again the dwellers in the dust, and to be made the messenger by the spirit from on high to restore the spirits and souls to their places, to the bodies that were decomposed underneath the dust. We read further: "and I will make thee swear (veashbe'akha) by the Lord, the God of heaven", the term veashbe'akha implying that the servant will be invested with the mystery of the seven (sheba') celestial lights which constitute the mystery of sublime perfection. Further: "that thou shalt not take a wife for my son of the daughters of the Canaanites." The "wife" is an allusion to the body lying underground, and "to my son" is an allusion to the soul, inasmuch as all the souls that issue from the celestial everflowing river are the children of the Holy One, blessed be He. The servant is thus bidden "not to take a wife for my son of the daughters of the Canaanites", or, in other words, not to take for a soul any of the bodies of the idolatrous nations whom the Holy One will in the future shake out of the Holy Land, as we read: "and the wicked be shaken out of it" (Job XXXVIII, 13), as one shakes dust from his garment. The servant is further bidden: "But thou shalt go unto my country, and to my kindred." "To my country" has already been explained; "to my kindred" is an allusion to Israel. Observe now what is written further: "And the servant took ten camels." The "servant" we have already identified; "ten camels" represent the ten grades over which the servant exercises dominion, and which are after the supernal pattern; "of the camels of his master", to wit, an exact pattern of the superior degrees, as already said; "having all goodly things of his master's in his hand", to wit, all the supernal spirits that emerge from the supernal luminaries; "and he arose and went to Aram-Naharaim", to wit, the spot in the Holy Land where Rachel wept at the time the Temple was destroyed. "And he made the camels to kneel down without the city by the well of water", that is, he fortified the energy of the souls before their entering into the bodies for their revival; "at the time of evening", to wit, the eve of Sabbath,

Zohar: Bereshith, Section 1, Page 182a

which is the sixth millennium, the same period as that alluded to in the text: "and to his laboul until the evening" (Ps. CIV, 23), also in the words: "for the shadows of the evening are stretched out" (Jer. VI, 4). We read further: "at the time that women go out to draw water", to wit, the time when those who drew the waters of the Torah will rise from the dead before the rest of mankind, in virtue of their having taken hold of the tree of life. Further: "and the daughters of the men of the city came out to draw water", to wit, the bodies will come forth, as we read: "and the earth will throw up the shades" (Is. XXVI, 19), implying that the earth will in future give up all the bodies lying therein, "to draw water", that is, to receive the soul in a perfected state. Further: "So let it come to pass, that the damsel to whom I shall say, Let down thy pitcher, that I may drink." It is one of our affirmations that every soul that occupied itself in this world in the study of the deep mysteries of Divine Wisdom, when it goes to heaven is raised to a high grade, high above those who remained in ignorance; and it is they who will rise from the dead first. The words, then, "Let down thy pitcher, etc." signify the inquiry which the servant will make of each soul regarding her occupation in this world. We read, then, "and she will say, Drink, and I will give thy camels drink also", that is, do thou drink first, and afterwards I will give drink to the othet grades, for although those grades drink from the same source, they ultimately derive their sustenance from the religious activity of the righteous who knew how to serve their Master properly, for it is the righteous who know how to supply proper sustenance to each grade. "The same be the woman", it says further, "that thou hast appointed for the son of my master"; that assuredly is the body destined for that superior soul. Observe that it has been said before that the desire of the male towards the female forms a soul, and the desire of the female towards the male rises upwards to unite with the soul and form one being. The woman is thus the body which is destined for the association of the soul that is derived from the male. These bodies, then, are destined to rise first, as we said already, and then all the others in the other lands will be raised in a complete state and will be renewed with the renewal of the moon, and the world will be restored to its primeval state, in allusion to which it is written: "Let the Lord rejoice in his works" (Ps. CIV, 31). Hence we read: "Behold, my servant will understand", that is, he will know how to restore the souls, each one to its place. "He shall be exalted and lifted up and shall be very high", from the side of all the superior grades as said above. The next verse says: "According as many were appalled at thee-so marred was his visage unlike that of a man" (Is. LII, 14). According to our exposition, when the Temple was destroyed and the Shekinah went into exile into strange lands, then "behold, their Erelim [Tr. note: A kind of angel.] cry without, the angels of peace weep bitterly" (Ibid. XXXIII, 7), for all wept and mourned for the Shekinah that was exiled from her place, and in the degree that she became altered from what she was, to the same degree her Master withdrew his light and became altered from what he was, as it is written: "The sun was darkened in his going forth" (Ibid. XIII, 10). Hence: "so marred was his visage.' According to another interpretation, the words, "so marred was his visage unlike that of a man" are illustrated by the verse: "I clothe the heavens with blackness, and I make sackcloth their covering" (Ibid. L, 3). For after the Temple was destroyed the heavens did not retain their former illumination. Esoterically speaking, benediction does not abide save where male and female are together, and since at that time

Zohar: Bereshith, Section 1, Page 182b

the male was not with her, all the souls that issued then were not the same as they had been when the sun was in union with the moon, as already said. This union is symbolized by the relation of Joseph to Jacob, as expressed in the verse, "These are the generations of Jacob: Joseph." This form of expression implies that Jacob's image was completely reproduced in Joseph, and that whatever happened to the one happened to the other also, the two being parallel and having the same esoteric symbolism.' AND JOSEPH BROUGHT EVIL REPORT OF THEM UNTO THEIR FATHER. This has been interpreted to mean that he accused them to his father of eating flesh cut from a living animal; he also accused the sons of Leah of having treated with contempt the sons of the handmaids. How, it may be asked, could they have done this, seeing that the sons of the handmaids were reckoned in the twelve tribes? Or how could they have eaten flesh from a living animal, seeing that this was distinctly forbidden to the sons of Noah in the words: "Only flesh with the life thereof, which is the blood thereof, shall ye not eat" (Gen. IX, 4)? The truth is, however, that it was only Joseph's talk, and he was punished for it. R. Judah said: 'The evil report of them that Joseph brought was that they cast their eyes on the daughters of the land, which was equivalent to providing sustenance to the unholy degrees that proceed from the unclean side.' NOW ISRAEL LOVED JOSEPH MORE THAN ALL HIS CHILDREN, BECAUSE HE WAS THE SON OF HIS OLD AGE; AND HE MADE HIM A COAT OF MANY COLOURS. Said R. Eleazar: 'It is written: "Come, my people, enter thou into thy chambers, and shut thy doors about thee; hide thyself for a little moment, until the indignation be overpast" (Is. XXVI, 20). God holds Israel in affection above the idolatrous nations, and on that account He warns them and puts them on their guard in all their deeds. There are three periods in a day during which the world is liable to chastisement, and at each of these periods it behoves a man to be specially on his guard. These are well known and are specified elsewhere. Furthermore, at a time when judgement is at work upon the world and death rages in a city, a man should not walk by himself in the open street, as already mentioned above, but he should shut himself in after the example of Noah, who shut himself within the ark so that he should not be met by the destroying angel. Hence: "Come, my people, enter into thy chambers, and shut thy doors about thee", so as not to be exposed to the destroying angel; "hide thyself for a little moment", until the indignation be overpast, as after the moment of judgement is passed the destroying angel has no more power to harm. And it is because God holds Israel in affection and draws them near to Himself that all the idolatrous nations hate Israel; for they see themselves kept at a distance whilst Israel are brought near. Similarly it was by reason of the love that Jacob showed towards Joseph above all his other sons that they conspired to slay him, though he was their own brother. How much greater, then, must be the enmity of the idolatrous nations towards Israel!' Observe the consequences that followed the excessive love shown to Joseph by his father: he was exiled from his father, and his father joined him in exile, and along with them

Zohar: Bereshith, Section 1, Page 183a

the Shekinah also went into exile. It is true that the exile was really the consequence of a divine decree; yet the proximate cause was the coat of many colours which he made for him specially. AND JOSEPH DREAMED A DREAM, ETC. On the subject of dreams, R. Hiya discoursed on the text: And he said: Hear now my words: If there be a prophet among you, I the Lord do make myself known unto him in a vision, I do speak with him in a dream (Num. XII, 6). 'God', he said, 'has brought into existence a series of grades, one higher than the other, one drawing sustenance from the other, some on the right, others on the left, all arranged in a perfect hierarchy. Now all the prophets drew their inspiration from one side, from the midst of two certain grades which they beheld in a "dull mirror", as it says: "I do make myself known unto him in a vision", the word "vision" denoting, as has been explained, a medium reflecting a variety of colours; and this is the "dull mirror". The dream, on the other hand, is a sixtieth part of prophecy, and so forms the sixth grade removed from prophecy, which is the grade of Gabriel, the supervisor of dreams. Now a normal dream proceeds from that grade, and hence there is not a dream that has not intermingled with it some spurious matter, so that it is a mixture of truth and falsehood. Hence it is that all dreams follow their interpretation, as it is written: "And it came to pass, as he interpreted to us, so it was" (Gen. XLI, 13); for since the dream contains both falsehood and truth, the word has power over it, and therefore it is advisable that every dream should be interpreted in a good sense.'

R. Hiya further discoursed on the text: In a dream, in a vision of the night, when deep sleep falleth upon men, in slumberings upon the bed; then he openeth the ears of men, and by their chastisement sealeth the decree (Job XXXIII, 15-16). 'When a man retires to rest,' he said, 'it behoves him first to acknowledge the Kingdom of Heaven [Tr. note: i.e. to recite the Shema.] and then to say a short prayer. For when a man goes to bed and sleeps, his soul leaves him and soars aloft. God then reveals to the soul through that grade which presides over the soul future events, or things which correspond to a man's own thoughts, so as to serve as an admonition to him. For no revelation comes to man when his body is in full vigour, but an angel communicates things to the soul, and the soul transmits them to the man; dreams, then, originate on high when souls leave the bodies, each one taking its own route. There is a graduated series of the intimations by which deeper knowledge is conveyed to men, dreams forming one grade, vision another grade, and prophecy a third grade, in a rising series. AND JOSEPH DREAMED A DREAM, AND HE TOLD IT TO HIS BRETHREN. AND THEY HATED HIM THE MORE FOR HIS DREAMS. From this we learn that a man should not tell his dream save to a friend, otherwise the listener may pervert the significance of the dream and cause delay in its fulfilment. Joseph communicated his dream to his brethren, and they caused its fulfilment to be delayed for twenty-two years. Thus we find it written: AND HE SAID UNTO THEM, HEAR, I PRAY YOU, THIS DREAM

Zohar: Bereshith, Section 1, Page 183b

WHICH I HAVE DREAMED. We see here how he begged his brethren to listen to him, and insisted on telling them his dream, which, had they given it another meaning, would have been fulfilled accordingly. But they said to him: "Shalt thou indeed reign over us? or shalt thou have dominion over us?" and with these words they sealed their own doom.

R. Hiya and R. Yose used to study with R. Simeon.

R. Hiya once put to him the following question: 'We have learnt that a dream uninterpreted is like a letter undeciphered. Does this mean that the dream comes true without the dreamer being conscious of it, or that it remains unfulfilled?' R. Simeon answered: 'The dream comes true, but without the dreamer being aware of it. For nothing happens in the world but what is made known in advance either by means of a dream or by means of a proclamation; as it has been affirmed, that before any event comes to pass in the world it is announced in heaven, whence it is broadcast into the world. So Scripture says: "For the Lord God will do nothing, but he revealeth his counsels unto his servants the prophets', (Amos. III, 7). This refers to the time when there were prophets in the world; when prophets were no more, their place was taken by the Sages, who, in a sense, even excelled the prophets; and in the absence of Sages things to come are revealed in dreams, and if not in dreams, through the medium of the birds of heaven; and so we have laid down.' AND HIS BRETHREN WENT TO FEED THEIR FATHER'S FLOCK IN SHECHEM. R. Simeon said: The dots on the top of the particle eth in this sentence indicate that the Shekinah accompanied them by reason of their being a band of ten. (They were only ten because Joseph was not with them and Benjamin remained at home on account of his tender age.) Hence, when they sold Joseph they were in the company of the Shekinah, and, furthermore, they associated the Shekinah with them in their oath (not to reveal the affair of Joseph); and until the fate of Joseph became known, the Shekinah did not rest on Jacob. The proof that the Shekinah accompanied the brethren is the verse of the Psalms which speaks of "the tribes of the Lord, a testimony unto Israel" (Ps. CXXII, 4), a title which shows that they were all of them righteous and devout, constituting the support of the whole world, both on high and below.' R. Simeon further discoursed on the text: I rejoiced when they said unto me: Let us go unto the house of the Lord (Ibid. CXXII, 1). 'This verse has been explained', he said, 'as follows. David was minded to build the House of God, but he was commanded to leave the task to his son, as we read: "Now it was in the heart of David my father to build a house for the name of the Lord... nevertheless thou shalt not build the house; but thy son that shall come forth out of thy loins, he shall build the house for my name" (I Kings VIII, 18-19). The whole of Israel knew of this and they used to say: "When is David going to die so that Solomon his son may arise and build the House, and we shall be able to say, 'Our feet are standing within thy gates, O Jerusalem' (Ps. CXXII, 2), for we will then go up and offer sacrifices?" But although David knew that they were impatient for his death, yet he rejoiced to hear them speak thus on account of his son, who would take his place in carrying out the command to build the House. David thus commenced to sing its praises and said: "Jerusalem that art builded as a city that is compact together" (Ibid. CXXII, 3). According to our teachers, God fashioned the lower Jerusalem on the model of the heavenly Jerusalem, the one exactly facing the other, as it is written: "the place, O Lord, which thou hast made for thee to dwell in, the Sanctuary, O Lord, which thy hands have established" (Ex. xv, 17). The expression "that art builded" indicates that God will in time to come cause the upper Jerusalem to descend below; this is further proved by the phrase "as a city that is compact (she-hubrah) together", where the term hubrah (lit. she is joined), written in the singular, indicates that the Mother has joined the Daughter and the two are become as one. We read further: "Whither the tribes went up", they being the support of the world and the upholding of the lower world, and even of the upper world, as it says: "even the tribes of the Lord, as a testimony unto Israel", the term "Israel" having its esoteric significance; for they, being the support of the lower world, act as a testimony to the upper world, and all in order "to give thanks unto the name of the Lord" (Ps. CXXII, 4), i.e. to acknowledge the name of God in all directions.'

Zohar: Bereshith, Section 1, Page 184a

AND ISRAEL SAID UNTO JOSEPH: DO NOT THY BRETHREN FEED THE FLOCK OF SHECHEM? COME, AND I WILL SEND THEE UNTO THEM. How came it that Jacob the perfect man, who loved Joseph above all his sons and knew that all his brethren hated him, sent him to them? The truth is that he harboured no suspicion of them, knowing them to be all righteous; but God brought all this about in order to fulfil the decree pronounced "between the pieces" (Gen. xv, 17). We have found it stated in ancient books that the sons of Jacob were anxious to obtain dominion over Joseph before he went down into Egypt, because they knew that if he should go down there first before they obtained dominion over him the Egyptians would obtain dominion over Israel in perpetuity; but by selling Joseph as a slave they made themselves his masters, and since he later on rose to power and the Egyptians became his slaves, Israel became masters of all. Joseph was the symbol of the heavenly covenant, and so long as he was alive the covenant of the Shekinah remained with Israel in perfect harmony, but as soon as Joseph departed the covenant of the Shekinah together with Israel was plunged into captivity, as it says: "Now there arose a new king over Egypt, who knew not Joseph" (Ex. I, 8). It was all fittingly ordained by Providence. AND A CERTAIN MAN FOUND HIM: this was Gabriel, of whom we read: "the man Gabriel, whom I had seen in the vision at the beginning ' (Dan. IX, 2 1). AND, BEHOLD, HE WAS WANDERING: indeed he was wandering both literally and metaphorically; he trusted his brethren and sought their affection but could not gain it, and he was looking for them but could not find them. Hence: AND THE MAN ASKED HIM, SAYING: WHAT SEEKEST THOU? AND HE SAID: I SEEK MY BRETHREN.... AND THE MAN SAID: THEY ARE DEPARTED HENCE, ETC. R. Judah discoursed on the text: O that thou wert as my brother, that sucked the breast of my mother! When I should find thee without, I would kiss thee; yea, and none would despise me (S. S. VIII, 1). 'The Companions', he said, 'interpret this verse as being addressed by the Community of Israel to the King to whom peace belongs. She said to Him: "O that thou wert as my brother", to wit, as Joseph towards his brethren, to whom he said: "Now, therefore, fear ye not; I will sustain you and your little ones" (Gen. L, 21), and whom he provided with food and fed in time of famine. According to another explanation, the phrase "as my brother" refers to Joseph, who was in the relation of a brother towards the Shekinah, with whom he was intimately associated–"that sucked the breast of my mother", this expresses the perfect affection between them; "when I should find thee witiout", to wit, in exile, in a strange land, "I would kiss thee", so that spirit should join spirit; "yea, and none would despise me", despite my dwelling in a strange land. Observe that although when Joseph fell into their hands they did not act towards him as brothers, yet when they fell into his hands he did act towards them as a brother, as it is written: "And he comforted them, and he spoke kindly unto them" (Gen. I, 21). AND THEY SAID ONE TO ANOTHER (lit. one man to his brother). These are Simeon and Levi, who were truly brothers in all respects, both being descended from the side of rigorous judgement; and hence it was that their anger was the anger that causes death in the world, as it says: "Cursed be their anger, for it was fierce, and their wrath, for it was cruel" (Ibid. XLIX, 7). For there are two species of anger. There is anger which is blessed on high and below, and is called "blessed" (barukh), as explained in connection with the sentence: "Blessed be Abram of God Most High, Maker of heaven and earth" (Ibid. XIV, 19); and there is anger which is accursed on high and is called "cursed" (arur), and regarding this it is written: "Cursed be thou from among all cattle, and from among all beasts of the field" (Ibid. III, 14), as well as "Cursed be their anger for it was fierce." This is the recondite significance of the two mounts Gerizim and Ebal set aside for the blessing and the curse (Deut. XI, 29), the two mounts corresponding to these two grades; and hence one is called cursed and the other blessed. Simeon and Levi both belonged to the side of severity, from which side, in its extreme manifestation, issues the anger which is under a curse. All anger issues from the side of rigorous judgement, but in two directions,

Zohar: Bereshith, Section 1, Page 184b

one referred to as blessed, the other as cursed. Similarly, from the side of Isaac there issued two sons, one of whom was blessed and the other cursed on high and below; the two separated, each going off towards his own side, the one making his abode in the Holy Land, the other on Mount Seir, being as he was "a cunning hunter, a man of the field" (Gen. xxv, 27). The latter had his home in the desert, in regions of waste and desolation, while the former "dwelt in tents" (Ibid.), all being fitly ordained. Hence it is that there are two grades, "blessed" and "cursed", each ranged on its own side. From the one issue all blessings in the upper and the lower worlds, all beneficence, all light, all deliverance, all redemption; whilst the other is the source of all curses, all wars and bloodshed, all desolation and evil, and all defilement.

R. Simeon said: 'It is written: I will wash my hands in innocency; so will I compass thine altar, O Lord (Ps. XXVI, 6). The inner implication of this verse has been explained as follows. Every man has a foretaste of death during the night, because the holy soul then leaves him, and the unclean spirit rests on the body and makes it unclean. When, however, the soul returns to the body, the pollution disappears, save from the man's hands, which retain it and thus remain unclean. Hence a man should not pass his hands over his eyes before washing them. When he has washed them, however, he becomes sanctified and is called holy. For this sanctification two vessels are required, one held above and the other placed beneath, so that he may be sanctified by the water poured on his hands from the vessel above. The lower vessel, then, is the vessel of uncleanness, receiving as it does the water of contamination, whilst the upper vessel is a medium of sanctification. The upper one is to be referred to as "blessed", the lower as "cursed". Further, the water of contamination should not be emptied in the house, in order that no one may come near it; for it forms a gathering-place for the elements of the unclean side, and so one may receive injury from the unclean water. Neither may a man pronounce a benediction before the pollution is removed from his hands. Thus, before he sanctifies his hands of a morning, a man is called unclean, and after that he is called clean. For this reason one should not allow water to be poured over his hands save by a man who has already washed his own hands, in harmony with the precept: "And the clean person shall sprinkle upon the unclean" (Num. XIX, 19). We see that the one with his hands washed is the clean person, the other the unclean. Similarly with the two vessels, the upper and the lower, the one being the holy vessel, the other the unholy. Nor is it permitted to put the polluted water to any use, or even to let it stay overnight in the house, but it must be emptied in a spot where people do not pass, as it is liable to cause harm through the unclean spirit that clings to it. It is quite permissible, however, to let it flow down a slope into the earth. It must not be given to witches, as by means of it they can do harm to people. One should, then, avoid this water, since it is water of curse, and the Holy One desires to purify Israel so that they may be holy, as it is written: "And I will sprinkle clean water upon you, and ye shall be clean; from all your uncleannesses, and from all your idols, will I cleanse you" (Ez. XXXVI, 25).' AND THEY TOOK HIM AND CAST HIM INTO THE PIT. R. Judah here discoursed on the text: The law of the Lord is perfect, restoring the soul (Ps. XIX, 8). 'The study of the Torah', he said, 'procures for a man life in this world and in the world to come, so that he gains the two worlds; and even he that studies the Torah for worldly motives and not purely for its own sake as he ought to, gains a good reward in this world, and escapes punishment in the other. The Scripture says: "Length of days is in her right hand; in her left hand are riches and honour" (Prov. III, 6). There is, indeed, length of days for him who devotes himself to the Torah for its own sake. For such a one there is length of days in the other world, where days are indeed days.

Zohar: Bereshith, Section 1, Page 185a

And further: "in her left hand are riches and honour", which means good reward in this world. Moreover, if a man has devoted himself to the Torah for its own sake, when he departs this world the Torah goes before him and proclaims his merit, and shields him against the emissaries of punishment. When a man's body is laid in the grave, the Torah keeps guard over it; it goes in front of his soul when it soars upwards, breaking through all barriers until the soul reaches its proper place; and it will stand by the man at the time when he is awakened at the resurrection of the dead, in order to defend him against any accusations. Thus Scripture further says: "When thou liest down, it shall watch over thee; and when thou awakest, it shall talk with thee" (Ibid. VI, 22). The "lying down" is an allusion to the time when man's body is lying in the grave and is being judged there; the Torah will then protect him; whilst "when thou awakest", that is, when the dead will rise from the dust, "it shall talk with thee", that is, plead thy cause.' R. Eleazar interpreted the clause "it shall talk with thee" to mean that when they rise from the grave the Torah will not be forgotten of them, but they will know it much as they did when they left this world. For their Torah will be preserved from that time, will penetrate within them, and will talk, as it were, within their very inwards; and moreover, they will be more adept than they were previously, so that points which formerly baffled them in spite of all their labour will now be fully comprehended by them, the Torah itself speaking within them. Hence: "when thou awakest, it will talk with thee".' R. Judah said: 'In a similar way, whoever devotes himself to the study of the Torah in this world will be privileged to study in the world to come; and so we affirm. On the other hand, the man who fails to study the Torah in this world, and so walks in darkness, when he leaves this world is taken and cast into Gehinnom, a nethermost place, where there will be none to pity him, a place called "tumultuous pit, miry clay" (Ps. XL, 3). Hence, of him who has not devoted himself to the study of the Torah in this world, but has besmirched himself with the offscourings of this world, it is written: "And they took him and cast him into the pit", that is, into Gehinnom, a place where those who have not laboured in the Torah are brought to judgement. "And the pit was empty", in the same way as he was empty: why so? "Because there was no water" (i.e. Torah) in him. Observe, too, how great is the punishment for neglect of the study of the Torah, seeing that Israel were not exiled from the Holy Land save for having abandoned the Torah, as it is written: "Who is the wise man that may understand this?... Wherefore is the land perished?... And the Lord saith: Because they have forsaken my law, etc." (Jer. IX, 11).'

R. Judah derived the same lesson from the verse: "Therefore my people are gone into captivity, for want of knowledge" (Is. v, 13), that is, because they have not applied themselves to the study of the Torah, which is the foundation of the upper and the lower worlds, as it says: "Were it not for my covenant enduring day and night, I would not have appointed the ordinances of heaven and earth" (Jer. XXXIII, 25). AND THEY CAST HIM INTO THE PIT. There is a hint here that they cast him ultimately among the Egyptians, a place where there was no sign of true faith. R. Isaac said: 'Seeing that the pit contained serpents and scorpions, how could Reuben have advised that Joseph should be cast into it in order that "he might deliver him out of their hand, to restore him to his father"? Had he no fear of the serpents and scorpions attacking Joseph? And if they did, how could he deliver him out of their hand, to restore him to his father? But the truth is that Reuben perceived the intense enmity of the brethren towards Joseph and how intent they were on killing him, and he therefore thought that it was better for him to fall into the pit of serpents and scorpions than to be delivered into the hands of enemies who would have no mercy on him. Hence the saying: "Rather should a man throw himself into a fire or a pit full of serpents and scorpions, than be delivered into the hands of his enemies."

Zohar: Bereshith, Section 1, Page 185b

The reason is that in a place infested with serpents and scorpions, if the man be righteous, God may possibly perform a miracle for him, or it may happen that the merits of his ancestors may stand him in good stead and he will be delivered. But of those who are delivered into the hands of their enemies, few indeed are able to escape. Hence the expression "that he might deliver him out of their hand", as much as to say "Let him be delivered, at any rate, out of their hand, and if he is to die in the pit, then it cannot be helped." Observe the great piety of Reuben. He knew well the ruthlessness of Simeon and Levi when acting and planning in conjunction, as witnessed by their treatment of Shechem, where they not only slew all the males, but took all their little ones and their wives, all their silver and gold, all their cattle and precious vessels, and everything else they found in the city, and even everything which was in the field, as we read: "and that which was in the city and that which was in the field they took" (Gen. XXXIV, 28). Reuben thus said to himself: "If such a great city as that could not escape them, should this youth fall into their hands they will not leave of him a single shred." Hence he said: "He must at all costs be rescued from them, since they will leave no sign of him for his father to see again; whereas here, if he is killed, his body, at any rate, will remain for me to bring back to my father." Hence the words: "to bring him back to his father", that is, even if he die there. Hence, too, Reuben's words: "The child is not", that is to say, not even a dead child did I find. Observe his tactfulness in saying "Let us not take his life," and not "Do not ye take his life." Now Reuben was absent when Joseph was sold, as the brethren had each in turn to attend one day on their father, and that day happened to be Reuben's turn. He was anxious lest on that day Joseph should disappear, and therefore at once HE RETURNED UNTO THE PIT. BUT BEHOLD JOSEPH WAS NOT IN THE PIT;–not even dead. AND HE RENT HIS CLOTHES. AND HE RETURNED UNTO HIS BRETHREN AND SAID: THE CHILD IS NOT, ETC. For even Reuben did not know that Joseph had been sold. As already said, the brothers associated the Shekinah with them in the oath of secrecy, and so Reuben did not learn of it until Joseph made himself known to his brethren. Reuben's attempt to save Joseph's life was all the more disinterested, because he knew that the birthright had been taken away from him and given to Joseph, for we thus find that Moses interceded on his behalf, praying: "Let Reuben live, and not die" (Deut. XXXIII, 6), i.e., let him live in this world and not die in the world to come; and this prayer was prompted by this action of Reuben and also by his repentance for that other action. [Tr. note: i.e. the affair of Bilhah.] For whoever repents of his sin, God preserves in this world and in the world to come. AND THEY TOOK JOSEPH'S COAT, AND THEY KILLED A HE-GOAT, ETC., the reason being, as has been laid down, that the blood of a he-goat resembles that of a human being. We learn from this passage how particular God is with the righteous, even when they act correctly. For although Jacob acted fittingly in bringing a he-goat to his father, who was of the side of severity, yet because he thereby deceived his father, he was punished through that other he-goat, the blood of which his sons brought for the purpose of deceiving him. Of Jacob it is written: "And she put the skins of the kids of the goats upon his hands, and upon the smooth of his neck" (Gen. XXVII, 16); correspondingly, we read of his sons: "and they dipped the coat in the blood", with the object of deceiving him. It was measure for measure. Likewise, there we read: "And Isaac trembled very exceedingly" (Ibid. 33), and as a punishment Jacob trembled when his sons uttered the words: "know now whether it is thy son's coat or not".

Zohar: Bereshith, Section 1, Page 186a

R. Hiya added: 'There it is written: "whether thou be my very son Esau or not?" (Ibid. 21): correspondingly, here it is written, "whether it is thy son's or not". We thus find that the Almighty is particular with the righteous to a hairbreadth.' R. Abba said: 'When the brethren perceived the pain they had caused their father, they were stricken with remorse and cast about to ransom Joseph at all costs, if so by they could discover his whereabouts. But when they found that they were unable to do so, they turned on Judah, who hitherto had been king over them, and deposed him from his high estate. Hence it is written: "And it came to pass at that time, that Judah went down from his brethren." '

R. Judah discoursed here on the text: The Lord also thundered in the heavens, and the Most High gave forth his voice; hailstones and coals of fire (Ps. XVIII, 14). 'When God', he said, 'created the world, He constructed for it seven pillars by which it was to be upheld. So Scripture says: "Wisdom hath builded her house, she hath hewn out her seven pillars" (Prov. IX, 1). These in turn are upheld by one grade from among them called "the Righteous One, the everlasting foundation" (Ibid. x, 25). Further, when the world was created, it was started from that spot which is the culmination and perfection of the world, the central point of the universe, which is identical with Zion, as it is written: "A psalm of Asaph. God, God the Lord hath spoken and called the earth from the rising of the sun unto the going down thereof. Out of Zion, the perfection of beauty, God hath shined forth" (Ps. L, 2). That is to say, God started the earth from Zion, from the spot where faith culminates in its full perfection. Zion is thus the citadel and central point of the universe, from which it began to be fashioned and from which the whole world is nourished. This lesson is esoterically indicated in our text. For Zion and Jerusalem, while one, represent two degrees, the one being the channel of judgement, the other of mercy; first there issues from one the sound of mercy, and afterwards there comes forth from the other the voice of judgement, the two forming the source from which the paths of judgement and mercy issue and diverge. Hence the expression "And the Lord also thundered in the heavens" indicates judgement, while "the Most High gave forth his voice" refers to mercy, and "hailstones and coals of fire" signify water and fire, that is, mercy and judgement commingled. 'Observe that when Judah was born, it is written: "and she left off bearing" (Gen. XXIX, 35), the reason being that Judah constituted the fourth of the four supports of the Heavenly Throne. But here it is written: AND JUDAH WENT DOWN FROM HIS BRETHREN, that is, from his position as their king, because Joseph had been taken down into Egypt, as explained. AND JUDAH SAW THERE A DAUGHTER OF A CERTAIN CANAANITE. The term Canaanite has been explained by the Companions. AND SHE CONCEIVED, AND BORE A SON; AND HE CALLED HIS NAME ER.

Judah had three sons, and the only one who survived was Shelah. R. Eleazar and R. Yose and R. Hiya were once walking together. Said R. Yose to R. Eleazar: 'Why is it that of the first son of Judah it is written: "and he called his name Er", whereas of the other two it is written: "and she called his name Onan", "and she called his name Shelah"?' R. Eleazar replied: 'There is a deep mystic allusion in these sentences, which explains all. Thus Judah going down from his brethren symbolizes the moon becoming obscured and descending from the perfected grade to another grade to which the serpent becomes associated, as is indicated in the statement: "and he turned into a certain Adullamite, whose name was Hirah". Then we read: "And she conceived, and bore a son; and he called his name Er." The name 'Er is a reversal of the letters ra' (evil), for he was evil, having issued from the side of the evil prompter. The accusative particle eth (the) inserted before his name likewise

Zohar: Bereshith, Section 1, Page 186b

hints at the emergence of another grade, that of impurity and defilement, from which grade Er was born. Nor was the defect made good until afterwards, when Shelah appeared. It says further: "And Er, Judah's first-born, was evil in the sight of the Lord", where the term "evil" finds its echo in the sentence: "for the imagination of man's heart is evil from his youth" (Gen. VIII, 21). Er was evil in that he shed blood, by spilling the seed on the ground, and therefore the Lord slew him. After that it is written: AND JUDAH SAID UNTO ONAN: Go IN UNTO THY BROTHER'S WIFE, ETC. R. Simeon

229

opened here a discourse with the text: I have roused up one from the north, and he is come, from the rising of the sun one that calleth upon my name; and he shall come upon rulers as upon mortar, and as the potter treadeth clay (Is. XLI, 25). 'How foolish', he said, 'are the sons of men who neither know nor care about the ways of the Almighty, their eyes being closed as in sleep. God made man after the supernal pattern, each limb corresponding to something in the scheme of Wisdom. For when the whole body of man had been duly shaped with all its members, God associated Himself with him and put a holy soul into him, so as to teach man to walk in the ways of the Torah and to observe His commandments in order that he might attain to his full perfection. Hence, while the holy soul is still within man's body, it is incumbent on him to multiply the image of the King in the world. There is herein an esoteric thought involved, namely, that just as the celestial stream flows on forever without ceasing, so must man see that his own river and spring shall not cease in this world. And so long as a man is unsuccessful in his purpose in this world, the Holy One, blessed be He, uproots him and replants him over and over again. Observe, then, the meaning of the words: "I have roused up one from the north, and he is come", where the rousing alludes to the rousing and stirring up of the desire of a man for mating in this world, which originates from the North, whilst the words "and he is come" allude to the holy soul which descends from on high, whence God sends it, and comes into this world to enter into a man, as said above. "From the rising of the sun" alludes to the place of that celestial ever-flowing river, whence the soul issues and is illumined: "and there come rulers as mortar" signifies the heavenly forces which cause a rousing in the souls above corresponding to the stirring of the man in his body. For it is for this purpose that God creates souls in couples and sends them down to the world, so that there may be companionship both on high and below, and the well-spring of all may be blessed. God made man that he should steadfastly walk in His ways, and never cut off his fount and well-spring; for if a man cuts off his well-spring on earth and causes it to dry up, it is as though he causes the waters of the celestial river to fail, as described in the words: "The waters fail from the sea, and the river is drained dry" (Job XIV, 11). For inasmuch as man has been established in this world after the pattern of the upper world, he whose well-spring ceases to produce through his not taking a wife is beyond remedy, and of him it is said: "That which is crooked cannot be made straight" (Eccl. I, 15). On the other hand, he who has taken a wife but has not been blessed with offspring can be redeemed by his near relative, that is, by his brother. He who dies without leaving children will not enter within the curtain of heaven and will have no share in the other world, and his soul will not be admitted to the place where all souls are gathered and his image will be cut off from there. Of such a one it is written: "And this soul will be cut off from before me." Such being the case, God has provided for such a man a redeemer

Zohar: Bereshith, Section 1, Page 187a

to redeem him out of the hands of the destructive angels, to wit, his brother who is near to him. So Scripture says: "If brethren dwell together, etc." (Deut. xxv, 5-10); also: "Go in unto thy brother's wife, and perform the duty of husband's brother unto her, etc." For the soul of such a man does not enter before the presence of the Holy One, blessed be He, but remains without, since he has not succeeded in radiating light in this world by means of the body. He who has not succeeded in this place must go to another place where he may have better fortune. When wood smoulders without any flame, if it is struck it flares up and throws out light. Man is compared to wood, as it says: "for the tree of the field is man" (Ibid. xx, 19). Now a man who eats and drinks and marries, but is not blessed with children, is like the wood that burns without giving off any light, that is, his soul has not been illumined in its present body but has remained in darkness. It is written: "He created it not a waste, he formed it to be inhabited" (Is. XLV, 18), that is, God made man for this purpose, and so dealt kindly with the world. Observe the Scriptural text: "And Abraham took another wife, and her name was Keturah" (Gen. xxv, 1). Herein is an allusion to the soul which after death comes to earth to be built up as before. Observe that of the body it is written: "And it pleased the Lord to crush him by disease; to see if his soul would offer itself in restitution, that he might see his seed, and prolong his days, and that the purpose of the Lord might prosper by his hand." (Is. LIII, 10). That is to say, if the soul desires to be rehabilitated then he must see seed, for the soul hovers round about and is ready to enter the seed of procreation, and thus "he will prolong his days, and the purpose of the Lord", namely the Torah, "will prosper in his hand". For although a man labours in the Torah day and night, yet if his source remains fruitless, he will find no place by which to enter within the heavenly curtain. As has been pointed out, a well of water, if not fed by its source and spring, is no well, since the well and the source are one and they have a joint symbolism. It is written: "It is vain for you that ye rise early, and sit up late, ye that eat the bread of sadness; so he giveth unto his beloved sleep" (Ps. CXXVII, 2). Precious, indeed, are the words of the Torah, each one containing sublime and holy mysteries, as has been affirmed, that when God gave the Torah to Israel, He gave it to them with all its sublime and holy treasures. The words: "It is vain for you that ye rise early" are addressed to those who are single, not exhibiting the proper union of male with female. In vain they rise early, as we read: "There is one that is alone, and he hath not a second... yet, there is no end of all his labour" (Eccl. IV, 8). In vain, too, they "sit up late", or, as we may translate, they "postpone rest", as woman is assuredly man's repose. They are addressed as "ye that eat the bread of sadness", for the man who has children eats his bread in good cheer and gladness of heart; but to him that has no children, the bread he eats is bread of sadness: "so he giveth unto his beloved sleep", the beloved being he whose wellspring is blessed, and to whom the Holy One vouchsafeth sleep in the other world, as we read: "and thou shalt lie down, and thy sleep shall be sweet" (Prov. III, 24), for he has a share in the world to come; the man will thus lie down and be blessed with the world to come. "There is one that is alone" (Eccl. IV, 8) is an allusion to the man who is improperly alone, without a wife; "and he hath not a second", no one to uphold him, no son to establish his name in Israel, or to bring him to his due meed; "yet there is no end of all his labour", as he is always labouring, day and night; "neither is his eye satisfied with riches" (Ibid.) and he has not the sense to reflect: "for whom, then, do I labour and bereave my soul

Zohar: Bereshith, Section 1, Page 187b

of pleasure?" (Ibid.) You may say that he has pleasure in that he eats and drinks and feasts every day; but it is not so, inasmuch as his soul (nefesh) does not share in his pleasure, so that assuredly he bereaves his soul of pleasure, of the blissful illumination of the world to come; for it is left stunted without attaining its full and proper growth. For God cares for His works, and so desires that a man should be set right and not perish from the world to come, as already said.'

R. Hiya put the following question: 'What is the position of a man who is just and upright and occupies himself with the study of the Torah day and night, and devotes himself wholly to the service of the Almighty, and yet is not blessed with children in this world despite all his effort, or who has children and they die–what is his position in the world to come?' R. Yose replied: 'His good deeds and the Torah will shield him in the world to come.' R. Isaac said: 'Of such it is written: "For thus saith the Lord concerning the eunuchs that keep my Sabbaths, and choose the things that please me, and hold fast my covenant: even unto them will I give in my house and within my walls a monument and a memorial, better than sons and daughters; I will give them an everlasting memorial that shall not be cut off" (Is. LVI, 4-5), so that these have a share in the world to come.' Said R. Yose: 'All this is perfectly correct. But what of the following problem? Suppose there is a perfectly righteous man who has all these qualities and duly perfects himself, yet dies without issue. Now, seeing that he will inherit his place in the world to come, will his wife require to marry his brother or not? If she has to do so, then the marriage will be purposeless, seeing that the other brother inherits his own place in the other world. The truth, however, is that she must still marry the brother, because we cannot say definitely whether the departed was really perfect or not. And in any case her second marriage is not purposeless, since it can serve to redeem some other righteous man who has died without children and has had no ransomer. The passage quoted above continues: "Two are better than one; because they have a good reward for their labour" (Eccl. IV, 9), alluding to those who have performed the duty of leaving children in this world, for whose sake they inherit a portion in the world to come. So God has planted trees in this world; if they prosper, well and good, and if not, He uproots them and replants them time after time. All the ways of the Holy One are thus for the purpose of achieving the good and the perfection of the world. ' Go IN UNTO THY BROTHER'S WIFE, AND PERFORM THE DUTY OF A HUSBAND'S BROTHER UNTO HER. Judah and all the other tribes were already cognisant of this duty, the main purpose of which is expressed in the sentence: "and raise up seed to thy brother", as that seed is needed for the purpose of putting things right by growing into human shape and form and thus preventing the stock from being severed from its root. And when all has been put right, then those concerned receive praisc in the other world, as the Holy One is pleased with them. Hence it says: "Wherefore I praised the dead that are already dead more than the living that are yet alive; but better than they both is he that hath not yet been, who hath not seen the evil work that is done under the sun" (Ibid. IV, 2-3). That is to say: I praised the dead that are already dead more than the living that have returned (from the other world) to the days of their youth; but better than they both is he that has not yet returned to the days of his youth, as he has no need to rectify and to suffer for his former sins; for the Holy One

Zohar: Bereshith, Section 1, Page 188a

has already given him a fitting place in the other world. Happy the portion of the just who walk in the way of truth. Of them it is written: "The righteous shall inherit the land" (Ps. XXXVII, 29). AND THE THING WHICH HE DID WAS EVIL IN THE SIGHT OF THE LORD; AND HE SLEW HIM ALSO. R. Hiya discoursed here on the text: In the morning sow thy seed, and in the evening withhold not thy hand; for thou knowest not which shall prosper, this or that, etc. (Eccl. XI, 6). 'It behoves a man', he said, 'to be well on his guard against sin, and to be heedful in his actions before the Holy One, blessed be He; for numerous messengers and chieftains roam about the world, spying out the works of the sons of man, to which they bear witness, and all of which are recorded in a book. Now of all the sins which defile a man, that which defiles him the most, both in this world and in the world to come, is the sin of spilling one's seed (semen). A man guilty of this sin will not enter within the Heavenly Curtain, and will not behold the presence of the Ancient of Days. So we learn from the recurrence of the word "evil" here and in the verse: "For thou art not a God that hath pleasure in wickedness; evil shall not sojourn with thee" (Ps. v, 5). It was on account of this sin, too, that the prophet said to the people, "your hands are full of blood" (Is. I, 15). Happy the portion of him who fears his Master, and is on his guard against the evil habit, keeping himself pure so as to persevere in the fear of his Master. Observe, then, the admonition saying: "In the morning sow thy seed." This alludes to the period when a man is in his prime and in the flower of youth, when he sets out to bring forth offspring from the woman destined for him. Then is the proper time for rearing children, as it says: "As arrows in the hand of a mighty man, so are the children of one's youth" (Ps. CXXVII, 4), as the father can then teach them the ways of the Holy One and so gain reward in the world to come, as it is written: "Happy is the man that hath his quiver full of them; they shall not be put to shame, when they speak with their enemies in the gate" (Ibid. 5), i.e. in the next world when the accusers bring their indictment against him, since there is no greater reward in the next world than that of the man who has trained his children in the fear of their Master and in the ways of the Torah. So it is written of Abraham: "For I have known him, that he will command his children and his household after him, that they may keep the way of the Lord, to do righteousness and justice" (Gen. XVIII, 19); and it was that merit which bestood him against all the accusers in the other world. Further: "and in the evening withhold not thy hand", that is to say, from begetting children even in old age, "for thou knowest not which shall prosper", that is which shall stand up in thy defence in the other world; and in regard to this it is written: "Lo, children are a heritage of the Lord" (Ps. CXXVII, 3), where the phrase "heritage of the Lord" is an allusion to the "bundle of souls" in the world to come, and the passage indicates that it is children that make a man worthy of entering that heritage of the Lord. Hence happy is the man who is blessed with them and who trains them in the ways of the Torah. AND SHE PUT OFF FROM HER THE GARMENTS OF HER WIDOWHOOD. Tamar was the daughter of a priest, and it can hardly be imagined that she set out with the intention of committing incest with her father-in-law, since she was by nature chaste and modest. She was indeed virtuous and did not prostitute herself, and it was out of her deeper knowledge and wisdom that she approached Judah, and a desire to act kindly and faithfully (towards the dead). And it was because her act was based on a deeper knowledge that God aided her and she straightway conceived. So that it was all ordained

Zohar: Bereshith, Section 1, Page 188b

from on high. If it is asked, why did not God cause those sons to be born from some other woman, the answer is that Tamar was necessary for this purpose, and not any other woman. There were two women from whom the seed of Judah was to be built up, from whom were to descend King David, King Solomon, and the Messiah, viz. Tamar and Ruth. These two women had much in common. Both lost their first husbands, and both took similar steps to replace them. Tamar enticed Judah because he was the next-of-kin to her sons who had died, and "she saw that Shelah was grown up, and she was not given unto him for wife". Ruth similarly enticed Boaz, as it says, "and she uncovered his feet and laid her down" (Ruth III, 7), and afterwards she bore him Obed. Now we do not ask why Obed was not born from another woman, for assuredly Ruth was necessary for that purpose to the exclusion of any other woman. From these two women, then, the seed of Judah was built up and brought to completion, and both of them acted piously, and had for their aim to do kindness toward the dead, for the proper establishment of the world subsequently. And this bears out our exposition of the verse "Wherefore I praise the dead that are already dead" (Eccl. IV, 2), for whilst their first husbands were alive there was no merit in them, but afterwards they were good for something, and so these two women exerted themselves to do kindness and truth with the dead; and God aided them in that work, and all was done fittingly. Happy is he who exerts himself in the study of the Torah day and night, as it says: "but thou shalt meditate therein day and night, that thou mayest observe to do according to all that is written therein; for then thou shalt make thy ways prosperous, etc." (Jos. I, 8). AND JOSEPH WAS BROUGHT DOWN TO EGYPT, AND POTIPHAR

BOUGHT HIM, ETC. The expression ' was brought down" indicates that God approved of the act, so as to bring to fulfilment the announcement made to Abram between the pieces: "thy seed shall be a stranger, etc." (Gen. xv, 13). AND POTIPHAR BOUGHT HIM, for a sinful purpose.

R. Hizkiah discoursed on the text: Who commandeth the sun, and it riseth not; and sealeth up the stars (Job IX, 7). 'God', he said, 'has set seven stars in the firmament, and each firmament contains numerous angels appointed to minister to the Holy One, blessed be He, each angel having his own service to perform before his Master. All attend to the service to which they have been appointed and each one knows his task. Some of them serve as messengers, having charge in this world of the works of men; others are appointed to chant to Him songs and hymns. But although this is their own particular charge, there is no host in heaven or in the stars or in the constellations but chants praises to the Holy One, blessed be He; for as soon as night falls three hosts of angels range themselves in three quarters of the universe; and in each quarter there are myriads upon myriads, all of whom have for their task

Zohar: Bereshith, Section 1, Page 189a

to chant praises to the Holy One. Over these three hosts there stands a sacred Hayah as chieftain. The chanting continues until daybreak. As soon as day breaks all those on the side of the South as well as the shining stars break out into song and praise to the Holy One, as we read: "When the morning stars sang together, and all the sons of God shouted for joy" (Job XXXVIII, 7), the morning stars being the stars of the South, the direction implied in the sentence: "And Abraham got up early in the morning" (Gen. XIX, 27), whilst the "sons of God" are those on the left side who merge themselves in the right. When daylight arrives Israel take up the song and offer praises to the Holy One three times a day, corresponding to the three watches of the night. Thus through the angels and Israel together the glory of God is proclaimed day and night with six litanies. The sacred Hayah that is in charge of the chantings of the night on high similarly presides over the chantings of Israel here below; and all is performed in proper order. In regard to this one it is also written: "She riseth also while it is yet night and giveth food to her household, and a portion to her maidens" (Prov. XXXI, 15), where the "household" alludes to the heavenly hosts, whilst the word "maidens" signifies Israel here below. The Holy One is thus extolled both on high and here below.' R. Simeon said: 'The clause "Who commandeth the sun, and it riseth not" applies to Joseph, whilst the sequel, "and sealeth up the stars", applies to his brethren, regarding whom he said, "And eleven stars bowed down to me."

Alternatively, "Who commandeth the sun" is an allusion to Jacob at the time his sons said to him: "Know now whether it is thy son's coat or not"; "that it shineth not" is a reference to the time when the Shekinah departed from him; whilst "sealeth up the stars" implies that through his sons Jacob's light was sealed and closed up, the sun for him was darkened and the stars did not shine–all because Joseph was separated from his father. And note that from the day on which Joseph disappeared Jacob abstained from marital intercourse and observed all the other rites of mourning until the day the good tidings of Joseph reached him.' F AND THE LORD WAS WITH JOSEPH, AND HE WAS A PROSPEROUS MAN; AND HE WAS IN THE HOUSE OF HIS MASTER THE EGYPTIAN. R. Yose quoted here the verse: "For the Lord loveth justice, and forsaketh not his saints; they are preserved forever" (Ps. XXXVII, 28). 'Observe', he said 'that wherever the righteous walk, God protects them and never abandons them, as David said: "Yea, though I walk through the valley of the shadow of death, I will fear no evil, for thou art with me; thy rod and staff they comfort me" (Ibid. XXIII, 4); wherever the righteous walk the Shekinah accompanies them and does not abandon them. Joseph walked through the valley of the shadow of death, having been brought down to Egypt, but the Shekinah was with him, as we read: "And the Lord was with Joseph", and by reason of the presence of the Shekinah all that he did prospered in his hand; so much so that if he had something in his hand and his master wanted something of a different kind, it changed in his hand to the kind his master wanted. Hence, it says "made to prosper in his hand", the reason being that the Lord was with him. Observe, too, that it is not written here, "And his master knew", but "And his master saw", signifying that he saw every day with his eyes the miracles God performed by the hand of Joseph; hence: "the Lord blessed the Egyptian's house for Joseph's sake". God guards the righteous, and for their sakes He guards also the wicked, so that the wicked receive blessings through the righteous. So we find it written: "The Lord blessed the house of Obededom... because of the ark of God" (II Sam. VI, 12). Others are sustained for the sake of those righteous, but they are not able to sustain or save themselves by their own merits. So Joseph, although his master was blessed for his sake, could not himself escape from him through his own merits and gain his freedom. He was even thrown afterwards into the dungeon, as we read: "His feet they hurt with fetters, his person was laid in iron" (Ps. cv, 18), until God liberated him and made him ruler over all the land of Egypt, and thus it is written: "and he forsaketh not his saints;

Zohar: Bereshith, Section 1, Page 189b

they are preserved forever." God shields the righteous in this world and in the world to come, as it is written: "So shall all those that take refuge in thee rejoice, they shall ever shout for joy, and thou shalt shelter them; let them also that love thy name exult in thee" (Ibid. v, 12).' AND IT CAME TO PASS AFTER THESE THINGS THAT HIS MASTER'S WIFE, ETC. R. Hiya discussed the text: Bless the Lord, ye angels of his, ye mighty in strength, that fulfil his word, hearkening unto the voice of his word (lbid. CIII, 20). 'How greatly', he said, 'it behoves a man to guard against sin and to pursue the straight path, so that the evil prompter, his daily assailant, should not lead him astray. And since he assails man perpetually, it behoves man to muster all his force against him and to entrench himself in the place of strength; for as the evil prompter is mighty, it behoves man to be mightier still; and those sons of men who do excel him in might are called "mighty in strength", dealing with him in his own coin, and they are "the angels of the Lord" who come from the side of Geburah (Might) to deal mightily with him. Such a one was Joseph, who was called "righteous" and guarded in purity the sign of the holy covenant which was imprinted upon him.' R. Eleazar said: 'The word "after" here alludes to the evil prompter, being the name of a grade, as we have laid down. Joseph exposed himself to his accusations because he used to pay great attention to his personal appearance. That gave the evil prompter an opening to say: "Behold, his father observes mourning for him, and he decks himself out and curls his hair!" Thus the bear was let loose, as it were, and set upon him.' AND IT CAME TO PASS AFTER THESE THINGS. When God surveys the world with intent to judge it, and finds there wicked people, then, in the words of the Scripture, "He shuts up the heaven, so that there shall be no rain, and the ground shall not yield her fruit" (Deut. XI, 17); through the sins of the sons of men heaven and earth are shut up and do not perform their functions. Now those who do not guard in purity the holy covenant cause a division between Israel and their Father in heaven. So Scripture says: "and ye turn aside and serve other gods, and worship them. He shut up the heaven, so that there shall be no rain" (Ibid. XI, 16-17); for to be false to the holy covenant is equivalent to bowing to another god. But when the holy covenant is properly guarded by mankind, God showers blessings from above on to this world, as we read: "A bounteous rain didst thou pour down, O God; thine inheritance and the weary one, thou confirmest it" (Ps. LXVIII, 10). "A bounteous (n'daboth, lit. favour) rain" is a rain of favour, at a time when the Community of Israel find favour in the eyes of the Almighty and He desires to shower upon them blessings; then "Thine inheritance", namely Israel, who are the inheritance of the Holy One, as it says: "Jacob the lot of his inheritance" (Deut. XXXII, 9), and "the weary one", to wit, the Community of Israel, which is weary in a strange land, which is parched, panting for drink, "with that rain of favour thou confirmest it". Hence heaven and earth with all their hosts are upheld by that covenant, as Scripture says: "If not for my covenant, day and night, the ordinances of heaven and earth were as though I had not made them" (Jer. XXXIII, 25). Hence it is first written: "And Joseph was of beautiful form, and fair to look upon", and immediately afterwards, "that his master's wife cast her eyes upon Joseph". AND IT CAME TO PASS, AS SHE SPOKE TO JOSEPH DAY BY DAY. R. Eleazar discoursed on the verse: To keep thee from the evil woman, etc. (Prov. VI, 24). 'Happy', he said, 'are the righteous who know the ways of the Almighty and follow them, since they devote themselves to the Torah day and night; for whoso devotes himself to the Torah day and night inherits two worlds, the upper world and the world

Zohar: Bereshith, Section 1, Page 190a

below. He inherits this world, even if he does not study the Torah for its own sake; and he inherits the other world, if he does study the Torah for its own sake. So it is written: "Length of days is in her right hand, in her left hand are riches and honour" (Ibid. III, 16); that is, whoever walks to the right of the Torah, for him she is length of life in the world to come, where he will be invested with the glory of the Torah, which is the truest glory and the crown of crowns; for the crown of the Torah is in the other world; but "in her left hand are riches and honour", to wit, in this world; even for him who does not study it for its own sake. When R. Hiya came from Babylonia to the Land of Israel he studied the Torah until his face shone like the sun, and when the students of the Torah stood up before him he would say: "This one studies the Torah for its own sake, this one does not study the Torah for its own sake." For the former he would pray that they should always retain that frame of mind and so merit the world to come; for the latter he prayed that their heart should be changed so that they should study the Torah for its own sake and merit life everlasting. One day he saw a certain disciple whose face was unnaturally pale. He said to himself: "This young man is undoubtedly assailed by sinful imaginations." So he took him in hand and interested him in the words of the Torah until he returned to a better frame of mind. From that day the disciple resolved not to give way any more to evil thoughts, but to study the Torah for its own sake.' R. Yose said: 'When a man perceives that evil thoughts are assailing him, he should study the Torah, and that will drive them away.' R. Eleazar said: 'When the evil side comes to seduce a man, he should draw it towards the Torah, and then it will quit him. For so we have learnt, that when the evil side stands up before the Almighty to accuse the world for its evil deeds, God in pity furnishes the sons of men with a device whereby to escape the accuser, so that he may not have power over them or their actions. This device consists in the study of the Torah, which will save them from the evil power, as it is written: "For the commandment is a lamp, and the teaching (Torah) is light, and reproofs of instruction are the way of life." The passage continues: "To keep thee from the evil woman, from the smoothness of the alien tongue" (Ibid. VI, 23-24), that is, from the side of uncleanness, or the other side, that is perpetually accusing the sons of men before the Almighty; and whilst it seduces men here below from the right path, it is busy on high pointing out the sins of men and indicting them, so that they may be given over into its power, in the same way as it acted towards Job. Especially at those periods when God sits in judgement on the world does it rise up to indict men and enumerate their sins. God, however, had compassion on Israel and provided them with a device for escaping from it, to wit, the trumpet (shofar) which is to be blown on New Year's Day, and the scapegoat which they give it on the Day of Atonement in order that it may leave them alone and occupy itself with its own portion. Of this it is written: "Her feet go down to death; her steps take hold on the nether world" (Ibid. v, 5); but of the true faith it says: "Her ways are ways of pleasantness, and all her paths are peace" (Ibid. III, 17). This refers to the ways and paths of the Torah. We have here the two opposing ways, the one of well-being, the other of death. Happy is the portion of Israel who cleave faithfully to the Holy One, who has afforded them a means of escape from all the other sides, because they are a holy people, His inheritance and portion. Happy are they in this world and in the world to come. When this evil side comes down and roams through the world and sees the works of mankind and how they all act perversely in the world, it ascends and accuses them, and were it not that the Almighty has compassion on the works of His hands, none would be left in the world on account of the accuser. Thus we read: "And it came to pass, as she spoke to Joseph day by day",

Zohar: Bereshith, Section 1, Page 190b

that is to say, the accuser ascends every day and brings ever so many evil reports and calumnies in order to destroy mankind; "but he hearkened not unto her", because He has compassion on the world; "to be by her", that is, to permit the accuser to exercise dominion over the world, which he cannot do without obtaining authorization. The virtuous man so guards his ways as to keep afar from him the evil prompter, as it is written: "And it came to pass, as she spoke to him day by day, that he hearkened not unto her"; for the unclean spirit, which is the same as the evil prompter, tries day by day to seduce man to lie by her, that is, to draw him into Gehinnom, to be with her there; for observe that once a man yields to that side he is more and more drawn towards it and defiles himself with it in this world and in the other world. This unclean side is ugly and filthy, and by it is punished he who goes astray from the Torah, and all those sinners that have no faith in the Holy One, blessed be He. It is further written: "And it came to pass on a certain day", to wit, the day in which the evil prompter is at large in the world, and comes to lead men astray; the day when the sons of men "come into the house to do their work", that is, to repent of their sins or study the Torah and carry out the commandments of the Torah, since man's proper work in this world is nothing else than the service of the Holy One. Hence it behoves him to be strong as a lion on every side, so that the other side should not get the mastery over him and should be powerless to seduce him. But when the evil prompter sees that there is no man to stand up against him and wage war with him, then "She caught him by the garment, saying: Lie with me", for when the evil prompter gains an ascendancy over a man, he decks him out with fine raiment and curls his hair and says "Lie with me", that is, attach yourself unto me. He that is righteous stands up to him and offers him battle; so Scripture says: "And he left his garment in her hand, and fled and got him out"-the righteous thus by an effort shakes him off and flees from him so that he should not have command over him any more.' R. Isaac said: 'The righteous will one day see the evil prompter in the form of a huge mountain and they will marvel at themselves, saying, How were we ever able to overthrow that mighty mountain? Contrariwise, to the wicked the evil prompter will appear like a thread as thin as a hair, and they will say in astonishment, How was it that we could not master so frail a thread as this? The righteous will weep for joy and the wicked will weep from anguish. And the Holy One will sweep the evil one off the earth, He will slaughter him before their eyes, so that his power will forever be gone from the world. The righteous will behold and rejoice, as it says: "Surely the righteous shall give thanks unto thy name, the upright shall dwell in thy presence" (Ps. CXL, 14).'

Zohar: Bereshith, Section 1, Page 191a

AND IT CAME TO PASS AFTER THESE THINGS, THAT THE BUTLER OF THE KING OF EGYPT AND HIS BAKER OFFENDED, ETC. R. Judah opened his discourse with the text: Will a lion roar in the forest when he hath no prey? win a young lion give forth his voice out of his den, if he has taken nothing? (Amos III, 4). 'It well boots a man', he said, 'to be assiduous in the worship of the Holy One, blessed be He, for then his fear and dread is upon every creature. For when God created the world, He made each creature in its proper likeness; and finally He created man in the supernal image and gave him dominion over all through this image. For as long as a man is alive the other creatures look up to him and, perceiving the supernal image, shake and tremble before him, as we read: "And the fear of you and the dread of you shall be upon every beast of the earth, and upon every fowl of the air, etc." (Gen. IX, 2). But this is only when they are aware of that image and soul in him (though R. Eleazar said that the image of the righteous does not change even when their soul (neshamah) is no longer in them). But when a man does not walk in the ways of the Torah, that divine image is altered, and the beasts of the field and the birds of the sky obtain power over him; because the divine image in him, the very form which makes him a man, is changed. Observe how God altered the order of nature in order to execute His purpose. For the form of Daniel was not altered even when he was thrown into the lions' den, and thus he was saved.' Said R. Hizkiah: 'If so, why is it said, "My God hath sent his angel, and hath shut the lions' mouths, and they have not hurt me" (Dan. VI, 23)?' R. Judah said in reply: 'The divine image of the righteous man is itself the very angel that shuts the mouths of the beasts and puts them in shackles so that they do not hurt him; hence Daniel's words: "My God hath sent his angel", to wit, the one who bears the imprint of all the images of the world, and he firmly fixed my image on me, thereby shutting the lions' mouths, and making them powerless over me. Hence man has to look well to his ways and paths, so as not to sin before his Master, and to preserve the image of Adam. Ezekiel guarded his mouth against forbidden food, as it is written: "Neither came there abhorred flesh into my mouth" (Ez. IV, 14), and for this he was dignified with the title "son of Adam". Of Daniel also it is written: "But Daniel purposed in his heart that he would not defile himself with the king's food, nor with the wine which he drank" (Dan. I, 8), in virtue of which he conserved the image of Adam; for all beings of the world fear the image of Adam, which is ruler and king over all.' Said

R. Yose: 'For this reason it behoves man to be on his guard against sin and to turn neither to the right nor to the left; and however careful he may be, he should still search himself daily for any sin. When a man rises in the morning two witnesses join him and follow him the whole day. When he opens his eyes, they say to him: "Let thine eyes look right on, and let thine eyelids look straight before thee" (Prov. IV, 25); when he gets up and makes ready to walk, they say to him: "Make plain the paths of thy feet, etc." (Ibid. 26). A man, therefore, should be on his guard against his sins the whole day and every day, and when night comes it behoves him to look back and examine all the actions he has done that day, so that he may repent himself. So David said: "And my sin is ever before me" (Ps. LI, 5), as an exhortation to repentance. Now, when Israel were in the Holy Land sin never clung to them, because the offerings which they offered up

Zohar: Bereshith, Section 1, Page 191b

made atonement for them. But now that they are exiled from the Land and the offerings have ceased, it is the Torah and good deeds that make atonement for them.'

R. Isaac remarked: 'So whosoever devotes himself to the study of the Torah and to the performance of good deeds enables the Community of Israel to raise its head in the midst of exile. Happy is the portion of those who study diligently the Torah day and night.'

Observe now how God regulates events in such a way as to raise aloft the head of the righteous; for in order that Joseph, who was found righteous before Him, might be exalted, He stirred his master to anger against his servants, as we read: "The butler of the king of Egypt and his baker offended their lord the king of Egypt"–all that Joseph the righteous might be exalted. And notice that it was through a dream that Joseph was brought low by his brethren, and it was through a dream that he was raised over his brethren and over the whole world. AND THEY DREAMED A DREAM, BOTH OF THEM, EACH MAN HIS DREAM, IN ONE NIGHT, EACH MAN ACCORDING TO THE INTERPRETATION OF HIS DREAM, ETC. Seeing that we have laid down that dreams follow their interpretation, it may be asked what made Joseph interpret the dream of one in a good sense and of the other in a bad sense. The explanation is that these dreams concerned Joseph himself, and, because he penetrated to the root of the matter, he gave to each dream the fitting interpretation so that everything should fall in its place. AND JOSEPH SAID UNTO THEM: DO NOT INTERPRETATIONS BELONG TO GOD? TELL IT ME, I PRAY YOU. Joseph used this formula because it is necessary before interpreting a dream to entrust the interpretation to the Holy One, since there, on high, is the shaping of all events, and His is the interpretation. Observe that the grade of dream is a low grade, the sixth from that of prophecy, and that its interpretation determines its effect, being itself embodied in speech and utterance. This is what is meant by Joseph's question: "Do not interpretations belong to God (Elohim)?" Assuredly to Elohim. Now observe the verse: "And the chief butler told his dream to Joseph, etc." R. Eleazar opened a discourse on the text: And it came to pass, when they were gone over, that Elijah said unto Elisha: Ask what I shall do for thee, before I am taken from thee. And Elisha said: I pray thee, let a double portion of thy spirit be upon me. 'The language used by Elijah here', he said, 'is not a little surprising, for surely it is only God who can grant whatever is asked of Him. And further, how could Elisha, knowing this, demand "Let a double portion of thy spirit be upon me"? But, indeed, this was surely not beyond the power of one who had a grip of heaven and earth and of the whole world, for assuredly God would perform the will of Elijah, as of all righteous men, as we read: "He will fulfil the desire of them that fear him" (Ps. CXLV, 19), and all the more when it was a question of Elijah bequeathing the holy spirit he possessed to Elisha, who was his own servant, and concerning whom God had said to him: "and Elisha, the son of Shaphat of Abel-mehulah shalt thou anoint to be prophet in thy room" (I Kings XIX, 16); hence Elisha was his heir by right. We may ask, however, how he could beg for a double portion of his spirit, which was more than Elijah possessed. What Elisha really asked, however, was not a double portion of the spirit, but the power to perform a double achievement with that same spirit. Elijah thereupon said: "Thou hast asked a hard thing; nevertheless, if thou see me when I am taken from thee, it shall be so unto thee; but if not, it shall not be so" (II Kings II, 10). By the words, "if thou see me" he meant: If thou canst penetrate to the true inwardness of the spirit that I bequeath thee at the moment I am taken from thee, it shall be so unto thee. For such essence of the spirit as he should discern while looking at Elijah he would fully grasp.

Zohar: Bereshith, Section 1, Page 192a

And so, whoever contemplates that which he learns from his master whilst at the same time seeing that wisdom reflected in his face, can thereby obtain an additional meed of spirit. So Joseph, in whatever he was about to do, used to contemplate in the spirit of wisdom the image of his father, and so he prospered and an augmentation of spirit came upon him with a higher illumination. When that sinner said to him: "behold, a vine was before me", Joseph was alarmed, not knowing what import it might have; but when he continued, "and in the vine were three branches", straightway Joseph's spirit was astir and received an influx of energy and illumination, because at the same time he gazed at the image of his father, and knew the meaning of the words he heard. We read, then, AND IN THE VINE WERE THREE BRANCHES. Said Joseph: 'This is assuredly tidings of unalloyed joy', since that vine was symbolic of the Community of Israel, and the three branches were the three higher grades ramifying from that vine, to wit, Priests, Levites, and Israelites: and AS IT WAS BUDDING ITS BLOSSOMS SHOT FORTH, that is, by virtue of those three orders the whole Community of Israel ascended and received the blessing from the Most High King: AND THE CLUSTERS THEREOF BROUGHT FORTH RIPE GRAPES, an allusion to the wine that is kept in store in its grapes since the six days of creation. [Tr. note: For the banqueting of the righteous in the world to come.] So far the dream was of good tidings for Joseph; the rest of the dream concerned solely the dreamer himself; for, indeed, some dreams there are which in part concern the dreamer himself and in part other people. In this connection we have been taught: To see white grapes in a dream is of good omen to the dreamer, but not black, the reason being that these two are emblems of two certain grades, one of the side of good, the other of the contrary side. Grapes in general are an allusion to faith, and hence they diverge within that category, one kind to the side of good and the other to the side of evil, the one requiring to be exorcised by prayer, the other betokening providential care. Observe that the wife of Adam pressed for him grapes and thereby brought death to him, and to the whole world. Noah, again, came upon those grapes and he was not duly circumspect, so it is written of

236

him: "And he drank of the wine, and he was drunken; and he was uncovered within his tent" (Gen. IX, 21). Of those same grapes the sons of Aaron drank, and they offered up sacrifices whilst under the influence of wine, as a result of which they died. Hence it is written: "their grapes are grapes of gall, their clusters are bitter" (Deut. XXXII, 32), referring to those grapes that caused all those ills; but the chief of the butlers saw in his dream the good grapes in that vineyard whence there ascends a pleasant and agreeable odour among the perfect grades in manner due. Thus Joseph, who penetrated to the root of the whole matter, interpreted the dream aright; for inasmuch as the dream contained good tidings for himself he interpreted the whole of it in a favourable sense, and so it was fulfilled. The text continues: WHEN THE CHIEF BAKER SAW THAT THE INTERPRETATION WAS GOOD, HE SAID UNTO JOSEPH: ALSO I SAW IN MY DREAM, AND BEHOLD, THREE BASKETS OF WHITE BREAD WERE ON MY HEAD. Cursed be the wicked whose actions are all fraught with evil intent, their utterances with malice. As soon as the chief baker opened his mouth with the word af (=anger) Joseph was affrighted, perceiving, as he did, that his words would be of evil import; and, indeed, in the words "and behold, three baskets of white bread upon my head" Joseph at once read the evil tidings of the destruction of the Temple and of the exile of Israel. For notice the rest of the dream, namely, "and the bilds did eat them out of the basket upon my head": this was a reference to the other nations who would assemble against Israel, slay them, devastate their dwellings, and scatter them into the four corners of the world. Joseph noted all this and knew that that dream concerned Israel at the time when they should sin before the King; he thus straightway interpreted it in an evil sense, which interpretation was fulfilled in the dreamer. Observe, then, that the two dreams belonged to two different grades: the one saw

Zohar: Bereshith, Section 1, Page 192b

the upper grade ascending and the moon in its fullness of light; the other saw the moon in darkness and under the domination of the evil serpent. Joseph therefore looked closely at that dream and interpreted it as of evil presage.

R. Judah opened a discourse on the verse: Create me a clean heart, O God, and renew a steadfast spirit within me (Ps. LI, 12). 'The term "a clean heart",' he said, 'finds its parallel in the passage: "Give thy servant therefore an understanding heart" (I Kings III, 9), and also in: "But he that is of merry heart hath a continual feast" (Prov. xv, 15). This is assuredly the clean heart which David asked for. "And renew a steadfast spirit within me" indicates the spirit spoken of in the passage: "and the spirit of God hovered over the face of the waters", this being, as has been pointed out, the spirit of the Messiah; the same is alluded to in the promise: "And a new spirit will I put within you" (Ez. XXXVI, 26). David thus prayed for that steadfast spirit, since on the sinister side there is the unclean spirit called the spirit of perverseness that leads people astray, that unclean spirit referred to in the statement: "The Lord hath mingled within her a spirit of perverseness" (Is. XIX, 14). David thus prayed: "and renew within me a spirit of steadfastness". The term "renew" also alludes to the renewal of the moon, a period which contains the assurance that David, King of Israel, is alive and in being.'

R. Eleazar and R. Yose were once walking on the road. Said R. Yose to R. Eleazar: 'We read: "And there came forth the spirit, and stood before the Lord, and said: I will entice him: And the Lord said unto him: Wherewith? And he said: I will go forth and will be a lying spirit in the mouth of all the prophets. And He said: Thou shalt entice him, and shalt prevail also; go forth and do so" (I Kings XXII, 21-22). According to tradition that was the spirit of Naboth the Jezreelite. Can, then, a soul which has once ascended to the upper world return to this world? Further, the words "I will go forth, and will be a lying spirit in his mouth" are very astonishing. And again, why was Ahab punished on account of Naboth, seeing that Samuel had so laid down the law to Israel, when he said to them: "And he will take your fields, and your vineyards, and your oliveyards, even the best of them" (I Sam. VIII, 14)? According to this, if Ahab took Naboth's vineyard, he was within his rights, and all the more so, seeing that he offered him in exchange another vineyard or its equivalent in gold, which he refused.' R. Eleazar said in reply: 'It is a proper question you ask. Observe that the traditional identification of that spirit with the spirit of Naboth does indeed raise a difficulty. For how could the spirit of Naboth stand up before the Almighty to ask permission to lie? If Naboth's was a righteous man, how could he ask permission to lie in the other world, the world of truth, seeing that even in this world it is the part of a righteous man to keep afar from falsehood? How much more so, then, in the upper world! On the other hand, if Naboth was not a righteous man, how could he have stood in the presence of the Almighty? But the truth is that Naboth was not righteous enough to stand in the presence of the Almighty, and that spirit was another one which has power in the world and continually ascends and stands before God, the same that leads people astray by means of falsehood. Now he who is accustomed to lying will always resort to lying, and hence he said: "I will go forth, and will be a lying spirit, etc.", to which the Holy One replied: "... go forth, and do so", as much as to say: "go hence and be off from here". This is in harmony with the Scriptural text: "He that speaketh falsehood shall not be established before mine eyes" (Ps. CI, 7). And in regard to the other difficulty–if Ahab took Naboth's vineyard, why did he kill him? It was just because he killed Naboth without cause, before expropriating his vineyard, that Ahab was punished. So it is written: "Hast thou killed, and also taken possession?" (I Kings XXI, 19). Great, indeed, is the number of those whom that lying spirit leads astray by means

237

of falsehood, dominating the world from many sides and through many activities. Hence King David supplicated that he might be guarded against him and removed from defilement, saying: "Create me a clean heart, O God; and renew a steadfast spirit within me", a steadfast spirit being the opposite of that other spirit. In sum, there are two grades, one sacred and the other defiled.'

R. Eleazar then opened a discourse on the text: And the Lord uttereth, his voice before his army; for his camp is very great, for he is mighty that executeth his word (Joel II, 11). He said: 'The expression" and the Lord" (V-Tetragrammaton), as we have laid down, everywhere indicates the Lord in conjunction with His Court of Justice; the "voice" here is the same as "the voice of words" (Deut. IV, 12) heard by the Israelites, where the term "words" again is identical with the same term in the verse "I am not a man of words" (Exod. IV, 10), the man of words being the man of God (Deut. XXXIII, 1); "before his army", to wit, Israel; "for his camp is very great", as it says: "Is there any number of his armies?" (Job xxv, 3),

Zohar: Bereshith, Section 1, Page 193a

inasmuch as the Holy One has ever so many chieftains and emissaries who are at hand to bring accusations against Israel, and therefore God goes before Israel in order to guard them, and so that their accusers should not prevail against them: "for he is mighty that executeth his word", to wit, the righteous man, who devotes himself to the study of the holy Torah day and night. Alternatively, the term "mighty" here is an epithet of the accuser, who appears frequently before the Almighty, and who is indeed mighty, strong as iron, hard as flint; and it is he that "executeth his word", as he first obtains authorization from above and then takes away man's soul here below. We read further: "For great is the day of the Lord and very terrible; and who can abide it?" (Joel II,11), inasmuch as He is ruler over all, most high and most mighty, all being subject to His dominion. Happy are the righteous in whom the Holy One constantly finds delight, so as to vouchsafe to them the world to come and to make them participators in the joy with which the righteous will one day exult in the Holy One, blessed be He, as it is written: "So shall all those who take refuge in thee rejoice, they shall ever shout for joy, and thou shalt shelter them, and that those that love thy name will exult in thee" (Ps. v, 12). Blessed be the Lord forevermore. Amen and Amen!'

MIQEZ

AND IT CAME TO PASS AT THE END. R. Hiya expounded the word "end" from the text: He setteth an end for darkness, and he searcheth out to the furthest bound; a stone of thick darkness and the shadow of death (Job XXVIII, 3). 'The end here mentioned is', he said, 'an allusion to the "end of the left", which, after roaming to and fro in the world, finally ascends and presents itself before the Holy One, blessed be He, to bring accusations against mankind. He "searcheth out to the furthest bound" (takhlith--destruction), inasmuch as all his works are never for good, but always for destruction and for the utter annihilation of the world. He is "a stone of stumbling" on which the wicked come to grief and which is found in "a land of thick darkness, as darkness itself" (Ibid. x, 22). For there is a "land of the living" on high, which is the Land of Israel, and a land below called "land of darkness'. The darkness and the shadow of death here mentioned are identical with the end that emerges from the side of darkness, which is also the "dross of gold". As we have laid down, it behoves the sons of men to take due thought of divine worship and to labour in the Torah day and night, so as to know how to serve the Holy One, blessed be He. The Torah herself summons man daily, saying: "Whoso is thoughtless, let him turn in hither, etc." (Prov. IX, 4-6). And whoever labours in the Torah and cleaves unto her is privileged to take hold of the tree of life, as it is written: "She is a tree of life to them that lay hold upon her" (Ibid. III, 18). And whoso takes hold upon the tree of life in this world will also keep hold on it in the world to come, since the grades assigned to souls in the next world correspond to their state on departing from this world. Now the tree of life ramifies into various degrees, all differing from one another, although forming a unity, in the shape of branches, leaves, bark, stock, and roots. All the faithful ones of Israel lay hold upon the tree of life, some grasping the stock, some the branches, some the leaves, and others, again, the roots. But those who exert themselves in the study of the Torah

Zohar: Bereshith, Section 1, Page 193b

grasp the very trunk of the tree, and so lay hold upon all; and so we affirm.' AND IT CAME TO PASS AT THE END. What does the term "end" signify? Said R' Simeon: 'It signifies the region wherein there is no remembering, which is identical with the end of the left. Why did it emerge at that moment? Because Joseph said: "But have me in thy remembrance when it shall be well with thee" (Gen. XL, 14). It was hardly becoming for Joseph the righteous to beg to be remembered by the chief butler; but he was led to do so by his dream, which he thought betokened remembrance. In this, however, he was mistaken, since all depended on God, and therefore the region of forgetfulness placed itself before him. Hence the Scripture, after saying, "Yet did not the chief butler remember Joseph" (Ibid. 23), adds the words "but forgot him", alluding to the region of forgetfulness, which is identical with the end of the side of darkness.' AT THE END OF TWO FULL YEARS. The two years were symbolic of the two grades, the grade of forgetfulness and the grade of remembrance to which it gave place, THAT PHARAOH DREAMED. AND, BEHOLD, HE STOOD BY THE RIVER. This dream was one that concerned Joseph himself, since the idea of river is closely connected with Joseph the righteous; and according to the lore of dreams a river seen in a dream is a presage of peace, for so it is written: "Behold, I will extend peace to her like a river" (Is. LXVI, 12).

R. Hiya opened a discourse on the text: The king by justice establisheth the land; but he that exacteth gifts overthroweth it (Prov. XXIX, 4). 'When God', he said, 'created the upper world, He so constituted it as to send forth celestial radiations in all directions, and He created the upper heaven and the upper earth in such a way that they should provide for the sustenance of the lower denizens. The "king" here is an allusion to the Holy One, blessed be He, while "justice" signifies Jacob, who forms the basis of the world, since the basis of the world is justice, which establishes the earth with all requirements and provides for its sustenance. Alternatively, the "king" is the Holy One, blessed be He, while "justice" refers to Joseph, who established the land, as it is written: "And all countries came into Egypt to Joseph to buy corn"; and because God chose for Himself Jacob, He caused Joseph to be ruler over the land.' R. Yose said: 'The "king" signifies Joseph, while the words "by justice establisheth the land" allude to Jacob, seeing that before Jacob arrived in Egypt the existence of the people was jeopardized by the famine; but as soon as Jacob set foot in Egypt the famine ceased through his merits and the world was made secure. Alternatively, the king who by justice establisheth the land is exemplified in King David, of whom it is written: "and David executed justice and righteousness unto all his people" (II Sam. VIII, 15); for David thereby upheld the world, which was preserved after him for the sake of his merits. "But he that exacteth gifts overthroweth it": this is exemplified in Rehoboam. For God for the sake of the righteous withholds punishment even when it has been decreed against the world; hence, during David's lifetime the land was upheld and after his death it was preserved for his sake, as we read: "and I will defend the city for mine own sake, and for my servant David's sake" (II Kings xx, 6). Similarly, during the lifetime of Jacob, as well as that of Joseph, no punishment was enforced against the world. Again, "he that exacteth gifts overthroweth it" is exemplified in Pharaoh, inasmuch as by hardening his heart before God he brought ruin on the land of Egypt, whereas before the land was preserved through Joseph in conjunction with Pharaoh's dreams.

Zohar: Bereshith, Section 1, Page 194a

AND, BEHOLD, THERE CAME UP OUT OF THE RIVER SEVEN KINE, WELL FAVOURED AND FATFLESHED; AND THEY FED IN THE REED GRASS. The river is mentioned because from it all the lower grades receive their blessings. For the (supernal) stream which flows perpetually waters and feeds the whole, and Joseph was himself the river by means of which the whole of Egypt was blessed. By that (upper) river seven grades are irrigated and blessed, they being "well favoured and fatfleshed", AND THEY FED IN THE REED GRASS (ahu). The word aku (meadow, or brotherhood) signifies that there is no separation between them. The number seven has everywhere a similar symbolism, e.g. the seven maidens and the seven chamberlains mentioned in the Book of Esther (Esther II, 9; I, 10). R. Isaac said that the seven good kine symbolize the superior grades, and the seven lean and ill-favoured kine other and lower grades; the former of the side of holiness, and the latter of the side of defilement. SEVEN EARS OF CORN. R. Judah said: 'The first seven ears were good, as they came from the right side, of which it is written "that it was good" (Gen. I, 4), and the second seven were ill, as being lower than the others; the first ones proceeded from the side of purity, and the others from the side of impurity. They all symbolized two series of grades corresponding with each other; and Pharaoh saw them all in his dream. R. Jesse remarked: 'Can it indeed be that the wicked Pharaoh was shown all these?' R. Judah in reply said: 'He only saw their counterparts rising in a corresponding series: he saw this through the medium of the lower grades. For, as we have learnt, what a man is shown in a dream corresponds to his own character, and his soul ascends just so far as to obtain for him the information suitable for his grade. Pharaoh thus saw as far as he was permitted to, see and no more.'
AND IT CAME TO PASS AT THE END. R.

Hizkiah quoted here the verse: To every thing there is a season, and a time to every purpose under the heaven (Eccl. III, 1). 'Forevery thing that the Almighty has made in the lower world,' he said, 'He has appointed a fixed term and limit. He has appointed a time for light and for darkness. He has fixed a term for the light of the other nations who are now the rulers of the world; and a term for the darkness of the exile of Israel who are now subjected to their rule. And so there is a term forevery purpose in the lower world.' According to another explanation, the word 'eth (time) is the name of an angelic power charged to see that everything takes place at its appointed time. AND IT CAME TO PASS IN THE MORNING THAT HIS SPIRIT WAS TROUBLED; AND HE SENT AND CALLED FOR ALL THE MAGICIANS OF EGYPT, AND ALL THE WISE MEN THEREOF. The word vatipo'em (and was troubled, akin to the word pa'am, time) indicates that the spirit kept on appearing to Pharaoh and leaving him, not staying with him long enough at any one time to enlighten him. The same was the case at first with Samson, of whom it is written: "And the spirit of the Lord began to move him in time beats (l'pha'amo)" (Jud. XIII, 25). In connection with Nebuchadnezzar it is written vatithpa'em (and was troubled) (Dan. II, 1), to indicate that the coming and going of the spirit was twice as rapid.

Zohar: Bereshith, Section 1, Page 194b

239

AND HE SENT AND CALLED FOR ALL THE MAGICIANS OF EGYPT AND ALL THE WISE MEN THEREOF, to wit, the bird-diviners. They all tried to make out the dream, but it baffled them. R. Isaac said: 'Although it has been affirmed that no man is shown anything in a dream save what falls within his own grade, it is different with kings, who are permitted to see more deeply than other men; for inasmuch as a king's grade is higher than that of other men, he is permitted to see that which falls within a higher grade than that of other men. So Scripture says: WHAT GOD IS ABOUT TO DO HE HATH SHOWN UNTO PHARAOH. whereas to other men God does not reveal what He is about to do, except to the prophets, saints, or sages of the generation. Now observe the words: ME HE RESTORED UNTO MINE OFFICE, AND HIM HE HANGED. From this we learn that a dream is determined by its interpretation, since the pronoun "he" can refer only to Joseph, indicating that it was Joseph who restored the one to his office, and hanged the other, through the medium of his interpretation. THEN PHARAOH SENT AND CALLED JOSEPH, AND THEY BROUGHT HIM QUICKLY (vayerizuhu) OUT OF THE DUNGEON. R. Abba discoursed on the verse: The Lord taketh pleasure (roze) in them that fear him, in those that wait for his mercy (Ps. CXLVII, 11). 'God indeed takes pleasure in the righteous', he said, 'because they promote peace in the upper world and in the lower world, and cause the bride to join her husband; and therefore God takes pleasure in those that fear Him and do His will. Those that wait for His mercy are they who study the Torah in the night time and thereby become associates of the Shekinah, and thus when the morning comes they wait for His mercy; for, as has been affirmed, whoso studies the Torah in the night time is looked upon graciously in the day time. So Scripture says: "By day the Lord will command His lovingkindness (or grace)"–for what reason? Because "in the night his song is with me" (Ps. XLII, 9). Hence: "The Lord takes pleasure in those that fear him", or, as we might translate more accurately, "appeases those that fear Him", like one friend with another. Similarly, of Joseph here it is written, vayerizuhu (and they brought him hastily), which admits of the rendering, "and they appeased him", when he was sad and woebegone, giving him words of good cheer that gladdened his heart and dissipated the gloom of the dungeon. Observe that just as his troubles commenced through his having been thrown into the pit, so it was through the pit that he finally was exalted.'

R. Simeon said: 'Before that incident (of Potiphar's wife), Joseph was not called righteous (zadiq); it was only after he stood the test of guarding the purity of the covenant that he was called righteous, and that the grade of the holy covenant was crowned through him, and having been with him in the first pit rose with him now; and thus it is written: "and they brought him quickly out of the pit"–he was raised from the pit and crowned by the well of living waters.' AND PHARAOH SENT AND (he) CALLED JOSEPH. Instead of "and called" we should have expected "to call for". The implied subject is, therefore, God, as in the verse "And he called to Moses" (Lev. I, 1), and this harmonizes with the words of the Psalmist: "Until the time that his word came to pass, the word of the Lord tested him" (Ps. cv, 19). AND HE CHANGED HIS RAIMENT, out of respect for royalty, as explained elsewhere. R. Eleazar quoted here the text: Israel also came into Egypt; and Jacob sojourned in the land of Ham (Ibid. 23). 'God,' he said, 'while accomplishing his decrees, yet directs events in such a manner as to soften their severity. For we have learned that but for the love which God bore to our ancestors, Jacob would have been brought down into Egypt in iron chains; but out of His love for the patriarchs He caused his son Joseph to be made ruler of the world; and so all the tribes went down into Egypt like people of distinction, and Jacob entered it like a king. In the verse: "Israel also came into Egypt; and Jacob sojourned in the land of Ham", we may take Israel to be an allusion to the Holy One, blessed be He, for it was for the sake of Jacob, who sojourned in the land of Ham, and his sons that the Shekinah came into Egypt. God thus arranged that

Zohar: Bereshith, Section 1, Page 195a

Joseph should first be brought into Egypt, as through his merit the covenant was confirmed with him, and made him ruler over all the land. In this connection it is written: "The King sent and loosed him; the ruler of peoples, and set him free" (Ibid. 20). According to R. Simeon, the word "ruler" in this sentence is the object of the verb "sent", and refers to the ruler of peoples, to wit, the angel-redeemer, who is the ruler of the earthly beings, and whom God sent to set Joseph free. GOD WILL GIVE PHARAOH AN ANSWER OF PEACE. This was a first greeting and an overture of peace. R. Abba said: 'The wicked Pharaoh said, "I know not the Lord" (Ex. v, 2), notwithstanding that he was the wisest of all the magicians; he knew, however, the name "God" (Elohim), seeing that he himself said: "Can we find such a man as this, a man in whom the spirit of God (Elohim) is?" But Moses came to him, not in the name of God (Elohim), but in the name of the Lord (Tetragrammaton), a name altogether beyond his apprehension.' R. Abba quoted in this connection: Who is like the Lord our God, that is enthroned on high, that looketh down low upon heaven and upon the earth (Ps. CXIII, 5–6). 'God', he said, 'is "enthroned on high", that is, He raises Himself high above His Throne of Glory and does not reveal Himself to the lower world at those times when no righteous men are to be found in the world. Contrariwise, He "looketh down low" when righteous men are found in the world, as then He descends in His grade so as to meet the lower beings and to take the world under His providential care. But when there are no righteous men in the world, He ascends aloft and hides His face from men, and deserts them, inasmuch as the righteous are the foundation and the mainstay of the world. Hence God did not reveal His Divine Name save to Israel alone, who are His portion and lot and heritage; and the rest of the world He apportioned to celestial chieftains, as we read: "When the Most High gave to the nations their inheritance. For the portion of the Lord is his people, Jacob the lot of his inheritance" (Deut. XXXII, 8-9).'

As R. Hiya and R. Yose were one day walking together, the latter said: 'I often puzzle over the language of Solomon in the book of Ecclesiastes, which I find exceedingly obscure; for instance, the words All things would wear a man out to tell; man cannot utter it, the eye is not satisfied with seeing, nor the ear filled with hearing (Eccl. I, 8). Why mention all these three organs? Having said that all things are more than mouth can utter, why add that "eye cannot see nor ear hear sufficiently"? The reason is, I presume, because eyes and ears function involuntarily; whereas the mouth is under a man's control, and so Koheleth teaches us that all three together cannot exhaust the universe.' Said R. Hiya: 'That is so. Man's mouth cannot utter, nor his eyes see, nor his ear hear the entirety of things; and yet "there is nothing new under the sun" (Ibid. I, 9). And observe that not even the disembodied spirits which the Holy One created under the sun are able to give utterance to all the things that are in the world, nor can their eye

Zohar: Bereshith, Section 1, Page 195b

see nor their ear hear all. Hence Solomon, who knew everything, spoke thus. Now, observe that all the doings of the world are controlled by vast numbers of spirits, but the people of the world know not and regard not what it is that upholds them. Even Solomon, the wisest of men, could not apprehend them.' He further discoursed on the verse: He hath made everything beautiful in its time; also he hath set the world in their heart, yet so that man cannotfind out the work that God hath done, etc. (Ibid. III, 11). 'How happy', he said, 'are those who labour in the Torah and thus learn to see with the eye of wisdom! Whatever God has formed in the world has its own controlling grade which directs it either for good or for evil. There are grades of the right and grades of the left. If a man goes to the right, whatever act he performs then becomes a directing grade on that side which helps him onward and procures him other helpers. But if he goes to the left, then whatever act he commits becomes a directing force on that side, and brings indictments against him, whilst leading him further into that side. Hence, whenever a man performs a good and proper act the chieftain of the right hand affords him help, and this is indicated in the expression "good in its time", that is, the act and its time become intimately bound up together; also "He hath set the world in their heart", that is, the whole world and all its works depend only on the will of man. Happy are those righteous who by their good deeds draw benefits upon themselves and upon the world, and who know how to attach themselves to the grade called "time of peace", and who in virtue of their righteousness in the lower world influence the grade called Kol (everything) to shine in its time ('eth). Woe to the sinners who know not the time-grade of any act and are not circumspect to perform their deeds in such a way as to benefit the world, and so that each deed of theirs should fall under the proper grade. Everything is thus dependent on man's free will, as it is written: "so that man cannot find out the work that God hath done from the beginning even to the end"; and inasmuch as it depends on a man's will whether his deeds are attached to the proper grade or to the improper one, the text continues: "I know that there is no good in them but to rejoice, and to perform good actions so long as they live" (Ibid. III, 12). That is to say, if a man's actions are not good, he has to rejoice at all their consequences and to give thanks for them to the Holy One and to do good actions as long as he lives; for since his own act brought evil upon him through the grade presiding over it, he has to rejoice at the punishment and to give thanks for it, seeing that he brought it on himself, like a bird blindly falling into the snare. So Scripture says: "For man also knoweth not his time; as the fishes that are taken in an evil net, and as the birds that are caught in the snare, even so are the sons of men snared in an evil time, when it falleth suddenly upon them" (Ibid. IX, 12). The expression "his time" ('eth) refers to the ministering angel called "time", who presides over each act a man performs, and is referred to in the statement "he hath made everything beautiful in its time". Hence they are "as the birds that are caught in the snare". Happy, then, are those who exert themselves in the study of the Torah and are intimate with the ways and paths of the Torah of the Most High King so as to follow the true way.'

Observe that a man ought never to begin his speech with an ill-omened utterance, as he does not know who will take it up, and he may come to grief over it. The righteous thus always begin their discourse with words of peace. So Joseph prefaced his address to Pharaoh with the words: "God will give Pharaoh an answer of peace." R. Judah said: 'It has been taught that the Holy One, blessed be He, is solicitous for the welfare of a king, as we read: "and he gave them a charge unto the children of Israel, and unto Pharaoh, King of Egypt" (Ex. VI, 13).'

Zohar: Bereshith, Section 1, Page 196a

R. Hiya said: 'Pharaoh wished to put Joseph to the test, and so changed the tenour of his dreams. But Joseph, knowing, as he did, the grades, saw clearly each object of the dream, and said, "thus and thus didst thou see", point by point. Hence it is written: AND PHARAOH SAID UNTO JOSEPH: FORASMUCH AS GOD HATH SHOWN THEE ALL THIS, THERE IS NONE SO DISCREET AND WISE AS THOU. As if to say: You seem to have been there at the time I dreamt my dream and to have seen the dream together with its interpretation." Said R. Isaac: 'If that be so, it would signify that Joseph told Pharaoh both his dream and its interpretation, as did Daniel to Nebuchadnezzar.' Said R. Hiya: 'Not so. Joseph gathered from Pharaoh's statement that he was speaking of certain grades, and was able to put him right on certain points, knowing the correct order of the grades. Whereas Daniel gathered nothing from Nebuchadnezzar's statement and told him outright both his dream and its interpretation. It is thus written: "Then was the secret revealed unto Daniel by a vision of the night" (Dan. II, 19), to wit, by Gabriel. There are six visions (corresponding to the six mentions of the word "vision" in Ezek. XLIII, 3). The vision of a dream is a reflection of a higher vision, and this again of a still higher, the whole forming a series called "visions of the night", through which all dreams are interpreted. Hence "he revealed the secret to Daniel in a vision of the night", that is to say, one of those grades revealed to him the dream and its interpretation. But Joseph divined the higher grades out of the words of Pharaoh. Hence Pharaoh gave him command over the whole land of Egypt, and in this way God restored to him what was his due. Joseph's mouth kept back from sinful kissing; correspondingly we read, "and according to the word of thy mouth shall my people be ruled"; Joseph's hand kept itself away from sinful touch, hence "Pharaoh took off his signet ring from his hand, and put it upon Joseph's hand"; Joseph's neck kept itself far from sinful embrace, so we read, "and he put a gold chain about his neck"; his body kept away from sin, hence "and he arrayed him in vestures of linen"; the foot did not ride in sin, so we read, "and he made him ride in the second chariot which he had"; and in virtue of the thought which Joseph kept pure he was called "discreet and wise of heart". So that all he received was his own due. It is then written: AND JOSEPH WENT OUT FROM THE PRESENCE OF PHARAOH, AND WENT THROUGHOUT ALL THE LAND OF EGYPT. R. Hizkiah said that he went through the land of Egypt to have his rule proclaimed, and also to collect the corn of the various districts. R. Eleazar said that he collected the corn to prevent it from rotting. R. Simeon said: 'God is ever moulding events so as to fulfil His promise. When God created the world He first provided all necessities and then brought man into the world, so that he found his food ready for him. So, too, with the promise made by God to Abraham in the words: "Know of a surety that thy seed shall be a stranger in a land that is not theirs... and afterwards shall they come out with great substance" (Gen. xv, 13-14). When Joseph came into Egypt he did not find there great substance, so God arranged to bring a famine on the world, with the result that all people brought their silver and gold into Egypt, so that the whole land of Egypt was filled with silver and gold; then, when great substance was amassed there, He brought Jacob into Egypt. For this is the way of the Almighty, to provide the cure before inflicting the wound. Thus here He first prepared great substance and then

Zohar: Bereshith, Section 1, Page 196b

brought Israel into exile. Observe that it was in virtue of being a righteous man that Joseph became the cause of Israel acquiring riches of silver and gold (Ps. cv, 37). All this came to Israel by the hand of the righteous, and all was for the purpose of making them worthy of the world to come. ' R. Simeon then took for his text the verse: Enjoy life with the wife whom thou lovest all the days of the life of thy vanity, etc. (Eccl. IX, 9). 'This verse', he said, 'has been thus esoterically explained. "Enjoy life" is an allusion to the life of the world to come, for happy is the man who is privileged to gain that life in its fulness; "with the wife whom thou lovest" is a reference to the Community of Israel, of whom it is written: "Yea, I have loved thee with an everlasting love" (Jer. XXXI, 3). When so? At the time when the Right side takes hold of her, as is implied in the concluding words: "Therefore with affection (hesed) have I drawn thee" (Ibid.); "all the days of thy vanity", inasmuch as she is bound up with life, with the world of the living, as opposed to this world, which is not the world of the living, since its denizens are "under the sun", where the lights of that (upper) sun do not reach, those lights which have departed from the world since the day when the Temple was destroyed, as is hinted in the verse: "The sun shall be darkened in his going forth" (Is. XIII, 10). "For that is thy portion in life": this alludes to the association of the sun with the moon, as it behoves us to bring the moon, as it were, into the sun and the sun into the moon so that there should be no separation between them, this being the portion of man by which he may enter the world to come. Then the passage continues: "Whatsoever thy hand findeth to do, do it with thy strength; for there is no work, nor device, nor knowledge, nor wisdom, in the grave, whither thou goest." This verse strikes one at first sight as surprising: is man indeed free to do "whatsoever his hand findeth to do"? But we must note the qualification in the phrase "do by thy strength", i.e. through the instrumentality of the higher soul of man (neshamah), which forms his strength, so as to gain through her this world and the world to come. Alternatively, "by thy strength" alludes to the wife mentioned above, she being a source of strength both for this world and the world to come. It thus behoves man to possess himself of that power in this world so as to be fortified by it in the next world; inasmuch as once a man departs this world he can do no more, and it is useless for him to say, "Henceforward I am going to perform good acts", for assuredly, "there is no work, nor device, nor knowledge, nor wisdom, in the grave, whither thou goest". If a man has not acquired merit in this world he will not acquire it any more in the other world, according to the dictum, "He who has not laid up provision for the journey from this world will have nothing to eat in the other world." There are, moreover, certain good deeds the fruits of which a man enjoys in this world whilst the principal remains for his enjoyment in the world to come. Observe that Joseph gained this world and the world to come in virtue of his determination to join himself to a God-fearing wife, as expressed in his words: "How can I do this great wickedness, and sin against God?" (Gen. XXXIX, 9). For this he rose to be a ruler in this world and gathered money for Israel, as we read, "Joseph gathered all the money that was found in the land of Egypt" (Ibid. XLVII, 14), and this was in the order of things, since the ever-flowing celestial river gathers within itself all things and is the repository of all riches. Everything thus happened according to plan: assuredly Joseph was predestined to rule over the kingdom. AND HE MADE HIM RIDE IN THE SECOND CHARIOT. God has made a second chariot for the Righteous One, by whom the world is nourished. For God has an upper chariot and a nether chariot. The nether chariot is the second chariot, and Joseph, having attained to the name of "righteous", was qualified to ride on the second chariot, like his prototype in the supernal world. AND THEY CRIED BEFORE HIM: ABRECH. The term "abrech" signifies the spot where the sun is joined to the moon, towards which all bow down. We read further: AND HE SET HIM OVER ALL, namely, over all the world, so that all the peoples acknowledged his rule.

Zohar: Bereshith, Section 1, Page 197a

Observe that God has made the earthly kingdom after the pattern of the heavenly kingdom, and whatever is done on earth has been preceded by its prototype in heaven. Now the dominion of the celestial kingdom was not perfect until it united itself to the patriarchs, since the Holy One intended that the supernal kingdom should be illumined from the grades symbolized by the patriarchs. And so when Joseph first went down into Egypt he drew after him the Shekinah, as the Shekinah only follows the Righteous One. Joseph was thus first drawn into Egypt, where he gathered up all the wealth of the world, and then came the Shekinah in company with all the tribes. And it was in virtue of having kept the purity of the covenant that Joseph was privileged to be crowned in his right place and merited the upper kingdom and the lower kingdom. Hence, to preserve the purity of the covenant is like observing the whole of the holy Torah, since the covenant is on a par with the whole Torah. NOW JACOB SAW THAT THERE WAS CORN IN EGYPT. R. Hiya discoursed on the verse: The burden of the word of the Lord concerning Israel. Thus saith the Lord who stretcheth forth the heavens, and layeth the foundation of the earth, and formeth the spirit of man within him (Zech. XII, 1). 'Certain points', he said, 'are to be noted in this verse. First, as to the import of the term "burden", here and in other passages. This term, wherever it introduces a judgement pronounced against other nations, has a favourable import, inasmuch as the prosperity of the idolatrous nations is, if one may say so, a burden for the Holy One. Hence a judgement pronounced against the idolaters removes, as it were, from Him the burden. Contrariwise, wherever the term "burden" introduces a decree of judgement against Israel, it has an unfavourable import, as it implies a burden put on the Holy One, blessed be He. Now, having said "who stretcheth forth the heavens, and layeth the foundation of the earth", what need is there for the text to add "and formeth the spirit of man", a fact which we know already? But in truth this points to a certain grade which forms the reservoir of all spirits and souls.' R. Simeon said: 'The words "within him" seem superfluous. But in truth this expression has a twofold recondite meaning. It bears allusion to that ever-flowing celestial river whence all the souls emerge and fly forth. For this purpose it gathers them in one central place or grade, and that grade "formeth the spirit of man within itself", like a woman who has conceived and forms the child within her womb from the moment of conception until it is fully developed; so the spirit remains within this grade until a man is created in the world to whom He assigns it. Alternatively, God "formeth the spirit of man" within him, to wit, in his body, literally. For when a man is created and God assigns him his soul, and he emerges into the light of day, the spirit within him finds no body in which to expand, and remains cramped in one corner, as it were; but with the growth and expansion of the body the spirit also grows and expands; and in response to its growing need it continues to receive from on high, in ever greater abundance, vigour and energy, which in its turn it infuses into the body. Further, the statement that the Holy One "formeth the spirit of man within him" indicates that the spirit needs sustenance in the same way as the body, and that as the body goes on developing, so is the spirit granted increased strength and energy.' Observe, that when Joseph was lost, Jacob was deprived of that increase of spirit through the departure of the Shekinah from him. But afterwards "the spirit of Jacob their father revived" (Gen. XLV, 27),

Zohar: Bereshith, Section 1, Page 197b

that is, it regained its former increase and growth.

[Note: The first eight lines of the Hebrew text do not appear in the English version]

R. Yose and R. Hizkiah were once travelling from Cappadocia to Lydda, and with them was a certain Judean driving an ass laden with clothes. Said R. Yose to R. Hizkiah: 'Repeat one of those excellent expositions of Scripture which you are wont to deliver daily before the Sacred Lamp.' R. Hizkiah then began to hold forth on the verse: Her ways are ways of pleasantness, and all her paths are peace (Prov. III, 17). 'These ways', he said, 'are the ways and paths of the Torah, as whoever walks in them is invested by the Holy One, blessed be He, with the grace of the Divine Presence as his constant accompaniment, and whoever follows her paths enjoys peace on high and below, peace in this world and in the world to come.' Said the Judean: 'A deeper meaning lies in this verse, like a coin in the corner of a box.' 'How do you know this?' they asked him. He said: 'I have heard the recondite explanation of this verse from my father.' He then continued to discourse thus. 'This verse contains a twofold idea, one suggested by the terms "ways" and "pleasantness", and the other by the terms "paths" and "peace". The "ways" are those mentioned in the passage, "who maketh a way in the sea" (Is. XLIII, 16). For the term "way" everywhere in Scripture denotes an open road, accessible to all. So the words "her ways are ways of pleasantness" allude to those ways which our patriarchs opened up and traversed on the great ocean, and which ramify in all directions to all quarters of the world; and by "pleasantness" is meant that pleasantness which issues from the other world, the source whence radiate all lamps in all directions. That felicity, that light which our patriarchs absorbed and inherited, is thus called "pleasantness". Or we can say that the world to come itself is called "pleasantness", because when it is awakened there is a stirring of all joy, all felicity, all illumination, and all freedom. Hence tradition tells us that when the Sabbath comes in, the sinners in Gehinnom have a respite and are granted ease and rest; and that at the termination of the Sabbath we have to call down the supernal joy upon us so that we may be delivered from the punishment that the sinners undergo from that moment onward; and this we do by reciting the verse: "And let the pleasantness of the Lord our God be upon us, etc." (Ps. xc, 17), an allusion to the supernal pleasantness which brings universal freedom. Now, as for the "paths", they denote the paths that proceed from on high and are all gathered into the single covenant which is named 'peace", meaning the peace of the household, and which carries those paths into the great ocean when it is agitated, and so gives it peace.' Observe that Joseph embodied the covenant of peace, and in consequence became ruler over the land of Egypt. Jacob, being deserted by the Shekinah, knew nothing of this, but nevertheless he had hopes [Tr. Note: This is a play on the term sheber=corn, which by a change of the diacritical point becomes seber=hope.] from the purchase of corn in Egypt, and he also foresaw calamity upon calamity [Tr. Note: Another play upon the term sheber, which, besides "corn", also signifies "calamity"] in his sons going down into Egypt. AND JACOH SAID TO HIS SONS: WHY SHOULD YE MAKE YOURSELVES CONSPICUOUS? meaning, in effect, "you should not pretend to be other than hungry and short of food". R. Hizkiah said: 'Assuredly there is here contained a recondite lesson, to wit, that when trouble is abroad in the world, and the world is in distress, a man should not show himself in the open road, in order that he may not be seized on account of his sins; and so it is affirmed. Alternatively we may explain that

Zohar: Bereshith, Section 1, Page 198a

for that very purpose God sent a famine into the world, namely that Jacob and his sons should go down into Egypt; and so Jacob saw the people bringing corn from Egypt, and thus knew that there was corn there. Or we may explain thus. When Isaac died, Jacob and Esau came to divide his inheritance. Esau renounced the inheritance of the (holy) land and all that it involved, and Jacob took up the whole, including the galuth. Hence he saw the calamity that awaited him in Egypt, where he and his sons would endure exile, and hence he said to his sons: "Why do you show yourselves off in presence of the supernal judgement? That is the way to bring the accuser down upon you." ‘ AND HE SAID: BEHOLD, I HAVE HEARD THAT THERE IS CORN IN EGYPT. GET YOU DOWN (redu) THITHER. It has already been pointed out that the numerical value of the term redu (RDU=210) amounts to the number of years Israel was in Egypt. AND JOSEPH WAS THE GOVERNOR OVER THE LAND, ETC. R. Jesse discoursed on the text: And now shall my head be lifted up above mine enemies round about me; and I will offer in his tabernacle sacrifices with trumpet-sound (Ps. XXVII, 6). ‘When God', he said, 'takes pleasure in a man, he raises him high above all his fellow-men and makes him chief over them all, so that all his enemies are subdued before him. King David was hated by his brothers and rejected by them, but God raised him high above all men. He had to flee from his father-in-law, but God made him ruler over the latter's whole kingdom and all knelt and prostrated themselves to him. Joseph, again, was rejected by his brothers, but afterwards they all knelt down and prostrated themselves before him, as we read: "And Joseph's brethren came, and bowed down to him with their faces to the earth." Alternatively we may suppose this verse to be spoken by the Community of Israel, whose head will one day be raised above Esau and all his lieutenants. Then Israel will "offer in his tabernacle sacrifices with trumpet-sound", or, rather, "sacrifices of breaking" (teru'ah) to wit, the broken spirit which is mentioned in the passage: "The sacrifices of God are a broken spirit" (Ibid. LI, 19), so as to cause severity to be removed from the world; "then I will sing, yea, I will sing praises unto the Lord", without ceasing, forevermore. According to another interpretation, it is the good prompter who says, "and now shall my head be lifted up above mine enemies round about me", to wit, above the evil prompter that surrounds man on every side and is his enemy throughout: "and I will offer in his tabernacle sacrifices with trumpet-sound", alluding to the study of the Torah, which has been given from the side of fire, as we read: "At his right hand was a fiery law unto them" (Deut. XXXIII, 2); for it is through the Torah that his head is lifted up and his enemies are broken before him, as it says: "Thou hast subdued unto me those that rose up against me" (Ps. XVIII, 40). According to another explanation it is King David who says, "And now shall my head be lifted up", namely, to be ranked among the patriarchs, as he had first to join the patriarchs before he became exalted and elevated. "Above mine enemies round about me": to wit, those on the left side, the accusers who sought to injure him; by his overcoming them the sun formed a junction with the moon, and a unity was effected. Observe now the passage: AND JOSEPH WAS THE GOVERNOR OVER THE LAND, which, in its deeper meaning, implies that the sun rules over the moon, gives her light and sustains her. We read further: HE IT WAS THAT SOLD TO ALL PEOPLE OF THE LAND. This alludes to the ever-flowing river whence all derive their nourishment and whence the souls of all men emerge. Hence all bow down toward that region, as nothing happens in the world that does not depend on mazzal, as explained elsewhere.

R. Eleazar here discoursed on the text: Wherefore should I fear in the days of evil the iniquity of my heels that compasseth me about? (Ps. XLIX, 6). 'There are', he said, 'three classes who fear, and know not what they fear, as we have laid down elsewhere. One kind is the man who has committed sins without realizing that they were sins, and he is therefore afraid of "days of evil", to wit, days that are under the jurisdiction of the

Zohar: Bereshith, Section 1, Page 198b

evil one, that is, the evil prompter, who on certain days is given authorization to lead astray all those who pollute their ways. For whoever enters the path of defilement is carried further along it. Those days, then, are called "days of evil", being assigned for the punishment of little sins which a man treads under his heels, [Tr. Note: i.e. Little peccadilloes which people are apt to overlook. An allusion to the term 'aqebai='footsteps, or lit. "heels".] as it were. Whoever, then, is habituated to those sins which men tread underfoot, as it were, is unaware of them and is constantly in fear. King David, however, was ever on his guard against these sins, and whenever he set out for battle he would closely examine himself to see that he was free from such sins, and he therefore was not afraid to go to war. Observe now the difference in the behaviour of four kings in going to war. David said: "Let me pursue mine enemies, and overtake them; neither let me turn back till they are consumed" (Ps. XVIII, 38). He dared to make this request because he guarded himself against those sins, and thus allowed no opening to his enemies to prevail against him. He therefore prayed only that he might pursue them continually, and had no fear that they might pursue him, or that his sins might cause him to fall into their hands. Asa was in greater fear, for though he also minutely examined himself for any sins, yet it was not with such care as David. His request, therefore, was that he might merely pursue his enemies, not overtake them himself, and that God should slay them for him. And so it came about, as we read: "So the Lord smote the Ethiopians before Asa, and before Judah; and the Ethiopians fled. And Asa and the people that were with him, etc." (II Chr. XIV, II-12). Whereas in regard to David it is written: "And David smote them from the twilight even unto the evening of the next day" (I Sam. xxx, 17). Jehoshaphat, again, in praying for help, said: "I am not able to pursue nor to slay them; but let me chant thy praises and do thou slay them." This was because he did not examine himself even to the same degree as Asa. And God did what he requested, as it is written: "And when they began to sing and praise, the Lord set liers-in-wait against the children of Ammon, Moab, and mount Seir, that were come against Judah; and they were smitten" (II Chr. xx, 22). Finally, Hezekiah felt himself able neither to sing praises, nor to pursue, nor to engage in war, the reason being that he feared the above-mentioned sins. It is thus written: "And it came to pass that night, that the angel of the Lord went forth, and smote in the camp of the Assyrians a hundred fourscore and five thousand; and when men arose early in the morning, behold, they were all dead corpses" (II Kings XIX, 35). That is, Hezekiah sat in his house, and lay in his bed, whilst God slew them. Now, if those righteous men were in so much fear on account of these sins, how much greater should be the fear of other men? Hence it behoves a man to be on his guard against those sins and to examine himself closely regarding them so as not to allow those "days of evil" which are without mercy to obtain dominion over him.' AND JOSEPH KNEW HIS BRETHREN. When they fell into his hands he had compassion on them, since he was completely virtuous. BUT THEY KNEW HIM NOT: these were Simeon and Levi, who came from the side of severity, and hence had no pity on him, inasmuch as all those imbued with severity take no pity on men when they fall into their hands.

Hence David said, "Wherefore should I fear?" indicating that naturally he ought to fear [Tr. Note: Al. that he had no reason to fear.]

Zohar: Bereshith, Section 1, Page 199a

those "days of evil", as previously stated. David continues: "The iniquity of my heels that compasseth me about." The word "heels" here, as in the passage, "and his hand had hold on Esau's heel" (Gen. xxv, 26) indicates those evil powers (forming as it were the heel of the Body) that are forever on the look out for the sins which a man constantly treads under his heels. These little sins are like "cords of vanity" (Is. v, 18), scarcely discernible, but which in time become as strong as "cart ropes", and thus cause a man to lose this world and the world to come. Happy are the righteous who know how to guard themselves against their sins and continually examine their deeds so that no accuser may rise up against them either in this world or in the world to come, the Torah being their guide and preparing the way before them. Of these it is written: "Her ways are ways of graciousness, and all her paths are peace." AND JOSEPH REMEMBERED THE DREAMS WHICH HE DREAMED OF THEM, ETC. R. Hiya quoted here the verse: Rejoice not when thy enemy falleth, and let not thy heart be glad when he stumbleth (Prov. XXIV, 17). 'God', he said, 'created man in order that he should make himself worthy of His glory and always serve Him and be occupied in the Torah day and night. For God takes pleasure in the Torah and gave it to Adam and taught it to him, so that he should know its ways. So it is written: "Then did he see it, and declare it; he established it, yea, and searched it out. And unto Adam he said: Behold, the fear of the Lord, that is wisdom; and to depart from evil is understanding" (Job XXVIII, 27-28). Adam, however, though he inquired into it, did not keep it, and transgressed the command of his Master and was punished for his sin. Similarly, all those who transgress one precept of the Torah are held to account for it. King Solomon, the wisest of men, transgressed one precept of the Torah, and for that he was dethroned and his son's inheritance was divided. What, then, must be the consequences of the transgression of the whole Torah! Now, since Joseph knew the Torah, having learnt it from his father, why when his brethren fell into his hands did he put them through all those ordeals? Far be it from us to think that it was out of a spirit of revenge that he heaped on them accusations: his only purpose was to make them bring with them his brother Benjamin, for whom his heart was longing; and, moreover, he did not let them come to grief, as we read later: "Then Joseph commanded them to fill their vessels with corn, etc." ' R. Judah said: 'After God created the moon He had her constantly before His eyes (Deut. XI, 12). In regard to this it is also written: "Then did he see it, and declare it (vayesaprah); he established it, yea, and searched it out" (Job XXVIII, 27). "He saw it" means that through His providence the sun is reflected in it. The term vayesaprah we may translate, "he made it like sapphire". "He established it" so that it should fall properly into twelve divisions, [Tr. Note: i.e. the division of the Holy Land according to the twelve tribes.] and be further distributed among seventy kingdoms, [Tr. Note: Corresponding to the seventy nations or languages among which the world was divided according to the enumeration given in Genesis, chap. x supported by seventy [Tr. Note: The editions read "seven".] celestial pillars, [Tr. Note: i.e. the seventy chieftains presiding over the seventy kingdoms of the world.] that it might be perfectly illumined. "And searched it out": to guard it with an eternal and never ceasing vigilance. And then He gave a warning to man, as we read further: "And unto man he said: Behold, the fear of the Lord, that is wisdom; and to depart from evil is understanding" (Ibid. XXVIII, 28), since wisdom is the means to attain to the fear of the Holy One, and understanding is the power by which to separate and keep away the refuse, and thus attain to a knowledge of and an insight into the glory of the Most High King.'

R. Yose once rose in the night to study the Torah, when there happened to be a certain Judean with him in the house. R. Yose began to expound the verse: Treasures of wickedness profit nothing; but righteousness delivereth from death (Prov. X, 2). 'There is no profit', he said, 'to those men who do not occupy themselves with the study of the Torah and follow only worldly affairs in order to amass treasures of wickedness, of which it is written: "And those riches perish by evil adventure" (Eccl. v, 2). But "righteousness delivereth from death" those who occupy themselves with the study of the Torah and know its ways; for the Torah is called the tree of life and is also called righteousness, as we read: "And it shall be righteousness unto us" (Deut. VI, 25). The word zedaqah (righteousness) here may also have its literal meaning of "charity".

Zohar: Bereshith, Section 1, Page 199b

The two meanings, Torah and charity, are however, in essence identical.' The Judean remarked: 'It bears also the meaning of peace.' R. Yose replied: 'Assuredly it is so.' The Judean then joined him and began to discourse on the text: He that tilleth the ground shall have plenty of bread; but he that followeth after vain things shall have poverty enough (Prov. XXXIII, 19). 'This verse', he said, 'presents a difficulty. For can it be supposed that King Solomon, the wisest man in the world, would have said that it behoves a man to devote himself to the tilling of the ground and to neglect the life everlasting? But there is an inward meaning therein.' The Judean then cited the verse: "And he put him into the Garden of Eden to dress it and keep it" (Gen. II, 15). 'This sentence, as has been explained,' he said, 'contains an allusion to the sacrifices, the object of the verb "to dress" being the higher King, and of "to keep" the lower King, the one embracing the upper world, the other the lower world, the one esoterically referred to in "remember", the other in "observe" [Tr. Note: An allusion to the two variants, "remember,' and "observe", in the text of the fourth Commandment, in Exodus and Deuteronomy.] Hence the "ground" here is an allusion to the Garden of Eden, which it behoves man to dress and to till so as to cause to flow upon it blessings from on high, whereby he himself will receive blessings along with it. Observe that the priest who blesses the people is blessed himself, as it says: "and I will bless them" [Tr. Note: i.e. the priests.] (Num. VI, 27). Hence, "He that tilleth the ground shall have plenty of bread", to wit, heavenly food, but "he that followeth after vain things", namely, he that cleaves to the other side, shall have poverty enough, assuredly.' R. Yose remarked: 'Happy art thou to be able to give such an exposition.' The Judean then followed with a discourse on the verse: A faithful man shall abound with blessings (Prov. XXVIII, 20). 'This speaks of the man', he said, 'who puts his trust in God, like R. Jesse the elder, who, although he had food for the day, would not prepare his meal before he had prayed for his daily bread to the Holy King; and he used to say, "We shall not eat before we obtain permission from the King." "But he that maketh haste to be rich shall not be unpunished" (Ibid.), because he refuses to devote himself to the Torah, which constitutes the life of this world and the life of the world to come. It being now the time to occupy ourselves with the study of the Torah, let us do so,' he said. He then began to discourse on the subject of dreams. 'We read, he said: AND JOSEPH REMEMBERED THE DREAMS WHICH HE DREAMED OF THEM. That is, when he saw them bowing to him, he called to mind his dream about their sheaves bowing to his sheaf. Further, one ought to remember a good dream, because, although there is no forgetfulness before the Holy One, yet if the man forgets the dream he also will be forgotten. A dream that is not remembered might as well not have been dreamt, and therefore a dream forgotten and gone from mind is never fulfilled. Joseph therefore kept his dream fresh in his memory, never forgetting it, so that it should come true, and he was constantly waiting for its fulfilment.

AND HE SAID TO THEM: YE ARE SPIES. Although he remembered his dream, he did not mention it to them, but only said, "Ye are spies." ' R. Yose discoursed on the verse: For a dream cometh through a multitude of business; and a fool's voice through a multitude of words (Eccl. v, 2). 'It has already been explained', he said, 'that dreams are under the charge of a hierarchy of custodians, so that some dreams are altogether true and others are a mixture of true and false. But to the truly righteous no false messages are ever communicated, but all they are told is true. Observe that of Daniel it is written: "Then to Daniel, in a vision of the night,

Zohar: Bereshith, Section 1, Page 200a

the secret was revealed" (Dan. II, 19), also: "Daniel had a dream and visions of his head upon his bed; then he wrote the dream" (Ibid. VII, 1). Had tie dream contained falsehood, it could not have been written down in the Scriptures. When the souls of the truly righteous ascend, nothing comes in contact with them save holy beings that communicate to them words of truth, words that can be relied upon never to prove false. There is, it is true, a tradition that King David never saw a happy dream, from which we should conclude that he was shown false things in his dreams. The truth is, however, that David was all his life engaged in making war, in shedding blood, and hence all his dreams were of misfortune, of destruction and ruin, of blood and shedding of blood, and not of peace. You may possibly also wonder how it is that a good man is often shown a bad dream. The explanation is that what he sees in such dreams is the evil that is to cleave to those who transgress the commands of the Torah and the punishments which will be meted out to them in the other world; and the good man sees all these in his dreams in order that the fear of his Master may constantly be upon him. So it says: "and God hath made it, that man should fear before him" (Eccl. III, 14), which has been explained to refer to bad dreams. This, then, is the reason why the righteous man is made to see a bad dream. We have learned that when a man has had a dream, he should unburden himself of it before men who are his friends so that they should express to him their good wishes and give utterance to words of good omen. Desire, which is Thought, is the beginning of all things, and Utterance is the completion; and so a deep symbolism will in this way have been effected, and all will have been made good. Thus a man's friends should affirm the good interpretation, and so all will be well. We see, then, that God communicates to each man by means of dreams of the degree and shade of colour conformable to the degree and shade of colour of the man himself.' The Judean remarked: 'Assuredly, it is only the good man that is made to see true dreams. When a man is in bed asleep, his soul leaves him and roams to and fro towards the upper world and enters as far as she can, and numerous bands of pure spirits who are traversing the world meet her. If she be worthy, she ascends on high and sees notable things, but if not, she falls into the hands of the other side, who communicate to her lying things, or things which are about to happen shortly. And when the man awakes, the soul communicates to him what she saw. The unjust man is thus shown a happy dream, but an untruthful one, so as to make him go further astray from the path of truth. For since he turned aside from the right path they defile him the more, as whoever sets out to purify himself is purified from above, and whoever sets out to defile himself is similarly defiled from above. This has already been expounded elsewhere.'

Thus R. Yose and the Judean discoursed until the morning dawned. R. Yose then remarked: 'Assuredly the reason that Joseph's name is not mentioned in connection with the standards of the tribes (v. Num. III) is that he exalted himself over his brethren.' Said the Judean: 'I have heard it said that Joseph derived from the world of the Male, whereas his brethren derived from the world of the Female; and it is for this leason that he was not included with them. It is thus written: WE ARE ALL ONE MAN'S SONS, where the word for "we" (anahnu) is written defectively nahnu, without the letter aleph. The aleph is the image of the male principle as against the beth, which is the image of the female principle; and since the brothers did not exhibit the symbolism of the covenant, the aleph was removed from them and they were left, as it were, of the female aspect in the company of the Shekinah. Afterwards, however, they said: "We are upright men" (Gen. XLII, 31), using the full form anahnu (we), containing the aleph, and without knowing it they were right, since Joseph was present with them. This view is further supported by the passage: "And they said: We thy servants are twelve brethren" (Ibid. 13): here clearly Joseph was included within the number twelve, and hence they similarly made use of the full form for "we are", namely anahnu, not the defective form nahnu.' R. Yose remarked: 'All these expositions we have just now given must be pleasing to God, since the Shekinah did not depart

Zohar: Bereshith, Section 1, Page 200b

from here in accordance with the verse: "Then they that fear the Lord spoke one with another; and the Lord hearkened, and heard, and a book of remembrance was written before him, for them that feared the Lord, and that thought upon his name" (Malachi, III, 16). ' AND HE PUT THEM ALTOGETHER INTO WARD THREE DAYS. Said R. Eleazar: 'Those three days correspond to the three days during which the men of Shechem were sick (Gen. XXXIV, 25). Observe that it is written here: AND JOSEPH SAID UNTO THEM THE THIRD DAY: THIS (zoth) DO AND LIVE, by which he showed them that he was not going to act towards them in the way they acted towards Shechem; for whereas they had first made the people of Shechem take upon them the sacred rite of the covenant, which is symbolized by the word zoth (this), and then had slain them to the last man, Joseph, on his part, said: "This (zoth) do and live"; why? "For I fear

247

God", and am guarding the sacredness of the covenant. All this procedure was only for the sake of Benjamin. AND THEY SAID ONE TO ANOTHER: WE ARE VERILY GUILTY CONCERNING OUR BROTHER, ETC. "One to another" (lit. a man to his brother) refers to Simeon and Levi, the same reference being contained in the words: "And they said one to another (lit. a man to his brother): Behold, this dreamer cometh" (Ibid. XXXVII, 19). Which is "man" and which is "brother"? "Man" must refer to Simeon, as in the passage: "And, behold, a man of the children of Israel came" (Num. xxv, 6). Simeon repented of his action and wept and felt remorse and said: "We are verily guilty"; and it was through his repentance that his emblem became the ox, the same as that of Joseph, of whom it is written: "His firstling bullock, majesty is his" (Deut. XXXIII, 17). And it was for that reason that we read AND HE TOOK SIMEON FROM AMONG THEM, for Joseph wished to separate him from the influence of Levi, as when the two were together they might find matter of charge against him. AND BOUND HIM BEFORE THEIR EYES. It has already been explained that only before their eyes did he have him bound, but after they departed he regaled him with food and drink. It must not be supposed that Joseph acted in the spirit of the verse, "If thine enemy be hungry, give him bread to eat, and if he be thirsty, give him water to drink, for thou wilt heap coals of fire upon his head" (Prov. xxv, 21). Joseph was too righteous a man for this. Far be it, then, from Joseph to have acted in that spirit. Indeed, he acted as a man to his brother, in true brotherly love without any other motive. And not only towards Simeon, but towards all his brethren he acted so, as it is written: THEN JOSEPH COMMANDED TO FILL THEIR VESSELS WITH CORN, AND TO GIVE THEM PROVISION FOR THE WAY; AND THUS IT WAS DONE UNTO THEM. All this he did in a spirit of brotherhood.'

R. Yose commenced a discourse on the verse: If they be peaceful and likewise many, and they will likewise be shorn, then he shall pass away; and though I have afflicted thee, I will afflict thee no more (Nahum I, 12). 'This verse', he said, 'has been expounded in the following manner. When a people live in peace, and harbour no quarrelsome persons in their midst, God has compassion on them, and rigorous justice is not invoked against them, even though they worship idols. This is in harmony with the verse, "Ephraim is joined in serving idols, let him alone" (Hos. IV, 17) [Tr. Note: i.e. albeit Ephraim are worshipping idols, since they are all joined together in peace and harmony, they will escape the rigour of justice.] In the expression "and they will likewise be shorn", the word "likewise" continues the thought of the word "peace" above, by adding to it charity, which is peace; for whoever promotes charity promotes peace, both in the upper world and in the lower world. "Those who are shorn" means those who allow themselves to be shorn of their substance, devoting it to charity: Concerning such the verse says: "and he (or it) shall pass away", not, as we should have

expected "they shall pass away", but "it shall pass away", namely, the wrathful judgement of heaven. The word "pass" is used in a similar connection in the verse "until indignation be overpast" (Is. XXVI, 20). The following is an alternative interpretation. "Thus saith the Lord: If they be perfect (shelemim)": this is an allusion to Israel, whom God favoured with the covenant which they were to guard constantly so as to be perfect on all sides, both on high and here below; for otherwise a man is defective in every respect. So it is written: "Walk before me, and be thou perfect" (Gen. XVII, 1), implying that Abram, before the sign of the covenant was confirmed in him, was defective. Hence: "if they be perfect they shall likewise be many", that is, if Israel observe this precept whereby they become perfect and do not remain in a state of incompleteness, they will in consequence increase

Zohar: Bereshith, Section 1, Page 201a

and multiply, inasmuch as souls do not descend into the world save through the covenant. The verse continues: "and so if they be circumcised it shall pass away", the last part referring to the taint of the uncircumcised state that attached to them before. The following is, again, another interpretation of the verse. "Thus saith the Lord: if they be perfect and likewise many": this is an allusion to the sons of Jacob, inasmuch as so long as they were in the presence of Joseph they were perfect in that they stood by him who kept the purity of the covenant. But when "they became separated", having gone and left Joseph and Simeon behind, then "He was wrathful", as then judgement was invoked on their account. The term 'abar (lit. pass) similarly indicates anger in the verse: "For the Lord will be full of wrath (ve'abar, lit. will pass through) in smiting the Egyptians" (Ex. XII, 23). Observe that there is severe judgement and mild judgement, and when mild judgement sucks, as it were, from severe judgement, it becomes itself harsh and formidable. When judgement is invoked against Israel, it is mild judgement that is exercised, such as has not been hardened by severe judgement. But when judgement is invoked against the idolatrous nations, mild judgement becomes hardened by the severity of judgement on high and is rendered terrible. It is thus written: "And the Lord will be full of wrath in smiting the Egyptians" (Ibid.), where the term ve'abar (lit. and He shall pass) indicates that He becomes full of wrath and indignation and takes hold of chastisement. (Note that when ten assemble together in Synagogue and one of them slips out, God is wrathful with him.) According to another interpretation, the second part of the verse says: "and likewise they", that is, the evil deeds of man, "will be removed, and it shall pass over". What shall pass over? R. Simeon said: 'When the soul leaves this world it has to pass through many trials before it reaches its place. And, finally, there is the ever-flowing river of fire which all souls have to pass and to bathe in, and who is he that can face it and pass through it without fear? But the soul of the righteous passes without fear and stands in His holy place; and the man who has

248

performed charity in this world, having given of his substance to charitable objects, of such a one it is written, "and he shall pass over", that is, he shall pass through that region without fear; and a herald will proclaim before that soul, "and though I have afflicted thee, I will afflict thee no more" (Nahum I, 12). For, whoever is worthy to pass through that region is exempt from any further ordeal whatever.'

It may be asked, what need was there to record all these incidents concerning Joseph and his brethren? The Torah, however, is the embodiment of truth and all its ways are ways of holiness, there being no word in the Torah that does not contain sublime and holy recondite truths and examples for man to lay to heart and follow. R. Yose began in this connection a discourse on the verse: Say not thou: I will requite evil; wait for the Lord, and he will save thee (Prov. xx, 22). 'Observe', he said, 'that the Holy One made man for the purpose that he should lay fast hold of the Torah and walk in the way of truth, towards the right side, and not towards the side of the left. And since they ought to go to the right, it behoves the sons of men to abound in love for each other, and banish enmity from their midst, so as not to weaken the right side, which is the spot to which Israel cleave. It is for this reason that there exist a good prompter and an evil prompter; and it behoves Israel to make the good prompter master over the evil prompter by means of good deeds. But when a man strays to the left, the evil prompter thereby gets the mastery over the good prompter, and after having been disabled is restored to strength through the man's sins, for this burden becomes strong only through man's sins. Hence it behoves man to see that the evil prompter does not become reinforced through his sins, inasmuch as it is the good prompter to whom more power should be given and not the evil prompter. Hence Scripture teaches us: "Say not thou: I will make complete the evil one (ashalmah ra'); wait for the Lord, and he will save thee." According to another interpretation, the verse teaches us first not to repay evil for good, inasmuch as "whoso rewardeth evil for good, evil shall not depart from his house" (Prov. XVII, 13); and, moreover, man must abstain even from repaying evil for evil, but must "wait for the Lord and he will save thee". This teaching was exemplified in Joseph the righteous, who abstained from repaying evil to his brethren when they fell into his hands. He addressed to himself the words, "wait for the Lord, and he will save thee", for he

Zohar: Bereshith, Section 1, Page 201b

feared the Holy One, blessed be He. He thus said to his brethren: THIS DO, AND LIVE.

R. Abba began a discourse on the verse: Counsel in the heart of a man is like deep water; but a man of understanding will draw it out (Ibid. xx, 5). 'The first clause of this verse', he said, 'may be applied to the Holy One, who with deep counsel moulded events by the hand of Joseph so as to execute his decree; "but a man of understanding will draw it out" is exemplified in Joseph, who revealed those deep things which the Holy One decreed on the world. Again, "Counsel in the heart of a man is like deep water" is exemplified in Judah at the time when he approached Joseph on behalf of Benjamin, as explained elsewhere, whereas "a man of understanding will draw it out" was exemplified in Joseph.' R. Abba was one day sitting at the gate of Lydda when he saw a man come and seat himself on a ledge overhanging the ground. Being weary from travelling, he fell asleep. R. Abba saw a serpent glide up towards the man, but, before it reached him, a branch fell from a tree and killed it. The man then woke up, and catching sight of the serpent in front of him stood up; and no sooner had he done so than the ledge gave way, and crashed into the hollow beneath it. R. Abba then approached him and said: 'Tell me, what have you done that God should perform two miracles for you?' The man replied: 'Never did anyone do an injury to me but that I made peace with him and forgave him. Moreover, if I could not make peace with him, I did not retire to rest before I forgave him together with all those who vexed me; nor was I at any time concerned about the evil the man did me; nay more, from that day onward I exerted myself to show kindness to such a man.' R. Abba then wept and said: 'This man's deeds excel even those of Joseph; for Joseph showed forbearance towards his own brethren, upon whom it was natural for him to have compassion; but this man did more, and it was thus befitting that the Holy One should work for him one miracle upon another.' R. Abba then began a discourse on the verse: He that walketh uprightly walketh securely; but he that perverteth his ways shall be known (yivade'a) (Ibid. x, 9). '"He that walketh uprightly",' he said, 'signifies the man that follows the ways of the Torah, and such a one "walketh securely", the malignant forces of the world being able to do him no harm; but "he that perverteth his ways" and turns aside from the way of truth "shall be known", to wit, he will become a marked man to all the executors of judgement, by whom his image will never be forgotten until the time when they will take him to the appointed place of retribution. But "him who walks in the way of truth" God takes under His cover so that he should not become known to nor recognized by the executioners of judgement. Happy are those who walk in the way of truth, and thus go about securely in the world without fear either in this world or in the world to come.' AND THE MEN WERE AFRAID, BECAUSE THEY WERE BROUGHT INTO JOSEPH'S HOUSE.

R. Yose said: Woe to the men who know not nor reflect on the ways of the Torah. Woe to them when God will call them to account for their actions and will raise the body and the soul to pay the penalty for all their deeds committed before the soul was separated from the body. That will be the Day of Judgement, on which the books are open and the prosecutors standing by. At that time the serpent will be on the alert to bite the man, quivering in all his limbs to leap upon him. The soul will then become separated from the body and will depart and be carried off to it knows not where. Alas for that day, a day of wrath and indignation! Hence it behoves man to contend daily with his evil prompter and to picture to himself the day when he will stand before the King to be judged, when they will lower him into the ground to rot there, whilst the soul will become separated

Zohar: Bereshith, Section 1, Page 202a

from him. We have been taught that it behoves man always to rouse the good prompter against the evil prompter; if the latter departs, well and good, but if not, the man should study the Torah, as there is nothing so well calculated to crush the evil prompter as the Torah; if he departs, well and good, but if not, let the man remind him of the day of death so as thereby to subdue him. This statement requires consideration. We know that the evil prompter and the angel of death are one and the same. How is it possible, then, that the angel of death should be cowed by the thought of the day of death, seeing that he himself is the slayer of the sons of men, and this is his joy, and in fact his whole purpose in leading men astray is to bring them to this? The truth, however, is that the purpose of bringing to mind the day of death is primarily to humble a man's heart, for the evil prompter dwells only in a place where pride and intoxication are rampant, but where he finds a broken spirit he leaves the man alone. Observe that the good prompter requires the joy of the Torah and the evil prompter the joy of wine and lewdness and arrogance. Hence a man should constantly be in fear of that great day, the Day of Judgement, the day of reckoning, when there will be none to defend him save his own good deeds which he performed in this world. If Joseph's brothers, who were all valiant men, were afraid when led by one youth into Joseph's house, how much greater will be man's fear when the Holy One, blessed be He, will cite him to judgement? Hence it behoves a man to strive his utmost in this world to fortify himself in the Almighty, and put his trust in Him; for then, although he may have sinned, if he repents with all sincerity, since his stronghold is in the Holy One, it will be as though he had not sinned. The brothers were afraid on account of their sin in having stolen Joseph, for had they not sinned they would not have had any cause to fear; for it is only a man's sins that break his courage and deprive him of strength, the reason being that the good prompter is at the same time unnerved, and left powerless to contend with the evil prompter. This is implied in the words: "What man is there that is fearful and faint-hearted?" (Deut. xx, 8), on account, that is, of sins which he may have committed, these being the ruin of a stout heart.

For many generations God exacted payment for the sins of the tribes, since nothing is forgotten of Him, but He exacts requital from generation to generation, and the sentence remains in force till it is fully paid. This is exemplified in the case of Hezekiah. Hezekiah sinned in exposing the mysteries of the Holy One, blessed be He, to the view of idolatrous nations. [Tr. Note: Is. XXXIX, 2: "and (he) showed them his treasure-house", which, according to the Cabbalists, is a reference to the Ark and the tables of the Ten Commandments.] God therefore sent him, through Isaiah, a message, saying: "Behold, the days come that all that is in thy house, and that which thy fathers laid up in store until this day shall be carried to Babylon, etc." (Is. XXXIX, 6). Through his sin in disclosing that which should have remained hidden, opportunity was given to the other side [Tr. Note: i.e. the K'liphoth, or shells, the sinister forces that avail themselves of every opening to contaminate and draw sustenance from any sacred region.] to obtain dominion over it. For, as explained already, blessing rests on that which remains undisclosed, but as soon as it is disclosed the other region obtains scope to exercise dominion over it. It is written: "All that honoured her despise her, because they have seen her nakedness" (Lament. I, 8). This is explained as follows. When Merodach Baladan, King of Babylon, sent a present to Jerusalem (Is. XXXIX, I) he sent a letter in which he first wrote, "Peace be unto Hezekiah King of Judah, and peace be unto the great

God, and peace be unto Jerusalem." But no sooner did the epistle leave his hands than he bethought himself that he had not done right in putting the greeting of the servant before that of his Master. So he rose from his throne, advanced three paces, took back his epistle and wrote another one in its place, headed thus: "Peace be unto the great God, peace be unto Jerusalem, and peace be unto Hezekiah." Thus was Jerusalem honoured;

Zohar: Bereshith, Section 1, Page 202b

but later, "all those that honoured her despised her", the reason being that "they have seen her nakedness", through the action of Hezekiah. Since, however, Hezekiah was very righteous, the punishment was postponed during his lifetime, but it was visited upon his descendants after him. Similarly, the guilt of the tribes did not bring its punishment until a later time, because the judgement from on high could not obtain power over them until an opportune time arrived. Hence, whoever is burdened by sins is constantly in fear, as it says: "and thou shalt fear night and day" (Deut. XXVIII, 66). AND HE LIFTED UP HIS EYES, AND SAW BENJAMIN HIS BROTHER, HIS MOTHER'S SON, ETC. R. Hiya began a discourse on the verse: Hope deferred maketh the heart sick; but desire fulfilled is a tree of life (Prov. XIII, 12). 'This', he said, 'bears out the traditional teaching to the effect that a man in praying to the Almighty should not observe too closely whether his prayer is answered or no, lest the numerous accusers who are about will come to scrutinize his deeds. The underlying meaning of the first part of the verse is that if a man thinks too much about whether his prayer will be answered, he provokes "sickness of heart", to wit, that spirit who is constantly shadowing him in his eagerness to indict him on high and below; but "desire fulfilled is a tree of life", that is, as tradition teaches us, whoever desires that the

Holy One, blessed be He, should accept his prayer, should be diligent in the study of the Torah, which is the tree of life, and thus desire is "fulfilled", or, more literally, "cometh" (baah). By "desire" is meant the grade that presides over all prayers and takes them up into the presence of the Most High King. The word "cometh" (baah) is used here as in the phrase, "In the evening she cometh" (Esther II, 14), and means that the desire comes up before the Most High King so as to fulfil the man's wish. Alternatively, "hope deferred maketh the heart sick" is an allusion to that other and wrong place in which man's prayer may be delayed whilst it passes from hand to hand and so fails to reach its destination, because it is passed from chieftain to chieftain and is brought down again into this world. "But desire fulfilled is a tree of life": this alludes to the hope that is not bandied about among those chieftains, but is granted to the man by God immediately; for if it is delayed among those chieftains it is exposed to the scrutiny and criticism of numerous accusers, who may prevent it from being granted. Not so is it with the hope that issues directly from the King's Court: this is granted to man at once, irrespective of his merits. Again, "hope deferred maketh the heart sick" is exemplified in Jacob, whose hope in regard to Joseph was deferred for a long time, while "desire fulfilled is a tree of life" is exemplified in the case of Benjamin, inasmuch as only a short time elapsed between Joseph's demand that he should be brought to him and his actual arrival, of which it is written, "And he lifted up his eyes, and saw Benjamin his brother, his mother's son." The words "his mother's son" in this passage indicate that Benjamin was the very image of his mother.' Said R. Yose: 'since it has already been written, "And Joseph saw Benjamin with them", why does the Scripture repeat "And he lifted up his eyes, and saw Benjamin his brother"? The truth is that the second time he saw something new: he foresaw through the holy spirit that Benjamin would have a portion along with his brethren in the Holy Land, and, moreover, that it would be in the portions of Benjamin and Judah that the Shekinah would rest, in that the Temple would be in their portion. [Tr. Note: Cf. T.B. Tractate Yoma, 12a: "A strip of land went forth from Judah's lot and entered into Benjamin's territory, and on this the Temple was built."] Hence he saw that Benjamin would be more closely connected with them than he himself.' AND JOSEPH MADE HASTE; FOR HIS HEART YEARNED TOWARD HIS BROTHER; AND HE SOUGHT WHERE To WEEP; AND HE ENTERED INTO HIS CHAMBER AND WEPT THERE. In connection with this, R. Hizkiah quoted the verse: The burden concerning the valley of vision. What aileth thee now that thou art wholly gone up to the house tops? (Is. XXII, 1). 'This verse', he said, 'has been expounded as alluding to the day on which the Temple was destroyed with fire by the enemies, when all the ministering priests went up

Zohar: Bereshith, Section 1, Page 203a

on the walls [Tr. Note: Al. the roofs.] of the Temple holding all its keys in their hands and exclaimed: "Until now we have been thy treasurers, now take back thine own." The Valley of Vision is an appellation of the Temple when the Shekinah dwelt in it, and when it was the source from which all drew their prophetic inspiration; for although the various prophets proclaimed their messages in various regions, they all drew their inspiration from the Temple. Hence the appellation "Valley of Vision". (The term hizayon (vision) has also been interpreted to signify "reflection of all the celestial hues".) The words "what aileth thee now, that thou art wholly gone up to the house tops?" allude to the Shekinah, who at the destruction of the Temple revisited all the spots where she had dwelt formerly and wept for her habitation and for Israel who had gone into exile and all those righteous ones and saints that perished there. God thereupon said to her: "What aileth thee, that thou art wholly gone up to the housetops?", the word "wholly" including together with the Shekinah all fhe legions and hosts that wept with her over the destruction of the Temple. The Shekinah replied with tears: "Thou that wast full of uproar, a tumultuous city, a joyous town, thy slain are not slain with the sword, nor dead in battle, etc. Therefore said I: Look away from me, I will weep bitterly" (Is. XXII, 4), as much as to say, "Seeing that my children have gone into exile and the Sanctuary is burnt, what is there left for me that I should linger here?" And the answer of the Holy One, blessed be He, as explained already elsewhere, was: "Refrain thy voice from weeping, etc." (Jer. XXXI, 16). Observe that from the time when the Temple was destroyed no day has passed without its curses. For as long as the Temple was in existence, Israel performed divine service, offering up burnt-offerings and other offerings, while the Shekinah in the Temple hovered over them like a mother hovering over her children, and so all faces were lit up, and all found blessing both above and here below, and no day passed without its blessings and its joys. Then Israel dwelt securely in their land and all the world was provisioned through them. But now that the Temple is destroyed and the Shekinah is in exile with Israel there is not a day but brings its curses, and the world is under a curse, and joylessness reigns on high and below. Nevertheless the Holy One, blessed be He, will in due time raise Israel from the dust and suffuse the world with joy. So Scripture says: "Even them will I bring to my holy mountain, and make them joyful in my house of prayer, etc." (Is. LVI, 7). And just as they went into exile with tears, as it is written, "she weepeth sore in the night, and her tears are on her cheeks" (Lam. I, 2), so shall they return with tears, as it is written, "they shall come with weeping and with supplications will I lead them" (Jer. XXXI, 9).' AS SOON AS THE MORNING WAS LIGHT, THE MEN WERE SENT AWAY, THEY AND THEIR ASSES. Said R. Eleazar:'Having said that the men were sent away, why does Scripture add "they and their asses"? The reason is to show that previously there had been no ground for their apprehension when they said, "and take us for bondmen, and our asses" (Gen. XLIII, 18). There is also an allusion to the

251

verse: "And Abraham rose early in the morning, and saddled his ass, etc." (Ibid. XXII, 3). It was that morning of Abraham that shone for the brethren to support them by its merits, so that, strong in the merit of Abraham, they went away in peace and were delivered from judgement. For at that moment the rigour of judgement was impending over them and would have exacted punishment from them but for the merit of that morning of Abraham.' R. Judah derived the same lesson from the verse, "And as the light of the morning, when the sun riseth, the morning without clouds; when through clear shining after rain, the tender grass springeth of the earth" (II Sam. XXXIII, 4). 'The "light of the morning" ', he said, 'is an allusion to the light of that morning of Abraham; "when the sun riseth" is an allusion to the sun that rose upon Jacob (Gen. XXXII, 32); "the morning without clouds" means that that morning was not very cloudy, but was "clear shining after rain", to wit, the rain that comes from the side of Isaac, which is the rain that causes the tender grass to spring from the earth. Alternatively we may explain that the light that shone on that morning when Abraham rose up

Zohar: Bereshith, Section 1, Page 203b

also shone when the sun rose upon Jacob, which was the morning without clouds, filled with light, and without any darkness; for as soon as morning dawns severity has no more any power, but is filled with light from the side of Abraham. The words "when through clear shining after rain" allude to Joseph the righteous one who brought rain upon the earth so as to cause grass and all other vegetation to spring forth.' Said R. Simeon: 'Observe this. As soon as night spreads its wings over the world, numerous angels of chastisement and accusers are let loose over the world and take command of it. But as soon as day breaks they all disappear, each one retiring to his own place.

Scripture thus says: "As soon as the morning was light", that is, in virtue of that morning on which Abraham rose early, "the men were sent away", to wit, the executioners of judgement, "and their asses", to wit, the legions that emanate from the side of impurity, who no longer show themselves or no more have any power as soon as dawn appears. For the supernal grades are divided into right and left, into grades of mercy and severity, constituting a hierarchy, some on the side of holiness and others on the side of impurity; but wherever the morning of Abraham awakens in the world, all the unclean grades disappear, exercising no more power, because they can have no existence on the right side but are confined to the left side. The Holy One, blessed be He, thus made night and day to dispose of every one to its own proper side.' R. Hiya discoursed on the verse: But even unto you that fear my name shall the sun of righteousness arise with healing in its wings (Malachi III, 20). 'God', he said, 'will at the proper time cause to shine on Israel that sun which he stored away at the time of the Creation, out of sight of sinners, as alluded to in the words: "But from the wicked their light is withholden" (Job XXXVIII, 15). This light, when it first emerged, radiated from one end of the world to the other; but when God contemplated the generation of Enoch and the generation of the Flood and the generation of the division of languages and all the sinners of the world, He stored it away. When Jacob appeared and wrestled with the chieftain of Esau, who struck against the hollow of his thigh so that he became lame, "the sun rose upon him" (Gen. XXXII, 32), to wit, that same sun that was stored away, in order, with its inherent healing powers, to heal him of his lameness. It is thus written: "And Jacob came perfect (shalem)" (Ibid. XXXIII, 18), to wit, perfect in body, inasmuch as he was made whole again. Likewise the Holy One, blessed be He, will in the future unsheathe that sun and cause it to shine upon Israel, as it says: "But unto you that fear my name shall the sun of righteousness arise", by which is meant the same sun that rose upon Jacob, who was made whole by it, "with healing in its wings", inasmuch as that sun will bring healing to all. For at the time when Israel will rise up from the dust, many lame and many blind will be among them, and so the Holy One will cause to shine upon them that sun with healing in its wings, by which they will be healed. The sun, then, will again radiate from one end of the world to the other, bringing healing to Israel, but the idolatrous nations will be consumed by it. Regarding Israel it is further written: "Then shall thy light break forth as the morning, and thy healing shall spring forth speedily; and thy righteousness shall go before thee, the glory of the Lord shall be thy rearward" (Is. LVIII, 8). Let us return to our subject. AND UNTO JOSEPH WERE BORN TWO SONS BEFORE THE YEAR OF THE FAMINE CAME, ETC. R. Isaac opened a discourse on the verse: And the remnant of Jacob shall be in the midst of many peoples as dew from the Lord, as showers upon the grass, that are not looked for from men, nor awaited at the hands of the sons of men (Micah v, 6). 'Observe', he said, 'that every day as soon as day breaks a certain bird wakes up on a tree in the Garden of Eden and calls three times in succession, whereupon the twig on which it sits stands upright, and then a herald cries aloud, saying: "To you the warning is given, O rulers of the world. There are those among you that see without seeing, that stand without knowing what supports them, and that regard not the glory of their Master."

Zohar: Bereshith, Section 1, Page 204a

The Torah is standing in their presence, but they occupy not themselves with it. It were better for them not to have been born. How can they exist without understanding? Woe to them when the days of evil will bestir themselves against them and extirpate them from the world! What are the "days of evil"? They are not the days of old age, inasmuch as for him who has children and grandchildren those are good days. These days of evil are those indicated in the verse, "Remember then thy creator in the days of thy youth, before the evil days come" (Eccl. XII, 1). The esoteric reference is as follows. When the Holy One, blessed be He, created the world, He created it by means of the letters of the Torah, all the letters of the Alphabet having presented themselves before Him until finally the letter Beth was chosen for the starting point. Moreover, the various Alphabets [Tr. Note: i.e. the various combinations of the Alphabet, based on a series of permutations, each one constituting, as it were, an Alphabet by itself.] in their variety of permutation presented themselves to participate in the Creation. But when it came to the turn of the Teth and the Resh to present themselves together, [Tr. Note: i.e. within the Alphabet called, from its initial letters, Albam. In this scheme the order is: Aleph, Lamed, Beth, Mim... Teth, Resh, etc.] the Teth refused to take its place; so God chid it, saying: "0 Teth, Teth, why, having come up, art thou loth to take thy place?" It replied: "Seeing that Thou hast placed me at the head of tob (good), how can I associate with the Resh, the initial of ra' (evil)?" God thereupon said to it: "Go to thy place, as thou hast need of the Resh. For man, whom I am about to create, will be composed of you both, but thou wilt be on his right whilst the other will be on his left." The two then took their places side by side. God, however, separated them by creating for each one special days and years, one set for the right and one for the left. Those of the right are called "days of good", and those of the left "days of evil". Hence Solomon's words: "before the evil days come", to wit, those days which encompass a man on account of the sins he commits. These days are also alluded to by the terms "days of famine" and "years of famine", and "days of plenty" and "years of plenty". The lesson to be derived from this is that the spring of the holy covenant should not be allowed to flow during the days of famine and the years of famine. Hence Joseph, the exemplar of the sacredness of the covenant, checked his fountain-head in the years of famine, and did not allow it to bring offspring into the world. This is incumbent on every man during years of famine.'

R. Simeon said: 'There is a deep idea contained here, namely, that if a man does not close his fountain when the year of famine has sway, then he causes a spirit from the other side to enter the child then born, and so enables the side of impurity to increase at the expense of the side of holiness. Hence, of those who do not observe such abstinence at such a time it is written: "They have dealt treacherously against the Lord, for they have begotten strange children, etc." (Hos. V. 7); for inasmuch as such children are called "strange children", assuredly the parents have dealt treacherously against the Lord. Thus happy is the portion of holy Israel who do not allow impurity to take the place of sacredness. And Scripture thus tells that "unto Joseph were born two sons before the year of famine came", inasmuch as from the time the famine overspread the land he closed his source so as not to give children to the unclean spirit and not to put impurity in the place of holiness. It behoves a man to wait for the Master of holiness to come and establish his sway, as it is written: "And I will wait for the Lord, that hideth his face from the house of Jacob, and I will look for him" (Is. VIII, 17).Happy are those righteous that know the ways of the Holy One, blessed be He, and keep the precepts of the Torah and follow them. Of them it is written: "For the ways of the Lord are right, and the just do walk in them, but transgressors do stumble therein" (Hos. XIV, 10), also: "But ye that did cleave unto the Lord your God are alive every one of you this day" (Deut. IV, 4).

Zohar: Bereshith, Section 1, Page 204b

[Note: The first four lines of the Hebrew text do not appear in the English translation}

God thus admonished Israel to sanctify themselves, in the words: "Ye shall be holy, for I the Lord your God am holy" (Lev. XIX, 2). The term Ani (I) here signifies the kingdom of heaven. Confronting this is the kingdom of idolatry, which is termed "another" (aher), regarding which it is written: "For thou shalt bow down to no other god, for the Lord whose name is Jealous, is a jealous God" (Ex. XXXIV, 14). Ani (I) is sovereign over this world and of the world to come, all being dependent on it, whereas the other one (aher), the side of impurity, the other side, has rule only in this world and none at all in the other world; and hence, whoever cleaves to that Ani (I) has a portion in this world and in the world to come; but he who cleaves to that aher (the other one) perishes from this world and has no portion in the world to come. He has, however, a portion in the world of impurity, as that other kingdom, the kingdom of idolatry, possesses innumerable emissaries through whom it exercises dominion over this world. Hence Elisha, known by the name of Aher (the other one), [Tr. Note: i.e. Elisha the son of Abuya, who through speculations in Greek philosophy was led into heresy, and for this was called by his colleagues Aher (the other one). T. B. Hagigah, 15a and 15b.] who went down and clung to that grade, was thrust out of the future world, and was not permitted to repent; hence his name Aher. It therefore beho~ es a man to keep himself afar from the side of impurity so as to gain this world and the world to come. Thus there are two sides, the one of beatitude, the other of curse, the one of plenty, the other of famine, each the opposite of the other. Hence at the time of famine a man should not bring any children into the world, as that would be giving children to another god, as already explained. Happy is the man who is heedful to walk in the way of truth and to cleave constantly to his Master, in harmony with that which is written: "and to him shalt thou cleave, and by his name shalt thou swear" (Deut. x, 20), where "swear" (tishabe'a) has a reference to the mystery of faith in the seven (shib'a) supernal grades with their corresponding grades below.'

R. Hiya and R. Yose were once walking together when they caught sight of a man wearing a talith; beneath it, however, they saw that he was armed. Said R. Hiya: 'This man is either exceedingly pious, or he is a dangerous hypocrite.' R. Yose answered: 'Our sainted teachers have said: Judge every man in a favourable sense. Furthermore, we have been taught that when a man sets out on a journey, he should prepare himself for three courses: for making presents, for fighting, and for prayer. Now that man is wearing a talith, which shows that he is ready for prayer, and he is carrying arms, so that he is prepared to fight; about the third thing we need not inquire.' When the man came up to them, they greeted him, but he did not respond.

R. Hiya remarked: 'We see now that he lacks one of the things with which he

Zohar: Bereshith, Section 1, Page 205a

should have been provided: he has not prepared himself for making presents, under which head is included the greeting of peace.' R. Yose replied: 'It may be that he is absorbed in prayer or is repeating his studies so as not to forget them.' They then all walked together for a time without the man speaking a word to them. R. Hiya and R. Yose at length turned aside from him and began discussing points of the Torah. As soon as the man noticed this he approached them and offered them greeting. He also said to them: 'What did you think of me when you gave me greeting and I did not respond?' Said R. Yose: 'I thought that you were engaged in prayer, or perhaps meditating over your studies.' He replied: 'May the Almighty judge you favourably as you have judged me. I will explain why I acted as I did. One day I was walking on the road when I met a man to whom I gave greeting. He happened to be a highwayman, and he fell upon me and molested me, and had I not stoutly resisted I would have come to no small harm. From that day onward I made a vow not to salute first any man save a righteous man, unless one whom I knew already, for fear lest he might set on me and overcome me. That it is forbidden to salute a sinner we know from the verse: "There is no peace, saith the Lord, concerning the wicked" (Is. XLVIII, 22). Now, when I saw you, and you saluted me, I suspected you because I did not notice about you any sign of religion, and besides, I was myself repeating my studies. But now that I see that you are righteous men, I have a plain road before me.' He then began a discourse on the verse: A Psalm of Asaph. Surely God is good to Israel, even to such as are pure in heart (Ps. LXXIII, 1). 'Observe', he said, 'that the Holy One, blessed be He, made a Right and a Left for the ruling of the world. The one is called "good", the other "evil", and He made man to be a combination of the two. The evil, then, which is identical with the left, embraces the idolatrous nations, and has been placed on their side, seeing that they are uncircumcised of heart and uncircumcised of flesh, so that they become defiled by it. But of Israel it is written: "Surely, God is good to Israel." Not, indeed, to all Israelites, but only to those who have not defiled themselves with that "evil", only to such as are "pure of heart". Surely "God is good to Israel", so that they may cleave to Him, and thereby Israel cleaves to the sublime mystery, to the mystery of Faith, so as to be perfectly united with God.' R. Yose then said: 'Happy are we that we did not suspect you falsely, seeing that it was the Holy One, blessed be He, that sent you to us.' R. Yose further said: 'Because He is good to Israel, Israel has a portion in this world and in the world to come, and is destined to see eye to eye the glorious vision, as it is written: "For they shall see, eye to eye, the Lord returning to Zion." ' Blessed be the Lord forevermore. Amen and Amen!

VAYIGASH

THEN JUDAH CAME NEAR UNTO HIM, ETC. R. Eleazar discoursed on the verse: For thou art our Father; for Abraham knoweth us not, and Israel doth not acknowledge us; thou, O Lord, art our Father, our Redeemer from everlasting is thy name (Is. LXIII, 16)....

[Tr. Note: The passage omitted is a repetition, in a shortened form, of pp. 2b, 3a.] He said:

Zohar: Bereshith, Section 1, Page 205b

[Note: The first twenty lines of the Hebrew text do not appear in the English translation as per the translator's note on page 205a]

'The word "thou" here refers to the grade by which the world was planned and created, and by which man was brought into the world. "For Abraham knoweth us not", inasmuch as, though life and death were in his hands, he did not show so much care for us as for Ishmael, on whose behalf he pleaded, "Oh, that Ishmael might live before thee!" (Gen. XVII, 18). Further: "Israel doth not acknowledge us", seeing that he left it to the divine grade to confer on his sons the blessings which he himself ought to have pronounced. Again, "Thou, O Lord, art our Father", as Thou art always standing by us to bless us and to watch over us like a father over his sons, to provide all their needs. "Our Redeemer from everlasting is thy name", God having been so called by Jacob when he said, "the angel who hath redeemed me" (Ibid. XLVIII, 16).'

One night when R. Isaac and R. Judah were sitting up studying the Torah, the former said: 'Tradition teaches us that when God created the world He created the lower world after the pattern of the upper world, and made the two the counterparts of each other, so that His glory is both on high and below.' Said R. Judah: 'Assuredly this is so, and He created man to be superior to all. Scripture thus says: "I, even I, have made the earth, and created man upon it" (Is. XLV, 12), that is to say, "I have made the earth for the sole purpose of creating man upon it"; since it depends upon man to complete the organic unity of the whole. It is written: "Thus saith God the Lord, he that creates the heavens, and stretcheth them forth, he that spreads forth the earth, and that which cometh out of it, he that giveth breath unto the people upon it, and spirit to them that walk therein" (Ibid. XL, 5). The first part of the verse refers to the Holy One, blessed be He, in His operations on high, as He "createth the heavens" and continually and at all times renews them. The "earth" here is an allusion to the holy land which constitutes the "bundle of life"; and it is this earth which "gives soul (neshamah, lit. breath) unto the people upon it." ' Said R. Isaac: 'The whole verse speaks of the upper world, as it is from thence that the soul of life emerges into that land; and that land, in its turn, is the reservoir from which issue souls for all. Observe that when the Holy One, blessed be He, created Adam, He gathered his earthly matter from the four corners of the world and fashioned him therefrom on the site of the Temple here below and drew to him a soul of life out of the Temple on high. Now the soul is a compound of three grades, and hence

Zohar: Bereshith, Section 1, Page 206a

it has three names, to wit, nefesh (vital principle), ruah (spirit), and neshamah (soul proper). Nefesh is the lowest of the three, ruah is a grade higher, whilst neshamah is the highest of all and dominates the others. These three grades are harmoniously combined in those men who have the good fortune to render service to their Master. For at first man possesses nefesh, which is a holy preparative for a higher stage. After he has achieved purity in the grade of nefesh he becomes fit to be crowned by the holy grade that rests upon it, namely ruah. When he has thus attained to the indwelling of nefesh and ruah, and qualified himself for the worship of his Master in the requisite manner, the neshamah, the holy superior grade that dominates all the others, takes up its abode with him and crowns him, so that he becomes complete and perfected on all sides; he becomes worthy of the world to come and is beloved of the Holy One, blessed be He; of him Scripture says: "To cause my beloved ones to inherit substance" (Prov. VIII, 21), the "beloved ones" being those who have attained to the holy neshamah.' R. Judah remarked: 'If that be so, how can we understand the verse in the account of the Flood: "All in whose nostrils was the soul of the spirit (nishmath-ruah) of life... died" (Gen. VII, 22)?' R. Isaac replied: 'This bears out what I said. Among the generation of the Flood no one was left that possessed the holy neshamah, as, for instance, Enoch or Jered or any of the other righteous who by their merits could have saved the earth from destruction, and i ts inhabitants f rom being exterminated. Scripture thus tells us that "all in whose nostrils was the soul of the spirit of life, of all those on dry land, died", that is to say, they had died already and departed this world, so that none was left to shield the world at that time. Observe that nefesh, ruah, and neshamah are an ascending series of grades. The lowest of them, nefesh, has its source in the perennial celestial stream, but it cannot exist permanently save with the help of ruah, which abides between fire and water. Ruah, in its turn, is sustained by neshamah, that higher grade above it, which is thus the source of both nefesh and ruah. When ruah receives its sustenance from neshamah, then nefesh receives it in turn through ruah, so that the three form a unity.' THEN JUDAH CAME NEAR UNTO HIM. This was an approach of one world to another so as to join together. For Judah was king and Joseph was king, and they came nearer and nearer to each other until they united. R. Judah opened a discourse on the text: For, lo, the kings assembled themselves, etc. (Ps. XLVIII, 5). 'This is an allusion', he said, 'to Judah and Joseph, who were both kings and joined together in an altercation. For Judah had gone surety for Benjamin and pledged himself to his father in respect of this world and the world to come, saying to his father: "I will be surety for him; of my hand shalt thou require him; if I bring him not unto thee, and set him before thee, then let me bear the blame all the days" (Gen. XLIII, 9), to wit, in this world and in the world to come. Hence he approached Joseph to reason with him regarding Benjamin, for fear lest he should be banned in this world and in the world to come. When Judah and Joseph hotly disputed, then all those that were present "saw, straightway they were amazed, they were affrighted, they hasted away. Trembling took hold of them there" (Ps. XLVIII, 6-7), as they feared lest they might kill or be killed, and all on account of Benjamin.'

Zohar: Bereshith, Section 1, Page 206b

[Note: The first three lines of the Hebrew text do not appear in the translation.]

R. Judah said: 'There is in this verse a recondite doctrine of faith, to wit, that when God is pleased with Israel and their union is crowned, then two worlds meet together in union, the one opening its store-house, and the other gathering in the contents. Thus, "lo, the kings assembled themselves", to wit, the two holy worlds, the upper world and the lower world.' R. Hiya said: 'The same effect is produced by the sacrifices, for when a sacrifice is offered up and each section receives its due, then there is a bond of union effected between all, and all faces are illumined. As for the words "they saw, straightway they were amazed", these cannot refer to the kings: they must refer to the accusers, whose whole joy lies in executing the sentence which has been committed to them. Hence, when the kings met together in amity and union, they, the accusers, "were amazed, they were affrighted, they hasted away"; they were subdued and passed out of the world; they had no dominion, and were left without any source of sustenance.' R. Eleazar said: 'The reason why Judah and no other came near to Joseph was because he went surety, as it says: "For thy servant became surety for the lad." Esoterically speaking, it was in the order of things that Judah and Joseph should thus meet, as Joseph was a Zaddik and Judah was a king, and so their union produced many benefits for the world: it was the cause of peace to all the tribes and between all the tribes, it was the cause of Jacob's spirit being fortified, as it says: "the spirit of Jacob their father revived" (Gen. XLV, 27). Hence, all both above and below conspired to bring them together.' R. Abba cited here the verse: "Fair in situation, the joy of the whole earth; even Mount Zion, the uttermost parts of the earth, the city of the great King" (Ps. XLVIII, 3), expounding it esoterically. '"Fair in situation"', he said, 'is an allusion to Joseph the Righteous, of whom it is said: "And Joseph was of beautiful form, and fair to look upon" (Gen. XXXIX, 6). He is called "the joy of the whole earth", as he is the joy and the gladness both of the upper and the lower world. He is also "Mount Zion, the uttermost part of the north", seeing that in his territory it was that the Tabernacle of Shiloh stood. "The city of the great King" is the place prepared to meet the Most High King, it being altogether the Holy of Holies, from whence there issue all light, all blessings, and all joy, to cause all faces to shine-the centre from which the Temple receives blessings, which in turn sends out blessings to all the world.'

R. Judah and R. Yose once met together in K'far-hannan, and whilst they were sitting in the inn there entered a certain man who had come with a laden ass.

R. Judah was then saying to R. Yose: 'Tradition tells us that King David used to sleep fitfully, like a horse. If so, how did David sleep till midnight, and not wake when a third of the night was passed?' R. Yose replied: 'When night-time arrived, David used to be sitting with the princes of his household dispensing justice and discussing the Torah, and afterwards he slept until midnight, when he would rise, and remain awake, absorbed in the service of his Master, singing songs of praise and hymns.'

Zohar: Bereshith, Section 1, Page 207a

The stranger here interposed, saying: 'Is your exposition correct? Hardly. The real truth of the matter is this. King David lives forever and ever. All his days he was on his guard so as not to have a foretaste of death, and therefore David, whose place is "living", only slept sixty breaths at a time. For up to the fifty-ninth breath the sleeper is still completely alive, but from that point he has a foretaste of death, and the spirit of impurity obtains power over him. King David therefore guarded himself so that the side of the unclean spirit should not obtain dominion over him. For the first sixty breathings less one are symbolic of heavenly life, of sublime breathings on high, on which life proper depends; they represent the mystery of life. But beyond that number they are associated with death. Hence King David measured out the night so as to remain in life and to prevent any foretaste of death coming over him. At midnight he was in his place, as he was anxious that at the arrival of midnight, when the holy Crown is awakened, he should not be found attached to another place, the place of death. For at midnight, when the supernal holiness is awakened, the man who remains asleep in his bed without regarding the glory of his Master falls under the spell of death and is attached to the other place. David thus rose up to contemplate continually the glory of his Master, who was a Living One like himself, and so never slept long enough to have a foretaste of death. He only slept like a horse, sixty breaths at a time.' R. Judah and R. Yose came up to him and kissed him. They asked him his name. He said: 'Hezekiah (lit. strengthened by God).' They said: 'May you be strong and may your knowledge of the Torah augment.'

When they sat down again, R. Judah said to the man: 'Having made a start, tell us more of the sublime mystical doctrines you alluded to.' The stranger then began to discourse on the verse: The Lord by wisdom founded the earth; by understanding he established the heavens (Prov. III, 19). 'When God', he said, 'created the world, He saw that it could not exist without the Torah, as this is the only source of all laws above and below, and on it alone are the upper and lower beings established. Hence, "the Lord by wisdom founded the earth; by understanding he established the heavens", inasmuch as it is through Wisdom that all things are enabled to exist in the universe, and from it all things proceed. An alternative exposition is as follows. "The Lord by wisdom founded the earth", that is, the upper world has been created through the higher Wisdom and the lower world through the lower Wisdom, so that all things came into being out of the higher Wisdom and the lower Wisdom. "By understanding he established the heavens"; literally, He establisheth (konen), to wit, day by day, without ceasing; they were not made complete at once, but He continues perfecting them each day. This is alluded to in the verse: "Yea, the heavens are not clean in his sight" (Job xv, 15). Think not that this verse implies any disparagement of the heavens. On the contrary, its purpose is to indicate their importance and the great love and affection in which God holds them, in that, notwithstanding that He is perfecting them every day, they are not yet deemed in His eyes to have reached the utmost perfection of which they are capable. In His great affection for them it is His delight to irradiate them continually and without ceasing, the world to come radiating day by day bright streams of light in order to make the heavens resplendent. Hence the heavens, pure as they are, in God's sight are not yet pure. Again, the heavens here symbolize the patriarchs, and the patriarchs find their centre in Jacob, who embraces them all, he being the choice of the patriarchs, and the one who causes light to radiate into the world. And after he was raised to the next world there issued from him a branch beauteous in appearance, from which radiate all illumination and all plenteousness. That branch is Joseph the Righteous, who gave the world abundance and by whom it was sustained. Thus whatever God does in the world has a deep symbolic significance and is all as it should be.' At this point R. Eleazar entered. As soon as he saw them he said: 'Assuredly, the Shekinah is here present. What have you been discussing?' They told him

Zohar: Bereshith, Section 1, Page 207b

all that had passed between them. He said: 'Assuredly, what he said was right. The first sixty respirations are those of life both above and below, but beyond these there are sixty other respirations that are of the side of death and over which hovers the grade of death. They are called "dormit", and contain a foretaste of death; King David, however, attached himself to the sixty respirations that are of life, after which he did not sleep any more. Thus he said: "I will not give sleep to mine eyes, nor slumber to my lids" (Ps. CXXXII, 4). Hence what the stranger said was correct, as David is living, belonging to the side of life and not to the side of death.'

So they sat together studying the Torah. R. Eleazar then discoursed on the verse: O Lord, God of my salvation, what time I cry in the night before thee (Ibid. LXXXVIII, 2). 'King David', he said, 'used to rise from his bed at midnight and study the Torah, and sang praises and hymns so as to cause joy to the King and the Matron. And this promoted the joy of faith throughout the earth. For at that time numberless celestial angels break joyously forth into song on high, and correspondingly praises should be sung here below; and whenever anyone offers up in the night praises on earth, the Holy One, blessed be He, finds pleasure in him, and all those holy angels that sing praises to the Holy One hearken to the one that sings praises to Him in the night on earth. When David wrote: "O Lord, God of my salvation, etc.", he said, in effect: "When is He my salvation? On that day when I rise up early in the night to offer thanksgiving to Thee; it is then that He is my salvation in the daytime." And observe further that whoever offers praises to his Master in the night is fortified in the daytime by the Right side, as a cord issues from the Right side which is drawn round him and by which he becomes strengthened. Hence again David said: "The dead praise not the Lord" (Ibid. cxv, 17), inasmuch as it is the due of the living to praise the Living One, but not of the dead. Hence "The dead praise not the Lord. But we will bless the Lord" (Ibid. 17), we who are alive and have no lot or part in the side of death. Hezekiah also said: "The living, the living, he shall praise thee, as I do this day" (Is. XXXVIII, 19), as the living has kinship with the living; King David is living, and hence he has kinship with the life principle of the universe. And he that has brought himself near to Him is alive, as it is written: "But ye that did cleave unto the Lord your God are alive every one of you this day" (Deut. IV, 4). It is also written: "And Benaiah the son of Jehoiada, the son of a living man [Tr. Note: According to the K'tib.] of Kabzeel" (II Sam. XXIII, 20).'

The Judean then followed with a discourse on the text: And thou shalt eat and be satisfied, and bless the Lord thy God (Deut. VIII, 10). 'Have we not to bless God', he asked, 'before we eat? Indeed, we have to get up early in the morning and recite His praises in proper order, and bless His name before we are allowed to salute any living person. Scripture also says: "Ye shall not eat with the blood" (Lev. XIX, 26), implying that it is forbidden to eat before pronouncing a benediction to one's Master. But the truth is that other benedictions are mainly concerned with the declaration of the unity of God, whereas the grace after meals is meant to show that along with him who says it the grade of faith is also satisfied, and hence it has to be recited in order that this grade may be satisfied and beatified and filled of joy from the celestial life, so that it may provide us with sustenance. For the providing of man's daily food is for the Holy One, blessed be He, as heavy a task as the cleaving of the Red Sea, because it depends upon mazzal and is not, as it were, under His jurisdiction until a benediction is pronounced to Him. Similarly, the arranging of marriages is a heavy task to Him. For when the holy mating takes place, all

Zohar: Bereshith, Section 1, Page 208a

the souls issue from that mazzal above which is identical with the everflowing river; and when there is desire in the lower for the higher, the souls fly down in pairs of male and female, after which their ruling grade separates them and sends each to its appointed place. But later on that presiding grade finds it hard to join them together in their original pairs, since they are now paired in accordance with men's conduct, and all depends now on a higher region. The providing of sustenance is compared to the cleaving of the Red Sea because this also depends on operations on high, ways and paths being opened and cleft in the sea in correspondence with the ways and paths on high. It is therefore necessary to offer blessings to the Power on high and to impart to Him reinforcement from below so that He may receive the heavenly blessings and the heavenly reinforcements in due measure. Hence it is written: "and thou shalt bless the Lord", the vocable eth (accusative particle) having a special significance (as pointing to that region). And toward that region it is necessary to show oneself satisfied and cheerful. Contrariwise, toward the other side, when it exercises sway over the world, one must show oneself hungry and famished, inasmuch as plenteousness does not then rule in the world. This, then, is the explanation of the verse: "And thou shalt eat and be satisfied, and bless the Lord thy God." ' Said R. Eleazar: 'This is truly so, and that is how men ought to act.' R. Judah said: 'Happy are those righteous whose coming together brings peace to the world, since they know how to effect unity. Before Joseph and Judah drew near each other there was no peace, but as soon as they did so they brought much peace into the world, and great joy both above and below, since as soon as Judah came near to Joseph all the tribes joined him.' THEN JOSEPH COULD NOT REFRAIN HIMSELF BEFORE ALL THEM THAT STOOD BY HIM. R. Hiya discoursed on the text: He hath scattered abroad; he hath given to the needy; his charity endureth forever (Ps. CXII, 9). 'Observe', he said, 'that God created the world and set man to be king over all. Now from the first man there have branched out different classes of men, righteous and wicked, foolish and wise, rich and poor; and among these each class can win credit for itself through the medium of the other, that is, the righteous through the wicked, the wise through the stupid, the rich through the poor. For it is by these means that a man becomes worthy of being joined to the tree of life; and what is more, the charity that he dispenses stands him forever in good stead, as it says: "his charity endureth forever".' Said R. Eleazar: 'When God created the world, He established it on one pillar the name of which is Righteous, as it is the Righteous One that upholds the world and that waters and sustains all that exists. So Scripture says: "And a river went out of Eden to water the garden; and from thence it was parted, and became four heads" (Gen. II, 10). The term "it was parted" signifies that the food and drink carried by that river is received in its entirety by the garden, and thence is scattered into the four quarters of the world; and many are they that wait to receive the drink and food from thence! So it is written: "The eyes of all wait for thee, and thou givest them their food in due season" (Ps. CXLV, 15). "But the wicked shall see, and be vexed" (Ibid. CXII, 10), namely, the idolatrous Kingdom. Observe that the Kingdom of Heaven is the Sanctuary designed to shelter all the needy under the shadow of the Shekinah; and the Righteous One is the charity-collector who dispenses to all, as it says: "He hath scattered abroad, he hath given to the needy." Hence, those who collect for charity receive as great a reward as those who give the charity all together. Thus the words: "Then Joseph could not refrain himself before all them that stood by him", refer to all those that stand and wait to receive food and drink from the Righteous One. In the sentence: "And there stood no

Zohar: Bereshith, Section 1, Page 208b

man with him, while Joseph made himself known unto his brethren", the term "with him" is an allusion to the Community of Israel, and "his brethren" refers to the other chariot-riders and legions referred to in the verse: "For my brethren and companions' sake" (Ibid. CXXII, 8). Or again: "And there stood no man with him" is a description of the time when the Holy One, blessed be He, will be mated with the Community of Israel. "While Joseph made himself known to his brethren": this again alludes to the time when the Holy One will join Himself to Israel, to the exclusion of the idolatrous nations.' R. Jesse expounded the verse as alluding to the time when the Holy One, blessed be He, will raise up the Community of Israel from the dust and will take vengeance on the idolatrous nations. Of that occasion it is thus written: "And of the peoples there was no man with me" (Is. LXIII, 3), which is analogous in phrasing to the passage "and there stood no man with him when Joseph made himself known to his brethren", and further: "and he bare them and carried them all the days of old" (Ibid. 9). R. Hizkiah said: 'It is written in one Psalm: "A song of ascents. Unto thee I lift up mine eyes, O thou that art enthroned in the heavens" (Ps. CXXIII, 1), and in another Psalm it is written: "I will lift up mine eyes unto the mountains" (Ibid. CXXI, 1). The difference has been expounded as follows. The latter speaks of heaven, whereas the former speaks of earth. Thus, "I will lift mine eyes unto the mountains", to wit, to the heavens above in order to draw down blessing from on high to below, to draw down blessings from those exalted mountains toward the Community of Israel; but then: "Unto thee I lift up mine eyes", in hoping and waiting for those blessings that descend from thence to here below. "O thou that art enthroned in the heavens": inasmuch as all might and strength is centred in heaven. For when the Jubilee opens the springs, all the gates of heaven are ready, and when the heaven receives all the lights that issue from the Jubilee, there flows down drink and food for the Community of Israel through the intermediary of one Righteous One. When this one moves towards her, many are those who stand and wait to be refreshed and to participate in the blessings from above, as Scripture says: "The young lions roar after their prey, and seek their food from God" (Ps. CIV, 2). But the Community of Israel rises in a recondite manner and receives dainties from her spouse in manner due. As to all those that stand round, they remain apart, as it says: "Then there was no man with him", and as it also says before: "and he cried: Cause every man to go out from me". Afterwards, however, when she has received dainties from her spouse, all the others are given drink and food, as it says: "They give drink to every beast of the field, the wild asses quench their thirst" (Ibid. CIV, 11).'

R. Yose opened a discourse on the subject of Elijah. 'There were', he said, 'two men who dared to expostulate with God: Moses and Elijah. Moses said: "Wherefore hast thou dealt ill with these people?" (Ex. v, 22); and Elijah said: "Hast thou also brought evil upon the widow with whom I sojourn, by slaying her son?" (I Kings, XVII, 20). Both used the term "evil" with the same recondite meaning. Moses said in effect: "Wherefore hast thou given licence to the side of evil to take the soul of that people?" Similarly Elijah said in effect: "Whoever preserves one soul in the world merits life and is worthy to lay hold of the tree of life; yet now the tree of death, the side of evil, has obtained power over the widow whom Thou hast commanded to sustain me." It may be asked, how could Moses and Elijah speak thus, seeing that evil is never done to man by the Almighty? The truth is that when a man walks on the right side, the protection of the Holy One, blessed be He, is constantly with him, so that the other side has no power over him, and the forces of evil are bowed before him, and cannot prevail over him. But as soon as the protection of the Holy One is withdrawn from him by reason

Zohar: Bereshith, Section 1, Page 209a

of his having attached himself to evil, that evil gains the mastery and advances to destroy him, being given authorization to take his soul.'

Said R. Hiya: 'Elijah was able to pronounce a doom with the full certainty that God would confirm it, as, for instance, that the heaven should not let fall rain or dew. How came it, then, that he felt afraid of Jezebel? How came it that at her threat to take his life (I Kings XIX, 2) he was filled with fear and fled for his life?' R. Yose said in reply: 'It has been laid down that the righteous should not put their Master to trouble by exposing themselves to an obvious danger. We find an example in Samuel, when he said: "How can I go? If Saul hear it, he will kill me" (I Sam. XVI, 2); and God therefore told him to take certain precautions (Ibid.). So it was with Elijah.' Said R. Yose, further: 'I have heard a special exposition of this matter as follows. When Jezebel threatened Elijah, it is not written that he "feared" (vayira), but he "saw" (vayar) (I Kings XIX, 3). What was it that he saw? He saw that the angel of death had followed him for a number of years, and he had not been delivered into his hand. Then the verse continues: vayelekh el nafsho (and he went for his life), which literally means, "and he went to (el) his soul", that is to say, he resorted to the foundation of his soul, or, in other words, he proceeded to attach himself to the tree of life. In connection with the phrase el nafsho (to his soul), I have heard,' he continued, 'the following recondite doctrine from R. Simeon. All the souls of mankind emerge from the everflowing celestial stream, from which they are received into the "bundle of life". Now, when a female becomes pregnant from a male, it is mostly the result of an equal and reciprocal desire, or less often of the predominating desire of the female. But when the desire of the male predominates, then the soul of the child that is born has unusual vitality, inasmuch as the whole of its being is the result of the desire and yearning for the tree of life. Hence Elijah, to whose birth that desire had contributed in a special degree, was gifted with special vitality, and did not die like other men. For his whole being was derived from the tree of life and not from the dust. He, therefore, without suffering death, as is the lot of other men, went up on high, as Scripture says: "and Elijah went up by a whirlwind into heaven" (II Kings II, 11). Observe the words: "behold, there appeared a chariot of fire, and horses of fire, etc." (Ibid.), which indicate that Elijah's spirit was stripped of its body, so that he departed not life in the manner of other men, but became a holy angel like other heavenly beings, carrying out divine messages in this world; for it is well established among us that the miracles which God performs in the world are carried out by his agency. Now observe that it is written further: "and he requested for himself (eth nafsho=his soul) to die" (I Kings XIX, 4). This implies that he turned to the tree wherein death lurks, and there God appeared unto him, as Scripture says: "Go forth, and stand upon the mount before the Lord... and after the earthquake a fire; but the Lord was not in the fire; and after the fire a still small voice" – referring to the very innermost point, which is the source of all illumination – "And it was so, when Elijah heard it, that he wrapped his face in his mantle.... And, behold, there came a voice unto him, and said: What doest thou here, Elijah? And he said: I have been very jealous for the Lord" (Ibid. XIX, 11-13). God said to him: "How long wilt thou continue to be jealous for me? Thou hast already closed fast the gate so as

Zohar: Bereshith, Section 1, Page 209b

to secure thyself from death, and the world will not be able to endure thee." Elijah replied: "for the children have forsaken thy covenant, etc." (Ibid. 14). The Holy One then said to him: "As thou livest, in whatever place the rite of the holy covenant (i.e. circumcision) will be performed, thou wilt be present." It is for this reason that at every performance of that rite a chair is set aside for Elijah, who is always there present. Observe what consequences followed Elijah's words, for it is written: "Yet will I leave seven thousand in Israel, all the knees which have not bowed unto Baal, and every mouth which hath not kissed him" (Ibid. XIX, 18). God said to him in effect: "Henceforth the world will not be able to tolerate thee along with my sons." So He commanded him, saying: "and Elisha the son of Shaphat of Abel-meholah shalt thou anoint to be prophet in thy room" (Ibid. 16), as much as to say: "There shall be another prophet for my children, and thou shalt go up to thy place." Observe that if a man is jealous for the Holy One, blessed be He, the angel of death has no power over him as he has over other men, and to him is given the covenant of peace, as it is said regarding Phinehas: "Wherefore say: Behold, I give unto him my covenant of peace" (Num. XXV, 12). AND HE FELL UPON HIS BROTHER BENJAMIN'S NECK, AND WEPT; AND BENJAMIN WEPT UPON HIS NECK. R. Isaac said: 'We expound this to indicate that Joseph wept on account of the destruction of the first Temple and of the second Temple.' R. Isaac proceeded to discourse on the verse: Thy neck is like the tower of David builded with turrets, whereon there hang a thousand shields, all the armour of the mighty men (S. S. IV, 4). 'The tower of David', he said, 'signifies the heavenly Jerusalem, of which it is written: "The name of the Lord is a strong tower; the righteous runneth into it, and is set up on high" (Prov. XVIII, 10), the phrase "on high" pointing to the tower above. "Thy neck" signifies the Temple below, which for its beauty is compared to the neck in the human body: as the neck gives symmetry and beauty to the body, so does the Temple to the whole world. "Builded with turrets" (talpiyoth, lit. mound of mouths), that is, a mound toward which all men turn their gaze when they open their mouths to offer prayer and praise. "Whereon there hang a thousand shields", alluding to the thousand cosmic reconstructions that are performed there. "All the armour of the mighty men", alluding to the angels of punishment that proceed from the side of severity. As a woman's ornaments are hung about her neck, so all the ornaments of the world are hung about the Temple. Similarly, in the passage, "To our very neck we are pursued" (Lam. v, 5), there is an allusion to the Temple. "We labour and have no rest" (Ibid.), that is, we have exerted ourselves to build the Temple twice, but the enemies have not permitted us to retain it, and it has not been rebuilt. Again, as the whole body perishes when the neck is destroyed, so as soon as the Temple was destroyed and its light extinguished, the whole world was plunged into darkness, and there was no light of sun or stars, either in heaven or on earth. Hence, Joseph wept on account of this. After he had wept for the Temple, he wept for the tribes that were to go into exile. For as soon as the Temple was destroyed, all the tribes were exiled and scattered among the nations. Scripture thus tells us: "And he kissed all his brethren, and wept upon them", that is to say, for them. He wept for all of them, for the twofold destruction of the Temple and for his brethren the ten tribes that went into exile and were scattered among the nations. AND AFTER THAT HIS BRETHREN TALKED WITH HIM. They, however, did not weep, because the Holy Spirit did not flash upon them as upon Joseph.' AND THE REPORT THEREOF WAS HEARD IN PHARAOH'S HOUSE. R. Abba opened a discourse on the verse: My soul yearneth, yea, even pineth for the courts of the Lord; my heart and my flesh sing for joy unto the living God (Ps. LXXXIV, 3). 'Observe', he said, 'that before offering his prayer to his Master, a man should first recite some thanksgiving. He should also pray before his Master in the proper time: in the morning to unite himself to the right side of the Holy One, blessed be He, and in the afternoon to the left side. It is incumbent on man to offer up prayer and supplication each day so as to unite himself with God. It has been laid down that in praying before his Master a man should not make his voice heard, as if he does so his prayer will not be accepted, for the reason that

Zohar: Bereshith, Section 1, Page 210a

prayer does not consist in audible voice nor is the voice prayer. Prayer consists in another voice attached to the voice which is heard. It thus behoves man to pray silently, to pray with that voice that is inaudible. It is thus written: "and the voice (veha-qol=and the report, lit. the voice) was heard", where the term qol is written defectively, without a vau, pointing to the inaudible voice, like that of Hannah's prayer, of which it is written: "but her voice could not be heard" (I Sam. I, 13). The prayer which the Holy One, blessed be He, accepts is that which is performed with earnestness and devotion and proper concentration of the mind on the unity of God.' R. Eleazar said: 'The silent voice is the supernal voice from which all other voices proceed. The statement "and the voice was heard", where the term qol (voice) is written without a vau, is an allusion to the voice which wept on account of the first Temple and the second Temple. The word "was heard' suggests the verse: "A voice was heard in Ramah" (Jer. XXXI, 15), where the word b'ramah (in Ramah, lit. on high) alludes to the upper world, to the world to come; for of that event it is indeed written: "And in that day did the Lord, the God of hosts, call to weeping, and to lamentation, etc." (Is. XXII, 12), so that the voice was heard in the height of heights. Therefore, too, Rachel wept for her children; she "refused to be comforted for her children, because he is not". It is not written "they are not" (einam), but "he is not" (einennu), which is an allusion to her Spouse; for if her Spouse were present with her, she would let herself be comforted for them, as they would not remain then in exile; but her Spouse not being with her she cannot be comforted. The "house of Par'oh" (Pharaoh) here is, again, an allusion to the Temple on high, that is, to the house that was stripped (par'oh= uncovering) and bared of all its light and radiance and its hidden treasures. When the Holy One, blessed be He, will raise that still voice from the dust and join the vau with it, then all that was lost to them in the time of exile will be restored, and they will feast on the supernal radiances that will stream with added brightness from the supernal world, as Scripture says: "And it shall come to pass in that day, that a great horn shall be blown; and they shall come that were lost in Assyria, and they that were dispersed in the land of Egypt; and they shall worship the Lord in the holy mountain at Jerusalem" (Ibid. XXVII, 13).' NOW THOU ART COMMANDED, THIS DO YE: TAKE YE WAGONS OUT OF THE LAND OF EGYPT, ETC. R. Hiya opened a discourse with the text: Rejoice ye with Jerusalem, and be glad with her, all ye that love her rejoice for joy with her, etc. (Ibid. LXVI, 10). 'When', he said, 'the Temple was destroyed and Israel on account of their sins were driven from their land, God removed Himself, as it were, to the height of heights and regarded not the destruction of the Temple nor the exile of His people, and so the Shekinah was exiled with them. When God again descended, He observed His House that was burnt down. He looked at His people and behold, they were in exile. He inquired concerning the Matron (Shekinah) and found that she had been driven out. Then, "in that day did the Lord, the God of hosts, call to weeping, and lamentation, and to baldness, and to girding with sackcloth" (Ibid. XXII, 12); and the Matron was called upon to "lament like a virgin girded with sackcloth for the husband of her youth" (Joel I, 8), because He had removed Himself from her and they were separated. The very heaven and the very earth lamented, as it is written: "I clothe the heaven with blackness, and I make sackcloth their covering" (Is. L, 3). The celestial angels all raised their voices in lamentation, as it says: "Behold, the angels cry without; the angels of peace weep bitterly" (Is. XXXIII, 7). The sun and the moon mourned and their light was darkened, as we read: "The sun shall be darkened in his going forth, etc." (Ibid. XIII, 10).

Zohar: Bereshith, Section 1, Page 210b

For what reason? Because the other side had obtained sway over the Holy Land.' R. Hiya further discoursed on the verse: And thou, son of man, thus saith the Lord God concerning the land of Israel: An end! the end is come upon the four corners of the land(Ezek. VII, 1). 'This verse', he said, 'contains a recondite idea. As has been stated, there is an end on the right and an end on the left. It is the end on the right which is alluded to in the expression "the land of Israel: an end!", while the expression, "the end is come" refers to the end on the left. The right end is the end of the good prompter; the left end is the end of the evil prompter; and when Israel's sins multiplied and increased, it was through this left end that the wicked kingdom obtained power and destroyed the House and Sanctuary of the Lord. Scripture thus says: "Thus saith the Lord God: An evil, a singular evil, behold, it cometh" (Ibid. 5). Heaven and earth thus lamented because dominion had been given to the left end. Now, seeing that the holy kingdom, the kingdom of heaven, has been overthrown and the wicked kingdom has prevailed, it behoves man to mourn with it and to abase himself with it, so that when it will be raised again and joy will be restored to the world, he may rejoice with it. Scripture thus says: "Rejoice for joy with her, all ye that mourn for her" (Is. LXVI, 10).' AND HE SAW THE WAGON'S, ETC. Egypt is called "a fair heifer" (Jer. XLVI, 20), and hence the word 'egloth (lit. wagons, or heifers) here may be an allusion to Egypt, indicating that a time will come when the Israelites, the bondsmen of Egypt, the fair heifer, will obtain dominion over it. R. Eleazar said: 'By means of the heifers Joseph intended to remind Jacob that when he was separated from him he had been studying with him the section of the heifer whose neck was to be broken (Deut. XXI, 4). Now this rite of the heifer whose neck was to be broken was carried out for a man found slain without its being known who had slain him. The heifer was thrown, as it were, to the evil spirits in order to ward them off and prevent them from obtaining dominion over the earth. Now all men depart life through the hands of the angel of death, except the one whose life has been taken by another man, before the angel of death had received permission to exercise his function upon him. The angel of death has thus cause to complain against the place of the murder, and therefore it was commanded that "the elders of that city shall bring down the heifer, etc." (Ibid. XXI, 4), so as to remove any indictment against that locality and to safeguard it against the power of the accuser. When Joseph left his father, he went without escort and without eating first; and when Jacob afterwards said "Joseph is surely torn", he added: "Nay, but I will go down to the grave to my son mourning" (Gen. XXXVII, 35), as much as to say: "It was I who was the cause of his death, and, moreover, I sent him off although I knew that his brethren hated him." All this Joseph hinted to him by sending the heifers.' Said R. Judah to R. Eleazar: 'But did not Joseph send the heifers by the command of Pharaoh, as it says: "And Joseph gave them heifers, according to the commandment of Pharaoh" (Ibid. XLV, 21)?' R. Eleazar replied: 'Pharaoh only gave the command at Joseph's request. Indeed, Jacob was not fully convinced of the tidings brought to him until he saw them, as Scripture says: "And when he saw the heifers that Joseph had sent him, the spirit of Jacob their father revived" (Ibid. 27).' R. Simeon remarked: 'First Scripture says: "and the spirit of Jacob revived", and immediately after: "And Israel said" (Ibid. 28). The Torah first calls him Jacob because the Shekinah departed from him when the brethren made her a party to the oath of secrecy with regard to the sale of Joseph; but now that the Shekinah returned he rose to the higher degree symbolized by Israel.'

Zohar: Bereshith, Section 1, Page 211a

AND HE SAID: I AM GOD, THE GOD OF THY FATHER... I WILL GO DOWN WITH THEE INTO EGYPT. This is an indication that the Shekinah accompanied him into exile; and wherever Israel were exiled the Shekinah followed them also into exile. Observe that Joseph sent his father six wagons, [Tr. note: Here the Zohar reverts to the accepted rendering of 'agaloth, namely, wagons.] an allusion to which is found in the "six covered wagons" presented by the princes to Moses (Num. VII, 3). According to another view, the number was sixty; but the two views are not contradictory. For, indeed, it is first written: "in the wagons which Joseph sent" (Gen. XLV, 27), and afterwards, "which Pharaoh sent" (Ibid. XLVI, 5), SO that the truth is that those which Joseph sent were of the proper number, which had a recondite significance, but the larger number which Pharaoh sent had no such numerical symbolism. AND JOSEPH MADE READY HIS CHARIOT. R. Isaac began a discourse on the verse: And over the heads of the living creatures (hayoth) there was the likeness of a firmament, like the colour of the terrible ice, stretched forth over their heads above (Ezek. I, 22). 'This verse', he said, 'has been explained as follows. There is a series of hayoth, one group higher than the other, and there is one above all which sets all the others in motion and causes them to transmit their light to one another. This supreme. Hayah has various faces which radiate to all the cardinal points, three on each side. There is besides a series of firmaments, one above the other, the highest one dominating all the others, which all turn their gaze towards it. So Scripture says: "And under the firmament were their wings conformable the one to the other, etc." (Ibid. 23), as they all rule over what has been committed to their charge. There being nine hayoth on each of the four sides of the universe, the total number is thirty-six. When they are all joined together, they form one impression symbolizing the one Name in an absolute unity. And when they are all ranged round the heavenly throne, then is realized the description given by the prophet: "And above the firmament that was over their heads was the likeness of a throne, as the appearance of a sapphire stone; and upon the likeness of the throne was a likeness as the appearance of a man above it" (Ibid. 26). Now the figures on that chariot culminate in that of man; and when the other figures are subordinared to this one so as to form a homogeneous chariot, then it may be said: "And Joseph made ready his chariot", Joseph representing the.Zaddik; further, "and went up to meet Israel his father, to Goshen", Israel typifying the supernal Adam, and Goshen (lit.

approaching) the coalescence of the two. The text continues: "and he presented himself unto him", symbolizing the reflection of the light of the sun on to the moon, whereby the moon is lit up and floods with its light all the dwellers of the lower world. Correspondingly, as long as the supernal sanctity rested on the lower Temple, that Temple was filled with an effulgence of light, and thus remained in its completeness, but subsequently the supernal sanctity was withdrawn and the Temple was destroyed, regarding which it is written: "and he wept on his neck a long while"; "he wept", on account of the Temple that was to be destroyed, and "a long while", on account of the last exile. When Jacob thus saw that all below was complete after the supernal pattern, he said: "Now let me die... that thou art yet alive", that is to say: since thou hast retained the holy covenant of Him

Zohar: Bereshith, Section 1, Page 211b

who is called the Living One of all eternity. The same is implied in Jacob's previous utterance: "It is enough; Joseph my son is yet alive." ' AND JACOB BLESSED PHARAOH. R. Yose cited in connection with this the verse: I have compared thee, O my love, to a steed in Pharaoh's chariot (S. S. I, 9). 'Observe', he said, 'that there are chariots of the left that belong to the other side, and there are chariots of the right that are under the aegis of supernal holiness; the latter are of grace, the former of severity. When the Holy One, blessed be He, executed justice on the Egyptians, every form of punishment which He inflicted on them was after the very pattern of those chariots, and after the very pattern of that other side: as that side slays and takes men's souls, so did the Holy One, blessed be He, as it says: "and the Lord slew all the first-born in the land of Egypt" (Ex. XIII, 15), and so with all the other punishments executed on the Egyptians. This is the implication of the words, "I compared thee, O my beloved, etc.", to wit, "I made thee equal to the other side in the power to slay." And what does Scripture say in regard to the future? "Who is this that cometh from Edom, with crimson garments from Bozrah? etc. (Is. LXIII, 1). AND ISRAEL DWELT IN THE LAND OF EGYPT, IN THE LAND OF GOSHEN; AND THEY GOT THEM POSSESSION THEREIN, AND WERE FRUITFUL, AND MULTIPLIED EXCEEDINGLY, and they got them possession, to wit, as a permanent possession, inasmuch as it belonged to them; and they were fruitful, and multiplied, assuredly so, seeing that they were relieved of all vexation and they enjoyed all the luxuries of the world. Blessed be the Lord forevermore. Amen and Amen!

[Tr. note: The first four and a half pages of this section (211b–216a) are declared by all the commentators to be an interpolation, containing much erroneous doctrine. Zohar: Bereshith, Section 1, Page 212a through 216a are omitted.

Note: The Hebrew text of these pages do not appear in our translation as explained in the translator's note above.]

VAYEHI

R. Hiya discoursed on the text: And thy people are all righteous, they shall inherit the land forever, etc. (Is. LX, 21). 'Israel', he said, 'have been favoured above all the Gentiles in being entitled by God righteous, that they may obtain an everlasting inheritance in the world to come, as it is written: "Then thou shalt delight in the Lord" (Is. LVIII, 14). Wherefore so? Because they attach themselves to the Body of the King, as it says: "Ye that cleave unto the Lord your God are alive every one of you this day" (Deut. IV, 4).' R. Isaac said: 'This text of R. Hiya contains a deep allusion for "the reapers in the field". [Tr. note: i.e. students of the esoteric doctrine.] For R. Simeon has laid down in the esoteric Agadah that the exalted inheritance of that other land is acquired by none save him who is called "righteous." For the Matron cleaves to the Righteous One and finds delight in him, and the Righteous One assuredly inherits the Matron. So God in His love for Israel called them righteous and they are therefore meet to inherit the Matron. The reason is that they are circumcised, according to the dictum: "Whoever is circumcised and enters into the covenant and observes it becomes attached to the Body of the King, and enters into the Righteous One", and they are therefore called righteous, and so "they shall forever inherit the land", to wit, the "land of the living". They are further called in the text "the branch of my planting", to wit, one of those shoots which God planted when He created the world, referred to in the verse, "And the Lord God planted a garden in Eden" (Gen. II, 8). According to another explanation, the words "And thy people are all righteous" refer to Jacob and his sons, who went down to Egypt among a stiff-necked people and all remained righteous, wherefore "they shall forever

Zohar: Bereshith, Section 1, Page 216b

inherit the land", since from there they went up to inherit the holy land.' AND JACOB LIVED IN THE LAND OF EGYPT. It is to be noted that this section is "closed", i.e. no space is left in the scroll of the Law between the beginning of this section (vayehi) and the end of the previous section (vayigash). Why is this? R. Jacob said: 'It is to indicate that when Jacob died the eyes of Israel became, as it were, closed, because then they really entered on the galuth and the Egyptians enslaved them.' R. Simeon said: 'It is to show that the words "and Jacob lived" are to be taken in close conjunction with the preceding sentence: "And Israel dwelt in the land of Egypt in the land of Goshen and they gat them possessions therein, and were fruitful, and multiplied exceedingly." That is to say, just as they lived in luxury and were short of nothing, so Jacob similarly had every comfort and was short of nothing. Hence it is said of him now that "he lived". For up to this time he had known nothing but trouble, but now he saw one of his sons in royal estate and the others virtuous and righteous, all living in the lap of luxury while he himself abode among them like good wine resting on its lees; so that now in reality he lived. SEVENTEEN YEARS. Why seventeen? R. Simeon said: 'Jacob's life was always one of hardship, but whenever he looked at Joseph he thought he saw his mother again, because Joseph closely resembled Rachel, and at such a time he forgot all his sorrows. When, however, Joseph was parted from him, this was a worse blow than all the previous ones, and he wept every day for the seventeen years that Joseph had been with him. Hence Providence compensated him with another seventeen years of Joseph's company, during which he lived in ease and luxury. Tradition tells us that all those seventeen years the Divine Presence rested upon him, and therefore they were called "life". So it says that when his sons told him that Joseph was alive, "the spirit of Jacob their father revived" (Gen. XLV, 27), for up to then the spirit had been dead within him and he had not been in a state to receive another in its place, since the spirit from above does not rest on an empty spot.' R. Yose said: 'The Shekinah does not rest on a place which is defective or disturbed, but only in a place properly prepared, a place of joyfulness. Hence all the years that Joseph was away and Jacob was in sadness, the Shekinah did not rest on him.' So we have learnt that R. Eleazar said in the name of R. Abba: 'It is written, "Serve the Lord with gladness, come before his presence with singing", to show that the service of God should be performed with joy.' This accords with what R. Eleazar has elsewhere said, that when Elisha desired the spirit to rest upon him, he said "and now bring me a minstrel" (II Kings III, 15).

R. Abba said: 'It has been laid down in a certain passage that the whole is derived from four sides, and that all the roots of the higher and lower beings are attached to them; and it has been further said that as one goes in another goes out, and as one is revealed another is concealed, and each one is linked to the next, and they are the origins of all.' R. Simeon said: 'There are three origins like the three patriarchs, and from them all the rest spread and extol the name to be crowned.'

R. Yose said: 'From the day that R. Simeon left the cave, nothing was concealed from the Companions, and things became clear to them as if they had been revealed that day on Mount Sinai. But after he died, then "the fountains of the deep and the windows of heaven

Zohar: Bereshith, Section 1, Page 217a

were closed", and the Companions could no longer get to the bottom of things, as shown by the following instance. One day R. Judah was sitting at the gate of Tiberias, and he saw two camels laden with bundles of clothes. One of the bundles fell down and a flock of birds flew to the spot. Before they could reach it, however, they dispersed. Then a number of other birds came up, and perched on the rock. The men threw stones and shouted at them but they would not go away. He heard a voice saying: "The crown of crowns is plunged in darkness and does not rest on the head of the Master." While he was still sitting, a man passed by and said: "You are not following the example of Abram, who, when the birds of prey came down upon the carcasses drove them away (Gen. xv, 11)." "I am doing so," said R. Judah, "but they will not go". The man turned his head away and said: "This man has not yet plucked the hairs from the head of his Master, nor shorn the Matron." R. Judah followed him three miles asking him to explain, but he would not, so that R. Judah was greatly perturbed. One day he fell asleep under a tree and dreamt that he saw four wings outstretched and R. Simeon ascending on them with a scroll of the Law, and also with all manner of books containing hidden expositions and Agadahs. They all ascended to heaven and were lost to his view. When he woke he said: 'Verily, since the death of R. Simeon wisdom has departed from the earth. Alas for the generation that has lost this precious jewel which used to illumine it and on which higher and lower beings were supported.' He came and told R. Abba, who clapped his hands on his head, saying: 'R. Simeon was the mill in which every day the goodly manna was ground. Now the mill and the manna have departed, and nothing is left of it in the world save as it were "one omerful put in a pot to be kept" (Ex. XVI, 33), that is, kept in a private place and not exposed. Who now can reveal mysteries or even know them?' R. Abba whispered to him: 'The man that you saw was assuredly Elijah, and he was not willing to reveal secrets in order that you may appreciate the worth of R. Simeon, and that his generation may weep for him.' He said to him: 'He indeed deserves to be wept. Woe is me that I did not depart this life with those three who died in the sacred chamber of R. Simeon, so as not to behold this generation that has been laid low.' He then said to him: 'Master, tell me. It is written: "And they shall take the gold and the blue and the purple and the scarlet and the fine linen" (Ex. XXVIII, 5). Why is there no mention here of silver, seeing that silver was also brought for an offering (v. Ex. xxv, 3)?' He replied: 'You might ask the same question with regard to copper, which also is mentioned in one place and not in the other. As the Sacred Lamp has revealed the answer, I also may reveal it.' He then discoursed as follows. 'It is written: "Mine is the silver and mine is the gold, saith the Lord" (Haggai II, 8). On many occasions we have pondered over the question, what holiness is there in these priestly garments? We have, however, been taught that there is holiness in every place, and that these garments are after the supernal pattern, as we have learnt: "There is a High Priest above and a high priest below, raiment of honour above and raiment of honour below." As for the omission of silver and copper, these were assigned to another place, as it is written, "All the pillars of the court round about shall be filleted with silver", and again, "and their sockets of brass" (Ex. XXVII, 17). These were the instruments for the service of the Tabernacle; but this raiment of honour was only to be used by the

High Priest and by no other.' AND THE TIME DREW NEAR THAT ISRAEL MUST DIE. R. Judah said: 'Alas, for the ignorance of mankind! They see not, neither do they hear,

Zohar: Bereshith, Section 1, Page 217b

nor know that every day the voice of a herald goes forth and resounds through two hundred and fifty worlds. We have learnt that when the herald goes forth one of these worlds shakes and trembles, and there issue from it two birds whose abode is beneath the tree wherein is the appearance of life and death, one towards the South and the other towards the North, one when the day dawns and one when it departs. Both proclaim what they hear from the herald. They then desire to return to their own place aloft, but their feet slip in the hollow of the great abyss and they are fastened there till midnight. Then the herald proclaims, and the sons of men are also "snared like birds caught in the trap".' R. Judah said: 'The day when a man's feet are caught and his time approaches to die is called "the day of the Lord", because then his spirit returns to Him. We have learnt that at that time a holy Crown, to wit, the seventh, is entrusted with his spirit, or, if he comes from the side of Might (Geburah) the eighth Crown; beyond that his days cannot be prolonged, as it says, "yet is their pride and labour but sorrow" (Ps. xc, 10); where there is no foundation the building cannot be firm.' R. Judah said: 'Happy are the righteous when God is pleased to take back their spirit to Himself. But if a man is not adjudged worthy, woe to his spirit, which has to be purified and to be prepared before it can be drawn to the Body of the King; and if it is not prepared, woe to it that it must roll about "like a stone in a sling" (cf. I Sam.). Further, we have learnt: "If the soul is worthy, great is the bliss reserved for it in the other world, as it is written, "No eye hath seen save thine, O Lord, what thou wilt do for him that trusts in thee" (Is. LXIV, 3).' R. Yose said: 'When a man's appointed time draws near, proclamation is made concerning him for thirty days, and even the birds of the heaven announce his doom; and if he is virtuous, his coming is announced for thirty days among the righteous in the Garden of Eden. We have learnt that during those thirty days his soul departs from him every night and ascends to the other world and sees its place there, and during those thirty days the man has not the same consciousness or control of his soul as previously.' R. Judah said: 'From the first arrival of those thirty days a man's shadow becomes faint and his form is not outlined clearly on the ground.'

R. Isaac one day sat himself at R. Judah's door in great sadness. The latter coming out and finding him in this condition said to him: 'What is the matter today?' He replied: 'I have come to ask you three things. One is that whenever you repeat any of my expositions of the Torah you should give them in my name. The second is that you should train my son Joseph in the Torah; and the third is that you should go every seven days and pray over my grave.' Said R. Judah: 'What makes you think you are going to die?' He answered: 'My soul has lately been leaving me in the night and not enlightening me with dreams as it used to do. Furthermore, when I bow down in the course of my prayers, I notice that my shadow does not appear on the wall, and I imagine the reason to be that the herald has gone forth and made proclamation regarding me.' R. Judah replied: 'I will carry out your requests. But I will ask you also

Zohar: Bereshith, Section 1, Page 218a

to reserve a place for me by your side in the other world, as we were together in this.' R. Isaac wept and said: 'I beg of you not to leave me for the rest of my days.' They then went to R. Simeon, whom they found studying the Torah. Raising his eyes, R. Simeon saw R. Isaac and the Angel of Death running and dancing before him, so going to the door, he took R. Isaac by the hand and said: 'I ordain that he who is wont to enter shall enter and he who is not wont shall not enter.' Thereupon R. Isaac and R. Judah entered and the Angel of Death was kept outside. R. Simeon looked at R. Isaac and saw that his time had not yet come, and that he had respite till the eighth hour of the day, so he made him sit down before him and study the Torah. R. Simeon then said to his son R. Eleazar: 'Sit by the door and speak with no one, and if anyone wants to come in, swear to him that he may not.' He then said to R. Isaac: 'Have you seen today the image of your father? For so we have learnt, that at the hour of a man's departure from the world, his father and his relatives gather round him, and he sees them and recognizes them, and likewise all with whom he associated in this world, and they accompany his soul to the place where it is to abide.' R. Isaac replied: 'So far I have not seen.' R. Simeon then arose and said: 'Sovereign of the Universe! R. Isaac is well known among us, and he is one of the seven eyes of the world here. Now that I hold him, give him to me.' A voice then went forth and said: 'The throne of his Master is near the wings of R. Simeon. Lo, he is thine, and he shall accompany thee when thou goest in to abide on thy throne.' R. Eleazar now saw the Angel of Death coming up, and said to him: 'The doom of death cannot fall in the place where R. Simeon is.' R. Simeon then said to his son: 'Come in here and take hold of R. Isaac, since I see that he is afraid.' R. Eleazar did so, and R. Simeon turned round and began to study. R. Isaac then fell asleep and saw his father in a dream. He said to him: 'My son, happy is thy portion both in this world and in the world to come. For among the leaves of the tree of life in the Garden of Eden there is placed a great tree, mighty in both worlds, which is R. Simeon, son of Yohai, and he shelters thee with his boughs.' Said R. Isaac to him: 'Father, what is my portion there?' He replied: 'Three days ago they roofed in thy chamber and prepared for thee, placing windows on all four sides to let light in upon thee, so that when I saw thy place I rejoiced, and said: Happy is thy portion; save that thy son has not yet learnt sufficient Torah. And behold now, twelve righteous

Companions were eager to visit thee, and when we were on the point of departing a voice went forth through all worlds saying "Ye companions that stand here, be proud of R. Simeon, for he has made a request and it has been granted to him." Nor is this [Tr. note: viz. that R. Isaac should live.] all, for there are here seventy crowned places belonging to him, and every place has doors opening to seventy worlds, and every world is open to seventy channels, and every channel is open to seventy supernal crowns, and from there paths are opened out to the Ancient and Inscrutable One, to give a view of that supernal delight which illumines and beatifies all, as it says, "to see the pleasantness of the Lord and to visit his temple".' Said R. Isaac: 'Father, how long am I granted to be in this world?' He answered: 'I am not permitted to tell, nor is this made known to a man. But in the great feast of R. Simeon, thou shalt prepare his table.' R. Isaac then awoke, his face full of smiles. R. Simeon, observing him, said: 'You have heard something, have you not?' 'Assuredly,' he replied; and he then told him his dream, and prostrated himself before him. It is related that from that day

Zohar: Bereshith, Section 1, Page 218b

R. Isaac diligently taught his son the Torah and always had him with him. When he went in to R. Simeon, he used to leave his son outside, and when he sat before R. Simeon he applied to himself the verse: "O Lord, I am oppressed, be thou my surety" (Is. XXXVIII, 14).

We have learnt that on the dread day when a man's time comes to depart from the world, four quarters of the world indict him, and punishments rise up from all four quarters, and four elements fall to quarrelling and seek to depart each to its own side. Then a herald goes forth and makes proclamation, which is heard in two hundred and seventy worlds. If the man is worthy, all the worlds welcome him with joy, but if not, alas for that man and his portion! We have learnt that when the herald makes proclamation, a flame goes forth from the North and passes through the "stream of fire", and divides itself to the four quarters of the world to burn the souls of sinners. It then goes forth and flies up and down till it alights between the wings of a black cock. The cock then flaps its wings and cries out at the threshold of the gate. The first time it cries: "Behold, the day cometh burning like a furnace, etc." (Mal. III, 19). The second time it cries: "For lo, he that formeth the mountains and createth the wind and declareth unto man what is his thought" (Amos IV, 13); that is the time when a man's deeds testify against him and he acknowledges them. The third time is when they come to remove his soul from him and the cock cries: "Who would not fear thee, King of the nations? For to thee doth it appertain, etc." (Jer. x, 7). Said R. Yose: 'Why must it be a black cock?' R. Judah replied: 'Whatever the Almighty does has a mystic significance. We have learnt that chastisement does not fall save upon a place which is akin to it. Now black is the symbol of the side of Judgement, and therefore when the flame goes forth, it strikes the wings of a black cock, as being the most appropriate. So when man's judgement hour is near, it commences to call to him, and no one knows save the patient himself, as we have learnt, that when a man is ill and his time is approaching to depart from the world a new spirit enters into him from above, in virtue of which he sees things which he could not see before, and then he departs from the world. So it is written: "For man shall not see me and live"; in their lifetime they may not see, but at the hour of death they may. We have further learnt that at the time of a man's death he is allowed to see his relatives and companions from the other world. If he is virtuous, they all rejoice before him and give him greeting, but if not, then he is recognized only by the sinners who every day are thrust down to Gehinnom. They are all in great gloom and begin and end their converse with "woe!". Raising his eyes, he beholds them like a flame shooting up from the fire, and he also exclaims "woe!". We have learnt that when a man's soul departs from him, all his relatives and companions in the other world join it and show it the place of delight and the place of torture. If he is virtuous he beholds his place and ascends and sits there and enjoys the delights of the other world. But if he is not virtuous, his soul remains in this world until his body is buried in the dust, and then the executioners take hold of him and drag him down to Dumah and to his appointed storey in Gehinhom.' R. Judah said: 'For seven days the soul goes to and fro from his house to his grave, and from his grave to his house, mourning for the body,

Zohar: Bereshith, Section 1, Page 219a

as it is written: "His flesh shall suffer pain for him, and his soul shall mourn for it" (Job XIV, 22), and it grieves to behold the sadness in the house. We have learnt that after seven days the body begins to decay, and the soul goes in to its place. It enters the cave of Machpelah, where it is allowed in up to a certain point according to its deserts. It then reaches the place of the Garden of Eden and meets the Cherubim and the flashing sword which is in the lower Garden of Eden, and if it is worthy to enter, it enters. We have learnt that four pillars [Tr. note: i.e. angels.] are waiting there with the form of a body in their hands, and with this it gleefully clothes itself and then remains in its appointed circle in the Garden of Eden for its allotted time. Then a herald makes proclamation and a pillar of three colours is brought forward, which is called "the habitation of Mount Zion" (Is. IV, 5). By means of this pillar it ascends to the gate of righteousness, in which are Zion and Jerusalem. If it is worthy to ascend further, then happy is its portion and lot that it becomes attached to the Body of the King. If it is not worthy to ascend further, then "he that is left in Zion and he that remaineth in Jerusalem shall be called holy" (Ibid. 3). But if it is privileged to ascend further, then it beholds the glory of the King, and enjoys the supernal delight from the place which is called Heaven. Happy he that is vouchsafed this grace.' R. Yose

265

said: 'There is a superior grace and an inferior grace. The superior grace is above the heavens, as it is written: "For great above the heaven is thy kindness" (Ps. CVIII, 5). Of the inferior grace it is written: "For great unto the heaven is thy kindness" (Ibid. LVII, 11), and to this class belong the "faithful kindnesses of David" (Is. LV, 3).'

R. Isaac once questioned R. Simeon with regard to the verse, "a joyful mother of children", saying: 'I know what is meant by the mother, but who are the children?'

R. Simeon answered: 'There are two children to God, one male and one female. The male he gave to Jacob, as it is written: "Israel is my son, my firstborn" (Ex. IV, 22). The female he gave to Abraham. The mother sits on the young and gives them suck; whence the precept, "Thou shalt not take the mother with the young." Our teachers have said: "A man should beware of sinfulness below lest thereby the mother should be parted from the children." But when men repent and act virtuously then the mother returns and shelters the young, and this is called "repentance" (t'shubah, lit. returning). Then, too, it can be said, "the mother of the children is joyful". Hence a man should not cease from propagating his kind till he has a son and a daughter.'

R. Isaac was not yet satisfied. 'The righteous', he said, 'desire no more than to "behold the pleasantness of the Lord" (Ps. XXVII, 4).' R. Simeon answered: 'It is all one, since this pleasantness comes from the Holy Ancient One to this heaven, and the desire of the righteous is fixed on that.' R. Simeon further said: 'It is written: "He hath cast down the earth from the heavens" (Lam. II, 1). For when the Almighty resolved to destroy the Temple and to banish Israel among the nations, He removed from before Him the upper earth, and when that earth was put away from Him, then the lower earth was laid waste and Israel were banished among the nations; whereupon the Community of Israel said: "My mother's sons were incensed against me" (S. S. I, 6), and that was the cause of my downfall.'

R. Yose was once walking with R. Hiya the son of Rab, and as they were going along he said to him: 'Do you see something over there?' 'I see a man in the river', he answered, 'and a bird on

Zohar: Bereshith, Section 1, Page 219b

his head with a piece of flesh which it is eating and tearing with its claws. The man is crying out something, but I cannot catch what he says.' Said the other: 'Let us go nearer and listen.' He said: 'I am afraid.' 'Why,' he said, 'do you think that this is a man here? This is some hint of Wisdom which God is sending us.' So they went nearer and they heard him saying: 'Crown, crown, two sons are kept outside, and there will be no peace or rest until the bird is thrown down in Carsarea.' R. Yose wept and said: 'Verily the Galuth is drawn out, and therefore the birds of heaven will not depart until the dominion of the idolatrous nations is removed from the earth, which will not be till the day when God will bring the world to judgement.' As they went on they heard a voice say: 'Let the flame of fire advance to chastise', whereupon a flame came forth and burnt the bird. Said R. Yose, 'God only banished Israel when there was no longer faith among them, for then, if one may say so, He was entirely forgotten.' R. Hiya said: 'What is the meaning of the verse: "He hath swallowed up death forever" (Is. xxv, 8)?' He said: 'When God shall arouse His right hand, then death shall be banished from the world. But He will not arouse His right hand till Israel give the impetus, to wit, by the Torah. At that time "the right hand of the Lord doeth valiantly" (Ps. CXVIII, 16), and "I shall not die but live" (Ibid. 17). We have learnt that when God is pleased with a righteous man and the herald makes proclamation concerning him thirty days among the righteous in the Garden of Eden, then all the righteous rejoice and go and crown his place in preparation for his coming to take up his abode among them. But if he is sinful, then the herald proclaims concerning him thirty days in Gehinnom, and all the sinners are sad and exclaim: "Woe, that a new punishment is to be executed on so-and-so", and the demons are ready to meet him. Woe to the wicked and woe to his neighbour!' Then they all exclaim: "Woe to the wicked, it shall be ill with him, for the reward of his hands shall be given to him' (Is. III, 11).' R. Isaac said: 'The word ra' (ill) in this passage refers especially to him who wilfully spills his seed, like Er the son of Judah. Such a one is thrust down lower than all the others in that world. All others have a chance to ascend, but not he. Is he even worse, it may be asked, than a murderer? Even so, because a murderer kills another man's children, but he kills his own, and he spills very much blood. Hence it is written of such a one particularly: "And that which he did was evil in the sight of the Lord" (Gen. XXXVIII, 10).' R. Judah said: 'Every sin admits of repentance barring this, and every sinner may hope to see the face of the Shekinah barring this one.' R. Isaac said: 'Happy are the righteous in this world and in the world to come; of them it is written: "And thy people are all righteous, they shall forever inherit the land (Is. LX, 21). [Tr. note: The translation of the three-and-a-half pages here omitted (219b–221b) will be found in the Zohar on Leviticus, 104b, to which they properly belong.]

AND THE DAYS DREW NEAR FOR ISRAEL TO DIE. R. Hiya said: 'Why is the name Israel used here in connection with his death, whereas above it says, "And Jacob lived, etc."?' R. Yose said in reply: 'Note here the word "days", which is somewhat peculiar, since a man only dies on one day, in fact, in one instant. The reason, however, is, as we have learnt, that when God desires to take back a man's spirit, all the days that he has lived in this world pass in review before Him. Happy, then, is the man whose days draw near before the King without reproach, not one of them being rejected because a sin was committed thereon. Hence the term "drawing near" is used of the righteous, because their days draw near before the King without reproach. But woe to the wicked whose days cannot so draw near, because they all passed in sin,

266

wherefore they are not recorded above, so that of them it is written: "The way of the wicked is like thick darkness, they know not on what they stumble" (Prov. IV, 19).

So here it says that the days of Israel "drew near", that is, without reproach and with unalloyed joy; and hence the name "Israel" is used, because it points to a greater perfection than the name Jacob.' R. Yose said: 'There are some righteous whose days when enumerated are put afar from the King, and others whose days are brought near to the King. It is they whose portion is blessed, and Israel was one of them.' AND HE CALLED HIS SON JOSEPH. R. Abba said: Joseph is called Jacob's son par excellence, because, as we have learnt, when Potiphar's wife tempted him, he lifted up his eyes and saw the image of his father (as it says, "and there was none of the men of the house there within" (Gen. XXXIX, 11), as much as to say, "but there was someone else"), and he thereupon resisted and withdrew. Hence it was that when Jacob came to bless his sons he said: "I know, my son, I know" (Gen. XLVIII, 19), repeating the word, as much as to say, "I know of the time when you proved in your own body that you were my son, and I also know that, as you say, this is the elder." Another explanation why he called him specially "my son" is that they closely resembled one another, so that whoever saw Joseph could testify that he was the son of Jacob.' R. Yose said that another reason was that he supported him and his family in his old age.

The reason why Jacob asked Joseph to bury him, and not any other of his sons, was that only Joseph had the power to take him out of Egypt. R. Yose said: 'Since Jacob knew that his descendants would be in bondage in Egypt, why did he not have himself buried there in order that his merit might shield them, which would have shown true parental solicitude? The truth is that, as tradition tells us, when Jacob was about to go down to Egypt he was afraid lest his descendants might be lost among the peoples and lest God might remove His Presence from him. Hence God said to him: "Fear not to go down to Egypt, for I will there make of thee a great nation" (Gen. XLVI, 3), and then, "I will go down with thee into Egypt" (Ibid. 4). Jacob was still afraid lest he should be buried there and not with his fathers, so God said to him: "I will also surely bring thee up again" (Ibid.), to wit, to be buried in the grave of thy ancestors. Hence he had various reasons for desiring to be taken out of Egypt. One was that the Egyptians should not make a god of him, since he foresaw that God would punish their gods. Another was because he knew that God would still keep his Presence among his descendants in the galuth. A third reason was that his body might rest in company with those of his ancestors, to be numbered with them and not with the sinners of Egypt, since, as we have learnt, Jacob reproduced the beauty of Adam, and his form was sublime and holy like that of the holy throne. Esoterically speaking, there is no separation among the patriarchs, and hence he said: "when I sleep with my fathers".'

Another reason why Jacob called Joseph "my son" was because he was from the first more intent on begetting him than any other of his sons, his whole thought having been devoted to Rachel.

Said R. Simeon: 'Man should take good heed not to sin or to transgress the will of his Master, because all his actions are recorded in a book and are reviewed by the holy King and revealed before Him; even his thoughts are present before God and do not escape Him. Now on the night when Jacob went in to Leah and she gave him the tokens which he had given to Rachel, he really thought she was Rachel, and God, to whom all secrets are revealed, allowed that thought to have effect, and so the birthright of Reuben was transferred to Joseph, that having been Jacob's first seed, and so Rachel came into her own inheritance. This, too, is why Leah called his name simply Reuben (=see a son) and not Reubeni (=see my son). We have learnt: "God knew that Jacob had no intent to sin before Him, and that he did not allow his thoughts to dwell on any other woman at that instant like the sinful, and therefore it is written: "And the sons of Jacob were twelve" (Gen. xxxv, 22).' For the sons of the sinners who act in this way are called by another name, which is known among the Companions. Hence "Jacob called to his son Joseph"– his real son, his son at the beginning and at the end.' PUT, I PRAY THEE, THY HAND UNDER MY THIGH.

R. Yose said: 'Jacob made him swear by the sign of the covenant which was stamped on his flesh, since the patriarchs assigned more importance to this than to anything else, and this covenant, too, is symbolized by Joseph.' R. Simeon said: 'We find the formula, "put thy hand under my thigh", in connection with both Abraham and Jacob, but not with Isaac, the reason being that Esau issued from him. Again, we may suppose Jacob's idea to have been: "Swear to me by that holy impress which has brought holy and faithful seed into the world and which has ever been preserved from defilement that you will not bury me among those unclean who have never guarded it, and of whom it is written, "whose flesh is the flesh of asses and their neighing the neighing of horses" (Ezek. XXIII, 20).' Why, it may be asked, was Joseph, who also guarded the covenant, buried among them? The answer is that it was to meet a special emergency, like the appearance of God to Ezekiel outside the Holy Land. God saw that if Joseph were removed from there, the Israelites would sink under the bondage; therefore He said: "Let his burial place be here in a spot which will not be defiled (for Joseph's coffin was thrown into the river), and so the Israelites will be able to endure the captivity.' R. Yose said: 'Jacob saw that he was fitted in every way to form part of the holy chariot like his fathers, but he thought it impossible that his body should be attached to his fathers if he was buried in Egypt.'

Seeing that the patriarchs were privileged to be buried in the cave of Machpelah with their wives,

Zohar: Bereshith, Section 1, Page 223a

why was Jacob buried with Leah and not with Rachel, who was the "foundation of the house"? The reason is that Leah bore more children from the holy stock. R. Judah said: 'Leah used to go out every day to the highway and weep for Jacob when she learnt that he was righteous, and prayed on his behalf, but Rachel never did so. Hence Leah was privileged to be buried with him, while Rachel's grave was set by the highway. The esoteric reason, as we have affirmed, is that the one typifies the disclosed and the other the undisclosed. Tradition tells us that the virtuous Leah prayed with many tears that she might be the portion of Jacob and not of the wicked Esau. Hence we have learnt that whoever prays with tears before the Almighty can procure the cancellation of any chastisement that has been decreed against him; for so Leah, though she had been assigned by divine decree to Esau, yet by her prayer succeeded in procuring the preference for Jacob and saved herself from being given to Esau.'

R. Isaac said: 'It is written: "And Solomon's wisdom excelled the wisdom of all the children of the East" (I Kings v, 9). What is the wisdom of the children of the East? Tradition tells us that it was the wisdom which they inherited from Abraham. For we read that Abraham "gave all that he had unto Isaac" (Gen. xxv, 5): this refers to the higher wisdom, which he possessed through the knowledge of the holy name of God. "But to the sons of the concubines which Abraham had Abraham gave gifts"; to wit, certain information about the lower crowns, and he settled them in "the east country" (Ibid.); and from that source the children of the East inherited wisdom.'

R. Simeon was once travelling from Cappadocia to Lydda accompanied by R. Abba and R. Judah. He was mounted and they were on foot. Tired with keeping pace with him, R. Abba exclaimed: 'Verily, "they that go after the Lord shall roar like a lion" (Hos. XI, 10).' R. Simeon then dismounted, saying: 'Truly, wisdom is not acquired by a man save when he sits and rests, as it says of Moses that he "sat on the mountain forty days" (Deut. IX, 9).' So they all sat down. R. Abba then asked him: 'What is the difference between the wisdom of Solomon and the wisdom of the children of the east and the wisdom of Egypt, mentioned in the same verse?' He replied: 'The secret of Solomon's wisdom was in the name of the moon when blessed from every side. In his days the moon was magnified and reached her fullness. A thousand mountains rose before her, and she blew them away with a puff. A thousand mighty rivers flowed before her, and she swallowed them at a draught. Her nails reached out in a thousand and seventy directions,

Zohar: Bereshith, Section 1, Page 223b

and her hands in twenty-four thousand, so that nothing could escape her. Thousands of bucklers clung to her hair. From between her feet went forth a youth [Tr. note: Metatron.] who stretched from one end of the world to the other with sixty clubs of fire, and who is also called "Enoch son of Jered." He was called "son of Jered" (lit. descent) in reference to the ten stages by which the Shekinah descended to the earth. Under him are stationed many Hayyoth, under which again is fastened the hair of the moon, which is called "the knobs of the sceptre". Her hands and feet take hold of it like a strong lion holding his prey. Her nails are those who call to mind the sins of men and inscribe them with all rigour and exactness. The offscourings of her nails are all those who do not cleave to the Body of the King and suck from the side of uncleanness, when the moon begins to diminish. Now, after Solomon had inherited the moon in its fullness, he also desired to inherit it in its defective state, and therefore he sought to acquire the knowledge of spirits and demons, so as to inherit the moon on every side. As for the wisdom of Egypt, this is the lower wisdom which is called "the handmaid behind the millstones", and which was also included in the wisdom of Solomon.' Said R. Abba: 'How thankful am I that I asked you this question, since I have received so illuminating an answer.' R. Simeon said further: 'With regard to Solomon's words, "What profit hath man in all his labour?" (Eccl. I, 3), these do not apply to labour in the study of the Torah, since the statement is qualified by the words, "wherein he laboureth under the sun", and the study of the Torah is above the sun.' Said R. Hiya: 'Study of the Torah which is prosecuted for worldly ends is also accounted "under the sun", as it does not ascend aloft '.

R. Eleazar said: 'Though a man should live a thousand years, yet at the time of his departure from the world it seems to him as if he had only lived a single day.' WHEN I SLEEP WITH MY FATHERS. Happy is the lot of the patriarchs that the Almighty has made them a holy chariot above and has taken delight in them to be crowned with them; hence it is written, "Only in thy fathers the Lord took delight" (Deut. x, 15).

R. Eleazar said:

Zohar: Bereshith, Section 1, Page 224a

'Jacob knew that he was to be crowned in his fathers and his fathers with him. Hence we have learnt regarding the graven letters that in the letter shin there are three strokes, one on one side and one on the other side and one combining them, and this is the allusion in the verse: "And the middle bar in the midst of the boards shall pass through from end to end" (Ex. XXVI, 28). Hence Jacob said: "I shall lie with my fathers".' R. Judah said: 'How deaf are men to the warnings of the Torah, and how blind are they to their own condition that they are not aware that on the day when a human being comes forth into the world, all the days that are assigned to him come forward and fly about the world and descend and warn the man, each day in its turn. And when a man has been so warned and yet sins against his Master, then the day on which he sinned ascends in shame and bears witness and stands by itself outside, and so it remains until the man repents. If he becomes virtuous it returns to its place, but if not, then it goes down and joins the outside spirit and returns to its house, and assumes the exact shape of that man in order to plague him and dwells with him continually in his house. If he is virtuous it proves a good companion, and if not, an evil companion. In either case, such days are missing from the full number and are not counted with the others. Woe to the man who has diminished the number of his days before the Almighty, and has not left days for himself with which to crown himself in the other world, and to approach the Holy King. For if he is worthy he ascends by means of those days, and they become a glorious vesture for his soul, those days in which he acted virtuously and did not sin. Woe to him that has diminished his days above, since when he comes to be clad in his days, those days that he spoilt by his sins are lacking, and his vesture is therefore defective; all the more so if there are many of them and he has nothing at all with which to clothe himself in the other world. Then woe to him and woe to his soul, since he is punished in Gehinnom for those days, many days for each, because when he departed from this world he had no days with which to clothe himself and no garment wherewith to cover himself. Happy are the righteous whose days are all stored up with the Holy King, and form glorious vestures with which they may robe themselves in the other world. This is the esoteric explanation of the verse, "and they knew that they were naked" (Gen. III, 7), that is to say, that the glorious raiment made of those days had been impaired and none of them was left to clothe themselves with. And so it was until Adam repented and God pardoned him and made him other garments, but not of his days, as it is written: "And God made Adam and his wife coats of skins and clothed them" (Gen. III, 21). Observe that of Abraham it says that "he came into days" (Gen. XXIV, 1), because when he departed this world he literally came into possession of his former days and was invested with them, his robe of glory being full and complete. Job, on the other hand, said of himself: "Naked came I out of my mother's womb and naked shall I return thither" (Job. I, 21), because no material was left wherewith to clothe himself. Our teachers have said: "Happy the righteous whose days are without reproach and remain for the world to come, so that after death they are all joined together and formed into

robes of glory through which they are privileged to enjoy the delights of the future world, and in which they are destined to come to life again. But woe for the sinners whose days are defective, so that there is not left from them wherewith to cover themselves when they depart from the world." We have further learnt that all the virtuous who have acquired a robe of glory through their days are crowned in the future world with crowns like those of the patriarchs, from the stream that flows continually into the Garden of Eden, and of them it is written, "the Lord shall lead thee continually and satisfy thy soul in dry places" (Is. LVIII, 11), but the wicked who have not acquired such a garment will be "like the heath in the desert that shall not see when good cometh, but inhabits the parched places in the wilderness" (Jer. XVII, 6).' R. Isaac said: 'Of all men Jacob had the fairest prospect, because he was entitled to a robe on account both of his own days and of those of his fathers; hence he said: "I shall lie with my fathers." ' R. Judah said: 'When Jacob went in to his father to obtain a blessing, he was wearing the garments of Esau; nevertheless the text says that Isaac smelt his garments (Gen. XXVII, 27), to indicate that he caught the odour of his raiment in the future world, and it was therefore that he blessed him. Hence, too, he said: "See the smell of my son is as the smell of a field which the Lord hath blessed", the reference being to the field of holy apples, in which every day drops dew from the place called heaven; hence he continued: "God give thee of the dew of the heaven." It has been taught that fifteen odours ascend every day from the Garden of Eden to perfume those precious garments in the other world.'

R. Judah asked how many garments there are. R. Eleazar said: 'The authorities differ on this point, but in truth there are three. One is for clothing the spirit (ruah) in the terrestrial Garden of Eden. A second, the most precious of all, is for investing the inner soul (neshamah) when among the bundle of the living in the circle of the King. The third is an outer garment which appears and disappears, and with which the vital soul (nefesh) is clothed. It flits about the world and on Sabbaths and New Moons it attaches itself to the spirit in the terrestrial paradise and learns from it certain things which it goes and makes known in this world. It has been taught that on Sabbaths and New Moons the soul (nefesh) makes two visits. First it joins the spirit among the perfumes of the terrestrial paradise, and then in company with the spirit it joins the higher soul in the "bundle of the living", and feasts itself on the glorious radiance coming from both sides. This is hinted in the expression "The Lord shall satisfy thy soul in bright places" (Is. LVIII, 11), the plural including both the outer radiance of the place of the spirit and the radiance within radiance which they enjoy by associating with the higher soul in the "bundle of the living".'

Said R. Simeon: 'When I visit the Companions in Babylon they come together to hear me, and I discourse to them openly, but they go and seal up my teaching under an iron padlock which makes it inaccessible to all. How often have I taught them the ways of the Garden of the King and the doctrine of the King! How often have I taught them all the degrees of the righteous in the future world! But they are all frightened to repeat

Zohar: Bereshith, Section 1, Page 225a

these things and only mumble them, on which account they are called "mumblers". However, I account this fear in them creditable, because they are denied the air and the spirit of the Holy Land and inhale the air and the spirit of an alien region. Further, too, the rainbow has appeared in their time, [Tr. note: The appearance of the rainbow, reminding God of His promise not to destroy the world, is a proof that there are no righteous who could protect the world by their merits alone. Vide T. B. Kethuboth, 77b.] and hence they are not worthy to behold the presence of Elijah, not to mention others. Their good fortune is that I am still alive to be the ensign and support of the world, for in my days the world will not be afflicted and the punishment of heaven will not fall upon it. After me there will not arise a generation like this one, and the world will be left without a protector, and insolence will be rampant both above and below–above on account of the insolence of those below, and their shamelessness. Mankind will cry and none will take heed; they will turn to every side and find no remedy. But one remedy there will be in the world and no more, to wit, in the place where there will be men devoting themselves to the study of the Torah, and where there will be a Scroll of the Law free from all error. When this will be taken out, the upper and lower denizens will bestir themselves, especially if the Holy Name is written in it in the fitting manner. As I have already taught, woe to the generation the members of which, high and low, do not rise when the Scroll of the Law is displayed Who shall come to its aid when the world is in distress and requires protection? Then it is necessary more than ever to display the Scroll of the Law. For when the world is in distress, and men go to the cemeteries to offer supplication, all the dead take note of the Scroll, since the soul goes and informs the spirit that the Scroll of the Law is in captivity through the distress of the world, and the living have come to supplicate. Then the spirit informs the higher soul (neshamah) and the higher soul informs the Almighty, who then takes note and has pity on the world, all because the Scroll of the Law has been banished from its place, and the living have come to supplicate by the graves of the dead. Alas for the generation that has need to remove the Scroll of the Law from one place to another, even from one synagogue to another, because they have nothing else to which to turn. Not all men know that the Shekinah at its last exile did not withdraw to heaven, but to "the wilderness, to an inn of travellers" (Jer. IX, 1), and that since then it is always to be found in the place where Israel is particularly in distress, and also wherever the Scroll is removed and high and low rise up before it.'

We have learnt that the soul is linked with the body twelve months in the grave, and they are judged together (this, however, does not apply to the souls of the righteous, as we have laid down), and it is present in the grave and is aware of the sufferings of the body.

It also knows the sufferings of the living, but does not intervene on their behalf. After twelve months it is clad in a certain vesture, and goes to and fro in the world, learning certain things from the spirit and interesting itself on behalf of the living who are in distress. But this is only when there is among them a virtuous man whose merit is properly recognized by them. For so we have learnt, that when a virtuous man is left in the world, he is known both among the living and the dead, and when the world is in great distress and he cannot deliver it, he makes the trouble known to the dead. And if there is not

Zohar: Bereshith, Section 1, Page 225b

such a one, then they take out the Scroll of the Law, and high and low accompany it, and it is incumbent on all at that time to do penance, for otherwise heaven will punish them. Even the spirits of the Garden of Eden intercede for them for the sake of the Scroll, as has been affirmed. Said R. Judah: 'Little do men know how God extends His mercy to them at all times and seasons. Three times a day a spirit enters the cave of Machpelah and breathes on the graves of the patriarchs, bringing them healing and strength. That spirit distils dew from on high, from the head of the King, the place of the supernal fathers, and when it reaches the lower patriarchs they awake. That dew, as we have learnt, comes down by degrees till it reaches the lower Garden of Eden, and becomes impregnated with its perfumes. Then a spirit containing two other spirits arises and traverses the spice–beds, and enters the door of the cave. Then the patriarchs awake, they and their spouses, and supplicate on behalf of their descendants. If the world is in distress on account of its sins, and the patriarchs sleep, the dew not descending from on high, then the remedy is to take out the Scroll of the Law. Then the soul tells the spirit, and the spirit tells the higher soul, and the higher soul tells God. God then takes His seat on the throne of mercy, and there issues from the Ancient Holy One a stream of dew of bdellium, which flows to the head of the King, so that the fathers are blessed. Then the dew flows to those sleepers, and all are blessed together, and God has mercy on the world. We have learnt that God does not show mercy to the world till He has informed the patriarchs, and for their sakes the world is blessed.' Said R. Yose: 'Assuredly this is so. And I have further found in the Book of King Solomon, that one which was called the "counsellor of all wisdom" (and Rab Hamnuna also said that the same thing had been revealed to him), that Rachel achieves more than all of them by standing at the parting of the ways at all times when the world is in need. This is symbolized by the fact that the ark and the mercy–seat and the Cherubim were in the territory of Benjamin, who was born by the wayside, the Shekinah being over all.' AND ISRAEL BOWED HIMSELF DOWN UPON THE BED'S HEAD. The "bed's head" is the Shekinah. Said R. Simeon: 'Not at all. The bed stands for the Shekinah, as in the verse, "Behold, it is the litter of Solomon" (S. S. III, 7). The "head of the bed" is the Foundation of the World who is the head of the sacred couch; and "that which is upon the head" is (the supernal) Israel who is established at the head of the bed. Hence, Israel bowed down to his appropriate grade. At this time he was not yet ill, as we see from the next verse, but because he knew that at the time he would rise to a supernal holy grade to become a perfect throne, therefore he bowed down to that supernal throne, the completion of the great and mighty tree, which was called by his name, to "Him who is over the Head of the bed".' R. Judah said: 'We have a dictum that if a man dies in foreign soil and

Zohar: Bereshith, Section 1, Page 226a

his body is buried in the Holy Land, to him may be applied the verse, "And ye came and defiled my land and my inheritance ye made an abomination" (Jer. II, 7). How, then, could Jacob ask to be buried in the grave of his fathers, seeing that he was dying on alien soil?' R. Judah said: 'Jacob was different, because the Shekinah was closely attached to him. Hence it is written, "I will go down with thee to Egypt" (Gen. XLVI, 4), to wit, to abide with thee in captivity; "and I will also surely bring thee up again" (Ibid.), to attach thy soul to Me, and to obtain burial for thy body in the graves of thy fathers-and this even though he departed life on an alien soil. He was further promised that Joseph should put his hand on his eyes, the reason being that God knew that he was the firstborn in intent, and that he was most attached to Joseph.'

What was the idea of this promise of putting his hands on his eyes? R. Yose said that it was as a sign of honour to Jacob, and to inform him that Joseph was alive and would be with him at his death. Said R. Hizkiah: 'I have learnt something about this which I hardly like to disclose, showing how wisdom is embodied in a common practice.' R. Abba clapped him on the shoulder, saying: 'Speak out and do not be afraid; in the days of R. Simeon there is no need for secrecy.' He then said: 'I have seen in the chapter of R. Jesse the Elder regarding customs, that if a man has a son, when he dies the son ought to put dust on his eyes at the time of his burial, and this is a mark of respect to him, being a sign that the world is now concealed from him, but his son inherits the world in his place. For the human eye represents the world with its various colours. The outer ring of white corresponds to the sea of Oceanus which surrounds the whole world. The next colour represents the land which is surrounded by the sea. A third colour in the middle of the eye corresponds to Jerusalem, which is in the centre of the world. Finally there is the pupil of the eye, which reflects the beholder and is the most precious part of all. This corresponds to Zion, which is the central point of the universe, in which the reflection of the whole world can be seen, and where is the abode of the Shekinah, which is the beauty and the cynosure of the world. Thus the eye is the heritage of the world, and so as the father leaves it the son inherits it.' Said R. Abba: 'You are quite right. But there is still a deeper significance in the practice, although men do not know it. For when a man departs from the world, his soul is still enclosed in him, and before his eyes are closed they see certain recondite things, as we have explained in connection with the verse, "For a man shall not see me and live", indicating that they see things in their death which they do not see in their life-time. Then it behoves those who are present to place their hands on his eyes and close them, and, as we have learnt in connection with customs and manners, if he has a son, it behoves the son in the first place to do so, as it is written, "And Joseph shall put his hand on thy eyes." The reason for the closing of the eyes is because some sight the reverse of holy might present itself, and it is not meet that the eyes which have just beheld a holy vision should now dwell on a sight of a different character. A further reason is that the soul is still attached to him in the house, and if the eye is left open, with that unholy vision still resting upon it, everything it looks upon is cursed; and this is not respectful to the eye, to allow it to gaze upon anything improper. The best sign of respect, therefore, is that a man's eyes should be closed by the hand of the son whom he has left behind him.'

For seven days the soul goes to and fro between the house and the grave, mourning for the body, and three times a day the soul and the body are chastised together, though no one perceives it. After that the body is thrust out and the soul is purified

Zohar: Bereshith, Section 1, Page 226b

in Gehinnom, whence it goes forth roaming about the world and visiting its grave until it acquires a vestment. After twelve months the whole is at rest; the body reposes in the dust and the soul is clad in its luminous vestment. The spirit regales itself in the Garden of Eden, and the higher soul (neshamah) ascends to the place where all delights are concentrated; and all three come together again at certain times. Alas for men that they look not to their foundation, and neglect the precepts of the Torah. For some of these precepts fashion a glorious garment above, and some a glorious garment below, and some a glorious garment in this world; and man requires them all. And they are made literally out of his days, as we have explained. R. Judah the Elder one day saw in a dream his own image illumined and radiating brightly in all directions. 'What is that?' he said; and the answer came: 'It is thy garment for thy habitation here'; whereupon he was in great joy.

R. Judah said: 'Every day the spirits of the righteous sit in rows in the Garden of Eden arrayed in their robes and praise God gloriously, as it is written: "Verily the righteous shall praise thy name the upright shall sit before thee." '

R. Abba said: 'When Jacob "bowed down to Him that is over the bed", as we have explained, and knew that he had reached the highest grade, and that his grade was on high with that of his fathers, and that he was the consummation of the whole, his heart was strengthened and he rejoiced in God's favour towards him. Hence it says, "And Jacob strengthened himself." '

R. Judah said: 'We learn in the Mishnah that judgement is pronounced on the world at four seasons: at Passover, in respect of produce; at Pentecost, in respect of fruit-trees; on New Year, when "all the denizens of the world pass before Him like a flock of sheep"; and on Tabernacles, when the rainfall is determined. This we have esoterically explained as follows. Passover is the time for the decision with regard to cereals, because on Passover Israel began to enter into the holy portion of the Almighty and to remove from themselves the leaven which symbolizes the powers who are appointed over the idol-worshipping nations and who are called "strange gods".

On Pentecost judgement is passed in respect of the fruit of the tree: this is the great and mighty tree which rears itself aloft. On New Year all pass before Him like a flock of sheep, because New Year (lit. head of the year) is the head of the King. On Tabernacles judgement is pronounced in respect of water, because this festival is the beginning of the right hand of the King, and therefore the rejoicing of water is universally diffused.'

Zohar: Bereshith, Section 1, Page 227a

R. Yose said: 'If we look closely, we find that in these periods both the three patriarchs and David can be found, and in these the world is judged. But in truth every day books are open and acts are recorded, though no one notices or inclines his ear, and the Torah testifies against man every day and a voice cries aloud: "Who is simple, let him turn in here", but no one listens. We have learnt that when a man rises in the morning witnesses stand by him and adjure him, but he pays no heed. His higher soul adjures him at all times and seasons. If he heeds her, it is well, but if not, then the books are open and the deeds recorded.' R. Hiya said: 'Happy are the righteous who have no fear of judgement, neither in this world nor in the future world, as it is written: "But the righteous is confident like a lion" (Prov. XXVIII, 1), and again, "the righteous shall inherit the earth" (Ps. XXXVII, 29).' R. Hizkiah, citing the verse, "And when the sun was going down, a deep sleep fell on Abram, etc." (Gen. XV, 12), said: 'This verse has been applied to the day of judgement, when man is removed from this world. For we have learnt that the day when man departs this world is the great day of judgement when the sun's light is withheld from the moon, as it is written, "or ever the sun be darkened" (Eccl. XII, 2). This is the holy neshamah which is withheld from man thirty days before he departs from the world. During that time he observes that he throws no shadow, the reason being that his neshamah is withheld from him. For it does not wait until he is on the point of dying, but even while he is still in his full vigour it passes out of him, and does not illumine the spirit, which in turn does not illumine the vital soul, so that his shadow no longer shows. From that day all proclaim his coming fate, even the birds of the heaven. When the spirit ceases to illumine the vital soul, the latter becomes weak and rejects food and all bodily enjoyments.' R. Judah said further: 'Also whenever a man is on a sick bed and is not able to say his prayers his neshamah leaves him, and the spirit does not illumine the soul until he is judged. If the judgement is favourable, then the neshamah returns to its place and illumines the whole. But when no trial is held, then the neshamah leaves him thirty days before his death and his shadow is withheld. We have learnt that when a man is judged above, his neshamah is brought to trial and she confesses all and testifies to all the thoughts of a man, but not to his deeds, since they are all recorded in a book. While the trial is going on, the body is in greater pain than at other times. If he is judged favourably, he obtains ease and a sweat breaks out over his body, and his neshamah returns to its place and illumines the whole; but a man never rises from his bed of sickness until he is judged above. How is it, then, it may be asked, that so many sinners and transgressors are alive and active? The reason is that God looks ahead, and if he sees that a man, though sinful now, may become virtuous subsequently, He judges him favourably, or it may be because he is destined to bear a son who will be virtuous. All God's judgements incline to beneficence, as it is written: "Have I any pleasure in the death of the wicked, saith the Lord God, and not rather that he should return from his way and live?" (Ezek. XVIII, 23). Sometimes, again, it is because the malady has run its course,

Zohar: Bereshith, Section 1, Page 227b

for illnesses have a fixed period, after which they depart, whether from the righteous or the wicked; and all is done in justice, as we have said.' AND ISRAEL SAW THE SONS OF JOSEPH, AND HE SAID: WHO ARE THESE? This verse seems to contradict the statement a little lower down that "the eyes of Israel were dim for age, so that he could not see". What this verse really means, however, is that he saw through the Holy Spirit those later descendants of Joseph, Jeroboam and his fraternity. Jeroboam made two golden calves and said: "These are thy gods, O Israel" (I Kings XII, 28). Hence Israel now said "Who are these", that is, who is he that will one day say "these" to idols. From this passage we learn that the righteous see into the distant future and God crowns them with His own crown. That God sees the future we learn from the verse: "And God saw all that he had made, and behold, it was very good" (Gen. I, 31), which means that He foresaw all that was to happen before it was commenced. In the same way all the generations of the world from one end to the other stand before Him before they come into the world, as it says, "He calleth the generations from the beginning" (Is. XLI, 4), i.e. from the Creation; all the souls that are to descend into the world stand before God before they descend in the form which they are to assume in this world, and are called by name. In the same way God shows the righteous all generations before they come into the world, as He showed them to Adam, as it is written: "This is the book of the generations of Adam" (Gen. v, 1), and also to Moses, as it says: "And he showed him all the land" (Deut. XXXIV,1), which we interpret to mean that God showed him all coming generations and leaders and prophets. So here with Israel. The words "who are these" have thus a double meaning (literal and metaphorical), and hence Joseph answered: "They are my sons whom God hath given me here." That Israel saw here through the Holy Spirit is proved by the words, "God hath let me see thy seed also", where the augmentative word "also" brings in his descendants, as we have explained. AND HE BLESSED JOSEPH AND SAID. This statement seems inaccurate, since on reading further we find that he did not bless Joseph at all, but only his sons. R. Yose solved the difficulty by stating that in blessing the sons Jacob blessed Joseph also, since the blessing of a man's sons is his own blessing. R. Eleazar said that the object of the verb "blessed" is the particle eth, which alludes to the sign of the covenant. When Joseph said "they are my sons", Jacob blessed that place which symbolizes the Covenant that Joseph kept. In the next words, "The God before whom my fathers Abraham and Isaac did walk", the word God alludes to the holy Covenant, and the elder patriarchs Abraham and Isaac were literally "before" this, because that place derives nourishment and sustenance from them. Jacob continued: THE GOD (Elohim) WHICH HATH FED ME. In repeating the word Elohim, he blessed that place with a reference to Elohim Hayyim (Living God), the source of life and of blessing. On that account he mentioned himself at this point, saying, "the God who blessed me", because all blessings that flow from the source of life are first received by Jacob, and thereupon this place is blessed, and all is made dependent on the male. From here we learn that wherever blessings are to be bestowed, God should be blessed first; otherwise the blessings will not be

Zohar: Bereshith, Section 1, Page 228a

fulfilled. The blessing which Isaac bestowed on Jacob is no exception to this rule, because he said first, "behold the smell of my son is like the smell of a field which the Lord hath blessed", where the field is an allusion to that field which is the source of blessings. Note that in the morning a man should first bless God and only then give his greeting to his fellow-men.

When Jacob was about to bless Joseph's sons, he saw by the Holy Spirit that Jeroboam the son of Nebat would issue from Ephraim, and he exclaimed, "Who are these?", the word "these" (eleh) being an allusion to idols. The reason is that besides the evil serpent there is one that rides on it, and when they are joined together they are called "these", and they visit the world with all their hosts. The Holy Spirit, on the other hand, is called "this", and is symbolized by the covenant of the holy imprint which is ever on a man's body. Hence we find written, "These also shall forget" (Is. XLIX, 15), and again, "For these I am weeping" (Ibid. 16), that sin being the cause to us of endless weeping; or alternatively, because this place was allowed to gain dominion over Israel and to destroy the Temple, the word "I" (ani) in this case referring to the Holy Spirit. It may be asked, on this hypothesis, what are we to make of the words "These are the words of the covenant"? The answer is that the word "these" is here also appropriate, because the words of the covenant are established by "these", since they are the abode of all curses, which await all who transgress the covenant. Similarly it is written, "These are the precepts which the Lord commanded", because the object of all the precepts is to purify man so that he should not stray from the right path and should keep far away from there. Hence, too, it is written, "These are the generations of Noah", because they included Ham the father of Canaan, who was accursed. The spirit of eleh is the "dross of gold". Aaron in the wilderness offered gold, which was his own affinity, since he was endowed with the strength of fire, and fire and gold are all one, but the unclean spirit which haunts the wilderness found at that time a place on which to fasten, and so Israel, after being freed at Mount Sinai from the primeval defilement which brought death into the world, afterwards incurred it again and brought death upon themselves and all their descendants. Hence, when Jacob saw in his mind's eye Jeroboam son of Nebat, who made an idol and said, "These are thy gods, O Israel", he trembled and said, "Who are these?". Hence when he came afterwards to bless them, he first blessed Elohim and then blessed them from that source. R. Judah discoursed here on the text: Then Hezekiah turned his face unto the wall and prayed unto the Lord (Is. XXXVIII, 2). He said: 'We have derived from this verse the lesson that a man in praying should stand near the wall, with nothing intervening between himself and the wall. Now the question may be asked, why does it say of Hezekiah in particular that he turned his face to the wall, and of no one else who offered prayer, though with no less devotion, as, for instance, Moses, of whom it is written that he "prayed to the Lord" (Ibid. XVII, 4), and he "cried to the Lord" (Ex. xv, 25)?

Zohar: Bereshith, Section 1, Page 228b

The reason is as follows. Hezekiah, as tradition tells us, was at that time not married and had no children. Isaiah therefore came to him and said: "Thou shalt die and not live", i.e. as tradition explains, "thou shalt die in this world and not live in the next world". For whoever has not laboured to beget children in this world is not established in the future world, and his soul is banished thence and can nowhere find rest; and this is the punishment referred to in the Law by the words, "They shall die childless" (Lev. xx, 20). Further, the Shekinah does not rest upon him at all. Hence Hezekiah "set his face to the wall", that is to say, he made a resolution to take a wife in order that the Shekinah, which is symbolized by a wall, might rest upon him, and hence the text continues, "and he prayed unto the Lord". From here we learn that anyone who is conscious of a sin for which he means to ask forgiveness should first form a resolution to cure himself of that sin and then offer his prayer, as it is written: "Let us search and try our ways" first, and then, "turn again unto the Lord" (Lam. III, 40). So Hezekiah, recognizing his fault, set his mind to put himself right with the Shekinah, the place against which he sinned. For all females are in the shelter of the Shekinah, and it abides with one who has a wife, but not with one who has none, and therefore Hezekiah first resolved to marry, and then offered his prayer. In regard to the actual language of his prayer, the words "Remember now, O Lord, I beseech thee, how I have walked before thee" allude to the fact of his having kept the holy covenant without defiling it; the words "in truth and with a perfect heart" denote that he clung to all the principles of faith which are comprised under the word "truth", and the words "and have done that which is good in thy sight" indicate that in praying he always concentrated his mind upon declaring the unity of God with full conviction. Finally, Hezekiah "wept sore", because there is no door which remains closed to tears.' THE ANGEL WHO REDEEMED ME FROM ALL EVIL. This is the angel who takes part in every deliverance. R. Eleazar said: 'After Jacob had mentally carried the blessings from the lower to the upper sphere, he then drew them from the upper to the lower. Thus he first said: "The God which hath fed me", and then, having set the blessings in that place, he said "the angel who redeemed me".' R. Eleazar further said: 'It is written: "For the Cherubim spread forth their wings over the place of the ark" (I Kings VIII, 7). The Cherubim were kept in their place miraculously, and three times a day they used to spread out their wings and cover the ark. They were a representation of the upper Cherubim and had the form of children, and they stood beneath that place on the right and the left. They were the first recipients of the blessings which flowed from above, and transmitted them further, and this is the meaning of the words, "the angel who blessed me", that is, the angel first received blessings from the beings above, and with them "blessed the lads", to wit, the Cherubim, and from them blessings were transmitted from the upper to the lower creatures.

Zohar: Bereshith, Section 1, Page 229a

R. Hiya discoursed on the verse: House and wealth are an inheritance from parents, but from the Lord is a prudent wife. (Prov. XIX, 14). 'When God gives a house and money to a man,' he said, 'sometimes he bequeaths the whole to his son, and therefore these things, although they are ultimately from God, may be called "inheritance of parents". But the possession of a good wife comes to man only from God. For God mates couples before they are born, and when a man is worthy he obtains a wife according to his deserts. Sometimes it happens that after the lot has been cast, that man perverts his ways, and then his mate is transferred to another until he rectifies his ways, or else until his time comes, and then the other is removed to make way for him and he comes into his own; and this is grievous in the sight of God, to remove one man to make way for another. Nor is it only a prudent wife who is from God. For if God has purposed to bestow benefits on a man, but he goes astray to the "other side", then from that other side to which he cleaves there shall come to him one who shall bring upon him all accusations and all ills. Hence of the wife who is not prudent Solomon said: "And I find that woman more bitter than death" (Eccl. VII, 26), because it is the man's sins which have drawn her on him. Hence, when God is pleased with a man, he provides for him a wife who is prudent, and redeems him from the other side. Hence Jacob said, "the angel who hath redeemed me from all wrong", meaning that a wife had not been assigned to him from the "other side", and that there was no defect in his seed, all of them being righteous and perfect.' SHALL BLESS THE CHILDREN. They were deserving of blessing because Joseph had kept the sign of the holy covenant. When Joseph said, "they are my sons whom God has given me here", he showed his father the sign of the covenant which he had kept, and therefore they were meet for blessing, and he also was deserving of blessing in abundance. Hence Jacob gave to the others only one blessing, but to Joseph many blessings, as it says, "the blessings of thy father... shall be upon the head of Joseph" (Gen. XLIX, 26).

R. Judah discoursed on the verse: Unto thee do I lift up mine eyes, O thou that sittest in the heavens (Ps. CXXIII, 1). He said: 'Prayer offered with true devotion is directed on high to the supernal recess, from whence issue all blessings and all freedom, to support the universe. It is attached above to the mystery of the supreme Wisdom, and it is attached below to him who sits on the throne of the patriarchs which is called heaven. Hence it is written here: "Who sits in the heavens." When the blessings issue from the supernal recess, they are all received by this place called heaven, and from thence they flow down till they come to the place called the "Righteous One the foundation of the world", from whence are blessed all the (heavenly) hosts and camps after their kind. All these heavenly legions are crowned by seventy-two lights, of which seventy [Tr. note: The seventy Chieftains] form a circle about the world, while in the midst of the circle is a certain point [Tr. note: The Shekinah.] from which the whole of the circumference is fed. The house of the holy of holies is the place

VAYEHI

for that spirit of all spirits, where lies hid the mystery of all mysteries, and when this removes, all move after it.'

As R. Hizkiah and R. Yose and R. Judah were once journeying together, R. Yose said: 'Let each one of us give some exposition of the Torah.' R. Judah thereupon began with the verse, "Remember not against us the iniquities of our forefathers, let thy tender mercies speedily prevent us" (Ps. LXXIX, 8). He said: 'God in His great love for Israel allows no one to sit in judgement on them save Himself, and when He tries them, He is filled with compassion for them like a father for his children, and when He finds they have done wrong, He removes their offences one by one until there are none left to place them in the power of the other side. Hence it says, "let thy mercies prevent us", because otherwise Israel would not be able to exist, in face of all the accusers and all the adversaries who are lying in wait for them above. Hence it continues "for we are very poor", that is, poor in good deeds in the sight of God. For were Israel rich in good deeds before God, idolatrous nations would not be able to exist in the world. It is Israel who enable other nations to hold their head high, because but for their sins the nations would be subdued before them. And, as we have already said, had not Israel by their sins brought the other side into the Holy Land, the idolatrous nations would not have gained possession of it, and Israel would not have been exiled from their land. Hence, because "we are brought very low", therefore "let thy tender mercies speedily prevent us".'

R. Yose discoursed on the verse: "Serve the Lord with gladness, come before his presence with singing" (Ps. c, 2). He said: 'The service of prayer offered by man to the Holy One, blessed be He, should be carried out with gladness and with singing, so that he may associate with him the Community of Israel; and then he should proclaim the unity in the fitting manner, as it says: "Know ye that the Lord he is God" (Ibid. 3). These two activities of gladness and song correspond to the two prayers of morning and afternoon, and to the two daily sacrifices-gladness in the morning and singing in the afternoon. The evening prayer, on the other hand, is optional, because at that time she (the Shekinah) is distributing sustenance to all her hosts, and it is not the time for blessing. In the daytime she is to be blessed from these two sides, morning and afternoon, out of gladness and singing, and at night time she divides the blessings among all in the fitting manner.'

R. Hizkiah took for his text the verse: "Let my prayer be established like incense before thee, the lifting of my hands like the evening oblation" (Ps. CXLI, 2). He said: 'It may be asked, why did David mention here the oblation of the evening rather than

of the morning? The answer may be given as follows. The offering of incense betokens joy, as it is written, "oil and incense rejoice the heart" (Prov. XXVII, 9). Hence the high priest, when he lit the candlestick, used to offer incense morning and evening (Ex. xxx, 7, 8); in the morning, because that is the natural season of joy, and in the evening to rejoice the left side, as befits. We see, then, that incense always betokened joy. Further, the incense links and unites upper and lower, and so removes death and wrath and accusation from the world and prevents them from prevailing over it; it was through the incense that Aaron stayed the plague. Hence the incense symbolizes universal joy and universal union. Now David offered the prayer we have quoted at the time of the afternoon oblation, when the world is under the aegis of justice, and he meant it to ascend and remove the wrath that was prevalent at that hour like the incense which removes wrath and accusation; hence he mentioned the "oblation of eventide", the time when punishment descends on the world. Observe that the Temple was burnt at the time of the evening oblation, as it is written: "Woe to us because the day hath declined and the shadows of evening stretch out" (Jer. VI, 3). The "shadows of evening" are the accusers and the punishments which are abroad at that hour. Hence we have learnt that a man should say the afternoon prayer with special devotion, even more than other prayers. Hence, too, it was that Isaac instituted the afternoon prayer, as we have already explained.'

As they proceeded they came to a mountain. Said R. Yose: 'This mountain is very formidable, let us keep clear of it.' Said R. Judah: 'If I were alone I should think the same, since we have learnt that he who travels alone makes his life forfeit. But this does not apply to three, all the more seeing that each one of us is worthy to be accompanied by the Shekinah.' Said R. Yose: 'But we have learnt that a man should not rely on a miracle, since even Samuel said: "How can I go? If Saul hear it, he will kill me" (I Sam. XVI, 2), and he was more worthy than we are.' He replied: 'Even so, he was by himself and the danger was obvious, whereas we are three and there is no danger actually in sight. For if it is evil spirits you are afraid of, we have learnt that they do not show themselves to three or harm them, and if it is robbers, there are none here, because this mountain is far from any inhabited spot, and people never pass here. The only thing we have to be afraid of is wild beasts. Scripture speaks of "the angel who redeemed me from all evil". This angel is the Shekinah, who continually accompanies a man and leaves him not so long as he keeps the precepts of the Law. Hence a man should be careful not to go on the road alone, that is to say, he should diligently keep the precepts of the Law in order that he may not be deserted by the Shekinah, and so be forced to go alone without the accompaniment of the Shekinah. Hence, before starting on a journey a man should first address his prayer to God in order that he may draw the Shekinah to himself, to be protected by it on the road and delivered from all harm. So Jacob, on setting out, said: "If God shall be with me", i.e. if the Shekinah will accompany me, "and keep me in this way" (Gen. XXVIII, 20), to deliver me from all harm. Now Jacob was alone

Zohar: Bereshith, Section 1, Page 230b

at that time, but the Shekinah went with him; all the more so then will it accompany the Companions who discourse on the Torah.' Said R. Yose: 'What are we to do? If we remain here we shall be overtaken by night; if we commence to ascend, the mountain is very high, and there is danger from wild beasts.' Said R. Judah: 'I am surprised at you, R. Yose.' He replied: 'We have learnt that a man should not rely on a miracle, for God does not perform miracles at all times.' He answered: 'That applies only when a man is by himself. But we are three, and words of Torah pass between us and the Shekinah is with us; therefore we have no need to fear.'

As they went on, they perceived on the mountain a rock in which was a cave. Said R. Judah: 'Let us go up to yonder rock, as I see there a cave.' So they went up there. Said R. Yose: 'Perhaps there are wild beasts in this cave which will attack us.' Said R. Judah to R. Hizkiah: 'Why is R. Yose so afraid? He is not a sinner that he should fear, and we read that "the righteous is bold like a lion" (Prov. XXVIII, 1).' R. Yose said: 'It is because we are willfully exposing ourselves to danger.' He replied: 'If that were so, you would be right, but there is no danger apparent here, and once we enter the cave no danger will follow us.' So they went into the cave. R. Judah then said: 'Let us divide the night into three watches, and let each one of us stand to his post in one of them, and let us all keep awake.'

R. Judah then commenced with the text: "Maskil to Ethan the Ezrahite" (Ps. LXXXIX, 1). He said: 'This psalm was uttered by our father Abraham when he devoted himself to the service of his Master and conferred on mankind the boon of teaching them to acknowledge God as ruler of the world; and he was called Ethan (lit. strong) because he clung strongly to God. "I will sing of the mercies of the Lord forever." Song comes from the side of the Left, not of Hesed (Mercy); so by this exordium the side of the Left was embraced in the Right. It was for this purpose (to combine Left with Right) that God tried Abraham, in order that he might be found to unite justice with mercy, and so be perfect. Hence he could say: "I will sing of the mercies of the Lord forever." He continued: "With my mouth will I make known thy faithfulness to all generations." This refers to the faithfulness of God in making Abraham known in the world and causing his name to be in the mouth of all creatures. God made known to Abraham the true principle of faith, and he thereupon realized that he was the foundation and support of the universe. For when God created the universe, He saw that it could not endure unless He stretched forth His right hand to it. For this world was created under the aegis of justice, and it was not established save by the right hand. Hence Abraham continued: "I said, the world is built up on mercy (hesed)", the first step in the building up of the world having been the light of the first day. Then on the second day the Left came into play and with it was established the heaven, as it says: "Thou establishest the heavens, thy faithfulness is in them." (This may also be explained to mean that the heavens were established by those mercies of the first day, and that the mystery of faith was established in them, the heavens being the bulwark of faith.) The text continues: "I have made a covenant with my chosen.' This covenant is the secret of faith. Or we may interpret the "chosen one" of

Zohar: Bereshith, Section 1, Page 231a

the Zaddik from whom issue blessings to all the lower creation, all the holy Hayyoth being blessed from the stream which flows forth to the lower world. "I have sworn unto David my servant", to wit, that he will always be established in this Zaddik, the foundation of the world, save in the time of galuth, when the flow of blessing is cut off, and faith is defective, and all joy is banished. During this period, at nightfall, joy no longer enters before the King. Yet, though rejoicings do not enter, angels stand outside and chant hymns, and at midnight when the impulse from below arrives on high, God arouses all the hosts of the heaven for lamentation and strikes the firmament, causing upper and lower worlds to quake; nor is there any respite save when those below commence to study the Torah. Then God and all those with Him listen with joy to that voice, and relief is felt. For on the day on which the Sanctuary below was destroyed, God swore that He would not enter the celestial Jerusalem until Israel should enter the earthly Jerusalem. Now all those singers stand outside and chant hymns in the three watches of the night and intone praises, and all the hosts of the heavens sing at night and Israel by day, nor is the sanctification recited above until it is recited by Israel below, and only then do all the hosts of heaven sanctify the holy name together. Hence, Israel are holy and are sanctified by upper and lower angels, since the sanctification of the holy name is complete only when uttered above and below together.'

R. Yose discoursed on the verse: Whereupon were the foundations thereof fastened? (Job XXXVIII, 6). He said: 'When God created the world, He established it on seven pillars, but upon what those pillars rest no one may know, since it is a recondite and inscrutable mystery. The world did not come into being until God took a certain stone, which is called the "foundation stone", and cast it into the abyss so that it held fast there, and from it the world was planted. This is the central point of the universe, and on this point stands the holy of holies. This is the stone referred to in the verses, "Who laid the corner-stone thereof" (Ibid. 6), "the stone of testing, the precious corner-stone" (Is. XXVIII, 16), and "the stone that the builders despise became the head of the corner" (Ps. CXVIII, 22). This stone is compounded of fire, water, and air, and rests on the abyss. Sometimes water flows from it and fills the deep. This stone is set as a sign in the centre of the world. It is referred to in the words, "And Jacob took a stone and set it as a pillar" (Gen. XXXI, 45). Not that he took this stone, which was created from the beginning, but he established it above and below, by making there a "house of God". This stone has on it seven eyes, as it is written, "On one stone seven eyes" (Zech. III, 9), and it is called "foundation stone", for one thing because the world was planted from it, and for another because God set it as a source of blessing to the world. Now at sunset, the Cherubim which stood in that place used to strike their wings together and spread them out, and when the sound of the beating of their wings was heard above, those angels who chanted hymns in the night began to sing, in order that the glory of God might ascend from below on high. The striking of the Cherubim's wings itself intoned the psalm, "Behold, bless ye the Lord, all ye servants of the Lord... lift up your hands to the sanctuary, etc." (Ps. CXXXIII). This was the signal for the heavenly angels to commence. At the second watch

Zohar: Bereshith, Section 1, Page 231b

the Cherubim again beat their wings, giving the signal to the angels of that watch. The psalm of the Cherubim this time was "They that trust in the Lord are like Mount Zion, etc." (Ps. cxxv). At the third watch the Cherubim beat their wings to the words "Hallelukah, praise, O servants of the Lord, praise the name of the Lord" (Ps. CXIII), and then the angels of the third watch commenced to sing, and also all the stars and constellations of the heaven, as it is written: "When the morning stars sung together and all the sons of God shouted for joy" (Job XXXVIII, 7), and also, "Praise him, all ye stars of light" (Ps. CXLVIII, 3), these being the radiant stars which are appointed to sing at dawn. After them Israel take up the chant below, and so the glory of God ascends both from below and from above, from Israel below in the day, and from the celestial angels above in the night, and so the name of God is fully praised on all sides. As for this stone that we have mentioned, all the angels above and Israel below take hold on it, and it ascends to be crowned in the midst of the patriarchs by day. At night the Holy One, blessed be He, comes to disport Himself with the righteous in the Garden of Eden. Blessed are those who stand at their posts and study the Torah at night, because God and all the righteous in the Garden of Eden listen to the voice of those sons of men who study the Torah.'

That stone we have mentioned is a goodly stone, and it is hinted at in the verse "And thou shalt set in it a setting of stone, four rows of stone" (Ex. XXVIII, 17), because there is another stone of which it is written "And I shall remove the heart of stone, etc." (Ezek. XXXVI, 26). The two tablets of stone were also hewn from this stone; and this was also called "the stone of Israel" (Gen. XLIX, 24), as has been explained. R. Hizkiah quoted the verse: "And the stone shall be according to the names of the children of Israel, twelve" (Ex. XXVIII, 21). He said: 'These are the precious supernal stones which are called "the stones of the place" (Gen. XXVIII, 11). They were "according to the names of the children of Israel" because just as there are twelve tribes below, so there are twelve tribes above, which are twelve precious stones; and therefore it is written: "Whither the tribes go up, even the tribes of the Lord, for a testimony unto Israel" (Ps. CXXII, 4), the reference being to the supernal Israel. Further, just as there are twelve hours in the day, so there are twelve hours in the night, in the day above and in the night below, each corresponding to each. These twelve hours of the night are divided into three sets, to each of which belong hierarchies of angels, which take their portion first. Hence, at midnight two ranks stand on one side and two on the other, and a celestial spirit goes forth between them and then all the trees in the garden break forth into song and God enters the garden, as it says: "Then do all the trees of the wood sing for joy before the Lord, for he cometh to judge the earth" (I Chron. XVI, 33), because judgement enters among them and the Garden of Eden is filled therewith. Then the north wind springs up, bringing joy in its train, and it blows through the spice trees and wafts their perfume, and the righteous put on their crowns and feast themselves on the brightness of the "pellucid mirror" - happy are they to be vouchsafed that celestial light! The light of this mirror shines on all sides, and each one of the righteous takes his appropriate portion, each according to his works in this world; and some of them are abashed because of the superior light obtained by their neighbours.

Zohar: Bereshith, Section 1, Page 232a

When night commences, numbers of officers of judgement arise and roam about the world, and the doors are closed, as we have affirmed. Thus at midnight the side of the north comes down and takes possession of the night until two-thirds of it have passed. Then the side of the south awakes until morning, and then both south and north take hold of it (the Shekinah). Then come Israel here below, and with their prayers and supplications raise it up until it ascends and hides itself among them, and receives blessings from the fountain-head.'

While they were sitting midnight arrived, and R. Judah said to R. Yose: 'Now the north wind awakes and the night is divided, and now is the time when the Holy One, blessed be He, longs for the voice of the righteous in this world, the voice of those who study the Torah. Now God is listening to us in this place; therefore let us not cease from discoursing on the Torah.' He then commenced: THE ANGEL WHO DELIVERED ME FROM ALL EVIL. This is the same as the one mentioned in the verse: "Behold I send an angel before thee, etc." (Ex. XXIII, 20), who, as we have laid down, is the deliverer of the world, the protector of mankind, and the one who procures blessings for all the world, he himself receiving them first. This angel is sometimes male, sometimes female. When he procures blessings for the world, he is male, resembling the male who provides blessings for the female. But when he comes to bring chastisement on the world he is called female, being, as it were, pregnant with the judgement. Similarly, in the words, "the flame of the sword which turned every way" (Gen III, 24), there is a reference to the angels who are God's messengers, and who turn themselves into different shapes, being sometimes female and sometimes male, sometimes messengers of judgement and sometimes of mercy. In the same way, this angel can take all colours like the rainbow, and treats the world correspondingly.

Zohar: Bereshith, Section 1, Page 232b

R. Yose discoursed on the verse: The king's strength also loveth judgement, thou dost establish equity, etc. (Ps. XCIX, 4) 'The king', he said, 'is God, who loves judgement and takes fast hold of it, because by judgement the earth is established. By judgement, too, the Community of Israel is confirmed and established, because from there it is sustained, and receives all its blessings. Hence all its desire and all its longing is for judgement. The words "Thou dost establish equity (mesharim, lit. straightnesses)" refer to the two cherubim below who render the world safe and habitable.'

R. Hizkiah discoursed on the verse: Praise ye the Lord (Hallelukah), praise, O ye servants of the Lord, praise the name of the Lord. 'The repetition of the word "praise" in this verse', he said, 'seems somewhat pointless, but there is a reason for it. We have been taught that a eulogy should not be extravagant, and that to ascribe to another merits which he does not possess is really to reproach him; and, therefore, in recounting the praises of a deceased person, we should say only what he deserves and no more, otherwise through trying to praise we shall really blame him. Now the word Hallelukah (lit. praise ye Kah) contains the highest of all the praises of the Lord, mentioning, as it does, the place to which no eye can penetrate, being most recondite and inscrutable. This is Kah, the name which is supreme above all. Hence this psalm commences with "Hallelukah", a word in which praise and name are combined. Further, the subject of the word "praise" is not specified, but just as the name Kah is undisclosed, so those who praise it are undisclosed, and so it is fitting that all should be undisclosed in the realm of the supreme mystery. But the psalmist then continues: "Praise, O ye servants of the Lord, praise the name of the Lord", because this is a place which is not undisclosed, a place which is called "Name". The first is completely undisclosed, the second half undisclosed, half disclosed, and therefore the psalmist specified those who praised that place, and said that they are "the servants of the Lord", who are meet to praise this place. The text continues "Blessed be (Yehi) the name of the Lord." The word yehi consists of the name Kah and the letter yod, and indicates the continuity between that supernal and inscrutable place which is Kah and the grade of the covenant which is the lower yod. For this reason the word yehi (let there be) in the account of the Creation, is used only of the upper productions, e.g. "let there be light", 'let there be a firmament", "let there be lights", but it is not used in connection with the

Zohar: Bereshith, Section 1, Page 233a

lower productions. So by this word the Holy Name is blessed in all. The text continues: "From the rising of the sun unto the going down thereof." The "rising" is the supernal place from which the sun derives light to shine over all, the place of the supernal and hidden fountainhead. The "setting" is the place to which faith is attached, from which blessings issue to all, and from which the world is sustained, as has been affirmed. The whole depends upon the impulse from below which is given by the service of the Lord when they bless the Holy Name, as we have said.'

By this time the morning had dawned, and so they came out of the cave, not having slept the whole night. They went on their way, and when they got beyond the hills they sat down and said their prayers. They then came to a village, where they stayed the whole day. At night they slept till midnight, when they rose to study the Torah. R. Judah began: AND HE BLESSED THEM ON THAT DAY, SAYING: IN THEE SHALL ISRAEL BLESS, SAYING. 'The expression that day" has an esoteric meaning, and signifies the grade which is in charge of blessings above, the "day" from the supernal place which is called "That" (Hu). Hence we translate "by the day of That", indicating that there is no separation between "day" and "That". The two signify an upper grade and a lower grade in conjunction. Thus Jacob blessed the sons of Joseph with the union of upper and lower in order that the blessings might be unalterable. He then completed the conjunction by saying, "in thee shall Israel bless". The name Israel here refers to the patriarch Israel. This Israel receives blessings from above and then blesses all through this lower grade. Hence he said "God make thee as Ephraim and Manasseh", putting Ephraim first because Ephraim were called Israel, as it is written: "Son of man, these bones are the whole house of Israel" (Ezek. XXXVII, 11), where the reference according to tradition is to the members of the tribe of Ephraim who were killed when they tried to break out of the captivity of Egypt before the time. For that reason, too, the tribe of Ephraim in the wilderness journeyed on the west. [Tr. note: Which was regarded as the side of the Shekinah.] Note that Israel blessed the sons of Joseph before he blessed his own sons, which shows that a man loves his grandchildren more than his children.' R. Yose said: 'It is written: "The Lord hath remembered us, he will bless, he will bless the house of Israel." The first "he will bless" refers to the men, and the "house of Israel" to the women, because the women derive blessings only from the blessings of the men. Alternatively, this lesson may be derived from the verse:

"He shall make atonement for himself and for his house" (Lev. XVI, 6)-for himself first and for his house afterwards. In this case we may interpret the words "He shall bless the house of Israel" to mean that God gives extra blessings to a man who is married, in order that his wife may be blessed through him,

Zohar: Bereshith, Section 1, Page 233b

and so he receives two portions, one for himself and one for his wife.'

R. Hizkiah discoursed on the verse: "Thine eyes did see mine imperfect substance, and in thy book they were all written, etc." (Ps. CXXXIX, 16). 'This verse', he said, 'has been frequently expounded. All the souls which came into existence when the world was created stand before God before coming down in that same form in which they afterwards appear in the world, since that bodily appearance of man which he had in this world is also found above. When this soul is about to descend into the world, it stands before God in the form which it is to assume in the world, and God adjures it to keep the precepts of the law and not to transgress them. Hence it says: "Thine eyes saw mine imperfect form" before it appeared in the world, "and in thy book they were all written", that is to say, all the souls in their forms are recorded in the book. The text proceeds: "The days are fashioned and there is not one among them", that is, there is not one day of them in this world which can stand before its Master as it should. For when a man is virtuous in this world his days are blessed above, from that place which is the measure of his days, mentioned in the verse, "Show me, O Lord, mine end, and what is the measure of my days" (Ps. XXXIX, 5). The "end" here is the "end of the right", which was united with David, and the "measure of my days" was the power in charge of his days.' R. Judah said: 'I have heard from R. Simeon that this verse refers to the days which were assigned to him out of the life of Adam, namely seventy years, since it has been affirmed that David had no life of his own, but Adam gave him seventy years of his life. David therefore prayed to know why it was that he had no life of his own, and continued, "Let me know how fleeting I am", that is to say, why, like the moon, I am without light of my own, unlike all those celestial lights which all have their own life. This is what David sought to know, but permission was not given to him. Observe that all celestial blessings were delivered to this grade to transmit to all creatures, and although it has no light of its own, all blessings and all joy and all goodness are contained in it and issue from it, and therefore is it called "the cup of blessing", or even simply "blessing", as it is written, "The blessing of the Lord maketh rich" (Prov. x, 22). Therefore it has a residue from all and is filled from all; it receives

Zohar: Bereshith, Section 1, Page 234a

of the supernal blessings to transmit them further.' Said R. Isaac: 'We know this from the fact that Jacob blessed the sons of Joseph from the place from which all blessings had been delivered into his hand to transmit.' AND JACOB CALLED TO HIS SONS AND SAID: GATHER YOURSELVES TOGETHER, ETC. R. Abba discoursed on the verse: He turned to the prayer of the lonely one and did not despise their prayer (Ps. CII, 18). He said: 'The use of the word "turned" here, instead of "hearkened" or "listened", is significant. The prayer of an individual man only enters before the Holy King with great difficulty, because before it can be crowned in its place God examines it closely and weighs the merits and defects of that individual. He does not so with the prayer of a congregation; for congregational prayers are offered by many who are not virtuous, and yet they all come before God and He does not regard their sins. Therefore it says, "God turns to the prayer of the solitary one" and weighs and considers it, and examines in what spirit it is offered and who is the man that offers it, and what is his conduct. Hence a man should pray with the congregation because "God does not despise their prayer", even though they do not all pray with devotion. According to another explanation, the word "solitary" here refers to an individual who is united with numbers, to wit, Jacob, who was united with two sides, and who called his sons and prayed for them that they might be acceptable above and not be destroyed in the captivity. When Jacob called his sons, Abraham and Isaac were there and the Shekinah with them, rejoicing in Jacob, and in the prospect of joining the patriarchs

Zohar: Bereshith, Section 1, Page 234b

and forming with them a chariot. When Jacob said to his sons, "I will tell you what will befall you in the latter end of days", a kind of sadness came over him and the Shekinah departed. His sons, however, raised their voices and said, "Hear, O Israel, etc.", and Jacob answered, "Blessed be the name of his glorious kingdom forever and ever", and on this proclamation of the unity the Shekinah returned to its place. AND JACOB CALLED. The word ' called ' signifies that he established them in their place above and below. Similarly, Moses "called Hosea son of Nun, Joshua" (Num. XIII, 16) to establish him in his proper place. There is a similar significance in the expressions "And he called his name Jacob" (Gen. xxv, 26) and "the God of Israel called him El" (Gen. XXXIII, 20). So, too, "I called from my sorrow unto the Lord" (Jonah, III, 7), signifying that one who praises his Master and addresses supplications to Him establishes his Master more firmly, by showing that all depends upon Him and not upon any other power. AND HE SAID. It has been laid down that "saying" means "thinking", as in the expression "And thou shalt say in thy heart" (Deut. VII, 17). ASSEMBLE YOURSELVES; that is, in complete harmony. AND I SHALL TELL YOU. The word "tell" (agidah) contains an allusion to the esoteric wisdom. He sought to reveal to them their final destiny. It may be asked, seeing that he did not reveal what he sought to reveal, why are his words, which were afterwards belied, recorded in the Scripture? The truth is that all that was needful to be revealed is completely stated, and there is a hidden meaning within, and so nothing in the Scripture is belied. In fact, everything is included in the Scripture, and there is no word or letter short in it. Jacob said all that was needful for him to say, but not all openly, and not a letter was short of what was required. R. Judah and R. Yose were one day sitting at the gate of Lydda. Said the latter: 'We are told that Jacob blessed his sons, but what are the blessings?' R. Judah answered: 'He did indeed bless them, as, for instance, "Judah, thee shall thy brethren praise", "Dan shall judge his people", "Out of Asher his bread shall be fat", and so forth; but what he sought to reveal to them he did not reveal, namely, the end. We have laid down that there is an end to the right and an end to the left, and he sought to reveal to them the end (of the left) in order that they might keep themselves

Zohar: Bereshith, Section 1, Page 235a

pure from uncleanness. What he revealed to them referred only to the time when they were in the Holy Land; later things were not stated openly, but are only hinted at in this section and in these blessings.' REUBEN, THOU ART MY FIRSTBORN, MY MIGHT AND THE BEGINNING OF MY STRENGTH. Why did Jacob begin with Reuben and not rather with Judah, who was the leader of the camps and also king? Further we see that he did not bless him, nay, that he removed blessings from him till Moses came and prayed for him, as it is written: "Let Reuben live and not die" (Deut. XXXIII, 6). The fact is, however, that he did bless him, but kept the blessing for its proper place. He was like a man who had a son, and when he was about to die was visited by the king, whereupon he said: "Let all my money remain in the king's hands on behalf of my son, and when the king sees that my son is worthy he will give it to him." So Jacob said: "Reuben, thou art my firstborn, the beloved of my soul; but thy blessings shall remain in the hand of the Holy King until He shall see that thou art worthy of them, because 'thou didst go after the sight of thine eyes, etc.'" (according to Chaldaic paraphrase of this passage).

R. Eleazar here discoursed on the verse: And he said to me: Prophesy unto the wind, etc. (Ezek. XXXVII, 9). 'There is a difficulty here,' he said, 'because the text continues: "Prophesy, son of man, and say to the wind", which seems a repetition. The truth is, however, that there is here an esoteric lesson. There are two adjurations here. One is to give the impulse from below, since if there is no impulse from below there is no stirring above. Hence the words "Prophesy unto the wind" indicate the impulse from below, and the words "Prophesy, son of man, and say" to the impulse from above; for even after the impulse is given from below, that which is above receives from that which is higher still, wherefore the verse continues "Thus saith the Lord." The text then goes on: "Come from the four winds, O breath." The four winds are south, east, north, and west, and the breath comes from the west through its conjunction with the others, and from this source issue spirits and souls to take shape in human form. The next word, "breathe", indicates taking from one side and giving to another, in the same way as the sea takes and gives, and therefore "is not full" (Eccl. I, 7).'

R. Eleazar put the following question to R. Simeon. 'Since it is known to God that men will die, why does He send souls down into the world?' He answered: 'This question has been discussed many times by the teachers, and they have answered it thus. God sends souls down to this world to declare His glory and takes them back afterwards. This mystery can be explained from the verse: "Drink water from thy cistern and flowing streams from the midst of thy well" (Prov. v, 15). As we have laid down, the term "cistern" designates the place from which the waters do not naturally flow. But they do flow when the soul is perfected in this world and ascends to the place to which it is attached, for then it is complete on all sides, above and below. When the soul ascends, the desire of the female is stirred towards the male, and then water flows from below upwards, and the cistern becomes a well of flowing waters, and then there is union-and foundation and desire and friendship and harmony, since through the soul of the righteous that place has been completed, and the supernal love and affection has been stirred to form a union.'

Observe that Reuben and all the rest of the twelve tribes were linked with the Shekinah, and when Jacob saw the Shekinah by him, he called to his twelve sons to join it. From the beginning of the world there was never so perfect a couch as that of Jacob when he was about

Zohar: Bereshith, Section 1, Page 235b

to depart from the world. Abraham was on his right, Isaac on his left, and he was lying between them with the Shekinah in front of him. When Jacob saw this, he called his sons and placed them round the Shekinah and arranged them in perfect order, so that the gathering was complete and many supernal chariots encompassed them. They then exclaimed: "Thine, O Lord, is the greatness and the power and the glory, etc." (I Chron. XXIX, 11), whereupon the sun joined the moon and the east drew near to the west, and the moon was illumined and attained fullness, and so, as tradition tells us, "Jacob our father did not die." When Jacob saw such perfection as had never been vouchsafed to any other man, he rejoiced and praised God and blessed each of his sons with the appropriate blessing.

R. Yose and R. Jesse were once walking together, when the latter said: 'We have learnt that all the sons of Jacob were arranged in proper order and were blessed each one with the appropriate blessing. What, then, are we to make of the verse: "Out of Asher his bread shall be fat"?' He answered: 'I do not know, because I have not learnt this from the Holy

Lamp. But let us both go to the Holy Lamp.' So they went, and when they came to R. Simeon they put their question to him. He said to them: 'Assuredly there is an esoteric meaning here. It is written: "Asher sat still at the haven of the sea, and abode by his creeks" (Judg. v, 17). He who dwells by the seashore has access to all luxuries, and Asher here signifies the supernal gate of Zedek (righteousness) when it receives blessings to transmit them to the world. This gate is always commissioned to send blessings to the world, and is called Asher, and it is one of the pillars upon which the world stands, and it repairs that place which is called "bread of affliction". This, then, is the meaning of the words "Out of Asher his bread is fat", that is to say, that which was bread of poverty becomes food of luxury, and hence the verse continues, "and he shall yield royal dainties": the giver here is the Community of Israel, by whom the king is fed with all luxuries, all blessings, all joy, and all goodness.' They said: 'If we had been born only to hear this, it would have been worthwhile.'

R. Hiya said: 'Reuben was entitled to all the rights of a firstborn, but they were all taken from him and the kingship was given to Judah, the birthright to Joseph, and the priesthood to Levi. Hence it is written: "Unstable as water, thou shalt not excel" (tothar, lit. be left over); that is, thou shalt not retain them. In calling him "my might and the beginning of my strength", Jacob blessed him and entrusted him to God. He was like a king's friend who desired that the king should treat his son well, so one day he went out with his son and said to the king: "This is my son, the beloved of my soul"; whereupon the king understood that he was asking him to treat his son well. So Jacob said of Reuben, "thou art my firstborn, etc.", thus commending him to the King. UNSTABLE AS WATER, THOU SHALT NOT HAVE THE EXCELLENCY. Here he indicated his subsequent fate, in not being left in the land, but cast outside. [Tr. note: Because the territory of Reuben was across the Jordan.] In return, there was an angel appointed over his border from the side of the supernal Tabernacle, which is in charge of Michael (according to others, Gabriel), and Reuben was next to this, although the kingship belonged to Judah. R. Simeon said: 'The sons of Reuben are destined to wage two wars. It is written here "my strength", alluding to the captivity of Egypt, and "the beginning of my strength", alluding to their entry into ths land of Canaan at the head of their brethren (Num. XXXII). The words "the excellency of dignity" (lit. removing) refer to the captivity of Assyria, which befell the sons of Gad and the sons of Reuben first of all; and they have suffered many evils without repenting up to now. The words "the excellency of power" refer to the time when the Messiah will appear, and they will go forth and make war and conquer all peoples, and mankind will tremble before them;

Zohar: Bereshith, Section 1, Page 236a

and they will endeavour to seize the kingship, but will not retain it, not in any quarter of the world, the reason being, as the text says, "because thou wentest up to thy father's bed", this being a reference to Jerusalem. The sons of Reuben have been scattered in captivity to all four quarters of the world, having been taken captive four times, one referred to in the words "my might", the second in the words "the beginning of my strength", the third in the words "excellency of dignity", and the fourth in the words "excellency of strength". Correspondingly, they are destined to make war in the four quarters of the world and to carry all before them, and to conquer many peoples and rule over them. Here was revealed his blessing, and what happened at that time and what was to happen when Israel entered the land, and what will happen at the time of the Messiah, as far as concerns Reuben. SIMEON AND LEVI ARE BRETHREN. R. Isaac said: He joined them to the left side of the Shekinah, since he saw deeds of vengeance which the world could not endure.' R. Yose said: 'Where is their blessing?' R. Isaac answered: 'Simeon was not meet for a blessing, since Jacob saw that he had wrought much evil; nor was Levi, because he came from the side of stern justice, and blessing did not attach to him. Even Moses did not bless him directly, but left it to the Almighty, as it is written: "Bless, Lord, his substance and accept the work of his hands" (Deut. XXXIII, 11). It is written: "Yonder is the sea, great and wide, wherein are things creeping innumerable, both small and great beasts" (Ps. CIV, 25). The "sea" refers to the Shekinah, which stood over Jacob when he was about to depart from the world. It is called "great and wide" because all the world was compressed into it. There were "creeping things innumerable", because numbers of celestial holy angels are found there; while the "small and great beasts" refer to the twelve tribes, the sons of Jacob, of whom one was called a hind, one a wolf, one a lion, and one a lamb.' R. Isaac said: 'First a lion, then a lamb, then a wolf, then a kid, and so forth, so that there should be great and small beasts.' R. Judah said: 'Simeon was an ox and came before Judah, who was a lion, and the Companions have laid down that they faced one another, one on the right and one on the left. It was as if a man had a vicious ox and said: Let us put the figure of a lion in his stall so that he shall see it and be afraid of it. Simeon was not meet for blessing, but Moses joined him to Judah, saying: "Hear, O Lord, the voice of Judah"; the word "hear" alluding to Simeon, at whose birth his mother said "For the Lord hath heard that I am hated." ' Said R. Judah: 'The blessing of Simeon and Levi was left by their father to Moses. Let us also leave this question to the Holy Lamp.' So they went and asked R. Simeon. He said: 'How glad I am you have asked me.' He then clapped his hands and wept, saying: 'Who shall ope thine eyes, thou holy mirror of faith! Thou hast excelled in thy lifetime all the sons of men, thou hast excelled them in thy death, when thy likeness is effaced. The keys of thy Master have ever been delivered into thy hands. Observe now. Jacob had four wives and begat sons from all of them.

281

Zohar: Bereshith, Section 1, Page 236b

When he was about to die the Shekinah stood over him. He sought to bless these two, but he was not able, being afraid of the Shekinah. He said: "What shall I do, seeing that both of them are from the side of stern judgement? And if I try to force the Shekinah, I shall not be able, for I have had four wives, which are a complete portion. I will leave them to the master of the house and he will do as he pleases." He also said: "I have taken my share of wives and children in this world and have had my fill; how, then, shall I press the matron more? I will therefore leave the matter to the master of the matron and he will do what he pleases without fear." Hence it is written: "Now this is the blessing wherewith Moses the man of God blessed" (Deut. XXXIII, 1). The term "man" here designates Moses as the master of the house and the master of the matron. Hence Moses blessed whom he pleased without fear, as we have affirmed.' O MY SOUL, COME NOT THOU INTO THEIR COUNCIL . R. Abba discoursed on the verse: The secret of the Lord is for them that fear him. '"The secret of the Lord"', he said, 'is the recondite doctrine of the Torah which God only gives to those who fear sin, and it is the sign of the holy covenant. Simeon and Levi insisted that the men of Shechem should circumcise themselves and accept this secret, and the Scripture tells us that it was "with guile". Later, Zimri, the son of Salu, who was of the tribe of Simeon, nullified this secret. Hence Jacob said: "Let not my soul enter into their secret" -that soul which entered into the supernal covenant above and was called ' the bundle of life'. UNTO THEIR ASSEMBLY, MY GLORY BE NOT THOU UNITED. This has been explained to refer to the assembly of Korah (Num. XVI, 1). "My honour" here refers to the honour of the people of Israel in general, and therefore their father did not bless them, but left them to Moses. I WILL DIVIDE THEM IN JACOB. R. Hiya said: 'From this verse we learn that these two tribes were never again united, and so it was meet, and there is no generation in which their punishment does not descend upon the world, and great is the number of beggars among them.' JUDAH, THEE SHALL THY BRETHEN PRAISE, THY HAND SHALL BE ON THE NECK OF THY ENEMIES.

R. Yose discoursed here on the verse: He made the moon for seasons (Ps. CIV, 19). 'God', he said, 'made the moon for us to sanctify by it new moons and new years. Now the moon never shines except from the reflection of the sun, and when the sun is aloft the moon does not appear, but only when the sun is gathered in does the moon rule the heavens, and the moon is of no account save when the sun is gathered in. God made both of them to give light and also "for signs", to wit, Sabbaths, "and for seasons", to wit, festivals, "and for days", to wit, new moons, "and for years", to wit, New Year days, so that the Gentiles should reckon by the sun and Israel by the moon. This accords with R. Eleazar's exposition of the verse: "Thou hast multiplied the nation, thou hast increased its joy" (Is. IX, 2), where he refers "nation" to Israel and "it" to the moon, which gained accession of light for the sake of Israel. Which are superior, Israel or the Gentiles? Assuredly, the moon

Zohar: Bereshith, Section 1, Page 237a

is highest, and the sun of the Gentiles is under this moon, and this sun derives light from this moon. See, then, the difference between Israel and the nations. Israel cling to the moon and are linked with the supernal sun, and are attached to the place which gives light to the supernal sun, as it is written: "But ye who cleave to the Lord, are alive every one of you this day" (Deut. IV, 4.' JUDAH, THEE SHALL THY BRETHREN PRAISE. R. Simeon said: 'The kingship was assigned to Judah; and hence Leah, as we have explained, said at the time of his birth: "This time I shall praise the Lord", because he was the fourth, the fourth leg of the throne. The letters yod, he', vau of his name are the impress of the supernal name, and they were completed by a daleth, which represents the second he, of the sacred name, so that this name is found completely in Judah's name. Hence "Thy brethren shall praise thee", because the kingship is meet to remain with thee. Verily, "Judah still walketh with God, and is faithful with the holy ones" (Hosea, XI, 12). These holy ones are the supernal angels, who all acknowledge him and call him faithful. Therefore he is first in everything, and king over all.' R. Simeon discoursed on the verse: "The all-honoured daughter of the king is within" (Ps. XLV, 14). 'The "all-honoured one" is the Community of Israel, who is called the daughter of the king, the supreme King, who is within, because there is another king who is not so far within. The "clothing" of this honoured daughter of the king is "inwrought with gold", because she is clothed and encompassed with supernal might (Geburah), which also is called "king". On this account the earth is established, namely, when she takes hold of judgement, and this we call "the kingdom of heaven". Judah took hold of this and inherited the kingdom of the earth.'

R. Judah and R. Isaac were once travelling together. Said R. Isaac: 'Let us discourse on the Torah as we go along.' He began with the text: And he drove out the man, and he placed at the east of the garden of Eden, etc. 'The word vayegaresh (and he drove out)', he said, 'may, the Companions have explained, be translated "and he divorced". The accusative particle eth here has an esoteric meaning. Adam was punished for his sin, and brought death upon himself and all the world, and caused that tree in regard to which he sinned to be driven out along with him and his descendants forever. It says further that God "placed the cherubim on the east of the garden of Eden"; these were the lower cherubim, for as there are cherubim above, so there are cherubim below, and he spread this tree over them. The "flame of a sword" refers to the flames of fire which issue from that flashing sword. It is said to "turn every way" because it sucks from two sides, and turns from one side to another. Another explanation is that the flames turn about, being sometimes men and sometimes women.' Said R. Judah: 'This is certainly correct, that Adam caused that tree through which he sinned to be driven out; and so, also, do other men, as it is written: "Through your transgressions your mother is sent away" (Is. L, 1). Still you are right, that the word eth refers to the perfection of man, and from that day the moon was impaired until Noah came and entered the ark. Then came sinners, and it was impaired again until Abraham came, and it was established perfectly through Jacob and his sons, and Judah came and took hold on it, and seized the kingship and took possession of it as an everlasting inheritance for himself and his sons after him.' JUDAH, THEE SHALL THY BRETHREN PRAISE. When Israel were at the Red Sea, they all praised him and entered after him into the sea. THY HAND SHALL BE ON THE NECK OF THY ENEMIES, as it says, "Judah shall go up first ' (Judg. I, 2). THE SONS OF THY FATHER SHALL BOW DOWN TO THEE: this includes all the other tribes, even though from other mothers. And even when Israel was split into two kingdoms, when the people went up to Jerusalem they used to bow down to the king there, because the kingship in Jerusalem

was derived from the holy kingdom. SHALL BOW DOWN BEFORE THEE. They only, but not other peoples, who will only bow down at the time of the Messiah. But here the expression only indicates Israel, all of whom would bow down to the Exilarch in Babylon, but not other peoples. JUDAH IS A LION'S WHELP: first he will be a whelp, and then a lion, corresponding to the transition from "lad" [Tr. note: i.e. Metatron.] to "man", as it is written: "The Lord is a man of war" (Ex. xv, 3). FROM THE PREY, MY SON, THOU ART GONE UP The word "prey" includes the angel of death, who preys upon mankind. From that prey the Shekinah shook itself free. It "stooped down" in the captivity of Babylon, it "couched" in the captivity of Edom, "as a lion" which is strong and as a "lioness" which is stronger. So Israel are strong, because though the Gentiles entice and oppress them, they adhere to their laws and their customs like a lion and a lioness. So, too, the Shekinah, which, although it is fallen, remains strong like a lion and a lioness. For just as these crouch only to spring upon their prey, which they smell from afar, so the Shekinah only crouches to take vengeance on idolaters and to spring upon them. WHO SHALL ROUSE HIM UP. He will not rise to take any petty vengeance. The word "who" (Mi) here indicates the supernal world, which has dominion over all; it is similarly used in the verse "From the womb of whom (Mi) came the ice" (Job XXXVIII, 29), as we have explained. THE SCEPTRE SHALL NOT DEPART FROM JUDAH, ETC. The word Shiloh, here, is spelt with both a yod and a he, to allude to the holy supernal name, Kah, by which the Shekinah shall rise; and this is also the allusion of Mi, as we have said. R. Hiya discoursed on the verse: The Lord shall keep thee from all evil, he shall keep thy soul. 'The words "He shall keep thee",' he said, 'refer to this world, and "he shall keep thy soul" to the next world. By "keeping in this world" is meant that a man is protected from many evil accusers who seek to bring charges against him and to cling fast to him. By preservation in the next world is meant, as we have explained, that when a man departs from this world, if he is virtuous his soul ascends and is crowned in its place, and if not, numbers of demons are at hand to drag him to Gehinnom and to deliver him into the hands of Duma, who has been made chief of demons, and who has twelve thousand myriads of attendants all charged to punish the souls of sinners. There are in Gehinnom seven circuits and seven gates, each with several gate-keepers under their own chief. The souls of sinners are delivered by Duma to those gate-keepers, who then close the gates of flaming fire. There are gates behind gates, the outer ones remaining open while the inner ones are closed. On Sabbath, however, they are all open, and the sinners go forth, as far as the outer gates, where they meet other souls which tarry there. When Sabbath goes out, a herald proclaims at each gate: "Let the wicked return to Sheol." Now God protects the souls of the righteous from being delivered into the hands of Duma, and that is the meaning of the words "he shall keep thy soul." '

BINDING HIS FOAL UNTO THE VINE. The vine is the Community of Israel, so called also in the verse: "Thou didst remove a vine from Egypt" (Ps. LXXX, 9). By "his foal" is meant the Messiah, who is destined to rule over all the hosts of the peoples, that is to say, the heavenly hosts who have charge of the Gentiles, and from whom they derive their strength. The Messiah will prevail over them, because this vine dominates all those lower crowns through which the Gentiles have dominion. This will be the victory above. Israel, who are "a choice vine", will conquer and destroy other hosts below; and the Messiah will prevail over all. Hence it is written of him that he will be "poor and riding on an ass and on a young ass's colt" (Zech. IX, 9). "Colt" and "ass" are two crowns by virtue of which the Gentiles have dominion, and they are from the left side, the side of uncleanness. It is strange that the Messiah should be called "poor". R. Simeon explained that it is because he has nothing of his own, and he is compared to the holy moon above, which has no light save from the sun. This Messiah will have dominion and will be established in his place. Below he is "poor", because he is of the side of the moon, and above he is poor, being a "mirror which does not radiate", "the bread of poverty". Yet withal he "rides upon an ass and upon a colt", to overthrow the strength of the Gentiles; and God will keep him firm. HE HATH WASHED HIS GARMENT IN WINE. With this may be compared the verse: "Who is this that cometh from Edom, with dyed garments from Bozrah?" (IS. LXIII, 1); and also: "I have trodden the winepress alone, etc." (Ibid. 3). "Wine" here alludes to the side of Geburah, of stern justice which will be visited on the idolatrous nations. AND HIS VESTURE IN THE BLOOD OF GRAPE. This is the lower-world tree, the judgement court which is called "grapes", in which the "wine" is kept. Thus the Messiah will be clothed in both to crush beneath him all the idolatrous peoples and kings.

R. Yose discoursed on the verse: "And on the vine were three branches, and it was as though it budded and its blossoms shot forth." 'How little', he said, 'do men care for the glory of their Master or pay heed to the words of the Torah! At first prophecy was vouchsafed to men, and through it they knew the glory of God. When prophecy ceased, they had a bath-kol, [Tr. note: t Lit. "daughter of a voice". According to the Rabbis, on certain occasions during the period of the Second Temple, a voice issued from heaven to give the Jewish people guidance or warning; and this was called by them bath-kol.] but now they have nothing but dreams. Dream is a lower grade, being one-sixtieth of prophecy, and it is vouchsafed to everyone, since it comes from the left side. It comes down in various grades, and is shown even to sinners and even to Gentiles. Sometimes the dream is carried by evil demons who make mock of men and show them false things; and sometimes it is sent to sinners and tells them things of importance. Now this sinner, Pharaoh's butler, saw a true dream. The vine represented the Community of Israel, which was called by the psalmist "this vine" (Ps. LXXX, 15). The three branches have the same reference as the three flocks of sheep which Jacob saw by the well. (Gen XXIX, 2). Its blossoming typifies the time of Solomon, when the moon was illumined. The buds represent the lower Jerusalem, or, according to another explanation, the grade which is over it and gives sustenance to it.

Zohar: Bereshith, Section 1, Page 238b

The clusters thereof brought forth ripe grapes, in which to keep the precious wine. All this was seen by that sinner. Further, he saw the cup of Pharaoh in his hands; this is the cup of confusion which sucks in from the court of judgement and which issued from the grapes that were given to Pharaoh; and he drank it as it was, on account of Israel. When Joseph heard this he rejoiced, remarking the truth which the dream contained, and therefore he gave it a good interpretation. Thus the words "binding his foal unto the vine" indicate that all the forces of the Gentiles are to be subdued beneath that vine, as we have said, their power being bound up and subdued.' R. Simeon said: 'There are two kinds of vine. There is the holy celestial vine, and there is the vine which is called "the vine of Sodom, the strange vine"; and therefore Israel is called "this vine". And when Israel sinned and abandoned "this vine", then it was said of them: "For from the vine of Sodom is their vine" (Deut. XXXIII, 32).'

As R. Judah and R. Isaac were once travelling together, the former said: 'Let us turn into this field, as it is more level.' They did so, and as they went along R. Judah said: 'It is written: "She is not afraid of the snow for her household, for all her household are clothed in scarlet." This verse has been expounded by our colleague, R. Hizkiah, who said that sinners are punished in Gehinnom twelve months, half with fire and half with snow. When they go into the fire, they say: "This is really Gehinnom." When they go into the snow, they say: "This is the real winter of the Almighty." They begin by exclaiming "Alas", and then they exclaim "Woe". The supreme punishment is with snow. Not so Israel, however, of whom it is written: "She is not afraid of the snow for her household", because "all her household are clothed with scarlet". The word shanim (scarlet) here may be read shnaim (two), referring to pairs of precepts such as circumcision and uncovering, fringes and phylacteries, mezuzahs and Hanukah lights, etc. The word "scarlet" may also be taken to indicate the robe of judgement, which is assumed for the punishment of idolaters. For one day God will put on a red robe and take a red sword to take vengeance on the ruddy one. [Tr. note: Esau.] This we learn from the verse: "Who is this that cometh from Edom with dyed garments, etc." ' R. Isaac said: 'We may also take the word shanim to mean "years", and to refer to the whole of past time, since the Community of Israel is the consummation of the ages and draws sustenance from all sides.'

As they were going along, they met a boy leading an ass on which an old man was riding. Said the old man to the boy: 'My son, repeat me a passage of Scripture.' He answered: 'I have more than one passage. But come down or let me ride in front of you, and I will repeat some to you.' He said: 'I am old and you are young, and I do not want to put myself on a level with you.' Said the boy: 'If so, why is it you ask me to recite my verses?' He said: 'To make the journey more agreeable.' Said the boy: 'This old man can go and hang himself. Ignoramus as he is, he must needs ride and will not descend to my level, forsooth!' So he left the old man and went his way. When R. Judah and R. Isaac came up, he joined them. They asked who he was, and he told them what had happened. Said R. Judah to him: 'You did quite rightly. Come with us and we will sit down over there and you will tell us something.' He said to them: 'I am very weary,

Zohar: Bereshith, Section 1, Page 239a

because I have not eaten today.' So they took out some food and gave him, and a miracle happened and they found a small stream of water under a tree from which he drank, and they also drank and sat down. The boy then quoted the text: "To David. Fret not thyself because of evil doers, neither be thou envious against them that work unrighteousness" (Ps. XXXVII, 1). He said: 'This is neither a song nor a prayer, but the superscription "To David" shows that it was spoken by the Holy Spirit, which thus admonished David: "Do not challenge the wicked, because thou knowest not if thou hast strength to prevail against him; perhaps he is a tree which has never been uprooted [Tr. note: i.e. perhaps his soul is the first time on earth and thine the second time.] and thou wilt be repulsed by him. Also, do not look at the works of those who do unrighteousness, so that thou shouldst not need to be indignant with them; for whoever sees their works and is not zealous for God transgresses three negative precepts, namely: "Thou shalt have no strange gods before me"; "Thou shalt not make to thee any graven image"; and "Thou shalt not bow down to them nor serve them." Therefore a man should keep away from them. That is why I have left the old man and taken a different path. Now that I have found you I will expound the Scripture in your presence.'

He then discoursed on the text: And he called unto Moses, etc. (Lev. I, 1). He said: 'The aleph of the word vayikra (and he called) is written small in the scroll, to show that this calling was not a perfect one, because it was only in the Tabernacle and in a strange land, perfection being only found in the Holy Land. Further, in the Tabernacle there was only the Shekinah, but in the land there was the complete union of Male and Female. When a king sits on his throne wearing the royal crown, he is called Great King, but when he comes down from his throne and visits his servant, he is called Little King. So God, as long as He is on high over all, is called Supreme King, but when He brings His abode below, He is simply King, not Supreme as before. The word "called", as we have learnt, means that he summoned him to his sanctuary. The "tent of meeting" (mo'ed=also appointed time) means the tent on which depends the reckoning of seasons, festivals, and sabbaths, this being none other than the moon. The word "saying" (lemor, lit. to say) indicates the disclosing of what hitherto was concealed; and so in all places where it occurs (e.g. "And God spoke unto Moses, saying"), it means that permission is given to disclose. It is written just before: "And they brought the tabernacle to Moses" (Ex. XXXIX, 33). The reason why the Israelites brought the Tabernacle to Moses when they had finished it was because God had shown him the whole plan of it on Mount Sinai; so now they brought it to him in order that he might see whether it corresponded to the plan which he had seen. It was as if a king had given orders for a palace to be built for his queen, and had charged the builders to make one room here and one there, here a bedchamber and there a sitting-room, and so when the builders finished they showed it all to the king. So the Israelites brought the Tabernacle to Moses, who was the "master of the house", the "man of God". When the sanctuary was finished, the queen invited the king to it, and invited also her husband, that is to say, Moses the master of the house. Hence Moses was able to "take the tent and pitch it outside" (Ex. XXXIII, 7),

Zohar: Bereshith, Section 1, Page 239b

a thing which no one else could possibly have done. The text continues: "And the Lord spoke to him", "the Lord" being another still higher grade.'

He further discoursed as follows. 'The text continues: When any man of you shall offer (Lev. I, 2). The word "man" (Adam) here indicates the union of the sun and the moon. "When he shall offer from you": this is a hint that he who desires to make his service of sacrifice truly acceptable should not be unmarried. "An offering to the Lord": this means that he should offer the whole for the purpose of uniting upper and lower. "From the cattle": to show man and beast as one. "From the oxen and from the sheep": these are the chariots which are clean. "Ye shall offer your offering": the "offering to the Lord" mentioned above was man, but "your offering" is from the cattle, from the herds and the flocks, to display the union of upper with lower and of lower with upper. If a king is sitting on a throne on a very high dais, then one who brings a present to the king has to mount from step to step until he reaches the top, the place where the king is sitting above all, and then it is known that that present is meant for the king. But when the present comes down from the top, then all know that the king is sending it from above to his friend who is below. So at first a man rises step by step from below upwards; this is "the offering of the Lord". Then he comes down step by step: and this is "your offering".' R. Isaac and R. Judah went up to him and kissed his forehead. They said: 'Blessed be God who has favoured us with this, blessed is God that these words have not been wasted on that old man.'

They then rose and went on. As they proceeded, they saw a vine in a garden. The boy then quoted the verse: "Binding his foal to the vine and his ass's colt to the choice vine." He said: 'The word oseri (binding) is written here with a superfluous yod, and the word 'iro (his colt) with he' instead of vau. Thus the Holy Name Kah is hinted here. Similarly with the words bni (colt) and sorekah (choice vine). All this is to show that just as there is a Holy Name to subdue the "foal", so there is a Holy Name to subdue another power, which is called "ass"; for if the Holy Name were not hinted here, they would devastate the world. The "vine", as we have said, is the Community of Israel. It is called vine because just as the vine will receive no graft from another tree, so the Community of Israel accepts no master but God, and therefore all other powers are subdued before her, and cannot obtain dominion over her. "He hath washed his garments in wine", even from the time of the Creation the reference being to the coming of the Messiah on earth. "Wine" indicates the left side, and "the blood of grapes" the left side below. The Messiah is destined

Zohar: Bereshith, Section 1, Page 240a

to rule above over all the forces of the idolatrous nations and to break their power above and below. We may also explain that as wine brings joyfulness and yet typifies judgement, so the Messiah will bring gladness to Israel, but judgement to the Gentiles. The "spirit of God which hovered over the face of the waters" (Gen. I, 2) is the spirit of the

Messiah, and from the time of the Creation he "washed his garments in celestial wine". "His eyes shall be red with wine": this is the intoxicating celestial wine from which the masters of the Torah drink. "And his teeth white with milk", because the Torah is both wine and milk, the Oral and the Written Law. It is written of wine that it "rejoiceth the heart of man" (Ps. CIV, 15). Wine at first brings gladness, being the place from which all gladness issues, but afterwards it brings punishment, because its end is the place where is gathered all punishment. Hence the verse continues: "And oil to make the face shine", to wit, from the place from which all gladness issues. It then says: "And bread that strengtheneth man's heart", bread being the support of mankind. It is not, however, the only support, because there is no night without day, and they must not be separated. If so, it may be asked, why did David say that "bread supports the heart of man"? The answer is that this is why he added the word "and" before "bread", to show that the others are included. Observe that grace after meals should not be said over an empty table, but there should be bread on it and a cup of wine, and the wine should be taken in the right hand, in order to join the Left hand to the Right, and in order that the bread should be blessed by them and linked with them, so that the whole should be linked together to bless the Holy Name fittingly. For the bread being joined with the wine, and the wine with the right hand, blessings rest on the world and the table is duly perfected.' Said R. Isaac: 'Had we come on this journey only to hear these words, it would have been worth our while.' R. Judah said: 'This lad has no right to know so much, and I am afraid he will not live long.' 'Why?' said R. Isaac. 'Because', he answered, 'he is able to see into a place which man has no right to look upon, and I am afraid that before he reaches maturity he will actually look and be punished for it.' The lad heard them and said: 'I have no fear of punishment, because when my father died he blessed me and prayed for me, and I know that the merit of my father will protect me.' They said to him: 'Who, then, is your father?' 'R. Judah, the son of Rab Hamnuna the Elder,' he replied. They then took him up and carried him on their shoulders three miles, applying to him the verse: "Out of the eater came forth meat, and out of the strong came forth sweetness" (Judg. xv, 14). The boy said to them: 'Since you have quoted the verse, expound it.' Said they to him: 'Since God has led us into the path of life, do you tell us.' He then began: 'We find a certain mystical allusion in this verse. The eater is the Zaddik, as it is written: "The Zaddik eats his fill" (Prov. XII, 25). By "his fill" is meant that he gives sufficiency to the place which is called the Soul of David. "From the eater comes forth food", for but for that Zaddik food would never come forth and the world could not exist. "Out of the strong came forth sweetness": this is Isaac, who blessed Jacob with the dew of heaven and the fatness of the earth. We may also explain that were it not for the rigour of justice there would come forth no honey, to wit, the Oral Law,

Zohar: Bereshith, Section 1, Page 240b

which comes forth from the Written Law, which is called "strong", as it is written: "The Lord shall give strength to his people" (Ps. XXIX, 11).' They went on together for three days till they reached the court where his mother lived. When she saw them she made preparations for them and they stayed with her two days. They then said farewell to him, and departed, and came and related everything to R. Simeon. He said: 'Truly, he has inherited the Torah, and if not for the merit of his fathers he would be punished from above. But for those who follow the Torah God has made it an inheritance to them and their descendants forever, as it is written: "But as for me, this is my covenant with them, saith the Lord, my spirit which is upon thee, etc." (Is. LIX, 21). ZEBULON SHALL DWELL AT THE HAVEN OF THE SEA, ETC. R. Abba discoursed on the verse: Gird thy sword upon thy thigh, O mighty One, thy glory and thy majesty. He said: 'Is this glory and majesty, to gird on weapons and to practise the use of them? To study the Torah and to fight battles in the Torah and to arm oneself with it–this is praiseworthy, this is glory and majesty. The truth of the matter, however, is this. God has given men the sign of a holy covenant, and imprinted it upon them for them to preserve and not impair in any way. He who impairs it is confronted with the sword which avenges the insult to the covenant. Now he who desires to preserve this place should brace himself up to meet the evil prompter, and when the latter assails him should set before his eyes this sword, which is girded on the thigh to punish those who impair this place. Hence it says: "Gird thy sword upon thy thigh, O mighty One." Such a one is called "mighty", and hence it is his "glory and majesty". Another explanation is that before setting out on a journey a man should prepare himself with prayer and arm himself with righteousness, which is the supernal sword, as it is written: "Righteousness shall go before him, and (then) he shall set his steps on the way" (Ps. LXXXV, 14). Now Zebulon used always to go out on the roads and highways and make war, and used first to arm himself with this celestial sword of prayer and supplication, and so he fought with peoples and overcame them. You may say that this was the function of Judah, so why is it assigned here to Zebulon?

Observe this. The twelve tribes are the adornment of the Matron. When Jacob was about to depart from the world, and saw that he was perfected on every side, with Abraham at his right, Isaac at his left, himself in the centre, and the Shekinah in front of him, he called his sons round him in order that both the lower and the upper might be fitly adorned. [Note: The last 12 lines of the Hebrew text do not appear in our translation.]

Zohar: Bereshith, Section 1, Page 241a

[Note: The beginning and ending passages of the Hebrew text do not appear in our translation.]

The twelve tribes correspond to the twelve oxen which were under the sea of bronze made by Solomon (I Kings VII, 23 seq.), three for each of the cardinal points. Three of them represented the right Arm, three the left Arm, three the right Thigh, and three the left Thigh. There were three tribes for each, because in each of these limbs there are three joints. And although this "adornment" was only complete with the number of six hundred thousand, yet already at the time of Jacob's death there were the seventy souls who had come down with him to Egypt and the very numerous progeny whom they had already produced in the seventeen years they had been there. Happy the portion of Jacob who was perfected above and below.

Zohar: Bereshith, Section 1, Page 241b

[Note: The first seven lines of the Hebrew text do not appear in our translation.]

R. Judah said: 'Zebulon and Issachar made an agreement that one should sit and study the Torah while the other went out and made money and supported him. So Zebulon used to traverse the seas with merchandise, and his territory was suitable for this, being on the sea coast. Hence it is written: "Rejoice, Zebulon, in thy going out, and Issachar in thy tents ' (Deut. XXXIII, 18).' HE SHALL DWELL AT THE HAVEN OF THE SEAS: that is to say, among those who sail the sea with merchandise. "At the haven of the seas": the plural "seas" is used, because although only one coast belonged to him, yet he dwelt by two. R. Yose said it is because traders from all other seas used to visit his coast. AND HE SHALL BE FOR A HAVEN OF SHIPS: that is, the place where all ships come to do trade. AND HIS BORDER SHALL BE UPON ZIDON. R. Hizkiah said: ' His territory stretched to the boundary of Zidon, and all merchants came to that place to trade.' R. Aha said: 'It is written: "Neither shalt thou suffer the salt of the covenant of thy God to be lacking from thy meal-offering; with all thine oblations thou shalt offer salt." Salt was to be used because it softens bitterness, and so mankind cannot do without it. Salt is the covenant upon which the world is established: hence it is called "the covenant of thy God".' R. Hiya said: 'It is written: "For God is righteous, he loves righteousness" (Ps. XI, 7). This is the salt in the sea, and he who separates them brings death upon himself. Hence it is written: "Thou shalt not suffer salt to be lacking." ' R. Aha said: 'The sea is all one, but it is called "seas" because in some places the water is clear (and in some turbid), in some sweet, and in some bitter; hence we speak of "seas".'

R. Abba was sitting one night and studying the Torah, when R. Yose came and knocked at his door. He said: 'When the prince sits with the chief, then true judgement is given.' So they sat down and studied the Torah. Meanwhile the son of their host got up and sat before them. He said to them: 'What is the meaning of the verse: "Ye will save alive my father and my mother, etc.", and just before, "And give me a true token" (Jos. II, 13-12)? What did Rahab ask of the spies?' R. Abba said: 'That is a good question; if you know an answer, tell me, my son.' He said: 'A further question arises from the fact that they gave her something which she did not ask for, since they said to her: "Thou shalt bind this line of scarlet thread in the window, etc." The explanation I have learnt is this. She asked for a sign of life, as it is written, "And ye will save alive my father, etc." She said: "A sign of life is only contained in the sign of truth, which is the letter Vau." In fact, as I have learnt, she asked for the sign of Moses. They, however, gave her a line of scarlet thread, because they said: "Moses is dead, and the sun is gathered in and the time has come for the moon to rule. Therefore we had better give you the sign of the moon, which is this line of scarlet thread. Thus the sign of Joshua shall be with you, because the moon is now in the ascendant." ' R. Abba and R. Yose rose

Zohar: Bereshith, Section 1, Page 242a

and kissed him, saying: 'Assuredly, you will one day be a head of a college or a great man in Israel'; and, in fact, he became R. Bun.

He then asked a further question, saying: 'Seeing that the twelve tribes were arranged below in the same order as above, why is Zebulon everywhere placed before Issachar in the blessings, although Issachar devoted himself to the Torah, which should always come first? The reason is that Zebulon took out of his own mouth and gave to Issachar. From this we learn that he who supports a student of the Torah is blessed from above and below, and not only so, but he is privileged to eat of two tables, a privilege granted to no other man. He is granted wealth in this world, and he is granted a portion in the next world. Hence it says of Zebulon, that "he shall dwell at the haven of the sea", that is to say, in this world, "and shall be for a haven of ships", in the future world.

He here quoted the verse: "I adjure you, O daughters of Jerusalem, by the roes and by the hinds of the fields, if you find my beloved, what will you tell him?" (S. S. v, 8). Why, it may be asked, should the Community of Israel speak thus, seeing that she is near to the king, like no other? The "daughters of Jerusalem", however, are the souls of the righteous, which are constantly near the King, and inform him every day of the requirements of the Matron. For so we have learnt, that when the soul comes down into the world, the Community of Israel makes it swear that it will tell the King her love for him in order to appease him. This appeasement is brought about when man unifies the Holy Name with his mouth, his heart and his soul, to link all together like flame with fire. According to another explanation, the "daughters of Jerusalem" are the twelve tribes, as we have learnt that Jerusalem is established on twelve rocks, three on each side (wherefore it is called Hayah (living one)), and these are called "the daughters of Jerusalem", and they testify to the King concerning the Community of Israel, as it is written: "The tribes of the Lord are a testimony unto Israel, to give thanks unto the name of the Lord" (Ps. CXXII, 4).' Said R. Judah: 'Happy are Israel who know the ways of God and of whom it is written: "For thou art a holy people unto the Lord thy God, and thee did the Lord choose, etc." (Deut. XIV, 2).' ISSACHAR IS A STRONG ASS COUCHING DOWN BETWEEN THE SHEEPFOLDS. R. Eleazar said: 'Why should Issachar, because he studied the Torah, be called an ass, rather than a horse, or a lion, or a leopard? The answer given is that the ass bears a burden patiently and does not kick like other animals, and is not fastidious and will lie down anywhere. So Issachar bears the burden of the Torah and does not kick against the Almighty, and is not fastidious and cares not for his own honour but for the honour of his Master. He therefore "couches between the sheepfolds", as we say of the student of the Torah that he is "willing to sleep on the ground" [Tr. note: v. Ethics of the Fathers, VI, 4.]. He also, in explanation of this verse, quoted the text: "To David. The Lord is my light and my salvation, whom shall I fear? The Lord is the strength of my life, of whom shall I be afraid?" (Ps. XXVII, 1). 'Those who study the Torah', he said, 'are beloved before God, so that they have no fear of evil hap, being protected above and below Nay more,

Zohar: Bereshith, Section 1, Page 242b

such a one subdues all evil haps and casts them down into the great abyss. At nightfall the doors are closed, and dogs and asses commence to roam about the world with permission to do damage. Men sleep on their beds and the souls of the righteous ascend to the bliss above. When the north wind awakes at midnight, then there is a holy stirring in the world, as has been explained in many places. Happy is he who rises at that hour and studies the Torah. For as soon as he begins, all those evil beings are cast by him into the great abyss and he binds the ass and throws him down into the dung-heap. Therefore Issachar, who was a student of the Torah, bound the ass and brought him down from the ladder which he had mounted to do injury to the world, and made him abide between the sheepfolds, that is, in the dung-heap.' AND HE SAW REST THAT IT WAS GOOD, AND THE LAND THAT IT WAS PLEASANT, AND HE BOWED HIS SHOULDER TO BEAR, AND BECAME A SERVANT UNDER TASK WORK. "Rest" here signifies the Written Law; "the land" signifies the Oral Law; "he bowed his shoulder to bear", namely the yoke of the Law, and to cleave to it day and night; and he "became a servant under task work", to be a worshipper of the Holy One, blessed be He, and to cleave to Him. R. Simeon and R. Yose and R. Hiya were once travelling from Upper Galilee to Tiberias. Said R. Simeon: 'Let us discuss the Torah as we go, for whoever is able to discuss the Torah and does not do so renders his life forfeit, and is further subjected to the burden of worldly cares and the domination of others. This we learn from the verse which says of Issachar that "he turned aside his shoulder from bearing,', that is to say, from bearing the yoke of the Law, and straightway "he became a servant under task work". Happy are those that study the Law, for they obtain favour above and below and every day win the inheritance of the future world, as it is written: "To cause them that love me to inherit substance (yesh)" (Prov. VIII, 21), which means the future world. For his waters never fail and he receives a good reward above such as is earned by no other man. This is hinted in the name of Issachar, which we may divide into yesh sachar (yesh is the reward), as much as to say, yesh (substance) is the reward of those who study the Torah.

It is written: "I beheld till thrones were placed and one that was ancient of days did sit, etc." (Dan. VII, 9). When the Temple was destroyed, two thrones fell, that is, two above and two below. Two above, because the lower was removed from the upper, the throne of Jacob from the throne of David, and the throne of David fell. The two thrones below are Jerusalem and the students of the Torah, the latter corresponding to the throne of Jacob and the former to the throne of David. Hence it says that "thrones" were cast down, and not merely one throne, and all on account of the neglect of the Torah. Observe that when the truly pious study the Torah, all the mighty ones of other peoples and other forces are humbled and their power broken, and they have no dominion in the world, and Israel are raised above all. But if not, the ass causes Israel to go into captivity and to fall into the hands of the peoples and to be ruled by them. Why is this? Because "he saw rest that it was good", and that he could obtain from it many comforts and enjoyments, and he perverted his path so as not to bear the yoke of the Torah, and therefore he "became a servant under task work".

Zohar: Bereshith, Section 1, Page 243a

Only through him was the knowledge of the Torah kept alive in Israel, as it says: "And of the sons of Issachar were those who had knowledge of the times, etc." (I Chron. XII, 32), and it was they who "caused all delights to be at our doors", to wit, the doors of synagogues and houses of study, "both new and old", because many old and new lessons of the Torah were brought to light by them to bring Israel near to their Father in heaven. "My beloved, I have kept hidden for thee": from this we learn that when one studies the Torah fittingly and knows how to draw the proper lessons from it, his words ascend to the throne of the King and the Community of Israel opens the gates before them and treasures them, and when God enters the Garden of Eden to disport Himself with the righteous, She brings them out before Him and God contemplates them and rejoices; and then God is crowned with noble crowns and rejoices in the Matron, and from that time the words are written in the book. Up to this point extends the sway of Judah, the arm that contained the strength of all sides, the three joints of the arm which enable it to prevail over all. DAN SHALL JUDGE HIS PEOPLE AS ONE OF THE TRIBES OF ISRAEL. R. Hiya said: 'We should have expected here, "Dan shall judge the tribes of Israel", or

"Dan shall judge the tribes of Israel as one." What is the meaning of "Dan shall judge his people"? We may explain as follows. Dan was the "rearward of the camps" (Num. x, 25), because he was the left thigh and went last. For after Judah and Reuben had set forth, the Levites and the Ark made an interval, as it were, and only after them did the standard of Ephraim set forth on the west, being the right thigh. We might have thought that Zebulon should have marched first, since it is written of him: "And his thigh is unto Zidon." But the truth is that Judah comprised all, being the lower kingdom, for just as the upper kingdom comprises all, so does the lower kingdom, both body and thigh, becoming thereby exceedingly strong. The first corps comprised Judah, the kingdom which derives from the side of Might (Geburah), combined with the right hand, the body and the thigh. The second corps was that of Reuben, who was on the south side, which is on the right, and all the power of the right was taken by Judah, because Reuben lost the kingship, and thus Judah was reinforced with the strength of Reuben. The third corps was that of Ephraim, who was the right thigh, which always goes before the left. Thus Dan, who was the left thigh, marched last. We read that "Solomon made a great throne of ivory" (I Kings x, 18). This throne was after the supernal pattern and contained all celestial figures, and therefore it is written: "And Solomon sat on the throne of the Lord as king" (I Chron. XXIX, 23), and so also "Solomon sat on the throne of David his father and his kingdom was established greatly" (I Kings II, 12), because the moon was at its full.' "Dan shall judge his people" at first, and then "the tribes of Israel as one", that is, as the one Being of the World.

Zohar: Bereshith, Section 1, Page 243b

This was realized in Samson, who single-handed wrought judgement on the world, and both judged and put to death without requiring a helper. R. Isaac said: 'Dan is compared to a serpent lying in wait in the way. But there is also a reference to another serpent above, lying in wait in ways and paths, from whom issue those who lie in wait for the sons of men on account of the sins which they cast behind their backs.' R. Hiya said: 'The primeval serpent above, before he is appeased with gladdening wine, is "a serpent by the way". As there is a "way" above, so there is a "way" below, and the sea is divided into various paths on every side. There is one path which has abundance of water and breeds many kinds of evil fishes, just as the waters below breed good and bad fishes. When they escape from the path of the sea, they appear like riders on horseback, and were it not that this serpent who is the rearward of all the tents lies in wait at the end of the path and drives them back, they would destroy the world. It is from the side of these that sorcerers come forth. Dan is called "a serpent by the way", because he that goes after the serpent repudiates the celestial household which is the supernal path that issues from above. To go after the serpent is like going to repudiate that celestial way, because from it the higher worlds are sustained. If it is asked why Dan is in this grade, the answer is given in the words, "That bites at the horse's heels", i.e. to protect all the camps. R. Eleazar said that he was one of the supports of the Throne, because on the throne of Solomon there was a serpent attached to his sceptre above the lions. It says of Samson that the "spirit of God began to move him in the camp of Dan" (Judg. XIII, 25). Samson was a Nazirite, and a man of huge strength, and he was a serpent in this world in face of the idolatrous nations, because he inherited the blessing of his ancestor Dan.' R. Hiya said: 'We know what a serpent is, but what is an adder (shephiphon)?' He answered: 'This word alludes to the practices of sorcerers, since it is written of Balaam that he went shephi (alone). If it is said that this was not properly the grade of Dan, that is true, but he was appointed over this grade to be the last side (of the Israelites' host), and this was his honour, since some officers of the king are appointed to one post and some to another, and all are honourable, and the king's throne is supported by all. Various paths and grades spread out beneath them, some for good and some for evil, and all help to support the throne. Therefore Dan was on the north side. In the hollow of the great abyss, which is on the north side, there are many demons endowed with power to do mischief in the world. Therefore Jacob prayed, saying, I HAVE WAITED FOR THY SALVATION, O LORD. He mentioned God's salvation here because he saw here the might of the serpent setting in motion chastisement.'

R. Yose and R. Hizkiah were once going to see R. Simeon in Cappadocia. Said R. Hizkiah: 'We have laid down that a man before praying should first pronounce God's praises. But what of the man who is in great distress and is in haste to pour out his prayer and is not able to pronounce the blessings of his Master fittingly?' He replied: 'That is no reason why the praise of his Master should be omitted. He should pronounce it, even

Zohar: Bereshith, Section 1, Page 244a

without proper devotion, and then say his prayer. Thus it is written: "A prayer of David. Hear, O Lord, righteousness, listen to my song" (Ps. XVII, 1)-first praise and then prayer. Of him who is able to pronounce the praise of his Master and does not do so, it is written: "Yea, when ye make many prayers I will not hear" (Is. I, 15).'

It is written: "The one lamb thou shalt offer in the morning, and the second lamb shalt thou offer at even" (Num. XXVIII, 4). Prayers have been ordained to correspond to the daily offerings. Through the impulse from below there is a stirring above, and through the impulse from above there is a stirring higher up still, until the impulse reaches the place where the lamp is to be lit and it is lit. Thus by the impulse of the smoke (of the sacrifice) from below, the lamp is kindled above, and when this is kindled all the other lamps are kindled and all the worlds are blessed from it. Thus the impulse of the sacrifice is the mainstay of the world and the blessing of all worlds. When the smoke commences to rise, the holy forms in charge of the world derive satisfaction, and are disposed thereby to stir the grades above them; and so the impulse rises until the King desires to associate with the Matron. Through the yearning of the lower world the lower waters flow forth to meet the upper waters, for the upper waters do not flow save from the impulse of the desire from below. Thus mutual desire is kindled and the lower waters flow to meet the upper waters, and worlds are blest, and all lamps are kindled, and upper and lower are endowed with blessings. Observe that the function of the priests and Levites is to unite the Left with the Right. Said R. Hizkiah: 'That is so, but I have been told that one rouses the Left and the other the Right, because the union of male and female is only brought about by Left and Right, as it says: "O that his left hand were under my head, and his right hand should embrace me" (S. S. II, 6). Then male and female are united, and there is mutual desire and worlds are blessed and upper and lower rejoice. Hence we see that the sacrifice is the support and the mainstay of the world, and the joy of upper and lower.' Said R. Yose: 'You are certainly right, and I had heard this before but had forgotten it. This, too, I have learnt, that nowadays prayer takes the place of sacrifice, and a man should fittingly pronounce the praise of his Master, and if not, his prayer is no prayer. The most perfect form of praising God is to unify the Holy Name in the fitting manner, for through this upper and lower are set in motion, and blessings flow to all worlds.' R. Hizkiah said: 'God placed Israel in exile among the nations in order that they might be blessed for their sake, for they do bring blessings from heaven to earth every day.'

As they were going along, they saw a snake wriggling on the path, so they turned aside. Another man then came up and the snake killed him. They looked back, and saw him dead, and said: 'Assuredly, that snake has performed the mission of his master. Blessed be God who has delivered us.' R. Yose thereupon quoted the verse: "Dan shall be a serpent in the way." 'This', he said, 'was in the days of Jeroboam, who, we are told, placed one of his golden calves in Dan (I Kings XII, 29). He placed it "on the way" in order to prevent the people from going up to Jerusalem; and thus Dan was to them "a serpent by the way", and also "an adder in the path", preventing Israel from going up to Jerusalem to celebrate their festivals and to bring sacrifices and worship there.

Zohar: Bereshith, Section 1, Page 244b

When Moses came to bless the tribes, he saw that Dan was linked to a serpent, and he changed it into a lion, as it says: "And to Dan he said: Dan is a lion's whelp that leapeth forth from Bashan" (Deut. XXXIII, 22), his object being to connect the beginning and end of the four standards with Judah, who was compared to a lion's whelp.' I WAIT FOR THY SALVATION, O LORD.

R. Hiya said: 'This refers to the time of Samson, of whom it was said: "He shall commence to save Israel from the hand of the Philistines" (Judg. XIII, 5).' R. Aha said: 'How could Jacob say "I wait", seeing that by that time he had been dead many years? The truth is, however, that the word "Israel" in the above passage has its esoteric-meaning.' Said R. Hiya: 'Assuredly that is so. Happy are the righteous who know how to study the Torah in such a way as to earn by it celestial life.' GAD A TROOP SHALL PRESS UPON HIM, BUT HE SHALL PRESS UPON THEIR HEEL. R. Jesse said: 'The conjunction of the two letters gimel and daleth indicates the issuing forth of troops and hosts, gimel giving and daleth receiving. [t r. note: Gimel (g'mul)=beneficence, and Daleth (dalluth)=poverty. The connection with armies is not clear.] That river which perennially flows from Eden supplies the needy, and therefore many hosts and many camps are sustained from here; and this is the significance of the name Gad, one producing and giving, and the other collecting and taking. R. Isaac said: 'Had Gad not been one of the sons of the handmaids, he would have risen to greater heights than all the rest. For the hour of his birth was propitious, but the flowing river departed at that moment, and therefore he had no share in the Holy Land and was removed from it.' R. Judah said: 'Reuben was in the same case, as it is written of him, "unstable as water, thou shalt not excel", which indicates that at his birth the waters stopped and did not flow. Neither Reuben nor Gad obtained a share in the Holy Land, but they provided troops and forces to conquer the land for Israel. The deficiency of Gad was made good in Asher, as it is written: "Out of Asher his bread shall be fat, etc." '

R. Eleazar and R. Abba once turned aside into a cave at Lydda to escape the heat of the sun. Said R. Abba: 'Let us now encompass this cave with words of the Torah.' R. Eleazar thereupon commenced with the verse: "Place me like a seal upon thy heart, like a seal upon thine arm... its coals are coals of fire, a very flame of the Lord" (S. S. VIII, 6). 'This verse', he said, 'has been much discussed. One night I was attending on my father, and I heard him say that the true devotion and yearning of the Community of Israel for God is only brought about by the souls of the righteous, who cause the flow of the lower waters towards the upper; and then there is perfect friendship and desire for mutual embrace to bring forth fruit. When they cleave to one another, in the fullness of her affection she says: "Set me as a seal upon thine heart." For, as the impress of a seal remains even after the seal is removed, so, says the Community of Israel, I shall cleave to thee, even though I am removed from thee and go

Zohar: Bereshith, Section 1, Page 245a

into captivity. Hence, "Set me as a seal upon thy heart" in order that my likeness may remain upon thee like the impress of a seal. "For love is strong as death": it is strong like the parting of the spirit from the body, as we have learnt that when man is about to depart from the world and sees strange things, his spirit courses through all his limbs and goes up and down like a boatman without oars who is tossed up and down on the sea and makes no progress. It then asks leave of each limb; and its separation is only effected with great violence. Such is the violence of the Community of Israel's love for God. "Jealousy is cruel as the grave." Love without jealousy is no true love. Hence we learn that a man should be jealous of his wife in order that his love for her may be perfect, for then he will not look at any other woman. Jealousy is compared to Sheol (the underworld), because just as the wicked are frightened of going down to Sheol, so is jealousy frightful in the eyes of one who loves and cannot bear to be parted from his beloved. Or we may also explain that just as when sinners are taken down to Sheol they are told the sins for which they are punished, so he who is jealous in demanding restitution reckons up all his grievances, and so his love becomes more firmly knit. "The flashes thereof are flashes of fire, the very flame of the Lord." This is the flame which is kindled and issues from the Shofar. It is the left hand, as it is written: "His left hand should be under my head" (S. S. VIII, 3). It is this which kindles the flame of love in the Community of Israel to the Holy One, blessed be He. Therefore "many waters cannot quench love", because when the right hand comes, although it is symbolized by water, it fans the fire of love and does not quench the flame of the left hand, as it is written: "And his right hand should embrace me." '

As they were sitting they heard R. Simeon coming up the road, with R. Judah and R. Isaac. When he approached the cave, R. Eleazar and R. Abba came out. R. Simeon said: 'I can see from the walls of the cave that the Shekinah is here.' So they all sat down. Said R. Simeon: 'What have you been discussing?' R. Abba replied: 'The love of the Community of Israel for God, and R. Eleazar applied to it the verse: "Set me as a seal upon thine heart, etc." ' Said R. Simeon: 'Eleazar, you have been scrutinizing the supernal love and affection.' He then fell into silence for a while. At last he said: 'Silence is good everywhere except in connection with the Torah. I have a certain gem which I do not desire to withhold from you. It is a profound thought which I have found in the book of Rab Hamnuna the Elder. It is this. Everywhere the male runs after the female and seeks to incite her love, but here we find the female courting the male and running after him, which it is not usually reckoned proper for the female to do. But there is here a deep mystery, much prized among the treasures of the king. There are three souls belonging to the celestial grades. The three are really four, because one is the supernal soul, which is not clearly discerned, even by the treasurer of the upper treasury, much less the lower. This is the soul of all souls, inscrutable and unknowable. Everything is dependent upon it, and it is veiled in a covering of exceeding brightness. It drops pearls which are linked together like the joints of the body, and it enters into them and displays through them its energy. It and they are one, and there is no separation between them. There is another, a female soul which is concealed in the midst of her hosts, to which is attached

Zohar: Bereshith, Section 1, Page 245b

the body, and through this body she shows her energy, like the soul in the human body. Those hosts are the counterpart of the hidden joints above. There is another soul, to wit, the souls of the righteous below. These come from those superior souls, the soul of the female and the soul of the male, and therefore the souls of the righteous are superior to all the heavenly hosts and camps. You may ask, if they are so transcendent from both sides, why do they come down to this world to be afterwards removed from it? Imagine a king who had a son whom he sent to a village to be brought up until he should learn the ways of the king's palace. When the king heard that his son was grown up, out of his love for him he sent the Matron his mother for him, and brought him into the palace, where he rejoiced with him every day. So the Holy One, blessed be He, had a son from the Matron, to wit, the celestial holy soul. He sent it to a village, to wit, to this world, to be brought up in it, and learn the ways of the king's palace. When the king found that his son had grown up, and that it was time to bring him to the palace, out of his love for him he sent the Matron for him and brought him into the palace. The soul does not depart from this world till the Matron has come for her and brought her into the king's palace, where she remains forever. And for all that, the inhabitants of the village weep for the parting of the king's son from them. There was one wise man among them who said: "Why are you weeping? Was he not the king's son, and is not his proper place in his father's palace and not among you?" So Moses, who was a wise man, saw the villagers weeping, and said to them: "Ye are sons of the Lord your God, ye shall not cut yourselves" (Deut. XIV, 1). Now, if the righteous all knew this, they would rejoice when their time arrives to depart from this world. For is it not a great honour for them that the Matron comes for their sakes to bring them to the King's palace, so that the King may rejoice in them every day? For God hath no delight save in the souls of the righteous. Now the love of the Community of Israel for God is excited only by the souls of the righteous here on earth, because they come from the side of the king, the side of the male. This excitement reaches the female and stirs her love; and in this way the male awakens the love and affection of the female, and the female is united in love with the male. In the same way, the desire of the female to pour forth lower waters to meet the upper waters is only aroused through the souls of the righteous. Happy, therefore, are the righteous in this world and in the world to come, since on them are established upper and lower beings. Hence it is written: "The righteous man is the foundation of the world" (Prov. x, 25). Esoterically speaking, the Zaddik is the foundation of the upper world and the foundation of the lower world, and the Community of Israel contains the Zaddik from above and from below. The righteous one from this side and the righteous one from that side inherit her, as it is written: "The righteous shall inherit the earth" (Ps. XXXVII, 29).

The Righteous One inherits this earth, and pours upon it blessings every day, and furnishes it with luxuries and delicacies in his flow. All this is hinted in the words: OUT OF ASHER HIS BREAD SHALL BE FAT, AND HE SHALL YIELD ROYAL DAINTIES. It is from the future world that the stream reaches this Righteous One which enables him to provide luxuries and delicacies to this earth, thus transforming it from "the bread of poverty" into "the bread of luxury".

Zohar: Bereshith, Section 1, Page 246a

The name "Asher" (lit. happy) signifies the place which all declare happy, to wit, the future world. In the expression "his bread" the reference of the word "his" is not specified; but we may divide the word lahmo (his bread) into lehem vau, that is, "the bread of vau" (which signifies the heavens); hence it is written: "Behold, I will rain bread from heaven for you" (Ex. XVI, 4). It is from thence that the tree of life is nourished and crowned, and when it receives this nourishment, then it "yields the dainties of the king". This king is the Community of Israel, who is fed therefrom by the hand of the Righteous One, the sacred grade of the sign of the covenant. In the book of Rab Hamnuna the Elder it says that the bread mentioned here is the Sabbath bread, which is double in quantity, as it is written in connection with the manna: "They gathered double bread" (Ex. XVI, 22); that is to say, bread from heaven and bread from earth, the one being "bread of luxury", the other "bread of poverty". For on Sabbath the lower bread was united with the upper bread, and one was blessed for the sake of the other. He further said that the Sabbath receives from the celestial Sabbath which flows forth and illumines all, and in this way bread is joined with bread and becomes double. NAPHTALI IS A HIND LET LOOSE, WHO GIVETH GOODLY WORDS. It has been affirmed that the upper world is of the male principle, and therefore whatever the Community of Israel causes to ascend on high must be male. We know this from the name of the offering ('olah, lit. going up), so called because it rises above the female. Hence it has to be a "male without blemish" (Lev. I, 3). By the words "without blemish" is meant that it must not be castrated. It may be objected that we find the words "without blemish" applied also to the female. This is true; nevertheless it does not alter the fact that the burnt-offering rises from the female to the male, and from this point upwards all is male, while from the female

Zohar: Bereshith, Section 1, Page 246b

downwards all is female. It may be said that there is a female principle above also. The truth is, however, that the whole body takes its description from the end of the body, which is male, although the beginning of the body is female. Here, however, both the beginning and end are female. Observe the recondite allusion in this matter. We see that Jacob blessed Joseph along with his brothers, but when God arranged the tribes under four standards He omitted Joseph and put Ephraim in his place. This cannot have been for any sin of Joseph's, but the reason is this. Joseph was the impress of the male, and since all the adornments of the Shekinah are female, Joseph was removed from the standards and Ephraim was appointed in his place. On this account he was stationed on the west, the side where the female abides, and the impress which is male was removed from her adornments. We thus see that all the twelve tribes are the adornment of the Shekinah after the supernal pattern, save for the grade of the Zaddik, who makes all the limbs male. WHO GIVETH GOODLY WORDS. The Voice speaks to the Utterance, there being no voice without utterance. This Voice is sent from a deep recess above in order to guide the Utterance, the two being related as general and particular. The Voice issues from the south and speaks to the west, inheriting two sides, and therefore Moses said to Naphtali: "Possess thou the west and the south" (Deut. XXXIII, 23). Observe that Thought is the beginning of all. This Thought is recondite and inscrutable, but when it expands it reaches the place where spirit abides and is then called Understanding (binah), which is not so recondite as the preceding. This spirit expands and produces a Voice composed of fire, water, and air, which corresponds to north, south, and east. This Voice embraces in itself all forces, and speaks to Utterance, and this shapes the word properly. When you examine the grades closely, you find that Thought, Understanding, Voice, Utterance are all one and the same, and there is no separation between them, and this is what is meant by the words: "The Lord is one and His Name is One." JOSEPH IS A FRUITFUL BOUGH, A FRUITFUL BOUGH BY A FOUNTAIN. The words fruitful bough are repeated to show that he is such both above and below. Observe that the holy kingdom does not attain its perfection as holy kingdom until it is joined with the patriarchs. Then its structure is completed from the upper world,

Zohar: Bereshith, Section 1, Page 247a

which is the world of the male. The upper world is called "seven years" because all the "seven years" [Tr. note: i.e. the seven Sefiroth.] are in it. The mnemonic of this is "and he built it seven years" (I Kings VI, 38). By means of this the lower world was built, which also is alluded to as "seven years". The mnemonic for this is "Seven days and seven days, fourteen days" (I Kings VIII, 66), the first seven being male and the second female. It is written: "Many daughters have done virtuously" (Prov. XXXI, 29). These are the twelve tribes who did valiantly. Hence it is written here: "The daughters advanced upon the wall"; that is to say, the daughters took part in the adornment of the Shekinah, but not the sons. BUT HIS BOW ABODE IN STRENGTH. This means that the bow which was his mate clothed him with strength and kept him firm, knowing that he would not go astray right or left in regard to his own proper grade of the sign of the covenant.

AND THE ARMS OF HIS HANDS WERE MADE STRONG: the word vayaphozu (were made strong) is akin to the word paz (fine gold), and indicates that his arms were adorned with precious jewels. BY THE HANDS OF THE MIGHTY ONE OF JACOB: these are the two sides to which Jacob held fast. FROM THENCE HE FED THE STONE OF ISRAEL: by him was supported that precious stone, as we have said. Or again, it may mean that that precious stone was sustained by these two sides which are north and south, and between which it was placed by the hands of the Righteous One.

Observe that Joseph received an extra blessing, as it is written: EVEN FROM THE GOD OF THY FATHER, HE SHALL HELP THEE. Jacob gave Joseph an inheritance above and below. The inheritance above was given in these words: "from the God of the father", the place called "heaven". He added: "And he shall help thee", to show that this place would not be exchanged for any other place, and his support would be from this place and from no other. AND WITH THE ALMIGHTY: this signifies another and lower grade, indicated by the word eth (with), from which issue blessings to the world.

Zohar: Bereshith, Section 1, Page 247b

[Note: The first seven lines of the Hebrew text do not appear in our translation.]

Up to this point the blessings were given in general; they were now particularized with the words: BLESSINGS OF HEAVEN ABOVE, ETC. THE BLESSINGS OF THY FATHER HAVE PREVAILED ABOVE THE BLESSINGS OF MY PROGENITORS.

This was so because Jacob inherited the cream of all more than the other patriarchs, he being perfect in all, and he gave all to Joseph. This was fitting, because the Righteous One takes all and inherits all, and all blessings are deposited with him. He first dispenses blessings above, and all the limbs of the body are disposed so as to receive them, and thus is brought into being the "river which goes forth from Eden". Why Eden (lit. delight)? Because whenever all the limbs are knit together in harmony and in mutual delight, from top to bottom, then they pour blessings upon it, and it becomes a river which flows forth, literally, from "delight". Or again, the word "Eden" may refer to the supreme Wisdom, from which the whole flows forth like a river until it reaches this grade, where all is turned to blessing. The two interpretations are practically the same. UNTO THE UTMOST BOUND OF THE

EVERLASTING HILLS. Or better, "unto the desire (ta'avath) of, etc." These everlasting hills are two females, one above and one below, each of whom is called 'olam (a world). The desire of all the limbs of the Body is for those two Mothers, from below to suck from the higher Mother, and from above to be linked with the lower Mother, both desires being in essence the same. Therefore, THEY SHALL ALL BE ON THE HEAD OF JOSEPH, so that the grade of the Righteous One should be blessed and receive all as befits. Happy are they who are called righteous, for only he is so called who observes this grade, this sign of the holy covenant. Happy are they in this world and in the world to come.

They now went out of the cave. Said R. Simeon: 'Let each one of us give some exposition as we go along.' R. Eleazar commenced with the next verse: BENJAMIN IS A WOLF THAT RAVINETH. Benjamin is called a wolf because he was imprinted in this form on the Throne, all animals great and small being delineated there. The throne which Solomon made contained similar designs. He is also called a wolf because the altar was in his territory, and the altar is called "wolf" because it consumed flesh every day. Again, we may translate: "Benjamin shall feed the wolf", to wit, the adversaries who are posted above to accuse, and who are all appeased by the sacrifice. IN THE MORNING HE SHALL DEVOUR THE PREY. This means that in the morning, when Abraham stirs in the world and it is the time of grace, the sacrifice brings appeasement and rises to the place called 'Ad (perpetuity). We may also translate "In the morning 'Ad shall eat", this being the supernal throne which is forever and ever ('ade 'ad). The smoke ascends and love is awakened above,

Zohar: Bereshith, Section 1, Page 248a

and a lamp is kindled and shines forth through this impulse from below. The priest is busy and the Levites sing praises joyfully, and wine is poured forth to be united with water (wine being good below to cause gladness to another wine above), and all is at work to link the Left with the Right. The bread, which is the "fine flour" used for royalty, and which gave the impulse, is received by the Left and the Right and joined to the Body. Then the supernal oil flows forth and is taken up by the hand of the Zaddik (hence the impulse must be given by means of fine flour and oil commingled, so that all should be linked together). So a complete unity is formed, with its resulting delight and the gratification which is gathered up by all the crowns. These all join together, and the moon is illumined through being joined with the sun, and there is universal delight. This is indeed "an offering for the Lord", and for no other. Hence, in the morning Ad shall eat and no other, until he has been sated and linked to his place. For first the Holy Name must be blessed and then others, and therefore it is forbidden to a man to bless his neighbour in the morning until he has blessed God.' AND AT EVEN HE SHALL DIVIDE THE SPOIL. The evening sacrifice was brought wholly to God, and the stirring ascended thither. And having received His blessing, He linked up all the other celestial powers and assigned to each its fitting blessings, so that worlds were gratified and upper and lower were blessed. This is hinted in the verse: "I have eaten my honeycomb with my honey" first of all; and afterwards He shares out among all and says: "Eat, O friends, drink, yea, drink abundantly, O beloved" (S. S. v, 1). Think not that the offering is brought to them or to any other power, but all is to the Lord, and He dispenses blessings to all the worlds.' Said R. Simeon: 'My son, you have said well. The whole object of the sacrifice is to set blessings in motion. First it is "an offering to the Lord" and no other, and then "you shall bring your offering" (i.e. carry away your gift), in that all worlds will be linked together and upper and lower will be blessed.' R. Abba then commenced with the next verse: ALL THESE ARE THE TWELVE TRIBES OF ISRAEL. 'The word "all" signifies that they were all attached irremovably to the place from which all blessings issue. The "twelve" refers to the twelve links of the adornments of the Matron, she being joined with them. AND THIS IT IS THAT THEIR FATHER SPAKE UNTO THEM AND BLESSED THEM.

The word "spake" indicates that in this place speech has scope. Further, we have here the union of upper with lower and of lower with upper. Below there is a union through the twelve tribes to which Zoth (this) was joined. The words "that he spoke" indicate the union of male and female. Thus there is a union on two sides, below and above. Finally, he united them in the place above, male and female together, as it is written: "Every one according to his blessing, etc." Similarly in the verse, "The Lord bless thee out of Zion, and see thou the good of Jerusalem, all the days of thy life" (Ps. CXXVII, 5), Zion is mentioned because from it issue blessings to water the garden, and then Jerusalem is mentioned to show that all blessings issue from male and female together. Similarly it is written: "The Lord bless thee and keep thee" (Num. VI, 24) – "bless" from the male, and "keep" from the female.'

Zohar: Bereshith, Section 1, Page 248b

R. Judah opened with the verse: AND WHEN JACOB MADE AN END OF CHARGING HIS SONS, ETC. We should have expected here "blessing" instead of "charging". What it means, however, is that he charged them to remain united with the Shekinah. He also charged them concerning the cave (of Machpelah), which is near the Garden of Eden, and where Adam was buried. That place was called Kiriath Arba (lit. city of four) because four couples were buried there -Adam and Eve, Abraham and Sarah, Isaac and Rebecca, Jacob and Leah. A difficulty arises here. We have learnt that the patriarchs are the "holy chariot", and a chariot consists of not less than four. We have further learnt that God joined King David with them so as to form a complete chariot. If so, then David ought to have been joined with them in the cave. The reason, however, why he was not buried with them was because a fitting place was prepared for him elsewhere, namely Zion. As for Adam, the patriarchs were buried with him because he was the first king, though the kingship was taken from him and given to David, who derived his seventy years from the years of Adam. As the patriarchs could not go on living till David appeared, he was assigned a fitting place elsewhere and was not buried with them.' HE GATHERED UP HIS FEET INTO THE BED. Since he was abiding in the place of the living, when he was about to depart from the world he gathered his feet into the bed. This is illustrated by the verse: "My soul yearns and longs for the courts of the Lord" (Ps. LXXXIV, 2). The Companions have explained this as follows. There are lower abodes and higher abodes. In the higher there are no dwellers, they being the inner room, but the outer rooms are called "courts of the Lord", because they are filled with love and desire for the female. When the soul departs, it turns wholly to the female, being united with it in whole-hearted desire. It is not said that Jacob died, but only that he "yielded up the ghost and was gathered unto his people". The words "he gathered up his feet into the bed" indicate that the sun was gathered in unto the moon. The sun does not die, but is gathered in from the world and goes to join the moon. When Jacob was gathered in, the moon was illumined, and the desire of the supernal sun was awakened for her, because when the sun departs, another sun arises and attaches itself to the first, and the moon is illumined.' Said R. Simeon: 'You are quite right. It has, however, been affirmed that above, the world of the male is joined with a lower one, which is the world of the female, and that the lower world is joined with the upper, and so one is the counterpart of the other. It has also been affirmed that there are two worlds, and although there are two females, one is supported by the male and one by the female. It is written: "The words of King Lemuel, the oracle which his mother taught him" (Prov. XXXI, 1). The secret meaning of this verse is not known. We may, however, render "the words which were spoken for the sake of El (God)

Zohar: Bereshith, Section 1, Page 249a

who is king". Observe that Jacob was gathered into the moon and through it produced fruit [Tr. note: i.e. souls.] in the world, and there is no generation without the fruit of Jacob, because he gave an impulse above. Happy is the portion of Jacob, since he was made perfect above and below, as it is written: "Fear not thou, O Jacob my servant, saith the Lord, for I am with thee" (Jer. XLVI, 28); it does not say "for thou art with me", but "for I am with thee", as has been pointed out.'

R. Isaac opened with the verse: AND THEY CAME TO THE THRESHING FLOOR OF ATAD. He said: What does it concern us that they came to the threshing floor of Atad, and why should there have been a great mourning there to the Egyptians? It has, however, been stated that as long as Jacob was in Egypt the land was blessed for his sake, and the Nile used to rise and water it, and, in fact, the famine ceased at his coming. Hence the Egyptians mourned for him.' R. Isaac here quoted the verse: "Who can utter the severities (geburoth) of the Lord or show forth all his praise?" (Ps. CXI, 2). 'We have here', he said, 'the unusual word yemallel (utter) instead of the more usual yedaber (speak). Such variations in the

Scripture are never without significance. So here, the word yemallel is akin to the word meliloth (cuttings), and is applied to the severities of the Lord because they are so numerous. Forevery sentence of punishment issues from there, and who is there who can annul one decree of those forcible acts which God performs? Or, again, we may take "utter" as being synonymous with "speak", and the meaning is that no man can recite the severities of the Lord, because they are innumerable, and there is no end to the officers of judgement. They can only be known by a recital which contains allusions of Wisdom, but not by straightforward speech. "Or show forth all his praise": for many are the grades which join in praise, hosts and camps without number, as it is written: "Can his hosts be counted?" See now, the Egyptians were all clever, and came from the side of Geburah. They knew countless hosts and camps and grades upon grades till they came to the lowest grades. Through their divinations they were aware that as long as Jacob was alive no people could gain dominion over his sons. They also knew that they would enslave Israel many times. When Jacob died they rejoiced, but looking farther afield, they foresaw the punishments which would issue from Atad, ([Tr. note: An allusion to the "mighty hand," with which God smote the Egyptians, the word atad having the same numerical value as yad (hand).] so when they came to this place "they lamented there with a very great and sore lamentation". And they rightly called it the "mourning of the Egyptians", because it was truly a mourning for them and for no others.'

R. Simeon made as though to depart, when he said: 'I see that on this day a house will fall in the town and bury two informers in its ruins. If I am in the town the house will not fall.' So they returned to the cave and sat down. R. Simeon then discoursed on the verse: Raise thy voice, O daughter of Gallim, etc. (Is. x, 30).

Zohar: Bereshith, Section 1, Page 249b

'This verse', he said, 'was addressed to the Community of Israel, which lauds God with the voice of praise. We learn from here that anyone who desires to praise God with singing should have an agreeable voice in order that those who listen may derive pleasure from hearing him; if not, he should not come forward to sing. The Levites were commanded to retire from service at the age of fifty (Num. VIII, 25), because at that age a man's voice begins to fail and is no longer so agreeable. The word Gallim (lit. heaps) indicates the future world, in which heaps of things are contained. The verse continues: "O listen, Laishah", this laishah (lit. lioness) signifies power to crush hostile forces, and when Israel sing praises then this listens. The verse continues: "Poor Anathoth." When the moon is full it is called "the field of apples", but when it is defective it is called "the field of Anathoth (poverty)". Hence, praise from below affords it wealth and completeness, and so David all his lifetime sought to provide this completeness by chanting hymns of praise below. When David died he left it complete, and Solomon received it at its full, since the moon had escaped from poverty and entered into riches. By means of this riches Solomon ruled over all the kings of the earth, and therefore "silver was not accounted for anything in the days of Solomon" (I Kings x, 21), but everything was of gold; and of that time it is written: "And he had dust of gold" (Job XXVIII, 6). For the sun shining on the dust of the mountain tops turned it into gold. From the rays of the sun beating on the mountains the dust

Zohar: Bereshith, Section 1, Page 250a

of the earth among the mountains became gold. And but for the wild beasts that roamed there, men would not have been poor. When Solomon observed this he called aloud: "All was from the dust" (Eccl. III, 20). Hence Solomon had no need to sing like David, save one song which is beloved of wealth, and is the jewel and favourite of all chants of praises, since it contains the praises recited by the Matron when she sits on the throne opposite the King. Everything was gold, and dust was joined with the left hand, on the side of love, and the sun clung to it and did not part from it. Solomon was hereby led into error. He saw that the moon had approached the sun and the right hand was embracing and the left hand under the head. Seeing this he said: "What need is there of the right hand here, seeing that they have drawn near to one another?" God then said to him: "I swear to thee that as thou hast rejected the right hand, thou shalt one day require the kindness (hesed) [Tr. note: which comes from the Right.] of men and shalt not obtain it." Straightway the sun parted from the moon, and the moon began to darken, and Solomon went begging and said: "I am Koheleth", and no one would show him kindness.

'It is written: "The old lion perishes without prey, and the young of the lioness are scattered" (Job IV, 11). When the lioness gives food, all the (heavenly) hosts come together and draw sustenance. But when she is without prey on account of the Galuth, then they are scattered to different sides. Hence, when the sacrifices were offered they were all supported and drew near together, as we have said. But now that there are no sacrifices, then indeed "the young of the lioness are scattered" Hence, there is no day without punishment, because upper and lower do not receive the proper impulse, as we have said. Now it is prayer which gives the proper impulse above and below, and through the blessings with which we bless God upper and lower are blessed. Hence worlds are blessed through the prayer of Israel. He who blesses God is blessed, and he who does not bless God is not blessed. Rab Hamnuna the Elder would not allow anyone else to take the cup of blessing, but he himself took it in his two hands and said the blessing. We have affirmed that the cup should be taken in the right hand, and not in the left. It is called "cup of salvations" (Ps. CXVI, 13), because through it blessings are drawn from the supernal salvations, and in it is collected the supernal wine. Also, the table over which the blessing is said should not be devoid of both bread and wine. The Community of Israel is called "cup of blessing", and therefore the cup should be raised both by the right hand and the left hand, so as to be set between.

Zohar: Bereshith, Section 1, Page 250b

It should be filled with wine, because of the wine of the Torah which issues from the future world. There is a mystic allusion in this cup of blessing to the holy chariot. The right and left hands correspond to the north and south, between which is "the couch of Solomon". He who says the blessing should fix his eye upon the cup to bless it with four blessings. Thus the cup contains the emblem of faith, north, south, east, and west, and so the holy chariot. There should be bread on the table in order that the lower bread may be blessed, and the "bread of poverty" may become the "bread of luxury". In this way the Community of Israel will be blessed in all four directions, above and below; above by the bread of blessing and the cup of blessing through which King David is joined to the patriarchs, and below, that bread should never be lacking from the Israelite's table.'

They all rose and kissed his hands, saying: "God be blessed who has brought us into the world to hear all this." They then left the cave and went on their way. When they reached the town, they saw a funeral procession for some men who had died through a house falling on them, and in whom were included some informers, as R. Simeon had said. R. Simeon quoted the text: "And they came to the threshing floor of Atad", saying: 'This is a hint of the passing of the dominion of the Egyptians to give place to the dominion of Israel; and hence it was that they "lamented with a very great and sore lamentation". So here also these people are not mourning for the Jews, although there are some Jews among the dead; and even these, had they been really Jews, would not have been killed, and since they have died God pardons their sins.

R. Simeon said: 'Although Jacob died in Egypt, yet his soul did not depart in a foreign land, since when he died his soul was straightway joined to its place. as we have stated. When Jacob entered the cave, all the perfumes of Eden filled it and a light went up from it and a lamp was kindled there. When the patriarchs went to Jacob in Egypt, to be with him, the light of the candle departed, but when Jacob entered the cave it returned. With his admission the cave obtained its full complement, and it never again received another occupant, nor will it ever receive one. The souls that are worthy pass before the patriarchs in the cave in order that they may awake and behold the seed which they have left in the world, and rejoice before the Almighty.'

R. Abba asked: 'What was the embalming of Jacob?' He said to him: 'Go and ask a physician. It says: "and Joseph commanded his servants the physicians to embalm his father, and the physicians embalmed Israel". Apparently, this embalming was like that of any other person. It cannot have been on account of the journey to Canaan, because Joseph also was embalmed and yet he was not taken out of the country. The real reason was that it was the custom to embalm kings in order to preserve their bodies. They were embalmed with very special oil mixed with spices. This was rubbed on them day after day for forty days. After that, the body could last for a very long time. For the air of the land of Canaan and of the land of Egypt corrupts the body

Zohar: Bereshith, Section 1, Page 251a

more rapidly than that of any other country. Hence they do this to preserve the body, embalming it within and without. They place the oil on the navel, and it enters into the body and draws out the inside, and thus preserves it inside and outside. It was fitting that Jacob's body should be so preserved, since he was the body of the patriarchs. Similarly Joseph, who was an emblem of the body, was preserved both in body and soul-in body, as it says "and they embalmed him", in soul, as it is written, "and he was put in a coffin in Egypt". The word vayisem (and he was put) is spelt with two yods, one of them to indicate an ark above which is called "the ark of the covenant", which Joseph inherited because he kept the covenant. There is also another hint in this expression, to wit, that although he died on a foreign soil, his soul was united with the Shekinah, the reason being that he was righteous, and every righteous one inherits the celestial holy land, as it is written: "And thy people are all righteous, they shall forever inherit the land, the branch of my planting, the work of my hands, that I may be glorified" (Is. LX, 21).'

Zohar Section 2: Exodus

Zohar: Shemoth, Section 2, Page 2a

SHEMOTH

NOW THESE ARE THE NAMES OF THE CHILDREN OF ISRAEL WHICH CAME INTO EGYPT EVERY MAN AND HIS HOUSEHOLD CAME WITH JACOB. It is written: And the wise shall be resplendent as the splendour (zohar) of the firmament, and they that turn many to righteousness shall be like the stars forever and ever (Dan. XII, 3). "The wise" are those who penetrate to the real essence of wisdom; "they shall be resplendent", i.e. illumined with the radiance of the supernal Wisdom; "as the splendour", this is the flashing of the Stream that goes forth from Eden (Gen. XI, 10), this being alluded to as "the firmament". There are suspended the stars, the planets, the sun and the moon, and all the radiant lights. The brightness of this firmament shines upon the Garden of Eden, and in the midst of the Garden stands the Tree of Life, whose branches spread over all forms and trees and spices in fitting vessels. All the beasts of the field and all the fowls of the air shelter beneath the branches of this Tree. The fruit of the Tree gives life to all. It is everlasting. The "other side" has no abode therein, but only the side of holiness. Blessed are they who taste thereof; they will live forever and ever, and it is they who are called "the wise", and they are vouchsafed life in this world as well as in the world to come..

The Tree rises to a height of five hundred parasangs, and its circumference is six myriads of parasangs. Within this Tree is a light [Tr. note: Tifereth.] out of which radiate certain colours: they come and go, never being at rest save in the Tree. Should they issue from it to show themselves in the brightness which does not shine of itself, [Tr. note: Malkuth.] they are not at rest but flit about. From this Tree went fortn twelve tribes, [Tr. note: The twelve 'obliquities' of Tifereth.] who had long been warmed by it, and they went down with this light that does not shine of itself into the exile of Egypt, accompanied by multitudes of heavenly hosts.

R. Simeon compared the Egyptian with the Babylonian exile, basing his remarks on the text: "The word of the Lord came (lit. coming came) to Ezekiel" (Ezek. 1, 3). 'Why', he said, 'the double expression "coming came"?

Zohar: Shemoth, Section 2, Page 2b

Moreover, if Ezekiel was indeed a faithful prophet, why did he disclose the whole of his vision? Is it right and meet for one whom the king has invited to his palace to reveal all the secrets which he has seen there? Now Ezekiel was indeed a faithful prophet, and whatever he saw he faithfully kept secret, and whatever he revealed he revealed by permission of the Holy One, blessed be He, and for proper reasons. Observe now that one who is accustomed to pain bears it patiently, but if one is not accustomed to pain and has always lived at ease, when pain comes upon him he really feels it keenly and deserves to be pitied. So when Israel went to Egypt they were inured to suffering, their father, the righteous Jacob, having been all his life a man of sorrows, and they could thus endure the exile patiently. But the exile of Babylon was a real torment for which there was weeping both in heaven and on earth, as it is written: "Behold, their heroes (angels) cried without, the angels of peace weeped bitterly" (Isa. XXXIII, 7); "by the rivers of Babylon, there we sat down, yea, we wept, when we remembered Zion" (Ps. CXXXVII, I): yea truly, all joined in the lamentation. They who had been brought up in royal luxury were now driven into exile with their necks yoked and their hands fettered; and when they reached the land of exile despair settled in their hearts, and they thought that they would never be raised up again, since God had deserted them. At that hour the Holy One called together all His heavenly hosts, His Family above, all the holy Chariots, the lower and the higher ranks, the whole celestial army, and spoke to them thus: "What do ye here? My beloved children are captives in Babylon, and do ye remain here? Arise, all of you, and go to them, and I will go with you." When the celestial Company arrived in Babylon, the heavens opened, and the holy spirit of prophecy descended upon Ezekiel, and he saw his wonderful vision, and proclaimed to the exiles: "Behold, your Master is here, and all the celestial beings have come down to be your companions." But they believed it not, and so he was compelled to disclose to them the whole of his heavenly vision. Then their joy was exceedingly great, and they recked not of the exile, knowing that the Lord Himself was in their midst. They were all filled with a perfect love of Him, ready to sacrifice themselves for the holiness of the All-Holy, blessed be He! This is the reason why the prophet disclosed to them all that he saw.

'We have been taught that wherever Israel went into captivity the Shekinah went with her. We learn this in the present instance from the expression "children of [the supernal] Israel", which we take here to refer to the heavenly hosts and chariots, which, we are told, "came with Jacob to Egypt".' R. Hiya cited in this connection the verse: Come with me from Lebanon, bride, with me from Lebanon! Look from the top of Amana, from the top of Senir and Hermon, from the lions' dens, from the mountains of the leopards. (S.S. IV, 8). 'This', he said, 'refers to the Community of Israel. When the Community of Israel left Egypt and went up to Mount Sinai to receive the Law, the Holy One said to her: "Come with Me, My bride, with Me, Lebanah (lit. white), thou moon who receivest thy light from the Sun!

Zohar: Shemoth, Section 2, Page 3a

Look (tashuri), a beautiful present (teshurah) wilt thou receive for thy children, from the top of Amana, from the realm of the supernal Faith (emunah)", the reference in the last word being to the.children of Israel when they said, "all that the Lord hath said we will do, and obey" (Ex. XXIV, 7), and who were then like angels, perfectly united, of whom the Psalmist sings, "bless ye the Lord, ye angels, mighty in strength, that do his commandments, hearkening unto the voice of his word" (Ps. ClII, 20). Thus Israel received a present "from the top of Senir and Hermon": i.e. from Mount Sinai, at the nether part of which they stood. Also "from the lions' dens": namely, the children of Seir, who refused the Law when offered to them. "From the mountains of the leopards": namely, the children of Ishmael, who likewise refused, as it is written, "The Lord came from Sinai, and rose up from Seir unto them; he shined forth from Mount Paran, and he came from the ten thousands of holy ones" (Deut. xxx, 2).And what is the meaning of "He came from the ten thousands of holy ones"? An ancient tradition explains it thus: when the Holy One was about to give the Law to Israel, hosts of angels protested with one voice, saying: "O Lord, our lord, how excellent is thy Name in all the earth! Give thy Glory (the Torah) to the heavens!" (Ps. VIII, I-2). In truth, they desired the Torah for themselves. Said the Holy One to them: "Has death any sway over you? Behold, in My Law death is the punishment for certain sins! Is robbery or theft known to you? In My Law it is written, 'Thou shalt not steal! Is there sexual desire among you? I have said, 'Thou shalt not commit adultery! Is it possible for you to lie? I have said, 'Thou shalt not bear false witness against thy neighbour! Can covetousness lodge with you? I have said, 'Thou shalt not covet! Of what service, then, will the Law be to you?" Straightway they sang in unison: "O Lord, our lord, how excellent is thy Name in all the earth" (ibid. 10). No more did they say, "give Thy glory to the heavens"!'.

R. Yose interpreted the above verse in the Song of Songs in connection with the descent of the.Shekinah to the Egyptian captivity. R. Simeon, however, found in it an allusion to the mystic union between Voice and Utterance. These should form one unity, without any separation whatever. They depend upon one another: no Voice without Utterance, and no Utterance without Voice. Essentially they both come from "Lebanon" (=lebanah, moon, symbolizing Wisdom). "Amana" represents the throat, out of which comes the breath to complete the hidden indication first given from "Lebanon". "From the top of Senir and Hermon" refers to the tongue; "from the lions' dens" suggests the teeth; "from the mountains of the.leopards" is symbolic of the lips, by which the Utterance is made complete.

R. Hiya applied to the Israelites who went down to Egypt the verse: "Eat thou not the bread of him that hath an evil eye, neither desire thou his dainties" (Prov. XXIII, 6). 'Indeed,' he said, 'the bread or any other boon offered by an evil-eyed man is not worth while partaking of or enjoying. Had the children of Israel, in going down into Egypt, not tasted the bread of the Egyptians they would not have remained there in exile, nor would the Egyptians have oppressed them.' Said R. Isaac: 'Was not that exile the fulfilment of a divine decree?' R. Hiya said in reply: 'That makes no difference, inasmuch as the decree did not mention Egypt in particular, only saying: "Thy seed shall be a stranger in a land that is not theirs" (Gen. XVI, 13)-not necessarily Egypt.' R. Isaac said: 'Though a man should have a vigorous appetite and be a hearty eater, yet if he encounters such an evil-eyed man, it were better for him to take his own life than partake of his bread.'

There are three types of men who drive away the Shekinah from the world, making it impossible for the Holy One, blessed be He, to fix His abode in the universe, and causing prayer to be unanswered.

Zohar: Shemoth, Section 2, Page 3b

One is he who cohabits with a woman in the days of her separation. There is no impurity comparable with this. He defiles himself and all connected with him. The child born of such a union is shapen in impurity, imbibes the spirit of impurity, and its whole life is founded on impurity. Next is he who lies with a heathen woman, for he profanes herewith the sacred sign of the covenant which constitutes the support of the sacred Name and the essence of faith. As soon as "the people committed whoredom" with the daughters of Moab, the anger of the Lord was kindled against Israel (Num. xxv, I-3). The leaders of the people, who did not endeavour to prevent them, were the first to be punished (ibid. 4), and in every generation it is the leaders who are made responsible for all the members of the community in regard to the profanation of the sign of the covenant, which is "sun and shield" (Ps. LXXXIV, 12): as the sun gives light to the world, so does the holy sign give light to the body, and as the shield protects, so does the holy sign protect. He who keeps it in purity is guarded from evil. But he who transfers this sign of holiness into a strange domain, breaks the commandment, "Thou shalt have no other gods but Me"; for to deny the king's seal is equivalent to denying the king himself. Next is he who purposely prevents the seed from coming to fruition, for he destroys the King's workmanship and so causes the Holy One to depart from the world. This sin is the cause of war, famine, and pestilence, and it prevents the Shekinah from finding any resting place in the world. For these abominations the spirit of holiness weeps. Woe to him who causes this: it were better that he had never been born. It was counted to the Israelites for righteousness that, although in exile in Egypt, they kept themselves free from these sins, and, moreover, fearlessly fulfilled the command to increase and multiply. This made them worthy to be liberated. R. Hiya found an indication of the purity of the Israelitish women in Egypt in the text:

Zohar: Shemoth, Section 2, Page 4a

"And he made the laver of brass, and the foot of it brass, of the looking-glasses of the women assembling at the door of the tent" (Ex. XXXVIII, 8). What was the merit of the women to have made them worthy of such honour that their looking-glasses should be used for the laver of the Tabernacle? Their ritual ablutions on the one hand, and their eagerness to attract their husbands on the other.

R. Eleazar and R. Yose were once walking together. Said R. Eleazar to R. Yose: 'Open thy mouth, and let thy words flow forth!' R. Yose replied: 'Will it please the master if I ask him to solve a certain difficulty for me? I have heard from the mouth of the "holy lamp" (R. Simeon b. Yohai) this interpretation of the words: "and these are the names of the children of Israel"-that they refer to the "Ancient Israel" (God)and to all the heavenly hosts and chariots who went into captivity with Jacob. I am, however, puzzled how to fit the words "a man and his household" in this verse into this interpretation.' R. Eleazar replied: 'What R. Simeon said is certainly correct. We have an esoteric doctrine that the receiver is, as it were, a "house" to the giver. This may be illustrated from the following verse: "And it came to pass when Solomon had finished the building of the house of the Lord and the king's house" (I K. IX, I). "The house of the Lord" is, of course, the Temple, which includes the outer courts, the porch, the antechambers, and the Temple itself: but the "king's house" is not, as you might think, the palace of Solomon, but the Holy of Holies, the innermost sanctum, the word "King" being here used in its absolute sense. For this King, although supreme, is, in relation to the Highest Point, the most hidden One, feminine, or receptive; but at the same time He is masculine, or active, in relation to the lower King; and this double relationship, to that which is above and that which is below, appertains to the whole supramundane world. It is in this symbolic sense that the angels are here called "his house".' AND THESE ARE THE NAMES. R. Yose connected these words with the words from the Song of Songs (IV, 12): "A closed garden is my sister bride, a closed spring, a sealed fountain." '"A closed garden" refers to the Community of Israel, for,' said R. Eleazar, 'as the garden has to be tended, ploughed, watered, and trimmed, so has the Community of Israel to be tended, nurtured, and trimmed. She is called "garden" and she is called "vineyard": "for the vineyard of the Lord of Hosts is Israel... and he fenced it and gathered out the stones thereof" (Isa. v, I-7).' Said R. Simeon:

[Tr. note: This paragraph belongs to the Tosefta (and is not found in our Hebrew text of the Zohar proper).]

We open our eyes
And straightway behold.
The holy chariot's
Swift-rolling wheels..
Voices of song.
Making lovely the air,
A joy to the heart,
A grace to the ear.
Thousand on thousand.
To trembling now fall.
As they sing and rejoice.
From below to above.
In tune with the song
Standing who stand.
Joined who are joined In multitudes thronging,
Four hundred and fifty. Thousands of beings.
Gifted with sight are they. Yet see and see not.
Two hosts them encompass.
As great as the first.
On the left hand is sorrow,
Is crying and moaning.

The Lords of Weeping.
Their dwelling here set;
Their being is judgement,
And chastisement their end.
The Judge is there ready.
And the books are open.
At this hour and moment.
The Lord of judgement.
Ascends to His Throne.
The singing ceases.
And silence falls.
Judgement begins.
The Lords of the right hand.
Who see and perceive.
And eighteen thousand.

Zohar: Shemoth, Section 2, Page 4b

Angelic companions.
Fearlessly sing.
And trumpets ring forth.
And a trembling begins.
Once again do thy sound. And the voices are silent.
Then rises the Lord.
From the Judgement throne;
On the throne of reconcilement
The Merciful now sits,
And utters the Name-. The holy, the blessed,. Source of mercy for men. And life-giving to all.
"Yod He Vau He" He cries;
Then murmurs anew. The song of the myriads, Of holy turning wheels.
In ecstasy they chant "Blessed be the Lord's glory.
From the place of His Shekinah".. The secret Garden
In worlds of light hidden-Two hundred and fifty Encompassing worlds-Where Shekinah's splendour
From splendour proceeding Its splendour sends forth
To the ends of creation, In the fulness of glory Is revealed in its beauty
To the eyes made seeing-The garden of Eden.
The Ancient, the Father, The Holy One speaks
His Name again pronouncing, "Yod He Vau He" again Gloriously crying.
Then speak the lightful Hosts Making brave music:
His thirteen paths of mercy They gladly proclaim.
Who sees those mighty ones High in the Heavens
Mighty in beauty? Who sees the Chariots Holy and glorious?
Who sees the Hosts in
The bright courts of glory Exalting and praising
In awe and in fear In joy and in wonder
The Holy One's Name?

Blessed are the souls of the righteous who perceive it! "There is none like unto thee, O Lord; thou art great and thy Name is great. Who would not be in awe of thee, thou king of the nations?" (Jer. x, 6-7).

Said R. Simeon: 'When the Shekinah went down to Egypt, a celestial "living being" (Hayah, cf. Ezek. 1, 5), called "Israel", in form like the patriarch Jacob, went down with Her, accompanied by forty-two heavenly attendants, each of whom bore a letter belonging to the Holy Name. They all descended with Jacob to Egypt, and hence it says "and these are the names of the children of Israel which came into Egypt... with Jacob".'

R. Judah asked R. Eleazar, the son of R. Simeon: 'As thou hast heard from thy father the mystical interpretation of this section of the Book of Exodus, tell me the significance of the words "a man and his household came with Jacob".' He replied: 'My father said that it refers to the various grades of angels, all of them celestial, but of whom the higher are called "men", and the lower "household" or "female", in the sense that the former are active while the latter are passive and receptive.'

When R. Isaac was once studying with R. Eleazar, the son of R. Simeon, he asked him: 'Did the Shekinah go down to Egypt with Jacob?' Said R. Eleazar: 'Surely! Did not God say to Jacob, "I will go down with thee into Egypt" (Gen. XLVI, 4)?' Said R. Isaac: 'See now, the Shekinah went down with Jacob into Egypt, but She also had with Her six hundred thousand holy Chariots (angelic beings), for it is written," and the children of Israel journeyed from Rameses to Succoth, about (lit. Iike) six hundred thousand on foot" (Ex. XII, 37). Now it does not say "six hundred", but "like" six hundred, etc., which suggests that there was an equal number of celestial beings who went out with them. The deeper meaning of the passage is as follows. When these holy Chariots and holy Hosts were about to leave Egypt, the children of Israel at once realized that it was for their sake that the celestial beings were detained, and therefore they hastened to get ready and leave as quickly as possible. Hence it says "they could not tarry" (Ex. XII, 39), not "they did not want to tarry". From this we learn that the expression "children of Israel" in all these passages refers to the celestial hosts. Moreover, it stands to reason that, as the Holy One promised Jacob that He would go down with him into Egypt, He would take His ministering angels with Him, for where the Master is there must His servants also be, and especially when we consider that even when Jacob was saved from Laban, "the angels of God met him" (Gen. XXXII, 2).'

Zohar: Shemoth, Section 2, Page 5a

[Note: The first 3 lines of the Hebrew text do not appear in our translation.]

R. Abba cited here the verse: "Come, behold the works of the Lord who hath made desolations in the earth" (Ps. XLVI, 8). 'The term shammoth (desolations)', he said, 'can also be read shemoth (names). This corroborates what R. Hiya said, namely, that whatever is in heaven, the Holy One, blessed be He, has made a counterpart thereof on earth. Thus, as there are hallowed names in heaven, so there are hallowed names on earth.' Said R. Yose: 'When Jacob went down to Egypt, sixty myriads of celestial angels accompanied him.' R. Judah illustrated from the verse: "Behold, it is the couch of Solomon, threescore mighty men are about it, of the mighty men of Israel" (S.S. III, 7), which he expounded thus: 'Six luminosities form a circle surrounding a seventh luminosity in the centre. The six on the circumference sustain the sixty valiant angels surrounding the "couch of Solomon". The "couch" is an allusion to the Shekinah, and "Solomon" refers to the "King to whom peace (shalom) belongs": "threescore mighty men are about it"—these are the sixty myriads of exalted angels, part of the army of the Shekinah which accompanied Jacob into Egypt.'

R. Hiya was once travelling from Usha to Lud, mounted on an ass, and R. Yose accompanied him on foot. R. Hiya dismounted, took R. Yose by the hand, and said: 'If men only knew what great honour was shown to Jacob when the Holy One said to him, "I will go down with thee to Egypt", they would lick the dust for three parasangs distance from his grave! For it has been said by the great Rabbis of old in connection with the verse, "And Moses went out to meet his father-in-law, and did obeisance" (Ex. XVIII, 7), that when Aaron saw Moses go, he also went, and so did Eleazar, and the princes, and the elders, and, in fact, all Israel went out to meet Jethro. For who could see Moses or the great ones go and not go himself? Thus because Moses went, all went. Now if Moses produced such an effect, how much more must God have done so when He said to Jacob "I will go down with thee to Egypt"?' As they were going along, R. Abba met them. Said R. Yose: 'Behold, the Shekinah is in our midst, as we have a great master of doctrine with us.' Said R. Abba: 'What were you discussing?' R. Yose replied: 'We were deducing that the angels went down with Israel to Egypt from the two verses "I will come down with thee into Egypt" and "These are the names, etc.".' Said R. Abba: 'I will give you a third. It says, "The word of the Lord came expressly unto Ezekiel... in the land of the Chaldeans by the river Chebar" (Ezek. 1, 3). Ezekiel, it is said, could not have been as faithful as Moses, of whom it is written, "He is faithful in all my house", for he revealed all the treasures of the King. But we have been instructed to beware of such thoughts about this prophet; on the contrary, he was a worthy prophet, and what he revealed he revealed with the permission of the Holy One, and he might have disclosed twice as much, because of the sad condition in which Israel found herself in Babylon, as has been explained already, and he had to prove to them that the Holy One would never leave His people in captivity without His Presence. Thus it goes without saying that when Jacob went down to Egypt, the Holy One, and His Shekinah, and all the holy heavenly beings, and all the Chariots, went down with him.'.

Zohar: Shemoth, Section 2, Page 5b

R. Judah said: 'If men only knew the love which God bears for Israel, they would roar like a lion till they could follow her! For when Jacob went down to Egypt, the Holy One called together all His celestial Family and said: "All of you must go down to Egypt, and I shall come with you!" Said the Shekinah: "Can hosts remain without a king?" Said He to Her: "Come with me from Lebanon, bride! With me from Lebanon! Look from the top of Amana, from the top of Senir and Hermon, from the lions' dens, from the mountains of the leopards" (S.S. IV, 8), i.e. "Come with Me from the Sanctuary above! Look from the tops of those who are the heads of the "Sons of Faith" (amanah=emunah)! Behold, they are about to receive from the mountain Hermon My Torah, which will be their shield in exile! Come from the lions' dens, the mountains of the leopards-the heathen nations who torment them with all manner of oppression".' R. Isaac applied the words, "Look from the top of Amana" to the Sanctuary above and to the Sanctuary below, according to the dictum of R. Judah, that the Shekinah never departed from the Western wall of the Temple. R. Judah applied the words, "From the lions' dens, etc.", to students of the Torah in the dens, i.e. in the synagogues and houses of study..

R. Hiya, as he was once studying with R. Simeon, asked him: 'Why does the Torah, in this passage (Ex. 1, 1-5), besides giving the total number of seventy souls, enumerate the twelve tribes by name? And further, why seventy?' R. Simeon replied: 'In order to bring out the contrast between the one nation and the seventy nations of the Gentiles in the world. What is more,' he went on, 'the principalities that preside over the seventy nations issue from twelve axes that stretch out to all points of the compass. This is the significance of the words, "He set the bounds of the peoples according to the number of the children of Israel" (Deut. XXXII, 8), and "For I have spread you abroad as the four winds of heaven" (Zech. II, 6): as the world cannot be without the four cardinal points, so cannot the nations be without Israel.' NOW THERE AROSE UP A NEW KING OVER EGYPT. R. Abba cited here the verse: Blessed are ye who sow above all waters, that send forth the feet of the ox and the ass (Isa. XXXII, 20). He said: 'Blessed are the children of Israel whom God hath chosen above all nations and brought near to Himself, as it is written, "The Lord hath chosen thee to be a peculiar people unto himself" (Deut. XIV, 2), and again, "For the Lord's portion is his people: Jacob is the lot of his inheritance" (Ibid. XXXII, 9). Israel cleaves to the Holy One, blessed be He, as it says "And ye who cleave to the Lord your God, ye are all alive.

Zohar: Shemoth, Section 2, Page 6a

today" (Ibid. IV, 4). They are worthy, in His sight, because they "sow above ('al) all waters", that is to say, they sow "according to righteousness" (Hos. x, 12), for of him who sows according to righteousness it is said: "For thy mercy is great above ('al) the heavens" (Ps. CVIII, 5). "Above the heavens" is identical with "above all waters", and refers to the world to come, and Israel sow a seed which is above all waters. The Book of R. Yeba the Elder remarks as follows: It is written "The matter is by the decree of the watchers, and the demand by the word of the holy ones" (Dan. IV, 14). All the judgements passed upon the world, and all decrees and decisions are stored in a certain palace, where seventy-two members of Sanhedrin deliberate upon them. The palace is called "the Palace of Acquittal", because the judges there lay stress on whatever can be pleaded in favour of the accused. Not so the "other side", where there is a place called "Accusation", because in that abode of the Serpent, the "Wife of whoredom", every effort is made to procure the condemnation of humanity, and to prejudice the servant in the eyes of the Master. Symbolically, the former is represented by "sweet, clear water"; the latter by "bitter water that causes the curse" (Num. v, 18). The decision concerning children, life, and livelihood, however, is not entrusted either to the "Temple of Acquittal" or to that of "Accusation" (being dependent on mazzal). Israel therefore, "sow above all waters", since their seed is established above. Further, they send away "the feet of the ox and the ass", i.e. the evil haps which are symbolized by the union of the ox and the ass (v. Zohar, Gen. 162b), and cleave to the "good side" of the supernal holy beings.. 'It says in the Book of R. Hamnuna the Elder, in connection with the words, "Now there arose a new king over Egypt", that all the nations of the world and all their kings become powerful only on account of Israel. Egypt, for instance, did not rule over the whole world before lsrael settled there. The same is true of Babylon, as well as of Edom (Rome). Before that all these nations were utterly insignificant and contemptible: Egypt is described as a "house of slaves" (Ex. xx, 2), Babylon as "a people who was not" (Isa. xx, II-13), and of Edom it says, "Behold, I have made thee small among the nations, thou art greatly despised" (Obad. 1, 2). It was entirely due to Israel that they became great. As soon as Israel was subjected to any of these nations, it immediately became all-powerful, since Israel singly are on a par with all the rest of the world. So when Israel went down to Egypt, straightway that country rose to supreme power. And this is the meaning of "Now there arose a new king", i.e. the supernal chieftain of Egypt rose up in strength and gained predominance over the chieftains of the other nations.

Zohar: Shemoth, Section 2, Page 6b

[Note: The first three lines of the Hebrew text do not appear in the translation.]

Then the words were fulfilled: "For three things the earth is disquieted... for a servant when he reigneth..." (Prov. xxx, 21).

R. Hiya said: 'Thirty days before a nation rises to power or before its downfall in this world, the event is proclaimed in the other world. Sometimes it is revealed through the mouths of little children, sometimes through simple folk, and sometimes through a bird. These proclaim it in the world, and yet no one notices them. If, however, a nation is deserving, the impending calamity is revealed to the righteous leaders of the people, in order that they may call the people to repent and return to the Lord while there is yet time.'.

As R. Eleazar was sitting one day at the gate of Lydda along with R. Abba, R. Judah, and R. Yose, R. Yose said: 'Listen, and I will tell you the sights which I have seen this morning. I rose early and beheld a bird which flew up three times and down once, exclaiming: "Ye celestials, ye angels of the higher sphere! In these days three heavenly Chieftains are raising up rulers on the earth. One is dislodged from his throne and made to pass through the Fiery Stream. He and his power are annihilated. But three mighty pillars of great height still stand upon the world." I threw a stone at the bird and cried: "Bird, bird! Tell me, who are the three who remain upright and the one whose power is taken from him?" He threw down to me three feathers from his right wing and one from his left wing. I know not what it all portends.' R. Eleazar took from R. Yose the feathers, smelt them, and lo, blood issued from his nostrils. Said he: 'Verily, three great rulers are now at Rome, and are about to bring evil upon Israel through the Romans.' Then he took the feather of the left wing, smelt it, and behold, black fire burst from it. He said: 'The power of the Egyptians is coming to an end; a Roman king is about to pass through the whole land of Egypt, appoint governors over it, and destroy buildings and erect new ones.' Then he threw the feathers on to the ground, and the three which were from the right wing fell on that which was from the left wing. As they were thus sitting, a young child passed by and recited the verse: "A burden concerning Egypt! Behold, the Lord rideth upon a swift cloud, and shall come into Egypt" (Isa. XIX, I). A second child passed by and declaimed: "And the land of Egypt shall be desolate" (Ezek. XXIX, 9). A third child passed by and recited: "Make thee instruments of captivity, O daughter of Egypt!" (Jer. XLVI, 19). Then they saw that the feather of the left wing was burning, but not the three feathers of the right wing. Said R. Eleazar: 'These two incidents, that of the bird and that of the children, are in truth but one–and they convey a prophecy from above. The Holy One, blessed be He, desired to reveal to us His hidden plans, as it is written, "Behold, the Lord will do nothing without revealing his secret to his servants the prophets" (Amos. III, 7). And the wise are greater than prophets, for on the prophets the holy spirit rests intermittently, but the wise He never leaves, as, although they know what is above and what is below, they keep it secret.' Said R. Yose: 'There are many wise, but the wisdom of R. Eleazar exceeds all.' Said R. Abba: 'If it were not for the sages the sons of men would comprehend neither God's Torah nor His commandments, and the spirit of man would not differ from the spirit of the beasts.' R. Isaac said: 'When the Holy One is about to chastise a nation He chastises first its celestial representative, as it is written, "The Lord shall punish the host of heaven in heaven and the kings of the earth upon the earth" (Isa. XXIV, 21). And what does the punishment consist in? He has to pass through the Fiery Stream, and then his power vanishes. Straightway it is proclaimed above,

Zohar: Shemoth, Section 2, Page 7a

and the proclamation resounds in all the heavens and reaches the ears of those who have dominion over this world. From them it issues and traverses the world, until it reaches birds and little children and simpleminded folk.' NOW THERE AROSE A NEW KING OVER EGYPT. According to R. Hiya he was really a new king, but according to R. Yose it was the same Pharaoh, only he made "new" decrees against Israel, forgetting all the benefits bestowed upon him by Joseph, as if "he did not know him".

R. Yose and R. Judah were once studying with R. Simeon. Said R. Judah: 'We have been taught that the expression "arose" suggests that Pharaoh "rose" on his own accord, viz. that he was not in the line of Egyptian kings, and was, in fact, not worthy to be king; he "rose" only because he was rich.' Said R. Simeon: 'Exactly as was the case with Ahasuerus, who also was not fitted for the kingship, but obtained it through his wealth.' R. Eleazar, R. Abba, and R. Yose were once walking from Tiberias to Sepphoris' On the way they met a Jew who started a conversation by quoting: "A burden upon Egypt. Behold, the Lord rideth upon a swift cloud and cometh into Egypt, and the godlings of Egypt shall flee from his presence" (Isa. XIX, I). 'Mark this,' he said. 'All the kings and all the nations of the world are as nothing before the Holy One, blessed be He (Dan. IV, 32). He only has to decide a thing and it is done. What, then, is the significance of the expression "cometh into Egypt"? Did He have to "come"? Yea, verily, He "came" for the sake of the Matrona (Shekinah), to take Her, as it were, by the hand and raise Her in glory, as He will also do when Israel's captivity in Edom (Rome) Will come to an end.' R. Yose remarked: 'If it was for the sake of the Matrona, why did He not "come" to Babylon, where the Shekinah was also in exile with Israel?' To this the Jew replied that according to tradition the reason why the Holy One did not reveal Himself fully by signs and wonders in Babylon was because the Israelites took to themselves foreign wives and profaned the sign of the holy Covenant. In Egypt, however, it was different: they entered it as pure sons of Israel, and left it as such. When the Edomitic exile comes to an end He shall manifest His glory in fulness and raise up His Spouse from the dust, saying to her: "Shake thyself from the dust; arise, sit down, O Jerusalem, loose thyself from the bands of thy neck, O captive daughter of Zion" (Isa. LII, 2). Who shall then stand against Him? It is written "And the godlings of Egypt shall flee from His presence." The "godlings" are not merely idols made of stone and wood, but celestial principalities and terrestrial divinities. Indeed, wherever Israel is in exile the Holy One watches them and demands an account from those peoples and their supernal representatives. Mark what is written! "Thus says the Lord, my people went down at the first to Egypt to sojourn there, and Assyria oppressed them for nothing" (Ibid. v. 4). The Holy One had a grave complaint against Assyria. "Behold what Assyria has done to me! Egypt I punished severely, although she treated my people with hospitality when they came to sojourn there, assigning to them the fat of the land, the land of Goshen; and even later, though they oppressed them, they did not take away the land from them nor anything belonging to them" (cf. Ex. IX, 6). But Assyria "oppressed them for nothing": they dragged

Zohar: Shemoth, Section 2, Page 7b

them to the other end of the earth and took their country away from them." Now if Egypt was punished, notwithstanding the kindness with which she treated Israel, especially at first, it can certainly be expected that Assyria and Edom, and, in fact, all the nations who have maltreated Israel, will receive their punishment from the Holy One, when He will manifest the glory of His Name to them, as it is written, "Thus will I magnify myself, and sanctify myself, and I will be known among many nations" (Ezek. XXXVIII, 23).

R. Simeon lifted up his hands and wept. 'Alas,' he said, 'for him who will live at that time! Yet happy he who will live at that time! When the Holy One comes to visit the "Hind" (Israel), he will examine who it is that remains loyal to her at that time, and then woe to him who shall not be found worthy, and of whom it shall be said, "I looked and there was none to help" (Isa. LXII, 23). Many sufferings shall then befall Israel. But happy he who will be found faithful at that time! For he shall see the joy-giving light of the King. Concerning that time it is proclaimed: "I will refine them as silver is refined, and will try them as gold is tried" (Zech. XIII, 9). Then shall pangs and travail overtake Israel, and all nations and their kings shall furiously rage together and take counsel against her. Thereupon a pillar of fire will be suspended from heaven to earth for forty days, visible to all nations. Then the Messiah will arise from the Garden of Eden, from that place which is called "The Bird's Nest". He will arise in the land of Galilee, and on that day the whole world shall be shaken and all the children of men shall seek refuge in caves and rocky places. Concerning that time it is written: "And they shall go into the holes of the rocks and into the caves of the earth, for fear of the Lord and for the glory of his majesty, when he ariseth to shake terribly the earth" (Isa. II, 19). "The glory of his majesty" refers to the Messiah when he shall reveal himself in the land of Galilee; for in this part of the Holy Land the desolation first began, and therefore he will manifest himself there first, and from there begin to war against the world. After the forty days, during which the pillar shall have stood between heaven and earth before the eyes of the whole world, and the Messiah shall have manifested himself, a star shall come forth from the East variegated in hue and shining brilliantly, and seven other stars shall surround it, and make war on it from all sides, three times a day for seventy days, before the eyes of the whole world. The one star shall fight against the seven with rays of fire flashing on every side, and it shall smite them until they are extinguished, evening after evening. But in the day they will appear again and fight before the eyes of the whole world, seventy days long. After the seventy days the one star shall vanish. Also the Messiah shall be hidden for twelve months in the pillar of fire, which shall return again, although it shall not be visible. After the twelve months the Messiah will be carried up to heaven in that pillar of fire and receive there power and dominion and the royal crown. When he descends, the pillar of fire will again be visible to the eyes of the world, and the Messiah will reveal himself, and mighty nations will gather round him, and he shall declare war against all the world. At that time the Holy One shall show forth his power before all the nations of the earth, and the Messiah shall be manifested throughout the whole universe, and all the kings will unite to fight against him, and even in Israel there will be found some wicked ones who shall join them in the fight against the Messiah. Then there will be darkness over all the world, and for fifteen days shall it continue, and many in Israel shall perish in that darkness. Concerning this darkness it is written: "Behold, darkness covers the earth and gross darkness the peoples" (Isa. LX, 2).'.

R. Simeon then discoursed on the verse:

Zohar: Shemoth, Section 2, Page 8a

"If a bird's nest chance to be before thee in the way in any tree, or on the ground, young ones or eggs, and the dam sitting upon the young... thou shalt in no wise let the dam go" (Deut. XXII, 6-7). 'This passage', he said, 'we interpret as an esoteric commandment in the Law, containing mysteries of doctrine, paths and ways known to the Fellowship and belonging to the thirty-two paths of the Torah.' Then, turning to R. Eleazar, his son, he said: 'At the time when the Messiah shall arise, there will be great wonders in the world. See now, in the lower Paradise there is a secret and unknown spot, broidered with many colours, in which a thousand palaces of longing are concealed. No one may enter it, except the Messiah, whose abode is in Paradise. The Garden is encompassed with multitudes of saints who look to the Messiah as their leader, along with many hosts and bands of the souls of the righteous there. On New Moons, festivals, and Sabbaths, he enters that place, in order to find joyous delight in those secret palaces. Behind those palaces there is another place, entirely hidden and undiscoverable. It is called "Eden", and no one may enter to behold it. Now the Messiah is hidden in its outskirts until a place is revealed to him which is called "the Bird's Nest". This is the place proclaimed by that Bird (the Shekinah) which flies about the Garden of Eden every day. In that place the effigies are woven of all the nations who band together against Israel. The Messiah enters that abode, lifts up his eyes and beholds the Fathers (Patriarchs) visiting the ruins of God's Sanctuary. He perceives mother Rachel, with tears upon her face; the Holy One, blessed be He, tries to comfort her, but she refuses to be comforted (Jer. XXXI, 14). Then the Messiah lifts up his voice and weeps, and the whole Garden of Eden quakes, and all the righteous and saints who are there break out in crying and lamentation with him. When the crying and weeping resound for the second time, the whole firmament above the Garden begins to shake, and the cry echoes from five hundred myriads of supernal hosts, until it reaches the highest Throne. Then the Holy One, blessed be He, beckons to that "Bird", which then enters its nest and comes to the Messiah, and flits about, uttering strange cries. Then from the holy Throne the Bird's Nest and the Messiah are summoned three times, and they both ascend into the heavenly places, and the Holy One swears to them to destroy the wicked kingdom (Rome) by the hand of the Messiah, to avenge Israel, and to give her all the good things which he has promised her. Then the Bird returns to her place. The Messiah, however, is hidden again in the same place as before.

'At the time when the Holy One shall arise to renew all worlds, and the letters of his Name shall shine in perfect union, the Yod with the He, and the He with the Vau, a mighty star will appear in the heavens of purple hue, which by day shall flame before the eyes of the whole world, filling the firmament with its light. And at that time shall a flame issue in the heavens from the north; and flame and star shall so face each other for forty days, and all men will marvel and be afraid. And when forty days shall have passed, the star and the flame shall war together in the sight of all, and the flame shall spread across the skies from the north, striving to overcome the star, and the rulers and peoples of the earth shall behold it with terror, and there will be confusion among them. But the star will remove to the south and vanquish the flame, and the flame shall daily be diminished until it be no more seen. Then shall the star cleave for itself bright paths in twelve directions which shall remain luminous in the skies for the term of twelve days. After a further twelve days trembling will seize the world, and at midday the sun will be darkened as it was darkened on the day when the holy Temple was destroyed, so that heaven and earth shall not be seen. Then out of the midst of thunder and lightning shall a voice be heard, causing the earth to quake and many hosts and principalities to perish. On the same day when that voice is heard throughout the world, a flame of fire shall appear burning in Great Rome (Constantinople);

Zohar: Shemoth, Section 2, Page 8b

it will consume many turrets and towers, and many are the great and mighty who shall perish then. All shall gather against her to destroy her, and no one will have hope to escape. From that day on, for twelve months, all the kings (of the world) will take counsel together and make many decrees to destroy Israel; and they shall prosper against him, as has been said. Blessed is he who shall live in that time, and blessed is he who shall not live in that time! And the whole world then will be in confusion. At the end of the twelve months the "sceptre of Judah", namely the Messiah, will arise, appearing from Paradise, and all the righteous will surround him and gird him with weapons of war on which are inscribed the letters of the Holy Name (Tetragrammaton). Then a voice will burst forth from the branches of the trees of Paradise: "Arise, O ye saints from above, and stand ye before the Messiah! For the time has come for the Hind to be united with her Spouse, and he must avenge her on the world and raise her from the dust". And all the saints from above will arise and gird the Messiah with weapons of war, Abraham at his right, Isaac at his left, Jacob in front of him, while Moses, the "faithful shepherd" of all these saints, shall dance at the head of them in Paradise. As soon as the Messiah has been installed by the saints in Paradise, he will enter again the place which is called "the Bird's Nest', there to behold the picture of the destruction of the Temple, and of all the saints who were done to death there. Then will he take from that place ten garments, the garments of holy zeal, and hide himself there for forty days, and no one shall be able to see him. At the end of those forty days a voice shall be heard from the highest throne calling the Bird's Nest and the Messiah who shall be hidden there. Thereupon he shall be carried aloft, and when the Holy One, blessed be He, shall behold the Messiah adorned with the garments of holy zeal and girded with weapons of war, he will take him and kiss him upon his brow. At that moment three hundred and ninety firmaments shall begin to shake. The Holy One shall command one of these firmaments, which has been kept in waiting since the six days of creation, to approach, and He shall take out from a certain temple in it a crown inscribed with holy names. It was with this crown that the Holy One adorned Himself when the Israelites crossed the Red Sea and He avenged Himself on all the chariots of Pharaoh and his horsemen. With this same crown will He crown King Messiah. As soon as he is crowned, the Holy One will take him and kiss him as before. All the holy multitude and the whole holy army will surround him and will bestow upon him many wonderful gifts, and he will be adorned by them all. Then will he enter into one of the temples and behold there all the upper angels, who are called "the mourners of Zion" because they continually weep over the destruction of the Holy Temple. These angels shall give him a robe of deep red in order that he may commence his work of revenge. The Holy One will again hide him in the "Bird's Nest" and he will remain there for thirty days. After the thirty days he will again be decked with those adornments from above and from below, and many holy beings will surround him. The whole world then shall see a light extending from the firmament to the earth, and continuing for seven days, and they will be amazed and not comprehend: only the wise will understand, they who are adepts in the mystic lore, blessed is their portion. All through the seven days the Messiah shall be crowned on earth. Where shall this be? "By the way", to wit, Rachel's grave, which is on the cross-road. To mother Rachel he will give glad tidings and comfort her, and now she will let herself be comforted, and will rise and kiss him. The light will then move from that place and shall stand over Jericho, the city of trees, and the Messiah will be hidden in the light of the "Bird's Nest" for twelve months. After the twelve months that light will stand between heaven and earth in the land of Galilee, where Israel's captivity began, and there will he reveal himself from the light of the "Bird's Nest", and return to his place. On that day the whole earth will be shaken from one end.

Zohar: Shemoth, Section 2, Page 9a

to the other, and thus the whole world will know that the Messiah has revealed himself in the land of Galilee. And all who are diligent in the study of the Torah-and there shall be few such in the world-will gather round him. His army will gain in strength through the merit of little infants at school, symbolized by the word ephroah-"young bird" (cf. Deut. XXII, 6). And if such will not be found at that time it will be through the merit of the sucklings, "the eggs" (Ibid), "those that are weaned from the milk, and drawn from the breasts" (Isa. XXII, 9), for whose sake the Shekinah dwells in the midst of Israel in exile, as indeed there will be few sages at that time. This is the implication of the words "And the dam sitting upon the young, or upon the eggs", which, allegorically interpreted, means that it does not depend upon the

Mother to free them from exile, but upon the Supreme King; for it is the young ones and the sucklings that will give strength to the Messiah, and then the Supernal Mother, which "sits upon them", will be stirred up towards Her Spouse. He will tarry for twelve months longer, and then he will appear and raise her from the dust: "I will raise up on that day the tabernacle of David that is fallen" (Amos IX, II). On that day the Messiah will begin to gather the captives from one end of the world to the other: "If any of thine be driven out unto the utmost parts of heaven, from thence will the Lord thy God gather thee" (Deut. xxx, 4). From that day on the Holy One will perform for Israel all the signs and wonders which He performed for them in Egypt: "As in the days of thy coming out of the land of Egypt, will I show unto him wonders" (Micah VII, 15)'.

Then said R. Simeon: 'Eleazar, my son! Thou canst find all this in the mystery of the thirty-two paths of the Holy Name. Before these wonders have taken place in the world, the mystery of the Holy Name will not be manifested in perfection and love will not be awakened: "Ye daughters of Jerusalem, I adjure you by the gazelles and by the hinds of the field, that ye stir not up, nor awake the love until she pleases" (Cant II, 7). The "gazelles" (zebaoth) symbolize the king, who is called Zebaoth; the "hinds" represent those other principalities and powers from below; "that ye stir not up, etc." refers to the "Right Hand" of the Holy One, called "Love"; "until she pleases", namely She (the Shekinah) who lies at present in the dust and in whom the King is well pleased. Blessed be he who will be found worthy to live at that time! Blessed will he be both in this world and in the world to come.'

R. Simeon then lifted up his hands in prayer to the Holy One, blessed be He. When he had finished his prayer, R. Eleazar his son and R. Abba seated themselves before him. As they were thus sitting they beheld the light of the day grow dim and a fiery flame sink in the Sea of Tiberias, and the whole place began mightily to tremble. Said R. Simeon: 'Verily, this is the time when the Holy One remembers His children and lets two drops fall into the great Sea. As they fall they meet the fiery ray and sink with it in the sea.' Then R. Simeon wept, and the disciples also. Said R. Simeon: 'Behold, I was moved a while ago to meditate on the mystery of the letters of the Holy Name, the mystery of His compassion over His children; but now it is fitting that I should reveal unto this generation something that no other man has been permitted to reveal. For the merit of this generation sustains the world until the Messiah shall appear.' He then bade R. Eleazar his son and R. Abba to stand up, and they did so. R. Simeon then wept a second time, and said: 'Alas! Who can endure to hear what I foresee! The exile will drag on; who shall be able to bear it? '

Then he also rose and spake thus: 'It is written, "O Lord our God, other lords beside thee dominated us, apart from thee do we make mention of thy Name" (Isa. XXVI, 13). This verse, apart from other interpretations, contains a profound doctrine of faith. Tetragrammaton Elohenu (Lord our God) is the source and beginning of supreme mysteries indeed; it is the sphere whence emanate all the burning lights, and where the whole mystery of Faith is centred: this Name dominates all. However, "other lords beside thee dominated us"; the people of Israel, who is destined to be ruled only by this supreme Name, is ruled in exile by the "other side". Yea, "apart from thee (beka) do we make mention of thy name". The name "by thee" BeKa (=22) symbolizes the Holy Name comprising twenty-two letters, and this is the name by which the Community of Israel is always blessed, as, for instance, "to whom thou swarest by thine own self" (beka, Ex. XXII, 13); "in thee (beka) shall Israel be blessed" (Gen. XLVIII, 20); "for in thee (beka) I can run through the troops" (Ps. XVIII, 19). At the period when there is perfection, peace, and harmony, the two names are not separated one from another, and it is forbidden

Zohar: Shemoth, Section 2, Page 9b

to separate them even in thought and imagination; but now in exile we do separate them, the Matrona from Her Spouse, as She (Shekinah) lies in dust (in exile with Israel). "Apart from thee" being far away from Thee, and being ruled by other powers, "we make mention of thy name" in separation, thy Name being separated from the Name expressed by Beka. All this in the days of exile; for the first exile began during the first Temple, and lasted seventy years, during which time the Mother (the Shekinah) did not brood over Israel, and there was a separation between the Yod and the He, the Yod ascending higher and higher to infinity (En Sof), and the holy Temple above-corresponding to the Temple below-did not send forth living waters, its source being cut off. The seventy years of the first exile corresponded to the seven years which it took to build the first Temple (I K. VI, 38). However, far be it from us to think that during that time the kingdom of Babylon had power in the heavens over Israel. The fact is that as long as the Temple stood there was a bright light descending from the Supernal Mother, but as soon as it was destroyed, through Israel's sin, and the kingdom of Babylon got the upper hand, that light was covered up and darkness prevailed here below and the angels below ceased from giving out light, and then the power symbolized by the letter Yod of the Holy Name ascended into the upper regions, into the Infinite, and thus during the whole seventy years of exile Israel had no divine light to guide her, and, truly, that was the essence of the exile. When, however, Babylon's power was taken away from her and Israel returned to the Holy Land, a light did shine for her, but it was not as bright as before, being only the emanation of the lower He since the whole of Israel did not return to purity to be a "peculiar people" as before. Therefore, the emanation of the supernal Yod did not descend to illumine in the same measure as before, but only a little. Hence Israel were involved in many wars until "the darkness covered the earth" and the lower He was darkened and fell to the ground, and the upper source was removed as before, and the second Temple was destroyed and all its twelve tribes went into exile in the kingdom of Edom. The He also went into exile there, and therefore the exile was prolonged.

'A mystery of mysteries has been revealed to them that are wise of heart. The He of the second Temple is in exile with her twelve tribes and their hosts. Twelve tribes form a great number, and because the mystery of the He is in them, the exile lasts during this whole number. Ten tribes are a thousand years, two tribes are two hundred years. At the conclusion of the twelve tribes (twelve hundred years) there will be darkness over Israel, until the Vau shall arise at the time of sixty-six years after the "twelve tribes", that isk after twelve hundred years of exile. And after the conclusion of the sixty-six years of the night- darkness, the words "And I shall remember my covenant with Jacob" (Lev. XXVI, 42) will begin to come to pass. From then the Holy One, blessed be He, shall begin to do signs and wonders,

Zohar: Shemoth, Section 2, Page 10a

as we have described. But over Israel those tribulations will come. After that King Messiah shall fight against the whole world, aided by the Right Hand of the Holy One. At the end of another sixty-six years the letters in the Holy Name shall be seen perfectly engraved above and below in manner due. After a further one hundred and thirty-two years He will begin "to take hold of the ends of the earth and shake off the wicked". The Holy Land will be purified, and the Holy One will raise the dead there and they shall rise in their hosts in the land of Galilee. At the end of a further hundred and forty- four years the remaining dead of Israel in other lands shall be raised, so that after altogether four hundred and eight years the world shall be re-inhabited and the evil principle (the "other side") driven out of it. Then the lower He (Shekinah) shall be filled from the upper spring (the highest Sephiroth), and be crowned and radiate in perfection until the Sabbath of the Lord arrives to gather souls in the joy of holiness throughout this whole seventh millennium. Then the holy spirits of the people of Israel at the fulness of time will be invested with new, holy bodies, and be called "Saints": "And it shall come to pass that he that is left in Zion and that remaineth in Jerusalem shall be called holy" (Isa. III, 4). These are the veiled mysteries.'

[Tr. note: The above calculation of the Messianic era rests on the supposition that of the seven millenniums of the present aeon, the seventh is to be considered as the Cosmic Sabbath, the sixth as the time of the Messiah, the fifth as the last (Edomitic or Roman) exile. The beginning of this exile is, according to the Zohar, 3828 years after Creation, hence with those 1200 years of exile the fifth millennium is completed. Sixty-six years later i.e. 5066 years after Creation (1306 C.E.), the signs of Redemption begin. 198 years later, i.e. 5264 after Creation (1504 C.E.), follows the "first resurrection", the second 144 years later, i.e. 1648 C.E. In the year 2240 the apocalyptic Sabbath begins. Cf. also Zohar, Gen. 116b, Deut. 249a.]

THERE AROSE UP A NEW KING. Said R. Yose: The Holy One creates each day new angels to be His emissaries to the world, as it is written, "He maketh his angels winds" (spirits) (Ps. CIV. 4). It does not say "He made", but "He maketh", because He makes them daily. At that time He appointed one to represent Egypt: "a new king", i.e. a new supernal representative; "who knew not Joseph", because Egypt's angel emanated from the sphere of Separation: since of the four "heads" into which the river that went out of Eden parted (Gen. II, 10), the first was the stream of Egypt (the Nile above, corresponding to the Nile below); and therefore "he knew not Joseph", who represents the sphere where is the abode of Unity, and which is called "Righteous."'

R. Eleazar and R. Yose once set forth upon a journey at dawn. Suddenly they beheld two stars which shot across the sky from either side. Said R. Eleazar: 'The time is now come when the morning stars do praise their Master: shooting forth in awe across the heavens, they prepare to glorify His Name in song, as it is written: "When the morning stars sing together" (Job XXXVIII, 7). Verily they sing in perfect unison, and in harmony do the sons of God shout for joy.' He then discoursed on the verse: To the musician. Upon the hind of the morning. A song of David (Ps. XXII, I). 'When the face of the east lightens', he said, 'and the darkness of the night is dispersed, an angel appears in the east, and from the south he draws a thread of light, and then the sun comes forth and, throwing open the casements of the sky, illumines the world. Then the "hind of the morning" comes, a red light enters into the darkness and it becomes day. And the light of the day draws that "hind" into itself. Now it is concerning that "hind" when it separates itself from the day, after it had been with it, that David sang. And the following verse:

Zohar: Shemoth, Section 2, Page 10b

"My God (Eli), my God, why hast thou forsaken me?"—suggests the cry over the "hind (ayala) of the morning", when she separates herself from the day.'

As they were thus walking, the day lightened and the time for prayer arrived. Said R. Eleazar: 'Let us pray, and then continue our journey.' They sat down and prayed, and then resumed their walk. On the way, R. Eleazar started to expound the following verse: There is a vanity (hebel, lit. breath) which is done upon the earth, that there be righteous men unto whom it happeneth according to the work of the wicked; again there are wicked men, to whom it happeneth according to the work of the righteous: I said that this also is vanity (Eccl. VIII, 14). 'This verse', he said, 'has been esoterically explained as follows. King Solomon, in this book, treated of seven "vanities" (habalim, lit. breaths) upon which the world stands, namely the seven pillars [Tr. note: i.e. Sefiroth.] which sustain the world in correspondence with the seven firmaments, which are called respectively Vilon, Rakia, Shehakim, Zebul, Ma'on, Machon, Araboth. It was concerning them that Solomon said: "Vanity of vanities, said Koheleth, all is vanity" (Ibid. 1, 1). As there are seven firmaments, with others cleaving to them and issuing from them, so there are seven habalim and others emanating from these, and Solomon in his wisdom referred to them all to convey the following esoteric lesson. There is a certain "breath" [Tr. note: Malkuth]. emanating from those supernal "breaths" upon which the world is sustained, closely connected with the earth and fed from it. It depends, in fact, on the souls of the righteous who have been gathered from the earth while still pure before they have committed any sin, and while their savour is still sweet: for instance, Enoch, of whom it is written, "And he was not, for God took him" (Gen. v, 24). God took him away before his time and had delight in him. And so it is with all the righteous, for we have been taught that the righteous are removed from this world before their time for one of two reasons: one for the sins of their generation, for when there is much sin in the world the righteous are penalized for its guilt; the second is that when the Holy One, blessed be He, is aware that they would commit a sin if they lived longer, He removes them before their time. And this is the meaning of the verse quoted above: "there are righteous to whom it happeneth according to the work of the wicked", as was the case with R. Akiba and his colleagues; the judgement from above came upon them, as if they had committed the sins and actions of the wicked. On the other hand, "there are wicked men to whom it happeneth according to the work of the righteous": they live in peace and comfort in this world, and the judgement does not come upon them, as if they performed the deeds of the righteous. Why so? Because the Holy One foresees that either they are about to repent, or that they will bring forth virtuous offspring, as, for instance, Terah, who brought forth Abraham, and Ahaz, who brought forth Hezekiah. Thus, as we have said, there is a "breath" (hebel) on one side as well as on the other, a "breath is made upon the earth" in order that the world may be sustained.

'Another interpretation of the verse is as follows. "Vanity is done upon the earth", for instance, when a "work of the wicked", the temptation to commit some sin, approaches the righteous and they remain steadfast in the fear of their Lord and refuse to defile themselves, like so many of whom we know who did the will of their Master and sinned not. On the other hand, "it happeneth that wicked men do the works of the righteous" on certain occasions, as, for instance, the Jew who belonged to a gang of robbers on a mountain, and who, whenever he saw a fellow Jew pass, warned him of the danger, so that R. Akiba applied to him the words of the second half of this verse; or the man

Zohar: Shemoth, Section 2, Page 11a

in the neighbourhood of R. Hiya who once seized a woman with the intention of violating her, but who, when she said to him "Honour thy Master and do not sin with me", mastered his passion and let her go. The Holy One has made both righteous and wicked, and, as He is glorified in this world by the works of the righteous, so is He glorified by the wicked when they happen to do a good deed: "He hath made everything beautiful in his time" (Eccl. III, 11). But woe to the sinner who makes himself wicked and cleaves obstinately to his sin!'

R. Eleazar further said: 'King Solomon, when wisdom was given to him, saw all "in the time of his hebel", i.e. in the time when the moon (the Holy Spirit) ruled. He saw the Righteous (Zaddik), the Pillar of the world, "perishing in his righteousness" in the time of the exile, for when Israel is in exile He is with them, and the supernal blessings do not reach Him. Thus "there is a righteous that perisheth in his righteousness" (Eccl. VII, 15). On the other hand, he saw "a wicked person that prolongeth his life in his evil" (Ibid.), namely Samael, who causes Edom (Rome) to continue in her prosperity through the help of his "Evil", his spouse, the loathsome Serpent. And the same applies to the prosperity of all the other kingdoms of this world; until the time when the Holy One, blessed be He, shall raise up from the dust "the booth of David that is fallen" (Amos IX, 11).' AND THERE WENT A MAN OF THE HOUSE OF LEVI. R. Yose discoursed here on the verse: "My beloved is gone down into his garden, to the beds of spices" (S.S. VI, 2). He said: 'The words "Into his garden" refer to the Community of Israel. She is a "bed of spices" filled with the savour of the world to come. In the hour when the Holy One descends into this Garden, the souls of all the righteous who are crowned there emit their perfume, as it says, "How much better is the smell of thy ointments than all spices" (S.S. IV, 10). These are they of whom R. Isaac has said: "All the souls of the righteous who have lived in this world, and all the souls who shall some day descend to dwell there, all these dwell in the earthly Garden (Paradise) in that shape which was or shall be their likeness on earth." This is a mystery which has been transmitted to the wise. The spirit which enters into the children of men, and which emanates from the Female (Malkuth) makes an impression after the fashion of a seal. That is to say, the form of the human body in this world is projected outwards, and takes the impress of the spirit from within. So when the spirit separates itself from the body it returns to the earthly Garden in the actual form and pattern of the body that was its garment during its sojourn in this world, and upon which it acted like a seal. Hence it says, "Set me as a seal" (Ibid. VIII, 6): as the seal presses from within and the mark of it appears outwards, so the spirit acts upon the body. But when it separates itself from the body and returns to the terrestrial Paradise, the aether there causes this impress in turn to project itself outwards, so that the spirit receives an outward shape in the likeness of the body in this world. The over-soul (neshamah), however, which issues from the Tree of Life (Tifereth), is fashioned there above in such a manner that it may ascend into the "Bundle of Life", in order to delight in the beauty of the Lord; as it says, "To behold the beauty of the Lord and to visit his temple" (Ps. XXVII, 4).' AND THERE WENT A MAN OF THE HOUSE OF LEVI. This refers to Gabriel, who is called "the Man" (Dan. IX, 2). "Of the house of Levi" is the Community of Israel, which proceeds from the "Left Side". "And took the daughter of Levi", namely the over-soul (neshamah); for we have been taught that in the hour when the body of a righteous one is born into the world,

Zohar: Shemoth, Section 2, Page 11b

the Holy One summons Gabriel, who takes from Paradise the soul ordained for that saint and commands her to descend into the body of him who is to be born in this world; and he, Gabriel, is thus appointed as guardian to that soul. But, it may be said, do we not know that the angel appointed to guard the spirits is called "Laila" (night)? How, then, can you say it is Gabriel? The answer is that both names are correct; for Gabriel comes from the "Left Side", and anyone who comes from that side bears also the other name, which signifies "night".

According to another explanation, "a man" here is Amram, and "the daughter of Levi" is Jochebed. A heavenly voice bade him unite himself with her, as through the son which should be born of them the time of the redemption of Israel would be brought near. And the Holy One came to his aid, for, as we have been taught, the Shekinah reposed upon the nuptial bed and the will of the two in their union was one with the will of the Shekinah. Therefore the Shekinah ceased not to abide with the fruit of that union. It is written: "Sanctify yourselves and be holy" (Lev. XI, 44), which signifies that when a person so sanctifies himself here below the Holy One adds His sanctification from above. As the two strove to unite themselves also with the Shekinah, She on her side united Herself with them in their union. Said R. Isaac: 'Blessed are those righteous ones whose whole desire is ever to be united with the Holy One in completeness and perfection! Inasmuch as they cleave unto Him will He also cleave unto them forever and ever. Woe unto the wicked, whose desire and attachment is turned away from Him! Not only do they keep aloof from Him, dwelling in separation, but they even unite themselves to that "other side". Thus Amram, who was faithful to the Holy One, became the father of Moses-him whom the Holy One never deserted, and with whom the Shekinah was ever united, blessed be he!' AND THE WOMAN CONCEIVED AND BARE A SON AND SHE SAW HIM THAT HE WAS GOOD. What mean the words "that he was good"? Said R. Hiya: 'She saw that even at his birth he was marked with the sign of the covenant, for the word "good" contains an allusion to the covenant, as it is written, "Say of the righteous one that he is good" (Isa. III, 10)' R. Yose said: 'She saw the light of the Shekinah playing round him: for when he was born this light filled the whole house, the word "good" here having the same reference as in the verse "and God saw the light that it was good" (Gen. I, 4).' AND SHE HID HIM THREE MONTHS. What does this signify? R. Judah says: 'This is a hint that Moses was not destined to perceive the Supernal Light until three months (after the Exodus) had passed, as it says "in the third month after the children of Israel were gone forth out of the land of Egypt, the same day came they into the wilderness of Sinai" (Ex. XIX, I). Only then was the Torah transmitted through him, and the Shekinah revealed, resting on him before the eyes of all, as it says, "and Moses went up unto God, and the Lord called him out of the mountain" (Ibid. v, 3).' AND WHEN SHE COULD NO LONGER HIDE HIM. During all that time his communing with the Holy One, blessed be He, was not manifest; but afterwards, "Moses spake, and God answered him by a voice" (Ex. XIX, 19). SHE TOOK FOR HIM AN ARK OF BULRUSHES: thereby prefiguring the Ark that contains the "Tables of the Covenant: AND DAUBED IT WITH SLIME AND WITH PITCH, prefiguring again the Ark which was overlaid within and without. R. Judah said that this was symbolic of the Torah in which the Holy One, blessed be He, laid down stringent rules [Tr. note: A play on the word homer, which means both 'slime, and (as a legal term) 'stringency.] in the form of precepts, positive and negative. AND SHE PUT THE CHILD THEREIN. This prefigures Israel, of whom it is written: "When Israel was a child then I loved him (Hos. XI, 1): AND LAID IT IN THE FLAGS (souph), alluding to the precepts of the Torah, which did not come into force until they entered the Land at the end (soph) of forty years. BY THE BRINK (sphath=lip) of the river, alluding to the instruction issuing from the lips of the teachers of law and statute.

The following is an alternative explanation of these verses: AND TOOK TO WIFE A DAUGHTER OF LEVI. This signifies the place which is filled with the brightness of moonlight. [Note: The last three lines of the Hebrew text on this page are not translated.] (Malkuth).

Zohar: Shemoth, Section 2, Page 12a

[Note: The first two lines of the Hebrew text on this page are not translated.]

AND SHE HID HIM THREE MONTHS. These are the three months in which the world is under the aegis of stern Justice, namely Tammuz, Ab, and Tebet. And what mean these words? They signify that before descending into this world Moses dwelt already in the upper regions, and therefore was united with the Shekinah from the moment of his birth. R. Simeon concluded from this that the spirits of the righteous exist in heaven before they come down into this world. AND WHEN SHE COULD NO LONGER HIDE HIM SHE TOOK FOR HIM AN ARK OF BULRUSHES. She guarded him with signs against the power of the fishes that swim in the ocean—that is, the evil spirits--"wherein are things creeping innumerable" (Ps. CIV, 25). She protected him from such harm by a precious covering composed of two colours, black and white (grace and might). She laid the child between these hues, in order that he might become familiar with them, and later ascend between them to receive the Torah. AND THE DAUGHTER OF PHARAOH CAME DOWN TO BATHE IN THE RIVER. She was the symbol of the power emanating from the "left side", which betokens severity; she thus bathed in the "river" and not in the "sea". AND HER MAIDENS WALKED ALONG BY THE RIVERSIDE: signifying all the legions that proceed from that side. AND SHE OPENED IT AND SHE SAW IT (vathir'ehu), THE CHILD. Why say "she saw it, the child" instead of simply "she saw the child"? Said R. Simeon: 'There is not a word in the Torah that does not contain sublime and precious mystical teachings. In regard to this passage, we have learned that the impress of the King and the Matrona was discernible in the child, an impress symbolized by the letters Vau and He. She thus straightway "had compassion on him". So far, the whole passage has allusions to heavenly matters; from this point the text concerns earthly occurrences, with the exception of the verse following. AND HIS SISTER STOOD AFAR OFF. Whose sister? The sister of Him Who calls the Community of Israel "My sister", in the verse "Open to me, my sister, my love!" (Cant. v, 2). "Afar off"-as it is written: "From far off hath the Lord appeared unto me" (Jer. XXXI, 2). From which it is evident that all the righteous are known by all in those higher regions before their souls descend into this world; how much more, then, Moses. We also learn from this that the souls of the righteous emanate from an upper region, as we have already stated. But there is also an esoteric lesson connected with it, namely, that the soul has a father and a mother, as the body has a father and a mother in this world. In fact, all things above and below proceed from Male and Female, as we have already derived from the words "Let the earth bring forth a living soul" (Gen. I, 24). "The earth" symbolizes the community of Israel; "a living soul"-the soul of the first, the supernal Man, as already explained.' Then came R. Abba to him, kissed him, and said: 'Verily, thou hast spoken well! It is so indeed. Blessed is Moses, the faithful Shepherd, more faithful than all the other prophets of the world.' There is still another interpretation of "and his sister stood afar off", namely, as symbolizing "Wisdom"-"say to wisdom, thou art my sister" (Prov. VII, 4).

Zohar: Shemoth, Section 2, Page 12b

Said R. Isaac: 'The attribute of Justice has never departed from the world, for whenever Israel sinned, stern Justice stood there as her accuser, and then "his sister (wisdom) stood afar off", without interfering. "And the daughter of Pharaoh came down to bathe in the river": i.e. as soon as Israel separates herself from the Torah, the attribute of Justice comes forth to "bathe" in the blood of Israel, because of the neglect of the Torah. "And her maidens walked along by the river's side": these are the nations who persecute Israel, because of her neglect of the Torah.' Said R. Judah: 'Man's fate depends in the last resort upon repentance and prayer, and especially prayer with tears; for there is no gate which tears cannot penetrate. It is written here: "And she opened it and saw the child", which, being interpreted, means that the Shekinah, who always hovers over Israel like a mother over her children, and pleads in her defence against her accuser, opened it "and saw the child, and behold the babe wept". The Shekinah saw the "child", the people of Israel, which is called "the child of delight" (Jer. XXXI, 20), in remorseful tears, pleading with the Holy One like a child with his father, and she "had compassion on him". She said: "This is one of the Hebrews' children", that is to say, of the Hebrews, who are gentle and tender-hearted, and not of the Gentiles, who are stiff-necked and stubborn of heart; they, the Hebrews, are tender-hearted and eager to return to their heavenly Master. "And she called the child's mother", who wept, as it is written: "In Rama was there a voice heard, lamentation, and weeping, and great mourning, Rachel weeping for her children, and would not be comforted" (Jer. XXXI, 14). The child wept, and the mother wept.' R. Judah continued: 'Concerning the future it says: "They will come with weeping, and with supplications will I lead them." For the sake of the weeping of Rachel, the child's mother, will they come and be gathered in from captivity.' R. Isaac said: 'The redemption of Israel depends only on weeping: when the effect of the tears of Esau, which he shed before his father on account of the birthright (Gen. XXVII, 38) shall have been exhausted, redemption will begin for Israel.' Said R. Yose: 'Esau's weeping brought Israel into captivity, and when their force is exhausted, Israel, through their tears, shall be delivered from him.' AND HE SAW AN EGYPTIAN SMITING A HEBREW. 'AND HE LOOKED HERE AND THERE (koh wa-koh). He looked for the fifty letters by which the Israelites proclaim the Divine Unity twice daily, but found no semblance of them expressed in the countenance of that man. Said R. Abba: 'He looked "here" to see whether there were any good works wrought by the man, and "there" to see whether a good son would issue from him. "And he saw that there was no man"; he saw through the holy spirit that no such good son would ever descend from him, for he was aware, as R. Abba has said, that there are many wicked parents who beget more good sons than righteous parents, and that a good son born of wicked parents is of special excellence, being pure out of impure, light out of darkness, wisdom out of folly. The word "saw" here indicates discernment through the holy spirit, and therefore he did not shrink from killing the Egyptian.

Now the Holy One, blessed be He, so ordered matters that Moses might come to the same well to which Jacob came. It says here: "And he sat down by ('al, lit. upon) a well" (Ibid. v, 15), and of Jacob it says, "And he looked, and behold, a well" (Gen. XIX, 2). This shows that although they belonged to the same degree (of sanctity), Moses in this ascended higher than Jacob.' As R. Yose and R. Isaac were once walking together, the former said: 'Was the well which both Jacob and Moses saw the same one which was digged by Abraham and Isaac?' Said R. Isaac: 'No! This well was created when the world was created, and its mouth was formed on the eve of the Sabbath of Creation, in the twilight.' [Tr. note: Cf. Pirke Aboth, v, 9.] That was the well which Jacob and Moses saw.'

Zohar: Shemoth, Section 2, Page 13a

NOW THE PRIEST OF MIDIAN HAD SEVEN DAUGHTERS Said R. Judah: 'If the well from which they drew the water was Jacob's well, how were Jethro's daughters able to draw water from it without difficulty? Was there not "upon the well's mouth a great stone" which had to be "rolled away" by the shepherds (Gen. XXIX, 2-3)?' Said R. Hiya: 'Jacob removed that stone from the well and did not put it back. From that time the water gushed forth, and there was no stone on the well, and thus Jethro's daughters were able to draw from it.'

R. Eleazar and R. Abba were once walking from Tiberias to Sepphoris. On the way a Jew joined them. Said R. Eleazar: 'Let each one of us expound some saying of the Torah!' He himself started by quoting the sentence: "Then said he unto me, prophesy unto the spirit, prophesy, son of man, and say to the spirit" (Ezek. XXXVII, 9). 'It may be asked, how could Ezekiel prophesy concerning the spirit, seeing that it is written: "No man hath power over the spirit to retain the spirit" (Eccl. VIII, 8)? Verily, man has no power over the spirit, but the Holy One has power over all things, and it was by His command that Ezekiel was prophesying. Besides, the spirit was embodied in material form in this world, and therefore he prophesied concerning it: "Come from the four winds, O spirit!"; namely from the region where it resides in the four foundations of the world.'

On hearing this the Jew jumped up. 'What is the matter?' asked R. Eleazar. The Jew replied: 'I see something.' 'And what is it?' He answered: 'If the spirit of man is endowed in Paradise with the form of the body which it is to assume in this world, should it not have been said: "Come from Paradise, O spirit!" and not "from the four winds"?' R. Eleazar replied: 'Before descending into this world the spirit ascends from the earthly Paradise to the Throne which stands on four pillars. There it draws its being from that Throne of the King, and only then does it descend to this world. As the body is collected from the four regions of the world, so is the spirit of man taken from the four pillars upon which the Throne is established.' 'The reason why I ran in front of you,' said the man, 'was because I beheld something from that side. One day I was walking in the desert and I beheld a tree, beautiful to look upon, and beneath it a cavern. I approached it and found that from the cavern issued a profusion of sweet odours. I plucked up courage and entered the cavern. I descended a number of steps which brought me to a place where there were many trees, and savours of overpowering sweetness. There I saw a man who held a sceptre in his hand, standing at a place where the trees parted. When he saw me he was astonished and came up to me. "Who art thou, and what doest thou here?" he demanded. I was frightened exceedingly and said: "Sir, I am one of the Fellowship. I noticed this place in the desert, and so I entered." Said he: "As thou art one of the Fellowship, take this bundle of writings and give it to the members of the Fellowship, to those who know the mystery of the spirits of the righteous ones." He then struck

Zohar: Shemoth, Section 2, Page 13b

me with the sceptre, and I fell asleep. In my sleep I saw crowds upon crowds arriving at that place, and the man touched them with the sceptre saying: "Take the path of the trees!" After going a little way they flew, in the air and I did not know to where. I also heard voices of great multitudes and knew not who they were. When I awoke I saw nothing, and I was in fear and trembling. Then I beheld the man again. He asked me: "Hast thou seen anything?" I told him what I had seen in my sleep. Said he: "These were the spirits of the righteous who go by that way in order to reach Paradise, and what thou hast heard are the voices of those who stand in the Garden in the likeness they are to wear in this world, expressing their great joy at the arrival of the spirits of the righteous who enter there. As the body is formed in this world from the combination of the four elements, so is the spirit formed in the Garden from the combination of the four winds that are in the Garden, and the spirit is enveloped there in the impress of the body's shape, and if it were not for the four winds, which are the airs of the Garden, the spirit would not have been clothed at all. These four winds are bound up with one another, and the spirit is shaped from them, as the body is shaped from the four elements. Therefore it says: 'Come from the four winds, O spirit!', namely from the four winds of Paradise from which thou art shaped. And now take this bundle of writings, and go thy way, and give it to the Fellowship." 'The Jew here finished, and R. Eleazar and his companions drew near and kissed him on his head. Said R. Eleazar: 'Blessed be the Merciful One Who sent thee here! Verily this is the true explanation of the subject, and God put that verse into my mouth.' Then the Jew gave them the bundle of writings. AS soon as R. Eleazar took it and opened it, a fiery vapour burst forth and enveloped him. He saw some things in it, and then the writing flew away from his hand. Then R. Eleazar wept, and said: 'Who can abide in the storehouse of the King? "Lord, who shall abide in thy tabernacle? Who shall dwell in thy holy hill?" (Ps. xv, 2). Blessed be the way and the hour in which this happened to me!' This incident made R. Eleazar glad for many days, but he said nothing to his colleagues. As they were proceeding, they passed a well from which they drank. Said R. Eleazar: 'Blessed

311

are the righteous! Jacob ran away from his brother, and chanced to find a well; as soon as it saw him, the waters recognized their master and ascended to meet him, and there he found his spouse. Moses felt assured when he saw that the water came up to him that there he would meet his future wife. Furthermore, the holy spirit never left him, and he knew by inspiration that Zipporah would be his wife. He thought: "To be sure, Jacob came to this same place and the waters came up towards him, and then a man came up and took him into his house and supplied him with all his needs: the same will happen to me".' Said the man who accompanied them: 'We have been taught that Jethro had been a heathen priest, and as soon as he saw that there was no truth in paganism he renounced it and ceased to worship the idols, and then his people excommunicated him, and when they saw his daughters they drove them away, for previously the shepherds used to pasture Jethro's flocks. When Moses saw through the holy spirit that the shepherds acted as they did on account of their idolatrous religion, he straightway stood up and helped the daughters and watered their flocks, acting wholly from zeal for God in all things.' Said to him R. Eleazar: 'Thou hast been so long with us, and yet we know not

Zohar: Shemoth, Section 2, Page 14a

thy name!' He replied: 'My name is Yoezer ben Jacob.' The colleagues came and kissed him. They said: 'Thou wert so long with us, and we knew thee not!' They walked together the whole day, and then accompanied him three miles on his way. AND THEY SAID, AN EGYPTIAN DELIVERED US FROM THE HAND OF THE SHEPHERDS. Said R. Hiya: The companions have affirmed that (in using the word "Egyptian") they spoke in a flash of inspiration, saying words of whose true import they themselves were not aware. They were indeed like a man dwelling in the desert who seldom tasted meat, but one day, when a bear pursuing a lamb passed his dwelling, he saved the lamb from the bear in order afterwards to slay it himself for food, so that it was the bear which was the means of supplying the man with meat. Even so it was due to the Egyptian whom Moses killed that Jethro's daughters were saved.'

The following is an alternative explanation of Ex. I, 11: AND THESE ARE THE NAMES OF THE CHILDREN OF ISRAEL. R. Judah opened with the words: "I am black but comely" (S.S. 1, 5). He said that they refer to the community of Israel, who is "black" because of her captivity, and "comely" because of the Torah and good works, for which she will be worthy to inherit the Jerusalem that is above. Although she is "as the tents of Kedar", i.e. "black" (kedar), she is "like the curtains of Solomon", i.e. she belongs to the King of perfect peace (shalom).

R. Hiya the Great once visited the masters of the (esoteric) lore to learn from them. He came to the house of R. Simeon ben Yohai and found it shut off by a curtain. R. Hiya felt bashful and said: 'I shall stand here and listen to what he says.' And he heard R. Simeon say: 'Flee away, my beloved, like the gazelle, or like a young hart on mountains of spices (S.S. VII, 14). This signifies the longing of Israel for the Holy One, blessed be He: she implores Him not to depart from her to a distance, but to be even as a gazelle and a young hart. These animals, unlike all others, do when running go but a little way, and then look back, turning their faces toward the place from which they came, then running on, do again turn round and look back. So the Israelites say to the Holy One, blessed be He: "If our sins have caused Thee to flee from us, may it be Thy pleasure to run like a gazelle or like a young hart, and look back on us!" And, indeed, is it not written: "And yet for all that, when they be in the land of their enemies, I will not cast them away, neither will I abhor them, to destroy them utterly" (Lev. XXVI, 44)? Furthermore, a gazelle sleeps with one eye closed and the other one open, and so Israel says to the Holy One, blessed be He, "Be unto me like a gazelle also in this"! Yea, verily, "He who keepeth Israel neither slumbereth nor sleepeth" (Ps. CXXI, 4).'

Hearing all this, R. Hiya said: 'Behold, supernal beings are present in this house, and do I stay outside? Woe is me.' And he commenced to weep. But R. Simeon, hearing him from within, said: 'Verily, the Shekinah is outside. Who will go out to bring Her in?' Said R. Eleazar his son: 'Though I burn, I shall not burn any more than the phoenix, for the Shekinah is there outside. Let her enter here, in order that the fire may be perfect.' Then he heard a voice: 'Not yet have the pillars been set up nor have the gates been fixed, and he is of those who are too young for the spices of Eden which are here.' So R. Eleazar did not go out. R. Hiya, still sitting without, sighed and recited: '"Turn, my beloved, and be thou like unto a gazelle, or like unto a young hart upon mountains of disruption" (S.S. 11, 17).' Then the dividing curtain opened, but R. Hiya did not enter. R. Simeon lifted up his eyes and said: 'He who is without has, by a clear sign, been permitted to enter, and do we remain here?' He stood up and lo, as he rose a fire began to move from the place where he stood to the place where R. Hiya was. Said R. Simeon: 'A spark of radiant light is without and I am here within.' R. Hiya could not open his mouth. When he entered, he dropped his eyes and looked not up. Said R. Simeon to R. Eleazar his son: 'Arise and pass thy hand over his mouth, for he is unaccustomed to these surroundings.' R. Eleazar arose and did so. Then R. Hiya opened his mouth and said: 'My eyes now see something they have not seen before. I have reached a height that I did not dream of. It is good to die in the fire kindled by the good gold, at the place where sparks fly on every side, each one ascending to three hundred

Zohar: Shemoth, Section 2, Page 14b

and seventy-five rows of angels, and each of which spreads itself to thousands and myriads, until they reach the Ancient of Days, who sits upon the Throne. The Throne trembles, and the trembling thereof penetrates through a hundred and sixty worlds until it reaches a place which is called "the delight of the righteous", and it is heard throughout all the firmaments. Then all they that are above and all that are below are greatly amazed, and cry as with one voice: "This is R. Simeon ben Yohai, the world-shaker; who can stand before him? When he opens his lips to expound the Torah, all the thrones, all the firmaments, all the angelic hosts, all who praise their Lord, do listen to his voice. No mouth is opened: all are silent, and not a sound is heard until his words break through all the firmaments above and below. But when he ends, then the song and the rejoicing of them who praise their Lord is such as was never before heard; it echoes through all the firmaments of Heaven-and all this on account of R. Simeon and his wisdom! They bow before their Master, the perfume of the spices from Eden ascends in sweetness to the Throne of the Ancient of Days-and all this on account of R. Simeon and his wisdom!".'

R. Simeon here discoursed as follows: 'In his going down into Egypt Jacob was accompanied by six angelic grades, each consisting of ten thousand myriads. Correspondingly Israel was made up of six grades, in correspondence to which again there are six steps to the supernal celestial Throne, and corresponding to them six steps to the lower celestial Throne. [Tr. note: Malkuth.] Observe that each grade was an epitome of ten grades, so that altogether there were sixty, indentical with the "threescore mighty men" that are round about the Shekinah. And these sixty, again, are the sixty myriads that accompanied Israel in their departure from exile and accompanied Jacob into exile.' R. Hiya asked him: 'But are there not seven grades, each an epitome of the ten grades, thus amounting to seventy?' R. Simeon said in reply: 'That number has no bearing on this matter, as we learn from the description of the candlestick, of which it says: "And there shall be six branches going out of the sides thereof: three branches of the candlestick out of the one side thereof, and three branches of the candlestick out of the other side thereof... And thou shalt make the lamps thereof seven" (Ex. xxv, 32). The central branch is not counted with the rest, as it says, "and they shall light the lamps thereof over against it" (Ibid.).'

As they sat thus, R. Eleazar asked his father, R. Simeon: 'For what purpose, and to what end, did the Holy One, blessed be He, allow Israel to go down to Egypt to be in exile there?' His father replied: 'Dost thou ask one question or two?' 'Two,' said R. Eleazar, 'why to Egypt, and why in exile?' Said R. Simeon: 'Stand up and take courage! In thy name shall this word be established above. Speak, my son, speak!' Then R. Eleazar opened his mouth and said: '"Threescore queens are they, and fourscore concubines, and virgins without number" (S.S. VI, 8). The "threescore queens" are allegorical of the celestial heroic angels that are of the host of Geburah, and that attach themselves to the "shells" (k'lifoth, i.e. baser elements) of the holy congregation of Israel. The "fourscore concubines" signify the lower "klifoth" that have dominion in this world, and whose power is to the higher powers as one to a hundred. The "virgins without number" are those angelic hosts of whom it is said, "Is there a number to his bands?" (Job. xxv, 3). And yet "My dove, my undefiled, is but one, she is the only one of her mother" (S.S. VI, 9), the Holy Shekinah, who proceeds from the twelve flashes of the radiance which illumines all things, and is called "Mother". And the Holy One, blessed be He, dealt according to this principle with the earth: He scattered the nations abroad in separation and appointed supernal chiefs over them, as it is written, "which the Lord hath imparted to all the nations under heaven" (Deut. VI, 19). But He took unto Himself the congregation of Israel to be His own portion and His own choice, as it is written, "For the Lord's portion is his people, Jacob is the lot of his inheritance" (Ibid. XXXII, 9). Thus it is clear that Israel is directly under God and none other; and He says of her: "My dove, my undefiled, is but one, she is the only one of her Mother." She is the only one of her Mother Shekinah who dwells in her midst. "Many daughters have done virtuously, but thou excellest them all" (Prov. XXXI, 29).'

There is a further esoteric meaning in this verse. We are told: "With ten Sayings the world was created" (Pirke Ab. v, 1). Yet, on examination they prove to be only three, viz. Wisdom, Understanding, and Knowledge. The world was created only for the sake of Israel. When the Holy One, blessed be He, desired to endow the earth with permanence, He formed Abraham in the mystery of Wisdom, Isaac in the mystery of Understanding, and Jacob in the mystery of Perception, that is to say, of Knowledge. Therefore it is said: "With wisdom is the house built, and by understanding it is established, and by knowledge shall the chambers be filled..." (Prov. XXIV, 4-5). At that hour the whole world came into perfection; and when the twelve Tribes were born to Jacob,

Zohar: Shemoth, Section 2, Page 15a

all things came to completion according to the supernal pattern ordained from the beginning. When the Holy One beheld the exceeding joy of this lower world at being completed after the fashion of the world above, He said: "Should they (the Israelites) mingle with the other nations, a blemish would be caused in all the worlds". What, then, did He do? He caused them to wander over the face of the earth and from one nation to another until, in Egypt, they fell among those of a stubborn race, who, deeming them but slaves, despised their customs and abhorred their ways, and would not mingle with them or have a part in them. Both male and female among the Egyptians loathed them, and thus the whole

Divine purpose could come into completion within the holy seed itself, whilst at the same time the guilt of the other nations became complete, as it is written: "In the fourth generation they (the children of Abraham) shall come hither again; for the iniquity of the Amorites is not yet full" (Gen. xv, 16). And when the Israelites came out of the bondage of Egypt, they came out as beings pure and holy, as it says: "The tribes of the Lord, the testimony of Israel" (Ps. CXXII, 4).'

Then R. Simeon approached his son, and kissing him he said: 'Remain, my son, standing at thy place, for the hour favours thee.' Then R. Simeon sat and listened while R. Eleazar, his son, stood and expounded mysteries of wisdom. And as he spoke his countenance was lit as by the radiance of the sun, and his words ascended to the starry heights and flitted across the firmament. They thus continued for a space of two days, neither eating nor drinking, and noticing neither day nor night. When they came forth they found that they had not tasted anything for two days. Said R. Simeon: 'We are told that Moses "was there with the Lord forty days and forty nights; he did neither eat bread, nor drink water" (Ex. XXIV, 28). If we, who but for a brief space were caught up into that rapture of Divine contemplation, forgot to eat and drink, how much more so Moses!'

When R. Hiya appeared before R. Judah the Saint and related this occurrence to him, R. Simeon ben Gamliel, R. Judah's father, said: 'R. Simeon ben Yohai is indeed a lion and his son likewise. He is different from all others of his kind. Of him it is written: "The lion hath roared, who will not fear?" (Amos III, 8). And if even the upper worlds do tremble before him, how much more then we? A man who has no need of fasting to proclaim his desires to the Almighty, and to have them fulfilled, since he decides and the Holy One, blessed be He, confirms his decision; or the Holy One deciding, he revokes the decision and it is annulled! As it is said: "There shall be one that ruleth over man, a righteous one ruling in the fear of the Lord" (2 Sam. XXIII, 3). The Holy One rules over man, but who rules over the Holy One? Surely, the Righteous! For it may even be from time to time that the Holy One proposes and the righteous disposes!'

R. Judah said: 'The Holy One, blessed be He, delights more in the prayer of the righteous than in any other thing soever; yet, though it please Him better than all else, He does not always grant their requests, nor do all that they ask. He sometimes refuses to fulfil their wish.'

It is recounted by the disciples that on one occasion when there was a shortage of rain, R. Eleazar decreed that the congregation should fast forty days. But no rain fell. Then R. Akiba prayed, and as he spake the words "Thou causest the wind to blow" so the wind blew, and when he said "and the rain to fall", lo, the rain fell. R. Eleazar was much chagrined at this. R. Akiba read his feelings in his looks, so he stood up and said to the congregation: 'I will tell you a parable. R. Eleazar is like unto one who is the king's own friend and dear companion: when he goes to the palace to entreat some favour, it is not granted at once, since the king so delights in his friend's presence that he keeps him by him as long as possible. I, on the other hand, am like the king's servant, whose requests are quickly granted, the king only desiring to get rid of him at once and be no more troubled; therefore he says: "Give the man what he wants at once, so that he should not have to enter my chamber!".' On hearing this, R. Eleazar was comforted. He said to him: 'Akiba, let me tell you what was shown to me in a dream in regard to the words, "Pray not for this people, neither lift up cry nor prayer for them, neither make intercession to me" (Jer. VII, 16). Twelve rows of pure balsam entered with him who wears breastplate and Ephod (i.e. the heavenly High Priest, the Intercessor, probably Metatron) when he prayed to the Holy One to have mercy upon the world, and yet he still is unanswered.' If so, why was R. Eleazar vexed? Because people did not know this.

Said R. Eleazar: 'Eighteen gardens of balsam are entered daily by the souls of the righteous, from which emanate forty-nine aromas,

Zohar: Shemoth, Section 2, Page 15b

reaching to the place called Eden-in correspondence with the forty-nine ways of interpreting the Torah, [Tr. note: Cf. Midrash Rabbah, Cant. 13a.] the forty-nine letters in the names of the twelve tribes, the forty-nine days' interval between the Exodus and the giving of the Law. Forty-nine holy days stand there, and each day waits for the instructions of the flashing stone set in the breastplate, and he who is adorned with the breastplate sits on a holy glorious throne. They look at the breastplate, and take the order from it either to enter or to depart. They lift up their eyes and behold a shining plate flashing towards six hundred and twenty sides on which the supernal holy Name is engraved.' Said R. Akiba to him: 'What is the meaning of the words, "I went down into the garden of nuts (Heb. nut)" (S.S. VI, 11)?' R. Eleazar replied: 'This garden is the one that goes out of Eden, namely the Shekinah; the "nut" is the supernal holy Chariot, namely the four heads into which the river parted (Gen. II, 10), like the walnut, which has four sections inside. "I went down" is used in the same sense as in the expression, "So-and-so went down to the Chariot" (i.e. penetrated to its inner meaning).' Said R. Akiba: 'In that case it ought to have said: "I went down into the nut"; why does it say, "into the garden of nuts"?' Said R. Eleazar: 'As it is the virtue of a nut to be closed in from all sides, so is the Chariot which goes out of the Garden (Paradise) hidden on all sides; as the four sections of the walnut are united at one side and separated at the other, so are all the parts of the Celestial Chariot united in perfect union, and yet each part fulfils a special purpose; one "compasses the whole land of Havilah,', and the other "compasses the whole land of Cush", etc.' Said R. Akiba:

314

'What is the symbolism of the moisture in the shell of the walnut?' R. Eleazar replied: 'Although the Scripture does not reveal it in this connection, it does in another connection. Almonds are sweet and also bitter, symbolizing condemnation and acquittal, although every instance in the Bible refers to condemnation only (cf. Jer. I, 11-12).' Said R. Akiba: 'Indeed, everything that the Holy One has made can teach us deep lessons, as it says, "The Lord hath made all things, to teach us wisdom) concerning himself" (Prov. XVI, 4).' R. Eleazar remarked: 'Rather quote the following verse: "And God saw every thing that He had made, and, behold, it was very good." The "very" suggests that we should learn the higher supernal wisdom from all that He made.' R. Judah said: 'That which God has made on earth corresponds to that which He made in heaven, and all things below are symbols of that which is above.' When R. Abba once saw a bird flying away from its nest in a tree, he wept, saying: 'If men only knew what this means, they would rend their garments for the knowledge which has perished from them. For as R. Yose says, "The trees which give mystic indications, like the carob and date tree, can all be grafted on one another. All that bear fruit have one secret nature, save the apple; all that do not bear fruit, save the willows of the brook, suck from one source; and all lowly shrubs, save the hyssop, are from one mother. Every kind of herb has its counterpart above. Therefore it is prohibited to "sow a field with mingled seed" (Lev. XIX, 19).

Zohar: Shemoth, Section 2, Page 16a

[Note: The Hebrew text from line 5 to line 38 does not appear in the translation.]

Now if it is true that all things have their counterparts in heaven, and God gives each one its name, how much more so is it true of the sons of Jacob, the holy Tribes, the pillars of the world! And this is the significance of the words "and these are the names", etc.' AND THESE ARE THE NAMES. Each time that R. Eleazar ben Arach came to this verse he wept. He said that when Israel went into exile all the souls of their progenitors gathered in the cave of Machpelah and cried: "Old man, the afflictions of thy children are terrible; they have to do the work of slaves and a heathen nation makes their lives unbearable." Immediately the spirit of Jacob was awakened. He asked permission to go to Egypt, and he went. Then the Holy One summoned all His celestial hosts and their leaders and they all accompanied Jacob and his sons. The tribes went down to Egypt with their father when they were alive and again when they were dead. Said R. Abba: 'Then the words were fulfilled: "As a father pitieth his children" (Ps. CIII, 13).'

R. Judah bar Shalom was once walking together with R. Abba. They arrived at a place where they decided to spend the night. After taking a meal they lay down to sleep, putting their heads on some raised ground under which was a grave. Before falling asleep they heard a voice from the grave, crying: 'Twelve years

Zohar: Shemoth, Section 2, Page 16b

have I been sleeping here, and only now do I wake, for I now see the image of my son.' R. Judah asked him who he was, and he said: 'I am a Jew, and lie under a ban, not being able to enter the higher regions because of the sorrows of my son, who was stolen by a heathen when he was very young, and is sorely maltreated.' Said R. Judah to him: 'Do the dead know of the sufferings of the living?' He replied: 'If it were not for us, the dead, who intercede before the angel of the grave for the living, they would not remain alive for half a day. I have awakened now, for I was told that my son would come here, but I know not whether alive or dead.' Then R. Judah asked him 'What do ye do in that other world?' The grave shook, and a voice was heard, saying: 'Go away! For at this moment my son is being beaten.' They ran from there for about half a mile and sat down until the morning. When they rose to go they saw a man running with blood streaming from his shoulders. They stopped him, and he told them what had happened to him. They asked him his name and he said: 'Lahma the son of Levi.' 'Why,' said they, 'that is the son of the dead man!' They were afraid to converse with him, neither did they return to the place of the grave. Said R Abba: 'That the prayers of the dead protect the living we learn from Caleb, who went to Hebron to beg for the intercession of the patriarchs (v. Num. XIII, 22).' R. Judah said: 'The Holy One gave two promises (lit. vows) to Jacob: one, that He Himself would go down and stay with him in exile; and the second, that He would let him come out of his grave to behold the joy of the holy host of celestial beings who would dwell with his children in their captivity; as it is written: "I will go down with thee into Egypt and I will surely bring thee up again" (Gen. XLVI, 4); "I will cause you to come up out of your graves" (Ezek. XXXVII, 12); "Whither the tribes go up" (Ps. CXXII, 5).' NOW THERE AROSE A NEW KING OVER EGYPT. R. Simeon said: 'As soon as Joseph died, the celestial representative of Egypt was given domination over all the other nations, as it says: "And Joseph died... and a new king arose", like one who rose to power from a lowly position. R. Tanhum said: 'Every nation has its own representative above, and when God elevates one He degrades another, and when He gives power to this one it is only on account of Israel, as it says: "Her adversaries have become chiefs" (Lam. 1, 5).' R. Isaac said: 'Israel singly is equivalent to all the other nations together; as seventy is the number of the nations, so seventy was the number of the children of Israel when they came into Egypt, and whoever rules over Israel rules over the whole world.' R. Huna said: 'Why is Israel subjected to all nations? In order that the world may be preserved through them, since they are on a par with the whole world. As God is One, so is Israel one, as it says: "And who is like thy people, one people on earth?" (2 Sam. VII, 23). And as His name is one and yet has seventy ramifications, so is Israel one, and yet divided into seventy.' R. Judah applied the words: "For three things the earth is disquieted... for a servant when he reigneth... and an handmaid that is heir to her mistress" (Prov. xxx, 21-22),

Zohar: Shemoth, Section 2, Page 17a

to Egypt and Ishmael (Islam). There is no nation so despised of the Holy One as Egypt, and yet he gave her dominion over Israel; while the "handmaid" is Hagar, who bare Ishmael, who tormented Israel so cruelly in the past, and still rules over her and persecutes her for her faith. In truth, the exile under Ishmael is the hardest of all exiles. Once, when going up to Jerusalem, R. Joshua saw an Arab and his son meet a Jew. The Arab said to his son: "See! There is a Jew whom God has rejected. Go and insult him. Spit in his face seven times, for he is of the seed of the exalted ones, and I know that the seventy nations shall be ruled by them". The boy went and took hold of the Jew's beard, whereupon R. Joshua said: "Mighty ones, mighty ones, I call upon the supernal ones to come down below!" And even before he had finished, the earth opened her mouth and swallowed up the Arabs.'

R. Isaac interpreted the verse "Until the day break and the shadows flee away, I will get me to the mountain of myrrh and to the hill of frankincense" (S.S. IV, 6) in connection with Israel's exile. 'She will be subjected by the nations until the "day" of the Gentiles, which is a thousand years, comes to an end–the "one day known to the Lord" (Zech. XIV, 7)– and "the shadows flee away", namely those who ruled over them. "I will get me", says the Holy One, "to the mountain of Moriah–Jerusalem–to drive away the heathen nations from there; and to the Sanctuary on Mount Zion, the joy of the whole earth." He will "take hold of the ends of the earth that the wicked might be shaken out of it" (Job XXXVIII, 13), as one shakes out the dust from a garment.' R. Yose said: 'Even before the day of the Gentiles be completed the Holy One will reveal Himself in the Jerusalem below to purify her from the abominations of the heathen, for R. Hiya has said that the domination of the Gentiles over Israel cannot last a day longer than a thousand years, which is the Holy One's One Day. Should it last longer, it will not be according to the King's will, but because Israel will not turn to Him in repentance, as it is written: "When thou shalt return unto the Lord... then the Lord thy God will turn thy captivity" (Deut. xxx, 1-4).' AND HE SAID UNTO HIS PEOPLE. Said R. Simeon: 'This refers to Egypt's principality in heaven. Note that this passage mostly speaks of "the king of Egypt", which refers to the celestial chieftain of Egypt; but where it says, "Pharaoh king of Egypt" the actual king is meant. "He said" means he put the idea into their minds that the representative in heaven of the children of Israel was mightier than theirs.' R. Isaac said: 'All the nations of the world derive their power from their celestial prototypes, but Israel only from God, therefore she is called "the people of the Lord".' R. Judah said: 'The Egyptians are here called "his (their representative's) people", and God says of Israel: "I have seen the affliction of my people" (Ex. III, 7): it is to be taken in the strictly literal sense, as it is written, "For all peoples walk every one in the name of its god, but we walk in the name of the Lord our God forever and ever" (Micah IV, 5).' R. Abba said: 'Instead of the peculiar expression "the people of the children of Israel", we should expect either "the people of Israel", or simply "the children of Israel". "Children of Israel", therefore, must refer to the angels, the children of the supernal Israel, and the Israelites were called by Pharaoh their people and not the people of the Lord.'

Zohar: Shemoth, Section 2, Page 17b

R. Johanan, being in the presence of R. Isaac, put to him the question: 'What made Balak say, "Behold, there is a people come out from Egypt" (Num. XXII, 5) instead of saying, "Behold, a people, to wit, the children of Israel"?' R. Isaac replied: 'Balak was a great sorcerer, and it is the way of sorcerers to avoid any doubtful statement. Thus, in mentioning a man they will never mention the name of his father, but that of his mother, for the reason that a man's maternal descent is beyond any doubt. They adopt this course because the demons scrutinize every word uttered to them, so that if it be a falsehood they communicate to the utterer lying information, but if it be truthful they communicate truthful information, at least about things that are to happen shortly. All the more is this the case when they are invoked to perform some action.' R. Aha said: 'Balak wished to show his contempt of Israel by his expression: "Behold, a people went forth from Egypt", as much as to say, "a people, whose origin we know not".'

R. Johanan said: 'Why are the nations of the celestial chieftains kept in safety and the people of the Holy One not?' R. Isaac replied: 'A poor man needs to take care of his goods, but not a rich one. Further, Israel belongs to the King who loves truth and justice, and therefore He punishes principally and first of all the members of His own family, in order that they may guard themselves from sin more than the outsiders, as it says: "Only you have I known from among all the families of the earth, therefore I will visit upon you all your iniquities" (Amos III, 2).'

R. Yose one day went for a walk with R. Aha bar Jacob. Neither spoke, but whereas R. Aha meditated on spiritual matters, R. Jose's mind was occupied with worldly things. As they were thus proceeding, R. Yose suddenly beheld a wild beast running after him. He said to R. Aha: 'Dost thou not see the beast running after me?' 'No,' replied R. Aha, 'I see nothing.' R. Yose ran, pursued by the beast. He fell, and blood gushed from his nose. Then he heard a voice say: "You only have I known, etc." Musing on these words, he said: 'If I have been punished because my mind was but for one moment separated from the Torah, what must await him who is forever apart from her! It is written, "Who led thee through that great and terrible wilderness, wherein were fiery serpents and scorpions" (Deut. VIII, 15). Why fiery serpents? To punish Israel should she separate herself from the Tree of Life, which is the Torah. God punishes the students of the Torah in order that they may not be separated from the Tree of Life even for a single moment.' AND HE SAID UNTO HIS PEOPLE. R. Isaac once drew near to the foot of a mountain, and there beheld a man sleeping under a tree. He sat down. Suddenly and without warning the earth began to quake violently and became full of fissures. The tree was uprooted and fell to the ground; and the man beneath it woke, and cried with a loud voice: 'O Jew, O Jew, weep and lament with mourning and sounds of sorrow! For even at this very moment a great supernal prince of the Gentiles is being appointed in Heaven, who will cause terrible misfortune to Israel. This quaking of the earth is meant as a portent and a warning to you.' At this R. Isaac fell a-trembling, and said: 'Verily, it is written, "For three things the earth is disquieted... for a servant when he reigneth, etc.", that is, when the supramundane principality, who was previously under another ruler, reigns, especially over Israel.' R. Hama bar Gurya said: 'When God allows Israel to fall under the oppression of the Gentiles He (God) weeps, as it is written, "My soul weeps in secret places" (Jer. XIII, 17).'

R. Judah once visited R. Eleazar. He found him sitting deep in thought, his hand pressed to his mouth in sadness. 'What are you thinking about?' he asked.

Zohar: Shemoth, Section 2, Page 18a

R. Eleazar replied: 'It says "In the light of the king's countenance there is life" (Prov. XVI, 15), but if our Master is cast down in spirit, and even sighing and weeping, what can his ministers do but follow His example? Therefore it is written, "Behold, their valiant ones (angels) cry without, the angels of peace weep bitterly" (Is. XXXIII, 7). Why do they cry? Because their Lord is within and they are without; because their Lord is in the inner chambers and they are in the outer courts. Why are they called "angels of peace"? Are there angels who are not of peace? Yea, verily! For there are emissaries both of stern judgement and of less stern judgement, and there are those whose attribute is justice mingled with mercy, and some who represent mercy only. It is these last who are called "Angels of peace". Of the lowest degree of heavenly beings it is written, "I clothe the heavens with blackness and I make sackcloth their covering" (Is. L, 3). But unto what end do the principalities of the Gentile nations cause God's children to suffer, seeing that it makes their Master grieve? They only carry out their office and they needs must do the will of their Lord.'

Said R. Dostai: 'When the children of the Holy One are delivered up to the rulers of the Gentiles, twelve celestial tribunals meet together and precipitate themselves into the great abyss, and all the ministering angels with all servitors cry in agony. Two tears fall then into the abyss. The higher angelic beings roll down below, and the lower are brought still lower to the measure of two hundred and forty degrees, for "The lion hath roared, who will not fear?" (Amos III, 8).' We have learned that at the time the Holy One, blessed be He, had given over Israel into the hand of the chieftain of Egypt, He decreed that seven hardships should be laid on them by the Egyptians These are enumerated in the verse saying: "And they made their lives bitter with hard service, etc." Correspondingly, He bestowed on them seven favours, as enumerated in the verse: "And the children of Israel were fruitful, and increased abundantly, and multiplied, and waxed mighty, very mighty, exceedingly so, and the land was filled with them." COME, LET US DEAL WISELY WITH THEM LEST THEY MULTIPLY (Ex. I,10). R. Judah said in the name of R. Isaac: 'Why did the Egyptians so desire to prevent Israel from multiplying, and what motive prompted their supernal representative to put such a desire into their hearts? Because he knew and made known to them that a son would be born to the Israelites through whom judgement should be brought upon the gods of Egypt; for, according to R. Johanan, when Moses said that God "will exercise judgement against all the gods of Egypt" (Ex. XII, I2), Duma, the celestial Prince of Egypt, ran away four hundred parasangs, and the Holy One said to him: "It is My decree!" In that hour his power and his dominion was taken from him, and he was banished, instead, to the lower regions and appointed over the realms of Gehenna, as judge of the souls of the wicked.' R. Judah said that he was appointed over the dead. R. Hanina said: 'It is written: "Upon their gods also the Lord executed judgements" (Num. XXXIII, 4). Can we speak of judgements being executed on gods made of silver or gold, of wood or stone?' R. Yose replied: 'Those made of silver and gold were melted of themselves, and the wooden rotted of themselves.' R. Eleazar said: 'The god of Egypt was the sheep, and so the Holy One, blessed be He, commanded to burn it in fire, so that its evil smell should go forth; and that it should be burnt with "its head with its legs and the inwards thereof" (Ex. XII, 9). And in addition, its bones were thrown into the market-place, a thing which distressed the Egyptians beyond all else. This was the "judgement" implied in the verse cited.' R. Judah said: '"Against their gods" refers in a literal sense to their Chieftains, in fulfilment of the prophecy: "The Lord will punish the host of the high heaven on high" (Is. XXIV, 21). The wise men among the Egyptians knew all this, and all the more so their Chieftain. Hence they said: "Come, let us deal wisely with them".' Said R. Johanan: 'They had many idols, but their chief god was the Nile,

Zohar: Shemoth, Section 2, Page 18b

and the Lord executed judgements on them all.' Said R. Abba: 'The exposition of R. Johanan is the correct and self-evident one. For we know that first the gods of a nation are punished and then the nation itself. So here, first the Nile and wood and stones were smitten, as Scripture says: "and there shall be blood throughout the land of Egypt, both in wood and stone" (Ex. XII, 19), the wood and stone being the very gods which the Egyptians worshipped.' R. Isaac remarked: 'But it is written, "the host of the high heaven on high", whereas the Nile was not on high.' Said R. Johanan: 'The greater part of its waters resemble their prototype on high.' R. Isaac said: 'First their Chieftain was smitten and then the rest of their gods.' R. Simeon, the son of R. Yose, said: 'The punishment of the Egyptian nation itself was accomplished at the sea, in regard to which it is written: "There remained not so much as one of them" (Ibid. XIV, 28), and before that, judgements were executed against their gods. Hence the words of Pharaoh, saying: "Come, let us deal wisely with them lest they multiply, and it come to pass that, when befalleth us any war, etc." There was here a premonition of what actually came to pass-"they also join themselves unto our enemies"-a premonition of the heavenly hosts that stood by the Israelites-"and fight against us" -a prediction of what Moses declared, saying: "The Lord will fight for you" (Ibid. XIV, 14) - "and get them up out of the land"- as in fact we read: "for the children of Israel went out with a high hand" (Ibid. XIV, 8).' AND THERE WENT A MAN OF THE HOUSE OF LEVI AND TOOK TO WIFE A DAUGHTER OF LEVI. R. Eleazar discoursed on the verse, "The Song of Songs of Solomon" (S.S. 1, I). He said: 'We have learnt that when the Holy One, blessed be He, was about to create the world, He was pleased to create the heaven with His right hand, and the earth with His left. He was also pleased to make a division of day and night, and He created angels appointed by His grace to chant hymns of praise by day, and others by night for the night watches. Thus it is said: "The Lord commandeth his grace in the daytime, and in the night his song with me" (Ps. XLII, 9). The former stand on the right hand, and the latter on the left, the latter hearkening to the song of the day and the former to the song of the night: and the singing they hear is the song of Israel, the holy.' R. Isaac said: 'Those that sing by night listen to the song of Israel by day, as it is written: "The companions hearken to thy voice" (S.S. VIII, 13).' Said R. Simeon: 'The angels of one degree with three divisions sing at night, and in darkness still their songs are heard, as it says, "She riseth while it is yet night, and giveth food to her household, and a portion to her maidens" (Prov. XXXI, 15).' R. Eleazar continued: 'On the first day ten things were created, and of these ten some belong to the day and its ways, and some to the night and the ways of the night. It is also known and believed that those angels who sing by night are the leaders of all other singers; and when on earth we living terrestrial creatures raise up our hearts in song, then those supernal beings gain an accession of knowledge, wisdom and understanding, so that they are enabled to perceive matters which even they had never before comprehended.' Said R. Nehemiah: 'Blessed is he who is worthy to perceive such singing, for, as we know and have been taught, he who is deemed worthy to comprehend this song becomes adept in doctrine and obtains wit to discern what has been and what will be. Solomon was found worthy of such knowledge, for thus taught R. Simeon: "David, peace be on him, was cognizant of it, and so could compose hymns and songs, many in number, in which he hinted concerning future events. He also became richly endowed with power in the holy spirit, understood matters appertaining to the Torah and to Divine wisdom, and obtained a mastery of the holy tongue. Solomon, however, was gifted with a still greater knowledge of that song: he penetrated into the essence of wisdom, and so he wrote many proverbs and made a book of the song itself. This is the meaning of his words, "I got me men singers (sharim) and women singers" (Eccl. II, 8); that is to say, he acquired the knowledge of the hymn sung by heavenly and terrestrial beings. And on account of this he called his book "The Song of Songs": the song of the supernal songs, the song containing all mysteries of the Torah and of Divine wisdom; the song wherein is power to penetrate into things that were and things that will be; the song sung by the supernal princes (sharim=sarim).'

Said R. Eleazar: 'Those heavenly princes stood in expectation until Levi was born; as soon as he was born they began to sing; as soon as Moses was born and Aaron was anointed high priest and the Levites were sanctified, the singing was perfected and the singers remained at their service.' He also said: 'At the hour when Levi was born, the heavenly choir began to sing: "O that thou wert as my brother that sucked the breast of my mother!

Zohar: Shemoth, Section 2, Page 19a

Should I find thee without, indeed I would kiss thee, and they would not despise me" (S.S. VIII, I). When the singers here below issued from the tribe of Levi and all of them were sanctified and entered into their service, and the two choirs, the heavenly and the earthly, were both hallowed, and sang in harmony so that the worlds were in unison and one King dwelt above them, then came Solomon and made a book of the hymning of the singers, wherein is enclosed heavenly wisdom.'

Said R. Judah: 'Why are the singers here below called Levites? Because they are joined closely (lava=to be joined to) to and united with (the singers) above in absolute unison. He who hears their singing, his soul is also joined closely to the upper world. Therefore Leah said (at the birth of Levi): "Now this time my husband will be joined unto me" (Gen. XXIX, 34).' Said R. Tanhum: 'The seed of Levi is always joined to the Shekinah: in Moses, Aaron, Miriam, and in all his descendants. Observe that when the supernal singers desired to minister, they could not actually perform their function before the brothers Moses and Aaron and their sister Miriam were born.

'We have a tradition that when Levi was born, the Holy One, blessed be He, took him and chose him from among all his brethren, and settled him in the land. He then begat Kehat, who begat Amram, who begat Aaron and Miriam. Amram separated himself from his wife and then took her again. At that hour the heavenly singers began to chant, but the Holy

One, blessed be He, rebuked them, and the chanting ceased, until He stretched out the line of His right hand (the attribute of Grace) towards Amram. Why was he called Amram? Because a people, higher than all the high ones ('am ram=high people), descended from him. And yet his name is not expressly mentioned (in connection with the birth of Moses). Why so? Because he secretly went away from his wife and secretly returned, so that no one should notice him. Wherefore it is written: "And there went a man"; it does not say "Amram". Likewise does it say: "And took to wife a daughter of Levi"; she also returned secretly, wherefore her name is not mentioned.' AND THERE WENT A MAN. R. Abahu said: This was Gabriel, who is called "man" in the verse, "And the man Gabriel" (Dan. IX, 21), and it was he who went and brought her (Amram's wife) back to him.' Said R. Judah: 'It was Amram himself, only his name is not mentioned because this going to rejoin his wife was not his own idea but was inspired from above.'

R. Isaac said: 'In regard to the birth of Aaron and Miriam it does not say anything concerning their parents' espousal, but in connection with the birth of Moses it says:" And took to wife a daughter of Levi", which shows that the Shekinah is called after Levi, and Amram was not worthy to beget Moses until he obtained a portion in the Shekinah, and then he begat Moses. Hence it is written: "And she saw him that he was good" (Ex. II, 2).' R. Eleazar said: 'Amram was blessed with a son who was found worthy to be addressed by the great Voice, as it is written, "And God answered him by a voice" (Ex. XIX, 19); and Amram himself had the privilege of being addressed by "the daughter of a voice" (bat kol, an echo of prophecy); "he took the daughter of Levi", that is to say, "the daughter of a voice". Therefore it is written, "and there went", meaning, he advanced from degree to degree until he reached this stage.'

We have been taught that when Moses was born the Holy One, blessed be He, attached His Name to him: it says of the child Moses, "he was good", and it says of God, "The Lord is good to all" (Ps. CXLV, 9) and "Taste and see that the Lord is good" (Ibid. XXIV, 9). AND IT CAME TO PASS IN THE COURSE OF THOSE MANY DAYS, ETC. (Ex. II, 23). R. Joshua of Saknin said: 'It was the end of their exile when their bondage was most severe. As soon as the appointed time of delivery came, "the king of Egypt died": i.e. the angelic Chieftain of Egypt was degraded from his high estate. As soon as he fell, the Holy One, blessed be He, remembered Israel and heard their prayer,' Said R. Judah: 'The proof of this is that immediately after the words "The king of Egypt died" the text continues "and the children of Israel sighed by reason of the bondage, and they cried, and their cry came up unto God", which shows that until then their crying had not been answered.' R. Eleazar said: 'Observe the loving-kindness of the Holy One, blessed be He. When He has pity on Israel He suppresses the attribute of Justice and thus lets her obtain mercy. This is the meaning of the saying (T.B. Ber. 59a): "The holy One, blessed be He, lets drop two tears into the Ocean". What are the two tears?' R. Yose said: 'This saying is not

Zohar: Shemoth, Section 2, Page 19b

authentic, for R. Kattina, when he heard it from a certain sorcerer, said to him "You are a liar".' Said R. Eleazar: 'There is no need for us to accept the words of a sorcerer, we have a definite statement that in the ten crowns of the King there are two tears of the Holy One, blessed be He, namely two measures of chastisement, which comes from both of these tears, as it says: "These two (desolation and destruction) have happened unto thee" (Isa. LI, 19). And when the Holy One remembers His children, He drops them into the great Sea, which is the Sea of Wisdom, in order to sweeten them, and He turns the attribute of Justice into the attribute of Mercy, and takes compassion on Israel.' Said R. Judah: 'We read later, "And behold the Egyptian marched after them" (Ex. XIV, 10). These words are referred by R. Yose to the angelic prince of Egypt; how, then, can you say that the "king of Egypt" here refers to this same prince?' Said R. Isaac: 'The later Scriptural saying, in fact, confirms the former, for it does not say "the king of Egypt marched after them", but "the Egyptian", because he was not king any longer, having fallen from his former dignity.'

R. Yose said: 'It is written: "Behold a day cometh to the Lord" (Zech. XIV, 1); and again, "But the day shall be one and it shall be known to the Lord" (Ibid. v, 7). Are we to suppose from this that the other days are not the Lord's? It is, however, as R. Abba has said: all the other days are given over to the angelic principalities of the nations, but there is one day which will be the day of the Holy One, blessed be He, in which He will judge the heathen nations, and when their principalities shall fall from their high estate. Of that day it is written: "And the Lord alone shall be exalted on that day" (Isa. II, 11).' R. Abba said: 'It is written: "for my sword is bathed in heaven" (Isa. XXXIV, 5), which refers to the Lord's judgement on the supernal princes, the "sword" being a symbol of judgement.' R. Abba further said: 'The sword is identical with the execution of judgement, as it is written, "and he saw the angel of the Lord standing between the earth and the heaven, having a drawn sword in his hand" (I Chron. XXI, 16). Now, can we imagine a drawn sword literally having been in the hand of the angel? But what it means is that he possessed the authorization to execute judgement.' Said R. Isaac: 'What do you make of the remark of R. Joshua, son of Levi, that "the angel of death once said to me: Were it not that I have regard for the dignity of mankind I would cut their throats as is done to an animal"?' R. Abba replied: 'This only means that he has authorization to execute judgement; and the same is meant by the phrase, "with his sword drawn in his hand" (Jos. v, 13).' 'If that be so, what is the meaning of "and he put his sword back into the sheath thereof" (I Chron. XXI, 27)?' Said R. Abba: 'It signifies that the power delegated to him was restored to its rightful possessor, to Him to whom authority belongs.' AND THE CHILDREN OF ISRAEL SIGHED. The sighing was in heaven for their sake. The "children of Israel" here are the supernal ones, namely those who carry on the divine service above.'

R. Isaac asked: 'When the Holy One, blessed be He, judges the family above (the angelic principalities), in what does the judgement consist?' R. Eleazar answered: 'He makes them pass through the fiery stream, and takes away from them their power as representatives of the nations and appoints the principalities representing other nations to rule instead of them.' 'But,' said R. Isaac, 'It says of the angelic world: "His ministers are a flaming fire" (Ps. CIV, 4) (and if so, what punishment is it for them to cross the fiery stream?).' To which R. Eleazar answered: 'There are different qualities of fire.'

R. Isaac said: 'We have to distinguish between the terms "sighing", "imploring", and "crying", all three of which are applied here to the children of Israel.' Said R. Judah: 'In fact they only implored and cried, as the sighing mentioned in the verse refers to the supernal beings.' 'What is the difference between imploring and crying?' Said R. Isaac: 'The former means prayer in actual words (Ps. XXXIX, 13; LXXXVIII, 14; XXX, 3), the latter crying without words. R. Judah

Zohar: Shemoth, Section 2, Page 20a

said: 'Hence crying is more poignant than all other expressions of grief, because it is entirely a matter of the heart, as it says, "Their heart cried unto the lord" (Lam. II, 18). This crying comes nearer to the Holy One, blessed be He, than imploring and praying in words, as it says, "If he (the orphan) cries unto me, I will surely hear his cry" (Ex. XXII, 20).' R. Berechiah said: 'When the Holy One, blessed be He, said to Samuel, "It repenteth me that I have set up Saul to be king", what did Samuel do? "IIe cried unto the Lord all night" (I Sam. xv, 11). He put aside everything and betook himself to crying, as this finds readiest access to the Holy One, blessed be He. Thus we read here: "Now therefore, behold, the cry of the children of Israel is come unto me" (Ex. III, 9). When one prays and weeps and cries so intensely that he is unable to find words to express his sorrow, his prayer is prayer in the truest sense, for it is in the heart, and shall never return unto him void.' Said R. Judah: 'Great is such crying in that it can effect a change in the divine sentence of judgement.' R. Isaac said: 'Great is such crying in that it dominates the supernal attribute of Justice.' Said R. Yose: 'Great is such crying in that it dominates both this world and the world to come, and makes man the heir of both, as it says, "They cried unto the Lord in their trouble and he delivered them out of their distresses" (Ps. CVII, 13). NOW MOSES KEPT THE FLOCK OF JETHRO HIS FATHERIN-LAW, THE PRIEST OF MIDIAN. R. Simeon discoursed here on the text: "My beloved is mine and I am his; he among the lilies tendeth his flock." He said: 'Alas for mankind, they neither heed nor know! When God designed to create the universe, His thought compassed all worlds at once, and by means of this thought were they all created, as it says, "In wisdom hast thou made them all" (Ps. CIV, 24). By this thought-which is His Wisdom-were this world and the world above created. He stretched forth His right hand and created the world above; He stretched forth His left hand and created this world, as it says, "Mine hand hath laid the foundation of the earth and my right hand hath spanned the heavens; when I call unto them they stand up together" (Isa. XLIX, 13). All were created in one moment. And He made this world corresponding to the world above, and everything which is above has its counterpart here below, and everything here below has its counterpart in the sea; and yet all constitute a unity. He created angels in the upper worlds, human beings in this world, and the Leviathan in the sea, "to couple the tent together, that it might be one" (Ex. XXXVI, 18). He chose the supernal beings and He chose Israel; He did not call the beings of the upper worlds "sons", but the Israelites He did call sons, as it says: "Sons are ye to the Lord your God" (Deut. XIV,1). He calls them "sons" and they call Him "father", "For thou art our father" (LXIII, 16). Hence it says: "I am my beloved's and my beloved is mine". He chose me and I chose Him also. "He among the lilies tendeth his flock": He feedeth among the lilies, although they are surrounded with thorns. Or again, as the lily is red and its juice is white, so does the Holy One, blessed be He, lead His world from the attribute of Justice to the attribute of Mercy, as it says: "Though your sins be as scarlet, they shall be as white as snow" (Isa. I, 18).'

R. Abba was once walking in company with R. Isaac. On the way they saw some lilies, and R. Abba plucked one. R. Yose met them. He said: 'Verily, the Shekinah is present here, for I see something in the hand of R. Abba which signifies that he has some great wisdom to impart, since I know that R. Abba would not have plucked this lily except with the view of teaching some esoteric lesson.' Said R. Abba: 'Sit down, my son, sit down.' They all sat down. R. Abba smelt the lily and said: 'What would the world be without smell? For I perceive that without smell the soul would pine away, and therefore we burn myrtle spices at the conclusion of the Sabbath.'

He then began to expound the verse: "My beloved is mine and I am my beloved's; he among the lilies tendeth his flock." 'What made me to belong to Him and Him to me? The fact that He feeds the world among lilies: as the lily has a sweet odour, is red, and yet turns white when pressed, and its aroma never evaporates, so the Holy One, blessed be He, guides the world. If it were not so, the world would cease to exist because of man's sin. Sin is red, as it says, "Though your sins be as scarlet";

Zohar: Shemoth, Section 2, Page 20b

320

man puts the sacrificial animal on fire, which is also red; the priest sprinkles the red blood round the altar, but the smoke ascending to heaven is white. Thus the red is turned to white: the attribute of Justice is turned into the attribute of Mercy. Red is indeed the symbol of rigorous justice, and therefore the priests of Baal "cut themselves... till the blood gushed out upon them" (I Kings XVIII, 28).' R. Isaac said: 'Red (blood) and white (fat) are offered for sacrifice, and the odour ascends from both. The spices of incense are in part red and in part white-frankincense is white, pure myrrh is red-and the odour ascends from red and white. Moreover, it is written, "To offer unto me the fat and the blood" (Ezek. XLIV, I5)-again white and red. Hence as a substitute for this (since the destruction of the Temple) man sacrifices his own fat and blood (by fasting) and so obtains atonement. As the lily, which is red and white, is turned entirely into white by means of fire, so the sacrificial animal is turned entirely into white (smoke) by means of fire. Also at the present time (when there are no sacrifices) when a man offers in his fast his fat and his blood, the sacrifice has to go through fire if it is to be turned into white (bring down mercy), for, said R. Judah, fasting weakens the limbs and causes the body to burn, and just then is the appropriate time to offer up the fat and the blood on that fire; and it is this which is called "an altar of atonement". That is why R. Eleazar, when fasting, used to pray: "It is known to Thee, O my God and God of my fathers, that I have offered unto Thee my fat and my blood, and that I have heated them in the warmth of my body's weakness. May it be Thy will that the breath coming out of my mouth at this hour should be counted unto me as if it were the odour ascending from the sacrifice brought on the altar by fire, and grant me favour." Therefore prayer was instituted to take the place of sacrifices, provided that it is offered with this sacrificial intention.'

We may also explain our text as follows. As thorns are scattered among the lilies, so does the Holy One, blessed be He, permit in His world the wicked to be found among the righteous, for, as without the thorns the lilies could not exist, so would the righteous go unrecognized in the world were it not for the wicked, as R. Judah said: "How are the righteous recognized? By contrast with the wicked I If it were not for the one, the other would not be known."

Another explanation is that God governs the world for the space of six (the lily, shoshana, has six, shesh, leaves) years (millenniums), and the seventh is the (Messianic) Sabbath of the Lord. AND MOSES TENDED THE FLOCK OF JETHRO HIS FATHER-IN-LAW, THE PRIEST OF MIDIAN. R. Hiya quoted in this connection the verse: "The Lord is my shepherd, I shall not want." 'As the shepherd', he said, 'leads the sheep to a good pasture by the water-springs, and deals with them tenderly, so it is written of the heavenly Shepherd, the Holy One, blessed be He, that "In pastures green He makes me lie, He leads me to the streams which run most pleasantly, my soul doth He restore".' Said R. Yose: 'A good shepherd keeps his flock in the open and will not let them stray into private ground, and so God keeps Israel in the straight path and will not let them turn right or left.' R. Yose also said: 'If a leader of Israel is a wise shepherd, he willingly takes upon himself the yoke of the Kingdom of Heaven and leads his flock in accordance with it; but if he is wise in his own conceit, "there is more hope of a fool than of him" (Prov. XXXVI, I2).' R. Judah said: 'Moses was a wise shepherd and knew how to treat his flock. He was like David, who was "tending the sheep" (I Sam. XVI, 11), and because he was very wise,

Zohar: Shemoth, Section 2, Page 21a

and treated his flock with great consideration and care, God made him king over all Israel. Why did Moses tend sheep and not oxen?' R. Judah said: 'Israel are called sheep, as it says: "And ye, my sheep, the sheep of my pasture, are men" (Ezek. XXXIV, 31), and again, "As the flock of holy things, as the flock of Jerusalem" (Ibid. XXXVI, 38). As the sheep sacrificed on the altar becomes a means of propitiation, enabling the sacrificer to inherit the world to come, so does Israel enable her leader, if he be a good shepherd, to inherit the world to come. As the shepherd tends with special care the newly-born lambs and carries them in his bosom, or gently leads them after their mother, and is compassionate with them, so must Israel's shepherd be compassionate and not cruel. Thus Moses said: "Thou sayest unto me, Carry them in thy bosom" (Num. XI, 12). As the good shepherd saves the sheep from wolves and lions, so does the good shepherd of Israel save them from pagan nations, from judgement here below and from judgement above, and prepares them for the life of the world to come. Just such a faithful shepherd was Moses, and the Holy One, blessed be He, foresaw that he would shepherd Israel as he shepherded Jethro's flock, the males as they required, and the females likewise according to their needs. Moreover, Moses "tended the flock of Jethro", not his own sheep, though he must have possessed some, for, as R. Yose remarked, "Jethro was a rich man, and, surely, he must have given to his son-in-law sheep and cattle!" Yet he did not tend his own sheep, for then people might have said, "he treats them so well because they are his own". Although Jethro was a "priest of Midian", that is to say, a pagan, yet because he was kind to Moses, the latter served him well and tended his flock with all due care in good and fat pasture.' AND HE LED THE FLOCK TO THE BACK OF THE WILDERNESS. Said R. Yose: 'From the time when Moses was born, the holy spirit never left him. He discerned by means of the holy spirit that that desert was sanctified and prepared by God as the place for Israel's acceptance of the yoke of the Kingdom of Heaven (the Sinaitic Law), therefore "He led the flock to the back of the wilderness"-not to the wilderness, as he did not wish them to tread that spot.' AND CAME TO THE MOUNTAIN OF GOD, TO HOREB. He came alone, without his flock. Said R. Yose: 'When a magnet becomes aware of a piece of iron, it instinctively leaps towards it.

So Moses, as soon as he saw the mountain, was attracted towards it.' R. Abba said: 'Verily, Moses and the mountain were prepared for one another even from the six days of Creation. On that day the mountain moved towards Moses, and seeing that Moses was about to ascend, it stopped, and both man and mountain were filled with joy.' Said R. Jannai: 'How did Moses know it was the mountain of God? Because he saw birds circling round it with outstretched wings, but never flying over it.' R. Isaac said: 'Moses saw birds flying towards him from the direction of the mountain and falling at his feet. This showed him plainly the character of the mountain, so he "led his flock to the back of the wilderness" and went up alone.' AND THE ANGEL OF THE LORD APPEARED UNTO HIM IN A FLAME OF FIRE OUT OF THE MIDST OF A BUSH. R. Tanhum said: 'It was the moment of the evening offering (minhah), a moment when the attribute of Justice is in the ascendant.' R. Johanan interposed, remarking: 'Is it not written: "By day the Lord will command his mercy" (Ps. XLII, 9), showing that mercy predominates as long as there is daylight?' Said R. Isaac: 'From sunrise until the sun declines westward it is called "day", and the attribute of Mercy is in the ascendant: after that it is called "evening", which is the time for the attribute of Severity. We derive the same lesson from the text: "Between the evenings ye shall eat flesh, and in the morning ye shall be filled with bread" (Ex. XVI, 12). "Between the evenings"-this is the time

Zohar: Shemoth, Section 2, Page 21b

of the sway of Severity-then "ye shall eat flesh", with the result, as the Scripture says, that "while the flesh was yet between their teeth, ere it was chewed, the anger of the Lord was kindled against the people" (Num. XI, 33), for between-the-evenings is under the sway of Severity" and in the morning ye shall be filled with bread", the morning being identified with Mercy, as Scripture says, "the mercy of God endureth all the day" (Ps. LII, 3), to wit, in the morning, as it says: "And God called the light day", referring to the morning.' R. Tanhum said: 'The one is symbolized by red, the other by white. The between-the-evenings period is red, so it is written, "between the evenings ye shall eat flesh"; whereas the morning hours are white, so it is written, "and in the morning ye shall be filled with bread".' R. Isaac cited the verse: "And the whole assembly of the congregation of Israel shall kill it between the evenings" (Ex. XII, 6), the reason being, he said, that that is the time for the execution of judgement. R. Judah said: 'This we derive from the ordinance concerning the two daily offerings, the one answering to the attribute of Mercy, the other to the attribute of Severity. So Scripture says, "The one lamb thou shalt offer in the morning" (Ex. XXIX, 39), where the designation "the one" signifies the special one, to wit, the one answering the attribute of Mercy; whereas the second lamb to be offered up between the evenings is associated with Severity, being analogous to the second day of Creation, of the works of which it is not said "that it was good".' Said R. Tanhum: 'It is for this reason that Isaac instituted the Afternoon-prayer (Minhah), namely, to mitigate the then ruling Severity; whereas Abraham instituted Morning-prayer, corresponding to the attribute of Mercy.' R. Isaac said: 'This idea may be derived from the verse saying: "Woe unto us, for the day declineth, for the shadows of the evening are stretched out!" (Jer. VI, 4), "the day declineth" being an allusion to the attribute of Mercy, and "the shadows of the evening" signifying the attribute of Severity.'

Our teachers have asked: 'Why at the time when Moses went up into Mount Sinai did the theophany take the form of a flaming fire, which is the symbol of Severity? The answer given by R. Jacob was: 'It was appropriate to the moment, which was one of Severity.' R. Yose said: 'It was symbolic of the events associated with that spot. For of this spot it is written: "and (he) came to the mountain of God, unto Horeb,', a place of which it is also written: "Also in Horeb ye made the Lord wroth" (Deut. IX, 8). It is written further: "And the angel of the Lord appeared unto him in a flame of fire out of the midst of a thorn-bush", as a symbol that the wicked are one day to become "as thorns cut down, that are burned in the fire,' (Isa. XXXIII, 12).' R. Judah said: 'We learn from here the mercifulness of the Holy One, blessed be He, towards the wicked. Thus it is written, "and, behold, the thorn-bush burned with fire", to wit, to execute judgement against the wicked: yet "the thorn-bush was not consumed", indicating that they will not be utterly exterminated. "Burning in fire" is certainly an allusion to the fire of Gehinnom; but "the thorn-bush was not consumed", to show that even so they will not be destroyed utterly.'

The following is an alternative explanation of these verses: AND THE ANGEL OF THE LORD APPEARED UNTO HIM IN A FLAME OF FIRE. Why in a flame of fire to Moses and not to other prophets? Said R. Judah: 'Moses was not like other prophets: fire had no dominion over him, as it is written: "And Moses drew near unto the thick clouds where God is" (Ex. xx, 21).' Said R. Abba: 'This peculiarity of Moses has to be explained in the light of the higher (esoteric) wisdom. He was "drawn out of the water" (Ex. I, 10) (i.e. the attribute of Hesed or Grace), and he who is drawn out of water has no fear of fire, and we have learnt that "from the place whence Moses was formed no other man was formed".' R. Johanan said: 'Moses was conversant with all ten degrees (of wisdom), as it is written: "He is faithful in all my house" (Num. XII, 7), and not merely "He is the faithful of my house". Blessed is the man to whom his Master testifies thus!' Said R. Dimi: 'But according to R. Joshua ben Levi, the words "no prophet arose in Israel like unto Moses" suggest that among the nations of the world there was one like unto him, namely Balaam.' The other replied: 'Truly, thou art right', and said no more. When R. Simeon appeared, they consulted him and he said: 'Shall resin be mixed with sweet-smelling balsam? (i.e. how can ye compare Balaam with Moses?) It is, however, true that Balaam was the counterpart of Moses. As the works of the one were from above, so were the other's from below. Moses wrought his works by means of the holy Crown of the All-highest King, Balaam by means of the unholy crowns from below. Hence, "The children of Israel slew Balaam the son of Beor, the soothsayer" (Jos. XIII, 22). And if thou desirest to know more, ask his ass!' R. Yose came and kissed his hand. He said: 'The desire of my heart has been fulfilled. For I see that there is a duality in the universe of upper and lower beings, Right and Left, Love and Justice, Israel and the heathen. Israel uses the upper, holy Crowns; the pagans the lower, unholy ones; Israel draws her life-substance from the Right, the heathen nations from the Left; and thus the superior prophets are separated from the inferior prophets-the prophets of holiness from the prophets of evil.' Said R. Judah:

Zohar: Shemoth, Section 2, Page 22a

'As Moses excelled all prophets in Israel in respect of the superior, holy prophecy, so Balaam excelled all other pagan prophets and soothsayers in respect of the inferior, unholy prophecy. In any case Moses was above, Balaam below, and there were numerous stages between them.'

R. Johanan said in the name of R. Isaac: 'Moses was anxious in his mind concerning Israel, lest they should succumb under their burdens, as it says, "He looked on their burdens" (Ex. II, 11). Therefore "the angel of the Lord appeared unto him in a flame of fire... and he looked and behold, the bush burned... and the bush was not consumed", to show that although their lives were made bitter with hard bondage, yet, like the bush, they would not be consumed. Blessed are the Israelites for that the Holy One, blessed be He, separated them from all nations and called them "children", as it says: "Children are ye to the Lord your God" (Deut. XIV. I).'

WAERA

AND GOD SPAKE UNTO MOSES, ETC. R. Abba began his reflections on this portion with the verse: Trust the Lord forever (lit. unto 'Ad), for in KAH Tetragrammaton is fashioning of worlds (lit. rock of ages) (Isa. XXVI, 4). 'All mankind', he said, 'should cleave to the Holy One, blessed be He, and put their trust in Him, in order that their strength should be drawn from the sphere called 'Ad [Tr. note:Tifereth.], which sustains the universe and binds it into an indissoluble whole. This 'Ad (lit. unto) is "the desire of the everlasting hills" (Gen. XLIX, 26), to wit, the two transcendent "Mothers", the year of Jubilee [Tr. note: Binah.] and the year of Remission [Tr. note: Malkuth.] (cf. Zohar, Gen. 247b); the desire of the former being to crown that sphere with glory, with the outpouring of blessings and wells of sweet water; whilst the longing of the other is to receive from 'Ad these same blessings and illuminations. Therefore it says, "Trust the Lord unto 'Ad" (i.e. contemplate the worlds of emanation only as far as the sphere 'Ad), for beyond that is a hidden region, so transcendent that it passes all understanding, the very source whence the worlds were designed and came into being. Up to this point only is it permissible to contemplate the Godhead, but not beyond, for it is wholly recondite. This is KAH Tetragrammaton, from whence all worlds were fashioned,' Said R. Judah: 'We have a direct Scriptural proof for this, for it says, "Ask of the days that are past... since the day that God created man upon earth, and ask from the one side of the heaven unto the other..." (Deut. IV, 32). Up to this point man may investigate, but no further.' Another explanation of this verse is as follows: Man must always trust the Holy One, blessed be He. He who trusts Him will never be confounded by the world (Ps. xxv, 2). He who depends entirely on the Holy Name is firmly established in the world, as the world itself is sustained by this Name: by the two letters JH (KAH) "the Lord

Zohar: Shemoth, Section 2, Page 22b

designed the worlds", this world and the world to come. This world was created by the attribute of Justice, and is sustained by the same attribute, in order that humanity should base its life on justice and not depart from the way of righteousness. AND ELOHIM SPAKE UNTO MOSES AND HE SAID TO HIM I AM Tetragrammaton. It is written above (v. 22): "And Moses said, Lord (Adonai), wherefore hast thou evil entreated this people?" What prophet could speak with such boldness as this save Moses, who knew that another and superior degree (viz. Tetragrammaton) was awaiting him? R. Isaac said: 'Moses, who was "faithful in God's house", addressed Him without fear and trembling, like a steward who has charge over the household.' According to another explanation, the words "And God spake and said unto him, I am Tetragrammaton" mean that the manifestation was in both attributes, in Justice and Mercy, both fitly framed and joined together. R. Simeon said that they were manifested not unitedly but successively, as is indicated by the expression, "And Elohim spake... and said unto him, I am Tetragrammaton": stage after stage. Said R. Yose: 'Moses would certainly have been punished for the boldness of his language had he not been "steward of the household" and man of God. He was like a man who had married the king's daughter, and having some contention with her, spoke harshly to her. She was about to answer him, when her father, the king, appeared. Seeing him, she stopped and he took up the word. He said to the husband: "Knowest thou not that I am the king, and the harsh words thou speakest against my daughter, thou speakest as it were against me?" So Moses complained against Adonai (the Shekinah) and was answered by Elohim (the King). AND I APPEARED, ETC. God was here like a king who had an unmarried daughter, and also had a personal friend. When he wanted to say something to the friend, he used to send his daughter to him to speak for him. Then the daughter was married, and on the day of her marriage the king proclaimed: "Call my daughter from now 'the Mistress, the Matrona'," and to her he said: "Until now I was wont to speak through thee to those who desired audience with me, but now I shall speak directly to thy husband, and he will transmit my messages." One day the husband spoke harshly to the princess in the king's presence, and before she could answer him the king took up the word. He said: "Am I not the king, with whom no one dared to speak but through my daughter, and have I not given my daughter to thee, and spoken with thee directly, a privilege not granted to any other?" Similarly God said to Moses: "Before the Shekinah was espoused I appeared to the Patriarchs as El Shaddai, and they could not speak directly with Me, only through My Daughter the Shekinah, and thou wast the first one to whom I spoke face to face, and now at the very outset thou darest in My Presence to speak to My Daughter in such a fashion!"

R. Yose interpreted the verse: "The earth is the Lord's and the fulness thereof, the universe, and they that dwell therein; for he hath founded it upon the seas, and established it upon the rivers" (Ps. XXIV, 2-3) in the following way. '"The earth" is the Holy Land of Israel, which is the first to imbibe sustenance and receive blessing from God, the rest of the world then receiving from it; "the seas" refer to

Zohar: Shemoth, Section 2, Page 23a

the seven pillars which are the foundation of the earth, and over which rules the Sea of Kinnereth (R. Judah, however, maintained that the latter is filled by the others); "the rivers" are connected with the "river which went out of Eden to water the garden" (Gen. II, 10). It is to be noticed that this Holy Land (the Shekinah) is called "the land of Israel". Why, then, did Jacob, who is Israel, not rule over it like Moses? The reason is-that already pointed out-that Jacob became the owner of the "house which is below" and left the "house which is above", though in the twelve tribes and in the seventy branches he made preparation herein for the "house which is above"; Moses, on the other hand, left the "house which is below" and took the "house which is above". The former experienced the Divine manifestation as "El Shaddai", but God did not speak with him in the higher grade designated by Tetragrammaton. AND I APPEARED UNTO ABRAHAM, UNTO ISAAC, AND (v) UNTO JACOB. The letter Vau in connection with Jacob is, according to R. Hiya, symbolic of the superiority of the Divine manifestation to Jacob over that which was vouchsafed to the other two: his is the unifying, harmonizing, grade; and yet he was not worthy to use it as Moses did. AND I HAVE ALSO ESTABLISHED MY COVENANT WITH THEM, TO GIVE THEM THE LAND OF CANAAN: as a reward for the covenant of circumcision; and only of those who are faithful members of this covenant can it be said that they "possess" the land, which is a heritage of the righteous, as it is written: "Thy people shall be all righteous, they shall possess the land" (Isa. LX, 21). Even Joseph was not called "righteous" before he guarded the sign of the covenant (at the time of temptation).

R. Eleazar once asked R. Simeon his father, in the presence of R. Abba: 'Why is it said here "I appeared", instead of "I spoke to Abraham, etc."?' R. Simeon replied: 'My son, this contains a deep mystery. Observe now. There are colours disclosed and undisclosed, this being a part of the mystery of Faith, but men neither know nor reflect on these matters. The visible colours were not perceived by any human being before the Patriarchs, Abraham, Isaac and Jacob. Therefore it says "and I appeared". And what are these visible colours? Those of El Shaddai, the reflection of higher colours. But these latter are hidden, and Moses alone perceived them. The Patriarchs, however, were not entirely ignorant of them; since they apprehended those undisclosed ones through the visible ones which they already knew. It is written: "And the wise shall be resplendent as the splendour of the firmament, and they that turn many to righteousness shall be like the stars forever and ever." The "wise" is he who by the power of his own contemplation attains to the perception of profound mysteries which cannot be expressed in words. The "firmament" is the "firmament of Moses" (his grade of Divine knowledge), which is set at the centre and whose splendour is veiled. This firmament is above that other which is non-resplendent and the colours of which are visible and not so bright as the invisible. There are four lights (i.e. Emanations), three of which are recondite and one disclosed. There is one which sheds light abroad (Hesed); one which shines for itself only (Geburah), being like the heavens in purity; one of purple hue which gathers light into itself (Tifereth); and one which is of itself lightless (Malkuth), but which looks up to the others and reflects them as a lamp reflects the sun. The first three are recondite and brood over the one which is

Zohar: Shemoth, Section 2, Page 23b

disclosed. (Of all this the eye is the symbol. In the eye three colours are visible, but none of these shines, because they are non-luminous. They are the parallel of those lights which are revealed; and it was by means of these visible colours that the Patriarchs were enabled to discern the colours which are luminous but invisible-that is, those colours of which Moses alone had cognizance, which were concealed from all others but revealed to him in that firmament to which he had attained, and which are above the visible colours.) To understand this mystery, close thine eye and press thine eyeball, and thou wilt discern radiating and luminous colours which can only be seen with closed eyes. [Tr. note: The colours thus seen are called luminous, because they are not attached to any material background. The idea seems to be that just as these can only be seen when the eye is closed, so the higher emanations can only be grasped when the mind completely abstracts itself from the perceptions of sense.] For this reason we say that Moses was possessed of the "luminous mirror", which is above the "nonluminous", which alone is vouchsafed to others. The Patriarchs, however, were able by means of the revealed colours to conceive of those that were concealed. This is the meaning of the words, "I appeared unto Abraham, etc ', namely, in those visible colours, "but by My Name Tetragrammaton was I not known to them", namely, in the supernal hidden luminous colours, which only Moses was privileged to behold. The closed eye sees the mirror of light: the open eye sees the mirror which is not luminous. Therefore in regard to the lightless mirror, the term "see" is used, because it is discernible, but in regard to the luminous mirror the term "know" is used, because it is in concealment.' Then came R. Eleazar and R. Abba and kissed R. Simeon's hand, and R. Abba wept and said: 'Alas for the world when thou, master, shalt be removed from it! It will become an orphan without thee; for who will then illumine the words of the Torah?' He then went on to quote David's greeting to Nabal: "Be well (lehai, lit. thus for life!), and peace be to thee, etc." 'Surely,' he said, 'David must have been aware of Nabal's wickedness, and how could he greet him thus? It was, however, New Year's day, the day when the Holy One judges the world, and David's intention in using both expressions, "Thus for life", and "and thou art peace", was to address Him from whom all life and all peace come, in order to make a fitting profession of faith. And greeting a righteous person with Shalom! (peace, harmony) is like greeting the Holy One Himself, especially when addressed to thee, O master, who in thine own person representest the harmony between the above and the below! But it is not allowed to greet thus a wicked person, and yet, if it be unavoidable, there is no insincerity involved in the phrase when outwardly addressed to the person concerned, but inwardly intended for God.'

R. Hezekiah discoursed on the verse: Blessed is the man unto whom the Lord imputeth not iniquity, and in whose spirit there is no guile (Ps. XXXII, 2). He said: 'How blind are the children of men who neither see nor perceive what the foundation is of their existence in the world! Behold, when the Holy One, blessed be He, created the world, He formed man in His own image, so disposing his capacities as to enable him to study the Torah and walk in His way. Therefore man was created from the dust of the lower Sanctuary; and the four winds of the world united at that place which afterwards was named the House of Holiness, and these four were then joined to the four elements of the lower world: fire, air, earth, and water. And when these winds and these elements were thus mingled, the Holy One, blessed be He, formed one body of wondrous perfection. Therefore it is plain that the substances composing man's body belong to two worlds, namely, the world below and the world above.' Said R. Simeon: 'The first four elements have a deep significance for the faithful: they are the progenitors of all worlds, and symbolize the mystery of the supernal Chariot of Holiness. Also the four elements of fire, air, earth, and water have a deep significance. From them come gold, silver, copper, and iron, and beneath these

Zohar: Shemoth, Section 2, Page 24a

other metals of a like kind. Mark well this! Fire, air, earth, and water are the sources and roots of all things above and below, and on them are all things grounded. And in each of the four winds these elements are found–fire in the North, air in the East, water in the South, earth in the West; and the four elements are united with the four winds–and all are one. Fire, water, air, and earth: gold, silver, copper, and iron; north, south, east, and west–these make altogether twelve; yet are they all one. Fire is in the left, at the side of the North, for fire has the energy of warmth, and the power of dryness is strong in it, and the North is just the reverse, and so the two are commingled. Water is in the right, in the side of the South, and the Holy One mixes the warmth and dryness of the South with the coldness and moisture of the water, and they become one as with the previous combination. The North is cold and moist, and its element, fire, hot and dry, and, contrariwise, the South is warm and dry, and its element, water, cold and moist, and so the Holy One mixes them. For water comes from the South, enters into the North, and flows again from the North; and fire comes out from the North, and enters into the South, and it is from the South that powerful heat goes out into the world. For the Holy One makes one borrow from the other as He sees right. In a similar fashion He proceeds with the air and the East. Observe now. Fire from one side, water from the other: there is opposition. Then comes the air (wind, spirit) between them and brings them together and they become one, as it is written: "And the spirit (air) of God brooded over the water" (Gen. 1, 2). For fire is aloft and water is on the surface of the earth, and air enters between them, unites both elements and makes peace between them. Earth has water, air, fire, above it and receives from all the three. Observe, further, that the East is warm and moist, and the air is warm and moist. Hence the warm-moist composite can take hold of both sides-with its warmth the fire, and with its moisture the water, and thus end the conflict between fire and water. The earth is cold and dry, therefore it can receive all the others - fire, water, and air - and all can accomplish their work in it. She receives from all of them, therefore through their influence can produce nourishment for the whole world. Now the side of the West, which is cold, unites with the North, which is cold and moist, for cold unites with cold, and from the other side, the dry, West unites with the South, which is warm and dry, and thus the West attaches itself to both sides. In the same fashion the South is united with the East on its warm side, and the East with the North in virtue of its moisture. Thus we find united: South-East, North-East, North-West, South-West, and all are contained in one another in mutual intermingling. In this way the North brings forth gold, which is produced by the side of the fire-power, as it is written,

"Gold cometh from the North" (Job. XXXVII, 22). For when fire joins with the earth gold is produced, as it is written: "As for the earth... it hath lumps of gold" (Ibid. XXXVIII, 5-6). When water is united with earth, the cold with the moist brings forth silver, and so the earth is united with two sides, gold and silver, and situated between them. Air joins to water and also

Zohar: Shemoth, Section 2, Page 24b

to fire and produces an amalgam which is "the colour of polished copper" (Ezek. 1, 7). As to the earth mentioned above, when it is by itself in its coldness and dryness it brings forth iron; therefore it says: "If the iron be blunt" (Eccl. x, 10). Earth, however, combines with all the other elements, and all work through it according to their several ways. For without earth there is no gold, no silver, no copper. For each element imparts of its character to the other to form a compound, and earth mingles with all, because the two sides, fire and water, are attached to it. Air also joins with it on account of those two, and acts upon it. Now we find that the earth, when united with them, brings forth also secondary products resembling their primary compounds. Thus corresponding to gold it brings forth the green dross which is subordinate to gold and resembles it; corresponding to silver, lead; corresponding to the superior copper, the inferior, tin; corresponding to iron, however, it brings forth only iron, and so it is said: "Iron with iron together" (Prov. XXVII, 17). 'Fire, air, water, and earth are originally all united one with the other, and there is no separation between them. But when the earth-dust began to generate its products were no longer united like the supernal elements, as it says: "From thence it was parted and became into four heads" (Gen. II, 10). In this was separation; for the earthy, when it generated in the power of the three upper elements, brought forth four streams, where precious stones are found. These precious stones are twelve in number, distributed in all the four cardinal directions, and corresponding to the twelve tribes of Israel: "And the stones shall be with the names of the children of Israel, twelve, according to their names" (Ex. XXVIII, 21). Observe that though all these supernal sides of which we spoke are united and bound up one with another, and form the foundation of things above and things below, yet is air (spirit) superior to them all, as it is the substance of all, without which nothing would live, and the soul exists only through the spirit, for if the air were to fail, even for a moment, the soul would not be. This is hinted in the words: "Also when the soul is without knowledge it is not good" (Prov. XIX, 2): soul without spirit "is not good", and cannot exist. Note, further, that those twelve stones correspond to the twelve oxen under the sea of brass which was in the Temple (I Kings VII, 25). Therefore the princes, the heads of the tribes, sacrificed twelve oxen (Num. VII, 3). All this is a deep mystery, and he who comprehends these words comprehends a mystery of the supernal wisdom, in which is the root of all things.'

R. Simeon concluded: 'See now the truth of R. Hezekiah's saying, that when the Holy One created man He took the dust of the lower Sanctuary, but for the making of his soul He chose the dust of the upper Sanctuary. Just as in the formation of man's body from the dust of the lower Sanctuary, three cosmic elements were combined, so in the formation of his soul from the dust of the upper Sanctuary, further elements, to the number of three, were mingled, and so man was completely formed. And this is the significance of the words: "Blessed is the man to whom the Lord imputeth not iniquity, and in whose spirit there is no guile." When does the Lord not impute iniquity? When there is no guile in his spirit. Moses was perfected to a higher degree than were the Patriarchs, since the Holy One spoke to him from a higher grade than to them, and Moses stood within the Palace of the King. Hence it says: "And I appeared unto Abraham, unto Isaac, and unto Jacob, by the name of EL SHADDAI, but by My name Tetragrammaton was I not known to them"; and so we affirm.' WHEREFORE SAY UNTO THE CHILDREN OF ISRAEL, I AM THE LORD, AND I WILL BRING YOU OUT FROM UNDER THE BURDENS OF THE EGYPTIANS, ETC. Said R. Judah: 'These words are in the wrong order, and should read, firstly, "I will redeem you", and then "I will bring you out". The reason, however, why bringing out is put first is that God desired to announce to them first the best promise of all.' To which R. Yose remarked: 'But does not the greatest promise of all come last, namely, "I will take you to me for a people and I will be

Zohar: Shemoth, Section 2, Page 25a

to you a God" (v. 7)?' R. Judah replied: 'Deliverance from Egypt was the chief concern of the people then, because they despaired of escaping on account of the magical arts with which the Egyptians held fast their prisoners; hence it came first in order in the proclamation, followed by the promise of deliverance from bondage once and for all, as they might have been afraid that the Egyptians would enslave them again. Then came the promise of redemption, namely, that He would not merely free them from Egypt and then leave them to themselves: this was followed by the proclamation that He would make them His people; and finally came the promise that He would bring them into their own land (v. 7).' [Note: At this point, the printed volumes, both Hebrew and English, contain a passage from the Raya Mehemna. Look below for page 25a.]

Zohar: Shemoth, Section 2, Page 25b

AND MOSES SPAKE SO UNTO THE CHILDREN OF ISRAEL, BUT THEY HEARKENED NOT UNTO MOSES FOR ANGUISH OF SPIRIT. What is the meaning of "anguish of spirit" (lit. shortness of breath)?

R. Judah interpreted the expression literally, "they had no rest from their labours, no time to breathe". But R. Simeon saw a mystical significance in the expression; the "Jubilee" (the world of Binah, the abode of transcendental "Freedom") was as yet not in manifestation to give them spiritual rest, and the later Spirit (Malkuth) was not yet able to exercise its functions, and so there was anguish to this Spirit. AND MOSES SPAKE BEFORE THE LORD, SAYING: BEHOLD, THE CHILDREN OF ISRAEL HAVE NOT HEARKENED UNTO ME, HOW THEN SHALL PHARAOH HEAR ME, WHO AM OF UNCIRCUMCISED LIPS? How did Moses dare say this? Had not the Holy One already promised him, when he said that he was not eloquent, that He "will be with his mouth" (Ex. IV, 10-12)? Or did the Holy One not keep His promise? However, there is here an inner meaning. Moses was then in the grade of "Voice", and the grade of "Utterance" was then in exile. Hence he said: "How shall Pharaoh hear me", seeing that my "utterance" is in bondage to him, I being only "voice", and lacking "utterance". Therefore God joined with him Aaron, who was "utterance" without "voice". When Moses came, the Voice appeared, but it was "a voice without speech". This lasted until Israel approached Mount Sinai to receive the Torah. Then the Voice was united with the Utterance, and the word was spoken, as it says, "and the Lord spake all these words" (Ex. xx, I). Then Moses was in full possession of the Word, Voice and Word being united. That was the cause of Moses' complaint (v. 23), that he lacked the word save at the time when it broke forth in complaint and "God spake to Moses" (VI, 2). On this occasion the word began to function, but it ceased again, as the time was not yet ripe; hence the verse continues, "and said to him, I am the Lord" (Ibid.). Only at the giving of the Law Moses was, as it were, healed of his impediment, when the Voice and the Utterance were united in him as their organ. Before that event the power which is Utterance guided Israel in the desert, but without expressing itself until they came to Sinai.

Zohar: Shemoth, Section 2, Page 26a

R. Judah interpreted in the same sense the verse from the Song of Songs (v, 5-6): "I rose up to open to my beloved, but my beloved hath withdrawn himself and was gone". As long as the Community of Israel is in exile the Voice is withdrawn from her and the Word does not function, as it says, "I am dumb with silence" (Ps. XXXIX, 3); and even when the Word does awaken, "my Beloved hath withdrawn Himself", i.e. it suddenly ceases, as it did at first with Moses.

The Voice went on: "And I appeared unto Abraham, unto Isaac, and unto Jacob." The "and" (the Vau) symbolizes Jacob's superiority over the others, according to R. Judah. Said R. Yose: 'What of the verse, "I am the God of Abraham and of Isaac" (Gen. XXVIII, 13)?' R. Judah replied: 'When that was said, Jacob was included in Isaac, who was blind at that time, and a blind man is counted dead; for as long as a person is alive, the Holy Name is not joined to his name (i.e. the God of so-and-so), therefore Jacob was included in Isaac and not directly mentioned; but Jacob being now dead, the Holy Name could be connected with him. "By El Shaddai", that is to say, through the "non-luminous mirror" not the "luminous". This, however, does not mean that they were conversant with the "Female" only and no higher grade, for it continues: "And I have also established my Covenant with them", indicating that the Covenant was united with the Female in their perception. He who has the privilege of being a member of the Covenant, inherits the Land, as it says, "I have established my covenant with them to give them the land of Canaan".' Said R. Simeon: 'It is written, "Be ye afraid of the sword, for wrath bringeth the punishments of the sword, that ye may know there is judgement". The "sword" is the one of which it says, "it shall avenge the covenant"; (Lev. XXVI, 25), it is the punishment awaiting him who nullifies the (sign) of the Covenant and thereby also the union of which it is a symbol. But he who brings the Covenant into its place and so guards it in purity becomes a channel of blessing both to the upper and lower worlds. Hence it says here, "Be ye afraid of the sword", for if this commandment does not awaken the sense of awe in a man, no other commandment will. Observe that as soon as the Israelites bestirred themselves to approach the Holy One and cried before Him, He "remembered His covenant". "Remembering" (Zachor) is always connected with the Covenant and its sign, for it is the awakening of the longing for union in the supernal spheres. Hence "I remembered my Covenant", to connect it with its proper place, and therefore "say unto the children of Israel, I am Tetragrammaton" (v. 6.)' AND THE LORD SPAKE UNTO MOSES AND AARON AND GAVE THEM A CHARGE UNTO THE CHILDREN OF ISRAEL AND UNTO PHARAOH. According to R. Yose, the charge consisted in this, that they should speak gently to Israel

Zohar: Shemoth, Section 2, Page 26b

and respectfully to Pharaoh. Gently to Israel, for, although for the time being they were slaves, yet they were of royal descent. For this reason the section dealing with the names of the heads of the tribal families comes immediately after this verse (vv. 14-25). R. Hiya says that this is to show that they did not change their customs nor intermarry with the natives. But according to R. Aha, the purpose is to introduce Moses and Aaron and to show that they were worthy to bring forth the people and to act as spokesmen before Pharaoh, for among the heads of the tribal families there were none like them. AND ELEAZAR, AARON'S SON, TOOK HIM ONE OF THE DAUGHTERS OF PUTIEL TO WIFE; AND SHE BARE HIM PHINEAS: THESE ARE THE HEADS OF THE FATHERS OF THE LEVITES ACCORDING TO THEIR FAMILIES. Why does it say "these are the heads" when the only one mentioned is Phineas? The truth is that because he saved thousands in Israel from the plague (v. Num. xxv, 8), by making atonement for the children of Israel and their chiefs, they are all included in him and he is referred to as "these". This expression also suggests that he in his own person compensated

327

for the loss of the heads of the Levites (Nadab and Abihu, v. Lev. x): they sinned and were burned, but their souls found their abode in Phineas. They separated the sign of the Covenant from its place (by leaving no issue), and he came and united it again, therefore the heritage and spirit of both of them were given to him. All this is suggested already here. In fact, Phineas is mentioned here because at first the Holy One, foreseeing that Aaron's two sons would impair the Covenant, did not desire to join Aaron with Moses in his mission, but then seeing that Phineas would restore the Covenant and repair the mischief caused by them, considered him to be after all worthy, as it is written concerning him: "These are that Aaron" (v. 26), meaning, "it is the same (worthy) Aaron". It is further written: "These are (lit. this is) that Aaron and Moses". The singular number "this" suggests the oneness of the two, the fusion of "wind" (=Moses, who symbolizes the Sephirah, Tifereth) with "water" (=Aaron, Grace); similarly the expression in the following verse (28): "These are (lit. this is) that Moses and Aaron" suggests the fusion of "water" with "wind".'

R. Eleazar and R. Abba once spent a night in an inn in Lydda. R. Eleazar expounded there the verse: "Know therefore this day and consider it in thine heart (lebabeka) that Tetragrammaton is God in heaven above and upon the earth beneath; there is none else" (Deut. IV, 39), as follows. 'The use of the form lebabeka instead of libka suggests a plural, "hearts"; and what Moses meant was this: "If thou desirest to know that Tetragrammaton and ELOHIM are one within the other and both are one, consider thine own 'hearts', i.e. thy two inclinations, the good and the evil, which are fused one with the other and form a unity".' He also said that sinners impair the supernal world by causing a separation between the "Right" and the "Left". They really cause harm only to themselves, as it is written, "He (Israel) hath corrupted himself (lo) that they are not (lo) his children; it is their blemish" (Deut. XXXII, 5). "Lo" (himself), and "lo" (not), in this verse suggest that they both cause and cause not: they cause, i.e. prevent the descent of blessings from above, as it is written: "and then the Lord's wrath be kindled against you and he shut up the heaven that there be no rain" (Deut. XI, I 7); and they cause not, as the heaven keeps the blessings to itself. Thus the sinners' separation of the good inclination from the evil one by consciously cleaving to evil separates, as it were, the divine attribute of Grace from that of Judgement, the Right from the Left. Consider the tribes: Judah

Zohar: Shemoth, Section 2, Page 27a

emanated from the Left and clave to the Right, in order to conquer nations and that his hand might be "in the neck of his enemies" (Gen. XLIX, 8). Had he not clung to the Right, he would not have broken down their armies. But does not the Left awaken Judgement? The truth is that when He judges Israel He pushes them away from Him with His "Left Hand" but brings them near to Him with His "Right Hand", but with the Gentiles it is just the opposite, as it is written, "Thy right hand, O Lord, is become glorious in power; thy right hand, O Lord, hath dashed in pieces the enemy" (Ex. xv, 6). Therefore Judah, who is of the Left, clave to the Right, and the other tribes of his company (v. Numbers II) also clung to the Right; Issachar, who devoted himself to study of the Torah, which comes from the Right (Deut. XXXIII, 2: "from his right hand went a fiery law for them"), and Zebulun, who supported Issachar in his studies by supplying his material needs (cf. Zohar, Gen. 241b), also clave to the Right. Therefore Judah effected a double union: north with water, left with right. Reuben, who sinned towards his father, started with the Right, joined the Left and clave to it, therefore all who belonged to his company were of the Left, viz. Simeon, symbolized by an ox (cf. Gen. XLIX, 6), of which it says: "The face of an ox on the left" (Ezek. 1, 10), and Gad, who represents the left thigh (v. Zohar, Gen. 241b). Here the south was fused with fire, right with left. Thus this is the meaning of the words, "Know therefore this day, etc.", to unite the Right with the Left and so to "know that Tetragrammaton is ELOHIM". Said R. Abba: 'Most assuredly so! "This Aaron and Moses"- "this Moses and Aaron"; wind fused with water, water with wind.' R. Abba expounded in a similar way the verse: "Thou shalt love Tetragrammaton thy God with all thy heart and with all thy soul and with all thy strength" (Deut. VI, 5). 'The holy unification', he said, 'is intimated here, and an earnest appeal is made to man to declare the unity of the Holy Name with a supreme love; viz. "with all thy heart" (lebabka, as above), i.e. with the right and the left, with the good and the evil inclinations; "and with all thy soul", with the soul of David, which is placed between them; "and with all thy strength", i.e. to unite in mind the two Names (Tetragrammaton and ELOHIM) in the transcendental sphere which passes all understanding. This is a perfect unification through the true love of God. Jacob, the unifier of sides (attributes), represents symbolically this love. This is the esoteric significance of the singular pronoun used in connection with Moses and Aaron: the two attributes which they represent are both fused into one, and there is no separation between them.' R. Judah found an example of the same thing in King David, who said of himself: "O, how I love thy Torah! It is my meditation all the day" (Ps. CIX, 97); "At midnight I rise to give thanks unto thee because of thy righteous judgements" (Ibid. v, 62). David guided his people like a shepherd so that they should not turn from the way of truth. During the day he studied the Law, in order to perfect himself in it, and at night he sang praises to the Holy One, blessed be He, until the morning, which he awakened, as he said: "Awake, my glory; awake, psaltery and harp; I wake up the morning." During the day he sought to administer justice in order to fuse the Left with the Right, and during the night he (sang praises) in order to make night also as it were a part of day. And observe that King David in his time brought all those "living creatures of the field" (Ps. CIV, 11) near the ocean, but as soon as Solomon obtained sway the ocean heaved up in its fulness and watered them. Which of them were the first to be given drink? It has already been stated that it was the huge supernal fishes, regarding which it is written, "and fill the waters in the seas" (Gen. I, 22). Said R.

Zohar: Shemoth, Section 2, Page 27b

Eleazar: 'Thirteen springs. [Tr. note: These are supposed to symbolize the forces of judgement which issue from the Sefirah Malkuth.] emerge in the upper world, on the right side, which give rise to thirteen deep streams. Of these streams, whilst some are rising others are falling, and their waters mingle with each other. These thirteen streams, issuing from thirteen springs, branch out besides into a thousand rivers, flowing in all directions, namely, four hundred and ninety-nine and a half to the one side, and four hundred and ninety-nine and a half to the other side, the remaining two half rivers being joined into one and metamorphosed into a Serpent, whose head is red as the rose, and whose scales are solid as iron, and who has fins by means of which he propels himself through all the rivers. When he raises his tail he strikes against all fishes coming in his way so that none of them dare stand in his path. His mouth emits a flaming fire. When he sets out to traverse the rivers, all the fishes fall a-trembling, take flight and precipitate themselves into the great ocean. Once every seventy years he crouches on the one side and once every seventy on the other side; the thousand rivers less one are thus filled with him. So he remains for a time; but when he bestirs himself there issues from him a strip of fire in his scales, which stand out and quiver, and the waters of the rivers become turbid and assume a dark-blue colour, and waves surge in every direction. He then lifts his tail and lashes with it upwards and downwards, so that everything flees before him; until finally a flame of fire is projected from the North and a proclamation goes forth, saying: "Arise, ye old females, [Tr. note: Alluding to Lilith, the night-demon, and her female retinue, According to the commentators, there is, besides old Lilith, also young Lilith, who is at the service of Asmodeus.] be scattered into all the four corners, for, behold, there is awakened the one who is about to put fetters on the jaws of the monster." So Scripture says: "And I will put hooks in thy jaws", etc. (Ezek. XXIX, 4). Then they all scatter, and the monster is seized and pierced through his jaws and thrust into the cavern of the great abyss, so that his power is broken. After that he is brought back to his rivers. This performance is repeated every seventy years in order to prevent him from doing damage to the heavenly regions and their foundations. For this we all give thanks and offer up praise, as it is written: "O come, let us bow down and bend the knee; let us kneel before the Lord our Maker" (Ps. xcv, 6). The superior dragons abide on high, to wit, those that were blessed, as we read: "And God blessed them" (Gen. I, 22). These rule over all the other fishes, of whom it is written, "and fill the waters in the seas" (Ibid.) Concerning this it is written: "How manifold are thy works, O Lord! In wisdom hast thou made them all" (Ps. CIV, 24).'

Zohar: Shemoth, Section 2, Page 28a

SAY UNTO AARON, TAKE THY ROD. Why Aaron's rod, and not that of Moses? Because Moses' rod was more sacred, as in the upper Paradise the Holy Name had been engraved on it, and it was not the desire of the Holy One that it should be defiled by coming into contact with the rods of the Egyptian magicians. There was, however, yet another reason, namely, that all those (impure) powers that come from the Left might be subdued by Aaron, whose grade is that of the Right.

R. Hiya asked R. Yose: 'As the Holy One knew that the Egyptian magicians were able to turn their rods into serpents, why did He command Moses and Aaron to perform this sign before Pharaoh? There was nothing wonderful in this to him.' R. Yose replied: 'Pharaoh's dominion originated with the Serpent, and therefore his punishment commenced with the serpent. When the magicians saw it they rejoiced because they knew that they could do the same, but then Aaron's serpent turned into a dry rod again, as it says, "and Aaron's rod swallowed up their rods" (Ex. VII, 12). Then they were astonished, realizing that there was a superior Power on earth. Thus Aaron showed in fact a double sign, one above and one below: one above, by showing to Pharaoh that there was a higher Serpent which ruled over theirs, and one below by making wood subdue their serpents. Do not think that the magicians' performance was mere make-believe: their rods actually did "become serpents" (Ibid.). It is written: "Behold, I am against thee, Pharaoh king of Egypt, the great dragon (tanin) that lies in the midst of his rivers" (Ezek. XXIX, 4). It is from there that the Egyptian magicians derived their power of witchcraft, but the source of their wisdom was the lowest of all grades.' Observe that their wisdom consisted in subjecting the lowest grades to higher grades, the chiefs of their dominion. These in turn derive their power from the Dragon underneath whom they are situated, as is indicated by the phrase, "who is behind the mill" (Ex. XI, 5).

R. Hiya was sitting one day by the gate of Usha when he saw a bird flying behind R. Eleazar. He said to him: 'It looks as if even when you walk in the streets everyone wants to follow you!' R. Eleazar turned his head and saw the bird, and then he said: 'It must have some message for me. The Holy One has many messengers, and not living creatures only, "For the stone crieth out of the wall and the beam out of the timber answereth it" (Hab. II, 11). How careful, therefore, should a man be not to sin before the Holy One, blessed be He, in secret, imagining that no one can testify against him: the stones and stocks of a man's own house shall cry out against him. Aaron's rod was a piece of dry wood, and yet the Holy One used it for His first sign in Egypt, performing through it two miracles: it swallowed up their serpents, and for a time was turned into a living being. Curse

Zohar: Shemoth, Section 2, Page 28b

[Note: the last 9 lines of the Hebrew text do not appear in our translation.]

on those who say that the Holy One will not raise the dead, because it seems to them an impossibility! Let those fools who are far from the Torah and from the Holy One think a little. Aaron had in his hand a rod made of dry wood, the Holy One turned it to be a living creature for a short time, with spirit and body; can He not also, then, at the time when He will gladden the world, turn into a new creation those bodies which once had spirits and holy souls in them, who kept the commandments and studied the Law day and night, and which He had hidden for a time in the earth?' Said R. Hiya: 'And what is more, from the words, "Thy dead ones will live" (Isa. XXVI, 19), it is evident that not only will there be a new creation, but that the very bodies which were dead will rise, for one bone in the body remains intact, not decaying in the earth, and on the Resurrection Day the Holy One will soften it and make it like leaven in dough, and it will rise and expand on all sides, and the whole body and all its members will be formed from it, and then the Holy One will put spirit into it.' Said R. Eleazar: 'Assuredly so. And the bone will be softened by the dew, as it says: "Thy dead ones shall live... for thy dew is the dew of plants" (Ibid.).' TAKE THY ROD AND STRETCH OUT THY HAND UPON THE WATERS OF EGYPT, UPON THEIR STREAMS, UPON THEIR RIVERS... THAT THEY MAY BECOME BLOOD. Said R. Judah: 'How was this possible? Could one rod so be stretched over all this extent? Moreover, it says later, "And seven days were fulfilled after the Lord had smitten the river" (v. 25), only mentioning the river, and leaving out the other waters of Egypt upon which Aaron had stretched out his hand. The explanation is that the reference is to the River Nile, for out of this all the other rivers, streams, ponds, and pools are filled, so that Aaron needed but to smite that river and all the other waters were smitten. The proof is that it says, "And the Egyptians could not drink of the water of the river" (v. 21).' R. Abba said: 'Observe that the lower waters diverge and spread on every side, but the upper waters draw together and are concentrated in one place,' [Tr. note: Yesod.] as it says: "Let the waters under the heaven be gathered together unto one place" (Gen. I, 9); and again, "And the gathering together of the waters called He seas" – as we have explained. The firmament in which the sun, the moon, the stars, and the plants are suspended is the great meeting place where the upper waters are gathered, and whence the earth, or lower world, is watered. She thereupon scatters and distributes these waters far and wide, in order that all things may be watered by them. When, however, chastisement impends over the world, then the lower world does not imbibe from that upper firmament of sun and moon, but from the "left side", concerning which it says: "The sword of the Lord is full of blood" (Isa. XXXIV, 6). Woe unto them who must drink from this cup! At such times the sea imbibes from both sides and divides itself into two parts, white and red (mercy and justice). Thus it was the lot of Egypt which was cast into the Nile, and the blow was inflicted both above and below. Therefore Israel drank water, but the Egyptians blood.

Zohar: Shemoth, Section 2, Page 29a

[Note: The first few lines of the Hebrew text do not appear in our translation.] 'Observe that when the Holy One, blessed be He, prepares to inflict chastisement upon the idolatrous nations, the "Left Side" awakens and changes the whiteness of the moon to blood; then the ponds and the pools below are also filled with blood. So the punishment of the unrighteous is indeed blood. Further, when the doom of blood impends upon a people, it is the blood of slaughter executed by another people whom God brings against them. But against Egypt the Holy One, blessed be He, did not choose to raise up another nation, lest Israel, who dwelt in her midst, might also suffer. Therefore He punished the Egyptians by causing their streams to be changed into blood so that they could not drink from them. And as Egypt's supramundane power was centred in the Nile, the Holy One enforced His will first on that principality, so that – the Nile being one of their divinities – their highest power might first of all be humbled. From the lesser idols also blood gushed out, as it is written: "And there may be blood throughout all the land of Egypt, both in vessels of wood and in vessels of stone" (Ibid.).'

R. Hiya arose one night to study the Torah, R. Yose the lesser, who was still a youth, being with him. R. Hiya began by quoting: "Go thy way, eat thy bread with joy, and drink thy wine with a merry heart; for God now accepteth thy works" (Eccles. IX, 7). He said: 'What made Solomon say this? Truly, all Solomon's words were uttered in wisdom, and when a man walks in the way of the Holy One, He draws near to him and gives him peace and rest, so that he enjoys his bread and his wine, the Holy One being well pleased with him and his work.' Then said the young man: 'If this is all that the words mean, where is their great wisdom?' R. Hiya replied: 'My son, cook thy meat well [Tr. note: Al. "When thou comest to ripeness"] and thou wilt understand.' Said the youth: 'Even without cooking [Tr. note: "Even before I ripen."] I understood the meaning thereof.' Said R. Hiya: 'How so?' He replied: 'I have once heard from my father that in this verse Solomon admonishes man to crown the Community of Israel with joy, which is the "Right Side", represented by bread, and then with wine, which is the "Left Side", in order that she may be firm in faith, since complete and perfect joy is in the union of "Right" and "Left"; and when she is between the two the world is full of blessing, bounty, righteousness, and grace. And all this is accomplished when the Holy One, blessed be He, is satisfied with the works of the children of men.' R. Hiya then went up to him, kissed him, and said: 'Assuredly, I had intended to say this, but purposely left it to thee; [Tr. note: Al. "on account of thee," i.e. thinking thee too young.] and now I perceive that the Holy One desires to crown thee with the Torah.'

R. Hiya then went on to expound the verse: SAY UNTO AARON, TAKE THY ROD, AND STRETCH OUT THY HAND OVER THE WATERS OF EGYPT. Why Aaron rather than Moses?' he asked. ' Because the Holy One, blessed be He, said: Aaron represents the principle of water, and the Left Side is eager to draw the waters for himself. It is thus befitting that Aaron, who himself emanates from that side, should stir it up to take possession of the waters, whereby they will turn into blood. Observe that the lowest of the grades was first smitten.' Said R. Simeon: 'The Holy One, blessed be He, began with the lowest grade, smiting each one in succession with every finger of His hand; and when He reached the highest He Himself passed through Egypt and slew all the firstborn of the land, as the firstborn represented the highest and choicest grade of all. Observe, further, that Pharaoh was the ruler of the waters, as it is written of him: "the great dragon that lieth in the midst of his rivers" (Ezek. XXIX, 3). For that reason the turning of his river into blood was the first plague. Then followed the frogs, who with mighty squealing and croaking entered the very entrails of the Egyptians. They emerged from the river on to the dry land, where they raised a noise all around until they fell dead in the interior of the houses. Esoterically speaking, the ten plagues were wrought by the mighty hand of the Almighty, by the hand that overpowered the grades

Zohar: Shemoth, Section 2, Page 29b

of the Egyptian divinities, and confused their minds so that they remained helpless. Observe that all their grades, as soon as they emerged into the open to accomplish something that could be seen by all, became powerless to do anything. This was due to the mighty hand which pressed on them.' AND THE RIVER SHALL SWARM WITH FROGS, WHICH SHALL GO UP AND COME INTO THINE HOUSE. R. Simeon quoted here the verse: "A voice is heard in Ramah, lamentation and bitter weeping, Rachel weeping for her children, because they were not" (Jer. XXXI, 15). 'The Community of Israel is called "Rachel", as it says, "As a sheep (rahel) before her shearers is dumb" (Isa. LIII, 7). Why dumb? Because when other nations rule over her the voice departs from her and she becomes dumb. "Ramah" (lit. high) refers to the Jerusalem which is above. "Rachel weeping for her children": as long as Israel is in exile, Rachel weeps, for she is their Mother. "She refuseth to be comforted over her children for he (singular) is not": it ought to be "they are not" (enam); why is the singular used? Because it refers to Israel's Spouse (God), who is her "Voice", and has departed from her and they live in separation. It was not once only that Rachel wept over Israel, but whenever they are in exile she weeps over them so. Because of this the Holy One gave the Egyptians another kind of "voice,', in the croaking of the frogs, who made a noise in their insides.' THEY SHALL COME INTO THY HOUSE AND THY SLEEPING-CHAMBER AND THY BED. The bed here is mentioned only in connection with Pharaoh, not with his servants and people. The reason is this. It is written concerning Sarah: "The princes of Pharaoh saw her and commended her before Pharaoh, and the woman was taken into Pharaoh's house" (Gen. XII, 15). The threefold repetition of "Pharaoh"

Zohar: Shemoth, Section 2, Page 30a

in this verse corresponds to the three Pharaohs, one in the time of Sarah, one in the time of Joseph, and one whom Moses punished with his rod. The first Pharaoh, seeing that Sarah was a beautiful woman, commanded his artists to make a likeness of her. They painted her picture on one of the walls of his bed-chamber, but he was not satisfied until they made a picture of her on wood, which he took with him to bed. Each successive Pharaoh used similarly to feast his eyes on that picture. For that reason Pharaoh was punished more severely than his subjects; the frogs entering even into his bed. R. Abba said: 'Israel praise God day and night, and in response the Holy One, blessed be He, remembered them in Egypt and brought against Pharaoh creatures that remain still neither day nor night, to wit, the frogs, whose sounds never cease, in punishment for his having made heavy the burden of the holy people, who cease not day or night to chant praises to the Holy One, blessed be He. Through the croaking of the frogs no one in Egypt could converse with his neighbour; through them the very soil became polluted, and babes and young children died from their chatter. Why, it may be asked, were the Egyptians not able to slay them? The explanation is that for every one an Egyptian attempted to kill with a stick or a stone, six came forth out of its belly, running hither and thither, so that people refrained from touching them. Observe that ever so many streams and rivers rise out of the Supernal Sea, which in their courses

Zohar: Shemoth, Section 2, Page 30b

divide and subdivide again into many other rivers and streams: and the portion that fell to the side of Egypt were waters swarming with such creatures. For all waters issuing from that sea breed various kinds of fishes, to wit, messengers sent into the world to carry out the will of their Master through the spirit of Wisdom. In regard to this a traditional text tells us that there are waters that breed wise men and other waters that breed foolish men, according to the various rivers that branch off into all sides. Now the Egyptian rivers breed masters of sorcery of various kinds, and of ten degrees, as enumerated in the verse, "one that useth divination, a soothsayer, or a charmer, or one that consulteth a ghost or a familiar spirit, or a necromancer" (Deut. XVIII, 10-11). Here we have ten species of sorcery. And at that time the Holy One, blessed be He, stretched forth His finger and disturbed the brooks and rivers of Egypt so that their fishes of wisdom were confounded: some waters turned into blood, others threw up small fishes of no account upon whom the spirit of sorcery never rested. Then there came upon them the plague called 'arob (lit. mixture, i.e. mixture of various beasts) which allegorically indicates that the Almighty confounded their magical arts so that their practitioners were not able to piece them together. Moreover, that confusion produced a mingling of a perverse and hybrid kind similar to those referred to in the words of Scripture, "thou shalt not sow thy field with two kinds of seed; neither shall there come upon thee a garment of two kinds of stuff mingled together" (Lev. XIX, 19). Many were then the legions that bestirred themselves above, but the Holy One, blessed be He, confounded them altogether; these mighty deeds which the Almighty performed in Egypt were accomplished by the raising of one of his hands against them, both on high and below. It was then that the wisdom of Egypt perished, as Scripture says: "and the wisdom of their wise men shall perish, and the understanding of their prudent men shall be hid" (Isa. XXIX, 14). Note further the pronouncement: "And I will confuse Egypt with Egypt" (Ibid. XIX, 2), that is to say, celestial Egypt with terrestrial Egypt. For the celestial legions are in charge of the terrestrial ones, and they both were altogether thrown in disorder. They were confused on high so that the Egyptians could not derive inspiration from the celestial sources as formerly. It was with this object that the Almighty brought on them the 'arob, or mixture and confusion, manifested in a mixed horde of beasts that assailed them; as well as the plague of vermin, engendered from the dust of the earth. Observe that whatever is engendered on earth grows through the stimulus of a celestial Chieftain who has charge over it, and that all on earth is shaped after a celestial pattern. There are on high seven firmaments, and seven zones of earth. Correspondingly, in the lower world there are seven graded firmaments and seven zones of earth. These, as the Companions have expounded, are arranged like the rungs of a ladder, rising one above the other, and each zone has ten divisions, so that there are seventy in all. Each one of these is presided over by a Chieftain, and these seventy Chieftains have under their charge the seventy nations of the earth. These seventy earth-divisions, again, border on and surround the Holy Land, as Scripture says: "Behold, it is the couch of Solomon; threescore mighty men are about, of the mighty men of Israel" (S.S. III, 7), there being, in addition to the threescore mentioned, ten concealed among their number. All these surround the Holy Land. This alludes to the upper world, and the same is reproduced in the lower world. Now at that time the Holy One, blessed be He, stretched forth His finger over the zone that was allotted to the Egyptians, and a fiery flame passed through the whole tract and dried up all the alluvial soil, with the result that the dust of the earth generated vermin. It was Aaron that smote the dust, in order to show that the right hand of the Holy One, blessed be He, breaks His enemies, as we read: "Thy right hand, O Lord, dasheth in pieces the enemy" (Ex. xv, 6). The same punishment is destined to be meted out by the Holy One, blessed be He, to Rome the great Metropolis, as it is written: "And the streams thereof shall be turned into pitch, and the dust thereof into brimstone" (Isa. XXXIV, 9). Thus "all the dust of the earth became vermin throughout all the land of Egypt".

R. Judah and R. Hiya were once walking together. Said R. Hiya: 'When members of the Fellowship

Zohar: Shemoth, Section 2, Page 31a

journey together they must be of one heart and mind, and should sinners or persons who have no place in the King's Palace chance to fall in with them, or to be in their company, they must separate from them. They should take example from Caleb, of whom it is written: "But my servant Caleb, because he had another spirit with him, and hath followed me fully..." (Num. XIV, 24). "Another spirit" signifies that Caleb separated himself from the other spies and went alone to Hebron in order to prostrate himself at the cave of Machpelah before the graves of the patriarchs; and Hebron was allotted to him as his inheritance, as it is written: "To him will I give the land that he hath trodden upon" (Deut. I, 36). And why was Hebron given to him? There is an esoteric reason for this, the same which also underlies David's connection with Hebron. For we find that when Saul died and David enquired of the Lord, "Shall I go up into any of the cities of Judah?", the answer was that he should go up into Hebron (2 Sam. II, 1). Now, since Saul was dead and David already the rightful king, why did he not at once proclaim his rule over the whole land? Why was it necessary for him to go to Hebron and there become anointed as king over Judah only for seven years, not being declared monarch over the whole of Israel till after the death of Ish-Bosheth? Truly, the Holy One, blessed be His Name, had a deep purpose in this. The holy kingdom could not be fully established without first attaching itself to the patriarchs in Hebron. When that contact was established the kingdom was firmly erected with support from the world above, whose symbol, in David's case, was "seven years". seven being the number of perfection, because it contains all. So when it is said of the Temple, "And he built it seven years", the same perfection is suggested. Now, David desired to build the perfect kingdom here below as a counterpart of the Kingdom above; but before he could achieve his desire he had to acquire power for the task by attaching himself to the patriarchs for "seven" years. Thus only was he enabled to establish his kingdom in perfection, in the fashion of the Kingdom of supernal light: a kingdom never to be shaken. And, guided by a similar inspiration, Caleb also went to Hebron.'

R. Yose and R. Hezekiah were once going from Cappadocia to Lydda, and with them was a Jew driving a donkey heavily laden. [Note: The last 13 lines of the Hebrew text do not appear in the translation.]

WAERA

Zohar: Shemoth, Section 2, Page 31b

[Note: The first 17 lines of the Hebrew text do not appear in the translation.]

On their way they arrived at a field where they noticed a number of animals dead and dying. They said: 'Undoubtedly, a cattle plague has broken out in this place.' The Judean then remarked as follows: 'The slaying of the flocks and herds in Egypt was of three kinds. One was through the murrain, one through the hail, and a third was limited to the firstborn. In regard to the first it is written: "Behold, the hand of the Lord is upon thy cattle which are in the field." Whereas previously it is written, "it is the finger of God" (Ex. VIII, I5), here it speaks of "the hand of the Lord", to wit, with all its five fingers, for the reason that five species of cattle were smitten, as enumerated in the passage, "upon the horses, upon the asses, upon the camels, upon the herds, and upon the flocks." They were smitten each one by one of the five fingers, and thus together by the hand of the Lord. Hence we read, "a very grievous murrain", signifying that the cattle died of themselves, suddenly and without any visible cause. Afterwards, as the Egyptians did not repent, the DeBeR (murrain) literally turned about its letters and became BaRaD (hail), which killed all those that survived. The difference between the two was that the former killed gently, and the latter with violence and with fury. Both, however, struck the same species, and by means of the five fingers.'

Zohar: Shemoth, Section 2, Page 32a

[Note: The first 9 lines of the Hebrew text do not appear in the translation.]

R. Yose and R. Hiya were walking together. Said R. Yose to R. Hiya: 'Why art thou silent? Without converse on holy matters the walk is not profitable.' R. Hiya burst into tears and said: 'It is written, "Sarai was barren, she had no child" (Gen. XI, 30). Alas, alas! Alas for the time when Hagar begat Ishmael!' Said R. Yose: 'Why? Did not Sarah afterwards conceive and bear a son of the holy stock?' R. Hiya answered: 'Thou seest and I see, but one may see more than another. And I have heard something from the mouth of R. Simeon, which makes me weep.' 'What is it?' 'I will tell you. Sarah was long in having a son of her own, and she said to Abraham: "I pray thee, go in unto my maid" (Gen. XVI, 2), and Hagar had a son by Abram, and Abram prayed to God: "O that Ishmael might live before thee!" Now, although the Holy One, blessed be He, promised Abraham that he would beget Isaac, yet Abraham was so attached to Ishmael, that the Holy One had to promise him: "As for Ishmael, I have heard thee: behold, I have blessed him... and I will make him a great nation" (Ibid. 20). Through his circumcision Ishmael entered into the holy covenant before Isaac was born. Now, for four hundred years the supramundane representative of Ishmael stood before the Holy One, blessed be He, and pleaded thus with him: "He who is circumcised, has he a portion in Thy Name?" "Yes." "But what then of Ishmael? Is he not circumcised? Why then has he no portion in Thy Name, like Isaac?" The Holy One answered: "Isaac was circumcised according to rule, [Tr. Note: i.e. with the peri'ah, or exposure of the flesh.] not so Ishmael; moreover the Israelites attach themselves to me from the eighth day of their birth, but the Ishmaelites for a long time are far from me." Said he: "Yet, as Ishmael has been circumcised, he ought to have a reward!', Woe, woe, that Ishmael was born into the world and was circumcised! What did the Holy One do? He banished the children of Ishmael from the heavenly communion and gave them instead a portion here below in the Holy Land, because of their circumcision. And they are destined to rule over the land a long time, so long as it is empty, just as their form of circumcision is empty and imperfect; and they will prevent Israel from returning to their own land until the merit of the children of Ishmael shall have become exhausted. And the sons of Ishmael will fight mighty battles in the world, and the sons of Edom will gather against them, and make war against them, some on land, others on sea, and some close to Jerusalem, and one shall prevail over the other, but the Holy Land will not be delivered to the sons of Edom. Then a nation from the furthest ends of the earth will rise against wicked Rome and fight against her for three months, and many nations will gather there and fall into the hands of that people, until all the sons of Edom will congregate against her from all the ends of the earth. Then the Holy One will rise against them, as it says: "A slaughter of the Lord in Bazrah and a great slaughter in the land of Edom" (Isa. XXXIV, 6). He will "take hold of the ends of the earth that the wicked might be shaken out of it" (Job XXXVIII, 13). He will wipe out the children of Ishmael from the Holy Land, and crush all the powers and principalities of the nations in the supramundane world, and only one power will remain above to rule over the nations of the world, namely the power representing Israel, as it is written: "The Lord is thy shadow at thy right hand" (Ps. CXXI, 5). For the Holy Name is at the Right, and the Torah is at the Right, and therefore all depends on the Right, and likewise the future salvation is at the Right, as it says: "Save with thy right hand" (Ps. LX, 7). Concerning that time it is written: "Then I will turn to the peoples a pure language that they may all call upon the name of the

Lord to serve him with one consent" (Haggai III, 9), and on that day "will the Lord be one and his name one" (Zech. XIV, 9). Blessed be the Lord forever and ever. Amen and amen.'

Zohar: Shemoth, Section 2, Page 32b

BO

AND THE LORD SAID UNTO MOSES, GO IN UNTO PHARAOH, FOR I HAVE HARDENED HIS HEART. R. Judah opened here with the verse: Blessed is the people that knows the joyful sound; O Lord, they shall walk in the light of thy countenance (Ps. LXXXIX, 16). He exclaimed: 'How important it is for man to walk in the ways of the Holy One, blessed be He, and keep the commandments of the Torah, that so he may be worthy of the world to come and triumph over all accusations, both on earth and in heaven! For as there are accusers of man here below, so there are also accusers above. But those who keep the commandments of the Torah and walk in righteousness, in fear of their Lord, will never lack intercessors in heaven, for is it not written: "If there be with him an angel-intercessor, one among a thousand... then he is gracious unto him, and saith, Deliver him from going down to the pit: I have found a ransom" (Job XXXIII, 23-24)?' Said R. Hiya to him: 'Why should man need an angel to intercede for him? Is it not written: "The Lord shall be thy confidence and shall keep thy foot from being taken" (Prov. III, 26); "The Lord shall keep thee from all evil" (Ps. CXXI, 7)? Yea, verily, the Holy One Himself beholdeth all that man does, whether it be good or evil, as it is written: "Can a man hide himself in secret places that I shall not see him?" (Jer. XXIII, 24).' R. Judah replied: 'Indeed, thou speakest truth! But it is also written that Satan said: "But put forth thine hand and touch his bone and his flesh", and that the Holy One Himself said to Satan, "And thou movest me against him" (Job II, 3-4); which proves that permission was given to the powers of the "other side" that they might so rise up against man on account of the deeds he had done in this world. And in all this the ways of the Holy One are hidden, and it is beyond me to follow them, for these are the statutes of the Holy One, which men must not examine too closely, save those who walk in the way of wisdom and so are in truth worthy to penetrate into the veiled paths of the Torah, and to comprehend the hidden truths contains therein.'

R. Eleazar then discoursed on the verse: And there was a day when the sons of God came to stand before the Lord, and Satan came also among them (Job I, 6). 'This "day" ', said he, 'was New Year's Day, on which the Holy One sits in judgement on the world. "The sons of God" are the supernal beings who are appointed to watch the actions of mankind. The expression "to stand before the Lord" is parallel to the verse, "All the hosts of heaven standing by him on his right hand and on his left" (I Kings XXII, 19). But in this verse it has a more special significance, viz. to make manifest the love of the Holy One for Israel. For these messengers who are appointed to watch over the works of men roam hither and thither throughout the world, gathering up the deeds of all creatures so that on New Year's Day, the day of judgement, they may stand before the Lord with their burden of accusations. Yet of all the peoples of the earth, it is only one – Israel – whose works are examined by them carefully and in detail, for the Israelites are the Holy One's children in a particular sense, and when their works are not according to the Divine purpose, they actually weaken the power of the Holy One Himself, but when they do His will they, as it were, increase His power and might-"give strength to God" (Ps. LXVIII, 35). Thus "the sons of God", the supernal messengers, when they "stand" with their accusations against Israel, stand also "against ('al) God". "And Satan came also among them." "Also" signifies that

Zohar: Shemoth, Section 2, Page 33a

he came with the set purpose of displaying his superior power as the greatest of all the celestial accusers and so making it difficult for Israel to obtain forgiveness. When the Holy One saw that they all came thus to accuse, "He said unto Satan, Whence comest thou? And Satan replied, From going to and fro in the land." Now we know that the control of all lands is entrusted to the supernal Chieftains, save that of the Land of Israel alone. Hence, when the Satan said "the land", God knew that he intended to accuse Israel, and therefore straightway asked him: "Hast thou considered my servant Job, that there is none like him in the earth? ", in order to divert him to another subject and make him leave Israel alone-like a shepherd who throws a lamb to a wolf in order to save the rest of the flock. Thereupon Satan left Israel and turned his attention to Job, saying: "Doth Job fear God for naught?", as if to say, "No wonder the servant fears the Master who gives him all that his heart desires! Remove thy providential care from him and then see what his fear and reverence will be worth!" Mark this! When in the hour of need something is thrown as a sop to the "other side"-like the lamb thrown to the wolf-the representative of the "other side" soon ceases to attack its original victim. This is the reason for the offering of a goat at the New Moon and on the Day of Atonement; for Satan occupies himself with these and leaves Israel in peace. Now the time had come for the "other side" to have its due from the whole seed of Abraham. For Satan had a case against Abraham for having brought as a sacrifice an animal instead of Isaac-an unlawful transaction, since it says, "he shall not alter it (an animal destined for sacrifice) nor change it" (Lev. XXVII, 10). His claim, therefore, was quite reasonable. Thus, from the time when Isaac was saved and an animal substituted for him as a sacrifice, the Holy One, blessed be He, apportioned unto Satan another branch of Abraham's family that he might accuse it, namely the (heathen) descendants of his brother Nahor, the family of Uz (and Job was from the land of Uz). Now Job was one of the closest counsellors of Pharaoh, and when the latter formed the intention of exterminating the children of Israel, Job advised him: "Do not kill them, but take their possessions from them and subject their bodies to severe toil." Then said the Holy One: "As thou livest, thou shalt be judged according to thine own judgements!" Therefore, when Satan said, "But put forth thine hand now and touch all that he has and touch his bone and his flesh" (V.11), the Lord

334

placed in his power all Job's possessions and his flesh, only bidding him to "save his soul" (v. 12)–that is, his life. It is true, the text says, "And thou movedst me against him to destroy him without cause" (Job. II, 3), which would seem to show that Job's sufferings were undeserved. We should, however, translate not "against him" (bo), but "in him", i.e. in his opinion, this being only Job's own idea, not the real fact.'

Zohar: Shemoth, Section 2, Page 33b

R. Abba here interposed, saying: 'All that is correct to a point, but we have been taught that Satan, the "old but foolish king" (Eccl. IV, 13), has the right to accuse only individuals, not humanity as a whole; for the judgement of the world is executed by the Holy One Himself, as it says concerning those who built the Tower of Babel: "And the Lord came down to see" (Gen. XI, 5.); also in connection with Sodom and Gomorra: "I will go down now and see" (Ibid. XVIII, 21); for the Holy One would not rest satisfied to condemn the world to perdition merely on the strength of the word of Satan, who is the great accuser and whose only desire is to destroy the world. The truth is, however, that on New Year's Day two "sides" stand before the Holy One, blessed be He, for the reception of mankind. Those men of whom good deeds and repentance can be recorded are privileged to be inscribed in the roll of that side which is life and which brings forth life, and whoever is on its side is inscribed for life; but those whose works are evil are assigned to the other side, which is death. Sometimes, however, it happens that the world is, as it were, exactly balanced between the two. Then if there is but one righteous person to turn the scale, the world is saved; but if one wicked, then the whole world is condemned to death. And in just such a condition were the affairs of men in the time of Job, when the Accuser "stood before the Lord", eager to denounce the world. Straightway the Holy One asked him: "Hast thou considered my servant Job?" And as soon as Satan heard this name, he concentrated all his attention upon him. For this reason we are taught that it is wrong to isolate oneself and be separated from the corporate community, since one is then liable to be singled out and accused in the upper realm. Therefore the Shunammite woman said, "I dwell among my people" (2 Kings IV, 13), meaning that she had no desire to separate herself from the majority, having dwelt hitherto among her people and being known above merely as one with them. Job, however, was known apart from his people: he was singled out; and this was Satan's opportunity. Said he: "Doth Job fear God for naught? Hast not thou made an hedge about him and about his house?..." (Job 1, 9-10), meaning, "Take away all the good things with which thou hast endowed him, and he will curse thee to thy face (v. 11): he will leave thee and become attached to the 'other side'. At present he eats thy bread; take that away and we shall soon see of what stuff he is made and to whom he will cleave!" Whereupon "the Lord said unto Satan, Behold, all that he hath is in thy hand" (v. I2). Thus permission was given to the Satan to persecute Job and to show that his motives were not really pure; for as soon as he was tried he left the right way and did not remain steadfast: "He did not sin with his lips" (II, 10), but he did sin in his mind, and later also in his speech. He did not, however, go so far as to attach himself to the "other side", as Satan had predicted. His trials lasted twelve months, for this is the space of time allotted to the "other side", as, according to tradition, sinners are judged in Gehenna for twelve months. And because Job did not attach himself to the "other side", "the Lord blessed the

Zohar: Shemoth, Section 2, Page 34a latter end of Job more than his beginning" (XLII, I2).

R. Simeon said: 'The Holy One, blessed be He, did not tempt Job in the same way as He tempted other righteous men; it does not say concerning him, as it says concerning Abraham (Gen. XXII, I), that God tempted him. Abraham led with his own hands his only begotten son to be sacrificed to the Holy One, but Job gave nothing to Him. Indeed, he was not bidden to do anything of the kind, as God knew that he would not be equal to the trial. He was merely delivered to the Accuser, and the Holy One spurred Satan, through the medium of the attribute of Justice, to test him, as it says: "Hast thou considered my servant Job? "...'

Said R. Simeon: 'It is written concerning Cain that he brought a sacrifice "at the end of days" (Gen. IV, 8), and we have laid down that this expression indicates the "other side" (v. Zohar, Gen. 62b). And of Abel it says that "he also brought of the firstlings of his flock and of the fat thereof" (Ibid. 4).The expression "he also" (gam hu) suggests that, unlike Cain, he brought his offering primarily to the Holy One, and spared only "the fat thereof" to the "other side"; whereas Cain offered primarily to the "other side", and gave only a part to the Holy One, and therefore his sacrifice was not accepted. Now we read in regard to Job that "his sons went and feasted... and sent and called for their three sisters to eat and to drink with them" (Job 1, 4). While they thus feasted and made merry the Accuser was daily present in their midst, but he could not prevail against them, as it is written: "Hast not thou made an hedge about him and about his house?" And when Job made sacrifices, he did not give Satan any part whatsoever, for it says, "He offered burnt-offerings according to the number of them all" (Ibid. 5), this being an offering which ascends ('olah) entirely on high, so that he gave no portion to the "other side". Had he done so, the Accuser would not have been able to prevail against him. Hence in the end he only took what was his due. As to the question which might be asked, why then did God allow Job to suffer thus, the answer would be that, had he given Satan his due, the "unholy side" would have separated itself from the holy, and so allowed the latter to ascend undisturbed into the highest spheres; but since he did not do so, the Holy One let justice be executed on him. Mark this! As Job kept evil separate from good and failed to fuse them, he was judged accordingly: first he experienced good, then what was evil, then again good. For man should be cognizant of both good and evil, and turn evil itself into good. This is a deep tenet of faith.'

R. Simeon continued: 'It is now fitting to reveal mysteries connected with that which is above and that which is below. Why is it written here, "Come (bo) unto Pharaoh"? Ought it not rather to have said "go" (lekh)? It is to indicate that the Holy One, blessed be He, guided Moses through a labyrinth right into the abode of a certain supernal mighty dragon-that is to say, Egypt's celestial representative, from whom many lesser dragons emanate. Moses was afraid to approach him, because his roots are in supernal regions, and he only approached his subsidiary streams. When the Holy One saw that Moses feared the dragon, and that none of the supernal messengers was able to overcome him, He proclaimed: "Behold, I am against thee, Pharaoh king of Egypt, the great dragon (tanim) that lieth in the midst of his rivers, which hath said: My river is my own, and I have made it for myself" (Ezek. XXIX, 3). Yea, truly, the Lord Himself had to war against this dragon, and no lesser being. This is the mystery of the "great dragon" for those who are familiar with the esoteric lore.' Said R. Simeon further: 'It is written: "And God created the great dragons (taninim) and every living creature that moveth, which the waters brought forth abundantly, after their kind" (Gen. 1, 21). This verse', he said, 'we have already discussed, but the words "He created the great dragons" contain a yet more special and particular mystery: they refer

Zohar: Shemoth, Section 2, Page 34b

to the Leviathan and his mate, which last was slain and is preserved by the Holy One for the regaling of the righteous (in the days of the Messiah). The great dragon reposes between nine rivers, the waters of which are turbulent; and there is a tenth river whose waters are calm, and into the depth of which the blessings of the waters of Paradise descend three times a year. Into this river the dragon enters, making there his habitation; and thence he sallies forth and swims down to the sea, and devours there fish of all kinds, and then returns again to the river. The nine swift rivers are banked by trees and fringed with flowers. The parent river issued from the Left Side and from it three drops fell into a certain channel, and each of the three was divided again into three, and every drop became a river. These are the nine rivers which flow through all the firmaments. And from the final moisture that remained when all the drops had issued forth yet another drop was formed, which issued gently, and of this drop was formed that tenth river, which flows calmly. Into this river also flows a drop from the blessings poured forth from the Right side by the "perennially flowing stream", and it is greater than all the rest. When the four rivers which flow out of the Garden of Eden divide, the one called Pison flows into and is fused with the calm tenth river of which we have spoken. Out of the calm river, thus augmented, are fed and filled all the other rivers; in each of which a dragon dwells, so that the number of the dragons is nine. And each of these nine has a hole in his head, and the great dragon as well, because each of them emits breath upwards and not downwards. It is written: "In the beginning God created..." and also "And God created the great dragons". This indicates that all the ten acts of Creation had their counterpart in these ten rivers, on each of which one of the dragons breathes heavily. Now, that great dragon, when he raises his fins, heaves up the waters around him, and all the earth is shaken and all the lesser dragons, and this takes place every seventy years.' Said R. Simeon: 'Verily, though the members of the Fellowship are students of the story of Creation, having knowledge of its wonders and perception of the paths of the Holy One, blessed be He, yet even among them there are few who know how to interpret it in connection with the mystery of the great dragon.

[Tr. Note: Here follows, in the original, an elaboration of the same theme belonging to a later section ("The Book of Concealed Mystery").] Zohar: Shemoth, Section 2, Page 35a[Note: The Hebrew text does not appear in the translation as explained in the Translator's note.] Zohar: Shemoth, Section 2, Page 35b [Note: The first 16 lines of the Hebrew text do not appear in the translation as explained in the Translator's note.]

FOR THE LORD WILL PASS THROUGH.... R. Yose commented on the expression, "The Lord shall see the blood... and pass over". 'Does God then', he said, 'require a sign? Are not all secrets revealed to Him? The explanation, however, is that only when a thought-be it good or evil-is translated into action, does it bring about its due result above, whether for reward or punishment, saving only the intention of idolatry, of which it says, "Take heed to yourselves that your heart be not deceived" (Deut. XI, 16).' As to the significance of the hyssop, R. Yose explained that all the streets and market-places of the Egyptians were filled with idols, and all their houses with implements of magic to link them with lower "crowns", and therefore it was necessary to purge the doors with the hyssop, in order that these powers might be exorcised; and this was done in three places, namely upon the lintel and the two side-posts. THEREFORE THE LORD WILL PASS OVER THE DOOR AND WILL NOT SUFFER THE DESTROYER TO COME IN UNTO YOUR HOUSES, because he will see the design of His Holy Name upon the door. Said R. Judah: 'But if so, why was blood only required, seeing that, as we have been taught, the divine attributes are symbolized by three colours, white, red, and a colour which is between the two and combines both?' R. Yose replied: 'The blood was of two kinds, that of circumcision and that of the Passover lamb, the former symbolizing mercy and the latter justice.' 'Not so,' rejoined R. Judah. 'It is even as we have been taught, that the Holy One made the blood a symbol of mercy, as if there were white in it, and therefore it says: "And when I passed by thee and saw thee polluted in thine own blood, I said unto thee: In thy blood live" (Ezek. XVI, 6). To this end was the door smeared with blood in three places, viz. on two sides and in the middle.' R. Hezekiah, however, held that two kinds of blood appeared on the doors to represent the two "crowns" which were manifested at that moment in the regions above. R. Yose maintained that it was one crown consisting of two sides blended,

Zohar: Shemoth, Section 2, Page 36a

viz. mercy and justice. Said R. Abba: 'In how many ways does the Holy One show His lovingkindness to His people! A man builds a house; says the Holy One to him: "Write My Name and put it upon thy door (mezuzah), and thou wilt sit inside thy house and I will sit outside thy door and protect thee!" And here, in connection with the Passover, He says: "You inscribe on your doors the sign of the mystery of My Faith and I shall protect you from the outside!" They inscribed the likeness of the Holy Name in the form of the letter He'. As the Holy Name was then turned from Mercy to Judgement, chastisement came into (God's) view at that time. Everything was turned into red, as a symbol of vengeance on Israel's enemy. Esoterically speaking, it is fitting to show below the colour corresponding to the state above, whether mercy or judgement. And as it was then even so shall it be in the future, as it says: "Who is this that cometh from Edom (=Rome), with dyed garments from Bozra?" (Isa. LXIII, I); for He will clothe Himself entirely in judgement to avenge His people.' AND NONE OF YOU SHALL GO OUT AT THE DOOR. The reason is found in the dictum of R. Isaac, that, when punishment impends over a place a man should not go out into the open, since, once the Destroyer is given leave, he does harm indiscriminately, and makes no distinction between the righteous and the unrighteous; therefore the people of God should hide themselves lest they be consumed in that vengeance which is the due of the Destroyer. R. Yose said that the same power which exercised judgement on the Egyptians was the agent of mercy to Israel, as it is written: "When I see the blood I will pass over you" (v. 13). For, as we have been taught, all the holy crowns above contain at one and the same time both judgement and mercy. R. Hezekiah drew the same inference from the verse, "And the Lord shall smite Egypt, smiting and healing" (Isa. XIX, 22), i.e. smiting the Egyptians and healing Israel, to wit, from the wound of circumcision, the phrase "the Lord will pass over the door" suggesting the "door" of the body, which is the place of circumcision. R. Simeon interpreted it in a similar way: at the moment when the night was divided and the Holy Crown (the Sefirah Kether) was moved to unite with the masculine principle which is the supernal Grace, for they never manifest themselves one without the other – one smote and the other healed. Also, "the Lord passed over the door": that door which is the opening of spirit and body. That circumcision is of such significance can be seen from Abraham: before he was circumcised he was, as it were, a closed vessel, impervious on all sides, but when he was circumcised, and the sign of the letter yod of the Holy Name was manifested in him, he became open to supernal influences, this being the inner meaning of the words, "he sat at the door of the tent in the heat of the day" (Gen. XVIII, I), i.e. of the supernal holy Tent. R. Eleazar said that when the yod was manifested he received the glad tidings that Grace was confirmed with Righteousness. R. Abba said it refers to the tenth crown (that of Grace), with which he was then endowed, as indicated by the words "in the heat of the day", namely at the time when Grace predominates. According to another explanation,

Zohar: Shemoth, Section 2, Page 36b

the word "pass" here signifies that God passed over the pleadings of the lower crowns, which were connected with certain celestial crowns, and loosened them from their foundations, and did constraint to Himself in order to execute judgement on them and to guard Israel. And so whenever the word "pass" is used of the Almighty, it means "constraining or forcing Himself", whether to exercise mercy or severity. [Tr. Note: This explanation is based on the use in Talmudic Hebrew of the expression "'abar'al middothav" (lit. passed beyond his usual qualities), to mean "forcing or constraining oneself".] l AND IT CAME TO PASS THAT AT MIDNIGHT THE LORD SMOTE ALL THE FIRSTBORN IN THE LAND OF EGYPT. R. Hiya and R. Yose were once journeying from Usha to Lydda, the former mounted on an ass. Said R. Yose: 'Let us pause awhile and pray, for the time of the afternoon prayer is at hand and we have been taught particularly never to neglect this prayer. Why so? Because severity is then dominant, and therefore a man should pay special heed to this prayer.' R. Hiya descended and they recited their prayers, after which they continued on their way. As they journeyed, evening drew on, and they saw that the sun was setting. Said R. Hiya: 'Why art thou silent?' R. Yose replied: 'I was reflecting that the condition of mankind depends entirely on their leaders: when these are worthy, the world and all in it prosper, but when they are unworthy, woe to the world and woe to the people!' Said R. Hiya: 'Indeed thou speakest the truth, for it is written, "I saw all Israel scattered upon the hills as sheep that have not a shepherd, and the Lord said, These have no master; let them return every man to his house in peace" (I Kings XXII, 17). Instead of "let them return to" (yashubu) we should expect the text to say "let them stay in" (yeshbu be-) their houses, since they had as yet not left them! The explanation is that, as we have been taught, when the head (in this case, the king of Israel) is unworthy, the people are punished for his guilt, as David expressed it: "Lo, I have sinned... but these sheep what have they done?" (2 Sam. XXIV, 17); but as "these have no master (because Ahab was punished for his disobedience and killed in the battle) let them return... in peace". Thus, when the head of the people is punished, the people escape punishment, for then the

337

attribute of Justice can claim no power over them (having already been appeased). And Jehoshaphat also would have been punished for joining Ahab had he not "cried out" (I Kings XXII, 32).'

As they thus proceeded on their journey, night came on. They said: 'What shall we do? Should we go on we shall be lost in the darkness, and to stay here may be dangerous.' So they turned off the road a little way, and sat down under a tree, keeping themselves awake by conversing on Scriptural subjects. At midnight they heard a sound, and lo, a hind passed by, crying loudly.

R. Hiya and R. Yose started up, trembling. Then they heard a voice, proclaiming in a loud tone: 'Ye who are awake, arise! Ye who are sleeping, wake! Ye worlds prepare to meet your Lord.' Said R. Hiya: 'It must now be just midnight, and this is the voice that "maketh the hinds to travail" (Ibid.). The esoteric significance of it is as follows. At the hour when the Lord thus shows Himself in the Garden, all the Garden assembles and keeps close to Eden, from whence the stream of life flows forth into numerous channels. The Garden is called "the Bundle of Life", and in it the pious are beatified with the light of the world to come. And at the hour when the Holy One, blessed be He, reveals Himself to these saints, a voice is heard, crying: "Awake, O north wind, come, O thou south, blow upon my garden, may its spices flow out. Let my beloved into his garden come, his pleasant fruit to eat" (S.S. IV, 16). The "pleasant fruit" signifies the sacrifices which are offered to the Holy One out of the soul-essence of the righteous. These offerings take place at midnight.'

After R. Hiya had spoken thus, he and R. Yose sat down. Said R. Yose: 'It has often seemed strange to me that the smiting of the Egyptian firstborn took place at midnight instead of by day, when its wonder would have been manifest to all; also that the firstborn of the "captives in the dungeon and the firstborn of the cattle" (Ex. XII, 29) died, and not the kings, princes, and warriors, as in the case of Sanherib, of whom it is written, "And the angel of the Lord slew in the camp of Assyria, etc." (2 Kings XIX, 35). On that occasion, tradition tells us, the whole camp consisted of kings, princes, and mighty men of war, so that one angel there must have shown

Zohar: Shemoth, Section 2, Page 37a

more power than was shown here by God Himself.' Said R. Hiya: 'This is a good question, which I am unable to answer. However, I have heard that R. Simeon ben Yochai is at present "purifying the streets of Tiberias" (cf. Midrash, Gen. R. 170a), therefore let us go to him.' They remained beneath the tree until the morning, and then set forth. When they reached the place where R. Simeon was, they found him sitting deep in study, with an Haggadic book in his hand. He was commenting on the verse: "All nations are before Him as nothing and they are counted to him as less than nothing" (Isa. XL, 17). 'The word "nothing",' he said, 'describes the religion of the pagans, who do not bring the heavenly and the earthly into union and adopt a faith of folly; and they are "counted less than nothing", like chaff blown about by the wind.' He also interpreted the verse: "God created the (eth) heavens and the (eth) earth" (Gen. I, I), referring the first eth to the Right Hand and the second to the Left Hand; and these two "stand together" (Isa. XLVIII, 13) through the agency of the Crown which is called zoth and which comprises both Mercy and Judgement. Thereupon R. Hiya said: 'Will our master allow us to explain why we have come? It is written: "and it came to pass that at midnight the Lord smote all the firstborn in the land of Egypt", and from what we have just heard we gather that this verse contains the same idea which you have been expressing, so that we have just come at the right time to consult you.' R. Simeon prefaced his answer with a reference to the verse: "Who is like unto the Lord our God who dwelleth on high, and yet humbleth himself to behold the things that are in heaven and earth?" (Ps. CXIII, 5), which he expounded thus: '"Who is like unto the Lord our God", who ascends to the highest spheres in order to be crowned with the supernal holy crown, the splendour of which is more resplendent than the glories of all lesser crowns; "and yet he humbleth himself" to descend from crown to crown, that is, from one sphere to another, from one abode of light to another, and each one lower than the last, and all this in order to exercise His providential care for the higher and lower worlds?' He then proceeded: 'Instead of "at midnight" in this passage we should have expected "about (ka-hazi) midnight", which was the phrase actually used by Moses when he predicted the event. Our colleagues, we know, explain that Moses used the word "about", so that, were the event not to occur at the exact second of midnight, the Egyptian astrologers should have no chance of calling him a liar. But this hardly solves the difficulty, for in that case he should not have put the expression in the mouth of the Lord (Ex. XI, 4). Another difficulty is that Moses, when speaking of the death of the firstborn, referred to the "firstborn of the maidservant that is behind the mill" (v. 5), yet in our verse we read of the "firstborn of the captive that was in the house of the pit". And on top of all comes your question, which is the last straw that breaks the camel's back. The whole subject, however, is explained esoterically among "the reapers of the field", for it contains a supreme mystery, having been proclaimed by the faithful prophet, even Moses, of whom it is written, "Thou art fairer than the children of men; grace is poured into thy lips; therefore God hath anointed thee with the oil of gladness

Zohar: Shemoth, Section 2, Page 37b

above thy fellows" (Ps. XLV, 3, 8). "Thou art fairer than the children of men" refers to Seth and Enoch; "grace is put into thy lips" means that Moses was greater than Noah and his sons; "therefore God hath blessed thee" signifies that he was above Abraham and Isaac; "oil of gladness" suggests that Moses was greater than Jacob; and "above thy fellows" that he was above all other prophets. Could a man so great, who ascended to degrees not attained by any other, have spoken with such a lack of precision? The truth, however, is as follows. It is written: "Who is this that cometh out of the wilderness like pillars of smoke?" (S.S. III, 6). This smoke symbolizes the Crown which is called Zoth (lit. this, i.e. the Sefirah Malkuth-Kingdom) and "Woman"; as it is written, "This (le-zoth) shall be called woman" (Gen. II, 23). This Crown which is called zoth rules over the middle of the night, so that it is able to be at one and the same moment white to Israel and black to the heathens; and so long as the night is not divided it cannot perform this function, as we learn from the case of Abraham, for whom, as we are told, "the night divided against them" (Gen. XIV, 15). So here, Moses used the expression ka-ha.zoth, meaning thereby "when the night is divided", knowing that it would not perform its function till then; but the latter expression "in the middle" (lit. half) means "in the second half", which is always the period when this zoth executes judgements. As to the references to the "firstborn behind the mill", and to the "firstborn of the captive and of the cattle", they relate to the three grades of impurity, with all their spirits and powers, higher and lower, with whom Pharaoh, being himself the wiliest of all his magicians, endeavoured to entangle the Israelites so subtly and so inextricably that they should never again be free. Here it was that the power of the Holy One, blessed be He, was revealed:

Zohar: Shemoth, Section 2, Page 38a

for He loosened all the bonds of impurity and broke all those "crowns" of magic, that His children might be liberated. Therefore it is written: "Who would not fear thee, O king of nations... forasmuch as among all the wise men of the nations and in all their kingdoms there is none like unto thee" (Jer. x, 7).'

Having spoken these things, R. Simeon wept, meditating on the greatness of the Lord; then he lifted up his voice, and said: "And so you thought this passage a bundle of contradictions! But verily, the significance of the Exodus is great indeed! For this reason the Holy One, blessed be He, frequently reminds Israel of her deliverance, as when He says: "Who hath brought thee out of the land of Egypt." (Ex. xx, 2). Now, as there are ten crowns above, so likewise there are ten such below; and all are concealed in the three grades symbolized by "the firstborn of Pharaoh", "the firstborn of the maidservant that is behind the mill", and "the firstborn of the cattle", by means of which Pharaoh sought to keep the Israelites captive forever. Blessed indeed are ye, Abraham, Isaac, and Jacob, for whose sake the knots of magic were loosed, because the Holy One, blessed be He, recollected in His mercy and lovingkindness the indissoluble bonds of your faithfulness, as it says: "And the Lord remembered his covenant with Abraham, with Isaac, and with Jacob" (Ibid. II, 24). Festivals, Sabbaths, and all days of moment in Israel have this "remembrance" for their object and basis, therefore the deliverance from Egypt is mentioned in connection with such days. Truly, this "remembrance" is the foundation and root of the whole Torah, the basis of all the commandments and of the real faith of Israel. Now, as to your question why the last act did not take place by day, the fact is that in this connection there is an apparent contradiction, since on the one hand we read, "today come ye out" (Ex. XII, 4), and on the other, "The Lord thy God brought thee out of Egypt at night" (Deut. XVI, I). However, it is true that Israel's essential redemption took place at night, because only at night does the Holy One exercise judgement, therefore it was night when the knots of sorcery were loosened and the bonds of darkness rent in twain; yet were they led out by day, before the eyes of the world, that all men might marvel at the works of the Lord; therefore they were freed "with a high hand, in front of all the Egyptians" (Num. XXXIII, 3).'

R. Simeon then ceased, and R. Hiya and R. Yose prostrated themselves before him and kissed his hand, saying, with tears in their eyes: 'Surely not only earthly creatures, but also celestial beings, look out from their abode to catch a sight of thee! The Holy One, blessed be He, built Jerusalem below as a counterpart of the Jerusalem above. He made the walls of the city and the gates thereof holy. None may enter the city unless the gates be opened for him, nor ascend unless the steps of the walls are firm. Who is able to open the gates of the city, who can fix the steps of the walls but R. Simeon ben Yochai? For it is he who opens the gates of the mysteries of wisdom, and fixes the ladder to the higher spheres! It is written, "Three times in the year all thy males shall be seen before the face of the Lord" (Ex. XXII, 17). Who then is this "face of the Lord"? None other than R. Simeon ben Yochai! And as to the reference to the "males" appearing before him, indeed only "the males of the males" (the truly manly, i.e. students of the esoteric lore) may draw near to him.'

R. Simeon continued: 'I have not yet finished answering your questions. You ask why the smiting of the firstborn took place at night. It was because then they were all at home, and not abroad in the fields. Further, tradition tells us that night was as bright as a day in Tamuz, therefore the whole Egyptian people could witness the mighty hand of the Holy One: "the night shined as the day; the darkness was as light"

Zohar: Shemoth, Section 2, Page 38b

(Ps. CXXXIX, 13). Nothing so miraculous was witnessed since the creation of the world. 'Come and see,' he said, 'it is written: "It is a night (leyl) of observations unto the Lord for bringing them out from the land of Egypt; this is that night (ha-layla) of the Lord, observations to all the children of Israel" (Ex. XII, 42). Now, why "observations" in plural, and "night" first in the masculine gender (layiil), and then in the feminine (layla)? To indicate the union which took place on that night between the Masculine and Feminine aspects in the Divine attributes, and also the same union which will take place in the future Redemption: "As in the days of thy coming out of Egypt will I show unto him marvellous things" (Micah VII, I 5).'

R. Hiya and R. Yose sat down and R. Simeon taught them the mysteries connected with the book of Leviticus, and they used to come every day and study with him. One day R. Simeon went out for a walk, and they, following, came upon him in a wood. They all sat down, and R. Simeon began to speak thus: 'It is written: "All things have I seen in the days of my vanity: there is a righteous man that perisheth in his righteousness, and there is a wicked man that prolongeth his life in wickedness" (Eccl. VII, I5). How could Solomon, the wisest among men, have spoken thus? He must have intended some inner meaning, for we see for ourselves that the ways of the Holy One, blessed be He, are not thus, for He "giveth every man according to his ways and according to the fruit of his works" (Jer. XVII, 10). But Solomon hinted here at two things. When the "eyes" of the Holy One "run to and fro through the whole earth" (Zech, IV, IO), and the world is full of sinners, their guilt is visited upon the one righteous of his generation, whereas God is patient with the wicked and waits for their repentance. If they do not repent, they are left without an intercessor, for "the righteous perisheth", i.e. he has been taken away from the world. It is on this account that the Rabbis have warned us to live only in a place which is the abode of men of pious deeds, and woe betide him who fixes his dwelling among the wicked! He will surely be "seized" for their sins! Conversely, when one lives among pious people one shares the reward of their goodness. Rab Hisda may serve as an example. Originally he lived among the Cappadocians, and suffered great poverty (cf. T. B. Shab. 140b) and many grievous ills; but when, after some time, he left those parts and removed to Sepphoris, all went well with him: he benefited both materially and spiritually, and he remarked, "all these blessings have come upon me because I have made my abode among people on whom the Holy One bestows His lovingkindness,'. There is, however, another explanation of the passage, arising out of another difficulty in the text. How could Solomon say, "All things have I seen in the days of my vanity (hebli)"? Did not Solomon attain to wisdom beyond all his contemporaries (I Kings v, 10, 11)? And did not his seven names–Solomon, Jedidiah, Agur, Jakeh, Ithiel, Lemuel, Koheleth (cf. Midrash Rabbah, Eccl. 1,2), correspond to the

Zohar: Shemoth, Section 2, Page 39a

seven supernal grades, the greatest of which is Koheleth, the essence of them all, signifying the supernal Holy Assembly of ten (Sephiroth)? Could he whose names thus symbolize grades of wisdom, and whose three books contain the whole essence of it-the Song of Songs representing Grace; Koleleth, Judgement; and Proverbs, Mercy-could such a one as he have said: "In the days of my vanity", and "vanity of vanities"? However, hebel is here to be understood in the literal sense, namely "breath", and conveys a very precious lesson. From the "breath" which issues out of the mouth the voice is formed, and according to the well-known dictum the world is upheld only by the merit of the "breath" of little school children who have not yet tasted sin. Breath is itself a mixture, being composed of air and moisture, and through it the world is carried on. Esoterically speaking, the breath of the little ones becomes "voice", and spreads throughout the whole universe, so that they become the guardians of the world. Solomon inherited this "breath" from his father, and through it he saw with clear vision. Hence he said, "I have seen all things in the days of my breath (hebel)". And what did he see? "The righteous perishing in his righteousness." That is to say, if this breath emanates from the sphere of Judgement, then "a righteous man perisheth in his righteousness"; but when the breath derives from the attribute of Mercy, then it may happen that "there is a wicked man that prolongeth his life". Therefore it says "in the days", and not "in the day", as it all depends on the "when" and the "whence" the "breath" emanates.'

As they thus sat listening to the master's expositions, they suddenly beheld smoke ascending and descending at a little distance, where there was a clearing in the wood. Said R. Simeon: 'The ground has been heated by the light from above, and now this field emits an aroma of all spices, passing sweet. Let us remain here, for the Shekinah is present with us. It is "the smell of the field which the Lord hath blessed" (Gen. XXVII, 27).' Presently he began to comment on this verse and referred to the tradition (cf. Midrash, Rab., Gen., LXV, 18; Zohar, Gen. 142b) that the "precious garments" which emitted a sweet odour when Jacob appeared before Isaac originally belonged to Adam, and in time came into the hands of Nimrod, "the mighty hunter", and finally to Esau, who was also a hunter. 'It has been remarked', he said, 'that these garments were made by the Holy One Himself (Gen. III, 21), by the agency of both Divine Names, Tetragrammaton and Elohim, which is more than can be said for heaven and earth, which were created only by Elohim (Gen. I, 1). It is rather difficult to understand how they came to Esau. For in the first place we are told that God made garments for Eve also (Ibid.), and what became of these? And surely Adam and Eve would have been

Zohar: Shemoth, Section 2, Page 39b

buried in them and not abandoned such a precious gift. The truth is, however, that no other human being ever wore those garments, which placed Adam and Eve on a par with supernal beings. And as for the "goodly raiment" which Rebekah put upon Jacob (Gen. XXVII, I5), this was royal apparel of silk and gold, which it is usual to keep in perfumes, and this is what lsaac smelt, and he said, "See the smell of my son" (Ibid. 27), because he knew that the smell was so sweet on account of him. How, it may be asked, did Isaac know of "the smell of the field which the Lord hath blessed" (Ibid.)? From two sources, which are essentially the same. It says, "and Isaac went out to meditate in the field" (Gen.

XXIV, 63). Why in the field? Did he not have a house or any other place in which to pray? The truth is that that field was actually the very one which Abraham bought from the sons of Heth, that field which was near the cave of Machpelah; and when Isaac passed it the Shekinah was present there and the field emitted holy heavenly aromas, and Isaac, recognizing the Presence, made it a regular place for his prayer. The second fact was that Isaac smelled the myrrh ascending from Mount Moriah. Thus, when Jacob approached him, the Paradisiacal savours brought back to him the recollection of the sweet odour he smelled in that field. ON THE TENTH DAY OF THIS MONTH THEY SHALL TAKE TO THEM A LAMB.

According to R. Abba, the tenth day was chosen because on this day the Jubilee illumines the Moon (i.e. Binah communicates light to Malkuth); for of the Jubilee it is written: "On the tenth day of this seventh month there shall be a day of atonement" (Lev. XXIII, 27). "They shall take a lamb." Why a lamb? Because it symbblized the power of the lowest "crown", which the Holy One broke, the "crown" to which all the other inferior "crowns" cling, forming the unholy triad signified by the phrase, "lambs, menservants, and womenservants", sent by Jacob to Esau, as a sop, as it were, to the evil powers which the latter represented. The Holy One said: "Do ye perform this act of slaughtering the Passover lamb, and I myself will nullify its power above. Do ye let it pass through fire (v. 8) here below, and I shall lead the impure principality which it represents through the fiery Stream." And why was the lamb to be tied up on the tenth day and slaughtered on the fourteenth? Because, according to R. Abba, the four days corresponded to the four hundred years that Israel was subjected to the power of Egypt. And why was the slaughter performed in the evening? Because that is the time when judgement predominates above and below, and also because it was at this time ("between the evenings") that Israel's exiles were foretold

Zohar: Shemoth, Section 2, Page 40a

to Abraham, as it is written: "And when the sun was going down, a deep sleep fell upon Abraham, and lo, a horror of great darkness fell upon him" (Gen. xv, I 2). "Horror" signifies one supernal "crown" which represents Egypt; "darkness" is a second such, representing Babylon; and "great" refers to the Edomite (Roman) exile, which was to be the hardest of all. Thus it is seen that the Israelites did not go out of Egypt until all the supernal powers and principalities which were Israel's enemies had been brought to nought; but when these things had come to pass the people were freed from their domination and brought under the holy and heavenly sway of the Holy One, blessed be He, and were joined to Him and to Him alone, as it is written: "For unto me the children of Israel are servants; they are my servants whom I brought forth out of the land of Egypt" (Lev. xxv, 55). Similarly, R. Simeon interpreted the verse: "Even the first day ye shall put away leaven (hamez) out of your houses, for whosoever eateth leavened bread (mahmezeth), etc." (Ex. XII, 15). Said he: 'Seor,hamez, and mahmezeth all mean one and the same thing, and are symbols of the same supernal grade, namely the powers appointed to represent all the other nations, which are pagan and enemies of Israel, and are termed variously "evil imagination", "foreign domination", "strange god", and "other gods".' Said God to Israel: 'All these years ye have been subject to an alien power, but now you are free men, you shall put away leaven, etc.' Said R. Judah: 'If so, why is leaven prohibited on these seven days only?' R. Simeon answered: 'This ceremony is only necessary when the Israelite requires to demonstrate the fact of his freedom. If a king raises a man to a high office, the latter will celebrate his elevation by rejoicing and donning costly festive garments for a few days; but subsequently he merely celebrates the anniversary as it comes round. The same is true of Israel: they, too, have each year their season of joy and gladness when they celebrate the high honour which the Holy One, blessed be He, showed them when He brought them out of the power of impurity into the invincible power of His holiness. Therefore it is written, "seven days ye shall eat mazoth (unleavened bread)".' Said R. Simeon further: 'The unleavened bread is called "the bread of poverty" (Deut. XVI, 3), because at that time the moon was not at full strength, the reason being that, although the Israelites were circumcised, the rite had not been completed by "peri'ah", and therefore the seal of the covenant was not revealed in its complete form. But later, when this completion had been achieved–namely at Marah, where Moses "made for them a statute and an ordinance" (Ex. xv, 25). the Holy One spake unto them, saying: "Until now ye have eaten the 'bread of poverty', but from now on your bread shall emanate from a far other region: 'I will rain bread from heaven for you'" (Ibid. XVI, 4). This phrase means literally "from heaven", that is, from the very centre of Grace, and not, as previously, from the blemished "Moon". Therefore the holy Israelites observe as a memorial the anniversary of the days when they came under the wings of the Shekinah, and eat the bread which emanates from Her. And why was the rite not brought to its completion in Egypt? Because the Exodus would then have been delayed until those who had undergone this operation had recovered.

Zohar: Shemoth, Section 2, Page 40b

Observe that when the Israelites were about to enter the Holy Land, Moses described it as "a land wherein thou shalt eat bread without scarceness" (Deut. VIII, 9), in contrast to the "bread of misery, of poverty", which was their food in Egypt, when the moon did not derive blessing and light from the sun, when she was not illumined by the Jubilee. And because they did not carry out the peritah in Egypt, the unification and harmonization of the Divine attributes was not manifested in its fulness. Why they continued to eat the "bread of poverty" in the land of Israel was in remembrance of Egypt.' R. Simeon also connected the words, "Also on the tenth day of this seventh month there shall be a day of atonement" (Lev. XXIII, 27), with the words, "In the tenth day of this month" (Ex. XII, 3), used in regard to the Passover lamb; for the one "tenth day" is dependent on the other.

[Tr. Note: From here to the end of the section (pp. 40b-43b) is from the Ray'a Mehemna, see below in this edition.]

BESHALAH

Zohar: Shemoth, Section 2, Page 44a

AND IT CAME TO PASS WHEN PHARAOH SENT AWAY THE PEOPLE, ETC R. Simeon discoursed here on the verse: "A prayer of Habakkuk the prophet upon shigionoth" (Hab. III, I). 'Why', he said, 'is this vision of Habakkuk designated "prayer", a title unique in the prophetic writings? Why do we find only a prayer of Habakkuk and not of Isaiah or Jeremiah? To explain this we must go back to the tradition which says that he was the son of the Shunammite woman who befriended Elisha, and that his name contains an allusion to Elisha's words,

Zohar: Shemoth, Section 2, Page 44b

"about this set time, according to the time of life, thou wilt embrace (hobeketh) a son" (2 Kings IV, 16). The promise was fulfilled, but the child subsequently died. Why? Because it was given to her and not to her husband; it came from the "feminine" region alone, and everything emanating from the feminine principle ends in death. Elisha, seeing that the child was dead, realized the reason; and therefore "he lay upon the child, and put his mouth upon his mouth, and his eyes upon his eyes, and his hands upon his hands, and he stretched himself upon the child, and the flesh of the child waxed warm" (Ibid. 34); that is to say, he connected him with another supernal region where there is an abundance of life, not uprooting the child from the former region, but awakening a new spirit from above and restoring his soul to him. "And the child sneezed seven times, and the child opened his eyes" (v. 35). Now this child became the prophet Habakkuk. The duplicate form of his name (Habakkuk instead of Habuk=embraced) suggests that he owed his life to two "embracings": one of

Zohar: Shemoth, Section 2, Page 45a

his mother (cf. v. 16), and one of Elisha, one coming from the sphere to which he was attached at first, and the other from the higher supernal grade. Hence his prophetic utterance took the form of a prayer, as issuing from the place to which he was first attached; and it was "upon shigionoth" (lit. errors), because the day on which his birth was announced was New Year's day, when the "errors" of mankind are judged by the Almighty. Hence, whenever the spirit of prophecy was stirred in him, he trembled, saying: "O Lord, I have the report of thee, and I am afraid" (Hab. III, 2). Therefore he prayed: "O Lord, revive thy work (i.e. himself) in the midst of the years... in wrath remember mercy" (Ibid.). Moreover, the fact that it does not say shegioth (errors), but shigionoth, shows that the reference is to the musical instruments, like "shigayon of David" (PS. VII, 1), which were used by all the prophets (except Moses, who was independent of external aids to prophecy), in order to enter into an ecstatic mood before receiving the spirit of prophecy (cf. I Sam. x, 5; 2 Kings III, 15), and Habakkuk needed the calming influence of music more than anybody.'

R. Simeon continued: 'When the children of Israel went out of Egypt their spirits were broken because of their past sufferings, and there was no energy left in them and no will to participate in the joy, singing and exultation of Moses and Miriam (Ex. xv, I-21). But when all those celestial hosts and chariots who accompanied the Shekinah on the way from Egypt began to sing and to praise the Lord for His glorious deeds, the Holy One awakened the spirits of the Israelites, putting new life into them, and they who had tasted death were healed by His touch, as it is written: "And the Lord went before them by day in a pillar of a cloud, to lead them the way; and by night in a pillar of fire, to give them light" (Ex. XIII, 21). All the ways emitted healing savours which entered into their bodies, and the singing of the celestial hosts entered into their souls, filling their spirits with joy and gladness. Pharaoh, however, and his hosts, and all the celestial principalities of Egypt and the other heathen nations, followed them from behind, until they reached Etham, on the edge of the wilderness.' AND IT CAME TO PASS... THAT GOD LED THEM NOT THROUGH THE WAY OF THE LAND OF THE PHILISTINES, FOR IT WAS NEAR. That is to say, they were in near danger of breaking the oath which had been administered to Abraham by Abimelech king of Gerar in the land of the Philistines, that he should deal with his people "according to the kindness that I have done unto thee" (Gen XXI, 23, 24).

Mark the wondrous punishment that overtook the enemies of Israel. On the night of the Exodus there were three slayings in Egypt. First, the firstborn killed whomsoever they could lay hands on; then, the Holy One executed His judgement at midnight; and, lastly, Pharaoh, on seeing the havoc wrought upon his own household, himself arose and with bitterness and fury smote those princes and nobles who had advised him to persecute Israel. He rose up at midnight; yea, even at the hour and moment when the Holy One Himself began His judgement (Ex. XII, 30), did Pharaoh likewise rise up in wrath, and kill his of ficers and nobles,

Zohar: Shemoth, Section 2, Page 45b

just as a dog, if hit with a stone, goes and bites another dog. Having done this, Pharaoh roamed through the market-places crying, "Rise up and get you forth from among my people" (Ibid. v, 31); and in fear he added, "and bless me also" (v. 32), as if to say, "let me live". Then, so eager was he to be rid of them that he himself accompanied them, as it says, "he sent the people away" (beshallach, lit. escorted). AND GOD LED THE PEOPLE ABOUT THROUGH THE WAY OF THE WILDERNESS OF THE RED SEA. This was to pave the way for the manifestation of the Divine power at the Red Sea. R. Judah asked: 'Why was it that when the children of Israel were still in Egypt, and were not yet circumcised, nor in full communion with the Holy One, He yet spoke of them as "my people" (Ex. v, 1), and "my firstborn Israel" (Ibid. IV, 22), whereas now that they were circumcised, and had duly sacrificed the Passover lamb, and were fully joined to the Holy One, they are referred to merely as "the people"? The answer is that they were spoken of–not only here, but in many other places (e.g. Ex. XXXII, 1, 35)—as "the people" because of the "mixed multitude,' which went out with them.'

R. Isaac and R. Judah were once journeying from Usha to Lud, and with them was a certain Yose driving a train of laden camels. On the way this Yose turned aside and misconducted himself with a heathen woman who was gathering herbs in a field near by. R. Isaac and R. Judah were greatly shocked, and the latter exclaimed: 'Let us abandon this journey, since God has given us a sign that we should not associate with this wicked man or have any further intercourse with him'. So they changed their course. On making inquiries they found that his mother was a heathen woman and that his father had been born in illegitimacy, and they blessed God for saving them from him. R. Isaac was reminded of the verse: "Fret not thyself because of the evildoers" (Ps. XXXVII, I). 'The evildoers,' he said, 'as opposed to "sinners" or "wicked men", are those who defile themselves and all who come into contact with them.' Said R. Judah: 'One must indeed beware of making friends (re'im) with the evildoers (mere'im), lest one should suffer for their deeds and be included in their judgement. Mark this. Were it not for that "mixed multitude", which joined and mingled with the Israelites, the sin of the "golden calf" would never have been perpetrated, and the children of Israel would not have had to suffer for it as they did. Nay, but for that sin Israel would have been, then and forever, that which the Holy One had ordained them to be; namely, pure as the angels and free from all evil: free from death and free from the dominion of earthly powers. But that sin brought upon them death and subjection, and through it the tablets were broken and many thousands were slain. All this came from their association with the "mixed multitude"; and it was on their account that they are called here not "children of Israel", nor "Israel", nor "my people", but simply "the people"' As for the expression in the same verse, "And the children of Israel went up harnessed out of the land of Egypt", this refers to the period before the "mixed multitude" joined them.' R. Yose objected that at the Red Sea Moses said to the Israelites, "the Egyptians whom ye have seen today ye shall see them again no more" (Ex. XIV, 13), and yet according to R. Isaac's interpretation they saw the "mixed multitude" every day. To this R. Judah answered that the "mixed multitude" were not Egyptians, but members of other peoples living in Egypt. Moreover, they had all been circumcised, and therefore would not in any case be called Egyptians. They were accepted as proselytes on the authority of Moses; for which reason

Zohar: Shemoth, Section 2, Page 46a

it says in a later passage, "Go, get thee down, for thy people which thou hast brought out of Egypt have corrupted themselves" (Ex. XXXII, 7).' AND THE CHILDREN OF ISRAEL WENT UP ARMED (hamushim). This signifies that the "mixed multitude" numbered one in every five (hamishah). According to R. Yose, for every five pure Israelites there was one who belonged to the mixed multitude. R. Judah said one in fifty (hamishim). R. Simeon saw in the word hamushim an allusion to the "Jubilee" which led them out of Egypt. For the same reason, fifty days had to pass before the Israelites received the Torah on Mount Sinai, since the Torah also emanated from that same region of the "Jubilee". AND MOSES TOOK THE BONES OF JOSEPH WITH HIM. Why did Moses do this rather than anyone else? Because Joseph was the leader in the descent into exile. Moreover, this was a sign of redemption to him, for Joseph "had strictly sworn the children of Israel" concerning it, the meaning of which has already been explained in another connection. Blessed be Moses, who, when the children of Israel were busy borrowing jewels from the Egyptians, saw to the fulfilment of the pledge given to Joseph! Some say that Joseph's coffin had been in the river Nile and Moses removed it from there by the power of the Holy Name; and that he also said: "Joseph, arise! The time of the redemption of Israel has arrived!" Some say that his body was buried among the kings of Egypt, and had to be removed from there. Others, again, hold that his body was put into the Nile in order that the Egyptians should not worship him as a god, and that Serah, the daughter of Asher, showed Moses the exact spot where it lay. [Tr. note: Cf. Midrash, Deut. Rabbah XI.] AND THE LORD WENT BEFORE THEM BY DAY. R. Yose discoursed upon the verse: To the chief musician, upon the hind of the morning (Ps. XXII, I). 'Great', he said, 'is the love which the Holy One, blessed be He, has lavished upon the Torah, in that all those who devote themselves to her are blessed for her sake. He who studies her diligently shall find favour in the upper and lower spheres, and the Holy One shall hearken to the words of such a one, and never leave him in this world or the world to come. The Torah must, however, be studied by day and by night, as Moses said to Joshua: "Thou shalt meditate therein day and night" (Joshua I, 8), and as it also says, "My covenant (shall be with thee) night and day" (Jer. XXXIII, 20). The night must be added to the day in order that the Holy Name may be with him in harmony and perfection. And as the day is not complete without the night, so the study of the Torah is not complete unless it is carried on by night as well as by day. The word "night" is commonly taken to include those evening hours which fall before midnight; but the real night only begins with the actual stroke of midnight, for at that moment the Holy One, blessed be He, enters the Garden of Eden in order to have joyous communion with the righteous. For this reason it behoves the pious man to rise also at that time, for then the Holy One and all the righteous in the Garden listen to his voice, as it is written, "Thou that dwellest in the gardens, the companions hearken to thy voice" (S.S. VIII, 3), and we refer this to the Community of Israel when she extols the Holy One by studying the Torah at night. Happy he who joins her in this praise! When morning dawns the Community of Israel still rejoices in her Lord, and He extends the sceptre of His grace over her and over every individual who participates in her rejoicings and communion with Him. It is on this account that the Community of Israel is known as "the hind of the morning".' Said R. Simeon: 'When the dawn is about to break the sky darkens: at that moment the Spouse enters her husband's chamber. On the other hand, when the sun is about to set, it grows light for an instant, and then night comes, and the light is removed, and all the gates are closed; asses begin to bray, and dogs bark. But with the midnight the King arises, and the Matrona sings, and the King draws nigh to the gate of the Palace, and knocks thereon, crying, "Open unto me, my sister, my love!" (S.S. v, 2), and He enters in, and has joyous communion with the souls of the righteous. Then is he indeed blessed who at that moment shall arise to study the Torah. For all those who dwell in the palace of the Matrona arise at that time to sing praises to the King, but the praise which ascends from this far-away world is the most pleasing of all to the Holy One. When the night passes and the dawn breaks, at that moment when the sky is darkened, the King and the Shekinah unite in joy, and He reveals celestial and hidden beauties to Her and all Her train, and presents them all with gifts. Blessed indeed is he who is numbered among them!' AND THE LORD WALKED BEFORE THEM BY DAY. The expression "and the Lord" means the Holy One, blessed be He, and His Council.

Zohar: Shemoth, Section 2, Page 46b

'This illustrates what we have been taught,' said R. Isaac, 'namely, that the Patriarchs were the Shekinah's chariot. Abraham is indicated by the words "walked before them by day"; Isaac by "in a pillar of cloud"; Jacob by "to lead them the way"; and David by the words "by night in a pillar of fire"; and all these four formed a supernal holy Chariot, for the assistance and guardianship of Israel, to the end that she might walk in harmony, completeness and peace, and that the Fathers might behold the redemption of their children. TO GO BY DAY AND BY NIGHT. Why had the children of Israel thus to go by night as well as by day like a pack of runaways? Had they not the Holy One Himself to protect and to lead them? The reason, however, was in order that the harmony of the whole (i.e. of the divine attributes of Mercy and Justice, symbolized by day and night) might be manifested in them. As for the "pillar of fire", it rose up at night to give light on either side, and it was as a beacon unto the Egyptians, luring them on to pursue, in order that the name of the Holy One, blessed be He, might be glorified in their overthrow. Also, it was to mislead the Egyptians into thinking that it was all a mere accident. Therefore it was that they went day and night.' Said R. Abba: 'Blessed are the Israelites for that the Holy One brought them out from Egypt in order that they might be His portion and possession! Observe that Israel gained freedom from the side of the "Jubilee"; since it shall be thus once again in the future time, as it is written, "And it shall come to pass in that day that the great trumpet shall be blown" (Isa. XXVII, 13). Moreover, on account of that supernal "Jubilee" they waited fifty days before receiving the Torah on Mount Sinai. And as they walked by day so they also walked by night, so that the days should be perfect; and still they went in ease and comfort. When they received the Law fifty days had passed, each consisting of day and night, and each being but the half of one whole. Thus, after they had journeyed for fifty complete days, the light of the fifty days of the Jubilee shone upon them.' AND IT WAS TOLD THE KING OF EGYPT By whom was it told?

According to R. Isaac, the magicians, who were Pharaoh's ministers, discovered by their dark arts that the Israelites walked both by day and by night, and concluded that they were running away, the more so as they also observed that they did not take the direct route, but went by a devious way, as it says, "And they returned and encamped before Pi-Hahiroth". AND HE TOOK SIX HUNDRED CHOSEN CHARIOTS. R. Yose said that this number corresponded to the number of the Israelites who went on foot-six hundred thousand footmen (EX. XII, 37). The "chosen chariots" were meant as a counterpart to the fighting men, who formed the flower of Israel, while "all the chariots of Egypt" corresponded to the "little ones" of the Israelites. Pharaoh acted entirely on the advice of his sorcerers and magicians. The word "warriors" (shalishim, from shelishi, third) signifies that every chariot contained three warriors, and this was planned with a deep purpose, that they might correspond to the Supernal grades (Sephiroth), which also go in threes (viz. right, left, and intermediary). According to R. Isaac, however, shalishim means simply "supervisors", as in the Aramaic translation (Targum). R. Hiya illustrated from the verse, "The Lord shall punish the host of the high ones on high, and the kings of the earth upon the earth" (Isa. XXIV, 21). 'When the Holy One', he said, 'shows favour unto the celestial representatives of a nation, granting them dominion and power, He deals similarly with the earthly nation which they represent; and when He lessens His favour and diminishes their power above, He does likewise below.'

[Note: The last 6 lines of the Hebrew text are omitted from the translation.]

BESHALAH

Zohar: Shemoth, Section 2, Page 47a

AND PHARAOH DREW NEAR. Said R. Yose: It has been pointed out that the word hikrib (drew near, lit. brought near) is in the causative form, signifying that he brought the Israelites near to God by repentance. So the Scripture says elsewhere, "O Lord, they have visited thee in trouble, they have poured out prayer when thy chastisement was upon them" (Isa. XXVI, 16), i.e. Israel do not turn to the Almighty when they are at ease, but only when they are "in trouble"; when He chastises them, then "they pour out prayer". They are like the dove in the story which took refuge from a hawk in the cleft of a rock and found a serpent there. They drew nigh unto the sea; but when they beheld how stormy it was, and how its waves roared and broke, fear overtook them. Then they looked back, and lo! there was Pharaoh with all his hosts and their manifold weapons! Their fear increased at this sight, and their terror knew no bounds. Then "they cried". Thus they came near to their heavenly Father, whose aid they invoked; and of this Pharaoh was indirectly the cause.'
AND MOSES SAID UNTO THE PEOPLE, FEAR YE NOT, STAND STILL AND SEE THE SALVATION OF THE LORD. Said R. Simeon: 'Blessed were the Israelites to have a shepherd like Moses! It is written: "Then he remembered the days of old, Moses his people" (Isa. LXIII, 11). This indicates that Moses was counted as of equal importance before the Lord with the whole people, and that the people's shepherd does not merely represent them, but actually is himself the people. If he is worthy, then is the whole people likewise worthy; and if he be not so, then is the whole people punished for his guilt, as we have shown on another occasion. "Stand still and see", i.e. "you have no occasion to fight, the Lord shall fight for you and ye shall hold your peace". On that night the Holy One gathered together His whole celestial Family to judge Israel, and had it not been for the merit and intercession of their ancestors they would not have been left unscathed.' R. Judah said: 'The merit of Jacob protected them from punishment, as it says, "If it were not for the Lord who was on our side, may Israel say" (Ps. CXXIV, 2), where the reference is to the patriarch Israel.' THE LORD SHALL FIGHT FOR YOU AND YE SHALL HOLD YOUR PEACE. R. Abba discoursed here on the verse: If thou turn away thy foot from the Sabbath, from doing thy pleasure on my holy day" (Isa. LVIII, 13). He said: 'Blessed are the Israelites that of all nations the Holy One singled them out for fellowship with Him and gave them, out of love, the Torah and the Sabbath! The Sabbath, the holiest of days, the most restful, the most joyous! The Sabbath, which is equal in significance to the whole Torah, so that he who keeps the Sabbath keeps, as it were, the whole Torah. "And call the Sabbath a delight" (Ibid.): a delight for the soul, and a delight for the body; a delight for those who are above, and a delight for those that are below. "And call the Sabbath." Call it, invite it, as one invites an honoured guest and prepares everything bounteously and concentrates one's attention on him,

Zohar: Shemoth, Section 2, Page 47b

"not doing one's own ways, nor finding one's own pleasure, nor speaking (profane) words" (Ibid.). For every word that man speaks, whether it be good or bad, causes a vibration in the higher spheres, and he who disturbs the Sabbath joy by uttering profane words causes a blemish in the holy day. When one has been invited to the king's banquet he would commit a great offence against the king if he were to neglect him in order to converse with some other person: the Sabbath is such a banquet. The weekdays must be devoted to all needful occupations, with their corresponding vibrations above; on the Sabbath, however, the vibration must be caused entirely by religious acts and words, by the sanctification of the day. Here, however, when Pharaoh was about to start the battle against Israel, the Holy One did not wish His people to start any movement from below, because the awakening was to come from above, namely, from their ancestors, the Patriarchs, whose meritorious intercessions stood before the Holy One. Hence Moses said: "The Lord shall fight for you, and ye shall hold your peace", which means, "ye need not utter a word to cause a vibration above: the initiative has already come from there." It may be noted that the initials of the words Tetragrammaton yilahem lakem-"the Lord shall fight for you"-make a part of the Holy Name (of the seventy-two letters), as the members of the Fellowship have pointed out.'

R. Yose and R. Judah were once walking together. Said R. Yose: 'We have been taught that the Name Tetragrammaton in every connection signifies mercy; even when it is related to war and judgement, the judgement is executed in mercy; but here we read, "Tetragrammaton shall fight for you", and yet the attribute of mercy was not manifested at all in the Egyptians' defeat, for "there remained not so much as one of them" (v. 28).' R. Judah replied by quoting a remark of R. Simeon on this subject, showing that here also mercy and kindness was manifested (in the execution of judgement). For when the Egyptians were drowned, the sea spat them out, while the earth refused to take in the bodies, until the Holy One, in order not to deprive them of the last honour, stretched out to the earth His right hand and commanded her to receive them, as is indicated by the words, "Thou stretchedst out thy right hand, the earth swallowed them" (xv, 12), Therefore the Israelites had to be silent, for had they caused an awakening from below, it was not the attribute of Mercy that they would have awakened, and so judgement would have been executed on the Egyptians without mercy, and the heavenly design would have been frustrated.' Said R. Yose: 'What of the verse: "And Tetragrammaton will come out and fight against those nations" (Zech. XIV, 3)?' R. Judah replied: 'There also mercy will be shown in that God will allow them to die without suffering. In fact, this Name always signifies judgement in mercy, except in one connection, namely the war of the future, of which it says: "The Lord shall go forth as a giant... like a man of war" (Isa. XLII, 13). But even here all that is meant is that the judgement will be exceptionally severe, and mercy will still be fused with it: the particle "ke" (like) has a qualifying effect, showing that the Lord is only compared to a "giant" and to a "man of war"; and although He will exercise judgement, He will have mercy on those whom He created.' AND THE LORD SAID UNTO MOSES, WHEREFORE CRIEST THOU UNTO ME? The significance of this question has been dealt with in the Book of Concealed Mystery, and the esoteric interpretation thereof belongs there. R. Judah connected this verse with the story of Jonah. 'We read there', he said, 'that "the Lord had prepared a great fish to swallow up Jonah" (Jonah III, 1). Now the word minah (prepared) means strictly "to allot as a portion", as, for instance, when it says, "the king allotted them a daily provision" (Dan. I, 5); therefore in this case it would seem more appropriate

Zohar: Shemoth, Section 2, Page 48a

to have said "and the Lord apportioned Jonah to the fish" than that the fish was prepared for Jonah. However, the fact is that the fish was a great boon to Jonah; for, once inside it, he was guarded from all the other fishes. Further, he beheld wondrous things there. He saw in the fish's belly an open space like unto the halls of a palace, and the two eyes of the fish shining like the sun at noon. Inside was a precious stone which illumined all around, and made visible to him all the wonders of the deep. If this was so, it may be asked, why does it say that he "called out of his affliction" (Ibid. II, 2), seeing that he was so well situated? The answer is, as R. Eleazar has told us, that when God saw Jonah enjoying himself with the sight, He said, "Was it for this that I brought thee in here", and straightway killed the fish. Then all the other fishes came round it and gnawed at its carcase from all sides so that Jonah found himself in dire straits, and it was then that he prayed "from out of the belly of sheol", to wit, of the dead fish. And the Holy One hearkened unto his prayer and brought the fish to life again, and lo! it arose from the sea and came up on to the land before the eyes of all, and it vomited out Jonah, and all saw the power of the Almighty. Now it is written, "And Jonah prayed unto the Lord his God out of the fish's belly"; i.e. to the grade of the Deity to which he was attached. Similarly here: "And the Lord said unto Moses: Why criest thou unto me?" (as much as to say, it is time to address a higher grade, viz. the Ancient of Days). And this is the significance of the words, "Speak unto the children of Israel that they go forward", i.e. from the grade they are at present addressing to a higher one.' BUT LIFT THOU UP THY ROD, AND STRETCH OUT THINE HAND OVER THE SEA, AND DIVIDE IT. This signifies: "Lift up thy rod, on which is engraved the Holy Name; stretch out thine hand with the side bearing this Holy Name, so that the waters, beholding it, may flee before the power that is in its letters. The other side of the rod will be used for other ends." Said R. Eleazar: 'How is it that the rod is termed sometimes "the rod of God" and sometimes "the rod of Moses"?' R. Simeon replied: 'In the book of R. Hamnuna the ancient it is rightly remarked that the two names are equivalent, the purpose of the rod in either case being to stir up the powers of Geburah (Might, or Judgement). "Thine hand" indicates the Left Hand, which is that connected with Geburah. Woe', R. Simeon continued, 'unto those who are deaf to the lessons of the Torah, which it proclaims to them every day. Water originates from the side of Geburah and issues thence. Now, therefore, that God desired to dry up the water, why did He bid Moses use his left hand? The answer is that Moses was bidden to "lift up his staff" to dry the waters, and to "stretch forth his hand" to bring them back on the Egyptians, through the agency of Geburah–the two operations being distinct. What is called here "sea" is later called "deeps" (Ex. xv, 8). This shows that God performed one miracle within another: causing the deeps to congeal in the heart of the sea, so that "the children of Israel went on dry land in the midst of the sea" (xv 8, 19).'

Zohar: Shemoth, Section 2, Page 48b

AND HE TOOK OFF THEIR CHARIOT WHEELS THAT THEY DRAVE THEM HEAVILY. R. Simeon discoursed on the verse: Now I beheld the living creatures (Hayoth), and behold one wheel upon the earth by the living creatures, with his four faces (Ezek. I, 15). 'This verse', he said, 'we can explain as follows. The Holy One reveals His dominion and power in all things, a power which shall never be shaken. He manifested His power in the Patriarchs, and particularly in Jacob. Now Jacob is united with the Tree of Life, over which death has no dominion, since in it all life is contained, emanating from it unto all those who are in perfect union with it. For this reason Jacob did not really die. He died in a physical sense when "he gathered up his feet into the bed" (Gen. XLIX, 33), which bed is mysteriously called "the bed of Solomon" (S.S. III, 7), the bed of the "strange woman" whose "feet go down to death" (Prov. v, 5). But of all the Fathers the Holy One chose Jacob to be the centre of perfection and fulfilment, as it is written: "Jacob whom I have chosen" (Isa. XLI, 8). Mark also this! All the supernal hosts with their cohorts and lightful chariots of celestial speed are joined one to another, grade to grade, the lower to the higher, each to its counterpart; and above them all a holy "Living being" (Hayah) (cf. Ezek. I) is set, and all those myriads of armies move and rest according to its will and direction. This is that Living Creature to which all Hayoth are linked, as each is also to each, all moving and swimming in the sea, concerning which it is written: "This is the great and wide sea, wherein are things creeping innumerable, both small and great beasts" (Ps. CIV, 25). Now, when the wheels of the sea arise all the boats which sail thereon do heave and toss, and air and waters are mightily stirred so that a great storm arises; and the fishes that dwell in the depths of the sea are whirled about by the violence of the tempest, and are buffeted towards the four corners of the earth, some to the east, and some to the west, some to the north, and some to the south; and there they are caught by the nets of fishermen, as they reach the ocean's shallower depths, where the sands of the shore slope down to meet the breakers of that sea. At that time the boats steer no course, either certain or uncharted, but only toss and heave in one place. At last a swift but subtle current arises amid the tumult of the stormy waters, and gradually their strife is stilled and peace descends upon the waves; then the boats steer a straight course for their bourne, and swerve not nor falter; concerning which it is written: "There go the ships; there is that Leviathan whom thou hast made to play therein" (Ibid. v, 26). And all the fishes of the sea gather to their places, and all the creatures rejoice over it and the Hayoth of the supernal fields, as it is written: "And all the beasts of the field play there" (Job XL, 20). Come and see! The likeness of that which is above is that which is below, and what is below is also in the sea, and the likeness of that which is above is that which is in the supernal sea, and what is below is also in the lower sea. As the higher sea has length and width and head and arms and hair and a body, so also the lower sea.' Said R. Simeon: 'How many chariots there are whose wheels run speedily, carrying the framework upon them without delay! Yet here "God made him drive heavily". We interpret these words of the heavenly chariot, which was the guardian angel of Egypt, and which then was rendered imperfect. There were many others dependent on this one, and when it lost its power the lower chariots lost their power, as it is written: "Behold, I will punish the multitude of No, and Pharaoh, and Egypt, with their gods, and their kings; even Pharaoh and all them that trust

in him" (Jer. XLVI, 25). At that time Egypt's Principality was superior to that of all other nations, but as soon as its power was broken, the power of all the other nations was also broken, as it is written: "Then the dukes of Edom were amazed, the mighty men of Moab, trembling took hold upon them..." (Ex. xv, 15). For they were all in Egypt's vassalage, and were linked with Egypt and were dependent on her for their existence, and therefore when they heard the mighty works of the Holy One in Egypt, they lost courage, and fear and trembling fell upon them. Verily, as soon as Egypt's power was broken above, the power of all those who were joined to her was also broken. Therefore it says: "and removed the wheel (ofan) of his chariots, not "wheels", signifying that when this was removed all the chariots dependent on it were unable to proceed. Happy are the Israelites who are linked to the Holy One who chose them to be His portion: "Ye who cleave to the Lord your God, ye are all alive today" (Deut. IV, 4). He brought them forth from the holy seed in order that they might be His portion, and therefore He gave them His Torah, the holy one, the supernal one, which was hidden for two thousand years before the creation of the world. He gave it to them out of love, so that they may cleave to it. Now all the supernal hosts and chariots are linked to one another, grades to grades, lower to higher, wheels within wheels: and a holy Hayah is over them all, and all the multitudinous hosts and powers are under her direction and control; when she moves they move, when she rests they rest. Therefore when the Holy One, blessed be He, desired to bring the hosts of Pharaoh down even unto the depths, He first removed that supernal influence which led and directed all the other powers and principalities. When that guardian was removed the others could not continue on their way, and as soon as their power was removed the guardian of Egypt lost his power as well, and had to pass through the Fiery Stream, and thus the dominion of Egypt came to nought. Therefore the Egyptians said: "Let us flee from the face of Israel" (V. 25).'

Said R. Isaac: 'In that hour when the Israelites drew near to the sea, the Holy One summoned unto Him the great angel appointed over the sea, and said: "When I created this My world I appointed thee over the sea, making at the same time a pact with the waters that they should divide for My children in their time of need. Now their hour of trial is come, and they must cross the sea." Hence it says, "and the sea returned to his strength", the word "leethano" (his strength) suggesting "lithnao" (his compact). And when the Israelites reached the shore and there beheld the waves of the sea heaving and tossing, and lifting up their eyes beheld so close behind them Pharaoh and all his hosts, they were grievously affrighted, therefore crying out unto the Lord. "Also the sea saw and fled" (Ps. CXIV, 3). What saw it, and why did it flee? It saw the coffin of Joseph, the man who "fled and went outside" (Gen. XXXIX, 12). We likewise read that the Egyptians said "Let us flee". Why said they so? Because they suddenly perceived the land of Egypt as it were on fire.'

R. Hiya and R. Yose were once walking in the desert. Said R. Hiya to R. Yose: 'Let me tell you something. When the Holy One, blessed be He, wishes to remove a certain nation from its dominion on earth, He first removes or casts down its celestial representative; but not before another such is appointed in the first one's stead, in order that there should be no break in their service in heaven,

as it is written: "He giveth it (the kingdom) to whomsoever he will" (Dan. IV, 14).' 'Quite so!' rejoined R. Yose. Then he took up the thread of their discourse thus: "It is written: O Lord our God, how glorious is thy name over all the earth, who hast set (asher tenah) thy glory above the heavens (Ps. VIII, 2). The words "asher tenah" (lit. which set) in the second half of the sentence are peculiar; we should expect either asher natata (which Thou hast set), or simply tenah (imperative, set) without the "asher" (which, who). In reality, however, this passage contains the mystery of the deepest "river" which flows out of Paradise; and the "asher" is a reference to "Ehye asher ehye"–"I shall be that which I shall be"; and of this river David prayed that it should manifest itself above the heavens, in order that all the worlds might be united in one perfection and harmony of joy, and the Matrona (the Shekinah) be crowned by the King, and all the strength of the heathen nations be made as nought, and their dominion be ended, and their greatness be cast down, and all their power and glory vanish, that every one who cleaves unto the Shekinah should lift up his head, perceiving the glory of the Lord and dwelling in the peace of His Kingdom.'

Whilst the two were thus conversing, they saw a man approaching, who carried a bundle on his shoulders. On perceiving him R. Hiya exclaimed: 'Let us hurry on, since this man may be a heathen, or an ignoramus, and it would be wrong for us to travel in his company.' R. Yose, however, said: 'Nay, rather let us sit down here and wait till he comes up with us, since he may be a great and wise man.' So they waited by the roadside. After some time the stranger drew near: when he reached them he paused and addressed them, saying: 'The way by which you are going is dangerous, except for a large company together. I know of a different way which would be better for you, and I feel it incumbent on me to tell you so as not to transgress the commandment: "Thou shalt not put a stumbling block before the blind" (Lev. XIX, 14), for you are, as it were, indeed blind in regard to this road and its danger, and may risk your lives.' Said R. Yose: 'Blessed be the Merciful One for causing us to wait here till thou camest by!' So they joined him, and he told them not to speak till they should have left the spot. He then led them by a different road. When they were at a safe distance from the place where they had halted he said: 'Once on a time two priests, one a scholar and the other an ignoramus, passed along that road; and the latter rose against the former and killed him. Since that time anyone who passes the spot where the crime was committed is in danger of his life, for all the brigands and felons that dwell among the mountains do congregate there, and lie in wait for passers by, and fall upon all that venture by that way, and rob and kill them: and the Holy One requires the blood of that priest every day.'

The stranger then began to expound the verse: As yet shall he (Sanherib) remain in Nob that day, he shall shake his hand against the mount of the daughter of Zion (Isa. x, 32). He said: 'This passage has already been interpreted by the masters of the academy, but I shall give you an esoteric interpretation which I have learnt. "That day." Which day? Now it is written: "And Aaron took Elisheba the daughter of Aminadab to wife" (Ex. VI, 23). This, allegorically interpreted, refers to the Community of Israel, in which Aaron is the "friend of the Bride", to prepare the house, to serve her, to lead her to the King, in order that she may unite herself with him. From that time every priest who ministered in the Sanctuary had the same office as Aaron (to unite Israel with God). Achimelech was a great high priest, and all the priests who ministered under him were "friends of the Matrona", and when they were killed by king Saul the Matrona remained alone without her friend, and there was none to minister to her, to prepare her "house", and to lead her to the union with the King. Hence, from that day she passed to the "Left Side", and it has ever been lying in wait to fall upon the world. It killed Saul and his sons, and the kingship passed from his line, and thousands and myriads of Israelites perished. And the guilt of that act hung over Israel until Sennacherib came and stirred it up again at Nob, the city of priests, the city of Achimelech. This is "the day-in Nob", the fateful day, when the Community of Israel lost her bridal "friend", when she remained without the "Right Hand" to join with the "Left", for the priest belongs to the Right Hand. "Gibea of Saul is fled" (Ibid.): Saul is mentioned because he killed the priests and was the cause of the Right Hand being uprooted from the world. So also here: since that priest was killed, no one dares pass this spot, lest he endanger his life.' Said R. Yose to R. Hiya: 'Did I not say, perhaps he is a great man?' Then he applied to him the words, "Blessed be the man that findeth wisdom and the man that getteth understanding" (Prov. III, 13), saying: 'Such are

Zohar: Shemoth, Section 2, Page 50a

we who found thee and acquired from thee a word of wisdom and were inspired with understanding to wait for thee! We are of those for whom the Holy One prepares a present when they are journeying, to wit, the manifestation of the Shekinah, as it says: "The path of the righteous is as the shining light, that shines more and more unto the perfect day" (Ibid. IV, 18).'

So they walked on. Then the man began to give an exposition of the verse: "A psalm of David. The earth is the Lord's and the fulness thereof; the world and they that dwell there" (Ps. XXIV, I, 2). 'Sometimes', he said, 'the title is "of David a psalm", and sometimes "a psalm of David". What is the difference? "Of David a psalm" signifies, as here, that David sang concerning the Community of Israel; but "a psalm of David" signifies that he sang concerning himself. "The earth is the Lord's and the fulness thereof" refers to the Community of Israel and all the multitudes who are attached to her and are called "fulness". "The world and they that dwell therein" refers to the lower world called tebel, which is under the aegis of Judgement, as it is written: "He will judge the world (tebel) in righteousness" (Ibid. IX,9). Whether as individuals, or nations, or the whole world, they are all linked to this sphere of judgement. Behold, Pharaoh imbibed from that source, so that he and his whole people perished. As soon as this judgement was awakened against him his celestial guardian was removed from his dominion, shaken in his power, and all whom he represented on earth fell with him. This is the significance of the words, "and he took off their chariots' wheel", to wit, He annulled the power of their supernal guardian, and the result was that all the Egyptians died in the sea. Why in the sea? Because the supernal "sea" was roused against them and they were delivered into its hands.' Said R. Hiy 1: 'Quite so. And therefore it says: "His chosen captains also were drowned in the sea of Suph" (the Red Sea), for "Suph" suggests "soph", an end, namely the end of the grades of the supernal powers.' Said R. Hiya: 'The expression "that they drave them heavily" (bi-kebeduth), in this verse, is a proof that man receives measure for measure. Pharaoh made his heart "heavy" (kabed), and the Holy One drave him "heavily".' AND THE EGYPTIANS (Mizraim) SAID, LET US FLEE FROM THE FACE OF ISRAEL. Mizraim here signifies the celestial chief who was in charge of Egypt. Said R. Yose: 'This presents a difficulty.For inasmuch as he was already removed from his dominion, how could he pursue the Israelites? But the truth is that in this sentence Mizraim signifies the Egyptians of this world, but in the second half of the verse, "for the Lord fighteth for them against the Egyptians", the term Mizraim refers to their chieftain on high. The verse thus amounts to saying that as their power was broken on high, so was their power broken below, and when the Egyptians perceived the overthrow of their celestial might and power, they said: "Let us flee from the face of Israel". Observe that when the Community of Israel bestirs itself, there is a stirring among all the legions attached to it, both on high and below, Israel rising above them all. For Israel derive their force from the body of the Tree of Life, and it is for this reason that Israel are attached to that Tree more closely than the idolatrous nations. And when they bestir themselves the power of all those who have sway over them is shattered. The celestial chieftain of Egypt oppressed Israel with all manner of hardship, but after he was crushed the lower kings were crushed with him. Hence the words of Scripture, "for the Lord fighteth them in Egypt", alluding to the celestial chieftains.'

Zohar: Shemoth, Section 2, Page 50b

R. Hiya applied to the Community of Israel the verse: "She is like the merchant's ship; she bringeth her food from afar" (Prov. XXXI, 14). 'The Community of Israel', he said, 'indeed brings her salvation from afar, to wit, from a certain grade that rests upon her, through which are transmitted all the streams that flow into the sea. To this grade they return, to be emptied into the sea once more, so that there should be a perpetual flow, as it says, "to the place whence the rivers go, there they return to go" (Eccl. I, 7), once more to the sea. The name of this grade is Zaddik.' R. Isaac said: 'There is still a higher sphere in which is contained and consummated the love-union of the Divine aspects which are never thereafter separated.' R. Judah asked: 'Who is worthy to know of it?' R. Isaac replied: 'He who has a portion in the world to come.'

Said R. Abba: 'How many thousands, how many myriads, of celestial cohorts surround the Holy One and follow in His train! Princes of supernal countenances are there, and beings full of eyes; lords of the sharp weapons, lords of the piercing cry, lords of the heralding trumpet, lords of mercy, lords of judgement; and above them the Lord has appointed the Matrona to minister before Him in the Palace. She for her own bodyguard has armed hosts of sixty different degrees. Holding their swords, they stand around Her. They come and go, entering and departing again on the errands of their Master. Each with his six wings outspread they circle the world in swift and silent flight. Before each of them coals of fire burn. Their garments are woven of flames from a bright and burning fire. A sharp flaming sword also is at the shoulder of each to guard

Zohar: Shemoth, Section 2, Page 51a

Her. Concerning these swords it is written: "The flaming sword which turned every way to keep the way of the tree of life" (Gen. III, 23). Now, what is "the way of the Tree of Life"? This is the great Matrona who is the way to the great and mighty Tree of Life. Concerning this it is written: "Behold the bed which is Solomon's; the three score valiant men are about it, of the valiant of Israel" (S.S. III, 7), namely, the Supernal Israel. "They all hold swords" (Ibid. 8), and when the Matrona moves they all move with her, as it is written: "and the angel of God, which went before the camp of Israel, removed and went behind them" (Ex. XIV, 19). Is, then, the Shekinah called "the angel of the Lord"? Assuredly! For thus said R. Simeon: "The Holy One prepared for Himself a holy Palace, a supernal Palace, a holy City, a supernal City, which is called 'Jerusalem, the holy city'. He who wishes to see the King, must enter through this holy City and thence take his way to the King: 'this is the gate of the Lord into which the righteous shall enter' (Ps. CXVIII, 20)." Every message which the King wishes to send out is sent through the Matrona, and, conversely, every message sent from the lower spheres to the King must first reach the Matrona, and from her it goes to the King. Thus the Matrona is the messenger between the upper regions and the lower. For this reason she is called "the angel (messenger) of God". It may be asked, is it consonant with the dignity of the King that the Matrona should declare war for him and receive petitions to him? The following parable may explain. A king married a noble lady, whose worth he esteemed so highly that in comparison with her he regarded all other women as a mere vulgar herd. "What shall I do to honour her?" he thought. "I will give her full control over the palace and over my whole household!" So he made a proclamation that all the king's business should pass through the hands of the queen. He also handed over to her all the weapons of war, all his military advisers and generals, all his regalia, and indeed all his treasures of every sort, and said: "From now anyone who wishes to speak to me must first make known his suit unto the queen." Similarly, the Holy One, blessed be He, out of His great love for the Community of Israel (represented by the Shekinah) has entrusted everything to her (i.e. the Shekinah), proclaiming all the other nations to be of no account in comparison with her. "There are threescore queens, and fourscore concubines, and virgins without number; but my dove, my undefiled is but one" (S.S. Vl, 8, 9). He resolved that His whole household be given into her keeping, and delivered to her all his armoury, all the lances, all the swords, all the bows, all the arrows, all the spears, all the catapults, all the citadels, and all weapons of warfare, the "sixty valiant men, the valiant of Israel". He said: "From now let My warfare be entrusted to Thee; My weapons, My fighters! From now Thou must guard them all. From now, he who wishes to speak to Me must first make known his concerns to Thee!" Hence "the angel of God went behind them." Why behind them? In order to face all the grades of fighting principalities and powers, all the hosts of celestial representatives of the enemy who had come to fight against Israel. For, as we have learnt, at that hour the greatest prince appointed to represent Egypt in the supernal spheres arrived and with him six hundred chariots, directed by six hundred angelic adversaries of Israel. That prince was Samael.

Zohar: Shemoth, Section 2, Page 51b

When did the Holy One requite him? In the battle of Sisera, when He rooted out all those chariots and delivered them unto the Matrona, as it is written, in the Song of Deborah: "The river Kishon swept them away, that ancient river, the river Kishon" (Jud. v, 21). And in the future all of them shall be delivered up, as it says: "Who is this that cometh from Edom...?" (Isa. LXIII, 1). And this indeed is the significance of the words: "And he went behind them"–that the Shekinah will uproot them all at the end of days.' AND THE PILLAR OF THE CLOUD REMOVED FROM BEFORE THEM AND STOOD BEHIND THEM. What was this pillar of cloud?

R. Yose said that it was the cloud which is always seen with the Shekinah, the cloud into which Moses entered (Ex. XXIV, 18). R. Abba said that it was that which supports the .Zaddik, coming from the side of Grace (Hesed), wherefore it went by day, while there was another cloud which went by night and was called "pillar of fire".' R. Simeon said that the pillar of cloud by day represented Abraham (Mercy), and the pillar of fire by night, Isaac (Severity), both attributes being united in the Shekinah, through the agency of the grade mentioned by R. Abba. 'The word "removed", in this sentence', he said, 'implies that there was a movement from Grace to Severity, for the time had arrived for the Holy One to clothe Himself with judgement.' R. Simeon further said that the "Moon"–the Shekinah–was then in her fulness and perfection, manifesting both attributes and representing in herself seventy-two holy Names according to the threefold order. [Tr. note: Of the letters of the three verses, Ex. XIV, 19-21, containing the mysterious Divine Name of seventy-two letters, and producing, when combined according to certain rules, no less than seventy-two other distinct names.] In virtue of the first order of letters, she clothed herself with the garment of Grace, shining with the resplendence of the light which the Supernal Father caused to shine for her; in virtue of the second she adorned herself with the implements of war, expressing Severity, and sixty "whips" of fire, emanating from the Supernal Mother. The third order of the letters represents Her in garments of purple, the adornment of the Holy Supernal Father, designated "Beauty" (Tiphereth), which is communicated to the Holy Son (i.e. the letter Vau in the Tetragrammaton) in seventy crowns from the side of the Father (Yod) and of the Mother (He,). We have been taught that from the side of Grace there are seventy-two witnesses; from the side of Severity, seventy-two scribes; from the side of Beauty, seventy-two colours of glory. In the transcendent sphere they are all linked one to the other, forming the Holy Name, the mystery of the Divine Chariot. Here (in the three verses, Ex. XIV, 19-21) are inscribed the patriarchs in unison, forming the Holy Name of seventy-two letters [Tr. note: each of these verses in the original contains 72 letters—a fact to which the Cabbalists attached a mystic significance.] of the three verses. And this is the order of their combination: the first verse (19) is to be written straight, for all its initial letters are found in Hesed; the second verse (20) is to be written backward, for all its second letters are found in Geburah; in this way Judgement may be roused, with all those powers that emanate from the left side. The letters of the third verse when written out show forth the colours which crown the Holy King; and all these letters are united in Him, and He is crowned with His diadems in the proper manner, like a king fully crowned. Here is the Holy Name engraved in seventy-two letters, which are crowned with the Fathers who are the supernal Holy Chariot. Should the question arise, why the third group is not to be written partly straightforward and partly backwards, so as to be in touch with both sides (as Tifereth is in touch with both Hesed and Geburah), we must picture a king who combines in himself the balance and harmony of all attributes, and therefore his countenance always shines like the sun, and he is serene because of his wholeness and perfection; but when he judges, he can condemn as well as acquit. A fool, seeing that the king's countenance is bright, thinks that there is nothing to be afraid of; but a wise man says to himself, "although the king's countenance shines, it is because he is perfect and combines benevolence with justice, and in that brightness judgement

Zohar: Shemoth, Section 2, Page 52a

is hidden, and therefore I must be careful". The Holy One is such a king. R. Judah found this idea expressed in the words: "I, the Lord, have not changed" (Mal. III, 6), meaning, "in Me all the attributes are harmoniously combined, the two aspects of mercy and severity are one in Me."

Said R. Simeon: 'Eleazar my son, observe this. When the Holy Ancient illumines the King, He crowns Him with supernal holy crowns. When these reach Him the Fathers are crowned, and there is completeness. Then the Matrona, participating in this celestial procession, is crowned by them all and is endowed with the power issuing from all of them.'

Said R. Isaac: 'When the Israelites encamped by the sea they saw many hosts,

Zohar: Shemoth, Section 2, Page 52b

many armies, many camps, above and below, all united against Israel, and in their distress they prayed unto the Lord. The sea was stormy, its waves roared, behind them were all those hosts, all those armies of the Egyptians, and above them were all those celestial foes; and they began to cry to God. Then "the Lord said unto Moses: Why criest thou unto me?" Then the Most Holy Ancient One appeared, and Mercy was manifested in all the upper worlds and all the lights were lit.' R. Isaac said: 'When the lights were lit the Sea began to exercise supreme judgements, and the upper and lower beings and powers were delivered unto its hands: hence the expression, "as difficult as the dividing of the Red Sea", because this depended on the Holy Ancient One.' Said R. Simeon: 'There is a certain hind on earth for which the Holy One, blessed be He, does many things: when she cries He hearkens to her afflictions and delivers her. When the world is in need of mercy, of water, she cries aloud and the Holy One answers her prayer. This is signified by the verse: "As the hind panteth after the water brooks, so panteth my soul after thee, O God" (Ps. XLII, 2). When she is about to bear a child and is in difficulty, she puts her head between her knees, and cries bitterly, and the Holy One sends a serpent which stings the place, and straightway deliverance comes to her.' R. Simeon, however, added: 'In this matter, "thou must not ask nor tempt the Lord".' THUS THE LORD SAVED ISRAEL... AND ISRAEL SAW THE EGYPTIAN(S) DEAD. God showed them Egypt's celestial chieftain passing through the fiery stream, which was at the shore of the Ocean. "Dead" means that he was deprived of his power. AND ISRAEL SAW THE GREAT HAND. R. Hiya said: 'Here was the Supernal Hand completed with all its fingers, and the Left Hand was included–as in its perfect manifestation it must ever be–in the five fingers of the Right Hand. For we have been taught that all is included in this Right Hand and all depends upon it, as it is written, "Thy right hand, O Lord, is become glorious in power; thy right hand, O Lord, hath dashed in pieces the enemy" (Ibid. xv, 6).' R. Isaac said: 'No one ever hardened his heart against the Lord to the same degree as Pharaoh.' Said R. Yose: 'What of Sihon and Og? Were they not equally hardened?' R. Isaac answered, that whereas they hardened their hearts against Israel, Pharaoh turned against the Lord Himself, although every day he witnessed His wonderful works. R.Judah said in the name of R. Isaac that Pharaoh was himself far wiser than all his sorcerers, yet by all the craft of his magic he could not divine there was a possibility of redemption for Israel: for he had knowledge of all the supernal sources inimical to the Israelites, but knew not that there was still another bond, the bond of Faith, which dominates all, and therefore he hardened his heart. According to R. Abba, it was the Holy Name which hardened Pharaoh's heart, for when Moses said to him: "Thus said Tetragrammaton,' this very Name hardened his heart: "And Tetragrammaton hardened the heart of Pharaoh", for with all his wisdom he was not aware that this Name has power on earth, and said: "Who is Tetragrammaton?" R. Yose remarked that later he did say: "I have sinned to Tetragrammaton, Tetragrammaton is the righteous" (Ex. IX, 27). R. Hiya said: 'Job was thinking of Pharaoh when he said, "It is all one thing, therefore I said: He destroyeth the perfect and the wicked" (Job IX, 22). The words "it is all one thing" have an esoteric meaning. They refer to a certain Crown also referred to in the verse, "My love, my undefiled is but one" (VI, 9), and when God judges by means of this Crown, then "He destroyeth the perfect and the wicked",

Zohar: Shemoth, Section 2, page 53a

for the righteous are then punished for the guilt of the wicked, as it is written: "He said to the angel that destroyed the people, It is enough" (2 Sam. XXIV, 16). Job, when he said these words, was thinking of his own fate in being made to suffer with the Egyptians, but he did not finish his observation.' Said R. Hiya: 'When Job saw how he suffered, he said: "If this is so, then God makes no distinction between wicked and righteous. Pharaoh hardened his heart, and said, 'Who is Tetragrammaton, whose voice I should hear?', and he deserved punishment; but I have not done anything of the kind, why should I have such a fate?" For it was of him that it is written, "He that feared the word of the Lord among the servants of Pharaoh." (Ex. IX, 22).' AND ISRAEL SAW THE GREAT HAND... AND THE PEOPLE FEARED THE LORD AND BELIEVED IN THE LORD AND MOSES HIS SERVANT. First they are called "Israel" and then "people"; why? R. Judah said: 'Israel here refers to the patriarch Jacob, who, having come with his children to Egypt, and having suffered the bitterness of exile with them, now actually saw, although he was dead, the vengeance wrought by the Holy One, blessed be He. The Lord said unto him: "Arise and behold what I am doing for thy children's sake, how I am bringing them out of the clutches of a mighty people." This tallies with what R. Jesse said, that when the Israelites went into exile to Egypt, fear and trembling came over Jacob, so that God had to say to him: "Fear not to go down to Egypt,' (Gen. XLVI, 3). Even then he was still afraid lest they might be exterminated there, so God reassured him by telling him that He Himself would go down with him to Egypt. Then he expressed his fear that he would not be buried with his fathers, nor witness the redemption of his children and the mighty works of the Lord. Then it was that the Holy One promised him "I will also surely bring thee up again", the emphatic expression indicating that he would be first brought up to be buried with his fathers and then again to witness Israel's redemption. R. Isaac found an added indication of this in the words: "Because he loved thy fathers... he brought thee out in his sight with his mighty power out of Egypt" (Deut. IV, 37); "in his sight" referring to Jacob. According to R. Hezekiah, however, "in his sight" (lit. countenance) refers to Abraham, of whom it says that he fell "on his countenance" when the Lord announced to him the birth of a son (Gen. XVII, 17), because it was hard for him to believe that a man of his age could be father to a newborn son, and the Holy One had to reassure him, revealing to him that he was destined to be the father of a great nation; and therefore, when the children of Israel went out from Egypt in their myriads, He let Abraham view their progress. R. Abba said that all the patriarchs were witnesses of the redemption. R. Eleazar finds this indicated in the above verse: "in his sight" referring to Jacob; "with his power" to Isaac; and "great" indicating Abraham. R. Simeon added that it is always for the sake of the patriarchs that the Lord redeems Israel, as it is written: "And I shall remember my covenant with Jacob, also my covenant with Isaac, and also my covenant with Abraham, and the land I shall remember" (Lev. XXVI, 42); the "land" representing King David, who completes a Chariot with the Patriarchs.

Zohar: Shemoth, Section 2, Page 53b

AND ISRAEL SAW THE GREAT HAND WHICH THE LORDS DID UPON THE EGYPTIANS. They had seen how God had smitten the Egyptians even before this; but only now did they behold the Hand of full five fingers, which hand is called "great" because it includes other "five fingers", namely those of the Left Hand, as we have already made clear, and every "finger" symbolizes many Divine powers and signs, by means of which all the grades of inimical celestial powers were brought to nought; and it is of this that the Israelites had a revelation at that moment by the sea shore. AND THEY BELIEVED IN THE LORD. Was it only then that they believed? Do we not read that "the people believed" as soon as it was proclaimed to them that the Lord intended to bring them out from Egypt (Ex. IV, 31)? Had they not seen before many mighty works of the Holy One in Egypt itself? Yes, but this statement concerning their belief refers particularly to what Moses told them: "Fear not, stand still and see the salvation of the Lord" (v. 13). 'How is it', asked R. Jesse, 'that after Moses had said to the people, "for the Egyptians whom ye have seen today, ye shall see them again no more forever" (Ibid.), we are now told that "Israel saw the Egyptians dead upon the sea shore" (v. 30)?' R. Yose, in answer, pointed out that after all they did not see them alive. This reply did not satisfy R. Jesse, nor R. Abba, who explained the verse thus: 'There is, according to our teaching, a world ('olam) above [Tr. note: Binah.] and a world below. [Tr. note: Malkuth] Now from the world above begins the kindling of lights which is afterwards completed in the world below, this world subsuming in itself all (the emanations). From this lower world issue punishments to mankind, and through it also God did wonders and miracles for Israel. And when this world was aroused to perform wonders, the Egyptians were through it cast into the sea at the same time that deliverance was wrought for Israel. Hence the words, "ye shall see them again no more forever" ('ad 'olam, lit. until a world), meaning, "ye shall not see them until that world ('olam) will be roused, and they will be delivered to judgement"; and as soon as that took place "Israel saw the Egyptians dead upon the sea shore... and they believed in the Lord and Moses His servant".' THEN SANG MOSES. R. Judah applied to Moses the words: "Before I formed thee in the belly I knew thee, and before thou camest forth out of the womb I sanctified thee, and I ordained thee a prophet unto the nations" (Jer. I, 5). 'Happy is the lot of Israel,' he said, 'that the Holy One, blessed be He, loved them more than any other nation, and out of the abundance of His love appointed to them a prophet of truth and a faithful shepherd, within whom He awakened the holy spirit more than in any other faithful prophet, communicating to him a part of His very self. Jacob dedicated the tribe of Levi to the Holy One, blessed be He, and as Levi was His in a special sense, He took him and crowned him with many crowns, and anointed him with the oil of the holy spirit from above, so that the holy spirit should issue forth to the world through him as from the representative of the holy faith. When the hour arrived at which Moses the faithful shepherd and prophet was to descend into this world, God brought forth a holy spirit from the depths of a sapphire stone in which it was hidden, and crowned it with crowns, and illumined it with two hundred and forty-eight lights, and stationed it before Him and gave over unto its charge the whole of His own Household, with the one hundred and seventy-three keys. Then He crowned it yet again with five diadems, each of which ascended and illumined a thousand worlds of lights and lamps stored in the secret treasures of the holy and highest King. Then the Holy One led it through all the lightful splendour of the Garden of Eden, and brought it to His Palace through all the ranks of the celestial legions. These were greatly amazed, and cried aloud: "Turn aside! For the Holy One has roused a Spirit to rule and to shake the worlds." One voice murmured: "Who is he, this stranger, in whose hands are all the keys?"

Zohar: Shemoth, Section 2, Page 54a

But another rebuked the first, and proclaimed: "Receive him in your midst! For on a day, and that right soon, he will descend to dwell among men, and the Torah, the most hidden treasure, shall be delivered into his hands to shake worlds both above and below." Then all trembled and followed Moses, saying: "Thou hast caused a man to ride over our heads; we went through fire and through water" (Ps. LXVI, 12). The letter Mim of the name of MoSHE drew nigh and crowned itself with its crown, and then crowned Moses with three hundred and twenty-five crowns, delivering also its keys into his hand. The letter Shin of the three Patriarchs crowned him with three holy crowns, and delivered into his keeping all the keys of the King and appointed him the faithful steward of the Household. The letter He drew nigh and crowned him with its crown. Then the spirit descended in one of the boats that sail on the great Sea, and received him in order to train him for sovereignty, and gave him, Moses, weapons with which to vanquish and punish Pharaoh and his whole land. And when he came down to earth in the seed of Levi, four hundred and twenty-five lights glittered before the face of the King, and four hundred and twenty-five esoteric formations of letters, expressing Divine mysteries, accompanied the spirit to its place. When he came forth into the world, the letter He of the Holy Name shone from his face, and the house wherein he dwelt was filled with his radiance. At that hour the Holy One proclaimed: "Before I had formed thee in the belly I knew thee; and before thou camest forth out of the womb I sanctified thee, and I made thee a prophet unto the nations." '

Said R. Isaac: 'At the moment when the Holy One slew the great chieftain of the Egyptians, and Moses and the children of Israel saw him, they began to sing.' THEN SANG MOSES AND THE CHILDREN OF ISRAEL THIS SONG UNTO THE LORD. Said R. Abba:

I have examined all the songs which Israel sang unto the Holy One, and I find that all of them began with "then" (az) (Cf Jos. x, 12; I Kings VIII, 12; Num. XXI, 17.) The reason for this is that all the wonders, and all the mighty deeds which were done to Israel when the light of the Holy Ancient One shone in His crowns, are engraved in the letters Aleph and Zain [Tr. note: Aleph symbolizes the first Sephirah, and Zain the seventh (after the first three), and when the light of the Crown - the first Sephirah - illumines the seventh, namely Malkuth-Kingdom, the power of God is manifested.]. Then there is song, the song of all sides. "Yashir" (lit. will sing): the tense suggests that this song fitted that occasion and will also fit the future Redemption, when it will again be sung by Israel. The expression "Moses and Israel" proves that the righteous of the past ages, although they have entered into the highest regions and are united with the "Bundle of life", will all rise again in bodily form and behold the signs and mighty works which the Holy One shall show to Israel, and sing this hymn.' R. Simeon established this fact by the following verse: "And it shall come to pass in that day that the Lord shall set his hand again the second time to recover the rest of his people" (Isa. XI, 11). '"The rest"', he said, 'are "the remnant", the righteous, like Eldad and Medad, who "remained" in the camp (Num. XI, 26), the righteous of whom it has been said that the world is sustained by them, who make themselves mere "remainders", as it were. It is they who will be brought to life again at the future Redemption. And why? Are they not already bound up with the "Bundle of life"? Why bring them down to earth again? Let the experience of the past give the answer. It has pleased the Holy One, in former time, to send down to earth those spirits and souls who belonged to the highest supernal grade. Should He not, then, let the spirits of the righteous men come down again in the future when He will make the crooked straight (i.e. redeem the world)? For, indeed, "there is not a righteous man upon earth that doeth good and sinneth not" (Eccl. VII, 20). And even the sinless ones who only died because of the "counsel of the Serpent" [Tr. note: T. B. Sabb. 55b, Benjamin, Amram, Jishai, and Kaleb, David's son, were sinless and died not for their own sins, but because of the "serpent's counsel", i.e. of "original sin"] will arise and be counsellors to the Messiah. "Moses and the children of Israel will sing this song." The same is implied in the words: "As in the days of thy going out of the land of Egypt will I show unto him marvellous things" (Micah VII, 15), where the "him" refers to Moses. Also: "I will show him the salvation of God" (Ps. L,24); "I will show him my salvation" (Ibid. XCI, 16).

Zohar: Shemoth, Section 2, page 54b

Moses and the children of Israel will then sing "this song unto the Lord": the song of the Matrona to the Holy One, blessed be He. We have been taught that every one who sings this hymn daily with true devotion will be worthy to sing it at the Redemption that is to be, for it refers both to the past world and to the future world; it contains confirmations of faith and mysteries relating to the days of the Messiah. The Shekinah will sing this song to the Lord, because the King will receive Her with a radiant countenance. R. Yose said that the Shekinah will praise the Lord for all the concentration of light and holiness which the Holy King shall direct towards her. Said R. Judah: 'If this is the song of the Shekinah, why does it say that Moses and the children of Israel sang it? Blessed were they that they knew how to praise Him for all the power and might which the Shekinah receives and shall receive from Him, the Holy King!' According to R. Abba, the singing is to be directed, not to any of the emanations of the Deity, but to the Holy King in His very essence, as it says, concerning the song of Moses and the children of Israel, that they sang "to the Lord". R. Yose said that the words "this song to the Lord" refer to the "river that issues forth from Eden" (Gen. II, 10), from which all the abundance of oil issues to kindle the lights; whereas the words, "I will sing unto the Lord" (Ibid.) refer to the Supernal Holy King. AND SPAKE, SAYING.: this repetition denotes that it is to be sung in all generations, in order that it should never be forgotten, for he who is worthy to sing this song in this world shall be worthy to sing it in the world to come, and to declare praises with it in the days of the Messiah, when the Community of Israel will rejoice in the Holy One. "Saying" means saying at the time of the Exodus, saying when Israel was in the Holy Land, saying in exile, saying when Israel will be redeemed, saying in the world to come. I WILL SING UNTO THE LORD. As stated above, they spoke in the name of the Shekinah, hence the singular. "To the Lord"—to the Holy King. For highly exalted is He (gaoh gaah): He ascends to be crowned with His crowns in order to dispense blessings, and perform wonderful works, and to be exalted in and through all; exalted in this world, exalted likewise in the world to come; exalted in order that He may crown Himself with His crowns and be glorified in perfect joy. THE HORSE AND HIS RIDER HATH HE THROWN INTO THE SEA. The dominion below and the dominion above, which are bound up the one with the other, have been delivered to that great "Sea" and that great sovereignty for punishment, as we have been taught that the Holy One does not exercise judgement below until He has done so above on the celestial representative of the particular nation, as it says: "The Lord shall punish the host of the high ones in the height (heaven) and the kings of the earth upon the earth" (Isa. XXIV, 21). R. Judah said: 'On thatnight extreme severity was roused, for the Matrona asked that all the hosts below and all the powers above should be delivered unto Her. And so they were.' R. Hiya discoursed on the verse: Thou hast beset me behind and before, and hast laid thine hand upon me (Ps. CXXXIX, 5). He said: 'How greatly is it incumbent on the children of men to glorify the Holy One, blessed be He! For when He created the world

Zohar: Shemoth, Section 2, page 55a

He looked on man and designed to make him to rule over all earthly things. He was of dual form and resembled both celestial and earthly beings. The Lord sent him down in splendour, so that when the lesser creatures beheld the glory of his state they fell down before him in awe, as it says: "And the fear of you and the dread of you shall be upon every beast of the earth and upon every fowl of the earth" (Gen. IX, 2). The Holy One brought him into the garden of His own planting, so that he might guard it and have endless joy and delight therein. A canopy of precious stones the Holy One also devised and fashioned to enfold man with glory: and the supernal angels rejoiced in his presence. Then the Lord gave him the commandment concerning the one tree: and, alas! man failed in his obedience and was not steadfast in the commandment of his Master. We find in the book of Enoch that after the Holy One, blessed be He, had transported Enoch to the supernal regions and shown him all the treasures of the King, both the celestial and the terrestrial, He permitted him to behold the Tree of Life and that Tree of which Adam was warned, and showed him the place where Adam had dwelt in the Garden of Eden, and Enoch perceived that if Adam had been obedient he would have so dwelt forever, having eternal life and perpetual joy in the glory of the Garden. But because he broke the commandment of his Lord, he was punished.' R. Isaac said: 'Adam was created as a double personality (male and female), as previously explained. "And he took one of his ribs..." (Gen. II, 21): He sawed him in two, and thus two persons were formed, one from the east and one from the west, as it says: "Thou hast beset me behind and before", i.e. from the west and from the east.' Said R. Hiya: 'What did the Holy One do? He formed the female, perfected her beauty exceedingly, and brought her to Adam, as it is written: "And the Lord God formed the side (zela', cf. Ex. XXVI, 20) which he had taken from man into a woman" (Ibid. 22).' R. Judah said: 'The Holy One gave to Adam a supernal soul and endowed it with wisdom and understanding that he might know all things. From which place did He take the soul? 'From the place whence the other holy souls emanate.' Thus R. Isaac. Said R. Judah: 'We learn this from the verse: "Let the earth bring forth the living soul after its kind" (Gen. II, 24). "The earth" signifies the place where the Sanctuary stood, and "living soul" refers to the soul of the first man.' R. Hiya said: 'Adam knew more of the supernal wisdom than the angels above; he was able to penetrate into all things and to be in closer union with his Master than any of the other beings in the universe. But when he sinned, all the springs of wisdom were closed to him: "And the Lord God sent him forth from the garden of Eden to till the ground" (Ibid III, 24).' Said R. Abba: 'The first man consisted of male and female, for it says: "Let us make man in our image after our likeness" (Ibid. I, 26), which indicates that male and female were originally created as one and separated afterwards. When it says, "the ground from whence he was taken" (Ibid.), the "ground" represents the feminine principle, and the Holy One associated with this to create man.' MY STRENGTH AND SONG IS KAH. R. Yose said: The Yod and the He in the Divine Name are mingled, and one is contained in the other and they are never separated, being forever united in love, being the source whence emanate all those streams and springs of blessing and satisfaction to the universe. The waters of these springs never "deceive" (Isa. LVIII, 11). Hence: "and He became my salvation", since for this purpose and unto this end the Holy King reveals His power below, and the Right Hand is moved to perform marvellous deeds.' THIS IS MY GOD AND I WILL MAKE HIM A HABITATION; THE GOD OF MY FATHER, AND I WILL EXALT HIM. "This is my God" refers to the Zaddik, from whom blessings emanate on the married state; "and I will make him a habitation" in the place where love is found, namely in the Sanctuary. "The God of my father, and I will exalt him" was said by Moses (the Levite) in regard to the supernal sphere whence the Levites derive, so that in this way there should be symmetry and perfection in that place. R. Isaac said that "and he became my salvation" refers to the Holy King, as in Isa. XII, 2.

Zohar: Shemoth, Section 2, page 55b

R. Hezekiah interpreted the verse: "A friend loveth at all times, and a brother is born for adversity" (Prov. XVII, 17), as follows. '"A friend" is the Holy One, of whom it is written, "Thine own friend and thy father's friend, forsake not" (Ibid. XXVII, 10). The Israelites are "brethren and friends" of the Holy One, and therefore when their enemies afflict them, God says, "For my brethren and friends' sake I will say, Peace be within thee" (Ps. CXXII, 9). He is a brother to meet the "adversity that is born".' Rabbi Judah refers the word "born" to the Holy One, for when one of His friends suffers tribulation through his enemies, the Holy King is roused in His strength to avenge him: His power is "born", that is, manifested. R. Yose said: 'How great should be man's love for the Holy One! Verily, love is the only true worship, and he who worships God in love is called "beloved" by Him.' There is an apparent contradiction in the two verses: "Thine own friend and thy father's friend forsake not", and "Withdraw thy foot from thy friend's house" (Ibid. xxv, 17). The members of the Fellowship have, however, explained it by applying the verses to different kinds of sacrifice. One should be diligent in sacrificing burnt-offerings and peace-offerings, but in regard to sin-offerings it is better to sin not, and so "withdraw thy foot from thy Friend's house", the Temple. Indeed, "thou must not forsake thy Friend", thou must worship Him, cleave to Him, keep His commandments, but "withdraw thy foot from thy evil impulse that he should not become thy master, withdraw it from thy house, namely from the holy soul which thy Friend has put into thee". The true worship of the Holy One, blessed be He, consists in loving Him above all and in all, as it is written: "Thou shalt love the Lord thy God" (Deut. VI, 5).

All the Israelites beheld at the sea what even the prophet Ezekiel was not privileged to see, and even the embryos in their mothers' wombs beheld the wonderful works of the Holy One, and sang praises to Him, saying: "This is my God and I extol Him; the God of my father and I exalt Him", namely the God of father Abraham. Said R. Yose: 'Does the God of Abraham need our exaltation? Is He not already exalted high above our comprehension?' R. Jesse replied: 'Yet man can and must exalt Him in the sense of uniting in his mind all the attributes in the Holy Name, for this is the supremest expression of worship.'

R. Judah sat one day at the feet of R. Simeon, and he began to expound the following verse: The voice of thy watchmen, they lifted up their voices, they shall sing altogether... when the Lord shall return to Zion (Isa. LII, 8). 'These "watchmen"', he said, 'are those who "watch" for the time when the Holy One will build His House once again. The use of the past tense "lifted", where we should rather have expected the future "shall lift", conveys the lesson that he who has lifted up his voice in weeping and lamentation over the destruction of the Temple shall be worthy to be numbered among those of whom it says "they shall sing altogether", and to enjoy the privilege of beholding the Holy One when He shall inhabit His House once more. The words "when the Lord returns (to) Zion" are to be understood as meaning "when the Lord brings back Zion". For when the earthly Jerusalem was destroyed, and the Community of Israel was scattered over the face of the earth, the Holy King drew Zion [Tr. note: According to the commentators, in this place Zion=Yesod.] up to Himself and stretched it out before Him, because the Community of Israel was banished. When, however, the Community of Israel shall be restored, the Holy King will restore Zion to its place, to unite itself with her in perfect bliss; and the children of Israel will sing: "He is my God, and I have prepared for Him an habitation." Concerning this it is written: "This is the Lord, we have waited for him, let us be glad and rejoice in his salvation" (Isa. xxv, 9) - meaning, literally, "in His own salvation". THE LORD IS A MAN OF WAR, THE LORD IS HIS NAME. R. Abba referred in connection with this verse to the words: "Therefore it is said in the book of the wars of Tetragrammaton: 'Vaheb in Supha, and in the brooks of Arnon'" (Num. XXI, 14). He said: 'How assiduously should one ponder on each word of the Torah, for there is not a single word in it which does not contain allusions to the Supernal Holy Name, not a word which does not contain many mysteries, many aspects, many roots, many branches.

Zohar: Shemoth, Section 2, page 56a

Where now is this "book of the wars of the Lord"? What is meant is, of course, the Torah, for, as the members of the Fellowship have pointed out, he who is engaged in the battle of the Torah, struggling to penetrate into her mysteries, will wrest from his struggles an abundance of peace. All other wars involve strife and destruction, but the war of the Torah is one of peace and love: "Vaheb in Supha" may be read "ahabah be-sophah", "love is in her end", for there is no love nor peace like this. The word "book" is used, and not "torah" as we might expect, for an esoteric reason, viz. that there is a divine sphere called "Book", as it says: "Seek ye out of the book of the Lord and read" (Isa. XXXIV, 16), on which all the mighty works of the Lord depend and from which they emanate. With this, God made war against a certain sphere at the end (soph) of the grades called Vaheb. God also fought against the "brooks", the subsidiary principalities attached to it. He waged war from the region called "Arnon", which is the sphere of the supernal marital union [Tr. note: Hokmah and Binah.] which is never dissolved. Therein it is rooted and spreads its branches to make war on every side and to manifest great and glorious power. When the mighty works of the Lord are roused and His battles begin to be waged, how many celestial warriors are stirred up to do martial deeds on every side! Then swords and spears are whetted, and mighty deeds begin. The sea grows stormy and the waves thereof rise mightily, and the boats toss on the heaving waters. Then the fray commences with catapults, spears, swords, and arrows, and the Lord takes command of His hosts to conduct the battle. Woe unto those against whom the Holy One declares war! "The Lord is a man of war." From the letters of this phrase lines of battle are formed against the wicked, the enemies of the Lord. These letters are known to the initiated, as has been explained elsewhere. In time to come the Holy One, blessed be He, will conduct a stupendous warfare against the heathen nations, to the glory of His Name: "Then shall the Lord go forth and fight against those nations" (Zech. XIV, 3); "Thus will I magnify myself and I will be known in the eyes of many nations"

(Ezek. XXVIII, 23).' PHARAOH'S CHARIOTS AND HIS MIGHT HE CAST INTO THE SEA AND THE CHOSEN ONES OF HIS KNIGHTS WERE DROWNED IN THE RED SEA. R. Judah said: When the Israelites were about to cross the sea, the Holy One said to the angel who is appointed over the sea: "Divide thy waters!" "Why?" said the angel. "So that My children may pass through." "Do they really deserve this redemption?" said the angel. "Wherein lies the difference between them and the Egyptians?" Said the Holy One: "I made this condition with the sea when I created the world!" Thereupon He exerted His power and the waters were piled up, wherefore it is written: "The waters saw thee, O God, the waters saw thee, they were afraid; the depths also were troubled" (Ps. LXXVII, 17). Then He said to the angel: "Exterminate all those hosts", and it then covered them, as it says, "the chariots of Pharaoh and his host he cast into the sea".'

Said R. Eleazar: 'Behold, how many chariots, how many hosts, the Holy One has formed above! How many camps, how many divisions! And all of them are

Zohar: Shemoth, Section 2, page 56b

linked to one another, all are chariots one to another, manifold grades, diverse and yet united! From the left side the chariots of the unholy principalities rise up. They also are linked one with the other, grade to grade, the greatest of them being, as we have already pointed out, "the firstborn of Pharaoh", whom the Holy One killed. All of these unholy powers are delivered unto the judgement of the Kingdom, the which is called "the great sea", in order that they may be uprooted each in his own grade, and be utterly cast down, and when they are broken above, all their counterparts below are also broken and lost in the "lower sea". As to the "captains" (shalishim) who were drowned in the Red Sea, it has already been made clear that all these grades consist of three (shalosh) attributes each (two and one, the triad, corresponding to the holy triad above). They were all delivered unto Her (the Shekinah's) hand, that their power might be broken. All the ten punishments which the Holy One brought on Egypt were achieved by the power of one "hand", for the "left hand" is included in the right, the ten fingers forming one entity in correspondence to the Ten expressions by which the Holy One is designated. Then came a punishment which was equal to all the rest, that of the sea: "The last one was the hardest" (Isa. VIII, 23). And in the future the Holy One will deal similarly with all the hosts, princes and chieftains of Edom (Rome), as it is written: "Who is he who cometh from Edom, with dyed garments from Bozrah? I that speak in righteousness, mighty to save" (Isa. LXIII, 1).' PHARAOH'S CHARIOTS AND MIGHT HE CAST INTO THE SEA. R. Isaac referred to the verse: "When he uttereth his voice, there is a multitude of waters in the heavens" (Jer. X, 13), and said: 'According to tradition, the Holy One created seven heavens, and in each heaven stars and planets are fixed. Arabot is above them all. The length of each heaven is such that it would take two hundred years to traverse, and the distance between each heaven and the next would take five hundred years to traverse. As for Arabot, one would need one thousand five hundred years to cover its whole length, and the selfsame number for traversing its breadth. All the heavens are lighted from the radiance of Arabot. Above Arabot is the heaven of the Hayoth, and above this latter sphere another heaven, brighter than all, as it is written: "And the likeness of the firmament upon the heads of the Hayoth" (Ezek. I, 22). And below there are many chariots at the right hand and at the left, of many grades, each with its own name. And beneath them are others, smaller and yet more varied, which are the smallest ranks of this celestial but unholy order; as it is written: "The sea is great... small beasts and great are there" (Ps. CIV, 25), as we have affirmed, that on the left side below there is a ruler, the "other side", attached to those above, but they are crushed by the great holy power, according to our interpretation of the words, "Pharaoh's chariots and his might he cast into the sea".' THY RIGHT HAND, O LORD, GLORIFIED IN POWER. R. Simeon said: 'In the hour when the morning breaks, the Hind (Shekinah) rises and starts from her place in order to enter the two hundred palaces of the King. When a man studies

Zohar: Shemoth, Section 2, page 57a

the Torah in solitude at midnight, at the hour when the north wind springs up and the Hind desires to be astir, he is taken with her into supernal realms, to appear before the King. When dawn brightens and he recites his prayers, and unifies the Holy Name in manner due, he is encircled with a thread of grace; he looks into the firmament, and a light of holy knowledge rests upon him. As the man is thus adorned and shrouded with light all things tremble before him, for he is called the son of the Holy One, the son of the King's Palace. Concerning him it is written, "The Lord is nigh to all who call upon him, to all that call upon him in truth" (Ps. CXLV, 18). The words "in truth" have the same significance as in the verse, "Thou wilt give truth to Jacob" (Micah VII, 20), "truth" here meaning the full knowledge which enables the worshipper perfectly to unite the letters of the Holy Name in prayer, which is indeed the true service of the Holy Name. He who knows how to unify thus the Holy Name establishes the one, the peculiar people in the world, as it is written: "And who is like thy people Israel, one people on earth?" (2 Sam. VIII, 23). Therefore it has been taught that a priest who knows not how to unify thus the Holy Name cannot perform proper service, for on the achievement of that unity hangs both celestial and terrestrial worship. The priest must, therefore, strive to concentrate heart and mind on the attainment of this unification, so that those above and those below may be blessed. And if a man comes to unify the Holy Name, but without proper concentration of mind and devotion of heart, to the end that the supernal and terrestrial hosts should be blessed thereby, then his prayer is rejected and all beings denounce him, and he is numbered with those of whom the

Holy One said, "When ye come to see (reading lir'oth instead of leraoth) my countenance (panim, lit. countenances), who hath required this from your hand, to tread my courts?" All the "countenances" of the King are hidden in the depths of darkness, but for those who know how perfectly to unite the Holy Name, all the walls of darkness are burst asunder, and the diverse "countenances" of the King are made manifest, and shine upon all, bringing blessing to heavenly and earthly beings. He who comes to unify the Holy Name must do so from the side of zoth (lit. "this", a name for the Shekinah), as it is written, "with this (be-zoth) shall Aaron come into the sanctuary" (Lev. XVI, 3), in order that the Zaddik and Righteousness may be perfectly united, and through this union all things may be blessed. But if he attempts to unify the Holy Name without bringing himself into the fitting frame of mind, if he come not in fear and love, then God says unto him: "Who hath required this (zoth) of your hand to tread my courts?" (Ibid.). No blessing appertains to such prayer; nay, rather, he who prays in such a fashion merely invokes upon himself and upon all things the attribute of Judgement. Now all light, all blessing, all joy, emanates from the "Right Hand" of the Holy One, blessed be He. Yet at the same time the "Left Hand" participates in the activities of the Right, just as in a human being, for though the right is the leader, yet when it is active the left becomes active likewise. When a man raises up his hand in prayer, his purpose is to bless God. But with God it is the reverse: when He raises up His right hand, then woe unto those below, yea, woe and tribulation; for then all blessing and support is removed from them. We learn this from the verse: "Thou stretchedst out thy right hand, the earth swallowed them" (Ex. xv, 12), meaning, that so soon as God raised His right hand they perished. (The Targum also renders, "Thou liftedst up Thy right hand".) When the Right Hand is in its place, the Left Hand is under its dominance, therefore stern justice can have no power among men. But if the Right Hand is lifted up, the Left remains alone, and stirs up mighty judgement in the world.' Each time that R. Simeon came to the words, "He hath drawn back his right hand,' (Lam. II, 3), he used to weep, interpreting them to mean that the Lord permitted the Left Hand to be powerful and to have sole dominion over the worlds, while the Right Hand remained in another place, far off. R. Simeon interpreted

Zohar: Shemoth, Section 2, page 57b

the words "hazaddik abad" (lit. "the righteous comes to grief", is lost, perishes (Isa. LVII, 1), in the sense that when the Temple was destroyed, of all the aspects of the King it was the one that is known as "Righteous" (Zaddik) that "lost", in a twofold sense. He lost because blessings no longer abode with Him as before; and He also lost because His spouse, the Community of Israel, was parted from Him. Thus the Righteous "lost" more than all. Moreover, concerning the time to be, which is the time of the Messiah, it is written: "Rejoice greatly, O daughter of Zion, shout, O daughter of Jerusalem, behold thy king cometh unto thee, he is righteous and saving himself (nosha')" (Zech. IX, 9). It does not say "moshia"'-"saving" or "a saviour", but "nosha'"-"being saved", literally. THY RIGHT HAND, O LORD, GLORIFIED IN POWER, THY RIGHT HAND DASHES IN PIECES THE ENEMY. The form "ne'ddari" (glorified) instead of "ne'ddar" suggests a plural, referring as it does to the joining of the Left Hand with the Right. Said R. Simeon: 'It is as we have explained. Just as man was divided physically, in order that he should receive a wife and both together form one body, so the Right Hand was divided, as it were, in order that it might take unto itself the Left and both become one, and therefore it is that God smites and heals with one and the same Hand. Note that this whole song has a reference both to the time of its composition and to the future; hence it does not say "hath dashed", but "dashes" (tirtaz, lit. will dash), i.e. when the Messiah shall arise. The same applies to the following verse: "In the fulness of thy majesty thou wilt overthrow (taharos) thine opponents; thou wilt send forth (teshalah) thy wrath; it will devour them like stubble." Thus the words, "Thy right hand, O Lord, glorified in power", refers to this time, to this world; the words "Thy right hand will dash the enemy" to the time of the Messiah; "In the fulness of thy majesty thou wilt overthrow thine opponents" to the time of Gog and Magog; "Thou wilt send forth thy wrath, it will devour them like stubble" to the time of the resurrection, of which it says, "and many of them that sleep in the dust of the earth shall awake, some to everlasting life, and some to shame and everlasting contempt" (Dan. XII, 2). Blessed are those who will be left in the world at that time t And who will they be? None will remain, except the circumcised who have accepted upon themselves the sign of the holy covenant and have entered into this holy covenant in its two parts, [Tr. note: i.e. the actual circumcision and the peri'ah, or folding back of the flesh.] as we have pointed out, and have guarded the covenant against contact with an alien sphere. These will remain and their names will be written "to life eternal", as it says: "And it shall come to pass that he that is left in Zion, and he that remaineth in Jerusalem, shall be called 'holy', even everyone that is written to life in Jerusalem" (Isa. IV, 3). "Zion" and "Jerusalem" symbolize the two grades (Foundation and Kingdom) into which he who will be circumcised shall enter. Such shall remain at that time, and the Holy One, blessed be He, will renew the world with them and rejoice together with them. Concerning that time it is written: "May the glory of the Lord remain forever; may the Lord rejoice in his works" (Ps. CIV, 31).'

R. Hiya once went to visit R. Eleazar, whom he found with R. Yose, the son of R. Simeon ben Lekunya, his father-in-law. As R. Eleazar raised his head he noticed R. Hiya. Said the latter: 'What is the meaning of the words, "Her ways are ways of pleasantness" (Prov. III, 17)?' He replied: 'How foolish are the sons of men that they neither know nor heed the

357

words of the Torah! These words are the "ways" by which one merits that "pleasantness of the Lord" of which the Psalmist speaks (Ps. XXVII, 5). As we have pointed out on another occasion, the Torah and her ways emanate from this "pleasantness".' Said R. Hiya: 'We have a tradition that when the Holy One, blessed be He, gave the Torah to Israel a light shone forth from that sphere which is called "Pleasantness", a light wherewith the Holy One crowned Himself, and from which were irradiated all worlds,

Zohar: Shemoth, Section 2, page 58a

all firmaments, and all crowns, and concerning which it is written: "Go forth, O ye daughters of Zion, and behold king Solomon with the crown wherewith his mother crowned him in the day of his espousals, and in the day of the gladness of his heart" (S. S. III, 11). When the building of the Temple was completed, the Holy One, blessed be He, crowned Himself with this crown and seated Himself on His Throne. But since the destruction of the Temple He has not donned this crown, and the "Pleasantness" is concealed and hidden.' Said R. Eleazar: 'When Moses entered the cloud (Ex. XXIV, 18), like a man traversing the region of the Spirit, a certain great angel, whose name, according to tradition, is Kemuel, and who is appointed guardian and chief over twelve thousand messengers, sought to attack him. Thereupon Moses opened his mouth and uttered the twelve letters of the Holy Name which the Holy One had taught him at the bush, and the angel departed from him to a distance of twelve thousand parasangs. And Moses walked in the midst of the cloud, his eyes flaming like coals of fire. Then another angel met him, greater and more eminent than the first. His name, according to tradition, is Hadraniel, and he is set above all the other angels and celestial cohorts, yea, is even removed from them by a distance of one thousand and sixty myriads of parasangs, and his voice, when he proclaims the will of the Lord, penetrates through two hundred thousand firmaments which are surrounded by a white fire. On seeing him, Moses was struck dumb with awe, and would have thrown himself down from the cloud, but the Holy One, blessed be He, admonished him, saying: "Moses, thou didst speak much with Me at the bush and didst desire that I should reveal to thee the Holy Name, and wast not afraid, and art thou now affrighted before one of My servants!" When Moses heard these words from the voice of his Master, he took courage; opening his mouth, he uttered the Supreme Name of seventy-two letters. At this, Hadraniel trembled, and drew near to Moses and cried: "Happy indeed is thy lot, O Moses, for that thou hast been vouchsafed knowledge such as is denied even to the supernal angels!" He then went along with Moses until they came to a mighty fire belonging to an angel whose name is Sandalphon, and who, as tradition tells us, is removed from his fellow angels through the magnitude of his splendour by a distance of five hundred years, and who stands behind the "curtain" of his Master, and out of the prayers of Israel weaves crowns for his Lord, and when such a crown is placed on the head of the Holy King, He receives Israel's supplications, and all the heavenly hosts begin to tremble in awe, and to shout: "Blessed be the glory of the Lord from his place" (Ezek. III, 12). Said Hadraniel to Moses: "Moses, I can no longer be with thee, lest the powerful fire of Sandalphon burn me". At that moment Moses began to quake with mighty dread, but the Holy One took hold of him and made him sit before Him and taught him the Torah, and spread over him the radiance of that "pleasantness", so that his countenance shone in all those firmaments and all the hosts of heaven trembled before him when he descended with the Torah. When the Israelites committed the sin of the Golden Calf below, the Holy One took away from Moses one thousand parts of that splendour, and the supernal angels and all those hosts came to burn him. When the Holy One said to him: "Go, get thee down, for thy people... have corrupted themselves" (Ex. XXXII, 7), Moses trembled and could not utter a word. Then he began to pray and intercede for Israel. Said the Holy One to him: "Moses lay hold of My Throne and gain courage therefrom!" And the Holy One rebuked all those hosts, and Moses took hold of the two tablets of stone and brought them down. Concerning this event it is written: "A wise man scaleth the city of the mighty, and bringeth down the strength of the confidence thereof" (Prov. XXI, 22). And from the remnants of that brightness Moses's countenance shone. Now, if merely because of this remnant of brightness the children of Israel could not steadfastly behold the face of Moses, how glorious must the splendour have been in its original state!' Said R. Hiya: 'The words, "Thy right hand, O Lord, glorified in power", refer to the Torah. This "right hand" does "dash in pieces the enemy"; for there is nothing which can break the power of the heathen nations save the power of the Torah, in the study of which Israel is absorbed. For as long as they are faithful students of the Torah the "Right Hand" is powerful and breaks down the domination of the heathen, and therefore the Torah is called "Strength", as it says, "The Lord will give strength to his people" (Ps. XXIX, 11). Contrariwise, when Israel neglects the Torah, the "Left Hand" predominates, and with it the power of heathendom and the nations rule over Israel and issue tyrannous decrees against them, and Israel is scattered among the nations, as it is written:

Zohar: Shemoth, Section 2, page 58b

"Why doeth the land perish and is burned up like a wilderness?... Because they have forsaken my Torah" (Jer. IX, 11-12).' Said R. Eleazar: 'It is indeed so. As long as the voices of the Israelites are heard in the synagogues and in the houses of study they are powerful: "the voice is the voice of Jacob"; but if not, then "the hand are the hands of Esau" (Gen. XXVII, 22), as has been explained on another occasion.' IN THE GREATNESS OF THINE EXCELLENCY (lit. uplifting) THOU OVERTHROWEST THEM THAT RISE UP AGAINST THEE. R. Hezekiah found here the same idea as in the verse: "Why standest thou afar off, O Lord? Why hidest thou thyself in time of trouble?" (Ps. x, 1). 'The sins of mankind,' he said, 'cause the Holy One to ascend higher and higher, and then men cry bitterly but without avail, because the Holy One has departed from the world, and they are unable to return to Him.' R. Isaac, however, applied these words to the time when the Holy One will adorn Himself with majesty in face of the nations who will gather against Him, of whom it says: "The kings of the earth set themselves, and the rulers take counsel together against the Lord and against his anointed" (Ps. II, 2). We are told that the seventy guardians of the nations will at that time gather from all sides with the armies of the whole world and start war against Jerusalem the holy city, and take counsel together against the Holy One. They will say: "Let us rise first against the Patron, and then against His people and against His sanctuary!" Then "He that sitteth in the heavens shall laugh; the Lord shall have them in derision" (v. 4). He will put on His majesty and shall dash them in pieces.' R. Abba said, in the name of R. Jesse the Elder-and R. Simeon made the same remark-that the Holy One will bring to life again all those kings who afflicted Israel and Jerusalem: Hadrian, Lupinus, Nebuchadnezzar, Sennacherib, and all the other kings of the nations who have destroyed His house, and set them up again as rulers, and they shall gather many nations, and then He will do vengeance and justice upon them near Jerusalem, as it is written: "And this shall be the plague wherewith the Lord will smite all the people that have fought against Jerusalem" (Zech. XIV, 12). On the other hand, here it says: "In the greatness of thy excellency Thou wilt overthrow thine opponents", which refers to the Messianic times; and so this song has an eternal significance. THE ENEMY SAID: I WILL PURSUE, I WILL OVERTAKE. "The enemy" is the celestial guardian of the Egyptians. When power was given to him over Israel, he desired to make an end of them, but the Holy One remembered the "Mountains of the world" (the Patriarchs), and these shielded them. And this applies to all the supernal guardians of the nations: they all have the same desire to do away with Israel, but the Holy One remembers the merit of the "Mountains of the world" and protects them. When Moses realized this, he sang praises to the Holy One, blessed be He, saying: WHO IS LIKE UNTO THEE AMONG THE GODS, O LORD? Said R. Simeon: 'There is a mighty and wondrous tree in the celestial sphere which supplies nourishment to beings above and below. It has twelve boundaries and stretches along the four sides of the world which encompass it. Seventy branches ascend from it and imbibe nourishment from its roots. Each branch, as the time arrives for it to be dominant, endeavours to drain the whole life of the tree, which is the essence of all the branches, and without which they would not exist. Israel clings to the main body of the tree, and when its time comes to be dominant

Zohar: Shemoth, Section 2, page 59a

it endeavours to protect the branches and to give peace to all. This is also symbolized by the seventy oxen offered on the feast of Tabernacles. Therefore it says: "Who is like unto thee among the gods (elim), O Lord?"; elim in the sense of "trees", as in the passage, "for ye shall be ashamed of the elim (terebinths) which ye desired" (Isa. I, 29). "Who among these is like unto Thee, Who hast pity on all? Among the surroundings of the tree is any like unto Thee, eager to be the guardian of all, even when it dominates them", not wishing to destroy them? "Who is like unto Thee, glorified in holiness?" Namely, in that supreme power called "Holiness", "power of the Lord", "pleasantness of the Lord", as already stated.'

"Who is like unto Thee?" R. Yose discoursed on the verse: "I have seen all the works that are done under the sun, and, behold, all is vanity and breaking of spirit" (Eccl. I, 14). 'How could Solomon,' he said, 'the wisest of men, say that all human actions are vanity? Can this be said of acts of righteousness and lovingkindness, of which it is written, "and the work of righteousness shall be peace" (Isa. XXXII, 17)? However, as has been pointed out, "all is vanity" refers to "works that are done under the sun," whilst "the work of righteousness" is above the sun. So far so good. But what, then, is the meaning of "all is breath (hebel) and breaking of spirit" in regard to the "works that are done under the sun"? Have we not been taught that "hebel" (breath) is the basis of the world above and the world below? It has been explained in the following way, and it is truly so. Every action done here below, if it is done with the intention of serving the Holy King, produces a "breath" in the world above, and there is no breath which has no voice; and this voice ascends and crowns itself in the supernal world and becomes an intercessor before the Holy One, blessed be He. Contrariwise, every action which is not done with this purpose becomes a "breath" which floats about in the world, and when the soul of the doer leaves his body, this "breath" rolls about like a stone in a sling, and it "breaks the spirit". The act done and the word spoken in the service of the Holy One, however, ascend high above the sun and become a holy breath, which is the seed sowed by man in that world, and is called zedakah (righteousness, lovingkindness), as it is written: "Sow for yourselves according to righteousness" (Hos. x, 12). This "breath" guides the departed soul and brings it into the region of the supernal glory, so that it is "bound with the bundle of life with the Lord" (I Sam. xxv, 29). It is concerning this that it is written: "Thy righteousness shall go before thee; the glory of the Lord shall gather thee up" (Isa. LVIII, 8). That which is called "the glory of the Lord" gathers up the souls of that holy breath, and this is indeed ease and comfort for them; but the other is called "breaking of spirit". Blessed are the righteous whose works are "above the sun" and who sow a seed of righteousness which makes them worthy to enter the world to come, and concerning whom it is written: "Unto you that fear my name shall the sun of righteousness arise with healing in his wings" (Mal. III, 20).' R. Simeon said: 'When the Temple was built below, it was built under the aegis of severity and wrath, as it is written: "For this city hath been to me as a provocation of my anger and of my fury from the day that they built it" (Jer. XXXII, 31); but in the time to come the Holy One will build it and restore it on another noble basis, called "Righteousness", as it is written: "In righteousness shalt thou be established" (Isa. LIV, 14), and therefore it will endure.

Zohar: Shemoth, Section 2, page 59b

THOU STRETCHEDST OUT THY HAND, THE EARTH SWALLOWED THEM. Said R. Isaac: The members of the Fellowship have remarked that when the Holy One brought the Egyptians dead out of the sea, He bade the earth "take them in", but she refused, until He stretched out His right hand and adjured her, and then she swallowed them.' R. Eleazar said that the "stretching out" of the "right hand" was to separate it from the "left" so that judgement might be executed. THOU LEADEST THROUGH THY MERCY THE PEOPLE WHOM THOU REDEEMEST; THOU GUIDEST THEM THROUGH THY MIGHT TO THY HOLY HABITATION. The divine attributes are indicated here in the same way as in the verse, "Thy right hand, and thine arm, and the light of thy countenance, because thou hast thy delight in them" (PS. XLIV, 4). "Thy right hand" corresponds to "thy mercy" and symbolizes Gedulah (Greatness); "thine arm", corresponding to "Thou guidest them through Thy might", stands for Geburah (Might); and "the light of Thy countenance", corresponding to "Thy holy habitation", indicates the Zaddik (Righteous One). FEAR AND DREAD FALL UPON THEM. R. Simeon interpreted the word aymathah (dread, instead of the usual aymah) as aymath he', "the fear of He" (i.e. the Shekinah), since there is no letter or word in the Torah that does not contain profound allusions. THOU WILT BRING AND PLANT THEM IN THE MOUNTAIN OF THINE INHERITANCE. The superfluous vau in tebiemo and wetitaemo ("Thou wilt bring and plant them") is an indication, given by the holy spirit, that these words refer to a later generation of Israelites who were circumcised by Joshua, and in whom the holy sign of the Divine Name was imprinted. They were qualified to inherit the land; for he who is circumcised and in whom the holy sign is revealed, and who guards it from profanation, is called "righteous", and "the righteous will inherit the land" (Isa. LX, 21). Truly, there is not a word or even a small letter in the Torah which does not contain profound allusions and holy indications. Happy is the lot of those who apprehend them! [Note: At this point, the printed volumes, both Hebrew and English, contain a passage from the Raya Mehemna. Look below for pages 59b-60a.]

Zohar: Shemoth, Section 2, Page 60a

Said R. Abba: 'Happy indeed are those who are worthy to sing this song in this world! They will be found worthy to sing it again in the world to come. This hymn is built up out of twenty-two engraved letters and of ten Words of Creation, [Tr. note: i.e. the thirty-two paths of wisdom.] and all are inscribed in the Holy Name, and are the completion and harmony of that Name. This, however, has already been explained.' Said R. Simeon: 'When the Israelites stood at the Red Sea and sang, the Holy One, blessed be He, revealed Himself to them with all His hosts and chariots, in order that they should know their King who had wrought all those signs and mighty works for them, and that each one of them should perceive of the Divine more than was vouchsafed to any prophet. Should anyone say that they did not know and did not cleave to the Supernal Wisdom, this song that they sang in perfect unison is a proof to the contrary; for how could they, without the inspiration of the Holy Spirit, have all sung together as if through one mouth? Yea, even the embryos in their mothers' wombs sang it in unison and beheld things that the prophet Ezekiel could not see. They all beheld the Divine glory eye to eye, and when their singing was ended their souls were so filled with joy and ecstasy that they refused to continue on their journey, desiring yet more perfect revelations of that glorious mystery. Then Moses said to the Holy One: "Thy children are loth to depart from the sea, because of their eagerness to behold Thee." What did the Holy One do? He hid His glory and transferred it from there to the wilderness, half disclosing it to them there. Moses bade them many times to proceed, but they refused, until he took hold of them and showed them the light of the glory of the Holy One in the wilderness. Concerning this it is written: "They went out into the wilderness of Shur" (v. 22), which, being interpreted, means that they went into the wilderness of "Beholding" (shur= to look round).' AND THEY WENT THREE DAYS IN THE WILDERNESS AND FOUND NO WATER. In Scripture "water" stands as a symbol for the Torah: "Ho, every one that thirsteth, come ye to the waters" (Isa. LV, 1). 'But', remarked R. Jesse, 'the time for the giving of the Torah was not yet, and how could they expect to find this "water" there?' Said R. Eleazar: 'They went out into the wilderness to see the glory of the Holy One, but could not, for He removed it from there. We learn from this that "water" is the symbol of the Torah, and the Holy One and the Torah are one.' Said R. Simeon: 'There in the wilderness a strange power, representing the nations of the world, the ruling spirit of the desert, appeared to them, but they soon discovered that it was not the radiance of their King's glory. Hence it says: AND WHEN THEY CAME TO MARAH THEY COULD NOT DRINK OF THE WATERS OF MARAH, FOR THEY WERE BITTER, and they did not feel the same "sweetness" in their souls as before. Moreover, this power came to act as an accuser against them. Then HE (Moses) CRIED UNTO THE LORD, AND THE LORD SHOWED HIM A TREE,

Zohar: Shemoth, Section 2, page 60b

360

WHICH, WHEN HE CAST IT INTO THE WATERS, THE WATERS WERE MADE SWEET. The tree is a symbol of the Torah, which is "a tree of life to those who lay hold upon her" (Prov. III, 18), and the Torah and the Holy One, blessed be He, are one.' R. Abba said: 'The "Tree" is a direct symbol of the Holy One, for it says: "The tree of the field is (the supernal) Adam" (Deut. XX, 19). The "field" is the "Field of the holy apples". Thus, when the light of their King's glory manifested itself to them, "the waters were made sweet", and the accuser became an intercessor.' THERE HE MADE FOR THEM A STATUTE AND ORDINANCE. Said R. Abba: 'At first, when the Israelites entered into the Covenant of the Holy One, there was something lacking in them, namely the final act of circumcision, the "peri'a", so that the holy sign was not manifested in them, but as soon as they arrived at this place they entered into both aspects of the holy sign, through the laying bare of its impress. These two aspects are symbolized by the two terms "statute" and "ordinance. AND THERE HE PROVED THEM: by this holy sign. In the book of R. Jesse the Elder there is a recondite interpretation of this tree (which God showed Moses). AND SAID: IF THOU WILT DILIGENTLY HEARKEN TO THE VOICE OF THE LORD THY GOD. And said. Who said? As it is not directly stated, it refers to the Holy One, blessed be He.

R. Hezekiah pointed to a similar expression in the passage: "And to Moses he said, Go up unto the Lord" (Ex. XXIV, 1). R. Yose said that from the context it is clear to whom the "he said" refers. Why, however, does the text continue, "if thou wilt hear the voice of the Lord thy God", instead of "My voice"? To indicate that voice to communion with which they had attained. R. Abba said: 'When the holy sign was manifested in them they entered into a dual holy state, as has been pointed out above; and having entered into these two holy conditions, they thereby entered into communion with two other holy conditions, so that they should not be deprived of any blessings from above, blessings emanating from the Holy King Himself. All this is indicated in the above verse: "and he said", namely the Holy King; "the voice of the Lord thy God" refers to the Shekinah as representing the Community of Israel; "wilt do what is right in His sight" refers to the Zaddik; "and will give ear to His commandment" refers to Nezah (Victory), while Hod (Majesty) is indicated in the words: "and keep all His statutes". Further, the words "I am the Lord that healeth thee" refer to the Holy King. From this we learn that he who guards the sign of the covenant rises eventually to the perception of the Holy King. R. Isaac said: 'He who is worthy of the perception of Zaddik is also worthy to perceive Nezah and Hod, the triad by which the Community of Israel is blessed; and he who is worthy of these reaches the perception of the Holy King, and so has communion with all four. In correspondence with these four grades the holy impress (of circumcision) has to be guarded from four things (intercourse with a menstruous woman, a bondwoman, a heathen woman, and a harlot). Once a man cleaves truly to the Holy King, then, "I will put none of these diseases upon thee which I have brought against the Egyptians: for I am the Lord that healeth thee". Observe with what tenderness and loving speeches the Holy One drew Israel to His Torah! He was indeed like unto a father tenderly leading his son to school, promising him good things.'

Zohar: Shemoth, Section 2, Pages 61a-61b

[Note: The Hebrew text does not have this passage up to the section on 62a beginning, "BEHOLD I WILL RAIN". The text that does appear in the Hebrew for page 61a corresponds to the end of the translation of 60b.] AND THE LORD SAID UNTO MOSES, BEHOLD I WILL RAIN BREAD FROM HEAVEN FOR YOU. R. Judah quoted here the verse: Blessed is he who considereth the poor: the Lord will deliver him in time of trouble (Ps. XLI, 2). 'These words', he said, 'have been applied to a man who is lying dangerously ill. Such a one is a prisoner of the King-his neck yoked and his feet in chains. On either side warders keep guard over him. His limbs war with one another, and he is unable to eat. But in his helplessness a guardian angel is appointed to watch over him and to intercede on his behalf before the King, recalling all his virtues and any good deed that he may have done. Happy is then the counsellor who teaches the afflicted one the way of life so that he may be delivered from judgement and be brought back to his Lord; he becomes an intercessor for him above. And what will be his reward? "The Lord will deliver him in time of trouble".'

R. Hiya said: 'I have often wondered at the words, "For the Lord heareth the poor" (Ps. LXIX, 34). Does He then hear only the poor?' R. Simeon replied: 'These words signify that the poor are indeed nearer to the King than all others, for it is written, "a broken and a contrite heart, O God, thou wilt not despise" (Ps. LI, 18) and no one in the world is so broken in heart as the poor man. Mark this! Most human beings appear before the Holy One in body and in soul, but the poor man presents himself before the Throne of the Most High in soul only, and the Holy One is nearer to the soul than to the body.'

At one time there lived in the neighborhood of R. Jesse a poor man of whom no one took any notice; and to beg he was ashamed.

One day he fell ill, and R. Jesse went to visit him. And as he sat by the sick man's bedside the Rabbi heard a voice saying: "Wheel, [Tr. note: i.e. the wheel of destiny.] wheel, a soul is flying to me before its rightful time has come! Woe unto his fellow townsmen that none were found among them to sustain him, that he might live!" R. Jesse, having heard these words, stood up and put into the mouth of the sick man the water of a certain herb, bidding him drink; and this made him so to sweat that the illness left him and he recovered. When R. Jesse came again to the house of that poor man the latter said: "By thy life, Rabbi! My soul had actually left my body and was conducted to the Palace of the King and brought before His Throne; and it would fain have remained there forever, only God desired to give thee the merit of restoring me to life. I heard them proclaim in the highest courts of Heaven: "R. Jesse's spirit shall have its abode in a holy chamber which the members of the Fellowship will occupy at their awakening", and three thrones were prepared for thee and for thy friends.' From that time the neighbours of the poor man looked after him. A similar tale is told of R. Isaac. One day he was walking along the highway when a poor man passed him, having in his hand half a mea (small coin) in silver. He said to R. Isaac: 'Save, I pray thee, my life and the life of my sons and daughters.' Said R. Isaac: 'How can I do this, seeing that I possess no more than half a mea?' 'Nevertheless,' the poor man replied, 'two half meas are better than one.' So R. Isaac took out his coin and gave it to the man. Later, R. Isaac dreamt that he was walking by the sea in a strange place, and some persons wanted to throw him into it, and then he saw R. Simeon stretching out his hand to him, and the poor man whom he had assisted came up and pulled him out, and brought him safe and sound to R. Simeon. When he awoke, the verse: "Blessed is he who considereth the poor: the Lord will deliver him in time of trouble" came automatically to his lips.

Every day dew from the Holy Ancient One drops into the "Lesser Countenance" and all the holy apple-fields are blessed. It also descends to those below; and it provides spiritual food for the holy angels, to each rank according to its capacity of perception. It was this food of which the Israelites partook in the wilderness: "each of them ate the food of celestial princes" (abirim) (Ps. LVIII, 26). Said R. Simeon: 'Even at this time there are those who partake of similar food, and that in a double measure. And who are they? Fellows of the mystic lore, who study the Torah day and night. See now, when the Israelites went out of Egypt into the desert, uniting themselves with the Holy King, when the sign of the Covenant was manifested in them in its fulness, they were granted a more spiritual, more supernal food than the "unleavened bread" which they ate immediately after they left Egypt; for of the manna it says: "I will rain bread from heaven for you." It was indeed heavenly food, emanating from the sphere called "heaven". But the sons of Wisdom, namely, the students of the Torah, derive their nourishment from a still higher region, the sphere of Wisdom, as it is written: "Wisdom keeps alive her owners" (Eccl. VII, 12).' 'If that is so,' asked R. Eleazar, 'why are they more frail than ordinary men?'

R. Simeon replied: 'That is a good question, and the answer is as follows. Ordinary food, by which the majority of people are nourished, is constituted of the elements of heaven and earth, and is therefore of a gross, material quality; the unleavened bread, which was eaten by the Israelites when they left Egypt, emanated from the sphere of "Judgement" and was somewhat subtler in quality; the manna was a still finer food, emanating from the sphere of "Heaven", and was assimilated by the soul more than by the body, "angels' bread"; but the food of those absorbed in the Torah nourishes only the soul and the spirit, but not the body, coming as it does from the sphere of "Wisdom", from the highest and most glorious supernal region. Hence it is hardly to be wondered at that Wisdom's children are more frail than other men, for they do not eat the food of the body at all.

Zohar: Shemoth, Section 2, page 62a

Truly, "Wisdom keeps alive her owners"! Blessed is that body which can derive benefit from the food of the soul!' R. Eleazar thereupon remarked: 'It is indeed so, but where do we find these foods in our days?' R. Simeon replied: 'This is also a good question, and the real answer is this. First, there is the food for the whole of humanity, natural food for ordinary men. Then there is the food which emanates from the sphere of "righteousness" (zedek), the food of the poor, which is turned into "beneficence" (zedakah), both to him who gives and to him who receives: "righteousness" is turned into "mercy" (hesed), and "a man of mercy does good to his own soul" (Prov. XI, 17). A more supernal food is the one by which sick people are nourished, the food of the Holy One, as it says: "The Lord will strengthen him upon the bed of languishing" (Ps. XLI, 4)—as it were sacrificial food, concerning which it says, "To sacrifice unto me fat and blood" (Ezek. XLIV, 15). Then there is the food of spirits and souls, a supernal, holy, and precious food, emanating from the "Pleasantness of the Lord". The subtlest and most precious food, however, is, as I have said, that by which the students devoted to the Torah are sustained; for the Torah emanates from the sphere of the Supernal Wisdom, and those whose minds are centred in her enter into the very essence of Wisdom, and their nourishment is derived from that holy source.' Then came R. Eleazar and kissed R. Simeon's hand, and said: 'I am truly blessed to hear such words! Blessed are the righteous who meditate on the Torah day and night I Blessed are they in this world, and blessed are they in the world to come! Truly, "He is thy life and the length of thy days" (Deut. xxx, 20).' BEHOLD, I WILL RAIN BREAD FROM HEAVEN FOR YOU. R. Yoco meditated here on the verse: "Thou openest thine hand and satisfiest every living thing according to thy will" (Ps. CXLV, 16). 'In the preceding verse,' he said, 'it is written: "The eyes of all wait upon thee, and thou givest them their meat in due season". All living beings wait upon, and lift up their eyes to the Holy One for food, but the "sons of Faith" must not merely wait, but also pray for their daily bread. Such prayer has the power of bringing blessing every day upon the Tree whence all nourishment for body and soul emanates. Thus even when he has a sufficiency of food, a man of faith ought to pray for "daily bread" in order that through him there may be each day an increase of blessing in heaven, and this is the meaning of the words, "Blessed be the Lord by day'. For this reason it is not right to cook food on one day for the next, so that one day should not interfere with another in regard to blessings above. Therefore it says concerning the manna: "The people shall go out and gather a day's portion every day" (Ex. XVI, 4); except on the sixth day, when they prepared for the Sabbath (Ibid. 5). Prayer for daily bread secures the favour of the Holy Ancient One, so that food is distributed to all, and the one who prays thus is indeed a "faithful son", a son through whose cooperation blessings are found in heaven. R. Abba dwelt on the verse: "The Lord taketh pleasure in them that fear him, in those that wait for his mercy" (Ps. CXLVII, 11). 'How much should one endeavour to walk in the way of the Holy King and in the ways of the Torah, in order to become the medium of blessing to all, to those above and to those below!

Zohar: Shemoth, Section 2, Page 62b

For the Lord dispenses favour (rozeh eth) to them that fear Him, and those who fear Him are those "that wait for His mercy", that is, who are entirely dependent on Him for their daily bread.' R. Jesse the Elder never used to prepare his meal before praying for it. He was wont to say: 'Let us ask the King first!' Then he would wait for some time and say: 'The time has arrived for the King to give us food; prepare the meal!' This is the way of those who fear the Lord and are afraid of sin. As for the ungodly, it is not so with them, for their ways are crooked: "Woe unto them that rise up early in the morning, that they may follow strong drink" (Isa. v, 11). But "The Lord taketh pleasure... in those that wait for His mercy"; and herein are the sons of faith different from others. Hence it is written: "The people shall gather a certain rate every day in his day, that I may prove them whether they will walk in my Torah or not." The peculiar expression "in his day" indicates that the sons of faith are known by their "daily" walking in the straight way of the Torah. R. Isaac found the same truth in the following verse: "The righteous eateth to the satisfaction of his soul" (Prov. XIII, 25), which he interpreted to mean: "The righteous has his meal only after he has satisfied his soul with prayer and study." Said R. Simeon: 'Observe that before the Holy One gave Israel the Torah He tried them to see who would be a son of faith and who would not be. How did He try them? By the manna. All those who were found to be sons of faith were signed with the sign of the crown of Grace by the Holy One Himself; and from those who were not found to be thus, this supernal crown was withheld.

'It has been said at that hour Israel was perfected below according to her prototype above, for it is written, "and they came to Elim, where were twelve wells of water and threescore and ten palm trees" (Ex. xv, 27). Now the Holy Tree [Tr. note: Tifereth.] spreads to twelve boundaries on the four quarters of the earth, and to seventy branches closely intertwined, so that what was above should have here its counterpart below. At that hour holy dew dropped down from the Hidden Most Ancient One and filled the head of the Lesser Countenance, the place which is called "Heaven". From this dew of the supernal holy light the manna descended, and in so doing dispersed itself into flakes and became solidified "as thin as the hoar frost on the ground" (Ex. XVI, 14). And all the sons of the Faith went out, gathered it, and praised the Holy Name for it. The manna diffused the scents of all the spices of the Garden of Eden, through which it had passed in descending. Each one found in the manna the taste he most desired; and as he ate he blessed the Supernal Holy King for His goodness, and was himself blessed with understanding of the Supernal Wisdom. Therefore that generation was called "the generation of knowledge". These were the sons of Faith, and to them was given the privilege of contemplating and comprehending the holy Torah. But of those who were not truly faithful it is written, "and the people roamed about (shatu) and gathered (the manna)" (Num. XI, 8). The word "shatu" (roamed about) indicates that these people allowed "stupidity" (shatuta) to enter into them, because they were not sons of Faith. And what do we read of them? "And they ground it in mills or beat it in a mortar" (Ibid.). Why should they have gone to all this trouble?

Zohar: Shemoth, Section 2, page 63a

Merely because they were not sons of Faith. They are the prototypes of all those who have no faith in the Holy One, blessed be He, and have no desire to meditate on His ways: they likewise labour day and night for food, in fear that they may be short of bread—all because they are not of the faithful. Thus "the people roamed about and gathered" and "ground it", making diverse foolish efforts and labouring greatly. And what did all their trouble avail them? Only this: "and the taste of it was the taste of fresh oil" (Ibid.). No other flavour rewarded them. Why? Because they were not sons of Faith. As to the actual taste of the manna, some say it was of paste mixed with oil; some, that it was only like paste in that it could be variously moulded and pounded; R. Judah said that it was indeed only the flavour of fresh oil.'

R. Isaac said: 'It is written: GATHER OF IT EVERY MAN ACCORDING TO HIS EATING (okhlo). Did, then, the one who ate little gather little, and the one who ate much gather much? Is it not written, "he that gathered much had nothing over, and he that gathered little had no lack" (Ex. XXVI, 18)? The term "okhlo", however, signifies that they gathered according to the number of the consumers. It was in this way. Two men would dispute concerning a servant, each one saying that she or he was his, and they would take their controversy to Moses that he might decide it. He would say to each: "How many persons have you in your family?" and having ascertained this, he commanded: "Tomorrow let everyone gather the manna according to the number of his people, and bring it all to me." Next morning they would come to Moses, and he counted for every person of each house an omer; having done which he found that one of the disputants had yet another omer over and above those which were the portion of the number of his household, which proved that the servant was his. Hence it says: "An omer for every man, according to the number of your persons" (V. 12).' AT EVEN THEN YE SHALL KNOW Said R. Yose: 'How were they to know? We may explain as follows. It has been taught that every day the judgements of the Holy One, blessed be He are manifested, and in the morning Grace predominates in the world, but at the time called "evening" Justice rules in the world, and for this reason, as we have learnt, Isaac instituted the afternoon prayer. Therefore it says: "In the evening ye shall know"; that is, when Judgement is awakened in the world you shall know that by the power of that Judgement God has brought you out from the land of Egypt; whereas "in the morning ye shall perceive the glory of the Lord", for all that time Grace is awakened in the world, and shall indeed bring down food for you, and "ye shall be given food to eat".' Said R. Hiya: 'Not so! The true meaning of the passage is the opposite, viz. that when the children of Israel said, "when we sat by the flesh pots, etc." (Ex. XVI, 3), then was awakened the attribute of Justice, symbolized by the "evening"; but nevertheless Grace also awakened with it, as it says, "ye shall know that the Lord brought you out of the land of Egypt", i.e. you shall know the Grace He showed you in the hour of judgement by bringing you out of Egypt. "In the morning you shall see the glory of the Lord"; and we know what is meant by "Glory". And why all this? For that He heareth your murmurings against the Lord.' Said R. Yose: 'The Holy One does not alter His judgements; it is the wicked in the world who turn Mercy to Judgement, as we have already made clear.'

R. Eleazar taught that in the coming age the righteous shall eat of this manna, but of a much higher quality, a quality which was never seen in this world, as it is written: "To behold the beauty of the Lord and to visit his Temple" (Ps. XXVII, 4); "Eye hath not seen. What he hath prepared for him that waiteth for him" (Isa. LXIV, 4).

R. Hezekiah discoursed on the verse: "A song of degrees. Out of the depth have I cried unto thee" (Ps. cxxx, 1, 2). 'This Psalm', he said, 'is anonymous, because

Zohar: Shemoth, Section 2, Page 63b

all men can apply it to themselves in all generations. Whoever prays before the Holy King must do so from the depths of his soul so that his heart may be wholly turned to God and his whole mind be concentrated upon his prayer. David had already said "I seek thee with my whole heart" (Ps. CXIX, 10). Why, then, should he now go further and say "out of the depths"? The reason is that when a man prays before the King he should concentrate mind and heart on the source of all sources, in order to draw blessings from the depth of the "Cistern", from the source of all life, from the "stream coming out of Eden" (Gen. II, 19), which "maketh glad the city of God" (Ps. XLVI, 5). Prayer is the drawing of this blessing from above to below; for when the Ancient One, the All-hidden, wishes to bless the universe, He lets His gifts of Grace congregate in that supernal depth, from where they are to be drawn, through human prayer, into the "Cistern", so that all the streams and brooks may be filled therefrom.' AND MOSES SAID UNTO THEM, LET NO MAN LEAVE OF IT UNTIL THE MORNING. R. Judah said: Every day the world is blessed through that superior day, the Seventh. For the six Days receive blessing from the seventh, and each dispenses the blessing so received on its own day, but not on the next. Hence the Israelites were commanded not to leave of the manna till the morning. The sixth day has more blessing than the rest, for on this day, as R. Eleazar has said, the Shekinah prepares the table for the King. Hence the sixth day has two portions, one for itself and one in preparation for the joy of the union of the King with the Shekinah, which takes place on Sabbath night, and from which all the six days of the week derive their blessing. For that reason the table has to be prepared on the Sabbath night, so that when the blessings descend from above they may find something on which to rest, as it were, for "no blessing rests on an empty table". Those who are aware of this mystery of the union of the Holy One with the Shekinah on Sabbath night consider, therefore, this time the most appropriate one for their own marital union.' SEE FOR THAT THE LORD HATH GIVEN YOU THE SABBATH. What is the meaning of the word "Sabbath"? The day in which all the other days rest, the day which comprises the other days, and from which they derive blessing. R. Yose said: 'The Community of Israel is also called "Sabbath", for she is God's spouse. That is why the Sabbath is called "Bride", and it is written, "Ye shall keep the Sabbath, for it is holy unto you" (Ex. XXXI, 13): it is holy to you, but not to other nations; "it is a sign between me and the children of Israel" (Ibid. v, 17): it is Israel's eternal heritage.' ABIDE YE EVERY MAN IN HIS PLACE, LET NO MAN GO OUT OF HIS PLACE ON THE SEVENTH DAY. This "place" is the "Place" where it is right to walk. The inner meaning of the word is as in the verse: "Put off thy shoes from off thy feet, for the place whereon thou standest is holy ground" (Ex. III, 5): the noted Place (i.e. stage of contemplation) where one is aware of the Supernal Glory. Therefore when man adorns himself with the supernal holy Crown (i.e. celebrates the Sabbath), he must take great care not to utter any word which might

Zohar: Shemoth, Section 2, Page 64a

profane the Sabbath, and similarly to guard his hands and also his feet, so as not to walk beyond the permissible limit of the two thousand cubits. Again, the "place" here refers to the glorious Place of Holiness, outside of which are "strange gods". "Blessed be the glory of the Lord" is the Supernal Glory; "from His place" is the terrestrial Glory. This is the secret of the Sabbatical Crown. Therefore: "let no man go out of his place on the seventh day". Blessed is the lot of him who is worthy of the glory of the Sabbath: blessed in this world and blessed in the world to come.

AND THE LORD SAID UNTO MOSES, GO ON BEFORE THE PEOPLE AND TAKE WITH THEE, ETC. R. Hiya began his interpretation by quoting the following verse: "The angel of the Lord encampeth round about them that fear him and delivereth them" (Ps. XXXIV, 8). He said: 'Blessed are the righteous, in that the Holy One is more concerned for their honour than for His own! See how He ignores those who scorn and blaspheme the Supernal! Sanherib, for instance, said: "Who are they among the gods of the countries... that the Lord should deliver Jerusalem out of mine hand?" (2 Kings XVIII, 35), and yet the Holy One exacted no requital from him; but as soon as he stretched out his hand against Hezekiah "the angel of the Lord smote in the camp of the Assyrians" (Ibid. v, 19). Jeroboam, the son of Nebat, worshipped heathen gods, brought incense and sacrificed to them, and yet God did not requite him for his sin; but when Iddo the prophet came to warn him, and Jeroboam stretched out his hand against him, then "his hand which he put up against him dried up and he could not pull it in again to him" (I Kings XIII, 4). Pharaoh scorned and blasphemed, and said: "Who is the Lord?" (Ex. v, 2), but the Holy One did not punish him until he refused to let Israel go, as it is written: "As yet exaltest thou thyself against my people... Behold tomorrow at this time I will cause it, etc. (Ex. IX, 17). And so it is always the case that the Holy One avenges the insult done to the righteous more than one offered to Himself. Here, however, when Moses said "They be almost ready to stone me" (Ex. XVII, 4), God said to him: "Moses, now is not the time to exact reparation for the insult done to thee. However, go before the people, and I shall see who will stretch out his hand against thee! Art thou in their power or in mine?" AND THE ROD WHEREWITH THOU SMOTEST THE RIVER TAKE IN THINE HAND. The rod was to be taken because it was inscribed with miracles, and the Holy Name was impressed on it. BEHOLD, I WILL STAND BEFORE THEE THERE UPON THE ROCK. This "rock" is the same as the one mentioned in the verse: "The rock, perfect is his work" (Deut. XXXII, 4); and, as the rod had formerly been a serpent, Moses here knew "the way of a serpent upon a rock" (Prov. xxx, 19). Said R. Judah: 'If that is so, what are we to make of the next words: "and thou shalt smite the rock and there shall come water out of it" (Ibid.)?' R. Hiya replied: 'Certainly it is so. Of all the names of the Holy One, blessed be He, there is not one which does not effect signs and wonders, producing all that the world needs.' 'But does it not say,' objected R. Judah, '"Behold, he smote the rock, and the waters gushed out" (Ps. cv, 41)?' R. Hiya replied: 'A strong hammer is known by the sparks it produces (i.e. a sharp mind is recognized by the problems it raises), and dost thou ask such a question? Listen. Everywhere "rock" symbolizes "Geburah" (Force), and when the Holy One wishes to wound and to smite, this "Geburah" is awakened and it is this that executes the act. Hence, we read: "The Rock smote, and the waters gushed out." Without this the waters would not have gushed out.' 'But,' said R. Judah, 'is it not written, "The Rock that begat thee thou hast neglected", or, as we interpret, "weakened" (Deut. XXXII, 18)?' R. Hiya replied: 'Surely! For if sinners knew that this Rock was going to be awakened and punish them, they would not sin; it is, however, weak in their estimation because they do not contemplate it nor observe its ways.'

R. Abba said: 'There are two Rocks: from the Supernal Rock emanates a lower Rock. That is to say, from the side of the "Mother" comes "Strength" (Geburah), as R. Eleazar has said, that, although the Supernal Mother does not in Herself signify Judgement, yet judgement issues from Her side, since

Geburah emanates from her. Therefore She is called "Supernal Rock". And in the same verse the words, "And hast forgotten God that formed thee" refer to the brightness of the Father, viz. the Supernal Grace.'

R. Abba further said: 'We know that "water" everywhere symbolizes God's kindness, "Grace", and yet the Holy One, blessed be He, on this occasion caused water to come from the "Rock" (the symbol of Judgement), though it ought to be connected with "Greatness" (=Grace). In this, however, consisted the "sign" and wonder of the Holy One: "Who turned the Rock into a pool" (Ps. CXIV, 8). "Turned" suggests that it is not the usual function of the rock to produce water. Therefore He caused water to come from the place below by means of the Supernal Rock. And what is the name of the place below? "Sela"', for it is written: "And thou shalt bring forth to them water out of the rock (sela')" (Num. xx, 8). And wherewith did this sela' bring forth water? By the power of the Supernal Rock.'

R. Simeon said: 'Moses in his Song, first said "The rock, perfect is his work" (Deut. XXXII, 4), referring to the occasion when water issued from the rock, doing the work of him who was called "perfect", namely Abraham (Gen. XVII, 1), who symbolizes Grace. But on the second occasion, when Moses tried to bring forth water from that rock (Num. xx), it did not turn to "perfection", because of Israel's sins; and in reference to this Moses said: "The Rock that begat thee thou hast weakened" (Deut. XXXII, 15), meaning, "thou hast weakened it from what it was to thee before; it does not now represent 'perfection' but 'judgement'; it is not now what it was when thou wast begotten as a people".'

Said R. Abba:' What did the Israelites mean when they said: IS THE LORD AMONG US OR NOT (ain, lit. nothing)? Were they so blind as not to know that He was in their midst? Did not the Shekinah encompass them and the clouds of glory surround them? Had they not seen the radiance of their King's glorious majesty at the sea? It is, however, as R. Simeon explained, that they desired to know whether the Divine manifestation which they had experienced was that of the Ancient One, the All-hidden One, the Transcendent, whose designation is Ayin (Nought), because He is above comprehension, or of the "Small Countenance", the Immanent designated Tetragrammaton. Hence the word "ayin" (nothing) is used here instead of "lo" (not). If so, it may be asked, why were they punished? Because they differentiated between these two aspects in God and "tempted the Lord"; for they said to themselves: "If it is the One, we shall pray in one way, and if it is the Other, we shall pray in another way".' THEN CAME AMALEK AND FOUGHT WITH ISRAEL IN REPHIDIM. R. Yose quoted in connection with this the following verse: Blessed are ye that sow beside all waters, that send forth thither the feet of the ox and the ass (Isa. XXXII, 20). 'Water', he said, 'has many symbolic meanings: there are many kinds of water. Blessed are the Israelites who "sow beside the water"—the water which is under the branches of the Holy One's Tree, a Tree great and mighty, containing food for the whole universe. This Tree is encompassed by twelve frontiers and adjoins all four sides of the world, and has seventy branches, and Israel is in the "body" of the Tree, and the seventy branches encompass her. This is symbolized by the "twelve wells of water and the threescore and ten palm trees", as we have often explained. But what do the words "and they encamped there by the water" signify? This. At that time the Israelites had control over the waters which are under the branches of that Tree, those which are called "the insolent waters,' (Ps. CXXIV, 5). And this is the meaning of the words, "blessed are ye that sow beside all waters, that send forth thither the feet of the ox and the ass", namely, the two "Crowns of the Left", to which are attached the pagan nations who are called "ox and ass". When the Israelites are worthy, then they dismiss these evil powers, and they have no dominion over them.' Said R. Abba: 'When the two (i.e. the ox and the ass) are united, the inhabitants of the world cannot stand up against them. For this reason

Zohar: Shemoth, Section 2, page 65a

it is prohibited to "plough with an ox and an ass together" (Deut. XXII, 10). From them, when united, emanates the power, called "dog", which is more insolent than all of them. Said the Holy One, blessed be He: "Ye said, 'is the Lord in our midst or not?' Behold, I will deliver you to the dog!", and straightway came Amalek.'

R. Judah said: 'It is written, "Amalek is the first of the nations; but his latter end shall be that he perish forever" (Num. XXIV, 20). Was, then, Amalek the first of the nations? Were there not many tribes, nations, and peoples in the world before Amalek came? But the meaning is that Amalek was the first nation who feared not to proclaim war against Israel, as it says, "and he feared not God" (Deut. XXIV, 18); whilst the other nations were filled with fear and trembling before Israel at the time of the Exodus, as it says: "The peoples heard and were afraid; trembling took hold of the inhabitants of Pelesheth" (Ex. xv, 14); in fact, apart from Amalek there was no nation that was not awestruck before the mighty works of the Holy One, blessed be He. Therefore "his latter end shall be that he perish forever".'

Said R. Eleazar: 'Observe that although the "Rock" (i.e. Geburah, Severity) dealt graciously with them in supplying them with water, yet it did not cease to perform its natural function, so that "Amalek came".' R. Abba discoursed on the verse: There is a sore evil which I have seen under the sun, namely, riches kept for the owners thereof to their hurt" (Eccl. v, 13). '"There is a sore evil." Are there then two kinds of evil, one that is sore, and another that is not sore? Yes, indeed! There is a particularly sore evil, for we have a tradition that from the Side of the Left emanate many emissaries of punishment who go down to the hollow of the great Sea, and then emerge in a body and, cleaving the air, advance upon the sons of men. Each one of them is called "evil", and it is to this that the words "there shall no evil befall thee" (Ps. xc, 10) refer. When a certain one of these "evils" befalls a man, it makes him miserly with his money, so that when a collector for charity or a poor man comes to him it strikes his hand saying, "do not impoverish yourself". It will not even let him buy food for himself. In fact, from the moment that that "evil" comes upon the man, he is "sore" like a sick man who can neither eat nor drink. King Solomon proclaimed in his wisdom: "There is an evil which I have seen under the sun... A man to whom God hath given riches, wealth, and honour, so that he wanteth nothing for his soul of all that he desireth, yet God giveth him no power to eat thereof, but a stranger eateth it" (Eccl. VI, 1-2). On the surface, the end of this verse would appear to contradict the beginning: if God has given him riches, etc., how can we say that he has no power over it? The meaning, however, is that he has no power over that "evil" to which he clings and entrusts himself, and therefore he is like a sick man who does not eat, nor drink, and he keeps his money tight until he leaves this world and another man comes and takes possession of it, and becomes its master.' We may also explain the verse as follows. When a young man who lives at ease in his father's house begins to make

Zohar: Shemoth, Section 2, page 65b

all sorts of complaints and demands, saying, "I want this, and I do not want that", he attaches himself to that "sore evil", and he will be punished both in this world and in the world to come. Concerning such a case, King Solomon said: "There is a sore evil... riches kept for the owners thereof to their hurt." Such was the case of the Israelites: the Holy One, blessed be He, carried them on eagles' wings, encircled them with the clouds of glory, made the Shekinah go before them, gave them manna to eat, and sweet water to drink, and yet they complained! Hence, "and Amalek came".

R. Simeon said: 'There is a deep allusion in the name "Rephidim". This war emanated from the attribute of Severe Judgement and it was a war above and a war below. The Holy One, as it were, said: "when Israel is worthy below My power prevails in the universe; but when Israel is found to be unworthy she weakens My power above, and the power of severe judgement predominates in the world.' So here, "Amalek came and fought with Israel in Rephidim", because the

Israelites were "weak" (raphe) in the study of the Torah, as we have explained on another occasion.' AND MOSES SAID UNTO JOSHUA, CHOOSE US OUT MEN, AND GO OUT, FIGHT WITH AMALEK. Why did Moses abstain from fighting the first battle which God Himself commanded? Because he was able to divine the true meaning of his Master's command. Hence he said: "I will prepare myself for the war above, and thou, Joshua, prepare thyself for the war below." This is the meaning of the words: "When Moses lifted up his hand, Israel prevailed" (Ibid. v, 11), namely Israel above. Therefore Moses did not participate in the war on earth, so that he might throw himself with greater zeal into the war in Heaven, and thus promote victory on earth. Said R. Simeon: 'Let us not think lightly of this war with Amalek. Verily, from the creation of the world until then, and since then till the coming of the Messiah, there has been and will be no war like that, nor can even the war of Gog and Magog be compared with it; and this not because of the mighty armies taking part in it, but because it was launched against all the attributes of the Holy One, blessed be He.' AND MOSES SAID TO JOSHUA. Why to him, who was then but a "youth" (Ex. XXXIII, 11)? Were there in Israel no greater warriors than Joshua? The reason was that Moses in his wisdom was aware that it was not going to be merely a battle against flesh and blood, but against Samael, who was coming down to assist Amalek. Now Joshua, "the youth", had reached at that time a high degree of spiritual perception, not, indeed, as high as Moses, who was united with the Shekinah, but his soul was, in fact, attached to the supernal region called "Youth" (=Metatron).

Zohar: Shemoth, Section 2, page 66a

Now when Moses perceived that Samael was going to fight for Amalek, he thought: "this young man, Joshua, will surely stand against him and prevail", and therefore he said unto him: "go and fight against Amalek! It is thy battle, the battle here below, and I will prepare myself for the battle above. Choose worthy men, righteous and the sons of the righteous, to accompany thee".' Said R. Simeon: 'At the moment when Joshua, the "young man", started out to fight Amalek, the "Young Man" above was stirred, and was equipped with weapons prepared by his "Mother" (the Shekinah) for the battle in order to "avenge the covenant" (cf. Lev. XXVI, 25) with the "sword" (Ex. XVII, 13). Moses equipped himself for the war above. "His hands were heavy" (Ibid. v, 12), that is to say, "weighty, honourable, holy hands", that had never been defiled, hands worthy to wage the war above. AND THEY TOOK A STONE AND PUT IT UNDER HIM AND HE SAT THEREON: to participate in the distress of Israel. AND AARON AND HUR STAYED UP HIS HANDS, THE ONE ON THE ONE SIDE, AND THE OTHER ON THE OTHER SIDE: AND HIS HANDS WERE STEADY (emunah, lit. faith). This cannot be taken in the literal sense; what it means is that Aaron represented his "side" (the attribute of Grace), Hur his "side" (the attribute of Strength), and Moses' hands between the two represented Faith. AND IT CAME TO PASS THAT WHEN MOSES HELD UP HIS HAND, ISRAEL PREVAILED, AND WHEN HE LET DOWN HIS HAND, AMALEK PREVAILED. "Hand 'here refers to the right hand, which he held up above the left, and so long as he did so, Israel, i.e. the Supernal Israel, prevailed; but when Israel below ceased praying Moses could not keep his hand up and "Amalek prevailed". From which we derive the lesson that, although the priest spreads out his hands at the sacrifice to make his mediation complete, yet Israel must co-operate with him in prayer. AND THE LORD SAID UNTO MOSES, WRITE THIS FOR A MEMORIAL IN THE BOOK, ETC. Note that in the previous verse it says, "And Joshua disabled (vayahlosh) Amalek and his people with the edge of the sword." Why is the word "disabled" used here instead of "slew"? Because the word halash has also another meaning, namely, "to cast lots" (cf. Isa. XIV, 2). Joshua did indeed first cast lots. [Tr. note: i.e. as to which of the multitude of nations that Amalek brought with him (vide infra) should first be put to the sword.] and then the sword, executing the vengenace of the covenant, slew them. WRITE THIS FOR A MEMORIAL: "this" in the first place, AND REHEARSE IT IN THE EARS OF JOSHUA, namely, that he is destined to slay other kings. FOR I WILL UTTERLY BLOT OUT (lit. for blotting out I will blot out); that is, both their celestial forces and their power here below: similarly THE REMEMBRANCE of them on high as well as below. Said R. Isaac: 'Here it is written: "For I will utterly blot out", whereas in another passage it says, "Thou shalt blot out the remembrance of Amalek" (Deut. xxv, 19). The Holy One, blessed be He, said in effect: "Ye shall blot out his remembrance on earth, and I will blot out his remembrance on high".' R. Yose said: 'Amalek brought with him other peoples, but all the rest were afraid to commence war against Israel. Hence Joshua cast lots which of them to slay.' AND MOSES BUILT AN ALTAR AND CALLED THE NAME OF IT Tetragrammaton NISSI (the Lord is my sign). He built an altar below to correspond to the Altar above.

Zohar: Shemoth, Section 2, page 66b

R. Yose said: 'The altar was intended to bring atonement and forgiveness to them. "He called the name", namely the name of the altar, "Tetragrammaton NISSI", just as Jacob called the altar which he built El Elohe Yisroel, "the God, the God of Israel" (Gen. XXXIII, 20).' He meant to indicate that the miracle was wrought for them because they had been properly circumcised, so that the sign of the Covenant was visibly imprinted upon them. Hence we learn that when a father performs the act of circumcision on his son, revealing the impress of the sign of the holy Covenant, the sacrificial act is, as it were, an altar of propitiation.

R. Yose said: 'How are we to understand the words, "and they saw the God of Israel" (Ex. XXIV, 10)? Who can see the Holy One? Is it not written: "No man can see Me and live"? It means that a rainbow appeared above them in radiant colours resplendent with the beauty of His grace. Therefore the saying that he who gazes at a rainbow gazes, as it were, at the Shekinah. For the same reason it is not right to look at the fingers of the priests when they spread out their hands to bless the people (the Shekinah "showing Herself through the lattice", i.e. through the priests' fingers).' R. Yose further said: 'They saw the light of the Shekinah, namely him who is called "the Youth" (Metratron-Henoch), and who ministers to the Shekinah in the heavenly Sanctuary. As for the "paved work of a sapphire brick" mentioned in the same verse, this was an impression of one of the bricks with which the Egyptians "embittered" the lives of the children of Israel (Ex. I, 14). There is a story concerning a Hebrew woman in Egypt who, when a child was born to her, being in fear of Pharaoh's decree, hid him under a brick. Then a hand was stretched out, took hold of the brick, and placed it under the "feet" of the Shekinah. There it remained until the earthly Temple was burned down. It is concerning this that it is written in the book of Lamentations (II, 1): "He remembered not his footstool in the day of his anger." Said R. Hiya: 'The radiance of the Sapphire extended towards seventy-two sides' (in accordance with the seventy-two Divine Names).

Zohar: Shemoth, Section 2, page 67a

[Note: The first 3 lines of the Hebrew text do not appear in the translation.]

THE LORD WILL HAVE WAR WITH AMALEK FROM GENERATION TO GENERATION. R. Judah said: There never was a generation of men, nor ever will be, in this world without this evil seed, and the Holy One, blessed be He, carries on His war against it. Of such is it written: "Let the sinners be consumed out of the earth, and let the wicked be no more. Bless thou the Lord, O my soul. Hallelukah!" (Ps. CIV, 35).'

JETHRO

NOW JETHRO, THE PRIEST OF MIDIAN, MOSES' FATHER-IN-LAW, HEARD OF ALL THAT GOD HAD DONE FOR MOSES AND FOR ISRAEL. R. Hezekiah opened here with a discourse on the verse: And Aaron lifted up his hand [Tr. note: So the k'tib.] toward the people and blessed them (Lev. IX, 22). 'The use of the word "hand" here', he said, 'in the singular indicates that he meant to lift up his right hand above his left; and this for a certain esoteric reason. We find, namely, in the book of King Solomon, that he who lifts up his hand towards heaven without any devotional intention to utter prayer or blessing will be cursed by ten celestial powers, the "ten potentates which are found in the city" (Eccl. VII, 19), namely, the ten supernal beings who are appointed over the "spreading of hands", to receive the blessings or prayers offered therewith, and to endow them with a power through which the holy name [Tr. note: Adonai] is glorified and blessed from below. And when, through the "spreading of hands", the name is blessed from below, it receives blessings from above also, and is thus glorified from all sides. And these "ten potentates" will then take of the blessings above, and pour them down upon him who is below. Therefore when man lifts up his hand to heaven, he must be careful that his intention should be to pray or bless or supplicate, for if he lifts them idly, [Tr. note: i.e. for cursing.] those powers that brood over the "spreading of hands" will curse him with two hundred and forty-eight curses. Of such a one it is written: "As he loved cursing, so let it come unto him" (Ps. CIX, 17). Moreover, the spirit of impurity rests on such hands, for it is wont to hover over an empty spot, and blessing does not rest there. Thus the hand must be lifted up to heaven only as an expression of prayer or of blessing. Indeed, this "spreading of hands" has a profound symbolical significance. When a man spreads out his hands and lifts them up in prayer and supplication, he may be said to glorify the Holy One in various ways. He symbolically [Tr. note: Because the pair of hands contain ten fingers] the ten Words (Sefiroth), thereby unifying the whole and duly blessing the Holy Name. He also, as it were, unites the inner Chariots and the outer Chariots, so that the Holy Name may be blessed from all sides, and all become one, both that which is above and that which is below. The ten powers of which we spake are the lower ten Words (Sefiroth), symbolized by the inscribed letters corresponding to those above, and they have charge, in the first instance, of the raising of the

Zohar: Shemoth, Section 2, page 67b

fingers in prayer. And when the whole side of holiness is united above, the "other sides" are subdued, and they also confess and praise the Holy King.

'Observe this. In the mystic doctrine of the Holy Name we speak of King and Priest, both above and below. The King above is the mystic Holy of Holies, [Tr. note: Binah.] and under him there is a Priest, the mystic Primeval Light, who ministers before him; he is the priest who is called "great" and is stationed at the right hand. There is a King below, in the likeness of the King above, who is king over all that is below; and under him there is a Priest who ministers to him: this is he whom we call Michael, the High Priest, who is at the right hand. All this constitutes the true object of faith, that of the side of holiness. On the "other side", the side which is not holy, there is also a king, the one who is called "an old king and a fool" (Eccl. IV, 13), and the priest, who is under him and ministers to him, is On (=aven, nothingness, idolatry); he is alluded to in the verse: "And Ephraim said, Yet I am become rich, I have found me out power", namely, the celestial unholy power which presided over the act of idolatry committed by Jeroboam (I Kings XII, 28), without which he would not have been able to succeed. Now, when this king and this priest of the "other side" are subdued, and their power broken, all the "other sides" follow suit, and are also subdued and broken, and acknowledge the sovereignty

368

of the Holy One, and in this way He alone rules above and below, as it is written: "And the Lord alone will be exalted in that day" (Isa. II, 11). In just the same way God broke here on earth the power of an "old and foolish king", namely Pharaoh, who, when Moses said to him, "The God of the Hebrews hath met with us", replied, "I know not the Lord," but when the Holy One, desiring that His Name should be glorified on earth as it is in heaven, punished him and his people, he came and acknowledged the Holy One. Subsequently his priest also, namely Jethro, the priest of On, i.e. idolatry, was also humbled, so that he came and acknowledged the Holy One, saying: "Blessed be the Lord, who hath delivered you.... Now I know that the Lord is greater than all the gods..." (Ex. XVIII, 10, 11). So when that king and that priest acknowledged the Holy One, blessed be He, and were humbled before Him, He was exalted above and below, and then, and then only did He give forth the Torah, as undisputed sovereign over all.'

R. Eleazar meditated on the words of the Psalm: "God be merciful unto us" (Ps. LXVII). Said he: [Tr. Note: There appears to be a lacuna here in the text.] 'King David rose and praised and thanked the Holy King. He was studying the Torah at the moment when the north wind rose and touched the strings of his harp, so that it made music. Now, what was the song of the harp? See now. When the Holy One moves towards the chariots and the hosts to give nourishment to all those supernal beings-as it is written, "She (the Shekinah) riseth while it is yet night and giveth food to her household and a portion to her maidens" (Prov. XXXI, 15)- all are filled with joy and song. They begin their hymning with the words: "God be merciful unto us and bless us, and cause His face to shine upon us"; and the north wind, when it awakens and breathes upon the world, sings: "That thy way may be known upon earth, thy salvation among all nations"; and the harp, when it is played upon by that wind, sings: "Let all peoples praise Thee, O God; let all the peoples praise Thee." As for David, when he was awakened and the Holy Spirit moved him, he sang: "Then shall the earth yield her increase, and God, even our God, shall bless us; God shall bless us, and all the ends of the earth shall fear him." This he sang so as to draw down the goodness of the Holy One from above to the earth below. Later David arranged all these songs into one psalm. The song of the harp ("Let all peoples praise thee") signifies that when the heathen nations acknowledge the Holy One, His glory is consummated above and below.

Zohar: Shemoth, Section 2, Page 68a

When Pharaoh acknowledged Him by saying: "The Lord is the righteous" (Ex. IX, 27), all other kings had to follow suit: "Then the dukes of Edom were terrified" (Ibid. XVI, 15); for Pharaoh was then the overlord of the whole world. Then came Jethro, that great and supreme priest of the whole pagan world, and confessed his faith in the Holy One, saying, "Now I know that the Lord is greater than all the gods"; then the Holy One was exalted in His glory above and below, and then it was that he gave the Torah in the completeness of his dominion.'

Said R. Simeon to R. Eleazar, his son: 'Concerning this, it is written: "Let all peoples praise thee, O Lord; let all peoples praise thee." Then R. Eleazar came and kissed his hand. But R. Abba wept and said: 'A father pitieth his children. Who will pity R. Eleazar and bring his words to completion except he have the Master's pity? How happy can we consider ourselves that we were privileged to hear these words so that we shall not be ashamed of our ignorance in the world to come! '

R. Abba continued: 'It does not say that Jethro was a priest of On, but of Midian.' R. Simeon replied: 'It is all one; at first the father-in-law of Joseph was called a "priest of On", and then "the father-in-law of Moses" was called a "priest of Midian", and both have the same symbolism, for both Moses and Joseph were in that grade symbolized by the two Vau's that are one.' Then R. Abba put his hands on his head, wept again, and said: 'The light of the Torah now reaches the highest throne in heaven. But who will light the lamp of the Torah when the Master shall have passed away? Woe to the world which will be orphaned without thee. However, the words of the Master will shine in the world until King Messiah appears, when "the earth shall be full of the knowledge of the Lord as the waters cover the sea" (Isa. XI, 9).' NOW JETHRO HEARD OF ALL THAT GOD (Elohim) HAD DONE FOR MOSES AND FOR ISRAEL, HIS PEOPLE, AND THAT THE LORD (Tetragrammaton) HAD BROUGHT ISRAEL OUT OF EGYPT. Said R. Hiya: 'We note that there is a transition in this verse from the name Elohim to the name Tetragrammaton. There is an inner reason for this. The first name indicates the Shekinah who protected Israel in exile, always being present with them and with Moses; and the second name signifies the supreme emanation which brought them out from Egypt, and is symbolically known as "Jubilee". According to another interpretation, "What God had done for Moses" refers to the time when he was thrown into the Nile and when he was saved from Pharaoh's sword, and "for Israel his people" to the time when "He heard the groaning".' R. Yose here quoted the verse: "He sent redemption unto his people; he hath commanded his covenant forever; holy and awful is his name" (Ps. CXI, 9). He pointed out that this and the following verse ("The fear of the Lord is the beginning of wisdom; a good understanding have all they that do his commandments; his praise endureth forever") each consists of three parts, the first letters of which are in alphabetical order, whilst the rest of the Psalm has but two such parts in each verse. And his explanation was that the last two verses between them complete the alphabet on six sides. The first corresponds to the three redemptions of Israel, apart from the Egyptian (i.e. Babylonian, Syrian, and the future one); the second to the three divisions of Scripture: Torah, Prophets and Sacred Writings. "He sent redemption unto His people", namely, when He redeemed Israel from the Egyptian exile; "He hath commanded His covenant forever", that is, when Jethro came and the Holy One received him into His Covenant and brought him near to Himself that he might worship Him. Since then all proselytes have been brought to rest under the wings of the Shekinah, and hereby "holy and awful is His Name", for the Holy Name is hallowed when the "other side" is subdued and broken, as in the case of Jethro.' NOW JETHRO... HEARD. Was Jethro the only one who heard of all that God had done? Does it not say, "Peoples heard, they were afraid" (Ex. xv, 14)? Indeed, the whole world did hear, yet Jethro alone

Zohar: Shemoth, Section 2, Page 68b

renounced idolatry and accepted the Holy One to worship Him.

Said R. Abba: 'We have frequently affirmed that whatever the Holy One has made, whether it be above or below, has a purpose: He is truth and His work is truth, and therefore no phenomenon in the world is to be spurned as of no account, since everything is formed according to a divine pattern, and therefore is of some necessity. Once, for example, R. Eleazar was walking along accompanied by R. Hezekiah, when they came across a snake. R. Hezekiah was about to kill it, but R. Eleazar said: 'Nay, leave it alone, do not kill it!' Said R. Hezekiah to him: 'But is it not a noxious creature which kills people?' To which R. Eleazar replied: 'It is written: "Doth the serpent bite without enchantment? (lit. whispering)" (Eccl. x, 11). The serpent does not bite unless it be whispered to from above and commanded to kill someone, so as to prevent that person from committing some evil; thus the very poison is used by the Holy One in order to perform some miracle. It is, in truth, all in His hands; it is all according to His plan, and if it had no purpose He would not have created it. And if it is wrong to despise anything in this world, how much more sinful must it be to think lightly of any word or act of the Holy One, blessed be He. It is written: "And God saw everything that He had made, and, behold, it was very good" (Gen. I, 31). The "living God" (Elohim Hayyim) purposed to give us light and to care for us in His Providence; and in His creation all are united, above and below, the "Right Side" and the "Left Side", the angel of life and the angel of death: all are part of His plan, and it is "very good"; it is all part of the same mystic doctrine, apprehended by those who contemplate the mystery of wisdom.

'It was Jethro who gave Moses sound advice concerning the administration of justice. And in this is contained an allusion to his confessing the Holy One, namely, in his awareness that "judgement is God's" (Deut. I, 17), and belongs not to the "other side", and that law and right were given to Israel and not to any of the heathen nations, as it is written: "He showeth his words unto Jacob, his statutes and his judgements unto Israel. He hath not dealt so with any nation; and as for his judgements, they have not known them" (Ps. CXLVII, 19, 20). So one must beware of despising anyone, since the words of an ordinary person may be of great consequence,

Zohar: Shemoth, Section 2, Page 69a

as it says of Moses that he "hearkened to the voice of his father-in-law, and did all that he had said (Ex. XVIII, 24).

R. Eleazar continued: 'It is written, "Therefore I shall praise thee, O Lord, among the nations, and sing praises unto thy name" (Ps. XVIII, 50). David said this under the prompting of the Holy Spirit, when he saw that the glory of the Holy One is not exalted and honoured in the world as it should be, unless other nations also contribute. It is true that the Holy One is glorified for Israel's sake alone; but while Israel are the foundation of the divine light from out of which issues forth light for the whole world, yet when heathen nations come to accept the glory of the Holy One and to worship Him, then the foundation of the light is strengthened, and all its rays are unified, and then the Holy One reigns above and below. This is exactly what happened when Jethro, the high priest of paganism, was converted to the worship of the true God of Israel: the whole world, hearing of the mighty works of the Holy One, and seeing that the great sage, Jethro, had been drawn to worship the God of Israel, gave up their idols, realizing their impotence, and in this way the glory of the Holy Name of God was exalted on all sides. For this reason the narrative concerning Jethro has been preserved in the Torah, with Jethro's name at the head.

'Pharaoh had as his counsellors three sages: Jethro, Balaam, and Job. Jethro, as already set forth, was the minister of worship, and there was no celestial Chieftain or star of which he did not know the appropriate cult. Balaam was an arch-sorcerer, in word and act. Job displayed pre-eminently the sense of religious awe and fear; for in the sphere of supramundane relationships, whether in the region of holiness or of unholiness ("the other side"), man cannot draw down the spirit from above and unite himself with it without a sense of fear and awe, the concentration of heart and mind, and self-effacement. Without this fear the worshipper, even if he be an idolater, cannot properly link his will to the power above; he will only be able to attain to some small sparks of that power and even these require concentration of will and a sense of fear. Jethro's religious activity had to be continuous, and independent of the needs of the worshippers; for, in order that he might be able to use the power when he needed to do so, he had always to be connected with it. Balaam clung to his mediums of sorcery, as we have stated, and Job, because of that overpowering sense of awe which was in him, when he saw the mighty works of the God of Israel in Egypt, turned to worship Him with the same amount of fear and awe. But Jethro was not converted until later. Only when the Israelites had actually left Egypt, when he realized that all the bonds by which the Egyptian magicians had attempted to retain Israel in their power were futile, and when he saw that the Egyptians themselves had all perished in the Red Sea, only then did he turn to worship the Holy One, blessed be He. Balaam, again, was not converted at all, for the impurity of the "other side" clung to him. Yet even he saw something of the Divine and the Holy, although from a distance, through the mist of his impurity and attachment to the "other side". For in the "other side" there is an admixture or outer ring of light which surrounds the darkness, as it is written: "A whirlwind came out of the north, a great cloud... and a brightness was about it" (Ezek. I, 4). And he saw this brightness from a distance but, as it were, through a partition; therefore, although he prophesied, he knew not what he prophesied: he looked at the light with a "closed eye" (Num. XXIV, 4), for there is no sphere of the "other side" that entirely lacks

Zohar: Shemoth, Section 2, Page 69b

some streak of light from the side of holiness, as even in a field of straw there are some grains of wheat, save only certain minor powers of special shamelessness and uncleanness. And it is this little spot of light which Balaam saw. Blessed is Moscs who moved in all the supernal holy regions, and who beheld that which it is not given to any other human being to behold. Moreover, as Balaam saw from a distance a small light from within the "other side", as it were through a partition, so Moses saw through the great light, as through a wall, a streak of darkness at its edge; but even he did not see it always, just as Balaam did not always see the streak of light. Happy was the lot of the faithful prophet Moses, for what is it that we read concerning him? "And an angel of the Lord appeared unto him in a flame of fire out of the midst of a bush" (Ex. III, 2). The bush was indeed in that region of holiness and clave to it, for all things cleave to one another, the pure and the impure, there is no purity except through impurity; a mystery which is expressed in the words: "a clean thing out of an unclean" (Job XIV, 4). The brain is contained in a shell, a shell which will not be broken until that time when the dead shall rise again. Then will the shell be broken and the light shine out into the world from the brain, without any covering on it. Blessed are the righteous in this world and in the world to come.' AND JETHRO TOOK ZIPPORAH AND HER TWO SONS. Why are they called "her two sons" and not "sons of Moses"? R. Hiya said because she had brought them up. R. Eleazar, however, explained it differently, saying that because Moses had united himself with a supernal sphere of holiness (the Shekinah), it would have been irreverent to call them "his sons", although they were in fact his sons, and later, when he had separated himself for the time being from the Shekinah, and went out to meet his father-in-law, we read: "And Jethro, Moses' father-in-law, came with his sons" (v. 5). Said R. Simeon: 'Eleazar, Eleazar! I see that the beginning of thy interpretation is quite right, but not the end. Certainly, because of the honour of the Shekinah, who was united with him at the time, it is written, "her sons", but when it says afterwards "his sons" it refers not to Moses but to Jethro, who begat sons after Moses had come to him, like Laban, who had no sons before Jacob came and dwelt in his house. For Moses' sake, and through his merit, did Jethro beget sons, whom he then brought with him to Moses, so that they might all enter together under the wings of the Shekinah. Therefore it says also in the following verse (6): "I, thy father-in-law, Jethro, am come unto thee, and thy wife, and her two sons with her." And that Jethro did have sons is definitely stated: "And the children of the Kenite, Moses' father-in-law..." (Judges I, 16), and he left his sons to be with Moses.'

Then R. Simeon went on to expound in connection with this theme the words of the prophet Isaiah (II, 3): "And many people shall go, and say, Come ye, and let us go up to the mountain of the Lord, to the house of the God of Jacob." 'A time will come', he said, 'when the heathen nations will wear their feet out to go and be brought under the wings of the Shekinah. "Let us go up", they will say- since all paganism is a descent, but cleaving to the Holy One is an ascent- "to the mountain of the Lord", i.e. the God of Abraham, who said: "In the mount of the Lord it shall be seen" (Gen. XXII, 14); for as the mountain is free to all to ascend, so is this holy place open to receive all comers. The verse continues: "to the house of the God of Jacob", because Jacob called the same place "a house of God" (Ibid. XXVIII, 17). Or, rather, it is called "mount" and is also called "house", although it is the same sphere of the Divine,

Zohar: Shemoth, Section 2, Page 70a

since it is a "mount" for the nations of the world, who have to ascend it if they desire to enter under the wings of the Shekinah, but a "house" to Israel, to whom the Shekinah stands in the relationship of a wife to a husband, united in love and joy, hovering over Israel like a mother over her children. Of Jethro we read: "And Jethro... came with his sons... to Moses into the desert." When it says "to Moses", why add "to the desert"? Because herein lay the whole significance of his coming; the "desert" symbolized the "mountain of the Lord", the place for the reception of proselytes; in other words, Jethro came to Moses with the intention of becoming a proselyte and entering under the wings of the Shekinah. Everyone who comes to this region called "Mountain" becomes a participant in this mystery, and is called "a proselyte of righteousness". However, although he is joined to this holy supernal sphere, yet is he called "Ger" (proselyte, lit. sojourner), a person living out of his own country, because he has left his own people and kin and taken up his abode in a new place. MOREOVER, THOU SHALT LOOK ABOUT AND CHOOSE OUT OF ALL THE PEOPLE, ABLE MEN. R. Isaac and R. Yose were one day studying the Torah in Tiberias. R. Simeon passed by and asked them what they were engaged upon. They answered him: 'The words which we have learned from thee, Master,' 'Which?' said he. They replied: 'It arises out of the verse: "This is the book of the generations of man; in the day when God created man, in the likeness of God made he him" (Gen. v, 1). We were taught,' they said, 'that this verse indicates that the Holy One showed to the first man all the future generations of mankind: all the leaders, all the sages of each period. We were further taught concerning the mystery contained in the words "this is the book" that there are two books, an upper and a lower book. The lower book is the "book of remembrance", and the upper one is called "this". And in order to show that the two are not separated, but form one, it is written "this is the book". There are two grades, male and female. For all the souls and spirits that enter human beings are alluded to in the words "generations of man (Adam)", for they all issue from the "Righteous One", and this is the "watering of the river that went out of Eden to water the garden" (Gen. II, 10). There is also another, a lower "Adam", alluded to in the words, "on the day that God created man (Adam)", in the same verse.

Zohar: Shemoth, Section 2, Page 70b

In regard to the upper Adam, the union of male and female is at first only distantly alluded to in the words "this is the book", but after they produced offspring they are called openly "Adam". Then it is said that God made man in the "likeness" of God. By the word "likeness" we are to understand a kind of mirror in which images appear momentarily and then pass away. According to another explanation, the word "likeness" refers to the union of male and female organs: and so the Master affirmed. Furthermore: "This is the book of the generations of Man", viz. the book which reveals the inner meaning of the features of man, so as to teach the knowledge of human nature. The character of man is revealed in the hair, the forehead, the eyes, the lips, the features of the face, the lines of the hands, and even the ears. By these seven can the different types of men be recognized. 'The Hair. A man with coarse, upstanding, wavy hair, is of a truculent disposition. His heart is as stiff as a die. His works are not upright. Have no fellowship with him. A man with very smooth, sleek and heavy-hanging hair, is a good companion, and one benefits from association with him. When left to himself he is not quite reliable. He cannot keep secrets

Zohar: Shemoth, Section 2, Page 71a

unless they are of great importance. His actions are sometimes good and sometimes the reverse.

'A man whose hair lies flat, yet is not sleek, is fearless and insolent. He has a strong desire to do good, for he perceives the beauty of goodness, but alas! his good intentions are never realized. In his old age he becomes God-fearing and pious. Great secrets are not to be entrusted to him, but he is safe enough with small ones. He can make much out of little and his words are listened to with respect. He is under the esoteric sign of the letter Zain, according to the scheme which our Master has taught us.

'A man whose hair is black and extremely glossy will succeed in all his doings, particularly in secular matters such as commerce, for instance. He is generous. But he prospers only as an individual; anyone associating himself with him will also have success, but not for long. He is also under the letter Zain.

'One whose hair is black but not glossy is not always successful in mundane affairs. It is good to associate oneself with him for a while in business matters. Should he be a student of the Torah he will succeed in his studies, and others who will join him will likewise succeed. He is a man who can keep a secret, but not for long. He is of a despondent nature, but will prevail against his enemies. He is under the sign of the letter Yod when it is not included in the letter Zain, but is numbered independently among the small letters.

'A man who is bald is successful in business, but is not straightforward. There is always a scarcity of food in his house. He is hypocritical; that is, when his baldness begins in youth. If he becomes bald in his old age he changes and becomes the opposite of what he was before, for good or for ill. This, however, only refers to the baldness which occurs on the forehead, at the spot where the phylactery is put on. Otherwise, it is not so. He is not

Zohar: Shemoth, Section 2, Page 71b

deceitful, but is given to backbiting and insinuation. He is occasionally sin-fearing. He is under the sign of the letter Zain when it includes the letter Yod. So much for the mysteries revealed by the different kinds of hair, mysteries revealed and entrusted only to those well versed in holy lore, those who comprehend the ways and mysteries of the Torah, by which they may find out the hidden propensities of men. 'The forehead. The secret of the forehead belongs under the sign of the letter Nun, which forms the completion of the letter Zain; sometimes this is included in the symbolism of Zain and sometimes it stands separately. 'A forehead which rises sharply upward from the nose, being straight and flat without any outward curve or rounding, indicates that its owner is somewhat thoughtless. Such a man will consider himself wise, though in reality he knows little. His temper will be quick, and his tongue like a serpent's. If his forehead has large uneven furrows when he speaks, but other lines on his forehead lie even, he is not a person to associate with save for a brief period. Whatever he plans or does is only for his own advantage; he cares for no one but himself. He is incapable of keeping any secret entrusted to him, and the saying, "A tale-bearer revealeth secrets" (Prov. XI, 13) is true of him; indeed, he cares not what he says. This type of person belongs to the mystery of the letter Nun when it is contained in the letter Zain. Such a one may be thought of as anything but reliable. 'A fine and rounded forehead indicates a man of great penetration, but whose judgement is sometimes clouded. He loves cheerfulness, and is kindhearted to all. He has high intellectual interests. Should he study the Torah he will become very proficient. When he speaks three large wrinkles appear on his forehead and three smaller ones above each eye. If when he is angry he weeps, he is better than he appears to be. In word and deed he is forthright and cares nothing for anyone. He will study the Torah with profit. Anyone

Zohar: Shemoth, Section 2, Page 72a

who allies himself with him will derive benefit from the association and will profit even in secular matters. He is not consistently pious. In legal affairs he will always be unlucky, and should therefore avoid such embroilments as far as possible. This type stands in the symbolism of the letter Nun alone when it is not included in the Zain. It is for this reason that he must shun legal matters, since he does not belong to the region of justice, but to that of love and mercy. 'A person whose forehead is large and yet unrounded - the kind of man who always bends his head, whether he stand or move-this type can be divided into two classes, both witless. The madness of the one is evident, apparent to all; such a person is an acknowledged idiot. On his forehead are four large wrinkles, which usually appear when he speaks. Sometimes, however, the skin of his forehead is stretched and the wrinkles are not evident, but other larger ones appear close to his eyes. He laughs for no reason, and at nothing. His mouth is large and loose. Such a man is of no worth or use. The other kind of madness included in this type is less apparent, and is unnoticeable in common intercourse. Such a man may pursue study with success, even the study of the Torah, though he will not take it up for its own sake, but only to make a show. He makes a great parade of his religion, to give the impression that he is deeply pious, but in reality he has no thought of God, but only of man. The one object of all his thoughts and behaviour is to draw attention to himself. This type, with its two distinct variants, also stands under the sign of the Nun when it is contained in the Zain. 'A large rounded forehead indicates one who is openminded and generally gifted. He can acquire any kind of knowledge, even without a teacher. His undertakings are uniformly successful, except when they are concerned with money matters, in which he sometimes comes to grief. He can infer great things from small; hence he is rightly called discerning. He is detached from the things of this world, and even when he knows that he will suffer

Zohar: Shemoth, Section 2, Page 72b

by not considering earthly matters he pays them no heed. He is tenderhearted. His forehead is deeply furrowed by two wrinkles, set high upon his brow, one over each eye. His forehead also has three long lines, and between his eyes is the double vertical furrow which signifies deep thought. He is always concerned with realities and not with appearances, because he does not care what men say about him. He is never afraid for long. He is very conciliatory. To outsiders his acts appear sometimes childish and sometimes wise. This type also stands in the sign of the Nun when it is separated and not included in the Zain. So much for the mystery connected with the study of the forehead. 'The eyes. The eyes are connected with the symbolism of the letter Samech. There are varieties of colour and of form. In the substances which go to compose the visible discernible eye are contained four colours. There is the white of the ball, which is common to all sorts of eyes. Enclosed within this white is the darker hue of the iris-thus white and dark are united. Included in this dark there is yet another shade, a bluish tinge; and the inmost circle of colour is black, this being the pupil. 'A man whose eyes are evenly set is straightforward and free from guile. A person with such eyes is always merry and full of jokes. He has good intentions, but seldom carries them out because of his fickleness. His mind is chiefly occupied with worldly things, but he has the capacity for spiritual matters if he should turn his thoughts towards them; therefore he should be encouraged in this direction. His eyebrows are long, slanting downward. In the midst of these several colours of the eye are sundry fine red veins, which are called the "small letters" of the eyes, because, when the colours shine,

Zohar: Shemoth, Section 2, Page 73a

their light causes the letters to be revealed in those veins to the initiated, these veins being formed in the shape of the letter Samech when it contains the letter He'. 'A man who has blue eyes set in white will be of a kindly disposition, but at the same time selfish. If the black is not noticeable in his eyes he will have strong desires, but not for evil, though he will not resist evil when it approaches. He can be trusted when he speaks of matters within his own knowledge, but not otherwise. He can keep a secret so long as it is a secret, but once it has leaked out he tells everything, since he does nothing perfectly. The colours of such an eye and the type to which its possessor conforms are contained in the mystery of the letter He' when contained in the letters Zain and Samech. 'He whose eyes are of a yellowish-blue colour has madness in his veins; he therefore suffers from megalomania and is grandiloquent in his manner and speech. In discussion he is easily defeated. He is not worthy to be instructed in the mystical meanings of the Torah, as he does not accept them meekly but becomes puffed up with his knowledge. This type belongs to the mystery of the letter He', which is included in the letter Zain only, being far removed from the letter Samech on account of his conceit. When such a man speaks, many wrinkles appear on his forehead. 'One whose eyes are pale with a certain admixture of a greenish hue is of an irascible disposition, but is also often kind-hearted enough. When angered, however, he becomes cruel. He cannot be entrusted with a secret. He belongs to the sign of the letter He' when it is included in the letter Samech. 'The man whose eyes are white and blue, with only a spot of black in them, can be trusted with secrets and makes good use of them. If he makes a good beginning in anything

he goes on prospering. His enemies cannot prevail against him, they can do him no evil, and eventually they are entirely subdued by him. He is under the sign of the letter Kaph when it is included in the letter Samech. 'So much for the mysteries concerning the eyes, which are revealed unto the wise. 'The lineaments of the countenance. For the masters of the inner wisdom the features of the face are not those which appear outwardly, but those within formed by internal forces; for the features of the face are moulded by the impress of the inner face which is concealed in the spirit residing within. This spirit produces outward traits which are recognizable to the wise, the true features being discernible from the spirit. Man has a spirit on which the letters of the alphabet are in a way designed. All these letters are enclosed in that spirit, and for a time the designs of those letters enter into the face; and as they enter, the face appears with the design of these letters upon it. But this semblance lasts for a short time only, save upon the faces of adepts in wisdom, on whom it is always visible. 'There is a place which is called "the world to come", from whence issues the mystery of the Torah with its alphabet of twenty-two letters, which is the essence of all things. Now that "river which goes out of Eden" carries all this along with it, so that when the spirits and the souls emerge therefrom they are all stamped with the imprint of those letters; the which, when the spirit of a man be thus stamped by it, makes also a certain impression on the face.' Said R. Simeon to them: 'If so, the likeness of the Mother is not impressed upon the form of that spirit.' They replied: 'This, Master, is the teaching which we have heard from thine own lips: The design of the letters proceeds from the side which is above, and the image of the Mother is impressed upon the spirit, while below the form of the letter is hidden in the spirit. The design of the Mother which is outwardly discernible follows the four prototypes- Man, Lion, Bull, and Eagle, in the Supernal Chariot, and the spirit projects the image of them all for a time, because whatsoever belongs to the domain of

the spirit thrusts itself forward and is both visible and invisible. All these forms are designed in the shape of the letters, and although they are hidden they are discerned for a short space by those who have eyes to see, by the wise who can comprehend the mystery of wisdom, to contemplate therein. Now, these are the four designs, their manifestations and significance: '1. When a man walks in the way of truth, those who know the mysteries of the inner wisdom can recognize him, because the inner spirit is duly prepared in him, and projects the full design of itself from within to without, from invisible to visible. And that design it is which becomes the outer form of a man. That is the design which is more perfect than any other. This design is the one which is made visible for a little unto the eyes of Wisdom and the children thereof. When one looks on the face of such a man one is moved to love him. On it is traced the design of four letters by means of a fine vein which is projected from the right side, and another vein, itself containing two more, which is projected from the left. These four signs severally form the four letters which make up the word edut (testimony). The sign of the first letter is represented by the vein which is on the right side, and each of the other three letters by one of the other three veins. This we find expressed in the words: "A testimony (edut) in Joseph" (Ps. LXXXI, 6), for everyone who looked upon him loved him, and he was perfected in love. In the seed of David the colours are reversed, and this it was that misled Samuel (I Sam. XVI, 7). Such a face contains all forms. Such a man is even-tempered, self-controlled, even when he is angered, and quickly appeased.

'2. When a man, not entirely bad, changes his ways and turns to the Lord, a good spirit begins to rest upon him, so that he is enabled to prevail against the evil that was in him, and for a time this new spirit thrusts itself forward into the expression of his face in the form of a lion. At a first casual examination his face would not inspire love, but gradually it becomes better comprehended and so better loved. When people look at him a sense of shame for his past misdeeds comes over him, for he feels that everyone knows his former evil ways, and the blood rushes to his face, and then again he turns pale. On his face are three veins, one on the right, one going up to the bridge of the nose, and a third which is joined thereto and branches downward from them. These veins form the shapes of the letters which are traced upon his face. They usually stand out prominently and quiver, but when he is penitent and gradually becomes accustomed to walking in the way of truth they subside. The mystery of these letters is contained in the word Karib (Koph, Resh, Yod, Beth, "near"), signifying that he had been far from holiness.

Although there are also other veins in his face, these do not protrude, except when he treads the paths of crookedness and iniquity. Here again the seed of David are the reverse of other men, first appearing in the form of Man and then in that of Lion, finally separating and taking the form of the "other side". '3. When a man deserts the ways of the Torah and follows ways of iniquity, the holy spirit, which formerly dwelt in his inner self, removes its influence from him and another spirit takes up its abode there, with another form which impresses itself on the outer lineaments and is there manifested to the vision of the wise in the form of an Ox. When they gaze at the person thus possessed, they mentally behold this form, and they observe in him two red, berry-like veins on the right side of the face, and three on the left. These are the symbolic letters of his type which shape themselves thus visibly in his face: one spherical and thin, the two others, also round, above it. The eyes of such a man are sunk deep in his head. The symbolic expression of these letters is as follows: The first vein is in the form of the letter Kaph, and the other two severally in that of Resh and Tau (Karet=to be cut off). The same letters are denoted by the veins on the left side of the face. Their significance is indicated by the words: "The shew (ha-Karath) of their countenance doth witness against them" (Isa. III, 9). These veins swell in the face more than all the others; but when the sinner repents and turns from the way of the left side back to the right hand of mercy and righteousness, that spirit whose form is the ox is subdued, and the spirit of holiness prevails; these thin veins then protrude no more, but recede into the inner reaches of the flesh and are lost sight of, and those which are the symbol of the good spirit become evident in their stead. With the seed of David the reverse was the case: first the lion held sway, and afterwards the ox. Two dark veins were made visible in his face, one on the right side of it and one on the left, which formed the two letters, Daleth and Ain; this being quite the reverse of other men. '4. This is the sign of a man who is perpetually in the state of making reparation for past misdeeds, making good the defects of his former life on earth. He is symbolized by the form of an eagle. His spirit is weak. No protuberant veins with a symbolic significance can be discerned in the lineaments of his countenance, since these were lost during the period of his former life. But this is the sign by which he can be recognized. His eyes do not sparkle even when he is joyful, because his spirit does not shine in the letters, and the spark of light which was in him in his former state has been extinguished. He does not belong to the grade of those whose character can be read in their faces. To him can be applied the words: "Wherefore I praise the dead which are already dead more than the living which are yet alive" (Eccl. IV, 2). The seed of David, however, is indicated in the words: "The secret of the Lord is with them that fear Him, to show them His covenant." 'Thus in the spirit of man, as we have shown, are inscribed letters which press through into visibility. To penetrate through these reflections to the inner symbols and to decipher those symbols aright is the privilege of the wise alone, that they may finally attain to knowledge of the spirit of which the symbols are the manifestation, through the esoteric significance of the words "This is the book" (Gen. v, 1). Through this all is revealed to them save that countenance which is to be judged by a different rule, according to the domination

Zohar: Shemoth, Section 2, Page 75b

of the spirit or the Lord of the spirit. Happy and blessed indeed are they to whom is entrusted knowledge of all these things! So much for the mystery of the countenance. 'The lips. The mystery of the lips belongs to the letter Pe' when it is included in the letter Samech. A man whose lips are big and thick is a tale-bearer, without shame or fear, a man of strife and mischief. He cannot keep a secret, but when he happens to be a student of the Torah he can for a time cover and keep hidden secret matters. His sign is the letter Pe' when it is included in the letter Resh, but not in Samech. He makes a show of being pious, but is not; one should not have any dealings with him, because all his words proceed out of his mouth alone, but not from his heart. 'Thick dry lips indicate a man of quick temper and insolence, intolerant, speaking evil of his fellows, without any sense of shame. He likes to mock and jeer at others. One should avoid a man of this kind. And when his whole face becomes hairy his evil tongue witnesses clearly against him. He is totally shameless, loving strife. In worldly matters he is apt to be successful. He is of a vengeful spirit, and relentless towards his enemies. Concerning him it is said: "A wicked man hardeneth his face" (Prov. XXI, 29). He stands under the sign of the letter Pe' alone when it is not included in the Samech, though it may sometimes be included in the letter Resh. 'The ears. Excessively large ears are a sign of stupidity in the heart and madness in the mind. Small shapely ears denote wisdom and sensibility, and their owner likes to try everything. His type is under the sign of the letter Yod when it is included in all the other letters. 'So much for the mysteries of the human physiognomy. Now we turn to other mysteries contained in the letters, but not set forth upon the countenance, being concerned with the apprehension of times and seasons: mysteries of which we are unworthy.' R. Simeon said: 'Ye are worthy in this world and ye are worthy in the world to come. Blessed are my eyes that will be worthy to see it all when I enter the world to come. For my soul calls to the Ancient of Days: "Thou preparest a table before me in the presence of my enemies; thou anointest my head with oil; my cup runneth over" (Ps. XXIII, 5). And the Holy One, blessed be He, calls concerning us: "Open ye the gates, that the righteous people which keepeth truth may enter in" (Isa. XXVI, 2).' Then they began to discourse on the verse: "And they (the Hayoth) had the hands of a man, under their wings, on their four sides" (Ezek. I, 8). 'This', said they, 'has been explained by the Fellowship as referring to the hands stretched out to receive penitents who return to God. But the expression "the hands of a man" also signifies all those forms and supernal mysteries which the Holy One has stamped upon man and ordered in his fingers outwardly and inwardly and in the "palm" (Kaph). When the Holy One created man He set in him all the images of the supernal mysteries of the world above, and all the images of the lower mysteries of the world below, and all are designed in man, who stands in the image of God, because he is called "the creation of the palm", and this is the mystery of the letter Kaph. Supernal mysteries and symbols are contained in this; the Ten Words, five belonging to the right side and five to the left, are all united in it as one mystery. Therefore it says: "I will also smite my one palm (kaph) upon the other" (Ezek. XXI, 17), meaning that the Lord will cause the two hands to be divided, so that blessing will depart from the world and the glory of Israel shall be given over to the nations. But when they are united as one, it is as it says: "One vessel (kaph, lit. palm) of ten shekels of gold" (Num. VII, 14). When they were united "God created Man in His own image." Man was in the Divine mind, in the inner mystery. God created him, male and female in one, "in the image of God", symbolized by the palm. For when man was created, what is it that is written concerning him? "Thou hast clothed me with skin and flesh, and hast fenced me with bones and sinews" (Job x, 11).

Zohar: Shemoth, Section 2, Page 76a

'What, then, is man? Does he consist solely of skin, flesh, bones and sinews? Nay, the essence of man is his soul; the skin, flesh, bones and sinews are but an outward covering, the mere garments, but they are not the man. When man departs (from this world) he divests himself of all these garments. The skin with which he covers himself, and all these bones and sinews, all have a symbolism in the mystery of the Supernal Wisdom, corresponding to that which is above. The symbolism of the skin is as the Master has taught us in connection with the words: "Who stretchest out the heaven like a curtain" (Ps. CIV, 2); and again: "Rams' skins, dyed red, and badgers' skins" (Ex. xxv, 5, in connection with the tabernacle). These skins are a garment which protects a garment, viz. the extension of the heavens, which is the outer garment (of the Divine). The curtains (of the Tabernacle) are the inner garments; corresponding to the skin upon the flesh. The bones and the sinews symbolize the Chariots and the celestial Hosts, which are inward. All these are garments upon that which is inward; which also is the mystery of the Supernal Man, who is the innermost. The same is found here below. Man is something inward, and his garments correspond to that which is above. The bones and sinews, as we have said, correspond to the Chariots and Hosts. The flesh is a covering to those hosts and chariots, and manifests itself outwardly, and is symbolically connected with the "other side" (the purely sensuous element). The skin, covering all, corresponds to the firmaments which cover all things. And all these are merely garments to clothe himself withal, for within is the essential man. Everything below corresponds to that which is above. This is the significance of the words: "And God created man in His own image; in the image of God created He him." Esoterically, the man below corresponds entirely to the Man above. Just as in the firmament, which covers the whole universe, we behold different shapes formed by the conjunction of stars and planets to make us aware of hidden things and deep mysteries; so upon the skin which covers our body and which is, as it were, the body's firmament, covering all, there are shapes and designs–the stars and planets of the body's firmament, the skin through which the wise of heart may behold the hidden things and the deep mysteries indicated by these shapes and expressed in the human form. Concerning this it is written: "The viewers of the heavens, the stargazers" (Is. XLVII, 13). But all this can only be discerned, in the case of the stars, in a clear sky, and, in man, when the face shines and is not clouded with anger, for then another rule applies. But when the faces of men are serene, and they are in their normal state, their shapes and lineaments reveal to the wise the inner thoughts and propensities of the mind. So by the lines of the hands and of the fingers it is possible to discern hidden facts of a man's personality. They are the shining stars which reveal the varieties of human types and their relationships to the upper treasures.' [Tr. Note: Here follows in the original a discourse on palmistry.]

Zohar: Shemoth, Section 2, Page 76b through 77b

[Note: The Hebrew text is not translated as explained in the Translator's note on page 76a]

Zohar: Shemoth, Section 2, Page 78a

[Note: The first 17 lines of the Hebrew text do not appear in the translation since they continue the discourse begun on page 76b]

MOREOVER THOU SHALT PROVIDE (lit. behold) OUT OF ALL THE PEOPLE, ETC.. Said R. Simeon: It does not say "thou shalt choose", but "thou shalt behold", namely, by means of the gift of inner sight of those characteristics which we have mentioned. All are indicated in this verse: "thou shalt look" refers to the hair; "of all the people" to the forehead; "for able men" to the face; "God-fearing" to the eyes; "men of truth" to the lips; and "hating covetousness" to the hands. All these are the signs by which to recognize men: signs, that is, to those on whom the spirit of wisdom rests. And yet Moses had no need of these signs, for we read: "And Moses chose able men out of all Israel" (V. 25); he chose them by the inspiration of the Holy Spirit, for we read: "When they have a matter, he cometh unto me" (v. 16); this "he" in the singular instead of "they" in the plural indicates that it refers to the Holy Spirit. So there was no necessity for him to use the gift of inner sight in order to find out who were the right persons: he knew at once whom to choose through the enlightenment of the Holy Spirit. Similarly Solomon, in all the legal cases brought before him, could give his decisions without the aid of any witnesses, because the Holy Spirit was present at his throne, and everyone coming near to it was overcome with fear and trembling. There was an invisible figure hidden in the throne, and when any one uttered a false plea it made a sound by which Solomon knew at once that the person was not telling the truth. But the Messiah will discern persons by their odour, for of him it says: "His scent will be in the fear of the Lord, and he shall not judge after the sight of his eyes, neither reprove after the hearing of his ears" (Isa. XI, 3). These three judged without witnesses and without warning; all others must judge according to the law, and must decide by the word of witnesses. The wise who are adepts in physiognomic lore must warn men and provide healing for their souls. Blessed are they in this world, and blessed in the world to come.' IN THE THIRD MONTH, WHEN THE CHILDREN OF ISRAEL WERE GONE FORTH OUT OF THE LAND OF EGYPT.... The third month is the one in which the celestial chief Uriel has sway. He has three hundred and sixty-five myriads of camps with him, corresponding to all the days of the year. All have three hundred and sixty-five keys of light issuing from the inner supernal sphere called "Hashmal" (v. Ezek. I, 4), which is hidden and veiled, in which the mysteries of the holy celestial letters of the Holy Name

Zohar: Shemoth, Section 2, Page 78b

are suspended. This "hashmal" receives the most supernal and recondite lights, and passes them on, so that all the camps receive those keys of the light [Tr. Note: Tifereth.] which issues forth from that sphere. And that light is contained in two lights, which yet are one. The first light [Tr. Note: Hesed] is white, too bright for the eye to behold. It is the light which is hidden away for the righteous in the world to come, as it is written: "Light is sown for the righteous" (Ps. xcvii, ii). The second light [Tr. Note: Geburah.] is one which gleams and sparkles redly. The two are united and become one. Uriel, the head of the angels, and all those hosts, partake of this light. As it is contained in two lights, it is called the "Twins". Therefore, in that month in which the Torah was given (Sivan), the constellation of the "Twins" rules, and from them issue lights of various grades below to illumine the world. Among all the other signs of the Zodiac there is not one possessing mouth or tongue, but this one has both, and the two are one. Therefore it is written in regard to the Torah: "And thou shalt meditate therein day and night" (Jos. I, 8), "day" corresponding to the tongue, and "night" corresponding to the mouth. And both these are one. Therefore the word teomim (twins), in connection with Jacob and Esau (Gen. xxv, 24), is written in a defective form, in order to indicate that Jacob alone is under the sign of this constellation. For Jacob had two months, Nisan and Iyar, as his, and is therefore within the symbolism of the "twins"; while Esau's months are Tamuz and Ab, and only nine days in Ab, so it can be seen that he is not included in the Twins. He separated himself and turned towards impurity, in chaos and desolation. And because Jacob is in the sign of the Twins the Torah was given to his children in the months of the Twins, being itself "twin", viz. written and oral; it was given in the third month (Sivan), symbolizing the treble Torah (Law, Prophets, Writings). R. Hiya said: 'At the time when the Israelites approached Mount Sinai, the Holy One gathered their families to Him and examined them as to their lineage, and He found them all of a holy seed, of genuine birth. So he said to Moses: "Now do I wish to give the Torah unto Israel. Draw them to Me by telling them of My love to their fathers and to themselves, and also concerning all the signs and wonders that I have manifested unto them. And thou shalt be My messenger." AND MOSES WENT UP UNTO GOD, AND THE LORD CALLED UNTO HIM OUT OF THE MOUNTAIN. He went to the region where the wings of the Shekinah are outspread, concerning which it is said: "He bowed the heavens and came down" (Ps. XVIII, 10). Said R. Judah: 'As long as the tracings of the Supernal King [Tr. Note: The emanations of the Godhead.] adhere to their proper places all worlds are impregnated with joy and all creation is upright and stable. Concerning this it is written: "And all the people among whom thou art shall see the work of the Lord that it will be terrible" (Ex. XXXIV, 10).' What is the meaning of "terrible"? Said R. Eleazar: 'It signifies the highest perfection of all, as in the expression: "A great, mighty, terrible God" (Deut. x, 17).

Zohar: Shemoth, Section 2, Page 79a

We have a boraitha to the same effect.' R. Yose once said: 'One day I stood before R. Judah the ancient. I asked him to explain to me the meaning of the words: "And he (Jacob) was afraid, and said, How terrible is this place!" What did he see there to call it terrible? His answer was: "Jacob saw manifested in that region the consummation of the holy faith, which corresponded to the reality above. And any place where such a consummation is revealed is called 'terrible'." I then asked him: "If that is so, why then does the Targum translate the word 'nora' (terrible) with 'fear' (d'hilu), and not with 'complete' (sh'lim)?" His answer was that there is no true fear and awe except in a place where there is completeness, as it is written "O fear the Lord, ye his saints, for there is no deficiency (mahsor) to them that fear him" (Ps. XXXIV, 10), and in the sphere where there is no deficiency, there is completeness.' A baraita also tells us that R. Yose once expounded the verse: Who hath ascended up into heaven, or descended? Who hath gathered the wind in his fists? Who hath bound the waters in a garment? Who hath established all the ends of the earth? What is his name, and what is his son's name? (Prov. xxx, 4). 'It is Moses who ascended up to heaven, as it says: "And Moses went up unto God." It is Aaron who gathered the wind in his fists, as it says: "His fist full of sweet incense" (Lev. XVI, 12). It is Elijah who "hath bound the waters in a garment", for he said: "There shall not be dew nor rain these years, but according to my word" (I Kings XVII, 1). And it is Abraham who "hath established all the ends of the earth", for it says concerning him: "These are the generations of the heavens and the earth when they were created (behibar'am)" (Gen. II, 4), the last word having the same letters as Abraham.' This was R. Jose's first interpretation. He then gave a different one, saying: '"Who hath ascended up into heaven?" The Holy One, of whom it says: "God hath ascended with a shout" (Ps. XLVII, 6). "Who hath gathered the wind in his fists?" The Holy One, "in whose hand is the soul of every living thing" (Job XII, 10). "Who hath bound the waters in a garment?" The Holy One, who "bindeth up the waters in his thick clouds" (Ibid. XXVI,8). "Who hath established all the ends of the earth?" The Holy One, of whom it says: "in the day when the Lord God made heaven and earth" (Gen. II, 4).' Finally, he affirmed that the words indicate the four knots (elements) of the universe: fire, air, water, earth. Said R. Jesse: 'It is evident that R. Jose's various applications of this verse are incompatible one with the other!' But when these interpretations came to the ears of R. Simeon, he put his hands on R. Jose's head and blessed him, saying: 'That which thou hast said is quite right. It is perfectly true, but whence hast thou these interpretations?' 'From my father, who heard it from R. Hamnuna the ancient,' replied R. Yose. One day R. Simeon sat at the gate of Sepphoris, when R. Jesse said to him: 'R. Yose applied the verse, "Who hath ascended, etc.", first to Moses, then to the Holy One, and finally to the four elements, and I saw that thou, Master, didst bless him!' Said R. Simeon: 'What he said was perfectly true. All the applications signify one and the same thing, since they all have their root and fulfilment in the Holy One, and they are all practically equivalent.' R. Jesse was deeply impressed by these words and said: 'Now I see that this is indeed so. And I have also heard it on another occasion from the mouth of the Master. But what is the meaning of the words, "And what is his son's name?" ' R. Simeon replied: 'The inner meaning of this I myself have taught my son, R. Eleazar.' 'I pray thee, tell it to me, for I did ask thee concerning it in a dream, but when I awoke I had forgotten thine answer.' 'And now, when I tell thee, wilt thou remember it?' 'I surely will,' replied R. Jesse, 'I always remember what my Mastor tells me.' Said R. Simeon: 'The words must be understood in the light of the expression, "My first-born son Israel" (Ex. IV, 22), and "Israel, in whom I am glorified" (Isa. XLIX, 3). "Israel" here refers to the supernal world, and it is this which is called "son". Whereupon R. Jesse replied: 'With all due respect to the Master, this is a secret which I already know.' But yet again he forgot it. He was much perturbed. But when he went into his house and lay down to sleep, he saw in his dream an haggadic book, wherein it was written: "Wisdom (Hokmah) and glory (Tifereth) in His sanctuary." When he awoke, he straightway went to R. Simeon, kissed his hand, and said: 'This night I saw in my dream an

Zohar: Shemoth, Section 2, Page 79b

haggadic book wherein were written the words: "Wisdom and glory in His sanctuary", "Wisdom" above, "Glory" below, and "in His sanctuary" at the side. This I saw in a dream, and I found it on my lips when I awoke.' Said R. Simeon to him: 'Until this time thou wast too young to join the company of the "reapers of the field", but now everything has been shown unto thee! Thus the meaning is: Wisdom (Hokmah) is His Name and Glory (Tifereth) the name of His son.' AND MOSES WENT UP UNTO GOD. Blessed indeed was Moses to have been worthy of this honour, to which the Torah herself testifies. Said R. Judah: 'See what a difference there is between Moses and other men: "Going up" in regard to ordinary men means "getting rich", "getting on", in honours, in office, in rank, etc. But Moses "went up unto God". Truly, he was blessed.' R. Yose remarked that this is one of the passages from which the members of the Fellowship derive the lesson that "he who comes to be purified is assisted from above": because Moses "went up unto God", therefore "the Lord called unto him out of the mountain". AND THE LORD CALLED UNTO HIM OUT OF THE MOUNTAIN, SAYING, THUS SHALT THOU SAY TO THE HOUSE OF JACOB, AND TELL THE CHILDREN OF ISRAEL. R. Isaac referred in this connection to the verse: "Blessed is the man whom thou choosest, and causest to approach unto thee, that he may dwell in thy courts" (Ps. LXV, 5). 'Blessed is the man', he said, 'whom the Holy One befriends and brings near to him to dwell in the holy Palace! He who is united with Him in worship has on him a sign inscribed from above to make it known that he is one who has been chosen by the Holy King to dwell in His courts. A man who has upon him such a sign can pass through all the supernal gates without let or hindrance.' R. Judah said: 'Blessed was Moses, concerning whom that verse was written! Of him we read: "And Moses drew near unto the thick darkness where God was" (Ex. xx, 21); and also, "Moses alone came nigh to the Lord, but they did not" (Ibid. XXIV, 2).' THUS SHALT THOU SAY TO THE HOUSE OF JACOB: this refers to the females; AND TELL THE CHILDREN OF ISRAEL: this means the males. R. Simeon connected the "thus" (Koh) in this verse with the "thus" in the ordinance of the priestly benediction: "Thus (Koh) shall ye bless" (Num. VI, 23); also with, "Thy saints bless Thee" (yebarakukah), which last word can be separated into two words: yebaraku Koh, "they bless with Koh" (i.e. the Sephirah Malkuth); "Saying" indicates the side of Justice (Severity), while "telling" indicates the side of Mercy, as in the verse: "And he declared (wa-yagged) unto you his covenant (mercy)" (Deut. IV, 13), and also in the declaration made by the Israelite on bringing the basket of firstfruits to the priest: "I proclaim (higgadti) this day unto the Lord thy God" (Ibid. XXVI, 3). Said R. Yose: 'As we have mentioned this verse, I should like to ask why it says "to the Lord thy God" instead of "the Lord our God"?' R. Simeon replied: 'This is not the only case where "thy" is used instead of "our". For instance: "the Lord thy God will bring thee into a good land" (Ibid. VIII, 7); "for the Lord thy God is a consuming fire" (Ibid. IV, 23). Moses himself, who used this expression, could not say "our" God, because, according to our dictum, "he who lives outside the Land of Israel is, as it were, without God." So he said to the children of Israel, who were going to settle in the Holy Land and to receive the Shekinah there, "thy God", but he could not well say "our God", since he was not to enter himself into the Holy Land.' 'But', retorted R. Yose, 'why did the Israelites have to say "thy God", seeing that they were already in the land?' R. Simeon's reply was that they had to proclaim that it was due to the Supernal Grace that they were so favoured by God and blessed with so many good things. All this they said to the priest who, as such, is connected with the attribute of Grace (forgiveness of sin and mediatorship)." Say to the house of Jacob" is the form fitting for them, "and tell the children of Israel" is the more perfect form fitting for them. For Jacob and Israel represent two grades (Malkuth and Tifereth), and though they unite into one, yet the complete product is termed Israel.

Zohar: Shemoth, Section 2, Page 80a

Hence "thou shalt tell the children of Israel", to reveal to them wisdom, and to tell them in the spirit of wisdom the grace and the truth which' the Holy One, blessed be He, has shown to them. R. Yose once told the following story: 'It chanced one day when I was out walking, accompanied by my son, R. Hiya, that we came upon a man collecting medicinal herbs. As we drew near to him I asked: "Tell us what these bundles of herbs are for?" He gave no reply, and did not even raise his head. Said I to R. Hiya, my son: "Certainly this man is either deaf or mad, or very wise." So we sat down near to him. When he had collected all the herbs and made them into bundles and covered each bundle with vine leaves, even to the last bundle of all, he turned to us, and said: "I see that ye are Jews, and it is said that the Jews are clever people. Yet, if I did not have pity on you, you would from henceforth have to shun the company of your fellows, for you become as lepers; because, as I perceive, the odour of one of these herbs has entered into your body, and it will cause you to be outcasts for three days. But now eat this garlic and you will be healed." We did as we were bid, and fell into a deep sleep. I awakened to find myself bathed in perspiration. Then the man said: "Now your God is with you indeed, for He has ordered it that you should find me and that the cure of your bodies should be accomplished through me." As we went along he said to us: "Every person must converse with his fellows according to the sex and class to which they belong." I was struck by this remark, and said to R. Hiya, my son: "This accords with the Scriptural verse: 'Thus shalt thou say to the house of Jacob, and tell the children of Israel."' Then the man said: "You probably wondered why I did not speak to you or pay you any apparent heed when you addressed me first. The reason is that my father was the greatest expert in herbs and their properties, and from him I learnt the powers and uses of every plant with healing properties, and I spend the whole year among them. Now with regard to the herb which ye saw me bind into bundles and cover with vine leaves. In a northern corner of my dwelling there is a place in which stands a millstone, from the hole of which a man emerges from time to time, and this man has two heads and carries a sharp sword in his hand. He strikes terror into the hearts of all who behold him, and, indeed, is the bane of our lives. On account of him I gathered this herb. Now follow me, and you shall see what virtue there is in it, and what the supreme God has revealed in the world, and how even the wise cannot surmise or fathom all His mysteries." So we followed him. On the way to his house we passed a hole in the ground in which the man deposited some of the herb. When he had done so, a serpent with an enormous head issued from the hole. The man took from his girdle a piece of cloth and bound the serpent as though it were a little lamb. We were much afraid, but the man said: "Follow me until we come to his abode"; and we followed him. Presently we reached his house, and there we saw the place of which he had spoken: in the dark, behind a wall. He took a candle and kindled a fire around the place where the millstone was set; then he said to us: "Do not be frightened at what ye see, and keep silence." As he said this he loosened the serpent's bonds and set him free, then ground some of the herb to powder and sprinkled this upon the serpent's head. Immediately the serpent descended into the opening of the millstone, and we suddenly heard a voice which made the whole place shake. We wanted to run away, being sore afraid, but the man took hold of our hands, saying: "Fear not, come close to me." Presently the serpent reappeared and we saw that it was dripping blood. Again it entered the opening of the millstone. After a short time a man with two heads issued from the opening, with the serpent wound about his neck. Three times he entered the opening of the millstone and emerged again, saying: "Chameleon, chameleon, woe to his mother who brought him there!" Then the millstone was torn from its place and man and serpent together were hurled out at our feet, where they fell down and died. We were terrified, but the man who had brought us there said: "Thus is manifested the power of the herb which I collected in your presence! This was the reason why I did not look up at you or speak even a word. If

Zohar: Shemoth, Section 2, Page 80b

men but knew the wisdom of all that the Holy One, blessed be He, has planted in the earth, and the power of all that is to be found in the world, they would proclaim the power of their Lord in His great wisdom. But the Holy One has purposely hidden this wisdom from men, in order that they should not turn from His way by trusting in that wisdom alone, forgetting Him." 'When I afterwards recounted the happenings of that day to R. Simeon, he said: "Surely, that was a wise man! For it is indeed as he said. Mark this! There is no grass or herb that grows in which God's wisdom is not greatly manifested and which cannot exert great influence in heaven. We may see this from the hyssop. Whenever the Holy One desires that men should purify themselves from defilement, he orders that hyssop be used as a means of purification. Now why is this? In order that the power above which is represented by that herb should be roused to exterminate the spirit of impurity, that the defiled one may be cleansed. And as to thee, I say: Blessed be the Merciful One who delivered thee." 'YE HAVE SEEN WHAT I DID UNTO THE EGYPTIANS. AND HOW I BARE YOU ON EAGLES'

WINGS. What do "eagles' wings" denote? According to R. Judah, the "eagles" are a symbol of mercy, as it says: "As an eagle stirreth up her nest, fluttereth over her young, spreadeth abroad her wings, taketh them, beareth them on her wings, so the Lord..." (Deut. XXXII, 11). As the eagle watches lovingly over its own young, but is cruel towards others, so does the Holy One manifest His loving mercy to Israel and His severe judgement to the heathen nations. R. Simeon

found the same indication in the verse: "The way of an eagle in the heavens" (Prov. xxx, 19). R. Eleazar once went from Cappadocia to Lydda, accompanied by R. Yose and R. Hiya. They had risen at sunrise, and as the light appeared, R. Hiya said: 'I see before me the vision of the prophet, "As for the likeness of their (the Hayoth) faces, they four had the face of a man and the face of a lion, on the right side; and they four had the face of an ox on the left side; they four also had the face of an eagle" (Ezek. I, 10). Thus the lion is on the right hand, the ox on the left; but what about the eagle?' R. Eleazar replied: 'It belongs to the sphere of the "child" (i.e. Mercy), for the eagle combines mercy and cruelty; and so God led Israel with love and dealt sternly with others, and the expression, "the way of an eagle in the heavens" is thus to be taken literally, for love (mercy) is, as it were, in the centre of heaven. Hence the lion is at the right, the ox at the left, and the eagle between, uniting them. As for "man", he comprises all, as it is written: "And upon the likeness of the throne was the likeness as the appearance of a man above upon it" (Ezek. I, 26).' AND IT CAME TO PASS ON THE THIRD DAY. R. Abba connected this with the following verse: "We have a little sister, and she hath no breasts; what shall we do to our sister in the day when she will be spoken for?" (S.S. VIII, 8). 'The "little sister" is the Community of Israel, who is called the Holy One's sister; "she hath no breasts", i.e. when they approached Mount Sinai she had no merits, no good works to protect her; "what shall we do to our sister?", when the Holy One shall reveal Himself on Mount Sinai to proclaim the words of the Torah, and her soul will fly away (out of fear).' Said R. Yose: 'When the Israelites approached Mount Sinai, on that night which followed the three days during which the people abstained from conjugal intercourse, the heavenly angels came and received them with brotherly affection. For as they are angels above, so are the Israelites angels below; as they sanctify the Supreme Name above, so do the Israelites sanctify it below. And the Israelites were crowned with seventy crowns on that night. Then it was that the angels said: "We have a little sister, and she hath no breasts. What shall we do to our sister? How should we honour her on the day when the Holy One will reveal Himself to give her the Torah?" 'R. Simeon said that when the Holy One came to reveal Himself

Zohar: Shemoth, Section 2, Page 81a

on Mount Sinai, He called together His whole celestial Family and said to them: "At present the Israelites are like children, they will not know how to deport themselves in My Presence. If I should reveal Myself to them in the attribute of Power (Geburah) they will not be able to bear it, but when I manifest Myself to them in love (Rahamim) they will accept My Law." Therefore the manifestation on Mount Sinai took place on the third day, which is the Day of love (Rahamim). In this manner did He reveal Himself first in Love; and then gave them the Torah from the side of Power; and that on the third day, for it is because of the "Three" that they are called Israel; and in the morning, in "a morning without clouds" (2 Sam. XXIII, 4), since had it been a cloudy morning darkness would have been found in it, and Grace would not have been revealed. And when does Grace reveal itself? In the morning: "The morning is light"; for as soon as the day breaks Grace is manifested and Judgement passes away, but when the light of morning does not enter the judgements do not vanish away, as it is written: "When the morning stars sing together, and all the sons of God shout for joy" (Job XXXVIII, 7; i.e. the angels of judgement shout for joy as long as night continues); but as soon as those stars set and the sun shines, behold there is "a morning without clouds", and Grace is awakened in the lower world.' R. Yose said: 'The Holy One began to reveal Himself on Mount Sinai "in the morning", and we have been taught that it took place when the merit of Abraham, who "rose up early in the morning" (to sacrifice Isaac, Gen. XXII, 3), was aroused. ' AND THERE WERE THUNDERINGS (voices) AND LIGHTNINGS AND A THICK CLOUD UPON THE MOUNT, AND THE VOICE OF THE TRUMPET EXCEEDING LOUD. Said, R. Abba: 'As koloth (voices) is written in a defective form, it indicates that there were two voices united as one, the one emanating from the other: air [Tr. Note: Tifereth.] from water [Tr. Note: Hesed.] and water from air, two that were one and one that was two.' R. Yose, however, was of the opinion that the defective form of the word, suggesting the singular, indicates that it is identical with the "great voice that did not cease" (Deut. v, 19), for all other Divine voices do break off sometimes, for, as we have been taught, four times a year the "Voice" ceases, and chastisement is sent into the world, but this great and mighty Voice [Tr. Note: Binah.] never stops and never abates of its full force. We have been taught also that this Voice is "the voice of voices", the voice which contains all other voices. R. Judah said: 'The "Voice" unites air, fire, and water, and one voice makes another; hence the plural "voices".' "And lightnings." Said R. Yose: 'Therefore it says: "He maketh lightnings for the rain" (Ps. cxxxv, 7), flame being combined with moisture in a supernatural union of love and affection.' R. Judah said that the Torah was given from the side of Power. Said R. Yose: 'In that case, it must have been given from the left side.' 'No,' replied R. Judah: 'the left was turned for the time into the right, for it is written: "From his right hand a fiery law to them" (Deut. XXXIII, 2). Contrariwise we read concerning Egypt's judgement: "Thy right hand, O Lord, glorified in power" (Ex. xv, 6); where the right hand has turned into the left (judgement).' "And a thick cloud upon the mount", that is, a mighty cloud which stayed in one spot without moving. "And the voice of the trumpet exceeding loud": this voice issued from the midst of the heavy cloud, as it is written, "When ye heard the voice out of the midst of the darkness" (Deut. v, 24). According to R. Judah, there were three grades of darkness: darkness, cloud, and thick clouds (araphel), and the voice came forth from out of their innermost depths. R. Yose said that the innermost was the one referred to in the words "with a great and ceaseless voice" (Deut. v, 19). Said R. Abba: 'It is written: "And all the people saw the thundering" (Ex. xx, 18). Surely it ought to be heard the thundering? We have, however, been taught that the "voices" were delineated, carved out, as it were, upon the threefold darkness, so that they could be apprehended as something visible, and they saw and heard all those wonderful things out of that darkness, cloud and cloudy darkness; and because they saw that sight they were irradiated with a supernal light, and perceived things beyond the ken of all succeeding generations, and saw face to face (Deut. v, 4).' And whence did they derive the power so to see? According to R. Yose, from the light of those voices, for there was not one of them but emitted light which made perceptible all things hidden and veiled, and even all the generations of men up to the days of King Messiah. Therefore it says: "And all the people saw the

Zohar: Shemoth, Section 2, Page 8lb

voices"; they did actually see them. The word koloth here is preceded by the particle eth, which, as usual, indicates that we are to understand another object in addition to the one mentioned: in this case another voice from below, which gathered into itself all the light [Tr. Note: Shekinah.] emanating from the other voices in which they saw, in sublime wisdom, all the celestial treasures and all the hidden mysteries which were never revealed to succeeding generations and will not be revealed until King Messiah comes, when "they shall see eye to eye" (Isa. LII, 8). In this latter passage (Ex. xx, 18) also we find "fire torches" mentioned instead of the "lightnings" of the former. Both, however, mean one and the same thing; when the lightnings are quite formed and ready to appear they are called "fire-torches" (lapidim). The "voice of the trumpet" mentioned in the same verse is, according to R. Judah, that voice which is itself called "trumpet" in reference to the Day of Atonement (Lev. xxv, 9). According to R. Simeon, the "voice of the trumpet" is the "word which proceedeth out of the mouth of the Lord" (Deut. VIII, 3), by which "man lives". It is greater and stronger than all lower voices. On it depends all; it is called "great voice", and also a "still thin voice" (I Kings XIX, 12), i.e. a clear though tiny light which illumines all things, but a "still voice" also because men must be filled with awe and silence to hear it, as it is written: "I said, I will take heed to my ways, that I sin not with my tongue; I will keep my mouth with a bridle" (Ps. XXXIX, 2). The text proceeds: "And when the people saw it, they trembled and stood afar off" (Ex. xx, 18). The same word (wa-yanu'u, they shook) is used here of the people as is used of the "posts of the door" in the Temple which moved when Isaiah saw his vision (Isa. VI, 4). And what do we read of Ezekiel when he saw the Presence? "And I looked, and, behold, a whirlwind came out of the north, a great cloud, and a fire infolding itself, and a brightness was about it, and out of the midst thereof as the colour of amber (hashmal), out of the midst of the fire" (Ezek. I, 4). The whirlwind, according to R. Yose, was symbolic of the breaking of the power of the four kingdoms. R. Judah added that according to tradition the strong wind which was stirred from the side of celestial Power (Geburah) came from the north, the special region hidden above, out of which justice emanates, as it does not say from "north", but from "the north". "The great cloud and a fire infolding itself" are the elements which awaken judgements three times a day from the region of Power. And what renders it endurable in spite of its severity? "The brightness" that surrounds it, the light which encircles it, so that the judgement is not too hard for men to bear.

Zohar: Shemoth, Section 2, Page 82a

R. Yose, the son of R. Judah, said that the Israelites at Mount Sinai saw more of the Divine than the prophet Ezekiel, and were all united with the supernal Wisdom. They saw five different grades of voices, by which five the Torah was given-the fifth being the "voice of the trumpet"-but Ezekiel saw but five lower degrees: whirlwind, great cloud, fire, the brightness, and the colour of amber. Said R. Eleazar: 'Of the Israelites it says: "Face to face hath the Lord spoken to you" (Deut. v, 4), but Ezekiel saw only a "likeness" (Ezek. I, 5), like one who looks through a partition.' Said R. Eleazar further; 'If the Israelites saw what no prophet ever saw, how much more true is this of Moses! How happy a lot was his, who "was there with the Lord" (Ex. xxxiv, 28), and with whom He spake "in sight but not in riddles" (Num. XII, 8)!' R. Yose drew attention to the expression used of Ezekiel, "The word of the Lord came (hayo haya) unto Ezekiel" (I, 3), indicating that his vision lasted but for a short space of time. R. Eleazar remarked that the expression hayo haya suggests that he both saw and did not see, heard and did not hear (i.e. his vision and hearing were imperfect): as he says, he saw something like hashmal, but not actually hashmal itself; but of the Israelites it is said: "They saw the voices": every one according to his grade actually saw; for there is a tradition that they stood in groups and divisions, and each one saw as befitted it. According to R. Simeon, the chiefs of the tribes stood by themselves, the women by themselves, and the leaders of the people by themselves, five grades at the right and five at the left, as it is written: "Ye stand this day all of you before the Lord your God; your captains of your tribes, your elders, and your officers, with all the men of Israel"- these were five grades at the right; "your little ones, your wives, the stranger that is in thy camp, from the hewer of thy wood unto the drawer of thy water" (Deut. XXIX, 9)-these were the five grades who stood at the left. All these grades corresponded to the ten celestial grades, and to the Ten Words (Decalogue), which are Israel's eternal possession, the essence of all the commandments, the good portion of Israel. We have been taught that when the Holy One revealed Himself on Mount Sinai all the Israelites saw the Divine manifestation as one sees a light streaming through the glass of a lamp, and by means of that light each one of them saw more than did the prophet Ezekiel, since those celestial voices were all revealed together, whilst to Ezekiel only the Shekinah was revealed in Her Chariot, and he but caught glimpses of it as though through many barriers. Said R. Judah: 'Blessed was Moses, concerning whom it says: "And the Lord came down upon Mount Sinai... and the Lord called Moses up to the top of the mount," and blessed was that generation concerning whom it says: "And the Lord came down upon Mount Sinai before the eyes of the whole people." As the Torah, however, was given from the Right Hand ("from his right hand went a fiery law for them", Deut. XXXIII, 2), what essential difference was there between the manifestation to the people and the manifestation to Ezekiel?' R. Yose replied: 'On Sinai the "Head" and the "Body" of the King were revealed, as it is written: "He bowed the heavens and came down" (2 Sam. XXII, 10); but to Ezekiel it was, as it were, only the "Hand" which was shown: "And the hand of the Lord was there upon him" (Ezek. I, 3). And even the "Hand" has two aspects, a higher and a lower. Observe that he says: "The heavens were opened and I saw visions (maroth) of God" (Ezek. I, 1). "Maroth" is written in a defective form, to indicate that he merely had a vision of the Shekinah.' Said R. Jesse: 'But is the Shekinah not a representation of the whole of the Deity?' R. Yose replied: 'The "Head" of the King is not to be compared to His "Feet", although both are in the "Body" of the King.' Observe that Isaiah said "I saw (eth) the Lord" (Isa. VI, 1), but Ezekiel said "I saw visions of God".' They meant, however, the same thing, and both belonged to the same grade (of spiritual perception).

Zohar: Shemoth, Section 2, Page 82b

Why, then, did Isaiah not give a detailed account of his visions, like Ezekiel? According to R. Yose, it was necessary that Ezekiel should speak in a detailed manner in order to impress the people in exile with the fact that the Holy One loved them, and that the Shekinah and Her Chariots had gone down into exile also, to be present with them. R. Hiya asked, why did the Shekinah reveal Herself in "the land of the Chaldeans" (Ezek. I, 3), of which it says: "Behold the land of the Chaldeans, a people which is not" (Isa. XXIII, 13, i.e. degraded)? If it was for Israel's sake, surely She could have been present among them without manifesting Herself in that inauspicious place? However, had She not revealed Herself the people would not have known that She was with them. Besides, the revelation took place "by the river Chebar" (Ezek. I, 3), by undefiled waters where impurity has no abode, that river being one of the four which issued from the Garden of Eden. [Tr. Note: v. Zohar, Genesis, 85a.] It was there, and nowhere else, then, that "the hand of the Lord was upon him," as is directly stated.

R. Hiya also expounded, in accordance with the esoteric teaching, Ezekiel's vision: "Out of the midst thereof came the likeness of four living creatures (Hayoth), and this was their appearance, they had the likeness of a man" (Ibid. v, 5), saying that there is a sacred Hall in which dwell four living Creatures, which are the most ancient celestial beings ministering to the Holy Ancient, and which constitute the essence of the Supernal Name; and that Ezekiel saw only the likeness of the supernal Chariots, because his beholding was from a region which was not very bright. He furthermore said that there are lower beings corresponding to these upper ones, and so throughout, and they are all linked one with another. Our teachers have laid down that Moses derived his prophetic vision from a bright mirror (cf. Midr. Lev. R., p. 145d), whereas the other prophets derived their vision from a dull mirror. So it is written concerning Ezekiel: "I saw visions of God", whereas in connection with the difference between Moses and all other prophets it says: "If there is a prophet among you, I the Lord will make Myself known to him in a vision My servant Moses is not so,

who is faithful in all my house: and with him I will speak mouth to mouth" (Num. XII, 7-8). R. Yose remarked that all the prophets are in comparison with Moses like females in comparison with males. The Lord did not speak to him in "riddles" (Ibid.), but showed him everything clearly. Blessed, indeed, was the generation in whose midst this prophet lived! Said R. Yose the son of R. Judah: 'The Israelites saw the splendour of the glory of their Lord face to face; and, moreover, there were neither blind, nor lame, nor deaf, among them: they all saw (Ex. xx, 18); they all stood (Ibid. XIX, 17); they all heard (Ibid. XIX, 8). And of the Messianic Age it says: "Then the eyes of the blind shall be opened, and the ears of the deaf shall be unstopped, then shall the lame man leap as an hart, and the tongue of the dumb sing" (Isa. xxxv, 5-6).' AND GOD SPAKE ALL THESE WORDS SAYING. R. Judah reflected here on the verse: "Who can utter the mighty acts of the Lord? Who can show forth all his praise?" (Ps. CVI, 2). Said he: 'In how many ways does the Torah testify to the glory of God and admonish man not to sin! How many are the forms in which it counsels him not to turn from the way, either to the right or to the left! And how numerous the signs which it scatters in his way to lead him back into the true path so that he may return to the Lord and receive forgiveness! We have been taught that the Holy One, blessed be He, gave six hundred and thirteen counsels unto man, in order that he might be perfect in attachment to his Lord, for the Holy King desires only his good, both in this world and in the world to come; but more especially in the world to come, since whatever good the Holy One bestows upon man in this world is taken from the sum of good which he is entitled to receive in the world to come. Why is this? Because, as we have been taught, the world to come is, as it were, God's own possession. This is not to say, of course, that this present world is not His also, but, as it has been said, it is like unto an antechamber in comparison with the hall itself; [Tr. Note: Pirke Aboth, IV, 21.] and the reward of a truly worthy man is taken from that which is God's very own, as it says of the tribe of Levi: "He shall have no possession among his brethren, for the Lord is his possession" (Deut. XVIII, 2). How happy is the lot of one who is accounted worthy of such a supernal heritage! He is indeed blessed in this world and in the "house" of this world, as well as in the world to come and in the heavenly holy House of that world, as it is written: "Even unto them I will give in my house and within my walls a place and a name..." (Isa. LVI, 5).

Zohar: Shemoth, Section 2, Page 83a

Blessed is he who is worthy to dwell with the King in His own House.' Said R. Simeon: 'Blessed is he who is worthy of that most inestimable privilege which is foretold in the words: "Then shalt thou delight thyself in the Lord" (Ibid. LVIII, 14). It does not say, "with the Lord", but "in the Lord", namely in the place from whence the upper and the lower worlds alike derive being, and to which they return, that sphere of which it is written: "I will lift up mine eyes unto the hills, from whence cometh my help" (Ps. CXXI, 2), and again: "and came to the Ancient of Days, and they brought him near before him" (Dan. VII, 13). The longing and delight of the righteous is to contemplate that splendour from whence all lights emanate, and all celestial crowns are illumined.' R. Simeon continued: 'We have expounded the closing words of this verse, "I will cause thee to ride upon the high places of the earth", to mean the supramundane world, called "heaven", and God is above this.' R. Abba said that "the Lord" here means Heaven, and the high places of the earth the "Land of the Living", consisting of Zion and Jerusalem which are above, the supernal heaven and the supernal earth. This, however, is quite in harmony with R. Simeon's interpretation, as it is all one celestial sphere. Then he said to R. Simeon: 'Would it please the Master to deign to interpret the whole verse, including the last words, "and feed thee with the heritage of Jacob thy father"?' R. Simeon then repeated what he had said before, and added that the last words are a reference to Isaac's blessing, "And God give thee of the dew of heaven" (Gen. XXVII, 28), this being "the heritage of Jacob". Now this blessing wherewith Isaac blessed Jacob was made in regard to that "heaven" of which we have spoken, and in these words he indicated that Jacob's children will rise again from the dead at the time of the Resurrection, by means of that heavenly dew, at the time when it shall issue forth from the Ancient of Days to the "Small of Countenance". R. Abba thought for a while, and said: 'Now everything is clear, and I see that there is even more significance in Isaac's blessing than I had thought.' AND GOD SPARE ALL THESE WORDS.

According to R. Simeon, the word "spake" denotes a proclamation. When the Holy One revealed Himself and began to speak, the celestial and the terrestrial beings began to tremble mightily, and the souls of the Israelites left their bodies because of their mighty dread. Then the Divine word descended from heaven, being on its way engraved upon the four winds of the universe; and then rose once more and again descended. When it rose up it drew from the mountains pure balsam

Zohar: Shemoth, Section 2, Page 83b

and was watered with the heavenly dew, and when it reached this earth it encompassed the Israelites and brought them back their souls. Then it encircled them again and impressed itself upon the tablets of stone, until the whole Ten Words were designed thereon. R. Simeon said further that every word contained all manner of legal implications and derivations, as well as all mysteries and hidden aspects; for each word was indeed like unto a treasure-house, full of all precious things. And though when one Word was uttered it sounded but as itself, yet when it was stamped upon the stone seventy different aspects were revealed in it, fifty crowns less one on the one side and fifty less one upon the other, [Tr. Note: i.e. the so-called "forty-nine aspects of clean and forty-nine of unclean, v. Midrash Rabba. Shir Ha-shirim, II, 4.] "like a hammer that breaketh the rock in pieces" (Jer. XXIII, 29), and all Israel saw eye to eye and rejoiced exceedingly; and the souls of all the children of Israel, past and present and to be, born and unborn, were present there, that all might accept the Torah given on Mount Sinai, as it is written: "Neither with you only do I make this covenant and this oath, out with him that standeth here... and also with him that is not with us here this day" (Deut. XXIX, 13, 14). And every one according to his grade saw and received the Words. AND GOD SPAKE. The word "God" (Elohim) here indicates that the proclamation emanated from the region of Power (Geburah); the next word, eth, that Geburah was joined with the Right Hand; the word kol (all), that the other Crowns were also associated; the word hadebarim (words), that the words issued continuously; the word haeleh (these), that they included all secret meanings, reasons, and penalties; and the word lemor (saying), that it was a heritage of all. Said R. Isaac: 'Why was the Torah given in fire and darkness? In order to show that he who is constantly and diligently occupied with the study of it will be saved from the fire of hell (Gehenna) and from the darkness of exile in heathen lands. It was the merit of Abraham which saved Israel from hell fire, as, according to tradition, the Holy One said to Abraham: "As long as thy children shall be absorbed in the ways of the Torah they will be saved from punishment, but should they turn from her and forget her paths the fire of hell will have dominion over them and they will be subjected by the nations of the earth." And Abraham pleaded: "Two punishments are surely too much; if it be Thy will, let them escape hell fire and rather go into exile." The Holy One replied: "So be it then." And so it was. For this reason it says: "Their rock had sold them, and the Lord had shut them up" (Deut. XXXII, 30), meaning that Abraham, their "rock", was the cause of their going into exile; "and the Lord had shut them up" because He accepted Abraham's petition and abode by his choice.' R. Judah said: 'Fifty days elapsed between the Exodus and the giving of the Law. Why was this? In order that the number of days should correspond to the number of years of the Jubilee, as it is written: "And ye shall hallow the fiftieth year and proclaim liberty..." (Lev. xxv, 10).' R. Simeon remarked that it was the Jubilee which led Israel out from Egypt; that is to say the divine liberation emanated from the side of Jubilee, and from the same side was judgement stirred up against the Egyptians. For this reason the deliverance from Egypt is mentioned fifty times in the Pentateuch in such expressions as "I have brought thee out

Zohar: Shemoth, Section 2, Page 84a

of the land of Egypt", "I have brought thee out with a strong hand", etc. R. Simeon further said: 'When the Israelites received the Torah the Jubilee crowned the Holy One, blessed be He, even as a king is crowned in the midst of his host, as it says, "Go forth, O ye daughters of Zion, and behold King Solomon with the crown wherewith his mother crowned him in the day of his espousals" (S.S. III, 11). Who is His "mother"? The Jubilee. And the Jubilee crowned itself with perfect joy, as it is written: "The mother of the children rejoiced" (Ps. CXIII).' R. Judah said: 'Concerning this it is written: "Thy father and thy mother shall be glad, and she that bore thee shall rejoice" (Prov. XXIII, 25).' Said R. Isaac: 'In the hour when the Holy One, blessed be He, revealed Himself on Mount Sinai, that mountain began mightily to shake and all the other hills and high places of the earth trembled in accord with it, so that they heaved and quaked until the Holy One stretched out His hand and calmed them, and a voice was heard: "What aileth thee, O thou sea, that thou fleddest, and thou Jordan that thou wast driven back? Ye mountains that ye skipped like rams, and ye hills like young sheep?" And the answer was: "Tremble, O earth, at the presence of the Lord, at the presence of the God of Jacob" (Ps. CXIV, 5-7). Now, "the Lord" in this verse refers to the "Mother" (Binah); "earth", to the "Mother" below (Malkuth); "the God of Jacob", to the Father (Hohmah), whose "firstborn son is Israel" (Ex. IV, 23), whom "his mother crowned in the day of his espousals": she crowned him with the symbolic colours, white, red, and green, in which all other colours are included, and in him they were all united.' According to R. Judah, the "crown" symbolizes Israel, who is God's glory, as it is written: "Israel, in whom I am glorified" (Isa. XLIX, 3); "and I will glorify the house of my glory" (Ibid. LX, 7). Said R. Isaac: 'The Torah was manifested in a black fire which was superimposed upon a white fire, signifying that by means of the Torah the "Right Hand" clasped the "Left Hand" that the two might be fused, as it is written: "from his right hand a fiery law to them" (Deut. XXXIII, 2).' Said R. Abba: 'When the smoke came out of Mount Sinai a fire ascended enveloped therein, so that its flames were of a blue colour. They flared high and dwindled again, and the smoke emitted all the aromas of Paradise, displaying itself in the colours of white, red, and black, as it says, "perfumed with myrrh and frankincense, with all powders of the merchant" (S.S. III, 6). It was the Shekinah who manifested Herself thus at the giving of the Law in the wilderness on Mount Sinai, as it says, "Who is this (zoth) that cometh up from the wilderness like pillars of smoke?" (Ibid.)' Said R. Judah: 'But surely it is not necessary to go so far afield to discover this. Have we not the direct statement that "Mount Sinai was altogether on a smoke, because the Lord descended upon it in fire, and the smoke thereof ascended as the smoke of a furnace" (Ex. XIX, 18)? Blessed were the people who beheld this wondrous thing and apprehended the mystery thereof!' Said R. Hiya: 'When the letters were engraved upon the two tablets of stone they were visible on both sides of the tablets. The tablets were of sapphire [Tr. Note: Heb. sanpirinon, prob. lapis-lazuli, v. Jastrow, s.v.] stone, and the letters were formed of white fire and covered again with black fire, and were engraved upon both sides.' According to R. Abba, the tablets were not engraved, but the letters fluttered on to them, being visible in two colours of fire, white and black, in order to demonstrate the union of Right and Left, as it is written, "length of days is in her right hand and in her left hand is riches and honour" (Prov. III, 16). But are we not told that "from his right hand (came) a fiery law to them" (Deut. XXXIII, 2)? The truth is that although the Torah emanated from the side of Power-that is the Left-the Left Side was included in the Right, and thus Justice was tempered by Mercy, which was symbolized by the two fires: white for Mercy, black for Power and Severity. It is written: "And the tablets were the work of God" (Ex. XXXII, 18). They were indeed so, for, as R. Judah said: 'The word ha-luhoth (the tablets) being written in a defective form, indicates that although they were two they appeared like one, and the Ten Words were engraved upon them, one section of five being included in, or superimposed on, the other five, so that they should be included in the emanations of the Right Side, that is, of Mercy; and in this way they were indeed the very "work of God".'

Zohar: Shemoth, Section 2, Page 84b

R. Isaac said: 'They were originally two sapphire stones which were rough-hewn, but the Holy One caused a wind to blow upon them, which smoothed them and transformed them into two tablets.' To this R. Judah demurred, maintaining that they only looked like sapphire, being in reality a new creation. 'This', he said, 'must be so, since it says that they were "the work of God".' To which R. Isaac retorted: 'But is not the sapphire, the most precious of all stones, itself a "work of God"? ' Said R. Judah: 'Why then does it say that these specially were a "work of God"? ' R. Isaac replied: 'It does not say that the stones were a special work of God, but the tablets; and the spelling of the word luhoth (without vau) suggests that the miraculousness was not so much in the stones themselves as in their formation as tablets, and in the writing.' Said R. Simeon: 'Both interpretations are correct. These two tablets existed from before Creation, but were perfected on the sixth day of Creation specially for this purpose; thus they were a special creation of the Holy One.' Of what were they formed? Of the supernal dew which issues from the Holy Ancient One, of which, when it was descending on the "Field of the Holy Apples", the Holy One took two drops, causing them to solidify and turn into two precious stones. Then He blew on them and they became flat like tablets. Thus both the stones and the writing were "a work of God", "written with the finger of God" (Deut. IX, 10). That "Finger" has the same symbolic significance as the "Finger of God" of which the Egyptian magicians spoke (Ex. VIII, 19), each "finger" expanding into ten until it becomes the complete hand, such as Israel saw at the sea.' Said R. Judah: 'When it says that the "writing was... graven upon the tablets" (Ex. XXXII, 16), it means that the tablets were pierced, so that the writing could be seen from either side; the writing formed an engraving within an engraving.' According to R. Abba, it was possible from one side to see the other side, and read the writing thereon. Said R. Eleazar: 'They were written miraculously in order that every man might discern that it was "God's writing", being unable to find any other explanation of this double appearance. Besides, if the tablets were pierced, as has been suggested, why does it not say that the writing was graven "in the tablets" instead of "upon the tablets"? The fact, however, is, as we have been taught, that five Words were written on the right and five on the left, and those of the left were included in those of the right, and from (within) the right one could see those of the left, so that all was on the right, and all were fused one with the other. He who stood at one side could see (therein) what was on the other side and read it, for we have been taught that the Left was turned into the Right. Thus it was, indeed, "the writing of God". What happened was this: he who stood on one side read, 'I am the Lord thy God", and out of these letters he could see the words, "Thou shalt not murder." Then he read, "Thou shalt not have (other gods)", and at the same time could see the words "Thou shalt not commit adultery". Then he went on reading, "Thou shalt not take the name of the Lord thy God in vain", and saw from the other side the words, "Thou shalt not steal", and so on. And conversely, if he looked at the other side.' AND MOSES WENT DOWN UNTO THE PEOPLE AND SAID UNTO THEM. R. Yose asked: What is the point of this remark, seeing that we are not told what he said?' R. Isaac replied: 'It is well known that when a person is expecting some great good fortune or misfortune to befall him, before the event happens he is in a state of great nervous tension and can hardly control himself; but once the best or the worst is known, he regains his equanimity. Now in this case Moses actually prepared the Israelites for the great event which was about to take place, and yet when it came it almost overwhelmed them, so we may imagine what would have happened if he had not prepared them. And this is the meaning of "he said": he told them what was going to happen so as to fortify them beforehand. And with all this, as has been already mentioned, they could not endure the revelation when it came, for, as R. Judah said in the name of R. Hiya, in the name of R. Yose: "When the Israelites heard the words of the Holy One, their souls flew from them and ascended up to the Throne of Glory in order to cleave to it. Said the Torah to the Holy One: 'Was it then for nothing and to no purpose that I was fashioned two thousand years before the creation of the world? Is it all in vain that in me is inscribed "Every man

Zohar: Shemoth, Section 2, Page 85a

of the children of Israel", "speak to the children of Israel", "the children of Israel are servants unto Me", "These are the children of Israel", and diverse other words of a like character? Where, then, are these children of Israel? At that hour the children of Israel received again the souls which had fled in the wake of the Divine splendour, for the Torah returned them every one to its own place; yea, she took hold of them and gave them back to their owners, each to the body which was its proper dwelling. This is the significance of the words: "The Torah of the Lord is perfect, returning (meshibath) the soul" (Ps. XIX, 7): "returning" in the literal sense.' There is a tradition concerning King Solomon, that when he first sat on his throne the Moon was in her fulness, as he was the fifteenth in descent from Abraham, the pedigree being Abraham, Isaac, Jacob, Judah, Perez, Hezron, Ram (Ruth IV, 19), Aminadab, Nahshon, Shalmon, Boaz, Obed, Jesse, David, Solomon. Therefore it is written: "Then Solomon sat on the throne of the Lord" (I Chr. XXIX, 23), and also "six ascents had the throne", thus being a replica of the Supernal Throne. In the days of Zedekiah, the Moon was in her wane, and the face of Israel was darkened. He was the fifteenth from Solomon, his pedigree being Rehoboam, Abiah, Asa, Jehoshaphat, Jehoram, Ahaziah, Joash, Amaziah, Uzziah, Jotham, Ahaz, Hezekiah, Manasseh, Amon, Josiah, Zedekiah. When Zedekiah came the Moon waned and remained thus, for it is written: "He (the king of Babylon) blinded the eyes of Zedekiah" (Jer. LII, 11). Then "He cast down from heaven unto the earth the beauty of Israel" (Lam. II, 1). The earth was removed far from the heaven and became dark. When the Israelites stood by Mount Sinai the Moon began to shine forth, as it is written: "He bowed the heavens and came down" (2 Sam. XXII, 10), meaning that the Sun approached the Moon, and the Moon began to shine, this being expressed in the words: "And on the east side toward the rising of the sun shall they of the standard of the camp of Judah pitch throughout their armies" (Num. II, 3). On Mount Sinai was Judah appointed chief in the kingdom. R. Isaac found this expressed in the words: "But Judah still ruleth with God, and is faithful with the saints" (Hos. XII, 1), which means, that when God was ruling in His Kingdom on Mount Sinai, Judah was ruling in his; when the Holy One said to Israel: "And ye shall be unto Me a kingdom of priests and a holy nation", Judah was found faithful and worthy to receive the kingdom, and therefore the Moon began to shine. I AM THE LORD THY GOD WHO BROUGHT THEE OUT OF THE LAND OF EGYPT. R. Eleazar referred to the verse: "My son, hear the instruction of thy father, and forsake not the Torah of thy mother" (Prov. I, 18). "'The instruction of thy father",' he said, 'refers to the Holy One; "the Torah of thy mother" to the Community of Israel.' According to R. Judah, "father" represents Wisdom (Hokhmah) and "mother" Understanding (Binah). Said R. Judah: 'Both interpretations mean one and the same thing, for we have been taught that the Torah emanated from the Supernal Wisdom.' R. Yose said that the Torah emanated from Understanding, for it says: "to perceive the words of understanding" and "forsake not the Torah of thy mother". Said R Judah: 'The Torah is an emanation of both Wisdom and Understanding, and combines the influence of both, for it says: "My son, hear the instruction of thy father, and forsake not the Torah of thy mother".' R. Abba said: 'It contains the influence of all the emanations, in virtue of containing those two: grace, judgement, and mercy, and every one required for perfection. When the King and the Matrona are in harmonious union all attributes are harmoniously united, and wherever these are found all the others are found as well.' R. Yose said: 'The "I" in the first commandment represents the Shekinah, as in "I will go down with thee to Egypt" (Gen. XLVI, 4).' R. Isaac said that after "I" there is a pause, and the next words, "the Lord is thy God", refer to the Holy One, blessed be He, identical with the "Heavens", as it is written: "Out of heaven he made thee to hear his voice" (Deut. IV, 36), and again, "Ye have seen that I have spoken to you from heaven" (Ex. xx, 22). The "who" (asher) which follows designates the sphere which all consider blessed (ashar)

Zohar: Shemoth, Section 2, Page 85b

The "bringing out of Egypt" designates the "Jubilee", as we have been taught that the "Jubilee" was the immediate cause of Israel's exodus from Egypt; for which reason this event is mentioned fifty times in the Torah. Fifty days passed from the Exodus to the Revelation on Sinai, and fifty years had to pass for the liberation of slaves. "From the house of slaves": as it is written: "The Lord smote all the firstborn of the land of Egypt" (Ex. XII, 29), which, as we have been taught, signifies the lower "crown" which the Egyptians worshipped. For, indeed, as there is a "House" above, so also there is a "house" below; a holy "house" above–"with wisdom is a house builded" (Prov. XXIV, 3)–and an unholy "house" below, a "house of slaves". We have been taught that when the "I" was proclaimed, all those commandments of the Torah which are united in the "Body" of the Supernal Holy King were comprised in it; for, indeed, all the commandments have their unifying centre in the "Body" of the King; some in the "Head", some in the "Trunk", some in the "Hands", and some in the "Feet", and none of them ever step out and become separate from the "Body" of the King or lose connection with it. He, therefore, who transgresses against even one of the commandments of the Torah is as though he transgressed against the "Body" of the King, as it is written: "And they shall go forth and look upon the carcases of the men that have transgressed against me" (Isa. LXVI, 24)–as it were, "against My very Self." Woe unto the sinners who break the words of the Torah- they know not what they do! And thus said R. Simeon: 'The Place against which a sin is committed itself reveals the sin. When a sin has been committed against the Holy One, it is He Himself who reveals it, as it is written: "The heaven shall reveal his iniquity and the earth shall rise up against him" (Job. xx, 27). "The heaven" signifies the Holy One; "the earth" the Community of Israel. We have also been taught that "heaven" reveals man's guilt and "earth" executes judgement on the sinners, as it is written: "The earth shall rise up against him." ' Said R. Yose: 'We have been taught in the name of R. Simeon that in the hour when the Torah was given to Israel Mother and children were together in perfect harmony, as it is written, "the mother of the children rejoiced" (Ps. XCIII, 9).' Thus "I" in this verse refers to the Shekinah, called "daughter" in the dictum "Abraham had a daughter, the Shekinah". "The Lord thy God" has the same reference as in the verse, "My firstborn son Israel" (Ex. IV, 22) (i.e. Tifereth); while the words "who hath brought thee out of the land of Egypt" refer to the mystery of "Jubilee" (the Mother). Thus the Mother was there and the Children were there, all in joy and completeness; so that we apply the verse "the Mother of the children rejoices". Hence we have learnt that a man should be careful not to sin lest he cause the Mother to depart from the Children.' R. Isaac said: 'All these expressions refer to the Holy One, blessed be He, and this is a thing disclosed to the "reapers of the field".' R. Eleazar said: 'From the fact that in one place it says: "In the beginning God created heaven and earth", and in another, "On the day when the Lord God made earth and heaven" (Gen. II, 4), it has been concluded that both heaven and earth were created as one; the Holy One stretched out His right hand and created the heaven, and then He stretched out His left hand and created the earth. Also, when it says: "And it shall come to pass on that day that I will answer the heavens, and they shall answer the earth" (Hos. II,21), it refers to the supernal heavens and to the supernal earth, the earth which is called "My footstool" (Isa. LXVI, 1). The significance whereof is that the heaven longed for the earth, that it might unite itself with her in the sphere called "Righteous", as it is written: "The righteous is the foundation of the world" (Prov. x, 25). From the head of the King to the place where this Righteous One commences flows a holy river,

Zohar: Shemoth, Section 2, Page 86a

the oil of anointment, which pours itself out in fulness of desire upon this earth; and the earth having received it therefrom nourishes all both above and below.' Said R. Isaac: 'We read: "And the Lord came down upon Mount Sinai" (Ex. XIX, 20); "He bowed the heavens and came down" (2 Sam. XXII, 10). Whither came He down? For the text tells us that He descended upon (lit. above) Mount Sinai and not on to Sinai.' R. Yose replied: 'He came down from grade to grade, from crown to crown, until He reached this "earth", and then the Moon shone and was revealed in completeness in the heavens. Hence it says, "He descended above Mount Sinai." What stands above Mount Sinai? Surely, the Shekinah.' THOU SHALT HAVE NO OTHER GODS BEFORE ME (lit. before My Face). Said R. Isaac: 'This prohibition of "other gods" does not include the Shekinah; "before My Face" does not include the "Faces of the King" (the Sephiroth), in which the Holy King manifests Himself, and which are His Name and identical with Him. That they are His name is shown by the verse: "I am Tetragrammaton, that is My Name" (Isa. XLII, 8). Thus He and His Name are one. Blessed be His Name forever and ever.' R. Simeon taught: 'Blessed are the Israelites, for that the Holy One calls them 'IMen" (Adam), as it is written, "Ye are my sheep; the sheep of my flock; ye are men" (Ezek. XXXIV, 31). Why are they called "men", in contradistinction to the heathen nations? Because they "cleave to the Lord their God" (Deut. IV, 4). When a Jewish child is circumcised he enters at once into the Abrahamitic covenant; and when he commences to keep the precepts of the Torah he enters into the grade of "man" and becomes attached to the "Body of the King" and so obtains the title of "man". Contrariwise Ishmael was a "wild man" (Gen. XVI, 12); he was only partly a "man": there were the beginnings of "manhood" in him, because he was circumcised, but this "manhood" did not come to fruition in him, because he did not receive the commandments of the Torah. But the seed of Israel, who were perfected in all things, they are "men" in the full sense: "For the Lord's portion is his people; Jacob is the lot of his inheritance" (Deut. XXXII, 9).' Said R. Yose: 'Therefore the graving and painting of all forms is permitted, except the human figure.' Said R. Isaac: 'The reason is, because when a human figure is represented in sculpture or painting, it is not only the body which is fashioned in the image of the person, but as it were the wholeness of the man is being reproduced, his inner form, namely his spirit, as well as his outer bodily form'; Said R. Judah 'This accords with the popular saying: "As the breath of the craftsman, so the shape of the vessel." 'R. Judah went once from Cappadocia to Lydda to see R. Simeon, who was sojourning there at that time, and R. Hezekiah accompanied him. Said R. Judah to R. Hezekiah: 'What R. Simeon taught us concerning the meaning of the term "wild man"

Zohar: Shemoth, Section 2, Page 86b

applied to Ishmael is perfectly true and quite clear, but what is the meaning of the second half of the verse: "and he shall dwell in the presence (lit. faces) of all his brethren"?' R. Hezekiah replied: 'I have heard no interpretation and I shall not give any, for it is written: "And this is the Torah which Moses set before the children of Israel" (Deut. IV, 44). What was set by Moses we can enunciate; what he did not set we cannot enunciate.' Then said R. Judah: 'It is written: "For he is thy life and the length of thy days" (Deut. xxx, 20). He who is worthy of the Torah and separates not himself from her is worthy of two lives: life in this world and life in the world to come. But he who separates himself from her separates himself from life. And he who separates himself from R. Simeon separates himself from all things. Here is a verse to which he has already opened a door, and yet we cannot enter it nor penetrate further without his aid; how much more difficult then will it be for us to enter into the more recondite words of the Torah! Woe to the generation from which R. Simeon will be removed! As long as we are in his presence the springs of the heart are open on every hand to the apprehension of truth, and everything is unfolded, but as soon as we separate ourselves from him we know nothing and all the springs are closed.' Said R. Hezekiah: 'It is written: "And he took of the spirit that was upon him (Moses) and gave it unto the seventy elders" (Num. XI, 25). It was like a light from which many lights are kindled, and which yet retains its brightness. R. Simeon is such a light; he illumines everyone and yet his light is not diminished, but remains steadfast in its full splendour.' They walked on until they reached the place where he was dwelling at the time. They found him absorbed in the study of the Torah. He was meditating aloud upon the verse: "A prayer of the afflicted (poor) when he is wrapped in darkness (languishing), and poureth out his complaint before the Lord" (Ps. CII, 1). He said: 'All prayers of Israel are effective, but the prayer of the poor man more so than all others. Why? Because it reaches the Crown of the King's Glory and becomes, as it were, a garland for His Head, and the Holy One clothes Himself with this prayer as with a garment. "When he is wrapped." He is not wrapped in garments, for he has none, being needy, but the word ya'atof has the same significance here as in the words, "the life of the young children that faint ('atuphim) for hunger" (Lam. II, 19). He "poureth out his complaint before the Lord". This is pleasing to the Lord, for the world is sustained by such. Woe unto him against whom a poor man complains to his Master! For the poor are nearest to the King. Concerning him the Lord says: "When he crieth unto me I will hear, for I am gracious" (Ex. XXII, 26), which signifies that the prayers of others are sometimes accepted and sometimes rejected, but the poor man's prayer is always answered. And why? Because the King dwells in broken vessels: "To this man will I look, even to him that is poor and of a contrite spirit" (Isa. LXVI, 2). "The Lord is near to those who are of a broken heart" (Ps. XXXIV, 19): "A broken and a contrite heart, O God, thou wilt not despise" (Ibid. LI, 19). Hence we have learnt that whosoever wrongs a poor man wrongs the

Shekinah. "For the Lord will plead their cause" (Prov. XXII, 23): their Protector is omnipotent; he needs no witnesses, no other judge, no pledge does he accept, except that of the soul: "and spoil the soul of those who spoil them (the poor)" (Ibid.).' He went on: '"A prayer of the poor...." Wherever the word "prayer" (tephillah) is mentioned, it signifies something precious, something which ascends to a supernal sphere-to the phylactery of the head worn by the King.' At this point R. Simeon turned his head and saw R. Judah and R. Hezekiah approaching him. When he had finished his reflections he looked at them, and said: 'You look as if you had lost something valuable.' 'Yes,' they replied, 'for the Master opened a precious door and yet we cannot enter into it.' 'And what is it?' said he. Said they: 'We refer to the verse concerning Ishmael: what is the meaning of the last words: "and he shall dwell upon the faces of all his brethren"? The beginning of the verse is clear to us, but what of this? We know not what the significance of these words is. The end does not seem to suit the beginning.' 'By your life!' replied R. Simeon, "both parts of the verse have one significance and point to the same truth. We know that the Holy One has many aspects (faces) in His manifestations to men: He manifests to some a beaming face, to others a gloomy one; to some a distant face,

Zohar: Shemoth, Section 2, Page 87a

to others one that is very near; to some an external, to others an inner, hidden aspect; to some from the right side, to others from the left. Blessed are the Israelites, for they are united with the uppermost "face" of the King, with the face wherein He and His Name are one. Contrariwise, the heathen nations are joined to the most distant "face", to the "lower face", and therefore they are at a great distance from the "Body" of the King. For we see that all those nations, like the Egyptians, for instance, who are related to Ishmael-for he had many brothers and relatives-were connected with the "lower", the "distant" faces of the Divine. Ishmael, however, when he was circumcised, had the privilege, for Abraham's sake, of having his dwelling-place and his portion in the sphere which dominated all those distant and lower faces, the faces of the Divine which are turned towards the other nations. Therefore it says of him: "His hand will be in all (kol) [Tr. Note: One of the lower grades of the Divine.]... and he shall dwell upon the faces of all his brethren", namely, he will be in a superior sphere to any of the other heathen nations; he will rule over all the "faces" that are below.' Then R. Judah and R. Hezekiah approached him and kissed his hands. Said R. Judah: 'This is an illustration of the proverb: "Wine settled on its lees and a bubbling spring are a wonderful combination." [Tr. Note: i.e. R. Simeon combines deliberate judgement with a perennial flow of learning.] Woe to the world when the Master will be removed from it! Blessed the generation that is privileged to hearken to his words! Blessed the generation in which he lives!' Said R. Hezekiah: 'But have we not been taught that a proselyte when circumcised is merely called a "proselyte of righteousness" and nothing more? Yet according to thy interpretation of this verse, Master, "his hand will be in all (kol)"?' R. Simeon replied: 'Quite so! Ishmael was not merely a "proselyte", he was a son of Abraham, a son of the holy man, to whom the Lord gave the promise: "As concerning Ishmael, behold... I have blessed him" (Gen. XVII, 20); which "blessing" has a reference to the statement, "And the Lord blessed Abraham in all things (kol)"; which again is connected with the promise to Ishmael that "his hand will be in all (kol)...." This indicates that proselytes from among other nations, Ishmael's kin, would be called "proselytes of righteousness", but the nation whom he himself represents should be above them, "he shall dwell above the faces of his brethren".' Said R. Judah: 'Hence the commandment to Israel: "Thou shalt have no other gods upon My face", meaning "Thou shalt even avoid conceiving Me in those aspects (faces) which form Ishmael's religion".' [Tr. Note: i.e. Mohammedanism.] THOU SHALT NOT MAKE UNTO THEE ANY GRAVEN IMAGE, OR ANY LIKENESS OF ANYTHING THAT IS IN HEAVEN ABOVE OR THAT IS IN THE EARTH BENEATH. We have already mentioned, in reference to this prohibition, the remark of R. Yose that 'all pictorial presentations are permitted, except that of a human countenance, because this countenance has dominion over all things'. R. Isaac applied to this commandment the maxim: "Suffer not thy mouth to cause thy flesh to sin" (Eccl. v, 5). 'How careful', he said, 'must one be not to err in regard to the meaning of the words of the Torah, and not to derive any doctrine from them which he has not learnt [from books] or heard from his teachers. He who gives his own interpretations of Scripture, not derived from these sources, transgresses against the commandment: "Thou shalt not make unto thee any graven image."

The Holy One will punish him in the world to come, when his soul shall desire to enter into her place. She will then be thrust away, and she will be cut off from that region which is "bound up with the bundle of life" wherein are the other souls. Concerning such a man it is written: "Wherefore should God be angry at thy voice?" (Ibid.), "voice" symbolizing the soul.' Said R. Hiya: 'It is for this reason that to this prohibition are added the words, "for I the Lord thy God am a jealous God". God is "jealous" above all for His Name, either because of the pictorial presentations wherewith His Name (character) is misrepresented, or because of the Torah when she is misinterpreted. For the Torah, as we have been taught, consists entirely of His Holy Name; in fact, every word written therein consists of and contains that Holy Name. Therefore one must beware of erring in regard to this Name and misrepresenting it. He who is false to the Supernal King will not be allowed to enter the King's Palace and will be driven away from the world to come.' R. Abba derived the same lesson from the words from this commandment: "Thou shalt not make... any graven image (pesel)", which he connected with the verse,

388

JETHRO

"Hew (pesal) thee two tables of stone" (Ex. XXXIV, 1), interpreting thus: "Thou shalt not 'hew' unto thee another Torah, which thou neither knowest [from books], nor hast learnt from thy master; for I the Lord thy God am a jealous God and shall punish thee in the world to come when thy soul shall long to enter into the spheres of glory and stand before My Presence." How many emissaries will then be ready to frustrate its desire and thrust it into Gehenna! [Tr. Note: Al. "To hiss at it and to gaze at it in Gehenna."] According to yet another interpretation, this commandment includes the prohibition against the profanation of the sign of the Abrahamitic covenant, which sign is a symbol of the Holy Name. By means of this sign Israel entered into the first Covenant and union with the Shekinah, and he who brings it into a foreign domain is false to the Holy One Himself. THOU SHALT NOT BOW DOWN TO THEM NOR WORSHIP THEM. As R. Eleazar was once walking in company with R. Hiya, the latter said: 'It is written: "When thou goes: out to war against thine enemies... and seest among the captives a beautiful woman... thou shalt bring her home to thine house" (Deut. XXI, 10, 11). How can this be? Is not intermarriage with heathens prohibited?' R. Eleazar replied: 'This only applied to the seven nations [Tr. Note: v. Deut. VII, 7.] when they were independent in their own land. But mark this. There is no woman among the heathen nations who is free from taint. Therefore the section concerning the captive woman is immediately followed by that of the rebellious son, to indicate that children born of such a union are far from good, the impurity of idolatry inherited by the mother being difficult to remove; all the more so if she has been already married, as the taint of her husband cleaves to her. Hence the command of Moses to exterminate the Midianite women who were the cause of Israel's downfall in the wilderness (Num. xxv, 1-9; XXXI, 15-19). Blessed is the man who keeps in purity this heritage (the Covenant), for in this holy possession he unites himself with the Holy One, blessed be He, especially if he keeps the commandments of the Torah! The Holy One then stretches out His Right Hand to receive him, and he cleaves to the Holy Body. Concerning this it says of Israel: "And ye who cleave to the Lord your God" (Deut. IV, 4); "Sons are ye to the Lord your God" (Ibid. XIV, 1): literally "sons", as it is also written: "My firstborn son Israel" (Ex. IV, 22); "Israel, in whom I am glorified" (Isa. XLIX, 3).' THOU SHALT NOT TAKE THE NAME OF THE LORD THY GOD IN VAIN. R. Simeon spoke in connection with this on the passage: "And Elisha said unto her, What shall I do for thee? Tell me, what hast thou in the house?" (2 Kings IV, 2). 'What Elisha meant', said he, 'was: "Hast thou nothing upon which the Divine blessing could rest?" For there is a dictum that it is prohibited to say grace after meals over an empty table, because the supernal blessing cannot rest on an empty place. It is therefore necessary to put a loaf or two on the table before saying grace, or at least the remnants of the former meal, in order that the blessing should not, as it were, be uttered "in emptiness". But when the woman said: "Thine handmaid hath not anything in the house, save a pot of oil" (Ibid.), the prophet replied: "Verily, this is fitted to receive a perfect blessing, as it is written: 'The good name (of God) can issue forth from good oil'" (Eccl. VIII, 1). For the Holy Name comes forth from "oil", to bless and to kindle new lights. What is this "oil"?' Said R. Isaac: 'It represents the same "good oil upon the head, that ran down upon the beard, even Aaron's beard" (Ps. CXXXIII, 2, the symbol of blessing, the instrument of which was the high priest).' R. Eleazar held that it represents the supernal mountains of pure balsam. R. Simeon interpreted the verse of Ecclesiastes thus: 'How good is the celestial name of the supernal holy lights, when they all radiate from the "good oil" we have mentioned! It is a sin to mention the Name of the Holy One in vain, in emptiness. A man who does that were better not to have been born.' According to R. Eleazar, this also means that one should not utter the Holy Name by itself, but only after a preceding word,

as in the Torah it only occurs for the first time after two words: Bereshit barah Elohim (In the beginning God created). Said R. Simeon: 'In the Torah the Holy Name is mentioned only in connection with a completed world: "On the day when Tetragrammaton Elohim made the heavens and the earth" (Gen. II, 4).' From all this it follows that one should not mention the Holy Name in vain, that is, in "emptiness". One should utter the Holy Name only within a blessing or a prayer. But he who takes the Name in vain, neither in a benediction nor in a prayer, will be punished when his soul will be leaving him: "for the Lord will not hold him guiltless that taketh His Name in vain". R. Yose further remarks in our Mishnah: 'What is the nature of blessing? It is the presence of the Holy Name in the blessing which makes it so significant, for this Name is the source of blessing to the whole universe. Therefore: "Thou shalt not take the Name of the Lord thy God in vain." 'REMEMBER THE SABBATH DAY, TO SANCTIFY IT. Said R. Isaac: 'It is written, "And God blessed the seventh day" (Gen. II, 3); and yet we read of the manna, "Six days ye shall gather it, but on the seventh day, the Sabbath, in it there shall be none" (Ex. XVI, 26). If there was no food on that day what blessing is attached to it? Yet we have been taught that all blessings from above and from below depend upon the seventh day. Why, then, was there no manna just on this day? The explanation is that all the six days of the transcendent world derive their blessings from it, and each supernal day sends forth nourishment to the world below from what it received from the seventh day. [Tr. Note: Here apparently=Binah.] Therefore he who has attained to the grade of Faith must needs prepare a table and a meal on the Sabbath eve (Friday) so that his table may be blessed all through the other six days of the week. For, indeed, at the time of the Sabbath preparation there is also prepared the blessing for all the six days that shall follow, for no blessing is found at an empty table. Thus one should make ready the table on Sabbath night with bread and other food.' R. Isaac added: 'Also on the Sabbath day.' Said R. Judah: 'One must regale oneself on this day with three meals, in order that this day may be one of satisfaction and refreshment.' Said R. Abba: 'One must do so in order that blessing may spread to those supernal days which receive their blessing from the seventh.' On this day the head of the "Little Face" is filled with the dew which descends from the Holy Ancient One, the Most Hidden One; He causes it to descend into the holy "Field of Apples" three times after the entrance of the Sabbath, in order that all unitedly may enjoy the blessing. Therefore it is necessary, not only for ourselves that we should have these three repasts during the day, but for all creation, for therein is consummated the true faith in the Holy Ancient One, the "Little Face", and the "Field of Apples", and we should rejoice and delight in all three. But he who lessens the number of the meals, as it were brings imperfection and blemish into the regions above, and great will his punishment be.' Said R. Simeon: 'When a man has completed the three meals on the Sabbath a voice proclaims concerning him: "Then shalt thou delight thyself in the Lord." This is in reference to one meal, in honour of the Ancient, the All Holy. Then it proclaims, "and I will cause thee to ride upon the high places of the earth"-this in reference to a second meal, in honour of the holy "Field of Apples"; then, "and feed thee with the heritage of Jacob thy father" (Isa. LVIII, 14)-completing the triad with a reference to the "Little Face". Correspondingly man should complete the number of three meals, and find joy and refreshment in all three and in each one of them separately, because this is a manifestation of perfected faith. Therefore the Sabbath is more precious than all other times and seasons and festivals, because it contains and unites all in itself, whereas no other festival or holy day does so.' Said R. Hiya: 'Because all things are found in the Sabbath it is mentioned three times in the story of Creation: "And on the seventh day God ended his work"; "and he rested on the seventh day"; "and God blessed the seventh day" (Gen. II, 2, 3).' R. Hamnuna the ancient, [Tr. Note: Al. R. Abba.] when he sat at his Sabbath meals, used to find joy in each one. Over one he would exclaim: 'This is the holy meal of the Holy Ancient One, the All-hidden.' Over another he would say: 'This is the meal of the Holy One, blessed be He.' And when he

Zohar: Shemoth, Section 2, Page 88b

came to the last one he would say: 'Complete the meals of the Faith.' R. Simeon used always to say when the time of the Sabbath meal arrived: 'Prepare ye the meal of the supernal Faith! Make ready the meal of the King!' Then he would sit with a glad heart. And as soon as he had finished the third meal it was proclaimed concerning him: 'Then shalt thou delight thyself in the Lord, and I will cause thee to ride upon the high places of the earth and feed thee with the heritage of Jacob thy father.' R. Eleazar asked his father, R. Simeon, in what order the three meals corresponded to the three divine grades. R. Simeon replied: 'Concerning the meal of Sabbath night (i.e. Friday night) it is written: "I will cause thee to ride upon the high places of the earth." In this night the Holy Matrona (Shekinah) is greatly blessed, and the whole "Field of Apples" also, and the man's table is blessed who partakes of his meal duly and with joy, and a new soul is added unto him. This night signifies the rejoicing of the Shekinah. Man therefore has to participate in Her joy and partake of Her meal. Concerning the second meal on the Sabbath day, it is written: "Then shalt thou delight thyself in the Lord"-that is, in the very Lord (Tetragrammaton); for at that hour the Holy Ancient One reveals Himself and all the worlds are irradiated with joy, and we, in participating in this meal, contribute to that joy. Concerning the third meal it is written: "And feed thee with the heritage of Jacob thy father." This is the meal of the "Little Face" who is then complete in harmonious perfection, from which perfection all the six days that are to come will receive blessing. Therefore one must wholeheartedly rejoice in these meals, and complete their number, for they are meals of the perfect Faith, the Faith of the holy seed of Israel, their supernal Faith, which is not that of the heathen nations: "A sign between me and the children of Israel" (Ex. XXXI, 17). And mark this. By these meals the children of Israel are distinguished as the King's sons, as belonging to the Palace, as sons of Faith; and he who abstains from one of these meals causes an incompleteness in the regions above; thus such a man testifies of himself that he is not one of the King's sons, not of the Palace, not of the holiness of Israel's seed, and he will be made to bear the burden of a threefold punishment in Gehenna. 'Also mark this. On all festivals and holy days a man must both rejoice himself and give joy to the poor. Should he regale himself only and not give a share to the poor, his punishment will be great. Concerning such a one it is written: "Behold, I will reprove your seed and spread dung upon your face, the dung of your solemn feasts" (Mal. II, 3). This particular verse, however, applies only to festivals, not to the Sabbath. Similarly, the words, "Your new moons and your appointed feasts my soul hateth" (Isa. I, 14), do not include the Sabbath. The unique character of the Sabbath is expressed in the words: "Between Me and the children of Israel." And because the Faith is centred in the Sabbath, man is given on this day an additional, a supernal soul, a soul in which is all perfection, according to the pattern of the world to come. What does the word "Sabbath" mean? The Name of the Holy One, the Name which is in perfect harmony at all sides.' [Tr. Note: This idea is based upon the mystic significance of the three letters of the word Sabbath, shin, beth, tau.] Said R. Yose: 'It is indeed so. Woe to him who does not help to complete the joy of the Holy King! And what is His joy? Those three meals of the Faith, the meals wherein Abraham, Isaac, and Jacob participate, and which express joy upon joy, the perfect Faith from all sides. On this day-so we have been taught-the Fathers crown themselves and all the Children imbibe power and light and joy, such as is unknown even on other festive days. On this day sinners find rest in Gehenna. On this day punishment is held back from the world. On this day the Torah crowns herself in perfect crowns. On this day joy and gladness resound throughout two hundred and fifty worlds. Mark also this. On all the six days of the week, when the hour of the afternoon prayer arrives, the attribute of Justice is in the ascendant, and punishment is at hand. But not so on the Sabbath. When the time of the Sabbath afternoon prayer arrives benign influences reign, the lovingkindness of the Holy Ancient One is manifested, all chastisements are kept in leash, and all is satisfaction and joy. In this time of satisfaction and goodwill Moses, the holy, faithful prophet, passed away from this world, in order that it should be known that he was not taken away through judgement, but that in the hour

Zohar: Shemoth, Section 2, Page 89a

of grace of the Holy Ancient One his soul ascended, to be hidden in Him. Therefore "no man knows of his sepulchre unto this day" (Deut. XXXIV, 6). As the Holy Ancient One is the All-hidden One, whom neither those above nor those below can comprehend, so was this soul of Moses hidden in the epiphany of God's good will at the hour of the Sabbath afternoon prayer. This soul is the most hidden of all hidden things in the world, and judgement has no dominion over it. Blessed is the lot of Moses. 'On this day the Torah crowns herself with all beauty, with all those commandments, with all those decrees and punishments for transgressions-in seventy branches of light which radiate on every hand. What it is to behold the little twigs which constantly emanate from each branch-five of which stand in the Tree itself, all the branches being comprised in it! What it is to behold the gates which open at all sides, and through which bursts forth in splendour and beauty the streaming, inexhaustible light! A voice is heard: "Awake, ye supernal saints! Awake, holy people, chosen from above and from below! Awake in joy to meet your Lord, awake in perfect joy! Prepare yourselves in the threefold joy of the three Patriarchs! Prepare yourselves for the Faith, the joy of joys! Happy are ye, O Israelites, holy in this world and holy in the world to come! This is your heritage over and above that of all heathen nations-"a sign between Me and you!" ' Said R. Judah: 'It is indeed thus. Hence: "Remember the sabbath day to sanctify it"; "Be ye holy, for I the Lord am holy" (Lev. XIX, 2); "Call the sabbath a delight, the holy of the Lord, honourable" (Isa. LVIII, 13).' All the souls of the righteous-so we have been taught-on this day are feasted on the delights of the Holy Ancient One, the All-hidden. A breath of this rapture is extended through all the worlds; it ascends and descends, and spreads abroad to all the children of the holy, to all the guardians of the Torah, so that they enjoy perfect rest, forgetting all cares, all penalties, all toil and drudgery. It is the day on which "the Lord giveth thee rest from thy sorrow, and from thy fear, and from the hard bondage wherein thou wast made to serve" (Isa. XIV, 3). Therefore the Sabbath is equal in importance to the whole Torah, and whosoever observes the Sabbath fulfils the whole Torah: "Blessed is the man that doeth this, and the son of man that layeth hold on it: that keepeth the sabbath from profaning it, and keepeth his hand from doing any evil" (Ibid. LVI, 2).' R. Judai one day met R. Simeon on the road, and he asked him to explain the words of the prophet: "For thus says the Lord unto the eunuchs that keep my sabbaths, and choose the things that please me, and take hold of my covenant; even unto them will I give in my house and within my walls a place and a name better than of sons and of daughters: I will give them an everlasting name that shall not be cut off" (Ibid. 4, 5). Said R. Simeon: 'Cappadocian! [Tr. Note: i.e. "rude fellow".] Get down from thy donkey and fasten it to a tree, or let him go behind, and do thou follow me! Holy Writ requires quiet and solemn contemplation.' He replied: 'It is for the Master's sake that I have undertaken this journey, and in following him I shall behold the Shekinah.' Then R. Simeon said: 'This subject has already been considered by the members of the Fellowship, but they have not explained it sufficiently. The "eunuchs" are, in fact, students of the Torah, who make themselves "eunuchs" during the six days of the week for the Torah's sake, and on Sabbath nights have their conjugal union, because they apprehend the supernal mystery of the right moment when the Matrona (Shekinah) is united with the King. Such adepts of the mystic lore concentrate their hearts on the Divine union, on the Faith of their Lord, and are blessed in their own union. Therefore it says: "that keep My Sabbaths", meaning "they keep them in their hearts", as in the expression: "But his (Joseph's) father kept the matter" (Gen. XXXVI, 11). They are "eunuchs', because they wait for the Sabbath, in order "to choose what pleaseth Me", namely His union with the Shekinah. Blessed is the man who is sanctified in this holiness, and comprehends this mystery. Mark this. It is written: "Six days shalt thou labour and do all

Zohar: Shemoth, Section 2, Page 89b

thy work, but the seventh day is the sabbath of the Lord thy God." "All thy work": during the six days of the week man has to work, and therefore those who are absorbed in the study of the Torah have their conjugal union at a time when they do not work, but when the Holy One works. And what is His work then? The union with the Shekinah, in order to bring forth holy souls into the world. For this reason the mystics sanctify themselves on this night in the holiness of their Lord with deep contemplation and concentration, and bring good and holy children into the world: children who turn neither to the right nor to the left, children of the King and the Queen: "Children are ye to the Lord your God" (Deut. XIV, 1)-His children in the most real sense. The world is sustained by the merit of these children of God, and when

391

the world is placed on its trial the Holy One looks on these His children and exercises His pity and mercy. They are "altogether a seed of truth" (Jer. II, 21): a holy, perfect seed, according to the promise, "Thou shalt give truth to Jacob" (Micah VII, 20), and "truth" being the Holy One Himself, it means that He enters into their very self.' Said R. Judai: 'Blessed be the Merciful One who sent me here! Blessed be He for that He has permitted me to hear thy words!' And he burst out weeping. 'Why dost thou weep?' R. Simeon asked. 'I weep', he said, "because I think: Woe to the children of the world whose ways are the ways of beasts, without knowledge and understanding! It would have been better for them not to have been created. Woe to the world when thou, Master, wilt be removed from it! For who will then unfold the mysteries of the Torah? Who will then comprehend and grasp her ways? ' Said R. Simeon: 'By thy life! The world belongs only to those who occupy themselves with the Torah and know its mysteries. The Rabbis were right in their hard judgement on those who are ignorant of the Torah and corrupt their ways, not knowing their right hand from their left; for they are indeed like cattle, and it is fitting to chastise them even on the Day of Atonement. Concerning their children it is written: "They are the children of whoredoms" (Hos. II, 6).' Said R. Judai: 'Master, there is a certain peculiarity in the words of this verse. It is written: "even unto them will I give in my house and within my walls a place and a name better than sons and daughters", and then "I will give him an everlasting name, etc., Why first "them" and then "him"?' R. Simeon replied: '"House" here is the celestial region of which it says concerning Moses, "He is faithful in all my house"; the "walls" are those of which it says: "Upon thy walls, O Jerusalem, I have set watchmen" (Isa. LXII, 6); "a place and a name" signify that they will draw holy souls from this celestial sphere which, in its harmonious perfection, is "better than sons and daughters"; and "to him", namely to this portion, God will give an "everlasting name". According to another explanation, "I will give him"-namely to him who comprehends this mystery, and knows how to concentrate on it with the right intention-"an everlasting name that shall not be cut off".' R. Simeon also explained on that occasion the reason why it is written: "Ye shall kindle no fire throughout your habitations upon the sabbath day" (Ex. xxv, 3). 'It is', he said, 'because fire symbolizes judgement. As to the fire of the sacrifices on the Sabbath day, it rises to hold in check judgement; for, as we have learnt, "there is a fire which consumes a fire": the fire of the altar consumes the fire of judgement. Therefore the Holy Ancient One reveals Himself on this day (Sabbath) more than on any other day, and when He reveals Himself judgement is not in evidence at all, and all the upper and lower celestial beings are in perfect joy, and judgement has no dominion. 'It is written: "For six days the Lord made heaven and earth" (Ex. XXXI, 17); it does not say "in six days", which indicates that the days themselves were a special creation. They are holy, supernal days, days in which the Holy Name is contained. Blessed are the Israelites more than all the heathen nations: of them it is written, "And ye who cleave to the Lord your God, ye are all alive today".'

Zohar: Shemoth, Section 2, Page 90a

HONOUR THY FATHER AND THY MOTHER. R. Hiya connected this command with the words: "And a river went out of Eden to water the garden" (Gen. II, 10). 'The "river" he said, is the issue of the fountain which flows perennially and from whence the whole Garden of Eden is watered, and this issue [Tr. Note: Tifereth.] of the holy fountain is called Ab-"Father".' R. Abba said that Eden itself [Tr. Note: Hokhmah.] is called Father, itself originating from the place called Ain (nought)-as we have laid down, that the place from which the Whole begins to take its being is designated both "Thou" and "Father", as it says: "For thou art our father" (Isa. LXIII, 16).' R. Eleazar applied the words "honour thy father" to the Holy One; "thy mother" to the Community of Israel; and the article eth to the Shekinah. R. Judah, however, held that, as "Father" and "Mother" in this commandment are not particularised, they include all aspects of the Divine, and the article eth between indicates all that is above and all that is below. R. Yose referred to R. Abba's remark that the sphere whence the "river" issues forth is called "Thou," and confirmed it by reference to the dictum: "What is hidden and has no beginning is designated 'He'; but the point where it begins to manifest itself is called 'Thou' and 'Father', and all are one." Blessed be His name forever and ever. Amen. Said R. Hezekiah: 'Verily, they are all one: "honour thy father", namely the Holy One, blessed be He; "and thy mother", the Community of Israel. Thus the commandment includes all, both that which is above and that which is below.' According to R. Isaac, it also includes teachers of the Torah, for they are the means of leading men to eternal life. R. Judah, however, held this to be included in the command to honour the Holy One, blessed be He. We have a dictum that the first five commandments include by implication the other five as well: in other words, in the first five the second five are engraved, five within five. How? Take the first commandment: "I am the Lord thy God." Does it not include the first of the second five? Indeed it does, for the murderer diminishes the likeness and image of his Master, man having been created "in the image of God", and it is also written: "And upon the likeness of the throne was the likeness as the appearance of a man upon it" (Ezek. I, 26). Said R. Hiya: 'It is written: "Whoso sheddeth man's blood, by man shall his blood be shed; for in the image of God made he man" (Gen. IX, 6). He who sheds the blood of a fellow-man is thus considered as diminishing the Divine archetype of man as well. Thus the first commandment, "I am the Lord thy God", contains the motive for the sixth, "Thou shalt not murder." The second commandment, "Thou shalt have no other gods", contains the motive for the seventh, "Thou shalt not commit adultery"; for the adulterer perfidiously lies against the Name of the Holy One which is impressed upon man, a sin comprising many other sins and entailing corresponding punishments. He who is unfaithful in this is unfaithful towards the King, as it is written: "They have dealt treacherously against the Lord, for they have begotten strange children" (Hos. v, 7). One is the result of the other. The third commandment, "Thou shalt not take the name of the Lord thy God in vain", corresponds to the eighth commandment, "Thou shalt not steal." For a thief is certainly inclined to swear falsely, as it is written: "Whoso is partner with a thief hateth his own soul, he heareth cursing and tells it not" (Prov. XXIX, 24). The fourth commandment, "Remember the sabbath day", corresponds to the ninth, "Thou shalt not bear false witness against thy neighbour"; for, as R. Yose said, the Sabbath is called a witness to God's creative activity, and man is required to testify to the fact that "in six days the Lord made heaven and earth, etc." Hence R. Yose said: 'God has "given truth to Jacob" (Micah VII, 20) in requiring Israel to keep the Sabbath; and he who bears false witness against his neighbour lies against the Sabbath-the witness of truth; and he who lies against the Sabbath lies against the whole Torah. The fifth commandment, "Honour thy father and thy mother", implies also the tenth, "Thou shalt not covet thy neighbour's wife"; for whosoever has a son born in adultery is "honoured" by him

Zohar: Shemoth, Section 2, Page 90b

on false pretences. Further, it is written in the fifth commandment "that thy days may be long upon the land which the Lord thy God giveth thee", as much as to say, "what He gives thee is thine-but covet not what is not thine". Thus the first five commandments imply the second five. Therefore: "From his right hand went a fiery law to them" (Deut. XXXIII, 2); for all was included in the five fingers of the Right Hand. Therefore also was the Torah proclaimed in five voices, corresponding to the five Books of the Torah.' R. Eleazar taught that in the Ten Words (Decalogue) all the other commandments were engraved, with all decrees and punishments, all laws concerning purity and impurity, all the branches and roots, all the trees and plants, heaven and earth, seas and oceans-in fact, all things. For the Torah is the Name of the Holy One, blessed be He. As the Name of the Holy One is engraved in the Ten Words (creative utterances) of Creation, so is the whole Torah engraved in the Ten Words (Decalogue), and these Ten Words are the Name of the Holy One, and the whole Torah is thus one Name, the Holy Name of God Himself. Blessed is he who is worthy of her, the Torah, for he will be worthy of the Holy Name. Said R. Yose: 'This means that he will be worthy of the Holy One Himself, as He and His Name are one. Blessed be His Name forever and ever. Amen.' YE SHALL NOT MAKE WITH ME (iti) GODS OF SILVER, NEITHER SHALL YE MAKE UNTO YOU GODS OF GOLD. R. Yose read iti (with me) as oti (me), and interpreted thus: 'Although "mine is the silver and mine the gold" (Hag. II, 8), ye shall not represent Me (oti) in silver and gold.'

R. Isaac connected the words, "Mine is the silver and mine the gold", with the verse: "For as much as there is none like unto thee, O Lord; thou art great and thy name is great in power" (Jer. x, 7). "Thou art great" corresponds, according to him, to "Mine is the silver"; "and Thy Name is great,' to "Mine the gold". These represent the two colours which are only visible in their full beauty when they are engraved in a certain place, namely Israel: "Israel, in whom I am glorified" (Isa. XLIX, 4). R. Judah illustrated from the verse: "I greatly rejoice in the Lord, my soul is joyful in my God; for He hath clothed me with the garments of salvation, he hath covered me with the robe of righteousness, as a bridegroom decketh himself with ornaments, and as a bride adorneth herself with her jewels" (Ibid. LXI, 10). He said: 'Blessed are the Israelites above all heathen nations, for that they have their joy in the Lord (Tetragrammaton, signifying Mercy) and their gladness in their God (Elohim, signifying Judgement). Thus does Israel say: "Whether He deals with us in Mercy or in Judgement we rejoice and are glad in Him." For these two attributes belong to His essential Being, as indicated by the words, "He hath clothed me with the garments of salvation (yesha)", namely with the garments consisting of colours in which one can have a perception, a beholding, of Him (shaah=to look). He says: "He who would behold Me must behold My colours (the attributes of Mercy and Justice)." And these two colours are indicated by the words, "as a bridegroom decketh himself with ornaments, and as a bride adorneth herself with her jewels". When these two colours are united their glory is such that all are aflame to behold their beauty.' R. Yose said that two kinds of joy are referred to in the words, "I greatly rejoice in the Lord", and one in the words, "my soul is joyful in my God". Said R. Judah: 'In each there is joy upon joy, but the joy which the Holy One shall vouchsafe unto Israel in the future will excel them all: "And the ransomed of the Lord shall return, and come to Zion with songs and everlasting joy upon their heads; they shall obtain joy and gladness" (Isa. xxxv, 10). "They shall return"; "they shall come with songs"; "everlasting joy upon their heads"; "they shall obtain joy and gladness"-the fourfold glad tidings corresponding to the four exiles of Israel among the nations (Egyptian, Assyrian, Babylonian, Roman). Therefore: "Ye shall say in that day, Praise the Lord, call upon his name, declare his doings among the peoples" (Isa. XII, 4).' [Tr. Note: 91a-93b belong to the Sitre Torah and the Raya Mehemna, and are too allusive to be made readily intelligible in a translation.] [Note: In connection with the previous note, see the "Raya Mehemna" menu choices for the Hebrew Zohar submenu. Look for pages 91b-93a. Also note the Hebrew text for these pages in the main Zohar volume.]

Zohar: Shemoth, Section 2, Page 91a=93b

[Note: The Hebrew text is not translated as explained in the Translator's note on page 90b]

Zohar: Shemoth, Section 2, Page 93b

[Note: The first 38 lines of the Hebrew text do not appear in the translation as explained in the Translator's note on page 90b] The Ten Words contain the essence of all the commandments, the essence of all celestial and terrestrial mysteries, the essence of the Ten Words of Creation. They were engraved on tables of stone, and all the hidden things were seen by the eyes and perceived by the minds of all Israel, everything being made clear to them. At that hour all the mysteries of the Torah, all the hidden things of heaven and earth, were unfolded before them and revealed to their eyes, for they

Zohar: Shemoth, Section 2, Page 94a

saw eye to eye the splendour of the glory of their Lord. Never before, since the Holy One created the world, had such a revelation of the Divine Glory taken place. Even the crossing of the Red Sea, where, as has been said, even a simple maid-servant saw more of the Divine than the prophet Ezekiel, was not so wonderful as this. For on this day all the earthly dross was removed from them and purged away, and their bodies became as lucent as the angels above when they are clothed in radiant garments for the accomplishment of their Master's errands; in which garments they penetrate fire without fear, as we read concerning the angel who appeared to Manoah (Jud. XIII, 20). And when all the fleshly impurity was removed from the Israelites their bodies became, as we have said, lucent as stars and their souls were as resplendent as the firmament, to receive the light. Such was the state of the Israelites when they beheld the glory of their Lord. It was not thus at the Red Sea, when the filth had not as yet been removed from them. There, at Mount Sinai, even the embryos in their mothers' wombs had some perception of their Lord's glory, and everyone received according to his grade of perception. On that day the Holy One, blessed be He, rejoiced more than on any previous day since He had created the world, for Creation had no proper basis before Israel received the Torah, as is implied in the words: "But for my covenant with day and night, I had not appointed the ordinances of heaven and earth" (Jer. XXXIII, 25). But when once Israel had received the Torah on Mount Sinai the world was duly and completely established, and heaven and earth received a proper foundation, and the glory of the Holy One was made known both above and below, and He was exalted over all. Concerning that day it is written: "The Lord is King, he hath put on glorious apparel; he hath put on his apparel, and girded himself with strength' (Ps. XCIII, 1). "Strength" signifies the Torah, as it is written: "The Lord giveth strength to his people; he blesseth his people with peace" (Ibid. XIX, 11). Blessed be the Lord forever. Amen and Amen.

MISHPATIM

AND THESE ARE THE JUDGEMENTS WHICH THOU SHALT SET BEFORE THEM. R. Simeon here introduced the subject of transmigration of souls, saying: 'Onkelos translates the above words as follows: "These are the judgements which thou shalt order before them". In other words, "These are the orders of the metempsychosis; the judgements of the souls, by which each of them receives its appropriate punishment." Associates, the time is now arrived to reveal diverse hidden and secret mysteries in regard to the transmigration of souls. IF THOU BUY AN HEBREW SERVANT, SIX YEARS HE SHALL SERVE.

When a soul is doomed to undergo transmigration, should it be one which has emanated from the side of the Servant, Metatron, who represents in himself six aspects, then the successive revolutions of that soul will not be more than six years (i.e. times) until it shall have completed the six stages which lead back to the region from whence it came. But if the soul has emanated from the sphere of the Shekinah Herself, who is symbolized by the number seven, it "shall go forth free", because its owner is righteous, and is not subjected to labour or servitude.' Now it chanced that while Rabbi Simeon spake these things

Zohar: Shemoth, Section 2, Page 94b

a certain "ancient one" came down to his side and said: 'If that be so, Master, where is the additional delight of the soul that emanates therefrom, indicated by the words, "In it thou shalt not do any work, thou nor thy son nor thy daughter nor thy manservant, etc." (Ex. xx, 10)? Rabbi Simeon replied: 'O venerable companion! Should a man of thy learning ask this? This verse assuredly speaks of the soul of the Righteous One, teaching us that even though she may have to undergo transmigration in any of these, even in a manservant or maidservant or in any animal, yet "in it thou shalt do no manner of work", or, what amounts to the same thing, "thou shalt not make him serve as a bondman". But, old man, the difficulty is this. Seeing that Sabbath is an only daughter, and that she is the mate of the Righteous One, what is meant by the words in our text, "if he take him another wife"?' He replied: 'These words refer to the weekdays.' 'What do these symbolize?' he asked. 'These', he said, 'are the bondmaid who is the body of the only daughter. Observe this. There is a soul which is called handmaid, and there is also a soul which is called the daughter of the king. Now as for the soul which is doomed to undergo transmigration, if she is the daughter of the Holy One, blessed be He, we cannot suppose that she is sold to an alien body that is under the domination of the evil spirit emanating from the side of Samael, since it is written: "I am the Lord, that is my name, and my glory will I not give to another" (Isa. XLII, 8). Nor is it to be thought that the body which harbours the daughter of the king shall be sold into the power of earthly crowns of defilement. Against this the Scripture says: "And the land shall not be sold in perpetuity" (Lev. xxv, 23). Which is the body of the King's daughter? Metatron; and this same body is identical with the handmaid of the Shekinah. Nevertheless, the soul that is the King's daughter is held prisoner therein, having to undergo transmigration. 'According to another interpretation, "man" here signifies the Holy One, blessed be He; "his daughter" denoting the Community of Israel, who emanates from the sphere of the "Only Daughter". The verse therefore indicates that when God delivers His people from the nations of the world "she shall not go out" as the menservants do, namely, as the children of Israel did when they left Egypt in haste. For at that time they were in the grade of "servants", represented by Metraton, who is but the bearer of the Shekinah; but in the days of the Messiah they shall "not go out with haste, nor go by flight" (Isa. LII, 12) from their captivity. See, now. When a human being is born into the world he is given a soul (nephesh) from the primordial "animal" sphere, the sphere of purity, the sphere of those who are designated "Holy Wheels"-namely, the supernal order of angels. If he is more fortunate he will be endowed with a spirit (ruah) which appertains to the sphere of the Holy.Hayoth. Should he possess still greater potential merit he is given a soul (neshamah) from the region of the Throne. These three grades of personality are the "maidservant", the "manservant", and the "bondwoman" of the King's daughter. And if the newly created being deserves still more, the soul which is put into his bodily form derives through a process of emanation (aziluth) from the sphere of the "Only Daughter", and is itself called "the King's daughter". If his merit is still greater he will be endowed with a spirit (ruah), deriving through emanation from the sphere of the "Central Pillar", and its owner is then called "The son of the Holy One", as it is written: "Sons are ye to the Lord your God" (Deut. XIV, 1). Should he be of even greater worth he is given a soul (neshamah) from the sphere of Father and Mother, concerning which it is written: "And he breathed into his nostrils the breath (nishmath) of life" (Gen. II, 7). What does "life" signify? It signifies the Divine Name YH; and therefore it is written of such souls: "Let the whole soul (all souls) praise KaH" (Ps. CL, 6). But if he should acquire still greater merit, the Holy Name Tetragrammaton is granted to him in its fulness-the letters Yod, He, Vau, He, representing Man in the sphere of the supernal Aziluth, and he is said to be "in the likeness of his Lord", and in him the words, "Have dominion over the fish of the sea, and over the fowl of the air, and over every living thing" (Gen. I, 28), are properly fulfilled: for his dominion is indeed over all the firmaments and over all the Wheels and Seraphim and Living Beings (Hayoth) and over all the hosts above and below. It is therefore concerning one who has attained to the sphere of the "Only Daughter" and has derived his soul from thence that it says, "She shall not go out as the menservants do".' R. Hiya and R. Yose met one night at the tower of Tyrus, and greatly enjoyed one another's company. Said R. Yose: 'How glad am I to behold the countenance of the Shekinah! For during the whole of my journey here I was molested by the chatter of an old carrier who pestered me with all sorts of foolish questions;

Zohar: Shemoth, Section 2, Page 95a

for example, "Which serpent is it that flies in the air whilst an ant lies undisturbed between its teeth? What is it that begins in union and ends in separation? Which eagle is it whose nest is in a tree that does not yet exist, and whose young ones are plundered by creatures who have not yet been created, and in a place which is not? What are those which when they ascend descend, and when they descend ascend? And what is it two of which are one and one of which is three? And who is the beautiful virgin who has no eyes and whose body is concealed and yet revealed; revealed in the morning and concealed during the day, and who is adorned with ornaments which do not exist?" So he went on plaguing me the whole of the way. But now I.shall have peace and quiet, and we can devote ourselves to discussing the Torah instead of wasting time in empty talk.' Said R. Hiya: 'Dost thou know anything of the old man?' R. Yose replied: 'I only know that there is nothing in him; for if there were, he would have expounded some text of Scripture, and the time spent on the road would not have been profitless.' 'Is the old man in this house?' asked R. Hiya. 'For sometimes it happens that in vessels that seem empty grains of gold can be discovered.' 'Yes,' replied R. Yose, 'he is here, preparing fodder for his donkey.' So they called the carrier and he came to them. The first thing the old man said was: 'Now the two have become three, and the three one!' Said R. Yose: 'Did I not tell thee that he only talks nonsense?' The old man seated himself and said: 'Sirs, it is only recently that I have become a carrier. I have a young son whom I send to school, and whom I wish to bring up in the study of the Torah; so whenever I see a scholar on my way I follow him in the hope of picking up some new idea in connection with the Torah; but today I have heard nothing new.' Said R. Yose: 'Of all the things I heard you say, one specially surprised me, because it showed exceptional folly in a man of your years, or else you did not know what you were saying.' Said the old man: 'What do you refer to?' Said R. Yose: 'That about the beautiful virgin and so forth.' Then the old man began thus: '"The Lord is on my side, I am not afraid; what can men do unto me?... It is better to trust in the Lord than to put any confidence in princes" (Ps. CXVIII, 6, 9). How good, how lovely, how precious, how supernal are the words of the Torah. Shall I tell them in the presence of scholars from whom so far I have not heard even one word of enlightenment? However, I feel impelled to speak, and surely there is no need to be shy in speaking of things spiritual to anyone, whether scholars or no.' The old man then drew his cloak round him, opened his mouth, and said: 'It is written: "If a priest's daughter be married unto a stranger, she may not eat of an offering of holy things" (Lev.

395

XXII, 12). Now this verse is followed by another verse: "But if the priest's daughter be a widow, or divorced, and have no child, and is returned unto her father's house, as in her youth, she shall eat of her father's meat, but there shall no stranger eat thereof" (Ibid. 18). These verses are plain enough in the literal sense, but the words of the Torah have also an esoteric significance, and every word therein contains hidden seeds of wisdom, comprehensible only to the wise who are familiar with the ways of the Torah. For, truly, the words of the Torah are not mere dreams. And even dreams have to be interpreted according to certain rules; how much more, then, is it necessary that the words of the Torah, the delight of the Holy King, be explained in accordance with the right way! And "the ways of the Lord are upright" (Hos. IV, 10). Now, "the priest's daughter" is the superior soul, the daughter of our father Abraham, the first of proselytes, who drew this soul from a supernal region.

Zohar: Shemoth, Section 2, Page 95b

And "a priest's daughter married unto a stranger" refers to the holy soul which emanates from a supernal region and enters into the hidden part of the Tree of Life. And when the breath of the supernal Priest has breathed souls into that Tree, those souls fly away from there and enter a certain treasure-house. Woe unto the world that knows not how to guard itself! Men draw down the soul along with their evil inclination, which is "the stranger", and this "priest's daughter", the soul, flies down to earth and finds her edifice in a "stranger"; and because it is the will of her Master, she enters there and bears the yoke, and cannot assert herself or become perfected in this world. So when she leaves this world she "may eat of an offering of holy things", like those souls which have perfected themselves in this world. There is still another significance to this verse: it is a great humiliation for the holy soul to enter into a "stranger", namely into a proselyte, for then she has to fly from Paradise into a habitation builded from an uncircumcised and unclean source. There is here, however, a still deeper mystery. Near to the pillar which supports the wheels where the souls are blown in there are two weighing scales, one at each side: these are the "weights of righteousness" and "weights of deception" which never cease to move, and souls rise and fall thereon, and appear and disappear. There are souls which are violently captured and oppressed when "man ruleth over man to his own hurt" (Eccl. VIII, 9). For this world is entirely directed by the "tree of knowledge of good and evil", and when human beings walk in the way of righteousness the scales are weighted on the side of good, and when they walk in the evil way they incline towards the evil side. And all souls found then on the scales are violently caught by the evil side. But this is "to its own hurt"; for these souls tread down and destroy all that they find on the evil side, just as the Philistines captured the holy Ark to their own hurt. And what becomes of these souls? In ancient books it is written that some of them become the souls of pious Gentiles and scholarly bastards of Jewish origin, who, because of their learning, are of a higher merit than even a high priest who has no divine knowledge, although by virtue of his office he enters into the Holy of Holies.' The old man here stopped and wept for a moment. The two companions were astonished but said nothing, and after a while he continued to speak on the following verse: IF SHE (the maidservant) PLEASE NOT HER MASTER, WHO HATH BETROTHED HER TO HIMSELF, THEN SHALL HE LET HER BE REDEEMED; BUT TO SELL HER TO A STRANGE NATION, HE SHALL HAVE NO POWER (V. 8). 'This passage', said he, 'continues the inner meaning of the "man who sells his daughter as a maidservant". It is written: "Who would not fear thee, O king of the nations? For it becometh thee, as among all the wise men of the nations, and in all their kingdoms, there is none like unto thee" (Jer. x, 7). How many people misunderstand this verse! They repeat the words, but the sense escapes them. Is the Holy One, blessed be He, the "King of the nations"? Is He not rather the King of Israel? Is it not written: "When the Most High divided to the nations their inheritance, when he separated the sons of men, he set the bounds of the peoples according to the number of the children of Israel. For the Lord's portion is his people" (Deut. XXXII, 8, 9), wherefore He is called the "King of Israel"? If the prophet here called God "King of the nations", he would be praising them more than they praise themselves, for they only claim to be in the charge of His ministers and servitors. The last part of the verse also contradicts this idea, for it says: "As among all the wise men of the nations... there is none like unto thee." Seeing that the other nations have so much to boast of, it is surprising that with this verse they do not ascend to the very heaven.

Zohar: Shemoth, Section 2, Page 96a

But in truth the Holy One, blessed be He, has blinded their eyes, and "all nations before him are as nothing, and they are counted to him less than nothing and vanity" (Isa. XL, 17). This is the real truth of the matter in their regard.' Said R. Hiya: 'And yet it is written: "God reigneth over the nations"!' The old man replied: 'I see that thou hast been behind their wall, and hast come forward to support them with this verse. I ought first to deal with my own difficulty; but since I have found thee in the way, I will first remove thee, and then go on to remove all other obstacles. See, now. All the Names of the Holy One, blessed be He, and all subsidiary Names, ramify in different directions and are encircled in each other, as it were, and yet branch out into various paths. Only one aspect is not so scattered: and that is the one definite and particular Name, which is the heritage of the one particular people, namely, the Name Tetragrammaton; for it is written: "For the portion of Tetragrammaton is His people"; "And ye who cleave to Tetragrammaton" (Deut. XXXII, 9, IV, 4), which signifies those that cleave to this very Name itself. Thus it is seen that this Name Tetragrammaton belongs only to

Israel. Above all the other names is one which spreads and separates itself towards many diverse ways and paths, to wit, Elohim. This name has been transmitted to the beings of this lower world, and has been shared among the Chieftains and ministering angels who guide other nations. Hence we read: "And Elohim came to Balaam by night" (Num. XXII, 20); "And Elohim came to Abimelech in the dream of the night" (Gen. xx, 3): and the same is true of all the principalities and powers appointed over the nations—all are included in this Name, yea, even their objects of worship find a place therein; and so it is this name and aspect of the Divinity which reigns over the nations, but not the peculiar Name, for in that they have no part, since it reigns over Israel only: the one nation, the holy nation. This, however, does not mean that the words, "Who would not fear thee, O King of the nations", are to be interpreted in this sense, namely, that He is the King of the nations in His attribute of Elohim, representing severity and justice; for, as I have pointed out, this Name signifies even the objects of pagan worship. Since, then, the wall on which you were leaning has been shaken, use a little subtlety to get to the true meaning of the words. This is: "Who is the king of the nations that would not fear thee?" The inversion of the order is similar to that found in the verse: "Praise ye the Lord. Praise ye servants of the Lord" (Ps. CXIII, 1), which does not mean that the servants of the Lord shall be praised, but is to be read as "Servants of the Lord, praise ye the Lord." 'The two companions rejoiced and wept, but said nothing. The old man also wept, even as he had done before. Then he went on: 'It is written: "And she (Sarah) said unto Abraham, Cast out the bondwoman and her son" (Gen. XXI, 10), which has been interpreted by the scholars to signify that Sarah desired to cleanse her house from idolatry, and that therefore Abraham was told: "In all that Sarah hath said unto thee, hearken unto her voice" (Ibid. v, 12). Now here we read, "And if a man sell his daughter to be a maidservant, she shall go out as the menservants do", which, being interpreted, means: When the soul is made to undergo transmigration because of the evil works of this world, when she is "sold" to be a "maidservant"-that is, delivered into the hands of the impure principle through the evil revolution of the wheel, so that she is wrenched violently away from the scale of souls -when her time thus comes to "go out", she shall not go out as the menservants do. And what sort of souls are these which are so violently despoiled and taken away? There is a mystery behind this. They are the souls of infants still at the breast. The Holy One, seeing that should they continue in this world they would lose their sweet savour, their aroma of purity, and, as it were, turn sour like vinegar, gathers them in their infancy while their savour is still sweet, and allows them to be wrenched away by that "maidservant", namely Lilith,

Zohar: Shemoth, Section 2, Page 96b

who, when they have been delivered into her power, gloatingly carries them away to other regions. Do not imagine that had they not been so removed they could have done any good in the world. For therefore it is written, "If she (the soul) pleases not her master", that is, the man in whom it is lodged will cause it to turn sour in course of time. Such a one is wrenched away, but no other. Yet, on the other hand, it does not mean that the Holy One has pre-ordained such a soul to be under the domination of impurity from the very day of her creation. Not at all! For in the revolution of the wheel, when the soul gives forth a good savour, "shall he let her be redeemed", namely, the Holy One will redeem her from her sore bondage and raise her unto the highest heights to be with Him. And it should not be imagined that because she had been once purloined by the impure power the Holy One will condemn her perpetually to enter into the bodies of pious Gentiles or scholarly bastards. No! "To sell her into a strange nation, he shall have no power." She will re-enter into the body of an Israelite and not into a stranger. And when she shall be redeemed from the bondage of the "wheel of impurity", "she shall not go out as the menservants do", but receive her crown with uplifted head. Nor is one to imagine that the "side of impurity" has put the soul in the child: for the impure power only snatched, as it were, at that soul and played with it until it entered into the body of that child. But the impure power visits the child occasionally and longs to possess his body. And after some time the Holy One takes into His own guardianship the soul, and the evil power attains mastery over the body. But eventually body and soul become the possession of the Holy One (in the Resurrection). '"She shall not go out as the menservants do." What does this mean? When the soul emerges from the scales, and the side of righteousness rejoices, the Holy One, blessed be He, stamps upon her the impress of a seal; and He likewise spreads about her His costly garment-namely the Holy Name Elohah. This is indicated by the words in the text, "be-bigdo bah" (when his garment is upon her, v. 8), for they signify the costly garment (beged) of the King. Therewith she is guarded and so cannot be delivered to a "strange nation", but only to Israel. Concerning this it is written: "He guards me like the days of Elohah" (Job. XXIX, 2). It is also of this mystery that we read here: "To sell her unto a strange nation he shall have no power, seeing he hath put his garment upon her." As long as this costly garment of the King adorns her, what power can the evil side have over her? Observe this. All men are in the power of the Holy King, and all have their allotted time in this world; but for this one there is no appointed time, and therefore it mocks at the evil spirits and gloats over them. Many admonitions to mankind are contained in these verses, and truly much good and excellent advice is to be found in all the words of the Torah, for they are all true and lead to further truth and are comprehended as such by the wise who know that path and walk therein. When the Holy One, blessed be He, came to create the world, it pleased Him to form all the souls which were destined to be allotted to the children of men, and each was shaped before him in the

397

very outline of the body she was afterwards to inhabit. He examined each one, and saw that some of them would corrupt their ways in the world. When the time of each was arrived, the Holy One summoned it, saying: "Go, descend into such and such a place, into such and such a body." But ofttimes it chanced that the soul would reply, "Lord of the world, I am satisfied to be here in this world, and desire not to leave it for some other place where I shall be enslaved and become soiled." Then would the Holy One respond: "From the very day of thy creation thou hast had no other destiny than to go into that world." At this the soul, seeing that it must obey, would descend against its will and enter into this world. The Torah, which counsels the whole world in the ways of truth, observed this, and proclaimed to mankind: "Behold, how the Holy One has pity upon you! He has sold to you for nothing His costly pearl, for you to use in this world, namely the holy soul." "If a man sell his daughter to be a maidservant"-that is, when the Holy One delivers His daughter, the holy soul, to be a maidservant, enslaved in bondage unto you,

Zohar: Shemoth, Section 2, Page 97a

I adjure you, when her time comes, let her "not go out as the menservants do", polluted by sins, but free, illumined, and pure, in order that her Master may be able to find joy in her, and to give her goodly reward in the splendours of Paradise, as it is written: "And he shall satisfy thy soul with brightness (zahzahoths lit. places lit by the sun)" (Isa. LVIII, 11); namely, when she shall ascend again thence, bright and pure. But should she "not please her Master", being polluted with sin, then woe to the body which has lost its soul forever! For when the souls ascend from this world in a bright and pure condition, they are entered into the King's archives, each one by name; and He says: "This is the soul of such a one: she belongs to the body which she left"; as it is written: "Who hath betrothed her to himself." But "if she pleased not her Master", that is, if she be polluted by sin and guilt, He does not again appoint that same body for her, and so she loses it forever, unless the person should be roused to repentance, for then "shall she be redeemed"-as it is written: "He will deliver his soul from going into the pit" (Job XXXIII, 28); which signifies that man is advised to redeem his own soul by repentance and amendment. In fact, the words "he shall redeem her" have a double significance: they point to man's own redemption of his soul by repentance, followed by the redemption from Gehenna effected by the Holy One. "To sell her unto a strange nation he shall have no power." Who is this "strange nation"? Hapless is the soul when she leaves this world after being attached to a man who has turned away from the right path. She desires to ascend to the heights, in the midst of the holy hosts; for holy hosts stand along the way to Paradise, and "strange" hosts line the other way, to Gehenna. If, then, the soul is worthy and wears the precious protecting garment, multitudes of holy hosts stand ready to join her and accompany her to Paradise. But if she hath not that garment, the "strange" hosts compel her to take the path which leads to Gehenna. Angels of destruction and confusion are they, who will gladly take their revenge on her. But "He shall have no power to sell her unto a strange nation", if "His garment is upon her", by which the Holy One guards her from the "strange nations" of the angels of destruction and despoilment. 'AND IF HE HAVE BETROTHED HER UNTO HIS SON, HE SHALL ACT TOWARDS HER AFTER THE MANNER OF DAUGHTERS. How careful should a man be not to walk in a crooked way in this world! For if he shall have proved himself worthy in this world, having guarded his soul with all care, then the Holy One, blessed be He, will be well pleased with him, and will praise him daily to His celestial Family, saying: "Behold the holy son whom I have in that lower world! See what acts he performed, how upright are his ways." And when such a soul leaves this world, pure, bright, and unsullied, the Holy One illumines her daily with innumerable radiances and proclaims concerning her: "This is the soul of my son so-and-so: let her be kept for the body which she has left." This is the significance of the words: "And if he have betrothed her unto his son, he shall act towards her after the manner of daughters." What is the meaning of these words, "after the manner of daughters"? This is a secret entrusted to the keeping of the wise alone, and here is the substance thereof. In the midst of a mighty rock, a most recondite firmament, there is set a Palace which is called the Palace of Love. This is the region wherein the treasures of the King are stored, and all His love-kisses are there. All souls beloved of the Holy One enter into that Palace. And when the King Himself appears, "Jacob kisses Rachel" (Gen. XXIX, 11), that is, the Lord discovers each holy soul, and takes each in turn up unto Himself, fondling and caressing her, "acting towards her after the manner of daughters", even as a father treats his beloved daughter, fondling and caressing her, and giving her presents. "Ear hath not heard, nor eye seen... what he doeth to him who waiteth for him" (Isa. LXIV, 3): as that "daughter", the soul, has done her work in this world, so will the Holy One "do" His work on her in the world to come.'

Zohar: Shemoth, Section 2, Page 97b

Then the old man prostrated himself in prayer, wept again, and continued: 'IF HE TAKE HIM.ANOTHER ONE, HER FOOD, HER RAIMENT, AND HER CONJUGAL COHABITATION SHALL HE NOT DIMINISH. What does it mean by saying, "If he take him another one"? Does it mean that the Holy One will give another soul in this world to the righteous, and not the same one which already had fulfilled in this world the will of her Master? Surely not: for what good tidings would that be for the righteous? However, it is written: "Then shall the dust return to the earth as it was and the spirit shall return unto God who gave it" (Eccl. XII, 7). Now this verse the scholars have applied to the destruction of the Temple: the dust [Tr. Note: The klifah, or evil spirit.] thereof did indeed return upon the earth, so that it reverted to the state in which it was when "the Canaanite was there" (Gen. XII, 6), and the spirit, namely the Shekinah, when she saw that her ten stages were completed and yet Israel did not repent, [Tr. Note: According to a tradition, the Shekinah departed from the Sanctuary at the time of the Exile in ten stages.] returned unto God, and since then the "other side" has had dominion over the Holy Land. All this has been established by the members of the Fellowship. Now the spirit (ruah) of a righteous man is adorned with its own form in the lower Paradise; and on sabbaths, festivals, and new-moons the spirits are crowned with new crowns, and ascend to the higher realms of Heaven. And as the Holy One deals with the supernal holy soul (neshamah) in the upper Paradise, so also He deals with this spirit in the lower Paradise: He brings it up before Him and says, "This spirit belongs to such and such a body." Then He crowns it with many crowns and finds His joy therein. This, however, does not mean that this occupation with the spirit interferes with the joy which the Holy One gives to the soul. "If he take him another one, her food, her raiment, and her conjugal cohabitation shall he not diminish." These are the three supreme Names which "no eye hath seen, apart from thee, O God" (Isa. LXIV, 8), all of whom are in the world to come and issue forth from thence. One is designated "sheerah" (her food), namely, the emanation of the radiance, the source of which is undiscoverable. It is the food which nourishes all and is called Tetragrammaton with the vowel points of Elohim. The second is called "her raiment": the King's garment which is spread over the soul and protects her always, another emanation of light. And what does the "conjugal cohabitation" stand for? This is the abundance of light and life of the world to come wherein is all bliss. It is Tetragrammaton Zebaoth who shines forth with all the hidden lights of the Tree of Life, and wherein is concealed the mystery of conjugal relations and whence it emanates. These three manifestations of the Divine Grace shall "not be diminished" to the soul, if she be worthy; but if she be not so, then she will not be crowned with any of them: "If he do not these three unto her"-because of the soul's unworthiness-"then shall she go out free without money (keseph)" (V. 11). That is to say, the soul is then pushed away without yearning (kisupha) for union with the supernal light, and without the joy of possessing it. 'So far we have dealt with the good counsel which the Torah gives to the children of men: the Torah, which abounds in good counsel. But now let us return to our former subject, namely to the supernal garment which the Holy One spreads over the soul as an armour of protection so that she should not be delivered to a "strange nation". "And if he hath betrothed her unto his son, he shall act towards her according to the rights of daughters." 'Associates,' said the old man, 'When ye shall draw nigh unto that rock upon which the whole world is sustained (R. Simeon), then shall ye tell him to remember the day of snow whereon beans were sown of fifty-two kinds and colours, [Tr. Note: Alluding to a discussion on the word ben (understanding), the numerical value of which is fifty-two] and having recalled that day to his mind, recall also the fact that on it we read the above verse: which, when ye have awakened in him the memory thereof, he will then unravel for you himself.' But the companions demurred to this, saying: 'Nay, we pray thee: he who began must himself continue!' Said he: 'So be it then! For I know that ye are wise and righteous scholars, worthy to be informed of all the mysteries which have been entrusted to the keeping of the faithful. I shall indeed interpret; but when ye remind him by that sign and token which I have given you, he will duly supplement and complete my words. We must now explain who is he that is called "son" to the Holy One, blessed be He. Come and see. A boy

Zohar: Shemoth, Section 2, Page 98a

who has reached the age of thirteen becomes a son of the Community of Israel and remains so until he is twenty. When he is twenty, if he be worthy he becomes a son of the Holy One, one of those of whom it is written, "Sons are ye to the Lord your God" (Deut. XIV, I). Thus, when David had reached his thirteenth year it was said concerning him: "The Lord said unto me, My son art thou, today have I begotten thee" (Ps. II, 7). What does this mean? It signifies that up till that time he was not in the state of sonship, and the supernal soul did not rest upon him, because he was in the years of immaturity ('orlah). But as soon as he reached the age when he became, being worthy, a son of the Community of Israel, he was, as it were, begotten anew: "Today have I begotten thee"-I and not the "other side" as hitherto: I alone. And when Solomon was twenty, what do we read concerning him? "I was a son of my father" (Prov. IV, 3), "father" referring to the Heavenly Father. Thus the words, "And if he have betrothed her unto his son" (in their mystical sense) refer to the time after the age of thirteen when a man emerges from the sphere of impurity to which he had been assigned. Then "he shall act towards her according to the rights of daughters". What is this? We have been taught that every day the Holy One, blessed be He, gazed steadfastly down from the celestial heights upon the young boy who is still held in the power of the unclean spirit ('orlah), noting how he gradually liberates himself therefrom: first by attending school, where he begins to weaken it, and then by going to the synagogue, where he masters it still further. What does the Holy One then do to the soul of such a one? He brings her into His Treasure-house, and bestows upon her rich, glorious and supernal gifts, and adorns her with noble ornaments until the time when the boy is thirteen years and upward, when He brings her under the bridal canopy. "And if he take him another". What do these words signify? Ah, they indeed contain a mystery of mysteries, such as is entrusted only to the wisest of the wise! One thing must be mentioned as a preliminary. On the Sabbath day, when the day is being sanctified, myriads of new souls emerge from the Tree of Life, and these are breathed into the denizens of earth and enter into them and remain in them during the whole of the Sabbath, and at the close of the Sabbath all these souls ascend once more to the regions of light, there to crown themselves with holy crowns of supernal brightness and splendour. And as at man's birth the Holy One provides him with a soul, so also does He provide him with this "other" soul specially for the Sabbath: at the same time not "diminishing" the food, raiment, etc., from his week-day soul.' Having arrived at this point in his exposition, the old man wept again and then exclaimed, addressing himself: 'Old man, old man! How long, how toilsomely hast thou laboured after the words of wisdom, that thou mightest grasp these holy mysteries; and now thou pourest them all out in a moment! And yet how was it possible for thee to hoard these words and not express them, seeing that the Scripture tells us, "Withhold not good from the owners thereof, when it is in the power of thine hand to do it" (Prov. III, 27)? Verily, wherever the truths of the Torah are expounded, the Holy One and the Community of Israel (the Shekinah) are present, "the owners" of the "good" side of the Tree of Knowledge of Good and Evil, who crown themselves with all the words of goodness and blessing which they hear spoken on earth. Old man, old man! Art thou, then, uncertain whether the Holy One and the Shekinah are present here, and whether those to whom thou speakest are worthy to hear these mysteries? Fear not! Hast thou not plunged unafraid into the midst of mighty battles, and art now afeared? Nay, nay, be not so: rather say what thou hast to say to the very end, since the Holy One and the Community of Israel are indeed here, for were it not so thou wouldst not have met with these men, nor even begun thy present discourse. So speak on, old man, speak on and have no fear!' He then commenced with the text: "O Lord my God, thou art very great; thou art clothed with majesty and beauty; who coverest thyself with light as with a garment; who stretchest out the heavens like a curtain; who layeth the beams of his chambers in the waters; who maketh the clouds his chariots; who walketh upon the wings of the wind; who maketh his angels spirits, his ministers a flaming fire" (Ps. CIV, I-3). 'The words "O Lord my God",' he said, 'signify the primary hypostasis (lit. beginning of faith), the emergence of the Thought [Tr. Note: Hokmah.] and the Future world, [Tr. Note: Binah.] an absolute unity without division. "Thou art great" refers to the beginning of actual creation, the first of the six primordial Days, the Right Side. The "very" symbolizes the Left Side. "Thou art clothed with majesty and beauty" signifies the two branches of the willows, [Tr. Note: Nezah and Hod.] of which more anon. When the Psalmist came to the Tree of Life [Tr. Note: Tifereth.] it hid itself and would not enter the series on account of that "very", to wit the "Left Side" of all the lower branches, including a certain bitter branch. [Tr. Note: Samael.] On account of this the Tree of Life hid itself and was loth to be included in the sum of these things until the Psalmist returned.to the subject and declared God's praise in another fashion, saying: "Who coverest thyself with light as with a garment"-to wit, with the light.

Zohar: Shemoth, Section 2, Page 98b

of the first day, and then, "Who stretchest out the heavens like a curtain", thus including the Left Side in the Right, so as to shine under the rubric of "heaven", while the "very" was discarded. Then the verse proceeds: "Who layeth the beams of his chambers in the waters": here we have the emergence in joy of the Tree of Life, the "River going out of Eden", with the two willow shoots, referred to in the words "upper chambers", rooted in its waters, so that it became "as a tree planted by the waters, that spreadeth out her roots by the river" (Jer. XVII, 8). This is also the allusion contained in the words: "The river, the channels thereof shall make glad the city of God" (Ps. XLVI, 8). What are these channels? They are the roots of the willows, which here are called "upper chambers". These and the roots and the channels-all are rooted in those waters of that mysterious river. "The clouds his chariots" in the next verse refers to Michael and Gabriel; "Who walketh upon the wings of the wind" to Raphael, who comes to give healing to the world. From that point on "he maketh his angels spirits, his ministers a flaming fire." Old man, old man! As thou art aware of all these things, fear not, but speak out boldly, and let the words of thy mouth spread light! ' The two friends rejoiced and listened in ecstasy and delight to the holy words. Said the old man: 'O ancient, O ancient, upon what a task hast thou entered! Thou hast plunged into the great sea, and now perforce must swim on till thou shalt have gained the farther shore! On, then! "And if he take him another.... "How many ancient mysteries never revealed before, regarding transmigration are indicated here! All the matters of which I am about to speak are perfect truth not deviating by one hair's-breadth from the path of truth. Now, in the first place I must remark that the souls of proselytes fly forth from Paradise in a very recondite manner. When the souls which proselytes have obtained from Paradise pass away from this world, to where do they return.? According to the traditional law, he who first seizes the possessions of a proselyte at the time of the latter's death becomes their rightful owner. In the same way, all the holy supernal souls which the Holy One has appointed for those that are below go out at certain times and seasons from their bodily owners and ascend.to their first home in order to enjoy the delights of Paradise. There they encounter the souls of proselytes, and whichever of them seizes on one claims it as its own. Each soul then clothes herself with that proselyte soul which she has claimed, and stands thus in Paradise, for there the souls must all be clothed. Not that they thereby forfeit any of the bliss which they enjoyed before, since it says "if he take unto him another, her food, etc." Still, when they ascend into the higher Paradise they remove these garments and are clothed only in their own radiance, for there no garb is worn.' Then the old man wept again as he had done before, and said to himself: 'Old man, old man, thou hast indeed reason to weep and to shed tears over every word; but the Holy One and His Holy Shekinah well know that what I say is said with all sincerity and devoutness, because they are the real source of every word uttered by me, and are crowned by it. All the holy souls which come down to this world to take up each its appropriate place in a human body array themselves with the souls of proselytes which they have appropriated, as we have explained; and they enter into the bodies of the holy seed of Israel wearing this garment to be served therewith in this world. When these garments draw to themselves the good things of this world these holy souls regale themselves with the aroma which they gather from the garments. Now, there is no work of the Holy One so recondite but he has recorded it in the Torah; and the Torah reveals it for an instant and then straightway clothes it with another garment, so that it is hidden there and does not show itself. But the wise, whose wisdom makes them full of eyes, pierce through the garment to the very essence of the word that is hidden thereby. And when the word.is momentarily revealed in that first instant of which we have spoken, those whose eyes are wise can see it, though it is so soon hidden again. In how many places does the Holy One insist that the holy seed should deal tenderly with the stranger, the proselyte! In the course of such passages a secret emerges from its sheath,

Zohar: Shemoth, Section 2, Page 99a

and as soon as it has been revealed returns thereto and once more conceals itself therein. That is to say, after repeating many times its injunctions concerning the treatment of the proselyte, the Scripture suddenly lays bare its hidden meaning by declaring: "For ye know the soul of the stranger" (i. e. proselyte, Ex. XXIII, 9). After this, however, the word retires again into its sheath, covers itself up, and hides itself again by adding: "For ye were strangers in the land of Egypt", imagining that because it covered itself up immediately, no one noticed it, to wit, this "soul" of the proselyte ' Then the old man expounded in connection with the subject of the soul and her garment the words: "And Moses went into the midst of the cloud and got him up into the mount" (Ex. XXIV, 18). 'Now what does the cloud signify?' he asked, and answered his own question, saying: 'There is a reference here to the words: "I set my bow in the cloud": namely, the rainbow, in reference to which we have learnt that it removed, as it were, its outer garment and gave it to Moses, who went up to the mountain with it and saw through it all the sights with which he was feasted there ' When the ancient one had reached this point he paused, and the two rabbis prostrated themselves before him, wept and said: 'Had we come into this world only in order to hear these thy words from thy mouth it were sufficient ' Said he: 'Associates, I did not begin to speak to you merely in order to tell you what I have told up till now, for, surely, an old man like myself would not limit himself to one saying, making a noise like a single coin in a jug. How many human beings live in confusion of mind, beholding not the way of truth whose dwelling is in the Torah, the Torah which calls them day by day to herself in love, but alas, they do not even turn their heads! It is indeed as I have said, that the Torah lets out a word, and emerges for a little from her sheath, and then hides herself again. But she does this only for those who understand and obey her. She is like unto a beautiful and stately damsel, who is hidden in a secluded chamber of a palace and who has a lover of whom no one knows but she. Out of his love for her he constantly passes by her gate, turning his eyes towards all sides to find her. She, knowing that he is always haunting the palace, what does she do? She opens a little door in her hidden palace, discloses for a moment her face to her lover, then swiftly hides it again. None but he notices it; but his heart and soul, and all that is in him are drawn to her, knowing as he does that she has revealed herself to him for a moment because she loves him. It is the same with the Torah, which reveals her hidden secrets only to those who love her. She knows that he who is wise of heart daily haunts the gates of her house. What does she do? She shows her face to him from her palace, making a sign of love to him, and straightway returns to her hiding place again. No one understands her message save he alone, and he is drawn to her with heart and soul and all his being. Thus the Torah reveals herself momentarily in love to her lovers in order to awaken fresh love in them. Now this is the way of the Torah. At first, when she begins to reveal herself to a man, she makes signs to him. Should he understand, well and good, but if not, then she sends for him and calls him "simpleton", saying to her messengers: "Tell that simpleton to come here and converse with me", as it is written: "Whoso is a simpleton let him turn in hither" (Prov. IX, 4). When he comes to her she begins to speak to him, first from behind the curtain which she has spread for him about her words suitable to his mode of understanding, so that he may progress little by little. This is called "Derasha" (Talmudic casuistry, namely the derivation of the traditional laws and usages from the letter of Scripture). Then she speaks to him from behind a thin veil of a finger mesh, discoursing riddles and parables, which go by the name of Haggadah. When at last he is familiar with her she shows herself to him face to face and converses with him concerning all her hidden mysteries and all the mysterious ways which have been secreted in her heart from time immemorial. Then such a man is

Zohar: Shemoth, Section 2, Page 99b

a true adept in the Torah, a "master of the house", since she has revealed to him all her mysteries, withholding and hiding nothing. She says to him: "Seest thou the sign, the hint, which I gave thee at first, how many mysteries it contains?" He realizes then that nothing may be added to nor taken from the words of the Torah, not even one sign or letter. Therefore men should follow the Torah with might and main in order that they may become her lovers, as has been described. '"And if he take him another" How many, and how wondrous, are the cycles of the soul as indicated in these words! Truly, all souls must undergo transmigration; but men do not perceive the ways of the Holy One, how the

401

revolving scale is set up and men are judged every day at all times, and how they are brought before the Tribunal, both before they enter into this world and after they leave it. They perceive not the many transmigrations and the many mysterious works which the Holy One accomplishes with many naked souls, and how many naked spirits roam about in the other world without being able to enter within the veil of the King's Palace. Many are the worlds through which they revolve, and each revolution is wondrous in many hidden ways, but men neither know nor perceive these things! Nor do they know how the souls roll about "like a stone inside a sling" (I Sam xxv, 29). Now, as we have begun to disclose these mysteries, it is opportune to reveal that all souls. (neshamah) emanate from a high and mighty Tree, from that "River which goes out of Eden" (Gen. II, 10), and all spirits (ruah) from another, smaller Tree-the souls from above and the spirits from below-and they unite after the fashion of male and female. And when they (soul and spirit) unite, they shine with a celestial light, and in their union they are designated "Lamp", as it says, "The lamp of the Lord is the soul of man" (Prov. xx, 27), NeR (lamp) being the abbreviation of Neshamah-Ruah (soul-spirit). Soul and spirit, the union of the masculine and the feminine, bring forth light, but if separate they do not give light The soul wraps herself in the spirit in order to occupy her station in the upper region, in the hidden Palace, as it is written: "For the spirit becomes a covering (ya'toph) before me and the souls which I have made" (Isa. LVII, I 6). There above, in the Garden, in the Palace, the soul wraps herself in the spirit in manner due And when the soul descends to the lower Paradise she wraps herself in another (lower) spirit (the soul of the proselyte), concerning which we have spoken above-a spirit which emanates from that lower Paradise and has his abode there. And the soul clothes herself in this world with all these various spirits, and so abides here. Now the spirit which has left this world without procreation and engendering of children undergoes. constant transmigration, finding no rest, and rolling about "like a stone inside a sling" until a "redeemer" [Tr. Note: The levir, or husband's brother. v. Deut. xxv, 8, 9] comes forward to redeem it and bring it back to the same "vessel" which it formerly used and to which it clave with heart and soul, as to its life's partner, in the union of spirit with spirit. This "redeemer" builds up that spirit again. For the spirit which was left by the deceased still clinging to that vessel has not been lost-since nothing is lost in the world-but it is still there and seeks to return to its basis; and so the "redeemer" brings it and builds it up again in its place, and it becomes a new creation, a new spirit in a new body. It may be said, "the spirit becomes the same as what it was": this is so, but it has not been built up save for the sake of the other spirit which was left in that vessel.

Zohar: Shemoth, Section 2, Page 100a

There is here a profound mystery. According to the Book of Enoch, this "building" is indeed constructed by the other spirit which was left in the "vessel,', and which draws after him the spirit which roams about in the air naked and alone; and these two spirits are welded together, and if the person is worthy to be built up again, the two spirits become one indeed, an organ in which a superior soul may wrap herself. For just as other men have a spirit which is seized by the over-soul and another higher spirit, and the holy over-soul is clothed with both, so here there are two spirits for the superior soul to wrap herself therewith, and for them another body (the child which is to be borne by the widow who married the near of kin), which is now built anew. 'Now the question arises, what becomes of the body of the man who died without issue? Is it lost because he was not worthy to bring forth a descendant? In that case it was in vain that he endeavoured to keep the commandments of the Torah: and even if he kept only one commandment, we know that "even the emptiest in Israel are full of good deeds as a pomegranate is full of grains" [Tr. Note: v. T. B. Chagigah, sub fin]. This body, although it was not found worthy to bring forth an issue, was yet able to fulfil other commandments, and should it all have been in vain? Friends friends! Open your eyes wide that ye may see more clearly, for I know that at present ye imagine that such bodies are mere figures in the void, incapable of sustained existence. It is, however, not so, and ye must beware of such thoughts. "Who can utter the mighty acts of the Lord? Who can show forth all his praise?" (Ps. CVI, 2). The body of the first husband is not lost: on the contrary, it will have an existence in the time to come, for it has already suffered a sufficiency of punishment, and the Holy One never curtails the reward of any creature which He has created, except of those who have entirely left the faith and in whom was no good whatsoever, and those who have not bowed down at the Modim [Tr. Note: Lit. "We give thanks": the opening word of one of the Eighteen Benedictions. Cf. T. B. Baba Kama, 16a] prayer, who are turned by the Holy One into other creatures, because that body will never again be built into the form of a man, and will not rise forever Not so these, however. What, then, does the Holy One do, if that spirit was worthy to be perfected in this world in the body of the other one? Observe now. The "redeemer" brings in his spirit, which mixes with the spirit already in the "vessel", with the result that there are three spirits there: one that was left there (by the deceased husband); one that is now naked but is drawn back there as to its basis (the spirit of the deceased husband); and one that the "redeemer" now brings in. This would seem to be impossible. But behold the mighty works of the Lord! The spirit which the "redeemer" brought in becomes the garment of the deceased's soul, taking the place of the proselyte's soul, and the naked spirit who has returned there to be built up becomes the covering for the supernal holy soul of the deceased. And the spirit which was left (by the deceased) cleaving to the "vessel" flies away from there, and the Holy One prepares for it a place in the mysterious region of the opening of the rock which is behind the walls of Paradise. There it is stored up and it enters eventually into the former body, together with which it will rise on the Resurrection. This is what I meant when I spoke of two that are one (or one that is two). That body, however, undergoes great punishment before the Resurrection, for, because it was not worthy to bring forth an issue, it was put into the earth in the region which adjoins Arqa. [Tr. Note: v. Zohar, Genesis 39b, 40a.] There it lies for a while, then it is removed to this world, then back again: it has no rest, except on Sabbaths, festivals, and new moons.

Zohar: Shemoth, Section 2, Page 100b

It is concerning such bodies that it is written: "And many of them that sleep in the dust of the earth shall awake, some to everlasting life and some to shame and everlasting contempt" (Dan. XII, 2); the latter are those who have not done their duty (by bearing children) in this world. There are the mighty works of the Supernal Holy King, who does not permit anything to perish, not even the breath of the mouth. He has a place for everything, and makes of it what He wills. Even a human word, yes, even the voice, is not void, but has its place and destination in the universe. This body which is built up again and emerges into the world as a new creation has no mate, and therefore the usual proclamation ("the daughter of so-and-so to so-and-so") [Tr. Note: v. T. B. Sotah, 2a] is not made about him from above. For his mate has been lost to him, the one whom he should have had becoming his mother, and his brother becoming his father (i. e. it is the brother of the deceased who died without issue, and his wife, to whom it is due that his body should be "built up" again) ' The old man now addressed himself again, saying: 'Old man, old man, what hast thou done? O, if thou hadst only been silent! Verily, thou hast launched thyself upon the great sea without rudder and without sail! What wilt thou do now? Wouldst thou fain ascend? Thou canst not Descend? It is impossible: the deep abyss will swallow thee up. What wilt thou do? O, old man, old man! Thou canst not turn back. Yet let not thy spirit or thy strength fail thee, for thou knowest that no other man in thy generation has ventured to sail in a little boat on the wide ocean as thou art doing. The son of Yohai knows how to guard his way, and even when he does enter into the deep dangerous waters of the high seas he first looks round him to see whether he will be able to cross; but thou, old man, didst not so. Now, old man, as thou art arrived at this pass, do not weaken in thy efforts, do not give up! Sail to the right and to the left, to the length and to the breadth, down into the depth, and up into the heights! Do not be afraid! Old man, old man, have courage! How many giants hast thou battled with, and how many battles hast thou won!' He wept, and then began again. 'It is written: "Go forth, O ye daughters of Zion, and behold King Solomon in the crown wherewith his mother crowned him in the day of his espousals, and in the day of the gladness of his heart" (S. S. III, 11). This verse has already been properly interpreted, and yet we may still ask, How is one to understand the words, "Go forth and behold King Solomon"? This title, we know, refers to the King of Peace, [Tr. Note: v. Zohar, Genesis, 29a] and who can behold Him who is high above the heavenly hosts in a region which "no eye hath seen apart from thee, O God" (Isa. LXIV, 3)? Him of whose glory the angels above ask: "Where is the place of His glory?" Observe, however, that the text does not say "and the crown", but "in the crown", from which we learn that he who sees the Crown beholds also the loveliness of the King of Peace. Then again, "wherewith his mother crowned him": She (the Shekinah) is sometimes called "Daughter", and sometimes "Sister", and here She is called "Mother". And She is indeed all these. He who penetrates into this mystery has imbibed precious wisdom. Now what shall I do? Should I explain? But such a veiled mystery ought not to be disclosed. Yet should I not explain, these good men will be orphaned of this mystery. The old man fell on his face and said: '"Into thine hand I deliver my spirit. Thou hast redeemed me, O Lord, the God of truth" (Ps. XXXI, 7). The vessel which was below, how can it be above? The husband who was above, how can he be below? His spouse become his mother! Wonder upon wonder! His brother become his father! If his real father were to redeem him that would be understood. But that his brother should become his father, is this not a wonder? This would indeed be topsy-turvydom: those that should be above are now below, and they that should be below are now above! However, "Blessed be the name of God forever and ever: for wisdom and might are his. And he changeth the times and the seasons. He knows what is in the darkness, and the light dwelleth with him" (Dan. II, 20-21). He who is in the light cannot see the darkness; but not so the Holy One, blessed be He;

Zohar: Shemoth, Section 2, Page 101a

although the light dwelleth with Him, He knows what is in the darkness. Out of the light He beholds the darkness and knows all that is there. The mystery of the soul and her revolutions is analogous to the mystery of the Divine Hypostases. [Tr. Note: i.e. in virtue of the fact that the Shekinah can be called sometimes "Daughter" and sometimes "Mother".] When a man reaches the age of thirteen he stands, as we have said, in the grade of sonship. When he is twenty, he reaches a higher grade, the grade of "Joseph": the realm of Masculinity, the sphere of Understanding. Now, at first, the man when he married the woman, was lord over the world of Femininity, over the "small tree" -for the Feminine is in the image of the Small Tree. But when he failed to have children with his wife, and died without leaving an issue, he was excluded from the world of Masculinity, and she, by marrying his brother, became, as it were, his mother (by bringing forth a successor to her deceased husband); and his brother, "the redeemer", becomes, as it were, his father and enters into the realm of Masculinity which was formerly his. Thus the Tree is turned upside down: what was above is now below, and what was below is now above. Oh, if only people knew the pain which the body of the men who died without children must undergo! There is no pain like unto the pain of the body that is in a state of frustration, when it has been uprooted from the sphere of Masculinity and transferred into that of Femininity. Concerning this, it is written: "If the priest's daughter (i.e. the soul) be a widow or divorced, and have no child, and is returned unto her father's house, as in her youth, she shall eat of her father's meat, but there shall no stranger eat thereof" (Lev. XXII, 13). We have already pointed out what "the priest's daughter" signifies. If she be a "widow" of the first body, "divorced" in not being able to penetrate into the courtyard of the King -for those who are not in the sphere of the Masculine realm have no part therein-"having no child", for if she had, she would not have sunk into the Feminine sphere, "and is returned unto her father's house", that is to say, unto the realm of Femininity (as that realm is called) where she previously was, then, if she be worthy, "she shall eat of her father's meat"

Zohar: Shemoth, Section 2, Page 101b

namely, participate in the joys of the Feminine realm, the supernal food coming down from above; but she is still a "stranger", not able to participate in the contemplative joy of the other righteous; she may not eat of "the holy things" (Ibid. v. 10), but may eat the Terumah (the meat of the heave-offering), because this symbolizes the Feminine sphere, and therefore she may eat only at night (v. 7). Whereas holy food which belongs to the world of Masculinity may be eaten only during the day. Therefore "Israel is holiness unto the Lord, the first fruits (the beginning) of his increase" (Jer. II, 3): the supernal beginning of the whole sphere of the Masculine is holy, and its further development in holiness is Israel. When spirits come to visit the graves, as they do at certain seasons, they do not visit the graves of these men, since they have not merited to rise to that region called "holiness", being only "strangers". Moreover, if that spirit did not succeed in doing its duty (by begetting children) in the period of transmigration, he may not even eat the Terumah, and is called "stranger" even in the lower world. 'So far concerning this mystery. Old man, old man! As thou hast started to sail on the wide sea, go on boldly in all directions and breast its waves! I have now to reveal something more. I said that the "redeemer", when he enters into the "vessel", lets his spirit cleave to that "vessel", so that nothing is lost, not even the breath of the mouth. This is quite correct. Old man, old man! If thou art to reveal mysteries, speak out without fear! What of other men, normal persons, who did procreate and then passed away from this world? We have said that the spirit of a man (the absconditus sponsus) is left in the woman who was his wife. Well, what becomes of it? Supposing she marries again, is it possible that two different spirits of two men should dwell together in one body? For there is no question of a "redeemer" in this case, as the first husband did have children. Is that spirit then entirely lost? Nay, this cannot be. The same problem arises even when the widow does not marry again. What becomes of her husband's spirit which cleaves to her? All this must now be explained. Old man, old man! See what thou hast done and what thou hast taken upon thyself! Arise, old man, and unfurl thy sail! Arise, old man, and humble thyself before thy Master!' He then continued: '"Lord, my heart is not haughty, nor mine eyes lofty: neither do I exercise myself (walk) in great matters, or in things too high for me" (Ps. CXXXI, 1). King David said this: he was a great king, supreme over all kings and rulers from east to west, and yet it never entered his mind to turn from the right path, for he was ever humble before the Lord. When he studied the Torah he summoned up all his strength like a lion, and his eyes looked down at the same time to the earth, out of awe to his Lord, and when he went about among the people he displayed no haughtiness Hence he said "my heart is not haughty, although I am a mighty king, nor mine eyes lofty, when I stand before Thee studying the Torah, and I do not walk in greatness or haughtiness when I go among the people." Now if David was thus humble, how much more must ordinary people be so! And I, how lowly and with what downcast eyes must I stand before the Holy King! Far be it from me to be puffed up when I deal with holy words of the Torah ' He wept and his tears trickled on to his beard. Said he: 'Old man, old man, feeble in strength, how fair are the tears on thy cheeks, like "the precious ointment that ran down upon the face of the good old man Aaron" (Ps. CXXXIII, 2). Say thy words, old man,

Zohar: Shemoth, Section 2, Page 102a

for the Holy King is here! 'What, then, becomes of the spirit of an ordinary man whose widow has married again? Come ye and see the wonderful and mighty works of the Holy King! Who can utter them? When the second husband's spirit enters into the body of the woman the spirit of the first husband contends with it, and they cannot dwell in peace together, so that the woman is never altogether happy with the second husband, because the spirit of the first one is always pricking her, his memory is always with her, causing her to weep and sigh over him. In fact, his spirit writhes within her like a serpent. And so it goes on for a long time. If the second spirit prevails over the first one, then the latter goes out. But if, as sometimes happens, the first conquers the second, it means the death of the second husband. Therefore we are taught that after a woman has been twice widowed no one should marry her again, for the angel of death has taken possession of her, though most people do not know this. Friends, I am aware that on this point you may well object that in that case the second husband's death was not in accordance with Divine judgement. It is not so, however. It is all decided by fair trial, whether the one spirit should prevail over the other or be at peace with it; but he who marries a widow is like unto one who ventures to brave the ocean during a storm without a rudder and without sails, and knows not whether he will cross safely or sink into the depths. 'Now I have said that when the second spirit prevails over the first, the latter deserts the body. But whither goeth it? What becomes of it? Old man, old man, what hast thou done? Thou didst intend to speak but little, and hast come as far as this! Thou hast entered a place into which no other human being has hitherto entered since the time of Doeg and Ahitophel, when four hundred questions were asked concerning a tower which was suspended in the air, and which no one could answer until Solomon came and made everything clear. [Tr. Note: v. T B. Sanhedrin, 106b.] Old man, old man! Thou hast commenced to reveal a profound secret. What hast thou done? Old man, old man! thou. shouldst indeed have considered beforehand and been careful of thy steps. Now there is no time to hide Old man, take fresh courage! The spirit that has left the body of the woman, where has it fled?' He wept again and said: 'Friends, the tears which I shed fall not on your account, but for fear of the Lord of the universe, that perchance I have revealed mysteries without permission. It is, however, known to the Holy One, blessed be He, that all I do, I am doing not for my own honour nor for the honour of my father, but because my sole desire is to serve Him. I discern the glory and honour of one of you in the other world; and as to the other one, I know that he is likewise worthy; at first this was not revealed to me, but now I see it clearly. Now where does the first spirit, having been thrust out by the second, go? It roams about in the world for some time, and then visits the grave of the man to whom it belongs, and then it flits about again in the world and reveals itself to men in their dreams, so that they behold in fancy the face of the deceased, who tells them various things after the manner of the original spirit from which this spirit is derived. For as the other spirit is roaming about the other world, so this one roams about this world, making communications to people, and it always visits that grave at the time when the spirits of the dead visit the graves of their bodies. Then the two spirits join one another, the one (the essential) using the other as its garment, and they ascend again. When the essential spirit reaches its place, it puts off its "garment", namely the second spirit, which latter is given a place either

Zohar: Shemoth, Section 2, Page 102b

within or without the palaces of Paradise, according to merit, there remaining hidden. And when the spirits visit this world and the dead attach themselves to the living they do it only through drawing down the essential spirit, which then wears the other as a garment. And should ye ask, "In that case the essential spirit of the first husband profits thereby, and the woman therefore has done him a favour in marrying again?" I would say it is not so, for had she not married again, and the spirit of the first husband not so been thrust out by that of the second, he would have profited in a different way: his spirit would not have had to roam about in the world and pay visits to the living. Should the question arise, "In that case her remarriage was her own decision and did not depend on a decree from above; why, then, didst thou say that it was providential and that one man should, as it were, be thrust out by the other and explain that the woman was indeed the preordained mate for the second husband and not for the first?" I would answer: "Indeed it is as I said: The spirit of the first husband is ejected by that of the second, just because it is the latter who was really intended from the first to be her consort, and not the first, and, conversely, if the second husband's spirit is pushed out by that of the first one, it shows that the first one was destined to be her only mate. Hence, he who marries a widow "knows not that it is with the peril of his life" (Prov. VII, 28), for he knows not whether she is predestined to be his real spouse. However, if the widow does not wish to marry again, even when the man who wishes to marry her is meant to be her ideal mate, the Holy One does not condemn her for that, and He prepares another wife for the man whom she had refused, and she is not brought before the heavenly tribunal for her refusal, even when she has no children, because the commandment concerning procreation is not obligatory for women. 'Now what happens to the spirit of a deceased husband whose widow does not marry again? It dwells in her for the first twelve months, visiting his soul (nephesh) every night at the grave, in depression and sadness, and after the twelve months it leaves her and stands before the gates of Paradise, but occasionally visits this world, namely the "vessel" from whence it went out And when the woman dies that spirit goes out to meet her, and clothes itself in her spirit, and so she comes into contact with her husband; and husband and wife shine together in the closest union. 'As we have come so far, we must now disclose the hidden paths of the Lord of the universe, which the children of men know not, though they are all within the way of truth, as it is written: "For the ways of the Lord are upright; the righteous shall walk in them, and the transgressors shall stumble therein" (Hos. XI, 10). The children of men neither know nor perceive how exalted are the deeds of the Holy One and how strange, yet withal according to the way of truth, turning neither to the right nor to the left. Those who undergo transmigration and are driven out from the other world (because they refused to propagate themselves) without feminine partners, how do they manage to find wives in this world, seeing that no female partner is preordained for them, as for other men? See how wondrous and exalted are the mighty works of God! We have been taught that over him who divorces his first wife the altar sheds tears. Why the altar? Because, as I have said on another occasion all women stand in the image and form of the altar, [Tr. Note: Because it symbolizes Malkuth, the sphere of feminine souls] for which reason they "inherit" the seven benedictions (used at the marriage sacrament), because they all have the "Community of Israel" (the Shekinah) as their prototype. Thus, when

Zohar: Shemoth, Section 2, Page 103a

a man divorces his wife he causes, as it were, a defect in the stone of the heavenly altar. Thus it is possible for the divorcements to unite themselves one with the other (i. e. the divorcement of the man's spirit in heaven and of the woman on earth). Concerning this mystery it says: "And hath written to her a bill of divorcement, and gave it in her hand, and sent her out of his house, and she departed from his house, and went and became another man's wife (Deut. XXIV, I). What is the significance of "another"? It points to the words, "and they shall shoot forth from another place" (Job VIII, 19), i.e. from the region of impurity. Thus the divorcements unite as one, the divorcement of this world and the divorcement of the other world For this woman who stood formerly in the likeness of the supernal form has now became attached to the low form. He is called "another" (aher), and he is called "latter", "last one" (ahron), as it says, "and if the last husband hate her" (Deut. XXIV, 3); "if the last husband die" (Ibid). Now, why is the second husband of the divorced woman called "last" and not "second"? It is as we have said, that it has a higher significance, he being "another" and also the "last". Now the stone rolls in the basket (i.e. there is a difficulty). First, why is he called "another" when the whole building (of the conjugal relationship with the first husband) has been destroyed and turned into dust? And then, why is he called "the last"? If he is the right person, well and good, but if not, there will be another development (and he will not be the last). But mark this. It is written: 'And God saw everything that he had made, and, behold, it was very good,' (Gen. 1, 31), and "good" here has been interpreted to refer to the angel of good, and "very" to the angel of death [Tr. Note: v. Midrash Rabba, in loco] Now the Holy One has prepared a remedy for all ills. It is written: "And a river went out of Eden to water the garden" (Gen. II, 10). This "river" never ceases to procreate and to spread itself and to bring forth fruit. But the "other god" (the principle of evil) is emasculated and has no desire to procreate, and does not multiply or bear fruit, for were he to bear fruit, he would reduce the whole world to chaos. Therefore man who causes the "other side" to multiply (by consciously rejecting the commandment of procreation) is called "an evil one", and will nevermore behold the race of the Shekinah, for it is written: "Evil dwelleth not with thee" (Ps. v. 5). A man who undergoes the metamorphosis of the soul, if he sins and joins the "other god" who produces no fruit and engenders no children, is therefore called "other"; the second husband who does likewise is called "the last one" by the Holy One, and not merely "the second", in order to avert an omen pointing to the destruction of the second building also. The Scripture itself teaches us this lesson, since it calls the second Temple "last". (Haggai II, 9), in order to avoid the omen. Therefore "the former husband who sent her away cannot take her again to be his wife, after that she is defiled" (Deut. XXIV, 4). It does not say "he should not", but "he cannot", because, as the woman has united herself with another man and been subjected to a lower grade, the Holy One is unwilling that the former husband should lower himself by uniting with a grade that is not his. And mark this. If that woman, having been divorced, did not marry again, even if she should have misconducted herself with many men, the husband, if he wishes, may take her back, but not when she has been legally married to another man. Once she has united herself with a lower grade, the first husband,

Zohar: Shemoth, Section 2, Page 103b

who belongs to the grade of "good", may not associate himself with her any longer nor spread on that side Other men may marry her, as perhaps she may find a proper mate again. A man who has children by his first wife, and brings such a woman into his house, unites himself with a flaming sword, in two ways: first, because two have already entered and been violently ejected, and now he is the third; and, secondly, how can he let his spirit enter into a vessel which has already been used by others, associate himself with her and cleave to her? It is not that he is prohibited to do so, but in doing it he chooses a bad companion to himself R. Levitas, from Kephar Oni, used to jeer and scoff at a person who married a woman of this sort, applying to her the words: "And she shall laugh at the last day" (Prov. XXX1, 25), meaning, the "last one" who unites himself with such a woman will be a laughing stock. 'Now we have to turn our attention to a great and noble spot which once was on the earth, being a very root and stock of truth, to wit, Obed the father of Jesse, the grandfather of David. It has been affirmed that he was such a "last one": how, then, could the root of truth (David) emanate from such a place? The fact, however, is that Obed worked and laboured at the root of the tree, until it was regenerated and made wholesome: it was therefore that he was called Obed (labourer, also "worshipper"), a name which no other man merited to bear. He came, he digged, he hoed round the root of the tree, he pressed out the bitterness from the branches and made wholesome the crown. Then came Jesse, his son, who further improved and invigorated it, and grafted it on to the branches of another stately tree, joining tree with tree so that they were intertwined. And when David came he found the branches entwined and knit together, and was thus enabled to attain dominion over the world. And all these things which came to pass had their cause and beginning in Obed ' Having spoken thus, the old man wept again and said: 'Old man, old man, did I not say that thou hadst plunged into the midst of the great sea? Now thou art indeed in the very midst of the mighty waves! Old man, old man, thou hast none to blame but thyself; hadst thou remained silent at the beginning all would have been well with thee, but now thou mayest not, and there is none to take hold of thine hand! Thou art alone. But arise, old man, and take courage! Obed remedied himself because he came out from the evil field in which were bad cisterns. Then came Jesse, his son, who improved and hoed round that tree and digged up that which was evil and that which was bitter likewise. This is a mystery of mysteries, and I know not with certainty whether or no to reveal it. Yet say on, old man! Yea, I shall certainly speak, if only in order that these two who shall hear me should be made fully cognizant of the other transmigrations of the souls of men. Now, Obed, as I have said, hoed round the root of the tree, so improving it somewhat; and yet, when King David came, he was left only with the lower, feminine tree, and had to receive life from another tree. Now, if he for whom the way was so well prepared had to develop thus, how much more so ordinary persons who undergo transmigration! Thus, then, it was with Perez, and with Boaz likewise. Obed was also thus. With regard to all of these, the tree emerged from the side of evil and was afterwards joined to the side of good, as we read that "Er, the firstborn of Judah, was wicked in the sight of the Lord" (Gen. XXXVIII, 7); so was Onan (Ibid. 9, 10); so also was Mahlon, although his evil was not so great. Thus, in all these there was a tincture of ill, from which, however, good eventually emerged; as it is written of David, their descendant: "goodly to look to", "and the Lord was with him" (I Sam. XVI, 12, 18). Thus the tree below was purified and remained so, so that "God ruled over the nations" (through the house of David). 'The grades of Israel took root in the supernal foundation from the beginning: Reuben, Simeon, Levi. But when it comes to Judah it says that Leah, his mother, said: "This time I will praise the lord . and she left off bearing" (Gen. XXIX, 35); concerning which it is written: "Sing, O barren, thou that didst not bear" (Isa. LIV, I). For when Judah was born the Feminine was united with the Masculine . Note: The last 4 lines of the Hebrew text are not translated]

Zohar: Shemoth, Section 2, Page 104a

[Note: The Hebrew text of this page does not appear in the translation.]

Zohar: Shemoth, Section 2, Page 104b

[Note: Only the last two lines of the Hebrew text appear in the translation.]

'All the twelve tribes represent on earth their celestial prototypes, and because they were in reality "sons" in this world, the Shekinah

Zohar: Shemoth, Section 2, Page 105a

was perfected in them in these twelve "lineaments" (boundaries) of Israel, which are called "Eleh" (these), as it says, "These (eleh) all are the tribes of Israel" (Gen. XLIX, 28), this word, in conjunction with Mi (Who?) forming the name Elohim, [Tr. Note: v. Zohar, Genesis 2a.] and so bringing the building to completion. On this account did the celestial representative of Esau say to Jacob: "Thy name shall be called no more Jacob, but Israel: for thou hast waged war with Elohim and with men and hast prevailed" (Gen. XXXII, 28), i.e. prevailed above, by means of the perfect and original structure, which is also indicated by the words "all these". Therefore Israel can never cease to be. If, God forbid, they should so cease to be, this Divine Name would be ended likewise, as it is written: "When they (the Canaanites) shall cut off our name from the earth, what wilt thou do unto thy great name?" (Josh. VII, 9). The "great Name" is the first building, the first Name, Elohim. And now, when Israel is in exile, the whole building has fallen, as it were. But in the time to come, when the Holy One shall redeem His children from exile, the "Mi" and the "Eleh", which when they were in exile were separated, will be united as one, and the Name Elohim be perfectly established and the world shall be healed. Therefore it is written: "Who (mi) are these (eleh) that fly as a cloud, and as the doves to their windows?" (Isa. LX, 8): the one Name, without any separation, namely Elohim. For because of the exile the Mi ascended, as it were, and left the building, and consequently the building fell, and the Name that was perfect, namely the supernal great Name that was from the beginning, fell. Therefore we pray in the synagogues that this Name may be restored as it was: "May His great Name be magnified and sanctified": "May the great Name be blessed." What is that "great Name"? It is the one that was in the beginning, the first of all, without whom there can be no building. The "Mi" will never be built up without the "Eleh". Therefore at that time (the Messianic age) the "Mi" and the "Eleh" "shall fly as a cloud", and the whole world shall see that the supernal Name has been restored to its perfection; and when the Name has been restored and built up again, then shall Israel rule over all, and all the other Names will be restored; for all the Names depend on that great Name, the first of all buildings. 'This mystery may be further explained as follows. When the Holy One created the world, before any other thing was built this Name was built, as it is written: "Lift up your eyes on high and see: who hath created these? (Mi barah eleh)" (Isa. XL, 26). He created His Name in its perfection, and when He created "Eleh" He created it with all the hosts appertaining to it, as it is written: "Who bringeth out their host by number (be-mispar)" (Ibid). What is the significance of "be-mispar"? The Holy One, blessed be He, has a son, whose glory shines from one end of the world to another. He is a great and mighty tree, whose head reaches heaven, and whose roots are set in the holy ground, and his name is "Mispar" and his place, is in the uppermost heaven, and below that heaven are five firmaments, and all these firmaments take this name for his sake, as it is written, "The heavens proclaim (mesaprim) the glory of God" (Ps XIX, I). Were it not for this "Mispar" there would be neither hosts nor offspring in any of the worlds Concerning this it is written: "Who can count the dust of Jacob and the number (Mispar) of the progeny of Israel?" (Num. XXXIII, 10). There are two indeed who did count these without the evil eye having any effect on them. The first "counted the dust of Jacob", the strong rocks, the holy rocks, whence issue waters to the world, concerning which it is written: "And thy seed shall be like the dust of the earth" (Gen. XXVIII, 11, 14); as the world is blessed for the sake of the dust, so will "all the nations of the earth be blessed in thy seed" (Ibid. XXII, 18). And the second shall "number the progeny of Jacob", the females, the pearls of the couch whereon Israel lay.

Zohar: Shemoth, Section 2, Page 105b

In the future (Messianic Age) "the flocks shall yet pass under one who counts" (Jer. XXXIII, 18). We know not who he shall be; but since at that time all will be in union without separation, there will be one "reckoner". Arise, old man;' he cried, 'awake, collect thy forces and breast the waves ' Then he continued: "Who can count the dust of Jacob and the number of the progeny of Israel?" When the Holy One shall arise to waken the dead, what will be the plight of those who went through transmigration several times and who have become two in one body, two fathers, two mothers, as we have seen? However, "Who (Mi) shall count the dust of Jacob?" The Lord will make all things straight and nothing will be lost. For so has been expounded the verse: "And many of them that sleep in the dust of the earth shall awake, some to everlasting life, and some to shame and everlasting contempt" (Dan. XII, 2). "The dust of the earth" is a reference similar to that explained in the Book of Enoch, that the associates saw the letters of which these words are composed, and a voice was heard, saying: "Awaken and sing, ye who dwell in the dust" (Isa XXVI, 19). The first edifice of the world (of the pre-resurrection period) will be as refuse in comparison with the second edifice (of the post-resurrection period), for this last will be perfected according to the Divine plan. Those that are worthy will awake to life in the world below, since they have not merited the world above; and those that are not worthy even of this will awaken to shame and everlasting contempt. As the "other side" will pass away from the world (there being no more evil principle or sin), the Holy One will leave these specimens of the past and evil world, who belonged to the stream which issued forth from that side, in order that all the children of the world may, in beholding them, be astonished. All this will be caused by those who suffered their fount to fail and produced no fruit here, having no wish to maintain the Holy Covenant. It is they who cause all this and all the transmigrations of which I spake. ' The old man was silent for a moment, and the companions wondered, not knowing whether it was day or night, whether they stood on their heads or their feet. Then the old man began again with the verse: "If thou buy an Hebrew servant, six years he shall serve, and in the seventh he shall go out for nothing" (v. 2). 'This verse', said he, 'proves what I have said. Observe, now. Every male before being born is in prototype in the world of Masculinity, and every female in the world of Femininity. Now, so long as a man serves the Holy One, blessed be He, he remains attached to the six first years (i.e. to the six "masculine" emanations); but if he withdraw himself from His service (by neglecting the commandment of procreation), then the Lord separates him from the six years of the world of Masculinity and he is delivered into bondage unto a man [Tr. Note: Metatron,] who does belong to the six sides, in order that he should serve him six years as a punishment for the supernal six years which he rejected. After that he descends lower and is attached to the world of Femininity: as he refused to take his rightful place in the Masculine world, let him now belong to that of the Female! The Female, the seventh year, comes and receives him, and from now on his part is in the world of Femininity. If he does not seek to fix himself therein, and refuses the redemption which it offers him (of making good his neglect), he descends still lower and joins the "other side". From now on he is finally severed both from the Masculine and, the Feminine worlds, and is held fast by the "servants" of the "other side", and he has to be branded and stigmatized, for every stigma comes from the "other side". However, when the Jubilee year arrives, he is freed from that power and begins to undergo transmigration once more, and returns to the world as he was before and is attached to the world of Femininity, but not to a still higher grade. If he be then worthy, he will bring into existence children all of whom will belong to the world of Femininity, symbolically expressed in the words: "The virgins, her companions shall be brought unto thee" (Ps. XLV, 15); it will be a sign of merit, for that he has made good his defect. But should he not be found worthy to procreate even after the Jubilee, he is made as though he were not, having been mercifully returned to this world and yet refusing the opportunity of reparation which was offered to him: "If he came by himself (be-gapo), he shall go out by himself" (v. 8), meaning: "If he enters this world single, without

Zohar: Shemoth, Section 2, Page 106a

offspring, not having previously desired the engendering of children, and even now leaving this world single, he departs even as a stone which is thrown from a sling, until it reaches the place which is called "the mighty rock", into which he enters. As soon as he is there, the breath of him who is the Single one (Samael), who had to be separated from his feminine counterpart (Lilith), and who walks after the manner of a serpent, breathes on him, and straightway he leaves that mighty rock and, wandering lonely forth, begins to roam the world until he shall find a "redeemer" through whose agency he can return to this earth. This is the significance of the words: "If he came by himself, he shall go out by himself"; the reference is to a man who refused to get married and beget children. But "if he get married" (Ibid), that is to say, if he had a wife but was not blessed with children, he is not thus driven out alone, for the Holy One does not let any creature remain unrewarded. "His wife shall go out with him": husband and wife both undergo transmigration and unite again as they were before. Such a man does not marry a divorced woman, but the woman who was previously his wife but did not then bear him children, in order that now both may gain merit by making good their deficiency. ʾThe text continues: "If his master have given him a wife, and she have borne him sons or daughters, the wife and her children shall be her master's and he shall go out by himself ' Scripture now returns to the former subject, namely to the case of a man who "went out" without a wife (that is, who never married at all), implying that the grade called "the seventh year" should redeem him. This "Seventh" is called "his master": the Master of the whole earth. And if this Master shall have pity on him and bring him back to this world by himself as he was, and give him a wife of the kind for whom the altar sheds tears (i e a woman divorced by a man whose first wife she was) and they unite, and she bears him sons and daughters, "the wife and her children shall be her master's", as has been explained. For, as he has made good his former omission, he is received by the Holy King, who restores him to the position intended for him. He is called a "repentant sinner", for he comes into the heritage of his original place in the ever-flowing celestial river. [Tr. Note: Which is the source of all souls.] There is no obstacle in the world that can stand in the way of repentance, and the word begapo (by himself) contains an allusion to the phrase: "upon the back of the highest (gape merome) places of the city" (Prov. IX, 3); that is to say: as Wisdom dwells in high and lofty places, so does the man who has repented of his sin attain an eminent position; therefore sinners who repent can enter where even the perfectly righteous are not admitted. Most assuredly the Holy One accepts every sinner who turns to Him. Such a one is set upon the way of life, and, notwithstanding his former stain, everything is put right and restored to its former position. Even when the Holy One has decreed most solemnly against a person, He forgives entirely where there is a perfect repentance. Thus we find it written concerning Jehoiachin: "As I live, says the Lord, if thou Coniah the son of Jehoiakim wert the signet upon my right hand, yet would I pluck thee hence. write ye this man childless" (Jer. XXII, 24-30); and yet, when he repented and turned again unto the Lord, we read: "And the sons of Jeconia, Assir, etc." (I Ch. III, 17), showing that after all he was not childless: which proves that repentance annuls all decrees and judgements, and breaks many an iron chain, and there is nothing that can stand against it. This is also indicated in the words: "And they shall go forth and look upon the carcases of the men that transgress against me" (Isa. LXVI, 24). It does not say: "who have transgressed", but "who transgress": namely those who go on transgressing without thinking of repentance; but as soon as they are penitent and remorseful for their sins the Holy One receives them again. The same applies here: this man (who rejected procreation), although he has sinned and impaired a vital part, when he repents and turns to Him the Holy One has pity on him and receives him again; for He is full

Zohar: Shemoth, Section 2, Page 106b

of mercy towards all His works, as it is written: "His tender mercies are over all his works" (Ps. CXLV, 9). His mercies extend even to animals and birds, still more to human beings who know how to praise their Lord. As David expressed it: "Many are thy tender mercies, O Lord: quicken me according to thy Judgement" (Ps. CXIX, I 56). Now, if His tender mercies are vouchsafed to sinners, how much more to righteous men! Who is it that needs healing? He who is sick. And who is sick if not the sinner? Therefore, when sinners turn to the Lord for healing and mercy, He stretches out His right hand to receive them. When God draws a man to Himself He draws him with His right hand, but when He pushes him away He does so with His left hand. [Tr. Note: Cf. T. B. Sanhedrin, 107b.] And even when the left hand pushes away, the right draws near, for the Holy One, blessed be He, does not withhold His tender mercy from sinners Observe how the Scripture says first, "And he went on frowardly in the way of his heart", and immediately afterwards, "I have seen his ways, and will heal him: I will lead him also and impart consolations. (nihumim) unto him and to his mourners" (Isa. LVII, 17, 18). This shows that even when sinners commit sin purposely, walking according to the desires of their own hearts, and heeding not the warnings of others, even for such, when they repent and begin to walk in the way of righteousness, is healing prepared. ʾNow this verse will repay a little closer consideration. The question is, does it refer to the living or to the dead? For the beginning and the end seem to conflict with one another, the first part referring to the living and the second to the dead. We may, however, interpret thus. As long as a man is alive and walks "frowardly in the way of his heart" because the evil inclination is strong in him, making it hard for him to repent and start a new life, the Holy One, seeing the wasted life of him who walks in the evil way, says: "I must give him strength. I see his ways of darkness, and I must open in his heart a way of repentance and bring healing to his soul." This is the meaning of "I will lead him"-like one who takes hold of somebody's hand and leads him out of darkness. As to the second part: "and impart consolations unto him and to his mourners", this language would naturally apply to the dead, and so indeed it does, for is not a sinner dead, even though he be alive? The meaning of the words, then, is as follows. Through the grace of God, when a person is thirteen years old, two angels are appointed over him, one at his right hand and one at his left. When he walks in the right way these angels rejoice over him and are glad, and joyfully cling to him, proclaiming before him: "Give honour to the King's image!" But when he turns from the path of rectitude and walks in crooked ways his angels mourn over him and turn away from him. Therefore, when the Holy One grants the sinner grace to repent and strength to accomplish his return to righteousness, "He imparts repentance to him, and consolations to his mourners" (nihumim in the double sense of "repentance" and "consolation"), and the man himself is truly and perfectly alive, being joined to the Tree of Life. And, being united with the Tree of Life, he is called "a man of repentance", for he is become a member of the Community of Israel, which is designated by the word "teshubah" (repentance, return), and "repentant sinners can enter even where the perfectly righteous are not admitted" 'King David said: "Against thee, thee only, have I sinned, and done this evil in thy sight" (Ps. LI, 5). The significance of this is as follows. It is possible to commit sins which are offences both against God and man; also one can commit sins which are offences against man but not against the Holy One; but there are also sins which are committed against the Holy One only David's sin was of this last kind. Perhaps, however, you will be inclined to question this, saying,

Zohar: Shemoth, Section 2, Page 107a

"But what of his sin with Bathsheba? Did he not sin against her husband–to whom she was now prohibited–as well as against the Holy One?" To this query there is an answer, and it is this. According to tradition Uriah, as was the custom with the warriors in Israel, gave his wife a bill of divorcement before he went out to battle, and so David did not sin against Uriah in the sense of perfidiously robbing him of his wife. And therefore we read: "And David comforted Bathsheba his wife" (2 Sam. XII, 24), which is a proof that she was considered as David's lawful wife, destined for him since the beginning of time, since the day whereon the world was created. Thus his sin was an offence against the Holy One alone. And in what did that offence consist? Not in that he commanded Joab to set Uriah in the forefront of the battle so that he might be killed–for David had a right to do that, as Uriah called Joab "my lord Joab" while in the king's presence, which was disrespectful (lese-majeste')–but because he did not kill him then, but let him be killed by the sword of the children of Ammon (Ibid. v. 24); for on every Ammonite sword was engraved a crooked serpent, the image of a dragon, which was their god. Said the Holy One to David: "Thou hast imparted strength to that abomination"; for when the sons of Ammon had killed Uriah and many other Israelites, and the sword of Ammon prevailed, it was as if the pagan god prevailed against the God of Israel. Nor does the title "Hittite" show that Uriah was not virtuous: he was merely called so after the place whence he came, as Jephthah was called "the Gileadite" (Judges XI, 1) because he was from Gilead. Thus the power of the abomination prevailed against the camp of God, and, David's hosts being in the very image of the supernal hosts, when he brought a stain upon the hosts below he caused, as it were, a stigma also on the hosts above. That was his sin, and therefore he said: "Against thee only have I sinned, and done evil in thine eyes"–"in thine eyes" literally, as much as to say that David was conscious that he had sinned against the omnipresent and all-penetrating eyes of God. "That thou mightest be justified in thy words, and be clear in thy judgements" (Ibid), and so I may not have any cause of saying that thou art wrong and I am right. The point of these words is as follows. We know that every man naturally uses the language of his occupation. Now David had been a king's jester, and so, though in sore distress and tribulation, when he found himself before the King, he reverted straightway to his quips and witticisms in order to entertain the King. He said: "Lord of the world! I said, Prove me, O Lord, and try me" (Ps. XXVI, 2), and Thou declaredst that I would not be able to withstand temptation. Therefore I have now sinned in order that Thou mayest be justified in Thy words, for if I did not so, my assertion would be proved true and Thy assertion refuted!" We have also been taught that David was not led away by his passions when he committed that sin with Bathsheba; for he said of himself: "My heart is hollowed within me" (Ps. CIX, 22),

Zohar: Shemoth, Section 2, Page 107b

and he meant by this: "There are two chambers in my heart, one containing blood, and the other spirit; the one which is filled with blood is the seat of the evil inclination, but my heart is void of that inclination, for I do not allow it to dwell there." Why, then, did David commit that sin? In order to give an opening to sinners so that they might be able to say: "King David sinned, but when he repented the Holy One forgave him; and if he was forgiven, there is still greater hope that common folk such as we shall receive forgiveness!" That is what David meant by saying: "I will teach transgressors thy ways, and sinners shall return unto thee" (Ps. LI, 14). It is also written of David that he "went up by the ascent of Mount Olivet, going up and weeping, and had his head covered, and he went barefoot" (2 Sam. xv, 30). He did this to show that he considered himself excommunicated, in order to receive his punishment, and his people kept away from him a distance of four cubits. Blessed is the servant who worshipped his Master thus, confessing his sin and turning back to Him with perfect repentance! See, now. The insulting behaviour of Shimei, the son of Gera (2 Sam. XVI, 5), towards David was worse than anything he had hitherto experienced, and yet David did not answer him a word, accepting the humiliation as deserved, and therefore his sins were forgiven him. 'It is here fitting to consider why Shimei, who was a scholar and a wise man, behaved to David as he did. The truth is that the words of insult and cursing which he uttered were not his own, but entered into his heart from another region (from heaven), for David's benefit, that he might repent with a perfect repentance, with a broken heart and with many tears before the Holy One. Therefore David said: "The Lord hath said unto him, Curse David" (Ibid. v. 10). He knew that the cursing and words of insult were inspired from above. Among the injunctions which David on his death-bed laid upon Solomon, two were of special importance: one concerning Joab and one concerning Shimei. Of Joab he said: "Moreover, thou knowest also what Joab the son of Zeruia did to me" (I Kings II, 5). The words "thou knowest" indicate that even Solomon ought not really to have known this, but since others knew of it David told him also. Concerning Shimei he said: "And behold, thou hast with thee Shimei, the son of Gera" (Ibid. v. 8). "With thee" means: "he is always with thee"; for he was Solomon's teacher. We read, "And the king sent and called for Shimei and said unto him, Build thee a house in Jerusalem" (Ibid. v. 36). Where, we may ask, was the great wisdom in this? It was, indeed, wiser than it seems. Solomon did all things in wisdom; he knew that Shimei was a wise man, and he said to himself: "I desire him to spread knowledge in the land, and he therefore must not go from Jerusalem, the centre." Another thing did Solomon see in his wisdom, for it says concerning Shimei that "he came forth (yoze yazo) and cursed" (2 Sam. XVI, 5), suggesting that there were two "comings forth": one from the house of study in order to meet David and abuse him, and the second from Jerusalem to Gath to meet his servants (I Kings II, 40); one to meet a king and the other to meet his own servants. And Solomon saw by means of the Holy Spirit the second "coming forth" of Shimei, and concerning this he said to him: "It shall be that on the day thou goest out, and passest over the brook Kidron, thou shalt know for certain that thou shalt surely die" (I Kings II, 37). Shimei "cast dust" at David (II Sam. XVI, 13), and Solomon referred to water when he prohibited him to cross the brook Kidron: dust and water were the means of testing the woman who was suspected of adultery (Num. v, 11-31), and these two symbols were in the mind of Solomon when he thought of Shimei, who maligned his father. In his charge to Solomon concerning this Shimei, David said: "And behold thou hast with thee Shimei. Which cursed me with a strong curse and I sware to him by the Lord saying, I will not put thee to death with the sword." Was Shimei, then, a fool to accept an oath like this, which forbade David only to kill him with a sword, but not with a spear or arrow? But this sentence can be taken in two ways. One is based on the saying of the son of the great fish

Zohar: Shemoth, Section 2, Page 108a

whose scales reached the highest clouds (i.e. whose wisdom was great), that when David swore he swore by his sword upon which was engraved the Ineffable Name (Tetragrammaton); and thus he swore to Shimei, as it is written: "I sware to him by the Lord (Tetragrammaton) I will not put thee to death (swearing) by the sword." But Solomon interpreted it differently. He said: "This man cursed my father with words; he shall die by means of a Word (Tetragrammaton)." And, in fact, he did not kill him with the actual sword, but with the Name. There is still, however, a difficulty, namely, that since David swore to him he ought not to have killed him, and that David said something with his lips which he did not mean in his heart. But the fact is that David did not kill him. [As to the question why he did not pardon him], it is well known that the members of the human body can receive foreign particles into themselves without real damage, except the heart, which cannot receive even a hair without being damaged; and in a sense David was, as it were, the heart of humanity and so very sensitive, yet he received such insults as surely ought not to have been left unpunished. Therefore he said: "For thou art a wise man and knowest what thou oughtest to do unto him" (I Kings II, 8). David in the same Psalm goes on to say: "For thou desirest not sacrifice, else would I give it; thou delightest not in burnt-offerings. The sacrifices of God are a broken spirit; a broken and a contrite heart, O God, thou wilt not despise" (vv. I 7, I 8). "Thou desirest not sacrifice" But has not the Holy One ordered sacrifices for the forgiveness of sin? It is to be noted, however, that David spake this in regard to the Divine Name Elohim, that is, the attribute of severe judgement: sacrifices must be brought to the Name Tetragrammaton, the attribute of Mercy, as this is the Name always mentioned in connection with the different kinds of sacrifices (Lev. I, 2; II, 1; III, 6), but to the Name Elohim the only sacrifice that can be offered is a broken spirit and a sorrowful heart, as it is written, "The sacrifices of Elohim are a broken spirit." For this reason a person who has had a bad dream must wear a sad and sorrowful demeanour, for he stands under the attribute of Elohim, and the sacrifice of the attribute of Justice must express itself through sadness and self-abasement, and such sadness is in itself sufficient fulfilment of the dream, and judgement will not exercise its sway over such a one, since he has brought the fitting sacrifice to the attribute of Judgement. When David says "A broken and contrite heart, O God, thou wilt not despise", he indicates that the Holy One, blessed be He, does despise a proud and arrogant heart. "Do good in thy good pleasure unto Zion; build thou the walls of Jerusalem" There is a double goodness mentioned here. For from the day whereon the Holy One occupied Himself with the building of the supernal Temple, even until this present time, that "goodness of His good pleasure" has not rested upon the edifice, and therefore it has not attained to complete perfection; but when this "good pleasure" shall be aroused the Lord will fill the edifice with such an array of lights that even the heavenly angels will not be able to look steadfastly upon it, and then the building, and indeed the whole work of the Holy One, blessed be He, shall be completed. The text continues: "Build thou the walls of Jerusalem." But has He then not built them already? Indeed, did He not begin to raise them at the time when He first began to be occupied with the building of the Temple? And if He has not built the walls, what need to say that He has not built the Temple? However, the Holy One, blessed be He, acts not as men. When human beings built the sanctuary here below, they first built the city walls for protection and then the sanctuary; but the Holy One will first build the Sanctuary and then, when He brings it down from heaven, and sets it in its rightful place, then "He will build the walls of Jerusalem"-the battlements of the Blessed City. Therefore David says first: "Do good in thy good pleasure unto Zion", and then: "Build

Zohar: Shemoth, Section 2, Page 108b

411

thou the walls of Jerusalem." A great and deep mystery is contained in these words. In all His other acts and deeds it may be noted that God made first that which is external and then that which is within; but with regard to the sanctuary the very reverse is the case. Although, for instance, He designed the brain first in thought, yet in fact the cranium comes first. For the shell in all cases emanates from the "other side", and what is of the "other side" always appears first; the husk is there to guard the fruit and then it is thrown away, as it says, "The wicked prepareth and the righteous shall put it on" (Job XXVII, 17): the husk is thrown away and a blessing is uttered on the Righteous One. But in regard to the future building of the Sanctuary, when the evil side shall become extinct and disappear from the face of the earth, this will not be necessary, as both the "brain" and the "husk" will be utterly His. First the "brain", signified by the words: "Do good in Thy good pleasure unto Zion"; and then the "husk": "Build thou the walls of Jerusalem"; signifying that in the time of the Kingdom of the Messiah the outer protective covering will no more be the powers of the "evil side", but, instead, the Holy One Himself; as it is written: "I will be unto her a wall of fire round about" (Zech. II, 5). Now, Israel is the supreme "brain" of the world. They were first in the mind of the Creator, and therefore it is that the heathen nations, who are but the "husk", gained the start of them, as it is written: "And these are the kings that reigned in the land of Edom, before there reigned any king over the children of Israel" (Gen. XXVII, 29). But in the future the Holy One will form the brain first without waiting for the husk, as it says: "Israel is holiness unto the Lord, the first fruit of His increase"; and because of this, "all that devour him shall be considered guilty, evil shall come upon them" (Jer. II, 3). "Then shalt thou be pleased with the sacrifices of righteousness" (Ps. LI, 20); for in that time all things will be perfectly united and the Holy Name shall also be united in its harmonious wholeness, and sacrifices will be offered to the united Names Tetragrammaton Elohim, and shall not be as in former days when Elohim had no part in the sacrifice-since, if it had had, all the powers of the "other side" would have been on the alert to participate. At that time, "Thou art great and doest wondrous things: thou art God alone" (Ps. LXXXVI, 10), and there will be no other God. It is concerning this time that it is written: "See now that I, even I, am He, and there is no god with me; I kill, and I make alive" (Deut. XXXII, 39). The double "I, I" indicates the absoluteness of the Divine Presence in the Messianic time, when the "other side" shall be vanquished and be no more seen; and even death, which until that time was connected with the "other side", will thenceforth be from Him directly, for those who have not yet experienced physical death, and He will raise them immediately; for nothing of that filth of sin which is the cause of death will remain in the world, and there will be a new world, fashioned and perfected by the hands of the Holy One, blessed be He. To return to the word begapo: the Targum (Aramaic) translation of this is "by himself", which is indeed correct. But gapo can also (in Aramaic) mean "wing", and we may therefore connect it with the dictum that the whole world is sustained upon one single "wing" of the Leviathan. The inner meaning is as follows. In the beginning the Holy One, blessed be He, created the Leviathan according to the two kinds, male and female; but whenever they moved the earth shook, and had the Holy One not castrated the male and cooled the sexual instincts of the female, they would eventually have brought the whole world into chaos and destruction. So, because of this, these monsters did not engender; therefore a man who does likewise-that is, who does not engender-if "he comes be-gapo, with one wing", is brought under the domination of that wing of the castrated Leviathan, and he "shall go out be-gapo": that is to say, he will be thrust out from the other world and never enter within the curtain. Mark this. It is written: "They will die as solitaries. (aririm) without offspring" (Lev. xx, 21). The word aririm is both masculine and feminine, indicating that a man who refuses to generate leaves the world in the sphere of femininity, although he first entered it in the sphere of masculinity. The Holy One, blessed be He, suffers not any man who has emasculated himself in this world to appear before Him, just as in a similar fashion no castrated animal was a permitted sacrifice (Lev. XXII, 24).

Zohar: Shemoth, Section 2, Page 109a

It is prohibited throughout all generations to castrate any creature which the Holy One has created, for castration appertains eternally and in all cases to the "other side". And when a person marries a woman and he or she refuses to generate, and so enter into the other world without having begotten any children, then "his wife shall go out with him": which signifies that he undergoes transmigration by himself as a male, and she by herself as a female. The text continues: "If his master have given him a wife, and she have borne him sons or daughters, the wife and her children shall be her master's, and he shall go out by himself." "His master" is "the Lord of the whole earth"; "have given him a wife": from this we learn that it is not in the discretion of man himself to take a wife, but that all things have to be "laid in the balance" (Ps. LXII, 10). And who is the woman whom the Master gives him in this case? One who was not actually intended to be his wife, but the wife of another whom he managed to anticipate in God's good graces, and his Master permitted him to have her because He foresaw that she would bear him children. Now when this man, having, as it were, produced fruit in a garden not rightfully his, shall come to the end of his earthly life, "the wife and her children shall be her Master's, and he shall go out by himself." Poor unfortunate! All his labour was thus in vain. He strove to bring forth fruit in an alien garden, in order to obey the dictates of his Master, and must perforce come out empty! Old man, old man! Confronted with such a problem as this, thou art indeed like unto a man lying helpless and powerless on the ground, who can only kick at the gate with his feet. But take courage, old man, and be not afeared. Now, why is it that this poor soul has perforce to go out from this world empty and alone? Is it because he had sown in a garden which was not his own? Surely not so, for was it not the Holy One Himself who gave him this garden? However, no deed is done by the Lord but has its reason and its justice; and as in all other cases, so also in this. He to whom the Holy One has given a wife, and who has generated with her, is not like others who undergo transmigration. One who in this world truly and humbly endeavoured to make the tree fruitful, but who did not succeed in his attempt, is not to be placed in the same category with one who consciously and willfully refused the duty of engendering children, so uprooting the tree, scattering its leaves, and wasting its fruit. He to whom the Master gave a wife in order that he might generate children did after all endeavour to enrich the tree, though he did not succeed. The Holy One, therefore, knowing his good intention, has pity on him and, after first collecting His own due, and taking what the fount formerly failed to produce, permits him to start anew, and labour for himself in order to make good his deficiency. In addition it must be remembered that the man has to undergo transmigration because he is not, in any case, of great merit: since if he were so he would not have had to pass into another form and live again upon the earth, but would at once have "a place better than sons and daughters". So much, then, for the mysteries contained in this verse. But, old man, old man, thou hast spoken of one whose work was in vain, and dost not observe that thou thyself hast uttered nought but vanity in all this discourse! For close on thy heels is a verse which overthrows all thy edifice, and thou imaginest that thou couldst swim the sea according to thy pleasure! What is this verse? "If the servant shall plainly say, I love my master, etc." Old man, old man, thou hast no strength, thy power is fled! What wilt thou do? Thou didst think that there would be none to pursue thee, and now, alas, this verse springs out from its ambush, leaping after thee like a gazelle in the field with thirteen bounds [Tr. Note: i.e. the thirteen words in the verse.] till it overtake thee. What wilt thou do, old man? Nay, be not downcast. Now must thou gather up thy strength, for until this day thou wert in very deed a mighty warrior. Old man, old man, remember that day of snow, when the beans of wisdom were sown, and mighty men

Zohar: Shemoth, Section 2, Page 109b

fought against thee, and thou didst prevail single-handed over thirteen men of might, each one of whom could slay a lion before breakfast. If thou couldst prevail against those giants, surely thou canst now conquer these thirteen, which are mere weaklings, being but words! On, then, and be bold. The expression "amor yomar" (if the servant saying shall say) has been interpreted by certain of the scholars according to its literal sense, i.e. that it indicates two sayings, one at the beginning and one at the end of the six years, before the seventh year has entered; for if he said it even a day after the commencement of the seventh year his words have no validity, as it says "the servant", that is, as long as he is still a servant, namely in the sixth year. And if he spake his words at the beginning of the six years but not at the end, then also his words have no validity. Our interpretation is that, if while he is still with this wife he prays daily to the Holy King, then he both begins and ends with supplication; and if he commences with prayer he shall be received with mercy. What does he say? "I love my Master, etc." Then the Holy One, blessed be He, receives him because of his repentance and his prayers. What, then, does He do for such a one? Instead of sending him back to this world to undergo punishment for the sins of his former life, the Holy One gives him instead into the hands of the celestial Tribunal, who judge him and deliver him unto the house of punishment. And the Holy One records how he was delivered to the Tribunal, and places on him a stigma by putting him under the domination of the Orlah (unclean spirits) [Tr. Note: Al. "and puts him under the domination of the Jubilee year"] for a certain period of time, after which his Master redeems him. But if the Jubilee should appear during the period of his stigmatization, then he is instantly set free-and this even though he should have been in captivity only one day when the Jubilee appeared-and is permitted to enter within the curtain ' Then the old man closed his eyes for a moment.

[Note: The last 26 lines of the Hebrew text do not appear in the translation.]

Zohar: Shemoth, Section 2, Page 110a-112a [Note: The Hebrew text of this page is omitted in the translation.]

Zohar: Shemoth, Section 2, Page 112b

[Note: The first 17 lines of the Hebrew text are omitted in the translation.]

He continued: 'Solomon said: "So I returned and considered all the oppressions ("oppressed") that are done under the sun, and behold the tears of such that were oppressed and they had no comforter" (Eccl. IV, 1). This verse has already been interpreted. But we have still to explain the words, "So I returned and saw" From whence did he return? Now, we have a tradition that Solomon was wont to rise each day at daybreak and turn his face towards the east, where he saw certain things-and then toward the south, where also he saw certain things, and finally, to the side of the north. He would stand thus with his head raised and his eyes half-closed until there would come towards him two pillars, one of fire and one of cloud, and borne upon this last an eagle, mighty in stature and strength, his right wing resting upon the fire, and his body and left wing upon the cloud. This eagle bore in his mouth two leaves. The pillar of cloud with the two leaves and the pillar of fire and the eagle upon them, would come and bow before Solomon. Then the eagle would bend down its head a little, and give him the leaves. Solomon would take and smell them, and by their odour could discern from whence they came, and recognize one leaf as belonging to him "who has his eyes shut", and the other to him "who has his eyes open" (cf. Num. xxv, 4). Now there were a number of things which King Solomon desired that these two beings should make known to him. What did he do? He sealed up his throne with a ring on which was engraved the Holy Name, drew forth from a hidden place another ring on which the Holy Name was also engraved, ascended unto the roof of his palace, seated himself upon the eagle's back, and so departed, attended both by fire and cloud. The eagle ascended into the heavens, and wherever he passed the earth below was darkened. The wiser sort in that part of the earth from whence the light was thus suddenly removed would know the cause and would say, "Assuredly that was King Solomon passing by!" but they knew not whither he went. The vulgar sort, however, would say, "Up there the clouds are moving, and that is why it grew dark so suddenly." The eagle would mount up even to the height of four hundred parasangs, until it reached at length the dark mountain, where is Tarmud in the wilderness; and there at last it would descend. Solomon would then lift up his head and see the dark mountain, and would learn therefrom all that it could teach him and also perceive that it was necessary to penetrate further; after which he would mount once more the back of the eagle and fly on as before until they entered into the depths of the mountains, in the midst of which grew an olive tree. When he was arrived at this spot Solomon would cry out with all his might: "Lord, thy hand is lifted up, they see not" (Isa. XXVI, 11). Then he would enter into that place until he reached those who abode there, and he would show them his ring, and there he gained all his knowledge of strange sciences (i.e. witchcraft). When they had told him all that he required he would

Zohar: Shemoth, Section 2, Page 113a

fly back to his palace in the same way that he came. Then, as he sat once more on his throne, he would reflect upon all that he had gone through, and would conceive ideas of profound wisdom; and it is in reference to such an occasion that he says: "So I returned and considered all the oppressions that are done under the sun." Could he then have viewed upon his journey all such as were oppressed? Hardly so; but he was referring to the little ones, to the sucklings snatched away from their mothers' breasts. Such as these are indeed "oppressed" from all sides: oppressed above in the celestial regions, and oppressed on earth below. There is none oppressed like those whose oppression is transmitted by heredity, concerning whom it is written: "He visits the sins of the fathers upon the children unto the third and fourth generations" (Ex. xx, 5). How is this? King Solomon loudly gives the answer when he says, "A man that is oppressed through the blood of his soul shall flee to the pit; no one will stay him" (Prov. XXVIII, 17). Since he is "oppressed with the blood of a soul" (i.e. has committed some grievous sin), either he or his son or his son's son will be "oppressed" (i.e. wronged) in the "balance"; he shall flee to the pit away from the place of righteousness and none shall stay him; because he has oppressed the blood of the soul he shall himself be oppressed by the other side, or his seed shall bear this oppression of retribution for him and on his account. Hence it says, "all the oppressed", as much as to say, "I have considered all those that are oppressed and all the manners of their oppression, and the reason of their being oppressed." Now, this class of oppressed ones are said to be "made under the sun", because their bodies were actually made before they were violently carried away, there being others who are never so much as fashioned on this earth, though spirits are waiting for them. Others, again, are "made", as it were, in defiance of the Almighty. Thus, when a man steals his neighbour's wife, either openly or secretly, and a child is born of such adulterous union, and the Holy One has perforce to fashion its body and give it form, then that child is indeed "an oppressed one who is made such", literally, in despite of the Almighty. Solomon reflected on this and said: "I consider the sad fate of these hapless oppressed ones who have been 'made', how they shed tears before the Holy One. They complain before Him and make moan, saying, When a person commits a sin he must assuredly die. But, Sovereign of the Universe, when a child is but one day old, shall he be judged?

Zohar: Shemoth, Section 2, Page 113b

These are "the tears of the oppressed ones, who have no comforter". There are many different kinds among them, but they all shed tears. Here is, for instance, a child born in incest. As soon as he emerges into the world he is separated from the community of the holy people, and the unfortunate bastard laments and sheds tears before the Holy One, and complains: "Lord of the world! If my parents have sinned, wherein is my guilt? I have ever striven to do only good works before Thee." But the greatest grief of all emanates from those "oppressed ones" that are but little sucklings which have been removed from their mothers' breasts. These can indeed cause the whole world to weep, and there are no tears like unto theirs, for these are tears which spring from the inmost and deepest recesses of the heart, causing the whole world to wonder and say: "The Holy One's judgements are forever righteous and all His paths are ways of truth. But why is it necessary that these poor little ones, who are blameless and without sin, should die? Where is now the true and righteous judgement of the Lord of the world? If they must die because of their parents' sins, then they certainly "have no comforter." However, the actual fact is that the tears of these "oppressed ones" intercede for and protect the living, and because of their innocence and the power of their intercession a place is eventually prepared for them such as even the perfect righteous cannot attain to or occupy; for the Holy One does in truth love them with a special and particular love, He unites Himself with them and prepares for them a supernal place, very near to Himself. It is concerning such that it is written: "Out of the mouth of babes and sucklings hast thou founded strength." What is it that they accomplish there and why went they thither? "Because of thin enemies, that thou mightest still the enemy and the avenger" (Ps. VIII, 3). And there is also another place prepared for sinners who repent. We have been taught (cf. Pirke Aboth, ch. v) that ten things were created upon the eve of the Sabbath in the twilight, at the time when the work of Creation was ended and the Sabbath not yet begun; among which are the shape of the written characters, the writing, and the tables of stone; for it is written: "And the tables were the work of God, and the writing was the writing of God, graven upon the tables" (Ex. XXXII, 16). Now it may be asked, what proof is there in this verse that these things were indeed created on the eve of the Sabbath, and not perhaps a thousand years later, or, maybe, when the Israelites stood at Mount Sinai? However, there can be no doubt that they were created on the eve of this Sabbath, for the following reason. In the whole account of the Creation (Gen. I) it is always the name Elohim which is used to denote God; but after the completion of the whole work God is called with the full name, Tetragrammaton Elohim (Gen. II, 4). For, although all things were created [Tr. Note: ie. in posse] in the power of the Name Elohim, that which was created was not actually made [Tr. Note: i.e. in esse.] until Sabbath eve, when "God ended the work which he had made" (Gen. 11, 2); that is to say, Creation only received its permanency with its completion through making. In the same sense it says concerning the tables of stone that they were "the work (ma'ase, lit. making) of God", which indicates that they were produced at the time when the consummation of the whole Creation took place through the act of God's "making"-and not in the later period concerning which the Name in its fulness is mentioned-"Tetragrammaton Elohim" (Gen. II, 4), and only herewith was the world placed upon a firm basis and permanently established. When Moses broke the tablets "under the mountain" (Ex XXXII, 19), the Ocean overflowed its borders and was on the point of inundating the whole world. When Moses saw how the waves were rising and threatening to overwhelm the universe, straightway he "took the calf which they had made and burnt it in the fire, and ground it to powder, and strawed it upon the water" (Ex. XXXII, 20). Then he stationed himself before the waters of the Ocean and said: "Waters, waters, what would ye?" And they answered: "Was not the world established by and on the merit of the Holy Words engraved upon the tablets? And now, because the Israelites have denied the Torah by making the golden calf, we desire to overwhelm the world." Then Moses answered them and said: "Behold, all that they have done in connection with the sin of the golden calf is delivered unto you; is it not enough that so many thousands of them have perished for their sin?" Straightway he "strawed it (the dust of the calf) upon the water". But even then the floods were not appeased. So he took from those angry seas a portion of water, and poured it upon the place where he had burned the calf, and then at last the Ocean was soothed and returned to its own bed. For in that wilderness there was no water, as it is written: "It is no place of seed neither is there any water to drink" (Num. xx, 5). Nor can the place whereon Moses strawed the powder have been Miriam's well, for assuredly Moses would never have permitted evil memories to pollute the place whose waters the Israelites would afterwards have had to drink. Besides, the Israelites only received their cistern when they came to the place Mattanah, as it is written: "Spring up, well . The princes digged the well. And from there to Mattanah" (Ibid. XXI, 17). [Tr. Note: v. T.B. Nedarim, 55a; Erubin, 54a.] As to the words "graven upon the tables" (harut'al ha-luhoth), it has already been pointed out that this phrase contains an allusion to heruth-that is, freedom. Freedom from what? From the angel of death, from subjection to the kingdoms of this world,

Zohar: Shemoth, Section 2, Page 114a

from all things earthly and from all things evil. And what is freedom? It is the seal of the world to come, in which is every kind of freedom. Had not the tablets been broken, the world would not have suffered as it subsequently did, and the Israelites would have been in the likeness of the supernal angels above. Therefore the Scripture proclaims: "the tablets were the work of God" (Elohim), from the time when the world was still under the aegis of the name Elohim, before the Sabbath had entered. The writing, too, was the "writing of God", black fire on white fire, and it was haruth (engraved) because the Jubilee proclaims freedom (heruth) to all worlds ' Having spoken these things, the old man paused a moment and then said: 'So far, my friends, and now no further! From now on ye shall know that the evil side has no power over you; and that I, Jebba the Ancient, have stood before you to utter these words ' The two Rabbis stood before him dumbfounded, like men waking out of their sleep. Then they prostrated themselves before him, and so remained, speechless and awestruck. After a while they wept. Finally R. Hiya found his voice again, and spake, saying: '"Set me as a seal upon thy heart, as a seal upon thine arm; for love is strong as death, zeal is hard as the sheol; the coals thereof are coals of fire, a blaze of Kah" (S. S. VIII, 6). When the Community of Israel cleaves to her Spouse she says: "Set me as a seal upon thy heart." The property of a seal is to leave its impress on the surface wherewith it has come into contact, and this impress naturally remains even after the seal has been removed. So the Community of Israel cries aloud unto her Spouse, saying: "Since I have cleaved to Thee, may my image remain engraven upon Thine heart, so that even when I myself must perforce be driven hither and thither in exile Thou mayst find my likeness there and remember me. May I thus cleave to Thee forever and not be forgotten of Thee." "For love is strong as death"-as the strength of the region where death dwells is the place called "eternal love". "Her coals are coals of fire." What are these coals? The diamonds and precious gems which are born of that fire. "A blaze of Kah"-the flame which issues out of the Supernal

World to unite itself with the Community of Israel and so bridge the gulf between Heaven and earth and unite both. Of this same quality of love do we also partake in regard to thee, and the coals of that very fire are set within our hearts, warming them towards thee. So may it be the will of the Holy One, blessed be He, that our image may be engraved upon thine heart forever, as thine is impressed upon ours!' Then the old man kissed and blessed them, and they departed. When they reached the dwelling of R. Simeon they recounted everything that had befallen them. R. Simeon was both delighted and amazed. He said: 'Blessed indeed are you in that ye were found worthy of all this! To think that you were in the presence of this supreme lion of wisdom with whom not even the greatest sages can be compared, and did not recognize him at once! I am astonished that you have escaped punishment for your disrespect towards him; it is evident that the Holy One desired to spare and save you ' Then he applied to them the verses: "And the path of the righteous is as the shining light, that shineth more and more unto the perfect day"; "When thou goest, thy steps shall not be straitened, and when thou runnest thou shalt not stumble" (Prov. IV, 12, 18); "and thy people shall be all righteous; they shall inherit the land forever, the branch of thy planting, the work of thy hands, that I may be glorified" (Isa. LX, 21). Thus ends the incident concerning R. Jebba the Ancient

Zohar: Shemoth, Section 2, Page 121a

[Tr. Note: The pages omitted belong to the Raya Mehemna.] [Note: the pages mentioned in the previous note were not translated.]

AND YE SHALL BE MEN OF HOLINESS UNTO ME; AND FLESH THAT IS TORN BY BEASTS IN THE FIELD YE SHALL NOT EAT; YE SHALL CAST IT TO THE DOG (XXII, 30). R. Judah quoted here the verse: "And wisdom, where shall it be found? And where is the place of understanding?" (Job XXVIII, I2). Said he: "Blessed are the Israelites for that the Holy One desires to honour them more than all the rest of mankind. At first He said unto them: "And ye shall be unto me a kingdom of priests" (Ex. XIX, 6). His great love to them was, however, not satisfied until he had added: "and a holy nation" (Ibid), which signifies a higher grade; His love was still not satisfied until He called them "a holy people" (Deut. XIV, 2), which is a still higher grade; and now He shows His endless love to them by calling upon them to be "men of holiness", which is the highest grade and destiny of all. For the Torah itself emanates from Wisdom, from the realm called "holiness", and Wisdom itself emanates from the region called "holy (lit. holiness) of holies" ' Said R. Isaac: 'The Jubilee is also designated "holiness", as it is written: "For it is the jubilee; it shall be holiness (kodesh) unto you" (Lev. XIV, I2). The Israelites who are destined to be "men of holiness" have a share in both (the Torah and the Jubilee). What is the difference in degree between "holy" and "holiness"?' Said R. Yose: 'The latter is the extremest, the utmost degree, but not so the former, for it is written: "And it shall come to pass that he that is left in Zion, and he that remaineth in Jerusalem, shall be called holy" (Isa. IV, 3), which signifies that the grade of "holy" is connected with that place (i.e. with the earthly Zion and Jerusalem),

Zohar: Shemoth, Section 2, Page 121b

whereas "holiness" is connected with a higher place.' R. Abba was once walking in company with R. Yose and R. Hiya. Said R. Hiya: 'How do we know that the expression, "and ye shall be unto Me men of holiness", signifies the highest grade?' Said R. Yose: 'All the companions have interpreted it well; it is truly so, for it is written: "Israel is holiness (kodesh) to the Lord, the beginning (reshith) of his increase; all that devour him shall be guilty" (Jer. II, 3). Israel is here designated "reshith", and Wisdom is also called "reshith", as it says, "The beginning (reshith) of wisdom is the fear of the Lord" (Ps. CXI, 10). And because Israel is called "holiness", the completion and harmony of all grades, they must not "eat flesh that is torn by beasts in the field"; they must not derive their nourishment from the side of severe judgement, but "cast it to the dogs", namely to the impudent and impure power on which judgement rests; so the people destined to be "men of holiness" should not be stained by the impurity of the principle of evil left in the flesh of the torn animal ' Once when R. Isaac was studying with R. Simeon, he asked him: 'What is the meaning of the last part of the verse quoted above (Jer. II, 3): "Israel is holiness to the Lord, all that devour him shall be guilty" (ye'shamu, will bear their guilt, i.e. will be punished)?' R. Simeon referred to the passages (Lev. XXII, 10, 14-16) where strangers eating of the holy things "lade themselves with guilt. (ashmah) of eating". 'Because Israel is called "holy", "holiness", all that "eat" him, that is to say, all the strange nations who try to devour and make an end of him are guilty of consuming something sacred ' Then R. Isaac came to him, kissed his hands, and said: 'It was worth coming here only to hear this! But, Master, if, as we have been taught, "holiness" is a higher degree than "being holy", how is one to explain "holy, holy, holy (kadosh) is the Lord Zebaoth"?' R. Simeon replied: 'When the triad (the holy, holy, holy) is united in one unity, it forms one "house", and that house is called "holiness "; it is the essence and core of the "holy"; and when Israel attain to the completeness and perfection of faith, they are called "holiness": "Holiness is Israel to the Lord"; "ye should be unto Me men of holiness" ' A certain legionary once asked R. Abba: 'Is it not written in your Law: "Flesh that is terepha (torn by beasts) ye should not eat: ye shall cast it to the dog"? Why, then, does it say: "He hath given tereph (food) to those that fear him" (Ps. CXI, 5)? Assuredly it ought rather to have said: "He gives tereph to the dog"! 'R. Abba replied: 'Fool (Reka)! Thinkest thou that tereph is the same as terepha? And even if we admit that it is the same, I say that God gave this prohibition only to those that fear His name, and therefore He gave it not to you, since He knows that you do not fear Him and will not keep His commandments; and so with all the restrictions of the Torah.' R. Eleazar taught that the peculiar expression, "men of holiness", contains a reference to the Jubilee, for there is a tradition that the Israelites came out from Egypt into freedom by means of the Jubilee, which is the source of all freedom, both early and everlasting. When they came out into freedom the Jubilee set them upon his wings, and they were called his men, his children. And of the Jubilee it says: "It is jubilee; holiness is it to you." Yea, verily, "to you". Therefore it says here: "Ye shall be unto Me men of holiness", that is, His men, these words having been spoken by the Holy One, blessed be He.

Zohar: Shemoth, Section 2, Page 122a

And therefore they become worthy to be known as "brethren of the Holy One", as it is written: "For my brethren and companions' sake, I will now say, Peace be within thee" (Ps. CXXII, 9). Later they were called "holiness" (Jer. Ibid), and not merely "men of holiness". We have been taught that because Israel is designated "holiness" no one is allowed to apply to his neighbour an insulting epithet or to bestow upon him a degrading nickname. The punishment for such an offence is indeed great. It is written: "Keep thy tongue from evil" (Ps. XXXI, 15). "From evil": for slander and malicious speech cause disease to enter into the world. Said R. Yose: 'He who offends his neighbour by giving him an insulting nickname or by addressing him in abusive terms will himself eventually suffer for offences which he has not committed ' In this connection R. Hiya also said in the name of R. Hezekiah: 'He who calls his neighbour "wicked" will be thrown into the very jaws of Gehenna. The only people whom one may legitimately call "wicked" are those who speak impudently and blasphemously against the Torah ' Once, when on a journey, R. Jesse passed close by a man who was cursing and reviling his neighbour; and the Rabbi said to him: "Thou behavest like a wicked one (rasha')." Those who were with R. Jesse, hearing his words, were shocked, thinking that he had assuredly committed a great offence; so they brought him before R. Judah to be judged. In defence he pleaded that he had not called the man "wicked", but only told him that he had behaved "like a wicked one." R. Judah was puzzled, and put the case before R. Eleazar, who said: 'The Rabbi has Scripture on his side, for do we not read: "The Lord was as an enemy" (Lam. II, 5)? which obviously does not mean that He actually became an enemy, for had that been the case Israel would certainly have been utterly annihilated. Similarly, we read: "How is she (Jerusalem) become as a widow" (Ibid. 1, 1), which signifies that she is indeed like unto a woman whose husband has gone away to a far country, but for whom she still waits.' Said R. Hiya: 'Is there not a better proof than all these, in fact, the standard example, namely: "And upon the likeness of the throne was the likeness as the appearance of a man" (Ezek. 1, 26)?' Said R. Isaac: 'Also it is written: "As the apple tree among the trees of the wood, so is my beloved among the sons" (S S. II, 3)–as an apple tree which has varied colours, red, white, and green combined in a unity ' Said R. Judah: 'Ah, had I come here only in order to hear these mystic revelations, it would have sufficed! It is also written: "And he that stumbled among them on that day shall be as David" (Zech. XII, 8). "As David", who said: "In my poverty I have prepared for the Lord an hundred thousand talents of gold."; "as David", who said of himself: "For I am poor and needy" (Ps. LXXXVI, I); yea, he called himself thus, who was king above all other earthly kings!' Said R. Abba: "And how blessed are the Israelites for that the Holy One does not call them "as holiness", but actually "holiness" itself, as it is written: "Holiness is Israel to the Lord"; and therefore: "all who devour him will be made to bear grievous punishment for their guilt." 'Said R. Yose: 'For what reason did God give Israel rules of judgement after He had given them the Ten Words (the Decalogue)? Because, as we have been taught, the Torah was given from the side of Power (Geburah), and therefore He desired to give them peace among themselves in order that the Torah should be observed under both of its aspects. For, as R. Abba has said in the name of R. Isaac, the world is sustained by Justice, as it was created by, and for, the principle of Justice. R. Abba also said that the words: "Execute judgement in the morning" (Jer. XXI, I2) mean that judges should sit in judgement "in the morning", that is, before they have had anything to eat or drink, since he who executes judgement after eating and drinking is not a true judge, as it is written: "Ye shall not eat with the blood" (Lev. XIX, 26), which means that a judge who eats before sitting in judgement is, as it were, guilty of shedding his neighbour's blood, for, indeed, he gives the "blood" of his neighbour to someone else. Now this is merely in reference to money matters; how much more, then, in criminal cases, when it is a question of life and death, should judges beware of eating and drinking before executing judgement!' Said R. Judah: 'He who betrays judgement betrays the supports of the King. And what are these? Those mentioned in the verse, "For I the Lord exercise lovingkindness, judgement, and righteousness" (Jer. IX, 25). All things depend upon these three ' R. Yose said: "These are the stays of the Throne, for it is written: "Righteousness and judgement are the establishment of thy throne" (Ps. LXXXIX, 15); and also "And in lovingkindness will the throne be established" (Isa. XVI, 5).

Zohar: Shemoth, Section 2, Page 122b [The Hebrew text of this page (taken from the Idra D'mishkana) is not translated.] Zohar: Shemoth, Section 2, Page 123a [The Hebrew text of this page is not translated.]

Zohar: Shemoth, Section 2, Page 123b

[Note: The first 36 lines of the Hebrew text are not translated.]

AND IN ALL THINGS THAT I HAVE SAID UNTO YOU TAKE YE HEED, ETC. Note the passive form tishameru (take heed, lit. ye shall be guarded). We may translate: "From the penalties which I have threatened for a breach of My service ye shall be guarded, so that no harm shall come to you", and therefore, MAKE NO MENTION OF THE NAME OF OTHER GODS. These words may also be expounded thus: 'Ye shall not bring it about that ye shall fall among the nations in a strange land so that there be fulfilled concerning you the words of Scripture: "and there shalt thou serve other gods, etc." (Deut. XXVIII, 36) R. Judah connected this text with the verses: "Hear, O my people, and I will admonish thee. . There shall no strange god be in thee.. I am the Lord thy God, who brought thee up out of the Land of Egypt, etc." (Ps. LXXXI, 9-11). 'These verses', he said, 'David uttered under the inspiration of the Holy Spirit, and they should be well pondered. "Hear, O My people", is a reminder of the repeated admonitions of the Torah and of the Holy One, blessed be He, to man, and all for the benefit of man, that he observe the commands of the Torah, for when one

Zohar: Shemoth, Section 2, Page 124a

observes the ordinances of the Torah and diligently studies it, it is as though he diligently studied the Divine Name. For the whole Torah is an enfolding of the one Divine Name, the most exalted Name, the Name that comprehends all other names; and hence if one diminishes it, even by a single letter, it is as though he made a gap in the Divine Name. Hence, according to our teaching, the words, "and make no mention of the name of other gods", signify "thou shalt not add to the Torah nor diminish from it" ' R. Hiya said: '"The name of other gods" signifies profane books which do not issue from the side of the Torah, and hence we are forbidden to study them: NEITHER LET IT BE HEARD OUT OF THY MOUTH, that is, we may not even mention them nor receive teaching from them, especially concerning the Torah. ' R. Judah expounded the passage as follows. 'For what reason is the precept concerning other gods closely followed by the precept, THE FEAST OF UNLEAVENED BREAD SHALT THOU KEEP? Because the nonobservance of this festival betokens lack of faith in the Holy One, blessed be He, since that festival is closely associated with Him ' R. Isaac said: 'It is the same with the other feasts and festivals, as they all are closely bound up with the most exalted Divine Name. Hence the dictum, that religious faith is closely bound up with the three festivals ' ALL THY MALES. Says R. Eleazar: Emphatically al l thy males", as they then receive blessings from the eternal spring. Hence the dictum that every circumcised Israelite is bound to appear before the Holy King so as to receive a blessing from the eternal spring. So Scripture says: "according to the blessing of the Lord thy God which he hath given thee" (Deut. XVI, 17), and here it is written: "before the Lord God", that is, from whence blessings pour and blessings are received. Happy is the portion of Israel above that of all other nations. On one occasion, when the Israelites were going up to celebrate the festival, a number of idolaters mingled with them. That year there was no blessing in the world. So they came to Rab Ham'nuna the Elder to consult him about the matter. He asked them: 'Did you see any portent of this beforehand?' They replied: 'We noticed on our return journey that everywhere the waters were dried up, and there was continuous cloud and darkness, so that the pilgrims could not proceed on their way. Furthermore, when we went in to show ourselves, the face of heaven was darkened ' R. Ham'nuna trembled and said: 'There is no doubt but either there are among you some who are uncircumcised or that idolaters mingled themselves in your company. For at that time blessings come into the world only through circumcised Israelites. The Holy One, blessed be He, looks at the sacred symbol and sends down the blessing,' The following year again a number of idolaters intruded themselves among the pilgrims who went up to Jerusalem. Then when the festive offerings were being joyfully eaten, the Israelites noticed those people covering their faces with their cloaks, and on further watching them they discovered that they did not pronounce a blessing over the meal, like all the others. This was communicated to the Court of Judges, who examined the strangers and asked them what kind of offering was that of which they had eaten a portion? As they could not give a satisfactory answer, further inquiries were made, and it was discovered that they were idolaters, and so they were put to death. The people said: "Blessed is the Merciful One who delivered His people, for assuredly blessing only rests on Israel, the holy seed, the children of Faith, the children of Truth." That year was one of rich blessing in the world, and the people exclaimed: "Surely the righteous shall give thanks unto thy name, etc." (Ps. CXL, 14). R. Hiya said: 'Through the merit of Israel circumcised their enemies have been subdued before them and their possessions inherited by them. Hence the verse: "Three times in the year shall all thy males appear, etc." (Ex. XXXIV, 23) is immediately followed by the verse: "For I will cast out nations before thee and enlarge thy borders" (Ibid. 24); for the Holy One, blessed be He, uproots one group of inhabitants and restores another, and therefore "shall all thy males appear before the Lord God"'.

Zohar: Shemoth, Section 2, Page 124b

THE LORD (Adon) GOD. R. Judah said: 'Sometimes the superior aspect of the Deity is called by the lower Name, at other times it is the lower aspect that is given the superior Name. Here, in the phrase "before the Lord God" (ha-ADoN Tetragrammaton), the lower term Adon (Lord) is expressive of the superior aspect. This matter has already been expounded, and expounded in various ways, which, however, all converge into one. Blessed be the Merciful One, blessed be His name forevermore!' BEHOLD, I SEND AN ANGEL BEFORE THEE. R. Isaac quoted in this connection the words: "Let him kiss me with the kisses of his mouth" (S S. 1, 2), and said: 'It is the Community of Israel who says this (to God). Why does she say "Let Him kiss me" instead of "Let Him love me"? Because, as we have been taught, kissing expresses the cleaving of spirit to spirit; therefore the mouth is the medium of kissing, for it is the organ of the spirit (breath). Hence he who dies by the kiss of God [Tr. Note: According to the Haggadah, Moses and certain other saints died "by the kiss of God".] is so united with another Spirit, with a Spirit which never separates from him. Therefore the Community of Israel prays: "Let Him kiss me with the kisses of His mouth", that His Spirit may be united with mine and never separate from it. The verse continues: "For thy love is better than wine" (Ibid). Why is the love of the Holy One compared with wine, which was the cause of Ephraim's degradation (Isa. XVIII, 27), and was prohibited to the priests at the time of service (Lev. x, 9)? Said R. Hiya: 'It is better even than the "wine of the Torah" 'R. Hezekiah said: 'It is better than the wine of which the Psalmist said that it "maketh glad the heart of man" (Ps. CIV, 15) ' R. Judah referred to the verse: "And Jacob kissed Rachel and lifted up his voice and wept" (Gen. XXIX, 11). Why did he weep? Because the intensity of his attachment to her overpowered him, and he found relief in tears. It is true, it also says of Esau that "he kissed him (Jacob) and they wept" (Gen. XXXIV, 4); but as has been said, the word wa-yishakehu (and he kissed him) has (masoretic) dots on it, to indicate the insincerity of Esau's kisses, [Tr. Note: Cf. Aboth de R. Nathan, XXXIII.] for there was no union of spirit with spirit there; and concerning him it is written: "The kisses of an enemy are abundant" (Prov. XXVII, 6; i.e. superfluous, burdensome); they are windy and betoken no attachment of spirit. As long as the Holy One was dwelling and moving in the midst of Israel there was a perfect union between Spirit and spirit; concerning which it is written: "And ye who cleave to the Lord your God, ye are all alive today" (Deut. IV, 4); they clave to one another in every possible manner, and were not separated. But when Moses heard the words, "Behold, I send an angel before thee", he knew that it meant separation, therefore he said: "If thy presence go not, carry us not up hence" (Ex. XXXIII, I 5). Said R. Abba: 'Note the verse that immediately precedes, viz, "The first of the firstfruits of thy land thou shalt bring into the house of the Lord Thy God. Thou shalt not seethe a kid in his mother's milk." The connection is as follows. This verse indicates that one may not mingle lower grades (the k'lifoth) with higher ones (sefiroth), lest the outer side should imbibe nourishment from the inner one, the one being from the side of impurity and the other from that of holiness. The "mother" here mentioned is the Community of Israel (the Shekinah), who is called Mother, and the "kid" symbolizes the principle of impurity. Therefore God said, "[Since you may indeed cause such separation] behold, I send My angel before thee". But Moses said: "I take this command [not to seethe a kid in its mother's milk] as a promise that Thou wilt not separate from us; therefore, 'if thy presence go not, carry us not up hence'." ' Said R. Eleazar: 'This the Holy One said in order to soothe the fears of Israel, because He loved them. He was like unto a king who always desired to walk with his son and never entrusted him to anybody else. The son once came to his father,

but felt chary of asking him to go out with him. The latter noticing it, said: "Captain So-and-so will accompany thee upon this way and will take care of thee"; then adding: "Beware of him" (v. 21), for he is somewhat quick-tempered. Then said the son: "If so, either I shall remain here or else thou must come with me; for I shall not separate myself from thee." In a similar fashion the Holy One first said: "Behold, I send an angel before thee, to keep thee in the way. Beware of him, and obey his voice, provoke him not." Then Moses said: "If Thy presence go not, carry us not up hence." 'When R. Simeon came, he found the Companions discussing this subject. Said he: 'Eleazar my son, thou hast spoken well, yet mark this. On this occasion (when God said that He would send an angel) Moses said nothing and did not object, because no separation was implied in the promise. [Tr. Note: i.e. because the Angel here denominates Malkuth.] I have already explained this to the companions. It is true, some understand it just in the opposite way, [Tr. Note: That the Angel here denominates Metatron.] but that is not according to the interpretation of the ancients (although at bottom there is no contradiction between the two). Here, as I have said, Moses did not object, but he did later, when the Holy One again said: "I will send an angel before thee" (Ex. XXXIII, 2), without saying anything more about him. But here we have the additional explanation concerning the character of the angel, for it says: "But if thou shalt indeed obey his (the angel's) voice and do all that I speak", indicating that God would speak through the angel; and similarly it continues, "Then will I be an enemy to thine enemies, and will afflict them that afflict thee", showing that everything depends upon him ' Said R. Judah: 'Should one say that on both occasions it is merely an angel that is referred to, then we have to say that Moses made no objection on the first occasion because he did not see an opportunity, but on the second occasion he did object, saying, "If Thy presence go not, carry us not up hence." ' To which R. Simeon remarked: 'The long and the short of it is that Moses did not desire that an angel should accompany them, therefore he said: "If now I have found grace in thy sight, O Lord, let my Lord, I pray thee, go among us" (Ex. XXYIV, 9) ' Said R. Judah: 'In regard to R. Abba's interpretation of the words: "Thou shalt not seethe a kid in his mother's milk" (v. supra), ought not this passage according to him to have read, "in the mother's" rather than "in his mother's"? For if the "kid" represents the spirit of impurity and the "mother" the Shekinah, dare one thus assert that the Community of Israel (the Shekinah) is the "mother" of the spirit of impurity-the Community of Israel, concerning whom R. Simeon has said that the Holy Mother is the very essence of Israel, part and parcel of her being, as it is written: "For the Lord's portion is his people" (Deut. XXXII, 9)?' R. Simeon replied: 'Your question is good, and yet R. Abba's remark is correct. See now. Two powers hold fast to the Shekinah, imbibing strength from Her strength, and clinging one to Her right hand and one to Her left. Therefore some incline towards the right and some towards the left, and all depend upon this holy "Mother". But the things of the Left are attached to this Mother only when she herself imbibes from the "other side", and the sanctuary is defiled and the mighty serpent begins to manifest himself. Then "the kid sucks of his mother's milk", and judgement is aroused. For this reason the Israelites hastened to bring the firstfruits, and when the priest had taken the basket of fruit from the hands of an Israelite and set it down before the altar, the latter would begin to recite the story of how Laban ("the Syrian", cf. Deut. XXVI, 5) came with his witchcraft to subject Jacob and his holy descendants, but did not succeed, and Israel was not delivered to the "other side" It is concerning this that it is written: "The first of the firstfruits of thy land thou shalt bring into the house of the Lord Thy God. Thou shalt not seethe the kid in his mother's milk", so that the "kid", namely the "other side", should not suck the milk of his "mother", and the sanctuary be not defiled, and the severe judgements be not roused. Therefore the holy seed is prohibited to eat flesh together with milk, [Tr. Note: v. Onkelos to Ex. XXIII, 19.] in order that a place in holiness should not be allotted to him who does not belong to it; for on this action the thing depends: the act below affects the activity above. Blessed are the Israelites above all the heathen nations for that their Lord says concerning them: "Ye are the children of the Lord your God"; "Thou art a holy people to the Lord thy God, and the Lord hath chosen thee to be a peculiar people unto himself above all the nations that are upon the earth" (Deut. XIV, I, 2). 'It is set forth in the mysteries of King Solomon's book that he who eats a composite of flesh and milk, or drinks milk shortly after eating meat, will appear for a space of forty days to the vision of the accusing angels in the aspect of a slaughtered goat, with myriads of impure powers

Zohar: Shemoth, Section 2, Page 125b

surrounding him, and he causes unholy judgements to be awakened in the world. And should he beget a son during those forty days, the latter will imbibe his soul and the breath of his spirit from the "other side". It says: "Ye shall sanctify yourself and ye shall be holy" (Lev. XI, 44), which signifies that he who endeavours to be holy is assisted from above, and, contrariwise, he who defiles himself is drawn on to defilement by the unholy powers, as it is written in the preceding verse (43): "Ye shall not make yourselves unclean. that ye shall be defiled" This is an impurity which is exceedingly gross, and which cannot be done away with by means of purification as can other defilements. Besides, such a person, having come to look, even in outer seeming, like a goat-as we have said-goes in constant fear of wild animals, for the human image has disappeared from both his inner and his outer aspects. R. Jesse used at one time to allow the eating of chicken with cheese or with milk. But R. Simeon said unto him: 'Thou must not permit this, lest thou thereby open the door to evil powers. Does one not say to a Nazarite: "Go away, go away, depart and come not near the vineyard!"? I say to thee, thou must not do this thing! If thou allowest such prohibited minglings of foods it is as though thou gavest wine unto a Nazarite. It is written: "Thou shalt not eat any abomination" (Deut. XIV, 3), where the word "any" includes every kind and sort of food which is forbidden ' There is a tradition that Daniel, Hananniah, Mishael and Azariah were delivered from their trials only because they had not defiled themselves with forbidden food. Said R. Judah: 'It is written: "And Daniel purposed in his heart that he would not defile himself with the portion of the king's meat" (Dan. I, 8), and there is a tradition that the wicked Nebuchadnezzar used, apart from the other strange dishes for which he had a partiality, to eat flesh with milk and cheese with meat. Because Daniel refrained from partaking of such food, when he was thrown into the lions' den, he attained fully to the image of the Lord, his perfected human form not changing to any other, so that the lions were struck with awe before him and did him no harm. On the other hand, when the wicked Nebuchadnezzar was deprived of his kingdom and he dwelt with the beasts of the field, his human countenance was taken away from him and from that day he did not bear the impress of a man, so that all the beasts of the field considered him as one of themselves, and would readily have devoured him, had it not been that it was decreed from heaven that he should become an object of derision to all men, just as he in his time had "scoffed at kings" (Hab. I, 10). It is written concerning Daniel and his companions that "at the end of ten days their countenances appeared fairer and fatter than the children which did eat the portion of the king's meat" (Dan. I, 5). This was because the image of their Lord was not removed from them, whereas from those others it was. What was the cause of this? The fact that they did not pollute themselves with the abomination of the prohibited food. Blessed are the Israelites who are called to be a "holy people"!' AND TO MOSES HE SAID, COME UP UNTO THE LORD. Who said this? The Shekinah. "Come up unto the Lord": as it is written, "And Moses went up to God" (Ex. XIX, 3). And for what other purpcse was Moses called up? To establish the covenant, for until that time it had not yet been completed because of the incomplete circumcision of the Israelites, as it is written: "There (at Marah) he made for them a statute and an ordinance" (Ex. xv, 25), these referring to the two acts connected with circumcision; "and there he proved them" (Ibid), that is, when the holy sign of the covenant was manifested in them. Then the covenant was established through Moses, as it is written: "And Moses took the blood and sprinkled it on the people, and said, Behold the blood of the covenant" (Ibid. XXIV, 8). R. Isaac drew attention to the verse: "And Moses took half of the blood and put it in basins; and half of the blood he sprinkled upon the altar" (Ibid. v, 6). 'The "upon" ', said he, 'is of special significance, indicating that the covenant was made with the highest grade ' AND WORSHIP YE AFAR OFF. The words afar off contain the same indication as in the verses, "The Lord appeared to me from afar" (Jer. XXXI, 2), and "and his sister stood afar off" (Ex. II, 4): namely, as R. Abba pointed out, that until that time the Moon (that is, the Shekinah) was on the wane, for Her light was obscured from before the eyes of the Israelites; but when that hour was arrived they were made more worthy of their holy portion, and established a holy covenant with Her and with the Holy One in all His aspects. Why did the Shekinah say to Moses, "Go up to the Lord"? In order that "Israel and I may now, through thy mediation, participate as one being in the Divine perfection, which has not been the case hitherto". So what did Moses do? He divided the blood into two parts: "half of the blood he sprinkled upon

Zohar: Shemoth, Section 2, Page 126a

the altar"–according to the significance which we have already revealed–and the other half he sprinkled upon the people and said: "behold the blood of the covenant, which the Lord hath made with you" (v. 8). HE PUT THE BLOOD IN BASINS. This is an allusion to the words: "Thy navel is a round basin" (S S. VII, 7), which is applied to the Shekinah. AND MOSES ALONE SHALL COME NEAR TO THE LORD. Happy was the lot of Moses in obtaining a privilege vouchsafed to no other mortal! The Israelites, too, attained to more exalted heights than ever before. In that hour they were established in the holy covenant, and given the glad tidings that a sanctuary should be erected in their midst, as it is written: "And let them make me a sanctuary, that I may dwell among them" (xxv, 8). AND THEY SAW THE GOD OF ISRAEL, AND THERE WAS UNDER HIS FEET AS IT WERE A PAVED WORK OF A SAPPHIRE STONE. Said R. Judah: 'It is written: "This thy stature is like to a palm tree" (S S. VII, 8). What love, indeed, has the Holy One bestowed upon the Community of Israel in that He never separates Himself from her, but is perpetually and perfectly united with her, even as a palm tree in which male and female are one in complete and continual union! See now. When Nadab and Abihu and the seventy elders "saw", what did they actually see? "They saw the God of Israel", that is to say, the Shekinah manifested Herself unto them ' But R. Yose interpreted the demonstrative pronoun eth in this verse ("and they saw eth the God of Israel") as denoting something more, over and above R. Judah's exposition, a kind of extra quality of enlightenment, as it were–although what they saw they saw from a distance. R. Isaac asked: [It says here, "Under his feet was as it were a work of sapphire stone, but Ezekiel said] "This is the living creature (Hayah) which I saw under the God of Israel by the river of Chebar" (Ezek. x, 20). Now, which Hayah is here indicated?' R. Yose replied in the name of R. Hiya that the reference is to the little Hayah. [Tr. Note: Metatron.] 'But is there then such a little Hayah?' 'Yes, assuredly there is. There is a little one and a superior one, [Tr. Note: Malkuth.] and there is also a very little one. [Tr. Note: Sandalphon.] As for the last part of the verse which is being treated, namely: "And under His feet as it were a paved work of a sapphire stone"–what was this which they saw? They beheld the precious stone with which the Holy One will build the future Sanctuary, as it is written: "I will lay thy stones with fair colours and lay thy foundations with sapphires" (Isa. LIV, 11) ' HE LAID NOT HIS HAND UPON THE NOBLES OF ISRAEL; AND THEY SAW GOD AND DID EAT AND DRINK. The nobles of Israel" refers to Nadab and Abihu: their punishment was postponed. R. Yose declared that these words were said in praise of them, for "they did eat and drink": that is to say, they feasted their eyes on this splendour. Said R. Judah: 'It was indeed a true partaking and a true nourishing, and a most veritable and perfect uniting with the supernal world. Oh, if they only had not later sinned!' R. Eleazar said: 'Israel also at that time [Tr. Note: The Zohar evidently adopts the view that the events recorded in this chapter (Ex. XXIV) took place before the giving of the Law. v. Rashi, ad loc.] became qualified for a revelation, and the Shekinah was united with them, and the making of the Covenant and the giving of the Torah all took place at one and the same time; and never again was such a sight vouchsafed to Israel. In the time which is to come the Holy One, blessed be He, will reveal Himself unto His children, so that they shall perceive His full glory eye to eye and face to face, as it is written: "For they shall see eye to eye when the Lord shall bring again Zion" (Isa. LII, 8); and it is also written: "And the glory of the Lord shall be revealed, and all flesh shall see it together" (Ibid. XL, 5) '

TERUMAH

AND THE LORD SPAKE UNTO MOSES SAYING, SPEAK UNTO THE CHILDREN OF ISRAEL THAT THEY TAKE ME A HEAVE OFFERING. R. Hiya, on coming to this portion, quoted the verse, "For Jacob hath chosen Kah unto himself, Israel is his costly possession" (Ps. cxxxv, 4). Said he: 'How beloved must Israel be to the Holy One, blessed be He, seeing that He has chosen them and desired to unite Himself with them and be bound up with them, making them a nation unique throughout all the world, as it is written: "Who is like unto thy people Israel, a unique people on earth?" (2 Sam. VII, 23). And they, too, have chosen Him and bound themselves up with Him, as it is written, "Jacob hath chosen Kah unto himself"

Zohar: Shemoth, Section 2, Page 126b

Yea, for over the other nations He appointed celestial principalities and powers, but reserved Israel for His own special portion ' R. Simeon discoursed on the text: "Who is this (zoth) that looketh forth as the morning, fair as the moon, clear as the sun and terrible as furnished with banners?" (S S. VI, 10). He said: 'The words "Who" and "This" denote the two worlds: the "Who" symbolizing the most supernal sphere, the unknowable beginning of all things, and "This" a lower sphere, the so-called "lower world"; and these two are indissolubly linked together. When they first unite, this lower world "looks forth as the dawn" when it is striving to become bright; when they draw closer, it is as "fair as the moon" when the sun's rays beat upon her; and finally it is "like the sun", when its moonlight becomes full. It is then "terrible as furnished with banners"; yea, mighty to protect all, furnished with power from the supernal world, through "Jacob", the "complete one", who united the two worlds as one. He united them above, and he united them below, and from him issued the twelve holy tribes after the supernal pattern. [Tr. Note: i.e. symbolizing the twelve permutations of the Tetragrammaton.] Jacob, who was "a man of completeness" (Gen. xxv, 27), brought harmony to the two worlds, as has been elsewhere explained. [Tr. Note: By marrying Leah and Rachel. v. Zohar, Genesis, 153b.] Other and lesser men, however, who follow Jacob's example (in marrying two sisters) merely "uncover nakedness" (i.e. dishonour the spirit of righteousness) both above and below, causing antagonism in both worlds, and engendering separation, as it is written: "Neither shalt thou take a wife to her sister in her life time to vex her" (Lev. XVIII, 18). And should it be pointed out that even Jacob was not spared this enmity in wives, as we read that "Rachel was jealous of Leah" (Gen. xxx, I), then would I answer: Surely so! and how could it be otherwise? For the whole longing and the most ardent desire of the lower world (symbolized by Rachel) is to be in all outer seeming like unto the upper world (symbolized by Leah), and to usurp its powers and reign in its stead. So not even Jacob could succeed in bringing perfect harmony into being between them. Other men, therefore (by marrying two sisters), will cause only enmity, separation and chaos, "removing the veil" from the hidden places in regard both to the world above and to the world below. "Who" and "This" are termed "sisters", because they are united in love and sisterly affection. They are also called "mother and daughter". And he who "uncovers their nakedness" shall find no portion in the world to come, nor any part in the Faith ' R. Simeon continued: 'We have a tradition that when the Holy One, blessed be He, created the world, He engraved in the midst of the mysterious, ineffable and most glorious lights, the letters Yod, He, Vau, He, which are in themselves the synthesis of all worlds both above and below. The upper was brought to completion by the influence symbolized by the letter Yod, representing the primordial supernal point which issued from the absolutely hidden and unknowable, the mysterious Limitless (En-Sof). Out of this unknowable issued a slender thread of light which was itself concealed and invisible, but which yet contained all other lights, and which received vibrations from That which does not vibrate and reflected light from That which diffused it not. This slender light in turn gave birth to another light wherein to disport and to conceal itself; and in this light were woven and fashioned six impressions which are not known save to that slender light when it goes in to hide itself and shine through the other light. The light which issues from the slender light is mighty and terrible, and it expands and becomes a world which illumines all succeeding worlds–a hidden and unknown world in which dwell six myriads of thousands of supernal powers and hosts. When the worlds were all completed

Zohar: Shemoth, Section 2, Page 127a

they were joined into a single organism, and are symbolized by the letter Vau (=six) when it is united with the veiled world. [Tr. Note: Yod, He.] And this is the esoteric meaning of the words, "For Jacob has chosen Kah unto himself." But when the Vau emerges self-contained from the Yod He, then "Israel attains to his costly possession": that is to say, to other men permission has not been granted to penetrate to the higher point (Binah), but only as far as the "costly possession" (Malkuth), which is a lower grade; and from this they can ascend higher in intention but not in actual attainment, as Jacob did ' R. Judah connected this text with the verse: "O, how (mah) great is thy goodness which thou hast hidden for them that fear thee; which thou hast wrought for them that trust in thee before the sons of men!" (Ps. XXXI, 20). 'This verse', said he, 'has been well enough expounded by the Companions; but the "holy lamp" (R. Simeon) found in it one of the deepest of the esoteric lessons. The supreme grade, esoterically known as "the supernal world", is designated "Mi" ("Who") and the lower grade known as "the lower world" is designated "Mah" ("What?", "How?"), and we have been taught that "Mah" contains an allusion to "meah" - "hundred"- because all the higher grades, when fully realized, are subsumed in it. Why is the world below called "Mah"? Because, although the emergence of the Supernal becomes manifest in that last of all the grades to a greater degree than at any previous stage, it is still mysterious: "What seest thou? What knowest thou?" As to the words "great is Thy goodness", these connote the Foundation of the world, as in the verse, "great goodness towards the house of Israel" (Isa. LXIII, 7). This is here said to be "hidden", because it has been stored away like the primordial light (which is called "good"). The verse continues: "Which Thou has wrought for those who trust in Thee". Yea, for in this Foundation is the fabrication of the whole, of all the world, of souls and spirits; this is the hidden force behind the creation of the (lower) heaven and earth, and this is also the hidden force behind the building of the Tabernacle, which was erected in the likeness both of the world above and of the world below. This is the significance of the words: "that they take me a heave offering": two grades [Tr. Note: Yesod and Malkuth] become united as one in the Tabernacle which is the emblem of that union ' R. Simeon, R. Eleazar, R. Abba, and R. Yose sat one day under a tree in a valley by the Lake of Genessareth. Said R. Simeon: 'How pleasant is the shade of these trees! Surely the beauty and peace of this place is worthy of being crowned with some exposition of the

Torah?' He then began to discourse, saying: 'It is written: "King Solomon made him a palanquin (apiryon) of the trees of Lebanon. He made the pillars thereof of silver, the bottom thereof of gold, the covering of it of purple, the midst thereof being paved with love by the daughters of Jerusalem" (S. S. III, 9, 10). This verse we interpret as follows. Apiryon symbolizes the Palace below which is formed in the likeness of the Palace above. This the Holy One, blessed be He, calls "The Garden of Eden", for He created it in order to satisfy His own ardent desire for joyous and continual communion with the souls of the righteous who have their abode there-these being those souls which have no bodies in this world. These all ascend and are crowned in that place of perfect delight, and have each their appointed places from whence they can perceive the "loveliness of the Lord", and partake of all the delicious streams of pure balsam (aparsamon). This aparsamon symbolizes the hidden Supernal Palace, whereas apiryon is the Palace below, which has no "stay" [Tr. Note: A play on the word semekh, which means both "support, and "the letter S (Aparsamon =apiryon+the letter samekh)] until it obtains it from the upper Palace

Zohar: Shemoth, Section 2, Page 127b

Now the streams of this aparsamon issue forth from the celestial sphere and the souls which have no earthly bodies ascend to imbibe from the light which emerges from them, and to revel therein. As for the souls who are clothed in bodily raiment and garmented with flesh, they ascend likewise and imbibe nourishment, but from the light of the sphere apiryon, for that is the region which appertains to them: which having done, they descend again. They both give and take. They emit sweet savours from the good works which they have wrought in this world, and they imbibe the aroma which was left in the Garden, and of which it is written: "as the savour of the field which the Lord had blessed" (Gen. XXVII, 27), the "field" being the Garden of Eden. And in this Garden all the souls appear, both those who dwell in earthly bodies and those whose sole being and joy is in the world above. The verse proceeds: "King Solomon made him": that is, He made it for His own glory. Should ye ask, But do not the souls of the righteous share the joy with Him? I would say, Most assuredly! For His joy would be as naught without them, since to have pleasure in their companionship is the very essence of His desire and delight. The term "King Solomon" refers to the King "to whom peace belongs"-namely, the Supernal King: and the term "king" by itself refers to the King Messiah. [Tr. note: v. Zohar, Gen. 29a.] "The trees of Lebanon" denotes those trees which the Holy One uprooted and planted in another place, as it is written: "the cedars of Lebanon which he hath planted" (Ps. CIV, 16). Of these trees the apiryon was built. And what are these trees, the "trees of Lebanon"? They are the six primordial Days of Creation. Now each of these Days performs in this apiryon [Tr. note: The world of Beriah or "creation".] the part which was assigned to it.

'By the first ordering, the primeval light which was afterwards stored away was taken from the Right Side and brought into the apiryon by means of a certain "Foundation", and performed its function therein. Afterwards the apiryon produced an image in the likeness of that original light, as is indicated by the words, "Let there be light, and there was light" (Gen. I, 3), the repetition of the word "light" denoting that the first light brought forth another light. This was the first day of the "trees of Lebanon".

'By the second ordering, there was drawn from the Left Side the division of waters through the stroke of a mighty fire, which entered into this apiryon and performed its function therein, dividing between the waters of the Right Side and those of the Left; and afterwards the apiryon brought forth an image in the likeness thereof. This was the second day of the "trees of Lebanon".

'By the third ordering, there was drawn from the sphere of the centre and the Right Side a certain third day which made peace in the world and from which were derived the seeds of all things. This performed its function in the apiryon, and brought forth various species, herbs and grasses and trees. Its likeness was left there, and the apiryon brought forth similar species, and this was the third day of the "trees of Lebanon".

'By the fourth ordering, the light of the sun was kindled to illumine the darkness of the apiryon, and it entered therein to give light, but did not perform its function till the fifth day. The apiryon produced in the likeness thereof, and this was the fourth day of those "trees of Lebanon".

'By the fifth ordering, there was produced a certain movement

Zohar: Shemoth, Section 2, Page 128a

in the waters, which laboured to bring forth the light of the ordering of the fourth day, and it performed its function in the apiryon and brought forth various species; and all remained in suspense until the sixth day, when the apiryon brought forth all that was stored in it, as it is written, "Let the earth bring forth living creature after its kind, etc." (Gen. 1, 24). This was the fifth day of the "trees of Lebanon".

'The sixth ordering was the day on which the apiryon came into completion, and apart from that sixth day of Creation it can have neither completion nor life-energy. But when that day was at length arrived the apiryon was completed, with many spirits, many souls, many beautiful virgins, [Tr. note: The Hekaloth.] privileged to abide in the Palace of the King. In the completion of this day the previous five days are completed also, and the upper and lower spheres are perfectly united in friendship, in joy, and in one ardent desire for the companionship of their King. Thus was the apiryon sanctified with supernal sanctifications and crowned with its crowns, until finally it was exalted with the Crown of Rest and was designated with a noble name, a name of holiness, to wit, Sabbath, which presages rest and peace, the perfect harmonization of all things both above and below. That is the significance of the words, "The King Solomon made him an apiryon out of the trees of Lebanon." He who is worthy of this Apiryon is worthy of all things, is worthy to repose in the peace of the Holy One's shadow, as it is written: "I sat down under his shadow with great delight" (S.S. II, 3). And now, as we ourselves here sit under the shadow of this peace, it behoves us to observe that we really abide in the shadow of the Holy One, within that Apiryon, and remain forever there: and we must crown this place with supernal crowns, so that the trees of that Apiryon may be induced to cover us with a shade yet more comforting.'

So they began to discourse upon holy and supernal matters. R. Simeon first spoke, saying: 'It is written: "They shall take me a heave offering: on the part of everyone whose heart is willing ye shall take my offering." "They shall take Me." This signifies that he who aspires towards piety and fellowship with the Holy One, blessed be He, must not be lax or remiss in his devotion, but must be ready and willing to bring sacrifices according to his strength: "according as the Lord God hath blessed thee" (Deut. XVI, 10). True, it is written, "Come ye, buy wine and milk without money and without price" (Isa. LV, 1), and this in reference to work on behalf of the Holy One. But this only indicates that, whereas knowledge of the Holy One and of His Torah can be acquired without price or fee, the doing of good works for the sake of Heaven requires sacrifice and must be "paid for" with full price; otherwise the doer is not worthy to draw down unto himself the spirit of holiness from above. In the book of sorcery from which Ashmedai taught King Solomon, it is written that he who desires to remove from himself the spirit of impurity and to subdue that spirit, must be prepared to pay in return for the fulfilment of his wishes whatever is demanded. For the spirit of impurity tempts the heart of man with many allurements, in order to take up its abode with him. But the spirit of holiness is not so: it demands a full price and strenuous effort, purification of one's self and one's dwelling, devotion of heart and soul; and even so one will be lucky to win it to take up its abode with him. Therefore one must beware and walk straitly according to the paths and ways of righteousness, turning neither to the right hand nor to the left; for otherwise, even if it had entered into a man, it will straightway depart from him, and thereafter it will indeed be passing hard to recall it again. Hence the expression, "Let them buy ("lakah" also means "to buy") unto Me". OF EVERY MAN: from everyone deserving the name of "man", that is, from everyone who prevails over his evil inclination. "That giveth it willingly, with his heart"-namely,

Zohar: Shemoth, Section 2, Page 128b

he with whom the Holy One is well pleased, for He-the Lord-is Himself the "Heart", as it is written: "My heart said to thee" (Ps. XXVII, 9); "the rock of my heart" (Ibid. LXXIII, 21) so also here, "Ye should take me a heave offering from him with whom I am well pleased", for there alone can the acceptable sacrifice be found, and in no other place soever. And how may one recognize a person with whom the Holy One is pleased and in whom He has His abode? When we observe that a man endeavours to serve the Holy One in joy, with his heart, soul and will, then we can be quite sure that the Shekinah has Her abode in him. Such a man is worthy to be well paid for his teaching and companionship. Therefore the ancients said: "Buy thee a companion" (i.e. teacher). [Tr. note: Pirke Aboth, I, 6.] Buy him for a good price, in order to merit the Shekinah's presence. Therefore also one must pursue and run after the sinner and "buy" him for a good price, in order that the filth of sin may be purged away from him and the spirit of impurity, the emanation of the "other side", be subdued. He who succeeds in redeeming such a sinner can justly consider himself the "creator" of the renewed and quickened soul, and such an act is the greatest praise (of God) imaginable, and it exalts the glory of the Holy One, blessed be He, more than any other circumstance or deed imaginable. Why so? Because by his action in turning the sinner from wickedness he helps to bring into subjection the "other side". Therefore it says of Aaron: "And he turned many from sin" (Mal. II, 6), and hence, "My covenant was with him, life and peace" (Ibid. 5). See now. He who seeks a sinner takes him by the hand, and induces him to give up his evil way, such a one is elevated as none other can be, yea, even with three particular deserts, namely by his causing the "other side" to be subdued, by magnifying the glory of the Holy One, and by sustaining, through the merit of his good works, the very equilibrium of the worlds, both the upper and the lower spheres. Concerning such a man it is written: "My covenant was with him: life and peace." He will be worthy to see his children's children; he is worthy to enjoy this world and the world to come, and none of the lords of judgement shall retain any power whatsoever over him to chastise him, either in this world or in the world to come. He will pass through twelve gates (of the firmament), and none will hinder him. Concerning such a one it is written: "His seed shall be mighty upon earth, the generation of the upright shall be blessed... His righteousness endureth forever. Unto the righteous there ariseth light in the darkness" (Ps. CXII, 2-4).

'In a certain Upper Chamber there are three colours which burn in one flame. The flame emanates from the South, which is the Right Side. The three mysterious colours which compose this flame proceed in three separate directions: one goes upward, one down, and one flickers, appearing and disappearing when the sun shines. The colour which ascends is the first to appear. It is of a whiteness more dazzling than any known. It enters into the flame and is a little absorbed into it, though without losing its identity. It rests upon the top of that Chamber, and when the Israelites enter the synagogues and pray, as soon as they are arrived at the end of the Geulah (Redemption) prayer- namely, at the "Blessed art Thou, O Lord, who redeemest Israel" and go straight on to the Amidah prayer- the white and lucent descends upon the top of the Chamber and weaves a crown of the prayers of the people; and a herald rises in Heavenly courts and proclaims: "Blessed are ye, holy people, for that ye perform (make) good (tob)l [Tr. note: H synonym for the Sefirah, Yesod or Zaddik.]before the face of the Holy One, blessed be He!" This is the inner significa of the words, "I have done what is good in thine eyes" (Isa. XXXVIII, 3): namely, that King Hezekiah connected by devotions "Redemption" with "Prayer". For when the praying people have reached the words "praises to the suprem God" (in the last hymn before the "Eighteen Benedictions") and the white brightness rests, as we have said, upon th top of that Chamber, the Zaddik is aroused to join the appropriate Place in love and joy, and all the "limbs" are united as one in one desire, the higher with the lower, and all the celestial lights sparkle and glow with divine supernal fire, and all are united in this Righteous who is designated "Good", as it is written, "Say ye to the righteous that he is good" (Isa. III, 10). And He unites them all in the silence of perfect joy, and kisses of friendship; and everything is united in the Chamber. And when the worshippers arrive at the prayer "Grant abundant peace" (at the end of the "Eighteen Benedictions"), the "River that goes out of Eden" does his service in this Assembly and all must take leave from the King, and no human being nor any other created thing may thereafter be found in that Presence, nor may any petitionary prayers be prayed then,

Zohar: Shemoth, Section 2, Page 129a

but one must "fall upon the countenance" (say propitiatory prayers). Why? Because that time is the time of service, and every being that dwells upon the earth must stand abashed before his Lord, covering his face in great awe, and let his soul join the service of the souls which are contained in that Chamber. Then the colour which descends hovers over the lower part of the Assembly, and another herald appears, like unto the first, and he cries with a loud voice: "Ye upper and lower beings! Bring witness of him who, by reclaiming sinners becomes a 'maker of souls', that he deserves to be crowned and is worthy to enter now into the presence of the King and the Matrona, because the King and the Matrona enquire after him!" Then two witnesses who are among the number of the "eyes of the Lord which run to and fro through the whole earth" (Zech. IV, 10), and who stand behind the curtain, emerge therefrom and testify, saying: "We testify indeed for that man." Blessed is his lot, for on his account his father shall be blessed and remembered into good, because he has re-made souls in the earthly sphere-souls even of sinners who had been captured by the "other side". Thus is the glory of the Holy One exalted in perfect joy. Then an angel appears who is the storekeeper of the celestial figures of the righteous, and this angel's name is Jehudiam because of his office ("over the people of the Jews") and he is crowned with a crown on which is engraven the Holy Name. The Holy One makes him a sign and he comes forward, bearing the image of the man who has reclaimed souls of sinners, and places it before the King and the Matrona. And I bring heaven and earth to witness that at that moment they deliver to him that figure; for there is no righteous person in the world whose image is not engraved in heaven under the authority of that angel. Seventy keys also are delivered into his hand-keys of all the treasures of the Lord. Then the King blesses that image with all the blessings wherewith He blessed Abraham when he reclaimed the souls of sinners. Then the Holy One, blessed be He, gives a sign to four groups of supernal beings, who take that image and show it seventy hidden worlds of which none are worthy except those who have reclaimed the souls of sinners. If only the sons of men knew and perceived what rewards follow the endeavours of the righteous to save sinners, they would assuredly run after them with the same ardour with which they run after life itself. A poor man's benefactor gains many good things, many supernal treasures, because he helps him to exist; but even he cannot be compared to him who endeavours to save the soul of a sinner. For the latter causes the breaking of the power of the "other side", of the "other gods"; he is the cause of the Holy One's exaltation on His Throne of Glory. He gives the sinner a new soul. Happy indeed is his lot!

'The second colour, which is both hidden and revealed, appears in its full glory at the moment when the Israelites are arrived at the Kedushah (Sanctus) of the Order of Prayer, [Tr. note: The Kedushah which occurs in the prayer, "And a redeemer shall come unto Zion."] for this is the sanctification which the children of Israel pronounce over and above those uttered by the supernal angels whose associates they are. This colour shows itself all the time that Israel are pronouncing that sanctification in order to defend the Israelites from the angels, who otherwise would take note of them and call down punishment upon them from above. Then a herald appears and proclaims with a loud voice: "Ye who are above and ye who are below, remove all such as are haughty because of their learning!" For we are taught that man must be humble in this world in regard to his knowledge of the Torah; only in the future world is the pride of learning permitted. In this Kedushah we must be on guard and hide our knowledge in quietness among ourselves, [Tr. note: By saying it in Aramaic.] more than in those which we say in company with the angels. [Tr. note:' The Kedushah in the benediction, "Fashioner of light", and the Kedushah in the Amidah.] in one of these we praise those self-same angels, and for this they permit us to pass through the upper gates.

Also we recite it

Zohar: Shemoth, Section 2, Page 129b

...nguage (Hebrew); for this reason, too, they permit us to pass through the heavenly gates; and by means ...tification we enter into still higher gates. It might be said that we deceive the angels by thus praising ...deception is permissible, for the heavenly angels are holier than we, and are able to derive and imbibe ...f holiness, and were we not to have an extra sanctification we would be unable to associate with them in ... or communion of praise, and the glory of the Holy One, blessed be He, would so be prevented from ...ompletion throughout both the upper and lower spheres at one and the same time. Therefore we endeavour ...rselves their associates, in order that the glory of the Holy One, blessed be He, may be exalted in all the ...he Kedushah which comes at the end [Tr. note: In the prayer, "And a redeemer shall come unto Zion."] is in ..., and this may be recited even by an individual-that is privately-but the Hebrew words of the Kedushah proper, ...is in Hebrew, must only be recited in a congregation of ten persons or more, because the Shekinah unites Herself ...the holy tongue, and all sanctifications with which the Shekinah is connected can be uttered only in the presence of ...least ten persons, for it is written: "And I shall be sanctified in the midst of the children of Israel" (Lev. XXII, 32). The ...erm "children of Israel" further implies that such a sanctification must be in the holy tongue, which is Israel's, the other nations speaking other languages. It may be objected: "Why, then, must the Kaddish, which is in Aramaic, be recited only in the presence of ten persons?" The answer is, that the sanctification expressed in the Kaddish is unlike the sanctification of the thrice-repeated "Holy, Holy, Holy", for this prayer, the Kaddish, ascends into all sides and all spheres both above and below, and to every side of Faith, [Tr. note: i.e. the Sefiroth.] and breaks down iron walls and weighty seals and all the shells [Tr. note: The k'lifoth.] and defences of evil, so that by its merits the glory of the Holy One, blessed be He, is more greatly exalted than through any other prayer, because it causes the power of the "other side" to wane and its empire to decline; and therefore it must be said in Aramaic, which is the language of the "other side", and one should respond in a loud voice and with a firm spirit: "Amen, May His great Name be blessed", in order that the power of the "other side" may be quelled and the Holy One be exalted in His glory above all things. And when the power of the "other side" is thus vanquished and broken by the power of holiness expressed in the Kaddish, then the Holy One is exalted in glory and remembers His children, and remembers His Name. So because of His exaltation this prayer must be recited in the presence of ten. Blessed forever is the holy people to whom the Holy One gave the holy Torah in order that they might be made worthy, by her aid, of the world to come.'

Then R. Simeon turned to the companions and said: 'Ye are worthy of the world to come; therefore, because we have begun to discourse upon matters concerned with the Crown of the supernal Kingdom, I shall continue to speak on your behalf in regard to the same subject, and the Holy One will assuredly reward you in the sphere of that Kingdom. And the breath of your mouths will ascend into heaven, as if ye yourselves had stirred up these words.' Then he continued, saying:

AND THIS IS THE OFFERINC WHICH YE SHALL TAKE OF THEM: GOLD AND SILVER AND BRASS. This verse applies both to the higher side, the side of holiness, and to the lower, the "other" side. Observe that when the Holy One created the world, He began to create from the side of silver, that is, Mercy, which is the right side, because that silver was above; but in the work of the Tabernacle, which was built according to its prototype (the universe), He began His creation from the left side and then proceeded to the right side, because the Tabernacle was from the left side.

'It is written: "Morning and evening and at noon will I pray and cry aloud" (Ps. LV, 17). We have referred on another occasion to this verse. It speaks of three seasons for prayer, and the companions have interpreted the significance of the three times in the following way' "Evening" is the mirror which has no radiance, "morning" the radiant mirror, while "noon" is symbolic of a place which should properly be called "darkness", because it adjoins the evening, only it is designated by the very opposite by a certain elegance of language, just as, on occasion, black

Zohar: Shemoth, Section 2, Page 130a

is called white, while sometimes white is called black; we read, for instance, of Moses' wife that she was black (Num. XII, 1), and Israel are compared to the Ethiopians (Amos IX, 7). The evening prayer is not obligatory, and there is no fixed time for it, because the evening is influenced by the "other side", which is dark and rules by night. The limbs and fatty portions of sacrifices used to be burnt on the altar in the evening, and from that moment numbers of groups of demons which issue and have sway by night receive their nourishment. It may be said, have we not been taught that the messengers of the "other side", of the spirit of impurity, had by rights no power in the Holy Land, and so if by this means the Israelites were to rouse them, would they not be doing something forbidden? The answer would be that the smoke of those parts was wont to ascend, not as the smoke of other sacrifices, which did ascend in a straight line heavenward: for these fumes rose and dispersed into a cavern in the North, where dwell all the hosts of evil spirits, and when the smoke arose, as we have said, as it floated upward in a crooked line towards that place, all those malevolent beings would feed on it, and so would remain where they were, dispersing not throughout the earth. One particular evil spirit was appointed over the others in that northerly cavern: his name was Synegoria, [Tr. note: Lit. "advocacy, justification. Perhaps a corruption for Sangorin (frorr. sanguis), "bloodthirsty".] and when the smoke began to ascend crookedly and to draw near, he and sixty thousand myriads of other spirits would rise up to meet it in order to imbibe nourishment therefrom. They would stand within their cavern and then pass through the door called "keri" (lit. defilement). It is to this door that there is an allusion in the words, "If ye walk contumaciously (in keri) unto me, then will I also walk contumaciously unto you" (Lev. XXVII, 24, 25); that is, the wrath and anger which come out from that door called Keri will be wreaked on those who walk contumaciously. These are the spirits who roam about by night. When the souls of the righteous emerge from the earth into the upper spaces in order to ascend heavenward, these same spirits also appear and contend with them, in order to prevent them from reaching and entering their heavenly habitation and rest. And, indeed, they bar the way to all save only the souls of the most supreme saints, which break through all firmaments and aethers until they reach the highest sphere. The demoniac hosts speak lying words to the children of men, disguising themselves in other forms, and seducing them till they defile themselves. But at the time when the limbs and the fat of the offerings were burnt, the smoke provided them a full repast of the kind suited to their station, and being busy with this they forgot to come forth and roam about the Holy Land. Now the evening prayer, as I have said, is not obligatory, because these bands of demons participate in the dominion of the night, and only Jacob was able to fix it. However, although the evening prayer is not legally obligatory, yet it has a protective influence against the terrors of the night, against the fear of Gehenna, for at night the wicked receive a punishment double that which is executed upon them by day. Therefore the Israelites introduce the evening prayer for weekdays with the verses: "And he is merciful, he forgiveth iniquity, and destroyeth not: yea, many a time he turneth his anger away, and doth not stir up all his wrath" (Ps. LXXVIII, 28). This is recited because of the fear of Gehenna. But on Sabbath, when there is no fear of the punishment of Gehenna nor of any judgement, one may not recite these verses lest he thus awaken the evil spirits, causing them to appear and become active. To counteract the fear of the accuser and slanderer of souls we conclude the Hashkibenu prayer ("Cause us, O Lord, to lie down in peace") with the words: "Blessed art Thou, O Lord, who guardest Thy people Israel forever. Amen". To counteract the fear of the many devils and accusers which are present in the night and have power to injure anyone who leaves his house at that time, we say: "Guard our going out and our coming in unto life and unto peace." From the fear of all these things we deliver in trust our bodies, souls and spirits to Heaven above, to the Supernal Kingdom which has dominion over all of them. Therefore we recite every night the evening prayers, performing all this to counteract the mysterious influences of the evil spirits now that there are no sacrifices to keep them at bay. At midnight, when the north wind awakens, it beats against all the abodes of those malevolent spirits, cracking in twain a gigantic mighty rock, the stronghold of the "other side", and rushes about everywhere, both above and below; and all

Zohar: Shemoth, Section 2, Page 130b

the evil demons return to their places, for their power is then broken and they have no influence. Then the Holy One, blessed be He, enters the Garden of Eden to have joyous fellowship with the righteous, as has been related before. When morning comes, the light of the lamp which rules the midnight hours hides before the light of the day. The morning has now full sway and dominion and the reign of the night is past. This is the morning of primaeval light, the morning which sheds beneficence throughout all the worlds. From it all celestial and terrestrial beings imbibe nourishment. It waters the Garden with supernal dews. It guards the whole Universe. Here is a mystery which is entrusted to "those who know the measures" of things spiritual. He who has to set out on a journey in the morning should rise at break of day and at a certain specially ordained moment turn and look towards the east. He will then behold a kind of letters which break through the surface of the sky, some ascending and some descending. These are flashed forth from those letters with which the heavens and the earth were created. If the watcher is cognizant of the mystery of the letters which form the mystic Holy Name of forty-two letters, and if he should in this hour be mindful of them with devout intent, with a loving heart, then will he behold in the luminous heaven six Yods, three upon the right side and three upon the left; also three Vaus, which ascend and descend and sparkle in the firmament. These are the number of the initial letters of the words of the priestly blessing. He should then say his morning prayers and set forth upon his journey, because, verily, the Shekinah Herself goes before him; happy is his lot! When morning arrives, a mysterious pillar appears in the South, in that portion of the firmament beneath which the Garden of Eden is stretched: this is a different pillar from the one which is in the midst of the Garden. The pillar set in the South flashes with the brightness of three colours, purple-woven. On that pillar there is a branch, on which three birds sit, chirping hymns of praise. One begins: "Hallelukah! Praise, O ye servants of the Lord, praise the Name of the Lord!" The second then takes up the chant thus: "Blessed be the Name of the Lord from this time forth and forevermore." Then the third sings: "From the rising of the sun until the going down of the same the Lord's Name is to be praised" (Ps. CXIII, 1-3). Then a herald proclaims: "Prepare yourselves, O ye supernal saints, who sing praises to your Lord! Prepare yourselves for the praisegiving of the day, when day separates itself from night! Happy is the lot of him who rises in the morning from the praise of the Torah which has engrossed him in the night watches." Then it is time for morning prayer. It is written: "The burden of Dumah. He calleth to me out of Seir, Watchman, what of the night? Watchman, what of the night? The watchman said, The morning cometh, and also the night: If ye will inquire, inquire ye: return, come" (Is. XXI, 11). This verse has been explained in references to Israel's exile in Seir (i.e. Edom=Rome). Israel says to the Holy One: "Watchman, what of the night?" meaning, "What will become of us in this exile, which is like the darkness of night?" Says the watchman, namely, the Holy One: "The morning hath come once (in the Egyptian exile) when I made My light to shine unto you, when I liberated you, when I ordained you for My service, when I gave you the Torah in order that you might achieve eternal life, but ye have forsaken My Torah", and therefore came also the "night" of this present exile. If ye will inquire from "the book of the Lord" (Ibid. XXXIV, 16) and read therein, ye will find there the reason and cause of your exile and the means of redemption. If you so inquire there, the Book will call upon you, "Return with a perfect repentance and come near to Me". A more esoteric explanation is as follows. First, in regard to the word "burden", it should be noted that there were six grades in the divine revelation to the prophets: "appearance" (mahzeh), "vision" (hazon), "revelation" (hezyon), "aspect" (hazuth), "word", and "burden". The first five aspects are all like unto the vision of one who beholds a reflection of light from behind a wall, and some of them are as the vision of one who sees the light of the sun through a lantern. But "burden" signifies that the light came with great difficulty, and was barely revealed. Here it was even a "burden of silence" (dumah), for which no words could be found. "He calleth to me from Seir." It does not say who calleth whom-whether the Holy One calls to the prophet, or the prophet to the Holy One. But there can be no doubt that the prophecy hints at the secret of faith, and that the faithful prophet is recording how the voice of the mystic object of faith called to him, to wit: "He calleth to me out of Seir".

Zohar: Shemoth, Section 2, Page 131a

Similarly it says elsewhere: "And he rose up out of Seir to them" (Deut. XXXIII, 2), not to Seir, the reason being that the mystic object of Faith is contained in grades within grades, each more recondite than the other; shell within shell, brain within brain. We have referred to this fact in regard to the vision of Ezekiel: "A whirlwind came out of the North, a great cloud, and a fire infolding itself, and a brightness was about it, and out of the midst thereof as the colour of amber, out of the midst of the fire. Also out of the midst thereof the likeness of four living creatures" (Ezek. I, 3-5). Grades within grades, as we have said. In the same manner the Holy One, blessed be He, revealed Himself to Israel: "He came from Sinai"-this was the most hidden grade of revelation; "He rose up from Seir unto them"-this was a second, a more open revelation, the shell nearest to the brain; "He shined forth from Mount Paran"-this was still another aspect of revelation. Then it says, "He came with ten thousands of holy beings" (cf. Deut. ibid.). This is the highest praise, that, although He revealed Himself in all these grades, yet the commencement of the revelation was from the place which is the root of all, to wit, "the thousands of holy beings"-the last supernal grade. So here, "Seir" is the grade cleaving to the highest. The "watchman" mentioned here is Metatron, the ruler of the night. It is written: "Watchman, what of the night (laylah)? Watchman, what of the night (lail)?" What is the difference between laylah and lail? They are one and the same, only in one part of the night the "other side" reigns and in the other it has no such sway; "lail" requires guarding, therefore it lacks the letter he at the end, it is the early part of the night before midnight, "the night (lail) of watchings" (EX. XII); from midnight on it is laylah (cf. Ps. CXXXIX, 13). "The watchman" here is Metatron, who said: "The morning cometh"-the morning prayer which rules the night. One must not suppose that it comes by itself, the male being so separated from the female, for it says, "And also the night": not so, for they are perpetually together and are never separated. And the voice proclaimed this: "The morning cometh and also the night." "Both are prepared for you. From now on if ye would pray your prayers, in supplication before the Holy King-do so. Return to your Lord, and come!" Even as a father is prepared to receive his prodigal children and to have mercy on them, the Holy One, morning and night, calls unto His children, saying: "Come!" Happy is the holy people whose Lord seeks them and beckons them to come unto Him. Because of that honouring and favour the holy people must unite and come to the Synagogue; and he who comes first unites himself with the Shekinah in one bond. Indeed, blessed is he who is found first in the Synagogue, for he stands in the grade of "Righteous" along with the very Shekinah Herself. This is the inner meaning of the words, "Those who seek me early will find me" (Prov. VIII, 17). He indeed reaches a high degree. But, it may be objected, we have been taught that when the Holy One, blessed be He, enters a Synagogue and finds there less than the ten requisite male persons, He is angry; how, then, canst thou say that the one who comes first is united with the Shekinah and is in the grade of "Righteous"? The following parable will explain. A King issued an order to the citizens of his capital, to meet him one and all at a certain place and at a certain time. While the rest were still making ready, one hastened to present himself at the appointed place. Then the King came and found him waiting. He asked him where the rest of the citizens were. The man answered: "My Lord King, I, as thou seest, have arrived first, but my fellow-townsmen are upon the road and will soon be here as well, according to Your Majesty's command". This pleased the King, and he entered into conversation with the man and became quite friendly with him. In the meantime

Zohar: Shemoth, Section 2, Page 131b

the others arrived and the King received them graciously and sent them away in peace. Now had no man been swift and prompt to obey the command of his lord, and to inform him of the near approach of his neighbours, would not the King have been much wroth? Similarly, when the Shekinah comes and finds in the Synagogue one person who has arrived there before anyone else, it is to Her even as though all were indeed present, for the Holy Shekinah joins company with him and together they wait for the others to come, that the prayers may be started. She becomes closely acquainted with him, and promotes him to the grade of "Righteous". But if no one had come in time, she would have said, "Why, when I came, was there no man?" (Isa. L, 2); and note that it does not say "there were no ten men," but "no man", meaning, "There was no one man waiting to unite himself with Me and become My companion and friend, to be a 'man of God' in the grade of Righteous." Moreover, if one day the favoured man is missing, She is greatly concerned, and makes inquiries about him, as it is written: "Who is among you that feareth the Lord, that obeyeth the voice of his servant...?" (Isa. L, 10). As we have pointed out, "His servant" is Metatron, who calls from "Seir" to men to repent and pray. Therefore, as we have said, he who comes early to the Synagogue merits the grade "Righteous".

'When morning comes and the congregation is assembled in the Synagogue, service must begin with hymns and psalms of David. We have already made clear that the purpose of the liturgy is to stir up Mercy and Lovingkindness both in the higher and lower range, to bring into being redemptive acts, and to awaken joy; and this was the essential significance of the Levitic service, namely to awaken love and joy above by means of song and praise. Woe unto him who engages in conversation of a secular nature in the Synagogue, for he causes separation, he weakens the Faith. Woe unto him, for he has no part in the God of Israel, since by his lack of awe before the Divine Presence he as much as denies the reality thereof, contemning the influence of the power which comes from above. For when Israel is occupied with the singing of psalms and hymns of praise and with prayer, three groups of supernal angels also assemble. One consists of holy beings who praise Him in the day-time, for there are also those who praise Him at night, in company with the Israelites; the second group consists of those holy angels who are always present in the midst of Israel at every Sanctus, and who have sway over all those celestial beings who are roused by Israel's sanctifications here below; the third celestial host is composed of those "virgins" whose office is to be maids of honour to the Shekinah, and to prepare Her to meet the King. These are the most supreme groups of angels, who join the worshippers in their singing of the Psalms of King David. When the Israelites have ended their singing of the Psalms of David, they sing the song of Moses ("The Song of the Sea"). Why do the Psalms of David come before the Song of the Sea? Does not the "written Torah" (the Pentateuch) take precedence of the Oral Law, and even of the Prophets and the Writings, of which latter the Psalms form a part? The reason is that just because of its importance above all other hymns and because the Community of Israel cannot be perfected except by means of the written Torah,

Zohar: Shemoth, Section 2, Page 132a

it must be recited in close proximity to the prayer said when seated. At the hour when the Song of the Sea is recited the Community of Israel is crowned with the crown wherewith the Holy One, in the time that is to be, will crown the King Messiah. That crown is engraved with Holy Names, those same Names which glittered as crowns of fire upon the head of the Holy One Himself on the day when Israel crossed the Sea and Pharaoh and his hosts were drowned therein. Therefore that song must be recited with special devoutness, and he who is able to recite this hymn in the present world will be found worthy to behold King Messiah in the hour of His crowning and to sing then this song of redemption. All this is beyond dispute.

'When the Yishtabah hymn is reached, the Holy One takes this crown and sets it before Him, and the Community of Israel prepares herself to meet her King. She must be attended by the thirteen attributes of the Divine Mercy wherewith she is blessed. These are the thirteen aspects of praise, enumerated during the course of that hymn: song, praise; hymn and psalm; strength and dominion; victory, power and greatness; adoration and glory; holiness-these together make twelve, and unto these is added Malkuth-sovereignty-which is the thirteenth, and whose office is to unite all the rest in one bond, for it (Sovereignty) receives blessings from the others. Because of these things the worshipper must concentrate his whole mind upon these thirteen attributes, and be careful not to disturb their sacred unity by conversing between the lines of the hymn. Anyone who should so disturb that unity by secular talk causes a flame to emerge from under the wings of the Cherubim, which cries out with a mighty voice: "Here is a man who has cut short the praise of the Holy One's majesty! Let him be himself cut short, so that he should not behold the glorious majesty of the Holy King!" as it is written: "And seeth not the majesty of the Lord" (Isa. XXVI, 10). For those thirteen attributes are the majesty of the Lord. From then on He is "the God to whom thanksgivings are due" (a part of the above hymn). He is the supernal King to whom perfect peace belongs; for all these praises come from the Community of Israel here below, a "song of songs" directed towards "Solomon" (Shelomoh), namely to the King to whom peace (shalom) belongs.

'Then follows the Yozer benediction: "Blessed art Thou... who formest light, and createst all things", the initial letters of the words of one verse of which contain the twenty-two letters of the Alphabet, the small letters, that is-for there are large letters and small, of which-the small ones represent the Divine activity in the lower world, and the large ones the world to come.

[Note: The last 20 lines of the Hebrew text do not appear in our translation.]

Zohar: Shemoth, Section 2, Page 132b

[Note: The Hebrew text on this page is not translated.]

Zohar: Shemoth, Section 2, Page 133a

[Note: The first 17 lines of the Hebrew text do not appear in our translation.]

'It is written: "And she (the Shunammite) said unto her husband, Behold now, I know that this is an holy man of God which passeth by us continually. Let us make a little chamber on the wall, and let us set before him a bed, and a table, and a stool, and a candlestick" (2 Kings IV, 9, 10). Here we have an allusion to the order of prayer. "Behold now, I know" refers to the concentration of mind during prayer; "that he is an holy man of God" refers to the supernal world which sitteth upon its Throne of Glory and from whence emanate all sanctifications and which sanctifies all worlds; "passeth by us continually" with the sanctification wherewith the worlds above are nourished, he also sanctifies us here below, for there can be no completion of the sanctification above without sanctification below, as it is written: "I shall be sanctified in the midst of the children of Israel" (Lev. XXII, 32). Therefore, "let us make a little chamber": let us have an ordered service as a stay for the Shekinah, who is called "wall", as in the verse, "And Hezekiah turned his face to the wall" (Isa. XXXVIII, 2). This stay created by our prayers and praises consists of a bed, a table, a stool, and a candlestick. By our evening prayers we provide Her with a bed; by our hymns of praise and by reciting the section of the sacrifice in the morning we provide Her with a table. By the morning prayers, which are said sitting, and with the proclamation of the Divine Unity (the Shema), we provide Her with a stool; and by means of those prayers which must be said standing ('Amidah) and of the Kaddish and Kedushah prayers and benedictions we provide Her with a candlestick. Blessed is the man who thus endeavours daily to give hospitality to the Holy One. Blessed is he in this world and blessed shall he be in the world to come. For these four groups of prayers equip the Shekinah with beauty, joy and lustre, to greet Her Spouse with delight and ecstasy day by day, through the worship of the holy people. The "bed" was given to Jacob to prepare, therefore he ordered the evening prayer; the "table" was prepared by King David in the Psalms which he wrote ("Thou preparest a table before me" (Ps. XXIII, 5)); the "stool" was prepared by Abraham, through his close union with the Lord, wherewith he benefited the souls of all the sons of men. The candlestick

Zohar: Shemoth, Section 2, Page 133b

was prepared by Isaac, who sanctified the Name of the Holy One before the eyes of the whole world, and lighted the supernal light in that sanctification. Therefore the Holy People must direct its mind towards the supernal world, and prepare for the Lord of the House a bed, a table, a stool, and a candlestick, in order that perfection and harmony may reign undisturbed every day, both above and below.

'At the time when Israel is proclaiming the unity-the mystery contained in the Shema-with a perfect intention, a light comes forth from the hidden supernal world, which divides into seventy lights, and those seventy lights into the seventy luminous branches of the Tree of Life. Then the Tree and all the other trees of the Garden of Eden emit sweet odours and praise their Lord, for at that time the Matrona prepares Herself to enter under the shade of the canopy, there to unite herself with her Spouse; and all the supernal potencies unite in one longing and one will to be united in perfect union, without any separation soever. Then the Spouse makes ready likewise to enter the Canopy in order to unite Himself with the Matrona. Therefore we proclaim loudly: "Hear, O Israel; prepare thyself, for thy Husband has come to receive thee." And also we say: "The Lord our God, the Lord is one", which signifies that the two are united as one, in a perfect and glorious union, without any flaw of separation to mar it. As soon as the Israelites say, "The Lord is One", to arouse the six aspects, these six unite each with each and ascend in one ardour of love and desire. The symbol of this is the letter Vau (because its numerical value is six) when it stands alone without being joined to any other letter. Then the Matrona makes herself ready with joy, and adorns herself with delight, and Her attendants accompany Her, and in hushed silence She encounters her Spouse; and Her handmaids proclaim, "Blessed be the Name of the Glory of His Kingdom forever and ever." These words are said in a whisper, for so she must be introduced to her Spouse. Blessed is the people which perceives these things, ordering its prayers in accordance with this mystery of the Faith! At the time when the Spouse is united with the Matrona a herald comes forth from the south, crying: "Awaken, O ye supernal hosts, and unfurl the banners of love in honour of your Lord!" Then one of the leaders of the celestial array-he whose name is Boel (God is in him)-stands forth, and in his hands are four keys which he obtained one from each of the four corners of the earth.

One key has upon it the sign of the letter Yod engraved; the second the letter He'; and the third the letter Vau; and these three keys he lays beneath the boughs of the Tree of Life. Then these three become one. Then the fourth and last key, which bears upon it the second letter He', joins the three which have become one. And all the angelic hosts enter by means of those keys into the Garden of Eden, where with one voice they proclaim the Divine unity at the selfsame moment as it is proclaimed here below. Then the Shekinah, the Bride, is conducted to the Palace of the King, Her Bridegroom, for now He stands complete in all His supernal goodness and can supply Her with all that She needs. Thus her attendants bring Her in unto Him in silence. Why in silence? In order that no "stranger" (evil potencies) should participate in her joy. As He united Himself above according to six aspects, so also She unites Herself below according to six other aspects, so that the oneness may be completed,

Zohar: Shemoth, Section 2, Page 134a

both above and below, as it is written: "The Lord will be One, and his Name One" (Zech. XIV, 9): Six words above- Shema Israel Tetragrammaton Elohenu Tetragrammaton ehad, corresponding to the six aspects, and six words below- baruk shem kebod malkuto le'olam waed (Blessed be the Name, etc.), corresponding to the six other aspects. The Lord is one above; and His Name is One below. We say this response silently, although it is a triumphant expression of the Oneness, because of the "evil eye", which still has power under the present dispensation; but in the future (Messianic Age) when the "evil eye" will have ceased to exist and will have no dominion whatsoever over this world, then we shall proclaim the Divine Unity and its full accomplishment openly and in a loud voice. At present, as the "other side" still cleaves to the Shekinah, She is not entirely One, and therefore, although even in this present time we proclaim the unity, we do so silently, symbolizing it by the letters of the word wa'ed (ever), which are equivalent by certain permutations to those of the word ehad (one). But in the time that is to be, when that other side shall be removed from the Shekinah and pass away from the world, then shall that unity be proclaimed openly. When She enters the canopy and is united with the Supernal King, then we awaken the joy of the Right and of the Left, as it is written: "Thou shalt love the Lord thy God with all thy heart", etc., that is, without any fear or foreboding, because the "other side" comes not near and has no power here. But whilst Her servants are bringing Her to the King they must keep a great and solemn silence. Of this Jacob is symbolic. Before his death, when he was about to speak of the "end of days" (and the Shekinah left him) he said to his sons: "Perchance some stain is attached to me or to my seed?" But they replied: "Nay, there is no such stain, nor is any fault found. Thine own heart is possessed only by the One, and as for us-we have no contact with the 'other side' or any of its evil minions; on the contrary we, like thyself, are united with the King alone, since all our will and intent has been to separate from the 'other side'." Then Jacob said: "Blessed be the Name of the glory of His Kingdom forever and ever." In that hour Jacob and his sons became for a space, as it were, living portraits here on earth of the Shekinah Herself. Jacob symbolized the six sides of the supernal world as a single whole, and his sons were shaped to the likeness of the six aspects as manifested in the lower world. Now he desired to reveal to them a certain "end", for, as we have pointed out elsewhere, [Tr. note: Zohar, Genesis, 62b] there is one "end of days" (kez ha-yamin), which refers to the Holy Kingdom, the mystery of Faith, the mystery of the King of Heaven; and another "end of days" (kez ha-yamim),

Zohar: Shemoth, Section 2, Page 134b

which is the mystery of the Guilty King, the "other King", ruler of the powers of darkness, and that end is called "the end of all flesh". Now when Jacob perceived that the Shekinah was withdrawing from him, he questioned his sons, as we have pointed out. And as Jacob and his sons proclaimed the union of the world above and the world below, so also must we. Blessed is he who concentrates his mind and will, with true humility and longing, upon this mystery. Blessed is he in this world and blessed shall he be in the world to come!' Said R. Hamnuna the Ancient: 'This stirring up of the unity has indeed been rightly and justly expounded, and that which we have just now heard is indeed very true; and in the future time these word's which we have now uttered will stand before the Ancient of Days and in no wise be abashed.'

He then began to expound this passage as follows. '"They shall take Me a heave offering." Here we have displayed an inclusive union of the above with the below, for it does not say "They shall take a heave offering", but "They shall take Me a heave offering", which denotes a fusion of the upper with the lower spheres. [Tr. note: i.e. Tifereth with Malkuth.] "On the part of everyone whose heart is willing ye should take my heave offering." The words "on the part of" seem at first sight to be superfluous, but in reality they contain a deep lesson for the masters of the esoteric lore. Blessed are the righteous who have learnt how to centre all their thoughts and desires on the Heavenly King, and whose aspirations are directed, not towards the vain and foolish toys of this world and its lusts, but to attaching themselves wholeheartedly to the world above in order to draw down the favour of the Lord Himself from heaven to earth. What is the place whence they receive this favour? It is a holy supernal region, whence emanate all holy wills and desires. This is known as "every man", who is identical with the "Righteous", the Lord of the House, whose love is always directed towards the Matrona, like a husband who loves his wife always. "Whose heart is willing": that is, His heart goes out to Her, and Her heart to Him. And although their mutual love is so great that they never separate, yet "ye shall take from Him My heave offering", meaning, "ye should take the Shekinah to dwell with you". The Holy One, blessed be He, unlike a human husband,

Zohar: Shemoth, Section 2, Page 135a

who would protest violently should anyone take from him the wife whom he so dearly loves, is greatly pleased when the Shekinah, whom He so loves, is "taken" from the supernal sphere, the abode of Love, to dwell below in the midst of

Israel. Happy is the lot of Israel and happy that of all those who are worthy of this. In that case, it might be asked, why does it say, "which ye should take from them" instead of "from Me"? Because the "from them" refers to these two Divine names or grades. Rabbi Yeba the Ancient suggested that meitam (from them) signifies meet M, from the sphere designated by the letter M; the mysterious sphere, the abode of the Righteous One, from whence He draws life to distribute to all the worlds. It is all one mystery, which has been entrusted to the wise. Happy is their lot! However, although they "take" Her (the Shekinah), they may do so only when her Spouse specially grants permission, and only in accordance with His will, in order that He may be worshipped in love. This is realized daily in the corporate liturgical services of Israel. Or "from them", again, can refer to the six supernal grades; or to the Seasons and Sabbaths. It amounts all to the same thing. GOLD AND SILVER, AND BRASS, AND BLUE AND PURPLE, AND SCARLET, AND FINE LINEN, AND GOATS' HAIR, AND RAMS' SKINS DYED RED, AND SEALSKINS, AND ACACIA WOOD. Gold symbolizes New Year's Day, the day of "gold", because it is a day of judgement, and the side of judgement, symbolized by gold, dominates it; as it is written, "gold cometh from the north" (Job XXXVII, 22), and "evil will be opened from the north" (Jer. Vl, 2). Silver symbolizes the Day of Atonement, when the sins of Israel are made "white as snow" (Isa. I, 18), for "on that day shall he make an atonement for you, to cleanse you, that ye may be clean from all your sins before the Lord" (Lev. XVI, 30). Brass is symbolic of the days of the Sacrifices of the Feast of Tabernacles, which alluded to the powers and principalities of the heathen nations, who are designated "mountains of brass". "Blue" (techeleth) corresponds to Passover, which established the dominance of the true object of Faith, symbolized by the colour blue, which could predominate only after the punishment of the firstborn of Egypt was accomplished. So all colours seen in dreams are of good omen, except blue. "Red-purple" (argaman) is connected with Pentecost, symbolizing the giving of the written Law, consisting of two sides, of the Right and of the Left, as it is written: "From his right hand went a fiery law unto them" (Deut. XXXIII, 2). "Scarlet" (tola'ath shani) is connected with the fifteenth day of Ab, a day on which the daughters of Israel used to walk forth in silken dresses. So far six symbolic elements have been enumerated; the rest symbolize the Ten Days of Repentance: [Tr. note: From New Year to the Day of Atonement.] fine linen, goats' hair, rams, skins dyed red, seal (tahash) skins, acacia wood, oil for the light, spices for the anointing oil and for the incense, beryls and set jewels. These are nine, corresponding to nine days of Repentance, and the Day of Atonement completes it and makes ten days.

'From all of these we take "the heave offering of the Lord" [Tr. note: Malkuth.] on each of these special seasons, in order that it may rest upon us: on Passover by means of the paschal lamb, on Tabernacles by means of the tabernacle, and so forth. The six Days are but a preparation for her. As they are united above in "One", so she is unified below in the mystery of "one", to correspond to them above. The Holy One, blessed be He, who is One above, does not take His seat upon the Throne of Glory, until She has entered within the mystery of the One in accordance with His very essence of Oneness, to be the One in One. This, as we have said, is the significance of the words: "The Lord is One, and His Name is One." It is the mystery of the Sabbath, which is united with the mystery

Zohar: Shemoth, Section 2, Page 135b

of the One so that it may be the organ of this Oneness.

'In the prayer before the entrance of the Sabbath the Throne of Glory is prepared for the Holy Heavenly King. And when the Sabbath arrives the Shekinah is in perfect union with Him and is separated from the "other side", and all the potencies of severe judgement are severed from Her, She being in closest union with the Holy Light and crowned with many crowns by the Holy King, and all the principalities of severity and all the lords of judgement flee from Her, and no other domination reigns in any of the worlds, and her countenance is illumined by the supernal light, and she is crowned here below by the Holy People, all of whom are invested with new souls. Then is the time for the commencement of prayer, when the worshippers bless Her with joy and gladness, saying, "Bless ye the Lord, the Blessed One!" (the beginning proper of the Sabbath Eve prayer). For the holy people cannot be allowed at this moment to begin with a verse that suggests judgement, as on weekdays, when "Bless ye" is preceded by "And He being merciful, forgiveth iniquity and destroyeth not", because the Shekinah is then entirely severed from the mystery of the "other side" and all the lords of judgement have separated themselves and passed away from Her, and he who rouses judgement in the lower spheres causes vibrations of doom and severity also in the celestial regions, and while this disturbing element is in evidence the Holy Throne cannot crown itself with the crown of holiness. Then the lords of judgement who have severed themselves for the time being from the rest of creation, hiding themselves away from all eyes in a deep and secret recess at the bottom of the sea, are roused to return to the celestial habitations, and they come back with violence and fury, so that the Holy Sphere, which requires above all rest and peace for the entrance of the Sabbath, is hard pressed by these potencies of judgement. So it is evident that we should not imagine that She (the Shekinah) is independent of our "rousings", for there is no vibration above of any sort but is caused by those which take place in the midst of Israel below, as we have already pointed out in connection with the expression "in the time appointed, on our solemn feast day"; it is not merely a feast day, but our feast day; that is to say, we effect a movement in the higher spheres by our prayers. Therefore the holy people, who are crowned with holy crowns of souls in order to awaken rest and peace above, may not order judgement there, but, on the contrary, must all consciously and with exceeding great love awaken blessings both above and below.

'The congregation respond: "Blessed is the Lord who is blessed forever and ever." The expression "who is blessed" indicates the streaming of blessings from the source of life to the place whence issue nourishment and bounty for all creatures. And why do we call this source "blessed"? Because it sustains and waters 'olam va'ed (lit. forever and ever), which is the Sabbath eve. In this way blessings are transmitted to this 'olam va'ed from the highest world, so that it attains its full perfection. Thus in this benediction, "blessed" represents the ultimate source whence all blessings emanate; [Tr. note: Hohmah.] "the Lord" is the centre [Tr. note: Tifereth.] of all the supernal sides; "who is blessed" represents the peace of the house, the fountain of the cistern, [Tr. note: Yesod]. providing completion and nourishment for all, while "forever and ever" refers to the world below, [Tr. note: Malkuth.] which needs these blessings: the "good oil" of "blessed", "the Lord", and "the Blessed One" is all for this 'olam va'ed. Therefore the whole congregation has to recite this every day; but on Sabbath eve it must be recited with special devotion and gladness, in order that the Sabbath may be fitly blessed by the holy people. When they begin to recite this benediction a voice is heard in all the heavens that are sanctified by the entrance of the Sabbath: "Blessed are ye, holy people, for that ye bless and sanctify on earth below, that thereby many supernal holy hosts

Zohar: Shemoth, Section 2, Page 136a

may be blessed and sanctified above." Blessed are they in this world and blessed are they in the world to come. The Israelites do not recite this benediction until they are crowned with the crowns of holy souls, as we have said before. Blessed is the people who is worthy of them in this world, so that it may merit them in the world to come. This, to the pious, is the night of conjugal unions, when they are thus crowned with new souls and new additional holy spirits, for, being in a state of supernal holy tranquility, they may then beget holy children.

'Here now is a mystery entrusted to the wise. At midnight on this night the Holy One is pleased to enter the Garden which is above. On weekdays at this time He enters the Garden of Eden which is below, in order to have joyous communion with the righteous who have their abode there; but on Sabbath He enters the Garden above. For on weekdays all the souls of the righteous abide in the Garden which is on the earth; but on Sabbath eve, all those hosts of holy angels who are appointed over the Lower Paradise bring up from that region the souls which dwell there into the firmament which is close to this Garden, where many holy chariots of fire await their coming, that they may escort these souls to the Paradise above, and bring them before the Throne of Glory. Whilst these souls are thus ascending, other souls are descending in a similar manner to become crowns to the holy people below. So their activity proceeds, some ascending and some descending. Do not, however, imagine that on this account the Paradise on earth remains empty and untenanted upon the Sabbath. Far from it! For, as we have said, while some souls go, others come, to wit, those souls who are being cleansed and purified during the six days of the week, but who are not yet sufficiently perfected to be able to abide in Paradise permanently, but on the Sabbath are permitted to enjoy its delights for a space, so that the place is never empty. This is symbolized by the removal and replacing of the "shew bread" (v. Leviticus XXIV, 5-9). Again, do not imagine that when the souls return to their earthly

Paradise at the end of the Sabbath they find it so overflowing with other souls that no place remains for them; for their abode becomes by some mysterious process much larger, being extended both in length, width and height, so that their presence makes no difference. There are also some souls which, having ascended to the highest sphere, never come down again. And in addition there are also those who ascend and descend continually to crown the holy people. In fact, on the Sabbath eve there is a veritable commotion of souls coming and going, ascending and descending. As for the innumerable holy Chariots which perpetually speed hither and thither, eye can scarce behold them for their radiant and glittering aspect! All the souls are full of joy and eagerness to become crowns for the holy people on earth, for the righteous in the lower Paradise. At last comes the moment when a voice proclaims throughout all the spheres: "Sanctified! Sanctified!" Then there is peace everywhere, perfect peace, even to the wicked in Gehenna, and all the souls crown themselves, some above, and some below. On Sabbath, at midnight, when the wise consummate their conjugal unions, at the time when they are sleeping peacefully in their beds, and their souls are eager to ascend and behold the glory of the King, the supernal spirits with which they crowned themselves at the sanctification of the Sabbath take those souls and bring them up unto the heights. These souls are there bathed in the spices of Paradise, and behold all that is within their capacity to behold. Then, when it is time to descend again, the supernal spirits accompany them until they reach safely their human habitations.

Zohar: Shemoth, Section 2, Page 136b

It is incumbent upon the wise to recite certain verses calculated to arouse that supernal holy spirit of the Sabbath coronation, as, for instance: "The spirit of the Lord God is upon me; for the Lord hath anointed me to preach good tidings to the meek; he hath sent me to bind up the broken-hearted, to proclaim liberty to the captives, etc." (Isa. LXI, I);

or, "Whithersoever the spirit was to go, they went, thither was their spirit to go; and the wheels were lifted up over against them: for the spirit of the living creature was in the wheels" (Ezek. I, 20), in order that the act of procreation may be effected in a spirit of Sabbath holiness, through the influence of the supernal Sabbatic spirit.'

When R. Hamnuna the Ancient used to come out from the river on a Friday afternoon, he was wont to rest a little on the bank, and raising his eyes in gladness, he would say that he sat there in order to behold the joyous sight of the heavenly angels ascending and descending. At each arrival of the Sabbath, he said, man is caught up into the world of souls. Happy is he who is aware of the mysteries of his Lord! And when the Sabbath day itself lightens, a spirit of tranquil joy ascends through all worlds. This is the significance of the Psalm (recited on Sabbath morning): "The heavens tell the glory of God; and the firmament proclaims his handiwork." ·What is meant by "Heaven"? That heaven in which the Supernal Name is made visible (shama-yim-heaven; shem-Name). What is the meaning of the word "tell" (mesaprim) P Assuredly not the mere telling of a tale. Far otherwise! It signifies that they are illumined from the flashing of the supernal Point and ascend in the Name which is contained in the light-stream of the supernal perfectness. They flash and lighten of themselves through the lightening and flashing of the Supernal Book; [Tr. note: Malkuth.] they lighten and flash towards all the sides which are attached to them, and each sphere retains unto itself a little of this light, for from that sapphire-like radiance every ring in the chain derives its light and radiance. For upon this day (Sabbath) the heavens are crowned and ascend in the power of the Holy Name more than on any other day. "His handiwork" is the supernal Dew which streams forth from all the hidden regions; it is "the work of His hands", and His self-fulfilment wherein He completes and perfects Himself on this day more than upon any other. This dew "streams down" (maggid in the Aramaic sense) from the Head of the King, with an abundance of blessing, the "firmament" here signifying the stream issuing from the Cistern, the "River which went out of Eden", which flows earthwards, as the stream of the Supernal Dew which gleams and flashes from all sides. This "firmament" draws it downward upon a current of love and desire, in order that it may water the field of bliss and joy at the entrance of the Sabbath. When that fair pearled Dew streameth down, the whole becomes full and complete in its holy letters acting through all their holy channels; since all is united to it, a path is opened to it to water and bless all below. "Day unto day"-one day to another, one ring or sphere unto its fellow. Here Scripture speaks in detail concerning the manner in which the heavens radiate sapphire brightness to that Glory, and how that "Firmament" of the supernal Dew causes the downward flow of the current. "Day unto day utters speech." Day unto day, grade unto grade, in order that the one should complete itself in the other, and one be illumined by the other from the luminous and sparkling radiance of the Sapphire which is reflected by the heavens back to the central glory. The word yabia' (uttereth) can be translated "hasteneth": they hasten to catch the light and the flashing one from another. The word OMeR (speech) indicates the letters and paths which proceed from the Father [Tr. note: Hokmah.] the Mother, [Tr. note: Binah.] and the head which issues from them, who is the firstborn Son. [Tr. note: ' Tifereth.] Aleph symbolizes the Father, and when it ascends and descends, the Mem unites itself with it, producing em, which signifies Mother; the resh is the Head (rosh =head), signifying Son. When these three unite the result is that they form "Word", "Speech". Thus the Father, the Mother, and the first born Son radiate one within the other in one union, which has its reign and duration upon the Sabbath. Thus all are united so as to become one, and therefore they hasten one to another that Omer, as a supernal reign, in order that all should be one. But when all has been conveyed down to that "firmament", then it diffuses light upon the "Glory of God" below that it may produce beings in the likeness of

Zohar: Shemoth, Section 2, Page 137a

the heavens which give light to that Glory. "And night unto night declareth knowledge." These are those "chariots" which form the body of the Throne; they are called "nights", as it is written: "My reins also instruct me in the nights" (Ps. XVI, 7). The upper chariot is called "Days" or "day unto day", the lower "Nights", or "night unto night". Ye-hawe (declares) may also mean "makes alive", to wit, produces the progeny of the heavens, "brings unto life" generations. "Knowledge" designates the mystery of the heavens: as the heavens have six sides, so also the generations which they bring into life in their likeness. Thus "day unto day" is included in a supernal sphere called "Word" (omer), and "night unto night" in the mystery of the Male, who gives light to her and whose name is "Knowledge". And because this "Word" is not like other words, but is a supernal mystery, Scripture comes back to it and says: "There is no word (omer) nor speeches, their voices are not heard" (v. 3). This "word" is a supreme mystery of supernal grades, where there are no voices nor speech, and which cannot be understood like the other grades which constitute the mystery of the Faith, and which are voices that can be heard. And yet "Their line is gone out through all the earth" (v. 4), although they are supernal mysteries which can never be perfectly comprehended, yet the current of their flow is downward. Because of this current, we have a true Faith in this world, and all mankind can discourse of the mystery of the Faith of the Holy One in connection with these grades, as if they were revealed to and not hidden from them. Therefore it says: "And their words to the end of the world" (Ibid.), which means that from the beginning to the end of the world the "wise of heart" discourse of those hidden grades although they cannot be comprehended. And how far are they comprehended? "In them hath he set a tent for the sun" (Ibid.), because the holy sun [Tr. note: ' Tifereth.] is as a tabernacle of all those supreme grades, and is as a light which has taken into itself all the hidden lights and the whole current of their extension, whereby Faith is manifested in the whole world. To grasp the Sun is equivalent to grasping all grades, because the sun is a "tent" including all and absorbing all; and he in turn lights up all the shining colours below. Hence "He is a bridegroom coming forth from his canopy (covering)" (v. 6), in the gleam and flash of those hidden lights which in strong yearning and desire give him tokens of their love, as to a bridegroom to whom all his friends give presents and gifts. And what is "his covering"? Eden, the "covering" which covers up all things. "He rejoiceth" from the side of the primeval light in which judgement has no place at all. "As a strong man" (gibbor)-from the side of "strength" (geburah); and note that it does not say here "a strong man", but "as a strong man", which means that Judgement is tempered by Mercy. Thus the sun gathers all together in one, in perfect devotion and love. "To run on the way", in order to nourish and complement the Moon on every side and make it possible for her to shed her light downwards. "His going forth is from the end of the heaven" (v. 7). He goes forth from the end of that supernal heaven, from the termination [Tr. note: Yesod.] of the Body, as it is written, "From one end of heaven to the other end of the heaven" (Deut. IV, 32); where the "one end" designates the upper world, and the "other end" its termination. "And his circuit unto the ends of it" (Ibid.): he (the sun) runs through all those holy regions that are capable

Zohar: Shemoth, Section 2, Page 137b

of being vivified and nourished by his rays. "And there is nothing hid from the heat thereof" (Ibid.): nothing is hidden from that radiance, for it is directed towards all together, to each according to its capacity of reception. When all are thus completed and vivified by the Sun, then the Moon is crowned in the likeness of the supernal perfect Mother in fifty gates. This is expressed in the following verse: "The Torah of the Lord is perfect, quickening the soul"; as she is perfect from all sides in the mystery of five grades, in the likeness of the supernal Mother, to whom belongs the mystery of the fifty. Therefore the Torah is introduced here in six parallel sentences of five words (in Hebrew) each, in order to complete the mystery of fifty. "The Torah of the Lord is perfect, quickening the soul" is five. "The testimony of the Lord is sure, making wise the simple" is five. "The statutes of the Lord are right, rejoicing the heart" is five. "The commandment of the Lord is clear, enlightening the eyes" is five. "The fear of the Lord is pure, enduring forever" is five. "The judgements of the Lord are true, righteous altogether" is five. All these sentences present themselves in five words each, after the semblance of the supernal Mother; six times, as the Tetragrammaton is mentioned in these verses six times, corresponding with the six supernal grades which form the mystery of the supernal heaven. So the Moon is completed in the realm of transcendence into that which it should be, and all this on the Sabbath day, upon which all is perfected in the mystery of the Sabbath above and below. On this day, therefore, radiance is increased everywhere. The heavens receive it from the source of life; and they then impart light and completeness to the supernal Glory from the mystery of the supernal Numberer (Sopher), the Father of all; then from the mystery of the Numbered (Sippur), the Supernal Mother; finally from the mystery of the Number (sepher). [Tr. note: v. Sefer Yezirah.] Therefore it says: "The heavens declare" (mesaprim), namely, as we have pointed out, in the mystery of these three Names which, on the Sabbath, reign supreme more than on other days. Therefore David uttered this Psalm of praise, through the Holy Spirit, in regard to the light and the effulgence of the Sabbath and its pre-eminence over the other days of the week because of the mystery of the Supernal Name which in it lightens up and radiates and sparkles in the spheres of holiness, and is completed above and below.

'Therefore the "Men of the Great Synagogue" have ordered that this Psalm of David should be the first one to be sung on the Sabbath day, since it refers to those particular "Heavens" which lighten all the others. Then follows (in the liturgy) that "river which goes out of Eden", alluded to in the Psalm which follows this one in the Sabbath service: "Rejoice in the Lord, O ye righteous" (Ps. XXXIII); for this "River" gathers into itself the whole mystery of the "heavens" and the source of life on this day, and the sun is perfected for its appointed task of the distribution of light. Then the Moon, when she separates herself from the "other side"-as on this day she does-in order to receive light from the sun, is alluded to in the Psalm following this one, namely (Ps. XXXIV): "Of David, when he changed his behaviour towards Abimelech." When the "other side" has separated itself from the "Moon", then the latter is united with the "Sun", and therefore this Psalm begins (acrostically) with the twenty-two letters of the Hebrew alphabet, signifying the merging of the Sun with the Moon. Then follows the union of the Matrona with Her Spouse: "A prayer of Moses, the man of God" (Ps. xc): He spreads out both His right and His left hands to receive Her and to unite Himself with Her in perfect union. Then follow other psalms of joy and ardent longing. "A psalm. Sing unto the Lord a new song, for he hath done marvellous things: his right hand and his holy arm hath wrought salvation for him" (Ps. XCVIII). This Psalm has been expounded elsewhere, and the Companions were perfectly correct in their assertion that it was chanted by the kine

Zohar: Shemoth, Section 2, Page 138a

who bore the sacred ark. [Tr. note: v Zohar, Genesis, 123a.] This corresponded to the mystery above: when the "living beings,' (Hayoth) lay hold of the Throne in order to raise it to the highest heights, then we sing this Psalm. As to the

435

question, why, then, is it called "new" when it is perpetually being repeated, the fact is that it is indeed a "new song" because it refers to the "new" moon at the time when she receives light from the sun. "His right hand and his holy arm hath wrought salvation for him": this denotes the rousing of the right and the left hand to receive Her (the Moon, signifying the Shekinah) when She arrives at "Beth Shemesh", the "House of the Sun", which hands receive and bear Her even as the kine bare the ark. This psalm of praise was therefore ordered to be chanted on the Sabbath by the "one people", namely the children of Israel. (Ps. XCII): "A song. A psalm for (to) the sabbath day. It is good to praise the Lord, to sing unto thy name, O most high. To proclaim thy lovingkindness in the morning and thy faithfulness in the nights." It has been established by the Companions that this hymn of praise was sung by the first man (Adam) after he had been driven out of the Garden of Eden, when the Sabbath drew nigh unto the Holy One and interceded for the created being. Then he sang this hymn in honour of the Sabbath which had delivered him. It is a hymn of praise sung by the world below to the world above, to a world which is altogether "Sabbath", the sphere of the "King whose is the peace". It is a hymn of the sabbath below unto the Sabbath above: the sabbath below, which is like night, sings to the Sabbath above, which is like day. In fact, whenever "Sabbath" is mentioned it refers to the "eve of the Sabbath" (i.e. the Shekinah), but when it says "the Sabbath day", it denotes the Supernal Sabbath (i.e. Tifereth). The former is symbolized by the Female, the latter by the Male. Thus "And the children of Israel should keep the Sabbath" (Ex. XXXI, 16) alludes to the Female, which is the night (layla), and "remember the Sabbath day" (Ibtd. xx, 8) alludes to the Male. Thus the sabbath here below sings a hymn to the Sabbath above. Therefore this psalm is anonymous, as we find everywhere where there is a reference to the world below (the Shekinah) that the Name is not actually mentioned, as, for example, "And he called unto Moses" (Lev. 1, I), "And to Moses he said, go up to the Lord" (Ex. XXIX, I). Since in this psalm reference is made to a higher sphere, therefore the divine name is not applied to the lower grade, just as a candle cannot shine in the sunlight. All the hymns sung in praise of and on the Sabbath are the aids to its ascension to supernal regions where it is crowned with supernal holy crowns above all other days.

'The Sabbath service continues with the prayer: "The soul of all living shall bless thy name, O Lord our God." The Companions have made some true observations on this prayer. [Tr. note: Zohar, Exodus, p.205b.] But the real truth is that on Sabbath it is incumbent on us to mention that soul [Tr. note: The "additional soul" given to the Israelite on Sabbath.] which emanates from "the Life of Worlds" (Yesod). And since this soul belongs to Him from whom all blessings proceed and in whom they are present, who wills to water and to bless that which is below, she is given permission to bless this Place. Thus the souls which fly forth from this "Living One" on the entrance of Sabbath do actually bless that Place in order to communicate blessings to the world below which is called the "Lower Name" (Malkuth). At the same time, the region whence those souls emanate blesses the Name from above, and so it receives blessings from below and from above, and is completed in all aspects. During other days she receives blessings from those souls which bless her from below; but on the Sabbath she receives blessings from those supernal souls which bless her with forty-five words according to the numerical value of the word Mah (What?) From the words "the soul of all living" to "the God of the first and last ages" there are forty-five words; from the words "were our mouths filled with song as the sea" to the words "and with us" are very nearly fifty words, corresponding to the Mi [Tr. note: "For the symbolic meaning of Mah and Mi, v. Zohar, Genesis, lb.] (numerical value=fifty). From here on follow other praises which resolve themselves in the number one hundred, the completion of all (to "the great God") and form one chariot.

Zohar: Shemoth, Section 2, Page 138b

Thus this hymn of praise and all the words contained in it are numerical symbols of the perfection of the Sabbath, and the perfection attained through it, according to the Divine purpose. Blessed is that people that has learnt how to conduct a service of praise in well-pleasing fashion! From here on follow prayers proper (connected with the Shema and the Amidah). It is written: "But be not thou, O Lord, far from me; my Hind (eyaluti), haste thee to help me" (Ps. VLXII, 20). These words did King David speak in that hour when he ordered that hymns of praise should be sung to the King, so that the unity of the Sun and the Moon should be accomplished. While he composed these praises, he said: "But be not thou far from me". The combination of "Thou" and "Lord" signifies the mystery of the one inseparable union. "Be not far": this refers to Her (the Shekinah) when she ascends to be crowned by her Spouse in the world above, and from thence to ascend still higher into the Infinite, to be united there, high, high, above. Therefore it says: "be not far", that is to say, do not ascend to such heights that will leave us without Thee. Therefore through this service of praise Israel seek to attach themselves closely to the Shekinah and her Glory, so that if this Glory should seek to rise aloft they may still cling to it and not allow it to abandon them. Therefore, also, the prayer proper (Amidah) is recited quietly, as one would speak confidentially with a King; for as long as Israel holds Him in confidential converse He cannot depart from her, leaving her alone. "My hind": even as the hind and the gazelle, though they flee to a far distance, yet soon return again to the place from which they went, so also the Holy One, blessed be He, even when He ascends into the unscalable heights of infinity, soon returns. Why so? Because Israel here below cling to Him, and being so attached to Him do not allow Him to forget them and abandon them. This is the significance of the prayer, "My hind, haste Thee to help me."

Therefore it behoves us to cling to the Holy One, blessed be He, in order so to speak to draw Him down from the heights, so that we should not be deserted by Him for an instant. Therefore, when we pass quickly from the Geulah (Redemption) benediction to the Prayer (Amidah or eighteen benedictions) we must, as it were, lay hold on Him, and lead Him apart, and converse with Him privately and in a still voice, in confidence, so that He should not depart far from us and leave us alone. Concerning this it is written: "And ye who cleave to the Lord your God, ye are all alive today" (Deut. IV, 4); "Blessed is the people who is in such a case; blessed is the people who has the Lord for its God" (Ps. CXLIV, 15).'

Having reached this point, R. Simeon rose and the Companions likewise, and they walked away from the tree in the valley. Said R. Eleazar unto R. Simeon his father as they journeyed on: 'Father, up to this point we have been sitting in the shadow of the Tree of Life in the Garden of Eden. Hereafter we must assuredly walk in the ways which guard this Tree.' R. Simeon replied: 'Begin thou first, while we are yet upon the way!'

R. Eleazar then explained to them the symbolic significance of colours and metals in connection with the Tabernacle. 'Gold is mentioned first because it is the emblem of the lower Power, or the Left Hand. Silver, which, on account of its whiteness, signifies Mercy, or the Right Hand, although it comes second here, is nevertheless the essential hue as regards the mystery of the Divine attributes in their manifestation to Israel, as it is written, "Mine is the silver and mine is the gold" (Haggai II, 8). It is also represented by the "cup of benediction" (the cup drunk after a meal) which, although it is taken up with both hands, is actually held only with the right hand. This is the esoteric meaning of the words "His left hand is under my head, and his right hand embraces me" (S.S. II, 6). Shining polished brass is a colour resembling gold, combining the colours of both gold and silver. Hence the "brazen altar was too small' (I Kings VIII, 64), because it symbolized the "smaller light which rules by night", while the golden altar symbolized "the greater light to rule the day" (Gen. 1, 16). Hyacinth (purple-blue),

Zohar: Shemoth, Section 2, Page 139a

which was used for the fringes, also denotes "judgement", or the Throne from which the judgement concerning capital offences is proclaimed. Therefore all colours seen in dreams are of good omen, with the exception of purple-blue, which denotes that the soul of the dreamer is being judged and the body is in danger of extermination. Much ardent prayer for mercy is needful to avert this portent. This colour symbolizes the Throne, concerning which it is written: "And above the firmament... was the likeness of a throne, as the appearance of a sapphire stone... and it had brightness round about" (Ezek. 1, 26-27). Because the fringes are made of a material of this colour, when the morning light begins to shine on them, they become greenish-blue like a leek, and from that moment the time of the recitation of the Shema begins. [Tr. note: v. T. B. Berachoth] For this reason capital cases may not be tried at night because that colour, blue, reigns, which has the power to snatch away souls without Judgement, since Judgement does not rule at that time. When morning comes and the Right Hand is roused, the brightness appears and reaches the dark blue, and then it becomes connected with another Throne. From this moment on it is time to recite the Shema. Argaman (reddish-purple) is a mixture of colours uniting as one. Tolaat shani (prop. worm of deep scarlet) symbolizes Israel: for as the worm's power to destroy exists only in its mouth, so does Israel's power lie in her mouth (i.e. prayer); and shani, being used in the plural (Prov. XXXI, 21), signifies that two (shne) colours are united to form one. It issues from the supernal Throne which rules over the dark blue from the right side, it is white and red, right and left. It represents Michael, the guardian of Israel (Dan. x, 21). "Fine linen", of six threads, symbolizes "Tarshish" (Gabriel). With these, two other are united: "goats' hair and rams' skins reddened": "goats' hair" denotes the lower outside power which protects (covers up) the inner power. All this is necessary and a place must be allowed for all, because they come from the sphere of gold (judgement); "rams' skins reddened", drawn from the two sides, left and right, to protect in another place. "And tahash (seal) skins": there is a species of this animal which flourishes on the "other side", in the wilderness and not in cultivated places, and this species is ritually "clean" and is the one here called tahash. The "acacia wood" symbolizes the Seraphim, for the word "standing" is applied to both of them (Ex. XXVI, 15; Isa. VI, 2). Then comes "oil for the candlestick", symbolizing the Holy Spirit. "Precious stones and stones to be set for the ephod and for the breastplate." These are holy stones, the foundation of the Sanctuary in holy chariots. They were set apart in the resplendent garments, for the High Priest to look upon and to remind him of the twelve Tribes. For that reason there were twelve stones, as has been pointed out. 'There are thirteen things enumerated apart from the stones, which, taken altogether, make twenty-five

Zohar: Shemoth, Section 2, Page 139b

in the supernal mystery of the union. Corresponding to these twenty-five, Moses chiseled twenty-five letters in writing the mystery of the Shema (the twenty-five Hebrew letters contained in the verse, "hear, O Israel, the Lord our God, the Lord is one"). Jacob wished to express the unity below and did so in the twenty-four letters of the response to the Shema: "Blessed be the Name of His glorious Kingdom forever and ever." He did not bring it up to twenty-five because the Tabernacle was not yet. But as soon as the Tabernacle was completed and the first Divine utterance was pronounced there, it contained twenty-five letters, to show that the Tabernacle was after the supernal pattern, as it is written, "And the Lord spake to him out of the tabernacle of the congregation" (Lev. 1, 1 - twenty-five letters in Hebrew). Thus the twenty-five things for the Tabernacle show forth the Sanctuary as a perfect and harmonious whole in accordance with the mystery of the twenty-five letters, as thou, our Master, hast taught us. This is the mystery of the whole Tabernacle and of everything appertaining to its construction. The number twenty-five corresponds with the twenty-two letters of the Alphabet, along with the Law, the Prophets and the Writings, which all form one whole sum and one mystery. When the Israelites proclaim the Unity, expressed in the mystery of the twenty-five letters of the Shema and in the twenty-four letters of the response, and each person in the congregations is doing this with devoutness, then all those letters unite as one and ascend as one unity. Then the forty-nine gates are opened which signify the mystery of the Jubilee. And when the gates are opened, the Holy One, blessed be He, regards each of such persons as though he had fulfilled the whole Torah-the Torah which can be viewed from forty-nine aspects. So it is necessary to concentrate heart and mind on both the twenty-five and the twenty-four letters and to raise them with the whole force of intention to the forty-nine gates, as we have said. Through concentration on this, one will concentrate on the Unity, for our Master has taught us that the "Hear, O Israel" and the "Blessed be the Name" are the summary of the whole Torah. Happy the lot of him who thus concentrates, for verily these contain the Torah in its entirety, above and below. It is the mystery of the complete Man, Male and Female, and is the secret of the whole Faith. In the debates in the schools of Shammai and of Hillel concerning the recitation of the Shema, the former held that the evening "Shema" should be recited in a reclining or resting position, and the morning "Shema" should be recited standing, their reason being that in the evening the Feminine aspect is included in the active energy and reign, while in the morning the Masculine aspect reigns exclusively in the supernal world, and it is therefore necessary to recite the Shema standing, as is done during the Prayer (Amidah) and at all times when the Masculine predominates. The school of Hillel, on the other hand, made no such distinction. If the said aspects (Male and Female) were each entirely by itself, it might be necessary to do so, but as we, by our concentration and intention, unite them in our consciousness during the recitation and response, in the forty-nine aspects, and raise them towards the forty-nine gates, we need not emphasize their separateness, but should rather concentrate on the fact that they are both one without any separation whatever: the Masculine in six words-"Hear, O Israel, etc.", and the Feminine in six—"Blessed be the Name", etc. And the rule is always according to the school of Hillel.'

R. Simeon lifted up his hand and blessed his son R. Eleazar. He then began to speak on the verse: "Who stirred up from the east him whom righteousness called to his foot?" (Isa. XLI, 2). 'This verse', he said, 'has been variously interpreted, but, esoterically considered, "Who" refers to the mystery of the supernal world, [Tr. note: Binah.]from whence the first revelation of the mystery of Faith is manifested, as we have already pointed out. Or again, the "Who" denotes that which is concealed, the absolutely impenetrable and undisclosed, and which begins to make its glory known from the region that is called "East", from which region the whole mystery of the Faith and light commences to be revealed. "Righteousness" reveals the Supernal Power and the reign of the Holy One, blessed be He, who delegates to that Righteousness authority to rule over all the worlds, to guide them and lead them towards perfection. For this reason does it go on to say: "Gave nations before him and made him rule over kings",

Zohar: Shemoth, Section 2, Page 140a

since all the kings of the world are under the authority of that "Righteousness", as it is written: "And he will judge the world in righteousness" (Ps. xcv, 13). Moreover, when it says "Righteousness calleth to his foot", the question is: Who calleth whom? The answer is that "Righteousness" calls to the resplendent mirror, which is ever bright and refulgent, as it is written: "Keep not thou silence, O God; hold not thy peace, and be not still, O God" (Psa. LXXXIII, I). Now the Holy One has let His light shine upon us on our way for the sake of my son Eleazar, who called down the supernal light upon us, and it has not waned. Happy is the lot of the righteous in this world and in the world to come.'

Then R. Abba discoursed on the text, "A psalm of David when he was in the wilderness of Judah" (Ps. LXIII, 1). 'Why', he said, 'is this psalm different from all others in that it alone mentions the place in which it was composed? However, this is not the only psalm where a particular motive for its composition is given. The superscription of one psalm runs: "Where he changed his behaviour before Abimelech" (Ps. XXXIV); and another (LIV) has: "When the Ziphim came and said to Saul, Doth not David hide himself with us?" The purpose of these headings is to proclaim the merit of David, showing that even when he was in distress and fleeing from his enemies he sang praises to the Holy One, blessed be He. True, it was the Holy Spirit that spoke through him, but had not David yearned continually for the Holy Spirit, it would not have rested upon him. It is always thus: the Holy Spirit will not descend upon a man unless he, from below, moves it to come. And David, as we have seen, in the greatest tribulation did not cease to sing hymns and to praise his Lord for all things. If I should be reminded of the difference between "A psalm of David" and "Of David a psalm", the former, as in the passage just discussed, signifying that the Holy Spirit gave the initiative, then I would say, be that as it may, if David had not prepared himself for the reception of the Holy Spirit, it would not have come upon him. "A psalm": this means the Holy Spirit. Why is it called so? Because it continually praises the Supernal King without ceasing. When David came,

438

the Holy Spirit found a "body" properly prepared, and so was able to sing through him in this world praises to the King, so that this world might be perfected to harmonize with the world above. "Of David": David, a complete, perfected, worthy man who never changed. "When he was in the wilderness of Judah": as we have said, although he was in great trouble, he sang praises. And what was the burden of his song? "O God, thou art my God: I seek thee: my soul thirsteth for thee, my flesh longeth for thee in a dry and thirsty land, where no water is, to see thy power and thy glory, so as I have seen thee in the sanctuary." "God" in a general sense; "My God" expresses David's individual grade of experience. In fact, there are three grades here: "God", "My God", "Thou". Yet, even though there are three designations, there is really only one grade, as all allude to the mystery of the Living God: "God" is the supernal One, the Living One; "My God" denotes His omnipotence "from one end of the heaven to the other end"; and "Thou" expresses the personal grade of David's awareness of this Presence. But, although all are one and are designated by one name, yet ashahreka (lit. I will seek Thee), may also be rendered (with allusion to shahar, black), "I will strengthen the light which shines darkly (the Shekinah)," for this does not shine until it is strengthened from below. And he who thus strengthens it becomes worthy of the white light, the light of the "refulgent mirror", and of the world to come. This mystery is expressed in the words: "And those that seek me (meshahrai) shall find me" (Prov. VIII, 17), namely those who, out of the blackness of the dawn, prepare a light. The double n in yimzaunni ("they shall find me") signifies that they will merit the two lights: the dim, blackish light of dawn and the white light of day: or, the mirror that is not refulgent and the mirror that is. Hence David said in effect: "I will prepare a light from the blackish dawn in order that the white light of day may shine on it'" "My soul thirsteth for Thee, my flesh longeth for Thee": as a starving man longs for food and drink. "In a dry and thirsty land, where no water is": in the desert, a place where holiness cannot dwell.

Zohar: Shemoth, Section 2, Page 140b

And we, Master, hunger and thirst for thee in this place; and as David longed to "behold God in holiness", so we long to drink in the words of the Master in his sanctuary (house of study).' Said R. Simeon to R. Abba: 'Let him who began continue.'

Then R. Abba spoke on the verse: "And they shall take me a heave offering." Said he: 'When the Holy One showed Moses the work of the Tabernacle, he was perplexed over its construction, as has been pointed out. Now comes the question, if it was to Moses alone that the Holy One gave the Terumah (heave-offering, i.e. the Shekinah), how could he have given her to others (i.e. communicated the Presence of God to the people), for it says that "the children of Israel should take a heave-offering"? We may answer by a parable. A King stood in the midst of his people, but his Queen was not with him. As long as she was absent the people did not feel secure and were somewhat uneasy. But as soon as the Queen arrived the whole people rejoiced, feeling that they were now safe. In like manner, although the Holy One, blessed be He, showed Israel many signs and wonders through Moses, they did not yet feel sure of themselves, but as soon as the Holy One said, "They shall take me a heave-offering that I may dwell in the midst of them" (v. 8), their confidence was at once firmly established and they rejoiced in the worship of the Holy One, blessed be He. Therefore it is written: "And it came to pass on the day that Moses had fully set up (kalloth) the tabernacle... that the princes of Israel brought their offerings...." (Num. VII, 1-3), namely on the day when the Bride (kallah) of Moses (Shekinah) came down to earth.

'Now the question might be asked: Wherever the expression "and it came to pass" occurs in Scripture, is it not always connected with something sad? And the answer would be that something sad occurred also on the day when the Tabernacle was completed and the Shekinah came down to earth. For a celestial Accuser stood at Her side who covered Her Face with a veil of thick darkness to prevent Her from finding Her way down to earth. And we have been taught that a thousand and five hundred myriads of accusing angels were round about Her for the same purpose. At the same time, also, a multitude of supernal angels rose up before the Throne of the Holy One, and said: "Lord of the world! All our splendour and all our refulgence emanates from the Shekinah of Thy Glory, and should She now descend to those below?" But in that hour, the Shekinah gathered up all her strength and, breaking through that darkness, like one breaking through strong barriers, came down to earth. As soon as they saw this they all cried together with a loud voice: "O Lord our God, how mighty is thy name in all the earth" (Ps. VIII, 1): "mighty", because She had thus broken through so many barriers and restraining hosts and had come down to earth to reign over all. All of which explains the use of the ominous expression, "and it came to pass", in connection with the completion of the Tabernacle, indicating the pain that was suffered by many celestial armies on the day when Moses' Bride (the Shekinah) came down to earth. Therefore it is said: "That they take Me a heave offering." Observe it does not say "Me and a heave offering", but "Me as a heave offering", to show that all is One, there is no separation, and the Tabernacle in its completion was in the likeness of that above: the one corresponded with the other in every detail, that the Shekinah might be located in it in all its aspects. Here in this world the Tabernacle was fashioned like unto the body which contains the spirit, and the Shekinah, which combines the upper with the lower, and which is the Holy Spirit, entered into this kind of body, so that the brain should dwell in a shell, all according to purpose. So the Holy Spirit becomes, as it were, a body to contain another spirit, subtle and luminous, and in this way all is contained one within the other, until it enters this world, which is the last external shell (klifah). The toughest husk is the one within the shell of this world, just as in a nut the outside shell is not the toughest, but the inner husk. So also above, the hard, withstanding shell is the other spirit which rules in the body; within it is a softer shell, within which again lies the brain.

'In the Holy Land, in connection with the Temple, things happened differently. The hard shell was broken in that spot and did not rule at all; it was broken there, and yawned asunder. And the opening thus made existed there as long as Israel worshipped

Zohar: Shemoth, Section 2, Page 141a

in manner due. Their sins, however, caused the two sides of the opening to draw together, until the shell became whole again. As soon as the shell closed up over the brain it ruled over Israel and drove them out from that place. Yet, in spite of this, the hard shell cannot rule in that holy spot, since it has no right there. If that is so, it may be asked, why is the Temple still in ruins, for all destruction comes only from the influence of that hard shell? The answer is that the destruction was indeed caused by that "side" when it closed over the brain, but the Holy One prevented it from ruling in that place, and when Israel had been driven out from there, the shell broke open as before. But because the holy people was no longer there, the opening was covered with a holy covering, a kind of thin curtain, to protect that spot and prevent the hard shell from closing over it again. This covering spreads over it from all sides. It is not possible for the holy ointment to descend upon the Land as formerly, as that thin covering prevents it, the Holy People being no longer there. Therefore it is that the ruined Temple has not been rebuilt. On the other hand, it is also impossible for the hard shell to rule there, because the thin covering prevents it from entirely closing over the brain. For this reason all the souls of members of other nations who live in the Holy Land, when they leave this world, are not accepted there, but are thrust out and are forced to roam about and go through many wanderings until they leave the Holy Land behind them and reach instead those impure regions where they belong. But all the Israelitish souls that leave this world from the Holy Land ascend from there, and that covering receives them into itself and through it they enter the Upper Holiness, because like always tends to like. And the souls of those Israelites who have departed from this world while still outside the confines of the Holy Land, and while in the power and dominion of that hard shell, wander hither and thither and roam about until they reach their appointed places. Happy is the lot of that man whose soul leaves this world in the domain of holiness, in the cavity provided by the Holy Land.

'He whose soul leaves him in the Holy Land, if his body is buried upon the day of his death, is in no way dominated by the spirit of impurity. Therefore it says of one who has been put to death by hanging that "his body shall not remain all night upon the tree, but thou shalt in any wise bury him that day, that thy land be not defiled" (Deut. XXI, 23), for at night the impure spirit is given permission to rule. However, although these last are given temporary power, they cannot exercise their sway within the boundaries of the Holy Land, because it is impossible for them to enter it unless they can come upon an organ or means of approach in the parts and fat of those sacrifices that are consumed at night for the purpose of feeding other (foreign) kinds. [Tr. note: v. supra. p. 129b-130a.] But even these portions were not left with the purpose of attracting evil potencies to the Holy Land, but rather, on the contrary, to entice them away from it, for, as has been said on another occasion, the smoke of these parts of the sacrifices was wont to ascend crookedly and drift away until it reached that hidden cavern in the North in which all the powers of the "other side" have their abode; into which cave the smoke would enter and all the demons and impure spirits be nourished thereby. But the smoke of those sacrifices which were burnt during the day ascended in a straight line unto its rightful place and all the proper spirits received nourishment from it. Over the bodies of the righteous, who were not seduced in this world by the lusts of the hard shell, the impure spirit has no power at all, because they did not associate themselves therewith. But just as the wicked in this life were seduced by that powerful shell of evil and its pleasures and practices, so are their bodies unclean after the soul has left them. The bodies of the righteous, because in this life

Zohar: Shemoth, Section 2, Page 141b

they took their delight in religious rejoicings and the meals and ceremonies of Sabbaths and festivals, are, as we have said, not in the power of the impure spirit at all, since they had no joy nor part in anything appertaining to it. Blessed is he who derived no pleasure therefrom at any time of his allotted mortal span! As for him whose soul left him outside the precincts of the Holy Land, his body is defiled by that impure spirit, which remains in it until it returns to the dust. And if such a body is brought into the Holy Land to be buried, to it applies the text, "And ye entered and defiled my land and made my heritage an abomination" (Jer. II, 7)-that is: "Into My Land over which the spirit of impurity has no power or dominion, ye have brought this your body wherein that very impure spirit has entrenched itself, to be buried in the hallowed soil! Ye defile My Land!" However, the Holy One, blessed be He, provides the land with a means of purging from this defilement: when such a body decomposes, the Holy One causes a wind to blow from above which thrusts the impure spirit outside, for He has compassion on His land. Joseph's body was never under the power of the impure spirit, although his soul left him when he was yet outside the Holy Land. Why had the "other side" no dominion over him? Because when he was alive he was never seduced by it. Yet he did not wish that his body should be taken for burial into the Holy Land, but only requested that his bones should be taken and deposited there. Jacob, again, did not die at all: his body remained intact and his spirit had no fear of the impure potencies, for his bed was filled with the perfection of the celestial light, in the brightness of the twelve tribes and of the seventy souls (which came into Egypt with him). Therefore he was not afraid of the "other side", and it had no power over him. Further, his body was in the likeness of the Supernal Form, for his beauty united all sides, and all the limbs of the first man-Adam-were united in him. Therefore Jacob said, "I will lie with my fathers, and thou shalt carry me out of Egypt" (Gen. XLVII, 30)- the whole body. Therefore also "the physicians embalmed Israel" in order that his body might remain intact, as was fitting. As to other men whose souls pass away in the Holy Land, their souls and bodies alike come to no harm.

'Three names has the soul of man: nephesh, ruah, neshamah. They are all comprised one within the other, yet they have three distinct abodes. Nephesh remains in the grave until the body is decomposed and turned into dust, during which time it flits about in this world, seeking to mingle with the living and to learn of their troubles; and in the hour of need it intercedes for them. Ruah enters the earthly Garden (of Eden) and there dons a likeness which is in the semblance of the body it tenanted in this world: that likeness being, as it were, a garment with which the spirit robes itself, so that it may enjoy the delights of the radiant Garden. On Sabbaths, New Moons and festivals it ascends unto higher regions, imbibes the joys thereof, and then returns to its place. Concerning this it is written: "And the spirit (ruah) returns to God who hath given it" (Eccl. XII, 7)-namely, at the special seasons and on the special occasions which we have enumerated. Neshamah ascends at once to her place, the region from whence she emanated, and for her sake the light is kindled to shine above. She never again descends to earth. In her is consummated the One who combines all sides, the upper and the lower. And as long as she has not ascended to be united with the Throne, the ruah cannot crown itself in the lower Garden, nor can the nephesh be at ease in its place; but when she ascends all the others find rest. Now when the children of men are in sorrow or trouble, and repair to the graves of the departed, then the nephesh is awakened and it wanders forth and rouses the ruah, which in turn rouses the Patriarchs, and then the neshamah. Then the Holy One, blessed be He, takes pity on the world. This matter has already been explained, although the doctrine of the neshamah has been put in a somewhat different form; but it all amounts to the same, and what we have said is entirely correct. Now if the neshamah is for one reason or another hindered from ascending to her rightful place, then the ruah, when it reaches the door of the Garden of Eden, finds it barred, and it cannot enter,

Zohar: Shemoth, Section 2, Page 142a

and so roams about unnoticed and forlorn; and as for the nephesh, it wanders about the world and beholds the body which was once its home devoured by worms and suffering the judgement of the grave, and it mourns therefor, as the Scripiure tells us: "But the flesh upon him shall have pain, and his soul within him shall mourn" (Job XIV, 22). Thus all suffer punishment, and so they remain until the neshamah is able to attain to her rightful sphere above. Once this is accomplished, however, both the others are united each with its sphere; for all three are one, forming one whole, united in a mystical bond, according to the prototype above, in which nephesh, ruah and neshamall constitute together one totality.

'The (supernal) Nephesh possesses in itself no light and cannot out of its own being engender it, and for this reason it is in close connection and deeply enmeshed with a certain Body, [Tr. note: Metatron.] which it fondles and sustains. It is concerning this Nephesh that it is written: "She giveth meat to her household and an appointed portion of labour to her maidens (Prov. XXXI, 15), the "house" denoting the Body, which she feeds, and the "maidens" the limbs of that Body. The (supernal) Ruah rides upon the Nephesh, dominates it, and enlightens it with supernal glory, as much as it can bear; this Nephesh is the throne or pedestal of this Ruah. The (supernal) Neshamah produces the Ruah, rules over it, and sheds upon it the light of life. The Ruah depends entirely upon the Neshamah and is lit up by its light and nourished by its celestial food, while the Nephesh is similarly dependent on the Ruah. But as long as that supernal Neshamah does not ascend unto the spring of the "Ancient of Ancients", the most Hidden of all hidden regions, there to be filled with the presence of Him whose glory is eternal as the waters of an unceasing and refreshing spring, so long must the Ruah be debarred from entering into that which is its own especial Paradise, namely, the Nephesh; and in all cases the abode of the Ruah is the Garden of Eden, while the Neshamah ascends aloft to the fountain-head, and the Nephesh takes up its abode in the body.

'Similarly in man below, the three are one yet separate. The neshamah ascends aloft to the fountain-head; the ruah enters the Garden of Eden- and the nephesh finds rest in the grave. It may be asked, what in our analogy corresponds above to the grave? The answer is that "the grave" in this case is the mighty klifah. In this respect the soul of man corresponds, and here, as elsewhere, the lower is after the pattern of the upper. Thus there are three grades of the soul distinct one from another, although they form one bond and one mystery. As long as the bones of their human habitation remain intact in the grave, the nephesh remains there also, though unwillingly.

'There is here a mystery which is entrusted only to such as perceive and know the way of truth and are afraid of sin. In the hour when the neshamah crowns herself above with the holy crown, and the ruah stands within the radiance of the supernal light to which it is admitted on Sabbaths, New Moons, and festivals, and when that same Ruah descends well satisfied from those feasts to enter into the Garden of Eden resplendent and radiant: in that hour the nephesh also rises up within the grave and assumes shape in the likeness of the form which it previously possessed when in the living body, and in virtue of this image all the bones arise and sing praises to the Holy One, blessed be He; as it is written: "All my bones shall say (tomarnah), O Lord, who is like unto thee?" (Ps. XXXV, 10). And had the eye but the power and permission to perceive such matters, it would behold on the nights of Sabbaths, New Moons, and festivals, a kind of figures singing and praising the Holy One above their graves. But the folly of the children of men prevents them from having any cognizance of these matters, since they neither know nor perceive what the foundation of their lives in the world is, and have no mind to be aware of the glory of the Supernal King in this world which they can see, not to speak of the world to come, which they see not; thus they have no perception of the basis of either, or of the inner meaning of these things.

'On New Year's Day, when the world is judged, and the Throne of Judgement stands by the Supernal King, every soul (nephesh) hovers about and intercedes for the living. On the night following the giving of judgement they roam about, endeavouring to discover what decisions have been made concerning the fate of men in the coming year; and sometimes they communicate their knowledge to the living in the form of a vision or dream, as it is written: "In a dream, in a vision of the night, when deep sleep falleth upon men... then he openeth the ears of men and sealeth their instructions" (Job XXXIII, 16): i.e. the soul puts its seal to words which it communicates to the sons of man that they may receive instruction or reproof. On the last night of the Feast of Tabernacles, when the final edicts are issued from the King, and the shadow is removed from those persons who are shortly to die,

Zohar: Shemoth, Section 2, Page 142b

a certain celestial officer named Yehudiam descends with myriads of followers and bears that shadow aloft; and the soul which we have mentioned roams about and sees the shadow and returns to its place, and announces to the rest of the dead: "Such and such an one is coming to be with us"-meaning the soul of whichever shadow has been most lately borne away by the angelic minions. If that deceased one be righteous and has lived a good life while in this world, all the dead rejoice; but if not, they all say: "Alas, alas! Woe, woe!" When the angels bring up the shadow, they deliver it to that faithful servant whose name is Metatron, and he takes it and brings it unto its due and rightful place, as it is written: "As a servant earnestly desireth the shadow" (Job VII, 2). From that hour on, a place is prepared for the neshamah of that man, and a place for his ruah in the Garden of Eden, and a place for his nephesh to rest in during its wanderings-for there is a certain nephesh which has no rest, concerning which it is written that "it shall be slung out, as out of the middle of a sling" (I Sam. xxv, 29), which nephesh wanders about in the world, having no rest either by day or by night, this being the greatest and direst punishment possible; and there is likewise a "nephesh" which is "cut off" together with the body, concerning which it is written: "and I will cut it off from its people" (Lev. XVII, 10): and there is also a nephesh which is not "cut off" together with the body, but is "cut off" from the place which, had it belonged to a worthy person, would have been its appointed place above, concerning which it is written: "that nephesh shall be cut off from my presence; I am the Lord" (Ibid. XXII, 3); "from My presence" means that the ruah does not rest on it any longer; and when that is so the nephesh can have no part in the heavenly bliss, nor have any cognizance of any of the matters which take place in the other world. Such a nephesh is like that appertaining to an animal.

'A nephesh which is destined eventually to find rest, when in the course of its wanderings it meets with Yehudiam, the chief angelic messenger, with all his princes, is taken by him through all the doors of the Garden of Eden and shown all the glories of the righteous and the splendours of its own ruah, and then it invests itself in all serenity with its ruah, and it perceives all that is going on in the supernal world. And when that ruah ascends to be crowned within its neshamah which is above, the nephesh joins the ruah and clings thereto with all its strength, and receives illumination from it, which causes it itself to shine, even as the moon borrows light from the sun. And that ruah then joins itself in the same wise to the neshamah, and the neshamah unites herself with the end of Thought, this being the mystery of the Nephesh which is above, and the Nephesh which is above unites itself with the Ruah which is above, and that Ruah again with its Neshamah, and that Neshamah with the Infinite (En-sof). Thus is achieved harmony, peace and union both above and below. This constitutes the attainment of the rest and quietude of the nephesh that is below, concerning which it is written: "But the soul (nephesh) of my lord shall be bound in the bundle of life with (et) the Lord thy God" (l Sam. xxv, 29); that is to say, in the union symbolized by et (the first and the last letters of the alphabet, signifying the union of all things), one being like unto another. For when the Moon-which is the symbol of the supernal Nephesh- descends, illumined with glory from all sides, then she in her turn illumines with her radiance all the chariots and all the camps, and unites them, so that they are formed into one complete body which shines forth resplendent with the steadfast brilliance of the supernal light. In the same way the lower nephesh, when it descends, similarly illumined from all sides-from the light of the neshamah and of the ruah-also illumines all the chariots and camps, namely the limbs and bones of its body, and forms them into one complete body which emits light. This is the significance of the words: "And he will satisfy with splendour (zahzahot) thy soul (Isa. LVIII, 11); and then He will make vigorous thy bones" (Ibid.): that is, they will be fashioned into one complete body which will emit light, and arise to give praises to the Holy One, as has been pointed out in connection with the words, "All my bones shall say, O Lord, who is like unto Thee?" This praising does indeed constitute the rest and delight of the nephesh, and is verily the completion of its joy. Blessed are the righteous who fear their Lord in this world, for they merit the threefold rest of saints in the world to come.'

Then came R. Simeon and blessed R. Abba, and said: 'Happy are ye, my sons, and happy am I who have been permitted to behold how many

Zohar: Shemoth, Section 2, Page 143a

supernal places are prepared which will shine for us in the world to come.' Then R. Simeon began to speak on the verse: "A song of degrees. They that trust in the Lord shall be as Mount Zion, which cannot be removed, but abideth forever" (Ps. cxxv, I). 'This verse', he said, 'has been variously interpreted, but its special significance is this: "A song of degrees" refers to the song which is sung by the supernal holy grades from the side of the celestial Might in harmony with the song of the Levites here below. There are "degrees" upon "degrees", and they worship in the mystery of the fifty years (Jubilee). "They that trust in the Lord" are the righteous which trust in their good works, as it is written: "The righteous trust (are bold) like the young lion" (Prov. XXVIII, 1). It might be objected that the righteous do not, in fact, trust in their own works, being, on the contrary, perpetually in a state of fear and trembling, like Abraham, of whom it says that he was afraid concerning Sarah (Gen. XII, 10-13); or Isaac, who was afraid (Ibid. XXVI, 7); or, again, like Jacob, who was likewise in fear (Ibid. XXXII, 8); and if these did not trust in their own good works, how much less cause for assurance have other righteous men! How, then, can it be said with any justice that "the righteous trust like the young lion"? We must observe, however, that they are compared to the young lion (Kephir), and not to the other kinds of lion, which are stronger. The young lion, although strong enough to hold his own, is, in comparison with the other kinds of lions, weak, and so does not trust his own strength. In the same manner the righteous, although confident of the power of their good works, yet do not trust in them more than the young lion in his strength. Therefore it says here: "They that trust in the Lord shall be as mount Zion", namely, they will be in the future dispensation, not merely like the young, or even the old, lion, but like mount Zion, immovable and without fear. And ye, my sons, sons of the saints above, your trust, your confidence, is indeed like unto mount Zion. Verily, blessed are ye in this world and in the world to come!

The companions now proceeded on their way, and by the time they reached the town it had grown dark. Said R. Simeon: 'As this day has shed light upon us while we were on our way, enabling us to make ourselves worthy of the world to come, so also will this night shed light upon us that we may through it become worthy of the world to come and crown the words of the day with those of the night in the presence of the Ancient of Days, for so perfect a day as this shall not occur again in all future generations. Happy indeed is our lot in this world, and happy in the world to come.' R. Simeon then repaired to his house, accompanied by R. Eleazar, R. Abba, and R. Yose. There they remained until midnight. Then R. Simeon said to the Companions: 'It is now time to crown the Holy Chariot which is above by our studies here below.' Then, turning to R. Yose, he said: 'Since no discourse from thee has been heard among us during the day, thou must now begin to illumine the night, for the time is now arrived in which it is auspicious and desirable that both higher and lower spheres should be illumined.'

R. Yose thereupon began to speak on the words: The song of songs, which is Solomon's (S.S.I, 1). Said he: 'This song King Solomon poured forth when the Temple was erected and all the worlds, above and below, had reached their perfect consummation. And although concerning the exact time of its singing there is some difference of opinion among the members of the Fellowship, we may be certain that it was not sung until that time of absolute completion, when the Moon-the Shekinah-came to her fulness and was revealed in the full perfection of her radiance, and when the Temple had been erected in the likeness of the Temple that is above. The Holy One, blessed be He, then experienced such joy as He had not known since the creation of the world. When Moses set up the Tabernacle in the wilderness, another such was raised in the heavenly spheres, as we learn from the words: "And it came to pass... that the Tabernacle was reared up", the reference being to the other Tabernacle, to that which was above, namely the Tabernacle of the "Young Man", Metatron, and nothing greater. But when the first Temple was completed another Temple was erected at the same time, which was the centre for all the worlds, shedding radiance upon all things and giving light to all the spheres. Then the world was firmly established, and all the supernal casements were opened to pour forth light, and all the worlds experienced such joy as had never been known to them before, and celestial and terrestrial beings alike broke forth in song. And the song which they sang is the "Song of Songs", or, as we might render, "Song of the Singers", of those musicians who chant to the Holy One, blessed be He.

Zohar: Shemoth, Section 2, Page 143b

King David sang "A song of degrees": King Solomon sang "the Song of Songs". Now what is the difference between the two? Do we not interpret both titles to signify one and the same thing? Verily, this is so, for both things are certainly one, but in the days of David all the singers of the spheres were not yet set in their rightful places to chant the praises of their King, because the Temple was not as yet in existence. For, as on earth, the levitic singers are divided into groups, so is it likewise above, and the upper correspond to the lower. But not before the Temple was erected did they assume these their due places, and the lamp [Tr. note: Malkuth.] which before gave no light began then to shed radiance abroad, and then this song was sung to the glory of the Supernal King, [Tr. note: Tifereth.] the "King to whom peace belongs". This song is superior to all the hymns of praise which had ever been sung before. The day on which this hymn was revealed on earth was perfect in all things, and therefore the song is holy of holies. [Tr. note: "R. Akiba says: 'All the Writings are holy, but the Song of Songs is holy of holies". T. B. Yadaim, III, 5.] It is written in the Book of Adam that on the day when the Temple would be erected the Patriarchs would awaken song both above and below. Not that they would sing themselves, but they would rouse to song those mighty singers who preside over all worlds. On that day, it is said, Jacob the "perfect" one arose and entered the Garden of Eden and caused it also to sing, and all the spices of the Garden likewise. He, therefore, it is who gave utterance to the song, since but for him the Garden would not have sung. This song comprises the whole Torah: it is a song in which those that are above and those that are below participate; a song formed in the likeness of the world above, which is the supernal Sabbath, a song through which the supernal Holy Name is crowned. Therefore it is holy of holies. Why so? Because all its words are instinct with love and joy. This is because the "cup of blessing" was then given with the Right Hand; and when this is so all is joy and love; therefore all the words of the Song of Songs are perfected with love and with joy. When the Right Hand was drawn back (at the destruction of the Temple (Lam. II, 3)), the "cup of blessing" was placed in the Left Hand, and therefore those that were above and those that were below broke out in lamentation, saying: "Where is the 'cup of blessing' of the supernal place which was wont to abide therein? It has been withdrawn and withheld from thee". Hence the Song of Songs, which emanated from the Right Side, is full of love and joy in all its words, but the Book of Lamentation, which marks the withdrawal of the Right Hand and the emergence of the Left, is full of complaint and lamentation. It may be asked, does not all joy and singing emanate from the Left Side, since the Levites who were the singers were from that side? The answer is that all joy which issues from the Left Side is due to the union of the Left with the Right. When the Right Hand combines with the Left, then the joy which belongs to the Right mitigates the turbulence of the Left, and is infused into the Left. But when the Right Hand is not active, the wrathfulness of the Left increases, and there is no joy. Then the cry rises "Ey kah": "what will become of the 'Cup of Blessing'?" It is retained in the Left Hand and the anger is hot and does not cool. No wonder, then, that there is lamentation and mourning. But the Song of Songs represents the "Cup of Blessing" when tendered by the Right Hand, and therefore all love and joy is found therein, as in no other song in the world. Therefore was this song aroused from the side of the Patriarchs.

'On the day when this song was revealed the Shekinah descended to earth, as it is written, "And the priests could not stand to minister because of the cloud." Why? Because "the glory of the Lord had filled the house of the Lord" (I Kings VIII, 11), On that day this hymn was revealed,

Zohar: Shemoth, Section 2, Page 144a

and Solomon sang in the power of the Holy Spirit this song wherein is to be found the summary of the whole Torah, of the whole work of Creation, of the mystery of the Patriarchs, of the story of the Egyptian exile, and the Exodus therefrom, and of the Song of the Sea. It is the quintessence of the Decalogue, of the Sinaitic covenant, of the significance of Israel's wanderings through the desert, until their arrival in the Promised Land and the building of the Temple. It contains the crowning of the Holy Name with love and joy, the prophecy of Israel's exile among the nations, of their redemption, of the resurrection of the dead, and of all else until that Day which is "Sabbath to the Lord". All that was, is, and shall be, is contained in it; and, indeed, even that which will take place on the "Seventh Day", which will be the "Lord's Sabbath", is indicated in this song. Therefore we are taught that he who recites a verse from the Song of Songs as a mere drinking song causes the Torah to dress in sackcloth and to complain before the Holy One, blessed be He: "Thy children have turned me into an amusement for a drinking bout." Yea, assuredly the Torah says this. Therefore it behoves the faithful to be wary, and to guard every word of the Song of Songs like a crown upon their heads. It may be asked, why, then, is the Song of Songs placed among the Hagiographa (which are not so sacred as the other two parts of Scripture)? The answer is, because it is the Hymn of Praise sung by the Community of Israel at the time when she is crowned above. Therefore no other hymn is so pleasing to the Holy One as this.

'We have been taught that the three words, Shir hashirim asher (Song of Songs which) connote the placing of the "cup of blessing" between the Right Hand and the Left, and its raising towards "the King to whom peace belongs", grace being thus carried higher and higher to the mystery of the En-Sof (Infinite). Again, the four words of the title correspond to the mystery of the perfect Holy Chariot (formed by the three patriarchs and David). Again, "song" stands for King David, the mover of song; "songs" for the Fathers, the high chiefs; "Solomon", for Him Who rides in this perfect Chariot [Tr. note: Binah.] This verse thus contains the inner meaning of the phrase, "from eternity to eternity", the mystery of the whole Faith. The whole is a perfect Chariot for That which is cognizable and That which is unknowable and which no one can apprehend. Therefore this verse was given in four words, containing the mystery of the complete Chariot as from four sides.

'Again, within this mystery there is another. We have been taught that if one sees grapes in a dream, if they be white, it is a good omen, but if they are black in colour, then, if the dream occur at a time when grapes are in season, they are of good significance, but if not, prayer is needed to avert the omen. Why this difference between white and black, between in season and out of season? Again, it has been said, that one who dreams that he has eaten black grapes can be certain

that he will enter the world to come. Why? The clue is to be found in the tradition that the forbidden fruit which was eaten by Adam and Eve was the grape, the fruit of the vine, [Tr. note: Cf. Bereshith Rabbah, XV, 8.] for it is written: "their grapes are grapes of gall" (Deut. XXXII, 32)—namely, the black grapes. Thus of the two kinds of grapes, black and white, when seen in a dream, the white signify something good because they emanate from, and are the product of, the side of life, but the black emanate from the side of death, and therefore one who in a dream sees or eats of such grapes requires special intercession. Again, why do black grapes portend good if dreamt of when in season? As we have already pointed out, when the dream is dreamed at the time when white grapes are in season naught but good is portended. Why so? Because at that time the whole world is made fair and joyous when they predominate, and both white and black fit into the scheme of things; but when the white grapes are not in season, and so have no special power, then the dream-appearance of the black grapes is a sign that the judgement of death hangs over the dreamer, and he needs to plead for mercy because he has beheld the fruit (lit. the tree) which caused Adam's sin, and in consequence of that sin death to himself and to the whole world. Here a problem arises which I would not mention were not the Master here. We have been taught that this world is formed on the pattern of the world above, and that whatever takes place in this earthly realm occurs also in the realm above. But when the serpent caused death to Adam in this world, what could have corresponded to that in the upper spheres?

Zohar: Shemoth, Section 2, Page 144b

One might say that the serpent causes the light of the Moon-the female aspect of the Deity-to be diminished for a time, and this is a kind of death. But why did the male also die? Besides, even as to the "Moon" or feminine aspect, we have been taught that the diminishing of her light was not due to the Serpent but to another cause, because she complained against the sun. [Tr. note: v. Zohar, Gen., p. 20a; Midrash Rabbah, ad loc]. Shall we say that her spouse shares the same fate? Can we imagine a defect in the highest? This is one of the mysteries of the Torah; but the Serpent did indeed cause a defect in all the worlds. Mark this. We have been taught that everything that the Holy One created, both above and below, He created in the mystery of male and female, and there is an infinity of grades in the supernal spheres, each differing from the other; and those grades which are of the same kind God framed and united in one "Body", in the mystery of the primordial Man. We have also been taught that on the second day of Creation, when the Gehenna was created, one body was formed in the mystery of Man, and those limbs that came near to the fire of Gehenna and were consumed returned to their original state, and this was because those limbs came near to that Serpent. This is the primordial Man who was enticed to the tent of the Serpent, and in this sense died, the Serpent causing him death because he came too near to him. Everywhere man is male and female, but the Holy Supernal Man rules over all and gives food and life to all. And withal this mighty Serpent withheld light from all. When it defiles the tabernacle the Female of that Man dies, and the Male dies and they return to their elemental state, and in this way lower and upper correspond. "If he ate of the black grapes he can feel confident that he will enter the world to come", because he has (symbolically) prevailed over and destroyed that place, and since he has removed the stubborn "shell", he has drawn near to the world to come, and none will gainsay him. In the same way there could be no song in the house of David until the "black grapes" had been subdued and removed, and then Solomon sang the "Song of Songs", as already mentioned.

'This canticle is superior to all that preceded it; for those which were sung by Solomon's predecessors ascended only to join with the company of the songs chanted by the angels, as, for instance, the "Song of degrees to David", which means "the song which the celestial grades sing to David", to solicit nourishment from him; or again, as we might translate, "a song of degrees for the sake of David", the great king who always praises the Great King. But when Solomon came, he sang a song which is high above even that of David, a song which is the very same as that sung by the great ones of the realms above, the pillars of the universe, in honour of the Supernal King who is the lord of all peace and harmony. Other men send up praises by means of lower Chariots, but King Solomon by means of higher Chariots. It may be asked, What of Moses, who ascended further than all other men in the grade of prophecy and love of the Holy One, blessed be He? Did his song also reach no further than the lower Chariots? The song which Moses uttered did indeed ascend on high, but the truth is, that although it was not on a level with the Canticle of King Solomon, whom no man equaled in poetry, Moses' song was praise and thanksgiving to the Supernal King who redeemed Israel and wrought many signs and wonders for them, both in Egypt and at the Red Sea; but King David and Solomon his son sang

Zohar: Shemoth, Section 2, Page 145a

with quite different purposes. David endeavoured to prepare the virgins (the celestial grades) and to adorn them for the Matrona's presence so that She and her maidens might be manifested in beauty and grace. When Solomon came he found that Matrona and the virgins thus adorned, so he in his turn aspired to lead the Bride to the Bridegroom. He brought the Bridegroom to the place where beneath the marriage canopy the Bride awaited Him, and drew them together with words of love, that they might be united as One, in one perfection, in perfect love. Therefore Solomon produced a more sublime song than all other men. Moses, by building the Tabernacle, brought about the union of the Matrona with the world here below, Solomon brought about the perfect union of the Matrona with the Bridegroom above: he first led Him to the Canopy, and then brought them both down to this world and prepared a habitation for them in the Sanctuary which he built. It might be asked, How could Moses bring down the Shekinah alone? Would not this cause separation above? The answer is that the Holy One first caused the Shekinah to be united with Moses, and She became, as it were, Moses' bride, as has already been pointed out. As soon as She was united with Moses, She descended to this world and united Herself with it, and She became firmly established in this world, as never before. But no man since Adam was first created has ever brought about love and union above except King Solomon, who, as we have said, first prepared that union and then invited the Bridegroom and the Bride to the House which he prepared for them. Blessed are David and Solomon his son who have furthered the Supernal Union. Since the day when the Holy One said to the Moon, Go and make Thyself small, She was never again joined! in perfect union with the Sun until Solomon came.

'Shir hashirim asher lishlomoh. Here are five grades which shall unite in the world to come: shir (song) is one; hashirim (songs) are two, which together make three; asher (which) is four; lishlomoh (Solomon's) is five. "Solomon" is in the fifth; for the fiftieth day is the mystery of the Jubilee. Mark now. Solomon would not have been able to bring about the union above had not union of the Shekinah with the world below been already completed in Her union with Moses; one could not have been without the other. All this is a supreme mystery, which yet is revealed to those of a wise heart. It is written concerning Solomon, that he "spake three thousand proverbs and his song was a thousand and five" (I Kings v, 12). This has been interpreted by the Companions to mean that every word that he uttered has three thousand allegorical meanings, as, for instance, his book Ecclesiastes (Koheleth), which has a profound esoteric meaning and is written in the fashion of an allegory. Verily, there is no word in this book which does not contain profound wisdom and allegorical significance, even unto the very least and smallest verse. R. Hamnuna the Ancient, for instance, when he came to the verse, "Rejoice, O young man, in thy youth, and let thy heart cheer thee in the days of thy youth, and walk in the ways of thine heart... but know thou that for all these things God will bring thee into judgement" (Eccl. XI, 9), used to weep, saying: "Verily, this verse is fittingly taken as an allegory, and who can enlarge on it? If it is to be taken literally, it expresses no more than a fact which we see with our eyes; but if, on the other hand, the passage contains esoteric wisdom, who can apprehend it?" ˙ Then he corrected himself and said: 'It is written, "These are the generations of Jacob: Joseph being seventeen years old, was feeding the flock with his brethren; and the young man was with the sons of Bilhah, and with the sons of Zilpah, his father's wives; and Joseph brought unto his father their evil report" (Gen. XXXVII, 2). The verse which we have just quoted from Ecclesiastes is an allegory on the esoteric meaning of this verse from the Pentateuch. "Rejoice, O young man," corresponds to "and the young man"; "and let thy heart cheer thee" to "was feeding the flock"; "in the days of thy youth" to "with the sons of Bilhah", etc.; "but know thou that for all these things" to "and Joseph brought unto his father their evil report"; "God will bring thee into judgement" corresponds to "These are the generations of Jacob: Joseph...." Joseph was here included in Jacob. Who can fully grasp the secrets of the Torah? This allegory branches off into three thousand other allegories which are yet all comprised

Zohar: Shemoth, Section 2, Page 145b

in this one, in which, as we see, Joseph was included in Jacob. The three thousand other veiled implications concern Abraham, Isaac, and Jacob, who are, however, all indicated in this allegory of the mystery of wisdom which is revealed only to the faithful. Here, too, how many pretended merchants are there, or serving men, who are really great men of learning? So, too, there is no end to the hidden meanings of wisdom. Hence it says: "And his song was a thousand and five": that is, as we have interpreted, "the song of every proverb". However, whether the "his" refers to Solomon or to the proverb, it is all the same, since the one was the author of the other. The "song" refers to the "Song of Songs". But does this song actually consist of a thousand and five? Assuredly! The "five" refers to the five gates and doors which open toward the "King whose is the peace". They are the five hundred years of the Tree of Life, the fifty years of the Jubilee. The "thousand" refers to the Tree of Life as such, to the Bridegroom who goes out from its side and takes possession of the five gates, in order to draw nigh unto the Bride and claim Her. The Day of the Holy One, blessed be He, is a thousand years, and this number symbolizes also the River which goes out of Eden. Joseph was called "Righteous" after the Moon, the Shekinah, according to a special agreement between her and the Holy One. Therefore, the Song of Songs is holy of holies, and there is no verse in this Canticle which does not contain the mystery of the "thousand and five". There are five grades contained in the title, as we have said. But why is the "thousand" not indicated? The truth is that this is hidden and will remain hidden until the Wife (the Shekinah) unites Herself with her Husband. Therefore

Solomon endeavoured to bring that "Thousand" to the Bride in secret, by the aid of the mysterious ring whereon is engraved the seal of the supernal wisdom (cf. Targum on Eccl. I, 7). As soon as he had completed the making of the Holy of Holies below, the mystery of the Holy of Holies above ascended and was hidden, so that the concealment of the Union might be complete above and below, according to the Divine purpose. "The Holy of Holies" above is the mystery of the Supernal Wisdom and Jubilee. Corresponding to this, the Bridegroom and the Bride inherit the inheritance of Father and Mother, but in a reversed manner. The inheritance of the Father passes to the Daughter in the ascension of the Holy Name, wherefore She is also called "Holy" and "Wisdom". The possession of the Mother is inherited by the Son, and is called "the Holies", because He takes all those supernal holy attributes and gathers them up unto Himself, and then takes them to the Bride. Therefore it says: "Song of Songs": "Song" corresponding to the "Holy" and "Songs" to the "Holies", in order that both these aspects may be fused into one whole in manner due. "Which is Solomon's": as has been already pointed out, this refers to the King "whose is the peace". Yet think not that this praise is His, for it ascends to a still more supernal realm. The mystery is as follows. When the Masculine and the Feminine are united as one under the Highest King, then that Supernal King ascends and is filled with all the sanctifications and benedictions, and pours them down below, this being His great pleasure, to be filled with such sanctifications and benedictions and to pour them down below. Therefore the significance of all our prayers and praises is that by means of them the upper Fountain may be filled; for when it is so filled and attains completeness, then the universe below, and all that appertains thereto, is filled also and receives completeness from the completion which has been consummated in the upper sphere. The world below cannot, indeed, be in a state of harmony except it receive that peace and perfection from above, even as the moon has no light in herself, but shines with the reflected radiance of the sun. All our prayers and intercessions have this purpose, namely, that the region from whence light issues may be invigorated; for then from its reflection all below is supplied. This is the whole significance of Solomon's Canticle, that "the King to whom peace belongs" may be invigorated, for when that is so, all is invigorated from His reflected glory, but otherwise there is no remedy for the moon.

Zohar: Shemoth, Section 2, Page 146a

AND THIS IS THE HEAVE-OFFERING. We have been told that at the revelation on Mount Sinai, when the Torah was given to Israel in Ten Words, each Word became a voice, and every voice was divided into seventy voices, all of which shone and sparkled before the eyes of all Israel, so that they saw eye to eye the splendour of His Glory, as it is written: "And all the people saw the voices" (Ex. xx, 18). Yea verily, they saw. The voice so formed warned each individual Israelite, saying: "Wilt thou accept me with all the commandments implicit in me?" To which the reply came: "Yes". Then the voice circled round his head once more, asking: "Wilt thou accept me with all the penalties attached to me in the Law?" And again he answered "Yes". Then the voice turned and kissed him on the mouth, as it is written: "Let him kiss me with the kisses of his mouth" (S.S. I, 2). And all that the Israelites saw then they beheld in one Light (the Shekinah) in which were focused all the other lights, and they yearned to possess it. Said the Holy One, blessed be He, unto them: "This light which ye have seen on Mount Sinai, in which all the colours of the other lights are combined, and which ye so desire, shall be yours: have it, take it unto yourselves!" And these colours which she combines are the gold, silver, brass, etc., mentioned here. [Tr. note: Gold symbolizing Severity, silver Grace, and brass Beauty.]

'Another interpretation of "Let him kiss me with the kisses of his mouth" is as follows' What prompted King Solomon, when recording words of love between the Upper and the Lower world, to begin with the words, "Let him kiss me"? The reason is, as has been laid down, that no other love

Zohar: Shemoth, Section 2, Page 146b

is like unto the ecstasy of the moment when spirit (ruah=breath) cleaves to spirit in a kiss, more especially a kiss on the mouth, which is the well of spirit (breath) and its medium. When mouth meets mouth, spirits unite the one with the other, and become one-one love. In the Book of the first R. Humnuna the Ancient it is said of this sentence, "the kiss of love expands in four directions (ruhoth), and these are unified in one, and this is part of the secret of Faith". The Four spirits ascend in four letters, these being the letters from which depends the Holy Name, and with it all things that are, both above and below. Also the hymning of the Song of Songs derives its meaning therefrom. And what are these four letters? A H B H (Love), which form a supernal chariot. They constitute the linking of all things into a perfect whole. These four letters are the four directions of the love and joy of all the limbs of the Body without any sadness at all. Four directions are there in the kiss, [Tr. note: ie. Four ways of combining the letters of the Holy Name.] each one fulfilling itself in union with the other. And when two spirits thus become mutually interlocked they form two which are as one, and thus the four form one perfect whole. When they separate, there is formed from these four a certain offspring, a spirit formed of four spirits which ascends and splits the firmaments until it reaches a palace which is called the "Palace of Love", because all love is centred there; and therefore this spirit is also called "Love". When that spirit ascends to this Palace, it incites the Palace to attach itself to that which is above. As we have said, there are four letters which proceed in four directions, and they are the letters which spell the word Love. Their fruit is Love. When they unite, one is active

447

towards one direction, another towards the opposite direction. First comes the letter Aleph (in A H B H). Then comes the letter He', which unites itself with the Aleph in love. From these two other letters issue Beth and He, and spirits are interlocked with spirits in love. Then the letters arise and float away in the breath of that spirit which ascended, and adorn themselves within it in the proper fashion. When love, thus consummated according to those four directions, ascends aloft, it meets with a celestial Chief who is appointed over one thousand nine hundred and ninety firmaments and over the outward flowing of the thirteen streams of pure balsam which descend from the mysterious supernal Dew. That outflow is called "Mighty Waters". This Chief tries to prevent the spirit from proceeding, but does not prevail, and it makes its way to the Palace of Love. Concerning this matter, Solomon speaks at the end of his Canticle, saying: "Many waters cannot quench love, neither can the floods drown it" (S.S. VIII, 7). This refers to the supernal waters which we have just mentioned-those that descend from the Supernal Dew-and to the thirteen streams of pure balsam. The Chief of whom we have spoken is an angel sent forth by the Holy One, blessed be He. He is lord over many celestial hosts. He wreathes crowns for his Lord, and this is the significance of his name, Akathriel (God-crowning); for he prepares crowns from the graven and inscribed Name Y H V H.J H Zebaoth. When that love spirit enters the Palace of Love the love-yearning for the supernal kisses is aroused, those concerning which it is written: "And Jacob kissed Rachel" (Gen. XXIX, 11), so that the kisses of the supernal love are duly brought forth, and they are the beginning of the awakening of all supernal love, attachment and union. For this reason the Hymn begins with the words: "Let him kiss me with the kisses of his mouth." Now who is "he"? He who is hidden within the supernal concealment. Can, then, the Most Recondite be the fount of kisses, and kiss that which is below? See now. The Most Recondite is beyond cognition, but reveals of Himself a tenuous and veiled brightness shining only along a narrow path which extends from Him, and this is the brightness that irradiates all. This is the starting-point of all esoteric mysteries, itself being unknowable. Or rather, it is sometimes indiscoverable, sometimes discoverable, but even were it wholly indiscoverable the impulse to the ascending of kisses still depends on it. And because He is veiled, the Canticle also begins with a veiled expression, "let him kiss me", to wit, Him who is veiled above. And with what

Zohar: Shemoth, Section 2, Page 147a

shall he kiss? With that supernal Chariot from which all colours depend, and in which all are united. Therefore it says, "With the kisses of his mouth". "For thy love is better than wine" (lit. good from wine): this denotes the Sun which gives light to the Moon from the radiance of those supernal kisses, which He gathers up and passes on to the Moon. And from whence is that light derived? From the "preserved wine", from the "wine" which is the joy of all joys. And who is this Wine which gives life and joy to all? Elohim Hayyim (Living God). Also the "Wine of the Name Tetragrammaton", the joy of love and mercy, the source of all life and joy.'

The Companions then came and kissed R. Yose on his head. R. Simeon wept, and said: 'I know for a certainty that the Holy Spirit from above has made itself manifest here.' They all wept with joy, and he continued: 'Blessed is this generation! There will be none other like unto it until King Messiah shall appear, when the Torah shall be restored to her ancient pride of place. Blessed are the righteous in this world and in the world to come!' AND THIS IS THE HEAVE-OFFERING WHICH YE SHALL TAKE FROM THEM. Said R. Eleazar: This verse has been interpreted and the inner mystery thereof explained. But there is evidently a contradiction between the above verse (where it says "That they take Me a heave-offering") and this. First it says, "take Me"; then "take My heaveoffering"; then "take from them". However, the whole meaning amounts to this: "Take Me (as) a heave-offering"- but who should take? The children of Israel. And from whom should they take? "From every man whose heart impels him", namely from the supernal angels above, upon whom this "Heave" (the Shekinah) is raised, those who do perpetually raise Her up to the Supernal King; and when Israel is worthy, they take Her from them and bring Her down. Who are those angels? The four who raise Her, and in whom the Heart (God) takes delight. Yet, though this "heave-offering" is borne aloft by them, "ye shall take" from them, in order to bring Her down to earth. How are they to do so, even in this dispensation? By the power of good works, prayer, and the keeping of the Law. But at the time when the Temple yet stood, it was by means of the colours that were manifested below, after the pattern of the colours above, through the sacrificial worship. Those colours drew down the Terumah (the Shekinah) to the lower spheres; that is to say, the colours which were below prevailed over those that were above, the former bringing down the latter, one entering into the other, the former becoming "bodies" for the latter. Therefore it says, "which ye shall take from them". GOLD, AND SILVER, ETC. Gold is included in Gabriel. The supernal gold is carried below by Gabriel, and seven kinds of gold separate themselves from it. "Silver" above is united with Michael below, and one rests on the other. "Brass" is also above; it originates from gold, because gold and five have the same symbolism. It is fire which brings forth brass, and from this power emanate supernal mysterious serpents (nehashim = nehosheth = brass) and Seraphim brought forth by fire (from saraph, to burn). Therefore brass is golden, lit with orange and red, like fire. It is contained in Noriel (Fire of God) and forms his body. Techeleth (purple blue) is contained in both brass and gold, and derives energy from both sides. It possesses great strength and nothing can obtain dominion over it. It forms the throne of the power of judgement, and is therefore called "Boel" ("In him is El", i.e. God as Power), as it is written: "And El (God) is angry every day" (Ps. VII, 12). But when men turn back to God with perfect repentance, his name is changed into Raphael (God heals): for he brings healing to assuage the pains of that bitter judgement.

Zohar: Shemoth, Section 2, Page 147b

In "purple-red" (Argaman) gold and silver are fused: Michael and Gabriel are intertwined with each other, and of this it is written: "He maketh peace among the dwellers on high" (Job xxv, 2). The two, being joined one with the other, become one body. There is "crimson" also above, contained in Uriel, like the former, to combine purple-blue and purple-red. Byssus also is above, contained, like the former, in the mystery of Raphael, in order that silver and gold may be united. So much for the mystery of the seven pillars [Tr. note: i.e. the seven angels symbolized by the seven colours.] above which are contained in the seven that are below.

'Assuredly, there is shell within shell for protection, or rather, as we have said, brain within brain. Thus there is goats' hair, as the shell which guards the brain. "Rams' skins reddened" symbolizes the mail-clad lords with the flaming eyes [Tr. note: Angels of chastisement.] – "And his eyes as lamps of fire" (Dan. x, 6). They are called outer "firmaments" within the "shell". "Tahash skins": these are powers which stand on the holy side but are not in union with it. As has been said above, Abraham begat a son by the "other" wife, whose name was Tahash (Gen. XXII, 24), a brother of Ishmael by his mother; so, just as there is a celestial representative of Esau, so likewise is there one of Ishmael. Ishmael's mother begat Tahash from Abraham. For, in spreading radiance on all things, the primordial light, as it shone forth on all sides, also shot forth sparks. When it was established, God stored it away. For whom? For the righteous. And why for them? In order that it might bring forth fruit through and in them. And so it indeed was, for they did bring forth fruit in the world, for Abraham and Sarah "made souls" (Gen. XII, 5) [Tr. note: v. Zohar, Genesis, 79a.], and as they made souls under the sign of holiness, so they also did under the sign of the "other side"; for, were it not for this impulse which Abraham implanted in the "other side", there would be no proselytes in the world. "Acacia wood" has already been explained as symbolizing the Seraphim, who "stand above it" (Isa. VI, 2); that is to say, above the Shell (v. supra). "Oil for the candle-stick." This symbolizes the supernal oil which emanates from above. It has two names: "The oil of the light" (Ex. XXXIX, 37), and the "oil for the light". The former is the one above; the latter the one below. The former never ceases to flow: it is always full of holiness and of blessing, and all lights and lamps are blessed and lit up from thence. The latter is sometimes full and sometimes otherwise. It is written: "And God made the two great lights: the great light to rule the day, and the small light to rule the night" (Gen. I, 16). This has been correctly interpreted by the Companions, but we may add the following. The "two great lights" refer to the "Oil of the light" and the "Oil for the light": the higher world and the lower world; the Masculine (Sun) and the Feminine (Moon), which, when they are manifested together, are both called by the masculine gender. Because the upper world is called "great", the lower world, which is united with it, is also called "great", but as soon as the above and the below part, and are separate, the one is called "great" and the other "small". Therefore the ancients said that "man should rather be a tail to lions than a head to foxes" (Pirke Aboth IV, 20). For the part bears the designation of the whole; since the tail of a lion is certainly lion, without any separation. Similarly, the head of a fox is still

Zohar: Shemoth, Section 2, Page 148a

fox. Thus, as we see, it first calls both the Sun and the Moon "great lights", but when the Moon has separated Herself from the Sun she is called "small", even as to be head to a fox is less than to be tail to a lion. Symbolically, therefore, the "oil of the Light" never ceases: it stands in the path of perpetual ascent, in order to rule by day, but the "oil for the light" is intermittent, and is called "small" on this account, and rules at night. The five materials of which the spices were composed (Ex. xxx, 34) were "for the anointing oil and for the incense". These two are really one with the "onyx stones", etc. Thus there are thirteen things connected with the construction of the Tabernacle. We may now revert to the former interpretation of their symbolism.

'It has been remarked that there are seven kinds of gold. Now, it might be thought that there is a mistake here, since gold denotes judgement and silver mercy, and yet gold appears to be reckoned as being above silver. There is, however, no mistake. Gold really does surpass all, but only that gold which is the seventh and the best of all the species of gold, and which is meant by the term "gold" here. It is the kind which shines and sparkles, dazzling the eyes, and he who gets hold of it hides it carefully. From it all other kinds emanate. And when is it called "gold"? When its radiance rises in the awe-inspiring glory of supernal joy to waft back to those below a measure of this holy joy. When it stands for the sign of judgement it changes colour to blue, dark blue, and red-indicating severe judgement. But its essential character is joy, and it ever ascends with joy and trembling to the supernal regions and awakens joyousness. The silver below is connected with the mystery of the Right Arm, while the Supernal Head is symbolized by gold, as it is written: "Thou art the head of gold" (Dan. II, 38). And when does silver find its consummation? When it is contained in gold, a mystery alluded to in the words, "Like apples of gold in pictures of silver" (Prov. xxv, 11). Thus silver comes back to gold, completing the circle. So there are indeed seven kinds of gold. Brass originates from gold, of which it is a degenerate form, and forms the Left Arm; purple-blue forms the Left Thigh; dark purple, included in the left, forms the Right Thigh. Byssus is the "River which issues forth" and which unifies all the six sides (shesh= byssus=shesh=six), and, as we have already pointed out, the same thing obtains below. Thus with this river there are seven corresponding to the seven cycles of the "Jubilee", and the "seven" of the years of release (Deut. xv, 9). Although there are six they are thirteen through the seventh. Thus the thirteenth is the head, which stands on the whole body below, which is above all the limbs and is of gold. What, now, is the difference between the two kinds of gold? The higher gold is in the symbol of the closed mystery, and its name is Zahab sagur, "shut-in-gold", that is, pure precious gold (I Kings VI, 20, 21), shut off and hidden from all, concealed from the eye, which has no power over it, but the gold below is more revealed." [Tr. note: This symbolism of metals evidently refers to the Sephirotic Tree, and it would require much space for the proper elucidation. What follows to the end of Page 148b is merely a disconnected fragment of a longer section, dealing with priestly and prophetic offices of Moses, Aaron, Samuel, and Jeremiah, and the differences between them, touching on the symbolism of gold, silver, brass, and the brazen serpent] [Note: The last 19 lines of the Hebrew text are not translated as explained by the Translator's note.]

Zohar: Shemoth, Section 2, Page 148b

[Note: The first 37 lines of the Hebrew text are not translated as explained by the Translator's note.]

It is written: "And God said, Let there be light, and there was light" (Gen. 1, 3). Said R. Yose: 'That light was hidden and kept in store for the righteous in the world to come, as already stated; for it is written, "A light is sown for the righteous" (Ps. XCVII, 11). Thus that light functioned in the world only on the first day of Creation; after that it was hidden away and no longer seen.' Said R. Judah: 'Had it been hidden away altogether,

Zohar: Shemoth, Section 2, Page 149a

the world would not have been able to exist for one moment. But it was only hidden like a seed which generates others, seeds and fruits, and the world is sustained by it. There is not a day that something does not emanate from that light to sustain all things, for it is with this that the Holy One nourishes the world. Moreover, whenever the Torah is studied by night, a little thread of this hidden light steals down and plays upon them that are absorbed in their study, wherefore it is written: "The Lord commandeth His lovingkindness in the daytime, and in the night his song is with me" (Ps. XLII, 9); this has already been expounded. On the day when the Tabernacle was set up on earth, what do we read concerning it? "And Moses was not able to enter into the tent of the congregation, because the cloud abode thereon" (Ex. XL, 35). What was that cloud? It was a thread from the side of the primordial light, which, issuing forth joyously, entered the Shekinah and descended into the Tabernacle below. After the first day of Creation it was never again made fully manifest, but it performs a function, renewing daily the work of Creation.'

R. Yose was once deep in study, R. Isaac and R. Hezekiah being with him. Said R. Isaac: 'We are aware that the structure of the Tabernacle corresponds to the structure of heaven and earth. The Companions have given us just a taste of this mystery, but not enough for a real mouthful.' Said R. Yose: 'Let us take our difficulties to the holy lamp (R. Simeon), for he is able to prepare savoury dishes such as the Holy Ancient One, the most hidden of all secret beings, has prepared for him, and which require no added flavour from anyone else. From his dishes one can eat and drink, and sate oneself as with all the delicacies of the world, and leave over. Of him can it be said, "So he set it before them, and they did eat, and left thereof according to the word of the Lord" (2 Kings IV, 44).' R. Yose continued: 'It is written: "And God gave Solomon wisdom as he promised him, and there was peace between Hiram and Solomon, and they two made a league together" (I Kings v, 26). This verse has been expounded in more than one place. The expression, "And God" (Va-Tetragrammaton) signifies agreement between the higher and lower spheres, namely, that He and His council are at one. "Gave wisdom", as one presents a gift to a beloved friend. "As He promised him"; that is to say, the gifts of wisdom, riches, peace and dominion. "And there was peace between Hiram and Solomon"; this indicates that they had a private code between them which other men did not understand. King Solomon realized that even in that most perfect of all generations it was not the will of the Supernal King that so much wisdom should be revealed by him, that the Torah which had hitherto been hidden should now be disclosed, because he opened a door to it. Hence, even though he did thus open the door, the full meaning of his words was yet undisclosed except to the wise, such as are worthy, and they, too, could only fumble with them and not express them clearly. But, in this generation of R. Simeon, the Holy One, blessed be He, is willing that for his sake these hidden mysteries shall be revealed through him. Therefore I am amazed at the scholars of this generation, that they neglect even for a moment to seek the presence of R. Simeon in order to study with him, as long as he is permitted to stay with us in this world. Nevertheless, wisdom shall not vanish from the world in this generation. Alas, for that generation from which he shall be taken away! The wise will then diminish and wisdom shall be forgotten.' Said R. Isaac: 'That is assuredly true. Once, when I was walking with him and he opened his mouth to expound the Torah, a pillar of cloud reaching from heaven to earth appeared and stood before us, and in it a great light shone, and I trembled exceedingly. Blessed is the man, I said, to whom in this world so much is vouchsafed. What is it that is written concerning Moses? "And all the people saw the pillar of cloud stand at the Tabernacle door; and all the people rose up and worshipped, every man at his tent door" (Ex. XXXIII, 10). Such a vision was fitting for a teacher like Moses, the faithful prophet, the greatest of all the prophets, and for that generation which received the Torah on Mount Sinai, and which had seen signs and wonders in Egypt and at the Red Sea. But in this generation it is the merit of R. Simeon alone that makes it possible for us to behold these wonders through him.'

Zohar: Shemoth, Section 2, Page 149b

AND PURPLE BLUE. Said R. Isaac: This colour is obtained from a fish of the Lake of Genessareth, which is in the territory of Zebulun. This colour had to appear in the Tabernacle for the following reason. It is written: "And God said, Let there be a firmament in the midst of the waters, and let it divide the waters from the waters" (Gen. 1, 6). That firmament was created on the second day, because this creative act comes from the Left Side (separation), and on this day, too, was Gehenna created from the dross of the fire of the Left side. Now the sea was dyed with that purple blue colour which symbolizes the Throne of Judgement That day also received water from the Right Side, which nevertheless did not emerge till the second day, in order that one (attribute) might be combined with and reinforced by the other. The light of the first day of Creation was the first of all the six lights. It came from the side of fire, as it is written: "And the light of Israel shall be for a fire" (Isa. X, 17). That "light of Israel" emanated from the Right Side, and was (yet) contained in the fire. Now, the first of those six days is (symbolically) water, but it performed the function not of water but of light, which is from the side of fire, which is of the second day, to make manifest that the Holy One created the world on the foundation of peace, and that everything has grown out of peace. Thus the first day performed all its operations from the Side of the second, and the second operated from the Side of the first day. Each functioned with the work of the other, to show that one was merged in the other. The third day was a synthesis of both the first and the second; therefore it says concerning the third day of Creation "And God saw that it was good" twice (Gen. 1, 10, 12). On this day the purple-blue was formed out of two other colours, red and black, the colours of the second day. The fiery red, which is the proper colour of the second day, is an attribute of Elohim, and it was assigned (in the Tabernacle) the colour of gold, which resembles it. When the red came down it plunged into the Sea, where it became dark blue, which is also an attribute of Elohim, but of an aspect less rigorous than the former. As for the black, it was formed as the residue of the original red when it came down below, for being as it were smelted, it formed round it a slimy element which was first an intense red, and finally was transformed into black. All these are transformations out of the primeval red; and all this was created on the second day and is designated "other gods". That black is so dark as to be almost indiscernible. The Holy Lamp put it this way. When the red was transformed into purple-blue, and the colours mixed, a scum was thrown off which sank to the depths and turned into mire and dirt, as it is written, "The wicked are like the troubled sea, when it cannot rest, whose waters cast up mire and dirt" (Isa. LVII, 20). And from that dirt of the Sea came that black which is dark, and not only dark but superlatively black-"Darkness upon the face of the deep" (Gen. I, 2). And why is it called "darkness"? Both because of its colour and because it darkens the face of Creation. It is both red and black, therefore it does not say of the second day of Creation, "And God saw that it was good". But have we not been taught that the words "And behold it was very good" (Gen. I, 31) include the Angel of Death? How, then, is it possible to say that it is because of him that it is not said of the second day that it was very good? Verily, herein is a mystery of mysteries. The Angel of Death is indeed good. Why so? Because, since all men know that one day they must die, many turn to repentance from fear of him before the Lord. Many fear the King because the lash looms before their eyes. Then is the lash indeed beneficial, making men good and virtuous and upright. Hence the Angel of Death is referred to as "very good".

Zohar: Shemoth, Section 2, Page 150a

'Concerning this mystery, the Holy Lamp (R. Simeon) gave us the following explanation: "And behold it was good" refers to the Angel of Life; "very" to the Angel of Death, for he is of greater importance. And why? When the Holy One, blessed be He, created the world, all was prepared for the coming of Man, who is the king of this world. Man was fashioned to walk in the straight way, as it is written: "God hath made man upright, but they have sought out many inventions" (Eccl. VII, 29). He made him upright, but he gave himself over to corruption and was therefore driven out of the Garden of Eden. This Garden was planted by the Holy One, blessed be He, on the earth with the full Name (Tetragrammaton Elohim), and made an exact likeness of its prototype, the Paradise above, and all supernal forms were fashioned and shaped in it, and the cherubs were there-not those carved in gold or any material that could be fashioned by human hands, but of supernal light, fashioned and broidered through the agency of the perfect Name of the Holy One. All the images and forms of all things in this world were there fashioned, all having the similitude of the things in this world. And this place is the abode of holy spirits, both of those that have come into this world, and also of those that have not yet come into this world. Those that are about to come are invested with garments and with faces and bodies like those in this world, and they gaze upon the glory of their Lord until the time comes for them to appear in the world. When they leave the Garden for that purpose, these spirits put off their celestial bodies and garments and take on the bodies and garments of this world; they henceforth make their abode in this world in the garments and bodies fashioned from the seed of procreation. So when the time comes for the spirit to leave this world again, it cannot do so until the Angel of Death has taken off the garment of this body. When that has been done, he again puts on that other garment in the Garden of Eden of which he had had to divest himself when he entered this world. And the whole joy of the spirit is in that celestial body. In it he rests and moves, and contemplates continually the supernal mysteries which, when he was in the earthly body, he could neither grasp nor understand. When the soul clothes herself with the garments of that world, what delights, what joys, she experiences! And who caused the body to be inhabited by the spirit? Why, he who took off the garment of flesh, the Angel of Death!

'God shows kindness to His creatures in not divesting them of their earthly garment until other garments, more precious and finer than these, are prepared for them. But the wicked, they who have never turned to their Lord with a perfect repentance- naked they came into this world, and naked they must return from it, and their souls go in shame to join the other souls in like plight, and they are judged in the earthly Gehenna by the fire from above. Some of them flutter upward after a time; these are the souls of the sinners who had intended to repent, but died before they had carried out their intentions. These are judged first in Gehenna and then flutter upward. See how great is the mercy of the Holy One towards His creatures! The most wicked sinner, if he have intended repentance, but dies without carrying out his resolve, is, it is true, punished for having gone out of this world without having repented, but his good intention is not lost, but it ascends to the Supernal King and there remains until the Holy One, seeing it, prepares for that soul a place of refuge in "Sheol", where it twitters repentance. For the good intention issues from before the Holy One, and, breaking all the strong gates of the habitations of Gehenna, reaches at last the place where that sinner lies. It smites him and awakens in him again that intention which he had had on earth,

Zohar: Shemoth, Section 2, Page 150b

causing the soul to struggle and ascend from the abode of Sheol. Truly, no good thought is ever lost from the remembrance of the Holy King. Therefore, blessed is he who nourishes good thoughts towards his Lord, for, even if he cannot put them into practice, the Holy One takes the will for the deed. This is the case with good thoughts. With evil thoughts, however, the will is not taken for the deed, save in the case of idolatry, as has been explained by the Companions. The wicked who had never given a thought to repentance go down to Sheol and never come out from thence, as it is written of them, "As the cloud is consumed and vanisheth away, so he that goeth down to sheol shall come up no more" (Job VII, 9). But, concerning those others who had intended to repent, it says, "The Lord killeth and maketh alive; He bringeth down to sheol and bringeth up" (I Sam. II, 6). '

Said R. Judah: 'Why are the sinners punished by the fire of Gehenna? Because the fire of Gehenna, which burns day and night, corresponds to the hot passion of sinfulness in man. There was once a period when for some time sin ceased to rule because it had been thrown into the iron ring in the abyss of the Ocean. During that period the fire of Gehenna went out and did not burn at all. When sinfulness returned, and again began to burn in the hearts of sinners, the fire of Gehenna was started again, for it is the heat of sinful passion in the hearts of sinners that kindles and keeps alight the fires of Gehenna, causing them to burn day and night without ceasing. Gehenna has seven doors which open into seven habitations; and there are also seven types of sinners: evildoers, worthless ones, sinners, the wicked, corrupters, mockers, and arrogant ones; and corresponding with them are the habitations in Gehenna, for each kind a particular place, all according to grade. And over each habitation a special angel is appointed, all being under the direction of Duma, who has thousands and myriads of angels under him, to punish sinners according to their deserts. The fire of the Gehenna which is below comes from the Gehenna which is above, and is kindled by the heat of the sinners in whom the evil inclination burns, and there all the piles burn. In Gehenna there are certain places and grades called "Boiling filth", where the filth of the souls that have been polluted by the filth of this world accumulates. There these souls are purified by fire and made white, and then they ascend towards the heavenly regions. Their filth remains behind and the evil grades, called "Boiling filth", are appointed over that filth and the fire of Gehenna rules over it. There are certain sinners who pollute themselves over and over again by their own sins and are never purified. They die without repentance, having sinned themselves and caused others to sin, being stiff-necked and never showing contrition before the Lord while in this world; these are they who are condemned to remain forever in this place of "boiling filth" and never leave it. Those who have corrupted their ways upon earth and recked not of the honour of their Lord in this world are condemned to remain there for all generations. On Sabbaths, New Moons, special seasons and festivals, the fire is extinguished there, and they have a respite from punishment, but, unlike sinners of a lesser degree who are accorded relief, they are not allowed to leave that place even on such days. As for those who, when on earth, profaned the Sabbath and the festivals, and recked not of the honour of their Lord, but openly profaned the holy days, these days, since they were not regarded in this world by these sinners, do not keep or guard them now in the other world; and so they have no rest.' Said R. Yose: 'Do not say this, for the truth is that there they are forced to keep the Sabbaths and festivals even against their will.' 'It is the heathen', rejoined R. Judah, 'who, not having been commanded to keep the Sabbath in this world, are there forced to keep it. Every Sabbath Eve, at the time of the sanctification of the day, heralds

452

are sent to proclaim throughout the length of Gehenna: "Cease from punishing the wicked! The Holy King is come; the Sabbath is about to be sanctified. He takes them all under His protection", and all chastisements cease and the wicked find rest for a space. But the fire of Gehenna never ceases to burn those souls who have never kept the Sabbath, and sinners there ask concerning them: "Wherein lies the difference between these and those? Why find these no rest?" And the lords of judgement make answer: "These are sinners who have denied the Holy One, blessed be He, and have broken the whole Law, because they kept not the Sabbath; therefore now have they no rest." Then all other kinds of sinners are allowed to come and see these, the tormented, for whom there is no rest. And a certain angel, named Santriel, goes away to fetch the body of such a sinner from the grave and brings it to Gehenna, holding it up before the eyes of all the sinners, that they may see how it has bred worms; and that soul has no rest in the fire of Gehenna. Then all the sinners of Gehenna swarm round it and call out: "This is such a one, a sinner, who regarded not the honour of his Lord! He denied the Holy One! He denied the whole Torah! Woe unto him! Better it were had he never been born that such punishment and disgrace should not have come upon him!" Concerning such it is written: "And they shall go forth and look upon the carcases of the men, that have transgressed against Me: for their worm shall not die, neither shall their fire be quenched; and they shall be an abhorring unto all flesh,' (Isa. LXVI, 24). "Their worm shall not die" refers to the body; "their fire shall not be quenched", to the soul; "an abhorring (deraon) unto all flesh"; that is to say, all the other sinners will say, "de-raon", we have seen enough of this horrible thing!' Said R. Yose: 'Quite true! For Sabbath is of equal importance with the whole Torah. The Torah is fire, therefore those who have broken it are doomed to be eternally burnt by the fire of Gehenna!' Said R. Judah; 'At the conclusion of the Sabbath that angel comes and takes back to the grave the worm-eaten body, and both the body and the soul are punished, each in its way. But this happens only when the body is still intact; if, on the other hand, it is decayed, it is not any longer punished, for the Holy One "doth not stir up all his wrath" (Ps. LXXXIII, 38).

'All sinners, as long as their bodies in the graves are intact, with all their limbs, are judged body and soul together, each in its own way; but as soon as the body is decayed, the punishing of the soul ceases. Those souls that are destined to leave Gehenna now leave it; those that are to have rest now find it, and those who are destined to become dust under the feet of the righteous become dust, each according to its deserts. How excellent a thing it is, therefore, both for the righteous as well as for sinners, when their bodies are in close contact with the earth so that decay can set in quickly and their punishment may not be prolonged through the continued existence of the body; for there is not one of the righteous who can escape the judgement of the grave, for the angel appointed over the graves stands over the body and punishes it daily. And if the righteous have to undergo this judgement of the grave, how much more so the wicked! But when the body decays, the judgement ceases in both cases. The only exceptions are those saints who are the pillars of the world, who merit that their souls immediately after death should ascend forthwith to the regions appointed for them. They, however, are few. It is the Destroying Angel who brings death to all people, except those who die in the Holy Land, to whom death comes by the Angel of Mercy who holds sway there.' Said R. Isaac: 'This being the case, wherein lay the superiority of Moses, Aaron and Miriam, concerning whom it is written that they died "by the mouth of the Lord", meaning that their death was not brought about by the Destroying Angel?' R. Judah replied:

'Truly, the greatness of these three and their superiority over all others is demonstrated by this, that, although they met their death outside the Holy Land, they, unlike their contemporaries, were not brought to it by the Destroying Angel, but by the Holy One Himself. But in the Holy Land itself, all who die do not die by the hand of the Destroying Angel, because that is the domain of the Holy One; concerning this it is written: "Thy dead shall revive, my dead bodies (nebelati) shall rise; awake and sing, ye that dwell in the. dust" (Isa. xxvi, 19). "Thy dead" refers to those who die in the Holy Land, who belong to Him alone and to no other power, for the "other side" has no power at all there; they are "Thy dead", namely, those of the Holy One. "My dead bodies" refers to those who die outside the Holy Land by the power of the "destroyer", so they are called nebelah, "dead body", defiling those who touch it. Forevery animal not slaughtered according to the rule is called nebelah, because slaughter is from the "other side", and as soon as it is improperly carried out the "other side" rests on it, and it is therefore dubbed nebelah, i.e. shamefulness, wickedness, folly; its name describing its character. Therefore, wherever the "other side" has power, it is called nebelah, and those who die outside the Holy Land, being under its power, are therefore called "dead bodies". "Awake and sing ye that dwell in dust"; "dwell" means that they are there but for a short period, and are not really dead but asleep, and have only to be awakened. This refers to those who are "asleep" in Hebron (the Patriarchs); therefore the expression used of them is "expire" (gawa), as of one gone into a trance from which he can be recalled. Thus the four pairs? the Patriarchs and their wives, who lie in Hebron, are asleep and not dead: their bodies are all intact, just as when they lived on earth, and they know the hidden mysteries more than any living being. They were hidden there at the gates of Paradise, and they are referred to in the words "dwell in dust". Truly, those whose souls went out of them as they dwelt in the Holy Land did not die by the power of the "other side", which has no power there, but by the Angel of Mercy, under whose care the Holy Land is.

'There is a place [Tr. note: Luz, cf. Bereshith Rabbah, 69.] in the world where that "Destroyer" has no power at all, where he is not permitted to enter, and those who live there do not die until they have left the town. And why has the Angel of Destruction no power there? It cannot be because it is not his domain, since even in the Holy Land, which is subject to no alien sway, people die. Nor can it be because it is a holy place, because there is no place so holy as the Holy Land. Nor can it be that it is on account of the merits of its builder, for there have been many men of greater merit.' Said R. Isaac: 'I have not heard any explanation of this, so I shall say nothing.' So they repaired to R. Simeon and asked him concerning this matter. Said he: 'It is indeed true that the Angel of Death has no power over that place, and the Holy One does not wish that anyone should ever die there. Nor should you think that before the town was built people in that place died. Not so. For, from the very beginning of the world God appointed this place to be thus, and to those who would penetrate into the mystery of wisdom there is in this a mystery of mysteries. When the Holy One, blessed be He, created the world, He did so by means of the secret power of letters. The letters were shaken about before Him and He created the world by the tracing of the Holy Name. The letters presented themselves for participation in the world's creation in a variety of permutations. [Tr. note: v. Zohar, Gen., 204a.] The Holy One said it must end with Yod, and the letter Teth remained hanging alone in the air above that place (Luz).

Zohar: Shemoth, Section 2, Page 152a

The light of the letter Teth is Life; therefore, anyone seeing this letter in a dream knows it is a good omen for him. Hence it is that death has no dominion over that place over which this letter hangs. When the Holy One desired the world to be firmly established, then took He a stone on which was engraved the mystery of the twenty-two letters of the Alphabet, and threw it into the waters. It drifted from place to place, but found nowhere to settle until it came to the Holy Land, and the waters followed it until it reached that spot where the Altar was to be established. There the stone sank, and the whole world was firmly established on it. It might be asked, if that place (Luz) is the place where life reigns, why was the Temple not built there, that it might give life also to those who dwell in Jerusalem? The answer is, that in that place abides one letter only, but in the Temple are all the letters by which it was miraculously built, after the manner and in the likeness of the whole Universe. Besides, the Holy Land gives life and expiation to those who are in the other world, but Luz gives life only to those who are in this world. Hence the purpose of the Temple was to obtain forgiveness of the sins of Israel, to make it possible for them to inherit the world to come. Mark this. The letter Teth signifies in all places the light of life; therefore the word "good" (tob) begins with this letter. The Angel of Destruction, when he comes to this letter, must flee, or, rather, he has not the power to approach it at all. This letter is the reverse of the letter Koph, [Tr. note: The first letter of Kelalah, curse.] which finds no resting place in the whole world. Now, as Teth dominates this place, so does koph dominate Gehenna. In the book of R. Hamnuna the Ancient it is written concerning the two letters Heth and Teth that they were not engraved upon the precious stones, those stones of perfection (on the High Priest's ephod), and the names of the Twelve Tribes inscribed on those stones do not contain these two letters, because together they would form the word Het' (sin). All the letters of the Alphabet hang in engraved mysteries of the Holy Names in the Temple place; also Heaven and Earth, and all that is above and below; yea, the Holy Name itself is engraved there. So it was in the Tabernacle also, because "Bezalel possessed such great wisdom that he knew how to combine those letters of the Alphabet by which heaven and earth were created", [Tr. note: T. B. Berakhoth, 55a.] and so, on account of his great wisdom, the building of the Tabernacle was entrusted to him, and he was set apart from among all the children of Israel. And as one was set apart above, so the Holy One wished that he should be set apart also below. As the Lord said unto Moses: "Behold I have called by name Bezalel the son of Uri, the son of Hur, of the tribe of Judah" (Ex. XXI, 2), so did Moses say unto the children of Israel: "Behold the Lord hath called by name Bezalel", etc. (Ibid. xxv, 30). Therefore his name was Bezalel, i.e. bezel El, "in the very shadow of God". And who is that one? The Righteous, who sits in the shadow of Him whose name is "The Highest God" (El elyon). So this one holds a position below corresponding to that of El above: as El "took six sides", so did the Righteous take six sides; as the El sends out light above, so does this Righteous shed light below; as that El is the synthesis of all the six dimensions, so is that Righteous. "The son of Uri"-the son of primeval light (or), which the Holy One created in the time of Creation. "The son of Hur"- the son of absolute freedom (herut); or "the son of the whitest (havra) of all colours". And he is appropriately "of the tribe of Judah".

'As we have already pointed out, all colours seen in dreams signify good things, with the exception of purple-blue (techeleth), and that is because it symbolizes the Throne from which souls are judged. But has it not some white in it? Truly; but when the judgement takes place it appears to be only purple-blue, as we have

Zohar: Shemoth, Section 2, Page 152b

said. The sight of that colour reminds a man that he must keep the commandments of his Lord. So it was with the Brazen Serpent in the wilderness: they who looked upon it were filled with awe and fear of the Holy One and kept themselves clear from sin, and therefore they were healed in that moment. And who was it that instilled in them fear of the Holy One? The instrument of punishment-that Serpent at which they so fixedly gazed. The same is true of "the thread of blue", that they were bidden to put upon the fringe of their garments (Zizith), concerning which it is written, "that ye may look upon it and remember all the commandments of the Lord" (Num. xv, 39). Therefore it was ordained that this colour should be in the Tabernacle.' Said R. Isaac: 'The Master has told us that this colour symbolizes the Throne when it becomes the seat of judgement. When, then, is it the seat of mercy?'

R. Simeon replied: 'When the Cherubim turn their faces the one towards the other, and gaze each into the face of the other, then all colours are merged- purple-blue becomes something else, and green or blue is turned into white. With the changing of colours judgement was changed into mercy, or vice versa. And so with all other colours. All depends on the way in which Israel orders her prayers; hence it is written: "Israel in whom I will be glorified" (lit. beautified) (Isa. XLIX, 3), to wit, in those colours which merge into one another and contain all beauty.' AND THOU SHALT MAKE A TABLE OF ACACIA WOOD. R. Isaac began: 'It is written: "When thou hast eaten and art full, then thou shalt bless the Lord thy God" (Deut. VIII, 10). How blessed are the Israelites, whom the Holy One has befriended above all nations and drawn near to Himself! It is for their sake that He nourished all nations; for, had it not been for them He would not have supplied the world with food. And now, when Israel is in exile, the Gentiles receive a double portion. When Israel dwelt in the Holy Land, the Holy One sent down food to them from a supernal region, the surplus of which was given to the heathen nations, but now it is just the reverse. He deals with them like a king with his servants. So long as the servants are obedient and loyal they are permitted to sit and eat with the king, and the remnants are thrown to the dogs; but when they are disobedient, and forget their loyal service, the king gives the food to the dogs and leaves them only the bones. The same is true of Israel: while they did the will of their Lord they ate from the King's table which He Himself had prepared for them, and they, out of the fullness of their joy, gave to the nations their surplus; but when Israel ceased to live according to the commands of their Lord they went into captivity and had to be content with that which the Gentiles left over. So it says: "Even thus shall the children of Israel eat their defiled bread among the Gentiles, whither I will drive them" (Ezek. IV, 13). Woe to the king's son, who is forced to wait at the servants' table to be fed upon the remnants! King David said: "Thou preparest a table before me in the presence of mine enemies; thou anointest my head with oil; my cup runneth over" (Ps. XXIII, 6). "Thou preparest a table": this is the meal of the king; "in the presence of mine enemies": this refers to the "dogs" who lie under the table waiting for the scraps while he sits with the king enjoying the meal: "Thou anointest my head with oil": this refers to the main part (the "head") of the meal, for all the rich oil and fat, and all the best portions of the food, are reserved for the king's friend, while that which is left is given to the scullions and the dogs. "My cup runneth over": the cup of the king's friend is ever filled up, even before he asks. The position of the children of Israel in regard to that of the Gentiles has ever been thus.'

R. Hiya once went to Tiberias to see R. Simeon, and R. Jacob, the son of Idi, and R. Jesse the younger accompanied him. On the way R. Jesse said to R. Hiya: 'I find very surprising the words of the Scripture, "But show kindness to the sons of Barzillai the Gileadite, and let them be of those that eat of thy table" (I Kings II, 7). Was this all the kindness that Solomon was to show him? Also it hardly accords with the dignity of a king that another person should eat with him

at the same table. The king should sit alone at his table, and his ministers by themselves at another table, somewhat lower.' R. Hiya replied: 'I have not heard any explanation of the matter, and therefore shall not say anything.' Then R. Abba asked R. Jacob: 'Hast thou heard aught concerning it?' He answered: 'If you who sip daily the richness of the most excellent oil (R. Simeon) have not heard anything, how can you expect me to know?' Then he asked R. Jesse: 'And hast thou heard anything?' He replied: 'Although I am but young, and have but lately been admitted to your company, and had no great teachers before, yet I have heard an explanation.' He then began by quoting the verse: "Who giveth good to all flesh: for his mercy endureth forever" (Ps. CXXXVI, 25). 'Why', said he, 'did David choose to end this great hymn of praise with this verse? Now there are three great channels above by which the Holy One, blessed be He, manifests Himself, which are His precious mystery: the brain, [Tr. note: Hokmah.] the heart, [Tr. note: Tifereth.] and the liver. [Tr. note: Malkuth.] These organs act above in the opposite manner from those below. Above it is the head which first receives nourishment, which it sends on to the heart, which eventually passes it on to the liver, which again gives sustenance to the lower members in due proportion. Here below it is the liver which comes first, which transfers the nourishment to the heart, in such a manner that it is that organ which receives the finest portions; then, when the heart is strengthened, it passes the nourishment on to the brain; while to the other parts of the body the liver apportions the amounts necessary. On a fast day, man sacrifices his food and drink to the supernal "Liver", and what is it that he thus sacrifices? His fatness, nourishing food, his blood, heart and soul; that "Liver" accepts it gladly, and in turn offers it to the "Heart" that reigns over it; in turn the "Heart" offers it to the "Brain", which rules over the whole body; then the "Liver" apportions to all the lower parts their share. At another time it is the Brain which receives first and gives to the Heart, which, again, gives to the Liver and the Liver to all the lower members; and when it distributes nourishment to this world it gives first to the heart, which on earth is the king; for the king must naturally be fed first. Blessed is he who is found worthy to eat at the King's table, for thus does he come first in the enjoyment of the bounty from above! This, then, was the significance of that kindness which David showed to the sons of Barzillai. Not that anyone sits actually at the table of the king. But those who eat along with the king, and at the same time, are in his favour and are reckoned as sitting at the same table with him.' Then R. Hiya came forward, kissed him on the brow, and said: 'Young thou art, but profound wisdom dwells already in thine heart.' In the meantime they discovered that R. Hezekiah had arrived. R. Hiya turned to him and said: 'Of a surety, the Holy One, blessed be He, will join this our company, for new thoughts upon the Torah will find utterance among us.' They then sat down to eat, and agreed that each should give some exposition of the Torah during the meal. Said R. Jesse: 'This which we eat is but a light repast, and yet it is called a "meal", a meal in which the Holy One participates, and concerning which it is written: "This is the table that is before the Lord" (Ezek. XLI, 22); for the words of the Torah will gather about this place.'

R. Hiya then began to discourse on the text: When thou hast eaten and art satisfed, then thou shalt bless the Lord thy God (Deut. VIII, 10). Said he: 'Should a man then bless the Lord only after he has filled his belly?

Nay, even if one eats but a morsel and counts it as a meal, that is called eating to satisfaction; for it is written, "Thou openest Thine hand and satisfiest the wish (will) of every living thing" (Ps. CXLV, 16). It is not written: '"Thou satisfiest with a substantial meal", but "the wish" or "the intention"; so it is not the quantity of food but the intention of the eater that "satisfies"; therefore it is necessary that at all times when we eat we should offer up our thanks in order that there may be joy above.'

R. Hezekiah spoke on the same words, saying: 'From these words also it is possible to deduce the rules that an intoxicated person is allowed to say the grace after meals. With prayers it is otherwise, for prayers ascend very high to the realm where there is neither eating nor drinking, and therefore prayers are best said on an empty stomach. But in that realm to which the benediction after meals enters, there is, as it were, both "eating and drinking", and from it emanates nourishment for us below. Therefore it is necessary to exhibit before it satiety and joy in the expression of grace after meals.'

R. Jesse then spoke on the words: AND THOU SHALT MAKE A TABLE OF ACACIA WOOD. Said he: This table stood in the Tabernacle, and there rested upon it the blessing from above, and from it issued nourishment to the whole world. Not for a moment was that Table to remain empty, since blessing does not rest upon an empty place. Therefore it was that the shew-bread had always to be renewed upon it each Sabbath (Lev. XXIV, 8), in order that the blessing from above might always rest upon it, and that food and blessing, because of it, might emanate from that table to all the tables of the world. So, too, should every man's table be when he says grace after meals; in order that the blessing from above should rest upon it, it should not be empty, as the Companions have indicated in connection with the words of Elisha to the widow: "Tell me, what hast thou in the house?" (2 Kings IV, 2). A table at which there is no converse pertaining to the words of the Torah is one concerning which it is written, "For all (their) tables are full of vomit and filthiness, without a place" (Isa. XXVIII, 8), and at such a table it is forbidden to say the benediction. There are two kinds of tables: there is the kind that is prepared for the Holy One above, and at which it is ever fitting that the Torah should be discoursed upon and the letters of the words of the Torah should be gathered in-the table concerning which it is written: "This is the table that is before the Lord" (Ezek. XLI, 22). And there is the table which has no part in the Torah, or in the holiness thereof, and which is called "full of filthiness"

-the table of "another god", which has no part in the mystery of the supernal God. That table, on the other hand, at which words of the Torah are spoken, is taken up by the Holy One, blessed be He, and becomes His own possession. Nay more, Suriya, the high angelic being, takes up all the holy words uttered at this table, and sets the form of it before the Holy One, and all the words, and the table also, are crowned before the Holy King, as is implied in the words "before the Lord". A man's table can purify him of all his sins. Blessed is the man whose table exhibits these two qualities-that from it words of the Torah ascend to the Holy One, and food goes forth to the poor. At the moment when such a table as this is being removed after the meal two angels appear, one at the right and one at the left. The one says: "This is a table belonging to the Holy King upon which such an one ordered his meal in His presence. May this table be continually full of supernal blessings, and may the Holy One pour upon it the richness of His bounty." And the other says: "This is a table of the Holy King which such an one had ordered before Him. It is blessed by those above and by those below. May it be set before the Ancient of Days both in this world and in the world to come." R. Abba, before the table was removed after a meal, was used to cover it up, saying: "Remove this table respectfully that it may not be put to shame before the King's messengers." A man's table, used rightly, secures for him participation in the bliss of the world to come, a sufficiency of nourishment in this world, and also additional power and excellency in the right place, and, withal, it causes him to be remembered favourably before the Ancient of Days. Happy the lot of such a man in this world and in the world to come.'

R. Jacob said: 'It is written, "And it came to pass, when all that knew him beforetime saw that, behold, he prophesied among the prophets, then the people said one to another, What is this that is come unto the son of Kish? Is Saul also among the prophets?" (I Sam. x, 11). Said he: 'Was not Saul already the chosen of the Lord, as it says, "See whom the Lord hath chosen" (Ibid. v. 24), i.e. already. Why, then, were they astonished that he prophesied? The reason was because the Holy One chose Saul to be a king, not a prophet; for no man ever, except Moses, was found worthy of combining the two functions of king and prophet. As to Samuel, he was certainly a prophet, as it says, "And all Israel knew that Samuel was established to be a prophet to the Lord", but besides being a prophet he was only a judge, not a king; otherwise the people would not have asked for a king. Therefore the people were astonished when Saul prophesied, because he had been chosen as king and not as prophet. If it should be asked, why, then, did the spirit of prophecy rest on him, the answer would be, that because the kingship is based on the inspiration of the Holy Spirit, he possessed the inspiration of prophecy before he became king; but as soon as he was made king, it was not the spirit of prophecy but the power to judge according to the truth that was bestowed upon him, and for which he had been chosen to be king. As long as he was among the prophets the spirit of prophecy rested on him, but when he left them, the spirit of prophecy departed from him. As for me, O that the inspiration of the Holy Spirit should come upon me, that I might be among the faithful prophets, the disciples of R. Simeon ben Yohai, before whom both supernals and terrestrials tremble in awe-and I that am now in your company stand in fear and trembling before you!'

Then he went on: '"Thou shalt make a table." This table was here below for setting the shew-bread upon. Now, which was of greater import, the table or the bread?

Zohar: Shemoth, Section 2, Page 154b

It might be thought that the bread was more important, since the table was needed to put the bread on, and besides, it was, in the very nature of things, beneath the bread. This, however, is not so: the table was the essential article, being, through its arrangement, the receptacle of blessing from above and of food for the whole universe. Indeed, from the secret influence of that Table emanated nourishment to the whole world, in proportion to the abundance poured out upon it from above. As for the bread, it was the fruit, the actual nourishment emanating from that Table, to show that theuniversal nourishment emanated from it-for wherethere is no vineyard there are no grapes, and where there is no tree there can be no fruit. So the Table was the essential and the shewbread was but the nourishment emanating from it. And the priests, from Sabbath to Sabbath, collected the fruit of the Table, to show that supernal nutriment emanated from the Table through the agency of that bread. And because the priests were permitted to eat the shew-bread, all the rest of their food and all that they drank was blessed, so that the "evil inclination" had no power to attack them-for, as a rule, the "evil inclination" is only present where there is much eating and drinking, as it is written: "Lest I be full and deny Thee, and say, Who is the Lord?" (Prov. xxx, 9); since it is from eating and drinking that the evil inclination gathers strength in a man's body. The bread which was taken from the table in the Tabernacle caused blessing to descend upon all the other food consumed by the priests, so that the evil impulse might have no power to attack them, and they could carry out their ministrations to the Holy One with perfect devotion. For the priests this was most necessary. The table had to be set up at the northern end, as it is written, "And thou shalt put up the table at the north side" (Ex. XXVI, 35), because the awakening of joy proceeds from thence. The Left Side (North) always receives from the Right Side, and rouses the Female, and the Right Side then draws Her to Himself, and She unites with Him. Water, which symbolizes joy, proceeds from the Right, then it bestows itself upon the Left, and so it is that water unites with the Left, communicating to it joy. All this is symbolized by the ritual washing of the hands before meals: the vessel containing the water is taken in the right hand and poured on to the left, not from left to right. Therefore the Table, as we have said, was set on the north side, for there was more fruit there, since joy was awakened there first. This is expressed in the words: "His left hand under my head, and his right hand embraces me" (S.S. II, 6). A man should sit down to table with a clean body, in order that God may be pleased with his meal and it may not be accounted "filth and refuse" for the impure side to reap any benefit therefrom. When one has eaten and is satisfied, it is necessary to give the scraps and the dregs to the "other side", and any particles left upon the hands after a meal must be washed away so that the "other side" may receive its due. Therefore the washing of the hands after a meal is an imperative duty and the water must be poured away into the place of guilt (hoba="duty" and "guilt"). Hence, no blessing is to be made over the washing of hands (after meals), since there can be no benediction in connection with that "side". So it is important that one should not give any of the food on the table to that "filth and vomit". The table in the Tabernacle was, as we have said, placed there in order that food should lie upon it and that nourishment should therefrom emanate to the whole world, and that is why

Zohar: Shemoth, Section 2, Page 155a

it was not permitted to remain empty, even for one moment. The other, the impure table, the table of emptiness, could have no place in the sanctuary. In the same manner, the table over which a man pronounces blessings for food must not be empty, for blessing cannot rest on emptiness. The bread which was set upon the Table of the Holy One took the form of tvelve loaves, and the symbolism of them has already been explained in connection with the mystery of the Countenance-for it was called "the bread of the Countenance" because all the nourishment and sustenance of the world emanated from this supernal Countenance. The "Bread of the Countenance" is the food of that "Countenance", and all the nourishment and plenty that the world contains emanates from that Countenance, and rests on that Table. And because the nourishment which it receives comes from that august Countenance, and from that self-same Countenance supplies all the others with sustenance, all of which was centred in that "bread", therefore was it put hot upon the table, and so, miraculously, was it also, [Tr. note: t Cf. T. B. Hagigah, 26b.] as has been inferred from the words "to put hot bread in the day when it was taken away" (I Sam. XXI, 6). And man must cherish the mysteries connected with his table, in all these aspects of which we have spoken on account of that Table.'

R. Eleazar then discoursed on the verse, LET THY GARMENTS BE ALWAYS WHITE, AND LET THY HEAD LACK NO OINTMENT (Eccl. IX, 8). This verse, said he, has been variously interpreted, but it may also be expounded thus. God created man in the mystery of Wisdom, and fashioned him with great art, and breathed into him the breath of life, so that he might know and comprehend the mysteries of wisdom, to apprehend the glory of his Lord; as it is written: "Everyone that is called by my name: for I have created (beratiw) him for my glory, I have formed (yezartiw) him, yea, I have made (asitiw) him" (Isa. XLIII, 7). "I have created him for my glory", literally, the inner meaning being that, as we have learnt, the glory of the holy Throne is fixed firmly and compactly in its place through the cooperation of the children of this world; that is, through the cooperation of righteous and saintly men, and those who know how to effect adjustments. So the words really mean: "I have created the world in order that, by means of their work, the righteous on earth may cause my glory to be established on mighty pillars to provide it with adornments and completion from below, that it may be exalted, through their merit." Beriah (creation, i.e. creative ideas) appertains to the left side; Yezirah (creative formation) appertains to the right side, as it is written, "Who formeth (yozer) light and createth (bore) darkness" (Isa. XLV, 7); while 'Asiyah (making, finishing) lies between them, as it is written, "I make ('ose) peace and create evil: I the Lord do ('ose) all these things" (Ibid.), and again, "He maketh ('ose) peace in his high places" (Job xxv, 2). Hence, because man is on the earth, and it is incumbent on him to establish firmly My glory, I have provided him with the same supports as the supernal Glory: as in it there are "creation", "formation", and "making", so of man it is written, "I have created him, I have formed him, yea, I have made him." Thus man is after the pattern of that supernal Glory that he may confirm it and make it complete on all sides. Blessed is the man whose works entitle him to be regarded thus. Concerning this it is written: "Let thy garments be always white", etc. And, as the Supernal Glory has no lack of "holy ointment", from the mystery of the world to come, the man whose works are "white" will not lack

Zohar: Shemoth, Section 2, Page 155b

this "holy ointment". Through what does a man merit participation in that supernal joy? Through his table: yea, when at his table he has satisfied the wants of the poor; as it is written: "If thou draw out thy soul to the hungry and satisfy the afflicted soul.... then shalt thou delight thyself in the Lord." (Isa. LVIII, 10-14). Such a man will the Holy One satisfy; he will anoint him with holy supernal "ointment", which ever streams upon that Supernal Glory.'

R. Yose and R. Hiya were walking together, and a certain merchant was walking behind them. Said R. Yose to R. Hiya: 'We must concentrate our thoughts upon the words of the Torah, for the Holy One goes before us, therefore it is time for us to do some service to Him on the way.' R. Hiya then began to speak on the words: It is time to act for the Lord, for they have made void thy Torah (Ps. CXIX, 126). He said: 'This verse has already been interpreted by the Companions, but the words may also be taken thus. "It is time to act for the Lord": whenever the Torah is observed and studied in the world, the Holy One, as it were, rejoices in His handiwork, and all the worlds which He has created, and the foundations of heaven and earth are consolidated; and what is more, He calleth into His presence the whole celestial family, saying unto them: "Behold my holy children on earth! Through their loving diligence is the Torah crowned in their midst. Behold those works of my hand of whom ye did say: "What is man that thou shouldst be mindful of him!" (Ps. VIII, 5 [Tr. note: v. Bereshith Rabba, ch. 8] And the celestial family, seeing the joy of the Lord in His people, begin to sing together: "And who is like thy people Israel, one nation on earth?" (2 Sam. VII, 23). When, however, the Israelites neglect the Torah, the very power of the Holy One is, as it were, weakened, as it is written: "The Rock that made him he (Israel) weakened" (Deut. XXXII, 15, according to an Haggadic interpretation), and then "all the hosts of heaven stand" (2 Chron. XVIII, 18) and accuse them. So "it is time to act for the Lord"; that is to say, the remnant of the righteous must gird up their loins and perform works of righteousness, so that in His armies and in His hosts the Lord may gain strength, because the greater number of the people "have made void thy Torah", and mankind will not occupy themselves seriously with it.' Said the merchant who followed them: 'May I be allowed to put to you a question?' Said R. Yose: 'Verily, our path is made straight before us. Ask thy question. 'Then said the man: 'Had it said "One must act", or "let us act", your explanation would have been fitting. But it says, "It is time to act". Besides, should it not have been "to act before the Lord"? Why does it say "for the Lord"?' Said R. Yose: 'In many ways is this journey of ours auspicious: one,

458

that we were first two and now we are three, and the Shekinah is present with us; secondly, I thought that thou wert a withered trunk, but I see thou art a green olive tree; and lastly, because thou hast asked a good question. And since thou hast begun, continue!' The man accordingly then went on as follows: '"It is time to act for the Lord for they have made void thy Torah." There are times and times--"a time to love and a time to hate" (Eccl. III, 8). There is a time which is above, the "time" which is a mystery of Faith, and this is called a "time of good will and grace". This always is the time for men to love the Lord, as it says: "Love the Lord thy God". But there is "another" time, the mystery of "other gods", a "time" which must be hated of man and its attraction guarded against. This is "the time to hate"; concerning which "time" it is written, "Speak unto Aaron thy brother, that he come not at all times unto the holy place (Lev. XVI, 2). The time when Israel diligently studies the Torah and keeps its commandments is the time that is within the mystery of the Holy Faith; it is fitly decked out and adorned with all its proper graces according to the eternal purpose. But the time when Israel neglects the Torah, making it void, is, as it were, a time of incompleteness, and has neither wholeness nor light. The verse is therefore to be interpreted: "There is a time which is still to be made or finished (la'asot), because at present it is incomplete, because Israel has made the Torah void"; for "time" is thus elevated or depressed according to the works of Israel.'

Then R. Yose and R. Hiya

Zohar: Shemoth, Section 2, Page 156a

kissed him on the brow, and R. Hiya said: 'Surely, we are not worthy that thou shouldst go behind us. Blessed is the road on which we were privileged to hear such words! Blessed is the generation which is contemporary with R. Simeon; for in it wisdom is found, even among the mountains!' The three then walked on, and the merchant said: 'It is written, But as for me, my prayer is unto thee, O Lord, in an acceptable time (time of good will): O God, in the abundance of thy mercy hear me, in the truth of thy salvation (Ps. LXIX, 14), and we are taught that the time when the congregation is occupied with prayer is called the time of good will. This is certainly the case, for the congregation in this way prepare the supports for this time, so that it becomes a time of "good will", propitious for the offering of petitions. "As for me, my prayer is unto thee, O Lord." These words contain the mystery of Unity: "as for me" indicates King David, the realm called "Redemption" (the name of the Benediction which follows the Shema), and "my prayer" refers to the "Prayer" (the 'Amidah), thus "joining the Redemption to the Prayer" without interruption, because they are both unified in the "time of good will". This prayer is recited during the Sabbath afternoon prayer, and not on weekdays, because the afternoon prayer on weekdays is the time when severe judgement is in the ascendant, and is not a time of "good will"; but on Sabbath "anger" is absent, and all the attributes are harmoniously united, and judgement, though it is roused, is mitigated by mercy. Hence it is necessary to recite this verse of unification in order to harmonize all the grades. It was at the time of Sabbath afternoon prayer that Moses passed away from this world. That was a time of good will above and of sorrow below, and for this reason the gates were closed from the time of the Sabbath afternoon prayer until the end of the Sabbath. Which gates? The gates of the houses of study, and they were closed in order to show that with the passing away of Moses, the Faithful Shepherd, the study of the Torah, for the time being, ceased. At that time the house of study of Moses was closed, needless, then, to say all others. If they were closed, would one expect that others should be open? If Moses' own Torah lamented over his death, who would not lament? For this reason are the gates of all the Houses of Study closed at this hour in perpetual memory of that sad occasion [Tr. note: v. Tosefoth to Menahoth, 30a.] and it is necessary for worshippers to repeat the "justification of the (Divine) judgement" contained in the verse, "Thy righteousness is like the mighty mountains: thy judgements are a great deep" (Ps. XXXVI, 7). There were three who passed away from this world at the time of Sabbath afternoon prayer- Moses, the supreme, faithful prophet; Joseph the righteous; and King David. Therefore three "justifications of the judgement" are recited at this time: [Tr. note: i.e. the Sabbath afternoon service, v. Prayer Book.] the first refers to Joseph the righteous, and is contained in the words, "Thy righteousness is like a mighty mountain, thy judgements are a great deep" for Joseph singly was comparable to the high mountains and to the mighty deep (cf. Gen. XLIX, 25, 26). Then comes Moses, the faithful prophet, to whom refer the word: "Thy righteousness, O God, reaches the heights, who hast done great things" (Ps. LXXI, 19), because he grasped both sides, the right and the left. Then comes King David, to whom refer the words, "Thy righteousness is an everlasting righteousness and thy law is the truth" (Ibid. CXIX, 142), for "everlasting" refers to David (cf. 2 Sam. VII, 16). Thus all was gathered in at that time, both the Written and the Oral Torahs, and therefore, at that time, the gates of the Torah were closed, and the gates of the whole world were also closed. When Joseph the righteous died, all the wells and springs were dried up, and the captivity (of Egypt) commenced for all the tribes. Then the celestial beings recited the verse: "Thy righteousness is like the mighty mountains", etc. On the death of Moses, the sun in his splendour was darkened and the Written Torah was locked up, that light of the luminous mirror. The Moon withdrew her light when King David died,

Zohar: Shemoth, Section 2, Page 156b

and the Oral Torah ceased to shine. Since that time the lights of the Torah have remained hidden, and controversy has increased over the Mishnah (i.e. the traditional Law), and the wise men dispute, and all the great thinkers are in confusion, so that to succeeding generations the joy of the Torah has been lost. When a great man dies the scholars proclaim a fast. Seeing, then, that the joy of the Written and Oral Torahs was gathered in at this hour, is it not fitting that the gates of the Torah should close then? This, then, is the reason why we repeat the three "justifications of judgement", as explained.'

R. Yose and R. Hiya rejoiced at his words and kissed him again, saying: 'Happy indeed is our lot on this path!' The stranger again spoke, taking as his text the verse: Wisdom strengtheneth the wise more than ten potentates which are in the city (Eccl. XII, 19). 'This', he said, 'refers to Moses. When he went up into Mount Sinai to receive the Torah, all those firmaments, and all those supernal hosts, began to tremble and spake unto the Lord of the Universe, saying: "Is not all our bliss and all our joy based on the Torah, and art Thou minded to send her down to earth?" And they gathered round Moses in order to consume him with fire, but Moses prevailed over them all, as the scholars have already set forth; [Tr. note: v. T.B. Shabb. 88b.] but there is more yet to be said. The man who gives himself up with ardour and diligence to the study of the Torah for her own sake will find in her a strong protection in time of need. From what region is it that he gains this strength? From the "ten rulers", the Ten Words of Creation which are written in the Torah, for these are supernal "potentates" by means of which man is strengthened both in this world and in the world to come. All mysteries, all commandments, and all wisdom, concerning both the higher and the lower, are dependent on them; all are included in them, and all is in the Torah. Blessed is the man who is occupied continually with the Torah, that through her he may gain power for the world to come. The "ten potentates" are also the ten aspects of Wisdom which are found in the Torah, contained in ten (Divine) Names, all included in one Name of twenty-two letters (of the Hebrew alphabet). Those mysteries of the world to come are imprinted in light such as no eye can look upon, nor can our imagination comprehend the measure of joy and delight which the Holy One, blessed be He, has in store for the righteous in the world to come, as it is written, "No eye hath seen it, O God, apart from thee, who has made it for those who wait for him" (Isa. LXIV, 4). Man's table enables him to attain to the delight of that other table: "he eats always at the king's table" (2 Sam. IX, 13), and as King David said, "Thou preparest a table before me" (Ps. XXIII, 4), which refers to the preparation of the Table in the other world for those from below; for this is the joy and delight of the soul in the world to come. But is there a table set for the souls in the world to come? Verily there is! In that world they eat of such food and with such satisfaction as the angels enjoy. And do the angels eat? Verily they do! Such as theirs was the food upon which the Israelites were fed in the wilderness. This food is symbolical of the Dew which emanates from above, from the mystery of the world to come. It is the food of the light of the oil of holy anointing; from it the righteous in the Garden of Eden derive their sustenance and are replete with joy. For in the Garden of Eden which is below the souls of the righteous put on a form which is like unto that which they had worn in this world; but on Sabbaths and holy days they put off this form like a garment and ascend to those heavenly regions where they may behold the Lord in His Glory, and where they may fully enjoy the supernal delights. Concerning this it is written: "And it shall come to pass that from one new moon to another, and from one Sabbath to another, shall all flesh come to worship before me, saith the Lord" (Isa. LXVI, 23). Is it "flesh", then, that will come? Ought it not to be written, "all spirits", or "all souls"? But the fact is that the Holy One created man in this world after the pattern of the supernal Glory above. This supernal Glory expands itself into spirit after spirit, and soul after soul,

Zohar: Shemoth, Section 2, Page 157a

until it reaches a region which it called "Body" [Tr. note: I Malkuth.] and into this "Body" the spirit from the Fountain of Life enters that is called "All"; for all the good and all the satisfaction and nourishment of the "Body" is in it. There is an allusion to this in the words: "Moreover, the advantage of the earth is in all" (Eccl. v, 9)-which "all" refers to the spirit of that "Body". Similarly, man in this world consists of a body, and the spirit which dominates it is in the likeness of that supernal Spirit which is called "All" and which rules over the "Body" above, and this is designated "all flesh"; therefore does it say: "all flesh shall come", and concerning that joy it is written, "No eye hath seen", etc.'

The Companions went on the way rejoicing, and when they had come to a certain mountain R. Hiya turned to the traveller and asked: 'What, then, is thy name?' He replied: 'Hanan' (Merciful). Said R. Hiya: 'May the Holy One be merciful to thee indeed, and hearken to thy voice when thou art in distress.' Said R. Yose: 'The sun is setting; behind this mountain there lies the village of Kephar Hanan. Let us thither and spend the night there to honour thy name.' On their arrival they entered an inn where a table was prepared for them with many viands. Said R. Hiya: 'Verily, this table has such a likeness to that of the world above, that it is meet for us to dignify and crown it with the words of the Torah.'

R. Yose began: 'It is written, "When thou hast eaten and art full, then thou shalt bless the Lord thy God for the good land which he hath given thee" (Deut. VIII, 10). It is evident from this verse that grace after meals is a duty in the Land of Israel; but whence do we know that it is a duty in other lands also? Now, when the Holy One created the world, He divided it into two parts: one part that should be habitable and the other a desert, the former on one side and the latter at the other. Then He redivided the habitable part in such a manner that it formed a circle, the centre of which is the Holy Land. The centre of the Holy Land is Jerusalem, and, again, the centre of Jerusalem is the Holy of Holies, to which all the

460

abundance of nourishment and all good things for the whole inhabited world flow in from above, and there is no place in this inhabited world that is not nourished and sustained from that source. The desert land He also divided, and there is no desert in the world so terrible and sinister as that where for forty long years Israel wandered, before its power was destroyed, of which it is written: "Who led thee through that great and terrible wilderness" (Deut. XIII, 15). There the "other side" reigned, and the children of Israel in despite of it traversed the desert forty years long, to break its power. Had they throughout that long period been worthy in heart and served the Holy One with faithfulness, the "other side" would have been wiped off the face of the earth; but they, time after time, provoked the Holy One to anger, and in like measure did the "other side" prevail, so that they became subject to its power. It might be remarked, "How came it, then, that Moses, who was the most worthy and faithful of all men, died there?" The answer would be: "Not so; the faithful Moses was not in the power of the "other side", for he died in Abarim (lit. quarrels. Deut. XXXII, 49). It was so called because the celestial principalities competed in wrath for it, but it was not given over to any of them, but was left as it was till Moses came and took possession of it, and there he was buried, and the Holy One alone attended to his burial and no one else, since it is written: "And (he) buried him in a valley" (Ibid. XXXIV, 6), without mention of a subject. Therefore Moses ruled alone over that place, and there was he buried, and in order to let all future generations know that those who died in the wilderness will rise again, He let their faithful shepherd abide among them, so that at the awakening of the resurrection in the world to come they may find themselves all together. It may be asked, If that wilderness consisted of what was left over from the power of the "other side", why did the Holy One command that the goat of the Day of Atonement should be sent to a mountain called Azazel (Lev. XVI, 8, 10, 26), and not to

Zohar: Shemoth, Section 2, Page 157b

a mountain in that wilderness in which Israel had sojourned? The answer is that the sojourn of the Israelites in that wilderness for forty years had broken its power, while, again, its power increased in a region where human feet had not ever trodden. And the mountain to which the goat was sent is a great and mighty rock, and below it are depths unplumbable, where man has never trodden. There the "other side" has power enough to consume his prey undisturbed, so that he leaves Israel alone and there is no one to bring accusations against them. The domain of the mystery of the Faith is in that very central point of the Holy Land which is in the Holy of Holies, the place where the Shekinah dwelt, and even though She dwells there no longer, and the Holy of Holies exists no more, yet for Her sake the whole world is still supplied with food, and nourishment and satisfaction ever stream forth, emanating from thence to all the inhabited regions of the world. Therefore, although Israel lives at present outside the Holy Land, yet it is owing to the power and worth of that Land that the world is supplied with food and subsistence. It is concerning this that it is written: "Thou shalt bless the Lord thy God for the good land which he hath given thee" (Deut. VIII, 10). Truly "the good land", since for its sake there is a sufficiency of nourishment for the whole world. When a man sits at his table and partakes of its plenty with joyous thanksgiving, he should at the same time let his mind dwell with sadness upon the holiness of that Land and of the Temple of the King which has been destroyed, and because of his sadness there, at the table, in the midst of his feasting, God regards him as a restorer of the House of the Holy One, and all the ruins of the Holy Temple. Happy is his lot!

'The Cup of Benediction (the cup of wine taken immediately after Grace has been recited at the conclusion of a meal) is only partaken of when there are (at least) three persons present at the table, because it is blessed through the mystery of the three Patriarchs. The cup must first be lifted by both hands, in order that it should be placed between the right and left grades, but afterwards it is left in the right alone, because it is blessed from that side. There have been ten things enumerated in connection with the Cup of Benediction, which is quite appropriate, since there are ten aspects of it, as the Companions have pointed out. It is necessary to look at the cup while reciting the benediction, because it is written, "The eyes of the Lord thy God are always upon it" (i.e. the Holy Land, Deut. XI, 12); therefore the thoughts must not be allowed to stray from the cup, but the eyes must be firmly fixed upon it. The Cup of Benediction is blessed by the very benediction which man pronounces over it to the Holy One, blessed be He, because it is the mystery of Faith, and therefore man must guard it with the utmost care, as the very essence of the King's Majesty, since for its sake is the table blessed. Also, when grace is recited, the table must not be empty, since "no blessing can rest on an empty table", as has been pointed out with reference to the words, "Tell me, what hast thou in the house?" (2 Kings IV, 2); in a word, the heavenly blessings come to rest only on a place that is complete. Esoterically this is expressed in the words: "In the hearts of all that are wise-hearted I have put wisdom" (Ex. XXI, 6, i.e. "he who hath, to him it shall be given"), and also in the words, "He giveth wisdom to the wise" (Dan. II, 21). The symbol for all this is the table of the "Bread of the Countenance", for it is written: "And thou shalt set upon the table bread of the Countenance before me always" (Ex. xxv, 30).' [Tr. note: From here to 159a belongs to Raya Mehemna.] [Note: This edition did not translate the Raya Mehemna passage mentioned in the previous note.]

Zohar: Shemoth, Section 2, Page 159a

AND LOOK THAT THOU MAKE THEM AFTER THEIR PATTERN WHICH WAS SHEWED THEE IN THE MOUNT. And again it is written: "And thou shalt rear up the Tabernacle according to the fashion thereof which was shewed thee in the mount" (Ex. XXVI, 30). R. Yose said: 'From this we see that the Holy One, blessed be He, actually gave Moses all the arrangements and all the shapes of the Tabernacle, each in its appropriate manner, and that he saw Metatron ministering to the High Priest within it. It may be said that, as the Tabernacle above was not erected until the Tabernacle below had been completed, that "youth" (Metatron) could not have served above before Divine worship had taken place in the earthly Tabernacle. It is true that the Tabernacle above was not actually erected before the one below; yet Moses saw a mirroring of the whole beforehand, and also Metatron, as he would be later when all was complete. The Holy One said to him: "Behold now, the Tabernacle and the 'Youth'; all is held in suspense until the Tabernacle below shall have been built." It should not be thought, however, that Metatron himself ministers; the fact is, that the Tabernacle belongs to him, and Michael, the High Priest, it is that serves there, within the Metatron's Tabernacle, mirroring the function of the Supernal High Priest above, serving within that other Tabernacle, that hidden one which never is revealed, which is connected with the mystery of the world to come. There are two celestial Tabernacles: the one, the supernal concealed Tabernacle, and the other, the Tabernacle of the Metatron. And there are also two priests: the one is the primeval Light, and the other Michael, the High Priest below.

[Tr. note: The passage which follows, to the beginning of 160b, deals with the symbolism of some letters and their significance as creative potencies, and does not lend itself to translation.]

Zohar: Shemoth, Section 2, Page 159b

Note: This Page is not translated as per note on Page 159a

Zohar: Shemoth, Section 2, Page 160a

Note: This Page is not translated as per note on Page 159a

Zohar: Shemoth, Section 2, Page 160b

R. Hiya and R. Yose were walking together. Said R. Yose: 'Let us now think on spiritual matters and talk on the words of the Torah.' He thereupon began by pointing out that three passages are introduced by the words, Hear, O Israel. "Hear O Israel, the Lord our God, the Lord is One" (Deut. VI, 4); "Hear, O Israel, this day thou hast become a people to the Lord thy God" (Ibid. XXVII, 9); and "Hear, O Israel, thou art to pass the Jordan this day" (Ibid. LX, I). 'Why', he said, 'did Moses commence in each of these cases with the word "hear"? In the first, indeed, the word seems appropriate, but what is its point in the other two cases? The truth is that in all three passages it is meant to teach a special lesson. This is obvious in the case of the first, where the word "hear" indicates the unity in the supernal Wisdom of what is above and what is below. The word Shema' consists of shem (name) and 'ain (seventy), indicating the combination of this Name and the other seventy from whence it derives blessing. At the recitation of the Shema', therefore, one must concentrate attention on this union of all the Divine names. For these seventy Names constitute the mystery of the supernal Chariot from whence that Name receives blessing and in which it is contained. Then comes the word Israel, referring, as we have learnt, to "Ancient Israel" (Tifereth), so that this emanation may also be included. So "Hear, O Israel," signifies the union of the Spouse with her Husband (i.e. Malkuth with Tifereth), so that all is in all, and all is one. As to the "hear" in the other two passages, it also has a special significance, though not so profound as in the first. "Hear, O Israel, this day thou hast become (nihyeta) a people". Why is not the usual form of the verb, hayita, used? To indicate that the Israelites are called "people" when their hearts are broken in order that they may worship the Lord, the word nihyeta having the same significance as in the verse, "And I Daniel was ended (nikyeti, i.e. fainted) and was sick... afterwards I rose up and did the King's business" (Dan. VIII, 27). Similarly, David said: "Hear me, my brethren and my people" (I Chron. XXVIII, 2), meaning, "If ye serve me of your own free will, ye are my brethren; but if not, ye are my people (i.e. subjects), to have your own will broken in order to serve me." The third passage is also on a lower plane. Neither of these two has the same significance as that which expresses the Unity and the acceptance by Israel of the yoke of the Kingdom of Heaven throughout all spheres, since, at the time of the recitation of the Shema, a man has to be prepared to proclaim the unity of the Divine Name and to accept the yoke of the Kingdom of Heaven. On the head of him who thus recites the Shema, to accept the yoke of the Kingdom of Heaven, the Shekinah rests-a witness to testify of him before the Holy King that twice daily does he declare the Unity of the Name, and thus, consciously, unite the Above and the Below. Therefore is the letter 'ain of the Shema written large, and also the daleth, of the ehad (one), which, when put together, make the word 'ed (witness): a witness before the Holy King. The mystery contained in the words, "The Lord our God, the Lord", the mystery of the Unity in three aspects (lit. "in three sides"), has often been referred to by the Holy Lamp (R. Simeon), and we are not permitted to enlarge upon what he has said. However, certain it is, that upon the head of the man who unifies

Zohar: Shemoth, Section 2, Page 161a

the Name of the Holy One above and below, the Shekinah descends to rest, and to bless him with seven blessings, and to proclaim concerning him: "Thou art my servant, Israel, in whom I am glorified" (Isa. XLIX, 3).'

R. Hiya then followed with an exposition of the verse: Thou hast been shown (har'eta) to know that the Lord he is God; there is none else beside him (Deut. IV, 35). 'What does this peculiar expression, "thou hast been shown to know", denote? When the Israelites came out of Egypt, at first they knew nothing of the true meaning of faith in the Holy One, blessed be He, because, while they were in captivity in Egypt, they had worshipped foreign gods and had forgotten the essentials of the Faith, that legacy which the Twelve Tribes had received from Father Jacob. So, when Moses came, he had to teach them that in the universe there is a supreme God. Then they were witnesses of all the signs and wonders connected with the crossing of the Red Sea, and more than that, of all the wonders that took place in Egypt itself before it; then, later, they experienced the mighty acts of God in connection with the manna and the water in the wilderness. And by and by the Torah was given to them, and, gradually, they learned the ways of the Holy One, blessed be He, until eventually they reached that point when the words quoted were said unto them. Moses said, in effect: "Till now I had to teach you as little children are taught"; thou "hast been shown to know", and thou hast learnt by now to know and penetrate into the mystery of the Faith, namely, this, that "the Lor0d (Tetragrammaton) He is God (Elohim)", which is no small matter, since concerning this it says: "know therefore this day and consider it in thine heart that the Lord he is God in heaven above and upon the earth beneath, there is none else" (Ibid. v. 39). The whole mystery of the Faith depends upon this; from this comes the knowledge of the mystery of mysteries, the secret of secrets. Tetragrammaton ELOHIM is a full Name, and the whole is one. Herein is a mystery of mysteries to the masters of the esoteric knowledge. And, indeed, blessed are they who endeavour to comprehend the Torah. When the Holy One resolved to create the world, He guided Himself by the Torah as by a plan, as has been pointed out [Tr. note: v. Zohar, Gen. 134a] in connection with the words "Then I was by him as amon" (Prov. VIII, 30), where the word amon (nursling) may also be read uman (architect). Was the Torah, then, an architect? Yes; for if a King resolves to build him a palace, without an architect and a plan how can he proceed? Nevertheless, when the palace has been built, it is attributed to the King: "here is the palace which the King has built", because his was the thought that thus has been realized. Similarly, when the Holy One, blessed be He, resolved to create the world, He looked into His plan, and, although, in a sense, it was the plan which brought the palace into being, it is not called by its name, but by that of the King. The Torah proclaims: "I was by Him an architect, through me He created the world!"-for the Torah preceded the creation of the world by two thousand years; and so, when He resolved to create the world He looked into the Torah, into its every creative word, and fashioned the world correspondingly; for all the words and all the actions of all the worlds are contained in the Torah. Therefore did the Holy One, blessed be He, look into it and create the world. That is why it says not merely "I was an architect", but "I was, alongside of Him, an architect". It may be asked, How can one be an architect with Him? God looked at His plan in this way. It is written in the Torah: "In the beginning God created the heavens and the earth"; He looked at this expression and created heaven and earth. In the Torah it is written: "Let there be light"; He looked at these words and created light; and in this manner was the whole world created. When the world was all thus created, nothing was yet established properly, until He had resolved to create man, in order that he might study the Torah, and, for his sake, the world should be firmly and properly established. Thus

Zohar: Shemoth, Section 2, Page 161b

it is that he who concentrates his mind on, and deeply penetrates into, the Torah, sustains the world; for, as the Holy One looked into the Torah and created the world, so man looks into the Torah and keeps the world alive. Hence the Torah is the cause of the world's creation, and also the power that maintains its existence. Therefore blessed is he who is devoted to the Torah, for he is the preserver of the world.

'When the Holy One resolved to create man, there appeared before His Mind potential man, in form and condition as he was to be in this world; and not he alone, but all human beings, before they enter this world, stand before Him in the same way, in that treasure-house of souls where, dressed in a semblance of their earthly forms, they await their entry into this world. When their time has arrived to descend to this world, the Holy One calls upon a certain emissary appointed over all the souls to go down, and says to him: "Go, bring hither to Me such and such a spirit", and on the instant that soul appears, clad in the form of this world, and is led forward by the angel that the Holy King may look upon it. Then does the Holy One warn that soul, when it shall have reached the earthly regions, to remember the Torah, and devote iself thereto, so that it may know Him and the mystery of Faith; for better were it for a man that he should never be born than not to know Him. Therefore is it presented before the Holy King, that afterwards it may know Him in this world, and be devoted to the Holy One in the mystery of the Faith. Concerning this it is written: "Thou hast been shown to know", that is, shown by the angel to the Holy One, in order to know, to understand, to penetrate in this world to the mystery of the Faith, the mystery of the Torah. And he who, having come into this world, does not study the Torah to know Him-better were it for him that he had never been born; since the only aim and object of the Holy One in sending man into this world is that he may know and understand that Tetragrammaton is Elohim. This is the sum of the whole mystery of the Faith, of the whole Torah, of all that is above and below, of the Written and Oral Torah, all together forming one unity. The essence of the mystery of Faith is to know that this is a complete Name. This knowledge that

Tetragrammaton is One with Elohim is indeed the synthesis of the whole Torah, both of the Written and of the Oral, for "Torah" stands for both, the former being symbolic of Tetragrammaton and the latter of Elohim. The Torah being the mystery of the Holy Name, it is therefore called by two names, one of which is general, and the other particular. The general is complemented by the particular, also the particular by the general, both combining to form one synthesis. In the Torah we find, therefore, the synthesis of the Above and the Below, for the one Name, Tetragrammaton, is above, while the other, Elohim, is below, one indicating the higher world and the other the lower. And therefore is it written: "Thou hast been shown to know that Tetragrammaton is Elohim."

Zohar: Shemoth, Section 2, Page 162a

This is the essence of all things, and it is necessary that man should perceive it in this world.'

R. Yose then discoursed as follows. 'According to one authority, the evening prayer is obligatory, [Tr. note: v. T. B. Berachoth, 27b] and it certainly is so, for the recital of the Shema is obligatory in the evening, and the unity of the Holy One is proclaimed at night as it is in the day, and the attribute of night is included in that of the day, and that of the day in the night, and one union is thus attained.

'It is written, "Thou shalt love the Lord thy God with all thy heart and with all thy soul", etc. (Deut. VI, 5). This has been interpreted by the Companions, but there is still a question to ask. If, in the recital of "Hear, O Israel," all is included, the Right and the Left, why is it necessary to recite afterwards the passages, "And thou shalt love" and "And it will come to pass if ye shall hearken diligently unto My commandments..."? Are they not already included in the proclamation of the Unity? The fact, however, is that in the Shema they are referred to generally, and then they are particularized, which also is necessary. [Tr. note Here follows in the original a passage on the symbolism of the phylacteries with reference to the Unity, which is practically a repetition in substance of Zohar, Exodus, 43a, b, and Genesis, 13b]. When this unity has been proclaimed in general terms, as from the head of the supernal Point, it was needful further to proclaim it from the mystery of the primeval light which is the beginning of all. Hence, "Thou shalt love" is the first outstretching of the right hand to love the Holy One, blessed be He, with that close attachment which the right hand symbolizes. If a man loves God, then God stretches out His right hand to him to receive

Zohar: Shemoth, Section 2, Page 162b

and welcome him with love. Everything in the world depends on the will; spirit rouses spirit, and the spirit in man turned yearningly in love to Him brings down the Divine Spirit. When a man's love to the Holy One is roused, the "right hand" is moved only by a threefold impulse, by "heart", "soul", and "might", for it does not say, "with all thy heart or with all thy soul", etc., but "and with all thy soul", etc.: all three are essential and necessary. Then does the Holy One respond and stir up His Right Hand towards that man, and He stretches it out to receive him, and He does indeed receive him; concerning which it is written: "The utterance of the Lord to my lord: Sit thou at my right hand" (Ps. CX, I); which verse has already been expounded as indicating the grade of nearness to the Holy One in which King David stood when he was united with Him by the Right Hand. There are in the section, "Thou shalt love the Lord thy God", etc. (Deut. VI, 4-9), thirteen commandments in regard to the Right Hand: "Thou shalt love the Lord thy God" is one; "with all thy heart" is two; "and with all thy soul" is three; "and with all thy possessions" is four; "And thou shalt inculcate them in thy children" is five; "and shalt talk of them" is six; "when thou sittest in thine house" is seven; "and when thou walkest by the way" is eight; "and when thou liest down" is nine; "and when thou risest up" is ten; "and thou shalt bind them for a sign upon thine hand" is eleven; "and they shall be as frontlets between thine eyes" is twelve; "and thou shalt write them upon the posts of thine house and on thy gates" is thirteen. All thirteen are included in the right hand, and the left is included in the right. All this is as it should be. And whenever the Left Hand is stirred up, the Right Hand first predominates in it. Therefore, if Israel is worthy, the Left Hand is embraced in the Right, for even when sometimes Judgement (Geburah) is roused, it is tempered by Grace; but if it should not be so, then the Right Hand is embraced in the Left, which means that the Left predominates, the Left always first awaking in love in the mystery of the Right, and only afterwards is its power to hurt strengthened as much as necessary. So it is everywhere, as has been noted by the Companions.'

Then came R. Hiya to him and kissed him, after which he began to speak on the following: MOREOVER THOU SHALT MAKE THE TABERNACLE WITH TEN PIECES OF TAPESTRY (Ex. XXVI, 1).

'Here', said he, 'again we have a symbolism of the Unity, for the Tabernacle was made up of many parts, and yet it says (v. 6), "and the tabernacle shall be one". Now, as the human body possesses many organs, higher and lower, some internal and not visible, others through that great and terrible wilderness" (Deut. XIII, 15). There the "other side" reigned, and the children of Israel in despite of it traversed the desert forty years long, to break its power. Had they throughout that long period been worthy in heart and served the Holy One with faithfulness, the "other side" would have been wiped off the face of the earth; but they, time after time, provoked the Holy One to anger, and in like measure did the "other side" prevail, so that they became subject to its power. It might be remarked, "How came it, then, that Moses, who was the most worthy and faithful of all men, died there?" The answer would be: "Not so; the faithful Moses was not in the power of the "other side", for he died in Abarim (lit. quarrels. Deut. XXXII, 49). It was so called because the celestial principalities competed in wrath for it, but it was not given over to any of them, but was left as it was till Moses came and took possession of it, and there he was buried, and the Holy One alone attended to his burial and no one else, since it is written: "And (he) buried him in a valley" (Ibid. XXXIV, 6), without mention of a subject. Therefore Moses ruled alone over that place, and there was he buried, and in order to let all future generations know that those who died in the wilderness will rise again, He let their faithful shepherd abide among them, so that at the awakening of the resurrection in the world to come they may find themselves all together. It may be asked, If that wilderness consisted of what was left over from the power of the "other side", why did the Holy One command that the goat of the Day of Atonement should be sent to a mountain called Azazel (Lev. XVI, 8, 10, 26), and not to

Zohar: Shemoth, Section 2, Page 163a

"With all thy soul"–the "all" includes all aspects of the soul, viz. nephesh, ruah, and neshamah. As to "with all thy possessions", these also have various aspects, each one different from the other. True love to the Holy One, blessed be He, consists in just this, that we give over to Him all our emotional, intellectual, and material faculties and possessions, and love Him. Should it be asked, How can a man love Him with the evil inclination? Is not the evil inclination the seducer, preventing man from approaching the Holy One to serve him? How, then, can man use the evil inclination as an instrument of love to God? The answer lies in this, that there can be no greater service done to the Holy One than to bring into subjection the "evil inclination" by the power of love to the Holy One, blessed be He. For, when it is subdued and its power broken by man in this way, then he becomes a true lover of the Holy One, since he has learnt how to make the "evil inclination" itself serve the Holy One. Here is a mystery entrusted to the masters of esoteric lore. All that the Holy One has made, both above and below, is for the purpose of manifesting His Glory and to make all things serve Him. Now, would a master permit his servant to work against him, and to continually lay plans to counteract his will? It is the will of the Holy One that men should worship Him and walk in the way of truth that they may be rewarded with many benefits. How, then, can an evil servant come and counteract the will of his Master by tempting man to walk in an evil way, seducing him from the good way and causing him to disobey the will of his Lord? But, indeed, the "evil inclination" also does through this the will of its Lord. It is as if a king had an only son whom he dearly loved, and just for that cause he warned him not to be enticed by bad women, saying that anyone defiled might not enter his palace. The son promised his father to do his will in love. Outside the palace, however, there lived a beautiful harlot. After a while the King thought: "I will see how far my son is devoted to me." So he sent to the woman and commanded her, saying: "Entice my son, for I wish to test his obedience to my will." So she used every blandishment to lure him into her embraces. But the son, being good, obeyed the commandment of his father. He refused her allurements and thrust her from him. Then did the father rejoice exceedingly, and, bringing him in to the innermost chamber of the palace, bestowed upon him gifts from his best treasures, and showed him every honour. And who was the cause of all this joy? The harlot! Is she to be praised or blamed for it? To be praised, surely, on all accounts, for on the one hand she fulfilled the king's command and carried out his plans for him, and on the other hand she caused the son to receive all the good gifts and deepened the king's love to his son. Therefore it is written, "And the Lord saw all that he had made, and behold it was very good", where the word "very" refers to the angel of death (i.e. the evil inclination). [Tr. note: v. Exodus, 68b.] Similarly, if it were not for this Accuser, the righteous would not possess the supernal treasures in the world to come. Happy, therefore, are they who, coming into conflict with the Tempter, prevail against him, for through him will they attain bliss, and all the good and desirable possessions of the world to come; concerning which it is written: "What eye hath not seen... he hath prepared for him that waiteth for him" (Isa. LXIV, 3). Happy are those, too, who have not come across him, for those sinners who encounter him allow themselves to be enticed by him. What profit is it, then, to the Tempter when the sinner obeys him?

Zohar: Shemoth, Section 2, Page 163b

Even if it profit him nothing, yet he is certainly doing the will of his Master, and, moreover, it gains him strength. He is not content until he has killed his victim, for then he gains strength and is satisfied; just as the angel of life gains strength when a man walks in the right way. May the Lord preserve us from becoming victims of the Tempter. Blessed are they who prevail against him, and thus become inheritors of the world to come and continually gain strength from the Holy King. Concerning such it is written: "Blessed is the man whose strength is in thee, in whose heart are the ways (to Zion)" (Ps. LXXXIV, 6). They are blessed in this world, and shall be blessed in the world to come.'

R. Yose, R. Judah, and R. Hiya, were riding together, when R. Eleazar suddenly met them. On seeing him they all alighted from their asses. Said R. Eleazar: 'Verily I behold the face of the Shekinah! For, to see the righteous and saintly of one's generation is to see the very face of the Shekinah. And why are these called the face of the Shekinah? Because in them is the Shekinah hidden: She is hidden in them, and they reveal Her. For they who are the friends of the Shekinah and are near to Her, are regarded as Her "face". And who are they? They are those with and by whom She adorns Herself in order to appear before the Supernal King. Now, as you are three, the Shekinah is surely in your midst!' He then forthwith began to expound these words of Jacob to Esau: "Take, I pray thee, my blessing that is brought to thee" (Gen. XXXIII, 11). 'When Jacob', said he, 'saw on that night the Accuser, Samael, he saw him in the form of Esau, and it was not until dawn was breaking that he recognized him as Samael. When the dawn broke, he looked at him closely, but even then he appeared at times to be the one and then the other. He then looked more closely still and he knew him for the celestial representative of Esau, and he prevailed against him. He said to Jacob, "Let me go, for the dawn breaketh" (Ibid. XXXII, 26), and the companions have already explained that he said this, because the moment had arrived when he, the representative of Esau, had to raise his voice in hymns to the Holy One. On this we may remark that indeed the power of Samael is only in the ascendant in the dark, as indicated in the words, "of fear in the night" (Ps. XCI, 5), namely, the fear of Gehenna; so it is that he rules at night alone. Hence he said, "Let me go, for the dawn breaketh", for when morning comes and his power is on the wane, he must depart, and he and his hosts must enter the recess of the abyss in the North, and they must remain until night breaks in on them, and the dogs are loosened from their chains and allowed to roam about till morning. That is why he pressed Jacob to let him go. In the same way Israel's exile has taken place at night, it is in fact called "night". The evil kingdom (Rome), the pagan power, rules over Israel until the morning shall again appear, and the Holy One, blessed be He, will cause the light to dawn again and the heathen power shall wane and at last disappear. Therefore it was that Esau's representative said, "Let me go, for the dawn breaketh". But Jacob held him, and his power weakened, because night had passed, so Jacob's strength increased, and he saw, in that angel, the image of Esau, but not quite clearly. Then the angel confirmed the blessings he had received. And what was it that Jacob afterwards said to Esau? "For therefore I have seen thy face, as though I had seen the face of God, and thou wast pleased with me" (Gen. XXXIII, 10). For he saw in Esau's face now the very image of Samael as he had appeared to him, for the realm to which a person belongs is revealed in his face. And ye, supernal saints, the Shekinah is in you, and your faces reflect the beauty of Her face. Blessed are ye!' Then said he also: 'If we were going in the same direction, I would be in your midst; but now, as ye must go one way, and I another, I will part from you with words

Zohar: Shemoth, Section 2, Page 164a of the Torah.'

Then he began to expound to them this verse: A song of degrees for Solomon (li-shelomoh). Except the Lord build the house, they labour in vain that build it; except the Lord guard the city, the watchman waketh but in vain (Ps. CXXVII, 1-2). Said he: 'Was it Solomon who composed this Psalm when he built the Temple? (for li-shelomoh could be understood to mean "of Solomon"). Not so. It was King David who composed it, about his son Solomon, when Nathan came to him (David) and told him that Solomon would build the Temple. Then King David showed unto his son Solomon, as a model, the celestial prototype of the Temple, and David himself, when he saw it and all the activities connected with it, as set forth in the celestial idea of it, sang this psalm concerning his son Solomon. There is also yet another interpretation, namely, that "for Solomon" (li-shelomoh) refers to Him "whose is the peace" (shalom), and this psalm is a hymn above all hymns, which ascends higher than all. "Except the Lord build the house": King David saw all the seven pillars upon which that house, the Universe, stands–for they stand row upon row–and above them all is the Master of the House, who advances with them, giving them power and strength, to each in turn. It is concerning this that King David said: "Except the King, whose is the peace, and who is the Master of the House, build the house, they labour in vain that build it"–that is to say, the pillars. Except the Lord–the King, whose is the peace–guard the city, "the watchman waketh but in vain". This is the pillar upon which the Universe stands, namely the "Righteous" who keeps waking guard over the City. The Tabernacle which Moses constructed had Joshua for its wakeful and constant guard; for he alone guarded it who is called the "young man", namely Joshua, of whom it says: "Joshua, the son of Nun, a young man, departed not out of the Tent" (Ex. XXXIII, 11). Later in its history it was another "young man" who guarded it, namely Samuel (I Sam. 11, 18), for the Tabernacle could be guarded only by a youth. The Temple, however, was guarded by the Holy One Himself, as it is written, "Except the Lord guard the City, the watchman waketh but in vain". And who is the watchman? The "young man", Metatron. And you, holy saints, ye are not guarded as the Tabernacle was guarded, but as the Temple was guarded, namely, by the Holy One Himself; for, whenever the righteous are on a journey the Holy One guards them continually, as it is written: "The Lord shall keep thy going out and thy coming in from now and forever" (Ps. CXXI, 9).' Then they accompanied him on his journey for a distance of three miles, and, parting from him, returned to their own way, and they were moved to quote these words concerning him. "For he shall give his angels charge over thee to keep thee in all thy ways. They shall bear thee up in their hands" (Ps. XCI, 11, I2); and "Thy father shall be glad and thy mother rejoice" (Prov. XXIII, 25).

AND THOU SHALT MAKE THE TABERNACLE WITH TEN PIECES OF TAPESTRY. R. Judah expounded in this connection the following verse: In the multitude of people is the king's honour, but in the want of people is the confusion of the prince (Prov. XIV, 28). Said he: 'It is the people of Israel that is referred to in the first clause, Israel who is called "a holy people to the Lord" (Deut. VII, 6). Their number swells to thousands and myriads, and when they attain such large numbers it is "to the King's honour", for those above and those below praise the name of the Supernal King, singing hymns to Him, for the sake of the Holy People, "the wise and understanding people, the great people" (cf. Deut. IV, 6).

But is it not written, "for ye are the fewest of all peoples" (Ibid. VII, 7)? Truly, "of all peoples" taken together, but not fewer than any individual people, for there is no nation in the world as numerous and mighty as Israel. But see how numerous are the Ishmaelites and the Edomites! That is so; but it must not be forgotten that all other peoples are intermixed with one another, unlike Israel, which is a pure and unadulterated race, "a holy people unto the Lord", chosen by Him. And therefore "in the multitude of the people is the King's honour", that is to say, the honour of the Supernal King, the Holy One, blessed be He. When

Zohar: Shemoth, Section 2, Page 164b

the Holy One enters the synagogue, and the people are united in prayer and sing together praises to the King, He is honoured and glorified, that is to say, the Holy King is strengthened to ascend in glory and beauty. On the other hand, "in the want of people is the confusion of the prince"; that is to say, when He enters a synagogue and finds no congregation come to pray and praise, all the celestial hosts and all the chieftains above are degraded from the high estate to which they were raised by the glorification of that King. For when the Israelites worship the Supernal King with prayer and praise, all the celestial hosts join them and sing in unison with them, and are strengthened by that holy exercise, that the Holy One may be exalted from above and from below in harmony; but when Israel does not assemble to worship the Lord, they lose this dignity, since they do not ascend and cannot praise their Master in fitting manner. Even if ten alone are present, the supernal hosts join them in their worship. The reason is that all the supports of that King are in the number ten, and therefore ten worshippers are sufficient if there are no more. Therefore, concerning the Tabernacle it says: "And thou shalt make the Tabernacle with ten ('eser) pieces of tapestry", ten being the number required for the full perfection of the Tabernacle. The shortened form of "ten" ('eser) is used here in order to show that the Shekinah herself is not included in the ten, since she broods above the congregation. So it is in all places where a shortened form is used for "ten", as, for instance, "It stood upon twelve (shne 'asar) oxen" (I Kings XII, 25), where the Shekinah was not included in the number, for it says: "and the sea (i.e. the Shekinah) was set above them" (Ibid.).'

R. Hiya discoursed on the words: Who coverest thyself with light as with a garment, who stretchest out the heavens like a curtain (yeri'ah) (Ps. CIV, 2). Said he: 'These words have been interpreted as follows: When the Holy One was about to create the world He robed Himself in the primordial light and created the heavens. At first the light was at the right and the darkness at the left. What, then, did the Holy One do? He merged the one into the other and from them formed the heavens: shamaim (heavens) is composed of esh and mayim (fire and water, i.e. right and left). He brought them together and harmonized them, and when they were united as one, He stretched them out like a curtain, and formed them into the letter vau. From this letter the light spread, so that "curtain" became "curtains", as it is written: "And thou shalt make the tabernacle with ten curtains." Seven firmaments are stretched out and stored in the supernal treasure-house, as has been explained, and over them is one firmament which has no colour and no place in the world of cognition, and is outside the range of contemplation; but, though hidden, it diffuses light to all and speeds them each on its fitting orbit. Beyond that firmament knowledge cannot penetrate, and man must close his mouth and not seek to reflect upon it. He who does so reflect is turned backwards, for it passes our knowledge. The ten curtains of the Tabernacle symbolized the ten firmaments, and their mystery can be comprehended only by the wise of heart' He who grasps this attains great wisdom and penetrates into the mysteries of the universe, for he contemplates

Zohar: Shemoth, Section 2, Page 165a

in this that which is above in the region to which every one of them is attached, except those two that are at the right and at the left, and which are hidden with the Shekinah.'

Said R. Yose: 'There are nine firmaments, and the Shekinah completes the number, bringing them up to ten. For if there are ten apart from the Shekinah, then She would be the eleventh, in addition to the ten. Thus really there are nine, and the nine days which come between New Year's Day and the Day of Atonement are a symbol of them: nine days, which are completed by the tenth. The same is true of the ten curtains in the Tabernacle, corresponding to the ten firmaments. Here is a mystery of mysteries, which none but the adepts in esoteric wisdom can fathom-one of those mysteries of the Holy Lamp (R. Simeon) who could expound the mystery of every firmament and of every being who officiates in each of them. There are seven firmaments above, and corresponding to them another seven below. There are seven firmaments in which the stars and planets have been placed to direct the world in its path. And in both, those above and those below, the seventh [Tr. note: Hesed.] is the most exalted, with the exception of the eighth, [Tr. note: Binah.] which stands above and directs them all.

'It is written: "Extol him that rideth upon araboth" (Ps. LXVIII, 4). Who is it that rides upon 'araboth, and what is meant by 'araboth? It is the seventh firmament, and it is called 'araboth (lit. mixtures) because it is composed of fire and water, from the region of the South and from the region of the North, being "mixed" from both these regions. And as 'Araboth is intrinsically the synthesis of all the other six firmaments, it forms intrinsically the Supernal Chariot. The Holy One, blessed be He, loves this firmament more than any of the other firmaments and delights in perfecting it with supernal beauty. Therefore does it say: "Extol Him that rideth upon 'Araboth... and rejoice before Him", Him that rideth upon that hidden, secret firmament, which is set upon the "Living beings" (Hayyoth). "And rejoice before Him." The expression "before" suggests, on the one hand, that no one can really have any conception of Him; and, on the other hand, that he who comes before that firmament must do so in joy, and not in sadness, for there all is pure joy with no trace of sadness or gloom. Therefore, when the High Priest was to stand before Him, in the Sanctuary, he had to enter that holy place with joy, and all things about him were to express joy. Therefore is it written: "Serve the Lord with joy, come before him with singing" (Ps. C, 2); for in His service there is no room for sadness. It may be asked, What if a man is deep in sorrow and tribulation, and has no heart to rejoice, and yet his trouble forces him to seek for compassion from the Heavenly King; is he to refrain from prayer because of his sorrow? What can he do? He cannot help being heavy-hearted? The answer is that "all gates have been closed since the destruction of the Temple, but the gates of tears have not been closed", and tears are the expression of sadness and sorrow. Those celestial beings who are appointed over those gates of tears break down all the iron locks and bars and let the tears pass through; so the prayers of those sorrowful ones penetrate through to the Holy King, and that Place is grieved by the man's sorrow, as it is written: "In all their afflictions he is afflicted" [Tr. note: Translation according to the Keri.] (Isa. LXIII, 9). Thus the prayer of the sorrowing does not return unto him void, but the Holy One takes pity

Zohar: Shemoth, Section 2, Page 165b

on him. Blessed is the man who in his prayers sheds tears before the Holy One. This is true even on the Sabbath, which must be a day of joy: when a person fasts on Sabbath he manifests sadness on the day when the supernal firmament reigns, that firmament which manifests itself in joy, yes, which is the very essence of joy, communicating joy to all. Yet if he fasts because of a sorrow, it delivers him from that punishment which had been decreed for him, as explained elsewhere. Hence it is written, "Extol Him that rideth upon (lit. in) Araboth"; that is to say, "Honour and glorify Him who rideth upon the Araboth, for there it is that perfect joy and gladness abide". "His Name is KAH", for that Name is connected with that realm. "And rejoice before Him", since one must not appear before Him in sadness, as we have pointed out.'

Said R. Eleazar: 'It ought to have been "who rideth upon ('al) araboth", why does it say "in (be) araboth"? Again: it ought to be, "He is in KAH", why does it say "in KAH is His Name"? It is because this verse refers to the Hidden of hidden ones, the most Ancient of all the ancients, the completely unknown and undisclosed. It may be said that, since He rideth in it, then in this sphere at least He does disclose Himself. Not so. What the verse tells us is that the Ancient of ancients "rideth in the araboth" in the sphere of KAH, which is the primordial mystery emanating from Him, namely the Ineffable Name KAH, which is not identical with Him, but is a kind of veil emanating from Him. This veil is His Name, it is His Chariot, and even that is not manifested.

Zohar: Shemoth, Section 2, Page 166a

to study the Torah. The innkeeper's daughter also rose and lit the lamp for them, and then, instead of leaving the room, stayed behind, but out of their sight, that she might listen to the words of the Torah. R. Yose began by speaking on the words: For the commandment is a lamp, and the Torah is a light, and reproofs of instruction are the way of life (Prov. VI, 23). 'This means', he said, 'that whoever endeavours to keep the commandments in this world will have a lamp lighted for him in the other world through each commandment which he fulfils, and he who studies the Torah will merit the supernal light from which that lamp is lit. For a lamp unlit has no value, and light without a lamp cannot shine, so the one has need of the other. The religious act is necessary to prepare the lamp, and study of the Torah is necessary to light the lamp. Blessed is he who takes it in hand both with light and lamp! "And reproofs of instruction are the way of life." The way of life by which man enters into the world to come consists in the reproofs and instructions which he receives in order that he may learn to keep away from the evil path and walk in the good way; or, again, we may translate, "reproofs of chastisement", which the Holy One brings upon man to purify him from his sins. Blessed is he who accepts them with gladness! Another interpretation of this verse is as follows: "The lamp of the commandment" is the lamp of David, that is, the Oral Torah. This is like a lamp which has continually to be trimmed and attended to in order to receive light from the Written Torah. For the Oral Torah (tradition) has no light in itself except that which it receives from the Written Torah, which is an actual source of illumination.'

When R. Yose had thus spoken, he turned round and caught sight of the innkeeper's daughter standing there behind them. He continued: '"For the commandment is a lamp." What sort of a lamp? The lamp which is the women's mitzvah (precept), the Sabbath light. For, although women have not the privilege of studying the Torah, men who have this privilege give that light to the lamp which it is the women's duty to light. To women goes the merit of preparing the lamp; to men, by the study of the Torah, the merit of supplying the light for the lamp.' When the woman heard these words she broke into sobs. In the meantime her father had also risen and come to join the company. Seeing his daughter in tears he inquired the reason. She told him what she had heard, and he too began to weep. Then said R. Yose to them: 'Thy son-in-law, the husband of this thy daughter, is, perchance, an ignorant man?' And he replied: 'Indeed, that is so. Therefore it is that my daughter and I must constantly weep. Once I observed him leap down from a high roof only that he might be present to hear the Kaddish prayer together with the congregation. Then it was that the thought entered my mind to give him my daughter to wife. This I did immediately after the congregation had left the synagogue that day. For, said I to myself, judging from the eager manner in which he leapt from the roof in order to hear the Kaddish, he will surely become one day a great scholar; although at that time he was but a youth and I had not known him before. But, in fact, he does not even know how to say Grace after meals. Even the recitation of the Shema I could not teach him.' R. Yose said to him: 'Make a change and take some other man as a husband for your daughter. Or perhaps he may yet have a son who will be a scholar.'

The young man had also by this time got up, and now leapt into the room and seated himself at the feet of the Rabbis. R. Yose looked on him long and earnestly, then said: 'I most certainly see that the light of the Torah will emanate into the world, either from this young man or from his descendants.' The young man smiled and said: 'My masters, may I be allowed to say a few words in your presence?'

Then he began: 'I am young, and ye are very old; wherefore I was afraid, and durst not shew you mine opinion (Job XXXII, 6). The pillars of the world have commented on these words. Elihu, who uttered them, was of the family of Ram (Ibid. 2), and it is said that he was a descendant of Abraham; and this is correct. He was also a priest and a descendant of the prophet Ezekiel, for of Elihu it says that he was the son of Barachel the Buzite (Ibid.), and of Ezekiel also it says he was "the son of Buzi the priest" (Ezek. I, 1). Should one, then, suppose that he came of contemptible stock (buz=contempt)? Not so, for he came of the kindred of Ram, the very highest (ram=high). Then why was he called the Buzite? Because he thought himself of low account in the presence of those

Zohar: Shemoth, Section 2, Page 166b

greater than himself. For that reason a most honourable name is given to him, expressing perfection, by which no other man has been called, namely "man" (Adam, cf. Ezek. II, 1). For this reason, too, it is emphasized that he was of the family of Ram. Now Elihu said: "Days should speak, and multitude of years should teach wisdom, but there is a spirit in man, and the inspiration of the Almighty giveth them understanding" (Job XXXII, 7, 8); in other words, at first he was too timid and shy to speak in the presence of older people. Of me the same is true. I had vowed not to speak on the Torah for two months. On this day that period ends; so now that you are here I will dare to open my mouth with the words of the Torah.'

Then began he to expound the words, "The commandment is a lamp." 'This', he said, 'refers to the Mishnah in the same way as the "Torah and the commandment" (Ex. XXIV, 12) mean the Written and the Oral Law respectively. And why is the Mishnah called a "lamp"? Because when she receives the two hundred and forty-eight organs from the Two Arms, she opens her two arms in order to gather them into her embrace, and so her two arms encompass them and the whole is called "lamp". "The Torah is a light" which kindles that lamp from the side of primordial light, which is of the Right Hand, because the Torah was given from the Right Hand (Deut. XXXIII, 2), although the Left was included in it to attain perfect harmony. This light is included in the two hundred and seven worlds which are concealed in the region of that light, and is spread throughout all of them. These worlds are under the hidden supernal Throne. There are three hundred and ten of them: two hundred and seven belong to the Right Hand and one hundred and three to the Left Hand. These are the worlds which are always prepared by the Holy One for the righteous, and from them spread treasures of precious things, which are stored away for the delight of the righteous in the world to come. Concerning them it is written: "That I may cause those that love me to inherit substance, and I will fill their treasures" (Prov. VIII, 21). "Eye hath not seen... what he shall do to those that wait for him" (Isa. LXIV, 3). Yesh, substance, indicates the three hundred and ten worlds (numerical value of Yesh) which are stored away under the world to come. The two hundred and seven (numerical value of 'or, light), which are of the Right Hand, are called "the primordial light", as the Left is also called "light", but not "primordial". The primordial light is destined to produce issue for the world to come. And not only in the world to come, but even now every day; for this world would not be able to exist at all if it were not for this light, as it is written, "For I have said, Mercy shall be built up forever" (Ps. LXXXIX, 3). It was this light that the Holy One sowed in the Garden of Eden, and through the agency of the Righteous, who is the Gardener of the Garden, He set it in rows; and He took it and sowed it as the seed of truth in rows in the Garden, where it grew, multiplied, and brought forth fruit which has nourished the world, as it is written: "A light sown to the righteous" (Ps. XCVII, 11). Thus all the worlds are nourished to repletion by that Gardener who is called "Righteous". Only when Israel is in exile does this light cease. In that time one might think "the waters fail from the sea, and the flood decayeth and drieth up" (Job. XIV, 11), so how can the world be sustained at all? Therefore it says that "a light is sown", that is to say, continually sown. Now from the time when the stream was cut off from the Garden, the Gardener has ceased to visit

Zohar: Shemoth, Section 2, Page 167a

it; but the light sows itself, bringing forth fruit out of itself, like a garden which brings forth without being sown, though it must be admitted that the issues and the fruit have no longer that perfection which they attained when the Gardener was present. So the significance of the words "and the Torah is a light" is this, that the Torah, which emanates from the region of primordial light, is continually being sown in the world and sends forth fruit without ceasing, and the world is nourished by it. "And reproofs of instruction are the way of life." There are two ways: a way of life and a way of death. The way of life can be recognized by "reproofs of instruction"; for the Holy One, desiring to guard the way of life, sets on it one who chastises and gives "reproof of instruction" to the children of the world. Who is this? It is that "flaming sword which turned every way, to keep the way of the tree of life" (Gen. III, 24). He who has experience of the "reproofs of instruction" will certainly endeavour to walk in that way of life where dwell those "reproofs". At first sight it would seem that the words "the reproofs of instruction are the way of life" contradict the beginning of the verse, but, interpreted as above, they contain the whole mystery of Faith. "The commandment is a lamp" contains the mystery of "keep"; "the Torah is a light" contains the mystery of "remember"; while "the reproofs of instruction are the way of life" refers to the prohibitions and penalties contained in the Torah. And all forms one mystery of Faith, and each of them is necessary to the other to produce a proper synthesis. Concerning the mystery of the light which kindles and produces the light in the lamp, it was said unto Aaron: "When thou lightest the lamps" (Num. VIII, 2); for he emanated from the region of that light. Concerning this, too, it is written: "Let there be light, and there was light" (Gen. I, 3). Why, it may be asked, was it necessary to repeat the word "light" in this verse? The answer is that the first "light" refers to the primordial light which is of the Right Hand, and is destined for the "end of days"; while the second "light" refers to the Left Hand, which issues from the Right. The next words, "And God saw the light that it was good" (Gen. 1, 4), refer to the pillar which, standing midway between them, unites both sides, and therefore when the unity of the three, right, left, and middle, was complete, "it was good", since there could be no completion until the third had appeared to remove the strife between Right and Left, as it is written, "And God separated between the light and between the darkness" (Ibid.). Since there were five grades which emanated from that primordial light, the word "light" is mentioned five times at the beginning of the account of Creation; all of these grades emanated from the Right Side and were included in it. When they were to be included in the Left Side they were symbolized by "water"; for which reason "water" also is mentioned five times (Gen. 1, 6-8). And when they were completed by the mystery of the middle, "firmament" is mentioned five times (Ibid.). And these three, light, water, firmament, are the three grades which include in themselves all five grades, and therefore are all mentioned five times.

'Here is a mystery of mysteries; namely, that in these three is the mystery of the human personality portrayed. Here there is first light, then water, then is a firmament formed in the midst of the waters. Similar is the formation of man at his birth. First he is the "seed" which is light, because it carries light to all the organs of the body. That "seed" which is light sheds itself abroad and becomes

Zohar: Shemoth, Section 2, Page 167b

"water", which in its moisture penetrates to all parts of the body; in which body, when it has taken shape, the diffusion of the water is solidified and is called "firmament". This is indicated by the words: "Let there be a firmament in the midst of the waters." As soon as the body has become clearly defined and purified, the moisture which is left becomes refuse, which leads astray mankind, both male and female. Having indicated the emergence of the Accuser, the text writes the word meoroth ("lights", Gen. I, 14) defectively, the consequence being the quinsy from which children suffer at the waning of the moon. After that (v. 15) meoroth is written in its full form, both lights being united as one. Where? In that "firmament of heaven"; for when the moon ascends and joins that firmament, then the lights are complete and perfect, without blemish.'

The young man here paused to smile, and then continued: 'All this that I have said concerning the mystery of man's formation through the light of that seed, which, being turned into water, spreads out and is formed into a firmament, all of this can be properly understood when referred to what goes on in the body of a female, where the seed is thus developed into the form of man. But if those five grades above mentioned are the form of Man [Tr. note: i.e. the Deity.] in what place was this form fashioned and spread out? We cannot say it was within the Female, [Tr. note: Binah.] that is the World-to-come, because no form or likeness was fashioned until the letters had emerged and taken shape; besides which, the World-to-come was the artificer. Nor can it have been the lower Female [Tr. note: Malkuth], for this was not yet, and when the form of Man emerged, his Female emerged with him, so his form could not have been shaped in her. Where, then, was that seed portrayed and engraved in order to become the form of Man? Herein is a profound mystery, viz. that the Archetypal Adam took shape and form without the cooperation of the Female, but a second Man was engraved and formed from the seed and energy of the first within a female. Archetypal Adam took shape and bodily image out of the substance of the Future World without the conjunction of male and female. Certain letters materialized within a measured outline, and the mystery of Adam was formed and shaped in them, these letters having proceeded in a direct line in their proper order from the mystery of primeval light. Only when the Female came to him with her adornments, and they turned face to face, was a desire conceived whereby within the Female a likeness of Adam was conceived and shaped. This was within the Female, but not so the first Adam, who was formed within the measured outline, as already said. A corresponding process took place on earth. We read: "And Adam knew his wife Eve, and she

470

conceived and bare Cain" (Gen. IV, 1). Together with Adam's energy it was that which had been left of the ape element in her that produced Cain. Therefore of Cain's birth it does not say, "And he begat" but "she bare a son". The reason for its saying of Abel also, "And she again bare his brother Abel", is that, although he was conceived of the Masculine side, yet the Accuser weakened Adam's power and energy. Now with the letter

Zohar: Shemoth, Section 2, Page 168a

koph (of Cain: koph also means an ape), the letters began to beget. As soon as the impurity was eliminated, the letter shin (of Sheth) began to come into operation, the union of the Masculine with the Feminine. Therefore it says "And he begat a son in his own likeness, after his image, and he called his name Sheth" (Gen. v, 3): he, and not she. Then the letters reversed and combining the aleph of Adam with the letter following the last in his name-nun-took vau also (but not he', because that is already found in Abel), and also the first letter of Sheth, and then the name Enosh came into being (v. 6). What is the difference between enosh (man) and adam (which also signifies "man")? Enosh (anash=to be sick) indicates that he had not the same strength as Adam; concerning which it is written:

"What is man (enosh) that thou shouldst magnify him?" (Job VII, 17). A weakening of the body, but a strengthening of the soul was the heritage left by Sheth to his son Enosh, a good heritage for his acceptance. The latter passed on a like heritage to his son. The letters now began again to reverse their order and to make straight again that which had become crooked. The son of Enosh was Kenan (v. 9), which (in Hebrew) has the same letters as Cain, with an additional letter to signify that humanity was healed from the curse of Cain. The son of Kenan was Mahalalel: the mem (m) was the last letter of Adam; the he and the lamed (l) are from Hebel (Abel), and, as the latter was not wicked like Cain, the letters of his name were not changed, with the exception of one, that is the second (the b), and it was altered to aleph in Mahalalel, in order to correct any defect that might have been left in him. And so, thus far was the world healed, and that which had become crooked was made straight from Enosh; only the guilt of Adam was not healed yet; that healing came only when Israel stood at Mount Sinai. But the crookedness of Cain and Abel was made good and healed. Yet the world continued to be full of trouble and sorrow until Noah came, concerning whom his father Lamech said: "This same shall comfort us concerning our work and the toil of our hands because of the ground which the Lord hath cursed" (Ibid. v. 29). The sin of Adam was not healed until the time when Israel stood at Mount Sinai and received the Torah, when the lamp and light became united together. And now, Masters, I may tell you that I am from Babylon, the son of Rab Saphra. Unhappily, I have not been able to know my father, so I came here to the Holy Land, and fearing lest the inhabitants of this land should be lions of wisdom and knowledge, I resolved in humility not to say one word concerning the Torah in the presence of anyone for two months. On this very day those two months have come to an end, and happy am I that today, too, ye have arrived here!"

He ceased, and R. Yose lifted up his voice and wept. They all then rose and kissed the young man on the brow. Said R. Yose: 'Blessed is our lot that we were found worthy to come this way so that we might listen to words concerning the Ancient of Days from thy mouth, words which until today it had not been granted to us to hear.' Then they all seated themselves again, and the youth said: 'Masters, as I have seen the sorrow that I have brought to this my father-in-law and to his daughter, who are filled with grief because I seem not to know how to recite the Grace after meals, so I must tell you that until I grasp the full significance of this prayer I determine not to consummate my marriage. For, although I could have been united with her without sin of any kind, yet I did not wish to deceive either her or her father about myself, as it was impossible for me to explain myself until the two months were passed.' R. Yose and R. Hiya, as well as the innkeeper and his daughter, now all wept together for joy. And R. Yose said: 'We pray thee, as thou hast begun, shed on us further the light of day. Blessed indeed are we that we came this way!'

Thus urged, the youth began to expound to them the Grace to be recited after meals. Said he: 'One verse says, "And thou shalt eat there before the Lord thy God" (Deut. XIV, 26), and another verse says, "Thou shalt rejoice before the Lord thy God" (Ibid. XXVI, 11). These verses could be fulfilled at the time when Israel dwelt in the Holy Land and appeared daily before the Holy One in the Temple, but in these days how can they be fulfilled? Who can now eat and rejoice before the Lord? However, it can be done. For when a meal is set before a man he should first recite the benediction, "He who bringeth forth bread..." (ha-mozi). Why ha-mozi and not simply mozi without the definite article (ha)? It is because from everything appertaining to the mystery of the hidden supernal world the letter he, is hidden away to show that it belongs to the unseen secret world,

Zohar: Shemoth, Section 2, Page 168b

whereas things more disclosed, and which belong to the world below, have this letter, as, for example, "Who bringeth out (ha-mozi) their hosts by number (i.e. the stars, Isa. XL. 26); "He that called (ha-koreh) for the waters of the sea" (Amos V. 8); these are things of the lower world. Now, as soon as a man recites the benediction over the bread, the Shekinah is there before he has well begun. The words, "Thou shalt eat there before the Lord", include the commandment to hold converse, while eating, on the words of the Torah, since the Holy One Himself is present, as it is written, "This is the table that is before the Lord" (Ezek. XLI, 22). And again it is written, "Thou shalt eat there before the Lord thy God". And when man is privileged to eat in the presence of his Lord, he must show his appreciation of this privilege by giving charity to the poor, feeding them, as his Lord in His bounty feeds him. And he who eats in the presence of the Holy King must take heed that no greedy person be present at the board, for greediness is of the "other side", as exemplified by Esau, who said to Jacob, "Let me devour (hal'iteni)" (Gen. xxv, 30), that is, greedily. This is characteristic of the "other side", as it is written, "the belly of the wicked shall want" (Prov. XIII, 25). "Thou shalt eat before the Lord thy God", not before the "other side". Nor is it fitting to hold a vain conversation at the table, except on such matters as appertain to the meal; the converse must be on sacred matters, since thereby, as it were, strength is given to the Lord, "And thou shalt rejoice before the Lord thy God", namely, with the "Cup of Benediction". When a man recites the benediction over this cup he must do so with joy, and with no trace of sadness. When he takes into his hands this cup, the Holy One is there beside him, and he must cover his head for joy, holding the cup, and saying–if there be at least three persons partaking of the meal–"Let us bless Him of whose bounty we have partaken, and in whose goodness we live". This response calls for a specially earnest concentration on the part of all towards the Ancient of Ancients, for which reason His Name is not directly mentioned. "In whose goodness", and not merely "by" or "from" whose goodness, that is to say, the Supernal Right Hand itself, while "from whose goodness" would symbolize a lower grade, [Tr. note: Zaddik.] which emanates from that Right Hand. For by this "goodness" was the universe constructed, and by it is it sustained. Why is it called both "goodness" and "grace" (hesed)? It is "goodness" when it contains all within itself, and has not yet expanded to descend below; it is "grace" when it descends to benefit all creatures without distinction, the good and the wicked. But that there is a subtle differentiation between them is clear from the expression, "truly goodness and grace shall follow me" (Ps. XXIII, 6). And in the grace after meals the phrase, "and in whose goodness we live" of the response is immediately followed by the words, "Who feedeth the whole world with thy goodness... with grace"; as it is written also, "Who giveth food to all flesh: for his grace endureth forever" (Ps. CXXXVI, 25). He truly feeds all, the righteous and the unrighteous. This is called "the blessing of the Right Hand". In the Grace after meals the "Left" is not referred to; and that is why the left hand does not assist the right hand in holding the Cup of Benediction. As soon as the benediction of the Right Hand has been said, the "Land of Life" has to be brought into contact with that Right Hand of God through our thanksgiving, so that the bounty of the Right Hand may fall upon that Land and nourish her in order that from her again all the world may be sustained and fed. Which is the reason why the "blessing for the land" comes next in order in the Grace after meals. It is necessary also to mention in it the Abrahamitic Covenant and the gift of the Torah–"for Thy covenant which Thou hast sealed in our flesh, and for Thy Torah which Thou hast taught us"–in order that it may be clearly shown that both the Covenant and the Torah are nourished by "Goodness", the covenant being the support of that "goodness". Hence for women it is not obligatory to say the Grace after meals. [Tr. note: v. T. B. Berakhoth, 20b, where the ruling seems to be different.] This section is concluded with the words: "Blessed art Thou, O Lord, for the land and for the food", in order that both the "land" and the "food" may be attached to "grace". The "land" is the land of life; the "food" the manifestation of grace, the extention of which is expressed in "praise" in the words, "We praise Thee, O Lord", that is, for all the signs and wonders that emanate from the side of "goodness".

Zohar: Shemoth, Section 2, Page 169a

Why is it that the Left has no part in the Grace? It is because "the other side" cannot participate in Israel's food, and if the Left Hand, that is Severity, were also to be roused by referring to this attribute of the Holy One during the Grace, the "other side" would thereby be roused, and he has sold his birthright to our father Jacob. When we wash our hands after meals we so give him his portion; and if the hands are unsoiled he gets a portion of the food which the hands have touched. So he has no portion with us; therefore we must not arouse the Left Hand at all in the Grace, otherwise the Accuser might become the possessor of a double portion, one below and one above, like a first-born; for Esau has sold his birthright to father Jacob, and his portion is below only, and there is nothing for him above. Israel takes his portion from above, but Esau takes from below only. Now, when the "Land of Life" has been blessed from the Right Side and received its nourishment from thence, we have to pray for mercy for all–"Have mercy, O Lord our God, upon Israel Thy people, upon Jerusalem Thy city, upon Zion the abiding place of Thy Glory", etc.; for from that stream of nourishment of the Land of Life do both we and the Sanctuary benefit, since the Sanctuary below will be rebuilt through that Mercy. And on Sabbath, when Judgement is not active, and in order that Victory and Beauty should both be included and united in Grace, we add to the Grace after meals the prayer that begins with the words: "Be pleased, O Lord our God, to fortify us with Thy commandments", so that both Victory and Beauty may be united in the "sure graces of David" (Isa. LV, 3), and "that there may be no trouble, grief or lamentation on the day of our rest". And corresponding to the petition "grant peace" which we offer in the Amidah, we say in Grace, "He who makes peace in his high heavens will bestow peace on us." We also say, "Who is good and doeth good"; for all proceeds from the "Right" side, and nothing from the "Left". He who recites the Grace after meals receives the blessings first of all, and a long life is his reward. It is written concerning him who takes the Cup and recites the Benediction: "I lift up the cup of salvations and call upon the name of the Lord"

(Ps. CXVI, 13). What do "salvations" imply? "Salvations" emanating from the Right Hand which saves from all accusers, as it is written: "His right hand saved him" (Ps. CXVI, 13); "May thy right hand save" (Ibid. LX, 7).'

Now day broke, and they all stood up and kissed the youth. Said R. Yose: 'Verily, this day is a day of joy, and we shall not depart hence until it has become a day of rejoicing and festivity for all the village. It will be a festival in which the Holy One, blessed be He, will participate.' Then they took the young woman and blessed her with many blessings; after which they bade her father prepare the house for the festivities. And all the inhabitants of that village came to the house and shared in the rejoicings, and they called her "Bride", and made merry with them the whole day. The young man, too, rejoiced with them in the words of the Torah, and when they were seated at the table he spoke on the following verse: "And thou shalt make the boards for the tabernacle of shittim wood standing" (Ex. XXVI, 15). 'These boards', he said, 'stood round the canopy serving the Bride (the Shekinah), so that within that canopy the Supernal Spirit could dwell. Therefore must the bride below (human bride) have a canopy, all beautiful with decorations prepared for her in order to honour the Bride above, who comes to be present to participate in the joy of the bride below. For this reason it is necessary that the canopy should be as beautiful as possible, and that the Supernal Bride should be invited to come and share in the joy. Just as at every celebration of the covenant of circumcision a beautiful chair must be prepared for the "man of zeal" (Elijah the prophet), since he is present there, so also at every wedding the canopy must be beautifully decorated in honour of the celestial Bride; for as below, so above: as the bride here below is blessed with seven benedictions, so is her prototype. [Tr. note: The Shekinah-Malkuth-who receives the fulness of blessing from the preceding Sefiroth] A woman who is being married is called "bride" only after the seven benedictions have been pronounced; and only then can there be conjugal union. All this is according to the pattern of what is above. These seven benedictions the Bride receives from the Spirit above,

Zohar: Shemoth, Section 2, Page 169b

from that realm whence all blessings come. But are there not, in fact, only six benedictions with which the (supernal) Bride is blessed? The last (the seventh), however, is the one which confirms all the rest. Most benedictions are pronounced over wine; why is this? Because wine symbolizes joy: the wine which is ever guarded in the grapes. Therefore the first benediction of the seven-"Blessed art Thou who createst the fruit of the vine"-is connected with the mystery of wine [Tr. note: Binah] which produces joy both above and below. The vine [Tr. note: Malkuth] takes all and brings forth fruit in the world. The first awakening of joy proceeds from the left side, as it is written: "His left hand under my head", and then "his right hand embraces me". And that Tree of Life [Tr. note: Tifereth] produces fruit through this awakening. Therefore this benediction over the fruit of the vine is the first of all. The second is: "Blessed art thou... Who hast created all things to Thy glory". This contains the mystery of the holy covenant, the joy of union. It takes all the blessings from the mystery of the Right Hand in order to produce fruit in that vine; for first that influx proceeds from above by way of the organs, and is then drawn to the sign of the holy covenant, to proceed thence to the vine. And this is of the Right Hand, for the fulness is found only in the right side: the Left Hand rouses the Right and the Right then operates. The Left is afterwards embraced in the Right and the Right in the Left in order that all may form the mystery of Man; hence the benediction, "Blessed art Thou... Creator of man", follows as the third in order, and therefore Jacob, the "middle pillar", was in the likeness of Man. The fourth benediction, "Blessed art Thou... who hast made man in Thine image, after Thy likeness, and hast prepared unto him, out of his very self, a perpetual fabric..."refers to the one pillar of the right thigh [Tr. note: Nezah] The fifth benediction is: "May she (Zion) who was barren (akarah) be exceeding glad and exult, when her children are gathered within her in joy", which means to say: May she who is the centre (akereth, from ikkar, substance) of the house rejoice when her children are gathered from the four corners of the world. This is the mystery of the other pillar which is united with the left thigh [Tr. note: Hod] in order to draw the children in love from all directions together, and set them between the knees; and in those two, wherein is the abode of the Prophets (the realm of Prophecy), is the joy of Her who is the basis of the house. Why is this her joy? Because the gathering together of the children, which is the fruit of the two willows, [Tr. Note: Nezah and Hod.] is effected only by the power of the Prophets. The sixth benediction is: "O make these loved companions greatly to rejoice, even as of old Thou didst gladden Thy creature in the Garden of Eden...." This is the region wherein goodwill, joy, and fellowship are found. It is the pillar of the whole universe, namely the "Righteous". The Righteous and Righteousness are the inseparable "beloved companions". Thus far there are six benedictions by which the bride is blessed. Now the seventh benediction is the synthesis of them all, and from it all the universe is blessed, because it comprises what is above and what is below, it is the epitome of the Ten creative Words, and therefore ten aspects of joy are found in this benediction: "Blessed art Thou... Who hast created joy and gladness, bridegroom and bride, mirth and exultation, love and brotherhood, peace and fellowship" in order that the bride may be the perfection of all. Blessed are the Israelites who are worthy to represent below that which is above. Concerning them it is written: "And who is like unto thy people Israel, a unique nation on the earth?" (2 Sam. VII, 23).'

Then they all rejoiced for that whole day in the words of the Torah, and the inhabitants of the town appointed the young man to be their head. On the next day R. Yose and R. Hiya rose and blessed them all, and departed on their way. As they came near to R. Simeon, he lifted up his eyes, and seeing them, said: 'Today did I behold you with the eyes of the spirit, and I saw that ye dwelt for two days and a night in the Tabernacle of that Youth, Metatron, and the Youth taught you of the supernal mysteries in the joy of the Torah. Blessed are ye, my children!' When they had told him all that had happened to them, he said: 'Happy are ye, and happy is my lot, for well do I recollect the day when his father, Rab Saphra, accompanied me on my way, and when I parted from him I blessed him with this blessing-that he might have a son who should be a scholar, but not that he himself should live to see it. Happy, my children, is your lot! Concerning you it is written: "And all thy children shall be taught of the Lord" (Isa. LIV, 13). There is, however, another interpretation of this verse. Does God teach all the children of the Israelites the Torah? Yes, indeed, for when these little ones learn, the Shekinah comes and lends to each of them power and energy to study; for without the help of the Holy One the strain on these babes would be too great.'

R. Simeon was one day together with R. Hiya at the gate of Lud, when a young boy approached them. Said R. Simeon: 'Verily, the Holy One, blessed be He, will in a few days embroil the kings of the earth with one another,

Zohar: Shemoth, Section 2, Page 170a

in order that while they fight, Israel may have a period of repose.' And the young boy remarked: 'This conflict has already begun, and much blood is being shed in the world.' Said R. Hiya: 'How does this young boy know this?' R. Simeon replied: 'Prophecy at times is lodged in the mouths of children, so that they prophesy even more than the prophets of old.' And the boy said: 'Why do you marvel that children have the spirit of prophecy, seeing that this is clearly foreshadowed in the Scriptures? It is written: "And all thy children shall be taught by the Lord." And, truly, when they are taught by the Lord they prophesy. Of all peoples it is only Israel of whose children it says that they shall be taught by the Lord, therefore out of them prophecy comes forth.' Hearing this, R. Simeon came up to the boy and kissed him, saying: 'I have never heard this idea till now.' AND THOU SHALT MAKE THE BOARDS FOR THE TABERNACLE OF SHITTIM WOOD STANDING.

Of the Seraphim also it says that they were "standing"; thus the boards of the Tabernacle corresponded to the Seraphim. It may be asked, Do not all the heavenly Hosts stand? Is it not written, "And I shall give thee walks among these (angels) that stand by" (Zech. III, 7)? "And all the hosts of heaven were standing" (I Kings XXII, 19)-because they have no joints?' [Tr. note: Cf. Bereshith Rabbah, 65.] It is indeed so, but the angels are sometimes called "Seraphim", and sometimes by other names, this name being applied to them all. [Tr. Note: i.e. as explained by Mikdash Melech. when they perform the office of Seraphim (lit. burning ones)] The verse has already been interpreted in its symbolic significance.

It is written: A psalm of David. The Lord is my shepherd, I shall not want (Ps. XXIII, 1). The difference between "a psalm of David" and "of David a psalm" has already been explained. In this psalm the Shekinah came first and rested upon the Psalmist, for, as has already been remarked, "a psalm of David" indicates that the first impulse proceeded from the Shekinah. But in this psalm David prays for nourishment, so that we should have thought the initiative would have come from him. The fact is that the Shekinah did indeed first urge David to sing this hymn to the King, to pray to Him for nourishment for Her, which She needs in order to supply food to the whole world; and it is her will that all mankind should pray for food, for when the Holy One wishes to send down to the world nourishment, She first receives it, She being the organ by which the whole world is sustained. Therefore, indeed, did She precede David in this psalm, and She rested upon him to inspire him in this prayer for food. "The Lord is my shepherd": as a shepherd leads his flock to those places where there is grass in abundance, in order to provide them with whatever they need, so does the Holy One also unto Me. Here is another interpretation. There is an ancient dictum that "to provide food for humanity costs the Holy One, blessed be He, as great a struggle as it did to divide the Red Sea". [Tr. note: T.B. Pes. 118b.] Here are two statements, both of deep significance. On the one hand, since everything done by the Holy One is done according to justice and truth, on which qualities the world is based, and as He always apportions a lot to all according to justice, both to the righteous and the wicked, and all that come into the world-as it is written, "for the Lord is righteous and loveth righteousness" (Ps. XI, 7)-He finds it difficult, when He sees so many wicked people and sinners, to supply them continually with nourishment. He deals with them not according to the rigour of the law, and nourishes and sustains them to the full extent of the supernal Grace which issues forth and descends upon all the beings of the world, and therewith He feeds them, one and all, righteous and saints, wicked and sinners, all creatures whatsoever, the beasts of the field and the fowls of the air, from the "horns of the buffaloes to the eggs of vermin". [Tr. note: v. T. B. Sabb. 107b.] There is nothing in the world to which His mercy does not extend, even though, on account of the evil works of men, this is all as difficult to Him as was the dividing of the Red Sea. But was that really difficult to Him? Is it not written: "He rebuketh the sea and maketh it dry" (Nahum I, 4)? "He that calleth for the waters of the sea and poureth them out upon the face of the earth" (Amos v, 8)? Is it not true of Him that as soon as

474

TERUMAH

He is resolved to do a thing all obstacles are as naught before Him? How was it that the dividing of the Red Sea was difficult to Him? This is the explanation. When the Israelites stood on the shore of the Red Sea and the Holy One was about to divide its waters for them, Rahab, the angel-prince of Egypt, appeared, and demanded justice from the Holy One. He stood before Him and said: "Lord of the world, why dost thou desire to punish Egypt and to divide the Red Sea for Israel? Have not all sinned against Thee? Thy ways are according to justice and truth. Those are idolaters and so are these. Those are murderers, so are these." Then was it difficult for Him to waive justice, and had not the Holy One called to mind Abraham's obedience in rising early (Gen. XXII, 3) to sacrifice his only son, they would all have perished in the Red Sea, because all that night God was weighing Israel in the scales of Justice, as we have been taught that the expression, "so that the one came not near the other all the night" (Ex. XIV, 20) indicates that the supernal angels appeared on that night to sing hymns of praise to the Holy One, and the Holy One said unto them: "The works of My hands are about to sink into the depths of the sea, and ye desire to sing unto Me hymns of praise?" But "it came to pass that in the morning watch the Lord looked..." (Ibid. v. 24); that is to say, He "looked" for Abraham's sake, He "looked" upon Abraham's merit, who "rose up early in the morning" to accomplish the will of the Holy One. Then it was that the waters "went back", they fled before Israel. Similarly, it has been stated [Tr. note: Cf. Lev. R. ch. VIII.] that "marriage unions are as difficult for (lit. before) the Holy One as was the dividing of the Red Sea". As at the dividing of the Red Sea those who stood on the one side of the sea were drowned, and the others were saved, so in marriages also there is weeping for some and singing for others; He allows one man to die and gives his wife to another man, and at times a bad man gets a good wife. These happenings are great mysteries, but it all conforms to justice, and all that the Companions have said on this subject is quite true; as is also that which they have stated concerning the difference between "before" (liphne, lit. the face of) and "from before" (miliphne). These matrimonial decisions are arranged by him who stands before the Holy One and ministers before Him. Therefore the aforementioned dictum does not run, "hard are unions to the Holy One", but "before (to the face of) the Holy One"; i.e. to him who is appointed over the arrangement of marriages and over the supply of food, since the power is not his, he is merely the administrator and under authority.

[Note: the last 14 lines of the Hebrew text do not appear in the translation]

[Note: the first 8 lines of the Hebrew text do not appear in the translation]

Now King David transmitted his prayer concerning nourishment to the realm above, since there the supply never ceases. Therefore he said: "The Lord is my shepherd, I shall not want", which was as much as to say, "my supply of nourishment cannot fail, since it issues from that stream which comes out of Eden and which never ceases to flow". Hence it is written, "a psalm of David", because the Shekinah gave him the impetus to pray and to praise. When that region receives nourishment from above, all those supernal beings who sanctify their Lord are thrilled and raise their wings when the Shekinah appears with that food, in order that they may not look upon Her. There are three battalions of them. The first proclaim "Holy!" and then call to the second while they raise their wings; and the second proclaim "Holy" and call to the third while raising their wings; and at last they all raise their wings and cry together: "Holy is the Lord of hosts, the whole earth is full of his glory" (Isa. VI, 3). So they are all joined to one another, and dovetail into one another, just as the boards of the Tabernacle were "bound to one another" (Ex. XXVI, 17). The boards stood ever upright and did not bend, just as the angels, the "standing ones", who, having no joints, never bend. As the boards had two holders which united one board with the next, so is one angel joined to the other: each one takes his own and his neighbour's wing, and so enfolded within each other they stand closely united. Of the Torah the same is true: the students both teach and learn from one another in perfect reciprocity. We read next: "He maketh me to lie down in pastures of tender green; he leadeth me beside the waters of rest; he quickeneth my soul". "Pastures of tender green" are those which lie round the supernal springs, from whence all nourishment emanates. These pastures are also called "the pastures of Jacob" (Lam. II, 2), and are called "green pastures" in contrast to those pastures which lie outside, the pastures of the desert" (Joel II, 22). It might be said: Is it not written, "Let the earth bring forth tender (green) grass" (Gen. I, 11), showing that "green" is applied also to what is below? The fact is that this "green" of earth emanates from those "pastures" above, germinating and flourishing through the life-giving energy supplied them from above. "He leadeth me beside the waters of rest." These "waters of rest" are those which come forth from that region which proceeds from Eden. "He quickeneth my soul", namely David's soul, which he desired to bring into contact with the sphere of his own grade whence it emanated. In these "waters of rest" the righteous will find rest in the world to come, as it is written: "And the Lord shall give thee rest constantly... and thou shalt be like a watered garden, and like a spring of water, whose waters fail not" (Isa. LVIII, 11). AND THOU SHALT MAKE FIFTY CLASPS OF BRASS. R. Eleazar and R. Abba were sitting together one evening, and when it grew dusk they went into a garden by the Lake of Tiberias. As they were going they saw two stars rush towards one another from different points in the sky, meet, and then disappear. Said R. Abba: 'How mighty are the works of the Holy One, blessed be He, in heaven above and in the earth below! Who can understand it, these two stars emerging from different directions, meeting, and disappearing?' R. Eleazar replied: 'And even if we had not seen these two stars, we have yet reflected

on them, as on many great works which the Holy One, blessed be He, is constantly performing.' He then went on to discourse on the verse, "Great is our Lord, and of great power; his understanding is without number" (infinite, Ps. CXLVII, 5). 'Great and strong, and sublime is, indeed, the Holy One', he said. 'But did we not always know that the Holy One is great and of infinite power? What honour does David pay to God here? Note, however, that in other psalms he says, "Great is Tetragrammaton" (Ps. CXLV, 3), but here he says, "great is our Lord" (adonenu). Why is this? It is because when he says, "Great is Tetragrammaton, and greatly to be praised", he is referring to the highest grade, while here it is of a lower grade that he speaks: "great is our Lord", which is parallel to "the Lord (adon) of the whole earth" (Joshua III, 13). What does it say in the preceding verse? "He counts the number of the stars, he calleth them all by their names" (Ps. CXLVII, 4). If all of mankind since the first man were to come together to count the stars, they would not succeed in numbering them, as it is written: "Look now toward heaven and tell the stars, if thou be able to number them" (Gen. xv, 5). But of the Holy One it says: "He counts the number of the stars; he calleth them by their names". Why is this? Because "Great is our Lord, and of great power; His understanding is without number." As the stars have no number except to Him, so is His understanding "without number" (absolutely). Mark this also. It is written: "Who bringeth out their host by numbers; he calleth them all by names" (Isa. XL, 26). The Holy One brings out all the hosts, camps, and stars, each one is called by its own name, and "not one faileth" (Ibid.). Over all these stars and constellations of the firmament there have been set chiefs, leaders, and ministers, whose duty is to serve the world each one according to his appointed station. And not the tiniest grass-blade on earth but has its own appointed star in heaven. Each star, too, has over it a being appointed who ministers before the Holy One as its representative, each according to his order. All the stars in the firmaments keep watch over this world: they are appointed to minister to every individual object in this world, to each object a star. Herbs and trees, grass and wild plants, cannot flourish and grow except from the influence of the stars who stand above them and gaze upon them face to face, each according to his fashion. Most of the planets and the starry hosts come out and shine at the commencement of the night, and they remain until three hours less a quarter after midnight. After that only a few appear. And all these stars do not shine and serve in vain. Some of them are busy the whole night long, enabling the plant over which they are appointed to grow and blossom forth. Some there are whose activities last only till midnight, operating on the object of their charge from the commencement of the night until that midnight hour. Others there are whose appointed task is quickly done each night, so soon as they have shown themselves in conjunction with the particular plant or grass which depends upon them. So the appearance of those stars which we observed was not without purpose. As soon as their purpose is fulfilled they are seen no more in this world, but they ascend to their appointed places above. In the Book of the higher Wisdom of the East, it says, speaking of certain stars which form a tail (sceptre) in the firmament, that on the earth there are herbs, of the kind that are called "elixirs of life", and precious stones, and fine gold, which forms within the breast of high mountains, under shallow water- which are all ruled by those comets by whose influence they grow and increase; it is the glance of that luminous tail which such stars trail after them across the sky that causes those things to flourish. Certain illnesses of men, as jaundice, can be cured through the patient's gazing upon shining steel, which is held before his eyes and rapidly moved from side to side, so that, like a comet's tail, it sends flashes of light into the face, thus healing the disease. Therefore all those objects over which such stars as these are appointed can have no proper development and growth unless the light of the comet actually passes over them, whereby they are enabled to renew their colour

and their energy according to their need. This must be true, since it is similarly indicated in the Book of King Solomon, in regard to the science of precious stones, that when these stones are denied the light and sparkle of certain stars, their development is retarded and they never reach their full perfection. And the Holy One, blessed be He, has ordered all things so that the world may be perfected and beautified, and accordingly it is written that the stars are "to give light upon earth" (Gen. I, 17), in all the things which the world needs for its perfection.'

'It is written: "And thou shalt make fifty clasps of brass"; and again it says, "And thou shalt make fifty clasps of gold" (Ex. XVI, 6), and we have been taught that he who never saw those clasps in the Tabernacle has not seen the light of the stars in heaven, for in appearance and colour they reminded all who looked upon them of the stars. Now there are stars in the heavens which have emerged from that firmament to which all the stars are attached. In that firmament there are one hundred latticed windows, some on the east and some on the south side of the firmament. At each window there is one star. And when the sun passes by these windows and lattices in the firmament he sends out flashing rays, and the stars catch up these rays and are coloured by them. Some take on the red of brass, some the yellow of gold; and for this reason some stars shine with a red, and some with a yellow gleam. The windows are divided into fifties, and, as we have said, in each one is a star. The windows in the east catch the yellow rays, while those in the south catch the red.

The stars which shine by night mingle with those that proceed from that firmament and they sparkle and shine, ruling over the elements of this world, some over brass, some over yellow gold, and these elements increase and develop through the power of the stars. These stars rule for the twenty-five and a half points of the night, which are in the division of an hour. Those stars which are appointed over brass are red, and they both shine and sparkle. When they shall have diffused their light three times towards the east, or five, or seven times, then the kings of the Gentiles will rise against the east, and from that region all gold and riches will disappear. When they sparkle, one, two, four, six, one after another, then fear and trembling will settle upon that region. When the rays will strike and subside, then strike and subside again, wars will arise in the world on that side, for there will be a vibration and stirring before the Holy One in connection with those angel-princes who have charge over the nations of the world. And so it will be on the other side also. Therefore I say, "Blessed be the name of God forever and ever: for wisdom and might are his. And He changeth the times and the seasons" (Dan. II, 20, 21). All things are in His hands, and He has liberated His holy people from the power and dominion of the stars and planets; for they have become objects of worship for the nations, but Jacob has no portion in them, because he belongs to Him who is the Creator of all things.

'There is a firmament high above all these firmaments, hidden, concealed, and the seal of the Tabernacle reigns over that firmament, which is called "Hall of the Tabernacle". There all those windows are to be found, on this side and on that, and it holds all the arrangements of the Tabernacle. Six of the windows are greater than all the others, and one, which is concealed, rules over them all. One of these seven is called "the window of light", and into it the star which the wise call Yad (hand) enters, which "hand" stretches out to the domain of the tribe of Judah. This does not mean that that tribe has any part in it, since the tribes of Israel are not under the dominion of the stars, and the tribe of Judah rules over that star, and not the star over it. But when members of this tribe became corrupted in their ways and turned away from the Holy One, then they began to divine their fate by contact with that window and the star that dwelt in it, saying: "It is the hand that conquers all the nations"; for concerning Judah it is written, "Thine hand shall be in the neck of thine enemies" (Gen. XLIX, 8), and they followed the star and worshipped it. Concerning which it is written: "And Judah did that which was evil in the sight of the Lord" (I Kings XIV, 22). When that star comes out it stretches out a hand with five rays, which are five fingers, which shine and sparkle in that window.

Zohar: Shemoth, Section 2, Page 172b

Sorcerers and astrologers are in fear and awe of this region, for when this star reigns they become confused and their predictions come to naught. It may be asked, If that firmament is hidden, how is it that they have knowledge concerning this star? The answer is that they have an outward sign from which they know when it is in the ascendant, and they fear it, and at such periods their incantations do not succeed. Thus it is that there have been times when people were lucky in connection with this star, and times again when they came to grief over it. For this reason the number of astrologers and sorcerers decreases in the world, because they become bewildered when their incantations and predictions fail. But the ancient astrologers knew of that star, and studied the outward sign which was disclosed to them.

'The second window is called "the window of the claw", because it has the form of a claw, and the star which enters into it is known to the wise as "Viper", since when this star reigns severe judgement prevails. It has a head like a viper lying in wait. From that window six hundred thousand myriads of spirits proceed, which spirits rule over the toe and fingernails of men when the nail-parings are thrown away instead of being burnt, for these nail-parings are used by the sorcerers for their divinations. All those who throw away their nail-parings, or use them for witchcraft while this star is in the ascendant, cause death, and increase the power of sorcery.

'The third window is called "Breastplate". A star enters into it, called "Bright Light". This is the one whose rays watch over every spirit, and rest, redemption, and goodness are in it, with no trace of the accusing element or severity. When it is in the ascendant all is repose and light, for peace, satisfaction and harmony prevail throughout the world.

'The fourth window is called "Chalice", and the star which enters into it is called by the wise "Cluster of cypress flowers", because it comes out like a cluster (eshkol) and spreads its rays in the form of the grapes. It awakens mercy in the world; it removes evil far off and brings the good near. Much procreation takes place in the world at this time. Men do not object to helping one another when required.

'The fifth window is that which is called "Cistern", because the star which enters it always "draws" like a bucket and is never at rest: the wise of heart can never discover its real nature, since it never remains still. They, therefore, only with great difficulty examine it and come to some conclusion about it.

'The sixth window is called Nagha (lit. brightness), and a star enters into it called Gazron, because when it reigns over the world it is a sign of judgement, which reveals itself in many severe decrees (gezeroth) and many punishments. Every day new decrees of evil are enacted against the world, and even before these have been completely carried out other fresh ones are enacted. In the present dispensation this star is not often in the ascendant, but when the days of the Messiah will draw nigh it will dominate the world, and as a consequence noxious beasts and diseases will rage in the world, evil haps will constantly be renewed, and Israel will be in great tribulation. But when they are thus oppressed in the darkness of exile the Holy One will cause the day to break for them "and the Kingdom and dominion, and the greatness of the Kingdom... shall be given to the people of the saints of the most High" (Dan. XII, 27), and the reign of the heathen nations will be terminated and Israel shall rule over them, and there will be fulfilment of the words, "Moreover the light of the moon shall be as the light of the sun" (Isa. xxx, 26), and then will this cause the seventh window to open to the whole world, whose star is the "Star of Jacob", concerning which Balaam said: "There shall come a star out of Jacob" (Num. XXIV, 17). This star will shine for forty days and forty nights, and when the Messiah shall be revealed and all the nations of the world shall gather around him, then will the verse of Scripture be fulfilled which says: "And in that day the root of Jesse which stands for an ensign of the peoples, to it shall the Gentiles seek: and his rest shall be glorious" (Isa. XI, 10).'

R. Simeon quoted here the verse: "But none saith, Where is God (Eloha) my maker who giveth songs in the night?" (Job xxxv, 10). Said he: 'The name "Eloha" here refers to Her who sings perpetual hymns of praise to the "King whose is the peace", who is like a lamp that never ceases to receive the light of supreme joy from the fulness

Zohar: Shemoth, Section 2, Page 173a

of His joy. Hence, "Who giveth songs in the night." All those stars which shine in heaven do sing and praise the Holy One, blessed be He, all the time that they are visible in the sky. And the angels above sing the praises of their Lord in successive watches of the night. By night various sides are active in different ways. At the beginning of the night, when darkness falls, all the evil spirits and powers scatter abroad and roam about the world, and the "other side" sets forth and inquires the way to the King from all the holy sides. As soon as the "other side" is roused to this activity here below, all human beings experience a foretaste of death in the midst of their sleep. As soon as the impure power separates itself from the realm above and descends to begin its rule here below, three groups of angels are formed who praise the Holy One in three night watches, one following another, as the Companions have pointed out. But whilst these sing hymns of praise to the Holy One, the "other side", as we have said, roams about here below, even into the uttermost parts of the earth. Until the "other side" has thus departed from the upper sphere, the angels of light cannot unite themselves with their Lord. This is a mystery comprehensible only to the wise. The angels above and the Israelites below both press upon the "other side" in order to oust it. The supernal angels, when they desire to be united with their Lord, cannot accomplish this until the "other side" has been expelled from the higher realms. What, then, do these celestial beings do? Sixty myriads of holy angels descend on to the earth and bring sleep to all the children thereof. Through this sleep they give this world to the "other side"– save only in the Land of Israel, where it has no sway. As soon, therefore, as it has left the angels they ascend before their Lord, and begin to sing praises. Similarly, Israel here below cannot unite themselves with their Lord until they have pushed the "other side" away from them, by giving it its due to keep it occupied. Then they, too, approach the Holy One, blessed be He, and thus the Accuser is finally found neither above nor below. It might be asked, That there is an accusation below is easy to understand, but what accusation can there be above? The truth is that the holy spirits cannot approach their Lord until the spirit of impurity has been banished from their midst, for holiness cannot be mixed with impurity, any more than the Israelites can be mingled with the heathen nations. Thus both regions, the celestial and the terrestrial, must expel the powers of unholiness before their inhabitants can approach and praise with joy and delight their Holy King. Therefore, when night falls and the holy supernal angels marshal themselves to approach Him, they first thrust out and banish the evil power. A king once had certain very precious stones which he kept locked away in a separate box in his palace. This king, in his wisdom, in order to keep prying eyes away from the casket, took a dangerous serpent and wound it round the box, thus effectually preventing anyone from stretching out his hand towards it. But the king had a great friend, and to him he said: "Whenever thou desirest to examine my gems, draw nigh without fear, and do such and such a thing to the serpent and he will be rendered harmless; then thou wilt be able to open the box and enjoy the sight of its contents." In like fashion the Holy One set about the inmost chamber of His Presence a serpent, the "other side". Now when the holy seraphic beings draw nigh with intent to enter the sphere of holiness, they come upon that serpent and are afraid lest they be defiled thereby. It may be asked: Since all angels are formed of fire, and fire cannot receive impurity, why are they afraid? The answer is indicated by the verse: "He maketh his angels spirits, his ministers a flaming fire" (Ps. CIV, 4). The first of these categories are those angels that stand outside while the second are those that stand within the innermost circle. Now those who encounter the serpent are "spirits", and that serpent is a spirit also. The spirit of impurity does not mingle

Zohar: Shemoth, Section 2, Page 173b

with the spirit of holiness, and therefore those angels that are called "spirits" cannot enter into the Holy Presence because of that spirit of impurity. Those angels, however, which are within are "fire", and that supernal holy fire ejects the impurity so that it cannot enter into the innermost place. Thus all combine to push out the impure power and prevent it from mingling with them; and, as we have said, the celestials can only begin to praise the Holy One after they have banished the "other side" from the heavenly courts.

Now, as we have said, the three watches of the night correspond to the hosts of angels when they divide themselves into three groups in order to sing praises to the Holy One. Therefore the conductor of them all is the "harp of David", for this never ceases to play, but constantly emits hymns of thanksgiving and praise before the Supernal King, and concerning this it is written: "Who giveth songs in the night". But how, it may be asked, can this be? You said that at the beginning of the night all the evil powers and spirits arise and wander over the face of the earth, and we have been taught that these all emerge from the side of the North; and you have said further that when the north wind awakens at midnight, those evil spirits and powers gather together from all the diverse parts of the earth in which they have been roaming and enter into a cavern in the Ocean. But, if that is the case, how can these evil spirits roam about in the side of the South at the beginning of the night, for then the South wind reigns? The answer, however, is that if it were not for the South, which keeps the evil power at bay and finally thrusts it away, that spirit of impurity would wipe out the whole world and none could withstand it. But when that "other side" is roused it is only in the West, which side rules at the beginning of the night, at which time the whole world is sunk in sleep. Therefore the Holy One prepared a healing medicine for the world in the way we have said. Blessed are the Israelites in this world and in the world to come, because the Holy One, blessed be He, has chosen them above all the other nations of the world.'

R. Eleazar and R. Abba entered the house and rested awhile. At midnight they got up to study the Torah. Said R. Abba: 'Verily, now is the time of the Holy One's favour, since we have often remarked that at the moment of midnight the Holy One, blessed be He, goes in unto the righteous in the Garden of Eden to have joyous fellowship with them. Blessed is he who is occupied with the study of the Torah at this time.' R. Eleazar asked: 'What is the manner of this joyous fellowship?' and continued, answering himself: 'At midnight the Holy One is roused in the love of the Left Hand towards the Community of Israel; for the arousing of love proceeds only from the Left Hand. The Community of Israel, however, has no gift through which to approach the King, nor any excellent worth in herself; only when He beholds the spirits of the righteous, crowned with many good works and with many acts of righteousness accomplished during the preceding day, He is more pleased with them than with all the savour of the sacrifices which the Israelites offer. Then a light breaks forth, and all the trees of the Garden of Eden begin to sing, and the righteous are crowned there with all the joys of the world to come. And when a man wakes at that time to study the Torah, he participates in the joy of the righteous in the Garden of Eden. A Divine Name engraved in thirty-two letters is then wrought into a garland for them, this being one of the mysteries of the righteous.'

R. Eleazar then began to discourse on the verse: Hallelukah. I will give thanks unto the Lord with my whole heart, in the council of the upright, and in the congregation (Ps. CXI, 1) Said he: '"Hallelukah" is, as has already been truly pointed out by the Companions, the most excellent of all the ten expressions of praise [Tr. note: Benediction, Hallel, prayer, song, psalm, melody, nezah, blessed, thanks, Hallelukah. Cf. Midrash Teh. 1.] used by David, since it embraces in one single word the Divine Name and the call to praise, and in addition that Name which it contains (KAH) is the epitome of the highest Holy Name. "I will give thanks unto the Lord with my whole heart (lebab)." Wherever King David composed an alphabetical

Zohar: Shemoth, Section 2, Page 174a

Psalm, as in this case, he intended to indicate the mystery of the twenty-two engraved letters of the Hebrew alphabet, which issue forth in the tracing of thirty-two paths. [Tr. note: The thirty-two paths of the primordial Wisdom.] There are letters which emanate from the mystery of the supernal world, and there are others which are formed on a smaller pattern. In this psalm we have the mystery of the alphabet which the upper world gives to the lower. Thus, in "I will give thanks to the Lord with my whole heart", the word lebab (heart) alludes to two hearts, the good and the evil inclination, both of which dwell in man; for one must thank the Holy One for all things, not only with one's good, but also with one's evil inclination. For from the side of the good inclination good comes to man, so he has to give thanks to Him who is good and who does good. From the evil inclination, again, comes seduction, and one must needs thank and praise the Holy One for all that comes to him, whether it be from one side or from the other. "In the council (mystery) of the upright and in the congregation." "In the mystery (sod) of the upright" is an allusion to the supernal holy angels who know and comprehend the mystery of the Holy One and are a part thereof; "the congregation" refers to the children of Israel when they congregate in tens to give thanks to the Holy One, blessed be He. Thus one has always to praise the Lord, for evil as for good, and to proclaim His wondrous deeds unto all men, for when these wonders are thus proclaimed, and His goodness, wisdom and majesty are lauded among all His creatures, then He is truly glorified in the world. Concerning this it is written: "and I shall be magnified and sanctified" (Ezek. XXXVIII, 23).'

R. Judah, commenting on the words, "Let the whole soul (neshamah) praise the Lord" (Ps. CL, 6), said: 'We have been taught that all souls emanate from one holy Body, and animate human beings. From what place (in the Body) do they come? From the place which is called "KAH" [Tr. note: Al. Yod="Hand"]. ' And what is the nature of that region?' Said R. Judah: 'It is written, "How manifold are thy works, O Lord! In wisdom hast thou made them all" (Ibid. CIV, 24); for, as we have learnt, in that wisdom, the spring of which divides into thirty-two rivers, all things that are, both above and below, were completed; it is called the "Holy Spirit", containing as it does all other spirits that are.' Said R. Isaac: 'When R. Simeon reflected on this subject, his eyes filled with tears, and he said: All the treasures of the Supernal King are disclosed by means of one key, which reveals in secret chambers supernal tracings. Who can comprehend what is hidden in the spring of wisdom? Moses revealed it not on the day whereon he made known other deep mysteries, although all things were revealed through him, save only in the hour when the Holy One, blessed be He, desired to receive him into the holy Council above, and to remove him and hide him away from men, as it is written: "I am a hundred and twenty years old today" (Deut. XXXI, 2). On that very day the span of his days was completed and the time of his entrance into that region was arrived, as it is written: "Behold, thy days have come near that thou must die" (Ibid. 14): "near" being meant literally. For Moses did not die. But is it not written, "And Moses died there"? The truth is, however, that although the departure of the righteous is always designated "death", this is only in reference to us. For over him who has attained completeness, and is a model of holy faith, death has no power, and so he does not, in fact, die. This was, for instance, the case with Jacob, in whom was the completeness of Faith, as may be confirmed from the words: "thy name shall not be called any more Jacob, but Israel shall be thy name" (Gen. xxxv, 10); "Israel" means the completion of all, as it is written, "And thou, O my servant Jacob, fear not, neither be dismayed, O Israel, for lo, I will save thee from afar, and thy seed from the land of their captivity..." (Jer. xxx, 10).' R. Judah derived the fact of Israel's completeness from the words "for I am with thee" (Ibid.). 'Happy', he said, 'was his lot in that his Lord spoke to him in this wise! It does not say, "for thou art with Me", but "for I am with thee"- that is to say, his Master came to unite His lot with His servant's, and to dwell with him.' R. Simeon said: 'It was well said by R. Abba that the verse, "and Jacob shall return and shall be in rest, and be quiet, and none shall make him afraid" (Ibid. II), signifies that Jacob shall return to be called by another name, as it is written: "Thy name shall no more be called Jacob, but Israel." There is, however, also another interpretation, as follows: "and Jacob shall return" -namely, to the place whence he was taken; "and be in rest"–while in this world; "and be quiet"–in the world to come; "and none shall make him afraid"–not even the Angel of Death. So we see that all perfection was in him.' Said R. Isaac: 'The Companions have proved the last point in another way, viz., from the words "and thy seed (shall return) from the land of their captivity"; just as his seed is alive, so also is he alive.'

Zohar: Shemoth, Section 2, Page 174b

AND THE MIDDLE BAR IN THE MIDST OF THE BOARDS SHALL PASS THROUGH FROM END TO END. R. Judah here quoted the verse, "Blessed art thou, O land, when thy king is the son of nobles, and thy princes eat in due time" (Eccl. x, 17). 'What', he said, 'precedes this? "Woe to thee, O land, when thy king is a child, and thy princes eat in the morning".' Said he: 'Woe unto mankind that they neglect the worship of their Lord, though He perpetually lavishes upon them His providential care, setting before them the precious treasure of the Torah, which they neglect. There are, as we have learnt, three cardinal duties which a man must fulfil towards his son, namely, circumcision, redemption of the first-born, and the finding of a wife; and all three God performs for Israel; circumcision, as it is written, "And the Lord shall circumcise thy heart" (Deut. xxx, 6); redemption, as it is written, "And the Lord thy God hath redeemed thee" (Deut. xv, 15); the finding of a wife, as it is written, "He created them male and female, and God blessed them and God said unto them, Be fruitful and multiply" (Gen. I, 27, 28). Moreover, he carried his children on his wings (Ex. XIX, 4).' Said R. Yose: 'All these benefits which He gave unto Israel were great, but the Torah is the greatest of all. For there is nothing which so ennobles a man, either in this world or in the world to come, as the Torah, concerning which it is written, "By me kings reign, and princes decree justice" (Prov. VIII, 15).

'We are told that when Rab Huna went to Palestine he found the students there discoursing on the verse, "And I will punish Bel in Babylon, and I will bring forth out of his mouth that which he had swallowed up, and the nations shall not flow together any more unto him" (Jer. LI, 44). They paid no attention to Rab Huna, as he was not known to them, being still young. When he entered the house of study, he found the students somewhat puzzled by the fact that Bel is given as the name of Nebuchadnezzar's god, whereas elsewhere we read, "But at the last Daniel came in before me, whose name was Belteshazzar, as the name of my god" (Dan. IV, 5); and also, as to the exact meaning of the words, "I will bring out of his mouth that which he hath swallowed up". Rab Huna thereupon stood up between the pillars and said: "Were I in my own place I would interpret this verse." But they took no notice of him. He stood up a second time and made the same remark. Then R. Judai bar Rab came to him and gave him a seat before him, saying: 'Speak, my son, for of the words of the Torah it says, "She (wisdom) crieth in the chief place of concourse" (Prov. I, 21).' Then Rab Huna began thus: 'We have been taught that in early times, before Jacob appeared, illness was unknown, and mankind were perfectly healthy until their time came, when they passed away without any previous sickness. When Jacob came he prayed to God, saying: "Lord of the world! May it please thee to grant that a man should first fall ill for two or three days, and then be gathered unto his people, in order that he may have time to put his house in order and repent of his sins." The Holy One replied: "It shall be so, and thou shalt be the pledge and the sign thereof." Therefore it is written concerning him, "And it came to pass after these things, that Joseph was told, Behold, thy father is sick" (Gen. XLVIII, 1)—this being

480

something new in the world. From the death of Jacob until the time of King Hezekiah, no man ever recovered from an illness, but of Hezekiah it is written, "In those days was Hezekiah sick unto death" (Isa. XXXVIII, 1), and later, "Then Hezekiah turned his face toward the wall and prayed unto the Lord" (V. 2). He said unto Him: "May it be Thy pleasure that men should be enabled to recover from their maladies, so that they may praise Thy Name and acknowledge Thee and turn unto Thee with perfect repentance, and thus be found worthy before Thee." And the Holy One replied: "So be it! And thou shalt be the first sign thereof." So Hezekiah experienced something which no human being had previously experienced, concerning which it is written: "The writing of Hezekiah King of Judah, and he had been sick, and was recovered of his sickness" (Ibid. v. 9). We are also told that on that day the sun went backward ten degrees. Merodach Baladan used to dine at the fourth hour (of the afternoon), having got up at the ninth hour. When he awoke on that day, he saw the sun still standing at the fourth hour! In great wrath he cried out to his attendants, saying: "What is this conspiracy that ye have devised to kill me by starvation?" "How,

master?" they inquired. "Have ye not let me sleep for the space of a day and the third part of a day?" said he. "Not so!" they replied. "What has happened is that the God of Hezekiah has performed two miracles this day: He has healed Hezekiah and brought back the sun unto this hour." Then said the King: "Is there in the whole world a greater god than mine?" They replied: "Yea, the God of Hezekiah." The King rose from his throne, and wrote: "Peace be to Hezekiah the King of Judah, peace be to his God, and peace be to Jerusalem, the holy city." Presently he again rose up from his throne, and retiring three steps as though in a king's presence, wrote: "Peace be to the great God in Jerusalem, peace be to Hezekiah the King of Judah, and peace be to Jerusalem the holy city." Then the Holy One spake to him and said: "Thou hast stepped back in my honour three paces. By thy life! three august kings who shall rule over the whole world will descend from thee!" And so it was. The first was Nebuchadnezzar. Of him Daniel says: "Thou art this head of gold, and after thee shall arise another kingdom inferior to thee, and another third kingdom of brass which shall bear rule over all the earth" (Dan. II, 38, 39). And it says further: "Nebuchadnezzar the king made an image of gold, whose height was three score cubits, and the breadth thereof six cubits" (Ibid. III, 1). Said Nebuchadnezzar: "The image which I saw in my dream had a head of gold on a body of silver, but I want to make an image all of gold and a golden crown on its head." And so we are told that on that day Nebuchadnezzar summoned all nations, peoples, and tongues, in order that they might worship that image, and he took one of the vessels of the Sanctuary on which the Holy Name was engraved and put it into the mouth of that image. Then he spoke boastful words until Daniel appeared, and came close to the image, and said: "I am an ambassador of the highest Lord: He has decreed through me that thou shouldst depart from here!" and uttered the Holy Name. Immediately the vessel departed and the image fell and broke in pieces. This, then, is the meaning of the words: "I will bring out of his mouth that which he hath swallowed up, and the nations shall not flow together any more unto him." ʻThen R. Judah stood up and kissed young Rab Huna on his head, and said: ʻHad I not drawn thee near to me, I should not have discovered thy wisdom.ʼ From that time the students treated him with great respect.

"Blessed art thou, O land, when thy king is the son of nobles, and thy princes eat in due time." R. Yose applied this verse to Moses when he brought out Israel from Egypt and made them a free people, for then they, the "princes", ate the Passover in due season (Ex. XI, 11). Said R. Simeon ben Yohai: "Have I not said that all the words of King Solomon are found within the holy Temple (i.e., have an esoteric significance)? What you have said is quite true, as far as it goes, and the application to Moses is quite feasible, but this particular verse soars into higher reaches, and is in the holy Temple. "Blessed art thou, O land, when thy king is the son of nobles." "Land" (erez), without any specific designation, refers to the earth (erez), as it is written: "He cast down from heaven unto the earth the beauty of Israel" (Lam. II, 1). This "earth" is one of the mysteries which are found within the crowns of the Holy King, for it is written: "On the day when the Lord God made earth and heaven" (Gen. II, 4). And this "earth" derives all its nourishment from the holy perfection called "heaven". And when the Holy One resolved to destroy His house and the Holy Land below, He first removed the "Holy Land" which is above-the celestial prototype-and cast it down from that grade where it had formerly imbibed nourishment from the holy Heaven, and then He caused the land below to be devastated: first He "cast down from heaven the earth", and then "He remembered not His footstool" (Ibid.). For there is a dictum concerning the Holy One's ways: "When He resolves to judge the world, He first executes judgement above, and then there follows the judgement below." First "the Lord shall punish the host of heaven in heaven", and then "the kings of the earth upon the earth" (cf. Isa. XXIV, 21)ʼ Said R. Simeon: ʻBlessed art thou, O Land (earth), that thy king is free (ben horin), and nourishes thee in plenty without fear of interference from the "other one" (Severity), all being nourished by that Supernal King. "And thy princes eat in due time", this "time" being that of which it is written: "In time it shall be said of Jacob and of Israel, What hath God wrought!" (Num. XXIII, 23). "Woe to thee, O land (earth), when thy king is a child", as the prophet threatened Israel with the words, "And I will give children to be their princes" (Isa. III, 4); for, indeed, woe unto the earth when it imbibes nourishment from the Left Side, the attribute of Severity, which is the symbolism of the words, "and thy princes eat in the morning", that is, have to imbibe the vapours of that early blackness

which reigns before the Light breaks and banishes all other rulers by the resplendence of its own majestic glory.'

R. Simeon, we are told, explained thus the words, "And the middle bar in the midst of the boards shall pass from one end to the other." '"The middle bar"', he said, 'signifies Jacob, the perfect saint, as we have pointed out on another occasion in connection with the characterization of Jacob as "a complete man, dwelling in tents" (Gen. xxv, 27). It does not say, "dwelling in a tent", but "dwelling in tents,', which denotes that he unified the two "tents" (of Severity and Mercy). The same implication may be found here: "The middle bar in the midst of the boards shall pass from one end to the other", uniting them. Jacob was perfect in regard to both sides, the Holy Ancient and the Microprosopus, and also to the supernal Grace and the supernal Power, harmonizing the two.' R. Simeon said further: 'I perceive that Wisdom ('Hokmah) is the totality of all the holy Sefiroth, and that supernal Grace (Hesed) emanates from Wisdom, and Power (Geburah), which is the prompter of severe judgement, from Understanding (Binah). Jacob harmonized both sides: the Fathers (Abraham and Isaac) signified the totality of all, and Jacob signified the union of the Fathers. We have learnt that Wisdom beat against the stones of the thirty-two Paths [Tr. note: i.e. the ten Sefiroth and the twenty-two letters of the Hebrew alphabet; cf. Sefer Yezirah.] and caused the wind to gather many waters into one place. Then fifty gates of understanding were opened. From the Paths emanated ten luminous crowns, and there were left twenty-two Paths. The wind whirled down those Paths and fifty Gates of Understanding were opened, and the twenty-two letters were engraved upon fifty gates of the Jubilee and were crowned with the seventy-two letters of the Holy Name. These opened out sideways in their turn and were crowned with the twenty-two crowns of Compassion which are contained in the Ancient of Days, who bestows light upon them, to each according to its place. Fifty engraved letters also were crowned with forty-two supernal letters of the Holy Name, by which heaven and earth were created. And eight gates were opened, which are the eight significations of Mercy, as it is written: "The Lord, the Lord God, merciful and gracious", etc. (Ex. XXXIV, 6-7), which emanate from the Holy Ancient and proceed to the Microprosopus, and they unite with those holy crowns, Supernal Wisdom and Understanding, taking Supernal Grace from the one side and Judgement or Power from the other. Then came the merit of Jacob and synthetized both and made them one, for he signifies supernal harmony.' R. Simeon added, so we are told, that on that account Jacob was called Israel, beeause "Jacob" symbolizes that which is below, "Israel" that which is above; "Jacob" betokens incompleteness, "Israel" is the completion of all. Said R. Judah: 'When Wisdom began to cause the shaping of Crowns, [Tr. note: i.e. Sefiroth.] with which Crown did it commence? With that which is called "Understanding" (Binah), for in Understanding all is contained; and therefore fifty gates are opened in its name, and thus it is found that all the letters and all the crowns are engraved in Wisdom. Therefore it is written: "Thou hast made them all in Wisdom" (Ps. CIV, 24). It is written: "Who hath measured the water in the hollow of his hand, and meted out heaven with the span, and comprehended the dust of the earth in a measure, and weighed the mountains in scales, and the hills in a balance?" (Isa. XL, 12). "The water" here symbolizes "Understanding".'

R. Eleazar referred it to "Grace", whereupon R. Simeon said to him: 'The two views are equivalent. "Heaven" symbolizes "Beauty" (Tifereth), and "dust" refers to "Power" (Geburah). "Mountains" refers to the other crowns which are called "Mountains of pure balsam", and "hills" alludes to somewhat lower chariots.'

Said R. Eleazar: 'It would seem that Jacob emanated from the region of severe Judgement, for Isaac laid hold on this attribute as his portion.' Said R. Simeon to him: 'But was this the only grade? Isaac emanated from Grace, surely, and so did all the Fathers. In fact, Judgement proceeds from Mercy, and Mercy from Judgement. Abraham inherited Mercy, and Isaac proceeded therefrom, but with the aura of Judgement about him; and Jacob in turn issued in Mercy from the midst of Judgement. So one quality emanates from another, each imbibes from each, and finally it is made manifest that all are one, and all depend on One, and the One is all in all. Blessed be His Name forever and ever.' Said R. Eleazar: 'It is evident that there can be no perfection except the one aspect be joined to the other and a third hold them together to harmonize and complete them, like Jacob in relation to Abraham and Isaac. That is why it is written: "And the middle bar in the midst of the boards shall be fastening from one end to the other." We have been taught that all this differentiation of the Divine Personality is from our side and relative to our knowledge, and that, above, all is one, all is set in one balance, unvarying and eternal, as it is written: "I the Lord change not" (Mal. III, 6).' Said R. Judah: 'All the heavenly lights are illumined from one and depend on one, and all the lights there form only one Light, and desire never to be separated, and he who does separate them in his mind is as though he separated himself from life eternal.' Said R. Isaac: 'It is written, "And I will give youths to be their princes, and babes shall rule over them" (Isa. III, 4). This is an allusion to the words, "And thou shalt make two cherubims of gold" (Ex. xxv, 18). It is also written: "The ark of the Lord which dwelleth between the cherubims" (I Sam. IV, 4); and again it is written, "And he rode upon a cherub" (2 Sam. XXII, 11). When He dwells in completeness, He "dwelleth between cherubims", but when the King is not established on His

Throne, He "rides" on "one" cherub. Said R. Yose: 'Woe unto the world when one cherub turns away his face from the other, for it is written, "And their faces shall look one to another" (Ex. xxv, 20); only then is there harmony in the world.' Said R. Isaac: 'We have been taught that the words, "The nakedness of thy father, or the nakedness of thy mother, shalt thou not uncover" (Lev. XVIII, 7) have an esoteric reference to supermundane relationships in addition to their obvious significance. Woe to him who "uncovers their nakedness" (by probing too deeply into the hidden mysteries of the inner aspects of the Divine Essence and the relationship of one to another). Similarly, it is written in regard to Jacob: "fastening from one end to the other". Happy is the lot of Israel, by whose praises the Holy One, blessed be He, is glorified even as He is glorified above: "Israel in whom I am glorified" (Isa. XLIX, 3).'

We have been taught that R. Isaac once said: 'In bygone times a person used to say to his neighbour, "Speak to me on a certain portion of the Torah and I will pay thee for it"; but in our days, even if one person says to another, "Study the Torah and I will reward thee with money for so doing", no one inclines his ears to listen, and none desires knowledge except those few saints of the Highest in whom the Holy One is glorified, and concerning whom it is written, "And thy people shall be all righteous, they shall inherit the land forever, the branch of my planting, the work of my hands, that I may be glorified" (Ibid. LX, 21).' THE HOOKS OF THE PILLARS AND THEIR FILLETS SHALL BE OF SILVER. Said R. Isaac: 'I presume that the "hooks of the pillars" symbolize all those who are attached to the supernal unifying pillars, [Tr. note: i.e. Nezah and Hod, who are attached to the three Sefiroth above them] and that all those who are below depend on them. What is the significance of the word vavim (hooks; also the letter vau, the numerical value of which is six)? Six within six (vv), all united and nourished by the Spine which is set over them. And we have learnt in the Book of the Hidden Mystery (Sifra di-zeniutha) this dictum: "Hooks above, hooks below (six above, six below), all comprehended in one meaning and one name, having one and the same significance." Now, what is this "Book of the Hidden Mystery"?' Said R. Simeon: 'It contains five sections which are to be found in the midst of a great Hall, and whose wisdom fills the whole earth.' Said R. Judah: 'If this book of wisdom is enclosed in that Hall, it is of more worth than any other tome.' 'Verily,' returned R. Simeon, 'it is so, for one who is used to passing in and out of the courts of wisdom, but not to one who rarely or never enters into that Hall. Once there was a man who dwelt among the mountains and was a complete stranger to the ways of townsfolk. He sowed wheat, but knew no better than to consume it in its natural condition. One day he went down into a city, and there a loaf of good bread was placed before him. He asked what it was, and was informed that it was bread and was meant to eat. He ate it and liked it. "What is it made of?" he said. They told him "Wheat". Later, he was given fine cake kneaded in oil. He tasted it, and again asked: "And this, of what is it made?" The same reply was made as before: "Of wheat". Finally, he was treated to some royal confectionery, flavoured with oil and honey. Once more he asked his question, and obtained the same reply. Then he said: "In sooth, I have all these at my command, because I eat the essential constituent of all, namely wheat." Thus,

Zohar: Shemoth, Section 2, Page 176b

through his untutored taste he remained a stranger to all these delicious flavours, and their enjoyment was lost to him. Even so it is with those who stop short at the general principles of knowledge because they are ignorant of the delights which may be derived from the further investigation and application of those principles.' [Tr. note: Pp. 177b-179a belong to the Sifra di-Zeniutha.]

Zohar: Shemoth, Section 2, Pages 177a-179b

[Note: These Pages belong to the Sifra di-Zeniutha and are not translated.]

TEZAWE

AND THOU SHALT COMMAND THE CHILDREN OF ISRAEL... AND THOU BRING NEAR UNTO THEE AARON THY BROTHER. Said R. Hiya: What is the significance of the expression "and thou" in these and other passages, e.g., "And thou shalt speak unto all that are of a wise heart" (XXVIII, 3); "And thou take unto thee principal spices" (Ex. xxx, 23)? In all cases it contains a reference to the supernal world, indicating that the Shekinah is joined with Moses.' Said R. Isaac: 'The upper and the lower lights, when united, are designated "and thou", as, for instance, in the passage, "and thou givest life to them all". Therefore it does not say merely "Command", "Take unto thee", "speak", etc., but prefixes the words "And thou", because at the time of the building of the Tabernacle the Sun united with the Moon, and all the divine aspects were merged into one Whole which should rest upon the holy place and bless the work of its construction.' R. Eleazar derived the same inference from the words: "Then wrought Bezalel... and every wise-hearted man, in whom the Lord put wisdom and understanding" (Ex. XXXVII, 1). Said R. Simeon: 'It can also be proved from the verse, "And thou shalt speak unto all that are of a wise heart, to him whom I have filled with the spirit of wisdom." Instead of "to him", we should have expected "to them", but the singular form refers to the "heart", which He has filled with the spirit of wisdom, as it is written: "And the spirit of the Lord shall rest upon him, the spirit of wisdom and understanding", etc. (Isa. XI, 2). Therefore it was necessary to say, "Him whom I have filled with the spirit of wisdom", in order to show that the Sun united with the Moon in an all-embracing completeness. For the same reason "and thou" is used in all the cases

483

which we have considered.' Said R. Eleazar: 'How, then, are all the passages beginning with "and thou" to be understood?' R. Simeon replied: 'In this way: "And thou bring near unto thee Aaron"-to join and unite with him in fitting manner the mystery of the Holy Name; "And thou shalt speak unto all that are of a wise heart": this indicates that none of them came to do the work of Aaron's vestments before the Holy Spirit spoke in them bidding them begin: "And thou shalt command the children of Israel that they bring pure oil... for the light"-this indicates that it was the Holy Spirit which urged them to do this and shed its light upon them that they might perform the work with all their heart; "And thou take unto thee principal spices"- this has the same significance as "And thou bring near unto thee Aaron". In fact, all the repetitions of the phrase "and thou" which occur in connection with the work of the Tabernacle contain this implication.'

R. Simeon spoke on the verse: "And thou, O Lord, be not far from me; O my strength, haste thou to help me" (Ps. XXII, 20). Said he: 'The two invocations, "And thou, O Lord", are in effect one. "Be not far", that is, do not soar away from us aloft, to remove the upper Light from the lower, for when the one separates from the other all light is darkened and removed from the world. For this cause, indeed, was the Temple destroyed in the time of Jeremiah, and although it was afterwards restored, that Light did not even then return to its place with the same fulness and perfection as before. The very name of that prophet signifies the "going up on high" (Jeremiah; lit. God shall be exalted) of the supernal light, and its continued absence from its place in the earthly sanctuary. Jeremiah himself was removed and never returned to his place, and the Temple was destroyed and the light was darkened; but Isaiah's very name ("The Salvation of the Lord") is the cause of future redemption and the return of the supernal light to its place and the restoration of the Temple and all the splendour and glory thereof. Therefore the names of these two prophets are thus differentiated, because the name is of great significance and potency, and the combination of letters one with the other operates either for good or for evil. Connected with this mystery is the combination of the letters of the holy names, and even the letters in themselves can be made to reveal supreme mysteries.

Zohar: Shemoth, Section 2 Page 180a-b

[Note This Page belongs to the Sifra di-Zeniutha and is not translated].

Zohar: Shemoth, Section 2, Page 181a

[Tr. note: The passage omitted (first 35 Hebrew lines) deals with the symbolism of the shapes of certain Hebrew letters, and is unsuitable for translation'.]

THAT HE MAY MINISTER UNTO ME IN THE PRIEST'S OFFICE. Said R. Simeon: 'Moses did not make use of the Moon until he was completed on all sides in the mystery of the vau (six), [Tr. note: i.e. until he obtained a perfect cognition of the Sefirah Tifereth.] as elsewhere explained. This is indicated by the superfluous vau at the end of le-khahano (to be a priest). The word li (to me) indicates that the vau (Tifereth) was to make use of the he (Malkuth), that all might be one. Blessed are the Israelites

Zohar: Shemoth, Section 2, Page 181b

who "entered and came out" and comprehended the mystery of the ways of the Torah, to walk in the way of truth. "From among the children of Israel", because only from there is unity possible, for the children of Israel stand here below as emissaries of the Most High, to open the gates, to shed light upon the ways, to kindle the radiance of the heavenly fire, to draw all things that are below near to them that are above, in order that all may become a unity. Therefore it is written: "And ye who cleave to the Lord your God, ye are all alive today".' R. Simeon further said: 'In all things there is a "drawing near" for him who understands how to accomplish the union and to worship the Lord, for when the sacrifice is offered in manner due, all grades are brought near as one unity, and the light of the Countenance is present in the world, in the Sanctuary, and the "other side" is subdued and covered in, and the side of holiness reigns in all as light and joy. But when the sacrifice is not offered in manner due, and the union is not effected, this Countenance is overcast and the light is not present, the Moon is in hiding, and the "other side" reigns, because there is no one who knows how to unify the Holy Name in the proper fashion.'

[Tr. note: Here follows in the original a passage about Job which is reproduced with only slight variations from Zohar, Exodus, 34a.]

Zohar: Shemoth, Section 2, Page 182a

'It is written: [Tr. note: The section from here to p. 187b seems to be out of place, and to belong properly to the portion Ki Tisa.] "Thou shalt not make to thee molten gods", and immediately after, "the feast of unleavened bread shalt thou keep" (Ex. XXXIV, 17, 18). What connection is there between the two precepts? We have been taught concerning this matter as follows: If one eats leaven during the Passover, it is as though he worshipped idols. For when Israel went out from Egypt they emerged from the dominion of the Egyptians, from that dominion which is called "leaven"; for the "evil inclination" operates in man and grows in him like leaven in the dough: it enters into him, and, little by little, extends its influence until his whole self is permeated by it. This is idolatry, concerning which it is written, "Let there be no strange god in thee" (Ps. LXXXI, 10).'

R. Judah discoursed in connection with this theme on the words: "Cease ye from man, whose breath (neshamah) is in his nostrils, for wherein is he to be accounted of?" (Isa. II, 22). 'This verse,' said he, 'has already been explained; but what is the particular significance of the expression, "cease ye from man"? Must one, then, avoid any intercourse with men? If that were so, there would be no social life whatsoever, and assuredly it was not thus ordained! It has, however, been expounded as applying to the man who rises up early to pay court to his neighbour (instead of going to prayers), which thought I have connected with another verse, namely: "He that blesseth his friend with a loud voice, rising early in the morning, it shall be counted a curse to him" (Prov. XXVII, 14). But although this explanation is satisfactory as far as it goes, the question still remains, What is the meaning of the expression, "Whose breath (neshamah) is in his nostrils"? It is this: the Holy One commands man to guard himself against those men who have turned from the good to the evil way, and have polluted their souls by the impurity of the "other side". For, when the Holy One created man, He made him on the supernal pattern and breathed into him a holy breath consisting of a triad, as has already been established, whose several names are nephesh, ruah, and neshamah, the highest being the neshamah, for it is the superior energy by means of which man can apprehend and keep the commandments of the Holy One. But when he lets his soul participate in the "strange worship", he defiles that soul and departs from the worship and the ways of his Lord. For these three aspects of the soul, nephesh, ruah, and neshamah, are all one, being merged one in the other on the pattern of the supernal mystery. And when we see a man who possesses all these three grades untarnished and firmly established therein, we may know that he is a complete man, a faithful servant of his Master; and with such a one we may safely associate in order to learn from him his way of life. And how is one to discern whether a person is one whose acquaintance is to be cultivated or shunned? By his temper; for by his demeanour when roused to anger can his character be discerned. If he guards the holy soul when he is wroth, in order that it may not be uprooted from its place, and supplanted by the "other side", then he is indeed a man, a servant of his Lord, complete and holy. But one who in his ire cares nothing for the welfare of his soul, uprooting it and letting it be replaced by the impure domination, such a man is a rebel against his Lord, one with whom we should shun contact of any kind, for he is one who, as it is written, "teareth his soul in his anger" (Job XVIII, 4) - he tears and uproots his soul in his heedless rage, and allows a "strange god" to usurp its place within him and to take possession of him in its stead. Thus the words, "Cease ye from a man whose soul is torn in his anger" (aph=anger as well as nostril), are obviously an injunction to refrain from intercourse with him who tears the holy soul and defiles it in his anger.

Zohar: Shemoth, Section 2, Page 182b

"For wherein (ba-meh) is he to be accounted for?"-such a one is "accounted" an "idol" (bamah, lit. "high place"), and to associate oneself with such a person is like associating with idolatry. And not only that: such a person has also uprooted holiness from its place and raised in its stead a "strange god" there; and as in regard to a "strange god" it is written: "Do not turn to idols" (Lev. XIX, 4), so it is prohibited to look on the face of such a person in his anger. As to the question, What about the anger of students of the Torah? that anger is good in all its aspects, since, as we have been taught, the Torah is fire, and it is she who kindles that holy anger in her devotees, as it is written, "Is not my word like as a fire? saith the Lord" (Jer. XXIII, 29). The anger of scholars is for offences against the Torah, it is in her honour, it is for the sake of the Holy One's glory and majesty. Therefore it says: "For the Lord thy God is a consuming fire, he is a zealous God" (Deut. IV, 24). But if a person becomes angry over purely secular matters, this is no service of God, and no sin that man commits is so literally idolatry as this, since it actually sets up an idol in the very heart of him who is angered: unto such a man one is forbidden to speak or draw nigh. Should one say, But, after all, this anger is only a momentary impulse from which he may soon repent- why, then, such severity as this? the answer would be, that in reality it is not thus, because he has uprooted the holiness of his soul from its place and the "other god" has entrenched himself therein, and will never leave him until by a great effort the person so afflicted completely purifies himself and roots out from his inner self that evil, and thereafter endeavours to sanctify himself afresh, and to draw down holiness from above upon himself; then only can there be a possibility of renewal and sanctification for him.' Said R. Yose to him: 'Why only a possibility of renewal and sanctification?'

R. Judah replied: 'Consider this: when a man uproots the holiness of his soul and is given admission to that "strange god" in its place-the "strange god" which is called "impure"-that man has become polluted and he pollutes everyone with whom he comes into contact, and holiness flees from him; and, holiness having once fled, whatever the person may do afterwards, it will not return to its place again.' Said R. Yose: 'And yet, how many who had defiled themselves are purified!' R. Judah replied: 'But anger, in contradistinction to sins which pollute only the body, pollutes also the soul and, in fact, the whole being. Therefore one must beware of such a man and must "keep the feast of unleavened bread", that is, the side of holiness within, and not exchange it for the "other side" to pollute oneself and others.

'"The feast of unleavened bread shalt thou keep (tishmor). Seven days shalt thou eat unleavened bread, as I have commanded thee" (Ex. XXXIV, 18). This is the sphere called shamor (keep=Kingdom, the "Feminine" emanation), therefore it says in regard to this feast, "keep". These "seven days" are not like the seven days of the feast of

Tabernacles, which latter are "upper" days (belonging to the world of "Understanding"), whilst the former are "lower" days (belonging to the world of "Kingdom"). Therefore, on the feast of Tabernacles the full "Hallel") [Tr. note: i.e. Ps. CXIII-CXVIII] in full. is recited, whilst on that of Passover (after the first day) only a part of it] [Tr. note: i.e. the same psalms with the omission of Ps. cxv, 1-11, and CXVI, 1-11.] is recited. It may be asked, After the feast of the Passover has been sanctified (on the first day), why is there a descent to a lower plane on the succeeding days? Is there not an ancient rule that "in holy things there must be continual progress upward, not regression downward"? Why, then, is not the "complete" Hallel said on the remaining six days of the feast? Why does the sanctification "come down" in these "lower" days? The answer would be as follows: It is written concerning the High Priest: "And he should make an atonement for himself and for his house" (Lev. XVI, 6); from which it is clear that he, being the medium of propitiation, must first make atonement on his own behalf and then be the means of atonement for his household. The same applies here: the grade of the Passover feast began to be sanctified first (on the first day), and having been sanctified itself required to sanctify its household, and for this reason it "came down". And what is the instrument of that sanctification? Israel which is below, when she counts the days of the Omer (from the second night of Passover until the night of Pentecost). And when these have been sanctified, this grade must be raised in order to ascend above, for when the house of the Matrona (Israel, the "bearer" of the Shekinah) is sanctified, it ascends to the upper region in order to unite itself with those "higher" days

Zohar: Shemoth, Section 2, Page 183a

above (on thc Fcast of Weeks). Therefore we have to count the days of the Omer standing, because these are "high" days. So, also, whenever a man enters into those "high" days, whether it be with prayers nr hymns of praise, he must pray or sing standing, his thighs taut, his feet firm, his body erect: the attitude. of a man, instinct with power, as distinct from the characteristic attitude of a woman, which is sitting. Another reason for standing is that the counting of the days of the Omer signifies praise-giving to the upper world. And because the counting of the Omer is part of the mystery of the world of Masculinity, therefore it is not obligatory for women; for it is only the men who are obliged to count, in order to unite all the attributes according to the Divine purpose. Similarly it is written (in regard to the pilgrimage to Jerusalem on the three festivals): "Three times in the year all thy males shall appear before the Lord God" (Ex. XXIII, 16)-males but not females, because the mystery of the Covenant applies to males but not to females; therefore the command to "appear" being bound up with that supernal mystery, women are not obliged to keep it. We have also learnt in this connection the mystery, that from every seven of those "high" days, one day of the lower days receives holiness, and that day is called Shabu'a (week), [Tr. note: Alluding to the fact that in the counting of the Omer the weeks are mentioned as well as the days] because it was sanctified by the seven "supernal" days. And so it is with all the sevens of the fifty days (between the second night of Passover and the night of Pentecost), or rather the forty-nine days, and as there are forty-nine supernal days, seven days below are sanctified, and every one of these days is called "week", because it ascends by means of those seven. Therefore it is written, "Seven complete weeks they shall be" (Lev. XXIII, 15). Because they (i.e. the "lower" days) are of the Feminine grade they are designated by a feminine form (sheba' instead of shib'ah). And when they have been sanctified by them (i.e. by the supernal days), and the "House" has been prepared, so that the Wife (the Shekinah) may be united with her Spouse, then it is called "The Feast of Weeks" (Pentecost), because of the "lower" days which have been hallowed by the "higher". Therefore it is written: "In your weeks" (Num. XXVIII, 26), because they are "yours", as Israel is also sanctified with them. Hence, when forty-nine days have been reached and passed, the fiftieth day, which reigns over them, symbolizes the mystery of the Torah (given on that day), which possesses forty-nine aspects; and this day, by means of the impulse from below, brought forth the Torah complete with forty-nine aspects.' R. Eleazar quoted in this connection the verse: "Yea, the sparrow hath found an house, and the swallow (deror) a nest for herself, where she may lay her young, at thy altars" (Ps. LXXXIV, 4). 'Of the birds of heaven,' he said, 'some make their dwellings outside (in the open) and some inside human habitations: as, for instance, the swallow, which makes her dwelling in a house, and is not afraid. Why? Because all call it "deror". And what, then, is the meaning of deror? Freedom, as it is written, "Ye should proclaim deror", and the Aramaic translation of deror is heru (Freedom). These swallows make a nest in a house and bring forth little ones and dwell in that house for fifty days and then separate and go each its own way and to whatsoever place it desires, all being free. Similarly, it is written: "And ye shall hallow the fiftieth year and proclaim freedom throughout all the land" (Lev. xxv, 10). Freedom emanates from this fiftieth year to all, and because of this the Torah which proceeded from that fiftieth day is called "Freedom". Concerning this it is written, "Graven (haruth) upon the tablets", which word haruth contains the same letters as heruth, which is Freedom, and the Decalogue, which is the essence of the Law, is thus given its due appellation, because whatever this supernal day brings forth is called "Freedom". It is the freedom of all things, of all spheres, of all worlds and of all created beings, both above and below.

'The children of Israel ate, when they left Egypt, two kinds of bread: one on their leaving, unleavened bread, the "bread of affliction"; and the other in the wilderness, "bread from heaven" (Ex. XVI, 4). Therefore the essential sacrifice of the day (Pentecost, when the Torah was given) was bread (Lev. XXIII, 17), and the others were additional to this, as it is written: "And ye shall offer with the bread some lambs", etc. (Ibid. 18), for this was the bread by means of which the Israelites were endowed with the superior wisdom of the Torah, and entered into her ways.

'Now one has to consider: On the Passover the Israelites emerged from their subsistence on the [spiritual] bread called "leaven"

Zohar: Shemoth, Section 2, Page 183b

to be nourished by the more honourable bread called Mazzah (unleavened). Now, when the Israelites were worthy (on the Day of Pentecost) to eat a more excellent bread, would it not have been more appropriate that the "leaven" should have been abolished altogether and not been in evidence at all? Why, then, was that sacrifice based chiefly on leavened bread, as it is written: "They (the two loaves) shall be baken with leaven" (Lev. XXIII, 17)? Moreover, on that day (Pentecost) the "evil inclination" (leaven) came to naught, and the Torah, called "Freedom", was then given. We may, however, explain by the following parable. A king had an only son who fell seriously ill. After a time the prince expressed a desire to eat, but he was forbidden to eat any food other than that prescribed by the physicians, and orders were given that for the set term of that diet no other viands should be found in the palace. All was carried out accordingly. But when the prince was come to the end of the period of his special diet the ban was lifted, and it was intimated that now he was free to eat whatsoever he fancied, since it would not harm him. Similarly, when the Israelites came out from Egypt they knew not the essence and mystery of the Faith. Said the Holy One: "Let them taste only the medicinal food, and before they have finished it be shown no other food soever." But when the mazzoth were finished, which was the medicine by means of which they were to enter and to comprehend the mystery of the Faith, then the Holy One proclaimed: "From now on they may see and eat leavened bread, because it cannot harm them"– especially on the Day of Pentecost, when the supernal bread, which is a cure of all ills, was prepared for them. Therefore leaven was offered to be burnt on the altar, [Tr. note: According to the Talmud, the two loaves of leaven were to be eaten by the priests.] and two other loaves were offered with it, and the leaven was burnt by the fire of the altar, and it could not reign over and do harm to Israel. Therefore holy Israel cleaves to the Holy One, blessed be He, on this day (Pentecost), and if the Israelites had but preserved the two sides (symbols) of the two loaves they would never have been subjected to chastisement.

'New Year's Day is a day of judgement for those who have not accepted the healing food, and have neglected the "medicine" of the Torah for the sake of another food, which is leaven. For on this day that "leaven" ascends and accuses mankind and speaks evil against all whom it can malign in any wise. And at that time the Holy One, blessed be He, sits in judgement over all and pronounces His decrees in regard to all the spheres. Therefore, when He gave the Torah to Israel He gave them to taste of that supernal bread of the celestial realm, namely, the manna, by means of which they were enabled to perceive and penetrate into the mysteries of the Torah and to walk in the straight path. However, this subject has been elucidated by the Companions, in connection with the mysteries to which we have already referred.'

R. Simeon and his son, R. Eleazar, were out walking one day, accompanied by R. Abba and R. Yose. As they went along, they beheld ahead of them an old man, who led by the hand a young child. R. Simeon, on perceiving them, exclaimed, turning to R. Abba: 'Assuredly, we shall hear new and instructive expositions from that old man.' So they walked on more quickly, and presently overtook the couple. When they approached the old man, R. Simeon said to him: 'Thou travellest in heavy garments. Who art thou?' The stranger replied: 'I am a Jew.' Said R. Simeon: 'Verily we shall hear new interpretations today from thee. Whence art thou?' The old man answered: 'I was wont until but lately to live retired from the world, a recluse in the desert, where I studied the Torah and meditated on sacred matters, but now I am come into the midst of the habitation of men, to sit in the shadow of the Holy One in these days of the seventh month.' R. Simeon rejoiced and said: 'Let us sit down, for verily the Holy One has sent thee to us. By thy life, we shall hear words from thy mouth of those which have been planted in the desert concerning this seventh month. But why art thou now so far from thy place of retirement, and why bent upon fixing thy dwelling elsewhere? The old man replied: 'From this question I can see that thou lackest not wisdom, and that indeed thy words reach the firmament of wisdom itself.' Then he began to speak as follows: 'It is written: "And in the wilderness where thou hast seen how that the Lord thy God bare thee as a man doth bear his son in all the way that ye went, until ye came unto this place" (Deut. I, 31). This verse ought surely to run: "And in the wilderness where the Lord thy God bare thee"; what is the significance of the words "where thou hast seen"? The answer is as follows. The Holy One led Israel tnrough a terrible wilderness "wherein were fiery serpents and scorpions" (Ibid. VIII, 15); indeed, the most fearful wilderness in the world. Why did He do this? Because in the hour when they left

Zohar: Shemoth, Section 2, Page 184a

Egypt and increased to the number of sixty myriad souls, the Holy Kingdom was strengthened and stood firm, high above all, and the Moon was illumined, and thus the wicked dominion, the "other side", was subdued, and the Holy One brought the Israelites out in order to lead them through the terrible wilderness, the very realm and domain of Samael the wicked, in order that the evil power might be broken and the ruler of the regions of darkness be crushed, that it might rear its head no more. Had the Israelites not sinned, the Holy One would have resolved to remove him altogether from the world. Therefore He led them through his very dominion and territory. But when they sinned the serpent stung them many a time, and then was fulfilled that which was written: "He shall bruise thy head (rosh) and thou shalt bruise his heel" (Gen. III, 15)- that is to say, Israel first (be-rosh) bruised his head, but because later they knew not how to guard themselves against him he finally smote them and they all fell dead in the wilderness, and then the other half of the verse was fulfilled: "and thou (i.e. the serpent) shalt bruise his heel". And forty years long were they chastised by him, which corresponded to the forty lashes of the judges. Therefore it says: "where thou hast seen". They saw with their own eyes the prince of the desert, a prisoner bound before them, and they took his lot and possession. And so I also separated myself from the haunts of men and departed to dwell in the desert in order to be able better to meditate upon the Torah and to subdue that "other side." Besides, the words of the Torah can best sink into the soul there in the desert, for there is no light except that which issues from darkness, for when that "other side" is subdued the Holy One is exalted in glory. In fact, there can be no true worship except it issue forth from darkness, and no true good except it proceed from evil. And when a man enters upon an evil way and then forsakes it the Holy One is exalted in glory. Hence the perfection of all things is attained when good and evil are first of all commingled, and then become all good, for there is no good so perfect as that which issues out of evil. The divine Glory is extolled and extended thereby, and therein lies the essence of perfect worship. And as for us, we remained in the desert throughout all the days of the year in order to subdue there that "other side", but now, when the time for the divine worship from the side of holiness has come, we return to an inhabited place where the worship of the Holy One is carried on. Moreover, now in the season of the New Year the time has come for that serpent to demand justice from the Holy One, and he rules there at present, and therefore we went away from there and are come to an inhabited place.'

The old man then proceeded to discourse on the verse: "Blow the trumpet in the new moon, in the time appointed on our solemn feast-day" (Ps. LXXXI, 4). He said: 'Now is the time when the mighty supernal judgement is awakened, and with it the "other side" also gathers force. And with this access of force it ascends and veils the Moon that She may no more shine, and She falls entirely under the influence of stern Justice. Then all the worlds and spheres come under the aegis of judgement, both celestial and terrestrial beings, and a herald makes proclamation throughout all the firmaments, saying: "Prepare the Throne of Judgement for the Lord of all, since He cometh to judge all worlds!" Here is a mystery which was revealed to us during our sojourn in the desert. Why is supernal justice roused to activity just on this day? Because all mysteries and all glorious sanctifications are centred in the mystery of seven. And the supernal Seventh, the upper world, called "the world to come", is the realm whence all lights derive their brightness. And when the time arrives when those blessings and sanctifications are to be renewed with fresh light, all the conditions in the different worlds are passed in review. Then all these preparations ascend from earth if they are fitting, but if not, then it is decreed that the Moon is not to shine till the sinners have been separated from the righteous. Then judgement is awakened, and from that judgement the "other side" gains strength, and the Accuser demands that the wicked should be delivered unto him-for concerning him it is written, "He searcheth out all extremities" (Job. XXVIII, 3); and he causes the light of the Moon to be concealed, as we have said. And why are the wicked not delivered into that Accuser's hands? Because it is not the will of the Holy One to destroy His handiwork. But that "other side" is encased in a powerful shell which cannot be broken, except by means of that counsel which the Holy One, blessed be He, gave to Israel when He said: "Blow the trumpet in the new moon, in the covering (ba-kese) of our solemn feast-day", in order to break that "covering" (kese) which prevents the Moon from shining. And when the Israelites blow the trumpet here below the voice thereof smites the air and breaks through all firmaments until it reaches the mighty rock which covers up the Moon through the evil power of the "other side", and when Satan, who has ascended and stands above, perceives that Mercy has been roused

Zohar: Shemoth, Section 2, Page 184b

he becomes confused, and the trumpet's voice causes the strength of the Accuser to depart from him, and the voice of judgement to be hushed and rigorous punishments to be revoked. And when Mercy is roused from below another supernal trumpet is roused and brings forth a voice, which is Mercy, in the upper sphere, and voice meets voice, and the awakening below causes an awakening above. If it should be asked, how the awakening below can have such an effect on the higher sphere, the answer is this. The lower world is always in a receptive state-being called "a good (precious) stone"- and the upper world only communicates to it according to the condition in which it is found at any given time. If it shows a smiling countenance, light and joy from the world above pour down upon it; but if it be sad and downcast, it receives the severity of judgement, as it is written, "Worship the Lord in joy" (Ps. c, 2), that the joy of man may draw down upon him supernal joy. So, too, does the lower sphere affect the upper: according to the degree of awakening below there is awakening and heavenly joy above. Therefore the Israelites haste to awaken the voice of the trumpet, which is compounded of fire, water, and wind, and all are made one and the voice ascends and strikes that "precious stone", which then receives the various colours of this voice and then draws down upon itself the attribute from above, according to the colour which it shows. And when it is duly prepared by this voice, Mercy issues from on high and rests upon it, so that it is enfolded in mercy, both above and below. Then is the "other side" thrown into confusion, and its power weakened, so that it lacks the strength to accuse, and the "precious stone" is lit up on both sides, from below and from above. And when is that light shed from the world above upon the ways of men? Verily, on the Day of Atonement. On that day the "precious stone" is illumined with the light from above, which emanates from the splendour of the world to come. Therefore Israel prepare a goat here below for the Day of Atonement and send it forth to that terrible desert which is under the dominion of the Accuser. That "other side" is the central point of the waste places of the world, just as the central point of the whole inhabited world is occupied by the "holy side", and therefore Jerusalem is in the centre of the inhabited world. The kingdom of heaven, which is the side of holiness, is fixed at two points, one its own and one belonging to the world to come. The upper point is hidden, and therefore it has two points. Under its own point is Jerusalem, the centre of the inhabited world. The point which takes from the hidden supernal Mother is the terrestrial Paradise, which is in the centre of the whole world. In the centre of this Paradise there is a hidden supernal point which is not manifested, and a pillar rises within that point from below, and from thence issue waters which spread to all four sides of the world. Thus there are three points which stand one upon the other, like the three sections of the Torah (Law, Prophets, Writings).

'Observe this: the goat which the Israelites sent down to Azazel, into that desert, was sent with the intention of giving to the "other side" a portion, so pacifying and keeping it occupied that it might not do harm to the sons of the Kingdom. But it may be objected: "Why, then, was it necessary to have two goats, one "to the Lord" and one to the "other side"? The answer to this question can be gathered from the following parable. A king once became angered with his son, and he called to that minister whose office it was to punish offenders that he might be at hand to chastise his son on the morrow. The minister, in high spirits, was overjoyed, and entered the palace to partake of food there. The prince, on seeing him, thought to himself: "Surely, that man comes here to no good purpose, but doubtless because my father is angry with me." So what did he do? He straightway went in unto his father and persuaded him to forgive him. Then the king commanded that a banquet should be prepared for him and his son, but that the minister should not be told thereof, for, he thought to himself, should he get wind of the repast which I have ordered

Zohar: Shemoth, Section 2, Page 185a

for myself and my son, he will disturb our meal. What, then, did the king do? He called to his chamberlain and said unto him: "Prepare first a meal for this minister, in order that he may imagine that I am showing him a mark of special favour by giving a banquet in his honour, and so be satisfied and depart, without knowing anything of the previous meal which I have commanded thee to prepare, and which we shall consume when he is gone. Therefore let him, as I have said, take his part and then go, that our joy may be complete and undisturbed." And so it was done. Now, if the king had not dealt thus with his minister and his son, the former would not have left the palace, and the feast of forgiveness would have been marred. Similarly, the Holy One said to Israel: "Prepare ye two goats, one for Me and one for that Accuser, in order that he may imagine that he is participating in My meal, but in reality may be quite unaware of the true meal of our joy. Let him take his part and go his way and leave My house." As the "supernal Mother", the world to come, comes down to dwell in the palace of the lower world in order that all faces should be lit up there, it is meet that the Accuser should not be found in its holy presence, neither he nor any other of the ministers of judgement, when it dispenses blessings and radiates light upon all things and freedom unto all creatures, and Israel takes of these blessings. For when the "world to come" enters into its palace, the lower world, and finds that it rejoices with its children in the most excellent meal, it blesses the table, and all the worlds are blessed, and all is joy and radiant looks. Therefore it says (in regard to the Day of Atonement):' 'That ye may be clean from all your sins before the Lord" (Lev. XVI, 30). It is written: "And Aaron shall cast lots upon the two goats, one lot for the Lord and the other lot for Azazel". This gives the Accuser great joy: that God should take a lot with him, and, as it were, invite him by the Holy One's own desire and invitation. But he little realizes how that the Lord heaps coals of fire on his head and upon the heads of all his legions. Haman, too, "went forth that day joyful and with a glad heart" (Esther v, 9)-namely, with that portion which was given him. But when the Supernal King comes in unto the Matrona She pleads before the King for Herself, for Her children, for Her people, and even when Israel is in exile, if they pray all this day long (on the Day of Atonement), She ascends unto the Supernal King and pleads for Her children, whereby all the punishments which the Holy One is about to inflict upon Edom (Rome) are decreed and fixed, and, in addition, those concerning the unsuspecting Accuser himself -for though he knows it not, he is destined to be done away with, as it is written, "And death will be swallowed up forever" (Isa. xxv, 8). So Esther said: "For we are sold, I and my people, to be destroyed... for the enemy could not countervail the king's damage" (Ibid. VII, 4). And then: "Haman was frightened before the presence of the King and the queen" (Ibid. VII, 6). Then radiant looks and perfect joy prevail, and Israel enters into freedom on that day. And from that day on freedom and joy reign manifestly over them, and the Holy One wills to associate Himself with them in joy thenceforward. And as the Israelites gave Satan a portion in order that he might leave them alone and in peace, so also did they give a portion to the pagan nations (the offering of seventy oxen on the Feast of Tabernacles for the seventy nations) in order that they might leave them alone here on earth below [Tr. note: The next two Page s in the original, dealing in further detail with the goat and the purifying effects of the Day of Atonement and the resulting joyousness of the Feast of Tabernacles, are made up mainly of fragments which belong in reality to other parts of the Zohar and occur in a more complete form elsewhere.]

Zohar: Shemoth, Section 2, Page 185b [Note: See Translator's note on Page 185a] Zohar: Shemoth, Section 2, Page 186a [Note: See Translator's note on Page 185a] Zohar: Shemoth, Section 2, Page 186b

[Note: See Translator's note on Page 185a] Zohar: Shemoth, Section 2, Page 187a

R. Simeon wept and rejoiced. Then they lifted up their eyes and saw five persons approaching, who were evidently disciples of the old man, since they followed him as though seeking to speak with him. They all rose and R. Simeon turned to him and said: 'And now, what is thy name?' He replied: 'Old Nehorai is my name: I am so known to distinguish me from another Nehorai who is among us.' R. Simeon and his companions then walked on with him a distance of three miles, accompanied by the five newcomers, to whom R. Simeon said: 'For what have you come here?' They answered: 'We came to find this old man, the waters of whose wisdom we imbibe in the desert.' Then came R. Simeon and kissed the old man and said: 'Nehorai is thy name, and light (nehara) dwells with thee indeed!' Then he turned to the Companions, and said: 'He revealeth the deep and secret things; and He knows what is in the darkness, and the light dwelleth with Him" (Dan. II, 22). Why does He reveal them? Because He knows what is in the darkness; for, were it not for darkness we would not know what light is. "And light dwelleth with Him." What light is that? It is the light

Zohar: Shemoth, Section 2, Page 187b

which is revealed out of darkness. And as to us, out of the darkness of the great wilderness this great light has risen to enlighten us. May the Merciful One let His light dwell with thee in this world and the world to come.' R. Simeon and his companions then journeyed with the old man for a further three miles, and then he asked him: 'Why did not thy five disciples accompany thee from the first?' He replied: 'I did not wish anyone to be troubled on my account, but from henceforth they shall go along with me, seeing that they have come.' Then they went their way, and R. Simeon his. Presently R. Abba said: 'Now we know the name of that ancient, but he departed without having learnt the name of the great Master with whom he conversed.' Said R. Simeon: 'I have learnt from him not to tell (without being asked).'

KI TISA

AND THE LORD SPAKE UNTO MOSES SAYING: WHEN THOU TAKEST THE SUM OF THE CHILDREN OF ISRAEL AFTER THEIR NUMBER, THEN SHALL THEY GIVE EVERY MAN AN EXPIATION FOR HIS SOUL UNTO THE LORD. It has been laid down that no blessing from above can rest on anything that is counted. Why, then, it may be asked, were the Israelites counted, as we read in this verse? The truth is that an expiation, a ransom, was obtained from them, and the counting did not begin until the whole of that ransom was collected and reckoned up. Moreover, first the Israelites were blessed, then counted, and then again blessed. On account of this double blessing "there was no plague among them" when they were numbered. And why should a plague come when the people are numbered? Because blessing does indeed not rest on what is numbered, and as soon as the power of the blessing has departed the "other side" takes possession and is able to do mischief. Therefore a ransom was taken in order that the counting should be applied to that and not to the people itself.

Zohar: Shemoth, Section 2, Page 188a

R. Yose and R. Hiya were once walking together. They went on until darkness fell. Then they sat down and conversed upon many subjects until dawn appeared, when they rose up once more and continued on their way. Said R. Hiya: 'Look at the East, how its face begins to lighten! Now all children of the East who inhabit the mountains of light will be worshipping the light which heralds the sun before it appears. For the sun himself has many votaries, but these are the worshippers of his harbinger, which they call "the god of the shining pearl", and their oath is by "Allah of the shining pearl". Yet say not that this worship is idle, for there is a wisdom in it known from former ancient days. When before the rising of the sun the light shines forth, the angel appointed to rule and guide the sun steps forth with the holy letters of the supernal blessed Name inscribed upon his brow, and in the power of those letters opens all the windows of Heaven and flies out. Then he enters into the aura of brightness which surrounds the sun and waits there till the sun himself arises to spread his light over the world. And the same angel who is the guardian of the sun is appointed also over gold and rubies; therefore the sun worshippers and the votaries of dawn worship that angel, and by certain spots and signs which they know from tradition and which they perceive in the sun, they find the place of gold and rubies.'

Said R. Yose 'How long will all these pagan worships continue! Surely, "falsehood has no feet on which to stand!" ' R. Hiya replied: 'It is written, "The lip of truth shall be established forever; but a lying tongue is but for a moment" (Prov. XII, 19). Now, if the objects of men's worship were themselves false, it would be as you say. But, in fact, the light and the splendour which we behold are true; the stars aloft in the firmament are true; because men, in their foolishness and lack of sense, mistake these things for God, and call them so, shall God destroy His own work? But in the time that is to be (the Messianic era), not the stars nor the sun will be destroyed, but they who persist in the worship thereof, and this, in fact, is just what the verse implies: "The lips of truth shall be established forever"-this refers to Israel, who is "the lip of truth", in that she proclaims: "Hear O Israel, the Lord our God, the Lord is one"-the very essence of truth; and the Shem'a concludes with the words, "I the Lord your God am truth". The second half of the verse we may translate not, "a lying tongue is but for a moment (reg'a)", but, more literally, "until I, Israel, shall find rest (argiy'ah) from my hard burden." For in time to come the lying tongue of those who call that thing "god" which is not God will be destroyed. But of Israel it is written: "This people have I formed for myself; they shall shew forth my praise" (Isa. XLIII, 21). I remember walking once with R. Eleazar, and meeting, while on the way, a Gentile worthy (hegemon). Said he to R. Eleazar: "You are well acquainted with the Jewish Holy Scriptures?" "I am," replied R. Eleazar. "You say, do you not," proceeded the Gentile, "that your Faith is truth and your Scriptures likewise, whereas our faith is a lie and our Scriptures a lie also? But it is written in your own Book: 'the lip of truth shall be established forever; but a lying tongue is but for a moment'. Now we have been established in our kingdom from ancient times; it has remained with us for generation after generation, and it is 'established forever'; whereas your kingdom was short-lived and was soon taken from you, and in you were fulfilled the words, 'the lying tongue is but for a moment'." Then said R. Eleazar unto him: "I see that you are well versed in Holy Scripture. A curse light

Zohar: Shemoth, Section 2, Page 188b

on you! Were it written, 'has been established', you would be right, but what it says is 'will be established', which means 'Truth will in the future be established, even if it is not established now'. At present 'the lip of lies' stands erect, and the 'lip of truth' lies prostrate. But in the future truth will rise erect and blossom forth from the midst of the earth." Said the Gentile to him: "You are indeed right, and blessed is the people which possesses the truth, and the Scripture thereof!" Later, I heard that he had become a Jew.'

They then went on till they came to a field, where they halted for prayer. After this they exclaimed: 'From now on let us unite ourselves with the Shekinah and discourse on the Torah as we go.' R. Yose then began by quoting the following verse: "Behold, all they that were incensed against thee shall be ashamed and confounded" (Isa. XLI, 11). Said he: 'The Holy One, blessed be He, will in the time to come bring to pass all those good things which He promised Israel through the true prophets, and in the hope of which Israel was able to suffer so much in exile. For were it not for those glorious promises which they see written in the Scripture, and which they await so eagerly, they would have had no strength wherewith to withstand the rigours of exile; but as it is, they repair to the houses of study, open the holy books, and read therein of all those good things which the Holy One has promised them, and are comforted in their exile. The other nations, however, mock and insult them, saying: "Where is your God? Where are all those good things which ye declare are promised to you and because of which all the nations of the world will be ashamed or confounded before you?" So it is written: "Hear the word of the Lord, ye that tremble at his word; your brethren that hate you, that cast you out as impure for my Name's sake, said, Let the Lord be glorified-that we may behold your joy!-they shall be ashamed" (Isa. LXVI, 5). "Ye that tremble at his word" are those who have endured much evil and many reproaches, one after another, as it is written, "We have heard a voice of trembling, of fear and not of peace" (Jer. xxx, 5). "Your brethren that hate you" are the sons of Esau-"those that cast you out as impure", as it says, "They cried unto them, Depart ye, it is unclean" (Lam. IV, 15), for no people in the world despises Israel so utterly, spitting in their faces with the utmost contempt, as do the sons of Edom, who say unto them: "Ye are all impure like a menstruant". "For my name's sake, let the Lord be glorified": they say, "We are children of the living God and His Name is glorified in us, we reign over the world because of him who is designated 'great'-as it says, 'Esau, her great (eldest) son' (Gen. XXVII, 15), and God is also called 'great' (Ps. CXL, 3), whereas ye are the smallest of all-'Jacob, her smallest son' (Gen. XXVII, 15); where, then, is your God? Where are all those good things which are to make you the envy of all other nations? We would greatly like to see that joy of yours of which you boast, saying, 'they will be ashamed'. (The Holy Spirit, however, echoes: 'They will be ashamed!')".' Said R. Hiya: 'It is indeed so; we see, nevertheless, as did also the great ones who were in this world in earlier years, that the exile is prolonged and that the son of David (the Messiah) has not yet appeared.' R. Yose replied: 'Yes. But what is it that enables Israel to endure their exile for so long? It is those promises which the Holy One has given them, as we have pointed out; so that when they go to the synagogues and houses of study and see all those consolations, all those comforting and sure hopes, they rejoice in their hearts and are able to endure all that comes upon them; otherwise they would not be able.' Said R. Hiya: 'True. And all depends on repentance. But shouldst thou imagine that they could at this time all together rouse themselves to repentance, I tell thee, no, they could not. Why? Because it is written: "And it shall come to pass, when all these things are come upon thee... and thou shalt call them to mind among all the nations whither the Lord thy God hath driven thee, and shalt return unto the Lord thy God... then the Lord thy God will turn thy captivity... and will return and gather thee from all the nations... If any of thine be driven out unto the utmost parts of the heaven, from thence will the Lord thy God gather thee..." (Deut. xxx, 1-5). As long as the whole implication of this passage remains unfulfilled, repentance cannot

Zohar: Shemoth, Section 2, Page 189a

show itself among them.' Said R. Yose: 'How hast thou closed up all ways and issues of escape against the benighted children of exile, leaving no loophole nor any ground for courage or hope! For there will assuredly be many-as there have been in all generations-who will wish neither the long exile nor the future reward, and will break loose from the precepts of the Torah and be absorbed in other nations! Not so. It says: "Like as a woman with child that draws near the time of her delivery is in pain and cries out in her pangs, so have we been before thee, O Lord" (Isa. XXVI, 17). Now the normal time of pregnancy is nine months, but it frequently happens that the child is born only a few days into the ninth month; yet all the pain and pangs take place in the ninth month, no matter whether the full time of pregnancy has elapsed. So also with Israel: Once they have tasted the pangs of exile, so soon as they repent they will be looked upon as though they had indeed endured all those things which are mentioned in Scripture, all the more so as really many tribulations have befallen them since the exile began.

'It is written: "When thou art in tribulation and all these things are come upon thee in the end of days" (Deut. IV, 30). The great love which the Holy One has bestowed upon Israel may be illustrated by the following parable. A king had an only son whom he loved dearly, and because he loved him he entrusted to the queen, his mother, the whole care of his upbringing and his instruction in the right manner of life. In course of time the son committed some misdeed which offended his father. The king punished him and then forgave him. But lo! The prince again offended, and this time the king was very wroth and expelled him from the palace in disgrace. The young man departed, but, instead of beginning a new life and adopting the path of virtue, so that his father, hearing of his plight, should long for his return, he said to himself: "Since I am out of my father's palace I can behave as I please", and he went and associated with harlots, polluting himself in their filth, and was always to be found in their company. The queen, his mother, inquired every day about him, so that she knew all about his doings from day to day, including his association with harlots, and she wept bitterly and grieved over her son. One day the king entered into her chamber and found her crying. He asked her: "Why weepest thou?" She replied: "Should I not weep when our son is away from the king's palace, consorting with harlots?" Said the king: "For thy sake I will let him come back, but thou must be responsible for him." She replied: "I will be." Said the king: "That being so, we must not fetch him publicly by day, since it would be a dishonour for us to visit brothels in search of him. Had he not so utterly disgraced himself, I would have gone to fetch him with great pomp at the head of all my army, with trumpets and songs of joy for our reconciliation, with a special bodyguard to escort him at his right and at his left, so that the whole world would be filled with awe and know that he is the king's son. But now that he has besmirched my honour, he must return secretly, that no one be aware of it." So the prince was brought back privily to the palace, and the king gave him over to his mother. After a time he misbehaved himself yet again. What then did the king do? He threw mother and son together out of the palace, saying: "Both of you must now be cast out and go, and suffer exile and punishment, for I know in my heart that, when ye shall suffer together, my son will really repent". Similarly, the Israelites are sons of the Holy King, who let them go down into captivity, in Egypt. Shouldst thou say, But at that time they had not sinned, the answer would be that what the Holy One had decreed (to Abraham) "between the pieces" (of the sacrifice, Gen. xv, 6-21) had to be fulfilled, and also Abraham's question, "Whereby shall I know that I shall inherit it?" (Ibid. v, 8), was a

Zohar: Shemoth, Section 2, Page 189b

cause of Israel's banishment in Egypt. However, until they went out from Egypt they were not yet a nation and did not appear in a fitting light. It is written: "As the rose among thorns so is my love among the daughters" (S.S. II, 2). The Holy One desired to shape Israel on the celestial pattern, so that there should be one rose on earth, even as it is in heaven. Now, the rose which gives out a sweet aroma, and is conspicuous among all other roses, is the one which grows among thorns. This is the nature of roses. Therefore He planted "rose-trees" to the number of seventy couples, each consisting of male and female, namely, the seventy souls descending from Jacob, and placed them all between the thorns. And these thorns, as soon as the roses were among them, brought forth branches and leaves and ruled over the world. When the Holy One came to pluck the rose from among the thorns, then the latter dried up and became worthless. When He went to gather this rose-that is to say, to bring His first-born son out from Egypt-the King came with many mighty angelic hosts with banners flying, and delivered His first-born out of bondage with many mighty deeds and brought him unto His Palace, and there he dwelt for a long time with the King. When he sinned against his Father he was reproved and punished by Him, as it is written: "And the anger of the Lord was against Israel, and he delivered them into the hands of the spoilers..." (Judges II, 14). And when he sinned again and rebelled against his Father he was driven out of the Father's house. Then what did the Israelites do? They saw that they were driven away to Babylon, so they became reckless and mixed freely with the heathen nations, took foreign women as their wives, and begat children from them. Withal, however, the "Holy Mother" (the Shekinah) pleaded their cause and protected them. And because Israel misbehaved thus, the Holy One said: "Let my son come out from his sojourn by himself, because he has profaned himself. It would be unseemly for Me to go there and bring him out Myself, manifesting signs and wonders as before." So they returned from Babylon alone and without assistance, without signs and wonders, but in separate groups, weary and poverty-stricken, and returned to the King's Palace in shame; and the "Holy Mother" was responsible for them. Then they sinned yet again. What did the Holy One do? He drove the son from out of His Palace, even as He had done the previous time, and his Mother with him, and He said: "From now on let the Mother and Her son suffer many afflictions together", as it is written. "For your transgressions was your mother sent away" (Isa. L, 1). And this is the significance of the words: "When thou art in tribulation and all these things are come upon thee in the end of days". What is "the end of days"? It designates the "Holy Mother" (Shekinah), with whom the children of Israel suffered together all the tribulations of exile. And if they only repent, even one suffering or one sorrow would be considered as equivalent to all the sufferings which were decreed as their portion; but if they do not so repent they will have to remain in exile until the "end" draws nigh to completion, yea, throughout the length of all its generations, as the Holy Lamp (R. Simeon) has told us, quoting the words: "And if it be not redeemed within the space of a full year, then the house that is in the walled city shall be established forever to him that bought it throughout his generations" (Lev. xxv, 30). Yea, verily, all depends upon repentance?' Said R. Hiya: 'Indeed, thou art right! And therefore the exile is prolonged, but the Holy One will accomplish all His promises to them at the "end of days", as it is written, "And it shall come to pass in the end of days that the mountain of the Lord's house shall be established in the top of the mountains, and shall be exalted above the hills, and all nations shall flow unto it" (Isa. II, 2). [Tr. note: Here in the original follows a passage dealing with the allusions to "Ancient Abraham" and "the Cup of Benediction" contained in the expressions "top of the mountains" and "end of days".]

Zohar: Shemoth, Section 2, Page 190a

[Note: Translation resumes with line 20 of Hebrew text]

In regard to the intimation which God gave to Moses, that although Israel will sin against Him in every generation He does not desire anyone to rise up and accuse them, what actual examples have we? One is the prophet Hosea, who first said, "The beginning of the word of the Lord by Hosea..." (Hosea I, 2), but soon after had to proclaim, "Yet the number of the children of Israel shall be as the sand of the sea..." (Ibid. II, 1), i.e. although he began with accusations he had afterwards to proclaim blessings. Therefore the prophet blessed them with many blessings in order to move them to repentance, to turn them to their Father in Heaven, and he ceased interceding until the Holy One forgave their sins and they were purified before Him. The same is true of Elijah. For what do we read concerning him? "And he came and sat down under a juniper tree, and he requested for himself that he might die" (I Kings XIX, 4). He said: "Lord of the world, Thou didst send a woman to Israel whose name was Deborah, and she caused them to repent, as it is written: 'until that I Deborah arose, that I arose a mother in Israel' (Judges v, 7); but I came and preached to them but did not succeed." As he was thus sitting beneath the tree, the Holy One revealed Himself to him and said: "What dost thou here, Elijah? At first thou didst show zeal on behalf of the Covenant, which when I observed I was glad for the sake of thy jealousy on My behalf, in regard to that Covenant, and so I took it with the consent of Moses and gave it to thee"-for it is written: "Wherefore say, Behold I give unto him (Phineas=Elijah) My Covenant: peace" (Num. xxv, 12)-"and now, as this Covenant of peace is thine, it is no longer right for thee to stand forth as an accuser of Israel: thou must let thy zeal lie fallow and leave the punishment of My people to Me, even as in the beginning, when it was mine, I left it in another hand, and did not accuse them." We have learnt that at that moment he lost the gift which Moses had given to him, for it says, "He went in the strength of that meat forty days and forty nights unto Horeb, the mount of God". Why did he go there? In order to demand the return of the Covenant from him who acquired it of old on the mount of God. Said Moses to him when he made this demand: 'Thou canst not receive it from me, go to the little ones in Israel (those who are about to be circumcised) and thou wilt benefit from them, and they will give it to thee." And he did as Moses bade him. [Tr. note: The text here seems to be defective.]

What kindness has the Holy One shown to Israel in every period of its history! Observe that it says: "O my people, what have I done unto thee?... and I sent before thee Moses, Aaron and Miriam" (Micah VI, 4). Now, there were many other prophets after Moses,

Zohar: Shemoth, Section 2, Page 190b

and so surely it ought to run: 'And I sent... Moses, Aaron, Eleazar, Phineas, Joshua, Elijah, Elisha, and ever so many other righteous men and saints." Why are only these three mentioned? Because what the Holy One meant was this: "My people, why do you not remember all the kindness that I have shown you in sending to you Moses, Aaron, and Miriam?" God was like a king who had a province and sent to it august governors to rule it, to lead the people, and to care for their welfare. Upon whom should fall the obligation of providing these high representatives of the king with their requirements, if not upon the inhabitants of that province? But with God it was the opposite. "I have sent unto you", says the Holy One, "Moses, who gave you manna to eat and led you and your children and your cattle, and exerted himself on your behalf, that all your wants might be satisfied. I have sent to you Aaron likewise, who brought to you clouds of glory wherewith to cover you as with a king's garment, who bathed you with the precious dew so that your garments and your sandals did not wear out, but were renewed every day. Also I have sent unto you Miriam, who brought a miraculous cistern to supply you with water from which you and your cattle drank and were refreshed. These three provided you all things needful for your existence and ye ate and drank and sat under their canopy of glory, but ye gave not anything to them--on the contrary, when they laboured on your behalf and took your burdens on their shoulders, ye rewarded them with insult and scorn." ' Said R. Yose: 'There never was a father as merciful and loving to his children as the Holy One to Israel. That lovingkindness is expressed in the words: "Blessed be the Lord that hath given rest unto his people... there hath not failed one word of all his good words which he promised" (I Kings VIII, 56). Observe His great mercy and love, how it is specially manifested in this passage. For had it merely said, "There hath not failed one word of all his words", it would have been better for the world and all the people thereof never to have been created; but as it says, "of all His good words", evil and punishment were not included, for the Lord prefers if possible to leave His intention of punishment unfulfilled.' And even when He threatens and raises the lash (to punish), the "Mother" (the Shekinah) comes and takes hold of His Right Arm so that the lash remains suspended, but does not descend, because both are of one counsel, He in threatening, and she in holding his hand. If you ask, Whence do we know all this? we answer, from the following clear statement. "And the Lord said to Moses: Go, get thee down, for thy people have corrupted themselves" (Ex. XXXII, 7). The Lord began to lift the lash, and Moses, not knowing the ways of the "Mother", was silent in fear. As soon as the Holy One perceived this, He pricked him and incited him by saying, "Now, therefore, let Me, that My wrath may wax hot against them." Moses divined immediately what this foreboded, and realized what he must do: so he seized the Holy One's arm, for it is written that he said, "Remember Abraham", etc. (Ibid. v. 13), on account of which the lash did not descend. But where was the "Mother", whose proper function it was to stay the Arm and prevent punishment? Why did She leave the task to Moses? I ask this question and am utterly baffled, knowing not what answer to give, until we repair to the Holy Lamp (R. Simeon).' When they came into his presence R. Simeon at once saw from their faces that something was troubling them. He said to them: 'Enter, my holy children! Come, O ye beloved sons of the King! Come, my cherished and dearly loved ones, ye who love one another!'-for R. Abba once said that Companions who love not one another pass away from the world before their time. All the Companions in the time of R. Simeon loved one another with heart and soul, and therefore in his generation the secrets were revealed; for he was wont to say that students of the Holy Torah who do not love one another cause a departure from the right path, and what is even more serious, cause a blemish in the very Torah itself, for the

Torah is the essence of love, brotherhood, and truth. Abraham loved Isaac, and Isaac loved Abraham. They embraced one another; and Jacob was held by both in love and fellowship, intermingling their spirits each with each. Therefore members of the fellowship follow that example in order not to cause any blemish in the Torah.

As we have said, R. Simeon, having observed a certain sign in the faces of the newcomers, welcomed them with words of love; and they answered him saying, 'Of a truth the spirit of prophecy rests upon the Holy Lamp, and so we should have known.' R. Simeon, having heard them, wept and said; 'This is one of those sayings whose significance was revealed to me in a whisper from the school of knowledge in Paradise itself, and which should not be repeated openly. Yet, in spite of all this, I will now reveal it unto you, O my beloved children, my children whom my soul loves! What else can I do? It was told to me in a whisper, but I will tell it to you openly, and when the days of the Messiah shall be come, when we shall see face to face,

Zohar: Shemoth, Section 2, Page 191a

all the "faces" will give their consent. Now, the sin which the "outsiders"-"the mixed multitude"-committed, and in which the holy people participated, was a sin against the "Holy Mother", the Shekinah, because they said, "Up, make us a god" (Elohim) (Ex. XXXII, 1)- Elohim, the Glory of Israel, She who rested upon them like a mother on her children. This is the secret contained in the words: "They changed their glory into the similitude of an ox that eateth grass" (Ps. CVI, 20). Yea, verily, that is the Glory of Israel: their Mother. Therefore it also says, "The glory has departed" (I Sam. IV, 22), because they caused the Shekinah to go into exile with them. They changed their glory with what? "The similitude of an ox." Herein lies a mystery. From out of the midst of the dregs of the wine, the dregs of evil, an Accuser emerges, the first Damager, in the form of a man approaching the Sanctuary. As soon as he passes on from there and desires to descend and wreak his evil will upon the earth he has to cover himself with a garment. Then he comes down with his hosts. And the first garment in which he clothes himself is the form of an ox. Therefore the first of those accusing demons is an ox. He is one of the "four principal damagers" [Tr. note: Cf. T. B. Baba Kama, ad init]. who come down to inflict misery on the world. All the three other damagers belong to and are under this first ox. What is the significance of "that eateth grass"? We have already explained it, but the essence of it is that those evil principalities have no portion in the residue of bread or of the seven kinds of wheat. Therefore the "Mother" was not there, and it would have been unfitting for Her to be there. But, knowing Her love and Her compassionate ways, the Father said to Moses: "My beloved son, both (of us) do ever concur in this counsel." This has been whispered to me secretly, and, as I have told you, it is not meant to be noised abroad lest the children should see that the lash is ready to descend, and so be ever in fear and trembling. However, God and the Shekinah are in one counsel, and rule according to the selfsame plan.' 'AND WHEN THE PEOPLE SAW THAT MOSES DELAYED (boshesh) TO COME DOWN OUT OF THE MOUNT. The word "people" denotes the "mixed multitude". And who were the "mixed multitude"? Were they Lydians, Ethiopians, or Cyprians? Were they not all Egyptians, and did they not all come from Egypt? If they had consisted of a mixture of many different nations, would not the plural verb 'alu (went up) have been used instead of the singular 'ala (Ex. XII, 38)? In fact, however, the "mixed multitude" consisted entirely of one people all the members of u,hich spoke one language: namely, all the sorcerers of Egypt and all its magicians, as it is written, "And the magicians of Egypt, they also did in like manner with their enchantments" (Ex. VII, 11); for they wanted to oppose the wonderful works of the Holy One, blessed be He. When they beheld the signs and the wonders which Moses wrought in Egypt they came to Moses to be converted. Said the Holy One to Moses: "Do not receive them!" Moses, however, replied: "Sovereign of the universe, now that they have seen Thy power they desire to accept our Faith, let them see Thy power every day and they will learn that there is no God like unto Thee." And Moses accepted them. And why, then, were they called "mixed multitude"? Because they consisted of all the grades of the Egyptian magicians, at their head being Jannes and Jambres. [Tr. note: Cf. Targum Jonathan, Ex. VII, 11] During the hours of the day these wizards practised their unholy arts, and from the time of the setting of the sun, the beginning of the second half of the sixth hour to the commencement of the second half of the ninth hour, they made observations of the heavens: the middle of the ninth hour being the "great evening" (ereb rab, which means both "great multitude" and "great evening"). The lesser magicians, however, did not thus: they made observation from the middle of the ninth hour until midnight. The chief wizards began at the time mentioned above because the nine hundred and ninety-five grades begin then to roam upon the mountains of darkness, and their spirit moved upon all those magicians in virtue of their witchcraft, and they did all that the latter asked of them, so that all the Egyptians had complete faith in them and called them "large evening", in contrast to the "small evening", which began from the middle of the tenth hour.

Zohar: Shemoth, Section 2, Page 191b

And because there were two "evenings", it speaks of the "large evening": that is, the chief magicians, who went out with the children of Israel from Egypt. Their wisdom was great. They studied the hours of the day and their significance, and they studied the grade of Moses and perceived that he was in all quarters in the number six (be-shesh) [Tr. note: Same letters as boshesh- delayed.], namely in the first six hours of the day, over which they had no power and could exercise no control, and also in the six supernal grades to which Moses was attached; and they realized that he was to come down from the Mount in the crowns of these six grades; but when the appointed time was come Moses had not yet returned. At once THE PEOPLE GATHERED THEMSELVES TOGETHER UNTO AARON. Why did the magicians gather themselves unto Aaron? In order that they might be included in the Right Side, while yet evoking the Left; so to Aaron they came, as he represented the Side of Mercy. 'AND SAID UNTO HIM: UP, MAKE US ELOHIM. Observe, that the whole time that Moses was in Egypt he did not once mention the name Elohim, but only Tetragrammaton, and therefore it was hard for Pharaoh, because through this the "other side" had no power and could not dominate the world. Now, however, the magicians sought after that divine Name, and therefore they said, "Make us Elohim", because we need the knowledge of just this aspect of the Divine Personality in order to strengthen our own side, which has hitherto been pushed away. WHICH SHALL GO BEFORE us. What did they mean by that? We see that all the good things and all the glory of the world belong to you-Israel-while we are pushed outside. We also want Elohim, who should walk before us as Tetragrammaton walketh before you, for our "side" has also the right and the power to walk before us, if we make proper preparation before it. Observe that all the clouds of glory which moved with the people in the wilderness covered only the children of Israel, and the cloud of Glory went before them, as it is written: "And the Lord walked before them by day". But this "mixed multitude", and all the cattle, walked on behind, outside the camp. Observe also this, that all the forty years that the Israelites walked in the wilderness no unclean object was permitted within that cloud-canopy. Therefore all the cattle, the grass eaters, remained outside together with those who tended them.' Said R. Eleazar: 'Father, in that case, that "mixed multitude" did not partake of the manna?' R. Simeon replied: 'Certainly not, indeed! They only had what the Israelites chose to give them, as one gives to a slave. And what part of the food did they eat? Of the husks which remained clinging to the millstones. Scripture proclaims it directly: "And the children of Israel ate the manna forty years long" (Ex. XVI, 35). Thus, until this time, the "mixed multitude" was kept down, but now they sought the performance of some act whereby they might strengthen the "other side", and they said, "either we become all of us one people so that we are included in you, or let us have one to walk before us, even as your God walks before you." Said Aaron: "It is not to be thought of that these should join with the holy people to become one with them, or that the holy should become mingled with them. It would be better to separate them entirely from the holy people until Moses comes back." Aaron verily meant to do all things for the best, only, alas! there were many in Israel who did associate

495

themselves with the others, if not in action at least in their hearts. Therefore, when Moses finally arrived, he had to purify the holy people from that sin, and he gave them that water (Ex. XXXIII, 20) to drink until they were all purified

Zohar: Shemoth, Section 2, Page 192a

and no dregs of unholiness were left in them. AND AARON SAID TO THEM, BREAK OFF THE GOLDEN EARRINGS (Ex. XXXII, 2). Did they have no other gold? Aaron's idea, however, was that while they were arguing with their wives and children time would be gained and Moses might return before harm was done. Observe how true the saying is: "Proselytes cause as much pain to Israel as a sore does to the flesh", particularly in this case, when they were not even genuine proselytes. AND ALL THE PEOPLE BRAKE OFF THE GOLDEN EARRINGS WHICH WERE IN THEIR EARS, AND BROUGHT THEM UNTO AARON.

What quantities of such earrings there must have been there! AND HE RECEIVED THEM AT THEIR HAND AND FASHIONED IT WITH A GRAVING-TOOL. Here itis plainly to be seen that Aaron did not guard himself against the two magicians who were the head of that "mixed multitude". One of these stood in front of him, and the other busied himself with his witchcraft. After the two sorcerers had hatched their plan they took the gold, one two-thirds and the other one-third, this being the method of that kind of magic.' At this point R. Simeon wept, and said 'O pious one! O holy one! O Aaron, thou anointed of the great God! Through thy piety many of the holy people have fallen, and this all because thou knewest not how to guard thyself! Alas! What did those sorcerers do? When the first six hours had passed and the scales of the day were even, they took that gold which they brake off their ears. Why did they break it off? Because he who desires to perform witchcraft must not consider the value of his possessions; and they thought, "the hour is now propitious for us, provided we do not waste time; therefore it is no time to worry about gold". At once, "All the people brake off the golden earrings", that is, they "brake" or tore their ears in their eagerness to take off the rings.' R. Simeon then wept again and said: 'O holy people, O holy people of God... Alas, alas!' Then he continued in tears: 'It is written: "And if the servant shall plainly say, I love my master... I will not go out free... then his master shall bore his ear..." (Ex. XXI, 5-6), and the Companions have commented: "the ear which heard on Mount Sinai the words, 'For the children of Israel are servants unto Me'-and not servants of servants-and which yet stoops to hearken to the words of tempters, causing its owner to shake off the yoke of the Kingdom of Heaven and sell himself to another man-such an ear must be bored." [Tr. note: v. Mechilta, ad loc.] And these sinners and evildoers, in their eagerness to return to their sinful ways, did not ask their wives and children, but broke their ears and threw off the yoke of heaven, forfeiting their right to any part in the Holy Name or the heritage of the holy people. What did they do, those two magicians? They divided that gold, as we have said: one took two-thirds and the other took one-third. They stood opposite the sun at the sixth hour. They manipulated the instruments of their sorcery and uttered their incantations. And when the seventh hour came they both lifted up their hands and placed them upon Aaron's hands, for it is written: "And he received them at their hand". There were thus only two from whom he "received them". As soon as he took the gold from their hand a voice proclaimed: "When the hand joins hand evil shall not be unpunished" (Prov. XI, 21), as Aaron said: "Thou knowest the people that they are set on evil" (Ex. XXXII, 22); that is, they brought evil into the world. The secret of it was that these wicked sorcerers, sons of wicked Balaam, grandsons of wicked Laban, perceived that the Cup of Benediction must be in the right hand, and that energy and power always emanate from the Right Side; so they thought in their hearts, "If the representative of the Right, namely the High Priest, should be on our side, then the power will properly and completely be ours." As soon as the seventh hour of the day was arrived they gave the gold instantly to Aaron. Now, had he but said to them, "Put the gold first on the ground and I will pick it up", their witchcraft would have had no effect whatever; but alas! he took it from their hand, wherefore Scripture complains: "And he received them at their hand!" See now the unhappy fate of Aaron! A prophet he, a sage, a holy man of God, and yet he could not guard himself! For had he only taken the gold from the ground all the magicians of the world could not have succeeded in their designs. AND FASHIONED IT WITH A GRAVING-TOOL. This does not mean, as people are apt to think, that he carved designs upon it with a graving-tool or chisel. What the text comes to show us is that Aaron was not sufficiently on his guard. For had he, even after taking it from their hands, thrown in on the ground, even if he had picked it up afterwards, this evil operation would not have

Zohar: Shemoth, Section 2, Page 192b

succeeded; but what he did was to put the whole of the gold into a bag, so keeping it hidden from view. This made the witchcraft effective. We have found in the Book of Enoch the following: "An only son [Tr. note: Aaron.] will be born unto Him of the White Head, [Tr. note The Supernal Priest] and when they of the asses' flesh [Tr. note: The mixed multitude, cf Ezek, XXIII, 20] shall come, they will mislead him through him who puts pearls into bells of gold without knowing what he does, and an image will be fashioned with a chisel." What does heret ("chisel"-or more literally "style") here signify? It alludes to the "style of a man (enosh)" (Isa. VIII, 1), namely, to the style of the wicked Enosh, the grandchild of Adam (Gen. v, 6), who corrupted the world by chiseling images and idols with that "style". Now, this is what occurred in the case of Aaron: first he threw the gold into a bag and hid it from view-which, as we have said, is an essential adjunct to all magical processes, for in their lore it is taught that anything which is to be made a public show of must first be covered up and hidden away; and conversely, what has to be hidden afterwards must first be shown to view. Now, my beloved children, the darlings of my soul! what shall I do? I must perforce disclose to you; but, I pray you, reveal it not again. In the side of holiness the true God (Elohim) reigns over the universe. He takes hold of three worlds–of Beriah (Creation), Yezirah (Formation), and ʿAsiyah (Completion)l; and we have in the verse under consideration an allusion to each one of those phases. "He received them at their hand" corresponds to beriah, since it symbolizes something as yet unfashioned; "and he fashioned it with a graving-tool" corresponds to yezirah; and then "he made it a golden calf". Ah, who has ever beheld such wily magicians, such crafty sorcerers as these! Now one may well ask, Is it not written that Aaron said: "I cast it unto the fire and then came out this calf"? Yet it is quite impossible to imagine that Aaron himself made that thing; in fact, it expressly states: "And he (Moses) took the calf which they made". Obviously, then, it was made by the unwitting power of those two actions of his: first, his having taken the gold from their hands, and secondly, his binding it up in a bag. It is only in a subsidiary sense that he can be said to have made it: were it not for those two actions, it would not have materialised. But when he took the gold from their hands they began their magical manipulations and incantations and so drew down the spirit of impurity from the "other side", and caused two spirits to come together, one male and the other female. The male was disguised in the form of an ox and the female in that of an ass, and these two became one. Why just these?

As to the ox, an explanation has already been given, but what of the ass? The reason for the inclusion of this beast in the symbolism of that unholy union is that concerning these Egyptian magicians we read: "the flesh of asses is their flesh" (Ezek. XXIII, 20); and through this we know that all those of the people of Israel who died because of that sin of the golden calf had sympathized with them in their hearts. And because there were two images, it says concerning the calf, "these are thy gods, O Israel". AND HE MADE IT A MOLTEN CALF. We are told that it weighed one hundred and twenty-five hundredweight (this figure being the numerical equivalent of the word massekah, "molten"); how, then, could he have taken them all from "their hands"? Could such a heavy weight possibly be lifted and held by human hands? The fact is, however, that they held in their hands only so much as filled them, and this portion represented the whole. It is written: "And when Aaron saw it, he built an altar before it". O holy man! strange that with all thy good intentions thou knewest not how to guard thyself! As soon as the gold was thrown into the fire the power of the "other side" was strengthened there, and the image of an ox emerged,

Zohar: Shemoth, Section 2, Page 193a

as already mentioned, through the two attractive forces of the "other side". At once "Aaron saw". What did he see? He saw that the "other side" had gained power, and immediately afterwards he built an altar; for had he not hastened so to do, the world would have been turned again into a waste. He was like a king's officer who sees that the highway is infested by a very formidable robber. He therefore persuaded the king to go forth on that road and then enticed the robber there. When the robber beheld the figure of the king before him he was seized with fear, and retreated. Similarly, Aaron, when he realized that the "other side" was gaining strength, grasped the one remedy left him and strengthened the side of holiness by making an altar. As soon as the "other side" saw the image of the king before it, it retreated and its power was weakened. Observe what Aaron proclaimed: "It is a feast (hag) to the Lord" (Ibid.). "A feast to the Lord", not to the calf. He laboured for the side of holiness, and summoned the people to the side of holiness. And this was the remedy which he hastened to apply, and failing which the world would have collapsed. And yet for all that "the anger of the Lord was roused against Aaron", although he himself had intended no evil. The Holy One said to him: "Aaron, those two magicians have drawn thee to do whatsoever they would. By thy life! Two of thy sons shall be struck down and die because of this sin." This is the implication of the words: "And the Lord was very angry with Aaron to have destroyed him" (Deut. IX, 20). Observe this: Aaron erected an altar before the Lord, and all that the calf symbolized retreated before it. Aaron's sons (Nadab and Abihu) erected the ensign of the "other side" before the face of the Lord ("strange fire") and the "Side of Holiness" retreated, as it is written, "And they offered strange fire before the Lord" (Lev. X, 1). They brought it unto His altar and were punished for this sin.

ʿAaron thought that in the meantime Moses would come back, and therefore Moses did not destroy the altar. For had it indeed been the case–as some think–that the altar was built in honour of the image, then surely Moses' first action should have been to destroy it, as the prophet Iddo, for instance, prophesied that the altar of Bethel would be destroyed (I Kings XIII). But here it was quite different, as I have made clear. Moses "took the calf which they made and burnt it in the fire and ground it to powder", but it does not say that he destroyed the altar. Observe that it says, "And Aaron proclaimed and said, Tomorrow is a feast of the Lord." The expression, "proclaimed and said" is used concerning Jonah (when he preached to the Ninevites, Jonah III, 4): and as there it denoted judgement, so does it also here. ʾTOMORROW IS A FEAST OF THE LORD. He prophesied in the spirit of that altar in order that judgement might come upon the iniquitous: "a feast of the Lord to exercise judgement upon you". The people suffered a threefold punishment: one wrought by the Lord (v. 35), one at the hands of the sons of Levi (v. 28), and one inflicted by Moses, when he made the children of Israel drink the water (v. 20). The night after they had drunk it they slept, but on the next day their bodies were all swollen and they died from the effects of that water. Mark also that the altar which Aaron made was intended for holiness, and dedicated unto the Lord, since it says that Moses "saw the calf and the dancing" (v. I 9), but it does not mention the altar, for Aaron knew very well that "he who sacrificeth unto any god, save unto the Lord only, he shall be utterly destroyed" (Ex. XXII, 20) and he was certainly saved by the good plan which he conceived, and all was done by him with a perfect and righteous intention.'

Said R. Eleazar: 'Father, it is indeed and truly so; and they who committed this sin were not genuine Israelites, but when Jeroboam put up the golden calves, were they not Israelites who worshipped them?'

R. Simeon replied: 'Truly so. But it has been explained thus. Jeroboam sinned and caused others to do likewise, for he sinned against the Kingdom. He reasoned thus: "I know well enough that the 'side of holiness' dwells only in the heart and centre of the world, namely in Jerusalem, and therefore I cannot draw down that side on to this region (Shechem). What, then, shall I do?" "Whereupon he took counsel and made two calves of gold" (I Kings VI, 28). He conceived a wicked design, thinking:

Zohar: Shemoth, Section 2, Page 193b

"The 'other side' can be drawn to every place, especially in this land (the Holy Land), where it is eager to dwell." But the "other side" could only be represented in the guise of an ox. Why, then, did he put up two calves? Because he thought, "In the wilderness dwelt those sorcerers of whom it says that 'their flesh is the flesh of asses'. Here are those two same evil spirits; let them be clothed in the manner appropriate to them, as male and female–male in Bethel and female in Dan". And so, indeed, it was. And since, as we are told, "The lips of the strange woman (idolatry) drop as an honeycomb", the Israelites were drawn with a special bewitchment towards the female of the kind, as it is written, "And the people went to (worship) before the one, unto Dan" (I Kings XII, 29). Therefore there were two calves, and Jeroboam attracted them unto the Holy Land, and this thing became a sin to him and to Israel, and he prevented blessings from coming down onto the world; and concerning him it is written, 'Whoso robbeth his father and his mother, and saith, It is no transgression, the same is the companion of a destroyer" (Prov. XXVIII, 24). Therefore, also, they were calves, because the first disguise or garment donned by the powers of the "other side" is an ox, as we have pointed out. And if it be asked why they were calves and not oxen, the answer is that it is ever thus with the demons of unholiness: they first appear in a diminutive form. Therefore, my beloved children, since they (the "mixed multitude") desired the aspect of Elohim, and the act (of the golden calf) was carried out with an intention in which the "side" of Elohim was kept in mind, that Holy Elohim, the "Mother" (the Shekinah), who doth ever keep back the Right Hand of the King (when He is about to punish His people) and holds up the lash, was not present there; so it was necessary for Moses to take Her place; and as soon as the Holy One awakened a certain uneasiness in him, he comprehended what it meant. Three times did the Holy One rouse this feeling in him, as it is written, "Now therefore let Me"; "that My wrath may wax hot against them and that I may consume them"; "and I will make of thee a great nation". Moses showed his wisdom in responding to these three intimations. He took hold of the Right Arm, which action corresponded to the first warning; he took hold of the Left Arm, and this corresponded to the second; he embraced the Body of the King, which corresponded to the last. And when he had embraced the "Body", and the two Arms, the one from this and the other from that side, He could not move to any side. This was Moses' wisdom: that he perceived, by means of the Lord's signs, which place to take hold of; and he did all things in wisdom.'

R. Eleazar and the Companions then approached him and kissed his hands. R. Abba was also present. Said he: 'Had I come into this world only to hear these words, it would have been worth while.' Then he wept, and said: 'Woe unto us, Master, when thou shalt depart from the world! Who will then light up for us the greater radiances of the Torah? This subject was hidden in darkness until now, but at last it has emerged and shines even unto the highest heavens. It is engraved upon the Throne of the King, the Holy One Himself rejoices in this discourse. Joy upon joy has been added before the face of the Holy King. Who will awaken words of wisdom in this world as thou dost?' [Tr. note: From here to the end of Ki Tisa is a verbal repetition of Zohar, Gen. 52a–53a ("Until he sinned... caused that imperfection")].

Zohar: Shemoth, Section 2, Page 194a

Note: This Page is not translated as per previous translator's note

Zohar: Shemoth, Section 2, Page 194b

Note: Hebrew text until beginning of Vayqhel is not translated as per translator's note supra

VAYAQHEL

AND MOSES ASSEMBLED ALL THE CONGREGATION OF THE CHILDREN OF ISRAEL, ETC. R. Hiya opened here a discourse on the text: "And Saul said unto the Kenites: Go depart", etc. (I Sam. xv, 6). 'Observe', he said, 'that in regard to Amalek it is written: "I remember that which Amalek did to Israel", etc. (Ibid. xv, 2). What is the reason that none of the wars waged by other nations against Israel was so displeasing to the Almighty as was the war waged against them by

Amalek? The reason, assuredly, is that the battle with Amalek was waged on both fronts, both on high and below; for at that time the evil serpent gathered all its forces both above and below. It is the way of a serpent to lie in wait on the cross-roads. So Amalek, the evil serpent of Israel, was lying in wait for them

Zohar: Shemoth, Section 2, Page 195a

on the cross-roads, as it is written: "how he set himself against him in the way" (Ibid.). He was lying in ambush on high in order to defile the Sanctuary, and below in order to defile Israel. This we deduce from the expression, "how he met thee by the way" (Deut. XXV, 18), where the term qar'kha is meant to suggest the kindred term in the passage, "If there be among you any man that is not clean by reason of that which chanceth him (miqre) by night" (Ibid. XXIII, 11). By using the term qar'kha, the text as much as says: "He has arrayed against thee that evil serpent from above that he may defile thee on all sides"; and were it not that Moses from above, and Joshua from below, put forth all their strength, Israel would not have prevailed against him. It is for this reason that the Holy One, blessed be He, cherished His enmity against him throughout all generations, inasmuch as he planned to uproot the sign of the covenant from its place. ([Tr. note: i.e. to lead Israel into ways of unchastity.]

'Our verse continues: "And Saul said to the Kenite." The Kenite, as we know, was Jethro. Now, how came the descendants of Jethro to have their abode alongside of Amalek? Was not Jericho their home? But the explanation is found in the verse: "And the children of the Kenite, Moses' father-in-law, went up out of the city of palm-trees (i.e. Jericho) with the children of Judah into the wilderness of Judah" (Judges I, 16); that is to say, when they left Jericho, they moved on as far as the border of Amalek, where they settled and remained until the time of King Saul, when, as we read, "the Kenites departed from among the Amalekites" (I Sam. xv, 6). They had to depart because, when the time comes to punish the guilty, the pious and just who are among them are first made responsible for their sins. This has already been made clear elsewhere. Similarly, if it had not been for the riffraff that became associated with Israel, the Israelites would not have incurred punishment for the sin of the golden calf. For, observe that first it is written here, "of every man whose heart makes him willing ye shall take my offering" (Ex. xxv, 2); to wit, of the whole body of the people, including the mixed multitude, as the Holy One, blessed be He, desired to have in the work of the Tabernacle the co-operation of all sections of the people, both the "brain" category and the "shell" category: all were charged with the performance of the work. Subsequently, however, the sections separated, each betaking itself to its own affinity, and so the mixed multitude made the golden calf and led astray numbers who afterwards died, and thus brought upon Israel death and slaughter. The Holy One, blessed be He, then said: "Henceforward the work of the Tabernacle shall be performed from the side of Israel only." Straightway "Moses assembled all the congregation of the children of Israel... Take ye from among you an offering unto the Lord" (Ibid. xxxv, 1-5). "From among you" emphatically, but not "from every man whose heart maketh him willing", as in the previous injunction. Furthermore, as no place of assembly is mentioned, the words, "And Moses assembled", etc., signify that, as the mixed multitude were mingled among the Israelites, Moses found it necessary to assemble the latter on one side so as to segregate them from the former.' AND MOSES AS SEMBLED. R. Abba cited in connection with this the verse: "Assemble the people, the men and the women and the little ones" (Deut. XXXI, 12). 'Just as there', he said, 'the gathering comprised the whole of Israel, so here also Moses assembled the whole of Israel; to wit, the six hundred thousand men.' R. Eleazar expounded our text in relation to Israel at the time when Moses descended from Mount Sinai, regarding which it is written: "And when Joshua heard the noise of the people as they shouted, he said unto Moses: There is a noise of war in the camp" (Ex. XXXII, 17). Is it possible that Joshua heard it and Moses did not hear it? The truth is that Moses knew already what had befallen, whilst Joshua only now became aware of it; and the word bere'oh (when they shouted) can read bera'ah, i.e. "in evil", as that tumult proceeded from the "other side" (synonymous with evil). For Joshua, who (as compared with Moses) was emblematic of the moon, apprehended the sound that proceeded from the evil side, and straightway "he said unto Moses: There is a noise of war in the camp". At that moment the two first tables of stone became too heavy for Moses' hands, as already stated elsewhere,

Zohar: Shemoth, Section 2, Page 195b

and dropped from them and broke. The reason was that the letters of the tables of stone flew away.

'Mark this. At the turn of the four seasons of the year a sound arises in the four quarters of the world through which the sinister side is stirred up, interposing between one sound and another, and at the same time obscuring the light that streams from on high. It is because the voice from above does not meet that from below that the left side is aroused and is able to insinuate itself between the two. That interposing sound is the sound or noise of war, the noise of the evil forces; and this is the meaning of the word bera'ah (in evil) [Tr. note: v. supra]. It was for that reason that only Joshua heard that noise but not Moses, for it proceeded from that evil power that impaired the light of the moon. Hence Joshua, who was the replica of the moon, perceived that noise, whereas Moses, who was the replica of the sun, did not perceive it. The light of all Israel was altogether darkened by reason of the evil power that took hold of them. But straightway the Holy One, blessed be He, forgave them their sins.' AND MOSES ASSEMBLED ALL THE CONGREGATION OF THE

CHILDREN OF ISRAEL, AND SAID UNTO THEM: THESE ARE THE WORDS, ETC. He took this step because the mixed multitude were now removed from them. R. Eleazar and R. Yose were sitting one night studying the Torah. When midnight arrived, the cock crew and so they pronounced the benediction [Tr. note: Blessed art Thou, O our God, King of the universe, who gavest the cock understanding to discern between day and night] R. Eleazar wept, and said: 'Observe this. The Holy One, blessed be He, has just smitten three hundred and ninety firmaments, and made them to shake and to tremble; He has wept on account of the destruction of the Temple, dropping two tears into the great ocean, as He bethought Himself of His children with weeping. For the night is divided into three courses which extend over a definite space of twelve hours, any additional hours being counted as belonging to the day and not to the night, which has just its own twelve hours. These three night courses are divided between three companies of angels. To the first company is assigned the period of the first four hours for the singing of the night hymn in praise of their Master. That hymn consists of the psalm, "The earth is the Lord's, and the fulness thereof... For he hath founded it upon the seas... who shall ascend into the mountain of the Lord?... He that hath clean hands, and a pure heart..." (Ps. XXIV, 1-6). Why that hymn? Because when the night spreads its wings over the world all human beings have a foretaste of death, so that their souls quit the bodies and soar upwards to heaven. Hence those angels are stationed there, and proclaim: "Who shall ascend into the mountain of the Lord?"; to wit, the Temple Mount; "and who shall stand in His holy place?", to wit, the court of the Israelites. [Tr. note: i.e. the Temple area, where non-priests of the male sex could enter.] For the Temple below has been constructed after the pattern of the Temple on high. Now, in each heaven there are various chieftains and commanders; and when the souls leave the body and attempt to enter heaven those that are unworthy are thrust aside by those angels, so that they roam to and fro in the world, being carried about by disembodied spirits who communicate to them lying statements, often mingled with a grain of truth, regarding events of the near future, as already explained elsewhere. But the righteous mount into heaven, where doors are opened for them through which they may enter the place called "the mount of the Lord", which is after the pattern of the Temple Mount below. From thence they penetrate within the place called "His holy place", where all the souls appear before their Master. After the same pattern, the place where Israel had to appear before the Holy One, blessed be He, [Tr. note: v. Ex. XXXIV, 23.] was called the Court of the Israelites. At the moment when the souls stand in that place there is joy before their Master, because by them the place called Holy of Holies becomes re-established: it is the place where are recorded all their deeds and their merits.

The second camp have assigned to them the second four hours of the night, but their chanting only continues until midnight, when the Holy One, blessed be He, enters the Garden of Eden. That company consists of the mourners for Zion, the same that wept for the destruction of the Temple. The litany of the middle four hours begins with: "By the rivers of Babylon, there we sat down, yea, we wept", etc. (Ps. CXXXVII, 1-9), the angels that chant it having themselves actually wept at the time by the rivers of Babylon together with Israel,

Zohar: Shemoth, Section 2, Page 196a]

as is clear from the words, "yea, we wept". We learn this also from the statement of the Scripture: "Behold, the angels cry without" (Isa. XXXIII, 7), the word "without" indicating Babylon; for that company of angels accompanied the Shekinah as far as Babylon, and there they wept together with Israel. Hence they commence their chanting with "By the rivers of Babylon" and conclude with "Remember, O Lord, against the children of Edom", etc. (Ps. CXXXVII, 7-9). The Holy One, blessed be He, then bestirs Himself and strikes the heavens, as already said, so that twelve thousand worlds quake, and He melts in tears, as it were. So Scripture says: "The Lord doth roar from on high, and utter his voice from his holy habitation; he dot mightily roar because of his fold" (Jer. xxv, 30). He remembers then Israel and drops two tears into the great ocean. At that moment a flame bursts forth in the North, and, impelled by a northerly wind, roams to and fro about the world. It is the moment of midnight, and the flame strikes against the wings of the cock. The cock then crows, and the Holy One, blessed be He, enters the Garden of Eden, for He finds no comfort until He goes there to have joyous communion with the souls of the righteous. This is the allegorical meaning of the verses: "for we are sold, I and my people. Then spoke the King... Who is he? And the King arose in his wrath from the banquet of wine and went into the palace garden", etc. (Esther VII, 4-7). At the moment when the Holy One, blessed be He, enters the Garden of Eden, all the trees of the garden, and all the souls of the righteous, break forth and chant: "Lift up your heads, O ye gates... Who is the King of glory?. Lift up your heads, O ye gates." (Ps. XXIV, 7-10). And when the souls of the righteous return to their bodies, all those angels lay hold of them and chant: "Behold, bless ye the Lord, all ye servants of the Lord" (Ibid. CXXXIV, 1). We have learned that this hymn is chanted by the third company of angels, who are occupied in song and praise during the last four hours of the night until daybreak, when all the stars and constellations, and all the superior angels who rule over the day, break forth in song and praise to their Master, this being alluded to in the words of the Scripture: "When the morning stars sang together, and all the sons of God shouted for joy" (Job XXXVIII, 7). Then when the sun appears in full daylight, Israel takes up the song below in unison with the sun above, as Scripture says: "They reverence thee at the appearance of the sun" (Ps. LXXII, 5). For the sun, on commencing his course, breaks forth into sweet melody, chanting: "O give thanks unto the Lord, call upon his name... Sing unto him, sing praises unto him..."

(Ibid. cv, 1-45).' Said R. Eleazar: 'Were mankind not so obtuse and insensitive, they would be thrilled to ecstasy by the exquisite melodiousness of the orb of the sun when he journeys forth singing praises to the Holy One, blessed be He.'

Whilst they were thus occupied in the study of the Torah the day broke. They then arose and came into the presence of R. Simeon. As soon as he saw them he said: 'Eleazar, my son! You, together with the Companions, must hide yourselves during the next three days, and not go out of doors, as the Angel of Death is now in the town with permission to do harm; and once such permission is given him he can lay hands on anyone that he sees. For if he catches sight of any man he ascends on high, brings an indictment against him, makes a record of his sins, and demands judgement from the Holy One, blessed be He, and he does not budge from thence until he obtains sentence against that man, after which, having received due permission, he proceeds to take his life.'

R. Simeon further said: 'I swear to you that the majority of people do not die before their time, but only those who know not how to take heed to themselves. For at the time when a dead body is taken from the house to the place of burial the Angel of Death haunts the abodes of the women. Why of the women? Because that has been his habit since the time that he seduced Eve, through whom he brought death upon the world. Hence, when he takes a man's life, and the males are accompanying the dead body, he mingles himself on the way among the women, and he has then the power to take the life of the sons of men. He looks on the way at the faces of those who come within his sight, from the time they carry the dead body out from his house to the place of burial until they return to their homes. It is on their account that he brings about the untimely death of many people. Regarding this it is written: "But there is that is swept away without justice" (Prov. XIII, 23). For he, the Angel of Death, ascends and brings accusations and recounts man's sins before the Holy One, blessed be He, so that the man is brought to judgement for those sins, and is removed from the world before his time. What is the remedy against this? When the dead body is carried to the place of burial, a man should turn

Zohar: Shemoth, Section 2, Page 196b

his face in another direction, and leave the women behind him. Should the latter pass in front he should turn round so as not to face them. Similarly, when they return from the place of burial he should not return by the way where the women are standing, and he should not look at them at all, but should turn a different way. It is because the sons of men do not know of this, and do not observe this, that the majority of people are brought up for judgement and are taken away before their time.'

Said R. Eleazar: 'If that is so, it were better for a man not at all to follow the dead to their resting place.' Said his father to him: 'Not so. For whoever takes heed unto himself in the manner just described is worthy of length of days, and still more of the world to come. Observe that it was not without cause that the ancients ordained the blowing of the trumpet at the time when the dead body is taken from the house to the place of burial. This was not instituted merely for the honour of the dead. Rather is its purpose to protect the living against the Angel of Death, so that he should not be able to indict them on high, and as a warning to us to guard themselves against him.' R. Simeon then discoursed on the verse: "And when ye go to war in your land against the adversary that oppresseth you, then ye shall sound an alarm with the trumpets", etc. (Num. x, 9). 'It has been explained', he said, 'that "the adversary" refers to the Angel of Death "that oppresseth" continually and takes the lives of the sons of men, and is eager to slay others. What is the remedy against him? "Then ye shall sound an alarm with the trumpets." For if on New Year's Day, the Day of Judgement in the Heavenly Court, when the Angel of Death descends here below so as to pry into men's deeds and ascends again in order to indict them—if at that time Israel, being aware that the Angel of Death is descending to earth and again ascending with the object of accusing them, anticipate him by blowing the trumpet so as to confuse him and so protect themselves against him, how much more so is this needful when the Angel of Death here below is executing judgement and taking the lives of men; and how much more still when people proceed to and return from the place of burial! For when the women walk in the funeral procession, the Angel of Death descends and places himself among them. So Scripture says: "Her feet go down to death" (Prov. v, 5), to wit, to the region called by the name of "death". It is thus that Eve brought death into the world. May the Merciful One save us! Observe the verse, saying: "So is the way of an adulterous woman; she eateth and wipeth her mouth, and saith, I have done no wickedness" (Ibid. xxx, 20). That verse has already been explained, but we may also interpret as follows: "The way of an adulterous woman" alludes to the Angel of Death, who is, indeed, called both by one name and the other; "she eateth and wipeth her mouth", to wit, he consumes the world by the conflagration which he kindles, taking men's lives before their time, "and saith, I have done no wickedness", since he invoked judgement against them, and they were found guilty, and thus died in accordance with justice. At the time when Israel made the calf and all those hosts died, the Angel of Death mingled himself among the women who were in the camp of Israel. As soon as Moses became aware of his presence among them he assembled all the male persons separately, and this is why Scripture says, "And Moses assembled all the congregation of the children of Israel", namely, the menfolk, whom he collected and set on one side. But the Angel of Death did not leave the women until the Tabernacle was erected, and even when the women were bringing their offerings to the Tabernacle he did not leave them until Moses, observing it, advised the menfolk not to come in company with them, and not to look at them face to face, but only over their

501

shoulders. Scripture thus says: "And they came, namely, the men" (Ex. xxxv, 22), the expression "and they came", instead of "and they brought" indicating that they did not come alongside of the women, but kept them behind, as the Angel of Death did not depart from them until the Tabernacle was erected.

'Note that the Angel of Death is not found among women if their number is less than seven, or less than ten. That is to say, if seven women are together he is found among them and invokes judgement against men; but if there are no less than ten, he even demands the penalty of death. And it is his presence among the women that is hinted at in the words, "And they came, namely, the men with the women" (Ibid.).' All that day, then, the Companions put themselves on their guard and absorbed themselves in the study of the Torah.

R. Simeon called attention to the verse: "And the Lord said unto Noah: Come thou and all thy house into the ark" (Gen. VII, 1). 'This verse', he said, 'has already been explained. But observe this. Could not the Holy One, blessed be He, have preserved Noah in some other way, as by putting him in some spot where the flood could not reach,

Zohar: Shemoth, Section 2, Page 197a

in the same way as we read, in connection with Gideon, that "it was dry upon the fleece only" (Judges VI, 40); or even have preserved him in the Land of Israel, of which it is written, "nor was it rained upon in the day of indignation" (Ezek. XXII, 24)? But the truth is that, as soon as the Destroying Angel comes down into this world, whoever does not shut himself in, but exposes himself to his view, forfeits his life, and thus destroys himself. We learn this from Lot, in connection with whom it is written: "Escape for thy life, look not behind thee" (Gen. XIX, 17). Why the warning "look not behind thee"? Because the Destroying Angel was stalking behind him, and had he turned his head and looked straight in the face of the angel, the latter would have been able to injure him. Hence it is written of Noah, "and the Lord shut him in" (Ibid. VII, 16), in order that Noah should not show himself before the Destroying Angel, and should so not fall into his power.' Now whilst the Companions were in concealment there died in the town thirteen men. R. Simeon said: 'Blessed be the Merciful One for that the Angel of Death did not look in your countenances!' AND MOSES ASSEMBLED ALL THE CONGREGATION OF THE CHILDREN OF ISRAEL, ETC. He repeated all over again the instructions concerning the making of the Tabernacle. R. Hiya said: 'It is all as has already been explained. The actual making of the Tabernacle was carried out by Israel alone, without the mixed multitude. For that mixed multitude drew down the Angel of Death into the world. As soon, therefore, as Moses observed him he threw out the mixed multitude and assembled the Israelites by themselves. This is the significance of the words, "And Moses assembled, etc." '

R. Simeon here expounded the verse: "Who hath ascended into heaven, and descended? Who hath gathered the wind in his fists? Who hath bound the waters in his garments? Who hath established all the ends of the earth? What is his name, and what is his son's name, if thou knowest?" (Prov. xxx, 4). 'This verse', he said, 'has already been explained. "Who hath ascended up into heaven?": this alludes to Moses, of whom it is written, "And unto Moses he said, Come up unto the Lord" (Ex. XXIV, 1). According to another interpretation, "Who ascended up into heaven" alludes to Elijah, of whom it is written, "and Elijah went up by a whirlwind into heaven" (2 Kings II, 11). It may be asked, How could Elijah have ascended into heaven, seeing that the heavens cannot endure even so much as a mustard seed of the matter of this world? How, then, can Scripture say, "and he ascended up by a whirlwind into heaven"? But it was with Elijah as with Moses. In connection with Moses it is first written: "And the Lord came down upon Mount Sinai" (Ex. XIX, 20), and further on it is written, "And Moses entered into the midst of the cloud, and went up into the mount" (Ibid. XXIV, 18). Now, inasmuch as the Holy One, blessed be He, was on Mount Sinai, regarding which it is written,

"And the appearance of the glory of the Lord was like devouring fire on the top of the mount" (Ibid. XXIV, 17), how could Moses have entered into His presence? The answer is found in the words, "and Moses entered into the midst of the cloud and went up into the mount". This shows that Moses enveloped himself in the cloud as in a garment, and, having thus wrapped himself round, he was able to draw near to the "fire of the glory of the Lord". In a similar way, Elijah, of whom it is written, "And Elijah went up by a whirlwind into heaven", entered into that whirlwind and enveloped himself in it as in a garment, and in this way ascended on high. The following recondite passage is found in the Book of Adam the First Man, in describing the generations of mankind: "A certain spirit will one day come down to earth and will clothe itself in an earthly body and will bear the name of Elijah. Whilst in that body he will soar aloft and, divesting himself of that body, enter within a whirlwind, where another and luminous body will have been prepared for him, so that he will be as an angel among angels' But whenever he will come down to earth he will invest himself again in the material body, which will remain in the lower world; and it is in this body that he will make himself visible on earth, whilst it is in the other body that he will appear on high." This is thus the recondite meaning of the words, "Who hath ascended up into heaven, and descended". There was no other man whose spirit ascended to heaven and then descended to earth except Elijah. According to another interpretation, "who hath ascended up into heaven" is an allusion to Elijah, whereas "and descended" alludes to Jonah, whom the fish caused to sink into the nethermost depths of the sea. Jonah was only made possible by Elijah. Elijah ascended and Jonah descended, and the one as well as the other "requested for himself that he might die". Further, "who hath bound the waters" alludes to Elijah, who bound up in a bundle, as it

502

were, all the waters of the world so that neither dew nor rain came down from heaven; "in his garment" alludes further to Elijah, who smote

with his mantle to perform his miracles. "Who hath gathered the wind (ruah=spirit) in his fists?" is again an allusion to Elijah, who restored the spirit of a man to his body; "Who hath established all the ends of the earth?" still alludes to Elijah, who, after he had restrained the waters and adjured the heavens not to let rain fall, afterwards, by means of his prayer, restored life to the world by bringing back the rain, which produced an abundance of food for all. "What is his name?" refers to Elijah; "and what is his son's name?" refers again to Elijah. "His name" refers to Elijah when he ascended on high, and "his son's name" refers to Elijah when he comes down to earth and becomes a messenger to perform miracles; he bears, then, the same name of Elijah. According to another exposition: "Who hath ascended up into heaven?" refers to the Holy One, blessed be He, the allusion being contained in the word Mi (Who?), as explained elsewhere. Here in this passage is contained the mystery of the Divine Chariot, consisting of the four directions of the world which are the four primordial elements, all of which depend on that supernal region called Mi (Who?), as already said.

'Observe this. When the hour arrives at which it pleases the Holy One, blessed be He, to unify the Supernal Chariot, [Tr. note: Al. "to combine the Supernal Chariot with the Lower Chariot".] a voice issues from that divine supernal region called Heaven to assemble all the saints beneath and all the holy chiefs and supernal legions, so that they should all be in readiness together. Thus Scripture says, "And Moses assembled", "Moses" being an allusion to Heaven; while the words "all the congregation of the children of Israel" allude to the twelve supernal holy legions. The next words, "and said unto them... This is the thing... Take ye from among you an offering unto the Lord", means, "prepare yourselves, all of you, to take and to bear upon you the glory of the Divine Throne so as to raise it aloft to the divine heights; appoint from among you those supernal glorified chiefs who shall take up that offering containing the mystery of the Divine Throne, in order to bring about a union with the "patriarchs", [Tr. note: Al. "with her spouse".] for the Matrona (i.e. the Shekinah) may not come to her Spouse except those youthful bridesmaids follow in her train until she is brought to Him, as it says, "The virgins her companions in her train being brought unto thee" (Ps. XLV, 15), to wit, that she may join her Spouse. The next words, "Whosoever is of a noble heart", are an allusion to the four superior legions that contain within themselves all the other legions; it is these who issue forth with the exalted patriarchs called "nobles", as in the passage, "which the nobles of the people delved" (Num. XXI, 18), indicating the patriarchs. The verse continues, "let him bring it". The singular, "him", where we should expect "them", indicates the merging of them all into a unity. In the next words, "the Lord's offering", the accusative particle eth indicates the inclusion of all the other supernal legions which were to be integrated into one unity; their number is twelve, symbolized by "gold, and silver, and brass; and blue, and purple, and scarlet, and fine linen, and goat's hair; and rams' skins dyed red, and sealskins, and acacia-wood; and oil for the light, and spices for the anointing oil, and for the sweet incense". These are the twelve supernal legions, which are all comprised under the four sacred Hayoth mentioned before. All these ascend towards the Divine Throne, so as to take her up on high that she may join her Spouse, and that He should be with Her in surpassing glory. The Most High King then seats Himself on the Divine Throne in perfect unison with His Spouse, and joy is thus diffused through the universe. (Observe that Scripture here mentions gold before silver, the reason being that this is the scale of values here below; but when it enumerates according to the scale of values in the Heavenly Chariot, Scripture commences from the right and proceeds to the left. So we find it written: "Mine is the silver, and Mine the gold" (Haggai II, 8), first silver and then gold, but here below the left comes first and then the right, as it is written, "gold, and silver, and brass".)

Now the phrase, "every noble-hearted", as already said, comprises those four legions who together are named noble-hearted; "the Lord's heave-offering" indicates the Divine Throne, so called because they raise it and cause it to ascend on high. [Tr. note: i.e. from the world of beriah to the world of aziluth]. And it is for this reason that Ezekiel, in his vision of the ascending Hayoth, failed to see what it was that they were taking up with them, since it was the Matrona rising to join the Most High King in hidden and supreme glory. "And let every wise-hearted among you come and make all that the Lord hath commanded." This is an allusion to the sixty well-springs that feed the world and so are enjoined to come and bring with them from the treasury of life, by executing the commands of the Holy One, so as to benefit the world.' TAKE YE FROM AMONG YOU AN OFFERING UNTO THE LORD. R. Judah discoursed on the verse: "Is it not to deal thy bread to the hungry...?" (Isa. LVIII, 7). 'Happy', he said, 'is the lot of him who happens to meet with a poor man, as the poor man is a present that God has sent him. Whoever receives that present with a cheerful countenance, happy is his portion. See now. Whoever takes compassion on a poor man and quickens his soul, the Holy One counts it to him as though he had created his soul. Hence, because Abraham took compassion on all men, God counted it to him as though he had created them, as it is written, "and the souls that they had made ('asu) in Horan" (Gen. XII, 5). The term "paros" (breaking) has also the significance of "spreading", it being incumbent on the host to spread for the poor man a table-cloth for the bread and other food offered. Again, the term "paros", in its significance of "breaking", teaches that it is the proper thing to cut the bread for the poor man into slices, so that he should not feel ashamed, and that there should be no stinting: "thy bread", says Scripture, thy emphatically, thine own property, but not that gotten by robbery or violence or theft; for, in that case, so far from its being a source of merit, it will be a reminder, woe to him! of his sins. Similarly, in our text it says: "Take ye from among you an offering", from among you emphatically, but not from what has been gotten by violence, robbery or theft.'

R. Hiya and R. Isaac and R. Yose were walking together on the road when R. Abba met them. Said R. Hiya: 'Assuredly the Shekinah is with us.' R. Abba, when he came up with them, expounded the verse: "Since the day that I brought forth my people Israel out of Egypt, I chose no city out of all the tribes of Israel to build a house, that my name might be there; but I chose David to be over my people Israel" (I Kings VIII, 16). 'This verse', he said, 'does not seem to be logically constructed. It begins, "I chose no city", and ends, "but I chose David", instead of, as we should expect, "but I chose Jerusalem". What connection have the two with each other? But the truth is, that when it is the pleasure of the Holy One, blessed be He, to build a city, He first considers who shall be the leader of its people, and not until then does He build the city and bring the people into it. The verse then says, in effect, "I chose no city until I had observed David to be fitting shepherd of Israel." For a city with all its inhabitants depends for its existence on the care of the people's shepherd and leader. If the latter be a good shepherd, it is well with him, well with the city, and well with the people; but if he be an evil shepherd, woe to him, woe to the city, and woe to the people!

'Thus, the Holy One, blessed be He, when He looked at the world and decided to build the city, first raised up David, as it says, "but I chose David", etc.'

'This is a new thought, what we have just heard', said his Companions.

R. Abba then further discoursed as follows. 'It is written, "Happy is he whose help is the God of Jacob, whose hope (sibro) is in the Lord his God" (PS. CXLVI, 5). Why "the God of Jacob", and not "the God of Abraham", or "the God of Isaac"? The reason is that Jacob placed his trust neither in his father nor in his mother when he fled from his brother and went on his way alone, penniless, as Scripture says, "for with my staff I passed over this Jordan" (Gen. XXXII, 11), but he put his trust in the Almighty, as it is written, "If God will be with me, and will keep me" (Ibid. XXVIII, 20); and he made all his requests only to the Holy One, blessed be He, who granted them to him. Further, the term "sibro" (whose hope) can also be read (by a change in the diacritical point) shibro (being bruised), pointing to the righteous who are content to be broken and bruised and to submit to tribulation upon tribulation, and all for the sake of "the Lord his God. So Scripture says: "Nay, but for thy sake are we killed all

Zohar: Shemoth, Section 2, Page 198b

the day" (Ps. XLIV, 23); and further, "Because for thy sake [Tr. note: The text of the Zohar wrongly quotes "we" instead of "I".] we have borne reproach" (Ibid. LXIX, 8). This was exemplified in Jacob, of whom it is written: "Now Jacob saw that there was crushing [Tr. note: Sheber= corn; also=crushing, breaking, misfortune.] in Egypt" (Gen. XLII, 1), indicating that Jacob foresaw the calamity of the exile that he would undergo in Egypt, but he placed his confidence in the Holy One, blessed be He. Similarly, the children of Jacob endured the calamity of exile, and yet did not deviate from the essence of the faith of their ancestors, the name of the Holy One, blessed be He, always having been, in the midst of the exile, on their lips. Hence the words of Moses: "and they shall say unto me: What (mah) is his name" (Ex. III, 13), signifying that the Israelites knew the Holy One, blessed be He, at no time having forgotten Him, but having suffered the pangs of exile for His sake. For the sake of this they merited redemption and great miracles and signs. Now, you exalted saints who endure bodily affliction in wandering from place to place for the sake of the Holy One, blessed be He, how much more are you worthy that miracles and acts of redemption should be performed for you, and that you should win the life of the world to come!'

They then proceeded on their journey together, and R. Abba then opened a discourse on the text: "Take ye from among you an offering unto the Lord, whosoever is of a willing heart let him bring it", etc. 'Observe', he said, 'that when a man wills to serve his Master, his desire is first generated in the heart, which is the basis and the active principle of the whole body. From thence the desire is diffused through all the members of the body, so that the desire of the rest of the members of the body, and the desire of the heart, unite into one whole and draw upon themselves the resplendence of the Shekinah to reside with them. Such a man becomes himself, as it were, a portion of the Holy One, blessed be He. Scripture thus says: "Take you from among you", or, in other words, "take you of your very selves, and become yourselves an offering and a portion for the Lord. And so that no one should say that this is not within man's power, observe the sentence saying, "whosoever is of a willing heart, let him bring it, the Lord's offering". Assuredly so, whosoever is of a willing heart may draw unto himself the Shekinah, may bring her (yebieha) from on high, may draw her from the supernal region to reside with him; and when she comes to reside with him, how many blessings, and how much riches, does she bring with her! So Scripture says, "gold, and silver, and brass", so that nothing is lacking for him of all the riches of the world. This', R. Abba concluded, 'is for the rest of mankind, but you exalted saints, "take from among you an offering unto the Lord". [Tr. note: i.e. the Shekinah is already among you, and you must raise Her on high.] Said R. Hiya: 'He who has begun to take an offering, let him continue in the work.'

R. Abba then discoursed on the text: "And the Lord (had) said unto the fish, and it vomited out Jonah upon the dry land" (Jonah II, 11). 'Where and when did God speak to the fish?' he asked. 'It was', he replied, 'at the time of Creation, when the Holy One, blessed be He, created the world; to wit, on the fifth day, when He created the fishes of the sea. Then He ordained and appointed a certain fish to swallow up Jonah and retain him in its body three days and three nights and then eject him. And not only in this case, but with all that He created did God make certain stipulations. Thus, on the first day, when He created the heavens, He stipulated with them that they should take up Elijah into heaven by a whirlwind, and so it was, as it is written, "and Elijah went up [Tr. note: And it does not say, "and God took up", by a special act.] by a whirlwind into heaven" (2 Kings II, 11). On the same day He created the light and stipulated with it that the sun should become darkened in Egypt three days, as it is written, "and there was a thick darkness in all the land of Egypt three days" (Ex. x, 22). On the second day He created the firmament to divide the waters from the waters, and in doing so He stipulated that they should separate between defilement and purity on behalf of Israel and be to them a means of cleansing, and so it was. On the third day He made the dry land emerge from the waters and caused the waters to be gathered together into one place, forming from them the sea, and He stipulated with it that it should allow the Israelites to pass through it on dry land and then overwhelm the Egyptians. And so it happened, as it is written, "and the sea returned to its strength when the morning appeared" (Ex. XIV, 27), where the term l'ethano (to its strength), by a transposition of letters, can be read litnao (to its stipulation). In addition, God stipulated with the earth that it should open its mouth on the occasion of the rebellion of Korah and swallow him up with all his company. And so it happened. On the fourth day he created the sun and the moon, and He stipulated with the sun that he should stand still in the midst of heaven in the days of Joshua.

Zohar: Shemoth, Section 2, Page 199a

He also stipulated with the stars that they should wage war against Sisera. On the fifth day He created the fishes of the sea and the birds of heaven. With the birds he stipulated that they should feed Elijah when he restrained the heaven from rain, as it is written: "and I have commanded the ravens to feed thee there" (I Kings XVII, 4); and He stipulated with the fishes of the sea to appoint one fish that should swallow up Jonah and then eject him. On the sixth day He created Adam and stipulated with him that a woman should descend from him who should sustain Elijah, as it is written, "Behold I have commanded a widow there to sustain thee" (Ibid. XVII, 9). Similarly, in regard to every unique phenomenon that has happened in the world, the Holy One, blessed be He, had predestined it from the time when the world was created. And so here the meaning of "And the Lord said to the fish" is that He had commanded it at the creation of the world.

'In the story of Jonah we have a representation of the whole of a man's career in this world. Jonah descending into the ship is symbolic of man's soul that descends into this world to enter into his body. Why is she called Jonah (lit. aggrieved)? Because as soon as she becomes partner with the body in this world she finds herself full of vexation. Man, then, is in this world as in a ship that is traversing the great ocean and is like to be broken, as it says, "so that the ship was like to be broken" (Jonah I, 4). Furthermore, man in this world commits sins, imagining that he can flee from the presence of his Master, who takes no notice of this world. The Almighty then rouses a furious tempest; to wit, man's doom, which constantly stands before the Holy One, blessed be He, and demands his punishment. It is this which assails the ship and calls to mind man's sins that it may seize him; and the man is thus caught by the tempest and is struck down by illness, just as Jonah "went down into the innermost part of the ship; and he lay, and was fast alseep". Although the man is thus prostrated, his soul does not exert itself to return to his Master in order to make good his omissions. So "the shipmaster came to him", to wit, the good prompter, who is the general steersman, "and said unto him: What meanest thou that thou sleepest? Arise, call upon thy God", etc.; it is not a time to sleep, as they are about to take thee up to be tried for all that thou hast done in this world. Repent of thy sins. Reflect on these things and return to thy Master. "What is thine occupation", wherein thou wast occupied in this world; and make confession concerning it before the Master; "and whence comest thou"; to wit, from a fetid drop, and so be not thou arrogant before him. "What is thy country"—reflect that from earth thou wast created and to earth thou wilt return; "and of what people art thou"; that is, reflect whether thou canst rely on merits of thy forbears to protect thee. When they bring him to judgement before the Heavenly Tribunal, that tempest, that is none other than the judgement doom which raged against him, demands from the King the punishment of all the King's prisoners, and then all the King's counsellors appear before Him one by one, and the Tribunal is set up. Some plead in defence of the accused, others against him. Should the man be found guilty, as in the case of Jonah, then "the men rowed hard to bring it to the land, but they could not"; so those who plead on his behalf find points in his favour and strive to restore him to this world, but they cannot; "for the sea grew more and more tempestuous against them", the prosecution storms and rages against him, and, convicting him of his sins, prevails against his defenders. Then three appointed messengers descend upon the man; one of them makes a record of all the good deeds and the misdeeds that he has performed in this world; one casts up the reckoning of his days; and the third is the one who has accompanied the man from the time when he was in his mother's womb. As already said, the doom summons is not appeased until "they took up Jonah", until they take him from the house to the place of burial. Then proclamation is made concerning him. If he was a righteous man, it runs, Render honour to the King's image! "He entereth into peace, they rest in their beds, each one that walketh in his uprightness" (Isa. LVII, 2).

Zohar: Shemoth, Section 2, Page 199b

But when a wicked man dies, the proclamation runs: Woe to that man, it would have been better for him had he never been born! Regarding such a man it is written, "and they cast him forth into the sea, and the sea ceased from its raging", that is, only after they have placed him in the grave, which is the place of judgement, does the judgement summons cease from its raging. For the fish that swallowed him is, in fact, the grave; and so "Jonah was in the belly of the fish", which is identified with "the belly of the underworld" (Sheol), as is proved by the passage, "Out of the belly of the underworld (sheol) cried I". "Three days and three nights": these are the three days that a man lies in his grave before his belly splits open. After three days it ejects the putrid matter on his face, saying: "Take back what thou gavest me; thou didst eat and drink all day and never didst thou give anything to the poor; all thy days were like feasts and holidays, whilst the poor remained hungry without partaking of any of thy food. Take back what thou gavest me." In regard to this it is written: "and I will spread dung upon your faces", etc. (Malachi II, 3). Again, after the lapse of three days, the man receives chastisement in each organ-in his eyes, his hands, and his feet. This continues for thirty days, during which time the soul and the body are chastised together. The soul therefore remains all that time on earth below, not ascending to her place, like a woman remaining apart all the days of her impurity. After that the soul ascends whilst the body is being decomposed in the earth, where it will lie until the time when the Holy One, blessed be He, will awaken the dead. A voice will then resound through the graves, proclaiming: "Awake and sing, ye that dwell in the dust, for thy dew is as the dew of light, and the earth shall cast forth the dead (rephaim)" (Isa. XXVI, 19). That will come to pass when the Angel of Death will depart from the world, as it is written: "He will destroy death forever, and the Lord God will wipe away tears from off all faces; and the reproach of his people will he take away from off all the earth" (Ibid. xxv, 8). It is of that occasion that it is written: "And the Lord spoke unto the fish, and it vomited out Jonah upon the dry land"; for as soon as that voice will resound among the graves they will all cast out the dead bodies that they contain. The term rephaim (the dead) being akin to the root, rapha (healing), indicates that the dead will be restored to their former physical condition. But, you may say, is it not written elsewhere, "the rephaim will not rise" (Ibid. XXVII, 14)? The truth is that all the dead will be restored to their former state whilst in the graves, but some of them will rise and others will not. Happy is the portion of Israel, of whom it is written, "My dead bodies shall arise" (Ibid. XXVII, 19). Thus in the narrative of that fish we find words of healing for the whole world. As soon as it swallowed Jonah it died, but after three days was restored to life and vomited him forth. In a similar way the Land of Israel will in the future first be stirred to new life, and afterwards "the earth will cast forth the dead".

'It has been affirmed that in quitting this world a man has to endure seven ordeals. The first is the judgement of heaven when the spirit leaves the body. The second is when his actions and utterances march in front of him and make proclamation concerning him. The third is when he is placed in the grave. The fourth is the ordeal of the grave itself. The fifth consists in his being consumed by the worms. The sixth is the suffering endured in Gehenna. The seventh ordeal is that his spirit is condemned to roam to and fro in the world, and is not able to find a resting place until his appointed tasks have been completed. Hence it behoves man continually to review his actions and to repent before his Master. When David reflected on these ordeals which a man has to endure he made haste to exclaim: "Bless the Lord, O my soul, and all my inward parts, bless his holy name" (Ps. CIII, 1), as much as to say: "Bless the Lord, O my soul, before thou quittest the world, whilst thou still inhabitest the body; and all my inward parts, all the members of the body that are in union with the spirit, whilst this union still lasts, hasten to bless His holy name, before the time will come when you will not be able to bless or to repent." David therefore repeats again: "Bless the Lord, O my soul, Hallelukah" (Ibid. CIII, 22).

R. Abba ceased, and the Companions approached him and kissed him on his head. R. Hiya then began a discourse on the text:

Zohar: Shemoth, Section 2, Page 200a

Take ye from among you an offering (t'rumah) unto the Lord. 'When God', he said, 'created the world, He did so for no other purpose than that Israel should one day come and receive the Torah. It was by means of the Torah that the world was created, and it is on the Torah that the world is established. So Scripture says: "Were it not for my covenant that endureth day and night, the ordinances of heaven and earth I would not have appointed" (Jer. XXXIV, 25). The Torah is length of life in this world and in the world to come. And he who labours in the Torah labours in the Palace of the Holy One, blessed be He, inasmuch as the supernal Temple of the Holy One is the Torah itself. And whenever a man labours in the Torah, there the Holy One, blessed be He, stands and listens to his voice, as it is written: "And the Lord hearkened, and heard, and a book of remembrance was written before him, for them that feared the Lord, and that thought upon his name" (Malachi III, 16); and that man escapes three ordeals: the ordeal of this world, the ordeal of the Angel of Death, who has no power over him, and the ordeal of Gehenna. What is the "book of remembrance"? It is an allusion to the duplicate Book which is at once above and below. [Tr. note: v Zohar, Ex. 70a.] The term "remembrance" is a designation of the region of the holy covenant and concentrates and gathers within itself the whole of the supernal life-energy. Hence, "book of remembrance" signifies the two grades that are yet one. [Tr. note: Malkuth and Yesod.] This is the underlying mystery of the "name Tetragrammaton", of which the Name is one and Tetragrammaton is one, yet the two are only one. For there is name and name. There is the name on high [Tr. note: Hohmah.] that is the sign of the unknown, of that which is above and outside all knowledge-it is the supernal point; and there is the name below which is expressive of the central point here below. So Scripture says: "from the one end of the heaven unto the other" (Deut. IV, 32), that is, from the supernal point that concentrates within itself all the supernal life-energy "unto the lower end of heaven", which bears the name "lower central point". [Tr. note: Malkuth.] This point is identical with the "book", and, being in the centre, it unites within itself all the world's directions; six directions come to a union in the supernal book which is above and over them, and six directions find their union again in the lower book which is above and over them; and the two, the supernal book and the lower book, constitute together the Law (Torah), the one the written Law, it being undisclosed and only to be revealed in the world to come, the other the oral Law. Of the written Law the writing is made, as it were, into a Palace of the central point, wherein the Law is concealed. The lower Law, on the other hand, is not embodied in writing, and hence is not constructed into a Palace for the central point beneath as is the superior Law for the supernal point. Hence, also, the oral Law is designated t'rumah (heave-offering, something separated), being apart and separated. I have further heard from the Sacred Lamp (R. Simeon) that the t'rumah is meant to be resolved into tre (two) and meah (hundred), indicating two out of a hundred. For the sum of the holy grades involved in the mystery of Faith, by which the Holy One, blessed be He, manifests Himself, amounts to ten, and these are also ten utterances. The whole thus amounts to a hundred; and so in bringing an offering [Tr. note: A side allusion to the heave-offering (t'rumah) due to the priest which, according to the Mishnah, normally consisted of a fiftieth part (2/100) of the produce.] we have to combine the lower central point with the supernal central point, so as to unite the Shekinah with her Spouse, these being the two of the hundred grades and sub-grades just mentioned.

'Observe too that every day a proclamation goes forth, saying, "O ye peoples, this thing depends on your own effort". And this is the sense of the words,

Zohar: Shemoth, Section 2, Page 200b

"Take ye from among you an offering unto the Lord", not as a burden, but "whosoever is of a willing heart let him bring her (yevieha)". [Tr. note: i.e. the Shekinah.] From this we learn that prayer offered with concentrated devotion by a man that fears his Master produces great effects on high, as already said elsewhere. First come the songs and hymns chanted by the angels on high, and the series of hymns recited by Israel here below. With these the Shekinah decks and adorns herself like a woman who prepares to meet her spouse. Then follows the recital of prayer. By virtue of the prayer they recite while sitting they adorn her bridesmaids and all her retinue. By the time "True and firm" [Tr. note: Benediction following the recital of Sh'ma and preceding the 'Amidah.] is reached, the bride with all her attendant damsels is fully arrayed. When the worshippers reach "who hast redeemed Israel", [Tr. note: Conclusion of above-mentioned benediction.] the whole assembly has to stand up. For at the moment "true and firm" is reached the bride's attendants accompany her towards the Most High King, but when it comes to "who hast redeemed Israel", the Holy and Most High King appears in His grades and comes out to receive her; and we must then stand on our feet in awe and trembling before the Most High King, as it is the moment when he stretches forth His right hand towards Her, and then puts His left hand under her head, then there is a mutual embracing and kisses. This comes to pass during the first three benedictions. It behoves, then, a man to concentrate his thoughts and to focus his mind on these great effects and on the ordering of the prayer. His mouth, his heart, his thoughts, must all work in unison. The Most High King and the Matrona being then in close and joyful embrace, whosoever has a petition to offer let him do so now, as it is an opportune moment. After having made his request of the King and the Matrona, he must then concentrate his thought and mind upon the last three benedictions so as to excite the inner delight, since by these benedictions the Shekinah is blessed with another embrace, in which he takes his departure. Withal, it should be his intention that the denizens of this world also should be blessed. The worshipper has next to fall on his face in token of surrender of his soul, among all the souls and spirits which the Shekinah at that moment collects in the "bundle of life". This I have heard among the mysteries expounded to me by the Sacred Lamp, who has not permitted me to reveal it save to you, o exalted saints. For whosoever surrenders his soul so at that moment will be bound in the bundle of life in this world and in the world to come. Moreover, it is important that the King and the Matrona should be united both above and below, and be crowned with a crown wrought of the souls above and the souls below; and whosoever concentrates his mind and heart on all this and surrenders his soul in complete devotion, the Holy One, blessed be He, names him "peace" below after the pattern of the peace above, as we read, "and the Lord called him peace" (Judges VI, 24). And when that man's soul quits this world it ascends and cleaves its way through all the heavens, and nothing can stop it, the Holy One, blessed be He, proclaiming: "He entereth into peace" (Isa. LVII, 2), and the Shekinah adding, "may they rest in their beds", etc. (Ibid.); and they open up for it

Zohar: Shemoth, Section 2, Page 201a

thirteen mountains of pure perfume, without let or hindrance. Hence, happy is the man who concentrates his thought on this. This, then, is the sense of "whosoever is of a willing heart, let him bring it, the Lord's offering", to wit, toward the Most High King.' R. Abba then lifted up his voice and said: 'Woe! O Rabbi Simeon! thou art living and we weep concerning thee; but we weep not for thee, we weep for the Companions and for the world. R. Simeon is like a bright lamp which throws light above and below. Alas for the world, for the time when the lower illumination will pass away and be absorbed in the upper illumination! Who will then diffuse through the world the light of the Torah?' R. Abba then rose and kissed R. Hiya, saying: 'You were in possession of these thoughts, hence the Holy One, blessed be He, sent me hither to become one of your company. Happy is my portion!'

R. Yose then followed with a discourse on the text: And let every wise-hearted man among you come and make, etc. 'This passage', he said, 'has already been expounded. When God said to Moses, "Get you wise men and men of discernment" (Deut. I, 13), the latter searched the whole of Israel but did not find men of discernment; it is thus written, "So I took the heads of your tribes, wise men, and full of knowledge" (Ibid. I, 15), without mentioning men of discernment. Assuredly the man of discernment (naban) is of a higher degree than the wise man (hakham). Even a pupil who gives new ideas to his teacher is called "wise". A wise man, then, it is true, knows for himself as much as is required, but the man of discernment apprehends the whole, knowing both his own point of view and that of others. The term "wisehearted" is used here because the seat of wisdom is the heart. As for the man of discernment, he apprehends the lower world and the upper world, his own being and the being of others.'

R. Yose further discoursed on the verse: "And He said unto me: Thou art my servant, Israel, in whom I will be glorified" (Isa. XLIX, 3). 'Observe', he said, 'that there is an outer and bodily worship of the Holy One, blessed be He, and an inner and spiritual worship which is the true and genuine worship. The body possesses twelve members that participate in rendering worship. These are the outer members of the body, but there are also twelve inner members whose act of worship is of benefit to the spirit. For this is the inner and precious worship of the Holy One, blessed be He, as expounded among the mysteries taught by R. Simeon, and as belonging to the mysteries of supernal wisdom known to the Companions, happy is their portion! Prayer is spiritual worship. Deep mysteries are attached to it, for men wot not that a man's prayer cleaves the ethereal spaces, cleaves the firmament, opens doors and ascends on high. At the moment of daybreak, when light emerges from darkness, a proclamation resounds through all the firmaments, saying: Make yourselves ready, ye sentinels at the doors, chiefs of the Palace-each one to his post! For the day-attendants are not the same as the night-attendants, the two groups replacing each other with the succession of day and night. This is alluded to in the passage, "the greater light for to rule the day", etc. (Gen. I, 16), "the rule of the day" and "the rule of the night" signifying the day-attendants and the night-attendants. When night arrives proclamation is made, saying: Make yourselves ready, O ye rulers of the night-each

Zohar: Shemoth, Section 2, Page 201b

one to his place! Similarly, when day breaks a proclamation goes forth: Make yourselves ready, ye rulers of the day-each one to his place! Each one thus, following the proclamation, is assigned his suitable place. The Shekinah then descends whilst Israel enter the Synagogue to offer praise to their Master in song and hymn. It behoves, then, every man, after equipping himself with emblems of holiness, [Tr. note: Fringes and phylacteries.] to attune his heart and his inner being for that act of worship and to say his prayers with devotion. For the words that he utters ascend on high, for the scrutiny of angelic supervisors. These abide in ethereal space on the four sides of the world. On the eastern side there is the chief supervisor, whose name is Gezardiya, and who is attended by a number of other chieftains, all awaiting the word of prayer that is about to ascend to the ethereal realm on that side. The moment it does so the supervisor takes it up. If it be fitly uttered, he, together with all the other chieftains, kisses that utterance and carries it aloft into the supernal firmament, where other chieftains are awaiting it. When kissing the utterance of prayer they say: "Happy are ye, O Israel, who know how to crown your Master with holy crowns. Happy is the mouth from which issued this utterance, this crown." Then the letters of the Divine Name that abide in the ethereal space soar upwards. That Divine Name is formed of twelve letters, and is the one by which Elijah flew to the ethereal regions until he reached heaven. This is indicated in the words that Obadiah spoke to Elijah, saying, "...that the spirit of the Lord (Tetragrammaton) will carry thee...." For it was that Name by which Elijah flew upwards, and it is that Name that rules the ethereal space. The letters, then, of the Name fly upwards with the prayer-utterance, in company with the chief who holds the keys of the ether, and all the other chiefs, until heaven is reached, where the prayer is taken in charge by another chief to carry it still higher. On the southern side there is another chieftain ruling over the ethereal space of that region and having under him a number of supervisors and officers. His name is Pesagniyah, and he is in charge of the keys of the ethereal space in that quarter. Now the prayer of persons in deep sorrow and anguish, if uttered with due devotion, ascends into that region and is taken up by the chief, who kisses it and pronounces over it the words, "The Holy One, blessed be He, be merciful towards thee and be filled with compassion on thy behalf." Then all the chieftains and officers administering that region accompany it upwards, along with the letters of the Divine Name-to wit, the Name of four letters that rule that region-until it reaches the heaven over that region. There it is taken in charge by the chief of that region. The name of the one in charge of the northerly region, who also has under his command a number of chieftains and officers, is Petahyah. He is appointed over that side to which prayers offered for deliverance from enemies ascend. If such a prayer be found worthy, the chief takes it up and kisses it. Then a spirit emerges out of the abyss in the North who makes proclamation through all the ethereal spaces, so that they all take up that prayer and carry it into heaven, all the while kissing it and exclaiming, "May thy Master cast thy enemy down before thee." It then ascends and cleaves the heavens. [Tr. note: Al. and ethereal spaces.] When it reaches the first heaven it is met by the chief of the West, whose name is Zebuliel, and who presides over numerous chieftains and officers that stand sentry over nine doors. The same Zebuliel would fain minister in that heaven in the daytime, but he is not permitted until moonlight appears, when he comes out with all those legions and chieftains. But when day breaks they all retire through one, the most prominent of the nine doors. Now any ascending prayer

Zohar: Shemoth, Section 2, Page 202a

enters through that door, and then all officers and chieftains, under the guidance of Zebuliel their chief, emerge through that door. They embrace it, and accompany it to the second heaven. That heaven is fitted with twelve gates, at the twelfth of which there stands a chief, named 'Anael, who is in command of numerous hosts and legions. And when the prayer arrives there that chief loudly orders all those doors to be opened, exclaiming, "Open ye the gates", etc. (Isa. XXVI, 2). All the gates then open, and the prayer enters through all the doors. Then arises a chief, ancient of days, who is placed at the northern side, and whose name is 'Azriel the Ancient, though sometimes he is called Mahniel (lit. mighty camp). This other name is given him because he commands sixty myriads of legions. All these legions are winged, part of them are full of eyes, and by their side are others full of ears. These are called "ears" because they listen to all those who pray in a whisper, from the heart, so that the prayer should not be overheard by anyone else. Only such a prayer is accepted by these "all-eared" legions, whereas a prayer that is heard by the ears of man is not listened to on high, and so remains unheard by anyone save by him who overheard it at first. Hence it behoves man to be careful not to let others hear his prayer. Furthermore, prayer becomes absorbed in the upper world, and the speech of the upper world should remain inaudible. Similarly, in the reading of the Book of the Law, while one reads, the other standing by him should be silent. For, if two read together faith is diminished, because voice and utterance are only one. For only a single voice and a single recital must be heard; so that if there are two voices and two utterances there is a diminution of Divine Faith. When the silent prayer soars aloft, all those sixty myriads of legions, all those "all-eye" and "all-ear" hosts, come forward and kiss it. So Scripture says: "The eyes of the Lord are toward the righteous, and his ears are open unto their cry" (Ps. XXXIV, 16), indicating the "all-eye" and the "all-ear" legions. From thence the prayer mounts to the third heaven, the chief of which is Gedariah, who has under him numerous officers and chiefs. He ministers three times a day in the presence of a ray of light that is constantly shooting up and down in that heaven without ever being still. And when the prayer mounts up there that ray descends and bows down before it. Then the chief of that heaven, after bowing down to the prayer, strikes with the ray of light against a mighty rock that is placed in the centre of that heaven, and there emerge from it three hundred and seventy-five legions that have been confined within it since the day the Torah came down to earth. They were so confined because they endeavoured to prevent the Torah descending on earth, and God rebuked and shut them up in the interior of that rock, whence they do not emerge save at the time when prayer ascends. They then break forth into song, chanting: "O Lord, our Lord, how glorious is thy name... above the heavens" (Ps. VIII, 2). They then bow to the prayer, after which it is crowned with supernal crowns and mounts up into the fourth heaven. Then comes forth the sun and Shamshiel (=mighty sun or sun of God) the chief enters that heaven accompanied by three hundred and sixty-five legions called days of the solar year, and they all crown that prayer with crowns of sweet perfume of the Garden of Eden. There it tarries until all those legions accompany it into the fifth heaven, the chief of which is Gadriel. This angel is in charge of the wars waged among the nations, but as soon as the prayer arives there a trembling seizes him with all his hosts so that

Zohar: Shemoth, Section 2, Page 202b

their strength is enfeebled; and they come forward and bow down to the prayer, and crown it and accompany it into the sixth heaven. There numerous hosts and legions come out to receive it and ascend with it until they reach a series of seventy gates in charge of a chief whose name is 'Anpiel. He crowns the prayer with seventy crowns. Then all the hosts and legions of all these heavens join together and take up that prayer, crowned with all these crowns, into the seventh heaven. Finally Sandalphon, the supreme chief, the keeper of all his Master's keys, introduces the prayer into the seven Palaces, to wit, the Palaces of the King. When the prayer enters there, decorated with all those crowns, it combines them all into one heavenly crown, each prayer according to its rank. And the name of the Holy One, blessed be He, is crowned on all sides, above and below, so that the whole forms a unity. Of this Scripture says: "Blessings are upon the head of the righteous" (Prov. x, 6). Happy is the portion of the man who knows the proper way in which to order his prayer. The Holy One, blessed be He, being glorified in such a prayer, awaits the completion of all the prayers of Israel, so that the whole is fitly harmonized, both the above and the below.

'So far we have spoken of prayer. But there are in addition certain precepts that are bound up, not with action, but with the words of prayer. These are in number six. The first is "to fear the glorious and awful Name" (Deut. XXVIII, 58); the second is "to love Him" (Ibid. x, 12); the third is to bless Him; the fourth is to proclaim His unity; the fifth enjoins the priests to bless the people; the sixth bids man to surrender his soul to Him. These six precepts are bound up with the words of prayer, just as there are other precepts that are connected with the action of prayer, such as those of the fringes and phylacteries. Now the injunction "to fear the Name" is accomplished by means of the hymns and songs that King David chanted, and of the sacrifices ordained by the Torah. For it behoves man to be filled thereby with fear of his Master, for those hymns belong to a region called "Fear" (yir'ah), [Tr. note: Malkuth.] and all the Hallelukahs are emblematic of the fear of the Holy One, [Tr. note: Because the word Hallelukah has the same numerical value as Elohim, signifying the attribute of Justice.] blessed be He; it thus behoves man to attune his mind to a spirit of awe in the recital of those hymns. In arriving at "Praised be" it behoves a man to concentrate his thoughts on the Holy One, blessed be He, in that benediction which reads: "Blessed art Thou... who formest light... Blessed art Thou, O Lord creator of the universe." The precept, "to love Him", is realized in the benediction commencing with "With abundant love", which is followed by the reading of "And thou shalt love the Lord thy God...", containing the mystery of the love of the Holy One, blessed be He. And we proclaim His unity when we recite "Hear, O Israel: the Lord our God, the Lord is One", as that declaration contains the secret of God's oneness. After the reading of these sections comes the passage wherein we mention our exodus from Egypt, in fulfilment of the injunction, "But thou shalt remember that thou wast a bondman in Egypt" (Deut. XXIV, 18). There follows the pronouncement of the blessing of the people by the priests in order to embrace all Israel at the moment when they receive blessings. For at that moment the Community of Israel receives blessings, and it is a propitious moment to surrender our souls to Him in the full willingness of our heart when we fall on our faces and recite the Psalm: "Unto Thee, O Lord, do I lift up my soul..." (Ps. xxv, 1), which should be the expression of our full and complete self-surrender to Him. These are the six precepts that are bound up with our daily prayer, and that comprise in a way the six hundred precepts of the Torah. If you ask, What of the thirteen left over, [Tr. note: There being, according to the Rabbinic reckoning, six hundred and thirteen precepts.] these are a category apart designed to draw upon us the thirteen attributes of mercy that comprise all the precepts. These are the six precepts by which prayer is embroidered. Happy is the portion of whoever concentrates his heart and will on them and realizes

Zohar: Shemoth, Section 2, Page 203a

them every day. With these precepts many others are interwoven, but at each particular passage it behoves man to concentrate his heart and will on the particular precept contained in that passage. Such a man is praised aloud in the words contained in the passage: "And He said unto me: Thou art My servant, Israel, in whom I will be glorified" (Isa. XLIX, 3).'

R. Yose ceased, and R. Abba went up to him and kissed him; and R. Isaac next began a discourse on the text: And Moses assembled all the congregation of the children of Israel, etc. 'The object', he said, 'of this assembling was to give them anew the law of the Sabbath. For the previous promulgation of the Sabbath before the Israelites made the golden calf was not observed by the mixed multitude. When they heard the words, "between Me and the children of Israel" (Ex. XXXI, 17), they said in protest: Are we then to be excluded from this? Straightway, "the people gathered themselves together unto Aaron", etc. (Ibid. XXXII, 1), and many were they that followed them. Then, after the guilty ones were put to death, Moses assembled the children of Israel separately and gave them the Sabbath anew, saying: "Six days shall work be done... Ye shall kindle no fire throughout your habitations upon the Sabbath day." Herein is involved the mystery of the Sabbath, the supreme mystery that is only revealed to those versed in the Supreme Wisdom. On the sixth day, when the time of evening arrives, a brilliant star appears in the north accompanied by seventy other stars. That star smites the others, absorbing them all into itself, so that one takes the place of seventy. The same star then becomes enlarged, and is made into a fiery mass, blazing on all sides. The flaming mass then extends itself round a thousand thousand mountains, becoming in the process a mere thread. After this the fiery mass draws out from within itself a variety of colours. The first is a green colour. When that colour appears, the fiery mass raises itself and plunges into the midst of the green colour, occupying the inner part of it. Then the fiery mass of the star attracts within itself the white colour. Then it ascends on high and plunges again in the midst of that colour, occupying its interior. The same is repeated with the whole gamut of colours, all of which it thrusts outside, concentrating itself more and, more in the middle until it approaches that hidden point to derive light therefrom.'

At this point R. Isaac quoted the verse: "And I looked, and, behold, a stormy wind came out of the north, a great cloud, with a fire flashing up, so that a brightness was round about it; and out of the midst thereof as the form of electrum (hashmal), out of the midst of the fire" (Ezek. I, 4). 'Ezekiel', he said, 'saw this vision with a completeness which is only possible when the above-mentioned star is in the ascendant. The "stormy wind" has been explained as being a reference to the storm that came to subdue the whole world before the wicked Nebuchadnezzar. But in reality the "stormy wind" is identical with the star that swallowed up the other seventy stars; and it is the same "stormy wind" that Elijah saw "rending the mountains and breaking in pieces the rocks" (1 Kings XIX, 11); it is, moreover, the force that continually protects the inward part as the membrane protects the brain. It is called "stormy wind" because it shakes the upper world and the lower worlds; it "came out of the north", from the side of which it is said, "Out of the north the evil shall break forth" (Jer. 1, 14), for many other sinister forces were united within that "stormy wind"; hence its origin was the north. "A great cloud": so called because it represents the dross of the gold that concentrates itself in the north and forms the central point of destruction; [Tr. note: v, p. 184b.] and being skilled in the arts of seduction it obtains power within the inhabited region, save in the Land of Israel, where, during the time Israel dwelt therein, it had no power; but after Israel sinned it obtained power, even in the Holy Land, as Scripture says: "He hath drawn back his right hand from before the enemy" (Lam. II, 3). "A great cloud" indicates the cloud of darkness that darkened the whole world. Observe the difference between this cloud and the other cloud. Of the other cloud

Zohar: Shemoth, Section 2, Page 203b

it is written: "And the cloud of the Lord was over them by day" (Num. x, 34), also, "and thy cloud standeth over them" (Ibid. XIV, 14), indicating the bright and luminous cloud wherein there are visible all varieties of light. But this cloud is the cloud of utter darkness that prevents any light whatever from penetrating through it. Really it is insignificant, but it is called a "great cloud" when it obtains sway. Alternatively, it is called "great", on account of its darkness, which is so intense that it hides and makes invisible all the sources of light, thus overshadowing the whole world. "With a fire flashing up" indicates the fire of rigorous judgement that never departs from it. "And a brightness was round about it": that is, although it is all that has been described, yet "a brightness was round about it". From here we learn that, although it is the very region of defilement, yet it is surrounded by a certain brightness, and hence we may not thrust it completely out; it possesses an aspect of holiness, and hence should not be treated with contempt, but should be allowed a part in the side of holiness. Rab Hamnuna the elder took this phrase interrogatively, thus: "is there a brightness round about it?", implying that it may be treated with contempt, since its brightness is concealed within it and is not visible from without. And because the brightness is within, the verse continues, "and out of the midst thereof", to wit, of the midst of that brightness, "as the form of hashmal" (electrum). The term hashmal has been interpreted as being composed of hash and mal, meaning Hayoth (order of angels), of quivering fire. [Tr. note: The term hashmal is resolved into hayoth (beasts), esh (fire), mallel (mutter or quiver).] From the Sacred Lamp (R. Simeon), however, we have heard in exposition of this the following most recondite doctrine. As long as the foreskin rests upon the sign of the holy covenant, the holy principle is prevented from disclosing the mystery of the convenantal sign. But when the bright light enters therein and separates between foreskin and holiness, the result is hash-mal, to wit, there is a speedy uncovering of circumcision. [Tr. note: Hash =speedy, mal=circumcision.]

'To resume. On the sixth day, when the evening approaches, that blazing fire we have mentioned plunges into the midst of the colours. It is then that Israel here below prepare themselves for the Sabbath, arrange their meals, and lay their tables, each one according to his means. Then a tongue of fire emerges and strikes against that flame, so that both of them are hurled down into the cavern of the great abyss. There they remain imprisoned. That tongue of fire is of the side of the Right, and it is in virtue of that that it sweeps away the blaze of fire and confines it to the great abyss, where it abides until the Sabbath ends. At the conclusion of the Sabbath it behoves every Israelite to pronounce a benediction over fire, so that the tongue of fire, under the force of that benediction, re-emerges, retaining its command over the flame, and keeping it in subjection all that night. Observe that the moment the Sabbath begins and that blaze of fire is imprisoned, all fires of the harmful kind are similarly hidden away and supressed, including even the fire of Gehinnom, so that the sinners obtain a respite. Indeed, there is then a period of rest for all, both in the upper worlds and in the lower worlds. At the conclusion of the Sabbath, when Israel say the blessing over the light, all the fires that were hidden away re-emerge and return each to its place. Now it is in order to prevent any other fire being awakened that the injunction is given: "Ye shall kindle no fire throughout your habitations upon the Sabbath day". But it may be asked, What about the fire on the altar? The following is the explanation. Immediately on the entrance of the Sabbath, proclamation is made in all the heavens, saying: Make ready, O ye Chariot teams and legions, to meet your Master! Following this there comes forth out of the south a spirit that spreads itself

Zohar: Shemoth, Section 2, Page 204a

over all those Chariot teams and legions of the side of the Right, who are wrapt with it as with a garment. That spirit is thus called "the solemn robe of the Sabbath". Then the tables of this world are prepared in a certain Palace. Happy is the portion of the man whose table here below appears there properly laid, everything prepared in the best manner, according to his means, so that he has no cause to feel ashamed.

'When the Sabbath comes in it is incumbent on the holy people to wash away from themselves the marks of their weekday labour. For what reason? Because during the weekdays a different spirit roams about and hovers over the people, and it is in order to divest himself of that spirit and invest himself with another spirit, a spirit sublime and holy, that he must wash away the stains of the workaday world. The inner meaning of this action is as follows. All the six days are concentrated within one sacred point, where they form a unity. There is another sextet of days that stand without and belong to the "other side". Now, for holy Israel, for all those who lead a holy life during all the week, all the six days become as one with those six days that are within and that are concentrated into that central point wherein they are kept and guarded. That point, again, is hidden during the six days, but at the entrance of the Sabbath it rises on high, where it is decorated and becomes unified with the whole cycle of days, all of whom become absorbed by it. Observe this. There are days and days. There are common weekdays, as said already: these exist on the fringe, and for other nations, but there are the Sabbath [Tr. note: i.e. Sabbath as signifying, in an extensive sense, week, but, according to the Zohar, of a sanctified nature, partaking of the sanctity of the Sabbath.] days, to wit, the weekdays as they exist for Israel. Now, when that point ascends, everything else is hidden away, it alone holding sway, and it assumes the name of Sabbath (SH a BB a TH). That name, apart from its simple meaning of "rest", has an esoteric significance associating that point with the Patriarchs. For the term SH a BB a TH is resolvable into the letter shin, betokening three, [Tr. note: To wit, by the three bars in its shape.] and the term B a TH, signifying daughter, the whole indicating that the Sabbath-point, when it rises in its resplendence as an only and beloved daughter, joined to the three Patriarchs, who together with her form a complete unity. We have thus SH in (symbolic of the three Patriarchs), and B a TH (symbolic of the beloved daughter, the Sabbath-point), together forming a unity expressed in SH ab B a TH. (There is also a higher Sabbath similarly made up of the Future World (Binah) and the Central Point, which is also called bath.) When that lower Sabbath-point ascends, comes into view and bedecks itself, a spirit of rejoicing is suffused through the upper and the lower worlds. In addition, during that night that point radiates its light and spreads forth its wings over the world, so that all other powers disappear and the world abides in a state of security. As for the Israelites, each one of them becomes the habitation of an additional soul, under the influence of which all sadness and gloom and irritation are forgotten, there being only joy and gladness diffused through both the upper and the lower worlds. In its descent, the additional soul bathes itself in the sweet perfumes of the Garden of Eden, after which it descends and rests upon the holy people. Happy are they when that spirit is stirred within them. At the time of the spirit's descent there accompany it into the Garden of Eden sixty Chariot teams in all their glory, facing towards the six directions. When it arrives in the Garden of Eden all the spirits and souls abiding therein bestir themselves to meet that Sabbath spirit, and a proclamation goes forth, saying: Happy are ye, O holy people of Israel, on whom your Master has bestowed

Zohar: Shemoth, Section 2, Page 204b

an additional spirit. Here is a most recondite doctrine only known to the initiated of the mystical Wisdom. This spirit is indeed the extension of the Sabbath-point, from which it grows out and diffuses itself into the world. This constitutes the true inwardness of the Sabbath here below; and this is specially alluded to in the injunction: "Wherefore the children of Israel shall guard the Sabbath" (Ex. XXXI, 16), where the particle eth is meant to include the additional spirit that requires special attention in order that it may remain with a man. The same is indicated in the clause, "that guards the Sabbath from profaning it" (Isa. LVI, 2). Within the mystery of the special spirit there is this further mystery, to wit, that it shares in all the enjoyments and delights that Israel partakes of on that day; hence it behoves us to afford it pleasure by partaking of food and drink three times, the three meals corresponding to the three grades of Divine Faith, as explained elsewhere. Happy is the portion of whoever affords it pleasure and delight on that day. During the six days of the week that spirit experiences a heavenly bliss radiated from the Ancient of Ancients. But on the Sabbath, after it descends and bathes itself in the Garden of Eden, it shares in the bodily pleasure derived from the meal of Faith, and is thus filled with the delights both of the superior world and the lower world. Insomuch, then, as it abides with man, it is necessary for him to guard it, conformably to the Scriptural injunction: "Wherefore the children of Israel shall guard the Sabbath" (Ex. XXXI, 16), the term "Sabbath" alluding to the terrestrial Sabbath-point, and the particle eth to the special spirit which is the expansion of the same Point. When that expansion brings an affluence of holiness and beatitudes from on high on to that point, there is an effulgence of light all around, and the spirit is illumined on all sides, the heavenly and the earthly. This is alluded to in the words, "It is a sign between me and the children of Israel" (Ibid. XXXI, 17), as much as to say: "It is a portion and a heritage shared between us jointly." The heavenly part of it consists of transcendental holy bliss and sublime delight in the resplendency of the Ancient of Ancients; whilst in the terrestrial part there is the physical enjoyment of the repasts. It behoves, therefore, a man to cheer that day with sumptuous food and drink, with noble raiment, and with whatever conduces to joyfulness. And when the terrestrial portion is duly decorated and is properly tended it ascends on high and becomes merged into one with the heavenly portion; so that the "Point" becomes an amalgam of the upper and the lower worlds, and a unification of all the elements. In the mystical book of King Solomon the following recondite doctrine, as expounded by the Holy Lamp, is found. The term vayinefash (and He rested) (Ibid.) may be resolved into vai (woe), nefesh (soul), that is, woe to the soul forlorn! Now we may well argue that it should rather be woe to the body that loses the special spirit with the departure of the Sabbath. But the truth is that man possesses a certain nefesh (psyche) that attracts to itself the special spirit on the eve of Sabbath, so that that spirit takes up its abode and resides within it the whole of the Sabbath. It thus becomes a superior nefesh, with greater power and resources than it possessed before. It is in reference to this that we have learned that the nefesh of every Israelite is decorated on the Sabbath day, that decoration consisting of the special spirit within them. But at the conclusion of the Sabbath that spirit departs, and then woe to the nefesh that is thus bereft. It has lost the heavenly crown and the holy energy it thereby possessed.

'Those initiated in the higher wisdom perform their marital duties on each Sabbath night. Concerning this, we put a question to the Holy Lamp, pointing out to him that it seems to contradict the known fact that the lower Crown receives what it receives [Tr. note: i.e. the souls from on high.] in the daytime, and in the night it distributes sustenance to all its host, as Scripture says: "She rises also while it is yet night, and giveth food to her household, and a portion to her maidens" (Prov. XXXI, 15). If this be so, how can we say the proper time for intercourse is on that night in particular? He replied: Assuredly, that is the proper time for marital intercourse, insomuch as that night distributes souls for those

Zohar: Shemoth, Section 2, Page 205a

initiated in the mystical Wisdom, and no other time is appropriate for this junction to be performed with all joy without any extraneous admixture, save that night when the souls are distributed to the wise, the righteous, and the pious. Each night, indeed, may be proper for it, and that at midnight, as explained elsewhere, but it behoves the initiated to limit themselves to that night. The reason is that one spirit hovers over the world during the other days of the week, but on Sabbath night another spirit, a sacred and sublime spirit, descends for the holy people. That spirit flows from the Ancient of Ancients and descends into the lower "Sabbath-point", bringing therein rest for all, whence it expands into all directions on high and below, as it says: "between Me and the children of Israel". Hence, for those men of wisdom the proper time for that function is when that holy and exalted spirit is diffused around them, since that same spirit draws after it in its descent here below all the holy souls, so that by its means the exalted saints transmit to their offspring those holy souls.

'Furthermore, as soon as that spirit hovers over the world, all the malignant spirits and the evil accusers of men vanish from the world. And so there is then no need to pray for protection, as Israel is then under the guardianship of that spirit, with the wings of the tabernacle of peace spread over them, so that they may be perfectly secure. There is, it is true, a traditional teaching which says that a man should not go out alone either on the night of the fourth day of the week or on the night of the Sabbath, and that at these times one has to be on one's guard; and this seems to contradict what has just been said, that on Sabbath night men are shielded from all evil accusers and need not therefore offer up a special prayer. Still, all this is assuredly correct. The fourth night of the week we have to be on our guard against them, for the reason that at the creation of the lights the moon was cursed, its light diminished, and occasion was thus given to bands of malignant roving spirits to exercise power that night; on Sabbath night, again, whilst these spirits scatter themselves in order to retire into the cavern of the abyss where they are powerless to harm, a solitary man must be on his guard against them, since, although they are deprived of power, now and then they show themselves, and so a solitary wayfarer has to be on his guard. If that be so, it was said, does it not betoken an inadequate degree of security? Not so, it was answered. On the Sabbath there is protection for the holy people, and the Holy One, on the entrance of the Sabbath, decorates every member of Israel with a crown-a holy crown, which every wearer must cherish and guard. Now, although the malignant spirits do not then frequent inhabited places, they often appear to a man that walks alone, and then his "lucky star" (mazzal) deserts him. It is therefore incumbent upon a man to decorate himself with the holy crown and to guard it. Howbeit, on that night the holy people are fully protected, since the tabernacle of peace overspreads them, and tradition tells us that the tabernacle of peace and the "other side" cannot coexist together. The Sabbath day is thus a day of universal joy and security, both in the upper and the lower worlds; and the lower light, radiating into the upper world, through the resplendency of the Sabbath crowns, is there intensified seventy-fold, so that the Ancient of Ancients bestirs Himself. Then at break of day the holy people proceed to Synagogue in a joyous spirit robed in their best, crowned with the celestial holy crown and endowed with the additional celestial spirit, and there they offer up praises in songs and hymns, which mount up on high, so that the upper and the lower worlds are filled with joy and are all decorated together. Then the celestial beings hold forth and say: "Happy are ye, O holy people on earth, through whom your Master is crowned, as well as all the sacred hosts." This day is the day of the soul and not of the body, exhibiting the sway of the "bundle of souls", when the upper and the lower beings are mated

Zohar: Shemoth, Section 2, Page 205b

together in virtue of the additional celestial spirit by which man is crowned.

'The prayer offered by the holy people on the Sabbath is of three parts, corresponding to the three Sabbaths, but being in essence only one. [Tr. note: i.e. the Sabbath of the Creation, the Sabbath on which the Torah was given, and the Sabbath of the Millennium.] Once the holy people enter the precincts of the Synagogue it is forbidden them to concern themselves with anything, even the requirements of the Synagogue, save words of thanksgiving and prayer and the study of the Torah; and whoever directs his mind to other and worldly matters profanes the Sabbath, and thus has no portion among the people of Israel. For such a one two angels are appointed on the day of Sabbath, who proclaim, saying: "Woe to So-and-so who has no portion in the Holy One, blessed be He." Hence it behoves the people to absorb themselves in prayer and songs and hymns to their Master, and in the study of the Torah. It is a day of the souls, a day in which the "bundle of the souls" is decorated by the praises offered to their Master. Hence on that day is recited the "Hymn of the Soul" which reads: "The soul of every living being shall bless Thy name, O Lord our God, and the spirit of all flesh...", as that day subsists solely by the spirit and soul, and not by the body. Another hymn that concerns the mystery of day, of the sacred sun that illumines it, is "... who formest light...", to wit, the illuminating light which affords sustenance and light for all the hosts and heavenly Chariots and stars and constellations, and all those who exercise sway over the world. Then follows a Hymn of the universe, couched in the words, "God, the Lord over all works...", an alphabetical hymn which contains the mystery of the twenty-two sacred celestial letters which are decorated with a crown made of the Patriarchs and the holy heavenly Chariot. Opposite to them are the twenty-two little letters of the lower world which enter in the daily hymn that reads: "The God, the blessed One, great in knowledge...". Herein the alphabet ranges over single words in succession, there being no space between the words; whereas in the Sabbath hymn, symbolic of the upper world, there is a wide space, significant of holy mysteries, between the successive letters. The seventh day thus chants a most sublime hymn, composed of the celestial letters, in praise of the Most High King, of Him who formed the world at the beginning. When this hymn mounts up on high, sixty celestial Chariots of those alluded to before, take it up from the holy people and ascend with it to where it is woven into a crown for the decoration of the many heavenly Chariots, and for all the righteous in the Garden of Eden, all of whom mount up with that hymn to the Divine Throne. There this hymn, recited by the whole of Israel, halts until the recital of the Sanctification (k'dushah) in the additional prayer (musaph). Thus is effected the complete union of the upper and the lower worlds. So much for this hymn-the gem of all hymns. Then follows the regular daily order of prayer up to "Moses rejoiced in the gift of his portion...." This expresses the joy of the supreme grade, the chief of the "Patriarchs", who rejoices in His portion when the Divine Throne approaches Him, and the two worlds are fused into one; again, it expresses the rejoicing of the Written Law on high in the Oral Law here below, and their fusion into one. To the joy at that union we have to add the joy of the holy people as expressed in the words: "May they rejoice in Thy kingdom, those who observe the Sabbath, and call the Sabbath a delight... O God and God of our fathers, accept our rest...." Now, the inwardness of the interrelationship between the Book of the Law (Sepher Torah) and that day has been expounded elsewhere. In this regard we have been taught as follows. It is written: "And they read in the book, in the Law of God, distinctly; and they gave the sense, and caused them to understand the reading" (Nehemiah VIII, 8). The inner implication of this verse is that the verse-divisions, the tonal accents, the Massoretic readings, and all the minutiae of the text with their profound mysteries, were all delivered to Moses on Sinai. It may be asked, If that is so, why are all these signs and notes, with all the mysteries they contain, absent from our most holy Scroll of Law? The explanation is as follows. When the Divine Throne was decorated and completed with the crown formed from the Written Law, all the points and tonal accents and Massoretic signs were hidden

Zohar: Shemoth, Section 2, Page 206a

in the interior of the Divine Throne; then all these signs were the means by which the Written Law fertilized the Oral Law, as a female is fertilized from the male. But the celestial letters remained in their original sanctity unaccompanied by any signs, and hence they have to appear in this guise in the Synagogue, seeing that the Divine Throne was decorated and sanctified by the Written Law in its bare letters. The celestial holiness is thus diffused through the whole, especially on the day of Sabbath. On that day seven persons are called up to take part in the public reading of the Law, corresponding to the seven voices [Tr. note: vide Ps. XXIX, which, according to the Midrash, refers to the giving of the Law.] amidst which the Torah was given; on the other festivals five persons read the Law, and on the Day of Atonement the number is six. All these regulations have a similar recondite significance. The number five corresponds to the five (divine) grades that come after the primordial Light, which are a symbol of the Law; six signifies the so-called "six directions", and seven corresponds to the seven voices: thus all have the same symbolism. On the day of New Moon a fourth is added to the three who are called up on an ordinary day, to symbolize the Sun that gives light at that time to the moon; and this is the inner significance of the additional sacrifice and the additional prayer (musaph) offered on that day. In the reading of the Law only one voice should be heard at a time. Both on the Sabbath and on other days when the Law is publicly read the holy people must have a Throne prepared in the form of a reading-desk with an ascent of six steps and no more, conformably to the passage saying, "and there were six steps to the throne" (2 Chron. XI, 18), and having one step above on which to place the Book of the Law, that it may be seen by the whole congregation. As soon as the Book of the Law is placed thereon the whole congregation below should assume an attitude of awe and fear, of trembling and quaking, as though they were at that moment standing beneath Mount Sinai to receive the Torah, and should give ear and listen attentively; for it is not permitted then to open one's mouth, even for discussing the Torah, still less other subjects. All must be in awe and fear, as though they were speechless. So Scripture says: "And when he opened it, all the people stood up" (Neh. VIII, 5); also, "And the ears of all the people were attentive unto the Book of the Law" (Ibid. VIII, 3). R. Simeon said: When the Book of the Law is taken out to be read before the congregation, the mercy-gates of heaven are opened and the attribute of Love is stirred up, and each one should then recite the following prayer: Blessed be the name of the Master of the universe, blessed be Thy crown and Thy place; may Thy favour accompany Thy people Israel forevermore, and manifest Thou to Thy people the redemption of Thy right hand in Thy Sanctuary so as to make us enjoy Thy goodly light and to accept our prayer in mercy. May it be Thy will to prolong our life in goodness, and may I, Thy servant, be counted among the righteous so that Thou have mercy upon me and guard me and all mine and all that are of Thy people Israel. Thou art He that nourisheth and sustaineth all, Thou art ruler over all, Thou art ruler over all kings, and the kingdom is Thine. I am the servant of the Holy One, blessed be He, and bow down before Him and before His glorious Torah at all times. Not in man do I put my trust, nor do I rely upon angels, but on the God of heaven, who is the God of truth and whose Torah is truth and whose prophets are true prophets: in Him do I put my trust and to His holy and glorious name do I sing praises. May it be Thy will to open my heart to Thy Law, and grant me male children, such as will do Thy will, and mayest Thou fulfil the desires of my heart and that of Thy people Israel, for whatever is good, for life, and for peace. Amen. It is forbidden for more than one at a time to read in the Book of the Law; the rest should listen attentively and in silence to the words coming from his mouth as though they were receiving them at that moment from Mount Sinai. Another person should stand next to the reader, but in silence, so that there should be heard one sole utterance, and not two. As the holy tongue stands alone, so its message must be delivered by one only; and for two to read simultaneously in the Book of the Law would be a lessening of Divine Faith and a lessening of the glory of the Torah. (Similarly, in reciting the translation, [Tr. note: It was formerly the custom that after each verse of the original the Aramaic translation (Targum) should be recited.] only one voice should be heard. The translation and the reading are related as the shell and the brain. [Tr. note: Al. as this world and the next world.]) All should be silent, one only reading, just as at Sinai, as we are told, "God spoke all these words, saying" (Ex. XX, 1), He being above and all the people beneath, as we read,

Zohar: Shemoth, Section 2, Page 206b

"and they stood at the nether part of the mount" (Ibid. XIX, 17). We also read, "And Moses went up unto God" (Ibid. XIX, 3). It behoves the reader to concentrate all his mind on the words he reads, and to realize that he is the messenger of his Master, charged with the duty of communicating these words to the whole congregation, he being in the place of heaven to them. Hence, whoever would go up to read in the Torah should previously rehearse his reading at home, or else not read at all. This we learn from the giving of the Law on Mount Sinai, of which we read, first, "Then did he see it and declare it; he prepared it, yea, and searched it out" (Job. XXVIII, 27), and then, "And unto man he said: Behold, the fear of the Lord, that is Wisdom" (Ibid. XXVIII, 28). It is forbidden to the reader to break off anywhere save where Moses indicated a pause. Neither may he in reading the portion of one week add part of the portion of another week. The inner reason of this is as follows. Each weekly lesson is at its conclusion adorned with a crown, and presents itself before God. At the conclusion of their yearly cycle they all present themselves, thus crowned, before the Holy One, blessed be He, each one announcing: I belong to the Sabbath so-and-so, and to congregation so-and-so. At that moment the angel Youfiel, the great chief, is called for, who presents himself accompanied by the fifty-three [Tr. note: The traditional division of the Pentateuch is into fifty-four sections. Some say that the sections Nizabim and Vayelekh are, by the Zohar, counted as one; others, that V'zoth Habbrakhah is here excluded, as not belonging to any Sabbath.] legions under his charge. These legions superintend the reading of the Law, each one having to preside over the reading on a particular Sabbath assigned to it. It is thus forbidden us to disarrange the Lessons and thereby cause the overlapping of one legion with another, even by so much as a hairbreadth, by so much as a single word or even a single letter; but each must be kept within its own limits as fixed by the Holy One, blessed be He. All the legions thus present themselves, each one standing guard over the weekly Lesson under its charge. Each portion thus decorated with a crown, after its reading has been completed by the congregation, is taken up by its superintending legion and brought before the presence of the Holy One, blessed be He, in all its several words. These words declare: "We are such-and-such a section, completed by such-and-such a congregation in such-and-such manner." If the reading of them has been completed in the proper manner, the words ascend and themselves are woven into a crown to adorn the Divine Throne, with its superintending legion standing guard over it. The same is repeated with each separate Sabbath lesson in turn until they are all joined and become interwoven into one single crown. Hence, happy is the portion of whoever completes the reading of the weekly portion of each and every Sabbath in the proper manner, and in accordance with the divisions fixed on high.

'On Sabbath we have to read in the Book of the Law twice: once in the morning and a second time at dusk. For the late afternoon is the time when judgement hangs over the world, hence it is necessary for us to intertwine the Left with the Right, [Tr. note: i.e. Rigour with Clemency.] seeing that the Torah proceeded from the two sides, as it is written: "At his right hand was a fiery law unto them" (Deut. XXXIII, 2), implying both the right and the left. Hence the reading of the Law at dusk should comprise ten verses or more, but not the entire portion, as the complete portion is of the right, and the right prevails only until the time of afternoon service. We have also to read the Law on the second and the fifth days of the week, as on these days the higher grades descend below, those grades that represent the main principles of the Torah. The esoteric significance of the matter is this. These superior grades represent one portion of the Torah, but from them there emanate nine grades, [Tr. note: The grades of Nezah, Hod, and Yesod, each with its three sections.] which form a unity, and hence have their counterpart in the nine persons called to read the Law: to wit, three on Sabbath at Minha, and three each on the second and the fifth days of the week. Similarly we read in the Book of R. Yeba the Venerable: "At Minha-time on Sabbath there is an awakening of the mysterious forces of the Left, and the lower 'Sabbath-Point' within that left side receives the mystery of the Torah. At that moment, therefore, it receives from the domination, as it were, of the left side, the side which is esoterically represented

Zohar: Shemoth, Section 2, Page 207a

by nine, and hence the nine persons who read the Law, to wit, six on weekdays and three on Sabbath at the moment when the left side bestirs itself." Happy is the portion of whoever is privileged to do honour to the Sabbath; happy is he in the two worlds, in this world and in the future world.

'It is written: "Let no man go out of his place on the seventh day" (Ex. XVI, 29). We have learned that the term "place" signifies the space wherein it is fitting for a man to walk; and esoterically it is the counterpart of the similar term in "Blessed be the glory of the Lord from his place" (Ezek. III, 12); also in "for the place whereon thou standest ', etc. (Ex. III, 5); it is a place well known on high, and we call it the place wherein is revealed the most high glory in heaven; and hence the warning to the man who is adorned with the holy heavenly crown not to "go out of his place on the seventh day", that is, not to speak of workaday matters, as that would be a profanation of the Sabbath, nor to do work with his hands, nor to walk beyond the limit of two thousand cubits. "Let no man go out of his place", to wit, the place of Holy Majesty, as beyond it is the place of strange gods. "Blessed be the glory of the Lord", to wit, His glory in the high heavens; "from His place", to wit, His glory in the lower world, the two together forming the Sabbath-crown. Hence, "let no one go out of his place". Blessed be He forever and to all eternity. It is written: "Behold, there is a place by me" (Ex. XXXIII, 21), a place, that is, concealed and hidden, eluding all inquiry, the place which is in the height of heights, the most high Temple, withdrawn from all cognition. But over against it is the lower place, referred to above. Thus there is "place" above and "place" below, and hence "let no man go out of his place on the seventh day". It is written: "And ye shall measure without the city for the east side two thousand cubits," etc. (Num. xxxv, 5). This verse contains sublime mysteries, indicated already elsewhere. It speaks of a higher and a lower region, the two thousand cubits extending on all sides. So the Shekinah does not hover anywhere outside the boundaries assigned to her.

'When the Sabbath begins to draw to a close Israel must draw it out as long as possible, for it is a great and exalted day, and the Shekinah, moreover, is our guest on that day, and so we must make every effort to detain the celestial guest as long as possible. Then, at the conclusion of the Sabbath, we commence prayers by reciting: "And He being merciful, forgiveth iniquity."

This verse is very appropriate for that night, because then Rigour resumes it sway, whereas it is not appropriate for reciting at the entrance of the Sabbath, since that Rigour is then completely withdrawn from the world. Then, when the congregation recite the passage beginning, "And let the pleasantness...", succeeding Sanctification, all the sinners in Gehinnom exclaim: "Happy are ye, O Israel! Happy are ye righteous men who observe the commands of the Torah! Alas for the wicked who did not succeed in observing the precepts of the Torah." Then appears Dumah, [Tr. note: The chief of the underworld.] and proclaims: "Let the wicked return to the nether-world, even all the nations that forget God" (Ibid. IX, 18). The wicked are then driven back by all the bands of demons into Gehinnom without anyone having compassion on them. Happy are those who observe the Sabbath in this world, and so enjoy the celestial delight vouchsafed to them from above, as already mentioned. On the other hand, he who keeps the Sabbath as a day of fasting provokes against himself two accusers who indict him before the Holy King. One is the holy Sabbatical super-spirit who is deprived of his due share of Sabbath-day delight; and the other is the angel named Sangariah, who has charge over those who observe a fast. These two accuse the man before the Holy King. For, since the lower spirit is deprived of its proper share of Sabbath delight, it is in a state of imperfection and therefore the corresponding spirit above is also in a state of imperfection, and the man thus deserves curses and punishments. If, however, he makes good on other occasions, so that the angel of

Zohar: Shemoth, Section 2, Page 207b

fasts finds satisfaction in the celestial bliss which he enjoys in the company of other guardian angels, his punishment is remitted. Suppose a king in the midst of his marriage festivities, in which all his subjects are invited to participate,

516

notices a man being led in chains to the place of punishment. Straightway he gives orders for the man to be released, so that all, without exception, may share in his rejoicings. Afterwards, the officers return and lead the man to the place of punishment. Similarly, the celestial officers come in due course and exact punishment of the man who caused a diminution of joy both in heaven and on earth by fasting on Sabbath. What, then, is his remedy? That he observe another fast to atone for his Sabbath fast; as he did away with the joy of Sabbath, so let him do away with the pleasure of weekdays. But if he banishes joy on Sabbath and indulges in it on weekdays, by fasting on the Sabbath and feasting on the following weekday, he will show that he thinks more of this world than of God, since he neglects the holy super-spirit of the Sabbath, and entertains the weekday spirit, which rests on the world afterwards. It is therefore incumbent on him to observe a fast on the first day of the week, the time when the ordinary weekday spirit resumes its sway, so that he may obtain healing by disregarding the everyday spirit. Happy is he who on earth rises to that sublime heavenly delight in the manner due. For this day is adorned with seventy crowns, and the Divine Name is perfected in all sides, and all the grades are illumined, and all is pervaded with joy, with blessing, and with an overflowing measure of holiness.

'The Sanctification (Kiddush), recited on the eve of the Sabbath, ushers in a holiness equal to that of the Sabbath of Creation, which was hallowed by the "thirty-two Paths of Wisdom" and "three holy apple-trees". [Tr. note: The three highest grades.] Hence, in the Sanctification ceremony we have to recite the passage: "And the heaven and the earth were finished... which God in creating had made" (Gen. II, 1-3), which contains an essential testimony to the work of creation. For this passage contains thirty-five words representing the "thirty-two Paths" and the three "holy apple-trees", which are represented by the three occurrences of the word "seventh" in the passage. This section also contains allusions to the upper world, the lower world, and the Divine Faith in all its compass. The word "Elohim" is mentioned three times, pointing to the lower world, the "Fear of Isaac" (Rigour), and the highest world, which is the Holy of Holies. Now, it behoves man to give testimony to this before his Master, gladly, joyfully, and with all his heart and mind. Thereby all our sins are atoned for. 'Next we recite the benediction, which runs: "Blessed art Thou, O Lord our God, King of the universe, who hast sanctified us by thy commandments and hast taken pleasure in us." This part of the recital balances the other part, called the testimony to Divine Faith, and so it also contains thirty-five words. Together we thus have seventy words, which are so many crowns by which the Eve of the Sabbath is adorned. Happy is the man who in his recital meditates over all this to the glory of his Master. The Sanctification (Kiddush) recital in the morning consists of the blessing over the cup of wine, to wit, "who createst the fruit of the vine", and no more. The reason of this is that then it is the day that sanctifies itself, whereas the Eve has to be sanctified by us with all the recital just mentioned. The Eve is only consecrated by the holy people on earth what time the supersoul descends on them; we thus have to sanctify it with special concentration of our thought on this. Contrariwise, the day makes itself holy, and Israel, being hallowed through prayers and supplications, sanctify themselves still further through the holiness of the day. Happy are the holy people of Israel who have inherited this day as an everlasting heritage.

'At the conclusion of the Sabbath we have to make "separation" between holy and profane, for the reason that at the moment the inferior spirits resume their sway over the world and all its doings; and so we have to demonstrate the existence of the Holy One in His holy place wrapt in holiness absolute, and to distinguish between the lower elements and most exalted Unity.

Zohar: Shemoth, Section 2, Page 208a

To do this, we recite a blessing over the light of fire. For, although all other fires are put out and hidden on the Sabbath, one fire still shows itself on this day, being included in the holiness of Sabbath; when this comes forth, all the other fires hide themselves. It is the fire of the altar upon which Isaac was to have been offered as a sacrifice. We have to say the blessing over the fire that burnt on the Sabbath, which is the fire that emanated from the celestial fire, the fire that carries fire; and when this is blessed, all other fires come forth and are assigned to their places. When we say the blessing over that fire, four legions of angels, called "lights of the fire", come down to be illuminated by this blessed fire. Therefore do we bend the four fingers of our right hand to catch the light of the lamp that is blessed, symbolic of the four legions, called "lights of the fire", who themselves are illumined by, and derive power from, a certain supernal Lamp. Those legions, moreover, are of the lower grades, and we bend thus our fingers before the light to show its supremacy. Contrariwise, in the recital of other blessings we have to raise our fingers, to show the supremacy of the supernal holy grades which rule over all, the Divine Name being by them crowned and sanctified, and which are illumined by the Supreme Lamp. But here we incline our fingers downwards against the light as a symbol of the lower grades which are illumined by the light of blessing, and so are called "Lights of the Fire". On all other days we praise the Almighty for having made the luminaries of "light" (or), in allusion to the supreme radiations of the primordial light which shed blessings and light over all grades together; whereas here we only mention the "lights of the fire" (esh). Now, inasmuch as these "lights of the fire" emanate from the fire over which the benediction was recited, why, one may ask, not say "lightest" instead of "createst"? The explanation is that at the entrance of the Sabbath all the lower grades and luminaries and potencies are absorbed by the Supreme Lamp and become invisible save for the one single point; and they remain in it the whole of the Sabbath day. Then, at the conclusion of the Sabbath the Almighty makes them appear one by one, as if created anew, in the same manner as at the first creation, and assigns each one to its place of domination. In the same manner, the supernal grades, called "luminaries of light", rule over the day and receive their light from the Supreme Lamp. When night falls, the Supreme Lamp gathers them up and absorbs them within itself until daybreak. As soon as Israel recites the blessing over the light of day the Supreme Lamp sends them forth fully radiant. We then thus bless the Lord "who formest (yozer) the luminaries", but not "createst" (bore). It is only at the conclusion of the Sabbath that we say "who createst the lights of the fire" in allusion to the lower grades. But both the upper and the lower grades are symbolized by our fingers. The finger-nails are of great importance in this symbolism. They are on the back of the fingers, and thus symbolize the Hinder Countenance, which needs to be illumined from that Lamp: it is called

Zohar: Shemoth, Section 2, Page 208b

"the back". Whereas the inner and nail-less side of the fingers symbolizes the Inner Countenance which is hidden. This symbolical action is based on the verse, "and thou shalt see my back; but my face shall not be seen" (Ex. XXXIII, 23). "My back" is represented by the outer and nail-part of the fingers which, when we say the blessing over the light, must be placed so as to catch that light; "but My face shall not be seen", and hence the inner side of the fingers symbolizing the Inner Countenance, need not face the light to be illumined by it, as their illumination emanates from no other source but the Supernal Lamp in the height of heights, which is utterly concealed and undisclosed. The outer and nail parts of the fingers must therefore be shown to the light, but the inner parts not. They are hidden and illumined from the hidden; innermost and illumined from the innermost; exalted and illumined from the highest. Happy is Israel in this world and in the world to come.

'It behoves us at the conclusion of the Sabbath to inhale the sweet odour of aromatic spices in order to fortify ourselves against the departure of the super-spirit, as by this departure a man's own soul is left forlorn and naked, as it were. In this regard it is written, "and he smelled the smell of his raiment" (Gen. XXVII, 27). This passage has already been expounded in a way. But observe further that the sweet smell provides sustenance for the soul, it being a substance which enters the soul but is too tenuous for absorption by the body. Now, the raiment here mentioned has been expounded as alluding to the garments of Adam the first man, those in which the Holy One arrayed him when He placed him in the Garden of Eden. When Adam sinned, however, he was stripped of these precious garments and was clothed in others instead. The original garments with which Adam was arrayed in the Garden of Eden were of the same kind as those in which the legions, called "hind-parts" (ahorayim), are arrayed, and bear the name of "nail-raiment". And so long as Adam remained in the Garden of Eden all those legions encompassed and guarded him so that no evil could come near him. But after he sinned he was stripped of those garments and clothed in profane garments, made out of vicious stuff and evil spirits, and the holy legions departed from him; and there was only left on him of the original covering the fingernails. These, however, have also an outer edge of impurity. For this reason we should not allow those nails with their impurity to grow; for as they keep growing so do the man's accusers multiply, and so does he himself sink every day into deeper melancholy. It behoves us, then, to cut them off, nor must we throw the cuttings away in a place where people pass, lest harm come to them. Now, all this is on the celestial pattern; for there also the "hinder" region is surrounded by the "other side". Later on, the Holy One made for Adam other garments out of the leaves of the terrestrial Garden of Eden. Now, those original garments, which were an emanation of the celestial Garden of Eden, emitted the sweet fragrances and aromas of the kind which calm and soothe the soul and make it happy. Isaac thus "smelled the smell of his raiment, and blessed him", as that fragrance calmed and soothed his soul and spirit. Hence, at the conclusion of the Sabbath we have to inhale the odour of sweet spices in order to restore our soul and counteract the effect of the loss of the superior spirit that has left it. The best odour for this purpose is that of the myrtle, as it is myrtle which sustains the holy place from which souls issue, and so in this world it is potent to uphold man's soul at the moment when it is deprived of its higher soul-companion. It was at the conclusion of the Sabbath that Adam was clothed in the garments of the terrestrial Paradise, the sweet odours and fragrance of which sustained his soul in the loss it suffered through the departure of the superior and glorified holy spirit. The myrtle thus assuredly sustains man's soul on earth as it does the souls on high-that superior spirit that descends into man on the Sabbath and fills his soul with joy. Thus this soul is raised to the state in which it will be in the future world,

Zohar: Shemoth, Section 2, Page 209a

for in the same measure as a man feasts and delights that spirit in this world will that spirit cause delight to the man in the future world. So Scripture says. "Then shalt thou delight thyself in the Lord", etc. (Isa. LVIII, 14), also, "and the Lord will... satisfy thy soul with brightness" (Ibid. 14). Whoever thus fully honours the Sabbath in the manner described, the Holy One, blessed be He, says to him: "Thou art my servant, Israel, in whom I will be glorified" (Ibid. XLIX, 3).'

R. Isaac now ceased, and R. Abba and the other Companions rose up and kissed him on his head. They all wept and said: 'Happy is our portion in that the Holy One, blessed be He, has led our feet on this path.' Said R. Abba: 'The Lord led me on this way so that I might join your company. Happy is my portion in having been thus privileged.' R. Abba further said to them: 'Let me relate to you what I saw. When I set out on my journey today I saw a light ahead of me which split into three separate lights. They all went in front of me and then disappeared. I said to myself: Assuredly, what I saw was the Shekinah. Happy is my portion. Now I know that those lights I saw were yourselves. Verily, you are the supernal lights and lamps to lighten this world and the world to come.' R. Abba continued, saying: 'Until now I did not know that all these hidden pearls were in your possession. And now that I see that all these words of yours have been uttered by the will and command of your Master, I know that they are all ascending this day to the Divine Throne, and that the Chief of the angels [Tr. note: Metatron] is taking them up and weaving them into crowns for his Master, and this very day sixty holy legions are adorned with crowns, made of the words uttered here this day, to the glory of the Divine Throne,' At this point he raised his eyes and noticed that the sun had gone down. 'Let us proceed to that village yonder,' he said, 'as it is the nearest to us in this desert.' So they went there and stayed there overnight. At midnight R. Abba, with the other Companions, arose in order to study the Torah. Said R. Abba: 'Now let us weave discourses which will be made into crowns for the righteous in Paradise, as now is the hour when the Holy One, blessed be He, and all the righteous in Paradise, listen to the voices of the righteous on earth.'

R. Abba then began to discourse on the verse: "The heavens are the heavens of the Lord, but the earth hath he given to the children of men" (Ps. cxv, 16). 'This verse', he said, 'contains a difficulty. For would it not have sufficed to say "the heavens are of the Lord"? Why, then, repeat the word "heavens", and say "the heavens are the heavens", etc.? But we account for it in this way. There are heavens and heavens; to wit, lower heavens with an earth beneath them, and upper heavens also having an earth beneath them. They constitute upper grades and lower grades, the two being counterparts of each other. The lower heavens are identical with the ten curtains, to which allusion is made in the words: "Who stretchest out the heavens like a curtain" (Ps. CIV, 2). The Holy One made them, with the legions that people them, to regulate the affairs of the lower earth. The ninth heaven propels all the lower heavens, which are harnessed to it, as it were, by a chain of links. (The tenth, however, is the chief of them all.) In each heaven are controlling angels, as far as the seventh; the rest are all illumined by the light that radiates from the Divine Throne, reaching the tenth heaven, whence it is extended towards the ninth and further to the eighth, whence it reaches those below. It is the light of the eighth which gives to each of the stars, when they are brought out to their places, its requisite light and force. In regard to this it is written: "He that bringeth out their host by number... by the greatness of might" (Isa. XL, 26), the term "greatness of might" referring to the supernal resplendency. Furthermore, there is in each heaven a chieftain who is in charge of a part of the world and a part of the earth, except the Land of Israel, which is not under the rule of any heaven or any other power but that of the Holy One, blessed be He, alone. But, it may be said, how can the sky over the Land of Israel be without effect, seeing that the Land of Israel receives rain and dew from heaven like any other land? The explanation is as follows. In the case of other lands,

Zohar: Shemoth, Section 2, Page 209b

the ruler in each heaven transmits of his power to the earth below through the medium of the heaven under his charge-of that power which he himself has received from the residue left of the supernal source. But the heaven which is over the Holy Land is not ruled by any chieftain or any other power, but is in the sole charge of the Holy One, blessed be He, who Himself directs the affairs of that land from that heaven. Each heaven is provided with a certain number of portals, and the charge of each chieftain extends from one portal to the next, and he may not encroach on the sphere of his fellow-chieftain by even so much as a hairbreadth, except he receive authorization to exercise dominion over his neighbour; when this happens one king on earth obtains power over another. There is, besides, in the centre of the whole of the heavens, a door called G'bilon; underneath that door are seventy other doors, with seventy chieftains keeping guard, at a distance from it of two thousand cubits, so that no one should come near it. From that door, again, there is a path mounting higher and ever higher until it reaches the Divine Throne. The same door gives access to all quarters of heaven as far as the gate called Magdon, [Tr. note: Al. Mandon] where is the end of the heaven that extends over the Land of Israel. All the seventy doors that are inscribed on the door called G'bilan, are called "gates of righteousness", being under the direct control of the Divine Throne, and no other power; and it is through those gates that the Holy One provides the Land of Israel with all that it needs; and it is from the residue of that provision that the Chieftains take and transmit to all the lower chieftains.

'In connection with the firmament that is above the lower Paradise there are sublime mysteries. When the Holy One was about to make the firmament, He took fire and water out of His Throne of Glory, fused them into one, and out of them made the lower firmament, which expanded until it reached the area of the Lower Paradise, where it halted. The Holy One, blessed be He, then took from the holy and supernal heaven fire and water of another kind, such as both are and are not, are both disclosed and undisclosed, and of them He made a further expanse of heaven which He spread over the lower Paradise where it joins the other firmament. That expanse of heaven, above the lower Paradise, displays four colours: white, red, green, and black, and correspondingly contains four doors in its four sides. These four openings form a passage for four light-radiations. On the right side two lights shine forth through two doors, one through the door of the right and one through the opposite. Within the light-radiation on the right a certain letter stands out with scintillating effulgence, to wit, the letter Mim. That letter moves up and down continually without ever resting at one point. Within the opposite light-radiation there similarly stands out with a scintillating effulgence the letter Resh, which on occasions, however, assumes the shape of the letter Beth. This similarly moves forever up and down, at times being revealed and at other times hidden. When the soul of a righteous man enters the Lower Paradise, these two letters emerge out of the midst of that radiation, and appear above that soul, where they continue to rise and fall. Then out of the same two doors there emerge from on high two legions, one under the charge of Michael the great prince, and the second under the great chieftain called Bael, who is the noble minister

Zohar: Shemoth, Section 2, Page 210a

called Raphael. These legions descend and pause above the soul, which they greet with the words: "Peace be thy coming, he entereth into peace, he entereth into peace!" The two letters then return to their place and become absorbed within the radiation that passes through those two doors. Similarly, through the other two doors, that on the left and on the west, there pass two light-radiations, out of which there project two other flaming and scintillating letters, to wit, a Gimel and a Nun; and when the two previous letters return to their own place these two flaming letters emerge from the midst of their surrounding illumination and appear above that soul. Then, again, emerging out of the other two portals, there come forth two other legions, one under the charge of the great chief Gabriel, and the other under that of the great chief Nuriel. These fix themselves above the soul whilst the letters return to their place. After that these two legions enter into a certain hidden Palace in the Garden, called Ahaloth (lit. aloes). Therein is the hidden store of the twelve varieties of sweet spices which Scripture enumerates, "Spikenard and saffron, calamus and cinnamon..." (S.S. IV, 14), these being the twelve varieties of spices of the Lower Paradise. Therein is also the repository of all the garments wherewith men's souls are invested, each according to its desert. On each garment all the good works that a man did in this world are inscribed, and in each case proclamation is made, saying: "This garment belongs to such a one"; after which the soul of the righteous in Paradise is clothed therewith, so as to become a replica of the man's personality whilst in this world. This takes place not less than thirty days after the man's death, inasmuch as for the first thirty days there is no soul but must undergo correction before entering Paradise, as already stated elsewhere. After purification it receives its garment, in virtue of which it is then assigned to its appropriate place. All the letters and legions then disappear. Now, the firmament over the Lower Paradise revolves twice a day under the impetus of the other firmament that is attached to it. That firmament, moreover, is inwrought with all the letters of the alphabet in various colours, each letter distilling of the heavenly dew over the Garden. It is in that dew that the souls bathe and recuperate after their previous immersion in the Nehar dinur (river of fire) for purification. That dew descends from no other source but from the midst of the letters that are graven in that firmament, these letters containing in miniature the whole of the Torah, and that firmament forming the esoteric aspect of the Torah, since it is made out of the fire and water of the Torah itself. Hence they drop their dew upon all those who in this world give themselves up to the study of the Torah for its own sake. The very words of their studies are inscribed in Paradise, whence they mount up to that firmament where they receive from those letters that dew on which the soul of the good man is nurtured. So Scripture says: "My doctrine shall drop as the rain, my speech shall distil as the dew" (Deut. XXXII, 2). In the centre of that firmament there is an opening directly facing the opening of the supernal Palace on high and forming the gateway through which the souls soar up from the Lower Paradise unto the Higher Paradise by way of a pillar that is fixed in the Lower Paradise reaching up to the door on high. There is, moreover, a column of light, formed of a combination of three lights of so many different colours, radiating upwards from the opening in the centre of that firmament, and thus illuminating that pillar with a many-hued light. Thus that firmament scintillates and flashes with a number of dazzling colours. The righteous are illumined by the reflection of that supernal resplendency, and on each New Moon the glory of the Shekinah as revealed in that firmament transcends that of other times. All the righteous then approach and prostrate themselves before it. Happy is the portion of whoever is found worthy of those garments wherein the righteous are clad in the Garden of Eden. Those garments are made out of the good deeds performed by

Zohar: Shemoth, Section 2, Page 210b

a man in this world in obedience to the commands of the Torah. In the Lower Paradise man's soul is thus sustained by these deeds and is clad in garments of glory made out of them. But when the soul mounts up on high through that portal of the firmament, other precious garments are provided for it of a more exalted order, made out of the zeal and devotion which characterized his study of the Torah and his prayer; for when that zeal mounts up on high a crown is made out of it for him to be crowned with, but some of it remains as the man's portion, out of which garments of light are made for the soul to be clad in when it has ascended on high. The former garments, as we have said, depend on his actions, but these depend on his devotion of spirit, so as to qualify their owner to join the company of holy angels and spirits. This is the correct exposition of the matter as the Holy Lamp learned it from Elijah. The garments of the Lower Paradise are made of man's actions; those of the celestia; Paradise of the devotion and earnestness of his spirit.

'It is written: "And a river went out of Eden to water the garden", etc. (Gen. II, 10). It is of importance to know the source and origin of the river that went out of Eden into the Lower Garden. Eden itself is most recondite, and no eye is permitted to discern it. The inner reason is that had the Lower Eden been allowed to be disclosed, the position of the Higher Eden also would have become discoverable. In order, therefore, that the Higher Eden should remain enveloped in holy mystery, the Lower Eden, from which a river went out, had also to be entirely hidden, and so it is undisclosed, even to the souls in the Garden of Eden itself. Now, as that river flows out of Eden to water the Garden, so from the portal in the centre of the Garden emerges a stream of light that divides into four sections, radiating in four directions, passing the four portals previously mentioned, and illuminating the inscribed letters. That fourfold beam issues from Eden, at the Lower Point that shines opposite the Celestial Point. That point is illumined, and is itself transmuted into Eden, the fount of the light. That Point itself is not given to any to see or know, but only the light radiating from it, before which the righteous in the Garden of Eden prostrate themselves, as already said. That Lower Point is in its turn Garden in relation to the Celestial Eden, a spot not given to any to know or to perceive. Concerning all this it is written: "No eye hath seen beside thee, O God" (Isa. LXIV, 3), which is an allusion to the holy Lower Point that alone has knowledge of the Lower Eden which is hidden in the Garden, there being none other that has knowledge of it. Again, "beside thee, O Elohim," alludes to the Higher Eden, which is identical with the mystery of the world to come, with the principle that knows the Lower Point, none other knowing it save Elohim, the One who ascends ever higher into the Boundless (En-soph).

'The river that goes forth out of the Lower Eden is a mystery only known to the initiated, and is alluded to in the words: "and he will satisfy thy soul in dry places (zahzahoth, al. with brightness)" (Isa. LVIII, 11). The soul that quits this dark world pants for the light of the upper world. Just as the thirsty man pants for water, so does the soul thirst for the brilliancy of the light of the Garden and the firmament. The souls sit there by that river that flows out of Eden; they find rest there whilst clad in the ethereal garments. Without those garments they would not be able to endure the dazzling light around them; but protected by this covering they are in comfort and drink their fill of that radiance without being overwhelmed by it. It is the river which renders the souls fit and able to feast on and to enjoy that radiance. The celestial river brings forth the souls who fly off into the Garden; the lower river in the terrestrial Garden, on the other hand, builds up the souls and makes them fit and able to enjoy those

Zohar: Shemoth, Section 2, Page 211a

radiances, and so to mount up to the celestial Paradise through the central opening of the firmament and by the pillar that stands in the centre of the Lower Paradise. That pillar is enveloped in cloud and smoke and bright flashes, the cloud and smoke encircling it from the outside in order to screen those mounting up into the Upper Paradise that they should not be seen by those remaining below. Herein is involved a most recondite doctrine. When the Holy One, blessed be He, desired to adorn the "Supreme Point" with Sabbaths and festivals and ceremonial days, He sent the Eagle with the four faces who fixed himself on the Temple called "Freedom" (d'ror). So in the Jubilee year we have to proclaim freedom, as we read, "and ye shall proclaim freedom (d'ror)" (Lev. xxv, 10). These four faces emit a sound inaudible to any save those souls that are worthy to ascend into the upper Paradise. These foregather there and are taken up by the four-faced eagle and made to mount by way of the central pillar. At that moment the other pillar goes up, the pillar of cloud and fire and smoke, with shining light in the interior (v. Isa. IV, 5). As soon as the souls arrive at the gate of the firmament the latter revolves three times round the Garden of Eden, producing thereby such sweet music that all the souls come forth and listen and behold the rising of the pillar of fire and cloud and smoke and shining brightness, before which they all prostrate themselves. After this the souls ascend through that portal until they enter within the Supreme Point, where they see wonderful sights, and in their ecstasy flit up and down, approaching each other and again retreating. The Supreme Point, on its side, yearns for them and adorns itself with radiance. Then one Righteous on high puts on garments of jealousy, as it were, surveys the effulgence and the gracefulness of the Supreme Point and its adornment, seizes it, raises it to Himself, so that radiance joins radiance and both become one. At that moment all the hosts of heaven break forth in chorus, saying: "Happy are ye, O righteous, who observe the Torah; happy are they who are assiduous in the study of the Torah, inasmuch as the joy of your Master is in you and the crown of your Master is fashioned by you." Now, after effulgence and effulgence have joined into one, a radiation of manifold hues descends to have converse with the souls of the righteous, and weaves them into a crown for the Divine Throne. Concerning this, then, Scripture says: "No eye beside thee hath seen what Elohim doth for those who wait for him" (Isa. LXIV, 3).'

R. Simeon said: 'It is written, "And over the heads of the living creatures there was the likeness of a firmament, like the colour of the terrible ice, stretched forth over their heads above" (Ezek. I, 22). This verse has already been expounded in a way. But there is a firmament and a firmament. There is a lower firmament that rests upon the four lower Holy Beasts, whence it extends and begins to take on the form of a female figure behind a male figure: this is esoterically implied in the passage, saying, "and thou shalt see my back, but my face shall not be seen" (Ex. DCXIII, 23), also in "Thou hast formed me aft and fore" (Ps. CXXXIX, 5), and again in the words, "and he took one of his ribs" (Gen. II, 21); and there is an upper firmament resting on the four upper Holy Beasts, whence it extends and takes on the figure of a male, very recondite. Of these two firmaments one is named "end of heaven", and the other, "from the end of heaven" (Deut. IV, 32). "The heads of the living creatures" refers to the four lower Holy Beasts who are inscribed above the four letters that are graven on the inner side of the four portals of the Garden of Eden. Now, although we said that the Lower Eden is on earth, and it is indeed so, nevertheless the subject is a most recondite one,

Zohar: Shemoth, Section 2, Page 211b

the fact being that the Supreme Point mentioned above has its part in the lower world as well as in the upper world, the Lower Garden being the portion of that Point through which it communes joyfully with the souls of the righteous on earth, and thus is filled both with celestial and terrestrial delight, communing above with the Righteous One and below with the product of the Righteous One (the souls of the righteous). The Garden is an emanation of the Point called Eden. "The heads of the living creatures", every one having four faces, that of a lion, an ox, an eagle, and that of a man, the latter embracing them all–as it says: "And the likeness of their faces was that of a man" (Ezek. I, 10)– are identical with the four "heads of the rivers" (Gen. II, 10); and it is they who support the Divine Throne; and out of the weight of that burden they ooze perspiration; and out of that perspiration there was formed the River of Fire (nehar dinur), of which it is written "a fiery stream issued and came forth from before him; thousand thousands ministered unto him" (Dan. VII, 10). The souls of men before ascending into Paradise are immersed in that "river of fire", where they are purged without being consumed. It is with the soul as with a garment made of the skin of a salamander. [Tr. note: A reptile believed to be engendered in fire, so that its skin was fireproof.] Such a garment, by reason of its having its origin in fire, can only be cleansed in fire, fire alone having the power to purge it of its impurities. For the soul indeed originated in fire, being an emanation from the Divine Throne, of which it is written, "his throne was fiery flames" (Ibid. VII, 9). So, in order to be purged of its impurities it has to pass through fire. Thus fire alone has the virtue of consuming every pollution in the soul, and making it emerge pure and white. Yet let it not be thought from this that the soul undergoes no penance. For, indeed, woe to the soul that has to endure a strange fire, although it thereby be purged and made white; and still more, woe to the soul which is greatly defiled, for that soul will have to pass twice through the fire in order to come out pure and white. At first the soul is taken to a spot called Ben-hinnom, so called because it is in the interior of Gehinnom, where souls are cleansed and purified before they enter the Lower Paradise. Two angel messengers stand at the gate of Paradise and call aloud to the chieftains who have charge of that spot in Gehinnom, summoning them to receive that soul, and during the whole process of purification they continue to utter aloud repeatedly the word "Hinnom". When the process is completed, the chieftains take the soul out of Gehinnom and lead it to the gate of Paradise, and say to the angel messengers standing there: "Hinnom (lit. here they are), behold, here is the soul that has come out pure and white." The soul is then brought into Paradise. Oh, how broken is that soul after her ordeal in the infernal fire! For, although it has descended from on high, yet when it reaches the earth below it is less rarefied, and it causes the soul intense suffering and leaves it enfeebled and broken. God then causes the rays of the sun to penetrate through the four openings of the firmament above Paradise and to shed its rays on that soul and heal it. Of this Scripture says: "But unto you that fear my name shall the sun of righteousness arise with healing in its wings" (Malachi III, 29). A second ordeal has to be undergone by the soul on its passage from Lower Paradise to Upper Paradise; for whilst in Lower Paradise it is not yet entirely purged of the materialities of this world, so as to be fit to ascend on high. They thus pass it through that "river of fire" from which it emerges completely purified and so comes before the presence of the Sovereign of the universe beatified [Tr. note: Al. purified.] in every aspect. Also the rays of the celestial light afford it healing. This is its final stage. At that stage the souls stand garbed in their raiment and adorned in their crowns before their Master. Happy is the portion

Zohar: Shemoth, Section 2, Page 212a

of the righteous in this world and in the world to come.

'The souls in Lower Paradise, on every New Moon and Sabbath day, go about and ascend to the spot called "Walls of Jerusalem", where there are a great many chieftains and legions mounting guard, as written: "I have set watchmen upon thy walls, O Jerusalem" (Isa. LXII, 6). They mount up as far as that spot, but do not enter it until their purging is complete.

There they prostrate themselves, drink in ecstatically of the celestial radiance, and then return into Paradise. They also at times go forth, roaming about the world and viewing the bodies of the sinners undergoing their punishment. So Scripture says: "And they shall go forth, and look upon the carcases of the men that have rebelled against me; for their worm shall not die, neither shall their fire be quenched; and they shall be an abhorring unto all flesh" (Ibid. LXVI, 24). They continue to roam about, casting their glance on those who are victims of pain and disease, who suffer for their belief in the unity of their Master. They then return and make all this known to the Messiah. When the Messiah hears of the great suffering of Israel in their dispersion, and of the wicked amongst them who seek not to know their Master, he weeps aloud on account of those wicked ones amongst them, as it is written: "But he was wounded because of our transgression, he was crushed because of our iniquities" (Ibid. LIII, 5). The souls then return to their place. The Messiah, on his part, enters a certain Hall in the Garden of Eden, called the Hall of the Afflicted. There he calls for all the diseases and pains and sufferings of Israel, bidding them settle on himself, which they do. And were it not that he thus eases the burden from Israel, taking it on himself, no one could endure the sufferings meted out to Israel in expiation on account of their neglect of the Torah. So Scripture says; "Surely our diseases he did bear", etc. (Ibid. LIII, 4). A similar function was performed by R. Eleazar here on earth. For, indeed, beyond number are the chastisements awaiting every man daily for the neglect of the Torah, all of which descended into the world at the time when the Torah was given. As long as Israel were in the Holy Land, by means of the Temple service and sacrifices they averted all evil diseases and afflictions from the world. Now it is the Messiah who is the means of averting them from mankind until the time when a man quits this world and receives his punishment, as already said. When a man's sins are so numerous that he has to pass through the nethermost compartments of Gehinnom in order to receive heavier punishment corresponding to the contamination of his soul, a more intense fire is kindled in order to consume that contamination. The destroying angels make use for this purpose of fiery rods, so as to expel that contamination. Woe to the soul that is subjected to such punishment! Happy are those who guard the precepts of the Torah!

'As already said, the Supreme Holy Point desires to hold converse with the spirits of the righteous, both on high and here below. It is at midnight that it descends below to converse with the spirits of the righteous and to fondle them as a mother fondles her children.

'The firmament overspreading the Garden of Eden is supported by the heads of the four Holy Beasts, who are symbolized by the four letters referred to above. There is, besides, a lower firmament on the pattern of the upper firmament. This firmament is embroidered with all divine colours, and it possesses four portals marked respectively by four scintillating letters. One portal is to the east, having stamped on it the letter aleph, which scintillates and constantly moves up and down. The second portal is on the north side with the letter daleth stamped on it,

Zohar: Shemoth, Section 2, Page 212b

which likewise scintillates, and without pause moves up and down. Its scintillation, however, is inconstant, as sometimes it flashes brightly and sometimes its light completely disappears. The third portal is on the west with the letter nun stamped on it, likewise scintillating. Finally, there is the fourth portal on the south, having stamped on it a point, the Lower Point, a tiny point, visible and yet not visible, to wit, the letter yod. The other letters of the alphabet are also stamped on that firmament, numbering altogether twenty-two, all adorned with crowns. The firmament revolves on the Living Beings, carrying with it letters arranged in a certain grouping which symbolizes the Divine Unity, viz. Aleph Teth, Beth Heth, Gimel Zain, Daleth Vau. These letters themselves symbolize other higher letters. When that firmament is illumined there become revealed four mystical groupings of letters, each composing the Divine Name, and together spelling out the thirty-two Paths of Wisdom. At that moment a dew descends from that firmament, distilled through the letters of the mystery of the Divine Name, which forms the food of all the celestial holy legions and hosts, who gather it up joyfully. When chastisement impends over the world, the first of each pair of these letters is absorbed, as it were, in the second, thus leaving only Teth, Heth, Zain, Vau (THZV). Then a voice from the north is stirred up so that all know that Rigour prevails over the world; at that moment, also, that firmament assumes a colour that comprehends all colours. When there is a movement in the eastern side of the firmament it embraces the aforesaid four four-faced Holy Beasts with the aforesaid letters, who all rise upward. The hidden letters then reappear, restoring the mystical letter-grouping of Aleph-Teth, Beth-Heth, Gimel-Zain, Daleth-Vau; the firmament is irradiated, a resounding voice proceeds from the letters, reaching the highest heavens, and celestial food and blessings and beatitudes are diffused again in plenty for those who come to partake of it. The letters then in their turn make the tour of the firmament until they reach the southern side; then they ascend, scintillating with a fiery gleam. Then in the centre of that firmament there is traced out a certain letter, to wit, Yod, followed by another three flaming letters, viz. He', Vau, He'. These letters swing up and down, sending out thirteen flames of fire. Then there descends a something which becomes absorbed in these letters, is adorned by them as with a crown, but remains undisclosed. Great joy is then among all the hosts and legions, hymns and praises ascend on high, the firmament begins a second time to rotate and revolve, and the aforementioned letters-'t, b.h, gz, dv- become absorbed in the supernal letters that contain the mystery of the Divine Name just mentioned, and these letters that were in the centre of the firmament, containing the mystery of the Divine Name are now traced out in the north side. They are traced out most faintly, and there is no one who can observe steadily that side. The celestial hosts then break forth in melodious song, reciting: "Blessed be the glory of the Lord from his place" (Ezek. III, 12).

Zohar: Shemoth, Section 2, Page 213a

And they repeat the same from all sides. As the firmament revolves, the volume of melodious sound, with the same refrain, goes up from all the numerous legions, at each of the four sides of the firmament. The firmament then becomes illumined with an exceedingly bright light, brighter than before, displaying, in a different mode, a colour composed of the whole range of colours; and the aforementioned Divine Name of four letters becomes augmented by an additional letter from on high, to wit, the letter Vau, resulting in V-Tetragrammaton (lit. and Tetragrammaton), expressive of both the male and female principles. Yet the Divine Name is not perfect except when it is composed of then in e letters, to wit, Tetragrammaton ELHYM (Elohim). When these letters are thus joined, that firmament shines with thirty-two lights, and all is joy, all is joined in one recondite union, both the upper and the lower world. In that same firmament, again, there is on the north side a flaming light that is never extinguished, to the right of which there are impressions of other letters, forming ten Sacred Names, in which are implicit seventy Names.

'By that firmament are borne along all the lower firmaments within the region of holiness as far as the boundary of the "other" firmaments belonging to the "other side". These latter are called "curtains of goats' hair", allusion to which is made in the verse, "And he made curtains of goats' hair for a tent over the tabernacle." For there are curtains and curtains. The "curtains of the tabernacle" are the counterpart of the firmaments spread over the Holy Beasts in the Holy Tabernacle; whereas the "curtains of goats hair" represent altogether different firmaments, those of the "other side". The former contain the mystery of the legions of the holy spirits; the latter represent the substance of mundane matter, of bodily appetites and actions, and hence form the outer covering of the inner firmaments similar to the shell that surrounds the brain. The latter are called "heavens of the Lord". Opposite to these lower heavens are the supernal heavens, heavens within heavens, called the "heavens of the Holy Beasts", in allusion to the supernal mighty Holy Beasts. They contain the mystery of the Torah, and on the highest heaven of all, namely, the eighth, [Tr. note: Binah.] there are engraved the twenty-two letters of the alphabet. That heaven is supported by the supernal Holy Beasts, and itself is of an essence entirely undisclosed, beyond any attribute of colour, whilst being itself the source and origin of all colours and all light. There is neither light nor darkness in it, but the souls of the righteous, as from behind a wall, discern the light which it sends forth and which illumines the supreme heaven, a light never ceasing, a light not to be known or grasped. There are lower heavens and upper heavens, both referred to in the passage, saying, "The heavens, heavens of the Lord" (Ps. cxv, 16), but this is the supremest heaven, raised

Zohar: Shemoth, Section 2, Page 213b

over them all. Up to this point some hint is given by the holy names by which the Holy One, blessed be He, is called, but beyond this point the discernment even of the wisest cannot pierce, and it is altogether outside the range of our faculties, excepting for one gleam of light, too minute to be dwelt on. Happy is the portion of whoever can penetrate into the mysteries of his Master and become absorbed into Him, as it were. Especially does a man achieve this when he offers up his prayer to his Master in intense devotion, his will then becoming as the flame inseparable from the coal, and his mind concentrated on the unity of the lower firmaments, to unify them by means of a lower name, then on the unity of the higher firmaments, and finally on the absorption of them all into that most high firmament. Whilst a man's mouth and lips are moving, his heart and will must soar to the height of heights, so as to acknowledge the unity of the whole in virtue of the mystery of mysteries in which all ideas, all wills and all thoughts find their goal, to wit, the mystery of the En-Sof (Infinite, Illimitable).

'We should repeat the same endeavour at each prayer, so as to adorn each day with the crown of the mystery of its corresponding supernal day, by means of our prayer. At night a man should represent to himself that he is about to quit this world, and that his soul will leave him and return to the Master of all. For every night the Supreme Point absorbs in itself the souls of the righteous. Here is a recondite truth for the initiate. The lower firmament, as mentioned above, is sustained by that Point. That firmament, moreover, is a fusion of the upper and the lower worlds, having its basis in the lower world, much as the dark flame of a lamp merges into the white flame above while having its basis below in a wick sunk in oil. So in the daytime that Point is essentially above, but in the night it is essentially below, becoming absorbed in the souls of the righteous, since at night all things return to their original root and source. So the soul mounts up, returning to its source, whilst the body lies still as a stone, thus reverting to its own source of origin. Whilst in that state the body is beset by the influences of the "other side", with the result that its hands become defiled and remain so until they are washed in the morning, as explained elsewhere. The souls of the righteous, in ascending in the night into their own celestial spheres, are woven into a crown, as it were, with which the Holy One, blessed be He, adorns Himself. There are night attendants who have charge of those souls, take them up on high and offer them up as an acceptable sacrifice to their Master. The supreme chieftain of those legions bears the name of Suriya, and each soul, as it passes through all the firmaments, is first brought before him, and he inhales its scent, as it says: "And he will inhale the scent of the fear of the Lord" (Isa. XI, 3). He takes them under his charge, and passes them on higher, until they arrive at the place of sacrifice. There all the souls are absorbed in the Supreme Point; as a woman conceives a child, so does the Supreme Point conceive them, experiencing a rapturous pleasure in absorbing in itself the souls with all their good deeds and Torah studies performed during the past day. The souls then re-emerge, that is to say, they are born anew, each soul being fresh and new as at its former birth. This is the inner meaning of the words, "They are new every morning; great is thy faithfulness" (Lam. III, 23). That is to say, "they (the souls) are new every morning",

because "great is thy faithfulness" to absorb them and then let them out as newly-born. Happy are the righteous in this world and in the world to come.'

By now day had broken, and R. Abba said: 'Let us rise and offer up praise to the Master of the World.' Then, after having recited their prayers, the Companions returned to him and said: 'Let him who began the discourse conclude it. Happy is our portion that we have been privileged to adorn the Holy One, blessed be He, with the crown of the recondite teachings of Wisdom.' R. Abba then began the following discourse:

AND BEZALEL MADE THE ARK OF ACACIA WOOD, ETC. 'The Holy Assembly', he said, 'have, indeed, already expounded the esoteric aspect of the Tabernacle. Yet there is still much here to ponder on, as its inner meaning is adorned with many mysteries of the teaching of Wisdom. The ark is one vessel with six sides, and it contains and conceals in its interior the Written Law that reaches out into the six directions of the creation. Again, the ark consists of five boards and an ark-cover, to symbolize the five books of the Pentateuch with the one grade that pervades them all, called the mystery of the covenant. Together, the six-sided ark and the Torah represent the inwardness of the nine grades that are summed up in the two Divine Names- Tetragrammaton, ELoHYM-whilst the ark-cover represents the most high heaven that surrounds all, covers up all, so that the whole remains undisclosed. Now we have to investigate the recondite significance of the ark. For there is ark and ark, one the opposite of the other. In connection with one,' continued R. Abba, 'it is written: "All this did Araunah the king give to the king", etc. (2 Sam. XXIV, 23). Now, even if we allow that Araunah was a king, yet seeing that David conquered Jerusalem and made it his own, as it says, "David took the stronghold of Zion", etc. (Ibid. v, 7-8), why did he need to buy the spot from Araunah with money? A simple explanation would be that although David was the ruler of Jerusalem, that spot was the heritage of Araunah, and so it could only be taken from him by his consent; in the same way as Ahab, although king and ruler in Israel, in order to acquire the vineyard of Naboth the Jesrealite, had first to obtain the latter's consent. But a deeper explanation is that Araunah indeed was king and ruler of that spot, and when the time came for it to pass out of his possession, this could only be effected at the cost of much blood and slaughter to Israel. Subsequently, when the Destroying Angel in the execution of his work of slaughter reached that spot he could not prevail there, and his strength was exhausted. It was, indeed, the spot where Isaac was bound on the altar that Abraham built; and so, when the Holy One looked at that place He was filled with compassion, as we read, "and as he was about to destroy, the Lord beheld, and he repented him of the evil" (I Chron. XXI, 15), meaning that He beheld there the binding of Isaac, and so had compassion on them, and straightway said to the Destroying Angel: "It is enough", etc. (Ibid.); the words, "it is enough", have the same import as the similar words in the passage, "Ye have dwelt long enough in this mountain" (Deut. I, 6), as much as to say: "This place has been long enough in thy possession; thou hast had it for many years, now return it to its rightful master." And for all that it could only be taken from him at a great sacrifice of life and money. What is the significance of the name "Araunah"? The same name is also written "Ornan" (I Chron. XXI, 15). So long as that place was in his possession he was called Araunah, a word of five letters, for in the case of such a niggard who represents the "other side", the addition of a letter implies a degradation, whereas for the side of holiness the diminution of the letters implies an added holiness.

Observe now that the holy side is called the ark (aron) of the covenant, and such an ark is appropriate for the placing therein of the bodily remains of a man. For this reason, when the holy and pious depart this world their bodies are placed in an ark, since the "other side" has not been provided with a body and has nothing in common with the body of Man. Of Joseph we find it written, "and he was put in a coffin (aron) in Egypt" (Gen. L, 26), where the word vayyisem (and he was put) is written with a double yod. For what reason? [Tr. note: Al. Observe that the "holy side" is called "ark of the covenant", that ark being a pit wherein is a receptacle for the Torah in its esoteric aspect, which aspect is the mystery of the image of the pure celestial Body. Corresponding to this, in the terrestrial world an ark has been provided wherein to place the earthly body that symbolizes Man, to wit, the body of him who has preserved the purity of the sign of the holy covenant. Hence the bodies of the holy and pious are placed in an ark, which is fitting only for such a one. Thus in connection with Joseph it is written: "and he was put in a coffin (aron)", etc.] Because he kept unimpaired the symbol of the holy covenant and therefore merited to be put into the ark.' R. Abba here wept, saying: 'Woe to mankind, that they are unaware of this disgrace! Alas, for their offence, in that everyone who wishes is placed in an ark! For this privilege should be reserved for those who are conscious that never in their lives have they transgressed against the sign of the covenant. To put anyone else into an ark is to desecrate it. There is a certain symbolism in this connection which makes it fitting for him and for no other; and woe to him who, notwithstanding his abuse of the sign of the covenant, is admitted into the ark-woe to him who abused it during life, woe to him who now abuses it when dead, woe to him for impairing the sign and the ark of the holy covenant, woe for the punishment to be exacted from him for his wrongs committed in this world and for that abuse of the ark! To this Scripture alludes in the words: "For the rod of wickedness shall not rest upon the lot of the righteous" (Ps. cxxv, 3). That is to say, when such a one comes up for judgement in the other world, and it is found that in addition to having impaired the sign of the holy covenant stamped on his body he also impaired the ark in the other world, he is excluded from any lot among the righteous and is put outside the category of man, and consequently of all those destined for everlasting life, and is delivered into the power of the "other side", the side which has no kinship with the mystery of the body of Man. When he is delivered into the power of that side, woe to him, since he is thrown into Gehinnom, whence he will not come out for all eternity. In allusion to such it is written: "And they shall go forth and look upon the carcases of the men that have rebelled against me", etc. (Isa. LXVI, 24). This doom, however, is only meted out to those who have not turned with a full repentance sufficient to wipe out all their misdeeds. But even after full repentance it is better for such a one not to be put into the ark, because as long as the body is in being the soul is under sentence and may not enter into its own place. But this is not so with the pious who are worthy to ascend, even whilst their bodies endure. Happy is their portion in this world and in the world to come. As regards the aforementioned sinners, there is no sin so grievous in the sight of the Holy One as the sin of perverting and impairing the sign of the holy covenant; and he who commits such an offence is excluded from the sight of the Shekinah.

'It is written here: "And Bezalel made the ark." Why did the wise men who made the Tabernacle not make the ark as well? The reason is that Bezalel represented the final part of the body, the symbol of the holy covenant which he kept pure, and hence it was his part to make the ark, which was, as it were, his own portion.' All the Companions then came near and kissed R. Abba. When they came to R. Simeon and repeated to him all the expositions they had heard during that walk he quoted the verse: "But the path of the righteous is as the light of dawn, that shineth more and more unto the perfect day" (Prov. IV, 18).

Zohar: Shemoth, Section 2, Page 215a

'This verse', he said, 'has been already expounded in a way, but there is still a deeper truth underlying it. "The path of the righteous" is the path of truth, the path the Holy One, blessed be He, delights in, the path along which the righteous proceed, with the Almighty, as it were, leading the way whilst all the heavenly legions come down to listen to their expositions and teachings; "as the light of dawn", that is, as a light that continues without ever fading, unlike the path of the wicked, of which it says: "The way of the wicked is as darkness" etc. (Ibid. 19). The following is an alternate comment. What is the difference between "path" (orah) and "way" (derekh)? A "path" is newly opened and still little trodden, whereas a "way" is a well-worn track, already traversed by many feet. Hence that whereon the righteous walk is called "path", since they are the pioneers who open up a new path for themselves; and even though others have preceded them, yet when they walk on it it becomes a new path, as though never trodden on by any before. For they metamorphose it in virtue of the many sublime and holy teachings with which they delight the Holy One. Moreover, the Shekinah now goes in that path, which she did not before. But "way", on the other hand, is a common road, open to all and trodden on, even by the wicked. This is hinted in the words, "Who maketh a way (derekh) in the sea" (Ibid. XLIII, 16), the word "way" being used because it is accessible to the "other side", the unwanted influence that exerts its power to defile the Tabernacle, and so the righteous are left to themselves, to rule over the region called "path" (orah), as already said. "Way" is thus open for all, for this "side" and its opposite, and you, O exalted saints,' concluded R. Simeon, 'you have entertained the heavenly Visitor (oreah), and sublime expositions have been uttered and displayed by you in the presence of the Ancient of Days. Happy is your portion!'

R. Simeon further discoursed, citing the verse: "And Joshua the son of Nun was full of the spirit of wisdom, for Moses had laid his hands upon him" (Deut. XXXIV, 9). 'In many places we have laid down', he said, 'that the face of Moses was as the face of the sun, whilst that of Joshua was like that of the moon. For the moon has no light of its own, but receives its light by reflection from the sun until it becomes full, when it may be said to reach its state of completeness. The completeness of the moon is when it is called "reflection" (d'muth), in relation to the supernal Sun called Tetragrammaton, for it receives this name only when it is complete, for it has many names according to its various manifestations. So when it is complete on all sides it is called Tetragrammaton, its completeness corresponding to the higher completeness. The Daughter, as it were, is the heiress of the Mother. This is the case on the fifteenth day of the month, and thus, "On the fifteenth day of this seventh month is the feast of Tabernacles" (Lev. XXIV, 34). It is also written, "Howbeit on the tenth day of this seventh month is the day of Atonement" (Ibid. 27), which has the same allusion. When the World-to-be is symbolized by all the Ten Utterances, and centred in this month, it is first named "ten", and afterwards when the moon is joined with them in completeness it is named "fifteen", the He (=5) joining the Yod (= 10), both forming the Divine Name YH. In the completed name Tetragrammaton there is a second He added, the first He' being associated with the supernal mystery, and the second symbolizing the Providence that provides the lower world with its sustenance. The moon is thus in its completeness, a completeness embracing the upper and the lower worlds, through the inner meaning of the Divine Name, all forming a unity of perfection. Joshua is the symbol of the fulness of the moon, he truly being the son of Nun, as the letter Nun is expressive of the recondite significance of the moon. And so "Joshua was full of the spirit of wisdom", full in the completeness of the Divine Name. For the Supreme Point, identical with the letter Yod, expanded and produced a Spirit, which Spirit produced a Temple. That Spirit then expanded further, and so became six directions. Having expanded through all these, it filled out and caused to come into being the Lower Temple. Thus

Zohar: Shemoth, Section 2, Page 215b

the Divine Name became manifest in a unity of completeness. "Joshua", then, "was full of the spirit of wisdom, for Moses had laid his hands upon him", that is, he poured out blessings upon him, and the well, so to speak became filled through him. And you,' concluded R. Simeon, 'you exalted saints, each one of you is filled with the spirit of wisdom and has attained the full phase of the mystic wisdom, inasmuch as the Holy One, blessed be He, found delight in you and had laid His hands upon you. Happy is my portion in that my eyes have seen this, to wit, the fulness of the spirit of wisdom that is in you.'

R. Simeon further discoursed, citing the verse: "Ye shall not eat with the blood; neither shall ye practise divination nor soothsaying" (Lev. XIX, 26). 'The esoteric teaching of this verse', he said, 'is that if a man eats before he has prayed, as it were, for his blood, it is as though he were practising divination and soothsaying. For in the night man's soul mounts up into heaven to gaze upon the mystery of the Divine Glory, each one according to its merits, and the body is thus left deriving its life-force solely from the blood. And although alive, the man has then a foretaste of death, that life-force being too sluggish to be reawakened on the return of the soul, so as to be able to receive it. For when man awakens from his sleep he is not in a state of purity, because, as explained elsewhere, the "other side" has sway wherever the soul is absent. He has first to purify himself with water, but even then, and although he may have been engaged in studying the Torah, the soul does not resume its former place and sway, and he is still sustained by the blood life-force alone, the force called nefesh (soul), which permeates the blood. It is only when he worships his Master in prayer that the blood-force resumes its normal position so that the soul regains its control in its own sphere. It is thus that man attains his proper and perfect condition, with the vital force (nefesh) beneath and the soul above. Hence, if a man prays before he eats he puts himself in a proper condition, but if he eats before he prays for his blood to resume its proper sphere, it is as though he were practising divination and soothsaying, seeing that it is the way of the diviner to elevate the "other side", and to degrade the side of holiness. The term m'nahesh (diviner) is related to nahash (serpent), and the diviner is so called because he gives himself over to the Serpent in order to obtain from him power and strength. Such a man is like one serving other gods, and so likewise is he who eats before prayer, worshipping the blood life-force instead of worshipping the Almighty in order to fortify the side of the soul, the side of holiness. Happy is your portion, O exalted saints', continued R. Simeon, 'in that through prayer man's body and soul are edified so that he becomes complete.

'Prayer works a fourfold process of upbuilding which is in essence one. First, it builds up him who prays; secondly, it builds up this world; there comes, third, the upbuilding of the upper world with all the heavenly hosts; the fourth process of upbuilding is wrought on the Divine Name, so that all the upper and lower regions are embraced in one edifying process, in the manner appropriate. First, as to man himself, it is incumbent on everyone to edify himself by means of meritorious action and holiness and sacrifices and burnt offerings. The upbuilding of this world is then effected when we recite the works of creation, praising the Almighty for each separate work through our reading of the Hallelukah Psalms, such as "Praise him, all ye stars of light, praise him, ye heavens of heavens", etc. (Ps. CXLVIII, 3-4). This is for the sustaining of this world. The third process is wrought on the

Zohar: Shemoth, Section 2, Page 216a

upper world with all its hosts upon hosts and legions upon legions. We thus recite: "Creator of ministering spirits... And the Ophanim and the holy Hayoth."

Finally comes the fourth process, wrought, as it were, on the Divine Name, which, by means of our prayer, becomes perfected. Happy is your portion', concluded R. Simeon, 'in this world and in the world to come. This is truly the effect of those precepts which you carry out by means of prayer.'

He further discoursed as follows. 'It is written: "Thou shalt fear the Lord thy God" (Deut. x, 20), and also, "and thou shalt fear thy God (m'elohekho, lit. from thy God)" (Lev. XIX, 14). Why in the latter passage is it written, "from thy God" and not simply "thy God", as in the former passage? The preposition "from", however, points to the place which is attached to the "brain" and surrounds it. That spot is the central fire that surrounds the innermost fire. For there are three varieties of fire in that connection. The first is the fire that receives fire with joy, the two meeting each other in love and joy; the second is that of which it is written, "and there was brightness (nogah) to the fire" (Ezek. I, 13); it is the inmost fire which is joyful at the presence of the other fire. Then comes the third fire which surrounds that brightness, and wherein resides the terror of Severity for the punishment of the wicked. Indeed, there is also a teaching that speaks of four varieties of fire-four that are in essence one. However, it is in the aforementioned fire that the terror of Severity resides. Hence "thou shalt fear (that which comes) from thy God", meaning: "Thy fear shall start from, or be inspired by, His punishment." Furthermore, we should combine fear with love, fear on one side and love on the other. We have to

527

fear on account of the punishment that proceeds from the one side for the transgression of the precepts of the Torah-for once this is begun, the side that inflicts it never relaxes until the transgressor is exterminated from this world and from the world to come. Man has thus to fear that fire which is the seat of fear. That fire spreads out into another fire outside, belonging to another object of fear, in regard to which it is written, "ye shall not fear the gods of the Amorites" (Judges VI, 10). But the aforementioned fire belongs to the holy side, and is the one that surrounds that brightness (nogah) mentioned before. The other and extraneous fire at times joins this fire, and at other times moves away from it. When it does join, it turns into darkness so as to darken and shut out the light of the other fires. After fear comes love. This is esoterically expressed by saying: "After fear has hovered over a man's head there awakens love, which belongs to the right side." For he who worships out of love attaches himself to a very sublime region and to the holiness of the "World-to-be", by reason of love ascending to the "right side" for its attachment and adornment. Think not, however, that worship coming from the side of fear is no worship at all. In truth it is worship highly to be prized. It does not ascend, however, so as to join the highest part of the supernal sphere. This is reserved for worship inspired by love, and he who worships in a spirit of love is the man destined for the future world. Happy is the portion of such a one in that he exercises dominion over the region of fear, love being the sole power dominating fear in virtue of its belonging to the recondite influence of the right. It is further essential in the performance of our worship to avow the unity of the name of the Holy One, blessed be He, and to avow the oneness of the upper and lower members and grades, and to combine them all in the spot to which they fittingly converge. This is the recondite significance of the declaration: "Hear, O Israel: The Lord our God, the Lord is one" (Deut. VI, 4). The term SHeMa' (hear) is esoterically analysed into SH e M (name) and the letter 'Ain (= 70), that is, one Name comprising seventy names whilst remaining a unity. "Israel" here signifies "Ancient Israel", in contrast to "Little Israel", of whom it is written: "When Israel was a child, then I loved him" (Hos. XI, 1). "Ancient Israel" symbolizes the union of the Shekinah with her Spouse, and in pronouncing that name we have to concentrate our mind on the principle of unity,

Zohar: Shemoth, Section 2, Page 216b

on the union of the two habitations; we have to put all our being, all the members of our body, our complete devotion, into that thought so as to rise and attach ourselves to the En-sof (Infinite), and thus achieve the oneness of the upper and the lower worlds. The words, "the Lord our God" are to reunite all the Members to the place from which they issued, which is the innermost Sanctuary. The same thought is continued in the words, "the Lord is one", in the recital of which we have to make our thoughts range throughout all the grades up to the Infinite (En-sof) in love and fear. This is the method of avowing the unity of God practised by Rab Hamnuna the Venerable, who learnt it from his father, who had it from his master, and so on, till it came from the mouth of Elijah. And it is the correct and proper method. The same Rab Hamnuna further said, that to concentrate the whole idea of unification in the term "one" (ehad) is a still better way; and it is for this reason that we dwell long over the enunciation of the word "one" (ehad), during which we effect the fusion into one of the upper and the lower worlds. As we have learnt, "one" alludes to above, below, and the four quarters of the universe, these being the supernal Chariot, so that all are embraced in a single unity reaching out to the En-sof (Infinite). After the recital of "Hear, O Israel...", we have to recite the section containing mention of the Exodus from Egypt (Num. xv, 37-41), for the reason that the Shekinah was in the Egyptian exile, and as long as She is in exile there is no union between the upper and the lower worlds. But the redemption from Egypt, attended by all those signs and wonders, set Her free; and that redemption has to be mentioned by us to show that though She was in chains She is now free, so as to join her heavenly Spouse. It is hence incumbent on us to let the recital of the Redemption be followed closely by our petitionary prayers, as a sign of perfect unity (between the divine aspects) without a rift and without any separation whatever. The mnemonic for this is: "neither shall they take a woman put away from her husband" (Lev. XXI, 7). But, you may say, is She not at present in exile, and so put away? This is not so. She is indeed in exile, but only for the sake of Israel, so as to dwell with them and to shield them, but She is not put away. Now the Shekinah appeared neither during the first Temple nor during the second Temple. In the second Temple, before Israel were driven into exile, She ascended on high, and only after the exile did She make Her abode with them. But She was never put away. Hence the importance of the first redemption, the one from Egypt which comprehended all the four redemptions. The esoteric exposition of the matter is as follows. When the Shekinah left the exile of Egypt, She besought the Holy One, blessed be He, that She might there and then be redeemed with a fourfold redemption, corresponding to the four exiles, so that She might remain free and not be put away any more. This request was granted and the exodus thus embraced for the Shekinah all the four redemptions. At

the moment, therefore, of Her union with Her heavenly Spouse there is need for the display, so to speak, of the redemption from Egypt, comprehending as it does the four redemptions. Hence, we have,

Zohar: Shemoth, Section 2, Page 217a

in the recital of that redemption, to repeat four times the term "true" before we reach the portion beginning with "Thou hast been the help of our fathers...", a prayer which is a firm support for all Israel. Then, in the course of the recital, "Thou hast been...", the term "true" recurs again four times, whereby we fortify, confirm and corroborate, as it were, the same four redemptions with the seal and signet of the King. Were not the four redemptions comprehended within the Exodus during the whole of the exile She would not obtain Her adornments so as to manifest the unity of the Divine Name. We have thus to make mention of the redemption from Egypt in every recital of Sanctification offered to the Holy One, blessed be He, forever and to all eternity. The inward significance of the Sanctification recitals is, as already stated, that thereby both the upper and the lower worlds, all grades, all the upper and lower legions, become sanctified. Herein are involved sublime mysteries through which the initiated discern the holiness of their Master. Happy is their portion! Happy is your portion," concluded R. Simeon, "and happy my eyes that they have witnessed the awakening of these holy words in this world, inasmuch as they are all inscribed in the world on high before the Holy King.'

He next discoursed on the verse: "Then they that fear the Lord spoke one with another; and the Lord hearkened, and heard, and a book of remembrance was written before him, for them that fear the Lord, and that thought upon his name" (Malachi III, 16). 'This verse', he said, 'presents a difficulty in using the word nidb'ru (lit. they were spoken) instead of dibbru (they spoke). What it signifies, however, is the repetition of the words spoken on earth in the upper world, by all the sacred hosts and legions. For the words of the holy Law spoken here below ascend on high, where multitudes come to meet them to take them up and present them before the Holy King, there to be adorned with many crowns woven of the supernal radiances. All these words, then, are self-spoken, as it were, before the Most High King. Whoever saw such joy, whoever witnessed such praises, as mount up into all those heavens at the moment those words ascend, whilst the Holy King looks on them and crowns Himself with them! They spring up and down, they settle, as it were, on His bosom for Him to disport Himself with them, whence they ascend toward His head and are woven there into a crown. Hence the words spoken by the Torah: "and I would be playing always before him" (Prov. VIII, 30), In the verse cited there is twice mention of "them that fear the Lord"; the first indicates the men themselves as they are here below, and the second their images as reflected in their words that ascend on high. This esoteric doctrine is found in the Book of Enoch, where it says that all the words of exposition uttered by the righteous on earth are adorned with crowns and are arrayed before the Holy One, blessed be He, who delights Himself with them. They then descend and come up again before His presence in the image of that righteous man who gave expression to them, and God then delights Himself with that image. The words, then, are inscribed in "a book of remembrance before Him", so as to endure forevermore. "And they that thought upon His name" is an allusion to those that meditate on the words of Torah in order thereby to cleave to their Master through an insight into the Divine Name, so as to know Him and become equipped with the wisdom of His name in their heart. It is written: "And above the firmament that was over their heads was as the appearance of a sapphire stone, the likeness of a throne" (Ezek. I, 26). This firmament', said R. Simeon, 'is the lower firmament, as you, Companions, have explained. Happy is my portion and happy is your portion, since as regards the supernal firmament there is no one who can ever discern it. Above that lower firmament, then, there is that "sapphire stone", that precious jewel by which it is adorned. It says, "the likeness of a throne", and not "the throne". For there is throne and throne. The term "the throne" would signify the Supernal Throne, which is undisclosed and beyond all knowledge and comprehension. Hence it says here "a throne", to wit, a lower throne. The verse cited continues: "and upon the likeness of the throne was a likeness as the appearance of a man" (Ibid.). Why say both "likeness" and "appearance" when "likeness" would be enough? The explanation is that the term "likeness" alludes to the higher glory, the image of Man; whereas the word "appearance" embraces the likenesses generated in his words of Torah exposition and mystic doctrines,

Zohar: Shemoth, Section 2, Page 217b

which ascend and are crowned on high, and afterwards assume the image of man, of those righteous ones who crown them, for the delight of the Holy One, blessed be He. And you, Companions, behold, the Holy One disports Himself now with those words you uttered, and you are standing now before your Master as represented by your holy images. For when I saw you and looked well at your inward forms, I saw that you were stamped with the mystical impress of Adam, and so I knew that your image is stationed on high. In this way the righteous are destined in the future to be distinguished in the eyes of all men, and to make their holy countenance manifest before all the world' It is thus written: "all that see them shall acknowledge them, that they are the seed that the Lord hath blessed" (Isa. LI, 9).'

At this point R. Simeon noticed R. Yose meditating worldly matters. Said he to him: 'Yose, arise and make complete your image, inasmuch as you are short of one letter.' R. Yose then rose up and joyously absorbed himself in expositions of the Torah. R. Simeon then looked at him again, and said: 'R. Yose, now you are whole before the Ancient of Days, and your image is complete.'

R. Simeon further discoursed, citing the verse: "And they made the plate (ziz) of the holy crown of pure gold", etc. (Ex. XXXIX, 30). 'Why was the plate called ziz (lit. gaze, peep)? Because it was a reflector, mirroring the character of any man gazing at it. For in that plate were graven the letters of the Divine Name, and when a righteous man appeared before it the letters so engraved bulged out and rose luminous from their sockets, from which a light shone on the man's face with a faint sparkling. For a moment the priest would notice the reflection of the letters on the man's face; but when he looked more closely he would see nothing more than a faint light, like the reflection of shining gold. But the first momentary glimpse that the priest caught was a sign to him that that man was pleasing to the Holy One, blessed be He, and that he was destined for the world to come, inasmuch as that light was an illumination from on high and a mark of divine favour. On the other hand, if a man's face failed to show any such sacred sign when he stood before the plate, then the priest knew that that man was an evildoer, and in need of atonement and intercession.'

R. Judah began a discourse on the verse: "Let thine eyes be on the field that they do reap, and go thou after them;... and when thou art athirst, go unto the vessels, and drink of that", etc. (Ruth II, 9). 'This verse', he said, 'raises a problem; for the point of it is not at all apparent.' R. Isaac interposed, saying: 'But are there not many more verses in Scripture which seem to be needless, and the purpose of which is not apparent, yet we know that they conceal within them deep esoterical doctrines.' Then R. Judah, resuming his discourse, said: 'As regards this verse, whoever just looks at it and does not study it deeply is like a man who looks at a dish without tasting it. In truth, there is an inner meaning in it, and it has been composed under the inspiration of the Holy Spirit. It amounts to this. Boaz, the Judge of Israel, observed the modesty of that righteous woman in that she did not turn her eyes hither and thither, but only looked straight in front of her, and that she had a benignant eye, and that there was no trace of impudence in her. He thus spoke in praise of her eyes. For there are eyes that throw a blight on any spot on which they are cast. But he observed in her a kindly eye, and he also saw that everything prospered in her hands, that the more she gleaned the more the gleaning in the field increased; and so Boaz recognized that the Holy Spirit hovered over her. Hence he thus addressed her, saying: "Let thine eyes be on the field that they do reap, and go thou after them", to wit, "after thine eyes". For the phrase "after them" cannot be construed as alluding to the gleaners, as if so it should have been written "and glean thou" instead of "and go thou". Boaz thus bade her "go after" her eyes, having observed that her eyes carried with them a blessing and were the cause of a manifold increase in the gleaning. "Other people", he as much as said, "are not

Zohar: Shemoth, Section 2, Page 218a

permitted to follow after their eyes, but thou mayest follow thine eyes, for they are the begetters of manifold blessings." The verse may also be explained as follows. Boaz saw, under the inspiration of the Holy Spirit, that great kings and rulers were destined to issue from her, they being called the "eyes" of the people, as in the passage: "And it shall be, if it be done in error through the eyes of the congregation" (Num. xv, 24), alluding to the Sanhedrin. For, as the members of the body must follow the eyes, which are the leaders of the body, so kings, members of the Sanhedrin, and other rulers, lead the way for the people to follow. This is thus what Boaz indicated in his words: "Let thine eyes be in the field". The term "field" is a reference to Zion and Jerusalem, as it is written: "Zion shall be plowed as a field" (Micah III, 12), and also, "as the smell of a field which the Lord hath blessed" (Gen. XXVII, 27), in allusion to Jerusalem. Hence, "Let thine eyes be on the field", that is, the rulers that were destined to come forth from her should have their centre only in Jerusalem. Boaz continued: "where they do reap", inasmuch as from that "field" all the peoples of the world would reap law and illumination, as Scripture says: "For out of Zion shall go forth the Law" (Isa. II, 3); "and go thou after them", meaning "after the virtuous deeds that I observed in thee". "Have I not charged the young men that they shall not touch thee": this can be taken literally, women being easily swayed. "And when thou art athirst": this is a euphemism, Boaz saying, in effect: "When thou conceivest a desire to attach thyself to a man in order to raise up seed", "go unto the vessels", to wit, to the righteous, who are called vessels, as it is written, "be ye clean, ye that bear the vessels of the Lord"(Isa. LII, 11); they are the vessels which mankind will in time to come bring as a present to King Messiah; they are the "vessels of the Lord", in whom the Holy One, blessed be He, rejoices; and although broken vessels, bruised in this world for the sake of observing the Torah, yet the Holy One makes use only of them: "attach thyself to such vessels", Boaz bade Ruth, "and drink", etc.'

R. Yose began a discourse on the verse: "And when Boaz had eaten and drunk, and his heart was merry", etc. (Ruth III, 7). 'His heart was merry,' he said, 'by reason of his having pronounced a benediction over his food; and there is, further, a deeper significance here, to wit, that whoever says a blessing after his meal satisfies his "heart", that which is by him alluded to in the words: "In thy behalf my heart hath said" (Ps. XXVII, 8), also in, "but God is the rock of my heart" (Ibid. LXXIII, 26). For, since the blessing offered up for one's food is precious before the Holy One, blessed be He, whoever pronounces such a blessing after he is satisfied does good and brings joy to "another region". So here "another region" derived enjoyment from the blessing after the meal that the righteous Boaz pronounced, and thus we read, "and his heart was merry". Why pronounce a blessing? It is because the sustenance of man is troublesome, so to speak, for the Almighty, but when the words of the benediction pronounced by a man after eating and drinking ascend on high, that place derives an enjoyment from those words, and so benefit is drawn from the food, both below and above. This is a recondite teaching known to the Companions. Furthermore, on weekdays "that region" enjoys only the words of the after-meal benediction that ascend on high. On Sabbath days, however, there is an enjoying on high of the very food enjoyed on earth by man in virtue of this being part of the holy joy of the Sabbath. There is thus here a merging of the heavenly and the earthly. This recondite teaching is indicated in the passage, "for all things come of thee, and of thine own have we given thee" (I Chron. XXIX, 14), alluding to the enjoyment in heaven of the holy joy in the Sabbath repasts partaken of below. Whoever pronounces the after-meal benediction must do so devotedly, and in a joyful mood unmingled with any tinge of sadness, inasmuch as in giving thanks he is giving of his own to someone else; and thus, as he gives thanks joyfully and unstintedly, so will sustenance be given to him joyfully and unstintedly. By the benedictions, each commencing with "Blessed art Thou", are sustained the four legions that rule over the four corners of the world. Hence we ought to recite them with heartiness. So Scripture says: "He that hath a bountiful eye shall be blessed, for he giveth of his bread to the poor" (Prov. XXII, 9),

Zohar: Shemoth, Section 2, Page 218b

where the term yeborakh (shall be blessed) can be read yebarekh (shall-or does-bless); and the verse thus amounts to saying that we should pronounce the after-meal blessing in a bountiful spirit, for through that blessing and our joyousness in uttering it we provide, as it were, sustenance for the poor, to wit, for that region [Tr. note: Malkuth.] that possesses naught of itself, but draws its sustenance from all sides and is made up from all sides. Now, these teachings have only been transmitted to the initiated who are conversant with the sublime mystical doctrines and with the paths of the Torah. Observe now that Boaz was bountiful of heart and free from all presumptuousness. It is thus written of him: "he went to lie down at the end of the heap of corn" (Ruth III, 7). This is esoterically elucidated by the passage: "Thy belly is like a heap of wheat" (S.S. VII, 3), and so we learn from here that whoever pronounces the after-meal grace joyfully and with devotion, when he quits this world there is a place prepared for him in the sacred and mysterious mansions. Happy is the man who gives heed to the precepts of his Master and knows their recondite significance, since there is no precept in the Torah but contains manifold sublime recondite teachings and radiances and resplendencies; but the sons of men know not nor give they heed to the glory of their Master. Happy is the portion of the righteous who are assiduous in the study of the Torah; happy are they in this world and in the world to come.

'Our sages have said that the arrogant and shameless have no portion in this world nor in the world to come. All the arrogant of Israel, when they gazed on the Plate, became contrite of heart and looked inwardly into their own deeds. For the Plate possessed miraculous powers, and thus was the means of making all who looked on it feel ashamed of their misdeeds. In this way the Plate secured atonement for the arrogant and the insolent. The letters of the Divine Name engraved on it stood out shining and flashing, and whoever looked at that flashing had to cast down his eyes in fear, and become contrite of heart, and thus the Plate effected their atonement. Of a similar potency was the Incense. For whoever smelled the smoke of the pillar that ascended from the "smoke-raiser" [Tr. note: One of the ingredients of the incense.] became cleansed of heart and intent on worshipping his Master: the taint of the evil spirit disappeared from him, leaving him to serve with single heart his Father in heaven. The Incense thus possessed the potency of breaking completely the evil spirit in man. As the Plate possessed miraculous powers, so did the Incense, nothing in the world having power to crush the "other side" like the Incense. Thus we read: "Take thy fire-pan, and put fire therein from off the altar, and lay incense thereon... for there is wrath gone out from the Lord: the plague is begun" (Num. XVII, 11). For there is nothing so beloved by the Holy One, blessed be He, as the Incense. It is able to banish sorcery and all evil influences from the house. Seeing that perfumes prepared by men possess the virtue to counteract, by their odour and fumes, the ill-effects of evil things, how much more so the Incense! It is a firmly established ordinance of the Holy One, blessed be He, that whoever reflects on and recites daily the section of the Incense will be saved from all evil things and sorceries in the world, from all mishaps and evil imaginings, from evil decrees and from death; and no harm will befall him that day, as the "other side" has no power over him. But it must be read with devotion.' R. Simeon remarked: 'Were people to know how precious the offering of the Incense is to the Holy One, blessed be He, they would take every word of the passage where it is enjoined and make it into a crown for their heads, as it were, a crown of gold. And whoever studies it ought to reflect deeply on the way it was carried out; and through the reciting of it daily with devotion a man merits a portion in this world and in the world to come, and keeps away death from himself and from the world, and is saved from all punishments in this world, from the "evil sides", from the punishment of Gehinnom, and from strange powers. When the pillar of smoke ascended from the burning Incense, the priest used to see the mystical letters of the Divine Name

Zohar: Shemoth, Section 2, Page 219a

ascending on high in that pillar. Then numerous holy legions would surround the pillar on all sides until it rose in the midst of light and gladness to the region where it diffused joy and knitted together the upper world and the lower world in a complete unity, thereby achieving atonement for the evil spirit in man and for idolatry, which is of the "other side".'

R. Simeon further discoursed on the verse: "And thou shalt make an altar (mizbeah) to burn incense upon" (Ex. XXX, 1). 'This verse', he said, 'raises a problem, for we find that there were two altars, namely, the altar of burnt-offering and the altar of incense, the former the outer altar and the latter the inner one. Now, why was the altar of incense called mizbeah (lit. slaughtering-place), seeing that it had no connection with animal slaughter? The explanation is that this altar was efficacious in defeating and subduing the numerous powers of the "other side", so as to make them powerless and unable to act as accusers. Hence the name mizbeah (place of slaughter). The "evil side", when it beheld the smoke of the incense ascending in a pillar, was subdued, and fled, and was quite unable to approach the Tabernacle. Now, because that joy was shared by no one beside the Holy One, blessed be He, by reason of this offering being so precious in His sight, that altar was placed in the innermost part of the Tabernacle, for it was the repository of blessings, and was therefore hidden from the eye of man. In regard to this, it is written: "And he stood between the dead and the living; and the plague was stayed" (Num. XVII, 13). For Aaron put the Angel of Death in chains so that he could not exercise dominion nor execute any judgement. It is a traditional teaching that wherever people recite with heartfelt devotion the portion relating to the incense there will be immunity from death and from injury; nor will any other nation have power over that place. The name, "altar to burn incense upon", further tells us that the altar had to be consecrated by the burning of incense. It further teaches us, in accordance with the Chaldaic rendering, that it is forbidden to burn incense anywhere save on coals of fire taken with the censer from this altar. Observe that whoever is pursued by Rigour needs the remedy of incense-burning to save him, as also repentance before his Master, this helping greatly to keep chastisement away from him. That will assuredly result if the man is accustomed to recite the incense-ordinance twice a day, in the morning and in the evening, corresponding to the precept, "And Aaron shall burn thereon incense of sweet spices; every morning... at dusk, he shall burn it" (Ex. xxx, 7-8). And this service, moreover, perpetually upholds the world, as is indicated in the phrase, "a perpetual incense before the Lord throughout your generations" (Ibid. 8); truly it is a means of upholding both the lower world and the upper world. Where the daily recital of the incense-burning does not take place, there heavenly judgements impend, many people die there, and other nations obtain dominion. Thus Scripture says, "a perpetual incense before the Lord" (Ibid.), indicating that it abides in the presence of the Lord, more than all other modes of worship, it being the most precious and beloved to the Holy One, blessed be He. Prayer, indeed, is the highest service of all, yet is incense-burning dear and acceptable to the Almighty. Observe the difference between prayer and incense-offering. Prayer has been instituted to take the place of the sacrifices that Israel used to offer, but none of the sacrifices had the same value as the incense. There is, further, this difference between the two. Prayer repairs damage which has been done, but incense does more- it strengthens, it binds together, it is the greatest light-bringer. It was incense that removed the evil taint (zuh'ma) and purified the Tabernacle, so that the whole was illumined, renewed, and knitted together into a combined whole. Hence the incense-recital must always precede our daily prayer as a means of removing the evil taint from the world, inasmuch as it acts as a daily therapeutic like the offering itself, in which God delighted. Now we find it written of Moses: "And the Lord said unto Moses: Take unto thee sweet spices, stacte", etc. (Ibid. xxx, 34). Why specifically in this place "unto thee"? It means "for thy sake", that is, "for thy satisfaction and gain". The purification of a woman redounds to the satisfaction of her husband. So, esoterically, we have thus to read that ordinance as saying: "Take unto thee sweet spice for the purpose of removing the evil taint, that the Shekinah and Her Spouse may be joined in sanctified union." Happy thus the portion

Zohar: Shemoth, Section 2, Page 219b

of Moses! Similarly do we read: "Take thee a bull calf for a sin offering" (Lev. IX, 2), an ordinance meant personally for Aaron to atone for the sin of the golden calf which he brought upon Israel. So here Moses was bidden "Take unto thee", that is, "take for thy benefit and use" the incense (q'toreth), which is potent to bind together (qatar), to illumine and to remove the evil taint. The Daleth is linked to the He', the He to the Vau, the Vau ascends and is adorned with the He, the He, is illumined by the Yod, and the whole ascends, reaching out to the En-sof (Infinite, Illimitable), so that there results one organic whole, interrelated under one principle, the most exalted of all. From thence and upward the whole is adorned as with a crown by the ineffableness of the En-sof; and the Divine Name in its mysteriousness is illumined and is adorned on all sides, and the worlds are all wrapt in joy, the lamps radiate their lights, and sustenance and blessing pour down on all the worlds. All this follows the hidden virtue of the incense, without which the evil taint would not be removed. All thus depends on it. Observe that the offering of the incense used to precede all other services, and hence its recital should be a prelude to our service of hymns and praises, as these latter do not ascend, nor is the required readjustment and unity achieved until the evil taint is removed. So Scripture says: "And he shall make atonement for the holy place... and because of their transgressions, even all their sins" (Lev. XVI, 16), first "atonement for the holy place" and then for "their transgressions". We, too, thus have first to remove the evil taint and purge the holy place, and then engage in song and hymn and prayer,' as already said. Happy are Israel in this world and in the world to come, inasmuch as they know how to effect adjustment on high and below; to achieve adjustment from the lower world upwards until the whole is bound together in the most sublime union. The process of adjustment performed in the lower world is by means of the impressed letters of the Ineffable Name by which the Holy One, blessed be He, is named.'

R. Simeon and R. Eleazar his son were one night sitting together studying the Torah. Said R. Eleazar to his father, R. Simeon: 'It is written: "Unto the woman he said: I will greatly multiply thy pain and thy travail, in pain thou shalt bring forth children; and thy desire shall be to thy husband", etc. (Gen. III, 16). We have learned that this passage contains a profound mystical teaching. One may comprehend this passage in its terrestrial significance, but what corresponds in the supernal world?' R. Simeon cited the verse: "As the hart panteth after the water brooks", etc. (Ps. XLII, 2). 'This verse has already been expounded,' he said. 'There is, however, a certain female animal that has under her daily charge a thousand keys, and that pants continually after the water brooks to drink and quench her thirst, of which it is thus written, "As the hart panteth after the water brooks." It is to be observed that this verse commences with a masculine subject, "hart" ('ayyal), and continues with a feminine predicate, tha'erog (she panteth). The recondite explanation of this is that it is an allusion to the male-female as one undivided and inseparable; and so it is the female part of the same that "panteth for the water brooks" and then becomes impregnated from the male element, and is in labour, coming under the scrutiny of Rigour. But at the moment when she is about to be delivered of offspring the Holy One, blessed be He, prepares for her a huge celestial serpent through whose bite she is safely delivered. And this is the hidden meaning of, "I will greatly multiply thy pain and thy travail", for she is in daily convulsions and pain because of the deeds of mankind: "in pain thou shalt bring forth children", a hidden allusion to the Serpent who casts a gloom over the faces of mankind; "and thy desire shall be to thy husband": this is in harmony with the expression, "she panteth for the water brooks"; "and he shall rule over thee": this has been already expounded elsewhere. Why all this? It was on account of the Moon's dissatisfaction with her state, in punishment for which, as tradition teaches us, her light was diminished, also her power was reduced so that she is beholden to what they grant her from outside. It may be asked, Why is the Serpent necessary in this connection? It is because it is he who opens the passage for the descent of souls into the world. For if he did not open the way, no soul would come down to animate a man's body in the world. So Scripture says, "sin coucheth at the door" (Gen. III, 7), alluding to the celestial door through which pass the souls at birth to emerge into this world. He, the Serpent, waits at that door. It is true, when the souls about to emerge are such as are to enter sanctified bodies, he is not present, having no dominion over such souls. But otherwise, the Serpent bites, and that spot is defiled and the soul passing through is unpurified. Herein is concealed a sublime mystical teaching. "In pain thou shalt bring forth children" is a mystical allusion to that Serpent, as it is

Zohar: Shemoth, Section 2, Page 220a

with him that She brings forth souls, since he is responsible for the body and she for the soul, and the two are combined. The Serpent is destined in the future to bring about the birth of the whole of the bodies before its own time comes, as Scripture says: "Before she travailed, she brought forth" (Isa. LXVI, 7). For, whereas the period of the serpent's gestation is seven years, that will be at the end of six. And at that hour, when he will have brought about their birth, he himself will die. Of this, Scripture says: "He will swallow up death forever" (Ibid. xxv, 8), also "Thy dead shall live, my dead bodies shall arise" (Ibid. XXVI, 19).' Said R. Simeon: 'At the time when the dead will be awakened and be in readiness for the resurrection in the Holy Land, legions upon legions will arise on the soil of Galilee, as it is there that the Messiah is destined to reveal himself. For that is the portion of Joseph, and it was the first part of the Holy Land to be destroyed, and it was thence that the exile of Israel and their dispersion among the nations began, as Scripture says, "but they are not grieved for the hurt of Joseph" (Amos VI, 6). Thus there they will rise up first, for the reason that it is the portion of him who was put in an ark, as it says, "and he was put in an ark in Egypt"(Gen. L, 26), and subsequently was buried in the Holy Land, as it says "And the bones of Joseph, which the children of Israel brought up out of Egypt, buried they in Shechem" (Jos. XXIV, 32); and he it was who kept the purity of the holy covenant symbol in a special degree. As soon as they will rise from the dead all those hosts will march, each man to the portion of his ancestors, as Scripture says, "and ye shall return every man unto his possession" (Lev. xxv, 10). They shall recognize each other, and God will clothe every one in embroidered garments; and they will all come and offer up thanksgiving to their Master in Jerusalem, where there will assemble multitudes upon multitudes. Jerusalem itself will spread out in all directions, to a further extent even than when the exiles returned there. When they assemble and offer up praises to their Master the Holy One, blessed be He, will rejoice in them. So Scripture says: "And they shall come and sing in the height of Zion, and shall flow unto the goodness of the Lord", etc. (Jer. XXXI, 12), namely, every one to his portion and the portion of his ancestors. And the possession of Israel will extend till it will reach Damietta of the Romans, and even there they will study the Torah. All this has already been stated, and it is in harmony with the Scriptural passage, saying: "Awake and sing, ye that dwell in the dust", etc. (Isa. XVI, 19). Blessed be the Lord forevermore! Amen and Amen!'

PQUEDE

THESE ARE THE ACCOUNTS OF THE TABERNACLE, EVEN THE TABERNACLE OF THE TESTIMONY, AS THEY WERE RENDERED ACCORDING TO THE COMMANDMENT OF MOSES, ETC. R. Hiya, in this connection, quoted the verse: "All the rivers run into the sea, yet the sea is not full" (Eccles. I, 7). 'Esoterically speaking', he said, 'all the rivers here allude to the sacred brooks and springs which, when filled, pour forth to supply the great ocean. This in turn, when so filled, flows over and affords drink to all the "beasts of the field". These are the lower Chariot group, for, after the ocean has drawn in all the waters it lets them out towards one side, namely, towards the lower Holy Chariots, giving them drink. Now, these are all numbered and noted by name, as we read: "He calleth them all by name" (Isa. XL, 26). Similarly, "These are the accounts of the tabernacle, even the tabernacle of the testimony".'

R. Yose cited here the verse: "Oh how abundant is thy goodness, which thou hast laid up for them that fear thee" (PS. XXXI, 20). 'How greatly incumbent', he said, 'it is on the sons of men to reflect on and to study the ways of the Holy One, blessed be He, inasmuch as day by day

Zohar: Shemoth, Section 2, Page 220b

a voice goes forth and proclaims: "O ye people of the world, take heed unto yourselves, close the gates of sin, keep away from the perilous net before your feet are caught in it!" A certain wheel [Tr. note: v. Zohar, Exodus, 95b.] is ever whirling continuously round and round. Woe to those whose feet lose their hold on the wheel, for then they fall into the Deep which is predestined for the evildoers of the world! Woe to those who fall, never to rise and enjoy the light that is stored up for the righteous in the world to come! Happy are the righteous in the world to come, for many are the effulgences treasured up for them, many the felicities reserved for them. The verse continues: "which thou hast wrought for them that take refuge in thee in the sight of the sons of men". The word "wrought" refers to the fact that God wrought the light as the medium for the creation of the world. "For them that take refuge in thee", to wit, for those who dwell underneath the shadow of the Holy One, blessed be He; "in the sight of the sons of men", inasmuch as it is the functioning of this light that makes possible the existence of mankind, who are sustained by it despite the fact that the light itself is stored away. Again, "which thou hast wrought", viz. as a medium for the construction of the world according to an orderly plan; and similar to the construction of the world was the construction of the Tabernacle. This is indicated by the similarity of the phrase, "these are the accounts of the tabernacle", and "these are the generations of the heaven and the earth". For all the generations of heaven and earth were produced by the energy of that treasured-up Light; and likewise, all that came within the "accounts of the tabernacle" was accomplished by the same energy. How do we know this? Because Scripture says, "And Bezalel, the son of Uri, the son of Hur, of the tribe of Judah", he being of the "right side"; "and with him was Oholiab", who was of the "left side", for the Tabernacle was made by the energy of both the right side and the left side, and was finally erected by Moses, who united the two.'

R. Eleazar discoursed on the verse: "And a throne is established through mercy, and there sitteth thereon in truth, in the tent of David, one that judgeth, and seeketh justice, and is ready in righteousness" (Isa. XVI, 5). 'This has been explained as follows', he said. 'When the Thought arose with glad purpose from the Most Recondite and Unknowable, that gladness impinged on the Thought, so that the latter entered more and more deeply until it was secluded in the interior of a certain supernal undisclosed Palace. [Tr. note: Binah.] It is from thence that there flow forth, first all the rivers of the "right side", and after them the others. On the "right side" it was that the Lower Throne was established, since the Holy One, blessed be He, established that Throne "through mercy, and there sitteth thereon in truth". The Throne is the bearer of the seal, the impress of which is Truth, and the Holy One sits on that Throne only in virtue of that seal; "in the tent of David", which is identical with the Lower Throne. "One that judgeth" is from the side of Rigour; "and seeketh judgement", from the side of Mercy; "and is ready in judgement", alluding to the Throne of Judgement, which is on earth. Similarly, the Tabernacle was established only on this side of Mercy, as already said; and thereby were adjusted all the affairs of the lower world.'

THESE ARE THE ACCOUNTS OF THE TABERNACLE, EVEN THE TABERNACLE OF THE TESTIMONY, AS THEY WERE RENDERED ACCORDING TO THE COMMANDMENT OF MOSES.

R. Simeon discoursed here on the verse: "In the beginning God created the heaven and the earth" (Gen. I, 1). 'This verse', he said,

Zohar: Shemoth, Section 2, Page 221a

'has been already expounded from various aspects. However, when the Holy One, blessed be He, created this world, He created it after the pattern of the supernal world. All the aspects of the upper world he established in the lower, so that the two worlds should be firmly knitted together. Furthermore, the Holy One, when about to create the world, used the Torah as a copy, and also the Divine Name, which is the epitome of the Torah, and by it firmly established the world. By three energies is the world upheld, to wit, by Wisdom, Understanding, and Knowledge. So Scripture says: "The Lord by wisdom founded the earth, by understanding he established the heavens. By his knowledge the depths were broken up" (Prov. III, 19-20). Observe that with the same three the Tabernacle was built, as it is written: "And I have filled him with the spirit of God, in wisdom and in understanding, and in knowledge" (Ex. XXXI, 3); and all these three are indicated in the story of Creation. Thus, "In the beginning" corresponds to Wisdom; "God created" hints at Understanding; "the heaven" to Knowledge. Similarly, in the account of the Tabernacle, "These are the accounts of the tabernacle" points to Wisdom; "even the tabernacle of testimony" points to Understanding; "as they were rendered according to the commandment of Moses" points to Knowledge. The two thus correspond to each other. Now, when God commanded Moses to make the Tabernacle, Moses stood bewildered, not knowing how to proceed until God showed him an actual representation of it. We thus read: "And see that thou make them after their pattern, which is being shown thee in the mount" (Ex. xxv, 40). We learn from the phrase, "after their pattern", that the Holy One showed Moses each single part of it in its exact supernal form, after which Moses constructed the earthly Tabernacle. Why does Scripture say, "which thou art shown (mor'eh) on the mount" instead of "which thou seest (roeh)"? By this we learn that Moses was shown through a dark glass, as it were, the reflection of all the parts of the Tabernacle as they existed on high, and as they were to be constructed here below. Moses, on surveying them, was somewhat perplexed, so God said to him: "O Moses, do thou follow thy indications and I will follow mine." Moses then commenced the work without misgiving.

'When he had completed the whole work it was necessary for him to make an inventory of all the parts in order that the Israelites should not say that there was a surplus of silver or gold which he was keeping back for himself. He had thus to render an account in the presence of Israel according to the injunction, "and ye shall be clear before the Lord and before Israel" (Num. XXXII, 22). Hence it is written: "These are the accounts of the tabernacle, even the tabernacle of the testimony." For, indeed, the Holy Spirit made the whole of Israel see the amount of gold and silver offered by them; and then rendered account of them, calling out: "All the gold that was used for the work... And the silver of them that were numbered in the congregation was a hundred talents...." For the Holy One, blessed be He, was well pleased with those artificers and thus desired to demonstrate their trustworthiness before all. When the work of the Tabernacle was completed, the "other side" began going to and fro to see if he could not find something wrong, but he could discover no ground to impugn the honesty of the artificers; and the Holy One, blessed be He, made him do obeisance to Moses, and forced him against his will to acknowledge the correctness of the accounts. The integrity of the artificers was thus revealed to all; and this is the inward significance of the sentence, "These are the accounts of the tabernacle". It is also written, "as they were rendered according to the commandment of Moses", which signifies that by the order of Moses a complete account was rendered of all that concerned the Tabernacle in the presence of himself and the whole of Israel.'

Zohar: Shemoth, Section 2, Page 221b

THESE ARE THE ACCOUNTS OF THE TABERNACLE, EVEN THE TABERNACLE OF TESTIMONY. The term "tabernacle" is mentioned twice: once in reference to the one on high, and once in reference to the one below. What constituted the "testimony"? In regard to this, Scripture says, "even the tribes of the Lord (YH), as a testimony unto Israel" (Ps. CXXII, 4), whence we learn that that Divine Name is a testimony unto Israel. Verily, these two letters render testimony in every place. Hence "tabernacle" is used as the symbol of this holy name. [Tr. note: Kah, which is the name of Binah.] To this allusion is made in the words, "and my testimony that I shall teach them" (Ibid. CXXXII, 12), inasmuch as it is a spot hidden and undisclosed beyond all other spots.

AS WAS RENDERED ACCORDING TO THE COMMANDMENT OF MOSES. This refers to the testimony, not to the Tabernacle, and we should render "which was entrusted to the mouth of Moses". For after the departure from this world of the patriarchs and all the heads of the tribes, to wit, the sons of Jacob, during Israel's sufferings in exile, the knowledge of the mystery of that supernal Divine Name was forgotten by them, the Name bound up with the testimony, the Name composed of those two letters which are the basis of heaven and earth, of high and low, and of all corners of the universe. But when Moses came, that Name was once more sought after and mentioned. For when he was near the thorn-bush he straightway asked concerning that Name, saying, "and they shall say to me, What is his name? what shall I say unto them?" (Ex. III, 13). It was there that that Name was entrusted to the mouth of Moses. We read further: THROUGH THE SERVICE OF THE LEVITES. The innersignificance of this is supplied by the passage: "But the Levite shall serve Hu (lit. He)" (Num. XVIII, 23), which is an emblem of the Holy Name. Therein is enclosed the mystery of the Divine Name, which is characterized by "He" (hu), and not "Thou" (atthah). The Tabernacle is thus fitly identified with the "service of the Levites". Or we may also say that the Tabernacle is the "service of the Levites", inasmuch as they carried it on their shoulders from place to place, as Scripture says: "But unto the sons of Kehath he gave none, because the service of the holy things belonged unto them: they bore them upon their shoulders" (Num. VII, 9).

THESE ARE THE ACCOUNTS OF THE TABERNACLE, EVEN THE TABERNACLE OF TESTIMONY. R. Abba began a discourse on the verse: "And it shall come to pass in that day, that the root of Jesse, that standeth for an ensign of the peoples, unto him shall the nations seek, and his resting-place shall be glorious" (Isa. XI, 10). 'In that day', he said, 'when peace will flourish in the world, the root of the Tree of Life will be confirmed, and from it shall all the terrestrial roots ramify and draw strength. "That standeth for an ensign of the people"; to wit, as a sign and symbol of the inwardness of the Divine Name. "Unto him shall the nations seek"; inasmuch as in him is contained the mystery of the Divine Name. The same is indicated in the words; "And many people shall go and say: Come ye, and let us go up to the mountain of the Lord", etc. (Ibid. II, 3). "And his resting-place shall be glorious", to wit, the Temple, of which it is written: "This is my resting-place forever" (Ps. CXXXII, 14). Now, the resting-place of the root of Jesse, which is called "the glory of the Lord", will never be within the bounds of numbering and calculation. For blessing rests not upon what is counted, but only on what is beyond number. Observe that that Tabernacle was subjected to an inventory, and hence it needed the prayer of Moses for blessings to rest upon it, as Scripture says: "And Moses blessed them" (Ex. XXXIX, 42).

What blessing did he pronounce? He said: "Let it be His will that blessing should rest on your handiwork." Yet blessings did not rest on that Tabernacle until Moses joined it to the heavenly Tabernacle. So Scripture says: "These are the accounts of the tabernacle, even the tabernacle of the testimony, as they were rendered according to the commandment of Moses." The last words indicate that without the supervision of Moses the accounts could not have been rendered.'

R. Abba continued: 'We find it written that the woman of Zarephath said to Elijah:

Zohar: Shemoth, Section 2, Page 222a

"As the Lord thy God liveth, I have not a cake, only a handful of meal in the jar, and a little oil in the cruse" (I Kings XVII, 12). Now, a "handful" forms a definite measure, hence it was not fitting that any blessing should rest upon the cruse. Nevertheless, we are told further: "For thus saith the Lord, the God of Israel: The jar of meal shall not be spent, neither shall the cruse of oil fail, until the day that the Lord will give rain upon the land" (Ibid. 14); and so it was. Now if that meal, though measured out and known to consist of a handful, yet did not fail to receive blessing in virtue of the word spoken by Elijah, how much the more so here, in regard to the Tabernacle of the testimony, notwithstanding its having been subjected to numbering, was it meet that blessings should rest on it since its inventory was made by Moses himself!'

THESE ARE THE ACCOUNTS OF THE TABERNACLE. R. Hezekiah adduced here the verse: "Draw not nigh hither, put off thy shoes from off thy feet, for the place whereon thou standest is holy ground" (Ex. III, 5). 'This verse', he said, 'has been explained as an injunction to Moses to separate from his wife so as to cleave to the Shekinah. The term "holy ground" denotes the Shekinah, to whom Moses attached himself at that moment. The Holy One, blessed be He, thus bound him to Himself in heavenly love and affection, made him, as it were, steward of the House, so that he had only to order and the Holy One would execute that decree, as when he said, "and the ground shall open her mouth", etc. (Num. XVI, 30), and we are told, "And it came to pass as he made an end of speaking... that the ground did cleave asunder" (Ibid. 31); or again, as when he said, "Rise up, O Lord... Return, O Lord" (Ibid. x, 35-36). It is thus written: "as they were counted (puqqad) under the commandment of Moses", for it was under the command of Moses that the whole was accomplished and the sum of it counted. The word piqude (numberings) here contains an allusion to the message which God gave to Moses, saying: "I have indeed taken count (paqod paqadti) of you" (Ex. III, 16). For it was Moses who constituted the voice that uttered the message which heralded the departure of Israel from exile.

AND BEZALEL, THE SON OF URI, THE SON OF HUR, OF THE TRIBE OF JUDAH, ETC. Said R. Judah: It has been laid down that Bezalel was of the "right side", and so it was he who perfected the whole work. Furthermore, since Judah was ruler and king over the rest of the tribes, it thus fell to a descendant of his to construct the Tabernacle. It has already been explained that the name Bezalel is a compound of two words, signifying "in the shadow of God", and thus indicates the "right side". Further, from this side Bezalel possessed himself of the wisdom to do all the work. AND WITH HIM WAS OHOLIAB, THE SON OF AHISAMACH, OF THE TRIBE OF DAN. Oholiab symbolized the "left side", the side of Rigour. The Tabernacle was thus made out of the two sides and upheld by both, so as to be a combination and a balancing of the Right and the Left.' R. Judah further cited in regard to this the verse: "Beautiful bowery, [Tr. note: The Zohar takes noph in its post-Biblical sense of branch, part of the tree] the joy of the whole earth; even Mount Zion, the uttermost parts of the north, the city of the great king" (Ps. XLVIII, 3). 'Observe', he said, 'that when the Holy One, blessed be He, was about to create the world, He detached one precious stone from underneath His Throne of Glory and plunged it into the Abyss, one end of it remaining fastened therein whilst the other end stood out above; and this other and superior head constituted the nucleus of the world, the point out of which the world started, spreading itself to right and left and into all directions, and by which it is sustained. That nucleus, that stone, is called sh'thyiah (foundation), as it was the starting-point of the world. The name sh'thyiah, furthermore, is a compound of shath (founded) and Kah (God), signifying that the Holy One, blessed be He, made it the foundation and starting-point of the world and all that is therein.

Zohar: Shemoth, Section 2, Page 222b

Now, the earth's expansion round the central point was completed in three concentric rings, each of a different hue and texture. The first ring, the nearest to the Point, is of the purest and most refined earth-material; the second expansion, surrounding the first, is of a less polished, less refined earth-material than the first, but is superior to the one surrounding it; the third expansion consists of the darkest and coarsest earth-material of all. Then, surrounding that expansion, come the waters of the ocean that surrounds the whole world. Thus the point is in the centre, and the various expansions encircle it. The first expansion embraces the Sanctuary and all its courts and enclosures and all its appurtenances, as well as the whole city of Jerusalem bounded by the wall; the second expansion embraces the whole of the Land of Israel, the Land which was declared holy; the third expansion comprehends the rest of the earth, the dwelling-place of all the other nations. Then comes the great ocean which surrounds the whole. The whole arrangement is symbolized by the structure of the human eye. For just as in the human eye there are three concentric layers surrounding a central point, which forms the focus of vision, so is the world's vision focused in the central point, consisting of the Holy of Holies and the Ark and the Mercy Seat. Hence the description, "a beautiful bowery, the joy of the whole earth", "beautiful" in its appearance, and radiating joy to the whole world. It is compared to a "bowery" because the beauty of a tree is displayed in its branches. Observe that true beauty and symmetry were not manifested in the world until the Tabernacle was finally erected and the Ark brought within the Holy of Holies. From that moment the world appeared at its best, it attained its just balance, and a way was opened through the Tabernacle and past the Ark up to that Point, that "beautiful bowery, the joy of the whole earth". When that point was reached the Ark broke forth, saying: "This is my resting-place forever; here will I dwell, for I have desired it" (Ps. CXXXII, 14).'

R. Jesse said: 'This verse was uttered by the Community of Israel when the Temple was built and the Ark entered into its place.' R. Hezekiah said: 'It is the Holy One, blessed be He, who utters this verse, applying it to the Community of Israel when the latter performs His will. For at such a time the Holy One, blessed be He, ascends His Throne of Glory, and has compassion on the world, and blessings and peace and love are there, so that He says: "This is my resting-place forever", etc. Now, observe that once the artisans had begun the work of the Tabernacle, it veritably completed itself of its own accord. This we learn from the words, "Thus was finished all the work of the tabernacle of the tent of meeting" (Ex. XXXIX, 32). The same happened in the creation of the world, of which it is likewise written: "And the heaven and the earth were finished" (Gen. II, 1). This, it is true, seems to conflict with the statement that "on the seventh day God finished his work which he had made" (Ibid. 2.) But the truth is, that although the several parts of the world completed themselves one by one, yet the world in its entirety was only completed and firmly established when the seventh day came. For then did the Holy One, blessed be He, with it knit together the world into a complete whole, so that it could be written, "And on the seventh day God finished his work which he had made." It was the same with the building of the Temple. The artisans having begun their work, it showed them what was to be done, as it were, before their eyes; it was traced out in their sight, and it completed itself of its own accord.' [Tr. note: v. Zohar, Gen. 74a.]

Zohar: Shemoth, Section 2, Page 223a

AND BEZALEL, THE SON OF URI, THE SON OF HUR. Tradition tells us that it was the Holy Spirit who made this announcement in the presence of Israel, proclaiming: "And Bezalel, the son of Uri, the son of Hur, of the tribe of Judah, made all that the Lord commanded Moses." AND WITH HIM WAS OHOLIAB, THE SON OF AHISAMACH.

From the expression, "and with him ('itto)", we learn that Oholiab never performed any work by himself, but always in association with Bezalel. Hence the words, "and with him", which proves that the left is always embraced within the right.

THESE ARE THE ACCOUNTS OF THE TABERNACLE, EVEN THE TABERNACLE OF THE TESTIMONY, AS THEY WERE RENDERED ACCORDING TO THE COMMANDMENT OF MOSES, ETC. R. Jesse said: 'The wise men having completed the Tabernacle, it was requisite that an account should be rendered of all the parts of the work. For what reason? Because as the account of each work was rendered, so did that work become firmly established in its place. Furthermore, as the Israelites had found delight at first in their voluntary offerings, so were they delighted in the accounts being rendered; and thus their delight helped to the confirming of the work. Now, it is written "these" and not "and these", this signifying that this account eclipsed all previous accounts rendered in the world, and was destined to outlive them, being the one by which the Tabernacle was sustained.' R. Jesse further discoursed on the verse: "And there shall be faithfulness in thy times, strength of salvation, wisdom and knowledge, and the fear of the Lord which is his treasure" (Isa. XXXIII, 6). 'We have been taught', he said, 'that whoever devotes himself to the study of the Torah in this world, and is able to appoint set times for it, must do so in "faithfulness", must direct his mind toward the Holy One, blessed be He, must study for Heaven's sake. The words "strength of salvation" indicate that he must fuse Rigour with Mercy. "Wisdom and Knowledge" are two qualities which merge into one another. "The fear of the Lord is his treasure"; to wit, the treasure which contains the qualities just mentioned. For the fear of the Lord collects all those "brooks" (of wisdom), and so becomes the receptacle of all. And when these treasures issue from it they do so under a vigilant count-taking. That process is thus called "faithfulness", as explained. Verily, if herein faithfulness has to be manifested, how much more so in workaday matters! The Holy One, blessed be He, therefore made the whole of Israel know the inwardness of faithfulness in all things that they performed.'

R. Yose and R. Isaac once were walking together when R. Yose remarked: 'The Holy One, blessed be He, indeed chose Bezalel from all Israel for the work of the Tabernacle. Why so?' R. Isaac replied: 'There is something in a name. It has been laid down that God has appointed certain names here on earth to be a crown to men and to enable them to achieve certain things.' R. Yose thereupon said: 'A more recondite explanation is as follows. Judah was of the "left side", but then attached himself to the "right side", and so the Tabernacle was begun from the "left side" and then was joined to the "right side", so that the whole was transformed into the "right". Reuben, on the other hand, began on the "right" but turned aside to the "left", and the other tribes of his company marched together with him, they also belonging to the "left". Hence Bezalel, who was of the tribe of Judah, and thus of the "right side", made the Tabernacle and completed it. As already said, the Holy One, blessed be He, took delight in him and chose him above all the rest for this work, and gave him wisdom and understanding and knowledge, inasmuch as he already was possessed of all wisdom of heart, as it is written: "and in the hearts of all that are wise hearted I have put wisdom" (Ex. XXXI, 6). For the Holy One, blessed be He, does not grant wisdom save to him that already has wisdom.' R. Simeon said: 'The name Bezalel was emblematic, and he was called so in virtue of his wisdom; esoterically the name is composed of b'zel-El (in the Shadow of God). In the verse, "As an apple tree among the trees of the wood... under its shadow I delighted to sit" (S.S. II, 3), the words, "under its shadow" (b'zilo), are an allusion to Bezalel, who made the Tabernacle, which is a delightful place wherein to sit, for it gives delight to the Community of Israel, and the Community of Israel sits under the shadow of God. Hence, "And Bezalel, the son of Uri, the son of Hur", "the son of Uri" denoting one of the right, and "the son of Hur" one of the left. And so, through him, full atonement was made for the sin of the Golden Calf.

ALL THE GOLD THAT WAS MADE: that is to say, that was destined for the purpose long before. FOR THE WORK IN ALL THE HOLY WORK; indicating that gold had to be used in the working out of each separate grade, for the reason that completeness can only be reached through the working together of Severity and Mercy. Hence gold had to go into all the work connected with the Sanctuary.

R. Abba, R. Yose, and R. Hizkiah were once sitting together studying the Torah. Said R. Hizkiah to R. Abba: 'Since we see that the Holy One, blessed be He, finds delight in dealing out stern judgement, tempering mercy therewith, why, then, does He withhold it from sinners?' R. Abba answered: 'Many mountains have been uprooted [Tr. note: Cf. the Talmudic phrase, "uprooter of mountains"=ingenious dialectician.] on this question. But the Sacred Lamp (R. Simeon) has revealed a number of truths in regard to this matter. Observe that the severity of judgement in which the Holy One, blessed be He, delights, is of the judgement fully clarified, the judgement that evokes clemency and gladness. But the sinners in this world are the embodiment of a judgement steeped in defilement, a judgement altogether displeasing to the Holy One, blessed be He. Hence He desires not to mingle holy judgement with defiled judgement until such time as the latter will be exterminated of itself and the sinner thus will be destroyed from the future world; by that very defiled judgement will he be destroyed from the world.'

R. Abba illustrated from the verse: "When the wicked spring up as the grass, and when all the workers of iniquity do blossom; it is that they may be destroyed forever" (Ps. XCII, 8). 'This verse', he said, 'apart from its more obvious meaning, is to be interpreted as follows. When the wicked spring up, it is but as grass, to wit, like grass that is withered in the parched soil, but revives somewhat at the approach of water, and like a felled tree that can still send forth twigs on either side, but can never regain its former foliage. So will the wicked be destroyed forever and be altogether uprooted. There is this further truth underlying this verse. It is, that the Holy One, blessed be He, is long-suffering with the wicked in this world, because this world is the portion of the "other side", whereas the world to come belongs to the side of holiness, is the portion of the righteous for them to abide therein adorned with the crown of the glory of their Master. These two sides are the counterparts of one another, the one

the side of holiness, the other that of defilement; the one destined for the righteous, the other for the wicked. Happy are those righteous who have no portion in this world but only in the world to come. Observe that all is predisposed and revealed before the Holy One, blessed be He. Even so was it with Balak and Balaam: although the motive of their action [Tr. note: Viz. the building of the altars and the offering of sacrifices.] was not the glory of Heaven, yet was all they did duly recorded before the Lord, who did not diminish aught of their reward in this world. Thus, through the power of the forty-two offerings which they brought on the seven altars, Balak and Balaam obtained for the time being dominion over Israel, so that twenty and four thousand Israelites died by the plague besides those who were slain, as we read: "Take all the chiefs of the people and hang them up unto the Lord in face of the sun. Slay ye every one his men that have joined themselves unto the Baal of Peor" (Num. XXV 4-5).' R. Simeon said: 'Observe that the forty-two offerings brought by Balaam and Balak were offerings diverted from the "other side" towards the Holy One, blessed be He, and so the "other side", which is called "curse", had to be repaid these offerings from Israel. This is the inner implication of the verse, "And he (Elisha) looked behind him and saw them" (2 Kings II, 24). That is to say, "behind him", meaning the "other side", which stands behind the Shekinah. He turned "and saw them" (the children), as being meet for punishment; "and cursed them in the name of the Lord" (Ibid.), inducing the Divine Name, as it were, to discharge the debt owing to the "other side", for the latter's offerings which had been diverted to Him. Thus all is made right before the Holy One, blessed be He, and not a single act is lost, whether for good or for evil. Take again the act of David in fleeing from before Saul. That was the cause of all the priests of Nob being destroyed, with the sole exception of Abiathar, the son of Zadok, and this in turn was the cause of many evils that befell Israel. Through it Saul and his sons were killed, and many thousands and myriads fell in Israel. But all the time the punishment to be exacted for that sin was hanging over David, until all his descendants perished in one day, with the sole exception of Joash, [Tr. note: V. 2 Kings, XI, 1-2]. who was stolen away from among the slain. Yet was that sin against Nob still awaiting expiation, as indicated in the words:

"There is still a day for a halt to be made at Nob" (Isa. x, 32). The same balancing of accounts is indicated in the words here, "All the gold ready-made (he'asui) for the work". What signifies the attribute "ready-made"? It signifies that God foresaw that the Israelites would give up their gold for the making of the Golden Calf, and so made them first give up their gold for the erection of the Tabernacle so as to make good the offering of the other gold. For had the Israelites still possessed all their gold at the time they made the Golden Calf, they would hardly have had to "break off the golden rings which were in their ears" (Ex. XXXII, 3). The offering of the gold for the Tabernacle was thus an atonement for the other gold. [Tr. note: There is here a lacuna in the text.] Hence, "And Bezalel, the son of Uri, the son of Hur, of the tribe of Judah", of the side of royalty, "made all that the Lord commanded Moses". For all the craftsmanship of the Tabernacle was achieved through these two, Bezalel performing all the work, and Moses afterwards putting the finishing touch. Moses and Bezalel were both parts, as it were, of one whole, Moses being above and Bezalel underneath, since the end of the body is also part of the body."

R. Yose gave a further exposition of the verse relating to Elisha which says: "And he went up from thence unto Beth-el; and as he was going up by the way, certain youths (ne'arim), little ones", etc. (2 Kings II, 23). 'The term ne'arim (youths)', he said, 'has been expounded to mean empty, [Tr. note: The root, N'R has this meaning only in post-Biblical Hebrew.] that is, empty of any words of the Torah and of any observance of the precepts of the Torah: "little ones",

Zohar: Shemoth, Section 2, Page 224b

to wit, of little faith, and such as were doomed in this world and in the world to come; "came forth out of the city" (Ibid.), that is, they abandoned the mystery of Divine Faith, the term "city" having the same implication here as in the passage, "and I will not enter the city" (Hos. XI, 9). [Tr. note: Al. the Divine Faith, which is called "city", as in the passage, "in the city of the Lord of hosts, in the city of our God" (Ps. XLVIII, 9)]. "And he looked behind him and saw them" (2 Kings II, 24); that is, he surveyed their future to see whether they would ever turn back from their evil ways, "and he saw them" as being such that were not ever to bring forth any good seed. Again, "and he saw them", that is, he recognized them as such as had been conceived on the night of the Day of Atonement; [Tr. note: When marital relations are forbidden.] straightway, therefore, "he cursed them in the name of the Lord" (Ibid.). Further, "And he turned behind him" signifies that having surveyed them in order to find out whether he would be punished for their sake or not, "he turned behind him", in other words, he found himself turned away and removed from such punishment. Parallel to it is the passage, "and Aaron turned" (Num. XI, 10), signifying that Aaron was turned away and shielded from Miriam's leprosy; "and he saw them", as being destined to perpetrate much evil in Israel. "And he turned behind him" further signifies that he turned his gaze behind the Shekinah, as it says of Lot's wife that she "looked back from behind him" (Gen. XIX, 26), meaning "from behind the Shekinah". Thus Elisha looked behind the Shekinah and discerned that their mothers had conceived them all on the night that presides over the atonement of the sins of Israel. Straightway "he cursed them in the name of the Lord". "And there came forth two bears" (2 Kings II, 24)-she bears, as indicated by the feminine numeral sh'tayim, big with offspring, "and tare forty and two children of them" (Ibid.), in correspondence, as has been explained, to the number of offerings brought by Balak.

'EVEN THE GOLD OF WAVING WAS. Why is the gold characterized as that of "waving"; and why is the silver not so characterized, although the brass is, as it says, "the brass of waving"? The reason is that "waving" signifies "rising upward", and thus distinguishes this gold from the lower and inferior gold. For all the grades and Chariots are of the superior plane, symbolized by the "gold of waving", and this same gold, the further it extends downwards the more it loses in colour, in virtue, and in brilliancy. Whilst in the heights above it is goodly gold in the mystery of its brilliancy, below it is the dross of itself and its refuse. Not so the silver, of which it is simply written, "And the silver of them that were numbered of the congregation". For silver retains its virtues, even in its extension downwards, although it does not remain in the same excellence; whereas gold, in its extension downwards, becomes coarser and coarser. [Tr. note: Gold, in the cabbalistic doctrine, is symbolic of Rigour, or Judgement, which in the higher regions exists in its purity, whilst the more it descends the more it is mingled with the dross of evil, sin, the "other side", or the evil Accuser, etc. But silver is symbolic of Mercy, which is not changed by its descent.] Hence the one had to be waved and raised to the heights, whilst the other had to be extended downwards and into all directions, since it retains its excellence everywhere.'

R. Yose then continued to discourse, citing the verse: "For the Lord God (Tetragrammaton ELOHIM) is a sun and a shield; the Lord giveth grace and glory; no good thing will he withhold from them that walk uprightly" (Ps. LXXXIV, 12). 'The "sun", he said, ' contains the mystery of the Divine Name Tetragrammaton, wherein is the abode of rest of all the grades, whereas "shield" contains the mystery of the Divine Name ELOHIM; the same is indicated in "I am thy shield" (Gen. XV, 1). The two together, sun and shield, constitute thus the mystery of the Divine Name complete: "the Lord giveth grace and glory", so that the whole should merge into a unity. "No good thing will he withhold from them that walk uprightly". This is in antithesis to the passage saying, "But from the wicked their light is withholden" (Job XXXVIII, 15), and is an allusion to the primordial light, of which it is written, "And God saw the light that it was good"

(Gen. I, 4), and so the Holy One, blessed be He, put it away and stored it up, as already said. He treasured it up and withdrew it so that the wicked may not enjoy it, neither in this world nor in the world to come. As for the righteous, "no good thing will he withhold from them that walk uprightly", alluding to that primordial light which "God saw that it was good". Thus that light needed not to ascend and be raised aloft, but only to be disclosed and extended, unlike the other, which is of the "left". This accounts for the one being characterized by "of the waving" and not the other. Hence it simply says: "And the silver of them that were numbered of the congregation was a hundred talents."

'Observe this. The "right side" is ever present in the world to sustain it, and to afford it light

and blessing. Hence the priest, inasmuch as he is of the "right side", is always in readiness to bless the people. For it is from the "right side" that all the blessings of the world do spring, and the priest takes by right the first share. The priest has thus been assigned to bless both the upper world and the lower. Observe that when the priest spreads his hands at the time he blesses the people, the Shekinah comes and hovers over him and endows him with power. [Tr. note: Lit. fills his hands.] When blessing, the priest raises his right hand above the left, so as to cause the right to prevail over the left. All the grades over which he spreads his hands are thus blessed from the source of all things, from the well called "Righteous". The source of all is the "future world", the sublime source which illumines all faces, whence are kindled all lamps. It has a counterpart in the source and spring of the well whence all the lower lamps and the lower lights are kindled and radiate. So one corresponds to the other. Hence, when the priest spreads out his hands and begins to pronounce the blessing over the people, the celestial benedictions flowing from the celestial source at once kindle the lamps, all faces are illumined, and the Community of Israel is adorned with celestial crowns, and all those blessings flow down from on high to below.

'Observe, then, that Moses gave the instructions and Bezalel carried them out, the two being in the esoterical relation of body and final part of body, which is the holy covenant symbol. The Tabernacle was thereby made the centre of the increase of Love and Unity. And the whole was performed in the mystery of the "right side". Hence, wherever the "right side" dominates the Evil Eye has no power. We thus read, "And the silver of them that were numbered of the congregation." [Tr. note: The Zohar seems to construe this phrase as: "the numbered silver of the congregation."] For that silver came from the right, and so all and everything were taken count of and numbered.'

R. Isaac put the following question to R. Simeon: 'Seeing that, as we have learnt, no blessing dwells in whatever is numbered or measured, why were all things connected with the Tabernacle made to be numbered?' R. Simeon replied: 'Wherever holiness abides, there, if the act of numbering proceeds from the side of holiness, blessing will abide continuously, and not pass away. This we learn from the tithe, which is a cause of blessing, the reason being that the act of counting is performed for a sacred purpose. How much more so, then, should that be with the Tabernacle, which was a sacred edifice and derived from the side of holiness! But it is not so with worldly matters, such as are not derived from the side of holiness; no blessing rests upon them if they are numbered. For then the "other side", that is, the Evil Eye, may obtain dominion over them; and wherever the Evil Eye rules there blessings cannot reach. Contrariwise, in holy affairs, through measuring and numbering blessings continuously increase. Hence, "And the silver of them that were counted of the congregation"; indeed, "counted", without fear of the Evil Eye, without fear of any evil consequences, as the blessings from above rested there upon all. Observe, likewise, that no evil eye had any power over the seed of Joseph, for the reason that Joseph came from the "right side", and this was the reason that the Tabernacle was made by Bezalel, who belonged to the same grade as Joseph, the grade exhibited in the purity of the holy covenant symbol.'

R. Abba and R. Aha and R. Yose were walking on the way from Tiberias to Sepphoris, when they caught sight of R. Eleazar, who was coming up in the company of R. Hiya. Said R. Abba: 'Truly, we are now going to have the company of the Shekinah.' They waited for them until they came up with them. Then R. Eleazar cited the verse: "The eyes of the Lord are toward the righteous, and his ears are open unto their cry" (Ps. XXXIV, 16). 'This verse', he said, 'presents a difficulty. It cannot mean that God's providence cares for the righteous for to endow them with the goods of this world, since, indeed, we see so many righteous in this world who cannot procure even so much sustenance as would satisfy the ravens of the air.

But there is a recondite meaning here. Observe that all beings of this world are known in the upper world, either to one side or to the other side. Those of the side of holiness are known to that side, whose watchful providence is ever towards them. Similarly those belonging to the side of defilement are known to that side, being under its continuous care. Now, when a man is under the care of the side of holiness, the "other side" will never come near him and is powerless to thrust him out of his place, or of whatever he is doing. Thus, "The eyes of the Lord are toward the righteous", etc., so that the "other side" is powerless to obtain rule over him. Now,' concluded R. Eleazar, 'the support of heaven is here with us, we are watched over from on high, and no power from the "other side", no evil thing, can rule over you.' Said R. Abba: 'Behold, we have learned that wherever the holy side hovers, there, despite its association with any act of numbering, blessings will never cease.' Said R. Eleazar: 'Assuredly it is so.' 'Now', rejoined R. Abba, 'behold, Israel is holy and comes from the side of holiness, as we read: "Israel is the Lord's hallowed portion" (Jer. II, 3); also, "ye shall be holy, for I the Lord your God am holy" (Lev. XIX, 2). Why, then, when David took a census of Israel did death rage among the people, as Scripture says: "So the Lord sent a pestilence upon Israel from the morning even to the time appointed" (2 Sam. XXII, 15)?' R. Eleazar said in reply: 'This was because he did not take from them shekels as a ransom in accordance with the injunction, "then shall they give every man a ransom for his soul unto the Lord, when thou numberest them; and there be no plague among them when thou numberest them" (Ex. xxx, 12) For that which is holy should give a holy ransom, and that holy ransom was not taken from them at the time. Observe that Israel is holy and not meet for numbering, and hence a ransom had to be taken from them, and this could be numbered whilst they themselves were not to be numbered. For holiness is the essence of the highest of grades; and just as to that highest degree of holiness there is attached a lower degree [Tr. note: Malkuth.] that admits of number and computation, so Israel, "the Lord's hallowed portion", have to give as ransom something of another degree of holiness, that admits of computation. Esoterically speaking, Israel is the tree that stands in the innermost. The ransom is of another kind of holiness, standing outside and admitting of computation. The latter is thus a shield to the former.'

The company then pursued their journey, and R. Eleazar began to discourse on the verse: "Yet the number of the children of Israel shall be as the sand of the sea, which cannot be measured nor numbered" (Hos. II, 1). 'The comparison to the sand of the sea', he said, 'is of a twofold aspect. First, just as when the sea rages and its waves hurl themselves forward to overwhelm the world, so soon as they encounter the sand of the shore their force is broken and they recede and rage no more, so the nations rage and fume and seek to overwhelm and flood the world; but when they behold Israel in close attachment to the Holy One, blessed be He, they recede, broken and powerless. Again, as the sand of the sea cannot be numbered or measured, so is Israel. Observe that there is somewhere a measuring hidden away and undisclosed, and similarly a hidden and undisclosed numbering, that measuring and that numbering upholding the upper world and the lower just because the basis of that measuring and of that numbering is beyond anyone's knowledge. This constitutes the all-in-all Divine Faith. Now, Israel on earth does not fall within the scope of number save through the side of something extraneous to themselves; thus it is their ransom that falls within the scope of number. Hence, when Israel are about to be numbered,

Zohar: Shemoth, Section 2, Page 226a

a ransom has to be taken from them, as already said. Thus, when David took a census of Israel without having taken from them a ransom, wrath was provoked and there perished of Israel many hosts and legions. This, then, is the significance of the words, "And the silver of them that were counted of the congregation... forevery one that passed over to them that are numbered". It was all consecrated to the work of the Tabernacle. It has been stated that the talents represented one category of number, whilst the shekels represented another category. For there are higher existences who come within a superior kind of number; and there are others who belong to a lower kind.'

R. Eleazar further discoursed on the verse; "A song of ascents; of Solomon. Except the Lord build the house, thy labour is in vain", etc. (Ps. CXXVII, 1). 'This verse', he said, 'was uttered by Solomon at the time when, having begun to build the Temple he became aware that the work proceeded of itself, as it were, in the hands of the labourers. "Except the Lord", he thus said, "build the house", etc. This alludes to the statement that "In the beginning God created heaven and earth" (Gen. I, 1), and tells us that the Holy One, blessed be He, created and garnished this world and fitted it out with all its requirements, thus making it a House. "They labour in vain that build it": this alludes to the streams that come forth and enter the House in order to furnish it with all its needs; try as they may, yet except the Lord of the supernal world make the House and put it in proper order, they labour in vain. "Except the Lord keep the city", etc. (Ibid.). This is in harmony with the verse: "The eyes of the Lord thy God are always upon it, from the beginning of the year even unto the end of the year" (Deut. XI, 12), indicating the providence by which it is guarded on all sides. And though it is also written, "Behold, it is the couch of Solomon; threescore mighty men are about it" (S.S. III, 7), all guarding it, this is "because of dread in the night" (Ibid. 8), to wit, the dread of Gehinnom that confronts it and tries to annihilate it. All thus are standing guard round about it. [Tr. note: The text here repeats the passage from Zohar, Genesis, 65a, commencing, "That unknowable light" to "is called En-Sof".] When the Thought is illumined, it remains undisclosed and unknowable, but it forms a centre of energies and of expansion in all directions. One outcome of that expansion is the Supernal World, the world of interrogation, as it were, or of the Supreme Utterance, the world called "Who?", alluded to in "Lift up your eyes on high, and see: Who hath created these?", or in other words, the creative utterance, the Word, created these; but subsequently it expanded and became the sea, symbolic of the lowest grade, and created a lower world after the pattern of the

Zohar: Shemoth, Section 2, Page 226b

upper, the two being the counterparts of each other. Hence the guarding of the universe is from above downwards, that is, from the upper world which was formed by the expansion of the Thought. We thus understand the meaning of the passage, saying, "Except the Lord keep the city, the watchman watcheth in vain", "the watchman" referring to the watchman of Israel, [Tr. note: i.e. Metatron, the chief of the angels.] since protection depends not on him but on the higher world. Note that the blue employed in the work of the Tabernacle symbolized the mystery of the upper world, the blue and the purple together symbolized the knitting together of the upper world and the lower.

AND OF THE THOUSAND SEVEN HUNDRED SEVENTY AND FIVE SHEKELS HE MADE HOOKS FOR THE PILLARS, AND OVERLAID THEIR CAPITALS, ETC. We have learned that these shekels escaped the memory of Moses, and he could not recall what use he had made of them until a Voice went forth and declared: "And of the thousand seven hundred seventy and five shekels he made hooks for the pillars", etc. In this connection, R. Hizkiah began a discourse on the verse: "While the king sat at his table, my spikenard sent forth its fragrance" (S.S. I, 12). 'This', he said, 'is an allusion to the Holy One, blessed be He, at the time when He gave the Torah to Israel, when He came to Sinai accompanied by multitudes of holy legions and all the supernal holy beings. The Torah was then given in the midst of flaming fire, itself being written in white fire upon black fire, the letters floating aloft in the air. The first letter of the Torah divided itself into seven hundred and seventy-five parts facing in all directions, all of which were visible aloft in the air within "the letter Vau, the letter which was traced out on every side of the world. These Vaus were upheld by pillars and the pillars were suspended by a miracle with all the Vaus on top of them. For the essence of the Torah is based on the Vau, and these Vaus, which constitute the mystery of the faith of the Torah, are all based on those pillars, which constitute in their turn the mysteries of the books of the Prophets. The supreme Vau is symbolic of the audible Voice, symbolic of the foundation of the Torah, for the Torah emerged from that inner Voice, called Great Voice, of which we read: "These words the Lord spake, etc., with a great voice, and it went on no more" (Deut. v, 22). Observe that that Great Voice is the root of all things, and is the essence of the Holy Divine Name. It is for this reason that it has been laid down that a man may not greet his friend before he has recited his prayer. This is the recondite significance of the verse: "He that blesseth his friend with a loud voice, rising early in the morning, it shall be counted a curse to him" (Prov. XXVII, 14); the prohibition only applies to a blessing that is joined with that which is emblematic of the "great voice", which is the main part of the Divine Name. The mystery of the Torah proceeds, then, from the Great Voice, which is identical with "the King", and "whilst the King sat at His table" alludes to the giving of the Law at Mount Sinai. "My spikenard sent forth

Zohar: Shemoth, Section 2, Page 227a

its fragrance" refers to the Community of Israel, who said: "All that the Lord hath spoken will we do, and obey" (Ex. XXIV, 7); by "the King" is meant the Most High King, as expounded.

'When the Holy One, blessed be He, was about to bring a flood on the world in order to destroy all flesh, He said to Noah: "It behoves thee to hide thyself, and not to be seen by the Destroyer lest he obtain dominion over thee and none will be able to shield thee." Subsequently, when the sacrifices brought by Noah were offered up, a fragrance was diffused in the world; but not so sweet as when, later on, Israel stood at Mount Sinai. Then the world was truly filled with a fragrance, and thus the Destroyer was no more to be seen. Indeed, the Holy One, blessed be He, was about to remove altogether the Destroyer from the world, when Israel, after the lapse of only a few days, committed a sin in making the Golden Calf; thus Scripture says: "And the children of Israel stripped themselves of their ornaments from Mount Horeb" (Ex. XXXIII, 6), "their ornaments" signifying the mysteries of the Divine Name with which the Holy One adorned them, but which were now removed from them. The Destroyer thus regained power over the world, inflicting punishment over it, as before.' R. Yose said: 'At the flood, what was there for the Destroyer to do, seeing that it was the waters that prevailed? The fact is that no punishment is ever meted out to the world but the Destroyer is in the midst of it all, busying himself among the judgements executed. Likewise here, while the flood wrought havoc, the Destroyer went about in its midst, and indeed "Flood" was his name. The Holy One, blessed be He, thus admonished Noah to hide himself and not let himself be seen.'

AND OF THE THOUSAND SEVEN HUNDRED SEVENTY AND FIVE SHEKELS HE MADE HOOKS (vavim) FOR THE PILLARS. R. Eleazar said: 'Why vavim (lit. Vaus)? Because the pillars were in the shape of the letter vau; the pillars were of silver, but their capitals were overlaid with gold. Forevery Vau is of the side of Mercy, and these were all known on high by number; and it is because they belonged to the side of Mercy that they are called Vavim (Vaus); and all besides depended on them. Now each Vau (vau-shaped pillar) consisted of both gold and silver (symbolic of Rigour and Mercy), and they were called "pillars", for the reason that they stood outside and underneath the Body.' Said R. Isaac: 'I was in doubt whether the work referred to in our verse was sacred or profane; for, indeed, there is ground for thinking that it speaks here of profane work from the occurrence of the word "thousand", which in the analogous passage, "Thou, O Solomon, shalt have the thousand" (S.S. VIII, 12), undoubtedly speaks of mundane things.' R. Eleazar said in reply: 'Not so. If these shekels were profane, no Vavim (vau-shaped pillars) would have been made of them. Further (in the Song of Songs), it only mentions "the thousand", no more, whereas here it is written: "the thousand seven hundred seventy and five". Now, what is profane has no share in the side of holiness, but belongs entirely to the "other side", to that of impurity. Thereon is based the separation (habdalah) which we have to make between the holy and the profane. Yet, for all that and despite their separateness, the holy contains a particle

Zohar: Shemoth, Section 2, Page 227b

of the "left side". Thus, "Thou, O Solomon, shalt have the thousand", signifies the thousand days of unholiness, to wit, the days of Exile (galuth). A thousand days there are of holiness, and, correspondingly, a thousand days of the "other side". The Companions have thus in regard to this remarked that the days of Exile alluded to are a thousand years; and although Israel may continue in exile longer than a thousand years, yet that will only be an extension of those thousand years designated by the term "thousand days". Hence it has been declared that the term Solomon (Sh'lama= possessor of peace), in the whole of the Song of Songs, is divine, with the exception of this one which is profane. Now, "the thousand", in reference to the Tabernacle, alludes to things holy, all the works of the Tabernacle being holy; hence of these shekalim "he made hooks for the pillars". Observe that it has been laid down that the letter vau, as we have stated elsewhere, symbolizes Mercy, and so wherever it is joined to the Divine Name it indicates an exercise of Mercy. We read, for instance, "And the Lord (V-Tetragrammaton) caused to rain upon Sodom" (Gen. XIX, 24), preceded by, "And the Lord (V-Tetragrammaton) said, Shall I hide from Abraham...?" (Ibid. XVIII, 17), indicating an exercise of Mercy and Rigour at one and the same time. This explains why, in the account of the Flood, the name Elohim (God) is used throughout, but never "and the Lord" (V-Tetragrammaton). [Tr. note: The text here repeats the passage from Zohar, Genesis, 64b, commencing: "We have been taught that the term" to "evil of eye".]

'It is written, "While the king sat at his table"; to wit, in the blissful company of Upper Paradise, which receives its plenitude of beatitudes by an undisclosed channel, and then distributes it into certain brooks; "My spikenard sent forth its fragrance" is an allusion to the hinder sea, which created the lower world after the pattern of the upper, so that a sweet savour of the upper world was diffused and a supernal light radiated throughout. Observe that when the fragrance of that spikenard is wafted on high, it is accompanied by an embrace of love, and the spikenard ascends to attach itself above; and all the sacred Chariots emit a fragrance that is woven into a crown for their adornment. Those sacred Chariots are called "maidens of song", alluded to in "upon Alamoth (maidens) of song" (Ps. XLVI, I), as well as in "and maidens without number". Of the same is written: "Is there any number of his armies" (Job xxv, 3).

HOOKS (vau-shaped tops) FOR THE PILLARS. The vau is symbolic of the male principle. All that exists and ascends with the dignity of anointing on high is of the male principle, which is typified by the vau, the symbol of heaven, which is male; whereas all below are called female. Hence all that proceed from the "left side" are of the side of the female; and it is they who have been appointed to preside over song, and continuously intone chants. This is indicated in "upon the Alamoth (maidens) of song". These come under the mystic symbolism of the letter he, and they bring forth many hosts after their kind through the mystic symbolism of the letter vau, the letter symbolic of the male principle upon whom falls the task of providing food for the female. Hence all those vavim (vaus) that Bezalel made over the pillars that represented the female principle. These spring from the mystery of the number thousand, which is a complete number, as well as seven hundred, also a complete number, and, further, from the number five and from seventy, all of which represent together one mystery. Thus, out of that mystery, and that number, he made the vavim (vaus); so all was made with a deep symbolism, and according to a certain calculation.'

Zohar: Shemoth, Section 2, Page 228a

AND THE BRASS OF THE WAVING WAS SEVENTY TALENTS. Said R. Judah: 'All this descends here below in the supernal image, containing the mystery of Faith. To the same pattern did Nebuchadnezzar make the image that he erected.' R. Yose said: 'It was not the image he made that was after the same pattern, but the image that he saw in his dream, an image made of gold, of silver and brass. Now, iron and clay were not worthy to enter into the work of the Tabernacle, but only those three metals. There is a recondite significance in the triad of metals. There were other materials that formed into tetrads, as the four fabrics consisting of blue, purple, scarlet, and fine linen, or the four rows of stones (in the breastplate).' R. Judah said: 'Some of them formed into threes, some into fours, some into twos, and again others were kept single. Nevertheless, an Order proper consists of a triad.

[Tr. note: The text here repeats the passage from Zohar, Gen. 159a, commencing: "There are three orders,' to "perfect unity" [159b]]

Zohar: Shemoth, Section 2, Page 228b

'The world is divided between forty-five varieties of light, seven of which are assigned to the seven abysses. Each light impinges on its Abyss, where there is a great rolling of stones, and penetrates into and pierces those stones so that water issues from them. The light impinges on the four sides of the Abyss, and then each light becomes entwined with the next and they join together and divide the waters, and all the seven lights overwhelm the seven Abysses, and hover over the darkness of the Abysses so that the light and darkness intermingle. Then the waters rush up and down, and there is a fusion of light and darkness and waters, from which emerge lights in which darkness is not intermingled. The lights then impinge on each other, with the result that they split into seventy-five channels of the Abyss along which waters course. Each channel roars with a sound peculiar to itself, so that there is a quivering of all the Abysses. At the sound of the roaring each Abyss calls to its neighbour, saying: "Divide thy waters". Thus Scripture says: "Deep calleth unto deep at the voice of thy cataracts" (Ps. XLII, 8). Underneath these there are the three hundred and sixty-five veins, some white, some black, some red, all of which intertwine and fuse into one colour. These veins are woven into seventeen nets, each of which is called a net of veins, and descend to the nethermost parts of the Abyss. Underneath these there are two nets of the appearance of iron and another two nets of the appearance of brass. Over above them there are two thrones, one on the right and one on the left. All these nets join into one, and water flows from these channels and enters the nets. As for the two thrones, one is the throne of the black firmament and the other of the variegated firmament. When the nets ascend, they go by the way of the throne of the black firmament, and when they descend they go by the way of the throne of the variegated firmament. The throne of the black firmament is on the right, and the throne of the variegated firmament is on the left. When the nets ascend by the throne of the black firmament, the throne of the firmament of the left lowers itself, and they descend by it, as the two thrones balance one another. Thus all the nets descend by means of them and enter into the nethermost parts of the Abyss. Then one of the thrones rises above all the Abysses and the other throne lowers itself underneath all the Abysses.

Zohar: Shemoth, Section 2, Page 229a

Between these two thrones whirl themselves all the Abysses, and all those channels are fixed between these two thrones. There are seventy-five channels, seven of which are higher than the rest, which, however, are attached to them, and all of them pass through the wheels of the two thrones on either side. Their waters course upwards and downwards. The downward-coursing waters form caves in the Abysses and cleave them asunder, while the upward-coursing waters enter into the caverns of the stones and continue rising until they fill them, which happens once in seven years. So far the seven varieties of lights with their profound symbolism.

'The "brass of waving", previously mentioned, represents the so-called "Brass-Mountains", and the "sockets of brass" represent the gates through which entrance is made to the King. Now of that brass were made all the ministering vessels of the altar. They are, indeed, ministers to the altar, because when the souls of men come up on the altar it is they that execute the service of the altar, and help it to perform its function, and hence they are named "vessels of the altar". All those "pins of the Tabernacle", and vessels, are specified by name as vessels of service, to serve in the Sanctuary. Hence they all stand as appointed chieftains and Chariot legions and heavenly spirits, each in its rank. They are, moreover, all numbered, their numbers being kept within certain Sacred Palaces. There is an interaction of gold and gold, silver and silver, brass and brass. The brass here below derives its power from the supernal brass, and so with the rest. Besides, all those varieties are interfused with each other, the clasps of gold binding together the curtains, the clasps of brass binding the Tabernacle, all being ranged opposite each other. Moreover, the clasps scintillated in the Tabernacle as the stars scintillate in the firmament, the fifty golden clasps and the fifty brazen clasps in rows facing each other. Also, out of the supernal light there was emitted a spark which penetrated within a dark speculum, that spark being a fusion of all colours of light and called "purple" (argaman). Then that "purple" impinged on that non-luminous light, causing it to emit another dull spark. The two were fused, and out of the fusion were formed the sacred robes in which Michael the High Priest was attired. When thus attired in these robes of glory he enters to minister in the Sanctuary, but not otherwise, just as we read of Moses that he "entered into the midst of the cloud, and went up into the mount" (Ex. XXIV, 18). We have learnt that Moses had first to attire himself in the cloud as in a robe, and only then could he go up into the mount, not otherwise. So the High Priest could not enter the Sanctuary unless robed in the priestly garments. And it is because they are emanations of the supernal mysteries, and are made after the supernal pattern, that they are called "residual garments" (bigde ha-s'rad), inasmuch as they were made of what has been left over of the supernal robes, of the residue of the ethereal celestial splendours, of the "blue" and "purple", the hues of the mystery of the Divine Name, called the Name Perfect, to wit, Tetragrammaton ELOHIM, as also of "scarlet red", thus comprising the colours, red, blue, and purple. Only thus clad could he enter into the innermost without being thrust out. All was made with a mystic significance, so that all things should bear the supernal pattern. Hence it is written: "The residual garments for ministering in the holy place" (Ibid. XXXIX, 41), for it is only when the supernal colours reside in them that Scripture says of them, "the holy garments

Zohar: Shemoth, Section 2, Page 229b

are they" (Lev. XVI, 4.) Of Israel, also, Scripture says: "Israel is the Lord's hallowed portion, the first-fruits of the increase" (Jer. II, 3), thus calling Israel holy, for the reason that in Israel are to be seen all shades of colour, as displayed by Priests, Levites, and Israelites; and these are the colours which may be exhibited in the inner holy place.

'Observe that man's soul does not ascend to appear before the Holy King unless she is first worthy to be attired in the supernal raiment. Likewise, the soul does not descend into this world until clad in the garments of this world. Similarly, the holy heavenly angels, of whom it is written, "Who makest thy angels into winds and thy ministers into flaming fire" (Ps. CIV, 4), when they have to execute a message in this world do not come down to it before they clothe themselves in the garments of this world. The attire thus has always to be in harmony with the place visited; and the soul, as we have said, can only ascend when clad in ethereal raiment. Adam in the Garden of Eden was attired in supernal raiment, of celestial radiancy. As soon as he was driven from the Garden of Eden and had need of forms suited to this world, "the Lord God", Scripture says, "made for Adam and for his wife garments of skin ('or), and clothed them" (Gen. III, 21). Formerly they were garments of light ('or), to wit, of the celestial light in which Adam ministered in the Garden of Eden. For, inasmuch as it is the resplendency of the celestial light that ministers in the Garden of Eden, when first man entered into the Garden, the Holy One, blessed be He, clothed him first in the raiment of that light. Otherwise he could not have entered there. When driven out, however, he had need of other garments; hence "garments of skin". So here also "they made residual garments to minister in the holy place", so as to enable the wearer to enter the Sanctuary. Now, it has been already taught that a man's good deeds done in this world draw from the celestial resplendency of light a garment with which he may be invested when in the next world he comes to appear before the Holy One, blessed be He. Appareled in that raiment, he is in a state of bliss and feasts his eyes on the radiant effulgence. So Scripture says: "To behold the graciousness of the Lord, and to visit early in his temple" (Ps. XXVII, 4). Man's soul is thus attired in the raiments of both worlds, the lower and the upper, thereby achieving perfection. Of this Scripture says: "Surely the righteous shall give thanks unto thy name"; to wit, in this world–"The upright shall dwell in thy presence" (Ibid. CXL, 14); namely, in the other world.'

AND HE MADE THE EPHOD OF GOLD. Said R. Yose: The ephod and the breastplate were inseparable, and we have laid down that in that place are fixed the twelve stones which bear the names of the twelve sons of Israel, to which, in their turn, correspond to the twelve supernal divisions. [Tr. note: The perrnutations of the letters of the Tetragrarnmaton.] This recondite symbolism underlies the passage, "Whither the tribes went up, the tribes of the Lord, as a testimony unto Israel, to give thanks unto the name of the Lord" (Ps. CXXII, 4). The reference here is to the twelve supernal tribes, they being the tribes of YH (the Lord), a name that is a testimony to Israel.' R. Hiya said: 'The term "tribes" is repeated here twice: first in allusion to the tribes here on earth, and secondly the supernal Tribes. "A testimony to Israel" bears esoteric reference to the supreme Divine Name that is called "testimony", of which Scripture says, "and my testimony that I shall teach them" (Ibid. CXXXII, 12). Now, these supernal twelve holy tribes were symbolized by the twelve sacred stones. For the twelve tribes below were the counterpart of those on high, and their names were all engraven on those stones, so that they were carried by the High Priest. When Jacob was on his way to Haran, Scripture says of him, "and he took some of the stones of the place, and put them under his head" (Gen. XXVIII, 11). These were the twelve sacred stones, which were made into one, as we read later, "and this stone" (Ibid. 22). All the twelve stones were absorbed in the one supreme sacred stone that is over them all, of which it is thus written, "and this stone

Zohar: Shemoth, Section 2, Page 230a

which I have set up for a pillar, shall be God's house" (Ibid). Hence the High Priest had to put them on his heart as a perpetual reminder of them, as Scripture says: "And Aaron shall bear the names of the children of Israel... upon his heart... for a memorial before the Lord continually" (Ex. XXVIII, 29). In all this the number twelve is of recondite significance: there are twelve stones of a supernal order in the upper world, concealed in a profound and holy mystery. These form the essence of the Torah; proceeding from a small, still voice, [Tr. note: Binah.] as said elsewhere. There is an order of another twelve hidden in a lower world, [Tr. note: The world of Creation.] after the pattern of the former, but which proceed from a different voice, designated Stone, as hinted in the words "from thence, from the Shepherd, the Stone of Israel" (Ibid. XLIX, 24). This is also the inner significance of the verse: "And thither were all the flocks gathered, and they rolled the stone... and put the stone again... in its place" (Ibid. XIX, 3). By the "stone" here is meant the Shekinah, called "tried stone", "the stone of Israel", which Israel roll along and take with them into exile, "and then put the stone again in its place". And so, after the name of the Shekinah all Israel are termed "stones". There are, moreover, stones and stones. There are stones which form the foundation of a house, of which Scripture says, "And the king commanded, and they quarried great stones, costly stones, to lay the foundation of the house with hewn stone" (I Kings v, 31); and there are precious supernal stones, to wit, those twelve stones. These are ranged in four orders, of three each, toward the four directions of the world. After the same pattern was the arrangement of the standards in the journey of the Israelites in the wilderness, where the twelve tribes were formed into groups of three each on each of the four cardinal points. Observe that when the High Priest was wearing the twelve stones fixed on the breastplate and the ephod, the Shekinah hovered over him. These twelve stones had engraved on them the names of the twelve tribes, each stone bearing the name of one of them. The letters were sunk, but when the stones shone they stood out and became luminous, spelling out what was required. Now, in all the names of the tribes the letters heth and teth were not to be found, for the reason that the tribes were without sin (HeT).' Said R. Hezekiah: 'This is reasonable as regards the heth, but not so in regard to the teth, since it is the initial of tob (good); and, further, we have learned that the letter teth seen in a dream is a good omen, since at the beginning of the Torah it is written, "And the Lord saw the light that it was good" (Gen. I, 4). Why, then, is that letter absent from the names of the tribes?' R. Hiya said in reply: 'It is because these two letters adjoin each other (in the alphabet), and, further, the teth is a letter hidden and withdrawn, as it is symbolic of the light that is above other lights, of the light of which it is written, "And the Lord saw the light that it was good". Hence it is the light of all the tribes together, and it could not be engraven on any of them. And, in addition, all the twelve tribes sprang from a certain undisclosed Apartment which is symbolized by the letter teth, and so, symbolizing as it does the undisclosed, this letter could not be made to be seen among them. Observe that all those stones possessed miraculous powers. Thus, when they became luminous, the face of the High Priest was likewise illumined, and at the same time the luminous letters stood out. The shining of the High Priest's face was a sign for all that the luminous letters were of a favourable significance; thereby it was known whether the High Priest was righteous or not.'

R. Abba was a frequent visitor to R. Simeon. He said to him once: 'In regard to the Urim and Thummim which were to be put in the breastplate (Ex. XXVIII, 30), we have learned that they were called Urim (=lights) because their words gave a clear and direct answer to the questions directed to them; and Thummim (tamim=perfect, complete) because their words were fulfilled to perfection. [Tr. note: v T. B. Yoma, 73.] Now, there seems to be something further to know in regard to this recondite subject.' Said R. Simeon: 'Assuredly so. Thus, the breastplate and the ephod correspond to the Urim and Thummim, and these again to the phylacteries (tefillin) and the knot of the phylacteries.'

R. Simeon here cited the verse: "And thou shalt see my back, but my face shall not be seen" (Ibid. XXXIII, 23). 'That means', he said, 'that the Holy One, blessed be He, made Moses see the knot of the phylacterie, [Tr. note: v. T. B. Menahoth, 35.] but not the phylacteries themselves. "My face" points to the phylacteries that contain the sublime mystery of thc Divine Name,

Zohar: Shemoth, Section 2, Page 230b

whereas "my back" involves the mystery contained in the knot of the phylacteries. As is well known to the Companions, the former denotes the shining speculum, the latter the dull speculum. So correspondingly Urim signifies the words illuminated, whereas Thummim points to the words in their fulfilment. The same mystical correlation is found between "voice" and "speech": for voice illumines the speech to be uttered, whereas speech brings the word to completion, and the two are indissolubly fused one with each other. The breastplate and the ephod', he concluded, 'correspond thus respectively to the "face" and the "back", the two being one and inseparable.' Said R. Abba: 'If that is so, and if he who separates them is called "one who separateth between familiar friends" (Prov. XVI, 28), how are we to explain the verse: "And it came to pass, when Abiathar, the son of Ahimelech, fled to David to Keilah, that he came down with an ephod in his hand" (I Sam. XXIII, 6), where the ephod is mentioned without the breastplate?' R. Simeon replied: 'The explanation assuredly is that the nearer a thing comes to the realm of the hidden and undisclosed, the less is it made mention of. So, contrariwise, what is nearer the realm of things revealed is to that degree more often mentioned, whereby the undisclosed is all the more covered, as it were. On the same principle, the Divine Name Sublime, the essence of the hidden and unrevealed, is never uttered, a name denoting the revealed being substituted for it. Thus the Name signifying the unrevealed is Tetragrammaton, but that signifying the revealed is ADNY (ADoNaY). The former is the way the Divine Name is written, the latter the way it is read. Thus it is throughout the Torah, which contains two sides: a disclosed and an undisclosed. And these two aspects are found in all things, both in this world and in the upper world.'

R. Simeon here adduced the verse: "Then said they unto him: Tell us, we pray thee, inasmuch as (ba'asher) thou art the cause that this evil is upon us, what is thine occupation?.. Then the men feared God exceedingly..." (Jonah I, 8-16). 'There is much', he said, 'to ponder over in this text. For, indeed, the men put to him their question with deep wisdom. Thus they wished to find out whether Jonah was of the seed of Joseph, at the sight of whose coffin the sea straightway divided itself and became dry land. So Scripture says: "The sea saw and fled" (Ps. CXIV, 3); that is, it saw him of whom it is written, "and he fled and got him out" (Gen. XXXIX, 12), and at once "the Jordan turned backward" (Ps. Ibid.). The men thus used the expression "inasmuch as" (ba'asher), thereby pointing to Joseph, who used a similar expression when he said, "inasmuch as thou art his wife" (Gen. XXXIX, 9); they thus said in effect, "If thou art of the seed of Joseph, pray that the sea may cease from its raging." They further used the expression "to whom?" (I'mi), an allusion to Jacob, in connection with whom it is written, "to whom belongest thou?" (Ibid. XXII, 17); they as much as said: "If thou art of the seed of Jacob who sent his message to Esau by holy angel messengers and in that way was saved from the calamity that threatened him, then pray to the Master that He may send His angel to save us from this calamity that threatens us, and if not"–they further asked–"What is thine occupation?" With what dost thou daily busy thyself? "and whence comest thou?" that is, Who were thy forefathers? "What is thy country?" Is it a country deserving punishment? Thus all the questions put by them had a good reason. "And he said unto them: I am a Hebrew, that is, from the seed of Abraham the Hebrew who sanctified the name of his master day by day; and I fear the Lord, the God of heaven", etc. They put their questions, cloaking their real meaning, but he answered them without disguise. Scripture then continues: "Then were the men exceedingly afraid." It was the Divine Name they heard that made them fear; for they all were aware of the miracles and mighty deeds that the Holy One, blessed be He, wrought on the sea. He further told them that he fled from the presence of the Holy One, blessed be He, and they thus asked him: "What is this that thou hast done?" that is, Why hast thou transgressed thy Master's command? Note that all these men, after they saw the miracles and mighty deeds that the Holy One, blessed be He, wrought for Jonah on the sea, became proselytes. For they all saw Jonah fall into the sea,

and the fish come up and swallow him; and then, when the same great fish emerged on the surface in the presence of them all and vomited him on dry land, they came up to him and declared themselves proselytes. This is borne out by the words of Jonah, saying: "They that regard lying vanities will forsake their own mercy" (Jonah II. 9). Observe, further, that they all became righteous proselytes and rose to be sages of the Law of the highest rank. For the Holy One, blessed be He, found delight in them, as in all those who come near to Him and sanctify His Name openly; for when His disclosed Name is sanctified, His undisclosed Name ascends His Throne of Glory. So Scripture says, "but I will be hallowed among the children of Israel" (Lev. XXII, 32).'

AND THEY BOUND THE BREASTPLATE BY THE RINGS THEREOF UNTO THE RINGS OF THE EPHOD WITH A THREAD OF BLUE. Why blue? Because it is an all-uniting colour, and thus is symbolic of the supernal mystery. "A golden bell and a pomegranate... and the sound thereof shall be heard when he goeth in unto the holy place before the Lord" (Ex. XXVIII, 34-35); it was necessary for the sound to be heard so that blessings might rest on the world by reason of the blessing pronounced by the priest on all. The "pomegranate" is a symbol of plenty, on account of its multitude of seeds.

AND HE MADE THE ROBE OF THE EPHOD OF WOVEN WORK, ALL OF BLUE. The significance of the blue colour consists in its being a reflection of the light of the Divine Throne, a light which is one with the white light. Said R. Simeon: 'All the priestly robes were emblematic of the supernal mystery, having been made after th.e celestial pattern. It may here be asked: Seeing that Michael was the High Priest and belonged to the "right side", why is Gabriel referred to as "the man clothed in linen" (Dan. XII, 7), seeing that such robes could only be worn by the High Priest? But the truth is that the "left" is always embraced within the "right", and hence Gabriel (although of the left) was clothed in these robes. Furthermore, Gabriel is the messenger for this world, hence he had to put on the garments of this world. The same has already been explained in regard to the soul which, whilst in the upper world, has to put on heavenly garments, but in descending below assumes lowly garments. Observe that the "robe of the ephod" was to cover the ephod when he put it on. It is written: "Thou hast formed me behind and before, and laid thy hand upon me" (Ps. CXXXIX, 4). Observe that at the creation of Adam the Holy One, blessed be He, made him male and female together, female behind and male before. Then He sawed them asunder and tricked out the woman and brought her to Adam; and when they were thus brought face to face, love was multiplied in the world and they brought forth offspring, a thing that was not yet before. But when Adam and his wife sinned and the serpent had intercourse with Eve and injected into her his venom, she bore Cain, whose image was in part derived from on high and in part from the venom of the unclean and low side. Hence it was the Serpent who brought death into the world, in that it was his side that was the cause of it. It is the way of the serpent to lie in wait to slay, and thus the one that sprang from him followed the same course. So Scripture says: "And it came to pass when they were in the field, that Cain rose up against Abel his brother, and slew him" (Gen. IV, 8). We find it written in the Ancient Books that in the act of slaying Abel, Cain bit him repeatedly

after the manner of the serpent, until he caused his soul to quit him. Abel was thus slain and his body resolved into its elements. Had not Cain been in part the offspring of the unclean side he would not have behaved so toward his brother. Adam, therefore, having seen Abel slain and Cain banished, said to himself: "Why henceforth should I bear children?" He then separated himself from his wife for a hundred and thirty years, during which period unclean female spirits conceived from him and bore spirits and demons, [Tr. note: v. T. B. Erubin, 18.] so-called "plagues of the children of men" (2 Sam. VII, 14). After that, Adam became jealous, rejoined his wife and begat Seth as we read, "and [he] begat a son in his own likeness, after his image; and called his name Seth" (Gen. v, 3); emphatically "in his own likeness, after his image", which did not happen before, that is, with the offspring born before that time. For previously intercourse with Adam was of another kind, but now the Holy One, blessed be He, brought Eve all beautified into the presence of Adam and they joined together face to face. Hence it is written, "this one shall be called woman" (Ibid. II, 23), to wit, this one and not any other. Observe that the ephod and breastplate were "behind and before", and so the Priest, when clothed in them, resembled the supernal pattern. As has already been said, when his face was illumined and the letters stood out brightly, then a message was thereby conveyed to him. For this reason the breastplate and the ephod were tied together; and although they had distinct functions, they had the same symbolism and were therefore united by the four rings that held them together, back and front. They thus symbolize the Chariots which are united from below to those above, and the whole symbolizes the Ofanim and Hayoth (Wheels and Sacred Beasts). It has already been explained that the verse, "In the beginning God created the heaven and the earth", means that the lower world was created after the pattern of the upper. Now, the Tabernacle below was likewise made after the pattern of the supernal Tabernacle in all its details. For the Tabernacle in all its works embraced all the works and achievements of the upper world and the lower, whereby the Shekinah was made to abide in the world, both in the higher spheres and the lower. Similarly, the Lower Paradise is made after the pattern of the Upper Paradise, and the latter contains all the varieties of forms and images to be found in the former. Hence the work of the Tabernacle, and that of heaven and earth, come under one and the same mystery. It is written: "Lift up your eyes on high, and see: who hath created these? He that bringeth out their hosts by number.... Not one faileth" (Isa. XL, 26). Are we to imagine from this that by lifting his eyes upwards a man can know and see what is not permitted to know and see? No. The true meaning of the passage is that whoever desires to reflect on and to obtain a knowledge of the works of the Holy One, blessed be He, let him lift his eyes upwards and gaze on the myriads of the hosts and legions of existences there, each different from the other, each mightier than the other. Then will he, while gazing, ask, "Who created these?" Indeed, as has already been expounded elsewhere, "Who created these?" amounts to saying that the whole of creation springs from a region that remains an everlasting "Who?" (Mi?), in that it remains undisclosed. "He that bringeth out their host by number", for inasmuch as that region is undisclosed it brings forth everything by means of the sound that issues from the trumpet, the sound that constitutes the "number" of all the celestial hosts and the sum of the whole of creation; and from thence also proceeds the mystery of sublime faith through all the supernal "sides", and then extending in grade after grade downwards, and widening out into numerous hosts after their kinds, all of whom are numbered, and "He calleth them all by name." The verse continues, "By the greatness of his might"—an allusion to the "right side", "for that he is strong in power"–alluding to the "left side", "no one faileth", this in allusion to the forces emanating from the two sides.

Zohar: Shemoth, Section 2, Page 232a

According to an alternative interpretation, the verse, "Lift up your eyes on high, and see: who hath created these?" contains an allusion to the erection and completion of the Tabernacle. For whoever then looked at the Tabernacle saw in it an epitome of the upper world and the lower; for all the works of the universe were contained in the equipment of the Tabernacle. Thus whoever gazed with attention at the clasps of the Tabernacle saw in their gleam the radiance of the stars, inasmuch as they were disposed in the same way as the stars in heaven.'

R. Simeon discoursed on the verses: "Hallelukah. Praise ye the Lord from the heaven... Praise him, ye heavens of heavens... Praise the Lord from the earth..." (Ps. CXLVIII, 1–8). 'This psalm', he said, 'was indited by David in honour of the mystery of the Divine Name, which is the supreme object of praises. There are two all-embracing songs of praise: this one, and the one contained in the last psalm, commencing: "Hallelukah. Praise God in his sanctuary" (Ibid. CL, 1–6). The latter psalm, however, contains a tenfold praise, alluding to ten musical instruments, but this one is a sevenfold hymn. The two, nevertheless, dwell on one and the same mystery, that of the Divine Name. This one begins, "Praise ye the Lord from the heaven", inasmuch as the heaven was the starting point of the six directions which expanded downwards from it. This is the limit within which it is permitted to man to investigate. So Scripture says: "For ask now of the days past, which were before thee, since the day that God created man upon the earth, and from the one end of heaven unto the other" (Deut. IV, 32), that is, so far art thou permitted to ask and investigate; but beyond it is not permitted to inquire, that being a sphere hidden and undisclosed. Hence, "praise ye the Lord from the heaven, praise him in the heights", these constituting the two directions, right and left, whence there was an expanding of all the others downwards in the mystery of the grades, till the development was complete. "Praise ye him, all his angels": these are the two supports on which the Body rests. These are here indicated by the term "angels" because, as the legs are, as it were, the messengers of man, moving about from place to place, so are the angels the messengers moving from place to place in the service of their Master, executing His messages. "Praise ye him, all his hosts," is an allusion to the region whence emanate all the supernal sacred hosts who are marked with the holy sign of the covenant. "Praise ye him, sun and moon, praise ye him, all ye stars of light", to wit all the heavenly luminaries, stars and constellations. Now the Psalmist returns to the height of heights, the place by which all is held fast, saying: "Praise him, ye heavens of heavens"; then again he turns to the earth, saying, "Praise the Lord from the earth", etc. Observe that the stars of the lower world exist by the energy they attract to themselves from the supernal mystery, since the whole of existence is based on the supernal archetype, as said elsewhere. Hence all the supernal stars and constellations are entrusted with the guidance of the world beneath them; and from thence there evolve a series of grades upon grades reaching out to the lower stars. All these have no power of their own whatever, but are under the power of the supernal world. Hence the words of Scripture: "Let now the astrologers, the stargazers... stand up and save thee" (Isa. XLVII, 13) indicating that the lower world is under the jurisdiction of the supernal world.'

AND THEY MADE THE TUNICS OF FINE LINEN (shesh)... AND THE MITRE OF FINE LINEN (shesh), ETC. R. Yose, in exposition of this, cited the verse: "And it shall come to pass in the end of days, that the mountain of the Lord's house shall be established on the top of the mountains", etc. (Isa. II, 2). 'That means', he said, 'that "in the end of days", when the Holy One, blessed be He, will visit the daughter of Jacob and raise her from the dust, when, further, the sun will be joined to the moon, then "the mountain of the Lord's house shall be established", to wit, Upper Jerusalem, which will be illumined by the radiation of the supernal light, which will then shine with sevenfold effulgence. So Scripture says:

"Moreover, the light of the moon shall be as the light of the sun, and the light of the sun shall be sevenfold, as the light of the seven days", etc. (Ibid. xxx, 26). "On the top of the mountains"

Zohar: Shemoth, Section 2, Page 232b

signifies the High Priest, who is the head of all, and symbolizes the "right side"; it is he who continuously beautifies the House, and by his benediction gives it a glad aspect. That House will thus be established and adorned by means of those robes made after the supernal pattern. The House being established by the "top of the mountains", that is, by the High Priest, will rear itself aloft, and merge its existence in the supernal realm, so that the world will be filled with an effulgence radiating from the light supernal; and so Scripture continues, "and [it] shall be exalted above the hills", to wit, above all the celestial hosts and legions, "and all nations shall flow into it". Observe this. When the priest here below spreads out his hands [to bless the people], a celestial light first emerges, then all the lamps are kindled, their lights radiating into each other and fusing into each other until the face of the Community of Israel is irradiated. All this comes to pass through the agency of the primordial light, which is the "High Priest". And the activity of the priest here below awakens a corresponding activity in the Priest on high. Thus "the mountain of the Lord's house shall be established on the top of the mountains... and all the nations shall flow unto it". For, whereas now all the other nations have Chieftains in heaven to rule them, at that time the Holy One, blessed be He, will remove those Chieftains and depose them from their sovereignty, as we read, "the Lord will punish the host of the high heaven on high" (Ibid. XXIV, 21). And when all these are removed the Holy One alone, blessed be He, shall be acknowledged mighty, as Scripture says: "And the Lord alone shall be exalted in that day" (Ibid. II, 11). And so the former passage continues: "And many peoples shall go and say: Come and let us go up to the mountain of the Lord, to the House of the God of Jacob" (Ibid. 3). All this will come to pass when the High Priest, the "top of the mountains", shall illumine her, by the mystery of the number six (shesh), signifying the six directions of the world.'

R. Eleazar and R. Isaac and R. Judah were once walking together on the road. Said R. Eleazar: 'It is time we drew to ourselves the company of the Shekinah; this will only be if She hears from us words of the Torah.' R. Judah then remarked: 'Let the chief begin.' R. Eleazar then began to discourse on the verse: "I am small and despised, yet have I not forgotten thy precepts" (Ps. CXIX, 141). 'King David', he said, 'sometimes extols himself, saying, for instance, "and [He] whose mercy to his anointed, to David and to his seed, forevermore" (Ibid. XVIII, 51); or, "The saying of David, the son of Jesse, and the saying of the man raised on high, the anointed of the God of Jacob" (2 Sam. XXIII, 1); and at other times he abases himself, saying, "for I am poor and needy" (Ps. LXXXVI, 1), or, as here: "I am small and despised." Now he also said of himself: "The stone which the builders rejected is become the chief corner-stone" (Ibid. CXVIII, 22). The truth is that when he found himself in peace and triumphant over his enemies, he extolled himself; but when he found himself oppressed and harassed by his enemies, he abased himself and called himself the poorest and the least of men. For at one time he would prevail over his enemies, and then he would again feel their pressure; but for all that he would always obtain dominion over them, and they were never able to discomfit him. Despite that, King David always humbled himself before the Holy One, blessed be He; for whoever abases himself before Him, He exalts above all other men. The Holy One, blessed be He, thus found David acceptable in this world and in the world to come-in this world, as it says, "For I will defend this city to save it, for mine own sake, and for my servant David's sake" (Isa. XXXVII, 35); and in the future world, as it says, "and [they] shall seek the Lord their God, and David their king; and shall come trembling unto the Lord and to his goodness in the end of days" (Hos. III, 5). David, indeed, was king in this world and will be king in the time to come; hence "the stone the builders rejected is become the chief corner-stone". For, when the sun turns away his face from the moon, and does not shine upon her, she has no light whatever and so does not shine, but is poverty-stricken and dark on all sides; but when the sun turns towards her and radiates his light upon her, then her face is illumined and she adorns herself for him as a woman for a man. She thus is then invested

Zohar: Shemoth, Section 2, Page 233a

with the dominion of the world. So David adorned himself after this very manner. Now he would appear poor and dejected, but then again he would be reveling in riches. Hence David's declaration, "I am small and despised, yet have I not forgotten thy precepts." It behoves, indeed, every man to follow this example and to humble himself in every respect so as to become a vessel in which the Holy One, blessed be He, may find delight. This lesson has also been expounded in connection with the phrase, "with him also that is of a contrite and humble spirit' (Isa. LVII, 15).'

R. Eleazar then continued: 'It is written, "And he brought me thither, and behold, there was a man, whose appearance was like the appearance of brass, with a line of flax in his hand, and a measuring reed; and he stood in the gate" (Ezek. XL, 3). Ezekiel saw in this prophetical vision a "man", but not "a man clothed in linen" (Dan. X, 5). For it is only when the angel is on an errand of severity that he is called "a man clothed in linen". Otherwise, he assumes various guises, appears in various attire conformably to the message he bears at the time being. Now, in the present vision "his appearance was like the appearance of brass", that is, he was clothed in the raiment formed of the "mountains of brass", and the "measuring reed" that he had in his hand was not the "Obscure Lamp" [Tr. note: Binah.] of the hidden and treasured-up light, but it was formed out of a solidified part, as it were, of the residue of light left by the "Obscure Lamp", what time that light mounted up to the heights and became engraven within the scintillating and undisclosed brightness. The "measuring reed", therefore, is used for measuring the dimensions of the lower sphere. [Tr. note: Beriah.] Now, there is a "measuring reed" and a "measuring line". All the measurements of Ezekiel were by the measuring reed, whereas in the work of the Tabernacle all was measured by the measuring line. This is also used for the measuring of the dimensions of this world after the pattern of the "cord" (employed in Ezekiel's Temple), inasmuch as in the process of its extension a knot was formed at every cubit length, which length became the standard measure for the purpose, called ammah (cubit). That "measuring line" thus bears the name of "cubit"; and that explains the wording, "The length of each curtain was eight and twenty by the cubit (ba-amah), and the breadth of each curtain four by the cubit" (Ex. XXXVI, 9), the singular," cubit", pointing to the fact that it was the cubit which measured on every side. Now this was a projection from the Supernal Lamp, the lower measurement being the counterpart of the higher. The miniature lower measurement embraces a thousand and five hundred facets, each facet expanding into twelve thousand cubits. Thus one cubit moved along, growing into a "measuring line", each cubit in its turn being newly revealed; and so it resulted in a length of eight-and-twenty "by the cubit" and a breadth of four "by the cubit". Hence the one cubit covered thirty-two spaces, symbolic of the thirty-two "Paths of Wisdom" that emanate from the supernal regions. Now the length (of the curtains) was formed into four sections of seven cubits each, the number seven expressing here the central mystical idea; similarly the thirty-two Paths are embraced within the seven, in their mystical symbolism of the Divine Name. So far in regard to this measurement, which was of a higher degree of holiness; for, indeed, there was another measured substance that was designed to be a covering to this, the external comprising the number thirty-four; whilst the internal was of the number thirty-two

Zohar: Shemoth, Section 2, Page 233b

[Note: Lines 5 through 11 of the Hebrew text are not included in our translation.]

and, moreover, being of a higher degree of holiness, it contained the sacred colours enumerated in the passage, "of fine twined linen, and blue, and purple, and scarlet" (Ibid. 8). The same lesson is indicated in the words, "I went down into the garden of nuts" (S.S. VI, 11). For, as the nut has a shell surrounding and protecting the kernel inside, so it is with everything sacred: the sacred principle occupies the interior, whilst the "other side" encircles it on the exterior. This is the inward meaning of "the wicked doth surround the righteous" (Habakkuk I, 4). The same is indicated in the very name EGVZ (nut). [Tr. note: The numerical value of EGVZ (1+3+6+7)=17. Similarly, HT (sin) (9+8=17) and TVB (the good) (9+6+2)=17.] Observe that the exterior, the more it is enlarged the more worthless it becomes. As a mnemonic we have the sacrifices of the Feast of Tabernacles, the number of which goes on diminishing with the increase of days. We thus find the same here. Of the inner curtain it is written: "And thou shalt make the tabernacle with ten curtains" (Ex. XXVI, 1); whereas for the outer ones the number was "eleven curtains" (Ibid. 7). Furthermore, of the outer curtains it says, "The length of each curtain shall be thirty cubits, and the breadth of each curtain four cubits" (Ibid. 8), the two numbers amounting together to thirty-four, a number symbolic of the lowest depth of poverty; [Tr. note: Since 34 is the numerical value of DaL (D =4, L=30), signifying the lowest extreme of poverty.] whereas the corresponding number in the ten curtains was thirty-two, a smaller number, but symbolizing the sublime mystery of the Faith, or the Divine Name. The lower is thus the higher, and the higher the lower. The former constitutes the interior, the latter the exterior. Now the same "measuring-line" went on expanding and thus measured the boards, concerning which it is written: "And he made the boards for the tabernacle of acacia-wood, standing up" (Ibid. XXXVI, 20). These symbolized the Seraphim, as indicated by the description "standing up", which is paralleled in "Seraphim were standing up" (Isa. VI, 2). Now, here it is written, "Ten cubits shall be the length of a board" (Ex. XXVI, 16), and not "ten by the cubit". This is because the boards represented the three triads with a single one hovering high above them. [Tr. note: i.e. the 10 Sefiroth, consisting of 3 groups of 3 each. with the Sefirah Kether (Crown) above them.] ‘ The number eleven and a half [Tr. note: i.e. the sum of 10 (the length of each board)+ 1 (the breadth).] has its recondite significance in that the boards symbolized a striving upwards, but not yet reaching to the degree of the Ophanim, [Tr. note: Lit. Wheels. An angelic order above that of Seraphim.] the half being expressive of incompleteness. This concerns the mystery of the Holy Chariot, for the twenty boards divide themselves into ten on this side and ten on the other, denoting a reaching out to the height of the sublime Seraphim. Then there is a further ascent in the holy region, denoted by the "middle bar" (Ibid. XXVI, 28). There is also an inward significance in the twenty boards in that they embrace the number 230. [Tr. note: i.e. Twenty times the length of each plus twenty times the breadth of each: (20x10)+(20x1)=230. The number 230 is the numerical value of certain sacred names.] The value of each prescribed measure has here its proper meaning. The curtains of the Tabernacle mentioned before stand for sublime mysteries, namely, the mystery of heaven, regarding which Scripture says: "Who stretchest out the heavens like a curtain" (Ps. CIV, 2). Now, of the two sets of curtains, the one expresses one aspect of the mystery whilst the other expresses another aspect of the same mystery. The whole is designed to teach us Wisdom in all its aspects and all its manifestations; and so that man may discern between good and evil, between what Wisdom teaches and what it rejects. The mystery of the basic measurement, as elsewhere laid down, embraces various objects. The Ark in its dimensions falls within the same recondite principle, in respect of what it received and what it possesses of its own.

Zohar: Shemoth, Section 2, Page 234a

We thus read: "two cubits and a half was the length of it" (Ex. XXXVII, 1). The one cubit on either side tells us about the Ark being the recipient from this side and from that side; whilst the half cubit in the centre represents what it had possessed of its own; and the same is indicated by the cubit and a half of its breadth and a cubit and a half of its height: each cubit speaks of what accrued to it, and each half of what is possessed already. For there must needs be something for something else to rest on, and hence the existing half in every account. There is a further recondite significance in that the Ark was inlaid with gold inside and outside so as to have its dimensions formed after the archetypal plan. The table was similarly measured by this archetypal scale. The dimensions of the Ark, however, were not used elsewhere, for reasons revealed to the wise. Similarly, all the other works of the Tabernacle were measured by the same cubit, with the exception of the breastplate, which was measured by the span. Now observe this. The tunic embraced the mystery of the "six" (shesh) [Tr. note: i.e. the six directions of the world. The homophone shesh=linen (of which the tunic was made) and also=six.] in that it symbolized the vesture designed for the setting right and investiture of all that comes within the "six" (directions of the world). So far the recondite significance of the "measuring-line". In the vision of Ezekiel, however, we find instead the "measuring-reed", for the reason that the House which he beheld was destined to remain forever in its place with the same walls, the same lines, the same entrances, the same doors, every part in accordance with prescribed measure. But in regard to the time to come, Scripture says: "And the side-chambers were broader as they wound higher and higher" (Ezek. XLI, 7). For immediately the building will be begun that "measuring-reed" will mount higher and higher in the length and in the breadth, so that the House will be extended on all sides, and no malign influence shall ever light on it. For at that time Severity will no more be found in the world; hence everything will remain firmly and immovably established, as Scripture says, "and [they will] be disquieted no more; neither shall the children of wickedness afflict them any more", etc. (2 Sam. VII, 10). And observe that all these measurements prescribed for this world had for their object the establishment of this world after the pattern of the upper world, so that the two should be knit together into one mystery. At the destined time, when the Holy One, blessed be He, will bestir Himself to renew the world, all the world will be found to express one mystery, and the glory of the Almighty will then be over all, in fulfilment of the verse, "In that day shall the Lord be one, and his name one" (Zech. XIV, 9).'

R. Judah followed with a discourse on the verse: "The counsel (sod) of the Lord is with them that fear him; and his covenant to make them know it" (Ps. xxv, 14).·'"The counsel" (sod),' [Tr. note: Sod in the Bible=counsel; in post-Biblical Hebrew = secret.] he said, 'alludes to the sublime mystical knowledge which remains hidden and undisclosed save for those that fear the Lord continuously and thus prove themselves worthy of these secrets and able to keep them. Observe that the world has been made and established by an engraving of forty-two letters, all of which are the adornment of the Divine Name. These letters combined and soared aloft and dived downwards, forming themselves into crowns in the four directions of the world, so that it might endure. They then went forth and created the upper world and the lower, the world of unification and the world of division. In the latter they are called "mountains of separation" (bather) (S.S. II, 17), which are watered when the south side begins to come near

Zohar: Shemoth, Section 2, Page 234b

them. The water flows with supernal energy and with ecstatic joy. Whilst the Thought mounts up with exulting joy out of the most Undisclosed One, there flows out of it a spark: the two then come into contact with each other, as explained elsewhere. [Tr. note: Zohar, Exodus, 220b.] These forty-two letters thus constitute the supernal mystical principle; by them were created the upper and the lower worlds, and they indeed constitute the basis and recondite significance of all the worlds. Thus is explained the verse, "The secret of the Lord is to them that fear him; and his covenant to make them know it", the first part alluding to the undisclosed engraven letters, whereas the latter speaks of the revealed. Now, it is written: "And thou shalt put in the breastplate of judgement the Urim and the Thummim" (Ex. XXVIII, 30). The term "Urim" (lit. light, illumination) signifies the luminous speculum, which consisted of the engravure of the Divine Name composed of forty-two letters by which the world was created; whereas the Thummim consisted of the non-luminous speculum made of the Divine Name as manifested in the twenty-two letters. The combination of the two is thus called Urim and Thummim. Observe that by the power of these sunken letters were the other letters, namely, the raised letters forming the names of the tribes, now illumined, now darkened. The letters of the Divine Name embrace the mystery of the Torah, and all the worlds are a projection of the mystery of those letters. The Torah begins with a Beth followed by an Aleph, [Tr. note: Allusion to B ereshith B ara E lohim (in the beginning God created).] indicating thereby that the world was created by the power of these letters, the Beth symbolizing the female principle and the Aleph the male principle, and both engendering, as it were, the group of the twenty-two letters. Thus we read, "In the beginning God created the (eth) heaven and the (eth) earth" (Gen. I, 1), where the particle eth (consisting of Aleph and

Tau) is a summary of the twenty-two letters by which the earth is nourished. [Tr. note: v. Zohar, Gen. 16b.] Now, the same letters were the instruments used in the building of the Tabernacle. This work was carried out by Bezalel for the reason that, as his very name (Bezel-El=in the shadow of God) implies, he had a knowledge of the various permutations of the letters, by the power of which heaven and earth were created. Without such knowledge Bezalel could not have accomplished the work of the Tabernacle; for, inasmuch as the celestial Tabernacle was made in all its parts by the mystical power of those letters, the lower Tabernacle could only be prepared by the power of the same letters. Bezalel was skilled in the various permutations of the Divine Name, and for each several part he employed the appropriate permutation of the letters. But when it came to the rearing up of the Tabernacle it was beyond his power, for the reason that the disposition of those letter-groups was entrusted to Moses alone, and hence

Zohar: Shemoth, Section 2, Page 235a

it was by Moses that the Tabernacle was erected. So Scripture says: "And Moses reared up... and [he] laid... and put in..." (Ex. XL, 18) Moses, but not Bezalel.'

R. Isaac then followed with a discourse on the verses: "O Lord, in thy strength the king rejoiceth; and in thy salvation how greatly doth he exult! Thou hast given him his heart's desire... he asked life of thee, thou gavest it to him, even length of days forever and ever" (Ps. XXI, 2-5). He said: 'David intended in this psalm to sing the praises of the Community of Israel by pointing out that the Holy One, blessed be He, is gladdened by means of the Torah, which is called "strength", as it is written, "The Lord will give strength unto the people" (Ibid. XXI, 11). The "king" in this verse refers to the Holy One, blessed be He, and the salvation mentioned is that of the Right. The verse continues: "He asked life of thee, thou gavest it to him, even length of days forever and ever". From here we learn that King David was not endowed with any life-duration at all of his own, but it was Adam who made him a gift of a portion of his life, consisting of seventy years. [Tr. note: v. Yalkut Hadash, 5b; Zohar, Gen. 55a.] He thus attained length of life, both in this world and in the world to come. "His glory is great", because the Holy One, blessed be He, is the greater of "the two great lights" (Gen. I, 16), but only "through thy salvation". The Psalm continues: "For thou makest him most blessed (lit. blessings) forever; thou makest him glad with joy in thy presence" (Ibid. XXI, 7), because He is the blessing of the whole world, the source of all blessing; similarly, it was said to Abram, "and be thou a blessing" (Gen. XII, 2): "Thou wilt make him glad with joy"; this refers to the time when the Holy One, blessed be He, will raise the Community of Israel from the dust and renew Her with the renewal of the moon in joy; "in thy presence", to wit, to abide joyfully in Thy presence, in the perfection which She will achieve in that time. For when the Sanctuary was destroyed it was emptied of all its fulness, as we read: "She that hath borne seven languisheth" (Jer. xv, 9), also, "I shall be filled with her that is laid waste" (Ezek. XXVI, 2). [Tr. note: v. T. B. Pesahim, 72b et passim. There is at this point a lacuna in the text.]

'Observe that when Moses was about to rear up the Tabernacle, he first surveyed each several part to see if it had been made properly, and only then did he rear it up; the several parts were one by one brought to him, this being the recondite idea of the verse, "the virgins her companions in her train being brought unto thee" (Ps. XLV, 15). So Scripture says: AND THEY BROUGHT THE TABERNACLE UNTO MOSES. They brought it to Moses as the time had come for his espousals; just as the bride is first brought to the bridegroom and then he enters unto her; so first they "brought the Tabernacle unto Moses" and then he entered into the tent of meeting. Indeed, it is written: AND MOSES WAS NOT ABLE TO ENTER INTO THE TENT OF MEETING, BECAUSE THE CLOUD ABODE THEREON, for the reason that She was then arraying herself in Her finery as a woman tires and bedecks herself to receive her husband; and at such a moment it is unseemly for the husband to enter unto her. Thus "Moses was not able to enter into the tent of meeting...", and they had to bring "the Tabernacle unto Moses".

Zohar: Shemoth, Section 2, Page 235b

Observe that throughout all the works about the Tabernacle the colour of blue was to play a part, as that colour summarized in its adornment the recondite significance of all the colours. Scripture thus says: AND THEY MADE THE PLATE OF THE HOLY CROWN OF PURE GOLD... AND THEY TIED UNTO IT A THREAD OF BLUE.

'The Tabernacle, in its recondite significance, reflected the supernal mysteries comprised within the Divine Name ADNY. The same significance is reflected by the Ark, of which it is written: "Behold, the ark of the covenant of the Lord (ADN) of all the earth" (Jos. III, 11), the term ADN being identical with the Divine Name ADNY. The name ADNY corresponds to the most sublime Divine Name Tetragrammaton, the Aleph of the one containing the same recondite meaning as the Yod of the other, the Daleth of the one corresponding to the He of the other, and so with the Nun and Vau, the Nun being emblematic of the male principle and the Vau of the female principle, but the two forming a complete whole; and so, too, with the Yod of the one and the He of the other. The several letters of the two Names, moreover, imply each other, complement each other, and together enfold one mystery. Now, the lower and earthly Tabernacle was the counterpart of the upper Tabernacle, whilst the latter in its turn is the counterpart of a higher Tabernacle, the most high of all. All of them, however, are implied within each other and form one complete whole, as it says: "that the tabernacle may be one whole" (Ex. XXVI, 6). The Tabernacle was erected by Moses, he alone being allowed to raise it up, as only a husband may raise up his wife. With the erection of the lower Tabernacle there was erected another Tabernacle on high. This is indicated in the words "the tabernacle was reared up (hukam)" (Ex. XL, 17), reared up, that is, by the hand of no man, but as out of the supernal undisclosed mystery in response to the mystical force indwelling in Moses that it might be perfected with him. It is written above: "And all the wise men that wrought

Zohar: Shemoth, Section 2, Page 236a

all the work of the sanctuary came", etc. (Ibid. XXXVI, 4). The "wise men that wrought" embrace the "right", the "left", and all the other sides constituting the ways and paths that lead into the sea and fill it. These wrought the supernal Tabernacle and perfected it. Likewise, the lower Tabernacle was wrought by Bezalel and Oholiab, the one of the right, the other of the left, followed by "every wisehearted man", all after the supernal pattern. On the day the Tabernacle was reared up death was removed from the world, that is, it was deprived of its dominion over the world. For, indeed, the entire extinction of the evil impulse will not come to pass until the coming of King Messiah, when the Holy One, blessed be He, will rejoice in His works and "he will swallow up death forever" (Isa. xxv, 8). Yet when the Tabernacle was reared up by the hand of Moses the power of the evil impulse was subdued so that it could not exercise dominion. At that time the power of Samael, the wielder of the fury of the "left side", was removed from the evil serpent, so that the latter was not able to dominate the world or attach himself to man and lead him astray.' R. Judah said: 'It is written: "And Moses used to take the tent and pitch it without the camp" (Ex. XXXIII, 7). The reason of this was that Moses did not wish that the "holy side" should rest in the midst of the side of defilement.' Said R. Eleazar: 'So long as the "holy side" rules, the side of defilement is powerless and bows before it. So we have learnt that so long as Jerusalem is in its fulness wicked, Tyre remains devastated.' [Tr. note: v. T.B. Pesahim 42b.]

R. Eleazar said: 'It is written: "And Rebekah lifted up her eyes, and when she saw Isaac, she alighted from the camel" (Gen. XXIV, 64). What is the significance of this verse that it should be written in the Torah? Is it merely to tell us that the sight of Isaac's good looks made her alight from the camel? The truth is that this verse contains a recondite meaning. Observe that when Rebekah encountered Isaac it was the time of Minha (afternoon prayer), a time when Rigour is at large in the world, and she discerned him as one who was of the region of fierce Rigour, a region symbolized by the camel (gamal), [Tr. note: The Zohar plays upon the Hebrew root GML, which as GaMaL =camel, and as GeMuL=reward, requitement, for good or evil deed.] and hence she leaned and slipped off that camel. This camel is all-devouring and all-exterminating, is always ready to inflict death on man. Hence, whenever a man sees a camel in his dream it signifies that death was decreed upon him, but he was delivered. Observe that the side of defilement is so designated by reason of it having brought death into the world. The same it was that seduced Adam and his wife, and Samael is the one that rides on it and leads the world astray, and brings about the death of every one. It was Adam who first drew him to himself, so that he became their seducer. Of this Solomon said, "and come not nigh the door of her house" (Prov. v, 8), for whoever comes nigh her house, she emerges, attaches herself, and is drawn unto him. Thus when Rebekah discerned Isaac as being of the side of Rigour, the side of the dross of gold, she straightway alighted from the camel so as to break herself loose from the Rigour and the dross. Observe

Zohar: Shemoth, Section 2, Page 236b

that when the Israelites committed the sin of the Golden Calf there was no reason why they should have made a calf rather than anything else of the evil side. But, indeed, they did not choose the Calf, but merely said: "Up, make us a god who shall go before us" (Ex. XXXII, 1); and Aaron intended to delay them. But the Calf was the appropriate form. For from the side of gold there emerged the dross, out of which spread in all directions all the forces of the "left side". All these forces have the red colour of gold, and are under the influence of the sun. For when the sun reaches his full strength he generates gold in the earth; and the Chieftain ruling under the force of the sun has the appearance of a calf, and is described as "the destruction (keteb) that wasteth at noonday" (Ps. XCI, 6). The red side, the defiled spirit, is the same as the Evil Serpent. On him there rides a male-female being, called eleh (these), so called for the reason that they appear everywhere in various guises. On the opposite side is the Holy Spirit, called zoth (this) [Tr. note: Allusion to Isa. LIX, 21: "this is My covenant with them".], pointing to the emblem of the holy covenant which is always found on man. The others, however, are called "these", wherefore it is written "yea, these [Tr. note: Allusion to the Golden Calf, v. Midrash Eikhoh, in loco.] may forget, yet will not I forget thee" (Isa. XLIX, 15). The same is alluded to in "For these things I weep" (Lam. I, 16), inasmuch as that sin was the cause of many weepings for Israel. Alternately, "For these I weep", to wit, for the dark forces of that region to whom was given the license to dominate over Israel and to destroy the Sanctuary. "These" (eleh) points thus to the powers of the unclean-side, and "I weep" points to the Holy Spirit, who is named "I". One might indeed urge against this, citing the words: "These (eleh) are the words of the covenant" (Deut. XXVIII, 69). [Tr. note: This is cited to prove that eleh (these) is associated with the good as well as evil.] But in truth, even here the word eleh (these) points to the curses awaiting him who will transgress "the words of the covenant". Similarly, in the passage, "These are the commandments, which the Lord commanded Moses" (Lev. XXVII, 34), the word "these" is a warning to man to purify himself by the observance of the precepts of the Torah and not to stray from the right path, but to keep afar from the evil powers. As regards "These are the generations of Noah" (Gen. VI, 9), the word eleh (these) is assuredly appropriate there, inasmuch as Noah begat Ham, the father of Canaan, in regard to whom it is written, "Cursed be Canaan" (Ibid. IX, 25). This, then, is the esoteric implication of eleh (these), pointing in our text to the dross and refuse of the gold. Now Aaron offered up the gold because he was of the side of fire, and gold is under the influence of the force of fire, the two being, as it were, one. The Unclean Spirit, whose haunting place is the desert, thus found at that moment an occasion to seize hold of him; and so, whereas Israel standing at Mount Sinai were purged of the primitive venom that the evil spirit injected into the world, thereby bringing death to all mankind, now the same evil spirit defiled them anew, took hold of them and brought again death to them and to all mankind and for all their generations to follow. Scripture so says: "I said: Ye are godlike beings. But ye shall die like men", etc. (Ps. LXXXII, 6-7). Aaron therefore had to purge himself afterwards during the seven sacred days, [Tr. note: v. Lev. VIII, 33.] and after that by means of a calf. [Tr. note: v. Ibid. IX, 2.] Observe that Aaron had to purge himself, for but for him the calf would not have emerged. For Aaron belonged to the "right side", he symbolized the strength of the sun, the source whence gold originates; and so the unclean spirit came down and insinuated itself, with the result that the Israelites were defiled, and Aaron also. Aaron was defiled through the emergence of the calf that belongs to the left side, as it says:

Zohar: Shemoth, Section 2, Page 237a

"and the face of the ox on the left side" (Ezek. I, 10). Thus, though Aaron was of the "right side", the "left side" was there in absorption, the side that gave occasion for the calf. In this way the unclean spirit prevailed and regained his former rule over the world. For Israel, through their sin, drew to themselves the evil impulse as formerly. And in order to purge themselves they needed to offer up a goat, inasmuch as the goat is the portion of the evil impulse, that is, the unclean spirit, as already said. It is written: "And they exchanged their glory for the likeness of an ox that eateth grass" (Ps. CVI, 20). This is an allusion to the calf that came from the "left side". "Their glory" signifies the Shekinah that led the way before them, but which they exchanged for something unclean. Thus will the slimy venom not pass out of the world until the time when the Holy One, blessed be He, will remove it, as it says: "and I will cause the unclean spirit to pass out of the earth" (Zech. XIII, 7).

'Now some sorcerers succeed in their art and others do not succeed, although they use the same practices, since the success of sorcery depends on the man himself. We have an example in Balaam, who was the very man for such arts, he being, as tradition tells us, blind in one eye, [Tr. note: v. Rashi ad Num. XXIV, 15.] and looking askance with the other. But of those who have to serve with the holy spirit it is written: "For whatsoever he be that hath a blemish, he shall not approach: a blind man or a lame" (Lev. XXI, 18). So here the way was paved for the unclean spirit to enter and obtain dominion. It found a desert utterly uninhabitable, as it is written, "wherein were serpents, fiery serpents, and scorpions", etc. (Deut. VIII, 15), a spot that belongs to his dominion, and that contained gold enough for his use. It also found in Aaron a medium through which to insinuate itself into the "right" side. Thus the place being in all ways suitable it emerged into the open, and the deed was done. So when Aaron wished to become purged, he offered up a calf so as to execute judgement, as it were, on the "evil side". Whereas before he brought forth the Calf to make it ruler, he afterwards offered up a calf in order to subdue the evil power, for once punishment is executed on the "left side" all the subordinate rulers of that side are subdued. In regard to this, Scripture says: "Eat not of it raw... but roast with fire, its head on its legs" (Ex. XII, 8), so as to break the evil power and subdue it, and so that all its subordinates should no more exercise rule. Similarly we read: "a red heifer, faultless", etc. (Num. XIX, 2). This had the same object, namely, to subdue all those sides of the unclean spirit.' Said R. Abba to R. Eleazar: 'But is not the heifer sacred and purifying? and how can this be?' R. Eleazar replied: 'Indeed, it is so. It has been expounded that it was an epitome of the four Kingdoms [Tr. note: v. Daniel VIII.] Thus, the "heifer" is Israel, of whom it is written, "For Israel is stubborn like a stubborn heifer" (Hos. IV, 16); "a red [heifer]" indicates the Kingdom of Babylonia, regarding which it says, "thou art the head of gold" (Dan. II, 38); "faultless" points to the Kingdom of Media; [Tr. note: An allusion to Cyrus, the liberator of the Babylonian Jews.] and "wherein is no blemish" indicates the Kingdom of Greece (who were near the true faith). "Upon which never came yoke" alludes to the Kingdom of Edom, [Tr. note: i.e. Rome.] which was never under the yoke of any other power. It is written: "Who can bring a clean thing out of an unclean? Not one" (Job. XIV, 4).

Zohar: Shemoth, Section 2, Page 237b

The heifer is such a thing; for first it was an unclean thing, [Tr. note: i.e. a symbol of the evil power that was to be destroyed.] but after judgement had been executed on her, after she had passed through the fire and was burned to ashes, she was transformed into a purifying agency. Hence all those who busied themselves with it became defiled, and even after it turned into ashes, before these were gathered and removed, it defiled all who handled them, as we read: "And he that gathereth the ashes of the heifer shall wash his clothes, and be unclean", etc. (Num. XIX, 10). But as soon as water was poured over the ashes they became clean-a clean thing out of an unclean. After the clean had emerged out of the unclean, whatever was allied to the unclean spirit fled. So now the Holy Spirit obtained dominion, and the unclean spirit was subjugated utterly. The latter received its punishment without the camp in harmony with the precept, "therefore shall thy camp be holy" (Deut. XXIII, 15).' R. Abba then approached and kissed R. Eleazar.

Said R. Simeon: 'All this is true, yet nevertheless the Holy One, blessed be He, has conferred power on the unclean spirit and it behoves man to subjugate him from all directions. Now I am about to reveal to you', he said, 'a mystery which is only permitted to be revealed to the superior saints. The Holy One, blessed be He, has conferred power upon the place which is the unclean spirit to have dominion over the world in many ways and to be enabled to inflict harm; we thus dare not treat him lightly, but we have to be on our guard against him lest he indict us, even in our holy actions. We have, therefore, a secret device, namely, to assign him a little space within our holy performances, since it is out of the source of holiness that he derives his power. Hence we are required to enclose inside the phylacteries a hair of a calf with one end jutting out and exposed to sight. This hair is incapable of communicating defilement, since it is smaller than a barley grain. [Tr. note: Allusion (apparently inexact) to Mishnah, Ahaloth III, 2.] Now, when the unclean spirit beholds this hair that is within the supremely holy, and thus finds that he has a portion therein, he will abstain from assailing the wearer and will be powerless to inflict evil on him, whether on high or below. Whereas if nothing is given him within what is holy he brings accusations, saying, that-and-that man who at the moment makes himself holy has done such-and-such a deed on such-and-such a day, and these-and-these are the sins he committed; so that the man will thus be brought to judgement and be punished. The Israelites, who were aware of this secret, used to adopt a similar device when they began to sanctify themselves on the Day of Atonement; they at once made provision for assigning the unclean spirit his portion, so that he should not accuse them nor bring to notice the sins of Israel. For when he presents himself to bring accusations against Israel, ever so many bands and hosts stand there ready to take up his word. Happy is the portion of him who is able to be on his guard so that his sins should not be brought to notice on high, and so that he should not be regarded with disfavour.' Meanwhile tears began to flow from R. Abba's eyes. Said R. Eleazar to him: "Abba, Abba, unloose thy girdle, and wipe the tears from thy face, inasmuch as the mystic doctrines of the Torah were entrusted to the righteous, as it is written: "The secret (sod) [Tr. note: Sod in Bib. Heb.=counsel, in post-Bib. =secret, mystery.] of the Lord is for them that fear him" (Ps. xxv, 14).'

Observe that on New Year's Day the world is the mysteries of the divine unification, and lift up this throne until they bring it unto "Moses". Thereby they draw unto themselves blessings from the very source brought to trial before the holy Judgement Seat; and there stands on one side the evil spirit who regards intently and makes a record of all those that are doomed to death. But at the moment

Zohar: Shemoth, Section 2, Page 238a

that Israel awakens mercy by means of the sound of the trumpet (shofar) he becomes altogether confused and distracted, and turns his gaze away from the doomed ones. This continues until some time after. [Tr. note: i.e. the eve of the Last day of Tabernacles.] Then all those under decree of death who have not repented of their sins are delivered into the hands of the evil power under a final order of death, which order is irrevocable. The whole of Israel together have thus to be on guard against him, and how much more so one who is by himself. We have thus to assign him at every New Moon a he-goat as his portion, so that he will abstain from acting as accuser. The sacred moon will thus draw sustenance in holiness and be fittingly renewed. The moon being renewed every month is thus called "na'ar" (youth), but the opposite force, which is forever immersed in defilement, is called "old and foolish king" (Eccles. IV, 13). Thus for holy Israel, the one nation united to God in holiness, the Holy One, blessed be He, has provided a means of escape from all the evil powers. Happy are they in this world and in the world to come. So Scripture says: "Thy people also shall be all righteous, they shall inherit the land forever; the branch of my planting, the work of my hands, wherein I glory" (Isa. LX, 21).

'AND THEY BROUGHT THE TABERNACLE UNTO MOSES, ETC. It is written: "And above the firmament" (Ezek. I, 26). This alludes to the firmament that is placed over the four Hayoth (Holy Animals) who are impinged on by the spirit of the Hayah (Holy Animal), by whose spirit they all rise aloft, as it says: "and when the Hayoth were lifted up from the earth, the Ofanim (Wheels) were lifted up beside them, for the spirit of the Hayah was in the Ofanim" (lbid. I, 21). It is when the space of that region, as it were, impinges on them that the four Hayoth rise and carry aloft the superior Hayah, bringing it to the Supernal Illumination. This is esoterically alluded to in the words, "The virgins her companions in her train being brought unto thee" (Ps. XLV, 15), the four Hayoth being so designated. These raise the Supernal Hayah higher and higher so as to uphold the Supernal Throne, as esoterically indicated in the words, "and [they] bore up the ark, and it was lifted up above the earth" (Gen. VII, 17). The same allusion can be found in the words, "And they brought the tabernacle unto Moses", Moses being a synonym of Adam. The Tabernacle is symbolic of all the members of the Body when suffused with a holy desire for the union of the male and female principles. So "they brought the tabernacle", since the bride is first to be brought to her spouse, who subsequently takes up his abode with her permanently.

'Again, the words, "And they brought the tabernacle to Moses" are an allusion to those who daily concentrate their minds [whilst reciting their prayers] on of life. Of this Scripture says: AND MOSES SAW ALL THE WORK.... AND MOSES

555

BLESSED THEM, the blessings thus flowing from the region that is of the grade of Moses. Thus the prayer of every man is scrutinized, whether it is recited with the proper concentration on divine unification

and if it is found to be so, then the man receives blessings from the fount of blessings. Thus, so soon as "they had done it, etc." "Moses blessed them', AND TIIEY BROUGHT THE TABERNACLE TO MOSES, inasmuch as he was the "master of the house", whom it behoved to supervise its arrangements and mysteries, which none else was permitted to observe and look upon. When they brought the tabernacle to Moses, they brought it in all its parts, each part to be fitted in its place, and all the parts to be joined together to form a whole. For when they attempted to do so themselves, they did not succeed; so they brought it to Moses, who straightway succeeded in joining the parts together, putting each in its place. So we read, "and Moses reared up the tabernacle", and also, "the tabernacle was reared up".

'Observe that when Moses was about to set up the tabernacle and to adjust all its parts and members, fitting them one into the other, all the components of the unclean, or "other" side, became enfeebled. For when the one side, the side of holiness, ascends in power, the unclean side relaxes, and similarly, when the other side ascends this side becomes feeble. When one is full the other is desolate, as with Jerusalem and Tyre. [Tr. note: Vide T. B. Pesahim, 42b.] Moses thus "reared up the tabernacle" so as to be fortified by the supernal power and not be overcome by the lower power. Moses, moreover, whose vision was through the "luminous glass", was the one needed for the rearing up of the tabernacle, that he might be enlightened by it and not by some inferior light, just as the moon must receive its light from the sun and not from any other source.

'Observe now, that the Community of Israel had to raise and attach itself to the sun.' In this connection R. Simeon expounded thus the verse: "This is the law of the burnt-offering ('olah); it is that which goes up..." (Lev. VI, 2). 'The burnt-offering symbolizes the ascent of the Community of Israel and her attachment [to the Holy One] within the World-to-come, so as to form a unity, and therefore She is called 'olah (ascending). It is thus written: "This is the law (Torah) of the burnt-offering ('olah)", to wit, the Written Law and the Oral Law, the two representing the unity of the male and female principles. She is called "the 'olah" because she ascends to the World-to-come, designated the holy of holies. Similarly, the burnt-offering ('olah) is holy of holies, and therefore it is killed northward [of the altar], since it is of the left side in that the Oral Law is not embraced save when the north side is awakened, as it says: "Let his left hand be under my head, and his right hand embrace me" (S.S. II, 6). The Oral Law then goes up in love, is entwined in the right and attached in the midst, and the whole becomes illumined from the esoteric source of the Holy of Holies, under the beneficent influence of the service of the priests, the song of the Levites, and the prayer of Israel.

'As already said, the burnt-offering, the most holy grade of offerings, is the emblem of the supernal spirit. For there are three spirits knit together: the lower spirit, designated the Holy Spirit; the intermediate spirit, called "spirit of wisdom and understanding", a name also borne by the lower spirit. But the spirit that proceeds out of the trumpet and is composed of fire and water is called "supernal spirit", since it is hidden and silent, and in it are concentrated all the holy spirits and all the illumined countenances. The burnt-offering was thus transmuted, as it were, into the very essence of that spirit, whereas its beast-part, the consumed fats, were food for the unclean side. Not so the other, or peace-offerings, which had in them the sides of the forces of Rigour, and hence were named "lesser holy offerings"; for they do not ascend as adornments to the height

of heights like the most holy offerings; and hence may be killed on any side of the altar.'

R. Simeon further expounded the verse: "Man and beast thou preservest, O Lord" (Ps. XXXVI, 7). 'Man', he said, 'comes from the side of Man, that is, from that of Adam, whereas beast comes from its own side, that of beast. Hence, "When a man brings from you an offering... of the cattle", etc. (Lev. I, 2), indicating that the offering is first from man, and then from the cattle, that is, the beast-part, both being necessary for our offering. Similarly, God at the Creation made man and beast together (on the same day). It may be said that birds are also eligible for offerings, and even for burnt-offerings, as we read, "And if his offering be a burnt-offering of fowls" (Lev. I, 14). Note, however, that of fowls, only turtle-doves and young pigeons are eligible for an offering, the qualifications of the two being opposite to each other; [Tr. note: According to T. B. Hulin, 22a-22b, there is a special age qualification for each, that of the turtle-dove comnnencing when that of the young pigeon had already terminated.] since the former is symbolic of the right, the latter of the left. This is indicated in "and let fowl ('of=flying creatures) fly", an esoteric allusion to the Heavenly Chariot by which the Holy spirit ascends upwards, the term "fowl" being symbolic of the right side, the same being Michael, and the term "let fly" of the left, the same being Gabriel, the two together forming a unity: to wit, that of the lower world with the upper world, or of the Spouse with Her Master. In the Ancient Books it is stated that the poor man [Tr. note: Whose offerings consist only of birds.] provides a portion only for the upper regions, but the truth is that even his portion is distributed both in the upper and the lower regions, each receiving the part appropriate to it. R. Eleazar asked of R. Simeon how far in the heights the burnt-offering reaches. In reply R. Simeon said: 'Even as far as En-Sof (without end) the Infinite, where is the union and consummation of all in complete mystery. En-Sof cannot be known, nor how it makes beginning or end, just as the zero number produces beginning and end. What is the beginning?

This is the supernal Point, the beginning of all, hidden in "Thought". And it makes the end which is called "the end of the matter" (Eccles. XII, 13). But beyond there is "no end"–neither intention nor light nor lamp; all the lights are dependent on it, but it cannot be reached. This is a Supreme Will, mysterious above all mysteries. It is Zero ('En). When the supreme Point and the World-to-come ascend, they catch no more than a scent of it…. This, however, [Tr. note: The text seems here to revert abruptly to the subject of the offering of the bird introduced above]. is not "a sweet savour", for such is furnished only by the combination of the three acceptable services of prayer, song, and offering, the whole symbolizing "man". It is this sweet odour which drives away the other side-a service performed by the hand of the priest, as it says: "Command Aaron

Zohar: Shemoth, Section 2, Page 239b

and his sons, saying" (Lev. XVII, 2), the term "command", as tradition tells us, alluding to idolatry. [Tr. note: v. T. B. Sanhedrin, 56b.] This signifies that the evil thought is removed from the holy principle, is separated along with the smoke and the burning fats, whilst the favoured part of the sacrifice ascends on high in its pure holiness. This is the work that was entrusted to the priests. It is true that the same term "command" is used in connection with the whole of Israel, as we read: "Command the children of Israel" (Num. XXVIII, 1). Israel, however, achieve the same work by means of prayer and obedience to the will of their Master. It is by this means that the evil is made powerless to rule over them; and this verse indicates how the Holy Spirit ascends ever higher whilst the spirit of defilement sinks to the lowest depths. Thus, what Israel achieves through prayer the priests achieve through the temple service. All this falls within the work of the priest, and thus is expounded the recondite doctrine of the co-operation (in the sacrifice) of "man and beast". Happy is the portion of the righteous in this world and in the world to come, in that they know the ways of the Torah and thus walk in the way of truth. Of them it is written: "O Lord, by these things", to wit, by the ways of the Torah, "men live" (Isa. XXXVIII, 16), to wit, in this world and in the world to come.

'According to another interpretation, the term "this is the law" refers to the Community of Israel, and the term ha'olah (that which ascends) to the evil thought that rises up in man's mind to turn him aside from the way of truth. The verse thus continues: "on its fire-wood upon the altar all night", signifying that the evil thought has to be consumed in fire so as not to allow it to grow. By the term "night" is meant the Community of Israel, which comes to purge man of the evil thought, and so "on its fire-wood" points to the "fiery stream" (n'har di-nur) (Dan. VII, 10), the place where the "unstable" (spirits) have to pass through the burning fire and be deprived of their power. When that happens, the Community of Israel, being the embodiment of the Holy Spirit, ascends on high. It is thus one of the recondite objects of the sacrifice to assign a portion of it as the share of the evil power so as to enable the Holy Spirit to rise on high, as symbolized in the rearing up of the Tabernacle.

'Observe that at the moment when the Tabernacle was erected, as also when the Temple (in Jerusalem) was built, the "other side" was subjugated and removed from the world; and that when the Tabernacle was erected by the hand of Moses the upper and the lower Tabernacles were erected together. Hence it is written: "And Moses reared up the tabernacle", signifying that the Tabernacle below was raised by Moses, as it were, to the height of heights; he raised up, in a sense, that which was fallen and lying low. The same will happen in the days to come, of which it is written: "In that day will I raise up the tabernacle of David that is fallen" (Amos IX, 11). [Note: The last seven lines of the Hebrew text do not appear in the translation]

Zohar: Shemoth, Section 2, Page 240a

[Note: The first six lines of the Hebrew text do not appear in the translation]

Observe that when Moses erected the Tabernacle, another Tabernacle, to wit, the celestial one, hidden and undisclosed, was simultaneously erected; and it was by the force of that upper Tabernacle that the lower one was made and held firm. As it was the hand of Moses that erected the lower Tabernacle, so was it the "grade" of Moses that simultaneously erected the celestial one. This is proved from the words: "And Moses reared up the (eth) tabernacle", where the particle (eth) signifies a twin Tabernacle.'

R. Yose said: 'How can Scripture say AND MOSES REARED UP THE TABERNACLE, seeing that that passage speaks of the setting up of its several parts, whilst the term "rearing-up" can only mean the completion of the whole by putting together of all its parts?' Said R. Isaac: 'Moses first set up the three sides of the Tabernacle, whereby the evil power was partly subjugated, and then completed the fourth side, so that the evil power was completely subjugated: a work that could only be done by Moses, and by no one else.

Observe, that when HE LAID ITS SOCKETS. Samael was shaken out of his place, together with his forty chariot-legions, and fled a distance of four hundred parasangs until he found refuge within the hidden abysmal cavern; and, as Moses "reared up its pillars" and made firm this "side", 'the pillars of the "other side" were loosened and fell down.' R. Isaac further discoursed on the verse: "In that day will I raise up the tabernacle of David that is fallen" (Amos IX, 11). 'It speaks of the day', he said, 'when the Almighty will execute divine justice upon the world and will visit their deeds upon the wicked of the world. For the Community of Israel cannot rise from the dust so long as the sinners from among Israel exist in the world. Thus the previous verse says: "All the sinners of my people shall die by the sword, that say: The evil shall not overtake nor confront us" (Ibid. 10); and this is immediately followed by the verse, saying: "In that day will I raise up the tabernacle... and close up their breaches, and I will raise up its ruins", where the plural "their" breaches can only point to "the sinners of My people" who form breaches in Israel, and so when "the sinners of My people shall die by the sword" those "breaches" will be closed up; "and I will raise up its ruins", to wit, the ruins of the tabernacle of David which was laid into ruins what time the wicked kingdom obtained dominion in the world. For, as we have learnt, of the two powers, as the one gathers strength the other languishes; as the one is filled the other is laid waste. So, until that day the wicked kingdom will be in power, but on that day the Holy One, blessed be He, will raise up the Holy Kingdom and "will raise up its ruins, and will build it as in the days of old" (Ibid.). This last is in allusion to: "Moreover the light of the moon shall be as the light of the sun, etc." (Isa. xxx, 26). AND MOSES REARED UP THE TABERNACLE, to wit, AND LAID ITS SOCKETS as a support underneath, and to enable the doors to revolve. "He laid them"; that is, he made them very firm, and at the same time the pillars of the "other side" were removed. Now we read: "Remember, O Lord, against the children of Edom the day of Jerusalem; who said: Rase it, rase it, even to the foundation thereof" (Ps. CXXXVII, 7). But God will in the future build the foundations of Jerusalem out of another substance which will prevail against all, to wit, out of sapphires, as it says, "and (I will) lay thy foundations with sapphires" (Isa. LV, 11). For these form firm and solid foundations without any weakness such as was in the former foundations. Over those stones

Zohar: Shemoth, Section 2, Page 240b

of the former foundations other nations could prevail, inasmuch as they lacked the light supernal; but these will possess the radiation from the supernal light and will be embedded in the abyss so that no one will be able to loosen them. These are the sapphires that will shed their light above and below. Nor should we think that the former foundations will then be discarded, for it is written: "Behold, I will set thy stones in antimony (pukh)", the term "set" (marbitz) signifying the repairing of the old broken stones. There are certain stones called pukh; the reason—so said R. Eleazar—only being known to the "reapers in the field". For we must not think for a moment that the stones of the foundations of Zion and Jerusalem fell into the power of the nations. In truth, they did not burn them, nor were they burnt, but they were all hidden and treasured up by the Holy One, blessed be He, without the loss of a single stone, and when God will again establish Jerusalem in its place, the ancient foundation-stones will return to their former positions; and no other (al. evil) eye will be able to rest on them save an eye painted with antimony (pukh). With such an eye one will be enabled to behold all the stones and foundations of Jerusalem set aright in their places. Similarly, all the other precious stones and stone edifices will be reared up in their former positions. Then "they shall see eye to eye the Lord returning [Tr. note: The Zohar takes here the verb shub (returning) in a transitive sense.] (to) Zion" (Ibid. LII, 8). Scripture speaks of the "Lord returning" for the reason that when other nations obtain rule over Zion, God removes her, as it were, and places her on high; but then He will restore her to her own place. Observe that if a thing is too bright for the eye to behold, the eye may yet look upon it if it is painted with certain substances. Hence, "Behold, I will set thy stones in pukh" [Tr. note: i.e. owing to the intense brilliancy of the stones, the eye could only look at them when shaded by certain paints like pukh (antimony).] Observe also that all the former foundations will in the future be in their former positions and the sapphire stones will be placed around them. Of the time that God will restore His House it is written: "He will swallow up death forever" (Ibid. xxv, 8); it will not be as at the time when Moses reared up the Tabernacle, but forever and for all generations. The Holy One, blessed be He, will then establish the Community of Israel, will raise up the pillars and the pins, and all the beams of the Sanctuary in their proper setting to endure forevermore. The "other side" will be swallowed up forever: "And the reproach of his people will he take away from off all the earth; for the Lord hath spoken it" (Ibid.). AND MOSES REARED UP THE TABERNACLE, AND LAID (vayiten) ITS SOCKETS. At the time when these pillars and supports were put into their places, the pillars and supports of the evil side were loosened and swept away from their places. Moses, as we have learnt, saw the wicked Samael advancing towards him with intent to bring accusations against him. But he overpowered him and bound him in fetters, and then reared up the tabernacle, and fixed its sockets. The term vayiten (and he laid) indicates the use of intense force, for no other man but Moses would have been able to overcome this antagonist and to fix the foundations in their place. It was on the first of Nisan that the Tabernacle was reared up, a season when the evil powers are let loose in the world; for in the days of Nisan, as the saying goes, "even when the ox has his head in the fodder basket, go up the roof" [Tr. note: T. P. Pesahim, 112.] Moses saw Samael going round and round him to confuse him, but he overpowered him. And whilst he began to set firmly the Tabernacle below, a corresponding work was begun

Zohar: Shemoth, Section 2, Page 241a

on high; there was opposite the earthly Tabernacle a heavenly Tabernacle, hidden and undisclosed, that radiated light on all sides, illuminating all the worlds. R. Yose asked R. Simeon: 'How is it that Scripture seems to speak of three

Tabernacles, in that it says: "And on the day that the tabernacle was reared up the cloud covered the tabernacle, even the tent of the testimony; and at even there was upon the tabernacle as it were the appearance of fire, until morning" (Num. IX, 15)? And further, why "tabernacle" rather than "house", inasmuch as a house was needed rather than a temporary abode?' R. Simeon prefaced his reply with the verse: "Thus saith the Lord: The heaven is my throne, etc." (Isa. LXVI, 1). 'Observe', he said, 'that the Holy One, blessed be He, found delight in Israel as His inheritance and portion, brought them near to Himself, and divided them into certain grades after the celestial model, so as to bring into one complete whole all the worlds, both the upper and the lower. Thus "the heaven is my throne" indicates the firmament wherein Jacob dwells, an exalted image, as it were, of the most high Divine Throne; [Tr. note: Al. "an exalted throne for the supernal sacred form."] "And the earth is My footstool", to wit, the firmament where King David abides to feast on the resplendency of the luminous glass; and since this resplendency is designed to be diffused downwards, the term "My footstool" is used. "The house that ye may build unto me" alludes to the Temple; and "the place that may be my resting-place" speaks of the Holy of Holies of the lower Temple. Now observe that all the time that the Israelites wandered in the desert they possessed a Tabernacle, which remained in existence until they came to Shiloh. This, then, is the allusion of the threefold mention of the word "tabernacle", that it went from one place to another, carrying a trail of light through all, but it was not a permanent resting-place. This only came about when the Temple was built in the days of King Solomon. Then was there indeed rest, both in the upper world and the lower; there were no more journeyings from place to place. The difference between "tabernacle" and "house" may be illustrated thus. In regard to the former we have to imagine a king who comes to visit his friend without bringing with him all his retinue, but only a few attendants, so as not to put his friend to trouble. But a "house" is a place where he comes to abide accompanied by his full retinue. The Temple, then, was designed as an ever-enduring resting-place for all the legions, all the symbols, all the solemn works, on the model of the celestial Temple; but the Tabernacle was the same, only on a small scale.

'Observe that when Moses was commanded to make the Tabernacle, he could not comprehend its design until God showed him an exact replica of every single part, a replica in white fire, in black fire, in red fire, and in green fire. Scripture thus says: "And see that thou make them after their pattern, which is being shown thee in the mount" (Ex. xxv, 40). Still Moses found the work difficult, and though he was shown it eye to eye, as it were, he was reluctant to undertake it. Now it cannot be that he lacked the skill or the knowledge for the work, for though Bezalel and Oholiab and the others with them did not see what Moses saw, yet it is written of them: "And Moses saw all the work, and, behold, they had done it, etc." (Ex. XXXIX, 43). How much more, then was Moses able to accomplish it! But the truth is that though Moses withdrew himself from the work of the Tabernacle, yet was the whole work done by his direction and under his supervision. Hence we read, "And see that thou make". According to an alternative exposition, Moses withdrew himself from the work of the Tabernacle, preferring to make way for someone else. So God said to him:

Zohar: Shemoth, Section 2, Page 241b

"See, I have called by name Bezalel... I have appointed with him Oholiab" (Ibid. XXXI, 1-6); and we read further: "And Bezalel and Oholiab and every wise-hearted man shall work" (Ibid. XXXVI, 1). For all that, seeing that the work was accomplished by and under his direction, it was as though he himself had done it. Moreover, it is the finishing of a work which is the decisive factor, and therefore we read: "And Moses reared up the tabernacle"; all those wise-hearted men attempted to rear it up but could not, the honour being left for Moses.' AND MOSES REARED UP THE TABERNACLE. R. Judah began a discourse on the verse: "Rejoice not against me, O mine enemy; though I have fallen, I have arisen, etc." (Micah VII, 8). 'It is the Community of Israel that says this', he said, 'in regard to the enmity of the wicked kingdom against the holy kingdom. "Though I have fallen" she says, "I have arisen", which is not so with any other kingdom, which once it falls never rises again. But the Community of Israel will rise again as she has risen before other times. She had fallen many times, was driven into exile, dwelt among enemies, and nations arose against Israel in an attempt to exterminate them, as it says: "They hold crafty converse against thy people.... They have said: Come, and let us cut them off from being a nation" (Ps. LXXXIII, 45). Yet, though all nations rose against them, God did not leave them in their hands, and if they did fall it was to rise again. And so at that future time when the Holy One, blessed be He, will raise her from the dust of the exile, the Community of Israel will say: "Rejoice not against me, O mine enemy; though I am fallen, I shall arise". Thus Israel arose from the Egyptian exile from which Moses brought them out with all the miracles and mighty deeds that the Almighty wrought for them. Hence it is written: "And Moses reared up the tabernacle", signifying that it was raised by Moses every time.'

R. Simeon discoursed in this connection on the verse: "When those went these went, and when those stood these stood" (Ezek. 1, 21). 'That means', he said, 'that when the Hayoth (living creatures) went the Ofanim (Wheels) also went, as we read, "and when the Hayoth went the Ofanim went hard by them" (Ibid. 19). For the movements of the Ofanim are only induced by the movements of the Hayoth, nor can they pause independently of the Hayoth, for the two move together as one. Now the celestial gate of the east is provided with twenty-four openings guarded by twenty-four sentinels who are surrounded by a flaming fire. There are at the entrance of the gate twenty-four sockets supporting twenty-four pillars. These pillars remain in their place and do not soar into space; they are thus designated "standing ones", in the verse: "I will give thee a place to walk among these standing ones" (Zech. III, 7). And as long as those pillars remain immobile those that are above them go to and fro through the world, survey things, and whatever they overhear they carry up on high. So Scripture says: "For a bird of the air shall carry the voice" (Eccles. x, 20). Now observe that the Ofanim (Wheels) are carried by the Hayoth (living creatures).

Zohar: Shemoth, Section 2, Page 242a

For that which is of a higher grade, though it seems to be carried by that which is of a lower grade, really carries it. It was the same with the Ark, which also carried its carriers. [Tr. note: T. B. Sotah, 35a.] We must distinguish between the Hayah, "the spirit of which was in the Ofanim", and the Hayoth, with which the Ofanim went. This one turned towards all four quarters of the globe. In regard to this it says: "This is the Hayah that I saw under the God of Israel by the river Chebar" (Ibid. x, 20); it is the same which forms a throne to the likeness of Man, and is below the superior holy Hayoth. For they are in grades, one above the other. The Throne immediately underneath the God of Israel is in the form of Jacob, and the Throne below in that of David; this is the one that turns to the four corners of the world. It follows that the spirit of the highest diffuses through the lower, and directs and guides the whole. There was similar direction in the lower world. Just as in connection with the upper world we read that "the spirit of the Hayah is in the Ofanim", so of the lower world it is written, "And Moses reared up the tabernacle", he being the guiding spirit below; wherefore it is written: "And he reared up, fixed, put."

'Observe that Moses set up thc Tabernacle in the recondite spirit of his own high grade; but the Temple that Solomon built was the recondite expression of the River that went forth from Eden, signifying homely peace and rest. The Tabernacle expressed love and affection, but not restfulness, whereas the Temple of Solomon meant rest, as it says, "he shall be a man of rest" (I Chron. XXII, 9). Each one builded according to his own grade.

'Moses first firmly established in the side of holiness the central Point which was hid in darkness and buried, and afterwards all the rest, which is but the enlargement of this Point. And if this Point had not been established first, all that spread from it could not have been established. This is referred to in the words, "he reared up the tabernacle". Moses then "set up its sockets" on either side to the number of a hundred, as it says, "a hundred talents, a talent for a socket" (Ex. XXXVIII, 27).

Zohar: Shemoth, Section 2, Page 242b

As already said, here it is not written "and he reared up", but "he laid" (vayiten) the sockets, for the reason that over above them there were placed other grades, riding one upon the other, as it were. At the moment when the central Point was reared up the evil power sank, but it was not wiped out altogether. That will come to pass in the future, as already said. As the one thus rose, so the other sank. When "he set up its sockets", the "holy side" began to gather force, whilst the forces of the "other side" plunged into the cavern of the Abyss. Had Israel not sinned, the evil powers could never more exercise sway in the world. But since Israel sinned, and thereby drew unto them the "other side" as of old, there is no remedy save to assign him his portion, esoterically speaking, in the sacrifices and libation-offerings. For this reason the burnt-offering is completely consumed in fire, so that the "other side" may be subjugated and the holy side may rise. Then the text repeats, "and he put in the bars thereof and he reared up its pillars", so that there should be rearing-up both at the beginning and the end, whereby the side of holiness was upraised and the evil side was weakened and forced down.

'The starting-point of the grades of the evil side, which is the beginning of the outside grade, assumes the shape of the head of a male riding on a camel. This is the starting-point of a thick darkness which spreads out. The darkness is caused by a smoke issuing in the midst of the fury of the evil side, which fury becomes intensified, begetting other furies, and furies upon furies, one riding on top of the other, and representing the male and the female principles. When the smoke begins to spread, through the pressure of the nucleus, it takes the form of a winding and dangerous serpent. The first result of its spreading is a grade which, after much moving up and down, settles into the grade called "shadow", being a shadow on the place called "death"; and when the two are combined they are called "the shadow of death". The lower and outer starting-point is enveloped in darkness and is far removed from the holy and central Point. The darkness round the lower point is black and yet not black, having no hue which can be discerned by the eye. It is of the same kind that prevailed in Egypt, regarding which it says: "they saw not one another, neither rose any from his place for three days" (Ex. x, 23); also, "even darkness which may be felt" (Ibid. 21).

Zohar: Shemoth, Section 2, Page 243a

Now this starting-point was ramified into seven grades. The first grade is a darkness that displays three hues: that of smoke, of fire, and that of blackness. The smoky hue is the apparition of the evil seducer who seduces mankind to stray from the path and to be rebellious. In allusion to such it is written: "There shall no strange god be in thee, neither shalt thou worship any strange god" (Ps. LXXXI, 9). The first half of the verse refers to the male principle, the second to the female principle. The fiery view is that aspect of the evil power which brings about slaughter, bloodshed, and destruction amongst mankind. For there is in the world causeless and purposeless slaughter and bloodshed, as well as slaughter and bloodshed in the course of war. The first proceeds from the male principle of the evil powers, the second from the female principle. The male aspect is concerned in mere bloodshed, whereas the female aspect is at the root of mutual wars of people against people; and all such wars proceed from the female principle. Finally, the black hue is the apparition of the evil power that presides over the infliction of wounds and bruises on the bodies of men as well as over crucifixions and strangulations.

Zohar: Shemoth, Section 2, Page 243b

"The second grade emerges out of the darkness and branches out into three hundred separate directions, although they all are absorbed within each other, as it were. They roam abroad to inflict evil on the world, to execute justice openly for sins committed by men in secret.

'The third grade is as a firmament that overspreads all the other grades.

Zohar: Shemoth, Section 2, Page 244a

The fourth grade is like a ruddy conflagration, and is also concerned with the shedding of blood among men. It gives the authority to the lower powers for the slaying of mankind. It is to the lower powers in the relation of soul to body. For the soul cannot act save through the medium of body. It is the aspect of the male, which can only act through the female principle, to wit, the lower powers.' [Tr. note: Here follows in the text a long dissertation on the Hekaloth (temples), or halls of the angels, which is not based on an exposition of the Scriptures.]

Zohar: Shemoth, Section 2, Pages 244b through 268b

[Note: These pages are not translated as per the translator's note on Page 244a, above]

Zohar: Shemoth, Section 2, Page 269a [Note: The first 39 lines of the Hebrew text do not appear in the translation]

THEN THE CLOUD COVERED THE TENT OF MEETING, whereby the Shekinah dwelt on the earth, and the unclean spirit, designated "end of all flesh", passed out of the world and disappeared into the cavern of the great abyss. The Holy Spirit had thus sole sway over the world, as Scripture says: "Then the cloud covered the tent of meeting". It is further written: AND MOSES WAS NOT ABLE TO ENTER INTO THE TENT OF MEETING, BECAUSE THE CLOUD ABODE THEREON, in other words, because the Holy Spirit hovered over the world and the unclean spirit passed out. The wicked, however, draw him again into the world, and if not for them he would completely disappear. But in the days to come the Holy One, blessed be He, will cause him to pass completely out of the world, as Scripture says: "He will swallow up death forever, and the Lord God will wipe away tears from off all faces; and the reproach of his people will he take away from off all the earth; for the Lord hath spoken it" (Isa. xxv, 8); also, "and (I will cause) the unclean spirit to pass out of the land" (Zech. XIII, 3). Blessed be the Lord forevermore. Amen and Amen. "The Lord will reign forever."

Zohar Section 3: Leviticus, Numbers, Deuteronomy

Zohar: Vayikra, Section 3, Page 2a

VAYIKRA

R. Eleazar began here with the verse, "Ask thee a sign [Tr. note: The Hebrew word is oth, which in Talmudic Hebrew commonly means "letter"] of the Lord thy God, ask it either in the depth or in the height above" (Isa. VII, 11). He said: 'We have compared the former with the latter generations, and found that the former were conversant with a higher wisdom by which they knew how to combine the letters that were given to Moses on Mount Sinai, and even the sinners of Israel knew a deep wisdom contained in the letters and the difference between higher and lower letters, and how to do things with them in this world. Forevery letter that was transmitted to Moses used to ascend as a crown upon the heads of the holy celestial Hayyoth, who with them flitted through the ether which is under the refined and unknowable supernal ether. There were large letters and small letters; the large letters came from the most high and hidden Temple (hekhal) and the smaller letters from another lower Temple; and both kinds were transmitted to Moses on Sinai, along with their occult combinations..

[Tr. note: The rest of this passage up to 3b ["And he called..."] deals mainly with the occult powers of various letters. The whole is omitted from the editiones majores of Mantua, Cremona, and Lublin.]

[Note: The last fifteen lines of the Hebrew text do not appear in the translation as explained in the previous translator's note]

Zohar: Vayikra, Section 3, Pages 2b–3a

[Note: The Hebrew text of these Pages do not appear in the translation as explained in the Translator's note on Page 2a]

Zohar: Vayikra, Section 3, Page 3b

[Note: The first 24 lines of the Hebrew text do not appear in the translation as explained in the Translator's note on Page 2a]

AND HE CALLED UNTO MOSES, AND THE LORD SPAKE UNTO HIM OUT OF THE TENT OF MEETING, SAYING. R. Hiya connected this with the verse, "I am come into my garden, my sister, my bride, I have eaten my honeycomb with my honey, I have drunk my wine with my milk, eat, O friends, etc." 'The first part of this verse', he said, 'does not seem to accord with the second. If a man invites another to eat, it is while the food is spread before him, not after he has eaten himself. The explanation, however, is this. On the day when the Tabernacle was set up on earth, another Tabernacle was set up aloft, and that day was one of joy to the Holy One, blessed be He. Moses, however, at that time, "was not able to enter the tent of meeting" (Ex. XL, 35), whereupon God said, "The Tabernacle has been raised by the hand of Moses, and shall he remain outside?" Straight-way, therefore, He called to Moses, saying, Moses, how does one dedicate a house? With a banquet, is it not? Therefore, "when any man of you offereth an oblation unto the Lord", etc. The verse can also be explained in the same connection as follows. The "garden" is the higher Garden of Eden, "My sister, my bride" is the Community of Israel, whose espousals were on that day consummated, all being blessed from the water of the supernal stream. Hence it says "I have gathered my myrrh with my spice, etc.",

Zohar: Vayikra, Section 3, Page 4a

while the words "eat, O friends, etc." indicate that all those beneath and all the branches were blessed and nourished when the others were blessed above. And wherewith are they all blessed and regaled? With the odour of the sacrifice. It was when the Community of Israel came down to make her abode on earth that God proclaimed this verse, because there was then blessing and joy in all worlds, and She was firmly established as a source of blessing to all. For when those Six [grades] are blessed, then all worlds are blessed, both below and above, and Israel draw blessing from all of them.'

R. Isaac said that the Holy One, blessed be He, was espoused to the Community of Israel only at the time when those Six drank their fill of the "stream that never fails". R. Judah said that the words, "Eat, O friends, drink, yea drink abundantly, O beloved", were addressed to all the lords of the loud battle-shout, who were then established and blessed because they all partook of the banquet of the King. For when the King came rejoicing he rejoiced the Matrona, and then they all ate and were glad. R. Abba said that the terms "friends" and "beloved" refer to the Six mentioned, who were bidden to drink and drink abundantly from that wine which slakes the thirst of all. R. Eleazar said that these terms refer to all the lower orders, since when those Six are blessed all beneath are blessed. R. Simeon said: 'All these explanations are good, but the real truth is that "friends" refers to those above and "beloved" to those below.' 'Who', asked R. Eleazar, 'are those above and those below?' 'This is a good question', he replied. 'Those in the higher realm who are fast friends and never separate are called "friends", whereas those below who unite only at certain times are called "beloved ones". Note that those in the higher realm are bidden only to eat and not to drink. For he who already has a cask of wine needs something to eat with it, and since in that realm is the precious "wine of creation", they are invited to eat, whereas those below who require liquid are invited to drink, for all shoots require to be watered from the deep stream.' Said R. Eleazar to him: 'The term "beloved" is the more endearing of the two: why, then, is it applied to those below?' He replied: 'Those who yearn for one another, but are not always together, are called "beloved", whereas those who are always together and never hidden or separated from one another are called "friends". In the inseparableness of the one set and the yearning of the other lies the completeness of the whole, for the blessing of the Community of Israel and the joy of all worlds.' R. Hizkiah applied the verse to the sacrifices, because they are the banquet which is brought before the King, and the accusers also partake of it and are satisfied, and so joy is diffused everywhere. R. Aha applied the verse to the time when the Shekinah entered the Tabernacle, blessing and joy being then universally diffused, and Israel being perfected and joined

Zohar: Vayikra, Section 3, Page 4b

to the Holy One, blessed be He, on earth, as it is written, "and they shall make me a sanctuary and I shall dwell among them" (Ex. xxv, 8). AND HE CALLED UNTO MOSES. R. Simeon connected this with the verse, "The flowers appear in the land, the time of the singing of birds (zamir) is come and the voice of the turtle is heard in our land" (S.S. II, 12). 'Why', he said, 'is the word "land" repeated in this verse? The reason is that the "flowers" here are the "shoots" which God plucked up and planted in another place, and whose blossoms appear on the "earth"—that earth which is fitly blessed by them, the holy earth, the supernal earth, the true earth. Then, too, the time of cutting-off (zamir) has drawn near, the time to destroy the dominion of the nations over Israel, when the Tabernacle was set up, "and the voice of the turtle was heard in our land", to wit, in the land which Joshua conquered for Israel. When the Tabernacle was set up, Moses stood outside, not venturing to enter without permission, until "one called unto Moses". Who was it that called? She to whom the house belonged, the bride who had authority over all the house.' AND THE LORD SPAKE TO HIM. This was He that is called Voice, and to whom Moses attached himself. R. Eleazar quoted here the verse: "Wherefore when I came was there no man, when I called was there none to answer?" (Isa. L, 2). 'Happy are Israel', he said, 'in that wherever they congregate God is among them and takes pride in them, as it says, "Israel in whom I will be glorified" (Ibid. XLIX, 3). Nay more, Israel attain to perfect faith on earth and Israel consummate the Holy Name. For when Israel are blameless in their conduct the Holy Name, so to speak, is whole, but when Israel are faulty in their conduct on earth, the Holy Name, if one may say so, is not whole above. For so we have learnt: "One went up and the other went down. The supernal Israel ascended aloft, the Community of Israel came down to earth. So they were parted from one another, and the Holy Name was left incomplete"; and all because the Community of Israel is in exile. Yet though Israel are in exile, the Holy One, blessed be He, is to be found among them, and precedes them to the synagogue, where he exclaims: "Return, ye backsliding children, I will heal your backslidings" (Jer. III, 22). And if none heed, then God says:

"Wherefore when I came was there no man, when I called was there none to answer?" So on the day when the Tabernacle was completed God came at once and rested thereon and straightway "called unto Moses and spake to him from the tent of meeting, saying". He made known to him how Israel would sin and how this tent of meeting would be "pledged" [Tr. note: A play on the words mischan, "tent", and mashcen (Aramnaic), "pledge".] for their sins and would not endure. There was, however, a remedy for this: "if a man should bring an offering to the Lord".'

R. Hizkiah once, when in the company of R. Simeon, asked him

Zohar: Vayikra, Section 3, Page 5a

what was the precise meaning of the term korban (offering). He replied: 'As is well known to the Companions, it means their "drawing near". [Tr. note: From karab, to draw near,] It refers to those holy Crowns which are all knit together and drawn near to one another until they all form a perfect unity to make whole the Holy Name. Hence it is written, "a korban to Tetragrammaton", meaning that the drawing near of those Crowns is to Tetragrammaton to unify properly the Holy Name so that mercy should be shown to all worlds, and rigour should not be aroused. Hence the name Tetragrammaton is used (in connection with the sacrifices), and not the name Elohim. ' Said R. Hizkiah: 'How glad I am that I asked this question, so as to receive such an explanation. But is it not written, "The sacrifices of Elohim are a broken spirit; a broken and contrite heart, Elohim, thou wilt not despise" (Ps. LI, 18)?' He replied: 'It does not say here "offering" (korban), but "sacrifices" (zibehe). It is for this reason that the sacrifices were killed on the north side of the altar, because that is the side of Geburah, which is designated Elohim, the purpose being to soften and break the spirit of severity, so that mercy may obtain the uppcr hand. It is meet, therefore, that a man should stand by the altar with a contrite spirit and repent of his misdeeds so that that stern spirit may be softened and mercy prevail over severity.'

WHEN ANY MAN OF YOU OFFERETH AN OBLATION UNTO THE LORD. R. Eleazar said: The words "of you" are inserted here to show that the word "man" (adam) does not refer to Adam, who also brought a sacrifice when God created the world, as explained elsewhere.' Said R. Simeon to him: 'You are quite right.' R. Abba discoursed here on the Psalm commencing: "A song, a psalm of the sons of Korah" (Ps. XLVIII). 'This psalm', he said, 'surpasses all the other hymns of praise, sung by the sons of Korah, being hymn upon hymn, a hymn with two facets, song and psalm. It was sung in praise of the Community of Israel. Wherein lies this praise? In the words, "Great is the Lord and highly to be praised, in the city of our God, in his holy mountain". For when is the Holy One, blessed be He, called great? When the Community of Israel is with Him; He is great "in the city of our God". We learn from this that the King without the Matrona is no king, nor is He great nor highly praised. Hence, whoever being male is without his female is bereft of all his praises and is not included in the category of "man", nor is he even worthy to be blessed. (So in the book of Rab Hamnuna the Elder we find it stated that Job was called "great" (Job 1, 3) only because of his wife, who was God–fearing like himself.) The praise of their espousals is contained in the next words, "Beautiful in elevation", the one referring to the Holy One, blessed be He, and the other to the Zaddik, this union being "the joy of the whole earth". "God hath made himself known in her palaces for a refuge": these are Nezah and Hod,

Zohar: Vayikra, Section 3, Page 5b

in which all blessings and joy are stored up, and from whence they issue through the agency of that grade which is called Zaddik. "For lo, the kings assembled themselves, they passed by together" these are all the crowns of the King together; and from this point the Psalm has a different reference.

'When a man rectifies his actions by means of the offering, all is firmly established and knit together in complete unity, as it is written, "when a man brings near", that is, unites what should be WHEN ANY MAN OF YOU OFFERETH. The term "man" (adam) excludes one who is not married, his offering being no offering and blessings not resting on him, either above or below. For he is deficient and is called "blemished", and nothing blemished may approach the altar. The proof is in the fate of Nadab and Abihu. Said R. Abba: 'The incense is the most excellent of all offerings, for through it are blessed both those above and those below. Therefore they were not worthy to bring this offering, because they were not married. It may still be asked, however, why were they burnt? The following parable will explain. A man came before the queen to inform her that the king intended to visit her and enjoy her company. He then presented himself to the king, who saw that he was physically defective. Said the king: "It comports not with my dignity that through the agency of this cripple I should be presented to the queen." Meanwhile the queen had prepared the room for the king. When she saw that the king was prevented from coming to her by that man, she ordered him to be put to death. So when Nadab and Abihu took the incense, the Matrona saw and rejoiced and prepared to meet the King. When the King, however, saw that they were defective, he did not wish to be introduced to her through them, and kept aloof. When the Matrona saw that through them the King kept aloof, straightway "a fire went forth from the Lord and consumed them". All this because a man who is not married is defective, and the holiness of the King flees from him.' OF THE CATTLE. This is the general term. OF THE HERD AND OF THE FLOCK: these are the particular terms. The Scripture particularizes those animals which are proper to eat. Those which are not proper to eat may not be brought as an offering. The difference between those that are proper and those that are not proper to eat is stated elsewhere. IF HIS OBLATION BE A BURNT

OFFERING. R. Hiya cited here the verse: "For my thoughts are not your thoughts, said the Lord" (Isa. LV, 8). 'The Thought of God', he said, 'is the fountain-head of all, and from that Thought spread forth ways and paths in which the Holy Name might be found and fittingly established. From that Thought, too, issued the stream of the Garden of Eden to water all. On that Thought depend all beings above and below, and from that Thought come the Written and the Oral Torahs. The thought of man is also the fountainhead of his life, and from it stretch ways and paths to pervert his ways in this world and in the next. From that thought issues the defilement of the evil inclination to work harm to him and to all, and from it come error and iniquity and presumptuous sin, idolatry, fornication and bloodshed; wherefore

Zohar: Vayikra, Section 3, Page 6a

it says, "my thoughts are not as your thoughts". Hence it says, first of all, "If his oblation be a burnt-offering", for the "burnt-offering" ('olah) has reference to "that which goeth up" ('olah) on the heart, to wit the thought, and therefore the first offering mentioned is the burnt-offering.'

R. Aha was once walking in company with R. Judah. As they were going along, R. Judah said: 'We have learnt that the "Virgin of Israel" is blessed from seven sources; yet the Scripture says, in reference to her, "And do thou, O son of man, raise a lament over the virgin of Israel", [Tr. note: This verse is not found in our text. Apparently the Zohar meant it for a paraphrase of Ezek. XIX, 1, "And do thou raise a lamentation over the princes of Israel".] and what is even worse, "The virgin of Israel is fallen, she shall no more rise" (Amos v, 2). It is true that this last verse has been explained by all the Companions as a message of comfort. [Tr. note: In T. B. Berachoth, the verse is explained thus: "She has fallen, but shall no more; rise, O virgin of Israel.',] This, however, can hardly be accepted, as the prophet himself calls it a lamentation (v. I).' Said R. Aha: 'I, too, have been perplexed with the same difficulty. I once came before R. Simeon looking very troubled. He said to me: "Your face shows that there is something on your mind." I said: "Truly my mind is as sad as my face." He said to me: "Tell me what it is." I said: "It is written, 'The virgin of Israel is fallen, she shall no more rise'. If a man is angry with his wife and she leaves him, shall she never return? If so, alas for the children who have been sent away with her!" He said to me: "Are you not content with what the Companions have said?" I replied: "I have heard their explanation, that it is really a message of comfort, but it does not satisfy me." He said: "What the Companions have said is quite right as far as it goes, but there is more to be said. Alas for the generation when the shepherds are gone and the sheep stray without knowing whither they are going! Truly this verse requires understanding, but it is all plain to those who can interpret the Torah fittingly. See now. In all the other exiles of Israel a term was set, at the end of which Israel returned to God and the Virgin of Israel came back to her place. But this last exile is not so, for she shall not return as on previous occasions, as is proved by this verse which says, 'The virgin of Israel is fallen, she shall rise no more.' Note that it is not written, 'I shall not raise her any more'. Imagine a king who was wroth with his queen and banished her from his palace for a certain time. When that time arrived she at once returned to the king. So it happened several times. Finally, however, she was banished from the king's palace for a very long time. Said the king: 'This time is not like the other times when she came back to me. This time I shall go with all my followers to find her.' When he came to her he found her in the dust.

Zohar: Vayikra, Section 3, Page 6b

Seeing her thus humiliated and yearning once more for her, the king took her by the hand, raised her up, and brought her to his palace, and swore to her that he would never part from her again. So the Community of Israel, on all previous occasions in which she was in exile, when the appointed time came, used to return of herself to the King; but in this exile the Holy One, blessed be He, will himself take her by the hand and raise her and comfort her and restore her to his palace. So it is written: 'In that day I will raise up the tabernacle of David that is fallen' (Amos IX, 11), the 'tabernacle of David' being identical with the 'Virgin of Israel'." Said R. Judah: 'Truly thou hast comforted and satisfied me, and this is the truth of the matter. And it reminds me of something similar which I had forgotten, of a saying of

R. Yose, that the Holy One, blessed be He, will one day make proclamation concerning the Community of Israel, saying "Shake thyself from the dust, arise, sit thee down, Jerusalem" (Isa. LII, 2), like a man taking his neighbour by the hand and saying, Pull yourself together, rise.' Said R. Aha to him: 'All the prophets use similar language. Thus it is written, "Arise, shine forth, for thy light is come", meaning that the King is here to be reconciled with her. And again, "Behold thy king cometh unto thee" (Zech. IX, 9): He shall come to thee to comfort thee, to raise thee, to repay thee all, to take thee into His palace and to espouse thee forevermore, as it is written: "And I shall betroth thee forever" (Hos. II, 19).'

As they went along they saw R. Abba approaching. They said: 'Here comes a master of wisdom; let us greet the Shekinah.' When, however, they came up, he himself slipped off the saddle and came down to the ground by them. He then began to discourse on the verse: "And there was the voice of a trumpet (shofar) exceedingly loud" (Ex. XIX, 16). 'The ancient scribes', he said, 'differed as to the correct intonation of this verse. Some punctuated it so as to read, "And there was a voice, the trumpet exceeding strong", making the voice and the trumpet two things, the trumpet being the signal for slaves to go forth to everlasting freedom. Some, again, made the voice and the trumpet one, this being the

565

great voice whence issued the Torah, which is called "strong", because there is no word in the Torah so apparently weak or feeble which when properly studied will not be found as strong as a hammer breaking the rock.

Zohar: Vayikra, Section 3, Page 7a

It is also written in the same passage: "Moses spake and God answered him by a voice" (Ibid. 19). This voice, as has been elsewhere explained, is the voice of Moses, the Voice to which Moses attached himself. It may be asked, does it not say further on that "God spoke" (Ibid. xx, I), and not Moses? Some explain that the reason was because the people said to Moses: "Speak thou with us and we will hear, but let not God speak with us" (Ibid. 19). But, in fact, there is no word in the Torah which Moses spoke on his own authority. Hence it says, "Moses spoke" with his own voice, "and God answered him with that mighty Voice", confirming what he said.'

They asked R. Abba to continue, so he went on with the verse: "But if a priest's daughter be a widow or divorced and have no child", etc. (Lev. XXII, 13). 'Blessed', he said, 'is the portion of Israel above that of all other nations, because God created the world only for their sake, that they might receive the Law on Mount Sinai and become pure and righteous in His sight. Now, when this world was made after the supernal pattern and that first man was planted in the earth whose stature reached to the heaven, God desired to draw down a holy soul from heaven to earth in order that they might be joined and linked together. And therefore "God formed man dust from the ground", etc. (Gen. II, 7), that he might join one with the other and himself be perfect. And therefore God created man male and female that he might be perfect. For when is man called complete after the supernal pattern? When he is joined with his mate in unity, in joy, and in affection, and there issue from their union a son and a daughter. Then is man complete below like the Holy Name above, and the Holy Name is attached to him. But if a man is not willing to complete the Holy Name below, it were better for him that he had not been born, for he has no portion at all in the Holy Name, and when his soul leaves him it never joins him again, because he diminished the likeness of his Master, until it has been wholly rectified, as it is written: "But if a priest's daughter be a widow or divorced", etc. "The priest's daughter" is the holy soul, called "daughter of the king", who issues from the union of the King and the Matrona, and is therefore the lower body consisting of male and female, there being a corresponding soul above. "If she shall be widowed" from that body to which she was united, "or divorced" from that portion of the Holy Name, because "she has no seed" to resemble therewith that which is above and to be linked to the Holy Name, then "she shall return" to be restored to her original state. Thereupon "she shall return to her father's house", that is, to the Holy One, blessed be He, "as in her youth", as at first, and "she shall eat of her father's bread", to partake of the delights of the King. But thenceforth "there shall no stranger eat thereof", that is, one who has not established the Holy Name below and who has no portion therein; such a one has no portion in the supernal delight wherein is true "eating",

Zohar: Vayikra, Section 3, Page 7b

and which is still in the place where it was when the savour of the sacrifices used to ascend. For when there is food below there is food above; it is as though a king were to prepare a banquet for himself and another for his servants, but were not to eat till his servants ate. Hence the expression "sweet savour" (lit. savour of pleasantness)– savour for the servants, pleasantness for the Lord. Hence we have learnt that Israel feed their Father in heaven. And who are they that eat of the banquet of the King? Who if not the souls of the righteous?'

R. Abba further discoursed on the verse: "Behold how good and how pleasant it is for brethren to dwell together in unity" (Ps. CXXXIII, l). 'Happy are Israel', he said, 'in that God gave them in the charge of no chief or messenger, and they are attached to Him and He is attached to them. And from His love for them He called them servants, as it is written: "For unto me the children of Israel are servants" (Lev. xxv, 55); and He further called them children, as it is written, "Ye are children of the Lord your God" (Deut. XIV, 1); and finally He called them brethren, as it is written, "For my brethren and companions' sakes" (Ps. CXXII, 8)' And because He called them "brethren", He desired to make his abode with them and not leave them. Also we may take the word "brethren" to indicate the Holy One, blessed be He, and the Community of Israel. So in the exposition of the verse, "Hear, O Israel, the Lord our God, the Lord is one", we have learnt that "one" signifies the Community of Israel who clings to the Holy One, blessed be He, since, as Rabbi Simeon said, the union of male and female is called "one", the Holy One, blessed be He, being called "one" only in the place where the Female also is, since the male without the female is called half the body, and half is not one. When, however, the two halves are united, they become one body and are called one. At the present day the Holy One, blessed be He, is not called "one". The inner reason is that the Community of Israel is in exile, and the Holy One, blessed be He, has ascended aloft and the union has been broken so that the Holy Name is not complete and is therefore not called "one ". When will it be called "one"? When the Matrona will be again with the King and they shall be united, when, in the words of the prophet, "the kingdom shall belong to Tetragrammaton", the kingdom referring to the Community of Israel, to whom kingship is attached. Then "in that day shall the Lord (Tetragrammaton) be one and his name one" (Zech. XIV, 9). The verse continues: "It is like the precious oil upon the head that ran down upon the beard." This is the oil of the anointing of holiness which streams forth from the Ancient Holy One and which is found in that supernal stream which gives to the children the wherewithal to kindle the lights. That oil trickles on to the head of the King and from the head to the holy and venerable beard, and from there it streams on to all the garments of splendour in which the King is arrayed, as it is written, "that came down upon the skirt of his garments". These are the Crowns of the King in which is found the Holy Name: and it is through them that all the bounty and all the joy of the various worlds come down to bless. And this "good oil"

Zohar: Vayikra, Section 3, Page 8a

was not available until the time when the service from below mounted on high so that they met one another.'

R. Aha and R. Judah lifted up their hands and thanked R. Abba. R. Aha then discoursed on the verse: "But God (Elohim) came to Abimelech in a dream of the night" (Gen. xx, 3). 'We also find that "Elohim" came to Balaam (Num. XXII, 9). How is it that "Elohim" came to Gentiles and not to Israel? The truth is, however, that, as we have learnt, the word "Elohim" in these passages refers to the celestial Power that was in charge of Abimelech or Balaam. So, when we read that Elohim said to Abimelech, "I also know", etc. (Gen. xx, 6), we interpret thus: "Although one higher than I am knows, yet I also know". Hence he continued: "And I also withheld thee from sinning against me." There is really no sinning against a [mere] celestial Power, but what he meant was that through the sins of a people on earth their guardian Power above is weakened, and deposed from his authority. We learn from this that through the sins of mankind injury is inflicted above, as it says, "And through your transgression your mother was put away" (Isa. L, 1). Hence an offering (korban) had to be brought in order to bring near (kareb) the upper world and the lower after they had been separated through the sins of men.'

R. Abba and R. Judah then came and thanked R. Aha. R. Judah then followed with the text: "Serve ye the Lord with gladness" (Ps. c, 1). 'We have learnt', he said, 'that all service of God must be performed with gladness and zest, otherwise it is not perfect. Now how is this possible in the case of the offering, which is brought as a sign of man's repentance for transgressing the precepts of the law? With what face can such a man stand before God? Surely only with a contrite spirit and sorrowful heart. Where, then, is the joy and shouting? The truth is, however, that this was provided by the priests and Levites: rejoicing was carried out by the priest because he is far from chastisement and must ever show a more joyful countenance than the rest of the people. The singing, again, was carried out by the Levites, whose function it was. So the priest stood by him

Zohar: Vayikra, Section 3, Page 8b

and found suitable words to unify in joy the Holy Name, while the Levites broke out into song. At the present day, when there are no offerings, if a man sins and returns to his Master with bitterness of heart, with sorrow, with weeping and contrition, how is he to provide joy and singing? The answer is an esoteric one. We have learnt: "A man should enter the synagogue to the extent of two gateways and then pray." This alludes to the words of David: "Lift up your heads, O ye gates" (Ps. XXIV, 7). These are Maon and Machon, the which are far within, the beginning of the grades Kindness (Hesed) and Fear (Pahad), and the gateways of the world. Therefore a man should in his prayer fix his mind on the Holy of Holies, which is the Holy Name, and then say his prayer. Others learn the same lesson thus: "Joy" is the Community of Israel, and Israel will one day come forth from the exile through this joy, as it is written, "For in joy ye shall go forth" (Isa. LV, 12), and therefore it says, "Serve ye the Lord with joy". It further says, "Come before him with song". This is the completion of the joy, for joy is in the heart and song in the mouth. This, then, is the fitting way for man to appear before his Master, and then it can be said to him, "Know that the Lord is God": he has now to unify the Holy Name and to link these two names so as to make them one, and this is the true service of the Holy One, blessed be He.' Said R. Aha and R. Abba to him: 'Assuredly it is so. Happy the righteous who study the Torah and know the ways of the Holy One, blessed be He.'

They accompanied R. Abba three miles. He quoted to them the verse: "But as for me, in the multitude of thy lovingkindness I will come into thy house", etc. (Ps. v, 8). 'This verse', he said, 'has been expounded to mean that before entering a house of prayer a man should consult Abraham, Isaac, and Jacob, who instituted prayers to the Holy One, blessed be He: Abraham as it is said, "I will come into thy house"; Isaac as it is said, "I will bow down toward thy holy temple"; Jacob as it says, "In thy fear". Of such a one it is written, "And he said to me, thou art my servant, Israel, in whom I shall be glorified" (Isa. XLIX, 3).' IF HIS OBLATION BE A BURNT OFFERING FROM THE HERD. R. Yose asked: 'Why should there be three kinds of burnt-offering-from the herd, from the flock, and from the fowl? Why is not one sufficient? The reason is that if a man can afford he brings an ox, and if he cannot afford an ox he brings a sheep, and if he cannot afford a sheep he brings a fowl; for God does not demand of a man more than he can perform.' R. Eleazar said: 'His offering was to correspond to his sin. A rich man puffed up with his wealth was to bring an ox, because his thoughts were likely to be the most sinful. A man of moderate means brought a sheep because he was not so prone to sin; while a poor man, who was the most timid of all, brought the smallest offering of all. And the offering of each was appraised by God at its true value.'

R. Eleazar asked R. Simeon, his father, the following question: 'We have learnt that famine comes to the world for three sins which are only found among the rich, because they are puffed up with their wealth, but not among the poor; how is it fair,

Zohar: Vayikra, Section 3, Page 9a

then, that God should slay the poor (by famine) and not the rich, for now they will sin still more?' He replied: 'This is a good question, and the Companions have answered as follows. Of all the sons of man, none are so near to the Supreme King as those vessels which He uses, to wit, "a broken and contrite heart" (Ps. LI, 18), "he that is of a contrite and humble spirit" (Isa. LVII, 15). Now, when there is a famine and the poor are punished and suffer, and they weep and cry before the King, and God draws them nearer than ever, as it is written, "For he hath not despised nor abhorred the affliction of the afflicted" (Ps. XXII, 25), God then visits the sin for which famine has come on the world. Woe, then, to the sinners who have caused this, when the King bestirs himself to take note of the voice of the poor. Heaven protect us from them and their vengeance, for so it is written, "I will surely hear his cry" (Ex. XXII, 23), "and my wrath shall wax hot, etc." (Ibid.).

'The offering of the poor man is a small one, because his heart is downcast, and therefore even if he harbours sinful thoughts he is forgiven because he is sufficiently punished by his own distress and that of his household. A rich man once brought an offering of two pigeons to the priest. On seeing them, the priest said: "This is not an offering for you." He went home very sad. His people asked him why he was so sad, and he said: "Because the priest would not take my offering." "What was it?" they said. He told them it was two pigeons. They said: "That is an offering for a poor man, not for you. You must bring a proper one." "What is that?" he asked. They replied: "An ox." "Is the mere thought of sin then so serious?" he said. "I vow that I will let no thought of sin enter my heart". From that day he used to spend the day in business, then go to bed at night, and on waking he used to call his brethren, and they taught him the Torah and he used to study it till daybreak. So, because he studied, they called him "the transformed Judah". One day R. Jesse the Elder found him dividing his money, half for the poor and half for merchandise to ship oversea, and after he had finished he sat down and studied the Torah.

'He expounded the verse: "And Saul said to the Kenites, etc." (2 Sam. xv, 6). 'The Kenites', he said, 'were the descendants of Jethro, the father-in-law of Moses, and were so called because they made for themselves a nest (ken) in the wilderness, in order to study the Torah; for the study of the Torah does not require luxuries or merchandise, but only labour day and night. Hence they left the luxuries of Jericho and removed to the wilderness. Now, of Jethro it is written, "And Jethro, Moses' father-in-law, took a burnt offering and sacrifices for God" (Ex. XVIII, 12). This shows that his offering

Zohar: Vayikra, Section 3, Page 9b

was highly esteemed in the sight of God, and therefore "Aaron and all the elders came to eat with Moses' father-in-law before God" (Ibid.); from which we learn that when one brings an offering with true devotion, God comes to meet him. Now the offering of a poor man is highly esteemed before God, because he brings two offerings: one the actual sacrifice, and the other his own flesh and blood, because, though he has nothing to eat himself, he yet brings an offering. A poor man can bring a little flour and make atonement; for just as his own flesh and blood were burning (with hunger), so the flour is heated with the oil smeared on it. Here, too, we learn that any man may bring an offering on a baking-pan or a frying-pan because it is heated in the same way as he heated his flesh and blood with his evil passions and set all his limbs on fire. The essence of the offering is that it is analogous to the sin, and that a man should offer to God his desires and passions, for this is more acceptable than all. Blessed are the righteous that they bring this offering every day. Yet withal, the actual offering is better, because it brings blessings on all worlds.'

'He further discoursed on the verse: "Blessed be the Lord out of Zion, who dwelleth at Jerusalem, hallelukah" (Ps. CXXXV, 21). He said: 'Is the Lord blessed from Zion? Is He not blessed from the recondite supernal stream? What it means, however, is that the Lord is blessed when the Moon is illumined by the Sun and they draw near one another. Or again, it may mean that the place from which it is known that the Holy One, blessed be He, is blessed is Zion, as it is written: "For there the Lord commanded the blessing, etc." (PS. CXXXIII, 3).' Said R. Jesse to him: 'Blessed art thou that thou hast attained to all this, and blessed are all those that study the Torah.' IF HIS OBLATION BE A SACRIFICE OF PEACE OFFERINGS. R. Judah discoursed here on the verse: "And God said, Let there be a firmament in the midst of the waters" (Gen. I, 6). 'When God created the world', he said, 'He created seven firmaments above, and in each one stars and constellations and ministers to serve, and Chariots one above the other to take upon themselves the yoke of the kingship of their Master. Some have six wings, some four wings; some have four faces, some two faces, and some one face; some are of fire, some of water, and some of air. The firmaments envelop one another like the skins of an onion, and every firmament trembles from the fear of its Master by whose command it moves or stops. Over all is the Holy One, blessed be He, who sustains all in His power and might. Similarly there are seven earths below,

Zohar: Vayikra, Section 3, Page 10a

one higher than the other, the Land of Israel being the highest of all and Jerusalem being the highest point in the whole inhabited world. Our colleagues who dwell in the South have seen all this in the books of the ancients and in the Book of Adam. Between each earth and the next is a firmament which divides them from one another. Hence they all have separate names, among them being the Garden of Eden and Gehinnom. The creatures in them also are different, corresponding to those above, some with two faces, some with four, and some with one; and their aspects also differ. But, it may be said, are not all men descended from Adam, and did Adam then go down to each of these earths and beget sons there? The truth is, however, that man is found only in this highest earth which is called Tebel (inhabited world), and which is attached to the upper firmament and to the supreme Name. Hence man is superior to all other creatures. For, just as above there is a highest firmament which is the throne of the Holy One, blessed be He, so below on this Tebel is the king of all, to wit, man. As for the lower creatures, they are produced from the moisture of the earth under the influence of the heavens, which brings forth creatures of various kinds, some with skins and some with shells- red, black, or white, and so forth, none of them enduring for more than ten years or so. In the Book of Rab Hamnuna the Elder it is explained further that all the inhabited world is circular like a ball, so that some are above and some below, and the strange appearances of certain races are due to the nature of the air, but they live as long as other men. Further, there is a part of the world where it is light when in another part it is dark, so that some have night while others have day. Also there is a place where it is always day and where there is no night save for a very short time. All this account which is found in the books of the ancients and in the Book of Adam is confirmed by Scripture, which says: "I will give thanks unto thee, for I am fearfully and wonderfully made, wonderful are thy works" (Ps. CXXXIX, 15), and again, "O Lord, how manifold are thy works" (Ps. CIV, 24). This mystery [Tr. note: ' That there are seven earths enveloping one another] has been entrusted to the masters of wisdom [Tr. note: The Cabbalists.] but is not known to those who mark out boundaries [Tr. note: The geographers.] Similarly the sea is full of different creatures, but in all worlds there is no ruler save man and God above him.'

R. Nehorai the Elder once went on a sea voyage. The ship was wrecked in a storm and all in it were drowned. He, however, by some miracle, went down to the bottom of the sea and found there an inhabited land where he saw strange human beings of diminutive size; they were reciting prayers, but he could not tell what they said. By another miracle he then came up again. He said: "Blessed are the righteous who study the Torah and know the most profound mysteries. Woe to those who dispute with them and do not accept their word." From that day, whenever he came into the house of study and heard the Torah being expounded, he would weep. When they asked him why he wept, he would say, "Because I was sceptical about the words of the Rabbis, and now I fear me for the judgement of the other world."

R. Judah, commenting on the verse, "Let there be a firmament in the midst of the waters", said: "Did not that firmament divide the upper from the lower waters there would be conflict between them. But

Zohar: Vayikra, Section 3, Page 10b

that firmament keeps the peace between them, and the world is established only on peace. God is also called "peace"; He is peace, His name is peace, and all is bound together in peace.' R. Abba said: 'I see that this supreme Holy Name is altogether peace and altogether one, and paths diverge from it in all directions. [Tr. note: The passage which follows in the text deals with the symbolism of the forms of the letters of the Divine Name, and also assigns the various names of the Deity to the various grades, as may be found in the table in the Appendix of this translation.]

Zohar: Vayikra, Section 3, Page 11a

[Note: The first 13 lines of the Hebrew text on this Page are not translated as explained in the Translator's note on Page 10b]

IF HIS OBLATION BE A SACRIFICE OF PEACE OFFERINGS. R. Abba here quoted the verse: "Awake, O north wind, and come thou south, blow upon my garden that the spices thereof may flow out" (S.S. IV, 15). 'The north wind', he said, 'refers to the burnt offerings which were killed on the north side (zafon) of the altar, because these atone for the thoughts which are in the recesses (mazpune) of a man's heart. The south wind refers to the peace offerings, which were killed on the south side of the altar, because they make peace between higher and lower, and between the various quarters of the world. Therefore the bringer also eats of them and has a share in them. Of all the offerings, none are so well beloved to God as the peace offerings, because they bring harmony to upper and lower. Superior to all, however, is the incense, because it is brought not for sin or trespass, but for joy, as it is written, "Oil and incense rejoice the heart" (Prov. XXVII, 9), according to our explanation. For this reason the incense was brought at the same time that the lamp was lit (Ex. xxx, 7). The peace offerings spread peace everywhere and allay strife and wrangling, but the incense fastens the bond of faith. [Tr. note: The passage which follows in the text resumes the discussion of the relation of the names of the Deity to the various grades, and suggests an alternative arrangement. This again is followed by a passage comparing the Ten Commandments to the ten "Words" of the Creation by a highly forced interpretation.]

Zohar: Vayikra, Section 3, Page 11b

[Note: The Hebrew text of this Page is not translated as explained in the previous footnote.]

Zohar: Vayikra, Section 3, Page 12a

[Note: The Hebrew text of this Page is not translated as explained in the previous footnote.]

Zohar: Vayikra, Section 3, Page 12b

[Note: The first 49 lines of the Hebrew text on this Page do not appear in the translation as explained in the previous footnotes.]

When R. Hizkiah was studying with R. Isaac, they once rose at midnight to study the Torah. R. Isaac discoursed on the verse: "Behold, bless ye the Lord, all ye servants of the Lord, which by night stand in the house of the Lord" (Ps. CXXXIV, l). 'This verse', he said, 'is a tribute to all true believers. And who are the true believers? Those who study the Torah and know how to unify the Holy Name in the fitting manner.

Zohar: Vayikra, Section 3, Page 13a

When a man rises at midnight to study the Torah and the North Wind awakes, then a certain Hind [Tr. note: The Shekinah.] arises and praises the Holy One, blessed be He. And with Her arise thousands and myriads [of angels] who all commence to praise the holy King. But they all fall into silence in order to listen to those who study the Torah, and they proclaim: "Behold, bless ye the Lord, all ye servants of the Lord", as much as to say, "You bless the Lord, you praise the holy King, you crown the King." And that Hind adorns herself with that man and stands before the King and says: "See the son with whom I am come before thee, with whom I approach thee." Their blessing is a real blessing, as it says, "Lift up your hands in (to) holiness" (Ibid.) What is "holiness"? The supernal Place from which issues the source of the "deep stream". When a man has come so far, they proclaim over him, "The Lord bless thee from Zion" (Ibid.); from the place in which the Community of Israel is blessed, from there He will furnish thee with blessings. Also, "thou shalt see the good of Jerusalem" (Ps. CXXVIII, 5), to wit, the blessings that reach it from the King through that holy grade of the Righteous One.' IF A SOUL SIN, ETC. R. Yose said: 'How greatly should men take heed not to sin before their Master, for every day a herald goes forth proclaiming, Turn your hearts, ye peoples, to the holy King, be on your guard against sin, arouse the holy soul which He has given you from the celestial holy place. For so we have learnt, that when the Holy One, blessed be He, draws forth a soul to send it down to earth, He impresses upon it many warnings and threats to keep His commandments, and He also takes it through a thousand and eight worlds to see the glory of those who have devoted themselves to the Torah, and who now stand before the King in a robe of splendour in the form which they possessed in this world, beholding the glory of the King and crowned with many diadems. When its time comes to descend to earth, it makes its abode in the terrestrial Paradise for thirty days to see the glory of the Master of the righteous, and then ascends to their abode above and afterwards comes down to earth.

Zohar: Vayikra, Section 3, Page 13b

Before it enters into the body of a man, the holy King crowns it with seven crowns. If it sins in this world and walks in darkness, the Torah is grieved for it and says, All this honour and all this perfection has the holy King delivered to the soul, and she has sinned before Him! And what if she does sin? We learn the answer', continued R. Yose, 'from the verse which says, "Until the day be cool and the shadows flee away" (S.S. II, 17). "Until the day be cool": this is a warning to the soul to repent and purify itself before the day of this world shall cool off and be followed by that awful day on which God shall call her to account when she departs from this world. "And the shadows flee away": this refers to the secret known to the Companions, that when a man's time comes to leave this world, his shadow deserts him. R. Eleazar says that man has two shadows, one larger and one smaller, and when they are together, then he is truly himself. Therefore a man should review his actions and rectify them before his Master and confess his sins, because God is called merciful and gracious, and He receives those who return to Him. Hence he should repent before the shadows flee away, for if he only does so when he is already under arrest, this is indeed repentance, but not so acceptable. For when the day arrives for the soul to depart from the world, the Holy One, blessed be He, looks sadly at her and says: "If a soul sin although it hath heard the voice of adjuration"—for did I not adjure her by My Name not to be false to Me, and testify against her when she went down to earth? "And he is a witness" (Ibid.): truly so, for many times I testified against him to keep my commandments. Therefore since the man is a witness, when he returns to the King and either "sees" or "knows"—sees, that is, his sins and ponders on them, or knows for certain that he has committed some transgression—then, "if he do not utter it", that is, if he do not confess his sins before his Master, when he leaves this world "he shall bear his iniquity". And if that is so, how shall the doors be opened to him and how shall he stand before his Master? Therefore it is written, "When a soul sinneth, etc." '

R. Abba cited the verse: "All this is come upon us, yet we have not forgotten thee, neither have our steps declined from thy way" (Ps. XLIV, 19). 'The word "this" ', he said, 'where we should have expected "these things", alludes to the celestial judgements; all these, says the Psalmist, have come upon us, and yet we have not forgotten the words of the Torah. From this we learn that whoever forgets the words of the Torah and is not willing to study is like one who forgets God, for all the Torah is the name of the Holy One, blessed be He. And whoever deals falsely with the sign of the holy covenant which is imprinted on him is like one who deals falsely with the name of the King, for the very name of the

King is stamped on him. Further, the Torah is bound up with this, and whoever keeps this covenant is like one who keeps the whole Torah, and whoever is false to it is like one who is false to the whole Torah. So, until Abraham was circumcised it was not written of him that he kept the whole Torah, but after he was circumcised it says of him: "Because Abraham obeyed my voice and kept my charge, my commandments, my statutes and my laws" (Gen. XXVI, 5). So, too, with Isaac

Zohar: Vayikra, Section 3, Page 14a

and Joseph, too, because he guarded this covenant, was rewarded with the ox, which is the first of offerings, as it says: "The firstling of his ox, majesty is his" (Deut. XXXIII, 17).' Said R. Judah to him: 'Why was he blessed with that which is of the left and not of the right, as it is written, "The face of an ox was on the left" (Ezek. I, 10)?' He replied: 'That he might avert the punishment of the sins of Jeroboam.' Said R. Judah: 'I have learnt a secret relating to this verse, that the word "ox" here alludes to a certain supernal grade, the partner of the one elsewhere called "cow", and that Joseph, because he guarded the covenant, became attached to these two grades.' Said R. Abba: 'This shows that whoever guards this sign attaches to himself these two grades to protect him and to crown him with heavenly glory.' R. Simeon said: 'A man who begets a son becomes linked with the Shekinah, which is the gateway to all the heavenly doors, the door which is linked with the Holy Name. Also, the blood which flows from the child is preserved before the Almighty, and when punishment impends over the world, God looks at that blood and delivers the world. We have learnt that through that blood the world is based on lovingkindness (hesed), and all worlds are established.' So R. Simeon expounded the words: "If not for my covenant day and night, etc." (Jer. XXXIII, 25), saying: 'There are two Crowns linked together, they being the gateway to all other Crowns; one is Justice and the other is Mercy, one male and one female, one white and one red. This covenant takes hold of both of them, lovingkindness and judgement, day and night. Hence it is called "day and night", because it takes hold on both. Thus he who is able to keep this covenant without fail and offends not against it all his days takes hold of day and night and is rewarded in two worlds, in this world and the world to come. Therefore Abraham was called "perfect" (Gen. XVII, 1), but not before he had attained both, day and night, and this was only after he was circumcised.'

Said R. Eleazar to him: 'We have learnt that when a proselyte is circumcised and enters under the wings of the Shekinah, he is called ger zedek (a proselyte of righteousness), but no more, which means that he is privileged to enter into

Zohar: Vayikra, Section 3, Page 14b

the crown of righteousness, and you say that he attains to "day and night"?' He replied: 'Eleazar, my son, you cannot compare one who comes from the holy root and the stock of truth to one who comes from an evil stock and from an abhorred root. Of Israel it is written, "I planted thee a noble vine, wholly a right seed" (Jer. II, 21), whereas of the idolatrous nations it is written, "whose flesh is as the flesh of asses and whose issue is like the issue of horses" (Ezek. XXIII, 20). Therefore Israel, who are holy, the seed of truth, the stock which has been established at Mount Sinai, where all their filth was removed from them, all enter into the covenant of day and night to be wholly perfected, but for the other nations it is hard to remove their pollution, even after three generations. Hence the expression, "proselyte of Zedek [Tr. note: i.e. they are attached only to this grade.] (righteousness)". 'And so', said Rab Hamnuna the Elder, 'Gentiles before they are circumcised abide in the lower crowns, which are not holy, and an impure spirit rests on them. When they are converted and circumcised, they abide in a holy crown which is above the lower crowns, and a holy spirit rests upon them. But the Israelites who are holy sons of holy parents who have been established at Mount Sinai and have entered into the perfect faith, so soon as they are circumcised attain to all.'

R. Yose said: 'It is written, "For this is as the waters of Noah unto me" (Isa. LIV, 9). Why have we here the expression "waters of Noah" and not "waters of the flood"? The reason is that when mankind are sinful and there is a righteous man in the world, God speaks with him in order that he may pray for mankind and obtain forgiveness for them. God first promises to save him alone and destroy the rest. Now the proper thing for a righteous man to do at such a time is to forget himself and espouse the cause of the whole world in order to appease God's wrath against them, as Moses did when Israel sinned. When God, however, said to Noah, "The end of all flesh is come

Zohar: Vayikra, Section 3, Page 15a

before me", Noah replied, "And what wilt thou do to me?", to which God replied, "I will establish my covenant with thee, make thee an ark of gopher wood". So Noah did not pray for the world, and the waters came down and destroyed mankind, and therefore they are called "the waters of Noah".'

R. Yose continued: 'What is the meaning of "this (zoth) is to me", in the verse quoted? Said the Holy One, blessed be He, The waters of Noah have caused me to reveal zoth in the world, as it is written, "zoth (this) is the sign of my covenant with them, my bow have I set in the heaven" (Gen. IX, 12, 13), as much as to say, there is none who heeds the glory of My Name which is alluded to by the word zoth. Hence it is one of the signs of a saintly and virtuous man that the rainbow does not appear in his days and the world does not require this sign while he is alive. Such a one is he who prays for the world and shields it, like Rabbi Simeon ben Yochai, in whose days the world never required the sign of the rainbow, for he was himself a sign. For if ever punishment was decreed against the world he could annul it. One day he was sitting at the gate of Lydda when he lifted up his eyes and saw the light of the sun darkened three times, and black and yellow spots appearing in the sun. He said to his son, R. Eleazar: 'Follow me, my son, and let us see what happens, for of a surety some punishment is decreed above, and God desires to let me know. For such a decree is kept in suspense thirty days, and God does not carry it out before making it known to the righteous, as it is written, "For the Lord will do nothing but he revealeth his secret to his servants the prophets" (Amos III, 7).' They came into a vineyard, where they saw a serpent advancing like a coil of fire along the ground. R. Simeon shook his garments and brought his hand down on the head of the serpent, which then came to a halt, though its tongue was still moving. He said to it: "Serpent, serpent, go and tell that supernal Serpent that R. Simeon is still alive." It then put its head into a hole in the ground. He said: "I ordain that just as this serpent has returned to its hole in the ground, so the supernal one shall return to the hollow of the great abyss." R. Simeon then began to pray. As they were praying they heard a voice say: "Ye ministers of evil, return to your place; ye band of ruffians, abide not in the world, for R. Simeon ben Yochai annuls your power. Happy art thou, R. Simeon, that thy Master is solicitous for thy honour at all times, above that of all other men." By this time he saw that the sun was shining again and the blackness had passed. He said: "Surely the world is safe again." He then went into his house and expounded the verse: "For the Lord is righteous, he loveth righteousness, the upright shall behold his face" (Ps. XI, 8). 'God', he said, 'loves to do righteous acts when the upright behold his face, that is, pray to him for their needs. According to a more esoteric explanation, the verse means that the 'days of antiquity' (yeme kedem) of the Ancient Unrevealed Holy One and the 'days of old' (yeme olam) of the Small of Countenance, which are called 'his face', see with direct glance the most precious of sights. For so we have learnt, that when the Holy One, blessed be He, looks upon the works of men and sees that they are good, then the Ancient Holy One is revealed in the Small of Countenance, and all the countenance of the latter beholds the hidden countenance and is wholly blessed, since they look at one another directly without turning to the right or left,

Zohar: Vayikra, Section 3, Page 15b

and they water one another until all worlds are blessed and all become one, so that 'the Lord is one and his name is one'. But when sin is rife in the world, the Ancient Holy One is hidden and they do not look at one another face to face, and punishment is let loose on the world and the thrones are cast down and the Ancient of Days is hidden and does not appear, so that sinners turn mercy into judgement.

'We have learnt as follows. From the side of the Mother issue emissaries of punishment who are armed with the clubs of Geburah (Severity), and prevail over Mercy, and then the worlds are defective and there is conflict between them. But when men amend their ways below, punishment is mitigated and removed, and mercy is awakened and prevails over the evil which arose from stern judgement, and then there is joy and consolation, as it is written, "And the Lord was comforted of the evil" (Ex. XXXII, 14). When judgement is mitigated, all the Crowns return to their places and the keys are restored to the Mother, and this is called repentance (teshubah, lit. returning), and the world is forgiven, since the Mother is in perfect joy.' [Tr. note: The passage which follows is written in so allusive a style that it would be hardly possible to convey its meaning by a translation. The point of it is that sin (especially the sin of unchastity) "uncovers the nakedness of the Mother (Binah)... and repentance is the covering-up again." The word teshubah (returning) is also explained to mean, "causing the light from the Ancient Holy One to return to the Small of Countenance".]

Zohar: Vayikra, Section 3, Page 16a

[Note: The first 34 lines of the Hebrew text are untranslated as explained in the Translator's note on Page 15b]

R. Abba was once sitting before R. Simeon, when R. Eleazar entered. R. Simeon thereupon quoted the verse: "The righteous shall flourish like the palm tree, etc." (Ps. XCII, 12). 'The palm', he said, 'is the slowest of all trees to mature, taking seventy years. The reason why the righteous is compared here to the palm tree is one which the Companions are reluctant to reveal, although it is indicated by the Scripture. It has to do with the exile f Babylon, when the Shekinah did not return to its home till seventy years had passed. The "righteous" here is the Holy One, blessed be He, as in the verse, "For the Lord is righteous, he loveth righteousness" (Ps. XI, 8). He is also compared to a cedar, as in the verse, "Excellent as the cedars" (S.S. 15). "He shall grow in Lebanon"; this is the supernal Eden, of which it is written, "No eye hath seen, O God, save thine" (Isa. LXIV, 4). This Cedar shall grow in that exalted place; and this shall be in the last exile, when God shall be like that cedar which is long in coming up, but once it comes up grows in a day, and at the beginning of the next day already provides a shade against the sun. "They shall be planted in the house of the Lord", at the time of the Messiah; "and flourish in the courts of our God, at the resurrection of the dead; "They shall still bring forth fruit in old age", on the day when the world will be waste, "and they shall be full of sap and green" afterwards;

Zohar: Vayikra, Section 3, Page 16b

[Note: Only the first 13 lines of the Hebrew text appear in the translation.]

and why all this? "To show that the Lord is upright, he is my rock and there is no unrighteousness in him." '

R. Simeon further discoursed on the verse: "A froward man scattereth abroad strife, and a whisperer separateth chief friends" (Prov. XVI, 28). "'The froward man scattereth abroad strife", as we have said, that sinners cause a blemish above; "and a whisperer separateth his friend", that is, he separateth the Matrona from the Holy One, blessed be He, so that He is not called One, for He is not called One save when they are in union. Woe to the wicked who cause separation above! And happy are the righteous who establish the upper realm, and happy are the penitent who restore all things to their places. Hence we have learnt that to the place reserved for penitents even the wholly righteous cannot attain. For the former are established in an exceeding high place, the place from which the Garden is watered, whereas the latter are established only in the place called "righteous". The former bring the water from the supernal place of the deep river to that place which is called "righteous", and the latter transmit it from that place where they abide to this world. Hence the former are higher and the latter lower. Happy is the lot of the penitent, and happy is the lot of the wholly righteous, since through them the world is able to exist.'

Zohar: Vayikra, Section 3, Page 17a

IF THE ANOINTED PRIEST SHALL SIN SO AS TO BRING GUILT ON THE PEOPLE. R. Abba cited here the verse: "Tell me, O thou whom my soul loveth... if thou know not, O fairest among women, go thy way forth, etc.' (S.S. I, 7, 8). 'The Companions', he said, 'have explained these verses in reference to Moses at the time when he departed from the world, as it says, "Let the Lord, the God of the spirits of all flesh, appoint a man over the congregation... who shall go out before them, etc." (Num. XXVII, 16). We may also, however, suppose them to be addressed by the Community of Israel to the Holy King. In the Book of Rab Hamnuna the Elder it is written that so long as the Community of Israel is in the Holy One, blessed be He, the latter, so to speak, is complete and pleased with himself from sucking the milk of the supernal Mother, and from that draught He waters all the others and gives them suck. We have learnt also that R. Simeon said that as long as the Community of Israel is in the Holy One, blessed be He, the latter is complete and joyful, and blessings abide in Him and issue from Him to all the others, but when the Community of Israel is not in the Holy One, blessed be He, then, as it were, blessings are withheld from Him and from all the others. The secret of the matter is that wherever male and female are not found together, blessings do not rest. Hence the Holy One, blessed be He, laments and weeps, as it says, "The Lord shall mightily roar over his fold" (Jer. xxv, 30). And when

Zohar: Vayikra, Section 3, Page 17b

the Community of Israel went into exile, she said to Him, "Tell me, O thou whom my soul loveth, how shalt thou feed thyself from the deep river that ever flows, how shalt thou feed thyself from the light of the supernal Eden, how shalt thou feed all the others that depend on thee, just as I too was fed from thee every day and water all those below, and Israel too were fed by me? And now how shall I be as one that is veiled, as one that fainteth without blessings for lack of the blessings that I require and have not? How shall I be able to lead without feeding the flocks of thy companions, to wit, Israel, the children of the patriarchs, who are a holy chariot above? To which the Holy One, blessed be He, answers: Leave this to me, for the secret thereof is with me. But if thou knowest not, here is a counsel for thee. Go thy way by the footsteps of the flock, to wit, the righteous who are trodden underfoot, and for whose sake I will give thee strength to rise, and feed thou thy kids, to wit, the school children for whose sake the world is preserved, and who give strength to the Community of Israel in exile, beside the shepherds' tents, the schools in which the Torah is ever to be found. Or the last words may be explained thus. When there are in the world righteous men and children learning the Torah, then the Community of Israel can exist with them in exile, but if not, God forbid, then neither She nor they can endure. And if there are any righteous, then they suffer first [for the sins of the age], and if not, then those kids for whose sake the world is preserved suffer first, and God takes them from the world although there is no sin in them. And not only this, but He also banishes from Himself the Community of Israel and She goes into exile. Hence it is written, "If the anointed High Priest shall sin so as to bring guilt on the people", or rather, "on account of the guilt of the people", the word yeheta (sin), meaning here "withhold his kindness and exercise judgement." 'R. Isaac cited the verse: "Remember Abraham, Isaac, and Israel thy servants" (Ex. XXXII, 13). 'Why', he asked, 'is it not written, "and Isaac"? The reason is, as we have learnt, that everywhere the "left" is embraced in the "right", and the right has been strengthened so that it can embrace the left, and therefore the word Isaac is not separated from Abraham. But the text goes on, "and Israel", because Jacob clasped both of them and was perfect in all. The verse proceeds: "To whom thou swarest by thy own self." God swore to the patriarchs by the Fathers [Tr. note: The highest grades.] above, by those who abide "in thee". "Which I said"; that is, "I willed", as in the verse: "The Lord said that he would dwell in the thick darkness" (I Kings VIII, 12). "And they shall inherit it forever" (lit. for a world): this is the supernal world to which this earth is attached and from which it is nourished, and if this earth is put away, why is it? Because of the iniquity of the people.' IF THE ANOINTED PRIEST SIN. R. Isaac said: This is the priest on earth who has been appointed for divine service. If a sin is found in him, then verily it brings guilt on the whole people, and woe to them who are relying upon him!

Zohar: Vayikra, Section 3, Page 18a

573

Similarly, if sin is found in the reader of a congregation, woe to those who are relying upon him!' R. Judah said: 'All the more so the priest, at whose hand all Israel and upper and lower beings are waiting to be blessed. For, as we have learnt, when the priest began to recite the formulas and to bring the offering, all were blessed and joyful. The Right began to waken, the Left was merged in the Right; all were linked together and united, so that through the priest heaven and earth were blessed. Hence he had to bring an offering for himself, that his sin might be atoned for.' Said R. Yose: 'We have learnt that through the priest a man's sin is atoned for when he brings the offering. But if the priest himself sins, who can bring an offering and atone for him, seeing that he is become corrupt and is not fit to be a source of blessing?' Said R. Judah: 'But is it not written, "And he shall make atonement for himself and for his house" (Lev. XVI, 6)?' Said R. Hiya: 'We know that the high priest was attached to a certain Place, and the deputy high priest and the ordinary priest to another. Therefore another priest had to bring his offering first that he might ascend to the Place to which he was by right attached, and there atone for his sin. If this is not enough, then the high priest brings his own offering, and then the angels all assemble to atone for his sin and the Holy King assents.'

Once as R. Eleazar and R. Abba were sitting together, the former said: 'I observe that my father will not listen to any man reading the prayers on New Year and the Day of Atonement unless he has watched him three days previously to purify him; for R. Simeon used to say, "Through the prayer of the man whom I have purified the world receives atonement." He was still more particular not to accept the shofar [Tr. note: The ram's horn blown on New Year.] blowing of any man who was not well acquainted with the rules of the shofar and their inner significance.

'On this day (of New Year) Isaac is crowned, and becomes the head of the patriarchs.' Said R. Abba: 'We read the portion of Isaac (Gen. XXI, XXII) on this day, because on this day he was bound below and was also united to the One above. R. Eleazar said: 'On this day Isaac crowned Abraham with glory, as it says, "And the Lord exalted (nissah, lit. proved) Abraham" (Gen. XXII, 1), because the Right Hand was completed and perfected.' R. Abba said: 'Had not the judgement of Isaac been passed through the place where Jacob abides and annulled there, it would have gone ill with the world. But when it entered into the place of Jacob, and Jacob laid hold

Zohar: Vayikra, Section 3, Page 18b

on it, then the fire sank and the heat was cooled. It is as if a man in a great passion seizes his weapons and goes out to kill someone, but a certain wise man meets him at the door and detains him, and while they are arguing with one another his anger cools down, and instead of going out to kill, he only goes out to reprove. Who was it on whom the man vented his passion? Surely the man who stood at the door! So the Holy One, blessed be He, said to Israel: "My sons, fear not, for I stand at the door; only brace yourselves up on this day and give Me strength." And through what? Through the shofar. For if the sound of the shofar is properly produced and listened to with devotion, then it mounts aloft and the patriarchs crown themselves with it and stand in the tent of Jacob. Hence strict attention should be paid to the sound of the shofar. Every sound of the shofar ascends to a different firmament, all the denizens of which give place to the sound, saying, "And the Lord uttereth his voice before his army" (Joel II, 11). And that voice remains in the firmament until another voice comes and joins it, and then they both ascend together to another firmament. And when all the voices from below are collected and ascend to the highest firmament where the Holy King is, they stand before the Holy King and then the thrones are set and another throne, that of Jacob, is firmly established. In the Book of Rab Hamnuna the Elder we find: Prayer and the sound of the shofar which are produced by a virtuous man with his heart and soul mount above, and the accusers above are thrust away before it and cannot face it. Happy are the righteous who know how to be truly devout before their Master and to establish the world on this day with the sound of the shofar; hence it is written, "Blessed is the people that know the joyful sound (of the shofar)" (Ps. LXXXIX, 15). On this day the congregation must look out for a man without blame who knows the ways of the King and how to honour Him, that he may pray for them and transmit the sound of the shofar to all worlds with concentration of thought, with wisdom, and with devotion, that through him chastisement may be removed from the world. Alas for those whose minister is not fitting, for through him their sins will be called to mind. But if he is truly virtuous, then the people are justified through him, and punishment is removed from them through him.' Said R. Eleazar: 'For this reason the priest and Levite were examined as to their character, and if they were not found satisfactory they were not allowed to minister. And so, too, with the members of the Sanhedrin before they were allowed to judge.' AND IF THE WHOLE CONGREGATION SHALL ERR, ETC. R. Simeon cited in this connection the verse: "Rise up, ye women that are at ease, and hear my voice, etc." (Isa. XXXII, 9). He said: 'A man should be ever solicitous for the honour of his Master in order that his son may be without flaw. For when God created man, He created

Zohar: Vayikra, Section 3, Page 19a

him without flaw, as it is written, "God made man upright" (yashar, lit. straight) (Eccles. VII, 20). The word "man" (adam) means male and female, the female being included in the male, and hence it says "upright". Now in the depth of the great abyss there is a certain hot fiery female spirit named Lilith, who at first cohabited with man. For when man was created and his body completed, a thousand spirits from the left side assembled round that body, each endeavouring to enter, until at last a cloud descended and drove them away and God said, "Let the earth bring forth a living soul" (Gen. I, 24), and it then brought forth a spirit to breathe into man, who thus became complete with two sides, as it says, "And he breathed in his nostrils the breath of life, and the man became a living soul" (Gen. II, 7). When man arose, his female was affixed to his side, and the holy spirit in him spread to each side, thus perfecting itself. Afterwards God sawed the man in two and fashioned his female and brought her to him like a bride to the canopy. When Lilith saw this she fled, and she is still in the cities of the sea coast trying to snare mankind. And when the Almighty will destroy the wicked Rome, He will settle Lilith among the ruins, since she is the ruin of the world, as it is written: "For there Lilith shall settle and find her a place of rest" (Isa. XXXIV, 14). In ancient books it says that she fled from man before this, but we have learnt differently, that she associated with man until this soul (neshamah) was placed in him, and then she fled to the seaside, where she tries to harm mankind.

'The remedy is this. When a man unites with his wife, he should sanctify his heart to his Master and say: "She that is wrapped in a robe is here. Thou shalt not enter nor take out; it is neither of thee nor of thy lot. Return, return, the sea is heaving, its waves await thee. I cleave to the holy portion, I am wrapped in the holiness of the King." He should then cover his head and the head of his wife for a short time. In the book which Ashmedai gave to King Solomon, it says that he should then sprinkle clean water round the bed. If a woman is suckling a child she should not join her husband while the child is awake, nor give it suck afterwards until time enough has elapsed for walking two miles, or one mile if the child cries for milk. If all this is done, Lilith will never be able to harm them. Happy are the righteous whom God has taught the secrets of the Torah, of heaven and earth, and all for the sake of the Torah, for whoever studies the Torah is crowned with the crowns of the holy Name, and knows secret ways and the mysteries of heaven and earth, and never comes to harm.

Zohar: Vayikra, Section 3, Page 19b

'Now on that day they were commanded concerning a certain tree and disobeyed the command. And because the woman sinned first it was decreed that the husband should rule over her. And from that time, whenever men sin before God those women from the side of severe judgement are charged to rule over them–those who are called "the flame of the revolving sword" (Gen. III, 24), which takes the shape sometimes of males and sometimes of females, as elsewhere stated. Alas for the world when those women have sway! When the prophet saw Israel perverting their ways and sinning before their Master, he exclaimed: "Ye women that are at ease, how can ye rest, how can ye sit idle in the world? Rise!" as has been explained elsewhere.'... [Tr. note: There is a lacuna here in the text.]

It was only said in the sense in which it was applied to Deborah. There is a dictum: Woe to the man at whose table the wife says grace. So when we read that "Deborah judged Israel at that time", we might exclaim, "Woe to the generation which could only find a female to be its judge!" See now. There were two women in the world who composed praises to God such as the men never equaled, namely, Hannah and Deborah. Hannah opened the gate of faith to the world in the words, "He raiseth up the poor from the dust, etc." (I Sam. II, 8). "To make them sit with princes": to wit, in the place where the princes, that is the patriarchs, sit above. According to another explanation, however, this refers to Samuel, who was placed on a par with Moses and Aaron. "And make them inherit a throne of glory": this refers to Samuel, who placed two kings on the throne. Or it may refer to God, who causes His servants to inherit His throne. "They that strive with the Lord shall be broken in pieces": that is to say, when judgement prevails over mercy, if then the Holy One, blessed be He, is blessed from the Source of the River, then mercy prevails and judgement is checked. "Against them he shall thunder in heaven": that is, when the dew from the Ancient Holy One shall rest upon Him and fills His head in the place called "heaven", then He breaks the power of mighty judgements. "And he shall give strength to his king": this is the Holy One, blessed be He; "and exalt the horn of his anointed": this is the Community of Israel. Deborah likewise praised the Holy King, as it is written: "Lord, when thou wentest forth out of Seir, when thou marchedst out of the field of Edom" (Judges V, 1)—speaking in the mystery of wisdom until she began to praise herself, saying, "Until that I Deborah arose, that I arose, a mother in Israel." Then the spirit of prophecy left her, so that she had to say to herself, "Awake, awake, Deborah, awake, awake, utter a song" (Ibid. 12). All this happened when the men were sinful and not worthy that the spirit of prophecy should rest upon them.'

Zohar: Vayikra, Section 3, Page 20a

AND IF THE WHOLE CONGREGATION OF ISRAEL SHALL ERR, ETC. This has been explained to mean, "err in interpreting the law". The "congregation" ('adath) refers to those who were in Jerusalem, from whence instruction went forth to all the people, so that if those who were there erred the whole people erred. AND THE THING BE HID FROM THE EYES OF THE ASSEMBLY: the eyes of the assembly are the Sanhedrin who were appointed over Israel.

R. Hiya and R. Yose were once walking together when the latter said: 'Let us expound words of the Torah, words of the Ancient of Days.' R. Hiya thereupon began with the verse: "I acknowledge my sin unto thee, etc." (Ps. XXXII, 5). He said: 'From this we learn that a man who conceals his sins and does not confess them before the Holy King and beg for mercy is not allowed to enter the door of repentance. But if he states them openly before God, then God has pity on him and mercy prevails over judgement, all the more so if he weeps, for tears open all doors. Thus the confession of sin brings honour to the King by making mercy prevail over judgement. There seems to be a certain redundancy of expression in this verse, as it would have been sufficient to say, "I will confess my transgressions to the Lord"; and here, too, we should have expected "to thee" instead of "to the Lord". But, indeed, these words, like all David's words, were uttered in the holy spirit. He was addressing the Kingdom of Heaven [Malkuth], for she is the intermediary between earth and heaven, and whoso has a petition of the King must make it known to her first. Hence David said: "I will acknowledge my sin to thee, the Kingdom of Heaven, and mine iniquity have I not hid from the Righteous One of the universe, and I said, I will confess my sin to the Lord, to wit, the Holy King to whom all peace belongs." Then it goes on: "And thou forgavest the iniquity of my sin"; this was in the highest realm, the place where the Ancient Holy One abides. Thus this verse includes all; and in the same way, whoever prays to the King should unify the Holy Name in his thought, ranging from lower to upper, and from upper to lower, and linking all together, and then his prayer will be granted.' Said R. Yose: 'Who has the skill to pray like King David, who used to keep watch at the gate of the King?' Said R. Hiya to him: 'Assuredly it is so, and therefore the Torah has taught us the ways

Zohar: Vayikra, Section 3, Page 20b

of the Holy King that we may know how to seek him, as it says, "After the Lord your God ye shall walk" (Deut. XIII, 4).'

R. Yose then discoursed on the verse: "A voice is heard in Ramah, lamentation and weeping, etc." (Jer. XXXI, 15). 'We have learnt', he said, 'that on the day when the Sanctuary on earth was laid waste and Israel went into captivity with millstones on their necks and their hands bound behind them, and the Community of Israel was banished from the house of her Husband to follow them, when She came down She said: "I will go in front and weep for my home and my children and my Husband." When she came down and saw her home devastated and the blood of saints spilled in its midst and the holy shrine and temple burnt, She lifted up her voice, and higher and lower angels fell a-quaking and the voice ascended to the place where the King abode, and the King was minded to turn the world into chaos again. Thereupon many armies and hosts went down to meet Her, but She would not accept consolation. Hence it is written, "A voice is heard in Ramah, Rachel weeping for her children because they are not"; or, as we should rather translate, "He is not" (enennu), referring to the Holy King who had gone aloft and was not in her midst.' R. Hiya asked: 'From what place did She begin to go into exile?' He replied: 'From the Sanctuary, where Her abode was. Afterwards She went all round the Land of Israel, and when She left it She came into the wilderness and remained there three days. She took Her armies and hosts and the denizens of the King's palace and exclaimed regarding herself: "How doth she sit solitary" (Lam. I, 1).' R. Hiya and R. Yose wept. Said R. Yose: 'Israel were not exiled from their land, nor was the Temple destroyed until they were all sinful before the King, the heads of the people being foremost in sin, as it says: "0 my people, they which lead thee cause thee to err, and destroy the way of thy paths" (Isa. III, 12): for, when the heads of the people sin, all the rest follow them.' R. Hiya learnt the same lesson from the verse, "And if the whole congregation of Israel shall err". 'Why do they err?' he said. 'Because "the thing is hidden from the eyes of the assembly", the "eyes" being the leaders whom all the rest follow.'

They then went on their way and came across a certain grassy sward, with a stream running past, so they sat down there. As they were sitting, a bird flew past them with a rustling noise. Said R. Hiya: 'Let us get up, for assuredly mountain-diggers [Tr. note: Al. "runners". The reference in either case is to robbers.] are here.' So they got up and went on. Turning their heads they saw robbers running after them. Providentially they saw in front of them a rock with a cave in it, so they went in and sat there the whole of that day and night.

R. Hiya discoursed on the verse: "Therefore fear not, O Jacob my servant... for lo, I will save thee from afar" (Jer. xxx, 10). 'The word "afar" here', he said, 'is used in the same sense as in the words, "From afar the Lord appeared unto me" (Ibid. XXXI, 3), and refers to the deep source of the River, the place where it issues forth. "Jacob shall return": Jacob is here a name of the Holy One, blessed be He, who will yet return to join the Community of Israel. "And shall be quiet": this refers to Yesod. "And at ease": to make his abode there. "And none shall make him afraid": of Isaac (Geburah).

Zohar: Vayikra, Section 3, Page 21a

And now the Holy One, blessed be He, has delivered us from afar and hidden us in this place in quiet and ease, and there is none to make us afraid; for when God does a miracle He does it completely.'

R. Yose discoursed on the verse: "And Barak said unto her, If thou wilt go with me then I will go, etc." (Judges IV, 8). He said: 'Barak reasoned thus: Because the holy spirit rests upon her I shall be delivered through her merit and shall come to no harm. Now if Barak could feel safe in dependence on a female, how much more so we who have the Torah with us, which is the name of the Holy King!'

So they remained in the cave all that day. When night came, the moon shone into the cave, and two merchants passed by with asses laden with wine and food for themselves. They said to one another: 'Let us stop here, and give food and drink to the asses, and go into the cave.' Said the other: 'Before we go in, explain this verse.' He said: 'Which one?' 'I refer', he said, 'to the verse, "I will praise thee forever because thou hast done" (Ps. LII, 10). Done what? It also says, "Because thou art good in the presence of thy saints" (Ibid.). Why only in their presence and not that of others?' He could not give him an answer. 'Alas', he said, 'that for the sake of my business I have neglected the Holy One, blessed be He.' R. Hiya and R. Yose, who heard them from the cave, rejoiced. 'Did not I tell you', said R. Hiya, 'that when God does a miracle He does not do it by halves?' So they went out, and R. Hiya immediately addressed them with the verse: "Peace, peace, to him that is far off and to him that is near" (Isa. LVII, 19). 'The near and the far', he said, 'are one and the same, namely, the penitent who was first far from God and has been brought near. Also, when a man is far from the Torah he is far from God, but if he draws near to the Torah, God draws him near to Himself. Now, therefore, join us and come into the cave.' So the merchants joined them, having first tethered their asses and given them food. Then they all went out to the mouth of the cave, and one of the merchants said: 'Since you are scholars, explain to us this verse: "I will give thee thanks forever because thou hast done [made] and I will hope, etc." ' R. Hiya answered: 'It means, because thou hast made the world; for because of this world which God has made and established, man must thank Him every day. As for the words, "for thou art good before thy saints", this is indeed so, since the name of the Holy One, blessed be He, is good before the righteous but not before the wicked, who spurn it every day and do not study the Torah.' Said the other: 'This is all very good, but I have heard a word from behind the wall, as they say, which I am afraid to disclose.' Thereupon R. Hiya and R. Yose said to him: 'Speak out, for the Torah is not an inheritance for one place only.' So he said to them: 'One day when I went to Lydda, on entering the town I stood behind the wall of a house in which was R. Simeon, and I heard him expound this verse, "I will praise thee because thou hast done", thus. The words "I will give praise to thee" were addressed by King David to the Holy One, blessed be He, for that last world which He has made [Malkuth]; for David attached himself to that world and through it attained to kingship. "I will wait on thy name, for it is good": this is the Holy One, blessed be He, when unified with that world which is called "good". And when is it called good? When it is in the presence of thy saints, or rather, "lovingkindnesses", [Tr. note: Reading hasadekha for hasidekha.] for when these are filled from the goodness of the stream issuing from the Ancient Holy One, then Yesod is called "good", and then He [Yesod] establishes this latter world and all is blessed. Hence David waited for this grade to illumine the world to which he was attached.' R. Hiya and R. Yose came up to him and kissed him on his head. Said R.

Zohar: Vayikra, Section 3, Page 21b

Hiya: 'Who shall cover thine eye in the dust, O R. Simeon, for thou art in thy place and thou shakest the highest mountains, and even the birds of the heaven rejoice at thy words. Alas for the world when thou shalt depart from it!'

The man resumed: 'At the same time I heard him expound the verse, "Now therefore, O God, hearken unto the prayer of thy servant and to his supplications... for my Lord's (Adonai) sake" (Dan. IX, 17). If this name were the highest, it would be in place here, as though one were to say, Do it for the sake of the king. But we know that this name signifies only the place of judgement, from which judgement issues to the world. Can a man say to a king, Do for the sake of thy servant or something less than thyself? The truth is, however, that this name prepares the house for the King and the sanctuary below, and when the sanctuary is established below, this name is established above; hence it is as though one said to the king, Build this house and this palace, that the Matrona may not have to abide without the palace.'

R. Hiya and R. Yose were beside themselves with gladness on that night. After they had eaten, the other merchant said: 'I will now tell you something on which I have been meditating this day, in connection with the verse, "A Psalm of David when he was in the wilderness of Judah" (Ps. LXIII, 1). David said this psalm when he was fleeing from his father-in-law. Why did he say, "Elohim, thou art my God" (Ibid. 2)? Because he was always attached to Geburah. He went on, "I will seek thee early." How, we may ask, could David seek God early in a distant land, when he was exiled from the land where the Shekinah abides? This shows, that though he was driven from there, he did not cease to seek the Holy One, blessed be He. "My soul thirsteth for thee", because my soul and my body yearn for thee that I may appear before thee and I am not able, being in a dry and weary land where no water is; for so any land is called where the Shekinah does not abide.'

Said R. Hiya and R. Yose: 'Verily, our way is made straight before us.' So they went into the cave and slept. At midnight they heard the cries of wild animals in the wilderness, so they got up. Said R. Hiya: 'It is time to assist the Community of Israel in praising the King. Let each of us say something which he has learnt of the Torah. So they all sat down and R. Hiya commenced with the text, "For the Chief Musician, set to Ayeleth Hashahar, a psalm of David" (Ps. XXII, 1). '"Ayeleth Hashahar (lit. hind of the morning)"', he said, 'is the Community of Israel, who is called "a loving hind and a pleasant doe" (Prov. v, 19). Is she then a hind of the morning only and not of all the day? What it means, however, is a hind from that place which is called "dawn", of which it says, "his going forth is as sure as the morning" (Hos. VI, 3). See now. When night falls, the doors of the upper world are closed, and those below fall to rest, and the distant ones (demons) awake and fly about and flit around the bodies of men, but if they see the likeness of the Holy King they are afraid, if men on their beds have thought about the Holy King. The souls of men ascend each according to

577

its desert, as explained elsewhere. At midnight a herald gives order and the gates are opened. Then a wind arises from the north and strikes

Zohar: Vayikra, Section 3, Page 22a

the harp of David, which then plays of itself and praises the King, and the Holy One, blessed be He, has joyous communion with the righteous in the Garden of Eden. Happy is he who awakes at that time and studies the Torah: he is called a companion of the Holy One, blessed be He, and of the Community of Israel. When day comes, a herald again gives order and the doors on the south side are opened, the stars and constellations awake, and the King takes his seat to hear his praises. Then the Community of Israel takes up those words and carries them aloft, and all the Companions cling to her wings, and the words come and rest in the bosom of the King. Then the King gives command, and they are all written in a book, and the names of those admitted into the palace are recorded in a book and a thread of grace is woven round them, which is the crown of the King, causing all beings above and below to be afraid of them, so that they enter without let or hindrance into all the gates of the King. And even when the executioners of judgement arise to punish the world, they do not touch such a one, because he bears the stamp of the King, which proclaims him to come from the palace of the King. Happy the lot of the righteous who study the Torah, especially at the time when the King longs for the words of the Torah! The secret of the matter is that the Community of Israel does not come into the King's presence save with the Torah. So as long as Israel in their own land studied the Torah the Community of Israel abode with them, but when they neglected the Torah she could not stay with them an instant. So when she presented herself to the King with the Torah she was full of strength and confidence and the Holy King rejoiced to meet her, but when she came without the Torah, then, as it were, her strength was enfeebled. Woe to those who cause weakness above, and happy those who study the Torah, especially at the time when it is needful to associate with it the Community of Israel. Of such a one God says, "Thou art my servant, Israel, in whom I will be glorified" (Isa. XLIX, 3).'

R. Yose discoursed on the verse: "The burden of Duma. One calleth unto me out of Seir, Watchman, what of the night?" (Isa. XXI, 11). 'This verse', he said, 'has already been expounded in many places, but it can also be interpreted as follows. To all the other exiles of Israel a term was set, and their duration was known beforehand, but the exile of Edom is "a burden of silence", for its term has not been disclosed. Says the Holy One, blessed be He: "One calls to Me from Seir": I have heard a voice from those who are oppressed and prostrate in the exile of Seir, [Tr. note: Edom=Rome.] saying, Watchman, what of the night?—asking Me what I have done with My Matrona. Thereupon the Holy One, blessed be He, assembles all His court and says: "See how My beloved children forget their own oppression and think only of the Matrona, saying to Me, Thou who art called Keeper, how dost Thou keep Thyself and Thy house?" Then the Holy One, blessed be He, answers them: "I have not forgotten My guardianship, for I will yet receive Her and be with Her." "The morning has come", for at first He ascended aloft to that morning which is ever ready for Him. Now it is time to be joined to "the night". The night, too, is ready, but for your sakes it has been delayed. And if you ask why, the answer is, "Return", to wit, in repentance, and then "come to Me" and we shall all place ourselves in a row and return to our place, as it is written, "And the Lord thy God will return with thy captivity

Zohar: Vayikra, Section 3, Page 22b

and will return and gather thee from all the peoples." The word "return" occurs here twice-once referring to the Holy One, blessed be He, and once to the Community of Israel.'

The merchant then discoursed on the verse; "When the morning stars sang together and all the sons of God shouted for joy" (Job XXXVIII, 7). 'When God', he said, 'comes to have joyous communion with the righteous in the Garden of Eden, everything in the lower (al. upper) world and all upper and lower angels arise to meet Him, and all the trees in the Garden break forth into song before Him, and even the birds of the earth utter praise before Him. Then a flame goes forth and strikes the wings of the cock, and it bursts into praise of the Holy King and calls to men to engage themselves in the study of the Law and in the praise of their Master and His service-happy the lot of those who

then rise from their beds to study the Torah! When the morning comes, the gates of the south are opened and healing goes forth to the world, and the east wind awakens and mercy prevails, and all the stars which are under the rule of that "morning" break out into song and praise the most high King, as it says, "when the morning stars sang together".'

The other merchant then discoursed on the verse: "As soon as the morning was light, the men were sent away" (Gen. XLIV, 3). He said: 'We have learnt that when morning comes and judgement passes away and lovingkindness seeks to awake, then all who come from that side hasten to their place to prepare blessings for the world; and this is the meaning of the words, "the morning is light", "light" being synonymous with "good". Note the following series of grades. "Night" is one grade, as we know. Then "morning light" is another grade, which we also know, a higher grade which always accompanies the other. The sun is a third grade known to us which establishes all and gives light to all. Thus the "morning light" receives light from the sun, and in turn gives light to the night, so that they are all linked with one another. When this "morning light" awakes, all men are gladdened and go about their business. And now that the day has dawned, it is time for us to go on our way.' So R. Hiya and R. Yose blessed them and kissed them on their heads and sped them on their way. Said R. Hiya to R. Yose: 'Blessed be God who has guided our steps aright! Verily, God sent these men to us. Blessed are they who study the Torah and do not neglect it for an instant!'

R. Hiya and R. Yose then left the cave and continued their journey. Said R. Yose: 'Verily, my heart goes out to those merchants.' R. Hiya said to him: 'I am not surprised at this incident, for in the days of R. Simeon even the birds utter wisdom, for his words are known above and below.' R. Hiya then quoted the verse: "And the Lord said unto Moses, Behold thou shalt sleep with thy fathers" (Deut. XXXI, 16). 'Mark this,' he said. 'As long as Moses was alive, he used to check Israel from sinning against God. And because Moses was among them, there shall not be a generation like that one till the Messiah comes, when they shall see the glory of God like him. As we have learnt, a handmaid saw at the Red Sea what even Ezekiel the prophet did not see. And if a handmaid saw that, how much more so their wives, their sons, the men themselves, the Sanhedrin, the princes, and especially Moses himself! And now when those merchants of the desert can pour forth such wisdom, how much more so the wise of the generation, how much more those who stand before R. Simeon and learn from him,

Zohar: Vayikra, Section 3, Page 23a

and how very much more R. Simeon himself, who is above all! Alas for the world when R. Simeon shall depart, and the fountains of wisdom shall be closed, and men shall seek wisdom and there will be none to impart it, and the Torah will be interpreted erroneously because there will be none who is acquainted with wisdom! Of that time it is written: "And if the whole congregation of Israel shall err." Why? Because "the thing is hidden from the eyes, to wit, the leaders, of the assembly".' Said R. Judah: 'God will one day reveal the hidden mysteries of the Torah, namely, at the time of the Messiah, because "the earth shall be full of the knowledge of the Lord like as the waters cover the sea" (Isa. XI, 9), and as it is written, "They shall teach no more every man his neighbour and every man his brother, saying, Know the Lord, for they shall all know me, from the least of them to the greatest of them" (Jer. XXXI, 34).' WHEN A RULER SINNETH, ETC. R. Isaac pointed out that the corresponding clauses referring to the high priest and the congregation begin with the word "if"--"if the anointed priest shall sin, etc." (Lev. IV, 3), "if the whole congregation of Israel shall err, etc." (Ibid. 13). 'The reason is', he said, 'that it is exceptional for the High Priest to sin, since he feels his responsibility to his Master and to Israel and to each individual. Similarly, it is very exceptional for the whole congregation to commit one and the same sin, for if some commit it, others will not. But a prince's heart is uplifted because of his power, and therefore he is almost bound to sin; hence it says here, "when", and not "if".' R. Judah illustrated from the verse: "And the princes brought the onyx stones and the stones to be set for the ephod and the breastplate" (Ex. xxxv, 27). 'Why', he asked, 'should it have been left for the princes to bring these things, seeing that the order had gone forth that "everyone willing of heart should bring the Lord's offering" (Ibid. 4), including "onyx stones and stones to be set for the ephod and the breastplate" (Ibid. 9)? The reason is that God said: Although the free-will offering is requested from all, yet leave these things to the princes. Why? Because they are borne on the breast of the High Priest. Let the princes whose heart is uplifted bring these stones which are worn on the heart of the High Priest, so that he may make atonement for their pride of heart. AND HE SHALL DO UNWITTINGLY ONE OF THE THINGS WHICH THE LORD HIS GOD HATH COMMANDED NOT TO BE DONE: that is, as stated elsewhere, if he transgresses a negative precept. IF HIS SIN BE MADE KNOWN TO HIM: because in the pride of his heart he did not notice his sin, but afterwards it was pointed out to him and he repented.'

R. Judah and R. Yose were sitting and studying the Torah one night. Said R. Judah: 'I observe that the Torah seems clearer by night than by day: how is this?' He replied: 'It is because the Written Law is explained by the Oral Law, and the Oral Law has sway by night and is more active then than by day. When, therefore, it holds sway, the Torah is clearer.' R. Yose continued: 'It is written, "But he said not, Where is the God my maker, who giveth songs in the night" (Job xxxv, 10). As already stated, when the north wind awakes at midnight, it strikes the wings of the cock, which looks to see what it is, and then for the sake of the honour of its Master calls aloud to the sons of men.

Zohar: Vayikra, Section 3, Page 23b

Then the faithful arise and give strength and power to the Community of Israel, and through this David and his sons inherit the kingdom for all generations. But if the cock calls and men continue to sleep in their beds and do not rise, then it claps its wings and says, Woe to so-and-so who contemns his Master, who deserts his Master, and heeds not His honour! When the day breaks a herald proclaims concerning him, "He did not say, Where is God my maker, who giveth songs in the night, so as to assist in those praises." What is the meaning of "my Maker"? If a man rises in the middle of the night and engages in the chanting of the Law-for the true singing is only at night-when day comes the Holy One, blessed be He, and the Community of Israel adorn him with a thread of grace to keep him safe from all harm and shed light upon him among both upper and lower beings, and they make him every day a new creature; hence the expression "my Maker" ('osai, lit. makers), referring to the Holy One and the Community of Israel, or according to another explanation, to Abraham and the Community of Israel.' IF ONE HATH MADE KNOWN TO HIM HIS SIN. If who has made known to him? And why is it not written, "if his sin is made known to him"? The truth is that the Holy One, blessed be

579

He, bids the Community of Israel to make known to a man the sin which he has committed. And how does she make it known to him? By chastisement. So, too, we have learnt: When a man sins before God and heeds not his sin to repent before his Master and throws it behind his back, then his soul goes up and testifies before the Holy One, blessed be He. Then the King bids the Community of Israel to "make known to him his sin", and to chastise him. And when chastisement comes upon him, then his spirit moves him to repent and he humbles himself and brings an offering; for it is through pride that he sins and forgets his sin. Said R. Yose: 'It is so assuredly, and so we find in the case of David that when he committed the sin with Bathsheba and forgot about it, God reminded him, saying, "Thou art the man" (2 Sam. XII, 7). But if a man wakes at night to study the Torah, then the Torah makes known to him his sin, and not through chastisement, but like a mother who gently chides her son, and he does not forget, but repents before his Master. It may be asked, seeing that David also used to rise at midnight to study, why was he warned by chastisement? The reason is that he transgressed against the very grade to which he was attached, and therefore he required to be chastised. His punishment, in fact, fitted his crime: he sinned against the holy Kingdom and Jerusalem, and therefore he was driven from Jerusalem and his kingdom was taken from him, until

Zohar: Vayikra, Section 3, Page 24a

he had made sufficient atonement.' R. Judah asked why David was punished at the hand of his son. R. Yose answered: 'As has been explained, because another man would have shown him no mercy.' 'But', said R. Judah, 'Absalom sought to kill his father and devised worse evil against him than a stranger would have done?' R. Yose said: 'I have not heard any answer to this.' Said R. Judah: ' I have heard an explanation, namely, that David sinned against Bath Sheba (lit. the daughter of seven), so God said, "Let the son of the daughter of a strange god come and avenge her." And who was this? Absalom, who was the son of a "fair captive" (v. Deut. XXI, 10 et seq.).' R. Yose then quoted the verse: "The Lord hath sworn by his right hand and by the arm of his strength" (Isa. LXII, 8). 'Whenever', he said, 'a man sins before God, there is a certain grade above which takes note of that sin to punish it; if the man repents, the sin is wiped out and judgement has no sway over him, but if not, that sin is inscribed with that grade. If he sins more, then another grade takes note of him and concurs with the previous grade, so that he requires a more fervent repentance. If he goes on sinning, further grades are added till the number of five is reached. When the Right Hand is thus completed, the Left Hand concurs with the Right and merges in it, and then there is no further room for repentance. When the final judgement is thus pronounced, five fingers are locked in five, the Right Hand in the Left, and therefore when God desires to pronounce the final judgement, then, "The Lord swears by his right hand and by the arm of his strength".'

[Note: The last 27 lines of the Hebrew text are not translated.]

Zohar: Vayikra, Section 3, Page 24b

[Note: The first 31 lines of the Hebrew text are not translated]

IF A SOUL (nefesh) COMMIT A TRESPASS. R. Isaac said: 'It has been pointed out that the word nefesh (soul) is here used advisedly. Happy are the righteous who have a superior portion in the Holy One, blessed be He, the holy portion, in the sanctities of the King, because they sanctify themselves with the holiness of their Master. For whoever sanctifies himself, the Holy One, blessed be He, sanctifies him, as it is written, "And ye shall sanctify yourselves and ye shall be holy" (Lev. XI, 44). If a man sanctifies himself below, heaven sanctifies him from above, and clothes him with a holy super-soul (neshamah), the inheritance of the Holy One, blessed be He, and the Community of Israel. It is these who are called "sons of the Holy One", as it is written, "sons are ye to the Lord your God" (Deut. xxv, 1). It is written, "Let the earth bring forth a living soul" (Gen. I, 24), this being the portion from which David inherited and became heir to the kingdom, as elsewhere explained. As has been stated, the soul is linked

Zohar: Vayikra, Section 3, Page 25a

with the spirit, and the spirit with the super-soul. Happy those who obtain this noble heritage! Alas for the wicked whose souls do not even win them this world, much less the world to come I Of them it is written, "And the souls of thine enemies shall he sling out as from the hollow of a sling" (I Sam. xxv, 29). For they wander about the world without finding a place to which to attach themselves, they are drawn into the side of impurity, and a herald proclaims of them: "then a soul commits a trespass, it defiles the sanctuary of the Lord, for it cannot enter into sanctity."

It may be asked, why is a goat brought as an offering (in this case), seeing that R. Simeon has said that a goat is an evil species, as its name indicates ('ez= 'az =impudent)? However, R. Simeon answered that there is a reason, because if a spirit of uncleanness passes over a man or he occupies himself with it, then a goat is his appropriate offering, as being akin to his sin. R. Simeon said further: 'Some are gifted with a supersoul (neshamah), some with the impulse of the spirit (ruah), and some only with an ordinary soul (nefesh). Those who attain no higher than the ordinary soul cling to the side of uncleanness, and when they sleep unclean sides (spirits) come and cling to them and show them things in dreams, partly true and partly false. Hence heathens also see true things sometimes in their dreams. Now those evil species are of three grades. The highest are suspended in the air. The lowest mock men in their dreams. The intermediate grade tell men things partly true and partly false, but if true, only relating to the immediate future. As for the higher grade of those who are suspended in the air, when the soul (nefesh) of a man seeks to prepare itself for the reception of the spirit (ruah), something issues from it and seeks to rise, and in so doing meets those spirits which tell it things that will happen both in the near and the more distant future, and it cleaves to that grade until it acquires spirit. When it has done so, the spirit issues forth and cleaves its way through rocks and mountains until it ascends among the holy angels, and there it learns many things before returning to its place. This is as far as man can attain in holiness until he is endowed with a super-soul (neshamah). When he acquires that super-soul, it ascends among the righteous who are bound up in the bundle of the living, and there it sees the delight of the King and regales itself with the supernal splendour. And when the holy Hind (Shekinah) awakes with the north wind, the soul comes down and that righteous one who has acquired it arises and strengthens himself like a lion in the study of the Torah till morning, and then he goes with that holy Hind to appear before the King to receive a thread of grace,

Zohar: Vayikra, Section 3, Page 25b

[Note: the first seven lines of the Hebrew text are not translated.] and he is crowned with her before the King. Blessed', said R. Simeon, 'are those who possess a super-soul, who study the Torah, who worship the Holy King. Woe to the sinners who do not cleave to their Master and have no portion in the Torah. For he who has no portion in the Torah has no portion either in the spirit or the super-soul, but he cleaves to the side of the evil species, having no portion in the holy King or in holiness. Woe to him when he shall leave this world, for he is a marked man to those evil species, pitiless dogs, emissaries of the fires of Gehenna. See now the difference between Israel and the nations. Even though an Israelite possess only an ordinary soul, yet a higher grade stands over him, and if he tries to acquire a spirit or super-soul, he can do so. But the heathen can never do so unless he becomes circumcised, when he acquires a soul from another place. If, however, an Israelite who is only in the grade of ordinary soul does not aspire to rise higher, his punishment is great. For there are men who cleave to that evil side because they are not endowed with more than this ordinary soul, and when this unclean spirit passes by them it rests upon them and they cleave to it. Thus their sin is from the side of that unclean spirit and their offering is a goat, a beast which comes from that side, and so is a fitting atonement.' Said R. Eleazar: 'It is written, "His body shall not remain all night on the tree... that thou defile not thy land" (Deut. XXI, 23). The reason is that the land is holy, and the unclean spirit must find no place in the holy land on which to rest. This being so, seeing that the spirit of uncleanness rests on this animal and it comes from the side of uncleanness, how can it be brought as an offering to the side of holiness?'

R. Simeon replied: 'You have asked well, my son. The answer is as follows. It is written, "The Lord thy God is a devouring fire" (Deut. IV, 24). The fire of the Holy One, blessed be He, feeds on another fire. There are angels which chant praises before the Holy One, and as soon as they finish are consumed in the flames of a devouring fire. Below, too, God has empowered the fire of the altar to consume all that side in its flames so that naught of it should be left in the world, and the man who brings the offering prevails over it, and through the savour of the sacrifice the side of the evil spirit departs from him and he obtains atonement.'

R. Aha was once walking along when R. Hiya and R. Yose met him. Said R. Aha: 'Verily, being now three, we are fitted to receive the presence of the Shekinah.' So they went along together. Said R. Aha; 'Let each one of us give a discourse on the Torah as we go.'

R. Hiya thereupon began with the verse: "Drop down, ye heavens, from above, and let the skies pour down righteousness" (Isa. xv, 8). 'This verse', he said, 'contains a mystery of wisdom which we have learnt from the Holy Lamp (R. Simeon). The words "drop down" refer to the side of rain, which brings nourishment to all. Therefore the eyes of all the world are turned to the Holy One, blessed be He, because He gives food to all. Yet think not that this depends on the place called "heaven", for so it is written here "from above"; the rain in sooth comes from "above", from the Ancient Holy One,

Zohar: Vayikra, Section 3, Page 26a

and not from the place called Heaven. "And let the skies pour down righteousness": since when the heavens receive this rain from the place above, then the skies pour down righteousness. What is meant by "skies" (shehakim)? The place where manna is ground (shahak) for the righteous, where Victory and Majesty grind manna for the place called Righteous, or, rather, for the two Righteous Ones Zaddik and Zedek. Then "the earth opens" (Ibid.) beneath, and mankind "are fruitful with salvation". "Righteousness springs forth together": mercy and kindness abound and man's food is provided, and so joy is added to joy and all worlds are blessed.' Said R. Aha: 'Had I come but to hear this, it would have been sufficient.'

R. Yose then discoursed on the verse: "My heart is towards the governors of Israel that offered themselves willingly among the people, bless ye the Lord" (Judges v, 9). 'If a man', he said, 'desires earnestly to pray that blessings should be poured on earth from above, he should concentrate his mind on that recondite Stream, the deepest recess of all, where is the very beginning of the union of Father and Mother (Hokmah and Binah). So it says here, "My heart is to the governors of Israel", to wit, to those, the Father and Mother, who trace out laws for the Holy Israel who flows out from between them. "That offer themselves willingly (mithnadevim) among the people": these are the Fathers who are called nedivim. Then, "bless ye the Lord", that blessings may flow from him below and fill the world. Happy are Israel that God pours down blessings upon them and listens to their prayer; of them it is written, "He hath regarded the prayer of the destitute and hath not despised their prayer" (Ps CII, 18).

ZAV

Hiya said: This fire is the fire of Isaac, who said (at the time of the binding), "Behold the fire and the wood" (Gen. XXII, 7), which perpetually exists. We have learnt that from the fire of Isaac there issue forth to the altar

[Note: The rest of this page in the Hebrew text does not appear in our translation.]

Zohar: Vayikra, Section 3, Page 26b [Note: This page in the Hebrew text does not appear in our translation.]

Zohar: Leviticus, Section 3, Page 27a [Note: The first 39 lines of the Hebrew text do not appear in our translation.]

[Tr. note: The opening passage of this section is repeated with minor variations from Zohar, Exodus, 238b ("The burnt offering symbolizes") to 239b ("of the Tabernacle").]

THE FIRE OF THE ALTAR SHALL BE KEPT BURNING THEREON. Said R. Aha: 'Why so? And why shall "the priest burn wood on it every morning"? Why the priest in particular? Have we not learnt that fire in every place symbolises judgement, whereas the priest is from the Right and is far from Judgement? The truth is, however, as we have learnt, that when a man inclines to sin before his Master, he burns himself in the flame of the evil imagination, which comes from the side of the unclean spirit,

Zohar: Vayikra, Section 3, Page 27b

so that the unclean spirit rests on him. Therefore certain offerings have been marked as coming from this side, so that the like may be offered on the altar. For that unclean spirit is not burnt away and removed either from a man or from the side from which it comes save through the fire on the altar; and the purpose of the priest is to prepare the fire to burn the evil species out of the world. Hence it is requisite that the fire should never be quenched or allowed to become too feeble to break the force of this alien power: wherefore it says, "It shall not go out'. And the priest is to put fire upon it every morning at the time when his own side is in the ascendant in order to mitigate stern judgement and keep away chastisement from the world. Regarding this we have learnt that there is a "fire consuming fire". The supernal fire consumes another fire, and similarly the fire of the altar consumes another fire. Therefore this fire must never go out, and the priest must trim it every day.

Zohar: Vayikra, Section 3, Page 28b [Note: The Hebrew text for this Page does not appear in our translation.]

Zohar: Vayikra, Section 3, Page 30a [Note: The first 11 lines of the Hebrew text do not appear in our translation.]

FIRE SHALL BE KEPT BURNING UPON THE ALTAR CONTINUALLY; IT SHALL NOT GO OUT. R. Hiya said: This fire is the fire of Isaac, who said (at the time of the binding), "Behold the fire and the wood" (Gen. XXII, 7), which perpetually exists. We have learnt that from the fire of Isaac there issue forth to the altar certain coals, one to the east side, one to the west side, one to the north side, and one to the south side. Now there is on the altar a footway with a certain number of steps, and the lowest step reaches to the abyss which is the highest of six, and when the coals mentioned above reach the four corners of the altar a spark shoots forth and descends to that highest abyss. In that place there are numerous hosts who proclaim "holy" with a loud voice, and on another side they say "holy" with a soft and wondrous voice, and on another side there are yet other hosts which say "holy". There are six hundred thousand myriads in each corner, all under one commander, and all clad in an ephod, who are there to carry out the service of the altar in correspondence with those on earth. In another place the waves of the sea roar and descend a certain number of degrees, and there other hosts proclaim with the voice of song: "Blessed be the glory of the Lord from his place" (Ezek. III, 12). Their song of praise is not stilled day or night, and all make melody. In another place are hosts who stand in fear and trembling. All look towards that supernal altar. When the fire of Isaac reaches the altar sparks fly about on every side, and from them many mighty beings are set aflame. And did not the priest stand by the altar and lay in order the wood, the world could not stand before them. From the sparks which issue the backs of those "living creatures" are set aflame (Ezek. I, 13). On the right side of those "living creatures" a certain wind stirs from above which blows upon that fire, so that it settles down with a steady flame and gives light to the hosts standing on the right side. Then on the left side rises a strong wind breaking the rocks which blows upon that fire and makes it burn fiercely, till it gives light to the hosts on that side. And so on all four sides for the four camps. But all are appeased when the priest goes up to the altar.'

R. Abba said: 'There are two altars below and two altars above. Of the latter one, the innermost of all,

Zohar: Vayikra, Section 3, Page 30b

is that on which is offered the inner fine incense, which is the bond of faith, and the most high Priest of all offers this incense with the bond of faith. This is called the Altar of Gold, the place where all the threads of faith are bound together. There is another altar called the Altar of Brass, which is more external and on which Michael the great chief brings the pleasing offering of the Holy One, blessed be He. On earth there are correspondingly the altar of gold and the altar of brass, on the one of which was offered incense and on the other fat and limbs. It is written, "Oil and incense rejoice the heart" (Prov. XXVII, 9), but not fat and limbs, although these, too, allay wrath. The altar which is the innermost of all, the linking of faith, is called "a still silent voice", and in relation to this the other altar is called the "outer" one. The inner one is called "the altar of the Lord" and the other one "the altar of brass". Said R. Abba: 'When Moses built an altar (Ex. XVII, 15), he meant it to correspond to that inner one, and therefore he called it "The Lord is my banner", because it was stamped with the sign of the holy covenant. This is the inner Altar, the "still silent voice", and on this "fire shall be burnt continually", that is, the perpetual Fire, the Fire of Isaac. The proper name for this is Adonai, but when the priest puts wood on the altar we call it by the name of mercy, Tetragrammaton; sometimes it answers to one and sometimes to the other.' R. Simeon said that there were two, the inner supported on the outer and fed from it, the two being thus linked together.

THIS IS THE OBLATION OF AARON. Said R. Hizkiah: 'How solicitous should men be for the honour of their Master, and how careful not to turn aside from the right way, forevery day punishment impends over the world, and man never knows when it may fall. If he sits in his house, judgement impends over him; if he goes abroad, judgement impends over him, and he does not know if he will return or not. Therefore he should in time beseech for mercy from the King, for every day judgement impends over the world, as it is written, "El (God) hath indignation every day" (Ps. VII, 12). Now the Companions have pointed out that the name El properly indicates lovingkindness; why, then, is it used here, and also in the expression El Gibbor (mighty God) (Isa. IX, 6)? The answer is that, as we have learnt, the wicked turn mercy into judgement, since in all the supernal crowns of the Holy King, mercy and judgement are intertwined.' Said R. Judah to him: 'This accounts for the expression El Gibbor; but what of "El hath indignation every day", which means that on every day He punishes, whether men are guilty or not?' He could not answer him, so they went and asked R. Simeon. He said: 'The Companions have explained that the name El indicates sometimes mercy and sometimes

Zohar: Vayikra, Section 3, Page 31a

judgement. If men are virtuous, El is there standing for lovingkindness, and if they are not deserving, El is there standing for severity and is called Gibbor. The real truth, however, is as follows. El everywhere stands for the light of the supernal Wisdom which exercises its influence every day, and without which the world could not stand a day before the heavy chastisements that arise every day against it. For El is indignant with them and thrusts them away and so establishes the world, which otherwise could not exist an instant. As for the expression El Gibbor, the whole verse in which this occurs is an epitome of the holy supernal faith. The word "Wonderful" alludes to the supernal Wisdom, which is wondrous and concealed beyond the reach of all; "Counsellor" is the supernal stream which issues forth perennially and counsels all and waters all; "EI" refers to Abraham, "Gibbor" to Isaac, and "Everlasting Father" to Jacob, who lays hold of both sides and attains perfection. The "Prince of Peace" is the Zaddik, who brings peace to the world, peace to the House, peace to the Matrona.' R. Hizkiah and R. Judah came and kissed his hands, and weeping with joy exclaimed: 'Happy are we that we asked this question. Happy is the generation in whose midst thou art!'

THIS (zeh) IS THE OBLATION OF AARON AND HIS SONS WHICH THEY SHALL OFFER UNTO THE LORD. Sinners cause the Holy One, blessed be He, to part from the Community of Israel; they separate zeh (this, masc.) from zoth (this, fem.), who should form one pair. So the holy Aaron comes with his sons, and through them they are brought together again, and zeh is united with zoth; hence it is written, "with this (bezoth) shall Aaron come to the holy place" (Lev. XVI, 3). You might ask, then, why is it not written here, zoth (this) is the offering of Aaron, to restore zoth to its place? The reason is that the priest commences from above, bringing the zeh to unite with the zoth-happy is his portion in this world and the next!

As R. Hiya and R. Yose were once going from Usha to Tiberias, the latter said: 'It is written, "Ye shall sanctify yourselves

Zohar: Vayikra, Section 3, Page 31b

and ye shall be holy" (Lev. XI, 44). We know that if a man sanctifies himself here below, he is further sanctified from above, and that if he defiles himself here below, he is further defiled from above. Now that he should be sanctified from above is fit and proper, since the holiness of his Master rests upon him; but from whence is he defiled? From above? And is there, then, defilement above?' R. Hiya replied: 'This is the meaning of what we have learnt, that any activity below stimulates a corresponding activity above. If the activity below is one of holiness, it stimulates holiness above to rest upon the doer and sanctify him. And if the man defiles himself below, a spirit of defilement is aroused above and comes and rests upon him, defiling him further. For there is no good or evil, holiness or defilement, which has not its root and source above. And just as action below stimulates action above, so words below stimulate words above-that is to say, decision couched in words. This word above is called "the word of the Lord"; for so we have learnt, that the word from below ascends and cleaves the firmaments until it reaches the place where it sets in motion either good or evil, according to its own character; hence it is written, "thou shalt keep thyself from every evil word (dabar)" (Deut. XXIII, 9).'

There [Tr. note: This passage, to "spoken and done" (p. 385), should properly be attached to Leviticus XXIII.] are four species in the lulab (palm-branch) which diverge into seven, and through their employment corresponding ones are roused above to benefit the world in various ways. And though the Community of Israel is one of these Seven, yet She is herself blessed from the other six and from the Stream which issues from the perennial source. The lower world is also blessed from them through this impulse, for when the Community of Israel is blessed by them all worlds are blessed. For this reason it was customary to go in procession round the altar on this festival (Tabernacles). [Tr. note: v. T. B. Succah.] We have learnt in the Book of Rab Hamnuna the Elder that the Powers which are in charge of these plants receive each one their blessings of joy above only at this time, and the gladness of those above and of these trees below is all at this season, and so when Israel lift up these branches, all is roused to activity at this time and the Community of Israel is blessed, so as to pour down blessings on the world. In Psalm XXIX, the "Voice of the Lord" is mentioned seven times, and R. Yose explained them thus: "The voice of the Lord is on the waters"; this is Abraham. "The voice of the Lord is in strength"; this is Isaac. "The voice of the Lord is in beauty"; this is Jacob. "The voice of the Lord breaketh the cedars"; this is Nezah (Victory). "The voice of the Lord heweth flames of fire"; this is Hod (Majesty). "The voice of the Lord causeth the wilderness to tremble"; this is Zaddik (Righteous One). And all bring blessings on to the world from the replenishment which they themselves receive. On all other days of the year these Seven are roused to activity by the prayer of men's mouth, but on this day it depends on action, and we require action, because at this season the whole year is blessed.

On the seventh day of Tabernacles the judgement of the world is finally sealed and the edicts are sent forth from the King, and God's might is aroused, and the "willows of the brook" [Tr. note: Nezah and Hod.] depend on it, and we require to awaken the might which sends the rain and to go round the altar seven times and sate it with the water of Isaac, because the well of Isaac is filled with water, and then all the world is blessed with water. We therefore pray that the rain-giving power may be manifested, and afterwards destroy willow twigs, since

Zohar: Vayikra, Section 3, Page 32a

judgement is closed on this day. R. Hiya said: 'In reference to this day, it is written: "And Isaac returned and dug the wells of water" (Gen. XXVI, 18). Isaac (symbolizing Geburah), having sat on the Throne of Judgement on the first day of the seventh month, now pours might upon the Community of Israel to set the waters in motion. Hence all depends on the appropriate action (of taking the four species).

On this day the idolatrous nations come to the end of their blessings and enter into judgement, and Israel come to the end of their punishments and enter into blessings. For on the next day (Eighth Day of Assembly) they are to rejoice in the King and to receive from Him blessings for all the year. This joy is reserved for Israel alone, and they are, as it were, the private guest of the king who can obtain any request which he makes. In reference to this it is written, "I love you, saith the Lord, and Esau I hate" (Mal. I, 2-3). Said R. Yose: 'We see that Esau is prosperous and dominant, with great cities and wide power, and yet you say, "And I have made his mountains desolate" (Ibid. 3)?' He replied: 'This is a frequent figure of speech. When the Holy King has pronounced a decree and placed it in his archives, the Scripture speaks of it as if it were already accomplished. And so with all the blessings which God has decreed for Israel, as it is written, "I, the Lord, have spoken and done" (Ezek. XVII, 24).

AND THIS IS THE LAW OF THE GUILT OFFERING. R. Isaac said: 'It has been explained that if this refers to what is below, then the other similar expressions ("this is the law of the meal offering", "this is the law of the sin offering", "this is the law of the peace offering") refer to what is below; and if this refers to what is above, then they also refer to what is above. Whoever engages in the study of the Torah obtains a portion in all and is attached to all sides and does not need to bring an offering for his soul, as has been explained.'

R. Isaac expounded the verse: "The priests said not, Where is the Lord, and they that handle the law knew me not; the shepherds also transgressed against me" (Jer. II, 8). 'By the "priests" here', he said, 'are meant the high priests who bring holy words to their place and proclaim each unity in the fitting way. "They that handle the law" are here the Levites who handle the harps which come from the side of the Law, and from whose side the Law was given and who are appointed to sing praises to the Holy King and complete His unity. The "shepherds" are the leaders of the people who care for them as a shepherd cares for his flock. These three classes must always be present by the offering, that it may be pleasing above and below and that blessings may be in all worlds. The priest brings the offering with intent to unify the Holy Name and to awaken the side to which he is attached. The Levites by their song endeavour to rouse the side to which they are attached

Zohar: Vayikra, Section 3, Page 32b

and to merge it in the side of the priest. The Israelite seeks to make his heart contrite and humble before God the Holy King, and so his sin is forgiven and there is joy above and below.'

R. Judah discoursed on the verse: "Who layeth the beams of his chambers in the waters", etc. (Ps. CIV, 3). 'When', he said, 'God created the world, He brought it forth from water and established it on water. He divided the waters in two, one half above and the other half below, and from each half created a world. Out of the lower half He made this world, which he established on this half of the waters, as it is written: "For he hath founded it upon the seas" (Ps. XXIV, 2). The upper half He took aloft, and made with it upper chambers, and on this half He established supernal holy beings made from the spirit which was detached from His mouth, as it is written, "And through the breath of his mouth all their hosts" (Ps. XXIII, 6). Among these he appointed some to sing His praises, fiery hosts, who sing praises in the morning and songs at even, all ceasing at night. Above them are hosts of a still more fiery nature who breathe fire and eat it, and then return to their places. In the other side there are abysses, one above the other, in all of which are executioners of judgement from the side of stern justice. In the lowest depth there are flames that burn flames, fires for the punishment of sinners issuing from the "river of fire", all fiery and flaming, situated between the higher and the lower. But when the smoke of the altar ascends, they leave that place where they were standing to destroy and annihilate, and the stream of flaming fire from the "river of fire" returns to its place and all enjoy the smoke from the altar when it goes straight towards the most high King. We have explained that it is the desire of each one to ascend above in order to please the Holy King, and Uriel appears there like a mighty lion crouching over his prey. When the priests and the Israelites saw this they rejoiced because they knew that the sacrifice was acceptable to the Holy King. Then another holy fire from above came down to meet the fire from below, and men trembled before their Master and repented. As a king to whom an acceptable present had been sent might say to his servant, Go and take this present which has been brought to me, so the Holy One, blessed be He, says to Uriel, Go and receive the present which my sons offer me. How great is the joy, how great the sweetness everywhere when the priest, the Levite and the bringer of the sacrifice are intent to bring the offering with perfect devotion! When, however, Israel were not virtuous or the sacrifice was not brought in the proper spirit, and was not accepted, they used to observe that the smoke did not ascend in a straight line, being blown aside by a wind from the hollow of the north, and they used to see the likeness of an impudent dog lying on the offering, and then they knew that it was not acceptable. As a king to whom an unworthy present has been brought might say, Take this present and give it to the dog, so when the offering was unacceptable it was given as a gift to the dog.

Zohar: Vayikra, Section 3, Page 33a

R. Judah said: 'When the fire went forth from the altar and consumed the offering (Lev. IX, 24), this was Uriel, who appeared in a flame on the altar;

Zohar: Vayikra, Section 3, Page 33b

and had it not been for the misfortune of the sons of Aaron, there would have been no day when God was more pleased with Israel from the time they left Egypt. And the death of the sons of Aaron was deserved for many reasons. One was that they offered incense at the wrong time-at a time when oil and incense were not together (i.e. not when the lamp was lit, v. Ex. xxx, 7). Another was that they thrust themselves forward in the place of their father. A third was that they were not married;

Zohar: Vayikra, Section 3, Page 34a

for such are not meet to bring blessings into the world. And a fourth was that they were intoxicated with wine.

THIS (zoth) IS THE ANOINTING PORTION OF AARON AND OF HIS SONS. R. Yose said: 'Zoth (Shekinah) indeed is the anointing portion of Aaron, for he brought of the oil of the supernal anointing and caused it to flow below; and by the hand of Aaron zoth was anointed with the holy anointing and drew blessing therefrom. From this oil blessings flow by the hand of the priest, and the priest causes it to flow below and anoints this zoth; hence, "this (zoth) is the anointing portion of Aaron, etc." '

TAKE AARON AND HIS SONS WITH HIM, AND THE GARMENTS. R. Hiya quoted here the verse: For with thee is the fountain of life, in thy light we shall see light" (Ps. XXXVI, 9). 'The fountain of life', he said, 'is the supernal oil which flows continually and is stored in the midst of that most high Wisdom, from which it never separates. It is the source which dispenses life to the supernal Tree and kindles the lights (of the emanations). And that tree is called the Tree of Life, because it is planted on account of that source of life. Therefore, too, "in thy light we shall see light"-in that light which is treasured for the righteous in the world to come, and with which Israel

Zohar: Vayikra, Section 3, Page 34b

will be illuminated. Or again, "with thee" may refer to the Holy One, blessed be He, who is a most high Tree in the midst of the Garden reaching out to all sides, because it clings to the source of life, which crowns it with supernal crowns all around the Garden like a mother who crowns her son.' R. Isaac said that the words refer to the High Priest above who corresponds to the high priest below. Therefore this Priest causes the supernal holy oil to flow down and kindle the lamps above. And just as the High Priest above is consummated with seven Days to be exalted above all, so there were seven days of consecration for the priest below, that lower might correspond to upper. The word for consecration (miluim, lit. filling) implies that they are completed by the priest, through being united with seven other days, for when the priest below bestirs himself, all above is stimulated through him, and blessings are spread above and below. R. Abba said that the reason why Moses anointed Aaron was because he was attached to the place which is the source of life, and Moses ministered all the seven days of the consecration to make all abide with Aaron.

When R. Hizkiah was once studying with R. Eleazar, he asked him: 'How many lights were created before the world was created?' He answered: 'Seven: namely, the light of the Torah, the light of Gehenna, the light of the Garden of Eden, the light of the Throne of Glory, the light of the Temple, the light of repentance, the light of the Messiah. Similarly seven lights were attached to Aaron, and he lit the lower lamps from the higher.' R. Eleazar quoted the verse: "All was from the dust" (Eccles. III, 20). 'We have learnt', he said, 'that everything is from the dust, even the orb of the sun. But from what dust? From that which is under the holy Throne of Glory. In the Book of Rab Yeba the Elder it says that paths went forth in all directions and then met again to give light, like dust that is thrown in all directions and yet returns again to the dust. The dust was that of the Sanctuary, which again was from the supernal dust.

'The Community of Israel is called "bride", as it says, "Thou art all fair, my love" (S.S. IV, 7). She is also called "a kingdom of priests" when blessed by the priests, since the priests enthrone her and give her power, making her queen over all the treasures and armoury of the King, over higher and lower, over the whole world.'

Zohar: Vayikra, Section 3, Section 2, Page 35a

R. Yose said: 'It is written, "He hath established his bond upon the earth (Amos IX, 6), namely, when the King joins her with all his holy Crowns in one company, for then She rules over all and shines above and below; and this at the time when the priest performs his service and brings the offering and burns the incense, uttering fitting prayer the while.' R. Yose said: 'When Aaron raised his hands, all raised with him, until the Community of Israel was blessed and higher and lower angels with her. Hence it says, "Blessed be the Lord out of Zion, who dwelleth in Jerusalem, Hallelukah" (Ps. CXXXV, 21).'

As R. Eleazar was once going from Cappadocia to Lydda, accompanied by R. Yose and R. Hizkiah, he began to discourse thus: 'It is written, "And I have put my words in thy mouth and have covered thee in the shadow of my hand" (Isa. LI, 16). We have been taught', he said, 'that if a man studies the words of the Torah and ever has them on his lips, God protects him and the Shekinah spreads her wings over him; nay more, he supports the world and God rejoices over him as if He had that day planted heaven and earth, as it says, "to plant heaven and to lay the foundations of the earth, and to say to Zion, thou art my people" (Ibid.); from this we learn that Israel are called Zion.' He further discoursed on the verse: "Bind the testimony, seal up the law among my disciples" (Isa. VIII, 16). 'The testimony is that of David, referred to in the verse, "My testimony that I shall teach them" (Ps. CXXXII, 12). The seal of the law and of all the abundance that flows from above is where? "In my disciples"; for there is the abundance gathered between the two pillars (Nezah and Hod) that stand there, and so all is tied firmly with one trusty knot. What, now, is the difference between those who study the Torah and faithful prophets? The former are ever superior, since they stand on a higher level. Those who study the Torah stand in a place called Tifereth (Beauty), which is the pillar of all faith, whereas the prophets stand lower in the place called Nezah (Victory) and Hod (Majesty); and those who merely speak in the spirit of holiness stand lower still. He who studies the Torah needs neither peace offerings nor burnt offerings, since the Torah is superior to all and the bond of faith; wherefore it is written "Her ways are ways of pleasantness and all her paths are peace" (Prov. III, 17), and also, "Great peace have they which love thy law and they have no occasion for stumbling" (Ps. CXIX, 165).'

As they were going along, they came across a man with three myrtle branches in his hand. They went up to him and said: 'What is this for?' He replied: 'To refresh the fainting one.' [Tr. note: The nefesh (soul), v. infra.] Said R. Eleazar: 'That is a good answer. But why three?' He replied: 'One for Abraham, one for Isaac, and one for Jacob; and I bind them together and smell them, because the scent refreshes the soul, and by this act of faith blessings are drawn down from above.' Said R. Eleazar: 'Happy is the lot

Zohar: Vayikra, Section 3 Page 35b

of Israel in this world and in the world to come. Mark now. The vital soul is only kept up by smell, and this smell brings to mind another, for when Sabbath departs and the additional soul departs, the soul and the spirit are separated and sad until the smell comes and unites them and makes them glad. In the same way all (attributes) are united by the smell of the sacrifice and the lamps are kindled and gladdened. If one lamp is placed above another and the lower one is lit, the smoke as it ascends kindles the upper one also. So the smoke of the sacrifices, as it ascends, kindles the supernal lamps till they all flame together and unite through this smell, so that there is "a sweet savour to the Lord". Thus the smell of the offering is the support of all and is produced by the priest who brings all together; and therefore seven days of fulfilment were completed in him in order that all may be blessed through his service, and there may be blessing and joy above and below.'

SHEMINI

AND IT CAME TO PASS ON THE EIGHTH DAY. R. Isaac said: 'Happy are Israel in that God has given them a holy Law which is the universal delight, the joy of the Holy One, blessed be He, and His recreation, as it is written, "and I was daily his delight" (Prov. VIII, 30). The Torah is all one name of the Holy One, blessed be He. By the Torah was the world created, as it is written, "And I was an artificer with him" (Ibid.). By the Torah, too, was man created, as it is written, "And God said, Let us make man" (Gen. I, 26). Said the Holy One, blessed be He, to the Torah: "I desire to create man." She replied: "This man is destined to sin and to provoke Thee unless Thou art long-suffering with him; how, then, shall he endure?" To which God replied: "I and thou shall maintain him, for not for nothing am I called 'long suffering'." ' R. Hiya said that the Oral and the Written Law together preserve mankind, as it is written: "Let us make man in our image, according to our likeness"-"image" having reference to the Masculine and "likeness" to the Feminine; and for this reason the Torah commences with the letter Beth (=2), as already explained. R. Isaac said: 'Why is the beth open on one side and closed on the other? To show that when a man comes

Zohar: Vayikra, Section 3 Page 36a

to attach himself to the Torah, it is open to receive him and to join with him; and when a man closes his eyes to it and walks in the other way, then it turns its closed side to him, according to the saying: "If thou leavest me one day, I will leave thee two days", until he returns to attach himself to it, never again to abandon it. Therefore the Torah makes the first approaches to men, proclaiming, "Unto you, O men, I call" (Prov. VIII, 4); and it is also written of her, "she crieth in the chief places of concourse, at the entering in of the gates" (Ibid. I, 21).' R. Judah said: 'The beth has two parallel lines and a third joining them. What do these signify? One for heaven, one for earth, and one for the Holy One, blessed be He, who unites and receives them.' R. Eleazar said: 'These represent three supernal and closely connected holy lights in which the whole Torah is comprised, and which provide the introduction to faith. Therefore to study the Torah is like studying the Holy Name, as we have said, that the Torah is all one holy supernal name. Therefore it commences with the letter beth, which symbolizes the holy name with three bonds of faith. All those who study the Torah cleave to the Holy One, blessed be He, and are crowned with the crowns of the Torah and beloved above and below, and God stretches out to them His right hand; and all the more to those who study at night, who, as we have stated, are associated with the Shekinah and joined with her. When morning comes the Holy One, blessed be He, winds round them a thread of grace to distinguish between the higher and the lower ranks, and all the stars of the morning, what time the Community of Israel and those who study the Torah come to appear before the King, break forth into song together, as it is written, "When the morning stars sing together and the sons of God shout for joy" (Job XXXVIII, 7).'

R. Eleazar was once travelling along a road on which R. Phineas ben Yair happened to be coming towards him. The ass on which R. Phineas was riding whinnied, and he said: 'Verily, from the note of gladness in the ass's voice, I see that I shall meet someone here.' When he emerged from under the brow of the hill he saw R. Eleazar approaching, and said: 'Assuredly, the omen of the ass's voice has been fulfilled.' R. Eleazar then came up to him and kissed him. He said to him: 'If you have the same destination as I have, let us join company, and if not, go your way.' He replied: 'Indeed, I was going to look for you, and since I have found you I will follow you and we can keep company.' R. Phineas then began a discourse on the verse: "The Lord shall bless thee out of Zion, and thou shalt see the good of Jerusalem" etc. (Ps. CXXVIII, 5). 'Why', he said, "from Zion "? Because there blessings repose, as it is written, "For there the Lord commanded the blessing, even life forevermore" (Ps. CXXXIII, 3). And for the sake of Zion Jerusalem is blessed and visited with mercy, and when Jerusalem is blessed all the people are blessed. The words "all the days of thy life" mean that the rainbow shall not be seen in thy days any more than in the days of thy father. "And see thy children to thy children", god-fearing, saintly and holy. "Peace upon Israel [Tr. note: The appearance of the rainbow was supposed to indicate a lack of virtue in the generation. Cf. Zohar, Gen. 225a.]": as who should say. "Peace upon the head of the king that he may lack nothing." So there is peace upon Israel when righteous men are in the world.'

R. Eleazar discoursed on the verse: "Children's children are the crown of old men, and the glory of children are their fathers" (Prov. XVII, 6). 'The word "children" ', he said, 'has its well-known esoteric meaning. "Children's children" are the other crowns of the King, and of them it says that—"the glory of children are their fathers", because the sons are only crowned through the fathers. From this we learn that the sons are only crowned and revived by the running Stream when the Fathers are crowned and blessed.'

Zohar: Vayikra, Section 3 Page 36b

As they were going along the time for prayer arrived, so they dismounted and said their prayers. While they were praying a serpent wound itself round the legs of the ass of R. Phineas, which thereupon uttered two cries. When they had finished praying R. Phineas said: 'I can understand my animal being in pain, because earlier in the day, while I was meditating on the Torah, it took me through some filth; hence now it is being hurt.' As they stood up they saw a snake coiled round its legs, whereupon R. Phineas said: "Snake, go and wind yourself round your own hole." At this the snake dissolved and fell into pieces. Said R. Eleazar: 'Is God so particular with the righteous?' He replied: 'Verily He is, and He takes note of all their errors, and desires to raise their holiness to a still higher level. This ass has been tormented because it did not guard my holiness, and this snake was a divine messenger. And how many agents has the Almighty, even beasts of the field and even idolaters, as it says, "The Lord shall bring a nation against thee from far, from the ends of the earth" (Deut. XXVIII, 49).' R. Eleazar asked: 'Does God ever make an Israelite His agent?' He replied: 'Yes: that is, a pious Israelite to punish a wicked one, but not one wicked one to punish another, save when he does so accidentally, as it is written, "but God deliver him into his hand" (Ex. XXI, 13), in order to punish both of them.' Said R. Eleazar: 'How does God use such Israelites and idolaters as His agents?' 'Has not your father told you?' said R. Phineas. 'I have never yet asked him,' he replied. R. Phineas thereupon began by quoting the verse: "When he giveth quietness who then can condemn?" etc. (Job XXXIV, 29). 'When God', he said, 'gives quietness and ease to a man, who is there that is authorized to injure and malign him? And when He withdraws His watchful providence from him, who can keep watch over him to protect him? And in this God's ways are "unto a man or a nation alike" – the same for the world or for a people or for an individual. For when men's actions are virtuous on earth, then the Right Hand of the Holy One, blessed be He, is active for them above, and many friends and protectors come forward on their behalf above on the right and on the left, and the Left Hand is subdued and kept under control. But when men's actions on earth are not virtuous, then the Left is awakened, and all those who come from the side of the left with it, and all become agents to inflict harm on men. For all who transgress the precepts of the Law receive a mark on their faces through which they are recognized by those who rise up from the side of the left. Hence serpents and idolaters, and all who come from the side of the left, are called "agents" in regard to those who bear this mark. Now Israelites, even if their actions are not virtuous, still come from the side of the right, but because the right has been paralysed by their actions the left has power over them, and those who come from the side of the left. Hence the agents chosen for punishing them are serpents and idolaters, and such-like who are from the side of the left, but not other Israelites, even sinners, because they are still from the side of the right. And if it happens that a sinful Israelite falls into the hand of another Israelite sinner, this is that they may both be punished and be purified by their punishment.' Said R. Eleazar: 'Whence do you derive all this?' He answered: 'From the incident of the concubine in Gibeah (Judges xx). For though the sinners there were Israelites, God was unwilling that other sinners of Israel should be the instruments for punishing them, and therefore numbers of them fell time after time until all the sinners in the attacking army had perished, and there were left in it only those

Zohar: Vayikra, Section 3 Page 37a

more righteous ones who could more appropriately execute the work. And even righteous Israelites are made the agents only when the two worlds, the upper and lower, are evenly balanced, and at that time [of the incident of Gibeah] they were not evenly balanced. Hence sinners of Israel are not made the agents of the King to punish other sinners of Israel, since they do not come from the side of the left. We may illustrate by the following parable. Certain men having offended against the king, an officer was charged to arrest and punish them. One clever fellow among them went and mixed himself with the officer's men. The officer, however, detected him and said: "Who said you could join us? Are you not one of those who have offended against the king? You shall be punished first." So Israel come from the side of the right and do not attach themselves to the left or mingle with it. Sometimes, however, through their sins they cause the Right to be weakened and the Left to be aroused, with all those that belong to it. Should, then, an Israelite try to insinuate himself among them, if they detect him they say: "Are you not one of those who come from the side of the right which is enfeebled because of their sins? Are you not one of those who have sinned against the king? Who allowed you to come amongst us?" So he is punished first. And King Solomon points openly to these people in the words: "What time one man hath power over another to his hurt" (Eccles. VIII, 9)—verily to his own hurt, because he is not the agent of the king and does not come from that side.' Said R. Eleazar: 'Verily it is so, since we have learnt that there is a left and there is a right, mercy and judgement, Israel to the right and the idolatrous nations to the left. Israel, although they sin and are humbled, yet they belong to the right and do not cleave to the left nor mingle with it. Therefore it is written, "Save thy right hand and answer us" (Ps. LX, 6), for when the Right Hand is exalted, Israel that cleave to it are exalted and crowned through it, and then the Left Hand and all who come from its side are humbled with it; hence it is written: "Thy right hand, O Lord, breaketh in pieces the enemy" (Ex. xv, 6).'

R. Eleazar then discoursed on the verse: "And it came to pass on the eighth day", etc. He said: 'This "eighth day" has reference to the preceding statement. "for he shall consecrate you seven days" (Lev. VIII, 33). Why seven days? Happy indeed are the priests who are crowned with the crowns of the holy King, and anointed with the holy oil, because thereby is put in motion the supernal oil which moistens all the Seven and from which the seven lamps are lit, this oil comprising them all, as we have learnt that there are six, and this is the consummation of all; hence, "seven days he shall consecrate you". Therefore, too, the Community of Israel is called "Bathsheba" (lit. daughter of seven), because She is the consummation of six others. After this septet had perfected the priests and crowned them and anointed them, when they reached the Community of Israel, which is the eighth, Aaron was commanded to offer a calf, to atone for the sin of that other calf which Aaron made, thereby sinning against the "cow", which is the eighth, the completion of the

588

guardians of Israel. Thus the priest is found complete in all, in the eight different vestments and in all crowns, complete above and below. Now, on all solemn occasions some act must be manifested, and therefore a ceremony was performed with Aaron below to produce a corresponding reaction above, and in this way worlds were blessed through the mediation of the priest. Aaron had to bring a calf for a sin-offering on account of the sin he had previously committed. Also a ram for a burnt-offering. Why a ram? Because of the ram of Isaac, who was a perfect burnt-offering, and this also was brought to make the sacrifice complete. Thus the calf was brought for its own sake and the ram to complete it

Zohar: Vayikra, Section 3 Page 37b

duly with the perfection of Isaac. Israel, who shared the sin of the priest, had to bring a similar offering, viz., "an ox and a ram for peace offerings, to sacrifice before the Lord", an ox for their sin and a ram to complete this place with the perfection of Isaac. The term "sin-offering" is not used in connection with Israel as with the priest, because Israel had already suffered their punishment in many places, and therefore God did not wish to mention their sin; hence it is written here, "for a peace offering" and not "for a sin-offering", as a sign of peace, to show that God had been reconciled with Israel in respect of this. Aaron, however, who had been saved from punishment through the prayer of Moses (v. Deut. IX, 20), and whose guilt still hung over him, had to bring a sin-offering, that his sin might be atoned for and that he should be purified and whole. On that day upper and lower beings reached their perfection, and there was peace everywhere in the joy of heaven and earth, and but for the tragedy of the sons of Aaron on that day there would have been no such joy above and below from the day that the Israelites came up from the Red Sea. On that day the sin of the Golden Calf was wiped out, and priests and people were cleansed of it. On that day all the accusers above were silenced, and they circled round Israel without being able to find any spot at which to attack them until the hour arrived when Nadab and Abihu rose up and spoilt the general joy, and wrath descended on the world. We have learnt that on that day it was the joy of the Community of Israel to be united [with her Spouse] by the bond of faith with all holy ties (for the incense binds all-hence its name), [Tr. note: Ketoreth, connected with katar, Aramaic for "bind"]. and they came and linked all the others together and left Her outside, and linked up something else.' Said R. Phineas to him: 'Do not say that they left her outside, but only that the Community of Israel was not united [to the rest] through them, [Tr. note: Because they were not married.] for wherever male and female are not found together, the Community of Israel does not abide. Therefore it is written, "With this shall Aaron come into the sanctuary" (Lev. XVI, 3), which was a warning to him that he should be male with female; and therefore a priest should not enter the sanctuary till he is married, in order that he may have a share in the union of the Community of Israel.' R. Yose referred in this connection to the verse: "As a lily among thorns, so is my love among the daughters" (S.S. II, 2). 'As has been explained,' he said, 'this verse is spoken by the Holy One, blessed be He, in praise of the Community of Israel in His love and desire for Her, and therefore it is a married man who should utter the praises of the Holy One, blessed be He, and of the Community of Israel. For, since he cleaves to his spouse and devotes his affection to her, when he comes to serve before the Holy God he awakens another love, that of the Holy One, blessed be He, for the Community of Israel. And for this the Holy One blesses him and the Community of Israel blesses him.

Zohar: Vayikra, Section 3 Page 38a

For the Community of Israel is blessed by the priest and the Israelite is blessed by the priest, and the priest is blessed by the Supernal Priest, as it is said: "And they shall put my name upon the children of Israel and I will bless them" (Num. VI, 27).'

It is written: "Remember, O Lord, thy tender mercies and thy lovingkindnesses, for they have been ever of old" (me'olam, lit. from the world, Ps. xxv, 6). "Mercies" here refers to Jacob and "lovingkindnesses to Abraham. God takes them from the world and raises them aloft, and makes of them a holy Chariot to shield the world. So God does with all the righteous. It may be asked, why is there no reference to Isaac here? He was left over to punish those who oppress his offspring, and is referred to in the verse, "Arouse thy might" (Ps. LXXX, 3); and again, "The Lord shall go forth as a mighty man, he shall stir up jealousy like a man of war" (Isa. XLII, 13). R. Hiya said: 'Jacob and Abraham we require to shield us, but Isaac's function is to make war, and therefore we do not desire him to be associated with them. We may also explain the words "for they are from the world" thus. When God created the world He took Isaac and created with him the world. He saw that it would not be able to endure, so He supported it with Abraham. He saw that it needed further support, so He took Jacob and joined him with Isaac. Hence the world is supported by Abraham and Jacob, and they are "from the world".'

[Tr. note: The text here inserts a passage which in substance is merely a repetition of p. 37a, 'R. Eleazar discoursed...,' to p. 37b, "something else".]

Zohar: Vayikra, Section 3 Page 38b

[Note: The first 15 lines of the Hebrew text do not appear in our translation.]

AND MOSES SAID UNTO ELEAZAR AND ITHAMAR, LET NOT THE HAIR OF YOUR HEADS GO LOOSE, ETC.... FOR THE ANOINTING OIL OF THE LORD IS UPON YOU. R. Abba said: 'All joy above derives from the Holy Oil, from which issue gladness and blessings to all the Lamps, and with the stream of which the Supernal Priest is crowned. Therefore the priest on earth on whom the anointing oil has flowed must display a smiling and joyful countenance, and there must be no blemish on his head or his attire or anywhere else, that he may not cause a blemish in another place. Hence had Eleazar and Ithamar allowed any blemish to appear at that moment on their heads or their garments they would not have been delivered, for it was a time of judgement. So we have learnt that when a plague is rife a man should not apply himself to any undertaking lest he become a marked man. Hence it is written, "lest ye die. But let your brethren the whole house of Israel bewail the burning", because they did not come from the side of the priests, and therefore would not be injured.'

R. Eleazar here adduced the verse: "And Aaron took him Elisheba, the daughter of Aminadab, the sister of Nahshon, to wife" (Ex. VI, 23). 'Aaron', he said, 'acted fitly, copying the supernal model. "Elisheba" was destined for Aaron from the time of the Creation, just as "Bathsheba" [Tr. note: v p. 37a.] was destined for David from the time of the Creation. Both are one, but the one name refers to judgement, the other to mercy. When she was joined with David, it was for judgement, to wage war and shed blood. Here with Aaron it was for peace, for joy, for gladness and blessing. Hence with David she is called Bathsheba, and with Aaron Elisheba: Elisheba (lit. to seven) to show that she was joined to Grace; Bathsheba (daughter of seven) to signify that she inherited royalty and power. [Tr. note: The text here introduces a brief digression on the esoteric significance of the "voice of the trumpet", the substance of which has already appeared elsewhere.]

Zohar: Vayikra, Section 3 Page 39a

Hence, "Aaron took Elisheba" to gratify her, to rejoice her, to join her with the King in a perfect union, that blessings might be diffused through all worlds by means of Aaron. Hence the priest must be ever smiling and joyful, since he is the instrument of joy and blessing, and in this way punishment, wrath and gloom are removed from him, that he may not be disqualified for the place to which he is linked.'

DRINK NO WINE NOR STRONG DRINK, THOU NOR THY SONS, ETC. R. Judah said: 'The fact that this injunction was given to the priests shows that Nadab and Abihu were under the influence of wine.' R. Hiya adduced here the verse: "Wine rejoiceth the heart of man" (Ps. CIV, 15). 'If', he said, 'the priest requires to be glad and smiling more than other men, why is he forbidden wine, which creates joy and smiles? The truth is that wine rejoices at first and saddens afterwards, and the priest must be glad throughout. Also wine is of the side of the Levites, but the side of the priests is pure and clear water.' R. Yose said: 'Each lends to the other, and therefore wine gladdens at first because it contains water, but afterwards it reverts to its own nature and brings gloom.' R. Abba said: 'Wine, oil and water issue from the same place. Water and oil, which are on the right, are taken by the priests, especially oil, which is joy first and last, as it is written: "Like the goodly oil upon the head that ran down upon the beard, even Aaron's beard" (Ps. CXXXIII, 2). Wine, which is on the left, is inherited by the Levites, that they may raise their voices in song and not be silent, for wine is never silent, but oil is always noiseless. The difference between them is this. Oil comes from the side of Thought, which is always silent and unheard, whereas wine, which is for raising the voice, comes from the side of the Mother. Therefore the priest, when he entered the Sanctuary to perform divine service, was forbidden to drink wine, because his service is carried out quietly.'

R. Judah and R. Isaac were once going from Be Merunia to Sepphoris, and with them was a youth leading an ass, on which was a jar of honey. Said R. Judah: 'Let us discourse on the Torah as we go.' R. Isaac began by quoting the verse: "And thy palate is like the best wine that goeth down smoothly for my beloved" (S.S. VII, 9). 'This wine', he said, 'is the wine of the Torah, which is in truth good, because there is another wine which is not good. But the wine of the Torah is good for all-good for this world and good for the world to come. This, too, is the wine that pleases the Holy One, blessed be He, more than all, and therefore he who quaffs deeply of the wine of the Torah will wake in the world to come and will come to life when God shall raise the righteous.' Said R. Judah: 'We have learnt that even in that world he will be able to study the Torah, as it is written, "He causeth to mutter the lips of the sleepers" (Ibid.).' The youth hereupon remarked: 'If it had been written, "thy palate is from the best wine", your explanation would have been correct, but it is written "like the best wine".' They looked at him, and R. Judah said: 'Speak on, for your remark is a good one.' He continued: 'I have heard that if a man who studies the Torah diligently allows his expositions to be heard and does not merely whisper them,

Zohar: Vayikra, Section 3 Page 39b

then he is like good wine, which also is not silent and causes the voice to be raised. When he departs from this world, then "my beloved goeth straight forward", turning neither to the right nor the left, and none interferes with him; and in that world, too, his lips mutter words of the Torah. I have further heard that this verse was addressed to the Community of Israel in her praise. It may be asked, who is it that praises her thus, for if it is the Holy One, blessed be He, we should expect "for me" instead of "for my beloved". However, the Holy One does in truth praise the Community of Israel thus, in response to Her praises. As She says, "His palate is sweet", He replies, "Thy palate is like the best wine", to wit, the wine that has been treasured from the Creation. "My beloved" is Isaac, who is called "beloved from the womb", and "straight forward" means, to unite the left with the right, through the joy diffused by that wine. Hence "causing to mutter the lips of the sleepers", because all are awakened with joy and blessing, and all worlds rejoice and rouse themselves to pour down blessings below.' R. Judah and R. Isaac approached him joyfully and kissed him. They said to him: 'What is your name?' He replied: 'Jesse.' They said: 'You shall be Rabbi Jesse: you shall become more famous than our colleague Rabbi Jesse who has departed from us.' They then said to him: 'Who is your father?' He replied: 'He is no longer alive. He used to teach me every day three expositions of the Torah, and every night three pieces of Aggadic lore, What I have just told you I learnt from my father, and now I live with a man who will not let me study, and makes me work all day, and so every day I go over again the things I learnt from my father.' They said to him: 'Does that man know anything of the Torah?' He replied: 'He does not. He is an old man and he cannot say Grace, and he has sons whom he does not send to school.' Said R. Judah: 'If that were not the case, I would go into that village to talk to him about you, but after what you tell me, it would be wrong of us to look at him. Leave your ass, therefore, and come along with us.' They then asked him who his father was. He replied: 'R. Zeira of Kfar Ramin.' On hearing this R. Judah wept and said: 'I was once in his house, and I learnt from him three things concerning the Cup of Benediction and two relating to the work of Creation.' Said R. Isaac: 'Seeing that we could learn from his son, how much more from himself!'

So they went along holding his hand until they came to a field where they sat down. They said to him: 'Tell us something that your father taught you concerning the work of Creation.' He thereupon discoursed on the verse: "And God created the great sea-monsters," etc. (Gen. I, 21). He said: 'The name Elohim is usually applied to the place of judgement, but here it is applied to the most high place from which judgements issue, for although it is intrinsically a place of Mercy, yet judgements issue from it and depend upon it. The "great sea-monsters" are the "Patriarchs", which are watered first and spread their roots throughout all. "And every living creature" (lit. living soul): this is the soul which the supernal Earth brought forth from the "living creature" (hayah), which is the highest of all, to wit, the soul of the first man which formed in its midst. "That moveth": this is the "living creature" (hayah) that moves about on all sides above and below. "Which the waters brought forth abundantly", namely the waters of that supernal stream which issues from Eden and waters the Tree there that it may spread its roots and provide food for all. "And every winged fowl after its kind": these are the holy angels whose function it is to sanctify the name of their Master every day, or to perform the messages of their Master in this world.' Said R. Judah: 'This is really too much for one so young to know, and I foresee that he will be removed to a place of eminence.' R. Isaac said:

Zohar: Vayikra, Section 3 Page 40a

'The "living creature that moveth" is the Hayah that is supreme above all, there being also another which is called by Scripture "earth". The expression here, "and let fowl multiply in the earth", means in the earth and not in the water, because the original stream flows on undivided up to that place which is called "earth" but from there, as it says, "it separates", etc. (Gen. II, 10); and the "fowl" mentioned are watered from this "earth".'

They then rose and went on their way, and R. Judah said: 'Let us take this youth into our company, and let each of us give some exposition of the Torah.' He then commenced with the verse: "Stay ye me with raisins, comfort me with apples", etc. (S.S. II, 5). He said: 'The Community of Israel speaks thus in exile. Support is needed by one who falls, and therefore the Community of Israel, of whom it is written, "she is fallen, she shall no more rise" (Amos v, 2), requires support, and she says, "Stay me". To whom does she say this? To her children who are in exile with her. And with what shall they support her? "With raisins": these are the "patriarchs", who are the first to be replenished with that good wine stored away from the Creation; and when they are replenished, blessings light upon her through the agency of a certain grade, namely the Righteous One, and so he who knows how to unify the Holy Name, even though blessings are not vouchsafed to the world, supports and stays the Community of Israel in exile. "Comfort me with apples": this is the same, and it also contains an inner meaning. Raisins intoxicate, but apples sober. Hence raisins to excite, and apples to see that the intoxication does not harm. And why all this? Because "I am sick of love" in the exile. He who unifies the Holy Name must fitly join Mercy with Justice, and this is what supports the Community of Israel in exile.'

R. Isaac took the verse: "Which did eat the fat of their sacrifices and drink the wine of their drink offering". He said: 'Happy are Israel in that they are holy, and God desired to sanctify them. All the life of this world that they inherit is derived from the World-to-come, because that is life both above and below, and the place where the "treasured wine" commences, and from which life and holiness issue. And Israel use wine on account of the wine of another Israel, for the supernal Israel derives life therefrom, and therefore they bless the Holy One with wine. Hence, when the idolater, who is unclean and defiles anyone who associates with him, touches the wine of Israel it becomes unclean and is forbidden; all the more the wine which he himself makes. All the practices of Israel are on the supernal pattern, and especially their offering of wine, which holds a very high rank, like the "treasured wine". Hence Israel drink the wine of Israel which has been made in holiness, as is fitting, just as the Israel above drinks of that holy wine, and they do not drink wine which has been made in defilement and from the side of defilement, for the spirit of uncleanness rests on it, and if one drinks it his spirit is defiled and he is not of the side of Israel and has no share in the World-to-come, which is the "treasured wine". Hence God is blessed with wine above all, because wine rejoices the Left side and in that joy merges itself in the Right, and when the whole becomes Right the Holy Name is glad, and blessings are everywhere diffused.'

Zohar: Vayikra, Section 3 Page 40b

The youth then followed, taking as his text: "The king by judgement establisheth the land, but a man of offerings overthroweth it" (Prov. XXIX, 4). 'The king here', he said, 'is the Holy One, blessed be He. "Judgement" is Jacob, who is the epitome of the patriarchs. "A man of offerings" is Esau, who used to ask questions about offerings, but never bring any. Or again, I can say that 'offerings" is the negation of judgement, being the elevation of mercy, and therefore "a man of offerings overthroweth it". But was not David "a man of offerings", and yet the land was established by him? This was because it is written of him, "the sure mercies of David"; as he clung to one quality, so did he cling to the other. All his days David strove that this "offering" should be united with judgement. Solomon came and wedded them together, so that the moon became full and the land was established. Zedekiah came and parted them, and the land was left without judgement, and the moon was impaired and the land was devastated. Note that oil was for the priests and wine for the Levites-not because they require wine, but from the "treasured wine" some comes to their side to link the whole together and make all worlds glad, right and left being found clasped together in them, so that they should be beloved of the true believers. Whoso concentrates his thought on this is perfect in this world and in the world to come, and all his days clings to repentance, the place where oil and wine are found. In this way he will not hanker after this world or its delights, for another kind of wealth is stored up for him, and he has a share in the future world, the place where oil and wine are stored. And he who loves this place does not require wealth or strive for it. Happy are the righteous who all their days strive after the celestial wealth of which it is written, "Gold and glass cannot equal it, neither shall the exchange thereof be jewels of fine gold" (Job XXVIII, 17).

He further discoursed on the verse: "And the Lord said unto Moses, Come up to me, and I will give thee... the law and the commandment which I have written to teach them" (Ex. XXIV, 12). 'The word lehorotham (to teach them) may be read lehoratham (to her that conceived them), the "them" referring to the law and the commandment. "She that conceived them" is the place of "treasured wine", because all writing of the Supernal Book commences there, and from thence issues the Torah which we call the Written Torah. The other Torah is called the Oral Torah (Torah of the mouth), the "mouth" being Knowledge which is the mouth of book and writing.

'It is written: "Take away the wicked from before the king and his throne shall be established in lovingkindness" (Prov. xxv, 3). When sinners are numerous in the world, the throne of the holy King is established in judgement and flames play around the world. But when the wicked are removed from the world, His throne is established in lovingkindness and not in judgement. This shows that the lower world depends on the higher, and the higher is disposed according to the conduct of the lower.

Zohar: Vayikra, Section 3 Page 41a

We further learn from this verse that when the priest enters the sanctuary he should enter with lovingkindness, of which the emblem is water, and not with wine, which is the emblem of severity.' R. Judah and R. Isaac then came and kissed his head, and from that day he never left R. Judah, and when he entered the House of Study, R. Judah used to rise before him, saying: 'I have learnt something from him, and it is fitting that I should show him respect.' Afterwards he became one of the Companions and they used to call him "R. Jesse the hammerhead that breaks rocks and makes the sparks fly in all directions", and R. Eleazar used to apply to him the verse: "Before I formed thee in the belly I knew thee" (Jer. I, 4).

AND THE LORD SPAKE UNTO MOSES AND TO AARON SAYING, THESE ARE THE LIVING THINGS WHICH YE SHALL EAT, ETC. Why was Aaron joined with Moses here? Because it was always his function to divide between the clean and the unclean. R. Abba expounded in this connection the verse: "What man is he that desireth life and loveth many days that he may see good?" (Ps. XXXIV, 13). 'Life here', he said, 'is the life which is called "the world to come", where true life abides. Similarly the "tree of life" means the tree that springs from that life and is planted therein. By "days" here is signified the name of the Holy King which is attached to the supernal days called "the days of the heaven over the earth". He who desires to have a portion in the higher life and to cleave to the supernal days should above all keep guard over his mouth and his tongue. He should preserve his mouth from food and drink which defile the soul and remove man from those supernal days and life, and he should keep his tongue from words of evil so as not to be defiled by them. Further, "mouth" and "tongue" are names given to supernal places, and therefore a man should be careful not to bring a stain on his mouth and tongue.'

THESE ARE THE LIVING THINGS WHICH YE SHALL EAT... AMONG ALL THE BEASTS. Why does it say first "living things" and then "beasts"? What it means is that as long as Israel keep their souls from impurity, then they will eat "living things" so as to be of a high grade of holiness and cleave to God's Name through rejecting the "beasts" which are not selected as clean. But if they do not keep themselves from unclean food and drink, then they shall cleave to another unclean place and be defiled by it. The eating, however, of the animals selected will be clean and will not defile them nor deprive them of a share in God's Name. Again, we may lay stress on the word zoth (this) and interpret: zoth (i.e. the Shekinah) confronts you to punish you if you defile your souls, because your souls are from her, and therefore she stands before you for good or ill. R. Eleazar said: 'Of all the beasts that are attached to one side you may eat, and of all that do not come from that side you may not eat. For there are beasts that come

Zohar: Vayikra, Section 3 Page 41b

from either side, and both sides have their signs. Hence, whoever eats of those that come from the unclean side defiles therewith himself and his soul, which comes from the side of purity.'

R. Simeon said: 'As there are ten Crowns of Faith above, so there are ten crowns of unclean sorcery below. All things on earth are attached either to one side or to the other. It may be asked, What of the goat in which dwells an unclean spirit, and is yet permitted? This is not really so, for if an unclean spirit dwelt in it, we should not be permitted to eat it. The fact is that the evil spirit passes through it and appears in front of it, but is not allowed to dwell in it. For when the evil spirit comes to take possession of it, another spirit passes by, and the evil spirit departs from it, though still appearing in front of it; and therefore it is not forbidden to us as food. Cattle, beasts, birds and fishes show signs of right or left, and whichever comes from the right we may eat and whichever comes from the left we may not eat, because an unclean spirit dwells in them; wherefore the holy spirit of Israel must not be mixed up with them, in order that they may remain holy and be recognized as such above and below. Happy is the portion of Israel in that the holy King delights in them and desires to sanctify and purify them above all others because they cling to Him. It is written, "Israel in whom I am glorified" (Isa. XLIX, 3). If the Holy One, blessed be He, takes pride in Israel, how can they go and defile themselves and cling to the other, unclean side? Therefore it is written, "Sanctify yourselves therefore and be ye holy, for I am holy"; he that is in the likeness of the king should not depart from the ways of the king. Happy the portion of Israel of whom it is written, "All that see them shall acknowledge them that they are the seed which the Lord hath blessed" (Isa. LXI, 9). Whoever eats of these unclean foods cleaves to the other side and defiles himself and shows that he has no portion in the most high God and comes not from His side, and if he departs in this state from this world he is seized by those who belong to the side of uncleanness, who punish him as a man spurned of his Master, and there is no healing to his defilement and he never escapes from it.' R. Yose said: 'King Solomon wrote in his wisdom: "All the labour of man is for his mouth" (Eccles. VI, 7). This signifies that all the punishment

Zohar: Vayikra, Section 3 Page 42a

which a man undergoes in the other world is on account of his mouth, because he did not guard it and through it defiled his soul.' R. Isaac said: 'For one to defile himself with unclean foods is like serving idols; just as he who serves idols quits the side of life and of the domain of holiness for another domain, so likewise he who eats unclean foods is defiled both in this world and the next, for these were assigned to the idolatrous peoples, who are already unclean and come from the side of uncleanness.'

R. Eleazar once said to his father: 'We have learnt that God will one day purify Israel; with what?' He answered: 'With that which is mentioned in the verse, "And I will sprinkle clean water upon you and ye shall be clean" (Ezek. XXXVI, 25). And when they are purified they shall be sanctified and called holy, as it is written, "Holy is Israel to the Lord" (Jer. II, 3). Happy are Israel of whom God has said: "Ye shall be holy for I am holy", because it is written, "And to him ye shall cleave" (Deut. x, 20).'

KI TAZRIA

AND THE LORD SPOKE UNTO MOSES SAYING, WHEN A WOMAN, ETC. R. Abba cited here the verse: "By night upon my bed I sought him", etc. (S.S. III, 1). 'This verse', he said, 'is spoken by the Community of Israel who in the exile lies in the dust, in an alien unclean land, and therefore complains of her bed and beseeches "him whom her soul loveth" to deliver her from thence. She "seeks him but finds him not", for it is not his way to unite

Zohar: Vayikra, Section 3, Page 42b

with her save in his temple. She "calls him and he answers not", for She dwells among other peoples, and only his sons hear his voice.' R. Isaac interpreted thus: '"I make plaint to him of my bed, that he may unite with me to gladden and bless me", for, as we have learnt, from the union of the King with the Community of Israel many righteous ones obtain a holy inheritance and many blessings accrue to the world.' R. Abba was once going from Kfar Kania to the cave of Lydda, along with R. Yose and R. Hiya. Said R. Yose: 'It is written: "A virtuous woman is a crown to her husband,' (Prov. XII, 4). The virtuous woman', he said 'is the Community of Israel, and "she that maketh ashamed" refers to the idolatrous nations whom God cannot abide, as it says "I abhorred them" (Lev. xx, 23).' Said R. Abba: 'Assuredly it is so; the Community of Israel is called a "woman of valour" (hayil) because she is the mistress of so many legions of valiant ones (hayalin).' R. Abba then said: 'Let each of us give some exposition of the Torah', and he himself commenced with the verse: "A virtuous woman who can find?" (Prov. XXXI, 10). 'The "virtuous woman", he said, 'is the Community of

593

Israel, as we have just explained. "Who shall find": who shall succeed in being wholly in her and always with her? "Far above rubies is her price" (michrah, lit. selling): those who do not truly and wholeheartedly cleave to her she sells into the hands of other peoples, and they are removed far from those precious holy pearls and have no share in them.' R. Hiya then expounded the next verse: "The heart of her husband trusteth in her, and she shall have no lack of spoil". 'The "husband",' he said, 'is the Holy One, blessed be He, who hath appointed her to govern the whole world and placed in her hands all his armoury and warriors; wherefore she "lacketh not spoil".' R. Yose took the next verse: "She doeth him good and not evil all the days of her life". 'She provides good for the world, for the temple of the King and those who frequent it. When is this? When those "days of the heaven" shine upon her and unite with her fitly, these being then the "days of her life", because the Tree of Life has sent to her life and shines upon her.' Said R. Abba: 'All this is well said, and all these verses can be applied to the Community of Israel.'

IF A WOMAN CONCEIVE SEED. We have learnt that if a woman conceives the seed first, the child is a male. Said R. Aha: 'But have we not learnt that God decrees whether the semen is to be male or female?'

R. Yose replied: 'Indeed, God distinguishes whether the germ itself comes from a male or female source, [Tr. note: According to the Zohar, the seed itself contains both a male and a female element. v. Zohar, Exodus, 161b.] and therefore He decrees whether the child is to be male or female.' R. Aha also asked why the word "conceive-seed" is used instead of merely "conceive".

R. Yose answered: 'A woman from the time she becomes pregnant till she is delivered can talk of nothing but the child she is to bear, whether it is to be a boy or a girl.'

R. Hizkiah adduced here the verse: "O Lord, how manifold are thy works" (Ps. CIV, 24). 'How manifold', he said, 'are the works of the Holy King in the world! He is like a man who takes in his hand a number of

bundles of seed and sows them all at once, and in time each kind comes up separately. So the Holy One, blessed be He, accomplished His work with wisdom; with wisdom He took all together and sowed them and afterwards they all issued each in its time, as it says: "In wisdom hast thou made them all".' R. Abba said: 'They were all secreted in Wisdom, and they did not issue into being save by certain paths alongside of Understanding (Binah), whence they become firmly established. Observe that when a man goes to unite with his wife in sanctity, his holy thought awakens a spirit compounded of male and female, and God signals to a messenger who is in charge of the conception of human beings and entrusts to him that spirit and informs him where to deposit it, and also lays various injunctions on the spirit itself. Then the spirit goes down to earth along with a certain form which bore its image above, and in that form it is created and goes about in this world; and so long as that form is with a man, he retains his form in this world.

'In the book of the sorceries of Asmodai we find that one who knows how to practise magic from the side of the left should rise by the light of the lamp and utter certain incantations and call the unclean sides by their names and prepare his forms for those whom he invites and say he is ready for their commands. Then that man passes out of the dominion of his Master and places himself in charge of the unclean side. And through his incantations two spirits appear in the shape of men which show him how to confer certain benefits or do certain kinds of harm at certain specified times. It is forbidden to a man to abandon any vessel of his house into the possession of the "other side", for many emissaries are in wait to punish such an act, and from that time blessings do not rest upon him-all the more if he assigns to the "other side" the most precious part of himself. For from that time he belongs to it, and when the time comes for the celestial form which has been given to him to depart from this world, the evil spirit to which he clung comes and takes it, and it is never again restored to him.

'When the soul is about to descend to this world, it first goes down to the terrestrial Garden of Eden and sees there the glory of the souls of the righteous, and then it goes down to Gehinnom and sees the wicked who cry "Woe, woe", and find no compassion. That holy form stands by him until he emerges into the world,

after which it keeps him company and grows up with him. Observe that all spirits are compounded of male and female, and when they go forth into the world they go forth as both male and female, and afterwards the two elements are separated. If a man is worthy they are afterwards united, and it is then that he truly meets his mate and there is a perfect union both in spirit and flesh. Hence it is written here: "When a woman conceives seed and bears a male", and not "male and female together", since on account of the ways of the world they are not united (at birth) as they were when they issued from on high, because the first man and his mate sinned before God. Therefore they are separated until, if a man is worthy, it pleases God to restore to him his mate. But if he is not worthy, she is given to another, and they bear children whom they should not.'

R. Eleazar said: 'This is not so. All at first comprise both male and female, and they are separated afterwards. But if the woman bears a male, they are then united from the side of the right, and if she bears a female, from the side of the left, this side being then predominant. Hence, if the male child issues from the side of the left, he is effeminate, but if from the side of the right, he has mastery over the female.

'Many myriads are brought forth at every hour, but they are not called souls until they are settled in a body, and this is only after thirty-three days.

SHE SHALL BE UNCLEAN SEVEN DAYS. Because for seven days spirits do not go in to abide with her; for seven days the spirit seeks for its place in the body, and only on the eighth day does it settle there so that body and soul may appear before the Matrona and unite with Her.

'AND SHE SHALL CONTINUE IN THE BLOOD OF HER PURIFYING THREE AND THIRTY DAYS. These are to allow the spirit to settle in the body. The three extra days are the first three after the circumcision, during which the child is in pain and the spirit cannot settle down in the body.

SHE SHALL TOUCH NO HALLOWED THING. Every day the Community of Israel takes from the household of the King food for the spirits of men and feeds

Zohar: Vayikra, Section 3, Page 44a

them in holiness, save for these, the spirits of which have not yet settled in the bodies. But after thirty-three days She tends them like all other human beings, because their spirits are united with their bodies as in all other men. In the case of a female double the number of days is required, because, as stated above, the side of the left is predominant, and therefore it takes twice as long in the case of a female for the spirit to be united with the body.'

R. Judah adduced here the verse: "There is none holy as the Lord, for there is none beside thee, neither is there any rock like our God" (I Sam. II, 2). 'Are there then other holy ones or other rocks besides the Lord? Yes, there are holy ones above, as it is written: "The demand is by the word of the holy ones" (Dan. IV, 14), and Israel are holy below, but none are holy like the Lord, because "there is none beside thee", that is, God's holiness is not like their holiness, for He does not require their holiness, but they could not be holy without Him. Also, "there is no rock (zur) like our God", or, as we may translate, "no fashioner like our God", as explained elsewhere; for the Holy One, blessed be He, shapes a form within a form, and finishes it and breathes into it the breath of life and brings it out into the open.'

R. Hiya and R. Aha were sitting one night with R. Abba. They rose at midnight to study the Torah, and when they went outside they saw a star strike another star three times and put out its light. They then heard two voices from different directions, one from the north above and one

Zohar: Vayikra, Section 3, Page 44b

below, which proclaimed: "Go now in to your places, now the hollow of the abyss is closed and the Holy One, blessed be He, goes into the Garden to have joyous communion with the righteous there". The voice then died away, and R. Aha and R. Abba turned their heads and said: 'Verily this is the hour when the Community of Israel arises to join the Holy King. Verily the Community of Israel meets the Holy One, blessed be He, only with song and praise until morning, and the King twines round her a thread of grace, and not round her alone but round all who accompany her. Let us go and join her.' So they all sat down.

R. Aha then discoursed on the verse: "And the Lord God said, It is not good that the man should be alone", etc. (Gen. II, 18). He said: 'Was man then alone? Is it not written, "male and female he created them", and we have learnt that man was created "with two faces"? What it means, however, is that the male did not concern himself with the female and had no support from her; she was at his side and they were like one from the back. Therefore God sawed him in two and separated the female from him and brought her to the man, so that they should be face to face. And when she was gathered in to man, then God blessed them, like the reader of the service who blesses the bride with seven blessings. Therefore he who unites with the wife of another impairs the union, for the union of the Community of Israel is with the Holy One, blessed be He, alone, whether it is a time with him of mercy or of judgement. He who joins with the wife of another is like one who denies the Holy One, blessed be He, and the Community of Israel, and therefore he does not obtain forgiveness by repentance until he departs from the world, until he enters repentant into the other world to receive his punishment.' R. Eleazar said: 'He who denies the Community of Israel is not received as a penitent until he has been punished in Gehinnom; all the more so if he denies both the Community of Israel and the Holy One, blessed be He, and all the more so if he caused God the trouble of forming a bastard in the wife of another.' R. Hiya said: 'It is written, "Whoso robbeth his father and his mother", etc. (Prov. XXVIII, 24). The "father" here', he said, 'is the Holy One, blessed be He, and the "mother" is the Community of Israel; and we have learnt, Whoever enjoys anything of this world without a blessing is like one who robs the Holy One and the Community of Israel. So he who has enjoyment of his wife without a blessing is like one who robs the Holy One and the Community of Israel, because their union is consummated by seven blessings. Further, he is "the companion of the destroyer" (Ibid.), because he impairs the celestial form and arrangement: all the more so, then, one who covets the wife of another to cleave to her.'

Zohar: Vayikra, Section 3, Page 45a

R. Abba then discoursed on the verse: "And he said, Let me go, for the day breaketh" (Gen. XXXII, 26)....

[Tr. note: Here follow in the text certain reflections on the conflict of Jacob and the angel which have appeared in substance elsewhere.] Why was not the angel able to prevail over Jacob? Because the sun had risen and his strength was crippled.... For when the light appears, all the emissaries of punishment are restrained, and then the Community of Israel communes with the Holy One, blessed be He, and that hour is a time of grace for all, and the King holds out to her and all who are with her his sceptre of the thread of grace so that they may be wholly united to the holy King. Observe this. When the Holy One, blessed be He, is in the company of the Community of Israel, if she first makes approaches to him and draws him towards her in the strength of her love and desire, then she is replenished from the side of the right and multitudes from the side of the right are found in all worlds. But if the Holy One, blessed be He, is the first to make advances and she

Zohar: Vayikra, Section 3, Page 45b

only rouses herself afterwards, then all is on the side of the female and many multitudes arise on the side of the left in all worlds. Hence it is written: "When a woman conceives seed and bears a male", etc., the lower world being on the model of the upper, and in all things a man should concentrate his thoughts above on the Holy One, blessed be He, that grace may abound in the world. Happy are the righteous who know how to concentrate their thoughts on the holy King; of them it is written: "Ye who cleave unto the Lord your God are all alive this day" (Deut. IV, 4).

WHEN A MAN SHALL HAVE IN THE SKIN OF HIS FLESH A RISING OR A SCAB OR A BRIGHT SPOT, ETC. R. Judah here cited the verse: "Look not upon me because I am swarthy, because the sun hath scorched me", etc. (S.S. 1, 6). 'When the Moon was hidden in the exile and she saw the yearning of Israel for her, she said, "Look not on me", meaning, "You cannot see me, because I am in darkness-for one thing because the sun has withdrawn his light from me, and for another because "the sons of my mother were incensed against me" (Ibid.), these being the emissaries of the side of severity. "They made me keeper of the vineyards", that is, of other nations, whereas "my own vineyard"-Israel-I cannot keep. Formerly I kept my own vineyard and through it the others were also kept; now I have to keep the others that my own may be kept among them.' As R. Hiya and R. Yose were once going along, they came to a field where there was a balsam tree on the right. Said R. Yose: 'A pall of smoke must come before our eyes; it is forbidden us to look upon any glad sight since the day when the Temple was destroyed.' He then expounded the verse: "The earth is the Lord's and the fulness thereof, the world and they that dwell therein" (Ps. XXIV, 1). 'This "earth" ', he said, 'is the holy earth which is called "the land of the living", while "the world" refers to other lands.' R. Hiya said: 'The "earth" is as you said; the "fulness thereof" is the souls of the righteous; the "world" is this earth, and "they that dwell therein" are mankind.' Said R. Yose: 'If so, what do you make of the next verse: "For he hath founded it upon the seas and established it upon the waters"?' He replied: 'Assuredly that "land of the living" is established upon the seas and rivers which issue from that supernal River that proceeds from Eden.'

As they were going along they came across a man standing under a tree whose face was full of the marks of blows. They noticed

Zohar: Vayikra, Section 3, Page 46a

that his face was all red from the blows. Said R. Hiya to him: 'Who are you?' He replied: 'I am a Jew.' Said R. Yose: 'He must be a sinner, as otherwise his face would not have all those marks, and these are not what are called "chastisements of love".' Said R. Hiya: 'Assuredly that is so, for the "chastisements of love" are hidden from view. So with the plague of leprosy, of those marks which are visible to all, it is written, "And the priest shall see and declare him unclean", for assuredly those come from the side of uncleanness and are not chastisements of love. In the same way, he who reproves his neighbour in love should not let other men hear in order that he may not be ashamed; and if he reproves him publicly he does not show true friendship. So God, in reproving a man, acts with him lovingly. At first He smites him inwardly. If he repents, well and good, but if not, he smites him under his garments, and this is called "chastisement of love". If he still does not repent, God smites him on his face where all can see, so that they may know that he is a sinner and not beloved of his Master.' The man thereupon said to them: 'You are in a conspiracy against me: of a surety you are of those who frequent the house of R. Simeon ben Yohai, who have no fear of anyone. If my sons were to come up, they would punish you for speaking thus loudly.' They said: 'The Law teaches us to do so, as it says, "Wisdom crieth in the chief places of concourse", etc. (Prov. I, 21). If we were to be afraid to speak words of the Torah before thee, we should be ashamed before God.' The man thereupon lifted up his hands and wept. Meanwhile his sons came up. The youngest one said: 'The support of heaven is here. King Solomon said: "All have I seen in the days of my vanity" (Eccl. VII, 15). In the days of King Solomon the moon was full, and Solomon was the wisest of men and he saw all: he saw "All" attached to the Moon and illuminating her like the sun. Now, when the righteous are numerous in the world, this "All" does not depart from the Sun, and receives all anointing and joy from above to unite with the Moon, for whose sake it is thus enriched. But when sinners are numerous in the world, and the Moon is darkened, the "Righteous One perisheth in his righteousness", that is, he loses all this as he cannot unite with the Moon. Then, too, all the side of the left is aroused, and the prosperity of sinners is prolonged;

hence it is written, "and there is a wicked man who prolongeth his life in his evildoing". Also we may interpret the words, "there is a righteous man that perisheth in his righteousness", to mean that when sinners multiply and judgement impends, the righteous man is seized for their sins, like my father, who has been punished for the sins of the townsfolk who are all law-breakers, because he did not chide them or try to stop them, taking as his guide the verse, "Quarrel not with evildoers, be not zealous against them that work unrighteousness".' His father said: 'In truth God has punished me for this, because I had the power to prevent them and I did not do so, and I did not reprove them either openly or secretly.' His other son then cited the verse: "And the Lord God formed man of the dust of the ground", etc. (Gen. II, 7). 'Man was formed with two inclinations, the good and the evil, one corresponding to Water and the other to Fire. The word "man" (adam) indicates a combination of male and female. The dust from which he was formed was that of the Holy Land, of the Sanctuary. "He breathed in his nostrils the breath of life": this is the holy soul which derives from the life above. "And the man became a living soul": he was provided with a holy soul from the supernal "living being" which the earth brought forth. Now, as long as that holy soul is attached to a man, he is beloved of his Master, he is guarded on all sides, he is marked out for good above and below, and the holy divine presence rests upon him. But if he perverts his ways the divine presence leaves him, the super-soul does not cling to him, and from the side of the evil serpent a spirit arises which can abide only in a place whence the heavenly holiness has departed, and so a man becomes defiled and his flesh, his facial appearance and his whole being, is distorted. Observe that because this "living soul" is holy, therefore when the holy land absorbs it, it is called "super-soul" (neshamah); it is this which ascends and speaks before the holy King and enters without let or hindrance in all gates, and therefore it is called "speaking spirit". [Tr. note: v. Targum Onkelos, in loco.] Hence the Torah proclaims, "Keep thy tongue from evil", etc. (Ps. XXXIV, 14), because if a man's lips and tongue speak evil words, those words mount aloft and all proclaim "keep away from the evil word of so-and-so, leave the path clear for the mighty serpent". Then the holy soul leaves him and is not able to speak: it is in shame and distress, and is not given a place as before. Hence it is written, "Whoso keepeth his mouth and his tongue keepeth his soul from troubles" (Prov. XXI, 23). For that soul which was vocal is reduced to silence on account of the evil word. Then the serpent gets ready, and when that evil word finds its way to him, then many spirits bestir themselves, and one spirit comes down from that side and finds the man who uttered the evil word, and lights upon him and defiles him, and he becomes leprous. And just as a man is punished for uttering an evil word, so he is punished for not uttering a good word when he had the opportunity, because he harms that speaking spirit which was prepared to speak both above and below in holiness. All the more so if the people walk in crooked ways and he is able to speak to them and reprove them and does not do so. So David said: "I held my peace from good and my trouble was stirred" (Ps. XXXIX, 3), alluding to his leprosy.'

R. Hiya and R. Yose then came and kissed him, and they kept together the whole of that journey.

WHEN A PLAGUE OF LEPROSY IS ON A MAN HE SHALL BE BROUGHT UNTO THE PRIEST. R. Yose said: 'The Companions have studied all the varieties of this plague, and the priest used to know which were chastisements of love and which were a sign that a man was rejected and spurned by his Master; for the plague lights upon mankind according to their works. It is written: "Incline not my heart to any evil thing, to be occupied in deeds of wickedness" (Ps. CXLI, 4).' Said R. Isaac: 'Does God then lead men astray into the ways of sin and evildoing? If so, how can the Torah say, "If thou hearkenest, if thou dost not hearken"? We should, however, translate: "Do not incline, O my heart, to an evil thing (word), for an evil word brings the plague of leprosy upon the world". The Companions have pointed out that the Aramaic translation of leprosy (segiru) means "shutting up", and indicates shutting up both above and below. In a similar sense it is written: "He hath defiled the sanctuary of the Lord" (Num. XIX, 20).' Said R. Eleazar: 'He defiles it because the Divine Presence departs from thence and the mighty serpent takes up his abode there and casts filth there and causes defilement, and all because of men's sins.'

AND IF A MAN'S HAIR BE FALLEN OFF HIS HEAD. R. Hiya cited here the verse: "Then I saw that wisdom excelleth folly as light excelleth darkness" (Eccl. II, 13).

'Where', he said, 'is the great wisdom in this remark of king Solomon? Does not anyone, even one who has no wisdom himself, know that wisdom is superior to folly as light to darkness, and why, therefore, does Solomon say, "Then I saw"? The truth, however, is that what is meant is that there is an excellence or profit to wisdom from folly itself, for if there were no folly, wisdom and its words would not be recognized. We have learnt that it is incumbent on a man when he learns wisdom to learn a little folly also, since there is a certain benefit to wisdom from it as there is to light from darkness. We have also learnt that this applies to the supernal Wisdom, for R. Simeon said to R. Abba: The supernal Wisdom does not illumine or become illumined save on account of the folly that arises from another place, and but for this it would have no superiority or excellence, and the profit of wisdom would not be discernible. So on earth, if there were no folly there would be no wisdom. Therefore did Rab Hamnuna the Elder, when he instructed the Companions in the secrets of wisdom, also give them a discourse full of folly, that wisdom might benefit therefrom. Therefore it is written: "More precious than wisdom and than honour is a little folly" (Eccl. x, 1).' R. Yose said: 'This means that a little folly reveals and displays the honour of wisdom and the glory of heaven more than anything else. So the benefit of light is only felt from its contrast with darkness, and similarly white is only known and valued from its contrast with black.' R. Isaac said: 'It is the same with sweet and bitter: a man does not know what sweet is until he tastes bitter.

Zohar: Vayikra, Section 3, Page 48a

'We have learnt: Man in the Scripture has four names– adam, geber, enosh, ish–and the highest of them is adam.' Said R. Judah: 'But is it not written, "When a man (adam) shall bring from you an offering" (Lev. I. 2), and who is it that requires to bring an offering? Is it not a sinner?' R. Isaac replied: 'The offering is the mainstay of the world, of upper and lower beings, the solace of the Almighty, and who is fitting to offer it? Surely this man who is called Adam.' Said R. Judah: 'If so, what of the verse, "When a man (adam) has on the skin of his flesh... and it become in the skin of his flesh the plague of leprosy"?' He replied: 'This one God desires to heal more than all others, and therefore it is written concerning him, "he shall be brought unto the priest"; it is the duty of anyone who sees him to bring him to the priest, in order that the holy image may not remain thus.' Said R. Judah: 'But it is written, "Now Moses the man (ish)"; why is he not called "adam"?' He replied: 'Because he was the "servant of the king", and therefore he is called ish in relation to the supernal Adam. But,' he said, 'why then is it written, "The Lord is a man (ish) of war"?' He replied: 'The secret of the Lord is to them that fear him.' Said R. Judah: 'I too am one of them, yet I have not been privileged to hear this.' Said the other: 'Go to R. Abba, for I learnt it from him only on condition that I should not tell.' So he went to

R. Abba, and found him discoursing and saying: 'When is there said to be completeness above? When the Holy One, blessed be He, sits on his throne. For so it is written: "And upon the likeness of the throne was the likeness as the appearance of a man (adam) upon it above" (Ezek. 1, 26); the term "adam" indicates wholeness and completeness.' Said R. Judah: 'God be blessed that I have found you discoursing thus. Tell me: is it not written, "The Lord is a man (ish) of war"?' Said R. Abba: 'Your question is a good one, and the answer is this. At the Red Sea there was not yet full consummation, and therefore God was called ish; but in the vision of Ezekiel there was full consummation, and therefore God was called adam.' '"The law of thy mouth is better to me than thousands of gold and silver" (Ps. CXIX, 72),' exclaimed R. Judah. 'But', he continued, 'it is also written, "O Lord, thou preservest man (adam) and beast" (Ps. XXXVI, 7). Should not the term ish be used here?' He said: 'This is analogous to the expression: "From the cedar which is in Lebanon to the hyssop that springeth out of the wall" (I Kings v, 13); it is the way of the Scripture in such cases to mention the two extremes.' 'But,' he went on, 'is it not written: "And there was no man (adam) to till the ground" (Gen. II, 5)?' He answered: 'Everything in the world was only made for the sake of man, and all things were kept back until he that was called Adam should appear, since his form was after the divine prototype, and when he was created all was complete.'

R. Yose said: 'The Hayoth which Ezekiel saw all had the form of man.' 'But', said R. Judah, 'it is written: "And the face of an eagle... and the face of a lion", etc.?'

Zohar: Vayikra, Section 3, Page 48b

He replied: 'All had the face of man, but in this face itself was seen the resemblance of an eagle, etc.'

R. Isaac said: 'Observe, that whoever is under the control of "adam" is called "ish", because the complete form of Adam was only reached from another previous form. For it has been taught in the profound mysteries of the Book of Concealed Wisdom that when man was created in the holy supernal form there came down with him two spirits from two sides, one from the right and one from the left, which between them formed the complete man. The one from the right was called the holy neshamah, as it says: "And he breathed in his nostrils the neshamah of life" (Gen. II, 7), while the other was called "living soul" (nefesh hayah). When man sinned there were formed from this spirit of the left creatures whose body was not complete, and these are called "the plagues of the sons of men", and they hear certain things on high which they communicate to those below. Now it has been taught: From the Lamp of Darkness [Tr. note: v. Zohar, Gen. 15a.] issued three hundred and twenty-five sparks traced out and linked together from the side of Geburah, and when these entered the Body it was called Ish.' Said R. Judah: 'Why so?' R. Isaac could not answer. So they went and asked R. Simeon, who replied: 'Because the lower judgements are attached to the hair of this one, [Tr. note: According to the anthropomorphic symbolism of the Sifra di-Zeniutha.] he is called "Stern Judgement", but when the hair is removed he becomes mitigated and the lower judgements are not held in readiness. Therefore he is called clean, as having emerged from the side of uncleanness, and here too it is written: "And if the hair of ish be fallen off his head, he is bald, he is clean." Similarly among men, if one is from the side of judgement and is liable to punishment, he is not purified until his hair is removed. So the Levites who came from this side were not purified until their hair was removed; and they required the Priests who came from the side of Lovingkindness to assist them, just as above when that Ish desires to be more exhilarated

Zohar: Vayikra, Section 3, Page 49a

the supernal Lovingkindness is displayed in him, and he becomes mitigated, and this Ish becomes merged in Adam.

AND IF HIS HAIR BE FALLEN OFF FROM THE FRONT PART OF HIS HEAD. This front part is what is called 'the face of wrath", and all who depend from that "face" are bold, stern and cruel. But when the "hair" is removed from the side of that "face", all these are removed and rendered powerless. For, as we have learnt, all those who depend from the "hair of the head" are superior to the others and not bold-faced like them. Hence the faces of the latter are red like fire from the flashing of the Lamp of Darkness.' Rabbi Isaac said: 'This plague is called "reddish-white" (Lev. XIII, 42); it is still a plague if the white is visible and the red has not disappeared. When, however, the whole has become white, mercy is present and judgement departs.'

Rabbi Abba said: 'Sometimes the Female is sullied by the sins of men and sometimes the Male, and the priest knew from which side the punishment came, and he also knew the sacrifices which ought to be brought, as it is written: "The sacrifices of Elohim (i.e. sacrifices to avert punishment) are a contrite spirit" (Ps. LI, 18).'

Zohar: Vayikra, Section 3, Page 49b

R. Yose quoted the verse: "O thou that hearest prayer, unto thee shall all flesh come" (Ps. LXV, 2). 'This means, at the time when the body is in pain from sickness and blows, and therefore it says "all flesh" and not "all spirit". Similarly it is written: "If there be a plague of leprosy in a man, he shall be brought unto the priest", the "priest" referring to the Holy One, blessed be He, since on Him depends all purification and holiness.' R. Isaac said: 'We have learnt as follows. "Plague" means stern judgement impending over the world. "Leprosy" means the shutting out from the world of the supernal light and goodness. "When it shall be in a man": this is he that is called "man". "He shall be brought unto the priest": this is the earthly priest, who is qualified to open what has been shut up and to kindle the lights, that blessings may through him be spread above and below, and the plague be removed and the light of mercy rest upon all.'

R. Abba said: 'I am struck by the way in which men neglect the honour of their Master. It is written concerning Israel: "I have separated you from the peoples to be mine" (Lev. xx, 26), and again, "Ye shall sanctify yourselves and be holy, for I the Lord am holy" (Ibid. 7). If they depart from God, where is their holiness, seeing that their thoughts are turned from Him? And Scripture cries to them saying: "Be not as the horse or as the mule which have no understanding" (Ps. XXXII, 9). In what are human beings distinguished from the horse and the mule? By sanctification and self-perfection. Hence the marital intercourse of human beings should be at fixed times, that they may concentrate their thoughts on cleaving to the Holy One, blessed be He. As has been pointed out, at midnight God enters the Garden of Eden to have communion with the righteous, and the Community of Israel praises the Holy One, blessed be He, and that is a propitious time to cleave to Him. But as for the Companions who study the Torah, the time of their intercourse is at the time of another intercourse, from Sabbath to Sabbath, [Tr. note: v. T.B. Ketuboth, 62b.] for that is the time when all above and below are blessed. But if men abandon Him and act like beasts, where are those holy souls which they derive from above? King Solomon also cries aloud: "Also without knowledge the soul is not good" (Prov. XIX, 2), for they draw upon themselves a soul that is not good from the "other side". He who is inflamed with the evil inclination and turns not his thoughts to God draws upon himself a soul which is not good. Therefore evil diseases light upon men and their appearance testifies that God has rejected them and will not heed them until they

Zohar: Vayikra, Section 3, Page 50a

amend their ways. Similarly it is written: "When ye be come into the land of Canaan... and I put a plague of leprosy in a house of the land of your possession", etc. (Lev. XIV, 34). God loved Israel and brought them into the Holy Land to place His divine presence among them and to make His abode with them, so that Israel should be holy above all other peoples. Now, when the women brought articles for the Tabernacle they used to specify what part each was for: "this is for the holy place, this for the curtain", and so forth, and each thing went to its place in holiness. Similarly, whenever anyone makes a thing for idolatrous worship, or the "other side", as soon as he mentions its name in connection with that thing, an unclean spirit rests upon it. Now the Canaanites were idolaters, and whenever they erected a building they used to utter certain idolatrous formulae, and a spirit of uncleanness rested on the building. But when the Israelites entered the land, God desired to purify them and sanctify the land and prepare a place for His divine presence, and so through that plague of leprosy they used to pull down buildings which had been erected in uncleanness. Now if they had done so merely that they might find hidden treasures, they would have replaced the stones afterwards; but the text says, "and they shall take out the stones... and he shall take other mortar", in order that the unclean spirit may pass away and the holiness return and the Shekinah abide in Israel. Therefore, when a man begins to set up a building he should declare that he is building for the service of God. Then the support of heaven is with him, and God assigns holiness to him and bids peace be with him. Otherwise he invites into his house the "other side"–all the more so if his inclination is to the "other side", for then, indeed, an unclean spirit will rest on the house, and that man will not leave this world until he has been punished in that house, and whoever dwells in it may come to hurt. If it is asked, How is one to know such a house? it is one in which the man who built it has come to harm, he or his family, whether through sickness or loss of money, he and two others after him. Better a man should fly to the mountains or live in a mud hut than dwell there. Therefore God had pity on Israel, who knew nothing of all those houses. He said: "You do not know, but I know them, and I will indicate them with the plague. There is a plague in the house; here is a greater plague which will drive it out." Hence "he shall break down the house, the stones thereof and the timber thereof." We may ask, since the uncleanness has gone, why should he break down the house? The reason is that as long as the house stands

Zohar: Vayikra, Section 3, Page 50b

it belongs to the "other side", and it may return. If that is the case in the Holy Land, how much more so in other lands!' Said R. Eleazar: 'Especially since that evil spirit calls his companions there, and even a hawk's talons could not scratch out the uncleanness from there. Therefore the Scripture says, "Woe unto him that buildeth his house by unrighteousness".'

R. Yose was once going into a house, and as he was crossing the threshold he heard a voice say: 'All now gather, here is one of our adversaries. Let us do him some hurt before he goes out again.' Another voice said: 'We cannot do him anything unless he takes up his abode here.' R. Yose drew back in great fear, saying: 'Assuredly, he who transgresses the words of the Companions endangers his life.' Said R. Hiya to him: 'But idolaters and other people live in such houses and come to no hurt?' He replied: 'They come from the same side as those spirits, but he that fears sin can be hurt by them. And even those others if they live there long will not come out in peace.' Said R. Hiya: 'But is it not written, "Their houses are safe from fear" (Job XXI, 9)?' He replied: 'It may be that they have taken them over from others, and that they were built originally in righteousness.'

THEN HE THAT OWNETH THE HOUSE SHALL COME AND TELL THE PRIEST, THERE SEEMETH TO ME TO BE AS IT WERE A PLAGUE IN THE HOUSE. The meaning of this verse is as follows. When this plague (of leprosy) enters, another (of uncleanness) is revealed, and they attack one another. Hence it says, "there seemeth" (lit. is seen) to me. Then the one that was concealed becomes visible and the one that was visible becomes hidden, and then reappears in the form of the leprosy, and this is what the owner "tells" the priest, who takes the hint. Then the priest comes, and the stones and wood are removed, and then the rest are blessed. Therefore it says, "Thou shalt build goodly houses and dwell therein" (Deut. VIII, 12); these are good, but the others were not good. 'But', said R. Judah, 'if that is so, what are we to make of the verse, "Houses full of all good things which thou filled not" (Deut. VI, 11)? How could they be full of good if an unclean spirit rested on them?'

R. Eleazar replied: 'It means, with money, with silver, with gold, and so forth: just as it is said elsewhere, "for the good of all the land of Egypt is yours", although all the houses of Egypt were full of magic and idolatry.' R. Simeon said: 'All this was indeed for the purpose of sanctifying the land and removing from it the unclean spirit, and when the house was destroyed he used to find in it money for building another, [Tr. note: v. Midrash Rabbah, in loco.] and so they were not distressed by the loss of the house, and besides, they dwelt there thenceforth in holiness.'

AND WHEN A MAN OR A WOMAN HATH IN THE SKIN OF THEIR FLESH BRIGHT SPOTS. R. Yose said: 'The "bright spot" is surrounded with many regulations as complicated as the wickerwork of a basket, all depending on the shade of colour.' R. Isaac said: 'Some authorities have formulated three hundred rules regarding the bright spot, and I learnt them all from my father. One black hair renders unclean, being like one witness; two render clean, being like two witnesses.' R. Hizkiah was once studying with R. Simeon. He said: 'It is written, "a reddish-white plague". This is a plague, because the white does not retain its purity.' R. Simeon said: 'Happy are Israel in that God desired to purify them, so that they should not come up for sentence before Him. For like always goes to like, red to red and white to white; right to right and left to left. Of Esau it is written, "and he came forth ruddy", and therefore his own kind rests upon him.'

Zohar: Vayikra, Section 3, Page 51a

It is true, David is also called "ruddy" (I Sam. XVI, 12), but whereas Esau's redness came from the "dross of gold", David's came from the brightness of gold. Observe that if there is first redness and then it turns whitish, this is a sign of the commencement of purifying. If white appears first, and then it reddens, this is a sign that uncleanness is commencing. The priest knew all these colours, and if the colour of cleanness appeared, he used to shut up the man to see if another colour would appear, and if not, he would declare him clean.'

As R. Isaac and R. Judah were once walking together, the latter remarked: 'It is written: "Elisha said to Gehazi, The leprosy of Naaman shall cleave unto thee and unto thy seed forever" (2 Kings v, 27). Now, if he sinned, why should his descendants be stricken?' R. Isaac replied: 'Elisha saw more than most prophets. He saw that Gehazi would never have virtuous offspring, and therefore he cursed all of them. Moreover, he said to him, I served Elijah faithfully, and therefore obtained two portions, but you, villain, have compromised me by swearing falsely and being covetous. You have transgressed the whole of the Law, and therefore deserve to die in this world and the next, but because you have served me, your death shall only be in this world and not in the next.'

R. Yose asked: 'Why should there be leprosy on wool and flax?' R. Isaac replied: 'It rests on all things and has sway over all. It is written, "She seeketh wool and flax", and therefore the sway of this plague which comes from this same supernal place extends over all, over these two articles, wool and flax.'

R. Isaac was once going to his father's home when he saw a man turning aside from the road with a load on his shoulders. He said to him: 'What is that bundle you have on your shoulders?' but the man gave him no answer. So he followed him till he saw him enter a cave. He went in after him and saw a cloud of smoke ascend from beneath the ground, while the man went into a hole and he lost sight of him. R. Isaac then left the cave in great fear. As he was sitting there, R. Judah and R. Hizkiah passed by. He went up to them and told them what had happened. Said R. Judah: 'Thank God for delivering you. That cave is where the lepers of Sarunia are, and all the inhabitants of that town are magicians and go into the desert to get black snakes ten years old or more, and through not being careful of them they become leprous, and all their magic arts are in that cave.' They then left the spot. On their way they came across a man who had with him a sick child tied to an ass. They asked him why the boy was tied. He replied: 'I live in a town of the Arameans, and my son here used to learn the Torah every day, and when he came home used to go over what he had learnt. Three years I lived in the same house and observed nothing wrong, but now one day when my son went into the house to repeat his lesson an evil spirit passed before him and distorted his eyes and his mouth and his hands, so that he is not able to speak. So I am going to the cave of the lepers of Sarunia to see if they can show me how to cure him.' R. Judah said to him:

Zohar: Vayikra, Section 3, Page 51b

'Do you know of any other person having come to harm in that house before?' He replied: 'I know that a long time ago a man did come to harm there, but people said that it was just an illness, while others said that it was the evil spirit of the house. Since then many people have been in the house without suffering any harm.' They said: 'This proves the truth of what the Companions said. Woe to those who disregard their words.' Said R. Judah: 'It is written, "Woe to him that buildeth his house without righteousness" (Jer. XXII, 13), because wherever there is righteousness all evil spirits fly from before it. Yet withal, whichever comes first to the place takes possession of it.' Said R. Hizkiah: 'If so, the holy Name is merely on a level with the unclean spirit?' He replied: 'Not so. If the holy spirit is there first, no evil spirits can appear there, much less approach. But if the evil spirit is there first, the holy Name does not rest upon it. Now when the plague of leprosy came, one had to purify the place and drive out the unclean spirit, and afterwards the house was taken down and built up again in holiness with the mention of the holy Name; and still other mortar had to be used and the foundation was removed two handbreadths. Nowadays, however, that the plague does not appear, there being thus no one able to drive out the evil spirit, what is the remedy? The best thing is to remove from the house, but if this cannot be done, it should be rebuilt with fresh wood and stones, and a little away from the previous spot, with the mention of the holy Name.' R. Isaac said to him: 'Why should one take all this trouble in these days, since it is written: "That which is crooked cannot be made straight" (Eccl. I, 15)? Since the destruction of the Temple there is no remedy; hence a man should be very careful.'

They said: 'Let us go along with this man and see.' Said R. Isaac: 'We may not. If we were going to a great and God-fearing man, like Naaman to Elisha, we could accompany him. But as he is going to such abandoned and godless people we must not.' 'But', said R. Judah, 'we have learnt that for healing sickness anything may be used save the wood of an Asherah?' [Tr. note: v. Deut. XVI, 21.] He replied: 'This too is idolatry.' So they went on their way. The man then entered the cave with his son, and left him there while he went out to tether his ass. Meanwhile a cloud of smoke came out and struck the boy on the head and killed him. When the father went in, he found him dead, so he took him and his ass, and on the next day came up with R. Isaac and R. Judah and R. Hizkiah. With many tears he related to them what had happened. Said R. Isaac: 'Did I not tell you many times that it was forbidden to enter there? Blessed are the righteous who walk in the way of truth in this world and in the next.' R. Eleazar said: 'In all his actions a man should have in mind the holy Name and declare that all is for the service of God, so that the "other side" should not rest on him, for this is ever lying in wait for man. Therefore it was that the warp and the woof used to become unclean

Zohar: Vayikra, Section 3, Page 52a
and the "other side" rested on them.'

R. Eleazar was once going to see his father-in-law, accompanied by R. Abba. He said: 'Let us discourse on the Torah as we go.' R. Eleazar then took as his text the verse: "Say, I pray thee, thou art my sister" (Gen. XII, 13). 'This', he said, 'is very strange. Can we believe that a God-fearing man like Abram should speak thus to his wife in order that he might be well treated? The truth is, however, that Abram relied on the merit of his wife, and not on his own merit, to procure for him the money of the heathen, for a man obtains money through the merit of his wife, as it is written: "House and riches are an inheritance from fathers, but a prudent wife is from the Lord" (Prov. XIX, 14). Further, he saw an angel going before her, who said to him: "Fear not, Abram, God sent me to procure for her the money of the heathen and to protect her from all harm". Hence Abram did not fear for his wife but for himself, since he saw the angel with her but not with himself. Therefore he said to her: "Say, I pray thee, that thou art my sister, that he (the angel) may do good to me in this world, and that my soul may live in the next world for thy sake, if thou departest not from the right way, for otherwise death awaits me in this world." '

R. Abba discoursed on the verse: "As in the day of thy coming forth from the land of Egypt will I show unto him marvellous things" (Mic. VII, 15). He said: 'God will one day bring deliverance to his sons as in the days when He sent to deliver Israel and inflicted plagues on Egypt for their sake. What is the difference between this deliverance and that of Egypt? The deliverance in Egypt was from one king and one country: here it will be from all the kings of the earth. Then God will be glorified in all the world, and all shall know His dominion, as it is written: "The Lord shall be king over the whole earth" (Zech. XIV, 9). And they shall bring Israel as an offering to the Holy One, blessed be He, as it is written, "And they shall bring all your brethren", etc. (Isa. LXVI, 20). Then the patriarchs shall rejoice to see the deliverance of their sons, and so it is written: "As in the days of thy going forth from Egypt I shall show him wonders." '

Zohar: Vayikra, Section 3, Page 52b

MEZORA'

AND THE LORD SPOKE UNTO MOSES SAYING, THIS SHALL BE THE LAW OF THE LEPER. R. Abba cited here the verse: "Be ye afraid of the sword, for wrath bringeth the punishments of the sword, that ye may know there is a judgement" (Job XIX, 29). 'Observe,' he said, 'that through the evil tongue of the serpent death came upon the world. The evil tongue is called a "sharp sword" (Ps. LVII, 5), and therefore it says, "Be ye afraid of the sword", to wit, of the evil tongue. Why? "For wrathful are the punishments of the sword", to wit, the sword of the Lord, "that ye may know there is a judgement", for he that hath a sword in his tongue is punished with the sword; hence it says, "this is the law of the leper".'

Zohar: Vayikra, Section 3, Page 53a

R. Eleazar said: 'When a man is on the point of leaving this world, his soul suffers many chastisements along with his body before they separate. Nor does the soul actually leave him until the Shekinah shows herself to him, and then the soul goes out in joy and love to meet the Shekinah. If he is righteous, he cleaves and attaches himself to her. But if not, then the Shekinah departs, and the soul is left behind, mourning for its separation from the body, like a cat which is driven away from the fire. Afterwards both are punished by the hand of Dumah. The body is punished in the grave and the soul in the fire of Gehinnom for the appointed period. When this is completed she rises from Gehinnom purified of her guilt like iron purified in the fire, and she is carried up to the lower Garden of Eden, where she is cleansed in the waters of Paradise and perfumed with its spices, and there she remains till the time comes for her to depart from the abode of the righteous. Then she is carried up stage after stage until she is brought near like a sacrifice to the altar. Hence it is written, "This shall be the law of the leper on the day of his cleansing: he shall be brought to the priest", to wit, to the angelic Priest above. This is the fate of a soul which has not been defiled overmuch in this world, and which can yet be healed in this way; but otherwise, "that which is crooked cannot be made straight".'

R. Isaac cited the verse: "The sun also ariseth and the sun goeth down" (Eccl. I, 5). 'When a man's soul (neshamah)', he said, 'is with him in this world, then it may be said of him that "the sun riseth and the sun goeth down". And when man departs from this world in a frame of repentance then "he hasteth to his place where he ariseth". To those who repent, God grants pardon for all sins save for the evil tongue, as it is written: "This shall be the law of the leper", the word mezorah (leper) being interpreted as mozi shem ra' (slanderer).' [Tr. note: Cf. T.B. Erekhin, 16a; Shab, 97a.]

R. Hiya said: 'Whoever spreads false reports, all his limbs become defiled and he is meet for shutting up, because his evil speech rises aloft and calls down an unclean spirit on him. So it says: "How is the faithful city become an harlot" (Isa. I, 21). Because Jerusalem uttered evil speech, God departed from her and a spirit of murderers abode in her. If that was the fate of Jerusalem the holy city, how much more so must it be that of ordinary men! Hence it says, "This shall be the law of the leper".' R. Judah said: 'Zoth (this) [Tr. note: The Shekinah.] indeed shall confront him to punish him for his evil speech.

'ON THE DAY OF HIS CLEANSING HE SHALL BE BROUGHT TO THE PRIEST. This shows that the prayer of an evil speaker does not ascend to the Almighty, but if he repents, then "on the day of his cleansing he shall be brought to the Priest". 'THEN THE PRIEST SHALL COMMAND TO TAKE FOR HIM THAT IS TO BE CLEANSED TWO LIVING CLEAN BIRDS, ETC. When R. Isaac and R. Yose were once studying with R. Simeon, they said to him: 'We know the symbolism of the cedar tree the shoots of which are transplanted in Lebanon, as has been expounded. But what is the point of the hyssop?' He replied: 'It is written here, "two living clean birds and cedar wood and scarlet

Zohar: Vayikra, Section 3, Page 53b

and hyssop". "Living" is a reference to two of the "living creatures" (Hayoth) that Ezekiel saw, denoting the place from which the true prophets draw inspiration. "Cedar wood" we have explained. "Scarlet" indicates the place of Severity, which is associated with him at first. "Hyssop" is the lesser Vau which gives sustenance to the Community of Israel. All these again rest upon him because he has been purified.'

602

R. Judah and R. Isaac were once travelling together. They stopped at a certain field to pray, and then went on. R. Judah then commenced a discourse on the Torah, taking for his text: "She is a tree of life to them that lay hold of her and happy is every one that retaineth her" (Prov. III, 18). 'The "tree of life" is the Torah, which is a great and mighty tree. It is called Torah (lit. showing) because it shows and reveals that which was hidden and unknown; and all life from above is comprised in it and issues from it. He that "takes hold" of the Torah takes hold of all, above and below. "They that retain her" are those who put the profit of merchandise into the purses of students of the Torah; such become worthy of having a progeny of faithful prophets. Such, too, "retain" her from the beginning, which is Wisdom, to the "end of the body", and become pillars of the faith.'

R. Isaac discoursed on the verse: "And he called unto Moses, and the Lord spake unto him out of the tent of meeting, saying" (Lev. I, 1). 'Who was it that called? The One who abides in the sanctuary. Moses was greater than Aaron, for Moses was the guest of the King, and Aaron was the guest of the Matrona. Just as a king might appoint for his queen a companion to attend to her and her house, and therefore the companion would never appear before the king without the queen, so of Aaron it is written, "With zoth (this, i.e. the Shekinah) shall Aaron come", etc. (Lev. XVI, 3). Moses, however, was invited as a guest by the King himself, and afterwards "the Lord spoke to him". All Aaron's discourse was for the purpose of bringing harmony between the King and the Queen, and therefore he made his dwelling with her to attend to her house, and for this he was perfected after the supernal model and was called "high priest". So he obtained all his requests of the King, and therefore it fell to him to purify all those who came before the Queen, so that there should be none

unclean among those who entered the sanctuary. Hence it is written: "And he shall take for him that is to be cleansed two birds", etc.'

R. Judah cited the verse: "He that sitteth in the heavens shall laugh, the Lord shall have them in derision" (Ps. II, 4). The word "laugh", he said, has reference to Isaac, who came from the side of wine, which first smiles and then rages and kills. So God is patient with the wicked: if they turn to Him, it is well, but if not, He destroys them from the future world and they have no share in it.'

R. Hiya discoursed on the verse: "Behold a day of the Lord cometh when thy spoil shall be divided in the midst of thee" (Zech. XIV, 1). 'This day', he said, 'has been fixed from the creation of the world for punishing the wicked and for God to take vengeance on those that afflict Israel. That day ever comes and stands before God, and calls upon Him to execute judgement on the heathen.' R. Isaac said: 'God has two Days: one that stays with Him and one that comes before Him, and with these He makes war on all. And when that Day comes to make war, it unites with another Day, and they join arms and make war on high and low, as it is written: "For there is a day to the Lord of Hosts upon all that is proud and haughty and upon all that is lifted up, and it shall be brought low" (Isa. II, 12).' R. Simeon drew a similar lesson from the verse: "And if a woman have an issue of her blood many days", etc. (Lev. xv, 25).' 'The "blood" is that referred to in the verse, "The sword of the Lord is filled with blood" (Isa. XXXIV, 6). "Not in the time of her impurity", as we have learnt, that the wicked bring punishment on the world before its time. "Or if she hath an issue beyond the time of her impurity": this implies an excess of punishment, as it is written, "I will chastise you still more seven times for your sins" (Lev. XXVI, 18). "All the days of the issue of her uncleanness": this means that the wicked with their sins pollute both themselves and the sanctuary, and bring an unclean spirit upon themselves; but in time to come God will purify Israel and remove from them the unclean spirit.'

Once, when R. Hizkiah was studying with R. Eleazar, they rose at midnight, and R. Eleazar discoursed on the verse: "On the day of good be of good cheer, and on the day of evil observe, for God hath made one to match the other" (Eccl. VII, 14). 'When God', he said, 'lavishes kindness on the world, a man should go abroad and show himself, for God's kindness then extends to all. Therefore a man should do kindness that kindness may be shown to him. But at the time when judgement impends over the world a man should not show himself abroad

nor walk alone, for when judgement impends over the world it impends over all, and will strike anyone it lights upon. Therefore on that day look carefully on all sides and go not abroad, for God hath made one to match the other; just as when kindness is abroad it extends to all, so when judgement is over the world it is over all. How many swords, then, suspended from the most high sword, issue forth and, seeing that highest sword red and bloody on all sides, decree punishments and set to work!'

R. Eleazar further discoursed on the verse: "Set me as a seal upon thy heart", etc. (S.S. VIII, 6). 'The Community of Israel says this to the Holy One, blessed be He. The seal is the seal of the phylacteries which a man places on his heart; for by so doing a man makes himself perfect after the supernal model. "For love is strong as death": there is nothing so hard in the world as the separation of the soul from the body when they have to part; and similar is the love of the Community of Israel for the Holy One, blessed be He. "Jealousy is as cruel as Sheol": of all the grades of Gehinnom there is none so hard as Sheol, and he who is jealous of a beloved one finds it harder to part than the Sheol, which is the hardest grade of Gehinnom. "The flashes thereof are flashes of fire": this is the fire that issues from the Shofar, compounded of air and water. And with that flame the Community of Israel sets on fire the world when she is passionate for the Holy One, blessed be He, and woe to him who crosses the path of that flame 1' R. Eleazar further discoursed on the verse: "Many waters cannot quench love", etc. (Ibid. 7). 'This', he said, 'is the Right Arm which desires to bind the phylactery on the Left Arm, in accordance with the verse, "that his right hand might embrace me" (S.S. II, 6). Or again, the "waters" may be the primordial stream from which issue other streams in every direction. "If a man were to give all the substance of his house for love, it would be utterly contemned": this means that if the Holy One, blessed be He, were to offer to the angels all the substance of His house in lieu of His uniting with the Community of Israel, they would contemn it,

Zohar: Vayikra, Section 3, Page 55a

since they have no joy save in the hour when the Community of Israel unites with the Holy One, blessed be He. When a man puts on the phylactery of the hand, he should stretch out his left arm as though to draw to him the Community of Israel and to embrace her with the right arm, so as to copy the supernal model, as it is written, "O that his left hand were under my head and his right hand embraced me" (S.S. II, 6), for then is that man wholly sanctified.'

R. Hizkiah spoke on the verse: "Hear righteousness, O Lord, attend unto my cry" (Ps. XVII, 1). He said: 'Beloved is the Community of Israel before the Holy One, blessed be He, and whenever she comes before Him, He is ready to receive her. Hence David said: "I am linked with the Community of Israel, being before Thee as She is, and therefore, hearken, O Lord, unto Righteousness first, and then give ear unto my prayer".' He continues: '"Without feigned lips." What is this? We have learnt that every word of prayer that issues from a man's mouth ascends aloft through all firmaments to a place where it is tested. If it is genuine, it is taken up before the Holy King to be fulfilled, but if not, it is rejected, and an alien spirit is evoked by it. So it is written of Joseph, "His feet they hurt with fetters... until the time that his word came", that is, until the word of Joseph's prayer came to heaven and was tested; and then, "the king sent and loosed him".'

Meanwhile day had arrived. Said R. Eleazar: 'It is now time for the Community of Israel to be united with her Spouse. Happy are the righteous who study the Torah by night and then come to unite themselves with the Holy One, blessed be He, and the Community of Israel.' R. Eleazar continued: 'It is written: "Thus shall ye separate the children of Israel from their uncleanness" (Lev. xv, 31). When an unclean spirit is roused below, it rouses another unclean spirit above which obtains permission to go down to the world, when the spirit of holiness which used to come down and smite it is no longer there. Then judgement confronts sinners, and there are two harmful spirits in the world, one of judgement and one of uncleanness.' Said R. Eleazar: 'Here I must say something that I have learnt from my father. Just as when an unclean spirit rests upon a house, God sends a plague of leprosy to attack it and so cause the house to be purified, so if a spirit of uncleanness rests on a man and God desires to purify him, He rouses a spirit of stern judgement which contends with that unclean spirit until

Zohar: Vayikra, Section 3, Page 55b

it is expelled. Nor does that spirit of judgement depart until it has loosened the bodily frame. Then at last is the man purified and freed from the unclean spirits. Therefore we have learnt that if a man wants to defile himself, heaven helps to defile him, [Tr. note: T.B. Yoma, 38b.] and woe to a man when an unclean spirit is found in him all his life, for this indeed shows that God desires to clear him out of the world (to come). Happy are the righteous on whom rests a spirit of holiness in this world and in the world to come'.

When it was full day they went on their way, and R. Eleazar discoursed on the verse: "And Jacob went on his way, and the angels of God met him" (Gen. XXXII, 1). 'Observe', he said, 'that all the time that Jacob was with Laban God did not speak with him (save at the very end, when he was about to depart), but as soon as he had left him the angels came to meet and to escort him. It says that the angels met him (bo, lit. in him), not that he met them. This is to indicate that they were some from the side of mercy and some from the side of judgement, and they met and were united "in him". Hence he called the place mahanaim (lit. two camps). It is written of Esau, "And the first came forth red" (Gen. xxv. 25). Though Esau came forth first, he was not really the elder, since at the time of procreation Isaac's thoughts were

Zohar: Vayikra, Section 3, Page 56a

first centred on mercy, represented by Jacob, and afterwards on judgement, represented by Esau. Hence Jacob was really created first. R. Judah used to teach as follows. Esau is called "first", and God is also called "first", as it is written, "I am the first and I am the last" (Isa. XLIV, 6). The "first" will one day punish the "first" and rebuild the other "first", to wit, "A glorious throne set on high from the first, the place of our Sanctuary" (Jer. XVII, 12). We have learnt: One day the walls of Jerusalem will reach on high to the throne of the King, as it is written, "At that time they shall call Jerusalem the throne of the Lord" (Jer. III, 17).'

AHARE MOTH

AND THE LORD SPOKE UNTO MOSES AFTER THE DEATH OF THE TWO SONS OF AARON. R. Judah said: Since it says here, "the Lord spoke unto Moses", why does it repeat in the next verse, "And the Lord said unto Moses, Speak to Aaron thy brother", etc.? The same question arises in other places (e.g. Lev. I, 1; Exodus XXIV, 1), and in all cases the answer is the same, that the reference is first to one grade (of the Deity) and then to another; but all are equivalent and come from one root.'

R. Isaac remarked: 'One verse says, "Serve the Lord with fear, and rejoice with trembling" (Ps. II, 11), and another verse says, "Serve the Lord with gladness, come before him with rejoicing" (Ps. c, 2). The apparent contradiction is explained as follows. When a man comes to serve his Master he should do so first in fear, and through that fear he will afterwards perform the precepts of the Law in joy. It says, "rejoice in trembling", because it is forbidden to a man to rejoice overmuch in this world, but in the words and the precepts of the Torah it is quite right that he should rejoice.' R. Abba said: 'The word "fear"

Zohar: Vayikra, Section 3, Page 56b

here esoterically alludes to the Holy One, blessed be He, as in the verse, "The fear of the Lord is the beginning of knowledge" (Prov. I, 7).' R. Eleazar said: 'If a man desires to serve his Master, from what place should he commence and in what place should he first aim at unifying the name of his Master? In "fear", with which the ascent heavenwards commences.'

Another interpretation is as follows. R. Yose said: 'Why does the text say, "after the death of the two sons of Aaron", and not "after the death of Nadab and Abihu", since we know they were his sons? The reason is to show that they had not yet emerged from the guardianship of their father, but they thrust themselves forward in his lifetime.'

R. Hiya said: 'One day I was on my way to visit R. Simeon to learn from him the portion of the Passover. In a certain mountain which I passed I saw some clefts in a rock and two men sitting in one. As I went along I caught the sound of their voices saying: "A song, a psalm of the sons of Korah." Why both song and psalm? We have learnt in the name of R. Simeon that this is a double song, and therefore superior to other songs. So, too, with the expressions, "A psalm, a song for the Sabbath day" (Ps. XCII, 1), or "Song of songs" (S.S. I, l): the doubling is a sign of pre-eminence. This is the song of the Holy One, blessed be He, which was sung by the sons of Korah, those who sat at the doorway of Gehinnom. [Tr. note: According to another reading, "regarding those who sat", etc. Cf. T.B. Baba Bathra, 74a.]

Therefore this Psalm is recited (in the morning prayers) on the second day of the week. I went up to them and asked them what they were doing in that place. They said: "We are pedlars, and two days in the week we go into a solitary place and study the Torah, because on other days people will not let us." I said to them: "Happy is your portion." They continued: "Whenever the righteous are removed from the world, punishment is removed from the world and the death of the righteous atones for the sins of the generation. Therefore we read the section dealing with the death of the sons of Aaron on the Day of Atonement that it may atone for the sins of Israel. God says: Recount the death of these righteous ones, and it will be accounted to you as if you brought an offering on that day to make atonement for you. For we have learnt that so long as Israel are in captivity, and cannot bring offerings on that day, the mention of the two sons of Aaron shall be their atonement. For so we have learnt, that Abihu was equal to his two brothers Eleazar and Ithamar, and Nadab to all together, and Nadab and Abihu were reckoned as equal to the seventy elders who were associated with Moses; and therefore their death was an atonement for Israel." '

Zohar: Vayikra, Section 3, Page 57a

R. Hizkiah quoted in this connection the verse: "Therefore thus saith the Lord to the house of Jacob who redeemed Abraham" (Isa. XXIX, 22). 'We might think', he said, 'that the words "to the house of Jacob" are misplaced, but really the verse is to be taken as it stands. For when Abram was cast into the furnace of the Chaldeans the angels said before God: How shall this one be delivered, seeing that he has no merit of his ancestors to rely upon? God replied: He shall be delivered for the sake of his sons. But, they said, Ishmael will issue from him? There is Isaac who will stretch forth his neck on the altar. But Esau will issue from him? There is Jacob who is the complete throne and all his sons who are perfect before me. They said: Assuredly through this merit Abraham shall be delivered. Hence it is written: "Jacob who redeemed Abraham,'. The verse continues: "Jacob shall not now be ashamed... but when he seeth his children the work of my hands", etc. The reference here in "his children" is to Hananiah, Mishael and Azariah, who cast themselves into the fiery furnace. We have learnt that when they were bound in order to be cast into the fire, each of them lifted up his voice and quoted a verse of Scripture in the presence of all the princes and rulers. Hananiah said: "The Lord is on my side, I will not fear what man can do to me", etc. (Ps. CXVIII, 6). Mishael said: "Therefore fear thou not, O Jacob my servant, saith the Lord", etc. (Jer. XXX, 10). When those present heard the name of Jacob they all laughed in scorn. Azariah said: "Hear, O Israel, the Lord our God the Lord is one" (Deut. VI, 4). At that moment God assembled His court and said to them: For the sake of which of those verses shall I deliver them? They replied: "They shall know that thou alone whose name is the Lord art most high over all the earth" (Ps. LXXXVII). God then turned to His Throne and said: With which of these verses shall I deliver them? The Throne replied: With the one at which they all laughed: as Jacob stood by Abraham in the furnace, so let him stand by these. Hence it is written in connection with them, "Not now shall Jacob be ashamed". Now why were these delivered? Because they prayed to God and unified His name in the fitting manner. The two sons of Aaron brought strange fire on the altar and did not unify God's name in the fitting manner, and therefore they were burnt.'

R. Isaac said: 'It is written here, "After the death of the two sons... and they died". Why this double mention of their death? One referring to their actual death, the other to their having no children, for he who has no children is counted as dead.' [Tr. note: T.B. Nedarim, 64b.] R. Abba derived the same lesson from this verse, "And Nadab and Abihu died... and they had no children and Eleazar and Ithamar ministered," etc. (Num. III, 4). He said further that they did not die like others who have no children: they died only their own death but not that of their souls,

Zohar: Vayikra, Section 3, Page 57b

because their souls entered into Phineas; wherefore it refers to Phineas as "these" (Ex. VI, 25). R. Eleazar said: 'For this reason whenever Phineas is mentioned he is always called "the son of Eleazar the son of Aaron the Priest" (v. Num. xxv, 7; Judges xx, 28). [Tr. note: The text here expounds the significance of the Yod with which the name Pinchas is written in Numbers xxv, 7, finding in it an indication that by his zeal in the matter of Zimri he rectified the misdeed of Nadab and Abihu, and reunited the letters of the Divine Name.]

'It has been taught in the name of R. Yose that on this day of Atonement it has been instituted that this portion should be read to atone for Israel in captivity. Hence we learn that if the chastisements of the Lord come upon a man, they are an atonement for his sins, and whoever sorrows for the sufferings of the righteous obtains pardon for his sins. Therefore on this day we read the portion commencing "after the death of the two sons of Aaron", that the people may hear and lament the loss of the righteous and obtain forgiveness for their sins. For whenever a man so laments and sheds tears for them, God proclaims of him, "thine iniquity is taken away and thy sin purged" (Isa. VI, 7). Also he may be assured that his sons will not die in his lifetime, and of him it is written, "he shall see seed, he shall prolong days (Isa. LIII, 19).'

R. Simeon said: 'I am amazed to see how little men pay heed to the will of their Master, and how they allow themselves to be wrapt in sleep until the day comes which will cover them with darkness, and when their Master will demand

Zohar: Vayikra, Section 3, Page 58a

reckoning from them. The Torah calls aloud to them, but none inclines his ear. Mark now that in future generations the Torah will be forgotten, and there will be none to close and open. Alas for that generation! There will be no generation like the present until the Messiah comes and knowledge shall be diffused throughout the world. It is written: "A river went forth from Eden" (Gen. II, 10). It has been laid down that the name of that river is Jubilee, but in the book of Rab Hamnuna the Elder it is called Life, because life issues thence to the world. We have also laid down that the great and mighty Tree in which is food for all is called the Tree of Life, because its roots are in that Life. We have learnt that that river sends forth deep streams with the oil of plenitude to water the Garden and feed the trees and the shoots. These streams flow on and unite in two pillars which are called Jachin and Boaz. Thence the streams flow on and come to rest in a grade called Zaddik, and from hence they flow further till they all are gathered into the place called Sea, which is the sea of Wisdom. But the current of that river never ceases, and therefore the streams flow back to the two pillars, Nezah. and Hod, whence they traverse that Zaddik to find there blessings and joy. The Matrona is called the "time" of the Zaddik, and therefore all who are fed below are fed from this place, as it is written: "The eyes of all wait on thee and thou givest them their meat in due season" (Ps. CXLV, 15). When these two are joined, all worlds have gladness and blessing, and there is peace among upper and lower beings. But when through the sins of this world there are no blessings from these streams, and the "time" sucks from the "other side", then judgement impends over the world and there is no peace. Now when mankind desire to be blessed, they can only be so through the priest, when he arouses his own Crown and blesses the Matrona, so that there are blessings in all worlds. We have learnt that at that time Moses inquired of God concerning this, saying: If the sons of men shall return to Thee, through whom shall they be blessed? and God replied: Do not ask Me. Speak to Aaron thy brother, for in his hands are delivered blessings above and below.'

R. Abba said: 'There are times when God is propitious and ready to dispense blessing to those that pray to Him, and times when He is not propitious and judgement is let loose on the world, and times when judgement is held in suspense. There are seasons in the year when grace is in the ascendant, and seasons when judgement is in the ascendant, and seasons when judgement is in the ascendant but held in suspense. Similarly with the months

Zohar: Vayikra, Section 3, Page 58b

and similarly with the days of the week, and even with the parts of each day and each hour. Therefore it is written: "There is a time forevery purpose" (Eccl. III, 1), and again, "My prayer is unto thee, O Lord, in an acceptable time" (Ps. LXIX, 14). Hence it says here: "Let him not come at every time to the Sanctuary".' R. Simeon said: 'This interpretation of the word "time" is quite correct and here God warned Aaron not to make the same mistake as his sons and try to associate a wrong "time" with the King, even if he should see that the control of the world has been committed for the time to the hands of another, and though he has the power to unify with it and bring it near to Holiness. [Tr. note: Al. "Yet it is not so far committed that this power should be united and brought near to Holiness (i.e. that its name should be linked with God as the name Adonay is).'"]

And if he wants to know with what he should enter, the answer is, with zoth (this=Shekinah), for that is the "time" which is attached to my name by the letter yod which is inscribed in my name. R. Yose taught: Verily it is as the Holy Lamp (R. Simeon) explained the verse, "He hath made everything (kol) beautiful in its time (be'itto)"; that is to say, "He hath made kol (Yesod) beautiful in 'eth (Malkuth), and none should interpose between them"; and therefore Aaron was warned that he should not come at every "time" into the Sanctuary, but only with zoth.'

Once when R. Eleazar was studying with his father he said to him: 'It is written of the sons of Aaron that a fire went forth from the Lord and consumed them, and also of the assembly of Korah that a fire went forth from the Lord and consumed them (Num. XVI, 35). Were they then in the same category?' R. Simeon replied: 'There is a difference, because of the assembly of Korah i t says that "they perished from the congregation", but this word is not used of the sons of Aaron.' He further asked him: 'Since it says, "let him not come at all times into the sanctuary", why does it not specify at which time he should come?' He replied: 'As we have explained, there was a certain time which was known to the priests, and here these words are inserted only as a warning to Aaron, as we have explained.' He replied: 'That is what I thought, only I wanted to make certain.' R. Simeon continued: 'Eleazar, my son, note that all the offerings were acceptable to God, but none so much as the incense, wherefore it was taken into the inmost shrine with the greatest privacy, and the severest punishment was inflicted for its misuse.' R. Simeon then expounded the verse: "In fragrance thine ointments are good" (S.S. I, 3). 'This fragrance is the odour of the incense, which is more subtle and intimate than any other, and when it ascends to unite with the anointing oil of the streams of the Source they stimulate one another, and then those oils are good for giving light, and the oil flows from grade to grade through those grades which are called the Holy Name; hence it is written, "therefore do maidens love thee" (Ibid.), where 'alamoth (maidens) may be read 'olamoth (worlds); and from thence blessings spread over all below.

Zohar: Vayikra, Section 3, Page 59a

And because this incense is bound up with the supernal ointment more closely it is more esteemed by the Almighty Holy One, blessed be He, than all offerings and sacrifices. The verse continues: "Draw me, we will run after thee". Therefore the Community of Israel says: "I am like incense and thou art like oil, draw me after thee, and we shall run, I and all my hosts. Let the King bring me to his chambers that we may all be glad and rejoice in thee".'

FOR I WILL APPEAR IN THE CLOUD UPON THE MERCY SEAT. R. Judah said: 'Happy are the righteous that God seeks to honour them. If a man rides on the horse of an earthly king he is put to death, but God let Elijah ride upon His, as it is written: "And Elijah went up in a whirlwind into heaven" (2 Kings II, 11); and He also took Moses into the cloud, though it is written here, "in the cloud I shall appear on the mercy seat". We have learnt that this was the place where the Cherubim abode. We have learnt that three times a day a miracle was accomplished with their wings. When the holiness of the King descended upon them they of themselves raised their wings and spread them out so as to cover the mercy seat. Then they folded their wings and stood rejoicing in the divine presence.' R. Abba said: 'The high priest did not see the divine presence when he entered the sanctuary, and but a cloud came down, and when it lighted on the mercy seat the Cherubim beat their wings together and broke out into song. What did they chant? "For great is the Lord and highly to be praised, he is to be feared above all gods" (Ps. XCVI, 4). When they spread out their wings they said: "For all the gods of the peoples are idols, but the Lord made the heavens" (Ibid. 5). And when they covered the mercy seat they said: "Before the Lord for he cometh to judge the earth, he shall judge the world with righteousness and the peoples with equity" (Ps. XCVIII, 9). Then the priest used to hear their voice in the sanctuary, and he put the incense in its place with all devotion in order that all might be blessed.' R. Yose said: 'The word "equity" (mesharim, lit. equities) in the above quoted verse indicates that the Cherubim were male and female.' R. Isaac said: 'From this we learn that where there is no union of male and female men are not worthy to behold the divine presence.'

Zohar: Vayikra, Section 3, Page 59b

It has been taught in the name of R. Yose: Once the people were short of rain and they sent a deputation to R. Simeon, R. Jesse, R. Hizkiah and the rest of the Companions. R. Simeon was on the point of going to visit R. Pinchas ben Jair, along with his son R. Eleazar. When he saw them he exclaimed: '"A song of ascents; Behold how good and how pleasant it is for brethren to dwell together in unity" (Ps. CXXXIII, 1). The expression "in unity",' he said, 'refers to the Cherubim. When their faces were turned to one another, it was well with the world—"how good and how pleasant", but when the male turned his face from the female, it was ill with the world. Now, too, I see that you are come because the male is not abiding with the female. If you have come only for this, return, because I see that on this day face will once more be turned to face. But if you have come to learn the Torah, stay with me.' They said: 'We have come for both purposes. Let, therefore, one of us go and take the good news to our fellows, and we will stay here with our Teacher.' As they went along he took as his text, "I am black but comely, O ye daughters of Jerusalem" (S.S. I, 5). 'The Community of Israel says to the Holy One, blessed be He: I am black in captivity but I am comely in religious practices, for although Israel are in exile they do not abandon these. "I am black like the tents of Kedar", to wit, the sons of Keturah, whose faces are always swarthy, and yet I am like the curtains of Solomon, like the brightness of the skies. "Look not upon me because I am swarthy." Why am I swarthy? Because the sun hath gazed hard on me, but not looked upon me to illumine me as he should have done. "My mother's sons were angry with me." These words are said by Israel, and refer to the Chieftains appointed over the other nations. Or they may still be spoken by the Community of Israel, and allude to the verse, "For he hath cast from earth to heaven the beauty of Israel" (Lam. II, 1). Or again, the words, "how good, how pleasant it is for brethren to dwell together in unity" may refer to the Companions when they sit together and there is no discord between them. At first they are like combatants who seek to kill one another, but afterwards they become friends and brothers. [Tr. note: v. T.B. Kiddushin, 30b.] Then God says: "Behold how good", etc., and He himself listens to them and delights in their converse. You, therefore, Companions that are gathered here, as you have been close friends hitherto, so may you never part until God shall give you glad greeting, and for your sake may there be peace in the world.'

They then went on their way till they reached R. Pinchas ben Jair. R. Pinchas came out and kissed him, saying: 'I am privileged to kiss the Shekinah.' He prepared for them couches with awnings. Said R. Simeon: 'The Torah does not require this.' So he removed them and they sat down. Said R. Pinchas: 'Before we eat let us hear something from the great Master, for R. Simeon always speaks his mind; he is a man who says what he has to say without fear of heaven or earth. He has no fear of heaven since God concurs

Zohar: Vayikra, Section 3, Page 60a

with him, and he is no more afraid of men than a lion of sheep.'

R. Simeon then turned to R. Eleazar his son, saying: 'Stand up and say something new in the presence of R. Pinchas and the rest of the Companions.' R. Eleazar thereupon arose and began with the text: "And the Lord spoke unto Moses after the death of the two sons of Aaron" (Lev. XVI, 1). 'This verse', he said, 'seems superfluous, seeing that the text proceeds, "And the Lord said to Moses, speak unto Aaron thy brother", which should properly be the beginning of the section. The explanation is this. When God gave the incense to Aaron, he desired that no other man should use it in his lifetime. He said to him: "Thou desirest to increase peace in the world. By thy hand shall peace be increased above. Therefore the incense of spices shall be delivered to thy hand from now onwards, and in thy lifetime no other shall use it." Nadab and Abihu, however, thrust themselves forward to offer it. We have learnt that Moses worried himself to find out what was the cause of their misfortune. Hence God spoke to him after their death and said to him: "The cause is that they 'drew near to the Lord', and thrust themselves forward in the lifetime of their father." Now if the sons of Aaron brought this upon themselves through thrusting themselves forward in the lifetime of their father, what should I deserve if I thrust myself forward before my father and R. Pinchas and the rest of the Companions?' Hearing this, R. Pinchas came up to him and kissed him and blessed him.

R. Simeon then discoursed on the verse: "Behold it is the litter of Solomon, threescore mighty men are round about it", etc. (S.S. III, 7). He said: 'The "litter" here is the throne of glory of the King, Solomon, the "king to whom all peace belongs". Threescore mighty men are round about it, clinging to its sides as emissaries from stern judgement; they are called the sixty rods of fire wherewith that Youth [Tr. note: Metatron.] is girt. On its right hand is a flashing sword, on its left hand coals of fire with seventy thousand consuming flames. Those threescore are armed with deadly weapons from the armoury of the supernal Might of the Holy One, blessed be He. They all "handle the sword and are expert in war": they are ever ready to execute judgement and are called the "lords of wailing and howling". And from whence do they receive all this? "From fear": that is, from the place called "the fear of Isaac". And when? "In the night": at the time when they are commissioned to execute judgement. We have learnt that a thousand and five hundred bearers of arms with authority to smite are attached to the side of those mighty ones. In the hands of him who is called "Youth" there are four mighty keys. Sea monsters go forth beneath the ship

Zohar: Vayikra, Section 3, Page 60b

of this mighty sea in four directions, and each has four aspects. A thousand rocks rise and sink every day from the tide of that sea. Afterwards they are uprooted from it and go to another sea. There is no number to those that cling to her hair. Two sons suck from her every day who are called "spies of the land", and two daughters are at her feet, and these cling to the sides of that litter. In her left hand are seventy branches that grow among the fishes of the sea, all red as a rose, and above them all is one of a still deeper red. This one goes up and down and all hide in her hair. When the master of the evil tongue comes down he becomes a serpent leaping over the hills and mountains until he finds prey to consume. Then he becomes mollified and his tongue turns to good. Israel furnish him with prey and then he returns to his place and enters into the hollow of the great abyss. When he ascends, there also ascend demons girt with spear and sword without number, who surround the sixty who are round the litter, so that myriads of myriads stand round this litter above, all being nurtured by it and doing obeisance to it, and below there go forth from it myriads who wander about the world until the trumpet blows and they assemble. These cling to the uncleanness of the nails. This litter embraces them all. Its feet take hold of the four corners of the world; it is found in heaven above and in the earth below. It is called Adonay, the lord of all, this name being inscribed among its hosts. Therefore the priest must concentrate his thought on heavenly things to unify the holy name from the fitting place. Hence we have learnt that Aaron was to come to the sanctuary with zoth. With this he was to bring the holiness to its place, and from this place man must fear God. Hence it is written, "O that they were wise, that they considered zoth" (Deut. XXXII, 29); that is to say, if men consider how zoth is surrounded by her hosts who stand ready before her to punish sinners, then at once they would "consider their latter end", be careful of their acts and not sin before the Holy One, blessed be He.' R. Simeon further said: 'If a man studies the Torah and guards this zoth, then zoth protects him and makes a covenant with him regarding his own covenant that it shall not depart from him or from his sons or his sons' sons forever, as it is written: "And as for me, this (zoth) is my covenant with them", etc.'

They then sat down to eat, and in the course of the meal R. Simeon said to the Companions: 'Let each one enunciate a new idea concerning the Torah at the table before R. Pinchas. '

R. Hizkiah then began with the text: "The Lord God hath given me the tongue of them that are taught, that I should know how to sustain with words him that is weary" (Isa. L, 4). 'Happy are Israel in that God has chosen them above all other peoples and called them "holy"

Zohar: Vayikra, Section 3, Page 61a

and given them as their portion union with the holy name. How do they effect this union? By their attainments in the Torah, for knowledge of the Torah means union with the Holy One, blessed be He. We have learnt in the presence of our Master: What is holiness? The consummation of the whole which is called Supernal Wisdom. From thence issue streams and fountains in all directions till they reach this zoth. And when this zoth is blessed from the supernal place called Holiness and Wisdom, it is called "the spirit of holiness"; and when mysteries of the Torah proceed from it, it is called "the language of holiness". When the holy oil flows to those two pillars [Tr. note: Nezah and Hod.] that are called "the disciples of the Lord", it is gathered in there, and when it issues thence through the grade called Yesod to this lesser Wisdom, it is called "the tongue of the disciples", and it goes forth to arouse the superior holy saints. Hence it is written, "The Lord has given me the tongue of disciples", and why? "To know how to sustain with words him that is weary". God gives this tongue to the Sacred Lamp, R. Simeon, nay more, He raises him higher and higher: therefore he speaks his mind openly without concealment.'

R. Jesse then took the text: "And the Lord gave Solomon wisdom as he had promised him, and there was peace between Hiram and Solomon" (I Kings v, 26). 'What is the connection between these two statements? The answer is this: "God gave Solomon wisdom"; and how did Solomon display this wisdom that God gave him? First in this way, that he made Hiram assume a more modest frame of mind. For we have been taught that Hiram at first set himself up as a god, as it is written: "Thou hast said, I am a god, I sit in the seat of God" (Ezek. XXVIII, 2). Solomon, however, with his wisdom induced him to give up these claims, and he deferred to him, and therefore it is written, "and there was peace between Hiram and Solomon". We have also learnt that R. Isaac said in the name of R. Judah that Solomon sent him a carriage which took him down to the seven circuits of Gehinnom and brought him up again. We have also learnt that Solomon inherited the Moon complete on all sides. So R. Simeon ben Yohai surpasses all others in wisdom, and none can rise save they make peace with him.'

R. Yose took as his text the verse: "O my dove that art in the clefts of the rock, in the covert of the steep place" (S.S. II, 14). 'The "dove" here is the Community of Israel, which like a dove never forsakes her mate, the Holy One, blessed be He. "In the clefts of the rock": these are the students of the Torah, who have no ease in this world. "In the covert of the steep place": these are the specially pious among them, the saintly and God-fearing, from whom the Divine Presence never departs. The Holy One, blessed be He, inquires concerning them of the Community of Israel, saying, "Let me see thy countenance, let me hear thy voice, for sweet is thy voice"; for above only the voice of those who study the Torah is heard. We have learnt that the likeness of all such is graven above before the Holy One, blessed be He, who delights Himself with them every day and watches them, and that voice rises and pierces its way through all firmaments until it stands before the Holy One, blessed be He. And now the Holy One, blessed be He, has graven the likeness of R. Simeon above, and his voice rises higher and higher and is crowned with a holy diadem, and God crowns him in all worlds and glories in him.'

R. Hiya took as his text: "That which is hath been already and that which is to be", etc. (Eccl. III, 15). 'This is explained by what we have learnt, that before God created this world He created others and destroyed them, until

Zohar: Vayikra, Section 3, Page 6lb

He consulted the Torah, and through it made the proper adjustments and became crowned. Thus all that was to be in this world was before Him fully prepared. We have learnt, too, that all men of all generations stood before Him in their likenesses before they came into the world, and even all the souls of men were traced out before Him in the firmament in the similitude of their shape in this world. All, too, that they afterwards learnt in this world they already knew before they came into it. All this, however, applies only to the truly virtuous. Those who did hot turn out virtuous in this world even there were far from the Holy One, blessed be He, being in the hollow of the abyss, whence they came down into the world before their time. And as they proved to be stiff-necked in this world, so, we have learnt, they were before they came into the world. They threw away the holy portion which was given them and went and defiled themselves with the hollow of the abyss and took their portion from thence and came down into the world before their time. If such a one deserves well afterwards and repents before his Master, he takes his own proper portion, namely, "that which hath been already". Now we may ask concerning the sons of Aaron, the like of whom were not in Israel, how they could perish from the world as they did. Where was their own merit, the merit of their father, the merit of Moses? We have, however, learnt from the Sacred Lamp that God was indeed solicitous for their honour, and so their bodies were burnt within but their souls did not perish. [Tr. note: v. T.B. Sabbath, 113b, where the reverse is stated.] Phineas, too, was already in existence who was to repair the damage; whence it is written, "that which is to be already was". We have learnt that all the truly virtuous before they come into the world are prepared above and called by their names. And R. Simeon ben Yohai from the first day of Creation was stationed before the Holy One, blessed be He, and God called him by his name, happy is his portion above and below!'

R. Abba took as his text the verse: "While the king sat at his table, my spikenard sent forth its fragrance" (S.S. I, 12). 'This has been applied by the Companions to the children of Israel when at the giving of the Law they sent forth a sweet fragrance which will bestead them in all generations by saying "we will do and we will hear". Or we may translate "my spikenard forsook its fragrance", applying the words to the making of the calf. There is, however, also an esoteric allusion in this verse. It says "A river went forth from Eden to water the garden" (Gen. II, 10). This stream first issues in a path which none knoweth. Then Eden joins with it in perfect union, and then fountains and streams issue and crown the holy Son, who thereupon assumes the inheritance of his Father and Mother, and the supernal King regales himself with royal delights. Then "my spikenard gives forth its fragrance": this is Yesod, who sends forth blessings at the union of the Holy King

Zohar: Vayikra, Section 3, Page 62a

and the Matrona, and so blessings are dispensed to all worlds and upper and lower are blessed. And now the Sacred Lamp is crowned with the crowns of that grade, and he and the Companions send up praises from earth to heaven wherewith She is crowned. Now blessings must be brought down from heaven on to the Companions through that grade. Let, therefore, R. Eleazar his son expound to us some of the profound ideas which he has learnt from his father.'

R. Eleazar then cited the verse: "And he looked and behold a well in a field," etc. (Gen. XXIX, 2). 'These verses', he said, 'have an esoteric meaning which I have learnt from my father. The "well" is the same as that of which it is written, "the well which princes digged" (the Shekinah). The three flocks lying by it are Nezah, Hod, and Yesod, and from them the well is ever full of blessings. "Out of that well they watered the flocks": this means that from it the lower worlds are sustained. "The stone upon the well's mouth was great": this is rigorous Judgement, which stands by it from the "other side" to suck from it. But "thither all the flocks gather": these are the six Crowns of the King, which gather together and draw blessings from the Head of the King and pour them upon her, and thereby they "roll away" the stern judgement and remove it from her. Then they "water the flock", that is, pour out blessings in that spot for higher and lower, and then "put the stone again upon the well's mouth in its place": that is to say, judgement returns to its place, because it is necessary for the upholding of the world. And now God has poured upon you blessings from the source of the stream, and from you all of this generation are blessed. Happy are ye in this world and in the world to come!'

R. Simeon then spoke on the verse: "Let the saints exult in glory, let them sing for joy upon their beds" (Ps. CXLIX, 5). 'We have learnt', he said, 'that the knot of faith is tied with thirteen attributes, and in addition the Torah is crowned with thirteen "measures", [rules of interpretation] and the holy name is crowned therewith. Similarly, when Jacob desired to bless his sons, he said that his sons should be blessed with the bond of faith; it is written, "all these are the tribes of Israel, twelve, and this (zoth)", etc. (Gen. XLIX, 28); thus there were thirteen, the Shekinah being joined with them. We have learnt that all those "measures" ascend and rest upon a certain head, and the pious inherit all that glory from above, as it is written, "Let the saints exult in glory", in this world, "and let them sing for joy upon their beds"-in the next world. "The high praises of God are in their mouths", to tie the bond of faith in fitting manner; and so "a two-edged sword is in their hand", to wit, the sword of the Holy One, blessed be He, which flashes with two judgements. Now R. Pinchas ben Jair is the crown of Lovingkindness, the high attribute, and therefore he inherits the glory from on high and ties the celestial and holy bond, the bond of faith. Happy is his portion in this world and in the world to come. Of this table it is said: "This is the table that is before the Lord" (Ezek. XLI, 22).' R. Pinchas then rose and kissed and blessed him, and R. Eleazar and all the Companions, and took the cup and said the benediction and the psalm, "Thou preparest a table before me in the presence of mine enemies" (Ps. XXIII, 5). All that day they gladdened themselves

Zohar: Vayikra, Section 3, Page 62b

with words of the Torah, and the joy of R. Simeon was great. R. Pinchas took R. Eleazar and did not leave him all that day and night, saying: 'All this great joy and gladness is of my portion, and they will make proclamation concerning me to that effect in the other world.'

When they rose to depart R. Pinchas would not at first let R. Eleazar go, but he accompanied R. Simeon and all the Companions on their way. As they went along R. Simeon said: 'It is time to work for the Lord.'

R. Abba came and asked him: It is written, AND AARON SHALL CAST LOTS UPON THE TWO GOATS. What, he asked, is the meaning of these lots, and why had Aaron to cast them?' R. Simeon began his reply by citing the verse: "And he took from them Simeon and bound him before their eyes" (Gen. XLII, 24) 'Why did Joseph take Simeon rather than any other one of the brothers? The reason was that Joseph said to himself: Simeon and Levi everywhere open the door to judgement. So it was with me and so it was with Shechem. It is therefore meet that I should take this one so that he should not rouse contention among all the tribes. The question has also been asked why Simeon associated himself with Levi rather than, say, with Reuben, who was also his full brother. The reason was that he saw that Levi came from the side of judgement and he himself was attached to the side of stern judgement. He therefore thought that if Levi joined him they would be able to conquer the world. What then did God do? He took Levi for his portion, and made Simeon isolated.

'We have learnt that on the side of the Mother there are two emissaries attached to her left hand who roam about the world to spy it out. Now Israel are God's portion, and from His great love for them He gave them one day in the year to cleanse and purify them from all their sins, and therefore on this day they are crowned and are safe from all executioners and all hostile emissaries. It is written that Aaron shall cast lots upon the two he-goats. Why is one of these for the Lord? Because God said, Let one abide by me and the other roam about the world; for if the two were combined the world would not be able to stand against them. The second one therefore goes forth, and when he finds Israel absorbed in religious service and pious deeds and all at peace with one another he can see no opportunity to bring a charge against them. We have learnt that there are many demons under his control, whose office it is to spy out the earth for those

Zohar: Vayikra, Section 3, Page 63a

who transgress the commands of the Law; but on that day there is no opening for any accusation against Israel. When that he-goat reaches the rock (of Azazel) there is great rejoicing and the emissary who went forth to accuse returns and declares the praises of Israel, the accuser becoming the defender. And not only on this day, but whenever Israel desire to be cleansed of their sins, God shows them how to restrain the accusers by means of the offerings which are brought before the Holy One, blessed be He, and then they cannot harm. But this day is more efficacious than all; and just as Israel appease all below, so all those who have accusations to bring (above) are appeased, though all the service is to the Holy One. We have learnt that at the hour of which it is written that Aaron should take the two he-goats, all those (accusers) above rouse themselves and seek to go forth into the world, and when Aaron brings near those below those above are also brought near. The lots are then produced for both sides; and as the priest casts lots below so the Priest casts lots above; and just as below one is left for the Holy One and one is thrust out to the wilderness, so above one remains with the Holy One, blessed be He, and one goes forth into the supernal wilderness; so the two are connected. It is written later:

AND AARON SHALL LAY HIS TWO HANDS ON THE HEAD OF THE LIVE GOAT AND CONFESS OVER HIM, ETC. He must use both hands in order that the Holy One may concur with him. The he-goat is called "live", to include the one above. The words "over him" mean that the sins shall all be left on the goat.' R. Abba asked how this could be reconciled with the verse which says, "And they shall no more sacrifice their sacrifices unto the he-goats after which they go a-whoring" (Lev. XVII, 7). He replied: 'It does not say there that they should not sacrifice he-goats, but to he-goats. So here, the goat bore on itself all their iniquities, but the offering was brought only to the Holy One, blessed be He, and through the offering upper and lower are appeased and judgement has no sway over Israel.

'AND SHALL SEND HIM AWAY BY THE HAND OF A MAN THAT IS IN READINESS. The words "in readiness" contain a hint that

Zohar: Vayikra, Section 3, Page 63b

forevery kind of action there are men specially fitted. There are some men specially fitted for the transmission of blessings, as, for instance, a man of "good eye". There are others, again, who are specially fitted for the transmission of curses, and curses light wherever they cast their eyes. Such was Balaam, who was the fitting instrument of evil and not of good, and even when he blessed his blessing was not confirmed, but all his curses were confirmed, because he had an evil eye. Hence, as we have learnt, a man should turn aside a hundred times in order to avoid a man with an evil eye. So here, "a man that is in readiness" means a man who is marked out by nature for this service. The priest was able to tell such a man because he had one eye slightly larger than the other, shaggy eyebrows, bluish eyes and a crooked glance. This was the kind of man fitted for such a task. In Gush Halba [Tr. note: =Gischala, in Galilee.] there was a man whose hands brought death to whatever they touched, and none would come near him. In Syria there was a man whose look always brought ill hap, even though he meant it for good. One day a man was walking in the street with a beaming countenance when this man looked at him and his eye was knocked out. Thus different men are fitted either for one thing or the other. Hence it is written, "He that hath a good eye shall be blessed" (Prov. XXII, 9), or, as we should rather read by a change in the vowelling (yebarech for yeborach), "shall bless". We have learnt that the man who took the goat to the wilderness used to go up on a mountain and push it down with both his hands, and before it was halfway down all its bones were broken, [Tr. note: v. T.B. Yoma, 67a.] and the man used to say: "So may the iniquities of thy people be wiped out", etc. And when the accuser of Israel was thus made into its advocate, the Holy One, blessed be He, took all the sins of Israel and all the records of them above and threw them into the place called "depths of the sea", as it is written: "Thou wilt cast all their sins into the depths of the sea" (Mic. VII, 19).

AND OF THE CONGREGATION OF THE PEOPLE OF ISRAEL HE SHALL TAKE TWO HE-GOATS FOR A SIN-OFFERING. This offering was to be taken from all of them, so as to make atonement for all of them,

Zohar: Vayikra, Section 3, Page 64a

and it was not sufficient that it should be taken from one individual. From whence, then, was it taken? They used to take the money for it from the boxes in the Temple court, [Tr. note: v. Mishnah, Shekalim, IV, 2.] which contained the contributions of all. The other goat, which was left to the Lord, was brought as a sin-offering first of all, being attached to a certain grade, and afterwards the other offerings were brought and Israel were left purified of all the sins which they had committed against God. On that day many doors were opened facing Israel to receive their prayers. On that day the priest was crowned with many crowns, and his service was more precious than at any other time, since he gave portions to all in those offerings of the Holy One, blessed be He. On that day lovingkindness was awakened in the world by the hand of the priest bringing offerings.'

Having gone some way, they sat down in a field and prayed. A fiery cloud came down and surrounded them. Said R. Simeon: 'We see that God's favour is in this place, so let us stay here'. They therefore sat down and discoursed on the Torah. R. Simeon quoted the text: "As cold waters to a thirsty soul, so is good news from a far country" (Prov. xxv, 25). 'King Solomon', he said, 'composed three books corresponding to three supernal attributes–the Song of Songs to Wisdom, Ecclesiastes to Understanding, and Proverbs to Knowledge. Why does Proverbs correspond to Knowledge? Because all its verses are in parallel form, one half balancing the other, and when we examine them we find that they can be placed in either order. Thus here we have two things, "cold waters" and a "good report", either of which may be compared to the other as a source of comfort and refreshment.' As they were sitting a man came up and told them that the wife of R. Simeon had recovered from her illness; and at the same time the Companions heard a voice saying that God had forgiven the transgressions of the generation. Said R. Simeon: 'This is a fulfilment of the verse about "a good report from a distant country"; it is as refreshing to the spirit as cool waters to a thirsty soul.' He then said: 'Let us rise and pursue our way, since God is performing miracles for us.' He then continued his exposition, saying: 'The "cold waters" mentioned here refer to the Torah, since he who studies the Torah and sates his soul with it will hear "a good report from a distant land", to wit, the promise of many good things in this world and the next from God, who was at first far from him, and also from the place where men were previously at enmity with him, from that place

Zohar: Vayikra, Section 3, Page 64b

greeting of peace shall be given to him.' AND HE SHALL GO OUT UNTO THE ALTAR THAT IS BEFORE THE LORD. R. Judah quoted here the verse: God, even God the Lord hath spoken, and called the earth from the rising of the sun unto the going down thereof" (Ps. L, 1) 'We have learnt', he said, 'that a thousand and five hundred and fifty myriads of choristers chant hymns to God when day breaks, and a thousand and five hundred and forty-eight at midday, and a thousand and five hundred and ninety myriads at the time which is called "between the evenings".' R. Yose said that when day dawns all the "lords of shouting" utter words of praise to greet it, because then all are exhilarated and judgement is mitigated. At that moment joy and blessing is in the world, and the Holy One, blessed be He, awakens Abraham [Tr. note: Hesed.] and has joyous communion with him, and gives him sway over the world. At the time called "between the evenings" all those angels called "masters of howling" are vocal, and contention is rife in the world. That is the time when the Holy One arouses Isaac [Tr. note: Geburah.] and rises to judge the guilty who transgress the precepts of the Law. Seven rivers of fire issue forth and descend on the heads of the wicked, along with burning coals of fire. Then Abraham returns to his place and the day departs and the sinners in Gehinnom groan as they say: "Woe unto us, for the day declineth, for the shadows of evening are stretched out" (Jer. VI, 4). At that time, therefore, a man should be careful not to omit the afternoon prayer. When night comes, those other fifteen hundred and forty-eight myriads are summoned from without the curtain and chant hymns, and then the underworld chastisements are aroused and roam about the world. These chant praises until midnight, a watch and a half. Then all the others assemble and sing psalms, after the north wind has risen and gone forth, until daylight comes and the morning rises, when joy and blessing return to the world.' R. Abba said that there are three leaders for all of the choirs. Over those who sing in the morning is appointed one named Heman, under whom there are many deputies for ordering their song. Over those of the evening there is appointed one named Jeduthun, who also has many deputies under him. At nighttime, when all from without the curtain arise, they are in disorder until midnight, when all gather together and the lead is taken by one called Asaph, to whom all the deputies are subordinate till morning comes. Then that "lad" [Tr. note: Metatron.] who sucks from his mother's breasts rises to purify them and enters to minister. That is a time of favour when the Matrona converses with the King, and the King stretches forth

Zohar: Vayikra, Section 3, Page 65a

a thread of blessing and winds it round the Matrona and all who are joined with her. These are they that study the Torah at nighttime after midnight. R. Simeon said: 'Happy he who comes with the Matrona at the hour when she goes to greet the King and to converse with Him, and He stretches out his right hand to receive her. This hour is called "the uttermost parts of the sea" (Ps. CXXXIX, 9), when her chastisements depart and she enters under the wings of the King, with all those that are attached to her. At that time the Patriarchs invite the Matrona and advance to converse with her, and the Holy One, blessed be He, joins them. Hence it is written: "God, even God the Lord hath spoken and called the earth", etc. The first "God" here (El) refers to the light of Wisdom which is called Lovingkindness; the second "God" (Elohim) to Might: and "the Lord" to Mercy.'

When R. Eleazar was once studying with his father he asked him why the name Tetragrammaton is sometimes pointed with the vowels of ELOHIM, and read so. R. Simeon answered: 'The name Tetragrammaton everywhere indicates mercy, but when the wicked turn mercy into judgement, then it is written Tetragrammaton and read Elohim. There is, however, a deeper explanation, as follows. There are three grades (of Judgement) which though essentially one can yet be distinguished. All plants and lamps are illumined and fired, watered and blessed from that perennial Stream in which all is comprised, and which is called the Mother of the Garden of Eden. In itself this is Mercy, but being called Mother it is also the source of Judgement. This is represented by the name Tetragrammaton read as ELOHIM, and this is the first grade. Then we have the grade of Geburah itself, which is properly called Elohim. Thirdly we have i Zedek (Righteousness), which is the final Crown and the Court of Justice of the King, and this is called Adonay, being also written so; and the Community of Israel is also called by this name.'

R. Eleazar then asked his father to explain to him the name EHYEH ASHER EHYEH (I am that I am). He said 'This name is all-comprehensive.

Zohar: Vayikra, Section 3, Page 65b

The first Ehyeh (I shall be) is the comprehensive framework of all when the paths are still obscure, and not yet marked out, and all is still undisclosed. When a beginning has been made and the Stream has started on its course, then it is called Asher Ehyeh (That which I shall be), meaning: Now I am ready to draw forth into being and create all, now I am the sum total of all individual things. "That I am": to wit, the Mother is pregnant and is ready to produce individual things and to reveal the supreme Name. We find it stated in the book of King Solomon that the Asher (That) is the link that completes the joyful union. Observe now how the divine utterance [Tr. note: In Ex. III, 14.] went from grade to grade to teach the secret of the holy name to Moses. First came Ehyeh (I shall be), the dark womb of all. Then Asher Ehyeh (That I Am), indicating the readiness of the Mother to beget all. Then, after the creation had commenced, came the name Ehyeh alone (Ibid.), as much as to say: Now it will bring forth and prepare all. Finally when all has been created and fixed in its place the name Ehyeh is abandoned and we have Tetragrammaton (Ibid. 15), an individual name signifying confirmation. Then it was that Moses knew the Holy Name, as it is both disclosed and undisclosed, and attained to an insight to which no other man has ever attained, happy is his portion!'

R. Eleazar came and kissed his hand. He said: 'Eleazar my son, from now onward be careful not to write the Holy Name save in the manner prescribed, since whoever does not know how to write the Holy Name in the manner prescribed so as to tie the bond of faith and unify the Holy Name, of him the Scripture says, "he hath despised the word of the Lord and hath broken his commandment", etc. (Num. xv, 31), even though he only left out one stroke from one letter. See, now, the Yod signifies the first framework of all, undisclosed from all sides. The Yod then produces the perennial stream indicated by He, and also a son and daughter, Vau and He, as explained elsewhere. Happy the lot of the righteous who know the profound secrets of the Holy King and are meet to give thanks to Him!'

R. Judah said: 'In the verse from the Psalms quoted above, the three names "God", "God", "the Lord" indicate the complete triad of the holy Patriarchs. God "called the earth", that the Community of Israel might perfect the gladness. And from what place does He join her? "Out of Zion the perfection of beauty" (Ps. L, 2). For, as we have learnt, Jerusalem is the centre of the earth and a (heavenly) place called Zion is above it, and from this place it is blessed,

Zohar: Vayikra, Section 3, Page 66a

and the two are indissolubly linked together.

AND HE SHALL GO OUT UNTO THE ALTAR WHICH IS BEFORE THE LORD, AND MAKE ATONEMENT FOR IT. We have learnt that just as the priest makes atonement below on this day, so also it is above, nor does the Priest above commence his service until the priest below has done so; for from below the sanctification of the Holy King commences to ascend, and then all worlds are one before the Holy One, blessed be He.' Said R. Judah: 'If Israel only knew why God visits their sins upon them more than those of other nations, they would perceive that He does not collect from them a hundredth part of His due. Many are the Chariots, Powers and Rulers that God has to serve Him. Now when He placed Israel in this world He crowned them with holy crowns and placed them in the holy land that they might devote themselves to His service, and He made all the celestials depend upon Israel, so that there is no joy or service before Him until Israel commence below; and when Israel neglect the service, it is suspended above, and there is no service either in earth or in heaven. And if this was so when Israel were in their own land, how much more so subsequently! If Israel but knew, says God, how many hosts and multitudes are held up through them, they would see that they are not worthy to survive for an instant. Therefore "the priest shall go out to the altar which is before the Lord" – this is the supernal Altar – and then "make atonement for it", and then "he shall come forth and offer his burnt offering and the burnt offering of the people" (v. 24).'

It is written: "And he shall make atonement for the holy place because of the uncleanness of the children of Israel" (v. 16). R. Eleazar said: 'The wicked cause imperfection above and arouse judgement and bring defilement on the Sanctuary, so that the mighty Serpent shows himself. So on this day the priest has to purify all and put on his holy crown so that the King may come to abide with the Matrona and to awaken joy and blessing in the world. Thus completeness both above and below can be realized only through the priest, when he awakens his own proper Crown. So when the joy of union comes to the King and the Matrona, all the ministers and attendants of the palace rejoice, and all the sins that they committed against the King are forgiven. Hence it is written, "No man shall be in the tent of meeting when he goeth in to make atonement in the holy place until he goeth out", to wit, when he goes in to unite them; and at that moment "he shall make atonement for himself and his house".'

R. Isaac said: 'When Israel are in captivity, God, if one may say so, is with them in captivity, for the Shekinah never leaves them. It was with them in Babylon and returned with them from the captivity; and for the sake of those righteous

who were left in the land it abode in the land, as it never left them.' R. Judah said: 'The Matrona returned to the King and everything was gloriously restored, and therefore they were called "the men of the great Synagogue". We have learnt that if Israel in exile show themselves deserving, God will have mercy on them and hasten to bring them forth from exile, and if not He keeps them there until the appointed time, [Tr. note: v. T.B. Sanhedrin, 98a.] and if when that comes they are still not worthy He has regard to the honour of His Name and does not forget them in exile, as it is written: "I shall remember my covenant with Jacob", etc. (Lev. XXVI, 42).' R. Isaac said: 'When the Holy King shall remember Israel for the sake of His Name and restore the Matrona to her place, then, as the Scripture says, "no man shall be in the tent of meeting when He comes to make atonement for the holy things", just as it is written of the priest when he went in to unify the Holy Name and to join the King with the Matrona.' R. Judah said: 'It has been taught that the priest entered into one degree and bathed his flesh. Then he left that grade and entered into another and bathed, making peace between the two. Thus at every step he had to perform some fitting ceremony, and wear corresponding garments, until he had properly completed the service, bringing blessing above and below. When all was linked together,

all faces were illumined. Then all fell on their faces and trembled and said, "Blessed be the name of his glorious kingdom forever and ever". Their voices joined that of the priest and he replied, "Ye shall be clean" (v. 30); only the High Priest said this, not the other priests or the people.

FROM ALL YOUR SINS SHALL YE BE CLEAN BEFORE THE LORD. It has been taught: From the beginning of the (seventh) month the books are opened and the judges sit in judgement, until the day which is called "the ninth of the month" (Lev. XXIII, 32), when all judgements are submitted to the Supreme Judge, and a Throne of mercy is set for the Holy King.

Then it is meet for Israel below to rejoice before their Master because on the next day He intends to try them from the holy throne of Mercy, of forgiveness, and to purify them from all the sins recorded in the books that are open before Him. Hence it is written, "from all your sins before the Lord".

'When the public recited this verse (in the Temple service) they went up to this point but no further, and none was permitted to say the word "Ye shall be clean" save the High Priest alone who was linking the Holy Name together through his utterance. When he had done so a voice came down and struck him and a word flowed into his mouth and he said "Ye shall be clean". He then performed his service and all the celestials that were left there were blessed. Then he bathed himself and washed his hands in preparation for another service, in which he was to enter into a place more holy than all. The other priests, the Levites and the people stood around him in three rows and lifted their hands over him in prayer, and a golden chain was tied to his leg. He took three steps and all the others came to a stand and followed him no further. He took three more steps and went round to his place; three more and he closed his eyes and linked himself with the upper world. He went into the inner place and heard the sound of the wings of the Cherubim chanting and beating their wings together. When he burnt the incense the sound ceased and they folded their wings quietly, if the priest was worthy and joy was found above. Here, too, at that moment there went forth a sweet odour as from hills of celestial pure balsam, and the scent was brought into his nostrils, gladdening his heart. Then all was silent and no accuser was found there. Then the priest offered his prayer with fervour and joy. When he finished, the Cherubim raised their wings again and resumed their chant. Then the priest knew that his service had been acceptable, and it was a time of joy for all, and the people knew that his prayer had been accepted. Happy the portion of the priest in that through him joy upon joy was diffused on that day both above and below!'

R. Hiya discoursed on the verse: "(With) my soul have I desired thee in the night, yea, with my spirit within me will I seek thee early" (Isa. XXVI, 9). 'It does not say here,' he remarked, "my soul desires thee", but "my soul I desire thee'. The explanation is, as we have learnt, that God is the soul and spirit of all, and Israel here calls Him so and says, "I desire thee in order to cleave to thee and I seek thee early to find thy favour".'

R. Yose said: 'When a man is asleep at night his soul goes and testifies to all that he has done during the day. Then the body says to the soul "I desire thee at night"

Zohar: Vayikra, Section 3, Page 67b

and to the spirit "I shall seek thee early". Alternatively, the Community of Israel says to the Holy One, blessed be He, "While I am in exile among the nations and withhold myself from all evil communication with them, my soul desires thee to restore me to my place, and although they subject my sons to all kinds of oppression the holy spirit does not depart from me nor do I cease to seek thee and do thy commandments.' R. Isaac said: 'Israel says before God: While my soul is still within me I desire thee at night (the exile), because at such time the soul is constrained to yearn for thee, and when the holy spirit awakens within me I shall seek thee early to do thy will.' R. Hizkiah said that "soul" refers to the Community of Israel and "spirit" to the Holy One, blessed be He.

When R. Abba was studying with R. Simeon, the latter once rose at midnight to study the Torah, and R. Eleazar and R. Abba rose with him. R. Simeon discoursed on the verse: "As a hind panteth after the water-courses so my soul panteth for thee, O Lord" (Ps. XLII, 2). 'Happy are Israel,' he said, 'for that God gave them the Holy Law and caused them to inherit holy souls from a holy place, that they might keep His commandments and delight themselves in His Law. For the Torah is called a delight, and this is what is meant by the saying that God comes to delight Himself with the righteous in the Garden of Eden, to wit, to regale Himself from the selfsame stream as the righteous. And whoever studies the Torah is privileged to delight himself along with

Zohar: Vayikra, Section 3, Page 68a

the righteous from the waters of this stream. So we are told here that the "hind", to wit, the Community of Israel, pants for the water brooks to receive a draught from the sources of the stream at the hands of the Righteous One. What are these sources? One is above, of which it is written, "And a river went forth from Eden to water the Garden", etc., and from there it flows forth and waters the Garden and all the streams issue from it and meet again in two sources called Nezah and Hod, and these pour forth water into that grade of Zaddik which goes forth from thence and waters the Garden. Observe that the soul and the spirit are inseparable. We have learnt that the perfect service offered by man to God consists in loving Him with his soul and his spirit. As these cleave to the body and the body loves them, so a man should cleave to God with the love of his soul and his spirit. Hence it says, "With my soul I have desired thee and with my spirit I seek thee early". It has been taught: Happy is the man who loves the Almighty with such a love; such are the truly virtuous for whose sake the world is established and who can annul all evil decrees both above and below. We have learnt that the virtuous man who with his soul and his spirit cleaves to the Holy King above with fitting love has power over the earth below, and whatever he decrees for the world is fulfilled, just as Elijah decreed concerning the rain. When the holy souls come down from heaven to earth and the virtuous of the world withdraw themselves from the King and the Matrona, few are they who at that time stand before the King and on whom the King deigns to look. For, as we have stated, at the time when God breathed spirit into all the hosts of the heavens, they all came into being and existence, but some were held back until the Holy One, blessed be He,

Zohar: Vayikra, Section 3, Page 68b

sent them below, and these have sway both above and below. Hence Elijah said: "As the Lord liveth before whom I have stood" (I Kings XVII, 1), not "before whom I am standing". Afterwards he returned to his place and ascended to his chamber, but the others do not ascend until they die, because they did not stand before God previously. Therefore Elijah and all those who cleave to the King were made messengers of the heavenly King, as we find in the book of Adam that all holy spirits above perform God's messages and all come from one place, whereas the souls of the righteous are of two degrees combined together, and therefore they ascend to a greater height. This applies to Enoch and Elijah. We have learnt that a hundred and twenty-five thousand grades of souls of the righteous were decided upon by the Almighty

615

before the world was created, and these are sent into this world in every generation and they fly about the world and are "bound in the bundle of the living", and through them God will resurrect the world.

YE SHALL AFFLICT YOUR SOULS, that Israel may be meritorious in the eyes of God and that their whole intent may be to cleave to Him so that their sins may be forgiven. The word "souls" (instead of "soul") indicates that one should eat and drink and feast on the ninth day so as to make the affliction double on the tenth.

FOR ON THIS DAY SHALL HE ATONE FOR YOU. This indicates, as we have learnt, that on this day the Ancient Holy One reveals himself to make atonement for the sins of all.'

R. Abba expounded in this connection the verse: "There was a little city and few men within it, and there came a great king against it and besieged it", etc. (Eccl. IX, 14, 15). 'The "little city",' he said, 'has here its well-known esoteric meaning (Malkuth); it is so called because it is the last and the lowest of all (the grades). There are "few men within it", for few are those who succeed in ascending to it and abiding in it. "A great king comes to it": this is the Holy One, blessed be He, who comes to unite with it, and He "surrounds it" with walls, "and builds great bulwarks for it", so that it is called "the holy city", and all the treasure of the King is placed there, and therefore it alone is crowned with all the diadems of the King. "He finds therein a poor wise man", or, as we should rather say, "a prudent (misken) wise man", a man crowned with the crowns of the Law and the precepts of the King, and endowed with wisdom to interpret aright the service of his Master. He "shall escape to that city in his wisdom", but "no man remembereth that man" to follow his example in keeping the precepts of the Law and studying the Torah.

Zohar: Vayikra, Section 3, Page 69a

"Then said I, Wisdom is better than strength", because in the other world none are permitted to enter save those truly virtuous who study the Torah day and night and are crowned with the precepts of the Law. "But the poor man's wisdom is despised and his words are not heard", since mankind pay no heed to him and have no desire to associate with him and listen to him. For so we have learnt, that to listen to the words of the Torah is like receiving it from Sinai, no matter from whom it comes, and he who inclines his ear to listen gives honour to the Holy King and to the Torah.'

One day, as the Companions were walking with R. Simeon, he said: 'I see all other peoples elevated and Israel degraded. What is the reason? Because the King has dismissed the Matrona and put the handmaid in her place. Who is the handmaid? This is the alien Crown whose firstborn God slew in Egypt.' R. Simeon wept, and continued: 'A king without a queen is no king. If a king cleaves to the handmaid of the queen, where is his honour? A voice will one day announce to the Matrona, "Rejoice greatly, O daughter of Zion, shout, O daughter of Jerusalem, for thy king cometh unto thee; he is just and having salvation", etc. (Zech. IX, 9); as if to say: The Righteous One (Zaddik) will be saved, he that was hitherto poor and riding on an ass, viz., as we have explained, the lower Crowns of the heathen nations whose firstborn God killed in Egypt. It is the Zaddik, as it were, who will be saved, because till now he was without Zedek (righteousness), but now they will be joined.' R. Isaac here asked R. Simeon to explain how it is that some say the world is founded on seven pillars and some on one pillar, to wit, the Zaddik. He replied: 'It is all the same. There are seven, but among these is one called Zaddik on which the rest are supported. Hence it is written: "The righteous one (Zaddik) is the foundation of the world" (Prov. x, 25). This handmaid', resumed R. Simeon, 'will one day rule over the holy land below as the Matrona once ruled over it, but the Holy One, blessed be He, will one day restore the Matrona to her place, and then who shall rejoice like the King and the Matrona?-the King, because he has returned to her and parted from the handmaid, and the Matrona because she will be once more united to the King. Hence it is written: "Rejoice exceedingly, O daughter of Zion", etc. Observe now that it is written, "This shall be to you a statute forever" (Lev. XVI, 29). This promise is a decree of the King, fixed and sealed.

Zohar: Vayikra, Section 3, Page 69b

IN THE SEVENTH MONTH ON THE TENTH DAY OF THE MONTH. The allusion of the "tenth" is as we have explained. We have learnt that on this day all joy and all illumination and all forgiveness depend on the Supernal Mother from whom issue all springs. Then all the lights shine with glad brightness until all is firmly established, and all judgements are also bathed in light and punishment is not inflicted.

It is written: "Howbeit (ach) on the tenth day of this seventh month is the day of atonement, and ye shall afflict your souls" (Lev. XXIII, 27). What is the force here of the word ach (only)? When used in connection with the Passover (Ex. XII, 15) we derive from it the lesson that on half of the day preceding the Passover the eating of leaven is permitted and on half it is forbidden. [Tr. note: v. T.B. Pesahim, 28b.] Shall we say that here also it teaches that half the day eating is permitted and half forbidden?' R. Simeon replied: 'It goes here with the words "ye shall afflict your souls", and signifies that the real affliction is only in the second half of the day.'

FOR ON THIS DAY HE SHALL ATONE FOR YOU. R. Eleazar said: 'We should expect here, "I shall atone for you". The "he", however, signifies that the Jubilee sends forth streams to water and replenish all on this day, and this "for you", to purify you from all sins, so that judgement should have no power over you.' R. Judah said: 'Happy are Israel in that God took pleasure in them and sought to purify them so that they might belong to his Palace and dwell therein.'

R. Judah cited here the verse: "A song of ascents. Out of the depths have I cried unto thee, O Lord" (Ps. CXXXI). 'We have learnt', he said, 'that when God was about to create man, He consulted the Torah and she warned Him that he would sin before Him and provoke Him. Therefore, before creating the world God created Repentance, saying to her: "I am about to create man, on condition that when they return to thee from their sins thou shalt be prepared to forgive their sins and make atonement for them". Hence at all times Repentance is close at hand to men, and when they repent of their sins it returns to God and makes atonement for all, and judgement is suppressed and all is put right. When is a man purified of his sin?' R. Isaac said: 'When he returns to the Most High King and prays

Zohar: Vayikra, Section 3, Page 70a

from the depths of his heart, as it is written, "From the depths I cried unto thee".' R. Abba said: 'There is a hidden place above, which is "the depth of the well", whence issue streams and sources in all directions. This profound depth is called Repentance, and he who desires to repent and to be purified of his sin should call upon God from this depth. We have learnt that when a man repented before his Master and brought his offering on the altar, and the priest made atonement for him and prayed for him, mercy was aroused and judgement mitigated and Repentance poured blessings on the issuing streams and all the lamps were blessed together, and the man was purified from his sin.'

(AFTER THE DOINGS OF THE LAND OF EGYPT IN WHICH YE DWELT SHALL YE NOT DO.) The Holy One, blessed be He, has produced ten holy crowns above wherewith He crowns and invests Himself, and He is they and they are He, being linked together like the flame and the coal. Corresponding to these are ten crowns beneath, which are not holy, and which cling to the uncleanness of the nails of a certain holy Crown called Wisdom, wherefore they are called "wisdoms". We have learnt that these ten species of wisdom came down to this world, and all were concentrated in Egypt, save one which spread through the rest of the world. [Tr. note: v. T.B. Kiddushin, 49b.] They are all species of sorcery, and through them the Egyptians were more skilled in sorcery than all other men. When the Egyptians desired to consort with the demons, they used to go out to certain high mountains and offer sacrifices and make trenches in the ground and pour some of the blood around the trenches and the rest into them and put flesh over it, and bring offerings to the demons. Then the demons used to collect and consort with them on the mountain. Israel, being subject to the Egyptians, learnt their ways and went astray after them; hence God said to them: "After the doings of the land of Egypt in which ye have dwelt shall ye not do", and also, "And they shall no more sacrifice their sacrifices unto the satyrs after whom they go a-whoring", since, as we have learnt, the demons used to appear to them in the form of he-goats. R. Hiya said: 'This is the last of the unholy crowns, as we have learnt.' R. Isaac said, in the name of R. Judah, that the souls of the wicked are the demons of this world. Said R. Yose: 'If so, the wicked are well off; where is their punishment in Gehinnom? Where is the evil in store for them in the other world?' R. Hiya replied: 'We have learnt and laid down that when the souls of the wicked leave this world many executioners of judgement await them and take them to Gehinnom, and subject them there to three tortures every day. Afterwards they go about the world in company with them and mislead the wicked, from whom repentance is withheld, and then return to Gehinnom and punish them there, and so every day'.

Zohar: Vayikra, Section 3, Page 70b

R. Isaac said: 'Happy are the righteous in this world and in the next, because they are altogether holy. Their body is holy, their soul is holy, their spirit is holy, their super-soul is holy of holies. These are three grades indissolubly united. If a man does well with his soul (nefesh), there descends upon him a certain crown called spirit (ruah), which stirs him to a deeper contemplation of the laws of the Holy King. If he does well with this spirit, he is invested with a noble holy crown called super-soul (neshamah), which can contemplate all.

'In the book of King Solomon it is written that God has made three abodes for the righteous. One is for the souls of the righteous which have not yet left this world and are still here, and when the world is in need of mercy and the living afflict themselves, these pray for mankind and go and inform those that sleep in Hebron, [Tr. note: The patriarchs.] who being thus awakened go into the terrestrial Paradise where are the souls of the righteous in their crowns of light, and take counsel of them and decide what shall be, and God carries out their desire and has pity on the world. These souls of the righteous are in this world to protect the living and know their troubles, and these are they of whom the Companions say that the dead know the sorrows of the world and the punishment of the wicked. The second rank belongs to the terrestrial Paradise. In it God has made excellent chambers after the pattern of those of this world and of the celestial world, and palaces of two colours without number and sweet-smelling herbs that grow afresh every day. In that place abides that which is called the "spirit" of the righteous, each one being clad in a precious garment after the pattern of this world and of the upper world. The third grade is that holy celestial abode which is called "the bundle of the living", where that holy superior grade called the super-soul (neshamah) regales itself with the supernal delights. Now we have learnt that when the world requires mercy and those righteous ones take note of it, that soul of theirs which is in the world to shield mankind flits about the world to tell the spirit, and the spirit ascends and tells the super-soul, and this tells the Holy One, blessed be He. Then God has pity on the world and the reverse process takes place, the super-soul telling the spirit and the spirit the soul. Thus when the world requires mercy, the living go and inform the spirits of the righteous and weep over their graves, in order that soul may cleave to soul,

Zohar: Vayikra, Section 3, Page 71a

and the souls of the righteous then come together and go and inform the sleepers of Hebron of the sorrows of the world, and then all enter the gateway of Paradise and inform the spirit, and those spirits which are crowned in Paradise like celestial angels join them and inform the super-soul, and this informs the Holy One, blessed be He, and God has mercy on the world for their sakes; and regarding this Solomon said: "Wherefore I praised the dead which are already dead more than the living that are still alive" (Eccl. IV, 2).'

Said R. Hiya: 'I wonder if anyone knows how to inform the dead besides us.' R. Abba replied: 'The sufferings of men tell them, the Torah tells them. For when there is none who knows how to do this, they take out the Scroll of the Law to the graveyard, and the dead are curious to know why it has been brought there; and then Duma informs them.' R. Yose added: 'They then know that the world is in trouble and the living are not meet nor know how to inform them. Then they all lament for the dishonour done to the Torah in bringing it to such a place. If men repent and weep with all their heart and return to God, then they all gather together and seek mercy and inform the sleepers of Hebron, as we have said. But if they do not repent, then woe to them for that they have assembled for nothing, and have caused the holy Torah to go into banishment without repentance, and they all go to remind God of their sins. Therefore men should not go thus to the graveyard without repentance and fasting.'

R. Abba said: 'There should be three fasts.' R. Yose, however, said that one is sufficient, namely on the same day, provided they are very contrite'.

R. Judah taught: One day R. Hizkiah and R. Jesse were going together when they came to Gischala, which they found in ruins. They sat down near to the graveyard, R. Jesse having in his hand the cylinder of a Scroll of the Law which had been torn. While they were sitting, a grave began to stir near them and to cry: Alas, alas, that the world is in sorrow, since the Scroll of the Law comes into exile hither, or else the living have come to mock us and to shame us with their Torah! R. Hizkiah and R. Jesse were greatly alarmed. Said the former: Who art thou? I am dead, was the reply, but I have been awakened by the Scroll of the Law. For once the world was in trouble and the living came here to awaken us with a Scroll of the Law, and I and my companions approached the sleepers of Hebron, and when they joined the spirits of the righteous in Paradise it was found that the Scroll of the Law which they brought before us was faulty and so belied the name of the King, there being a superfluous vau in one place. So the spirit said that since they had belied the name of the King they would not return to them, and they thrust me and my companions out of the assembly, until a certain elder who was among them went and brought the Scroll of Rab Hamnuna the Elder. Then R. Eleazar the son of R. Simeon who was buried with us awoke and entreated for them in Paradise and the world was healed. And from the day that they caused R. Eleazar to leave his grave with us and join his father there is none of us that has wakened to stand before the sleepers of Hebron, for we remember with fear the day when they rejected me and my companions. And now that you have come to us with a Scroll of the Law in your hands, I presume that the world is in trouble and therefore I am in fear and trembling as I think: Who will go and tell those sainted ones, the sleepers of Hebron. R. Jesse thereupon let go of the stick of the Scroll and R. Hizkiah said: God forbid, the world is not in trouble, and we have not come on that account.

R. Hizkiah and R. Jesse then rose and went on their way. 'Verily,' they said, 'when there are no righteous in the world, the world is sustained only by the Scroll of the Law.'

R. Jesse asked: 'Why, when rain is wanted, do we go to the graveyards, seeing that it is

Zohar: Vayikra, Section 3, Page 7lb

forbidden to "inquire of the dead" (Deut. XVIII, 11)?' He replied: 'You have not yet seen the "wing of the Bird of Eden". [Tr. note: R. Simeon.] The "dead" here are those of the sinners of the heathens who are forever dead, but of Israel who are truly virtuous Solomon says that "they have died aforetime", but now they are living. Further, when other peoples visit their dead, they do so with divinations to summon demons to them, but Israel go with repentance before the Lord, with a contrite heart and with fasting, in order that the holy souls may beseech mercy for them. Therefore we have learnt that the righteous man, even when he departs from this world, does not really disappear from any world, since he is to be found in all of them more than in his lifetime. For in his lifetime he is only in this world, but afterwards he is in three worlds. So we find that Abigail said to David: "May the soul (nefesh) of my lord be bound in the bundle of life" (I Sam. xxv, 29); she did not say "super-soul" (neshamah), because all three are bound together, and so even the nefesh of the righteous is in "the bundle of the living".'

R. Eleazar said: 'The Companions have laid down that it is forbidden to remove a Scroll of the Law even from one synagogue to another, all the more to bring it out into the street. Why then do we do so when praying for rain?' R. Judah replied: 'As we have explained, that the dead may be awakened and entreat for the world.'

R. Abba said: 'The Shekinah also was driven from place to place until she said: "O that I had in the wilderness a lodging place of wayfaring men", etc. (Jer. IX, 1). So here, the Scroll is first taken from synagogue to synagogue, then

618

into the street, then to "the wilderness, the lodging place of wayfaring men".' R. Judah said: 'In Babylon they are afraid to take it even from synagogue to synagogue.' It has been taught that R. Simeon said to the Companions: 'In my days the world will not require this.' R. Yose said to him: 'The righteous shield the world in their lifetime, and after their death even more than in their life. For so God said (to King Hezekiah): "I will defend this city to save it for my own sake and for my servant David's sake" (Isa. XXXVII, 35), but in David's lifetime He did not say so.'

R. Judah said: 'Why does God put David here on a par with Himself? Because David was found worthy to be attached to the Holy Chariot of the Patriarchs, and therefore all is one.

Zohar: Vayikra, Section 3, Page 72a [Note: The Hebrew text does not appear in our translation.]

Zohar: Vayikra, Section 3, Page 72b [Note: The first 5 lines of the Hebrew text are not found in our translation]

R. Isaac said: 'The Egyptians used to serve the power called "handmaid" and the Canaanites the power called "the captive which is behind the mill", and all used to misuse holy words and practise their arts therewith; therefore the Israelites were commanded: "After the doings of the land of Egypt shall ye not do", etc.' R. Judah said that they caused evil demons to rule over the land, as it says, "and the land was defiled". We have learnt that one day God will purify His land of all the uncleanness wherewith the heathen have defiled it, like one who cleans a garment, and will cast out all those that are buried in the holy land, and purify it from the "other side", since, if one may say so, it went a-whoring after the Chieftains of the peoples and received their uncleanness. R. Simeon purified the streets of Tiberias, removing all dead bodies from there.' [Tr. note: v. T. B. Sabbath, 33b, 34a.] R. Judah said: 'Happy he whose lot it is during his lifetime to abide in the holy land; for such a one draws down the dew from the heavens above upon the earth, and whoever is attached to this holy land in his lifetime becomes attached afterwards to a supernal holy land. But of those who do not live there but are brought there to be buried, the Scripture says: "Ye have made my inheritance an abomination" (Jer. II, 7). His spirit leaves him in a strange land and his body comes to rest in the holy land; he turns holy into profane and profane into holy. But if one dies in the holy land his sins are forgiven and he is taken under the wings of the Shekinah. Further, if he is worthy, he continually draws to himself a holy spirit, but he that lives in a strange land draws to himself a strange spirit. We have learnt that when R. Hamnuna the Elder went up to Eretz Israel he was accompanied by twelve members of his academy. He said to them: If I go on this way it is not for myself, but to restore the pledge [Tr. note: His soul.] to its owner. We have learnt that all who do not attain to this in their lifetime restore the pledge of their Master to another'. R. Isaac said: 'Consequently, if anyone takes those evil spirits or foreign powers into the land it becomes defiled, and woe to that man and his soul, because the holy land does not receive him again.'

MY JUDGEMENTS SHALL YE DO AND MY STATUTES SHALL YE KEEP. R. Abba said: Happy are Israel in that God has chosen them above all peoples, and for the sake of His love has given them true laws, planted in them the tree of life, and made His divine Presence abide with them. Why? Because Israel are stamped with the holy impress on their flesh, and they are marked as being His and belonging to His temple. Therefore all who are not stamped with the holy sign

Zohar: Vayikra, Section 3, Page 73a

on their flesh are not His, and they are marked as coming from the side of uncleanness, and it is forbidden to associate with them or to converse with them on matters of the Holy One, blessed be He. It is also forbidden to impart to them knowledge of the Torah, because the Torah consists wholly of the name of the Holy One, blessed be He, and every letter of it is bound up with that Name.' R. Simeon said: 'We are told in regard to the paschal lamb that no stranger who is uncircumcised may eat it. If this is so with the paschal lamb because it is the symbol of some holy thing, how much more must it be so with the Torah, which is holy of holies.'

R. Eleazar once said to his father: 'We have learnt that it is forbidden to teach the Torah to a heathen, and the Companions in Babylon have well connected this rule with the text, "He hath not dealt so with any nation" (Ps. CXLVII, 20). But in the preceding verse, why, after saying, "He sheweth his word unto Jacob" does it add "His statutes and his judgements to Israel"?' He replied: 'Eleazar, God has given this holy celestial portion to Israel and not to the nations. And Israel themselves are in two grades, corresponding to the two grades of the Torah, the disclosed and the undisclosed. To all who have been circumcised and stamped with the holy impress, we impart those things in the Torah which are on the surface, the letters and the plain contents and the precepts, and no more. This is indicated in the words, "He telleth his words to Jacob". But if the Israelite rises to a higher grade, then "His statutes and his judgements to Israel": these are the allegories of the Torah and the hidden paths of the Torah and the secrets of the Torah, which should only be revealed to those of a higher degree. But to impart even a little letter to one who is not circumcised is like destroying the world and repudiating the Holy Name of the Holy One, blessed be He. Hence it is written, "This is the law which Moses set before the children of Israel" (Deut. IV, 44), and not before other peoples. Peace be upon the fathers of the world, Hillel and Shammai, who thus dealt with Onkelos [Tr. note: The reputed author of the Aramaic version of the Pentateuch.] and refused to impart to him any knowledge of the Torah until he was circumcised. See now. The very first thing taught to children, the Aleph Beth, transcends the comprehension and the mind of man, and even of the higher and highest angels, because the Holy Name is concealed in the letters. A thousand and four hundred and five worlds are suspended from the point of the aleph, and seventy-two holy names traced in their full spelling, which uphold heaven and earth, upper and lower beings, and the Throne of the King, are suspended along the stroke of the aleph, while the mystery of Wisdom and the hidden paths and the deep rivers and the ten Words all issue from the lower point of the aleph. From this point aleph begins to extend into beth, and there is no end to the wisdom that is here inscribed. Therefore

Zohar: Vayikra, Section 3, Page 73b

the Torah is the support of all and the link that binds all in faith, and he who is circumcised is attached to that link and he who is not circumcised is not. Of such it is written, "No stranger shall eat of the holy thing" (Lev. XXII, 10), for an unclean spirit comes from his side and mingles itself with the holiness. Blessed be the Merciful One who has separated Israel from them and their uncleanness.' R. Eleazar then came and kissed his hands.

R. Hizkiah said: 'It is written, "God will not forsake his people for the sake of his great name" (I Sam. XII, 22), since Israel is linked to God, and by what? By the holy impress on their flesh. We have learnt that the Torah is called "covenant", and God is called "covenant", and this impress is called "covenant", and so all is inseparably linked together.' R. Jesse asked whence we derive the statement that God is called covenant. He replied: 'From the text, "And he remembered for them his covenant" (Ps. CVI, 45), as has been explained.

'The "statutes" mentioned above are ordinances of the King, and the "judgements" are the edicts of the Torah.' R. Judah said that all those ordinances which come from the place called "Righteousness" are called "my statutes", and they are the edicts of the King, and those that come from the place called "judgement" are called his "judgements", the judgements of the King who is enthroned in the place where two sections, judgement and mercy, meet. We have learnt that even though one is circumcised, if he does not carry out the precepts of the Torah he is like a heathen in all respects, and it is forbidden to teach him the precepts of the Torah. He is called "an altar of stones" because of the hardness of his heart, and therefore his circumcision does not avail him aught.

Zohar: Vayikra, Section 3, Page 74a

[Note: The first 12 lines of the Hebrew text are not found in our translation]

THE NAKEDNESS OF THY FATHER AND THE NAKEDNESS OF THY MOTHER SHALT THOU NOT UNCOVER. R' Hiya cited the verse: "As the apple tree among the trees of the wood, so is my beloved among the sons" (S.S. II, 3). 'Why', he said, 'does the Community of Israel praise God by comparing Him to an apple tree? Because it combines all excellences. As it is healing for all, so is God healing for all; as it combines two colours, so God combines two attributes; as the apple has a more delicate scent than other trees, so of God it is written, "His scent is like Lebanon" (Hosea, XIV, 5); as the apple has a sweet taste, so of God it is written, "His mouth is most sweet" (S.S. v, 16). And the Holy One, blessed be He, praises the Community of Israel by comparing her to a lily, for reasons which have been explained elsewhere.' R. Judah said: 'When the righteous abound in the world, the Community of Israel emits sweet odours and is blessed in the Holy King and her face shines. But when the wicked abound she does not send forth good odours, and she receives a bitter taste from the other side, and her face is darkened.' R. Yose said: 'Of the time when the righteous abound it is said, "His left hand is under my head and his right hand doth embrace me" (S.S. II, 6). But of the time when sinners abound it is written, "He hath drawn back his right hand" (Lam. II, 3).' R. Hizkiah said: 'The King separates from the Matrona, and in regard to this it is written, "the nakedness of thy father and thy mother shalt thou not uncover".'

When R. Eleazar was once studying with his father he said: 'If an Advocate comes down to the world, he is to be found in the Matrona, and if there is an Accuser who assails the world, it is the Matrona that he assails. Why is this?' He replied with a parable. 'A king once had a son from a queen. As long as the son was obedient to the king the latter consorted with the queen. But when the son was not obedient to the king he separated from the queen. So it is', he said, 'with the Holy One, blessed be He, and the Community of Israel. As long as Israel perform the will of God the Holy One makes His abode with the Community of Israel. But when Israel do not perform the will of God He does not make His abode with the Community of Israel, because Israel is the firstborn of the Holy One, blessed be He, and the Community of Israel is their mother. All the time that Israel is kept away from the temple of the king, the Matrona, if one may say so, is kept away with them. Why is this? Because the Matrona did not in time apply the lash to this son to keep him in the right path. For the King never punishes his son, but leaves it in the hand of the Matrona to punish him and to lead him in the straight way before the King.

Zohar: Vayikra, Section 3, Page 74b

It is written, "A wise son maketh a glad father, but a foolish son is the heaviness of his mother" (Prov. x, 1). As long as this son goes in the right way and is wise he rejoices his father, the Holy King, but if he perverts his way he is the heaviness of his mother, to wit, the Community of Israel. Never was there such joy before the Holy One, blessed be He, as on the day when Solomon attained to wisdom and composed the Song of Songs. Then was the face of the Matrona brightened, and the King came to make his abode with her, so that she became more beautiful and exalted than ever. Why was this? Because she had produced this wise son for the world. [Tr. note: Al. "King".] When she produced Solomon

620

she produced all Israel, and all were in high degrees, virtuous like Solomon, and God rejoiced in them and they in Him. On the day when Solomon completed the temple below the Matrona prepared the house above, and they made their abode together and her face was bright with perfect joy, and then there was gladness for all above and below. But when this son does not conform to the will of the King, then there is uncovering of nakedness on all sides, because the King parts from the Matrona and the Matrona is kept away from the palace; for is not their separation a kind of nakedness? Hence it is written, "the nakedness of thy father and thy mother shalt thou not uncover".

Zohar: Vayikra, Section 3, Page 75a

[Note: The first 18 lines of the Hebrew text are not found in our translation]

THE NAKEDNESS OF THY FATHER'S WIFE SHALT THOU NOT UNCOVER. Who is meant by thy father's wife? Said R. Simeon: 'We have learnt: As long as the Matrona is with the King and giveth suck to thee, she is called "thy mother". Now, however, that she is banished with thee and is removed from the King, she is called "thy father's wife". She is his wife, because he has not divorced her, although she is in exile. Therefore the text enjoins concerning her twice-once in reference to the time when she is still with the King and is called "thy mother", and once in reference to the time when she is banished from the King's palace and is called the wife of the King. Although she is far from him, thou shalt not cause her to remove from thee, lest thine enemies gain dominion over thee and she do not protect thee in the captivity. Hence "thou shalt not uncover the nakedness of thy father's wife". Why? Because "it is thy father's nakedness": because although she is removed from the King, yet he is constantly watching over her, and therefore thou must be careful before her and not sin against her.'

R. Simeon here quoted the verse: "For the Lord thy God walketh in the midst of thy camp to deliver thee", etc. (Deut. XXIII, 14). 'This', he said, 'refers to the Shekinah, which is in the midst of Israel, and especially in the captivity, to protect them continually and on all sides from all other peoples, that they should not destroy them. For so it has been taught, that

Zohar: Vayikra, Section 3, Page 75b

the enemies of Israel have no power over them until Israel weaken the might of the Shekinah in face of the Chieftains who are appointed over the other nations. Then only the latter have power over them and enact cruel decrees against them. But when they return in repentance to her she breaks the power of all those Chieftains and of the enemies of Israel and avenges them on all. Hence "thy camp shall be holy": a man must not defile himself by sin and transgress the commands of the Law. We have learnt that there are two hundred and forty-eight members in the human body, and all are defiled when he is defiled, that is, when he is minded to be defiled. We have learnt that for three things Israel are kept in captivity: because they pay scant respect to the Shekinah in their exile, because they turn their faces away from the Shekinah, and because they defile themselves in the presence of the Shekinah.'

THE NAKEDNESS OF THY SISTER... THOU SHALT NOT UNCOVER. R. Abba was once going from Cappadocia to Lydda in company with R. Yose. As they were going they saw a man approaching with a mark on his face. Said R. Abba: 'Let us leave this road, because that man's face testifies that he has transgressed one of the precepts of the Law against illicit intercourse.' Said R. Yose: 'Suppose this mark was on him from his boyhood; how can it show that he has transgressed by illicit intercourse?' R. Abba replied: 'I can see that he has by his face.' R. Abba then called him and said: 'Tell me, what is that mark on your face?' He replied: 'I beg of you, do not punish me further, because my sins have caused this. 'How is that?' said R. Abba. He replied: 'I was once travelling with my sister, and we turned in to an inn, where I drank much wine. All that night I was in company with my sister. When I got up in the morning I found the host quarrelling with another man. I interposed between them and received blows from both, one on one side and one on the other, and was severely wounded, but was saved by a doctor who was living among us.' R. Abba asked who the doctor was, and he replied: 'It was R. Simlai.' 'What medicine did he give you?' asked R. Abba. He replied: 'Spiritual healing. From that day I repented, and every day I looked at myself in a mirror and wept before the Almighty for my sin, and from those tears my face was healed.' Said R. Abba: 'Were it not that you might cease repenting, I would cause that scar to be removed from your face. However, I will say over you the verse, "And thine iniquity is taken away and thy sin purged" (Isa. VI, 7). Repeat that three times.' He repeated it three times and the mark vanished; whereupon R. Abba said: 'In sooth, your Master was fain to remove it from you, which shows that you have truly repented.' He said: 'I vow from this day to study the Torah day and night.' R. Abba asked him what his name was, and he said 'Eleazar'. Said R. Abba: 'Eleazar, God is thy help; as thy name is so art thou.' He then sent him away with a blessing.

Some time after, R. Abba, as he was on his way to R. Simeon, went into the town where this man lived. He found him expounding the verse: "A brutish man knoweth not, neither doth a fool understand this" (Ps. XCII, 6). 'How stupid', he said, 'are mankind that they take no pains to know the ways of the Almighty by which the world is maintained. What prevents them? Their stupidity, because they do not study the Torah; for if they were to study the Torah they would know the ways of the Holy One, blessed be He. "A fool doth not understand this": to wit,

Zohar: Vayikra, Section 3, Page 76a

621

the ways of "this" (zoth, the Shekinah), in the world, how it judges the world. For they only see the punishments of this zoth alighting on the righteous and not alighting on the wicked who transgress the precepts of the Torah, and who inherit this world in every direction, as it is written, "the wicked spring as the grass". Nor should we know better, did not King David enlighten us in the second part of the verse, saying, "It is that they shall be destroyed forever"; that is, to be destroyed in the other world, where they shall be dust under the feet of the righteous.' He further discoursed on the verse: "My leanness riseth up against me, it testifieth to my face" (Job XVI, 8). 'Observe', he said, 'that if a man transgresses the precepts of the Law, the Torah itself goes up and down and makes marks on that man's face so that all both above and below look at him and heap curses on his head. We have learnt that all the eyes of the Lord which go to and fro in the world to observe the ways of mankind look well at the face of that man and exclaim: Alas, alas! Alas for him in this world, alas for him in the world to come. Keep away from So-and-so because his face testifies against him that an unclean spirit rests upon him. If during the days that that testimony is upon his face he begets a son, he instils in him a spirit from the unclean side; and such become the shameless sinners of the generation, to whom their Master allows scope in this world in order to destroy them in the next. But if a man is virtuous and studies the Torah day and night, then God weaves around him a thread of grace and sets a mark on his face which makes all afraid of him both above and below.' Said R. Abba to him: 'All this is very true; from whence have you learnt it?' He replied: 'So I have been taught, and I have also been taught that this evil heritage is transmitted to all his sons, if they do not repent, for repentance overcomes everything. For this remedy was given me once when I bore a mark on my face, until one day as I was going along I met a certain saintly man through whom this mark was removed from me.' 'What is your name?' asked R. Abba. He replied: 'My name is Eleazar', and he divided it into El ezer (God is help). Said R. Abba to him: 'Blessed be God that I have been privileged to see thee thus. Blessed art thou in this world and the next. I am the man who met you.' He thereupon prostrated himself before him and brought him into his house and prepared for him special bread and flesh from a fatted calf.

After they finished eating the man said: 'Rabbi, I want you to tell me something. I have a red heifer, the mother of the calf the flesh of which we have just eaten. One day before it had calved I was going with it to the pasture when a man met me and said to me: What is the name of that cow? I replied that I had never given it a name. He said: It will be called Bathsheba the mother of Solomon if you shall succeed in repenting. Before I could turn my head he was gone, and I thought his remark very ridiculous.

Zohar: Vayikra, Section 3, Page 76b

Now, however, that I have become a student of the Torah I have been thinking again over that remark, but since R. Simlai departed this world there has been none who can enlighten us on questions of the Torah like him, and I am afraid to put forth any opinion of my own which I have not learnt from a teacher, and I can see that there is a hidden meaning in this remark though I do not understand it.' 'Truly', replied R. Abba, 'it has a hidden meaning with reference both to the upper and the lower world. A certain divine grade is called Bath sheba (daughter of seven in the mystery of Wisdom, and is symbolized by the seven kine, the seven burnings, the seven sprinklings, the seven washings, the seven unclean, the seven clean, the seven priests. [Tr. note: The reference is, apparently, to the section of the Red Heifer, Num. XIX] [Tr. note: V. T. B. Erubin, 18b.] This was the hidden meaning in that man's remark.' He said: 'Thank God for granting me to hear this, and for giving me His greeting of peace, and bringing me near to Him when I was far away.' Said R. Abba to him: '"Peace be unto thee and peace to thy house and peace to all that thou hast" (I Sam. xxv, 6).'

THOU SHALT NOT UNCOVER THE NAKEDNESS OF THY FATHER'S SISTER. We have learnt elsewhere that Adam separated from his wife a hundred and thirty years2 after Cain killed Abel. R. Yose said: 'When death was decreed for him and for all mankind, he said: Why should I beget children for confusion? and he therefore separated from his wife. Then two female spirits used to come to him and they bore from him. Their offspring were demons and were called "plagues of the children of men". We have learnt that when man came down to earth in the supernal likeness all who saw him, both higher and lower beings, came to him and made him king of this world. Eve bore Cain from the filth of the serpent, and therefore from him were descended all the wicked generations, and from his side is the abode of spirits and demons. Therefore all spirits and demons are half of the class of human beings below and half of the class of angels above. So, too, those that were born from Adam afterwards were half of the lower and half of the upper sphere. After these were born from Adam, he begat from those spirits daughters with the beauty of the heavenly beings and also with the beauty of the lower beings, so that the sons of God went astray after them. One male came into the world from the side of the spirit of the side of Cain, and they called him Tubal Cain. A female came with him who was called Naamah, from whom issued other spirits and demons; these hover in the air and tell things to those others below. This Tubal Cain produced weapons of war, and this Naamah clung to her own side, and she still exists, having her abode among the waves of the great sea. She goes forth and makes sport with men and conceives from them through their lustful dreams. From that lust she becomes pregnant and brings forth further species in the world. The sons whom she bears from human beings show themselves to the females of mankind, who become pregnant from them and bring forth spirits, and they all go to the ancient Lilith, who brings them up. She goes out into the world and seeks

Zohar: Vayikra, Section 3, Page 77a

her little ones, and when she sees little children she cleaves to them in order to kill them and to insinuate herself into their spirits. There are, however, three holy spirits which fly in front of her and take that spirit from her and set it before the Holy One, blessed be He, and there they are taught before Him. Thus they guard that child and she cannot hurt him. But if a man is not holy, and draws upon himself a spirit from the unclean side, she comes and makes sport with that child, and if she kills him she enters into his spirit and never leaves it. You may say: What about those others whom she has killed, although the three angels confronted her and took from her their spirits? Since they were not on the side of uncleanness, why had she power to kill them? This happens when a man does not sanctify himself, but yet does not purposely try to defile himself nor actually do so. In such cases she has power over the body but not the spirit. Sometimes it happens that Naamah goes forth to have intercourse with men and a man is linked with her in lust, and then suddenly wakes and clasps his wife though his mind is still full of the lust of his dream. In that case the son so born is of the side of Naamah, and when Lilith goes forth she sees him and knows what has happened, and brings him up like the other children of Naamah, and he is often with her, and she does not kill him. This is the man who receives a blemish on every New Moon. For Lilith never gives them up, but at every New Moon she goes forth and visits all those whom she has brought up and makes sport with them; hence this man receives a blemish at that time. These things King Solomon revealed in the book of Asmodai, and we find therein a thousand and four hundred and five manners of defilement which can affect mankind. Alas for mankind that they close their eyes and observe not nor take any heed how they are preserved in the world! Counsel and healing are before them but they heed not, for they cannot deliver themselves save by the counsel of the Torah, as it is written: "Ye shall sanctify yourselves and ye shall be holy, for I am the Lord your God."

'We have learnt that when Cain and Abel were removed, Adam returned to his wife and was clothed with a fresh spirit and begat Seth, with whom commenced the generations of righteous men in the world. God showed lovingkindness to the world, and with each one a female was born to populate the world, after the supernal pattern. For so we have affirmed in the secret doctrine of the Mishnah, that "if a man taketh his sister, his father's daughter or his mother's daughter, it is hesed" (lit. Iovingkindness); truly so, and after hesed had appeared, roots and stocks came forth from beneath the highest, and branches spread and that which was near receded afar. This was at the beginning, in the hidden development of the world, but subsequently human beings who behave so "shall be cut off before the eyes of the children of their people".

Zohar: Vayikra, Section 3, Page 77b

[Note: The first 3 lines of the Hebrew text are not found in our translation]

'We have learnt that the upper He was conceived from the love of its inseparable companion Yod, and brought forth Vau. When this Vau came forth, its mate came forth with it. Lovingkindness came and parted them, and there came forth roots from beneath the Highest, and branches spread and grew and the lower He, was produced. It spread its branches higher and higher until it joined the upper tree and Vau was linked with He. Who caused this? Hesed. But the union of Yod with the upper He is not caused by Hesed but by mazzal (lit. Iuck). In this way Yod is linked with He, He with Vau, Vau with He, and He, with all, and all forms one entity, of which the elements are never to be separated. He who causes separation between them, as it were, lays waste the world and is called "the nakedness of all". In time to come God will restore the Shekinah to its place, and there will be a complete union, as it is written: "On that day the Lord shall be one and his name one" (Zech. XIV, 9). It may be said: Is He not now one? No; for now through sinners He is not really one; for the Matrona is removed from the King and they are not united, and the supernal Mother is removed from the King and does not give suck to Him, because the King without the Matrona is not invested with His crowns as before. But when He joins the Matrona, who crowns Him with many resplendent crowns, then the supernal Mother will also crown Him in fitting manner. But now that the King is not with the Matrona, the Supernal Mother keeps her crowns and withholds from Him the waters of the Stream and He is not joined with Her. Therefore, as it were, He is not one. But when the Matrona shall return to the place of the temple and the King shall be wedded with her, then all will be joined together without separation, and regarding this it is written, "On that day the Lord shall be one and his name one". Then "saviours shall come up on Mount Zion to judge the mount of Esau" (Obad. I, 21), as it has been taught: R. Simeon said, The Matrona will not enter her temple in joy until the kingdom of Esau has been brought to judgement and she has taken vengeance on it for causing all this. Therefore "they shall judge the mount of Esau" first, and then "the kingdom shall be the Lord's" (Ibid.), the kingdom being the Matrona.'

THE NAKEDNESS OF THY FATHER'S BROTHER THOU SHALT NOT UNCOVER. R. Judah taught that this refers to Israel below, and "the mother's sister" to Jerusalem below; for it was for these sins that Israel was destined to go into exile among the peoples and the earthly Jerusalem to be destroyed. Concerning this we have learnt that God showed His love for Israel by calling them brothers, as it is written, "For my brethren and companions' sake I will speak peace concerning thee" (Ps. CXXII, 8), the esoteric meaning of which is as follows, as explained by R. Simeon in the name of R. Judah. The word "companion" refers to one who never parts, and so the supernal Mother is called "companion" because the love of the Father never departs from her,

Zohar: Vayikra, Section 3, Page 78a

whereas the lower Mother is called "bride" (daughter-in-law) and "sister". In this passage it refers to her as "the daughter of thy father" and "the daughter of thy mother". If she is from the side of the Father she is called Wisdom (Hokhmah), and if from the side of the Mother she is called Understanding (Binah); and in either case she is from both the Father and the Mother; and this is hinted in the words "born at home", to wit from the side of the Father, "or born abroad", to wit, from the side of the Mother. R. Abba, however, said that "born at home" means coming from the River that issues from Eden, and "born abroad" from the Small of Countenance. R. Judah said that Israel are called "brothers" to the Holy One, blessed be He, because His love never departs from them. The earthly Jerusalem is called "thy mother's sister". It is written, "Jerusalem that art builded as a city that is compact together" (Ps. CXXII, 3). It is so called because the King is joined to it from six sides and all the crowns of the King are comprised in it. "Whither the tribes went up, even the tribes of KAH": these are the twelve boundaries which spread from that great and mighty Tree, and which it inherited from the side of the Father and the Mother. "For there are set thrones for judgement, thrones for the house of David": that he may inherit the holy kingdom, he and his sons for all generations. Thus this is a hymn which David composed concerning the holy supernal kingdom. R. Hizkiah said: 'The whole has a supernal reference, to show that he who impairs below impairs above. It is written "The nakedness of thy daughter-in-law thou shalt not uncover". If the disciples of the wise who know the inner meaning of this commit an offence below, then, as it were, they cause a blemish in the Bride above; but in regard to the mass of men the verse has its literal significance, and for this sin the Shekinah departs from them.'

Zohar: Vayikra, Section 3, Page 78b

R. Simeon said to R. Eleazar: 'See now. These twenty-two letters which are inscribed in the Torah are all illustrated in the Ten Creative Utterances. Each of those ten, which are the crowns of the King, is traced in certain letters. Hence the Holy Name is disguised under other letters and each Utterance lends to the one above it certain letters, so that they are comprised in one another. Therefore we trace the Holy Name in other letters not its own, one set being concealed in the other, though all are linked together. He who desires to know the combinations of the holy names must know the letters which are inscribed in each crown and then combine them. I myself trace them from the profound book of Solomon, and so I am able to do it and reveal them to the Companions. Blessed are the righteous in this world and the next, because God desires to honour them and reveals to them profound secrets of the Holy Name which He does not reveal to the celestial holy ones (angels). And therefore Moses was able to crown himself among those holy ones and they were not able to touch him, though they are like a burning flame and coals of fire. For otherwise how could Moses have stood among them? When God commenced to speak with Moses, the latter desired to know His holy names, disclosed and undisclosed, each one in fitting manner, and thus he came closer and learnt more than any other man. When Moses entered into the cloud and came among the angels, one named Gazarniel came up to him with flames of fire, with flashing eyes and burning wings, and sought to wound him. Then Moses mentioned a certain holy name which was traced with twelve letters, and the angel was utterly confused; and so with all the others.

'THOU SHALT NOT UNCOVER THE NAKEDNESS OF A WOMAN AND HER DAUGHTER. We have explained these prohibitions to refer to the adornments of the Matrona, but they also have their literal meaning because they are necessary for the right ordering of society, and if a man transgresses one of them, woe for him and woe for his soul, because he uncovers other nakednesses. We have learnt that the last of the Ten Commandments, "Thou shalt not covet thy neighbour's wife", comprises all the others, and he who covets his neighbour's wife is like one transgressing the whole of the Law. Nothing, however, can stand in the way of repentance, especially if a man receives his punishment, like King David.' R. Yose said: 'We have learnt that if a man sins and gives up the fruit of his sin, his repentance brings him to a higher grade than before; but if he does not give up the fruit of his sin, his repentance does not avail him. If that is the case, it may be asked why did not David part from Bathsheba?' He replied: 'Bathsheba was his by right, and he only took his own, her husband having died. For it has been taught that Bathsheba was destined for David from the Creation, and what kept her from him was his marrying the daughter of King Saul. On that day Uriah obtained her by a special grace, though she was not really his. Afterwards David came and took his own; and it was because David anticipated matters by killing Uriah that God was displeased with him, and He punished him that he might be established in the supernal holy kingdom.'

I AM THE LORD. R. Yose taught: 'This means, "I am the Lord who will one day bestow a good reward on the righteous in the time to come; I am the Lord who will one day punish the wicked in the time to come". It is written, "I kill and make alive" (Deut. XXXII, 39); although

I am in the attribute of mercy, the wicked turn me to the attribute of judgement.' R. Simeon said: 'Sinners cause imperfection above, as we have explained.'

THOU SHALT NOT APPROACH A WOMAN TO UNCOVER HER NAKEDNESS AS LONG AS SHE IS IMPURE BY HER UNCLEANNESS. R. Judah taught: The generation of whom R. Simeon is one are all righteous, saintly and fearful of sin, and the Shekinah abides among them as among no other generation. Therefore these things are stated openly and not concealed, whereas in former generations supernal mysteries could not be revealed, and those who knew them were afraid to utter them. For when R. Simeon expounded the mysteries of this verse all the Companions were in tears, and his meaning was clear to them. For one day R. Jesse mockingly repeated R. Simeon's words, "An egg of truth [Tr. note: The primordial Yod.] which issues from a bird which abides in fire and bursts forth on four sides; two go forth from there, one is depressed and one overflows into a great sea".' R. Abba said to him: 'You have turned sacred into profane before R. Simeon.' Said R. Simeon: 'Before the egg breaks open, you shall depart from this world; and so it came to pass in the Chamber of R. Simeon. [Tr. note: v. Zohar, Numbers, 144a.] We have learnt that in the days of R. Simeon one man used to say to another: Open thy mouth that thy words may spread light. In the holy Chamber it was said: Here it is fitting to reveal what concerns this subject. When the mighty Serpent above rouses himself on account of the sins of the generation, he joins himself to the Female and injects filth into her. Then the Male parts from her because she is defiled, and it is not fitting for the Male to approach her, for pity would be if he were defiled with her. We have learnt that a hundred and twenty-five species of uncleanness came down into the world and are connected with the side of the mighty Serpent, and twenty-seven chiefs of them attach themselves to females and cling to them. Alas, then, for a man who touches such a woman at that time, for through this sin he awakens the supernal Serpent and casts filth into a holy place, and punishments are let loose on the world and all is defiled. We have learnt that the Serpent injected twenty-four kinds of uncleanness into the female when he was joined to her, so that twenty-four punishments are roused above and twenty-four below. The hair and the nails grow, and therefore when a woman comes to purify herself she must cut off the hair which grew in the days of her uncleanness and cut her nails with all the filth that clings to them. For, as we have learnt, the filth of the nails arouses another filth, and therefore they must be hidden away. [Tr. note: v. T. B. Moed Katon, 18a; Niddah, 17a.] He who hides them away completely, as it were, awakens lovingkindness in the world, for they even provide opportunity for sorcerers to exercise their magic on account of the demons attached to them,

and a person stepping on them with his foot or his shoe may come to harm. If this is true of this remnant of a remnant of filth, how much more of the woman who was joined with the Serpent! Alas for the world which inherited that filth from her! Therefore it is written, "To a woman in the separation of her uncleanness thou shalt not draw near". Happy the generation in which R. Simeon lived! To it the words apply, "Happy art thou O land, when thy king is a free man". This is R. Simeon, who holds his head erect to expound doctrine and fears not, like a free man who says what he wants to say without fear.'

R. Simeon said: 'It is written: "And it shall come to pass that from one new moon to another, and from one Sabbath to another", etc. (Isa. LXVI, 23). Why is "new moon" put side by side with "Sabbath"? Because both are of one grade, being the time when one is joined to the other. On Sabbath there is joy and an additional soul, because the Ancient One reveals Himself and the wedlock is prepared. So, too, at the renewal of the moon, because the sun illumines her with the joyful light of the Ancient One above. Therefore the offering of new moon is an atonement above.

'It is written, "The burnt offering of the Sabbath beside ('al, lit. upon) the continual burnt offering" (Num. XXVIII, 10). The word 'al here signifies that the thought should be directed to the very highest more than on other days. Similarly it is written, "And Hannah prayed to ('al, lit. upon) the Lord" (I Sam. I, 19), because children depend upon the holy mazzal, as we have pointed out.' R. Yose found R. Abba similarly interpreting the words, "Cast thy burden upon the Lord" (Ps. LV, 23), because food also depends on mazzal. R. Judah expounded similarly the verse, "For this ('al zoth) let every one that is godly pray to thee" (Ibid. XXXII, 6): verily, to that which is above zoth.

R. Isaac said: 'Happy are the righteous in that many precious treasures are stored up for them in the other world, where God will have joyous converse with them, as we have laid down. Happy their portion in this world and the

next, as it is written: "But let all those that put their trust in thee rejoice, let them ever shout for joy because thou defendest them, let them also that love thy name be joyful in thee" (Ps. v, 12).'

KEDOSHIM

YE SHALL BE HOLY, ETC. R. Eleazar cited here the text: "Be ye not as the horse or as the mule which have no understanding", etc. (Ps. XXXII, 9). 'How often', he said, 'does the Torah warn men, how often does it cry aloud on all sides to rouse them, yet they all sleep in their sins [Tr. note: Al. "in their dens".] and heed not! With what face will they rise on the day of judgement when the Most High King will visit upon them their neglect of the Torah in not listening to her call, since they are full of blemishes and know not the faith of the Heavenly King. Alas for them and for their souls! For the Torah has warned them saying: "Whoso is simple let him turn in hither; as for him that is void of understanding (lit. heart), she saith to him" (Prov. IX, 4). Why is he called "void of heart"? Because he has no faith; since he who does not study the Torah has no faith and is wholly blemished. It is the supernal Torah which "saith to him", and calls him "void of heart". Similarly we have learnt that if a man does not study the Torah it is forbidden to go near him, to associate with him, to do business with him, all the more so to walk in the road with him. We have learnt that if a man walks abroad and no words of Torah accompany him, his life is forfeit; still more one who goes with a man who has no faith and heeds neither the honour of his Master nor his own, being regardless of his soul. Hence it is written: "Be not as the horse or as the mule", etc. Happy are the righteous who study the Torah and know the ways of the Holy One, blessed be He, and sanctify themselves with the holiness of the King and become holy throughout, thereby drawing down a holy spirit from above, so that all their children are truly virtuous and are called "sons of the king". Woe to the wicked who are shameless and do shameless deeds, for which their children inherit an unclean soul from the unclean side. "Be not like a horse or a mule", which are lustful above other creatures, for "they which have no understanding" fall a prey to the "dogs which are greedy and can never have enough" (Isa. LVI, 11), and which are ready to "shepherd them that have no understanding" (Ibid.)

Zohar: Vayikra, Section 3, Page 80b

into Gehinnom. Why does all this come upon them? Because they do not duly sanctify themselves in wedlock. God said: Of all peoples I desired to attach to myself only Israel; hence, "Ye shall be holy".'

YE SHALL BE HOLY FOR I THE LORD AM HOLY. R. Isaac cited here the verse: "Ah land of the rustling of wings", etc. (Isa. XVIII, 1). 'When God', he said, 'came to create the world and reveal what was hidden in the depths and disclose light out of darkness, they were all wrapped in one another, and therefore light emerged from darkness and from the impenetrable came forth the profound. So, too, from good issues evil and from mercy issues judgement, and all are intertwined, the good impulse and the evil impulse, right and left, Israel and other peoples, white and black–all depend on one another.' Said R. Isaac in the name of R. Judah: 'The whole world is like a garland of variegated flowers; when it is tried, it is judged with judgement mingled with mercy; otherwise it could not stand an instant. We have learnt that when judgement is suspended over the world and righteousness is crowned with its judgements, many winged messengers arise to meet the lords of stern judgement and to obtain sway over the world, and they spread their wings on both sides to overshadow the earth, which is then called "the land of the rustling of wings".' R. Judah said: 'I perceive that all mankind are shameless save the truly virtuous. So, if one may say so, it is throughout: if one commences to purify himself he is supported from above and similarly if he commences to defile himself. [Tr. note: v. T.B. Yoma, 38b.]

As R. Yose was once on the road he met R. Hiya and said to him: 'In reference to the verse, "Therefore I have sworn to the house of Eli that the iniquity of Eli's house shall not be purged with sacrifice nor offering forevert" (I Sam. III, 4), the Companions, you know, have stated that it will not be purged with sacrifices nor offering, but it can be purged with words of Torah. [Tr. note: v. T.B. Rosh Hashanah, 18a.] Why is this? Because the words of the Torah rise above all offerings.' He replied: 'This is truly so, and if a man studies the Torah it benefits him more than all sacrifices and burnt-offerings, and even though punishment has been decreed against him from above it is annulled. Therefore it is that words of the Torah are not susceptible to uncleanness, [Tr. note: v. T.B. Berachoth, 22a.] because it can itself purify those who are unclean. We know this from the verse: "The fear of the Lord is clean, enduring forever" (Ps. XIX, 9).' Said R. Yose: 'But it says here "the fear of the Lord", and not "the Torah"?' He replied: 'It means the same thing, because the Torah comes from the side of Geburah (Might).' Said R. Yose: 'Rather derive it from here: "The fear of the Lord is the beginning of wisdom" (Ibid. CXI, 10). It is written: "The fear of the Lord is pure", and the Torah is called "holiness", as it is written, "I the Lord am holy", and the Torah is the supernal holy Name. Therefore

Zohar: Vayikra, Section 3, Page 81a

he who studies it is first purified and then sanctified. We have learnt that the holiness of the Torah surpasses all other sanctifications, and the holiness of the superior recondite wisdom is highest of all.' He said to him: 'There is no Torah without wisdom and no wisdom without Torah, both being in the same grade, the root of the Torah being in the supernal Wisdom by which it is sustained. As they were going along they came across a man riding on a horse through a garden, and as he raised his hand he broke off the branch of a tree. Said R. Yose: 'This illustrates the verse: "Ye shall sanctify yourselves and become holy"; if a man sanctifies himself below, he is further sanctified above.'

R. Abba taught: 'This section sums up the whole Torah, and is the seal of truth. In this section are contained profound mysteries of the Torah relative to the Ten Commandments and divine decrees and penalties and precepts, so that when the Companions came to this section they used to rejoice.'

Said R. Abba: 'Why does the section of "holiness" follow immediately upon the section dealing with sexual offences? Because we have learnt that whoever preserves himself from these offences shows that he was begotten in holiness; all the more so if he sanctifies himself with the holiness of his Master. The Companions have indicated the proper time of marital intercourse for all classes. He who desires to sanctify himself according to the will of his Master should not have intercourse save from midnight onwards, or at midnight, for at that time the Holy One, blessed be He, is in the Garden of Eden, and greater holiness is abroad, wherefore it is a time for a man to sanctify himself. This is the rule for the ordinary man. But students who know the ways of the Torah should rise at midnight to study and to join themselves with the Community of Israel to praise the holy name and the holy King; and their time of intercourse is at that hour on the night of the Sabbath [Tr. note: v. T.B. Ketuboth, 62b.] when grace abounds, that they may obtain favour from the Community of Israel and the Holy One, blessed be He, and those are called holy.'

R. Abba quoted here the verse: "Who is like thy people Israel, one nation in the earth?" (I Sam. VII, 23). 'God', he said, 'chose Israel alone of all peoples, and made them one unique nation in the world and called them "one nation", after His own name. He gave them many precepts to be crowned withal, including the phylacteries of the head and the arm, wherewith a man becomes one and complete. For he is only called "one" when he is complete, and not if he is defective, and therefore God is called One when He is consummated with the Patriarchs and the Community of Israel. When, therefore, the Israelite puts on his phylacteries and wraps himself in the fringed garment, he is crowned with holy crowns after the supernal pattern and is called "one", and it is fitting that One should come and attend to one. And when is a man called "one"? When he is male with female and is sanctified with a high holiness and is bent upon sanctification;

Zohar: Vayikra, Section 3, Page 81b

then alone he is called one without blemish. Therefore a man should rejoice with his wife at that hour to bind her in affection to him, and they should both have the same intent. When they are thus united, they form one soul and one body: one soul through their affection, and one body, as we have learnt, that if a man is not married he is, as it were, divided in halves, and only when male and female are joined do they become one body. Then God rests upon "one" and lodges a holy spirit in it: and such are called "the sons of God", as has been said.'

YE SHALL FEAR EVERY MAN HIS MOTHER AND HIS FATHER, ETC, The fear of mother and father is here put side by side with the keeping of the Sabbath. Said R. Yose: 'It is all one; he who fears one keeps the other. Why is the mother here placed before the father? As we have learnt, because she has not so much power as the father.' R. Isaac connected this with the preceding words, "ye shall be holy": when a man comes to sanctify himself together with his wife, it is the female who deserves the greater credit for that sanctification, and therefore the mother is placed first here.' R. Judah pointed out that in another place the father is placed before the mother, the object being to indicate that both contributed equally to producing the son. The verse continues: AND YE SHALL KEEP MY SABBATHS, to show that one precept is of equal weight with the other.

Zohar: Vayikra, Section 3, Page 82a

[Note: The first 3 lines of the Hebrew text do not appear in our translation.]

R. Simeon said: 'When a man sanctifies himself below, as, for instance, the Companions who sanctify themselves from Sabbath to Sabbath at the hour of the supernal wedlock, when grace abounds and blessings are at hand, then all cleave together, the soul of Sabbath and the body that has been prepared for Sabbath. Therefore it is written, "Ye shall fear every one his mother and his father", who form one wedlock in the body at that hour which has been sanctified. "Ye shall keep my sabbaths": the plural refers to the upper and the lower Sabbath which invite the soul to that body from that supernal wedlock. We may also translate "Ye shall wait for my sabbaths", this being an admonition to those who wait for their marital intercourse from Sabbath to Sabbath, as it is written, "the eunuchs who keep my sabbaths" (Isa. LVI, 4), for so we may call the Companions who emasculate themselves all the other days of the week in order to labour in the study of the Torah and wait from Sabbath to Sabbath. We may also take "father and mother" here to refer to the Body, and "my sabbaths" to the Soul, both of which cleave together.'

Zohar: Vayikra, Section 3, Page 83b

TURN YE NOT UNTO IDOLS NOR MAKE TO YOURSELVES MOLTEN GODS. R. Hiya adduced in this connection the verse: "Turn not unto the stubbornness of this people" (Deut. IX, 27). 'How', he said, 'could Moses address such a request to the Almighty who observes all things and passes all deeds in judgement? The answer is as follows. If a man performs a religious action, that action ascends and stands before the Almighty and says: I am from So-and-so who has performed me; and God then sets it before Him that He may look upon it all the day and treat the doer well for its sake. Similarly, if a man transgresses a precept of the Law, that action ascends and stands before the Almighty and says: I am from So-and-so who has performed me; and God sets that action where the sight of it will remind him to destroy that man. But if the man repents, then He removes that sin to where He will not observe it. Hence Moses said to God: "Turn not to the wickedness of this people, nor to their wickedness nor to their sin".'

R. Yose the younger once went in to see R. Simeon and found him expounding the verse: "And the man said: The woman whom thou gavest to be with me, she gave me of the tree and I did eat" (Gen. III, 12). 'The expression "with me",' he said, 'indicates that Adam and Eve were created together with one body.' Said R. Yose to him: 'If so, what of the words of Hannah to Eli: "I am the woman who stood with thee here" (I Sam. I, 26)?' He replied: 'It does not say here "was given".' 'But,' said the other, 'what of the verse, "And the Lord God said, It is not good that the man should be alone, I will make him an help meet for him" (Gen. II, 18), which implies that she was not made until then?' He replied: 'Adam was indeed alone in so far as he had no support from his female, because she was fixed in his side, as we have explained. Hence God did not say "I will create a help", but "I will make", that is, fashion; and so God did by taking one of his sides and fashioning it and bringing it to him. Then Adam cohabited with his wife, and she became a support to him.

'We have learnt that the beauty of Adam was like an emanation from the supernal effulgence, and the beauty of Eve such that no creature could look steadily at her. Even Adam could not look steadily at her until they had sinned and their beauty had been diminished. Then only did Adam gaze steadfastly at her and "know" her. We have learnt that it is forbidden to a man to gaze at the beauty of a woman [Tr. note: v. T.B. Berachoth, 24a et passim.] lest evil thoughts should be provoked in him and he should be incited

Zohar: Vayikra, Section 3, Page 84a

to something worse.' When R. Simeon went through the town, followed by the Companions, if he saw a beautiful woman he used to lower his eyes and say to the Companions, Do not turn. Whoever gazes at the beauty of a woman by day will have lustful thoughts at night, and if these gain the better of him he will transgress the precept, "Ye shall not make to yourselves molten gods". And if he has intercourse with his wife while under the influence of those imaginings, the children born from such union are called "molten gods". R. Abba said: 'It is forbidden to a man to fix his gaze upon heathen idols and upon Gentile women, or to receive benefit or healing from them.'

R. Abba discoursed on the verse: "Turn unto me and have mercy upon me, give thy strength unto thy servant" (PS. LXXXVI, 15). 'Had God, then', he said, 'nothing more beautiful than David to turn to? It is, however, as we have learnt, that God has another David who is in command of many celestial hosts and legions: and when God desires to be gracious to the world He looks upon this David with a smiling countenance, and he in turn sheds light and grace upon the world through his beauty, his head being a skull of gold broidered with seven ornaments of gold. And through God's great love for him, He tells him to turn his eyes towards Him and look at Him, because they are very beautiful; and when he does so, His heart is, as it were, pierced with shafts of supernal love. And for the sake of that celestial David, beautiful, beloved and desired of God, David said: "Turn to me and be gracious unto me". Similarly, when Isaac said to Jacob, "Behold the smell of my son is as the smell of a field which the Lord hath blessed", this, we are told, was because the Garden of Eden entered with Jacob. Here, too, we may ask, how could the Garden of Eden enter with him, seeing that it is of immense extent in length and breadth, with many compartments and residences? The truth is that God has another holy Garden of which He is specially fond, and which He guards Himself and which He appoints to be continually with the righteous; and this it was that entered with Jacob. Similarly when we are told that the whole land of Israel came and folded itself under Abram, [Tr. note: v. Midrash Rabbah on Genesis XIII, 15.] this refers to another holy supernal land which God has and which is also called "the land of Israel". This is below the grade of Jacob and has been transmitted by God to Israel out of His love for them to abide with them and to lead and protect them, and it is called "the land of the living".

'It is forbidden to a man to gaze upon a place which God loathes, and even on one which God loves. For instance, it is forbidden to gaze upon the rainbow, [Tr. note: v. T.B. Hagigah, 16a.] because it is the mirror of the supernal form. It is forbidden to a man to gaze upon the sign of the covenant upon him, because this is emblematic of the Righteous One of the world. It is forbidden to gaze upon the fingers of the priests when they spread out their hands to bless the congregation, [Tr. note: v. Ibid.] because the glory of the most high King rests there. If one must not gaze at a holy place,

Zohar: Vayikra, Section 3, Page 84b

how much less may he at an unclean and loathsome one! Therefore, "turn not to the idols".' R. Isaac said: 'If it is forbidden to look at them, how much more to worship them!

The injunctions in this section correspond to those in the Ten Commandments. Thus: "Ye shall not turn to the idols" corresponds to "Thou shalt have no other gods before me"; "nor make to yourselves molten gods" to "thou shalt not make unto thee any graven image"; "I am the Lord your God" to "I am the Lord thy God"; "ye shall fear every one his mother and his father" to "honour thy father and thy mother"; "and ye shall keep my sabbaths" to "remember the Sabbath day to keep it holy"; "ye shall not swear by my name falsely" to "thou shalt not take the name of the Lord thy God in vain"; "ye shall not steal" to "thou shalt not steal"; "neither shall ye deal falsely nor lie to one another" to "thou shalt not bear false witness against thy neighbour '; "the adulterer and the adulteress shall surely be put to death" (xx, 10) to "thou shalt not commit adultery"; "neither shalt thou stand against the blood of thy neighbour" to "thou shalt not murder". Thus the Law is summed up in this section.' R. Hiya asked: 'Why in the Ten Commandments is the singular (thou) used and here the plural (you)? Because in the whole of their existence Israel were never so united in heart and

628

mind in devotion to God as on that day when they stood before Mount Sinai; hence they were addressed there as a single individual, but later they were not so single-hearted.'

R. Eleazar once went to pay a visit to R. Yose ben R. Simeon ben Lakunia, his father-in-law, accompanied by R. Hiya and R. Yose. On reaching a certain field they sat down under a tree, and R. Eleazar said: 'Let each of us give a discourse on the Torah.' He himself commenced with the text: "Yet I am the Lord thy God from the land of Egypt, and thou shalt know no god but me" (Hos. XIII, 4). He said: 'Was God then their king only from the land of Egypt and not previously? Did not Jacob say to his sons, "Remove the strange gods from your midst" (Gen. xxxv, 2)? The truth is that Israel never paid such recognition to the glory of God as in the land of Egypt, where they were so bitterly oppressed and yet did not change their customs; nay more, they saw every day much magic and sorcery which might have seduced them, and yet they turned aside neither to the right nor to the left, although they did not actually know much of the glory of God, but only adhered to the customs of their fathers. Afterwards they saw many wonders and miracles, and therefore God said to them, "I am the Lord thy God from the land of Egypt", where His glory was revealed to them by the sea, and they saw the brightness of His glory face to face, so that they should not say it was another God who spoke with them, but should know that it was the same one who brought them out of the land of Egypt, whom they had seen in the land of Egypt, who had slain their enemies there and wrought the ten plagues there.'

He further discoursed on the verse: THOU SHALT NOT OPPRESS THY NEIGHBOUR, NOR ROB HIM; THE WAGES OF A HIRED SERVANT SHALL NOT ABIDE WITH THEE ALL NIGHT UNTIL MORNING. 'The reason for this last injunction is to be found in the verse, "In his day thou shalt give him his hire, and the sun shall not go down upon him" (Deut. XXIV, 15): that is to say, that thou be not gathered in from the world on his account before thy time cometh. From this we learn another thing, that if one restores the soul of a poor man, even

Zohar: Vayikra, Section 3, Page 85a

if his time has arrived to depart from the world, God restores his soul and gives him a further lease of life. To withhold the wage of a poor man is like taking his life and the life of his household. As he diminishes their souls, so God diminishes his days, and cuts off his soul from the other world. For all the breaths which issue from his mouth for the whole of that day ascend and stand before the Almighty, and afterwards his soul and the souls of his household ascend and stand in those breaths. Thus, even if length of days and many blessings had been decreed for that man, they are all withdrawn, nor does his soul mount aloft. Therefore R. Abba said: God save us from them and from their plaint! And the same is true even if it is a rich man, and his right is withheld from him. Hence R. Hamnuna, when a hired worker had finished his work, used to give him his wage and say to him: Take your soul which you have entrusted to my hand! Take your deposit! And even if the other asked him to keep it for him, he was unwilling to do so, saying: It is not fitting that your body shall be deposited with me, still less then your soul, which should be deposited only with God. Why is it written, "On his day thou shalt give him his hire"? Because every day is under the surveillance of another, a supernal Day, and if he does not give him his soul on that day, it is as if he impairs that supernal Day.'

R. Hiya discoursed on the next verse: THOU SHALT NOT CURSE THE DEAF NOR PUT A STUMBLING BLOCK BEFORE THE BLIND. 'This verse can be taken literally, but all this section has also other significations, and each set is connected with the other. See now. If a man curses his neighbour in his presence, it is as if he spills his blood When, however, he curses him not in his presence, the voice of his words ascends, and is joined by many emissaries of judgement until the place of the great abyss is aroused Woe, therefore, to him who lets an evil word issue from his mouth. The words, "thou shalt not put a stumbling block before the blind" we interpret of one who leads another into sin, [Tr. note: v. T.B. Moed Katon, 17a.] and also of one who strikes his grown-up son; or again, of one who not being competent gives decisions on points of Jewish law, because he causes his fellow-man to come to grief in the future world. For we have learnt that he who walks straightly in the path of the Torah and who studies it in the fitting manner has ever a goodly portion in the world to come, since the word of Torah which issues from his lips flits about the world and goes aloft, where many angels join it, and it is crowned with a holy crown and bathed in the light of the world to come, so that there proceeds from it a celestial light which crowns him during the whole of the day. But if a man studies the Torah not in the true and

Zohar: Vayikra, Section 3, Page 85b

proper manner, his words stray from the path and no angels join them, but they are thrust away by all and find no resting place. Who is the cause of this? The one who led him astray from the right path. If a man, however, desires to study the Torah and cannot find a proper teacher, and yet out of his love for the Torah he pores over it and babbles it ignorantly, all his words ascend and God rejoices in them and plants them around the River, where they grow into mighty trees and are called "willows of the brook". Happy are those who know the ways of the Torah and study it in the proper manner, for they plant trees of life which are superior to all healing medicines. Therefore it says, "The law of truth was in his mouth" (Mal. II, 6). For there is a law which is not of truth, namely, of him who gives decisions without being qualified, and one who learns from him learns something which is not truth. None the less it behoves a man to learn Torah, even from one who is not qualified, in order that thus his interest may be aroused and he may eventually learn from one who is qualified and walk in the straight path of the Torah.'

R. Yose then discoursed on the next verse: YE SHALL DO NO UNRIGHTEOUSNESS IN JUDGEMENT, ETC. IN RIGHTEOUSNESS SHALT THOU JUDGE THY NEIGHBOUR. 'Two grades are here mentioned, "judgement" and "righteousness". What is the difference between them? One is mercy and one judgement, and one is established by the other. When "righteousness" is aroused it deals out sentence to all impartially without indulgence; but when "judgement" is aroused, clemency is also in it. I might then think that judgement alone should be used; therefore the verse says, "In righteousness shalt thou judge thy neighbour", not sentencing one and passing over another, but treating all equally. Should, then, righteousness alone be used? No: the verse tells us "thou shalt judge", implying that both must be together. Why so? Because God is there, and therefore the trial must be without flaw: as he does below, so does God do above. For God sets up His throne of judgement when the judges sit on earth, and it is from there that God's Throne is established, that Throne consisting of righteousness and judgement. Hence if a judge offends against these, he, as it were, impairs the Throne of the King, and then God leaves the judges and does not remain among them.'

Zohar: Vayikra, Section 3, Page 86a

[Note: The first 6 lines of the Hebrew text are not found in our translation]

They then rose, and as they went along R. Eleazar cited the verse: THOU SHALT NOT GO UP AND DOWN AS A TALE-BEARER AMONG THY PEOPLE, ETC. All these rules', he said, 'have been commented on by the Companions. Let us, however, also give some exposition of this section. It is written: YE SHALL KEEP MY STATUTES. THOU SHALT NOT LET THY CATTLE GENDER WITH A DIVERSE KIND, ETC. It is written: "Ye are my witnesses said the Lord, and my servant whom I have chosen" (Isa. XLIII, 10). Israel are called witnesses and the heaven and earth are called witnesses, as it says, "I testify against you heaven and earth" (Deut. xxx, 19). Israel witness against one another and heaven and earth against all. Observe now. When God created the world, He assigned all things to their respective sides, and appointed over them celestial powers, so that there is not even a tiny herb without such a supervisor, [Tr. note: v. Bereshith Rabbah, 10.] and whatever they do is done through the power of that heavenly control, and all are rigidly assigned, and none

Zohar: Vayikra, Section 3, Page 86b

leaves its appointed sphere. All are guided by another superior regulation which gives to each its portion, which comes from the heavens, and all together are called "the statutes of the heavens". Hence it is written, "Ye shall keep my statutes", because each power is appointed over a certain sphere in the world in virtue of a certain statute. Therefore it is forbidden to confound species and mate them one with another, because this dislodges the heavenly power from its place and is a defiance of the celestial household. The word kilaim (divers kinds) may be connected with kele (prison), and it also bears the meaning of preventing, indicating that one who does this prevents the celestial powers from carrying out their function, and throws them into confusion. As has been said, he alters the commands of the King, and exchanges the Tree of Life, by which all is perfected and on which faith depends, for another place.

'We have learnt that in all things a man should act after the supernal model and perform the right thing, and that if he alters it he draws upon himself something which he would better have avoided. When a man does things below in the right way, he draws upon himself a celestial holy spirit. But if he does things in a crooked way, he draws upon himself another spirit which leads him astray to an evil side. What brings upon him this evil spirit? The action which he exhibited in the other side. Such is he who joins wool and flax. (In the case of the fringes, however, this is allowed, [Tr. note: v. T.B. Yebamoth, 4a et passim.] because when making these a man is in the category of completeness, and therefore he does no wrong.) But if one joins them when he is not in the category of completeness, he brings an unwelcome spirit on himself. We have a proof of this in Cain and Abel, because they came from different sides; therefore the offering of Cain was rejected for that of Abel. Another proof is in the prohibition to plough with an ox and an ass, which are names given to two different sides. These must not be mingled together, lest the junction should harm the world, whereas he who keeps them separate benefits the world. So, too, he who keeps flax and wool separate.

Zohar: Vayikra, Section 3, Page 87a

Cain was of the type of kilaim because he came partly from another side which was not of the species of Adam and Eve; and his offering also came from that side. In the case of Abel the two sides were joined in the womb of Eve, and because they were joined no benefit came to the world from them and they perished. Hence he who makes this union arouses both sides together and may come to harm, and a wrong spirit rests on him. Israel, however, ought to call down upon themselves a holy spirit, so as to be at peace in this world and the next. Therefore the High Priest on the Day of Atonement wore only linen garments when he came to clear away the ashes from the altar (Lev. VI, 10), because the burnt-offering is an atonement for evil thoughts; but when he went into the Sanctuary, the place where there was completeness and all services of completeness, it mattered not if he wore wool and flax together, because there all the different celestial species were found together in harmony, and similarly all kinds of holy vessels were there in combination, after the supernal model.

R. Hiya followed him with a discourse on the text: WHEN YE SHALL HAVE COME INTO THE LAND AND SHALL HAVE PLANTED ALL MANNER OF TREES FOR FOOD... IN THE FOURTH YEAR ALL THE FRUIT THEREOF SHALL BE HOLY, FOR GIVING PRAISE UNTO THE LORD. 'Observe', he said, 'that the tree only produces fruit from the earth, which is its true source, nor does the earth produce the fruit save through another power above it, just as the female only produces issue from the energy of the male. Now, that fruit does not reach its complete state until three years have passed, nor is any power appointed over it above until it has reached its complete state. Then, too, the earth is established with it, and the establishment of both constitutes completeness. Similarly the progeny of a woman does not reach completeness till her third delivery, and therefore Levi was chosen from all the sons of Jacob, being the third to his mother who was established with him. Thus after three years a power is appointed over the fruit above, and in the fourth year "all its fruit is holy for giving praise" to the Holy One, blessed be He. For in the fourth year

Zohar: Vayikra, Section 3, Page 87b

the Community of Israel becomes united with the Holy One, blessed be He, and then celestial powers are appointed over the world, an appropriate one for each object. Thenceforward all products are blessed and are permitted to be eaten, since all are in their complete state, in regard both to heaven and to earth. Till that time it is forbidden to eat of them; and he who eats of them is like one who has no share in the Holy One, blessed be He, and in the Community of Israel, since that fruit is as yet under no holy celestial control, nor is the strength of the earth established in it, so that he who eats of it shows that he has no portion either above or below, and if he makes a blessing over it, it is an idle blessing.'

R. Yose then said: 'The succeeding verses are to be taken in their literal meaning, but some remarks may be made on the verse: THOU SHALT RISE UP BEFORE THE HOARY HEAD, AND HONOUR THE FACE OF AN OLD MAN. The "hoary head" refers to the Torah, and a man should rise before the Scroll of the Torah. When R. Hamnuna the Elder saw a Scroll of the Law, he used to rise and say, "Thou shalt rise up before the hoary head". Similarly a man should rise before a man of learning, because he exhibits the holy supernal image and is emblematic of the supernal Priest. Further we may derive from the verse the lesson that we should rise up to do good deeds before old age comes upon us; for there is not much credit to a man in doing this when he is old and cannot do evil any more; but it is an honour to him if he is good while still in his prime.'

Said R. Eleazar: 'In very truth this way of ours is made straight before us, and it is the way of the Holy One, blessed be He. For "God knows the way of the righteous" (Ps. I, 6), to benefit them and protect them. Therefore when a man goes forth on the way he should see that that is the way of the Holy One, blessed be He, and should obtain His companionship.

Zohar: Vayikra, Section 3, Page 88a

Of such a way it is written: "The path of the righteous is as the shining light that shineth more and more unto the perfect day" (Prov. IV, 18).'

EMOR

AND THE LORD SAID UNTO MOSES, SPEAK UNTO THE PRIESTS THE SONS OF AARON AND SAY UNTO THEM, THERE SHALL NONE DEFILE HIMSELF FOR THE DEAD AMONG HIS PEOPLE. R. Yose said: 'What is the connection of this with the verse that immediately precedes, "A man also or a woman that hath a familiar spirit or that is a wizard shall be put to death" (Lev. xx, 27)? It is this: that having admonished the Israelites to sanctify themselves, the Scripture now admonishes the priests to sanctify themselves specially. Later, too, it admonishes the Levites (Num. XVIII, 21 et seq.), so that all should become holy and pure. The priests are designated here "the sons of Aaron", to show that they are something more than merely the sons of Levi, Aaron being the starting point of the priesthood because God chose him to make peace in the world, his conduct having entitled him to this distinction, since all his days he strove to promote peace in the world, so that God appointed him to bring peace to the celestial family also.

THERE SHALL NONE DEFILE HIMSELF FOR THE DEAD AMONG HIS PEOPLE. Observe that when a man is on his deathbed and on the point of departing for the other world, three messengers are sent to him, and he sees what other men cannot see in this world. That day is a day of heavenly judgement on which the King demands back his deposit. Happy the man who can restore the deposit just as it was lodged within him; for if it has been defiled with the impurity of the body, what will he say to the owner of the deposit? He sees the angel of death standing before him with his sword drawn, and all his limbs are relaxed, nor is anything so hard for the soul as its separation from the body. Before a man dies he beholds the Divine Presence, towards which the soul goes out in great yearning;

Zohar: Vayikra, Section 3, Page 88b

and after it has left the body what other soul will cleave to it? This we have discussed elsewhere. After the soul has left the body and the body remains without breath, it is forbidden to keep it unburied. [Tr. note: v. T.B. Moed Katon, 28a; Baba Kama, 82b.] For a dead body which is left unburied for twenty-four hours causes a weakness in the limbs of the Chariot and prevents God's design from being fulfilled; for perhaps God decreed that he should undergo a transmigration at once on the day that he died, which would be better for him, but as long as the body is not buried the soul cannot go into the presence of the Holy One nor be transferred into another body. For a soul cannot enter a second body till the first is buried, just as it is not fitting for a man to take a second wife before the first is buried. Another reason why the body should be buried on the same day is that when the soul departs from the body it cannot enter the other world until it is invested with another body formed of light. (So Llijah had two bodies, one in which he appeared on earth, and one in which he appeared among celestial angels.) So long as the body remains unburied the soul suffers pain and an unclean spirit rests upon the body, and therefore the body should not be kept over night, because by night the unclean spirit spreads over the earth, seeking for a body without a soul to defile it further. Therefore the priest was warned "not to defile himself for the dead among his people".' R. Isaac said that the word "say" here signifies "say quietly", just as all the operations of the priests were carried out in quietness; and the repetition "say" and "thou shalt say" is to give emphasis to the injunction that they should not defile themselves, since he who ministers in a holy place should be holy throughout. As we have said, the body without the spirit is unclean, and the desire of unclean spirits is for the bodies of Israel, since now that the holy spirit has been emptied out of them they want to be joined to a holy vessel. The priests who are additionally holy must not defile themselves at all, since "the oil of the anointment of the Lord is upon him".'

Zohar: Vayikra, Section 3, Page 89a

R. Isaac also said: 'The priest who stands here below is emblematic of the Priest above, and therefore he must be in a superior grade of holiness.'

AND FOR HIS SISTER A VIRGIN THAT IS NEAR UNTO HIM. R. Abba quoted here the verse: "Who is this that cometh from Edom, with dyed garments from Bozrah?" (Isa. LXIII, 1). 'God', he said, 'will one day put on garments of vengeance to chastise Edom for having destroyed His house and burnt His Temple and driven the Community of Israel into exile among the nations. He will wreak vengeance on them until all the mountains are full of the slain of the nations, when he will summon all birds of the air and the beasts of the field and they shall feast on them, the beasts twelve months and the birds seven years, and the earth shall not bear the stench thereof. God shall come from Bozrah, because from there the world's hosts went forth to war against Jerusalem, and they began to burn the Temple, and the children of Edom threw down the walls and destroyed the foundations. God will be "glorious in his apparel", His robes of vengeance, and "marching in the greatness of his strength". Said the Israelites to Isaiah: "Who is he that shall do all this?" He replied: "I that speak in righteousness, mighty to save". And why all this? Because "for his sister a virgin that is near unto him, which hath had no husband", to wit, for the Community of Israel who does not belong to the portion of Esau, for her He may be defiled, to wit, in those garments of vengeance with which He will stain himself among all those hosts.'

THEY SHALL NOT MAKE BALDNESS UPON THEIR HEAD. R. Yose said: 'The reason is that on the head of the supernal Priest is the holy oil of anointing, the removal of which would cause baldness; and therefore the priest below must perform an action symbolical of this."

[Tr. note: Here follows in the original a passage expanding this idea in the highly allusive and untranslatable style of the Midrash Hane'elam.]

Zohar: Vayikra, Section 3, Page 89b

(AND HE THAT IS THE HIGH PRIEST AMONG HIS BRETHREN, ETC.) R. Abba here quoted the verse: To thee, O Lord, belongeth righteousness, but unto us confusion of face" (Dan. IX, 7). '"Righteousness"', he said, 'refers to the place to which all the shining faces are attached, as it is attached to them; and "confusion of face" refers to the place from which the shining faces are removed. Therefore the High Priest should always present a face bright and shining and more joyful than others, seeing that he symbolizes the higher grade.

Zohar: Vayikra, Section 3, Page 90a

[Note: The first 23 lines of the Hebrew text are not found in our translation]

'HE SHALL NOT PROFANE HIS SEED AMONG HIS PEOPLE. Whoever discharges his semen without purpose will never be allowed to behold the divine Presence, [Tr. note: v. T.B. Niddah, 13a.] and such a one is called wicked. This is not the case, however, if a man's wife does not conceive; still, a man should pray that God should provide him a fitting vessel so that his seed should not be spoilt. For he who discharges his seed into a vessel that is not fitting spoils his seed; and if this is the case with ordinary men, how much more so with the priest who is the counterpart on earth of the supernal holiness. AMONG HIS PEOPLE: that is to say, this is a disgrace, a defect among his people. FOR I AM THE LORD WHICH SANCTIFY HIM: I am He that sanctifies him every day, and therefore he must not spoil his seed nor must any blemish be found in him. He must be holy throughout, so that the Holy One may be served by a holy one.

Zohar: Vayikra, Section 3, Page 90b

And because God is served by the hand of the priest, who is holy, the priest is served by one who is sanctified by his purity, to wit, the Levite. The ordinary man, too, is served [Tr. note: i.e. should have water poured over his hands, v. Shulhan Aruch.] by one who has already sanctified himself, and thus Israel are set apart in holiness to serve the Holy One, blessed be He.'

He further expounded the verse: "Salvation is the Lord's; thy blessing be upon thy people" (Ps. III, 9). 'We have learnt', he said, 'that wherever Israel go into exile the Shekinah goes with them. [Tr. note: v. T.B. Megillah, 29a.] When, therefore, they will come forth from captivity, who will be delivered? Israel or God? The answer is given in the verse, "Salvation is the Lord's". And when will this be? When "thy blessing is upon thy people, selah", to take them out of captivity and deal well with them.'

WHOEVER HE BE OF THY SEED THROUGHOUT THEIR GENERATIONS THAT HATH A BLEMISH. R. Isaac said: 'Whoever has a blemish is not fitted to serve before the Holy One, as we have laid down, that whoever has a blemish has no true faith, and his blemish bears witness against him.' R. Eleazar was once sitting in the room of his father-in-law, and he complained that his eyes were watering. A man happened to pass by who had lost one eye. 'Let us ask him,' said the father-in-law. He replied: 'He is blemished, and therefore not to be trusted.' 'Still let us ask him,' said the other. So they said to him: 'Who is mightiest in the world?' He replied: 'A rich man; and I shall remain with him through all.' Said R. Eleazar: 'His words show that he has no religious faith in him.' He then discoursed on the verse: "For the law and for the testimony; if they speak not according to this word" (Isa. VIII, 20). "'Law" here', he said, 'signifies the Written Law, and "testimony" the Oral Law. The Oral Law does not rest in a blemished place, because it is fashioned from the Written Law. Hence the text says "Bind up the testimony" (Ibid. 16), because there in the Oral Law is the bundle of life, and the knot of faith is tied up with the testimony above, and thence diverse paths through all the worlds. "Seal the law among my disciples" (Ibid.) Where is the seal of the Written Law? In "my disciples", that is, the prophets. The whole is established only in its completeness, and holiness rests on it only when it is complete, when part is joined with part and there is no empty place. Hence no man with a blemish must draw near to serve, nor must a sacrifice with a blemish be offered. But surely it may be said, God abides only in a broken place, a broken vessel, as it is written, "With him that is of a contrite and humble spirit" (Isa. LVII, 15)? That is so, for this place is more perfect than all, when a man humbles himself so that the grandeur of all, the heavenly grandeur may rest upon him. But it is not written

Zohar: Vayikra, Section 3, Page 91a

"with the blind and crippled". If a man humbles himself, God raises him. Therefore the priest must above all others be complete and not show any blemish, and therefore the Scripture warns the priests saying, "whoever of thy seed hath a blemish", etc.' He further quoted the verse: "And when ye offer the blind for sacrifice, is it no evil?" etc. (Mal. I, 8). In those days the Israelites used to appoint priests with blemishes to serve at the altar and in the Sanctuary, saying: What does it matter to God if it is this one or another? It is no evil. And God answered them with their own words: It is no evil! "Present it now unto thy governor, will he be pleased with thee or will he accept thy person?" (Ibid.) If any one of you wanted to make a present to the king, would he send it by the hand of a man who was deformed? How then can you set before Me a man with a blemish to present your gift? Such a gift is given to the dog.' R. Yose said: 'God will one day make Israel whole so that there shall be none with a blemish among them, in order that they may adorn the world as a man's garments adorn his body. Observe that when the dead rise from the dust, they will leave it as they entered; if they went into it lame or blind, they shall rise from it lame or blind, in order that it should not be said that it is another who has risen. Afterwards, however, God will heal them and they will be whole before Him and the world will be whole. [Tr. note: Cf. T.B. Sanhedrin, 91a.]

WHEN A BULLOCK OR A SHEEP OR A GOAT IS BROUGHT FORTH, THEN IT SHALL BE SEVEN DAYS UNDER THE DAM. R. Yose said: 'It is written, "Man and beast thou preservest, O Lord" (Ps. XXXVI, 7): that is to say, in mercy God preserves both in equal measure. The law of the beast and the law of the man is the same; man is to be circumcised on the eighth day, and the beast shall be seven days under its dam and from the eighth day it shall be accepted for an offering made by fire unto the Lord.' R. Hiya said: 'Israel from the eighth day cleave to God and are impressed with His name and become His, but the other peoples do not cleave to Him nor conform to His rules, and they remove from themselves the holy impress until

Zohar: Vayikra, Section 3, Page 91b

they cleave to the other side which is not holy. When God came to give the Law to Israel, before doing so He summoned the children of Esau and said to them: Do you desire to accept the Law? [Tr. note: v. T.B. Abodah Zara, 2b.] At that moment the earth quaked and was fain to enter into the cavern of the great deep. She said: Sovereign of the Universe, is that which was a plaything of delight for two thousand years before the universe was created to be presented to the uncircumcised who are not stamped with thy covenant? Whereupon the Holy One, blessed be He, answered: Throne, throne, let a thousand such peoples perish before the covenant of the Law is presented to them. Hence it is written, "Lord, when thou wentest forth out of Seir, when thou marchedst out of the field of Edom, the earth trembled" (Jud. v, 4), because the Law is not to be given save to one who bears on himself the holy covenant. And he who teaches the Torah to one who is not circumcised is false to two covenants, [Tr. note: v. T.B. Hagigah, 13a.] to the covenant of the Zaddik and the covenant of the Community of Israel, since the Torah was given to this place and to no other.' R. Abba said that he is false to three supernal places, the Law, the Prophets, and the Holy Writings.' R. Hiya said: 'When God revealed himself on Mount Sinai to give the Law to Israel, the earth reclined and rested at ease, as it says, "the earth feared and was still" (Ps. LXXVI, 9).

'Observe that when a child is born, a power from above is not appointed to watch over it until it is circumcised. When the child is circumcised, some supernal activity is stirred in connection with it. If he proceeds to the study of the Torah, the activity is heightened. If he is able to keep the precepts of the Law, the activity is still further heightened. If he advances so far as to marry and beget children and teach them the ways of the Holy King, then he is a complete man. Contrariwise, the beast from the moment of its birth is under the same supervision as throughout its life. Therefore it is written, "when a bullock or a sheep or a goat is born", not "a calf or a lamb or a kid", to show that what it has at the end it has at the moment of birth. It is to be seven days under its dam in order that that power may be settled and firmly established in it. For this it is necessary that one sabbath should pass over it; and then "it is acceptable for an offering made by fire unto the Lord".'

[Note: The last line of the Hebrew text is not found in our translation]

Zohar: Vayikra, Section 3, Page 92a

[Note: The first 30 lines of the Hebrew text are not found in our translation]

AND WHETHER IT BE AN OX OR A SHEEP, YE SHALL NOT KILL IT AND ITS YOUNG BOTH ON ONE DAY. R. Yose said 'This must be taken to refer to the mother, since the young goes after the mother and not the father, [Tr. note: v. T.B. Hullin, 78b, where two views are given.] nor do we know which it is. Why must not both be killed on one day?' R. Judah said: 'If it is to avoid giving pain to the animal, we could kill one in one place and the other in another, or one somewhat later than the other.' He replied: 'Some actually allow this, but this is not correct; the prohibition relates to the whole of the same day. Observe now that we have learnt that "a fast is as good for a dream as fire for flax", [Tr. note: T.B. Taanith, 12b.] but it must be on the same day, because every day below is controlled by a day above, and therefore if the man fasts, that day does not pass till the adverse decree is annulled, but if he puts it off to another day, then the control belongs to that day. Thus over every day below is appointed a day above, and a man should take heed not to impair that day. Now the act below stimulates a corresponding activity above.

Zohar: Vayikra, Section 3, Page 92b

Thus if a man does kindness on earth, he awakens lovingkindness above, and it rests upon that day which is crowned therewith through him. Similarly if he performs a deed of mercy, he crowns that day with mercy and it becomes his protector in the hour of need. So, too, if he performs a cruel action, he has a corresponding effect on that day and impairs it, so that subsequently it becomes cruel to him and tries to destroy him, giving him measure for measure. Israel are withheld from cruelty more than all other peoples, and must not manifest any deed of the kind, since many watchful eyes are upon them.'

R. Simeon said: 'When God resolves to punish the world with famine, He makes the proclamation Himself, and not by the hand of a herald, as in the case of all other punishments. [Tr. note: v. T.B. Taanith, 2a.] From that moment it is forbidden to a man who still has plenty to make a show of it, since in so doing he defies the word of the King and, as it were, drives the emissaries of the King from their place. Therefore it was that Jacob said to his sons when the famine came, "Do not show yourselves off", as much as to say: Why do you cause blemish both above and below, and belie the word of the king and all his emissaries? For Jacob still had much corn, and yet he only desired to "buy among those that came", so that no blame should attach to his actions. So, too, when Aaron blessed the people he raised his right hand above his left, so that the action below should stimulate a corresponding action above.'

Zohar: Vayikra, Section 3, Page 93a

THE SET FEASTS OF THE LORD WHICH YE SHALL PROCLAIM TO BE HOLY CONVOCATIONS. R. Isaac said: It is written, "And God called the light day" (Gen. I, 5). Does this mean that the light called day exists by itself? No, for it says, "and the darkness he called night". Does this mean that each exists separately?

Zohar: Vayikra, Section 3, Page 93b

No, for it says, "And there was evening and there was morning one day". This shows that there is no day without night and no night without day, and on account of their interlocking they are called one. Similarly the Holy One, blessed be He, and the Community of Israel are called one when together, but not when parted; and so now that the Community of Israel is in exile, she is, as it were, not called one, and will only be called one when Israel emerge from captivity. Similarly it says: "These are the appointed feasts of the Lord which ye shall proclaim" (lit. call), that is, invite all to one place so that all shall form one, and Israel below shall be one nation on the earth. And how will they be called one? Through the earthly Jerusalem, as it is written, "And who is like thy people Israel one nation in the earth" (2 Sam. VII, 23), since they are only called one when wedded to this "earth", after the supernal pattern.'

HOLY CONVOCATIONS. R. Isaac cited here the verse: "Unto thee my heart said, Seek ye my face; thy face, Lord, will I seek" (Ps. XXVII, 8). 'We can explain this verse', he said, by supposing that King David was speaking here on behalf of the Community of Israel, thus: "For Thy sake my heart says to mankind: Seek ye my face, to wit, the Crowns of the King which are one with the King"; and David was more qualified than any other man to speak thus in the name of the Community of Israel because he was closely attached to Her. We may also interpret the word "face" to refer to the appointed seasons and festivals, all of which were invited by David to the place called "holy", in order to crown each of them on its day and its appointed time, that all might draw from that most profound source from which issue streams and fountains. Therefore they are called "invited to holiness"- invited to that place called "holiness" to be crowned with it and draw from it that all may be sanctified together and joy may be found among them. R. Abba said that "holy convocations" means "invited by holiness", and when they are invited by this, they are invited by the Stream that issues forth perennially. We may compare it to a king who, having invited people to a banquet, sets before them all manner of dishes and opens for them casks of well flavoured wine, for he who invites invites to eat and drink. So the "holy convocations", since they are invited to the banquet of the King, are invited to partake of the good wine which has long been kept in store. Israel, too, are called "holiness", because they are invited by the holiness above; therefore they should prepare a banquet and rejoice, since for them it is fitting.

Zohar: Vayikra, Section 3, Page 94a

THESE ARE THE SET FEASTS OF THE LORD. R. Simeon said: 'They are from the Lord (Tetragrammaton), because He is the link between those (grades) above and those below, all being united through Him. Why? Because just as the King inherits the Father and Mother and is attached to their holiness, so all those that are attached to the King are to be invited to that supernal place called "holiness" in order that they mav all be united. Hence they are called first "set feasts of the Lord", and then "holy convocations".

WHICH YE SHALL PROCLAIM IN THEIR APPOINTED SEASON. Israel have two portions in them-whether from the side of the King, since Israel "cleave to the Lord", or from the side of Holiness, since they are called "men of holiness". Therefore (says the Scripture), for you it is fitting to invite them and to prepare a joyful feast before them and rejoice in them: for one who invites a guest must show him a smiling face to crown his visit therewith. Imagine a king who invites an honoured guest and says to his court: All other days you are each in his house doing his work there, or in business or in the field, save only on my special day which you devote to rejoicing with me. Now I have invited a very honoured guest, and I desire that you should engage in no work in the house or in business or in the field, but that you should all come together as on my special day and prepare to meet that guest with smiles, with joy and with praises. So God said to Israel: All other days you are engaged in work and in business, save on my special day (the Sabbath). Now I have invited a very honoured guest, and do you therefore receive him with smiles and prepare for him a special table as on my own day. Hence it says: "You shall call (i.e. invite) them in their appointed time". See now. When Israel below rejoice in those festivals and sing praises to the Holy One, blessed be He, and prepare a table and put on their best garments, the angels in heaven ask: What do Israel mean by this, and God answers them: They have a distinguished guest on this day. But, they say, is he not Thy guest, from the place called Holiness? He replies: And are not Israel holy and called holy, so that it is meet for them to invite My guest--alike from My side, because they cling to Me, and from the side of holiness, since it is written, "Israel are holy to the Lord". Assuredly the guest is theirs. Then they all break forth with the words, "Happy is the people that is in such a case".

' There are three that are invited from Holiness, and no more-the Feast of Unleavened Bread, the Feast of Weeks, and the Feast of Tabernacles.' 'But', said R. Abba to him, 'is not Sabbath also invited from Holiness?' 'No,' he replied, 'for two reasons. One is that Sabbath is itself called holiness, and the other is that Sabbath has the right of entry by inheritance. Hence all the rest are invited and link themselves with Sabbath and crown themselves with it, but the Sabbath is not invited. It is like a son who enters the house of his father and mother and eats there whenever he desires. A king, we will say, had a son whom he fondly loved, and to whom he assigned a number of companions. One day he said: It would be a good thing to invite my son's companions and to show my affection and esteem for them. So he invited the companions, but the son did not need an invitation, since he could go into his father's house and eat and drink there whenever he wished.'

Zohar: Vayikra, Section 3, Page 94b

It is written here: SIX DAYS SHALL WORK BE DONE. R. Yose said: 'The six Days made the heaven and the earth, each performing its own work, and therefore they are called the six workdays.' Said R. Isaac: 'Why then are they called the six "ordinary" days?' 'Because now', replied R. Yose, 'the world is carried on by their agent, [Tr. note: Metatron.] and therefore they are called "ordinary" or "profane".' R. Hiya said 'It is because work may be done on them. For that reason they are not called holy, and what is not called holy is called ordinary. Hence the Companions have laid down that we should say at the close of Sabbath, "who divideth between holy and profane", the separation consisting in the fact that holiness is something apart, and the rest issue from it. Hence these are for work. And there is a time when these too are to be kept, namely, when they are invited, from Holiness'. [Tr. note: i.e. when the festivals fall on them.] R. Judah said: 'The joy and the observance of the Sabbath are superior to that of all the others, because this day is crowned with the Father and the Mother, and is invested with an additional holiness; wherefore it is a day of joy for higher and lower, and full of blessings in all worlds. On this day, too, there is rest for higher and lower, and even for the sinners in Gehinnom. Suppose a king made a feast in honour of his only son, during which he placed a crown upon him and invested him with supreme authority. There would be universal joy, so that the governor of a prison who had in his charge men condemned to stripes and execution, would, in honour of the king's celebration, release them, so that day is the day of the King's rejoicing with the Matrona. Of the joy of Father and Mother in Him, of the rejoicing of higher and lower. In the joy of the King all must rejoice, and there must be no suffering then. On this day the sons of the King must prepare three meals for their table for the honour of the King, as we have laid down. But if a festival or appointed time occurs on it, a man need not prepare two tables for each meal, one for Sabbath and one for the guest: there is sufficient at the King's table for the guest who has come.' R. Eleazar asked: 'If the guest arrives at the time of the third Sabbath meal, [Tr. note: i.e. if the third meal is prolonged until the evening which commences a festival.] do we waive it nor not? If we waive it, then the guest is debarred from the table of the King. If we do not waive it, then the banquet of the King is itself deficient.' R. Simeon his father replied: 'The case is like that of a king on whom a guest happened to call, so he took food and put it before him, so that although the king did not eat with him, yet he ate from the food of the king. In the household of R. Hamnuna the Elder, however, they used to pay no attention to the guest at this time, but later they used to set a table for the guest.' 'But,' said R. Eleazar, 'how is it possible not to set the king's banquet before the guest, seeing that if the fourteenth day of Nisan falls on a Sabbath, the banquet of the king is waived in favour of the Passover, although it is not yet a guest.' He replied:

Zohar: Vayikra, Section 3, Page 95a

'There are indeed a number of reasons why the banquet of the King is waived on account of the Passover-one, that a man should come hungry to the unleavened bread and bitter herbs, and, again, there is no bread after midday, and a table without bread is not complete. However, I myself have always been particular not to waive the third Sabbath meal even when the Sabbath happens to be the eve of Passover.

On this day (of Sabbath) the holy Field of Apples is blessed, and higher and lower are blessed, and this day is the link of the (two branches of the) Torah.' R. Abba said: 'R. Simeon, when the Sabbath meal was removed, used to arrange his table and meditate on the Construction of the Chariot, [Tr. note: i.e. the relation of God to the universe, as set forth in the first chapter of Ezekiel.] and say, Here is the banquet of the King, let Him come and partake with me. Therefore Sabbath is superior to all feasts and appointed seasons, and is called "holy" and not "holy convocation".' R. Judah said: 'New Year and the Day of Atonement are not called "holy convocations", because there is no joy on them, they being days of judgement. But the three festivals are times of gladness when Israel have joyous communion with the Holy One, blessed be He. On the Sabbath all sorrow and vexation and trouble is forgotten because it is the day of the espousals of the King, when an additional soul is imparted (to men) as in the future world. R. Isaac asked R. Judah: 'Why have we learnt that Sabbath is to be remembered over wine?' He replied: 'Because wine represents the joy of the Torah, and the wine of the Torah is the universal joy.'

IN THE FIRST MONTH ON THE FOURTEENTH DAY OF THE MONTH. R. Hiya adduced here the verse: "I was asleep but my heart waked, it is the voice of my beloved that knocketh", etc. (S.S. II, 2). 'Says the Community of Israel: I was asleep in the captivity of Egypt, when my children were sore oppressed, but my heart was awake to preserve them so that they should not perish under the oppression. "The voice of my beloved", the Holy One, blessed be He, saying, Open to me an opening no bigger than the eye of a needle, and I will open to thee the supernal gates. "Open to me, my sister", because thou art the door through which there is entrance to Me; if thou openest not, I am closed. Thus it was that when the Holy One, blessed be He, slew the firstborn in Egypt, at that very time Israel entered into the covenant of the holy sign, and linked themselves with the Community of Israel, by means of the blood which they displayed on the door- the blood of the paschal lamb and the blood of the circumcision, one on one side and one on the other, and one between, to show their faith. On the fourteenth day, too, they removed the leaven and Israel emerged from the sphere of an alien power and clung to the unleavened,

Zohar: Vayikra, Section 3, Page 95b

which is a holy bond, and later they became linked to a still higher realm of faith called "heaven".

AND ON THE FIFTEENTH DAY OF THE SAME MONTH. At the hour of wedlock, when the moon is in full union with the sun and the lower crowns are not found in such numbers in the world (for the evil species abound at new moon and spread throughout the world, but when the moon enjoys the full light of the sun they all withdraw to a certain place and the sanctifications of the King are aroused), of that time it is written, "a night of vigils for the Lord", for then the holy wedlock takes place which is protection for all.' R. Abba said: 'Therefore the adornment of the bride is on that day, and at night is the visiting of the house. Woe to those that are not of the household when the two Torahs come to unite, woe to them that are not present! Therefore holy Israel prepare for them the house all that day, and through them the visitors enter, and they rejoice and sing gleefully.' Said R. Yose: 'The verse says as much distinctly in the word "vigils", which implies two-the union of the moon with the sun. It is "for all the children of Israel for their generations", since from that time they were linked to the holy Name and emerged from the dominion of another power. Therefore on the fourteenth day they prepare themselves and remove leaven from among them and enrol themselves under holy power, and then the bridegroom and the bride are crowned with the crowns of the Supernal Mother, and a man should show that he is free.'

R. Yose asked: 'What is the meaning of the four cups of wine drunk on this night?' R. Abba replied: 'The Companions have explained that they correspond to the four expressions of deliverance, [Tr. note: In Exodus VI, 2–8, v. Shemoth Rabbah, 6.] but a better explanation is given in the book of R. Jesse the Elder, which says that it is because the holy wedlock takes place on this night, and this is consummated in four unions. When this wedlock takes place we partake in the joy of all, and therefore this night is different from all other nights and it behoves us to form the Name in all four. Further, we call those four "deliverances", because this last grade [Tr. note: Malkuth.] is called "deliverer", and that only on account of another higher grade which illumines it, and that one does not do so save through the agency of two more which are above it, so that in all there are four deliverances.'

R. Judah asked R. Abba: 'Seeing that the seven days of Passover are all days of joy, why do we not say the complete Hallel on all of them, as on Tabernacles?' He replied: 'Because at this point Israel were not yet linked with the supernal world to such an extent as they were to be later. Therefore on this night (the first night of Passover) when there is the divine wedlock and universal joy in which Israel participate, we say the whole Hallel as a sign of completeness. But afterwards we do not say the whole, because Israel were not yet linked with those four higher grades, since the holy sign was not yet displayed on their flesh, and they had not yet received the Torah; whereas on Tabernacles all had been completed and the joy was more complete.'

Zohar: Vayikra, Section 3, Page 96a

[Note: The first 4 lines of the Hebrew text are not found in our translation]

Said R. Judah to him: 'All this is quite correct, and this is the second time I hear it, but I had forgotten. Now I should like to know another thing. Why is it that Passover and Tabernacles consist of seven days, but not the Feast of Weeks, which really ought to more than the others?' He replied: 'It is written: "Who is like thy people Israel one nation in the earth?" (2 Sam. VII, 23). Now why are Israel called "one" here rather than in any other place? It is because the text is here speaking in praise of Israel, because it is the pride of Israel to be one. The reason is that the junction of upper and lower takes place at the spot called "Israel", which is linked with what is above and what is below, and with the Community of Israel: wherefore the whole is called one, and in this spot faith becomes manifest and complete union and supernal holy unity. The Tree of Life is also called one, and its day therefore is one, and therefore we have Passover and Tabernacles and this in the middle, and this is the honour of the Torah that it should have this one day and no more.' R. Isaac said: 'Israel will in the future chant joyful hymns of praise to the Holy One, blessed be He, like those which they chanted on the night of the Passover when the Community of Israel was hallowed with the sanctity of the King, as it is written: "Ye shall have a song as in the night when the holy feast was kept" (Isa. xxx, 29).

AND ON THE DAY OF THE FIRSTFRUITS WHEN YE BRING A NEW OFFERING TO THE LORD IN YOUR WEEKS, ETC. UP to this time Israel were bringing "the produce of the earth", that is to say, an earthly product (barley), literally, and they occupied themselves therewith and found therein their link (with the divine). God said: I gave you manna in the wilderness from the place which is called "heaven", and now you bring before me barley (for the Omer). The truth is that this offering had the same significance as the offering brought by the wife of the jealous husband, which was also of barley, and was to show that the Community of Israel was not unfaithful to the Holy King.

Zohar: Vayikra, Section 3, Page 96b

[Note: The first 9 lines of the Hebrew text do not appear in our translation.]

This was brought for seven full weeks, and then the Holy King came to join the Community of Israel and the Torah was given to Israel.

[Note: The last 47 lines of the Hebrew text do not appear in our translation.]

Zohar: Vayikra, Section 3, Page 97a

[Note: Only the last 3 lines of the Hebrew text appear in our translation.]

AND YE SHALL COUNT TO YOU FROM THE MORROW AFTER THE SABBATH. Observe that when Israel were in Egypt they were under an alien domination and they were t rammelled with uncleanness like a woman in the days of her uncleanness. When they were circumcised, they entered into the holy portion which is called "covenant",

Zohar: Vayikra, Section 3, Page 97b

and thereupon the uncleanness left them as the blood of uncleanness leaves a woman. Just as a woman then has to count seven days, so now God bade the Israelites count days for purity. They were to count "for themselves", so as to be purified with supernal holy waters, and then to be attached to the King and to receive the Torah. The woman had to count seven days, the people seven weeks. Why seven weeks? That they might be worthy to be cleansed by the waters of that stream which is called "living waters," and from which issue seven Sabbaths. When Israel drew near to Mount Sinai, that dew that descends from the supemal Point came down in its fullness and purified them so that their filth left them and they became attached to the Holy King and the Community of Israel and received the Torah, as we have explained. Observe that any man who does not count those seven complete weeks so as to qualify himself for purity is not called "pure" and is not in the class of "pure", nor is he worthy to have a portion in the Torah. But if a man has reached this day in purity and has not lost count, then it behoves him on this night to study the Torah and to preserve the special purity to which he has attained on this night. We have learnt

Zohar: Vayikra, Section 3, Page 98a

that the Torah which he ought to study on this night is the Oral Law, and afterwards in daytime the Written Law can come and he can attach himself to it, so that both may be interlocked above. Then proclamation is made concerning him, saying, "And as for me, this is my covenant with them, saith the Lord; my spirit which is upon thee and my words which I have put in thy mouth", etc. (Isa. LIX, 21). Therefore the pious ones of old used not to sleep on this night, but they used to study the Torah and say, Let us acquire a holy inheritance for ourselves and our sons in two worlds. On that night the Community of Israel is crowned above them, and comes to join the Holy King, and both are crowned above the heads of those who are worthy of this. When the Companions gathered round him on this night, R. Simeon used to say: 'Let us go and prepare the ornaments of the Bride, that tomorrow she may appear before the King fitly adorned and bedecked. Happy the portion of the Companions when the King shall inquire of the Matrona who has arranged her adornments and illumined her crowns. For there is none in the world who knows how to arrange the jewels of the Bride like the Companions, happy is their portion in this world and in the world to come! Now the Companions adorn the Bride, but who prepares the King on this night for his visit to the Matrona? It is the Holy Stream, the deepest of all streams, the Supernal Mother, as it says, "Go forth, ye daughters of Zion, and behold King Solomon in the crown wherewith his mother hath crowned him in the day of his espousals" (S.S. III, 11). After she has prepared the King and crowned him, she goes to purify the Matrona and those that are with her. Imagine a king who had an only son whom he united in marriage to a noble lady. What did his mother do? All that night she spent in her storeroom, and she brought forth therefrom a noble crown set with seventy

Zohar: Vayikra, Section 3, Page 98b

precious stones to crown him with; she brought forth silken garments and clad him therewith and adorned him royally. Then she went to the bride and saw how her maidens were arranging her crown and her garments and her jewels. She said to them: I have prepared a bath with flowing water perfumed with all manner of sweet scents to purify my daughter-in-law. Let my daughter-in-law, the lady of my son, come with all her maidens that they may purify themselves in the place of flowing water which I have prepared for them, and then they can robe her with all her ornaments. Tomorrow when my son comes to wed the lady he will prepare a palace for all and his abode shall be among you. So it is with the Holy King and the Matrona and the Companions, whose dwelling shall thus be together inseparably. as it is written, "Lord, who shall sojourn in thy tabernacle?... He that walketh uprightly and worketh righteousness" (Ps. xv, I, 2); these are they that array the Matrona in her jewels, her raiment and her crowns.

IN THE SEVENTH MONTH IN THE FIRST DAY OF THE MONTH. R. Isaac said: 'Blessed are Israel in that God has drawn them near to Him from a far place, as it says, "And Joshua said unto the people, Thus saith the Lord, the God of Israel, Your fathers dwelt of old beyond the River" (Joshua XXIV, 2), and a little further on it says, "And I took your father Abraham from beyond the River" (Ibid. 3). Now these verses require consideration. Did not the Israelites, and still more Joshua, know all this?

Zohar: Vayikra, Section 3, Page 99a

Then why did God tell it to them? The inner meaning, however, is this. Great kindness did God show Israel in choosing the patriarchs and making them a supernal holy chariot for his glory and bringing them forth from the supernal precious holy River, the lamp of all lamps, that he might be crowned with them. Also it says, "I took your father Abraham from beyond the River" (Ibid. 4), because Abraham did not cleave to that River as Isaac clave to his side. Now, although this River is not judgement, yet chastisements issue from its side, and when Isaac takes hold of his sons, then higher and lower angels assemble for judgement, and the throne of judgement is set up and the Holy King takes his seat thereon and judges worlds. Then is the time to "blow up the trumpet on the new moon, at the appointed time on our solemn feast day" (PS. LXXXI, 4): for happy are Israel who know how to remove the throne of judgement and set up the throne of mercy; and wherewith? With the shofar.' R. Abba, as he was once studying with R. Simeon, said to him: 'Many times have I inquired concerning the significance of the shofar, but I have never yet received a satisfactory answer.' R. Simeon replied: 'The true explanation is this. Why Israel have to use a ram's horn on this day and not any other is this, that we know to what place the horn belongs, and we do not desire to awaken judgement. For, as we have learnt, by word and deed we have to awaken secret powers. Now when the supernal Shofar, in which is the illumination of all, removes itself and does not shine upon the sons, then judgement is awakened and the thrones are set up for judgement,

Zohar: Vayikra, Section 3, Page 99b

and Isaac strengthens and prepares himself for judgement. But when this Shofar rouses itself and men repent of their sins, it behoves them to blow the shofar below, and the sound thereof ascends on high and awakens another supernal Shofar, and so mercy is awakened and judgement is removed. We must produce from this shofar below various sounds to arouse all the voices that are contained in the supernal Shofar, and therefore we not only use the shofar on this day but arrange the blasts in a number of series.

'With the first blast the voice goes forth and makes its way upwards to the firmaments, breaking through lofty mountains till it reaches Abraham, on whose head it rests so that he awakes and prepares himself for the throne, where the Father and Mother appoint him to his station. Then there goes up a second mighty blast to break down wrath, being itself of broken notes, and all chastisements that stand in its way as it ascends to Isaac are broken. Then Isaac awakens and beholds Abraham preparing the throne and standing before it, and then he also is chastened and his severity is abated. And on this he who blows the shofar should concentrate his mind, so as to break the strength of stern judgement. With the third blast the voice issues and ascends and cleaves the firmaments, till it reaches the head of Jacob,

Zohar: Vayikra, Section 3, Page 100a

who thereupon awakens and sees Abraham ready on the other side. Then both take hold of Isaac, one on one side and one on the other, so that his violence cannot break forth. These three blasts form one series.

'In the next series a voice goes forth and ascends and takes hold of Abraham and brings him down to the place where the harshness of Isaac abides and sets Abraham in the midst thereof. With the second blast goes forth a broken voice, not so powerful as the first; not that it is weaker, but because it does not approach Isaac like the previous one, but only the lower court, which is weaker; and they all see Abraham among them and are humbled. With the third blast a voice issues and rises till it forms a crown on the head of Jacob, whom it brings down to the place where those powers of judgement are, so that Abraham faces them on one side and Jacob on the other, and they being in the middle are rendered more lenient. These form the second series.

'The last series has to take them back to their places and to place Isaac between them as before, since it is necessary to fix him in his place so that he should not leave it in his violent mood. In this way all punishments are kept in check and mercy is awakened. This is the purpose which these blasts should serve, being accompanied by repentance before God. Thus when Israel produce the blasts of the shofar with proper devotion, the supernal Shofar returns and crowns Jacob so that all is properly arranged. Another throne is set up and joy is universally diffused and God has mercy on the world. Happy are Israel who know how to divert

Zohar: Vayikra, Section 3, Page 100b

their Master from justice to mercy and to be the instruments for establishing all worlds. Corresponding to the three series of blasts three books are opened above on this day, and just as mercy is awakened and punishments are restrained and put back in their place above, so below in the same way harsh punishments are kept back and removed from the world. And what are these? These are the irremediably wicked who are inscribed at once for death.' Said R. Abba: 'Assuredly this is the true explanation of the matter. Blessed be

God that I asked for and obtained this instruction.' R. Judah said: 'It is written, A MEMORIAL OF BLOWING OF TRUMPETS. We make a memorial by the concentration of our mind and thought. Israel make a memorial below by an appropriate ceremony, so as to arouse a corresponding reaction above.'

R. Eleazar said: 'This day is called "the concealing (keseh) for the day of our feast", because the moon is still covered and does not shine. [Tr. note: Cf. T.B. Rosh Hashanah, 8b.] Through what then will it shine? Through repentance and the sound of the shofar, as it is written, "Blessed is the people that know the trumpet sound, because, O Lord, they shall walk in the light of thy countenance" (Ps. LXXXIX, 15). On this day the moon is covered, and it does not shine until the tenth day, when Israel turn with a perfect repentance, so that the supernal Mother gives light to her. Hence this day is called the day of atonements (kipturim), because two lights are shedding illumination, since the higher lamp is illumining the lower. For on this day the Moon receives illumination from the supernal Light and not from the light of the Sun.'

R. Abba sent to inquire of R. Simeon: 'When is the union of the Community of Israel with the Holy King?' He answered him with the verse: "And moreover she is indeed my sister the daughter of my father, but not the daughter of my mother" (Gen. xx, 12). R. Abba lifted up his voice and wept, saying: 'My master, my master, holy lamp, alas for the world when thou shalt depart from it, alas for the generation which shall be orphaned of thee!' R. Hiya said to R. Abba: 'What means this answer that he sent you?' He replied: 'The union of the King with the Matrona is only when she is illumined from the supernal Father, when she is called holy. Then indeed she is "my sister the daughter of my father", but not "of my mother", since it is from the Father that she derives this name.'

R. Abba said: 'On New Year Adam was created and was brought to trial before his Master and

Zohar: Vayikra, Section 3, Page 101a

repented and was pardoned by the Almighty. He said to him: Adam, thou shalt be a sign to thy descendants for all generations. On this day they are brought to trial, and if they repent I will pardon them and remove from the Throne of Judgement and sit on the Throne of Mercy and have mercy on them.'

HOWBEIT ON THE TENTH DAY OF THIS SEVENTH MONTH IS THE DAY OF ATONEMENT; IT SHALL BE AN HOLY CONVOCATION UNTO YOU. R. Hiya quoted here the verse: "A Psalm of David, Maschil. Blessed is he whose transgression is forgiven, whose sin is covered" (Ps. XXXII, 1). 'What', he said, 'is meant by Maschil? The waters that give wisdom to those who seek to find that place which is called maschil (lit. he that giveth heed). And because it is called so, forgiveness and complete freedom depend on it. What is meant by "whose sin is covered"? As we have explained, that sin which he commits before God and, concealing it from men, confesses to God. Observe that when a man commits a sin once and twice and three times, and does not repent, his sins are exposed and are published above and below, and heralds go before him and proclaim, Keep away from So-and-so, who is scorned of his Master, scorned above and scorned below, Woe to him that he has impaired the likeness of his Master, woe to him that he has not regarded the honour of his Master. When, however, a man walks in the way of his Master and occupies himself with His service, if then he should happen to commit a sin, all screen him, higher and lower, and he is called "one whose sin is covered". ' Said R. Abba to him: 'All this is quite correct, but you have not yet got to the root of the matter. There are two recondite teachings in this expression. One is this. We have learnt that the good deeds which a man does in this world fashion for him a precious and noble garment wherewith to cover himself. Now when a man has laid up a store of good deeds and then falls into evil ways, if God observes that his bad deeds outweigh the good and that he is wicked enough to regret all the good deeds that he did at first, [Tr. note: v. T.B. Kiddushin 40b.] then he is entirely lost both in this world and in the other. What, then, does God do with the good deeds which he performed at first? For though the wicked sinner perishes, the good deeds that he performed do not perish. If, then, there is a righteous man who walks in the ways of the King and is preparing his garment from his works, but before he has completed it he departs from this world, God completes it from the deeds which have been lost to that wicked sinner for him to array himself therewith in the other world, as it is written, "He (the wicked man) shall prepare it, but the just shall put it on" (Job XXVII, 17). Hence he may be said to be "covered from sin", that is, from the sins of the wicked. Another lesson is this, that the sin of this righteous man is hidden in what are called "the depths of the sea", just as one who falls into the depths of the sea can never be found, because the waters cover him.

Zohar: Vayikra, Section 3, Page 101b

What are these "depths of the sea"? It is a deep mystery, which R. Simeon has explained. All those that come from the violent side and are attached to the "evil species," the lower crowns, like Azazel on the Day of Atonement, are called the "depths (m'zuloth=clarifying region) of the sea", since they draw the impurities off the holy sea in the same way as the fire purifies silver, drawing off its dross. All the sins are thus dropped into it. For this reason it is also called "Sin" (hetaah, lit. failure), inasmuch as it takes away, especially on this day, the defilement of the soul and of the body, to wit, the sins committed through the evil prompting which is called filthy and disgusting.'

R. Yose said: 'It is written, "And he shall put on the two he-goats lots". This would seem to be a great honour for Azazel. Have you ever seen a slave cast lots with his master? Usually the servant takes only what his master gives him. The fact, however, is that because Samael is ready on this day with his accusations, and so that he should not have any grievance, he is given a portion in this way. This lot used to come up of itself. For so said R. Judah in the name of R. Isaac: We find a great wonder in the lot. The lot which Joshua cast used of itself to say, This is the portion of Judah, this is the portion of Benjamin, etc. And so here, too, when the priest placed his hands in position, the lots used to leap up and come down in their places, as it is written, "The goat on which hath gone up the lot for the Lord".

'Not on this occasion only, but whenever accusation is prepared and permission is given to the accuser it behoves us to set before him something with which he may occupy himself and so leave Israel alone. The Companions have noted in connection with the words of the Satan "from going to and fro in the earth" (Job I, 7), that, when the Israelites were about to cross the Red Sea, he said, I have gone to and fro through the Holy Land and I have seen that these are not worthy to enter it. If Thou wilt here execute judgement on the Egyptians, how do the Israelites differ from them? [Tr. note: v. Yalkut Reubeni on Beshalah.] Either let them all die together, or let them all return to Egypt. And further, didst Thou not say, "they shall serve them four hundred years", and only two hundred and ten of the number are past? Thereupon God said: 'What am I to do? This one must have some sop thrown to him. I will give him something with which to occupy himself so as to leave my sons. I have someone for the purpose. Straightway God said to him, "Hast thou considered my servant Job?", and straightway the Satan sought to discredit him, saying, "Does Job fear God for nothing?". Imagine a shepherd seeking to take his flock across a river, when he sees a wolf about to fall on them. What shall I do? he says. While I am carrying the lambs across, he will fall on the sheep. Then he catches sight among the flock of a ram from the fields, strong and powerful. I will throw this one to him, he says, and while they are struggling I will take all the flock across and save them. So God said: Here is a strong and powerful ram, I will throw it to him, and while he is busy with it my sons shall cross and not be attacked. Thus while the Satan was busy with Job he left Israel alone and they were not accused. So on the Day of Atonement also the informer is ready to spy out the land, and we must send him something with which he may occupy himself. So there is a saying, Give some wine to the menial of the king's palace and he will praise thee to the king, and if not he will malign thee to him, and it may be that the officers of the king will take up his words and the king will execute judgement.' R.

Zohar: Vayikra, Section 3, Page 102a

Isaac said: 'Give the fool who stands before the king some wine and tell him all the faults and errors thou hast committed and he will come and praise thee and say that there is not another in the world like thee. So here the informer is ever before the king, and Israel present him a gift along with a list of all the faults and wrongs which they have done, and he comes and praises Israel and becomes their defender, and God puts all on the head of the wicked of his own people.' Said R. Yose: 'Woe to the people of Esau at the time when Israel send that he-goat to the Informer who is their Chieftain, since for its sake he comes and praises Israel and God diverts all those sins on to the head of his people.' Said R. Judah: 'If the heathen knew of that he-goat, they would not leave Israel alive a single day. All that day Satan is occupied with that goat, and therefore God makes atonement for Israel and purifies them from all their sins and they are not accused before Him. Afterwards the Satan comes and praises Israel and the accuser becomes defender and departs. Then God says to the seventy Chiefs that surround His throne, Do you see how this Informer is always seeking to attack my sons? A certain goat has been sent to him with a tablet recording all their sins and errors which they have committed before me, and he has accepted it. Then they all agree that those sins should be discharged on the head of his own people.' R. Abba said: 'At first all those sins cleave to him, and afterwards they are discharged upon the head of his people.

'On this day the priest is crowned with superior crowns and stands between heavenly and earthly beings and makes atonement for himself and his house and the priests and the sanctuary and all Israel. We have learnt that at the moment when he enters with the blood of the bullock he concentrates his thoughts on the highest principle of faith and sprinkles with his finger, as it is written, "and he shall sprinkle it upon the mercy-seat and before the mercy-seat" He used to dip the top of his finger in the blood and sprinkle, going lower and lower each time, at the side of the mercy-seat. He began to count one [Tr. note: v. T.B. Yoma, 53b]-the first "one" by itself, one being the sum of all, the glory of all, the goal of all, the beginning of all. Then "one and one", joined together in love and friendship inseparable. When he had passed this "and one" which is the mother of all, he began to count in pairs, saying, "one and two", "one and three", "one and four", "one and five", "one and six", "one and seven", so as to draw down this "one" which is the supernal Mother by certain grades to the crown of the lower Mother [Tr. note: Al. "to illumine the lower Mother".] and to draw deep rivers from their place to the Community of Israel. Hence on this day two luminaries diffuse light together, the supernal Mother giving light to the lower Mother.' R. Isaac said: 'A cord was tied to the feet of the High Priest before he entered the Holy of Holies, so that if he died suddenly within they should be able to draw him out. They used to know by a certain thread of scarlet if the priest had been successful in his intercessions. If its colour did not change, they knew that the priest within was not free from sin, but if he was to issue in peace, it was known by the thread changing its colour to white, when there was rejoicing above and below. If it did not, however, all were distressed, knowing that their prayer had not been accepted.' [Tr. note: v.. T.B. Yoma, 39a.] R. Judah said: 'When he went in and closed his eyes so as not to see what he had no right to see, and heard the voice of the Cherubim chanting praises, he knew that all was in joy and that he would come out in peace, and another sign was if his words came forth joyfully, so as to be accepted and blessed.'

Zohar: Vayikra, Section 3, Page 102b

R. Eleazar asked R. Simeon: 'Why is this day attached only to this grade? Surely it should more than any other day be in the grade where the King abides?' He replied: 'Eleazar, my son, you have asked a good question. The reason is this. The Holy King has left his temple and house in the hands of the Matrona and has left his sons with her that she may guide them and chastise them and abide in their midst, so that if they are virtuous the Matrona enters with joy and honour

into the presence of the King. If, however, they are not deserving, She and they are sent into exile according to our interpretation of the text, "and through your transgression your mother is sent away" (Isa. L, 1). Hence one day is appointed in the year for examining them. When this day comes the supernal Mother, in whose hand is all freedom, comes to examine Israel, and Israel prepare themselves on this day with many prayers and services and fastings to make themselves worthy. Then is freedom granted to them from the place where all freedom abides, through the hand of the Matrona. And when she sees the sons of the King, her sons who are entrusted to her hands, all virtuous without sin or guilt, She joins the King with smiles, with gladness, and with perfect love, because she has trained up fitting sons for the supreme King. But if they are not found as they should be on this day, woe to them and woe to their emissaries, for the Matrona is removed from the King and the supreme Mother departs and no freedom proceeds from her to any world. Happy are Israel whom the Holy One, blessed be He, has taught His ways that they may be delivered from judgement and

641

found deserving before Him. Hence it is written: "For on that day he shall make atonement for you" (Lev. XVI, 30), and "I shall sprinkle on you purifying waters" (Ezek. XXXVI, 25).'

HOWBEIT ON THE FIFTEENTH DAY OF THE SEVENTH MONTH. R. Yose asked R. Abba: 'What is the meaning of these fifteen days?' He replied: 'Assuredly they contain a deep mystery. Observe that both above and below each day proceeds on its own path and remains in its own place and performs its own function. The first group of ten belongs to the Community of Israel, while the five are of the King, because in the fifth grade (from the Matrona) the King sits upon his throne. Then the Father shines upon the Mother and fifty gates are illumined from Her to shed light upon the fifth. And should you say that the Matrona is the seventh, this is because the King completes the Patriarchs. Therefore the seventh is the day on which the King is fully crowned and inherits from the Father and Mother, who are joined together. Hence both come to the same thing.'

R. Judah discoursed here on the verse: "And the Canaanite the king of Arad heard" (Num. XXI, 1). 'We have learnt', [Tr. note: v. T.B. Taanith, 9a.] he said, 'that three notable gifts were conferred upon Israel through the three brethren, Moses, Aaron, and Miriam. The manna was given to them for the merit of Moses, the clouds of glory for the merit of Aaron, and the well for the merit of Miriam.

Zohar: Vayikra, Section 3, Page 103a

[Note: The first 6 lines of the Hebrew text are not found in our translation]

When Miriam died the well was taken from them, as it is written, "And Miriam died, and there was no water for the congregation" (Num. xx, 1, 2). Another well which was with Israel also desired to depart, but when it saw six clouds that hovered over them it remained attached to them. When Aaron died the clouds departed and the cloud of the well with them, until Moses came and brought them back.' R. Isaac said: 'Why was this honour conferred upon Aaron? Because he was linked with clouds and he linked them all together, so that they were all blessed through him. For in addition to all the lovingkindness that God did with Israel, He linked with them seven precious clouds which He also linked with the Community of Israel, whose cloud was linked with seven others, and Israel traversed the wilderness protected by all of them. They all form a bond of faith, and therefore Israel were bidden to dwell in booths seven days, so that the Israelite may show that he is dwelling in the shadow of faith. As long as Aaron was alive, Israel were in the shadow of faith under those clouds. When Aaron died, a cloud on the right departed and the rest departed with it, and the weakness of Israel was exposed, and straightway the king of Arad heard that the clouds had departed [Tr. note: Cf. T.B. Taanith, ibid.] and the great explorer to whom they were all linked was dead.' R. Isaac observed that the King of Arad dwelt in the south, and the spies also brought back word that Amalek dwelt in the south (Num. XIII, 20), to awe the people, because Amalek had struck the first blow at them. R. Abba said: Why is the Canaanite mentioned here? Because Canaan was a slave of slaves (Gen. IX, 25), and this shows that he who withdraws himself from the shadow of faith deserves to be a slave to the slave of slaves. Hence "all that are homeborn in Israel shall dwell in booths"; everyone who is of the holy root and stock of Israel shall dwell in a booth under the shadow of faith. Shall he that is not of the holy stock withdraw himself from the shadow of faith? We are told that Eleazar the servant of Abraham was a Canaanite, but because he served Abraham, who sat under the shadow of faith, he was delivered from the curse of Canaan and was even called "blessed", as it is written, "Come in, thou blessed of the Lord" (Gen. XXIV, 31). Thus whoever abides under the shadow of faith acquires freedom for himself and his descendants in perpetuity, and is blessed with a noble blessing, but he who withdraws from the shadow of faith brings captivity upon himself and for his children, as it is written, "And he took some of them captive".

Zohar: Vayikra, Section 3, Page 103b

YE SHALL DWELL IN BOOTHS. The word succoth (booths) is written without a vau, to show that there is one cloud to which all the others are linked. R. Eleazar cited here the verse: "Thus saith the Lord, I remember for thee the kindness of thy youth", etc. (Jer. II, 2). 'This verse', he said, 'refers to the Community of Israel at the time when She went in the wilderness with Israel. The "kindness" (hesed) is the cloud of Aaron which carried along with it five others which were linked with thee and shone for thee. "The love of thine espousals": when they adorned and perfected thee like a bird. And all this for what? That thou mightest "go after me in the wilderness, in a land not sown". Observe that when a man sits in this abode of the shadow of faith, the Shekinah spreads her wings over him from above and Abraham and five other righteous ones make their abode with him.' R. Abba said: 'Abraham and five righteous ones and David with them. Hence it is written, "In booths ye shall dwell seven days", as much as to say, "Ye seven days shall dwell in booths", and a man should rejoice each day of the festival with these guests who abide with him.' R. Abba further pointed out that first it says "ye shall dwell" and then "they shall dwell". The first refers to the guests, and therefore Rab Hamnuna the Elder, when he entered the booth, used to stand at the door inside and say, Let us invite the guests and prepare a table, and he used to stand up and greet them, saying, In booths ye shall dwell, O seven days. Sit, most exalted guests, sit; sit, guests of faith, sit. He would then raise his hands in joy and say, Happy is our portion, happy is the portion of Israel, as it is written, "For the portion of the Lord is his people", and then he took his seat. The second "dwell" refers to human beings; for he who has a portion in the holy land and people sits in the shadow of faith to receive the guests so as to rejoice in this world and the next. He must also gladden the poor, because the portion of those guests whom he invites must go to the poor. And if a man sits in the shadow of faith and invites these guests and does not give them their portion, they all hold aloof from him, saying "Eat thou not the bread of him that hath an evil eye" (Prov. XXIII, 6). That table which he prepares is his own and not God's. Alas for him when those guests leave his table.' R. Abba further said: 'Abraham always used to stand at the cross roads to invite guests to his table. [Tr. note: v. T.B. Sotah, 10b.] Now when a man invites him and all the righteous and King David and does not give them their portion, Abraham rises from the table and exclaims, "Depart, I pray you, from the tents of these wicked men" (Num. XVI, 26), and all rise and follow him. Isaac says, "The belly of the wicked shall want" (Prov. XIII, 26). Jacob says, "The morsel thou hast eaten thou shalt vomit up" (Ibid. XXIII, 8). The other righteous ones say, "For all tables are full of vomit and uncleanness" (Isa. XXVIII, 8). David says. [Tr. note: There is here a lacuna in the text.] In those ten days during which David judges the world, that man is judged who has treated him more ungratefully than Nabal.' R. Eleazar said: 'The Torah does not demand of a man more than he can perform, as it says, "Each one man shall give as he is able,' (Deut. XVI, 7). A man should not say, I will first satisfy myself with food and drink, and what is left I shall give to the poor, but the first of everything must be for the guests. And if he gladdens ihe guests and satisfies them, God rejoices with him and Abraham proclaims over him, "Then shalt thou delight thyself in the Lord", etc. (Isa. LVIII, 14). Isaac proclaims, "No weapon that is formed against thee shall prosper" (Ibid. LIV, 17).' R. Simeon said: 'This verse is said by King David, because all royal weapons of war have been handed to David. What Isaac says is, "His seed shall be mighty on the earth" (Ps. CXII, 2). Jacob proclaims, "Then shall thy light break forth as the morning" (Isa. LVIII, 8). The other righteous say, "The Lord shall guide thee continually and satisfy thy soul in dry places" (Ibid. 11). Happy the lot of the man who attains ta all this!'

AND YE SHALL TAKE YOU ON THE FIRST DAY THE FRUIT OF GOODLY TREES. R. Simeon quoted here the verse: "Every one that is called by my name, for my glory I have created him, I have formed him, yea I have made him" (Isa. LXIII, 7). '"Every one that is called by my name": this is man whom God has created in His likeness and whom He calls by His own name when he does truth and justice, as it is written, "Thou shalt not revile the judges" (Elohim, Ex. XXII, 28). "I have formed him, yea I have made him": as has been explained, the words "Let us make man in our image, after our likeness" refer to the time of wedlock, namely, the union of "image" and "likeness", so that man issued from Male and Female. In the Book of King Solomon it is written that at the hour of wedded union

on earth, God sends a certain form with the figure of a human being which hovers over the union, and if a man's eye were capable of such a thing it would see such a form over his head. The child is created in that form, and before that form stands over a man's head the child is not created, that form being prepared for it before it issues into the world. In that form it grows up, in that form it goes about, as it is written, "Surely every man walketh in a form" (zelem, Ps. XXXIX, 9). This form is from on high. When the spirits go forth from their places, each one stands before the Holy King with its adornments, with the countenance which it is to wear in this world; and from that adornment comes forth this form (zelem). Thus it is the third from the spirit, and it comes down first to this world at the time of wedded union, from which it is never absent. In the case of Israel, who are holy, this zelem is holy and from a holy place. But for the heathens it comes from the "evil species", from the side of uncleanness. Therefore a man should not mix his form with that of a heathen, because the one is holy and the other unclean. [Tr. note: From here to the end of the paragraph is inserted from Zohar, Genesis, 220a, whither it has been transposed in the text.] This explains why the dead body of an Israelite defiles while the dead body of a heathen does not defile. For when an Israelite dies, all the sanctifications of his Master depart from him, and that holy form and holy spirit leave him and his body is left unclean. But the contrary is the case with the heathen: his form and spirit are unclean in him when he is alive, but when he dies they leave him, and his body, though unclean itself, does not propagate uncleanness. Observe that when judgement is aroused, and God sits upon the throne of judgement to judge the world, a man should betake himself to repentance and amend his ways, since on this day the sentences are written. If a man repents in time, his sentence is torn up. If not, he still has a chance on the Day of Atonement. If still his repentance is not perfect, his sentence is suspended till the last day, the eighth of the Feast of Tabernacles, after which the sentences are no more returned to the court of the King. The sign is that a man's shadows depart from him.'

ON THE EIGHTH DAY SHALL BE AN HOLY CONVOCATION UNTO YOU. This is because this day is from the King alone, it is his day of rejoicing in Israel. A king invites some guests, and while they are there all the household attend on them. When they depart the king says to his household, Till now I and you have all of us been attending to the guests; now I and you will rejoice together for one day' So God said: Up to now you have been bringing sacrifices for the other peoples, now bring one for yourselves. The guests of faith are with the King continually and all assemble before him on the day of the King's rejoicing. On this day Jacob is at the head of the rejoicing. Therefore it is written: "Happy art thou, O Israel, who is like unto thee? (Deut. XXXIII, 29).

THAT THEY BRING UNTO THEE PURE OLIVE OIL BEATEN FOR THE LIGHT. Why does this section follow the section of the festivals? Because there are lamps above in which burns the supernal oil, and through Israel both higher and lower are blessed and the lamps are lit.

Zohar: Vayikra, Section 3, Page 105a

R. Abba quoted here the verse: "Be glad in the Lord and rejoice, ye righteous" (Ps. XXII, 11). '"Be glad in the Lord", when judgement is repressed and mercy is aroused. Then "the righteous", that is, Zaddik and Zedek, bless and rejoice all worlds. Then "Exult, ye upright of heart": these are the sons of faith who are linked with them. In all things some action is required below to arouse the activity above. For observe: he who says that no action is needed or no audible utterance, a curse light on such a one! This section confutes him, of the lighting of the lights, for through this act there is a kindling above and a rejoicing above and below and a proper linking of both.' R. Judah said: 'The altar below rouses another altar, above, the priest below rouses another Priest, above.'

R. Yose and R. Isaac were once walking together when the former said: 'It is written, "Thou shalt call the Sabbath a delight and the holy of the Lord honourable, and shalt honour it, not doing thine own ways" (Isa. LVIII, 13). So far I understand. But what is the meaning of the next words: "Nor finding thine own pleasure, nor speaking thine own words"? What derogation is there in this for the Sabbath?' He replied: 'Truly it is derogatory. For there is no word which issues from the mouth of a man but has a voice which rises aloft and awakens something else, namely that which is called "ordinary" above, belonging to the ordinary days. Now if the ordinary is awakened on the holy day, it is counted something derogatory above, and the Holy One and the Community of Israel ask: Who is this that seeks to break up our union, who is it that seeks the ordinary here? The Ancient Holy One appears not and rests not on the ordinary. For this reason it is permitted on Sabbath to think about ordinary things, because mere thinking produces no effect, but if a word issues from a man's mouth it becomes a voice and rises aloft and breaks through ethers and firmaments and arouses something else. Therefore it says, "Not to find thine own pleasure nor speaking thine own word". But if a man utters a holy word of the Torah, it rises aloft and arouses the saints of the King, who set a crown on its head, so that there is rejoicing above and below.' 'Assuredly it is so,' said R. Yose, 'and so I have already heard. But tell me, if a man fasts on Sabbath, does he do anything derogatory to the Sabbath or not? How can you say he does not, seeing that he neglects the repasts of faith, and his punishment must be great, since he does away with the joy of the Sabbath.' He replied: 'I have heard that on the contrary this is he who is more remarked above than any other. For this day is one of supreme joy above and below, joy of all joys, the joy of faith, on which even sinners in Gehinnom have respite. Now when this man is seen to be without joy and without rest, different from all others above and below, they all ask, What is the cause of So-and-so being in sorrow? And when the Ancient Holy One is revealed on this day and the prayer of this sorrowful one rises and stands before Him, then all the punishments decreed against him are cancelled, even if the Court of the King has concurred in the sentence, because when the Ancient One is revealed all freedom and all joy is present. Hence, as we have learnt, the sentence of "seventy years" is annulled, the "seventy years" being the seventy crowns of the king in which He is revealed. All this, however, is only

Zohar: Vayikra, Section 3, Page 105b

when a man is warned in a dream on the night of Sabbath. Imagine a king who makes a wedding feast for his son and orders all to rejoice. All therefore rejoice, but one man is in sorrow because he is chained for execution. When the king comes he sees all rejoicing as he ordained, but he lifts up his eyes and sees one man chained and sorrowing. Why, he says, should all rejoice in the espousals of my son and this one be chained for execution? And straightway he orders him to be released. So with him who fasts on Sabbath when all the world is rejoicing: when the Holy Ancient One is disclosed, even though all those "seventy years" have concurred in his sentence, it is wholly annulled. If on other days it is possible to procure annulment, how much more on Sabbath? For every day has its own power, and if a man fasts on account of a dream, before the day ends his sentence is annulled; not, however, if it is of the "seventy years", unless on Sabbath. Hence he has to fast on that day and not on another, for one day has no power over the next, each being responsible only for what happens in itself. Hence a man should not postpone his fast from one day to another. Observe, too, that a man is not warned in a dream without reason. Woe to him who has no warning dreams; he is called "evil", as it is written: "He that is not visited (in a dream) is evil" (Prov. XIX, 23).'

AND THE SON OF AN ISRAELITISH WOMAN WHOSE FATHER WAS AN EGYPTIAN WENT OUT. R. Judah said: 'He went out from the sphere of the portion of Israel, from the sphere of the whole, from the sphere of faith. AND THEY STROVE TOGETHER: From this we learn that he who comes from a polluted seed is ultimately exposed before all. What is the cause? The defilement of the evil portion in him, since he has no portion in the whole body of Israel.'

(AND THE SON OF THE ISRAELITISH WOMAN BLASPHEMED THE NAME.) R. Hiya quoted here the verse: "It is the glory of God to conceal a thing" (Prov. xxv, 2). 'This means', he said, 'that it is not permitted to a man to disclose mysteries which are not meant to be disclosed, and which the Ancient of Days has hidden, as it is written, "To eat sufficiently, but to conceal the Ancient One" (Isa. XXIII, 18). "To eat sufficiently"—until that place which is permitted, but no further. Or we may also take the words to refer to R. Simeon and his generation, the Companions who know how to walk in the path of faith, like the generation of R. Simeon and his colleagues, but such things are to be concealed from other generations which are not fitted to "eat a sufficiency". In the days of R. Simeon a man would say to his companion, Open thy mouth and let thy words give light, but after his death they said, "Let not thy mouth cause thy flesh to sin" (Eccl. v, 6).

Zohar: Vayikra, Section 3, Page 106a

AND HIS MOTHER'S NAME, ETC. Up to this point his mother's name was concealed, but now that he had uttered blasphemy his mother's name is mentioned.' Said R. Abba: 'Were it not that the Sacred Lamp is still alive, I would not reveal this, since it is not meant to be revealed save to those who are among the reapers of the field: a curse light on those who want to reveal to those who should not know! The Israelitish man mentioned here was the son of another woman, and his father was the husband of Shelomith. When an Egyptian came to her in the middle of the night and he returned home and became aware of it, he separated from her and took another wife. Hence one is called "the Israelitish man" and the other "the son of the Israelitish woman". Now if they quarreled, how came the Holy Name to be involved? The reason was that the Israelitish man reviled the other's mother, and the latter took the He from the Holy Name and cursed with it to defend his mother; hence the word nakab (lit. hollowed) is used, to show that he separated the letters of the Holy Name. But all this is only for "the reapers of the field".'

(AND THEY PUT HIM IN WARD.) R. Isaac said: Besides insulting his mother, he mentioned that his father was the man whom Moses had slain with the Holy Name, and therefore it was that "they brought him to Moses", since Moses was concerned in the matter. When Moses perceived who it was, straightway "they put him in ward", and so both father and son fell by the hand of Moses.'

WHOEVER CURSETH HIS GOD SHALL BEAR HIS SIN. R. Isaac quoted here the verse: "There shall no strange god be in thee, neither shalt thou worship any strange god" (Ps. LXXXI, 9). 'The "strange god"', he said,

Zohar: Vayikra, Section 3, Page 106b

'mentioned in the first clause refers to the evil prompting, for if a man links himself with this, a "strange god" enters into him, for straightway he breaks the commandments of the Torah, and so he comes to abandon the faith in the Holy Name and to bow down to false gods. Hence the verse tells us that "if there is no strange god in thee, through the evil prompting, then thou shalt not come to bow down to a strange god". Hence if a man only "curses his god", in which case he may plead that he is referring only to that evil prompting which abides in him, and we do not know whether he is speaking truly or not, he shall merely "bear his iniquity"; but "he that uttereth the name of the Lord shall be put to death".' Said R. Judah: 'If that is so, it should say, "his sin shall be forgiven", not "he shall bear his sin".' He replied: 'We must suppose him to say "my god", without specifying.' Said R. Hiya: 'Certainly in that case he shall bear his iniquity, but if he pronounces the name of the Lord he shall be put to death, because on this all faith depends and he can make no excuse.'

R. Yose said: 'Assuredly it is so, that this name is the basis of the faith of higher and lower, and all worlds are established on it. On one tiny letter are suspended thousands of thousands and myriads of myriads of delectable worlds, as we have learnt that these letters are linked with one another, and thousands and myriads of celestials depend on each one, and there is wrapped in them that which is not grasped by higher or lower.'

R. Hizkiah cited the verse: "No hand shall touch it, for he shall surely be stoned or shot through", etc. (Ex. XIX, 13). 'Now if', he said, 'this was to be the penalty for touching a mere mountain like Sinai because the glory of the Holy King was revealed on it, what must happen to one who touches the King? And if this was to happen to one who touched the mountain, even respectfully, what must happen to one who touches the King insultingly?' R. Jesse cited the verse: "Draw not nigh hither, put off thy shoes from off thy feet", etc. (Ex. III, 5). 'If', he said, 'this could be said to Moses, from whom the holy halo never departed from the day that he was born, and who drew near in reverence and holiness, what would be said to one who draws near to the King insultingly?'

R. Abba said: 'When Israel were in Egypt, they were acquainted with the Chieftains who are appointed over the various nations of the world, and each of them feared one or other of them. When they were linked with the bond of faith and God brought them near to His service, they abandoned those powers for the higher faith. Therefore they were commanded, "Whoever curseth his god", etc., as much as to say: Although the service of these is strange worship, yet I have appointed them to control the world, and therefore whoever curses or insults them must bear his iniquity. But "he that blasphemeth the name of the Lord shall be put to death".'

R. Simeon was once going along accompanied by R. Eleazar, R. Abba, R. Hiya, R. Yose, and R. Judah. They came to a certain watercourse, and R. Yose slipped down in his clothes into the water. He said:

Zohar: Vayikra, Section 3, Page 107a

'I wish this water channel had never been here.' Said R. Simeon to him: 'You must not say that. This is for the service of the world, and it is forbidden to revile a ministrant of the Holy One, blessed be He, especially those loyal servants of his. They are appointed by Providence. It is written that "God saw all that he had made, and behold it was very good" (Gen. I, 31), even serpents and scorpions and fleas and all things that appear to be pests-all these are for the service of the world, though men know it not.' [Tr. note: s. T.B. Shabbath, 77b.] As they went along, they saw a snake crawling in front of them. Said R. Simeon: Assuredly this creature is there to perform some miracle for us. The snake quickly crept in front of them and wound itself round a basilisk in the middle of the path. They then struggled together until both were killed. When they came up to them they found them lying dead in the road and R. Simeon said: 'Blessed be God for performing for us this miracle, for if anyone had looked upon this creature while it was alive, or had been looked upon by it, he would not have escaped harm, much less if he had approached it. Thus God makes all things His agents and we must not revile anything that He has made.'

R. Simeon discoursed on the verse: "I am a rose of Sharon, a lily of the valleys" (S.S. II, 1). 'How beloved', he said, 'is the Community of Israel to the Holy One, blessed be He, so that He continually praises Her and She continually praises Him, having many chants and hymns in store for the King. The Community of Israel is called the rose of Sharon because she flowers beautifully in the Garden of Eden, and the lily of the valleys because she desires to be watered from the deep stream, the source of rivers, as it is said, "Sharon is like an Arabah" (dry land). She is also called the lily of the valleys because she is at the lowest point of all. At first she is a rose with yellowish leaves, afterwards a lily with two colours, white and red, a lily with six leaves, a lily which changes from one colour to another. When she seeks to unite with the King she is called "rose", but after she has joined him with her kisses she is called "lily".

'Observe that when God created man and invested him with high honour, He required of him to cleave to Him in order that he might be unique and single-hearted, cleaving to the One by the bond of single-minded faith wherewith all is linked together. Afterwards they turned aside from the way of faith and abandoned the unique tree which is high above all trees and clung to the place which is ever changing from colour to colour, from good to bad and bad to good, and came down from on high and clung below to the ever changeable and abandoned the supreme and changeless One. Hence their hearts alternated between good and bad: sometimes they deserved mercy and sometimes punishment,

Zohar: Vayikra, Section 3, Page 107b

according to that to which they clave. Said the Holy One, blessed be He: Man, thou hast abandoned life and clung to death; verily death is before thee. Therefore death was decreed for him and for all the world. Now if Adam sinned, what was the sin of the rest of the world? For it cannot be said that all creatures came and ate of the forbidden tree. No. What happened was that when man stood upright, all creatures saw him and feared him and followed him like slaves. So when he said to them, "Come, let us bow down to the Lord who made us", they all went after him. And when they saw man bowing down to the other place and cleaving to it, they again followed him, and thus he brought death on himself and all the world. Thus Adam alternated between various colours, good and bad, commotion and rest, judgement and mercy, life and death: never constant in one, through the influence of that place, which is therefore called "the flame of a sword which turns every way", from this side to that, from good to evil, from mercy to judgement, from peace to war. The Supreme King, however, in compassion on the works of his hands, warned them saying, "From the tree of knowledge of good and evil ye shall not eat". Man, however, did not listen, and followed his wife and was banished forever, for woman can attain to this place but no further, and woman brought death on all. But in days to come "the days of my people shall be as the days of the tree" (Isa. LXV, 22)-like that tree of which we know. Of that time it is written, "He hath swallowed up death forever, and the Lord God hath wiped away tears from all faces" (Ibid. xxv, 8).'

BEHAR

AND THE LORD SPAKE UNTO MOSES... THEN SHALL THE LAND KEEP A SABBATH UNTO THE LORD. R. Eleazar introduced this portion with a discourse on the verse: "This is the law of the burnt-offering, the burnt-offering shall be", etc. (Lev. VI, 2). 'We have explained this verse', he said, 'to refer to the Community of Israel when she ascends to join the Holy King in perfect union. When night enters and the gates are closed, the lower judgements are aroused in the world, and asses, she-asses and dogs wander about; that is to say, the asses of their own accord, but the she-asses and dogs only if human beings practise sorceries with them. Then all men sleep, and a fire is kindled on the lower altar without [the curtain]. At midnight the north wind awakes, and from the lower altar there goes forth a flame of fire, and the gates are opened and the lower judgements shrink back into their holes. The flame of fire in its passage parts and travels in many directions and enters

Zohar: Vayikra, Section 3, Page 108a

under the wings of the cock, which thereupon crows. Then the Holy One, blessed be He, enters the company of the righteous, and the Community of Israel utters His praises until morning, when they are found to be discoursing on a certain secret. The daybreak is a time for flames and judgements, but then Abraham awakens and there is rest for all.

Now when Israel entered the promised land, there were no lower judgements in it, and the Community of Israel was at ease in it upon the wings of the Cherubim, for Israel did not go to rest until they had brought the evening sacrifice and so caused judgements to depart. When the burnt-offering burnt on the altar, there was ease and comfort throughout, and the Spouse was with her Husband. Hence it is written, "and the earth shall rest a sabbath for the Lord"; for such it was literally.'

R. Eleazar further quoted here the verse: "If thou buy an Hebrew servant, six years shall he serve" (Ex. XXI, 2). 'Every Israelite', he said, 'who is circumcised and bears on him the holy impress has relief in the sabbatical year, because it belongs of right to him to find rest therein: and this is called "the Sabbath of the land". Truly there is freedom and rest in it; as the Sabbath is rest for all, so the sabbatical year is rest for all, for the spirit and the body. Observe that the He denotes rest for higher and lower-the higher He for the higher and the lower for the lower. The higher He is seven years seven times, the lower He is seven years only; the one is a sabbatical year, the other a Jubilee; and when closely scrutinized, both are found to be one.

'In this rest of the land slaves are also required to partake. Hence it is written, "In the seventh year he shall go out free for nothing" (Ex. XXI, 2). What is meant by "for nothing"? The words have the same inner meaning as in the verse, "We remember the fish which we did eat in Egypt for nought" (Num. XI, 5)-that is to say, without pronouncing a blessing; for in Egypt the yoke of heaven was not upon them. What is the yoke of the kingdom of heaven? Just as an ox is put under a yoke in order that it may be of use, and otherwise it never does any work, so a man must first accept the yoke and then perform religious service: and without it he will not be able to serve God. This yoke will not rest upon one who is subject to another, and therefore slaves are exempt from the yoke of the kingdom of heaven. And if they are exempt from this yoke, they are exempt from all the rest of the religion, and therefore Israel ate in Egypt "for nothing". Here, too, the slave shall go forth to freedom, although so far all that he did was "for nothing", without the yoke of heaven, and he shall have rest. Later when he is free and has rest, he receives a yoke from the place which brought him forth to freedom. And if a man refuses to go forth to freedom, he impairs that place, since he leaves the yoke of the kingdom of heaven and accepts the yoke of a master. Therefore "his master shall bring him to Elohim"- to the place which he impairs, "and bring him to the door or the doorpost",

Zohar: Vayikra, Section 3, Page 108b

since this place is the gateway to the higher world. And since he was minded to impair that place, a blemish is left in his body, as it is written, "And his master shall bore his ear through". And since Israel at Mount Sinai placed "doing" before "hearing", therefore "hearing" is attached to this sabbatical year.

'It is written: "Six years thou shalt sow thy land and in the seventh year thou shalt let it rest", etc. Why so? "That the poor of thy people may eat" (Ibid.). For the poor are attached to that place, and therefore let them eat. Hence he that loves the poor brings peace to the Community of Israel and increases blessing in the world, and brings joy and strength to the place which is called Righteousness that it may pour down blessing on the Community of Israel.'

Zohar: Vayikra, Section 3, Page 110b

AND IF YE SAY, WHAT SHALL WE EAT, ETC. R. Judah cited here the verse: "Trust in the Lord and do good, dwell in the land and follow after faithfulness" (Ps. XXXVII, 3). 'Observe', he said, 'that, as we have learnt, the deed below arouses the activity above, as it says, "and ye shall do (lit. make) them", as much as to say, by your action below you make those above. Hence it says here, "Do (i.e. make) good", "good" being a reference to the Zaddik. When you do this, then that "good" is aroused, and then you may "dwell in the land and follow after faithfulness". The "earth" referred to here is the supernal earth, with which none can abide save he first arouse this "good"; but if he does that he may dwell in its midst and eat its fruit and delight in it. And the same meaning is in the words "follow after faithfulness". We may also take these words to mean, "Concentrate all thy thought upon Her". For if thou arousest not this good to meet Her, bestirrest thyself not to meet Her, this good departs from Her and thou canst not approach Her, as thou canst not approach a burning furnace, and if thou dost approach it will be in fear, like one who is afraid of death, for then a fire burns to consume the world. But if this "good" advances to meet Her and abides in Her, then thou needest not to fear, and then "thou shalt decree a thing and it shall be established unto thee and light shall shine upon thy ways" (Job XXII, 28). For the sons of faith bend Her to their will every day. Who are the sons of faith? Those who arouse this "good" to meet Her, and do not spare their substance, knowing that the Holy One, blessed be He, will give them more, because they set in motion blessings before Him. Hence "if ye say, What shall we eat in the seventh year?" the answer is, "I will command my blessing upon you in the sixth year"; just as it is written elsewhere: "See that the Lord... giveth you on the sixth day the bread of two days" (Ex. XVI, 29).'

As R. Yose and R. Hiya were once travelling together, they saw in front of them two other men going along. They saw a man come up to them and say, I beg of you, give me some food, if only a piece of bread, because for two days I have been wandering in the wilderness without tasting anything. One of the two men thereupon took out the food which he had brought with him for the journey and gave him to eat and drink. Said his companion to him: 'What will you do for food, for I am going to eat my own?' He replied: 'Do I want to eat yours?' The poor man ate up all that he had save some bread, and this he gave him for the road. Said R. Hiya: 'God did not desire that this good deed should be done by us.' R. Yose replied: 'Perhaps that man was doomed to some punishment, and God sent this man to him so as to deliver him.' They resumed their journey, and soon after the man who had given his food became faint. Said his companion to him: 'Did I not

tell you not to give your bread away?' R. Hiya then said to R. Yose: 'We have bread, let us give him some.' Said R. Yose to him: 'Do you want to undo the merit of his good deed? Let us watch a little, for assuredly the pallor of death is on this man's face, and God prepared some merit for him in order to deliver him.' Meanwhile the man fell asleep under a tree and his companion left him. R. Yose and R. Hiya then saw a fiery adder by him. 'Alas for that man,' said R. Hiya; 'surely he will now be killed.' R. Yose replied: 'He deserves that a miracle should be done on his behalf.' At that point a snake came down from the tree with intent to kill the man, but the adder attacked and killed it, and then turned its head and departed. Said R. Yose: 'Did I not tell you that God desired to perform a miracle for him, and that you should not exhaust his merit?' The man then woke up and began to go. R. Hiya and R. Yose came up to him and gave him food. When he had eaten they informed him of the miracle which God had performed for him. R. Yose then quoted the verse: "Trust in the Lord and do good, dwell in the land and follow after faithfulness" (Ps. XXXVII, 3). 'Happy', he said, 'is the man who does good with what he hath, because he arouseth good for the Community of Israel, to wit, with righteousness. [Tr. note: Zedakah, i.e. charity.] Hence it is written, "Righteousness delivereth from death" (Prov. X, 2). Why so? Because righteousness is the tree of life, and it rouses itself against the tree of death and takes those who are attached to it and delivers them from death. And what rouses it to do so? You must say, the charity which that man does; as it were, he performs it above also.'

BEHUKOTHAI

IF YE WALK IN MY STATUTES, ETC. R. Hiya introduced this section with a discourse on the verse: "O my people, remember what Balak king of Moab consulted, and what Balaam the son of Beor answered him" (Micah VI, 5). 'Happy', he said, 'is the people whose Master exhorts them thus, as though to say, Although you go astray from the ways of My people, My ways, yet ye are My people, and I do not desire to requite you according to your deeds.' R. Isaac said: 'Happy the portion of the people whose Master says to them, "O my people, what have I done to thee and wherein have I wearied thee?" (Ibid. 3).' R. Yose said: 'God said to Israel, "Remember now (I pray you)". We cry every day with tears and wailing, "Remember, O Lord, what is come upon us" (Lam. v, 1), "Remember, O Lord, against the children of Edom" (Ps. CXXXVII, 7), and He says to us, "I pray you, remember now", and we pay no heed; therefore when we cry He pays no heed to us.' R. Judah said: 'In truth God does heed us and remember us, otherwise Israel would not be able to stand a single day in captivity, for so it is written, "And yet for all that when they be in the land of their enemies", etc. (Lev. XXVI, 44).

God does not requite us according to our deeds.

'Balak was a greater master of magic arts than Balaam. For just as the celestial holiness can be aroused both by act and by word on our part, so can they that come from the side of uncleanness. Balaam was the greatest of sorcerers, but Balak was still greater. Balaam was greater in divination, but Balak in sorcery. For sorcery depends on actions, but divination on utterances and observations. Not so holy Israel, whose whole endeavour is to draw upon themselves the spirit of holiness, wherefore it is written, "For there is no divination against Israel nor enchantment against Jacob" (Num. XXIII, 23). Because Balaam was more powerful with his mouth than all diviners and in the observation of the great Serpent, therefore Balak wished to combine his own sorcery with his divination. Said God to him: Wretch, my sons have anticipated you. They have something which prevents all evil sides and species and sorceries from coming near them, to wit, the tent of assembly and the holy vessels and the utensils of the Sanctuary and the incense of spices, which allays all wrath and anger, both above and below, and the daily sacrifices and the two altars and the table and the shew-bread and the laver and its base, and many utensils to serve the utterance of the mouth, the ark and the two tablets of the Law and Aaron to make atonement for the people with his prayer every day. When the wicked Balaam saw all this he said: "For there is no divination against Israel nor sorcery against Israel". Why? Because "the Lord his God is with him, and the pleasure of the King is in him". Therefore, "My people, I beseech you to remember the time when Balak and Balaam joined forces to destroy you, but did not succeed because I took hold of you as a father takes hold of his son, not letting him fall into the hand of another." The verse continues, "From Shittim to Gilgal". Why are these places mentioned? As much as to say: Remember that when you let go your hold upon me, then in Shittim "the people ate and bowed down to their gods" (Num. XXV, 2), and in Gilgal "they sacrificed bullocks" (Hos. XII, 11), and then your enemies prevailed over you. Why all this? "That you might know the righteous deeds of the Lord", all those kindnesses that I did to you when you kept hold on Me, and I allowed nothing in the world to dominate you and neither the higher nor lower wrath nor the evil species were able to touch you. "And he said to them: Tarry here this night, and I will bring you word again as the Lord shall speak unto me." Observe that when the sun goes down and all the gates are closed and night falls and it grows dark, many dogs are loosened from their chains and go wandering about the world. There are many Chieftains who guide them and one supreme Chieftain from the side of the Left. That wicked Balaam gained access to this supreme Chieftain by his sorceries, which he practised in the night when he was at the head of all his company, and then he made known his requests to him.

Zohar: Vayikra, Section 3, Page 113a

The word Elohim is used in connection with Balaam as with Laban and with Abimelech, because this is a name of general application, being used of idols under the title of "other gods", which includes these Chieftains also. So this wicked Balaam summoned the Chieftain to him and he came to him. It may be said that he was with him by day (when he was with Balak). The truth is, however, that at that hour he only made observations by means of his divinations to fix the right hour, and when it says, "he went not as at other times to meet with enchantments" (Ibid. XXIV, 1), this signifies that he tried to fix the hour, but was not able as on other days, because he saw that there was no great wrath in the world and knew that "it was good in the eyes of the Lord to bless Israel" (Ibid.). For when burning wrath is rife the Left is aroused, and the wicked Balaam knew how to take hold of the left side so as to curse; but on this occasion he looked and saw that the wrath was not there.

'IF YE WALK IN MY STATUTES. This is the place from which depend the decrees of the Law, whereas "judgements" signifies another and higher place to which this statute is attached; and the two, "statute" and "judgement", are connected both on the higher and the lower plane. All the commandments and decrees and sanctifications of the Torah are attached to these, because one is the Written Torah and the other the Oral Torah. Both are intertwined and form one entity, and this is the sum of the Holy Name, so that he who transgresses against the commandments of the law in effect impairs the Holy Name.

'AND YE SHALL DO (MAKE) THEM. After walk and "keep" have been mentioned, why does it also say "do"? Because he who "keeps" the precepts of the Law and "walks" in God's ways, if one may say so, "makes" Him who is above. Also it says, "You shall make them", because the two aspects (of statute and judgement) are both aroused through you and join together so that the Holy Name is consummated.' Similarly, R. Simeon commented on the verse, "And David made him a name" (2 Sam. VIII, 23). 'Did, then, David really make it?' he asked. 'What it means is that because David walked in the way of the Torah and carried out the precepts of the Torah and exercised his royal power in the fitting manner, he, as it were, "made" a Name on high. No other king was so worthy to accomplish

Zohar: Vayikra, Section 3, Page 113b

this as David, because he used to rise at midnight and praise the Holy One, blessed be He, until the Holy Name ascended on its throne at the hour when the light of day appeared. In the same sense it is written here, "and ye shall make them"; and if ye strive to establish thus the Holy Name, all those blessings from above shall abide firmly with you. Similarly it is written: "And they shall keep the way of the Lord to do justice and judgement" (Gen. XVIII, 19), to signify that he who keeps the ways of the Torah, as it were, "makes" justice and judgement. And who are these? The Holy One, blessed be He.' R. Simeon here wept and exclaimed: 'Alas for mankind that they know not and heed not the honour of their Master! Who is it that "makes" the Holy Name every day? You must say, he that gives charity to-the poor. As we know, the poor man takes hold of judgement and all his food is judgement, the place that is called Zedek (righteousness). Hence he that gives charity (zedakah) to the poor makes the Holy Name complete as it should be above, since zedakah is the tree of life, and when it gives to Zedek the Holy Name becomes complete. Hence he who sets this activity in motion from below, as it were, fully makes the Holy Name. It has been stated elsewhere which is the place of the poor man. [Tr. note: Viz. the Shekinah.] Why is it so? Because the poor man has not anything of his own, save what is given him, and the moon has no light save what is given her by the sun. Why is a poor man counted as dead? Because he is found in the place of death. [Tr. note: The Shekinah being called "the tree of death".] Therefore, if one has pity on him and gives him charity, the tree of life rests upon him, as it says, "Zedakah (charity) delivereth from death" (Prov. x, 2). This applies only to charity done for its own sake, for then the doer links together zedakah with zedek so that the whole forms the Holy Name, since zedek is not established without zedakah.'

AND I SHALL GIVE PEACE IN THE LAND, AND YE SHALL LIE DOWN AND NONE SHALL MAKE YOU AFRAID. R. Yose cited here the verse: "Stand in awe and sin not", etc. (Ps. IV, 5). 'When night has fallen', he said, 'and men have gone to bed, many emissaries of the law arise and go about the world, and it behoves men to tremble in awe before the Holy One, blessed be He, in order that they may be delivered from them. And a man should be careful not to make any reference to them with his lips so as not to draw their attention to him. Hence it is written, "Commune with your own heart upon your bed" (Ibid.) Hence, when Israel are virtuous it is written of them, "I shall give peace in the land".

649

This means peace above, where the Holy One, blessed be He, comes to join the Community of Israel. Then "ye shall lie down and none shall make you afraid". Why so? Because "I shall cause evil beasts to cease out of the land".

These beasts are the evil species below, namely Iggereth bath Mahalath with all her company. She it is by night, but in the day the men who come from her side, in reference to whom it is written, "neither shall the sword go through your land".' R. Abba said: 'We have explained that this includes even a sword of peace, like that of Pharaoh Necho. King Josiah interpreted the verse thus, but as we have learnt, he was made to suffer for the sins of Israel. Here a difficulty arises, since we have learnt that if the head of the people is good, they are all delivered for his sake, and if the head is not good the whole people is made to suffer for his sake. Now seeing that Josiah was a good king and acted rightly, why had he to suffer for the sins of Israel? The reason was because he did not exercise control over Israel, since he thought that they were all virtuous like himself, and though Jeremiah told him that they were not, he did not believe him. Another reason was that the Moon's light was fading and it was seeking to disappear.

AND I WILL SET MY TABERNACLE AMONG YOU. My tabernacle" (mishcani) means the Shekinah; the word can also be rendered "my pledge", which was taken back for the sins of Israel. Once a man was very fond of a friend of his and said to him: I am so fond of you that I am going to stay with you. Said the other: How do I know that you will stay with me? So he took all his most precious belongings and brought them to him, saying: Here is a pledge to you that I shall never leave you. So God sought to abide with Israel, and He therefore took his most desirable possession and sent it down to Israel, saying: Here is my pledge to you that I shall never leave you. And although the Holy One, blessed be He, has departed from us, He has left his pledge in our hands, and we keep that treasure of His, so that if He wants His pledge He must come and abide with us.

'AND MY SOUL SHALL NOT ABHOR YOU. Suppose now the man is so fond of his friend that he wants to live with him, then he takes his bed to his house, saying: Here is my bed in thy house so that I shall have no need to leave thee. So the Holy One, blessed be He, said: Here is my bed in your house, and therefore you shall know that I shall not leave you.

AND I WILL WALK AMONG YOU AND BE YOUR GOD. Since my pledge is with you, of a surety you will know that I walk with you, as it is written, "For the Lord thy God walketh in the midst of thy camp to deliver thee and to give up thine enemies before thee" (Deut. XXIII, 14).' Once, when R. Isaac and R. Judah were in a village near the Lake of Tiberias, they rose at midnight and R. Isaac said to R. Judah: 'Let us discourse on the Torah, for though we are in such a place as this, we ought not to go away from the Tree of Life.' R. Judah then expounded the verse: "Now Moses took the tent and pitched it without the camp" (Ex. XXIII, 7). Why did he do so? Said Moses: Since Israel have denied the Holy One, blessed be He, and have exchanged His glory for another, let His pledge here be in the hands of a faithful keeper until we see with whom it will be left. He said to Joshua: Thou shalt be the man of trust between God and Israel, and the pledge shall be entrusted to thee, until we see

with whom it shall be left. Why to Joshua? Because he stood to Moses in the relation of the moon to the sun, [Tr. note: Cf. T.B. Baba Bathra, 75a.] and he was a fitting person to hold the pledge, and therefore it is written, "Joshua the son of Nun, a young man, departed not out of the camp" (Ibid. 11). Said the Holy One, blessed be He, to Moses: Moses, this is not right. I have given my pledge to them, and even though they have sinned against me, it must remain with them. Therefore return my pledge to them, and for its sake I will not abandon them wherever they are. Therefore wherever Israel go into exile the Shekinah is with them, and therefore it is written, "And I will set my tabernacle among you".'

R. Isaac adduced the verse: "My beloved is like a doe or a young hart, behold he standeth behind our wall", etc. (S.S. II, 9). 'Happy', he said, 'are Israel to whom it has been granted that this pledge should be with them from the supreme King, for though they are in exile, the Holy One, blessed be He, comes at the beginning of every month and on every Sabbath and festival to take note of them and to look at his pledge which is with them, his most precious possession. He is like a king whose queen has offended him so that he has expelled her from the palace. What does she do? She takes the king's son, his pride and his darling; and because the king is still fond of her he leaves him with her. When the king yearns for the queen and her son, he climbs up roofs and goes down steps to peep at them through chinks in walls, and when he obtains a glimpse of them he weeps behind the wall and then departs. So Israel, though they have gone forth from the king's palace, have not lost that pledge, which the King has left with them because He still loves them, and when He yearns for them He goes up on roofs and steps to gain a sight of them through the chinks of the wall, as it says, "He looketh in at the windows, he glanceth through the lattice", in the synagogues and houses of learning. Therefore Israel should rejoice on the day on which they know this, and say, "This is the day on which the Lord hath wrought, we will rejoice and be glad in it" (Ps. CXVIII, 24).'

AND IF YE SHALL REJECT MY STATUTES, ETC. R. Yose adduced here the verse: "My son, despise not the chastening of the Lord, neither be weary of his reproof" (Prov. III, 11). 'Israel', he said, 'are beloved to God, and therefore God is fain to reprove them and to lead them in the right path as a loving father leads his son, and because of his love he always has the rod in his hand to keep him in the right path and to prevent him from straying to the right or the left. But from him whom He loves not and hates God withdraws His reproof and His rod; and so we interpret the verse, "I have loved you, saith the Lord... but Esau I hated" (Mal. I, 2). The word takuz (be weary) in the above-quoted verse may be connected with kozim (thorns), for the reproof is like a thorn in a man's flesh, and yet he should not flee from it. When righteousness arises with its judgements, many are the shining emissaries who bestir themselves on the right hand and on the left, with many rods of fire, coal and flame, with which they traverse the world and smite the sons of men. Under them are many other emissaries, lords of the thirty-nine strokes, who come down and smite and ascend and receive authorization, who enter

Zohar: Vayikra, Section 3, Page 115a

into the hollow of the great deep where they become painted with flames and a burning fire is attached to them and they issue forth like burning coals. Hence it is written, "I shall chastise you still more (lit. I will add to chastise you) seven times for your sins", that is to say, I will give additional power to the chastisers to chastise, up to seven times for your sins. It may be asked: How can this be, seeing that if God were to collect His due, the world could not endure for an instant? The truth is that this "seven" refers to the Sabbatical Year which is so called: "seven" will chastise you.'

AND I ALSO WILL CHASTISE YOU SEVEN TIMES FOR YOUR SINS. R. Abba said: 'This means that I will rouse this Seven against you. Observe the deep love of the Holy One, blessed be He, for Israel. We may compare Him to a king who had a dearly beloved son who repeatedly offended against him. At length one day the king said: All these days I have chastised thee and thou hast not hearkened. What shall I do to thee? If I banish thee from the land and depose thee from the kingdom, perhaps bears or wolves or robbers will attack thee and destroy thee. Therefore I and thou together will leave the land. So God said to Israel: What shall I do to you? Behold I have smitten you and ye have not inclined your ears. I have sent against you smiters and burners and ye have not hearkened. If I send you out of the land alone, I fear for the many bears and wolves who may rise against you and drive you from the earth. What, then, shall I do? I and you will leave the land and go in exile: yet think not that I shall abandon you, for "I also" shall be with you. For "Seven" shall be banished with you: the Matrona shall leave her temple with you, and all will be desolate, both my temple and yours. Hence I too will be with you, and therefore when Israel emerge from captivity, God will return with them.'

As R. Hiya and R. Yose were journeying together, they came to a cave in a field and R. Hiya asked R. Yose: 'Why is it written "These are the words of the covenant which the Lord commanded Moses to make with the children of Israel, besides the covenant which he made with them in Horeb" (Deut. XXVIII, 69)? It should be: These are the words of the adjuration, should it not?' He replied: 'Both were words of a covenant, for

Zohar: Vayikra, Section 3, Page 115b

although the later ones were not from the mouth of God (but of Moses), yet they were words of a covenant, since both good and evil are foreshadowed in them, good from the side of Zaddik and evil from the side of judgement, which is Zedek, and Zaddik and Zedek are called "Covenant". Hence these words are words of a covenant.'

AND YET FOR ALL THAT, WHEN THEY BE IN THE LAND OF THEIR ENEMIES I WILL NOT REJECT THEM, NEITHER WILL I ABHOR THEM TO DESTROY THEM UTTERLY AND TO BREAK MY COVENANT WITH THEM. R. Yose said: '"When they be" means when they are all together. "I will not reject them, neither will I abhor them", so as not to be associated with them. "To break my covenant with them": for if I shall not redeem them, my covenant will be divided.' Said R. Hiya: 'I have heard the following from R. Eleazar. The expression "I will not reject them or abhor them to destroy them" is somewhat strange: we should expect, "I will not smite them or slay them". What it means, however, is this. One who is hated of another is abhorred and rejected of him, but God will not reject Israel, because the beloved of His soul is among them, and for her sake all of them are beloved of Him. If a man loves a woman who lives in a street of tanners, if she were not there he would never go into it, but because she is there it seems to him like a street of spice makers where all the sweet scents of the world are to be found. So "even when they are in the land of their enemies", which is the street of tanners, "I will not abhor or reject them", because of that bride in their midst, the beloved of my soul who abides there.'

Said R. Yose: 'If I had only come to hear this, it would have been worth my while. It is written,' he continued, '"A son honoureth his father" (Mal. I, 6). We have learnt that when the father is alive it is the son's duty to honour him with food and drink. Is he free from the obligation of honouring him after his death? Not so, since it is written, "Honour thy father" (Ex. XX, 12). If the son walks in the crooked path, of a surety he brings dishonour and shame on his father. But if he walks in the straight path and his deeds are upright, then he confers honour on him both in this world among men and in the next world with God, who gives him a special throne of honour. An example is R. Eleazar, who honoured his father in his lifetime and now has made him more honoured in the next world after his death as the progenitor of holy sons and a holy stock.'

Zohar: Section 3, Bemidbar, Page 117a

BEMIDBAR

AND THE LORD SPAKE UNTO MOSES IN THE WILDERNESS OF SINAI, IN THE TENT OF MEETING, ETC. R. Abba cited here the verse: "And God created man in his own image, in the image of God created he him", etc. (Gen. I, 27). 'We have already explained', he said, 'that when the Holy One, blessed be He, created man, He made him in the image of the higher and the lower grades, so that he epitomised the whole, and his light shone forth from one end of the world to the other, and the whole of creation feared him. It is necessary, however, to look deeper into this verse. For since Scripture says "And God created man in his own image", why repeat "in the image of God created he him"? But what it signifies is a two-foldness of grades, of male and female comprised within the man, which made him a duality of prosopa, so that he was complete in all respects, and he contemplated in wisdom both what was above and what was below. But once he sinned his prosopa diminished, wisdom departed from him, and he could survey only the affairs of his body. He then begat offspring partaking both of the higher and of the lower nature, but the world was not settled by either of them until Adam begat a son called Seth, [Tr. note: Sheth = foundation.] by whom the world was made complete. [Tr. note: Al. with whom the world was planted. v. Mid. R. Num. XIV, 12; Cant. VIII, 9.] Yet was not the lower world finally completed, nor was it firmly established until Abraham appeared, until Abraham took hold of it by the right hand as one upholds with his right hand one who is falling. Then came Isaac, who seized the world by the left hand, establishing it still more firmly. When Jacob came, he held the world by the centre of the body, uniting the two sides, whereby the world became firm and immovable. With all that it did not take deep root until there were born the twelve tribes and their offspring, numbering seventy souls. Nor yet was the world finally completed until Israel received the Torah on Mount Sinai and the Tabernacle was set up. All worlds were then finally established and perfected, and higher and lower creatures were properly based. The Torah and the Tabernacle thus having been established, the Holy One, blessed be He, desired to take a muster, as it were,

Zohar: Bemidbar, Section 3, Page 117b

of the forces of the Torah and the forces of the Tabernacle. For a thing cannot be finally settled in its place until its name has been called and it has been assigned there. We thus see here that the Holy One, blessed be He, decided on an enumeration of the forces of the Torah and of those of the Tabernacle, these two being in essence one and inseparable on the celestial model. Their forces were thus enumerated and noted, excepting some who did not enter into the count. Therefore it is written that "the Lord spake unto Moses in the wilderness of Sinai, in the tent of meeting', the two corresponding one to the Torah and the other to the Tabernacle. Both were "in the first day of the second month", the two being one. That month, besides, is called Ziv (=brightness, splendour), in allusion to the brightness of the moon of that month in that year, by reason that then the worlds altogether found themselves in completion.

AFTER THEY HAD COME OUT OF THE LAND OF EGYPT: this emphasizes the fact that Israel's exodus from Egypt took place in the first month.' R. Isaac cited here the verses: "The Lord hath been mindful of us, he will bless... the house of Israel... the house of Aaron... them that fear the Lord, both small and great. The Lord increase you" (Ps. CXV, 12-14). 'The first "he will bless",' he said, 'refers to the men who were numbered, and whom the Lord blesses and "increases more and more". Observe this. Whoever speaks in praise of his companion or of his children or his substance, should also bless him and shower blessings on him. We learn this from Moses, who, after saying "And, behold, ye are this day as the stars of the heaven for multitude" (Deut. I, 10), continued, "The Lord, the God of your fathers, make you a thousand so many more as ye are" (Ibid. 11), and then confirmed his words by adding "and bless you, as he hath promised you" (Ibid.). But he who, recounting his neighbour's good points, omits to bless him, will be the first to incur heavenly displeasure. Whereas he who does so bless will receive blessings from above. The man's blessing, moreover, must be given not grudgingly, but generously and with a good heart, as God above all desires man's good heart. [Tr. note: v. T.B. Sanhedrin, 107a.] How much more so must this be the case when a man offers praise to the Holy One, blessed be He! So Scripture says: "And thou shalt love the Lord thy God with all thy heart", etc. (Ibid. VI, 5). Now it has been laid down that the heavenly blessing does not rest on anything enumerated. How, then, is it that the Israelites were enumerated? Because the enumeration was by means of a ransom taken from them. The Israelites were thus first blessed, then their ransoms were counted, and that was followed again by a blessing given to them. The blessings, before and after, were a shield against death, which is ready to attack wherever there is enumeration. Should the blessing be removed, the "other side" may swoop down and inflict harm. The text continues: "He will bless the house of Israel", indicating the women who were not included in the enumeration, "He will bless the house of Aaron", who pronounce the blessing on Israel generously and out of goodness of heart and love. "The house of Aaron": again including their women. "He will bless them that fear the Lord", alluding to the Levites, all of whom are blessed, because they fear the Lord. "Both small and great": that is, even those who were not included in the enumeration. Observe that at no other enumeration were the Israelites blessed as at this one, which was intended in especial to be attended by a blessing and to put the finishing touch to all worlds.'

Zohar: Bemidbar, Section 3, Page 118a

R. Judah used to be much in the company of R. Simeon. Once he asked him: 'Which region is it whence blessings go forth to Israel?' R. Simeon replied: 'Woe to the world in that its people do not ponder or reflect on the glory of the Most High King. Observe this. When Israel are found worthy before the Holy One, blessed be He, and are with Him in a certain sacred celestial tree which contains the food of the whole world, then He is blessed from the repository of all the blessings, and Israel below are blessed from the place from which all blessings come, as it says: "Then Lord bless thee out of Zion" (Ps. CXXXIV, 3), also, "Like the dew of Hermon that cometh down upon the mountains of Zion; for there the Lord commanded the blessing, even life forever" (Ibid. CXXXIII, 3). This same is, too, the shining light of the world of which Scripture says: "Out of Zion the perfection of beauty, God hath shined forth" (Ibid. L, 2). It is the light which, when once it shines, will shine for all the worlds. When that light will awaken, the whole will be one common fellowship, under the reign of universal love and universal peace. There will be peace in heaven and peace on earth. So Scripture says: "Peace be within thy walls, and prosperity within thy palaces" (Ps. CXXII, 7).'

EVERY MAN WITH HIS OWN STANDARD, ACCORDING TO THE ENSIGNS, BY THEIR FATHER'S HOUSES, SHALL THE CHILDREN OF ISRAEL PITCH. R. Eleazar began a discourse, citing the verse: "Rejoice ye with Jerusalem, and be glad in her, all ye that love her", etc. (Isa. LXVI, 10). 'How beloved', he said, 'is the Torah before the Holy One, blessed be He, inasmuch as wherever words of the Torah are heard the Holy One, blessed be He, listens together with all His hosts. Indeed, He comes to lodge with the one that gives utterance to those words, as Scripture says: "In every place where I cause my name to be mentioned", etc. (Ex. XX, 21). Moreover, the enemies of such a man fall down before him, as said elsewhere. Observe this', he continued. 'The precepts of the Torah are exalted essences on high. Whenever a man fulfils one of the precepts, that precept presents itself, all adorned, before the Holy One, blessed be He, saying: So-and-so fulfilled me and I proceed from him. That man, thus, as he roused that precept below, caused a stirring on high, and brought about peace on high and below. Of this Scripture says: "Or else let him take hold of my strength, that he make peace with me; yea, let him make peace with me" (Isa. XXVII, 5); twice "peace", to wit, peace on high and peace below. Happy is the portion of the man who observes the precepts of the Torah. The text cited above says: "Rejoice ye with Jerusalem", etc., inasmuch as at no time is there joy save when Israel is established in the Holy Land, where the Wife is joined to her Spouse, diffusing thereby world-embracing joy, both on high and below. But when Israel is not in the Holy Land, a man is forbidden to display joy or gladness, as Scripture says: "Rejoice ye with Jerusalem, and be glad in her", to wit, only when within her.' R. Abba once saw a man making merry in the house of some Babylonian officers. R. Abba struck at him, citing the words: "Rejoice ye with Jerusalem", etc., which teaches us that only when Jerusalem is in joy is it permissible for us to rejoice. In harmony with this idea, R. Eleazar reconciled the two seemingly contradictory verses, one of which says "Serve the Lord with gladness" (Ps. C, 2), whilst the other says, "Serve the Lord with fear, and rejoice with trembling" (Ibid. II, 11). 'The former', he explained, 'speaks of the time when Israel dwells in the Holy Land, whilst the latter refers to the time of their dwelling in a strange land. Or we may also say that "serve the Lord in fear" speaks to the Community of Israel at a time when She is in exile among the nations.' R. Judah adduced in opposition to this the verse, "For ye shall go out with joy" (Isa. LV, 12), which seems to show that the Community of Israel will be in joy whilst still in exile. R. Eleazar, in reply, said: 'The truth is that so long as She is in exile and lies in the dust there will be no real gladness. But only when the Holy One, blessed be He, will raise Her from the dust, saying, "Shake thyself from the dust", etc. (Isa. LII, 2), "Arise, shine", etc. (Ibid. LX, 1), and the people will assemble together, then there will be gladness indeed, gladness for all. Then indeed "ye shall go out with joy"; then indeed numerous hosts will go forth to meet the Matrona, sharing in the joy of her espousals with the King. Scripture thus says: "The mountains and the hills shall break forth", etc. (Ibid. LV, 12); also, "For the Lord will go before you, and the God of Israel will be your rearward" (Ibid. LII, 12).

Zohar: Bemidbar, Section 3, Page 118b

EVERY MAN WITH HIS OWN STANDARD, ACCORDING TO THE ENSIGNS... [Tr. note: There is here a lacuna in the text.] This signifies the four camps of the Community of Israel, comprising the twelve tribes, forming twelve boundaries enclosing Her, all on the celestial model. Of this Scripture says: "Whither the tribes went up" (PS. CXXII, 4), to wit, the twelve tribes, the twelve lower boundaries: "even the tribes of YH, as a testimony unto Israel" (Ibid.), inasmuch as of a truth YH is the attestor of Israel. This we see in their names, as Hareuben Y (the Reubenite), Hashimeon Y (the Simeonite), and so on. Assuredly it is so, inasmuch as a sacred celestial Tree traced out its boundaries through them, as expounded elsewhere. We find Scripture saying: "As for the likeness of their faces, they had the face of a man; and they four had the face of a lion on the right side", etc. (Ezek. I, 10). The image of man, that is, was combined with all of them. The faces turned toward the four cardinal points, each with its own likeness, but all combined with the likeness of man. Michael was on the right, Gabriel on the left, Uriel in front, and Raphael behind, while the Shekinah was hovering over them all. Thus there were two on each side with the Shekinah in the centre. This model was followed here below, namely, two on either side with YH in the centre; for as soon as two standards had commenced to march, then "the tent of meeting, the camp of the Levites, journeyed", and then two others set forth. First "the standard of the camp of the children of Judah set forward" (Num. x, 14), corresponding to the camp of Uriel; the camp of Reuben corresponded to the camp of Michael; the one was toward the south, the other toward the east, symbolic of the southeast of the altar. Then the camp of Dan toward the north, corresponding to the camp of Gabriel, and the camp of Ephraim to the west, corresponding to the camp of Raphael. This is symbolic of the north-west of the altar. The whole was linked together and was unified in the Divine Name, which is both the starting-point and the consummation of all existence. Thus the Yod, symbolic of the east, is the starting-point of light which moves on toward the south; the He, is symbolic of the south and the north. Thus, YH (the Yod and the He') is the upholder of the south and the north; whilst the Vau is the centre, and is significant of the male child. Hence the dictum, "Whoever places his bed between north and south will have male children born to him". [Tr. note: T.B. Berachoth, 5b.] Then the last He denotes the west. The south is thus interlinked with the east, which constitutes the starting-point of the sun. Hence we have learnt that it is the side of the Father to which is attached the supernal Hesed (Mercy), and the side of the Mother from which depends Geburah (Might). So are the corners of the altar circled (by the priest when sprinkling the blood), beginning with southeast, as the strength of the south resides in the east, the starting-point of the sun; followed by the east-north, since the south in its turn gives its light to the north, the north being enfolded in the south, as the left hand is clasped in the right; there follows north-west, the west, symbolised by the last He, deriving from the north; finally, west-south, the west thus proceeding to be embraced, as it were, by the south; in the same way as the south depends on the east, from which it derives its strength, so the west is embraced by the south, as it says: "Let his left hand be under my head, and his right hand embrace me" (S.S. II, 6). The right signifies the south, and the left the north. This mystery we are taught by the Holy One, blessed be He, who thus places His bed between the north and the south, and so has man to do-as my father taught me-in order that he may have male children born to him. In all his deeds

Zohar: Bemidbar, Section 3, Page 119a

it behoves a man to imitate the celestial model, and to realize that according to the nature of a deed below there is a responsive stirring on high.' R. Phineas, having heard this discourse, kissed R. Eleazar. He wept and laughed, saying: 'Happy is my portion in this world and in the world to come.' The same R. Phineas then quoted the verse: "The Lord is my light and my salvation, whom shall I fear?", etc. (Ps. XXVII, 1). 'When a man', he said, 'turns his eyes to the heavenly light, he will be illumined by the light that God will cause to shine upon him, and he will fear no one, either in the upper worlds or the lower. So Scripture says: "But upon thee the Lord will arise, and his glory shall be upon thee" (Isa. LX, 2); "The Lord is the stronghold of my life" (Ps. XXVII, 1), for when the Almighty takes hold on a man he will have no fear in the other world of any of the executors of judgement. So I,' said R. Phineas, 'having taken hold of thee and of thy father, have no fear of anything in this world or in the other world. It is concerning such a one as thou that it is written: "Let thy father and thy mother be glad, and let her that bore thee rejoice" (Prov. XXIII, 25). "Thy father" is the Holy One, blessed be He, and "thy mother" is an allusion to the Community of Israel, while "her that bore thee" refers to thy mother here below. As for thy father, R. Simeon, where is his joy referred to? In a separate verse, saying: "The father of the righteous will greatly rejoice, and he that begetteth a wise child will have joy of him" (Ibid. 24), where by "the father of the righteous" is meant the Holy One, blessed be He, and "the begetter of a wise child" refers to thy father here below.'

R. Eleazar cited the verse: "In thy hand I commit my spirit; thou hast redeemed me, O Lord, thou God of truth" (Ps. XXXI, 6). 'This statement', he said, 'is somewhat surprising; for have you ever seen a man committing anything into the hand of the King? But, assuredly, happy is the man who walks in the paths of the Most Holy King and does not sin before Him. For as soon as night falls the Tree of Death dominates the world and the Tree of Life ascends to the height of heights. And since the Tree of Death has sole rule of the world, all the people in it have a foretaste of death. It is therefore incumbent upon man to make haste and meet the Tree of Death and deposit his soul with it, as a man deposits a pledge with his creditor. For, although the debt exceeds the value of the pledge, yet the creditor does not distrain on him because he has the pledge, but otherwise he will exact his debt. So all the souls of man are taken by the Tree of Death in deposit, and all have a taste of death. Now although their sins are excessive, and they do not deserve to receive back their souls, and the Tree has really no right to give them back, [Tr. note: Being the attribute of Judgement. yet they are returned to men at the moment the Tree of Life awakens in the world, to wit, the moment when dawn breaks. The Tree of Death then departs, and people come to life again by reason of the Tree of Life. It is true that many men wake during the night, but this, too, is the work of the Tree of Life. This happens in accordance with what is written, "to see if there were any man of understanding that did seek after God" (Ibid. XIV, 2); for thereby is removed any excuse that man might plead, saying: "Had I been in control of my soul in the night, I would have laboured in the study of the Law".' Said R. Judah: 'This is rightly explained in regard to Israel; but what about the other nations to whom we see the same thing happens?' R. Eleazar replied: 'That is a good remark.' He then discoursed (concerning the other nations), citing the verse: "How shall I curse, whom EL (God) hath not cursed, and how shall I execrate, whom the Lord hath not execrated?" (Num. XXIII, 8). 'Observe', he said, 'that the lower world is modelled on the upper world. On high there is a Right and a

Left; so below there are Israel and the idolatrous nations, the former on the right, attached to the holiness of the Holy King, the latter on the left, on the side of the unclean spirit. The grades are linked one with another,

Zohar: Bemidbar, Section 3, Page 119b

all depending finally on the one at the head, and the tail has to move in accordance with the head. Balaam could avail himself of all the lower grades, but he saw that even the lowest was still guided by the head. Hence his declaration: "How shall I curse, whom EL hath not cursed?", because the superior Head did not exercise rigour in those days. It is true that El denotes Goodness and Mercy, but it also expresses Rigour, as it says, "and El (God) hath indignation every day" (Ps. VII, I2). As for the compound "El-Shaddai", this signifies the God who put a limit to the universe. [Tr. note: SHaDaY (Shaddai)=He who... enough; i.e. He who, at the proper moment, put a limit to the expanding universe at the Creation by the word of command: "Enough!", v. T.B. Hagigah, 12a.] Hence "How shall I curse, whom El hath not cursed?". For, as the Head moves, so does the Tail.' [Tr. note: This is in reply to the question of R. Judah as to how men of other nations awake during the night.] R. Eleazar wept. He discoursed on the verse: "The sound thereof shall go like the serpents", etc. (Jer. XLVI, 22). 'At the present time,' he said, 'when Israel is in exile, he is assuredly as the serpent. For when the serpent presses its head into the sand its tail flies upwards, being master, as it were, and lashing out at anyone near him; so Israel in exile has his head bowed down into the dust whilst the tail obtains the mastery. But although the head is bowed down into the sand, it is the same head, and that directs and rules the movements of the tail; and so at the present time it is indeed the other nations, who are attached to the tail, that rise on high, have the mastery and are lashing out, whilst the head is bowed down into the dust, as it says, "The virgin of Israel is fallen, she shall no more rise" (Amos v, 2); yet it is the head that directs the tail in its motions, as it says: "They made me keeper of the vineyards" (S.S. I, 6), to wit, of the idolatrous nations, which are the tail.' R. Judah then came and kissed the hands of R. Eleazar, saying: 'Had I never asked you any other question but only this, my gain would already be great in that now I know how the sway of the idolatrous nations is being directed. Happy is the portion of Israel, in regard to whom it is written: "For the Lord hath chosen Jacob unto himself, and Israel for his own treasure" (Ps. cxxxv, 4).' R. Eleazar asked him what was meant by "for his own treasure". R. Judah replied: 'The three patriarchs are called "treasure", both on high and here below; so are the priests, the Levites, and the Israelites; it is all one, and this is indicated in the words, "Then ye shall be mine own treasure from among all peoples" (Ex. XIX, 5).'

THEN THE TENT OF MEETING, WITH THE CAMP OF THE LEVITES. THE STANDARD OF THE CAMP OF EPHRAIM, ACCORDING TO THEIR HOSTS, SHALL BE ON THE WEST SIDE. This was because the Shekinah is in the west. [Tr. note: v. T.B. Baba Bathra, 25a] In this regard it is written: "And he blessed them that day, saying, By thee shall Israel bless, saying. And he set Ephraim before Manasseh" (Gen. XLVIII, 20). It is not written "shall be blessed", but "shall bless", as much as to say: Holy Israel will not bless the world save by invoking Thee, [Tr. note: Referring to the Shekinah.] who art in the west. This shows that Jacob then saw the Shekinah. It is true that it is written, "the eyes of Israel were dim for age, so that he could not see" (Ibid. 10), but it also says, "putting his hands crosswise" (Ibid. 14). That is, he first raised up his right hand, but the Shekinah turned it toward Ephraim, and having caught the scent of the Shekinah, as it were, over his head, he said: By Thee will Israel bless. He saw then that the Shekinah is in the west. The reason for this, as has been explained, is that She may be between north and south, in an attitude of nuptial union, with the north supporting Her beneath Her head and the south embracing Her. So says Scripture: "Let his left hand be under my head, and his right hand embrace me". There is a dictum: "Whoever recites the Psalm Praise of David (Ps. CXLV) thrice daily may be assured that he is destined for the world to come". [Tr. note: T.B. Berakoth, 4b.]

Zohar: Bemidbar, Section 3, Page 120a

This is because thereby we symbolize daily the union that is effected between north and south. Thus in the morning a man takes upon himself the yoke of heaven by reciting the Psalm headed "Praise of David", followed by ten "Hallelukahs", to wit, the five Psalms each commencing with "Hallelukah" and ending with "Hallelukah", with the very last of them containing ten, times the expression "praise ye" (Ibid. CL). Then follows the Song of Moses, which contains all praises, and whereby a man takes upon himself the yoke of the Holy Kingdom. Then at the end of the Service he places Her in Hesed at the end of the prayer proper, to be sanctified therewith. Then the same Psalm is repeated at Minha (Afternoon Prayer), when Vigour is in the ascendant and Rigour prevails alongside the south. Thus unification is effected all along between north and south; and whoever co-ordinates daily his prayers in this way is assuredly destined for the world to come. Thus ON THE WEST SIDE SHALL BE THE STANDARD OF THE CAMP OF EPHRAIM, that is, lying between north and south; with the standard of the camp of Reuben on the south, and the standard of the camp of Dan on the north, Ephraim is found on the west between the two, between north and south, all on the heavenly pattern. The following is a mystery known to those who inhabit the south, and has been sent to us by our "brethren who arrange the lamps". 'That ye may effect unification by means of the intertwined mysteries that are of the shape of the celestial intertwining, accept upon yourselves the first thing every day the yoke of the Holy Kingdom; thereby will ye enter into the holy intertwining of the south. These encircle the sides of the world until they become bound up in one knot, but keep firm hold of the south and there abide.' R. Eleazar then asked his father, R. Simeon, for a mnemonic suggestive of this method of effecting unification. In reply his father mentioned the manner in which the priest goes round the altar, regarding which the Mishnah-Code says: "And [the priest] came to the south-eastern, then to the north-eastern, the north-western, and the south-western horn". [Tr. note: Mishnah Zebahim v, 3.] R. Eleazar then asked: 'How could one come to the south before taking upon oneself the yoke of the Kingdom of Heaven?' R. Simeon, in reply, said: 'Just so. It says [literally] "and he came to the horn of south-east", that is, first to the horn, symbolic of the yoke of the Kingdom of Heaven, and then to the south-east, symbolic of the Tree of Life. And whoever accomplishes

Zohar: Bemidbar, Section 3, Page 120b

unification in the proper way as just indicated, happy is his portion in this world and in the world to come, and, moreover, in such a one the Holy One, blessed be He, glorifies Himself. Concerning such a one, Scripture says: "And he said unto me, Thou art my servant, Israel, in whom I will be glorified" (Isa. XLIX, 3).'

R. Simeon began a discourse, citing the verse: "[A Psalm] of David. Unto thee, O Lord, do I lift my soul. O my God, in thee have I trusted", etc. (Ps. xxv, 1-22). 'Why did David', he asked, 'compose this Psalm in an alphabetic acrostic, and besides, why is the letter Vau absent therefrom? Why, again, has this Psalm been prescribed as the "falling-on-one's-face prayer"? [Tr. note: This in accordance with the Sephardi ritual. v. Common Prayer Book, ed. Gaster. The Ashkenazi ritual prescribes Psalm VI.] Now the solution of all this is based on an esoteric doctrine known to the Companions, which is as follows. When night falls the Nethertree, from which death issues, spreads its branches so as to cover the whole of the universe. And so darkness prevails, and all the people of the world have a foretaste of death. And every man hastens to surrender his soul into His Hand as a trust. And inasmuch as He takes them in trust He returns each one to her owner in the morning. Thus, as each morning arrives, man, having received back his deposit, ought to render blessings to the Holy One, blessed be He, who is trustworthy above all. Then, having risen, a man goes to Synagogue, adorns himself with phylacteries and enwraps himself in a garment provided with fringes, then he first purifies himself by the [recital of the regulations concerning the] sacrifices, then follows the recital of the hymns of David by which he accepts upon himself the yoke of the Kingdom of Heaven. After that comes the prayer said sitting, followed by the prayer said standing, the two being knit together into one. Observe the inwardness of the matter, to wit, that although prayer is performed by speech and verbal utterance, its efficacy springs primarily from the preparatory actions performed. First action, then prayer-utterance corresponding to that action. Thus a man has in the first place to cleanse himself [by ablution], then accepts upon himself the Heavenly Yoke symbolized in the act of spreading over his head the fringed robe. Then he makes tight on himself the knot expressive of unification, to wit, the phylacteries, consisting of the phylactery of the head and that of the hand, the latter on the left hand over against the heart, in consonance with the Scriptural verses, saying: "Let his left hand be under my head", etc. (S.S. II, 6), and "Set me as a seal upon thy heart, as a seal upon thy arm" (Ibid. VIII, 6). So far the preparatory actions. Then corresponding to these, man, in entering Synagogue, first cleanses himself by the [recital of the regulations concerning the] sacrifices; then he accepts upon himself the Heavenly Yoke by the recital of the hymns of King David. Then comes the prayer said sitting, which corresponds to the arm-phylactery, followed by the prayer said standing, which corresponds to the head-phylactery. So prayer is made up of both action and speech, and when the action is faulty speech does not find a spot to rest in; such prayer is not prayer, and the man offering it is defective in the upper world and the lower. The main thing is to perform the act and to give utterance to words in coordination with it; this is perfect prayer. Woe to him who spoils his prayer, the worship of his Master. Of such a one Scripture says: "When ye come to appear before me... yea, when ye make many prayers, I will not hear" (Isa. I, 12-15). Observe this. Both upper and lower worlds are blessed through the man who performs his prayer in a union of action and word, and thus effects a unification. And so with the conclusion of the prayer said standing, a man has to assume the appearance of one who has departed this world in that he has separated himself from the Tree of Life. Now he has to be gathered towards that Tree of Death and fall on his face and say: "Unto thee, O Lord, do I lift up my soul. "

As much as to say: "Before,

Zohar: Bemidbar, Section 3, Page 121a

I gave Thee my soul in trust, now that I have effected unification and performed act and word in befitting manner and have confessed my sins, behold, here is my soul which I surrender to Thee completely." A man must then look upon himself as having departed this world, his soul having been surrendered to the region of death. This is the reason that that Psalm does not contain the letter Vau, since that letter is symbolic of the Tree of Life, whereas that Psalm is concerned with the Tree of Death. For there are sins which are beyond forgiveness until a man departs this world, of which Scripture says: "Surely this iniquity shall not be expiated by you till ye die" (Isa. XXII, 14), so that man has given himself over, as it were, to death, and delivered his soul into that region, not merely in trust as during the night, but as though he had actually departed this world. This service must be performed by the man with full devotion of heart, and then the Holy One, blessed be He, will take pity on him and forgive his sins. Happy is the man who knows how to persuade, as it were, and how to offer worship to his Master with devotion of will and heart. Woe to him who comes to persuade his Master with an absent heart and without true intent in the way described in the words: "But they beguiled him with their mouth, and lied unto him with their tongue. For their heart was not steadfast with him" (Isa. LXXVIII, 36-37). Such a one may recite: "Unto Thee, O Lord, do I lift up my soul...", but all his words proceed from an absent heart; and this causes him to be removed from the world before his allotted days, at a moment when that Tree bestirs itself in the world to execute judgement. Hence it is incumbent on man to cleave heart and soul to his Master, and not to come to Him with deceitfulness. Of such a one Scripture says: "He that speaketh falsehood shall not be established before mine eyes" (Ibid. CI, 7). Being interpreted, this means that when a man prepares himself for this, but with a heart remote from the Holy One, blessed be He, a Voice proclaims, saying: He will not be established before Mine eyes. All the more is this so when a man comes to effect unification of the Divine Name, but does not do so in the proper manner. Happy is the portion of the righteous in this world and in the world to come. Of them it is written, "and they shall come, and shall see my glory", etc. (Isa. LXVI, 18); and again, "Surely the righteous shall give thanks unto thy name", etc. (Ps. CXL, 14).' R. Eleazar then approached and kissed his father's hand, saying: 'Had I not come into the world for aught else but to hear these words it would have sufficed me.' Said R. Judah: 'Happy is our portion and the portion of Israel who cleave to the Holy One, blessed be He. So Scripture says: "But ye that did cleave", etc. (Deut. IV, 4); and again, "Thy people also shall be all righteous", etc. (Isa. LX, 21).'

NASO

AND THE LORD SPAKE UNTO MOSES, SAYING: TAKE THE SUM OF THE SONS OF GERSHON, ETC. R. Abba began a discourse on the verse: "Happy is the man unto whom the Lord counteth not iniquity, and in whose spirit there is no guile" (Ps. XXXII, 2). 'The two halves of this verse', he said, 'do not seem to hang together, [Tr. note: The first half implies that there is iniquity in him, the second that there is not.] but it has been explained thus. At the time of the Afternoon Prayer (Minha) Rigour prevails over the world. For it was Isaac who instituted Afternoon Prayer, and so supreme Force prevails then and the Left aspect is diffused. This continues until night bestirs itself. Then all the keepers of the outer gates of the universe bestir themselves and spread about, and all mankind have a foretaste of death. At the precise moment of midnight the Left aspect bestirs itself again as before, the Divine Rose [Tr. note: i.e. the Shekinah.] diffuses a sweet odour, and breaks forth into loud praise-giving, then ascends and rests Her head on the Left Arm,

Zohar: Bemidbar, Section 3, Page 121b

which is extended to receive Her. Then proclamation goes forth into the world, announcing that it is the time for awakening and chanting praises to the King. A chorus of praises then breaks forth, accompanied by a sweet odour permeating the whole. Happy is the portion of whoever awakens then to effect this espousal. When morning comes round and the Right aspect awakens and embraces Her, then the wedlock is complete. Observe that when mankind lie asleep and experience a foretaste of death, the soul of each ascends on high and to an assigned region. There she is examined concerning all the actions she performed during the day. These are recorded on a tablet. Indeed, the soul then gives evidence concerning man's works, and concerning each word that issued from his mouth. Should that word be an appropriate word, a holy word of Torah study or of prayer, it will cleave its way through the heavens until it reaches an assigned place. There it halts until night falls, when the soul ascends, seizes that word and presents it to the King. An improper word, however, a word uttered by an evil tongue, goes up to its assigned spot, where it is put on record, charging the man with the commission of a sin. Of this Scripture says: "Keep the doors of thy mouth from her that lieth in thy bosom" [Tr. note: i.e. the soul.] (Micah VII, 5). Hence the Psalm says: "Happy is the man unto whom the Lord counteth not iniquity", to wit, the man "in whose spirit there is no guile".'

[Note: The last 7 lines of the Hebrew text are not found in our translation]

Zohar: Bemidbar, Section 3, Page 122a

[Note: The first 20 lines of the Hebrew text are not found in our translation]

R. Isaac and R. Judah were walking together on the road leading from Usha to Lud. Said R. Judah: 'Let us discourse on the Torah whilst walking.' R. Judah then cited the verse: "And if a man shall open a pit, or if a man shall dig a pit... the owner of the pit shall make it good", etc. (Ex. XXI, 33-34). 'If that man', he said, 'has to make good, how much more so he who brings the whole world into disfavour by his sins. And I do, indeed, find it strange, that having brought the world into disfavour a man can make restitution by penitence, as Scripture says: WHEN A MAN OR WOMAN SHALL COMMIT ANY SIN... THEN THEY SHALL CONFESS THEIR... AND HE SHALL MAKE RESTITUTION, ETC. The truth, however, is that through man's penitence the Almighty Himself, as it were, rectifies on high the wrong committed, and thus the world is put right again.' R. Isaac then cited the verse: "In thy distress, when all these things are come upon thee, in the end of days, thou wilt return.... For the Lord thy God is a merciful God", etc. (Deut. IV, 30-31). 'We learn from here', he said, 'that penitence is of most effect before Rigour lights upon the world. For once it does so it strongly entrenches itself, and who can remove it? Indeed,

Zohar: Bemidbar, Section 3, Page 122b

it will not depart until restitution is made, followed by penitence; and then only is the world again put right. Now the phrase "in the end of days" points to the Community of Israel who is in exile and shares Israel's distress. For this reason, the Holy One, blessed be He, although he has sent Rigour into the world, desires that Israel should repent so that He may do good to them in this world and in the world to come. For nothing can withstand the power of repentance. Proper repentance is only effected by a surrender of one's soul, so that she is taken away in a state of repentance. One sinner in the world brings about the destruction of many. Woe to the sinner, woe to his neighbour! We see this in the case of Jonah. Through his refusing to carry the message of his Master, how many people would have been destroyed on his account in the sea! So they all turned on him and carried out on him the sentence of sea-drowning, whereby they were all saved. The Holy One, blessed be He, however, had mercy on him and so brought about the deliverance of multitudes of people. This happened after Jonah returned to his Master out of the midst of his affliction, as we read: "I called out of my affliction unto the Lord, and he answered me" (Jonah II, 3).'

Zohar: Bemidbar, Section 3, Page 124a

IF ANY MAN'S WIFE (lit. man, man, if his wife) GO ASIDE, AND COMMIT A TRESPASS (lit. trespass a trespass) AGAINST HIM, ETC. R. Eleazar said: 'Why twice, man, man'? It speaks of a man who has behaved as a man should, following the admonition: "Drink waters out of thy own cistern", etc. (Prov. v, 15). Why, again, the double expression "trespass a trespass"? It points, on the one hand, to the Community of Israel, and, on the other, to her Spouse. We thus read further: THEN SHALL THE MAN BRING HIS WIFE UNTO THE PRIEST, for the reason that the priest is the "best man", so to speak, of the Matrona. Again, she has to be brought to the priest, although in regard to any sacrifice we read: "And he shall kill the bullock before the Lord" (Lev. I, 5), signifying that a layman ought to kill it and not a priest, he being forbidden [Tr. note: This is contrary to the Mishnah, which does not forbid, but makes it optional for the priest.] to execute judgement so as not to impair the region to which he belongs. Here, however, the priest alone is the fit person for the performance, he being the "best man" of the Matrona, and all the women of Israel are blessed by the medium of the Community of Israel. Therefore it is that the woman here on earth at her marriage has conferred upon her seven benedictions, in that she is bound up with the Community of Israel. It is the priest alone, and no outsider, who arranges all the service of the Matrona and attends closely to all that is needed. Hence the priest functions here, and no other. And, in fact, it is not judgement that the priest executes in this matter, but, on the contrary, he promotes peace in the world and increases lovingkindness. For should the woman be found innocent, the priest will have promoted peace between them, and, moreover, she will conceive a male child, [Tr. note: Cf. T.B. Sotah, 26a.] which is also a means of bringing peace. Should she, however, not be found innocent, it is not the priest that will have doomed her, but it will be the Divine Name which she invoked falsely that will have probed and doomed her. Observe that the priest does not obtrude himself into the affair, but when she presents herself before him to clear herself

Zohar: Bemidbar, Section 3, Page 124b

he questions her once and twice, and then performs a ceremony in order to restore peace. The priest writes the Divine Name once in a straightforward way and then upside down, [Tr. note: AHAH Tetragrammaton] symbolic of Mercy and Rigour intertwined. If she be proved innocent the letters signifying Mercy remain, and those pointing to Rigour disappear. But if she be not as she should be, Mercy departs and Rigour is left, and judgement is executed.'

R. Eleazar adduced here the verse: "And when they came to Marah, they could not drink the waters of Marah, for they were bitter There he made for them a statute and an ordinance, and there he proved them" (Ex. xv, 23-25). 'I wonder', he said, 'how it is that people take so little trouble to understand the words of the Torah. Here, for example, one should really inquire what is the point of the words "There he made for them... and there he proved them". But the inward significance of the water mentioned here is this. The Egyptians claimed to be the parents of the children of Israel, and many among the Israelites suspected their wives in the matter. So the Holy One, blessed be He, brought them to that place, where He desired to put them to the test. Thus when Moses cried to the Lord he was told: Write down the Divine Name, cast it into the water, and let all of them, women and men, be tested, so that no evil report should remain in regard to My children; and until they all be probed I will not cause My Name to rest upon them. Straightway "the Lord shewed him a tree, and he cast it into the waters", the tree being thus identical with the Divine Name the priest has to write for the testing of the wife of an Israelite. Thus "There he made for them a statute and an ordinance, and there he proved them". Now it may be asked: This was properly done for the women, but why include the men? But, indeed, the men also had to be probed to show that they had not contaminated themselves with Egyptian women, in the same way as the women had to be probed to show that they had kept themselves uncontaminated by Egyptian men, all the time they were among them. And all, male and female, were proved to be pure, were found to be the seed of Israel, holy and pure. Then

Zohar: Bemidbar, Section 3, Page 125a

the Holy One, blessed be He, caused His Name to dwell among them. Hence assuredly it was by the waters "there that he. proved them". Similarly here it is through water that the priest proves the woman, and through the Divine Name.'

AND OF THE DUST THAT IS ON THE FLOOR OF THE TABERNACLE. We find it written: "all are of the dust, and all return to dust" (Eccl. III, 20). There is a teaching concerning this, saying that even the orb of the sun is of the dust, all the more so then the sons of men.' Said R. Yose: 'If it were written here "and of the dust" and no more, this remark would be relevant; but since it says, "and of the dust that is on the floor of the tabernacle", it seems to point to something else. Indeed, it points to the verse, saying: "He makes his sword in the form of dust" (Isa. XLI, 2). This verse speaks of the archers and catapult throwers, symbolic of rigorous judgement. Similarly here "the floor of the tabernacle", which is connected with elements underneath. The priest then puts it into the water, "the water of bitterness that causes the curse". This refers to the Divine Name when it is in Rigour, and for this reason the waters of the sea are bitter. For the Sacred Sea has many sweet rivers flowing into it, yet since it presents the world's judgement its waters are bitter, since universal death is attached to it. Yet when these waters flow outwards they are sweet. The sea, besides, exhibits a variety of colours. Now it is when the Serpent injects into it its venom that its waters become bitter and accursed; and therefore the priest has to go through his performance below, and recite an adjuration, so that judgement may be executed. If the woman is proved pure, these waters enter her body,

turn into sweet waters, act as a cleansing force, and remain there until she becomes pregnant. Their effect is that a male child is born, one comely and pure and without any blemish. But if not, these waters enter her, causing her to smell the odour of the venom, and are transmuted into a serpent. Her punishment is thus of the same nature as her sin, and her shame is openly revealed. Happy is the portion of Israel in whom the Holy One, blessed be He, delights and whom He desires to purify.'

R. Hizkiah discoursed on the verse: "Thy wife shall be as a fruitful vine in the innermost parts of thy house" (Ps. CXXVIII, 3). 'As a vine cannot receive any graft but of its own kind, so a woman in Israel, after the example of the turtle dove, only accepts her own spouse. She is thus fruitful, spreading her branches on all sides. And where? "In the innermost parts of thy house", and not abroad, in the marketplace, so as not to be false to the supreme covenant. Of the false wife Solomon says: "She forsaketh the lord of her youth, and forgetteth the covenant of her God" (Prov. II, 17), indicating the place called "covenant" to which she is attached. This is the meaning of "the innermost parts of thy house".' R. Hizkiah further said: 'Cursed be the man who allows his wife to let the hair of her head be seen. This is one of the rules of modesty in the house. A woman who exposes her hair for self-adornment brings poverty on her household, renders her children of no account in their generation, and causes an evil spirit to abide on her house. If this is so when the woman does this in the house, how much more is it when in the open road; and ever so much more so does all this result from another kind of shamelessness.' Said R. Judah: 'The hair of the head

of a woman being exposed leads to Hair of another kind being exposed and impaired. Hence a woman should not let her hair be seen, even by the beams of her house, much less in the open. Observe that as the rule is most strict in the case of a man's hair, [Tr. note: The reference apparently is to the Nazirite.] so is it with a woman's. Consider the harm a woman's hair brings about. It brings a curse on her husband, it causes poverty, it causes something besides to happen to her household, it causes the inferiority of her children. May the Merciful One deliver us from their impudence! A woman thus should cover her hair in the four corners of her house. When she does this, then "thy children like olive plants" (Ps. ibid.). As the olive does not shed its leaves either in winter or summer, but ever retains its superiority over other trees, so her children will excel all other children; her husband, moreover, will receive blessings from above and from below, will be blessed with riches, with children and children's children. So the Psalm continues: "Behold, surely, thus shall the man be blessed.... And see thy children's children. Peace be upon Israel" (Ibid. 4-6).'

WHEN EITHER MAN OR WOMAN SHALL CLEARLY UTTER A VOW, ETC. R. Eleazar began a discourse on the verse: "Wherefore, when I came, was there no man?" etc. (Isa. L, 2). 'How beloved', he said, 'are Israel before the Holy One, blessed be He, in that wherever they dwell He is found among them, for He never withdraws His love from them. We find it written: "And let them make me a sanctuary, that I may dwell among them" (Ex. xxv, 8). That is, any sanctuary whatever, inasmuch as any Synagogue, wherever situated, is called sanctuary, and the Shekinah hastens to the Synagogue (before the worshippers). Happy is the man who is of the first ten to enter Synagogue, since they form something complete, and are the first to be sanctified by the Shekinah. But it is necessary that the ten should come together at the same time and not in sections, so as not to delay the completion of the body in its members. So did the Holy One, blessed be He, make man all at one time, and establish all his members in one act. So we read: "Hath he not made thee and established thee?" (Deut. XXXII, 6). So when the Shekinah goes early to the Synagogue she desires ten to be there at the same time so that a completed body should be formed with every member in its place. Those that come later are the mere "adornments of the body". But when the people do not arrive together the Holy One, blessed be He, exclaims: "Wherefore, when I came, was there no man?" [Tr. note: v. T.B. Berachoth, 6b.] For inasmuch as the single members are not together there is no complete body, and so that is "no man". Observe that the moment the body is made complete here below a supernal holiness comes and enters that body, and so the lower world is in truth transformed after the pattern of the upper world. Thus it is incumbent on all not to open their mouths to talk of worldly matters, seeing that Israel then are at their completest and holiest. Happy is their portion!

'WHEN A MAN SHALL CLEARLY UTTER (yaflee=shall separate) A VOW; that is, when a man shall place himself apart from the rest of the world, to sanctify himself on the pattern on high and thus to be found perfect. For whoever sets out to purify himself is assisted from above. [Tr. note: v. T.B. Yoma, 38b.] When one wishes to sanctify himself, they spread on him a sanctity derived from that of the Holy One, blessed be He....' [Tr. note: There is here a lacuna in the text.]

R. Abba discoursed on the verse: "[A Psalm] of David bless the Lord, O my soul, and all that is within me, bless his holy name" (Ps. CIII, 1). 'How much', he said, 'it behoves a man to study and reflect on the service of his Master! Forevery day a proclamation goes forth, saying: "How long, ye thoughtless, will ye love thoughtlessness?' etc. (Prov. I, 22); "Return, ye backsliding children, I will heal your backslidings" (Jer. III, 22), but there is no one who inclines his ear; the Torah makes proclamation before the people and none pay regard. Observe this. A man walks about in the world thinking that it is his perpetual possession and that he will abide therein from generation to generation. But even while he walks he is being put in chains; while he sits he is being tried in the conclave among the other prisoners. If there be an advocate on his side he is delivered from punishment. So Scripture says: "If there be for him an angel, an intercessor, one among a thousand, to vouch for man's uprightness; then he is gracious unto him, and saith ', etc. (Job XXXIII, 23). Who

Zohar: Bemidbar, Section 3, Page 126b

is his advocate? It is man's good works that stand by him at the moment of need. Should no advocate be found for him, he is declared guilty and is sentenced to be removed from the world. At that moment, whilst lying bound in the chains of the King, lifting his eyes he sees two beings near him who write down all that he did in this world and every word that ever went forth from his mouth. Of all this he has to give an account, as it is written: "For, lo, he that formeth the mountains, and createth the wind, and declareth unto man what is his thought (siho=speech)'. [Tr. note: v. T.B. Hagigah, 5b.] He admits all this, since the works which he did are there present to testify against him and to be inscribed in his presence; they do not leave him until the time that he is adjudged guilty on their account in the other world. Observe that all a man's works in this world are ready to testify against him: they do not vanish. And when he is led to his grave they all go before him; and three heralds, one in front, one to his right, and one to his left, proclaim: "Behold So-and-so who rebelled against his Master, who rebelled on high and here below, who rebelled against the Torah and against its commandments. Behold his actions, behold his utterances. It were better he had not been created!" When he arrives at his burial place, all the dead quake in their places on account of him, saying: "Woe, woe, that this man is buried among us!" His deeds and words precede him, enter the grave and stand over the body, whilst his spirit hovers to and fro mourning over the body. So soon as the man is hidden away in the tomb, [the angel] Dumah advances accompanied by three judges who are appointed to sit in judgement over the newly-buried; these hold in their hands fiery rods and submit to examination the spirit and the body together. Woe to [the victim of] that judgement! Woe for his deeds at the time when he is caught in the fetters of the King, if no advocate is found on his behalf! The King's officer advances towards his feet holding in his hand a sharp sword. The man lifts up his eyes, and sees the walls of his house in a blaze of fire, kindled by himself. Presently he sees before him one full of eyes all over, [Tr. note: i.e. the Angel of Death, v. T.B. Abodah Zaroh, 20b.] and clothed in fiery garments. (This may indeed be so, inasmuch as many a man meets an angel in the road, whilst other passers-by do not see him.) You may ask, since it is written, "Who maketh spirits (winds) [Tr. note: Ruhoth—winds or spirits.] his angels" (Ps. CIV), how can an angel be visible? It has, however, been explained that when an angel descends to earth he assumes the guise of man, and in this guise he makes himself visible to this man or the other. Otherwise mankind could not endure any sight of him. All the more does this apply to this one, to whom all the world must come. He instils three drops with his sword, and so on, as the Companions have expounded elsewhere. At the sight of him the man's body falls a-trembling, and his heart throbs, this being the king of the whole body, and the spirit passes along through the members of the body, taking leave of each one in turn, like a man taking leave of his neighbour when departing for another place. Woe, it exclaims, for the man's deeds! There is no remedy for such a man unless he repents in time. Until the last moment the man is in fear, attempts to hide himself, but is not able. Seeing his helplessness he opens his eyes and gazes at the Angel of Death with open eyes, and surrenders himself, body and soul. It is the moment of the Great Judgement to which man is subjected to in this world. As the spirit makes its journey through the body and takes leave of each separate member and parts from it, that member immediately dies. When the spirit is about to depart, having thus taken leave of the whole body, the Shekinah stands over the body and the spirit straightway flies off. Happy is the portion of whoever cleaves to Her! Woe to the sinners who keep afar from Her! Indeed, what a number of ordeals man has to undergo in passing out of this world! First comes the ordeal from on high, at the moment when the spirit leaves the body, just mentioned. Then comes his ordeal when his actions and utterances precede him and make proclamation concerning him. Another ordeal is when he enters the tomb.

Zohar: Bemidbar, Section 3, Page 127a

One more is in the tomb itself. He afterwards undergoes an ordeal at the hands of the worms. There is then the ordeal of Gehinnom. And finally there is the ordeal undergone by the spirit when it roams to and fro through the world, finding no resting-place until its tasks are accomplished. Man has thus to pass through seven ordeals. Hence it behoves man while in this world to fear his Master and minutely to examine daily his works and to repent of any misdeeds before his Maker. So King David, in reflecting on the ordeals man has to undergo on departing this world, made haste to exclaim, "Bless the Lord, O my soul" (Ps. CIII, 1); to wit: Do it before thou leavest this world, and whilst thou art in the body; "and all that is within me, bless his holy name" (Ibid.), in other words: Ye bodily members who are associated with the spirit, whilst that spirit is with you, make haste to bless the Divine Name in advance of the time when ye will be unable to bless Him and offer up thanks. Observe then the words: When a man shall separate himself by uttering a vow, the vow of a Nazirite, etc., referring to him who makes haste whilst in this world, to consecrate himself to his Master. He shall abstain from wine and strong drink... nor eat fresh grapes, etc. The question here arises, why should the Nazirite, in addition to wine, be forbidden also grapes, seeing that the priest, who is also enjoined to "drink no wine nor strong drink" (Lev. x, 9), is yet permitted to eat grapes. There is, however, a recondite idea involved in this. It is a known thing that the tree of Adam's transgression was a vine, the fruits of which, wine, strong drink and grapes, belong together to the side of the left. Hence the Nazirite has to keep altogether away from them. The Book of Rab Hamnuna the Elder supports this exposition. There we read in reference to the injunction, he shall let the locks of hair of his head grow long, that the letting of the hair of his head and beard grow long and the abstention from wine and strong drink and grapes is for the reason that all these belong to the left side and they are, moreover, unhairy: the wine is the Superior Mother, the strong drink is a product of the wine and is unhairy. It belongs to the region of the Levites, and hence the Levites were enjoined to "cause a razor to pass over all their flesh" (Num. VIII, 7). The grapes are the Lower Mother, which gathers in herself both the wine and the strong drink. The Nazirite therefore has to abstain from the whole of the left side, so that none of their works should be seen in him. And the grapes grow no hair nor beard, symbolic, as it were, of the female, who has to remove her hair before having relations with the male, and who is by nature beardless. Hence the Nazirite has to let grow his hair, including his beard. Now Samson, although a Nazirite of God, was punished because he married the daughter of a strange god, so that instead of associating himself with his own he debased his holiness by mingling with the daughter of a strange god. It is held by some that he will have no portion in the world to come, for the reason that he said: "Let me die with the Philistines" (Jud. XVI, 30), and thus placed his portion among those of the Philistines.

Zohar: Bemidbar, Section 3, Page 127b

Now in regard to the Levites it says: "And thus shalt thou do unto them to cleanse them: sprinkle the water of purification upon them, and let them cause a razor to pass over all their flesh" (Num. VIII, 7). After the hair has been removed and all the details performed, the Levite is designated "pure", but not "holy". But the Nazirite, having abstained from the side of rigour, is designated "holy" and not simply "pure". So Scripture says: All the days of his vow of Naziriteship...in which he consecrateth himself unto the Lord, he shall be holy, he shall let the locks of the hair of his head grow long. This is explained by the passage, "and the hair of his head [was] like pure wool" [Tr. note: i.e. white, the symbol of mercy.] (Dan. VII, 9), inasmuch as the Nazirite in this regard resembles the celestial pattern.' R. Judah said: 'It is indeed by his hair that the Nazirite is distinguished as holy. This is in allusion to "his locks are curled" (S.S. v, 11).' A teaching of R. Simeon says: 'Did men but understand the inner significance of the Scriptural passages regarding the hair, they would acquire a knowledge of their Master by means of the Superior Wisdom.'

[Tr. note: Here follows in the text the Idra Rabba; v. Appendix.]

Zohar: Bemidbar, Section 3, Page 145a

SPEAK UNTO AARON AND UNTO HIS SONS, SAYING: ON THIS WISE YE SHALL BLESS, ETC. R. Isaac quoted here the verse: "But the grace (hesed) of the Lord is from everlasting to everlasting upon them that fear him, and his righteousness unto children's children" (Ps. CII, 17). 'How great', he said, 'is the virtue of fear in the esteem of the Almighty, inasmuch as fear embraces humility, and humility embraces a state of grace (h'siduth)! Hence, whoever is possessed of fear of sin is possessed of all those virtues; but whoever does not fear Heaven possesses neither humility nor the state of grace. There is a teaching: Whoever emerges from the stage of fear and robes himself in humility, attains thereby a higher degree, as it says, "The fear of the Lord is the heel of humility" [Tr. note: E.V. "The reward of humility and the fear of the Lord is..."] (Prov. XXII, 4). Whoever is possessed of the fear of Heaven is rewarded with humility, and he who is possessed of humility is rewarded with the state of grace; so that fear of the Heaven leads to both of these. We have been taught: Whoever has attained the degree of grace is designated "angel"

Zohar: Bemidbar, Section 3, Page 145b

of the Lord of hosts, as we read: "For the priest's lips should keep knowledge, and they should seek the law at his mouth; for he is the angel of the Lord of hosts" (Malachi II, 7). Wherewith did the priest merit to be called "angel of the Lord of hosts"?' Said R. Judah: 'As the angel of the Lord of hosts is a priest on high, so is the priest below an angel of the Lord of hosts. The angel of the Lord of hosts on high is Michael the great prince who issues from the celestial Grace (hesed) and is the celestial High-priest. So the High-priest on earth is called "angel of the Lord of hosts" by reason that he belongs to the side of Grace. He has attained that degree through fear of God. Scripture thus says: "And the grace of the Lord is from everlasting to everlasting (lit. world to world) upon them that fear him". What means "from world to world"? Said R. Isaac: 'As it has been established in the exposition of the Holy Assembly; [Tr. note: The Idra Rabba.] it alludes to the two worlds.' R. Hiya objected: 'If so, it should have been written "from the world to the world".' Said R. Eleazar: 'It is an allusion to the celestial Adam and the earthly Adam. "Upon those who fear Him", inasmuch as whoever fears sin is called "Adam" (Man).' Said R. Judah: 'But there is a teaching that the term "Adam" signifies the conjunction of male and female?' R. Eleazar in reply said: 'Assuredly so. He who achieves for himself the union of male and female is called Adam, and in this way has the fear of sin. He attains, moreover, to the virtue of humility, and even the degree of grace. Contrariwise, he who remains without that union possesses neither fear nor humility nor the state of grace. So Scripture says: "For I have said: The world is built by Grace" (Ibid. LXXXIX, 3), to wit, by Adam, who denotes the union of male and female. Again: "And the grace of the Lord is from world to world" is an allusion to the priests who proceed from the side of Grace and have obtained this inheritance that descends from the upper world to the lower. "Upon those who fear him", to wit, the priests here below, regarding whom it is written, "and [he shall] make atonement for himself, and for his house" (Lev. XVI, 6), by means of which house (i.e. wife) he falls within the category of Adam. The Psalmist continues: "and his righteousness unto children's children", in allusion to the priest who was rewarded with children's children. Hence the teaching: A priest who has no wife is forbidden to perform the service, as it is written, "and he shall make atonement for himself and for his house".' R. Isaac said that the reason is because the Shekinah does not abide with one who is not married, and the priest in especial must be one with whom the Shekinah abides. Along with the Shekinah there rests on the priests Hesed (Grace), and they are called hasidim (grace-endowed), and as such it behoves them to bless the people. So Scripture says: "And thy saints (hasidim) shall bless thee" (Ps. CXLV, 10); also, "Thy Thummim and thy Urim be with thy saintly one (hasid)".

'"On this wise ye shall bless", to wit, in the holy tongue; "on this wise", to wit, in fear and in humility.' R. Abba said: 'We have learned that KoH (on this wise) is the name of the Power whence all judgements come into action.

Zohar: Bemidbar, Section 3, Page 146a

But when Hesed (Grace) is joined to Koh the latter is sweetened. Hence the priest, who is derived from Hesed, is entrusted with Koh to have it blessed and sweetened. Thus the command was "On this wise (KoH) ye shall bless", that is, by the influence of Hesed ye shall fill with blessing and make sweet the power of Koh in its relation to Israel, so that Rigour should not prevail. 'It says: "On this wise ye shall bless the children of Israel, saying (amor) unto them". It is not written "ye shall say unto them", parallel to "ye shall bless".' R. Judah taught that we have therefore to construe it thus: If they will be worthy, then [the blessing is] to them, but if not, then there is merely saying.

R. Isaac discoursed on the verse: "And I Daniel alone saw the vision; for the men that were with me saw not the vision", etc. (Dan. x, 7). 'There is a tradition', he said, 'that those men were prophets, to wit, Haggai, Zechariah and Malachi, whereas Daniel himself was not a prophet. There was thus a reversal of the relation of holy and common. For they, the holy men, were seized with fear and were not able to see the vision, whereas he, a common man, did see without fear. This is explained, however, by the verse: "Though a host should encamp against me, my heart shall not fear; though war should rise up against me, in this (zoth) I will be confident" (Ps. XXVI, 3). The word "this" (zoth) is an allusion to the Providence presiding over David's inheritance that will ensure it for him and will execute vengeance on his behalf. There is a teaching that the Holy One, blessed be He, prepared for David a Holy Chariot, adorned with the holy superior crowns of the Patriarchs. That remained an inheritance for David, and his kingdom was reserved in perpetuity for his descendants. This kingdom had its counterpart on high, and fortified by that heavenly kingdom the rulership of the House of David will never depart from it throughout all generations. So that whenever the crown of Kingship in any way bestirs itself for a descendant of David there is no one who can stand up against him. The reason thus why "Daniel alone saw the vision" was because he was a descendant of David, as we read: "Now among these were, of the children of Judah, Daniel, Hananiah", etc. (Ibid. I, 6); he saw the vision and rejoiced in that it was of the side of the inherited possession which was the lot and portion of his fathers; it was his own, and thus he could endure it, whereas others could not.'

R. Simeon said: 'When KoH bestirs itself in its rigour, mankind cannot stand against it. But when the priests spread out their hands, which are derived from Hesed (Grace), celestial Grace bestirs itself in response and allies itself to KoH, whereby the latter is sweetened, as it were, and in this way the priests, with shining faces, pronounce the blessing on Israel, so that judgement of Rigour is removed from them.

'TO THE CHILDREN OF ISRAEL, and not the other nations. Only the priest is empowered to pronounce the blessing, and no other, since he is under Hesed (Grace) and is called Hasid (grace-endowed), and it is said, "and Thy hasidim shall bless thee (yevarehu-Koh)" (Ps. CXLIX, 10), to wit, they will cause KoH to join in the blessing. ON THIS WISE YE SHALL BLESS: to wit, by the ineffable Name and in the holy tongue.' R. Judah said: 'When the priest below stands up and spreads out his hands, all the celestial sacred Crowns bestir themselves and make ready to receive blessings, and draw sustenance unto themselves from the depth of the Well, the never-ceasing Well whence blessings ever flow forth for all worlds; these Crowns drink in, as it were, all the blessings. At that moment there is a whisper followed by silence throughout the universe. So when a king is about to join his queen, all his attendants are agog and a whisper runs through them: Behold, the King is about to meet his Matrona. Here the Matrona is the Community of Israel.' R. Isaac said: 'The priest [in pronouncing the benediction] has to raise his right hand higher than his left hand, for the reason that the right is higher in estimation than the left.

'There is a teaching: The priest who is about to spread forth his hands [for the benediction] needs an inflow of holiness

Zohar: Bemidbar, Section 3, Page 146b

in addition to his own; he must therefore have his hands washed by one who is himself holy, to wit, a Levite, of whose order it is written: "And thou shalt sanctify the Levites". [Tr. note: These words are not to be found in our texts.] Thus the priest may not receive the sanctification of the washing of hands from any commoner who is not himself sanctified. It may be asked, why only a Levite? Why should not the priest be sanctified by the hands of another priest? The answer is, because the other priest would not be complete, but the Levite is complete, being qualified for his own service, and he is also designated "cleansed", as it says, "and cleanse them" (Num. VIII, 6). Tradition, again, teaches us that the priest, in the spreading forth of his hands, should not have his fingers joined close together, for it is requisite that the sacred Crowns should receive the blessing each one apart in a manner proper to each, because the letters of the Divine Name require also to be kept distinct and not to run into each other.' R. Isaac said: 'The Holy One, blessed be He, desired that the upper beings should be blessed, in order that the lower beings should draw down the blessing from above, and, on the other hand, that the most holy beings above should reciprocally draw to themselves the blessings through the lower beings who are the most holy here below, as we read, "and thy godly ones shall bless thee" (Ps. CXLV, 10). R. Judah said: 'If a priest is ignorant of this inward significance of the blessing and does not know whom he blesses or what his blessing connotes, his blessing is naught. So Scripture says: "For the priest's lips should keep knowledge, and they should seek the law at his mouth; for he is the messenger of the Lord of hosts" (Mal. II, 17). That is, the upper beings should seek at his mouth the Torah, to wit, the Written Law and the Oral Law, which are bound up with the two celestial Crowns called by the same names; they do so because he is "the messenger of the Lord of hosts". So the priest, as tradition tells us, needs to think with devotion on the inward and elevated significance of the words uttered whereby the unification of the Divine Name is achieved.'

R. Simeon cited the following from the Book of Mystery. 'The Divine Name has both a revealed and an undisclosed form. In its revealed form it is written Tetragrammaton, but in its undisclosed form it is written in other letters, this undisclosed form representing the most Recondite of all.' R. Judah said: 'Even the revealed form of the Name is hidden under other letters, [Tr. note: i.e. ADNY (ADoNaY).] in order to screen more effectively the most Recondite of all. For it behoves the priest to concentrate on the various permutations of the Divine Name, and to call down the mercies of all the Attributes through the two Crowns of mercy. [Tr. note: Viz. Mah, Adonay.] In these letters of this Name are concealed twenty-two attributes of Mercy, viz. thirteen of the Ancient One, Most Recondite of all, and nine of the Microprosopus (Lesser Figure); but they all combine in one composite Name, on which the priest concentrated his mind when he spread forth his hands, a name containing twenty-two engraven letters. We have learnt that when reverence was prevalent among mankind, the ineffable Name was openly enunciated in the hearing of all, but after irreverence became widespread it was concealed under other letters. Therefore at the time when the Name was disclosed, the priest would concentrate his mind on its deep and inner meaning, and he would utter the Name in such a way as to accord with that meaning. But when irreverence became common in the world he would conceal all within the written letters. Observe that the twenty-two letters

Zohar: Bemidbar, Section 3, Page 147a

were uttered by Moses in two sections. The first time [Tr. note: Ex. XXXIV, 6.] he uttered thirteen attributes of the Ancient of Ancients, the Most Undisclosed, so as to bring them down to the region where Rigour rules and subdue it. The second time [Tr. note: Num. XIV, 18.] he uttered nine attributes of Mercy which are inherent in the Microprosopus (Lesser Figure) and which are radiated from the light of the Ancient and Undisclosed One. All this the priest combined together when he spread forth his hands to bless the people, so that all the worlds received the blessings from the side of the mercies which are drawn from the Ancient and Most Undisclosed One. It is for this reason that in the command it says simply "saying" (amor), instead of the definite form "say" (imru), this being a reference to the hidden letters within the words of blessing. Again, the word AMoR has in its letters the numerical value of two hundred and forty-eight less one, equal to the number of the bodily members of man, excepting the one member on which all the rest depend. All these members thus receive the priestly blessing as expressed in the three verses.'

R. Yose said: 'One day I was sitting in the presence of R. Eleazar, the son of R. Simeon, when I asked him the import of David's words, saying: "Man and beast thou preservest, O Lord" (Ps. XXXVI, 7). "Man" is plain enough, I said, but why associate with him "beast"? He replied: It is as much as to say: If they are worthy they are of the category of man, if not they are of that of beast. I said to him: Rabbi, I would like a deeper exposition. He then said: Observe that the Holy One, blessed be He, called Israel "Adam" (Man), in virtue of their being of the celestial pattern, and He also called them "beast". So we read in one and the same verse, "And ye my sheep, the sheep of my pasture, are men (Adam)" (Ezek. XXXIV, 31): thus Israel is called both sheep, which is beast, and man (Adam). Hence "man and beast the Lord preserveth". Furthermore, when they are virtuous they are "Adam", of the celestial pattern, otherwise they are called "beast", but both receive the blessing at one and the same time, the celestial Adam and the earthly beast. Observe that no blessing is found here below until it comes into existence on high. But so soon as it comes into existence on high it is found below. The same correspondence exists whether for good or for ill. In regard to good, Scripture says: "I will respond to the heavens, and they shall respond to the earth" (Hos. II. 23); in regard to ill, we read: "the Lord will punish the host of the high heaven on high, and the kings of the earth upon the earth" (Isa. XXIV, 21).' R. Judah remarked: 'It is for this reason that it is written "say to them", without specification, implying that the blessing embraces the upper world and the lower together; and similarly it first says "thus" (Koh), and then the children of Israel". THE LORD BLESS THEE, to wit, on high, AND KEEP THEE, here below; THE LORD MAKE HIS FACE TO SHINE UPON THEE, to wit, on high, AND BE GRACIOUS UNTO THEE, here below; THE LORD SHOW FAVOUR UNTO THEE, on high, AND GIVE THEE PEACE, below.' R. Abba said: 'They all are blessed together by the twenty-two engraven letters of the Divine Name that are embraced within the priestly blessing. They symbolize, moreover, Mercy within Mercy, with the entire absence of Rigour. As for the words "yisa... panav" (the Lord lift up His countenance), it may also be translated, "the Lord remove and put away His anger", so that Rigour will be entirely absent. There is a teaching in the name of R. Yose, saying: When the priest spreads forth his hands it is forbidden to look at them, [Tr. note: v. T.B. Hagigah, 16a.] for the reason that the Shekinah is hovering over his hands.

R. Isaac remarked: 'Inasmuch as one is unable to see the Shekinah, as it says, "for man shall not see me and live" (Ex. XXXIII, 2), to wit, not whilst alive but only in death, what matters it then if one looks at the priest's hands?' Said R. Yose: 'It matters because the Divine Name is reflected in the fingers of the priest's hands, so that although people cannot see the Shekinah they ought not to look towards the hands of the priests, as that would indicate irreverence towards the Shekinah. We have learnt that when the priests hold their hands outspread [in blessing], the congregation should be in fear and awe, and realize that it is a time of favour in all the worlds when the upper and lower worlds are being blessed, and there is everywhere an absence of Rigour. It is a moment when the undisclosed aspect of the Ancient of Ancients is being revealed as Microprosopus (Lesser-Figure), and thus peace prevails then everywhere.

Zohar: Bemidbar, Section 3, Page 147b

[Note: The first 3 lines of the Hebrew text are not found in our translation]

A teacher taught in the presence of R. Simeon: Whoever is in distress on account of a dream should

recite during the time the priests spread forth their hands the following: [Tr. note: T.B. Berachoth, 55a.] "O Master of the world, I am Thine and my dreams are Thine...." For that is a propitious moment, and if one then offers up prayer in his distress, Rigour is turned for him into Mercy.'

SO THEY SHALL PUT MY NAME UPON THE CHILDREN OF ISRAEL. R. Judah said that the term samu (put) conveys the idea of orderly arrangement, as the priests are therein bidden to arrange by their blessing the Crowns of the right to the right, and the Crowns of the left to the left, without confusing them, so that the upper world and the lower will receive the blessing. If they follow this, then I WILL BLESS THEM, a blessing extended to the priests themselves, as we read: "And blessed be every one that blesseth thee" (Gen. XXVII, 29), also, "And I will bless them that bless thee" (Ibid. XII, 3). We are told that a priest not beloved by the people ought not to take part in blessing the people. On one occasion, when a priest went up and spread forth his hands, before he completed the blessing he turned into a heap of bones. This happened to him because there was no love between him and the people. Then another priest went up and pronounced the blessing, and so the day passed without harm. A priest who loves not the people, or whom they love not, may not pronounce the blessing. So Scripture says: "He that hath a bountiful eye shall be blessed" (Prov. XXII, 9), where the word YeBoRaKH (shall be blessed) can also be read YeBaReKH (shall bless).' R. Isaac said: 'Note that the wicked Balaam, when he was entrusted with the task of blessing Israel, fixed on them an evil eye so as to prevent the blessing from being fulfilled. So Scripture says: "The saying of Balaam the son of Beor" (Num. XXIV, 3), that is, the son of the most hateful enemy of Israel; "and the saying of the man whose eye is closed" [Tr. note: By a change from right to left of the diacritical point, the word shethum (opened) is read sethum (closed).] (Ibid.): that means that he closed his benevolent eye so that the blessing should be of no effect.' R. Judah remarked: 'This is assuredly so, as indeed we find that a real blessing is associated with the opening of the eye. Thus it is written, "Open thine eyes" (Dan. IX, 18), that is, in order to bless. So R. Hamnuna the Elder's blessing for anyone took the form of "May the Holy One, blessed be He, keep His eyes open on thee".' R. Isaac continued: 'Thus the blessing pronounced by the priest with a benevolent eye is effective, but if it is not given with a benevolent eye, of such it is written: "Eat thou not the bread of him that hath an evil eye, neither desire thou his dainties" (Prov. XXIII, 6), to wit, in no wise seek any blessing from such a man.' Said R. Yose: 'Observe the verse: "Nevertheless the Lord thy God would not hearken unto Balaam" (Deut. XXIII, 6). Now we should have expected rather "to hearken unto Balak" instead of "unto Balaam", seeing that Balak was the instigator of the whole attempt. But the reason why Balaam is mentioned is because he closed his eye in order to make his blessing of no effect.' R. Yose said: 'The Holy One, blessed be He, said in effect to Balaam: "Wretch! Thou hast closed thine eye in order that My children should not receive any blessing. I, however, will open thine eyes and so I will turn all thy utterances into blessings." So we read: "But the Lord thy God turned the curse into a blessing unto thee, because the Lord thy God loved thee" (Ibid.). It has been taught: How beloved are Israel before the Holy One, blessed be He, in that the upper beings are only blessed for the sake of Israel. Thus R. Judah said in the name of R. Hiya, who had it from R. Yose: 'The Holy One, blessed be He, swore that he would not enter the heavenly Jerusalem save after Israel had entered the earthly Jerusalem, as it is said: "[I am] the holy one in the midst of thee, and I will not come into the city" (Hos. XI, 9). That means that so long as the Shekinah is here in exile the Name on high is not complete, the arrangements [of the Divine Powers] are not properly effected, [Tr. note: i.e. there is friction between the Grades, v. Appendix.] and, if it were possible to say so,

Zohar: Bemidbar, Section 3, Page 148a

the Holy Name is left impaired.' R. Abba was once going toward Lud when he met R. Zeira, the son of Rab. Said R. Zeira: 'Now do I behold the presence of the Shekinah, and whoever beholds the presence of the Shekinah ought to quicken his pace and follow Her. So we read: "And let us know and pursue to know the Lord" (Ibid. VI, 3); also, "And many peoples shall go and say: Come ye and let us go up to the mountain of the Lord... for out of Zion shall go forth the law" (Isa. II, 3). I thus desire to follow thee and taste of some of the good things that ye learn daily in the Holy Assembly. [Tr. note: i.e. the full assembly of R. Simeon and the Companions.] Now,' he asked, 'it is written: "And he believed in the Lord, and he counted it to him for righteousness" (Gen. xv, 6). Does it mean that the Holy One counted it to Abraham, or that Abraham counted it to the Holy One? I myself', he said, 'heard that it means that the Holy One counted it to Abraham, but this does not satisfy me.' Said R. Abba: 'It is indeed not so. Observe that it is written, "and he counted it" (vayahsh'veha), but not "and he counted to him" (vayahshov lo). This assuredly means that Abraham counted it to the Holy One, blessed be He. It has been taught on this point as follows. It is written: "And he brought him forth abroad" (Ibid. 5), to wit, the Holy One, blessed be He, said to Abraham in effect: [Tr. note: v. T.B. Shabbath, 156a.] Give up thy astrological speculations; this is not the way to acquire a knowledge of My Name. Thou seest, but I see also. Abram, it is true, is not to beget children, but Abraham will beget children. Henceforth follow another direction. "So (KoH) shall thy seed be" (Ibid.). The word KoH is expressive of the tenth sacred Crown of the King by which His Name may be known; it is the Crown through which rigorous judgements are set in motion. At that moment Abraham became filled with joy, inasmuch as the good tidings came to him through the medium of KoH, for although rigorous judgements are stirred up thence, yet "Abraham counted it", to wit, the Crown, source of Rigour, "for righteousness": that is, he realized that the very Rigour was turned for him into Mercy. Now, in the command "On this wise (KoH) shall ye bless", it is signified that for the sake of Israel the very KoH is to be blessed by the priest, so that Israel will be blessed below, and thus blessing will be diffused through the universe. As for the time to come, it is written, "The Lord bless thee out of Zion..." (Ps. CXXXIV, 3); as well as, "Blessed be the Lord out of Zion, who dwelleth at Jerusalem" (Ibid. cxxxv, 21).'

AND IT CAME TO PASS ON THE DAY THAT MOSES HAD MADE AN END (Khalloth), ETC. R. Yose taught: This was the day when the bride [Tr. note: Khalloth (= ending) suggests Khallah (= bride = Shekinah).] entered under the canopy, and it was by the hands of Moses that she entered there.' R. Judah remarked: 'And did She then delay until that time to enter into Her place? Is it not written: "And Moses was not able to enter the tent of meeting", etc. (Ex. XL, 35)?' Said R. Isaac: 'The Torah is not written in chronological order. [Tr. note: v. T.B. Pesahim, 6b, et passim.] Again, "Khalloth" (making an end) is the same as "Khallath" (the bride of) Moses. Assuredly she was the "khallah", bride of Moses. So we learn that R. Simeon explained the verse: "Thou hast ascended on high; thou hast led captivity captive", etc. (Ps. LXVIII, 19), as follows. When the Holy One, blessed be He, said to Moses, "Put off thy shoes from off thy feet" (Ex. III, 5), the mountain shook. Said Michael to the Holy One, blessed be He: Lord of the Universe! Art Thou about to annihilate man? Is it not written, "Male and female created he them, and blessed them" (Gen. v, 2), so that blessing is only found in the association of male and female? But now Thou biddest him to separate from his wife. The Holy One replied: Indeed, Moses has already fulfilled the command of bearing children. Now I desire him to espouse, as it were, the Shekinah, and thus for his sake the Shekinah will descend to dwell with him. This is what is meant by "Thou hast ascended on high; Thou hast led captivity captive", to wit, the Shekinah, who was, as it were, espoused to thee. In regard to Joshua, whose face shone as the face of the moon, [Tr. note: Cf. T.B. Baba Bathra, 75a.] it is written: "Put off thy shoe (singular) from off thy foot" (Jos. v, 15), for the reason that he separated himself from his wife only at certain times, inasmuch as the Shekinah was not espoused to him in the same degree, he not being so much deserving of her. So it is written: "And Joshua fell on his face to the earth" (Ibid. v, 14). But here we read of her being the bride of (KHLLTH) Moses in all truth. Happy was the portion of Moses, whose Master delighted in his glory above all the rest of mankind.'

AND THE LORD SAID UNTO MOSES: EACH PRINCE ON HIS DAY. 'The word layom (=to the day)', said R. Judah, 'is an allusion to the celestial Days which were dedicated

Zohar: Bemidbar, Section 3, Page 148b

to be blessed by the twelve delimited areas; [Tr. note: The twelve permutations of the Tetragrammaton.] and each one was put right and dedicated by means of a blessing through the days here below. We have learnt that all are blessed through the celestial altar. All are blessed, even the lower world, even the other nations of the world.' R. Simeon said: 'If not for the sacrifices offered by these twelve princes, the world could not stand against the twelve princes of Ishmael, of whom it is written, "twelve princes according to their nations" (Gen. xxv, 16). Hence "each prince on the day"; and whatever he offered was after the celestial pattern, so that all should receive the blessing. THE RAMS SIXTY, THE HE-GOATS SIXTY, representing the threescore mighty men about it" (S.S. III, 7), which belong to the side of Strength. ONE GOLDEN SPOON OF TEN GOLDEN SHEKELS, etc. Based on this, it was declared: Happy is the portion of the righteous on whom the Holy One, blessed be He, pours blessings, and unto whose prayer He hearkens. Regarding them it is written: "When he hath regarded the prayer of the destitute, and hath not despised -their prayer" (Ps. CII, 18).'

BEHA'ALOTHEKHA

AND THE LORD SPOKE UNTO MOSES, SAYING: SPEAK UNTO AARON, AND SAY UNTO HIM: WHEN THOU LIGHTEST THE LAMPS. R. Judah discoursed here on the verse: "Which is as a bridegroom coming out of his chamber", etc. (Ps. XIX, 6). 'Happy is the portion of Israel', he said, 'in whom the Holy One, blessed be He, delights and to whom He gave the Torah of truth, the Tree of Life, whoever takes hold of which achieves life in this world and in the world to come. Now the Tree of Life extends from above downward, and it is the Sun which illumines all. Its radiance commences at the top and extends through the whole trunk in a straight line. It is composed of two sides, one to the north, one to the south, one to the right, and one to the left. When the trunk shines, first the right arm of the tree is illumined, and from its intensity the left side catches the light. The "chamber" from which he goes forth is the starting-point of light, referred to also in the words of the next verse, "from the end of the heaven", which is, indeed, the starting-point of all. From that point he goes forth veritably as a bridegroom to meet his bride, the beloved of his soul, whom he receives with outstretched arm. The sun proceeds and makes his way toward the west; when the west is approached the north side bestirs itself to come forward to meet it, and joins it. Then "he rejoices as a strong man to run his course" (Ps. ibid.), so as to shed his light on the moon. Now the words WHEN THOU LIGHTEST THE LAMPS contain an allusion to the celestial all of which are lit up together from the radiance of the sun.' [Tr. note: There seems to be a lacuna here in the text.]

R. Abba began a discourse with the verse: "Happy is the people that know the joyful shout; they walk, O Lord, in the light of thy countenance" (Ps. LXXXIX, 16). 'Happy', he said, 'are Israel to whom the Holy One, blessed be He, gave the Holy Law

Zohar: Bemidbar, Section 3, Page 149a

and whom He taught His ways, how to cleave unto Him and observe the precepts of the Torah whereby to merit the world to come; and whom He brought near to Himself at the time when they went forth from Egypt. For then He took them away from a strange dominion and caused them to be united to His Name. Then they were called "the children of Israel", to wit, free men entirely emancipated from any strange power, and united to His Name that is supreme over all, that rules over the upper beings and the lower; and out of His love for them He designated them "Israel my firstborn" (Ex. IV, 22), on the celestial pattern. Then He slew every firstborn on high and below, set free the bondmen and prisoners, the upper and the lower ones, so as to free Israel completely. Hence the Holy One, blessed be He, did not send an angel or a seraph, but performed the deed Himself. Furthermore, He alone, being all-knowing, could distinguish and discern and set free the bondmen, things not within the power of any messenger but only within His own. Now on that night when the Holy One, blessed be He, was about to slay all those firstborn, the angels came forward to sing their song of praise before Him. He said to them: "This is not the time for it, as another song my children on earth are about to sing." Then at the division of the night the north wind bestirred itself, and the Holy One, blessed be He, executed judgement and Israel broke forth in loud songs of praise. Then He made them free men, freed from every bondage; and the angels and all the celestial hosts hearkened unto the voice of Israel. After Israel had circumcised themselves they marked their houses with that blood and with the blood of the paschal lamb in three spots, to wit, "the lintel and the two side-posts" (Ibid. XII, 22). For when the destroying angel went forth and saw the mark of the holy sign on that door he had compassion on Israel, as it is written: "the Lord will compassionately pass over the door" (Ibid. 23). There is a certain difficulty here. For since the Holy One Himself was to come and slay in the land of Egypt, what need was there for a sign on the door, seeing that all is revealed before Him? Further, what signifies "and [He] will not suffer the destroyer" (Ibid.)? We should have expected "and [He] will not destroy". But the truth is as follows. It is written, and "the Lord smote all the firstborn in the land of Egypt" (Ibid. 29). Now "and the Lord" (V-Tetragrammaton) everywhere denotes "He together with His tribunal", and on any such occasion it behoves man to exhibit some visible act in order to be saved. It is thus of importance to have sacrifices offered on the altar so as to keep at a distance the Destroyer during a service. The same applies to the New-Year Day, the Day of Judgement, when the lords of the evil tongue rise up against Israel; it is then that we need prayer and supplication, and, in addition, some outward and visible act. This act consists in blowing the trumpet, the sound of which wakes into action another trumpet. We thereby bring about the working of Mercy and Rigour at one and the same time, like the celestial trumpet that emits a combined sound. Our object is to awaken Mercy and to bring about the subjection of the Masters of Rigour so that they may be impotent on that day. And so when the powers of Mercy are awakened, all the celestial lamps are lit on both sides, and then "In the light of the King's countenance is life" (Prov. XVI, 15). So at the moment when the priest is about to kindle the lamps here below and offers up the perfumed incense, the celestial lights are kindled and all is linked together so that joy and gladness pervade all the worlds. So Scripture says: "Ointment and perfume rejoice the heart" (Prov. XXVII, 9). This, then, is the full import of "When thou lightest the lamps".'

R. Eleazar, R. Yose and R. Isaac once on their travels came to the mountains of Kurdistan. As they approached them R. Eleazar raised his eyes and saw some tall and forbidding cliffs, and they were all filled with fear. Said R. Eleazar to his Companions: 'Had my father been here I should not have feared, but all the same, as we are three and are discussing words of the Torah, there is no place here for the divine Rigour.' R. Eleazar then quoted the verse: "And the ark rested in the seventh month, on the seventeenth day of the month, on the mountains of Ararat" etc. (Gen. VIII, 4). 'How precious', he said, 'are the words of the Torah, seeing that each particular word contains sublime mystical teachings, the Torah itself being designated the sublime general rule. Now, one of the thirteen exegetical principles by which the Law is expounded reads: "If anything is included in a general proposition and is then made the subject of a special statement, that which is predicated of it is not to be understood as limited to itself alone, but is to be applied to the whole of the general proposition." So it is with the Torah itself. It

Zohar: Bemidbar, Section 3, Page 149b

is itself the supernal all-comprehensive Rule, yet in addition does each particular narrative, seemingly a mere story or fact, standing outside the all-comprehensive Rule of the Torah, teach us not only its own limited lesson, but supernal ideas and recondite doctrines applicable to the whole of the all-comprehensive Rule of the Torah. Thus when we read that "the ark rested in the seventh month, on the seventeenth day of the month, upon the mountains of Ararat", we assuredly find here a particular statement, apparently a superfluous detail; for what matters it to us whether the ark rested in this or in the other place so long as it rested somewhere? Yet does it contain teaching applicable to the whole principle of the Torah. And happy are Israel to whom was given the sublime Torah, the Torah of truth. Perdition take anyone who maintains that any narrative in the Torah comes merely to tell us a piece of history and nothing more! If that were so, the Torah would not be what it assuredly is, to wit, the supernal Law, the Law of truth. Now if it is not dignified for a king of flesh and blood to engage in common talk, much less to write it down, is it conceivable that the most high King, the Holy One, blessed be He, was short of sacred subjects with which to fill the Torah, so that He had to collect such commonplace topics as the anecdotes of Esau, and Hagar, Laban's talks to Jacob, the words of Balaam and his ass, those of Balak, and of Zimri, and suchlike, and make of them a Torah? If so, why is it called the "Law of truth"? Why do we read "The law of the Lord is perfect.... The testimony of the Lord is sure. The ordinances of the Lord are true.... More to be desired are they than gold, yea, than much fine gold" (Ps. XIX, 8-11)? But assuredly each word of the Torah signifies sublime things, so that this or that narrative, besides its meaning in and for itself, throws light on the all-comprehensive Rule of the Torah. See now what the resting of the ark comes to teach us. At the time when Rigour impends over the world and the Holy One, blessed be He, sits on His throne of Judgement to judge the world, within that Throne, in the King's chest, there are deposited ever so many records, notes and books, so that nothing is forgotten by the King. That Throne attains its full significance only in the seventh month, on the Day of Judgement, when all the people of the world pass before it for scrutiny. "The Ark" thus "rested in the seventh month", on the world's Day of Judgement, "on the mountains of Ararat", that is, attended by the lords of Rigour, the lords of the hostile shout. Many are the executioners who bestir themselves on that day and place themselves underneath the Throne to take part in the world's judgement. Israel on that day offer up prayer and supplication before Him, they blow the trumpet, and the Holy One, blessed be He, takes compassion on them and changes Rigour into Mercy. Then all the upper and the lower beings proclaim: "Happy is the people that know the joyful shout" (Ps. LXXXIX, 16). Hence, on that day, whoever blows the trumpet should know the root of the matter, so as to concentrate his mind on the meaning of the blowing and to perform

667

it with understanding. Thus, "happy is the people that know the joyful shout", and not merely "that sound the joyful shout".'

The Companions then proceeded on their journey the whole day. When night fell they ascended to a spot where they found a cave. Said R. Eleazar: 'Let one of us enter inside the cave if haply he find there a more convenient spot.' R. Yose entered and noticed therein an inner cave lit by a lamp, and he heard a voice speaking thus: "When thou lightest the lamps the seven lamps shall give light in front of the candlestick". Here (said the voice) the Community of Israel receives the light whilst the supernal Mother

Zohar: Bemidbar, Section 3, Page 150a

is crowned, and all the lamps are illumined from Her. In Her are two small flames, companions of the King, as it were, which kindle all the lights on high and below.' R. Yose, on hearing this, rejoiced, and reported it to R. Eleazar, who said to him: 'Let us enter therein, for the Holy One, blessed be He, seems to have appointed for us this day as one on which a miracle should happen to us.' When they entered their eyes met there two men engaged in the study of the Torah. R. Eleazar proclaimed: '"How precious is thy lovingkindness, O God! and the children of men take refuge in the shadow of thy wings" (Ps. XXXVI, 8).' The two men stood up, then they all sat down in joyful mood. Said R. Eleazar: 'The Holy One, blessed be He, has shown us lovingkindness in letting us find you in this spot. Now, light the lamps!'

R. Yose then began the following discourse: When thou lightest the lamps. 'The term beha'alothekha (when thou lightest) has here its literal meaning [to wit, when thou makest ascend], inasmuch as the verse speaks here of the services performed by the priest, the two which form a unity, to wit, those of the oil and the incense, so that "Oil and perfume rejoice the heart" (Prov. XXVII, 9). So Scripture says: "And Aaron shall burn thereon incense... when he dresseth the lamps....

And when Aaron lighteth the lamps at dusk he shall burn it" (Ex. xxx, 7-8). Why the term b'hetivo (when he dresseth, lit.=when he maketh good)?' R. Judah said that this points to the idea contained in "but he that is of a merry (lit. good) heart hath a continual feast" (Prov. XV, 15), whilst the expression "when he maketh ascend" (b'ha'aloth) points to the exaltation of the supernal beings after having drunk their fill of the waters of the River, so that blessings and joy are diffused throughout.' Said R. Aha: 'When the Most Profound illumes the River, and the River so illumined flows on in a straight path-of such a moment it is written, "when he makes ascend", in that from the Most Profound there issue the causes that come from the supernal side of the Most Profound which is called

Thought. The two terms ["make ascend" and "make good"] thus signify one and the same thing. At that moment the Community of Israel is blessed and blessings are diffused throughout the worlds.

[Note: The last 27 lines of the Hebrew text do not appear in our translation.]

Zohar: Bemidbar, Section 3, Page 150b [Note: The Hebrew text for this entire page does not appear in our translation.]

Zohar: Bemidbar, Section 3, Page 151a [Note: The translation begins with the concluding lines of the Hebrew text.]

R. Eleazar said: 'This section, dealing with the ceremonies of the candlestick, is a repetition of another section dealing with the same. The reason for the repetition is as follows. Having recorded the offerings brought on the altar by the Princes, and all the ceremony of its dedication, Scripture records the service of the candlestick, which was a finishing touch ministered by Aaron, inasmuch as it was through Aaron that the supernal candlestick with all its lamps was lighted. Observe that the altar had to be dedicated and perfected by the twelve Princes, representing the twelve tribes, who were ranged on four sides carrying four standards. It was all on the supernal pattern, to wit, the candlestick

Zohar: Bemidbar, Section 3, Page 151b

with its seven lamps to be lighted by the hand of the priest. Candlestick and the inner altar together minister to the joy of the whole of existence, as Scripture says: "Ointment and perfume rejoice the heart" (Prov. XXVII, 9). For of the two altars, the inner one [on which the incense was offered] radiated its force to the outer one, the one assigned for other offerings; and it is by meditating on the inner altar that one obtains a knowledge of the Supernal Wisdom, which is concealed within the words ADoNaY Tetragrammaton. Hence the incense had to be offered up only when the oil had been poured in the lamps. The following is found in the Book of King Solomon. The incense has the virtue of diffusing joy and putting away death. For whereas Judgement prevails on the exterior, joy and illumination, on the other hand, proceed from the interior, the seat of all happiness. So when this bestirs itself all Judgement is removed and is powerless. The incense thus has the virtue of annulling death and binds all together, and was therefore offered on the interior altar. Take the Levites. This indicates that it was needful to cleanse them and draw them on that they might be linked to their own proper place. For they symbolize the Left Arm, identical with the side of Judgement, and whoever proceeds from the side of Judgement ought not to let his hair grow, as he thereby strengthens Judgement in the world. For the same reason a woman may not have her hair exposed to view, but it behoves her to cover her head and keep her hair concealed. When this is done, all those who proceed from the side of Judgement are blessed; and thus is explained the significance of the command saying: And thus shalt thou do unto them to cleanse them... and let them cause a razor to pass over all their flesh....

Furthermore, the Levites could not take up their post until the priest had offered them up for a wave-offering, inasmuch as it is the right that has to lead the left.' Said R. Simeon: The Levites, on entering into their assigned places, had to bring as an offering two bullocks, symbolic of the left side, as they themselves were of the left side. On the other hand, power and adjustment are vested in the priest, inasmuch as the power of the body is chiefly displayed in the right arm. The priest was therefore the right arm of all Israel, charged to set right Israel and all the world. Nevertheless he, together with the left side, was part of the body, the body being the all-in-all.

'THIS IS THAT WHICH PERTAINETH UNTO THE LEVITES, ETC. Observe that the Levite enters on his service when twenty-five years old, and remains in his service for twenty five years until he reaches the age of fifty. When he reaches the fifty-year grade the strong fire within him is cooled down, and in such a state he cannot but impair the spot to which he is attached. Besides, his singing voice no longer serves him so well, whereas that voice ought not to be impaired, but should constantly gain in vigour; and since the Levite stands in the region of Strength (Geburah), no feebleness whatever can be permitted to attach to him.'

AND THE LORD SPOKE TO MOSES IN THE WILDERNESS OF SINAI, ETC. Said R. Abba: 'Why was the command regarding the paschal lamb repeated here after it had been given them once whilst they were still in Egypt? The reason is that the Israelites thought that that command was intended only for the one year in Egypt and not for future years. Hence,

Zohar: Bemidbar, Section 3, Page 152a

"in the wilderness of Sinai... of the second year": the command was renewed to indicate that it was to be kept throughout the generations. "In the first month of the second year" contains a sublime mystery. The month signifies the Moon, [Tr. note: Malkuth.] and the year points to the Sun [Tr. note: Tifereth.] that sheds his rays on the Moon. Thus it happened at the time when all the precepts of the Torah were delivered to Israel.' Said R. Simeon: 'Alas for the man who regards the Torah as a book of mere tales and everyday matters! If that were so, we, even we could compose a torah dealing with everyday affairs, and of even greater excellence. Nay, even the princes of the world possess books of greater worth which we could use as a model for composing some such torah. The Torah, however, contains in all its words supernal truths and sublime mysteries. Observe the perfect balancing of the upper and the lower worlds. Israel here below is balanced by the angels on high, of whom it says: "who makest thy angels into winds" (Ps. CIV, 4). For the angels in descending on earth put on themselves earthly garments, as otherwise they could not stay in this world, nor could the world endure them. Now, if thus it is with the angels, how much more so must it be with the Torah—the Torah that created them, that created all the worlds and is the means by which these are sustained. Thus had the Torah not clothed herself in garments of this world the world could not endure it. The stories of the Torah are thus only her outer garments, and whoever looks upon that garment as being the Torah itself, woe to that man-such a one will have no portion in the next world. David thus said: "Open thou mine eyes, that I may behold wondrous things out of thy law" (Ps. CXIX, 18), to wit, the things that are beneath the garment. Observe this. The garments worn by a man are the most visible part of him, and senseless people looking at the man do not seem to see more in him than the garments. But in truth the pride of the garments is the body of the man, and the pride of the body is the soul. Similarly the Torah has a body made up of the precepts of the Torah, called gufe torah (bodies, main principles of the Torah), and that body is enveloped in garments made up of worldly narrations. The senseless people only see the garment, the mere narrations; those who are somewhat wiser penetrate as far as the body. But the really wise, the servants of the most high King, those who stood on Mount Sinai, penetrate right through to the soul, the root principle of all, namely, to the real Torah. In the future the same are destined to penetrate even to the super-soul (soul of the soul) of the Torah. Observe that in a similar way in the supernal world there is garment, body, soul and super-soul. The heavens and their hosts are the outer garment, the Community of Israel is the body which receives the soul, to wit, the "Glory of Israel"; and the super-soul is the Ancient Holy One. All these are interlocked within each other. Woe to the sinners who consider the Torah as mere worldly tales, who only see its outer garment; happy are the righteous who fix their gaze on the Torah proper Wine cannot be kept save in a jar; so the Torah needs an outer garment. These are the stories and narratives, but it behoves us to penetrate beneath them.

[Note: The last 3 lines of the Hebrew text are not found in our translation]

Zohar: Bemidbar, Section 3, Page 152b

IF ANY MAN (lit. a man, a man) OF YOU... SHALL BE UNCLEAN, ETC. What signifies the repetition of the term "a man"? It signifies "a man who is a man", that is, who is otherwise worthy of the name "man", and fit to receive the supernal soul, but who has allowed himself to be blemished and defiled so that the Shekinah cannot abide with him. We read further: OR BE IN A JOURNEY AFAR OFF. There is a dot over the resh of the word rehokah (afar off) to indicate that if a man sullies himself here, they sully him on high. He is thus "in a journey afar off", far away from the region and the path which the seed of Israel have chosen.' R. Isaac remarked: 'Is it not written, "If a man... shall be unclean... or be in a journey afar off", thus signifying two different cases?' Said R. Yose: 'Just so. The former speaks of a man not yet defiled on high, whilst the latter refers to one who has been thus defiled. Neither upon the one nor upon the other, Scripture implies, can holiness rest, and so neither may offer up the paschal lamb at the time when the rest of Israel offer it up. As for the secondary paschal lamb, the man is only permitted to offer it after he has purified himself and repaired his defect. Israel, however, who offered the Passover in its proper time, stand in a higher degree in that they receive the beneficences of the Moon and the Sun [Tr. note: Malkuth and Tifereth.] together.'

[Note: The last 8 lines of the Hebrew text are not found in our translation]

Zohar: Bemidbar, Section 3, Page 153a

[Note: The Hebrew text of this page is not found in our translation]

Zohar: Bemidbar, Section 3, Page 153b

AND ON THE DAY THAT THE TABERNACLE WAS REARED UP. R. Hiya cited here the verse: "He hath scattered abroad, he hath given to the needy, his righteousness stands forever" (PS. CXII, 9). 'The term "scattered" here', he said, 'is to be interpreted in the light of the saying: "There is that scattereth, and increaseth all the more" (Prov. XI, 24), that is, increaseth in riches, increases in life. Besides, the term nosaf (increaseth) has the secondary meaning of "gathering in", thus pointing to the region of death. The verse thus says that such a man draws to himself, where death would otherwise have been, an increase of life from on high.' R. Judah said, in the name of R. Hiya: 'This verse testifies that whoever gives to the poor induces the Tree of Life to add of itself to the Tree of Death, [Tr. note: The Shekinah.] so that life and joy prevail on high, and so that that man, whenever in need, has the Tree of Life to stand by him and the Tree of Death to shield him. The verse continues, "and his charity [Tr. note: zidkatho=his righteousness; in later Hebrew=his charity.] standeth forever", that is, it stands by him to provide him with life and strength; as he has awakened life, so will the two Trees stand by him to shield him and grant him an increase of life.'

[Note: The following passage does not appear in our Hebrew text.]

R. Abba said: 'Every time the tabernacle was set up by the hands of men there was a day of universal joy, and the sacred Oil was poured into the lamps, and these all shed their light abroad, and those who brought this about won redemption for themselves in this world and life in the next. Thus "righteousness delivereth from death".'

Zohar: Bemidbar, Section 3, Page 154a [Note: The first 10 lines of the Hebrew text are not found in our translation]

MAKE UNTO THEE TWO TRUMPETS OF SILVER, ETC. R. Simeon adduced here the verse: "And when the Hayoth (living creatures) went, the wheels went hard by them; and when the Hayoth were lifted up from the bottom the wheels were lifted up" (Ezek. I, 19). 'The Hayoth', he said, 'are borne along by the supernal power; and so were the movements of the tribes below who bore on their standards the likenesses of the Hayoth, that of Lion, Eagle, Ox, Man. Angels attended each of the standards. The first standard bore the likeness of Lion and was attended by Michael, who had under him two chieftains, Zophiel and Zadkiel. When these set out numerous armed hosts moved in unison on the right-hand side whilst the sun on the left illumined them. The Lion put forth his right hand and summoned to himself all his hosts, to wit, three hundred and seventy thousand lions, and they all assembled round him. When this Lion roars all the firmaments and all their hosts and legions quiver and shake. The Fiery River blazes forth and sinks a thousand and five hundred stages to the lower Gehinnom. Then all the sinners in the Gehinnom shake and tremble and burn in the fire. So Scripture says: "The lion hath roared, who will not fear?" (Amos III, 8). A second roar he emits, which is taken up by his entourage of three hundred and seventy thousand lions. Then he puts forth his left hand, when all the "masters of Rigour" here below are seized with fear and are bowed down underneath that hand. So we read: "Thy hand shall be on the neck of thy enemies" (Gen. XLIX, 8). Each of the Hayoth had four wings formed of white flaming fire, as well as four faces turned towards the four cardinal points, all illumined by the white light of the sun; the one turned to the east was illumined with a joyous light, the one towards the west with a concentrated light, the one towards the north was within the penumbra of the sun. These contained three groups. [Tr. note: Corresponding to the three tribes under each standard.] One numbered seventy-four thousand and six hundred. These were of the higher grades. There were, besides, a long succession of lower grades. These were innumerable. The second group contained fifty-four thousand and four hundred besides

Zohar: Bemidbar, Section 3, Page 154b

those of the lower grades, who were innumerable. The third group, which followed behind, contained fifty-seven thousand and four hundred. So soon as the first standard began to march the tabernacle was taken down, and all the Levites chanted hymns, and the lords of praise were all ranged there "for the spirit of the Hayoth was in the Ophanim (Wheels)". The second standard bore on it the Eagle, symbolic of the angel Uriel, and was ranged on the south. Two chieftains accompanied him, namely, Shamshiel and Hasdiel. When the Eagle arose all the winged forces went in front, accompanied by innumerable hosts on all sides. When he set off he put forth his right pinion, and gathered unto him all his hosts to the number of three hundred and fifty thousand. Three groups belonged to that standard; the first contained forty-six thousand and five hundred, the second fifty-nine thousand and three hundred, and the third fifty-four thousand six hundred and fifty. Two heralds, emerging out of these two flanks, marched in front of all these hosts. At their proclamation there assembled all hosts and legions, living creatures, small and large. All the firmaments indeed moved forward along with these hosts in front of the tabernacle. We thus read: "And when the Hayoth went, the Ophanim went hard by them". Then follows the third standard to the north. It had for its ensign Ox and was accompanied by the angel Gabriel and his two chieftains, Kafziel and Hizkiel. The Ox, being of the left side, has horns between his two eyes, which flame as it were with burning fire; he gores and tramples with his feet ruthlessly. When he moos there emerge out of the hollow of the great abyss numerous spirits of wrath who proceed in front in a chorus of shrieking. Seven fiery rivers flow in front of him, and when thirsty he draws up a whole riverful at one gulp. Yet this river is straightway filled again as before, unfailingly. And were it not for a stream of water from the region of the lion quenching the fiery coals, the world could not endure. It is a region where the sun never rises, and where numberless spirits roam about in the darkness, and the fire of the burning river is itself dark and black. You may wonder that there should be such things as fire of various hues, white, black, red and of double hue, but indeed it is so. Thus we have learnt that the Torah was written with black fire on white fire.

Zohar: Bemidbar, Section 3, Page 155a

Now the third standard also had under it three divisions. One contained sixty-two thousand and seven hundred; the second forty-one thousand and five hundred; whilst the third contained fifty-three thousand and four hundred. All this besides all the other grades scattered all around them, grades upon grades innumerable, as well as lower grades, executioners, who have the impudence of a dog and bite like an ass. Woe to whoever finds himself near them and under their judgement! On the fourth side the fourth standard, on the west, had for its symbol Man, the angel Raphael, [Tr. note: Whose chief function, as his name (RaFA=to cure) denotes, was the healing of men.] with whom there is healing. Blessed are Israel in whose glory the Holy One, blessed be He, delights, and to whom He assigned a portion above all other nations and in whose praise He glorifies Himself, as we read: "And he said unto me, Thou art my servant", etc. (Isa. XLIX, 3).'

AND IT CAME TO PASS WHEN THE ARK SET FORWARD. R. Eleazar said: 'What is the meaning of the inverted letter Nun introduced here twice? [Tr. note: In the Massoretic text there are inserted here two isolated Nuns, turned upside down and sideways, one preceding and the other following the two verses beginning with our text.] We explain it thus. We read a little before: "And the ark of the covenant of the Lord went before them three days' journey, to seek a resting-place for them,'. Now, as soon as the ark set off the Nun [Tr. note: i.e. the Shekinah symbolized by this letter.] accompanied it, with its face turned towards Israel. The Shekinah ever hovered over the ark, but the love of the Holy One, blessed be He, towards Israel was such that even though they strayed from the straight path He would not forsake them, but always turned His countenance towards them, for otherwise they could not endure in the world. So that whilst "the ark... went before them three days' journey", the Nun (symbol of the Shekinah) remained inseparable from it, and accompanied it, yet turned her face away from the ark and towards Israel, like a young hart that, whilst going, turns its face towards its starting-point. Thus when Moses said, "Rise, O Lord...", implying "do not forsake us, turn Thy face towards us", the Nun turned round facing Israel in the manner of one turning his face towards his beloved friend. "And when it rested" the Nun turned its face again towards the ark.' Said R. Simeon: 'O Eleazar, assuredly it is as you said, saving that when the ark rested the Shekinah did not turn her countenance away from Israel. This is clearly shown by the second Nun, which is also of an inverted shape. The truth is that when Moses said "Return, O Lord", and the ark rested, the Shekinah turned back and stood on the other side of the ark, [Tr. note: i.e. instead of between the ark and Israel, as during the journey.] but her countenance turned both

Zohar: Bemidbar, Section 3, Page 155b

towards Israel and towards the ark. Israel, however, caused afterwards the turning away of the Shekinah from them. So we read: And the people were as murmurers (K'mithonnim)." [Tr. note: A play upon the Hebrew word, which contains two Nuns of ordinary shape, their faces, as it were, being away from Israel.] Said R. Eleazar: 'What I said I found in the Book of R. Yeba the Elder.' R. Simeon replied: 'What he said is rightly said, but you will find my exposition in the book of R. Hamnuna the Elder, and this is assuredly the right exposition.'

NOW THE MANNA WAS LIKE CORIANDER (gad) SEED. Said R. Yose: 'The term gad (lit. troops) signifies that the manna had the virtue of inducing propagation. It implies further that in the same way as the seed of Gad took their portion in another land, [Tr. note: i.e. outside the border of the Holy Land proper, in Transjordan.] so the manna hovered over Israel outside the Holy Land. We may also explain the words to mean that it was white in appearance, like coriander seed, and coagulated when it reached the atmosphere, and was transmuted into material substance [Tr. note: i.e. out of its ethereal state.] inside the body. [Tr. note: Al. "it was absorbed by the body", i.e. without leaving any waste, as with material food. v. T.B. Yoma, 75b.] AND THE APPEARANCE THEREOF AS THE APPEARANCE OF BDELLIUM, to wit, it was white in colour like bdellium, this being the colour of the Right in the supernal sphere.'

AND IF THOU (at) DEAL THUS WITH ME. R. Isaac asked: 'For what reason did Moses make use of the feminine form at (thou) instead of the masculine atta? The reason is', he explained, 'that Moses directed his words towards the realm of

671

death, the realm associated with the female principle. Therefore he said "Kill me, I pray thee, out of hand', an invocation to the Tree of Death. Hence the feminine at.

AND THE LORD SAID UNTO MOSES: GATHER UNTO ME SEVENTY MEN.... The Holy One, blessed be He, in effect said to him: On every such occasion you wish to die, [Tr. note: Allusion to "blot me, I pray thee out of thy book..." (Ex. XXXII, 32), in connection with the Golden Calf.] so "I will take of the spirit which is upon thee, and will put it upon them". Observe that Moses was here made to know that he would die [in the wilderness] and not enter into the Land, as, in fact, Eldad and Medad announced. [Tr. note: v. T.B. Sanhedrin, 17a.] This is a lesson that in time of wrath a man ought not to utter anything in the nature of a curse against himself, inasmuch as ever so many malignant powers are standing by, ready to take up that utterance. On the other occasion, when Moses prayed for death to himself [Tr. note: Viz. in connection with the Golden Calf.] his request was not taken up, for the reason that Moses meant it all for the benefit of Israel. Here, on the other hand, Moses only gave vent to his anger and anguish of heart; his words, therefore, were taken up, and Eldad and Medad, who remained in the camp, announced, "Moses will be gathered in and Joshua will bring Israel into the Land". This made Joshua jealous for the sake of Moses, and so he came to him and said, "My lord Moses, restrain them", or, as we might also render, "withhold from them these words". But Moses, regardless of his own glory, did not consent. Observe the meekness evinced in the reply of Moses: "Art thou jealous for my sake?" Happy is the portion of Moses, who rose high above the highest prophets (al. the prophets of the world).' R. Judah remarked: 'All the prophets were to Moses like the moon to the sun.'

One night R. Abba was sitting and studying the Torah, R. Yose and R. Hizkiah being with him. Said R. Yose: 'How obtuse are mankind that they have no regard whatever for the things of the other world.' Said R. Abba: 'This is caused by the badness of their heart, which spreads through all the members of the body.' He then cited the verse: "There is an evil which I have seen under the sun, and it is heavy upon man" (Eccl. VI, 1). 'The evil here referred to', he said, 'is the evil residing in the hardened heart that longs to obtain dominion in affairs of this world, but is altogether regardless of the other world. Scripture continues: "a man to whom God giveth riches, wealth and honour..." (Ibid. 2). There is here an apparent contradiction, since it first says, "so that he wanteth nothing for his soul of all that he desireth", and then goes on, "yet God giveth him not power to eat thereof". If he is in want of nothing for himself, how can we say that God gives him not power to eat thereof? There is, however, an inner meaning here as in all the words of Solomon, and although we have to take note also of the outer garb, we must look deeper into the meaning of this verse, which is as follows. There is a man to whom

Zohar: Bemidbar, Section 3, Page 156a

the Holy One, blessed be He, gives a certain riches which he may enjoy in the next world and which may remain with him as a capital, to wit, the ever-enduring capital, which consists of the realm of the bundle of souls. It is thus incumbent on man to reserve and leave behind him that capital, which he will receive after he has left this world. This capital is indeed the Tree of Life belonging to the other world, the fruit of which alone has any place or room in this world. The good man thus enjoys its fruit in this world whilst the capital remains for him for the other world, where he obtains the superior celestial life. But if a man has sullied himself and followed his selfish desires, and "wanted nothing", that is, abstained from gratifying no desire, then that Tree remains apart and will not acknowledge him on high, for "God giveth him not power to eat thereof" and to have the reward of that riches, "but a stranger eateth it", as we read elsewhere: "He may prepare it, but the just shall put it on" (Job XXVII, 17). It thus behoves man to use what the Holy One, blessed be He, has given him so as thereby to merit the next world. He will thus enjoy of it in this world and have the capital left for the next world to be bound up in the bundle of life.' Said R. Yose: 'Assuredly it is so.' R. Yose further said: 'It is written: AND IF THOU DEAL THUS WITH ME, KILL ME, I PRAY THEE, OUT OF HAND.... Is it likely', he asked, 'that Moses, the meekest of men, should have wished death for himself just because the Israelites asked him for food?' R. Abba said in reply: 'There is a deep mystery here which I have learnt. Moses did no evil in His sight, and his asking for death was not by reason of Israel's asking for food. Mark now, that Moses was attached to a high grade to which no other prophet attained. And so when the Holy One, blessed be He, said to him, "Behold, I will cause to rain bread from heaven for you" (Ex. XVI, 4), he rejoiced, saying: Verily, there is completeness found in me, seeing that it is for my sake that the manna is now provided for Israel. But when Moses saw that they lowered themselves again to the other grade, and asked for flesh, "If so", he said, "my own grade must be blemished, since it was for my sake that the Israelites have the manna in the wilderness." He therefore besought death for himself rather than fall from his high grade. So the Lord said unto him: GATHER UNTO ME SEVENTY MEN, reassuring him thereby that his grade was not blemished, adding thus, AND I WILL TAKE OF THE SPIRIT THAT IS UPON THEE, AND WILL PUT IT UPON THEM, inasmuch as they all are of the degree of the Moon, and so need the Sun [Tr. note: i.e. Moses.] to illumine them; and so this food would not descend for the sake of Moses. Happy the portion of Moses, whom the Holy One, blessed be He, desires to honour, and whom He loves above all other prophets, communicating with him without an intermediary, as it says, "With him do I speak mouth to mouth".

'AND MOSES CRIED UNTO THE LORD SAYING: HEAL HER NOW, O GOD, I BESEECH THEE. In this prayer is involved the mystery of the Divine Name formed of eleven letters, and Moses did not wish to lengthen his prayer further, for the reason that, since it concerned his own, [Tr. note: i.e. his own sister.] he was unwilling

Zohar: Bemidbar, Section 3, Page 156b

to trouble the King, as it were, overmuch. Therefore God was solicitous for the honour of Moses; and, indeed, everywhere He is more solicitous for the honour of the righteous than for His own.'

SHELAH LECHA

AND THE LORD SPAKE UNTO MOSES SAYING, SEND THEE MEN TO SPY OUT THE LAND OF CANAAN, ETC. R. Hiya here cited the verse: "Hast thou caused the dayspring to know his place", etc. (Job XXXVIII, 12). 'Note', he said, 'that Moses was the sun, and when he desired to enter the land, God said to him, Moses, when the light of the sun arrives, the moon

Zohar: Bemidbar, Section 3, Page 157a

is embraced in it, but the sun and the moon cannot shine together; the moon cannot shine till the sun is gathered in. Now thou art not permitted to enter, but if thou wouldst fain know of the land, send thee man who will inform thee. For Moses already knew at this time that he was not to enter the land, and since he wanted to know of it before he departed, he sent the spies. When they failed to bring him back a proper report, he did not send again, but waited till God showed him the land.

'The first instruction that Moses gave to the spies was to inquire "whether there were trees in it or no". Moses in fact knew already, and what he really referred to was the Tree of Life, of which the proper place is the terrestrial Garden of Eden. He said: If this tree is in it, I shall enter, but if not, I shall not be able to enter. Observe that there are two Trees, [Tr. note: Tifereth and Malkuth.] one higher and one lower, in the one of which is life and in the other death, and he who confuses them brings death upon himself in this world and has no portion in the world to come.' Said R. Isaac: 'Moses took to himself the Tree of Life, and therefore he wished to know whether it was in the land or not.'

SEND THEE MEN. R. Judah quoted here the verse: "Like the coolness of snow in the day of harvest, so is a faithful messenger to one who sends him, he refresheth the soul of his master" (Prov. xxv, 13). "'The faithful messenger" is exemplified in Caleb and Phineas, who were sent by Joshua and brought back the Shekinah to abide in Israel. But those whom Moses sent were a source of weeping to future generations, and caused many thousands to perish from Israel.'

As R. Hizkiah and R. Jesse were once walking together, the latter said: 'I see from your looks that some thought is troubling you.' He replied: 'I am pondering on the verse: "For that which befalleth the sons of man befalleth beasts, even one thing befalleth them" (Eccl. III, 19). This saying of the wise Solomon troubles me, because it seems to give an opening to the unbelievers.'

Zohar: Bemidbar, Section 3, Page 157b

'That is assuredly so,' he replied. At that moment a man came up to them and asked them for water, as he was thirsty and weary from the heat of the sun. They asked him who he was. He replied that he was a Jew. 'Have you studied the Torah?' they asked. He replied: 'Instead of talking with you, I can go up to that hill and find water there and drink.' R. Jesse thereupon brought out a flask full of water and gave it to him. When he had drunk, they said: 'We will go up there with you for water.' So they went up to the rock and found there a trickling stream from which they filled a bottle. They then sat down, and the man said to them: 'You just now asked me if I had studied the Torah. I have done so through a son of mine whom I have put under a teacher, and from whom I have gained some knowledge of the Torah.' R. Hizkiah said to him: 'If it is through your son, well and good; but I see that for the solution of our problem we shall have to look somewhere else.' The man said: 'Let me hear it, since sometimes in the beggar's wallet one finds a pearl.' They then quoted to him the verse of Solomon. He said to them: 'Wherein are you different from all other men who also do not know?' They replied: 'Wherein then?' He then said: 'That is the way in which Solomon meant this verse. He was not saying it in his own name like the rest of the book, but was repeating what is said by worldly fools, that "the hap of man and the hap of the beast", etc.; that is to say, that this world is the sport of chance, and there is no Providence, but "the hap of man and the hap of beast is the same". When Solomon observed this, he called those fools themselves "cattle", as it says in the next verse, "I said in my heart concerning this saying of the sons of men that God should put them on one side and that (the faithful) should see that they are cattle for themselves". A curse on those cattle, on those fools, on those faithless unbelievers! Better they had never come into the world! What did Solomon answer them? "Who knows the spirit of the sons of man which goeth upwards and the spirit of the beast which goeth downwards to the earth?" Who of those fools that wot not of the honour of the supreme King knows that the spirit of the sons of man goes upwards to a supernal, precious and holy place to be nourished by the supernal brightness of the Holy King and to be included in the "bundle of the living", while the spirit of the beast goes downwards to the earth, and not to that place where is every man of those of whom it is written, "In the image of God he made man"? How can those foolish unbelievers say that there is one spirit to all? They shall be like chaff before the wind, and will be left in Gehinnom and not ascend for all generations.'

R. Hizkiah and R. Jesse thereupon came and kissed him on his head, saying: 'All this you knew and we were not aware! Blessed the hour in which we met thee!'

Zohar: Bemidbar, Section 3, Page 158a

He then proceeded: 'This is not the only instance of such a usage. There is, for instance, the verse: "This is evil in all that is done under the sun, for there is one hap to all" (Ibid. IX, 3): as much as to say, "What the evil man says is, There is one hap to all". And he goes on: "For he who chooses (the future world) does naught, [Tr. note: Translating the Kethib of Eccl. IX, 4.] for we are well assured that for all the living there is trust", and also that a live dog is better than a dead lion.' They said to him: 'Would you mind if we join you, and you should accompany us?' He replied: 'Were I to do so, the Torah would call me a fool, and, moreover, I should render my life forfeit.' 'Why so', they asked. 'Because', he said, 'I am a messenger, and King Solomon said, "He cutteth short his own legs, and drinketh in damage who sendeth words by the hand of a fool" (Prov. XXVI, 6). For the spies, because they did not prove trusty and faithful messengers forfeited their lives both in this world and the next.' He then embraced them and departed. R. Hizkiah and R. Yose also went their way, and meeting some men they inquired about the stranger. They were told that he was R. Haggai and one of the leading Companions, and that the Companions in Babylon had sent him to make some inquiries of R. Simeon and the other Companions. Said R. Jesse: 'Assuredly this is the R. Haggai who was always unwilling to let it be known that he is a scholar, and therefore it was that he told us that he learnt the Torah through his son. Verily he is a faithful messenger, and happy is the man who has committed his message to him. So, too, Eleazar, the servant of Abraham, was accursed in virtue of being a Canaanite, but because he was a faithful messenger he escaped from his curse and was blessed in the name of the Lord (Gen. XXIV, 31). ALL OF THEM MEN. They were all virtuous, but they were misled by a false reasoning. They said: If Israel enter the land, we will be superseded, since it is only in the wilderness that we are accounted worthy to be leaders, and this was what caused their death and the death of all who followed them.

Zohar: Bemidbar, Section 3, Page 158b [Note: The first 8 lines of the Hebrew text are not found in our translation]

AND MOSES CALLED HOSHEA THE SON OF NUN JOSHUA: As much as to say: May KAH save thee from them!' R. Abba said: 'As he was being sent for the purpose of entering the land, it was requisite that he should be perfect, to wit, through the Shekinah, for up to that time he had been called "a lad", and therefore Moses joined the Shekinah with him. And though we find the name Joshua before this in the text (e.g. Ex. XVII, 9; XXXIII, 11), it is there used in anticipation.'

WHETHER THERE ARE TREES (lit. tree) IN IT OR NOT (ayin). Said R. Hiya: 'Did not Moses know that there were trees in it, seeing that God had told him that it was a land flowing with milk and honey?' R. Simeon said: 'What he said was this: "If you see that the produce of the land is like that of other lands, then the Tree of Life is in it, but it does not derive from a still higher place. But if you see that its produce is superior to that of all the rest of the world, then you will know that that difference originates from the Ancient Holy One who is called ayin (nothing), and you will know the answer to the question once asked by the Israelites, "whether the Lord is in our midst or ayin" (Ex. XVII, 7).'

AND THEY WENT UP IN THE SOUTH AND (HE) CAME TO HEBRON. It should surely be "they came"?'

R. Yose said: 'The reference is to Caleb, who went to pray over the graves of the patriarchs. Caleb said: Joshua has been blessed by Moses with support from heaven, and can therefore be delivered from these. What shall I do? He therefore conceived the idea of praying on the graves of the patriarchs in order to keep clear of the evil counsel of the other spies.' R. Isaac said: 'That which was more distinguished than all of them went in within him;

Zohar: Bemidbar, Section 3, Page 159a

the Shekinah entered the land in Caleb in order to bring tidings to the patriarchs that the time had arrived for their descendants to come into the land which God had sworn to give them.

AND THERE WERE AHIMAN, ETC. We have learnt that Ahiman, Sheshai and Talmai were of the descendants of the giants whom God cast down upon the earth and who begat children from the daughters of men.'

AND THEY CAME TO THE BROOK OF ESHCOL. As R. Judah was once walking along with R. Abba, he said to him: 'I should like to ask you one question. Seeing that God knew that man was destined to sin and to be condemned to death, why did He create him? That He knew this is proved by the fact that in the Torah, which existed two thousand years before the universe, we find it already written, "When a man shall die in a tent", and so forth. Why does God want man in this world, seeing that if he studies the Torah he dies, and if he does not study he also dies, all going one way.' He replied: 'What business have you with the ways and the decrees of your Master? What you are permitted to know and to inquire into, that you may ask, and as for what you are not permitted to know, it is written: "Suffer not thy mouth to cause thy flesh to sin" (Eccl. v, 6).' He said to him: 'If that is the case, all the Torah is secret and recondite, since it is the Holy Name, and if so we have no permission to ask and inquire?' He replied: 'The Torah is both hidden and revealed, and the Holy Name is also hidden and revealed, as it is written, "The hidden things belong to the Lord our God, and the revealed things are for us and for our children" (Deut. XXIX, 29). The revealed things we may inquire into, but the

674

hidden things are for the Lord alone. Hence men are not permitted to utter secret things and divulge them, save only the Holy Lamp, R. Simeon, since the Holy One, blessed be He, has concurred with him, and because his generation is distinguished both on high and below, and therefore things are divulged through him, and there shall be no such another generation till the Messiah comes. Now, as for your question. The Holy One, blessed be He, has three words in which He is enshrouded. The first [Tr. note: Aziluth.] is a supernal recondite one which is known only to Him who is concealed therein. The second [Tr. note: Beriah.] one is linked with the first and is the one from which the Holy One, blessed be He, is known. The third [Tr. note: Yezirah.] is a lower one in which is found separation, and in this abide the celestial angels, and the Holy One, blessed be He, is both in it and not in it, so that all ask, "Where is the place of his glory?" Similarly man has

Zohar: Bemidbar, Section 3, Page 159b

three worlds. The first is the one which is called "the world of separation", in which man both is and is not; as we look at him he departs and vanishes. The second is the world which is linked with the higher world, being the terrestrial Garden of Eden, while the third is a hidden recondite and unknowable world. Now the first world is a stepping-stone to the others, and did not man sin he would not have a taste of death when he is about to enter those other worlds and when the spirit is divested of the body. But as it is, the spirit has to be cleansed in the "stream of fire" to receive its punishment, and then it enters the terrestrial Garden of Eden, and it is furnished with a robe of light resembling its appearance in this world, and therewith it is equipped, and then its abode is there continually, and on New Moons and Sabbaths it attaches itself to the super-soul and ascends aloft. This is the essence of the matter, and so it is with all save the sinners who are cut off from all worlds if they do not effect repentance.' Said R. Judah: 'Blessed be God that I put this question and gained this knowledge.'

R. Simeon said: 'All this section (Num. XIII) can be expounded esoterically. God praises the Torah and says: "Walk in My ways and devote yourselves to My service, and I will bring you in to good and noble worlds." To men who will not believe this God says: "Go and spy out that good and desirable land." They say: "How are we to spy it out and to find out all this?' Therefore it is written: "Go up here in the south": study the Torah, and from it you will know that the land is before you. "And ye shall see the land what it is": from it you shall see the world of that inheritance into which I am bringing you. "And the people that dwell in it": those are the righteous in the Garden of Eden who stand in rows in the celestial glory. "Whether he is strong or weak": through this you shall see whether they attained to all this when they conquered their evil inclination or no, or when they clung fast to the Torah to study it night and day, or if they relaxed their hold on it and still attained to all this. "Whether they be many or few": whether they be many that devote themselves to my service and cling to the Torah in order to attain to all this or not. "And what is the land, whether it is fat or lean": from the Torah ye shall discover what is the nature of that other world, whether it confers in abundance heavenly bliss on those that dwell there or withholds from them anything. "Whether there are in it trees or no": whether the Tree of Life is therein for all eternity, and whether the "bundle of the living" is there or not.

Zohar: Bemidbar, Section 3, Page 160a

"And they went up by the south": men go up therein halfheartedly, like one working for nothing, since they think it brings no reward and they see that the riches of this world are lost through it, until "he comes to Hebron", that is, he comes to read and re-read it. "And there were Ahiman, Sheshai and Talmai": there they see great contrasts, unclean and clean, forbidden and permitted, punishments and rewards. "And they came to the brook of Eshcol": these are the words of Agadah which strengthen faith. "And they cut from there a branch": they teach from there general principles which rejoice the true believers and show them how all is reduced to one principle without deviation. But the sceptical and those who do not learn the Torah for its own sake find deviation, as it says, "and they carried it on upon a pole between two". Then, "they returned from spying out the land": they turn from the way of truth and return to the evil side, saying: What use is this? Till this day we have derived no benefit; we have laboured for nothing. We have made ourselves laughing-stocks, and as for the other world, who can make himself worthy to enter it? We have laboured and toiled to find out what is the portion of that world, and "indeed it is flowing with milk and honey"; that other world is indeed good. "Howbeit the people are fierce": he that would study must be strong-minded so as to disregard this world, and therefore he should be well provided with money, and also a strong body, since the study of the Torah weakens a man's strength. And should a man say that with all this he will still manage, "Amalek dwells in the south land": the evil inclination, the seducer of man, is always in his body, "and the Hivite and the Amorite": many are the accusers there to prevent a man entering into that world; so who can attain it? Thus "they spread an evil report of the land". What say then the faithful? "If the Lord delight in us, he will give it to us": if a man seeks with all his heart to serve God, only the heart is required;

Zohar: Bemidbar, Section 3, Page 160b

only "rebel not against the Lord": he should not rebel against the Torah, for the Torah demands not wealth nor vessels of gold or silver. "Neither fear ye the people of the land": for if a broken body will study the Torah, it will find healing therein. "For they are bread for us": those accusers themselves provide every day food for those who study the Torah.' AND THEY CAME UNTO THE VALLEY OF ESHCOL. R. Abba said: 'They cut off the cluster, and when they came to raise it they were not able, nor even to move it, but Caleb and Joshua came and lifted it. While joined to the tree it was called a "branch", but afterwards a "staff". Through this Joshua and Caleb knew that they were destined to enter into the land and obtain a portion in it. On the way the others plotted against them, so Caleb addressed the branch, saying: Fruit, fruit, if for thee we are to be killed, why should we have thee? Straightway it lightened itself and they gave it to them.' R. Eleazar said: 'They did not give it to any other, but when they came back to the Israelites they gave it to them, and withdrew into the background.' R. Isaac said: 'When they came into the presence of the Anakim they displayed before them the staff of Moses and so were delivered.' R. Judah said: 'We have a tradition that Moses transmitted to them the Holy Name, and through this they were delivered.' R. Hiya said: 'The giants were called by three names: Nefilim, Anakim, Refaim. Their original name was Nefilim, and when they associated with the daughters of men they were called Anakim, and then when they went about the world and neglected the Heavenly One they were called Refaim. They lived to a great age until at last half their body became paralysed while the other half remained vigorous. They would then take a certain herb and throw it into their mouths and die, and because they thus killed themselves they were called Refaim.' R. Isaac said that they used to drown themselves in the sea, as it is written, "The Refaim are slain beneath the waters" (Job XXVI, 5). R. Simeon said: 'Had Israel entered the land under the sign of

Zohar: Bemidbar, Section 3, Page 161a

the evil tongue, they would not have endured an instant. Observe how much evil was wrought by the evil tongue: it called forth the decree that our ancestors should not enter the land, those that uttered it died, and weeping was decreed for succeeding generations. Their calumny of the Holy Land was, as it were, a calumny of the Almighty, and therefore God was indignant on account of this, and all Israel would have been destroyed but for the prayer of Moses.

AND THEY TOLD HIM: the word "told" (sapper) means "explaining in detail". WE CAME: as much as to say, "We entered into that land of which you were always singing the praises'. AND SURELY IT FLOWETH WITH MILK AND HONEY: R. Isaac said that if a man wants to deceive he should first say something true so that he may be believed. R. Hiya, however, said that what they meant was, "We came into the land which you praised so much and which you said was flowing with milk and honey, and this is its fruit! If this is the inheritance which God is giving to Israel and for which they have endured such sufferings, there is fruit in Egypt twice as good.

HOWBEIT THE PEOPLE THAT DWELL IN THE LAND ARE FIERCE: as a rule the best warriors are stationed outside the towns to protect the roads, but here even those who dwell in the cities are mighty men. AND THE CITIES ARE FORTIFIED: even if all the kings of the world were to assemble against them, they could make no impression on them. R. Yose said: 'The worst of their calumnies was that AMALEK DWELLS IN THE LAND OF THE SOUTH: so when a man has been bitten by a snake, if people want to frighten him they say, There is a snake here. So they said: That one that made war on you before is here, and where? In the land of the south, by which you have to enter. Straightway ALL THE CONGREGATION LIFTED UP THEIR VOICE AND CRIED: they doomed that night to be one of weeping for all generations. 'AND NOW, I PRAY THEE, LET THE POWER OF THE LORD BE GREAT. Observe that when God created man, He formed him on the supernal pattern, and placed his strength and power in the middle of the body where the heart is. Now the heart

Zohar: Bemidbar, Section 3, Page 161b

is closely attached to a place above it, to wit, the brain. In a similar way did God fashion the world. He placed the ocean round about the inhabited world, and the habitation of the seventy nations round about Jerusalem. Jerusalem itself is round about the Temple Mount, and the Temple Mount round about the courts of the Israelites, and the courts of the Israelites round about the Chamber of Hewn Stone where the Great Sanhedrin used to sit, and this again was round the place of the altar, and the place of the altar round the court, and the court round the Temple proper, and the Temple round the Holy of Holies, where the Shekinah used to abide, and there was the heart of the whole world, and the whole world was nourished from there, while this heart itself was nourished from the brain and the two were linked together. Similarly in a higher sphere, in the mystery of the supernal King. The Stream of Fire is round about many camps, which again are round certain Ministers, who in turn surround the four Chariots, which again surround the Holy City, which rests upon them. Thus ultimately it is found that all is nourished from the supernal hidden Brain, and when examined all are found to be linked together. Now when the Hidden Ancient One illumines the Brain, and the Brain the Heart by the way of "the pleasantness of the Lord", then this is the "power of the Lord"; and Moses now prayed that it might be magnified and ascend higher and higher, and then be drawn doun below. As THOU HAST SPOKEN: as we have explained. SAYING: that is, that all future generations should learn to use this address in the time of trouble, namely, THE LORD IS SLOW TO ANGER, ETC. R. Isaac asked: 'Why is "truth" not mentioned here (among the attributes)?' R. Hiya answered: 'Because they caused it to depart through having spoken falsely; they were thus punished with measure for measure.'

[Tr. note: There is here a lacuna in the text.]... with one another things that they had not been able to discuss previously. They went out through that door and sat down in a garden under some trees. They said: 'Now that we are here and see all this, if we die here we shall certainly enter the future world.' So they sat there and fell asleep, until the guardian came

Zohar: Bemidbar, Section 3, Page 162a

and woke them, saying: 'Rise and go forth into the outer garden'. So they went out and found the Masters of Holy Writ expounding the verse, IN THIS WILDERNESS THEY SHALL BE CONSUMED: but not (they said) in any other place. AND THERE THEY SHALL DIE: but not in any other place. This speaks of the bodies, but in regard to their souls they shall be like the denizens of the Garden.

The guardian then told them to leave the garden, and they went out with him. He said to them: 'Did you hear anything from that grade?' They replied: 'We heard a voice say, "He who interrupts shall be interrupted, he who shortens shall be shortened, he who shortens shall be lengthened".' 'Did you understand what it meant,' he asked, and they answered, 'No'. He said to them: 'Did you observe a mighty eagle, and a boy who gathered herbs? R. Ilai of Nisibis and his son once came here and saw this cave, and when they went into it they could not endure the darkness and died. The boy stands every day before Bezalel when he comes down from the heavenly Academy and says three things. "He who interrupts shall be interrupted": that is, if one interrupts his study of the Torah to speak of idle matters, his life shall be interrupted in this world and his judgement awaits him in the other world. "He who shortens shall be shortened": if one shortens his "Amen", and does not draw it out, his life shall be shortened. "He who shortens shall be lengthened": the first syllable of ehad (one) [Tr. note: In the Shema.] should be uttered very rapidly and not dwelt on at all; and if one does so, his life will be prolonged.' They said to him: 'He also said: "They are two, and one is joined to them, making three, and when they are three they are one".' He said to them: 'These are the two names "Lord" in the Shema; [Tr. note: "Hear, O Israel, the Lord our God, the Lord is one."] "our God" is, as it were, the signature, and when they are joined they form one.' They said to him: 'He also said: "They are two and have become one; when he has sway he flies on the wings of the wind and traverses two hundred thousand and hides himself".' He said to them: 'These are the two cherubim on which the Holy One, blessed be He, used to ride, but from the day that Joseph has been hidden from his brethren one has been hidden away in two hundred thousand worlds, and He who was wont to ride upon it has hidden himself. Now go forth from here.'

They went forth and the guardian gave them a rose, and the mouth of the cave closed, leaving nothing visible. They saw the eagle come down from a tree and enter another cave. They smelt the rose and entered there, and the eagle said to them: 'Enter, ye truly virtuous, for yours is the first society I have enjoyed since I came here.' They went in and came to another garden along with the eagle. When they came to the Masters of the Mishnah the eagle took the form of a man in a resplendent robe like theirs and sat down with them. He said to them: 'Pay honour to the scholars of the Mishnah who have come here, since their teacher showed us many wonderful things here.' One of them said to them: 'Have you a token?' They said: 'Yes', and brought out the two roses. They smelt them and said to them: 'Sit, members of the Academy, sit, ye truly virtuous.' Then they took hold of them and they sat down and learnt thirty rules that they did not know before, and other mysteries of the Torah.

They then went back to the Masters of Holy Writ and found them expounding the verse: "I said, Ye are gods, and all of you sons of the Most High" (Ps. LXXXII, 6). 'This', they said, 'is what God said when Israel at Mount Sinai said "we will do" before "we will hear", [Tr. note: v. Ex. XXIV, 7] but when they followed their evil imagination He said, "Verily like Adam ye shall die"; like Adam, that is, whose death drew him down to the dust in order that the evil imagination in him might be wiped out; for it is that evil imagination which died and was consumed within him.'

Zohar: Bemidbar, Section 3, Page 162b

An old man who was at their head said: 'Here, too, it is written: AND YOUR CARCASES SHALL FALL IN THIS WILDERNESS. What is meant by "carcases"? The evil imagination. "In this wilderness they shall be consumed" (v. 35), to wit, these carcases, and there they shall die, because it is the will of the Holy One, blessed be He, to destroy those carcases from the world.'

R. Ilai said to them: 'Ye truly virtuous, enter and see, for permission is given you to enter as far as the place where the curtain is hung, happy is your lot!' So they arose and went to a place where there were Masters of the Agadah, [Tr. note: i.e. the Cabbalah.] their faces shining like the sun. 'Who are these,' they asked. He replied: 'These are the Masters of the Agadah who every day see the true splendour of the Torah. They stood there and heard many new expositions of the Torah, but they were not permitted to join with them. R. Ilai said to them: 'Come into another place and you will see.' They went into another garden and saw there people digging graves and dying immediately, and coming to life again with holy, luminous bodies. 'What does this mean?' they asked. He replied: 'They do this every day. As soon as they lie in the dust the evil taint which they received at first is consumed and they rise at once with new and luminous bodies, those

677

in which they stood at Mount Sinai. As you see them, so they stood at Mount Sinai, with bodies free from all taint; but when they drew upon themselves the evil imagination, they were changed into other bodies.'

A voice then came forth saying: 'Go, assemble, since Aholiab is in his place and all the thrones before him.' So the others all flew away and they were left alone under the trees of the garden. They saw a door and went in through it, and they then saw a temple, in which they went and sat down. Two young men were there. They lifted up their eyes and saw a tent embroidered with all sorts of figures in various colours, and over it a curtain of flashing light too dazzling to behold. They also heard a voice saying: 'Bezalel is the fourth of the supernal lights... ' [Tr. note: Here follow in the text a number of similar enigmatic utterances.] When the voice ceased the two youths said to them: 'Have you a token?' They said 'Yes', and brought out the two roses. They smelt them and said: 'Sit here till you shall hear two profound mysteries from the head of the Academy, which you must always keep secret.' They promised to do so. (Said R. Simeon: 'They wrote down all that they had seen, but when they came to this point they said, "I will take heed to my ways that I sin not with my tongue" (Ps. XXXIX, 2): I asked my father about those two words and he said to me: I swear to you, my son, those two words could build worlds and destroy worlds in the hands of one who knew how to use them.') When they had heard those two words the two youths said: 'Go out, go out, you are not permitted to hear any more.' One of them brought out an apple and said: 'Smell this'. They did so and went out, and forgot nothing of all they had seen.

Another guardian then came and said to them: 'Companions, R. Ilai has sent me to bid you wait here at the entrance of the cave till he comes and tells you notable things which you have not heard before; for he has asked

Zohar: Bemidbar, Section 3, Page 163a

permission from the Academy to reveal to you certain things.' So they went out and waited at the entrance of the cave, discussing with one another what they had seen and heard there. At last R. Ilai came, resplendent like the sun. They said to him: 'Have you heard any new exposition?' He said: 'Assuredly so, and permission has been given to me to tell you.' So they gathered together at the mouth of the cave and sat down. He said to them: 'Happy are you to have been shown by your Master the like of the other world. Are you not afraid?' They said: 'Assuredly, we can no longer feel like other human beings, being so amazed at all we have seen in this mountain.' He said to them: 'Do you see those rocks? They are the Heads of the Academies of this people in the wilderness, and they enjoy now privileges which they did not enjoy when they were alive. On New Moons and Sabbaths and festivals these Heads of Academies gather to the rock of Aaron the priest and throng round him and enter into his academy, and there they are renewed with the purity of the holy dew which descends upon his head and the oil of anointment which flows upon him, and along with him they are all renewed with the rejuvenation of the beloved of the Holy King, so that this is called the Academy of Love, and He sustains the whole Academy secretly [Tr. note: The text seems here to be imperfect.]... flashing like eagles' wings in the Academy of light, and this is the Academy of Moses. All stand without and no one enters save Aaron alone, but occasionally one or other of them is called by name. No one can see Moses, because a veil overspreads his face and seven clouds of glory surround him. Aaron stands within the curtain below Moses, the curtain half separating them, and all the Heads of the Academies remain outside of this curtain. All the rest remain outside of the clouds. The more illuminating the exposition given of the Torah, the more those clouds are lit up, and they become more and more transparent until the veil becomes visible, and from the midst of that veil they see a light brighter than that of all other lights, and this is the face of Moses. No one actually sees his face, but only the light which proceeds from the veil behind all the clouds. Moses makes a remark to Aaron, and Aaron explains it to the Heads of the Academies. How does he explain it? With all those founts of wisdom which were closed to him when the time of Joshua came. Now he restores them with wonderful streams that flow from each word. Similarly all the virtuous women of that generation come to Miriam. Then they all ascend like pillars of smoke in this wilderness. That day is called the day of the marriage celebration. The women on the eves of Sabbaths and festivals all come to Miriam to gain knowledge of the Sovereign of the Universe. Happy is that generation above all other generations. When they emerge from the Academy of Moses they fly to the Academy of the firmament, and those who are qualified fly to the highest Academy. Of that generation it is written: "Happy is the people that is in such a case, yea, happy is the people whose God is the Lord" (Ps. CXLIV, 15).'

[Note: The last 13 lines of the Hebrew text do not appear in our translation.]

[Tr. note: From here to p. 174a the text is fragmentary, and it is not easy to find a connecting thread.]

Zohar: Bemidbar, Section 3, Pages 163b–173b

[Note: These pages do not appear in our Hebrew text as explained in the translator's note on page 163a.]

Zohar: Bemidbar, Section 3, Page 174a

[Note: Most of this page does not appear in our Hebrew text as explained in the translator's note on page 163a.]

AND THE LORD SAID TO MOSES, SPEAK UNTO THE CHILDREN OF ISRAEL... THAT THEY MAKE THEMSELVES FRINGES ON THE CORNERS OF THEIR GARMENTS, ETC. R. Hizkiah adduced here the verse: "And he showed me Joshua the high priest", etc. (Zech. III, 1).

Zohar: Bemidbar, Section 3, Page 174b

[Only the last 4 lines of the Hebrew text appear in our translation.]

'What did he see? He saw him standing before the angel.' R. Isaac said: 'What does this tell us? That every man who in this world does not wrap himself in the ceremonial garb and clothe himself therewith, when he enters the other world is covered with a filthy garment and is brought up for trial. Many are the garments prepared for man in this world, and he who does not acquire the garment of religious observance is in the next world clad in a garment which is known to the masters of Gehinnom, and woe to the man who is clad therein, for he is seized by

Zohar: Bemidbar, Section 3, Page 175a

many officers of judgement and dragged down to Gehinnom, and therefore King Solomon cried aloud, "At all times let thy garments be white".'

Zohar: Bemidbar, Section 3, Page 175b

R. Judah said: 'God has appointed many witnesses to give man warning. When he rises in the morning and begins to move, the witnesses stand before him and say: "He shall keep the feet of his saints" (I Sam. II, 9), and "keep thy feet when thou goest" (Eccl. IV, 17). When he opens his eyes to observe the world, the witnesses say: "Thine eyes shall look right on" (Prov. IV, 25). When he begins to speak the witnesses say: "Keep thy tongue from evil" (Ps. XXXIV, 14). When he begins to transact business they say: "Depart from evil and do good" (Ibid. 15). If he listens to them, well and good, but if not, then they all testify against him above. But if he desires to labour in the service of the Almighty, they all become his advocates in the hour of need. When, therefore, he rises in the morning, he should recite a number of blessings. He then puts the phylactery on his head and he knows he has the Holy Name impressed on his head. When he stretches out his arm he sees it bound with the knot of the Holy Name. When he puts on the ceremonial garment he sees in the four corners four kings issuing to meet four. Four true witnesses of the King are suspended from the four corners like grapes from a cluster. Like seven couriers are the seven windings of blue round each one, which may be increased up to thirteen, but not more.' R. Isaac said that if there are seven, they are symbolical of the Shekinah, and if thirteen, of the thirteen attributes. R. Isaac said that the threads indicate how the four sides of the world are suspended from that special place which controls all as the heart the body. R. Judah said: 'The Holy One, blessed be

He, thus signifies that whoever wishes to walk in the fear of Him should follow after this heart and after the eyes that are above it, but "ye shall not go astray after your heart and your eyes".'

Zohar: Bemidbar, Section 3, Page 176a

R. Hiya said: 'Why is the exodus from Egypt mentioned in this passage? Because when they went forth from Egypt God brought them into this portion (of the commandments), and therefore He admonished them thus.'

KORAH

NOW KORAH THE SON OF IZHAR THE SON OF KEHATH THE SON OF LEVI, ETC. He who makes the right left and the left right, as it were, lays waste the world. Now Aaron represented the right and the Levites the left, and Korah sought to make the right and the left change places, and therefore he was punished. Further, the evil tongue was also found in him, and for that also he was punished. R. Judah said: 'The left should always be embraced in the right. Korah sought to change the order fixed both above and below, and therefore he perished both above and below. 'TOOK. What did he take? He took an evil counsel for himself. If one runs after that which is not his, it flies from him, and what is more, he loses his own as well. So Korah pursued that which was not his, and he lost his own without obtaining the other. Korah quarreled with peace, and he who quarrels with peace quarrels with the Holy Name,

Zohar: Bemidbar, Section 3, Page 176b

because the Holy Name is called peace.' R. Yose said: 'The Torah is also peace, as it is written: "And all her paths are peace" (Prov. III, 17). Korah tried to upset peace on high and below, and therefore he was punished both on high and below.' AND THEY ROSE UP BEFORE MOSES, ETC. R. Simeon said: 'The earthly kingdom is on the pattern of the heavenly kingdom. All those supernal Crowns to which the Holy Name is attached are summoned from a place called Holiness, and just as the higher Holiness summons them, so the lower Holiness summons its hosts to be crowned and exalted therewith. And just as its hosts are above, so are the rulers of the people below. Hence they are described here as "called to the assembly". They are also called here "men of name", but not "men of the Lord", because they came from the side of Geburah, but they arrogated more to themselves and banded together in contention.

'IN THE MORNING THE LORD WILL SHOW WHO ARE HIS AND WHO ARE HOLY. Why "morning", and why holy, rather than "pure"? Moses meant this: In the morning the Crown of Priest is active, and if you are priests, then in the morning perform the service of the morning and the Lord will make known who is His-that is to say, the Levite-and who is the holy one-that is to say, the priest-and he shall bring near to Himself. The test will only be made by "Morning". If it is meet for you to remain on the side of Judgement, then Morning will not endure you, for it is not the time of Judgement. But if it is meet for you to remain on the side of Grace, then as it is the time thereof, you shall remain with it and it will accept you. In virtue of what? Of the incense, since the incense requires the "best man" to form the

679

link and union; and the "best man" is the priest. Therefore the man whom the Lord shall choose, he shall be "holy", and not only "pure".

'AND THEY FELL ON THEIR FACES AND SAID, O GOD, THE GOD OF THE SPIRITS OF ALL FLESH. Moses and Aaron at this point risked their lives, since "falling on one's face" always means a supplication to the place of the Tree of Death, [Tr. note: The Shekinah.] the place where is the bundle of all souls, to which they ascend and from which they issue.'

Zohar: Bemidbar, Section 3, Page 177a [Note: The first 27 lines of the Hebrew text do not appear in our translation.]

AND MOSES SAID UNTO AARON, TAKE THY CENSER, ETC. R. Hiya adduced here the verse: "The wrath of the king is as messengers of death, but a wise man will pacify it" (Prov. XVI, 14). 'How careful men should be', he said, 'to abstain from sin and to watch their actions, for at many periods the world is judged and every day deeds are placed in the balance and examined on high and recorded before the Almighty; and when the deeds of men are not approved before the King, wrath arises and judgement is awakened. But if when the executioners of judgement are ready to strike and wrath impends, there is found in the generation a righteous man who is inscribed above, then God looks upon him and His wrath is mollified. He is like a king who is angry with his servants and sends for the executioner to punish them, but meanwhile the king's friend enters and stands before him, and when the king sees him his face lights up, and when he begins to speak he is glad. So when the executioner comes and sees the king all smiling, he goes away and does not execute judgement, and then the king's friend intercedes for his servants and procures forgiveness for them. So here, when Moses saw wrath

Zohar: Bemidbar, Section 3, Page 177b

impending he at once told Aaron, who was the "friend" of the Matrona, to take the incense, which increases peace in the world and binds the knot of faith, which is the joy of higher and lower and effects the removal of wrath.' R. Eleazar said: 'It is written "Cut ye not off the tribe of the families of the Kohathites from among the Levites" (Num. IV, 18), because they are the main stock of the Levites, and further, "This do unto them that they may live". This means that the priest had to regulate them, since although they were near to the holiness they were not to enter save with the regulation of the priest, who knew exactly how far they could go in, and when the holy vessels began to be covered another covering also began, and it was forbidden them to see. For things done quietly are the province of the priests and not of the Levites, whose function it was to raise the voice in song. Hence, when judgements begin to assail the world from the side of the Left, the Right Hand must bring appeasement with the incense, which makes no sound. Observe that when that other altar commences to grow restive because there are no righteous, the inner altar intervenes with it and judgements are allayed. Hence AARON TOOK AS MOSES SPAKE, AND RAN INTO THE MIDST OF THE ASSEMBLY, AND HE PUT ON THE INCENSE, which belongs to the inner precinct symbolizing the Priest, and so HE MADE ATONEMENT FOR THE PEOPLE AND HE STOOD BETWEEN THE DEAD AND THE LIVING, between the Tree of Life and the Tree of Death. Then the Right Hand drew them near one to another and the plague was stayed. Happy the lot of the priest who has power above and below and brings peace above and below!' As R. Eleazar was once standing before his father, R. Simeon, he quoted to him the verse: "See life with the wife whom thou lovest all the days of the life of thy vanity" (Eccl. IX, 9). 'This', he said, 'is a hint to a man that he should unite Life with this place, [Tr. note: i.e. Tifereth with Malkuth.] the measure of day with the measure of night. All Solomon's words', he went on, 'are written in wisdom, yet it would seem that here he is giving the rein to worldliness, and equally in the words that follow: "Whatsoever thy hand findeth to do, do with thy might, for there is no work nor device", etc. How could the wise Solomon

Zohar: Bemidbar, Section 3, Page 178a

speak thus? But, indeed, all the words of Solomon have a deep inner significance. What is indicated here is that a man should always merge the left in the right, and all his actions should be controlled by the right. Thus we interpret, "all that thy hand findeth to do" of the left, and "that do with thy might" of the right. When a man is careful that all his acts should be towards the right side, and that he should include the left in the right, then God dwells within him in this world and brings him into the next world. A man should not say, When I reach that world I will seek mercy of the King and repent before him, for "there is no work or device or knowledge or wisdom" after a man departs from this world, but if a man desires that the Holy King should illumine him for that world and give him a share in the world to come, he should strive in this world to place his actions in the sphere of the right. Or we may also explain that there is no work nor device nor knowledge nor wisdom in Sheol. There are storeys in Gehinnom, one above another; there is Sheol and below it Abadon. From Sheol it is possible to come up again, but not from Abadon. Now those who have good works in this world, or reckoning or knowledge or wisdom, when they pass by to observe the sinners in Gehinnom and hear them crying out from the grade of Sheol, are not left there, but ascend aloft to the place of illumination and delight where God comes to have converse with the righteous in the Garden of Eden. BUT THE LEVITES SHALL DO THE SERVICE OF THE TENT OF MEETING. At the time of the Creation the world was not completed and established until man emerged in his complete form as the consummation of all and the (seventh) day was sanctified and the holy throne was set for the King.

At the moment when the day was about to be sanctified the spirits of the demons issued forth, but the day was sanctified before their bodies were created, and so the world was left deficient.

Zohar: Bemidbar, Section 3, Page 178b

When Israel were sanctified and all their grades completed with the Levites on the left side, then this deficiency of the world on the left side was made good, and all was then subordinated to the right and the world was freed from defect. Hence it says "the Levite shall do", i.e. "make" or "complete". We may also translate, "And the Levite shall serve hu (him)", the reference being to the Ancient One, and the Levite typifying Judgement, but for which men would not rise to the higher faith, nor study the Torah, nor carry out the precepts of the Torah for the service of the Holy King.'

[Note: The last 12 lines of the Hebrew text do not appear in our translation.]

Zohar: Bemidbar, Section 3, Page 179b

HUKKATH

AND THE LORD SPAKE UNTO MOSES AND UNTO AARON SAYING, THIS (zoth) IS THE STATUTE OF THE LAW WHICH THE LORD HATH COMMANDED, SAYING. R. Yose said: 'This passage commences simply, "This is the statute of the law", but in another passage we find, "Now this (ve-zoth) is the law which Moses set before the children of Israel" (Deut. IV. 44). Why this difference? As we have learnt, because the addition of the vau (now) indicates the complete union of all, of the Community of Israel with the Holy One, blessed be He; and such is the essence of the Torah. But where this vau is absent, there we have only the "statute of the Law" and not the Law itself.' When R. Simeon and R. Eleazar and R. Abba and R. Isaac were once in the house of R. Phineas ben Jair, the latter asked R. Simeon to give some new exposition of the section commencing: "This is the statute of the law". R. Simeon, however,

Zohar: Bemidbar, Section 3, Page 180a

called on R. Eleazar. The latter thereupon discoursed on the text: "Now this was the custom in former time in Israel concerning redeeming and concerning exchanging, to confirm all things", etc. (Ruth IV, 7). 'This verse', he said, 'raises a problem. If the ancients adopted this custom on the basis of the Torah, and later generations abolished it, how could they do so, seeing that to abolish a thing laid down in the Torah is like laying waste the whole world? If, again, it was not an injunction of the Torah, but a mere custom, why was a shoe chosen for the purpose? The truth is that this was enjoined originally by the Torah, and because the ancients were pious and virtuous this thing was revealed to them, but when sinners multiplied the thing was done in a different way, in order to conceal matters which have a high mystic significance. Now when God said to Moses, "Draw not nigh hither" (Ex. III, 5), He also said, "Put off thy shoes from off thy feet"; and it has been explained that by these words He enjoined him to part from his wife and attach himself to another wife of holy supernal radiance, to wit the Shekinah, and the drawing off of the shoe removed him from this world and placed him in another world. Similarly with a dead man who has departed from the world without children. The Shekinah does not gather him in, and he is driven to and fro about the world, but God has pity on him and bids his brother redeem him so that he may be set right by means of other dust. Now if that redeemer is not willing to establish seed for his brother in this world, he must tie a shoe on his foot and the wife must loosen it and take it to herself. Why was a shoe chosen for this purpose? Because the shoe was the support of the dead man in this world, and the woman, by taking it, signifies that the dead man who was wandering about among the living will now through that shoe no longer wander about among them. She must dash the shoe on the ground to show that she has laid to rest the body of the dead, and God then, or after a time, has pity on him and receives him into the future world. Therefore it was that whoever desired to confirm an undertaking took off his shoe and gave it to his neighbour. This was beforetime in Israel when they were pious and holy, but when sinners multiplied they concealed the matter under another form, using the corner of a garment.

Zohar: Bemidbar, Section 3, Page 180b [Note: The first 10 lines of the Hebrew text do not appear in our translation.]

A RED HEIFER, ETC. The heifer receives from Ox, who is on the left, and is therefore used to purify. "Red" symbolizes the sentence of judgement. "Without spot" symbolizes lenient judgement. "Wherein is no blemish" indicates the Shekinah.' AND YE SHALL GIVE HER UNTO ELEAZAR THE PRIEST. Why to him and not to Aaron? Because Aaron was the friend of the Matrona, and also because Aaron came not from the side of Pure, but from the side of Holy; for only he is called pure who emerges out of impurity. The key to the whole passage is in the words, "for a water of impurity, it is a sin-offering" (v. 9). For all the lower judgements, and all that come from the side of uncleanness, when it sucks from the "other side" sitting in judgement bestir themselves and haunt the world, but when all this ceremony of the heifer is performed on earth, and cedar wood, etc.', is thrown into it,

Zohar: Bemidbar, Section 3, Page 181a

then their strength is enfeebled and wherever they are they are crushed and weakened, since their power also appears to them in this form (of an ox), and they no longer stay with a man, and he is purified.'

[Note: the rest of this page in the Hebrew does not appear in the translation.]

Zohar: Bemidbar, Section 3, Page 181b

AND THE CHILDREN OF ISRAEL, EVEN THE WHOLE CONGREGATION, CAME INTO THE WILDERNESS OF ZIN. R. Judah said: 'Why is the section of the red heifer followed immediately by the statement of the death of Miriam? To show that just as judgement was executed on this heifer to purify the unclean, so judgement was executed on Miriam to purify the world. When Miriam departed, the well which accompanied Israel in the wilderness also departed. Therefore THERE WAS NO WATER FOR THE CONGREGATION, because the well had departed both above and below. Then the right hand was broken, as it says, "Let Aaron be gathered to his people", and finally the sun was darkened, when God said to Moses, "And die in the mountain", etc. There never was a generation like that in which Moses was present along with Aaron and Miriam. And think not that there was the like in the days of Solomon, for in the days of Solomon the Moon held sway but the Sun was gathered in, whereas in the days of Moses the Moon was gathered in but the Sun held sway. It is written: "And the sun ariseth and the sun goeth down" (Eccl. 1, 5). This signifies, as we have explained, that when the Israelites came forth from Egypt the Sun [Tr. note: Tifereth.] shone for them and not the Moon, but it went down in the wilderness. To where, then, was it gathered in? "Unto its place", in order to give light to the Moon. So it was with Moses, and that is the point of the verse, "What profit is there to a man from all his labour", etc. (Ibid. 3). The "man" here is Joshua, who laboured to give Israel possession of the land and yet did not succeed in bringing the Moon to fullness, because he laboured for Israel "under the sun", that is, on a lower plane than the sun of Moses, and he did not really take his place. That being so, what was his glory, seeing that he did not reach perfection on either side (either of the sun or of the moon)?

Zohar: Bemidbar, Section 3, Page 182a

R. Simeon said: 'What is "under the sun"? This is the moon; and whoever attaches himself to the moon without the sun, his labour is "under the sun" assuredly; and this was the original sin of the world; and hence it says, "What profit is there to man in all his labour, to wit, to the first Adam and all who have followed him.' LET AARON BE GATHERED UNTO HIS PEOPLE, ETC. R. Hiya adduced here the verse: "Wherefore I praised the dead which are already dead", etc. (Eccl. IV, 2).

Zohar: Bemidbar, Section 3, Page 182b

'How could King Solomon praise the dead more than the living, seeing that only he is called "living" who walks in the way of truth in this world, while the wicked man who does not walk in the way of truth is called "dead"? We must, however, look at the words which follow, "which are already dead". This refers to one who has already died but who has the opportunity to return to this world in order that he may rectify (his previous life); verily this one is more to be praised than the other dead, because he has received his punishment, and he is more to be praised than the living who have not yet received their punishment. Such a one is called "dead" because he has had a taste of death, and although he is in this world he is dead and has returned from the dead; whereas "the living who are still alive" have not yet had a taste of death, and have not received their punishment and do not know if they will be worthy of the other world or not. Observe, further, that the virtuous who are thought worthy to be "bound up in the bundle of the living" are privileged to see the glory of the supernal holy King, and their abode is higher than that of all the holy angels, while those who have not merited to ascend so high are assigned a lower place according to their deserts. They are stationed in the lower Eden, which is called "lower Wisdom", and between which and the higher Eden there is a difference as between darkness and light. These, then, are they whom Solomon called "the living who are still alive", but the others "who have already died" and who have received their punishment once and twice are in a higher grade than they, and are called refined silver which has been purified of its dross. "And better than both is he which hath not yet been"; this refers to the spirit, which remains above and which delays to come down to earth, since it has not to receive any punishment, and it is nurtured with that supernal food above.

Zohar: Bemidbar, Section 3, Page 183a

[Or, again, we may explain that] best of all is he that has not separated from God and is concealed in obscurity, the pious saintly ones that keep the precepts of the Law and study the Torah day and night: such a one reaches a higher grade than all other men, and all envy his canopy. Now when God said to Moses, "Let Aaron be gathered to his people", he was greatly distressed, as he knew that his right hand was being broken, and he trembled greatly, until God said to him, "Take Aaron and Eleazar his son", as if to say: "Moses, see, I have prepared for thee another right hand". And for all that, Eleazar did not completely fill the place of his father, since the clouds of glory departed on Aaron's death and did not return save for the merit of Moses, and not of Eleazar.

AND MOSES DID AS THE LORD COMMANDED, ETC. Why did they go up "in the sight of all the congregation"? Aaron was most dearly beloved of all the people, and therefore, so that they should not say that he was laid out by Moses, they all saw when he stripped Aaron of the garments and put them on Eleazar. Why was Moses chosen for this task? Because Moses had put them on Aaron when he was invested with the priesthood; so now he stripped him of what he had given him, while God stripped him of what He had given him, Moses stripping without and God within. God prepared for Aaron a bed and a candlestick of gold with a light, taken from the candlestick which he used to light twice a day, and He closed the mouth of the cave and they descended.' R. Judah said: 'The mouth of the cave was left open and all Israel saw Aaron lying there and the light burning before him and his bed being taken out and in, with a cloud resting on it, and then they knew that Aaron was dead, besides which they saw that the clouds of glory had departed. Therefore all the house of Israel, men, women and children, wept for Aaron because he was most beloved of all.' R. Simeon said: 'Why were not these three holy brethren buried in one place? Some say that each was buried in a place where Israel was destined to be in danger, so as to protect them, but in truth each died in the fitting place, Miriam in Kadesh, between the north and the south, Aaron on the right side, and Moses in his fitting place, which was connected [by underground passages] both with the mountain where Aaron died and with the grave of Miriam.

Zohar: Bemidbar, Section 3, Page 183b

[Note: The first 11 lines of the Hebrew text do not appear in our translation.]

AND THE PEOPLE SPAKE AGAINST GOD AND AGAINST MOSES. That is to say, they spoke against God and wrangled with Moses. WHEREFORE HAVE YE BROUGHT US UP: they put all faces [i.e. God and Moses] on the same level. Therefore there were sent among them serpents that burnt them like fire, and the fire entered their bodies and they fell dead.

THAT IS THE WELL WHEREOF THE LORD SAID UNTO MOSES, GATHER THE PEOPLE, ETC. This well never left them. It may be asked, How could they all draw from it? It issued into twelve streams and a channel went forth in every direction, and when Israel encamped and required water they used to stand by it and recite this song: "Ascend, O well, bring up thy waters to provide water for all, so that they may be watered from thee". So, too, they sang the praises of the well: "The well which the princes digged", etc. All that they said in its praise was true, and from this we learn that if one wishes to set in motion the powers above, whether through action or words, he produces no effect if that action or word is not as it should be. All people go to synagogue to influence the powers above, but few know how to do it. God is near to all who know how to call upon Him and to set powers in motion in the proper manner, but if they do not know how to call upon Him He is not near. So here, the Israelites spoke words of truth so as to set in motion

Zohar: Bemidbar, Section 3, Page 184a

[Note: The translation of this page does not conform entirely to the Hebrew text.]

this well, and before they did this it would not move. So also with magicians who get the "evil species" to serve them, if they do not employ the right formulas to draw them, they do not stir. So it says, "They called on the name of Baal", etc. (I Kings XVIII, 26), yet they availed nothing, for one thing because it was not permitted to them to bring fire down from heaven, and for another because they did not use the right invocation, since God confused them, as it says, "Thou didst turn their heart backwards" (Ibid. 37).' R. Simeon said: 'Here I must tell you something. Whoever knows how to perform the correct ceremony and recite the proper words can certainly influence the Holy One, blessed be He. If so, it may be asked, what is the superiority of the righteous who know the root of the matter and can concentrate their minds and thoughts more than the others who do not know this? The truth is that those who do not know the basis of the ceremony, and perform it only as a matter of rote, draw down to themselves an influence from behind the shoulders of the Holy One, blessed be He, which is only called "Providence", but those who do know draw forth blessings from the place which is called "Thought" until upper and lower beings are blessed and the Holy Name is blessed through them. Happy are they in that God is near them and ready to answer when they call.

'AND THE LORD SAID TO MOSES, DO NOT FEAR HIM. Og was one of those who clave to Abraham and were circumcised with him. Hence Moses was afraid that he would not be able to overcome the sign which Abraham had impressed upon him. Therefore God said to him, "Do not fear him (otho)", as much as to say, Do not fear that sign (oth) which is upon him, because he has impaired that sign of his, and whoever impairs his sign deserves to be annihilated.

Zohar: Bemidbar, Section 3, Page 184b

Therefore Israel destroyed him entirely, with his sons and all his people, as it is written: "And they smote him and his sons and all his people".'

BALAK

AND BALAK THE SON OF ZIPPOR SAW, ETC. What did he see? He saw both through the window of wisdom and with his physical eyes. The tails of the skirts of the stars are the windows of wisdom, and there is one window through which the very essence of wisdom can be seen. So Balak saw with his own particular wisdom. He was the "son of a bird", [Tr. note: Zippor means, in Hebrew, "bird".] for he used birds for all his magic arts. He used to mark a bird plucking a herb or flying through the air, and on his performing certain rites and incantations that bird would come to him with grass in its mouth and he would put it in a cage. He would tie knots before it and it would tell him certain things. He would perform his magic arts and the bird would chirp and fly away to the "open of eye" and tell him, and then return. One day he performed his arts and took the bird, and it flew away but did not return. He was greatly distressed, until he saw it coming with a fiery flame following it and burning its wings. Then he saw strange things and became afraid of Israel. The name of that bird is known, but none can make use of it for magic arts with the same effect as Balak. All his wisdom was through that bird. He covered his head and crawled before it, saying "The people", and the bird answered "Israel". He said "exceedingly" and the bird answered "numerous". Seventy times they thus chirped to one another, with the result that he was seized with fear, as it says: "And Moab was sore afraid of the people, for they were many". In the descriptions of the magic of the ancient Kasdiel we find that they used to make a bird of this kind at stated times out of silver mingled with gold. Its head was of gold, its mouth of silver; its wings of polished brass mixed with silver; its body of gold, the dots on its wings of silver, and its legs of gold. They used to place in its mouth a tongue of that known bird and set it in a window which they used to open to face the sun, or at night to face the moon, and then they used to tie knots and do magical rites and adjure the sun, or at night the moon;

Zohar: Bemidbar, Section 3, Page 185a

and so they used to do for seven days. From that time the tongue used to quiver in the bird's mouth, and they used to prick it with a needle, when it would utter wonderful things of itself. Balak knew all things through this bird, and therefore he was called "son of the Bird".

It is written: "The Lord said, I will bring again from Bashan, I will bring again from the depths of the sea" (Ps. LXVIII, 23). God's words are true and can be relied upon, for what He says is done. In time to come God will arouse and bring back from Bashan all those who were killed and devoured by the wild beasts of prey. For there is in the world an abode of all great beasts, and lofty mountains where they hide. The mighty Og was among the wild asses of the wilderness, and his strength was there because he was the king of Bashan. No king could make war against him, till Moses came and did so. Sihon was the colt of the wilderness, and the reliance of Moab was upon him. When Israel destroyed the city of Sihon, a herald traversed the kingdom of heaven saying: "Assemble, ye rulers of all the peoples, and see how the kingdom of the Amorite has been laid waste". At that time all the Governors of the seven nations (of Canaan) gathered together and sought to restore the kingdom to its former condition. But when they saw the power of Moses they turned back. Hence it is written: "Therefore the rulers said, Come ye to Heshbon, let the city of Sihon be built and established" (Num. XXI, 27). But when they saw the might of Moses they said: "A fire has gone out of Heshbon, a flame from the city of Sihon". Why did they use both names? They said: All paths and ways are closed by the power of their leader. If we should say, Let Heshbon be rebuilt, behold, a fire has gone out of Heshbon; and if we say merely "the city of Sihon", behold, a flame has issued from the city of Sihon. Since that flame of fire is there, none can prevail against it to restore the place to its former condition; on every side we are prohibited. Therefore, "Woe is thee, Moab"; he that was thy shield has been crushed. Seeing this, "Moab was sore afraid of the people"-more than of death, because they saw that Israel prevailed above and below, over their Chieftains and Rulers above, and over their chieftains and rulers below. Israel, in fact, was the "great one", the elder and the holy one, and not Esau.

[Note: The last 7 lines of the Hebrew text are not found in our translation]

Zohar: Bemidbar, Section 3, Page 185b

[Note: The first 3 lines of the Hebrew text are not found in our translation]

AND MOAB SAID UNTO THE ELDERS OF MIDIAN, ETC. R. Hiya spoke on the verse: "And he showed me Joshua the high priest standing before the angel of the Lord" (Zech. III, 1). 'How careful', he said, 'should a man be of his ways in this world, to walk in the way of truth, because all his actions are recorded in writing before the King! The gatekeepers are ready, the witnesses are at hand, the prosecutors are well prepared, the judge is waiting to receive the evidence, and those who have charges to bring are bestirring themselves, and it is not known whether they will come from the right or the left. For when the spirits of men leave this world many are the accusers who stand up against them, and heralds to proclaim the result of the trial, whether good or bad, as it has been taught: Man is sentenced many times in this world, both during his lifetime and after, but God's mercies are over all and He does not desire to judge men according to their works, as David said: "If thou, KAH, shouldst mark iniquities, Lord, who should stand?" (Ps. cxxx, 3). In this verse David mentioned three degrees of mercy. If one's sins are so numerous that they are marked by KAH, then there is "the Lord", who stands for mercy: and if even this name which stands for mercy arises to chastise, and all grades are sealed in judgement, there is still one grade to which we can turn, since all healing comes from it, and this will have pity on us: this is MI (Who). Therefore it says here, "Who shall stand?", since all the ways of mercy and repentance open out from it. Now Joshua the son of Jehozedek was a perfectly righteous man, a man who penetrated to the innermost shrine, who was admitted to the Heavenly Academy. All the members of the Academy assembled to consider his case. For it is the rule there that when one is brought to be tried a herald proclaims: All members of the Academy enter the secret chamber. Then the Court assembles and the spirit of the man to be tried is brought up by two officers, and placed near a pillar of flashing flame which stands there and which is kept in shape by a current of air blowing on it. Now if any have on earth studied the Torah and given original explanations, their words have been immediately reported to the members of the Academy. They all now come to see him. If his word was a fitting one, happy is he, for he is crowned with many radiant crowns by all the members of the Academy. If, however, his word was of another kind, alas for his disgrace. They thrust him outside, and he stands within the pillar until he is taken to his punishment. Heaven preserve us! Others there are who are taken up there when the Holy One, blessed be He, is arguing with the members of the Academy and says: Who shall decide? Here is So-and-so, who will decide. And so they take him up there and he decides that matter in dispute between God and the members of the Academy. Others are taken up there to be chastised in order to become cleansed and purified.' Said R. Yose to him: 'If so, then a man departs this world without judgement; and if he departs after judgement, why is he judged a second time?' He replied: 'What I have learnt is that a man does indeed depart this world in judgement, but before he enters the place set aside for the righteous he is taken up to be tried (again) before the Heavenly Academy, the official of Gehinnom standing there in order to pervert the judgement, if possible. Happy is he who emerges from the trial successfully; otherwise the officer of Gehinnom seizes him so soon as he is delivered into his power, and hurls him down to nether regions like a stone

Zohar: Bemidbar, Section 3, Page 186a

from a sling, and there he receives his punishment according to his sentence. Similarly Joshua the high priest was taken up for trial to that Heavenly Academy when he departed this world. He was "standing before the angel of the Lord": this is the "youth", [Tr. note: Metatron.] the head of the Academy, who pronounces sentence on all. The "Satan" is he who has charge of the souls in Gehinnom, who ever craves for more and says "give, give", more souls to Gehinnom. Then, "The Lord said unto Satan, The Lord rebuke thee, Satan, and the Lord rebuke thee...." Why two rebukes here? One for Dumah and one for him who comes out of Gehinnom to lead astray. That higher Satan, as we have stated elsewhere, goes down to earth in the form of an ox, and all those wicked spirits which have been condemned to Gehinnom he licks up in one moment and hands over to Dumah after he has swallowed them. Therefore it was that Moab said to the elders of Midian, "Now shall this multitude lick up all that is round about us as the ox licketh up the grass of the field", since it is known that the ox is there to do evil to all mankind.' Said R. Yose: 'If so, Balak was clever?' He replied: 'Certainly; and he had to know all the ways of that ox, as otherwise he would not have been able to practise his magic arts.'

Once, when R. Isaac and R. Judah were on a journey, they came to a place called Kfar Sachnin, where Rab Hamnuna the Elder used to live. They put up at the house of his wife. She had a young son who was still at school, and when he came from school and saw the strangers his mother said to him: 'Go up to these distinguished gentlemen that you may obtain a blessing from them'. He began to approach, but suddenly turned back, saying to his mother: 'I don't want to go near them, because they have not recited the Shema this day, and I have been taught that if one does not recite the Shema at the proper time, he is under a ban the whole of that day.' When the others heard him they were amazed, and they lifted up their hands and blessed him. They said: 'Indeed this is so; today we were busy looking after an engaged couple who had no means of their own, and were therefore delaying their marriage. There was no one to provide for them, so we did so, and so omitted to say the Shema at the proper time, since if a man is engaged on one mizvah (religious precept) he is exempt from performing another (which might interfere with it).' They then asked him how he knew. He replied: 'I knew by the smell of your clothes when I came near you.' In great surprise they sat down, washed their hands and broke bread. R. Judah's hands were dirty, but he commenced to say the blessing before he had poured water on them. Said the boy to them: 'If you are the disciples of R. Shemaya the Saint, you ought not to say a blessing with dirty hands, as this renders one liable to death.' He then began a discourse on the verse: "When they go in to the tent of meeting they shall wash with water, that they die not" (Ex. XXX, 20). 'We learn from this text', he said, 'that one who is not careful on this point and appears before the King with soiled hands is liable to the death penalty. The reason is that a man's hands are stationed in the highest heights. It is written: "And thou shalt make bars of acacia wood, five for the boards of the one side of the tabernacle, and five for the boards of the other side" (Ibid. XXVI, 26), and it is further written, "And the middle bar in the midst of the boards shall pass from end to end" (Ibid. 27). Now it must not be thought that this middle bar is not included in the five mentioned previously; it was one of the five, being the middle one with two on each side, symbolical of Moses,

Zohar: Bemidbar, Section 3, Page 186b

the most important of all, as the rest depended on it. To these the five fingers of the hand correspond, and therefore all the blessings of the priest are made with separated fingers. If so much significance is attached to them is it not right that they should be clean when a blessing of God is said over them, seeing that through them and what they stand for the Holy Name is blessed? Seeing, therefore, that you are so wise, why did you not take heed of this and listen to R. Shemaya the Saint, who said that all dirt and all stains betake themselves to the "other side", which derives sustenance from them, and therefore it is a religious duty to wash the hands after a meal?'

They were dumbfounded, and could say nothing. R. Judah asked the boy what was the name of his father. The boy was silent for a moment, then went to his mother and kissed her saying: 'Mother, these wise men have asked me the name of my father; shall I tell them?' His mother said: 'Have you tested them?' He replied: 'I have tested them and not found them satisfactory.' His mother then whispered something to him, and he went back to them and said: 'You asked about my father. He has departed this world, but whenever holy saints travel on the road he follows them in the form of a pedlar. If you are sainted holy ones, how is it that you did not find him following you? The truth is that I saw through you before, and now I see through you again, since my father never observes a wise man on the road without following him with his ass in order to carry the yoke of the Torah. Since my father did not deign to follow you, I will not tell you who was my father.' Said R. Judah to R. Isaac: 'Methinks that this child is no son of man.'

They ate their meal, while the boy gave expositions of the Torah. Having finished they said: 'Come, let us say grace.' He said to them: 'You have spoken well, since the Holy Name is not to be blessed with this blessing unless permission is asked.' He then cited the verse: "I will bless the Lord at all times" (Ps. XXXIV, 2). He said: 'The permissive form abarechah (let me bless) is used, because when a man sits at table the Shekinah is there and the "other side" is there. If a man invites the company to bless the Holy One the Shekinah takes her place above to receive the blessings, and the "other side" is kept down. But if a man does not invite the company to bless, the "other side" hears and pushes in that he may have a share in that blessing. It may be asked, why is not such an invitation necessary in the case of other blessings (over food)? The fact is that the character of the thing over which the grace is said is itself an invitation. For instance, if one says grace over fruit, that fruit is itself an invitation, and the "other side" has no share in it. For previously (in the three years of "uncircumcision") it was in the power of the "other side", and no blessing could be said over it. But when it has emerged from the power of the "other side" it may be eaten and a blessing is said over it, and this is itself the invitation to the blessing. You may still ask, Seeing that similarly for the grace after meals the cup of benediction is the invitation, why should one have to say, Come, let us say grace? The reason is that when one drank earlier in the meal he said the blessing "Creator of the fruit of the vine", which was an invitation, and now for the grace after meals we require a change for another invitation, since this cup is for God and not for food.' Said R. Judah: 'Happy is our lot, for

Zohar: Bemidbar, Section 3, Page 187a

never till this moment have I heard these things. Assuredly I say that this is no son of man.'

He said to him: 'My son, messenger of the Lord and His beloved, in regard to what you said before about the bars, there are many bars but only two hands.' He replied: 'This bears out the saying: From a man's mouth one can tell who he is. However, since you did not pay attention, I will explain. It says: "the wise man's eyes are in his head" (Eccl. II, 14). Where, it may be asked, should they be if not in his head? What it means, however, is this. We have learnt that a man should not go four cubits with his head uncovered, the reason being that the Shekinah rests on the head. Now a wise man's eyes are directed to his head, to that which rests on his head, and then he knows that the light which is kindled on his head requires oil, which consists in good deeds, and therefore the eyes of a wise man are towards his head, and no other place. You being wise men, on whose head certainly the Shekinah rests, why did you not mark what is written, "Thou shalt make bars for the boards of one side... and thou shalt make bars for the boards of the second side", but there is no mention of a third and fourth side, since the first and the second are the important ones?' They came and kissed him again. R. Judah wept and said: 'R. Simeon, happy is thy portion, happy is thy generation, since for thy sake even schoolchildren are like lofty and mighty mountains.' His mother came and said to them: 'I beg of you, sirs, look not on my son save with a benignant eye.' They said to her: 'Happy is thy portion! Thou art a goodly woman, a woman selected from all others, for the Holy One, blessed be He, has selected thy portion and raised thy standard above that of all other women.' The boy said: 'I am not afraid of any evil eye, since I am the son of a great and precious fish, [Tr. note: A play on the name Hamnuna and the word nuna, the Aramaic for "fish".] and fishes are not susceptible to the evil eye.' They said: 'My son, messenger of the Lord, there is no evil eye in us, nor are we from the side of the evil eye. May the Holy One protect thee with his wings!'

He then began to discourse on the verse: "The angel which hath redeemed me from all evil bless the lads" (Gen. XLVIII, 16). 'These words', he said, 'were uttered by Jacob in the spirit of holiness, and therefore they must contain some mystery of wisdom. "Angel" is here one of the names of the Shekinah, applied to her when she is a messenger from on high and receives radiance from the supernal mirror, for then she is blessed by the Father and Mother, who say to her: Daughter, go, mind thy house, attend to thy house; go and feed them, go to the lower world where thy household wait for sustenance from thee; here is all which they require. Then she is "angel". True, she is in many places called "angel" when she does not come to give sustenance to worlds, and further she gives sustenance not in this name but in that of "the Lord". She is, however, called "angel" when she is sent by the Father and Mother, and "Lord" when she rests on the two Cherubim. When she first appeared to Moses she was called "angel", but to Jacob she appeared only under the figure of Rachel, as it is written, "And Rachel came with the sheep".

Zohar: Bemidbar, Section 3, Page 187b

To Abraham again she appeared as "Adonay", as it is written, "And Adonay appeared to him in the plains of Mamre" (Gen. XVIII, 1), because at that time he had accepted the covenant, and what had been concealed from him till then was now revealed. Jacob called her "angel" when he was about to depart from the world, because at that moment he was about to inherit her. "Who redeemed me from all evil": because he never drew near the side of evil, and evil never had dominion over him. "Bless the lads": Jacob was speaking like a man who goes into a new house and gives his orders for furnishing and decorating it, "the lads" referring to those who are appointed to be the channels of blessing to the world, to wit, the two Cherubim. "And let my name be named on them": with these words he set his house in order and rose to his proper grade to be united with the supernal Jacob. When those "lads" are duly blessed, then "they swarm like fishes in the midst of the earth". Fishes multiply in the sea and die as soon as they are brought to dry land, but these, although they come from the Great Sea, have their increase in the midst of the earth.'

They came and kissed him again and said: 'Come, let us say grace.' He said: 'I will say grace, because all that you have heard so far has been from me, so I will fulfil in myself the verse, "He that hath a bountiful eye shall be blessed" (Prov. XXII, 9), which we may also read as "shall bless". Why? "Because he hath given of his bread to the poor". Of the bread and food of my Torah have ye eaten.' Said R. Judah: 'Son beloved of the Lord, we have learnt that the host breaks bread and the guest says grace.' He replied: 'Neither am I host nor you guests, but I have found a text which I will carry out. For, indeed, I am "bountiful of eye", seeing that without being asked I have spoken till now, and you have eaten my bread and food'. He then took the cup of benediction and said grace. His hands shook as he held the cup, and when he came to "for the earth and for the food", he exclaimed, "I will lift up the cup of salvation and call on the name of the Lord", and he placed the cup down and took it up again in his right hand and resumed. When he finished he said: 'May it please God that the life of one of these may be prolonged from the Tree of Life, on which all life depends, and may the Holy One, blessed be He, be surety for him, and may he find an additional surety for himself below.' He then closed his eyes an instant, and then opening them, said: 'Companions, peace to you from the Lord of good, to whom belongs the whole world.'

In great wonder they wept and blessed him. They stayed there overnight, and in the morning

Zohar: Bemidbar, Section 3, Page 188a

rose early and departed. When they came to R. Simeon they told him all that had happened. R. Simeon wondered greatly and said: 'He is a mighty rock, and is worthy of this and even of more than one can imagine. He is the son of R. Hamnuna the Elder.' R. Eleazar was greatly excited and said: 'I must go to see that bright lamp.' Said R. Simeon: 'His name will not be known in the world, because there is something very exceptional about him. It is the light of the anointing of his father which shines on him, and this secret is not divulged among the Companions.'

One day the Companions were sitting arguing with one another—R. Eleazar and R. Abba, and R. Hiya and R. Yose, and the other Companions. They said: 'It is written, "Vex not Moab neither contend with him", etc., Moab and Ammon being spared because of Ruth and Naama, who were destined to issue from them. Now,' they asked, 'seeing that Zipporah, the wife of Moses, was from Midian, and Jethro and his sons, who were most virtuous, came from Midian, and Moses lived in Midian, was not Midian in fairness even more deserving to be spared than Moab and Ammon?' R. Simeon replied: 'A tree from which figs have still to be gathered is not like one from which they have been already gathered.' Said R. Eleazar: 'But even if the figs have been gathered, credit is due to the tree?' He replied: 'If a man has not yet gathered figs from a tree, he watches it so that no harm should come to it on account of the figs which it is still to bear. But once he has gathered the figs, he leaves it and no longer watches it. So God protected Moab, which had still to yield its figs, but not Midian, which had already yielded them: and this in spite of the fact that here it was Moab who took the first step, as it says: "And Moab said to the elders of Midian".'

R. Eleazar once went to see R. Yose b. R. Simeon b. R. Lakunia, his father-in-law. He was accompanied by R. Abba and R. Yose, and on the way they discussed points of Torah. Said R. Abba: 'Why did the Israelites treat the Moabites differently from the Ammonites, for, as we have learnt, in the presence of the former they brandished their weapons as if they meant to attack them, whereas against the Ammonites they made no display of military force?' R. Eleazar gave the answer that the younger daughter of Lot, from whom Ammon came, was more modest than the elder from whom Moab came. As they were going along, R. Eleazar suddenly remembered that boy, so they went three parasangs out of their way to get to that spot. They arranged to lodge in the house, and when they went in they found the boy sitting there and a table being laid before him. When he saw them he came up to them and said: 'Enter, holy saints, enter, ye shoots of the world to come, who are praised above and below, to meet whom even the fishes of the sea come up on the dry land.' R. Eleazar went to him and kissed him on his head. Then he again kissed him on his mouth. He said: 'The first kiss is for the fishes that leave the sea and come up on the dry land. The second was for the spawn of the fishes which produce good increase in the world.' Said the boy: 'From the smell of your garments I can see that Ammon and Moab have been attacking you; how did you escape them? You had no weapons, and yet you went in confidence without fear.'

Zohar: Bemidbar, Section 3, Page 188b

R. Eleazar and R. Abba and the Companions were in amazement. Said R. Abba: 'Blessed is this journey and happy is our lot that we have been privileged to see this.' They went on preparing the table, and the boy said: 'Holy sages, do you desire the bread of ease without warfare, or the bread of warfare?' R. Eleazar replied: 'Beloved son, dear and holy, so we desire. We are practised in all weapons of war, and we know how to use the sword and the bow and the lance and the sling, but thou art young and hast not yet seen how mighty warriors contend in battle.' The boy rejoiced and said: 'In truth I have not seen, but it is written: "Let not him that girdeth on boast like him that putteth off".' They then laid the table with all requirements. Said R. Eleazar: 'How I rejoice over this youngster, and how many new points will be brought out at this table! Therefore I said that I knew that his heart was being agitated by the holy spirit like a bell.' Said the boy: 'He that desires bread at the point of the sword, let him eat.' R. Eleazar drew him near to him and said: 'Because you boasted, you must commence the fight.' 'But', said the boy, 'I said at first that the fighting would be after the meal. Now, however, whoever wants fine flour must bring his weapons in his hands.' R. Eleazar replied: 'It is most fitting for you to give us a taste of your weapons.'

The boy then took the text: "It shall be that when ye eat of the bread of the land, ye shall offer up an heave offering unto the Lord" (Num. xv, 19). 'This verse refers to the Omer of waving (tenufah). What is tenufah? We may read it Tenu feh, "Give a mouth", the mouth being symbolic of the honour which we have to give to the Holy One, blessed be He. Hence the Omer had to be lifted up to show that we give to God this "mouth", since the chief praise of the Supreme King is when Israel prepare for him this honour and give glory to the King. Why was the Omer from barley and not from wheat? Because barley ripens first, whereas wheat is the more perfect food, being symbolical of the elimination of sin by the substitution of hittah (wheat) for het (sin). You, Companions, who have not attended on R.

Zohar: Bemidbar, Section 3, Page 189a

Shemaya the Saint, say that in the five kinds of corn there is no share for the "other side", but in truth in whatever rots in the ground there is a share for the other side, namely the chaff and the straw. These are represented by the heth and the teth of hittah, and so wheat, in virtue of the he, is the most perfect of plants, and wheat is the plant with which Adam sinned.' Said R. Eleazar: 'Assuredly, it is so.' The boy proceeded: 'The Holy Land is under the control of the Holy One, blessed be He, and no other power can enter there. How was the land tested to see whether it remained faithful and did not attach itself to any other power? By the bringing of an offering of barley, like the suspected wife.' [Tr. note: Num. v.] Said R. Abba: 'Of a surety thy sword is sharp.' The boy replied: 'I am prepared with shield and buckler to protect myself.' He said: 'There is no other power that can enter the Holy Land. Whence, then, come chaff and straw there?' The boy replied: 'It is written, "And God created man in his image... and God said to them, Be fruitful and multiply", etc. (Gen. I, 27, 28). Shall we say that if the serpent had not had intercourse with Eve there would have been no generations in the world, or if Israel had not sinned with the calf they would have had no posterity? The fact is that had not the serpent had intercourse with Eve, Adam would have produced progeny at once, in accordance with the verse just quoted, and that progeny would have been perfectly pure without any defilement. So here, the Holy Land, into which no alien power can enter, produces straw and chaff, but not from that side, but outside the Land the straw and chaff are from the "other side", which dogs holiness as a monkey dogs a man.' R. Eleazar and the Companions thereupon went and kissed him, and he said: 'I fancy that I have made good use of the weapons of war, the bread of the table.' Said R. Eleazar: 'Indeed it is so, and all weapons of war prosper in thy hands.'

He then discoursed on the verse: "And in the vine were three branches", etc. (Gen. XL, 10). 'We have learnt', he said, 'that there are seven firmaments which are six and also five. All issue from the ancient holy supernal Wine, which Jacob presses from a certain Vine. Therefore it was that Jacob presented to Isaac the wine which was fitting for him. That wine proceeds from grade to grade up to Joseph the Righteous, who is David the Faithful.

Zohar: Bemidbar, Section 3, Page 189b

This Vine is the one that is recognized as holy, in contrast to another which is called the "strange vine", the grapes of which are hard and biter. But this is the vine from which all the holy ones drew the taste of old and good wine, the wine in which Jacob poured water so that all who knew the taste of wine could drink it with relish. When this vine came near the Shekinah it put forth three branches. Then it "was as though it budded", like a bride bedecking herself, and it entered in the love and the joy of that wine to the place where joy abides. Then "its blossoms shot forth": its love went out to its beloved and it began to sing in love. Then were those tender grapes ripened and filled with the good old wine into which Jacob had poured water. Therefore one who blesses over wine should pour some water into it, since the blessing, "Have mercy, O Lord, upon thy people Israel", should not be said save with water in the wine.' R. Eleazar and R. Abba were amazed. They said: 'Holy angel, messenger from above, thy wine has conquered in the mystery of the holy spirit.' They all came and kissed him, and R. Eleazar said: 'Blessed be God for sending me here.' The boy then said: 'Bread and wine are the essence of the meal, all the rest being subsidiary. The Torah is begging of you, saying: "Come, eat ye of my bread and drink of the wine I have mingled" (Prov. IX, 5). Since the Torah calls you, you must obey her behest.' They said: 'That is assuredly so.' So they sat and ate and rejoiced with him.

After they had finished eating they still lingered at the table, and the boy discoursed further, on the verse: "And Moab said to the elders of Midian". 'It does not say, "the elders of Moab",' he said, 'but simply "Moab": the younger took counsel of the elders. What counsel did they give them? They gave a counsel which redounded to their own hurt. They said to Moab: We have reared a curse among us, namely Moses their chief, through a certain priest who was among us, who brought him up in his house and gave him his daughter to wife. Nay more, he gave him money and sent him to Egypt to destroy all the land, and he and all his household followed him. If we can uproot that chief of theirs, all his people will be immediately uprooted. All the nefarious plan of Peor was from Midian. On their advice they hired Balaam, and when they saw that Balaam could not prevail, they adopted another plan and prostituted their daughters and wives more than Moab. They planned

Zohar: Bemidbar, Section 3, Page 190a

with their prince that he should prostitute his daughter, thinking to catch Moses in their net. They invested her with all kinds of magic in order to catch their chief, but God "turns the wise backwards". They foresaw that a chief of the Israelites would be caught in their net, but they did not understand what they foresaw. They enjoined her not to unite herself with any man save Moses. She said to them: How shall I know him? They said: Join the man before whom you see all others rise, but no other. When Zimri, son of Salu, came, fifty-nine thousand of the tribe of Simeon rose before him, as he was their prince. She thought he was Moses and joined him. When all the rest saw this they did likewise, with the consequences that we know. Thus all was from Midian, and therefore Midian was punished. God said to Moses, "Avenge the children of Israel of the Midianites" (Num. XXXI, 1), as though to say: For thee this is fitting and proper. Moab I leave until two pearls shall have issued from them. David the son of Jesse shall punish Moab and wash the pot clean of the filth of Peor, as it says, "Moab is my washpot" (Ps. LX, 9). With all this the sinners of Moab did not desist from their wickedness. In a later generation, when they saw that Joshua and all the elders for whom miracles might have been performed were dead, they said: Now we have a chance, and so they went and joined Amalek, saying, Remember what the children of Israel and Moses their chief, and Joshua their disciple did to you, trying to destroy you. Now is the time when they have no one to shield them, and we will join you. So it is written, "The Midianites came up and the Amalekites and the children of the East" (Judges VI, 3), and again, "Because of Midian the children of Israel made themselves the dens", etc. (Ibid. 2). No one did them as much harm as Midian. Hence Moses told the Israelites: "God said to me, Vex not Moab" (Deut. II, 9); that is to say, this injunction was laid upon Moses but not on any other, on David, for instance. In fact, Joshua and the elders who survived him were also forbidden to attack Moab because they were all members of the Beth Din of Moses, and what was forbidden to Moses was forbidden to them, and also because the precious pearls had not yet issued from them. For Ruth was in the days of the Judges. She was the daughter of Eglon, King of Moab, and when Eglon was killed by Ehud they appointed another king, and his daughter was left in charge of a guardian. When Elimelech came to the field of Moab she married his son. She was not made a Jewess by Elimelech, but she learnt all the ways of his house and the rules about food, and when she went with Naomi, then she was converted. Naamah came from the children of Ammon in the days of David. Then the holy spirit rested on David, saying: David, when I measured out all the earth and cast lots, then "Israel was the lot of his inheritance", and I remember what Moab did to them. Hence it is written that David "measured them with the line"; All who were of that tribe and deserving of death the line seized. Midian was destroyed by Gideon, so that none were left of the seed which harmed Israel with counsel or in any other way. God cherishes enmity against all who harm Israel and takes vengeance on them, but if anything good for the world is destined to issue from them, He

Zohar: Bemidbar, Section 3, Page 190b

bears with them until that good has come forth, and then He punishes them.' Said R. Eleazar: 'This is indeed so, and all this is correct.' Said the boy: 'Now do you Companions prepare your weapons and join combat.' R. Eleazar then discoursed on the verse: "Bless the Lord, ye angels, ye mighty of his", etc. (Ps. CIII, 20). 'King David', he said, 'here invited the hosts of heaven which are the stars and constellations to bless the Holy One, joining his own soul with them, wherefore he concluded the Psalm with the words, "Bless the Lord, O my soul". Before Israel came, the heavenly angels used to serve with the performance of ceremonies. When Israel at Mount Sinai said, "We will do and we will hearken", performance was taken from the ministering angels and confined to the land of Israel alone. Hence it says, first, "Mighty in strength that fulfil his words", and then, "To hearken". Happy are Israel who took performance from them and carried it out themselves.' Said the boy to him: 'Be on your guard and have your weapon ready. Did Israel take this honour and no other?' He replied: 'I have found this and no other.' Said the boy to him: 'Your sword is of no avail, or you do not wield it properly. Leave the sword to one who knows how to use it. The highest term of praise which has been entrusted to the ministering angels-not by themselves, but only in conjunction with Israel-is "Holy", but benediction is committed to them when alone, as also to Israel. Not so "holy", for they say the sanctification only in conjunction with Israel. Before Israel sanctify below they cannot sanctify above; hence the great honour of Israel is that they say the sanctification below by themselves.' Said R. Eleazar: 'This is indeed so, and all this has been established. We have also explained that three sanctifications were entrusted to Israel below, from the verse: "And ye shall sanctify yourselves and be holy, for I the Lord am holy" (Lev. XI, 44, and XX, 26).' Said the boy: 'Quite so, but you did not remember your lance till I took it from your shoulder and put it in your hand. Now remember that the lance is in your hand. Return to where you left off.' R. Eleazar then resumed: 'We were speaking of benediction. What is the meaning of "bless ye"? The drawing of blessings from the place from which all blessings issue until they become a blessing through the abundance of the drawing, and from the abundance of waters in that blessing straightway they swarm with fishes of all kinds. The angels who dwell in the heavenly abodes say simply "Bless the Lord", but we who dwell below say "Bless eth the Lord", because we need to draw this eth [Tr. note: The Shekinah.] down upon us, and through it we enter the presence of the King. And since we draw this eth down upon us, we have at the same time to say prayers and praises, and therefore it is forbidden to greet any man until one has said his prayers, and if he does so he draws a "high place" down upon himself instead of this eth.' Said the boy to him: 'Of a truth I see that your weapons are good; be mindful of them and do not forget them. Assuredly the might of a warrior lies

Zohar: Bemidbar, Section 3, Page 191a

in his lance and sword. But what is the meaning of "mighty in strength that fulfil his word, hearkening unto the voice of his word"?' Said R. Eleazar: 'I have already explained.' Said the boy: 'I see that your arm has become faint. Now it is time not to hold back, but to sling from the catapult stone after stone.'

He then cited the verse: "I am black but comely, O ye daughters of Jerusalem" (S.S. I, 5). 'This means that when she (the Moon) is very lovesick for her Beloved, she shrinks to nothing until only a dot is left of her, and she is hidden from all her hosts and camps. Then she says, I am black, like the letter yod, in which there is no white space, and I have no room to shelter you under my wings; therefore "do not look at me", for ye cannot see me at all. What then do her mighty warriors do? They roar like lions, until their voice is heard by the Beloved above, and He knows that his Beloved is lovesick like himself, so that none of her beauty can be seen, and so through the voices of those warriors of hers her Beloved comes forth from his palace with many gifts and presents, with spices and incense, and comes to her and finds her black and shrunken, without form or beauty. He then draws near to her and embraces and kisses her until she gradually revives from the scents and spices, and her joy in having her Beloved with her, and she is built up and recovers her full form and beauty. And this was brought about by the might and power of her doughty warriors. Hence it is written, "Mighty in strength that fulfil his word". And then when they have restored her to her form and beauty they and all the other hosts wait attentively for her words, and she is like a king in the midst of his army. In the same way below, when there are sinners in the generation, she hides herself and diminishes herself till only a dot is left, until the mighty ones, the truly virtuous, come and as it were restore her, so that she gradually brightens and recovers her form and beauty and becomes as before.' The Companions came and kissed him, saying: 'Had even the prophet Ezekiel said this, the world would have wondered.' The boy then said: 'I will say the grace.' They said: 'Do so, for to you it is fitting.' He said: 'How holy you are, how many blessings await you from the holy Mother because ye have not refused to let me say the grace! We have learnt that it is the duty of every one to say grace. If he cannot himself, his wife or his sons can say it for him, but a curse light on the man who does not know how to say grace himself and has to ask his wife or children. If he knows, he must train his son and give him the cup of benediction. And if he does not, then we say of him, "He that withholds his son shall be cursed to the holy Mother" (Prov. XI, 26), but as I am the only son of my mother, give me the cup and I will bless the Holy King who has brought to my mother's house men of worth before whom I can utter powerful discourse. Before I say grace, however, I will expound properly the verse

Zohar: Bemidbar, Section 3, Page 191b

I have quoted. The word yikbuhu (curse him) means properly "pronounce distinctly": that is, they will set forth his sins distinctly to the holy Mother. We may also translate, "he who withholds blessings from the Son", whom the Father and Mother have crowned and blessed with many blessings, and concerning whom they commanded, "Kiss the son lest he be angry" (Ps. II, 12), since he is invested both with judgement and with mercy. The last part of the verse we may translate, "He who gives blessing to the Head breaks the power of the "other side". Now, Companions, let us say grace.' They handed him the cup and he said grace, and the Companions rejoiced more than they had ever done since the wedding of R. Eleazar. They blessed the boy with all their hearts, and he said to them: 'You should not depart save with words of the Torah.' He then expounded for them the verse: "And the Lord went before them by day in a pillar of cloud" (Ex. XIII, 21). 'We should', he said, 'render thus: And the Lord, that is, the Shekinah, was there, but day, that is Abraham (hesed) went before them by day, while the Bride went before them by night, as it is written, "and by night in a pillar of fire to give light to them"–each one at the fitting time. And as for you, Companions, may night and day ever be before you.'

They kissed and blessed him as before and went their way. When they came to R. Simeon they told him what had happened. He was greatly astonished, and said: 'This is indeed excellent, but he will not make a name. When a thin stick burns it burns only for a little time. It is written, "His seed shall be mighty upon earth, the generation of the upright shall be blessed" (Ps. CXII, 2). When a man is mighty on the earth, mighty in the Torah and in control of his passions, then his light goes forth and is continued through many generations.' 'But', said R. Abba, 'we see children who say wonderful things and afterwards become very eminent.' He replied: 'When a child says one or two wonderful things by

690

accident, then we may be confident that he will one day teach the Torah in Israel. But the same cannot be said of this one whose light is already complete. And besides, the Holy One, blessed be He, desires to smell this apple.

Happy are the righteous, of whom it is written "And the remnant that is escaped of the house of Judah shall again take root downwards and bear fruit upward" (2 Kings XIX, 30). His father who has departed this world is a root below in the Academy of the firmament, and he shall bear fruit above in the highest Academy. Were it not that I would fain not oppose the Holy One, blessed be He, whose desire is to savour him, none should have dominion over him. As it is, may it be God's will that his mother should have no trouble from him'. And so it came to pass. AND HE SENT MESSENGERS UNTO BALAAM THE SON OF BEOR. There are here twenty-eight words corresponding to the twenty-eight degrees of the sorceries of the bird. It may be asked, Why did Balak commence with Balaam so abruptly? He should have first ingratiated himself with him and then told him what he wanted. The truth is', said R. Yose, 'that we see from here that Balak knew the disposition of that bad man, that he was always craving for honour and had no pleasure save in doing evil. Balak, through his sorceries, knew that the grades of Moses were very high, and he knew by the same means that the grades of Balaam corresponded. Pethor, to which he sent, was the town of Balaam; it was so called because Balaam used to prepare a table (pethor) there with food and drink for the evil sides, as is the custom of those who practise magic, in order to bring together the evil spirits to answer their inquiries.'

He then cited the verse: "And thou shalt make a table of acacia wood" (Ex. xxv, 23), and again, "Thou shalt put upon the table shew bread", etc. 'God desired all those holy vessels to be made in order that the holy spirit might be drawn down from heaven to earth. Similarly the wicked Balaam prepared one for the other side, with bread which is called "abominable bread".

'It is written, "Lord, when thou wentest forth out of Seir, when thou marchedst out of the field of Edom, the earth trembled", etc. (Jud. v, 4). This refers to the fact that before God gave the Law to Israel He offered it to the children of Esau and the children of Ishmael, and they would not accept it. The question may be asked—and there is no sin in scrutinising the language of the Law minutely—when God went to Seir, to what prophet of the children of Esau did He reveal himself? And similarly when He went to Paran, to what prophet of them did He reveal himself? We cannot say that He was revealed to all of them, for we find no such thing save in the case of Israel, and that by the hand of Moses. Further, in the verse, "The Lord came from Sinai and shone forth from Mount Seir", etc. (Deut. XXXIII, 2), it should be "came to Sinai", "shone to Seir", etc.' When R. Simeon came, he asked him. He said: 'This question has been answered as follows. "God came from Sinai" to reveal Himself to the Israelites. "He shone forth

from Seir", that is, from the refusal of the children of Esau to receive the Law; from this Israel derived additional light and love. So, too, with Mount Paran, from the refusal of the children of Ishmael. As for your question, through whom was He revealed to Esau and Ishmael, this is a profound mystery which is to be revealed through you. The Torah issued from the mystic Head of the King. When it came to the Left Arm the Holy One, blessed be He, saw some vicious blood that had collected there. He said: I must cleanse and purify this arm, since if this vicious blood is not lessened it will damage all. He therefore summoned Samael and said to him: Dost thou desire my Law? What is written in it, he asked? He replied, taking a test passage: "Thou shalt not kill". Whereupon Samael said: Heaven save us. This Torah is thine, and let it remain thine. I do not want it. He then besought Him, saying: Master of the Universe, if Thou givest it to me, all dominion will vanish, for it is based upon slaughter, on the star of Mars, and if there are no wars it will pass away from the world. Master of the Universe, take Thy Law, and let me have no portion in it. But, if it please Thee, there is the people of the sons of Jacob, for them it is fitting. He thought to do them a mischief: If they receive this, he said, assuredly they will vanish from the world and will never have dominion. God said to him: Thou art the firstborn and for thee it is fitting. He replied: He has my birthright, as it was sold to him and I consented. Then God said: Since thou desirest no portion in it, leave it entirely. He replied: Good. He then said: This being so, give me an advice how I shall induce the children of Jacob to accept it. He said: Master of the Universe, it is necessary to offer some inducement to them. Take some light from the light of the powers of the heavens and put it upon them, and for this they will receive it, and give them some of mine first. He then took off some of the light with which he was covered and gave it to Him to give to Israel. Hence it says, "He shone forth to them from Seir", Seir being a name of Samael. Having thus cleared away the bad blood from the Left Arm, God turned to the Right Arm and saw it in the same state. So He called Rahab and said: Dost thou desire my Law? He asked what was written in it. God again selected a crucial passage and said: "Thou shalt not commit adultery". He exclaimed: Alas for me, if God shall give me this inheritance, since it will destroy all my dominion, for I have received the blessing of the waters, of the fishes of the sea, to whom it was said: Be fruitful and multiply, etc. He began to beseech the Almighty, saying: Master of the Universe, two sons came forth from Abraham, there are the sons of Isaac, give to them, for them it beseems. He said: I cannot, for thou art the firstborn, and to thee it belongs. He commenced to implore Him, saying: Master of the Universe, let my birthright be his, and this extra light which I inherit on this account take and give to them. And God did so; wherefore it is written, "He shined forth from Mount Paran". When He had taken these gifts for Israel from those great Chiefs, He summoned all

Zohar: Bemidbar, Section 3, Page 193a

the myriads of holiness who are appointed to rule the other nations and they gave Him the same reply, and from all of them He received gifts to give to Israel. He was like a physician who had a phial full of some elixir of life which he desired to keep for his son. He was a clever man, and he said to himself: I have bad servants in my house; if they know that I intend to give to my son this present, they will be jealous of him and seek to kill him. What did he do therefore? He took a little poison and smeared it round the edge of the phial. He then called his servants and said to them: You are faithful servants, do you want to try that drug? They said: Let us see what it is. They just took a taste, and they had scarcely smelt it when they came near dying. They said to themselves: If he gives this poison to his son, he will certainly die, and we shall inherit our master. They said to him: Master, this medicine is fitted only for your son. We remit to you the reward of our labour, which you can give to him as a present so that he may take the medicine. So God, being a wise physician, knew that if He gave the Torah to Israel without telling them they would every day pursue them and klll them for it, but in this way He made them give presents and gifts so that Israel should accept it, and Moses received all of them to give to Israel, as it is written: "Thou has ascended on high, thou hast taken captives" (Ps. LXVIII, 19), and in this way Israel inherited the Torah without any opposition or challenge. These gifts and presents which they received are their ornament, and therefore death and the other side had no dominion over them till they sinned, when, as it says, "they took off their ornaments from Mount Sinai" (Ex. XXXIII, 6). Whenever Israel return to their father in heaven those ornaments are restored to them and they are invested with them, and in the time to come all will be returned.'

R. Yose said: 'It says, "Lord, when thou didst go forth from Seir the earth shook". Why did it shake? Because it desired to return to chaos when it saw that God had offered the Torah to all peoples and they had not accepted it and only Israel was left, and it was thought that Israel would refuse like the other nations. When, however, they said, "We will do and we will hearken", it became calm again. Observe that because Israel said "we will do", they are not afraid of anything that magicians may do with their arts. One reason is this, and another is because when God brought them out of Egypt He broke before them all kinds of magic and divination so they cannot prevail against them. When Balak came he knew this, and therefore he sent messengers to Balaam that he might prepare a table and seek counsel therefrom.' R. Eleazar and R. Abba were once going to see R. Yose, son of R. Simeon b. Lakunia, the father-in-law of R. Eleazar. They rose at midnight and sat down to study the Torah. Said R. Eleazar: 'Now is the hour when the Holy One, blessed be He, goes into the Garden of Eden to have joyous converse with the righteous there.' Said R. Abba: 'What is this joyous converse?' R. Eleazar replied: 'This is a profound mystery,

Zohar: Bemidbar, Section 3, Page 193b

concealed with the Unknown.' Said R. Abba: 'Were, then, the great ones of former days relying on an empty fantasy, and did they not try to find out on what they were established in this world, and what they were to expect in the next?' R. Eleazar then commenced to discourse on the verse: "O Lord, thou art my God, I will exalt thee, I will praise thy name, for thou hast done wonderful things" (Isa. xxv, 1). 'This verse', he said, 'contains the mystery of faith. "Lord" is the supreme mystery, the beginning of the supernal Point, the recondite and unknowable. "My God" refers to the still small Voice which is the first subject of interrogation, and is also the supernal Priest. We have further laid down that there are three places each of which is called "thou". "I will exalt thee": all together. "I will praise thy name": in fitting manner, this being the known Name. "For thou hast done wonderful things,': this is the secondary light with which is invested the hidden ancient primordial light, the supreme grade, the primordial Adam. Rab Hamnuma the Elder said that "wonderful things" is a grade of the wonders of wisdom, to wit, "a path which no bird of prey knoweth" (Job XXVIII, 7). The "counsels of old" are the two willow twigs [Tr. note: Nezah and Hod.] whence comes all the counsel of the prophets. "Faithfulness and truth" are two things which are one, the river and the garden; the one issues from Eden and the other is watered from it. Thus we have here the whole mystery of faith.'

R. Eleazar said: 'Who killed the wicked Balaam, and how was he killed?' R. Isaac replied: 'Phineas and his comrades killed him, as it says, "they slew on their slain". For we have learnt that through his magic arts in the city of Midian he became able to fly in the air, he and the kings of Midian, and it was the holy frontlet and the prayer of Phineas that brought them down on their slain.' Said R. Eleazar: 'I know all this.' R. Simeon then said: 'Eleazar, Balaam was a powerful adversary, as it says, "There arose not a prophet in Israel like Moses", but-so we explain-there did arise among the Gentiles, to wit, Balaam, who was supreme among the lower Crowns as Moses among the upper Crowns. How, then, were they able to kill him? The answer is to be gathered from a remark of the Book of the Wisdom of King Solomon. There are three signs in a man: paleness is a sign of anger, talking is a sign of folly, and self-praise is a sign of ignorance. It is true that it says, "Let a stranger praise thee and not thy own mouth" (Prov. XXVII, 2), and we alter this to "Let a stranger praise thee, and if not, thine own mouth", but that only means that if thou art not known, discourse on the Torah so that through the opening of thy mouth in the Torah men should know who thou art and praise thee. But the wicked Balaam praised himself in everything, and deceived people as well. He made much of little; for all that he said of himself referred only to the unclean grades, and though it was true, it did not mean much, though whoever heard it imagined that he surpassed all the prophets of the world. When, for instance, he said, "Which heareth the words of God and knoweth

the knowledge of the Almighty", who that heard would not think that there was no true prophet like him? Certainly it was true; but only with reference to the grades to which he was attached. He heard the words of a god-the one who is called "another god", and he knew the knowledge of the most high, that is, the highest of the grades of uncleanness, those who direct the boat and the tempest. There are forty-nine of them, and the steersman is the highest of them all. Thus he praised himself vaguely, and while speaking truthfully he yet misled people. So when he said, "Who seeth the vision of the Almighty", the hearers thought that he saw something which no other could see, but what he saw was only one of the branches that issue from Shaddai. What was that vision? Uzza and Azael, who were "falling down and having eyes open".

Now where was Balaam at that time? Seeing that he said, "Now I am going to my people", how can he have been in Midian? The truth is, however, that when he saw that twenty-two thousand of Israel fell through his counsel, he stayed there and demanded his reward; and while he was staying there Phineas and his captains of the host came there. When he saw Phineas he flew up into the air with his two sons, Yunus and Yamburus. But these, you will say, died at the time when the golden calf was made? (We learn this from the words of the text, "there died of the people about three thousand" (Ex. XXXII, 28), the word "about" indicating that these two were reckoned as equal to three thousand men.) That wretch, however, being acquainted with every kind of enchantment, took also those of his sons, and with them commenced to fly away. When Phineas saw a man in the air flying away, he shouted to his soldiers: Is anyone able to fly after him, for it is Balaam? Then Zilya, of the tribe of Dan, arose and seized the Domination that rules over enchantments and flew after him. When Balaam saw him he changed his direction in the air and broke through five ethers

and vanished from view. Zilya was then sorely vexed, not knowing what to do. Phineas thereupon called out: Shade of the dragons which overshadow all serpents, turn thy tresses. Straightway he revealed his path and Zilya approached him and both came down in front of Phineas. This is referred to in the blessing of Jacob (Gen. XLIX, 17): "Dan shall be a serpent in the way"-this is Samson: "an adder in the path"-this is Zilya; "that biteth the horses' heels"-this is Ira the companion of David; "so that his rider falleth backward"-this is Shiryah, who is destined to come with the Messiah of Ephraim, and who will wreak vengeance on other nations; and then it will be time to expect the deliverance of Israel, as it says, "For thy salvation I hope, O Lord". When Balaam came down in front of Phineas, he said to him: Wretch, how many evil haps hast thou brought upon the holy people! He then said to Zilya: Kill him, but not with the Name, for it is not meet that the divine sanctity should be mentioned over him, so that his soul in leaving him should not be united with matters of holy grades, and his prayer be fulfilled: "May my soul die the death of the righteous" (Num. XXIII, 10). He then tried to kill him in many ways, but did not succeed, until he took a sword on which was engraved a snake on each side. Said Phineas: Kill him with his own weapon. And then he did kill him; for such is the way of that side, he who follows it is killed by it and it is with his soul when it departs from him, and he is punished in the other world and never finds burial, and his bones rot and become noxious serpents, and even the worms that eat his body become serpents. We have found in the Book of Asmodai which he gave to King Solomon, that anyone who desires to make powerful enchantments, if he knows the rock where Balaam fell, will find there snakes formed from the bones of that wicked one, and if he kills one he can make certain enchantments with its head and others with its body, and others again with its tail, there being three kinds in each one. One of the questions which the Queen of Sheba asked Solomon was how to take hold of the bone of the serpent of three enchantments. From that point, Eleazar my son, God did other things with that sinner, and these are secret mysteries which should not be revealed, only in order that the Companions here should know the hidden ways of the world I have revealed them.'

[Note: The last 3lines of the Hebrew text are not found in our translation]

[Note: The first 2 lines of the Hebrew text are not found in our translation]

COME NOW, THEREFORE, I PRAY THEE, CURSE ME THIS PEOPLE, ETC. R. Abba discoursed on the verse: "A prayer of the afflicted when he is overwhelmed" (Ps. CII, 1). He said: 'There are three to whom prayers are ascribed in the Scripture, viz., Moses and David and the afflicted one. We also find, it is true, "A prayer of Habakkuk the prophet", but when we examine this we find that it is a praise giving to the Almighty for having revived him and performed miracles for him. The "prayer of Moses" is one such as no other man ever offered. The "prayer of David" (Ps. LXXXVI) is one such as no other king ever offered. Yet the prayer of the poor man is the most excellent of all, and takes precedence of the prayer of Moses or of David, or of any other man. The reason is that the poor man is broken of heart, and it is written, "God is near to the broken of heart" (Ps. XXIV, 19). The poor man always expostulates with God, yet God listens and hears his words. When he prays He opens all the windows of the firmament, and all other prayers which ascend aloft have to make way for that of the broken-hearted poor man. God says, as it were: Let all other prayers wait, and let this one enter before me. I require here no court to judge between us, let his complaint come before Me and I and he will be alone. And so God alone attends to those complaints, as it is written, "and poureth out his complaint before the Lord". Truly, "before the Lord". All the hosts of heaven ask one another: With what is the Holy One, blessed be He, engaged? They answer: He is engaged eagerly with His own vessels. None of them know what is done with that prayer of the poor man and with all his complaints. But when he pours out his tears with expostulation before the Almighty, God desires nothing so much as to receive them. Now David saw that all the windows and all the gates of heaven were opened to the poor man, and there was no other to whose prayer God gave ear so readily, so he made himself a poor man and a beggar, he stripped himself of his royal garment and sat on the ground like a beggar and uttered his prayer. Hence it says, "A prayer of David. Bow down thine ear, O Lord, and answer me"; why? "for I am poor and needy" (Ps. LXXXVI, 1). Said the Almighty to him: David, art thou not a king, the ruler over mighty kings, and thou makest thyself a pauper and a beggar? Straightway he gave his prayer another turn, and leaving the pose of a pauper he said: "Preserve my soul, for I am pious"; and in truth, all these features were in David.' Said R. Eleazar to him: 'What you have said is quite right; and withal [Tr. note: Al. therefore.] a man in praying should make himself poor and needy in order that his prayer may enter along with that of the rest of the poor, for the doorkeepers allow none to enter so readily as the poor, since they can even enter without asking permission. So if a man puts himself in the position of the poor, his prayer ascends and meets the other prayers of the poor and ascends with them and enters as one of them and is favourably received before the King. 'King David placed himself in four categories. He placed himself among the poor; he placed himself among the pious; he placed himself among the servants; and he placed himself among those who are ready to sacrifice themselves and their lives for the sanctification of God's Name. He placed himself among the poor, as it is written, "For I am poor and needy". He placed himself among the pious, as it is written, "Preserve my soul, for I am pious". For a man should not consider himself wicked; nor can it be objected that if so he will never tell of his sins, for when he makes confession of his sins then he is pious, since he comes to make repentance; he removes himself from the evil side in the uncleanness of which he abode until now, and cleaves to the right hand which is outstretched to receive him. Nor should you think that God does not receive him till he makes full confession of all the sins that he has committed since he was born, for if so, what of those

Zohar: Bemidbar, Section 3, Page 195b

that are concealed from him? The truth is that he need only recount those that he remembers, and if he concentrates his attention on these, all the others follow them, just as in searching for leaven we do not peer into every nook and cranny, but if we have searched as far as the eye can see, the rest is reckoned as cleared away along with this. So also the priest declared the leper clean if he could observe no mark on him without peering too closely. So a man need not recount all his sins since the day he was born, or those which are concealed from him. Hence David placed himself among the saints. He placed himself among the servants, as it is written, "Save thy servant, O thou my God". He placed himself among those who are ready to sacrifice themselves for the sanctification of God's Name, as it is written, "Rejoice the soul of thy servant, for unto thee, O Lord, do I lift up my soul" (Ibid. 4). All these four characters did King David assume before his Master.'

R. Eleazar said: 'I lift up my hand in prayer before the Holy King, for we have learnt that it is forbidden for a man to raise his hand above him save in prayer and blessing and supplication, since the fingers of man have an important significance-and so I do now, and say that if any man shall arrange his service thus before his Master and sincerely carry out this purpose, his prayer shall not return unanswered. At first he must make himself a servant to arrange a service of praise and song before Him. Again he becomes a servant to recite the standing-up prayer, and once more after saying his prayer. Therefore David called himself "servant" three times in this psalm, as it says, "Save thy servant, thou my God", "Rejoice the soul of thy servant", and "Give strength to thy servant". Next a man should place himself among those who are ready to sacrifice themselves for the sanctification of God's Name, by reciting with proper devotion the formula of the unity, "Hear, O Israel". Then he must make himself poor, when he knocks at the doors of the highest heights in saying the prayer "true and certain", and proceed thus to the Amidah prayer, so that he, in saying it, should feel himself broken-hearted, poor and needy. Then he should place himself among the saints by recounting his sins in the prayer "hearkening to prayer", for so the individual should do in order to cling to the right hand which is stretched forth to receive sinners who repent We have learnt that when a man has sincerely prayed in these four styles, God is pleased and stretches forth His right hand over him when he comes to the third servant, and says of him, "Thou art my servant". Assuredly the prayer

Zohar: Bemidbar, Section 3, Page 196a

of such a man shall never return unanswered.' R. Abba came and kissed him. He said: 'This is what we call "more desirable than gold and much fine gold" (Ps. XIX, 10). How sweet are the time-honoured words which the ancients have strung together! When we taste them we are unable to eat any other food. Assuredly it is so, and the Scripture proves that there are three servants who are mentioned in one place-two as you have said, and the third for the Holy One, blessed be He, to crown Himself withal.'

R. Eleazar then discoursed on the verse: "Who is among you that feareth the Lord, that hearkeneth to the voice of his servant" (Isa. L, 10). 'This verse', he said, 'has been explained by the Companions to refer to one who is accustomed to go to synagogue to pray and one day does not come. Then God inquires of him, saying: "Who is among you that feareth the Lord, that hearkeneth to the voice (of) his servant": that is to say, who is wont to hear himself called servant, the name given in honour by the Almighty, the "voice" being heard in all the firmaments that this is the servant of the Holy King. "He that walketh in darkness and hath no light": before Israel gather in their synagogues for prayer, the "other side" closes up all the supernal lights and prevents them from diffusing themselves over the worlds. Three times in the day, however, the other sides, male and female, go and wander over the world, and that is the time which is fitting for prayer, because then there is no accuser there at all. And while they are wandering over "mountains of darkness", the windows of the upper lights are opened and they come forth and rest in the synagogues upon the heads of those who are praying there, and God inquires of him who is not there and says: Alas for So-and-so who was wont to be here and is now going in darkness and has moved away from the light-"he hath no light"; how many good things he has lost! But if he were there "he would trust in the name of the Lord", in the circle of the first Servant, "and stay upon his God", in the mystery of the second Servant.' Said R. Simeon: 'Eleazar, my son, of a surety the spirit of prophecy rests upon thee.' R. Abba said: 'Lion, son of lion, who can stand before them when they roar to take prey? All lions are strong, but these above all. But from other lions it is hard to rescue prey, whereas from these it is easy, for when they snatch they give to all.'

[Note: The last 4 lines of the Hebrew text are not found in our translation]

Zohar: Bemidbar, Section 3, Page 196b

R. Eleazar said: 'Of a truth there is a hidden reference in the name Zippor. It is written, "Yea the sparrow (zippor) hath found her a house, and the swallow a nest for herself" (Ps. LXXXIV, 4). Would King David have said this of a mere sparrow? The reference, however, is to what we have learnt: How beloved are souls (neshamoth) before the Holy One, blessed be He. This does not mean all souls, but the souls of the righteous whose abode is there with Him. We have learnt that there are three walls to the Garden of Eden, and between each pair many souls and spirits walk about and enjoy the perfumes from within, though they are not permitted to enter. On certain days in the year, in the months of Nisan and Tishri, those spirits assemble in a certain place on the walls of the garden, where they look like chirping birds every morning. This chirping is praise given to the Almighty, and prayer for the life of human beings, because in those days Israel are all busy with performing the commandments and precepts of the Lord of the universe.' Said R. Simeon: 'Eleazar, so far very good, since in truth those spirits are there, but what will you make of "and the swallow a nest for herself"?' He replied: 'What I have learnt is that this is the holy super-soul that goes aloft to a hidden place which no eye but God's has seen.' Said R. Simeon: 'Eleazar, truly all this is correct, and so it is in the lower Garden of Eden as you have said. The "sparrows" are the holy spirits that are privileged to enter and then come out again, and these "find a house", each one its appropriate chamber, and nevertheless they are all jealous of the canopy of their comrades, those that have freedom from all. God shows them a certain hidden palace, "which no eye has seen but thine, O God", and which is called "the bird's nest". From there are woven crowns for the Messiah in the time to come, and three times a year God holds converse with those righteous and shows them that hidden palace which is not known even to all the righteous there. "Who hath put her young with thine altars": these are the righteous whose merit has been perfected with holy sons learned in both Torahs in this world, and who are called two altars crowned before the Holy King, since the merit of their sons in this world shields them and crowns them there. Now continue thy discourse, since we did not mean to shame thee.' R. Eleazar then proceeded: 'The "bird" is Jethro and the "swallow" indicates his sons, who used to be in the Chamber of hewn stone (in the Temple) teaching the Torah and giving decisions on religious matters. At first they left the comfort of their homes in Midian to dwell in the wilderness, but when God saw that their yearning was for the Torah, He drew them from there and made them a "house" in the Chamber of hewn stone. The "swallow" here is the same as the "bird". This is why the name of Balak's father, Zippor, is mentioned here, though we do not find this with other (heathen) kings. Jethro abandoned idolatry and came to join Israel, and for this he was banished and

Zohar: Bemidbar, Section 3, Page 197a

persecuted. Balak, who was of his descendants, abandoned his path. When the elders of Moab and the elders of Midian, who were brothers in idolatry, saw that whereas Jethro and his son had clung to the Shekinah, this one had abandoned it, they came and made him king over them, as it is written, "And Balak son of Zippor was king of Moab at that time". Hence he is specially mentioned as being the son of Zippor, as if to say that this was not worthy of him. It says that "he saw". We should have expected "he heard". What did he see? He saw that he was destined to fall into the hands of the Israelites, after Israel had first fallen into his hands.'

R. Abba discoursed on the passage beginning: "If thou know not, O thou fairest among women", etc. (S.S. I, 8). 'The Community of Israel', he said, 'is she that gathers in from all the camps above, and holds in all that she gathers, letting it escape only by drops like dew, because there is not sufficient faith below. For if She were to find faith as it is found in her, She would pour the light on every side without restraint, and they would give to her also gifts and presents without stint. But it is those of the lower world who restrain them and restrain her, and therefore she is called Azereth (the restrainer). Nevertheless, as a mother gives to her sons in secret and unbeknown, so she does with her children, Israel. We have learnt from the Sacred Lamp that when She ascends to receive delights and dainties, if then there is a blemish in Israel She is separated from her Spouse a fixed number of days. Then it is known above that there is a blemish in Israel and the Left awakens and lets down a thread below. Then Samael quickly rouses himself to assail the world, as it says, "And he called Esau his elder (lit. great) son" (Gen. XXVII, 1). He is indeed great with the camps of the "other side" and he steers all the ships of the sea of accusations with the evil breeze to sink them in the depths of the sea. Now when the Holy One, blessed be He, is in merciful mood, He gives to him all the sins of Israel and he casts them into the depths of the sea-for so his camps are called-and they take them and flow with them to all other peoples. Are, then, the sins and guilt of Israel scattered among their people? The truth is that they wait for gifts from above like a dog at a table, and when God takes all the sins of Israel and throws them to them, they think that He is diverting from Israel the gifts which He intended to give them, and giving to them instead, and they straightway rejoice and throw them to the other peoples. Observe now. The Community of Israel says first, "Black am I and comely", humbling herself before the Holy King. Then She inquires of Him, saying: "Where feedest thou thy flock, where makest thou it to rest at noon?" The two "where"s hint at the two destructions of the Temple. The word "feed" refers to the captivity of Babylon, which lasted but a short time, and the word "causest to lie down" to the captivity of Edom, which is long drawn out. We might also translate, "where does she feed and cause to lie down", making Her refer to Herself as if to say: How can she cause dew to drop upon them from the heat of midday? Also when Israel cry out because of their oppression

Zohar: Bemidbar, Section 3, Page 197b

and the taunts of their enemies and yet they praise and bless God for all their tribulations, (She says) I "sit as one that is veiled" and cannot work wonders for them or avenge them. Then He answers Her: "If thou knowest not, O thou fairest among women", how to gather strength in captivity and to defend thy children, "go thy way forth by the footsteps of the flock": these are the school children who learn the Torah, "and feed thy kids": these are the infants who are snatched away from this world to the Academy on high which is "beside the shepherds' tents". This is the Academy of Metatron where are all the mighty of the world and all those who guide men in the laws of permitted and forbidden.' R. Eleazar interrupted, saying: 'The "footsteps of the sheep" are the students who have come later into the world and find the Torah clearly expounded, and yet manage to find new expositions every day, and the Shekinah rests on them and listens to their words.' R. Abba said: 'That is indeed so, but it comes to the same thing. Why does it say here, "O thou fairest among women", seeing that she called herself "black"? He says to Her: "Thou art the fairest of women", the fairest of all the grades. Or it may mean that He approves of the kindnesses which she did for her sons in secret, just as a father is glad when a mother is secretly merciful to his children, even though their conduct has not been good.'

R. Abba here broke off to say: 'I find rather surprising the words of the Scripture, "If a man have a stubborn and rebellious son... then shall his father and his mother lay hold of him", etc. (Deut. XXI, 19), concerning which we have learnt that when God told Moses to write this, Moses said: Sovereign of the Universe, omit this; is there any father that would do so to his son? Now Moses saw in wisdom what God would later do to Israel, and therefore he said, Omit this. God, however, said to him, Write and receive thy reward; though thou knowest I know more; what thou seest I will attend to; examine the Scripture and thou wilt find. God then nodded to Yofiel, the teacher of the Law, who said to Moses, I will expound this verse: "When a man shall have": this is the Holy One, blessed be He, who is called "a man of war". "A son": this is Israel. "Stubborn and rebellious", as it is written, "For Israel hath behaved himself stubbornly like a stubborn heifer" (Hos. IV, 16). "Which will not obey the voice of his father nor the voice of his mother": these are the Holy One, blessed be He, and the Community of Israel. "Though they chasten him", as it says, "Yet the Lord testified unto Israel and unto Judah by the hand of every prophet" (2 Kings XVII, 13). "Then shall his father and mother take hold of him", with one accord, "and bring him out unto the elders of his city and unto the gate of his place": "the elders of his city" are the ancient and primeval Days.

Zohar: Bemidbar, Section 3, Page 198a

"And they shall say, This our son": assuredly our son, and not the son of other peoples. "He is a riotous liver and a drunkard". Why are these last words added now? Because what caused Israel to be rebellious against their Father in heaven was because they were riotous and drunken among other nations, as it is written, "They mingled themselves with the nations and learnt their works" (Ps. CVI, 35). Therefore, "the men of his city shall stone him with stones":

these are the other peoples who hurled stones at them and cast down their walls and towers and did not help them at all. When Moses heard this, he wrote this section. And with all this, "thou fairest of women, go thy way forth by the footsteps of the flock": these are the synagogues and houses of study; "and feed thy kids": these are the young school children who know not the taste of sin; "beside the shepherds' tents": these are the teachers of children and the heads of academies. We may also refer this to the kings of the Amorites whose land the Israelites took for pasture for their cattle. When Balak heard that so valuable a land had been turned by the Israelites into pasture, he began to take active steps and associated with himself Balaam.'

COME NOW, THEREFORE, I PRAY THEE, AND CURSE ME THIS PEOPLE. R. Eleazar said: 'That villain said to himself: In truth, now is the propitious hour for me to do what I desire. He saw, but he did not see properly. He saw that many thousands of Israel would through him fall in a short time, and therefore he said "now". He said, Till now there was no one in the world who could prevail against them, because of the protector who was with them, but now that the time is propitious, let us make war against them. FOR THEY ARE TOO MIGHTY FOR ME. In what battle had he up to now tested their might

that he could say this? The truth is that he was far-sighted, and saw King David, the descendant of Ruth the Moabitess, mighty as a lion, fighting many battles and conquering Moab, and placing them under his feet. Hence he said, "He is mighty", meaning a certain king who will issue from them. He went on: "Perhaps I shall be able to smite him", or, as we might translate, "Perhaps I might prevail on thee so that we should diminish him", depriving the mighty lion of this limb before that king comes into the world, so that he should not drive Moab out of his territory.'

CURSE (arah) FOR ME. R. Abba said: 'Balak used two expressions to Balaam, arah (curse) and kaboh (imprecate). What is the difference? The word arah means cursing by the use of herbs and snakes' heads. When he saw that Balaam had more power in his mouth, he said kaboh. Yet all the same Balak did not neglect enchantments, but took all manner of herbs and snakes' heads and put them in a pot, which he buried under the ground fifteen hundred cubits down. When David came he dug down fifteen hundred cubits and brought up water from the depths and poured it on the altar. That was when he said, "Moab is my washpot" (PS. LX, 10), that is, I have washed clean the pot of Moab. He went on: "Over Edom I cast my shoe". This also had reference to a much earlier event, when Esau said to Jacob, "Make me swallow, I pray thee, some of that red stuff", and David now said, "I will stuff my shoe down his throat". He also said: "Over Philistia I will blow the trumpet", because Philistines were from the "other side", and for the "other side" the blowing of the trumpet was required, as it is written, "And when ye go to war in your land ye shall sound an alarm with the trumpet" (Num. x, 9).'

R. Hizkiah cited here the verse: "And righteousness shall be the girdle of his loins and faithfulness the girdle of his reins" (Isa. XI, 5). 'The second part of this verse', he said, 'seems at first to be a mere repetition of the first, but this is not so. Though "righteousness" and "faithfulness" are much the same, and represent the same grade, yet there is a distinction between the two. When this grade wields stern judgement and receives power from the left side, then it is called "righteousness". It is "faithfulness" when truth is joined with it, and then there is joy and all faces smile. Then there is pardon for all, and the souls even of sinners, since they are given in trust, are restored in mercy. Similarly, there is a distinction between "loins" and "reins", the former being the upper and the latter the lower part. Hence for valour and for war "righteousness" is the girdle of his "loins", while for mercy and for kindness "faithfulness" is the girdle of his "reins". Thus with one and the same grade he will judge in two directions, one being mercy

for Israel and the other chastisement for the other nations. Also when Israel went forth from Egypt they were girt with these two girdles, one for war and one for peace. 'THAT I MAY DRIVE THEM FROM THE EARTH. When Balak took counsel of Balaam', he said, 'That grade to which they are attached is assuredly from the earth. Therefore if I drive them from this earth, I shall be able to do all that I desire. Wherein does their strength lie? In deeds and words. You have words and I have deeds. 'FOR I KNOW THAT HE WHOM THOU BLESSEST, ETC. From where did he know? As has been explained, from the help he gave to Sihon. But in truth, he knew it from his own wisdom. 'WHOM THOU BLESSEST IS BLESSED. Why should he mention blessing, seeing that he wanted him for cursing? This is a question which I could not solve till R. Eleazar came and expounded the verse: "I will bless eth the Lord" (Ps. XXXIV, 2). Who is it that requires blessings from those on earth? Eth, because it is connected with them as the flame with the wick. Said that sinner: That grade of theirs is attached to them because of the blessings which they address to it every day. You have power to bless that grade and so detach it from them, and by this we shall prevail against them.'

He then discoursed on the verse: "Therefore fear thou not, O Jacob my servant, saith the Lord, neither be dismayed, O Israel... for I am with thee", etc. (Jer. xxx, 10, 11). 'The word "thou" here', he said, 'contains a reference to the Ark of the Covenant, which is the grade that went into captivity with her sons, the holy people. As has been pointed out, it does not say here, "for thou art with me", but "for I am with thee". The word kalah (full end) occurs twice here. The first time it is written hard (for I will make kalah with all the nations), and the second soft (I will not make khalah of thee). From this', said R. Hamnuna the ancient, 'we can learn that the oppression of Israel brings benefit to them, and that the ease of the other nations brings evil to them. For the word kalah can be read

Zohar: Bemidbar, Section 3, Page 199b

kallah (bride) while khalah can only mean destruction and annihilation. The verse continues: "But I will correct thee with judgement" (lit. for judgement). God provides remedies for Israel before they appear for judgement. What are these remedies? On every occasion God punishes Israel little by little in each generation, so that when they come to the great day of judgement when the dead shall arise, judgement shall have no power over them. "And will in no wise leave thee unpunished". What is the meaning of this? When Israel are by themselves and do not come up for judgement with the other peoples, God is lenient with them and makes atonement for them. But when they come up with the other peoples, God knows that Samael, the guardian of Esau, will come to call to mind their sins, and therefore He provides a remedy for them and for each sin He smites them and purifies them with chastisements little by little, but does not clear them out of the world. When they come up for judgement Samael brings up many records against them, but God brings forth the records of the sufferings which they have endured for each sin, so that they are all wiped off without any indulgence. Then Samael has no more power and can do nothing to them and he vanishes from the world with all his followers and peoples. Similarly the words of King David: "For lo, the wicked bend the bow, they make ready their arrow upon the string" (Ps. XI, 2), although explained as referring to Shebna and Joach, the officers of Hezekiah, can also be applied to this Samael and his company, whose whole object is to harm Israel. Balak and Balaam chose that path, and, as we have said, made an evil partnership.' R. Simeon said: 'Let Balak and Balaam rot in hell. They took evil counsel together against the Protector, whom they thought to remove by means of deed and word. Said that wicked one: The ancients tried and did not succeed. The generation of the Tower of Babel tried but could not, because though they had deeds the word of the mouth was lacking, as their tongues were confused. But thy mouth is sharp and thy tongue is ready for either course. That side which thou desirest to remove is removed by thy mouth and tongue, and that side which thou desirest to curse by the power of thy mouth is cursed.

Zohar: Bemidbar, Section 3, Page 200a

Therefore I will do the enchantments, and do thou complete all with thy mouth. He, however, did not know that God "removeth the speech of the trusty and taketh away the understanding of the elders" (Job XII, 20). "He removeth the speech of the trusty", as from the generation of the Tower of Babel, whose speech He confused, "and taketh away the understanding of the elders", to wit, of Balak and Balaam. Observe that all the acts of the wicked Balaam were dictated by pride and arrogance. Both offered sacrifices, as it says, "And Balak and Balaam offered" (XXIII, 2), and it was Balak who prepared all the altars, yet Balaam said, "I have prepared the seven altars, and I have offered a bullock and a ram on every altar" (Ibid. 4). Said God to him: Villain, I know all, but return to Balak, and thou needest not to speak with him, but thus shalt thou say. Hence it says, "He taketh away the understanding of the wise".

'AND HE SAID TO THEM, LODGE HERE THIS NIGHT. Because night is the time of the "other side" for enchanters, when the evil sides are at large in the world. AS THE LORD SHALL SPEAK UNTO ME. He made a boast of the Name of the Lord. AND THE PRINCES OF MOAB ABODE WITH BALAAM. Those of Midian, however, left and would not stay with him; and they would have done well to separate from him altogether, as then they would not have been smitten at the end; for it was through his advice that they sent their women to the Israelites. Or, again, we may say that the princes of Moab did better by staying, for they thereby showed respect for the word of the Lord, and for this they were rewarded afterwards, whereas the princes of Midian showed that they had no desire to hear the word of the Lord, and for this they were punished afterwards.

'In that night he used enchantments and divinations until he called down to himself a spirit from above, as it says, AND AN ELOHIM CAME TO BALAAM: this was his grade from the "other side", of the Left. AND SAID, WHAT MEN ARE THESE WITH THEE? Being of the other side, of the Left, he needed to ask. The Companions, however, say that God made trial of him by thus speaking to him. There were three who were thus tried: Hezekiah, Ezekiel, and Balaam, and only Ezekiel gave the right answer, for when God asked him, "Shall these bones live?" he replied, "O Lord God, thou knowest" (Ezek. XXXVII, 3). Hezekiah, however, when God said to him, "Whence come these men?" replied, "They have come to me from a far land, from Babylon" (2 Kings xx, 14). And so Balaam now answered, "Balak son of Zippor King of Moab sent to me", as much as to say: I am highly esteemed in the eyes of kings and rulers. A certain Kuthean said to R. Eleazar: I discern a superiority in Balaam over Moses, for of Moses it says, "And the Lord called unto Moses", but of Balaam it says,

Zohar: Bemidbar, Section 3, Page 200b

"And God met Balaam, And God came to Balaam'. He replied: A king was once sitting on his throne in his palace when a leper came to the gate. Who is knocking at the gate? he asked. They said: A certain leper. He said: He must not enter here and defile the palace. I know that if I tell this to a messenger he will take no notice, and my son will come in and be defiled by contact with him. I will therefore go and threaten him so that he shall go away from the abode of my son and not defile him. So the king got up and went to him and threatened him, saying: Leper, leper, keep away from the path of my son, and if not I will tell the sons of my handmaidens to cut you in pieces. Then the friend of the king called at the door. Who is it? said the king. They replied: Your friend, So-and-so. He said: It is my friend, the beloved of my soul; no other voice shall call him in save mine. The king then cried out saying: Enter, beloved of my soul, my own friend; prepare the palace that I may converse with him. So when Balaam, who was rejected of men like a leper, called at the gate of the King, the latter, on hearing, said: The unclean leper shall not enter and defile my palace. It is necessary for me to go and threaten him so that he shall not approach the gate of my son and not defile him. Therefore it says, "God came to Balaam". He said to him: Leper, leper, "thou shalt not go with them, thou shalt not curse the people for he is blessed". You shall not come near my people either for good or for evil, being wholly unclean. But of Moses it is written, "He called unto Moses", with the voice of the King and not through a messenger, "from the tent of meeting", from the holy palace which higher and lower angels desire to approach but are not allowed.

'BALAK SON OF ZIPPOR KING OF MOAB. Above (v. 4) Balak was called "king to Moab", to show that he was only appointed king for the emergency, not like "the first king of Moab" (Num. XXI, 26), who was an hereditary monarch. Balaam, however, out of his pride called him "king of Moab", as if to say: See how great a king sends to me!'

R. Phineas was once going to see his daughter, the wife of R. Simeon, who was ill. He was accompanied by the Companions, and was riding on his ass. On his way he met two Arabs, and said to them: 'Has a voice ever been heard in this field?' They replied: 'About former times we cannot say, but we know that in our own time there used to be robbers who waylaid men in this field and they once fell on some Jews with intent to cut them down, when there was heard from a distance in this field the voice of an ass braying twice, and a flame of fire came into the field and burnt them, so that the Jews escaped.' He said to them: 'Arabs, Arabs, for the sake of this information that you have given me you shall be delivered this day from other robbers who are lying in wait for you on the way.' R. Phineas wept, and said: 'Sovereign of the Universe, thou hast caused this miracle to befall on my behalf, and those Jews were delivered and I knew it not. It is written, "To him who alone doeth great wonders, for his mercy endureth forever" (Ps. CXXXVI, 4). How much kindness does God do for men, and how many miracles does He cause to befall for them, and no one knows save He! A man will rise in the morning and a snake comes to kill him and he treads on the snake and kills it without knowing, but God alone knows. A man goes on the road and robbers are in wait for him, and another comes and takes his place and he is delivered, and does not know the kindness that God has wrought with him or the miracle He has done on his behalf. God alone does it and knows it.' He then said to the Companions: 'Companions,

what I really wanted to learn from the Arabs who frequent this field was whether they have heard the voice of the Companions who study the Torah, for R. Simeon and R. Eleazar and the rest of the Companions are in front of us without knowing of us, and I was asking those Arabs about them, because I know that the voice of R. Simeon shakes the field and the rocks; they, however, have told me something I did not know.'

As they were going along the Arabs returned to him and said: 'Old man, old man, you asked us concerning bygone days but not concerning this day in which we have seen wonder on wonder. We have seen five men sitting together and one old man among them, and we saw the birds collecting and spreading their wings over his head, some going and others coming, so that there was always a shade over their heads, and as the old man raised his voice they were listening.' He said: 'That was what I wanted to know; Arabs, Arabs, may you have all the good fortune on this journey that you desire. You have told me two things which have given me joy.' They then proceeded on their way. Said the Companions to him: 'How are we to find the place where R. Simeon is?' He replied: 'Leave it to the Master of the steps of my beast, who will guide its steps thither.' He then gave the rein to his ass, which thereupon turned aside from the road two miles, after which it commenced to bray three times. R. Phineas dismounted and said: 'Let us prepare ourselves to meet the presence of the day, for now great faces and small faces will come out to us.' R. Simeon heard the braying of the ass and said to the Companions: 'Let us rise, for the voice of the ass of the pious elder has reached us.' R. Simeon thereupon rose and the Companions also.

R. Simeon cited the verse: "A psalm. O sing unto the Lord a new song, for he hath done marvellous things" (Ps. XCVII, 1). 'The tonal accent on the word mizmor (psalm) here', he said, 'shows that this psalm has some special distinction. Who was it that uttered this song? It was the kine (that bore the ark from the house of Obed Edom) in their lowing. Whom did they call upon to "sing"? All the Chariots, all the Chieftains, all the grades (of angels) who had come thither to meet the Ark. The word for "song" here is the masculine form, shir, whereas Moses designated his song by the feminine form, shirah (Deut. XXXI, 32). The reason is that in the time of Moses only the Ark itself was coming forth from captivity, but here the Ark was coming forth with what was deposited in it. "For he hath done marvellous things": this refers to what was done to the Philistines and their idols. "His right hand hath wrought salvation for him": that is, for the psalm itself and the holy spirit concealed in it. His right hand takes hold of this psalm and does not leave it in the hand of another. In the words "taking hold with the right hand" the comparison is to a father who draws his son to his breast in front of him so as to protect him, as though to say: Who shall touch my son? But when the son does wrong the father takes hold of the son by the shoulders and pushes him away, and so it is written, "He hath drawn back his right hand before the enemy" (Lam. II, 3). Here, however, it says, "His right hand and his holy arm hath wrought salvation for him"—he being held fast in two arms. Now if those kine for which miracles were an unusual thing, being vouchsafed to them only on that occasion, uttered this song in their lowing, how much more must we say that the braying of the ass of the pious elder signifies a song of praise! Nor think, Companions, that this has not been the manner of this ass from the time the world was created. For if this was the case with the ass of the wicked Balaam, how much more must it be so with the ass of R.

Zohar: Bemidbar, Section 3, Page 201b

Phineas ben Jair! Now it is time, Companions, to reveal something. When you are told that the mouth of the ass was created on the eve of Sabbath at twilight, [Tr. note: v. T.B. Aboth v.] do you think that its mouth was open from that time, or that God made stipulation with it from that time? Not so; there is here a mystery which has been transmitted to the wise who pay not heed to folly. The mouth of the ass is the grade of the asses, that supernal one from the side of the females who rested on that ass and spoke over it. When God created that grade called "the mouth of the ass" He enclosed it in the hollow of the great deep and kept it there till that day, and when the time came He opened the hollow and it came forth and rested on the ass and spoke. So when it says that "the earth opened its mouth" (Num. XVI, 32), this refers to Dumah. The mouth of the ass was called Kadriel and the mouth of the well was called Yahadriel. These three "mouths" were created on the eve of the Sabbath. But at the hour when God sanctified the day there came up a Mouth which is superior to all other mouths, namely, that day which was exalted and sanctified in all, and was called "the mouth of the Lord".'

They now caught sight of R. Phineas coming towards them. When he came up he kissed R. Simeon, saying: 'I kiss the mouth of the Lord, I catch the perfume of His Garden.' They all rejoiced and sat down. Thereupon all the birds that were making a shadow over them flew away in all directions. R. Simeon turned his head and called after them, saying: 'Birds of heaven, have ye no respect for your master who is here?' They thereupon remained still, not moving from their place, but not drawing nearer. Said R. Phineas: 'Tell them to go their ways, since they are not permitted to return to us.' Said R. Simeon: 'I know that God desires to perform a miracle for us. Birds, birds, go your ways, and tell him who is in control of you that at first he was his own master, but now he is not his own master, but we are leaving him for the day of the rock when enmity will arise between two mighty ones and they will not unite.' The birds then scattered and went. Meanwhile they found three trees spreading their branches over them in three directions and a stream of water flowing in front of them. All the Companions rejoiced at this, as did also R. Phineas and R. Simeon. Said R. Phineas: 'It was a great trouble for those birds at first, and we do not desire to give pain to living creatures, since it is written, "and his mercies are on all his works" (Ps. CXLV, 9).' R. Simeon replied: 'I did not trouble them, but if God was kind to us, we cannot reject His gifts.' They then sat down under the tree and drank of the water and refreshed themselves.

R. Phineas then discoursed on the verse: "A fountain of gardens, a well of living waters and flowing streams from Lebanon" (S.S. IV, 15). 'Are there not then', he said, 'other fountains besides those of the gardens? There is, however, a difference in the benefit they confer. If a fountain gushes forth in the wilderness, in a dry place, it is serviceable to one who sits by it and drinks from it. But how good and precious is a fountain of gardens, for it benefits herbs and plants, and he who draws near to it derives benefit not only from the water but also from the herbs and plants. That fountain is bedecked in all ways, having many fragrant flowers around it, so that it is truly a "well of living waters". Now it has been explained that it is the Community of Israel who is called "a fountain of gardens". The Holy One, blessed be He, has five gardens in which He delights himself, and there is one hidden and secret fountain which waters all of them, and all produce fruit and flowers. There is one garden below them which is guarded on all sides, and below this are other gardens which produce fruit and flowers after their kinds. This garden transforms itself and becomes according to need either a fountain or a well to water them; for there is a difference between waters flowing

Zohar: Bemidbar, Section 3, Page 202a

of themselves and waters drawn by irrigation. And just as drops of water gradually become a fountain, so those five sources that issue from Lebanon drip gradually into this fountain. What is meant by "flowing streams from Lebanon"? Those five sources that issue from Lebanon above become "streams", for when they become a fountain water issues from it, drop by drop, sweet water that refreshes the soul. So God has wrought for us a miracle in this place, and I apply this verse to this fountain.'

He then discoursed on the verse: "When thou shalt besiege a city a long time in making war against it to take it", etc. (Deut. XX, 19). 'How goodly, he said, 'are the ways and paths of the Torah, since it is full of good counsel for man, and every word of it radiates light in many directions. This verse can be taken literally, and it can be expounded homiletically, and it contains also a lesson of the higher wisdom. He who constantly occupies himself with the Torah is compared by the Psalmist to "a tree planted by streams of water" (Ps. I, 3). Just as a tree has roots, bark, sap, branches, leaves, flowers and fruit, seven kinds in all, so the Torah has the literal meaning, the homiletical meaning, the mystery of wisdom, numerical values, hidden mysteries, still deeper mysteries, and the laws of fit and unfit, forbidden and permitted, and clean and unclean. From this point branches spread out in all directions, and to one who knows it in this way it is indeed like a tree, and if not he is not truly wise. Observe how beloved are those who study the Torah before the Holy One, blessed be He, for even when chastisement impends over the world and permission is given to the destroyer to destroy, the Holy One, blessed be He, charges him concerning them, saying: "When thou shalt besiege a city", because of their numerous sins against Me, for which they have been adjudged guilty, "for many days", that is to say, three successive days, so that the thing is known in the town, then I will charge thee concerning the sons of My house, "Thou shalt not destroy the tree thereof": this is the learned man in the town, who is a tree of life, a tree that produces fruit. Or, again, we may explain it of one who gives good counsel to the townspeople, telling them how they may escape from punishment, and teaches them the way in which they should go. Therefore "thou shalt not destroy its tree by wielding an axe against it", that is, by inflicting punishment upon him and brandishing the flaming sword over him, which slays other men. The verse then continues, "For from it thou eatest". Now we cannot possibly apply this to the destroyer, so we must translate, "for from it she eats", to wit, that mighty rock from which issue all great and holy spirits, for the holy spirit has no pleasure in this world save from the Torah of that pious one, who, if one may say so, sustains her and gives her food in this world more than all sacrifices. Since the Temple has been destroyed and the sacrifices have ceased, the Holy One, blessed be He, has only those words of the Torah which this man expounds. Therefore "it thou shalt not cut down',: be careful not to touch him, "for man is the

tree of the field"; this one is called "man", being known as such above and below; he is the mighty tree of that field which the Lord hath blessed. "To be besieged of thee": these words are connected with the earlier part of the verse, "thou shalt not destroy its tree", namely, him who gave advice to the townspeople and prepared them to withstand a siege before thee, counselling them to amend and to blow the trumpet for repentance, to avoid thee and come before God. "In siege": this is the place to which higher and lower angels cannot enter, but where repentant sinners may enter. If they accept this advice then I pardon them their sins and they are received into favour before Me. Happy, therefore, are those who study the Torah, for they are great in this world. See what God has done, how He has planted these trees, not one only, but three spreading their branches on all sides. May it be the will of heaven that these trees shall never depart from this place, nor this fountain. And in truth those trees and that fountain are still there, and men call it "the plantation of R. Phineas b. Jair".'

R. Simeon then discoursed on the verse: "And he lifted up his eyes and saw the women and the children, and said: Who are these with thee? And he said, The children which God hath graciously given thy servant" (Gen. XXXIII, 5). 'The wicked Esau', he said, 'had his eye on women, and therefore Jacob took precautions against him, putting in front the handmaids and then their children, for whom he had more regard, then Leah and her children behind her, and then Rachel, and behind her Joseph. But when they drew near and bowed down, it says that "Joseph came near and Rachel", putting Joseph first. This indicates that Joseph, being a good and loving son, was afraid for his mother, and so kept her behind him and covered her with his arms and his body, so that Esau should not look at her. Now it says of Balaam that "he lifted up his eyes and saw Israel dwelling according to their tribes" (Num. XXIV, 2). The tribe of Joseph and the tribe of Benjamin were there: the tribe of Joseph, over whom the evil eye has no power, and the tribe of Benjamin, who also has no fear of the evil eye. Now Balaam had said: I will cross this line which is of no account and look well at them. Rachel was there, and when she saw that his eye was sharpened to do them hurt, she went forth and spread her wings over them and covered her sons. Hence it says, "The spirit of the God came upon him" (Ibid.), to wit, upon Israel, whom He was protecting, and straightway Balaam retired. So at first the son protected the mother and later the mother protected the sons; for so God had said at the time when he saved his mother from the eye of the wicked Esau. To return to our text: the words "And he lifted up his eyes and saw the women" contain a mystery of wisdom. On the Day of Atonement, when mankind is on trial and Israel repent before the Almighty to obtain forgiveness of their sins, and the Accuser comes forward to destroy them, they send him a gift and he becomes their advocate. He lifts up his eyes and sees the Israelites all fasting and barefoot, along with their wives and children, and pure and stainless,

and he says, "Who are these with thee?", referring to the children, as much as to say: I understand you, the grown-ups, fasting because you have sinned against the King; but what are these children doing here? Then the holy spirit answers him: "They are the children which God hath graciously given to thy servant", to wit, to that officer of thine to put them to death though guilty of no sin. When He hears the mention of those children, he at once goes up to the Holy One, blessed be He, and says: Sovereign of the Universe, all Thy ways are justice and truth. Now if punishment impends over Israel it is because of their sins. But their children who have not sinned—why hast Thou delivered them up to be slain without guilt? God then takes note of his words and has mercy on them, and at that time there is no whooping-cough among the children. The Accuser is then jealous of his subordinate, saying: To me God has given those who are clad in sin and guilt, and to my subordinate He has delivered children without sin who know not the taste of guilt. Straightway he goes to rescue them from his hands that he should have no power over them. Thus the holy spirit rescues them from the hand of the servant. Then it "passes before them" when the prayers of Israel ascend on this day before the Holy One, blessed be He, and "bows down seven times", corresponding to the seven grades above it, so as to include them with it, "until he reaches his brother", the grade of Mercy, to whom it makes known the distress of their sons below, and then both enter the secret and hidden palace of the Day of Atonement, their Mother, and beseech pardon for Israel. So now with the wise children here to whom God has communicated the secrets of the Torah to be crowned and perfected therewith, the evil eye has no power over them because of the good eye, the holy spirit of R. Phineas which rests upon them.' R. Phineas then approached and kissed him, saying: 'Had I taken this journey only to hear these words it would have been worth my while. Blessed is this journey which led me to thee, and God is here who has agreed with us. This well is a symbol of the supernal Well which is hidden and concealed. These three trees represent the three cedars which are called the Cedars of Lebanon, the emblem of the Patriarchs. Happy is our portion at this hour'. The trees then inclined themselves, one over the head of R. Simeon, one over the head of R. Phineas, and one over the head of R. Eleazar, while the branches spread on every side over the heads of the Companions. R. Phineas wept for joy, saying: 'Happy is my lot and blessed my eyes that see this. I rejoice not only for myself and for thee, but also for our son, R. Eleazar, who is esteemed before the Holy King as one of us.' He then arose and kissed him, and R. Simeon said: 'Eleazar, stand up and repeat before thy Master His words.'

R. Eleazar then rose

Zohar: Bemidbar, Section 3, Page 203b

and opened a discourse on the verse: "O my people, remember now what Balak king of Moab consulted", etc. (Mich. VI, 3). 'God', he said, 'is merciful to his sons like a father to his son. A father beats his son and yet he does not leave his evil ways. He rebukes him, and still he does not listen to him. Says the father to himself: I will no longer treat my son as I have done hitherto. When I beat him, his head is hurt and his pain is my pain. When I rebuke him, his face becomes distorted. What, then, shall I do? I will go and plead with him, and speak gently to him so that he will not be vexed. So God tries all ways with Israel. He begins to beat them, but they pay no attention; he rebukes them and they pay no attention. He then says: I see that my beating has hurt their head. Alas, because I also feel their pain, as it is written, "In all their trouble he had trouble" (Isa. LXIII, 9). If I rebuke them, their looks are distorted, as it is written, "Their visage is blacker than a coal, they are not known in the streets" (Lam. IV, 8). Now, therefore, I will plead with them gently, "My people, what have I done with thee and wherein have I wearied thee?" My son, my only one, beloved of my soul, see what I have done for thee. I have made thee ruler over all the inmates of my palace; I have made thee ruler over all the kings of the world; and if I have done aught different to thee, "testify against me. My people, remember, I pray thee, what Balak king of Moab counselled", etc.'

[Note: The last 35 lines of the Hebrew text are not found in our translation]

Zohar: Bemidbar, Section 3, Page 204a

[Note: The first 27 lines of the Hebrew text are not found in our translation]

R. Eleazar discoursed on the verse: "O Lord, in the morning shalt thou hear my voice", etc. (Ps. v, 4). 'When daylight comes', he said, 'that "Morning" of Abraham awakes, and then is a time of grace for all, both virtuous and wicked, and therefore it is the hour to offer prayer to the Holy King, since all the prisoners of the King then have respite. And most of all is it the time for those who repent to offer their prayer before the Holy King, because at that hour a certain Chieftain named Raphael goes forth to the side of the South having all manner of healing medicines in his hand, and from the side of the South comes forth a certain spirit which meets that keeper of the medicines. When the prayer reaches the Holy One, blessed be He, He enjoins His court not to hear accusations, because life is in His hand and not in theirs. And since it is a time of grace, God desires to justify that man if he is engaged in prayer or repentance. At that time the twittering of birds is heard praising and lauding the Holy One, blessed be He, and the Hind of the morning awakes and says: "How great is thy goodness which thou hast laid up for them that fear thee" (Ps. XXXI, 19). Then that emissary goes forth and does all that he was enjoined. When we said that he had medicaments in his hand, this was not quite correct, as really they are only in the hand of the King. But when God ordains healing for that man, the emissary goes forth and all the accusers who bring sicknesses fear him, and then that spirit that journeyed from the South is handed to that man, and thus there is healing, though all is in the hands of the Holy One, blessed be He. Our text continues: "In the morning will I order my prayer unto thee and keep watch". Why is the word "morning" repeated? One refers to the morning of Abraham and the other to the morning of Joseph.

Zohar: Bemidbar, Section 3, Page 204b

The words "I will order" mean, I will prepare thy lamp to give light, and refer to the morning of Joseph. Why does David say, "I will keep watch"? Surely all men watch and hope for the kindness of God, and even the beasts of the field? I inquired concerning this, and was given the following answer, and it is a right one, and very recondite. The first light that God created was so bright that the worlds could not endure it. God therefore made another light as a vestment to this one, and so with all the other lights, until all the worlds could endure the light without being dissolved. Hence grades were evolved and lights were wrapped in one another until they reached this "morning of Joseph", which was a substratum to all the higher lights. And since all the higher lights converge on it, its brightness goes forth from one end of the world to the other, so that the worlds below cannot endure. David therefore came and prepared this lamp as a covering to this "morning of Joseph", so as to preserve the lower worlds, and therefore he said, "I will prepare the morning for thee and" (as we might translate the word azapeh) "overlay it".' R. Abba came and kissed him, saying: 'Had I made the journey only to hear this it would have repaid me.'

As they were going along a pigeon approached R. Eleazar and commenced cooing in front of him. He said: 'Worthy dove, thou wast ever a faithful messenger, go and tell him that the Companions are coming and I am with them, and a miracle will be performed for him in three days, and he should not be afraid as we are approaching him in joy.' He replied again, saying: 'I am not very glad; in fact, I am sore distressed on account of a certain full pomegranate which has been sacrificed for him, and Yose is his name'. The dove went on in front and the Companions left them. Said R. Abba: 'I am greatly amazed at what I see.' He said to him: 'This dove came to me on a message from R. Yose, my father-in-law, who is lying ill, and I know from this pigeon that he has been delivered, and a substitute has been found for him, and he has been healed'. As they went along a raven came and stood before them, croaking loudly. R. Eleazar 'said: 'For this thou art here, and for this thou art come; go thy way, for I know already.' Said R. Eleazar: 'Companions, let us proceed and do an office of kindness with a pomegranate that was full of juice, R. Yose of Pekiin was his name, for he has departed from this world and there is no one to attend to him, and he is near us.' So they turned aside and went there.

When the townsfolk saw them, they all came out to meet them. The Companions then went into the house of R. Yose of Pekiin. He had a young son who would let no one approach the bed of his father as he lay dead, but he himself kept close to him and wept over him, putting his mouth to his mouth. He exclaimed: 'Sovereign of the Universe, it is written in the Torah, "If a bird's nest chance to be before thee... thou shalt surely let the dam go" (Deut. XXII, 6). Sovereign of the Universe,' he said with sobs, fulfill this word. We were two children to my father and mother, I and my younger sister. Thou shouldst have taken us and fulfilled the injunction of the Torah. And if Thou shouldst say, It is written "mother" and not "father", he was both, father and mother, for my mother has died and Thou didst take her from her children. Now the father who was our protector has been taken from the children; where is the justice?' R. Eleazar and the Companions wept to hear the tears and sobs of the boy. R. Eleazar started to quote the verse, "The heaven for height and the earth for depth" (Prov. xxv, 3), but before he could complete it a pillar of fire parted them, while the child still had his lips pressed to the mouth of his father. Said R. Eleazar: 'Either God desires to work a miracle, or He desires no other man to attend to him; but in any case I cannot bear the words and the tears of this child.' As they sat they heard a voice

Zohar: Bemidbar, Section 3, Page 205a

say: 'Happy art thou, R. Yose, for the words of this young kid have ascended to the throne of the Holy King and sentence has been passed and God has assigned thirteen men to the Angel of Death in thy place, and an addition has been made to thy years so that thou mayest teach the Torah to this excellent kid, beloved before the Holy One, blessed be He.' R. Eleazar and the Companions rose and would not let anyone stay in the house. Forthwith they saw that pillar of fire depart and R. Yose opened his eyes, the boy's lips still being pressed close to his. Said R. Eleazar: 'Happy is our lot that we have seen the resurrection of the dead with our own eyes'. They drew near to him and found the boy sleeping like one dead to the world. They said: 'Happy is thy portion, R. Yose, and blessed is God who has wrought a miracle for thee for the weeping and sobbing of thy son. For the sake of his beautiful words with which he has knocked at the gate of heaven and of his tears they have added years to thy life.' They then lifted up the boy and kissed him, weeping for joy, and they took him out of the house to another house, and were careful not to tell him at once. They remained there three days, and expounded many points of the Torah with R. Yose. Said R. Yose to the Companions: 'I am not permitted to reveal what I saw in the other world till twelve years have passed. But the three hundred and sixty-five tears which my son shed have all been counted before the Almighty, and I assure you, Companions, that when he quoted that verse three hundred thousand chairs in the Academy of the firmament were shaken, and all stood before the Holy King and besought mercy for me and offered themselves as surety for me. And God was filled with mercy towards me, being well pleased with those words and his offer to sacrifice himself for me. There was one Guardian who said: Sovereign of the Universe, it is written, "Out of the mouth of babes and sucklings hast thou established strength" (Ps. VIII, 3). May it please Thee for the merit of the Torah and for the merit of that child who offered his life for his father, that Thou mayest spare him so that he be delivered. So He assigned him thirteen men in my place and gave him a pledge to save me from this sentence. Then God called the Angel of Death and commanded him to return for me in twenty-two years. And so, Companions, because God saw that you are truly virtuous, He wrought a miracle before your eyes.'

R. Yose then discoursed on the verse: "The Lord killeth and maketh alive, he bringeth down to the grave and bringeth Up" (I Sam. II, 6). 'This verse', he said, 'raises a difficulty. Can it be said that the Lord killeth, seeing that this name is the elixir of life to all? We have, however, to ask how He kills. You might think it is by merely departing from a man, because so long as He is with him all the Accusers of the world cannot harm him, but so soon as He leaves him they at once have power over him and he dies. This, however, is not the real meaning. Who is it really that the Lord kills? It is that influence of the evil "other side". So soon as the influence of the evil side sees the splendour of the glory of the Holy One, blessed be He, it dies straightway and cannot survive an instant. And so soon as that influence of the "other side" dies, at once God "brings to life". Whom does He bring to life? The influence of the spirit of holiness which comes from the side of holiness. All this the Holy One, blessed be He, does at one and the same time. As for the words "He bringeth down to the grave and bringeth up", this means that He takes that spirit of holiness down to Sheol and there baptizes it to purify it, after which it ascends to its rightful place in the Garden of Eden. Now, Companions, at the time when I departed from the world, my spirit left me and slept for a little while till God revived me, my body being dead. When my son uttered those words, his soul flew away and met my soul as it was coming up from its purification to a certain place where its sentence was pronounced, and they gave me twenty-two years of life for the sake of the tears

Zohar: Bemidbar, Section 3, Page 205b

and words of my son. From this time forward I must occupy myself only with what I have seen, and not with the affairs of this world, since God desires that naught of what I have seen should be forgotten by me.'

He then discoursed on the verse: "The Lord hath chastened me sore", etc. (Ps. CXVIII, 18). 'David said this in reference to all that had befallen him in this world, to his having been pursued and taken refuge in the land of Moab and the land of the Philistines, in order to strengthen his assurance of the other world. He said: If I have sinned in this world I have been smitten in this world and received my punishment and been purified, and nothing of my punishment is left for the next world after death. Hence assuredly "God has chastened me" in this world, "but he hath not given me over to death" in the next world. So I, too, have been purified once in this world, and from now onward I must be careful that I do not incur disgrace in the world to come.'

His son then discoursed on the verse: "Our father died in the wilderness, and he was not among the company", etc. (Num. XXVII, 3). 'Why did the daughters of Zelopehad so particularly state that their father had died in the wilderness, seeing that so many thousands of others had also died in the wilderness? Men are at a loss to explain this, and some say he was the man who gathered sticks on the Sabbath, and others say other things, but what I have learnt is this [which] my father taught it me on the day when he fell ill. We must take the word midbar (wilderness) here in the sense of "saying". Zelopehad was one of the principal men of the sons of Joseph, but because he did not know the ways of the Torah sufficiently he did not become their prince. His fault was that he was not careful of his speech and his tongue in front of Moses. Hence, because he sinned in his speech against Moses, his daughters thought that Moses bore a grudge against him, and therefore they drew near "before Moses and Eleazar and all the princes", and spoke with Moses only in their presence, because they were afraid of his anger. From this we learn that one who is afraid of a judge should bring a large audience before him in order that they may hear him judge and he may be afraid of them and conduct the case properly. Otherwise, he should not be allowed to conduct the case. They did not know that Moses "was exceedingly meek, above all the men on the face of the earth" (Num. XII, 3). When Moses observed that a whole gathering of the leading men of Israel and all the heads of the fathers and all the princes were assembled round him, he at once resigned the case, and so it says, "And Moses brought their cause before the Lord" (Num. XXVII, 5), as if to say: This case is not for me. This shows the modesty of Moses, for other judges would not act so.' R. Eleazar and the Companions were delighted, and the boy continued: 'The tonal accent (zarka) on the word "our father" resembles in shape a serpent drawing its tail into its mouth, being an indication of the One who presides over him above; for "he died in the wilderness" through the utterance of his mouth.' At this point the boy became frightened and clung to his father's neck, weeping and saying: 'Zelopehad died through words, and thou, father, hast been restored to this world through words.' His father in turn kissed

Zohar: Bemidbar, Section 3, Page 206a

and embraced him, and R. Eleazar and the Companions all wept, and his father with them, and they lifted him up and kissed him on his mouth and his head and his hands. R. Eleazar said to him: 'My son, since you have said so much, tell us what is meant by "but he died in his own sin".' He replied: 'It means, by the sin of that serpent. And what is that? The speech of the mouth.' R. Eleazar then clasped him tightly to his breast, and all the Companions wept. He said to them: 'Rabbis, leave me here with my father because my spirit is not yet properly restored.' R. Eleazar then asked R. Yose how many years and days old the boy was. He replied: 'I beg of you, Companions, not to ask this, because five years have not yet passed over him.' 'God forbid,' said R. Eleazar; 'I desire to turn only a good eye on him, and your five years are "the five years in which will be no ploughing or reaping" (Gen. XLV, 6), an omen that you shall never reap him.' Said

R. Eleazar to R. Abba: 'Let us stay here seven days, till the house becomes settled, because for seven days after the soul has left the body it goes about naked, and now though it has returned it will not be settled in its place till after seven days.' R. Abba replied: 'It is written, "Thou shalt surely open thine hand unto thy brother, thy poor, thy needy, and to thy poor in thy land" (Deut. xv, 11), and we have learnt that this is a lesson that one should not abandon his own poor to give to another. Now R. Yose, your father-in-law, is sick; let us go and visit him, and when we return we will go in here, and all the time we are going and returning on this journey we shall see the resurrection of the dead.' Said

R. Eleazar: 'That is assuredly so.' So they kissed the boy and blessed him and departed. Said R. Abba: 'I am amazed at the young children of this generation, what capacities they show, being already mighty and lofty rocks.' R. Eleazar replied: 'Blessed is my father, the master of this generation. In his days God has been pleased to establish His two Academies and to create for us a great and noble academy, for there shall not be another generation like this till the Messiah shall come.' So they went their way. As they were going, R. Abba said: 'We have learnt that for eleven things the plague of leprosy comes upon a man, and these are they: for idolatry, for cursing the Name, for fornication, for stealing, for slander, for false witness, for perversion of justice, for false swearing, for encroaching on the property of a neighbour, for harbouring evil designs, and for fomenting quarrels between brothers. Some add also, for the evil eye.

[Note: The last 20 lines of the Hebrew text are not found in our translation]

Zohar: Bemidbar, Section 3, Page 206b

[Note: The first 29 lines of the Hebrew text are not found in our translation]

All these were found in the wicked Balaam. Fornication and idolatry, as it is written, "Behold these caused the children of Israel to commit trespass against the Lord through the counsel of Balaam in the matter of Peor" (Num. XXXI, 16). False witness, as it is written, "Balaam the son of Peor sayeth... which knoweth the knowledge of the Most High" (Ibid. XXIV, 16), while he did not know even the knowledge of his ass. He perverted judgement, as it is written, "Come and I will advertise thee" (Ibid. 14). He encroached on a domain which did not belong to him, as it is written, "And I offered oxen and rams on the altar", and also, "The seven altars I have prepared" (Ibid. XXIII, 4). He fomented discord between brothers, between Israel and their Father in heaven. As for slander, there was no other to equal him. And so with the rest.'

R. Yose quoted the verse: "Eat thou not the bread of him that hath an evil eye" (Prov. XXIII, 6). 'This', he said, 'is Balaam who blessed Israel. "Neither desire thou his dainties": this was Balak, whose burnt offerings were not accepted by the Almighty. When Balak observed that Sihon and Og had been killed and their land taken away, he foresaw in his wisdom that he and five princes of Midian and his people would fall by the hand of Israel, and not knowing what to make of it he approached Balaam, whose power was in his mouth, just as the power of Israel was in its mouth. Balaam was even more anxious to attack them than Balak. The knowledge which he acquired was at night time, because the lower crowns and the asses are at large only in the first watch of the night. Therefore he had an ass to attract

Zohar: Bemidbar, Section 3, Page 207a

the asses to her in the early part of the night. It is true that it says, "Elohim came to Balaam in the night", but we have explained this to refer to the Chieftain appointed over them. It was on this account that Balaam said to the princes of Balak, "Tarry here this night". Balaam went to his she-ass and performed his rites and uttered his spells, and the ass then told him and he did the requisite act for that spirit to rest upon him. Then someone came and told him things through the agency of the ass. It may be asked, if he told him in one night, "Thou shalt not go with them", why did he try a second time? The fact is that these powers are subject to a higher control, and we have learnt, "In the way in which a man desires to go he is led". At first he was told, "Thou shalt not go with them". When God saw that he was bent on going, He said to him, "Arise, go with them, only the thing that I tell thee", etc. 'All that night, therefore, Balaam was pondering and saying in his mind: What honour is it for me if I am tied to someone else? He cast about all that night and found no side in which he should be his own master save that of his ass. R. Isaac has told us in the name of R. Judah, that among those lower crowns there is a right and a left, on the left side being she-asses. R. Yose said that those of the right are all merged in one called "ass", and that is the ass of which it is written, "thou shalt not plough with an ox and an ass together" (Deut. XXII, 10), and that is also the ass which the King Messiah shall control, as we have explained. There are ten on the right and ten on the left which are included in kesem (divination), and ten others on the right and ten others on the left which are included in nahash (enchantment), and therefore it is written, "For there is no enchantment with Jacob and no divination with Israel" (Num. XXIII, 23); why? Because "the Lord his God is with him". Balaam, therefore, finding no way out save through his ass, straightway ROSE UP IN THE MORNING AND SADDLED HIS ASS to attain his own ends and the ends of Balak through it. And therefore "the anger of God was kindled because he went", as much as to say, because he was following his own bent and breaking loose from the one who said to him, "only the thing which I shall tell thee", etc. Said the Holy One, blessed be He, to him:

Zohar: Bemidbar, Section 3, Page 207b

Sinner, thou makest ready thy weapon to escape from my control; I will show thee that thou and thy ass are in my power. Straightway THE ANGEL OF THE LORD PLACED HIMSELF IN THE WAY. Said R. Abba: He left his own function to take up the function of another, for this was an angel of mercy, and this bears out what R. Simeon said, that sinners turn mercy into judgement.'

R. Eleazar, however, said: 'The angel did not change, nor did he leave his own function, but because he was from the side of mercy and stood in his way he nullified his wisdom and frustrated his intention. Thus he was "an adversary to him", but to others he was not an adversary.' 'We have learnt', R. Simeon said, 'how clever was Balaam with his enchantments above all others, because when he sought to escape from the control of the Holy One, blessed be He, he found no means save the ass, and therefore "he loaded his ass" with all the enchantments and divinations that he knew of in order to curse Israel. Straightway, "the anger of God was kindled because he was going". What did God do? He sent an angel of mercy to meet him and to nullify his enchantments. Note that here for the first time in this passage the name "Lord" is mentioned, showing that this was an angel of mercy sent to frustrate his wisdom and to turn his ass aside from the way, namely, that way on which he was bent on going. Said the Holy One, blessed be He: Sinner, thou hast loaded thy ass with thy enchantments to bring down all kinds of punishments on my sons; I will turn thy load into something else; and straightway He sent the angel of mercy to stand in his way.'

AND THE ASS SAW THE ANGEL OF THE LORD, ETC. Said R. Isaac: 'Why did she see while Balaam, who was so wise, did not see?' R. Yose replied: 'It was not to be thought of that that sinner should behold the vision of holiness.' Said the other: 'What, then, are we to make of the words, "Falling down and having his eyes open" (Num. XXIV, 4)?' 'Regarding that', he said, 'I have not heard anything, so I can give no explanation.' Said R. Isaac: 'I have heard that when it was proper for him to behold, he used to fall down and see, but now it was not proper for him to behold.' 'If that is so,' said the other, 'he was in a grade superior to that of all the true prophets, since when falling with open eyes he beheld the glory of the Holy One, blessed be He. R. Simeon, however, has told us that through his enchantments Balaam knew only the lower Crowns beneath, and was entitled only a "diviner". And R. Simeon also said that through one vision which he was granted exceptionally, as it says, "And the Lord opened the eyes of Balaam", his eyes were stricken. How, then, can you say that he saw with open eyes and gazed on the glory of God?' He said: 'I simply answered your question. Both your statement and mine require to be cleared up. Of a truth the mysteries of the Torah are deep, and not to be penetrated, and therefore one should not make any statement about the Torah until he has heard and understood it properly.' They therefore went to R. Simeon and laid the matter before him. In reply he cited to them the verse: "What is man that thou art mindful of him, and the son of man that thou visitest him?" (Ps. VIII, 5). 'The exposition of this verse', he said, 'is that it was uttered by those in charge of the world at the time when God expressed His intention of creating man. He called together various companies of heavenly angels and stationed them before Him. He said to them: I desire to create man. They exclaimed, "Man abideth not in honour", etc. (Ps. XLIX, 13). God thereupon put forth His finger and burnt them. He then set other groups before Him, and said: I desire to create man. They exclaimed,

Zohar: Bemidbar, Section 3, Page 208a

"What is man that thou shouldst remember him?" What is the character of this man, they asked. He replied: Man will be in our image, and his wisdom will be superior to yours. When He had created man and he sinned and obtained a pardon, Uzza and Azael approached Him and said: We can plead justification against Thee, since the man whom Thou hast made has sinned against Thee. He said to them: Had you been with them you would have sinned equally, and He cast them down from their high estate in heaven. Now to come to your question. How are we to explain Balaam's saying of himself, "Falling and with eyes open"? For if this was merely an empty boast, how comes a false statement in the Torah? And if it is true, how could that sinner attain to a degree higher than that of all the true prophets, especially as the holiness from above rests only on a spot qualified to receive it? The fact is, however, that after God cast Uzza and Azael down from their holy place, they went astray after the womenfolk and seduced the world also. It may seem strange that being angels they were able to abide upon the earth. The truth is, however, that when they were cast down the celestial light which used to sustain them left them and they were changed to another grade through the influence of the air of this world. Similarly the manna which came down for the Israelites in the wilderness originated in the celestial dew from the most recondite spot, and at first its light would radiate to all worlds and the "field of apples", and the heavenly angels drew sustenance from it, but when it approached the earth it became materialized through the influence of the air of this world and lost its brightness, becoming only like "coriander seed'. Now when God saw that these fallen angels were seducing the world, He bound them in chains of iron to a mountain of darkness. Uzza He bound at the bottom of the mountain and covered his face with darkness because he struggled and resisted, but Azael, who did not resist, He set by the side of the mountain where a little light penetrated. Men who know where they are located seek them out, and they teach them enchantments and sorceries and divinations. These mountains of darkness are called the "mountains of the East,' and therefore Balaam said: "From Aram hath Balak brought me, from the mountains of the

East", because they both learnt their sorceries there. Now Uzza and Azael used to tell those men who came to them some of the notable things which they knew in former times when they were on high, and to speak about the holy world in which they used to be. Hence Balaam said of himself: "He saith, which heareth the words of God"-not the voice of God, but those things which he was told by those who had been in the assembly of the Holy King. He went on: "And knoweth the knowledge of the Most High", meaning that he knew the hour when punishment impended over the world and could determine it with his enchantments. "Which seeth the vision of the Almighty": this vision consisted of the "fallen and the open of eyes", that is Uzza, who is called "fallen" because he was placed in the darkest depth, since after falling from heaven he fell a second time, and Azael, who is called "open of eye" because he was not enveloped in complete darkness.

Zohar: Bemidbar, Section 3, Page 208b

Balaam called both of them "the vision of the Almighty". At that time he was the only man left in the world who associated with them, and every day he used to be shut up in those mountains with them.' Said R. Simeon: 'How often have I repeated this, and yet the Companions do not pay attention, that the Holy One, blessed be He, does not let His divine presence rest save in a place which is meet that it should rest therein. Happy is the portion of Israel in that God has sanctified them that He may abide among them, as it is written, "For the Lord thy God walketh in the midst of thy camp", etc. (Deut. XXIII, 14). Happy, too, is the portion of the true prophets who are holy and are permitted to make use of the celestial holiness.

AND THE ASS SAW THE ANGEL OF THE LORD STANDING IN THE WAY: in that way which Balaam had chosen. WITH HIS SWORD DRAWN IN HIS HAND. If the angel went to meet the ass, why did he require a sword, and if he went to meet Balaam, why did his ass see and not he himself? All, however, was arranged by Providence. The angel was sent by Providence to lead the ass out of that way in which it was being driven, and to thwart Balaam in order to punish him for wanting to go his own way.' R. Yose said: 'The question now arises, if his words came from the side of the lower crowns and not from another side, why is it written, "And God (Elohim) came to Balaam?"'

R. Isaac replied: 'What we have learnt is that Elohim in this passage designates an angel, being the place that comes from the side of stern judgement, to which is attached the strength and power of those lower crowns which were employed by Balaam. Hence it says, "And Elohim came to Balaam", etc., because sometimes the angel is called by the superior name.

AND THE ASS TURNED ASIDE OUT OF THE WAY. That is, from the way of stern judgement against Israel. How did Balaam see that she had turned aside?' Said R. Simeon: 'Even on the way he sought to do harm to Israel through the power of his ass, and when he saw that he was not succeeding he smote it with his staff, which is a symbol of stern judgement. AND WENT IN THE FIELD: in the straight path on the side of "field". AND BALAAM SMOTE THE ASS TO TURN HER INTO THE WAY: that is, to turn her out of that way of the field. When he saw he was not able, then "he smote the ass with a staff", as has been explained.' AND THE ANGEL OF THE LORD STOOD, ETC. Said R. Abba: 'These verses have

Zohar: Bemidbar, Section 3, Page 209a

a profound symbolical meaning, and it was not for nothing that the angel went forth to appear to an ass and to meet it now here and now there. All was designed by the Holy One, blessed be He, to protect Israel from the domination of the evil species. We have learnt that from the side of the Mother when she is crowned there issue in her crowns fifteen hundred sides graven in her ornaments. When She desires to unite with the King she is crowned with a diadem of four colours, which flash to all four sides of the world, each one three times, making twelve graven boundaries. On the top of the crown there are four walls with towers, on each of which are three doors fixed in precious stones on each side. Under the crown are bells of gold, a bell on this side and a bell on that, and a pomegranate in which are a thousand bells, each one flashing white and red. This pomegranate is divided into four quarters and is open so that the bells can be seen. There are three hundred and twenty-five bells on each side, and all four sides of the world are illumined with the radiance of each quarter. There are four wheels on the four corners to bear the crown. Their voice is heard through all the firmaments, and at the sweet sound of them all the hosts of heaven are excited and inquire of one another until they all say: Blessed is the glory of the Lord from His place. When the King joins the Matrona, this crown ascends and settles on the head of the Matrona. Then there comes down a supernal crown studded with all kinds of precious stones and with garlands of lilies around it. It comes with six wheels to the six sides of the world, borne by six wings of eagles. In its quarters are fifty grapes round about traced by the supreme Mother, set with precious stones, white and red and green and black and blue and purple, six hundred and thirteen corners to each side. There are a thousand and six hundred turrets on each side, moistened by the supernal Mother with her oil of anointing. Then the Mother silently sends down noble gifts and fixes them in that crown, which thereupon lets fall streams of oil of holy anointing on the head of the King, whence it flows down on to his precious beard and from there on to the garments of the King. Then the supernal Mother crowns Him with that crown and spreads over Him and the Matrona precious garments. Then there is joy among all the sons of the King, to wit, those who come from the sides of Israel, since none associate with them save Israel, who are of their household, so that the blessings which issue from them are for Israel. Israel take all and send a portion thereof to the other peoples, who thence derive their sustenance. We have learnt that from between the sides of the portions of the Chieftains of the other peoples there goes forth

Zohar: Bemidbar, Section 3, Page 209b

a narrow path whence is drawn a portion to those lower ones, and thence it spreads to many sides, and this is called the "residue", which issues from the side of the Holy Land, and thus the whole world drinks from the residue of the Holy Land. And not only the heathen peoples, but also those lower Crowns drink therefrom. This is indicated here by the expression, "a hollow way between the vineyards", the path of the Princes of the other peoples, from which they are blessed. Therefore when the angel saw that Balaam had made his ass turn aside into that path, straightway he STOOD IN THE HOLLOW WAY BETWEEN THE VINEYARDS, in order that the other heathen peoples and the lower Crowns should not furnish him assistance. There was A FENCE ON THIS SIDE AND A FENCE ON THAT SIDE.

'Said R. Abba: 'The angel would not have been able to block up the path had he not received assistance from the Holy One, blessed be He, and the Community of Israel.' R. Judah said it was the Torah that assisted him. Then the ass THRUST HERSELF INTO THE WALL, the "wall" here symbolizing the protector that guarded them. Also, instead of assisting Balaam she "pressed his foot against the wall", hinting the same thing to him. Then HE SMOTE HER AGAIN, on this side, AND THE ANGEL OF THE LORD WENT FURTHER AND STOOD IN A NARROW PLACE, thus closing all paths to her, so that she could not assist Balaam in any way at all. Then SHE LAY DOWN UNDER BALAAM, and BALAAM'S ANGER WAS KINDLED AND HE SMOTE HER WITH A STAFF, as we have explained. 'AND THE LORD OPENED THE MOUTH OF THE ASS. R. Isaac said: 'What did she say that was of any consequence either to Balaam or to herself or to Israel?' R. Yose replied: 'She made him ridiculous in the eyes of the nobles who were with him. When they came to Balak they said: Have you sent to honour that fool? You will find nothing in him or his words. Thus through the words of the ass he became degraded.' R. Hiya said: 'Had not the ass spoken thus, Balaam would not have given up his attempt, but through the words of the ass he knew that his power was broken.' R. Abba asked: 'Why does it say here that "God opened the mouth of the ass", while in an analogous passage it says that "the earth opened its mouth" (Num. XVI, 32).' 'The reason', he said, 'is that there Moses decreed the opening and the earth carried out his injunction, for it would not be fitting that God should do so, but here there was no one who gave the order, but it was the will of God, and therefore it is written that "God opened the mouth of the ass".'

R. Judah said: 'We have carefully examined this section and these words, and we find that they are not words of any consequence. Yet after it says that "God opened the mouth of the ass", those words ought to have been words of profundity and wisdom. Why, then, did God trouble to open its mouth for merely such words?' R. Abba replied: 'Assuredly, through those words we learn the mind of Balaam, that he was not worthy for the holy spirit to rest on him, and we learn that there was no power in his ass to do either good

Zohar: Bemidbar, Section 3, Page 210a

or harm. We also learn from this ass that animals are not capable of receiving a rational mind. SHE SAID UNTO BALAAM, WHAT HAVE I DONE UNTO THEE. As much as to say: Was it in my power to do good or evil? Not so, for beasts can only do as they are directed. And that beast, too, though it struck a deeper note, was still in the power of Balaam. AND BALAAM SAID UNTO THE ASS, BECAUSE THOU HAST MOCKED ME. He ought to have laughed at her, but he answered her in her own tone, and it was then that they mocked him and he became contemptible in their eyes, and they knew that he was a fool. They said: He pretends he can kill peoples with his mouth, and yet he cannot kill his ass without a sword. We learn from here that beasts are not capable of receiving another spirit. For should men say: If only beasts could speak, what they would have to tell the world, learn from this ass of Balaam; for God opened her mouth, and see what she said!'

AND IT CAME TO PASS IN THE MORNING THAT BALAK TOOK BALAAM, ETC. R. Isaac said: Balak was cleverer at enchantments than Balaam, only he did not know how to fix on the right hour for cursing. AND HE BROUGHT HIM UP TO THE HIGH PLACES OF BAAL. He examined by his enchantments from what side he could best attack them, and he found that they would one day make high places and serve Baal. He saw the princes of the people and their king serving him. Straightway he said: BUILD ME HERE SEVEN ALTARS. R. Yose and R. Judah differed as to the significance of this number. One said it corresponded to the seven built by the patriarchs. The other said that it was based on cosmological grounds, because the portion of Israel is attached to seven grades. A man had a friend who was left to him from his father, and on account of whom men were afraid to attack him. One day a man wanted to pick a quarrel with him, but he was afraid lest the friend protect him. He therefore sent a present to the friend. Said the latter: What does this man want with me? It must be because of the son of my friend. I will therefore not accept this gift, but give it to the dogs. So when Balaam desired to attack Israel, seeing that he would not be able to prevail against them on account of their friend, he began to prepare a gift for him. Whereupon God said: Sinner, what have I to do with you? You want to attack my son;

here is your gift for my dogs. So it says, "God met Balaam", the word vayikkar (met) having the connotation of "uncleanness" and also of "uprooting".'

Zohar: Bemidbar, Section 3, Page 210b

R. Simeon said: 'The loathsomeness of Balaam may be seen from the fact that in all the section it never says, "The Lord said" or "spoke" to Balaam. What it says is, "The Lord placed a word in the mouth of Balaam", like one who places a bit in the mouth of an ass. God said to him: Sinner, think not that through you the blessing of my sons will be confirmed or otherwise. They do not require you; but return to Balak, and when you open your mouth, it will not be to say your own words, but Koh [Tr. note: The Shekinah.] (thus) will speak out of your mouth.'

COME CURSE ME JACOB. R. Yose said: This means: Cast them down from the grade in which they stand, for then they will be uprooted from the world. COME, PROVOKE ISRAEL; that is, the supernal Israel, so that wrath may be aroused. FOR FROM THE TOP OF THE ROCKS I SEE HIM.' R. Isaac said: These are the patriarchs. AND FROM THE HILLS I BEHOLD HIM: these are the matriarchs. From neither side can they be cursed.' R. Yose said: 'It means: Who can prevail against Israel, since he is attached to the source whence all rocks, that is, all forceful deeds, issue. LO IT IS A PEOPLE THAT DWELL ALONE: as it is written, "The Lord did lead him alone" (Deut. XXXII, 12). WHO CAN COUNT THE DUST OF JACOB: this dust ' is the place whence the first man was created, and from that dust issue many hosts and camps, many flames and arrows and catapults and lances and swords. OR NUMBER THE FOURTH PART OF ISRAEL: this refers to David, who was the fourth foot of the Throne.

[Note: The last 3 lines of the Hebrew text are not found in our translation]

Zohar: Bemidbar, Section 3, Page 211a

BEHOLD THE PEOPLE RISETH UP AS A LIONESS. What people is strong like Israel? When the day dawns the Israelite rises like a lion refreshed for the service of his Master with songs and praises, and then occupies himself with the Torah all day. And before he lies down at night he sanctifies the supreme Name and declares its kingship above and below. How many officers of judgement are bound hand and foot before them when they open their mouths on their beds with "Hear, O Israel," and seek compassion from the Holy King with many appropriate Scriptural verses!' R. Abba said: 'This people will one day rise against all the heathen peoples like a mighty lion and throw themselves on them. It is the way of the lion to lie down with his prey, but this people will not lie down till he has eaten of the prey. Or, again, we may explain, "he riseth up as a lioness" to offer burnt-offerings and sacrifices before their king on the altar. "He shall not lie down": these are the sacrifices of the night, like the burnt-offerings. AND DRINK THE BLOOD OF THE SLAIN: because God makes war upon their enemies.' R. Eleazar said: 'What is the meaning of "he shall not lie down"? It means that when a man walks in the precepts of his Master he never

[Note: The last 31 lines of the Hebrew text are not found in our translation]

Zohar: Bemidbar, Section 3, Page 211b

lies down upon his bed at night before he has killed a thousand and a hundred and twenty-five of those evil species that abide with him.' R. Hizkiah said: 'Corresponding to the three times that Balaam smote his ass and directed it by his sorceries, Israel were blessed three times.' R. Hiya said that Israel were blessed three times correspondingly by having to appear three times before the Holy King.

AND WHEN BALAAM SAW THAT IT PLEASED THE LORD TO BLESS ISRAEL, HE WENT NOT AS AT THE OTHER TIMES TO MEET WITH ENCHANTMENTS. R. Yose said: The first two times he went with all his enchantments. When he saw what was God's purpose, and that he was only the mouthpiece of Koh, he sought to look upon them with the evil eye. He scrutinized the two grades of Jacob and Israel to see through which he could harm them with his enchantments, and that is why all the blessings were bestowed both upon Jacob and Israel. Having, therefore, abandoned his enchantments, he began under another impulse to praise Israel, the impulse of a certain spirit from the side of the left under which were made fast those species and enchantments of his.' Said R. Eleazar: 'We have learnt that even at that time the spirit of holiness did not rest on him.' Said R. Yose to him: 'Why, then, is it written on this occasion that "the spirit of the Lord came upon him", which we do not find before?' He replied: 'It is written, "He that hath a bountiful eye shall be blessed" (Prov. XXII, 9), or, as we read, "shall bless", and Balaam had an evil eye like no other. Now there is a saying that if a man is taking his child through the street and is afraid of the evil eye, he should cover his head with his scarf, and then he will be safe from the evil eye. So here, when Balaam saw that he was not able to harm Israel with his enchantments and sorceries, he sought to look upon them with the evil eye, and therefore "he set his face towards the wilderness", that is, as the Targum renders, to the calf which they made in the wilderness, in order to find some opening for doing them harm, and had not God provided in advance some remedy for them, he would have destroyed them with the glance of his eye. What was this remedy? It is indicated in the words, "And there was upon him the spirit of God"-upon him, that is, upon Israel; as when a man spreads his scarf over the head of a child in order that the evil eye should not injure him. Then he began to say: "How goodly are thy tents, O Jacob". Observe that anyone who desires to look at anything with the evil eye has first to praise and laud the thing whieh he desires to curse with the evil eye, as by saying: "See how good this is, how beautiful this is". So here he said: How goodly are thy tents, how many

Zohar: Bemidbar, Section 3, Page 212a

goodly shoots spring from them, resembling those which God planted in the Garden of Eden. He was like a man who, seeing another with beautiful hands, takes hold of them and begins to praise them, saying: How fair and beautiful they are! See these fingers of divine form! Then he goes on: Would that these hands were encased in precious stones and in purple in my box that I might have the use of them! So Balaam, after beginning to praise them went on: "Let water flow from his buckets", or as we may read, from his poor ones (dalav), as much as to say: Let this fair shoot, the shoot of the Torah, come only from the poor among them. God said to him: Wretch, thine eyes cannot harm them, since the veil of holiness is over them. Then he went on: "God bringeth him forth out of Egypt", etc.: the whole world cannot harm them because a mighty power from above takes hold of them.' R. Eleazar said: 'No man was so skilled in inflicting harm as Balaam. For at first he was in Egypt, and through him the Egyptians fastened upon the Israelites fetters from which they thought they would never escape. Balaam therefore now said: How can I harm them, seeing that it was I who devised that they should not escape from the bondage of Egypt forever. But "God brought them out of Egypt", and no enchanters could prevail against them. BEHOLD I GO UNTO MY PEOPLE. When the Israelites left Egypt, and Balaam heard that all his enchantments and divinations and magical fetters had not availed anything, he began to tear his flesh and pluck out his hair, and he then betook himself to the "mountains of darkness". Now when a man first approaches those mountains Azael, who is called "open of eye", sees him and tells Uzza. Then they give a shout and certain huge flaming beasts gather to them. They send to meet the visitor a little creature like a cat with a serpent's head and two tails and tiny legs. When the man sees it he covers his face and throws in its face some ashes from the burning of a white cock which he has brought with him, and it then accompanies him to the top of the chains. This top is stuck in the ground and the chain extends thence to the abyss, where it is made fast to a pole stuck in there. When the man reaches the chain he strikes it three times. The others thereupon call him and he falls on his knees and closes his eyes till he reaches them. Then he sits before them with all the beasts around him, and when he opens his eyes and sees them he trembles and falls on his face before them. They then teach him enchantments and divinations and he remains with them

Zohar: Bemidbar, Section 3, Page 212b

fifty days. When the time comes for him to depart the small creature and the beasts go before him till he emerges from the mountains and from the thick darkness. When Balaam came to them, he informed them of what had happened and he sought means of assailing Israel so as to bring them back to Egypt, but God confounded all his wisdom. Now, too, when he saw that he could not harm Israel, without waiting to be asked he gave Balak counsel, namely, regarding the women, as we learn from what Moses said later, "Behold these caused the children of Israel through the counsel of Balaam", etc. (Num. XXXI, 16). God therefore showed to that power which rules over enchantments the end of days, and that is how Balaam came to speak of far-off events, for the words were really spoken by the power which controlled him.

I SEE HIM BUT NOT NOW: since some of these things were fulfilled at that time and some later, while some are left for the Messiah. We have learnt that God will one day build Jerusalem and display a certain fixed star flashing with seventy streamers and seventy flames in the midst of the firmament, and it will shine and flash for seventy days. It will appear on the sixth day of the week on the twenty-fifth of the sixth month, and will disappear on the seventh day after seventy days. On the first day it will be seen in the city of Rome, and on that day three lofty walls of that city shall fall and a mighty palace shall be overthrown, and the ruler of that city shall die. Then that star will become visible throughout the whole world. In that time mighty wars will arise in all quarters of the world, and no faith shall be found among men. When that star shines in the midst of the firmament, a certain powerful king shall arise who will seek domination over all kings and make war on two sides and prevail against them. On the day when the star disappears the Holy Land will be shaken over an area of forty-five miles all round the place where the Temple used to be, and a cave will be laid open beneath the ground from which shall issue a mighty fire to consume the world. From that cave shall spread a great and noble branch which will rule over all the world and to which shall be given the kingship, and the heavenly saints shall gather to it. Then will the King Messiah appear and the kingship shall be given to him. Mankind will then suffer one calamity after another, and the enemies of Israel will prevail, but the spirit of the Messiah shall rise against them and destroy the sinful Edom and burn in fire the land of Seir. Hence it is written, "And Edom shall be a possession, Seir also shall be a possession of his which were his enemies, while Israel doth valiantly". And in that time the Holy One, blessed be He, shall raise the dead of his people, and death shall be forgotten of them.' R. Abba said: 'Why is it written, "For in joy ye shall go out" (Isa. LV, 12)? Because when Israel go out from captivity the Shekinah will go forth with them and they with Her.

Zohar: Bemidbar, Section 3, Page 213a

PINHAS

[Tr. NOTE. From the beginning of the section Pinhas to the end of the Zohar, a large portion of the text in the original is taken up by the Raya Mehemna; hence the frequency of the omissions in the translation. On the section Mattoth there is only a short piece of Zohar of too allusive a nature to be made intelligible in a translation. There is no Zohar at all on the sections Mas'e, Debarim, Ekeb, Re'eh, Shofetim, Ki Teze, Ki Tabo, Nizabim, and Vezoth Haberakah.]

PHINEAS THE SON OF ELEAZAR THE SON OF AARON THE PRIEST. R. Simeon said: 'Israel deserved to be destroyed at that time, and were only saved by that deed of Phineas.' Said R. Simeon: 'If a man receives a soul in the course of its transmigration and it does not properly fit into him, he as it were belies his trust to the King, and I apply to him the verse: "If he find something lost and deny it and swear falsely" (Lev. VI, 3). We have learnt that a completely righteous man is not thrust aside, but one who is not completely righteous may be thrust aside. A completely righteous man is one who does not receive migratory souls out of their course, who builds on his own inheritance, and digs his wells and plants his trees there. The righteous one who is not completely so builds on another's inheritance: he labours but does not know if what he produces will remain his. In respect of himself he is called good and righteous, but not in respect of that inheritance. He is like a man who builds a fair building, but when he examines the foundation he finds that it is sloping and crooked. His building in itself is good,

Zohar: Bemidbar, Section 3, Page 213b

but in respect of its foundation it is bad, and therefore is not called a perfect building. Note that if one is zealous for the name of the Holy One, blessed be He, even though he is not qualified for greatness, he nevertheless obtains it. Phineas at that time was not qualified for greatness, but because he was zealous for the name of his Master he rose to the greatest heights, and all was made right in him [Tr. note: i.e. the souls of Nadab and Abihu entered into him, s. infra.], and he was invested with the high priesthood. Hence the word "son" is mentioned in connection with him twice.

[Note: The last 52 lines of the Hebrew text are not found in our translation]

Zohar: Bemidbar, Section 3, Page 214a [Note: The first 10 lines of the Hebrew text are not found in our translation]

Phineas merited reward in this world and in the next. He was granted to outlive all those who went forth from Egypt and won the high priesthood for himself and his descendants. Now it is a rule that a priest who kills a human being becomes disqualified for the priesthood, and therefore by rights Phineas should have been disqualified. But because he was jealous for the Holy One, blessed be He, the priesthood was assigned to him and to his descendants in perpetuity.'

As R. Eleazar and R. Yose were once walking in the wilderness, R. Yose said: 'When it says of Phineas, "Behold I give him my covenant of peace", it means peace from the Angel of Death, so that he should never have power over him and that he should not suffer his chastisements. As for the tradition that Phineas did not die, the truth is that he did not die like other men, and he outlived all his generation, because he kept hold of this supernal covenant, and when he departed from the world it was with celestial yearning and beauteous attachment.' R. Eleazar cited the verse: "And he showed me Joshua the high priest standing before the angel of the Lord", etc. (Zech. III, 1). 'The "filthy garments", as explained elsewhere, are those with which the spirit was clad in this world. It has been asked: When a man is doomed to Gehinnom, what are the garments with which they invest him? And the answer is given in the words, "Now Joshua was clothed with filthy garments, and standing before the angel" (Ibid. 3). This was the angel appointed over Gehinnom, and from this we can learn that the evil deeds of a man make for him these filthy garments, and so God said afterwards to him: "Behold, I have caused thine iniquity to pass from thee and I have clothed thee with rich apparel"; he was clothed in other proper garments through which a man may see the glory of the Shekinah. So Phineas did not depart from this world until there were prepared for him other garments pleasing to the spirit for the next world.'

Zohar: Bemidbar, Section 3, Page 214b

[Note: This Hebrew text does not appear in our translation.]

Zohar: Bemidbar, Section 3, Page 215a

[Note: This Hebrew text does not appear in our translation.]

Zohar: Bemidbar, Section 3, Page 215b

[Note: This Hebrew text does not appear in our translation.]

Zohar: Bemidbar, Section 3, Page 217a

[Note: The translation is only of the first 15 lines of the Hebrew text.]

As R. Simeon was once studying this portion, his son, R. Eleazar, came and asked him: 'What is the connection of Nadab and Abihu with Phineas? If Phineas had not been born when they died and had afterwards come into the world and taken their place, I could understand, but he was alive at the time, and his soul was already in its place?' He replied: 'My son, there is a deep mystery here. When they departed from the world they were not sheltered under the wings of the holy Rock, because they had no children, and they were therefore not fitted for the high priesthood. Now when Phineas rose up against the adulterers, when he saw all the hosts of the tribe of Simeon gathering around him, his soul fled from him, and then two souls which were flying about naked joined it and they all became one and thus united entered into him, so that he took the place of Nadab and Abihu to become high priest, and therefore it is written, "Phineas son of Eleazar son".'

R. Hiya expounded the verse: "He causeth grass to grow for the cattle" (Ps. CIV, 14). 'The "grass",' he said, 'refers to the sixty thousand myriads of angels who were created on the second day of the Creation, being all of flaming fire; and they are called "grass" because they are constantly being cut down and restored. They are food for the "Cattle", over which rules the "Man".'

Zohar: Bemidbar, Section 3, Page 217b [Note: the first 13 lines of the Hebrew text are not translated.]

R. Abba and R. Yose once rose at midnight to study the Torah. As they were sitting they saw a shadow hovering over them and going to and fro in the house, and they marvelled greatly. Said R. Abba: 'Yose, my son, I will tell you what once happened to me with the Sacred Lamp. Once we were walking in the Valley of Ono, studying the Torah.

Zohar: Bemidbar, Section 3, Page 218a

To escape the heat of the sun we sat down in the hollow of a rock. I said to him: Why is it that whenever sinners multiply in the world and punishment impends over the world, the virtuous among them are smitten for them, as we have learnt, that for the guilt of the generation the holy and righteous are seized upon? Why should this be? If because they do not reprove mankind for their evil deeds, how many are there who do reprove but are not listened to (though the righteous do humble themselves before them)? If it is in order that there may be no one to shield them, let them not die and let them not be seized for their sins, since it is a satisfaction to the righteous to see their destruction. He replied: It is true that for the guilt of the generation the righteous are seized upon, but we may explain this on the analogy of the limbs of the body. When all the limbs are in pain and suffering from sickness one limb has to be smitten in order that all may be healed. Which is the one? The arm. The arm is smitten and blood is drawn from it, and this is healing for all the limbs of the body. So men are like limbs of one body. When God desires to give healing to the world He smites one righteous man among them with disease and suffering, and through him gives healing to all, as it is written, "But he was wounded for our transgressions, he was bruised for our iniquities... and with his stripes we are healed" (Isa. LIII, 5). A righteous man is never afflicted save to bring healing to his generation and to make atonement for it, for the "other side" prefers that punishment should light upon the virtuous man rather than on any other, for then it cares not for the whole world on account of the joy it finds in having power over him. Yet withal another virtuous man may attain to dominion in this world and the next; he is "righteous

Zohar: Bemidbar, Section 3, Page 218b

and it is well with him", because God does not care to make atonement with him for the world. I said to him: If all suffered alike, I could understand, but we see a righteous man in one place who is sick and suffering, and a righteous man in another who enjoys all the good things of the world. He replied: One or two of them are enough, since God does not desire to smite all of them, just as it is sufficient to let blood from one arm; only if the sickness becomes very severe is it necessary to let blood from two arms, and so here, if the world becomes very sinful all the virtuous are smitten to heal all the generation, but otherwise one is smitten and the rest are left in peace. When the people are healed the righteous are healed with them, but sometimes all their days are passed in suffering to protect the people, and when they die all are healed.

'We arose and went on our way, the sun becoming stronger and more oppressive. We saw some trees in the wilderness with water underneath, and we sat down in the shade of one of them. I asked him: How is it that of all peoples of the world, only the Jews sway to and fro when they study the Torah, a habit which seems to come natural to them, and they are unable to keep still? He replied: You have reminded me of a very deep idea which very few people know. He pondered for a moment and wept. Then he continued: Alas for mankind who go about l i ke cattle without understanding. This thing alone is sufficient to distinguish the holy souls of Israel from the souls of heathen peoples. The souls of Israel have been hewn from the Holy Lamp, as is written, "The spirit of man is the lamp of the Lord" (Prov. xx, 27). Now once this lamp has been kindled from

Zohar: Bemidbar, Section 3, Page 219a

the supernal Torah, the light upon it never ceases for an instant, like the flame of a wick which is never still for an instant. So when an Israelite has said one word of the Torah, a light is kindled and he cannot keep still but sways to and fro like the flame of a wick. But the souls of heathens are like the burning of stubble, which gives no flame, and therefore they keep still like wood burning without a flame.' Said R. Yose: 'That is a good explanation; happy am I to have heard this.'

Zohar: Bemidbar, Section 3, Page 219b [Note: This page of the Hebrew text is not translated.]

Zohar: Bemidbar, Section 3, Page 220a [Note: the first 4 lines of the Hebrew text are not translated.]

The shadow returned as before and went to and fro in the house in the shape of a man. R. Abba fell on his face. R. Yose said: 'I remember that I once saw R. Phineas b. Jair in this place standing in this spot and discoursing on the verse, "Phineas son of Eleazar son of Aaron the priest", etc. God at that time, he said, was debating how to give this \covenant to Phineas, because it belonged of right to Moses, and it would be an insult to him to give it to anyone else unless he consented. God therefore commenced to speak with Moses, saying: Phineas son of Eleazar son of Aaron the priest. Said Moses: Sovereign of the Universe, what of him? He replied: Thou didst risk thy life many times to save Israel from destruction, and now he has turned My wrath away from the children of Israel. Moses thereupon said: What wilt Thou of me? All is in Thy hand. He replied: Nay, all is in thy hand. Tell him that it (the Shekinah) will abide in him. Moses replied: I am willing with all my heart that it should be with him. God then said: Declare aloud that thou deliverest it to him with all thy heart. Hence we read in the text, "Say, Behold I (viz. Moses) give unto him my covenant", and not, "Say to him". Yet think not that it was taken away from Moses: it was like a light from which another is kindled without loss to itself.'

The shade then came and sat down and kissed him. They heard a voice saying: Make way, make way for R. Phineas b. Jair, who is with you, as we have learnt: Any place in which a righteous man has given some new explanation of the Torah he visits when he is in the other world, especially when there are in it other righteous men discoursing on the Torah. So R. Phineas b. Jair came to revisit his place and found those righteous men repeating his own remark. R. Abba gave a further exposition in the name of R. Phineas b. Jair of the text: "Whatsoever thy hand findeth to do, do it with thy might" (Eccl. IX, 10). 'It is fitting for a man', he said, 'that while the lamp is burning over his head he should strive to do the will of his Master, because the light of that lamp is the might that rests upon him, as it is written, "And now I pray thee, let the power of the Lord be great" (Num. XIV, 17). The "power of the Lord" is the might that rests on the heads of the righteous, and of all who strive to carry out the will of their Master, and therefore we have learnt that when one makes the response, "Amen, may his great name be blessed", he should do so with all the might of his limbs, because through that effort he awakens that supernal holy might and breaks the power and might of the "other side".

Zohar: Bemidbar, Section 3, Page 220b

The verse continues: "Because there is no work nor device nor knowledge nor wisdom in the grave whither thou goest". In that "might", however, there is work, namely, effort in this world, which is called "the world of work"; "device" in the world that depends on speech, "knowledge" of the "six sides", which are called "the world of Thought", and wisdom on which all depends. Hence a man who does not labour with his "might" in this world to bring it into "work and device and knowledge and wisdom", will eventually enter into Gehinnom, where there is no work nor device nor knowledge nor wisdom. For all men go down to Sheol, but they come up again at once, save those sinners who never harboured thoughts of repentance, and who go down and do not come up. Even the completely righteous go down there, but they only go down in order to bring up certain sinners from there, to wit, those who thought of repenting in this world, but were not able to do so in time before they departed from it. The righteous go down and bring these up.' Said R. Abba to R. Yose: 'How fair is the jewel that you obtained from the company of the holy saint who is with us t! would add that assuredly it is not right to send a woman to stay in another place until her husband gives her permission. Her husband must therefore first be told and persuaded to give her permission. So God persuaded Moses to say, "Behold, I give him my covenant of peace", and until Moses gave it permission to go there it would not go. Similarly the Righteous One of the world gives Her permission to abide among the righteous ones of this world; in the evening She comes in to her spouse, and in the morning She returns to the righteous of this world, but She is ever in the charge of her Spouse. So Moses gave the gift to Phineas on condition that it should be subsequently restored; and it was through this covenant that Phineas obtained the high priesthood, and without it he would not have been linked to the grade of the priesthood.'

R. Abba said: 'I remember a certain thing which I heard from the Sacred Lamp, and which he said in the name of R. Eleazar. One day a certain clever non-Jew came to him and said: Old man, old man, I want to ask three questions

Zohar: Bemidbar, Section 3, Page 221a

of you. One is, how can you maintain that another Temple will be built for you, whereas only two were destined to be built, the first and the second. A third and a fourth you will not find mentioned in the Scripture, but it is written, "Greater shall be the glory of this latter house than of the first" (Haggai II, 9). Again, you maintain that you are nearer to the King than all other peoples. Now, one who is near to the King is ever in joy and free from sorrow and oppression, but you are ever in sorrow and oppression and anguish, more than all the rest of mankind, whereas we never suffer sorrow or oppression or anguish at all. This shows that we are near to the King and you are far away. Again, you do not eat nebelah and terefah, [Tr. note: Flesh of animals not killed according to Jewish rites.] in order to protect your health, but we eat whatever we like and we are healthy and strong, whereas you who do not eat are all weak and sickly beyond other peoples. You are a people who are wholly hated of your God. Old man, old man, don't say anything to me, for I will not listen to you. R. Eleazar raised his eyes and looked at him, and he became a heap of bones. When his wrath subsided he turned his head and wept, saying: "O Lord, our Lord, how excellent is thy name in all the earth" (Ps. VIII, 2). How mighty is the power of the Holy Name, and how beloved are the words of the Torah, since there is nothing at all which cannot be found in the Torah, and there is not a single word of the Torah which does not issue from the mouth of the Holy One, blessed be He. These questions which that wretch put to me I also one day asked Elijah, and he told me that

713

they had been raised in the celestial Academy before the Holy One, blessed be He. The answer given was as follows. When Israel left Egypt, God desired to make them on earth like ministering angels above, and to build for them a holy house which was to be brought down from the heaven of the firmaments, and to plant Israel as a holy shoot after the pattern of the celestial prototype. Thus it is written, "Thou shalt bring them in and plant them in the mountain of thine inheritance, the place, O Lord, which thou hast made for thee to dwell in" - this is the first Temple - "the sanctuary, O Lord, which thy hands have established" (Ex. xv, 17) - this is the second Temple; and both were to have been the work of the Almighty. But as they provoked God in the wilderness they died there and God brought their children into the land, and the house was built by human hands, and therefore it did not endure. In the days of Ezra also on account of their sins they were forced to build it themselves and therefore it did not endure. All this time the first building planned by God had not yet been set up. Now of the future time it is written, "The Lord buildeth Jerusalem" (Ps. CXLVII, 2). He and no other. It is for this building that we are waiting, not a human structure which cannot endure. The Holy One, blessed be He, will send down to us the first House and the second House together, the first in concealment and the second openly. The second will be revealed to show all the world the handiwork of the Holy One, blessed be He, in perfect joy and gladness. The first, which will be concealed, will ascend high over that which is revealed, and all the world will see the clouds of glory surrounding the one which is revealed and enveloping the first one which ascends to the height of the glorious heavens. It is for that building that we are waiting. Even the future city of Jerusalem will not be the work of human hands, all the more so then the Temple, God's habitation. This work should have been completed when Israel first went forth from Egypt, but it has been deferred to the end of days in the last deliverance.

Zohar: Bemidbar, Section 3, Page 221b

As for the second question, assuredly we are nearer to the supernal King than all other peoples. God has made Israel as it were the heart of all mankind, and as the limbs cannot endure for a moment without the heart, so the other nations cannot endure without Israel. And what the heart is among the limbs, such is Israel among the nations. The heart is tender and weak, and it alone feels sorrow and distress, since in it alone is intelligence. The other limbs are distant from the king, which is the wisdom and intelligence situate in the brain, but the heart is near. So Israel is near to the Holy King, while the other nations are far away. Similarly in regard to the third question, Israel being the heart, which is tender and delicate and king of the members, takes for its food only the most purified part of all the blood, and leaves the remnant for the other members, which are not particular. They are therefore strong, as we see, but they also suffer from boils and from other ailments from which the heart is quite free. So God takes to himself Israel, who are clean and pure without any blemish.'

NOW THE NAME OF THE MAN OF ISRAEL THAT WAS SLAIN, WHO WAS SLAIN WITH THE MIDIANITISH WOMAN. R. Isaac said: 'We should have expected the text to run "whom Phineas slew". The reason why it is put in this way is because God, having raised Phineas to the high priesthood, did not wish to associate his name with the killing of a man, which does not beseem a high priest.'

R. Simeon was once going from Cappadocia to Lydda with R. Judah. R. Phineas b. Jair was coming the other way with two men behind him. Suddenly the ass of R. Phineas came to a stop and would not budge. Said R. Phineas: 'Let him be, he must have scented some newcomers here, or a miracle is to be wrought for us.' While they were there R. Simeon emerged from behind a rock, and the ass immediately began to move forward. 'Did I not tell you', said R. Phineas, 'that he scented some newcomers?' He got down and embraced him, saying: 'I saw in a dream the Shekinah coming to me and giving me beautiful presents. Now I see it.' R. Simeon said: 'From the sound of your ass's hoofs I know that you are wholly joyful.' Said R. Phineas: 'Let us sit down in a suitable spot, since the words of the Torah require coolness.' They found a spring of water and a tree and sat down. R. Phineas said: 'I was reflecting that, in the resurrection of the dead, God will reverse the way of this world so that what is now first will then be last. We know this from the bones which God revived by the hand of Ezekiel, as it is written first, "And the bones drew near, each bone to his fellow", and then,

Zohar: Bemidbar, Section 3, Page 222a

"And I saw, and behold there were sinews on them and flesh came up and skin formed on them above, but there was no breath in them" (Ezek. XXXVII, 7, 8). Thus we see that what a man is divested of here first will there be last, for here the breath is lost first and then the skin and then the flesh and then the bones.' Said R. Simeon: 'The ancients also marveled at this. But the truth is that these bones which God revived were treated in an exceptional manner. What will really happen is indicated in the verse: "Remember now that thou hast made me like clay and will restore me to dust", and then, "Wilt thou not pour me out like milk and congeal me like cheese?" (Job x, 9, 10). At the time of the resurrection of the dead, God will melt that bone which remains of a man [for all time] and pour it out like milk and then congeal it and shape it like a cheese, and then skin and flesh and bones and sinews will be drawn over it, and lastly the spirit of life will be put into them, as it says, "and thy charge preserved my spirit" (Ibid.), the words "thy charge" referring to the Matrona of the King, in whose charge are all spirits and by whom they are preserved.' R. Phineas wept, and said: 'Did I not tell you that the Shekinah gave me beautiful presents? Happy is my lot to have seen and heard this.'

He then said: 'So much for that bone, but what about the other bones that will then be in existence?' He replied: 'They will all be put together with that bone and made into one dough and shaped with it. '

Zohar: Bemidbar, Section 3, Page 224a-226b

[Note: The Hebrew text of these pages do not appear in our translation.]

Zohar: Bemidbar, Section 3, Page 231a

R. Judah said: 'Pray tell us some of your fine ideas on the New Year.' R. Simeon thereupon discoursed on the verse: "And it fell on a day, and the sons of God came", etc. (Job I, 6). 'The expression, "And it fell on a day",' he said, 'always refers to a day on which there is trouble, here, the New Year. The "sons of God" are the great Beth Din, the seventy Chieftains who always surround the King. "To stand before the Lord": this indicates that sentence is first passed on those who do not heed the honour of the Holy Name to save it from being profaned in the world. The ancient pillars of the world were divided in opinion in regard to Job, some holding that he was of the saints of the Gentiles, and some that he was of the saints of Israel, and that he was smitten to make atonement for the sins of the world. On that day of New Year seventy seats are set for hearing the judgement of the world, some inclining to the right to acquit and some to the left to condemn.

[Note: The Hebrew text of this page does not correspond fully to the translation.]

Zohar: Bemidbar, Section 3, Page 231b-236a

[Note: The Hebrew text of these pages do not appear in our translation.]

Zohar: Bemidbar, Section 3, Page 236b

[Note: The first 36 lines of the Hebrew text do not appear in our translation.]

Now Phineas stood before the stern judgement of Isaac to shield the world and to close the breach, and therefore Phineas here corresponds to Isaac, [Tr. note: The reference is to the fact that there is here in the text an extra yod in the name Pinhas, which makes it numerically equivalent to Yitzhak (viz. 198).] and here the Left was united with the Right.

HE TURNED BACK MY ANGER, ETC. We have here mentioned the three chiefs of Gehinnom, "Destruction", "Anger", and "Wrath". When he saw the wrath stretching forth from the side of Isaac, he invested himself with [the might of] Isaac and seized that wrath like a man who

Zohar: Bemidbar, Section 3, Page 237a

takes hold of another and turns him back. And this was FROM THE CHILDREN OF ISRAEL, for he saw that Wrath coming down upon the children of Israel. He saw the letter mim descending upon them, which is the sign of the Angel of Death, so he snatched it and drew it to him and at once the Angel of Death drew back. It may be asked, How can it be said that Phineas turned back the wrath of God from Israel seeing that so many died of the plague? The fact is, however, that not one of the children of Israel died save from the tribe of Simeon, for when the mixed multitude came they associated with the women of the tribe of Simeon after they had become proselytes and bore sons from them; and of these some died on account of the golden calf, some by plague, and some now. And because Israel and all the holy seed kept themselves clear, they were now numbered to show that not one of them was missing. In the same way all those that died at the time of the calf were from the mixed multitude, and to show this Moses was afterwards commanded to assemble "all the congregation of the children of Israel" (Ex. xxxv, I), and to take from them only the free-will offering.' R. Eleazar said: 'Father, this would be a very good explanation if there were not something which conflicts with it.' He said to him, 'My son, say it.' He replied: 'It is written, "And Israel was joined (vayizamed) to Baal Peor" (Num. xxv, 3), which we explain to mean, "like the ornament (zamid) on a man's arm".' He replied: 'Eleazar, that is true; Israel were joined to Baal Peor. But I did not say that Israel were clear of that sin, but that they were not condemned to death.' He rejoined: 'But it is written, "Take the heads of the people and hang them". 'Yes,' he replied, 'the heads of the people, but not the heads of the children of Israel. Hence it is written, "And Israel were joined to Baal Peor", that is, only lightly, but it goes on to say, "And the people ate and worshipped" (Ibid. 2), but not "the children of Israel".

Zohar: Bemidbar, Section 3, Page 237b-239b

[Note: The Hebrew text does not appear in our translation.]

Zohar: Bemidbar, Section 3, Page 240a

[Note: The first two paragraphs of Hebrew text do not appear in our translation.]

COMMAND THE CHILDREN OF ISRAEL AND SAY UNTO THEM, MY OBLATION, MY FOOD FOR MY OFFERINGS, ETC. It is written: "Hath the Lord as great delight in burnt offerings and sacrifices as in obeying the voice of the Lord?" (I Sam. xv, 22). It is not God's desire that a man should sin and bring an offering to atone for his sin; the offering brought without sin is the perfect offering.' R. Abba cited here the verse: "The sacrifices of God are a broken spirit", etc. (Ps. LI, 18). 'This verse', he said, 'has been explained as showing that God does not desire a sacrifice from man for his sin, but a contrite spirit. I have heard from the Sacred Lamp that when a man is inclined to defile himself with sin, he draws down upon himself a spirit from the side of uncleanness which has complete sway over him, but if a man makes an effort to purify himself he is helped to do so. When the Temple existed and he brought his offering, his atonement was held in suspense until he had repented and broken the pride of that spirit and humbled it, and then his offering was favourably accepted, but if not, it was given to the dogs.' R. Eleazar said: 'There is a mystery relating to the offering in the verse, "I have come to my garden, my sister, my bride... eat, O friends, drink, O beloved" (S.S. v, 1), which I have seen in the book of Enoch.' Said R. Simeon: 'Tell us what you have seen

Zohar: Bemidbar, Section 3, Page 240b

and heard.' He said: 'God says, "I have come into my garden" because all offerings when they ascend go into the Garden of Eden at the beginning of the sacrifice when a man confesses his sins over it, and, as it were, his own blood is poured out on the altar. Now, it may be asked, How do the holy spirits find enjoyment in this, and what is the reason for the offering of an animal? Would it not be more reasonable that a man should humble himself and repent? The inner reason is that there is an animal which sprawls over a thousand mountains the produce of which it eats every day, and concerning it we have learnt: "There is a beast which consumes beasts made of fire, all of which it licks up at one swoop, and it swallows at one draught as much water as flows down the Jordan in six years". Now all these are the basis and foundation of these beasts of the earth, because the spirit is spread from them below, and that spirit is formed below in the beasts, and so when a man sins he brings a beast for an offering and that bestial spirit rises and returns to its place and all that belong to that species come together and feast on the flesh and the blood which is the vestment of this spirit, and so become advocates on behalf of that man. Therefore it is that an offering is brought from the animal.' R. Simeon said to him: 'That explains the offering of the animal, but what of the offering of birds?' He replied: 'I have not seen nor heard anything different from this of the beasts.' He said: 'Eleazar, my son, you have spoken well, but the mysteries of the offerings are many and should only be revealed to the truly virtuous. The sacrifices do in fact contain a hidden reference to the holy Beasts (Hayoth). Four forms are engraved on the Throne-of an ox, of an eagle, of a lion, and of a man. From those archetypal forms myriads without number are spread above and below. From the "face of an ox" a spirit is spread to four species closely connected, namely, bullocks, sheep, he-goats, and rams. These are appointed for offerings; and because those holy powers which spread from the "face of an ox" are akin to them, they draw near to their foundation and partake of that foundation and vestment of theirs in the same way as the holy Shekinah derives satisfaction from the spirits of the righteous. From the "face of an eagle" a spirit is spread to the birds in two directions, right and left, and therefore not all birds of the clean side are brought for offerings, but only pigeons and turtle doves, which are faithful to their mates

Zohar: Bemidbar, Section 3, Page 241a

more than all other birds, and are preyed upon but do not prey; and so those holy spirits come down and partake of their basis and foundation. You may ask how the little that comes from this pigeon or turtle dove can be shared among countless powers, and the same may be asked of a single animal. The answer is that it is in the same way as a little light fills the whole world or a thin stick will light a conflagration. So much for the offering from two of the sides engraved on the Throne. And in reality there is an offering from the other two also, although it does not seem so. When the sacrifice is completed, the Lion comes down and enters into the fire and feasts himself. Also the supernal Man derives benefit from the earthly man, who offers there his spirit and soul, and so each kind partakes of its own kind and basis. In the same way the priest who unifies the Holy Name is brought near to the supernal Priest, the Levites with their song rejoice that side to which they belong, and the lay Israelites, who offer prayers alongside of the sacrifice, awaken the supernal holy Israel. Thus the lower grades arouse the upper grades, but none of them is permitted to eat or to have any enjoyment of the sacrifice until the supreme King has eaten and given them permission. All this is hinted in the verses, "I have gathered my myrrh with my spice, I have eaten my honeycomb with my honey, I have drunk my wine with my milk; eat, O friends, drink, yea, drink abundantly, O beloved"'

Zohar: Bemidbar, Section 3, Page 241b

This is the real secret and mystery of the sacrifices.'

[Tr. NOTE:From the beginning of the section Pinhas to the end of the Zohar, a large portion of the text in the original is taken up by the Raya Mehemna; hence the frequency of the omissions in the translation. On the section Mattoth there is only a short piece of Zohar of too allusive a nature to be made intelligible in a translation. There is no Zohar at all on the sections Mas'e, Debarim, Ekeb, Re'eh, Shofetim, Ki Teze, Ki Tabo, Nizabim, and Vezoth Haberakah.]

Zohar: Bemidbar, Section 3, Pages 242a, 244a-b, 246a-b, 247a-b, 248a-b, 249a-b, 250a-b, 251a-b, 252a, 253b, 254a-b, 258b, 259a-b. Note: No translation appears for this Hebrew text as explained in the Translator's note above.]

Zohar: Devarim, Section 3, Page 260a

VAETHHANAN

AND I BESOUGHT THE LORD AT THAT TIME SAYING, O LORD GOD, THOU HAST BEGUN TO SHOW THY SERVANT, ETC. R. Yose adduced here the verse: "And Hezekiah turned his face to the wall and prayed to the Lord" (Isa. XXXVIII, 2).

'How great', he said, 'is the power of the Torah, and how it is exalted above all, since he who occupies himself with the Torah fears no adversaries either above or below, nor any evil haps of the world, because he is attached to the Tree of Life and eats therefrom every day. For the Torah teaches man how to walk in the right way, it gives him counsel how to return to his Master, so that even if sentence of death has been passed on him it is annulled and removed from him and impends not over him. Therefore he should occupy himself with the Torah day and night and never depart from it: for if he banishes the Torah from him or departs from it, it is as though he parted from life. Now it is a good counsel for a man that when he goes to his bed at night he should take upon himself the yoke of the heavenly kingdom with a perfect heart and hasten to entrust to God his soul. The reason, as we have explained, is that all the world then has a foretaste of death, as the tree of death is then present in the world, and all the spirits of men then leave them and ascend and are delivered to Him, but because they are given in trust they afterwards return to their places. Now when the north wind awakes at midnight and a herald goes forth, and the Holy One, blessed be He, enters the Garden of Eden to have joyous communion with the souls of the righteous, then all the sons of the Matrona, and all the denizens of the palace, prepare to sing praises to the Holy King, and then all the souls that were entrusted to her hand are returned to their owners; and most men awake at that time. Those who belong to the supernal Palace rise up in vigour and betake themselves to praise giving in accordance with the Torah and join the Community of Israel until the day is light. When the morning comes, She and all who belong to the Palace go to visit the Holy King, they being called the sons of the King and of the Matrona, as has been explained. When the morning comes, a man should cleanse himself and gird on his weapons [Tr. note: i.e. fringes and phylacteries.] to pay suit to the Holy King. For in the night he paid suit to the Matrona, and now he should come with the Matrona to unite her with the King. He goes to the synagogue, he purifies himself with [the recital of the] offerings, he repeats the praises of King David; he has the phylacteries on his hand and his head, and the fringes at his side; he says "A psalm of David", and offers his prayer before his Master. While he says this he must stand like the heavenly angels, [Tr. note: v. T.B. Berachoth, 10b.] who are also called "those who stand", and concentrate all his thoughts on his Master as he offers his petition. Note that when a man arises at midnight to study the Torah a herald proclaims concerning him: "Behold, bless ye the Lord all ye servants of the Lord which stand in the house of the Lord by night" (Ps. CXXXIV, 1), and now when he stands in prayer the herald proclaims over him, "And I will give thee places to walk among them that stand" (Zech. III, 7). When he has finished his prayer with devotion before his Master, as already said, he should deliver his soul with complete renunciation to the rightful place. Thus there is good counsel for men for all occasions.

Zohar: Devarim, Section 3, Page 260b

When prayer is being offered, all the words that a man has emitted from his mouth during his prayer mount aloft and cleave their way through ethers and firmaments until they reach their destination, where they are formed into a crown on the head of the King. The Companions have agreed that the prayer directed by man to the Almighty should be of the nature of supplication. [Tr. note: Ibid, 2 lb, Aboth II.] We know this from Moses, of whom it is said, "And I besought the Lord" (Deut. III, 23); this is the best kind of prayer. When a man stands in prayer he should keep his feet together, [Tr. note: T.B. Berachoth, 10b.] and cover his head, and he should also shade his eyes so as not to look at the Shekinah. In the Book of R. Hamnuna the Elder it says that if a man opens his eyes at the time of prayer or does not cast them on the ground he brings the Angel of Death on to himself before his time, and when his soul leaves him he will not behold the face of the Shekinah, nor will he die by a (divine) kiss. If one contemns the Shekinah, he himself is contemned in the hour of need, as it says, "Them that honour me I shall honour, and they that despise me shall be lightly esteemed" (I Sam. II, 30). This is he that looks at the Shekinah at the time of prayer. In fact, of course, one cannot look at the Shekinah; but what he should do is to know that the Shekinah is before him, and therefore there should be nothing interposing between him and the wall.

'Before a man stands in prayer he should first recite the praise of his Master and then offer his supplication. So Moses first said, THOU HAST BEGUN, ETC., and then LET ME GO OVER, I PRAY THEE. '

R. Judah said: 'Why did Moses say first "Lord" (Adonay) and then "God" (Tetragrammaton)? Because this is the proper order from the lower to the higher, so as to combine the measure of day with night, and of night with day, and to unite all fitly together.

THOU HAST BEGUN TO SHOW THY SERVANT. Why is "beginning" mentioned here? Because Moses indeed made a new beginning in the world by being complete in all. It is true that Jacob was also complete and in him the tree was completed below after the pattern above. Yet there was that in Moses which was not in any other man, since his perfection radiated to many thousands and myriads of Israel in the Tabernacle, the priests, the Levites, the twelve tribes with their chieftains, the seventy members of the Sanhedrin-in fact, with the perfect body, Aaron being at the right, Nahshon at the left, he himself in the centre, as it says here "thy greatness", referring to Aaron, and "thy strong hand", referring to Nahshon. Thus Moses was a new beginning in the world. And if you ask, Who is the termination? the answer is, the King Messiah, for then there shall be such perfection in the world as had not been for all generations before. For then there shall be completeness above and below, and all worlds shall be united in one bond, as it is written, "On that day the Lord shall be one and his name one" (Zech. XIV, 9).'

AND THE LORD SAID UNTO ME, LET IT SUFFICE THEE, SPEAK NO MORE, ETC. R. Hiya said: 'God said to Moses, It is enough for thee that thou hast been united with the Shekinah; thou canst advance no further.' R. Isaac said: 'Long enough hast thou enjoyed the light of the sun that was with thee; thou canst not do so any more, for the time of the moon is come, and the moon cannot shine till the sun is gathered in. Therefore "Charge Joshua and encourage him and strengthen him"; thou who art the sun must give light to the moon.' [Tr. note: v. T.B. Baba Bathra, 75a.]

BUT YE THAT DID CLEAVE UNTO THE LORD YOUR GOD, ETC. R. Yose said: 'Happy is the people whom God chose from all the heathens and took for His portion and blessed with His own blessing, the blessing of His Name. All other peoples God has placed under the charge of Chieftains who have control of them, but Israel the Holy One, blessed be He, has taken for His own portion to be united to Him, and He has given them His holy Law that they may be joined to His Name.'

Zohar: Devarim, Section 3, Page 261a

AND THE LORD SPAKE UNTO YOU OUT OF THE MIDST OF THE FIRE: YE HEARD THE VOICE OF WORDS, ETC. R. Eleazar said: 'What is meant by "the voice of words"? It means, the Voice which is also called Utterance, because all utterance proceeds from it. Hence also it says "ye heard" [and not "saw"], because "hearing" corresponds to "utterance".

BUT YE SAW NO FORM. They were not like Moses, of whom it says, "And he beholdeth the form of the Lord". Or we may say that "form" refers to the inner Voice which was not seen at all. ONLY YE HEARD A VOICE: this is the other voice, which we mentioned above. Hence there is a higher He and a lower He; the higher He is "the great voice which did not cease", the flow of which never ceases, and all those "voices" were in it when the Torah was given to Israel. Now what is called "the repetition of the law" (Deuteronomy) was said by Moses in his own name. For the supreme Wisdom is called the summation of the Torah, and from it all issues through that inner Voice. Eventually it comes to rest in the place called "the Tree of Life", wherefrom depend the general and the particular, the Written Law and the Oral Law. And to show that both are one, the later (of the Ten) Commandments are in this version connected with one another by "and".'

R. Yose said: 'Why do we find here both "thou shalt not covet" and "thou shalt not desire"? Because they are two different grades. A man covets things which it is in his power to obtain (wrongfully), and through coveting he does try to obtain them. A man can desire things even if he sees no way of obtaining them.

GO THOU NEAR AND HEAR, ETC. When the Law was given to Israel, all the Voices were present and the Holy One, blessed be He, was sitting on His throne, and one was seen within another, and the utterance of each came forth from the one above it, wherefore it is said, "The Lord spake to you face to face in the mount out of the midst of the fire" (Deut. v, 4), which means that the utterance came forth from the midst of fire and flame, which thrust it forth by the force of spirit and water; and fire, spirit and water all issued from the trumpet which contained them all. Israel were terrified and drew back, and therefore they said: Do thou speak to us; we do not desire to be spoken to by the mighty Power from on high, but only from the place of the Female, not higher. Said Moses to them: Of a truth ye have weakened my power, and also another power. For had not Israel drawn back and had they listened to

Zohar: Devarim, Section 3, Page 261b

the remaining words as to the first, [Tr. note: According to the Rabbis, the Israelites heard the first two commandments directly from God, the rest from Moses. T.B. Maccoth, 24a.] the world would never have been laid waste subsequently and they would have endured for generations upon generations. For at the first moment they did die, for so it had to be on account of the tree of death, but after they revived and stood up God desired to bring them up to the Tree of Life, which is above the tree of death, that they might endure forever, but they drew back and were not willing; therefore was the power of Moses weakened and another power with him. Said the Holy One, blessed be He: I desired to establish you in an exalted place that ye might cleave to life, but ye desired the place of the Female. Therefore Go, SAY TO THEM, RETURN TO YOUR TENTS: let each one go to his female and join her. And with all this, since Israel acted thus only through the pious awe that was upon them, nothing worse was said of them than "O that there were such an heart in them that they would fear me", etc. From this we learn that if a man, though doing an action which in itself is bad, does not turn his mind and intent to the evil side, punishment does not fall upon him as on another man, and God does not impute it to him for evil.

'BUT AS FOR THEE, STAND THOU HERE BY ME. From this point Moses parted from his wife completely and attached himself to another higher place, of the male and not of the female. Happy the lot of Moses the faithful prophet who was favoured with the highest grades to which no other man ever attained, wherefore he was called "good". But was not David also called "good"? Of David it says that he was "goodly to look upon": his goodness was in the appearance, but Moses was absolutely good.'

R. Judah said: 'A man should place God before him in all his acts. When a man walks abroad he should have three objects in view, the highest of which is prayer, and higher even than prayer is the converse of two or three companions on matters of the Torah, for they shall come to no harm, since the Shekinah accompanies them.' Thus R. Eleazar and R. Hiya were once walking together, and R. Eleazar said: 'It is written, "And the Lord God made for Adam and his wife coats of skins" (Gen. III, 22). Were they then divested of that skin till then? Yes, for they were robes of glory.' Said R. Hiya: 'Surely they did not deserve even coats of skin. For you cannot say that this was before they sinned, since it is after they sinned that it is written, "And the Lord God made them coats of skins" '. He replied: 'At first they were like heavenly creatures, and divested of the earthly type, and heavenly light played around them. After they sinned they became of the type of this world, and the heavenly character was taken away from them, and then God made them coats of skin and clothed them with the character of this world. None the less the beauty of those garments was incomparable. It is further written, "And the eyes of both of them were opened" (Gen. III, 7), that is, to see the squalor of this world, which they did not notice before since their eyes were turned aloft. So of the future time it is written, "And I will bring the blind by a way that they know not", etc. (Isa. XLII, 16), which means that God will open eyes that are not wise to contemplate

Zohar: Devarim, Section 3, Page 262a

supernal wisdom and to attain to heights which they could not attain in this world, that they may know their Master. Happy are the righteous who are deemed worthy of this wisdom, since there is no wisdom like that wisdom, nor knowledge like that knowledge, nor attachment like that attachment.' As they were going along they saw some robbers following them with intent to harm them. R. Eleazar looked at them and two serpents came out and killed them, whereupon R. Eleazar said: Blessed be the Merciful One who has saved us.

'We have learnt as a profound mystery in the Book of Hidden Wisdom that three hollows of inscribed letters are disclosed in the Cranium of the Small of Countenance, and we have further learnt that there are three Brains enclosed in these hollows, but through the influence of the uppermost and hidden brain of the Ancient Holy One which spreads through that Small of Countenance they become four Brains. These spread throughout the whole of the Body, and these are the four compartments of the phylacteries which the Holy One, blessed be He, puts on. Therefore a man should put on the phylacteries every day, because they are the supernal Holy Name in its inscribed letters. The first compartment of the phylacteries contains the passage, "Sanctify unto me every firstborn", which typifies the highest brain, to wit, Wisdom. The second compartment contains the passage commencing "And it shall come to pass when the Lord thy God bringeth thee".' R. Judah said: 'This typifies the brain which opens out through fifty gates, which in turn correspond to the numerous places where the going forth from Egypt is mentioned in the Pentateuch We have learnt in the Book of R. Hamnuna the Ancient that God burst open many gates above and below which were closed with chains in order to bring forth Israel, for from the gates of that brain all other gates are unlocked and opened. Had not the gates of that brain been first opened, the others could never have been opened to execute judgement and to bring forth Israel from bondage. All is closed up in that which is called the Supernal Mother, whence power is derived to the Lower Mother. This one comes forth from the Supernal Mother, who is the second compartment, which is called the He of the Holy Name which opens out through fifty gates, and from this issues a spirit to one of the Nostrils. We have learnt, too, that the Jubilee in which slaves go forth to freedom is attached to this Brain, and the fifty days of the Jubilee further correspond to the fifty days of the Omer. Thus He stands for the appeasement of the spirit and its going forth to freedom, and thus the going forth from Egypt depends on this compartment and on the letter He of the Holy Name, as has been explained. Observe that from the side of the Father issues Lovingkindness and from the side of the Mother Force, and the Holy One, blessed be He, grasps both and crowns himself therewith as the letter Vau.

Zohar: Devarim, Section 3, Page 262b

The third compartment contains the passage commencing, "Hear, O Israel", the reference being to the patriarch Israel. R. Simeon, however, says that the reference is to the supernal Israel crowned from the side of his Father, to wit, Abraham, and crowned from the side of his Mother, to wit, Isaac. We have learnt that he who loves the King does lovingkindness with all, and all the more so if he asks for no reward, which is a "kindness of truth", through which he increases lovingkindness in the world. Hence this passage goes on, "Thou shalt love". The fourth compartment contains the passage commencing, "And it shall come to pass if ye diligently hearken". This passage contains the words, "Take heed to yourselves... and the anger of the Lord be kindled against you", and this compartment typifies Might and stern judgement, and it comes from the side of the supernal Mother; for we have learnt that although She Herself is not judgement, yet from Her side issues judgement and force. These four does Vau take and crown himself therewith, and these are the phylacteries which the Holy One, blessed be He, puts on. We have learnt that this Vau ascends and assumes his crowns and grasps both sides and is crowned with all, and therefore Vau is the centre of all above and below to display complete Wisdom on all sides.'

R. Abba learnt: It is written, "Only the Lord had a delight in thy fathers" (Deut. x, 15). Commenting on this, R. Simeon said that the patriarchs are the holy chariot above. As there is a holy chariot below, so there is a holy chariot above. And what is this? As we have said, the holy chariot is the name given to the Whole, all being linked together and made one. But the fathers are only three, and the chariot has four wheels. Who is the fourth? It says: "And he chose their seed after them"; this includes David, who is the fourth to complete the holy chariot, as we have learnt: The patriarchs are the consummation of the whole, and the Body was completed through them and made one. Then King David came and perfected the whole and made firm the body and perfected it. R. Isaac said: 'As the patriarchs merited to be crowned with the holy chariot, so did David merit to be adorned with the fourth support of the chariot.' R. Judah said: 'It is written of David, "He was ruddy and withal fair of eyes". The "ruddiness" typifies his occupation (as a man of war), while "with fair of eyes" refers to the patriarchs. Note that while Jerusalem and Zion correspond respectively to Judgement and Mercy, yet it is written, "The city of David, that is Zion" (I Kings VIII, 1).

'We have learnt: Vau takes those upper ones that we have mentioned, and those are the phylacteries which the Holy One, blessed be He, puts on, and therefore a man should take a pride in them. Of such a one it is written, "And all the people of the earth shall see that thou art called by the name of the Lord" (Deut. XXVIII, 10)—literally. These are the phylactery of the head. The phylactery of the arm is the left, which is called "strong", and inherits from the "strong".

Zohar: Devarim, Section 3, Page 263a

Therefore the second He', which is the left, takes the four which are one body and entwined in one another, to wit, Tifereth, Nezah, Hod, and Yesod.' Said R. Hiya: 'If that is so, this is what is meant by "Thou shalt see my back" (Ex. XXXIII, 23), which, as we have learnt, means the knot of the phylacteries.' He replied: 'So we have explained, and this is the truth of the matter, and therefore a strap hangs down below to show that all below are sustained by this, and therefore it is called a "sign", as it is written, "And it shall be for a sign upon thy hand".'

HEAR, ISRAEL. R. Yesa said: 'This is the patriarch Israel.' R. Isaac said: '"Israel" here has the same meaning as "heavens" in the verses "Hear, O heavens" (Isa. I, 2), and "Give ear, O heavens" (Deut. XXXII, 1). "The Lord" here indicates the starting-point of all, in the radiance of the Holy Ancient One, and this is what is called "Father". "Our God" is the deep source of the streams and founts that flow forth to all. "The Lord" again is the body of the Tree, the completion of the roots. "One" is the Community of Israel. All form one whole linked together without division.' R. Isaac learnt: 'The holy supernal chariot consists of the four compartments of the phylacteries which are put on by Vau, as already explained. There is another holy chariot of four other compartments united into one which are put on by the second He', as already stated.'

Zohar: Devarim, Section 3, Page 265a

[Note: The first 12 lines of the Hebrew text do not appear in our translation.]

R. Simeon said: 'When a man rises at midnight and gets up and studies the Torah till daylight, and when the daylight comes he puts the phylacteries with the holy impress on his head and his arm, and covers himself with his fringed robe, and as he issues from the door of his house he passes the mezuzah containing the imprint of the Holy Name on the post of his door, then four holy angels join him and issue with him from the door of his house and accompany him to the synagogue and proclaim before him: Give honour to the image of the Holy King, give honour to the son of the King, to the precious countenance of the King. A holy spirit rests on him and proclaims: "Israel in whom I will be glorified" (Isa. XLIX, 3), and then ascends aloft and testifies concerning him before the Holy King. Then the Most High King orders the names of all the children of His palace, of all those that acknowledge Him, to be written before Him, as it says, "And it was written in the book of remembrance before him, for them that feared the Lord and that thought upon his name" (Mal. III, 16). The word hoshebei (that thought upon) can also be taken in the sense of "making designs"—designs of the phylacteries with their compartments, their straps and their writing; designs of the fringes with their threads and the thread of blue; and designs of the mezuzah, all for the sake of God's Name. God then glories in them and proclaims through all worlds: See what my son has done in my world. He, however, who leaves his house to go to the synagogue without the phylacteries on his head or fringes on his garment and who yet says, I will bow down to Thy holy temple in Thy fear—of him God says: Where is my fear? he is bearing false witness.'

R. Yose said: 'Happy the portion of Moses who attached himself to a higher grade than all the other faithful prophets. For in connection with the verse, "Moses spoke and God answered him with a voice" (Ex. XIX, 19), we have learnt that this voice was the voice of Moses, the Voice to which he was attached through his superiority over all the other prophets. And because he was attached to this higher grade he was able to say to Israel, "The Lord thy God", namely, the grade called Shekinah which abode in their midst.' R. Simeon further said: 'We have learnt that the curses in Leviticus were uttered by Moses as coming from the mouth of the divine Might, but those in Deuteronomy were uttered by him as from the mouth of himself. What is meant by "as from the mouth of himself",'? Can it be thought that Moses said a single word of the Law of himself? No: what it refers to is the Voice to which he was attached, which is called "himself", so that one set of curses were uttered from the mouth of the divine Might and the other of that grade to which he attained in virtue of his superiority over the other prophets. Hence, while in all other places he says "Thy God", here (in the Shema) he says "Our God".

'Note how diligent men should be to devote themselves to the service of their Master so as to win eternal life. Under the throne of the Holy King there are supernal chambers; and in that place of the throne there is fastened a mezuzah to deliver men from executioners of justice

Zohar: Devarim, Section 3, Page 265b

who are ready to assail them in the other world. Similarly did God do to Israel, giving them precepts of the Law which they may observe to deliver themselves from many assailants and accusers that are on the watch for men every day.' R. Hiya said: 'If a man wishes to guard his steps, he should not step over water that has been poured out in front of a door, because a certain demon abides between the two posts of the door with his face to the door seeing all that goes on inside, and therefore a man should not pour water between the two doorposts.' (R. Isaac, however, said that if it is clean water it does not matter, provided it has not been poured out in contumely.) The reason is that he is authorized to do harm, and if he turns his head to the house everything on which he looks will be cursed. He has three hundred and sixty-five assistants, corresponding to the number of the days of the year, and all go forth with a man when he leaves his house.' R. Eleazar said: 'Against all this God desired to protect Israel, and therefore a man should inscribe on the door of his house the Holy Name in which all faith is summed up. For wherever the Holy Name is the evil species cannot come and are not able to accuse a man. The place of the door of the supernal House is called mezuzah, which is a necessary part of the house, and from it flee the emissaries of justice and punishment. Correspondingly when on earth a man affixes a mezuzah to his door with his Holy Name inscribed in it, such a one is crowned with the crowns of his Master and no "evil species" come near to the door of his house.'

As R. Abba was once coming away from a visit to R. Simeon he was met by R. Isaac, who exclaimed: 'Who is coming? The master of light, the man who all day has been cleaving to a consuming fire. Behold, light abides with him.' R. Abba said to him: 'We have learnt that a man should go to pay his respects to the Shekinah every Sabbath and New Moon, and who is meant? His teacher. All the more, then, is it incumbent on all people to pay their respects to the Sacred Lamp.' Said R. Isaac: 'I will turn back with you and pay my respects to the Shekinah and [meanwhile] taste of those excellent words of which you have tasted.' R. Abba then commenced a discourse on the verse: "A song of degrees, Unto thee do I lift up mine eyes, O thou that sittest in the heavens" (Ps. CXXIII, 1). 'The author of this psalm is not mentioned, and in all such cases we suppose the holy spirit to have uttered it concerning Israel in captivity. We have laid down that whoever desires to offer his supplication before the Holy King should pray from the lowest depth that blessing should be poured down below. This is indicated by the superfluous yod in the word hayoshebi (who sittest), the yod being the lowest of all; and therefore through it one should pray that blessings be poured down to the place called "heaven", that all may be fed from it. For when blessings are drawn from that spot most remote of all and collected in the place called heaven, then blessings abound among both higher and lower beings. "As the eyes of servants look unto the hand of their master": these are the Chieftains of the other peoples who are fed only from the remnants, the overhanging branches of the tree to which Israel cling, and when Israel receive blessings from that place they are all blessed from Israel. "As the eyes of a maiden unto the hand of her mistress": this, as already stated, is the handmaiden whose host God slew in Egypt, since she has no power of her own save when it is drawn to her from the Land of Israel, which itself

Zohar: Devarim, Section 3, Page 266a

is called "mistress". From the direction of this handmaiden issue many officials of judgement who bring accusations against Israel, but the Holy One, blessed be He, protects Israel from them as a father protects his son. God says to Israel: "Many are the accusers looking out for you, but be diligent in mv service and I will protect you without, while within you will sleep safely in your beds. Now when the evil species come to the door of a man's house, and they raise their eyes and see the Holy Name written outside the mezuzah, namely Shaddai, which has power over all of them, they flee away in fear of it and do not come near the door.' Said R. Isaac to him: 'If that is so, a man should inscribe only this name on his door; why all the section?' He replied: 'This is quite right, because this name is crowned only with all those letters, and when the whole section is written this name is crowned with its crowns and the King goes forth with all his hosts stamped with the impress of the King, and they all flee from him in fear.' R. Abba said: 'Many holy hosts are present when a man fixes a mezuzah on his door, and they all proclaim, "This is the gate of the Lord", etc. (Ps. CXVIII, 20). Happy is the portion of Israel, for then Israel know that they are the sons of the Holy King, for all bear His stamp. They are stamped on their bodies with the holy impress; their garments bear the stamp of a religious precept; [Tr. note: The fringes.] their heads are stamped with the compartments of the phylacteries with the name of their Master; their hands are stamped with the straps of holiness; their feet with the ceremonial shoes; [Tr. note: The shoe used in the ceremony of halizah.] without they bear the stamp of the [precepts connected with] sowing and reaping, and in their houses that of the mezuzah at their doorway. Thus in all ways they are stamped as the sons of the Most High King.'

As they proceeded R. Abba said: 'What is the meaning of the verse: "They have forsaken me the fountain of living waters to hew out to them cisterns, broken cisterns that cannot hold the water" (Jer. II, 13)? This', he said, 'refers to one who is false to the sign of the holy impress. And how is he false to it? By letting it enter into an alien domain, which is called "broken cisterns". For so the idolatrous peoples are called, but Israel's God is called "a fountain of living waters". For the perennially flowing Stream waters all the Garden and replenishes every place, as we have already pointed out, until it comes to that place in the Garden which is called "the fountain of living waters", whence are sustained all creatures above and below. But all the sides of the Left Side are not watered from that Stream of running water because they are of the side of the other peoples, and they are called "broken cisterns". Hence he who is false to the holy impress cleaves to the "broken cisterns which do not hold the waters," because they do not enter into them, whereas he that is able to guard it is granted to drink of the waters of that stream in the world to come, and causes that supernal Well to be filled so as to pour forth blessings to higher and lower; happy is he in this world and the next: of him it is written, "And thou shalt be like a watered garden and like a spring of water whose waters fail not" (Isa. LVIII, 11). Woe to him who is false to the holy impress, for he is false

Zohar: Devarim, Section 3, Page 266b

to the most high Name, nay more, he causes blessing to be withheld from that Well, and we apply to him the words, "he hath brought up an evil name on a virgin of Israel" (Deut. XXII, 19); for so R. Simeon has expounded, that one who brings a false charge against his first wife and brings an evil name upon her is like one who casts aspersions on high. This, again, is in conformity with what R. Hiya said in the name of R. Yose, that a virgin inherits seven blessings, but not a woman who is married again; she, however, inherits the blessing of Boaz and Ruth.'

They came to a field where they saw a number of trees, and sat down beneath them. R. Abba said: 'Here is clear air for expositions of the Torah; let us stay here.' He then began a discourse on the verse: "And it shall come to pass in that day that a great trumpet shall be blown; and they shall come which were ready to perish in the land of Assyria, and they that were outcasts in the land of Egypt" (Isa. XXVII, 13). 'What is meant', he said, 'by "that day"? It is that day which shall be known to the Holy One, blessed be He, as it is written, "But it shall be one day which is known unto the Lord" (Zech. XIV, 7), or again, "In that day when Gog shall come against the land of Israel" (Ezek. XXXVIII, 19). "A great trumpet shall be blown"? What difference does it make whether it will be great or small? It refers, however, to that great trumpet through which slaves go forth to freedom; this is the trumpet of the supernal Jubilee, and it is very mighty, and when it is aroused all freedom is set in motion, and it is called "the great trumpet". "They that are perishing in the land of Assyria": because those who live in an alien land suck from an alien power, and, as it were, do not abide in the faith. They are lost from all sides, for when Israel dwell in the Holy Land they are ever virtuous in all, both above and below. According to another explanation, "those that are perishing" are the Zaddik and the Community of Israel. These are also called "lost", as it is written, "Wherefore perisheth the land" (Jer. IX, 12), to wit, the Community of Israel. The Zaddik, as it is written, "The righteous (Zaddik) perisheth" (Isa. LVII, 1). If it is asked, Whence are they to "come", the answer is, the Community of Israel from exile, and the Zaddik, as it is written, "When the Lord returneth with (eth) the captivity of Zion" (Ps. CXXVI, 1), which, as we have explained, means that He will return to His place and join the Community of Israel. "And they shall bow down to the Lord on the holy mountain, Jerusalem": this means, if we may say so, that Israel will not go out of captivity save with the Shekinah.'

R. Abba further discoursed on the verse: "The Lord shall keep thy going out and thy coming in from this time forth and forevermore" (Ps. CXXI, 8). He said: 'That God shall keep thy going forth we understand; but what need is there to say, "thy coming in"? For when a man goes into his house he is in no danger? What it means, however, is that he who affixes the holy sign to his house with the words of the Holy Name is protected against all danger. The one who dwells at the door of his house accompanies him when he issues forth, and when he returns it proclaims before him: Have a care for the honour of the image of the Holy King-all this on account of the Holy Name which is impressed on his door, so that not only is a man protected in his house, but God protects him both when he goes out and when he comes in, as it is written, "The Lord shall keep thy going out and thy coming in", etc. But as for the evil spirit that abides between the doorposts,

Zohar: Devarim, Section 3, Page 267a

woe to the man who does not know how to guard against it by impressing on the door of his house the Holy Name that it may be with him, for this spirit has three hundred and sixty-five assistants, one for every day of the year, which accuse him above and below, trying to mislead him by day and troubling his dreams by night. When he goes out they accuse him; when he comes in they place their hands on his shoulders and say: Woe to So-and-so who has thrown off the control of his Master, woe to him in this world and in the world to come! Therefore the sons of the true faith should be stamped throughout with the impress of their Master to scare away all the sides of the "evil species", that they may be protected in this world and the next.'

AND THOU SHALT LOVE THE LORD THY GOD. R. Yose adduced here the verse: "Now, therefore, what do I here, saith the Lord, seeing that my people is taken away for nought" (Isa. LII, 5). 'This', he said, 'shows the love of God for Israel, for although their sins caused Him to depart from them, and they were scattered among the nations, yet He avenges their wrong. When Israel were in their land, God used to delight Himself in His garden and draw near to Israel and hear their voice and glory in them. But since through their sins Israel have been banished from their land, the Holy One, blessed be He, does not enter His garden nor take delight in it, and He even exclaims, "What do I here, saith the Lord?" Since the day that Israel were banished from their land there has been no joy before the Holy One, blessed be He. Therefore because of the love which God shows to Israel it is written, "thou shalt love the Lord thy God", which means that man should bind himself to Him with very strong love, and that all service performed by man to God should be with love, since there is no service like the love of the Holy One, blessed be He.' R. Abba said: 'These words are the epitome of the whole Law, since the Ten Commandments are summed up here, as the Companions have explained. Nothing is so beloved of God as that a man should love Him in the fitting manner. How is this? As it is written, "with all thy heart", which includes two hearts, one good and one evil; "with all thy soul", one good and one evil; [Tr. note: T.B. Berachoth, 54a.] and "with all thy might". What lesson can be learnt from the word "all" here?' R. Eleazar said: 'The word "might" refers to money, and "all" means both money which comes to a man from inheritance and money which a man earns himself.' R. Abba said: 'To return to the words "and thou shalt love": one who loves God is crowned with lovingkindness on all sides and does lovingkindness throughout, sparing neither his person nor his money. We know this from Abraham, who in his love for his Master spared neither his heart nor his life nor his money. He paid no heed to his own desires because of his love for his Master; he spared not his wife, and was ready to sacrifice his son because of his love for his Master; and he sacrificed his money also by standing at the cross-roads and providing food for all comers' Therefore he was crowned with the crown of lovingkindness. Whoever is attached in love to his Master is deemed worthy of the same, and what is more, all worlds are blessed for his sake.'

Once when R. Yose was ill, R. Abba and R. Judah and R. Isaac went to see him. They found him asleep lying on his face. When he awoke they perceived that his face was wreathed in smiles. Said R. Abba to him: 'Have you seen some notable thing?'

Zohar: Devarim, Section 3, Page 267b

'Assuredly so,' he replied, 'for my soul went aloft and I saw the glory of those who have sacrificed themselves for the sanctity of their Master, how they were given thirteen streams of pure balsam, and how the Holy One, blessed be He, held joyous converse with them. I saw things which I am not permitted to tell. I asked for whom was this honour, and they replied: For those who loved their Master in the other world. My soul and my heart were illumined with what I saw, and therefore my face was wreathed in smiles.' R. Abba said: 'Happy is thy portion. The Torah testifies of them saying, "Eye hath not seen, O God, beside thee what he shall do for him that waiteth for him" (Isa. LXIV, 4).' R. Judah said to him: 'The Companions have already asked: Why is it written here, "he shall do", and not "thou shalt do"?' He replied: 'The reason is to be found in the inner meaning of the words, "To behold the beauty of the Lord and to inquire in his temple" (Ps. XXVII, 4). The "beauty of the Lord", as we have explained, is that which comes from the Ancient Holy One, and wherewith the Holy One, blessed be He, delights himself. So here, "he shall do" refers to the Ancient Hidden One on whom it depends.' He said: 'Assuredly it is so. Happy those to whom the love of their Master cleaves; there is no limit to their portion in the other world.' R. Isaac said: 'Many are the abodes of the righteous in the other world, one above another, and highest of all that of those to whom was attached the love of their Master, for their abode is linked with the palace that surpasses all, the Holy One, blessed be He, being crowned in this one. This Palace is called Love, and it is established for the sake of love. So it is too with the Holy Name, the forms of the letters of which are linked together, so that the whole is called "love"; wherefore he who loves his Master is linked to that Love. Hence it is written, "And thou shalt love the Lord thy God".'

AND THESE WORDS SHALL BE, ETC. R. Isaac adduced here the verse: "All my bones shall say, Lord, who is like unto thee, who delivereth the poor from him that is too strong for him, yea, the poor and the needy from him that spoileth him" (Ps. XXXV, 10). 'This verse', he said, 'refers to the time when the Holy One, blessed be He, will revive the dead, at which time He will prepare the bones and bring each one near to its fellow, as it says, "And the bones came together, bone to his bone" (Ezek. XXXVI, 7). They will then sing a psalm, namely, "O Lord, who is like thee", etc. And this song will be superior to that which the Israelites chanted by the Red Sea, for there they mentioned the Holy Name only after three words, as it is written, "Who-is like-unto-thee among-the-mighty, O Lord", but here they will put the Holy Name first. "He delivereth the poor from him that is too strong for him". This means that God delivers the good prompting from the evil prompting; for the evil prompting is hard like stone, whereas the good prompting is tender like flesh. What does the evil prompting resemble? When it first comes to associate itself with a man it is like iron before it is placed in the fire, but afterwards like iron when it is heated and becomes wholly like fire.' R. Hiya said: 'The evil prompting is at first like a wayfarer who comes to the door of a house and, finding that there is no one to stop him, goes into the house and becomes a guest. Finding that there is still no one to stop him he takes liberties and acts as the master [Tr. note: v. Bereshith Rabba, 22b.]

Zohar: Devarim, Section 3, Page 268a

until the whole house is subject to him. From where do we learn this? From the story of David and Nathan. Nathan first said, "There came a traveller to the rich man"—a mere traveller who passes the door without any intention of staying there and meaning to proceed on his way. So the evil prompting when it first approaches a man prompts him to a petty sin, being still but a chance visitor. Then the text goes on, "to prepare for the guest that came to him". So the evil prompting incites him to greater sins one day or two days like a guest who stays in a house one or two days. Next it says, "And dressed it for the man (ish) that was come to him" (the word ish meaning "master", as in "the man, the master of the land" (Gen. XLII, 30)). So the evil prompting becomes the "master of the house" in respect of the man, who is now bound to his service, and he does with him what he likes. Hence a man should ever carry about with him words of Torah in order that the evil prompting may be subdued by them, since there is no opponent of the evil prompting like words of Torah; wherefore it is written, "And these words shall be upon thy heart" (lebabeka), that is, upon both thy promptings, the good prompting that it may be crowned with them and the evil prompting that it may be subdued by them.' R. Judah asked: 'Why does the good prompting need them?' He replied: 'The good prompting is crowned by them, and the evil prompting, if it sees that a man does not repent nor seek to study the Torah, goes above and points out his guilt.'

When R. Simeon came, he said: 'Assuredly in the section of the Shema are hinted the Ten Commandments, as already stated elsewhere, in the words "and these words shall be". There are also ten commandments here corresponding to the other ten. They are as follows: (1) "Thou shalt teach them diligently to thy children", (2) "And thou shalt speak of them", (3) "When thou sittest in thy house", (4) "And when thou goest by the way", (5) "And when thou liest down", (6) "And when thou risest up", (7) "And thou shalt bind them for a sign on thy hand", (8) "And they shall be for frontlets between thine eyes", (9) "And thou shalt write them upon the doorposts of thy house"' (10) "And upon thy gates". Hence this section is a fundamental portion of the Law; blessed is he who recites it completely twice every day, since then the Holy Name is fitly sanctified in his mouth.'

R. Aha once rose after midnight with R. Eleazar to study the Torah. R. Eleazar cited the verse: "For it is thy life and the length of thy days" (Deut. XXXII, 47). 'Observe', he said, 'that above all the stipulations which God made with Israel when they entered the Holy Land was the stipulation that they should study the Torah. Why so? Because the Divine Presence finds a home in the land only through the Torah, and it finds a home above only through the Torah. For so my father has said: The Oral Law has been made known only for the sake of the Written Law, and the Shekinah finds a home above and below only through the Torah.' As they were sitting, R. Simeon bent his head and said: 'Assuredly it is so, and this secret I have found in the Book of R. Hamnuna the Ancient, who applied to the Community of Israel the verse: "Her food, her raiment, and her duty of marriage shall he not diminish" (Ex. XXI, 10); and if they are withheld from her, then it is written, "She shall go out for nothing without money". He that withholds the Torah from her is like one who withholds the raiment of his wife from her, so that she is left as a widow without being a widow.'

They sat and studied the Torah till daylight, when they resumed their journey. As they went along they saw a man going on the road with his head shrouded. When they came near him they found that he was muttering

Zohar: Devarim, Section 3, Page 268b

with his lips, and he made no answer to their greeting. Said R. Eleazar: 'Of a surety this man is consulting his Master.' R. Eleazar and R. Aha sat down and said their prayers, while the man stood upright in another place. They went on their way and the man went another way. Said R. Eleazar: 'Either that man is a fool or an evildoer.' He then said 'Let us occupy ourselves with the Torah, for it is time.' Before he could commence, the man came up to them. Said R. Eleazar: 'We must not interrupt our study, for he who studies the Torah becomes worthy of obtaining the heavenly inheritance in the glory of the supernal Holy King, and also of an inheritance in this world, which is called "the glory of the Lord". For when a man walks in the path of rectitude before the Holy One, and occupies himself with the Torah, he inherits that "glory of the Lord" for himself, and he has many protectors and advocates above who point out his merits before the Holy King, but if a man does not study the Torah nor walk in the way of his Master, then God appoints for him an accuser, who flies about in the air but does not at first go aloft, in case that man will repent of his sins. When he sees that he does not repent, and does not seek to study the Torah, he goes aloft and points out his guilt.'

He then discoursed on the verse: "And if the family of Egypt go not up and come not, neither upon them shall be the plague", etc. (Zech. XIV, 18). Why does it not say here, "not upon them shall be the rain", as in the case of all the other peoples? It is because, as the Companions have pointed out, the land of Egypt does not require rain, and therefore another punishment was decreed against them. But the Holy Land was ever watered from the heavens, and therefore when Israel studied the Torah it was watered properly, and he who withheld Torah from it was like one withholding good from heaven.'

They went into a cave which was by the road, and the man went in with them. They sat down, and the man opened a discourse on the verse, "And the Lord spake unto Moses face to face", etc. (Ex. XXXIII, 11). 'This verse', he said, 'does not seem to hang together properly; first it says, "God spake to Moses face to face", then, "Moses returned to the camp", then, "And his minister Joshua the son of Nun, a young man", etc. What does it mean?' Said R. Eleazar: 'Verily God

724

desired to honour us, for now we are associated with the Shekinah, which has not departed from us. Let him who has opened the discourse continue it.' The man then proceeded: 'Moses was separated by many degrees from all the other prophets, who bore the same relation to him as an ape to a human being. Other prophets beheld visions in a glass that did not illumine, and even so they did not venture to lift up their eyes and gaze above, but were like Daniel, who said, "I was fallen into a deep sleep on my face, and my face was upon the ground" (Dan. x, 9); nor was their message given to them in clear terms. Not so was Moses, the faithful prophet: he saw his vision in a luminous glass [Tr. note: T.B. Yebamoth, 49b.] and still stood upright, and he dared to raise his head and gaze upwards, like one to whom his neighbour says: Lift up your head and look me in the face in order that you may know what I say. So Moses raised his head without fear and gazed

Zohar: Devarim, Section 3, Page 269a

at the brightness of the supernal glory without losing his senses like the other prophets, who when they prophesied were bereft of their faculties and became transformed and knew nothing at all of this world. Not so Moses, for even while he was in that exalted grade he did not lose his faculties, and straightway after gazing on the brightness of the heavenly glory he "returned to the camp" to speak to them concerning all their requirements, and his mind was as clear as before, and more so. "His minister Joshua the son of Nun, a young man", derived instruction from "the tent", [Tr. note: The Shekinah.] where he learnt to contemplate in the holy spirit. So long as he was with Moses he used to learn and derive instruction from "the tent" without fear, but after Moses departed from him and he was left alone, then we read of him that "he fell on his face on the ground and did worship" (Joshua V, 14), not being able to gaze even on the messenger of God; how much less so then on another place. There was a man with whom a king entrusted vessels of gold and precious stones. As long as they were with him the man's servant was able to handle them and examine them. When, however, the man died, the king would not leave anything with the servant and took back his deposit. Alas, exclaimed the servant, for what I have lost! When my master was alive I had the handling of all these. So while Moses was alive Joshua used to suck every day from the "tent" without fear, but when Moses died, then Joshua "fell on his face". So I, being in your company, will examine the words of the Torah and not be afraid. When, however, I leave you, I shall not be able to examine them by myself. He then continued:

AND THOU SHALT TEACH THEM DILIGENTLY TO THY CHILDREN AND SHALT TALK OF THEM, ETC. A man should sharpen the intellect of his son on the words of the Torah like a two-edged sword, so that he should not be dull. THOU SHALT TALK OF THEM. Every word of the Torah has each its separate way. A man should conduct and guide himself by them so as not to turn aside right or left. WHEN THOU SITTEST IN THY HOUSE. A man should conduct himself with due propriety in his house, so as to set an example to his household, and he should also be gentle with them and not overawe them. AND WHEN THOU WALKEST BY THE WAY: to guide himself by the precepts of the Law and to direct himself by them in the fitting manner, and to prepare himself like Jacob for gift, for battle, and for prayer. AND WHEN THOU LIEST DOWN: to conduct himself in the fear of his Master, in holiness and humility, so as not to be bold of face towards his Master. AND WHEN THOU RISEST UP: to give praises to his Master for having restored his soul, in spite of his many sins before his Master, who, however, shows him lovingkindness and restores the soul to his body.

AND THOU SHALT BIND THEM FOR A SIGN UPON THY HAND. Our colleagues who dwell in the South have explained the inner meaning of the four compartments of the phylacteries in their own way, viz., that the passage "sanctify to me every firstborn" is to correspond to the Supernal Crown (Kether); "and it shall come to pass when the Lord bringeth thee" to Wisdom; "hear, O Israel," to Binah; and "and it shall come to pass if thou hearkenest diligently" to Hesed. Then they are all combined in one on the left arm which is called Strength (Geburah). We, however, do not accept this view, because the Supreme Crown comprises all and is not reckoned (among the grades). Further, the section "and it shall come to pass

Zohar: Devarim, Section 3, Page 269b

when the Lord bringeth thee" is connected with the going forth from Egypt, and so with that place in which is freedom for slaves. [Tr. note: Binah.] Hence our colleagues are not right. We commence from Wisdom, and we hold that the Holy One, blessed be He, wears them, four above, four below, four in the place of the brain, and four in the place where the heart is, because one is linked with the other. Man should crown himself with them, because they form the supernal Holy Name, and whoever crowns himself with the supernal Holy Crown is called king on earth as the Holy One, blessed be He, is king in the firmament. AND THOU SHALT WRITE THEM ON THE DOORPOSTS OF THY HOUSE AND ON THY GATES in order that a man may be found complete in all, complete in the precepts of his Master, inscribed above and inscribed below. Happy is the portion of Israel.'

R. Eleazar then discoursed as follows. 'We find sometimes the expression "Thus saith the Lord of Hosts", and sometimes "Thus saith the Lord God". What is the difference? A message opening with the words "Thus saith the Lord of Hosts" is one of mercy, whereas a message opening with Thus saith the Lord God" is one of judgement. The reason is that in the first case the Koh (thus) [Tr. note: A name of the Shekinah.] is blessed from the Zaddik and Nezah and Hod, which are called "the Lord of Hosts", and therefore the message is delivered in gentleness, since it comes from the place thereof. But in the other case it sucks from the side of judgement, from the side of the supernal Geburah; and I have learnt from my father that it is then judgement with mercy. Thus the prophet was careful to give the source of his message, and the sons of the true faith knew whence it depended.'

R. Aha then discoursed on the verse: "Curse ye Meroz, saith the angel of the Lord", etc. (Judges v, 23). 'This verse', he said, 'contains a profound mystery. When the Holy King handed over his house to the Matrona, he placed in her hands all kinds of weapons and engines of war, and put Her in command of all his warriors who are called "the mighty men of Israel, expert in war" (S.S. III, 7, 8); for when the Holy One, blessed be He, makes war, it is with these that He does so. We have learnt that when the Israelites vowed to uncover the holy impress on their flesh, [Tr. note: At the time of circumcision.] then that "sword that executeth the vengeance of the covenant" collected all its forces and armament to make war with Sisera, and the stars poured down fire from heaven, as it says, "The stars from their courses fought with Sisera" (Jud. v, 20). For God said to them: Be ready to execute the vengeance of my sons. I am going to exact a twofold vengeance from the enemy, once for the six hundred chariots which he lent the Egyptians to make war against Israel, and again for their oppression of my sons till now. Therefore they were judged with two punishments, one of fire and one of water. Among the stars was one which did not come to assist in the work of vengeance, and it was cursed forever, so that when it commences to shine the other stars come and swallow it up with all its attendant stars, and they all vanish. Hence it says, "Curse ye Meroz, saith the angel of the Lord". It may be asked, Has an angel the right to say this? This, however, is the one of whom it is written, "And the angel of the Lord that went before the camp of Israel removed", etc. (Ex. XIV, 19), for to him belong

Zohar: Devarim, Section 3, Page 270a

all wars, and this is also the one whom Jacob called "The angel that delivered me" (Gen. XLVIII, 16). This one, too, will be supreme and glorious in the time to come, and through him the Holy Name will be magnified, and the Holy One, blessed be He, will take vengeance of the peoples.'

They went on until they came to R. Simeon, who on seeing them said: 'Behold, the Shekinah is here; of a truth we must show gratitude to the Shekinah.' He then discoursed on the verse: "Lo, it is yet high day", etc. (Gen. XXIX, 7). 'This verse', he said, 'has been expounded to signify that when Israel shall turn in repentance before the Holy One, blessed be He, through the merit of the Torah they shall return to the Holy Land and be gathered from exile. For the captivity of Israel is only one day and no more. If, therefore, they do not repent, God says: Behold it is still high day, it is not time that the cattle should be gathered together, without merits or good deeds to their credit. You have, however, a remedy: "Water the sheep": study the Torah and drink of its waters, "and go and feed" in a restful spot, the desirable place of your inheritance. Or, again, we may take the "day" mentioned here to refer to the "day of discomfiture, of treading down, and of perplexity" (Isa. XXII, 5), when the Temple was destroyed and Israel went into captivity, and on account of their evil deeds that day is prolonged and drawn out. Therefore "water the sheep", as we have explained, with words of the Torah, for through the merit of the Torah Israel will escape from captivity. What do Israel reply? "We cannot, until all the flocks be gathered together", that is, until the other supernal Days be gathered together, "so that they may roll the stone", roll away the stern judgement of that Day which commands the mouth of the "Well" that is in captivity with us. When that Well is released and the stone will no longer dominate it, then "we shall water the sheep". At the end of days God will restore Israel to the Holy Land and gather them from exile. This "end of days" is the "latter end of days" frequently mentioned in Scripture, which is also a name for the Community of Israel in exile. With this the Holy One, blessed be He, will execute vengeance, and He will also restore it to its place, as it is written, "And it shall come to pass in the latter end of days that the mountain of the Lord's house shall be established", etc. (Isa. II, 2). Just as when the Temple was destroyed the shadows commenced to fall, as it is written, "Woe unto us for the day declineth, for the shadows of evening are stretched out" (Jer. VI, 4), so at the end of the captivity the shadows will commence to pass. The extent of that shadow will be six fists and a half, measured by the hand of a man who is a man among men. The mnemonic for this mystery among the Companions is the verse, "For we are but of yesterday and know nothing, because our days upon earth are but a shadow" (Job VIII, 9): that is to say: We are but from yesterday in captivity, and we did not know that the shadow is for God to settle us upon the land. Happy he that sees it and happy he that does not see it. Woe to him who will be at hand when the mighty lion seeks to join his mate, still more when they actually do join. Of that time it is written, "The lion roareth, who will not fear", etc. (Amos. III, 8). Of that time it is also written, "And the Lord God will turn thy captivity", etc. (Deut. xxx, 3): the Community of Israel will return from exile and the Zaddik will return to occupy his place.'

Zohar: Section 3, Devarim, Page 270b, 274a, 275a–b
[Note: The Hebrew text does not appear in our translation.]
Zohar: Section 3, Devarim, Page 283a

VAYELECH

AND MOSES WENT AND SPAKE THESE WORDS UNTO ALL ISRAEL. R. Hizkiah cited here the verse: "That caused his glorious arm to go at the right hand of Moses, that divided the water before them" (Isa. LXIII, 12). 'Happy', he said, 'are Israel in that God chose them, and because He chose them He called them sons,

firstborn, holy, brothers, and came down to dwell among them and sought to establish them after the supernal pattern, and spread over them seven clouds of glory. Three holy brethren accompanied them, Moses, Aaron and Miriam, and for their sakes God gave them precious gifts. All the days of Aaron the clouds of glory did not depart from Israel, and Aaron, as we have stated, was the right hand of Israel, and therefore it is written, "that caused his glorious arm to go at the right hand of Moses": this refers to Aaron. Therefore Aaron being dead it says now that Moses "went", like a body without an arm, as it says, "and they went without strength before the enemy" (Lam. I, 5).

'All the days of Moses the children of Israel ate bread from heaven, but as soon as Joshua came "the manna ceased on the next day... and they ate of the produce of the land" (Joshua v, 12). What is the difference between them? One is from the higher source and the other from the lower. As long as Moses was alive the orb of the sun was in the ascendant and illumined the world, but as soon as Moses departed the orb of the sun was gathered in and the moon came forth. We have learnt that when God said to Moses, "Behold my angel shall go before thee" (Ex. XXIII, 23), Moses said, "Shall the radiance of the sun be gathered in and the moon lead us? I desire not the orb of the moon, but that of the sun". Then the orb of the sun shone forth and Moses became like the orb of the sun to Israel; and when Moses was gathered in the orb of the sun was gathered in and the moon shone and Joshua used the light of the moon. Alas for this degradation!

'AND HE SAID TO THEM, I AM AN HUNDRED AND TWENTY YEARS OLD THIS DAY. This bears out what R. Eleazar said, that the sun illumined Israel for forty years and was then gathered in, and the moon commenced to shine.' R. Simeon said: 'This accords with the verse: "There is that is destroyed without justice" (Prov. XIII, 23), which has caused some difficulty to the Companions. The explanation is this. It has already been stated that all spirits issue from heaven in pairs, male and female, and then separate. Sometimes the spirit of the female goes forth before the male which is her mate, and as long as the time of the male has not come to be united with her another can come and marry her, but when the time of the first one arrives to marry her, when Zedek (Righteousness) arises to visit the sins of the world, this other that married her is gathered in and the first comes and marries her. And even though his works were not particularly evil, he is gathered in before his time and not in accordance with judgement, and the doom of Zedek lights on him for his sins because the time of the other to whom she belongs has come.' R. Eleazar asked: 'Why should he die? Cannot God separate them and let the other come and give her to him?' He replied: 'This is the kindness that God does with a man, that he should not see his wife in the hand of another. Observe, too, that if the first

is not deserving, even though the woman is his by rights, the other is not removed to make way for him. In the same way Saul obtained the kingdom, because the time of David, to whom it rightfully belonged, had not yet come. But when David's time arrived to come into his own, Zedek arose and gathered in Saul on account of his sins, and he had to make way for David. If it is asked, Could not Saul have lost the kingdom without also dying, the answer is that God did him a kindness in gathering him in while he was yet king so that he should not see his servant ruling over him and taking what was formerly his. So here too. Therefore a man should pray to God that he be not thrust out to make way for another. So, too, God said to Moses: Do you want to overturn the world? Have you ever seen the sun serving the moon? Have you ever seen the moon shining when the sun is still high? BEHOLD THY DAYS APPROACH THAT THOU MUST DIE, CALL JOSHUA; let the sun be gathered in and the moon rule. Nay more, if thou enterest the land the moon will be gathered in before thee and have no sway. The time has come for the dominion of the moon, but it cannot rule while thou art in the world.

THAT I MAY GIVE HIM A CHARGE. We find, in fact, that God gave no charge to Joshua, but only to Moses. Why, then, does it say, "that I may give him a charge"? What it means is this. God said to Moses: Although thou liest with thy fathers, thou wilt still be existing to give light to the moon, just as the sun even after it has set continues to give light to the moon. Therefore I will charge Joshua to be illumined, and therefore it says also, "command Joshua and encourage him" (Deut. III, 28): charge him, that is, to give light.

FOR THOU SHALT BRING THE CHILDREN OF ISRAEL. And previously (v. 7) it says, "thou shalt come with this people". Why this variation? One was to announce to him that he would enter the land and remain on it, the other that he would have sway over Israel.'

R. Simeon discoursed on the verse: "From the uttermost part of the earth have we heard songs, glory to the righteous", etc. (Isa. XXIV, 16). 'These songs are the praises uttered by the Community of Israel before the Holy One, blessed be He, at night, at the time when He holds joyous converse with the righteous in the Garden of Eden. When is this? From midnight onwards. And for what purpose? To be united with the Holy One, blessed be He, and to be sanctified with the same holiness. The verse continues: "I pine away, I pine away, woe is me. The treacherous dealers have dealt treacherously". Woe is me for the generation and for the world! For all are false to Him, and their children inherit their treachery and add to it their own, and so become defective both above and below. When Isaiah saw this, he gathered all who feared sin and taught them the way of holiness and the sanctity of the King that their sons might be holy; and therefore the sons they bore were called after his name, wherefore it says, "Behold I and the children whom the Lord hath given me are for signs and wonders in Israel" (Isa. VIII, 18). Another explanation of this verse ("From the uttermost part of the earth", etc.) is that when the Israelites came into the land with the Ark of the holy covenant before them, they heard from one side of the land the sound of joyful praises and the voice of sweet singers who were singing in the land. And this redounded to the praise of Moses, that wherever the ark rested in the land they heard a voice saying, "This is the law which Moses set before the children of Israel". But woe is me that the traitors have dealt treacherously, that Israel are destined to be false to God and to be uprooted from the land, and because their children persist in their falsehood they will be uprooted a second time until their guilt will be expiated in a foreign land.

THAT IT MAY BE THERE FOR A WITNESS AGAINST THEE. Three things [are recorded in Scripture as] having been made witnesses, namely, the well of Isaac, the lot, and the stone which Joshua set up. This song, however, is the best witness of all.' Said R. Isaac: 'If so, there are four?' He replied: 'The term "witness" is not specifically applied to the lot in Scripture, though it says "by the mouth of the lot shall their inheritance be divided', (Num. XXVI, 55).'

AND MOSES SPAKE THE WORDS OF THIS SONG UNTIL THEY WERE FINISHED. R. Eleazar asked: Why does it say here, "the words of this song" and not simply "this song"? The reason is that all the words which Moses spoke were traced with the name of the Holy One, blessed be He, and then every word came to Moses to be traced by him and remained before him. How is it, it may be asked, that for the song of Solomon the masculine term shir (song) is used, and for the song of Moses the feminine term shirah? Seeing that, as we have learnt, all the other prophets were in comparison to Moses like an ape compared to a man, should not Moses have said shir and the other shirah?

Zohar: Devarim, Section 3, Page 285a

The answer is that Moses was speaking not for himself but for Israel.' R. Simeon said: 'This is not so, but the truth is that this itself is a proof of the superiority of Moses. For Moses went up, from the lower to the higher, but they came down, from the higher to the lower. Moses said shirah, which is the song of the Matrona in honour of the King, and he was attached to the King. They said shir, which is the song of the King in honour of the Matrona, and they were attached to the Matrona; and thus the superiority of Moses was here displayed. We may also say that Moses used the term "shirah" to connect his words with the place from which judgement could be visited on them, since he had already said, "For I know their imagination", etc. (v. 21), and also, "For I know that after my death", etc. (v. 29). We find it also written, however, "And David spake unto the Lord the words of this song (shirah, 2 Sam. XXII, 1). It is to the honour of David that he attained to this grade of inditing a shirah from the lower to the higher. This was towards the end of his days, when he had reached a higher stage of perfection. And why was he worthy to indite such a hymn, from the lower to the higher, at the end of his days? Because he had peace on all sides, as it is written, "On the day that the Lord delivered him from the hand of all his enemies" (Ibid.).'

R. Simeon said: 'What is the most perfect hymn? One that is addressed both by the lower to the higher and by the higher to the lower, and which then combines the two. From whose example do we know this? From this song of Moses. First the lower addresses the higher in the words, "For I will call on the name of the Lord", and again, "Ascribe greatness to our God", the reference being to the Most High King. Afterwards he traces the degrees from higher to lower, as it is written, "righteous and upright". Finally the knot of faith is tied in the words "he is". This should be the example forevery man in arranging the praises of his Master. At first he should ascend from the lower to the higher till he carries the honour of his Master to the place whence issues the stream of the most recondite fountain. Then he draws it downwards from that moistening stream to each grade in turn down to the lowest grade, so that blessings are drawn to all from on high. Then he has to knit all firmly together with the knot of faith, and this is the man who honours the name of his Master by unifying the Holy Name. Of such a one it is written, "Them that honour me I will honour" (I Sam. II, 30), that is, them that honour Me in this world I will honour in the next. "But", the verse goes on, "they that despise me shall be lightly esteemed". This applies to one who does not know how to unify the Holy Name, to bind the knot of faith, and to bring blessings to the proper place; for whoever does not know how to honour the name of his Master were better not to have been born. R. Judah says that these words apply to one who does not answer "Amen" with devotion, since we have learnt: Greater is he that answers "Amen" than he that says the blessing. [Tr. note: T.B. Berachoth, 57b.] For so we have explained in the presence of R. Simeon, that Amen draws blessings from the Source to the King and from the King to the Matrona; in the inscribed letters of R. Eleazar, from A to M and from M to N. and when the blessings come to N. from there

Zohar: Devarim, Section 3, Page 285b

they issue forth to higher and lower and spread through all, and a voice proclaims, "Drink from the stream of blessings that So-and-so the servant of the Holy King has sent forth". And when Israel below are careful to answer "Amen" with fitting devotion, many doors of blessing are opened for them above, many blessings are spread through all worlds, and great is the joy throughout. For this Israel receive a reward in this world and in the next. In this world because when Israel are oppressed and offer up prayer a voice proclaims in all worlds, "Open ye the gates that the righteous nation which keepeth truth may enter in" (Isa. XXVI, 2): as Israel open for you gates of blessing, so open the gates for them and let their prayer be received for deliverance from their oppressors. In the next world what is their reward? That when a man who was careful to answer Amen departs from this world, his soul ascends and they proclaim before him: Open the gates before him [Tr. note: V. T.B. Shabbath, 119b.] as he opened gates every day by being careful to answer Amen. But if one hears a blessing from the reader and is not careful to answer Amen, what is his punishment? As he did not open blessings below, so they do not open for him above, and when he leaves this world they proclaim before him: Close the gates in the face of So-and-so that he enter not, and do not receive him woe to him and to his soul! We have learnt that the sinners of Gehinnom are in different storeys, and that Gehinnom has a number of gates corresponding to those of the Garden of Eden, each with its own name. There is one storey lower than all the rest which consists of a storey on a storey, and this is called the nether Sheol, "sheol,' being one storey and "nether" another below it. We have learnt that he who descends to Abadon,

Zohar: Devarim, Section 3, Page 286a

which is called "nether", never ascends again, and he is called "a man who has been wiped out from all worlds". To this place they take down those who scorn to answer Amen, and for all the amens which they have neglected they are judged in Gehinnom and taken down to that lowest storey which has no outlet, and from which they never ascend. Of such it is written, "As the cloud is consumed and withereth away, so he that goeth down to Sheol shall come up no more" (Job VII, 9); this refers to that nether storey.' R. Yose cited the verse: "For my people have committed two evils: they have forsaken me, the fountain of living waters, and have hewed them out cisterns, broken cisterns, that can hold no water" (Jer. II, 13). '"They have forsaken me", by refusing to sanctify the name of the Holy One, blessed be He, with Amen; and their punishment is "to hew out broken cisterns", by being taken down to Gehinnom storey after storey till they reach Abadon, which is called "nether". But if one sanctifies the name of the Holy One, blessed be He, by answering Amen with all his heart, he ascends grade after grade till he is regaled with that World-to-come which perennially issues forth.'

R. Eleazar said: 'Israel will one day indite a chant from the lower to the higher and from the higher to the lower and tie the knot of faith, as it is written, "Then shall Israel sing (yashir) this song" (Num. XXI, 17), from the lower to the higher. "Spring up, O well, sing ye to it": that is, ascend to thy place to unite with thy Spouse. This is from the lower to the higher; then from the higher to the lower in the words, "The well which the princes digged"-for it was begotten of the Father and the Mother, "which the nobles of the people delved", as a place for the King to join her with blessings. And through what shall be their union?" "With the sceptre": this is Yesod; "And with their staves": these are Nezak and Hod. Thus we have from the higher to the lower. Then the song proceeds: "And from the wilderness to Mattanah and from Mattanah to Nahaliel and from Nahaliel to Bamoth": this is the complete bond of faith, the permanent bond wherein is all.'

R. Yose said: 'Israel will one day utter a complete song comprising all other songs, as it says: "And in that day shall ye say, Give thanks unto the Lord, call upon his name, declare his doings among the peoples" (Isa. XII, 4).'

HA'AZINU

GIVE EAR, YE HEAVENS, AND I WILL SPEAK, ETC. R. Judah cited here the verse: "I opened to my beloved, but my beloved had withdrawn himself and was gone", etc. (S.S. v, 6). 'And just before this it is written, "I was asleep but my heart waked" (Ibid. 2). Said the Community of Israel: I was asleep to the precepts of the Law when I went in the wilderness, but my heart was awake to enter the land so as to perform them, since they all are meant for the land. "It is the voice of my beloved that knocketh": this is Moses, who administered many reproofs

Zohar: Devarim, Section 3, Page 286b

and rebukes, as it says, "These are the words", etc. (Deut. I, 1), "Ye were rebellious", etc. (Ibid. IX, 24). Yet withal he spoke only in love for Israel, as it says, "Ye are a holy people", etc. (Ibid. VII, 6). Said the Israelites: When we were about to enter into the land and to receive precepts of the Law, then "my beloved withdrew himself and was gone", for "Moses the servant of the Lord died there". "I sought him but I could not find him", as it is written, "There arose not a prophet like Moses". "I called him but he gave me no answer", for there was no generation like that of Moses, one to whose voice God hearkened and for whom He did such wonders and miracles. R. Isaac said: "I rose to open to my beloved": this was in the days of Moses, during the whole of which there was no need of angel or messenger to guide Israel. "My beloved had withdrawn himself and was gone": this was in the days of Joshua, as it is written, "Nay, but as captain of the host of the Lord am I now come" (Joshua v, 14). Moses heard the voice of the holy supernal King without trembling; "I came in the days of Moses thy master but he would not accept me". Then did the children of Israel realize the greatness of Moses; they sought the Holy One, blessed be He, but He was no longer at hand for them as in the days of Moses.'

GIVE EAR, YE HEAVENS, AND I WILL SPEAK. R. Hiya said: 'Blessed is Moses in that he was superior to all other prophets. For Isaiah being further removed from the King said only, "Hear, heavens", but Moses being nearer to the King [Tr. note: v. Yalkut, Is. 1.] said, "Give ear". We have learnt that when Isaiah said "Hear, heavens, and give ear, earth", many translucent angels sought to break his head and a voice came forth saying: Who is this that seeks to throw the world into confusion; and he therefore made haste to say: I do this not of myself, but "the Lord speaketh". In regard to Moses, however, it says, "Hear, ye heavens, and I will speak"–I, and no other, "and let the earth hear my voice"–mine and no others.' R. Yose said: 'There is a further difference between Moses and Isaiah in that Moses said, "Give ear, the heavens", that is, those highest heavens which are called the name of the Holy One, blessed be He, and further, "and let the earth hear", the upper earth, the land of the living. But Isaiah said only "heaven" and "earth", meaning the lower heaven and earth, and withal he was nearly punished.'

R. Isaac discoursed on the verse: "As the apple tree among the trees of the wood, so is my beloved among the sons" (S.S. II, 3). 'Just as the apple is superior in its colouring to all other fruits, so the Holy One, blessed be He, is distinguished from all forces, higher and lower. Observe that the Holy One, blessed be He, is compared to the apple, which has three colours, and the Community of Israel to the lily, which has two, red and white.'

Zohar: Devarim, Section 3, Page 287a

R. Judah said: 'The Holy One, blessed be He, is called Heaven, and because He is called heaven, therefore all the seven firmaments which are included under this name when they are joined together are also called heaven and are called the name of the Holy One, blessed be He.'

R. Yose asked: 'Why is this discourse called "song"?' R. Isaac answered: 'Just as

Zohar: Devarim, Section 3, Page 287b

a song is drawn from heaven to earth by the holy spirit, so these words were drawn from heaven to earth by the holy spirit. Observe that Moses made a long exordium saying, "Give ear, ye heavens, and hear, O earth, let my discourse drop as the dew", etc. Why all this? "Because I will call on the name of the Lord". We have learnt that when Moses said "Give ear, ye heavens, and I will speak", all worlds were shaken. A voice came forth and said: Moses, why dost thou shake the world, being but a mortal? He replied: Because I will call on the name of the Lord. Forthwith they were silent and listened to his words.'

[Tr. note: Here in the original follows the Idra Zuta, v. Appendix.]

Zohar: Devarim, Section 3, Page 296b

R. Yose said: 'God first called Israel "holy", as it is written, "For thou art a holy people", etc. (Deut. XIV, 2). Then He called them "holiness", as it is written, "Israel is holiness (kodesh) to the Lord, the first fruits

Zohar: Devarim, Section 3, Page 297a

of his increase" (Jer. II, 3). What is the difference between the two terms?' R. Abba said: '"Holiness" is higher than all, for so we have learnt that when all sanctities are combined they are called "holiness", and all assemble together to that place which is called "holiness".' R. Eleazar said: 'The beginning and end of all is comprised in "holiness", and the supreme Wisdom is called "holiness", and when this Wisdom shines forth the wisdom of Solomon is illumined, the Moon being then at the full. When it is illumined from Yesod we call it "holiness" when this illumines her fully, but when it is not illumined completely we call it "the spirit of holiness". And when it is blessed from Yesod and gives suck to all below, we call it Mother, and we call them "holinesses", and so it becomes "holy of holies".'

FOR I WILL PROCLAIM THE NAME OF THE LORD, ETC. R. Abba said: '"Ascribe ye greatness" refers to Gedulah; "The Rock, his work is perfect" to Geburah; "For all his ways are judgement" to Tifereth; "a God of faithfulness" to Nezah; "and without iniquity" to Hod; "just" to Yesod; "and right" to Zedek; "is he" completes the holy name of the Holy One, blessed be He.' R. Yose said: 'Then only did Moses reveal this name to the children of Israel, as it is written, "I am an hundred and twenty years old this day", etc. (Deut. XXXI, 2). From this we learn that one in whom resides divine wisdom, when his time arrives to depart from the world, should reveal that wisdom to those among whom is the holy spirit. If he does not, we apply to him the words, "Withhold not good from them to whom it is due when it is in the power of thine hand to do it" (Prov. III, 27).' R. Hiya said: 'The end of this verse makes fast the knot of faith in the word "he", as if to say "He is all, He is one without division", and all the others mentioned are not diverse but are all united in One, who is, was, and will be. Happy is he who calls upon the King and knows how to call upon him fittingly. But if one calls without knowing to whom he calls, the Holy One, blessed be He, is far from him, as it is written, "God is near to all who call upon him, (to wit) to all who call upon him in truth" (Ps. CXLV, 18). Is there, then, one who calls upon Him in falsehood?' Said R. Abba: 'Yes; he that calls and knows not to whom he calls.

'THEY HAVE CORRUPTED THEMSELVES, THEY ARE NOT HIS CHILDREN, IT IS THEIR BLEMISH. We have learnt: Sinners, if one may say so, create a blemish above,

Zohar: Devarim, Section 3, Page 297b

[Note: The last 16 lines of the Hebrew text do not appear in our translation.]

in that through them all the divine adornments are not in their proper condition.' Said R. Yose: 'What is the blemish? That the Fathers do not obtain full blessing from the watering of the Stream, and even less of course the Children.' Similarly R. Simeon said: 'When sinners are numerous in the world, the Holy Name, if one may say so, is not blessed in the world, but when sinners are not numerous, the Holy Name is blessed in the world.' R. Abba said: 'This text also says so explicitly. Who is the cause of the corruption here mentioned? "A perverse and crooked generation." Hence, after Moses had expressed the Holy Name in fitting manner, closing with the words, "just and right is he", he went on, "but they corrupted themselves being not his sons", etc. Why? Because they were a perverse and crooked generation.

DO YE THUS REQUITE THE LORD, to wit, for all those kindnesses that He has shown thee.' R. Eleazar said: 'Blessed are Israel above all heathen peoples, because although they have provoked their Master, the Holy One, blessed be He, was fain not to abandon them. For in every place to which they have been exiled the Holy One, blessed be He, is with them in their banishment, as it is written, "And yet for all that, when they be in the land of their enemies I will not reject them", etc. (Lev. XXVI, 44). Now how great is the love of the Holy One, blessed be He, for Israel, for although they brought exile upon themselves the Shekinah never leaves them, as it says, "and this (zoth) also (is with them) when they are in the land of their enemies". A king had a son who provoked him so that he condemned him to depart from him and to go to a distant land. The Queen on hearing this said: Seeing that my son is going to a distant land and the King casts him out of his palace, I will not leave him, but either we will both return together to the palace or both will dwell together in another land. In course of time the King sought the Queen and did not find her, because she had gone with her son. He said: Since the Queen is there, let them both return. But it is the Queen whom the King seeks out first, and for her sake he seeks out his son, as it is written, "I have heard the groaning of the children of Israel". Why? Because "I remember my Covenant" (Ex. VI, 5).'

Zohar: Devarim, Section 3, Page 298a

As R. Isaac was once journeying on the road, R. Hiya met him. He said to him: 'I see from the look of your face that your abode is with the Shekinah. Why is it written, "And I am come down to deliver them out of the hand of the Egyptians"? Surely it should be, "And I shall come down"? It means, however, "I went down at first", namely, when Jacob went down to Egypt; I then went down to deliver them from the hand of the Egyptians, since otherwise they could not have endured the captivity; and so it says, "I am with him in trouble, I will deliver him and honour him" (Ps. XCI, 15).' He replied: 'Of a truth wherever Israel dwell the Holy One, blessed be He, is among them, and wherever the wise of the generation walk the Holy One, blessed be He, walks with them. How do we know? From Jacob, of whom it is written, "And Jacob went on his way" (Gen. XXII, 1), and then, "And Jacob said when he saw them, This is God's host". Now let us join one another and proceed, as I know we are going to the same place, to pay our respects to the Shekinah.' 'Assuredly so,' replied the other. As they went along, R. Hiya said: 'It is written, "These are the generations of the heavens and the earth" (Gen. II, 4). "The heavens" includes the Holy One, blessed be He, and "the earth" includes the Holy One, blessed be He, and all that is lower is called "the generations of the heavens". We have learnt that this world was created with He' and the future world with Vau. From the Head of the King the streams issue forth to Binah, and thence they flow to all corners until finally they are collected in the place called the Great Sea, whence issue generations for all.' Said R. Isaac: 'When we studied with R. Simeon, all this was set forth explicitly and not by way of allusion.' He replied: 'R. Simeon is not like other men, for they are to him as the other prophets to Moses.'

As they went along, R. Hiya asked R. Isaac the meaning of the verse: "Can a woman forget her sucking child, that she should not have compassion on the son of her womb?" (Isa. LXIX, 15)'. Said the other: 'If in the company of the colleagues we could find no proper explanation for it, how can I say?' He thereupon said: 'I once caught a hint of the meaning as I was going along the road, but I do not know who said it or exactly what he meant. For seven days I was troubled by this and did not eat anything, and now I am going to the Sacred Lamp in case he may be able to remind me.' Said R. Isaac: 'Perhaps it was the day when R. Eleazar was going to his father-in-law, and I was with him, and I can remember. For thus said R. Eleazar in the name of his father: Israel said before the Holy One, blessed be He: Since the day that we fell into captivity God has forsaken and forgotten us, as it is written, "But Zion said, The Lord hath forgotten me" (Ibid. 14). Whereupon the Shekinah replied: "Can a woman forget her sucking child, that she should not have compassion on the son

Zohar: Devarim, Section 3, Page 298b

of her womb?" "Yea, these may forget"—to wit, those mentioned in the verse, "These are the generations of heaven and earth", "yet will not I forget thee". This shows that the Holy One, blessed be He, will not forsake Israel forever. Further, there is a deep mystery here, since God said that "these" things are attached to His name, and just as the Holy

One, blessed be He, cannot forget His name, which is all, so He does not forget Israel, who are attached to His very name.' R. Hiya thereupon became excited and said: 'In truth that is the thing. Blessed be God that I reminded you, so that now I know what it was and who said it. I ran four miles that day and could not find out who it was.' R. Isaac said: 'I heard it because I went into a cave where R. Eleazar was resting.'

REMEMBER THE DAYS OF OLD, CONSIDER THE YEARS OF MANY GENERATIONS. R. Abba said: 'The days of old" are the six Days in which God made the world; and these Days know and are acquainted with all the years of the world, and all generations up to this generation to which we ourselves belong. ASK THY FATHER AND HE WILL SHOW THEE: this is the Holy One, blessed be He, who will reveal to thee the hidden depths of Wisdom, to wit, that when those six Days constructed the universe they did so only for thy sake that thou mightest come and perform the Law, as we have learnt, that God made a condition with creation that if when Israel came they would accept the Torah it should stand, and if not that it should revert to chaos. Therefore God assigned other peoples to Chieftains and Overseers, but of you it is written, FOR THE LORD'S PORTION IS HIS PEOPLE, JACOB IS THE LOT OF HIS INHERITANCE, since He assigned them to no Potentate or Angel or Chieftain, but took them for his own portion. Where did He find them? IN A DESERT LAND AND IN A WASTE HOWLING WILDERNESS, as it is written, "Terah the father of Abraham... and I took your father Abraham", etc. (Joshua XXIV, 2, 3); and from there He guided Israel in every generation, never separating from them.'

AS AN EAGLE THAT STIRRETH UP HER NEST. R.Yose said: 'There is no creature so devoted to her young as the eagle, being as kind to them as it is cruel to others. THE LORD ALONE DID LEAD HIM AND THERE WAS NO STRANGE GOD WITH HIM: He alone, as it is written, "And the Lord went before them", etc. (Ex. XIII, 21), and they were not led by an angel or any other Chieftain such as are called "strange god".'

O THAT THEY WERE WISE, THAT THEY UNDERSTOOD THIS. R. Yose said: 'All the verses of this section are reproofs addressed by Moses to Israel, with the exception of the Holy Name which he disclosed at the beginning of his discourse.' R. Abba said: 'Even his reproofs are included in the holy name, since there is no word in the Torah which is not comprised in the holy name. That the name

Zohar: Devarim, Section 3, Page 299a

of the Holy One, blessed be He, however, might be inscribed in this section, we have had to wait till here, where it is indeed written, "O that they were wise, that they understood this (zoth)", meaning that if Israel knew how zoth takes hold of judgement to punish sinners "they would consider their latter end", and take heed to be faithful to her. Or we may explain that She is united with Israel when they keep the precepts of the Torah and dwell with Her in peace, and then they know that this zoth is on their side to help them to punish their enemies. Israel who are the least of nations will then know "how one should chase a thousand and two put ten thousand to flight".

EXCEPT THEIR ROCK HAD SOLD THEM AND THE LORD HAD DELIVERED THEM UP. Why so?

Because "Of the Rock that begat thee thou art unmindful" (v. 18), and the divine adornments are not in their proper place.' R. Judah said: 'The "rock" here is Abraham, who said, "Let Israel be condemned to exile rather than to Gehinnom", and God consented, so that whenever Israel sin they are sent into captivity and their enemies rule over them.' R. Judah said: 'Why did Moses reprove Israel thus in this song? Because they were about to enter into the land where the Shekinah would dwell in their midst.' R. Isaac said: 'When the prophet said, "The Lord hath a controversy with Judah, and will punish Jacob according to his ways" (Hosea XII, 2), the nations of the world exulted, saying: "Now they will be utterly destroyed". But when God saw them rejoicing, He changed His mind, and it is written, "In the womb he took his brother by the heel", etc. (Hos. XII, 4). A woman had a quarrel with her son, and went to complain against him to the court. When she saw the judge condemning prisoners to stripes, to crucifying, to burning, she said: Alas, what shall I do with my son? When the judge was ready he said to her: Tell me what I shall do with your son. She said: I was only shouting.' HE FOUND HIM IN A DESERT LAND AND IN THE WASTE HOWLING WILDERNESS. Assuredly he afterwards made all those "shells" [Tr. note: The klifoth.] subservient to him.

'Up to this point this section was transcribed in the Book of Kartana the physician. Then in a note to this verse were set down all the precautions that a wise physician should take for a person laid up in his sickness, among the prisoners of the King, for the service of his Master, the Lord of the Universe. When the wise physician goes in to him, he "finds him in a desert land and in the waste howling wilderness". Are we to say that because God has commanded him to be seized, no one should seek to help him? Not so, for David said, "Blessed is he that considereth the poor" (Ps. XLI, 2), and the "poor" is one confined to a bed of sickness. What, then, is the wise physician to do? He "compasses him about", finding means to protect him against the things that injure him, by letting blood and removing the bad blood from him. "He cares for him", examining the cause of the disease, and taking steps that it should not grow worse. Then "he keeps him as the apple of his eye", that he may be careful to prescribe for him the proper medicines, since if he makes a mistake in a single particular God imputes it to him as if he were to shed blood, for, although that man is among the prisoners of the King, yet God desires that his fellow man should tend him and help to release him from the prison. He used to say thus: God passes sentence on human beings above, whether for death or

Zohar: Devarim, Section 3, Page 299b

banishment or confiscation of goods or imprisonment. He who is liable to confiscation of goods falls ill and is not healed until he pays all that is decreed against him. When he has paid his money penalty he is healed and goes out from his prison, and therefore it is fitting that one should assist him to pay his fine and be released. He who is liable to uprooting is seized and thrown into the prison until he is completely uprooted, though sometimes he is uprooted only from his limbs or from one of them and is then released. But one who is liable to death cannot save himself by any ransom whatever. Hence a wise physician must do his best first to provide him a healing for his body, and if he cannot do this he must try to find a healing for his soul. This is the physician whom God assists both in this world and in the next.' R. Eleazar said: 'I never heard before of this physician and this book, save once when a certain merchant told me that he had heard his father say that in his days there was a physician who on looking at a patient would say: This one wlll live, or this one will die. He was said to be a virtuous God-fearing man, and if a patient could not afford to get what he prescribed he would give him out of his own pocket. It was said, too, that there was no physician so skilful as he, and that he accomplished more with his prayer than with his hands. I fancy this was that same physician. Said that merchant: His book is indeed in my possession, as I inherited it from my father's father, and all the words of that book are founded upon hidden meanings of the Torah, and I have discovered profound secrets in it and many remedies which he said should not be administered save by one who was God-fearing, they being of those which were employed by Balaam, who used to utter an incantation over a sickness and heal it forthwith. All this he explained in that book, saying: This is forbidden and this is permitted to one who fears sin, since, as he said, the cure of many illnesses depends on the incantation. These are from the side of enchantment, some of them from the side of magic. All those which it is forbidden to pronounce with the mouth or to do with the hands were set down, and we found that certain diseases i t was necessary to excommunicate, which was a great wonder to us.' R. Eleazar and the Companions were greatly interested to hear this. Said R. Eleazar: 'If I had that book I would see what it says, and I vow that I would show it to the Sacred Lamp'. We have learnt that R. Eleazar said: I had that book for twelve months and I found in it many illuminating things. When I came to the incantations of Balaam I was in some perplexity. One day I uttered one in a certain place, and letters went up and down and a voice said to me in a dream: Why dost thou enter into a domain which is not thine and not thy concern? When I woke I was sore displeased with the hidden mysteries there. I sent to a certain Jew named R. Yose, son of R. Judah, and gave him the book. In the secrets of Balaam I had found some of the names of the angels which Balak sent to him, but not set down in the proper manner. I also, however, found a number of remedies which were based on arrangements of texts and secret mysteries of the Torah, and saw that they consisted of pious remarks and prayers and supplications to the Almighty. It must not be thought, however, that he performed healing with verses of the Scripture or with mysteries of the Torah; far from it. He used to pronounce mysteries of the Torah, and thereby he discovered secret healings the like of which I have never seen. I said: Blessed be God who has imparted to man of the supernal wisdom. I also took some of the words of Balaam, from which I could see that there never was a sorcerer like him. I said: Blessed be God for removing sorcery from the world, so that men should not be led astray from the fear of the Holy One, blessed be He.

Zohar: Section 3, Devarim, Page 300a

[Note: From here until page 309b, in the Hebrew, begins a section called Tosafoth. Since this is not part of the main Zohar, it is not translated.]

Zohar – Raya Mehemna – The Faithful Shepherd

Zohar: Shemoth, Raya Mehemna, Page 25a

AND I WILL TAKE YOU TO ME FOR A PEOPLE AND I WILL BE TO YOU A GOD, AND YE SHALL KNOW THAT I AM THE LORD YOUR GOD. This is the first of all commandments, the root of all precepts of the Law: the knowledge of God in a general way, namely that there is a Supernal Ruler, Lord of the universe and of all life, Creator of heaven and earth and all their hosts. But this general knowledge of God must lead on to a particular knowledge of Him. This is the inner meaning of man being "male and female together'. When the Israelites were about to come out of Egypt they had no knowledge of the Holy One, blessed be He, and Moses had to teach them the first principle of Divine knowledge. Without this doctrine they would not have believed in all those signs and wonders which they were about to experience. At the end of the forty years in the desert, after having been instructed by Moses in all the commandments, both in those which are directly connected with the Holy Land and in those which are not, he taught them in an individual, particular way, the knowledge of God, as it says: "Know therefore this day and consider it in thine heart that the Lord he is God in heaven above and in the earth beneath; there is none else" (Deut. IV, 39). "That the Lord (Tetragrammaton) is God (ELOHIM), this is the particular aspect of cognition. This particular mode of knowledge is essentially identical with the general concept of God as Creator and Lord. Should the question arise: Is not "the fear of the Lord the beginning of wisdom" (Prov. 1, 7, i.e. the first commandment)? the answer would be that the fear of the Lord (which is connected with the commandments) must precede the second, the particular grade of knowledge, although, of course, one has to fear the Lord even before one has an intellectual knowledge of Him in His revelational individual aspects. Thus the ultimate and whole duty of man is to know the Holy One, blessed be He, in a general and in a particular way. The verse, "I am the first, and I am the last" (Isa. XLIV, 7) has a symbolic reference to this twofold mode of knowledge; "I am the first," to the general apprehension of Him, and "I am the last," to the particular, and these two are one. As a result of a proper knowledge of God as Creator and Lord, the two hundred and forty-eight organs of the human body become organs of the two hundred and forty-eight positive commandments of the Law, and man's life becomes something complete and harmonious, and the particular, individual, knowledge of God causes salvation and blessing to enter into every day of the three hundred and sixty-five days of the year (corresponding to the three hundred and sixty-five negative commandments). For as it is above so it is below: as all the supernal "days" are filled with blessing by the (heavenly) Man, so are the days here below filled with blessing through the agency of Man (i.e. the righteous). Blessed are the Israelites in this world through having the commandments of the Torah! The word "Man" is applied to them only, but not to the heathen (Ezek. XXXIV, 31), therefore they must endeavour to keep the commandments with zeal and diligence, that all may become one in the inner meaning of Man. When the Holy One gave Israel the Torah on Mount Sinai, his first word was "Anokhi", I. This "Anokhi" contains many mysteries; here, however, we are concerned with the fact that it is the first of all commandments, the root of all precepts of the Law: "I am the Lord'. This is the general axiom. The particular is "thy God". The same is true of "The Lord thy God is a consuming fire." (Deut. IV, 24).

Zohar: Shemoth, Raya Mehemna, Page 25b

[Note: The translation for this page appears above, together with the translation for page 25a.]

Zohar: Shemoth, Raya Mehemna, Page 40b

AND THE PEOPLE TOOK THEIR DOUGH BEFORE IT WAS LEAVENED. On the strength of this is founded the precept that the leaven should be burned on the Passover Eve. "Leaven," and "unleaven" symbolize the evil and the good inclinations in man.

It is obligatory for every Israelite to relate the story of the Exodus on the Passover night. He who does so fervently and joyously, telling the tale with a high heart, shall be found worthy to rejoice in the Shekinah in the world to come, for rejoicing brings forth rejoicing; and the joy of Israel causes the Holy One Himself to be glad, so that He calls together all the Family above and says unto them: "Come ye and hearken unto the praises which My children bring unto Me! Behold how they rejoice in My Redemption!" Then all the angels and supernal beings gather round and observe Israel, how she sings and rejoices because of her Lord's own Redemption—and seeing the rejoicings below, the supernal beings also break into jubilation for that the Holy One possesses on earth a people so holy, whose joy in the Redemption of their Lord is so great and so powerful. For all that terrestrial rejoicing increases the power of the Lord and His hosts in the regions above, just as an earthly king gains strength from the praises of his subjects, the fame of his glory being thus spread throughout the world.

Zohar: Shemoth, Raya Mehemna, Page 41a

And similarly a man should acknowledge and proclaim any wonder that God has wrought for him. This should he do, not in order that the Omniscient should become aware of all His wonderful acts, since to Him all things of the past, as well as of the future, are already known, but rather in order that the praises may ascend even unto the highest spheres and awaken among the supernal beings a responsive outburst of praise and worshipful delight in the faithfulness of His people and in the invincible greatness of His glory, who is Himself rejoiced at the rejoicings of His people and His heavenly hosts. Conversely, with the confession of sin: the Holy One is aware of all man's sins and needs no reminder thereof; yet, since Satan, the supernal adversary and accuser, continually lies in wait, ever ready to bring man's sins before the Holy One, it is but a natural precaution to hasten on in advance of him, making full confession of one's sins, so that the Accuser, when he comes, may find himself anticipated and left without ground for his denunciations, and so be discouraged and leave his intended victim alone. Then, should the sinner carry out his repentance fully, he will be fully exonerated, and all will be well; and if not, Satan will thus obtain a just opportunity to rise up against the impious one, saying: "Here is a man who has had the audacity to appear before Thee, and yet has rebelled against his Lord!" Therefore man should at all times beware lest he falter in his fealty, and strive ever to be found a faithful servant before the Holy One, blessed be He. Then follows the command that we should eat unleavened bread during Passover, it being a memorial, throughout the generations, of the true secret of Faith. For, as already stated elsewhere, Israel at that time emerged from the association with idolatry and entered into the mystery of Faith. THIS IS THE ORDINANCE OF THE PASSOVER: THERE SHALL NO STRANGER EAT THEREOF. This commandment is a memorial of the Passover of Egypt. The lamb had to be kept from the tenth day of the month, because on that date the moon begins to increase her light until the fifteenth day, when she is in her full strength. The lamb was slaughtered on the fourteenth, "between the evenings", namely at an hour when judgement hangs over the world. It signified the removal of the impurity from the holy sign (of the circumcision). Therefore "no uncircumcised person should eat thereof" (v. 48); for this sacrifice was brought by sons of the covenant, in order to break down the power of the "other side", to remove the "foreskin," from the sign of the holy covenant. When the Holy One came to Egypt He saw the blood of the Passover lamb smeared on the door, as well as the blood of the covenant, and the doors purged with hyssop, in order, as has already been explained, that the powers of impurity might be exorcised at the time of the supreme redemption of Israel. This memorial of the past redemption is, however, at the same time a sign and a token of the future Redemption, when the Holy One will "slaughter" the evil inclination once and for all.

Zohar: Shemoth, Raya Mehemna, Page 41b

And because He killed all the firstborn of the "other side", He ordered that the firstborn of Israel should be redeemed, so that nothing of that "side" should cleave to them. In all things He watched over Israel like a father over his children. WITH BITTER HERBS THEY SHALL EAT IT... NEITHER SHALL YE BREAK A BONE THEREOF. The bitter herbs signify the Shekinah's exile with Israel in all their bitter afflictions in Egypt. Why were the bones of the Passover lamb not allowed to be broken? So that the dogs might drag them about, and the Egyptians be thus made to realize the nothingness of that which they worshipped, and so be put to shame, and the Holy One be glorified. SANCTIFY UNTO ME ALL THE FIRSTBORN. The am haarez (ordinary man) requires redemption from the power of the evil impulse, which is his lord and master, as Jacob averred when he said: "Let my lord (Esau=evil) pass over before his servant" (Gen. XXXIII, 14). In this world the "evil impulse" is indeed the lord, because of the multitude of sins and evils which attack the body of man; as it has been truly said: "The righteous is judged by the good impulse, the sinner by the evil impulse, and the intermediate, he who is between these two extremes, is judged by both". Thus, he who is of the intermediate sort is a "brother,' to the good as well as to the evil impulse, as Esau, the evil one, said to Jacob: "My brother, keep that thou hast unto thyself" (Gen. XXXIII, 9) When, however, there is a preponderance of meritorious works, the spirit breaks down the two "night watches of asses and dogs" and he ascends to the morning watch wherein resides man, and becomes master of his animal nature. As for the intermediate person, a war is continually being waged between the principalities of justification and of condemnation to gain control of him; and when the side of condemnation sees that it cannot prevail against him, it tries to make him forget all his Torah, by transferring him into one of the seven regions of forgetfulness. For when a man is about to be born into the world the angel Gabriel wrestles with the dust of which man is formed, and inculcates into the potential man seventy languages, which, however, he retains not when he enters into this world, since the evil impulse wipes them out from his mind, so that the battle between the conflicting principles begins even before the man is born. Before all this, there are four angels which descend with him if he comes of pious stock. One of the four angels will be Michael, in remembrance of Abraham; one Gabriel, in remembrance of Isaac; one Nuriel, in remembrance of Jacob; and one Raphael, in remembrance of Adam; and the good impulse hovers over him. But if he himself is unworthy and possesses no heritage of righteousness to assist him, four powers of evil shall be his companions when he enters into this world, namely, Anger, Destruction, Depravity, and Wrath; and the evil impulse hovers over him to become his judge in the world to come. This explains the aforesaid saying, that, "the wicked is judged by the evil inclination, the righteous by the good, and the intermediate by good and evil mingled". In the case of the last-mentioned, Gabriel, who represents the good impulse,

Zohar: Shemoth, Raya Mehemna, Page 42a

and Samael, who represents the evil, become his judges. For every man who is compounded of the four elements is accompanied by four angels on his right hand and four on his left, those already named; and from the side of his body

Metatron presses close to him at the right and Samael at the left. Now all men are formed of the four elements, but on the order in which these elements are found-that is, the order of the planets with which each man is connected-depends the order of the angels who accompany him, and also the potential characteristics of the man. Thus, if his ruling planet be the Lion, Michael will lead, and be followed by Gabriel, and after him Raphael, and lastly Nuriel. If, however, his planet is the Ox, first comes Gabriel, then Michael, then Nuriel, then Raphael. If the Eagle be the planet by which he is influenced, Nuriel will be first, then Michael, followed first by Gabriel and then by Raphael. And should his planet be Man, then will Raphael lead, with Michael, Gabriel and Nuriel coming after in the order named. Now all aspects of Michael are of the attribute of mercy. A man whose leading angel is Michael will be benevolent, he will be pious and wise; but all this applies only if he is a student of the Torah, for if he is not so he will be the very reverse of all this, since he will be formed after the evil inclination; he will be stupid and unfeeling, without benevolence or worth-for no ignorant man can be truly pious. Should a man be from the side of Gabriel, his attributes will all partake chiefly of the quality of justice: he will stand up courageously against the wicked; he will prevail over his own evil inclinations, will abhor sin and cleave unto all things righteous, and he will become a judge by profession; but again, all this will only come to pass if he study the Torah with diligence and attain proficiency; should he neglect this, he will be as strong in iniquity as otherwise in holiness; he will rejoice in the tribulations of the righteous; he will be hard in his condemnations, bold in evildoing, with no fear of sin; he will have a red face, and will be of the type of Esau-a blood-shedder. He whose planet is the Eagle possesses neither the attribute of mercy nor that of justice in a marked degree, but is either moderately good or moderately bad, as his good or evil inclination obtains influence over him, as his countenance reveals, red and white being blended therein. He who is under the guidance of the planet Man combines in himself-in so far as he derives his characteristics from the good side-all the good qualities: he is wise and pious, strong in intellectual apprehension, sin-fearing, full of excellent virtues; and the colour of his countenance is dark. But if he is governed by the principle of evil, he will be full of bad qualities. Now if a man's evil actions predominate, all the (angelic) hosts of the good prompting will leave him and those of the evil prompting obtain control, and Samael will become completely master of him and ruler over all the members of his body-Samael and his whole band. On the other hand, should his good actions be plentiful, all his evil concomitants will be removed, and his good inclinations permeate his whole being, so that the powers of holiness may obtain entire sway over him and the holy name Tetragrammaton will rule over him. Should he by nature belong to the class of intermediaries, the heavenly hosts will be ranged at his right hand and on his left, the one side accusing and the other defending, and his ultimate salvation or destruction will depend on the relative strength of these conflicting celestial hosts, for whichever wins will claim him, be it for justice or for mercy. Therefore it has been said that man should always imagine that the fate of the whole world depends upon him. Now he who emanates from the side of Michael is called "firstborn". Michael's grade is white silver, and therefore the redemption of the firstborn is silver: five sel 'as, according to the numerical value of the letter he' in Abraham. Should such a man be successful in the study of the Torah, then a letter yod is added to him, which symbolizes holiness: for with the numerical value of yod-namely ten-the firstborn of cattle had to be redeemed. And when a man shall have reached this degree of holiness, then the words "Israel is holy to the Lord" (Jer. II, 3) can indeed be applied to him. Now all the supernal holy beings (hayoth) are called according to the letters of the Holy Name, as it is written, "Every one that is called by my name, I have created him for my glory, I have formed him, yea, I have made him" (Isa. XLIII, 7). And not only these celestial creatures themselves, but also all lesser creatures created through the instrumentality of these holy beings are stamped with this name in order that it may proclaim Him who created it. The Yod is the symbol of the head of all creatures—the two He's represent the five fingers of the right hand and the left; the Vau is the symbol of the body. Yet God says, "to whom then will ye liken me that I should be equal to him?" (Ibid. XL, 25), which means, "among all created things there is none that could be likened to Me even among the number of those whom I have created in the likeness of the signs of My Name; for I can efface the form and then create newly again and yet again, but there is no god above Me who could efface

Zohar: Shemoth, Raya Mehemna, Page 42b

My likeness". Should one ask: "Is it not written, Ye saw no manner of similitude?" the answer would be: "Truly we did behold him under a certain similitude, for is it not written, 'and the similitude of the Lord should he (Moses) behold, (Num. XII, 8)?' But only in the similitude which Moses beheld was the Lord revealed, not in any other similitude of any creature formed by His signs. Hence it is written: "To whom then will ye liken God? Or what likeness will ye compare unto him?" (Isa. XL, 18). Even that "similitude" was a likeness of the Holy One, blessed be He, not in His own place, for that cannot be penetrated, but in the aspect of the King when He shows forth His power to rule over the whole of His creation, appearing, therefore, to each of His creatures according to the capacity of each to comprehend Him, as it is written: "And through the prophets I am represented in similitudes" (Hos. XII, 11). And therefore He says: "Although I represent Myself to you in your own likeness, to whom will ye liken Me that I should be equal to him?" For in the beginning, before shape and form had been created, He was without form and similitude. Therefore it is forbidden to one who apprehends Him as He is before creation to picture Him under any form or shape whatsoever, not even by His letters He and Vau, nor by the whole of His Holy Name, nor by any letter or sign soever. The words, "For ye saw no manner of similitude" thus mean, "Ye saw nothing which could be represented by any form or shape, nothing which ye could present or simulate by any finite conception". But when He had created the form of supernal Man it was to Him as a chariot, and He descended on it, to be known according to the style "Tetragrammaton", in order that He might be known by His attributes and perceived in each attribute separately. For this reason He let Himself be called "El, Elohim, Shaddai, Zebaoth, and Tetragrammaton", each being a symbol to men of His various Divine attributes, that it may be made manifest that the world is sustained by mercy and by justice, according to the works of men. Had the brightness of the glory of the Holy One, blessed be His Name, not been shed over the whole of His creation, how could He have been perceived even by the wise? He would have remained unapprehendable, and the words "The whole earth is full of his glory" (Isa. VI, 3) could never be spoken with truth. But woe unto the man who should presume to compare the Lord with any attribute, even one which is His own, much less any human created form, "whose foundation is in the dust," (Job IV, 19), and whose products are frail creatures, soon vanishing, soon forgotten. The only conception of the Holy One, blessed be He, which man dare frame is of His sovereignty over some particular attribute or over creation as a whole. And if we perceive Him not under those manifestations, there is left neither attribute, nor similitude, nor form in Him; even as the sea, whose waters have neither form nor tangibility in themselves, but only when they are spread over a certain vessel which is the earth. On the basis of this fact we can calculate thus: The source of the sea is one. A current issues from it with a revolution which is Yod. The source is one and the current makes two. Next it makes a great basin, like a channel dug in the earth, which is filled by the waters which emanate from the source. It is this basin which we know as "Sea": this is the third factor involved. This large basin is split up into seven channels, which are like so many long tubes. Thus the waters are conveyed from the sea into these seven channels. The source, the current, the sea, and the seven channels form together the number ten. Should the master who constructed these tubes come to break them up, then the waters return to their source, and there remains nought but broken vessels, dry, without water. It is thus that the Cause of causes has brought forth the ten Sephiroth, and called the Crown the "Source", an inexhaustible fount of light, wherefore He designates Himself "En-sof", Limitless. He has neither shape nor form, and there is no vessel that could contain Him, no means to comprehend Him. It is in this sense that it has been said, "Search not the things that are too hard for thee, and seek not the thing which is hidden from thee" (Ben Sira, 320-324). Then He formed a vessel, small as the letter Yod, which is filled from Him, and He called it "Wisdom-gushing Fountain", and Himself in virtue of it "wise". Afterwards He made a large vessel and called it "Sea" and designated it "Understanding" (Binah) and Himself in virtue of it "understanding". He is both "wise" and "understanding" in His own essence: for Wisdom does not merit the title by itself, but only through Him who is wise and who has filled it from His "fountain"; and Understanding does not merit the title by itself, but only through Him who filled it from His own essence: if He were to depart from it it would be turned into aridity. In regard to this it is written, "As the waters fail from the sea, and the flood decayeth and drieth up" (Job XIV, 11). Finally, "He smites (the sea) into seven streams" (Isa. XI, 15), i.e. He diverts it into seven precious vessels, and calls them "Greatness", "Strength", "Beauty", "Victory", "Majesty", "Foundation", "Sovereignty"; and Himself He calls "great" in the "Greatness", "strong" in the "Strength", "beauteous" in "Beauty", "victorious" in "Victory"; in "Majesty" He calls His Name "the beauty of our Fashioner" and in "Foundation" "righteous" (cf. Prov. x, 25). In "Foundation" He sustains all things: all vessels and all worlds.

Zohar: Shemoth, Raya Mehemna, Page 43a

Finally, in "Sovereignty" He calls Himself "King", whose is "the greatness, the strength, the beauty, the victory, the majesty; for all that is in the heaven and in the earth is thine. Thine is the kingdom, O Lord, and thou art exalted as head above all" (I Chr. XXIX, 11). All things are in His power, whether He wills to lessen the number of vessels or to increase the light which springs from them, or whether He wills the contrary. Above Him, however, there is no god who could increase or lessen. Then He created ministering beings to those vessels: one throne supported on four columns and six steps to the throne: ten altogether. And the whole throne is like the chalice of benediction, in regard to which ten things are formulated, in harmony with the Torah which was given in Ten Words (Decalogue), and with the Ten Words by which the world was created. Then He prepared for the throne angelic hierarchies to serve Him: malachim (angels), erelim, seraphim, hayoth (living beings), ophanim, hamshalim, elim, elohim, be'ne (sons of) elohim, ishim (supernal "men"). To these He appointed as ministers Samael and all his groups-these are like clouds to ride upon when He descends to earth: they are like horses. That the clouds are called "chariots" is expressed in the words, "Behold the Lord rideth upon a swift cloud, and shall come into Egypt" (Isa. XIX, 1). Thus the Egyptians saw their Chieftain like a horse bearing the chariot of the Holy One, and straightway "the idols of Egypt were moved at His presence, and the heart of Egypt melted in the midst of it" (Ibid.), i.e. they were "moved" from their "faith" in their own Chieftain. AND EVERY FIRSTLING OF AN ASS THOU SHALT REDEEM WITH A LAMB, AND IF THOU WILT NOT REDEEM IT... THOU SHALT BREAK HIS NECK. The ass and the lamb symbolize the evil and the good inclinations. The very evil can be turned into good by repentance: the "ass" must be redeemed by a "lamb". In other words, even if a man is an "ass", a spiritual ignoramus, he can be redeemed from the exile of darkness and be included in the redemption of Israel, "the scattered sheep" (Jer. L, 17). But if he does not repent, "thou shalt break his neck", meaning, he belongs to the stiff necked ones who will be blotted out from the Book of Life, for concerning such unrepentant sinners it is written: "Whosoever hath sinned against me, him will I blot out of my book" (Ex. XXII, 33). AND IT SHALL BE FOR A TOKEN UPON THINE HAND AND FOR FRONTLETS BETWEEN THINE EYES. This commandment has also another significance besides being a Divine ordinance, for the phylacteries are signs and means of sanctification, symbols of the beauty of the supernal colours. It is written: "And thou shalt do that what is right and good." "Right" here indicates the phylactery of the hand, which has to be supplemented by and joined with the phylactery of the forehead. The four Biblical sections (Ex. XIII, 1-10, 11-16; Deut. VI, 4-9, XI, 13-21) are in the head-phylactery in four compartments, but in the hand-phylactery in one, for the latter has nothing of itself but what it receives from above (the head). This mystery is expressed in the words, "all rivers run into the sea" (Eccl. 1, 7). And because it draws the influx of Divine light from that which is above, it is called tephillah (entreaty, prayer, the traditional name for phylactery); and because it derives holiness, it is called kedushah, and it also symbolizes "Sovereignty", "Kingdom", the Kingdom of God in its completeness. The symbolism of the four sections has been explained in various places. The first of them (Ex. XIII, 1-10)

Zohar: Shemoth, Raya Mehemna, Page 43b

is of supreme significance, containing all the four divisions of the supernal light which emanates from Ain (lit. "nothing", the hidden, unapproachable, transcendent). Each word in the verse, "sanctify unto Me all the firstborn" stands for something connected with the Divine attributes: "sanctify" is related to the hidden region of supernal Holiness, the mystery of the Wisdom which comes from above; "unto Me" refers to Binah-Understanding, the Mystery of the supernal world, the inner Hall-as it is written, "unto Me are the children of Israel slaves"; "unto Me belongs every firstborn"; "ye shall be unto Me a precious people"-all these are connected with Binah. "All" signifies Grace: grace above and grace below; "firstborn" has a symbolic reference to "Israel my firstborn" (Ex. IV, 22), who represents all the sides and all the colours. These four words, esoterically considered, contain all the truths which are given in greater detail in the four Scripture sections written on the parchment scrolls of the phylacteries. Thus the first section is a summary of all the four. The second section (Ex. XIII, 11-16), referring, as it does, to the Exodus from Egypt, symbolizes the freedom of the "Jubilee", and represents Binah. The third section, the Shema, contains the mystery of the right side, called "The Supernal Grace", for it effects the union of all things extending unto the four quarters of the universe; and the Holy One, blessed be He, through the medium of this attribute, brings forth order and harmony in the whole universe, a harmony which extends even to the lowest depths. By this attribute of Grace the Holy One created the world, when He wrapped Himself in the garment of light. This Supernal Grace is the Unifier. For this reason the section of the Shema is joined to that of "And it shall be"; for the act which makes each day a unity and likewise forms the whole sum of separate days into the perfect whole, is the fact of following the Divine Will in knowledge and action; and through this act alone (of concentration on the union during prayer and the recitation of the Shema) can that union of which we have frequently spoken be attained: that is, the union of each day, the union which is expressed in the sentence: "Hear, O Israel, Tetragrammaton Elohenu Tetragrammaton is one". These three are one. How can the three Names be one? Only through the perception of Faith: in the vision of the Holy Spirit, in the beholding of the hidden eyes alone. The mystery of the audible voice is similar to this, for though it is one yet it consists of three elements-fire, air, and water, which have, however, become one in the mystery of the voice. Even so it is with the mystery of the threefold Divine manifestations designated by Tetragrammaton Elohenu Tetragrammaton -three modes which yet form one unity. This is the significance of the voice which man produces in the act of unification, when his intent is to unify all from the En-sof to the end of creation. This is the daily unification, the secret of which has been revealed in the holy spirit. There are many kinds of unification, and all are appropriate, one involving the other, but the one which is effected on earth by the symbolism of the voice is the most appropriate.

The fourth section (Deut. XI, 13-21) contains the mystery of rigorous Judgement: "Take heed to yourselves that your heart be not deceived" (v. 16). We have already dealt with the symbolism of the relationship of the two phylacteries to one another. The strap that is passed through the head-phylactery ends at the back of the head in a knot representing the letter Daleth (D. in Shaddai), and concerning it it is written: "And thou shalt see My hinder-parts", for all is tied up there in one knot. The strap that is passed through the hand-phylactery is fastened in a knot in the shape of the letter Yod, the sign of the mystery of the holy covenant, to which we have frequently referred. It is all a part of one mystery. Blessed are the Israelites for being made aware of this mystery. It is essential that every man should put on the phylacteries daily, in order that he may achieve the likeness of the supernal Prototype, and then "all the people of the earth shall see that thou art called by the name of the Lord, and they shall be afraid of thee" (Deut. XXVIII, 10).

Zohar: Shemoth, Raya Mehemna, Page 59b

THE PLACE WHICH THOU HAST MADE FOR THY DWELLING-PLACE, LORD, FOR THE SANCTUARY, LORD, WHICH THY HANDS PREPARED.

[Tr. note: This passage, down to "ordinary field", is from the Ray'a Mehemna.] This implies the necessity of building a sanctuary below, corresponding to the Sanctuary above, wherein the Holy One is daily served and worshipped. Now prayer itself has the character of service, and is called so. A synagogue should be a handsome structure, beautifully decorated, for it is an earthly copy of a heavenly prototype. The Temple below had its counterpart in the Temple above, and everything there, holy vessels and holy ministers, corresponded to something above. The same was true of the Tabernacle which Moses erected in the desert. And a synagogue must have the same object: it must be a true house of prayer. A sanctuary must have windows, as Daniel had in his upper chamber where he prayed (Dan. VI, 11) corresponding to the "windows" in heaven, as it is written: "My beloved... he looketh forth at the windows, showing himself through the lattice" (S.S. II, 9). We might think that it is more proper to pray in the open air in order to allow the spirit a free ascent. This, however, is not so! There must be a house to correspond to the "House" above. Besides, prayer and the spirit must issue forth from a narrow, limited space, in a straight line towards Jerusalem,

Zohar: Shemoth, Raya Mehemna, Page 60a

without deviating right or left. This is symbolized by the sound of the Shophar, which is thrust forth in a straight line from a narrow opening and breaks through the firmaments in order to stir up the Spirit above. It is true, we are told, that "Isaac did meditate in the field" (Gen. XXIV, 63); but there are special reasons for this; and besides, the field where he prayed was not an ordinary field.

Zohar: Shemoth, Raya Mehemna, Page 91b, 92a-b, 93a, 114a-b, 115a-b, 116a-b, 117a-b, 118a-b, 119a-b, 120a-b
[Note: The Hebrew text is not translated as explained in the Translator's note on page 157b of the main Zohar text, section 2.]
Zohar: Shemoth, Raya Mehemna, Page 121a
Zohar: Shemoth, Raya Mehemna, Page 134b [Note: The Hebrew text for this page is apparently not translated.]
Zohar: Shemoth, Raya Mehemna, Page 157b, 158a-b, 159a
[Note: The Hebrew text is not translated as explained in the Translator's note on page 157b of the main Zohar text, section 2.]
Zohar: Shemoth, Raya Mehemna, Page 187b [Note: The Hebrew text for this page is apparently not translated.]
Zohar: Shemoth, Raya Mehemna, Page 188a [Note: The Hebrew text for this page is apparently not translated.]

Zohar Appendix I

ON THE ZOHARIC EXPOSITION OF THE FIRST CHAPTER OF GENESIS

From page 15a onwards the Zohar consists mainly of a verse-by-verse exposition of the Pentateuch of the type known in Hebrew literature as Midrash. The discursive style of the work, and the amount of extraneous matter which has been intercalated in the original text, render this fact liable to be overlooked; and it has therefore been one of the objects of the translation to keep it clearly before the reader's eye.

The Zoharic expositions of the Scripture are frequently, if not usually, difficult to follow, on account partly of their far-fetched character, partly of their technical language, partly of the abrupt and even uncouth manner in which they are expressed. The point which the Zohar desires to make is often highly elusive, and not to be grasped without close and attentive scrutiny. Particularly can we apply this remark to the expositions of the first chapter of Genesis contained in pages 15a-22a and 29a-31a of the original text. On these passages there rests a special and exceptional obscurity which, it is to be feared, the translation has done little to dispel. It seems, therefore, advisable to add some observations setting forth the views by which the translators have sought to guide themselves through the intricacies of these pages, and which have determined their version of many obscure passages. An endeavour to understand these pages is all the more necessary as we may surmise a priori that they contain some of the most important teaching of the Zohar; and we do indeed find on examination that they are capable of yielding light on two of the most fundamental tenets of the Zohar- the distinction of the divine grades and the potency of the sacred Name, and so of providing the key to the whole of its esoteric doctrine.

One of the most characteristic ideas of the Zohar is that God, while essentially one, is yet found in various grades or degrees. These 'grades' turn out on examination to be degrees of creative power, arranged in descending or ascending order according to the sphere in which each one functions and the stage of development which it postulates in the created universe, and which thus constitutes, so to speak, its 'opposite number'. Thus the highest grade corresponds to sheer nothingness, and the lowest grade to the conscious soul of man (the neshamah). The creative power in itself is conceived as 'thought', which in the process of creation becomes 'light' or 'illumination'. The primal light is utterly beyond human (or even angelic) comprehension. But as the grades descend, the 'lights' (which form, as it were, a vestment to one another) swim into human ken, until between the lowest grade and the conscious soul of man a close communion is established.

The main purpose of the Zoharic exposition of the first chapter of Genesis, in so far as it is contained in the pages mentioned, seems to be to derive this doctrine from (or read it into) the text of the Scripture. The way in which the Scripture is made to yield the desired meaning is more or less as follows.

The first grade. the 'Most Mysterious and Recondite', indistinguishable from the En-Sof (limitless, uncharacterisable), and corresponding to absolute nothingness in the work of creation-is not directly mentioned in the Scripture, unless it is alluded to by the letter beth (=in) of the word bereshith, implying that it went, so to speak, into itself, and so made a start. This start consists in a 'flash' (zohar), which thus releases the creative powers of the 'limitless'.

From this 'inwardness" resulted a point or focus capable of infinite development and expansion; this is called in the Scripture Reshith (beginning), and it is identified by the Zohar with Hokmah (Wisdom), the architect of the creation. This is the second grade.

The next word, 'created', according to the Zohar, denotes in this place the expansion of Reshith, which produced a 'palace' or 'house' containing in itself the germ of creation. This place is called in the Scripture Elohim, and it constitutes the third grade, the artificer of the creation. By the

Zohar it is called more specifically Elohim Hayyim (living God), the word Elohim being a generic name for all the grades. Its creative powers or faculties are pictured as 'letters' or 'seed', and are divided into an active and a passive principle. The active principle is called in the Scripture 'heaven', and is identified by the Zohar with the 'Voice'. The passive principle is called in the Scripture 'earth', and in v. 2 it is identified with the primordial elements of the terrestrial, the celestial, and the spiritual worlds (v, page 39b).

Up to this point there has been no clear differentiation between creator and created: the creation has not yet emerged from the realm of potentiality. From this point, however, the two are distinguished, the creator using and the created obeying the Voice. This is indicated in the Scriptural words, 'And God said'. The Voice henceforth issues in a series of maamaroth (creative utterances) which shape the material universe, or, in the language of the Zohar, 'imprint and inscribe letters'. With the new developments of the creation there issue new grades of the Godhead, which are called by the Scripture 'days' (v, page 39b).

The first maamar, according to the Zohar, produced light in three grades, one called light, the second firmament, and the third darkness. The first seems to be regarded as the light of mind, the second as that of light proper, and the third as that of fire. The first is called by the Zohar right, the second centre, and the third left. The first vanished as soon as it appeared, so that the second became the right. This is apparently derived from the verse: 'And God saw the light (i.e. the centre) that it was good, and God divided between the light (i.e. the right) and the darkness.' The centre was thereupon given continued existence in a category of time called day, and the darkness in a category of time called night. To produce these is the function of the next grade, called in the Scripture 'one day', and by the Zohar Right, or sometimes Hesed (Kindness).

In some way not specified in the Zohar, the 'light' and the 'darkness' of the first day became 'upper waters' containing, in solution as it were, 'lower waters'. The second maamar created an instrument for separating or liberating the lower waters from the upper. This instrument is called 'firmament' or 'expansion' (a different firmament from that mentioned in connection with the first day). The upper waters are characterised after separation as 'male', and the lower as 'female'. To effect this separation is the function of the next grade, called in Scripture 'third day', and by the Zohar Left or Geburah (Force).

The next maamar gave a certain flow or direction to the upper and lower waters, so that they should meet in ' one plaee' in a kind of sexual union, the result of which is to enable the 'earth' or 'dry land' to appear. This means that, as a result of the meeting of the upper and lower waters, the existence of the earth is rendered possible. To confirm this possibility a new maamar produced the 'Throne of Glory' with its attendant angels, figuratively referred to in the Scripture as 'the earth putting forth verdure and fruit tree' (pages 18a, 19b). To effect the union between the waters and to guide the 'Throne of Glory' is the function of the grade called in the Scripture 'third day', and by the Zohar He 'Olmin (Life of Worlds).

The next maamar produced a 'membrane for the brain' in the shape of a lower firmament containing heavenly luminaries which reflected the upper light, and served as a kind of screen to the 'Throne of Glory'. These luminaries are, properly speaking, not those which are visible to the human eye, but sentient beings which stand to these in the same relation as the human soul to the body. The chief of them are the sun and the moon, which were originally equal in status. They are charged 'to give light upon the earth', i.e. to determine the forms and characters of all beings on the earth. To procure for these luminaries their light and energy is the function of the grade called in Scripture 'fourth day'.

Having pursued the development of the grades up to this point, the Zohar, on page 22a, goes off on to quite a different tack, nor does it anywhere complete the exposition of the first chapter of Genesis on these lines. In later passages, however, we find frequent references to a grade called Zaddik Yesod 'Olam (the Righteous One, the Foundation of the World), which upholds God's covenant with the earth and procures sustenance for the living beings upon it. As it is also called 'ninth', we may without hesitation identify it with the 'sixth day' of the Scripture.

On page 29a the Zohar reverts to the beginning of the first chapter in order to define the position of what it calls the 'Female'. If this part of the Zohar is to be brought into harmony with the preceding part, then this 'Female' can only be the tenth grade, corresponding to the 'seventh day' in the Biblical account. The function of the 'Female', according to the Zohar, is to reproduce in a new medium the work of the original creative force. This medium is called 'the lower heaven and earth', and the work itself 'the lower world'. What exactly is meant by these terms is not specified, but we may surmise that in reality the medium of the 'Female' is the human consciousness, and the 'lower world' stands to the 'upper world' in this connection in the relation of phenomenon to noumenon; or, in Kantian language, that the 'upper world' is the Ding an sich and the 'lower world' the human idea of it.

The development of the grades, according to the Zohar, corresponds not only to the development of the created universe, but also to the emergence of a certain name, which is their unifying element. It is a postulate of the Zohar that the Biblical name Tetragrammaton-the so-called tetragrammaton-has an intimate, if unspecified, connection with the primordial Thought. It is the chosen instrument for rendering the Thought intelligible or realisable to the human mind. It is regarded as having been 'in' the Thought from the first, and its emergence into external or objective existence is stated to have been one of the purposes of the creation (page 29a). According to the Zohar, it emerged in various stages, each of which is symbolised by one or more of its constituent letters and is associated with the emergence of one or other of the grades. Thus with the grade Reshith emerged the letter Yod; with the next grade, Elohim Hayyim, the letter He, called the first or upper He; with the heavens, the letter Vau; with the earth, the second, or lower He; with the first day the combination of the letters Yod, He; with the second day, the combination of the letters Vau, He; while with the third day all the four letters were combined. The resultant Name is the absolute One or unit of being, representing on the one side the first integration of the Thought, and on the other the ultimate discoverable cause of existence (v, page 18b).

The above explanation, while leaving much obscure, will perhaps suffice to give a general idea of what the Zohar has in mind in this exposition of the first chapter of Genesis, to bring the whole, as it were, into focus, and exhibit the purpose which runs through it. It remains to complete the picture of the grades by bringing them into connection with the Sefiroth of the Cabbalah and with the names of the Deity used in the Scripture.

It is worthy of note that the Zohar rarely uses either the term Sefirah or the names of the Sefiroth current in the Cabbalistic literature. Where these names do occur, it is usually in passages which on other grounds may be suspected of belonging properly not to the Zohar but to one or other of the allied works (e.g, page 21b). Nevertheless, there is an exact correspondence between the Zoharic grades and the Cabbalistic Sefiroth, and they could be interchanged with one another (as indeed they are by most of the Zoharic commentators) without causing any confusion. Similarly there is, according to the Zohar, a correspondence between the designations of the grades found in the first chapter of Genesis and the names of the Deity scattered throughout the Scripture. This fourfold correspondence may be conveniently exhibited in the form of a table giving (a) the designation of each grade in the first chapter of Genesis; (b) the special Zoharic names of each grade; (c) the corresponding name of the Deity in the Scripture; (d) the corresponding Sefirah.

TABLE SHOWING THE CORRESPONDENCE OF THE GRADES WITH THE SEFIROTH, ETC.

Designation in Genesis 1 B' (In)	Zoharic Appellatives Most Mysterious and Recondite; King	Names of Deity Ehyeh	Sefiroth Kether (Crown)
Reshith (Beginning)	First Point; Wisdom; Father	Asher (or Asher Ehyeh)	Hokmah (Wisdom)
Elohim (God) (Heaven and Earth)	Palace; Elohim Hayyim; Mother	Tetragrammaton	Binah (Understanding)
One Day	Right; Kindness	El Gadol	'Hesed (Kindness)
Second Day	Left; Force	Elohim	Geburah (Force)
Third Day	Life of Worlds; Central Column	Tetragrammaton	Tifereth (Beauty)
Fourth Day		Zebaoth (?)	Nezah (Victory)
Fifth Day		Shaddai (?)	Hod (Majesty)
Sixth Day	Righteous One; Foundation of the World	El (?)	Yesod (Foundation)
Seventh Day	Female	Adonay	Malkuth (Kingship)

Zohar Appendix II

THE COSMIC SCHEME OF THE ZOHAR

In the terminology of the Zohar, a prominent part is played by three pairs of correlative terms which, taken from the language of ordinary life, are frequently used by it with an esoteric significance. These pairs are male and female; (b) right and left; and (c) upper and lower. These terms are worthy of special consideration, because they embody, more than any others, the cosmology of the Zohar, and so lie at the root of its philosophy and ethics; and what is more, a proper understanding of them will be found to afford a clue to some of the most puzzling symbolism of the Zohar.

Male and Female. These terms are applied by the Zohar in a mystic sense to certain generative pairs-the one member imparting and the other receiving-the union of which is holy. The first of such pairs are the two primordial grades of the Godhead indicated in the first verse of Genesis by the words Reshith and Elohim, and commonly designated by the Zohar Father and Mother, and by the Cabbala Wisdom (Hokmah) and Understanding (Binah). The Father imparts to the Mother the plan or design of creation, and the product is the creative instrument, the Voice. The Voice, again, indicated, according to the Zohar, by the word 'heavens' in the first verse of Genesis, combines with the inchoate material called 'earth', as male with female, to produce the six days of Creation. A little lower in the scale, a male and female pair is constituted by the 'upper waters' and 'lower waters', which produce the vegetative power of the earth. The chain of holiness is completed in the union of the first human pair.

The terms male and female are further applied to the 'upper' and 'lower' worlds in a sense which will be considered later.

Right and Left. The terms 'right' and 'left' are used by the Zohar, first of the twin qualities of the Godhead, Kindness and Rigour, and then of the instruments by means of which these qualities are exercised. This distinction assumes in the Zohar many ramifications which will be best understood if we trace it to its basis in the Biblical text, as follows.

The second verse of Genesis, according to the Zohar, describes what might be called the first approaches to one another of heaven and earth, which produced not actual 'being', but a kind of 'being-about-to-be'. The earth in this stage is said to have been of two qualities: (a) 'formless' (tohu), and (b) 'inchoate' (bohu). Correspondingly, the heaven was of two qualities: (a) 'darkness on the face of the deep' (t'hom, identified by the Zohar with tohu), and (b) 'the spirit of God moving over the face of the waters' (identified by the Zohar with bohu).

Thus the material of creation was of two qualities, and correspondingly the product was of two qualities. From the 'spirit of God hovering over the waters' issued light, characterized as 'good', and forming the content of the first day under the aegis of the divine attribute of Hesed (kindness, or mercy). From the 'darkness on the face of the deep' issued the firmament, not characterized as good, and forming the content of the second day under the aegis of the divine attribute of Geburah (force, or rigour). Though luminous in itself, the firmament is dark by the side of the primordial light. And the fact that the formula 'God saw that it was good' is omitted from the account of the second day may be taken as a sign that the work of that day was not devoid of evil.

The whole of this exposition is not found in the Zohar as we have it, but it fits in with the general scheme of the Zohar, and it does at least explain why, in the Zohar, evil and darkness are so often associated with the grade of the second day, and why that grade is always supposed to be in latent if not open conflict with the grade of the first day. Certain it is that we have a constant contrast between Hesed, light, good, on the one side, and Geburah, darkness, evil, on the other. Why these two sides are called respectively right and left is not explicitly stated in the Zohar. We may find a reason in the Biblical verse: 'O that his left hand were under my head and his right hand were embracing me' (S. S. II, 6), which in various places in the Zohar is applied to the relations of the grades Hesed and Geburah to the Shekinah.

(c). Upper and Lower. The terms 'upper' and 'lower' are frequently used in a more or less popular sense in the Zohar, to indicate the distinction between heaven and earth, between God and angels, between angels and men, between the future world and this world, and so forth. More specially, the term 'upper' is sometimes applied to the three primary grades of the Godhead to distinguish them from the seven secondary grades. There is, however, a further highly characteristic use of the terms which demands more particular consideration.

The Zohar, as has been explained in the Appendix to Vol. I, draws a distinction between the seventh of the secondary grades and the preceding six, corresponding to the distinction drawn in the first chapter of Genesis between the seventh day and the preceding six. The essence of this distinction, according to the Zohar, is that the six grades are active creative or controlling forces, whereas the seventh is by comparison passive, merely reflecting the work of the others. It is what might be called the self-consciousness or introspective faculty of the Godhead. It thus stands to the others in the relation of the moon to the sun, and is therefore frequently designated 'moon' without more ado. It is also regarded as 'female' in relation to the other grades, which thus become 'male'. The world reflected in this 'moon', which is also the Shekinah, is 'lower' in relation to the actual, real world of the other six grades. But it is of this reflected world that the soul (neshamah) of man forms a part, or at any rate an emanation; and hence the extraordinary importance which is attached to it in the Zohar. The 'upper world', though complete in itself, is regarded as lacking its final consummation without the lower (a hint of this is found by the Zohar in the letter beth with which Genesis commences), and hence the relation between the two worlds is often pictured by the Zohar in language of eroticism based on the Song of Songs.

Zohar Appendix III

The Divine Nomenclature of The Zohar

The reader of the Zohar, whether in the original or a translation, hardly needs to be told that with the mere understanding of the words he can in a great many passages by no means be sure of having penetrated to the sense. The Zohar has a way of using ordinary terms, including well-known proper names, in a sense peculiar to itself, often, too, when the reader, if not on his guard, might not suspect this; it deals largely in allegories of a very far-fetched and intricate character; and therefore a great part of it cannot be understood without some kind of a key. The appendices and glossaries in the first two volumes aimed only at giving such help as would make the main outlines of the Zohar intelligible. Now that the whole work of the translation has been completed, it seems proper to endeavour to provide a more effective clue to its mysteries.

Now, if there is one feature more than another which distinguishes the Zohar, it is the great variety of expressions which it uses to designate God and the divine essence in general. Not merely does it divide the Godhead into grades, but it has a number of names for each grade, besides other names which, strictly speaking, lie outside of the ideology of the grades. For the proper understanding of the Zohar nothing is more essential than the accurate distinguishing of these names; and an Appendix dealing with this matter in a systematic fashion will probably be found the most succinct means of providing a key, if not to the whole, at any rate to a great part of the Zohar, while it will incidentally afford occasion for a critique within limits of the theology of the Zohar, which is the aspect of it most likely to be of interest to the modern reader.

The Three Approaches to God

An attentive study of the Zohar from this point of view reveals in it a complexity of a peculiar kind. It exhibits three distinct approaches to the God idea springing from distinct psychological needs and ministering to distinct religious requirements, yet all based upon the study of the Hebrew Scriptures and all consonant with Jewish faith and practice. The object of the Zohar in this field may in all cases be said to be the bringing of the individual Jew into communion with God. This, however, may be effected in three ways, according as the appeal is made to his sentiment of prayer and devotion, to his ethical impulse, or to his philosophical spirit. The Zohar recognizes-or postulates-that the individual may be materially assisted in this endeavour by being provided with suitable designations under which to represent to himself the Deity. It further recognizes the need of harmonizing these representations and showing how their diversity is consistent with the essential unity of God; and for this purpose further sets of designations are brought into play. Thus we find in the Zohar on the one hand three designations-or rather, sets of designations, for each has an alternative-which constitute what may be called the standard names of God, according as communion is sought by means of any one of the three approaches mentioned above; and on the other hand, a number of other designations grouped round these and serving to correlate them, and bring them, so to speak, into one frame. We may now proceed to specify these designations and the various aspects of the divine essence to which they are applied.

To designate God as the recipient of the Israelite's prayers and the object of his devotions, the Zohar commonly uses a term which the reader would not immediately suspect to have a divine significance, namely 'Community of Israel'. This term corresponds to what present-day writers call the 'national' or 'tribal' or 'particularist' God of Israel. Belief in such a God is based purely on historical grounds, especially on the election of the patriarchs. God as the 'Community of Israel' is the protector and guardian of the people of Israel in this world. In this capacity God is not only personal, but also localized. He is with the children of Israel wherever they are, whether in their own land or in exile. This union was first effected at Mount Sinai; it was consummated by the building of the Temple, and was not broken even by the destruction of the Temple. But since that event God's protection of Israel is naturally much less efficacious. It will however, be restored to its former vigour in time to come, on the advent of the Messiah, which is frequently predicted in the Zohar with great circumstantiality.

If we ask, how does God manifest His presence in Israel, the answer is, through the Divine Light, the Shekinah. This light is the connecting link between the divine and the non-divine. For, according to the Zohar, God, the protector of Israel, is borne along by four Hayyoth or Holy Beasts, constituting His throne, and these are borne on other angelic beings, which again rest on higher firmaments, under which is the lowest heaven, to which belongs the earth and all its creatures. [Tr. note: It will be noticed that this hierarchy corresponds closely to the four 'worlds' of the Cabbalists-of Emanation, Creation, Formation and Completion. In the Zohar itself the worlds of Aziluth and Beriah are mentioned only occasionally, the others hardly at all.] Through this hierarchy an emanation of the Divine Presence is conveyed to earth, just as, on the other hand, the prayer of human beings is conveyed up to heaven. The Shekinah originally rested on the Tabernacle and Temple, but even now it accompanies the wise, especially when three study together.

The 'throne of God', consisting of the Hayyoth, is the instrument of God's providence on earth. For the Hayyoth are pictured as having each a human face, but with the aspect respectively of a man, a lion, an ox and an eagle. According, therefore, to the aspect through which he is looked upon from on high will be the providential care which a man receives here on earth. Here, too, intermediate beings come into play, and round this conception of the Godhead revolves most of the angelology of the Zohar. All this constitutes the more popular portion of the Zohar. Its Biblical basis is to be found in the first chapter of Ezekiel. It is essentially imaginative in character, and its main purpose is to afford consolation and encouragement to Israel in exile by assuring them that God's protection is still with them, as evidenced by the fact that the name 'Community of Israel' has both a human and a divine application.

As the promoter of man's moral strivings, God is usually termed in the Zohar 'The Holy One, blessed be He'. In this capacity God is regarded as the source of animate life, as the creator of species, as the vitalizing force in the universe. Man knows of God in this aspect through his own neshamah, the consciousness-based primarily on his neshimah (breathing power)-of his own individuality, the super-soul, the deeper self which transcends his ruah (spirit, intellectual faculties), and nefesh (physical vitality'). Through his neshamah man is capable of direct communion with the Holy One, blessed be He, and also of ethical and moral perfection or the reverse. The Israelites possess in the precepts of their Torah the instrument for achieving this perfection, and in proportion as they do so or fail to do so, their neshamah is rewarded or punished after their death. The place of reward is called the Garden of Eden, of punishment, Gehinnom. As the dispenser of reward and punishment after death, God is called the 'Holy King'. Another name given to God from this point of view is the 'Tree of Life', in the branches of which the souls of the righteous are figured as resting. Hence, when an Israelite carries out the Torah, he is said to be cleaving to the Tree of Life. Round this conception of God as the Holy One, blessed be He, revolves the whole Zoharic doctrine of the moral life, of reward and punishment, of heaven and hell and their respective denizens, and of the incarnation and transmigration of souls. This part of the Zohar is predominantly emotional in tone, and the God-idea which it embodies may be said to be based on an effort of introspection, or on what in German philosophical language would be called a Lebensanschauung. Its Scriptural basis is the second chapter of Genesis.

The Zohar is not content to base the religious life merely on the emotional side of man's nature. It seeks an approach to God, not only introspectively, from the starting-point of a Lebensanschauung, but also extraspectively, from the starting-point of a Weltanschavung. The designation given to God for this purpose is 'Ancient Holy One'. This name designates God regarded as the First Cause of all existence and all movement. God m this aspect is purely impersonal, a fact somewhat veiled by the designation and of which the writers of the Zohar seem frequently to lose sight. It is, however, clearly brought out in another expression frequently used to describe God in this aspect, viz. 'That Hidden and Undisclosed' (or equivalent terms). It is a postulate of the Zohar that this First Cause is a kind of algebraical x, which for the sake of intellectual satisfaction must be sought for, but which can never be found. This attitude is summed up in the Zoharic interpretation of the Biblical text, 'See who created these' (Isa. XL, 26). The aspect of 'these'-the perceptible universe-points to the existence of a First Cause, but on inquiring into it we can get no further than the interrogation 'Who?' since the pursuit of an ultimate cause can be carried on to 'en sof ', without limit. In order, therefore, to find a beginning we posit an 'Ancient One' who differs from the 'Ancient Holy One' in being not absolutely absolute, so to speak, but containing the possibility of producing or becoming the non-absolute.

As the precepts of the Torah furnish man with the complete guide to the life of righteousness and moral improvement, so the first chapter of Genesis furnishes the complete guide to the quest of the Absolute. When pursued under such guidance, this quest is called hokhmah, wisdom, and constitutes the highest form of human activity, the mark of perfection in man. Naturally, in the eyes of the Zohar this quest is fundamentally a theological rather than a metaphysical activity, since the First Cause is ex hypothesi regarded as God, and has by some means or other to be identified not only with the personal God who enjoins the moral life, but also with the localized God who dwells among and protects the people of Israel. Hokhmah forms a link between man and the First Cause because hokhmah also governs the relation of cause and effect throughout the universe. And as the divine hokhmah determines the consequences to the soul of human conduct, so the human hokhmah embraces of necessity the moral life. Thus there can, in the system of the Zohar, be no conflict between philosophy and the moral law.

The Correlation of The Three Approaches

From what has been said above, it will be seen that it is possible to distinguish three strata in the Zohar regarded as a theological work, which we may designate the devotional, the ethical, and the philosophical, and which address themselves primarily to the imagination, the emotions, and the intellect respectively. Each of these strata is, so to speak, dominated by its own designation for the Deity, representing God under a distinct aspect-in the one case as both personal and local, in the second as personal but not local, in the third as neither personal nor local. But the Zohar is not content to leave these aspects side by side, like the Scottish clergyman who commenced a prayer with the words, 'O Thou who art our eternal hope and ultimate hypothesis'. A great part of it-perhaps the most important-is taken up with an endeavour to correlate them by expressing each in the terms of the others. This involves a wide extension of the designations of God, which we have now to consider.

We have seen above that the providential care of Israel in this world is exercised, according to the Zohar, by God qua 'Community of Israel', while the recompensing of souls in the other world is carried out by God qua 'the Holy King'. Now, these two activities are pictured by the Zohar as being the same relation to each other as the management of the royal household to the management of the affairs of State. If the latter is assigned to the King, naturally the former is assigned to the Queen. Hence the Community of Israel is brought into relation with the Holy King by being designated the Matrona, or Queen, and they are pictured as consorting together in ziwwug, or wedlock. The pious are fancifully pictured as, by means of their prayers and studies, preparing the Matrona for the union, and partaking in Her joy. Apparently this is possible even at the present time -a doctrine which it is not altogether easy to reconcile with the statement frequently made in the Zohar, that since the destruction of the Temple there has been 'separation' between the King and the Matrona.

Another way of bringing these two aspects into relationship is to picture the Community of Israel as the moon reflecting the light of the Holy One, blessed be He, who is the sun. Strictly speaking, we should compare them as sun light and moon light, and the moon, the opaque reflecting body, is formed by the souls of the righteous. God's activity in sending souls down to this world and resuscitating them in the next is like the light of the sun. But His providential care of Israel in this world, superadded to His care for their souls, is like the light of the moon, which is the light of the sun conveyed to a place to which it does not properly belong. And just as the moon is not always equally bright, so the Community of Israel is not always equally beneficent. It is the wicked who 'impair' the Moon, causing the Sun's light to be withdrawn from it, while the righteous restore it to fulness. In this way, then, King and Queen, and Sun and Moon are all designations in the Zohar of various aspects of the Godhead.

The question now arises, how does the Zohar unify the First Cause with the Holy One, blessed be He, and the Community of Israel? The answer is, through the doctrine of the grades (v. Appendix to Vol. 1). This is in essence the same as what is usually called by the Cabbalists the doctrine of the Sefiroth, but it is enunciated in the Zohar in a manner specially adapted for the purpose it has in view and with its own peculiar theological terminology.

When the Zohar speaks of 'grades', there is no question that ordinarily it means grades of the Godhead, and specifically of the Godhead regarded as First Cause. Seeing that it enumerates ten such grades, it in effect posits ten First Causes. This is apparently a contradiction in terms, and it must be admitted that the Zohar, while positing that the ten grades are in essence one, does habitually speak of them as if they were distinct entities capable of forming all sorts of relations with one another. The favourite method adopted by the Zohar for expressing their unity in diversity, or vice versa, is by picturing them as members of a human body or features of a human head; this method is elaborated in the 'Book of Concealed Wisdom' and in the two Idras. This, however, affords no satisfactory answer to our problem; for while it would be permissible, if we had some rational explanation, to illustrate it by the figure of the human frame, it is surely somewhat 'preposterous' (in the literal sense of the term) to seize on the figure of the human frame first and leave its precise application to be filled in afterwards.

Another explanation which is only adumbrated in the Zohar, but which is found more clearly expressed in other parts of the Cabbalistic literature, and has been adopted by Cordoveiro in his Pardes Rimmonim, is as follows. The First Cause is compared to a luminary shining on to a reflecting glass which in turn throws its light on to another from which it is cast on to a third, and so on through nine reflecting glasses (or it may be ten, for there is a difference of opinion as to whether the original light is reckoned among the ten or not). In this way there are ten lights of various grades of intensity which are yet all the same light. This figure explains the fact that there can be a gradation in the extent to which the human mind comprehends the First Cause. But it fails to explain the objective division of the First Cause into ten, which is certainly posited in the Cabbala, because it does not provide us with anything to which we can attach the figure of the reflecting glasses.

It would be possible to find such a basis of comparison in certain 'worlds' of which mention is made in the Zohar. We frequently come across such phrases as, 'there is rejoicing in all worlds', or 'all worlds are knit together'. Now, in later Cabbalistic works there is no doubt that by 'worlds' in such a connection would be meant the four 'worlds' of Aziluth, Beriah, Yezirah and 'Asiah (v. Introduction). But, as we have seen, the Zohar does not seem to be really familiar with this idea, and certainly it hardly seems in place in the contexts where these expressions occur. It makes much better sense if we regard 'worlds' in these contexts as the 'opposite numbers' of the various grades, as the effects of the various manifestations of the First Cause. After all, if the First Cause is tenfold, it stands to reason that the universe must also be tenfold; and we may take this to be the doctrine of the Zohar, though it is nowhere expressly stated. [Tr. note: of course, the three inferior 'worlds, of the Cabbalists would be contained in these worlds, though how exactly they are to be distributed is not easy to determine.]

This supposition, however, only carries the difficulty back a stage, and we have still to ask, how are we to understand the simultaneous existence of various worlds? The key can perhaps be found in the Zoharic conception of the primordial 'Days'. Of the ten grades, six–from the fourth to the ninth–are regarded as functioning each within its own 'day'. Now it is obvious that these 'days' are not successive, since all the grades are evidently functioning concurrently. We must suppose, therefore, that when the Zohar says there are six 'days', what it means is that there are six kinds of time, what we might call six 'tempos' of existence, and in relation to each of these the First Cause assumes a different aspect, exhibits a different manifestation, becomes, in the Zoharic language, a different grade of itself. If we ask, how are we to imagine different kinds of time, it would be hard to find anything in the Zohar throwing light on this point, but it is not difficult to provide an answer, if we regard time as something not objectively perceived, but as subjectively felt. It might fairly be held that the animate world feels time in a manner different from the inanimate, and the higher branches of the animate world in a manner different from the lower. In this way the conception of various 'worlds' each with its own First Cause, yet all forming one, would become intelligible.

The 'day' as a definite kind of time, presupposes the existence of 'heaven and earth', that is, of an active cause and a material on which it works, originally one but differentiated by the action of the First Cause as a preliminary to the creation of 'worlds'. In this preliminary stage itself the Zohar distinguishes three grades, which it commonly refers to in a group as 'The Patriarchs'. It impresses upon us that these grades are totally beyond the realm of human comprehension, but this does not prevent it from speaking about them quite familiarly. The third of them is frequently called 'the Jubilee', a word which is meant to indicate the passage of timelessness into time, or, it may be, vice versa. The relation of the six Days of Heaven and Earth to the primordial First Cause is expressed by comparing them to six saplings trained in a nursery and subsequently planted out, the mnemonic being the verse of the Psalms, 'The trees of the Lord, the cedars of Lebanon which he hath planted' (Ps. CIV, 16).

The names given to the grades are the same as those given in Cabbalist literature to the Sefiroth: Kether, Hokhmah, Binah, then Hesed, etc. For Wisdom and Understanding one can perceive a certain reason; the rest seem more or less fanciful, and no reason for them is given in the Zohar. It should be observed that, strictly speaking, all these are names of God, regarded as first cause. That the Zohar always keeps this fact in mind it would not be safe to assert; it is hardly possible in many places to avoid the impression that we are dealing with a plurality of divinities, or again with mere attributes of the Deity. But either supposition reduces the Cabbalistic system to nonsense.

As there are grades prior to 'heaven and earth' and the six grades functioning in them, so there is a grade posterior to heaven and earth. Whence comes the energy which constitutes this 'day'? This is a question to which it is difficult to find an answer in the Zohar. We might say, however, that it is constituted by a kind of reflex action, and consists in the activity of the First Cause in being conscious of itself and all that it has accomplished. This would explain why the specific function of the Seventh Day is to unite the human soul or consciousness (neshamah) with the body, and why, being outside of 'heaven and earth', it occupies a position apart from the previous six grades.

After what has been said it will not be difficult to understand how the conception of God as First Cause can be made to embrace the conceptions of God as Ruler of the world and Protector of Israel. The sixth grade, Tifereth or Beauty, is the one which functions in the third of the six days of creation, and therefore stands in the relation of First Cause to the earth as the basis of all animate existence and all activity of propagation. There is, therefore, obvious ground for identifying this grade with the Holy One, blessed be He, the dispenser of vital powers and the arbiter of life and death in both worlds. When the Ancient Holy One and the Holy One, blessed be He, are thus correlated, they are distinguished as Arich Anpin (Makroprosopus, lit. long of nostrils, i.e. long-suffering, forbearing), and Ze'er Anpin (Microprosopus, lit. small of nostrils, i.e. hasty), the reason being that suffering and pain issue directly from the latter, but not from the former.

If the Holy One, blessed be He, can be identified with the sixth grade, Tifereth, with equal right the Community of Israel can be identified with the tenth grade, Malkuth. The latter is the first cause of union of the human soul with the body; the former is God regarded as immanent in the human soul. A further resemblance lies in the fact that Malkuth, lying outside of the sphere of 'heaven and earth', acts only with a kind of borrowed energy, or, in the language of the Zohar, 'has no light of its own', while the Community of Israel also is regarded as but a moon shining with a borrowed light. Hence the transition from one to the other is easy and natural.

The connection between the various designations of God employed by the Zohar may be illustrated by the following figure. Imagine a long hall divided into three sections, of which one bears the title 'Community of Israel', the second 'Matrona', and the third 'Malkuth'. The first section is open to the heavens; the second section has a somewhat lofty roof; the third a much lower roof. The roof of the second section forms the floor of another hall which extends over the third section also. That part of it which covers the second section of the lower hall, the Matrona, is entitled 'Holy King' and is open to the heavens; that part of it which extends over Malkuth is called Tifereth, and it has three storeys underneath it between itself and Malkuth and five storeys above it, of which the topmost-or it may be the three highest-is open to the heavens. If a man desires to have communion with God, he must enter the lowest hall, but he has his choice between its three sections. If he is content to base his belief in God on the teaching of tradition, he can immediately find communion with God through prayer and devotional exercises. If he seeks to base his belief on the consciousness of his neshamah, or higher self, then devotion is only a first stage and true communion is attained only by ethical practice. If, finally, he bases his belief on philosophical speculation, then even ethical practice is only the fifth of ten stages of intellectual cultivation which he has to pass through in order to attain his goal.

To complete this sketch of the divine nomenclature of the Zohar two things are still necessary. One is to fit into the above scheme the three pairs of categories to which attention was called in the Appendix to Vol. II, namely, Upper and Lower, Male and Female, and Right and Left. The second is to discuss the place occupied in the Zoharic system by the Holy Name or Tetragrammaton.

The Designations and The Categories

Upper and Lower. According to the Zohar, the grades, as the name implies, constitute a hierarchy, each one being superior to the one which follows. The reason is that the activity of each is conditioned by the activity of the one above it, but not vice versa. This is expressed in Zoharic language by saying that each one sucks from the one above it. Hence the terms 'upper' and 'lower' applied to the grades are relative, save that the lowest grade is 'lower' and the highest grade 'upper' par excellence. It is no doubt in virtue of this conditioning that the Zohar lays down that whatever takes place 'above' also takes place 'below', since it is natural that the same First Cause working in different media should produce parallel results.

Male and Female. While each grade is responsible for its own world, in certain cases it is regarded as having received the seed thereof from the grade above, to which it accordingly stands in the relation of female to male. Thus the grades of Wisdom and Understanding are regarded as male and female in regard to the primordial 'heaven and earth' which are, properly speaking, the 'world' of the latter, and hence these two grades are commonly designated 'Father' and 'Mother'. Again, the world of the grade Hesed is commonly known as 'upper waters' and that of the grade Geburah as 'lower waters', the former being a fluid element and the latter fiery. These are regarded as being respectively 'male' and 'female', and out of their union issues the earthly element. The grades themselves, however, Hesed and Geburah, are not distinguished as male and female. Further, the lowest grade, Malkuth, is regarded as female in respect of the six grades of 'heaven and earth', and is often referred to simply as 'The Female'. More specifically, it forms a pair with the grade Yesod (Foundation) immediately above it. The two, when thus conjoined, are usually designated Zaddik (Righteous One), and Zedek (Righteousness), and out of their interaction issues the neshamah as the soul of man.

Right and Left. The distinction between 'right' and 'left' in the Zohar is of particular importance because it is the keystone of the Zoharic theory of good and evil. It is also more elusive and difficult to explain than the other categories. This is due to the fact that these terms are found on examination to embody three sets of ideas which in themselves are in reality quite distinct.

In one sense, 'right and left' seem to be used in the Zohar simply as a variation of 'male and female'. Hokhmah, being 'male', is on the right, and Binah, being 'female', is on the left. Similarly, Hesed, being responsible for the 'male waters', is on the right, and Geburah, being responsible for the 'female waters', is on the left. The supreme grade, Kether, being beyond the division of male and female, is pictured as being in the centre. Similarly, Tifereth, which effects the union between male and female waters, is also placed in the centre. Thus it is possible to speak of a 'straight line' from Kether to Tifereth, and to designate Tifereth the 'central pillar'.

A second use of the terms 'right and left' is based on the identification of the grade Tifereth with the Holy King, the Ruler and Judge of the world. The Holy King as judge can exercise either clemency or rigour, and it is a not unnatural figure to say that He exercises clemency with His right hand and rigour with His left. Now, as we have seen, the 'world' of the grade Tifereth, namely the earthly element capable of producing life, is formed by a union of the fluid and fiery elements which constitute the 'worlds' of Hesed and Geburah. It is assumed by the Zohar that the world of bliss which is reserved for the souls of the righteous after death in some way derives from the grade of Hesed and its element, while the world of punishment reserved for the souls of the wicked derives from Geburah and its element. Hence, by a natural transference, Hesed becomes the Right Arm and Geburah the Left Arm. A further elaboration of this idea is to regard Hesed and Geburah as two judges advocating respectively acquittal and condemnation, while Tifereth turns the scale. When thus grouped the three grades are designated Abraham, Isaac and Jacob.

The distinction between 'right' and 'left' in the Zohar corresponds, not only to the distinction between reward and punishment in the next world, but also between good and evil, and specifically moral good and evil in this world. Samael, the power of evil, the tempter, the accuser, the evil Serpent, is placed on the left and is identified with the grade Geburah. Now Samael is represented as the opponent not of Hesed but of Tifereth. He is the Great Dragon, who on New Year swallows the Moon, that is, prevents the union of the Matrona with the Holy King, until Israel by their sacrifice on the Day of Atonement induce him to desist. He also, by means of his minions, Lilith and others, seduces men to defile their souls, contrary to the desire of the Holy King [Tr. note: It may be noted here that the Zohar distinguishes the zelem (form) and demuth (likeness) of man (v. Genesis I, 26) as 'left' and 'right', and identifies the demuth with the neshamah. Thus one aspect of the distinction between right and left in the Zohar is a conflict between Samael and the Holy King. This conflict is obviously a very different thing from the conflict of view between Hesed and Geburah, though described in the same terms, and if we ask how it arises, the answer is by no means easy to find in the Zohar. A possible explanation is as follows. It has been mentioned above that each grade is regarded as 'sucking' from the one above it. Now it is not unnatural to suppose that the one which is 'sucked' should offer a certain resistance to the process, so that two opposite tendencies are always at work. This would seem to be implied in the somewhat obscure interpretation given by the Zohar to a text which it frequently quotes as containing a fundamental principle with reference to the grades, viz. 'To the place whence the rivers came, thither they are ever returning' (Eccl. I, 7). On this principle there should be a conflict between all the adjacent grades; but we may suppose that the reason why the Zohar dwells on the conflict between Samael and the Holy King is because of its importance for the salvation of man's soul and the welfare of the people of Israel.]

The Divine Name

It remains to say a few words on the place occupied by the Holy Name, the Tetragrammaton, in the scheme of the Zohar. In the Cabbalistic doctrine the name formed by the four Hebrew letters yod, he, vau, he, has a special and intimate connection with the grade of Tifereth, of which it is in the strict sense the proper name. We must understand this to mean that if one could grasp with sufficient clearness the nature of the grade Tifereth, especially as the originator of the neshamah, he would automatically perceive that this is the fitting appellation which should be given to it. To this grade of comprehension Moses and the other prophets actually rose, and this was the basis of their inspiration. There is, however, a difference between the inspiration of Moses and that of the other prophets. Moses was able to grasp the connection between the grade and the Name fully and clearly, but the others only through a haze, as it were, since their comprehension only reached fully to the two inferior grades of Nezah and Hod, the two 'pillars' or 'willows of the brook', as they are fancifully called.

Apart from its importance as a vocable, the Tetragrammaton has a deep significance for the Zohar as a written word, through the symbolism of its individual letters and their shapes and qualities. Thus the point of the Yod symbolizes the grade Kether; the Yod itself stands for Hokhmah the Father, and the first He' for Binah, the Mother. The Vau, having the numerical value of six, symbolizes the 'six ends', the grades of the six days, and more particularly Tifereth, the centre of this group. The second He' naturally symbolizes Malkuth. Since the shape of the Vau combines features of the Yod and the He', it is fancifully referred to as the 'son' of these letters, and this designation of 'son' is sometimes transferred to the grade Tifereth which it represents, although we do not find that Tifereth as a grade is particularly associated with Hokhmah and Binah. Thus the Tetragrammaton in its letters sums up the whole doctrine of the grades, while as a name it is the pivot of the entire Holy Writ; and the Zohar therefore does not hesitate to declare that 'the whole of the Torah is the Holy Name'.

-MAURICE SIMON

Glossary

ADAM. The Sefiroth, or divine grades, represented as a man, e.g. Hesed the right arm, Hod the left thigh, etc. Tr. note: For the Sefiroth and divine grades, see Appendix I.

AGADAHS. Homilies and discourses of the Rabbis.

AMIDAH. The principal part of all the three daily prayers, to be recited quietly and in a standing posture.

ANCIENT OF DAYS. The highest of the Grades of the Godhead.

APPLE FIELD. A name for the Garden of Eden.

ARMS. The divine grades Hesed (Right Arm) and Geburah (Left Arm) (v. Adam).

ARQA. One of the seven levels of the earth.

BEAUTY OF ISRAEL. The Sefirah Tifereth.

BODY. The Sefirah Tifereth.

CENTRAL PILLAR. A name for the Sefirah Tifereth, which unites the Right and the Left.

CHARIOT. That which God directly controls.

CHIEFTAINS. The celestial chiefs and guardians attached to the various nations of the earth.

COMMUNITY OF ISRAEL. The Shekinah in its connection with the people of Israel.

COVENANT. The sign of circumcision (v. Genesis XVII).

CROWNED. Glorified.

DAUGHTER. Same as Female (q.v.).

DISCLOSED. The divine grades following the first three.

DROSS OF GOLD. The k'lifoth, outer shells or lower-grade spirits.

DUMA. The spirit in charge of Gehinnom. EL SHADDAI. God Almighty.

FATHER. he second of the divine grades (v. Appendix).

FEMALE. The last of the divine grades, synonymous with the Shekinah (v. Appendix).

FIELD OF APPLE-TREES. The Garden of Eden. FIRE. The emblem of the grade Geburah.

FOUNDATION (Yesod). The ninth Sefirah, also called Zaddik.

FOUNDATION OF WORLD. A synonym for the Zaddik (q.v.).

GEBURAH (lit. force, might). The presiding grade of the left side, the source of rigour and chastisement (v. Appendix).

GEDULAH (lit. greatness). Another name for the Sefirah Hesed.

GEHINNOM. Hell.

GRADE. Any degree in the scale of being; often=angel or demon.

HANUKAH. The Feast of Dedication.

HAYYAH (lit. animal). The highest grade of angel.

HOLY ONE. A name commonly applied to God in the aspect of Tifereth (q.v.).

HUSBAND. The divine grade called. Hokmah (Wisdom).

ISRAEL. A name given to the highest of the divine grades.

JUBILEE. The supernal world; Moses as distinguished from Jacob.

KING. The highest of the divine grades.

KLIFOTH (lit. 'shells' or 'husks'). The powers of evil. LAD. A synonym for Metatron (q.s.).

LAND OF LIFE. The Future World.

LEBANON (Trees or Cedars of). The Six Days of creation with their associated grades.

LEFT. The side of Geburah (v. Appendix).

LESSER COUNTENANCE. The Sefirah Tifereth – (Kether being the 'long countenance').

MALE. The upper world in its relation to the Shekinah (v. Appendix).

MALKUTH (lit. sovereignty). The tenth Sefirah: esp., the Shekinah in connection with Tifereth (q.v.).

MASTER OF THE HOUSEHOLD. Moses.

MATRON. One of the names of the Shekinah.

MAZZAL (lit. constellation, luck). The allotted portion of a human being.

METATRON. The chief of the Chieftains (q.v.), the power charged with the sustenance of mankind.

METATRON. [alt.] The head of the 'world of creation', called also the 'servant' or the 'body' of the Shekinah.

MEZUZAH (lit. doorpost). A scroll containing Biblical verses attached to a doorpost (v. Deut. VI, 9).

MIRROR. The source of the prophetic faculty in one or other of the firmaments, luminous for Moses, dim for others.

MOON. One of the names of the Shekinah (v. Appendix).

MOTHER. The third of the divine grades (v. Appendix).

NEFESH. The vital principle, the lowest of the three grades of the soul.

NESHAMAH. The moral consciousness, the highest of the three grades of the soul.

NORTH. The side of Geburah.

ONKELOS. The reputed translator of the Chaldaic version of the Pentateuch.

ORLAH (lit. foreskin). The condition of being unreceptive of the Shekinah.

PATRIARCHS. The three highest of the divine grades. PRINCE OF THE WORLD. Metratron (g.v.).

RED. The symbolic colour of the divine attribute of judgement or severity.

RIGHT. The side of Hesed (v. Appendix).

RIGHTEOUS (Zaddik). The ninth Sefirah, also called Foundation'.

RIGHTEOUS ONE (v. Zaddik).

RUAH (lit. spirit). The intellectual faculty, the middle of the three grades of the soul.

SABBATICAL YEAR. The seven secondary divine grades; a name applied to Jacob when compared with Moses.

SACRED LAMP. R. Simeon b. Yohai.

SHEKINAH (lit. neighbourhood, abiding). The Divine Presence (v. Appendix).

SHEMA (lit. hear). The proclamation of the unity of God, commencing with 'Hear, O Israel' (v, Deut. VI, 4).

SHEOL. The under world.

SOUTH. The side of the divine attribute of mercy.

SUN. The upper world in relation to the Shekinah (v. Appendix).

TALITH. A garment with fringes (v. Num. xv, 38).

THIGHS. The divine grades Nezah (Victory), and Hod (Majesty) (v. Adam).

TIFERETH (lit. beauty). The sixth Sefirah, often symbolized by the sun, also by the Tree of Life with twelve roots and seventy branches.

TORAH. The Law of Moses, especially the esoteric doctrine.

UNDISCLOSED. The three highest of the divine grades.

VAU. The sixth letter of the Hebrew alphabet and third of the sacred Name, symbolizing the original heavens.

VOICE. The instrument of the Creation, identified with the original heavens.

WATER. The symbol of the divine attribute of.Hesed (kindness or mercy).

WELL. The supernal source of being.

WHITE. The symbolical colour of the divine attribute of mercy or kindness (Hesed).

WIFE. The divine grade called Elohim or Binah (understanding).

WINE. The symbol of the divine attribute of rigour or severity (Geburah).

WISDOM. The esoteric doctrine of the divine grades. YESOD (v. Foundation).

YOD. The tenth letter of the Hebrew alphabet.

ZADDIK (lit. righteous). The divine grade associated with the covenant.

ZADDIK [alt.] (v. Righteous).

Made in the USA
Las Vegas, NV
25 February 2024

86265641R00411